TROUBLESHOOTING, MAINTAINING, and REPAIRING PCs

TROUBLESHOOTING, MAINTAINING, and REPAIRING PCs

SECOND EDITION

STEPHEN J. BIGELOW

McGraw-Hill

New York San Francisco Washington, D.C. Auckland Bogotá
Caracas Lisbon London Madrid Mexico City Milan
Montreal New Delhi San Juan Singapore
Sydney Tokyo Toronto

Library of Congress Cataloging-in-Publication Data

Bigelow, Stephen J.
   Troubleshooting, maintaining, and repairing PCs / Stephen J.
Bigelow, — 2nd ed.
     p. cm.
     Includes Index.
     ISBN (invalid) 0-00-791373-3 (direct mail version). — ISBN
0-07-913732-6 (trade)
      1. Microcomputers—Maintenance and repair. 2. IBM-compatible
computers—Maintenance and repair. I. Title.
    TK7887.B553 1998
    621.39'16'0288—dc21   98-20453
                                          CIP

McGraw-Hill

A Division of The **McGraw·Hill** *Companies*

   3 4 5 6 7 8 9 0   DOC/DOC   9 0 3 2 1 0 9 8

P/N 006885-2
Part of ISBN 0-07-913732-6

*The sponsoring editor for this book was Scott Grillo, the editing supervisor was Andrew
Yoder, and the production supervisor was Clare B. Stanley. It was set in Times New Ro-
man by Lisa M. Mellott through the services of Barry E. Brown (Broker—Editing, Design
and Production).*

Printed and bound by R. R. Donnelley & Sons Company.

McGraw-Hill books are available at special quantity discounts to use as premiums and
sales promotions, or for use in corporate training programs. For more information, please
write to the Director of Special Sales, McGraw-Hill, 11 West 19th Street, New York, NY
10011. Or contact your local bookstore.

This book was printed on acid-free paper.

CONTENTS
AT A GLANCE

1 Inside today's desktop and tower   *UPDATED*
2 Inside today's monitors
3 Operating systems and the boot process   *UPDATED*
4 The pre-service checkout   *UPDATED*
5 Batteries
6 BIOS   *UPDATED*
7 CD-ROM and CD-R drives   *UPDATED*
8 Chipsets   *UPDATED*
9 CMOS   *UPDATED*
10 Conflict troubleshooting   *UPDATED*
11 CPU identification and troubleshooting   *UPDATED*
12 Disk-compression troubleshooting   *UPDATED*
13 Drive-adapter reference   *UPDATED*
14 DVD drives   *NEW*
15 Error codes   *NEW*
16 Floppy drives   *MORE SYMPTOMS*
17 Hard drives   *UPDATED*
18 ISA/EISA bus operations
19 Joysticks and game ports   *MORE SYMPTOMS*
20 Keyboards   *MORE SYMPTOMS*
21 Laser/LED printers   *UPDATED*
22 MCA bus operations
23 Memory troubleshooting   *UPDATED*
24 Memory managers   *NEW*
25 Mice and trackballs   *MORE SYMPTOMS*
26 Modems and fax cards   *UPDATED*
27 Monitor troubleshooting   *UPDATED*
28 Motherboard troubleshooting   *UPDATED*
29 Overlay software troubleshooting   *NEW*
30 Other interfaces and technologies   *NEW*
31 Parallel-port (Centronics) troubleshooting
32 PC cards and peripherals   *UPDATED*
33 PCI bus operations
34 Pen systems and touchpads   *MORE SYMPTOMS*
35 Plug-and-Play configuration and troubleshooting   *NEW*

36 Power switching supplies
37 High-voltage power supplies
38 Removable media drives   *NEW*
39 SCSI systems and troubleshooting   *UPDATED*
40 Serial (RS-232) port troubleshooting
41 Sound boards   *UPDATED*
42 Tape drives   *UPDATED*
43 Video adapters and accelerators   *UPDATED*
44 Video capture/PC-TV boards   *UPDATED*
45 Virus symptoms and countermeasures   *UPDATED*
46 VL bus operations
47 Floppy drive testing and alignment
48 Monitor testing and alignment
49 Preventive maintenance   *NEW*

Appendix A: MPC standards for the PC

Appendix B: ASCII Chart

Appendix C: DOS error messages   *NEW*

Appendix D: PC Newsgroups   *NEW*

Appendix E: Windows 95 Shortcuts   *NEW*

Appendix F: Forms

Appendix G: The A+ Checklist   *NEW*

Appendix H: PC standards chart   *NEW*

CONTENTS

Disclaimer and cautions *xxxi*

Introduction *xxxiii*

FAQ "Getting the Most From This Book" *xxxvii*

List of figures *xlv*

List of tables *li*

Symptoms at a glance *lvii*

Chapter 1   Inside today's desktop and tower *1*

Under the hood   *2*
   Enclosure   *2*
   Power supply   *6*
   Motherboard   *6*
   Drives   *9*
   Expansion boards   *11*

Notes for disassembly and re-assembly   *19*
   The value of data   *19*
   Opening the system   *19*
   Closing the system   *20*
   Tips for working inside a desktop or tower PC   *21*

Standardized form factors   *22*
   ATX form factor   *22*
   NLX form factor   *25*

Further study   *27*

Chapter 2   Inside today's monitors *29*

Monitor assembly   *30*
   Enclosure   *30*
   CRT   *31*
   CRT drive board   *33*
   Raster drive board   *34*
   Power supply   *35*

Working with on-screen controls   *35*
   Basic controls   *35*
   Advanced controls   *37*

Notes on monitor disassembly and reassembly   *39*
   Discharging the CRT   *39*
   Removing sub-assemblies   *40*

Replacing sub-assemblies   *40*
Tips for working with a monitor   *41*
Further study   *41*

Chapter 3   Operating systems and the boot process   **43**

The PC hierarchy   *44*
Hardware   *44*
BIOS   *45*
Operating System   *45*
Applications   *46*

Understanding popular OS features   *46*
MS-DOS 6.22   *48*
PC-DOS 7.0   *49*
Windows 95   *50*
OS/2 Warp 4.x   *50*
Windows CE   *51*
Windows NT (Workstation)   *51*
Windows 98   *53*

A closer look at MS-DOS   *55*
IO.SYS   *55*
MSDOS.SYS   *56*
IO.SYS and MSDOS.SYS variations under Windows 95   *56*
Adjusting MSDOS.SYS under MS-DOS 7.x   *57*
COMMAND.COM   *59*
Recognizing and dealing with OS problems   *62*

The boot process   *63*
Applying power   *63*
The bootstrap   *63*
Core tests   *63*
POST   *64*
Finding the OS   *65*
Loading the OS   *66*
Establishing the environment   *66*
Creating a DOS boot disk   *67*

Further study   *68*

Chapter 4   The pre-service checkout   **69**

The universal troubleshooting process   *70*
Define your symptoms   *70*
Identify and isolate   *71*
Replace   *71*
Re-test   *72*

The spare parts dilemma   *72*
Parts are always changing   *72*
Inventory costs money   *73*
A better strategy   *73*

Benchmarking the PC   *73*
Avoiding benchmark problems   *74*
Obtaining benchmarks   *74*

Viruses and computer service   *79*
Computer viruses explained   *79*

The tell-tale signs   *80*
Anti-virus software   *81*
Sterilizing your shop   *81*

Quick-start bench testing   *83*
The system doesn't start at all   *84*
The system starts but won't initialize   *86*
The system starts but crashes/reboots intermittently   *87*
After an upgrade   *88*
Windows 95 boot symptoms   *89*

Further study   *93*

Chapter 5   Batteries   **94**

A battery primer   *95*
Battery ratings   *95*
Charging   *95*

Backup batteries   *97*
Lithium batteries   *97*
Backup battery replacement   *99*
Troubleshooting backup-battery problems   *100*

Mobile batteries   *102*
Nickel-cadmium   *102*
Nickel metal-hydride   *104*
Lithium-ion and zinc-air   *105*
Recognizing rechargeable battery failures   *105*
Conserving mobile battery power   *105*
Troubleshooting mobile battery problems   *106*

Battery recycling   *110*
Further study   *110*

Chapter 6   BIOS   **111**

A look inside the motherboard BIOS   *112*
POST   *112*
Setup   *113*
System service routines   *113*

BIOS features   *115*
Determining features from BIOS ID strings   *118*

BIOS and boot sequences   *121*
American Megatrends   *121*
Phoenix Technologies   *122*

BIOS shortcomings and compatibility issues   *124*
Device drivers   *124*
"Flash" laziness   *125*
BIOS shadowing   *125*
Direct control   *125*
BIOS bugs   *126*
The year 2000 (Y2K) problem   *126*

Troubleshooting BIOS error messages   *128*
General BIOS error messages   *128*
PCI error messages   *136*

Further study   *137*

Chapter 7   CD-ROM and CD-R drives   138

Understanding CD media   *139*
   CD data   *140*
   EFM and data storage   *142*
   Caring for compact discs   *143*
   Caring for recordable CDs   *143*

CD-ROM/CD-R standards and characteristics   *144*
   High Sierra   *144*
   ISO 9660   *145*
   CD-ROM standards ("Books")   *145*
   The multi-spin drive   *145*
   The MPC   *146*
   Effects of CD-ROM caching   *147*
   Bootable CD-ROM (El Torito)   *147*
   "Orange Book certified" media   *147*
   Multisession CDs   *148*
   Fixation vs. finalization   *148*
   Disc-at-Once   *148*
   Track-at-Once   *149*
   Incremental and packet writing   *149*

Drive construction   *149*
   CD-ROM mechanics   *149*
   CD-ROM electronics   *152*

Understanding the software   *153*
   Device drivers   *153*
   MSCDEX.EXE   *154*

Creating a bootable CD   *154*
   Making the CD   *156*
   Making the bootable image file   *156*
   Make a booting catalog file   *157*
   Create the ISO 9660 image file   *157*
   Modify the ISO 9660 image file   *157*
   Burn the ISO file to CD-R   *158*
   Test the bootable CD   *159*

Troubleshooting CD-ROM drives   *159*

Troubleshooting CD-R drives   *169*
   CD-recording issues   *170*
   Typical compatibility problems   *172*
   CD-R symptoms   *172*

Further study   *177*
   CD-related newsgroups   *178*

Chapter 8   Chipsets   179

AMD chipsets   *181*
   AMD-640 chipset   *182*
   More on the AMD-640 System Controller (Northbridge)   *184*
   More on the AMD-645 Peripheral Bus Controller (Southbridge)   *184*

Intel chipsets   *185*
   Intel 430 VX Pentium chipset   *185*
   Intel 430 TX Pentium chipset   *186*
   Intel 430 HX Pentium chipset   *187*
   Intel 430 FX Pentium chipset   *187*

Intel 430 MX mobile Pentium chipset   *188*
Intel 440 FX Pentium Pro/II chipset   *188*
Intel 450 GX/KX Pentium Pro chipset   *190*
Intel 440 LX Pentium II chipset   *190*

VIA chipsets   *191*
VIA Apollo P6 chipset   *191*
VIA Apollo VP3 chipset   *191*
VIA Apollo VP2 chipset   *192*
VIA Apollo VPX/97 chipset   *193*
VIA Apollo VP-1 chipset   *193*
VIA Apollo Master chipset   *194*

SiS chipsets   *195*
OPTi chipsets   *195*
OPTi Discovery chipset   *197*
OPTi Vendetta chipset   *197*
FireStar chipset   *197*

Legacy and support ICs   *198*
Further study   *206*

Chapter 9   CMOS   *207*
What CMOS does   *208*
The CMOS map   *208*
Configuring the CMOS Setup   *213*
Entering CMOS Setup   *213*
Basic CMOS optimization tactics   *215*
Configuring the standard CMOS setup   *215*
Configuring the advanced CMOS setup   *217*
Configuring the advanced Chipset setup   *222*
Configuring Plug and Play/PCI   *229*
Configuring power management   *242*

Making use of "Auto-configuration"   *243*
BIOS defaults   *243*
Power-on defaults   *243*

Backing up CMOS RAM   *243*
CMOS maintenance and troubleshooting   *244*
Typical CMOS-related symptoms   *244*
CMOS password troubleshooting   *248*
CMOS battery maintenance   *250*

Further study   *250*

Chapter 10   Conflict troubleshooting   *251*
Understanding system resources   *252*
Interrupts   *252*
DMA channels   *254*
I/O areas   *255*
Memory assignments   *255*
Index of typical assignments   *261*

Recognizing and dealing with conflicts   *262*
Confirming and resolving conflicts   *263*
Dealing with software conflicts   *263*
Dealing with hardware conflicts   *264*
Conflict troubleshooting with Windows 95   *264*

The role of Plug-and-Play (PnP)   277
Keep your notes   278
Further study   278

Chapter 11   CPU identification and troubleshooting   279

The basic CPU   287
The busses   287
Addressing modes   288
Modern CPU concepts   288
The P-rating (PR) system   289
CPU sockets   289
CISC vs. RISC CPUs   291
Pipelining   291
Branch prediction   291
Superscalar execution   292
Dynamic execution   292
The Intel CPUs   292
8086/8088 (1978/1979)   292
80186 (1980)   298
80286 (1982)   298
80386 (1985-1990)   298
80486 (1989–1994)   299
Pentium (1993-current)   300
Pentium Pro (1995-current)   301
Pentium MMX (1997-current)   311
Pentium II (1997-current)   312
The AMD CPUs   313
Am486DX series (1994-1995)   313
Am5x86 (1995-current)   314
K5 series (1996-current)   314
K6 series (1997-current)   314
The Cyrix CPUs   315
6x86 series (1995-current)   315
MediaGX (1996-current)   316
6x86MX (M2) (1997-current)   317
CPU overclocking   317
Requirements for overclocking   318
Potential pitfalls   319
Overclocking the system   319
Special notes for 75 and 83MHz bus speeds   322
Overclocking notes for the Intel Pentium   322
Overclocking notes for the Intel Pentium Pro   322
Overclocking notes for the Cyrix/IBM 6x86   324
Overclocking the AMD K5   324
Tips for controlling heat   324
Troubleshooting CPU problems   325
General symptoms and solutions   325
Cyrix 6x86 issues   329
Overclocking troubleshooting   331
Troubleshooting a diagnostic failure after installing an Intel math co-processor   332
Troubleshooting an arithmetic test failure   333
Troubleshooting an environment test failure   333

Intel diagnostics conformance test failure with Intel387(TM)
    SL math co-processor   *333*
Intel387 DX math co-processor recognized as an Intel287TM
    XL math co-processor   *333*
Intel387 math co-processor recognized as an Intel287 math co-processor   *334*
System integrity diagnostic test failure   *334*
"CHKCOP has found" and locks up   *334*
CHKCOP 2.0 fails divide test   *334*
CHKCOP seems faster on an Intel287 math co-processor   *334*
System diagnostics and the Intel287 XL math co-processor   *335*
Intel387 DX and inboard Intel287 math module and IBM advanced diagnostics   *335*
Troubleshooting failure to boot after installing an Intel math co-processor   *335*
Weiteck co-processor not installed   *336*
OS2 1107 error   *336*
162 error in IBM PS/2 model 50, 60, and 70   *337*
"Configuration error" after removing 80287 from IBM PC/AT   *337*
Further study   *337*
    Newsgroups   *338*

Chapter 12   Disk-compression troubleshooting   ***339***
Concepts of compression   *340*
    Disk space allocation   *340*
    Data compression   *341*
    The compression system   *341*
    Factors that effect compression   *343*
Before and after compression   *343*
    Scan the disk for physical defects   *343*
    Defragment the disk and check free space   *344*
    Check the disk for file defects   *344*
    Check the memory   *344*
    Install the compression utility   *344*
    Create a bootable disk   *345*
    DBLSPACE.INI and DRVSPACE.INI file settings   *345*
    Removing DOS doublespace or drivespace manually   *349*
Troubleshooting compressed drives   *351*
    Troubleshooting Windows 95 DriveSpace   *351*
    Troubleshooting DOS DoubleSpace and DriveSpace   *360*
    Troubleshooting DOS Stacker   *371*
Further study   *381*

Chapter 13   Drive-adapter reference   ***382***
ST506/412   *383*
    ST506/412 features and architecture   *384*
    Cabling the ST506/412 interface   *387*
    Low-level formatting an ST506/412 drive   *387*
    Partitioning and high-level formatting   *388*
    The fate of ST506/412   *389*
ESDI   *389*
    ESDI features and architecture   *389*
    Cabling the ESDI drive system   *392*
    Low-level formatting an ESDI drive   *392*
    Partitioning and high-level formatting   *393*
    The fate of ESDI   *394*

IDE   *394*
   IDE features and architecture   *394*
   Cabling the IDE/EIDE interface   *397*
   Low-level formatting an IDE/EIDE drive   *398*
   BIOS support of IDE   *399*
   The role of ATAPI   *399*
EIDE   *399*
   Understanding the 528MB IDE limit   *400*
   Understanding LBA   *401*
   Drive support   *401*
   Data-transfer rates   *402*
   Installing an EIDE system   *403*
   Adapter configuration jumpers   *406*
   Software installation cautions   *407*
Ultra-ATA   *407*
   Implementing an Ultra-ATA system   *407*
   Ultra-ATA compatibility and configuration issues   *408*
Troubleshooting a drive adapter   *408*
Further study   *416*

Chapter 14   DVD drives   **417**
The potential of DVD   *418*
Specifications and standards   *419*
   Access time   *419*
   Data transfer rates   *419*
   Books and standards   *420*
   Data formats   *420*
   Audio and video standards   *420*
   CD compatibility   *421*
DVD media   *421*
   Caring for a DVD disc   *422*
DVD drives   *424*
   Inside the drive   *425*
   Region code control   *426*
The MPEG-2 decoder board   *426*
   A look at MPEG-2   *428*
   Notes on Dolby AC-3   *428*
   Decoder board connections   *428*
Basic DVD/MPEG-2 troubleshooting   *429*
Further study   *434*

Chapter 15   Error codes   **435**
IBM diagnostic codes   *436*
   Reading the codes   *436*
   Troubleshooting with diagnostic codes   *462*
Beep codes   *464*
POST codes   *469*
   Interpreting the POST codes   *470*
The POST board   *556*
   I/O ports   *557*
   Interpreting the LEDs   *557*

Beep/POST troubleshooting   *558*
Further study   *560*

Chapter 16   Floppy drives   *561*

Magnetic-storage concepts   *562*
  Media   *562*
  Magnetic recording principles   *563*
  Data and disk organization   *565*
  Media problems   *567*
Drive construction   *568*
  Drive electronics   *570*
  Physical interface   *572*
Troubleshooting floppy disk systems   *574*
  Repair vs. replace   *574*
  Preliminary testing   *574*
Further study   *580*

Chapter 17   Hard drives   *581*

Drive concepts   *582*
  Platters and media   *582*
  Air flow and head flight   *583*
  Data-density characteristics   *585*
  Latency   *585*
  Tracks, sectors, and cylinders   *586*
  Zoned recording   *588*
  Sector sparing (defect management)   *588*
  Landing zone   *589*
  Interleave   *589*
  Write precompensation   *590*
  Drive parameters and translation   *590*
  Start time   *591*
  Power-mode definitions   *592*
  SMART command set   *592*
  IDE/EIDE hard-drive concepts   *592*
  Data-transfer rates   *594*
  Block-mode transfers   *595*
  Bus mastering   *595*
  Drive caching   *597*
Drive construction   *598*
  Frame   *598*
  Platters   *598*
  Read/Write heads   *600*
  Head actuators   *602*
  Spindle motor   *603*
  Drive electronics   *603*
Concepts of drive formatting   *605*
  Low-level formatting   *605*
  Partitioning   *605*
  High-level (DOS) formatting   *606*
File systems and tips   *606*
  FAT basics   *606*
  FAT 16   *607*

Partitioning large hard drives   *608*
FAT 32   *609*
Partitioning and formatting for FAT 32   *610*
Understanding drive-capacity limits   *611*
Cylinder limits in BIOS   *612*
Partition limits in the operating system   *612*
Overcoming capacity limits   *612*
Drive testing and troubleshooting   *614*
HDD-controller BIOS error codes   *615*
Troubleshooting "DOS Compatibility Mode" problems   *616*
Symptoms and solutions   *617*
Further study   *632*
Usenet FAQ   *632*

Chapter 18   ISA/EISA bus operations   *633*
Industry-standard architecture (ISA)   *634*
8-bit ISA   *634*
Knowing the XT signals   *635*
16-bit ISA   *636*
Knowing the AT signals   *636*
Potential problems mixing 8-bit and 16-bit ISA boards   *638*
Extended industry-standard architecture (EISA)   *639*
Knowing the EISA signals   *641*
Configuring an EISA system   *641*
General bus troubleshooting   *642*
Further study   *642*

Chapter 19   Joysticks and game ports   *643*
Understanding the game-port system   *644*
Inside the joystick   *644*
Adapting a second joystick   *646*
Digital joysticks (game pads)   *647*
Joystick calibration   *647*
Joystick drift   *648*
Cleaning joysticks   *649*
Joysticks and Windows 95   *649*
Troubleshooting joysticks and game ports   *650*
Joystick eliminator plug   *650*
Adapting IDC connectors   *651*
Sound cards and Y-adapter problems   *651*
Further study   *656*

Chapter 20   Keyboards   *657*
Keyboard construction   *658*
Key codes   *660*
Keyboard interfaces   *660*
Dvorak keyboards   *662*
Converting to Dvorak keyboards   *662*
Keyboard cleaning and maintenance   *663*
Correcting problem keyboards   *664*
Vacuum cleaners and keyboards   *664*
Replacing the <Space Bar>   *665*

Preventing the problems   *665*
Dealing with large objects   *666*
Dealing with spills   *666*
Disabling a keyboard   *666*
Keyboard troubleshooting   *667*
Further study   *672*

Chapter 21   Laser/LED printers   *673*

Understanding EP operation   *674*
Cleaning   *675*
Charging   *676*
Writing   *677*
Developing   *677*
Transfer   *678*
Fusing   *679*
Understanding writing mechanisms   *680*
Lasers   *680*
LEDs   *682*
The EP cartridge   *683*
Protecting an EP cartridge   *684*
Laser/LED printer troubleshooting   *684*
Controller (logic) symptoms   *686*
Registration symptoms   *701*
Laser/scanner symptoms   *703*
Drive and transmission symptoms   *708*
HVPS symptoms   *710*
Fusing symptoms   *713*
Corona (charge roller) symptoms   *717*
Miscellaneous symptoms   *721*
Further study   *727*
Webpages   *727*
Usenet newsgroups   *727*

Chapter 22   MCA bus operations   *728*

MCA bus configuration and signals   *729*
MCA layout   *729*
Knowing the MCA signals   *730*
PS/2 reference and diagnostic disks   *735*
Clearing a 55sx password   *735*
Dealing with PS/2 "165" errors (.ADF files)   *736*
General bus troubleshooting   *737*
Further study   *737*
Usenet newsgroup   *737*

Chapter 23   Memory troubleshooting   *738*

Essential memory concepts   *739*
Memory organization   *739*
Memory signals   *740*
Memory package styles and structures   *741*
Add-on memory devices   *741*
Megabytes and memory layout   *743*
Memory organization   *759*

Conventional memory   *759*
Extended memory   *759*
Expanded memory   *770*
Upper memory area (UMA)   *770*
High memory   *771*
Memory considerations   *771*
Memory speed and wait states   *771*
Determining memory speed   *772*
Presence detect (PD)   *773*
Understanding memory "refresh"   *773*
Memory types   *774*
Memory techniques   *777*
The issue of parity   *779*
The parity principle   *779*
Even vs. odd   *779*
The problems with parity   *779*
Circumventing parity   *780*
Abuse and detection of fake memory   *780*
Alternative error correction   *781*
Memory installation and options   *781*
Getting the right amount   *782*
Filling banks   *782*
Bank requirements   *783*
Recycling older memory devices   *785*
Memory speed   *785*
Memory type   *785*
SIMM stackers   *785*
Mixing "composite" and "non-composite" SIMMs   *786*
Remounting and rebuilding memory   *786*
Memory troubleshooting   *786*
Memory test equipment   *786*
Repairing SIMM sockets   *788*
Contact corrosion   *788*
Parity errors   *788*
Troubleshooting classic XT memory   *789*
Troubleshooting classic AT memory   *790*
Troubleshooting contemporary memory errors   *790*
Further study   *796*

Chapter 24   Memory managers   **797**
Making the most of conventional memory   *798*
Protect the configuration   *799*
Optimizations for CONFIG.SYS   *799*
Optimizations for AUTOEXEC.BAT   *804*
Reviewing your results with MEM   *805*
Mix and match   *805*
Adjusting the memory environment for DOS programs under Windows 95   *806*
Troubleshooting typical optimization problems   *806*
Troubleshooting QEMM   *808*
Troubleshooting HIMEM/EMM386   *817*
Troubleshooting 386MAX   *823*
Further Study   *826*

Chapter 25   Mice and trackballs   ***827***

The mouse   *828*
   Mouse gestures   *828*
   Mouse construction   *829*
   Mechanical sensors   *830*
   Opto-mechanical sensors   *831*
The trackball   *832*
   Trackball construction   *832*
Cleaning a pointing device   *832*
Troubleshooting a pointing device   *834*
   Mouse/trackball interfaces   *834*
   Mouse driver software issues   *835*
   MouseKeys under Windows 95   *835*
   Symptoms   *838*
Further Study   *844*

Chapter 26   Modems and fax cards   ***845***

Basic modem construction and operation   *846*
   The internal modem   *846*
   The external modem   *847*
   Advanced modem features   *848*
   Modem commands   *849*
   Modem initialization strings   *862*
   Modem modes   *868*
   Modem negotiation   *868*
   Reading the lights   *871*
Understanding signal modulation   *871*
   BPS vs. baud rate   *872*
   Modulation schemes   *872*
Signaling standards   *873*
   Bell standards   *873*
   ITU (CCITT) standards   *874*
   MNP standards   *876*
   File-transfer protocols   *878*
Modem troubleshooting   *879*
   Checking the command processor   *880*
   Checking the dialer and telephone line   *882*
   Typical communication problems   *882*
   Symptoms   *885*
Further Study   *899*

Chapter 27   Monitor troubleshooting   ***900***

Monitor specifications and characteristics   *901*
   CRT   *902*
   Pixels and resolution   *902*
   Triads and dot pitch   *902*
   Shadow and slot masks   *903*
   Convergence   *904*
   Pincushion and barrel distortion   *904*
   Horizontal scanning, vertical scanning, raster, and retrace   *904*
   Interlacing   *906*
   Bandwidth   *907*

Swim, jitter, and drift   *907*
Video signal   *908*
Synchronization and polarity   *908*
The color circuits   *908*
Video drive circuits   *908*
Vertical drive circuit   *909*
Horizontal drive circuit   *912*
The flyback circuit   *913*
Construction   *914*
Troubleshooting a CRT   *915*
Inside the CRT   *915*
Identifying CRT problems   *917*
Correcting shorts   *919*
CRT testers/rejuvenators   *920*
Troubleshooting a color monitor   *920*
Wrapping it up   *921*
Post-repair testing and alignment   *921*
Symptoms   *921*
Further Study   *931*

Chapter 28   Motherboard troubleshooting   **932**

Active, passive, and modular   *932*
Understanding the motherboard   *933*
Socket 7, Socket 8, or Slot 1   *934*
AT, ATX, and NLX   *935*
Learning your way around   *935*
Troubleshooting a motherboard   *945*
Repair vs. replace   *945*
Start with the basics   *946*
Symptoms   *947*
Further Study   *959*

Chapter 29   Overlay software troubleshooting   **961**

Disk Manager troubleshooting   *962*
EZ-Drive troubleshooting   *965*
Drive Rocket troubleshooting   *969*
Further Study   *971*

Chapter 30   Other interfaces and technologies   **972**

ACPI (Advanced Configuration and Power Interface)   *973*
Implementing ACPI   *974*
AGP (Accelerated Graphics Port)   *974*
AGP and PCI   *975*
Implementing AGP   *978*
APM (Advanced Power Management)   *978*
The parts of APM   *978*
Implementing APM   *981*
Device Bay   *981*
Implementing Device Bay   *981*
DMI (Desktop Management Interface)   *981*
Each device is identified   *982*
Implementing DMI   *982*

I²O (Intelligent I/O)   *983*
   I²O in operation   *983*
   Implementing I²O   *984*
Instant ON   *984*
   Implementing Instant ON   *985*
IrDA (Infrared Data Association)   *985*
   IrDA standards   *986*
   Limitations to IrDA   *986*
   Implementing IrDA   *986*
SMBus (System Management Bus) and Smart Battery   *986*
   The "smart battery"   *987*
   Implementing SMBus   *988*
USB (Universal Serial Bus)   *988*
   USB operations   *988*
   Implementing USB   *989*
Further Study   *989*

Chapter 31   Parallel-port (Centronics) troubleshooting   991
Understanding the parallel port   *992*
   Addresses and interrupts   *993*
   Parallel-port signals   *993*
   Port operation   *996*
   Advanced parallel ports   *996*
   IEEE 1284 modes   *998*
   ECP/EPP cable quality   *999*
   IEEE 1284 issues   *999*
Troubleshooting the parallel port   *999*
   Tips to fix parallel ports   *1000*
   Symptoms   *1001*
Further Study   *1003*

Chapter 32   PC Cards and peripherals   1004
Understanding the PC Card   *1005*
   Making it work   *1006*
   Enablers   *1008*
   Card types   *1009*
   CardBus and Zoomed Video   *1010*
   Inside the card   *1010*
   Hot insertion and removal   *1011*
   Understanding attribute memory   *1011*
   Connections   *1012*
PC Card applications   *1015*
   PC Card problems   *1016*
   Today's cards   *1016*
   Installing a PC Card   *1017*
Optimizing memory in PC Card systems   *1020*
   Remove any unnecessary drivers   *1020*
   Recover unused memory areas   *1021*
   Utilize any PCMCIA reserved window   *1021*
   Change the driver loading order   *1022*
Troubleshooting PC Card problems   *1023*
Further Study   *1041*
   Newsgroup   *1041*

Chapter 33   PCI bus operations   1042

PCI bus configuration and signals   1043
  PCI bus layout   1044
  Knowing the PCI signals   1047
General bus troubleshooting   1047
Further Study   1048

Chapter 34   Pen systems and touchpads   1049

Understanding pen digitizers   1051
  Resistive digitizers   1051
  Capacitive pen digitizers   1053
  Capacitive touchpad digitizers   1053
  Electromagnetic digitizers   1054
A pen environment   1056
  Gestures   1057
  Glyphs   1057
Troubleshooting pen systems   1058
  Cleaning a pen-tablet or touchpad   1058
  Ink and video drivers   1059
  Pen tips and batteries   1059
  Pen-tablet symptoms   1059
  Touchpad symptoms   1067
Further Study   1069

Chapter 35   Plug-and-Play configuration
and troubleshooting   1070

Understanding PnP under Windows 95   1071
  PnP devices   1071
  PnP BIOS   1071
  PnP operating system   1072
  An overview of PnP behavior   1072
  Device types and identification   1073
  Detection vs. enumeration   1073
  Legacy devices   1080
Enabling PnP under DOS   1081
  The PnP configuration driver   1081
  The PnP configuration utility   1082
  BLASTER variables   1082
  Potential problems with generic PnP configuration software   1082
  Potential problems with manufacturer's PnP software   1083
  Handling PnP configuration issues under DOS   1083
Managing and troubleshooting PnP devices   1084
  Installing PnP devices   1084
  Installing legacy devices   1085
  Updating device drivers   1085
  Installing modems manually   1085
  Installing printers manually   1086
  Disabling a device   1086
  Removing a device   1087
  Symptoms   1087
Further Study   1097

Chapter 36   Switching Power Supplies   *1098*

Understanding switching supplies   *1099*
    Concepts of switching regulation   *1099*
Connecting the power supply   *1101*
    AT-style power connections   *1102*
    Drive power connections   *1102*
    ATX/NLX-style power connections   *1103*
    Optional ATX/NLX power connector   *1104*
    Voltage tolerances   *1105*
Troubleshooting switching power supplies   *1106*
    Tips for power-supply service   *1106*
    An example power supply   *1106*
    Symptoms   *1107*
Further Study   *1109*

Chapter 37   High-voltage Power Supplies   *1110*

Backlight power supplies   *1110*
    Inverter principles   *1111*
    Troubleshooting backlight supplies   *1111*
CRT flyback supplies   *1113*
    Troubleshooting flyback supplies   *1113*
Further Study   *1115*

Chapter 38   Removable media drives   *1116*

Iomega Zip drive   *1117*
    Zip drive troubleshooting   *1117*
Iomega Ditto drive   *1125*
    Ditto demands   *1125*
    Ditto drive troubleshooting   *1125*
Iomega Bernoulli drives   *1129*
    Bernoulli notes   *1129*
    Bernoulli drive troubleshooting   *1129*
SyQuest drives   *1135*
    SyQuest drive troubleshooting   *1136*
Further Study   *1140*

Chapter 39   SCSI systems and troubleshooting   *1141*

Understanding SCSI concepts   *1142*
    Device independence   *1142*
    SCSI variations   *1143*
    Initiators and targets   *1144*
    Synchronous and asynchronous   *1145*
    Disconnect and reconnect   *1145*
    Single-ended and differential   *1145*
    Terminators   *1146*
    SCSI IDs   *1146*
    Bus configurations   *1147*
Understanding SCSI bus operation   *1148*
    Negotiation   *1151*
    Information   *1152*

Upgrading a PC for SCSI   1152
   SCSI peripherals   1152
   SCSI host adapter   1153
   SCSI cables and terminators   1154
   SCSI drivers   1154
   Tips for a smooth upgrade   1154
   Configure and install the SCSI adapter   1155
   Configure and install the SCSI peripheral   1156
   Cabling and termination   1156
   Real-mode SCSI driver issues   1158
   Tips for Windows 95 SCSI drivers   1159
Troubleshooting the SCSI system   1159
   Isolating trouble spots   1160
   General troubleshooting tips   1161
   Symptoms   1162
Further Study   1168

Chapter 40   Serial (RS232) port troubleshooting   **1170**
Understanding asynchronous communication   1171
   The data frame   1171
   Signal levels   1173
   Baud vs. BPS   1173
Understanding the serial port   1174
   Addresses and Interrupts   1175
   DTE vs. DCE   1176
Serial-port signals   1177
   Tx and Rx   1178
   RTS and CTS   1178
   DTR and DSR   1178
   DCD   1178
IrDA port issues   1178
   Installing the IrDA driver(s)   1179
   Removing the IrDA driver(s)   1179
   IrDA tips   1180
Troubleshooting the serial port   1181
   Serial port conflicts   1181
   Match the settings   1182
   Frame it right   1182
   Finding a port address with Debug   1182
   General symptoms   1183
Further Study   1185

Chapter 41   Sound boards   **1186**
Understanding sound boards   1187
   The recording process   1187
   The playback process   1188
   The concept of "sampling"   1188
   Data bits vs. sound quality   1189
   The role of MIDI   1190
   Inside a sound board   1191
Knowing the benchmarks   1192
   Decibels   1192
   Frequency response   1192

Signal-to-noise ratio   *1193*
Total harmonic distortion   *1193*
Intermodulation distortion   *1194*
Sensitivity   *1194*
Gain   *1194*

Using microphones   *1194*
Microphone types   *1195*
Phantom power   *1195*
Choosing a microphone   *1195*

Troubleshooting a sound board   *1196*
Drivers and driver order   *1196*
Full-duplex drivers   *1196*
.WAV playback problems under Windows 95   *1197*
Symptoms   *1200*

Further Study   *1209*

Chapter 42   Tape drives   *1210*
Understanding tape media   *1211*
Quarter-inch cartridge   *1212*
QIC cartridge details   *1213*
QIC minicartridge details   *1213*
QIC tape compatibility   *1215*
Travan tape cartridges   *1215*
Helical-scan tapes   *1216*

Tape drive construction   *1218*
Mechanical construction   *1218*
Electronic circuitry   *1220*

Drive and tape maintenance   *1221*
Drive cleaning   *1221*
Autoloader cleaning   *1221*
Tape maintenance   *1223*
Errors due to cleaning neglect   *1224*
Media problems and DAT drives   *1225*
Recommended cleaning frequency for DAT drives   *1225*

Freeing caught tapes   *1226*
The power trick   *1226*
Rescuing the tape   *1226*

Tape-drive troubleshooting   *1229*
Sense codes and tape drives   *1230*
Symptoms   *1232*

Further Study   *1243*

Chapter 43   Video adapters and accelerators   *1244*
Understanding conventional video adapters   *1245*
Text vs. graphics   *1246*
ROM BIOS (Video BIOS)   *1247*

Reviewing video display hardware   *1247*
MDA (Monochrome Display Adapter—1981)   *1249*
CGA (Color Graphics Adapter—1981)   *1249*
EGA (Enhanced Graphics Adapter—1984)   *1250*
PGA (Professional Graphics Adapter—1984)   *1251*
MCGA (Multi-Color Graphics Array—1987)   *1251*
VGA (Video Graphics Array—1987)   *1252*

8514 (1987)   *1252*
SVGA (Super Video Graphics Array)   *1253*
XGA (1990)   *1253*
Understanding graphics accelerators   *1254*
Video speed factors   *1258*
3D graphics-accelerator issues   *1261*
The 3D process   *1261*
Key 3D-speed issues   *1262*
Improving 3D performance through hardware   *1263*
Understanding DirectX   *1266*
Pieces of a puzzle   *1266*
More on DirectDraw   *1267*
More on DirectSound   *1268*
More on DirectInput   *1269*
More on Direct3D   *1269*
More on DirectPlay   *1269*
Determining the installed version of DirectX   *1270*
Video feature connectors   *1270*
AMI multimedia channel   *1271*
Troubleshooting video adapters   *1274*
Isolating the problem area   *1274*
Unusual hardware issues   *1276*
Clock speed and the VL bus   *1276*
"SLC" motherboards and the VL bus   *1276*
8514/A and COM4 conflicts   *1277*
ATI Mach, S3 Vision/Trio, and COM4 conflicts   *1277*
Award video BIOS glitch   *1277*
Symptoms   *1277*
Further Study   *1288*

Chapter 44   Video capture/PC-TV boards   *1289*
Understanding video-capture boards   *1290*
How a capture board works   *1290*
The capture process   *1292*
The role of a CODEC   *1292*
Intel Indeo video   *1293*
Making the most of video capture   *1294*
Image window size   *1294*
Image frame rate   *1294*
Video source quality   *1295*
Color   *1296*
Lighting   *1296*
Camera techniques   *1296*
Understanding PC-TV boards   *1297*
Displaying TV video in a window   *1297*
Video overlay mode   *1298*
Primary surface mode   *1299*
Decoding Intercast broadcasts   *1299*
Troubleshooting video capture and PC-TV boards   *1300*
Effects of hardware conflicts in video capture   *1300*
Troubleshooting tips   *1301*
Installation symptoms   *1302*
Video-capture symptoms   *1304*

Capture/TV application symptoms   *1310*
Video playback symptoms   *1311*
MPEG/PC-TV board troubleshooting   *1314*
Further study   *1317*

Chapter 45   Virus symptoms and countermeasures   *1318*

Understanding virulent software   *1319*
Software bugs   *1319*
Trojan horses   *1319*
Software chameleons   *1320*
Software bombs   *1320*
Logic bombs   *1320*
Time bombs   *1320*
Replicators   *1325*
Worms   *1326*
Viruses   *1326*
Types of viruses   *1326*
Command processor infection   *1326*
Boot sector infection   *1327*
Executable-file infection   *1327*
File-specific infection   *1328*
Memory-resident infection   *1329*
Multipartite infection   *1329*
Macro viruses   *1329*
Virus myths   *1329*
Protecting the PC   *1331*
Recognizing an infection   *1332*
Dealing with an infection   *1334*
Learning about specific viruses   *1335*
Understanding anti-virus tools   *1335*
Vaccines   *1335*
File comparisons   *1336*
Antidotes   *1336*
Signature scanners   *1337*
Memory-resident utilities   *1337*
Disk mappers   *1338*
Troubleshooting anti-virus tools   *1338*
Preventing macro viruses   *1338*
Symptoms   *1339*
Further Study   *1341*

Chapter 46   VL bus operations   *1342*

VL bus configuration and signals   *1343*
VL bus layout   *1344*
Knowing the VL signals   *1346*
General bus troubleshooting   *1346*
VL-specific issues   *1347*
Further Study   *1348*

Chapter 47   Floppy drive testing and alignment   *1349*

Understanding alignment problems   *1350*
Recognizing the problems   *1350*

Repair vs. replace   *1351*
Tips to reduce floppy drive problems   *1351*
Using alignment tools   *1352*
Advanced tools   *1352*
Aligning the Drive   *1353*
Drive cleaning   *1353*
Clamping   *1353*
Spindle speed   *1355*
Track 00 test   *1355*
Radial alignment   *1356*
Azimuth alignment   *1357*
Head step   *1357*
Hysteresis   *1358*
Head width   *1359*
Further Study   *1360*

Chapter 48   Monitor testing and alignment   *1361*
Before you begin   *1362*
Testing vs. alignment   *1362*
Know the warranty   *1362*
Getting from here to there   *1363*
High-voltage cautions   *1363*
The mirror trick   *1364*
Making an adjustment   *1364*
Tests and procedures   *1365*
High-voltage test and regulation   *1366*
Screen control   *1366*
Focus   *1367*
Dynamic pincushion   *1367*
Horizontal phase   *1368*
Horizontal and vertical centering   *1369*
Horizontal and vertical size (height and width)   *1369*
Horizontal and vertical linearity   *1370*
Static convergence   *1371*
Dynamic convergence   *1372*
Color purity   *1374*
Color drive   *1375*
Cleaning and vacuuming   *1376*
Further Study   *1376*

Chapter 49   Preventive maintenance   *1377*
Protecting your data   *1378*
Step 1: File backups   *1378*
Step 2: CMOS backups   *1380*
Cleaning   *1380*
Step 3: Clean the case   *1381*
Step 4: Clean the air intake   *1381*
Step 5: Clean the speakers   *1381*
Step 6: Clean the keyboard   *1382*
Step 7: Clean the monitor   *1382*
Step 8: Clean the mouse   *1382*

External check   *1383*
    Step 9: Check external cables   *1383*
    Step 10: Clean the floppy drive   *1383*
    Step 11: Clean the tape drive   *1384*
    Step 12: Check the CD tray   *1384*
    Step 13: Check the sound system   *1385*
    Step 14: Check color purity   *1385*
Internal check   *1386*
    Step 15: Check the fans   *1386*
    Step 16: Clean fans and filters   *1386*
    Step 17: Check expansion boards   *1386*
    Step 18: Check internal cables   *1387*
    Step 19: Check memory   *1387*
    Step 20: Check the CPU   *1387*
    Step 21: Check drive mounting   *1388*
Drive check   *1388*
    Step 22: Update the boot disk   *1388*
    Step 23: Run ScanDisk   *1389*
    Step 24: Run Defrag   *1389*
Preventive maintenance troubleshooting   *1389*
Further Study   *1390*

Appendix A: MPC standards for the PC   **1393**

Appendix B: ASCII Chart   **1395**

Appendix C: DOS error messages   **1398**

Appendix D: PC Newsgroups   **1404**

Appendix E: Windows shortcut keys   **1406**

Appendix F: Forms   **1409**

Appendix G: The A+ checklist   **1414**

Appendix H: PC standards chart   **1418**

Index   **1421**

DISCLAIMER

AND CAUTIONS

It is important that you read and understand the following information. Please read it carefully!

Personal Risk and Limits of Liability

The repair of personal computers and their peripherals involves some amount of personal risk. Use extreme caution when working with AC and high-voltage power sources. Every reasonable effort has been made to identify and reduce areas of personal risk. You are instructed to read this book carefully before attempting the procedures discussed. If you are uncomfortable following the procedures that are outlined in this book, do not attempt them —refer your service to qualified service personnel.

Neither the author, the publisher, nor anyone directly or indirectly connected with the publication of this book and accompanying computer software shall make any warranty either expressed or implied, with regard to this material, including, but not limited to, the implied warranties of quality, merchantability, and fitness for any particular purpose. Further, neither the author, publisher, nor anyone directly or indirectly connected with the publication of this book and computer software shall be liable for errors or omissions contained herein, or for incidental or consequential damages, injuries, or financial or material losses resulting from the use, or inability to use, the material and software contained herein. This material and software is provided as-is, and the reader bears all responsibilities and risks connected with its use.

Virus Warning

Although the software included with this book was thoroughly checked for viruses before publication, you are strongly advised to inspect all new software, including this book's companion software, for the presence of computer viruses before executing the software. Anti-virus software can be obtained through commercial and shareware sources. Neither the author, publisher, nor anyone directly or indirectly connected with this book assume any liability whatsoever for incidental or consequential damages, financial loss, or material loss, resulting from the occurrence of computer viruses on your system or network. You use this software at your own risk.

Vendor Warning

The products, materials, equipment, manufacturers, service providers, and distributors listed and presented in this book are shown for reference purposes only. Their mention and use in this book shall not be construed as an endorsement of any individual or organization, nor the quality of their products or services, nor their performance or business integrity. The author, publisher, and anyone directly or indirectly associated with the production of this book expressly disclaim all liability whatsoever for any financial or material losses or incidental or consequential damages that might occur from contacting or doing business with any such organization or individual.

INTRODUCTION: A BOOK
FOR CHANGING TIMES

It used to be that when a PC failed, it wound up sitting on a test bench surrounded by a battalion of test equipment. An experienced technician would be hovering over the PC, logic probe or test leads in-hand. They relied on their knowledge of electronics and microprocessor operations to track the problem to a faulty IC or passive component that could then be replaced with relatively simple soldering tools. There were few add-ons or peripherals to worry about, and only 1MB of memory or so to work with. The few expansion devices that did exist were often plagued by compatibility problems and proprietary interfaces.

Times certainly have changed. Today's PC is largely an collection of very inexpensive subassemblies, many of which are now manufactured in the Pacific Rim and assembled in high volumes at factories around the world. The diverse array of peripherals that are now available (e.g., tape drives, PC cards, CD-ROMs, pointing devices, etc.) enjoy a remarkable level of hardware compatibility using well-established interface schemes (e.g., SCSI, EIDE, USB, or PCI). The labor cost involved in a component-level repair today is usually more expensive than the cost of a replacement assembly. There is little doubt that the day of component-level PC repair is over.

However, PCs still fail in ways that continue to exhaust even the most patient mind. When you realize that there are now well over 100 million PCs in operation (and growing at an astonishing rate each year), you can see that effective troubleshooting requires more than simply an arbitrary swapping of boards and drives. Now, more than ever, efficient and cost-effective troubleshooting requires an understanding of PC hardware and operating systems, along with a keen knowledge of symptoms and diagnostics. Setting up, optimizing, and upgrading a PC are three other important areas that demand the attention of today's technician.

Inside This Edition

This book is intended for the modern computer enthusiast, working technician, or PC student. It is not designed to explain computer theory; there are already plenty of theory books out there. Instead, this book is designed to be a hands-on desktop (or workbench) reference for PC repair, maintenance, and upgrading. This book concentrates on the symptoms and problem areas that occur in every area of the modern PC, as well as proper diagnosis of problems. Resources, glossaries, and problems to consider are included on the CD for almost every chapter making the book ideal for classroom or home study. The first edition proved to be extremely popular, but this second edition is packed with improvements, just a few of which are highlighted below:

■ This second edition greatly expands much of the troubleshooting and reference information throughout the original edition of the book, and adds 8 new chapters. There are over 1000 symptoms and solutions completely updated and revised (compared to just over 400 in the first edition). Many chapters have been rewritten, and all have been reviewed and revised.

■ Section 1 has been re-named "Getting Started," and chapters 1, 2, 3, 4, 5, and 7 from the first edition have been summarized and moved to the Companion CD area as "The Technician's Primer." This is located in the BOOKTEXT sub-directory. Students and readers interested in additional troubleshooting background information will find this material particularly useful.

■ Now, a "Student Workbook," composed of 3 to 5 questions and answers for each chapter, is included. This "Student Workbook" is located on the Companion CD in the BOOK-TEXT subdirectory as a Microsoft Word 7.0 .DOC file. Students and instructors alike will find great value in this "Student Workbook" for classroom or self-paced instruction.

■ Each chapter now includes a number of web addresses for further study. This should give the book an added value for classroom instruction and an aid to self-paced study.

■ The diagnostic diskette included with the first edition is now replaced with the DLS Diagnostic CD II that contains over 150 ready-to-go shareware diagnostics and utilities.

■ Original chapters 9, 23, and 43 have been reorganized into a new chapter 15 entitled "Error codes," which will make locating beep codes, POST codes, and diagnostic codes much easier.

This book is meant to be a lifeline and a resource to help you repair your PC, keep it running, and get the most out of it. More than 1000 PC problems are fully detailed and explained. There are references to hundreds more POST and diagnostic codes to help you identify even the most obscure problems. But the support you'll find here goes far beyond these book pages. You'll find an entire CD-ROM full of power-tools—shareware and freeware diagnostics and utilities designed to help you identify even the peskiest PC problems. This is one of the only PC hardware books to bundle so many diagnostic software products with the text.

Subscribe to *The PC Toolbox*

Many readers also complain that PC books suffer from a limited "life-span." All too often, a book is dated as soon as it is placed on bookstore shelves. You can avoid this kind of "technical obsolescence" by subscribing to our #1 newsletter; *The PC Toolbox*. Stay informed of the latest hands-on service articles, optimization techniques, and find the answers to your PC questions. Even if you don't fix computers for a living, a subscription can save you hundreds of dollars in shop costs. You can find the ad and order form for *The PC Toolbox* at the back of this book.

Test Your Knowledge

Worried about keeping yourself employable? Go for the Dynamic Learning Systems Technician's Certificate II. As the purchaser of this book, you can take the electronic DLS Technician's Examination included at the back of the book. Those readers that pass will receive a certificate showing your mastery of the material in this book. But the certificate is not just for framing—readers who successfully complete the examination are much better prepared to tackle the industry-recognized A+ examination, and even move on to acquire certification through the ETA (Electronic Technician's Association). The test file is contained on the accompanying CD.

I'm Interested in Your Success

I've taken a lot of time and effort to see that this edition is the most comprehensive and understandable book on PC/peripheral repair available. If you have any questions or comments about the book, please don't hesitate to contact me.

Contacting Dynamic Learning Systems

Whether you're an experienced technician, or just starting to tinker with your new PC, I am interested in your success. Every possible measure was taken to ensure a thorough and comprehensive book. Your comments, suggestions, and questions about this book are welcome at any time, as well as any troubleshooting experiences that you may wish to share. Feel free to write to me directly, or contact me through via e-mail. Be sure to check the book's FAQ section.

Dynamic Learning Systems
Attn: Stephen J. Bigelow
P.O. Box 282
Jefferson, MA 01522 USA
e-mail: sbigelow@cerfnet.com
web: http://www.dlspubs.com

FAQ:

"GETTING THE MOST FROM THIS BOOK"

General Book Information

Q. I have a question or comment about the book. How can I contact you?

A. We welcome any questions or comments regarding this book. Feel free to send an e-mail to: sbigelow@cerfnet.com. It might take a few days to respond, depending on our mail volume. If you'd prefer to contact us by mail, write to: Dynamic Learning Systems, P.O. Box 282, Jefferson, MA 01522 USA. Our fax number is 508-829-6819.

Q. Do you help folks troubleshoot their PCs? Do you offer any kind of technical or telephone support?

A. The answer to your question is "yes and no." Yes, we do welcome troubleshooting questions via e-mail at: sbigelow@cerfnet.com, by fax, or by mail (see "Contacting Dynamic Learning Systems"). However, we do not run a live tech support hotline. Inquiries are gladly answered, but only on a time-available basis; it might take several days or longer to research and formulate a reply (depending on our mail volume). As a result, we cannot provide emergency troubleshooting help or respond to immediate requests for advice. We reserve the right to refuse or reject inquiries at our discretion.

Q. What a long title! Just what is the difference between troubleshooting, maintaining, and repairing? Aren't they all the same?

A. No, they're not the same, but they're close; it's really a matter of semantics. "Troubleshooting" is really a process of determining the problem, "maintaining" is an on-going activity focusing on keeping the PC running smoothly, and "repairing" is the actual fixing of the problem.

Q. I see the terms "new," "more symptoms," and "updated" in the Contents at a Glance section. What do these terms mean for the book?

A. Although the entire book has been reviewed and enhanced, you should be aware of some notable sections. Chapters marked with "updated" have been substantially improved or rewritten with a great deal of additional information. Chapters marked "new" are completely new to this edition of the book. Chapters marked "more symptoms" have been tweaked as necessary, but contain a number of new symptoms.

Q. What new material does this book have that your first edition does not?

A. This edition of the book is a substantial improvement over the first one, with over 1000 symptoms and 150 shareware/freeware utilities. Many chapters have been expanded and updated, and a number of new chapters have been added. See the Contents at a Glance section.

Q. I see a lot of cryptic "http" and/or "www" references used at the ends of each chapter and in tables throughout the book. What are these designations, and how do I use them?

A. There are "universal resource locators" (or URLs) which point to Internet Web pages that contain extra details and information from manufacturers or organizations. You can usually "jump" from each site to other related sites as well, expanding your access to information over the Internet.

Q. What are the "glossary," "contacts," and "chapter questions" on the CD?

A. This edition of the book contains a comprehensive glossary, list of company contacts, and some challenging chapter questions. Unfortunately, there wasn't enough room in the book to publish all of this information, so we placed these sections on the companion CD.

Q. What is this "CD Technicians Primer" on the companion CD, and why isn't it in the book?

A. The "CD Technician's Primer" is actually the first few chapters of the first edition which was not included in the second edition because of space constraints. There was just too much new troubleshooting information in the second edition.

Q. Why are the glossary and chapter questions on the CD instead of in the book?

A. There just wasn't enough space in the book to include the glossary "CD Glossary" and chapter questions "CD Questions."

Q. I'm a college instructor and I want to use this book for my class. What resources do you have here for students and instructors?

A. A number of resources are available for students and instructors. Some text files are on the CD: a glossary, some questions (a student workbook), and a list of company contact addresses. The first few chapters from the first edition are included on CD as a "CD Technicians Primer." A number of topic-related Web sites are listed at the end of each chapter. We've updated the DLS Technician's Certificate II to 200 questions. The PC Toolbox is available to all subscribers, and you'll find MONITORS and PRINTERS utilities right on the Companion CD, along with over 150 other software utilities.

Q. I want to recommend this as the standard PC course textbook for my school, and we often plan lectures with excepts from the book. Do I need to request permissions each time we take an excerpt?

A. Qualified educational institutions which use the book must make a single request in writing using the institution's letterhead stating what you want to excerpt. You will get a prompt reply which entitles you to use excerpts from the book subject to the following limitations; you can't post excerpts online, you can't sell excerpts to students, and you can't distribute excerpts electronically (i.e., downloadable text files).

Using the Book Productively

Q. I've been trying to access a web site you listed in the book but I keep getting an error saying that there's "no such site" or that the Web browser can't connect. What good is that?

A. This is a fair complaint, but it is also a reality of today's Internet. Although we've made every effort to provide current contact information, it's not always possible to stay "up to the minute" with the fast and furious changes occurring on the Internet. Web sites appear, change URLs, and sometimes disappear with little or no warning. Unfortunately, little can be done about this issue, except to try cross-referencing the desired company or contact through a search engine, such as Yahoo, Alta Vista, or Excite.

Q. You said I could download a patch or update from a manufacturer's Web site, but I've been searching this web site for hours and I STILL can't find a trace of the patch or update. What can I do now?

A. Web sites are a mixed blessing; they can change dynamically with up-to-the-minute information, but needed information and important support resources can also disappear without a trace at the whim of a webmaster. If you cannot track down a patch or update file from a particular manufacturer's Web site, we can only suggest that you e-mail the webmaster or technical support department (there's almost always an e-mail link through a Web site) and inquire directly with them. They might direct you to the proper web page URL, another Web site, an FTP site, a BBS, or some other resource that may allow you to obtain the desired file.

Q. I want to certify my knowledge in PC technology and repair. What kind of certifications should I pursue?

A. Several options are available to new technicians; start by taking the DLS Technician's Certificate II (see the following section). This is an inexpensive and informal option for testing your troubleshooting knowledge. The next step up is the A+ exam, which is an industry-recognized certification that employers do look at when evaluating a new candidate. Also, you should seriously consider other prime industry certifications, such as ETA, as your career expands.

Q. I'm pretty new to PCs and I want to be sure that I don't mess up my system. How can I protect myself from making mistakes?

A. The best way to protect yourself from "messing up" your system is to make a complete backup of everything on the hard drive(s) before proceeding with a repair or upgrade.

Q. I use this book for a lot of troubleshooting, but is there any way to track down symptoms fast instead of paging through the entire book?

A. We've taken steps to simplify your reference of symptoms. See the "Symptoms at a Glance" section of the book.

Q. Is there any way to find topics quickly without wading through the Table of Contents?

A. We've taken steps to simplify your reference of the book's contents. See the "Contents at a Glance" section of the book.

Q.   Why aren't any anti-virus programs on the accompanying CD? There are so many.

A.   Although a great deal of anti-virus software is available, it often grows obsolete quickly. As a result, the decision was made to avoid anti-virus software on the companion CD. Instead, you'll find URLs pointing to a wealth of anti-virus shareware available for download, as well as links to major commercial anti-virus products. Hopefully, this will help you get the most from your anti-virus strategy.

The Book's Companion CD

Q.   What's on the CD?

A.   We've really pulled out all the stops to bring you a value-packed CD. It contains more than 150 programs for diagnostics and utilities, along with a glossary, contact list, and student workbook of questions and answers. It also includes a technician's primer with content from the first edition of the book (all supplemental text is contained in the BOOKTEXT subdirectory on the CD).

Q.   I don't understand how to install/use a particular software product. Can I call you for support?

A.   No! Aside from the MONITORS and PRINTERS utilities (which are Dynamic Learning Systems products), neither Dynamic Learning Systems nor McGraw-Hill can provide technical support for any of the software on the DLS Diagnostic CD II. If you have any questions about installing or using a piece of software which is not answered in the product's documentation, you must refer to the author of the particular software for support or product registration.

Q.   My DLS Diagnostic CD II is missing or damaged. Can I get another from you? How can I get another?

A.   McGraw-Hill is the publisher of the book and the CD. Dynamic Learning Systems does not provide warranty or replacement service for the CD. You'll need to return the book to your place of purchase for a new book/CD or contact McGraw-Hill's Customer Support department as instructed in the CD's warranty page at the rear of the book.

Q.   I've seen so much about computer viruses lately. How do I know that the programs and documents on the companion CD are virus-free?

A.   First, every program has been checked for viruses using current anti-virus software before being compressed and mastered to the companion CD. But don't take our word for it! Be sure to check all software (from any source) with a current virus checker before executing it for the first time. You can unzip a program without risk of infection, but be sure to check the decompressed files before launching the actual program.

Q.   How do I use the software on the CD?

A.   See Chapter 1 for general guidelines on installing a program to hard disk or floppy. If you still cannot get the program installed or running, you must refer to the respective program author.

Q.   I tried one of the programs from the CD on my system, but the program won't work. What's wrong?

A. It is possible that the particular utility you are using is not compatible with the PC you're using it on, or the combination of hardware installed in the PC. Try a different utility, or check with the program author to see if there is an update or patch which can help you overcome the problem.

Q. I'm so disappointed in the CD; there are few (if any) Windows 95 diagnostics. Why is everything DOS? DOS is dead, isn't it?

A. It's really a matter of philosophy. Windows 95 demands that much (really all) of the PC hardware be working in the first place; otherwise, Windows 95 won't even load. This would prevent you from loading Windows 95 utilities. DOS offers a simple and safe operating-system environment, which can run utilities while demanding an absolute minimum of system resources.

Q. Shareware costs money to register. You don't expect me to register everything that's on this CD do you?

A. Absolutely not! Shareware works on the "try before you buy" principle, so the idea is that you can use the software on your CD for a limited period of time to see if it works for you. If you choose to continue using the software (and want the benefits provided when you register the software), then you should consider registering the software. You may register as many or as few programs as you wish depending on your needs.

Q. I can't decompress the MONITORS and PRINTERS programs on the CD. Why not?

A. Unlike the other software on this CD, the MONITORS and PRINTERS utilities are not shareware. They are fully functional commercial software products that have been included on the CD, but have been encrypted. To use MONITORS or PRINTERS, you need to buy the "unlock code" from Dynamic Learning Systems at 508-829-6744 (see the order form at the back of the book).

The DLS Technician's Certificate II

Q. I want to take the A+ test. Will this exam help me to take the A+ exam successfully?

A. Yes. Although the DLS Technician's Certificate II exam is not a direct reflection of the A+ exam, we've received a great deal of positive feedback from readers who have taken the A+ exam after passing the DLS Technician's Certificate exam and found that the exam has made the A+ exam easier.

Q. What's the DLS Technician's Certificate II exam and why should I take it?

A. The DLS Technician's Certificate II is the next-generation exam from Dynamic Learning Systems, designed to aid PC enthusiasts and technicians in learning the issues involved in troubleshooting and maintenance. If you're serious about troubleshooting, consider taking the exam—especially as a "warm up" for the A+ exam. The exam is located on the accompanying CD.

Q. How much does it cost, and what do I get?

A. The A+ exam is a 200 question multiple choice troubleshooting test with a one-time processing fee of $35.00. If you fail the exam, you can retake it again as many times as necessary for no additional fee. When you pass the exam, you'll receive your graded test, along with a certificate suitable for framing.

Q. What if I fail the exam?

A. No problem, you'll get a new set of answer sheets, and you can try again until you pass. There are no additional fees to re-take the exam.

Q. What's different between the original exam and this one?

A. This second generation of the DLS Technician's Certificate exam uses 200 multiple-choice questions. Overall, the exam has been revised to keep pace with advances in PC technology.

Q. I've already taken the original DLS Technician's Certificate. Why should I take this test too?

A. You'll find that many new questions and issues are covered by the exam, which has been extensively updated to keep pace with the advances in PC technology. If you've already taken the exam from the original edition of the book, you can test your knowledge and keep it current for a very reasonable price.

The PC Toolbox Newsletter

Q. What is the newsletter all about? What does it cover?

A. *The PC Toolbox* newsletter is a semi-monthly (6 issues/year) newsletter focusing on troubleshooting all aspects of the PC and peripherals. You'll find this to be an exceptional supplement to the book.

Q. I'm interested in *The PC Toolbox* newsletter. Is there any way I can get a sample copy to look over before I choose to subscribe?

A. Yes, we're always pleased to send along a complementary copy for individual reviews. All we need is a brief request mailed, faxed, or e-mailed to Dynamic Learning Systems with your full name, mailing address, and daytime telephone number. Please, help us conserve resources by limiting your request to one per person. Remember that if you choose to subscribe, every subscription is backed by a 90-day unconditional money-back guarantee.

Q. I teach at a college/university, and I'm interested in purchasing a number of subscriptions for my class. Do you offer any discounts?

A. Yes, Dynamic Learning Systems can provide a quantity of newsletters to qualified educational organizations on either a "one-time" basis (for free), or on an ongoing basis (for a nominal charge). Submit your request on official institution letterhead via mail or fax. Be sure to indicate the desired quantity, shipping information, and your direct contact information. Dynamic Learning Systems will respond promptly with a quote.

Placing Orders with Dynamic Learning Systems

Q. I'm interested in ordering software or a subscription to *The PC Toolbox* newsletter, but I live outside of the U.S. What are the prices for international orders?

A.   The prices listed in this book are global. There are no surcharges or extra fees for orders placed from outside of the U.S. However, all payments must be in U.S. dollars (USD).

Q.   Do you take American Express?

A.   No, Dynamic Learning Systems only accepts Visa or MasterCard purchases at this time. If you do not have a credit card, you may mail your order form (see the order form in the back of the book) along with a check or money order made out to Dynamic Learning Systems.

Q.   How long does it take to receive my order(s)?

A.   It depends on how you order. Dynamic Learning Systems processes all orders within 48 hours and ships all newsletters and software via first-class mail (for domestic U.S. orders), or air mail (for all orders placed outside of the U.S.). The general delivery guidelines are below:

- Mail orders placed from within the U.S.   2 weeks
- Fax/phone orders placed from within the U.S.   1 week
- Mail orders placed within the western hemisphere   3 weeks
- Fax orders placed within the western hemisphere   2 weeks
- Mail orders placed from outside of the western hemisphere   4 weeks
- Fax orders placed from outside of the western hemisphere   3 weeks

Q.   I'm uncomfortable sending a check or money order for a lot of money. How do I know the order will get to you promptly?

A.   We get this question a lot—especially from customers outside of the U.S. If you have any question at all about your mail service to Dynamic Learning Systems, you should send the order as a "registered" letter (your local post office can assist you with this). This requires a signature from the DLS employee that receives the order and provides proof that the order was received.

LIST OF
FIGURES

Figure 1-1   A selection of PC enclosures. COMPUTER CASES DESIGNED AND MANUFACTURED BY OLSON METAL PRODUCTS, SEGUIN, TX

Figure 1-2   The layout of a typical desktop PC.

Figure 1-3   The layout of a typical tower PC.

Figure 1-4   An Olson Baby AT case. COMPUTER CASES DESIGNED AND MANUFACTURED BY OLSON METAL PRODUCTS, SEGUIN, TX

Figure 1-5   An Olson Slimline chassis. COMPUTER CASES DESIGNED AND MANUFACTURED BY OLSON METAL PRODUCTS, SEGUIN, TX

Figure 1-6   A modern motherboard assembly. INTEL CORPORATION

Figure 1-7   The front appearance of typical PC drives.

Figure 1-8   A comparison of typical video board layouts.

Figure 1-9   A typical SCSI controller board. COPYRIGHT 1995 FUTURE DOMAIN CORPORATION. REPRINTED WITH PERMISSION

Figure 1-10   A comparison of common communication ports.

Figure 1-11   The layout of a typical sound board.

Figure 1-12   The layout of a typical MPEG-2 decoder board.

Figure 1-13   The layout of a dual game-port board.

Figure 1-14   The layout of an ATX motherboard.

Figure 1-15   The layout of an ATX I/O port panel.

Figure 1-16   A comparison of full AT, baby AT, and ATX mounting.

Figure 1-17   The layout of an NLX motherboard.

Figure 1-18   A view of NLX riser, motherboard, and back panel.

Figure 2-1   A modern PC monitor. CTX INTERNATIONAL, INC.

Figure 2-2   Exploded diagram of a Tandy VGM220 monitor. TANDY CORPORATION

Figure 2-3   The diagram of a typical color CRT assembly.

Figure 2-4   The relationship of a shadow mask and color phosphors.

Figure 2-5   Basic on-screen monitor adjustments.

Figure 2-6   Advanced on-screen monitor adjustments.

Figure 2-7   Discharging an unpowered CRT before servicing.

Figure 3-1   A standard PC hierarchy.

Figure 3-2   A look inside the MSDOS.SYS file.

Figure 4-1   The universal troubleshooting procedure.

Figure 5-1   A Rayovac computer clock battery. COURTESY OF RAYOVAC CORPORATION

Figure 5-2   A cross section of a lithium coin cell.

Figure 5-3   A cross section of a NiCd battery.

Figure 5-4   Battery terminals for an IBM ThinkPad battery pack.

Figure 6-1   The main sections of a typical BIOS.

Figure 7-1   A Smart and Friendly CD-R 4006. COURTESY OF SMART AND FRIENDLY

Figure 7-2   A cross-sectional diagram of CD media.

Figure 7-3   A close-up view of a CD spiral track pattern.
Figure 7-4   Reading a typical compact disc.
Figure 7-5   The eight-to-fourteen modulation (EFM) technique in action.
Figure 7-6   An exploded diagram of a CD-ROM drive.
Figure 7-7   An exploded diagram of a CD "drive engine."
Figure 7-8   Underside view of a typical BC-7C assembly.
Figure 7-9   An electronics block diagram for a typical CD-ROM drive.

Figure 8-1   An Intel 440LX chipset. INTEL CORPORATION

Figure 10-1   The Windows 95 Device Manager.
Figure 10-2   Device properties highlighting the Device Usage.
Figure 10-3   Device properties highlighting Resource Settings.

Figure 11-1   An Intel Pentium II processor. INTEL CORPORATION
Figure 11-2   A diagram of a generic CPU.
Figure 11-3   A comparison of major CPU socket configurations.

Figure 12-1   A hard disk drive before and after compression.

Figure 13-1   A selection of drive adapter boards. COPYRIGHT © 1995 FUTURE DOMAIN CORPORATION.
                REPRINTED WITH PERMISSION
Figure 13-2   The connector layout for an ST506/412 drive.
Figure 13-3   The control cabling for an ST506/412 drive.
Figure 13-4   The connector layout for an IDE/EIDE drive.
Figure 13-5   The data and control cabling for an IDE/EIDE drive.

Figure 14-1   A DVD-ROM drive.
Figure 14-2   A comparison between DVD and CD data density.
Figure 14-3   The layers and sides in DVD discs.
Figure 14-4   A front view of a DVD-ROM drive.
Figure 14-5   A rear view of a DVD-ROM drive.
Figure 14-6   Looking into the top of a DVD drive.
Figure 14-7   Looking at the bottom of a DVD drive.
Figure 14-8   An MPEG-2 board for DVD video and audio playback.
Figure 14-9   The decoder board connections.
Figure 14-10   The DVD-ROM drive entry under the *Device manager*.
Figure 14-11   The DVD-ROM *Properties* dialog.

Figure 15-1   The POSTProbe from Micro2000. MICRO2000, INC.

Figure 16-1   An NEC FD1138H floppy drive. NEC TECHNOLOGIES, INC.
Figure 16-2   Flux transitions in floppy disks.
Figure 16-3   Floppy-drive recording principles.
Figure 16-4   An exploded diagram of a floppy-disk drive assembly. TEAC AMERICA, INC.
Figure 16-5   Underside view of a floppy-drive spindle-motor assembly. TEAC AMERICA, INC.
Figure 16-6   A typical floppy drive mail logic/interface board. TEAC AMERICA, INC.
Figure 16-7   A detailed view of a R/W head and stepping motor. TEAC AMERICA, INC.
Figure 16-8   A block diagram of a floppy drive.
Figure 16-9   A diagram of a standard 34-pin floppy-drive interface.
Figure 16-10   A DriveProbe screen display for automatic drive testing. ACCURITE TECHNOLOGIES, INC.

Figure 17-1   A contemporary hard-drive unit. NEC TECHNOLOGIES, INC.
Figure 17-2   A Maxtor hard drive. MAXTOR CORPORATION
Figure 17-3   Air-flow patterns in a hard drive. MAXTOR CORPORATION
Figure 17-4   A comparison between foreign objects on a hard-drive platter.
Figure 17-5   Data organization on a hard drive.
Figure 17-6   An example of cylinder skewing.

Figure 17-7   A typical hard-drive sector layout. MAXTOR CORPORATION
Figure 17-8   A cache control algorithm. MAXTOR CORPORATION
Figure 17-9   An exploded diagram of a Quantum hard drive. QUANTUM CORPORATION
Figure 17-10   A close-up view of a head actuator assembly. MAXTOR CORPORATION
Figure 17-11   A block diagram of a high-performance Quantum drive system. QUANTUM CORPORATION

Figure 18-1   A diagram of 8-bit and 16-bit ISA slots.
Figure 18-2   A diagram of a 32-bit EISA slot.

Figure 19-1   A general-purpose analog joystick. SUNCOM TECHNOLOGIES
Figure 19-2   Simplified diagram of a game-port system.
Figure 19-3   Wiring diagram for a dual joystick port.
Figure 19-4   A typical "Nintendo-style" digital joystick.
Figure 19-5   A simple "joystick eliminator" plug for game-port testing.

Figure 20-1   A Cherry G83-3000 keyboard. CHERRY ELECTRICAL PRODUCTS
Figure 20-2   A mechanical switch assembly.
Figure 20-3   A membrane switch assembly.
Figure 20-4   A simplified diagram of a keyboard matrix.
Figure 20-5   Keyboard interface connectors.
Figure 20-6   QWERTY vs. Dvorak keyboards.
Figure 20-7   A Curtis anti-static keyboard mat. CURTIS, A DIVISION OF ROLODEX, SECAUCUS, NJ 07094

Figure 21-1   A cross section of an HP LaserJet-type printer. HEWLETT-PACKARD COMPANY
Figure 21-2   Cleaning an EP drum.
Figure 21-3   Erasing all charges from an EP drum.
Figure 21-4   Placing a uniform charge on the EP drum.
Figure 21-5   Developing the latent drum image with toner.
Figure 21-6   Transferring the developed image to paper.
Figure 21-7   Fusing the toner image to the page.
Figure 21-8   A simplified diagram of a generic writing mechanism.
Figure 21-9   A LaserJet-type laser scanning assembly.
Figure 21-10   An exploded view of an HP EP cartridge. HEWLETT-PACKARD COMPANY
Figure 21-11   Diagram of an EP main controller board. TANDY CORPORATION
Figure 21-12   Recognizing main controller board faults.
Figure 21-13   A diagram of an EP mechanical controller board. TANDY CORPORATION
Figure 21-14   Recognizing pickup/registration faults.
Figure 21-15   Writing with a laser beam. TANDY CORPORATION
Figure 21-16   Recognizing laser/scanner faults.
Figure 21-17   An EP mechanical system. TANDY CORPORATION
Figure 21-18   Recognizing drive or transmission problems.
Figure 21-19   Recognizing high-voltage power-supply problems.
Figure 21-20   The fusing-unit temperature control loop.
Figure 21-21   Recognizing fusing system faults.
Figure 21-22   Recognizing a corona or charge roller fault.
Figure 21-23   Paper-tray ID switch system.
Figure 21-24   The operation of a paper sensing arm.
Figure 21-25   The operation of a low-toner sensor.
Figure 21-26   Recognizing miscellaneous faults.

Figure 22-1   The various elements of an MCA bus.

Figure 23-1   Simplified diagram of a memory array.
Figure 23-2   A diagram of a typical memory IC.
Figure 23-3   A comparison of SIMMs and DIMMs.
Figure 23-4   Conventional and upper memory in a typical PC.
Figure 23-5   Major cache system components.
Figure 23-6   The SIMCHECK main unit. INNOVENTIONS, INC.

Figure 23-7   The SIMCHECK PS/2 SIMM adapter. INNOVENTIONS, INC.
Figure 23-8   The SIMCHECK Static RAM unit. INNOVENTIONS, INC.

Figure 24-1   A simple, but inefficient, CONFIG.SYS file.
Figure 24-2   A reasonably optimized CONFIG.SYS file.
Figure 24-3   A typical AUTOEXEC.BAT file using the LOADHIGH command.
Figure 24-4   A breakdown of memory utilization using the DOS MEM /C function.
Figure 24-5   The *Advanced program settings* dialog.

Figure 25-1   A Logitech MouseMan. LOGITECH, INC.
Figure 25-2   The internal construction of a basic mouse.
Figure 25-3   The Crystal Mouse from Suncom Technologies. SUNCOM TECHNOLOGIES
Figure 25-4   The sensor layout for an opto-mechanical mouse or trackball.
Figure 25-5   A Curtis mouse cleaning kit. CURTIS, A DIVISION OF ROLODEX, SECACUS, NJ 07094
Figure 25-6   Controlling the Windows 95 MouseKeys feature.
Figure 25-7   Configuring MouseKeys operation.

Figure 26-1   A block diagram of an internal modem.
Figure 26-2   A block diagram of an external modem.
Figure 26-3   Testing the command processor in the terminal window.

Figure 27-1   A CTX EX910 color monitor. CTX INTERNATIONAL, INC.
Figure 27-2   Arranging color phosphors in a triad.
Figure 27-3   The importance of convergence in a color monitor.
Figure 27-4   The effects of pincushion and barrel distortion.
Figure 27-5   Forming a screen image on a CRT.
Figure 27-6   Interlaced vs. non-interlaced scanning.
Figure 27-7   Block diagram of a color (VGA) monitor.
Figure 27-8   The schematic of a VGM-220 video circuit. TANDY CORPORATION
Figure 27-9   The schematic of a VGM-220 main (raster) circuit. TANDY CORPORATION
Figure 27-10   A wiring diagram for the VGM-220. TANDY CORPORATION
Figure 27-11   A cross section of a color CRT.

Figure 28-1   The motherboard assembly for a Tandy 1500HD laptop. TANDY CORPORATION
Figure 28-2   The AMI Atlas PCI motherboard. AMERICAN MEGATRENDS, INC.
Figure 28-3   An Intel ATX Slot 1 motherboard. INTEL CORPORATION
Figure 28-4   An Intel NLX Slot 1 motherboard. INTEL CORPORATION
Figure 28-5   An Intel PD440FX motherboard layout. INTEL CORPORATION
Figure 28-6   The connector pinouts of an Intel PD440FX motherboard. INTEL CORPORATION
Figure 28-7   The connector layout of a typical ATX back panel.
Figure 28-8   Front-panel header layout for a typical ATX motherboard.

Figure 30-1   The basic block diagram of an AGP implementation.
Figure 30-2   The block diagram of an APM configuration.
Figure 30-3   The block diagram of an SMBus/smart battery system.
Figure 30-4   A typical USB port layout.

Figure 31-1   The block diagram of a bi-directional parallel port.
Figure 31-2   A typical parallel-cable assembly.
Figure 31-3   A typical parallel-port timing diagram.

Figure 32-1   A PC card SCSI adapter for mobile computers. COPYRIGHT 1995 FUTURE DOMAIN CORPO-
          RATION. REPRINTED WITH PERMISSION
Figure 32-2   Basic PC card dimensions.
Figure 32-3   Simplified PC card architecture.
Figure 32-4   A commercial PC card drive for desktop or tower PCs. QUATECH
Figure 32-5   A comparison of PC card thicknesses.
Figure 32-6   An internal view of the PC card ATA drive. MAXTOR CORPORATION

Figure 32-7   A PCMCIA header diagram.
Figure 32-8   Typical PC-card connector products. AMP INC.

Figure 33-1   PCI local bus diagrams.

Figure 34-1   A popular pen-based tablet. ACECAD
Figure 34-2   A popular touchpad assembly. CIRQUE
Figure 34-3   A single-layer resistive digitizer.
Figure 34-4   A dual-layer resistive digitizer.
Figure 34-5   A capacitive (electrostatic) digitizer.
Figure 34-6   An electromagnetic (RF) digitizer.
Figure 34-7   A comparison of typical pen gestures.

Figure 36-1   A block diagram of a switching power supply.
Figure 36-2   A simplified diagram of a switching power supply.
Figure 36-3   A simplified schematic of an IC-based switching power supply.
Figure 36-4   AT-style motherboard power connections.
Figure 36-5   An ATX/NLX-style motherboard power connector.
Figure 36-6   An optional ATX/NLX motherboard power connector.
Figure 36-7   A complete IC-based switching power supply.

Figure 37-1   Locating the LCD backlight inverter.
Figure 37-2   A basic backlight inverter circuit.
Figure 37-3   A high-voltage schematic fragment from Tandy VGM-220 monitor. TANDY CORPORA-TION

Figure 39-1   SCSI adapter boards. COPYRIGHT © 1995 FUTURE DOMAIN CORPORATION. REPRINTED WITH PERMISSION
Figure 39-2   Terminating an internal SCSI adapter and hard drive.
Figure 39-3   Terminating an internal SCSI adapter, HDD, and CD-ROM.
Figure 39-4   Terminating an external SCSI device.
Figure 39-5   Terminating mixed internal and external SCSI devices.

Figure 40-1   A typical data frame.
Figure 40-2   The block diagram of a UART.
Figure 40-3   Serial-port connectors.

Figure 41-1   A Logitech SoundMan Wave sound board. COPYRIGHT © 1995 LOGITECH CORPORATION
Figure 41-2   The sound-board recording process.
Figure 41-3   The sound-board playback process.
Figure 41-4   The concept of "sampling rate."
Figure 41-5   The path of MIDI signals through the PC.
Figure 41-6   The simplified block diagram of a sound board.
Figure 41-7   A sample sound-board frequency-response curve.
Figure 41-8   The *Audio* tab under the *Multimedia properties* dialog.
Figure 41-9   The multimedia *Volume control* applet.

Figure 42-1   Typical internal and external tape drives. COPYRIGHT © 1995 MOUNTAIN NETWORK SOLU-TIONS, INC.
Figure 42-2   A typical tape minicartridge.
Figure 42-3   A typical QIC tape cartridge.
Figure 42-4   The helical-scan tape configuration.
Figure 42-5   The concept of azimuth angle.
Figure 42-6   An example of a helical-scan tape path.
Figure 42-7   An exploded diagram of a Teac tape drive. TEAC AMERICA, INC.
Figure 42-8   A block diagram of a Teac tape drive. TEAC AMERICA, INC.
Figure 42-9   Manually cleaning a tape drive.
Figure 42-10   A carriage view of a Teac tape drive. TEAC AMERICA, INC.

Figure 42-11   An underside view of a tape-drive mechanism. TEAC AMERICA, INC.
Figure 42-12   A Teac tape drive with drive motors removed. TEAC AMERICA, INC.
Figure 42-13   A close-up view of a carriage load/unload mechanism. TEAC AMERICA, INC.

Figure 43-1   A typical video-adapter board.
Figure 43-2   The block diagram of a frame buffer video adapter.
Figure 43-3   The pinout of an MDA video connector.
Figure 43-4   The pinout of a CGA video connector.
Figure 43-5   The pinout of an EGA video connector.
Figure 43-6   The pinout of a VGA/MCGA/SVGA video connector.
Figure 43-7   A typical video accelerator board.
Figure 43-8   The block diagram of a video accelerator board.
Figure 43-9   A typical video-feature connector.

Figure 44-1   A typical PC-TV/video-capture board. INTEL CORPORATION
Figure 44-2   A block diagram of an integrated video capture/VGA board.
Figure 44-3   Typical video-capture board connections.
Figure 44-4   The audio/video capture and playback map.
Figure 44-5   A typical PC-TV board.
Figure 44-6   Locating *PCI to ISA bridge* in the *Device manager*.

Figure 46-1   A simplified drawing of a VL card and bus.

Figure 47-1   A Teac FD-235 3.5" floppy drive. TEAC AMERICA, INC.
Figure 47-2   The DriveProbe automatic drive test display. ACCURITE TECHNOLOGIES, INC.
Figure 47-3   DriveProbe: the advanced edition. ACCURITE TECHNOLOGIES, INC.
Figure 47-4   The screen display from a DriveProbe eccentricity test. ACCURITE TECHNOLOGIES, INC.
Figure 47-5   The screen display from a DriveProbe motor speed test. ACCURITE TECHNOLOGIES, INC.
Figure 47-6   The screen display from a DriveProbe radial alignment test. ACCURITE TECHNOLOGIES, INC.
Figure 47-7   The screen display from a DriveProbe azimuth alignment test. ACCURITE TECHNOLOGIES, INC.
Figure 47-8   The screen display from a DriveProbe index-to-data test. ACCURITE TECHNOLOGIES, INC.
Figure 47-9   The screen display from a DriveProbe hysteresis test. ACCURITE TECHNOLOGIES, INC.
Figure 47-10   The screen display from a DriveProbe head-width test. ACCURITE TECHNOLOGIES, INC.

Figure 48-1   Mark a starting point before starting an adjustment.
Figure 48-2   A typical main PC board for a monitor.
Figure 48-3   A high-voltage regulation test pattern.
Figure 48-4   The screen focus test pattern.
Figure 48-5   The phase test pattern.
Figure 48-6   The linearity test pattern.
Figure 48-7   A typical convergence ring assembly.
Figure 48-8   Calibrating dynamic convergence.
Figure 48-9   Typical locations of color banding (color distortion).

Figure 49-1   Manually cleaning a floppy drive.

LIST OF

TABLES

Table 1-1   Typical video resolution and pixel depth.

Table 3-1   A partial listing of contemporary operating systems.
Table 3-2   A comparison of system requirements for major operating systems.
Table 3-3   An index of external/transient MS-DOS commands.
Table 3-4   An index of internal/resident MS-DOS commands.

Table 4-1   An index of computer benchmarks.
Table 4-2   The pinouts of ATX and Baby AT power connectors.

Table 5-1   A comparison of mobile battery features.
Table 5-2   Status indicators for an IBM ThinkPad computer.

Table 6-1   A summary of BIOS services.
Table 6-2   Award EliteBIOS features.
Table 6-3   Microid Research Mr. BIOS features.

Table 7-1   A sample of eight-to-fourteen modulation codes.
Table 7-2   The data transfer rates for CD-ROM drives.
Table 7-3   MSCDEX command-line switches.

Table 8-1   Detailed chipset manuals and technical information.
Table 8-2   A summary of motherboard chipset components.
Table 8-3   AMD-640 chipset features at a glance.
Table 8-4   Intel Pentium/MMX chipset features at a glance.
Table 8-5   Intel Pentium Pro/II chipset features at a glance.
Table 8-6   Intel Pentium II chipset features at a glance.
Table 8-7   VIA Apollo P6 chipset features at a glance.
Table 8-8   VIA Apollo VP3 chipset features at a glance.
Table 8-9   VIA Apollo VP2 chipset features at a glance.
Table 8-10   VIA Apollo VPX/97 chipset features at a glance.
Table 8-11   VIA Apollo VP-1 chipset features at a glance.
Table 8-12   VIA Apollo Master chipset features at a glance.
Table 8-13   SiS5597 chipset features at a glance.
Table 8-14   SiS5596 chipset features at a glance.
Table 8-15   SiS5571 chipset features at a glance.
Table 8-16   SiS551X chipset features at a glance.
Table 8-17   SiS85C49X chipset features at a glance.
Table 8-18   A brief listing of legacy and support ICs.

Table 9-1   A typical CMOS RAM map.
Table 9-2   Typical CMOS setup key sequences.
Table 9-3   A list of CMOS RAM/RTC power pins.

Table 10-1   XT and AT interrupt assignments.
Table 10-2   XT and AT DMA assignments.
Table 10-3   XT/AT I/O port addresses.
Table 10-4   I/O port variations for PS/2 systems.
Table 10-5   Modern AT I/O assignments.
Table 10-6   Modern Pentium PC memory map.
Table 10-7   Typical device assignments.

Table 11-1   Historical index of PC CPUs and MCPs.
Table 11-2   Compatibility details for major CPU sockets.
Table 11-3   Comparison of commercial PC CPUs.
Table 11-4   Comparison of Pentium performance ratings.
Table 11-5   Detailed CPU manuals and technical information.
Table 11-6   S-spec numbers for Pentium and Pentium MMX processors.
Table 11-7   Comparison of Pentium Pro performance ratings.
Table 11-8   S-spec numbers for Pentium Pro processors.
Table 11-9   Comparison of Pentium II performance ratings.
Table 11-10   S-spec numbers for Pentium II processors.
Table 11-11   Comparison of AMD K5 performance ratings.
Table 11-12   Clock settings for the Cyrix 6x86 family.
Table 11-13   Generic 486 overclocking suggestions.
Table 11-14   Generic Pentium/6x86 overclocking suggestions.
Table 11-15   Pentium overclocking options.
Table 11-16   Pentium Pro overclocking options.

Table 12-1   Typical compression ratios.
Table 12-2   DoubleSpace file versions with and without Microsoft Plus!
Table 12-3   Programs known to interfere with CVF operation.
Table 12-4   Disabling all device drivers, except for STACKER.COM and SWAP.COM.
Table 12-5   Typical STACVOL header sizes.

Table 13-1   The pinout for an ST506/412 control cable.
Table 13-2   The pinout for an ST506/412 data cable.
Table 13-3   The pinout for an ESDI control cable.
Table 13-4   The pinout for an ESDI data cable.
Table 13-5   The pinout for an IDE/EIDE signal cable.
Table 13-6   The pinout for an IDE XT-type signal cable.
Table 13-7   CHS values vs. drive size.
Table 13-8   PIO and DMA data transfer modes.

Table 14-1   CD technology timeline.
Table 14-2   Specifications of DVD and CD media.
Table 14-3   DVD region codes.

Table 15-1   IBM diagnostic codes.
Table 15-2   AMI beep codes.
Table 15-3   AST beep codes.
Table 15-4   Compaq beep codes.
Table 15-5   IBM desktop beep codes.
Table 15-6   IBM ThinkPad beep codes.
Table 15-7   Mylex beep codes.
Table 15-8   Mylex 386 beep codes.
Table 15-9   Phoenix Beep Codes for ISA/MCA/EISA POST.
Table 15-10   Quadtel beep codes.
Table 15-11   POST codes for ACER BIOS.
Table 15-12   POST codes for ALR BIOS.
Table 15-13   POST codes for AMI BIOS (prior to April 1990).
Table 15-14   POST codes for AMI BIOS (after April 1990).
Table 15-15   POST codes for AMI BIOS version 2.2x.

Table 15-16   POST codes for AMI PLUS BIOS.
Table 15-17   POST codes for AMI Color BIOS.
Table 15-18   POST codes for AMI EZ-Flex BIOS.
Table 15-19   POST codes for Arche Legacy BIOS.
Table 15-20   POST codes for AST BIOS.
Table 15-21   POST codes for AT&T BIOS.
Table 15-22   POST codes for Award XT BIOS.
Table 15-23   POST codes for Award XT BIOS version 3.1.
Table 15-24   POST codes for Award AT BIOS version 3.0.
Table 15-25   POST codes for Award AT BIOS version 3.1.
Table 15-26   POST codes for Award AT BIOS version 3.3.
Table 15-27   POST codes for Award AT/EISA BIOS version 4.0.
Table 15-28   POST codes for Award EISA BIOS.
Table 15-29   POST codes for Award Plug-and-Play BIOS.
Table 15-30   POST codes for Award EliteBIOS 4.5x.
Table 15-31   POST codes for Chips & Technologies BIOS.
Table 15-32   POST codes for general Compaq BIOS.
Table 15-33   POST codes for Compaq i286 Deskpro BIOS.
Table 15-34   POST codes for Compaq i386 Deskpro BIOS.
Table 15-35   POST codes for Compaq i486 Deskpro BIOS.
Table 15-36   POST codes for Compaq Video BIOS.
Table 15-37   POST codes for Dell BIOS.
Table 15-38   POST codes for DTK BIOS.
Table 15-39   POST codes for Eurosoft/Mylex BIOS.
Table 15-40   POST codes for Eurosoft 4.71 BIOS.
Table 15-41   POST codes for Mylex BIOS.
Table 15-42   POST codes for Faraday A-Tease BIOS.
Table 15-43   POST codes for IBM XT BIOS.
Table 15-44   POST codes for IBM AT BIOS.
Table 15-45   POST codes for IBM PS/2 BIOS.
Table 15-46   POST codes for Landmark JumpStart XT BIOS.
Table 15-47   POST codes for Landmark JumpStart AT BIOS.
Table 15-48   POST codes for Landmark SuperSoft AT BIOS.
Table 15-49   POST codes for Microid Research BIOS 1.0A.
Table 15-50   POST and beep codes for contemporary Microid Research BIOS.
Table 15-51   POST codes for Microid Research 3.4x BIOS.
Table 15-52   POST codes for NCR PC6 (XT) BIOS.
Table 15-53   POST codes for NCR AT BIOS.
Table 15-54   POST codes for NCR PC916 BIOS.
Table 15-55   POST codes for Olivetti 1076/AT&T BIOS.
Table 15-56   POST codes for Olivetti M20 BIOS.
Table 15-57   POST codes for Olivetti M24/AT&T BIOS.
Table 15-58   POST codes for Olivetti PS/2 BIOS.
Table 15-59   POST codes for Philips BIOS.
Table 15-60   POST codes for Phoenix Technologies XT 2.52 BIOS.
Table 15-61   POST codes for Phoenix Technologies ISA/EISA/MCA BIOS.
Table 15-62   POST codes for PhoenixBIOS 4.0.
Table 15-63   POST codes for Quadtel XT BIOS.
Table 15-64   POST codes for Quadtel AT 3.00 BIOS.
Table 15-65   POST codes for Tandon Type A BIOS.
Table 15-66   POST codes for Tandon Type B BIOS.
Table 15-67   POST codes for Tandon i486 EISA BIOS.
Table 15-68   POST codes for Zenith Orion 4.1E BIOS.

Table 16-1   A comparison of floppy-disk drive specifications.

Table 17-1   A comparison of drive parameters vs. capacity.
Table 17-2   Typical reported drive capacities.
Table 17-3   Data transfer speeds vs. PIO modes.

Table 17-4   Data transfer speeds vs. DMA modes.
Table 17-5   A comparison between form factor and actual drive dimensions.
Table 17-6   Partition size vs. cluster size for FAT 16 partitions.
Table 17-7   Partition size vs. cluster size for FAT 32 partitions.
Table 17-8   Possible CMOS workarounds for huge hard drives.
Table 17-9   Common HDD controller error codes.
Table 17-10   Typical DEBUG command strings for LL formatting.

Table 18-1   The ISA 8-bit (XT) bus pinout.
Table 18-2   The ISA 16-bit (AT) bus pinout.
Table 18-3   The EISA 16/32-bit bus pinout.

Table 19-1   The pinout for a standard joystick port.
Table 19-2   The pinout for a joystick Y adapter.
Table 19-3   The pinout for an Amiga-type game pad.
Table 19-4   The pinout for a sound-board joystick cable adapter.
Table 19-5   The pinout for a sound-board compatible joystick Y adapter.

Table 20-1   Standard scan codes for U.S. keyboards.

Table 21-1   An index of printer manufacturers.
Table 21-2   HP LaserJet family messages and error codes.
Table 21-3   Typical tray switch configurations.

Table 22-1   MCA 16-bit bus pinout.
Table 22-2   MCA 32-bit bus pinout.
Table 22-3   PS/2 reference and diagnostic disk FTP addresses.

Table 23-1   The pinout of a standard 30-pin SIMM.
Table 23-2   The pinout of a standard 72-pin SIMM.
Table 23-3   The pinout of a 72-pin ECC SIMM.
Table 23-4   The pinout for an older 144-pin small-outline (SO) DIMM.
Table 23-5   The pinout of a 168-pin unbuffered DRAM DIMM.
Table 23-6   The pinout of a 168-pin unbuffered SDRAM DIMM.
Table 23-7   72-pin SIMM identification guidelines.
Table 23-8   Real-mode memory map of a typical PC.
Table 23-9   CPUs, wait states, and memory speed.
Table 23-10   Index of presence detect (PD) signals.
Table 23-11   CPUs vs. memory bank size.
Table 23-12   Memory combinations for a typical motherboard.
Table 23-13   Index of IBM PC/XT error codes.
Table 23-14   200-series error codes.
Table 23-15   Classic AT error codes.

Table 24-1   Syntax and command-line switches for HIMEM.
Table 24-2   Syntax and command-line switches for EMM386.
Table 24-3   Version designations for EMM386.
Table 24-4   Protected-mode exception errors for EMM386.

Table 25-1   The pinout of a serial mouse port (Logitech).
Table 25-2   The pinout of a bus mouse port (Logitech).
Table 25-3   The pinout of a PS/2 mouse port (Logitech).
Table 25-4   Command-line switches for Microsoft mouse driver 9.0x.

Table 26-1   The index of the AT command set.
Table 26-2   The list of typical modem result codes.
Table 26-3   An index of S-register assignments.
Table 26-4   An index of modem initialization strings.

Table 26-5   Connect sequences for V.22bis and V.32 modems.
Table 26-6   A comparison of popular UARTs.

Table 27-1   Scan rates vs. monitor resolution.
Table 27-2   Typical CRT pin designations.

Table 28-1   A CD-ROM audio connector pinout.
Table 28-2   Telephony connector pinouts.
Table 28-3   Wavetable connector pinout.
Table 28-4   Line-in connector pinout.
Table 28-5   ATX power connector pinout.
Table 28-6   GP I/O connector pinout.
Table 28-7   Front-panel header assignments.
Table 28-8   Yamaha wavetable module connector pinouts.

Table 30-1   The pinout for an AGP slot.
Table 30-2   APM system conditions.

Table 31-1   The pinouts for a Centronics-type parallel cable.

Table 32-1   Typical function ID entries for CISTPL_FUNCID.
Table 32-2   Pin assignments for PC card and CardBus interfaces.
Table 32-3   DOS PC card drivers.
Table 32-4   Windows PC card drivers.
Table 32-5   PC card software vs. application.

Table 33-1   Features of a PCI bus architecture.
Table 33-2   PCI bus pinout: 5 volt and 3.3 volt (Rev. 2.0)

Table 35-1   Microsoft PnP device identification codes.

Table 38-1   A listing of native Iomega ASPI drivers.
Table 38-2   Command-line options for ASPIPPA3.SYS.
Table 38-3   ASPIPPA3.SYS error messages.
Table 38-4   SyQuest error codes for SQ555, SQ5110C, and 5200C drives.

Table 39-1   A comparison of SCSI variations.
Table 39-2   The pinout of a standard single-ended A cable.
Table 39-3   The pinout of a standard differential A cable.
Table 39-4   The pinout of a standard single-ended P cable.
Table 39-5   The pinout of a standard differential P cable.

Table 40-1   Typical serial port addresses and IRQ assignments.
Table 40-2   Typical UART register address offsets.
Table 40-3   Serial-port connector pinouts (at the PC end).

Table 42-1   QIC standards for full-size cartridges.
Table 42-2   QIC standards for minicartridges.
Table 42-3   QIC tape compatibility.
Table 42-4   Travan tape specifications.
Table 42-5   An index of SCSI tape-drive sense codes.
Table 42-6   An index of media and hardware error-sense codes.

Table 43-1   An index of video modes.
Table 43-2   A listing of popular 2D and 3D video chipsets.
Table 43-3   The pinout for a video-feature connector.
Table 43-4   AMI multimedia channel pinout (standard VFC mode).
Table 43-5   AMI multimedia channel pinout (DVS mode).

Table 43-6   AMI multimedia channel pinout (MDP mode).

Table 43-7   AMI multimedia channel pinout (MPP mode).

Table 44-1   Altering memory allocation for a PC-TV board.

Table 45-1   Activation dates of many known computer viruses.

Table 46-1   VL bus pinout (Rev. 2.0).

Table 48-1   Typical backup power capacities.

Table 49-1   A summary of PC preventative maintenance periods.

SYMPTOMS
AT A GLANCE

Symptom	Description	Chapter	Page
none	*C000 ROM error*	3	66
none	*Video ROM error*	3	66
none	*XXXX ROM error*	3	66
none	*Diskette boot record error*	3	67
none	*Non-system disk or disk error*	3	67
none	*Disk boot failure*	3	67
none	*No boot device available*	3	67
none	*ROM BASIC error*	3	67
none	*Invalid partition table*	3	67
none	*Error loading operating system*	3	67
none	*Missing operating system*	3	68
Symptom 4-1	*There is no power light, and you cannot hear any cooling fan*	4	84
Symptom 4-2	*There is no power light, but you hear the cooling fan running*	4	84
Symptom 4-3	*The power light is on, but there is no apparent system activity*	4	84
Symptom 4-4	*The power light is on, but you hear two or more beeps*	4	86
Symptom 4-5	*The power light is on, but the system hangs during initialization*	4	86
Symptom 4-6	*You see a message indicating a CMOS setup problem*	4	86
Symptom 4-7	*You see no drive light activity*	4	86
Symptom 4-8	*The drive light remains on continuously*	4	87
Symptom 4-9	*You see normal system activity, but there is no video*	4	87
Symptom 4-10	*The system randomly crashes/reboots for no apparent reason*	4	87
Symptom 4-11	*The system fails to boot, freezes during boot, or freezes during operation for no apparent reason*	4	88
Symptom 4-12	*The system fails to recognize its upgrade device*	4	88
Symptom 4-13	*One or more applications ail to function as expected after an upgrade*	4	89
Symptom 4-14	*The Windows 95 boot drive is no longer bootable after restoring data with the DOS backup utility*	4	89
Symptom 4-15	*Windows 95 will not boot and ScanDisk reports bad clusters that it cannot repair*	4	89
Symptom 4-16	*You see a "Bad or missing <filename>" error on startup*	4	90

Symptom	Description	Chapter	Page
Symptom 4-17	*Windows 95 reports damaged or missing files, or a "VxD error"*	4	90
Symptom 4-18	*After installing Windows 95, you can't boot from a different drive*	4	90
Symptom 4-19	*Windows 95 Registry files are missing*	4	90
Symptom 4-20	*During the Windows 95 boot, I get an "Invalid System Disk" error*	4	91
Symptom 4-21	*Windows 95 will not install on a compressed drive*	4	91
Symptom 4-22	*The drive indicates that it is in "MS-DOS compatibility mode"*	4	91
Symptom 4-23	*Disabling protected-mode disk driver(s), hides the partition table when FDISK is used*	4	92
Symptom 4-24	*You cannot achieve 32-bit disk access under Windows 95*	4	92
Symptom 4-25	*Windows 95 does not recognize a new device*	4	92
Symptom 4-26	*Windows 95 malfunctions when installed over Disk Manager*	4	92
Symptom 4-27	*You have problems using a manufacturer-specific hard-disk driver (such as Western Digital's FastTrack driver WDCDRV.386) for 32-bit access under Windows 95*	4	92
Symptom 5-1	*You see an error such as: "System hardware does not match CMOS configuration"*	5	101
Symptom 5-2	*You notice corrosion from the CMOS battery on the battery holder and motherboard*	5	101
Symptom 5-3	*The system configuration is lost intermittently*	5	101
Symptom 5-4	*The backup battery goes dead frequently*	5	102
Symptom 5-5	*You see a "161" error or a message that indicates that the system battery is dead*	5	102
Symptom 5-6	*The battery pack does not charge*	5	107
Symptom 5-7	*The system does not run on battery power, but runs properly from main (ac) power*	5	108
Symptom 5-8	*The system suffers from a short battery life*	5	108
Symptom 5-9	*The battery pack becomes extremely hot during charging*	5	109
Symptom 5-10	*The computer quits without producing a low-battery warning*	5	109
Symptom 6-1	*8042 Gate—A20 error*	6	128
Symptom 6-2	*BIOS ROM checksum error—system halted*	6	128
Symptom 6-3	*Cache memory bad, do not enable cache*	6	128
Symptom 6-4	*CMOS battery failed*	6	128
Symptom 6-5	*CMOS battery state low*	6	129
Symptom 6-6	*CMOS checksum error—defaults loaded*	6	129
Symptom 6-7	*CMOS display type mismatch*	6	129
Symptom 6-8	*CMOS memory size mismatch*	6	129
Symptom 6-9	*CMOS system options not set*	6	129
Symptom 6-10	*CPU at nnn*	6	129
Symptom 6-11	*Data error*	6	129
Symptom 6-12	*Decreasing available memory*	6	129

Symptom	Description	Chapter	Page
Symptom 6-13	*Diskette drive 0 (or 1) seek failure*	6	129
Symptom 6-14	*Diskette read failure*	6	129
Symptom 6-15	*Diskette subsystem reset failed*	6	130
Symptom 6-16	*Display switch is set incorrectly*	6	130
Symptom 6-17	*DMA (or DMA #1 or DMA #2) error*	6	130
Symptom 6-18	*DMA bus time-out*	6	130
Symptom 6-19	*Drive not ready*	6	130
Symptom 6-20	*Floppy disk(s) fail*	6	130
Symptom 6-21	*Hard-disk configuration error*	6	130
Symptom 6-22	*Hard-disk controller failure*	6	130
Symptom 6-23	*Hard-disk(s) diagnosis fail*	6	130
Symptom 6-24	*Hard-disk failure*	6	131
Symptom 6-25	*Hard-disk drive-read failure*	6	131
Symptom 6-26	*Incompatible processors: CPU0 (or CPU1) is B0 step or below*	6	131
Symptom 6-27	*Incompatible processors: cache sizes different*	6	131
Symptom 6-28	*Insert bootable media*	6	131
Symptom 6-29	*INTR #1 (or INTR #2) error*	6	131
Symptom 6-30	*Invalid boot diskette*	6	131
Symptom 6-31	*Invalid configuration information—please run SETUP program*	6	131
Symptom 6-32	*I/O card parity error at xxxxx*	6	131
Symptom 6-33	*Keyboard clock-line failure*	6	131
Symptom 6-34	*Keyboard controller failure*	6	132
Symptom 6-35	*Keyboard data-line failure*	6	132
Symptom 6-36	*Keyboard error or no keyboard present*	6	132
Symptom 6-37	*Keyboard is locked out—unlock the key*	6	132
Symptom 6-38	*Keyboard stuck key failure*	6	132
Symptom 6-39	*Memory address-line failure at <address>, read <value> expecting <value>*	6	132
Symptom 6-40	*Memory data line failure at <address>, read <value> expecting <value>*	6	132
Symptom 6-41	*Memory double word logic failure at <address>, read <value> expecting <value>*	6	132
Symptom 6-42	*Memory odd/even logic failure at <address>, read <value> expecting <value>*	6	132
Symptom 6-43	*Memory parity failure at <address>, read <value> expecting <value>*	6	133
Symptom 6-44	*Memory write/read failure at <address>, read <value> expecting <value>*	6	133
Symptom 6-45	*Memory size in CMOS invalid*	6	133
Symptom 6-46	*No boot device available*	6	133
Symptom 6-47	*No boot sector on hard-disk drive*	6	133
Symptom 6-48	*No timer tick interrupt*	6	133
Symptom 6-49	*Non-system disk or disk error*	6	133
Symptom 6-50	*Not a boot diskette*	6	133
Symptom 6-51	*Off-board parity error*	6	133

Symptom	Description	Chapter	Page
Symptom 6-52	*On-board parity error*	6	134
Symptom 6-53	*Override enabled—defaults loaded*	6	134
Symptom 6-54	*Parity error*	6	134
Symptom 6-55	*Plug-and-Play configuration error*	6	134
Symptom 6-56	*Press <TAB> to show POST screen*	6	134
Symptom 6-57	*Primary master hard disk fail*	6	134
Symptom 6-58	*Primary slave hard disk fail*	6	134
Symptom 6-59	*Resuming from disk*	6	134
Symptom 6-60	*Secondary master hard disk fail*	6	134
Symptom 6-61	*Secondary slave hard disk fail*	6	134
Symptom 6-62	*Shutdown failure*	6	135
Symptom 6-63	*Terminator/processor card not installed*	6	135
Symptom 6-64	*Time-of-day clock stopped*	6	135
Symptom 6-65	*Time or date in CMOS is invalid*	6	135
Symptom 6-66	*Timer chip counter 2 failed*	6	135
Symptom 6-67	*Unexpected interrupt in protected mode*	6	135
Symptom 6-68	*Warning—Thermal probes failed*	6	135
Symptom 6-69	*Warning—Temperature is too high*	6	135
Symptom 6-70	*Bad PnP serial ID checksum*	6	136
Symptom 6-71	*Floppy-disk controller resource conflict*	6	136
Symptom 6-72	*NVRAM checksum error, NVRAM cleared*	6	136
Symptom 6-73	*NVRAM cleared by jumper*	6	136
Symptom 6-74	*NVRAM data invalid, NVRAM cleared*	6	136
Symptom 6-75	*Parallel-port resource conflict*	6	136
Symptom 6-76	*PCI error log is full*	6	136
Symptom 6-77	*PCI I/O port conflict*	6	136
Symptom 6-78	*PCI IRQ conflict*	6	136
Symptom 6-79	*PCI memory conflict*	6	136
Symptom 6-80	*Primary boot device not found*	6	137
Symptom 6-81	*Primary IDE-controller resource conflict*	6	137
Symptom 6-82	*Primary input device not found*	6	137
Symptom 6-83	*Secondary IDE-controller resource conflict*	6	137
Symptom 6-84	*"Static device resource conflict" or "System board device resource conflict"*	6	137
Symptom 7-1	*The drive has trouble accepting or rejecting a CD*	7	159
Symptom 7-2	*The optical read head does not seek*	7	159
Symptom 7-3	*The disc cannot be read*	7	160
Symptom 7-4	*The disc does not turn*	7	160
Symptom 7-5	*The optical head cannot focus its laser beam*	7	160
Symptom 7-6	*No audio is generated by the drive*	7	161
Symptom 7-7	*Audio is not being played by the sound card*	7	161
Symptom 7-8	*You see a "Wrong DOS version" error message when attempting to load MSCDEX*	7	161
Symptom 7-9	*You cannot access the CD-ROM drive letter*	7	162
Symptom 7-10	*An error appears when trying to load the low-level CD-ROM driver*	7	162

Symptom	Description	Chapter	Page
Symptom 7-11	An error appears, such as "Error: not ready reading from drive D:"	7	162
Symptom 7-12	SmartDrive is not caching the CD-ROM properly	7	162
Symptom 7-13	The CD-ROM drivers will not install properly on a drive using compression software	7	163
Symptom 7-14	You see an error indicating that the CD-ROM drive is not found	7	163
Symptom 7-15	After installing the CD-ROM drivers, the system reports significantly less available RAM	7	163
Symptom 7-16	In a new installation, the driver fails to load successfully for the proprietary interface card	7	163
Symptom 7-17	The CD-ROM driver loads, but you see an error, such as "CDR101" (drive not ready) or "CDR103" (CD-ROM disk not HIGH SIERRA or ISO)	7	164
Symptom 7-18	You are having trouble setting up more than one CD-ROM drive	7	164
Symptom 7-19	Your CD-ROM drive refuses to work with an IDE port	7	164
Symptom 7-20	You cannot get the CD-ROM drive to run properly when mounted vertically	7	164
Symptom 7-21	The SCSI CD-ROM drive refuses to work when connected to an Adaptec SCSI interface	7	164
Symptom 7-22	You see a "No drives found" error when the CD-ROM driver line is executed in CONFIG.SYS	7	165
Symptom 7-23	The CD-ROM LCD displays an error code	7	165
Symptom 7-24	When a SCSI CD-ROM drive is connected to a SCSI adapter, the system hangs when the SCSI BIOS starts	7	165
Symptom 7-25	You see an error, such as "Unable to detect ATAPI IDE CD-ROM drive, device driver not loaded"	7	165
Symptom 7-26	The CD-ROM drive door will not open once the 40-pin IDE signal cable is connected	7	166
Symptom 7-27	You are using an old CD-ROM and can play CD audio, but you cannot access directories or other computer data from a CD	7	166
Symptom 7-28	The front-panel controls of your SCSI CD-ROM drive do not appear to work under Windows 95	7	166
Symptom 7-29	You cannot change the CD-ROM drive letter under Windows 95	7	166
Symptom 7-30	You installed Windows 95 from a CD-ROM disc using DOS drivers, but when you removed the real-mode CD-ROM drivers from CONFIG.SYS, the CD-ROM no longer works	7	167
Symptom 7-31	Your CD-ROM drive's parallel port-to-SCSI interface worked with Windows 3.1x, but does not work under Windows 95	7	167
Symptom 7-32	You see a message that the: "CD-ROM can run, but results might not be as expected"	7	168
Symptom 7-33	The CD-ROM works fine in DOS or Windows 3.1x, but sound or video appears choppy under Windows 95	7	168
Symptom 7-34	You can't read a Video CD-I disc in Windows '95 using any ATAPI/IDE CD-ROM drive	7	168

Symptom	Description	Chapter	Page
Symptom 7-35	An IDE CD-ROM is not detected on a 486 PCI motherboard	7	168
Symptom 7-36	An IDE CD-ROM is not detected when "slaved" to an IBM hard drive	7	169
Symptom 7-37	The CD-ROM drive will not read or run CD Plus or Enhanced CD titles	7	169
Symptom 7-38	You notice that the LED indicator on the CD-ROM is always on	7	169
Symptom 7-39	You cannot play CD audio on a particular CD-ROM under Windows 95	7	169
Symptom 7-40	Absorption control error <xxx>	7	173
Symptom 7-41	Application code error	7	173
Symptom 7-42	Bad ASPI open	7	173
Symptom 7-43	Buffer underrun at sector <xxx>	7	173
Symptom 7-44	Current disc already contains a closed audio session	7	173
Symptom 7-45	Current disc contains a session that is not closed	7	174
Symptom 7-46	The currently selected source CD-ROM drive or CD recorder cannot read audio in digital format	7	174
Symptom 7-47	Data overrun/underrun	7	174
Symptom 7-48	Destination disc is smaller than the source disc	7	174
Symptom 7-49	Disc already contains tracks and/or sessions that are incompatible with the requested operation	7	174
Symptom 7-50	Disc is write-protected	7	174
Symptom 7-51	Error 175-xx-xx-xx	7	174
Symptom 7-52	Error 220-01-xx-xx	7	174
Symptom 7-53	Error 220-06-xx-xx	7	174
Symptom 7-54	Error reading the Table of Contents (TOC) or Program Memory Area (PMA) from the disc	7	175
Symptom 7-55	General-protection fault	7	175
Symptom 7-56	Invalid logical block address	7	175
Symptom 7-57	Last two blocks stripped	7	175
Symptom 7-58	"MSCDEX" errors are being encountered	7	175
Symptom 7-59	MS-DOS or Windows cannot find the CD-R drive	7	175
Symptom 7-60	No write data (buffer empty)	7	175
Symptom 7-61	Read file error	7	176
Symptom 7-62	Selected disc image file was not prepared for the current disc	7	176
Symptom 7-63	Selected disc track is longer than the image file	7	176
Symptom 7-64	Selected disc track is shorter than the image file	7	176
Symptom 7-65	The "disc in" light on the drive does not blink after you turn on the computer	7	176
Symptom 7-66	Write emergency	7	176
Symptom 7-67	The CD-R is recognized by Windows 95, but it will not function as a normal CD-ROM drive	7	177
Symptom 7-68	You cannot read CD-R (gold) discs in some ordinary CD-ROM drives	7	177
Symptom 9-1	Changes to CMOS are not saved after rebooting the PC	9	244
Symptom 9-2	The system appears to be performing poorly	9	244

Symptom	Description	Chapter	Page
Symptom 9-3	*CMOS mismatch errors occur*	9	245
Symptom 9-4	*Some drives are not detected during boot*	9	245
Symptom 9-5	*The system boots from the hard drive, even though there is a bootable floppy disk in the drive*	9	245
Symptom 9-6	*Power-management features are not available*	9	245
Symptom 9-7	*PnP support is not available or PnP devices do not function properly*	9	246
Symptom 9-8	*Devices in some PCI slots are not recognized or not working properly*	9	246
Symptom 9-9	*You cannot enter CMOS setup—even though the correct key combination is used*	9	246
Symptom 9-10	*The system crashes or locks up frequently*	9	246
Symptom 9-11	*COM ports don't work*	9	247
Symptom 9-12	*The RTC doesn't keep proper time over a month*	9	247
Symptom 9-13	*The RTC doesn't keep time while system power is off*	9	247
Symptom 9-14	*You see an "Invalid system configuration data" error*	9	247
Symptom 9-15	*You encounter "CMOS checksum" errors after updating a flash BIOS*	9	248
Symptom 9-16	*You notice that only some CMOS Setup entries are corrupted when running a particular application*	9	248
Symptom 11-1	*The system is completely dead (the system power LED lights properly)*	11	325
Symptom 11-2	*A beep code or I/O POST code indicates a possible CPU fault*	11	326
Symptom 11-3	*The system boots with no problem, but crashes or freezes when certain applications are run*	11	326
Symptom 11-4	*The system boots with no problem, but crashes or freezes after several minutes of operation (regardless of the application being run)*	11	326
Symptom 11-5	*An older system refuses to run properly when the CPU's internal (L1) cache is enabled*	11	327
Symptom 11-6	*You cannot run a 3.45-V CPU in a 5-V motherboard—even though an appropriate voltage regulator module is being used*	11	327
Symptom 11-7	*A system malfunctions under HIMEM.SYS or DOS4GW.EXE after installing a new CPU*	11	327
Symptom 11-8	*The system runs fine, but reports the wrong type of CPU*	11	327
Symptom 11-9	*After reconfiguring a VL motherboard for a faster CPU, the VESA VL video card no longer functions*	11	328
Symptom 11-10	*Some software locks up on systems running 5x86 processors*	11	328
Symptom 11-11	*The Windows 95 Device Manager identifies the CPU incorrectly*	11	328
Symptom 11-12	*The heatsink/fan will not secure properly*	11	328
Symptom 11-13	*The Cyrix 6x86 system crashes or freezes after some period of operation*	11	330
Symptom 11-14	*The Cyrix 6x86 system crashes and refuses to restart*	11	330
Symptom 11-15	*The Cyrix 6x86 performs poorly under Window NT 4.0*	11	330

Symptom	Description	Chapter	Page
Symptom 11-16	*Quake (or another graphics-intensive program) doesn't run nearly as well on a Cyrix 6x86 system as it does with a similar Pentium system*	11	330
Symptom 11-17	*A Cyrix 6x86 CPU won't work on your motherboard*	11	331
Symptom 11-18	*The performance degrades when using a Cyrix 6x86 under Windows 3.1x or Windows 95*	11	331
Symptom 11-19	*The system does not boot up at all after reconfiguring the system for overclocking*	11	331
Symptom 11-20	*The system starts after overclocking, but locks up or crashes after some short period of time*	11	332
Symptom 11-21	*Memory errors occur after increasing the bus speed for overclocking*	11	332
Symptom 11-22	*After reconfiguring for overclocking, the system works, but you see a rash of CPU failures*	11	332
Symptom 11-23	*After reconfiguring for overclocking, you find that some expansion board or other hardware is no longer recognized or working*	11	332
Symptom 11-24	*After reconfiguring for overclocking, a number of recent files are corrupt, inaccessible, or missing. In effect, the system is not stable*	11	332
Symptom 12-1	*A DoubleGuard error code occurs*	12	352
Symptom 12-2	*A FAT 32 drive cannot be compressed*	12	352
Symptom 12-3	*The system is caught in a reboot loop after installing DriveSpace*	12	352
Symptom 12-4	*The DriveSpace real-mode driver cannot be removed by Windows 95*	12	354
Symptom 12-5	*DriveSpace does not restart in mini-Windows mode*	12	355
Symptom 12-6	*The MINI.CAB file is missing or corrupt*	12	356
Symptom 12-7	*A DRVSPACE 125 error occurs when using DriveSpace 3*	12	356
Symptom 12-8	*The DriveSpace VxD and real-mode driver are mismatched*	12	357
Symptom 12-9	*Windows 95 detects a compressed drive-access error*	12	357
Symptom 12-10	*Windows 95 cannot delete a compressed drive*	12	359
Symptom 12-11	*DriveSpace for Windows 95 reports that drive C: contains errors that must be corrected*	12	359
Symptom 12-12	*Some applications do not run properly on a DoubleSpace-compressed drive*	12	360
Symptom 12-13	*A "CVF is damaged" error message appears when the system starts*	12	361
Symptom 12-14	*A DoubleGuard alert appears in DOS*	12	361
Symptom 12-15	*Free space is exhausted on a compressed drive*	12	361
Symptom 12-16	*Free space is exhausted on the host drive*	12	362
Symptom 12-17	*Estimated compression ratio cannot be changed*	12	362
Symptom 12-18	*Compressed drive size cannot be reduced*	12	363
Symptom 12-19	*DEFRAG fails to fully defragment the drive*	12	363
Symptom 12-20	*You see a "Swap File is Corrupt" error message when starting Windows 3.1x*	12	363
Symptom 12-21	*You cannot access compressed drive(s) after booting from a system disk created by the Windows 3.1x*	12	364

Symptom	Description	Chapter	Page
Symptom 12-22	*The compressed drive is too fragmented to resize*	12	364
Symptom 12-23	*An error writing to the CVF occurs during defragmenting*	12	366
Symptom 12-24	*DoubleSpace or DriveSpace does not work properly on systems with Promise Technologies VL IDE controller cards*	12	366
Symptom 12-25	*The disk-compression program has used all reserved memory*	12	366
Symptom 12-26	*A compression error indicates that drive <X> is not available*	12	367
Symptom 12-27	*DIR /C fails to report the file-compression ratio*	12	367
Symptom 12-28	*FORMAT overwrites the CVF on a floppy disk*	12	368
Symptom 12-29	*The system hangs when a SCSI driver is loaded after DBLSPACE.SYS*	12	368
Symptom 12-30	*The compressed disk cannot be mounted in a BackPack drive*	12	368
Symptom 12-31	*DOS compression restarts the computer and loops endlessly*	12	368
Symptom 12-32	*You cannot use compression on a drive partitioned with Disk Manager*	12	369
Symptom 12-33	*Compression software mounts a Bernoulli disk as non-removable*	12	369
Symptom 12-34	*DriveSpace reports an "incompatible version" error*	12	369
Symptom 12-35	*DRIVER.SYS causes an "insert diskette" error when compression software is running*	12	369
Symptom 12-36	*A compressed drive refuses to mount after installing RAMDrive*	12	369
Symptom 12-37	*A compressed SCSI drive doesn't mount at startup*	12	370
Symptom 12-38	*DoubleSpace cannot copy the DBLSPACE.INF file*	12	370
Symptom 12-39	*EZTape hangs or produces an error with a compressed drive*	12	370
Symptom 12-40	*Compression software hangs the system with a DTC 3280 SCSI drive*	12	370
Symptom 12-41	*A compression error indicates cross-linked files between C: and C:*	12	371
Symptom 12-42	*Compression software indicates an "R6003—Integer Divide by Zero" error*	12	371
Symptom 12-43	*An error message appears, indicating "Lost sector groups"*	12	372
Symptom 12-44	*The error message "Size mismatch, existing installation" appears*	12	372
Symptom 12-45	*An error message appears, such as "The drive is too fragmented"*	12	373
Symptom 12-46	*The Stacker drive does not update or HCONVERT hangs up*	12	373
Symptom 12-47	*"Setup error #2002" appears*	12	374
Symptom 12-48	*After converting a DoubleSpace or SuperStor /DS drive to Stacker, no additional space is detected*	12	374
Symptom 12-49	*When using the Stacker CHECK utility, you see an error message indicating that the File Allocation Tables are not identical*	12	374

Symptom	Description	Chapter	Page
Symptom 12-50	*SDEFRAG errors 109/110, 120, or 170 are encountered*	12	375
Symptom 12-51	*"SDEFRAG/OPTIMIZER error 101" occurs*	12	376
Symptom 12-52	*While running the Stacker CHECK utility, a "Not enough disk space to save header" error appears*	12	376
Symptom 12-53	*The uncompress process fails*	12	377
Symptom 12-54	*The error message appears: "Not a Stacker STACVOL file—NOT MOUNTED" or "Invalid # reserved sectors—NOT MOUNTED"*	12	379
Symptom 12-55	*An error message appears: "CHECK I/O Access Denied: Error 27"*	12	379
Symptom 13-1	*The drive adapter software will not install properly*	13	408
Symptom 13-2	*The controller will not support a drive with more than 1024 cylinders*	13	409
Symptom 13-3	*Loading a disk driver causes the system to hang or generate a "Bad or missing COMMAND.COM" error*	13	409
Symptom 13-4	*Drive performance is poor—data transfer rates are slow*	13	409
Symptom 13-5	*The PC refuses to boot after a drive adapter is installed*	13	410
Symptom 13-6	*Windows generates a "Validation Failed 03,3F" error*	13	410
Symptom 13-7	*Windows hangs or fails to load files after loading the EIDE driver*	13	410
Symptom 13-8	*After replacing a drive adapter with a different model, the hard drive is no longer recognized*	13	410
Symptom 13-9	*A fatal error is generated when running DEBUG*	13	411
Symptom 13-10	*Trouble occurs when formatting ESDI drives over 670MB using an older drive adapter*	13	411
Symptom 13-11	*When low-level ESDI formatting, a "Fatal error R/W head" message appears*	13	411
Symptom 13-12	*After installing a new ESDI drive adapter, you cannot install Novell*	13	411
Symptom 13-13	*System problems occur after installing a VL drive adapter*	13	411
Symptom 13-14	*You cannot enable 32-bit Disk Access under Windows 3.1x*	13	412
Symptom 13-15	*The EIDE drive adapter's secondary port refuses to work*	13	412
Symptom 13-16	*The drive adapter's BIOS doesn't load*	13	413
Symptom 13-17	*The drive adapter BIOS loads, but the system hangs up*	13	413
Symptom 13-18	*The ATAPI CD-ROM is not recognized as the "slave" device versus an EIDE "master"*	13	413
Symptom 13-19	*Hard drives are not recognized on the secondary drive controller channel*	13	413
Symptom 13-20	*The drive adapter can only support 528MB per disk*	13	414
Symptom 13-21	*You get a "code 10" error relative to the drive adapter*	13	414
Symptom 13-22	*You encounter mouse problems after changing the drive adapter*	13	415
Symptom 13-23	*You cannot run Norton Anti-Virus 95 with Promise drive adapters*	13	415

Symptom	Description	Chapter	Page
Symptom 13-24	*The system hangs after counting through system memory*	13	415
Symptom 13-25	*After replacing/upgrading a drive adapter, the system hangs intermittently during use*	13	415
Symptom 13-26	*Errors occur when reading or writing to floppies after replacing/upgrading a drive adapter*	13	416
Symptom 14-1	*The DVD drivers refuse to install*	14	430
Symptom 14-2	*The DVD drive isn't detected*	14	431
Symptom 14-3	*The DVD motorized tray won't open or close*	14	431
Symptom 14-4	*There is no audio when playing an audio CD*	14	431
Symptom 14-5	*There is no DVD audio while playing a movie or other multimedia presentation*	14	431
Symptom 14-6	*Video quality appears poor*	14	431
Symptom 14-7	*The video image is distorted when trying to play an MPEG file*	14	432
Symptom 14-8	*The picture is beginning to occasionally pixelize or "break apart"*	14	432
Symptom 14-9	*The DVD-ROM light flashes regularly without a disc inserted*	14	432
Symptom 14-10	*An "Disk playback unauthorized" error message appears*	14	432
Symptom 14-11	*An error indicates that the DVD device driver could not be loaded*	14	432
Symptom 14-12	*You see an error, such as "Cannot open <filename>, video and audio glitches might occur"*	14	432
Symptom 14-13	*The display turns magenta (red) when attempting to adjust the DVD video overlay feature*	14	433
Symptom 14-14	*The DVD drive cannot read CD-R or Photo CD discs*	14	433
Symptom 15-1	*The power and cooling fan(s) are on, but nothing else happens*	15	558
Symptom 15-2	*After power-up, you hear the fan change pitch noticeably (a chirping sound might also be coming from the supply)*	15	558
Symptom 15-3	*You see one or more POST board power LEDs off, very dim, or flickering*	15	559
Symptom 15-4	*The Reset LED remains on (the POST display will probably remain blank)*	15	559
Symptom 15-5	*One or more activity LEDs is out (the POST display will probably remain blank)*	15	559
Symptom 15-6	*You hear a beep code pattern from the system speaker, but no POST codes are displayed*	15	559
Symptom 15-7	*The POST display stops at some code (the system probably hangs up)*	15	560
Symptom 15-8	*A POST or beep code indicates a video problem (there is no monitor display)*	15	560
Symptom 15-9	*A POST or beep code indicates a drive or controller problem*	15	560
Symptom 16-1	*The floppy drive is completely dead*	16	574
Symptom 16-2	*The floppy drive rotates a disk, but will not seek to the desired track*	16	575

Symptom	Description	Chapter	Page
Symptom 16-3	*The floppy drive heads seek properly, but the spindle does not turn*	16	576
Symptom 16-4	*The floppy drive will not read from/write to the diskette*	16	577
Symptom 16-5	*The drive is able to write to a write-protected disk*	16	577
Symptom 16-6	*The drive can only recognize either high- or double-density media, but not both*	16	578
Symptom 16-7	*Double-density (720KB) 3.5" disks are not working properly when formatted as high-density (1.44MB) disks*	16	578
Symptom 16-8	*DOS reports an error, such as "Cannot Read From Drive A:" even though a diskette is fully inserted in the drive, and the drive LED indicates*	16	578
Symptom 16-9	*When a new diskette is inserted in the drive, a directory from a previous diskette appears*	16	579
Symptom 16-10	*The 3.5" high-density floppy disk cannot format high-density diskettes (but can read and write to them just fine)*	16	579
Symptom 16-11	*An XT-class PC cannot be upgraded with a 3.5" floppy disk*	16	579
Symptom 16-12	*The floppy drives cannot be "swapped" so that A: becomes B: and B: becomes A:*	16	579
Symptom 16-13	*When using a combination floppy drive (called a combo drive), one of the drives does not work, but the other works fine*	16	580
Symptom 16-14	*No jumpers are available on the floppy disk, so it is impossible to change settings*	16	580
Symptom 16-15	*The floppy drive activity LED stays on as soon as the computer is powered up*	16	580
Symptom 17-1	*The hard drive is completely dead*	17	618
Symptom 17-2	*You see drive activity, but the computer will not boot from the hard drive*	17	618
Symptom 17-3	*One or more subdirectories appear lost or damaged*	17	619
Symptom 17-4	*Errors occur during drive reads or writes*	17	619
Symptom 17-5	*The hard drive was formatted accidentally*	17	619
Symptom 17-6	*A file has been deleted accidentally*	17	619
Symptom 17-7	*The hard drive's root directory is damaged*	17	619
Symptom 17-8	*Hard-drive performance appears to be slowing down over time*	17	620
Symptom 17-9	*The hard drive accesses correctly, but the drive light stays on continuously*	17	620
Symptom 17-10	*The hard drive is not accessible and the drive light stays on continuously*	17	620
Symptom 17-11	*A "No fixed disk present" error message appears on the monitor*	17	620
Symptom 17-12	*The drive spins up, but the system fails to recognize it*	17	621
Symptom 17-13	*The IDE drive spins up when power is applied, then rapidly spins down again*	17	621
Symptom 17-14	*A "Sector not found" error message appears on the monitor*	17	621

Symptom	Description	Chapter	Page
Symptom 17-15	A "1780 or 1781 ERROR" appears on the monitor	17	622
Symptom 17-16	A "1790 or 1791 ERROR" appears on the monitor	17	622
Symptom 17-17	A "1701 ERROR" appears on the monitor	17	622
Symptom 17-18	The system reports random data, seek, or format errors	17	623
Symptom 17-19	A "Bad or Missing Command Interpreter" error message appears	17	623
Symptom 17-20	An "Error reading drive C:" error message appears	17	623
Symptom 17-21	A "Track 0 not found" error message appears	17	624
Symptom 17-22	Software diagnostics indicate an average access time that is longer than specified for the drive	17	624
Symptom 17-23	Software diagnostics indicate a slower data transfer rate than specified	17	624
Symptom 17-24	The low-level format operation is taking too long or it hangs up the system	17	625
Symptom 17-25	The low-level format utility is not accessible from the DEBUG address	17	625
Symptom 17-26	The low-level format process regularly hangs up on a specific head/cylinder/sector	17	626
Symptom 17-27	The FDISK procedure hangs up or fails to create or save partition record for the drive(s)	17	626
Symptom 17-28	A "Hard disk controller failure" message appears or a large number of defects occur in the last logical partition	17	626
Symptom 17-29	The high-level (DOS) format process takes too long	17	627
Symptom 17-30	The IDE drive (<528MB) does not partition or format to full capacity	17	627
Symptom 17-31	The EIDE drive (>528MB) does not partition or format to full capacity	17	627
Symptom 17-32	"Disk boot failure," "Non-system disk," or "No ROM basic—SYSTEM HALTED" error messages appear	17	627
Symptom 17-33	The hard drive in a PC is suffering frequent breakdowns (i.e., between 6 to 12 months)	17	628
Symptom 17-34	A hard-drive controller is replaced, but during initialization, the system displays error messages, such as "Hard disk failure" or "Not a recognized drive type"	17	628
Symptom 17-35	A new hard drive is installed, but it will not boot, or a message appears, such as: "HDD controller failure"	17	628
Symptom 17-36	Disk Manager is installed to a hard drive, but is formatted back to 528MB when DOS is reinstalled	17	628
Symptom 17-37	ScanDisk reports some bad sectors, but cannot map them out during a surface analysis	17	629
Symptom 17-38	The drive will work as a primary drive, but not as a secondary (or vice versa)	17	629
Symptom 17-39	32-bit access does not work under Windows 3.1x	17	630
Symptom 17-40	Drive diagnostics reveal a great deal of wasted space on the drive	17	630
Symptom 17-41	A Y-adapter fails to work	17	630
Symptom 17-42	During the POST, the drive begins to spin-up and produces a sharp noise	17	630

Symptom	Description	Chapter	Page
Symptom 17-43	*Opening a folder under Windows 95 seems to take a long time*	17	630
Symptom 17-44	*The hard drive is infected by a bootblock virus*	17	631
Symptom 17-45	*An "Incorrect DOS version" error appears*	17	631
Symptom 17-46	*A "File allocation table bad" error appears*	17	631
Symptom 17-47	*DOS requires a "volume label," but the label is corrupt*	17	631
Symptom 19-1	*The joystick does not respond*	19	652
Symptom 19-2	*Joystick performance is erratic or choppy*	19	652
Symptom 19-3	*The joystick is sending incorrect information to the system—the joystick appears to be drifting*	19	653
Symptom 19-4	*The basic X/Y, two-button features of the joystick work, but the hat switch, throttle controls, and supplemental buttons do not seem to respond*	19	653
Symptom 19-5	*A "Joystick not connected" error appears under Windows 95*	19	653
Symptom 19-6	*The joystick drifts frequently and requires recalibration*	19	653
Symptom 19-7	*The joystick handle has lost tension—it no longer "snaps" back to the center*	19	654
Symptom 19-8	*The joystick responds, but refuses to accept a calibration*	19	654
Symptom 19-9	*The hat switch and buttons on a joystick work only intermittently (if at all).*	19	654
Symptom 19-10	*When downloading FCS (or calibration) files to a joystick, the line saying: "Put switch into calibrate" doesn't change when the download switch is moved*	19	654
Symptom 19-11	*To download a calibration file, you need to rock the red switch back and forth a number of times (or hit the <Enter> key a number of times) to get it to 100%*	19	654
Symptom 19-12	*A joystick cannot be used with a PC using a sound card with an ESS or OPTi chipset*	19	655
Symptom 19-13	*The joystick port is not removed when the sound card is removed*	19	655
Symptom 19-14	*The "jumperless" joystick port cannot be disabled*	19	655
Symptom 20-1	*During initialization, an error message indicates that no keyboard is connected*	20	667
Symptom 20-2	*During initialization, an error message indicates that the keyboard lock is on*	20	667
Symptom 20-3	*The keyboard is completely dead—no keys appear to function at all*	20	668
Symptom 20-4	*The keyboard is acting erratically*	20	668
Symptom 20-5	*The keyboard is acting erratically. One or more keys might be stuck or repeating*	20	669
Symptom 20-6	*A "KBC Error" (or similar) is displayed during system startup*	20	669
Symptom 20-7	*Macros cannot be cleared from a programmable keyboard*	20	669
Symptom 20-8	*The keyboard keys are not functioning as expected*	20	669

Symptom	Description	Chapter	Page
Symptom 20-9	*Some keys on a programmable keyboard will not remap to their default state*	20	670
Symptom 20-10	*A wireless keyboard types random characters*	20	670
Symptom 20-11	*The wireless keyboard beeps while typing*	20	670
Symptom 20-12	*Typed characters do not appear, but the cursor moves*	20	670
Symptom 20-13	*Some function keys and Windows keys might not work some PC configurations*	20	670
Symptom 20-14	*One or more Windows-specific keys don't work*	20	671
Symptom 20-15	*Remote-control programs don't work after installing keyboard drivers*	20	671
Symptom 20-16	*On a PS/2 system, you encounter keyboard errors, even though the keyboard driver loads successfully*	20	671
Symptom 20-17	*Assigned key sounds do not work*	20	671
Symptom 20-18	*You cannot use Windows-specific keys to start task-switching software other than TASKSW16.EXE*	20	671
Symptom 20-19	*The NumLock feature might not activate when the NumLock key is pressed*	20	672
Symptom 21-1	*The printer's LCD shows a "CPU error"*	21	686
Symptom 21-2	*The printer's LCD shows a "ROM checksum Error"*	21	686
Symptom 21-3	*The printer's LCD shows a "RAM R/W error," a "Memory error," or other memory defect*	21	696
Symptom 21-4	*The printer's LCD shows a "Memory overflow" error*	21	697
Symptom 21-5	*The printer's LCD shows a "Print overrun" error*	21	697
Symptom 21-6	*The printer reports an "I/O protocol error"*	21	697
Symptom 21-7	*The image is composed of "garbage" and disassociated symbols*	21	698
Symptom 21-8	*The image appears "stitched"*	21	698
Symptom 21-9	*The image appears elongated and "stitched"*	21	700
Symptom 21-10	*Portions of the image are disassociated like a "jigsaw puzzle"*	21	700
Symptom 21-11	*The image appears to be shifted down very significantly*	21	700
Symptom 21-12	*The image appears "rasterized" with no intelligible information*	21	700
Symptom 21-13	*The image is blacked out with white horizontal lines*	21	701
Symptom 21-14	*The image is incorrectly sized along the vertical axis*	21	701
Symptom 21-15	*The print contains lines of print—usually in the lower half of the page—that appear smudged*	21	701
Symptom 21-16	*There is no apparent top margin*	21	702
Symptom 21-17	*Pronounced smudging is at the top of the image (generally near the top margin)*	21	702
Symptom 21-18	*Too much margin space is on top of the image*	21	703
Symptom 21-19	*The image is "skewed" (not square with the page)*	21	703
Symptom 21-20	*Right-hand text appears missing or distorted*	21	704
Symptom 21-21	*Horizontal black lines are spaced randomly through the print*	21	704
Symptom 21-22	*The printer's LCD reports a "polygon motor synchronization error"*	21	705

Symptom	Description	Chapter	Page
Symptom 21-23	*One or more vertical white bands is in the image*	21	706
Symptom 21-24	*A white, jagged band is in the image*	21	706
Symptom 21-25	*Repetitive waves are in the image*	21	706
Symptom 21-26	*Worsening waves are in the image*	21	707
Symptom 21-27	*The image appears washed out—little or no intelligible information is in the image*	21	707
Symptom 21-28	*The print appears "jeweled"*	21	707
Symptom 21-29	*The print regularly "smudges"*	21	707
Symptom 21-30	*The print is blacked out with white horizontal lines*	21	708
Symptom 21-31	*The image forms correctly, except for random white gaps that appear horizontally across the page*	21	708
Symptom 21-32	*Gaps and overlaps are in the print*	21	708
Symptom 21-33	*The print has a "roller-coaster" appearance*	21	710
Symptom 21-34	*The image is highly compressed in the vertical axis*	21	710
Symptom 21-35	*The printer's LCD displays a "high-voltage error"*	21	710
Symptom 21-36	*The image is visible, but the printout is darkened*	21	711
Symptom 21-37	*Random black splotches are in the image*	21	711
Symptom 21-38	*"Graping" is in the image*	21	711
Symptom 21-39	*The image appears, but it contains heavy black bands*	21	712
Symptom 21-40	*The image appears fuzzy—letters and graphics appear "smudged" or "out of focus"*	21	712
Symptom 21-41	*Weakly developed areas are in the image*	21	712
Symptom 21-42	*The image appears washed out*	21	712
Symptom 21-43	*The page is blacked out*	21	713
Symptom 21-44	*The printer's LCD indicates a "heater error" or other type of fusing temperature malfunction*	21	713
Symptom 21-45	*Print appears smeared or fused improperly*	21	715
Symptom 21-46	*The print is smudged in narrow, horizontal bands*	21	715
Symptom 21-47	*Wide, horizontal areas of print are smudged*	21	716
Symptom 21-48	*Dark creases are in the print*	21	716
Symptom 21-49	*Little or no fusing is on one side of the image*	21	716
Symptom 21-50	*Pages are completely blacked out, and might appear blotched with an undefined border*	21	717
Symptom 21-51	*Print is very faint*	21	717
Symptom 21-52	*Print is just slightly faint*	21	718
Symptom 21-53	*One or more vertical black streaks are in the print*	21	719
Symptom 21-54	*One or more vertical white streaks are in the print*	21	719
Symptom 21-55	*The print appears "scalloped"*	21	720
Symptom 21-56	*The print contains columns of horizontal "tic" marks*	21	720
Symptom 21-57	*The print appears speckled*	21	720
Symptom 21-58	*Light/white splotches are in the image*	21	720
Symptom 21-59	*Light/white zones are spread through the image*	21	721
Symptom 21-60	*The printer never leaves its warm-up mode*	21	721
Symptom 21-61	*A "Paper out" message appears*	21	721
Symptom 21-62	*A "Printer open" message appears*	21	723

Symptom	Description	Chapter	Page
Symptom 21-63	*A "No EP cartridge" message appears*	21	724
Symptom 21-64	*A "Toner low" message appears constantly or the error never appears*	21	724
Symptom 21-65	*The printer's LCD displays a "fan motor error" or similar fault*	21	725
Symptom 21-66	*Ghosting is in the image*	21	725
Symptom 21-67	*The print appears fogged or blurred*	21	726
Symptom 21-68	*Nothing happens when power is turned on*	21	726
Symptom 23-1	*You see a 1055 201 or 2055 201 error message*	23	790
Symptom 23-2	*You see a "Parity check 1" error message*	23	790
Symptom 23-3	*You see a "XXYY 201" error message*	23	790
Symptom 23-4	*You see a "Parity error 1" error message*	23	790
Symptom 23-5	*The number "164" displayed on the monitor*	23	792
Symptom 23-6	*You see an "Incorrect memory size" error message*	23	792
Symptom 23-7	*You see a "ROM error" message displayed on the monitor*	23	793
Symptom 23-8	*New memory is installed, but the system refuses to recognize it*	23	793
Symptom 23-9	*New memory has been installed or replaced, and the system refuses to boot*	23	793
Symptom 23-10	*You see an "XXXX Optional ROM Bad, Checksum = YYYY" error message*	23	793
Symptom 23-11	*You see a general RAM error with fault addresses listed*	23	794
Symptom 23-12	*You see a "Cache Memory Failure—Disabling Cache" error*	23	795
Symptom 23-13	*You see a "Decreasing Available Memory" error message*	23	795
Symptom 23-14	*You are encountering a memory error with HIMEM.SYS under DOS*	23	795
Symptom 23-15	*Memory devices from various vendors refuse to work together*	23	795
Symptom 23-16	*Windows 95 "Protection" errors occur after adding SIMMs/DIMMs*	23	795
Symptom 24-1	*You see an error message from a driver or TSR when attempting to relocate it*	24	807
Symptom 24-2	*The system locks up when a program is relocated*	24	807
Symptom 24-3	*A device driver small enough for the available UMA fails to load there*	24	808
Symptom 24-4	*A program works erratically or improperly when loaded into the UMA*	24	808
Symptom 24-5	*Nothing is being loaded into the UMA*	24	808
Symptom 24-6	*The message appears: "Address wrap at xxxx"*	24	808
Symptom 24-7	*The error appears: "NOUSERAM=xxxxx-yyyyy"*	24	808
Symptom 24-8	*The error appears: "Invalid USERAM due to memory cache!"*	24	809
Symptom 24-9	*QEMM 8.0x refuses to function properly under Windows 95 on an IBM ThinkPad*	24	809

Symptom	Description	Chapter	Page
Symptom 24-10	*The error appears: "QEMM386: Cannot load because there is not enough memory"*	24	809
Symptom 24-11	*The error appears: "QEMM386: Cannot load because the processor is already in Virtual 86 mode"*	24	809
Symptom 24-12	*The error appears: "QEMM386: Cannot load because an expanded memory manager is already loaded"*	24	810
Symptom 24-13	*The error appears: "QEMM386: Unknown Microchannel Adapter ID: XXXX"*	24	810
Symptom 24-14	*The error appears: "QEMM386: Cannot find file MCA.ADL"*	24	810
Symptom 24-15	*The error appears: "QEMM38452 Cannot load because this is not an 80386"*	24	810
Symptom 24-16	*The error appears: "QEMM386: Cannot load because there is no room for a page frame"*	24	811
Symptom 24-17	*The error appears: "QEMM386: Cannot load because QEMM is already loaded"*	24	811
Symptom 24-18	*The error appears: "QEMM386: Disabling Stealth ROM:F because the page frame does not overlap any ROM"*	24	811
Symptom 24-19	*The error appears: "QEMM386: Disabling Stealth ROM:M because there is no page frame"*	24	811
Symptom 24-20	*The error appears: "QEMM386: Disabling stealth because QEMM could not locate the ROM handler for INT xx"*	24	812
Symptom 24-21	*The error appears: "Cannot load because QEMM is not registered. Run the INSTALL program to register"*	24	812
Symptom 24-22	*You see the errors: "CONTEXTS is no longer a QEMM parameter!," or "NAMES is no longer a QEMM parameter!"*	24	812
Symptom 24-23	*The error appears: "LOADHI: The high memory chain is corrupted"*	24	812
Symptom 24-24	*The error appears: "LOADHI: Cannot write to log file"*	24	813
Symptom 24-25	*The error appears: "Stealth ROM is being disabled because it cannot find ROM handler 05 76"*	24	813
Symptom 24-26	*The system will hang when attempting to use Colorado Tape Backup*	24	813
Symptom 24-27	*There is no specific error message, but Optimize won't complete*	24	813
Symptom 24-28	*After Optimize is complete, you see the error; "Fixed disk parameter error or BIOS error"*	24	813
Symptom 24-29	*Optimize won't complete on a PC with a Plextor 6X CD-ROM and Adaptec 1515 SCSI controller*	24	813
Symptom 24-30	*An NEC UltraLite Versa PC suffers Exception 13 errors in the Exxxh range*	24	814
Symptom 24-31	*A Philips CD Recorder (i.e. CDD200) fails to function if you put the USERAM=1M:32M parameter on the QEMM386.SYS line in CONFIG.SYS*	24	814
Symptom 24-32	*QEMM 8.0x refuses to complete an optimization on a Compaq computer*	24	814
Symptom 24-33	*XtraDrive cannot be installed on the desired drive*	24	814

Symptom	Description	Chapter	Page
Symptom 24-34	*QEMM cannot be installed on a system with XtraDrive*	24	814
Symptom 24-35	*The XtraDrive device driver cannot be installed into high RAM*	24	815
Symptom 24-36	*The error appears: "This program is attempting to access the disk via the page frame"*	24	815
Symptom 24-37	*Windows 95 hangs on the opening logo screen or your video display appears distorted*	24	815
Symptom 24-38	*After accepting the Optimize results, the system gets caught in a loop and eventually stops in a Windows protection fault 14*	24	815
Symptom 24-39	*An error appears: "Configuration too large for memory" while running Optimize under Windows 95*	24	815
Symptom 24-40	*Floppy-drive problems occur after installing QEMM*	24	816
Symptom 24-41	*Using the RAM parameter with QEMM causes an IBM ThinkPad to hang*	24	816
Symptom 24-42	*Problems occur when loading programs high, the system hangs, or there is other odd behavior from TSRs, device drivers, or PC cards*	24	817
Symptom 24-43	*QEMM generates an Exception 6, 12, or 13 error*	24	817
Symptom 24-44	*Systems with Disk Manager fail to Optimize properly*	24	817
Symptom 24-45	*System hangs using HIMEM /TESTMEM*	24	817
Symptom 24-46	*A20 gate problems occur when installing HIMEM*	24	818
Symptom 24-47	*A general error or system problem occurs with EMM386*	24	818
Symptom 24-48	*An error appears: "Unable to set page frame base address—EMS unavailable"*	24	819
Symptom 24-49	*An error appears: "Size of expanded memory pool adjusted"*	24	819
Symptom 24-50	*Windows 3.x cannot provide EMS when using the NOEMS switch*	24	820
Symptom 24-51	*EMM386 locks up the computer*	24	820
Symptom 24-52	*An error appears: "Insufficient memory for UMBs or virtual HMA"*	24	821
Symptom 24-53	*An error appears: "Unable to create page frame"*	24	821
Symptom 24-54	*An error appears: "EMM386 Privileged Operation Error #01"*	24	822
Symptom 24-55	*An error appears: "EMM386 Not Installed—Unable to set page frame base address"*	24	822
Symptom 24-56	*An AT&T 6386E system hangs with a RAM option in EMM386*	24	822
Symptom 24-57	*A Plus Hardcard II is very slow with EMM386*	24	823
Symptom 24-58	*Exception errors occur with EMM386*	24	823
Symptom 24-59	*The Qualitas DOSMAX utility doesn't function as expected*	24	823
Symptom 24-60	*The error appears: "Error 1014: Disk cache or other file I/O software using EMS memory"*	24	824
Symptom 24-61	*The error appears: "VxD Error: Unable to provide DOSMAX features"*	24	824
Symptom 24-62	*The error appears: "VxD Error: Qpopup is not running"*	24	825
Symptom 24-63	*The error appears: "Error 1021: Qualitas MAX stacks required for DOSMAX support"*	24	825

Symptom	Description	Chapter	Page
Symptom 24-64	The error appears: "Error 1011: Bus master disk subsystem detected that requires Qcache or other compliant disk cache to be loaded"	24	825
Symptom 24-65	The error appears: "Error 2035: V86 RAM page(s) in use"	24	825
Symptom 24-66	The error appears: "Error 1020: 386MAX.SYS version mismatch"	24	825
Symptom 24-67	Video problems or conflicts occur while using MAX	24	825
Symptom 25-1	The mouse cursor appears, but it only moves erratically as the ball moves (if at all)	25	838
Symptom 25-2	One or both buttons function erratically (if at all)	25	839
Symptom 25-3	The screen cursor appears on the display, but it does not move	25	839
Symptom 25-4	The mouse/trackball device driver fails to load	25	839
Symptom 25-5	You see a "General Protection Fault" after installing a new mouse and driver under Windows	25	840
Symptom 25-6	You see an error: "This pointer device requires a newer version"	25	840
Symptom 25-7	You see an error: "Mouse port disabled or mouse not present"	25	840
Symptom 25-8	The mouse works for a few minutes, then stops	25	840
Symptom 25-9	You attempt a doubleclick but get quadrupleclick, or you attempt a singleclick and get a doubleclick	25	841
Symptom 25-10	A single mouse click works, but doubleclick doesn't	25	841
Symptom 25-11	A PS/2 mouse is not detected by a notebook PC under Windows 95	25	841
Symptom 25-12	Mouse pointer options are not saved	25	841
Symptom 25-13	Clicking the right mouse button doesn't start the default context menus of Windows 95	25	842
Symptom 25-14	The modem won't start after installing new mouse software	25	842
Symptom 25-15	A two-button "First Mouse" refuses to work on a Packard Bell system	25	843
Symptom 25-16	A Logitech three-button mouse refuses to work on a Packard Bell computer	25	843
Symptom 25-17	The mouse pointer moves only vertically	25	843
Symptom 26-1	The PC (or communication software) refuses to recognize the modem	26	885
Symptom 26-2	The modem appears to be functioning properly, but you can't see what you are typing	26	885
Symptom 26-3	The modem appears to be functioning properly, but you see double characters print while typing	26	885
Symptom 26-4	The modem will not answer at the customer's site, but it works fine in the shop	26	886
Symptom 26-5	Your modem is receiving or transmitting garbage, or is having great difficulty displaying anything at all	26	886
Symptom 26-6	The modem is connected and turned on, but the modem is not responding	26	887
Symptom 26-7	The modem will not pick up phone line	26	887

Symptom	Description	Chapter	Page
Symptom 26-8	The modem appears to work fine, but prints garbage whenever it's supposed to show IBM text graphics, such as boxes or ANSI graphics	26	887
Symptom 26-9	Strange character groups, such as "[0m," frequently appear in the text	26	887
Symptom 26-10	The modem makes audible "clicking" noises when hooked to phone line	26	888
Symptom 26-11	The modem is having difficulty connecting to another modem	26	888
Symptom 26-12	The modem starts dialing before it draws dialtone	26	888
Symptom 26-13	The modem has trouble sending or receiving when the system's power-saving features are turned on	26	889
Symptom 26-14	You see an error, such as: "Already on line" or "Carrier already established"	26	889
Symptom 26-15	The modem refuses to answer the incoming line	26	889
Symptom 26-16	The modem switches into the command mode intermittently	26	889
Symptom 26-17	Your current modem won't connect at 2400bps with a 2400bps modem	26	889
Symptom 26-18	The communications software is reporting many Cyclic Redundancy Check (CRC) errors and low Characters Per Second (CPS) transfers	26	890
Symptom 26-19	Errors are constantly occurring in your V.17 fax transmissions	26	890
Symptom 26-20	During installation, a modem setup program cannot find the internal modem	26	890
Symptom 26-21	After installing a new internal modem, the system mouse driver no longer loads or the mouse behaves erratically	26	890
Symptom 26-22	After installing modem driver software, Windows locks up or crashes	26	891
Symptom 26-23	DOS communication software works fine, but Windows communication software will not	26	891
Symptom 26-24	You cannot get the modem's "distinctive-ring" feature to work	26	891
Symptom 26-25	You cannot get the modem's "Caller ID" feature to work	26	892
Symptom 26-26	You cannot recall previous "Caller ID" data	26	892
Symptom 26-27	The modem will not provide synchronous communication	26	893
Symptom 26-28	The modem appears to be set up and configured properly, but it is experiencing data loss	26	894
Symptom 26-29	When running modem software, an error appears, such as: "Can't run on a Plug-and-Play ready system"	26	894
Symptom 26-30	The modem appears to be setup and configured properly, but it regularly connects at slower speeds than it is capable of	26	894
Symptom 26-31	Windows 95 insists on assigning the modem to COM5	26	895
Symptom 26-32	You cannot get the modem to work with a Winsock, but conventional BBS or CompuServe connections work fine	26	896

Symptom	Description	Chapter	Page
Symptom 26-33	*You are having trouble configuring the modem for hardware and software flow control*	26	896
Symptom 26-34	*The modem will not establish a connection through a cellular telephone*	26	896
Symptom 26-35	*The modem will not fax properly through a cellular telephone*	26	896
Symptom 26-36	*Windows 95 recognizes the modem, but 16-bit communications software will not see it*	26	896
Symptom 26-37	*DOS ICU software is installed, but it will not allow the modem to be configured on COM1 or COM2*	26	897
Symptom 26-38	*The modem's flash ROM update will not install because it cannot recognize the modem's current firmware version*	26	897
Symptom 26-39	*The modem establishes connections properly, but it frequently drops connections*	26	897
Symptom 26-40	*When selecting a modem in your communication software, your particular modem is not listed*	26	898
Symptom 26-41	*It seems to take the modem an unusually long time to hang up*	26	898
Symptom 26-42	*The modem is configured as COM4 (IRQ3) under Windows 95, but the modem refuses to work*	26	898
Symptom 26-43	*When auto-detect tries to add a new modem at COM2, Windows 95 locks up*	26	898
Symptom 26-44	*HyperTerminal works using PCMCIA support under Windows 95, but no 16-bit communication programs work*	26	898
Symptom 26-45	*A Winmodem installed correctly and responds to AT commands fine, but whenever you call out, the modem makes a 9600 V.34 connection*	26	899
Symptom 26-46	*Windows 95 never detected the Winmodem*	26	899
Symptom 27-1	*The heater opens in the CRT*	27	917
Symptom 27-2	*Heater shorts to a cathode in the CRT*	27	917
Symptom 27-3	*Cathode shorts to the control grid in the CRT*	27	918
Symptom 27-4	*One or more colors appear weak*	27	918
Symptom 27-5	*CRT phosphors appear aged or worn*	27	918
Symptom 27-6	*The CRT suffers from bad cutoff (a.k.a. bad gamma)*	27	918
Symptom 27-7	*The control grid in the CRT is open*	27	919
Symptom 27-8	*The CRT screen grid is open*	27	919
Symptom 27-9	*The CRT focus grid is open*	27	919
Symptom 27-10	*The control grid shorts to the screen grid in the CRT*	27	919
Symptom 27-11	*The image is saturated with red or appears greenish-blue (cyan)*	27	921
Symptom 27-12	*The image is saturated with blue or appears yellow*	27	922
Symptom 27-13	*The image is saturated with green or appears bluish-red (magenta)*	27	922
Symptom 27-14	*Raster is present, but there is no image*	27	923
Symptom 27-15	*A single horizontal line appears in the middle of the display*	27	923
Symptom 27-16	*Only the upper or lower half of an image appears*	27	924

Symptom	Description	Chapter	Page
Symptom 27-17	*A single vertical line appears along the middle of the display*	27	924
Symptom 27-18	*There is no image and no raster*	27	924
Symptom 27-19	*The image is too compressed or too expanded*	27	925
Symptom 27-20	*The displayed characters appear to be distorted*	27	925
Symptom 27-21	*The display appears wavy*	27	926
Symptom 27-22	*The display is too bright or too dim*	27	926
Symptom 27-23	*Visible raster scan lines are in the display*	27	926
Symptom 27-24	*Colors bleed or smear*	27	926
Symptom 27-25	*Colors appear to change when the monitor is warm*	27	927
Symptom 27-26	*An image appears distorted in 350- or 400-line mode*	27	927
Symptom 27-27	*The fine detail of high-resolution graphic images appears a bit fuzzy*	27	928
Symptom 27-28	*The display changes color, flickers, or cuts out when the video cable is moved*	27	928
Symptom 27-29	*The image expands in the horizontal direction when the monitor gets warm*	27	928
Symptom 27-30	*The image shrinks in the horizontal direction when the monitor gets warm*	27	928
Symptom 27-31	*High-voltage fails after the monitor is warm*	27	929
Symptom 27-32	*The image blooms intermittently*	27	929
Symptom 27-33	*The image appears out of focus*	27	929
Symptom 27-34	*The image appears to flip or scroll horizontally*	27	930
Symptom 27-35	*The image appears to flip or scroll vertically*	27	930
Symptom 27-36	*The image appears to shake or oscillate in size*	27	930
Symptom 28-1	*A motherboard failure is reported, but goes away when the PC's outer cover is removed*	28	947
Symptom 28-2	*The POST (or your software diagnostic) reports a CPU fault*	28	947
Symptom 28-3	*The POST (or your software diagnostic) reports a problem with the floating-point unit*	28	947
Symptom 28-4	*The POST (or your software diagnostic) reports a BIOS ROM checksum error*	28	948
Symptom 28-5	*The POST (or software diagnostic) reports a timer (PIT) failure, an RTC update problem, or a refresh failure*	28	948
Symptom 28-6	*The POST (or software diagnostic) reports an interrupt controller (PIC) failure*	28	948
Symptom 28-7	*The POST (or software diagnostic) reports a DMA controller (DMAC) failure*	28	949
Symptom 28-8	*The POST (or software diagnostic) reports a KBC fault*	28	949
Symptom 28-9	*A keyboard error is reported, but a new keyboard has no effect*	28	949
Symptom 28-10	*The POST (or software diagnostic) reports a CMOS or RTC fault*	28	949
Symptom 28-11	*The POST (or software diagnostic) reports a fault in the first 64KB of RAM*	28	949
Symptom 28-12	*The MCP does not work properly when installed on a motherboard when external caching is enabled*	28	950
Symptom 28-13	*A "jumperless motherboard" receives incorrect CPU Soft Menu settings, and now refuses to boot*	28	950

Symptom	Description	Chapter	Page
Symptom 28-14	*When installing two 64MB SIMMs, only 32MB of RAM are displayed when the computer is turned on*	28	950
Symptom 28-15	*A Creative Labs PnP sound board refuses to work on one motherboard, but the board works just fine on another motherboard*	28	950
Symptom 28-16	*The system CD-ROM drive refuses to work once an IDE bus master driver is installed*	28	951
Symptom 28-17	*You cannot get an AMD 5x86 133MHz CPU to run on your motherboard*	28	951
Symptom 28-18	*You cannot get a Cyrix 5x86 CPU to run on your motherboard*	28	951
Symptom 28-19	*You see the error message "System Resource Conflict" on the AMI BIOS POST display*	28	951
Symptom 28-20	*The system hangs after using MEMMAKER under DOS*	28	951
Symptom 28-21	*The Power management icon does not appear in the Windows 95 Control panel*	28	951
Symptom 28-22	*Systems with a Western Digital 1.6GB HDD fail to boot even through BIOS recognized the presence of HDD*	28	951
Symptom 28-23	*After installing Windows 95, the system can no longer find the CD-ROM drive on the secondary IDE channel*	28	952
Symptom 28-24	*The system hangs up or crashes when the chipset-specific PCI-IDE DOS driver is loaded*	28	952
Symptom 28-25	*The Pentium motherboard is unusually picky about which SIMMs it will accept*	28	952
Symptom 28-26	*You experience a problem with pipeline burst cache*	28	952
Symptom 28-27	*You get no display or the system refuses to boot because of the keyboard controller*	28	952
Symptom 28-28	*Your customer forgets their password*	28	952
Symptom 28-29	*You encounter problems with Western Digital hard drives (the drives work on other systems)*	28	953
Symptom 28-30	*You encounter memory parity errors at bootup*	28	954
Symptom 28-31	*You flash a BIOS, but now you get no video*	28	954
Symptom 28-32	*You are trying to use a PnP sound card and PnP modem together on the same system, but you're getting hardware conflicts*	28	954
Symptom 28-33	*After setting the DRAM speed to 70 nS in the Advanced chipset setup, the system crashes or refuses to boot*	28	954
Symptom 28-34	*32MB (or more) of memory is installed, and the BIOS counts it all during POST, but you only see 16MB in the CMOS setup screen*	28	954
Symptom 28-35	*You move a working IDE drive from an older 386/486 system to your new Pentium system, but the system no longer works*	28	954
Symptom 28-36	*Windows 95 locks up when you install a Diamond Stealth Video 3200 board and an Intel EtherExpress Pro 10/100 network card*	28	955
Symptom 28-37	*You install an Intel Pentium P55C (MMX) 200MHz CPU, and you set the CPU speed jumper(s) for 200MHz, but the system still reports 166MHz*	28	955

Symptom	Description	Chapter	Page
Symptom 28-38	*The system frequently locks up or crashes after installing a Cyrix 6x86 CPU*	28	955
Symptom 28-39	*After installing a Pentium 120MHz motherboard, you get "registry corruption" or "out of memory" errors from Windows 95*	28	955
Symptom 28-40	*The motherboard fails to "auto-detect" the hard drive parameters*	28	955
Symptom 28-41	*The motherboard refuses to detect the SCSI controller during bootup*	28	956
Symptom 28-42	*A Cyrix 6x86 CPU will not run on a particular motherboard*	28	956
Symptom 28-43	*The system can only count up to and recognize 8MB of RAM, although the system can accommodate even more*	28	956
Symptom 28-44	*When four 8MB SIMMs are installed in the system (32MB), the system only counts up to 24MB*	28	956
Symptom 28-45	*Gold-plated SIMMs do not work properly in tin-plated sockets*	28	956
Symptom 28-46	*Even though all peripherals in the system are SCSI, Windows 95 will continue to detect the PCI IDE controller*	28	956
Symptom 28-47	*An "EISA CMOS configuration error" occurs when the system starts*	28	957
Symptom 28-48	*The SMP (dual processor) mode refuses to run in Windows NT*	28	957
Symptom 28-49	*When attempting to upgrade your flash BIOS, an "insufficient memory" error occurs*	28	957
Symptom 28-50	*A prolonged "Updating ESCD" message appears each time that the system boots*	28	957
Symptom 28-51	*A yellow (!) sign appears over the USB port in the* Device manager	28	957
Symptom 28-52	*The* Device manager *under Windows 95 indicates four COM ports (at unusual IRQs and I/O addresses), but only two physical ports are on the motherboard*	28	957
Symptom 28-53	*The performance of a motherboard with an AMD K5 CPU seems extremely poor*	28	957
Symptom 28-54	*The system hangs up after installing a Cyrix 6x86 CPU*	28	957
Symptom 28-55	*When attempting to upgrade the BIOS version, a key sequence, such as <Ctrl>+<Home>, cannot be used to reboot the PC in order to start the flash process*	28	958
Symptom 28-56	*A particular SVGA board refuses to work on a particular motherboard*	28	958
Symptom 28-57	*When the on-board printer port is set to 3BCh (and EPP/SPP mode) and another parallel port add-on card is set to 378h or 278h, the BIOS only recognizes the add-on card*	28	958
Symptom 28-58	*With 32MB of RAM on the motherboard, Checkit 3.0 causes the system to reboot when performing DRAM tests*	28	958
Symptom 28-59	*The IBM Blue Lighting CPU will not run on a motherboard that should support it*	28	958

Symptom	Description	Chapter	Page
Symptom 28-60	When using a benchmark program, such as SYSINFO, the "Overall Performance" rating of a Pentium 100 system marks better than a Pentium-120 system	28	958
Symptom 28-61	Parallel-port devices do not work on your motherboard	28	958
Symptom 28-62	Some configurations of memory provide less performance than others	28	959
Symptom 28-63	The performance does not improve when enabling PCI/IDE bus mastering	28	959
Symptom 28-64	The BIOS banner displayed on power-on is showing the wrong motherboard model	28	959
Symptom 28-65	The Pentium P55CM BIOS shows a 150MHz CPU— even though the CPU is a 166MHz model	28	959
Symptom 28-66	"Static device resource conflict" error message occurs after the system memory count when using the P55CM CPU	28	959
Symptom 29-1	You are having difficulty installing Ontrack's Disk Manager software from the B: drive	29	962
Symptom 29-2	Windows 95 reports that the system is operating in "DOS Compatibility Mode"	29	962
Symptom 29-3	Disk Manager does not appear to function properly with Windows 95	29	962
Symptom 29-4	When using Disk Manager 6.0x, Windows 95 reports operating in the "DOS Compatibility Mode"	29	962
Symptom 29-5	You encounter trouble with the disk driver (such as WDCDRV.386) for 32-bit disk access in Windows 95	29	963
Symptom 29-6	When installing a new, large drive (and reinstalling Disk Manager to the new drive), you encounter errors with cluster sizes	29	963
Symptom 29-7	Disk Manager fails to identify the hard drive correctly	29	963
Symptom 29-8	You have problems removing Disk Manager	29	963
Symptom 29-9	You find "Out of disk space" errors after loading as little as 800MB of data onto a 1GB drive	29	963
Symptom 29-10	Disk Manager appears to conflict with other programs in conventional memory	29	963
Symptom 29-11	Disk Manager installed properly and responded as expected, but after installing DOS 6.2, the drive ended up at 504MB	29	964
Symptom 29-12	Disk Manager installed and ran properly, but now you get a "DDO integrity error" and cannot access the hard drive	29	964
Symptom 29-13	You can only get 16-bit file access on the secondary ("slave") drive formatted with Disk Manager	29	964
Symptom 29-14	Drive letters are all switched around when booting from a bootable diskette	29	964
Symptom 29-15	You have trouble creating a floppy so that you can boot from a diskette and still have the DDO load	29	965
Symptom 29-16	You encounter problems using certain utilities on your hard drive	29	965
Symptom 29-17	EZ-Drive refuses to work properly with the system's VLB IDE controller	29	965

Symptom	Description	Chapter	Page
Symptom 29-18	*The keyboard or mouse does not function normally after exiting Windows on an EZ-Drive system*	29	966
Symptom 29-19	*With EZ-Drive installed on the system, QEMM 7.5 will not load in stealth mode*	29	966
Symptom 29-20	*Windows crashes with EZ-Drive installed on my drive*	29	966
Symptom 29-21	*You have trouble removing EZ-Drive from the system*	29	966
Symptom 29-22	*You see an error message, such as: "No IDE drive installed"*	29	966
Symptom 29-23	*You have trouble removing EZ-Drive from a system with available LBA support*	29	967
Symptom 29-24	*You keep getting the message "Hold down the CTRL key . . ."*	29	967
Symptom 29-25	*The system hangs after booting directly from non-system disk*	29	968
Symptom 29-26	*You encounter an: "Unrecognized DBR" message from EZ-Drive*	29	968
Symptom 29-27	*You cannot get EZ-Drive to work on some PS/1 and PS/2 systems*	29	968
Symptom 29-28	*Windows 95 reports a problem with the MH32BIT.386 driver*	29	969
Symptom 29-29	*After removing EZ-Drive, the data on a hard drive is inaccessible*	29	969
Symptom 29-30	*The <Alt> + <T> function was accidentally invoked under Disk Manager and the DDO could not be recovered through EZ-Drive*	29	969
Symptom 29-31	*When running Drive Rocket, the QEMM Stealth ROM feature indicates: "Disabling Stealth ROM," then reports a reference to INT 76*	29	969
Symptom 29-32	*During installation, Drive Rocket produces an error, which says that it can't recognize the driver*	29	969
Symptom 29-33	*Drive Rocket cannot be removed*	29	970
Symptom 29-34	*Drive Rocket refuses to identify the hard drive correctly*	29	970
Symptom 29-35	*You have trouble loading Drive Rocket into high memory*	29	970
Symptom 29-36	*Drive Rocket reports a −35% increase*	29	970
Symptom 29-37	*You encounter a GPF when working with the Control Panel in Windows 3.1x*	29	970
Symptom 31-1	*You hear a beep code or see a POST error, indicating a parallel port error*	31	1001
Symptom 31-2	*A 9xx parallel adapter is displayed on the XT or early AT system*	31	1001
Symptom 31-3	*The computer initializes properly, but the peripheral (printer) does not work*	31	1001
Symptom 31-4	*The peripheral (printer) will not go on-line*	31	1002
Symptom 31-5	*Data is randomly lost or garbled*	31	1002
Symptom 31-6	*You see a continuous "paper out" error—even though paper is available and the printer's paper sensor works properly*	31	1003
Symptom 32-1	*The SRAM or flash card looses its memory when powered down or removed from the system*	32	1024

Symptom	Description	Chapter	Page
Symptom 32-2	*You are unable to access a memory card for reading. You might not be able to write to the card, either*	32	1024
Symptom 32-3	*You see an error message indicating that a PCMCIA card will not install or is not recognized*	32	1025
Symptom 32-4	*Even though a desired card is installed, an error message or warning is displayed, asking you to insert the card*	32	1025
Symptom 32-5	*You encounter a number of card-service errors or other problems when anti-virus programs are used*	32	1025
Symptom 32-6	*There are no pop-up displays when a PC card is inserted or removed*	32	1026
Symptom 32-7	*The application locks up when a PC card is inserted or removed*	32	1026
Symptom 32-8	*The fax/modem card works fine in DOS, but refuses to work in Windows 95*	32	1026
Symptom 32-9	*The mouse/trackball locks up or acts strangely after a fax/modem card is installed*	32	1026
Symptom 32-10	*My peripheral (e.g., sound card, scanner, etc.) no longer works now that the PC Card is installed*	32	1026
Symptom 32-11	*The PCMCIA CardSoft enabler software won't install*	32	1027
Symptom 32-12	*When installing a PC Card, (such as a fax/modem card), you find that the desired COM port or IRQ is not available*	32	1027
Symptom 32-13	*You don't hear the proper number of beeps when inserting a PCMCIA card*	32	1027
Symptom 32-14	*The card's configuration refuses to accept memory addresses (if needed)*	32	1027
Symptom 32-15	*Other programs stop working or change their behavior after the card software is installed*	32	1027
Symptom 32-16	*When starting a client driver under Windows 95, the message "Client registration failed" appears*	32	1027
Symptom 32-17	*The PC Card will not configure properly. An I/O Address conflict message is displayed*	32	1028
Symptom 32-18	*My system hangs when card services loads*	32	1028
Symptom 32-19	*An "Invalid command-line switch" message is displayed when loading services or client drivers*	32	1029
Symptom 32-20	*You have a Xircom Combo card (i.e., fax/modem and LAN) and cannot get it to work with standard card-manager software*	32	1029
Symptom 32-21	*You get a "Abort, Retry, Ignore" message when accessing an ATA PC Card*	32	1029
Symptom 32-22	*You can't get any sound from the PC Card sound device or you get an error message saying that it can't talk to card services*	32	1029
Symptom 32-23	*When you insert a Practical Peripherals PractiCard 14,400bps modem (revision A) in a PCMCIA slot, the modem might not be initialized*	32	1029
Symptom 32-24	*The SRAM card refuses to work*	32	1029
Symptom 32-25	*When you first install your PC Card software, you get the error message: "No PCMCIA controller found"*	32	1029

Symptom	Description	Chapter	Page
Symptom 32-26	When a program attempts to identify or check the status of a PC Card modem, the program might stop responding (or cause the computer to hang) if the modem has been powered off using power-management features	32	1030
Symptom 32-27	When you eject a PC Card network adapter from a CardBus socket without stopping the card in PC Card properties, your computer might restart	32	1030
Symptom 32-28	After a multi-function PCMCIA adapter is installed, the adapter might appear as a "parent" node below a "child" node in the Windows 95 Device manager	32	1030
Symptom 32-29	After a second boot with a CardBus PCMCIA controller installed in your computer, the Device manager might display a red "X" for one or more PCMCIA sockets on your system	32	1030
Symptom 32-30	After installing Windows 95 OSR2, the Device manager might display a PCIC-compatible PCMCIA controller as a conflicting resource (an exclamation point in a yellow circle)	32	1031
Symptom 32-31	When using a 3COM Elnk3 PCMCIA network card and a Xircom CE2ps PCMCIA network card together on a DEC HiNote Ultra CT475 computer, the Xircom card is not recognized	32	1031
Symptom 32-32	When you use the Suspend command on certain Gateway laptop computers, battery power continues to drain	32	1031
Symptom 32-33	When you insert a Hayes Optima 14.4 PCMCIA modem into a PC Card socket, you hear a single (low) tone (or other indication) that the PCMCIA modem has not been recognized	32	1031
Symptom 32-34	When you use the Windows 95 Compression Agent with a removable PCMCIA hard disk, the Compression Agent might restart continuously at 10% finished	32	1031
Symptom 32-35	When you start Windows 95 with a PCMCIA hard disk inserted in the computer's PCMCIA slot, the hard disk seems to be recognized, but might not be available in Windows 95	32	1032
Symptom 32-36	When you insert a PCMCIA disk drive into a PCMCIA slot, your computer beeps (indicating that the PCMCIA card is recognized), but the disk drive is unavailable in Windows 95	32	1032
Symptom 32-37	When you attempt to dial under Windows 95 using an Integrated Services Digital Network (ISDN) connection, your computer might hang	32	1032
Symptom 32-38	When you try to send a fax from a cellular phone using Microsoft Exchange and a Motorola Power 14.4 PCMCIA modem, your fax feature might not work	32	1032
Symptom 32-39	When you run Windows 95 on a Dell Latitude XP Notebook computer with a port replicator, PC Card services might not be available	32	1033
Symptom 32-40	When you try to undock a laptop computer with a PCMCIA card installed in a Databook PCMCIA controller socket, you might receive the following error message: "The computer failed to undock"	32	1034

Symptom	Description	Chapter	Page
Symptom 32-41	*When you insert a PCMCIA SRAM or flash memory card into a Windows 95 computer that has been configured to use protected-mode PCMCIA card drivers, there might be no drive letter in My Computer or Windows Explorer associated with the PCMCIA card*	32	1034
Symptom 32-42	*You are logged on without a password*	32	1034
Symptom 32-43	*You have trouble with incompatible NDIS driver versions*	32	1035
Symptom 32-44	*You can't set up the PCMCIA slot in an AT&T Globalyst 130 laptop*	32	1035
Symptom 32-45	*When you are using a Motorola Power 14.4 cellular modem with Windows 95, you might not be able to dial the second time you try to use the modem*	32	1036
Symptom 32-46	*A PCMCIA token-ring network adapter refuses to work in the computer*	32	1036
Symptom 32-47	*You restart the computer improperly after installing PCMCIA drivers*	32	1037
Symptom 32-48	*In System Agent, the Last Result column for a ScanDisk task might report "Check was stopped because of an error"*	32	1037
Symptom 32-49	*When you start Windows 95 on a Zenith ZDS 1762 laptop computer, the computer might stop responding (hang) while Windows 95 is running the CONFIG.SYS file*	32	1037
Symptom 32-50	*When you use the Suspend feature on a Dell Latitude XP laptop computer connected to a port replicator, your PCMCIA devices might not reactivate when you exit the Suspend mode*	32	1037
Symptom 32-51	*You have trouble using similar cards simultaneously*	32	1037
Symptom 32-52	*The Zenith Zplayer PCMCIA CD-ROM adapter does not function correctly using Windows 95 32-bit drivers*	32	1038
Symptom 32-53	*On a computer with only one PCMCIA socket, Windows 95 cannot set up a new PCMCIA card if the original PCMCIA card is being used to access the Windows 95 source files*	32	1038
Symptom 32-54	*You cannot format an SRAM card using the Windows 95 graphical user interface because the Full and quick format options are not available*	32	1038
Symptom 32-55	*After you dock or undock a Compaq Elite laptop computer, the computer's PCMCIA devices might stop working*	32	1038
Symptom 32-56	*When you set up Windows 95, it will not install more than one PCMCIA network adapter correctly*	32	1039
Symptom 32-57	*When you try to connect to a network using an IBM token-ring PCMCIA network card on an Omnibook 600 computer, you are unable to view any resources*	32	1039
Symptom 32-58	*When you run ScanDisk, the "Select the drive you want to check for errors" box might or might not show drives that exist*	32	1039
Symptom 32-59	*When you insert a Xircom CE2 PCMCIA network adapter card, the card might not work and the computer might not be connected to the network*	32	1039

Symptom	Description	Chapter	Page
Symptom 32-60	PCMCIA cards are not configuring properly on your Compaq computer	32	1039
Symptom 32-61	When the system boots up, you see the error message "Divide overflow" before entering Windows 95—this forces you to boot Windows 95 in safe mode	32	1040
Symptom 32-62	Your PC Card client drivers refuse to load and an error message appears when starting Windows 95	32	1040
Symptom 32-63	PCMCIA cards are not configuring properly on IBM Thinkpads	32	1040
Symptom 32-64	The computer produces a single, low beep when the PCMCIA card is inserted, but the PC Card icon shows no information about the socket, and the Stop feature shows the "Device cannot be removed" error	32	1040
Symptom 32-65	Windows 95 does not recognize the parameters of the PCMCIA note disk	32	1040
Symptom 34-1	The pen seems to operate intermittently as it moves along the surface	34	1059
Symptom 34-2	The pen or tablet does not appear to respond at all	34	1060
Symptom 34-3	Ink appears on the LCD as the pen moves, but ink is not exactly under the pen	34	1060
Symptom 34-4	The pen-computer locks up or suffers other strange problems once the RF digitizer has been repaired or replaced	34	1061
Symptom 34-5	As you write, no "ink" appears on the display, but the characters are recognized and translated properly	34	1061
Symptom 34-6	The DOS pen driver(s) will not load as the system initializes	34	1061
Symptom 34-7	The pen buttons do not work correctly in your software	34	1061
Symptom 34-8	The pen tablet does not work in Windows	34	1062
Symptom 34-9	Windows locks-up or the tablet fails to respond	34	1062
Symptom 34-10	The cursor is too sensitive or not sensitive enough to pen movement	34	1062
Symptom 34-11	The cursor seems to "jitter" or leave spikes when drawing	34	1062
Symptom 34-12	No matter what "stroke width" is chosen in the drawing application, only thin, narrow lines appear when drawing on the pen tablet	34	1062
Symptom 34-13	After installing the latest pen tablet drivers for Windows 95, you get an: "Invalid Dynamic Link call to a .DLL file" error once the PC restarts	34	1063
Symptom 34-14	Installing the pen tablet on a Packard Bell PC results in various errors	34	1063
Symptom 34-15	The pen cursor moves, but everything is reversed	34	1064
Symptom 34-16	The pen is not "selecting" or "inking"	34	1064
Symptom 34-17	The cursor flickers in Windows 95	34	1064
Symptom 34-18	The cursor is moving, selecting items, or otherwise behaving strangely—even though the pen is not touching the tablet	34	1064
Symptom 34-19	There is no "inking" and handwriting recognition doesn't work	34	1065
Symptom 34-20	The pen does not work properly in Microsoft Word using Windows 95 Pen Computing	34	1065

Symptom	Description	Chapter	Page
Symptom 34-21	An "Invalid VxD dynamic link call" error occurs when trying to install pen-tablet software under Windows 95	34	1065
Symptom 34-22	An error appears: "VxD not present: either Windows 95 is running in safe mode or xxx.VxD is not installed correctly"	34	1066
Symptom 34-23	The pen tablet works intermittently on a laptop	34	1066
Symptom 34-24	After installing a pen-tablet driver, the cursor moves very slowly	34	1066
Symptom 34-25	After installing a pen-tablet driver, SCSI devices are no longer present	34	1067
Symptom 34-26	When you place a pen against the tablet surface, the cursor jumps to the top left corner of the screen	34	1067
Symptom 34-27	After installing a pen-tablet driver, .AVI files do not open	34	1067
Symptom 34-28	You notice that the system slows after installing touchpad drivers in Windows 95	34	1067
Symptom 34-29	The touchpad cursor freezes in the center of the screen after installing the driver(s)	34	1068
Symptom 34-30	The touchpad and software were installed, but it refuses to operate—the mouse continues to operate	34	1069
Symptom 35-1	Windows 95 fails to recognize the computer as "Plug and Play"	35	1087
Symptom 35-2	The IRQ conflicts with PCI display adapters	35	1088
Symptom 35-3	The resources for disabled devices are not freed	35	1088
Symptom 35-4	An AST PnP BIOS is not registered as PnP	35	1088
Symptom 35-5	A PnP ISA adapter is not recognized automatically	35	1088
Symptom 35-6	The computer no longer operates properly after docking or undocking	35	1089
Symptom 35-7	Serial PnP devices are not recognized when an adapter is used to connect them	35	1089
Symptom 35-8	Windows 95 Setup hangs up when detecting SCSI controllers	35	1089
Symptom 35-9	After installing an HP OfficeJet 300 printer, a "Fatal exception error" occurs each time you run the Add new hardware wizard	35	1090
Symptom 35-10	The PS/2 mouse is disabled after installing an ISA PnP device	35	1090
Symptom 35-11	When running the Add new hardware wizard, it doesn't detect a device that has been removed in Device manager on a multiple-profile system	35	1090
Symptom 35-12	An extra serial port is displayed in the Device manager	35	1090
Symptom 35-13	Windows 95 cannot setup with a PnP program active	35	1090
Symptom 35-14	An IBM ThinkPad doesn't support PnP under Windows 95	35	1091
Symptom 35-15	A PnP pointing device is not detected	35	1092
Symptom 35-16	The PnP printer is re-detected every time Windows 95 starts	35	1092
Symptom 35-17	After installing Windows 95, none of the APM features were installed	35	1093

Symptom	Description	Chapter	Page
Symptom 35-18	*The* Device manager *reports a "PCI-to-ISA bridge conflict"*	35	1094
Symptom 35-19	*The PnP BIOS is disabled on a laptop or notebook computer*	35	1094
Symptom 35-20	*The sound device on a DEC HiNote Ultra isn't working*	35	1094
Symptom 35-21	*Device resources are not updated in a "forced" configuration*	35	1095
Symptom 35-22	*Restarting the computer causes the PC to hang*	35	1095
Symptom 35-23	*Adding a PCI device to a Dell Dimension causes the system to hang in Windows 95*	35	1095
Symptom 35-24	*You cannot configure disabled devices in the* Device manager	35	1096
Symptom 35-25	*A Toshiba T4900 laptop doesn't switch from LCD to external monitor*	35	1096
Symptom 35-26	*A third port is detected with a CMD PCI dual-port IDE controller*	35	1096
Symptom 36-1	*The PC or peripheral is completely dead—no power indicators are lit*	36	1107
Symptom 36-2	*Supply operation is intermittent—device operation cuts in and out with the supply*	36	1108
Symptom 37-1	*The backlight appears inoperative.*	37	1112
Symptom 37-2	*Anode high-voltage measures very low—it has no raster and no picture, or a vertical line is against the raster*	37	1114
Symptom 38-1	*An Iomega Zip drive displays a* Floppy-disk *icon under* Windows 95	38	1117
Symptom 38-2	*The SCSI Zip drive has no drive letter under* Windows 95	38	1117
Symptom 38-3	*The parallel-port Zip drive has no drive letter under* Windows 95	38	1118
Symptom 38-4	*The system hangs when installing drivers for* Windows 95	38	1119
Symptom 38-5	*After installing a Zip drive, you find the other drives in the system are using the DOS-compatibility mode*	38	1119
Symptom 38-6	*The Zip drive takes over the CD-ROM drive letter in* Windows 95	38	1120
Symptom 38-7	*Duplicate Zip drive letters appear*	38	1120
Symptom 38-8	*A Zip guest locks up or cannot locate the drive or adapter*	38	1120
Symptom 38-9	*You encounter Zip drive letter problems under DOS*	38	1121
Symptom 38-10	*The GUEST utility cannot find an available drive letter*	38	1122
Symptom 38-11	*System recovery fails after the Zip Tools setup process is complete*	38	1122
Symptom 38-12	*Error messages, such as: "Can't find Zip tools disk" or "No drive letters added," appear when using Zip parallel-port drives*	38	1122
Symptom 38-13	*Windows 3.11 allows network drive letter to conflict with Zip drive letter*	38	1123
Symptom 38-14	*The Zip drive setup could not find a Zip Tools disk for Zip parallel-port drives*	38	1123

Symptom	Description	Chapter	Page
Symptom 38-15	*You cannot print while using a ZIP drive*	38	1123
Symptom 38-16	*Problems occur while installing a Zip SCSI drive*	38	1124
Symptom 38-17	*The drive letter is lost each time the PC is turned off*	38	1125
Symptom 38-18	*The internal Ditto tape drive is not detected when running from a floppy-disk controller*	38	1125
Symptom 38-19	*The internal Ditto drive is not detected when running from a Ditto Dash accelerator card*	38	1126
Symptom 38-20	*The internal Ditto drive takes longer to backup than expected and the drive regularly spins back and forth*	38	1126
Symptom 38-21	*The Ditto parallel-port drive is not detected under DOS or Windows 3.1x*	38	1126
Symptom 38-22	*The internal Ditto drive does not find any catalogs during a restore*	38	1127
Symptom 38-23	*The Ditto drive encounters many corrected errors during a compare*	38	1127
Symptom 38-24	*A "Fatal exception error" occurs with the Ditto drive*	38	1128
Symptom 38-25	*The Ditto drive is not restoring selected files*	38	1128
Symptom 38-26	*The error: "The drive received an invalid command" appears when using a Ditto drive*	38	1129
Symptom 38-27	*The Iomega Bernoulli drive has a floppy icon in Windows 95*	38	1129
Symptom 38-28	*The Iomega Bernoulli SCSI drive does not have a drive letter in Windows 95*	38	1130
Symptom 38-29	*The parallel-port (or PPA-3) adapter does not have a drive letter in Windows 95*	38	1130
Symptom 38-30	*The Bernoulli drive takes over the CD-ROM's drive letter in Windows 95*	38	1131
Symptom 38-31	*An "Invalid drive specification" error occurs after installing an Iomega SCSI drive*	38	1131
Symptom 38-32	*An "Invalid Unit Reading Drive <x>" error occurs*	38	1131
Symptom 38-33	*Problems occur when using the Iomega parallel-port interface (PPA-3) with a Bernoulli drive*	38	1132
Symptom 38-34	*The Iomega PPA3 locks up on installation*	38	1133
Symptom 38-35	*SCSI communication problems occur*	38	1134
Symptom 38-36	*The IDE Bernoulli drive receives two drive letters*	38	1134
Symptom 38-37	*Using an Iomega PC2X 8-bit Bernoulli controller might cause the system to crash*	38	1134
Symptom 38-38	*The compressed removable-media drive(s) are not automatically mounted on startup*	38	1135
Symptom 38-39	*Problems occur when running Iomega Jaz Tools under Windows 95*	38	1135
Symptom 38-40	*Removable-media IDE drives have problems in Windows 95*	38	1136
Symptom 38-41	*Problems are encountered with SyQuest drives and Future Domain SCSI adapters*	38	1136
Symptom 38-42	*Problems are encountered with SyQuest drives and NCR SCSI adapters*	38	1137
Symptom 38-43	*Problems are encountered with SyQuest drives and Rancho Technology SCSI adapters*	38	1137

Symptom	Description	Chapter	Page
Symptom 38-44	*Problems occur with Packard-Bell multimedia PCs and SyQuest drives*	38	1138
Symptom 38-45	*Problems occur using BusLogic SCSI adapters and SyQuest drives*	38	1138
Symptom 38-46	*Problems occur when using Qlogic SCSI adapters and SyQuest drives*	38	1138
Symptom 38-47	*Problems occur when using an IBM MicroChannel SCSI controller and SyQuest drive*	38	1138
Symptom 38-48	*Problems occur when using Data Technology Corporation (DTC) SCSI adapters and SyQuest drives*	38	1139
Symptom 38-49	*The lights on the SyQuest drive are blinking in a regular pattern*	38	1139
Symptom 39-1	*After initial SCSI installation, the system will not boot from the floppy drive*	39	1162
Symptom 39-2	*The system will not boot from the SCSI hard drive*	39	1162
Symptom 39-3	*The SCSI drive fails to respond with an alternate HDD as the boot drive*	39	1163
Symptom 39-4	*The SCSI drive fails to respond with another SCSI drive as the boot drive*	39	1163
Symptom 39-5	*The system works erratically.*	39	1163
Symptom 39-6	*A 096xxxx error code appears*	39	1164
Symptom 39-7	*A 112xxxx error code appears*	39	1164
Symptom 39-8	*A 113xxxx error code appears*	39	1164
Symptom 39-9	*A 210xxxx error code appears*	39	1164
Symptom 39-10	*A SCSI device refuses to function with the SCSI adapter—even though both the adapter and device check properly*	39	1164
Symptom 39-11	*A "No SCSI controller present" error message appears*	39	1165
Symptom 39-12	*The PCI SCSI host adapter is not recognized and the SCSI BIOS banner is not displayed*	39	1165
Symptom 39-13	*During boot-up, a "Host-adapter configuration error" message appears*	39	1165
Symptom 39-14	*An error message, such as "No SCSI functions in use, " appears*	39	1165
Symptom 39-15	*An error message, such as "No boot record found," appears*	39	1166
Symptom 39-16	*An error, such as "Device fails to respond—No devices in use. Driver load aborted," appears*	39	1166
Symptom 39-17	*An error, such as "Unknown SCSI device" or "Waiting for SCSI device," appears*	39	1166
Symptom 39-18	*An error, such as "CMD failure XX," appears*	39	1166
Symptom 39-19	*After the SCSI adapter BIOS header appears, a message, such as "Checking for SCSI target 0 LUN 0," appears*	39	1166
Symptom 39-20	*The system hangs up when the SCSI BIOS header appears*	39	1166
Symptom 39-21	*The SCSI BIOS header is displayed during system startup, then the message appears: "Host adapter diagnostic error"*	39	1167

Symptom	Description	Chapter	Page
Symptom 39-22	*When a VL bus SCSI adapter is installed, the system hangs at startup*	39	1167
Symptom 39-23	*When upgrading a VL bus system CPU to a faster model, the system locks up with a SCSI VL card installed or won't boot from the SCSI HDD*	39	1167
Symptom 39-24	*The VL SCSI adapter won't work with an "SLC" type CPU*	39	1167
Symptom 39-25	*When running the Qualitas 386MAX memory-manager software on ISA or VL systems with an SCSI host adapter, the system crashes when booting*	39	1168
Symptom 39-26	*When installing an EISA SCSI adapter and running the EISA configuration utility, you see an "EISA configuration slot mismatch" or "board not found in slot x" error*	39	1168
Symptom 39-27	*An EISA SCSI adapter can't be configured in enhanced mode*	39	1168
Symptom 40-1	*You hear a beep code or see a POST error, which indicates a serial-port fault*	40	1183
Symptom 40-2	*An 11xx or 12xx serial adapter error is displayed*	40	1183
Symptom 40-3	*The computer initializes properly, but the serial peripheral does not work*	40	1184
Symptom 40-4	*Data is randomly lost or garbled*	40	1184
Symptom 40-5	*LapLink does not recognize the IR COM port*	40	1184
Symptom 40-6	*Problems occur when maintaining an IR connection in the daylight*	40	1185
Symptom 41-1	*A noticeable buzz or hum is being produced in one or both speakers*	41	1200
Symptom 41-2	*No sound is produced by the speaker(s)*	41	1200
Symptom 41-3	*CD audio will not play through the sound card*	41	1201
Symptom 41-4	*An error, such as "No interrupt vector available" appears*	41	1201
Symptom 41-5	*It has no MIDI output*	41	1201
Symptom 41-6	*Sound play is jerky*	41	1201
Symptom 41-7	*An error, such as "Out of environment space" appears*	41	1201
Symptom 41-8	*Regular "clicks," "stutters," or "hiccups" occur during the playback of speech*	41	1202
Symptom 41-9	*The joystick is not working or not working properly on all systems*	41	1202
Symptom 41-10	*The sound board is installed and everything works properly, but now the printer does not seem to work*	41	1202
Symptom 41-11	*The following error message appears: "Error MMSYSTEM 337: The specified MIDI device is already in use"*	41	1202
Symptom 41-12	*The following error message appears: "Error: Wave device already in use when trying to play wave files while a MIDI file is playing"*	41	1202
Symptom 41-13	*You hear "pops" and "clicks" when recording sound under Windows 95*	41	1203
Symptom 41-14	*You notice high-frequency distortion in one or possibly in both channels*	41	1203

Symptom	Description	Chapter	Page
Symptom 41-15	*You hear "pops" and "clicks" when playing back pre-recorded files under Windows 95*	41	1203
Symptom 41-16	*"Pops" and "clicks" are audible on new recordings only, pre-existing files sound clean*	41	1203
Symptom 41-17	*"Pops" and "clicks" occur when playing back or recording any sound file*	41	1204
Symptom 41-18	*The sound board plays back fine, but it will not record*	41	1204
Symptom 41-19	*A DMA error is produced when using a sound board with an Adaptec 2842 controller in the system*	41	1204
Symptom 41-20	*A DMA error is produced when using a sound board with an Adaptec 1542 controller in the system*	41	1204
Symptom 41-21	*The sound card will not play or record—the system just locks up when either is attempted*	41	1204
Symptom 41-22	*The sound card will record, but will not playback*	41	1204
Symptom 41-23	*The sound application or editor produces a significant number of DMA errors*	41	1205
Symptom 41-24	*The sound board will not record in DOS*	41	1205
Symptom 41-25	*When recording sound, the system locks up if a key other than the recorder's "hot-keys" are pushed*	41	1205
Symptom 41-26	*After the sound board driver is loaded, Windows locks up when starting or exiting*	41	1205
Symptom 41-27	*When using Windows sound-editing software, the sound board refuses to enter the "digital" mode—always switching back to the analog mode*	41	1205
Symptom 41-28	*The microphone records at very low levels (or not at all)*	41	1206
Symptom 41-29	*The sound card isn't working in full-duplex mode*	41	1206
Symptom 41-30	*DMA errors occur using an older sound board and an Adaptec 1542*	41	1207
Symptom 41-31	*Hard-disk recording problems occur under Windows 95*	41	1207
Symptom 41-32	*The microphone records only at very low levels or not at all*	41	1208
Symptom 41-33	*The dynamic microphone clips terribly, and recordings are noisy and faint*	41	1208
Symptom 41-34	*Trouble occurs when using Creative Labs or Labtec microphones with your (non-Creative Labs) sound board*	41	1209
Symptom 41-35	*Static is at the remote end when talking through a voice application, such as WebPhone*	41	1209
Symptom 42-1	*The tape drive does not work at all*	42	1232
Symptom 42-2	*The tape does not read or write, but the tape and head seem to move properly*	42	1233
Symptom 42-3	*The R/W head does not step from track to track*	42	1234
Symptom 42-4	*The tape does not move or its speed does not remain constant*	42	1234
Symptom 42-5	*There are problems in loading or ejecting the tape*	42	1236
Symptom 42-6	*The drive writes to write-protected tapes*	42	1236
Symptom 42-7	*The drive does not recognize the beginning or end of the tape*	42	1237
Symptom 42-8	*A software program using a hardware copy-protection device on the parallel port locks up*	42	1237

Symptom	Description	Chapter	Page
Symptom 42-9	*The backup software indicates "Too many bad sectors" on the tape*	42	1237
Symptom 42-10	*The tape backup software produces a "Tape drive error XX," where XX is a specific fault type*	42	1237
Symptom 42-11	*The tape drive is not found by the backup software*	42	1238
Symptom 42-12	*The tape drive works in DOS, but refuses to work in Windows 95*	42	1238
Symptom 42-13	*The backup software generates an overlay error, such as "Could not open file: QBACKUP.OVL"*	42	1238
Symptom 42-14	*An error occurs when using older versions of backup software (e.g., "General tape failure: 187")*	42	1239
Symptom 42-15	*"Media errors," "bad block errors," "system errors," or "lock-ups" occur*	42	1239
Symptom 42-16	*During initialization under DOS or Windows, the SCSI tape driver (e.g., BPASPI.SYS) reports the error: "An ASPI drive was not found"*	42	1239
Symptom 42-17	*When using a Colorado Trakker tape drive, you cannot get the drive to save or restore files reliably*	42	1239
Symptom 42-18	*It takes much longer than you expect to perform a backup*	42	1240
Symptom 42-19	*When you try to format a DT-350 tape in a Conner 250 tape drive, the following message appears: "Errors occurred during this operation"*	42	1240
Symptom 42-20	*When you try to perform a backup, restore, or compare operation in Microsoft Backup, or close Backup after performing one of these operations, the following error message appears: "Microsoft Backup has encountered a serious error in the Memory Manager. Quit and restart Backup, and then try again"*	42	1240
Symptom 42-21	*The QIC-3020 formatted tape is not recognized by tape drive for writing*	42	1241
Symptom 42-22	*The backup software does not auto-skip busy files*	42	1241
Symptom 42-23	*The floppy-port tape drive cannot be connected to a floppy controller*	42	1241
Symptom 42-24	*An error message, such as: "DMA setting specified for this device might be incorrect" appears*	42	1241
Symptom 42-25	*The tape drive makes no sound when a minicartridge is inserted*	42	1241
Symptom 42-26	*An error message, such as: "File not found in file set directory," appears*	42	1242
Symptom 42-27	*Formatting the minicartridge lasts from 7 to 18 hours*	42	1242
Symptom 42-28	*You experience low capacity, or slow read and writes to your tape drive*	42	1242
Symptom 42-29	*A parsing or logic error occurs*	42	1242
Symptom 42-30	*Space runs out during DOS backups*	42	1242
Symptom 42-31	*Excessive "shoe shining" occurs during backups*	42	1243
Symptom 43-1	*The computer is on, but there is no display*	43	1277
Symptom 43-2	*There is no display and you hear a series of beeps when the PC initializes*	43	1278
Symptom 43-3	*Large, blank bands are at the top and bottom of the display in some screen modes, but not in others*	43	1278

Symptom	Description	Chapter	Page
Symptom 43-4	*The display image rolls*	43	1278
Symptom 43-5	*An error message appears on system startup indicating an invalid system configuration*	43	1279
Symptom 43-6	*Garbage appears on the screen or the system hangs up*	43	1279
Symptom 43-7	*When returning to Windows from a DOS application, the Windows screen "splits" from top to bottom*	43	1280
Symptom 43-8	*The system hangs up during initialization, some characters might be missing from the display, or the screen colors might be incorrect*	43	1280
Symptom 43-9	*Your system is generating DMA errors with a VGA board in the system and video BIOS shadowing disabled*	43	1281
Symptom 43-10	*The system hangs up using a 16-bit VGA board and one or more 8-bit controllers*	43	1281
Symptom 43-11	*You have trouble sizing or positioning the display, or you see error messages, such as "Mode not supported" or "Insufficient memory"*	43	1281
Symptom 43-12	*You frequently encounter GPFs when using QuickTime for Windows 1.1*	43	1281
Symptom 43-13	*The video board will not boot up when used in a particular motherboard*	43	1281
Symptom 43-14	*Diagnostics refuse to show all of the available video modes for a particular board—even though all video RAM was properly detected, or the board refuses to operate in some video modes*	43	1282
Symptom 43-15	*The characters shown in the display appear fuzzy*	43	1282
Symptom 43-16	*Pixels appear "dropped" behind the mouse cursor, and graphic images appear to break up under Windows*	43	1282
Symptom 43-17	*Video-related conflicts occur in Packard Bell systems*	43	1282
Symptom 43-18	*The text appears in an odd color*	43	1282
Symptom 43-19	*When an application is started (under Windows), the opening display appears "scrambled"*	43	1283
Symptom 43-20	*The display colors change when exiting from a DOS shell under Windows*	43	1283
Symptom 43-21	*The computer locks up or crashes when starting an .AVI file*	43	1283
Symptom 43-22	*The computer is running very slowly (poor performance) and the hard drive light is continuously lit*	43	1283
Symptom 43-23	*The .AVI files have distorted colors or "grainy" playback*	43	1283
Symptom 43-24	*The PCI video board will not work under Windows unless the system's PCI SCSI devices are disconnected*	43	1283
Symptom 43-25	*Boot problems occur after a new video board has been installed*	43	1284
Symptom 43-26	*Boot problems occur when a PCI video board is installed*	43	1284
Symptom 43-27	*The monitor overscans when entering a DOS shell from Windows*	43	1284
Symptom 43-28	*An intermittent "Divide by zero" error occurs*	43	1284
Symptom 43-29	*During MPEG playback, the display flickers, shows low refresh rates, or appears to be in an interlaced mode*	43	1284

Symptom	Description	Chapter	Page
Symptom 43-30	An error, such as "There is an undetectable problem in loading the specified device driver" occurs when starting an MPEG player or other video tool	43	1285
Symptom 43-31	On video boards with TV tuners, the TV window is blurry or fuzzy at 1024-x-768 (or higher) resolutions	43	1285
Symptom 43-32	On video boards with TV tuners, the reception does not appear as good as that of an ordinary TV	43	1285
Symptom 43-33	Errors appear, such as "Insufficient video memory"	43	1285
Symptom 43-34	The PCI video board is not working properly. A BIOS conflict is occurring with PCI interrupt 1Ah	43	1285
Symptom 43-35	Video corruption or sporadic system rebooting occurs when using an SLC-type motherboard	43	1286
Symptom 43-36	Video playback experiences long pauses while the hard drive thrashes excessively	43	1286
Symptom 43-37	The loop-through feature of your video board cannot be used	43	1286
Symptom 43-38	Windows appears with a "black box" cursor and/or icons that fail to appear on the screen	43	1286
Symptom 43-39	Video problems occur or the system locks up while using an anti-virus program	43	1286
Symptom 43-40	An error indicates that not enough memory is available for playback or re-sizing of the playback window	43	1286
Symptom 43-41	The video board refuses to accept a particular video mode	43	1287
Symptom 43-42	The video system cannot lock memory using QEMM and linear video memory	43	1287
Symptom 43-43	The video system cannot lock memory under Windows or the system hangs	43	1287
Symptom 43-44	Other devices don't work properly after the PCI video card is installed	43	1287
Symptom 43-45	A Windows 95 game doesn't start or runs slower than normal	43	1287
Symptom 44-1	Problems occur when installing the S-Video cable	44	1302
Symptom 44-2	Even though a valid video source is available, vertical multi-colored lines appear in the capture application window	44	1302
Symptom 44-3	Even though a valid video source is available, only black appears in the capture application window	44	1302
Symptom 44-4	During installation, the error "Unable to locate an available interrupt" appears	44	1303
Symptom 44-5	The capture board cannot be initialized because of a lack of available IRQs	44	1303
Symptom 44-6	When starting the capture utility, the error "Unable to initialize a capture device" appears	44	1303
Symptom 44-7	Colors appear washed out or bleeding	44	1304
Symptom 44-8	The video signal appears to be weak or washed out even though the video signal source is acceptable	44	1304
Symptom 44-9	"Vertical sync" error appears when trying to capture	44	1304
Symptom 44-10	Up to 50% of small frames are being dropped (large frames appear to capture properly)	44	1304

Symptom	Description	Chapter	Page
Symptom 44-11	*When capturing video, the corresponding screen image appears broken-up or jerky*	44	1305
Symptom 44-12	*The video-capture board is working, but captures are occurring very slowly*	44	1305
Symptom 44-13	*The Super Compressor option cannot be used in Video for Windows*	44	1305
Symptom 44-14	*More than one frame of motion video can't be captured*	44	1305
Symptom 44-15	*The color video being captured is shown as black and white*	44	1306
Symptom 44-16	*The video image shown in the VIDCAP capture window appears torn or bent at the top*	44	1306
Symptom 44-17	*When capturing video, an error appears: "No frames captured. Confirm that vertical sync interrupts are configured and enabled"*	44	1306
Symptom 44-18	*Artifacts appear when capturing video at high data rates*	44	1307
Symptom 44-19	*Artifacts appear when capturing video using certain PCI graphics cards*	44	1307
Symptom 44-20	*Systems with SiS 5596 or 5511 PCI chipsets lock up when using a video-capture device*	44	1307
Symptom 44-21	*Systems lockup when running video-capture devices on PCs with Phoenix BIOS*	44	1308
Symptom 44-22	*You cannot use the capture device on a system with a SiS PCI chipset*	44	1308
Symptom 44-23	*The capture device cannot be used on a system with an S3 chipset-based video card*	44	1308
Symptom 44-24	*A gray background is in the live video window display*	44	1309
Symptom 44-25	*The video device locks up in 8-bit (256 color) display modes*	44	1310
Symptom 44-26	*Bitmap or still-image files can't be imported into the Intel DVP 4.0 application*	44	1310
Symptom 44-27	*Intercast viewer can't be started*	44	1310
Symptom 44-28	*You only receive incomplete Intercast broadcast Web page displays on the PC-TV card*	44	1310
Symptom 44-29	*Intercast broadcast Web pages are missing*	44	1310
Symptom 44-30	*An error indicates that the computer can't find a .DLL file when trying to run the PC-TV application*	44	1310
Symptom 44-31	*An error appears, such as: "The following entry should be in your system.ini file: [drivers] Msvideo= stlthcap.drv"*	44	1311
Symptom 44-32	*The error "MMTASK ERROR > GPF IR30.DLL 0003:0B85" appears when trying to play a captured file*	44	1311
Symptom 44-33	*The video playback is choppy or contains dropped frames*	44	1311
Symptom 44-34	*An initial flash of color appears when playing back video files*	44	1311
Symptom 44-35	*No sound is heard during playback*	44	1312
Symptom 44-36	*When playing video, the system locks up when power-management features are enabled*	44	1312

Symptom	Description	Chapter	Page
Symptom 44-37	*The system locks up when changing resolutions or color depths while using MPEG playback or video-capture functions*	44	1312
Symptom 44-38	*Sound gaps occur and the image appears choppy during playback*	44	1312
Symptom 44-39	*Blue or green flesh tones are in the live video and MPEG playback*	44	1313
Symptom 44-40	*An MPEG movie clip cannot be scaled to full screen when using 16.7 million colors*	44	1313
Symptom 44-41	*The video looks grainy (or otherwise poor quality) when playing back or recording*	44	1313
Symptom 44-42	*With Active Movie installed, the MPEG options do not show up as a device under Media Player*	44	1313
Symptom 44-43	*The error: "No suitable DirectDraw provider" appears*	44	1314
Symptom 44-44	*The PC locks up when using the PC-TV in full-screen mode*	44	1314
Symptom 44-45	*TV images move only very slowly in an Intercast viewer*	44	1315
Symptom 44-46	*Bad or improper colors appear in the PC-TV window*	44	1315
Symptom 44-47	*The system locks up when using S3 Vision 968 or 868-based video adapters*	44	1315
Symptom 44-48	*You cannot tune the PC-TV card above channel 13*	44	1315
Symptom 44-49	*The PC-TV picture suffers from poor quality*	44	1316
Symptom 44-50	*The TV picture displays a blue screen*	44	1316
Symptom 44-51	*Snapshots taken from a PC-TV board don't display correctly*	44	1316
Symptom 44-52	*The display flickers when using a PC-TV device*	44	1316
Symptom 44-53	*Only channels 5 and 6 are available, and they are only in black and white*	44	1317
Symptom 44-54	*The television picture is green*	44	1317
Symptom 44-55	*All channels are available, but 14 and 15*	44	1317
Symptom 45-1	*You cannot run more than one anti-virus product at a time*	45	1339
Symptom 45-2	*Your anti-virus tool does not function or causes other drivers to malfunction*	45	1339
Symptom 45-3	*You notice that your anti-virus tool is slowing disk access dramatically, or it locks up under Windows*	45	1339
Symptom 45-4	*The anti-virus tool is reporting false alarms*	45	1339
Symptom 45-5	*The memory-resident anti-virus tool cannot be removed*	45	1339
Symptom 45-6	*The virus scanner is only scanning files very slowly*	45	1339
Symptom 45-7	*The virus scanner seems to conflict with the boot sector when it scans*	45	1339
Symptom 45-8	*You receive a "Cannot load device drivers error" from the virus scanner*	45	1340
Symptom 45-9	*An "Insufficient memory" message appears when the virus scanner is loading under Windows 95*	45	1340
Symptom 45-10	*A "Cannot create events" error appears when the virus scanner is loading*	45	1340
Symptom 49-1	*No CD audio is audible through the CD-ROM headphone jack or no sound is emanating from the system speakers*	49	1389

Symptom	Description	Chapter	Page
Symptom 49-2	*The system no longer boots correctly or key feature(s) no longer work correctly*	49	1390
DOS Errors	*Abort, Retry, Fail*	C	1398
DOS Errors	*Access Denied*	C	1398
DOS Errors	*Bad Command Or File Name*	C	1399
DOS Errors	*Bad Or Missing Command Interpreter*	C	1399
DOS Errors	*Bad Or Missing File Name*	C	1399
DOS Errors	*Cannot Find A Device File That May Be Needed To Run Windows*	C	1399
DOS Errors	*Cannot Find System Files*	C	1400
DOS Errors	*Directory Already Exists*	C	1400
DOS Errors	*Disk Full*	C	1400
DOS Errors	*Drive A: Does Not Exist*	C	1400
DOS Errors	*Duplicate File Name Or File(s) Not Found*	C	1400
DOS Errors	*Existing Format Differs From That Specified*	C	1400
DOS Errors	*File Cannot Be Copied Onto Itself*	C	1400
DOS Errors	*File Creation Error*	C	1400
DOS Errors	*File Exists*	C	1401
DOS Errors	*File Not Found*	C	1401
DOS Errors	*Formatting While Copying*	C	1401
DOS Errors	*Help Not Available For This Command*	C	1401
DOS Errors	*Incorrect DOS Version*	C	1401
DOS Errors	*Insert System Disk*	C	1401
DOS Errors	*Insufficient Disk Space*	C	1401
DOS Errors	*Insufficient Memory*	C	1401
DOS Errors	*Invalid Date/Invalid Time*	C	1401
DOS Errors	*Invalid Directory*	C	1401
DOS Errors	*Invalid Drive In Search Path*	C	1401
DOS Errors	*Invalid Drive Specification*	C	1402
DOS Errors	*Invalid Filename*	C	1402
DOS Errors	*Invalid Media Type*	C	1402
DOS Errors	*Invalid Parameter*	C	1402
DOS Errors	*Non-System Disk Or Disk Error—Replace And Strike Any Key*	C	1402
DOS Errors	*Out Of Memory*	C	1402
DOS Errors	*Path Not Found*	C	1402
DOS Errors	*Proceed With Format (Y/N)?*	C	1403
DOS Errors	*Read Error*	C	1403
DOS Errors	*Stack Overflow—System Halted*	C	1403
DOS Errors	*Syntax Error*	C	1403
DOS Errors	*Terminate Batch Job (Y/N)?*	C	1403
DOS Errors	*This Disk Cannot Be Unformatted*	C	1403
DOS Errors	*Too Many Open Files*	C	1403
DOS Errors	*Write-Protect Error*	C	1403

INSIDE TODAY'S
DESKTOP AND TOWER

CONTENTS AT A GLANCE

Under the Hood
  Enclosure
  Power supply
  Motherboard
  Drives
  Expansion boards

Notes for Disassembly and Re-assembly
  The value of data
  Opening the system

Closing the system
Tips for working inside a desktop or
  tower PC

Standardized Form Factors
  ATX form factor
  NLX form factor

Further Study

To upgrade or troubleshoot a PC effectively, a technician must be familiar with the general mechanical and physical aspects of the PC. They must be able to disassemble the unit quickly (without causing damage to the case or internal assemblies in the process), then accurately identify each sub-assembly, expansion board, and connector. Once a diagnosis and repair has been completed, the technician must be able to re-assemble the PC and its enclosures (again without damaging assemblies or enclosures). This chapter is designed to provide you with a guided tour of the typical desktop and tower PC (Fig. 1-1), point out the various operating sub-assemblies, and offer a series of assembly guidelines.

FIGURE 1-1   A selection of PC enclosures. Computer cases designed and manufactured by Olson Metal Products, Seguin, TX

Under the Hood

The first step is to look at the generic components you'll expect to find in a desktop or tower system. Figure 1-2 illustrates an exposed view of a desktop PC. Although it might look crowded at first glance, you will see that there are actually only a handful of sub-assemblies to deal with. With a little practice, identifying various assemblies should become almost automatic. An average tower system is illustrated in Fig. 1-3. With few exceptions, desktop and tower PCs incorporate seven key items; the enclosure, the power supply, the motherboard, a floppy disk drive, a hard disk drive, a video adapter, and a drive controller. The following sections detail each item. Feel free to skip directly to related chapters later in the book for more detailed definitions and descriptions.

ENCLOSURE

The *enclosure* is the most obvious and least glamorous element of a PC. Yet, the enclosure serves some very important functions. First, the enclosure (such as the Olson Baby AT case of Fig. 1-4) forms the mechanical foundation (chassis) of every PC. Every other sub-assembly is bolted securely to this chassis. Second, the chassis is electrically grounded through the power supply. Grounding prevents the buildup or discharge of static electricity from damaging other sub-assemblies. Whenever you work inside of a PC, be sure to use a properly grounded anti-static wrist strap to prevent electrostatic discharge from your body from accidentally damaging circuitry inside the system. If you do not have an anti-static wrist strap handy, you can discharge yourself on the PC's metal chassis as long as the power supply is plugged in. However, because you are strongly urged to protect yourself by unplugging the power supply ac, do not rely on the chassis to discharge

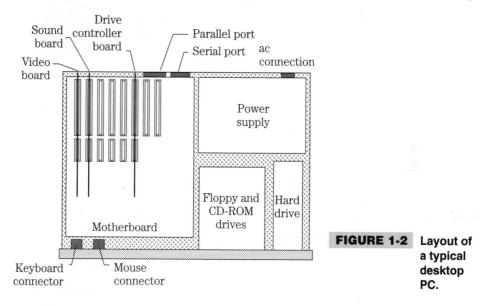

FIGURE 1-2 Layout of a typical desktop PC.

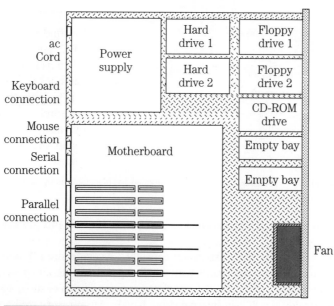

FIGURE 1-3 Layout of a typical tower PC.

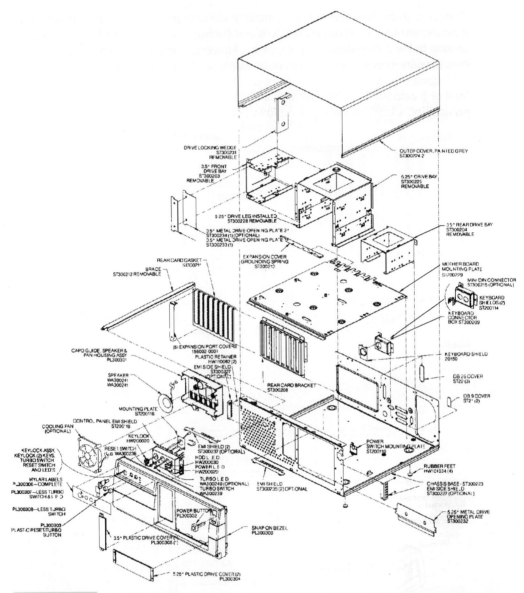

FIGURE 1-4   **An Olson Baby AT case.** Computer cases designed and manufactured by Olson Metal
Products, Seguin, TX

you. Grounding also prevents a serious shock or fire hazard if ac should come in contact
with the metal case.

The enclosure also limits the PC's expansion capacity. Average-sized desktop enclosures typically offer room for motherboards with 6 to 8 expansion slots, and provide space
for 3 or 4 drives—two drives mounted in front slots (or external drive bays), and one or
two drives mounted inside the PC (in internal drive bays). An average-sized enclosure,
such as this, allows a fair amount of space to expand the system as your customer's needs

change. Unfortunately, the push toward smaller PCs has led to the use of smaller, more-confined enclosures. Small (or low-profile) enclosures (such as the Olson Slimline Chassis in Fig. 1-5) restrict the size of the motherboard, which results in fewer expansion slots (usually 4 to 6), and allows room for only 1 to 3 drives.

The great advantage to tower enclosures is their larger physical size. Towers usually offer 4 or 5 external drive bays, as well as 3 or 4 internal bays. To accommodate such expandability, a large power supply (250 to 300 watts) is often included. Tower cases can

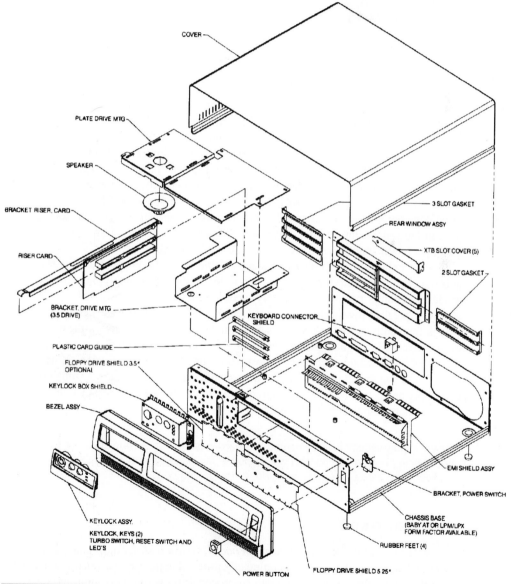

COVER

PLATE DRIVE MTG

SPEAKER

BRACKET RISER, CARD

RISER CARD

3 SLOT GASKET

REAR WINDOW ASSY

XTB SLOT COVER (5)

2 SLOT GASKET

BRACKET, DRIVE MTG
(3.5 DRIVE)

KEYBOARD CONNECTOR
SHIELD

PLASTIC CARD GUIDE

FLOPPY DRIVE SHIELD 3.5"
OPTIONAL

KEYLOCK BOX SHIELD

BEZEL ASSY

EMI SHIELD ASSY

BRACKET, POWER SWITCH

CHASSIS BASE
(BABY AT OR LPM/LPX
FORM FACTOR AVAILABLE)

RUBBER FEET (4)

KEYLOCK ASSY.

KEYLOCK, KEYS (2)
TURBO SWITCH, RESET SWITCH AND
LED'S

POWER BUTTON

FLOPPY DRIVE SHIELD 5.25"

FIGURE 1-5 **An Olson Slimline chassis.** Computer cases designed and manufactured by Olson Metal Products, Seguin, TX

also fit larger motherboards, which tend to support a greater number of expansion slots. The higher power demands of a tower system result in greater heat generation. Towers compensate for heat by providing one or more internal fans to force air into the enclosure. If a second internal fan is included, it generally works in conjunction with the first fan to exhaust heated air. For example, you'll often find tower systems with two fans—one in the lower front to force in cooler air and one in the upper rear to exhaust heated air. If only one fan is used, it will usually be located in the upper rear of the chassis to exhaust heated air.

POWER SUPPLY

The power supply is the silver box that is usually located in the rear right quarter of the enclosure. Ac enters the supply through the ac line cord, which is connected at the rear of the enclosure. A supply then produces a series of dc outputs that power the motherboard and drives. The importance of a power supply is easy enough to understand, but its implications for system integrity and expandability might not be as obvious.

Power supplies sustain a great deal of electrical stress in normal everyday operation. The conversion of ac into dc results in substantial heat, which is why so many power supplies are equipped with a cooling fan. Surges, spikes, and other anomalies that plague ac power distribution (especially in underdeveloped regions of the world) also find their way into PC power supplies, where damage can occur. The quality of a power supply's design and components and design dictate how long it will last in operation. A quality supply will resist power problems and tolerate the rigors of normal operation, but a sub-standard supply can fail spontaneously after only a few months of operation. When replacing or upgrading a power supply, be sure to choose a reliable model.

Power supplies also limit a system's expandability. Every element used in the PC requires a certain amount of power (marked *W* for *watts*). The supply must be capable of producing enough power to adequately meet the system's demand. An under-powered supply (typical in low-profile systems) or a supply overloaded by excessive expansion (which frequently occurs in tower systems) might not be able to support the power needs of the system. Inadequate power results in very strange system behavior such as unpredictable system lockups, random memory faults, or disk-access problems. When replacing a power supply, be certain that the new supply can provide at least as much power as the supply being replaced. When upgrading a supply, choose a supply that offers at least 50 watts more than the original supply.

> Power supply assemblies are generally regarded as extremely safe because it is virtually impossible to come into contact with exposed high-energy circuitry. Still, exercise care and common sense whenever working with a running power supply.

MOTHERBOARD

The *motherboard* (also known as the *main board*, *system board*, *backplane board*, or *planar board*) holds the majority of a computer's processing power. As a minimum, a motherboard contains the system CPU, math co-processor (now routinely built into the CPU), clock/timing circuits, RAM, cache, BIOS ROM, serial port(s), parallel port, and expansion

FIGURE 1-6 **A modern motherboard assembly.** Intel Corporation

slots. Each portion of the motherboard is tied together with interconnecting logic circuitry. Some advanced motherboards also include circuitry to handle drive and video interfaces. You can identify the motherboard easily as shown in Fig. 1-6—it is the single large printed circuit board located just off of the enclosure's base.

As you might expect, it is the motherboard more than any other element of the PC that defines the performance (and performance limitations) of any given computer system. This is the reason why motherboard upgrades are so popular, and often provide such stunning improvements to a PC. Let's break motherboard limitations down into the following nine categories:

CPU type A CPU is responsible for processing each instruction and virtually all of the data needed by the computer (whether the instruction is for BIOS, the operating system, or an application). The type of CPU limits the PC's overall processing power. For example, a PC with a Pentium II CPU runs Windows 95 much better than a PC with a "classic" Pentium CPU. Also, a Pentium MMX CPU will generally handle graphics-intensive applications better than a "classic" Pentium CPU.

CPU speed Even when CPUs are the same, clock speed (measured in MHz) effects performance. For example, a PC with a "classic" Pentium 166MHz CPU will run faster than a PC with a "classic" Pentium 120MHz CPU.

CPU upgrade potential Because CPUs have a finite processing limit, it follows that upgrading the CPU will improve system processing. Although this is great in theory, you can't just place any old CPU in the CPU socket and expect the motherboard to work. Any motherboard is limited to using a handful of current CPU versions. For example, Intel's recent AN430TX motherboard supports Pentium processors at 90, 100, 120, 133, 150, 166, and 200MHz, as well as Pentium MMX processors running at 166, 200, and 233MHz. By comparison, Intel's new NX440LX motherboard supports Pentium II microprocessors operating at 233, 266, and 300MHz. Changing the processor type and speed requires changes in several jumper settings.

Memory slots The sheer amount of memory that can be added to the motherboard will indirectly affect system performance because of a reduced dependence on virtual memory (a swap file on the hard drive). Memory is added in the form of SIMMs (Single In-line Memory Modules) or DIMMs (Dual In-line Memory Modules). Motherboards that can accept more or larger-capacity memory modules will support more memory. It is not uncommon today to find motherboards that will support 512MB of RAM (equal to the storage capacity of older hard drives).

Memory types The type of memory will also have an effect on motherboard (and system) performance. Faster memory will improve system performance. DRAM remains the slowest type of PC memory, and is usually used in older systems or video boards. EDO RAM is faster than ordinary DRAM, and is now commonplace in PCs. SDRAM is measurably faster than EDO RAM, and is appearing in high-to-mid-range PC applications. By the time you read this book, SDRAM should be common. RDRAM is an emerging memory type that should gain broad acceptance in the next few years. It is not necessary for you to understand what these memory types are yet; just understand that memory performance and system performance are related.

Cache memory Traditional RAM is much slower than a CPU—so slow that the CPU must insert pauses (or "wait states") for memory to catch up. Cache is a technique of improving memory performance by keeping a limited amount of frequently used information in VERY fast cache RAM. If the needed information is found, the CPU reads the cache at full speed (and performance is improved because less time is wasted). By making the cache larger, it is possible to hold more "frequently used" data. Older motherboards used from 128KB to 256KB of cache. Current motherboards use 512KB to 1MB of cache RAM.

Chipsets A chipset is a set of highly optimized, tightly inter-related ICs which, taken together, handle virtually all of the support functions for a motherboard. As new CPUs and hardware features are crammed into a PC, new chipsets must be developed to implement those functions. For example, the Intel 430HX chipset supports the Pentium CPU and EDO RAM. Their 430VX chipset supports use of the Pentium CPU, the Universal Serial

Bus, and SDRAM. By comparison, the Intel 440LX chipset supports the Pentium II CPU, an accelerated graphics port, SDRAM, and an Ultra DMA-33 drive interface.

System BIOS The BIOS ROM contained on the motherboard also limits the system's capabilities, although such limits are not always drastic or obvious. BIOS is a set of small programs recorded onto ROM ICs that allow the operating system (such as MS-DOS or Windows) to interact with memory and the various drives and devices in the system. Although the BIOS versions produced today are generally quite uniform, older BIOS ICs might not support some of the new features that we now expect from computers. For example, many systems using i286-based motherboards do not support the format process for 3.5" 1.44MB floppy disk drives directly, as newer systems do, or your BIOS might not support new bootable CD-ROM drives (using the "El Torito" standard). Overcoming BIOS limitations is often a matter of upgrading the BIOS program or upgrading the motherboard entirely.

Expansion slots Each motherboard offers a fixed number of expansion slots. The number of expansion slots limits the number of features and devices that can be added to the system. Internal modems, scanner boards, video boards, drive-controller boards, sound boards, network cards, and SCSI controllers are only some of the devices competing for expansion space in your PC. The fewer slots that are available, the less a system can be expanded. The type of expansion slots also influences expandability and performance. Classical motherboard designs offer a mix of 8-bit XT and 16-bit ISA slots. More recent motherboards have added one or two slots to accommodate enhanced expansion technologies, such as the VL bus for improved video boards, and a second VL slot might be available for an improved drive or network adapter. Today, motherboards typically incorporate two or three PCI slots for high-performance network, video, or drive-controller boards (the remainder of available expansion slots will generally be 16-bit ISA slots).

DRIVES

The modern PC would be entirely useless without long-term, high-volume storage, as well as the ability to transfer files between PCs. Drives represent a variety of devices used for storing or retrieving relatively large amounts of information. Floppy-disk drives (FDDs), hard-disk drives (HDDs), and CD-ROM drives are the three most popular drive types for desktop and tower PCs, although Iomega Zip drives (resembling 3.5" floppy drives) and tape drives are occasionally used. CD recorders and DVD-ROM drives are now common in current PCs. Even PC card "drives" are finding their way into desktop/tower systems. Figure 1-7 illustrates the standard profile for each drive.

Floppy-disk drives (FDD) Floppy disks have gone through several incarnations (5.25" 360KB, 5.25" 1.2MB, 3.5" 720KB, and 3.5" 1.44MB) since they first appeared in the IBM PC. But in spite of its limited storage capacity, the floppy drive remains the traditional PC drive, which is universally accepted in virtually every PC manufactured since 1982. Floppy disks use only one light to indicate drive activity.

Iomega "Zip" drives Combining magnetic and optical storage technologies, Iomega has developed a 3.5" drive capable of storing up to 100MB on a single "Zip" disk. Over

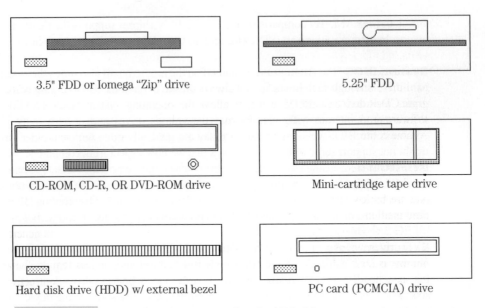

3.5" FDD or Iomega "Zip" drive

5.25" FDD

CD-ROM, CD-R, OR DVD-ROM drive

Mini-cartridge tape drive

Hard disk drive (HDD) w/ external bezel

PC card (PCMCIA) drive

FIGURE 1-7 The front appearance of typical PC drives.

the last few years, the Zip drive has proven to be an inexpensive and handy storage system—so much so that some PC manufacturers now include Zip drives as standard equipment in their new systems. At first glance, the Zip disk and drive could easily be mistaken for a floppy disk drive.

CD-ROM drives Originally developed for the music industry as a digital replacement for aging phonographs, the CD-ROM quickly found a place in modern PCs. One optical disc can store up to 650MB of programs, data, or other media, such as Kodak photos and digital audio. Although their storage capacity is now dated when compared to multi-gigabyte hard drives, CD-ROM drives are standard equipment in all modern PCs. CD-ROM drives use a "load/eject" button, a volume control (to adjust CD audio), and a single activity light.

Tape drives Tape drives offer a significant amount of storage capacity using relatively inexpensive tape media. However, tape devices are slow, hot, and noisy, so they have largely been relegated to occasional system backup chores. Tape drives use two lights: one as a power indicator and another as a drive activity light.

Hard-disk drives (HDD) The hard drive is truly the icon of the personal computer. Magnetic storage technology has evolved at a staggering pace, and the slow 100MB to 200MB hard drives of 10 years ago have been replaced by lightning-fast 4GB and 5GB hard drives. The hard drive has provided the PC industry with huge, fast, reliable, and quiet storage mechanisms for just pennies per megabyte. This upward spiral of hard-drive capacity shows no signs of slowing. Hard drives are standard equipment on all PCs and are the preferred boot device for quick loading of even the largest operating systems. The hard drive typically uses only one light to indicate drive activity.

CD-R drives CDs have been around for years, but recording your own CD has been prohibited by proprietary (and hideously expensive) hardware and software. In the last few years, CD-R drives have plummeted in price. Although hardly standard equipment, the combination of falling prices, improved reliability, more extensive PC resources (i.e., RAM, hard-drive space, and faster CPUs) and good intuitive Windows 95 authoring software has made CD-R drives an attractive option for such tasks as software backups, file archiving, and software product prototyping. CD-R drives use a "load/eject" button, drive activity light, and volume control. They also sport a second activity light to show when the drive is writing.

DVD-ROM drives The DVD drive represents the next step in the evolution of optical storage for the PC. DVD discs can offer up to 17GB of storage on a single disc the size of a CD (yet are backward-compatible with almost all existing CD-ROM standards). They are an ideal medium for the distribution of audio and video multimedia (when combined with a PCI MPEG-2 decoder board), as well as unimaginable volumes of data. The first generations of DVD drives, which appeared in mid-1997, only read DVD discs, but future iterations of DVD (known as *DVD-R* and *DVD-RAM*) will be able to record blank DVD discs. DVD-ROM drives use a "load/eject" button, a volume control (to adjust CD audio), and a single activity light.

PC card drives With the explosive growth of portable computers, the use of desktop PC card (formerly referred to as *PCMCIA cards*) "drives" is increasing to support the easy transfer of files between laptop and desktop systems. At first glance, the PC card drive appears much like a 3.5" floppy drive, although the card opening is thicker and narrower. The term *drive* is a bit of a misnomer here because the PC card drive is entirely electronic—there are no moving parts, except for the electrical card connector and a simple card-ejection mechanism. PC card drives are relatively rare, and are most often encountered on PC platforms used for data acquisition or post-processing from remote data-gathering PCs. A mechanical lever ejects the PC card, and a single light is used to indicate drive activity.

Drives are typically located in the front right quarter of the desktop enclosure. Each drive is secured into an available drive bay within the enclosure. There are two types of drive bays that you should be familiar with: internal and external. The external drive bay allows a drive to be mounted facing the outside world. Floppy, CD-ROM, CD-R, DVD-ROM, PC card, and tape drives rely on the availability of external drive bays. After all, what good is the drive if you can't insert or remove the media? On the other hand, hard-disk drives use non-removable media. This means the drive can be mounted in an internal (or non-accessible) bay. A typical desktop PC offers two external and two internal bays. The external bays usually hold a 3.5" FDD and a CD-ROM. The internal drive bay(s) are typically reserved for one or two hard drives. Larger desktop cases might offer additional external bays. Tower cases can easily support a full range of external drives mounted along the upper front of the enclosure. A tower's internal drive bays can handle another three or four hard drives.

EXPANSION BOARDS

Although many PCs today incorporate video, sound, and FDD/HDD controller circuitry directly on the motherboard, those circuits can often be disabled when expansion boards are used. In fact, many such "integrated" controllers are eventually disabled so that video and drive systems can be upgraded with more advanced expansion boards. In most cases, you should expect to find at least a video board plugged into an expansion slot. The video board will often be accompanied by an FDD/HDD controller board. Of course, there will probably be additional boards in the system as well. This part of the chapter is intended to help you identify each category of expansion board on-sight.

Video boards Video adapter circuits (whether implemented on the motherboard or on an expansion board) are designed to convert raw graphic data traveling over the system bus into pixel data that can be displayed by a monitor. Without the monitor attached, however, the video adapter can only be identified through its video port connector. Figure 1-8 compares the four major generations of video adapters: MDA, CGA, EGA, and VGA. Remember that the illustrations shown in Fig. 1-8 are typical examples—some video board designs might not follow these layouts exactly. Chapter 43 describes video adapter standards and service in more detail.

The Monochrome Display Adapter (MDA) is the oldest video adapter board, and few are still in service. MDA boards are noted for their use of a 25-pin parallel port included with the 9-pin video connector. You might find MDA boards used in IBM PC/XTs or compatible systems. The Color Graphics Adapter (CGA) is roughly the same vintage as MDA and it is the first graphics adapter to introduce color to PC displays. A CGA board can often be identified by a round RCA-type feature connector located just above a 9-pin video connector. Like the MDA boards, CGA is long-since obsolete. Many of the older systems that used CGA boards have been scrapped, or have been upgraded to later video systems. The Enhanced Graphics Adapter (EGA) offers more colors and higher display

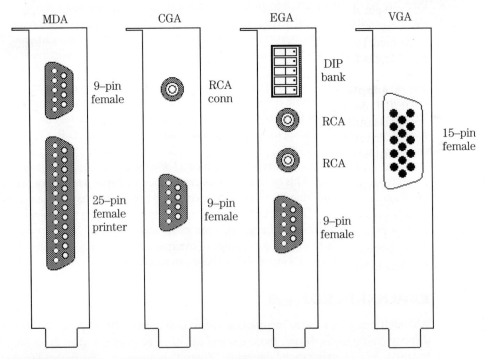

FIGURE 1-8 Comparison of typical video board layouts.

TABLE 1-1 TYPICAL VIDEO RESOLUTION AND PIXEL DEPTH

RESOLUTION	BITS/PIXEL (2 MB)	BITS/PIXEL (4 MB)	BITS/PIXEL (8 MB)
640 × 480	8, 16, 24, 32	8, 16, 24, 32	8, 16, 24, 32
800 × 600	8, 16, 24, 32	8, 16, 24, 32	8, 16, 24, 32
1024 × 768	8, 16	8, 16, 24, 32	8, 16, 24, 32
1152 × 864	8, 16	8, 16, 24, 32	8, 16, 24, 32
1280 × 1024	8	8, 16, 24	8, 16, 24, 32
1600 × 1200	8	8, 16	8,16,24

NOTE: 8 bits/pixel = 256 colors
16 bits/pixel = 655,36 colors ("high color" mode)
24 bits/pixel = 16 million colors ("true color" mode)
32 bits/pixel = 4 billion colors (usually reserved for scanning)

resolution than CGA. You can identify an EGA board by its small bank of DIP switches located above two RCA-type feature connectors and a 9-pin video connector.

The *Video Graphics Array (VGA)* board marked a departure from previous video systems. VGA abandoned logic-level video signals (on/off signaling) in favor of analog video levels. Thus, primary colors could be "mixed" together to provide many more color combinations than ever before—up to 262,144 possible colors for ordinary VGA. You can easily identify a VGA connector as a 15-pin high-density connector (15 pins stuffed into a 9-pin shell). SVGA (or Super VGA) extends the capabilities of VGA by adding more resolutions and color depths allowing as many as 16 million colors (known as *true color* mode) to be displayed at one time. Table 1-1 compares the common resolutions and color depths for a typical SVGA video board.

Drive adapters The term *drive adapter* is usually applied to floppy drive controller, EIDE/IDE drive controller, and tape-drive accelerator boards. As a rule, SCSI adapters are not classified as "drive adapters" because a SCSI adapter can handle other peripherals besides drives. Drive controllers are easily identified by tracing drive signal cables from the particular drive back to the supporting controller.

Notice the signal "headers" that connect to the individual ribbon cables. The 34-pin header is marked *FDD* or *Floppy*, and is always connected to the floppy drive(s). The 40-pin headers are marked "EIDE" and "IDE," respectively, or "HDD1" and "HDD2," and are always connected to EIDE/IDE hard drives. The first hard drive port is often designed for EIDE drives, and the second hard-drive port is designed for older IDE drives (though many new controllers support EIDE drives on both drive ports). Chapter 13 outlines drive adapters in more detail.

If there is only one hard drive port on the controller (marked *HDD* or *Hard*), chances are very good that the controller is an older IDE-only controller board. Do not attempt to use EIDE drives on IDE ports. The 40-pin interface will work (and you won't damage the drive), but you cannot partition and format the full capacity of the drive without drive overlay software, such as EZ-Drive.

You should also be able to identify "proprietary" drive adapters—most notably for early (non-IDE) CD-ROM drives. The earliest CD-ROM adapters used stand-alone controller boards, but these were quickly replaced by one or more proprietary controller ports built right into popular sound boards, such as the Creative Labs "Sound Blaster" series. Notice that there are often several connectors: a 44-pin connector for a Mitsumi CD-ROM, a 36-pin connector for a Sony CD-ROM, and a 44-pin interface for a Creative-brand CD-ROM. You would then use a jumper to select the desired port, depending on which CD-ROM came packaged with the sound board.

The real trick comes with 40-pin CD-ROM interfaces—it's impossible to tell by sight if the port is IDE or proprietary. Still, you can use the following rule. Older sound boards with a 40-pin CD-ROM interface are almost always proprietary, and the port will often share space with other proprietary interfaces nearby. Newer sound boards with a 40-pin CD-ROM interface sitting by itself (with no other proprietary ports nearby) are almost always standard IDE.

> An IDE interface on a sound board is a "true" IDE port. It should support any other IDE drive (i.e., older IDE hard drives or IDE tape backups) without problems.

SCSI adapters The Small-Computer System Interface (SCSI) offers impressive expandability by allowing SCSI-compatible devices (SCSI hard drives, SCSI CD-ROMs, SCSI tape drives, SCSI scanners, etc.) to all be connected together over the same daisy-chained cable. There are several ways to detect the presence of a SCSI adapter. First, you will see a screen message generated by the SCSI adapter BIOS when the PC initializes. You can also confirm the presence of a SCSI adapter by identifying the interconnecting cables. Internally, SCSI cables are 50-pin or 68-pin ribbon cables. Figure 1-9 illustrates a SCSI adapter with a 50-pin SCSI header. Because many SCSI adapters can handle both internal and external devices, the adapter will have an external 50-pin D-type connector available. If the SCSI adapter also includes a 34-pin header, the adapter is providing a standard floppy drive port. You might need to disable any such floppy port because there is probably a working floppy port elsewhere in the system (i.e., on the motherboard or drive-controller board). Chapter 39 covers SCSI concepts and troubleshooting in great detail.

Ports and modems PCs are rarely any use in a vacuum—they must be able to communicate with devices in the "outside world." PC communication is accomplished through the use of parallel or serial ports, and you should recognize such ports on sight. Traditionally, parallel ports allow the PC to drive printers, but with improvements in parallel-port performance, new peripherals are available which can operate through a parallel port (i.e., parallel-port tape drives, hard drives, and CD-ROM drives). Such devices are particularly handy when they must be moved between several machines. A parallel port is implemented as a 25-pin (female) connector (Fig. 1-10). Although older PCs included parallel ports as part of the MDA video board (Fig. 1-8) or as a stand-alone expansion board, virtually all current PCs incorporate at least one parallel port directly on the motherboard. You'll find much more about parallel ports in Chapter 31.

FIGURE 1-9   **A typical SCSI controller board.** Copyright ©1995 Future Domain
Corporation. Reprinted with permission.

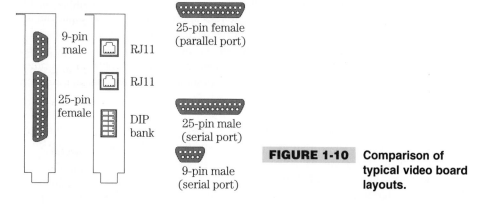

FIGURE 1-10   **Comparison of typical video board layouts.**

Given the tremendous appeal of inexpensive online resources, such as AOL and the
Internet, serial communication has evolved substantially over the last decade. As a result,
you will likely find one or two serial ports located on the PC (Fig. 1-10). Older PCs typically implement a single serial (or RS-232) port as a 25-pin D-type (male) connector. Do
not confuse this with 25-pin D-type female connectors, which are used for parallel ports!
Because most serial communication can be accomplished with far fewer than 25 pins, most
PC manufacturers now use a 9-pin D-type male connector instead of the 25-pin D-type

male connector. Newer systems offer two 9-pin D-type male serial ports directly on the motherboard. When implemented on a stand-alone expansion board, you will often find a 9-pin D-type male serial port combined with a 25-pin D-type female parallel port. Chapter 40 covers serial ports in detail.

To communicate over a telephone line, serial signals must be translated into tones that can be carried within the frequency bandwidth of an ordinary voice telephone line. Returning signals must also be decoded into serial signals. The device that performs this PC-telephone line interface is called a *modem*. External modems are stand-alone devices which attach to an available serial port. Internal modems, however, are quite popular, and combine the circuitry for a serial port and modem on a single expansion board. You can usually identify an internal modem board by its two RJ11 (phone jack) connectors. Notice that one jack is for the telephone line itself, and the second connector is a "feed-through" that can be connected to any standard telephone. Modems are covered in Chapter 26.

Sound boards The acceptance of sound boards in everyday PCs has been simply staggering. What started as a novel means of moving beyond the limitations of PC speakers has quickly evolved into a low-cost, CD-quality stereo playback/recording system. Even business applications are embracing sound cards for presentations and simple speech-recognition tasks. Sound cards are firmly established as an essential part of every PC used for educational, game, and multimedia applications. Fortunately, sound boards are relatively easy to recognize (Fig. 1-11).

The giveaway here is the volume control knob. Sound cards are the only devices that currently require such manual adjustments. Three miniature jacks are also included. The line input jack allows pre-recorded sound (i.e., output from tape player, CD player, or synthesizer) to be digitized and recorded by the sound board. The microphone input supports recording from an ordinary 600-Í microphone. The stereo output is the main output for the board, where digitized voice and music files are reproduced. An output can drive amplified speakers or an interim stereo amplifier deck. Your particular sound board might have slightly different features. The sound board shown in Fig. 1-11 offers a 15-pin D-type female connector. This feature connector is designed to serve double-duty as either a joystick port or a MIDI interface. Chapter 41 covers sound-board concepts and troubleshooting in detail.

MPEG decoder boards Although a DVD-ROM drive requires a "standard" interface (i.e., SCSI or EIDE) for normal programs and data, DVD video and audio do not use this data path. There are two reasons for this. First, the data required to reproduce real-time video and audio would bog-down—even the fastest PC when transferred across a standard drive interface. Second, video and audio data are highly compressed using MPEG standards, so even if the PC wasn't bogged down by the compressed data, the decompression process would load-down the system with processing overhead. To play DVD audio and video, DVD-ROM drives require a stand-alone, hardware-based MPEG-2 decoder board (Fig. 1-12). The MPEG-2 decoder board works independently of the drive-controller system, video system, and sound system.

There are five major connections on the MPEG-2 decoder board: an analog input jack, an analog output jack, a digital output jack, a monitor connector, and a video input connector. The analog input is rarely (if ever) used in normal operations, but it might be handy for mix-

Sound board

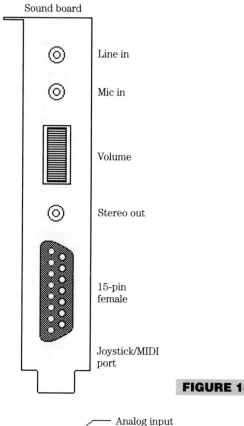

Line in

Mic in

Volume

Stereo out

15-pin
female

Joystick/MIDI
port

FIGURE 1-11 Layout of a typical sound board.

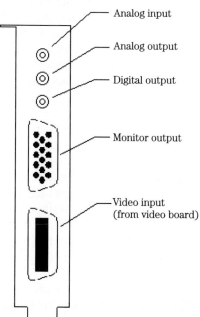

Analog input

Analog output

Digital output

Monitor output

Video input
(from video board)

FIGURE 1-12 Layout of a typical
MPEG-2 decoder board.

ing in an auxiliary audio signal to the decoder board. The analog output signal provides the master audio signal, which is fed to the line input of your existing sound board. The advantage of using a line input is that you don't need a volume control on the decoder board. Instead, you can set the line input volume through your sound board's "mixer" applet. When you play a DVD video, any audio will continue to play through your sound board and speakers. The digital output is intended to drive an external Dolby digital device, so you will probably not be using the digital output in most basic PC setups.

The MPEG-2 decoder board will now drive your VGA/SVGA monitor through the monitor connector. This is important because the decoded video stream is converted to RGB information, and fed to the monitor directly—this avoids having to pass the video data across the PCI bus to your video card. The normal output from your video card is looped from your video board to the decoder card; while the decoder board is idle, your normal video signal is just "passed through" the MPEG-2 board to the monitor.

Joystick adapters The use of PC games and simulators often requires the use of an analog joystick. Joysticks are connected to one of two 15-pin D-type female connectors on the joystick adapter (also called the *game port*). Figure 1-13 illustrates the typical layout for a joystick adapter. Because two connectors are usually included, an adapter can

Gameport

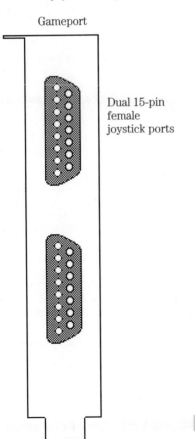

Dual 15-pin
female
joystick ports

FIGURE 1-13   Layout of a dual game-port
board.

support two analog joysticks. Another hallmark of a joystick adapter is its small size—typically an 8-bit (or half-slot) board. Chapter 19 outlines joystick and game port installation and troubleshooting.

Notes for Disassembly and Re-assembly

All to often, the mechanics of PC repair—taking the system apart and putting it back together again—are overlooked or treated as an afterthought. As you saw in the first part of this chapter, PC assemblies are not terribly complicated, but a careless or rushed approach to the repair can do more harm than good. Lost parts and collateral damage to the system are certain ways to lose a customer (and perhaps open yourself to legal recourse). The following section outlines a set of considerations that can help ensure a speedy, top-quality repair effort.

THE VALUE OF DATA

It is a fact of modern computing that the data contained on a customer's hard drive(s) is usually more valuable than the PC hardware itself. If your customer is an entrepreneur or corporate client, you can expect that the system contains valuable accounting, technical, reference, design, or operations information that is vital to their business. As a consequence, you should make it a priority to protect yourself from any potential liability issues connected with your customer's data. Even if the drives are causing the problem, a customer might hold you responsible if you are unable to restore or recover their precious information. Start a consistent regimen of written and oral precautions. Such precautions should include (but are not limited to):

- Always advise your customers to backup their systems regularly. Before the customer brings in their system, advise them to perform a complete backup of their drives, if possible.
- Always advise your customers to check their backups—a backup is useless if it can't be restored.
- When a customer delivers a system for repair, be sure that they sign a work order. Work orders should expressly give you authority and permission to work on the customer's system, outline such things as your hourly rate, labor minimums for evaluation and service, and show all applicable disclaimers. Your work order should include a strong disclaimer expressly relieving you of any and all liability for the contents of any magnetic media (i.e., hard drives) in the system. If you attempt data recovery, the disclaimer should also disclaim any warranty or guarantee of results—that way, you're not liable if you are unable to recover vital files. Because liability issues vary from state to state and country to country, a local attorney can advise you on specific wording.

OPENING THE SYSTEM

Most desktop and tower systems use a metal chassis covered by a painted metal cover or shroud that is secured with a series of screws. There are often nine screws—two on either side of the enclosure, and five at the rear of the chassis. Although this pattern covers many of the desktop PCs in service, you are likely to encounter a number of variations. You might find that instead of bolting screws in from the sides, the screws might be bolted in from the bottom. There might also be more or fewer screws in the rear of the chassis. Only on very rare occasions will you find screws used to secure the enclosure at its front—the molded plastic housing used on most desktop PCs does not accommodate screws without spoiling the finished "look."

Tower cases are a bit different. The metal shroud also uses about nine screws—all secured from the rear. The bottom and front edges of the enclosure are typically bent inward to "interlock" with the chassis when seated properly. This approach allows the entire enclosure to fit securely along the whole chassis while using only a minimum of screws. Enclosures that do not interlock, however, might require screws along the bottom and front edges. As a general rule, PC enclosure manufacturers tend to minimize the use of visible screws in order to enhance a "seamless" appearance—this is why most screws are relegated to the back chassis.

There are three factors to keep in mind when removing screws and other mounting hardware. First, be extremely careful not to mark or gouge the painted metal enclosure. Customers are rightfully possessive of their PC investment; putting a scratch or dent in an enclosure is tantamount to dinging their new car (a careless reputation is very bad for business). Be equally careful of the enclosure after removing and setting it aside. Second, store the screws in a safe, organized place. The old "egg carton" trick might seem cliché, but it really does work. Of course, you are free to use plastic bags or organizer boxes, as well—the idea here is to keep screws and other hardware off the work surface (unless you enjoy picking them up off the floor). Third, take note of each screw as you remove it, and keep groups of screws separated. This allows you to put the right screws back into the corresponding locations. Because most enclosures use screws of equal size and length, this is rarely an issue at this phase of disassembly. But as you dismantle other sub-assemblies for upgrade or repair, keeping track of hardware becomes an important concern.

Use care when sliding the enclosure away. Metal inserts or reinforcements welded to the cover can easily catch on ribbon cables or other wiring. This can result in damage to the cable, and damage to whatever the cable is attached to. The rule here is simple: Force nothing! If you encounter any resistance at all, stop and search for the obstruction carefully—it's faster to clear an obstruction than to replace a damaged cable.

CLOSING THE SYSTEM

After your repair or upgrade is complete, you will need to close the system. Before sliding the enclosure back into place, however, make it a point to check the PC carefully. Be sure that every sub-assembly is installed and secured into place with the proper screws and hardware—leftover parts are unacceptable. A little care in organizing and sorting hardware during disassembly really pay off here. Remember to re-attach power and signal cables as required. Each cable must be installed properly and completely (in its correct orientation). Take time to route each signal cable with care and avoid jamming them into the system haphazardly. Careless cable runs stand a good chance of being caught and damaged by the enclosure during re-assembly, or the next time the system needs to be disassembled. Properly routed cables also reduce the chance of signal problems (such as noise or crosstalk) that can result in unstable long-term operation. Also check the installation of any auxiliary cables, such as CD-ROM sound cables, the speaker cable, and the keylock cable.

Once the system components are re-assembled securely, you can apply power to the PC and run final diagnostics to test the system. When the system checks properly, you can slide the enclosure into place (being careful not to damage any cables or wiring) and secure the enclosure with its full complement of screws.

TIPS FOR WORKING INSIDE A DESKTOP OR TOWER PC

Whether you're troubleshooting, upgrading, or building your own PC from scratch, there's no doubt that you'll get plenty of hands-on time inside desktop and tower PCs. Unfortunately, many potential problems can be overlooked (or even caused) while working inside a PC. The following tips should help you make the most of your PC experience and minimize the chances of collateral problems:

■ *Be extremely careful of any sharp edges along the metal cover, or inside the metal chassis itself* Case manufacturers often save costs by omitting such production steps as burr removal and dulling sharp edges.

■ *Be sure that the chassis assembly is tight* All chassis are not created equal—some stand solid as a house, and others can seem to sway freely. Take note of the chassis condition and tighten the chassis, if necessary.

■ *Watch your vents and fans for good air flow* Be sure that the fan blades, grills, and any intake and exhaust filters are kept clean. Check to see that all fans are working.

■ *Watch for dust and debris* When you're examining the enclosure, check for accumulations of dust or other debris. Dust is generally a thermal insulator and electrical conductor, and can easily block the flow of air inside a chassis, so it is important to avoid accumulations of dust and debris wherever possible.

■ *Choose a new chassis with care* Replacing a chassis (or building a new PC from scratch) is an exciting, but time-consuming effort, so plan for adequate expansion in terms of drive bays, expansion slot openings, power supply capacity, and drive power cables.

■ *Go with standardized cases, power supplies, and motherboards* New PC systems have largely abandoned the use of "AT"-style cases (i.e., Baby AT or Full AT) in favor of ATX or NLX versions. As you'll see in the following sections, standard dimensioning ensures that cases, motherboards, and power supplies will all fit together.

■ *Keep drives mounted snugly* All PC drives (whether in an internal or external drive bay) should be mounted with at least four screws. Fewer screws can allow the drive to vibrate, and this can shorten the drive's working life. Be sure that all four screws are in place and secure, but do not over-tighten the screws. Over-tightening can actually warp a drive's internal frame and cause premature failures as well.

■ *Carefully mount the motherboard* Under no circumstances should you ever flex a motherboard or install it in such a way that it is uneven. See that no metal edges or standoffs touch the motherboard, and the motherboard should not sit flush against any part of the PC chassis.

■ *Check your cables closely* There are a myriad of cables inside a PC. Make it a point to check the installation and routing of each cable. Each end of a cable should be installed evenly and completely. Cables should be run (where possible) to minimize any interruptions to air flow.

■ *Check your expansion boards* Whenever you're working inside a PC, be sure that any expansion boards inside the system are inserted evenly and completely into their bus slots. Often, exchanging external cables can accidentally wiggle a card loose—resulting in possible system problems. Also see that each expansion board is secured with a screw in the PC chassis.

■ *Check your memory devices* While you're in the system, take a look at the memory devices. Be sure that each SIMM or DIMM module is clipped securely into place (especially if you're replacing or upgrading memory). If your motherboard uses COAST (cache-on-a-stick) modules for cache RAM, also see that the COAST module is installed properly.

■ *Check the CPU heatsink/fan* Chances are that your CPU is fitted with a heatsink/fan assembly. Check to see that the heatsink is attached securely to the CPU, and verify that the fan portion of the assembly is working once the system is powered up.

Standardized Form Factors

Traditional PC chassis have always been somewhat of a "hit or miss" proposition. You'd choose cases, power supplies, and motherboards, and hope that everything would fit properly. All too often, screw holes won't line up, and you'd be forced to return assemblies, or "kluge" the assemblies together—aligning as many screw holes as possible, and ignoring, clipping, or removing standoffs outright. Over the last few years, the PC industry has come together to develop a set of standard dimensions for key PC components (cases, motherboards, and power supplies). The two current standards are known as *ATX* and *NLX*. This part of the chapter looks at both of these standards in more detail.

> The use of new "form factors" does not have any bearing on the capabilities or performance of any new PC—only the dimensions of the motherboard, case, and power supply are affected.

ATX FORM FACTOR

The version 2.01 ATX form factor (Fig. 1-14) is the first true effort to standardize the major assemblies of a PC. In addition to the use of well-established mounting holes, the ATX approach makes several key improvements to the layout of a system. The CPU is relocated to a position on the motherboard which will not interfere with the use of full-length expansion boards (a common complaint of baby/full AT motherboard users). Because full-length cards can now be used in all the slots, it won't be necessary to shuffle expansion cards around to avoid interfering with the CPU. The CPU itself can also be upgraded without having to remove expansion cards. SIMM and DIMM connectors are also located away from drive bays and expansion slots for easier access. The use of rear I/O ports (Fig. 1-15) and front-panel connections have been standardized on the ATX motherboard, which simplifies case design and reduces the wiring on the motherboard. Integrated drive-controller connections are now located closer to the drive bays to reduce drive cable

Expansion slots

I/O ports

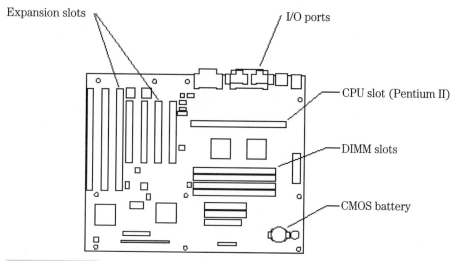

CPU slot (Pentium II)

DIMM slots

CMOS battery

FIGURE 1-14   Layout of an ATX motherboard.

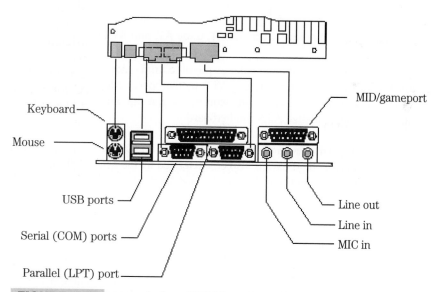

Keyboard

Mouse

MID/gameport

USB ports

Serial (COM) ports

Parallel (LPT) port

Line out

Line in

MIC in

FIGURE 1-15   Layout of an ATX I/O port panel.

lengths and reduce clutter. The ATX power supply provides power (including a native 3.3 V) through a single 20-pin cable, rather than the two 6-pin cables used in traditional baby/full AT systems. Finally, the ATX case design is configured to be cooled by a single fan located in the ATX power supply. This not only simplifies the case and reduces power demands, but it makes the system quieter.

ATX motherboard sizes   A full-size ATX board is 12" wide × 9.6" deep (305 mm × 244 mm). The Mini-ATX board is 11.2" × 8.2" (284 mm × 208 mm). Designers have at-

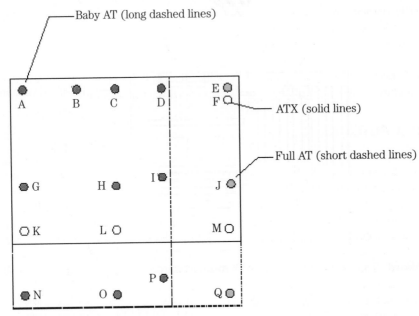

FIGURE 1-16   Comparison of full AT, baby AT, and ATX mounting.

tempted to use as many mounting holes as possible from older baby/full AT-style mother-boards to allow existing chassis to use ATX motherboards with a minimum of modification. Figure 1-16 illustrates a comparison between a full AT motherboard, a baby AT motherboard, and a full-size ATX motherboard.

ATX motherboard connectors Aside from the board size and placement of mounting holes, an ATX motherboard is also characterized by the general placement of various connectors. The listing outlines the major connectors:

- Expansion slots (PCI/ISA) are located at the rear left of the motherboard.
- The power input connector is placed along the right edge of the board (near CPU).
- Drive signal connectors are located along the front edge of the board near the drive bays.
- Front-panel I/O connectors (i.e., power switch and LED) are located along the front edge of the board—usually to the right of the expansion slots.
- Back-panel I/O connectors (i.e., COM ports, parallel port, USB port, etc.) are all located on a single panel to the right rear of the motherboard.
- Memory-module connectors are located between the CPU and expansion slots, or between the CPU and drive-signal connectors (usually visible on inspection).
- The CPU is usually located on the right side of the motherboard in front of the back-panel I/O connectors.

ATX power supply An ATX power supply is about 6.1" long, 5.7" wide, and 3.5" deep—roughly equivalent to a PS/2 power-supply footprint. The supply must generate the four traditional PC voltage levels (+5 V, –5 V, +12 V, –12 V), as well as a 3.3-V level to better support low-voltage logic being used in modern PCs. Power is provided to the motherboard through a single 20-pin connector. A single exhaust fan assembly located in the supply must be capable of maintaining a minimum air flow of 23 CFM.

ATX case The only real distinguishing characteristic of an ATX case is the rear opening that corresponds to the motherboard's back-panel I/O connector plate.

NLX FORM FACTOR

The version 1.2 NLX form factor (Fig. 1-17) is one of the newest dimensioning specifications for modern PCs. NLX is specifically designed to accommodate "low-profile" PC systems, while providing superior management for heat control and easy maintainability. The key to the NLX configuration is not the motherboard, but a riser board. The vertical riser board connects directly to the power supply (not the motherboard), and holds all of the expansion boards horizontally. The riser board also holds the drive cable connectors (i.e., floppy connectors and hard-drive connectors), which previously resided on the motherboard. This means that the NLX motherboard has no cables to be attached or removed when servicing the NLX system. An NLX motherboard can simply be "undocked" from the system's riser card, and another one can be installed in a matter of moments. A wide area for back panel I/O connectors is provided on the rear of the NLX motherboard, which allows for a large variety of high-end ports, such as TV, sound, gameports, etc. NLX motherboards are also some of the first to support the Accelerated Graphics Port (AGP) for better graphics performance on PCs. The CPU is placed toward the front of the NLX

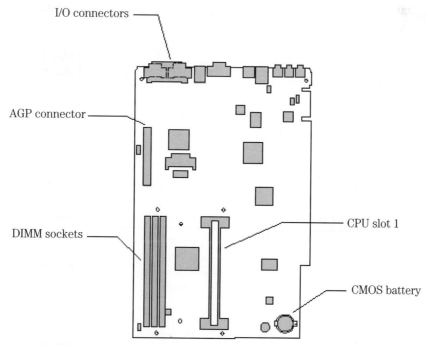

FIGURE 1-17 Layout of an NLX motherboard.

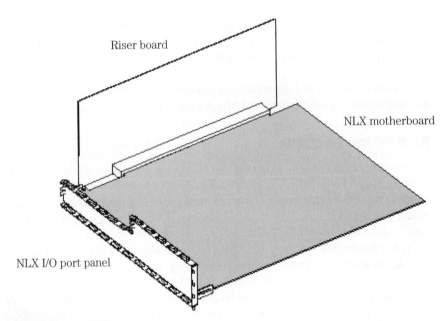

FIGURE 1-18   View of NLX riser, motherboard, and back panel.

motherboard (close to the fan) to ensure better system cooling. You can get a better view of the NLX riser, motherboard, and back panel in Fig. 1-18.

NLX motherboard sizes   NLX motherboards are not as straightforward as ATX units. The NLX specification defines motherboards of 9.0" × 13.6" (maximum) and 8.0" × 10.0" (minimum)—this means an NLX motherboard might run anywhere between these two sizes, and an NLX case must be able to support all possible sizes, although the typical NLX motherboard dimensions will be as follows:

- 8.0" × 10.0"
- 9.0" × 10.0"
- 8.0" × 11.2"
- 9.0" × 11.2"
- 8.0" × 13.6"
- 9.0" × 13.6"

NLX motherboard connectors   Perhaps the most noticeable difference between an NLX motherboard and other motherboards is the apparent lack of expansion-board connectors and drive-port connectors, which have been implemented on the riser card. You'll also notice the presence of a 340-pin card-edge connector, which interfaces to the riser card. The list outlines the disposition of important connections:

- Expansion slots (PCI/ISA) are located on the riser card in a horizontal orientation.
- The power-input connector is attached to the riser card.
- Drive-signal connectors are attached to the riser card.

- Back-panel I/O connectors (i.e., COM ports, parallel port, USB port, etc.) are all located on a single panel to the right rear of the motherboard. This back panel occupies the entire rear of the motherboard.
- Memory-module connectors are typically located somewhere between the CPU and expansion slots, or behind the CPU toward the rear of the motherboard.
- The CPU is usually located on the left front side of the motherboard in direct proximity to an NLX case intake fan.
- The Accelerated Graphics Port (AGP) connector is located along the left side of the motherboard several inches from the left rear corner of the motherboard.

NLX power supply An NLX power supply uses the same dimensions as an ATX power supply (about 6.1" long, 5.7" wide, and 3.5" deep). The supply must generate the four traditional PC voltage levels (+5 V, –5 V, +12 V, –12 V), as well as a 3.3-V level to better support low-voltage logic being used in modern PCs. Power is provided to the riser card through a single 20-pin connector. A single exhaust fan assembly located in the supply must be capable of maintaining a minimum air flow of 23 CFM.

NLX case The only real distinguishing characteristic of an NLX case is the long rear opening corresponding to the motherboard's back-panel I/O connector plate. There might also be hinged access or other provision to ease the installation or replacement of NLX motherboards. An additional inlet fan is located in the front left part of the chassis to aid in cooling the CPU.

Further Study

That's it for Chapter 1. Be sure to review the glossary and chapter questions on the accompanying CD. If you have access to the Internet, point your Web browser to some of these contacts:

AGP Implementers' Forum: **http://www.agpforum.org/**

Amtrade Products: **http://www.amtrade.com**

ATX information: **http://www.teleport.com/˜7Eatx/**

Enlight: **http://www.enlightcorp.com.tw**

Fong Kai Industrial: **http://www.fkusa.com**

Intel chipsets: **http://developer.intel.com/design/pcisets/**

Intel's AN430TX motherboard: **http://developer.intel.com/design/motherbd/an/index.htm**

Intel's NX440LX motherboard: **http://developer.intel.com/design/motherbd/nx/index.htm**

InWin Development: **http://www.in-win.com**

Iomega: **http://www.iomega.com**

NLX information: **http://www.teleport.com/˜7Enlx/**

ProCase: **http://www.procase.com.tw/68.htm**

The Intel AGP Web site: **http://developer.intel.com/pc-supp/platform/agfxport/**

INSIDE

TODAY'S

MONITORS

CONTENTS AT A GLANCE

Monitor Assembly
Enclosure
CRT
CRT drive board
Raster drive board
Power supply

Working With On-Screen Controls
Basic controls
Advanced controls

Notes on Monitor Disassembly and Reassembly
Discharging the CRT
Removing sub-assemblies
Replacing sub-assemblies
Tips for working with a monitor

Further Study

The ability to display images and information has evolved right along with CPUs, memory, hard-drive space, and all of the other computer attributes that are associated with PC performance. Although the essential principles of a monitor have remained virtually unchanged, the small, drab monochrome displays of just a decade ago have been almost entirely replaced by flicker-free, high-resolution monitors capable of producing photo-realistic color images (Fig. 2-1). Today's monitor is more than just an output device—it has become our window into the complex virtual world created by computers. This chapter shows you what is inside the typical color monitor, and provides some guidelines for monitor disassembly and re-assembly.

FIGURE 2-1 **A modern PC monitor.** CTX International, Inc.

Monitor Assembly

As you can see from Fig. 2-2, a typical computer monitor is not terribly complicated. Compared to notebook computers and low-profile desktop systems, the monitor assembly is spacious. This is not an accident—monitors require substantial amounts of energy for operation. Much of this energy is dissipated as heat. Extra space prevents a buildup of heat from damaging the monitor's circuitry, and heat is allowed to escape through ventilation slots in the enclosure. Another reason for ample enclosure space is to ensure ample high-voltage insulation. Some monitors generate up to 30 kV during normal operation (sometimes more for very large monitors), and normal plastic-wire insulation is hardly sufficient to ensure safety. High-voltage insulation and plenty of unobstructed space keep high-voltage from arcing to other circuits. The typical monitor can be broken down into five sections; the enclosure, the CRT, a CRT drive board (or "video drive" board), a raster drive board, and a power supply.

ENCLOSURE

Monitor enclosures are built as two pieces, The front enclosure (marked *3*) is used to mount the CRT and degaussing coil. This is bolted to a frame (marked *12*), which forms the base of the monitor. Once other circuit boards are attached to the frame, the rear enclosure (marked *17*) forms a shroud over almost all of the monitor. In most cases, the rear enclosure can be freed by removing four screws (marked *18*), as shown in Fig. 2-2. A few monitor enclosures are held together by plastic latches in addition to screws. If the rear enclosure does not slide away easily, suspect the presence of snap-in latches or extra screws installed into the frame from the bottom.

CRT

Although color monitors rely on extra video circuitry to process color signals, it is the design and construction of the CRT itself (marked CRT in Fig. 2-2) that really makes color

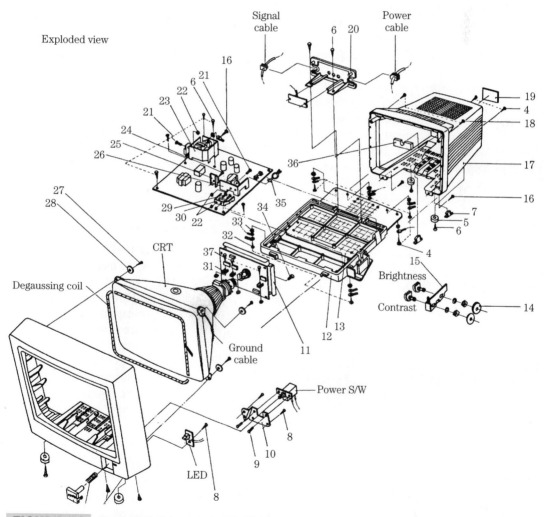

FIGURE 2-2   Exploded diagram of a Tandy VGM200 monitor. Tandy Corporation

monitors possible. The basic principles of a color CRT (Fig. 2-3) are very similar to a monochrome monitor—electrons "boil" off the cathode and are accelerated toward the phosphor-coated front face by a high positive potential. Color CRTs use three cathodes and video control grids—one for each of the three primary colors. Control (brightness), screen, and focus grids serve the same purpose as they do in monochrome CRTs. The *control grid* regulates the overall brightness of the electron beams, the *screen grid* begins accelerating the electron beams toward the front screen, and the *focus grid* narrows the beams. Once the electron beams are focused, vertical and horizontal deflection coils (or deflection yokes) apply magnetic force to direct the beams around the screen.

You will notice a *shadow mask* added to the color CRT. A shadow mask is a thin plate of metal that contains thousands of microscopic perforations—one perforation for each screen pixel. The mask is placed in close proximity to the phosphor face. There is also a substantial difference in the screen phosphors. Where a monochrome CRT uses a homogeneous layer of phosphor across the entire face, a color CRT uses phosphor triads, as shown in Fig. 2-4 (the distance between the shadow mask and phosphor screen is shown greatly exaggerated). Red, green, and blue phosphor dots are arranged in sets so that the red, green, and blue electron beams will strike the corresponding phosphor. In actual operation, the color dots are so close together that each triad appears as a single point (or pixel). A degaussing coil (shown in Fig. 2-2) mounted in front of the CRT works to keep the shadow mask demagnetized.

Color CRTs must also be more precise in how the three electron beams are directed around the screen. Because there are now three phosphors instead of just one, it is critical that each electron beam strike only its corresponding phosphor color—not adjoining phosphors. This is known as *color purity*. A *purity magnet* added to the CRT yoke helps to adjust fine beam positioning. By using a *shadow mask*, the electron beams are only allowed

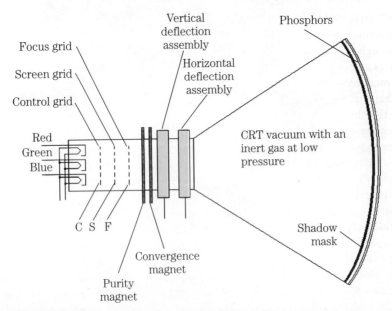

FIGURE 2-3 Diagram of a typical color CRT assembly.

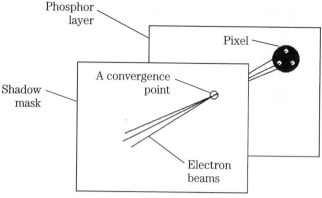

Phosphor layer

Pixel

Shadow mask

A convergence point

Electron beams

*Sizes and distances are NOT shown to scale

FIGURE 2-4 The relationship of a shadow mask and color phosphors.

to reach the phosphors where there are holes in the mask. Also realize that each of the three electron beams must converge at each hole in the shadow mask. A convergence magnet added to the CRT yoke adjusts beam convergence in the display center (known as *static convergence*), and a convergence coil driven by the raster circuitry optimizes beam convergence at the edges of the display (known as dynamic convergence). It is this delicate balance of purity and convergence adjustments, as well as the presence of a shadow mask, that give today's color monitors such rich, precise color.

CRT DRIVE BOARD

The CRT drive board (marked *31* in Fig. 2-2) attaches directly to the CRT pins through a circular connector. Control (brightness), screen, and focus grid voltages are applied to the CRT through this board. The CRT drive board also contains the red, green, and blue video amplifiers and drivers. Because more CRT drive circuitry is needed for a color monitor than a monochrome monitor, the CRT drive board for a color monitor is usually much larger than that of a monochrome monitor. Once the monitor is unplugged and discharged, be sure that this board is attached evenly and securely to the CRT. The CRT drive circuit regulates the strength of each electron beam by adjusting signal strength on the corresponding video control grid in the CRT. The CRT drive circuit must convert a small video signal (usually no more than 0.7 V) into a signal large enough to drive the CRT (typically around 50 V). For color monitors with three analog video lines, three separate video drive circuits are required.

Problems can strike the CRT drive circuits in a number of ways, but there are clues to help guide your way. If the display disappears, but the raster remains (*raster* is that dim haze you see by turning up the monitor's brightness), the video signal might have failed at the video adapter board in your PC. If there is suddenly not enough (or far too much) red, green, or blue in the displayed image, the corresponding DAC (digital-to-analog converter) on the video adapter might have failed, or the corresponding CRT drive circuit in the monitor might have broken down. Try a known-good monitor. If the correct image appears, you know the video adapter is producing the desired output, and the original monitor is probably defective. If no display appears on a known-good monitor, suspect the video adapter board in your PC. If the screen is black, suffers from fixed brightness (with or without video input), or loses focus, one or more grids in the CRT might have shorted and failed. Refer to Chapter 27 for detailed instructions on monitor troubleshooting.

RASTER DRIVE BOARD

The main raster board contains the vertical raster, horizontal raster, and high-voltage circuits that actually drive the CRT and direct the electron beam(s) around the screen. Depending on the design of your particular monitor, the raster board might contain part or all of the power supply circuit as well, along with some microcontroller-driven circuitry to operate on-screen monitor adjustments. Just about all monitors mount the raster board directly to the frame horizontally below the CRT neck. This assembly can be difficult to remove because it is obstructed by the CRT neck and yoke, as well as the interconnecting wiring that connects to the power supply, front-panel controls, and flyback transformer.

The vertical drive circuit is used to operate the vertical deflection yoke. This is accomplished with a vertical sweep oscillator, which is little more than a free-running oscillator set to run at either 60 or 70/72 Hz (depending on the design of the particular monitor). When the oscillator is triggered, it produces a sawtooth wave—the start of the sawtooth wave corresponds to the top of the screen, although the end of the sawtooth wave corresponds to the bottom of the screen. When the sawtooth cycle is complete, there is a blank period for blanking and retrace. One vertical sweep will be accomplished in less than $\frac{1}{60}$ of a second (or $\frac{1}{70}$ or $\frac{1}{72}$ of a second depending on the monitor).

Trouble with the vertical drive circuit usually strikes the vertical output driver circuit. If part of the driver should fail, either the upper or lower half of the image will disappear. If the entire driver should fail, the screen image will compress to a straight horizontal line in the center of the screen (there would be no vertical deflection—only horizontal deflection). Another problem is vertical oversweep, which elongates the picture to the extent where it "wraps back" on itself in the lower portion of the screen. The area where the vertical image oversweeps will appear with a whitish haze and is typically the fault of the vertical oscillator circuit.

The horizontal drive circuit is the second part of the color monitor's raster circuit, and it is designed to operate the horizontal deflection yoke. This is accomplished with a horizontal oscillator, which is little more than a free-running oscillator set to run at a frequency between 15kHz and 48kHz. A CGA monitor will typically use a horizontal sweep frequency of about 15.75kHz. The actual oscillator might be based on a transistor, but is usually designed around an integrated circuit, which is more stable at the higher frequencies that are needed. When a horizontal synchronization trigger pulse is received from the video adapter board, the oscillator is forced to fire. When the oscillator is triggered, it produces a square wave. The start of the square wave corresponds to the left side of the screen. When the cycle is complete, there is a blank period for blanking and retrace. At an operating frequency of 31.5kHz, one horizontal sweep will be accomplished in about 31.7 ms.

Trouble with the horizontal drive circuit usually strikes the horizontal output drive circuit because that is the circuit that sustains the greatest stress in the monitor. If the drive circuit should fail, the entire image will disappear because high-voltage generation will also be affected. Unfortunately, a fault in the horizontal oscillator will also result in an image loss because high-voltage generation depends on a satisfactory horizontal pulse. If the horizontal oscillator or amplifier fails, high-voltage fails as well, and the image becomes too faint to see—this makes troubleshooting horizontal problems a bit more difficult than troubleshooting vertical problems.

The high-voltage system is actually part of the horizontal drive circuit. A monitor's power supply generates relatively low voltages (usually not much higher than 140 V). This means that the high positive potential needed to excite the CRT's anode is not developed in the power supply. Instead, the 15 to 30 kV or more needed to power a CRT anode is generated from the horizontal output. The amplified, high-frequency pulse signal generated by the horizontal driver circuit is provided to the primary winding of a device known as the *FlyBack Transformer (FBT)*. The FBT produces the high voltage. The principle is similar to the ignition system used in automobiles.

POWER SUPPLY

The power supply is typically a hand-sized assembly that converts ac into several dc voltage levels (usually +135, +20, +12, +6.3, and +87 Vdc) that will be needed by other monitor circuits. The ac itself might be filtered and fused by a separate small assembly near the monitor's base. If there is no stand-alone power-supply board in your particular monitor, the supply is probably incorporated into the raster board. As you saw earlier, the only voltage that is not produced in the power supply is the high-voltage source. A stand-alone power supply is typically mounted vertically to the frame. The metal frame not only provides a rigid mounting platform, but it serves as a chassis common, and it helps to contain RF signals generated by the monitor.

Working With On-Screen Controls

PC monitors have traditionally been analog devices that used manually adjusted controls to configure proper operation. However, as monitor sizes, viewing areas, and resolutions continue to increase, users demand more control over the image's appearance. The use of microcontrollers in large, modern monitors allows many display adjustments to be made through the front control panel, which otherwise would require a tedious and time-consuming internal alignment. Such changes can then be easily saved in the monitor's internal memory. Because adjustments can be set for major resolutions independently, the monitor can "remember" your optimum display configuration for your most frequently used display modes—there is almost no "tinkering" with the monitor each time you change a screen mode. On-screen controls are listed through a series of icons that indicate the general action of each control. Figure 2-5 illustrates some of the most popular icons for basic on-screen monitor adjustments.

BASIC CONTROLS

The basic on-screen controls might seem overwhelming at first glance—that's understandable because most PC users never get to use more than "brightness" and "contrast" knobs. Still, the basic controls are designed to help you set the overall image position and quality for your current display mode.

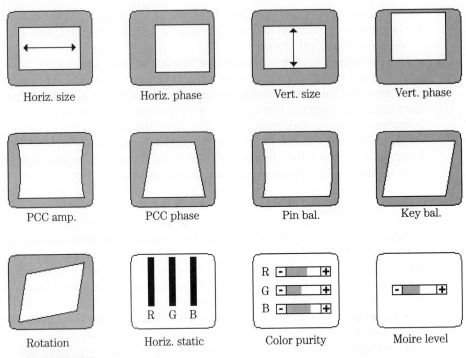

Horiz. size	Horiz. phase	Vert. size	Vert. phase
PCC amp.	PCC phase	Pin bal.	Key bal.
Rotation	Horiz. static	Color purity	Moire level

FIGURE 2-5   Basic on-screen monitor adjustments.

Some of these adjustments can cause severe image distortion if set improperly. Before making any adjustments (aside from contrast and brightness), be sure to note the starting level of each adjustment or find the "factory default" button, which can restore default levels automatically.

Horizontal size (also called _H-size_)   This makes the image fatter or thinner. If the image is too wide (where one or both ends are "lost" beyond the edges of the display area), you can use the H-size control to pull the image inside the display area.

Horizontal phase (also called _H-phase_ or _H-posi_)   This control lets you position the image left or right in the display area. For example, if the image is too far to the right, use H-phase to shift the image to the left. You might use H-phase and H-size alternately to size the image properly.

Vertical size (also called _V-size_)   This makes the image taller or shorter. If the image is too tall (where one or both ends are "lost" beyond the top and bottom of the display area), you can use the V-size control to pull the image inside the display area.

Vertical phase (also called _V-phase_ or _V-posi_)   This control lets you position the image higher or lower in the display area. For example, if the image is too low, use V-phase to shift the image upward. You might use V-phase and V-size alternately to size the image properly.

PCC amp (also called *pincushion adjustment*)   Use this control to straighten the left and right sides of the image. If the PCC control is set too low, the image will bow outward. If the PCC control is set too high, the image will draw inward. Ideally, the sides of the image should be straight.

PCC phase (also called *trapezoidal adjustment*)   Use this control to make the image perfectly rectangular. If the adjustment is set too low, the top of the image will be narrower than the bottom. If the adjustment is set too high, the top of the image will be wider than the bottom.

Pin balance (also called *curvature adjustment*)   Use this adjustment also to straighten the image. If the control is too high, the image might curve to the left. If the image is too low, the image might curve to the right. Notice that this is not a pincushion (PCC amp) adjustment because the left and right sides of the image are affected in the same direction.

Key balance (also called *slant control* or *tilt adjustment*)   Use this adjustment also to straighten the image. If the control is set too high, the top of the image might be pulled right and the bottom of the image might be pulled left. If the control is set too low, the top of the image might be pulled left, and the bottom of the image might be pulled right.

Rotation (also called *twist adjustment*)   This control effects the rotation of the entire image in the display. Ideally, the image should appear straight in the display—the two bottom corners of the image should be exactly the same distance from the desk.

Horizontal static (also called *color alignment*)   Use this control to adjust the alignment of the red, green, and blue electron beams.

Color purity (also called *color balance*)   Ideally, white should be a "pure" white—containing the exact same amounts of red, green, and blue. However, age might affect CRT color guns and video driver levels, so you can tweak the RGB settings to restore color purity.

Moire level   Moire is a form of distortion that occurs when certain conditions of resolution, dot pitch, screen size, and image coloring are met. The moire pattern usually appears as wavy or elliptical patterns. Use the Moire-level control to adjust the amount of moire distortion that might appear in an image.

ADVANCED CONTROLS

The advanced on-screen image adjustments are often quite similar to the basic adjustments, but advanced adjustments allow more precise and subtle corrections—especially in

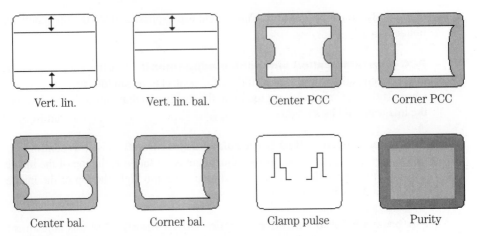

FIGURE 2-6   Advanced on-screen monitor adjustments.

the corners of an image, which are the most difficult to set correctly. Figure 2-6 highlights the advanced controls that you'll encounter most frequently.

Vertical linearity (also called *V-lin*)   Linearity is the geometric "correctness" of the display. For example, if there is an image of small colored boxes the same size throughout, each box should "appear" to be the same size. If not, linearity might be a problem. The linearity control adjusts linearity in the vertical direction.

Vertical linearity balance (also called *V-lin balance*)   The linearity-balance control effectively centers the linearity of the display's vertical axis. For example, it might be necessary to shift the linearity balance when changing linearity to avoid making uniform linearity changes across the entire display.

Center PCC (also called *center pincushion*)   This precision adjustment allows you to tweak the pincushion adjustment near the vertical center of the image, instead of across the entire left and right sides of the image. This adjustment should only be used when there is limited pincushioning around the middle of the image.

Corner PCC (also called *corner pincushion*)   This precision adjustment allows you to tweak the pincushion adjustment near the corners of image, instead of across the entire left and right sides of the image. This adjustment should only be used when there is limited pincushioning around the edges of the image.

Center balance   This feature (similar to pin balance) adjusts the curvature of the left and right sides of the display near the vertical center of the image, instead of across the entire image. Use this adjustment to correct minor curvature in the center of the image.

Corner balance   This feature (similar to pin balance) adjusts the curvature of the left and right sides of the display at the corners of the image, instead of across the entire image. Use this adjustment to correct minor curvature at the corners of the image.

Clamp pulse position   This feature is not needed with RGB inputs, such as those provided by your 15-pin video cable, but might be needed when using Sync-on-Green signals through a BNC connector. Clamp-pulse controls allow you to eliminate the excessive green or white background that can occur when using Sync-on-Green or external sync signals at the monitor.

Purity   This feature allows you to adjust the color purity—or color "uniformity" of the display. Do not adjust this level unless it is absolutely necessary.

Notes on Monitor Disassembly and Reassembly

The process of monitor disassembly is remarkably straightforward. In most cases, only the rear enclosure must be removed to expose the entire inner workings of the monitor. The rear enclosure itself is typically held in place with only four screws (additional screws can be inserted at the bottom). On some occasions, you might also encounter a number of plastic latches, but this is rare. After removing the rear enclosure, you will see the bell and neck of the CRT, the CRT drive board, the raster board, and the power supply (if a separate supply is used).

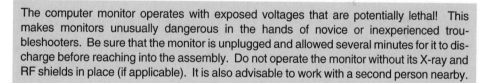

The computer monitor operates with exposed voltages that are potentially lethal! This makes monitors unusually dangerous in the hands of novice or inexperienced troubleshooters. Be sure that the monitor is unplugged and allowed several minutes for it to discharge before reaching into the assembly. Do not operate the monitor without its X-ray and RF shields in place (if applicable). It is also advisable to work with a second person nearby.

You should take note of any metal shrouds or coverings that are included with the monitor assembly. Metal shielding serves two very important purposes. First, the oscillators and amplifiers in a monitor produce radio-frequency (RF) signals that have the potential to interfere with radio and TV reception. The presence of metal shields or screens helps to attenuate any such interference, so always make it a point to replace shields securely before testing or operating the monitor. Second, large CRTs (larger than 17") use very high voltages (25 kV or higher) at the CRT anode. With such high potentials, X-radiation becomes a serious concern. CRTs with lower anode voltages can usually contain X-rays with lead in the CRT glass. Metal shields are added to the larger CRTs as supplemental shielding to stop X-rays from escaping the monitor enclosure. When X-ray shielding is removed, it is vital that it be replaced before the monitor is tested and returned to service. X-ray shields will usually be clearly marked when you remove the monitor's rear cover.

DISCHARGING THE CRT

Before removing any wiring or boards from the monitor, it is important that the CRT is fully discharged. Even though unplugging the monitor will prevent ac and high-voltage

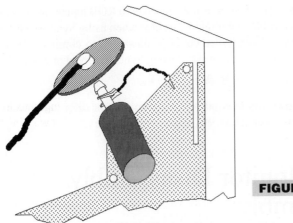

FIGURE 2-7 Discharging an unpowered CRT before servicing.

electrocution, there might still be enough high-voltage charge stored in the CRT to provide a fair kick to the careless. Be sure that the monitor is turned off and allow several minutes for the ac supply to discharge. Use a regular-blade screwdriver with a heavy-duty alligator clip attached between the screwdriver shaft and the metal chassis. Gently insert the screwdriver blade under the high-voltage anode cap as shown in Fig. 2-7. You will probably hear a mild crackle as the CRT is grounded. Do not rotate the screwdriver or force it in the CRT—remember that the CRT is a glass assembly and that excessive force can damage it easily. Once the crackling stops, remove the screwdriver and unplug the monitor's ac cord. The assembly should now be safe to work on.

REMOVING SUB-ASSEMBLIES

Removing boards is often a simple matter. The CRT drive board is simply plugged into the CRT through a circular connector. Rock the video board back and forth gently to pull it away from the CRT. The raster board is typically mounted to the frame with several screws. After the screws are removed, the raster board should be free. When removing any board, be sure to make a careful note of each connector's location and orientation. A CRT is held in place with a metal bracket bolted to the front enclosure. Unfortunately, replacing the CRT usually means removing the video and raster boards along with the frame. If you must place the monitor (or front enclosure alone) face-down onto a work surface, be sure to use a layer of soft towels or foam to prevent scratches to the front enclosure or CRT.

REPLACING SUB-ASSEMBLIES

The most important rule to remember when exchanging a board or CRT is to use an exact replacement part. Monitors are precisely timed, high-energy systems—so "close" doesn't count. An improper replacement assembly might cause the monitor to malfunction, or might it work only for a limited amount of time. When re-assembling a monitor, be extremely careful of the wiring interconnecting each board and the CRT. Be sure that all wiring and connectors are installed properly and completely. Loose connectors can cause erratic or intermittent operation. Pay close attention to wire paths—do not allow wiring to be pinched under boards or against the metal chassis. Finally, re-install any RF or X-ray shielding that might have been removed during the repair.

TIPS FOR WORKING WITH A MONITOR

Of all the PC peripherals, monitors are perhaps the most potentially dangerous in careless hands. The tips listed will help protect you from injury, and get the most working life from your monitor investment:

- For best monitor images, always keep the 15-pin video cable secured to the video adapter board. Also avoid using monitor cable extensions, which can cause image ghosting.
- Use simple, ammonia-based cleaners to clean the monitor case, but never spray cleaner onto the monitor—only onto the cleaning cloth.
- CRT coatings (i.e. anti-glare coatings) can be extremely sensitive to chemicals, so never use any sort of cleaner other than demineralized water to clean the CRT. Remember to wet the cleaning cloth—not the CRT.
- Monitors use convection for cooling. Be sure to keep all of the vent openings on the monitor case unobstructed and free of dust and debris. Vacuum out any accumulations of dust within the monitor.
- When working on a monitor, always use a soft pillow or plush towel to cushion the CRT and avoid scratches.
- Monitors can contain potentially dangerous voltages. Be sure to keep the monitor turned off and unplugged before working inside it. Discharge the CRT's high-voltage anode before performing any service.
- Do not use metal tools when working inside a monitor—especially when attempting to make alignments.
- When reassembling a monitor, be extremely careful to avoid damaging wiring and connectors.
- Monitors (especially large monitors) are extremely sensitive to the influences of magnetic fields. Be sure to keep any motorized or magnetic devices well clear of the monitor. Even unshielded multimedia speakers can adversely affect the monitor.
- Monitors are particularly heavy devices, so be very careful when lifting a monitor. Lift from the knees—not from the back. Hold the CRT face toward your chest.

Further Study

This concludes Chapter 2. Be sure to review the glossary and chapter questions on the accompanying CD. If you have access to the Internet, point your Web browser to some of these contacts:

Anatek Corporation: **http://www.anatekcorp.com**

CTX: **http://www.ctxintl.com/**

NEC: **http://www.nec.com**

Sony: **http://www.ita.sel.sony.com/support/displays/**

Viewsonic: **http://www.viewsonic.com/desk/desk.htm**

OPERATING SYSTEMS

AND THE

BOOT PROCESS

CONTENTS AT A GLANCE

The PC Hiararchy
  Hardware
  BIOS
  Operating system
  Applications

Understanding Popular OS Features
  MS-DOS 6.22
  PC-DOS 7.0
  Windows 95
  OS/2
  Windows CE
  Windows NT (workstation)
  Windows 98

A Closer Look at MS-DOS
  IO.SYS
  MSDOS.SYS
  IO.SYS and MSDOS.SYs variations
    under Windows 95

Adjusting MSDOS.SYS under
  MS-DOS 7.x
COMMAND.COM
Recognizing and dealing with OS
  problems

The Boot Process
  Applying power
  The boot strap
  Core tests
  Post
  Finding the OS
  Loading the OS
  Establishing the environment
  Creating a DOS boot disk

Further Study

As a technician, it is vital for you to understand the relationship between PC hardware and software. In the early days of computers, hardware was typically the center of attention. Since early software was written for a specific computer (such as a DEC PDP system or IBM Vax), and early computers were very limited in their storage and processing capacity, software often arrived as an "afterthought" (we still see software development lagging behind hardware advances to this day). With the introduction of personal computers in the mid-1970s, designers realized that a wide selection of software would be needed to make PCs attractive. Instead of writing software specifically for particular machines, a uniform environment would be needed to manage system resources and launch applications. In this way, applications would be portable between systems whose hardware resources would otherwise be incompatible. This "uniform applications environment" became known as the *Operating System (OS)*. When IBM designed the PC, they chose to license a simple operating system from a fledgling company called *Microsoft*—and the rest is history.

Although this book is dedicated to dealing with PC hardware (because it is the hardware that "breaks"), you must realize that the operating system has a profound effect on PC resources, and how those resources are allocated to individual software applications. This is especially true of the more sophisticated operating systems, such as Windows 95 and OS/2 Warp. Every good technician is sensitive to the fact that problems with an OS will result in problems with PC performance. This chapter explains the relationship between PC hardware and software, illustrates some of the major features found in typical operating systems, and walks you through a typical PC boot process.

The PC Hierarchy

Before digging into the operating system itself, you should understand the complex (and often frustrating) relationship between computer hardware and software. As shown in Fig. 3-1.

HARDWARE

As you might expect, hardware forms the core of a PC hierarchy—there is no computer without the hardware. The hardware includes all of the circuits, drives, expansion boards,

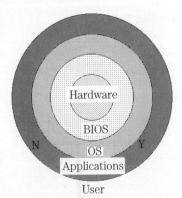

FIGURE 3-1   A standard PC hierarchy.

power supplies, peripheral devices, and their interconnecting wiring or cables. This extends not only to the PC itself, but to monitors, keyboards, pointing devices, printers, etc. By sending digital information to various ports or addresses in memory, it is possible to manipulate almost anything attached to the system CPU. Unfortunately, controlling PC hardware is a difficult process, which requires an intimate knowledge of a PC's electronic architecture. How is it that Microsoft can sell an operating system that works on an i286-based AT, as well as a new Pentium-based system? Because each PC manufacturer designs their circuitry (especially motherboard circuitry) differently, it is virtually impossible to create a "universal" operating system without some sort of interface between the one standard OS and the myriad variations of hardware in the marketplace. This interface is accomplished by the *Basic Input/Output System (BIOS)*.

BIOS

Simply put, a BIOS is a set of small programs (or services) that are designed to operate each major PC subsystem (i.e., video, disk, keyboard, and so on). Each of these BIOS Services is invoked by a set of standard calls—originally developed by IBM—which are made from the operating system. When the operating system requests a standard BIOS service, the particular BIOS program will perform the appropriate function tailored to the particular hardware. Thus, each PC design requires its own BIOS. Using this methodology, BIOS acts as a "glue," which allows diverse (and older) hardware to operate with a single uniform OS. In addition to services, the BIOS runs a power-on self-test (POST) program each time the PC is initialized. POST checks the major subsystems before attempting to load an operating system.

Because BIOS is specific to each PC design, BIOS resides on the motherboard in the form of a read-only memory (ROM) IC, although newer systems use electrically rewritable (or "flash") ROMs, which allow the BIOS to be updated without having to replace the BIOS ROM IC. You might see BIOS referred to as *firmware*, rather than software, because software is permanently recorded on an IC. As you might imagine, the efficiency and accuracy of BIOS code will have a profound impact on the overall operation of a PC—better BIOS routines will result in superior system performance, while clumsy, inefficient BIOS routines can easily bog a system down. Bugs (software errors) in BIOS can have very serious consequences for the system (such as lost files and system lockups).

OPERATING SYSTEM

The operating system serves two very important functions in the modern PC. First, an OS interacts with, and provides an extension to the BIOS. This extension provides applications with a rich selection of high-level file handling and disk-control functions. It is this large number of disk-related functions, which added the term *disk* to *operating system* (i.e., *disk operating system, DOS*). When an application needs to perform disk access or file handling, the DOS layer performs most of the work. By providing access to a library of frequently used functions through DOS, application programs can be written without the need to incorporate the code for such complex functions into each application itself. In actual operation, the OS and BIOS work closely together to give an application easy access to system resources.

Second, an OS forms an "environment" (or shell) through which applications can be executed, and provides a user interface allowing you and your customers to interact with the PC. MS-DOS uses a keyboard driven, command-line interface signified by the command-line prompt (such as C:>_), which we have become so familiar with. By contrast, the Windows family of operating systems provides a *Graphical User Interface (GUI)* relying on symbols and icons that are selected with a mouse or other pointing device.

APPLICATIONS

Ultimately, the aim of a computer is to execute applications (such as games, word processors, spreadsheets, etc.). An OS loads and allows the user to launch the desired application(s). As the application requires system resources during run-time, it will make an appropriate call to DOS or BIOS, which in turn will access the needed function and return any needed information to the calling application. The actual dynamics of such an exchange is more complex than described here, but you get the general idea. Now that you have seen an overview of the typical PC hierarchy and understand how each layer interacts with one another, it is time to take a closer look at the OS layer itself.

Understanding Popular OS Features

There are many different operating systems written for today's computers. The range and complexity of operating systems spans the entire spectrum of features and complexity—some are large, complex, commercial giants (such as Windows 95 and Windows NT), and others are small, freely distributed packages (like FreeBSD). Other operating systems are tailored for such features as real-time operation, true or high-performance multitasking, or networking. New specialized operating systems are regularly being introduced to support particular systems, such as process control, manufacturing, or other "mission critical" needs. Table 3-1 offers a partial listing of today's available operating systems. As a technician, you should understand the important features of today's operating systems, and why

TABLE 3-1 PARTIAL LISTING OF CONTEMPORARY OPERATING SYSTEMS

OPERATING SYSTEM	PURPOSE/EMPHASIS	FURTHER STUDY
A/UX	–	http://jagubox.gsfc.nasa.gov/aux/
AROS	replacement for Amiga OS	http://194.51.182.14/
BeOS	Mac/Pentium/Alpha OS	http://www.teleport.com/~pdxbug/Main.html
CHORUS	for communication devices	http://www.chorus.com/
Coherent UNIX	UNIX variant	comp.os.coherent
CP/M	precursor to DOS	comp.os.cpm
CTOS	networking OS	www.dogstar.com/Sirius/Menu/TechLibrary.NewsletterExerpts.html
DR-DOS v6.0	DOS from Novell	http://support.novell.com/Ftp/Updates/dsktop/drdos60/Date0.html
FreeBSD	free UNIX variant	http://www.freebsd.org/

TABLE 3-1   PARTIAL LISTING OF CONTEMPORARY OPERATING SYSTEMS (CONTINUED)

OPERATING SYSTEM	PURPOSE/EMPHASIS	FURTHER STUDY
GEOS	OS from GeoWorks	http://users.bergen.org/~edwdig/geos/
GNU	free UNIX variant	http://www.delorie.com/gnu/
Grasshopper	OS for persistent systems	http://www.gh.cs.su.oz.au/Grasshopper/index.html
Helios	real-time embedded OS	http://www.perihelion.co.uk/spg.html
HP/UX 10.x	a Unix variant from HP	http://eigen.ee.ualberta.ca/
IBM OS/2 v4.x	commercial GUI OS from IBM	http://www.software.ibm.com/os/warp/
Inferno	networking OS	http://207.121.184.224/
Linux	free UNIX variant	http://www.linux.org/
LynxOS	real-time OS	comp.os/lynx
Mach 4.x	small multi-processor OS	www.cs.cmu.edu/afs/cs.cmu.edu/project/mach/public/www/mach.html
Macintosh OS 8	OS for Macintosh systems	http://www.macos.apple.com/
MaxMinix	Minix variant for Mac systems	http://www.mcs.drexel.edu/~gbpliner/macminix/
Magic Cap	communication-based OS	http://www.genmagic.com/MagicCap/index.html
Minix	small free UNIX variant	http://www.cs.vu.nl/~ast/minix.html
MkLinux	Mach-based Linux for Apples	http://www.mklinux.apple.com/
MS-DOS v6.x	commercial DOS from MS	http://www.microsoft.com/kb/default.asp
Multics	time-sharing OS	ftp://ftp.stratus.com/pub/vos/multics/tvv/multics.html
NetBSD 1.2	free UNIV variant	http://www.netbsd.org/
Netware v4.x	networking OS from Novell	http://www.novell.com/intranetware/products/
NeXTStep	networking OS	http://www.omnigroup.com/Documentation/NEXTSTEP/Guide.html
Novell-DOS v7.0	DOS version from Novell	http://www.novell.ru:8080/Ftp/Updates/dsktop/ndos7/Alpha0.html
OpenStep 4.0	open platform OS	http://www.stepwise.com/
OSF/1	DEC OS for Alpha	http://wsspinfo.cern.ch/file/osfsp
PC-DOS v7.0	DOS version from IBM	http://www.software.ibm.com/os/warp/pspinfo/pcdos.html
Plan9	distributed computing OS	http://www.ecf.toronto.edu/plan9/
QNX	real-time OS	http://www.qnx.com/
Rhapsody	Macintosh OS	http://www.stepwise.com/
SCO Unix	a UNIX variant from SCO	http://www.sco.com/
Solaris 2.5	a UNIX variant from Sun	http://www.lafayette.edu/~mulliga/SUN/
Unix	the classic workstation OS	http://www.unix.digital.com/
UnixWare	a UNIX variant from SCO	http://www.sco.com/

TABLE 3-1   PARTIAL LISTING OF CONTEMPORARY OPERATING SYSTEMS (CONTINUED)

OPERATING SYSTEM	PURPOSE/EMPHASIS	FURTHER STUDY
VMS (OpenVMS)	the classic mainframe OS	http://www.levitte.org/~ava/index.htmix
Windows 95	commercial GUI PS OS	http://www.microsoft.com/products/prodref/426_ov.htm
Windows 98	commercial GUI PC OS	http://www.microsoft.com/windows98/info/w98overview.htm
Windows CE	version for hand-held PCs	http://www.microsoft.com/products/prodref/120_ov.htm
Windows NT v4.0	commercial networking OS	http://www.microsoft.com/products/prodref/428_ov.htm
X Window System	a UNIX variant	http://www.rahul.net/kenton/xsites.html
Xinu	multi-tasking OS	http://willow.canberra.edu.au/~chrisc/xinu.html

TABLE 3-2   COMPARISON OF SYSTEM REQUIREMENTS FOR MAJOR OPERATING SYSTEMS

FEATURE	DOS	WINDOWS 95	WINDOWS NT
PC platform	any	486/25MHz	486/25MHz Alpha MIPS R4X00 PowerPC
RAM	1024KB	8MB	16–32MB
Install drive	1.44MB	CD-ROM	CD-ROM
Hard drive	6MB	40–45MB	110MB
Display	mono text	VGA	VGA
Mouse	optional	required	required

one OS might be selected over another. The following sections offer some highlights of the major commercial operating systems offered by Microsoft and IBM.

MS-DOS 6.22

MS-DOS 6.22 is the last "stand-alone" command-line operating system designed by Microsoft for the PC, and is generally considered to be one of the most versatile and reliable DOS-type OS ever released by Microsoft. Numerous safety features and enhancements are designed to provide the safest possible computing environment of any MS-DOS version. The most notable features are outlined, as follows. Table 3-2 highlights the system requirements for MS-DOS 6.22.

■ *DriveSpace and DoubleGuard* DriveSpace now integrates disk compression into the operating system supporting both hard disks and floppy disks. DriveSpace includes DoubleGuard safety checking, which protects data by verifying data integrity before writing to the disk.

- *MemMaker* MemMaker is a memory-optimization program designed to free conventional memory by moving device drivers and memory-resident programs from conventional memory into the *Upper Memory Area (UMA)*.
- *Backup* Backup is a utility for backing up your hard drive. MS-DOS 6.22 includes a version of Backup for both DOS and Windows 3.1x.
- *Anti-Virus* The Anti-Virus utility can identify and remove more than 1000 different computer viruses. MS-DOS 6.22 includes a version of Anti-Virus for both DOS and Windows 3.1x.
- *Undelete* The Undelete feature allows you to recover deleted files. MS-DOS 6.22 includes a version of Undelete for both DOS and Windows 3.1x.
- *ScanDisk* MS-DOS 6.22 includes the latest version of ScanDisk, which detects, diagnoses, and repairs disk errors on uncompressed drives and DriveSpace-compressed drives. ScanDisk can repair file-system errors (such as cross-linked files and lost clusters) and physical disk errors.
- *MultiConfig* MultiConfig allows you to define more than one configuration in your CONFIG.SYS file. If your CONFIG.SYS file defines multiple configurations, MS-DOS displays a menu that enables you to choose the configuration you want to use each time you boot the computer.
- *Interactive Start* The interactive start feature gives you the ability to bypass startup commands when you turn on your computer by pressing the <F8> key. This allows you to choose which CONFIG.SYS and AUTOEXEC.BAT commands MS-DOS should carry out.
- *Defrag* MS-DOS 6.22 includes the latest version of Defrag, which reorganizes files on your hard disk to minimize the time it takes your computer to access them.
- *SmartDrive* The SmartDrive program included with MS-DOS 6.22 speeds up your computer by using a disk cache, which stores information being read from your hard disk or CD-ROM drive. SmartDrive can also be set to cache information being written to your hard disk.
- *Interlink* The Interlink feature enables you to easily transfer files between computers. With Interlink and a cable, you can access information on another computer without using floppy disks to copy data from one computer to another.

PC-DOS 7.0

PC-DOS is IBM's answer to MS-DOS. Early versions of PC-DOS were actually licensed to IBM from Microsoft, but the two giants eventually parted company, and IBM continued the development of PC-DOS under their own banner. Today, PC-DOS 7.0 is roughly equivalent in features and performance to MS-DOS 6.22—including disk compression, anti-virus software, and limited networking features. System requirements are about the same, but PC-DOS 7.0 includes PCMCIA support, a DOS file-update feature (to keep files synchronized between PCs), and a high-level programming language called *REXX*.

- *Improved utilities* There are numerous enhancements to DOS and Windows utilities including Central Point's Backup Utility, Phoenix Technology's PCMCIA support utility, and the RAMBoost Memory Optimizer.
- *Anti-Virus* PC-DOS 7.0 includes IBM AntiVirus, which checks for more than 2100 viruses.

- *Stacker* Stacker 4.0 disk compression delivers an excellent mix of compression and performance.
- *File Update* A new PC DOS File Update feature automatically synchronizes files between your desktop and notebook PCs so they're always up to date.
- *REXX* PC-DOS 7.0 includes a new integrated REXX high-level programming language.

WINDOWS 95

Microsoft released Windows 95 in August of 1995 as the major upgrade to Windows 3.1x. Windows 95 was designed to offer superior performance while taking advantage of emerging PC hardware, such as Plug-and-Play, power conservation, PCI bus architecture, etc. Windows 95 runs most Windows 3.1x and DOS programs, but also supports improved features, such as a built-in uninstaller, dial-up networking, multitasking, and long file names. Though aging, Windows 95 is currently the most popular commercial OS for the personal computer.

- *Taskbar* The Taskbar acts as a "home base," where you can start programs (with the *Start* button) and keep track of what programs have been launched. You can use the Taskbar to switch between programs (as needed) for convenient multitasking.
- *Windows Explorer* The traditional File Manager of earlier Windows versions has been replaced by Windows Explorer for browsing through and managing your files, drives, and network connections.
- *Active right mouse button* Use the RMB to accomplish many common tasks quickly and easily. Click almost anything in Windows 95 with your right mouse button to see a context-sensitive menu of options.
- *Long file names* Windows 95 supports long file names (up to 250 characters) to make your files and folders easier to organize and find. File names can now have sensible titles.
- *Shortcuts* Easily create links for easy access to important files, folders, drives, programs, or Web sites.
- *Multitasking* Windows 95 offers improved multitasking capabilities, which truly allow the system to handle multiple tasks simultaneously without system interruptions.
- *Plug-and-Play* The Plug-and-Play feature allows you to insert the card for a hardware device into your computer, and Windows automatically recognizes and sets up the hardware for you.
- *Dial-Up Networking* Dial-Up Networking allows easy access to online resources (such as Internet), and supports communication between connected PCs.

OS/2 WARP 4.X

OS/2 Warp has long been IBM's premier OS. Originally co-developed with Microsoft, OS/2 development continued in-house after IBM and Microsoft ceased their cooperative ventures. OS/2 is a GUI-based operating system capable of running most Windows and DOS software, as well as native OS/2 applications in a true multitasking environment. OS/2 Warp 4.x focuses on network operations and connectivity—including built-in

Internet applications—and offers an advantage over competing operating systems with its use of voice input controls. In spite of these advantages, OS/2 is noted for a surprising lack of hardware support. For example, it can be surprisingly difficult to find suitable OS/2 drivers for such devices as CD-ROM drives and sound boards.

- *Software compatibility* OS/2 runs DOS and most Windows 3.1x applications, along with native OS/2 and Java applications. OS/2 also supports such features as TrueType, OpenGL, OpenDOC, Open32, and Plug-and-Play.
- *Connectivity* OS/2 is particularly noted for its strong network connectivity.
- *Reliability* True multitasking environment is well suited to critical applications, and OS/2 is relatively crash-proof when compared to Windows 95 and NT.
- *Systems management* OS/2 offers powerful system-management features including Desktop Management Interface (DMI) support.
- *Speech recognition* OS/2 includes VoiceType for OS/2 Warp speech-recognition software.

WINDOWS CE

Windows CE is designed to serve as an operating system for a broad range of communications, entertainment, and mobile-computing devices. It also enables new types of non-PC business and consumer devices that can communicate with each other, share information with Windows-based PCs, and connect to the Internet (i.e., "wallet" PCs, digital information pagers, cellular smart phones, DVD players, and Internet "Web phones." The first hand-held PC products based on Windows CE began shipping in November 1996. It is important that Windows CE is strictly released as an OEM product, and cannot be purchased through retail channels.

- *Companion applications* The Windows CE operating system supports Windows CE-based companion applications that share or synchronize information with their counterparts for Windows.
- *Internet Explorer* Windows CE includes a version of Internet Explorer, which offers built-in Web access for many types of communications, entertainment and mobile-computing devices.
- *Windows development environment* The Windows CE development environment supports a comprehensive and expandable subset of Win32 APIs, and uses familiar off-the-shelf development tools. This will hopefully ensure a strong aftermarket for Windows CE applications.
- *Communication with Windows-based PCs* Windows CE can seamlessly synchronize, communicate, and exchange information with Windows-based PCs.

WINDOWS NT (WORKSTATION)

Windows NT represents Microsoft's emphasis on business communication and networking. Although the "look and feel" of Windows NT might seem quite similar to Windows 95, NT incorporates a powerful suite of networking and Internet-related features backed up by detailed security, cryptography, and system policies configurations. Windows NT also abandons "DOS-mode" support. There is no doubt that Windows NT represents one of the most complex and versatile operating systems now in service for business and networking environments.

- *Management and control*   Windows NT includes remote-management and troubleshooting tools, and allows administrators to implement policies and standards for system-wide desktop configurations.
- *Windows NT Explorer*   The Windows NT tool for browsing and managing files, drive, and network connections. It displays your computer's contents as a hierarchy, or "tree," allowing you to see the contents of each drive, folder, and network connection.
- *Task Manager*   An integrated tool for managing applications and tasks. The Task Manager maintains detailed information on each application and process running on the desktop. It also provides an effective way to terminate applications and processes that are not responding.
- *Internet Explorer*   Windows NT Workstation comes with Internet Explorer, which gives you full support to explore the Internet.
- *Peer Web Services*   Peer Web Services (PWS) enables easy publication of personal Web pages, and lets systems share that Web information over Intranets. It's also ideal for developing, testing, and staging Web applications and content.
- *Client Support for PPTP*   Point-to-Point Tunneling Protocol (PPTP) provides a secure path to use public data networks (such as the Internet) to create virtual private networks. PPTP allows you to safely transmit confidential communications over the Internet.
- *WINS and DNS integration*   Windows NT takes advantage of the integration between Windows Internet Name Service (WINS) and Domain Name System (DNS) to provide a form of dynamic DNS that makes it easier to connect to network resources.
- *Client support for NDS*   Windows NT Workstation includes an improved version of Client Services for NetWare that supports Novell NetWare Directory Services (NDS). This enables users to log on to Novell NetWare 4.x servers running DNS to access files and print resources.
- *Dial-Up Networking multilink channel aggregation*   Dial-Up Networking now provides channel aggregation that enables users to combine all available dial-up lines to achieve higher transfer speeds. For example, you can combine two or more PPP ISDN B channels to achieve speeds of up to 128KB.
- *Windows messaging client*   This universal e-mail inbox that you can use with many different e-mail systems. It includes full Messaging API (MAPI) 1.0 support. You can send, receive, organize, and store e-mail and file-system objects.
- *System policies and user profiles*   System policies are used to provide a standardized, controlled desktop environment for users. User profiles contain all user-definable settings, and can be stored on a Windows NT Server, so a user can receive the same desktop, regardless of their location.
- *Setup manager*   This Windows NT utility assists administrators in creating installation scripts, and reduces the time and effort of deploying Windows NT.
- *Dial-Up Networking*   Improved Dial-Up Networking provides the ability to easily and automatically dial-up on demand.

- *Hardware profiles* Windows NT hardware profiles allow you to have different computer settings depending on the environment in which a computer is being used, and makes it easier to use computers in different configurations (i.e., docked and undocked laptop configurations).
- *Multimedia APIs* Windows NT supports the multimedia APIs found in Windows 95: DirectDraw, DirectInput, DirectPlay, and DirectSound. Supporting these APIs allows developers to simultaneously create games and other applications for both platforms.
- *Telephony APIs* Telephony API (TAPI) integrates telephones and PCs. Using the TAPI interface, communications applications can ask for access to a modem or telephone device, allowing them to be shared.
- *Cryptography APIs* Windows NT includes a set of encryption APIs that allow developers to easily create applications that work securely over non-secure networks (such as the Internet).
- *Distributed COM* Distributed COM (DCOM) support provides the infrastructure that allows DCOM applications (also known as *Network OLE*) to communicate across networks without needing to redevelop applications.

WINDOWS 98

With the many new hardware standards and features being developed for the PC, Windows 95 is becoming hard-pressed to make the fullest use of system resources. Windows 98 (previously code-named *Memphis*) builds on Windows 95 by adding a rich suite of refinements and improvements to a full 32-bit operating system. New wizards, utilities, and resources work proactively to keep systems running more smoothly. Performance is faster for many common tasks such as application loading, system startup, and shut down. Full integration with the Internet's Web aids online work and system versatility. As of this writing, Windows 98 has entered the Beta 2 phase, and should be released around the second quarter of 1998. The following notes outline some of the features planned for Windows 98:

- *Disk Defragmenter Optimization wizard* The new Disk Defragmenter Optimization wizard uses the process of disk defragmentation to increase the speed with which your most frequently used applications run.
- *Windows 98 HelpDesk* Windows 98 HelpDesk is the first step in resolving a technical support issue. It links you to local and Internet resources (including Online Help, Troubleshooting Wizards, Knowledge Base, Technical Support for Windows home page, Windows Update Manager, and the Windows 98 Web-based Bug Reporting Tool).
- *Windows System Update* The Windows System Update feature helps ensure that you are using the latest drivers and file systems available. The new Web-based service scans your system to determine what hardware and software you have installed, then compares that information to a back-end database to determine whether there are newer drivers or system files available. If there are newer drivers or system files, the service can automatically install the drivers.
- *System File Checker* A System File Checker utility provides an easy way to verify that the Windows 98 system files (*.DLL, *.COM, *.VXD, *.DRV, *.OCX, *.INF, *.HLP,

etc.) have not been modified or corrupted. The utility also provides an easy mechanism for restoring the original versions of system files that have changed.

■ *System Troubleshooter* The System Troubleshooter utility automates the routine troubleshooting steps used by support personnel and users when diagnosing issues with the Windows configuration.

■ *Dr. Watson utility* Windows 98 includes an enhanced version of the Dr. Watson utility. When a software fault occurs (general-protection fault, hang, etc.), Dr. Watson will intercept it and indicate what software failed (and why). Dr. Watson also collects detailed information about the state of your system at the time the fault occurred.

■ *Backup utility* A new backup applet supports SCSI tape devices and makes backing up your data easier and more versatile.

■ *Faster shutdown* The time it takes to shutdown the system has been dramatically reduced in Windows 98.

■ *Broadcast architecture* With a TV tuner board installed, Windows 98 allows a PC to receive and display television and other data distributed over the broadcast networks, including enhanced television programs (which combine standard television with HTML information related to the programs).

■ *Support for new hardware* Windows 98 provides support for an array of innovations that have occurred in computer hardware over the last few years. Some of the major hardware standards supported by Windows 98 include: Universal Serial Bus (USB), IEEE 1394, Accelerated Graphics Port (AGP), Advanced Configuration and Power Interface (ACPI), and Digital Video Disc (DVD).

■ *Display configuration enhancements* Display setting enhancements provide support for dynamically changing screen resolution and color depth. Adapter refresh rates can also be set with most newer display driver chipsets.

■ *ActiveMovie* Windows 98 supports a new media-streaming architecture called ActiveMovie that delivers high-quality video playback of popular media types, including MPEG audio, .WAV audio, MPEG video, AVI video, and Apple QuickTime video.

■ *Support for Intel MMX processors* Provides support for software that uses the Pentium Multimedia Extensions (MMX) for fast audio and video support on the next generation of Pentium processor.

■ *FAT32* FAT32 is an improved version of the FAT file system that allows disks over two gigabytes to be formatted as a single drive. FAT32 also uses smaller clusters than FAT drives, resulting in a more efficient use of space on large disks.

■ *Power-management improvements* Windows 98 includes support for the Advanced Configuration and Power Interface (ACPI), and support for the Advanced Power Management (APM) 1.2 extensions including: Disk spindown, PCMCIA modem power down, and resume on ring.

■ *Multiple display support* Multiple display support allows you to use multiple monitors and/or multiple graphics adapters on a single PC.

■ *Remote Access Server* Windows 98 includes all of the components necessary to enable your desktop to act as a dial-up server. This allows dial-up clients to remotely connect to a Windows 98 machine for local resource access.

■ *PCMCIA enhancements* There have been several enhancements to Windows 98 for PCMCIA support, including support for PC Card32 (Cardbus) for implementing high-bandwidth applications, such as video capture and 100Mbps networking. There is support for PC Cards that operate at 3.3 V and there is support for multifunction PC Cards (such as LAN and Modem, or SCSI and sound) to operate on a single physical PC Card.

■ *Support for Infrared Data Association (IrDA) 3.0* Windows 98 supports IrDA for wireless connectivity—users can easily connect to peripheral devices or other PCs without using connecting cables. Infrared-equipped laptop or desktop computers have the capability of networking, transferring files, and printing wirelessly with other IrDA-compatible infrared devices.

■ *Dial-Up Networking improvements* The Dial-Up Networking included with Windows 98 has been updated to support such features as dial-up scripting and support for multilink channel aggregation, which enables users to combine all available dial-up lines to achieve higher transfer speeds.

■ *Support for Point-to-Point Tunneling Protocol (PPTP)* The Point-to-Point Tunneling Protocol (PPTP) provides a way to use public data networks (such as the Internet) to create virtual private networks connecting client PCs with servers. PPTP offers protocol encapsulation to support multiple protocols via TCP/IP connections and data encryption for privacy, making it safer to send information over non-secure networks.

■ *Distributed Component Object Model (DCOM)* Distributed COM (DCOM) in Windows 98 (and Windows NT 4.0) provides the infrastructure that allows DCOM applications (the technology formally known as *Network OLE*) to communicate across networks without needing to redevelop applications.

■ *Support for NetWare Directory Services (NDS)* Windows 98 includes Client Services for NetWare that support Novell NetWare Directory Services (NDS). This enables Windows 98 users to log on to Novell NetWare 4.x servers running NDS to access files and print resources.

A Closer Look at MS-DOS

The operating system provides I/O resources to application programs, as well as an environment that can be used to execute programs or interact with the operating system. To accomplish these two tasks, MS-DOS uses three files: IO.SYS, MSDOS.SYS, and COMMAND.COM. Notice that the myriad of other files shipped with MS-DOS are technically not part of the operating system itself, but are instead a library of utilities intended to help you optimize and maintain the system. The following sections examine each of the three core MS-DOS files in more detail. Remember that loading and running an operating system properly relies on adequate processing, memory, and disk-system resources.

IO.SYS

The IO.SYS file provides many of the low-level routines (or drivers) that interact with BIOS. Some versions of IO.SYS are customized by original equipment manufacturers (OEMs) to supplement the particular BIOS for their system. However, OS customization is rare today because it leads to system incompatibilities. In addition to low-level drivers, IO.SYS contains a system initialization routine. The entire contents of the file (except for the system initialization routine) is kept in low memory throughout system operation. IO.SYS is a file assigned with a hidden-file attribute, so you will not see the file when searching a bootable disk with an ordinary *DIR* command. Although Microsoft uses the filename IO.SYS, other OS makers might use a different name. For example, the corresponding file name in IBM's PC-DOS is *IBMBIO.COM*.

In order for a disk (floppy or hard disk) to be bootable under MS-DOS 3.x or 4.x, IO.SYS must be the first file in the disk directory, and it must occupy at least the first available cluster on the disk (usually cluster 2). This is the disk's OS volume boot sector. Of course, subsequent clusters containing IO.SYS can be placed anywhere in the disk, just like any other ordinary file. MS-DOS 5.x (and later) eliminate this requirement and allows IO.SYS to be placed in any root directory location anywhere on the disk. When disk access begins during the boot process, the bootable drive's boot sector is read, which loads IO.SYS into memory and gives it control of the system. Once IO.SYS is running, the boot process can continue, as you will learn later in this chapter. If this file is missing or corrupt, you will see some type of boot failure message or the system might lock up.

MSDOS.SYS

This is the core of MS-DOS versions up through 6.22. The MSDOS.SYS file is listed second in the boot disk's directory, and is the second file to be loaded during the boot process. It contains the routines that handle OS disk and file access. Like IO.SYS, the MSDOS.SYS file is loaded into low memory, where it resides throughout the system's operation. If the file is missing or corrupt, you will see some kind of boot failure message or the system might lock up.

IO.SYS AND MSDOS.SYS VARIATIONS UNDER WINDOWS 95

With the introduction of Windows 95, the classic DOS files have been redesigned to streamline the boot process. Windows 95 places all of the functions found in IO.SYS and MSDOS.SYS into a single hidden file, called *IO.SYS* (this file might be renamed *WINBOOT.SYS* if you start the PC with a previous OS). Most of the options formerly set with entries in the CONFIG.SYS file are now incorporated into Windows 95's IO.SYS. The settings that are selected with IO.SYS can be superseded by entries in a CONFIG.SYS file, but the defaults used with IO.SYS are listed:

■ dos=high	DOS components are automatically loaded into high memory
■ himem.sys	The real-mode memory manager is loaded
■ ifshlp.sys	The file system-enhancement utility is loaded
■ setver.exe	The MS-DOS version utility is loaded
■ files=60	File-handle buffers are allocated
■ lastdrive=z	Specifies the last drive letter available for assignment
■ buffers=30	File buffers are allocated
■ stacks=9,256	Stack frames are created
■ shell=command.com	Sets the desired command processor
■ fcbs=4	Sets the maximum number of file control blocks

Few of the default settings in IO.SYS are really needed by Windows 95, but they are included to provide a level of backward compatibility with pre-existing system configurations.

The MSDOS.SYS file has also been dramatically altered under Windows 95. Where older versions of MS-DOS relied on MSDOS.SYS for disk and file code, all of that functionality has been worked into IO.SYS. MSDOS.SYS under Windows 95 is now little more than a text .INI file that is used to configure the boot properties of Windows, and list important paths to key Windows files (including the registry).

ADJUSTING MSDOS.SYS UNDER MS-DOS 7.X

Windows 95 essentially eliminates the function of the MSDOS.SYS file—replacing it instead with a text file used to tailor the startup process. Normally, there is little need to access the MSDOS.SYS file, but you might be faced with the need to adjust the Windows 95 boot process. This part of the chapter takes you inside the MSDOS.SYS file for MS-DOS 7.x (Windows 95), and illustrates the various options you can use to enhance the Windows 95 platform. A typical example of an MSDOS.SYS file is shown in Fig. 3-2.

> Notice that MSDOS.SYS must be longer than 1024 bytes in length. Otherwise, Windows 95 will fail to load. Do not alter or remove the "x" lines in MSDOS.SYS.

There are two main sections to the MSDOS.SYS file: the [Paths] section, and the [Options] section. Paths defines the directory paths to major Windows file areas, while

```
[Paths]
WinDir=C:\WINDOWS
WinBootDir=C:\WINDOWS
HostWinBootDrv=C

[Options]
BootMulti=1
BootGUI=1
;
;The following lines are required for compatibility with other programs.
;Do not remove them (MSDOS.SYS needs to be >1024 bytes).
;xxxxxxxxxxxxxxxxxxxxxxxxxxxxxxxxxxxxxxxxxxxxxxxxxxxxxxxxxxxxxxxxxxxxxxa
;xxxxxxxxxxxxxxxxxxxxxxxxxxxxxxxxxxxxxxxxxxxxxxxxxxxxxxxxxxxxxxxxxxxxxxb
;xxxxxxxxxxxxxxxxxxxxxxxxxxxxxxxxxxxxxxxxxxxxxxxxxxxxxxxxxxxxxxxxxxxxxxc
;xxxxxxxxxxxxxxxxxxxxxxxxxxxxxxxxxxxxxxxxxxxxxxxxxxxxxxxxxxxxxxxxxxxxxxd
;xxxxxxxxxxxxxxxxxxxxxxxxxxxxxxxxxxxxxxxxxxxxxxxxxxxxxxxxxxxxxxxxxxxxxxe
;xxxxxxxxxxxxxxxxxxxxxxxxxxxxxxxxxxxxxxxxxxxxxxxxxxxxxxxxxxxxxxxxxxxxxxf
;xxxxxxxxxxxxxxxxxxxxxxxxxxxxxxxxxxxxxxxxxxxxxxxxxxxxxxxxxxxxxxxxxxxxxxg
;xxxxxxxxxxxxxxxxxxxxxxxxxxxxxxxxxxxxxxxxxxxxxxxxxxxxxxxxxxxxxxxxxxxxxxh
;xxxxxxxxxxxxxxxxxxxxxxxxxxxxxxxxxxxxxxxxxxxxxxxxxxxxxxxxxxxxxxxxxxxxxxi
;xxxxxxxxxxxxxxxxxxxxxxxxxxxxxxxxxxxxxxxxxxxxxxxxxxxxxxxxxxxxxxxxxxxxxxj
;xxxxxxxxxxxxxxxxxxxxxxxxxxxxxxxxxxxxxxxxxxxxxxxxxxxxxxxxxxxxxxxxxxxxxxk
;xxxxxxxxxxxxxxxxxxxxxxxxxxxxxxxxxxxxxxxxxxxxxxxxxxxxxxxxxxxxxxxxxxxxxxl
;xxxxxxxxxxxxxxxxxxxxxxxxxxxxxxxxxxxxxxxxxxxxxxxxxxxxxxxxxxxxxxxxxxxxxxm
;xxxxxxxxxxxxxxxxxxxxxxxxxxxxxxxxxxxxxxxxxxxxxxxxxxxxxxxxxxxxxxxxxxxxxxn
;xxxxxxxxxxxxxxxxxxxxxxxxxxxxxxxxxxxxxxxxxxxxxxxxxxxxxxxxxxxxxxxxxxxxxxo
;xxxxxxxxxxxxxxxxxxxxxxxxxxxxxxxxxxxxxxxxxxxxxxxxxxxxxxxxxxxxxxxxxxxxxxp
;xxxxxxxxxxxxxxxxxxxxxxxxxxxxxxxxxxxxxxxxxxxxxxxxxxxxxxxxxxxxxxxxxxxxxxq
;xxxxxxxxxxxxxxxxxxxxxxxxxxxxxxxxxxxxxxxxxxxxxxxxxxxxxxxxxxxxxxxxxxxxxxr
;xxxxxxxxxxxxxxxxxxxxxxxxxxxxxxxxxxxxxxxxxxxxxxxxxxxxxxxxxxxxxxxxxxxxxxs
Network=1
```

FIGURE 3-2 **A look inside the MSDOS.SYS file.**

Options allow you to configure many of the available attributes used to boot a Windows 95 system. The Options are listed:

[Paths]

WinDir=
Indicates the location of the Windows 95 directory specified during Setup.

WinBootDir=
Indicates the location of the necessary startup files. The default is the directory specified during the Setup process (i.e., C :\WINDOWS).

HostWinBootDrv=c   Indicates the location of the boot drive root directory.

[Options]

BootMulti=
This enables dual-boot capabilities. The default is 0. Setting this value to 1 enables the ability to start MS-DOS by pressing <F4>, or by pressing <F8> to use the Windows Startup menu.

BootGUI=
This enables automatic graphical startup into Windows 95. The default is 1.

BootMenu=
This enables automatic display of the Windows 95 Startup menu (the user must press <F8> to see the menu). The default is 0. Setting this value to 1 eliminates the need to press <F8> to see the menu.

BootKeys=
This enables the startup option keys (i.e., F5, F6, and F8). The default is 1.

BootWin=
This enables Windows 95 as the default operating system. Setting this value to 0 disables Windows 95 as the default (useful only with MS-DOS version 5 or 6.x on the computer). The default is 1.

BootDelay=n
This sets the initial startup delay to n seconds (default is 2). A BootKeys=0 entry disables the delay. The only purpose of the delay is to give the user sufficient time to press <F8> after the Starting Windows message appears.

BootFailSafe=
This enables Safe Mode for system startup. The default is 0.

BootMenuDefault=#   This sets the default menu item on the Windows Startup menu; the default is 3 for a computer with no networking components and 4 for a networked computer.

BootMenuDelay=#
This sets the number of seconds to display the Windows Startup menu before running the default menu item. The default is 30 seconds.

Logo=
This enables display of the Windows 95 logo. The default is 1. Setting this value to 0 also avoids hooking a variety of interrupts that can create incompatibilities with certain memory managers from other vendors.

BootWarn=
This enables the Safe Mode startup warning. The default is 1.

DblSpace=
This enables automatic loading of DBLSPACE.BIN. The default is 1.

DrvSpace=	This enables automatic loading of DRVSPACE.BIN. The default is 1.
DoubleBuffer=	This enables loading of a double-buffering driver for a SCSI controller. The default is 0. Setting this value to 1 enables double-buffering (if required by the SCSI controller).
LoadTop=	This enables the loading of COMMAND.COM or DRVSPACE.BIN at the top of 640KB memory. The default is 1. Set this value to 0 with Novell NetWare or any software that makes assumptions about what is used in specific memory areas.
Network=	This enables Safe mode with networking as a menu option. The default is 1 for computers with networking installed. This value should be 0 if network software components are not installed.

If Windows 95 is installed in its own directory, the earlier version of MS-DOS is preserved on the hard disk. If you set BootMulti=1 in MSDOS.SYS, you can start the earlier version of MS-DOS by pressing <F4> when starting Windows 95.

COMMAND.COM

The COMMAND.COM file serves as the MS-DOS shell and command processor. This is the program that you are interacting with at the command-line prompt. COMMAND.COM is the third file loaded when a PC boots, and it is stored in low memory, along with IO.SYS and MSDOS.SYS. The number of commands that you have available depend on the version of MS-DOS in use. MS-DOS uses two types of commands in normal operation: resident and transient.

Resident commands (also called *internal commands*) are procedures that are coded directly into COMMAND.COM. As a result, resident commands execute almost immediately when called from the command line. CLS and DIR are two typical resident commands. Transient commands (also called *external commands*) represent a broader and more powerful group of commands. However, transient commands are not loaded with COMMAND.COM. Instead, the commands are available as small .COM or .EXE utility files in the DOS directory (such as DEBUG and EMM386). Transient commands must be loaded from the disk and executed each time they are needed. By pulling out complex commands as separate utilities, the size of COMMAND.COM can be kept relatively small. A table of transient (external) commands for MS-DOS are shown in Table 3-3 and the resident (internal) commands for MS-DOS are listed in Table 3-4.

TABLE 3-3 AN INDEX OF EXTERNAL/TRANSIENT MS-DOS COMMANDS											
COMMAND	2.0	2.1	3.0 3.1	3.2	3.3	4.0	5.0	6.0	6.2	6.21 6.22	7.0 7.1
APPEND					*	*	*	*	*	*	
ASSIGN	*	*	*	*	*	*	*				

TABLE 3-3   AN INDEX OF EXTERNAL/TRANSIENT MS-DOS COMMANDS (CONTINUED)

COMMAND	2.0	2.1	3.0 3.1	3.2	3.3	4.0	5.0	6.0	6.2	6.21 6.22	7.0 7.1
ATTRIB			*	*	*	*	*	*		*	*
BACKUP	*	*	*	*	*	*	*				
BASIC	*	*	*	*							
BASICA	*	*	*	*							
CHKDSK	*	*	*	*	*	*	*	*	*	*	*
CHOICE								*	*	*	*
COMMAND	*	*	*	*	*	*	*	*	*	*	*
COMP	*	*	*	*	*	*	*				
DBLSPACE								*	*		
DEBUG	*	*	*	*	*	*	*	*	*	*	*
DEFRAG								*	*	*	*
DELTREE								*	*	*	
DISKCOMP	*	*	*	*	*	*	*	*	*	*	*
DISKCOPY	*	*	*	*	*	*	*	*	*	*	*
DOSKEY								*	*	*	*
DOSSHELL						*		*	*		
DOSSWAP								*	*		
DRVSPACE										*	*
EDIT							*	*	*	*	*
EDLIN	*	*	*	*	*	*	*				
EMM386							*	*	*	*	*
EXE2BIN		*	*	*	*	*	*				
EXPAND							*	*	*	*	*
FASTHELP								*	*	*	
FASTOPEN					*	*	*	*	*	*	
FC					*	*	*	*	*	*	*
FDISK	*	*	*	*	*	*	*	*	*	*	*
FILESYS						*					
FIND	*	*	*	*	*	*	*	*	*	*	*
FORMAT	*	*	*	*	*	*	*	*	*	*	*
GRAFTABL			*	*	*	*	*				
GRAPHICS	*	*	*	*	*	*	*	*	*	*	
GWBASIC					*	*					
HELP							*	*	*	*	
IFSFUNC						*					
INTERLINK								*	*	*	
INTERSVR								*	*	*	
JOIN				*	*	*	*				
KEYB					*	*	*	*	*	*	*
KEYBFR			*	*							
KEYBGR			*	*							

TABLE 3-3   AN INDEX OF EXTERNAL/TRANSIENT MS-DOS COMMANDS (CONTINUED)

COMMAND	2.0	2.1	3.0 3.1	3.2	3.3	4.0	5.0	6.0	6.2	6.21 6.22	7.0 7.1
KEYBIT			*	*							
KEYBSP			*	*							
KEYBUK			*	*							
LABEL			*	*	*	*	*	*	*	*	*
LINK	*	*	*	*	*	*					
LOADFIX							*	*	*	*	*
MEM						*	*	*	*	*	*
MEMMAKER								*	*	*	
MIRROR							*				
MODE	*	*	*	*	*	*	*	*	*	*	*
MORE	*	*	*	*	*	*	*	*	*	*	*
MOVE								*	*	*	*
MSBACK								*	*	*	
MSCDEX								*	*	*	
MSD								*	*	*	
MWAV								*	*	*	
MWAVTSR								*	*	*	
MWBACKUP								*	*	*	
MWUNDEL								*	*	*	
NLSFUNC					*	*	*	*	*	*	*
POWER								*	*	*	
PRINT	*	*	*	*	*	*	*	*	*	*	
QBASIC							*	*	*	*	
RECOVER	*	*	*	*	*	*	*				
REPLACE			*		*	*	*	*	*	*	
RESTORE	*	*	*	*	*	*	*	*	*	*	
SCANDISK								*	*	*	*
SELECT			*	*	*	*					
SETVER							*	*	*	*	*
SHARE			*	*	*	*	*	*	*	*	
SIZER								*	*	*	
SMARTDRV								*	*	*	
SMARTMON								*	*		
SORT	*	*	*	*	*	*	*	*	*	*	*
SUBST				*	*	*	*	*	*	*	*
SYS	*	*	*	*	*	*	*	*	*	*	*
TREE	*	*	*	*	*	*	*	*	*	*	*
UNDELETE							*	*	*	*	
UNFORMAT							*	*	*	*	
VSAFE								*	*	*	
XCOPY					*	*	*	*	*	*	*

TABLE 3-4   AN INDEX OF INTERNAL/RESIDENT MS-DOS COMMANDS

	2.0	2.1	3.0	3.1	3.2	3.3	4.X	5.X	6.X	7.X
CD/CHDIR	*	*	*	*	*	*	*	*	*	*
CHCP							*	*	*	*
CLS	*	*	*	*	*	*	*	*	*	*
COPY	*	*	*	*	*	*	*	*	*	*
CTTY	*	*	*	*	*	*	*	*	*	*
DATE	*	*	*	*	*	*	*	*	*	*
DEL/ERASE	*	*	*	*	*	*	*	*	*	*
DIR	*	*	*	*	*	*	*	*	*	*
EXT			*	*	*	*	*	*	*	*
EXPAND								*	*	
LOADHIGH/LH								*	*	*
MD/MKDIR	*	*	*	*	*	*	*	*	*	*
PATH	*	*	*	*	*	*	*	*	*	*
PROMPT	*	*	*	*	*	*	*	*	*	*
RD/RMDIR	*	*	*	*	*	*	*	*	*	*
REN/RENAME	*	*	*	*	*	*	*	*	*	*
SET	*	*	*	*	*	*	*	*	*	*
TIME	*	*	*	*	*	*	*	*	*	*
TYPE	*	*	*	*	*	*	*	*	*	*
VER			*	*	*	*	*	*	*	*
VERIFY	*	*	*	*	*	*	*	*	*	*
VOL	*	*	*	*	*	*	*	*	*	*

RECOGNIZING AND DEALING WITH OS PROBLEMS

Because the operating system is an integral part of the PC, any problems with using or upgrading the OS can adversely affect system operation. Software does not fail like hardware—once software is loaded and running, it will not eventually break down from heat or physical stress. Unfortunately, software is hardly perfect. Upgrading from one OS to another can upset the system's operation, and bugs in the operating system can result in unforeseen operation that might totally destroy a system's reliability.

Virtually all versions of operating systems have bugs in them—especially in early releases. In most cases, such bugs are found in the transient commands that are run from the command line, rather than in the three core files (IO.SYS, MSDOS.SYS, and COMMAND.COM). Even the latest stand-alone version of MD-DOS (6.22) has endured several incarnations since its initial release as 6.0. As a technician, you should be sensitive to the version of DOS (and Windows) being used by your customer. Whenever the customer complains of trouble using a DOS utility (such as BACKUP or EMM386), or complains of difficulties using particular software under DOS, one of your first steps should be to ensure that the version in use is appropriate. If it has been updated, you should try the new release. Remember that a software fault can manifest itself as a hardware problem—that is, the hardware might malfunction or refuse to respond. Check with the OS maker to find their newest releases and fixes. Microsoft maintains an extensive Web site for the support of their operating systems. Check in regularly to find error reports and upgrades.

Another concern for technicians is dealing with old versions of an OS. Remember that part of the task of an OS is to manage system resources (i.e., disk space, memory, and so on). New OS versions, such as MS-DOS 5.0 and later, do a much better job of disk and memory management than MS-DOS 4.x and earlier. Should you recommend an upgrade to your customer? As a general rule, any MS-DOS version older than 5.0 is worth upgrading to MS-DOS 6.22—especially if your customer is planning to keep or upgrade the PC. If the MS-DOS version is 5.0 or later, the only good reason to upgrade would be to take advantage of advanced utilities, such as MemMaker or DoubleSpace, which have been refined and included with MS-DOS 6.22. If the PC hardware will support an upgrade to Windows 95 or Windows 98, it should also be considered as a potential OS upgrade.

The Boot Process

Computer initialization is a process—not en event. From the moment that power is applied until the system sits idle at the command-line prompt or graphical desktop, the PC boot process is a sequence of predictable steps that verify the system and prepare it for operation. By understanding each step in system initialization, you can develop a real appreciation for the way that hardware and software relate to one another—you also stand a much better chance of identifying and resolving problems when a system fails to boot properly. This part of the chapter provides a step-by-step review of a typical PC boot process.

APPLYING POWER

PC initialization starts when you turn the system on. If all output voltages from the power supply are valid, the supply generates a Power Good (PG) logic signal. It can take between 100 ms and 500 ms for the supply to generate a PG signal. When the motherboard timer IC receives the PG signal, the timer stops forcing a Reset signal to the CPU. At this point, the CPU starts processing.

THE BOOTSTRAP

The very first operation performed by a CPU is to fetch an instruction from address FFFF:0000h. Because this address is almost at the end of available ROM space, the instruction is almost always a jump command (JMP) followed by the actual BIOS ROM starting address. By making all CPUs start at the same point, the BIOS ROM can then send program control anywhere in the particular ROM (and each ROM is usually different). This initial search of address FFFF:0000h and the subsequent re-direction of the CPU is traditionally referred to as the *bootstrap* in which the PC "pulls itself up by its bootstraps"—or gets itself going. Today, we have shortened the term to *boot*, and have broadened its meaning to include the entire initialization process.

CORE TESTS

The core tests are part of the overall *Power-On Self-Test (POST)* sequence, which is the most important use of a system BIOS during initialization. As you might expect, allowing the system to initialize and run with flaws in the motherboard, memory, or drive systems can have catastrophic consequences for files in memory or on disk. To ensure system integrity, a set of hardware-specific self-test routines checks the major motherboard components, and identifies the presence of any other specialized BIOS ICs in the system (i.e., drive-controller BIOS, video BIOS, SCSI BIOS, and so on).

BIOS starts with a test of the motherboard hardware such as the CPU, math co-processor, timer ICs, *Direct Memory Access (DMA)* controllers, and *interrupt (IRQ)* controllers. If an error is detected in this early phase of testing, a series of beeps (or beep codes) are produced. By knowing the BIOS manufacturer and the beep code, you can determine the nature of the problem. Chapter 15 deals with beep and error codes in more detail. Beep codes are used because the video system has not been initialized.

Next, BIOS looks for the presence of a video ROM between memory locations C000:0000h through C780:000h. In just about all systems, the search will reveal a video BIOS ROM on a video adapter board, plugged into an available expansion slot. If a video BIOS is found, its contents are evaluated with a checksum test. If the test is successful, control is transferred to the video BIOS, which loads and initializes the video adapter. When initialization is complete, you will see a cursor on the screen and control returns to the system BIOS. If no external video adapter BIOS is located, the system BIOS will provide an initialization routine for the motherboard's video adapter and a cursor will also appear. Once the video system initializes, you are likely to see a bit of text on the display identifying the system or video BIOS ROM maker and revision level. If the checksum test fails, you will see an error message such as: C000 ROM Error or Video ROM Error. Initialization will usually halt right there.

Now that the video system is ready, system BIOS will scan memory from C800:0000h through DF80:0000h in 2KB increments to search for any other ROMs that might be on other adapter cards in the system. If other ROMs are found, their contents are tested and run. As each supplemental ROM is executed, they will show manufacturer and revision ID information. In some cases, a supplemental (or "adapter") ROM might alter an existing BIOS ROM routine. For example, an Ultra DMA/33 drive-controller board with its own on-board ROM will replace the motherboard's older drive routines. When a ROM fails the checksum test, you will see an error message such as: "XXXX ROM Error." The *XXXX* indicates the segment address where the faulty ROM was detected. If a faulty ROM is detected, system initialization will usually halt.

POST

BIOS then checks the memory location at 0000:0472h. This address contains a flag that determines whether the initialization is a cold start (power first applied) or a warm start (reset button or <Ctrl>+<Alt>+<Del> key combination). A value of 1234h at this address indicates a warm start—in which case, the (POST) routine is skipped. If any other value is found at that location, a cold start is assumed, and the full POST routine will be executed.

The full POST checks many of the other higher-level functions on the motherboard, memory, keyboard, video adapter, floppy drive, math co-processor, printer port, serial port, hard drive, and other sub-systems. Dozens of tests are performed by the POST. When an error is encountered, the single-byte POST code is written to I/O port 80h, where it might be read by a POST-code reader. In other cases, you might see an error message on the display (and system initialization will halt). Remember that POST codes and their meanings will vary slightly between BIOS manufacturers. If the POST completes successfully, the system will respond with a single beep from the speaker. Chapter 15 covers I/O port POST codes.

FINDING THE OS

The system now needs to load an operating system (usually DOS or Windows 95). The first step here is to have the BIOS search for a DOS volume boot sector (VBS) on the A: drive. If there is no disk in the drive, you will see the drive light illuminate briefly, and then BIOS will search the next drive in the boot order (usually drive C:). If a disk is in drive A:, BIOS will load sector 1 (head 0, cylinder 0) from the disk's DOS volume boot sector into memory, starting at 0000:7C00h. There are a number of potential problems when attempting to load the VBS. Otherwise, the first program in the directory (IO.SYS) will begin to load, followed by MSDOS.SYS.

- ■ If the first byte of the DOS VBS is less than 06h (or if the first byte is greater than or equal to 06h and next nine words of the sector contain the same data pattern), you will see an error message similar to: "Diskette boot record error."
- ■ If the IO.SYS and MSDOS.SYS are not the first two files in the directory (or some other problem is encountered in loading), you'll see an error such as: "Non-system disk or disk error."
- ■ If the boot sector on the diskette is corrupted and cannot be read (DOS 3.3 or earlier), you'll probably get a *Disk boot* failure message.

If the OS cannot be loaded from any floppy drive, the system will search the first fixed drive (hard drive). Hard drives are a bit more involved than floppy disks. BIOS loads sector 1 (head 0, cylinder 0) from the hard drive's master partition boot sector (called the *master boot sector, MBS*) into memory, starting at 0000:7C00h, and the last two bytes of the sector are checked. If the final two bytes of the master-partition boot sector are not 55h and AAh respectively, the boot sector is invalid, and you will see an error message similar to: "No boot device available and system initialization will halt." Other systems might depict the error differently or attempt to load ROM BASIC. If the BIOS attempts to load ROM BASIC and there is no such feature in the BIOS, you'll see a ROM BASIC error message.

Otherwise, the disk will search for and identify any extended partitions (up to 24 total partitions). Once any extended partitions have been identified, the drive's original boot sector will search for a boot-indicator byte, marking a partition as active and bootable. If none of the partitions are marked as bootable (or if more than one partition is marked bootable), a disk error message will be displayed such as: "Invalid partition table." Some older BIOS versions might attempt to load ROM BASIC, but will generate an error message in most cases anyway.

When an active bootable partition is found in the master partition boot sector, the DOS *Volume Boot Sector (VBS)* from the bootable partition is loaded into memory and tested. If the DOS VBS cannot be read, you will see an error message similar to: "Error loading operating system." When the DOS volume boot sector does load, the last two bytes are tested for a signature of 55h and AAh, respectively. If these signature bytes are missing, you will see an error message such as: "Missing operating system." Under either error condition, system initialization will halt.

After the signature bytes are identified, the DOS volume boot sector (now in memory) is executed as if it were a program. This "program" checks the root directory to ensure that IO.SYS and MSDOS.SYS (or IBMBIO.COM and IBMDOS.COM) are available. In older MS-DOS versions, IO.SYS and MSDOS.SYS have to be the first two directory entries. If the DOS volume boot sector was created with MS-DOS 3.3 (or earlier) and the two startup files are not the first two files in the directory (or there is an error in loading the files), the system will produce an error code, such as: "Non-system disk or disk error." If the boot sector is corrupt, you might see a message like: "Disk boot failure."

LOADING THE OS

If no problems are detected in the disk's DOS volume boot sector, IO.SYS (or IBM-BIO.COM) is loaded and executed. If Windows 95 is on the system, IO.SYS might be re-named *WINBOOT.SYS*, which will be executed instead. IO.SYS contains extensions to BIOS that start low-level device drivers for such things as the keyboard, printer, and block devices. Remember that IO.SYS also contains initialization code that is only needed during system startup. A copy of this initialization code is placed at the top of conventional memory which takes over initialization. The next step is to load MSDOS.SYS (or IBM-DOS.COM), which is loaded so that it overlaps the part of IO.SYS containing the initialization code. MSDOS.SYS (the MS-DOS kernel) is then executed to initialize base device drivers, detect system status, reset the disk system, initialize devices (such as the printer and serial port), and set up system-default parameters. The MS-DOS essentials are now loaded and control returns to the IO.SYS/WINBOOT.SYS initialization code in memory.

> For Windows 95 systems, IO.SYS (or WINBOOT.SYS) combines the functions of IO.SYS and MSDOS.SYS.

ESTABLISHING THE ENVIRONMENT

If a CONFIG.SYS file is present, it is opened and read by IO.SYS/WINBOOT.SYS. The DEVICE statements are processed first in the order they appear, then INSTALL statements are processed in the order they appear. A SHELL statement is handled next. If no SHELL statement is present, the COMMAND.COM processor is loaded. When COMMAND.COM is loaded, it overwrites the initialization code left over from IO.SYS (which is now no longer needed). Under Windows 95, COMMAND.COM is loaded only if an AUTOEXEC.BAT file is present to process the AUTOEXEC.BAT statements. Finally, all other statements in CONFIG.SYS are processed, and WINBOOT.SYS also looks for the SYSTEM.DAT registry file.

When an AUTOEXEC.BAT file is present, COMMAND.COM (which now has control of the system) will load and execute the batch file. After the batch-file processing is complete, the familiar DOS prompt will appear. If there is no AUTOEXEC.BAT in the root directory, COMMAND.COM will request the current date and time, then show the DOS prompt. You can now launch applications or use any available OS commands. AU-TOEXEC.BAT can also call a shell (such as Windows 3.1x) or start an application. Under Windows 95, IO.SYS/WINBOOT.SYS automatically loads HIMEM.SYS, IFSHLP.SYS, and SETVER.EXE, then loads the WIN.COM kernel to officially start Windows 95.

CREATING A DOS BOOT DISK

The most persistent problem with PC troubleshooting is that it can be difficult to boot a system successfully—especially if there are hard-drive problems. This makes it particularly important to have a bootable floppy diskette on hand. The two means of creating a boot disk are: automatically (through an existing Windows 95 platform) or manually (through a DOS 6.22 platform). In either case, you're going to need access to a running PC with an operating system that is similar to the version you plan to install on the new PC.

Windows 95 Windows 95 comes with an automatic "Startup Disk" maker. If you have access to a Windows 95 system, use the following procedure to create a DOS 7.x startup disk:

- Label a blank diskette and insert it into your floppy drive.
- Click on *Start*, *Settings*, and *Control Panel*.
- Doubleclick on the *Add/remove programs* icon.
- Select the *Startup disk* tab.
- Click on *Create disk*.
- The utility will remind you to insert a diskette, then prepare the disk automatically. When the preparation is complete, test the diskette.

The preparation process takes several minutes, and will copy the following files to your diskette: ATTRIB, CHKDSK, COMMAND, DEBUG, DRVSPACE.BIN, EDIT, FDISK, FORMAT, REGEDIT, SCANDISK, SYS, and UNINSTAL. All of these files are DOS 7.x-based files, so you can run them from the A: prompt.

> The Windows 95 FDISK utility has been reported to have a bug that can cause problems when creating more than one partition on the same drive. Later releases of Windows 95 (i.e., OSR 2) claim to have corrected this issue, but if you encounter problems with FDISK, use the DOS 6.22 version.

DOS 6.22 If you don't have access to a system with Windows 95 already, you'll need to make a boot disk manually using DOS 6.22 utilities. Create a bootable diskette by using the SYS feature, such as:

```
C:\DOS\> SYS A:        <Enter>
```

or use the *Format* command to make a bootable diskette like:

```
C:\DOS\> FORMAT A: /S    <Enter>
```

Once the diskette is bootable, copy the following DOS utilities (usually from the DOS directory): FDISK, FORMAT, SYS, MEM, DEFRAG, SCANDISK, EDIT, HIMEM, EMM386, and EDIT. You might not need all of these utilities, but it can be handy to have them on-hand in case you need to check a disk or memory.

Further Study

That concludes Chapter 3. Be sure to review the glossary and chapter questions on the accompanying CD. If you have access to the Internet, point your Web browser to some of the following contacts (also check out some of the URLs listed in Table 3-1):

IBM: **http://www.software.ibm.com/os/warp/warp-client/**

Microsoft: **http://www.microsoft.com**

Novell: **http://www.novell.com**

V Communications (System Commander): **http://www.v-com.com**

THE

PRE-SERVICE

CHECKOUT

CONTENTS AT A GLANCE

The Universal Troubleshooting Process
Define your symptoms
Identify and isolate
Replace
Re-test

The Spare Parts Dilemma
Parts are always changing
Inventory costs money
A better Strategy

Benchmarking the PC
Avoiding benchmark problems
Obtaining benchmarks

Viruses and Computer Service
Computer viruses explained
The tell-tale signs
Anti-virus software
Sterilizing your shop

Quick-Start Bench Testing
The symptom doesn't start at all
The system starts but won't initialize
The system starts but crashes/
    reboots intermittently
After an upgrade
Windows 95 boot symptoms

Further Study

As a PC technician, you must understand a basic rule of business—time is money. Whether you are the boss or work for someone else, the ability to identify and isolate a PC or peripheral fault quickly and decisively is a crucial element to your success. It requires a keen eye, some common sense, and a little bit of intuition. It also requires an understanding of the troubleshooting process, and a reliable plan of action. Even though the number of PC configurations and setups are virtually unlimited, the methodology used to approach each repair is always about the same. This chapter is intended to illustrate the concepts of basic troubleshooting and show you how to apply a suite of cause-and-effect relationships that will help you narrow the problem down before you even take a screwdriver to the enclosure. By applying a consistent technique, you can shave precious time from every repair.

The Universal Troubleshooting Process

Regardless of how complex your particular computer or peripheral device might be, a dependable troubleshooting procedure can be broken down into four basic steps (Fig. 4-1): define your symptoms, identify and isolate the potential source (or location) of your problem, replace the suspected sub-assembly, and re-test the unit thoroughly to be sure that you have solved the problem. If you have not solved the problem, start again from Step #1. This is a "universal" procedure that you can apply to any sort of troubleshooting—not just for personal computer equipment.

DEFINE YOUR SYMPTOMS

When a PC breaks down, the cause might be as simple as a loose wire or connector, or as complicated as an IC or sub-assembly failure. Before you open your tool box, you must have a firm understanding of all the symptoms. Think about the symptoms carefully—for example:

- Is the disk or tape inserted properly?
- Is the power or activity LED lit?
- Does this problem occur only when the computer is tapped or moved?

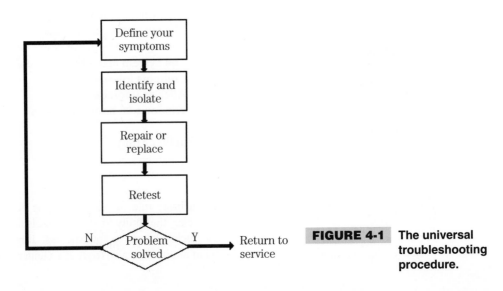

FIGURE 4-1   **The universal troubleshooting procedure.**

By recognizing and understanding your symptoms, it can be much easier to trace a problem to the appropriate assembly or component. Take the time to write down as many symptoms as you can. This note-taking might seem tedious now, but once you have begun your repair, a written record of symptoms and circumstances will help to keep you focused on the task at hand. It will also help to jog your memory if you must explain the symptoms to someone else at a later date. As a professional troubleshooter, you must often log problems or otherwise document your activities anyway.

IDENTIFY AND ISOLATE

Before you try to isolate a problem within a piece of computer hardware, you must first be sure that the equipment itself is causing the problem. In many circumstances, this will be fairly obvious, but some situations might appear ambiguous (i.e., there is no power, no DOS prompt, etc.). Always remember that a PC works because of an intimate mingling of hardware and software. A faulty or improperly configured piece of software can cause confusing system errors. Chapter 3 touched on some of the problems that operating systems can encounter.

When you are confident that the failure lies in your system's hardware, you can begin to identify possible problem areas. Because this book is designed to deal with sub-assembly troubleshooting, start your diagnostics there. The troubleshooting procedures throughout this book will guide you through the major sections of today's popular PC components and peripherals, and aid you in deciding which sub-assembly might be at fault. When you have identified a potential problem area, you can begin the actual repair process and swap the suspect sub-assembly.

REPLACE

Because computers and their peripherals are designed as collections of sub-assemblies, it is almost always easier to replace a sub-assembly outright, rather than attempt to troubleshoot the sub-assembly to its component level. Even if you had the time, documentation, and test equipment to isolate a defective component, many complex parts are proprietary, so it is highly unlikely that you would be able to obtain replacement components without a significant hassle. The labor and frustration factor involved in such an endeavor is often just as expensive as replacing the entire sub-assembly to begin with (perhaps even more expensive). On the other hand, manufacturers and their distributors often stock a selection of sub-assemblies and supplies. You might need to know the manufacturer's part number for the sub-assembly to obtain a new one.

During a repair, you might reach a roadblock that requires you to leave your equipment for a day or two, or maybe longer. This generally happens after an order has been placed for new parts, and you are waiting for those parts to come in. Make it a point to reassemble your system as much as possible before leaving it. Gather any loose parts in plastic bags, seal them shut, and mark them clearly. If you are working with electronic circuitry, be sure to use good-quality anti-static boxes or bags for storage. Partial re-assembly (combined with careful notes) will help you remember how the unit goes together later on.

Another problem with the fast technological progress we enjoy is that parts rarely stay on the shelf long. That video board you bought last year is no longer available, is it? How about that 4× CD-ROM drive you put in some time back? Today, there's something newer and faster in its place. When a PC fails and you need to replace a broken device, chances are that you'll need to upgrade simply because you cannot obtain an identical replacement device. From this standpoint, upgrading is often a proxy of troubleshooting and repair.

RE-TEST

When a repair is finally complete, the system must be reassembled carefully before testing it. All guards, housings, cables, and shields must be replaced before final testing. If symptoms persist, you will have to reevaluate the symptoms and narrow the problem to another part of the equipment. If normal operation is restored (or greatly improved), test the computer's various functions. When you can verify that the symptoms have stopped during actual operation, the equipment can be returned to service. As a general rule, it is wise to let the system run for at least 24 hours to ensure that the replacement sub-assembly will not fail prematurely. This is known as letting the system *burn in*.

Check your CD for the burn-in utilities 486TST.ZIP and BURNIN43.ZIP.

Do not be discouraged if the equipment still malfunctions. Perhaps you missed a jumper setting or DIP switch, or maybe software settings and device drivers need to be updated to accommodate the replacement sub-assembly. If you get stuck, simply walk away, clear your head, and start again by defining the current symptoms. Never continue with a repair if you are tired or frustrated—tomorrow is another day. Even the most experienced troubleshooters get overwhelmed from time to time. You should also realize that there might be more than one bad assembly to deal with. Remember that a PC is just a collection of assemblies, and each assembly is a collection of parts. Normally, everything works together, but when one assembly fails, it might cause one or more interconnected assemblies to fail as well.

The Spare Parts Dilemma

Once a problem is isolated, technicians face another problem: the availability of spare parts. Novice technicians often ask what kinds and quantity of spare parts they should keep on hand. The best answer to give here is simply: none at all. The reason for this somewhat drastic answer is best explained by the two realities of PC service:

PARTS ARE ALWAYS CHANGING

After only 15 years or so, the PC is in its sixth CPU generation (with such devices as the AMD K6 and Intel Pentium II). As a result, a new generation matures every 24 to 36 months (although the newer generations have been arriving in 18 to 24 months). Even the "standardized" products, such as CD-ROM drives, have proliferated in different speeds and versions (8, 10×, 12×, 16×, and even 20× speeds). Once production stops for a drive or board, stock rarely remains for very long. You see, even if you know what the problem is, the chances of your locating an exact replacement part are often quite slim if the part is more than two years old. Notice the word *exact*—this is the key word in PC repair. This is the reason why so many repairs involve an upgrade. For example, why replace a failed EGA board with another EGA board when you can install an SVGA board (which is typically EGA compatible) for the same price or less? Choosing the "right" parts to stock is like hitting a moving target, so don't bother.

INVENTORY COSTS MONEY

Financial considerations also play a big role in choosing parts. For computer enthusiasts or novice technicians just tinkering in their spare time, the expense and space demands required for inventory are simply out of the question. Even for more serious businesses, inventory can burden the bottom line.

A BETTER STRATEGY

Unless you are in the business of selling replacement parts and upgrade components yourself, don't waste your money and space stocking parts that are going to be obsolete in less than 24 months. Rather than worry about stocking parts yourself, work to develop your contacts with computer parts stores and superstores that specialize in PC parts and sub-assemblies—let them stock the parts for you. Because parts stores generally have an inside line with distributors and manufacturers, parts that they do not stock can often be ordered for you. Even many reputable mail-order firms can provide parts in under 48 hours with today's delivery services.

Benchmarking the PC

We all know that today's personal computers are capable of astounding performance. If you doubt that, consider any of the current 3D games, such as Quake II or Monster Truck Madness. However, it is often important to quantify the performance of a system. Just saying that a PC is "faster" than another system is simply not enough—we must often apply a number to that performance to measure the improvements offered by an upgrade, or to objectively compare the performance of various systems. Benchmarks are used to test and report the performance of a PC by running a set of well-defined tasks on the system. A benchmark program has several different uses in the PC industry depending on what you're needs are:

- *System comparisons* Benchmarks are often used to compare a system to one or more competing machines (or to compare a newer system to older machines). Just flip through any issue of *PC Magazine* or *Byte*, and you'll see a flurry of PC ads all quoting numerical performance numbers backed up by benchmarks. You might also run a benchmark to establish the overall performance of a new system before making a purchase decision.
- *Upgrade improvements* Benchmarks are frequently used to gauge the value of an upgrade. By running the benchmark before and after the upgrade process, you can get a numerical assessment of just how much that new CPU, RAM, drive, or motherboard might have improved (or hindered) system performance.
- *Diagnostics* Benchmarks sometimes have role in system diagnostics. Systems that are performing poorly can be benchmarked as key components are checked or reconfigured. This helps the technician isolate and correct performance problems far more reliably than simple "visual" observations.

AVOIDING BENCHMARK PROBLEMS

One of the most serious problems encountered with benchmarks is the integrity of their numbers. You've probably heard that "statistics can lie," and the same thing is true of benchmarks. In order for benchmarks to provide you with reliable results, you must take some precautions:

■ *Note the complete system configuration* When you run a benchmark and achieve a result, be sure to note the entire system configuration (i.e., CPU, RAM, cache, OS version, etc.).

■ *Run the same benchmark on every system* Benchmarks are still software, and the way in which benchmark code is written can impact the way it produces results on a given computer. Often, two different versions of the same benchmark will yield two different results. When you use benchmarks for comparisons between systems, be sure to use the same program and version number.

■ *Minimize hardware differences between hardware platforms* A computer is an assembly of many interdependent sub-assemblies (i.e., motherboard, drive controllers, drives, CPU, etc.), but when a benchmark is run to compare a difference between systems, that difference can be masked by other elements in the system. For example, suppose you're using a benchmark to test the hard-drive data transfer on two systems. Different hard drives and drive controllers will yield different results (that's expected). However, even if you're using identical drives and controllers, other differences between the systems (such as BIOS versions, TSRs, OS differences, or motherboard chipsets) can also influence different results.

■ *Run the benchmarks under the same load* The results generated by a benchmark do not guarantee that same level of performance under "real-world" applications. This was one of the flaws of early computer benchmarking—small, tightly written benchmark code resulted in artificially high performance, but the system still performed poorly when real applications were used. Use benchmarks that make use of (or simulate) actual programs, or otherwise simulate your true workload.

OBTAINING BENCHMARKS

Benchmarks have been around since the earliest computers, and there are now a vast array of benchmark products to measure all aspects of the PC—as well as measure more specialized issues, such as networking, real-time systems, and UNIX (or other operating system) platforms. Table 4-1 highlights a cross-section of computer benchmarks for your reference. In many cases, the table includes a URL or FTP site where you can obtain source code for the benchmark, or download the complete benchmark program. Today, Ziff Davis and CMP publish a suite of freeware benchmark utilities that have become standard tools for end users and technicians alike.

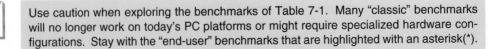

Use caution when exploring the benchmarks of Table 7-1. Many "classic" benchmarks will no longer work on today's PC platforms or might require specialized hardware configurations. Stay with the "end-user" benchmarks that are highlighted with an asterisk(*).

TABLE 4-1 AN INDEX OF COMPUTER BENCHMARKS

BENCHMARK	DESCRIPTION/PURPOSE	SOURCE/APPLET AVAILABILITY
007 (ODBMS)	designed to simulate a CAD/CAM environment	ftp.cs.wisc.edu/007
3D WinBench 97*	PC 3D system benchmark	http://www8.zdnet.com/ pcmag/pclabs/bench/ bench3d.htm
3D-Bench	PC 3D graphics benchmark	http://www.sysopt.com/ 3dbench.html
		http://www.sysopt.com/ cbench.html
AIM	overall performance and multitasking throughput	—
BatteryMark*	mobile PC battery benchmark	http://www8.zdnet.com/ pcmag/pclabs/bench/ benchbm.htm
Bonnie	bottleneck checking	—
Busperf	PC bus-performance benchmark	http://www.sysopt.com/ pub/busperf.zip
Byte	UNIX performance	—
CacheChk	PC cache-checking benchmark	http://www.sysopt.com/ cachk4.html
CompTest	general PC benchmark	ftp://oak.oakland.edu/Sim Tel/msdos/sysinfo/ ctest259.zip
CPU2	floating-point benchmark (UNIX/VMS)	ftp://swedishchef.lerc.nasa. gov/drlabs/cpu/ (select cpu2.unix.tar.Z or cpu2.vms.tar.Z)
Dhrystone MIPS	short test for system programming	ftp.nosc.mil/pub/aburto
Fhourstones	integer-only benchmark	ftp.nosc.mil:pub/aburto/ c4.shar
Flops	MFLOP rating benchmark	ftp.nosc.mil/pub/aburto
Hanoi	recursive-function benchmark	ftp.nosc.mil/pub/aburto
Hartstone	real-time benchmark	ftp.sei.cmu.edu/pub/hart-stone
Heapsort	array-sorting benchmark	ftp.nosc.mil/pub/aburto
IOBENCH	multistream benchmark	—
IOZONE	read/write test	—
JMark*	PC Java virtual machine benchmark	http://www8.zdnet.com/ pcmag/pclabs/bench/ benchjm.htm
Khornerstone	multipurpose benchmark	—
LFK (Livermore Loops)	general-performance testing	netlib.att.com/netlib/ benchmark/livermore
LINPACK	algebraic processing	netlib.att.com/netlib/ benchmark/linpack

TABLE 4-1 AN INDEX OF COMPUTER BENCHMARKS (CONTINUED)

BENCHMARK	DESCRIPTION/PURPOSE	SOURCE/APPLET AVAILABILITY
Matrix Multiply	matrix multiplication benchmark	ftp.nosc.mil/pub/aburto
MUSBUS	—	monu1.cc.monash.edu.au/pub/musbus.sh
NAS Kernels	computational fluid dynamics	ftp.cs.wisc.edu/wwt/Misc/NAS
NetBench*	PC networking benchmark	http://www8.zdnet.com/pcmag/pclabs/bench/benchnb.htm
Netperf	networking performance	ftp://ftp.cup.hp.com/dist/networking/benchmarks
Nettest	networking performance	—
Nhfsstone	file-server performance	—
PERFECT	—	—
RhosettaStone	—	eos.arc.nasa.gov
ServerBench*	PC network-server benchmark	http://www8.zdnet.com.pcmag/pclabs/bench/benchsb.htm
Sieve of Eratosthenes	integer testing	otis.stanford.edu/pub/benchmarks/c/small/sieve.c
SLALOM	—	tantalus.al.iastate.edu/pub/Slalom/
SPEC	CPU-intensive benchmarks	ftp.nosc.mil/pub/aburto
SSBA	UNIX performance	ftp.inria.fr:/system/bench-mark/SSBA/ssba1.22F.tar.Z
Stanford	compares RISC/CISC	—
SYSmark	app/OS-based benchmark	—
TFFTDP	FFT benchmark	ftp.nosc.mil/pub/aburto
TPC A/B/C	POS benchmark	—
ttcp	TCP/UDP performance	—
VidSpeed	PC video benchmark	http://www.sysopt.com/pub/vidspd40.zip
WebBench*	PC Internet-browser benchmark	http://www8.zdnet.com/pcmag/pclabs/bench/benchweb.htm
Whetstone	floating-point benchmark	netlib.att.com/netlib/bench-mark/whetstone
WinBench 97*	PC subsystem benchmarks	http://www8.zdnet.com/pcmag/pclabs/bench/benchwb.htm
Winstone*	overall Windows 95/NT benchmark	http://www8.zdnet.com/pcmag/pclabs/bench/benchw97.htm
Wintach	Windows benchmark	ftp://ftp.winsite.com/pub/pc/win3/util/wintch12.zip

TABLE 4-1 AN INDEX OF COMPUTER BENCHMARKS (CONTINUED)		
BENCHMARK	**DESCRIPTION/PURPOSE**	**SOURCE/APPLET AVAILABILITY**
Wintune 97*	overall PC Windows 95 benchmark	http://www.winmag.com/soft-ware/wt97.htm
WPI Benchmarks	general benchmarks	wpi.wpi.edu
Xstone	general benchmarks	netcom.com/pub/micromed/uploads/xstones.summary.z

*See below for a more detailed description

Winstone 97   Winstone 97 is a 32-bit Windows benchmark test used to gauge a PC's overall performance under Windows 95 or Windows NT. Winstone has two components: business and high-end. The *business Winstone* test measures the time a PC requires to execute a set of application scripts that exercise eight best-selling applications—it then weights the test timings and converts it to a relative score (the score is relative to the performance of a Gateway 486DX2/66 with 16MB of RAM, whose score is defined as 10). The *high-end Winstone* measures the time a PC takes to execute a set of application scripts that exercise six applications in CAD, applications development, image editing, and 3-D visualization. These tests weight a given machine's timings equally, derive a composite number, and convert this number to a relative score (the score is relative to the performance of a Dell Pentium/100 system with 32MB of RAM, whose score is defined as 10).

WinBench 97   WinBench 97 is a more hardware-oriented utility that provides a detailed measure of graphics, disk, processor, CD-ROM, and video-playback performance under Windows 95 and Windows NT. WinBench produces two graphics. WinMark 97 scores that reflect performance of a machine's graphics subsystem: the business graphics WinMark 97 score reflects performance when running the typical business applications. The high-end graphics WinMark 97 score reflects performance when running the corresponding test applications. WinBench also tests disk-subsystem performance, producing a business-disk WinMark 97 score, and a high-end disk WinMark 97 score.

WinBench 97 also provides two scores indicating the speed of a processor subsystem (including CPU, secondary cache, and system RAM). The CPUmark32 score reflects the speed of a PC's processor subsystem under a 32-bit operating system, and the CPUmark16 score reflects the speed of this subsystem under a 16-bit operating system. WinBench 97 includes CD-ROM tests based on a profile of six of today's most popular Windows CD-ROMs (including sequential-read tests, access-time tests, and CPU utilization tests). A variety of CD video-playback tests report performance replaying a number of video clips.

3D WinBench 97   3D WinBench 97 is a specialized benchmarking utility that measures the performance of a 3D graphics subsystem (including the Direct3D software, the monitor, the graphics adapter, the graphics driver, and the bus used to carry information from the graphics adapter to and from the processor subsystem). You can use 3D WinBench 97 to test hardware graphics adapters, drivers, and the value of such processor-enhancement technologies as MMX.

BatteryMark BatteryMark 2.0 uses a combination of hardware and software to measure the battery life of notebook computers under real-world conditions (the hardware used in BatteryMark 2.0 is the same ZDigit II device required by version 1.0). BatteryMark exercises a different 32-bit software workload engines for processor, disk, and graphics tasks. BatteryMark mixes these workloads together and adds periodic breaks in the work that reflect the way users pause while working. BatteryMark 2.0 works with *Advanced Power Management (APM)* under Windows 95.

NetBench NetBench 5.01 is our benchmark test for checking the performance of network file servers. NetBench provides a way to measure, analyze, and predict how a file server will handle network file I/O requests. It monitors the response of the server as multiple clients request data, and reports the server's total throughput. To test application servers, you should use the ServerBench utility instead.

ServerBench ServerBench 4.0 is the latest version of Ziff-Davis' standard benchmark for measuring the performance of servers in a true client/server environment. Server-Bench clients make requests of an application that runs on the server—the server's ability to service those requests is reported in transactions per second. ServerBench 4.0 runs on IBM's OS/2 Warp Server, Microsoft's Windows NT Server 4.0 (for both Digital Alpha and x86-compatible processors), Novell's NetWare 4.11, Sun's Solaris 2.5 on SPARC, and SCO's OpenServer Release 5 and UnixWare 2.1. To test network file servers, use the NetBench utility instead.

WebBench WebBench 1.1 is the Ziff Davis benchmark test for checking performance of Web-server hardware and software. Standard test suites produce two overall scores for the server: requests per second and throughput (as measured in bytes per second). WebBench includes static testing (which involves only HTML pages), and dynamic testing (including CGI executables, Internet Server API libraries, and Netscape Server API dynamic link libraries.

JMark JMark 1.01 is a suite of 11 synthetic benchmark tests for evaluating the performance of Java virtual machines. The JMark 1.01 suite simulates a number of important tests of Java functionality. It includes Java versions of a number of classic benchmark test algorithms, as well as tests designed to measure graphics performance in a GUI environment. You can download JMark 1.01 from Ziff Davis, or run the tests online within your browser.

Wintune 97 Wintune 1.0 for Windows 95/NT is a recent benchmark entry from CMP, the publishers of *Windows Magazine*. Wintune 97 is an overall benchmark to measure Windows 95/NT performance. It has a fast user interface that allows the program to load much faster than the earlier Wintune 95, and will now support testing of the latest Pentium II systems. Wintune 97 tests video systems on the fastest new computers at full-screen resolution.

 Check your CD for the benchmarking utility JBENCH.EXE.

Viruses and Computer Service

Few developments in the personal computer field have caused more concern and alarm than the computer virus. Although viruses do not physically damage computer hardware, they can irrevocably destroy vital data, disable your PC (or shutdown a network), and propagate to other systems through networks, disk swapping, and on-line services. Even though virus infiltration is generally regarded as rare, a good PC technician will always protect themselves (and their customers) by checking the system for viruses before and after using their diagnostic disks on the PC. A careful process of virus isolation can detect viruses on the customer's system before any hardware-level work is done. Virus-isolation tactics also prevent your diagnostic disks from becoming infected—and subsequently transferring the virus to other systems (for which you might be legally liable). This section of the chapter outlines a virus-screening procedure for PCs. Chapter 45 covers the symptoms and countermeasures for viruses in more detail.

COMPUTER VIRUSES EXPLAINED

There have been many attempts to define a computer virus, and most definitions have a great deal of technical merit. For the purposes of this book, however, you can consider a virus to be some length of computer code (a program or program fragment) that performs one or more—often destructive—functions and replicates itself wherever possible to other disks and systems. Because viruses generally want to escape detection, they might often hide by copying themselves as hidden, system, or read-only files. However, this only prevents casual detection. More-elaborate viruses affect the boot sector code on floppy and hard disks, or attach themselves to other executable programs. Each time that the infected program is executed, the virus has a chance to wreak havoc. Still other viruses infect the partition table. Most viruses exhibit a code sequence that can be detected. Many virus scanners work by checking the contents of memory and disk files for such virus "signatures." As viruses become more complex, however, viruses are using encryption techniques to escape detection. Encryption changes the virus "signature" each time the virus replicates itself—for a well-designed virus, this can make detection extremely difficult.

Just as a biological virus is an unwanted (and sometimes deadly) organism in a body, "viral" code in software can lead to a slow, agonizing death for your customer's data. In actuality, few viruses immediately crash a system (with notable exceptions, such as the much-publicized Michealangelo virus). Most viruses make only small changes each time they are executed and create a pattern of chronic problems. This slow manifestation gives viruses a chance to replicate—infecting backups and floppy disks, which are frequently swapped to infect other systems.

Frequent system backups are an effective protection against computer viruses because you can restore files damaged by viruses. Even if the backup is infected, the infected files can often be cleaned once they are restored from the backup.

THE TELL-TALE SIGNS

Viruses are especially dangerous because you are rarely aware of their presence until it is too late and the damage is already done. However, there are a number of behaviors that might suggest the presence of a virus in your system. Once again, remember that one of the best protections against viruses (or other drive failures) is to maintain regular backups of your data. None of these symptoms alone guarantee the presence of a virus (there are other reasons why such symptoms can occur), but when symptoms do surface, it is always worth running an anti-virus checker just to be safe. The following symptoms are typical of virus activity:

■ *The hard drive is running out of disk space for no apparent reason* Some viruses multiply by attaching copies of themselves to .EXE and .COM files—often multiple times. This increases the file size of infected files (sometimes dramatically) and consumes more disk space. If left unchecked, files can grow until the disk runs short of space. However, disk space can also be gobbled up by many CAD, graphics, and multimedia applications, such as video-capture systems. Be aware of what kind of applications are on the disk.

■ *You notice that various .EXE and .COM programs have increased in size for no reason* This is a classic indicator of a virus at work. Few rational people make keep track of file sizes, but dates can be a giveaway. For example, if most of the files in a sub-directory are dated six months ago when the package was installed, but the main .EXE file is dated yesterday, it's time to run that virus checker.

■ *You notice substantial hard-drive activity, but were not expecting it* It is hardly unusual to see the drive-indicator LED register activity when programs are loaded and run. In disk-intensive systems, such as Windows 95, you should expect to see extensive drive activity because of swap-file operation. However, you should not expect to see regular or substantial disk activity when the system is idle. If the drive runs for no apparent reason—especially under MS-DOS—run the virus checker.

■ *System performance has slowed down noticeably* This symptom is usually coupled with low drive space, and it might very well be the result of a filled and fragmented disk, such as those found in systems that deal with CAD and multimedia applications. Run the virus checker first. If no virus is detected, try eliminating any un-needed files and defragment the drive completely.

■ *Files have been lost or corrupted for no apparent reason, or there are an unusual number of access problems* Under ordinary circumstances, files should not be lost or corrupted on a hard drive. Even though bad sectors will crop up on extremely rare occasions, you should expect the drive to run properly. Virus infiltration can interrupt the flow of data to and from the drives and result in file errors. Such errors might occur randomly or they might be quite consistent. You might see error messages, such as "Error in .EXE file." Regular errors might even simulate a drive failure. Try running a virus checker before running a diagnostic, such as ScanDisk. Inadequate power problems can also have an effect on drive reliability.

■ *The system locks up frequently or without explanation* Faulty applications and corrupted files can freeze a system. Memory and motherboard problems can also result in system lockups. Although viruses rarely manifest themselves in this fashion, it is possible that random or consistent system lockups might suggest a virus (or virus damage to key files).

■ *There are unexplained problems with system memory or memory allocation* Although there might be one or more memory defects, it is quite common for viruses to exist in memory, where other files can be infected. In some cases, this can affect the amount of free memory available to other applications. You might see error messages such as: "Program too big to fit in memory." If you are having trouble with free memory or memory allocation, run a virus checker that performs a thorough memory check. If the system checks clear of viruses, you can run diagnostics to check the memory.

ANTI-VIRUS SOFTWARE

In the race between good and evil, evil usually has the head start. As a result, anti-virus detection and elimination packages are constantly trying to keep up with new viruses and their variations (in addition to dealing with more than 2000 virus strains that have already been identified). This leads to an important conclusion about anti-virus software—they all quickly become obsolete. Even though first-class shareware and commercial packages can be quite comprehensive, they must all be updated frequently. Some of the most notable anti-virus products are found in Symantec's Norton Anti-Virus and VirusScan from McAfee and Associates. If you use MS-DOS 6.0 or later, you already own Microsoft Anti-Virus (MSAV).

Another important factor in anti-virus programs is their inability to successfully remove all viruses from executable (.EXE) files. Files with a .COM extension are simply reflections of memory, but .EXE files contain header information that is easily damaged by a virus (and are subsequently unrecoverable). It is always worth trying to eliminate the virus—if the .EXE header is damaged, you've lost nothing in the attempt, and you can reload the damaged .EXE file from a backup or its original distribution disks, if necessary. Remember that there is no better protection against viruses and other hardware faults than keeping regular backups. It is better to restore an infected backup and clean it, than to forego backups entirely.

STERILIZING YOUR SHOP

Sterilization starts by assuming that all machines coming in for service are infected with a virus. You should assume the possibility of an infection—even if the complaint is something innocent (i.e., the keyboard is "acting up"). This section of the chapter shows you how to create anti-virus work disks that will be used to boot and check the systems brought in for service. Guard your master anti-virus disks by placing them somewhere ELSE besides the shop. That way they won't be infected accidentally. Immediately write-protect your work disks! Also, be ready to discard your work disks frequently. Replacing a 50-cent work disk is much cheaper than having to scan and clean every disk in your shop! If possible, write-protect work disks, too. If the anti-virus software, DOS, and the DISKCOPY program can all fit, you should use double-density disks, rather than high-density disks. Double-density disks can be used in high-density drives (but not vice versa).

Routine, pre-service virus scanning makes good sense. It will save time by detecting virus-related problems right away. You won't waste time disassembling cabinets and troubleshooting hardware. Also, eliminating viruses are much easier than reformatting or replacing the hard drive (a devastating choice if your customer has no current backup). Reformatting a hard drive on a system with a virus might not solve the problem and result in a callback. On the other hand, not wiping out your customer's entire drive is a sure way to make a friend. Finally, pre-service virus checking is quick—the computer is on the bench anyway. Sticking in a disk and turning on the computer is all the labor required.

> In the procedure, it is assumed that your floppy disk is A:, your main hard drive is C:, and your CD-ROM (if installed) is D:. If your particular system is configured differently, please substitute the correct drive letters.

1 Start at the DOS command line. You should exit Windows or Windows 95 before proceeding.

2 Ensure that your system is virus-free. Run a current virus checker, which checks for the most important types of viruses—including memory-resident viruses. Once the system is clean, you can proceed.

3 Format 10 floppy disks as bootable (system) disks. If your diskettes are totally blank, use the FORMAT command, such as:

```
C:\DOS\> format a:   <Enter>
```

Next, make the diskettes bootable by transferring system files. Use the SYS command to make the diskettes bootable, such as:

```
C:\DOS\> sys a:     <Enter>
```

If you purchase your diskettes pre-formatted, simply use the SYS command.

4 Test a diskette. Reboot your computer and see that the system will boot successfully to the A: DOS prompt. If so, you have created simple boot disks (you need only test one disk), but other steps are required to complete a virus-checking disk.

5 Copy the virus checker to your first bootable floppy disk. Virus checkers are typically self-contained, single-file tools, such as Norton's NAV.EXE, Microsoft's MSAV.EXE, or the shareware tool FPROT.EXE. Copy the necessary executable file(s) to your diskette.

6 Create an AUTOEXEC.BAT file that will start the virus checker. Ideally, you want the virus checker to start automatically, so create a simple AUTOEXEC.BAT file that will start the virus checker. For example, MSAV.EXE could use a command line such as:

```
a:\msav.exe
```

You might also add command line arguments to streamline the virus checker even further. Save the AUTOEXEC.BAT file to your floppy disk.

7 Test the diskette again. Reboot the system with your master anti-virus floppy disk. The system should boot "clean"—with no drivers or TSRs loaded that might confuse the virus checker—and the anti-virus program should load. Depending on exactly which virus checker and command line options you choose, the checker might run through a complete scan automatically, or you might have to manually start testing from the program's menu.

8 Duplicate the original disk to the other work disks. Use the DOS DISKCOPY command to duplicate your original virus-checking diskette to the other nine diskettes you have prepared. You might have to swap back and forth between the source (original) and target (new) diskettes several times. When the new diskette is done, DISKCOPY will ask if you want to repeat the procedure.

9 Mark the diskettes carefully. You have just created a batch of anti-virus work disks. They should be immediately write-protected, and kept together as a set.

> Step 8 instructs you to create 10 copies of the virus-checking software. Even though the disks are exclusively for your use and you will only use one disk at a time, this kind of "multiple duplication" might violate the license agreement for your anti-virus software. Be sure that your license allows multiple copies of the software before proceeding.

Using the virus work disks Whenever a PC comes in for service, use one of your anti-virus work disks to boot and check the system first before trying a boot disk or diagnostic disk. Professionals always create anti-virus diskettes in batches because the diskettes are disposable. That is, if a virus is detected and cleaned, the diskette that detected the infection should be destroyed, and you should boot the system with a new work disk to locate any other instances of the same virus or any different viruses. This might seem radical, but it is cheap insurance against cross-contamination of the diskette. Once a system is booted with a work disk and checks clean, you can put that work disk away, and boot the system again with a diagnostic or boot disk as required. It is also advisable to check the PC for viruses again once the repair is complete.

Problems with anti-virus tools The protocol outlined should help to protect you (and your customer) from virus attacks. Still, there are two situations where trouble can occur. First, viruses are proliferating with the aid of powerful new programming languages and vast avenues of distribution, such as the Internet. You will need to update your virus work disks regularly with the very latest anti-virus software. Too often, technicians buy an anti-virus package and continue to use it for years. The software certainly remains adept at detecting the viruses that it was designed for, but it does not take into account the many new strains that crop up regularly. As a result, older virus checkers might allow newer viruses to pass undetected.

Second, technicians tend to get cheap with their floppy disks. If a work disk detects and eliminates a virus, it should be considered contaminated, and you should throw it away. Start again with a fresh work diskette. Continue checking and eradicating viruses until the system checks clean. The 50 cents or so that the diskette is worth is not worth the risk of contracting the virus.

Quick-Start Bench Testing

Many problems can plague the PC, but perhaps the most troubling problems occur during startup—when the computer fails to start at all or does not start completely. Startup problems make it almost impossible to use diagnostics or other utilities to help isolate problems. Since Windows 95, even more difficulties can develop. This part of the chapter offers you a series of possible "quick start" explanations for full and partial system failures.

THE SYSTEM DOESN'T START AT ALL

Symptom 4-1. There is no power light, and you cannot hear any cooling fan Chances are that there is insufficient power to the computer. Use a voltmeter and confirm that there is adequate ac voltage at the wall outlet. Check the ac cord next—it might be loose or disconnected. See that the power switch is turned on and connected properly. Check the power-supply fuse(s). The main fuse might have opened. Replace any failed fuse.

> If you replace a main fuse and the fuse continues to fail, you might have a serious fault in the power supply. Try replacing the power supply.

Symptom 4-2. There is no power light, but you hear the cooling fan running This usually means that some level of ac power is reaching the system. Use a voltmeter and confirm that there is adequate ac voltage at the wall outlet. Unusually low ac voltages (such as during "brownout" conditions) can cause the power supply to malfunction. Verify that the power-supply cables are attached properly and securely to the motherboard. Use a voltmeter to verify that each output from the power supply is correct. Table 4-2 illustrates the proper voltage for each wire/color. If any output is very low or absent (especially the +5-volt output), replace the power supply. Finally, use a voltmeter and verify that the *Power good* (or *PwrOK*) signal is +5 V. If this signal is below 1.0 V, it might inhibit the CPU from running by forcing a *Reset* condition. Because the *Power good* signal is generated by the power supply, try replacing the power supply.

Symptom 4-3. The power light is on, but there is no apparent system activity Check the power-supply voltages. Use a voltmeter to verify that each output from the power supply is correct. Table 4-2 lists the proper voltage for each wire color. If any output is very low or absent (especially the 5-V output), replace the power supply. Use a voltmeter and verify that the *Power good* (or *PwrOK*) signal is +5 V. If this signal is below 1.0 V, it might inhibit the CPU from running by forcing a continuous *Reset* condition. Because the *Power good* signal is generated by the power supply, try replacing the power supply.

Check to see that the CPU is cool, that the heatsink/fan assembly is fitted on correctly, and that the CPU itself is inserted properly and completely into its socket. Check the CPU socket—if the CPU is seated in a *Zero Insertion Force (ZIF)* socket, be sure that the socket's tension lever is closed and locked into place. If there is a separate math co-processor on the motherboard (i286 and i386 systems), be sure that the MCP is inserted properly and completely into its socket. Next, check the expansion boards and be sure that all expansion boards are seated properly. Any boards that are not secured properly, or that are inserted unevenly, can short bus signals and prevent the PC from starting. Check the motherboard for shorts. Inspect the motherboard at every metal standoff and see that no metal traces are being shorted against a standoff or screw. You might want to free the motherboard and see if the system starts. If it does, use non-conductive spacers (such as a small piece of manila folder) to insulate the motherboard from each metal standoff. If the system still fails to start (and all voltages from the power supply are correct), replace the motherboard.

TABLE 4-2 PINOUTS OF ATX AND BABY AT POWER CONNECTORS

ATX POWER CONNECTOR

COLOR	VOLTAGE	PIN
Orange	+3.3 Vdc	1
Orange	+3.3 Vdc	2
Black	GND	3
Red	+5 Vdc	4
Black	GND	5
Red	+5 Vdc	6
Black	GND	7
Gray	PwrOK	8
Purple	+5V standby	9
Yellow	+12 Vdc	10
Orange (22AWG)	+3.3 Vdc	11
Brown (22AWG)	3.3 V sense	11
Blue	−12 Vdc	12
Black	GND	13
Green	PS-ON	14
Black	GND	15
Black	GND	16
Black	GND	17
White	−5 Vdc	18
Red	+5 Vdc	19
Red	+5 Vdc	20

BABY AT POWER CONNECTORS

COLOR	VOLTAGE	PIN
Orange	PwrOK	1 (P8)
Red	+5 Vdc	2 (P8)
Yellow	+12 dc	3 (P8)
Blue	−12 Vdc	4 (P8)
Black	GND	5 (P8)
Black	GND	6 (P8)
Black	GND	1 (P9)
Black	GND	2 (P9)
White	−5 Vdc	3 (P9)
Red	+5 Vdc	4 (P9)
Red	+5 Vdc	5 (P9)
Red	+5 Vdc	6 (P9)

THE SYSTEM STARTS BUT WON'T INITIALIZE

Symptom 4-4. The power light is on, but you hear two or more beeps There is no video. Check the video board first. Video problems can easily halt the initialization process. Turn off and unplug the PC, then be sure that your video board is inserted completely into its expansion slot. Consider the beep code itself—a catastrophic fault has been detected in the *Power On Self-Test (POST)* before the video system could be initialized. BIOS makers use different numbers and patterns of beeps to indicate failures. You can determine the exact failure by finding the BIOS maker (usually marked on the motherboard BIOS IC), then finding the error message in Chapter 15. In the vast majority of cases, the fault will be traced to the CPU, RAM, motherboard circuitry, video controller, or drive controller.

Symptom 4-5. The power light is on, but the system hangs during initialization Video might be active, but there might be no text in the display. The *Power On Self-Test (POST)* has detected a fault, and is unable to continue with the initialization process. BIOS makers mark the completion of each POST step by writing single-byte hexadecimal completion codes to port 80h. Turn off and unplug the PC, then insert a POST board to read the completion codes. Reboot the computer and find the last code to be written before the initialization stops—that is the likely point of failure. You can determine the meaning of that POST code by finding the BIOS maker (usually displayed in the initial moments of power-up), then locating the corresponding error message in Chapter 15. Without a POST board available, it will be extremely difficult to identify the problem.

Symptom 4-6. You see a message indicating a CMOS setup problem The system parameters entered into CMOS RAM do not match the hardware configuration found during the POST. Enter your setup routine. If you are working on an older system (early i386 and i286 systems), you will probably need to boot the PC from a setup disk. If there is no setup disk available, you might be able to find a suitable routine at one of the sites at: **oak.oakland.edu:/SimTel/msdos/at** or **ftp.uu.net:/systems/msdos/simtel/at.**

If you can't get a CMOS setup utility online, try CMOSER11.ZIP or GSETUP31.ZIP on the CD.

Review each entry in the CMOS setup—especially things like drive parameters and installed memory—and be sure that the CMOS entries accurately reflect the actual hardware installed on your system. If not, correct the error(s), save your changes, and reboot the system. Finally, test the CMOS battery. See if CMOS RAM will hold its contents by turning off the PC, waiting several minutes, then rebooting the PC. If setup problems persist, and you find that the values you entered have been lost, change the CMOS backup battery.

Symptom 4-7. You see no drive light activity The boot drive cannot be located. The most frequent cause of drive problems is power connections. Inspect the 4-pin power cable and see that it is attached properly and completely to the drive. Check the power-supply voltages next. Use a voltmeter and verify that the +5- and +12-V levels (especially +12 V) are correct at the 4-pin connector. If either voltage is low or absent, replace the power supply. Locate the wide ribbon cable that connects to the drive and be sure that it is attached correctly and completely at the drive and controller ends. Look for any scrapes or nicks along the cable that might cause problems. Start the CMOS setup. If you are working on an older system (early i386 and i286 systems), you will probably need to boot the PC from a setup disk. If no setup disk is available, you might be able to find a suitable routine at: **oak.oakland.edu:/SimTel/msdos/at** or **ftp.uu.net:/systems/msdos/simtel/at**.

Check the CMOS setup next. Review the drive parameters entered in the CMOS setup, and be sure that the CMOS entries accurately reflect the actual boot drive installed on your system. If not, correct the error(s), save your changes, and reboot the system. Also, be sure that the drive-controller board is installed properly and completely in its expansion slot, and see that any jumpers are set correctly. Try booting the system from your boot floppy. If the system successfully boots to the A: prompt, your problem is limited to the hard-drive system. Now try switching to the C: drive. If the drive responds (and you can access its information), there might be a problem with the boot sector. Try a package, such as PC Tools or Norton Utilities, to try and "fix" the boot sector. If you can't access the hard drive, try a diagnostic to check the drive controller and drive. Check for boot-sector viruses. A boot-sector virus can render the hard drive unbootable. If you haven't checked for viruses yet, use your anti-virus work disk now, and focus on boot-sector problems. If you cannot determine the problem at this point, try replacing the drive with a known-good working drive. Remember that you will have to change the CMOS setup parameters to accommodate the new drive. If all else fails, try a new drive-controller board.

Symptom 4-8. The drive light remains on continuously The boot drive cannot be located. This typically happens if the signal cable is inserted backwards at one end. In most cases, this type of problem happens after replacing a drive or upgrading a controller. Be sure that the cable is inserted in the correct orientation at both the drive and controller ends. If you cannot determine the problem at this point, try replacing the drive with a known-good working drive. Remember that you will have to change the CMOS setup parameters to accommodate the new drive. If all else fails, try a new drive-controller board.

Symptom 4-9. You see normal system activity, but there is no video Be sure that the monitor is plugged in and turned on. This type of oversight is really more common than you might think. Be sure that the monitor works (you might want to try the monitor on a known-good system). If the monitor fails on a known-good system, replace the monitor. Next, trace the monitor cable to its connection at the video board and verify that the connector is inserted securely. Check the video board. It is possible that the video board has failed. If the problem persists, replace the video board.

THE SYSTEM STARTS BUT CRASHES/ REBOOTS INTERMITTENTLY

Symptom 4-10. The system randomly crashes/reboots for no apparent reason Check for viruses first. Some viruses (especially memory-resident viruses) can cause the PC to crash or reboot unexpectedly. If you haven't run your virus checker yet, do so now. Check the power-supply cables and verify that they are attached properly and securely to the motherboard. Use a voltmeter to verify that each output from the power supply is correct, as outlined in Table 4-2. If any output is low (especially the +5-V output), replace the power supply.

With all power off, check to see that the CPU is cool, that the heatsink/fan assembly is fitted on correctly, and that the CPU itself is inserted properly and completely into its socket. If the CPU overheats, it will stall—taking the entire system with it. If the CPU is seated in a *Zero Insertion Force (ZIF)* socket, be sure that the socket's tension lever is closed and locked into place. Also be sure that all SIMMs are seated properly in their holders and locked into place. You might try removing each SIMM, cleaning the contacts, and re-installing the SIMMs.

Be sure that all expansion boards are seated properly. Any boards that are not secured properly or that are inserted unevenly, can short bus signals and cause spurious reboots. If you've recently installed new expansion hardware, be sure that there are no hardware conflicts between interrupts, DMA channels, or I/O addresses. Inspect the motherboard at every metal standoff and see that no metal traces are being shorted against a standoff or screw. You might want to free the motherboard and see if the crashes or reboots go away. If so, use non-conductive spacers (such as a small piece of manila folder) to insulate the motherboard from each metal standoff. If the system continues to crash or reboot (and all voltages from the power supply are correct), replace the motherboard.

AFTER AN UPGRADE

Symptom 4-11. The system fails to boot, freezes during boot, or freezes during operation for no apparent reason This is the classic sign of a hardware conflict. A PC is designed with a limited number of resources (i.e., memory, I/O addresses, IRQ lines, DMA channels, etc.). For the PC to function properly, each device added to the system must use its own unique resources. For example, no two devices can use the same IRQ, DMA, or I/O resources. When such an overlap of resources occurs, the PC can easily malfunction and freeze. Unfortunately, it is virtually impossible to predict when the malfunction will occur, so a conflict can manifest itself early (any time during the boot process) or later on (after DOS is loaded) while an application is running.

Resolving a conflict is not difficult, but it requires patience and attention to detail. Examine the upgrade and its adapter board, and check the IRQ, DMA, and I/O address settings of other boards in the system. Make sure that the upgrade hardware is set to use resources that are not in use by other devices already in the system. For example, some motherboards offer built-in video-controller circuits. Before another video adapter can be added to the system, the motherboard video adapter must be disabled—usually with a single motherboard jumper. Some sophisticated adapter boards (especially high-end video adapters and video-capture boards) require the use of extra memory space. If memory exclusions are needed, be sure that the appropriate entries are made in CONFIG.SYS and AUTOEXEC.BAT files. If memory exclusions are not followed, multiple devices might attempt to use the same memory space and result in a conflict.

Symptom 4-12. The system fails to recognize its upgrade device Even if the hardware is installed in a system correctly, the PC might not recognize the upgrade device(s) without the proper software loaded. A great example of this is the CD-ROM drive. It is a simple matter to install the drive and its adapter board, but the PC will not even recognize the drive unless the low-level CD-ROM device driver is added to CONFIG.SYS and the MS-DOS CD-ROM driver (MSCDEX) is included in AUTOEXEC.BAT. If the

PC is running in a stable fashion, but it does not recognize the expansion hardware, be sure that you have loaded all required software correctly.

If you are mixing and matching existing sub-assemblies from new and old systems, be sure that each device is fully compatible with the PC. Incompatibilities between vintages and manufacturers can lead to operational problems. For example, adding a 3.5" floppy drive to an i286 AT system can result in problems because the older BIOS could not format 3.5" high-density (1.44MB) floppy disks. A DOS utility (such as DRIVER.SYS) is needed to correct this deficiency.

It is also possible that the upgrade device might simply be defective or installed incorrectly. Open the system and doublecheck your installation. Pay particular attention to any cables, connectors, or drive jumpers. When you confirm that the hardware and software installation is correct, suspect a hardware defect. Try the upgrade in another system if possible. If the problem persists when you attempt the upgrade on another PC, one or more elements of the upgrade hardware are probably defective. Return it to the vendor for a prompt refund or replacement. If the upgrade works on another system, the original system might be incompatible with the upgrade or you might have missed a jumper or DIP switch setting on the motherboard.

Symptom 4-13. One or more applications fail to function as expected after an upgrade This is not uncommon among video adapter and sound board upgrades. Often, applications are configured to work with various sets of hardware. When that hardware is altered, the particular application(s) might no longer run properly (this is especially true under Windows). The best way to address this problem is to check and change the hardware configuration for each affected application. Most DOS applications come with a setup utility. You can adjust most Windows configurations under the *Control panel* icon. Under Windows 95, you can access system-configuration settings under the *System* icon under the *Control panel*.

WINDOWS 95 BOOT SYMPTOMS

Symptom 4-14. The Windows 95 boot drive is no longer bootable after restoring data with the DOS backup utility This happens frequently when a replacement drive is installed, and you attempt to restore the Windows 95 backup data. Unfortunately, the DOS version of backup is not configured to restore system files. Start backup and restore your root directory with "System Files," "Hidden Files," and "Read-Only Files" checked. Next, boot the system from an MS-DOS 6.x upgrade setup disk #1 or a Windows 95 startup disk, then use the SYS command to make the hard drive bootable such as:

```
A:\> sys c:    <Enter>
```

You should then be able to restore the remainder of your files. When backing up a Windows 95 system, your best approach is to use the Windows 95 Backup program. Once the new drive is installed, partitioned, and formatted, install a new copy of Windows 95, start Windows 95 backup, then restore the remaining files to the drive.

Symptom 4-15. Windows 95 will not boot and ScanDisk reports bad clusters that it cannot repair This is a problem encountered with Western Digital hard drives. If your WD drive fails in this way, you can recover the drive, but you will lose all information on it. Backup as much information from the drive as possible before proceeding:

- Download the Western Digital service files WDATIDE.EXE and WD_CLEAR.EXE from WD at: **http://www.wdc.com/**. You can also get these files from AOL by typing keyword *WDC*.
- Copy these files to a "clean" boot floppy diskette.
- Boot to DOS from a "clean" diskette (no CONFIG.SYS or AUTOEXEC.BAT files) and run WD_CLEAR.EXE. This utility clears all data on the media (and destroys all data).
- Next, run the WDATIDE.EXE utility to perform a comprehensive surface scan.
- Repartition and reformat the drive, then restore your data.

Symptom 4-16. You see a "Bad or missing <filename>" error on startup A file used by Windows 95 during startup has probably become corrupt. Locate the file mentioned in the error message. If you can find the file, erase it and try re-installing it from original Windows 95 disks or CD.

Symptom 4-17. Windows 95 reports damaged or missing files, or a "VxD error" During startup, Windows 95 depends on several key files being available. If a key file is damaged or missing, Windows 95 will not function properly (if it loads at all). Run Windows 95 setup again and select the *Verify* option in *Safe recovery* to replace the missing or damaged file(s).

Symptom 4-18. After installing Windows 95, you can't boot from a different drive The Windows 95 setup program checks all hard disks to find just one that contains the 80h designator in the DriveNumber field of a boot sector. Windows 95 will typically force the first drive to be bootable and prevent other drives from booting. However, there are two ways to correct the problem after Windows 95 is installed:

- Use the version of FDISK included with Windows 95 to set the primary active partition.
- Use a disk-editor utility to change a disk's DriveNumber field so that you can boot from that hard disk.

Symptom 4-19. Windows 95 Registry files are missing There are two registry files: USER.DAT and SYSTEM.DAT. They are also backed up automatically as USER.DA0 and SYSTEM.DA0. If a .DAT file is missing, Windows 95 will automatically load the corresponding .DA0 file. If both the .DAT and .DA0 registry files are missing or corrupt, Windows 95 will start in the *Safe mode* offering to restore the Registry. However, this cannot be accomplished without a backup. Either restore the *Registry* files from a tape or diskette backup, or run Windows 95 Setup to create a new Registry. Unfortunately, restoring an old registry or creating a new registry from scratch will reload programs and re-add hardware to restore the system to its original state—a long and difficult procedure. Use the following DOS procedure to backup the Registry files to a floppy disk:

```
attrib -r -s -h system.da?
attrib -r -s -h user.da?
copy system.da? A:\
```

```
copy user.da? A:\
attrib +r +s +h system.da?
attrib +r +s +h user.da?
```

Symptom 4-20. During the Windows 95 boot, I get an "Invalid System Disk" error This often happens during the first reboot during Windows 95 setup, or when you boot from the startup disk. When you see a message such as "Invalid system disk. Replace the disk, and then press any key." There might be several possible problems. First, your disk might be infected with a boot-sector virus. Run your anti-virus work disk and check closely for boot sector viruses. Windows 95 setup might also fail if there is anti-virus software running as a TSR, or your BIOS has enabled boot-sector protection. Be sure that any boot-sector protection is turned off before installing Windows 95. Check for disk-overlay software—Windows 95 might not detect overlay software such as Disk Manager, EZ-Drive, or DrivePro, and overwrite the master boot record (MBR). See the documentation that accompanies your particular management software for recovering the MBR. To re-install the Windows 95 system files, follow these steps:

1 Boot the system using the Windows 95 Emergency Boot Disk.
2 At the MS-DOS command prompt, type the following lines:
```
c:
cd\windows\command
attrib c:\msdos.sys -h -s -r
ren c:\msdos.sys c:\msdos.xxx
a:
sys c:
del c:\msdos.sys
ren c:\msdos.xxx c:\msdos.sys
attrib c:\msdos.sys +r +s +h
```
3 Remove the Emergency Boot Disk and reboot the system.

Symptom 4-21. Windows 95 will not install on a compressed drive You are probably using an old version of the compression software, which Windows 95 does not recognize. Although Windows 95 should be compatible with all versions of SuperStor, it does require version 2.0 or later of Stacker. Be sure that your compression software is recent and see that there is enough free space on the host drive to support Windows 95 installation. If you have the PlusPack for Windows 95, you should be able to install DriveSpace 3 for best Windows 95 support.

Symptom 4-22. The drive indicates that it is in "MS-DOS compatibility mode" For some reason, Windows 95 is using a real-mode (DOS) driver instead of a protected-mode (32-bit) driver. Be sure that any software related to the hard drive (especially hard-disk drivers) are using the protected-mode versions. Windows 95 should install equivalent protected-mode software, but you might need to contact the drive manufacturer and obtain the latest Windows 95 drivers. If you are using Disk Manager, be sure that you're using version 6.0 or later. You can get the latest patch (DMPATCH.EXE) from the Ontrack web site at: **http://www.ontrack.com/**. Finally, check your motherboard BIOS—Windows 95 might use DOS-compatibility mode on large EIDE hard disks (hard disks with more than 1024 cylinders) in some computers. This might occur because of an invalid drive geometry translation in the system ROM BIOS that prevents the protected-mode IDE device driver from being loaded. Contact your system manufacturer for information about obtaining an updated BIOS.

Symptom 4-23. Disabling protected-mode disk driver(s), hides the partition table when FDISK is used As with Symptom 4-22, there are problems preventing 32-bit operation of your hard drive(s). Do NOT use the "Disable all 32-bit protected-mode disk drivers" option. Instead, upgrade your motherboard BIOS to a later version.

Symptom 4-24. You cannot achieve 32-bit disk access under Windows 95 If the Windows 95 system refuses to allow 32-bit disk access, there might be a conflict between the motherboard CMOS setup entries and the BIOS on your EIDE controller. For example, if both BIOS have settings for *Logical Block Addressing (LBA)*, be sure that only one entry is in use.

Symptom 4-25. Windows 95 does not recognize a new device In some cases, Windows 95 is unable to recognize a new device. When this happens, check to see if there is a hardware conflict between the device and other devices in the system (you can see conflicts represented in the Device Manager with small yellow exclamation marks). Also be sure that any necessary drivers have been installed properly. If problems continue, remove the new device through your Device Manager, and reinstall it through the *Add new hardware* wizard.

Symptom 4-26. Windows 95 malfunctions when installed over Disk Manager Disk Manager should typically be compatible with Windows 95, but there are some points to remember. Check your Disk Manager version first. If you are using Disk Manager, be sure that you're using version 6.0 or later. You can get the latest patch (DM-PATCH.EXE) from the Ontrack Web site at: **http://www.ontrack.com/**. Check the slave drive with Disk Manager. Although the Windows 95 file system is supposed to work properly with a slave drive only using Disk Manager, there are some circumstances where problems can occur:

- When a Windows 3.1x virtual driver replaces the Windows 95 protected-mode driver (such as WDCDRV.386).
- When the cylinder count in CMOS for the slave drive is greater than 1024 cylinders.
- When the motherboard CMOS settings for the slave drive are set to *Auto-detect*.

Symptom 4-27. You have problems using a manufacturer-specific hard-disk driver (such as Western Digital's FastTrack driver WDCDRV.386) for 32-bit access under Windows 95 Generally speaking, Windows 95 has 32-bit protected-mode drivers for a wide variety of EIDE devices—in actuality, you should not need a manufacturer-specific driver. If Windows 95 has not removed all references to the driver from SYSTEM.INI, you should edit the file and remove those references manually, then reboot the system. Be sure to make a backup copy of SYSTEM.INI before editing it.

Further Study

That's it for Chapter 4. Because this is the last chapter of this section, take some time to review the glossary and chapter questions on the accompanying CD. If you have access to the Internet, set your Web browser to some of the following contacts:

Symantec: **http://www.symantec.com**

McAfee and Associates: **http://www.mcafee.com**

IBM Setup routines: **oak.oakland.edu:/SimTel/msdos/at**, or **http.uu.net:/systems/msdos/simtel/at**

Ontrack Software: **http://www.ontrack.com/**

Ziff Davis benchmark site: **http://www8.zdnet.com/pcmag/pclabs/bench/**

Benchmarking news group: **comp.benchmarks**

5

BATTERIES

CONTENTS AT A GLANCE

A Battery Primer
   Battery ratings
   Charging

Backup Batteries
   Lithium batteries
   Backup battery replacement
   Troubleshooting backup-battery
      problems

Mobile Batteries
   Nickel-cadmium

Nickel metal-hydride
Lithium-ion and zinc-air
Recognizing rechargeable battery
   failures
Conserving mobile battery power
Troubleshooting mobile battery
   problems

Battery Recycling

Further Study

Of all the elements in a PC, few are as overlooked and ignored as the battery. Batteries play an important role in all PCs by maintaining the system's configuration data while main ac power is turned off (just imagine how inconvenient it would be to re-enter the entire system setup in CMOS before being able to use the system each time). For portable systems such as notebook and sub-notebook PCs, battery packs also provide main power for the entire system. This chapter outlines the technologies and operating characteristics of today's battery families and illustrates a selection of battery-related problems that can plague a PC.

A Battery Primer

The battery is perhaps the most common and dependable source of power ever developed. It is an electrochemical device that uses two dissimilar metals (called *electrodes*) that are immersed or encapsulated in a chemical catalyst (*electrolyte*). The chemical reaction that occurs in a battery causes a voltage differential to be developed across its electrodes. When a battery is attached to a circuit, the battery provides current. The more current required by a load, the faster a chemical reaction will occur. As the chemical reaction continues, electrodes are consumed. As a result of this chemical consumption, the battery will eventually wear out. It is important to realize that a battery and a cell are not necessarily the same. A cell is the basic element of a battery, however, a battery might be made up of several individual cells.

For some batteries, the chemical reaction is irreversible. When the battery is dead, it must be discarded. These are known as *non-rechargeable (primary) batteries*. Most PCs use primary-type batteries to sustain the CMOS setup. However, some types of batteries can be recharged. By applying current to the battery from an external source (i.e., a battery charger), the expended chemical reaction can be almost entirely reversed. Such rechargeable batteries are referred to as *secondary batteries*. Secondary batteries are used to supply main power for all mobile computers.

BATTERY RATINGS

Batteries carry two important ratings: cell voltage and ampere-hours (Ah). *Cell voltage* refers to the cell's working voltage. Most everyday cells operate around +1.5 Vdc, but can range from +1.2 to +3.0 Vdc, depending on the particular battery chemistry in use. The ampere-hour rating is a bit more involved, but it reflects the "energy storage capacity" of a battery. A large Ah rating suggests a high-capacity battery, and vice versa.

As an example, suppose your battery is rated for 2 Ah. Ideally, you should be able to draw 2 amps from the battery for 1 hour before it is exhausted. However, you should also be able to draw 1 amp for 2 hours, 0.5 amps for 4 hours, 0.1 amps for 20 hours, etc. Keep in mind that the ampere-hour relationship is not always precisely linear. Higher current loads might shorten battery life to less than that expected by the ampere-hour rating, but small loads might allow slightly more battery life than expected. Regardless of the ampere-hour rating, all batteries have an upper current limit—attempting to draw excess current can destroy the battery. Physically large batteries can usually supply more current (and last longer) than smaller batteries. Another way to express a battery's energy capacity is in Watt-hours per kilogram (Wh/kg) or Watt-hours per pound (Wh/lb). For example, a 1 kg battery rated at 60 Wh could provide 60 W of power for 1 hour, 30 W of power for 2 hours, 10 W of power for 6 hours, etc.

CHARGING

In its simplest sense, *charging* is the replacement of electrical energy to batteries whose stored chemical energy has been discharged. By applying an electrical current to a discharged battery over a given period of time, it is possible to cause a chemical recombination at the battery's electrodes, which will restore most of the cell's spent potential. Essentially, you must back-feed the battery at a known, controlled rate.

Recharging only works for secondary cells, such as nickel-cadmium or nickel metal-hydride batteries. Attempting to recharge a primary battery will quickly destroy it.

Before you dive into an overview of charging circuits and troubleshooting, you must understand the concept of C. The term C designates the normal current capacity of a battery (in amperes). In most circumstances, the value of C is the same as the ampere-hour current level. For example, a battery rated for 1300 mAh (1.30 Ah) would be considered to have a C value of 1.30 amps. A battery rated for 700 mAh (0.70 Ah) would have a C of 0.70 amps. Charging rates are based upon fractions or multiples of C.

To charge a battery, you must apply a reverse voltage, which will cause the appropriate amount of charging current to flow back into the battery. Ideally, the battery should be charged at a rate of $0.1C$. For batteries with a C of 500 mA (0.5 A), $0.1C$ would be 50 mA (0.05 A). At $0.1C$, the battery could be left connected in the charger indefinitely without damage. Low-current charge rates, such as $0.1C$, are sometimes referred to as a *slow charge* or *trickle charge*. Slow charging produces the least physical or thermal stress within a battery and ensures the maximum possible number of charge/discharge cycles.

Many current secondary batteries can be charged well above the $0.1C$ rate. The quick charge approach uses current levels of $0.3C$ (three times the rate of a slow charge) to recharge the cell in 4 to 6 hours. For a battery with a C of 600 mA (0.60 A), the $0.1C$ charging rate would be 60 mA (0.06 A), but the quick charge rate would be 180 mA (0.18 A). However, the quick charging process runs the risk of overcharging a battery. Once a battery is fully recharged, additional current at or above the quick-charge rate causes temperature and pressure buildups within the cell. In extreme cases, a severely overcharged cell might rupture and be destroyed. When quick charging, the $0.3C$ charging rate should be used only long enough to restore the bulk of a cell's energy. The rate should be reduced to $0.1C$ (or less) for continuous operation.

New NiCd and NiMH battery designs allow for an even faster charge of 1 hour. The 1-hour charge uses a rate of $1.5C$ - 1.5 times the amount of current that the cell is intended to provide. A battery with a C of 1400 mA (1.4 A) would use a 1-hour charge rate of 2100 mA (2.1 A). Remember that only specially designed secondary cells can be safely charged in 1 hour or less. With 1-hour charging, current control and timing become crucial issues. The battery-charging current must be reduced as soon as the cell approaches its full charge or catastrophic battery failure will almost certainly result. Rapid charging causes substantial temperature and pressure increases that eventually take their toll on the cell's working life. You should expect the working life of any cell to be curtailed when it is regularly operated in a 1-hour charge mode.

The *constant-current charger* is designed to automatically compensate for changes in battery terminal voltage to maintain charging current at a constant level. Constant-current charging is very efficient, but it is not adjustable. If the charger were set to deliver substantial charging currents, the battery pack could charge quickly, but the pack could eventually be damaged by overcharging. The charger could be set to a lower level for safe charging (perhaps $0.1C$), but the low charging rate means very long charge times for a battery pack (10 hours or more). Such limitations make constant-current chargers ill-suited for use in mobile computers. Instead, constant-current chargers are typically used in stand-alone battery-pack charging units.

A more effective approach for portable computers is a variable-current (constant-voltage) scheme. When a battery is deeply discharged and its terminal voltage is low, there will be a substantial difference between the power-supply source and battery voltage level. This difference results in a sizable current flow to the battery. Charging usually starts out around the $0.5C$ to $0.3C$ rate for fast charge operation. As the battery takes on a charge, its terminal voltage increases. Higher battery voltage reduces the difference between the supply and battery—current flow into the battery decreases. When the battery pack reaches full charge, there is almost no voltage difference between the charger and battery, so only a small amount of current trickles into the battery. Current flow might reach levels as low as $0.05C$.

Backup Batteries

When IBM released its PC/AT in the early 1980s, one of the many design changes over the older PC/XT was the elimination of DIP switches that were used to set the system configuration. Instead of discrete physical switches, PC designers chose to set system parameters using bit sequences stored in small areas of low-power static RAM. Because it would be necessary to maintain the contents of this RAM even when system power was off, designers chose to use RAM ICs based on *Complementary Metal-Oxide Semiconductor (CMOS)* fabrication. This memory became known as *CMOS RAM*. CMOS RAM can be maintained for years using only a single small battery or battery pack incorporated onto the motherboard (Fig. 5-1), called a *CMOS backup battery*.

Mobile computers, such as IBM's ThinkPad series, often use additional batteries to serve as a "standby" power source. These standby batteries are rechargeable battery packs, frequently used to supplement the main battery in mobile computers. Traditionally, you'd need to shut down a laptop and replace a main battery pack, then reboot the system to keep working. If the main battery pack failed, you'd lose any work in progress (and perhaps corrupt important files). With a standby power source, the system can automatically enter a "suspend" mode, where almost no power is used, but files and data can be kept active in memory. You can then replace the main battery and leave the "suspend" mode to keep working without the time and trouble to reboot and reload your applications. If the main battery should fail, the standby batteries can keep your work intact for up to several days until you can exchange the main battery pack, or find an ac outlet for a battery eliminator.

LITHIUM BATTERIES

Lithium/manganese-dioxide (Li/MnO2 or simply "lithium") batteries are commonly used as CMOS backup batteries. Lithium batteries use a layer of lithium as the anode, a specially formulated manganese-dioxide alloy as the cathode, and a conductive organic electrolyte. Depending on the overall size and shape of the cell, a lithium battery can supply +3.0 Vdc at up to 330 Wh/kg of energy density. Lithium cells also offer a 5-year shelf life with almost no loss of power. Although their energy density is quite high, lithium cells offer only low ampere-hour ratings between 70 mAh (0.70 Ah) and 1300 mAh (1.30 Ah). Limited Ah ratings allow lithium cells to maintain an almost constant output voltage over a long working life.

FIGURE 5-1 A Rayovac Computer Clock battery. Courtesy of Rayovac Corp.

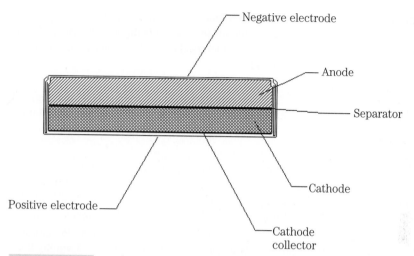

FIGURE 5-2   Cross-section of a lithium coin cell.

The classic type of lithium "coin cell" design is shown in Fig. 5-2. The typical coin cell is designed in two halves, with a lithium anode at the top and a manganese-dioxide cathode layer on the bottom. Both halves are separated by a thin membrane containing a conductive electrolyte. The finished electrochemical assembly is then packaged into a small metal can. The lid forms the negative electrode, while the side walls and bottom of the coin form the positive electrode. The lid is physically isolated from the rest of the metal can by a thin insulating grommet—thus, the coin cell is not sealed. A grommet keeps moisture and contaminants out, yet will allow any pressure buildup to escape the battery.

BACKUP BATTERY REPLACEMENT

Battery life has a finite limit. Eventually, all backup batteries will discharge to the point where they can no longer sustain the system. When the battery finally does fail, CMOS information is lost. The next time you attempt to turn the PC on, the system will generate an error code or message indicating that the system configuration does not match the CMOS setup information. The loss of a CMOS setup suddenly leaves a system disabled until new (and correct) CMOS information is entered. This presents a serious problem for most PC users because few users bother to backup or record their CMOS setup. As you might imagine, it then becomes an exercise in frustration to load the setup routine and re-construct the system setup from scratch.

Fortunately, you can do two things to avoid this problem. First, make it a point to replace the backup battery every two years (no more than three years). If you change the backup battery for a customer, note the battery part number and replacement date on a sticker, then place the sticker inside the PC enclosure. You might also note the next replacement date on your customer's bill. Second, backup the system CMOS entries before replacing the battery. You can note the entries on paper (using the form included in the appendix of this book) and tape the page inside the enclosure, or you can use a shareware utility to backup CMOS contents as a disk file. CMOS backup as a disk file is quick and easy, and the file can be restored in a matter of seconds. A backup utility is especially handy when no setup disk is available for the system being worked on. Make it a point to keep the backup current as system parameters change. Otherwise, you would be restoring information that is no longer valid.

There are a number of CMOS backup/restore utilities for you to choose from. Check out CMOS.ZIP, CMOSRAM2.ZIP, AUTOCMOS.ZIP, and CMOS93CD.ZIP on the companion CD.

The actual process of backup battery replacement is simply a matter or removing the old battery and inserting a new one. Because the battery is often located prominently on the motherboard, it is possible to replace a backup battery with system power applied (this lets the system maintain its CMOS settings). However, working inside a "hot" system is against the safety protocols have been established for this book, so be sure to record the CMOS settings on floppy disk or paper first, then power down and unplug the PC before opening it. Replace the battery, then restart the PC and reload the CMOS settings from disk or paper. Replacing the backup battery in a notebook or sub-notebook PC is sometimes easier because the battery is usually accessible from a small panel on the bottom enclosure (you do not have to disassemble the notebook enclosures to replace the battery). Even with easy access, you should make it a point to remove power before replacing the battery.

If you act quickly when replacing the CMOS backup battery, there might be enough of a latent charge in CMOS RAM where the contents will remain intact for several minutes. However, each motherboard is designed differently, and there is no guarantee how long CMOS RAM contents might remain intact once the battery is removed. Always be prepared to restore CMOS settings from scratch before removing the CMOS backup battery.

TROUBLESHOOTING BACKUP-BATTERY PROBLEMS

Lithium CMOS backup batteries are typically rugged and reliable devices, whose greatest threat is simply old age. Because lithium cells are the primary type, they cannot be recharged, so they must be replaced. Under most circumstances, only a few symptoms occur for the majority of backup battery problems.

Checking the CMOS backup battery It is usually a simple matter to check the CMOS backup battery. Power down the system and expose the motherboard. Locate the CMOS backup battery and find the two battery terminals leading from the battery to the motherboard. Measure the voltage between those two terminals—you should read between 2.5 to 3.7 Vdc. If the backup battery voltage is correct, there might be a software program or motherboard failure. If the backup battery reads low, replace the battery. If the battery discharges again quickly, there is a problem on the motherboard, which is shorting the CMOS backup battery.

Do not remove the CMOS backup battery from the motherboard—this will clear your CMOS configuration and make it difficult for the system to boot until the CMOS settings are restored.

Symptom 5-1. You see an error such as: "System hardware does not match CMOS configuration" For some reason(s), the BIOS has identified different hardware than that listed in the CMOS setup, or the CMOS RAM contents have been lost. Start by checking your CMOS RAM contents through the CMOS setup routine. Make sure that the CMOS setup is configured properly (configuration errors can happen frequently when new drives or RAM is added to the system). Remember to save your changes to CMOS RAM before exiting the setup routine. If the CMOS RAM contents won't hold, check the battery connector to see that the battery is secure. A loose or corroded battery connector might effectively "disconnect" the battery—even if the battery is working perfectly. If the CMOS RAM contents still won't hold, you should replace the CMOS backup battery outright. When replacing the battery, be sure to install the new battery in the proper orientation, and verify that it is secure in its connector.

This error often happens when RAM is added to the system—even though there is no entry for installed RAM anywhere in the CMOS setup. Try to "exit savings changes"—even though you might not have actually changed any settings.

Symptom 5-2. You notice corrosion from the CMOS battery on the battery holder and motherboard This frequently occurs with older motherboards (i.e., i386 and i486 vintage motherboards) that have been stored for prolonged periods. The battery has ruptured and leaked onto the holder or onto the motherboard itself. Batteries are very caustic to metals, and chances are that any traces or solder connections that have come in contact with the battery leakage have been ruined. Unfortunately, this also means that the motherboard has been ruined and must be replaced.

If you're planning to remove and store a motherboard for any period of time, take a <PrintScreen> of all CMOS setup pages before removing the motherboard, then store the old motherboard with the battery removed. You might place the battery in a small, heavy-gauge plastic bag at the bottom of the motherboard's anti-static box. When resurrecting the motherboard later, you can replace the battery and restore the CMOS settings from your printed record.

Symptom 5-3. The system configuration is lost intermittently A lithium battery generally produces a very stable output voltage until the very end of its operating life. When the battery finally dies, it tends to be a permanent event. When a system loses its setup configuration without warning, but seems to hold the configuration once it is restored, the problem could be a lose or intermittent connection. Turn the PC off and unplug it. Check the battery and be sure it is inserted correctly and completely in its holder. A coin cell should fit snugly. If the cell is loose, gently tighten the holder's prongs to hold the cell more securely. Be sure to remove any corrosion or debris that might be interfering with the contact. High-quality electrical contact cleaner on a moistened swab is particularly effective at cleaning contacts. When the battery is attached by a short cable, see that the cable is not broken or frayed, and be sure that it is inserted properly into its receptacle. If problems persist, replace the CMOS backup battery.

Symptom 5-4. The backup battery goes dead frequently This rare and perplexing problem is often difficult to detect because it might only manifest itself several times per year. Ideally, a lithium coin cell should last for several years (perhaps three years, or longer). A lithium or alkaline battery pack can last five years or longer. If a system loses its setup more than once a year because of battery failures, it is very likely that an error in the motherboard design is draining the backup batteries faster than normal. Unfortunately, the only way to really be sure is to replace the motherboard with a different or updated version. Before suggesting this option to your customer, you might wish to contact technical support for the original motherboard manufacturer and find out if similar cases have been reported. If so, find if there is a fix or correction that will rectify the problem.

Symptom 5-5. You see a "161" error or a message that indicates that the system battery is dead Depending on the particular system you are working with, there might also be a message indicating that the CMOS setup does not match the system configuration. In either case, the backup battery has probably failed and should be replaced. Remember to turn off the system before replacing the battery. Once the backup battery is replaced, restart the system. You will likely receive a message that the CMOS setup does not match the system configuration. Restore the configuration from paper notes or a file backup. The system should now function normally.

Mobile Batteries

Besides providing power to backup the system's configuration, notebook and sub-notebook computers rely on batteries for main power when operating away from ac. Such power is typically provided from a battery pack installed from the bottom or side of the computer. The requirements for battery packs are ever-more stringent—packs have to provide as much power for as long as today's technology will allow, yet be as light and small as possible. Further, today's battery packs must be quickly rechargeable, and offer a long working life through hundreds of recharging cycles. The three battery technologies best suited to these requirements are nickel-cadmium, nickel metal-hydride, and lithium-ion.

NICKEL-CADMIUM

The *Nickel-Cadmium (NiCd) battery* is one of the most cost-effective power sources in mass production today. Large NiCd battery packs have been widely used in mobile computers (primarily laptops and notebooks) as a main power source. Because NiCd cells can be manufactured in almost limitless shapes and sizes, they are ideal for systems requiring unusual battery configurations. Although NiCd batteries initially cost more than primary batteries, they can be recharged often—usually recovering their initial cost many times over.

Nickel-cadmium batteries are secondary (rechargeable) devices using an anode of nickel hydroxide and a cathode consisting of a specially formulated cadmium compound (Fig. 5-3). The electrolyte is made of potassium hydroxide. NiCd cells can supply up to +1.2 Vdc

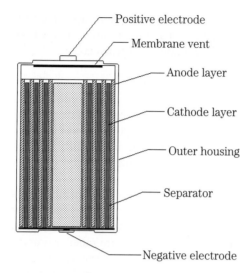

Positive electrode

Membrane vent

Anode layer

Cathode layer

Outer housing

Separator

Negative electrode

FIGURE 5-3 **Cross-section of a NiCd battery.**

each with ampere-hour ratings from 500 mAh (0.50 Ah) to 2300 mAh (2.30 Ah). Energy densities in NiCd cells can approach 50 Wh/kg (23 Wh/lb). Respectable ampere-hour ratings allow NiCd cells to supply sizable amounts of current, but their inherently low energy density means that NiCds must be recharged fairly often.

The NiCd *memory effect* is a unique phenomenon that is not entirely understood. In operation, a NiCd battery can develop a "memory" that limits either the capacity or terminal voltage of a cell. As you might expect, either limit can result in problems with the battery. *Voltage memory* is generally caused by prolonged charging over a period of weeks and months. High ambient temperatures and high charging currents can accelerate this condition. In effect, the battery is charged for so long, or at such a high rate or temperature, that the efficiency of the electro-chemical reaction is impaired. As a result, the battery suffers from low terminal voltage.

The *memory capacity* problem is probably more widely recognized, and is usually expressed as the loss of a NiCd's ability to deliver its full power capacity. The generally accepted cause of capacity problems is the result of frequent partial battery discharge, followed by a full recharge. Over several such cycles, the battery "learns" that only a portion of its capacity is used. This renders the battery unable to deliver a full discharge when needed. Although the chemical reason for memory capacity is not fully understood, it is believed to be caused by oxidation reactions, which temporarily coat the electrodes with non-reactive chemical compounds. Fortunately, the memory effect is usually temporary, and can usually be cleared by forcing the battery through several full discharge/recharge cycles. If you are in the habit of using your notebook or laptop PC until you receive low-battery warnings, you will probably not have to worry about NiCd memory problems. It is interesting that the newer nickel metal-hydride batteries do not seem to suffer from memory problems.

NiCd cells also have a very limited charged life when sitting idle. Although alkaline and lithium cells can hold close to their original charge for years, NiCds will lose approximately 25% to 35% of their remaining charge each month. After several months of inactivity, a NiCd battery pack will need to be recharged before use. As a general rule, you should fully recharge any new or rarely used NiCd battery or battery pack prior to use. Today, NiCd batteries have largely been phased out of mobile computer use in favor of NiMH and Li-ion batteries. Table 5-1 illustrates a comparison of mobile battery features.

NICKEL METAL-HYDRIDE

Nickel metal-hydride (NiMH) batteries are a somewhat newer type of rechargeable battery designed to offer substantially greater energy density than NiCd cells for mobile computer applications. Since their introduction in 1990, NiMH cells have already undergone some substantial improvements and cost reductions that have made NiMH the dominant type of battery for mobile computers.

NiMH batteries are remarkably similar in construction and operating principle to NiCds. A positive electrode of nickel-hydroxide remains the same as that used in NiCds, but the negative electrode replaces cadmium with a metal-hydroxide alloy. When combined with a uniquely formulated electrolyte, NiMH cells are rated to provide at least 40% more capacity than similarly sized NiCd cells. NiMH batteries can provide +1.2 Vdc with discharge ratings from 800 mAh (0.80 Ah) to more than 2400 mAh (2.40 Ah) at continuous discharge currents of 9 A or more. Energy densities can exceed 80 Wh/kg (38.1 Wh/lb). This means a NiMH battery can power a laptop and support additional features (i.e., a larger active-matrix color display) for longer periods of time. NiMH batteries do not seem to suffer the "memory effects" that plague NiCd batteries, but NiMH has a shelf life of only a few days—so you'll need to keep your NiMH batteries fully charged before traveling.

TABLE 5-1   A COMPARISON OF MOBILE BATTERY FEATURES

		TODAY'S RECHARGEABLE BATTERIES		NEWER BATTERY TECHNOLOGIES	
Battery Feature	Battery Need	NiCd	NiMH	Li-ion	Zinc-air
Portability	Lightweight (high energy density)	45 watt hours/kg	70 watt hours/kg	115 watt hours/kg	220 watt hours/kg
Full day operation*	High energy storage (for a 1.5-lb. battery)	30 watt hours	48 watt hours	60 watt hours (1.15 lbs)**	150 watt hours
Conven-ience*	Long operating time between charges	1.5 to 2.5 hours	2.5 to 4 hours	3 to 5 hours	8 to 12 hours

*Assumes a full-function notebook operating between 12 and 20 watts
**Safety and performance considerations currently limit lithium-ion implementations to 60-watt hour battery packs

LITHIUM-ION AND ZINC-AIR

Lithium-ion (Li-ion) batteries are a relatively recent development, but they are now readily available for the newest mobile computers. The formulation of the Li-ion battery allows 20 to 30% more running time than a similarly sized NiMH battery (at about 115 Wh/kg), and retains a charge for a long time while "on the shelf". Li-ion batteries are also free of the "memory effects" found in NiCd batteries and will last through well over 1200 recharge cycles.

Zinc-air batteries are a new development in mobile battery design; the batteries now appearing in the field offer almost twice the energy density of Li-ion batteries (at a whopping 220 Wh/kg). In actuality, however, zinc-air batteries have proven extremely large and heavy. They are also quite expensive. These factors have kept zinc-air batteries out of most small mobile systems. Still, the high energy potential of zinc-air will keep development active. Over the next few years, Li-ion and zinc-air batteries should become the major power sources for mobile systems.

RECOGNIZING RECHARGEABLE BATTERY FAILURES

Rechargeable batteries can and do fail eventually. The process of discharge and recharge generates physical stress in the battery, which will eventually wear it out. In general, a NiCd battery will last from about three to five years (through 500 to 1500 complete charge cycles). However, proper charging in a cool environment can extend battery life much further (up to as much as 10,000 complete charge cycles have been reported). Over the life of a rechargeable cell, microscopic "whiskers" of conductive compounds develop between the electrodes. Ultimately, these deposits work to short-circuit the cell. Although "zapping" techniques have been developed using brief surges of current to remove these deposits, such techniques are very risky because the battery stands a good chance of exploding. Another failure mode is the premature loss of liquid electrolyte during high-current or high-temperature charging. Improperly designed "quick-charge" chargers can drive a battery so hard that electrolyte starts to corrode the battery's pressure relief vent. If the vent is damaged or frozen in the open position, electrolyte will continue to evaporate, and the battery will fail.

CONSERVING MOBILE BATTERY POWER

Battery life is affected by the current drawn by a computer—greater current draw results in shorter battery life, and vice versa. A large portion of battery troubleshooting is to ensure that your system setup is adequate. The following steps should help you to optimize battery life:

■ Take advantage of such special power modes as *Suspend* or *Hibernation*. These modes use very little power and should be selected when you'll be away from the running laptop for any period of time.
■ Remove or disable any unnecessary devices in the laptop. For example, you might not need that PCMCIA modem card or sound card during that flight cross-country, so remove the card. If you can disable unneeded devices (i.e., shut down power to the built-in infrared communication unit), that will also save substantial power.

- Use the lowest screen brightness that you are comfortable with by adjusting the display's brightness and contrast control(s).
- Backlights gobble up substantial amounts of power, so set a short time-out interval for the backlight (one or two minutes is often a good selection).
- Light characters and images on a dark background generally consumes less power than dark characters or images on a light background. Try setting your screen mode to a "light on dark" configuration. If you're using Windows 95, select a dark color scheme.
- The hard-disk drive is another major power user—not only by spinning, but during spinup as well. Select a moderate time-out interval for the hard drive (not so long that it spins forever and not so short that it is constantly starting). Otherwise, you will waste more power constantly spinning up the drive than you save by turning it off. Also, constant starting and stopping can reduce the life expectancy of the drive.
- RAM consumes much less power than hard drives, so try setting up a disk cache or RAM disk to reduce the number of disk accesses. This allows the hard drive to shut down fairly quickly and not require access for a relatively long period of time.
- Microprocessor speed can be a serious drain on battery power. If your laptop computer allows you to select processor speed, use the slowest speed possible for all but the most demanding applications. Most word processors and conventional DOS utility software runs just fine with slower processor speeds.
- Most mobile batteries have trouble retaining their full charge capacity when left unused for prolonged periods of time. For example, IBM tests suggest that after a one-year shelf life at room temperature, a Li-ion battery retained 95% of its original capacity (about 90% for NiMH). If you purchase several batteries for a mobile computer, be sure to alternate the use of each battery.

TROUBLESHOOTING MOBILE BATTERY PROBLEMS

When discussing batteries as main power sources, not only are the batteries or battery pack involved, but a whole host of other circuitry is included as well (such as battery charging, battery protection, and power-management circuits). As a result, you should understand that problems running or charging the battery might be originating outside of the battery compartment itself. Because batteries power notebook and sub-notebook systems, trouble might be on the motherboard (where most charging and power management functions are located).

Checking the battery pack When the battery refuses to take or hold a charge, it will often be necessary for you to verify the integrity of your mobile battery. The following steps outline the procedure:

1 Power down the laptop or notebook computer and remove the battery pack, according to the instructions for your particular system.

2 Once the battery pack is removed, measure the voltage between battery terminals. If there are more than two terminals (as in Fig. 5-4 for an IBM ThinkPad battery), be sure to measure across the proper two terminals. For the example of Fig. 5-4, you would measure across pins 1 and 4. If you read 0 Vdc, the battery pack is defective and should be replaced.

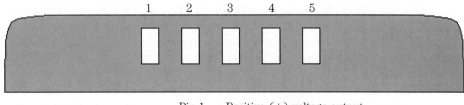

Pin 1   Positive (+) voltage output
Pin 2   Send terminal
Pin 3   Thermal feedback signal
Pin 4   Ground (−)
Pin 5   Select terminal

FIGURE 5-4   **Battery terminals for an IBM ThinkPad battery pack.**

The remaining pins on the battery pack are used for thermal sensors and other communication between the mobile PC and the battery.

3 If the voltage across the battery terminals is less than the optimum value (usually less than +11.0 Vdc), the battery pack has been discharged through self-discharge (being left on the shelf) or use in the PC. Recharge the battery pack. If the voltage is still less than what the fully charged voltage should be after recharging, replace the battery pack.

4 If the voltage is more than +11.0 Vdc, measure the resistance between the thermal sensor and ground terminals (pins 3 and 4 in Fig. 5-4). The resistance should be about 4 to 30 kÍ. If the resistance is not correct, the thermal sensor has failed. This can make it impossible to charge the battery properly, so replace the battery pack.

5 If the resistance is correct, the battery-charging circuit has probably failed.

Symptom 5-6.   The battery pack does not charge   In this type of situation, the computer might run fine from the ac-powered supply, and the system might very well run from its on-board battery when the ac-powered supply is removed. However, the battery pack does not appear to charge when the ac supply is connected and running. Without a charge, the battery will eventually go dead. Remember that some computers will not recharge their battery packs while the system is on—the computer might have to be turned off with the ac supply connected for the battery pack to charge. Refer to the user manual for your particular system to review the correct charging protocol.

Your clue to the charging situation comes from the computer's battery-status indicator. Most notebook/laptop systems incorporate a multicolor LED or an LCD status bar to show battery information. For example, the LED might be red when the small-computer is operating from its internal battery. A yellow color might appear when the ac-powered supply is connected to indicate the battery is charging. The LED might turn green when the battery is fully charged. If the battery-status indicator fails to show a charging color when the ac-powered supply is being used, that is often a good sign of trouble. Table 5-2 lists the status indicators for an IBM ThinkPad (check the user manual for your particular computer).

Check the battery pack with all computer power off. Be sure that the battery pack is inserted properly and completely into its compartment. Also check any cabling and connectors that attach the battery pack to the charging circuit. Loose or corroded connectors, as well as faulty cable wiring, can prevent energy from the ac-powered supply from reaching the battery. Re-seat any loose connectors and re-attach any loose wiring that you might find.

After you are confident of your connections, you should trace the charging voltage from the ac-powered supply to the battery terminals. If charging voltage does not reach the battery, the battery can never charge. Set your multimeter to measure dc voltage (probably in the 10- to 20-Vdc range) and measure the voltage across your battery pack. You should read some voltage below the pack's rated voltage because the battery pack is somewhat discharged. Now, connect the computer's ac-powered supply and measure voltage across your battery pack again. If charging voltage is available to the battery, your voltage reading should climb above the battery pack's rated voltage. If charging still does not seem to take place, try replacing the battery pack, which might be worn out or damaged. If charging voltage is not available to your battery pack, the charging circuit is probably faulty. Replace the charging circuit. Because the charging circuit is typically located on the motherboard, it might be necessary to replace the entire motherboard assembly.

Symptom 5-7. The system does not run on battery power, but runs properly from main (ac) power This symptom usually suggests that your computer runs fine whenever the ac-powered supply is being used, but the system will not run from battery power alone. The system might or might not initialize, depending on the extent of the problem. Before you disassemble the computer or attempt any sort of repair, be sure that you have a fully charged battery pack in the system. Remove the battery pack and measure the voltage across its terminals. You should read approximately the battery voltage marked on the pack. A measurably lower voltage might indicate that the battery is not fully charged. Try a different battery pack or try to let the battery pack recharge. The charging process might take several hours on older systems, but newer small-computer battery systems can charge in an hour or so. If the discharged battery pack does not seem to charge, refer to Symptom 5-6.

When you have a fully charged battery, check to be sure that it is inserted completely and connected properly. Inspect any wiring and connectors that attach the battery pack to its load circuit. Faulty wiring, corroded connections, or loose connectors can cut off the battery pack entirely. At this point, it is safe to assume that battery power is not reaching the laptop circuit(s). In this event, the battery charging/protection circuit might be defective and should be replaced. If the circuit is incorporated into the motherboard, the motherboard should be replaced.

Symptom 5-8. The system suffers from a short battery life Today's small-computers are designed to squeeze up to 6 hours of operation (or more) from every charge.

TABLE 5-2 STATUS INDICATORS FOR AN IBM THINKPAD COMPUTER		
MODE	**COLOR**	**MEANING**
Charging	Green	Battery fully charged
	Orange	Battery charging
	Blinking orange	Battery needs charging
Conservation	Green	Computer is in suspend mode
	Blinking green	Computer is entering suspend mode or hibernation mode, or resuming normal operation.
Status	Green	Power on

Most systems get at least 2 hours from a charge. Short battery life can present a perplexing problem—especially if you do a great deal of computing on the road. All other computer functions are assumed to be normal.

Begin your investigation by inspecting the battery pack itself. Check for any damaged batteries. Be sure that the battery pack is inserted properly into the computer, and see that its connections and wiring are clean and intact. Try replacing the battery pack. Remember that rechargeable batteries do not last forever—typical NiCd packs are usually good for about 800 cycles, NiMH packs are often suitable for 500 cycles, and Li-ion packs are usually rated for 1200 cycles. Fast-charge battery packs are subject to the greatest abuse and can suffer the shortest life spans. It is possible that one or more cells in the battery pack might have failed. The battery pack might also have developed a "memory" problem. Try several cycles of completely discharging and recharging the pack. If the problem remains, replace the battery pack.

The computer's configuration itself can largely determine the amount of running time that is available from each charge. The CPU, the display (and its backlight), the hard drive, floppy drive/CD-ROM drive access each consume substantial amounts of power. Many mobile computers are designed to shut down each major power consumer after some preset period of disuse. For example, an LCD screen might shut off if there is no keyboard activity after two minutes, or the hard drive might stop spinning after three minutes if there is no hard drive access, etc. Even reducing CPU clock speed during periods of inactivity will reduce power consumption. The amount of time required before shutdown can usually be adjusted through setup routines in the computer or through the operating system. See the previous "Conserving mobile battery power" section.

Symptom 5-9. The battery pack becomes extremely hot during charging

As you learned earlier in the chapter, current must be applied to a battery from an external source to restore battery charge. When a battery receives significant charging current (during or after the charging process), its temperature will begin to rise. Temperature rise continues as long as current is applied. If high charging current continues unabated, battery temperature might climb high enough to actually damage the cells. Even under the best circumstances, prolonged high-temperature conditions can shorten the working life of a battery pack. Today's high-current charging circuits must be carefully controlled to ensure a full, rapid battery charge, but prevent excessive temperature rise and damage.

Battery packs or compartments are fitted with a thermistor (a temperature-sensitive resistor). When the battery pack is fully charged, the thermistor responds to the subsequent temperature increase and signals charging circuitry to reduce or stop its charging current. In this way, temperature is used to detect when full charge had been reached. It is normal for most battery packs to become a bit warm during the charging process—especially packs that use fast-charge currents. However, the cell(s) should not give off an obnoxious odor or become too hot to touch. Hot batteries are likely to be damaged. In many cases, the thermistor (or thermistor's signal-conditioning circuitry) has failed and is no longer shutting down charge current. Try another battery pack. If the new pack also becomes very hot, the fault is in the charging circuit, which should be replaced. If the new pack remains cooler, the fault is probably in the original battery pack.

Symptom 5-10. The computer quits without producing a low-battery warning

Computers are rarely subtle in regard to low-power warnings. Once a battery pack falls below a certain voltage threshold, the computer initiates a series of unmistakable audible (and sometimes visual) queues that tell you there are only minutes of power remaining. Such a warning affords you a last-minute opportunity to save your work and switch over to ac power, if possible. If you choose to ignore a low-power warning, the system will soon reach a minimum working level and crash on its own—whether you like it or not.

Mobile computers measure their battery voltage levels constantly. A custom IC on the motherboard is typically given the task of watching over battery voltage. When voltage falls below a fixed preset level, the detector IC produces a logic alarm signal. The alarm, in turn, drives an interrupt to the CPU, or passes the signal to a power-management IC, which then deals with the CPU or system controller. Once the alarm condition reaches the CPU, the computer typically initiates a series of tones, flashes a "power" LED, or sometimes both (see Table 5-2).

Most PCs produce at least one beep during initialization to test the internal speaker. If you do not hear this beep, the speaker or its driving circuit might be damaged. Try replacing the speaker, then try replacing the motherboard. When an audible beep is heard during initialization, there is probably a fault in the computer's battery-detection or power-management circuits. Try cleaning the battery contacts first, then try replacing the motherboard.

Battery Recycling

Most types of batteries use metals and electrolyte chemicals, which are harmful to the environment. As a consequence, many states and provinces have enacted legislation that prohibits the dumping or discarding of batteries (especially lead-acid, NiCd, and alkaline). NiMH and lithium batteries are somewhat less toxic, but can also often be recycled. To help support a cleaner environment, many vendors who sell PC batteries are accepting returns of the old defective batteries, which are then recycled. For example, IBM supports the Reusable Battery Recycling Center (at 770-984-0708). 1-800-Batteries (another major battery vendor) accepts returns (at 408-879-1930).

Further Study

That concludes Chapter 5. Be sure to review the glossary and chapter questions on the accompanying CD. If you have access to the Internet, point your Web browser to some of these contacts:

Direct Power: **http://www.dpp.com/index.html**

1-800-BATTERIES: **http://www.800batteries.com/index2.html**

Duracell: **http://www.duracell.com/**

Energizer: **http://www.energizer.com/**

Tadiran: **http://www.tadiranbat.com/**

Rayovac: **http://www.rayovac.com/**

6

BIOS

CONTENTS AT A GLANCE

A Look Inside the Motherboard BIOS
  POST
  Setup
  System service routines

BIOS Features
  Determining features from BIOS ID
    strings

BIOS and Boot Sequences
  American megatrends
  Phoenix technologies

Bios Shortcomings and Compatibility Issues
  Device drivers
  "Flash" laziness
  BIOS shadowing
  Direct control
  BIOS bugs
  The year 2000 (Y2K) problem

Troubleshooting BIOS Error Messages
  General bios error messages
  pci error messages

Further Study

Although every personal computer uses the same essential sub-assemblies, each sub-assembly is designed a bit differently. This is especially true of the processing components contained on a motherboard—this is understandable, given the tremendous speed at which PC components and technology are advancing. Unfortunately, variations in hardware make it difficult to use a single standard operating system. Instead of tailoring an operating system (and applications) to specific computers, a *Basic Input/Output System (BIOS)* is added on ROM ICs to provide an interface between the raw PC hardware and the standardized operating system—BIOS gives an OS access to a standard set of functions. As a result, every system uses a slightly different BIOS, but each BIOS contains the same set of functions which an OS can interface to. This chapter explains the internal workings of a typical BIOS, illustrates some means of identifying BIOS versions, and shows you the many features that a modern BIOS must support.

Of course, BIOS is not limited solely to the motherboard, although most BIOS versions carry enough routines to support video and drive-controller operations—in addition to other motherboard features. But, what happens when a new video card is developed that the system BIOS does not know how to work with or when an advanced drive-controller board becomes available? It is common in computer design to include a BIOS ROM for major sub-systems, such as video and drive control. One of the early steps of system initialization is to check for the presence of other valid BIOS ROMs located in upper memory (between 640KB and 1024KB). These are usually referred to as "expansion" or *adapter BIOS*. When another BIOS is located, it is also checksum-tested and used by the PC. In general, a PC can be fitted with up to five or more BIOS ROMs:

■ System (motherboard) BIOS
■ Video BIOS
■ Drive-controller BIOS
■ Network-adapter board BIOS
■ SCSI-adapter BIOS

A Look Inside the Motherboard BIOS

The typical BIOS ROM occupies 128KB of space in the system's *Upper Memory Area (UMA)* from E0000h to FFFFFh (within the PC's first MB of memory). Contrary to popular belief, BIOS is not a single program, but an arsenal of individual programs—most quite small. In general, BIOS contains three sections (Fig. 6-1): the POST, the CMOS setup routine, and the System services routines. The particular section of BIOS code that is executed depends on the computer's state, and its activities at any given moment.

POST

Although many novice technicians are aware that POST checks the system, few are aware that POST actually manages the entire system startup. The Power-On Self-Test handles

FIGURE 6-1 The main sections of a typical BIOS.

virtually all of the initialization activities for a PC. POST performs a low-level diagnostic and reliability test of the main processing components—including ROM programs and system RAM. It tests the CPU, initializes the motherboard's chipset, checks the 128 bytes of CMOS for system-configuration data, and sets up an index of interrupt vectors for the CPU from 0000h to 02FFh. POST then sets up a BIOS Stack Area from 0300h to 03FFh, loads the BIOS Data Area (BDA) in low memory 0400h to 04FFh, detects any optional equipment (adapter BIOS ROMs) in the system, and proceeds to boot the operating system.

SETUP

The hardware configuration for any given computer is maintained in a small amount of CMOS RAM, and a CMOS setup routine is required in order for you to access the system's configuration. Older i286 and i386 systems provided the CMOS setup routine as a separate utility included with the system on a floppy disk. In most cases, the "setup disk" was promptly misplaced or discarded. Starting with late-model i386 and later systems, the CMOS setup routine has been integrated into the motherboard BIOS itself. The actual CMOS setup program can vary tremendously between system manufacturers and motherboards, so there is no one standard for just what settings can be controlled or where those entries are located. Check Chapter 9 for a detailed discussion of typical CMOS entries and their meanings.

SYSTEM SERVICE ROUTINES

The *system services* (also referred to as *BIOS services*) are a set of individual functions that form the layer between hardware and the operating system. Services are called through the use of interrupts. An interrupt essentially causes the CPU to stop whatever it was working on and sends program control to another address in memory, which usually starts a subroutine designed specifically to deal with the particular interrupt. When the interrupt-handling routine is complete, the CPU's original state is restored, and control is returned to where the PC left off before the interrupt occurred. A wide range of interrupts can attract the attention of a CPU, and interrupts can be produced from three major sources: the CPU itself, a hardware condition, and a software condition. Table 6-1 lists 56 standard interrupts found in a typical BIOS. Remember that the BIOS used in your particular system might offer more or fewer functions, depending on its vintage.

TABLE 6-1 SUMMARY OF BIOS SERVICES

INT CODE	TYPE	SERVICE DESCRIPTION
00h	Processor	Divide by zero
01h	Processor	Single step
02h	Processor	Non-maskable interrupt (NMI)
03h	Processor	Breakpoint
04h	Processor	Arithmetic overflow
05h	Software	Print screen
06h	Processor	Invalid op-code

TABLE 6-1 SUMMARY OF BIOS SERVICES (CONTINUED)

INT CODE	TYPE	SERVICE DESCRIPTION
07h	Processor	Co-processor not available
08h	Hardware	System-timer service routine
09h	Hardware	Keyboard-device service routine
0Ah	Hardware	Cascade from 2nd programmable interrupt controller
0Bh	Hardware	Serial-port service (COM2)
0Ch	Hardware	Serial-port service (COM1)
0Dh	Hardware	Parallel-printer service (LPT2)
0Eh	Hardware	Floppy-disk drive service
0Fh	Hardware	Parallel-printer service (LPT1)
10h	Software	Video service routine
11h	Software	Equipment-list service routine
12h	Software	Memory-size service routine
13h	Software	Hard-disk drive service
14h	Software	Serial-communication service routines
15h	Software	System-services support routines
16h	Software	Keyboard-support service routines
17h	Software	Parallel-printer support services
18h	Software	Load and run ROM BASIC
19h	Software	DOS loading routine
1Ah	Software	Real-time clock service routines
1Bh	Software	<CTRL><BREAK> service routine
1Ch	Software	User timer service routines
1Dh	Software	Video-control parameter table
1Eh	Software	Floppy-disk parameter table
1Fh	Software	Video-graphics character table
20h–3Fh	Software	DOS interrupt points
40h	Software	Floppy-disk revector routine
41h	Software	Hard-disk drive C: parameter table
42h	Software	EGA-default video driver
43h	Software	Video graphic characters
44h	Software	Novell NetWare API
45h	Software	Not used
46h	Software	Hard-disk drive D: parameter table
47h–49h	Software	Not used
4Ah	Software	User alarm
4Bh–63h	Software	Not used
64h	Software	Novell NetWare IPX
65h–66h	Software	Not used
67h	Software	EMS support routines
68h–6Fh	Software	Not used
70h	Hardware	Real-time clock
71h	Hardware	Redirect interrupt cascade

TABLE 6-1   SUMMARY OF BIOS SERVICES (CONTINUED)

INT CODE	TYPE	SERVICE DESCRIPTION
72h–74h	Hardware	Reserved, do not use
75h	Hardware	Math co-processor exception
76h	Hardware	Hard disk support
77h	Hardware	Suspend request
78h–79h	Software	Not used
7Ah	Software	Novell NewWare API
78h–BFh	Software	Not used

Interrupts produced by the CPU itself (known as *processor interrupts*) are often the result of an unusual, unexpected, or erroneous program result. For example, if a program tries to divide a number by zero, the CPU will generate INT 00h, which causes a "Divide by zero" error message. There are five processor interrupts (00h to 04h).

The hardware interrupts are generated when a device is in need of the CPU's attention to perform a certain task. Hardware interrupts are invoked by asserting a logic level on a physical interrupt request (IRQ) line. The CPU suspends its activities and executes the interrupt-handling routine. When the interrupt handler is finished, the CPU resumes normal operation. For example, each time a keyboard key is pressed, the keyboard buffer asserts a logic line corresponding to INT 09h (IRQ 1). This invokes a keyboard-handling routine. PC/AT-compatible systems typically provide 16 hardware interrupts (IRQ 0 to IRQ 15), which correspond to INT 08h to 0Fh and 70h to 77h, respectively.

Software interrupts are generated when a hardware device must be checked or manipulated by the PC. The *Print screen* function is a prime example of a software interrupt. When the *Print screen* button is pressed on the keyboard, an INT 05h is generated. The interrupt routine dumps the contents of its video character buffer to the printer port.

BIOS Features

PC technology is constantly advancing in CPU's, chipsets, memory, video, drives, etc. As the hardware continues to advance, the BIOS must also advance to keep pace with the resources emerging on today's systems. As a result, it is important for you to recognize the key features that are included in a modern BIOS. You do not need to understand the details of each feature right now, but you should at least recognize a "current" BIOS by reviewing its feature set. Table 6-2 lists the specifications for an Award Software EliteBIOS. The feature set for Mr. BIOS (Microid Research) is shown in Table 6-3. Although many of the features listed in Tables 6-2 and 6-3 might seem a bit incidental, the core features of a modern BIOS can be broken down into several major areas:

■ *CPU support* BIOS should support a rich range of CPUs, preferably from such CPU makers as Intel, AMD, and Cyrix. Look for Pentium, Pentium MMX, Pentium Pro, and Pentium II support (although one BIOS will probably not support all of these CPU families).

■ *Chipset support* The BIOS should support the latest chipset families (such as Intel's 430TX chipset). Chipset support is crucial because it allows motherboard designers to implement other features, such as USB and advanced memory.

■ *Memory support* The BIOS should be able to auto-size and support the most modern forms of memory (i.e., EDO and SDRAM). Memory error checking (parity and ECC) should also be supported.

■ *ACPI/APM support* The BIOS should be fully compliant with the *Advanced Configuration and Power Interface (ACPI)* specification (revision 1.0), and supports APM BIOS specifications through version 1.2. Power management is important for mobile systems, and is widely used in desktop/tower systems to reduce energy waste.

■ *Drive support* The BIOS must support large EIDE/Ultra-ATA hard drives (over 1024 cylinders) with very fast data-transfer modes, such as PIO Modes 0-4 and Ultra DMA/33.

■ *PC 97 support* The BIOS should be compliant with the current Microsoft PC 97 BIOS requirements.

■ *I2O support* The BIOS might support I2O (Intelligent I/O), which allows the dynamic assignment of ports and resources for I/O devices in the PC.

■ *Boot versatility support* The BIOS should be able to boot from a number of different drives, and include the BIOS Boot Specification for *Initial Program Load (IPL) devices*. This currently supports booting from up to four IDE drives (including CD-ROM drives), SCSI drives, and network cards.

■ *Plug-and-Play support* The BIOS must detect and configure PnP devices during POST. The BIOS also communicates with Windows 95 to determine system resources. Support of Microsoft's AML permits compatibility with PnP capability in future Windows operating systems (such as Windows 98/NT).

■ *PCI support* The BIOS must support Intel's Peripheral Component Interconnect (PCI) bus specification (version 2.1), including PCI-to-PCI and PCI-to-ISA bridging.

■ *USB support* The BIOS should support both Universal and Open HCI standards. It should maintain full core compatibility and providing Legacy support for USB hardware and multi-layered USB hubs.

TABLE 6-2 AWARD ELITEBIOS FEATURES

Industy-Standards Support	ACPI, PCI, DMI, USB, EISA, VUMA
	Plug and Play
	PC Card (PCMCIA)
	Legacy PC adapters
CPU Support	Intel, AMD, Cyrix, IBM, and TI
	Low-power SMM & SMI
	Multiple processors (SMP)
Chipset Support	ACC, ALI, Intel, OPTi, PicoPower, SiS, UMC, and VIA
Bus Support	PCI, ISA, EISA, and VLB
	PCI-to-PCI & PCI-to-ISA bridging
Power Management	ACPI 1.0, APM 1.2
Plug-and-Play	Resource allocation for PCI & PnP/Legacy ISA

TABLE 6-2 AWARD ELITEBIOS FEATURES (CONTINUED)

Operating System Support	DOS/Windows 3.x Windows 95/NT OS/2 Warp Novell NetWare SCO UNIX
Flash Support	Boot block BIOS for fault recovery
Drive Support	HDD/FDD and CD-ROM ATAPI Selectable boot drive options, including CD-ROM, LS-120, SCSI, and Iomega ZIP drives Auto-IDE detection "Fast" DMA and Ultra DMA support EIDE PIO modes 0–4 Hard drives over 8.4 GB supported
Memory Management	RAM support up to 4 GB Auto-memory chipset sizing Auto-sizing for cache mapping System and video BIOS shadowing Memory parity check ECC support
Additional Support	Bus-mastering support Fast gate A20 support PS/2-style mouse support Combo-I/O controller support HDD LBA-mode support
Security Support	Boot-sector virus protection Multi-level password protection

TABLE 6-3 MICROID RESEARCH MR. BIOS FEATURES

Password Security	Setup only Powerup/setup Bootup/setup H/W switch master override
Boot Sequence	Boot any drive A-F Screen prompt or AutoSearch boot Programmable boot-delay (0–30 sec) Memory priming: full test or quick scan
Fixed Disk Support	Enhanced IDE support LBA and CHS translations EDPT table support IBM/Microsoft INT 13 Extensions 8 Disks max. (each to 137GB) Name any disk C: Boot SCSI (ahead of IDE) Fast-ATA support ATA Mode 4/5 (to 20MB/s) Built in IDE drivers (AD12, CMD, OPTI, etc.) Raid-O disk striping Data-transfer modes: 32-bit, block, polling, etc. Auto-configure IDE drives

TABLE 6-3 MICROID RESEARCH MR. BIOS FEATURES (CONTINUED)

Floppy Support	Handles over 1024 cylinders Two-user programmable drive types Built-in low-level format utility 4-floppy support: 360KB to 2.88MB 4-floppy/tape drives max. Configurable slow/fast step-rate Enhanced floppy support Name any floppy A:
Plug-and-Play Support	Auto resource steering Windows 95 compatible
ATAPI and Removal IDE Support	CD-ROM recognition SyQuest and ejectable media support
I/O Port Support	Dynamic port mapping in SETUP 4 serial, 4 parallel ports supported SPP, Bi-dir, EPP and ECP modes USB support
Power Management	APM for Windows and DOS VESA DPMS video management SMI and STPCLK, all x86's
Video Support	Automatic detection (no jumpers needed) Dual monitor management Mono-VGA compatibility
Keyboard & Mouse Support	XT, AT, PS/2 83 to 102-key keyboards supported XT/AT auto-switch compatibility Selectable boot-up NumLock state Programmable typematic rates Automatic PS/2 mouse recognition
Cache Support	586 write back support AutoDetection & AutoSizing Full SRAM/TagRAM cache testing Enable/disable via Setup utility On-the-fly hot-key cache control Cacheable/non-cache regions
Memory Support	Support Up to 4 GB View memory map in Setup Auto-scan: 256–16MB DRAMs
Shadow-RAM Support	E000,F000 (system ROMs); 64K granularity C000-DFFF (video, adapters): 16K granularity Each block: read/write or write protect Setup: view present ROMs and vacancies
Automatic Configuration Support	PCI configuration Memory wait states AT bus speed Cache wait states AutoDetection of Cyrix CPU cache XT/AT/PS2 keyboard selection

DETERMINING FEATURES FROM BIOS ID STRINGS

Ordinarily, the BIOS forms a "transparent" layer between the operating system and PC hardware—you're not even supposed to know the BIOS is there. In actuality, however, the BIOS can be a root cause of many incompatibilities and problems in the PC, and you must often be able to determine as much information about the BIOS as possible when checking for known BIOS problems or upgrades. When a PC starts and the video system is initialized, a BIOS "banner" is typically the first item to appear. The BIOS banner usually lists the BIOS manufacturer and copyright date, then provides a ID string. A great deal of information is encoded into most BIOS ID strings, and this part of the chapter will help you decode many of those cryptic ID codes.

If you simply need to extract the copyright date from your BIOS, try the BIOS.ZIP utility on the companion CD.

Older AMI BIOS AMI BIOS prior to the Hi-Flex line often used a "4/4/6" pattern of BIOS information, such as:

```
ABBB  CCCC  DDEEFF  GG
```

- **A**—*BIOS options* Particular options included with the BIOS: (D) diagnostics, (S) setup, (E) extended setup.
- **BBB**—*Chipset or motherboard code* A 3-character code used to identify the corresponding chipset or motherboard.
- **CCCC**—*Reference number* A manufacturer's license reference number.
- **DD**—*BIOS Date Month*
- **EE**—*BIOS Date Day*
- **FF**—*BIOS Date Year*
- **GG**—*Keyboard-controller version number* The BIOS and KBC must work together properly. This number indicates the KBC version designed to work with this BIOS.

AMI Hi-Flex line 1 BIOS ID strings following this format are typically associated with AMI Hi-Flex BIOS. These types of AMI BIOS used several different BIOS ID strings at boot time, and the following line is typically shown first:

```
AB  CCDD  EEEEEE  FGHIJKLM  NNOOPP  QQQQQQQQ  R
```

- **A**—*Processor type* Defines the vintage of CPU the BIOS is intended for: (0) 8088 or 8086, (1) 80286, (2) 80386, (3) 80386SX, (4) 80486, or (5) Pentium.
- **B**—*Size of BIOS* Indicates the BIOS ROM size: (0) 64KB ROM or (1) 128KB ROM.
- **CC**—*Major version number*
- **DD**—*Minor version number*
- **EEEEEE**—*Reference number* A number typically used only by the BIOS maker.
- **F**—*Halt on POST error* Details whether the POST will stop if an error is encountered or not: (0) no or (1) yes.
- **G**—*Initialize CMOS in every boot* Details whether the CMOS will be initialized at boot time: (0) no or (1) yes.
- **H**—*Block pins 22 and 23 of the keyboard controller* (0) no or (1) yes.
- **I**—*Mouse support in BIOS/keyboard controller* (0) no or (1) yes.
- **J**—*Wait for <F1> if error found* (0) no or (1) yes.
- **K**—*Display floppy error during POST* (0) no or (1) yes.
- **L**—*Display video error during POST* (0) no or (1) yes.
- **M**—*Display keyboard error during POST* (0) no or (1) yes.

- **NN**—*BIOS Date Month*
- **OO**—*BIOS Date Day*
- **PP**—*BIOS Date Year*
- **QQQQQQQQ**—*Chipset identification/BIOS name* This designation is intended to identify the chipset supported by this BIOS.
- **R**—*Keyboard-controller version number* The BIOS and KBC must work together properly. This number indicates the KBC version designed to work with this BIOS.

AMI Hi-Flex line 2 BIOS ID strings following this format are typically associated with AMI Hi-Flex BIOS. These types of AMI BIOS used several different BIOS ID strings at boot time, and the following line is typically shown second:

```
AAB  C  DDDD  EE  FF  GGGG  HH  II  JJJ
```

- **AA**—*KBC pin number* Defines the pin number used for KBC clock switching
- **B**—*KBC pin function* Defines the function performed by the KBC clock-switching pin: (H) switches clock to high speed or (L) switches clock to low speed.
- **C**—*Switching enable* Sets clock switching through chipset registers: (0) disable or (1) enable.
- **DDDD**—*Port address to switch clock high*
- **EE**—*Data value to switch clock high*
- **FF**—*Mask value to switch clock high*
- **GGGG**—*Port address to switch clock low*
- **HH**—*Data value to switch clock low*
- **II**—*Mask value to switch clock low*
- **JJJ**—*Turbo pin* The pin number for Turbo Switch input.

AMI Hi-Flex line 3 BIOS ID strings following this format are typically associated with AMI Hi-Flex BIOS. These types of AMI BIOS used several different BIOS ID strings at boot time, and the following line is typically shown third:

```
AAB  C  DDD  EE  FF  GGGG  HH  II  JJ  K  L
```

- **AA**—*Keyboard-controller pin* Designates the lines used for cache control.
- **B**—*Cache control* Indicates whether high signal on cache control pin enables or disables cache: (H) enable or (L) disable.
- **C**—*Controller signal* Indicates if the high signal if used on the keyboard controller pin: (0) false or (1) true.
- **DDD**—*Cache control through chipset registers* (0) cache control off or (1) cache control on.
- **EE**—*Port address* To enable cache through special port.
- **FF**—*Data value* To enable cache through special port.
- **GGGG**—*Mask value* To enable cache through special port.
- **HH**—*Port address* To disable cache through special port.
- **II**—*Data value* To disable cache through special port
- **JJ**—*Mask value* To disable cache through special port.
- **K**—*Pin number* For resetting the 82335 memory controller.
- **L**—*BIOS modified flag* Incremented each time BIOS is modified.

BIOS and Boot Sequences

The next step in understanding the BIOS is to recognize how it boots—the series of steps that take a PC from power-on to the point where it's loading an operating system. Each BIOS is written a bit differently, and might have more or less steps than comparable BIOS versions. This part of the chapter looks at the boot sequences for AMI and Phoenix BIOS.

AMERICAN MEGATRENDS

American Megatrends is renowned for their BIOS, PC diagnostics, and motherboards. AMI BIOS performs a fairly comprehensive suite of 24 steps to check and initialize the PC. The general AMI BIOS POST procedure is:

1 *Disable the NMI* BIOS disables the non-maskable interrupt line to the CPU. A failure here is suggestive of a problem with the CMOS RAM IC or its associated circuitry.
2 *Power-on delay* The system resets the soft and hard reset bits. A fault here indicates a problem with the keyboard-controller IC or system clock-generator IC.
3 *Initialize chipsets* BIOS initializes any particular motherboard chipsets (such as the Intel or VIA chipsets) that might be present in the system. A problem here might be caused by the BIOS, the clock-generator IC, or the chipset itself.
4 *Reset determination* The system reads the reset bits in the keyboard controller to determine whether a hard or soft reset (cold or warm boot) is required. A failure here might be caused by the BIOS or keyboard-controller IC.
5 *BIOS ROM checksum* The system performs a checksum test of ROM contents and adds a factory preset value that should make the total equal to 00h If this total does not equal 00h, the BIOS ROM is defective.
6 *Keyboard test* The system tests the keyboard controller. A fault here is likely the keyboard-controller IC.
7 *CMOS shutdown check* BIOS tests the shutdown byte in CMOS RAM, calculates the CMOS checksum, and updates the CMOS diagnostic byte. The system then initializes a small CMOS area in conventional memory and updates the date and time. A problem here is likely in the RTC/CMOS IC or the CMOS backup battery.
8 *Controller disable* BIOS now disables the DMA and IRQ controller ICs before proceeding. A fault at this point suggests trouble in the respective controller.
9 *Disable video* BIOS disables the video-controller IC. If this procedure fails, the trouble is probably in the video adapter board.
10 *Detect memory* The system proceeds to check the amount of memory available. BIOS measures system memory in 64KB blocks. A problem here might be in the memory IC(s).
11 *PIT test* BIOS tests the programmable interrupt timer (PIT) vital for memory refresh. A problem with the PIT test might reflect a fault in the PIT IC or in the RTC IC.
12 *Check memory refresh* BIOS now uses the PIT to try refreshing memory. A failure indicates that the problem is with the PIT IC.
13 *Check low address lines* The system checks the first 16 address lines controlling the first 64KB of RAM. A problem with this test typically means a fault in an address line.

14 *Check low 64KB RAM* The system now checks the first 64KB of system RAM. This is vital because this area must hold information that is crucial for system initialization. A problem here is usually the result of a bad RAM IC.

15 *Initialize support ICs* BIOS proceeds to initialize the *Programmable Interrupt Timer (PIT)*, the *Programmable Interrupt Controller (PIC)*, and the *Direct Memory-Access (DMA)* ICs. A fault here would be located in one of those locations.

16 *Load INT vector table* BIOS loads the system's interrupt vector table into the first 2KB of system RAM.

17 *Check the KeyBoard Controller (KBC)* BIOS reads the keyboard-controller buffer at I/O port 60h. A problem here indicates a fault in the keyboard-controller IC.

18 *Video tests* The system checks for the type of video adapter in use, then tests and initializes the video memory and adapter. A problem with this test typically indicates a fault with the video memory or adapter, respectively. After a successful video test, the video system will be operational.

19 *Load the BDA* The system now loads the *BIOS Data Area (BDA)* into conventional memory.

20 *Test memory* BIOS checks all memory below 1MB. A problem here is typically the fault of one or more RAM ICs, the keyboard-controller IC, or a bad data line.

21 *Check DMA registers* BIOS performs a register-level check of the DMA controller(s) using binary test patterns. A problem here is often caused by a failure of the DMA IC(s).

22 *Check the keyboard* The system performs a final check of the keyboard interface. An error at this point is usually the fault of the keyboard.

23 *Perform high-level tests* This step involves a whole suite of tests that check such high-level devices as the floppy and hard disks, serial adapters, parallel adapters, mouse adapter, etc. The number and complexity of these tests vary with the BIOS version. When an error occurs, a corresponding text message will be displayed. If the system hardware does not match the setup shown in the CMOS setup, a corresponding error code will be displayed.

24 *Load the OS* At this point, BIOS triggers INT 19h, which is the routine that loads an operating system. An error here generally results in an error message, such as "Non-system disk."

PHOENIX TECHNOLOGIES

Phoenix Technologies is one of the premier BIOS manufacturers for IBM-compatible PCs. Phoenix is known for their extensive POST and versatility with OEMs. A typical Phoenix BIOS performs essentially the same steps as an AMI BIOS, but the several variations are:

1 *Check the CPU* The registers and control lines of the CPU are checked. Any problems will usually be the result of a faulty CPU or clock IC.

2 *Test CMOS RAM* The CMOS IC is tested. A fault is usually caused by a failure of the RTC/CMOS IC.

3 *BIOS ROM checksum* A checksum is performed on the BIOS ROM. If the calculated checksum does not match the factory-set value, an error is generated. A checksum problem is typically the result of a faulty BIOS ROM. Try replacing the BIOS ROM.

4 *Test chipset(s)* The system checks any chipsets (such as the Intel or VIA chipsets) for proper operation with the BIOS. A problem here is typically caused by a fault in the chipset. Replace the motherboard.

5 *Test PIT* The *Programmable Interrupt Controller (PIT)* is tested to ensure that all interrupt requests are handled properly. A problem here indicates that the PIT IC is defective.

6 *Test DMA* The *Direct Memory Access (DMA)* controller is tested next. A fault at this point is typically caused by the CPU, the DMA IC, or an address-line problem.

7 *Test base 64KB memory* BIOS checks the lowest 64KB of system RAM. A problem here is caused by a fault in memory, or an address-line problem.

8 *Check serial and parallel ports* The system checks the presence of serial- and parallel-port hardware, and I/O data areas are assigned for any devices found.

9 *Test PIC* The *Programmable Interrupt Controller (PIC)* is tested to see that proper interrupt levels can be generated. A problem here is typically caused by a fault in the PIC IC.

10 *Check KeyBoard Controller (KBC)* The keyboard controller IC is tested for proper operation. If a problem occurs, the keyboard controller is likely defective.

11 *Verify CMOS data* Data within the CMOS is checked for validity. If the extended area returns a failure, CMOS data has probably been setup incorrectly. However, continuous failures typically represent a faulty RTC/CMOS IC.

12 *Verify video system* Video RAM is tested, then the video controller is located, tested, and initialized. A fault is usually the result of a defective video controller. If the controller is located on an expansion board, try replacing the video board.

13 *Test RTC* The *Real-Time Clock (RTC)* is tested next and each frequency output is verified. A problem here is usually caused by a fault in the RTC, PIT, or system crystal.

14 *Test CPU in protected mode* The CPU is switched to protected mode and returned to POST at the point indicated in CMOS RAM offset 0Fh. When this step fails, the CPU, keyboard-controller IC, CMOS IC, or address line(s) might be at fault.

15 *Verify PIC 2* Counter #2 is tested on the PIC IC. If this test fails, the PIC IC is likely defective.

16 *Check NMI* The NMI is checked to be sure it is active. A problem here often indicates trouble with the CMOS IC, but it could also reflect problems in the BIOS ROM, PIC IC, or CPU.

17 *Check the keyboard* The keyboard buffer and controller are checked

18 *Check the mouse* BIOS initializes the mouse (if present) through the keyboard controller. A fault is usually caused in the mouse-adapter circuit.

19 *Check system RAM* All remaining system RAM is tested in 64KB blocks. Trouble usually means a defective memory IC.

20 *Test disk controller* Fixed- and floppy-disk controllers are checked using standard BIOS calls. Problems here are usually the result of defective controllers or faulty drives. If the controllers are installed on expansion boards, you can try replacing the respective expansion board.

21 *Set shadow RAM areas* The system looks at CMOS to find which ROM(s) will be shadowed into RAM. Problems here are often caused by a faulty adapter ROM or problems in RAM.

22 *Check extended ROMs* BIOS looks for signatures of 55AAh in memory which indicate the presence of additional ROMs. The system then performs a checksum test on each ROM. A problem with this step generally indicates trouble with the extended ROM or related adapter circuitry.

23 *Test cache controller* The external cache-controller IC is tested. A problem is usually caused by a fault in the cache-controller IC itself or by a defect in cache memory.

24 *Test CPU cache* The internal cache present in the CPU is tested. A problem here is almost always caused by a CPU fault.

25 *Check hardware adapters* BIOS proceeds to check the high-level sub-systems, such as the video system, floppy disk, hard disk, I/O adapters, serial ports, and parallel ports. Problems usually reflect a fault with the respective adapter or with an invalid CMOS setup.

26 *Load the OS* At this point, BIOS triggers INT 19h which is the routine that loads an operating system. An error here generally results in an error message, such as "Non-system disk."

BIOS Shortcomings and Compatibility Issues

No matter how much time and effort are put into BIOS development, there are still many times when BIOS can come up short. Before you start troubleshooting, you should have an understanding of the places where BIOS is weakest.

DEVICE DRIVERS

As you might expect, no BIOS can possibly address every piece of hardware in the PC marketplace or keep pace with the rapid advances of those devices that a BIOS does support. As a result, PC designers have devised a way to augment BIOS through the use of device drivers. Traditional CD-ROMs are an excellent example. A number of CD-ROM designs are in use today—each CD-ROM and their corresponding adapter board use their own (often proprietary) circuitry to operate the drive and interface it to the PC bus. Neither the CD-ROM application, DOS, or BIOS are capable of identifying the drive or interface. To get around this, a low-level device driver is loaded into conventional memory from disk once the PC initializes. The low-level device driver translates a set of standard DOS calls into the instructions necessary to operate the adapter and drive. An extension of DOS (MSCDEX for MS-DOS-based systems) is also loaded into memory after the low-level driver. The DOS extension works seamlessly with MSDOS.SYS to provide applications with a standard set of software-interrupt CD-ROM services. Generally speaking, device drivers all serve to supplement BIOS. Video, SCSI, and network adapters all make use of device drivers at some level.

The newest BIOS versions do support bootable CD-ROM drives, which adhere to the "El Torito" standard.

"FLASH" LAZINESS

The broad acceptance of "flash" memory allows BIOS to be reprogrammed "in-system," through the use of a downloadable program. There is no need to open the PC or exchange BIOS ICs. This offers BIOS makers a great deal of versatility in the development of new BIOS, but it can also foster an attitude of laziness. Given the astounding speed at which new developments are proliferating, BIOS makers are under a great deal of pressure to create ever-more powerful and diverse BIOS. With traditional BIOS, programmers needed to create solid, well-tested code because replacing thousands of BIOS ICs in the field is an expensive and cumbersome task. Now that BIOS can be quickly updated with relatively simple software, BIOS programmers can sometimes take the "release-it-and-patch-it-later" attitude. As a rule, BIOS code is still quite solid, but you should be aware that the potential for BIOS problems and oversights are now much higher than in years past.

BIOS SHADOWING

Another problem with BIOS ICs is their inherently slow speed. BIOS is typically recorded onto "flash" ROM ICs (older BIOS used conventional ROM ICs or other programmable ROM ICs). These devices are necessary because BIOS data must be maintained even when power is removed. Unfortunately, permanent-storage ICs, such as these, have hideously slow access times (150 ns to 200 ns), when compared to the fast RAM used in today's PCs (50 ns to 70 ns). When you consider that the services stored in a BIOS ROM are used almost continuously, it is easy to see that each delay is additive—the net result is an overall reduction in PC performance.

   To overcome this limitation, it would be necessary to accelerate the access time of BIOS ROM. However, this is not too likely, given the current state of semiconductor technology, so PC designers do the next best thing: *ROM shadowing*. The process of "shadowing" basically copies ROM contents from the BIOS IC into available RAM in the upper memory area. Once the copy is complete, the system will work from the copy, rather than the original. This allows BIOS routines to take advantage of faster RAM. Not only system BIOS, but all BIOS can be shadowed. Video BIOS is particularly popular for shadowing. ROM shadowing can typically be turned on or off through the CMOS setup routine.

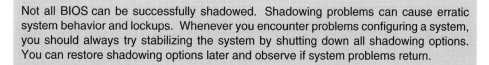

Not all BIOS can be successfully shadowed. Shadowing problems can cause erratic system behavior and lockups. Whenever you encounter problems configuring a system, you should always try stabilizing the system by shutting down all shadowing options. You can restore shadowing options later and observe if system problems return.

DIRECT CONTROL

In the race to wring every last clock-tick of performance from a PC, even the most elegantly written BIOS is simply too slow for high-performance applications. If the application could work with PC hardware directly, system performance (especially disk and video sub-systems) could be substantially improved. Writing directly to hardware is hardly new—pre-IBM PCs relied on direct application control. The use of BIOS was included by IBM to ensure that variations in PC hardware would still remain compatible with operating system and application software. As it turns out, today's PC hardware functions are remarkably standardized (even though the actual components can vary dramatically). With this broad base of relatively standard features, software developers are reviving the direct-control approach and ignoring the use of BIOS services in favor of routines written into the application. The trouble with this approach is that direct hardware control might not work on all system configurations, and any changes to the system hardware (i.e., upgrade or replacement parts) might cause the PC to malfunction when the particular application is executed.

BIOS BUGS

As with all software-based products, BIOS code is subject to accidental errors or omissions (software bugs). When BIOS is developed, it is replicated by the thousands and purchased by motherboard manufacturers who incorporate the BIOS into their motherboards. If a bug is present in the BIOS, the system will typically lock-up or crash unexpectedly, or during a certain operation. Because the same BIOS might be used in several motherboards, the bug might not manifest itself in all cases. As one example, some users of AMI BIOS (dated 04/09/90 or earlier) reported problems with the keyboard controller when running Windows or OS/2. As you can imagine, BIOS bugs are particularly frustrating. If an application contains a bug, you can turn the application off. Unfortunately, you cannot turn the BIOS off, so the only way to correct a bug in BIOS is to update the BIOS IC, "flash" the BIOS with an updated BIOS file, or replace the entire motherboard.

When investigating a customer complaint for a PC, you might wish to check with the BIOS manufacturer (through technical support, fax-back service, or CompuServe forum) and find if there have been any problems with the BIOS when used in the particular motherboard (i.e., a Phoenix BIOS in an Intel motherboard). If your symptoms match other symptoms that have been reported, a quick BIOS upgrade might save the day for your customer.

THE YEAR 2000 (Y2K) PROBLEM

The turn of the century is approaching, and with it comes a perplexing problem with file dates. Traditional OS and applications use two-digit year designations (i.e., 1998 would be shown as "98"). The problem is that not all PC hardware or applications are suitable to move into the new century because they cannot properly handle the "roll-over" of year designations such as "00" for 2000, "01" for 2001, etc. This is known as the *year 2000 problem*.

As far as the PC hardware is concerned, Y2K problems are with the *Real-Time Clock (RTC)*, and its relation to the internal DOS clock device driver (CLOCK$), which is actually a counter and not a real clock at all. You can verify if your system has an RTC problem by setting the date and time to 11:57pm (or 23:57) on December 31, 1999, and leaving the machine running to see what happens when it reaches 2000. DOS copes with the problem quite easily, but if you turn the power off and reboot, you might see a system date starting somewhere in 1980. The date 01/01/1980 is usually set if your CMOS contents are lost and 01/04/1980 is set if an out-of-range date is encountered.

The reason for this discrepancy is the interaction between the RTC and DOS clocks. The RTC is part of the CMOS RAM chip that maintains the system BIOS settings, and is kept intact by a backup battery. Some of the older RTC chips cannot keep track of the centuries by themselves, so a byte is used in the CMOS to do the job instead. Also, the RTC timing components are "trimmed" at the factory to a certain tolerance (typically, ±20 seconds a month), which will only be adhered to if the desired operating environment is maintained (i.e., temperature and humidity).

By contrast, the DOS device driver (CLOCK$) only interrogates the RTC (via the BIOS) when the machine starts, then proceeds to ignore it as long as the PC is running. The date supplied is converted to the number of days since January 1, 1980 and the number of seconds since midnight of the current day. The number of seconds since midnight is stored in the counter by the BIOS; when DOS needs to read the clock, the BIOS is called to read the counter and the number of ticks is converted back to seconds. If the counter goes past midnight, it is reset to zero by the BIOS, and the first call after that is told that the day has advanced. As a result, if more than 24 hours has elapsed between calls, there is no way that DOS can tell which day it is.

> That is why there is often a time difference between your watch and your PC at the end of the day; the system clock has to compete for attention with other devices, and is often reprogrammed by games or other applications which use it for their own timing purposes. Being interrupt driven, the system clock's accuracy depends on system activity.

As DOS operates between 1980 and 2099, it can figure out that 00 equates to 2000 (although DOS might have problems if the RTC specifically hands it a date of 1900 or any other incompatible date). In practice, the BIOS converts the date as well—some correct the time automatically at boot and supply DOS with 2000 instead of a hardware date of 1900. However, other BIOS cannot produce a date later than 1999 (i.e., Award BIOS 4.5G prior to November 1995 can only accept dates between 1994 and 1999).

Most new BIOS and RTC versions (released after 1996) are designed to deal with the year 2000 properly. But you will need to test older systems for rollover capability—especially as the year 2000 approaches. If your owner's manual doesn't mention this issue, and you can't call the computer manufacturer for clarification, take these steps:

■ Set the time on your computer to three minutes before midnight (23:57:00) and the date to December 31, 1999.
■ Turn your computer off and wait for five minutes.
■ Turn your computer on, booting from a "clean" floppy disk (DOS only with no CONFIG.SYS or AUTOEXEC.BAT files). Check the date.
■ If the date is correct, you're all set.
■ If the date is incorrect, try entering the correct date in CMOS setup (remember to exit saving your changes), then reboot the system. If the new dates hold after adjusting the CMOS setup, you're all set.
■ If the date is still incorrect after a reboot or if you find that you need to reset the system date every day, you'll need to upgrade the system BIOS.
■ If the date problems persist after upgrading the BIOS, you might need a new RTC (or upgrade the motherboard).

> Even if the BIOS and RTC are functioning properly for Y2K service, the operating system and applications must also be written to support dates after January 1, 2000.

Troubleshooting BIOS Error Messages

You've got to be familiar with the myriad of error messages that a system can generate. Each time you start the PC, the *Power-On Self Test (POST)* initiates a comprehensive series of tests to verify the computer's hardware. Traditionally, the POST generates two types or error messages: beep codes, and POST codes. Beep codes are generated through the PC speaker before the video system has properly initialized. POST codes are single-byte hexadecimal characters written to I/O port 80h (or other I/O port) as each POST test is started. You can read the POST code using a POST reader card. By matching the beep code or POST code to your particular BIOS, you can determine the exact fault. See Chapter 15 for a comprehensive set of error codes.

The problem with beep codes and POST codes are their cryptic nature—you need a detailed code listing to match the code to the fault. However, current generations of BIOS and operating systems are starting to use more "user-friendly" error messages. By displaying complete error messages (rather than simple codes), a great deal of guesswork is removed from the troubleshooting process. Remember that BIOS error messages are designed to enhance (rather than replace) beep and POST codes. Also notice that unlike beep codes and POST codes, many BIOS error messages are not fatal—that is, the system will continue to run after the error has been generated.

GENERAL BIOS ERROR MESSAGES

The following list outlines many of the most common BIOS error messages, explains their intended meaning, and suggests some corrective action. The list is a compilation developed from a variety of different systems and is presented in alphabetical order.

Symptom 6-1. 8042 Gate—A20 error There is a fault using gate A20 to access memory over 1MB. One or more SIMMs might be loose or the keyboard controller might have failed. Check that each of the SIMMs are installed securely. Try replacing the keyboard controller or replace the entire motherboard, if necessary.

Symptom 6-2. BIOS ROM checksum error—system halted The checksum of the BIOS code in the BIOS chip is incorrect—this is a fatal problem, indicating the BIOS code might have become corrupt. You will need to replace the motherboard BIOS before the system will initialize.

Symptom 6-3. Cache memory bad, do not enable cache POST has determined that your cache memory is defective. Do not attempt to enable the cache in your system. You should replace the cache RAM at your earliest opportunity. Until then, you might notice a decline in system performance.

Symptom 6-4. CMOS battery failed The CMOS battery is no longer functional. You will need to replace the CMOS battery as soon as possible. If you haven't yet lost CMOS contents, take a <PrintScreen> of each CMOS setup page immediately to record the setup configuration.

Symptom 6-5. CMOS battery state low The CMOS battery power is getting low. Record your CMOS settings as soon as possible, then replace the CMOS battery promptly.

Symptom 6-6. CMOS checksum error—defaults loaded CMOS RAM has become corrupt, so the CMOS checksum is incorrect. The system loads the default equipment configuration in an effort to ensure that the system can start. This error might have been caused by a weak battery. Check the CMOS backup battery and replace it, if necessary.

Symptom 6-7. CMOS display type mismatch The video type indicated in CMOS RAM is not the one detected by the BIOS. Check your CMOS setup and be sure that the correct video type is selected (usually "VGA"). Remember to save your changes before exiting and rebooting.

Symptom 6-8. CMOS memory size mismatch The amount of memory recorded in the CMOS setup configuration does not match the memory detected by the POST. If you have added new memory, start your CMOS setup and make the appropriate corrections (or simply "save changes and reboot"—even though you change nothing). If you've made no changes to the system, try rebooting the computer. If the error appears again, some of your memory might have failed. Try a systematic replacement to locate a defective SIMM.

Symptom 6-9. CMOS system options not set The values stored in CMOS RAM are either corrupted or nonexistent. Check your CMOS backup battery and replace it if necessary. Enter the CMOS setup routine and reload any missing or corrupted entries. Remember to save your changes before exiting and rebooting.

Symptom 6-10. CPU at nnn Displays the running speed of the CPU (where *nnn* is the speed in MHz). This is not an error, but a measurement. If the displayed speed is known to be different than the actual clock speed, you should check the motherboard's clock settings and multipliers, or suspect an error in BIOS speed detection (you might need to update the BIOS).

Symptom 6-11. Data error The diskette or hard-disk drive that you are accessing cannot read the data. One or more sectors on the disk(ette) might be corrupted. If you are using MS-DOS, run the CHKDSK or ScanDisk utility to check the file structure of the diskette or hard-disk drive.

Symptom 6-12. Decreasing available memory An error has been detected in memory and the "available memory" is being reduced below the point at which the fault was detected. Either a SIMM has failed or one or more SIMMs might be improperly seated.

Symptom 6-13. Diskette drive 0 (or 1) seek failure Your floppy drive was unable to seek to the desired track. A cable might be loose, or the CMOS setup information might not match your actual floppy drive. Check your CMOS setup, check your signal cable, and replace the floppy drive, if necessary.

Symptom 6-14. Diskette read failure The system was unable to read from a floppy disk. This is usually caused by a dirty read/write heads, a loose signal cable, or a defective floppy disk. Try cleaning the read/write heads, try a different diskette, check the floppy signal cable, and replace the floppy drive, if necessary.

Symptom 6-15. Diskette subsystem reset failed The PC was unable to access the floppy-drive system. The diskette drive controller might be faulty. Be sure that the drive controller is seated properly in its bus slot and that all cables are attached securely. Try the drive controller in another slot and replace the drive controller, if necessary.

Symptom 6-16. Display switch is set incorrectly Some motherboards provide a display switch that can be set to either monochrome or color. This message indicates the switch is set to a different setting than indicated in CMOS setup. Determine which video setting is correct, then either turn off the system and change the motherboard jumper, or enter CMOS setup and change the video selection.

Symptom 6-17. DMA (or DMA #1 or DMA #2) error A serious fault has occurred in the DMA-controller system of your motherboard. In virtually all cases, the motherboard will have to be replaced (unless you can replace the DMA controller).

Symptom 6-18. DMA bus time-out A device has driven the bus signal for more than 7.8 microseconds. This might be a random fault, but chances are that a device in the PC has failed. Try removing expansion devices first. Otherwise, replace the motherboard.

Symptom 6-19. Drive not ready No diskette is in the drive. Be sure that the valid diskette is secure in the drive before continuing.

Symptom 6-20. Floppy disk(s) fail The PC cannot find or initialize the floppy-drive controller or the floppy drive itself. Be sure that the drive controller is installed correctly (you might try a different expansion slot). If no floppy drives are installed, be sure that the *Diskette drive* entries in CMOS setup are set to *None* or *Not installed*.

Symptom 6-21. Hard-disk configuration error The system could not initialize the hard drive in the expected fashion. This is often caused by an incorrect configuration in the CMOS setup. Be sure that the correct hard-drive geometry is entered for the drive (or try "auto-detecting" the drive). If the problem persists, try replacing the hard drive.

Symptom 6-22. Hard-disk controller failure There is a problem with the hard-drive system—either the hard drive or drive controller has failed. Check the drive controller first and be sure it's seated properly in its bus slot. Try a different bus slot. Check that all the drive cables are secure. Be sure that the hard drive is spinning up. Try a new drive controller and try a different hard drive, if necessary.

Symptom 6-23. Hard disk(s) diagnosis fail Your BIOS might run specific disk diagnostic routines. This type of message appears if one or more hard disks return an error when those diagnostics are run. In most cases, the drive itself is installed improperly or is defective. Check the drive installation, and replace the drive, if necessary.

Symptom 6-24. Hard disk failure The hard drive failed initialization, which usually suggests that the drive has failed. Be sure that the drive signal cable is attached properly, and see that the drive spins up, then replace the hard drive, if necessary.

Symptom 6-25. Hard-disk drive read failure The drive cannot read from the hard drive, which usually suggests that the drive has failed. Be sure that the drive signal cable is attached properly and see that the drive spins up, then replace the hard drive, if necessary.

Symptom 6-26. Incompatible processor: CPU0 (or CPU1) is B0 step or below You have installed an old version of a CPU that is not supported by the BIOS. In a single-microprocessor system, *CPU0* refers to the system board microprocessor; in a dual-microprocessor system, it refers to the secondary microprocessor on the add-in card. The CPU1 message appears only on a dual-microprocessor system and it always refers to the system-board microprocessor. Replace the microprocessor with a current version of the microprocessor.

Symptom 6-27. Incompatible processors: cache sizes different This message appears for a dual-microprocessor system if the CPUs use differing L2 cache sizes. Replace one of the microprocessors to make the L2 cache sizes match.

Symptom 6-28. Insert bootable media The BIOS cannot find a bootable media. Insert a bootable floppy diskette or bootable CD, or switch to a known-good bootable drive.

Symptom 6-29. INTR #1 (or INTR #2) error A serious fault has occurred with your interrupt controller on the motherboard. In virtually all cases, the motherboard will have to be replaced entirely.

Symptom 6-30. Invalid boot diskette The BIOS can read the disk in floppy drive A:, but cannot boot the system from it. Use another known-good boot disk or try booting from a different drive.

Symptom 6-31. Invalid configuration information—please run SETUP program The system-configuration information in your CMOS setup does not match the hardware configuration detected by the POST. Enter the CMOS setup program and correct the system configuration information. Remember to save your changes before exiting and rebooting.

Symptom 6-32. I/O card parity error at xxxxx An expansion card failed. If the address can be determined, it is displayed as *xxxxx*. If not, the message is "I/O card parity error ????" In either case, you'll need to find and replace the defective expansion card.

Symptom 6-33. Keyboard clock-line failure BIOS has not detected the keyboard clock signal when testing the keyboard. Often, the keyboard connector is loose or the keyboard is defective. Check the keyboard cable and try another keyboard, if necessary. If the problem persists, the keyboard controller might have failed. Try replacing the keyboard-controller IC or replace the entire motherboard.

Symptom 6-34. Keyboard controller failure The keyboard controller on the motherboard is not responding as expected. Start by checking the keyboard connection and try a different keyboard. If the problem persists, the keyboard controller might have failed. Try replacing the keyboard-controller IC or replace the entire motherboard.

Symptom 6-35. Keyboard data-line failure BIOS has not detected the keyboard data signal when testing the keyboard. Often, the keyboard connector is loose or the keyboard is defective. Check the keyboard cable and try another keyboard, if necessary. If the problem persists, the keyboard controller might have failed. Try replacing the keyboard-controller IC or replace the entire motherboard.

Symptom 6-36. Keyboard error or no keyboard present The system cannot initialize the keyboard. Be sure that the keyboard is attached correctly and see that no keys are pressed during POST. To purposely configure the system without a keyboard (i.e., if you're setting up a server), you can configure the CMOS setup to ignore the keyboard.

Symptom 6-37. Keyboard is locked out—unlock the key If your system comes fitted with a key lock switch, be sure that the switch is set to the "unlocked" position. If there is no key lock switch (or the switch is set properly), one or more keys might be pressed or shorted on the keyboard. Try a new keyboard.

Symptom 6-38. Keyboard stuck key failure In almost all cases, this is a keyboard problem. POST has determined that one or more keys on the keyboard are stuck. Be sure that nothing is resting on the keyboard and see that no paper clips or staples have fallen into the keyboard. Try a different keyboard.

Symptom 6-39. Memory address line failure at <address>, read <value> expecting <value> An error has occurred in the address decoding circuitry used in memory. In many cases, one or more SIMMs might be improperly seated. Check that all SIMMs are installed correctly. If the problem continues, try systematic replacement to locate a defective SIMM. If you cannot find a defective SIMM, there is likely a problem elsewhere on the motherboard. Replace the motherboard.

Symptom 6-40. Memory data line failure at <address>, read <value> expecting <value> An error has been encountered in memory. In virtually all cases, one or more SIMMs might be faulty or improperly seated. Be sure that every SIMM is seated correctly and try a systematic replacement to locate a defective SIMM.

Symptom 6-41. Memory double word logic failure at <address>, read <value> expecting <value> An error has been encountered in memory. In virtually all cases, one or more SIMMs might be faulty or improperly seated. Be sure that every SIMM is seated correctly and try a systematic replacement to locate a defective SIMM.

Symptom 6-42. Memory odd/even logic failure at <address>, read <value> expecting <value> An error has been encountered in memory. In virtually all cases, one or more SIMMs might be faulty or improperly seated. Be sure that every SIMM is seated correctly and try a systematic replacement to locate a defective SIMM.

Symptom 6-43. Memory parity failure at <address>, read <value> expecting <value> An error has been encountered in memory. In virtually all cases, one or more SIMMs might be faulty or improperly seated. Be sure that every SIMM is seated correctly and try a systematic replacement to locate a defective SIMM.

Symptom 6-44. Memory write/read failure at <address>, read <value> expecting <value> An error has been encountered in memory. In virtually all cases, one or more SIMMs might be faulty or improperly seated. Be sure that every SIMM is seated correctly and try a systematic replacement to locate a defective SIMM.

Symptom 6-45. Memory size in CMOS invalid The amount of memory recorded in the CMOS setup configuration does not match the memory detected by the POST. If you have added new memory, start your CMOS setup and make the appropriate corrections. If you've made no changes to the system, try rebooting the computer. If the error appears again, some of your memory might have failed. Try a systematic replacement to locate a defective SIMM.

Symptom 6-46. No boot device available The computer cannot find a viable diskette or hard drive—typically because the drives have not been entered properly into CMOS. Enter the CMOS setup program and configure the proper drive information. You should also verify that your diskette or hard drive has been prepared as bootable.

Symptom 6-47. No boot sector on hard-disk drive The PC is refusing to boot from the hard drive. This is usually because the drive is not configured properly. Check the CMOS setup and verify that the correct drive information has been entered (or select "auto-detect"). Also be sure to partition the drive with an active bootable partition, and format it as a bootable device. If the problem continues, try replacing the hard drive.

Symptom 6-48. No timer tick interrupt The interrupt timer on the motherboard has failed. This fatal error will probably require you to replace the motherboard.

Symptom 6-49. Non-system disk or disk error The diskette in drive A: or (your hard drive) does not have a bootable operating system installed on it. If you're booting from a floppy drive, make the diskette bootable. If you're booting from a hard drive, be sure that the drive is partitioned and formatted for bootable operation.

Symptom 6-50. Not a boot diskette There is no operating system on the diskette. Boot the computer with a diskette that contains an operating system.

Symptom 6-51. Off-board parity error A parity error is in memory installed in an expansion slot (i.e., a SIMM on the video adapter). The format is: OFF BOARD PARITY ERROR ADDR (HEX) = (XXXX), where *XXXX* is the hex address where the error occurred. Chances are that the memory installed at the error address has failed.

Symptom 6-52. On-board parity error There is a parity error in memory installed on the motherboard in one of the SIMM slots. The format is: ON BOARD PARITY ERROR ADDR (HEX) = (XXXX), where *XXXX* is the hex address where the error occurred. Chances are that the memory installed at the error address has failed.

Symptom 6-53. Override enabled—defaults loaded If the system cannot boot using the current CMOS configuration for any reason, the BIOS can override the current configuration using a set of defaults designed for the most stable, minimal-performance system operations. The CMOS might be ignored if the CMOS RAM checksum is wrong or if a critical piece of CMOS information is missing, which would otherwise cause a fatal error.

Symptom 6-54. Parity error A parity error has occurred in system memory at an unknown address. Chances are that memory has failed. Try a systematic "check and replace" approach to isolate the replace the defective memory component.

Symptom 6-55. Plug-and-Play configuration error The system has encountered a problem in trying to configure one or more expansion cards. Start the CMOS setup routine and check that any PnP options have been set correctly. If any "configuration utilities" are included with your particular system, try running those utilities to resolve any configuration issues.

Symptom 6-56. Press <TAB> to show POST screen Some system OEMs (such as Acer) might replace the normal BIOS POST display with their own proprietary display—usually a graphic logo. When the BIOS displays this message, the operator is able to switch between the OEM display and the default POST display. This can be helpful for troubleshooting purposes.

Symptom 6-57. Primary master hard disk fail POST detects an error in the primary ("master") hard drive on the primary EIDE controller channel. Doublecheck the drive's installation, jumpering, and cable connections. Otherwise, replace the drive outright.

Symptom 6-58. Primary slave hard disk fail POST detects an error in the secondary ("slave") hard drive on the primary EIDE controller channel. Doublecheck the drive's installation, jumpering, and cable connections. Otherwise, replace the drive outright.

Symptom 6-59. Resuming from disk Award BIOS offers a save-to-disk feature for notebook computers. This message might appear when the operator re-starts the system after a save-to-disk shut down. You will almost never find this type of message on a desktop or tower system.

Symptom 6-60. Secondary master hard disk fail POST detects an error in the primary ("master") hard drive on the secondary IDE controller channel. Doublecheck the drive's installation, jumpering, and cable connections. Otherwise, replace the drive outright.

Symptom 6-61. Secondary slave hard disk fail POST detects an error in the secondary ("slave") hard drive on the secondary IDE controller channel. Doublecheck the drive's installation, jumpering, and cable connections. Otherwise, replace the drive outright.

Symptom 6-62. Shutdown failure A serious fault is on the motherboard—usually associated with the CMOS RAM/RTC function. In most cases, you'll need to replace the motherboard outright.

Symptom 6-63. Terminator/processor card not installed This error occurs with dual-CPU systems when neither a "terminator" card nor a secondary microprocessor card is installed in the secondary card connector. Be sure that either a terminator card or a secondary microprocessor card is installed in the connector. Install the appropriate card and start the system again.

Symptom 6-64. Time-of-day clock stopped The *Real-Time Clock (RTC)* has stopped. The CMOS battery might be dead (or almost dead). Enter the CMOS setup and correct the date and time. If the trouble continues, try replacing the CMOS backup battery.

Symptom 6-65. Time or date in CMOS is invalid The time or date displayed in the CMOS setup does not match the system clock. This can happen often under Windows 95 (or other operating systems), which can "desynchronize" system clock. Enter the CMOS setup utility and correct the date and time. If the problem re-occurs, you might be able to determine a specific application that is causing the problem.

Symptom 6-66. Timer chip counter 2 failed A serious fault is on the motherboard—probably caused by a failure of a *Programmable Interrupt Timer (PIT)*. In most cases, you'll need to replace the motherboard outright.

Symptom 6-67. Unexpected interrupt in protected mode An interrupt has occurred unexpectedly. Loose or poorly inserted SIMMs can cause such a problem, so start by checking and reinstalling the SIMMs. A faulty keyboard controller can also result in interrupt problems. Try replacing the keyboard controller, if possible, or replace the entire motherboard.

Symptom 6-68. Warning—Thermal probes failed This error is usually found in Pentium Pro systems with one or two thermal probes. At system start-up, the BIOS has detected that one or both of the thermal probes in the computer are not operational. You can continue to use the system, but be aware that the temperature probe(s) are disabled— a processor overheat condition will not shut down the system. You will probably have to replace the motherboard to correct this fault.

The Pentium Pro has a built-in thermocouple that halts microprocessor operation if the CPU exceeds its rated temperature.

Symptom 6-69. Warning—Temperature is too high During system start-up, the BIOS has detected that one or both microprocessors are overheated. This can happen if you try to restart the system too soon after a thermal shutdown. After displaying this message, the BIOS halts the processes and turns off the system. Let the system cool down before attempting to restart it.

PCI ERROR MESSAGES

Symptom 6-70. Bad PnP serial ID checksum The serial ID checksum of a Plug-and-Play card is invalid. Try replacing the offending expansion card.

Symptom 6-71. Floppy-disk controller resource conflict The floppy-disk controller has requested a resource that is already in use by another device. Try freeing the resources that are requested by the PnP system.

Symptom 6-72. NVRAM checksum error, NVRAM cleared The *Extended System Configuration Data (ESCD)* was reinitialized because of an NVRAM checksum error. Try rerunning the *ISA Configuration Utility (ICU)*. If the problem persists, replace the NVRAM IC or replace the motherboard.

Symptom 6-73. NVRAM cleared by jumper The "Clear CMOS" jumper on the motherboard has been moved to the *Clear* position and the system has been initialized. CMOS RAM and ESCD have been cleared, and now must be reconfigured.

Symptom 6-74. NVRAM data invalid, NVRAM cleared Invalid data has been found in the ESCD (which might mean that you have changed devices in the system). When this message is displayed, the BIOS has already rewritten the ESCD with current configuration data. Try rebooting the system.

Symptom 6-75. Parallel-port resource conflict The parallel port requested a resource that is already in use by another device. Try freeing the resources requested by the PnP system.

Symptom 6-76. PCI error log is full More than 15 PCI conflict errors have been detected, and no additional PCI errors can be logged. Deal with the PCI errors already contained in the log to reduce the total number of errors.

Symptom 6-77. PCI I/O port conflict Two devices requested the same I/O address, resulting in a conflict. Try freeing the resources needed to allow both devices to be configured properly.

Symptom 6-78. PCI IRQ conflict Two devices requested the same IRQ, resulting in a conflict. Try freeing the IRQs needed to allow both devices to be configured properly.

Symptom 6-79. PCI memory conflict Two devices requested the same memory resource, resulting in a conflict. Try freeing the memory needed to allow both devices to be configured properly.

Symptom 6-80. Primary boot device not found The designated primary boot device (hard-disk drive, floppy-disk drive, or CD-ROM drive) could not be found. Check the installation and configuration of each boot device.

Symptom 6-81. Primary IDE-controller resource conflict The primary IDE controller has requested a resource that is already in use. Try freeing the resources that are needed to allow the IDE controller to operate.

Symptom 6-82. Primary input device not found The designated primary input device, such as the keyboard or mouse (or other device if input is redirected), could not be found. Check the installation and configuration of all your input devices. Be sure that the input devices are also enabled in CMOS setup.

Symptom 6-83. Secondary IDE-controller resource conflict The secondary IDE controller has requested a resource that is already in use. Try freeing the resources that are needed to allow the IDE controller to operate.

Symptom 6-84. "Static device resource conflict" or "System board device resource conflict" A non-Plug and Play ISA card has requested a resource that is already in use. Try reconfiguring the ISA card to use other resources or try freeing the resources needed by the ISA card.

Further Study

This finishes up Chapter 6. Be sure to review the glossary and chapter questions on the accompanying CD. If you have access to the Internet, point your Web browser to some of these contacts:

American Megatrends: **http://www.megatrends.com**

Award BIOS: **http://www.award.com**

Hardware IC newsgroup: **comp.sys.ibm.pc.hardware.chips**

IBM SurePath BIOS page: **http://www.surepath.ibm.com/**

MicroFirmware: **http://www.firmware.com/catalog2.htm**

Microid Research (Mr. BIOS): **http://www.mrbios.com/**

SystemSoft: **http://www.systemsoft.com**

Unicore: **http://www.unicore.com/**

Year 2000 reference: **http://www.year2000.com (or http://www.sbhs.com/y2k)**

7

CD-ROM AND
CD-R DRIVES

CONTENTS AT A GLANCE

Understanding CD Media
CD data
EFM and data storage
Caring for compact discs
Caring for recordable cds

CD-ROM/CD-R Standards and Characteristics
High sierra
ISO 9660
CD-ROM standards ("books")
The multi-spin drive
The MPC
Effects of CD-ROM caching
Bootable CD-ROM (el torito)
"Orange book certified" media
Multisession CDs
Fixation vs. finalization
Disc-at-once
Track-at-once
Incremental and packet writing

Drive Construction
CD-ROM mechanics

CD-ROM electronics

Understanding the Software
Device drivers
MSCDEX.EXE

Creating a Bootable CD
Making the CD
Making the bootable image file
Make a booting catalog file
Create the ISO 9660 image file
Modify the ISO 9660 image file
Burn the ISO file to CD-R
Test the bootable CD

Troubleshooting CD-ROM Drives

Troubleshooting CD-R Drives
CD-recording issues
Typical compatibility problems
CD-R symptoms

Further Study
CD-related newsgroups

The *compact disc (CD)* first appeared in the commercial marketplace in early 1982. Sony and Philips developed the CD as a joint venture and envisioned it as a reliable, high-quality replacement for aging phonograph technology. With the introduction of the audio CD, designers demonstrated that huge amounts of information can be stored simply and very inexpensively on common, non-magnetic media. Unlike previous recording media, the CD recorded data in *digital* form through the use of physical "pits" and "lands" in the disc. The digital approach allowed excellent stereo sound quality, which does not degrade each time the disc is played, but also attracted the attention of PC designers, who saw CDs as a natural solution for all types of computer information (i.e., text, graphics, programs, video clips, audio files, etc.). The CD-ROM drive is now standard equipment on both desktop and mobile PC systems.

Although CD-ROM drives bring a great deal of reliable storage potential to the PC, it has not been possible to record CDs on the desktop—the technology required to create audio and computer CDs has traditionally been terribly complex and expensive, and limited by PC computing power of the day. Since the early 1990s, *CD recorder (CD-R)* technology has steadily become more reliable and economical. Today, virtually any Pentium-based PC with a SCSI bus and 1GB or more of hard drive space can support a CD-R drive for under $500 (U.S.). This chapter explains the technologies and troubleshooting techniques for CD-ROM and CD-R drives (Fig. 7-1).

Understanding CD Media

CDs are mass-produced by stamping the pattern of pits and lands onto a molded polycarbonate disc (known as a *substrate*). This stamping process (much like the stamping used to produce vinyl records) places the data on the disc. But the disc is not yet readable—several

FIGURE 7-1   **A Smart and Friendly CD-R 4006.** Courtesy of Smart and Friendly

finish steps must be performed to transform a clear plastic disc into viable, data-carrying media. The clear polycarbonate disc is given a silvered (reflective) coating so that it will reflect laser light. Silvering coats all parts of the disc side (pits and lands) equally. After silvering, the disc is coated with a tough, scratch-resistant lacquer that seals the disc from the elements (especially oxygen, which will oxidize and ruin the reflective coating). Finally, a label can be silk-screened onto the finished disc before it is tested and packaged. Figure 7-2 illustrates each of these layers in a cross-sectional diagram.

Recordable media appears very similar to "pressed" CD media (Fig. 7-2), but with two important variations. First, the polycarbonate CD-R substrate is pre-formed with a track spiral into which data will be written during recording. The substrate is then coated with a greenish translucent layer, and backed with a reflective layer of gold before protective lacquer is applied over the gold. These translucent and gold layers allow the recorded pits and lands to be read back after recording.

CD DATA

CDs are not segregated into concentric tracks and sectors as magnetic media is. Instead, CDs are recorded as a single, continuous spiral track running from the spindle to the lead-out area. Figure 7-3 shows the spiral pattern recorded on a CD. The inset illustrates the relationship between the pits and lands. Each pit is about 0.12 μm (micrometers) deep and 0.6 μm wide. Pits and lands can range from 0.9 to 3.3 μm in length. Approximately 1.6 μm are between each iteration of the spiral. Given these microscopic dimensions, a CD-ROM disc offers about 16,000 tracks per inch (TPI).

During playback, CDs use a highly focused laser beam and laser detector to sense the presence or absence of pits. Figure 7-4 illustrates the reading behavior. The laser/detector pair is mounted on a carriage, which follows the spiral track across the CD. A laser is directed at the underside of the CD, where it penetrates more than 1 mm of clear plastic before shining on the reflective surface. When laser light strikes a land, the light is reflected toward the detector, which, in turn, produces a very strong output signal. As laser light

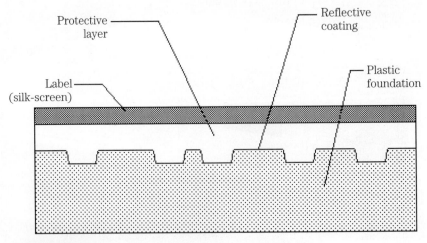

FIGURE 7-2   **Cross-sectional diagram of CD media.**

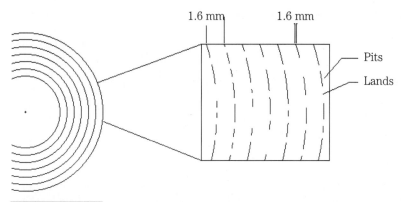

1.6 mm   1.6 mm

Pits

Lands

FIGURE 7-3   Close-up view of a CD spiral track pattern.

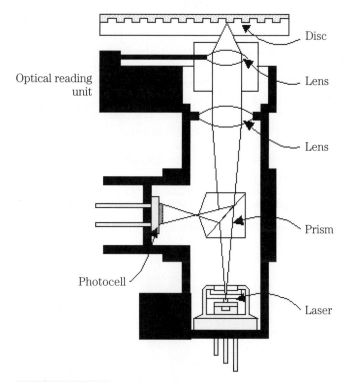

Disc

Optical reading
unit

Lens

Lens

Prism

Photocell

Laser

FIGURE 7-4   Reading a typical compact disc.

strikes a pit, the light is slightly out of focus. As a result, most of the incoming laser energy is scattered away in all directions, so very little output signal is generated by the detector. As with floppy and hard drives, the transition from pit to land (and back again) corresponds to binary levels, not the presence or absence of a pit or land. The analog light signal returned by the detector must be converted to logic levels and decoded. A process known as *Eight-to-Fourteen Modulation (EFM)* is very common with CD-ROMs.

EFM AND DATA STORAGE

A complex decoding process is necessary to convert the arcane sequence of pits and lands into meaningful binary information. The technique of EFM is used with CD-ROMs. For hard-disk drives, such techniques as 2,7 RLL encoding can be used to place a large number of bits into a limited number of flux transitions. The same is true for CDs using EFM. User data, error-correction information, address information, and synchronization patterns are all contained in a bit stream that is represented by pits and lands.

Magnetic media encodes bits as flux transitions—not the discrete orientation of any magnetic area. The same concept holds true with CD-ROMs, where binary 1s and 0s do not correspond to pits or lands. A binary 1 is represented wherever a transition (pit to land or land to pit) occurs. The length of a pit or land represents the number of binary 0s. Figure 7-5 illustrates this concept. The EFM encoding technique equates each byte (8 bits) with a 14-bit sequence (called a *symbol*), where each binary 1 must be separated by at least two binary 0s. Table 7-1 shows part of the EFM conversion. Three bits are added to merge each 14-bit symbol together.

A CD-ROM *frame* is composed of 24 synchronization bits, 14 control bits, 24 of the 14-bit data symbols you saw previously, and eight complete 14-bit *Error-Correction (EC) symbols*. Each symbol is separated by an additional three merge bits, bringing the total number of bits in the frame to 588. Thus, 24 bytes of data is represented by 588 bits on a CD-ROM, expressed as a number of pits and lands. There are 98 frames in a data block, so each block carries (98 × 24) = 2048 bytes (2352 with error correction, synchronization, and address bytes). The basic CD-ROM can deliver 153.6KB of data (75 blocks) per second to its host controller.

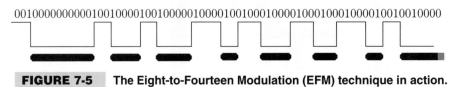

FIGURE 7-5   The Eight-to-Fourteen Modulation (EFM) technique in action.

TABLE 7-1 A SAMPLE OF EIGHT-TO-FOURTEEN MODULATION CODES		
NUMBER	**BINARY PATTERN**	**EFM PATTERN**
0	00000000	01001000100000
1	00000001	10000100000000
2	00000010	10010000100000
3	00000011	10001000100000
4	00000100	01000100000000
5	00000101	00000100010000
6	00000110	00010000100000
7	00000111	00100100000000
8	00001000	01001001000000
9	00001001	10000001000000
10	00001010	10010001000000

Remember that the CD-ROM disc is recorded as one continuous spiral track running around the disk, so ordinary sector and track ID information that is associated with magnetic disks does not apply very well. Instead, information is divided in terms of 0 to 59 minutes, and 0 to 59 seconds recorded at the beginning of each block. A CD-ROM (like an audio CD) can hold up to 79 minutes of data. However, many CD-ROMs tend to limit this to 60 minutes because the last 14 minutes of data is encoded in the outer 5 mm of disk space, which is the most difficult to manufacture and keep clean in everyday use. There are 270,000 blocks of data in 60 minutes. At 2048 data bytes per block, the disk's capacity is 552,950,000 bytes (553MB). If all 79 minutes are used, 681,984,000 bytes (681MB) will be available in 333,000 blocks. Most CD-ROMs run between 553 and 650MB in normal production.

CARING FOR COMPACT DISCS

A compact disc is a remarkably reliable long-term storage media (conservative expectations place the life estimates of a current CD at about 100 years. However, the longevity of a CD is affected by its storage and handling—a faulty CD can cause file and data errors that you might otherwise interpret as a defect in the drive itself. Here are some tips to help protect and maintain the disc itself:

- *Don't bend the disc* Polycarbonate is a forgiving material, but you risk cracking or snapping (and thus ruining) the disc.
- *Don't heat the disk* Remember, the disc is plastic. Leaving it by a heater or on the dashboard of your car might cause it to melt.
- *Don't scratch the disc* Laser wavelengths have a tendency to "look past" minor scratches, but a major scratch can cause problems. Be especially careful of circular scratches (one that follows the spiral track). A circular scratch can easily wipe out entire segments of data, which would be unrecoverable.
- *Don't use chemicals on the disc* Chemicals containing solvents, such as ammonia, benzene, acetone, carbon tetrachloride, or chlorinated cleaners, can easily damage the disc's plastic surface.

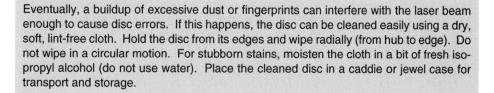

Eventually, a buildup of excessive dust or fingerprints can interfere with the laser beam enough to cause disc errors. If this happens, the disc can be cleaned easily using a dry, soft, lint-free cloth. Hold the disc from its edges and wipe radially (from hub to edge). Do not wipe in a circular motion. For stubborn stains, moisten the cloth in a bit of fresh isopropyl alcohol (do not use water). Place the cleaned disc in a caddie or jewel case for transport and storage.

CARING FOR RECORDABLE CDS

As a rule, recordable CDs are as rugged and reliable as ordinary "pressed" CDs. Still, you should exercise some rules in the careful handling and storage of recordable media:

- *Maintain a comfortable environment* Don't expose recordable discs to sunlight or other strong light for long periods of time. Also avoid high heat and humidity, which can damage the physical disc. Always keep blank or recorded media in clean "jewel" cases for best protection.

- *Don't write on the disc* Don't use alcohol-based pens to write on discs—the ink might eventually eat through the top (lacquer) surface and damage your data. Also don't use ball-point or other sharp-tipped pens because you might scratch right through the lacquer surface and damage the reflective gold layer (and ruin your data).
- *Don't use labels on the disc* Don't put labels on discs unless they are expressly designed for recordable CDs. The glue might eat through the lacquer surface just as some inks do, and/or the label might unbalance the disc and cause problems in reading it back or recording subsequent sessions. Never try to remove a label—you might tear off the lacquer and some of the reflecting surface.
- *Watch your media quality* Many different brands of recordable CD media are now available. Quality varies from brand to brand (and even from batch to batch within a given brand). If you have repeated problems that can be traced to the blank media you are using, try using a different brand or even a different batch of the same brand.
- *Don't use Kodak Photo CDs* Avoid the use of Kodak Photo CDs on everyday CD recorders. Kodak Photo CDs are designed to be used only with Kodak Photo CD professional workstations. Although the discs are inexpensive, they have a protection bit that prevents them from being written on many CD recorders. When you attempt to write these discs on the recorders, which recognize the protection bit, you will receive an error message.

CD-ROM/CD-R Standards and Characteristics

Like so many other PC peripheral devices, the early CD-ROM faced a serious problem of industry standardization. Just recording the data to a CD is not enough; the data must be recorded in a way that any CD-ROM drive can read. Standards for CD-ROM data and formats were developed by consortiums of influential PC manufacturers and interested CD-ROM publishers. Ultimately, this kind of industry-wide cooperation has made the CD-ROM one of the most uniform and standardized peripherals in the PC market. With the broad introduction of CD recorders into the marketplace, it is also important for you to understand the major concepts and operations of CD recorders. This part of the chapter explains many of the key ideas needed to master CD-ROM and CD-R drives.

HIGH SIERRA

In 1984 (before the general release of CD-ROM), the PC industry realized that there must be a standard method of reading a disc's *Volume Table of Contents (VTOC)*. Otherwise, the CD-ROM market would become extremely fragmented as various (incompatible) standards vied for acceptance. PC manufacturers, prospective CD publishers, and software developers met at the High Sierra Hotel in Lake Tahoe, CA to begin developing just such a uniform standard. By 1986, the CD-ROM standard file format (dubbed the *High Sierra format*) was accepted and approved. High Sierra remained the standard for several years, but has since been replaced by ISO 9660.

ISO 9660

High Sierra was certainly a workable format, but it was primarily a domestic U.S. development. When placed before the *International Standards Organization (ISO)*, High Sierra was tweaked and refined to meet international needs. After international review, High Sierra was absorbed (with only few changes) into the ISO 9660 standard. Although many technicians refer to High Sierra and ISO 9660 interchangeably, you should understand that the two standards are not the same. For the purposes of this book, ISO 9660 is the current CD-ROM file format, and all CD recorders are capable of recording a disc in the ISO 9660 format.

By adhering to ISO 9660, CD-ROM drive makers can write software drivers (and use MSCDEX under MS-DOS) to enable a PC to read the CD's VTOC. ISO 9660 also allows a CD-ROM disc to be accessed by any computer system and CD-ROM drive that follows the standard. Of course, just because a disc is recognized does not mean that it can be used. For example, an ISO 9660-compliant Mac can access a ISO 9660 MPC disc, but the files on the disc cannot be used by the Mac.

CD-ROM STANDARDS ("BOOKS")

When Philips and Sony defined the proprietary standards that became CD audio and CD-ROM, the documents were bound in different colored covers. By tradition, each color now represents a different level of standardization. *Red Book* (a.k.a. *Compact Disc Digital Audio Standard: CEI IEC 908*) defines the media, recording and mastering process, and the player design for CD audio. When you listen to your favorite audio CD, you are enjoying the benefits of the Red Book standard. CDs conforming to Red Book standards will usually have the words "digital audio" printed below the disc logo. Today, Red Book audio might be combined with programs and other PC data on the same disc.

The *Yellow Book* standard (*ISO 10149:1989*) makes CD-ROM possible by defining the additional error-correction data needed on the disc, and the detection hardware and firmware needed in the drive. When a disc conforms to Yellow Book, it will usually be marked "data storage" beneath the disc logo. Mode 1 Yellow Book is the typical operating mode that supports computer data. Mode 2 Yellow Book (also known as the *XA format*) supports compressed audio data and video/picture data. The Yellow Book standards build on the Red Book, so virtually all CD-ROM drives are capable of playing back CD audio.

The *Orange Book* (a.k.a. *Recordable Compact Disc Standard*) is the key to CD recorders, and it extends the basic Red and Yellow Book standards by providing specifications for recordable products, such as *(Part 1) Magneto-Optical (MO) drives* and *(Part 2) write-once CD-R drives*. The *Green Book* standard defines an array of supplemental standards for data recording, and provides an outline for a specific computer system that supports *CD-I (Compact Disc-Interactive)*. Interactive kiosks and information systems using CD-I discs are based on Green Book standards. *Blue Book* is the standard for laser discs and their players. The *White Book* standards define CD-ROM video.

THE MULTI-SPIN DRIVE

The Red Book standard defines CD audio as a stream of data that flows from the player mechanism to the amplifier (or other audio-manipulation circuit) at a rate of 150KB/sec. This data

TABLE 7-2 DATA TRANSFER RATES FOR CD-ROM DRIVES

SPEED	CD-ROM (MODE 1) 2048 BYTES/BLOCK	DATA TRANSFER RATE CD-ROM (MODE 2) 2336 BYTES/BLOCK	CD-I XA (FORM 2) 2324 BYTES/BLOCK
1×	153.6KB/s (0.15MB/s)	175.2KB/s (0.17MB/s)	174.3KB/s (0.17MB/s)
2×	307.2KB/s (0.3MB/s)	350.4KB/s (0.35MB/s)	348.6KB/s (0.34MB/s)
4×	614.4KB/s (0.61MB/s)	700.8KB/s (0.70MB/s)	697.2KB/s (0.69MB/s)
6×	921.6KB/s (0.92MB/s)	1051.2KB/s (1.05MB/s)	1045.8KB/s (1.04MB/s)
8×	1200KB/s (1.2MB/s)	1401.6KB/s (1.40MB/s)	1394.4KB/s (1.39MB/s)
10×	1500KB/s (1.5MB/s)	1752.0KB/s (1.75MB/s)	1743.0KB/s (1.74MB/s)
12×	1800KB/s (1.8MB/s)	2102.4KB/s (2.10MB/s)	2091.6KB/s (2.09MB/s)
14×	2100KB/s (2.1MB/s)	2452.8KB/s (2.45MB/s)	2440.2KB/s (2.44MB/s)
16×	2400KB/s (2.4MB/s)	2803.2KB/s (2.80MB/s)	2788.8KB/s (2.78MB/s)
18×	2700KB/s (2.7MB/s)	3153.6KB/s (3.15MB/s)	3137.4KB/s (3.13MB/s)
20×	3000KB/s (3.0MB/s)	3504.0KB/s (3.50MB/s)	3486.0KB/s (3.48MB/s)
22×	3300KB/s (3.3MB/s)	3854.4KB/s (3.85MB/s)	3834.6KB/s (3.83MB/s)
24×	3600KB/s (3.6MB/s)	4204.8KB/s (4.20MB/s)	4183.2KB/s (4.18MB/s)

rate was chosen to take music off the disc for truest reproduction. When the Yellow Book was developed to address CD-ROMs, this basic data rate was carried over. Designers soon learned that computer data can be transferred much faster than Red Book audio information, so the multi-spin (or multi-speed) drive was developed to work with Red Book audio at the normal 150KB/sec rate, but run faster for Yellow Book data to multiply the data throughput.

The first common multi-spin drives available were "2×" drives. By running at 2× the normal data-transfer speed, data throughput can be doubled from 150KB/sec to 300KB/sec. If Red Book audio is encountered, the drive speed drops back to 150KB/sec. Increased data transfer rates make a real difference in CD-ROM performance—especially for data-intensive applications such as audio/video clips. CD-ROM drives with "4×" transfer speed (600KB/sec) can transfer data four times faster than a Red Book drive. Table 7-2 lists the average data rates for current CD-ROM drives.

THE MPC

One of the most fundamental problems of writing software for PCs is the tremendous variability in the possible hardware and software configurations of individual machines. The selection of CPUs, motherboard chipsets, DOS versions, available memory, graphics resolutions, drive space, and other peripherals make the idea of a "standard" PC almost meaningless. Most software developers in the PC market use a base (or minimal) PC configuration to ensure that a product will run properly in a "minimal" machine. CD-ROM "multimedia" products have intensified these performance issues because of the unusually heavy demands posed by real-time audio and graphics. Microsoft assembled some of the largest PC manufacturers to create the *Multimedia Personal Computer (MPC)* standard. By adhering to the MPC specification, software developers and consumers can anticipate the minimal capacity needed to run multimedia products.

Appendix A outlines the three levels of MPC standards for the personal computer.

EFFECTS OF CD-ROM CACHING

The limiting factor of a CD-ROM is its data-transfer rate. Even a fast multi-spin CD-ROM takes a fairly substantial amount of time to load programs and files into memory—this causes system delays during CD-ROM access. If the PC could predict the data needed from a CD and load that data into RAM or virtual memory (i.e., the hard drive) during background operations, the effective performance of a CD-ROM drive can be enhanced dramatically. CD-ROM caching utilities provide a "look-ahead" ability that enables CD-ROMs to continue transferring information in anticipation of use.

However, CD-ROM caching is a mixed blessing. The utilities required for caching must reside in conventional memory (or be loaded into upper memory). In systems that are already strained by the CD-ROM drivers and other device drivers, which have become so commonplace on PC platforms, adding a cache might prohibit some large DOS programs from running. Remember this when evaluating CD-ROM caches for yourself or your customers.

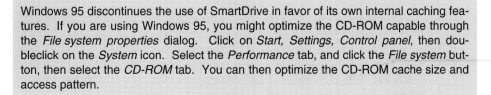

Windows 95 discontinues the use of SmartDrive in favor of its own internal caching features. If you are using Windows 95, you might optimize the CD-ROM capable through the *File system properties* dialog. Click on *Start, Settings, Control panel*, then doubleclick on the *System* icon. Select the *Performance* tab, and click the *File system* button, then select the *CD-ROM* tab. You can then optimize the CD-ROM cache size and access pattern.

BOOTABLE CD-ROM (EL TORITO)

Traditionally, CD-ROM drives have not been bootable devices. Because the CD-ROM drive needs software drivers, the PC always had to boot first to load the drivers. This invariably required a bootable hard drive or floppy drive. When building a new system, this required you to boot from a floppy disk, install DOS and the CD-ROM drivers, then pop in your Windows 95 CD for setup. In early 1995, the "El Torito" standard was finalized, which provides the hardware and software specifications needed to implement a bootable CD-ROM. You need three elements to implement a bootable CD-ROM:

- A bootable CD-ROM drive mechanism (almost always fitted with an EIDE/IDE interface).
- A BIOS that supports the bootable CD-ROM (now common on many new motherboards).
- A CD with boot code and an operating system on it. If you don't already have a bootable (or "system") CD, see "Creating a bootable CD" later in this chapter.

"ORANGE BOOK CERTIFIED" MEDIA

The Orange Book (Part II) is the primary specification for CD-R media, and all CD-R media should meet the Orange Book criteria for recordability and playback. Philips and Sony (the originators of the Orange Book specification) provide Orange Book certification of CD-R media. CD-R media that is not "Orange Book certified" should generally be avoided.

MULTISESSION CDS

One of the problems with recording early CDs was that once the CD was written, it could not be appended. This means if 123MB of data is written to a CD, the remaining 527MB of storage potential on the disc is lost. CD developers sought a means of adding new data to a CD that has been previously recorded. This *multisession capability* means that a CD could be written in terms of "sessions," and subsequent sessions can be linked to previous sessions—allowing the CD to be systematically filled.

A CD-R drive that supports multisession recording can write a disc that will have multiple sessions linked together—each session containing its own lead-in, program, and lead-out areas. In effect, each session is treated as a different CD. Any multisession-capable CD-ROM can access the data in any session. By comparison, a "pressed" CD-ROM or a CD-R written in "Disc at Once" mode contains only one lead-in area, program area, and lead-out area.

> Some older CD-ROM drives that are not multisession-capable can only read the first session of a multisession disc.

FIXATION VS. FINALIZATION

Each session written to a disc (whether multisession or single session) must be "fixed" before the session can be read. *Fixation* is the process of writing the session's lead-in and lead-out information to the disc. This process finishes a writing session and creates a table of contents. Fixation is required before a CD-ROM or CD-Audio player can play the disc. Discs that are "fixated for append" can have additional sessions recorded later (each with their own session lead-in and lead-out) creating a multisession disc. When a disc is finalized, the absolute lead-in and lead-out for the entire disc is written, along with information that tells the reader not to look for subsequent sessions. This final *Table Of Contents (TOC)* conforms to the ISO 9660 file standard.

DISC-AT-ONCE

The *disc-at-once* CD writing mode requires data to be written continuously without any interruptions, until the entire data set is transferred to the CD-R. The complete lead-in, program, and lead-out are written in a single writing process. All of the information to be recorded needs to be staged on the computer's hard disk prior to recording in the disc-at-once mode. This eliminates the linking and run-in and run-out blocks associated with multisession and packet-recording modes (which often are interpreted as uncorrectable errors during the glass-mastering process).

> This mode is usually preferred for discs that are sent to a CD-ROM replication facility when CD-R is the source media.

TRACK-AT-ONCE

The *track-at-once* writing mode is the key to multisession capability, and it allows a session to be written in a number of discrete write events, called *tracks* because the written sessions contain complete "tracks" of information. The disc might be removed from the writer and read in another writer (given proper software) before the session is fixated.

INCREMENTAL AND PACKET WRITING

Track-at-once writing is a form of incremental write that mandates a minimum track length of 300 blocks and a maximum of 99 tracks per disc. A track written "at once" has 150 blocks of overhead for run-in, run-out, pre-gap, and linking purposes. On the other hand, *packet write* is a method, where several write events are allowed within a track, thus reducing the demands of overhead data. Each writing "packet" is bounded by seven blocks of data: four for run-in, two for run-out, and one for linking.

Drive Construction

Now that you have an understanding of CD-ROM/CD-R media and standards, it is time to review a drive in some detail. CD-ROM/CD-R drives are impressive pieces of engineering. The drive must be able to accept standard-sized disks from a variety of sources (each disk might contain an assortment of unknown surface imperfections). The drive must then spin the disk at a *Constant Linear Velocity (CLV)*—that is, the disk speed varies inversely with the tracking radius. As tracking approaches the disk edge, disk speed slows, and vice versa. Keep in mind that CLV is different than the *Constant Angular Velocity (CAV)* method used by floppy and hard drives, which moves the media at a constant speed. The purpose of CLV is to ensure that CD data is read at a constant rate. A drive must be able to follow the spiral data path on a spinning CD-ROM, accurate to within less than 1 Êm along the disk's radius. The drive electronics must be able to detect and correct any unforeseen data errors in real time, operate reliably over a long working life, and be available for a low price that computer users have come to expect.

CD-ROM MECHANICS

You can begin to appreciate how a CD drive achieves its features by reviewing the exploded diagram of Fig. 7-6. At the center of the drive is a cast aluminum or rigid stainless-steel frame assembly. As with other drives, the frame is the single primary structure for mounting the drive's mechanical and electronic components. The front bezel, lid, volume control, and eject button attach to the frame, providing the drive with its clean cosmetic appearance, and offering a fixed reference slot for CD insertion and removal. Many drives use a sliding tray, so the front bezel (and the way it is attached) will not be the same for every drive.

The drive's electronics package has been split into several PC board assemblies: the main PC board, which handles drive control and interfacing, and the headphone PC board, which simply provides an audio amplifier and jack for headphones. The bulk of the

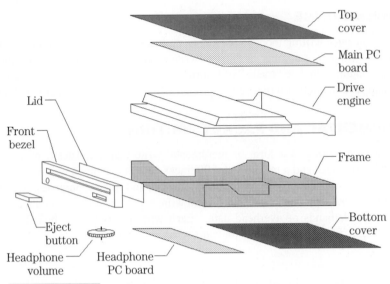

FIGURE 7-6   Exploded diagram of a CD-ROM drive.

drive's actual physical work, however, is performed by a main CD subassembly, called a *drive engine*, which is often manufactured by only a few companies. As a result, many of the diverse CD-ROM drives on the market actually use identical "engines" to hold/eject, spin, and read the disk. This interchangeability is part of the genius of CD-ROM drives—a single sub-assembly performs 80% of the work. Sony, Philips, and Toshiba are the major manufacturers of CD-ROM engines, but other companies, such as IBM and Ikka, are also producing engines.

A typical drive engine is shown in Fig. 7-7. The upper view of the engine features a series of mechanisms that accept, clamp, and eject the disk. The foundation of this engine is the BC-7C assembly. It acts as a sub-frame, which everything else is mounted to. Notice that the sub-frame is shock-mounted with four rubber feet to cushion the engine from minor bumps and ordinary handling. Even with such mounting, a CD-ROM drive is a delicate and fragile mechanism. The slider assembly, loading chassis assembly, and the cover shield provide the mechanical action needed to accept the disk and clamp it into place over the drive spindle, as well as to free the disk and eject it on demand. A number of levers and oil dampers provide a slow, smooth mechanical action when motion occurs. A motor/gear assembly drives the load/unload mechanics.

The serious work of spinning and reading a disk is handled under the engine (Fig. 7-8). A spindle motor is mounted on the sub-frame and connected to a spindle motor PC board. A thrust retainer helps keep the spindle motor turning smoothly. The most crucial part of the CD engine is the optical device that contains the 780-nm (nanometer) 0.6-mW gallium aluminum arsenide (GaAlAs) laser diode and detector, along with the optical focus and tracking components. The optical device slides along two guide rails and shines through an exposed hole in the sub-frame. This combination of device mounting and guide rails is called a *sled*.

A sled must be made to follow the spiral data track along the disk. Although floppy disks (using clearly defined concentric tracks) can easily use a stepping motor to position the head assembly, a CD drive ideally requires a linear motor to act much like the voice coil motor used to position hard-drive R/W heads. By altering the signal driving a sled motor and constantly measuring and adjusting the sled's position, a sled can be made to track very smoothly along a disk—free from the sudden, jerky motion of stepping motors.

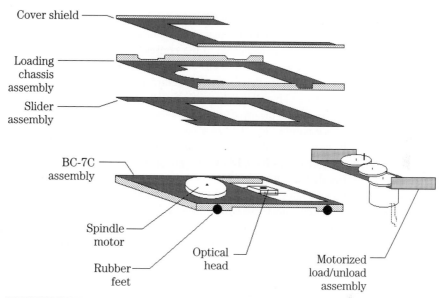

FIGURE 7-7   Exploded diagram of a CD "drive engine."

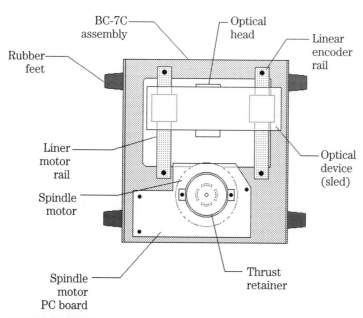

FIGURE 7-8   Underside view of a typical BC-7C assembly.

Some CD drives still use stepping motors with an extremely fine-pitch lead screw to position the sled. The drive's main PC board is responsible for managing these operations.

CD-ROM ELECTRONICS

The electronics package used in a typical CD-ROM drive is illustrated in Fig. 7-9. The electronics package can be divided into two major areas: the controller section and the drive section. The controller section is dedicated to the peripheral interface—its connection to the adapter board. Much of the reason for a CD-ROM's electronic sophistication can be traced to the controller section. Notice that the controller circuitry shown in Fig. 7-9 is dedicated to handling a SCSI interface. This allows the unit's "intelligence" to be located right in the drive itself. You need only connect the drive to a system-level interface board (a SCSI adapter) and set the drive's device number to establish a working system. Most current, low-cost CD-ROM drives will use an EIDE/IDE interface (the same interface used for hard drives).

The drive section manages the CD-ROM's physical operations (i.e., load/unload, spin the disk, move the sled, etc.), as well as data decoding (EFM) and error correction. Drive circuitry converts an analog output from the laser diode into an EFM signal, which is, in turn, decoded into binary data and *Cross-Interleaved Reed-Solomon Code (CIRC)* information. A drive-controller IC and servo-processor IC are responsible for directing laser focus, tracking, sled motor control (and feedback), spindle motor control (and feedback), and loading/unloading motor control.

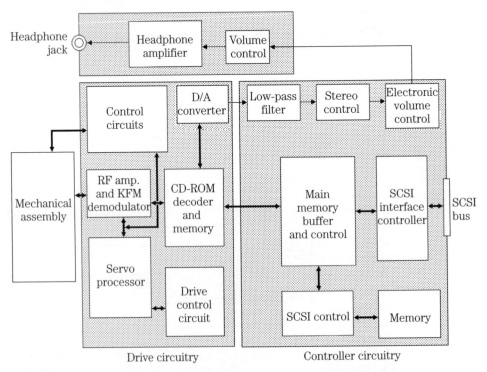

FIGURE 7-9   Electronics block diagram for a typical CD-ROM drive.

When it comes to CD drive electronics, treat the diagram of Fig. 7-9 more as a guideline than as an absolute. There are quite a few different iterations of drive electronics and interfaces. Although many manufacturers use SCSI interfaces, most systems the EIDE/IDE system-level interface, and several manufacturers implement proprietary interfaces (in some cases, these are often subtle, non-standard variations of SCSI or IDE interfaces). Obtain manufacturer's service data wherever possible for specific information on your particular drive.

Understanding the Software

Hardware alone is not enough to implement a CD-ROM or CD-R drive. In an ideal world, BIOS and MS-DOS would provide the software support to handle the drive, but in actuality, the variations between CD-ROM designs and interfaces make it impractical to provide low-level BIOS services. Manufacturers provide a hardware-specific device driver used to communicate with the CD-ROM and interface. An MS-DOS extension (MSCDEX) provides file handling and logical drive letter support. This part of the chapter explains the operations and features of CD-ROM device drivers and MSCDEX.

DEVICE DRIVERS

A low-level device driver allows programs to access the CD-ROM or CD-R drive properly at the register (hardware) level. Because most CD-ROM/CD-R drives are designed differently, they require different device drivers. If you change or upgrade the drive at any point, the device driver must be upgraded as well. A typical device driver uses a .SYS extension, and is initiated by adding its command line to the PC's CONFIG.SYS file, such as:

```
DEVICE=HITACHIA.SYS /D:MSCD000 /N:1 /P:300
```

The *DEVICE* command can be replaced by the *DEVICEHIGH* command if you have available space in the *Upper Memory Area (UMA)*.

A CD-ROM/CD-R device driver will typically have three command line switches associated with it. These parameters are needed to ensure that the driver installs properly. For the previous example command line, the /D switch is the name used by the driver when it is installed in the system's device table. This name must be unique, and matched by the /D switch in the MSCDEX.EXE command line (covered later). The /N switch is the number of CD-ROM drives attached to the interface card. The default is 1 (which is typical for most general-purpose systems). Finally, the /P switch is the I/O port address where the drive's adapter card resides. As you might expect, the port address should match the port address on the physical interface. If there is no /P switch, the default is 0300h.

An additional wrinkle when using CD recorders is that virtually all internal CD-R drives use the SCSI interface. This means the PC must be fitted with a SCSI adapter, and configured with an ASPI driver in order to allow the SCSI adapter to interface to the drive (this is also true if you're using a SCSI CD-ROM drive). A typical ASPI driver entry would appear in CONFIG.SYS, such as:

```
DEVICE=C:\SCSI\ASPIPPA3.SYS /L=001
```

If no SCSI hard drives are in the system, the SCSI adapter's on-board BIOS ROM can usually be disabled.

MSCDEX.EXE

MS-DOS was developed in a time when no one anticipated that large files would be accessible to a PC, and it is severely limited in the file sizes that it can handle. With the development of CD-ROMs, Microsoft created an extension to MS-DOS that allows software publishers to access 650MB CDs in a standard fashion—the *Microsoft CD-ROM Extensions (MSCDEX)*. As with most software, MSCDEX offers some vital features (and a few limitations), but it is required by a vast majority of CD-ROM/CD-R products. Obtaining MSCDEX is not a problem—it is generally provided on the same disk containing the CD-ROM's low-level device driver. New versions of MSCDEX can be obtained from the Microsoft Web site (**http://www.microsoft.com**) or from the Microsoft forum on CompuServe (GO MSL-1).

In operation, MSCDEX is loaded in the AUTOEXEC.BAT file. It should be loaded after any mouse driver, and loaded before any MENU, SHELL, DOSSHELL, or WIN line. It should also be loaded before any .BAT file is started. If a .BAT file loads a network, MSCDEX must be included in the batch file after the network driver. Further, MSCDEX must be loaded after that network driver with the /S (share) switch to hook into the network driver chain. If you want to use the MS-DOS drive caching software (SmartDrive) to buffer the CD-ROM drive(s), load MSCDEX before SmartDrive. The MSCDEX /M (number of buffers) switch can be set to 0 when using SmartDrive. If you find that SmartDrive is interfering with such MPC applications as Video for Windows, you can load SmartDrive before MSCDEX, and set the /M switch to at least 2. When loading MSCDEX, remember that the MSCDEX /D switch MUST match the /D label used in the low-level driver. Otherwise, MSCDEX will not load. If SETVER is loaded in the CONFIG.SYS file, be sure to use the latest version of MSCDEX.

Although the vast majority of CD-ROM bundles include installation routines that automate the installation process for the low-level driver and MSCDEX, you should understand the various command-line switches (Table 7-3) that make MSCDEX operate. Understanding these switches might help you to overcome setup problems.

Creating a Bootable CD

With the acceptance of the "El Torito" standard for IDE CD-ROM drives, it is now possible to boot your PC from a CD and load an operating system without a floppy or hard drive. The problem is in obtaining bootable CDs to begin with. Many new computers are

TABLE 7-3 MSCDEX COMMAND LINE SWITCHES

/D:x	Device Name	The label used by the low-level device driver when it loads. MSCDEX must match this label for the device driver and MSCDEX to work together. A typical label is MSCD000.
/M:x	Buffers Allocated	The number of 2KB buffers allocated to the CD-ROM drives. There are typically 8 buffers (16KB) for a single drive and 4 buffers for each additional drive. This number can be set to 1 or 2 of conventional memory when space is at a premium.
/L:x	Drive Letter	This is the optional drive letter for the CD-ROM. If this is not specified, the drive will be automatically assigned to the first available letter (usually D:). There must be a LASTDRIVE= entry in CONFIG.SYS to use a letter higher than the default letter. When choosing a letter for the LASTDRIVE entry, do not use Z. Otherwise, network drives might not install after MSCDEX.
/N	Verbose Option	This switch forces MSCDEX to show memory usage statistics on the display each time the system boots.
/S	Share Option	This switch is used with CD-ROM installations in network systems.
/K	Kanji Option	Instructs MSCDEX to use Kanji (Japanese) file types on the CD, if present.
/E	Expanded Mem.	Allows MSCDEX to use expanded memory for buffers. There must be an expanded memory driver running (i.e., EMM386.EXE) with enough available space to use it.

being sold with a "system disc," which can boot and load an operating system, but it is rare for users to bring in their bootable CDs with the system when service is required. If you have a CD-R drive and some readily available software tools, you can actually make a bootable CD yourself. This part of the chapter covers the procedure used to create a bootable CD. Before you can create a bootable CD, you will need a system (or access to a system) with the following hardware and software tools:

- An "El Torito-capable" IDE or SCSI CD-ROM drive (with their standard IDE/SCSI interfaces).
- An "El Torito-capable" motherboard or SCSI adapter BIOS that supports booting from bootable CDs.
- A hexadecimal editor utility. If you have Norton Utilities (version 8.0 or Windows 95), the DISKEDIT.EXE utility is preferred.
- A bootable floppy disk (MS-DOS 6.2x or DOS 7.0 of Windows 95). You might also use a bootable hard drive.
- A hard-disk drive with ample speed and space to hold an ISO 9660 image file for the bootable CD. A SCSI disk is preferred, but a fast EIDE hard drive will also work. At least 650MB of free space should be on the HDD for the image file.
- A CD-R drive (almost always SCSI).
- Any CD-R software that can make an ISO 9660 image file. For example, you could use Adaptec's Easy CD Pro for Windows 95.
- A blank CD-R disc (you can't make a multisession CD bootable).

Creating a bootable CD is a rather lengthy and sophisticated procedure that requires some knowledge of editing hexadecimal files and creating ISO image files. You might choose to seek the advice and guidance of more experienced personnel before proceeding on your own.

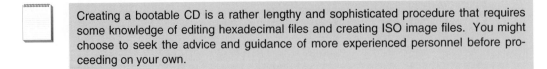

If you need a hex editor, try HW16V210.ZIP on the Companion CD.

MAKING THE CD

To boot from a CD, a *Boot Volume Descriptor (BVD)* must be located at sector 17 of the CD. The BVD is a string of hex codes. Somewhere in those hex codes, a series of 4 bytes must list the starting address of the *Booting Catalog (BC)*. The BC is another set of hex codes that describe several different aspects of the CD. Again, it must have a sequence of 4 bytes that indicates the starting address of a bootable image file.

The actual process of making a bootable CD consists of roughly five steps. First, make an image file of the bootable floppy (or hard) disk with the hex editor (i.e., DISK EDIT.EXE). Name the file OSBOOT.IMG. Next, make a booting catalog file, named BOOTCAT.BIN. Third, make an ISO 9660 image file that contains the previous two files—as well as other files and directories to be written to the CD. Edit the ISO file using the hex editor. Finally, burn that ISO 9660 image file to the blank CD-R disc.

MAKING THE BOOTABLE IMAGE FILE

Before making a bootable image file of your floppy (or hard) disk, pay particular attention to your CD-ROM drivers. If you create a bootable CD without the CD-ROM drivers and MSCDEX, you'll simply create an "image" if the A: (or C:) drive. This will allow you to boot from the CD, but the other files and directories on the CD will not be accessible because the CD-ROM drivers will not be loaded. You must include the CD-ROM drivers if you wish the other (non-booting) files on the CD to be available after the boot process has finished. In fact, some more experienced technicians have developed a multi-boot menu in CONFIG.SYS, which allows them to select low-level CD-ROM drivers for many possible drives (this allows the same bootable CD to be accessible on many different drives). If you're using Norton's DISKEDIT.EXE, follow the steps below to create an image file:

1 Select *Object*, *Drive*, then A: (or B: or C:, depending on what bootable disk you care to take an image from) .

2 Select *Object*, *Physical sector*, and *OK*.

3 Select *Tools*, *Write object to*, then choose *To a file*.

4 Enter the file name (i.e., OSBOOT.IMG), then select *Yes* to save the file.

Remember that the actual file used to boot the CD is just an image of another bootable drive. The other files "outside" the bootable image file (after the CD has booted) can only be found after the CD-ROM drivers have been loaded by an appropriate CONFIG.SYS and AU-TOEXEC.BAT file.

MAKE A BOOTING CATALOG FILE

The next step is to create a booting catalog file. No tool does this automatically, so you'll have to handle this manually. Create a hex file (call it BOOTCAT.BIN) using your hex editor. The file should be 2048 bytes long. Use DISKEDIT (or your own hex editor) to edit the BOOTCAT.BIN file like this:

```
01 00 00 00 00 00 00 00 00 00 00 00 00 00 00 00
00 00 00 00 00 00 00 00 00 00 00 00 AA 55 55 AA
88 02 00 00 00 00 01 00 BB
```

The rest of this file must be filled with hex 00. The last "BB" in the file has no meaning, and will be changed later. It's just used to mark the place where the OSBOOT.IMB file address should go.

CREATE THE ISO 9660 IMAGE FILE

Now you must create an ISO 9660-compatible file that contains our booting catalog, the bootable image file, and any other files and directories that you want to be on the bootable CD. You can use virtually any CD-R authoring software you wish (e.g., Easy CD Pro for Windows 95). Most CD-R authoring software now uses a "drag-and-drop" interface for defining the files that will be placed on the CD. The order in which files are "dragged and dropped" into the workspace is the order in which they will be written. Make the booting catalog (BOOTCAT.BIN) your first file on the CD-R, then make the bootable image file (OSBOOT.IMG) your second file on the CD-R. After that, you can simply "drag-and-drop" any other files and directories that will be written on the CD.

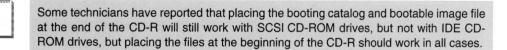

Some technicians have reported that placing the booting catalog and bootable image file at the end of the CD-R will still work with SCSI CD-ROM drives, but not with IDE CD-ROM drives, but placing the files at the beginning of the CD-R should work in all cases.

Once you have all the desired files defined for the new bootable CD, go ahead and generate the ISO 9660 image file to your hard drive (keep in mind that there must be sufficient space on the hard drive to hold the entire image file—up to 650MB).

MODIFY THE ISO 9660 IMAGE FILE

This is perhaps the trickiest part of the process because you will use your hex editor to modify the ISO 9660 image file before burning the file to a blank CD-R disc. Start DISKEDIT.EXE (or whatever other hex editor you're using), then load the image file you just created. Depending on the amount of material you added to the image file, it can be quite lengthy.

1 Find the ASCII string in "BOOTCAT." Put your active cursor at the "B," then move the cursor up 2 lines and right 1 space. Write down the next 4 bytes. For example, if you move the cursor and the next four bytes read 15 00 00 00, then write down "15 00 00 00" on a sheet of paper for later use.

2 Find the ASCII string in "OSBOOT." Put your active cursor at the "O," then move the cursor up two lines and right one space. Write down the next four bytes. For example, if you move the cursor and the next four bytes read "16 00 00 00," then write down "16 00 00 00" on a sheet of paper for later use.

3 Find the Hex string "AA 55 55 AA." It is located in the sector occupied by the BOOT-CAT.BIN file. You will find a "BB" (where you placed it) in the third row of this sector. From this place, fill in the four bytes obtained from finding the "OSBOOT" ASCII string (i.e., 16 00 00 00). For example, the line that said:

```
88 02 00 00 00 00 01 00 BB 00 00 00
```

should be changed to:

```
88 02 00 00 00 00 01 00 16 00 00 00
```

> That "02' in the second byte of this row means that it's a 1.44MB floppy bootable image. If you use other media for the bootable image, change it to: 01 for a 1.2MB floppy disk, 02 for a 1.44MB floppy disk, 03 for a 2.88MB floppy disk, or 04 for a hard disk.

4 Edit sector 17 of the ISO file. Go back to the beginning (sector 0) of this ISO image file, then press PageDown key to offset 34816 (decimal). This is the beginning of sector 17. Replace the hex codes from the beginning of this sector with the following:

```
00 43 44 30 30 31 01 45 4C 20 54 4F 52 49 54 4F
20 53 50 45 43 49 46 49 43 41 54 49 4F 4E 00 00
00 00 00 00 00 00 00 00 00 00 00 00 00 00 00 00
00 00 00 00 00 00 00 00 00 00 00 00 00 00 00 00
00 00 00 00 00 00 00 BB
```

The ASCII area should now say ".CD001.EL TORITO SPECIFICATION." Notice the "BB" in the 5th row from the beginning of this sector. It's the beginning place to put the address codes of BOOTCAT.BIN. From this place, fill in the four bytes obtained from finding the "BOOTCAT" ASCII string (i.e., 15 00 00 00). For example, the line that said:

```
00 00 00 00 00 00 00 BB 00 00 00
```

should be changed to:

```
00 00 00 00 00 00 00 15 00 00 00
```

The rest of this sector (ended at offset 36863) should be replaced by "00."

BURN THE ISO FILE TO CD-R

At this point, use your CD-R authoring tool to "burn" the modified ISO 9660 image file to the CD-R disc. The writing process might take from several minutes to as much as an hour, depending on the amount of programs and data being transferred to the disc. If you want extra safety, have the authoring software test the writing process for proper data transfer before starting to write.

TEST THE BOOTABLE CD

For an IDE CD-ROM, you just have to change the setting of booting sequence in BIOS to "CDROM, C:, A:," then reboot the PC with the bootable CD in CD-ROM drive. For SCSI CD-ROM drives, the booting sequence of the motherboard BIOS should be changed to "SCSI, IDE." If the BIOS doesn't have this option, you'll just have to temporarily set all the IDE HDD entries to "none" or "not installed." Next, enter the BIOS setting of your SCSI card. For example, in Adaptec's AHA 2940U, go into "Advanced Configuration Options," enable the options: "Host Adapter BIOS (Configuration Utility Reserve BIOS Space)" and "BIOS Support for Bootable CD-ROM." Then reboot the PC with the bootable CD in the drive.

If you like the idea of creating your own bootable CDs, but don't like the idea of editing hex code manually, try the following utilities on the Companion CD: MKBTCD1.ZIP, BOOTISO.ZIP, and BCD.ZIP.

Troubleshooting CD-ROM Drives

Although the vast majority of CD-ROM problems are caused by software or setup problems, the drives themselves are delicate and unforgiving devices. Considering that their prices have plummeted over the last few years (and still continue to drop), there is little economic sense in attempting a lengthy repair. When a fault occurs in the drive or in its adapter board, your best course is typically to replace the defective drive outright.

The companion CD contains a number of CD-ROM testing/caching utilities. Check out CDCP10.ZIP, CDQCK120.ZIP, and CDSPEED.ZIP.

Symptom 7-1. The drive has trouble accepting or rejecting a CD This problem is typical of motorized CD-ROM drives, where the disc is accepted into a slot or placed in a motorized tray. Before performing any disassembly, check the assembly through the CD slot for any obvious obstructions. If nothing is obvious, expose the assembly and check each linkage and motor drive gear very carefully. Carefully remove or free any obstruction. Be gentle when working around the load/unload assembly. Notice how it is shock mounted in four places.

Disconnect the geared dc motor assembly and try moving the load/unload mechanism by hand. If you feel any resistance or obstruction, you should track it down by eye and by feel. Replace any worn or damaged part of the mechanism, or replace the entire load/unload assembly. Also check the geared motor for any damage or obstruction. Broken or slipping gear teeth can interfere with the transfer of force from motor to mechanism. Replace any damaged gears or replace the entire geared assembly. You might also simply replace the CD-ROM drive mechanism outright.

Symptom 7-2. The optical read head does not seek An optical head is used to identify pits and lands along a CD-ROM, and to track the spiral data pattern as the head moves across the disk. The optical head must move very slowly and smoothly to ensure accurate tracking. Head movement is accomplished using a linear stepping motor (or linear actuator) to shift the optical assembly in microscopic increments—head travel appears perfectly smooth to the unaided eye. Check the drive for any damaged parts of obstructions. When the optical head fails to seek, the easiest and fastest fix is simply to replace the CD-ROM mechanism outright.

Symptom 7-3. The disc cannot be read This type of problem might result in a DOS level "sector not found" or "drive not ready" error. Before you reach for your tools, however, check the CD itself to ensure that it is the right format, inserted properly, and physically clean. Cleanliness is very important to a CD. Although the laser will often "look past" any surface defects in a disc, the presence of dust or debris on a disc surface can produce serious tracking (and read) errors. Try a different disc to confirm the problem. If a new or different disc reads properly, the trouble might indeed be in (or on) the original disc itself. Not only the disc must be clean, but the head optics must also be clear. Gently dust or clean the head optics, as suggested by your drive's particular manufacturer.

If read problems persist, check the physical interface cable between the drive and its adapter board. Be sure that the cable is connected correctly and completely. Many CD drives use SCSI interfaces—if you are using multiple SCSI devices from the same controller card and other SCSI devices are operating properly, the SCSI controller board is probably intact. If other SCSI devices are also malfunctioning, try a new SCSI host controller board. At this point, either the drive's optical head or electronics are defective. Your best course here is to replace the drive. If problems persist on a drive with a proprietary interface, replace the adapter board.

Symptom 7-4. The disc does not turn The disc must turn at a *Constant Linear Velocity (CLV)* that is directed and regulated by the spindle. If the disc is not spinning during access, check to be sure that the disc is seated properly, and is not jammed or obstructed. Before beginning a repair, review your drive installation and setup carefully to ensure that the drive is properly configured for operation. If the drive's BUSY LED comes on when drive access is attempted (you might also see a corresponding DOS error message), the drive spindle system is probably defective. If the computer does not recognize the CD drive (i.e., "invalid drive specification"), there might be a setup or configuration problem (either the low-level device driver or MSCDEX might not have loaded properly). If your particular drive provides you with instructions for cleaning the optical head aperture, perform that cleaning operation and try the drive again. A fouled optical head can sometimes upset spindle operation. If operation does not improve, replace the CD-ROM drive mechanism.

Symptom 7-5. The optical head cannot focus its laser beam As you saw earlier in this chapter, a CD-ROM drive must focus its laser beam to microscopic precision to properly read the pits and lands of a disk. To compensate for the minute fluctuations in disc flatness, the optical head mounts its objective lens into a small focusing mechanism, which is little more than a miniature voice-coil actuator—the lens does not have to move very much at all to maintain precise focus. If focus is out or not well maintained, the laser detector might produce erroneous signals. This might result in DOS drive error messages.

If random, but consistent, DOS errors appear, check the disc to be sure that it is optically clean—dust and fingerprints can result in serious access problems. Try another disc. If a new disc continues to perform badly, try cleaning the optical aperture with clean (photography grade) air. If problems persist, the optical system is probably damaged or defective. Replace the CD-ROM drive mechanism outright.

Symptom 7-6. No audio is generated by the drive Many CD-ROM drives are capable of not only reading computer data, but reading and reproducing music and sounds under computer control. Audio CDs can often be played in available CD-ROM drives through headphones or speakers. Start your investigation by testing the headphones or speakers in another sound source, such as a stereo. Once you have confirmed that the speakers or headphones are working reliably, check the drive's audio volume setting, which is usually available through the front bezel. Set the volume to a good average place (perhaps mid-range). Be sure that the disk you are trying to play actually contains valid Red Book audio. Check any software required to operate the CD drive's audio output (usually set with a "mixer applet") to be sure that it is installed and loaded as expected. CD-ROMs will not play audio CDs without an audio driver. Also check the line output, which would drive amplified speakers or stereo inputs. If speakers work through the line output but headphones or speakers do not work through the front bezel connector, the volume control or output audio amplifier might be defective. If the headphone output continues to fail, replace the headphone PC board or replace the entire CD-ROM drive outright.

Symptom 7-7. Audio is not being played by the sound card Normally, the sound card will not play Red Book audio from a CD—that is usually fed directly to the CD's headphone or line output. However, audio can be channeled to the sound board for playback. Most CDs offer an audio connector that allows audio signals to be fed directly to the sound board. If this "CD audio cable" is missing or defective, Red Book audio will not play through the sound board. Check or replace the cable. If the cable is intact (and audio is available from the CD-ROM headphone output), check the sound board's configuration for any "mixer" applet (see that any control for CD audio is turned up, and remember to save any changes). If problems persist, replace the sound board. If the CD audio cable is intact (and audio is not available from the CD-ROM headphone output), the audio amplifier circuit in the CD-ROM is probably defective—replace the CD-ROM drive.

Symptom 7-8. You see a "Wrong DOS version" error message when attempting to load MSCDEX You are running MS-DOS 4, 5, or 6 with a version of MSCDEX which does not support it. The solution is then to change to the correct version of MSCDEX. The version compatibility for MSCDEX is:

- v1.01 14,913 bytes (No ISO9660 support—High Sierra support only)
- v2.00 18,307 bytes (High Sierra and ISO9660 support for DOS 3.1-3.3)
- v2.10 19,943 bytes (DOS 3.1-3.3 and 4.0—DOS 5.x support provided with SETVER)
- v2.20 25,413 bytes (same as above with Win 3.x support—changes in audio support)
- v2.21 25,431 bytes (DOS 3.1-5.0 support with enhanced control under Win 3.1)
- v2.22 25,377 bytes (DOS 3.1-6.0 & higher with Win 3.1 support)
- v2.23 25,361 bytes (DOS 3.1-6.2 and Win 3.1 support—supplied with MSDOS 6.2)

When using MS-DOS 5.x to 6.1, you will need to add the SETVER utility to CONFIG.SYS to use MSCDEX v2.10 or v2.20 properly (i.e., DEVICE = C:\DOS\SETVER.EXE).

SETVER is used to tell programs that they are running under a different version of DOS than DOS 5.0. This is important because MSCDEX (v2.10 and v2.20) refuses to work with DOS versions higher than 4.0. SETVER is used to fool MSCDEX into working with higher versions of DOS. In some versions of DOS 5.0 (such as Compaq DOS 5.0), you will need to add an entry to SETVER for MSCDEX (i.e., SETVER MSCDEX.EXE 4.00). This entry modifies SETVER without changing the file size or date.

Symptom 7-9. You cannot access the CD-ROM drive letter You might see an error message, such as "Invalid drive specification." This is typically a problem with the CD-ROM drivers. The MS-DOS extension MSCDEX has probably not loaded. Switch to the DOS sub-directory and use the MEM /C function to check the loaded drivers and TSRs. If you see the low-level driver and MSCDEX displayed in the driver list, check the CD-ROM hardware. Be sure that the data cable between the drive and adapter board in inserted properly and completely. If problems persist, try replacing the adapter board. If you do not see the low-level driver and MSCDEX shown in the driver list, inspect your CONFIG.SYS and AUTOEXEC.BAT files. Check that the drivers are included in the startup files to begin with. Be sure that the label used in the /D switch is the same for both the low-level driver and MSCDEX. If the label is not the same, MSCDEX will not load. If you are using MS-DOS 5.0, be sure that the SETVER utility is loaded. You could also try updating MSCEDX to v2.30.

Symptom 7-10. An error appears when trying to load the low-level CD-ROM driver Check that you are using the proper low-level device driver for your CD-ROM drive. If you are swapping the drive or adapter board, you probably need to load a new driver. If the driver fails to load with original hardware, the adapter board might have failed or its jumper settings might not match those in the driver's command line switches. Check the signal cable running between the drive and adapter board. If the cable is crimped or scuffed, try replacing the cable. Next, try replacing the adapter board. If problems persist, try replacing the CD-ROM drive mechanism itself.

Symptom 7-11. An error appears, such as "Error: not ready reading from drive D:" Check that a suitable disc is inserted in the drive and that the drive is closed properly. Be sure that the low-level device driver and MSCDEX are loaded correctly. If the drivers do not load, the problem might be with the adapter board or drive mechanism itself. Also check that the data cable between the drive and adapter is connected properly and completely. If problems persist, suspect that a weakness is in the PC power supply (especially if the system is heavily loaded or upgraded). Try a larger supply in the system. If problems persist, replace the CD-ROM drive. If a new drive does not correct the problem, try a different interface adapter.

Symptom 7-12. SmartDrive is not caching the CD-ROM properly The version of SmartDrive supplied with DOS 6.2x provides three forms of caching, although older forms of SmartDrive (such as the ones distributed with Windows 3.1, DOS 6.0 and 6.1) will not adequately cache CD-ROM drives. The BUFFERS statement also does not help caching. So, if you are looking to SmartDrive for CD-ROM cache, you should be using the version distributed with DOS 6.2x. You should also set BUFFERS=10,0 in the CONFIG.SYS file, and the SmartDrive command line should come after MSCDEX. When using SmartDrive, you can change the buffers setting in the MSCDEX command line (/M) to 0. This allows you to save 2KB per buffer.

> SmartDrive is not used by Windows 95, which uses its own CD-caching scheme. Try disabling SmartDrive when running under Windows 95.

Symptom 7-13. The CD-ROM drivers will not install properly on a drive using compression software This is usually because you booted from a floppy disk and attempted to install drivers without loading the compression software first. Before doing anything else, check the loading order—allow your system to boot from the hard drive before installing the CD-ROM drivers. This allows the compression software to assign all drive letters. As an alternative, boot from a compression-aware floppy disk. If you must boot the system from a floppy disk, be sure that the diskette is configured to be fully compatible with the compression software being used.

Symptom 7-14. You see an error indicating that the CD-ROM drive is not found This type of problem might also appear as loading problems with the low-level driver. There are several possible reasons why the drive hardware cannot be found. Check the power connector first and be sure that the 4-pin power connector is inserted properly and completely. If the drive is being powered by a Y-connector, be sure that any interim connections are secure. Use a voltmeter and measure the +5-V (pin 4) and +12-V (pin 1) levels. If either voltage (especially the +12-V supply) is unusually low or absent, replace the power supply. Check the signal connector next and see that the drive's signal interface cable is connected securely at both the drive and controller. If the cable is visibly worn or damaged, try a new one.

Inspect the drive interface adapter and be sure that the adapter's IRQ, DMA, and I/O address settings are correct. They must also match with the command line switches used with the low-level driver. If the adapter is for a CD-ROM alone, you might also try installing the adapter in a different bus slot. If your CD-ROM uses a SCSI interface, be sure that the SCSI bus is properly terminated at both ends. If problems persist, replace the drive adapter.

Symptom 7-15. After installing the CD-ROM drivers, system reports significantly less available RAM This is usually a caching issue with CD-ROM driver software, and you might need to adjust the CD-ROM driver software accordingly. This type of problem has been documented with Teac CD-ROM drives and CORELCDX.COM software. If the software offers a command line switch to change the amount of XMS allocated, reduce the number to 512 or 256. Check with tech support for your particular drive for the exact command line switch settings.

Symptom 7-16. In a new installation, the driver fails to load successfully for the proprietary interface card In almost all cases, the interface card has been configured improperly. Check the drive adapter card first. Be sure that the drive adapter is configured with the correct IRQ, DMA, and I/O address settings, and check for hardware conflicts with other devices in the system. In some cases, you might simply enter the drive maker (i.e., Teac) as the interface type during driver installation. Be sure that the interface is set properly for the system and your particular drive. Check the driver's command line next—the driver's command-line switches should correctly reflect the drive adapter's configuration.

Symptom 7-17. The CD-ROM driver loads, but you see an error, such as: "CDR101" (drive not ready), or: "CDR103" (CD-ROM disk not HIGH SIERRA or ISO) You are using a very old version of the low-level driver or MSCDEX. Check your driver version (it might be outdated). Contact the drive manufacturer's tech support and see that you have the very latest version of the low-level driver. For very old drives, a later "generic" driver might be available. Check your version of MSCDEX next. Because low-level drivers are often bundled with MSCDEX, you might also be stuck with an old version of MSCDEX. You can usually download a current version of MSCDEX from the same place you get an updated low-level driver, or download it from Microsoft at: **http://www.microsoft.com.**

Symptom 7-18. You are having trouble setting up more than one CD-ROM drive You must be concerned about hardware and software issues. Check the drive adapter first—be sure that the drive adapter will support more than one CD-ROM on the same channel. If not, you will have to install another drive adapter to support the new CD-ROM drive. Low-level drivers present another problem because you will need to have one copy of a low-level driver loaded in CONFIG.SYS—one for each drive. Be sure that the command line switches for each driver match the hardware settings of the corresponding drive adapter. Finally, check your copy of MSCDEX. You need only one copy of MSCDEX in AUTOEXEC.BAT, but the "/D:" switch must appear twice—once for each drive ID.

Symptom 7-19. Your CD-ROM drive refuses to work with an IDE port The drive might use a non-standard port (other than IDE). Try replacing the drive adapter board. You must connect the CD-ROM drive to a compatible drive adapter. If the drive is proprietary, it will not interface to a regular IDE port. It might be necessary to purchase a drive adapter specifically for the CD-ROM drive.

Symptom 7-20. You cannot get the CD-ROM drive to run properly when mounted vertically CD-ROM drives with "open" drive trays cannot be mounted vertically—disc tracking simply will not work correctly. The only CD-ROM drives that can be mounted vertically are those with caddies, but you should check with those manufacturers before proceeding with vertical mounting.

Symptom 7-21. The SCSI CD-ROM drive refuses to work when connected to an Adaptec SCSI interface Other drives are working fine. This is a common type of problem among SCSI adapters, and is particularly recognized with Adaptec boards because of their great popularity. In most cases, the Adaptec drivers are the wrong version or are corrupted. Try turning off *Sync negotiations* on the Adaptec SCSI interface, and reboot the system. Your SCSI drivers might also be buggy or outdated. Check with Adaptec technical support (**http://www.adaptec.com**) to determine if you should use a later driver version instead.

Symptom 7-22. You see a "No drives found" error when the CD-ROM driver line is executed in CONFIG.SYS In most cases, the driver command-line switches do not match the hardware configuration of the drive adapter. Your low-level driver might be missing or incomplete. Open CONFIG.SYS into a word processor and see that the low-level driver has a complete and accurate command line. See that any command line switches are set correctly. Check the MSCDEX command line next. Open AUTOEXEC.BAT into a word processor and see that the MSCDEX command line is accurate and complete. Also confirm that any MSCDEX command-line switches are set correctly. If you are using SmartDrive with DOS 6.0 or later, try adding the /U switch to the end of your SmartDrive command line in AUTOEXEC.BAT. Check for hardware conflicts. Be sure that no other hardware devices are in the system that might be conflicting with the CD-ROM drive controller. If problems persist, replace the drive controller.

Symptom 7-23. The CD-ROM LCD displays an error code Even without knowing the particular meaning of every possible error message, you can be assured that most CD-based error messages can be traced to the following causes (in order of ease):

- *Bad caddy* The CD caddy is damaged or inserted incorrectly. The CD might also be inserted into the caddy improperly.
- *Bad mounting* The drive is mounted improperly or mounting screws are shorting out the drive's electronics.
- *Bad power* Check that +12 and +5 V are powering the CD-ROM drive. Low power might indicate that your system requires a new or larger supply.
- *Bad drive* Internal diagnostics have detected a fault in the CD-ROM drive. Try replacing the drive.
- *Bad drive controller* Drive diagnostics have detected a fault in the drive controller. Try replacing the drive controller or SCSI adapter (whichever interface you're using).

Symptom 7-24. When a SCSI CD-ROM drive is connected to a SCSI adapter, the system hangs when the SCSI BIOS starts In most cases, the CD-ROM drive supports Plug and Play, but the SCSI controller's BIOS does not. Disable the SCSI BIOS through a jumper on the controller (or remove the SCSI BIOS IC entirely) and use a SCSI driver in CONFIG.SYS instead. You might need to download a low-level SCSI driver from the adapter manufacturer.

Symptom 7-25. You see an error, such as: "Unable to detect ATAPI IDE CD-ROM drive, device driver not loaded" You have a problem with the configuration of your IDE/EIDE controller hardware. Check the signal cable first, and be sure that the 40-pin signal cable is attached properly between the drive and controller. IDE CD-ROM drives are typically installed on a secondary 40-pin IDE port. Be sure that no other device is using the same IRQ or I/O address as your secondary IDE port. Finally, be sure that any command-line switches for the low-level driver in CONFIG.SYS correspond to the controller's hardware settings.

Symptom 7-26. The CD-ROM drive door will not open once the 40-pin IDE signal cable is connected You should only need power to operate the drive door. If the door stops when the signal cable is attached, check for some possible problems. Check the power connector first and be sure that both +5 and +12 V are available at the power connector. See that the power connector is attached securely to the back of the CD-ROM drive. Check the IDE signal cable next—the 40-pin signal cable is probably reversed at either the drive or controller. Try a different signal cable. Also be sure that the 40-pin IDE drive is plugged into a "true" IDE port—not a proprietary (non-IDE 40-pin) port. If problems persist, try a known-good CD-ROM drive.

Symptom 7-27. You are using an old CD-ROM and can play CD audio, but you cannot access directories or other computer data from a CD Older, proprietary CD-ROM drives often used two low-level drivers—one for audio and one for data. You probably only have one of the drivers installed. Check your low-level drivers first, and see that any necessary low-level drivers are loaded in the CONFIG.SYS file. Also see that any command-line switches are set properly. Some older sound boards with integrated, proprietary CD-ROM drive controllers might not work properly with the drivers required for your older CD-ROM drive. You might have to alter the proprietary controller's IRQ, DMA, or I/O settings (and update the driver's command-line switches) until you find a combination where the driver and controller will work together.

Symptom 7-28. The front-panel controls of your SCSI CD-ROM drive do not appear to work under Windows 95 Those same controls appear to work fine in DOS. Windows 95 uses SCSI commands to poll removable media devices every two seconds to see if the status has changed. Because SCSI commands to the CD-ROM generally have higher priority than front-panel controls, the front-panel controls might appear to be disabled under Windows 95. Try pressing the front-panel controls repeatedly. You might be able to correct this issue by disabling the CD-ROM polling under Windows 95.

Symptom 7-29. You cannot change the CD-ROM drive letter under Windows 95 You need to change the drive's settings under the *Device manager*:

- Open the *Control panel* and select the *System* icon.
- Once the *System properties* dialog opens, click on the *Device manager* page.
- Locate the entry for the CD-ROM. Click on the + sign to expand the list of CD-ROM devices.
- Doubleclick on the desired CD-ROM.
- Once the CD-ROM drive's *Properties* dialog appears, choose the *Settings* page.
- Locate the current drive letter assignment box and enter the new drive designation. Multiple letters are needed only when a SCSI device is implementing LUN addressing (i.e., multidisc changers).
- Click on the *OK* button to save your changes.
- Click on the *OK* button to close the *Device manager*.
- A *System settings change* window should appear. Click on the *Yes* button to reboot the system so that the changes can take effect, or click on the *No* button so that you can make more changes to other CD-ROMs before rebooting system. Changes will not become effective until the system is rebooted.

Symptom 7-30. You installed Windows 95 from a CD-ROM disc using DOS drivers, but when you removed the real-mode CD-ROM drivers from CON-FIG.SYS, the CD-ROM no longer works You need to enable protected-mode drivers by running the *Add new hardware* wizard from the *Control panel*:

- Boot Windows 95 using the real-mode drivers for your CD-ROM and its interface.
- Open the *Control panel* and select the *Add new hardware* icon.
- Proceed to add new hardware, but do not let Windows 95 attempt to "auto-detect" the new hardware. Use the diskette with protected-mode drivers for the new installation.
- When the new software is installed, Windows 95 will tell you that it must reboot before the hardware will be available—do not reboot yet.
- Open a word processor, such as Notepad, and edit the CONFIG.SYS and AU-TOEXEC.BAT files to REMark out the real-mode drivers for your CD and the reference to MSCDEX.
- Shut down Windows 95, then power down the system.
- Check that the CD-ROM interface is set to use the resources assigned by Windows 95.
- Reboot the system. Your protected-mode drivers should now load normally.

Symptom 7-31.   Your CD-ROM drive's parallel port-to-SCSI interface worked with Windows 3.1x, but does not work under Windows 95 This problem is typical of the NEC CD-EPPSCSI01 interface, and is usually caused by a problem with the driver's assessment of your parallel-port type (i.e., bi-directional, unidirectional, or enhanced parallel port). Start your CMOS setup routine first and see what mode your parallel port is set to operate in. Be sure it is set to a mode that is compatible with your parallel-port drive. Next, update your version of MSCDEX. Change the MSCDEX command line in AUTOEXEC.BAT to load from the C:\WINDOWS\CONTROL\ directory, and remove the /L:x parameter from the end of the MSCDEX command line (if present). Finally, cold boot the computer. Because typical parallel port-to-SCSI interfaces get their power from the SCSI device, the external drive must be powered up first. If you're using real-mode drivers for the interface, place a switch at the end of the interface's command line that tells the driver what mode your parallel port is operating in. For example, the Trantor T358 driver (MA358.SYS) uses the following switches (yours will probably be different):

- /m02 :for unidirectional mode (also known as *standard* or *output only*)
- /m04 :for bi-directional mode (also known as *PS/2 mode*)
- /m08 :for enhanced mode

As an alternative, disable your real-mode drivers. Remove or REMark out any references to the interface's real-mode drivers in CONFIG.SYS, then remove or disable the MSCDEX command line in AUTOEXEC.BAT. Start Windows 95, open the *Control panel*, select the *System* icon, then choose the *Device manager* page. Find the SCSI adapter settings and expand the "SCSI controllers" branch of the device tree. Select the device identification line for your parallel port-to-SCSI interface, then click on the *Properties* button. Click on the *Settings* page. In the *Adapter settings* dialog box, type in the same parameter that would have been used if you were using real-mode drivers. Click on the *OK* buttons to save your changes, then select *Yes* to reboot the system. If problems persist, check the technical support for your parallel port-to-SCSI adapter and see if there are any known problems with your particular setup, or if any updated drivers are available for download.

Symptom 7-32. You see a message that the: "CD-ROM can run, but results might not be as expected" This simply means that Windows 95 is using real-mode drivers. If protected-mode drivers are available for the CD-ROM drive, you should use those instead.

Symptom 7-33.   The CD-ROM works fine in DOS or Windows 3.1x, but sound or video appears choppy under Windows 95 Several factors can affect CD-ROM performance under Windows 95. Windows 95 performance (and stability) is severely degraded by real-mode drivers, so start by removing or disabling any real-mode drivers. Try installing the protected-mode drivers for your CD-ROM drive instead. If protected-mode drivers are not available for your drive, you might consider upgrading the CD-ROM hardware.

Also, avoid using DOS or Windows 3.1x applications under Windows 95. Real-mode applications run under Windows 95 can also cripple performance. Try exiting any DOS or Windows 3.1x applications that might be running on the Windows 95 desktop. Also exit unneeded Windows 95 applications because additional applications take a toll on processing power. Exit any Windows 95 applications that might be running in the background. Finally, reboot the system to ensure that Windows 95 has the maximum amount of resources available before running your CD-ROM application.

Symptom 7-34. You can't read a Video CD-I disc in Windows 95 using any ATAPI/IDE CD-ROM drive The built-in ATAPI driver in Windows 95 cannot read raw data in 32-bit disk-access mode. Such symptoms can also happen to any ATAPI/IDE-compatible CD-ROM as long as they are using the built-in ATAPI driver in Windows 95. You should update the CD-ROM's ATAPI driver to a current manufacturer-specific version. As another alternative, you can use the following procedure:

1 Disable the 32-bit disk-access feature of Windows 95.
2 Under the Windows 95 *Desktop*, click *Start* and choose *Settings* and *Control panel*.
3 Click on *System* icon and select the *Performance* option.
4 Choose *File system* and select the *Troubleshooting* option.
5 At the *Troubleshooting* dialog, click on "Disable all 32-bit disk access."
6 Edit AUTOEXEC.BAT and append the following line (where {path} is the path name of your Windows 95 software):

```
C:\{path}\COMMAND\MSCDEX.EXE /D:MSCD000
```

Symptom 7-35. An IDE CD-ROM is not detected on a 486 PCI motherboard This is a known problem when using Aztech CD-ROM drives and 486 PCI motherboards with SIS 82C497 chipsets. The motherboard bus noise is far too high, which results in the misinterpretation of the IDE interface handshaking signals (namely DASP,PDIAG). As a consequence, the CD-ROM drive sometimes (or always) is not detected. You might be able to resolve this problem by connecting the IDE CD-ROM drive as a "slave" device to the hard disk—although you might need to slow the hard drive's data-transfer mode to accommodate the slower CD-ROM drive.

Symptom 7-36. An IDE CD-ROM is not detected when "slaved" to an IBM hard drive This is a known problem with Aztech IDE CD-ROM drives and IBM Dala 3450 hard drives. The pulse width for the drive-detection signal (DASP) is not long enough for the CD-ROM to identify itself properly. This results in the improper detection of an Aztech IDE CD-ROM. You should make the CD-ROM drive a master device on its own IDE channel, or (if possible) upgrade the CD-ROM drive's firmware to utilize more reliable timing. If the CD-ROM manufacturer has no firmware upgrades available, and you cannot reconfigure the CD-ROM on another IDE channel, you'll need to replace the CD-ROM or hard drive.

Symptom 7-37. The CD-ROM drive will not read or run CD Plus or Enhanced CD titles This is a known problem with Acer CD-ROM models: 625A, 645A, 655A, 665A, 525E, 743E, 747E, and 767E. The CD Plus (or Enhanced CD) titles use a new data format that was recently released by Sony. The new format is for interactive CD titles that incorporate video clips and music, and the data structures on these CDs cannot be recognized by these CD-ROM drive models. In this case, you'll need to upgrade the CD-ROM drive outright to a newer model that can accommodate newer file types.

Symptom 7-38. You notice that the LED indicator on the CD-ROM is always on The drive seems to be working properly. This is not necessarily a problem. Some CD-ROM drive models (such as the Acer 600 series) use the LED indicator as a "ready" light instead of as a "busy" light. Whenever a CD is loaded in the drive, the LED will be lit, and will remain lit whether the drive is being accessed or not. This feature tells the user whether or not a CD-ROM disc is currently loaded in the drive by simply checking the LED. The CD-ROM drive might have a jumper that allows you to switch the indicator light from "Ready" mode to "Busy" mode.

Symptom 7-39. You cannot play CD-audio on a particular CD-ROM under Windows 95 Replacing the CD-ROM resolves the problem. This is a known incompatibility issue with Acer 525E CD-ROM drives and Windows 95 (this does not affect the integrity of programs and data). Windows 95 will mute the CD-audio on this and many other brands of double-speed IDE CD-ROMs. If you cannot obtain a patch directly from Microsoft or the CD-ROM manufacturer, your only real alternative is to replace the CD-ROM drive.

Troubleshooting CD-R Drives

Prices for CD recorders (or CD-Rs) have tumbled over the first half of 1997—recorders that would have cost thousands of dollars just a couple of years ago can now be purchased for just $400 to $600 (U.S.). These low prices, combined with readily available units from Philips, Sony, Hi-Val, Smart and Friendly, and other manufacturers, means that CD-Rs have begun appearing in desktop and tower systems. CD recorders offer some exciting potentials for computer users. Not only are CD-Rs ideal for file backup and archiving purposes, but

CD-Rs support data-intensive uses, such as photo albums, personal clipart libraries, customized multimedia productions, and high-volume file distribution.

However, CD recorders present some special problems for the typical PC. Virtually all CD-R units use the SCSI interface to handle more consistent data transfer from the system to the drive. Installing a CD-R might require the addition (and expense) of a SCSI adapter and driver software. CD recording demands a substantial commitment of hard-drive space (perhaps as much as 1GB) to create an image file for recording (an "image file" basically converts the data to be recorded into the "pits" and "lands" that must be encoded to the blank disc). So if you're tight on drive space, you might also need another hard drive to support the CD-R. Finally, CD-Rs require a constant and uninterrupted flow of data during the recording process. If the CD-R data buffer empties, the recording process will halt, and your blank CD will be ruined. This means that you need fast hard drives and a high-performance interface (i.e., PIO Mode 4). This part of the chapter explains some of the problems associated with installing and using a CD-R, and illustrates a series of troubleshooting symptoms and solutions.

CD-RECORDING ISSUES

Writing data to recordable compact disc is a complex process that demands a great deal from your PC's hardware and software—most of this complexity is hidden by the power of the CD authoring program, but you should be aware of a number of important factors that can influence the success of CD recording.

File sizes The sheer amount of data being written to the CD is less important than the individual file sizes—the recorder might have trouble locating and opening the files quickly enough to send them smoothly to the CD recorder, where fewer large files are typically problem-free.

System interruptions Any interruption in the flow of data is fatal to CD recording, so be sure that your CONFIG.SYS and AUTOEXEC.BAT files do not load any TSR utilities, which might periodically interrupt the computer's drive operations. Utilities, such as screen savers, calendar alarms or reminders, and incoming faxes are just a few "features" that will interrupt disc writing. If the PC is part of a network, you should temporarily disable network sharing so that no one tries to access the files you're trying to write to the CD.

Hard disk The hard drive is a crucial component of the CD-R system because you must create a sizable "image file," which will then be sent to the CD-R. Consider three major issues when choosing your hard drive: speed, file fragmentation, and thermal calibration.

■ *Speed* To write a virtual "image file" to a compact disc, the hard disk from which you are writing must have a transfer rate fast enough to keep the CD-R drive buffer full. This usually means an average hard disk access time of 19 ms or less. It would also help to use a high-performance drive interface, such as EIDE or SCSI-2.
■ *Fragmentation* This issue is also related to speed. Searching all over a very fragmented hard disk for image file data can cause drive operations to slow down. In many cases, a badly fragmented hard drive cannot support CD-R operations. Be sure to defragment your hard drive before creating an image file.

■ *Thermal calibration* All hard disks periodically perform an automatic thermal calibration to ensure proper performance. Calibration interrupts hard-disk operations for as much as 1.5 seconds. Some hard disks force a calibration at fixed intervals (even if the disk is in use), causing interruptions that are fatal to CD writing. This problem is particularly noticeable when the image file is large, and the writing process takes longer. If you can select a new hard drive to support CD-R operations, choose a drive with "intelligent" thermal calibration, which will postpone recalibration until the drive is idle.

■ *CD recorder speed* Many current CD recorders are capable of writing at 2× or 4× the standard writing/playback speed of 150KB/s (75 sectors/s). Recording speed is simply a matter of how fast the bits are inscribed by the laser on the disc surface, and has nothing to do with how fast you read them back or how much data you can fit on the disc. However, higher recording speeds can accomplish a writing process in a shorter period of time. Faster recording speeds are certainly a time saver, but it also means that larger recording buffers are required (and those buffers empty faster). As a consequence, faster recorders demand a faster hard drive and interface to support data transfer. In most cases, "buffer underrun" type problems can often be corrected by slowing down the recording process, rather than upgrading the drive system.

When you write a real ISO image file from hard disk to CD, speed is rarely a problem because the image is already one gigantic file in which the files and structures are already in order and divided into CD-ROM sectors, so it is only necessary to stream data off the hard drive to the CD recorder. When you write from a "virtual" image, things get trickier because a "virtual" image is little more than a list. The CD authoring program must consult the virtual image database to find out where each file should go in the image and where each file is actually stored on hard disk. The authoring software must then open the file and divide it into CD-ROM sectors—all while sending data to the CD recorder in a smooth, continuous stream. Locating and opening each file is often the more time-consuming part of the recording process (which is why "on-the-fly" writing is more difficult when you have many small files).

CD recorder buffer All CD recorders have a small amount of on-board buffer memory. The CD recorder's buffer helps to ensure that data is always ready to be written because extra data is stored as it arrives from the computer. The size of the buffer is crucial to trouble-free writing—a slow-down or interruption in the transfer of data from the computer will not interrupt writing so long as the buffer is not completely emptied. The larger the buffer, the more safety margin you have in case of interruptions. If your CD recorder has a very small buffer and your hard disk is slow, you might find it difficult (or impossible) to write virtual images on-the-fly to CD. When this occurs, you can make a real ISO image file on the hard disk and record to CD from that, use a faster hard disk sub-system, or upgrade your CD recorder's buffer (if possible).

If you want to write a virtual image on-the-fly to CD, and you have a slow hard disk, it is generally safest to write at 1× speed. Otherwise, create a real ISO image file first and record from that. In most situations where your hardware configuration is adequate (a fast, defragmented hard disk, few small files, and a good-sized CD recording buffer), you can successfully write virtual images straight to CD. However, it's always best to test first and create a real ISO image file only if necessary.

TYPICAL COMPATIBILITY PROBLEMS

Even when CDs record perfectly, it is not always possible to read them correctly in other drives. The following notes highlight three common compatibility issues.

Problems reading recordable CDs Recordable CDs frequently cannot be read in ordinary CD-ROM drives. If the CD can be read when used on the CD-R, but not on a standard CD-ROM drive, check in disc-recording utility to be sure that the session containing the data you just wrote is closed—CD-ROM drives cannot read data from a session that is not closed.

If your recorded disc is ejected, you receive an error message or you have any random problems accessing files from the recorded disc, the problem might be that your CD-ROM drive is not well calibrated to read recorded CDs. Try the disc on another CD-ROM drive.

If you recorded the disc using DOS filenames, but there are difficulties in reading back the recorded CD with DOS or Windows, you might have an older version of MSCDEX (before version 2.23) on your system. Check your MSCDEX version and update it, if necessary.

Problems reading multisession CDs If you can only see data recorded in the first session on the CD—not in subsequent sessions—the disc might have been recorded in CD-ROM (Mode 1) format, but your multi-session CD-ROM drive only recognizes CD-ROM XA (Mode 2) multi-session CDs. If this happens, you might need to re-record the disc in the correct mode. Of course, your CD-ROM drive must support multi-session operation in the first place. If you can only see data recorded in the last session, you might have forgotten to link your new data with data previously recorded on the CD. Refer to the instructions for your CD recorder and review the steps required to create a multi-session CD.

CD-ROM drive incompatibility with recordable CDs Sometimes, it seems that you wrote a CD without trouble and can read it properly on your CD-R, but when you put the disc in a standard CD-ROM drive, the disc is ejected, or you see error messages, such as "No CD-ROM" or "Drive not ready," or you have random problems accessing some files or directories. You might also find that the problems disappear when reading the CD on a different CD-ROM drive.

At first, you might suspect a problem with the original CD-ROM drive, but this might be caused by compatibility problems with some CD-ROM drives (especially older ones) and recorded CDs. Some CD-ROM drive lasers are not calibrated to read recordable CDs (often the surface is different from that of factory-pressed CDs). If your CD-ROM drive reads mass-produced (silver) CDs but not recordable CDs, check with the CD-ROM drive manufacturer to determine whether this is the problem. In some cases, a drive upgrade might be available to resolve the problem.

The combination of blank disc brand and CD recorder can also make a difference. Use blank CD media that has been recommended by the CD-R manufacturer.

CD-R SYMPTOMS

CD recorders are subject to a large number of potential errors during operation. Many typical recording errors are listed. In most cases, the error is not terribly complex and it can be corrected in just a few minutes once the nature of the problem is understood. Keep in mind that the actual error message depends on the CD recorder software in use, so your actual error messages might vary just a bit.

Symptom 7-40. Absorption control error <xxx> This error most often means that there is a slight problem writing to a recordable disc—perhaps caused by a smear or speck of dust. It does not necessarily mean that your data has not been correctly recorded. A sector address is usually given so that you can (if you wish) verify the data in and around that sector. When writing is completed, try cleaning the disc (on the non-label side) gently with a lint-free cloth. If the error occurs again, try a new disc.

Symptom 7-41. Application code error This error typically occurs when you try to write Kodak recordable CDs (Photo CDs) on non-Kodak CD recorders. These discs have a protection bit that is recognized only by the Kodak CD-R—all other recorders will not record these discs. In this case, you'll need to use "standard" blank CDs.

Symptom 7-42. Bad ASPI open The CD-R ASPI driver is bad or missing, and the SCSI CD-R cannot be found. Check the installation of your CD-R drive and SCSI adapter, then check the driver installation. Try reinstalling the SCSI driver(s).

Symptom 7-43. Buffer underrun at sector <xxx> Once an image file is generated, CD writing is a real-time process that must run constantly at the selected recording speed—without interruptions. The CD recorder's buffer is constantly filled with data from the hard drive waiting to be written. This "buffering" action ensures that small slowdowns or interruptions in the flow of data from the computer do not interrupt writing.

The "buffer underrun" message indicates that the flow of data from hard disk to CD recorder was interrupted long enough for the CD recorder's buffer to be emptied, and writing was halted. If this occurs during an actual write operation, rather than a test, your CD might be damaged.

To avoid buffer underruns, you should remove as much processing load as possible from the system. For example, be sure that no screen savers or other *Terminate and Stay Resident (TSR)* programs are active (they can momentarily interrupt operations). Close as many open windows as possible. See that your working hard disk cannot be accessed via a network.

Also, the CD recorder's position in the SCSI chain—or the cable length between the computer and CD recorder—might cause data slowdowns. Try connecting the CD recorder as the first peripheral in the SCSI chain (if not done already), and use a shorter SCSI cable (if possible) between the CD recorder and the SCSI host adapter.

Symptom 7-44. Current disc already contains a closed audio session Under the Red Book standard for audio CDs, all audio tracks must be written in a single session. If you add audio tracks in more than one session, playback results will be unpredictable. Most CD-ROM drives will playback all audio tracks on a CD—even if they are recorded in several different sessions, but most home and car CD players can only playback the tracks in the first session. If you continue and record audio in a different session, you might have problems reading subsequent audio sessions.

Symptom 7-45. Current disc contains a session that is not closed In actuality, CD-ROM drives can only read back one data track per session, so avoid recording another data track in an open session. Be sure to close the session before writing additional data to the disc.

Symptom 7-46.   The currently selected source CD-ROM drive or CD recorder cannot read audio in digital format This is more of a warning than a fault. Reading audio tracks in "digital format" is not the same as playing the music, and few CD-ROM drives are able to read audio tracks in digital format (only Red Book format).

Symptom 7-47. Data overrun/underrun The SCSI host adapter has reported an error that is almost always caused by improper termination or a bad SCSI cable. Recheck the installation of your SCSI adapter, cabling, and termination.

Symptom 7-48. Destination disc is smaller than the source disc This error commonly occurs when you're trying to duplicate an existing CD to the CD-R. There is not enough room on the recordable CD to copy the source CD. Try recording to a blank CD. Use 74-minute media instead of 60-minute media. Some CDs cannot be copied because of the TOC (Table of Contents) overhead in CD recorders, and also because of the calibration zone overhead.

Symptom 7-49. Disc already contains tracks and/or sessions that are incompatible with the requested operation This error appears if you are trying to add data in a format that is different from the data format already on the disc. For example, you'll see this type of error when trying to add a CD-ROM XA session to a disc that already contains a standard CD-ROM session. A disc containing multiple formats is unreadable, so you are not allowed to record the different session type.

Symptom 7-50. Disc is write-protected You are attempting to write to a disc that has already been closed. Use a fresh blank disc for writing.

Symptom 7-51. Error 175-xx-xx-xx This error code often indicates a "buffer underrun." See the Symptom 7-50.

Symptom 7-52. Error 220-01-xx-xx This error code often indicates that some of your software cannot communicate with a SCSI device—possibly because your SCSI bus was reset. In many cases, this is caused by conflicts between real-mode and protected-mode SCSI drivers working in a Windows 95 system. Try REMming out any real-mode SCSI drivers in your CONFIG.SYS file (the protected-mode drivers provided for Windows 95 should be sufficient on their own).

Symptom 7-53.   Error 220-06-xx-xx This error code often indicates a SCSI Selection Time-out error, which indicates a SCSI setup problem—usually with the SCSI host adapter. Contact your SCSI host-adapter manufacturer for detailed installation and testing instructions.

Symptom 7-54. Error reading the *Table of Contents (TOC)* or *Program Memory Area (PMA)* from the disc This recordable disc is defective, or has been damaged (probably during a previous write operation). Do not write to this disc. Unfortunately, you can do very little, except discard the defective disc.

Symptom 7-55. General-protection fault This type of problem has been identified with the Adaptec AHAr-152× family of SCSI host adapters, and is caused by outdated driver software. You can solve this problem by upgrading to version 3.1 or later of Adaptec's EZ-SCSI software. If you're not using Adaptec software, check for current drivers for whatever adapter you're using.

Symptom 7-56. Invalid logical block address This error message usually means that the CD mastering software has requested a data block from the hard disk, which either does not exist or is illegal (this might suggest that your hard disk is corrupted). Exit the CD mastering software and run ScanDisk and Defrag to check and reorganize your hard drive.

Symptom 7-57. Last two blocks stripped This message appears when copying a track to hard disk if the track you are reading was created as multi-session compliant (following the Orange Book standard). This is because a multi-session track is always followed by two run-out blocks. These are included in the count of the total size (in blocks) of the track, but do not contain data and cannot be read back. This message appears to alert you just in case you notice that you got two blocks fewer than were reported for the Read Length. Don't panic—you haven't lost any data.

Symptom 7-58. "MSCDEX" errors are being encountered Early versions of MSCDEX (prior to v.2.23) had problems with filenames containing "illegal" ASCII characters, such as a hyphen. If a directory contains a filename with an "illegal" ASCII character, you can still see all the files by doing a directory (DIR) from DOS, or you can open the illegally named file. However, one or more files listed after the illegal one might not be accessible or might give errors. You should update MSCDEX to the latest available version.

Symptom 7-59. MS-DOS or Windows cannot find the CD-R drive There are several possible reasons why the CD-R drive cannot be found by software. First, turn the computer off and wait at least 15 seconds. Be sure that the SCSI adapter card is firmly seated and secured to the computer case. The SCSI adapter must also be properly configured. Check the SCSI cable and see that it is properly attached to the adapter and drive. Turn the computer on. If problems persist, be sure that the correct SCSI drivers are installed and that any command line switches are set correctly.

Symptom 7-60. No write data (buffer empty) The flow of data to the CD-R drive must be extremely regular so that its working buffer is never empty when it prepares to write a block of information to disc. This message indicates that the flow of data from the hard disk to the CD recorder has been interrupted (similar to the "Buffer underrun" error). Ensure that no screen savers, other TSR utilities, or unneeded open windows are active, which might momentarily interrupt operations. Your working hard disk should not be accessible over a network.

The CD recorder's position in the SCSI chain, or the length of cabling between the SCSI adapter and CD recorder might also cause data slowdowns. Try connecting the CD recorder as the first device in the SCSI chain (you might need to re-terminate the SCSI chain), and keep the SCSI cable as short as possible.

Windows 3.1x requires the use of a RAM cache to manage the flow of data. SmartDrive (the caching utility supplied with Windows 3.1x) is necessary for writing virtual images on-the-fly to CD. However, when writing a real ISO image from hard disk to CD, it might cause a buffer underrun. If a buffer underrun occurs during testing or writing of a real ISO 9660 image under Windows 3.1x, exit to the DOS shell and type the following:

```
smartdrv x-
```

where *x* is the letter of the hard drive from which you will write the ISO image. This disables SmartDrive for the specified drive so that CD writing can proceed smoothly.

Symptom 7-61. Read file error A file referenced by the virtual image database cannot be located or accessed. Be sure that the suspect file is not being used by you or by someone else on a network.

Symptom 7-62. The selected disc image file was not prepared for the current disc This type of error message occurs if you prepared the disc image file for a blank CD, but are now trying to record it to a CD already containing data, (or vice versa). In either case, you would wind up writing a CD that couldn't be read because the CD addresses calculated for the disc image are wrong for that actual CD. If you are given the option of writing anyway, select "No" to abort because it is very unlikely that the writing operation would yield a readable CD.

Symptom 7-63. The selected disc track is longer than the image file The disc-verify process fails immediately because the source ISO 9660 image file and the actual ISO 9660 track on CD are not the same size—the disc track is actually longer than the image file, which could indicate that the CD-R drive is defective.

Symptom 7-64. The selected disc track is shorter than the image file The disc-verify process fails immediately because the source ISO 9660 image file and the actual ISO 9660 track on CD are not the same size—the disc track is actually shorter than the image file, which could indicate that the CD-R drive is defective.

Symptom 7-65. The "disc in" light on the drive does not blink after you turn on the computer In virtually all cases, no power is reaching the CD-R drive. For internal CD-R drives, be sure that the computer's 4-pin power cable is properly connected to the CD-R drive unit. For external CD-R drives, be sure that the power cord is properly connected to the back of the CD-R drive unit and is plugged into a grounded power outlet. Be sure the power switch on the back of the drive is on. Refer to your CD-R drive's installation guide for more detailed information.

Symptom 7-66. Write emergency This error occurs if the drive is interrupted during a write action. It is commonly seen when writing Red Book audio, but it can also occur with data. For example, one typical reason for a write emergency is dust particles that cause the laser to jump off track.

Symptom 7-67. The CD-R is recognized by Windows 95, but it will not function as a normal CD-ROM drive The drive appears normally in the Windows 95 *Device manager*. The driver that is operating the CD-R drive might not allow the drive to function as a normal CD-ROM reader. For example, this is a known problem with the Philips CDD2000 CD-R. Check to see if an updated Windows 95 CD-R driver is available to overcome this limitation. If not, you might need to replace the CD-R drive with an upgraded model whose drivers do support CD-ROM-type functionality.

Symptom 7-68. You cannot read CD-R (gold) discs in some ordinary CD-ROM drives This is actually a very complex issue because a number of important factors can affect the way that a CD is read. Laser calibration plays a big role. Some CD-ROM drive lasers are not calibrated to read recordable discs (whose recorded surface is slightly different from that of "pressed" discs). If your CD-ROM drive reads mass-produced (silver) CDs, but not recordable CDs, check with the CD-ROM drive manufacturer to determine whether laser calibration is the problem. You might be able to return the CD-ROM drive for factory recalibration or replace the CD-ROM drive with a model that is better calibrated for reading both CD-ROM and CD-R discs.

Fast CD-ROM drive operations might be another problem. For some CD-ROM models to work as fast as they do, they must perform unconventional operations, such as a laser calibration in the lead-out area to determine the approximate position of several tracks. With some CD recorders, the session lead-out is not recorded correctly, which can cause problems with gold-disc compatibility.

The CD-R authoring software can be a problem. Any authoring software can sometimes produce incorrect tracks because of bugs or recording glitches. A good way to check whether incompatibility problems lie with the originating software is to test the same gold disc on several CD-ROM drives. If one drive is capable of reading the gold disc back correctly, chances are that the problem was not in the recording process.

Finally, consider your version of MSCDEX. Although MSCDEX (the Microsoft extension for reading CD-ROMs) will allow non-ISO legal characters in filenames, versions of MSCDEX prior to 2.23 have a problem in dealing with filenames that contain the hyphen. If a directory contains a filename with a hyphen in it, you will be able to see all the files by doing a DIR from DOS. But any files listed after the file with the illegal name are not accessible—when trying to open them, you would get a "file not found" message. MSCDEX 2.23 appears to have fixed this bug.

Further Study

This concludes Chapter 7. Be sure to review the glossary and chapter questions on the accompanying CD. If you have access to the Internet, point your Web browser to some of these contacts:

AcerOpen: **http://www.acercomponents.com/POL_CD-Drives.htm**

Adaptec: **http://www.adaptec.com/cdrec/** (CD Creator 2.x and Adaptec's Easy CD Creator Deluxe 3.0)

Aztech: **http://www.aztech.com.sg/c&t/spec_cd.htm**

CDR Publisher: **http://www.cdr1.com**

CeQuadrat: **http://www.cequadrat.com/** (WinOnCD 3.0 software)

El Torito specification: **http://www.ptltd.com/techs/specs.html**

Philips: **http://www.pps.philips.com**

Smart and Friendly: **http://www.smartandfriendly.com**

Teac America: **http://www.teac.com/dsp/dsp.html**

CD-RELATED NEWSGROUPS

alt.cd-rom

alt.cd-rom.reviews

comp.publish.cdrom.hardware

comp.publish.cdrom.multimedia

comp.publish.cdrom.software

comp.sys.ibm.pc.hardware.cd-rom

8

CHIPSETS

CONTENTS AT A GLANCE

AMD Chipset
  AMD-640 chipset
  More on the AMD-640 system
    controller (Northbridge)
  More on the AMD-645 peripheral
    bus controller (Southbridge)

Intel Chipsets
  Intel 430 VX Pentium chipset
  Intel 430 TX Pentium chipset
  Intel 430 HX Pentium chipset
  Intel 430 FX Pentium chipset
  Intel 430 MX mobile Pentium
    chipset
  Intel 440 FX Pentium Pro/II chipset
  Intel 450 GX/KX Pentium Pro
    chipset
  Intel 440 LX Pentium II chipset

VIA Chipsets
  Via Apollo P6 chipset
  Via Apollo VP3 chipset
  Via Apollo VP2 chipset
  Via Apollo VPX/97 chipset
  Via Apollo VP-1 chipset
  Via Apollo Master chipset

SiS Chipsets

OPTi Chipsets
  OPTi discovery chipset
  OPTi Vendetta chipset
  FireStar chipset

Legacy and Support ICs

Further Study

In the early days of the PC, motherboards (and pretty much every other device) were designed and built with discrete logic gates. If you were around in the days of the PC/XT and PC/AT, you probably remember the huge motherboards packed with over 150 to 200 individual ICs. Discrete ICs demanded a lot of power, and took up lots of room. It didn't take designers long to realize that "standard" functions of the PC (like floppy drive interface circuits, DMA controllers, or programmable interrupt controllers) could be integrated onto Application-Specific ICs (or ASICs). With the use of ASICs, PCs were able to drop their chip count, reduce construction costs, and reduce power requirements.

But there are also performance advantages to such high levels of integration. Combining logic circuitry onto a single IC dramatically shortens the signal paths, and allows the circuit to operate at higher speeds. By optimizing the signal paths within the IC itself, performance could be improved even further. Designers quickly saw that they could integrate all the core logic needed to facilitate a complete PC in just a few highly integrated ICs. Because these chips were specifically designed to be used as a set on the motherboard, they were dubbed the *chipset* (Fig. 8-1).

Today, chipsets play a leading role in the design and fabrication of modern personal computers. Where early motherboards could use hundreds of ICs, you'd be hard-pressed to find more than 20 ICs on a current motherboard. In fact, chipsets are so important that new chipsets must be developed to support each new feature or CPU. For example, you'll find that Intel's 430 TX chipset supports features, such as SDRAM, dual CPUs, ACPI, and Ultra DMA—but the venerable 430 HX chipset does not. As a result, motherboards with a 430 HX chipset would have to be replaced with a motherboard using the 430 TX chipset

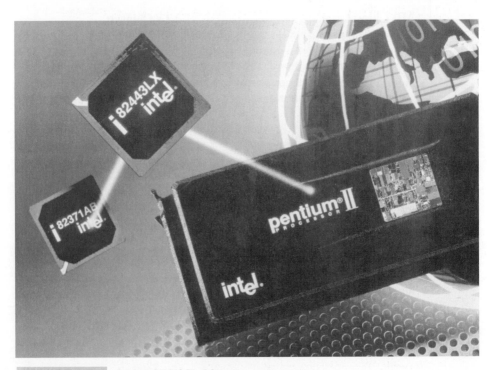

FIGURE 8-1   **An Intel 440LX chipset.** Intel Corporation

TABLE 8-1 DETAILED CHIPSET MANUALS AND TECHNICAL INFORMATION

AMD 640 chipset:	http://www.amd.com/K6/k6docs/pdf/21090c.pdf
Intel 430 FX Pentium chipset:	http://developer.intel.com/design/pcisets/datashts/290518.htm
Intel 430 HX Pentium chipset:	http://developer.intel.com/design/pcisets/datashts/290551.htm
Intel 430 VX Pentium chipset:	http://developer.intel.com/design/pcisets/datashts/290553.htm
Intel 430 TX Pentium chipset:	http://developer.intel.com/design/pcisets/datashts/290559.htm
Intel 450 GX/KX Pentium Pro chipset:	http://developer.intel.com/design/pcisets/datashts/290523.htm
Intel 440FX Pentium Pro chipset:	http://developer.intel.com/design/pcisets/datashts/290549.htm
Intel 440LX Pentium Pro chipset:	http://developer.intel.com/design/pcisets/datashts/290564.htm
Intel 430MX mobile Pentium chipset:	http://developer.intel.com/design/pcisets/datashts/290525.htm
VIA VT82C590 Apollo VP2:	http://www.via.com.tw/vp2586a.pdf
VIA VT82C595:	http://www.via.com.tw/595.pdf
VIA VT82C586B:	http://www.via.com.tw/586b.pdf
VIA VT82C580 Apollo VPX:	http://www.via.com.tw/vpx586a.pdf
VIA VT82C580 Apollo VPX/97:	http://www.via.com.tw/580vpx.pdf
VIA VT82C580 Apollo VP-1:	http://www.via.com.tw/apollovp.pdf
VIA VT82C570M Apollo VP Master:	http://www.via.com.tw/apollovp.pdf
VIA VT82C496 Pluto:	http://www.via.com.tw/496pluto.pdf
SiS chipset family	http://www.sisworld.com/
OPTi Vendetta	ftp://ftp.opti.com/pub/chipsets/system/vendetta/index.htm

before those features would be available. Ultimately, the overall features and capabilities of your PC are largely defined by the motherboard chipset (sometimes called *core logic*). This chapter is intended to familiarize you with many of the current chipsets in use today. If you want detailed technical information about today's chipsets, you can usually download the complete manual from the chipset manufacturer's Web site (in Adobe Acrobat's .PDF format). Table 8-1 lists the URLs for many chipset manuals.

The companion CD offers several utilities for the detection of core logic chipsets. For older motherboards, try SHOWS174.ZIP. For more recent systems, use CONF810E.ZIP, which also provides a complete assessment of system information (highly recommended).

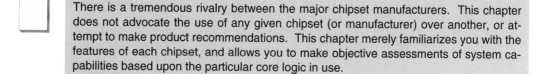

There is a tremendous rivalry between the major chipset manufacturers. This chapter does not advocate the use of any given chipset (or manufacturer) over another, or attempt to make product recommendations. This chapter merely familiarizes you with the features of each chipset, and allows you to make objective assessments of system capabilities based upon the particular core logic in use.

AMD Chipsets

Although AMD (Advanced Micro Devices) is certainly no stranger to the CPU arena, they are relative newcomers to the chipset market. Traditionally, AMD relied on other chipset makers to support their line of CPUs (i.e., the 5x85, K5, and K6). However, not all chipset makers provided the optimum support for AMD's products. As a consequence, AMD has developed the 640 chipset for use with their K6 CPU.

AMD-640 CHIPSET

The AMD-640 chipset features two devices: the AMD-640 system controller, and the AMD-645 peripheral bus controller (Table 8-2). Working together, these chips can deliver numerous high-performance features that accelerate multimedia applications (especially those designed for MMX-type processors). The AMD-640 system controller has been optimized to accelerate AMD-K6 processor transactions, and also incorporates support for SDRAM (Synchronous DRAM)—the most recent development in the evolution of main system memory. The AMD-645 peripheral bus controller features support for Ultra DMA/33, which allows the ATA/IDE interface to provide a 33MB/s data transfer rate. System performance is further increased with Type F DMA, which provides a 5× improvement over standard DMA transfers. Type F DMA reduces the system bus requirements for DMA transfers, providing the CPU with greater access to the ISA bus (less of a bottleneck during data transfers). Perhaps most important for AMD, the 640 chipset is backward-compatible with existing AMD and Intel CPUs.

TABLE 8-2 SUMMARY OF MOTHERBOARD CHIPSET COMPONENTS

MASTER CHIPSET	COMPONENT	#NEEDED	FUNCTION
AMD-640	AMD-640	1	System controller
	AMD-645	1	Peripheral bus controller
Intel 430 VX (Triton II*)	82437VX	1	System controller
	82371SB	1	PCI ISA IDE Xcelerator (PIIX3)
	82438VX	2	Data path unit
Intel 430 TX	82439TX	1	System controller
	82371AB	1	PCI ISA IDE Xcelerator (PIIX4)
Intel 430 HX (Triton II*)	82439HX	1	System controller
	82371SB	1	PCI I/O IDE Xcelerator (PIIX3)
Intel 430 FX (Triton*)	82437FX	1	System controller
	82371FB	1	SA bridge, PCI/ISA/IDE Xcelerator (PIIX)
	82438FX	2	Data path unit
Intel 430 MX	82437MX	1	System controller
	82438MX	2	Data path units
	82371MX	1	PCI I/O IDE Xcelerator (MPIIX)
Intel 440 FX (Natoma*)	82441FX	1	PCI and memory controller
	82442FX	1	Data bus accelerator
	82371SB	1	PCI ISA IDE Xcelerator (PIIX3)
Intel 450 KX (Orion*)	82451KX	4	Memory interface component
	82452KX	1	Data path unit
	82453KX	1	Data controller
	82454KX	1 or 2	PCI bridge
Intel 450 GX (Orion*)	82451GX	4	Memory interface component
	82452GX	1	Data path unit
	82453GX	1	Data controller
	82454GX	1 or 2	PCI bridge

TABLE 8-2 SUMMARY OF MOTHERBOARD CHIPSET COMPONENTS (CONTINUED)

MASTER CHIPSET	COMPONENT	#NEEDED	FUNCTION
Intel 440 LX	82443LX	1	PCI AGP System controller
	82371AB	1	PCI ISA IDE Xcelerator (PIIX4)
VIA Apollo P6	VT82C685VP	1	System controller
	VT82C586	1	PCI/ISA/IDE/USB controller
	VT82C687	1	Memory controller
VIA Apollo VP3	VT82C597	1	System controller
	VT82C586B	1	PCI/IDE/USB controller
VIA Apollo VP2/97	VT82C595	1	System controller
	VT82C586B	1	PCI/IDE/USB controller
VIA Apollo VPX/97	VT82C585VPX	1	System controller
	VT82C586B	1	PCI/ISA/IDE/USB controller (97-compliant)
	or VT82C586A	1	PCI/ISA/IDE/USB controller (non-97)
	VT82C587VP	2	Share frame buffers
VIA Apollo VP-1	VT82C585VP	1	System controller
	VT82C586	1	PCI/IDE/ISA/USB controller
	VT82C587VP	2	Share frame buffers
VIA Apollo Master	VT82C575M	1	System controller
	VT82C576M	1	PCI/ISA/IDE controller
	VT82C577M	2	Frame buffers
	VT82C416	1	Support controller
SiS 5597 (Jedi)	5597	1	Integrated system controller
SiS 5596	5596	1	System controller
	5513	1	USB controller
SiS 5571 (Trinity)	5571	1	Integrated system controller
SiS 551X	5511	1	System controller
	5512	1	Bus controller
	5513	1	USB controller
SiS 85C49X (486)	85C496	1	System controller
	85C497	1	Bus controller
OPTi Discovery	82C650	1	System Controller
	82C651	1	Bus controller
	82C652	1	Auxiliary PCI bus controller
OPTi Vendetta	82C750	1	Integrated system controller
OPTi Fire Star	82C700	1	Integrated system controller

TYPICAL CHIPSET FUNCTION DESIGNATIONS

- APIC: Advance Programmable Interrupt Controller
- DBX: Data Bus Accelerator
- DC: Data Controller
- DP: Data Path
- DPU: Data Path Unit
- B: ISA Bridge
- MIC: Memory Interface Component
- PB: PCI Bridge
- PIIX: PCI ISA IDE Xcelerator

TABLE 8-2 SUMMARY OF MOTHERBOARD CHIPSET COMPONENTS (CONTINUED)

MASTER CHIPSET	COMPONENT	#NEEDED	FUNCTION

- PMC: PCI and Memory Controller
- PRMC: Power Management Controller
- SC: System Controller
- SMBA: Shared Memory Buffer Architecture
- UMA: Unified Memory Architecture
- USBC: Universal Serial Bus Controller

*Intel chipset code names are strictly unofficial, and Intel does not even acknowledge the use of code names.

MORE ON THE AMD-640 SYSTEM CONTROLLER (NORTHBRIDGE)

The AMD-640 system controller features the 64-bit Socket 7 interface, integrated write-back cache controller, system memory controller, and PCI bus controller. The Socket 7 interface has been optimized for the AMD-K6 processor—providing 3-1-1-1-1-1-1-1 transfer timing for both read and write transactions from PBSRAM (Pipeline Burst Static RAM) at 66 MHz. The memory controller features a data-buffering design that uses four cache lines (16 quad words or QW) of processor-to-DRAM or cache-to-DRAM write buffering with concurrent write-back capability to accelerate write-back and write-miss cycles. The integrated PCI bus controller features concurrent processor and PCI operation through a five-double word (or DW) posted write buffer design. PCI concurrency with DRAM or cache memory is achieved through a 48-double word post write buffer and 26-double word prefetch buffer.

The AMD-640 design also uses byte-merging, which optimizes processor-to-PCI throughput and reduces PCI bus traffic by converting consecutive processor addresses into burst PCI cycles. The controller minimizes PCI initiator read latency and DRAM access using techniques, such as snoop ahead, snoop filtering, forwarding cache write-backs to the PCI initiator, and merging L1 write-backs into the PCI-posted write buffers. The integrated PCI controller supports enhanced PCI bus commands, such as Memory-Read-Line, Memory-Read-Multiple, and Memory-Write-Invalidate. These features allow a PCI initiator to achieve the full 133-Mbps burst-transfer rate. The integrated PCI bus controller is fully compatible with the PCI local bus specification (revision 2.1). Table 8-3 offers the AMD-640 chipset features at a glance.

MORE ON THE AMD-645 PERIPHERAL BUS CONTROLLER (SOUTHBRIDGE)

The AMD-645 peripheral bus controller features an integrated ISA bus controller, enhanced master mode PCI EIDE controller with Ultra DMA/33 technology, ACPI-compatible Power Management Unit, USB controller, PS2-compatible keyboard/mouse controller, and Real-Time Clock (RTC) with extended 256-byte CMOS RAM. The on-chip EIDE controller has a dual-channel DMA engine with capability of interlaced dual-channel commands. High-bandwidth PCI transfers are achieved by an enhanced 16 double-word data FIFO with full scatter and gather capability. The integrated USB controller features a root hub with two ports having 18-level-deep data FIFOs and built-in physical layer transceivers. The USB controller also offers backward compatibility with legacy keyboard and PS/2 mouse support. The AMD-645 peripheral bus controller meets Microsoft Windows 95 Plug-and-Play requirements with steerable PCI interrupts, ISA interrupts, and DMA channels. The integrated power management unit is compliant with ACPI and APM, and provides dedicated input pins for external modem ring indication and power-on, five general-purpose I/O pins with option for I2C port, and 16 general-purpose pins that can be programmed as inputs or outputs.

Intel Chipsets

The Intel corporation provided the 8086 CPU that went into the first PC, and has led the way in CPU development ever since. Though competitors like AMD and Cyrix are narrowing the performance gap, Intel has managed to retain the lead in fast, high-performance CPUs, like the Pentium II. Because Intel is the first to release new CPUs, they are also ideally positioned to develop the chipsets to complement those CPUs. Intel is also a frequent collaborator with Microsoft in the proposal of new industry initiatives (such as ACPI and AGP), so they often have a head-start in supporting those initiatives. Intel offers a wide range of chipsets.

INTEL 430 VX PENTIUM CHIPSET

The Intel 430 VX chipset (also referred to as the "Triton II" chipset) is used in relatively recent Pentium-based PCs that are designed for low-end or end-user applications (e.g., multimedia, games, and personal productivity software). The 430 VX chipset integrates support for the Universal Serial Bus (USB) standard, so home users can add a wide variety of Plug-and-Play digital input devices, such as mice, keyboards, joysticks, scanners, and cameras. The 430 VX supports concurrent PCI architecture, which maximizes system

---

TABLE 8-3 AMD-640 CHIPSET FEATURES AT A GLANCE

- Optimized for the AMD-K6 processor
- Provides SDRAM, EDO RAM, and FPM RAM support
- Offers PCI concurrency
- Supports Ultra DMA/33
- Includes Data path units
- Includes PS/2 keyboard/mouse controller
- Includes RTC
- Backward compatible with other AMD and non-AMD processors
- Offers USB support
- Supports ACPI
- Includes Plug-and-Play support

performance with simultaneous activity on the CPU, PCI, and ISA buses. This generally improves video and audio performance for multimedia applications, and allows more high-speed peripherals in the systems without impacting the performance of the PCI bus. Improved EDO memory support, faster timing, and support for Synchronous DRAM (SDRAM) are also included. Memory support also allows the Shared Memory Buffer Architecture (SMBA) option. The Intel 430VX PCIset consists of the 82437VX system controller, two 82438VX data paths, and the 82371SB PCI ISA IDE Xcelerator (PIIX3).

Although the 430 VX is generally considered to be a good performer, some features are noticeably absent. There is no support for multiple CPUs, and no support for ECC. The chipset will only handle up to 128MB of RAM (but only 64MB are cacheable). RAM timing is also a bit slower than the 430 HX, so 430 TX systems tend to be a bit slower—even when SDRAM is installed. Table 8-4 outlines the features of the 430 VX chipset.

INTEL 430 TX PENTIUM CHIPSET

The 430 TX chipset optimizes the capabilities of the Intel Pentium processor with MMX technology (Pentium MMX), and has found "dual-duty" in both desktop and mobile PCs.

TABLE 8-4 INTEL PENTIUM/MMX CHIPSET FEATURES AT A GLANCE

CHIPSET	430 VX	430 TX	430 HX	430 FX	430 MX
Processor	Pentium	Pentium	Pentium	Pentium	Pentium
Voltage	3.3 V(I/O)	3.3 V(I/O)	3.3 V(I/O)	3.3 V(I/O)	3.3 V(I/O)
Dual CPUs	No	No	Yes	No	No
Refresh	CAS-before-RAS	CAS-before-RAS	CAS-before-RAS	RAS Only	CAS-before- RAS
RAS Lines	5	6	8	5	4
64-Mbit Support	No	Yes	Yes	No	No
Max Memory Size	128MB	256MB	512MB	128MB	128MB
Memory Types	SDRAM/EDO/FPM	SDRAM/EDO/FPM	EDO/FPM	EDO/SPM	EDO/SPM
SDRAM (CL=2)	6-1-1-1	6-1-1-1	N/A	N/A	N/A
EDO (66 MHz)	6-2-2-2	5-2-2-2	5-2-2-2	7-2-2-2	7-2-2-2
MA Buffers	Integrated	Integrated	Integrated	External	External
ECC/Parity	No	No	Yes	No	No
L2 Cache Type	Async, DRAM, Pburst	Pburst	Pburst	Async, Burst, Pburst	Async, Burst, Pburst
Cacheability	64MB	64MB	512MB	64MB	64MB
PCI Support	PCI 2.1	PCI 2.1	PCI 2.1	PCI 2.0	PCI 2.0
Concurrent PCI	Yes	Yes	Yes	No	No
MTT	Yes	Yes	Yes	No	No
SMBA Support	Yes	No	No	No	No
Bridge Type	PIIX3	PIIX4	PIIX3	PIIX	MPIIX
USB Support	Yes	Yes	Yes	No	No
IDE Support	BMIDE	Ultra DMA	BMIDE	BMIDE	Normal IDE
RTC	ßExternal	Integrated	External	External	External
Power Mgt.	N/A	ACPI	N/A	N/A	SMI, APM
I/O Mgt.	N/A	SM Bus/GPIO	N/A	N/A	N/A

Reduced power consumption enables new applications by delivering mobile-style power management to the desktop. The 430 TX chipset features Dynamic Power Management Architecture (DPMA)—extending the battery life of mobile computers, and enabling new power-efficient desktop models. Support for the Advanced Configuration and Power Interface (ACPI) also improves power management.

The 430 TX also supports the Ultra DMA disk drive protocol with the enhancements required for faster performance of today's multimedia applications. For higher memory throughput, the chip set supports Synchronous DRAM (or a mix of SDRAM and EDO RAM). Concurrent PCI support is available for the first time in a mobile PCI chip set, enabling faster and smoother video and audio performance. There is also support for the Universal Serial Bus (USB). With the "outside the box" Plug-and-Play capabilities of USB, the 430 TX chipset helps the integration of multimedia, I/O peripherals, and digital imaging devices.

The 430 TX also implements a full System Management Bus (SMBus) host controller with three-wire interface—through which the system can communicate with simple monitoring controllers. For example, "Smart Battery" devices can provide information to the power-management charging system via the SMBus. The user can then be informed of the current battery state, along with an accurate prediction of the available operating time (or remaining time to fully charge the battery). Table 8-4 compares the features of the 430 TX.

The 430 TX chipset is a two-chip solution consisting of the 82439TX system controller, and the 82371AB PCI ISA IDE Xcelerator. The 430 TX forms a host-to-PCI bridge, provides the second level (L2) cache control, and offers a full 64-bit data path to main memory. The system controller integrates the cache and main memory DRAM control functions, and provides bus control for transfers between the CPU, cache, main memory, and the PCI bus. The L2 cache controller supports write-back cache for cache sizes of 256KB and 512KB (cache-less designs are also supported).

INTEL 430 HX PENTIUM CHIPSET

The venerable 430 HX chipset (unofficially dubbed "Triton II") is perhaps the most well-known and well-respected Pentium chipset ever produced. With uncompromised EDO RAM timing, the 430 HX matches the performance of an asynchronous L2 cache-based system (without the cache). It supports 64Mbit DRAM, and offers 8 RAS lines (for up to 512MB of system memory). Memory address buffers are built into the system controller. Integrated deep-posting and FIFO buffers enable concurrent activity on both sides of the system controller and data paths for improved CPU utilization. ECC and parity memory support are integrated into the chip set, along with dual CPU support. The 430 HX supports concurrent PCI architecture and the Universal Serial Bus (USB). The 430 HX chipset consists of the 82439HX system controller and the 82371SB PCI I/O IDE Xcelerator (PIIX3). Table 8-4 lists the features of the 430 HX.

INTEL 430 FX PENTIUM CHIPSET

The 430 FX chipset (or "Triton" as it is unofficially known) was the first Intel Pentium chipset to become extremely successful—so successful, in fact, that it is largely deemed to be the undoing of other competitors like ETEQ, UMC, and ALI. It was also the first x86-type chipset using EDO RAM (and is responsible for EDO now being a standard RAM type). Although the 430 FX is now obsolete, it is still considered to be a decent performer. Table 8-4 lists the specifications for the 430 FX chipset.

The 430 FX chipset consists of the 82437FX system controller, two 82438FX Data Paths, and the 82371FB PCI ISA IDE Xcelerator (or PIIX). The chipset forms a host-to-PCI bridge, provides second level (L2) cache control, and supports a full 64-bit data path to main memory. The system controller integrates the cache and main memory DRAM control functions, and provides bus control for transfers between the CPU, cache, main memory, and the PCI bus. The L2 cache controller supports a write-back cache for cache sizes of 256KB and 512KB (cache-less designs are also supported). Cache memory can be implemented with either standard, burst, or pipelined burst SRAMs. An external Tag RAM is used for the address tag, and an internal Tag RAM handles the cache line status bits. The system controller supports up to 128MB of main memory. An optimized PCI interface allows the CPU to sustain a high bandwidth to the graphics frame buffer at all frequencies. Using the snoop-ahead feature, the system controller allows PCI masters to achieve full PCI bandwidth. The data paths provide the connections between the CPU/cache, main memory, and PCI bus.

INTEL 430 MX MOBILE PENTIUM CHIPSET

The 430 MX chipset is the first of Intel's complete mobile chipset solutions for the Pentium processor. The 430 MX uses many architectural innovations developed for the 430 FX chipset designed for desktop computers, and was designed for such uses as ProShare, high-speed Ethernet, and audio/graphic-intensive applications. The 430 MX chipset is ideally suited for any application that requires a faster bus (from 25 to 33MHz) for greater performance.

The 430 MX supports EDO RAM and pipelined-burst SRAM. Its architecture provides greater than 100 MB/s PCI data streaming. The highly integrated Mode 4 local bus IDE controller improves the operation of fast hard drives. In addition, its integrated Plug-and-Play port makes systems easier to use and increases performance by transforming ISA motherboard peripherals into pseudo-PCI devices. As a mobile chipset, the 430 MX benefits from Advanced Power Management (APM) support.

The 430 MX chipset consists of the 82437MX system controller, two 82438MX data paths, and the 82371MX PCI I/O IDE Xcelerator (or MPIIX). The 430 MX forms a host-to-PCI bridge, provides the second level (L2) cache control, and supports a full 64-bit data path to main memory. The 82371MX MPIIX provides the bridge between the PCI bus and the ISA-like Extended I/O expansion bus. In addition, the 82371MX has an IDE interface that supports two IDE devices—providing an interface for IDE hard disks and CD-ROM drives. The MPIIX integrates many common I/O functions used in ISA-based PC systems—a seven-channel DMA controller, two 82C59 interrupt controllers, a 8254 timer/counter, Intel SMM power management support, and control logic for NMI generation. Chip-select decoding is provided for the BIOS, real-time clock, and keyboard controller. Edge/level interrupts and interrupt steering are supported for PCI Plug-and-Play compatibility.

INTEL 440 FX PENTIUM PRO/II CHIPSET

The 440 FX chipset (unofficially referred to as the "Natoma" chipset) is a highly integrated solution for supporting Pentium II and Pentium Pro processors in mainstream business systems. This second-generation chipset optimizes system performance for 32-bit application software in 32-bit operating system environments, and will support multiple CPUs. Based on concurrent PCI architecture, the 440 FX chipset includes a multi-transaction timer (MTT) for enhanced video transfer and higher frame rates, and a passive release mechanism for improved MPEG and audio performance. There is also enhanced write performance for full utilization of write buffers (to improve host-based processing applications) and PCI-delayed transactions to ensure CPU-to-ISA write control compatibility with the PCI 2.1 specification.

The 440 FX chipset is slated for compact designs implemented in a four-layer board (in either the ATX, baby AT, or LPX form factors). The chipset supports up to 1GB maximum memory size using flexible memory options including EDO RAM. Memory is further enhanced with ECC support. The 440 FX also utilizes the PIIX3—allowing motherboards to use the same I/O subsystems as those used with the 430 HX and 430 VX. Universal Serial Bus (USB) support allows for Plug-and-Play connectivity "outside the box," and Bus Master IDE (BMIDE) handles access for fast hard drives. Table 8-5 lists the features for a 440 FX chipset. The 440 FX chipset consists of the 82441FX PCI and memory controller, the 82442FX data bus accelerator, and the 82371SB PCI ISA IDE Xcelerator (or PIIX3).

TABLE 8-5   INTEL PENTIUM PRO/II CHIPSET FEATURES AT A GLANCE

CHIPSET	440 FX	450 GX	450 KX
Processor	Pentium Pro Pentium II	Pentium Pro	Pentium Pro
Voltage	GTL+	GTL+	GTL+
Dual CPUs	Yes	Up to quad processor	Yes
Refresh	RAS only or CAS-before-RAS	CAS-before-RAS	CAS-before-RAS
RAS Lines	8	16	8
64-Mbit Support	Yes	Yes	Yes
Max Memory Size	1GB	8GB	1GB
Memory Types	EDO/FPM/BEDO	FPM	FPM
Memory Interleave	No	4-way, 2-way, non	2-way, non
ECC/Parity	Yes	Yes*	Yes*
PCI Support	PCI 2.1	PCI 2.0	PCI 2.0
Concurrent PCI	Yes	N/A	N/A
MTT	Yes	No	No
SMBA Support	No	No	No
Bridge Type	PIIX3	Not included	Not included
USB Support	Yes	N/A**	N/A**
IDE Support	BMIDE	N/A***	N/A***
RTC	External	N/A	N/A
Power Mgt.	SMM	SMM	SMM
I/O Mgt.	N/A	N/A	N/A

Notes:
*ECC only on memory and parity on host bus
**Some motherboard implementations include the 82371SB, which is capable of USB
***Some motherboard implementations include the 82371FB, which is capable of bus master IDE

INTEL 450 GX/KX PENTIUM PRO CHIPSET

The 450 GX chipset (known as the "Orion" chipset) is designed to support Pentium Pro processor servers and scientific systems—especially those which use multiple CPUs (up to four). By comparison, the 450 KX (also sometimes referred to as "Orion") is aimed at designers of workstations and high-performance desktops with one or two CPUs. In actuality, the 450 GX/KX chipsets are rarely used because of the many features the chipsets lack. Neither supports concurrent PCI, USB, or any form of I/O management. When compared with other contemporary chipsets, the 450 GX/KX are simply not as competitive as the more recent 440 FX chipset. Table 8-5 highlights the features of the 450 GX/KX chipset.

INTEL 440 LX PENTIUM II CHIPSET

The 440 LX chipset is the first in a series of AGP (Accelerated Graphics Port) chipsets from Intel designed to optimize the performance of a Pentium II processor. This is seen as a major new computing platform for small business, large business, and home users alike. The 440 LX chipset with AGP extends the system bandwidth to the graphics controller, and optimizes the system bandwidth and concurrency with the implementation of Quad Port Acceleration (QPA). QPA provides four-port concurrent arbitration of the processor bus, graphics bus, PCI bus, and SDRAM.

The 440 LX chipset also offers advanced power management and fast resume from powered-down states through Advanced Configuration and Power Interface (ACPI). This enables local power down operation, with remote wake up for off-hours maintenance. Application performance for 3D graphics are improved. AGP gives PCs the capability to handle memory-intensive 3D graphics applications, providing the faster performance and enabling larger textures out of main memory—resulting in more life-like image detail.

The 82443LX PCI AGP system controller integrates a host-to-PCI bridge, optimized DRAM controller and data path, and an Accelerated Graphics Port (AGP) interface into a single chip. The I/O subsystem portion of the 440 LX is the 82371AB, which provides an ISA bridge, a PCI ISA IDE Xcelerator (PIIX4), and USB controller. Table 8-6 lists the features for the 440LX chipset.

TABLE 8-6 INTEL PENTIUM II CHIPSET FEATURES AT A GLANCE	
CHIPSET	**440 LX**
Processor	Pentium II
Voltage	GTL+
Dual CPUs	Yes
DRAMRefresh	CAS-before-RAS
RAS Lines	8
64 Mbit Support	Yes
Max. Memory Size	1GB EDO, 512MB SDRAM
Memory Types	EDO/SDRAM
Memory Interleave	No

TABLE 8-6 INTEL PENTIUM II CHIPSET FEATURES AT A GLANCE (CONTINUED)	
CHIPSET	440 LX
ECC/Parity	Yes
PCI Support	PCI 2.1
Concurrent PCI	Yes
AGP compliant	Yes
1× Support	Yes
2× Support	Yes
PIPE	Yes
SEA	Yes
MTT	Yes
SMBA Support	No
Bridge Type	PIIX4
USB Support	Yes
IDE Support	BMIDE and Ultra DMA/33
RTC	Integrated
Power Mgt.	SMM and ACPI
I/O Mgt.	SMBus/GP10

VIA Chipsets

Founded in 1987, VIA is perhaps the greatest threat to Intel's dominance of the chipset market. Their line of Apollo chipsets has provided an effective alternative for the support of Intel Pentium/MMX/Pro, AMD K5 and K6, and Cyrix 6x86 and M2 CPUs. VIA chipsets are generally recognized as full-featured, high-performance solutions that are used on many motherboards. VIA also produces a selection of network and peripheral controller ICs for computer applications.

VIA APOLLO P6 CHIPSET

VIA's VT82C680 Apollo P6 is a high-performance energy-efficient chipset for PCI/ISA desktop and notebook PC systems based on 64-bit Intel Pentium Pro processors. The chipset supports multiple Pentium Pro configurations (based on Intel GTL+), and handles up to 66MHz external CPU bus speed. The chipset also supports the Pentium Pro CPU multi-phase protocols for split transactions and eight level deep in-order queue for optimal CPU throughput. The DRAM and PCI bus are also independently powered so that each of the buses can be run at 3.3 V or 5 V (the ISA bus always runs at 5 V). The main features of the Apollo P6 chipset are listed in Table 8-7.

VIA APOLLO VP3 CHIPSET

The Apollo VP3 is a high-performance, two-chip chipset for the implementation of AGP, PCI, and ISA bus architectures in desktop and notebook PC systems, based on 64-bit Socket-

7 CPUs (including Intel Pentium and Pentium MMX, AMD K5 and K6, and Cyrix/IBM 6x86 and 6x86MX processors). The Apollo VP3 chipset consists of the VT82C597 system controller and the VT82C586B PCI-to-ISA bridge. The VT82C597 system controller provides superior performance between the CPU, optional synchronous cache, DRAM, AGP bus, and the PCI bus with pipelined, burst, and concurrent operation. The VT82C597 complies with the Accelerated Graphics Port Specification 1.0 and features a 66MHz master system bus. It is interesting to notice that the VP3 chipset is one of the few that provide AGP support for non-Pentium Pro processors. The key features for the chipset are shown in Table 8-8.

VIA APOLLO VP2 CHIPSET

The two-chip VIA Apollo VP2/97 is the industry's most highly integrated, high-performance Socket 7 compliant chipset. With ECC, Microsoft PC-97 compliance, SDRAM, 512MB DRAM, and 2MB cache support, the VP2/97 offers remarkable versatility for Intel Pentium, Pentium MMX, Cyrix/IBM 6x86 and 6x86MX, and AMD K5 and K6 MMX processors.

The Apollo VP2/97 builds on the VIA VT82C580VP Apollo VP (widely recognized as a leading Socket 7 chipset). Additional performance related features include a fast DRAM

TABLE 8-7 VIA APOLLO P6 CHIPSET FEATURES AT A GLANCE

■ Highly integrated 3-chip solution
■ Fast DRAM controller
■ Intelligent PCI bus controller
■ Enhanced master-mode PCI IDE controller
■ Plug-and-Play controller with two Windows 95-compliant Plug-and-Play ports
■ Integrated USB interface with hub and dual function ports
■ Integrated power management, providing normal, doze, sleep suspend and conserve modes
■ GTL+ bus-driver/receiver compatible with Intel fast DRAM controller specifications
■ Up to 1GB of banked DRAM

TABLE 8-8 VIA APOLLO VP3 CHIPSET FEATURES AT A GLANCE

■ PC-97 compatible using VT82C586B with ACPI power management.
■ Includes Ultra-DMA/33, EIDE, USB, and Keyboard/PS2-mouse interfaces.
■ Includes RTC/CMOS on-chip.
■ Supports 64-bit Socket 7 CPUs, 64-bit system memory, 32-bit PCI, and 32-bit AGP interfaces.
■ 3.3-V and sub-3.3-V interface to CPU.
■ 3.3-V (5-V tolerant) DRAM, AGP, and PCI interface.
■ AGP v1.0 compliant.
■ PCI buses are synchronous to host CPU bus.
■ 33MHz operation on the primary PCI bus.
■ 66MHz PCI operation on the AGP bus.
■ Concurrent CPU and AGP access.
■ Supports FPM RAM, EDO RAM, and SDRAM.

TABLE 8-9 VIA APOLLO VP2 CHIPSET FEATURES AT A GLANCE

- PC-97 compliance includes an extension to ACPI/OnNow.
- Integrated Universal Serial Bus controller.
- Enhanced master-mode PCI IDE controller with extension to Ultra-DMA/33.
- Support for up to 512MB DRAM with ECC.
- DRAM controller with FPM/EDO/SDRAM support in mixed combinations of 32-bit or 64-bit data bus widths.
- Intelligent PCI bus controller offering concurrent PCI master/CPU/IDE operations, and zero wait-state PCI master and slave burst-transfer rates.
- Integrated KeyBoard Controller (KBC) and Real-Time Clock (RTC).
- Supports Pentium, Pentium MMX, Cyrix 6x86 and M2, and AMD K5 and K6 MMX.
- Advanced cache controller with burst synchronous cache SRAM support up to 2MB.
- Plug-and-Play controller and PCI-to-ISA bridge.

controller with support for SDRAM, EDO, BEDO, and FPM DRAM types in mixed combinations with 32-/64-bit data bus widths and row and column addressing, a deeper buffer with enhanced performance, an intelligent PCI bus controller with concurrent PCI master/CPU/IDE operations, and zero-wait-state PCI master and slave burst transfer rates. The Apollo VP2/97 features the VIA VT82C586B PCI-IDE controller chip, which supports ACPI/OnNow, Ultra-DMA/33, and USB technologies. Table 8-9 lists the main features of the chipset.

VIA APOLLO VPX/97 CHIPSET

The VIA VT82C580VPX Apollo VPX/97 core logic chipset is a high-performance four-chip solution for Socket 7 main boards supporting Intel Pentium, Pentium MMX, Cyrix/IBM 6x86 and 6x86MX, and AMD K5 and K6 MMX processors. To enable proper implementation of the Cyrix/IBM 6x86 200+ processor, the chipset features an asynchronous CPU bus that operates at either 66 or 75MHz speeds. Apollo VPX/97 also supports the Cyrix/IBM linear burst mode.

The Apollo VPX/97 features a fast DRAM controller with support for SDRAM, EDO, BEDO and FPM DRAM types in mixed combinations of 32- or 64-bit data bus widths. Additional features include a deeper buffer with enhanced performance, an intelligent PCI bus controller with concurrent PCI master/CPU/IDE operations, and zero-wait-state PCI master and slave burst transfer rates. There is support for up to 2MB of L2 cache, and up to 512MB of DRAM. The VIA Apollo VPX/97 features the VIA VT82C586B PCI-IDE controller chip that complies with the Microsoft PC-97 industry standard by supporting ACPI/OnNow, Ultra-DMA/33, and USB technologies. Table 8-10 lists the key features of the Apollo VPX/97.

VIA APOLLO VP-1 CHIPSET

The VT82C580VP Apollo VP-1 is a four-chip solution for PCI/ISA desktop and notebook PCs based on Pentium, AMD K5x86, and Cyrix 6x86 CPUs. Apollo VP-1 features functions designed to bypass conventional board-level bottlenecks (including burst and normal EDO RAM, FPM RAM, and SDRAM support, burst SRAM and cache module support, and an on-board dual-channel enhanced-master-mode PCI IDE controller that supports up to four Enhanced IDE (EIDE) devices. The VIA Apollo VP-1 chipset consists of one VT82C585VP system controller, a VT82C586 PCI/IDE/ISA/USB controller, and two VT82C587VP share frame buffers. The features of the VP-1 are listed in Table 8-11.

VIA APOLLO MASTER CHIPSET

The VT82C570M Apollo Master is an older chipset for PCI/ISA desktop PCs, based on Intel Pentium, AMD K5x86, and Cyrix 6x86 CPUs. The VIA Apollo Master consists of a VT82C575M system controller, a VT82C576M PCI/ISA/IDE controller, two VT82C577M frame buffers, and a VT82C416 support IC. Few features would now be considered "advanced," but Table 8-12 lists the main features.

TABLE 8-10 VIA APOLLO VPX/97 CHIPSET FEATURES AT A GLANCE

- Asynchronous CPU bus, which is operational at either 66/75MHz.
- PC-97 compliance includes extension to ACPI/OnNow.
- Integrated Universal Serial Bus controller.
- Enhanced master-mode PCI IDE controller with extension to Ultra-DMA/33.
- Support for up to 512MB DRAM.
- DRAM controller with FPM/EDO/SDRAM support in mixed combinations with 32-bit or 64-bit data bus widths.
- Intelligent PCI bus controller offering concurrent PCI master/CPU/IDE operations, and zero-wait-state PCI master and slave burst-transfer rates.
- Integrated Keyboard Controller (KBC) and Real-Time Clock (RTC).
- Supports the Pentium, Pentium MMX, Cyrix 6x86 and M2, and AMD K5 and K6 MMX.
- Advanced cache controller with burst synchronous cache SRAM supports up to 2MB.
- Integrated Plug-and-Play controller and PCI-to-ISA bridge.
- Multiple processor support.

TABLE 8-11 VIA APOLLO VP-1 CHIPSET FEATURES AT A GLANCE

- PCI/ISA "Green PC" ready
- Integrated Universal Serial Bus support and intelligent PCI Bus controller.
- Unified Memory Architecture includes SDRAM and BEDO support.
- Fast DRAM Controller with support for various DRAM modes (32-bit or 64-bit data width).
- Enhanced master-mode IDE controller with support for up to four devices.
- Integrated cache controller.
- Shared frame buffers.
- Integrated Plug-and-Play controller and Power-Management Unit.
- Integrated PCI-to-ISA bridge.

TABLE 8-12 VIA APOLLO MASTER CHIPSET FEATURES AT A GLANCE

- PCI/ISA "green" chipset.
- Fast DRAM controller.
- Master-mode PCI bus controller.
- Enhanced master-mode PCI IDE controller supports up to four devices.
- Windows 95 Plug-and-Play compliant.
- Power-Management Unit.
- Supports Intel Pentium, AMD K5, and Cyrix 6x86 CPUs.
- Synchronous ISA bus controller.

TABLE 8-13 SIS5597 CHIPSET FEATURES AT A GLANCE

- Single-chip solution with the 5597 (Jedi chip).
- Pentium/PCI/ISA low-cost core logic with integrated VGA controller.
- 64-bit PCI/Host graphic and video accelerator.
- Meets PC-97 and ACPI requirements.
- PCI Burst Write.
- Supports the universal serial bus.
- Integrated Direct-Draw hardware accelerator.
- 85Hz vertical refresh rate.

SiS Chipsets

SiS is another major manufacturer of chipsets that support core logic (motherboards), as well as mobile PCs and multimedia applications. Although SiS is a bit behind VIA and Intel in chipset development, they are rather unique in the inclusion of video-accelerator hardware into the chipset (particularly in their later products). This makes SiS chipsets particularly appealing to entry-level PCs, where minimizing cost is very important. Because SiS products are not as widely used as other chipsets, you'll find summaries of SiS chipset features in the following tables:

- SiS5597 chipset; Table 8-13
- SiS5596 chipset; Table 8-14
- SiS5571 chipset; Table 8-15
- SiS551X chipset; Table 8-16
- SiS85C49X chipset; Table 8-17

OPTi Chipsets

Founded in 1989, OPTi is a well-known supplier of core logic and multimedia chipsets to manufacturers of desktop and mobile computer products worldwide. Although the

TABLE 8-14 SIS5596 CHIPSET FEATURES AT A GLANCE

■ Two-chip solution with the 5596 and 5513.

■ Pentium low-cost core logic with integrated VGA controller.

■ Supports Intel Pentium CPUs (and other compatible CPUs) at 66/60/50MHz.

■ Integrated high-performance video/graphics accelerator.

■ Integrated L2 cache controller supporting up to 1MB of L2 cache.

■ Integrated high-performance DRAM controller (FPM and EDO RAM).

■ Supports up to 512MB of main system memory.

■ Integrated PCI bus support.

■ Supports super-high-resolution graphic modes up to 1280 × 1024.

■ Supports a "virtual screen" up to 2048 × 2048.

■ Microsoft Video for Windows-compliant.

TABLE 8-15 SIS5571 CHIPSET FEATURES AT A GLANCE

■ Pentium/PCI/ISA high-performance core logic.

■ Single-chip solution with the 5571 (Trinity chip).

■ Supports Intel Pentium CPUs (and other compatible CPUs) at 66/60/50 MHz.

■ Integrated L2 cache controller supporting up to 1MB of L2 cache.

■ Integrated high-performance DRAM controller supporting up to 384MB of main system memory.

■ Concurrent CPU and PCI operations.

■ Integrated post-write buffers and read prefetch buffers to increase system performance.

■ Supports five external PCI masters.

■ Includes an enhanced PCI IDE master/slave controller.

■ Integrated universal serial bus controller.

■ ISA-compatible and Fast Type-F DMA cycles supported.

TABLE 8-16 SIS551X CHIPSET FEATURES AT A GLANCE

■ Pentium/PCI/ISA core logic.

■ Three-chip solution with the 5511, 5512, and 5513.

■ Supports Intel Pentium CPUs (and other compatible CPUs) at 66/60/50MHz.

■ Integrated second-level (L2) cache controller.

■ Integrated DRAM controller.

■ Provides high-performance PCI arbiter and integrated PCI bridge.

■ Supports the full 64-bit Pentium data bus.

■ Provides 32-bit interface to the PCI bus.

■ Includes enhanced DMA functions and integrated interrupt controllers.

■ Integrated KeyBoard Controller (KBC) and Real-Time Clock (RTC).

■ Includes a fast PCI IDE master/slave controller.

■ Includes a USB interface.

■ On-board Plug-and-Play support.

TABLE 8-17 SIS85C49X CHIPSET FEATURES AT A GLANCE

- 486 PCI/ISA core logic chipset.
- A two-chip solution using the 85C496 and 85C497.
- Supports the Intel 486 (and other compatible CPUs) at 50/40/33/25MHz.
- Includes an L2 cache controller and DRAM controller.
- Supports VESA bus specification Rev 2.0p.
- Supports PCI bus specification Rev 2.0.
- Supports up to four external PCI masters.

chipsets by Intel and VIA have pushed OPTi into the background, they continue to produce some respected motherboard chipsets.

OPTI DISCOVERY CHIPSET

The OPTi Discovery chipset (82C650/651) provides a highly integrated solution for a wide range of fully compatible, high-performance PC platforms, based on the Intel Pentium Pro processor. The Discovery chipset is comprised of two chips, the 82C650 system controller, and the 82C651 bus controller (and an optional third chip—the 82C652—which provides an auxiliary PCI bus that can be used as the AGP port). It provides 64-bit core logic, integrated PCI (revision 2.1), support for a second host-to-PCI device (the 82C652), support for all popular memory technologies, sophisticated power management features, as well as optional support for Unified Memory Architecture (UMA) and the Accelerated Graphics Port (AGP). The deep buffers and several levels of pipelining minimize system level latencies and maximize/sustain throughputs for all the major subsystems. Support for parity/ECC protection provides enhanced levels of fault tolerance to greatly improve the reliability of the system.

OPTI VENDETTA CHIPSET

The OPTi Vendetta (82C750) single-chip core logic unit provides a highly integrated solution for high-performance PC platforms. It supports the Intel 3.3-V Pentium, Cyrix 6x86, and AMD 5K86. In addition to supporting a wide range or platform designs, the 82C750 feature set also includes audio and one-game-port functionality, common architecture support, isolated primary/secondary Ultra-DMA IDE support, and dual USB ports. This makes the Vendetta an ideal choice for multimedia-based end-user systems.

FIRESTAR CHIPSET

OPTi's FireStar single-chip core logic combines high-performance features with space-saving design ideal for mobile applications. This solution is based on the Intel 3.3-V and 2.5-V (split voltage) Pentium MMX, Cyrix M2, and AMD K6 processors. FireStar also allows FPM DRAM, EDO DRAM, or Synchronous DRAM (SDRAM) as options when designing the system. The highly concurrent cycles and deep-buffering features of FireStar also improve the system's performance. For power-management applications, FireStar offers power-saving modes for extended battery life and provides true CPU-temperature monitoring. In STPGNT mode, CPU power consumption can be reduced by 80%. In STPCLK mode, CPU power consumption can be reduced by as much as 99%. FireStar also features advanced fail-safe thermal management, full peripheral activity tracking and power-off control, Advanced Configuration and Power Interface (ACPI) support, and Advanced Power Management (APM), as well as "suspend to memory" and "suspend to disk" power-management options.

Legacy and Support ICs

Although this chapter is intended to highlight many of the most popular motherboard chipsets in use today, there are a great many more older chips and chipsets still in the field. The myriad of 386 and 486-class systems still in service almost guarantee that you'll encounter these "legacy" chips sooner or later. It is almost impossible to adequately list all the chips and chipsets that have been used in PCs throughout the years, but Table 8-18 attempts to cover the more popular devices (as well as other support ICs, which might still be in use).

TABLE 8-18 A BRIEF LISTING OF LEGACY AND SUPPORT ICS

ACC 82010 Chipset (i286/i386 systems motherboard chipset)

IC	FUNCTION
ACC2000	Integrated peripheral controller
ACC2100	System controller
ACC2210	Data bus buffer
ACC2220	Address bus buffer

ACC 82020 Chipset (i286/i386 systems motherboard chipset)

IC	FUNCTION
ACC2000	Integrated peripheral controller
ACC2120	Enhanced system controller
ACC2210	Data bus buffer
ACC2220	Address bus buffer
ACC2300	Page-interleaved memory controller
ACC2500	System controller
ACC2030	Single-chip i286 system controller
ACC2035	Single-chip i386SX system controller

TABLE 8-18 A BRIEF LISTING OF LEGACY AND SUPPORT ICS (CONTINUED)

Acer Labs (motherboard chipsets)

IC	FUNCTION
M1521-A/1523	Aladdin III
M1541/1533	Aladdin IV

Chips & Technologies CS8230 Chipset (CHIPset i286 motherboard chipset)

IC	FUNCTION
82C201	System controller
82C202	RAM/ROM decoder and I/O controller
82C203	High-address bus buffer
82C204	Low-address bus buffer
82C205	Data bus buffer and parity generator

Chips & Technologies CS8221 Chipset (NEAT i286 motherboard chipset)

IC	FUNCTION
82C211	System controller and extended CMOS RAM control logic
82C212	I/O and memory decode logic
82C215	Parity logic and bus buffers
82C206	Integrated peripheral controller

Chips & Technologies CS8233 Chipset (PEAK i386 motherboard chipset)

IC	FUNCTION
82C311	CPU, cache, DRAM controller
82C316	Peripheral controller
82C315	Bus controller
82C452	Super VGA controller
82C601	Single-chip peripheral controller
82C765	Single-chip floppy-disk controller

Chips & Technologies CB8291/CB8295 Chipset (ELEAT i286/i386 motherboard chipsets)

IC	FUNCTION
82C235	SCAT system controller
82C450	1MB DRAM VGA graphics controller
82C451	Integrated VGA graphics controller
82C710	Universal peripheral controller
82C711	Universal peripheral controller II

Chips & Technologies CS8230/CS8231 Chipset (i386DX motherboard chipsets)

IC	FUNCTION
82C206	Integrated peripheral controller
82C301	Bus controller

TABLE 8-18 A BRIEF LISTING OF LEGACY AND SUPPORT ICS (CONTINUED)

82C302	Page/interleave memory controller
82C303	High-address bus buffer
82C304	Low-address bus buffer
82C305	Data bus buffers
82C306	Control buffer
82C307	Cache/DRAM controller

Chips & Technologies CS8238 Chipset (i386DX motherboard chipset for MCA bus systems)

IC	FUNCTION
82C226	System peripheral controller
82C233	DMA controller
82C321	CPU/microchannel controller
82C322	Page interleave/EMS controller
82C325	Data bus buffer

Chips & Technologies CS8281 Chipset (NEATsx i386SX motherboard chipset)

IC	FUNCTION
82C206	Integrated peripherals controller
82C215	Data and address buffer
82C811	CPU and bus controller
82C812	Page interleave/EMS controller

Chips & Technologies CS8285 Chipset (PEAKset/SX i386SX motherboard chipset)

IC	FUNCTION
82C235	System controller
82C835	Cache controller

Chips & Technologies CS82310 Chipset (PEAKset i386DX/i486SX/i486DX motherboard chipset)

IC	FUNCTION
82C351	CPU/cache/DRAM controller
82C355	Data buffer
82C356	Integrated peripheral controller

Chips & Technologies CHIPS 280 Chipset (PS/2 Model 80 i386DX motherboard chipset for MCA bus)

IC	FUNCTION
82C226	Page interleave/EMS controller
82C233	DMA controller
82C321	CPU/microchannel controller
82C322	Page interleave/EMS controller
82C325	Data bus buffer and controller

TABLE 8-18 A BRIEF LISTING OF LEGACY AND SUPPORT ICS (CONTINUED)

82C450	1MB DRAM VGA graphics controller
82C607	Multi-function controller

ETEQ Microsystems 82C390SX Chipset (Panda i386DX motherboard chipset)

IC	FUNCTION
82C390SX	CPU, cache, and DRAM controller

ETEQ Microsystems 82C4901/82C4902 Chipset (Bengal i386DX motherboard chipset)

IC	FUNCTION
82C4901	CPU, cache, and DRAM controller
82C4902	Data bugger and MCP interface controller

ETEQ Microsystems ET2000 Chipset (i386DX/i486SX/i486DX motherboard chipset for EISA bus)

IC	FUNCTION
ET2001	EISA bus controller
ET2002	EISA data buffer
ET2003	EISA integrated peripheral controller
ET2004	EISA cache/memory controller

ETEQ Microsystems ET6000 Chipset (Cheetah i486SX motherboard chipset)

IC	FUNCTION
ET6000	System controller

Faraday FE3600B Chipset (motherboard chipset)

IC	FUNCTION
FE3001	System controller
FE3010	Peripheral controller
FE3021	Address bus and memory control logic
FE3031	Parity and data bus controller

Integrated Technology Express (motherboard chipsets)

IC	FUNCTION
IT8330G	Platinum
IT8331G	Platinum plus

Intel 82350/DT EISA Chipset (i386DX/i486SX/i486DX chipset for EISA bus)

IC	FUNCTION
82077	Floppy-disk controller
82352	EISA bus buffer

TABLE 8-18   A BRIEF LISTING OF LEGACY AND SUPPORT ICS (CONTINUED)

82353	Advanced data path
82357	Integrated peripheral controller
82358	EISA bus controller
82359	DRAM controller

Intel Peripheral Controllers (other ICs)

IC	FUNCTION
8206	Error detection and correction unit
8207	Dual-port dynamic RAM controller
82078	Single-chip floppy-disk controller
82091AA	Advanced integrated peripheral (AIP)
82350	EISA chip set
82351	Local I/O EISA support peripheral (LIO.E)
82355	Bus master interface controller (BMIC)
82C08	Dynamic RAM controller
82C54	Programmable interval timer
82C55A	Programmable peripheral interface

OPTI Chipset (i286/i386 motherboard chipset)

IC	FUNCTION
82C381	System and cache memory controller
82C382	Direct-mapped page-interleaved memory controller

OPTI 386WB Chipset (i386DX motherboard chipset)

IC	FUNCTION
82C206	Integrated peripheral controller
82C391	System controller
82C392	Data bus controller

OPTI 486SXWB Chipset (i486SX motherboard chipset)

IC	FUNCTION
82C206	Integrated peripheral controller
82C392	Data bus controller
83C493	System controller

OPTI 386/486WB Chipset (i386DX/i486SX/i486DX motherboard chipset for EISA bus)

IC	FUNCTION
82C681	EISA bus controller
82C682	Memory/cache controller
82C686	Integrated peripheral controller
82C687	Data bus controller

TABLE 8-18   A BRIEF LISTING OF LEGACY AND SUPPORT ICS (CONTINUED)

OPTi Other Support ICs

IC	FUNCTION
82C566/7/8-MAX	Viper Max chipset
82C814	Mobile PC docking controller
82C824	PC card controller
92C178	PCI/LCD controller
82C931	Audio controller

SiS Other Support ICs

IC		FUNCTION
5581	SiS5581	Core logic (Jessie chip)
6204	SiS6204	ISA video controller
6205	SiS6205	High-performance PCI 2D graphics and video accelerator
6225	SiS6225	MPEG1 PCI/2D graphics and video accelerator
6226	SiS6226	MPEG2 PCI/AGP/2D graphics and video accelerator
6326	SiS6326	MPEG2 PCI/AGP/3D graphics and video accelerator
5107	SiS5107	Hot docking controller
5131	SiS5131	PCMCIA/ISA controller
5120	SiS5120	Single chip notebook solution
8132	SiS8132	128KB pipelined burst SRAM
8164	SiS8164	256KB pipelined burst SRAM

Suntec Chipset (i286 motherboard chipset)

IC	FUNCTION
ST62C201	System bus controller
ST62C202	Memory controller
ST62C008	Integrated peripheral controller
ST62C010	Address bus controller
ST62BC001	System controller
ST62BC002	High address controller
ST62BC003	Low address controller
ST62BC004	Data buffer
ST62C005	I/O control, DMA page register
ST62C006	Integrated peripheral controller

Suntec Chipset (i286/i386SX motherboard chipset)

IC	FUNCTION
GS62C101	System, data bus, timer, and interrupt controller
GS62C102	Memory, DMA, and I/O controller

TABLE 8-18   A BRIEF LISTING OF LEGACY AND SUPPORT ICS (CONTINUED)

Symphony Labs HAYDN AT Chipset (i386SX/i386DX/i486SX/i486SLC/i486DX motherboard chipset)

IC	FUNCTION
SL82C362	Bus controller
SL82C461	System controller
SL82C465	Cache controller

Symphony Labs Mozart Chipset (i386SX/DX/i486SX/SLC/DX motherboard chipset for EISA bus)

IC	FUNCTION
SL82C471	CPU, cache, and DRAM controller
SL82C472	EISA bus controller
SL82C473	EISA DMA controller

Western Digital Chipset (motherboard chipset)

IC	FUNCTION
75C10	Single-chip 286 AT controller
75C20	Floppy-drive, hard-drive, and real-time clock controller
75C30	Serial- and parallel-port controller
76C10	High-speed single i286 system controller
WD6000	System, interrupt, and timer controller
WD6010	DMA, reset, and parity controller
WD6020	Address and data bus controller
WD6036	DRAM/cache memory controller

VIA Chipset (FLEXSET motherboard chipset)

IC	FUNCTION
SL9011	System controller
SL9020	Data bus controller
SL9023	Address controller
SL9030	Integrated peripheral controller
SL9090	Universal clock IC
SL9095	Power-management IC
SL9151	i286 page-interleave memory controller
SL9152	i286 system and memory controller
SL9250	i386SX Page-mode memory controller
SL9251	i386SX Page-interleave memory controller
SL9252	i386SX System and memory controller
SL9350	i386DX Page-mode memory controller
SL9351	i386DX Page-mode memory controller
SL9352	i386DX System and memory controller

TABLE 8-18 A BRIEF LISTING OF LEGACY AND SUPPORT ICS (CONTINUED)

VIA Other Support ICs

IC	FUNCTION
VT86C100	Rhine fast ethernet controller (10/100 BaseT)
VT86C926	Amazon PCI 10BaseT fast ethernet controller
VT86C916	Nile ISA 10BaseT fast ethernet controller
VT83C572	PCI-to-USB bridge
VT83C469	PCMCIA socket controller
VT83C465	PCMCIA controller
VT8225	Clock generator
VT82C887	Real-Time Clock (RTC)
VT82C885	Real-Time Clock (RTC)
VT82C42	KeyBoard Controller (KBC)

VLSI Technology Chipset (TOPCAT i286/i386SX motherboard chipset)

IC	FUNCTION
VL82C331	ISA bus controller
VL82C320	System controller
VL82C106	Multi-function controller

VLSI Technology Chipset (TOPCAT i386DX motherboard chipset)

IC	FUNCTION
VL82C106	Multi-function controller
VL82C311	ISA bus controller
VL82C322	Data buffer
VL82C330	System controller

VLSI Technology Chipset (VL82CPCAT-16/20 motherboard chipset)

IC	FUNCTION
VL82C100	Peripheral controller
VL82C201	System controller
VL82C202	Memory controller
VL82C203	Address buffer
VL82C204	Data buffer

VLSI Other Support ICs

IC	FUNCTION
Polaris	Alpha system controller
VAS96031	Pier 39 PCI-to-Mac I/O bridge controller
VL82C829	Songbird 3D audio accelerator
VMS110	16-bit DES coprocessor

TABLE 8-18 A BRIEF LISTING OF LEGACY AND SUPPORT ICS (CONTINUED)

VES2030	MPEG 2 transport demultiplexer subsystem
ACTIS	Actis single-chip VLSI ISDN data processor
ENDEC+	Fiber-channel ENDEC
Firefly	Chipset fiber-channel ASSP solution
GSM	GSM power and flexibility in a single chip
RubyII	Advanced communication processor
SC2000	Universal timeslot interchange
SC4000	Universal timeslot interchange
VCS94250	Apollo serial storage architecture
VIP	Single-chip VLSI ISDN subscriber processor
VN567200	VN567200 ATM Quad Uni

Zilog Chipset (motherboard chipset)

IC	FUNCTION
P90	System, interrupt, DMA, clock, and refresh controller
P91	Memory controller
P92	Address and data-bus controllers

Zymos Chipset (motherboard chipset)

IC	FUNCTION
POACH/XTB	Single-chip XT controller
POACH1	System clock, bus controller, interrupt controller, and RTC
POACH2	DMA, timer, refresh, and I/O controller
POACH4	Single-chip XT controller
POACH6	High-speed i386DX/i486 system controller
POACH7	System clock, bus controller, interrupt controller, and RTC
POACH8	DMA, timer, refresh, and I/O controller

Further Study

This finishes up Chapter 8. Be sure to review the glossary and chapter questions on the accompanying CD. If you have access to the Internet, take some time to review a few of the chipset makers:

AMD: **http://www.amd.com**

Intel: **http://developer.intel.com/design/pcisets/**

VIA: **http://www.via.com.tw/**

SIS: **http://www.sisworld.com/**

Opti: **http://www.opti.com**

VLSI: **http://www.vlsi.com**

9

CMOS

CONTENTS AT A GLANCE

What CMOS Does
  The CMOS map

Configuring the CMOS Setup
  Entering CMOS setup
  Basic CMOS optimization tactics
  Configuring the standard CMOS
    setup
  Configuring the advanced CMOS
    setup
  Configuring the advanced chipset
    setup
  Configuring Plug and Play/PCI
  Configuring Power Management

Making Use Of "Auto-configuration"
  BIOS defaults
  Power-on defaults

Backing Up CMOS RAM

CMOS Maintenance and Troubleshooting
  Typical CMOS-related symptoms
  CMOS password troubleshooting
  CMOS battery maintenance

Further Study

With the introduction of their PC/AT computer, IBM abandoned the configuration DIP switches that had been used for the PC/XT. Rather than limit the system's configuration options, IBM chose to store the system's setup parameters in a small, low-power RAM IC called the *CMOS RAM* (in actuality, CMOS RAM is typically combined on the same IC with the real-time clock, RTC). In effect, the discrete switches of the XT were replaced with logical "switches" of each CMOS bit (after all, a bit can be high or low, just as a switch can be on or off). When an AT-type computer starts, its system attributes—stored in the CMOS RAM—are read by the BIOS. BIOS then uses those attributes during normal system operation. As a result, it is vitally important that the correct settings be used when configuring a system. Otherwise, system problems could result. This chapter explains a broad selection of CMOS parameters in detail, then provides some guidelines for proper CMOS optimization and battery maintenance.

Many PC enthusiasts (and even experienced technicians) use the terms *BIOS* and *CMOS* interchangeably. However, BIOS and CMOS RAM are not the same thing, although the two are intimately related. *BIOS* refers to the firmware instructions located on the BIOS ROM, and *CMOS* refers to the low-power RAM that is holding the system's setup parameters. BIOS reads the CMOS RAM into memory at start time, and provides the "setup" routine that allows you to change the contents of CMOS, but the CMOS RAM/RTC device is a totally different IC.

What CMOS Does

In simplest terms, CMOS RAM is nothing more than some amount of very low-power static RAM. Older CMOS RAM devices offered 64 bytes, and later implementations provide an extra 64 bytes (128 bytes total). The latest motherboards use 256 bytes to store the CMOS setup along with ESCD (Extended System Configuration Data) information needed by the PC's plug-and-play system. For the purposes of this book, a 128-byte CMOS system is considered. Because RAM is lost when system power is removed, a battery is added to the PC to continue to provide power to the CMOS RAM (and RTC). This CMOS battery backup keeps the date, time, and system parameters intact until you turn the system on again. Of course, if the battery should fail, the system will lose its date, time, and all of its setup parameters. Many a tear has been shed trying to reconstruct lost system parameters by trial and error. You will learn about CMOS backup techniques later in this chapter.

THE CMOS MAP

To truly appreciate the importance of CMOS RAM, you should understand the contents of a typical CMOS RAM IC, as shown in Table 9-1. You will find that a standard 128-byte ISA-compatible CMOS is divided into four fairly distinct sections: 16 bytes of real-time clock data (00h–0Fh), 32 bytes of ISA configuration data (10h–2Fh), 16 bytes of BIOS-specific configuration data (30h–3Fh), and 64 bytes of extended CMOS data (40h–7Fh). Additional CMOS RAM is typically used as the ESCD (and is inaccessible through the typical CMOS setup).

TABLE 9-1   A TYPICAL CMOS RAM MAP

OFFSET	DESCRIPTION
00h	*RTC Seconds* Contains the seconds value of current time.
01h	*RTC Seconds Alarm* Contains the seconds value for the RTC alarm.
02h	*RTC Minutes* Contains the minutes value of current time.
03h	*RTC Minutes Alarm* Contains the minutes value for the RTC alarm.

TABLE 9-1	A TYPICAL CMOS RAM MAP (CONTINUED)

OFFSET	DESCRIPTION
04h	*RTC Hours* Contains the hours value of current time.
05h	*RTC Hours Alarm* Contains the hours value for the RTC alarm.
06h	*RTC Day of Week* Contains the current day of the week.
07h	*RTC Date Day* Contains day value of current date.
08h	*RTC Date Month* Contains month value of current date.
09h	*RTC Date Year* Contains year value of current date.

04h (continued)

OFFSET	DESCRIPTION	
0Ah	*Status Register A* Various bits that define:	
	Bit 7	Update progress flag
	Bit 6–4	Time-base frequency setting
	Bit 3–0	Interrupt-rate selection
0Bh	*Status Register B* Various bits that define:	
	Bit 7	Halt cycle to set clock
	Bit 6	Periodic interrupt disable/enable
	Bit 5	Alarm interrupt disable/enable
	Bit 4	Update ended interrupt disable/enable
	Bit 3	Square-wave rate disable/enable
	Bit 2	Date and time format (BCD/binary)
	Bit 1	Hour mode (12/24)
	Bit 0	Daylight savings disable/enable
0Ch	*Status Register C* Read-only flags indicating system-status conditions.	
0Dh	*Statuc Register D* Valid CMOS RAM flag on bit 7 (battery-condition flag).	
0Eh	*Diagnostic Status Flags* Various bits that define:	
	Bit 7	RTC IC power invalid/valid
	Bit 6	CMOS RAM checksum invalid/valid
	Bit 5	CMOS RAM configuration mismatch/match
	Bit 4	CMOS RAM memory-size mismatch/match
	Bit 3	Hard disk C: initialization failed/passed
	Bit 2	Time status is invalid/valid
	Bit 1–0	reserved . . . should be 0
0Fh	*CMOS Shutdown Status* Allows the CPU to reset after switching from protected to real-mode addressing. The shutdown code is written here so that after reset, the CPU will know the reason for the reset.	
	00h	Normal POST execution
	01h	Chipset initialization for return to real mode
	02h–03h	Internal BIOS use
	04h	Jump to bootstrap code
	05h	User-defined shutdown. Jump to pointer at 40:67h. Interrupt controller and math co-processor are initialized.
	06h	Jump to pointer at 40:67h
	07h	Return to INT 15 function 87h
	08h	Return to POST memory test
	09h	INT 18 finction 87h block-move shutdown request
	0Ah	User-defined shutdown. Jump to pointer at 40:67h. Interrupt controller and math co-processor are not initialized.
10h	*Floppy Drive Type* Defines drives A: and B:	
	Bits 7–4	Drive A: type
	0h	No drive
	1h	360KB drive
	2h	1.2MB drive
	3h	730KB drive
	4h	1.44MB drive
	5h	2.88MB drive

TABLE 9-1   A TYPICAL CMOS RAM MAP (CONTINUED)

OFFSET	DESCRIPTION
	Bits 3–0 Drive B: type
	0h No drive
	1h 360KB drive
	2h 1.2MB drive
	3h 730KB drive
	4h 1.44MB drive
	5h 2.88MB drive
11h	*System Configuration Settings* Various bits that define:
	Bit 7 Mouse support disable/enable
	Bit 6 Memory test above 1MB disable/enable
	Bit 5 Memory test-tick sound disable/enable
	Bit 4 Memory parity-error check disable/enable
	Bit 3 Setup utility trigger display disable/enable
	Bit 2 Hard-disk type 47 RAM area (0:300h or upper 1KB of DOS area)
	Bit 1 Wait for <F1> if any error message disable/enable
	Bit 0 System boot up with NumLock (off/on)
12h	*Hard Disk Type ID*
	Bits 7–4 Hard–disk drive C: type
	0000h No drive installed
	0001h Type 1
	.....
	1110h Type 14
	1111h Type 16–47 (defined later in 1Ah)
	Bits 3–0 Hard-disk drive D: type
	0000h No drive installed
	0001h Type 1
	.....
	1110h Type 14
	1111h Type 16–47 (defined later in 19h)
13h	*Typematic Parameters*
	Bit 7 Typematic rate programming disabled/enabled
	Bits 6–5 Typematic rate delay
	Bits 4–2 Typematic rate
14h	*Equipment Parameters* Lists a selection of equipment parameters.
	Bits 7–6 Number of floppy drives.
	00h No drives
	01h One drive
	10h Two drives
	Bits 5–4 Monitor type
	00h Not CGA or MDA
	01h 40×25 CGA
	10h 80×25 CGA
	11h MDA
	Bit 3 Display adapter installed/not installed
	Bit 2 Keyboard installed/not installed
	Bit 1 Math co-processor installed/absent
	Bit 0 Always set to 1
15h	*Base Memory* (in 1KB increments) Least-significant byte
16h	*Base Memory* (in 1KB increments) Most-significant byte
17h	*Extended Memory* (in 1KB increments) Least-significant byte
18h	*Extended Memory* (in 1KB increments) Most-significant byte

TABLE 9-1   A TYPICAL CMOS RAM MAP (CONTINUED)

OFFSET	DESCRIPTION
19h	*Hard Disk C:* Type (16–46) 10h to 2Eh Type 16 to 46 respectively
1Ah	*Hard Disk D:* Type (16–46) 10h to 2Eh Type 16 to 46 respectively
1Bh	*User-Defined Drive C:* Number of Cylinders Least-significant byte
1Ch	*User-Defined Drive C:* Number of Cylinders Most-significant byte
1Dh	*User-Defined Drive C:* Number of Heads
1Eh	*User-Defined Drive C:* Write Precomp. Cylinder Least-significant byte
1Fh	*User-Defined Drive C:* Write Precomp. Cylinder Most-significant byte
20h	*User-Defined Drive C:* Control Byte
21h	*User-Defined Drive C:* Landing Zone Least-significant byte
22h	*User-Defined Drive C:* Landing Zone Most-significant byte
23h	*User-Defined Drive C:* Number of Sectors
24h	*User-Defined Drive D:* Number of Cylinders Least-significant byte
25h	*User-Defined Drive D:* Number of Cylinders Most-significant byte
26h	*User-Defined Drive D:* Number of Heads
27h	*User-Defined Drive D:* Write Precomp. Cylinder Least-significant byte
28h	*User-Defined Drive D:* Write Precomp. Cylinder Most-significant byte
29h	*User-Defined Drive D:* Control Byte
2Ah	*User-Defined Drive D:* Landing Zone Least-significant byte
2Bh	*User-Defined Drive D:* Landing Zone Most-significant byte
2Ch	*User-Defined Drive D:* Number of Sectors
2Dh	*System Operational Flags* Bit 7 Weitek processor present/absent Bit 6 Floppy-drive seek at boot enable/disable Bit 5 System boot sequence (C: then A: / A; then C:) Bit 4 System boot CPU speed high/low Bit 3 External cache enable/disable Bit 2 Internal cache enable/disable Bit 1 Fast Gate A20 operation enable/disable Bit 0 Turbo switch function enable/disable
2Eh	*Standard CMOS Checksum* Most-significant byte
2Fh	*Standard CMOS Checksum* Least-significant byte
30h	*Extended Memory Found by BIOS* Least-significant byte
31h	*Extended Memory Found by BIOS* Most-significant byte
32h	*Century Byte* BCD value for century of current date.
33h	*Information Flags* Various bytes that define: Bit 7 BIOS length (64KB/128KB) Bits 6–1 reserved . . . should be set to 0 Bit 0 POST cache test passed/failed
34h	*BIOS and Shadow Option Flags* Bit 7 Boot sector virus protection disabled/enabled Bit 6 Password checking option disabled/enabled Bit 5 Adapter ROM shadow C800h (16KB) disabled/enabled Bit 4 Adapter ROM shadow CC00h (16KB) disabled/enabled Bit 3 Adapter ROM shadow D000h (16KB) disabled/enabled Bit 2 Adapter ROM shadow D400h (16KB) disabled/enabled

TABLE 9-1   A TYPICAL CMOS RAM MAP (CONTINUED)

OFFSET	DESCRIPTION
	Bit 1 Adapter ROM shadow D800h (16KB) disabled/enabled
	Bit 0 Adapter ROM shadow DC00h (16KB) disabled/enabled
35h	*BIOS and Shadow Option Flags*
	Bit 7 Adapter ROM shadow E000h (16KB) disabled/enabled
	Bit 6 Adapter ROM shadow E400h (16KB) disabled/enabled
	Bit 5 Adapter ROM shadow E800h (16KB) disabled/enabled
	Bit 4 Adapter ROM shadow EC00h (16KB) disabled/enabled
	Bit 3 System ROM shadow F000h (64KB) disabled/enabled
	Bit 2 Video ROM shadow C000h (16KB) disabled/enabled
	Bit 1 Video ROM shadow C400h (16KB) disabled/enabled
	Bit 0 Numeric processor test disabled/enabled
36h	*Chipset-specific Information*
37h	*Password Seed and Color Option* Variables used for password control.
	Bits 7–4 Password seed (do not change)
	Bits 3–0 Setup screen color palette
	07h White on black
	70h Black on white
	17h White on blue
	20h Black on green
	30h Black on turquoise
	47h White on red
	57h White on magenta
	60h Black on brown
38h–3Dh	*Encrypted Password* (do not change).
3Eh	*MSB of Extended CMOS checksum*
3Fh	*LSB of Extended CMOS checksum*
40h	*Model Number Byte*
41h	*1st serial number byte*
42h	*2nd serial number byte*
43h	*3rd serial number byte*
44h	*4th serial number byte*
45h	*5th serial number byte*
46h	*6th serial number byte*
47h	*CRC Byte*
48h	*Century Byte*
49h	*Date Alarm*
4Ah	*Extended Control Register 4A*
4Bh	*Extended Control Register 4B*
4Ch–4Dh	*Reserved*
4Eh	*RTC Address—2*
4Fh	*RTC Address—3*
50h	*Extended RAM Address - LSB*
51h	*Extended RAM Address - MSB*
52h	*Reserved*
53h	*Extended RAM Data Port*
54h–5Dh	*Reserved*

TABLE 9-1 A TYPICAL CMOS RAM MAP (CONTINUED)	
OFFSET	**DESCRIPTION**
5Eh	*RTC Write Counter*
5Fh–7Fh	*Reserved*

Configuring the CMOS Setup

As you might expect, CMOS data does not simply materialize out of the ether—it must be entered manually (initially by the system manufacturer, and later by you or your customers) through a "setup routine." Early AT-compatible PCs relied on a disk-based setup utility—that is, you needed to boot the computer from a floppy disk containing the CMOS setup utility. The great danger with a setup disk is that the disk might fail and leave you without a setup disk, or you might lose the setup disk as the system changes hands or falls into disuse. If you find yourself with a setup disk, be sure to make a backup copy of it as soon as possible. Late-model 386 and subsequent systems abandon the use of "setup disks" and incorporate the setup utility onto the BIOS. When the setup routine is resident in the system, you can usually access the setup during system initialization by pressing one or more keys simultaneously (such as <Del> or <Ctrl>+<F1>). This part of the chapter is intended to familiarize you with the options found in current CMOS setup programs, and illustrate the typical defaults.

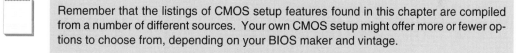

Remember that the listings of CMOS setup features found in this chapter are compiled from a number of different sources. Your own CMOS setup might offer more or fewer options to choose from, depending on your BIOS maker and vintage.

ENTERING CMOS SETUP

The first trick in configuring your CMOS setup is to launch the setup utility. BIOS manufacturers are rarely consistent when it comes to accessing the setup utility. In most cases, you can only launch Setup in the first few moments after the system boots—a note on the display will usually indicate the correct key or key combination such as:

```
Press <F1> to enter Setup...
```

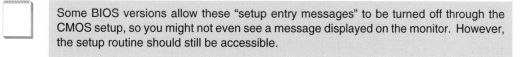

Some BIOS versions allow these "setup entry messages" to be turned off through the CMOS setup, so you might not even see a message displayed on the monitor. However, the setup routine should still be accessible.

Unfortunately, there are about as many key combinations as there are BIOS makers, and knowing the proper key combinations for every system can be an exercise in frustration. Table 9-2 lists the known key combinations for many popular BIOS and system types. When you're stuck and cannot enter CMOS with any of the key combinations in Table 9-2,

TABLE 9-2   TYPICAL CMOS SETUP KEY SEQUENCES

BIOS/SYSTEM	KEY OR KEY SEQUENCE
AMI BIOS	<Del> key during the POST
Award BIOS	<Ctrl>+<Alt>+<Esc>
DTK BIOS	<Esc> key during the POST
IBM PS/2 BIOS	<Ctrl>+<Alt>+<Ins> after <Ctrl>+<Alt>+<Del>
Phoenix BIOS	<Ctrl>+<Alt>+<Esc> or <Ctrl>+<Alt>+<S>
ALR PC	hit <F2> (for PCI systems) or <Ctrl>+<Alt>+<Esc> (for non-PCI systems)
Compaq PCs	hit <F10>
Gateway 2000 PC	hit <F1>
Sony PC	hit <F3> while the PC is starting (you see the Sony logo), then hit <F1>

you might be able to "force" the CMOS setup routine by causing a configuration change (such as removing a SIMM or two). This sometimes causes a CMOS error and allows you to proceed to the setup routine.

> Some new motherboard designs allow access to CMOS setup to be disabled through a motherboard jumper. If you absolutely cannot access the Setup using a proper key combination or a forced configuration change, check the motherboard to see if Setup access has been disabled.

Of course, if you've got a 286 or early 386 model PC sitting on your workbench, you'll need a "setup disk" to load the CMOS setup utility. If you've actually got a setup disk for the system, consider yourself lucky—they are usually the first things to be lost. If you need a setup utility, you might be able to download a suitable third-party freeware utility from:

http://oak.oakland.edu:/SimTel/msdos/at
ftp.uu.net:/systems/msdos/simtel/at

If you find yourself working with a GRiD system, you can probably get a setup utility from:

http://support.tandy.com/grid.html
http://www.ast.com/americas/files.htm

For IBM PS/2 systems, you can get a setup utility from the IBM site at:

http://www.pc.ibm.com/files.html

Finally, setup utilities for Panasonic computers are available on the Web at:

http://www.panasonic.com/host/support/

BASIC CMOS OPTIMIZATION TACTICS

As PCs have continued to evolve, the ever-increasing variety of memory types, busses, PC initiatives, and system architectures has forced BIOS makers to provide more and more entries in the CMOS setup. Today, there are dozens of possible setup entries in any given BIOS—each yielding hundreds of potential combinations. This variety makes it very difficult to select the optimum settings for a system. However, if you're really just interested in getting the most from your Setup, the following points might come in handy:

- *Check the basics* Be sure that all standard CMOS settings correspond to the installed components of your system. For instance, you should verify the date, time, available memory (if possible), hard disks, and floppy disks (see "Configuring the standard CMOS setup").
- *Enable all system cache* Be sure that all your cache memory (both internal and external) is enabled. Of course, you must have internal (L1) and external (L2) cache memory present in the system—which is always the case for systems less than five years old (see "Configuring the advanced CMOS setup").
- *Minimize RAM wait-states* Be sure that the wait-state values used for your main system RAM are set at the minimum possible. You must be careful here because if values are too low, your system might freeze (hang up). For more information, check out "Configuring the advanced chipset setup."
- *Enable ROM shadowing* As a minimum, you should shadow your video and system ROM. On older systems, this might improve performance significantly. Newer systems (with faster "flash" ROM devices) might not benefit as much from shadowing (see "Configuring the advanced CMOS setup").
- *Enable power management* Be sure to use the power-management features supported by your BIOS. Proper power management will conserve electricity and can extend the working life of many of the system components (see "Configuring power management").
- *Optimize drive access.* Hard-disk data-transfer speeds are a major bottleneck for system performance. Use the fastest data transfer protocol that your hard-disk system will support (e.g., PIO Mode 4 or Ultra-DMA/33). Remember that both the drive and drive controller must support the chosen data transfer protocol. If the hard-drive system supports Bus Mastering IDE (BMIDE), you might consider using that to improve drive performance on multitasking or disk-intensive systems.

CONFIGURING THE STANDARD CMOS SETUP

The "standard CMOS setup" usually comprises one screen of basic data about your system's date, time, and attached devices (primarily floppy and hard drives). It is important for you to get this data correct because the system will refuse to boot unless it is aware of all the drives installed.

Date and time Use these settings to change the date and time of the system clock.

RTC devices are notoriously inaccurate devices. Depending of the quality of the motherboard, you should expect to lose (or gain) several seconds per month. You should periodically check the date and time, and correct it as necessary.

Daylight savings When enabled, this feature allows the RTC to automatically adapt to the Daylight Savings scheme (which is removing one hour on the last Sunday of October and adding one hour on the last Sunday of April). As a rule, this can be enabled. Otherwise, you'll need to correct for Daylight Savings manually.

Hard disk C: This number is the BIOS drive table number of your primary (master) hard drive. In virtually all cases today, this number is 47 (user defined), which means that you must specify the drive specs according to your hard drive manual. SCSI drives in the "C:" position should be set to "none" or "not installed." Typically, six parameters define your hard drive:

- *Cyl* The number of cylinders (tracks) on your hard disk.
- *Heads* The number of heads in the hard disk.
- *WPre* This setting specifies the cylinder where write precompensation begins, and uses additional energy to write the "compensated" cylinders. Today, WPre is essentially useless. Set it either to –1 or the maximum number of cylinders on the drive. For EIDE/IDE hard drives, it is not necessary to enter a WPre cylinder.
- *LZ* This setting specifies the cylinder used as the landing zone for older drives without an "auto parking" feature. Today, LZ is essentially useless. Set it either to 0 or the maximum number of cylinders on the drive.
- *Sect/Trk* This setting specifies the number of Sectors Per Track (SPT). It is often 17 for MFM drives, and 26 for RLL drives. Modern types of drives use "zoned recording," and the number of sectors per track will vary (increasing on the outer tracks). There is usually one "translation number" provided for the drive.
- *Size* The total drive size is automatically calculated according the number of cylinders, heads, and sectors entered. The number is given in MB, according to the formula: ($Hds \times Cyl \times Sect \times 512$)/1048.

Hard disk D: This number is the BIOS drive table number of your secondary (slave) hard drive. In virtually all cases today, this number is 47 (user defined), which means that you must specify the drive specs according to your hard drive manual. SCSI drives set to the "D:" position should be set to "none" or "not installed." The six parameters that define your hard drive are listed.

If your drive controller supports four hard drives, you might find an additional two hard drive entries (e.g., hard disk E: and hard disk F:). These would be a "secondary master" and "secondary slave" drive.

When installing two drives on the same channel, be sure to set the drive's "master/slave" jumpers properly.

Translation mode IDE drives with less than 528MB are typically set as CHS (cylinder/head/sector), but EIDE, Fast-ATA and Ultra-ATA drives use LBA (logical block addressing) instead.

If you alter a drive's translation mode after the drive has been partitioned and formatted, the data contained on the drive will be inaccessible. You'll need to repartition and refor- mat the drive.

Floppy drive A: Set this entry to reflect the type of floppy drive installed for drive A:. In most cases, the drive will be 1.44MB 3.5", although a few systems use a 2.88MB 3.5" floppy. Older systems use 720KB 3.5", 1.2MB 5.25", or even 360KB 5.25" floppy drives.

Floppy drive B: Set this entry to reflect the type of floppy drive installed for drive B:. The typical selections for a floppy drive are shown.

Primary display This entry specifies the general type of display you are using. The most frequent selection for older systems is VGA/PGA/EGA, although current systems shorten this to simply *VGA*. If you have an older black/white display, select *Mono* or *Her- cules*. If your video adapter card is text only, select *MDA*.

Keyboard This sets whether or not a keyboard is attached. In virtually all cases, the proper entry is *installed*. If *not installed*, the BIOS will pass the keyboard test in the POST, allowing a PC to boot without a keyboard without the BIOS producing a keyboard error (most commonly encountered in file servers, printer servers, and so on).

CONFIGURING THE ADVANCED CMOS SETUP

The advanced CMOS setup contains the settings needed to tweak your boot characteris- tics, and optimize the performance of memory and cache. Most of the options here are not vital to the system's proper operation, but can help you tailor the system to your particular tastes and needs.

Typematic rate programming This feature enables the typematic rate programming of the keyboard, which determines how a keyboard will respond if a key is held down. If enabled, a key will repeat automatically if it is held down. If disabled, the key will not re- peat. This feature is often disabled.

Not all keyboards support typematic rate programming. This feature must be disabled if the keyboard doesn't support it.

Typematic rate delay This sets the initial delay (in ms) before a key starts repeating (this is how long you've got to press a key before it starts repeating). A setting of 500 ms (0.5 s) is recommended.

Typematic rate This is how fast the key will repeat (in characters per second or CPS). A typical setting is 15CPS.

Above 1MB memory test Enable this feature if you want the system to check the memory above 1MB for errors. The HIMEM.SYS driver for DOS 6.2 verifies the XMS anyway, so the test would be redundant in this case. For faster boot performance, leave the feature disabled.

Memory test tick sound   When enabled, this feature generates a sequence of audible tones ("ticks") as the memory test executes. It also provides an audible confirmation of your CPU clock speed/turbo switch setting. The idea is that an experienced user can hear if something is wrong with the system just by the tick sound pattern. However, because PCs now have much more memory than before, this setting is not used that frequently. If the noise is annoying, disable the test. If you cannot hear the test when it's enabled, check the speaker.

Memory parity error check   This feature controls the parity checking of your system's memory. Parity checking can help improve the integrity of data in memory. When enabled, parity checking will generate an error, such as "Parity error at 0AB5:00BE System halted" if an error is detected. Otherwise, errors in memory will go undetected—possible corrupting and crashing the system. If you're using parity memory on the system, enable parity checking. If you're using non-parity memory on your system, parity checking must be disabled.

> Besides being caused by data errors, parity errors can also be caused by insufficient wait-states, or mixing slower memory with faster memory components.

Hard-disk type 47 RAM area   This selection allows you to choose the location of the Type 47 HDD data area in memory. The BIOS has to place the HD type 47 data somewhere in memory. You can choose between DOS memory or the I/O address space at 0:300h. DOS memory is valuable (you only have 640KB to work with), so you should try to use the I/O space instead. However, there might be some peripheral that needs this area too (i.e., a sound card or network card). Notice that this feature is redundant if BIOS is shadowed (except possibly for very old BIOS).

Wait for <F1> if any error   If enabled, the system will halt and wait for <F1> keyboard input before proceeding. If disabled, the system will simply continue after displaying an error message without waiting for any keyboard input. Disable the feature if you want the system to operate as a server (without a keyboard). Otherwise, you can enable the feature.

System boot up NumLock   This specifies whether you want the NumLock key to be activated at boot up. You are free to keep this feature enabled or disabled, as your personal tastes dictate.

Numeric processor test   This feature will test the math co-processor. 486DX, DX2, DX4, and all Pentium-class CPUs use a built-in co-processor, and this test should be enabled (otherwise, the co-processor function might not be enabled). 486SX, 486DLC, 486SLC, and all previous CPUs use a separate math co-processor, and you should set this feature, depending on whether a co-processor is present or not.

Weitek co-processor This feature is normally found on older 386 motherboards from a period when Weitek co-processors were popular. This high-performance co-processor has two to three times the performance of the comparable Intel co-processors. Weitek uses some RAM address space, so memory from this region must be remapped elsewhere. If you have a 386 system with a Weitek unit, enable the feature. If you do not have a Weitek unit, disable the feature. This setting is normally found on 386 motherboards.

Floppy drive seek at boot This feature selects whether a floppy drive will be checked at boot time. Keep this feature disabled for faster booting and reduced damage to floppy R/W heads. Enable this feature if you want to boot from a floppy disk (important for "booting clean" and running diagnostic utilities).

> Disabling the floppy drive, changing the system boot sequence, and setting a CMOS password are good techniques for adding some security to a PC.

System boot sequence This feature controls the order in which system drives are checked for an operating system. A:, C: is the typical sequence, but C:, A: can be selected for faster booting. Modern BIOS also supports booting from other items, such as the CD-ROM (which meet the "El Torito" bootable CD-ROM specification), and SCSI drives (even while EIDE/IDE drives are in the system).

System boot up CPU speed This is commonly referred to as the *turbo mode*, and it allows you to specify what processor speed the system will boot to. The typical settings are High and Low. High speed is recommended for best performance, but if you encounter booting problems, you should try the Low speed.

External cache memory This feature allows you to enable or disable the external (L2) cache in the system. If L2 cache is in the system (virtually all 486 and Pentium-class systems use L2 cache), be sure that this feature is enabled for best performance. If there is no L2 cache, keep this feature disabled. Enabling the L2 cache when there is no cache in the system might cause the PC to lock up.

Internal cache memory This feature allows you to enable or disable the internal (L1) cache in the CPU. If there is L1 cache in the system (all 486 and Pentium-class CPUs use L1 cache), be sure that this feature is enabled for best performance. If there is no L1 cache (or you have reason to believe that the CPU's L1 cache is damaged), keep this feature disabled. Enabling the L1 cache when there is no cache in the CPU might cause the PC to lock up. This feature might also be presented as *CPU internal cache*.

> Some CMOS setup utilities combine the cache control into a single entry, such as *Cache Memory*, and allows you to select *Disabled*, *Internal Cache Only*, or *Both Enabled*.

Fast gate A20 option This relates to the first 64KB of extended memory (A0 to A19), known as the *High Memory Area (HMA)*. This option controls the use of the A20 address line to access memory above 1MB. Normally, all RAM access above 1MB is handled through the A20 gate in the keyboard controller chip (e.g., 8042 or 8742). In virtually all cases, this option should be enabled. Disabling this option might make it impossible to access memory over 1MB.

Turbo switch function This feature enables or disables the turbo switch. This setting is now rarely used in modern systems because PCs are always run at their top speed (there is no need to slow down a PC artificially). If there is a turbo switch in the system, keep this feature enabled. Otherwise, disable this feature.

Shadow memory cacheable "Shadowing" is the process of copying ROM to RAM. Once the ROM contents are copied into RAM, its performance can often be increased even further by making that RAM space cacheable. You can enable this feature to cache shadow memory, or disable it to prevent caching of shadow memory. Shadow caching is usually a good idea for DOS and Windows-based platforms, and it should be enabled. But Linux and other Unix-like operating systems will not benefit from this feature, and it can remain disabled.

Password checking option This option controls whether a password is used to access the system, or access the CMOS setup, or both. When enabled, you'll need to set a password, then enter the appropriate password(s), as required. Always remember to note your password(s) in a safe place, and change your passwords frequently. If you forget a password, or encounter a system with a password option in place, see the section "CMOS password troubleshooting" at the end of this chapter.

Video ROM shadow C000, 32K Memory hidden in the "I/O hole" of 0x0A0000h to 0x0FFFFFh might be used to "shadow" video ROM, where the contents of the video ROM are copied into RAM, and the faster RAM copy is used instead. It is generally recommended to enable this feature, although systems with faster "flash" video BIOS might not see as much performance benefit. You should disable video ROM shadowing if you need to update a "flash" video BIOS, or if you're using a memory-resident utility to shadow the video BIOS. Notice that video ROM shadowing might also cause some operating systems or applications to lock up.

Adaptor ROM shadow C800,16K This feature enables shadowing for other adapter ROMs at C800h (e.g., SCSI or network controller BIOS) that might be in the system. If there are no other adapter devices in the system, keep this feature disabled.

Adaptor ROM shadow CC00,16K This feature enables shadowing for other adapter ROMs that might be in the system at CC00h. This feature is often disabled by default because some hard-drive adapters use the CC00h address.

Adaptor ROM shadow D000,16K This feature enables shadowing for other adapter ROMs that might be in the system at D000h. This is the default address for most network adapters, so should usually be disabled unless there is a network adapter in the system, or some other known device with ROM at D000h.

Adaptor ROM shadow D400,16K   This feature enables shadowing for other adapter ROMs that might be in the system at D400h. Because some special controllers (e.g., controllers that support four floppy drives) often use this space, the default is often set disabled.

Adaptor ROM shadow D800,16K   This feature enables shadowing for other adapter ROMs that might be in the system at D800h. The default is often disabled unless there is a known ROM in the system at that address.

Adaptor ROM shadow DC00,16K   This feature enables shadowing for other adapter ROMs that might be in the system at DC00h. The default is often disabled unless there is a known ROM in the system at that address.

Adaptor ROM shadow E000,16K   This feature enables shadowing for other adapter ROMs that might be in the system at E000h. The default is often disabled unless there is a known ROM in the system at that address.

Adaptor ROM shadow E400,16K   This feature enables shadowing for other adapter ROMs that might be in the system at E400h. The default is often disabled unless there is a known ROM in the system at that address.

Adaptor ROM shadow E800,16K   This feature enables shadowing for other adapter ROMs that might be in the system at E800h. The default is often disabled unless there is a known ROM in the system at that address.

Adaptor ROM shadow EC00,16K   This feature enables shadowing for other adapter ROMs that might be in the system at EC00h. The default is often disabled unless there is a known ROM in the system at that address. SCSI adapter BIOS ROMs are often set to this address.

> Some recent forms of SCSI controllers use writeable addresses, and should not be shadowed or cached. Check for such warnings or cautions in the SCSI controller manual before attempting to shadow the SCSI BIOS ROM.

System ROM shadow F000, 64K   Memory hidden in the "I/O hole" of 0x0A0000h to 0x0FFFFFh might be used to "shadow" the system ROM, where the contents of the motherboard BIOS ROM are copied into RAM, and the faster RAM copy is used instead. It is generally recommended to enable this feature, although systems with faster "flash" motherboard BIOS might not see as much performance benefit. You should disable motherboard ROM shadowing if you need to update a "flash" motherboard BIOS, or if you're using some memory-resident utility to shadow the BIOS. Notice that motherboard ROM shadowing might also cause some operating systems (other than DOS or Windows) or applications to lock up.

BootSector virus protection   This is a relatively new feature in BIOS that provides a warning whenever any software attempts to write to the disk's boot sector—a main target for computer viruses. You can generally keep this feature enabled unless you're installing a new operating system (like Windows 95), which needs to write to the boot sector during installation. You can disable the BootSector virus protection before installing the OS, then re-enable the feature afterward.

CONFIGURING THE ADVANCED CHIPSET SETUP

As you probably noted from Chapter 8, the core logic (or chipset) is responsible for providing many of the advanced features that we take for granted in today's PCs. As a consequence, there are a tremendous number of variables involved in the proper configuration of a chipset. This part of the CMOS setup allows you to tweak the performance of your chipset (namely memory operations, memory refresh options, data bus performance, cache enhancements, etc.).

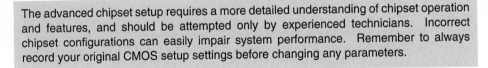

The advanced chipset setup requires a more detailed understanding of chipset operation and features, and should be attempted only by experienced technicians. Incorrect chipset configurations can easily impair system performance. Remember to always record your original CMOS setup settings before changing any parameters.

Automatic configuration When enabled, this feature allows the BIOS to automatically set the settings in the advanced chipset setup (e.g., clock divider, wait states, etc.). If you're uncertain about configuring the advanced chipset features, keep this feature enabled. Disable this feature if you're going to make manual changes to the chipset setup. You might have to disable this feature if some highly specialized adapter cards are used in the system.

Keyboard reset control This feature enables the <Ctrl>+<Alt>+<Del> warm reboot. Disable this feature if you want to prohibit this kind of warm reboot.

Hidden refresh This feature allows the RAM refresh memory cycles to take place in memory banks not used by your CPU at this time—instead of with the normal refresh cycles, which are executed every time that the interrupt DRQ0 is called (every 15 ms). There are typically three types of refresh schemes: cycle steal, cycle stretch, or hidden refresh. Cycle steal actually steals a clock cycle from the CPU to do the refresh. Cycle stretch delays a cycle from the processor to do the refresh (because it only occurs every 4 ms or so, it's an improvement from cycle steal). Hidden refresh simply refreshes idle memory banks. Most systems enable hidden refresh by default, but some memory supports hidden refresh better than others. Try hidden refresh. If the computer crashes or locks up, disable the hidden refresh.

Slow refresh This option reduces the frequency of RAM refresh. This increases system performance slightly because of the reduced contention between the CPU and refresh circuitry, but not all RAM necessarily support these reduced refresh rates (in which case, you will get parity errors and system crashes). Many systems enable the slow refresh by default.

Here's a tip for mobile PC users—refresh cycles take power, so using slow refresh to reduce the number of refresh cycles can save power.

Concurrent refresh This feature enables both the processor and the refresh hardware to have access to the memory at the same time. If this feature is disabled, the processor has to wait until the refresh hardware has finished, and this can slow system performance slightly. Many systems enable concurrent refresh by default.

Burst refresh When enabled, this feature performs several refresh cycles at once. This feature can normally be enabled.

DRAM burst at 4 refresh This is a slight variation of burst refresh, where the refresh is occurring in bursts of four. This feature can normally be enabled.

Hi-speed refresh (or fast refresh) When enabled, this feature causes refresh cycles to occur at higher frequencies to accomplish a refresh cycle in a shorter period. When combined with such features as burst refresh, the overall system performance can improve. Not all types of memory can support fast refresh, and it uses more power than slow refresh.

Staggered refresh When enabled, refresh is performed on memory banks sequentially. This results in less power consumption, and less interference between memory banks. Many systems enable staggered refresh by default.

Slow memory refresh divider If you can extend the refresh cycles of your system (using such techniques as slow refresh), you can free more CPU time, and system performance improves. This feature allows you to select a divider, which slows the refresh cycles. If you slow the refresh too much, you'll get parity errors and system crashes.

Decoupled refresh option This feature enables the ISA bus and the RAM to refresh separately. Because refreshing the ISA bus is a slower process, separating the refresh cycles this way causes less strain on the CPU. This option is often enabled.

Refresh value The lower this value is, the better the performance.

Refresh RAS active time This is the amount of active time needed for row address strobe during refresh. Lower entries are usually better.

Single ALE enable Address Latch Enable (ALE) is an ISA bus signal (pin B28) that indicates that a valid address is posted on the bus, and this bus is used to communicate with 8- and 16-bit peripheral cards. Some chipsets have the capability to support an enhanced mode, in which multiple ALE assertions might be made during a single bus cycle. Single ALE Enable enables or disables this capability. Because this feature might slow the video bus if enabled, it is generally set as disabled (no).

AT bus clock selection (or AT bus clock source) This selects a division of the CPU clock (or system clock) so it can approximate the ISA/EISA bus clock of 8.33MHz.

The settings are in terms of CLK/x, (or CLKIN/x and CLK2/x), where x might have values like 2, 3, 4, or 5. CLK represents your bus processor speed. For example, 486DX33, 486DX2/66, and 486DX3/99 all use a 33MHz bus speed, and should have a divider value of 4 for an ISA speed of 8.25MHz. For 286 and 386 processors, CLK is half the speed of the CPU. Here are some typical settings:

CLK/2: all 286 and 386 systems
CLK/3: SX/DX16, DX20, DX25, DX2/50, DX4/100
CLK/4: SX/DX33, DX2/66, DX3/99
CLK/5: DX40, DX2/80
CLK/6: DX50, DX2/100
CLK/7: 60MHz bus
CLK/8: 66MHz bus

The bus speed doesn't have to be precisely 8.33MHz, but that's what to shoot for. An improper setting might cause significant decrease in performance. If the divider is too high, the ISA bus speed will be too low (below 8.33MHz), and the ISA devices will perform poorly. If the divider is too low, the ISA bus speed will be too high (above 8.33MHz), and the ISA devices might malfunction.

Bus mode This feature selects the clock mode that is used to drive the bus. In synchronous mode, the CPU clock is used to drive the bus. In asynchronous mode, the ATCLK is used. In most cases, the synchronous mode is selected.

AT cycle wait-state This entry indicates the number of wait-states inserted whenever an operation is performed with the AT bus. You might need some additional wait-states if old ISA cards are used—especially if they are used together with fast adapter cards. Too many wait-states will reduce bus performance, and too few wait-states can cause bus errors and system lock ups.

16-bit memory, I/O wait-state This entry lists the number of wait-states inserted with 16-bit memory and I/O operations. Too many wait-states will reduce bus performance, and too few wait-states can cause bus errors and system lock ups.

8-bit memory, I/O wait-state This entry lists the number of wait-states inserted with 8-bit memory and I/O operations. Too many wait-states will reduce bus performance, and too few wait-states can cause bus errors and system lock ups.

16-bit I/O recovery time This is an additional delay time inserted after every 16-bit operation. This is sometimes needed to support older 16-bit devices, and the value is added to the minimum delay inserted after every AT bus cycle.

Fast AT cycle When enabled, this feature might speed-up data-transfer rates with ISA cards (and can have an important effect on ISA video boards).

ISA IRQs This entry informs the PCI cards of IRQs used by ISA cards so that the PCI cards will not attempt to assign those "legacy" resources.

DMA wait-states This entry lists the number of wait-states inserted before direct memory access (DMA) is attempted. Lower numbers (fewer wait-states) result in better DMA performance.

DMA clock source This entry indicates the source of the DMA clock, which is used for DMA transfers. This setting will affect DMA performance for any peripheral (like floppy, tape, network, and SCSI adapters) using DMA. The maximum is 5MHz.

E0000 ROM belongs to ATBUS This entry indicates if the E0000h area (upper memory) belongs to the motherboard DRAM or to the AT bus. For most systems, enabled (yes) is recommended.

Memory remapping This feature remaps the memory used by the BIOS (A0000h to FFFFFh or 384KB) above the 1MB limit. If enabled, you cannot shadow video and system BIOS. In many cases, you should set this feature to disabled.

Fast decode enable This refers to some hardware that monitors the commands sent to the keyboard-controller chip. The original AT used special codes not processed by the keyboard itself to control the switching of the 286 processor back from protected mode to real mode. The 286 itself had no hardware to do this, so they actually have to reset the CPU to switch back. PC makers added a few logic chips to monitor the commands sent to the keyboard controller chip, and when the "reset CPU" code was detected, the logic chips did an immediate reset. This "fast decode" of the keyboard reset command allowed OS/2 and Windows to switch between real and protected modes faster, and allowed much better performance. You will generally find this entry on 286 and early 386 systems because newer processors DO have hardware instructions for switching between modes.

If you find this entry on a current system, the *fast decode enable* command is probably defines a bit differently. The design of the original AT bus made it very difficult to mix 8-bit and 16-bit RAM or ROM within the same 128K block of high address space. An 8-bit BIOS ROM on a VGA card forced all other peripherals using the C000h-DFFFh range to also use 8 bits. By doing an "early decode" of the high address lines, along with the 8/16-bit select flag, the I/O bus could then use mixed 8- and 16-bit peripherals. In both cases, you should probably have this feature enabled.

Extended I/O decode The normal range of I/O addresses is 0–0x3FFh using only 10 address bits. With this feature enabled, the system will support a 16-bit I/O-address bus allowing a 64KB I/O space using. Most motherboards or I/O adapters can be decoded only by 10 address bits, so this feature can usually be left disabled.

I/O recovery time The I/O recovery time is the number of wait-states to be inserted between two consecutive I/O operations (generally specified as a two-number pair, such as 5/3). The first number is the number of wait-states to insert for an 8-bit operation, the second is the number of wait-states for a 16-bit operation. In general, this feature can be disabled. If the AT bus clock is running fast (over 8.33MHz), or you're using slow peripherals, it might be necessary to enable I/O recovery time starting with a value like "5/3."

A few BIOS versions specify an "I/O setup time" (or "AT bus (I/O) command delay"). It is specified similarly to I/O recovery time, but is a delay before starting an I/O operation, rather than a delay between I/O operations.

IDE multi-block mode (also called IDE block mode) This feature enables IDE drives to transfer several sectors per interrupt. Six modes are possible:

- Mode 0 (standard mode transferring a single sector at a time)
- Mode 1 (no interrupts)
- Mode 2 (sectors are transferred in a single burst)
- Mode 3 (speeds up to 11.1 MB/s—sometimes abbreviated as *32-bit mode*)
- Mode 4 (up to 16.7 MB/s)
- Mode 5 (up to 20 MB/s—not used in actual drive implementations)

The important attribute for block mode is the number of sectors per interrupt. The maximum number of sectors per interrupt is often (but not always) related to the drive's buffer size. If this setting is not set properly, communication with COM ports might not work. If the block size (sectors/interrupt) is set too large, you might experience serial port overruns and CRC errors. To fix this, decrease the block size or disable block mode altogether.

IDE DMA transfer mode This defines the means by which DMA transfers are executed. The three typical settings are disabled, type B (for EISA), and standard (for PCI). Standard is the fastest, but might cause problems with IDE CD-ROMs. The standard type is Type F.

IDE multiple sector mode When IDE DMA transfer mode is enabled, this feature sets the number of sectors per burst (with a maximum of 64). Problems might occur with COM ports if this setting is configured improperly.

IDE 32-bit transfer When enabled, the read/write performance of the hard disk is faster. When disabled, only 16-bit data transfers are possible. Enable this feature, if possible.

Extended DMA registers With a standard AT-type computer, DMA support is only provided for the first 16MB of system RAM. With this feature enabled, DMA support will be extended for up to 4GB of RAM. In most cases, this feature can be left disabled.

Cache read option (often called the *SRAM Read Wait-State* or *Cache Read Hit Burst*) This specifies the number of clocks needed to load four 32-bit words into a CPU internal cache (typically specified as clocks per word). A timing of "2-1-1-1" indicates five clocks to load the four words, and is the theoretical minimum for current high-end CPUs (486DX, 486SX, 486DX2, 486DX4, and Pentium). This timing determines the number of wait-states for the cache RAM in normal and burst transfers (the latter for 486 systems only). Timing of "4-1-1-1" is usually recommended, but the faster timing that a computer can support, the better.

Cache write option This is the same as "cache read option," but it is used to control cache write timing.

Fast cache read/write Allows enhanced cache performance through memory inter-leaving techniques, so enable this feature if you have two banks of cache (64KB or 256KB).

Cache wait state This feature is used to introduce additional wait states for cache op-erations. Like conventional memory, fewer wait states will result in better cache perfor-mance (but it will demand faster cache). An entry of "0" will provide optimum performance, but "1" wait-state might be required for bus speeds higher than 33MHz.

Tag RAM includes dirty When enabled, the cache is not replaced during cycles, sim-ply overwritten. This results in a performance increase. However, the maximum range of cacheable memory is cut in half because a bit is needed as a "dirty bit" tag. In general, you can leave this feature disabled unless you have little system RAM.

Non-cacheable block-1 size The non-cacheable region is intended for a memory-mapped I/O device that isn't supposed to be cached. For example, some video cards can present all video memory at 15MB to 16MB, so the software doesn't have to bank-switch. If the non-cacheable region covers actual RAM memory you are using, expect a signifi-cant performance decrease for accesses to that area. If the non-cacheable region covers only non-existent memory addresses, there should be no performance hit. If you are using devices that should not be cached, enable this feature to set aside some memory from caching. Otherwise, you can leave this entry disabled.

Non-cacheable block-1 base Enter the base address of the area you don't want to cache. It must be a multiple of the non-cacheable block-1 size selected above. When dis-abled, set this to 0KB.

Non-cacheable block-2 size This is the same function as "non-cacheable block-1 size," and it is normally left disabled.

Non-cacheable block-2 base This is the same as "non-cacheable block-1 base," and it is usually set to 0KB.

Cacheable RAM address range Chipsets usually allow memory to be cached just up to 16 or 32MB. This is to limit the number of memory address bits that need to be saved in the cache together with its contents. Set this entry to the lowest possible value. For ex-ample, if you only have 4MB of RAM, select 4MB—don't enter 16MB if you only have 8MB installed.

Video BIOS area cacheable This feature can enable or disable caching the video BIOS. Caching the video BIOS can often enhance video performance, but with many of today's accelerated video cards, it might be necessary to prevent caching.

Memory read wait-state (or "DRAM read wait-states") The CPU is often much faster than RAM, and it is necessary to introduce wait-states to allow the slower RAM to "catch up" to the CPU. Each wait-state effectively adds 30 ns of RAM speed. Fewer wait-states result in better system performance, and the ideal number of wait-states is "0" (though "1" wait-state is typically required). The number of wait states necessary is approximately

[*RAM speed in ns* + 10) × *Clock speed in MHz*/1000 – 2. If there are too many wait-states, system performance will suffer. If there are too few wait states, parity errors and system crashes will occur.

Memory write wait state (or DRAM write wait-states) This is the same as "memory read wait state," but it applies to RAM writing.

> Some BIOS versions combine these two options as the "DRAM wait states." In this case, the number of read and write wait states must be equal.

DRAM CAS timing delay DRAM is organized into rows and columns, and accessed through strobe lines. The CPU activates a *Row Access Strobe (RAS)* line to find the row containing the required data, then a *Column Access Strobe (CAS)* line specifies the column. As a result RAS and CAS signals are used to identify a location in a DRAM chip. When using slow RAM, it might be necessary to introduce a delay into the CAS timing. The default is no CAS delay.

DRAM refresh method This feature selects the refresh method used for RAM. The options are "RAS only" and "CAS before RAS." Most current systems use "CAS-before-RAS" timing by default.

RAS precharge time This is the time interval during which the row address strobe (RAS) signal to DRAM is held low for normal read and write cycles. This is the minimum interval between completing one read or write and starting another from the same (non-page mode) DRAM. Advanced techniques, such as memory interleaving or the use of Page Mode DRAM, are often used to avoid this delay. The RAS Precharge value is typically about the same as the RAM access time. For a 33MHz CPU, an entry of 4 is a good choice, but lower values should be selected for slower speeds.

RAS active time This is the amount of time a RAS signal can be kept open for multiple accesses. Higher figures will improve system performance.

RAS-to-CAS delay time This is the amount of time a CAS is performed after a RAS. Lower figures are better for system performance, but some DRAM will not support low figures.

CAS-before-RAS When enabled, this option reduces refresh cycles and power consumption.

CAS width in read cycle This feature expresses the number of wait-states for the CPU to read DRAM. Lower figures are better for system performance.

Interleave mode When enabled, the system will use an "interleaved" approach to access system memory. If the motherboard is not designed to support interleaved memory (or used an advanced form of high-performance memory), this option should be disabled.

Fast page-mode DRAM When enabled, this feature speeds up memory access for FPM DRAM. When memory access occurs in the same memory "page," the overhead of RAS and CAS sequences are not necessary, and memory performance is improved.

CONFIGURING PLUG AND PLAY/PCI

Plug-and-Play (PnP) and the PCI (Peripheral Component Interconnect) bus are two tightly related features designed to ease the configuration burden of PC devices, and provide those devices with a high-performance bus capable of working directly with the CPU and main memory. However, Plug-and-Play and PCI features must be configured properly in BIOS in order to ensure trouble-free operation. This part of the chapter explains the options used to configure PCI slots and PnP behavior.

Latency timer (PCI clocks) This entry controls the length of time an agent on the PCI bus can hold the bus when another device has requested it. Because the PCI bus runs faster than the ISA bus, the PCI bus must be slowed during interactions with it. This setting allows you to define how long the PCI bus will delay for a transaction between the given PCI slot and the ISA bus. This number depends on the PCI master device in use, and it ranges from 0 to 255. The default is often 66, but 40 is a good place to start. Smaller values result in faster access to the bus (with better response times), but bandwidth and data throughput become lower. Normally, you'd leave this setting alone, unless you're working with latent-sensitive devices (e.g., audio cards or network cards with small buffers).

PCI Slot x INTx Use this entry to assign PCI interrupts (INT#s) to specific PCI slots.

■ *Edge/level select* Once an interrupt is assigned with "PCI slot x INTx," this option programs PCI IRQs to single-edge or logic-level triggering modes. Most PCI cards use level triggering, but most ISA cards use edge triggering. However, try selecting edge triggering for PCI IDE.

PCI device, slot 1/2/3 This feature enables I/O and memory cycle decoding for PCI slots. There are three options: enable (enables the device as a slave PCI device), en master (enables the device as a master PCI device), and use default latency timer. If this is enabled (yes) you don't need to set the latency timer value.

Slot X using INT# This entry selects an interrupt (INT#) channel for a PCI slot, and there are four (A, B, C, and D) for each one. That is, each PCI bus slot supports interrupts A, B, C and D. INT#A is allocated automatically, and you would only use #B, #C, and #D if the PCI card needs to use more than one (PCI) interrupt service. For example, select #D if your PCI card needs four interrupts. Often, it is simplest to use the auto mode.

Xth available IRQ This feature selects (or "maps") an IRQ for one of the available INT#s (A, B, C, or D). There are 10 selections (3, 4, 5, 6, 7, 9, 10, 11, 12, 14, and 15). *1st available IRQ* means that the BIOS will assign this IRQ to the first PCI slots (order is 1, 2, 3, and 4), etc. *N/A* means the particular IRQ has been assigned to the ISA bus. It is, therefore, not available to a PCI slot.

PCI IRQ activated by This lists the method by which the PCI bus recognizes an IRQ request (level or edge). Use the default entries unless advised otherwise by your PCI device manufacturer, or if you have a PCI device that only recognizes one of these methods.

Configuration mode This entry sets the method by which information about "legacy" cards is conveyed to the system:

■ *Use ICU* The BIOS depends on information provided by plug-and-play software (such as the configuration manager or ISA configuration utility). Only select this if you have the utilities needed.
■ *Use setup utility* The BIOS depends on information provided in the CMOS setup routine—don't use configuration utilities.

ISA shared memory size This option sets a block of system memory that will not be shadowed. This feature should normally be disabled, unless you have an ISA card that uses the upper memory area. If you enable this feature, you'll also need to configure the following:

■ *ISA shared memory base address* Enter the base address here. If you choose 64K, you can only choose D000h or lower.

IRQ 3-IRQ 15 These entries are used to list what IRQs are in use (or reserved) by ISA "legacy" cards. If you don't use specific IRQs, set the respective entries to *Available*. Otherwise, set *Used by ISA card*, which means that nothing else can use it.

PCI IDE prefetch buffers This feature allows you to enable or disable a set of prefetch buffers in the PCI IDE controller. You might need to disable this feature with an operating system (like Windows NT) that doesn't use the BIOS to access the hard disk, and doesn't disable interrupts when completing a programmed I/O operation. Disabling also prevents errors with faulty PCI-IDE interface chips that can corrupt data on the hard disk (as can happen with true 32-bit operating systems). You can usually leave this feature disabled.

PCI IDE second channel Disable this feature if you're not using the second channel on the PCI IDE card. This frees up IRQ 15. Otherwise, you will lose IRQ 15 on the ISA slots.

PCI IDE IRQ map to This option allows you to configure your system to the type of IDE disk controller. The device is assumed to be ISA. If you have a PCI IDE controller, this setting allows you to specify which slot has the controller and which PCI INT# (A, B, C, or D) is associated with the connected hard drives. Notice that this refers to the hard disk, rather than individual partitions. Because each IDE controller supports two drives, you can select the INT# for each. Also notice that the primary channel has a lower interrupt than the secondary channel. There are four modes:

■ *PCI-auto* If the IDE is detected by the BIOS on one of the PCI slots, then the appropriate INT# channel will be assigned to IRQ 14.
■ *PCI-slot X* If the IDE is not detected, you can manually select the slot.

- *Primary IDE INT#, secondary IDE INT#* This assigns two INT# channels for primary and secondary channels (if supported).
- *ISA* This option assigns no IRQs to PCI slots. Use this mode for PCI IDE cards that connect IRQs 14 and 15 directly from an ISA slot using a table from a legacy paddle board.

PCI bus parking This is a sort of bus mastering; a device parking on the PCI bus has full control of the bus for a short time. This feature improves performance when that device is being used, but excludes others. Try enabling this feature with network cards and hard-disk controllers.

IDE buffer for DOS and Windows When enabled, this feature provides IDE read-ahead and posted-write buffers so that you can increase throughput to and from IDE devices by buffering reads and writes. However, this feature might actually slow older devices, so it should be disabled.

IDE master (slave) PIO mode This option changes the IDE data-transfer speed; Mode 0–4 or Auto. Rather than have the BIOS issue commands to affect transfers to or from the disk drive, PIO allows the BIOS to tell the controller what it wants, then lets the controller and the CPU perform the complete task by themselves. Modes 1–4 are available for EIDE systems, but are set to *Auto* for an automatic configuration.

HCLK PCICLK This entry allows you to set the host CLK / PCI CLK divider. The options are: *AUTO, 1–1,* and *1–1.5.*

PCI-ISA BCLK divider This entry allows you to set the PCI bus CLK / ISA bus CLK divider. The options are: *AUTO, PCICLK1/3, PCICLK1/2,* and *PCICLK1/4.*

PCI write-byte-merge (sometimes called *CPU-to-PCI byte merge*) When enabled, this allows data sent from the CPU to the PCI bus to be held in a buffer. The chipset will then write the data in the buffer to the PCI bus, when appropriate.

CPU-to-PCI read buffer (sometimes called *PCI-to-CPU write buffer*) When enabled, up to four double-words (DW) can be read from the PCI bus without interrupting the CPU. When disabled, a write buffer is not used, and the CPU read cycle will not be completed until the PCI bus signals that it is ready to receive the data. Enabling the buffer is best for system performance.

CPU-to-PCI read line When enabled (On), more time will be allocated for data setup with faster CPUs. This feature might only be required if you add an Intel OverDrive processor to your 486-class system.

CPU-to-PCI read burst When enabled (On), the PCI bus will interpret CPU read cycles as the PCI burst protocol, meaning that back-to-back sequential CPU memory read cycles addressed to the PCI will be translated into fast PCI burst memory cycles. Performance is improved, but some non-standard PCI adapters (e.g., VGA adapters) might experience problems.

PCI-to-DRAM buffer When enabled, this feature improves PCI-to-DRAM performance by allowing data to be stored if a destination is busy. Buffers are needed for this feature because the PCI bus is separate from the CPU.

Latency for CPU-to-PCI write This is the delay time before a CPU writes data to the PCI bus.

PCI cycle cache hit This option defines how the cache is refreshed during PCI operation. Normal refresh will produce a cache refresh during normal PCI cycles. Fast refresh will produce a cache refresh without a PCI cycle for CAS. Fast performance is usually better.

Use default latency timer value This option determines whether the default value for the latency timer will be loaded, or the succeeding latency timer value will be used. If *Yes* is selected (default), no further programming is needed for the latency timer value.

Latency timer value This is the maximum number of PCI bus clocks that the master might burst. A longer latency time provides the CPU with more of a chance to control the bus.

Latency from ADS# status This feature allows you to configure how long the CPU waits for the Address Data Status (ADS). It determines the CPU-to-PCI post write speed. When set to $3T$, this is $5T$ for each double word. With $2T$ (default), it is $4T$ per double word. For a quad word (Qword) PCI memory write, the rate is $7T$ ($2T$) or $8T$ ($3T$). The default should be correct, but if you add a faster CPU to your system, you might find it necessary to increase it. The choices are: $3T$—three CPU clocks, or $2T$—two CPU clocks (Default).

PCI master latency This option sets the time that a PCI master can control the bus. If your PCI master controls the bus for too long, there is less time for the CPU to control it. A longer latency time gives the CPU more time to control the PCI bus.

Max. burstable range This is the maximum bursting length for each asserting FRAME#. Longer burst durations should improve performance.

CPU-to-PCI burst memory write When enabled, back-to-back sequential CPU memory write cycles to PCI are translated to PCI burst memory write cycles. Otherwise, each single write to PCI will have an associated FRAME# sequence. Keeping this feature enabled is best for performance, but some non-standard PCI cards (e.g., VGA adapters) might have problems.

CPU-to-PCI post memory write This feature enables up to four double-words (Dwords) of data to be posted to PCI. Otherwise, not only is buffering disabled, but completion of CPU writes is limited (the CPU write does not complete until the PCI transaction completes). Keeping this feature enabled is best for performance.

CPU-to-PCI write buffer Same as "CPU-to-PCI read buffer," only for writing.

PCI-to-ISA write buffer   When enabled, the system will temporarily write data to a buffer so that the CPU is not interrupted. When disabled, the memory write cycle for the PCI bus will be direct to the slower ISA bus. As a result, keeping this feature enabled is best for performance.

DMA line buffer   This feature allows DMA data to be stored in a buffer so that PCI bus operations are not interrupted. Disabled means that the line buffer for DMA is in single-transaction mode. Enabled allows it to operate in an 8-byte transaction mode for greater efficiency. This feature should be enabled for best system performance.

ISA master line buffer   ISA master buffers are designed to isolate the slower ISA I/O operations from the PCI bus for better performance. Keeping this feature disabled means that the buffer for ISA master transaction is in single-mode. Enabling this feature means that it is in 8-byte mode, which increases the ISA master's performance.

CPU/PCI post write delay   This is the delay time before the CPU writes data into the PCI bus.

Post write CAS active   This is the pulse width of the CAS# signal when the PCI master writes to DRAM.

PCI master accesses shadow RAM   This feature enables the shadowing of a ROM on a PCI master for better performance.

Enable master   This feature enables the selected device as a PCI bus master, and checks whether the card is capable of performing as a PCI master.

AT/ISA bus clock frequency   This is the AT bus speed in a PCI system. Select a divisor, which will give you a bus speed closest to 8.33MHz (depending on the speed of the PCI bus).

Base I/O address   This entry lists the base of the I/O address range from which the PCI-device resource requests are satisfied.

Base memory address   This entry lists the base of the 32-bit memory address range from which the PCI device resource requests are satisfied.

Parity   When enabled, this feature allows parity checking of PCI devices.

ISA linear frame buffer   This feature enables a buffer if you use an ISA card that features a linear frame buffer (i.e., a second video card for AutoCAD). The buffer address will be set automatically.

ISA VGA frame buffer size (or *ISA LFB size*)   This feature allows you to use a VGA frame buffer and 16MB of RAM at the same time; the system will allow access to the graphics card through a "hole" in its own memory map. In other words, access to addresses within this "hole" will be directed to the ISA bus instead of main memory. This feature should be set to *Disabled* unless you're using an ISA card with more than 64KB of memory that needs to be accessed by the CPU, and you are not using the plug-

and-play utilities. If you have less than 8MB of memory or use MS-DOS, this feature will be ignored.

Residence of VGA card   This option lists whether the VGA card resides on a PCI or VL bus. Today, the default is PCI.

Memory map hole start/end address   This entry determines where the hole starts, and depends on the ISA LFB size. If you can change it, the base address should be 16MB minus the buffer size. See "ISA VGA frame buffer size."

Memory hole size   This entry defines the size of the memory "hole." Options are *1MB*, *2MB*, *4MB*, *8MB*, and *Disabled*. These are the amounts below 16MB that are assigned to the AT bus, and reserved for ISA cards.

Memory hole start address   This entry defines where the memory "hole" starts. The selections are from 1MB to 15MB. This entry is not used if *Memory hole* is disabled.

Byte merging   This feature allows writes to sequential memory addresses to be merged into one PCI-to-memory operation, which increases performance for older applications that write to video memory in bytes, rather than words. This feature is not supported well on all PCI video cards. Enable this feature unless you encounter graphics problems.

Byte merge support (a variation of byte merging)   Eight- or 16-bit data traveling from the CPU to the PCI bus is held in a buffer where it is accumulated or merged, into 32-bit data, providing faster overall performance. In this case, enabling this feature means that CPU-PCI writes are buffered.

Multimedia mode   This feature enables or disables palette snooping for multimedia cards.

Video palette snoop   This feature controls how a PCI graphics card can "snoop" write cycles to an ISA video card's color palette registers. Snooping essentially means interfering with a device. This is a powerful performance option; only disable it if: an ISA card connects to a PCI graphics card through a VESA connector, the ISA card connects to a color monitor and the ISA card uses the RAMDAC on the PCI card, and palette snooping (RAMDAC shadowing) is not operative on the PCI card.

PCI/VGA palette snoop   This feature alters the VGA palette setting while graphic signals pass through the feature connector of the PCI VGA card and are processed by the MPEG card. VGA snooping is used by multimedia video devices (e.g., video capture boards) to look ahead at the video controller (VGA device) to see what color palette is currently in use. Enable this feature if you have MPEG connections through the VGA feature connector (this means that you can adjust PCI/VGA palettes). Otherwise, go ahead and disable the feature.

Snoop filter (or *cache snoop filter*)   This feature saves the need for multiple inquiries to the same line as if it was checked previously. When enabled, cache snoop filters ensure data integrity (cache coherency) while reducing the snoop frequency to a minimum.

E8000 32K accessible This 64KB area of upper memory is used for BIOS purposes on PS/2s, 32-bit operating systems, and plug-and-play. This setting allows the second 32KB page to be used for other purposes when not needed (in the same way that the first 32KB page of the F range is usable after boot up has finished).

PCI arbiter mode Devices gain access to the PCI bus through arbitration. There are two modes: mode 1 (default) and mode 2. The idea is to minimize the time it takes to gain control of the bus and move data. Generally, mode 1 should be sufficient, but try mode 2 if you encounter problems with PCI bus access.

Stop CPU when PCI flush When this feature is enabled, the CPU will be stopped when the PCI bus is being flushed of data. Disabling this feature (default) allows the CPU to continue processing, giving somewhat greater system performance.

Stop CPU at PCI master When this feature is enabled, the CPU will be stopped when the PCI bus master is operating on the bus. Disabling this feature (default) allows the CPU to continue processing, providing somewhat greater system performance.

I/O cycle recovery When enabled, the PCI bus will be allowed a recovery period for back-to-back I/O (which slows back-to-back data transfers)—it's like adding wait-states to the PCI bus, so disable this feature (default) for best performance.

I/O recovery period This feature sets the length of time for the "I/O cycle recovery." The range is from 0 to 1.75 μs in 0.25-μs intervals.

Action when W_Buffer full This feature sets the behavior of the system when the write buffer is full. By default, the system will immediately retry (rather than wait for it to be emptied).

Fast back-to-back When this feature is enabled, the PCI bus will interpret CPU read cycles as the PCI burst protocol, meaning that back-to-back sequential CPU memory read cycles addressed to the PCI will be translated into the fast PCI burst memory cycles. By default, the feature is enabled.

CPU-pipelined function This feature allows the system controller to signal the CPU for a new memory address—even before all data transfers for the current cycle are complete. This results in increased data throughput. The default is usually disabled, so pipelining off.

Primary frame buffer When this feature is enabled, the system can use unreserved memory as a primary frame buffer. Unlike the VGA frame buffer, this would reduce over-all available RAM for applications. The default is usually disabled.

M1445RDYJ to CPURDYJ This feature determines whether the *PCI Ready* signal is to be synchronized by the CPU clock's ready signal or bypassed (default).

VESA master cycle ADSJ This feature allows you to increase the length of time the VESA master has to decode bus commands. Typical choices are *Normal* (default) and *Long*.

LDEVJ check point delay This feature allows you to select how much time is allocated for checking bus cycle commands. These commands must be decoded to determine whether a local bus device access signal (LDEVJ) is being sent, or an ISA device is being addressed. Increasing the delay increases stability (especially in the VESA subsystem) while very slightly degrading the performance of the ISA sub-system. Settings are in terms of the feedback clock rate (FBCLK2) used in the cache/memory control interface:

1 FBCLK2 = One clock
2 FBCLK2 = Two clocks (default)
3 FBCLK2 = Three clocks

CPU dynamic fast cycle This feature gives you faster access to the ISA bus. When the CPU issues a bus cycle, the PCI bus examines the command to determine if a PCI agent claims it. If not, then an ISA bus cycle is initiated. The dynamic-fast cycle then allows for faster access to the ISA bus by decreasing the latency (or delay) between the original CPU command and the beginning of the ISA cycle.

CPU memory sample point This feature allows you to select the cycle check point (which is where memory decoding and cache hit/miss checking occurs). Each selection indicates that the check occurs at the end of a CPU cycle, with one wait-state indicating more time for checking to take place than zero wait states. A longer check time allows for greater stability at the expense of some performance.

LDEV# check point The VESA local device (LDEV#) check point is where the VL-bus device decodes the bus commands and checks for errors, within the bus cycle itself:

0 Bus cycle point T1 (default)
1 During the first T2
2 During second T2
3 During third T2

Local memory check point This entry allows you to select between two techniques for decoding and error checking local bus writes to DRAM during a memory cycle:

Slow = Extra wait state; better checking (default)
Fast = No extra wait state used

FRAMEJ generation When the PCI-VL bus bridge is acting as a PCI master and receiving data from the CPU, a fast CPU-to-PCI buffer will be enabled if this selection is also enabled. Using the buffer allows the CPU to complete a write—even though the data has not been delivered to the PCI bus. This reduces the number of CPU cycles involved and speeds overall processing:

Normal Buffering not employed (default)
Fast Buffer used for CPU-to-PCI writes

PCI-to-CPU write pending   This feature sets the behavior of the system when the write buffer is full. By default, the system will immediately retry (but you can set it to wait for the buffer to be emptied before retrying).

Delay for SCSI/HDD (also sometimes called *SCSI boot delay*)   This is the length of time (in seconds) that the BIOS will wait for the SCSI hard disk to be ready for operation. If the hard drive is not ready, the PCI SCSI BIOS might not detect the hard drive correctly. The range is from 0 to 60 seconds.

Master IOCHRDY   When this feature is enabled, it allows the system to monitor for a VESA master request to generate an I/O channel-ready (IOCHRDY) signal.

VGA type   This entry is used when the video BIOS is being shadowed. The BIOS uses this information to determine which bus to use. Choices are *Standard* (default), *PCI*, and *ISA/VESA*.

PCI master timing mode   This entry gives you the ability to choose between two timing modes: *0* (default) and *1*.

PCI arbit. rotate priority   Typically, the system manages (or arbitrates) access to the PCI bus on a first-come-first-served basis. When priority is rotated, once a device gains control of the bus, it is assigned the lowest priority and every other device is moved up one in the priority queue. This helps to prevent any one device from monopolizing the PCI bus.

I/O cycle post write   When this feature is enabled (default), data being written during an I/O cycle will be buffered for faster performance.

PCI post write fast   When this feature is enabled (default), data being written during an PCI cycle will be buffered for faster performance.

CPU master post-W/R buffer   When the CPU operates as a bus master for either memory access or I/O, this entry controls its ability to use a high-speed posted write buffer. Choices are *N/A*, *1*, *2*, and *4* (default).

CPU master post-W/R burst mode   When the CPU operates as a bus master for either memory access or I/O, this entry controls its ability to use a high-speed burst mode for posted writes to a buffer.

CPU master fast interface   This entry enables or disables what is known as a "fast back-to-back" interface when the CPU operates as a bus master. When enabled, consecutive reads/writes are interpreted as the CPU high-performance burst mode.

PCI master post-W/R buffer   When a PCI device operates as a bus master for either memory access or I/O, this entry controls its use of a high-speed posted write buffer. Choices are *N/A*, *1*, *2*, and *4* (default).

PCI master burst mode When a PCI device operates as a bus master for either memory access or I/O, this entry controls its use of a high-speed burst mode for posted writes to a buffer.

PCI master fast interface This feature enables or disables what is known as a *fast back-to-back interface* when a PCI device operates as a bus master. When enabled, consecutive reads/writes are interpreted as the PCI high-performance burst mode.

CPU master DEVSEL# time out When the CPU initiates a master cycle using an address (target) which has not been mapped to PCI/VESA or ISA space, the system will monitor the DEVSEL (device select) pin for a period of time to see if any device claims the cycle. This entry allows you to determine how long the system will wait before timing-out. Choices are *3 PCICLK, 4 PCICLK, 5 PCICLK*, and *6 PCICLK* (default).

PCI master DEVSEL# time out When a PCI device initiates a master cycle using an address (target) which has not been mapped to PCI/VESA or ISA space, the system will monitor the DEVSEL (device select) pin for a period of time to see if any device claims the cycle. This entry allows you to determine how long the system will wait before timing out. Choices are *3 PCICLK, 4 PCICLK* (default), *5 PCICLK*, and *6 PCICLK*.

IRQ line If you have installed a device requiring an IRQ service into the given PCI slot, use this entry to inform the PCI bus which IRQ it should initiate. Choices range from *IRQ 3* through *IRQ 15*.

Fast back-to-back cycle When this feature is enabled, the PCI bus will interpret CPU read or write cycles as PCI burst protocol, meaning that back-to-back sequential CPU memory read/write cycles addressed to the PCI will be translated into fast PCI burst memory cycles.

State machines The chipset uses four state machines to manage specific CPU and/or PCI operations. Each can be thought of as a highly optimized process center designed to handle specific operations. Generally, each operation involves a master device and the bus it wishes to use. The four state machines are: CPU master to CPU bus (CC), CPU master to PCI bus (CP), PCI master to PCI bus (PP), and PCI master to CPU bus (PC). Each state machine has the following settings:

- *Address 0 WS* This refers to the length of time the system will delay while the transaction address is decoded. When enabled, there will be no delay.
- *Data write 0 WS* The length of time that the system will delay while data is being written to the target address. When enabled, there will be no delay.
- *Data read 0 WS* The length of time the system will delay while data is being read from the target address. When enabled, there will be no delay.

On-board PCI/SCSI BIOS You should enable this feature if your system motherboard has a built-in SCSI controller attached to the PCI bus, and you want to boot from it.

PCI I/O start address The I/O devices make themselves accessible by occupying an address space. This allows you to make additional room for older ISA devices by defining the I/O start address for the PCI devices.

Memory start address This feature is for devices with their own memory, which use part of the CPU's memory address space, allowing you to determine the starting point in memory where PCI device memory will be mapped.

VGA 128K range attribute When this feature is enabled, it allows the chipset to apply features, such as CPU-to-PCI byte merge, and CPU-to-PCI prefetch to be applied to VGA memory range A0000H–BFFFFH. When enabled, the VGA receives CPU-to-PCI functions. When disabled, the system retains the standard VGA interface.

CPU-to-PCI write posting The Intel 450GX/KX "Orion" chipset maintains its own internal read and write buffers, which are used to help compensate for the speed differences between the CPU and the PCI bus. When this feature is enabled, writes from the CPU to the PCI bus will be buffered. When disabled (default), the writes will not be buffered, and the CPU will be forced to wait until the write is completed.

CPU read multiple prefetch A prefetch occurs during a process (e.g., reading from the PCI bus or memory) when the chipset peeks at the next instruction and actually begins the next read. The Intel 450GX/KX "Orion" chipset has four read lines. A multiple prefetch means that the chipset can initiate more than one prefetch during a process. By default, the feature is disabled.

CPU line read multiple A line read means that the CPU is reading a full cache line. When a cache line is full, it holds 32 bytes (eight DWORDS) of data. Because the line is full, the system knows exactly how much data it will be reading and doesn't need to wait for an end-of-data signal, freeing it to do other things. When this feature is enabled, the system is allowed to read more than one full cache line at a time. The default is disabled.

CPU line read prefetch When this feature is enabled, the system is allowed to prefetch the next read instruction and initiate the next process.

CPU line read This feature enables or disables (default) full CPU line reads.

CPU burst write assembly The Intel 450GX/KX "Orion" chipset maintains four posted write buffers. When this feature is enabled, the chipset can assemble long PCI bursts from the data held in them. By default, the feature is disabled.

VGA performance mode When this feature is enabled, the VGA memory range of A0000–B0000 will use a special set of performance features. This feature has little or no effect using video modes beyond the standard VGA most commonly used for Windows, OS/2, UNIX, etc., but this memory range is heavily used by such games as DOOM.

Snoop ahead This feature is only applicable if the cache is enabled. When enabled, PCI bus masters can monitor the VGA palette registers for direct writes and translate them into PCI burst protocol for greater speed, which can enhance the performance of multimedia video.

DMA line buffer mode This feature allows DMA data to be stored in a buffer so as not to interrupt the PCI bus. When the Standard mode is selected, the line buffer is in single-transaction mode. When the Enhanced mode is selected, the feature allows it to operate in 8-byte transaction mode.

Master arbitration protocol This is the method by which the PCI bus determines which bus master device gains access to the bus.

PCI clock frequency This entry allows you to set the clock rate for the PCI bus, which can operate from 0 to 33MHz. *CPUCLK/3* means that the PCI bus was operating at 11MHz (33/3 = 11). The typical entries are:

CPUCLK/1.5   CPU speed/1.5 (default)
CPUCLK/3   CPU speed/3
14MHz   14MHz
CPUCLK/2   CPU speed/2

Max. burstable range This feature sets the size of the maximum range of contiguous memory, which can be addressed by a burst from the PCI bus.

I/O recovery time This is a programmed delay, which allows the PCI bus to exchange data with the slower ISA bus without data errors. Settings are in fractions of the PCI BCL:

 2 BCLK = Two BCLKS (default)
 4 BCLK = Four BCLKS
 8 BCLK = Eight BCLKS
12 BCLK = Twelve BCLKS

PCI concurrency When enabled, this means that more than one PCI device can be active at a time. With Intel chipsets, it allocates memory bus cycles to a PCI controller while an ISA operation (such as bus mastered DMA) is taking place, which normally requires constant attention. This involves turning on additional read and write buffering in the chipset. The PCI bus can also obtain access cycles for small data transfers without the delays caused by re-negotiatiating bus access for each part of the transfer, so the feature is meant to improve performance and consistency.

PCI streaming Data is typically moved to and from memory and between devices in discrete chunks of limited sizes because the CPU is involved. On the PCI bus, data can be "streamed"—that is, much larger chunks can be moved without the CPU being used. This feature should be enabled for best performance.

PCI bursting When this feature is enabled, consecutive writes from CPU will be regarded as a PCI burst cycle. This feature should normally be enabled.

PCI (IDE) bursting   This is similar to "PCI bursting," but this one enables burst-mode access to video memory over the PCI bus. The CPU provides the first address, and consecutive data is transferred at one word per clock. The device must support burst mode.

Burst copy-back option   When this feature is enabled, if a cache miss occurs, the chipset will initiate a second burst cache line fill from main memory to the cache—the goal being to maintain the status of the cache.

Preempt PCI master option   When this feature is enabled, PCI bus operations can be preempted by certain system operations, such as DRAM refresh, etc. Otherwise, they can take place concurrently.

IBC DEVSEL# decoding   This feature allows you to set the type of decoding used by the ISA Bridge Controller (IBC) to determine which device to select. The longer the decoding cycle, the better chance the IBC has to correctly decode the commands. Choices are *Fast*, *Medium*, and *Slow* (default).

Keyboard controller clock   This entry sets the speed of the keyboard controller (PCICLKI = PCI bus speed). Typical options are:

7.16 MHz Default
PCICLKI/2   1/2 PCICLKI
PCICLKI/3   1/3 PCICLKI
PCICLKI/4   1/4 PCICLKI

CPU pipeline function   This feature allows the system controller to signal the CPU for a new memory address even before all data transfers for the current cycle are complete, resulting in increased throughput. *Enabled* means that address pipelining is active.

PCI dynamic decoding   When this feature is enabled, the system can remember the PCI command, which has just been requested. If subsequent commands fall within the same address space, the cycle will be automatically interpreted as a PCI command.

Master retry timer   This feature sets how long the CPU master will attempt a PCI cycle before the cycle is unmasked (terminated). The choices are measured in PCICLKs, which the PCI timer controls. Values are *10* (default), *18*, *34*, or *66 PCICLKs*.

PCI pre-snoop   Pre-snooping is a technique by which a PCI master can continue to burst to the local memory until a 4K page boundary is reached, rather than just a line boundary. This feature can be enabled.

CPU/PCI write phase   This feature determines the turnaround between the address and data phases of the CPU master to PCI slave writes. Choices are *1 LCLK* (default) or *0 LCLK*.

PCI preempt timer   This entry sets the length of time before one PCI master preempts another when a service request has been pending. Typical entries are:

Disabled   No preemption (default)
260 LCLKs   Preempt after 260 LCLKs

132 LCLKs	Preempt after 132 LCLKs
68 LCLKs	Preempt after 68 LCLKs
36 LCLKs	Preempt after 36 LCLKs
20 LCLKs	Preempt after 20 LCLKs
12 LCLKs	Preempt after 12 LCLKs
5 LCLKs	Preempt after 5 LCLKs

CPU-to-PCI POST/BURST

Data from the CPU to the PCI bus can be posted (buffered by the controller) and/or burst. This entry sets the methods used:

- *POST/CON.BURST* Posting and bursting supported (default).
- *NONE/NONE* Neither supported.
- *POST/NONE* Posting, but not bursting, supported.

PCI CLK This feature determines whether the PCI clock is tightly synchronized with the CPU clock, or is asynchronous. If your CPU, motherboard, and PCI bus are running at multiple speeds of each other (e.g., Pentium 120, 60MHz, and 30MHz PCI bus), choose to synchronize.

CONFIGURING POWER MANAGEMENT

Energy is expensive, and in a world of dwindling energy reserves and escalating energy demands, PCs are often required to work longer hours and pack in more features, yet be energy efficient. Today's PCs use far less energy than their early counterparts—largely because there are fewer components—but also because PCs use a wide range of energy-saving techniques that are designed to reduce power demands as the system remains idle for a time (these are collectively known as *green PCs*). Most power-management features are selectable through the CMOS setup. This part of the chapter illustrates how to deal with typical power management features.

Doze timer This feature sets the time delay before the system will reduce 80% of its activity. 10 to 20 minutes is usually the preferred time.

Green timer of main board This feature allows you to set the time before a CPU of an idle system will shut down. The usual options are Disabled or a time interval ranging from 1 to 15 minutes. As a rule, 5 to 10 minutes is recommended.

HDD standby timer This feature sets the time after which the hard disk of an HDD-idle system (no HDD access) will shut down (or "spin down"). 10 to 20 minutes is usually the preferred time.

Standby timer This feature sets the time delay before the system will reduce 92% of its activity. 30 to 45 minutes is usually the preferred time.

Suspend timer This feature sets the time after which the system goes into the most inactive state possible (which is 99%). Once this state is entered, the system will require a warm-up period so that the CPU, hard disk, and monitor might go online. 45 to 60 minutes is usually the preferred time.

System slow down   This feature will slow the CPU clock dramatically after the timer has elapsed—reducing CPU heating and saving a great deal of power. A time anywhere from 30 to 60 minutes is usually acceptable.

Making Use of "Auto-configuration"

All recent motherboards now provide an auto-configuration option—taking most BIOS setup problems out of the technician's hands. In the majority of cases, an "auto-configured" BIOS will work just fine. But you must remember that "auto-configuration" is not an optimization of the system's setup, but rather a set of efficient settings that should ensure a working system. You will have to disable this setting if you want to tweak the CMOS setup yourself (otherwise, your settings will be ignored). If you're stuck with CMOS settings, you should be able to get the system running by using system defaults. You can work with two levels of default: BIOS defaults and power-on defaults.

BIOS DEFAULTS

BIOS defaults might not be (and usually aren't) tuned for your particular motherboard or chipset, but they give a reasonable chance of getting the system to boot. The BIOS default settings are also a good place to start fine-tuning your system. BIOS defaults can also recover your setup if you enter completely unacceptable values in CMOS setup and the system refuses to boot. Of course, you'll have to start optimizing all over again.

POWER-ON DEFAULTS

When powering up the system, the BIOS puts the system into the most conservative state possible—turbo off, all caches disabled, all wait states set to maximum, etc. This ensures that you can always enter CMOS setup. This mode is particularly useful if the settings returned by BIOS defaults fail. If the system still refuses to boot, then there is a serious hardware issue with the motherboard (or elsewhere in the system) that you will need to address first.

Backing Up CMOS RAM

Taken all together, CMOS settings are hardly intuitive—determining the proper settings for optimum system performance requires an understanding of each CMOS variable, and a detailed knowledge of the individual system. Unfortunately, most end users (and many technicians) are not familiar enough with the intricacies of any given PC, or the meaning of each setup entry, to adequately reconstruct the CMOS setup should the backup battery ever fail. When the battery does fail (it will eventually), it might take an unprepared user (or unfortunate technician) hours to rediscover settings that otherwise could be entered in a matter of minutes. This is the real tragedy—with just a few minutes of advance planning,

CMOS contents can be backed-up with complete safely. The two methods of backing-up CMOS contents are hard copy backup, and file backup.

Hard copy backup is just as the name implies—CMOS contents are recorded on paper, which is filed away or taped to the inside of the PC enclosure. The simplest method of hard copy backup is to connect the PC to a printer and capture a <Print Screen> of each data screen. This provides a fast, simple, and permanent record. On the other hand, it might take several minutes to restore the configuration. If there is no printer available, you can photocopy and complete the CMOS setup form included in Appendix F.

File backup is a fairly new alternative, which uses a small utility to copy CMOS RAM contents to a data file (usually on floppy disk), then restore the file to CMOS RAM addresses later, as needed. Shareware utilities, such as CMOS_RAM, are ideal for this kind of support. When saving a CMOS RAM file, be sure to save it to a floppy disk because losing CMOS contents will often disable the hard drive. The advantage of a backup file is speed—CMOS contents can be restored in a matter of moments.

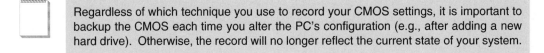

Regardless of which technique you use to record your CMOS settings, it is important to backup the CMOS each time you alter the PC's configuration (e.g., after adding a new hard drive). Otherwise, the record will no longer reflect the current state of your system.

Several CMOS backup/restore tools are on the companion CD. Try CMOS.ZIP or CMOSRAM2.ZIP.

CMOS Maintenance and Troubleshooting

Although it is very rare for CMOS RAM/RTC devices to fail, there are many circumstances where CMOS contents might be lost or corrupted, and system performance might be compromised by a poorly configured CMOS setup. Beyond the traditional beep and POST codes that suggest a CMOS problem (Chapter 19) or the more recent BIOS error messages (Chapter 9), a wide range of PC symptoms can indicate an improperly or incompletely configured CMOS. This part of the chapter is intended to identify a series of symptoms that can suggest CMOS setup problems and offer suggestions for corrective action.

TYPICAL CMOS-RELATED SYMPTOMS

Symptom 9-1. Changes to CMOS are not saved after rebooting the PC In virtually all cases, you have exited the CMOS setup routine incorrectly. This is a very common oversight (especially given the proliferation of different BIOS versions and CMOS setup routines). Try making your changes again, then be sure to "Save, then Exit, and Reboot."

Symptom 9-2. The system appears to be performing poorly The system must also be stable—if it crashes frequently, or certain devices refuse to work, you might be dealing with a system conflict in hardware or software. Use a diagnostic tool, such as

MSD (in DOS) or the Device Manager (in Windows 95), to help identify possible points of conflict.

If the system is free of hardware or software conflicts, you can focus on performance. "Performance" is often a subjective evaluation, and should first be verified using a benchmark test compared to other similar PCs (identical systems, if possible). If you find that your particular system is performing below its optimum level, suspect a CMOS setup problem. In some cases, the CMOS RAM might have been loaded with its "power on" or "auto-configuration" defaults. Although defaults will almost always allow the system to function, it will rarely offer top performance. Check the advanced CMOS and chipset setup pages (particularly the memory, cache, and bus-speed related entries). Refer to the "Basic CMOS optimization tactics" section.

Symptom 9-3. CMOS mismatch errors occur These errors occur when the PC equipment found during the POST does not match equipment listed in CMOS. In most cases, the CMOS backup battery has failed and should be replaced. You can then load the CMOS defaults and tweak the setup as necessary to optimize the system (an easy task if you've got a record of the CMOS settings). Otherwise, refer to the "Basic CMOS optimization tactics" section.

> If you've cleared the CMOS setup (using a "clear" jumper on the motherboard), be sure that you've reset the jumper so as not to continue clearing the CMOS RAM.

Symptom 9-4. Some drives are not detected during boot This happens most often with hard drives or other devices in the Basic CMOS setup page. In some cases, the device simply might not be listed or entered properly (e.g., you might have forgotten to enter your newly installed hard drive or floppy drive in the CMOS setup). In other cases, the drive might need more time to initialize at boot time. Try increasing the "boot delay" or disabling any "quick boot" feature that might be in use.

Symptom 9-5. The system boots from the hard drive—even though there is a bootable floppy disk in the drive Notice that the system still boots and runs properly. The floppy disk is fully accessible (if not, check the floppy drive, power, and signal cables). This type of issue is usually not a problem, but is caused instead by an improper boot sequence. Most BIOS versions allow the PC to search through several different drives to locate an operating system, and will boot from the first suitable drive where an operating system is found. Chances are that your boot sequence is set to "C: A:," where the C: drive is checked first. Because the C: drive is connected and functional, the A: drive will simply be ignored. To boot from the A: drive, you'll need to change the boot sequence to something like "*A: C:.*" Remember to save any changes before exiting the CMOS setup.

Symptom 9-6. Power-management features are not available First, be sure that your BIOS supports power management to begin with. Modern PC power management is typically handled by a combination of BIOS and the operating system (e.g., APM under Windows 95). However, power management must be supported by BIOS and enabled under the CMOS setup in order for the operating system to make use of it. If you can't use power management (or it is not available in the Windows 95 Device Manager under *System* *devices*), it probably isn't enabled in the CMOS setup. Check the *Power Management* page of your CMOS setup (or the *Advanced Chipset Setup*) and be sure that power-management features are enabled. You might also want to review and adjust the various device time-outs, as required. When you restart the operating system, you should then be able to configure the corresponding power-management features.

Symptom 9-7. PnP support is not available, or PnP devices do not function properly First, be sure that your BIOS supports Plug-and-Play (PnP) standards to begin with. If not, you'll need to use a DOS ISA configuration utility (or ICU) to support any PnP devices in the system. Also be sure that you're using an operating system that supports PnP (e.g., Windows 95).

If you can't get support for PnP devices, be sure that PnP support is enabled in the CMOS setup, and verify that PnP-related settings (such as *Configuration mode* or *IRQ3-IRQ15*) are all configured properly. If necessary, try loading the BIOS defaults for your CMOS setup, which should give you baseline PnP support if your BIOS and OS supports it. Be sure to record your original CMOS settings before attempting to load defaults.

Symptom 9-8. Devices in some PCI slots are not recognized or not working properly First, be sure that your motherboard supports PCI (Peripheral Component Interconnect) slots, and verify that there is in fact at least one PCI adapter board in the system. There are simply a proliferation of PCI-related configuration settings in the PnP/PCI area of a CMOS setup, so it is extremely difficult to suggest any one probable oversight. If you cannot get PCI devices to work (or work properly), try loading the BIOS defaults for your CMOS setup, which should provide you baseline PCI support. Be sure to record your original CMOS settings before attempting to load defaults.

Symptom 9-9. You cannot enter CMOS setup even though the correct key combination is used Be sure that you're pressing that key combination quickly enough—many BIOS versions only allow a few moments during POST to enter CMOS setup. Once the operating system begins to load, you'll need to reboot. Also verify that you are using the correct key or key combination. It is also possible that access to CMOS setup has been disabled through a motherboard jumper. Refer to the documentation for your particular motherboard and locate the "CMOS access" jumper. The jumper (if it exists) should be in the position that allows access.

Be careful that you don't accidentally confuse this access jumper with the "CMOS clear" jumper—the two serve completely different purposes.

Symptom 9-10 The system crashes or locks up frequently. There are many reasons for a PC to crash or lock up—everything from a hardware fault to a bad driver to a software bug can interfere with normal system operation. Before you check the CMOS setup, run a DOS diagnostic to verify that the system hardware is performing properly, and check that there is no hardware conflict in the system. Then check the Device Manager and look for any signs of conflicting or inoperative devices (marked with yellow or red exclamation marks). If the system runs properly when DOS is booted "clean" or Windows

95 is started in the "safe mode," there might be a buggy or conflicting driver (or TSR) that is interfering with system operation.

If problems persist, there might be any of several different problems in the CMOS setup. Typical oversights include insufficient wait states, memory-speed mismatches (e.g., mixing 60- and 70-ns memory), and enabling cache (L1 or L2) when there is no such cache in the system. Review your system configuration very carefully. It is also possible that shadowing and snooping features can interfere with system operation. Try systematically disabling video ROM shadowing, motherboard ROM shadowing, and other shadowing options. Then, try disabling video palette snoop and other snooping or "pre-snoop" options.

If problems still continue, try loading the BIOS defaults into CMOS. The defaults should ensure some level of hardware stability, but you'll still need to optimize the CMOS setup manually for best performance.

Symptom 9-11. COM ports don't work Assuming that the COM ports are installed and configured properly, operating problems can sometimes be traced to "IDE block mode" or "IDE multiple sector mode" issues. Try disabling the "Block mode" or "Multiple sector mode," or scale back the block mode to a lower level.

Symptom 9-12. The RTC doesn't keep proper time over a month This is a very common problem for real-time clock (RTC) units. RTCs are notoriously inaccurate devices anyway—often straying by as much as several minutes per month. Some "third tier" RTCs (or units burdened by heavy interrupt activity) might be off by more than several minutes per week (or even more). Very little can be done to correct this kind of poor time keeping other than to replace the motherboard with one using a better-quality RTC (hardly an economical solution), or use a "time-correcting utility," which compensates for the RTCs drift.

Several "time correction" utilities on the companion CD might help you to tame finicky RTCs. Try out FIXCLOCK.ZIP and RITM25.ZIP.

Symptom 9-13. The RTC doesn't keep time while system power is off Time seems maintained while system power is on, but the RTC appears to stop while the system is turned off. This is often a classic sign of CMOS backup battery failure. Because the RTC usually takes a bit more power than the CMOS RAM—and CMOS RAM can be maintained by a latent change—this kind of "clock stall" is often the first sign that the CMOS battery is failing. Record your CMOS setup and replace the CMOS battery at your earliest opportunity.

Symptom 9-14. You see an "Invalid system configuration data" error This type of error often means that there is a problem with the Extended System Configuration Data (ESCD). This is a storage space for the configuration data in a Plug-and-Play system. Once you have configured your system properly, the Plug-and-Play BIOS uses your ESCD to load the same configuration from one boot to the next. If this error message is displayed, take these steps:

1 Go into *Setup* and find a field labeled *Reset configuration data*.
2 Set this field to *Yes*.

3 Save and exit the CMOS setup program. The system restarts and clears the ESCD during POST.

4 Run whatever PnP configuration tool is appropriate for your system.

- If you have Windows 95 (a Plug-and-Play operating system), just restart your computer. Windows 95 will automatically configure your system and load the ESCD with the new data.
- If you don't have Windows 95, run the DOS ICU (ISA Configuration Utility) to reset the ESCD.

Symptom 9-15. You encounter "CMOS checksum" errors after updating a flash BIOS Flashing a BIOS IC will typically require you to clear the CMOS setup and reconfigure the *Setup* again from scratch. Most current motherboards offer a "Clear CMOS" jumper, which can be used to wipe out all the CMOS settings—this is sometimes referred to as a *CMOS clear* or *CMOS NVRAM clear*. Try clearing the CMOS RAM, then load the BIOS defaults. At that point, the errors should stop, and you might need to optimize the CMOS setup entries to tweak the system. If you documented the original CMOS setup entries with <Print Screen> before upgrading the BIOS, you should be able to reset key entries in a matter of minutes. Remember to save your changes when exiting.

Symptom 9-16. You notice that only some CMOS setup entries are corrupted when running a particular application This kind of error sometimes happens with several games and other programs on the market that access memory locations used by CMOS RAM and the BIOS Data Area (BDA), which are shadowed into the Upper Memory Area. This can alter or corrupt at least some CMOS locations. One solution is to contact the program maker and see if there is a patch or fix that will prevent CMOS access. Another solution to this problem is to exclude the C000h to CFFFh range in the EMM386 device line in your CONFIG.SYS file. This prevents programs from accessing the section of memory that the BIOS uses for shadowing. Here is an example:

```
DEVICE=C:\DOS\EMM386.EXE X=C000-CFFF
```

CMOS PASSWORD TROUBLESHOOTING

Passwords are usually regarded as a necessary evil—a means of keeping out the malicious and the curious. However, passwords also cause their share of problems. As systems are passed from person to person or department to department, passwords often become lost or forgotten. This means the system won't start. The trick with all system passwords is that they are stored in CMOS RAM. If you can clear the CMOS RAM, you can effectively disable the password protection. In actuality, any means of clearing the CMOS will work, but you know as well as I do that you don't have a backup of your CMOS settings (go ahead, admit it), and choosing "default" settings doesn't always work. Before you start "slashing and burning" your CMOS setup, start small and work your way up.

- *Does anybody know the password?* Check with friends, colleagues, supervisors—someone might know the password. This will save you a lot of hassle, and you can always disable the password in CMOS setup once you're in. If you're using an AMI BIOS and the password feature has been enabled (but no new password has been entered), try "AMI." For Award BIOS, you can try "BIOSTAR" or "AWARD_SW." There's no guarantee such defaults will work, but it's worth a try.

■ *Check for a password clear jumper.* Crack open the case and take a look at the motherboard. There's probably a jumper that will clear the password without wiping out the entire CMOS setup. In some cases, the jumper is even marked "clear password" (so much for security). If you can find such a jumper, set it, then boot the system. After the system boots, power down, and reset the jumper. Your password should now be clear.

■ *Force a configuration change.* This is one of my personal favorites. Try taking out a SIMM and power up the PC. In many cases, the BIOS will recognize the configuration change and generate an error like: "CMOS Mismatch—Press <F1> for Setup." This gets you into CMOS, where you can disable the password without clearing the CMOS RAM entirely. You'll have to save your changes and reboot. Remember that when you finally replace that SIMM, you'll probably see another CMOS error—just go back into CMOS and do a quick correction.

■ *Clear the CMOS RAM.* There's no doubt that this is your least desirable choice. There are several ways to clear the CMOS. Look for a motherboard jumper that says "CMOS clear" or has some similar marking. Set the jumper and power up the system. When you see a message indicating that CMOS is clear, or that default settings have been loaded, power down the PC and reset the jumper (the password is now gone). You can then restart the PC and reconfigure your CMOS setup.

■ If you can't find the proper jumper, remove the CMOS battery and wait for the CMOS RAM to clear. As a rule, you should wait for at least 30 minutes, but I've seen CMOS RAM hold a latent charge for days. To accelerate the process, you can short a 10-kΩ resistor across the empty battery terminals (be sure to turn the power off first). If that doesn't work, you can use the same resistor to short the CMOS RAM power pins directly, as shown in Table 9-3. Again, remember that all system power should be off before you do this.

■ Once your CMOS RAM is clear, you will need to restore the setup (probably starting with defaults). After the CMOS is restored, be sure to take a <Print Screen> of each setup page and keep them with the PC's documentation.

TABLE 9-3 LIST OF CMOS RAM/RTC POWER PINS

BRAND	PART	SHORT PIN #S
Benchmarq	BQ3258S	12 and 20
Benchmarq	BQ3287AMT	12 and 21
Benchmarq	BQ3287MT	Cannot clear (replace the IC)
C&T	P82C206	12 and 32
Dallas	DS1287	Cannot clear (replace the IC)
Dallas	DS1287A	12 and 21
Dallas	DS12885S	12 and 20
Hitachi	HD146818AP	12 and 24
Motorola	MC146818AP	12 and 24
OPTi	F82C206	3 and 26
Samsung	KS82C6818A	12 and 24

CMOS BATTERY MAINTENANCE

Ordinarily, the RTC/CMOS IC requires no maintenance. However, the backup battery will need to be replaced on a fairly regular basis (often every few years). Before replacing the battery (or battery pack), be sure that you have a valid CMOS backup—either on paper or floppy disk. Turn off system power, unplug the system, and remove the battery. This will cause the CMOS RAM IC to lose its contents. Discard the original battery and install the new one according to the system manufacturer's instructions. Secure the battery and re-start the system. When the system boots, go directly to the CMOS setup routine and restore each setting. If you have CMOS information recorded in a file, boot the system from a floppy disk and use the CMOS backup/restore utility to restore the file. You should then be able to restart the system as if nothing had ever happened.

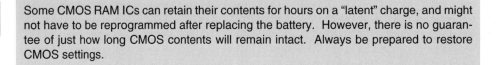

Some CMOS RAM ICs can retain their contents for hours on a "latent" charge, and might not have to be reprogrammed after replacing the battery. However, there is no guarantee of just how long CMOS contents will remain intact. Always be prepared to restore CMOS settings.

If you're going to be storing old (replaced) motherboards for any period of time, make it a point to remove the CMOS backup battery first. Batteries tend to be very safe and reliable, but there are many instances where they can and do leak. Because batteries use an acid-based electrolyte, battery leakage can easily damage battery contacts, or spill over onto the motherboard itself—damaging circuit traces and ruining the motherboard beyond repair.

Further Study

That's it for Chapter 9. Be sure to review the glossary and chapter questions on the accompanying CD. If you have access to the Internet, take some time to review a few of these BIOS and CMOS/RTC makers:

American Megatrends: **http://www.megatrends.com**

Award BIOS: **http://www.award.com**

Dallas Semicon.: **http://www.dalsemi.com/DocControl/Overviews.web/PnP_RTC/ overview.html**

MicroFirmware: **http://www.firmware.com/catalog2.htm**

IBM SurePath BIOS page: **http://www.surepath.ibm.com/**

Mr. BIOS: **http://www.mrbios.com/**

Unicore: **http://www.unicore.com/**

10

CONFLICT TROUBLESHOOTING

CONTENTS AT A GLANCE

Understanding System Resources
  Interrupts
  DMA channels
  I/O areas
  Memory assignments
  Index of typical assignments

Recognizing and Dealing with Conflicts
Confirming and resolving conflicts

Dealing with software conflicts
Dealing with hardware conflicts
Conflict troubleshooting with
 Windows 95
The role of Plug-and-Play (PnP)
Keep your notes

Further Study

The incredible acceptance and popularity of the PC largely results from the use of an "open architecture." An open architecture allows any manufacturer to develop new devices (e.g., video boards, modems, sound boards, etc.) that will work in conjunction with the PC. When a new expansion board is added to the PC, the board uses of various system resources in order to obtain CPU time and transfer data across the expansion bus. Ultimately, each board that is added to the system requires unique resources. No two devices can use the same resources—otherwise, a hardware conflict will result. Low-level software (such as device drivers and TSRs) that uses system resources can also conflict with one another during normal operation. This chapter explains system resources, then shows you how to detect and correct conflicts that can arise in both hardware and software.

Understanding System Resources

The key to understanding and eliminating conflicts is to understand the importance of each system resource that is available to you. PCs provide three types of resources: interrupts, DMA channels, and I/O areas. Many controllers and network devices also utilize BIOS, which requires memory space. Do not underestimate the importance of these areas—conflicts can occur anywhere, and carry dire consequences for a system.

INTERRUPTS

An interrupt is probably the most well-known and understood type of resource. Interrupts are used to demand attention from the CPU. This allows a device or sub-system to work in the background until a particular event occurs that requires system processing. Such an event might include receiving a character at the serial port, striking a key on the keyboard, or any number of other real-world situations. An interrupt is invoked by asserting a logic level on one of the physical interrupt request (IRQ) lines that are accessible through any of the motherboard's expansion bus slots. AT-compatible PCs provide 16 IRQ lines (noted IRQ 0 to IRQ 15). Table 10-1 illustrates the IRQ assignments for classic XT and current AT systems. These lines run from pins on the expansion bus connector or key ICs on the motherboard to Programmable Interrupt Controllers (PICs) on the motherboard. The output signals generated by a PIC triggers the CPU interrupt. Keep in mind that Table 10-1 covers hardware interrupts only. There are also a proliferation of processor and software-generated interrupts.

The use of IRQ 2 in an AT system deserves a bit of explanation. An AT uses IRQ 2 right on the motherboard, which means that the expansion bus pin for IRQ 2 is now empty. Instead of leaving this pin unused, IRQ 9 from the AT extended slot is wired to the pin previously occupied by IRQ 2. In other words, IRQ 9 is being redirected to IRQ 2. Any AT expansion device set to use IRQ 2 is actually using IRQ 9. Of course, the vector interrupt table is adjusted to compensate for this slight of hand.

After an interrupt is triggered, an interrupt-handling routine saves the current CPU register states to a small area of memory (called the *stack*), then directs the CPU to the interrupt vector table. The interrupt vector table is a list of program locations that correspond to each interrupt. When an interrupt occurs, the CPU will jump to the interrupt handler routine at the location specified in the interrupt vector table and execute the routine. In most cases, the interrupt handler is a device driver associated with the board generating the interrupt. For example, an IRQ from a network card will likely call a network device driver to operate the card. For a hard-disk controller, an IRQ calls the BIOS ROM code that operates the drive. When the handling routine is finished, the CPU's original register contents are "popped" from the stack, and the CPU picks up from where it left off without interruption.

As a technician, it is not vital that you understand precisely how interrupts are initialized and enabled, but you should know the basic terminology. The term *assigned* simply means that a device is set to produce a particular IRQ signal. For example, a typical hard-drive controller board is assigned to IRQ 14. Assignments are usually made with one or more jumpers or DIP switches, or are configured automatically through the use of Plug-and-Play (PnP). Next, interrupts can be selectively enabled or disabled under software control. An "enabled" interrupt is an interrupt where the PIC has been programmed to pass on an IRQ to the CPU. Just because an interrupt is enabled does not mean that there

TABLE 10-1 XT AND AT INTERRUPT ASSIGNMENTS

IBM PC/XT

IRQ	FUNCTION
0	System timer IC
1	Keyboard-controller IC
2	unused
3	Serial port 2 (COM2: 2F8h–2FFh and COM4: 2E8h–2EFh)
4	Serial port 1 (COM1: 3F8h–3FFh and COM3: 3E8h–3EFh)
5	XT hard-disk controller board
6	Floppy-disk controller board
7	Parallel port 1 (LPT1: 3BCh [mono] or 378h [color])

IBM PC/AT

IRQ	FUNCTION
0	System timer IC
1	Keyboard-controller IC
2	Second IRQ controller IC
3	Serial port 2 (COM2: 2F8h–2FFh and COM4: 2E8h–2EFh)
4	Serial port 1 (COM1: 3F8h–3FFh and COM3: 3E8h–3EFh)
5	Parallel port 2 (LPT2: 378h or 278h)
6	Floppy-disk controller
7	Parallel port 1 (LPT1: 3BCh [mono] or 378h [color])
8	Real-time clock (RTC)
9	unused (redirected to IRQ 2)
10	USB (on systems so equipped—can be disabled)
11	Windows sound system (on systems so equipped—can be disabled)
12	Motherboard mouse port (PS/2 port)
13	Math co-processor
14	Primary AT/IDE hard-disk controller
15	Secondary AT/IDE hard-disk controller (on systems so equipped—can be disabled)

are any devices assigned to it. Finally, an "active" interrupt is a line where real IRQs are being generated. Notice that *active* does not mean assigned or enabled.

Interrupts are an effective and reliable means of signaling the CPU, but the conventional ISA bus architecture—used in virtually all PCs—does not provide a means of determining which slot contains the board that called the interrupt. As a result, interrupts cannot be shared by multiple devices. In other words, no two devices can be actively generating interrupt requests on the same IRQ line at the same time. If more than one device is assigned to the same interrupt line, a hardware conflict can occur. In most circumstances, a conflict will prevent the newly installed board (or other previously installed boards) from working. In some cases, a hardware conflict can hang up the entire system.

The MCA (Micro Channel Architecture) and EISA (Extended ISA) busses overcome this IRQ sharing limitation, but MCA was never widely accepted in the PC industry because the slots are not backwardly compatible with the well-established base of ISA boards. EISA bus slots are backwardly compatible with ISA boards, but an ISA board in an EISA slot was still faced with the same IRQ limitations.

DMA CHANNELS

The CPU is very adept at moving data. It can transfer data between memory locations, I/O locations, or from memory to I/O and back with equal ease. However, PC designers realized that transferring large amounts of data (one word at a time) through the CPU is a hideous waste of CPU time. After all, the CPU really isn't processing anything during a data move, just shuttling data from one place to another. If there was a way to "off-load" such redundant tasks from the CPU, data could be moved faster than would be possible with CPU intervention. Direct Memory Access (DMA) is a technique designed to move large amounts of data from memory to an I/O location, or vice versa, without the direct intervention by the CPU. In theory, the DMA controller IC acts as a stand-alone "data processor," leaving the CPU free to handle other tasks.

A DMA transfer starts with a DMA Request (DRQ) signal generated by the requesting device (such as the floppy-disk controller board). If the channel has been previously enabled through software drivers or BIOS routines, the request will reach the corresponding DMA controller IC on the motherboard. The DMA controller will then send a HOLD request to the CPU, which responds with a Hold Acknowledge (HLDA) signal. When the DMA controller receives the HLDA signal, it instructs the bus controller to effectively disconnect the CPU from the expansion bus and allow the DMA controller IC to take control of the bus itself. The DMA controller sends a DMA Acknowledge (DACK) signal to the requesting device, and the transfer process can begin. Up to 64KB can be moved during a single DMA transfer. After the transfer is done, the DMA controller will reconnect the CPU and drop its HOLD request—the CPU then continues with whatever it was doing without interruption.

Table 10-2 illustrates the use of DMA channels for both classic XT and current AT systems. Twice as many DMA channels are available in an AT than an XT, but you might wonder why the AT commits fewer channels. The issue is DMA performance. DMA was developed when CPUs ran at 4.77MHz, and is artificially limited to 4MHz operation. When CPUs began to work at 8MHz and higher, CPU transfers (redundant as they are) actually became faster than a DMA channel. As a result, the AT has many channels available, but only the floppy drive controller and other limited-performance devices (such as sound cards) continue to use DMA. In an AT system, DMA channel 4 serves as a cascade line linking DMA controller ICs.

As with interrupts, a DMA channel is selected by setting a physical jumper or DIP switch on the particular expansion board (or through Plug-and-Play). When the board is installed in an expansion slot, the channel setting establishes a connection between the board and DMA controller IC. Often, accompanying software drivers must use a command line switch that points to the corresponding hardware DMA assignment. Also, DMA channels can not be shared between two or more devices. Although DMA sharing is possible in theory, it is extremely difficult to implement. If more than one device attempts to use the same DMA channel at the same time, a conflict will result.

TABLE 10-2 XT AND AT DMA ASSIGNMENTS

IBM PC/XT

DMA	FUNCTION
0	Dynamic RAM refresh
1	Unused
2	Floppy-disk controller board
3	XT hard-disk controller board

IBM PC/AT

DMA	TRADITIONAL FUNCTION	CURRENT FUNCTION(S)
0	Dynamic RAM refresh	Audio system
1	Unused	Audio system or parallel port
2	Floppy-disk controller	Floppy-disk controller
3	Unused	ECP parallel-port or audio system
4	Reserved (used internally)	Reserved (used internally)
5	Unused	Unused
6	Unused	Unused
7	Unused	Unused

I/O AREAS

Both XT and AT computers provide space for I/O (input/output) ports. An I/O port acts very much like a memory address, but it is not for storage. Instead, an I/O port provides the means for a PC to communicate directly with a device—allowing the PC to efficiently pass commands and data between the system and various expansion devices. Each device must be assigned to a unique address (or address range). Table 10-3 lists the typical I/O port assignments for classic XT and classic AT systems. PS/2 systems use many of the same address assignments, but also add some wrinkles of their own (as shown in Table 10-4). Finally, the I/O scheme for a modern Pentium system (with a 430TX-based motherboard) is listed in Table 10-5.

I/O assignments are generally made manually by setting jumpers or DIP switches on the expansion device itself, or automatically through the use of Plug-and-Play. As with other system resources, it is vitally important that no two devices use the same I/O port(s) at the same time. If one or more I/O addresses overlap, a hardware conflict will result. Commands meant for one device might be erroneously interpreted by another. Remember that although many expansion devices can be set at a variety of addresses, some devices cannot.

MEMORY ASSIGNMENTS

Memory is another vital resource for the PC. Although early devices relied on the assignment of IRQ, DMA channels, and I/O ports, a growing number of modern devices (e.g.,

TABLE 10-3 XT/AT I/O PORT ADDRESSES

Classic IBM PC/XT systems

000h–00Fh	8237 DMA IC—channels 0–3
020h–021h	8259 Programmable interrupt controller IC
040h–043h	8253 System timer IC
060h–063h	8255 Programmable peripheral interface IC
070h,071h	Real-time clock/CMOS, NMI mask
080h	POST code port
081h–083h, 087h	DMA page registers (0–3)
0A0h	NMI mask register
0C0h–0CFh	Reserved
0E0h–0EFh	Reserved
0F0h–0FFh	Math co-processor
108h–12Fh	Reserved
130h–13Fh	Available
140h–14Fh	Available
150h–1EFh	Reserved
200h–207h	Game ports
208h–20Bh	Available
20Ch–20Dh	Reserved
20Eh–21Eh	Available
21Fh	Reserved
220h–22Fh	Available
230h–23Fh	Available
240h–247h	Available
250h–277h	Available
278h–27Fh	Parallel port 2 or 3 (LPT2 or LPT3)
280h–2AFh	Available
2B0h–2DFh	Alternate EGA ports
2E1h	GPIB port 0 (Adapter 0)
2E2h–2E3h	Data acquisition port 0 (Adapter 0)
2E4h–2E7h	Available
2E8h–2EFh	Serial port 4 (COM4)
2F8h–2FFh	Serial port 2 (COM2)
300h–31Fh	IBM prototype card
320h–323h	Primary XT HDD controller
324h–327h	Secondary XT HDD controller
328h–32Fh	Available
330h	Available
340h	Available
350h–35Fh	Available
360h–363h	Network card ports (low I/O)
364h–367h	Reserved
368h–36Ah	Network card ports (high I/O)
36Ch–36Fh	Reserved

TABLE 10-3   XT/AT I/O PORT ADDRESSES (CONTINUED)

370h–377h	Secondary FDD controller
378h–37Fh	Parallel port 1 or 2 (LPT1 or LPT2)
380h–38Ch	SDLC 2 (or Bisync 1) ports
390h–393h	Cluster ports (Adapter 0)
394h–3A9h	Available
3A0h–3ACh	SDLC 1 (or Bisync 2) ports
3B0h–3BFh	MDA (monochrome video) port
3BCh–3BFh	First LPT port of monochrome video board
3C0h–3CFh	EGA port
3D0h–3DFh	CGA port
3E0h–3E7h	Available
3E8h–3EFh	Serial port 3 (COM3)
3F0h–3F7h	Primary FDD controller
3F8h–3FFh	Serial port 1 (COM1)

Classic IBM PC/AT systems

000h–00Fh	DMA controller IC #1 (channels 0–3)
020h–03Fh	Programmable interrupt controller (PIC) IC #1
040h–05Fh	System timer IC
060h	Keyboard/mouse controller
061h	System-board I/O port
064h	Keyboard/mouse-controller IC
070h–07Fh	RTC port and NMI mask port
080h	POST code port
081h–08Fh	DMA page registers
0A0h–0BFh	Programmable interrupt controller IC #2
0C0h–0DEh	DMA controller IC #2 (channels 4–7)
0F0h–0F8h	Math co-processor ports
1F0h–1F8h	Hard-disk controller ports
108h–12Fh	Available
130h–13Fh	Available
140h–14Fh	Available
150h–15Fh	Available
170h–177h	Secondary HDD controller
1F0h–1F7h	Primary HDD controller
200h–207h	Game port
208h–20Bh	Available
20Ch–20Dh	Reserved
20Eh–21Eh	Available
21Fh	Reserved
220h–2FFh	Available
230h–23Fh	Available
240h–247h	Available
250h–277h	Available
278h–27Fh	Parallel printer 2 (LPT2)

TABLE 10-3 XT/AT I/O PORT ADDRESSES (CONTINUED)

280h–2AFh	Available
2B0h–2DFh	Alternate EGA ports
2E0h–2E7h	GPIB (Adapter 0)
2E8h–2EFh	Serial port 4 (COM4)
2F8h–2FFh	Serial port 2 (COM2)
300h–31Fh	Available
320h–32Fh	Available
330h	Available
340h	Available
350h–35Fh	Available
360h–363h	Network card port (low I/O)
364h–367h	Reserved
368h–36Ah	Network card port (high I/O)
36Ch–36Fh	Reserved
370h–377h	Secondary FDD controller
378h–37Fh	Parallel printer 1 (LPT1)
380h–38Ch	SDLC 2 (or Bisync 1) port
390h–393h	Cluster ports
394h–3A9h	Available
3A0h–3ACh	SDLC 1 (or Bisync 2) port
3B0h–3BFh	Monochrome display adapter (MDA) port
3BCh–3BFh	Parallel printer 3 (LPT3)
3C0h–3CFh	Enhanced graphics adapter (EGA) port
3D0h–3DFh	Color craphics adapter (CGA) port
3E0h–3E7h	Available
3E8h–3EFh	Serial port 3 (COM3)
3F0h–3F7h	Primary FDD controller
3F8h–3FFh	Serial port 1 (COM1)

TABLE 10-4 I/O PORT VARIATIONS FOR PS/2 SYSTEMS

061h–06Fh	System-control port B
090h	Central-arbitration control port
091h	Card-select feedback
092h	System-control port A
094h	System-board enable/setup register
096h	Adapter enable/setup register
100h–107h	PS/2 programmable-option select
3220h–3227h	COM2
3228h–322Fh	COM3
4220h–3227h	COM4
4228h–322Fh	COM5
5220h–3227h	COM6
5228h–322Fh	COM7

TABLE 10-5   MODERN AT I/O ASSIGNMENTS

Based on current Pentium system (430TX chipset)

0000h–000Fh	PIIX4—DMA 1
0020h–0021h	PIIX4—Interrupt controller 1
002Eh–002Fh	Super I/O controller configuration registers
0040h–0043h	PIIX4—Counter/timer 1
0048h–004Bh	PIIX4—Counter/timer 2
0060h	Keyboard-controller byte—Reset IRQ
0061h	PIIX4—NMI, speaker control
0064h	Keyboard controller, CMD/STAT byte
0070h	(Bit 7) PIIX4—Enable NMI
0070h	(Bits 6-0) PIIX4—real-time clock, address
0071h	PIIX4—Real-time clock, data
0078h	Reserved—board configuration
0079h	Reserved—board configuration
0081h–008Fh	PIIX4—DMA page registers
00A0h–00A1h	PIIX4—interrupt controller 2
00B2h–00B3h	APM control
00C0h–00DEh	PIIX4—DMA 2
00F0h	Reset numeric error
0170h–0177h	Secondary IDE controller channel
01F0h–01F7h	Primary IDE controller channel
0200h–0207h	Audio/game port
0220h–022Fh	Audio (Sound Blaster compatible)
0240h–024Fh	Audio (Sound Blaster compatible)
0278h–027Fh	LPT2
0290h–0297h	Management extension hardware
02E8h–02EFh	COM4/video (8514A)
02F8h–02FFh	COM2
0300h–0301h	MPU-401 (MIDI)
0330h–0331h	MPU-401 (MIDI)
0332h–0333h	MPU-401 (MIDI)
0334h–0335h	MPU-401 (MIDI)
0376h	Secondary IDE channel command port
0377h	Secondary floppy-channel command port
0378h–037Fh	LPT1
0388h–038Dh	AdLib (FM synthesizer)
03B4h–03B5h	Video (VGA)
03BAh	Video (VGA)
03BCh–03BFh	LPT3
03C0h–03CAh	Video (VGA)
03CCh	Video (VGA)
03CEh–03CFh	Video (VGA)
03D4h–03D5h	Video (VGA)
03DAh	Video (VGA)

TABLE 10-5 MODERN AT I/O ASSIGNMENTS (CONTINUED)

03E8h–03EFh	COM3
03F0h–03F5h	Primary floppy channel
03F6h	Primary IDE channel command port
03F7h	Primary floppy-channel command port
03F8h–03FFh	COM1
04D0h–04D1h	Edge/level-triggered PIC
0530h–0537h	Windows sound system
0604h–060Bh	Windows sound system
LPT n + 400h	ECP port, LPT n base address + 400h
0CF8h–0CFBh	PCI-configuration address register
0CF9h	Turbo and reset-control register
0CFCh–0CFFh	PCI configuration data register
0E80h–0E87h	Windows sound system
0F40h–0F47h	Windows sound system
0F86h–0F87h	Yamaha OPL3-SA configuration
FF00h–FF07h	IDE bus-master register
FFA0h–FFA7	Primary bus-master IDE registers
FFA8h–FFAFh	Secondary bus-master IDE registers

TABLE 10-6 MODERN PENTIUM PC MEMORY MAP

Based on a 430TX/440LX or equivalent chipset.

ADDRESS RANGE (DECIMAL)	ADDRESS RANGE (HEX)	SIZE	DESCRIPTION
1024K–262144K	100000–10000000	255MB	Extended memory
960K–1024K	F0000–FFFFF	64KB	BIOS
944K–960K	EC000–EFFFF	16KB	Boot block (available as UMB)
936K–944K	EA000–EBFFF	8KB	ESCD (PnP/DMI configuration)
932K–936K	E9000–E9FFF	4KB	Reserved for BIOS
928K–932K	E8000–E8FFF	4KB	OEM logo or scan user flash
896K–928K	E0000–E7FFF	32KB	POST BIOS (available as UMB)
800K–896K	C8000–DFFFF	96KB	Available high DOS memory
640K–800K	A0000–C7FFF	160KB	Video memory and BIOS
639K–640K	9FC00–9FFFF	1KB	Extended BIOS data
512K–639K	80000–9FBFF	127KB	Extended conventional memory
0K–512K	00000–7FFFF	512KB	Conventional memory

SCSI controllers, network cards, video boards, modems, etc.), are demanding memory space for the support of each device's on-board BIOS ROM. No two ROMs can overlap in their addresses—otherwise, a conflict will occur. Table 10-6 lists a memory map for a modern PC using an Intel 430 or 440 type of chipset (or equivalent).

INDEX OF TYPICAL ASSIGNMENTS

Now that you've got a handle on the way resources are allocated, it's time to put some of that information to work. Table 10-7 presents a cross-section of typical devices and ports found in today's PCs, and it lists the standard resource assignments most often associated with them. It might assist you in spotting potential conflicts before installing new devices. Notice that you might encounter any combination of resources listed in the table for a given device.

TABLE 10-7 TYPICAL DEVICE ASSIGNMENTS

DEVICE		IRQS	DMA CHANNELS	I/O ADDRESSES
AdLib Sound Device				228h
				238h
				239h
				289h
				388h
				389h
Aria Synthesizers				280h–288h
				290h–298h
				2A0h–2A8h
				2B0h–2B8h
Drive Controllers	FDD1	6	2	03F0h–03F5h
	FDD2	6	2	370h–377h
	HDD1	14		01F0h–01F7h
	HDD2	15		0170h–0177h
Gameport Adapters				201–211h
Internal Ports	COM1	4		03F8h–03FFh
	COM2	3		02F8h–02FFh
	COM3	4		03E8h–03EFh
	COM4	3		02E8h–02EFh
	LPT1	7		0378h–037Fh
	LPT2	5		0278h–027Fh
	LPT3	5		03BCh–03BFh
	PS/2 Mouse	12		064h
MPU-401 (MIDI)				300h
(IRQ shared with Sound Blaster)				320h
				330h
Network Interface Cards (NICs)		2	1	280h–283h
		3	3	280h–2FFh
		4	5	2A0h–2A3h
		5	7	2A0h–2BFh
		7		300h–303h
		10		300h–31Fh
		11		320h–323h
				320h–33Fh
				340h–343h
				340h–35Fh
				360h–363h
				360h–37Fh
Reserved System Resources		0	0	
		1	2	
			4	

TABLE 10-7 TYPICAL DEVICE ASSIGNMENTS (CONTINUED)

DEVICE	IRQS	DMA CHANNELS	I/O ADDRESSES
SCSI Host Adapters	10	3	130h–14Fh
	11	5	140h–15Fh
	14		220h–23Fh
	15		330h–34Fh
			340h–35Fh
Sound Blaster	5	1	220h–22Eh
(DMA playback)	7	3	240h–24Eh
	9	5	
	10	7	
	11		
Windows Sound System	5	0	530h
(DMA playback)	7	1	E80h
	9		3530h–F48h
	10		
	11		

Recognizing and Dealing with Conflicts

Fortunately, conflicts are almost always the result of a PC upgrade gone awry. Thus, a technician can be alerted to the possibility of a system conflict by applying the Last Upgrade rule. The rule consists of three parts:

1 A piece of hardware and/or software has been added to the system very recently.
2 The trouble occurred after a piece of hardware and/or software was added to the system.
3 The system was working fine before the hardware and/or software was added.

If all three of these common-sense factors are true, chances are very good that you are faced with a hardware or software conflict. Unlike most other types of PC problems, which tend to be specific to the faulty sub-assembly, conflicts usually manifest themselves as much more general and perplexing problems. The following symptoms are typical of serious hardware or software conflicts:

■ The system locks up during initialization.
■ The system locks up during a particular application.
■ The system locks up when a particular device (e.g., a TWAIN scanner) is used.
■ The system locks up randomly or without warning regardless of the application.
■ The system might not crash, but the device that was added might not function (even though it seems properly configured). Devices that were in the system previously might still work correctly.
■ The system might not crash, but a device or application that was working previously no longer seems to function. The newly added device (and accompanying software) might not work properly.

What makes these problems so generic is that the severity and frequency of a fault, as well as the point at which the fault occurs, depends on such factors as the particular devices that are conflicting, the resource(s) that are conflicting among the devices (i.e., IRQs, DMAs, or I/O addresses), and the function being performed by the PC when the conflict manifests itself. Because every PC is equipped and configured a bit differently, it is virtually impossible to predict a conflict's symptoms more precisely.

CONFIRMING AND RESOLVING CONFLICTS

Recognizing the possibility of a conflict is one thing, proving and correcting it is another issue entirely. However, there are some very effective tactics at your disposal. The first rule of conflict resolution is Last In First Out (or LIFO). The LIFO principle basically says that the fastest means of overcoming a conflict problem is to remove the hardware or software that resulted in the conflict. In other words, if you install board X and board Y ceases to function, board X is probably conflicting with the system, so removing board X should restore board Y to normal operation. The same concept holds true for software. If you add a new application to your system, then find that an existing application fails to work properly, the new application is likely at fault. Unfortunately, removing the offending element is not enough. You still have to install the new device or software in such a way that it will no longer conflict in the system.

Several "system reporting tools" are on the companion CD, which can help you identify the resources in use (and avoid accidental resource conflicts because of configuration mistakes). Try CONF810E.ZIP, SNOOP330.ZIP, or SYSINF.ZIP on the companion CD.

DEALING WITH SOFTWARE CONFLICTS

Two types of software can cause conflicts in a typical PC: TSRs and device drivers. TSRs (sometimes called "popup utilities") load into memory, usually during initialization, and wait until a system event (e.g., a modem ring or a keyboard "hot key" combination). There are no DOS or system rules that define how such utilities should be written. As a result, many tend to conflict with application programs (and even with DOS itself). If you suspect that such a popup utility is causing the problem, find its reference in the AUTOEXEC.BAT file and disable it by placing the command REM in front of its command line (e.g., REM C:\UTILS\NEWMENU.EXE /A:360 /D:3). The REM command turns the line into a "REMark," which can easily be removed later if you choose to restore the line. Remember to reboot the computer so that your changes will take effect.

Device drivers present another potential problem. Most hardware upgrades require the addition of one or more device drivers. Such drivers are called from the CONFIG.SYS file during system initialization (or loaded with Windows), and use a series of command-line parameters to specify the system resources that are being used. This is often necessary to ensure that the driver operates its associated hardware properly. if the command line options used for the device driver do not match the hardware settings (or overlap the settings of another device driver), system problems can result. If you suspect that a device driver is causing the problem, find its reference in the CONFIG.SYS file and disable it by placing the command REM in front of its command line (e.g., *REM DEVICE = C:\DRI-VERS\NEWDRIVE.SYS /A360 /I:5*). The REM command turns the line into a "REMark," which can easily be removed later if you choose to restore the line. Remember that disabling the device driver in this fashion will prevent the associated hardware from working, but if the problem clears, you can work with the driver settings until the problem is resolved. Remember to reboot the computer so that your changes will take effect.

Finally, consider the possibility that the offending software has a bug. Try contacting the software manufacturer. There might be a fix or undocumented feature that you are unaware of. There might also be a patch or update that will solve the problem.

DEALING WITH HARDWARE CONFLICTS

A PC user recently added a CD-ROM and adapter board to their system. The installation went flawlessly using the defaults—a 10-minute job. Several days later, when attempting to backup the system, the user noticed that the parallel port tape backup did not respond (although the printer that had been connected to the parallel port was working fine). The user tried booting the system from a "clean" bootable floppy disk (no CONFIG.SYS or AUTOEXEC.BAT files to eliminate the device drivers), but the problem remained. After a bit of consideration, the user powered down the system, removed the CD-ROM adapter board, and booted the system from a "clean" bootable floppy disk. Sure enough, the parallel port tape backup started working again.

Stories such as this remind technicians that hardware conflicts are not always the monstrous, system-smashing mistakes that they are made out to be. In many cases, conflicts have subtle, non-catastrophic consequences. Because the CD-ROM was the last device to be added, it was the first to be removed. It took about 5 minutes to realize and remove the problem. However, removing the problem is only part of conflict troubleshooting—re-installing the device without a conflict is the real challenge.

Ideally, the way to correct a conflict would be to alter the conflicting setting. That's dynamite in theory, but another thing in real life. The trick is that you need to know what resources are in use and which ones are free. Unfortunately, there are only two ways to find out. On one hand, you can track down the user manual for every board in the system, then inspect each board individually to find the settings, then work accordingly. This will work (assuming that you have the documentation), but it is cumbersome and time consuming. As an alternative, you can use a resource testing tool, such as the Discovery Card by AllMicro, Inc. The Discovery Card plugs into a 16-bit ISA slot and uses a series of LEDs to display each IRQ and DMA channel in use. Any LED not illuminated is an available resource. It is then simply a matter of setting your expansion hardware to an IRQ and DMA channel that is not illuminated. Remember that you might have to alter the command line switches of any device drivers. The only resources not illustrated by the Discovery Card are I/O addresses, but because most I/O ports are reserved for particular functions (as you saw in Tables 10-3 to 10-5), you can typically locate an unused I/O port with a minimum of effort.

CONFLICT TROUBLESHOOTING WITH WINDOWS 95

One of the biggest problems with conflict troubleshooting is that every conflict situation is a bit different. Variations in PC equipment and available resources often reduce conflict troubleshooting to a "hit or miss" process. Fortunately, conflict troubleshooting can be accomplished quickly and easily using the tools provided by Windows 95 (namely the Device Manager). This part of the chapter provides a step-by-step process that you can use for conflict resolution under Windows 95.

The following steps should be read like a flow chart and you'll find many references that will take you back and forth to various steps throughout this section.

Step 1: Getting started   Start the Device Manager in Windows 95:

1 Click the *Start* button, then click *Settings,* then select *Control panel.*
2 Double-click the *System* icon, then click on the *Device manager* tab (Fig. 10-1).
3 Be sure that *View devices by type* is selected.

If the hardware that has the conflict isn't visible in the list, click the plust sign (+) next to the type of hardware.

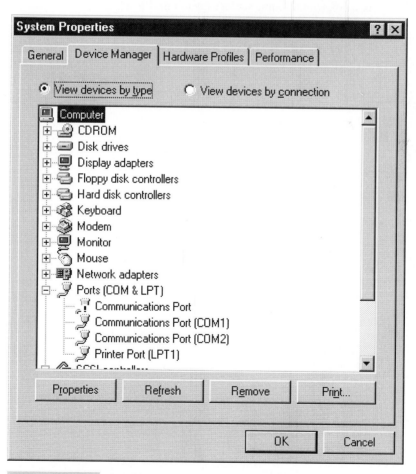

FIGURE 10-1   **The Windows 95 Device Manager.** Intel Corporation

Determine if the device was installed twice. Is the device you were installing (or that suffers from the conflict) listed twice in *Device manager*?

■ If the device is listed only once, go to Step 2.
■ If the device is listed twice and there is only supposed to be one such device in the system, go to Step 3.
■ If the device is listed twice, but there are supposed to be two such devices in the system, go to Step 2.

Step 2: Device listed only once View the resource settings for the conflicting device:

1 Double-click on the hardware that shows a conflict.
2 In the *Device usage* area (such as Fig. 10-2), be sure that there is a check in the box next to the configuration marked "Current." If the box isn't checked, check the box now.
3 Click the *Resources* tab.

Do you see a box with resource settings (as in Fig. 10-3)?

■ If the box with resource settings appears, go to Step 4.
■ If the *Set configuration manually* button appears instead, go to Step 5.
■ If the device doesn't have a Resources tab, go to Step 6.

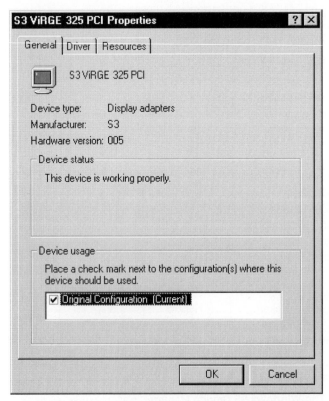

FIGURE 10-2 Device properties highlighting the Device Usage.

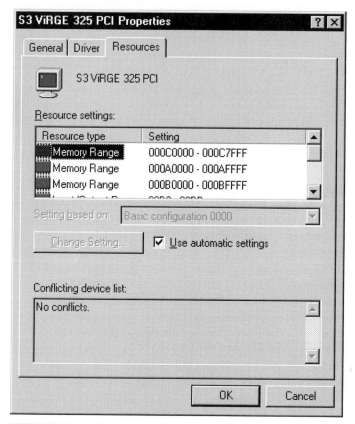

FIGURE 10-3   Device properties highlighting Resource
Settings.

Step 3: Device listed twice   Remove all of the duplicated device(s), and install
again:

1 Remove each duplicate item from the hardware list. Click its name, and then click *Remove*. When you are finished, no instances of the conflicting hardware should be listed.
2 Click *OK*.
3 Now (while still within the *Control panel*), double-click on the *Add new hardware* icon. If you see a message that you already have a wizard open, click *Finish* in that wizard, and then click the button in this step to start a new wizard.
4 Click *Next*.
5 Click the option to automatically detect your hardware, and then click *Next*. Continue until you finish the wizard.

Did this fix the problem?

■ If the conflict no longer appears, this should correct the problem, and you should be done. Exit the *Control panel* and restart Windows 95.
■ If the conflict still appears, go to Step 2.

Step 4: Resource settings appear Identify exactly which resources are causing the conflict:

1 In the *Conflicting device list* box, identify the hardware that is using conflicting resources.

Is more than one resource conflict listed?

- If more than one resource conflict is listed, go to Step 7.
- If only one conflict is listed, go to Step 8.
- If no conflicts are listed, or if one or more indications show *System reserved* as the conflict, go to Step 9.

Step 5: Manual button appears Determine why the resources are not displayed:

1 When the *Resources* tab shows a *Set configuration manually* button, it is either because the device has a conflict or other problem and is disabled, or because the resource settings used by this device are working properly, but they don't match any of the known configurations.
2 You can tell which situation applies by reading the text above the button.

Which text message do you see?

- If you see a message that says; "The device is conflicting, or the device is not currently enabled or has a problem," then go to Step 10.
- If you see a message that says; "The resource settings don't match any known configurations," there is no further solution to the problem. You should probably remove the conflicting device.

Step 6: There is no *Resources* tab You have probably chosen the wrong device. Select the correct device:

1 Click *Cancel* to return to the hardware list.
2 Carefully double-click the hardware that has a conflict.
3 In the *Device usage* area, be sure that there is a check in the box next to the configuration marked "Current." If the box isn't checked, check it now.
4 Click the *Resources* tab.

Do you see a box with resource settings now?

- If the box with resource settings now appears, go to Step 4.
- If you see a *Set configuration manually* button, go to Step 5.
- If the resource settings still do not appear, there is no further solution to the problem. You should probably remove the conflicting device.

Step 7: More than one conflict is listed At this point, you should determine just how many devices are listed as being conflicting.

- If you only see one device causing all the conflicts, go to Step 11.
- If more than one device is causing the conflicts, go to Step 12.

Step 8: Only one conflict is listed Look for a resource setting that doesn't conflict:

1 In the *Resource settings* box, double-click the icon next to the resource setting that is conflicting. If you see a message that says "You must clear the Use Automatic Settings box before you can change a resource setting," click *OK* to close the message, and then clear the *Use automatic settings* box.

2 Scroll through the available resource settings.

3 For each setting, look at the *Conflicting device list* box to see if it conflicts with any other hardware.

4 If you find a free setting, click *OK*.

Did you find a setting that doesn't conflict with any other hardware?

■ If you can find a setting which does not conflict, go to Step 13.
■ If you cannot find a setting that does not conflict, go to Step 14.
■ If you see a message stating that the resource setting cannot be modified, go to Step 15.

Step 9: No conflicts are listed If there are no conflicts listed in the *Conflicting device list* box, either you are not viewing resources for the correct device, or the conflict has already been resolved (you need to restart your computer to allow Windows 95 to configure the hardware). Look at the top of the dialog box to see if you are viewing resources for the correct device.

There is no further solution to this problem. If restarting Windows 95 does not clear the problem, you might simply need to remove the conflicting device.

Step 10: The device is conflicting Now you need to identify which hardware is conflicting:

1 Click *Set configuration manually*.

2 In the *Conflicting device list* box, identify the other hardware that is using the conflicting resources.

Is more than one resource conflict listed?

■ If more than one resource conflict is listed, go to Step 16.
■ If only one resource conflict is listed, go to Step 17.
■ If no conflicts are listed, go to Step 9.

Step 11: Only one device is conflicting Do you want to disable the device that is causing all the conflicts?

■ If you wish to disable the conflicting device, go to Step 18.
■ If you must use the hardware that is causing the conflicts, go to Step 17.

Step 12: More than one device is conflicting Look for resource settings that don't conflict:

1 In the *Resource settings* box, double-click the icon next to a resource setting that is conflicting. If you see a message that says "You must clear the Use Automatic Settings box before you can change a resource setting," click *OK* to close the message, and then clear the *Use automatic settings* box.

2 Scroll through the available resource setting.

3 For each setting, look in the *Conflicting device list* box to see if it conflicts with any other hardware.

4 When you find a free setting, click *OK.*

5 Repeat steps 1 through 4 for each conflicting resource.

Did you find a free setting for each conflicting resource?

■ If you do find free settings for each conflicting resource, go to Step 19.

■ If some (or all) resources are still conflicting, go to Step 20.

■ If you see a message indicating that the resource setting cannot be modified, go to Step 15.

Step 13: There is a free setting   When a free setting is available, change the configuration:

1 Enter the new setting value.

2 Make a note of the old and new settings to refer to later.

3 Click *OK.* If you see a message prompting you to restart your computer, click *No.*

> Depending on the type of hardware you have, you might have to change the jumpers on your hardware card to match the new setting(s) or you might have to run a configuration utility provided by your hardware manufacturer. If the jumper settings on your card aren't set properly, your hardware will not work—even if you resolved the conflict correctly. Refer to your hardware documentation for instructions on changing jumpers.

Restart your computer:

1 Click *OK.*

2 You might see a message prompting you to restart your computer. Click *No.*

3 Click the *Start* button, click *Shut down,* then click *Yes.*

4 When Windows says it is safe to do so, turn off your computer so that you can configure the hardware devices that you've changed.

This should correct the problem, and the hardware conflict should now be resolved once the PC is restarted.

Step 14: All other settings conflict   Identify hardware you no longer need:

1 Scroll through the available resource settings.

2 When a conflict appears in the *Conflicting device list* box, determine whether you still need to use the device that is causing the conflict.

Can you identify a hardware device that you no longer need to use?

■ If you can disable the conflicting device, go to Step 21.

■ If you cannot disable the conflicting device, go to Step 22.

Step 15: Resource settings cannot be modified View the resources for the other device:

1 In the *Conflicting device list* box, make a note of which device is using the resource that cannot be modified.

2 Click *Cancel.*

3 In the hardware list, find and double-click the device that is using the resource.

Does this device have a Resources tab?

■ If a *Resources* tab is available, go to Step 23.

■ If a *Resources* tab is not available, go to Step 24.

Step 16: There is more than one conflict How many devices are listed as conflicting?

■ If only one device is causing the conflicts, go to Step 11.

■ If more than one device is causing the conflicts, go to Step 12.

Step 17: There is only one conflict Look for a resource setting that doesn't conflict:

1 In the *Resource settings* box, double-click the icon next to the resource setting that is conflicting. If you see a message that says "You must clear the Use Automatic Settings box before you can change a resource setting," click *OK* to close the message, then clear the *Use automatic settings* box.

2 Scroll through the available resource settings.

3 For each setting, look in the *Conflicting device list* box to see if it conflicts with any other hardware.

4 If you find a free setting, click *OK*.

Did you find a setting that doesn't conflict with any other hardware?

■ If you manage to find a setting that does not conflict, go to Step 13.

■ If you see a message indicating that the resource setting cannot be modified, go to Step 15.

■ If all other settings conflict with other hardware, there is no further solution to the problem, and you should probably remove the conflicting device.

Step 18: Disable conflicting hardware Determine how to best disable the conflicting hardware:

1 On the hardware list, double-click the hardware that you want to disable. If you do not see the hardware list, click *Cancel* until you return to it.

2 In the *Device usage* area, click the box next to the configuration marked "Current" to remove the check mark.

3 Click the *Resources* tab. If there is a *Set configuration manually* button, Windows 95 can disable and free up resources used by this hardware without your removing its card from your computer.

Do you see a *Set configuration manually* button?

■ If the button exists, you can effectively disable the device, so go to Step 19.
■ If the button is not available, go to Step 25.

Step 19: Resources now set without conflicts Print out a report for each device you changed:

1 In the hardware list, click a device whose resource settings you changed while resolving the conflict. If you do not see the hardware list, click *OK* until you return to it.
2 Click *Print*.
3 Click the second option to print the selected class or device.
4 Click *OK*.
5 Repeat steps 1 through 4 for each device that you changed during this troubleshooting process.

This should correct the problem, and you should be done.

Step 20: Some resources are still conflicting Set resources to conflict with only one device:

1 Double-click a resource that is still conflicting. If you see a message that says "You must clear the *Use automatic settings* box before you can change a resource setting," click *OK* to close the message, then clear the *Use automatic settings* box.
2 Scroll through the available resource settings. For each value, write down the setting and the name of the hardware it conflicts with. Then click *Cancel*.
3 Repeat steps 1 and 2 for each conflicting resource.
4 Looking at the list, see if you can change the resource settings so that they conflict with only one device—preferably one you could disable.

Are all conflicts with one device?

■ If all the conflicts are with only one device, go to Step 11.
■ If resources still conflict with more than one device, there is no further solution to the problem, and you should probably remove the conflicting device.

Step 21: Disable the unneeded device Determine whether the hardware you want to disable is Plug-and-Play:

1 Select each resource setting that conflicts with the hardware you will disable, and then click *OK*.
2 When the message appears saying the setting conflicts with another device, click *Yes* to continue.

3 Click *OK* until you return to the hardware list.

4 Click the plus sign (+) next to the type of hardware that you want to disable.

5 Double-click the hardware that you want to disable.

6 In the *Device usage* area, click the box next to the configuration marked "Current" to remove the check mark.

7 Click the *Resources* tab.

8 If there is a *Set configuration manually* button, Windows 95 can disable and free up resources used by this hardware without your removing its card from your computer.

Do you see a *Set configuration manually* button?

- If the button exists, you can effectively disable the device, so go to Step 19.
- If the button is not available, go to Step 25.

Step 22: All devices are in use Write down a list of all devices using resources:

1 Scroll through the resource settings. On a piece of paper, write down the name of each piece of conflicting hardware and its setting.

2 Click *Cancel* until you return to the hardware list.

Rearrange resource settings for conflicting hardware:

1 On the hardware list, click the plus sign (+) next to the hardware type for the first item on your written list.

2 Double-click the hardware.

3 Click the *Resources* tab.

4 Double-click the resource setting that you wrote down. If you see a message that says "You must clear the *Use automatic settings* box before you can change a resource setting," click *OK* to close the message, then clear the *Use automatic settings* box.

5 Scroll through the available resource settings. For each setting, look in the *Conflicting device list* box to see if it conflicts with any other hardware.

6 If you find a free setting other than the one you wrote down, write down the new values, and continue.

7 If you do not find a free setting, repeat steps 1 through 5 until you run out of hardware to try or you find a free setting.

Did you find a free resource setting?

- If you found free resources, go to Step 26.
- If you could not locate free resources, go to Step 27.

Step 23: Resource information is available Check to see if the device can use a different resource:

1 Click the *Resources* tab.

2 In the *Resource settings* box, double-click the resource setting that you need to free for the other device. If you see a message that says "You must clear the Use Automatic Settings box before you can change a resource setting," click *OK* to close the message, then clear the *Use automatic settings* box.

3 Scroll through the available resource settings.

4 For each setting, look in the *Conflicting device list* box to see if it conflicts with any other hardware.

5 If you find a free setting, click *OK*. If you see a message prompting you to restart your computer, click *No*.

Did you find a free resource setting?

■ If *Yes*, go to Step 28.
■ If *No* (or the settings cannot be modified), go to Step 29.

Step 24: Resource information is not available   Decide which device you should disable. Because both devices need to use the same resource setting, you must decide which device you want to use. You must disable and/or remove the other device.

It probably is easier to remove the device that had the original conflict. If you choose to remove the other device, you might see a message stating that you still have a conflict after completing the procedure. Just restart the procedure and continue resolving the conflict.

Which device would you like to disable?

■ If you'd rather disable the original device, go to Step 30.
■ If you'd rather disable the other conflicting device, go to Step 31.

Step 25: Manual button not available   Disable the conflicting hardware by removing it:

1 On the hardware list, click the plus sign (+) next to the type of hardware that you want to disable. If you do not see the hardware list, click *Cancel* until you return to it.

2 Click the hardware you want to disable.

3 Click *Remove*.

Go to Step 19.

Step 26: Free resources found   Change the resource settings to utilize the free resources:

1 Save the new setting by clicking *OK*, then clicking *OK* again.

2 If you see a message about restarting your computer, click *No*.

3 Double-click the hardware that first had the conflict.

4 Click the *Resources* tab.

5 Double-click the resource that is conflicting. If you see a message that says "You must clear the Use Automatic Settings box before you can change a resource setting," click *OK* to close the message, then clear the *Use automatic settings* box.

6 Change the resource setting to the value you just freed. The *Conflicting device list* box might show a conflict with the other hardware that you just changed.

7 Click *OK*. If you see a message, click *Yes* to continue.

Go to Step 19.

Step 27: No free resources available   You must disable some hardware to relieve the conflict. Do you want to disable the hardware that caused the original conflict?

■ If you want to disable the hardware that originally caused the conflict, go to Step 18.
■ If you must use all of the hardware in the system, there is no further solution to the problem because the conflict cannot be resolved.

Step 28: Free setting found   Determine whether there are any remaining conflicts:

1 Click *OK* to return to the hardware list.
2 Double-click the device that had the original conflict.
3 Click the *Resources* tab.
4 See if there are any remaining conflicts listed in the *Conflicting device list* box.

> If the conflict you just resolved is listed, you can ignore it. It will no longer conflict after you restart your computer later.

Are there still conflicts listed?

■ If all the resources are now set without any conflicts, go to Step 19.
■ If some or all of the resources are still conflicting, go to Step 20.

Step 29: No free setting found   You must decide which device to disable. Because both devices need to use the same resource setting, you must decide which device you want to use. You must disable and remove the other device.

   It probably is easier to remove the device that had the original conflict at this point. If you choose to remove the other device, you might see a message telling you that you still have a conflict after you finish and restart your computer. Just restart this procedure and continue resolving the conflict.

   Which device would you like to disable?

■ If you choose to disable the device with the original conflict, go to Step 30.
■ If you choose disable the other device that it is conflicting with, go to Step 31.

Step 30: Disable original conflicting device   Determine whether you have to remove the card to disable the hardware:

1 On the hardware list, double-click the hardware that you want to disable. If you do not see the hardware list, click *Cancel* until you return to it.
2 In the *Device usage* area, be sure that there is a check in the box next to the configuration marked "Current." If the box isn't checked, check it now.
3 Click the *Resources* tab. If there is a *Set configuration manually* button, Windows 95 can free up resources for this hardware without your removing its card from your computer.

When you see a *Set configuration manually* button: If you do see that button, and there are no resource settings listed in the box, you'll need to restart your computer.

1 Click *OK*, then click *OK* again.
2 You might be prompted to restart your computer. Click *Yes*.

When you don't see a *Set configuration manually* button: if no button is available, you'll need to disable the physical hardware by removing it from the system.

1 On the hardware list, click the plus sign (+) next to the type of hardware that you want to disable. If you do not see the hardware list, click *Cancel* until you return to it.
2 Click the hardware you want to disable.
3 Click *Remove*, then click *OK*.
4 You might be prompted to restart your computer. You will have to remove the card for this hardware from your computer, so you need to shut down instead of restarting. Click *No*.
5 Click the *Start* button, click *Shut down*, then click *Yes*. When the message says it is safe to do so, turn off your computer and remove the card from your computer.
6 Restart your PC and check if your problem has been resolved.

This should correct the conflict and complete your troubleshooting procedure.

Step 31: Disable other conflicting device Determine whether you have to re-move the card to disable the hardware:

1 On the hardware list, double-click the hardware that you want to disable. If you do not see the hardware list, click *Cancel* until you return to it.
2 In the *Device usage* area, click the box next to the configuration marked "Current" to re-move the check mark.
3 Click the *Resources* tab. If there is a *Set configuration manually* button, Windows 95 can free up resources for this hardware without your removing its card from your computer.

Do you see a *Set configuration manually* button?

■ If you see the button, go to Step 32.
■ If you don't see the button, go to Step 33.

Step 32: Disable the other device Determine whether there are any remaining conflicts:

1 Click *OK* to return to the hardware list.
2 Double-click the device that had the original conflict.
3 Click the *Resources* tab.
4 See if there are any remaining conflicts listed in the *Conflicting device list* box. If the conflict you just resolved is listed, you can ignore it. It will no longer conflict after you restart your computer later.

Are there still conflicts listed?

■ If there are no further conflicts, go to Step 19.
■ If one or more conflicts are still listed, go to Step 34.

Step 33: Remove the other device   Disable hardware by removing it:

1 On the hardware list, click the plus sign (+) next to the type of hardware that you want to disable. If you do not see the hardware list, click *Cancel* until you return to it.
2 Click the hardware you want to disable.
3 Click *Remove*.

Go to Step 19.

Step 34: There are still some conflicts   Try setting resources to conflict with only one device:

1 Double-click a resource that is still conflicting. If you see a message that says "You must clear the *Use automatic settings* box before you can change a resource setting," click *OK* to close the message, then clear the *Use automatic settings* box.
2 Scroll through the available resource settings. For each value, write down the setting and the name of the hardware it conflicts with, then click *Cancel*.
3 Repeat steps 1 and 2 for each conflicting resource.
4 Looking at the list, see if you can change the resource settings so that they conflict with only one device—preferably one you could disable.

Are all conflicts now with one device?

■ When all the conflicts are with only one device, go to Step 11.
■ If the resources still conflict with more than one device (or cannot be changed), there is no further solution to this problem, and you should probably remove the conflicting device.

THE ROLE OF PLUG-AND-PLAY (PNP)

Traditional PCs used devices that required manual configuration—each IRQ, DMA, I/O port, and memory address space had to be specifically set through jumpers on the particular device. If you accidentally configured two or more devices to use the same resource, a conflict would result. This would require you to isolate the offending device(s), identify available resources, and reconfigure the offending device(s) manually. Taken together, this was often a cumbersome and time-consuming process.

In the early 1990s, PC designers realized that it was possible to automate the process of resource allocation each time the system initializes. This way, a device needs only to be installed, and the system would handle its configuration without the assistance or intervention of the installer. This concept became known as "Plug-and-Play" (PnP), and it is now standard in the PC arena. PnP systems require three elements to function:

■ PnP-compliant devices (such as video boards, modems, drive controllers, and so on).
■ PnP-compliant BIOS (now used in all Pentium-class systems).
■ PnP-compliant operating systems (like Windows 95).

When the PnP system works properly, a PnP device can be installed in an available expansion slot on a PnP-supported motherboard (with a PnP BIOS). When Windows 95 starts, it recognizes the new PnP device, assigns resources, then attempts to install the proper protected-mode driver (which could be installed from manufacturer's floppy disk or a Windows 95 installation CD). Thereafter, the system "remembers" the new device and reconfigures it each time the system starts. Ideally, if the PnP device is ever removed, Windows 95 would automatically clear the device from its "system," and free the resources for other devices.

However, if any of these elements are missing, devices will not be "auto-configured." For example, PnP won't work under DOS (though there are DOS PnP drivers that can be used to initialize PnP devices). Older, jumper-configured devices (called *legacy devices*) also won't support PnP, and resources need to be reserved for legacy devices to prevent the PnP system from ignoring them entirely.

> PnP "auto-configuration" information is stored in the Extended System Configuration Data (ESCD) area, and is cleared when the CMOS RAM is cleared or lost.

KEEP YOUR NOTES

Once you have determined the IRQ, DMA, and I/O settings that are in use, a thorough technician will note each setting on paper, then tape the notes inside the system's enclosure. This extra step will greatly ease future expansion and troubleshooting. To make your note-taking process even faster, you can photocopy and use the System Setup Form included in the Appendix of this book.

Further Study

That concludes Chapter 10. Be sure to review the glossary and chapter questions on the accompanying CD. If you have access to the Internet, take some time to review a few of the resources listed:

Data Depot: **http://www.datadepo.com/datadepo.htm**

Download MSD 2.11 **http://support.microsoft.com/download/support/mslfiles GA0363.EXE**

The Discovery Card: **http://www.ffg.com/pcproductsdiscover.html**

Windsor Technologies: **http://www.windsortech.com**

CPU IDENTIFICATION AND TROUBLESHOOTING

CONTENTS AT A GLANCE

The Basic CPU
The busses
Addressing modes

Modern CPU Concepts
The p-rating (pr) system
CPU sockets
CISC vs. RISC CPUs
Pipelining
Branch prediction
Superscalar execution
Dynamic execution

The Intel CPUs
8086/8088 (1978/1979)
80186 (1980)
80286 (1982)
80386 (1985–1990)
80486 (1989–1994)
Pentium (1993–current)
Pentium Pro (1995–current)
Pentium MMX (1997–current)
Pentium II (1997–current)

The AMD CPUs
AM486DX series (1994–1995)
AM5X86 (1995–current)
K5 series (1996–current)
K6 series (1997–current)

The Cyrix CPUs
6X86 series (1995–current)
Mediagx (1996–current)
6X86MX (M2) (1997–current)

CPU Overclocking
Requirements for overclocking
Potential pitfalls
Overclocking the system
Special notes for 75 and 83MHz bus
  speeds
Overclocking notes for the Intel
  Pentium
Overclocking notes for the Intel
  Pentium Pro

CONTENTS AT A GLANCE (Continued)

Overclocking notes for the
   Cyrix/IBM 6X86
Overclocking the AMD K5
Tips for controlling heat

Troubleshooting CPU Problems
General symptoms and solutions
Cyrix 6X86 issues
Overclocking troubleshooting
Troubleshooting a diagnostic
   failure after installing an Intel
   math co-processor
Math co-processor
   troubleshooting—older devices
Troubleshooting an arithmetic test
   failure
Troubleshooting an environment
   test failure
Intel diagnostics conformance test
   failure with Intel387(TM) SL math
   co-processor
Intel387 DX math co-processor
   recognized as an Intel287TM XL
   math co-processor

Intel387 math co-processor
   recognized as an Intel287 math
   co-processor
System integrity diagnostic test
   failure
"Chkcop has found" and locks up
Chkcop 2.0 fails divide test
Chkcop seems faster on an Intel287
   math co-processor
System diagnostics and the Intel287
   XL math co-processor
Intel387 DX and inboard Intel287
   math module and IBM advanced
   diagnostics
Troubleshooting failure to boot after
   installing an Intel math co-processor
Weitek co-processor not installed
OS2 1107 error
162 error in IBM PS/2 model 50, 60,
   and 70
"Configuration error" after removing
   80287 from IBM PC/AT

Further Study
Newsgroups

The *Central Processing Unit* (also called a *CPU, microprocessor,* or simply a *processor*) has become one of the most important developments ever realized in integrated circuit technology (Fig. 11-1). On the surface, a CPU is a rather boring device—in spite of its relative complexity, a typical CPU only performs three general functions: mathematical calculations, logical comparisons, and data manipulation. This isn't a very big repertoire for a device carrying millions of transistors. When you look deeper, however, you realize that it is not the number of functions that makes a CPU so remarkable, but that each function is carried out as part of a program that the CPU reads and follows. By changing the program, the activities of a CPU could be completely re-arranged without modifying the computer's circuitry.

Once the concept of a generic central-processing function was born, designers realized that the same system could be used to solve an incredibly diverse array of problems (given the right set of instructions). This was the quantum leap in thinking that gave birth to the computer, and created the two domains that we know today as *hardware* and *software*. As you might have guessed, the idea of central processing is hardly new. The very earliest computers of the late 1940s and 1950s applied these concepts to simple programs stored

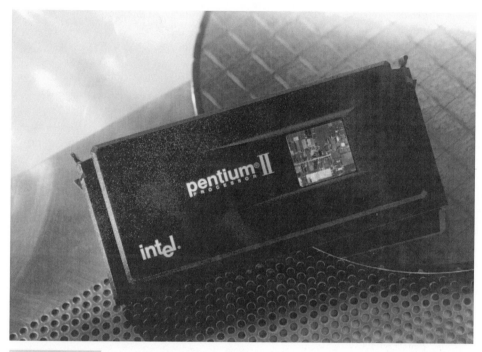

FIGURE 11-1   An Intel Premium II processor. Intel Corporation

on punched cards or paper tape. The mainframe and minicomputers of the 1960s and 1970s also followed the central-processing concept. However, it was the integration of central-processing functions onto a single IC (the microprocessor) in the mid-1970s that made the first "personal" computers possible, and spawned the explosive developments in CPU speed and performance that we have seen ever since.

Although a CPU can handle mathematical calculations, the CPU itself was not (until recently) designed to handle floating-point math as an internal function. Of course, floating-point math was possible through software emulation, but the performance of such an approach was unacceptable for math-intensive applications (such as CAD and scientific programs). To deal with high-performance floating-point math in hardware, a *Math Co-Processor (MCP)* or *Numerical Processing Unit (NPU)* was developed to work in conjunction with the CPU. Although the classic MCP was implemented as a stand-alone device, newer generations of CPU incorporate the MCP's functions right into the CPU itself.

The CPU is closely related to the overall speed and performance of personal computers. As a technician, you should understand the essential specifications and characteristics of CPUs. This chapter is intended to provide some insights into CPU evolution and capabilities, and illustrate some of the problems that can manifest themselves in microprocessor operation. Table 11-1 provides a "quick index" of CPUs used in personal computers.

TABLE 11-1   HISTORICAL* INDEX OF PC CPUs AND MCPs

Microprocessors
Intel i4004 CPU
Intel i4040 CPU
Intel i8008 CPU
Intel i8080/i8080A CPU
Zilog Z80 CPU
Intel i8085A/i8085AH CPU
Intel i8086A/i80C86A CPU
Intel i8088A/i80C88A CPU
AMD Am8086/Am80C86 CPU
AMD Am8088/Am80C88 CPU
Harris HS80C86/883 CPU
Harris HS80C88/883 CPU
Siemens SAB8086 CPU
Siemens SAB8088 CPU
Hitachi H80C88 CPU
Intel i80186/i80C186 CPU
Intel i80188/i80C188 CPU
AMD Am80L186 CPU
AMD Am80Li88 CPU
AMD Am186EM CPU
NEC V30 CPU
NEC V20 CPU
Siemens SAB80186 CPU
Siemens SAB80188 CPU
Intel i80886 CPU
Intel i80286 CPU
AMD Am80286/Am80C286 CPU
Harris 80C286 CPU
Siemens SAB80286 CPU
Fujutsi 80286 CPU
Kruger 80286 CPU
Intel i80386 CPU
Intel i80386/i80386DX CPU
Intel i80386SX CPU
Intel i80386SL CPU
Intel RapidCAD CPU
Intel i80376 microprocessor
Intel i386SX microprocessor
Intel i386CX microprocessor
Intel i386EX microprocessor
AMD Am386DX CPU
AMD Am386DXL CPU
AMD Am386DXLV CPU

TABLE 11-1 HISTORICAL* INDEX OF PC CPUs AND MCPs (CONTINUED)

AMD Am386SX CPU

AMD Am386SXL CPU

AMD Am386SXLV CPU

AMD Am386DE CPU

AMD Am386SE CPU

AMD Am386EM CPU

IBM 386SLC CPU

Chips & Technologies Super386 38600DX CPU

Chips & Technologies 38605DX CPU

Chips & Technologies 38600SX CPU

IBM 486DLC CPU

IBM 486DLC2 CPU

IBM 486SLC CPU

IBM 486SLC2 CPU

IBM 486BLX CPU (Blue Lightning)

IBM 486BLX2 CPU (Blue Lightning)

IBM 486BLX3 CPU (Blue Lightning)

Cyrix Cx486DLC CPU

Cyrix Cx486SLC CPU

Cyrix Cx486SLC/e CPU

Cyrix Cx486SLC/e-V CPU

Cyrix Cx486DLC / Cx486SLC CPU incompatibilities

Cyrix Cx486DLC2 CPU

Cyrix Cx486SLC2 CPU

Cyrix Cx486DRx CPU

Cyrix Cx486SRx CPU

Cyrix Cx486DRx2 CPU

Cyrix Cx486SRx2 CPU

Cyrix Cx486DRu CPU

Cyrix Cx486SRu CPU

Cyrix Cx486DRu2 CPU

Cyrix Cx486SRu2 CPU

Texas Instruments TI486DLC CPU

Texas Instruments TI486SLC CPU

Texas Instruments TI486SXL-S-GA CPU (Potomac)

Texas Instruments TI486SXL-VS-GA CPU (Potomac)

Texas Instruments TI486SXL2-S-GA CPU (Potomac)

Texas Instruments TI486SXL2-VS-GA CPU (Potomac)

Texas Instruments TI486SXLC-PAF CPU (Potomac)

Texas Instruments TI486SXLC-V-PAF CPU (Potomac)

Texas Instruments TI486SXLC2-PAF CPU (Potomac)

Texas Instruments TI486SXLC2-V-PAF CPU (Potomac)

Intel i80486DX CPU

Intel i80486SL CPU

Intel i80486DXL CPU

TABLE 11-1   HISTORICAL* INDEX OF PC CPUs AND MCPs (CONTINUED)

Intel i80486SX CPU

Intel i80486SXL CPU

Intel i80486DX2 P24 CPU

Intel i80486DX4 P24C CPU

Intel i80486SX2 CPU

AMD Am486DX CPU

AMD Am486DXL CPU

AMD Am486DXLV CPU

AMD Am486DX2 CPU

AMD Am486DXL2 CPU

AMD Am486DX4 CPU

AMD Am486SX CPU

AMD Am486SXLV CPU

AMD Am486SX2 CPU

AMD Am486SE CPU

AMD Am486DX4 SE CPU

AMD Am5x86 CPU

IBM 80486DX CPU

IBM 80486SX CPU

IBM 80486BLDX2 CPU (Blue Lightning)

Cyrix FasCache Cx486D CPU

Cyrix FasCache Cx486S CPU

Cyrix FasCache Cx486S/e CPU

Cyrix FasCache Cx486S-V CPU

Cyrix FasCache Cx486S2 CPU

Cyrix FasCache Cx486S2/e CPU

Cyrix FasCache Cx486S2-V CPU

Cyrix FasCache Cx486DX CPU

Cyrix FasCache Cx486DX-V33 CPU

Cyrix FasCache Cx486DX2 CPU

Cyrix FasCache Cx486DX2-V33 CPU

Cyrix FasCache Cx486DX2-V CPU

Cyrix FasCache Cx486DX4 CPU

Cyrix 5x86 CPU

Texas Instruments TI486SXL-GA CPU (Potomac)

Texas Instruments TI486SXL-V-GA CPU (Potomac)

Texas Instruments TI486SXL2-GA CPU (Potomac)

Texas Instruments TI486SXL2-V-GA CPU (Potomac)

Texas Instruments TI486DX2 CPU

Texas Instruments TI486DX4 CPU

SGS-Thomson ST486DX2 CPU

UMC (486) U5S CPU

UMC (486) U5SD CPU

UMC (486) U5SF CPU

TABLE 11-1   HISTORICAL* INDEX OF PC CPUs AND MCPs (CONTINUED)

UMC (486) U5SLV CPU

UMC (486) U5FLV CPU

UMC U486DX2 CPU

UMC U486SX2 CPU

Intel i80486DX2 CPU for Intel i80486DX CPU (ODPR)

Intel i80486DX2 CPU for Intel i80486SX CPU (ODPR)

Intel i80486DX2 CPU for Intel i80486DX CPU (ODP)

Intel i80486DX2 CPU for Intel i80486SX CPU (ODP)

Intel i80486DX4 CPU for Intel i80486DX CPU,Intel i80486DX2 CPU (ODP)

Intel Pentium P24T CPU (ODP)

Intel Pentium P24CT CPU (ODP)

Cyrix Overdrive CPU

Intel Pentium P5 CPU

Intel Pentium P54C CPU

Intel Pentium P55C CPU

Intel Pentium P54M CPU

Intel Pentium P55CT CPU

AMD 5k86 K5 CPU (K86 series)

AMD 5k86 SSA/5 CPU (K86 series)

Cyrix 5x86 CPU

NexGen Nx586/Nx587 CPU chipset

Intel Pentium Pro P6 CPU

Intel Pentium Pro P6L CPU

Intel Overdrive P6 CPU

Intel Overdrive P6T CPU

IBM 6x86 CPU

IBM 6x86L CPU

Cyrix 6x86 CPU

NexGen Nx686 CPU

Intel Pentium/MMX CPU

Intel Pentium II CPU

AMD K6 CPU

Cyrix M2 CPU

DEC DECchip-210 Alpha CPU

DEC DECchip-211 Alpha CPU

MIPS R4000 CPU

MIPS R4200 CPU

MIPS R4400 CPU

MIPS Orion R4600 CPU

IBM, Motorola PowerPC CPU

Sun Sparc CPU

HP PA CPU (Precision Architecture)

Motorola MC6800 CPU

Motorola MC6802 CPU

TABLE 11-1   HISTORICAL* INDEX OF PC CPUs AND MCPs (CONTINUED)

Motorola MC68HC11 CPU

Motorola MC6809 CPU

Motorola MC68000 CPU

Motorola MC68008 CPU

Motorola MC68302 CPU

Motorola MC68010 CPU

Motorola MC68340 microprocessor

Motorola MC68020 CPU

Motorola MC68030 CPU

Motorola MC68040 CPU

Motorola MC68LC040 CPU

Motorola MC68040V CPU

Motorola MC68050 CPU

Motorola MC68060 CPU

Math Co-processors

Intel i8087 NPX

Intel i80287 NPX

AMD Am80C287 NPX

AMD Am80EC287 NPX

Cyrix Cx287 NPX

Intel i80187 NPX

Intel i80287XL NPX

Cyrix FasMath Cx82S87 NPX

IIT IIT-2C87 NPX

Intel i80387 NPX

Intel i80387DX NPX

Intel i80387SX NPX

Intel i80387SL Mobile NPX

Intel i80X87SL Mobile NPX

Chips & Technologies SuperMath 38700DX NPX

Chips & Technologies SuperMath 38700SX NPX

Cyrix FasMath Cx83D87 NPX

Cyrix FasMath Cx387+ NPX

Cyrix FasMath EMC87 NPX

Cyrix FasMath 83S87 NPX

Cyrix Cx387DX NPX

Cyrix Cx387SX NPX

IIT IIT-3C87 NPX

IIT IIT-3C87SX NPX

IIT IIT-XC87DLX2 NPX

ULSI MathCo 83C87 NPX

ULSI MathCo 83S87 NPX

Weitek Abacus 1167 NPX

TABLE 11-1   HISTORICAL* INDEX OF PC CPUs AND MCPs (CONTINUED)
Weitek Abacus 3167 NPX
RISE 80387 NPX
Symphony Laboratories 80387 NPX
Cyrix Cx4C87DLC NPX
IIT IIT-4C87 NPX
IIT IIT-4C87DLC NPX
Intel i80487SX NPX
Intel i80487 NPX
Cyrix Cx487S NPX
Weitek Abacus 4167 NPX

*This list is presented from oldest to newest devices

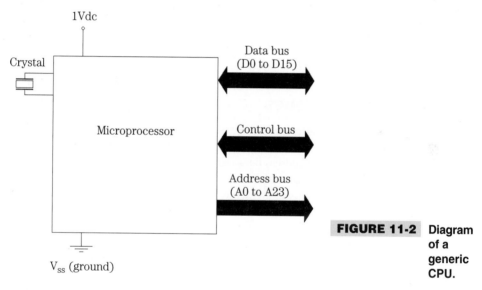

FIGURE 11-2 Diagram of a generic CPU.

The Basic CPU

A generic microprocessor can be represented by a block diagram, such as the one in Fig. 11-2. As you can see, there are several sets of signals (or busses) that you should be familiar with: the data bus, the address bus, and the control bus. These three busses allow the CPU to communicate with the other elements of the PC and control its operations.

THE BUSSES

The data bus carries information to and from the CPU, and it is perhaps the most familiar yardstick of CPU performance. The number of wires in the bus represents the number of bits (or data volume) that can be carried at any point in time. Data lines are typically labeled with a "D" prefix (e.g., D0, D1, D2, Dn, etc.). The size of a data bus is typically 8,

16, 32, or 64 bits. As you might expect, larger data busses are preferred because it allows more data to be transferred faster.

For the CPU to read or write data, it must be able to specify the precise I/O port or location in system memory. "Locations" are defined through the use of an address bus. The number of bits in the address bus represent the number of physical locations that the CPU can access. For example, a CPU with 20 address lines can address 220 (1048576) bytes. A CPU with 25 address lines can address 224 (16777216) bytes, etc. Address lines are generally represented with an "A" prefix (e.g., A0, A1, A19, etc.).

Control signals are used to synchronize and coordinate the operation of a CPU with other devices in the computer. Although the number and use of each control signal varies a bit from generation to generation, most control signals fall into several categories:

- Reading or writing functions (to memory or I/O locations)
- Interrupt channels
- CPU test and reset
- Bus arbitration and control
- DMA control
- CPU status
- Parity checking
- Cache operation

ADDRESSING MODES

When you consider a microprocessor, you must also consider the means it uses to address its memory. As you will see later in this chapter, the original Intel CPUs (such as the 8088 and 8086) used only 20 address lines (labeled *A0* to *A19*). With 20 address lines, the CPU can access only one million addresses (actually 1048576 addresses). Technically, this was not a problem, and DOS was written to work within this 1MB of space. Unfortunately, when newer CPUs were designed to break the 1MB memory barrier, DOS was stuck with this 1MB limitation (although more sophisticated software, such as DOS extenders and extended memory managers, allow DOS programs to access memory areas above 1MB).

To maintain backward compatibility with older CPUs, newer CPUs can operate in one of two modes. In the real-mode, a CPU behaves like an 8088/8086, and will only access up to 1MB. DOS and DOS programs operate in the real-mode exclusively. Newer operating systems (such as Windows 95 and OS/2) allow a CPU to utilize all of its address lines when accessing memory. This is known as *protected-mode operation*. Protected-mode operation not only supports much greater amounts of physical memory, but it also supports virtual memory. When a program calls for more memory than actually exists in a system, the CPU is able to swap code between memory and the hard drive—in effect, the hard drive can be used to simulate extra RAM. The software running on a CPU in protected-mode could be far more sophisticated than real-mode programs.

Modern CPU Concepts

There is a lot more to CPU technology than just busses and addressing modes—in fact, entire books are written on CPUs. We won't get into many of those concepts in this book, but there are a wide range of concepts that you should understand when working with to-day's PCs.

THE P-RATING (PR) SYSTEM

CPUs are traditionally classified by their clock speed. For example, a 233MHz Pentium is generally regarded as a better performing CPU than a 166MHz Pentium. However, this presents unique and perplexing marketing problems for competing CPU manufacturers—even though Intel continues to lead CPU development, other CPU makers (such as AMD and Cyrix) are keeping the pressure on by packing more performance into fewer clock cycles. Unfortunately, it is difficult for an ordinary user to understand that a non-Intel CPU at a given clock speed can perform as well as an Intel processor at another clock speed. In early 1996, Cyrix, IBM Microelectronics, and SGS Thomson (all Intel competitors) gathered to create the P-rating (or PR) system for describing their CPUs. By using a "PR" designation, a CPU can be equated to an Intel Pentium. As an example, the AMD 133MHz Am5x86 processor is marked PR75, and performs comparably to an Intel 75MHz Pentium. When the rating includes a "+" or "++" suffix (e.g., PR75++), it means that the CPU is delivering better performance than the corresponding Intel part. P ratings are determined through a method of direct comparison:

- The Winstone 96 benchmark is run on a specifically configured PC system powered by a Pentium processor of a given clock speed.
- The Pentium processor is removed from the system and replaced with a competing processor. The Winstone 96 benchmark is run again and a second Winstone score is obtained from the same system now running the competing processor. The system configuration remains identical, and all peripherals are carefully documented.
- The competing processor is assigned the highest P-rating at which it delivers Winstone scores equal to or greater than a given Pentium. For example, if an AMD K5 processor delivers performance equal to or better than a 90MHz Pentium, it receives a P-rating of 90.

CPU SOCKETS

Another important idea in CPU development and upgradeability is the concept of "sockets." Each generation of CPU uses a different number of pins (and pin assignments), so a different physical socket must be used on the motherboard to accommodate each new generation of processor. Early CPUs were not readily interchangeable, and upgrading a CPU typically meant upgrading the motherboard. With the introduction of the i486 CPUs, the notion of "OverDrive" processors became popular—replacing an existing CPU with a pin-compatible replacement processor that operated at higher internal clock speeds to enhance system performance. Table 11-2 shows that the earliest "sockets" were designated Socket 1 for early 486SX and DX processors (you can see the corresponding sockets illustrated in Fig. 11-3). As CPUs advanced, socket types proliferated to support an ever-growing selection of compatible processors.

Today, the most common type of socket is Socket 7. Socket 7 motherboards support most Pentium-type processors (i.e., Intel Pentium, Intel Pentium MMX, AMD K5, AMD K6, Cyrix 6x86, and Cyrix 6x86MX). By setting the proper clock speed and multiplier, a Socket 7 motherboard can support a variety of Pentium-type CPUs without making any

TABLE 11-2 COMPATIBILITY DETAILS FOR MAJOR CPU SOCKETS

SOCKET	PINS	VOLTS	CPU	COMPATIBLE OVERDRIVE PROCESSOR(S)	
Socket 1	169	5 V	486 SX	BOXDX4ODP75	BOXDX4ODP100
			486 DX	BOXDX4ODPR75	BOXDX4ODPR100
Socket 2	238	5 V	486 SX	BOXDX4ODP75	BOXDX4ODP100
			486 DX	BOXDX4ODPR75	BOXDX4ODPR100
			486 DX2	BOXPODP5V63	BOXPODP5V83
Socket 3	237	3 V/5 V	486 SX	BOXDX4ODP75	BOXDX4ODPR75
			486 DX	BOXDX4ODP100	BOXDX4ODPR100
			486 DX2	BOXPODP5V63	BOXPODP5V83
			486 DX4	N/a	
Socket 4	273	5 V	60/66MHz Pentium	BOXPODP5V133	
Socket 5	320	3 V	75/90/100MHz Pentium	BOXPODP3V125	
				BOXPODP3V150	
				BOXPODP3V166	
Socket 6	235	3 V	486 DX4	N/a	
Socket 7	321	2.5 V/3.3 V	75/90/100MHz Pentium	BOXPODP3V125	
				BOXPODP3V150	
				BOXPODP3V166	
Socket 8	387	2.5 V	Pentium Pro	N/a	
Slot 1	242	N/A	Pentium II	N/a	

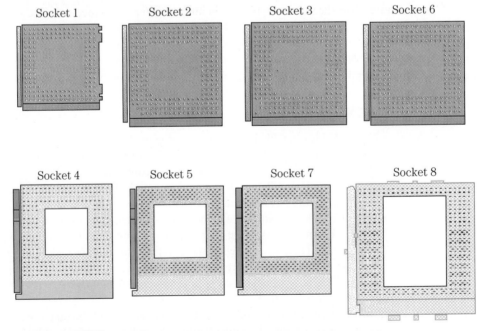

FIGURE 11-3 Comparison of major CPU socket configurations.

other hardware changes. It is this kind of versatility that has made sockets so important, and extended the working life of current PCs by providing an upgrade path for CPUs.

CISC VS. RISC CPUS

You might sometimes see processors referred to as "CISC" or "RISC" processors. Traditional CPUs are based on a Complex Instruction Set Computing (CISC) architecture. This approach allows any number of instructions to be used in the CPU, and the CPU must provide all of the internal circuitry needed to process each instruction. Because each new instruction requires many new transistors for processing, CISC offers versatility at the expense of CPU performance. CISC CPUs (such as Intel Pentium MMX and AMD K6 devices) are typically used in general-purpose desktop and mobile computers. By comparison, a Reduced Instruction Set Computing (RISC) architecture uses a limited number of very powerful instructions. This requires less transistors in the CPU for processing, and generally results in faster CPU performance with far lower power consumption. However, RISC processors are often less versatile than their CISC counterparts. CISC CPUs appear in dedicated peripheral devices, such as laser printers. Designers are still trying to develop processors that combine CISC versatility with RISC performance, although a number of RISC CPUs (like the DEC Alpha or MIPS Orion 4600 devices) appear in high-end workstations.

PIPELINING

CPUs process instructions and generate results through a complex series of transistor switches inside the CPU die itself (just like any other logic IC). Early CPUs processed one instruction at a time—that is, an instruction was fetched and processed completely, then a new instruction was fetched. Processing could be accomplished in several clock cycles (the exact number of clock cycles depended on the particular instruction). Simple instructions could be processed in two or three clocks, while complex instructions might demand as much as seven or eight clocks.

The pipelining technique (also called *instruction pipelining*) allows a new instruction to start processing while a current instruction is still being processed. This way, a CPU can actually work on several instructions during the same clock cycle. In other words, for any given clock cycle, there might be several instructions "in the pipeline." Pipelining lets the CPU make use of execution resources that would otherwise sit idle while an instruction is being completed. Still, the CPU can only finish (generate results for) one instruction per clock cycle.

BRANCH PREDICTION

Because pipelined CPUs must fetch the next instruction before they have completely executed the previous instruction, this presents a processing dilemma—if the previous instruction was a branch (an "if/then" statement), then the next instruction fetch could have been from the wrong place. Branch prediction is a technique that attempts to infer the proper address of the next instruction while knowing only the current one. If the improper branch is predicted (called a *mispredict*), the proper branch must be determined, and this can cause delays that impair processing performance. As a consequence, the branch prediction feature of a modern CPU must be extremely powerful.

SUPERSCALAR EXECUTION

Traditional CPUs used a single "execution engine" to process instructions. Even if the CPU supports instruction pipelining, the CPU can only generate results for one instruction for any given clock cycle. By adding more than one "execution engine" to the CPU, designers have provided the CPU with an ability to process more than one instruction per clock. These are known as *superscalar processors*. For example, the Pentium Pro processor uses two execution "pipes" (dubbed *U* and *V*). By combining pipelining with the multiple execution engines of a superscalar architecture, CPUs are making extremely efficient use of every clock cycle.

DYNAMIC EXECUTION

Even the fastest CPU executes instructions in the order that they are written within the particular program. This means an improperly or inefficiently written program can reduce the processing efficiency of the CPU. In many cases, even well-written code can become impaired during the software assembly and linking process. The dynamic execution technique allows the processor to evaluate the program's flow and "choose" the best order in which to process instructions. When implemented properly, this "selective reordering" of instructions allows the CPU to make even better use of its processing resources—and aids overall CPU performance.

The Intel CPUs

There is little doubt that Intel Corporation has been a driving force behind the personal computer revolution. Each new generation of microprocessor represents not just mediocre improvements in processing speed, but technological leaps in execution efficiency, raw speed, data throughput, and design enhancements (such as dynamic execution). This part of the chapter provides a historical overview of Intel microprocessors and compares their characteristics. You can find a breakdown of Intel CPU specifications in Table 11-3.

8086/8088 (1978/1979)

The 29,000-transistor 8086 marked the first 16-bit microprocessor—that is, there are 16 data bits available from the CPU itself. This immediately offered twice the data throughput of earlier 8-bit CPUs. Each of the 24 registers in the 8086/8088 is expanded to 16 bits, rather than just 8. Twenty address lines allow direct access to 1,048,576 bytes (1MB) of external system memory. Although 1MB of RAM is considered almost negligible today, IC designers at the time never suspected that more than 1MB would ever be needed. Both the 8086 and 8088 (as well as all subsequent Intel CPUs) can address 64KB of I/O space (as opposed to RAM space). The 8086 was available for four clock speeds; 5MHz, 6MHz, 8MHz, and 10MHz. Three clock speeds allowed the 8086 to process 0.33, 0.66, and 0.75 MIPS (Millions of Instructions Per Second), respectively. The 8088 was only available in 5MHz and 8MHz versions (for 0.33 and 0.75 MIPS, respectively), but its rather unique multiplexing nature reduces its data bandwidth to only 2MB/s.

TABLE 11-3 COMPARISON OF COMMERCIAL PC CPUs

PROCESSOR	SHIP DATE	BITS	CLOCK (MHZ)	SPEC-92 INF/FP	SPEC-95 INT/FP	UNITS/ ISSUE	PIPE STAGES INT/DST/FP	CACHE KB/ASSOC	VDD (V)	POWER (PEAK)	TRANSISTORS (MILLIONS)
Pre-i386 Processors											
Intel 8086	1978	16	10			1/1	1/1/na		5.0		0.029
Intel 80186	1982	16				1/1	1/1/na		5.0		
Intel 80286	1982	16	12			1/1	1/1/na		5.0		0.134
i386 Series											
Intel i386DX	1985	32	16			1/1			5.0		0.275
Intel i386DX	1989	32	33	9.4/		1/1			5.0		0.275
Intel i386SX	1988	32	16			1/1	4/na/na		5.0		0.275
Intel i386SX	1992	32	33	6.2/3.3		1/1	4/na/na		5.0	2 W	0.275
Intel i386SL	1990	32	25			1/1	4/na/na		5.0		0.855
i486 Series											
Intel i486DX	1989	32	33	22.4/		2/1	5/na/5	8/4	5.0		1.2
Intel i486DX	1991	32	50	33.4/14.5		2/1	5/na/5	8/4	5.0	5 W	1.2
Intel i486SX	1991	32	25	12/		2/1	5/na/5		5.0		1.185
Intel i486SX	1992	32	33	15.9/		2/1	5/na/5		5.0		0.9
Intel i486SL	1992	32	33			2/1	5/na/5				1.4
Intel i486DX2	1992	32	66	39.6/18.8		2/1	5/na/5	8/4	5.0	7 W	1.2
Intel i486DX4	1994	32	100	55/27		2/1	5/na/5	16/4	3.3	4 W	1.6
Classic Pentium (note 1)											
Intel P5	1993	32	66	78/63.6		3/2	5/na/8	8/8 2/2	5.0	16 W	3.1
Intel P54C	1994	32	100	122/93.2	3.3/2.8	3/2	5/na/8	8/8 2/2	3.3	5.0 W	3.1
Intel P54CQS	1995	32	120	157/108	3.8/3.0	3/2	5/na/8	8/8 2/2	3.3	10.0 W	3.1
Intel P54CS	1995	32	133	174/121	4.2/3.3	3/2	5/na/8	8/8 2/2	3.3		3.1

TABLE 11-3 COMPARISON OF COMMERCIAL PC CPUs (CONTINUED)

PROCESSOR	SHIP DATE	BITS	CLOCK (MHZ)	SPEC-92 INF/FP	SPEC-95 INT/FP	UNITS/ ISSUE	PIPE STAGES INT/DST/FP	CACHE KB/ASSOC	VDD (V)	POWER (PEAK)	TRANSISTORS (MILLIONS)
Intel P54CS	1996	32	150	181/125	4.3/3.3	3/2	5/na/8	8/8 2/2	3.3		3.1
Intel P54CS	1996	32	166	198/138	4.8/3.7	3/2	5/na/8	8/8 2/2	3.3		3.1
Intel P54CS	1996	32	200		5.5/4.2	3/2	5/na/8	8/8 2/2	3.45		3.1
Mobile Pentium											
Intel P54VRT	1994	32	75	89.1/68.5	2.4/2.1	3/2	5/na/8	8/8 2/2	2.9	5.2 W	3.1
Intel P54VRT	1994	32	90	110/84.4	2.9/2.5	3/2	5/na/8	8/8 2/2	2.9	6.5 W	3.1
Intel P54VRT	1996	32	120	157/108	3.8/3.0	3/2	5/na/8	8/8 2/2	2.9		3.1
Intel P54VRT	1996	32	133	174/121	4.2/3.3	3/2	5/na/8	8/8 2/2	2.9	3.3 W	3.1
Intel P54VRT	1996	32	150		4.6/3.3	3/2	5/na/8	8/8 2/2	3.1	3.8 W	3.1
Pentium MMX											
Intel P55C	1997	32	166		5.6/4.3	5/2	6/na/8	16/16 4/4	2.8		4.5
Intel P55C	1997	32	200		6.4/4.7	5/2	6/na/8	16/16 4/4	2.8	15.7 W	4.5
Intel P55C	1997	32	233		7.1/5.2	5/2	6/na/8	16/16 4/4	2.8	17 W	4.5
Intel P55C	1997	32	266		5.6/4.3	5/2	6/na/8	16/16 4/4	2.8		4.5
Mobile Pentium MMX											
Intel P55VRT	1997	32	166		5.6/4.3	5/2	6/na/8	16/16 4/4	2.45	7.8 W	4.5
Intel P55VRT	1997	32	200		6.4/4.7	5/2	6/na/8	16/16 4/4	1.8	3.4 W	4.5
Intel P55VRT	1997	32	233		7.1/5.2	5/2	6/na/8	16/16 4/4	1.8	3.9 W	4.5
Pentium Pro Series											
Intel P6	1995	32	150	245/220	6.1/5.4	7/3	14/14/16	8/8	3.1	29.2 W	5.5
Intel P6	1995	32	180		7.3/6.1	7/3	14/14/16	8/8	3.3		5.5
Intel P6	1995	32	200	320/283	8.2/6.8	7/3	14/14/16	8/8	3.3	35 W	5.5

TABLE 11-3 COMPARISON OF COMMERCIAL PC CPUs (CONTINUED)

PROCESSOR	SHIP DATE	BITS	CLOCK (MHZ)	SPEC-92 INF/FP	SPEC-95 INT/FP	UNITS/ ISSUE	PIPE STAGES INT/DST/FP	CACHE KB/ASSOC	VDD (V)	POWER (PEAK)	TRANSISTORS (MILLIONS)
Intel P6	1996	32	166	293/261	7.3/6.2	7/3	14/14/16	8/8	3.3	29.4 W	5.5
Intel P6	1996	32	200		8.7/6.7	7/3	14/14/16	8/8	3.3		5.5
Intel P6	1997	32	200		8.7/6.8	7/3	14/14/16	8/8	3.3		5.5
Pentium II (Klamath) Series											
Intel Pentium II	1997	32	233		9.5/6.4	7/3		16/16	2.8		7.5
Intel Pentium II	1997	32	266		10.8/6.9	7/3		16/16	2.8		7.5
Intel Pentium II	1997	32	300		11.9/8.6	7/3		16/16	2.8		7.5
Upcoming Pentium Processors											
Deschutes	1997	32	350		~14/~11			16/16			
P68	1998	No information available									
Merced (P7)	1999	64									
Early AMD Processors											
Am386	1990	No information available									
Am486	1995	32	120			2/1				3 W	
Am5x86	1995	32	133			2/1		16			
AMD 5k86 Series											
Am5k86	1995	32	75	(PR75)		6/4	5/5/5	16/8 4/4	3.5		4.3
Am5k86	1995	32	90	(PR90)		6/4	5/5/5	16/8 4/4	3.5		4.3
Am5x86	1996	32	100	(PR100)		6/4	5/5/5	16/8 4/4	3.5		4.3
AMD K5 Series											
AMD K5	1996	32	90	(PR120)		6/4	5/5/5	16/8 4/4	3.5		4.3

TABLE 11-3 COMPARISON OF COMMERCIAL PC CPUs (CONTINUED)

PROCESSOR	SHIP DATE	BITS	CLOCK (MHZ)	SPEC-92 INF/FP	SPEC-95 INT/FP	UNITS/ ISSUE	PIPE STAGES INT/DST/FP	CACHE KB/ASSOC	VDD (V)	POWER (PEAK)	TRANSISTORS (MILLIONS)
AMD K5	1996	32	100	(PR133)		6/4	5/5/5	16/8 4/4	3.5	14 W	4.3
AMD K5	1997	32	117	(PR166)		6/4	5/5/5	16/8 4/4	3.5		4.3
AMD K6 Series											
AMD K6	1997	32	166			7/6	6/7/7	32/32 2/2	2.9	17.2 W	8.8
AMD K6	1997	32	200			7/6	6/7/7	32/32 2/2	2.9	20 W	8.8
AMD K6	1997	32	233			7/6	6/7/7	32/32 2/2	3.2	28.3 W	8.8
AMD K6	1997	32	266			7/6	6/7/7	32/32 2/2	8.8		
Cyrix/IBM 486 Series											
486SLC	1992	32				1/1					0.6
486DX4	1993	32	100			2/1		8/4	3.0		1.1
Cyrix/IBM 5x86 Series											
5x86 (M1sc)	1995	32	100			2/1	6/6/?	16/4	3.45	3.5 W	2.0
5x86 (M1sc)	1995	32	120			2/1	6/6/?	16/4	3.3		2.0
Cyrix/IBM MediaGX Series											
5gx86	1996	32	120			2/1	6/6/?	16/4	3.3		2.4
5gx86	1997	32	133			2/1	6/6/?	16/4	3.3		2.4
5gx86	1997	32	150	(PR150)		2/1	6/6/?	16/4	3.3		2.4
Cyrix/IBM 6x86 (M1) Series											
6x86 (M1)	1995	32	100			3/2	7/7/?	16/4	3.3	10 W	3.0
6x86 (M1)	1995	32	120			3/2	7/7/?	16/4	3.3		3.0
6x86 (M1R)	1996	32	100	(PR120)		3/2	7/7/?	16/4	3.3/2.8		3.0

TABLE 11-3 COMPARISON OF COMMERCIAL PC CPUs (CONTINUED)

PROCESSOR	SHIP DATE	BITS	CLOCK (MHZ)	SPEC-92 INF/FP	SPEC-95 INT/FP	UNITS/ ISSUE	PIPE STAGES INT/DST/FP	CACHE KB/ASSOC	VDD (V)	POWER (PEAK)	TRANSISTORS (MILLIONS)
6x86 (M1R)	1996	32	110	(PR133)		3/2	7/7/?	16/4	3.3/2.8		3.0
6x86 (M1R)	1996	32	120	(PR150)		3/2	7/7/?	16/4	3.3/2.8		3.0
6x86 (M1R)	1996	32	133	(PR166)		3/2	7/7/?	16/4	3.3/2.8		3.0
6x86 (M1R)	1996	32	150	(PR200)		3/2	7/7/?	16/4	3.3/2.8		3.0
Cyrix/IBM 6x86MX (M2) Series											
6x86MX (M2)	1997	32	150	(PR166)		3/2	7/7/?	64/4	2.9		6.0
6x86MX (M2)	1997	32	166	(PR200)		3/2	7/7/?	64/4	2.9		6.0
6x86MX (M2)	1997	32	188	(PR233)		3/2	7/7/?	64/4	2.9		6.0
6x86MX (M2)	1997	32	225	(PR266)		3/2	7/7/?	64/4	2.9		6.0
6x86MX (M2)	1998	32	250	(PR300)		3/2	7/7/?	64/4	2.9		6.0
Upcoming Cyrix Processors											
M3	98	No information available									
Nexgen (AMD) Processors											
Nx586	1995	32	93			5/1	7/9/na	16/16	4.0		3.5
Nx586	1995	32	133			5/1	7/9/?	16/16	3.6	16 W	
IDT Series											
IDT C6	1997	32	200			3/1	5/5/?	32/32 2/2			5.4

NOTES: int - integer; fp - floating point; ldst - long word register; kb - kilobyte or KB; Assoc - Associative memory

Even though Pentium-type processors use a 64-bit external data bus, the internal data bus is still 32 bits.

For all intents and purposes, the 8088 is identical to the 8086. They are exactly the same microprocessor—with only one exception: the 8088 multiplexes (time-shares) 8 of the 16 address lines between the address bus and the data bus. If you look at the pinout of an 8088, you will see only 8 data lines available to the outside world (D8 to D15). During one part of a bus cycle, the lower 8 address lines serve as the lower 8 data bits (D0 to D7). During another part of the bus cycle, those 8 shared bits are used as the lower 8 bits of the address bus (A0 to A7). Both CPUs are designed to work with the 8087 MCP.

80186 (1980)

The 16-bit 80186 built on the x86 foundation to offer additional features, such as an internal clock generator, system controller, interrupt controller, Direct Memory Access (DMA) controller, and timer/counter circuitry right on the CPU itself. No Intel CPU before or since has offered so much integration in a single CPU. The x186 was also first to abandon 5MHz clock speeds in favor of 8MHz, 10MHz, and 12.5MHz. Aside from these advances, however, the x186 remained similar to the 8086/8088 with 24 registers and 20 address lines to access up to 1MB of RAM. The x186 were used as CPUs in embedded applications and never saw service in personal computers. The limitations of the early x86 architecture in the PC demanded a much faster CPU capable of accessing far more than 1MB of RAM.

80286 (1982)

The 24-register, 134,000-transistor 80286 CPU (first used in the IBM PC/AT and compatibles) offered some substantial advantages over older CPUs. Design advances allow the i286 to operate at 1.2 MIPS, 1.5 MIPS, and 2.66 MIPS (for 8, 10, and 12.5MHz, respectively). The i286 also breaks the 1MB RAM barrier by offering 24 address lines, instead of 20, which allow it to directly address 16MB of RAM. In addition to 16MB of directly accessible RAM, the i286 can handle up to 1GB (gigabytes) of virtual memory, which allows blocks of program code and data to be swapped between the i286's real memory (up to 16MB) and a secondary (or "virtual") storage location, such as a hard disk. To maintain backward compatibility with the 8086/8088, which can only address 1MB of RAM, the i286 can operate in a real mode. One of the great failings of the i286 is that it can switch from real-mode to protected-mode, but it cannot switch back to real-mode without a warm reboot of the system. The i286 uses a stand-alone math co-processor, the 80287.

80386 (1985–1990)

The next major microprocessor released by Intel was the 275,000-transistor, 32-register, 80386DX CPU in 1985. With a full 32-bit data bus, data throughput is immediately double that of the 80286. The 16, 20, 25, and 33MHz versions allow data throughput up to 50MB/s and processing power up to 11.4 MIPS at 33MHz. A full 32-bit address bus allows direct access to an unprecedented 4GB of RAM in addition to a staggering 64 TB (tera bytes) of virtual memory capacity. The i386 was the first Intel CPU to enhance processing through the use of instruction pipelining, which allows the CPU to start working on a new instruction while waiting for the current instruction to finish. A new operating mode (called the *virtual real-mode*) enables the CPU to run several real-mode sessions simultaneously under operating systems such as Windows.

Intel took a small step backward in 1988 to produce the 80386SX CPU. The i386SX uses 24 address lines for 16MB of addressable RAM and an external data bus of 16 bits, instead of a full 32 bits from the DX. Correspondingly, the processing power for the i386SX is only 3.6 MIPS at 33MHz. In spite of these compromises, this offered a significantly less-expensive CPU, which helped to propagate the i386 family into desktop and portable computers. Aside from changes to the address and bus width, the i386 architecture is virtually unchanged from that of the i386DX.

By 1990, Intel integrated the i386 into an 855,000-transistor, low-power version, called the *80386SL*. The i386SL incorporated an ISA-compatible chip set along with power-management circuitry that optimized the i386 for use in mobile computers. The i386SL resembled the i386SX version in its 24 address lines and 16-bit external data bus.

Each member of the i386 family uses stand-alone math co-processors (80387DX, 80387SX, and 80387SL, respectively). All versions of the 80386 can switch between real-mode and protected-mode, as needed, so they will run the same software as (and are backwardly compatible with) the 80286 and the 8086/8088.

80486 (1989–1994)

The consistent push for higher speed and performance resulted in the development of Intel's 1.2 million-transistor, 29-register, 32-bit microprocessor, called the *80486DX*, in 1989. The i486DX provides full 32-bit addressing for access to 4GB of physical RAM and up to 64TB (tera bytes) of virtual memory. The i486DX offers twice the performance of the i386DX with 26.9 MIPS at 33MHz. Two initial versions (25 and 33MHz) were available.

As with the i386 family, the i486 series uses pipelining to improve instruction execution, but the i486 series also adds 8KB of cache memory right on the IC. Cache saves memory access time by predicting the next instructions that will be needed by the CPU and loading them into the cache memory before the CPU actually needs them. If the needed instruction is indeed in cache, the CPU can access the information from cache without wasting time waiting for memory access. Another improvement of the i486DX is the inclusion of a floating-point unit (an MCP) in the CPU itself, rather than requiring a separate co-processor IC. This is not true of all members of the i486 family, however. A third departure for the i486DX is that it is offered in 5- and 3-V versions. The 3-V version is intended for laptop, notebook, and other low-power mobile computing applications.

Finally, the i486DX is upgradeable. Up to 1989/1990, personal computers were limited by their CPU—when the CPU became obsolete, so did the computer (more specifically the motherboard). This traditionally forced the computer user to purchase new computers (or upgrade the motherboard) every few years to utilize current technology. The architecture of the i486 is intended to support CPU upgrades where a future CPU using a faster internal clock can be inserted into the existing system. Intel has dubbed this as "OverDrive" technology. While OverDrive performance is not as high as a newer PC would be, it is much less expensive, and allows computer users to protect their computer investments for a longer period of time. It is vital to note that not all i486 versions are upgradeable, and the CPU socket on the motherboard itself must be designed specifically to accept an OverDrive CPU (see the "CPU sockets" section).

The i486DX was only the first in a long line of variations from Intel. In 1991, Intel released the 80486SX and the 80486DX/50. Both the i486SX and i486DX/50 offer 32-bit addressing, a 32-bit data path, and 8KB of on-chip cache memory. The i486SX takes a small step backward from the i486DX by removing the math co-processor and offering slower versions at 16, 20, 25, and 33MHz. At 33MHz, the i486SX is rated at 20.2 MIPS. Such design compromises reduced the cost and power dissipation of the i486SX, which accelerated its acceptance into desktop and portable computers. The i486SX is upgradeable with an OverDrive CPU (if the computer's motherboard is designed to accept an OverDrive CPU), is compatible with an 80487 CPU/MCP, and the i486SX is available in 5- and 3-V versions. The i486DX/50 operates at a clock speed of 50MHz, where it performs at 41.1 MIPS. The i486DX/50 does integrate an on-board math co-processor, but it is not OverDrive upgradeable, and it is not available in a 3-V version.

The first wave of OverDrive CPUs arrived in 1992 with the introduction of the 80486DX2/50 and the 80486DX2/66. The "2" along with the "DX" indicates that the IC is using an internal clock that is double the frequency of the system. The i486DX2/50 actually runs in a 25MHz system, yet the CPU performs at 40.5 MIPS. The i486DX2/66 runs in a 33MHz system, but it runs internally at 54.5 MIPS. The slower system speed allowed the CPU to work directly with existing PC motherboard designs. Both OverDrive CPUs offer on-board math co-processors, and are themselves upgradeable to even faster OverDrive versions. The i486DX2/50 is available in 5- and 3-V versions, but the i486DX2/66 is only available in the 5-V version.

In 1992, Intel produced a highly integrated, low-power version of the 80486, called the *80486SL*. Its 32-bit data bus, 32-bit address bus, 8KB of on-board cache, and integrated math co-processor make it virtually identical to other i486 CPUs, but the SL uses 1.4 million transistors. The extra circuitry provides a low-power management capability that optimize the SL for mobile computers. The i486SL is available in 25 and 33MHz versions, as well as 3- and 5-V designs. At 33MHz, the i486SL operates at 26.9 MIPS.

Intel rounded out its i486 family in 1993 with the introduction of three other CPU models: the 80486DX2/40, the 80486SX/SL-enhanced, and the 80486DX/SL-enhanced. The i486DX2/40 is the third OverDrive CPU intended to run in 20MHz PCs, while the CPU's internal clock runs at 40MHz and performs at 21.1 MIPS. The i486SX/SL (26.9 MIPS at 33MHz) and i486DX/SL (26.9 MIPS at 33MHz) are identical to their original SX and DX versions, but the SL enhancement provides power management capability intended to support portable computers, such as notebook and sub-notebook computers.

By 1994, Intel was finishing its work with the i486 series with the DX4 OverDrive processors. Contrary to the DX4 designation, these 3.3-V OverDrive devices are clock triplers—so an i486DX4/100 actually runs at a motherboard clock speed of 33MHz. It is important to note that all versions of the 80486 will run the same software, and are backwardly compatible with all CPUs back to the 8086/8088.

PENTIUM (1993–CURRENT)

By 1992, the i486 series had become well-entrenched in everyday desktop computing, and Intel was already laying the groundwork for its next generation of CPU. Although most users expected Intel to continue with its traditional numbering scheme and dub its next CPU the 80586, legal conflicts regarding trademarking forced Intel to use a name which it could trademark and call its own. In 1993, the 3.21 million-transistor Pentium microprocessor (dubbed "P5" or P54 series) was introduced to eager PC manufacturers. The Pentium retains the 32-bit address bus width of the i486 family. With 32 address bits, the

TABLE 11-4 COMPARISON OF PENTIUM PERFORMANCE RATINGS

PENTIUM PROCESSOR (MHZ)	ICOMP® INDEX 2.0	EXTERNAL BUS FREQUENCY (MHZ)	BUS/CORE RATIO	UPGRADABILITY WITH A PENTIUM OVERDRIVE
200	142	66	1/3	No
166	127	66	2/5	Yes
150	114	60	2/5	Yes
133	111	66	1/2	Yes
120	100	60	1/2	Yes
100	90	66 or 50	2/3 or 1/2	Yes
90	81	60	2/3	Yes
75	67	50	2/3	Yes

Pentium can directly address 4GB of RAM, and can access up to 64TB of virtual memory. The 64-bit external data bus width can handle twice the data throughput of the i486s. At 60MHz, the Pentium performs at 100 MIPS, and 66MHz yields 111.6 MIPS (twice the processing power of the i486DX2/66). Table 11-4 shows a comparison of Pentium performance ratings in versions from 75MHz to 200MHz. All versions of the Pentium include an on-board math co-processor, and are intended to be compatible with future OverDrive designs.

The Pentium uses two 8KB caches—one for instructions and another for data. A dual pipelining technique allows the Pentium to actually work on more than one instruction per clock cycle. Another substantial improvement in the Pentium's design include on-board power-management features (similar to the i486SL line), allowing it to be used effectively in portable computers. Early Pentium models started at 5 V, but all models starting at about 100MHz (P54C) use 3.3 V or less. Finally, the Pentium is fully backward-compatible with all software written for the 8086/8088 and later CPUs. As of this writing, Intel has released various versions of the Pentium up to 200MHz. Faster versions are unlikely because of more powerful processors, such as the Pentium MMX, Pentium Pro, and Pentium II. For technicians who want the nitty-gritty details on Pentium operation, you can download the Pentium processor manuals from the Internet, as listed in Table 11-5.

The number of Pentium versions and features has simply proliferated over the last few years—so much so that it is extremely difficult to tell whether a motherboard is configured properly for a given CPU. However, you can use the S-spec rating marked on each Pentium or Pentium MMX processor to reveal key operating characteristics of the particular CPU. Table 11-6 presents the S-specs for Pentium and Pentium MMX processors.

PENTIUM PRO (1995–CURRENT)

Even though the Pentium has proven adept at handling 16- and 32-bit operating systems, designers continued to seek ways to optimize the Pentium for 32-bit performance—especially for such operating systems Windows NT, and the then-emerging Windows 95. The Pentium Pro (dubbed *P6* or *PPro*) evolved as an "optimized" Pentium intended to support "business

TABLE 11-5 DETAILED CPU MANUALS AND TECHNICAL INFORMATION

Pentium processor manuals: **http://developer.intel.com/design/pentium/manuals/**

Pentium MMX manuals: **http://developer.intel.com/design/mmx/manuals/**

Pentium Pro processor manuals: **http://developer.intel.com/design/pro/manuals/**

Pentium II manuals: **http://developer.intel.com/design/PentiumII/manuals/**

Am486DX2 manual: **http://developer.intel.com/design/PentiumII/manuals/**

Ama486DX2 manual: **http://www.amd.com/products/cpg/techdocs/datasheets/19200d.pdf**

Am486DX4 manual: **http://www.amd.com/products/cpg/techdocs/datasheets/19160d.pdf**

5x85 manual: **http://www.amd.com/products/cpg/techdocs/datasheets/19751c.pdf**

K5 manual: **http://www.amd.com/products/cpg/techdocss/appnotes/18524c.pdf**

K6 manual: **http://www.amd.com/K6/k6docs/pdf/20695e.pdf**

6x86 processor manuals: **http://www.cyrix.com/process/hardwrdc/6x-dbk1.htm**

Cyrix MediaGX: no technical manuals available, check **www.cyrix.com**

6x86MX manuals: **http://www.cyrix.com/process/hardwrdc/6xMx-dbk.htm**

TABLE 11-6 S-SPEC NUMBERS FOR PENTIUM AND PENTIUM MMX PROCESSORS

S-SPEC	MANUFACTURER'S STEP	SPEED (MHZ) CORE / BUS	COMMENTS
Q016	mxA3	150/60	ES, TCP (note 11)
Q017	mxA3	166/66	ES, TCP (note 11)
Q018	xA3	200/66	ES, PPGA (note 12)
Q019	xA3	166/66	ES, PPGA (note 12)
Q020	xA3	150/60	ES, PPGA (note 12)
Q024	mcC0	150/60	TCP/VRT (notes 2, 4)
Q040	mcC0	150/60	SPGA/VRT (notes 2, 4)
Q0540	B1	75/50	ES
Q0541	B1	75/50	ES
Q0542	B1	90/60	STD
Q0543	B1	90/60	DP
Q0563	B1	100/66	STD
Q0587	B1	100/66	VR
Q0601	B1	75/50	TCP mobile
Q0606	B3	75/50	TCP mobile
Q061	mxA3	150/60	ES, PPGA (note 11)
Q0611	B3	90/60	STD
Q0612	B3	90/60	VR
Q0613	B1	90/60	VR
Q0614	B1	100/66	VR
Q062	mxA3	166/66	ES, PPGA (note 11)
Q0628	B3	90/60	STD
Q0653	B5	90/60	STD
Q0654	B5	90/60	VR

TABLE 11-6 S-SPEC NUMBERS FOR PENTIUM AND PENTIUM MMX PROCESSORS (CONTINUED)

S-SPEC	MANUFACTURER'S STEP	SPEED (MHZ) CORE / BUS	COMMENTS
Q0655	B5	90/60	MD
Q0656	B5	100/66	MD
Q0657	B5	100/66	VR, MD
Q0658	B5	100/66	VRE/MD
Q0666	B5	75/50	STD
Q0677	B3	100/66	VRE/MD
Q0686	mA1	75/50	VRT, TCP (notes 4, 2)
Q0689	mA1	75/50	VRT, SPGA (notes 4, 2)
Q0694	mA1	90/60	VRT, TCP (notes 4, 2)
Q0695	mA1	90/60	VRT, SPGA (notes 4, 2)
Q0697	C2	100/50 or 66	STD
Q0698	C2	100/50 or 66	VRE/MD
Q0699	C2	90/60	STD
Q0700	C2	75/50	STD
Q0704	B5	75/50	TCP mobile
Q0707	B5	120/60	VRE/MD (note 1)
Q0708	B5	120/60	STD (note 1)
Q0711	C2	120/60	VRE/MD
Q0725	C2	75/50	TCP mobile
Q0732	C2	120/60	VRE/MD
Q0733	C2	133/66	MD
Q0749	C2	75/50	MD
Q0751	C2	133/66	MD
Q0772	cB1	133/66	STD/no kit (notes 4, 3)
Q0773	cB1	133/66	STD (note 4)
Q0774	cB1	133/66	VRE/MD, no kit (notes 4, 3)
Q0775	C2	133/66	VRE/MD
Q0776	cB1	120/60	STD/no kit (notes 4, 3)
Q0779	mcB1	120/60	VRT, TCP (notes 4, 2)
Q0783	E0	90/60	STD
Q0784	E0	100/50 or 66	STD
Q0785	E0	120/60	VRE
Q0808	mcB1	120/60	3.3 V, SPGA (note 4)
Q0835	cC0	150/60	STD
Q0836	cC0	166/66	VRE/no kit (note 3)
Q0837	E0	75/50	STD
Q0841	cC0	166/66	VRE
Q0843	cC0	133/66	STD/no kit (note 3)
Q0844	cC0	133/66	STD
Q0846	E0	75/50	TCP mobile
Q0848	mA4	75/50	VRT, TCP (notes 2, 4)
Q0849	mA4	90/60	VRT, TCP (notes 2, 4)

TABLE 11-6 S-SPEC NUMBERS FOR PENTIUM AND PENTIUM MMX PROCESSORS (CONTINUED)

S-SPEC	MANUFACTURER'S STEP	SPEED (MHZ) CORE / BUS	COMMENTS
Q0850	mA4	100/66	VRT, TCP (notes 2, 4)
Q0851	mA4	75/50	VRT, SPGA (notes 2, 4)
Q0852	mA4	90/60	VRT, SPGA (notes 2, 4)
Q0853	mA4	100/66	VRT, SPGA (notes 2, 4)
Q0878	cC0	150/60	STD, PPGA (note 9)
Q0879	mcC0	120/60	TCP/VRT (notes 2, 4)
Q0880	mcC0	120/60	SPGA 3.1 V (note 4)
Q0881	mcC0	133/66	TCP/VRT (notes 2, 4)
Q0882	mcC0	133/66	SPGA 3.1 V (note 4)
Q0884	mcB1	100/66	VRT, TCP (notes 4, 2)
Q0886	cC0	166/66	VRE, PPGA (note 9)
Q0887	mcC0	100/66	TCP/VRT (notes 2, 4)
Q0890	cC0	166/66	VRE, PPGA (note 9)
Q0906	mcC0	150/60	TCP 3.1 V (note 4)
Q0949	cC0	166/66	VRE, PPGA (notes 8, 9)
Q0951	cC0	200/66	VRE, PPGA (note 8, 9)
Q0951F	cC0	200/66	VRE, PPGA (note 9, 10)
Q115	mxB1	166/66	ES, TCP (note 11)
Q116	mxB1	150/60	ES, TCP (note 11)
Q124	xB1	200/66	ES, PPGA (note 12)
Q125	xB1	166/66	ES, PPGA (note 12)
Q126	xB1	166/66	ES, SPGA (note 12)
Q127	mxB1	166/66	ES, PPGA (note 11)
Q128	mxB1	150/60	ES, PPGA (note 11)
Q129	mxB1	133/66	ES, PPGA (note 11)
Q130	mxB1	133/66	ES, TCP (note 11)
Q140	xB1	233/66	ES, PPGA (note 12)
S106J	cB1	133/66	STD/no kit (notes 4, 7, 3)
SK079	C2	75/50	TCP mobile
SK086	C2	120/60	VRE/MD
SK089	mA1	75/50	VRT, TCP (notes 4, 2)
SK090	mA1	90/60	VRT, TCP (notes 4, 2)
SK091	mA1	75/50	VRT, SPGA (notes 4, 2)
SK092	mA1	90/60	VRT, SPGA (notes 4, 2)
SK098	C2	133/66	MD
SK106	cB1	133/66	STD/no kit (notes 4, 3)
SK107	cB1	133/66	STD (note 4)
SK110	cB1	120/60	STD/no kit (notes 4, 3)
SK113	mcB1	120/60	VRT, TCP (notes 4, 2)
SK118	mcB1	120/60	VRT, TCP (notes 4, 7, 2)

TABLE 11-6 S-SPEC NUMBERS FOR PENTIUM AND PENTIUM MMX PROCESSORS (CONTINUED)

S-SPEC	MANUFACTURER'S STEP	SPEED (MHZ) CORE / BUS	COMMENTS
SK119	mA4	75/50	VRT, TCP (notes 2, 4)
SK120	mA4	90/60	VRT, TCP (notes 2, 4)
SK121	mA4	100/66	VRT, TCP (notes 2, 4)
SK122	mA4	75/50	VRT, SPGA (notes 2, 4)
SK123	mA4	90/60	VRT, SPGA (notes 2, 4)
SK124	mA4	100/66	VRT, SPGA (notes 2, 4)
SL22F	mxA3	166/66	TCP (note 11)
SL22G	mxA3	150/60	TCP (note 11)
SL22M	cC0	120/60	STD (note 6)
SL22Q	cC0	133/66	STD (note 6)
SL239	xA3	166/66	SPGA (note 12)
SL23R	xA3	166/66	PPGA (note 5, 9, 12)
SL23S	xA3	200/66	PPGA (notes 5, 9, 12)
SL23T	xA3	166/66	SPGA (note 6, 12)
SL23V	xB1	166/66	PPGA (notes 6, 9, 12)
SL23W	xB1	200/66	PPGA (notes 6, 9, 12)
SL23X	xB1	166/66	SPGA (notes 6, 12)
SL23Z	mxA3	166/66	PPGA (note 11)
SL246	mxA3	150/60	PPGA (note 11)
SL24Q	cC0	200/66	VRE, PPGA, no kit (notes 3, 8, 9, 13)
SL24R	cC0	166/66	VRE, no kit (notes 3, 13)
SL25H	cC0	200/66	VRE, PPGA (notes 6, 9)
SL25J	cC0	120/60	STD (note 5)
SL25L	cC0	133/66	STD (note 5)
SL25M	xA3	166/66	PPGA (note 6, 9, 12)
SL25N	xA3	200/66	PPGA (notes 6, 9, 12)
SL26H	xA3	166/66	PPGA (notes 12, 13)
SL26J	xA3	200/66	PPGA (notes 12, 13, 15)
SL26Q	xA3	200/66	PPGA (notes 5, 9, 12, 13)
SL26T	mxB1	166/66	TCP (note 11)
SL26U	mxB1	150/60	TCP (note 11)
SL26V	xA3	166/66	SPGA (notes 12, 13)
SL274	xA3	200/66	PPGA (notes 6, 9, 12, 13)
SL27A	mxB1	166/66	PPGA (note 11)
SL27B	mxB1	150/60	PPGA (note 11)
SL27C	mxB1	133/66	PPGA (note 11)
SL27D	mxB1	133/66	TCP (note 11)
SL27H	xB1	166/66	PPGA (note 12)
SL27J	xB1	200/66	PPGA (note 12)
SL27K	xB1	166/66	SPGA (note 12)
SL27S	xB1	233/66	PPGA (note 12)

TABLE 11-6 S-SPEC NUMBERS FOR PENTIUM AND PENTIUM MMX PROCESSORS (CONTINUED)

S-SPEC	MANUFACTURER'S STEP	SPEED (MHZ) CORE / BUS	COMMENTS
SL293	xB1	233/66	PPGA (notes 6, 9, 12)
SL2BM	xB1	233/66	PPGA (notes 5, 9, 12)
SL2FP	xB1	166/66	PPGA (notes 5, 9, 12)
SL2FQ	xB1	200/66	PPGA (notes 5, 9, 12)
SL2HX	xB1	166/66	SPGA (notes 5, 12)
SU031	C2	90/60	STD (note 6)
SU032	C2	100/50 or 66	STD (note 6)
SU033	C2	120/60	VRE/MD (note 6)
SU038	cB1	133/66	STD/no kit (notes 4, 6, 3)
SU070	C2	75/50	STD (note 6)
SU071	cC0	150/60	STD (note 6)
SU072	cC0	166/66	VRE, no kit (note 3, 6)
SU073	cC0	133/66	STD/ no kit (notes 3, 6)
SU097	E0	75/50	STD (note 5)
SU098	E0	75/50	STD (note 6)
SU099	E0	100/50 or 66	STD (note 6)
SU100	E0	120/60	STD (note 6)
SU110	E0	100/50 or 66	STD (note 5)
SU114	cC0	200/66	VRE, PPGA (notes 5, 8, 9, 14)
SX874	B1	90/60	DP, STD
SX879	B1	90/60	STD
SX885	B1	90/60	MD
SX886	B1	100/66	MD
SX909	B1	90/60	VR
SX910	B1	100/66	VR, MD
SX921	B3	90/60	MD
SX922	B3	90/60	VR
SX923	B3	90/60	STD
SX942	B3	90/60	DP, STD
SX943	B3	90/60	DP, VR
SX944	B3	90/60	DP, MD
SX951	B3	75/50	TCP mobile
SX957	B5	90/60	STD
SX958	B5	90/60	VR
SX959	B5	90/60	MD
SX960	B3	100/66	VRE/MD
SX961	B5	75/50	STD
SX962	B5	100/66	VRE/MD
SX963	C2	100/50 or 66	STD

TABLE 11-6   S-SPEC NUMBERS FOR PENTIUM AND PENTIUM MMX PROCESSORS (CONTINUED)

S-SPEC	MANUFACTURER'S STEP	SPEED (MHZ) CORE / BUS	COMMENTS
SX968	C2	90/60	STD
SX969	C2	75/50	STD
SX970	C2	100/50 or 66	VRE/MD
SX975	B5	75/50	TCP mobile
SX994	C2	120/60	VRE/MD
SX998	C2	75/50	MD
SX999	mcB1	120/60	3.3 V, SPGA (note 4)
SY005	E0	75/50	STD
SY006	E0	90/60	STD
SY007	E0	100/50 or 66	STD
SY009	E0	75/50	TCP mobile
SY015	cC0	150/60	STD
SY016	cC0	166/66	VRE, no kit (note 3)
SY017	cC0	166/66	VRE
SY019	mcC0	133/66	TCP/VRT (notes 2, 4)
SY020	mcC0	100/66	TCP/VRT (notes 2, 4)
SY021	mcC0	120/60	TCP/VRT (notes 2, 4)
SY022	cC0	133/66	STD/no kit (note 3)
SY023	cC0	133/66	STD
SY027	mcC0	120/60	SPGA 3.1 V (note 4)
SY028	mcC0	133/66	SPGA 3.1 V (note 4)
SY029	mcB1	100/66	VRT, TCP (notes 4, 2)
SY030	mcC0	120/60	SPGA 3.3 V (note 4)
SY033	E0	120/60	STD
SY037	cC0	166/66	VRE, PPGA (notes 8, 9)
SY043	mcC0	150/60	TCP 3.1 V (note 4)
SY044	cC0	200/66	VRE, PPGA (note 9)
SY045	cC0	200/66	VRE, PPGA (notes 8, 9, 15)
SY046	mcC0	100/66	SPGA 3.1 V (note 4)
SY056	mcC0	75/50	TCP/VRT (notes 2, 4)
SY058	mcC0	150/60	SPGA/VRT (notes 2, 4)
SY059	xA3	166/66	PPGA (note 12)
SY060	xA3	200/66	PPGA (note 12)
SY061	mcC0	150/60	TCP/VRT (notes 2, 4)
SY062	cC0	120/60	STD
SZ951	B3	90/60	STD (note 5)
SZ977	B5	75/50	STD (note 5)
SZ978	B5	90/60	STD (note 5)
SZ994	C2	75/50	STD (note 5)

TABLE 11-6 S-SPEC NUMBERS FOR PENTIUM AND PENTIUM MMX PROCESSORS (CONTINUED)

S-SPEC	MANUFACTURER'S STEP	SPEED (MHZ) CORE / BUS	COMMENTS
SZ995	C2	90/60	STD (note 5)
SZ996	C2	100/50 or 66	STD (note 5)

NOTES:

■ *PPGA, TCP,* and *SPGA* are all case styles.

■ *ES* means "engineering sample."

■ *DP* means for use in a "dual processor" configuration only.

■ *Mobile* means the CPU was developed for mobile operation.

■ *MD* means designed to accommodate "minimum timing."

■ *VR* means "voltage reduced" (3.3–3.465 V).

■ *VRE* means the CPU uses 3.4–3.6 V.

■ *VRT* means the CPU uses "split voltage" (2.8 V/3.3 V).

■ *STD* means "standard part" using normal timing and 3.135–3.6 V.

1. $T^{CASE} = 60°C$.

2. VRT (Voltage-Reduction Technology): The V_{CC} for I/O is 3.3 V, but the core V_{CC} (accounting for about 90% of power usage) is reduced to 2.9 V to reduce power consumption and heating.

3. "No kit" means that part meets the specifications (but is not tested) to support 82498/82493 and 82497/82492 cache timings.

4. The cB1 step is logically equivalent to the C2-step, but on a different manufacturing process. The mcB1 step is logically equivalent to the cB1 step (except it does not support DP, APIC or FRC). The mcB1, mA1, mA4, and mcC0-steps also use VRT (see note 2) and are available in the TCP and/or SPGA package, primarily to support mobile applications. The mxA3 is logically equivalent to the xA3 step (except it does not support DP or APIC). All mobile steps are distinguished by an additional "m" prefix, for "mobile." All steps of the Pentium MMX are distinguished by an additional "x" prefix.

5. This is a boxed Pentium processor *without* an attached fan heatsink.

6. This is a boxed Pentium processor *with* an attached fan heatsink.

7. These parts do not support boundary scan testing. S106J was previously marked (and is the same as) SK106J.

8. DP, FRC, and APIC features are not supported on these parts.

9. These parts are packaged in the Plastic Pin Grid Array (PPGA) package.

10. Some Q0951F units are marked on the bottom side with spec number Q0951 and with an additional line immediately underneath spelling out "Full Feature" to properly identify the unit.

11. This is a mobile Pentium MMX with a core operating voltage of 2.285 V – 2.665 V.

12. This is a desktop Pentium MMX with a core operating voltage of 2.7 V – 2.9 V.

13. The part may run only at the maximum specified frequency. A 200MHz unit might be run at 200MHz +0/–5MHz (195 – 200MHz) and a 166MHz can be run at 166 MHz +0/–5MHz (161 – 166MHz).

14. SU114 units are marked on the bottom side with a VMU code of "VSS." This is incorrect—the proper code should read "VSU" because the units do not support DP, FRC, or APIC features. This spec number has been discontinued and is replaced by spec number SY045.

15. This part ships as a boxed processor with an unattached fan heatsink.

systems," such as high-end desktop workstations and network servers. The P6 processors range from 150MHz to 200MHz, and can handle multiprocessing in systems up to four CPUs.

The Pentium Pro uses dynamic execution to improve its performance, and uses two separate 8KB L1 caches—one for data, and one for instructions. Another major improvement in the Pentium Pro is its use of up to 1MB of on-board L2 cache. This maximizes the P6's performance without relying on the motherboard to supply L2 cache. You can see the use of L1 and L2 cache and Pentium Pro family performance in Table 11-7.

Although not as prolific as the "classic" Pentium and Pentium MMX, there are still a number of Pentium Pro versions and features to contend with—this can make it difficult to determine the proper motherboard configuration for a given P6. However, you can use the S-spec rating marked on each Pentium Pro processor to reveal key operating characteristics of the particular CPU. Table 11-8 presents the S-specs for Pentium Pro processors.

TABLE 11-7 COMPARISON OF PENTIUM PRO PERFORMANCE RATINGS

CORE FREQUENCY	OPERATING VOLTAGE	L2 CACHE SIZE	L1 INST./DATA CACHE SIZE	DYNAMIC EXECUTION	SPECINT95	SPECFP95
150 MHz	3.1 V	256KB	8KB/8KB	Yes	6.08	5.42
166 MHz	3.3 V	512KB	8KB/8KB	Yes	7.11	6.21
180 MHz	3.3 V	256KB	8KB/8KB	Yes	7.29	6.08
200 MHz	3.3 V	256KB	8KB/8KB	Yes	8.09	6.75
200 MHz	3.3 V	512KB	8KB/8KB	Yes	n/a	n/a
200 MHz	3.3 V	1MB	8KB/8KB	Yes	n/a	n/a

TABLE 11-8 S-SPEC NUMBERS FOR PENTIUM PRO PROCESSORS

S-SPEC	MANUFACTURER'S STEP	L2 SIZE (KB)	SPEED (MHZ) CORE / BUS	COMMENTS
Q008	sB1	512	166/66	Note 4
Q009	sB1	512	166/66	Note 4
Q010	sB1	512	200/66	Note 4
Q011	sB1	512	200/66	Note 4
Q033	sB1	256	180/60	Note 4
Q034	sB1	256	200/66	Note 4
Q035	sB1	256	180/60	Note 4
Q036	sB1	256	200/66	Note 7
Q076	sA1	256	133/66	Notes 3, 4
Q0812	B0	256	133/66	Notes 3, 4
Q0813	B0	256	150/60	Notes 3, 4
Q0815	B0	256	133/66	Notes 3, 4
Q0816	B0	256	150/60	Notes 3, 4
SY002	B0	256	150/60	Note 3
SY011	B0	256	150/60	
SY014	B0	256	150/60	
Q0822	C0	256	150/60	Notes 3, 4
Q0825	C0	256	150/60	Note 4
Q0826	C0	256	150/60	Note 4
SY010	C0	256	150/60	

TABLE 11-8 S-SPEC NUMBERS FOR PENTIUM PRO PROCESSORS (CONTINUED)

S-SPEC	MANUFACTURER'S STEP	L2 SIZE (KB)	SPEED (MHZ) CORE / BUS	COMMENTS
Q0858	sA0	256	180/60	Notes 2, 4
Q0859	sA0	256	200/66	Notes 2, 4
Q0860	sA0	256	180/60	Notes 2, 4, 5
Q0861	sA0	256	200/66	Notes 2, 4, 5
Q0864	sA0	512	166/66	Notes 2, 4, 6
Q0865	sA0	512	200/66	Notes 2, 4, 6
Q0873	sA0	256	180/60	Notes 2, 4
Q0874	sA0	256	200/66	Notes 2, 4
Q0910	sA0	256	180/60	Note 2
SY012	sA0	256	180/60	Note 2
SY013	sA0	256	200/66	Note 2
Q076	sA1	256	200/66	Note 7
Q0871	sA1	256	180/60	Note 4
Q0872	sA1	256	200/66	Note 4
Q0907	sA1	256	180/60	Note 4
Q0908	sA1	256	200/66	Note 4
Q0909	sA1	256	200/66	Note 4
Q0918	sA1	512	166/66	Notes 4, 6
Q0920	sA1	512	200/66	Notes 4, 6
Q0924	sA1	512	200/66	Notes 4, 6
Q0929	sA1	512	166/66	Note 4
Q932	sA1	512	200/66	Note 4
Q935	sA1	512	166/66	Note 4
Q936	sA1	512	200/66	Note 4
SL245	sA1	256	200/66	Note 7
SL247	sA1	256	200/66	Note 7
SU103	sA1	256	180/60	
SU104	sA1	256	200/66	
SY031	sA1	256	180/60	
SY032	sA1	256	200/66	
SY034	sA1	512	166/66	
SY039	sA1	256	180/60	
SY040	sA1	256	200/66	
SY047	sA1	512	166/66	
SY048	sA1	512	200/66	
Q008	sB1	512	166/66	Note 4
Q009	sB1	512	166/66	Note 4
Q010	sB1	512	200/66	Note 4
Q011	sB1	512	200/66	Note 4
Q033	sB1	256	180/60	Note 4
Q034	sB1	256	200/66	Note 4
Q035	sB1	256	180/60	Note 4

TABLE 11-8 S-SPEC NUMBERS FOR PENTIUM PRO PROCESSORS (CONTINUED)				
S-SPEC	MANUFACTURER'S STEP	L2 SIZE (KB)	SPEED (MHZ) CORE / BUS	COMMENTS
Q036	sB1	256	200/66	Note 4
Q083	sB1	256	200/66	Note 7
Q084	sB1	256	200/66	Note 7
SL22S	sB1	256	180/60	
SL22T	sB1	256	200/66	
SL22U	sB1	256	180/60	
SL22V	sB1	256	200/66	
SL22X	sB1	512	166/66	
SL22Z	sB1	512	200/66	
SL23L	sB1	256	180/60	
SL23M	sB1	256	200/66	
SL254	sB1	256	200/66	Note 7
SL255	sB1	256	200/66	Note 7

NOTES:

1. L2 Cache refers to the silicon revision of the 256KB or 512KB on-chip L2 cache.
2. The sA0 step is logically equivalent to the C0 step, but on a different manufacturing process.
3. The VID pins are not supported on these parts.
4. These are engineering samples only.
5. The VID pins are functional but not tested on these parts.
6. These sample parts are equipped with a pre-production 512KB L2 cache.
7. These components have additional specification changes associated with them:
    a) Primary voltage = 3.5 V ± 5%
    b) Max. thermal design power = 39.4 W @ 200MHz, 256K L2
    c) Current = 11.9A
    d) The VID pins are not supported on these parts.
    e) T9 = *Minimum GTL + Input hold time* = 0.9 ns
    f) *Minimum non-GTL + Input high voltage* = 2.2 V

PENTIUM MMX (1997–CURRENT)

The data-processing demands imposed by "multimedia" applications continue to be a burden to most PCs—especially for graphics-intensive games and other video applications. In 1997, Intel released an important enhancement to the Pentium, known as *MultiMedia eXtensions (MMX)*. By streamlining and improving the existing Pentium architecture, and adding 57 new "MMX instructions," the Pentium MMX seems poised as the premier mid-range CPU into the late 1990s. With current speeds at 166MHz (iCOMP 2.0 = 160), 200MHz (iCOMP 2.0 = 182), and 233MHz (iCOMP 2.0 = 203), the Pentium MMX can typically execute existing software 10 to 20% faster than "classic" Pentium processors at the same clock speed. When using software written specifically for "MMX instructions," the PC can deliver higher color depths and higher resolutions, while still maintaining high frame rates for rendering and video.

The Pentium MMX has doubled code and data caches to 16KB each. Larger separate internal caches improve performance by reducing the average memory access time and providing fast access to recently used instructions and data. The data cache supports a write-back (or write-through on a line-by-line basis) policy for memory updates. Pentium MMX processors also use improved dynamic branch prediction to boost performance by predicting the most likely set of instructions to be executed.

Many other features are included in the Pentium MMX line. The superscalar architecture is capable of executing two integer instructions in parallel in a single clock cycle for improved integer-processing performance. A pipelined *Floating-Point Unit (FPU)* supporting 32-bit, 64-bit, and 80-bit formats is capable of executing two floating-point instructions in a single clock. An additional instruction pipe has been added to further improve instruction processing. A pool of four write buffers is now shared between the dual pipelines to improve memory write performance. Also, a multiprocessor interrupt controller is on the chip to allow low-cost symmetric multiprocessing (SMP), and SL technology power-management features for efficient power control. Table 11-6 lists the S-spec numbers for Pentium MMX processors.

PENTIUM II (1997–CURRENT)

With the Pentium MMX and Pentium Pro processors firmly entrenched in the PC community, Intel sought to combine the best features of both—the software performance of the Pentium Pro and the multimedia performance of the Pentium MMX. The result appeared in 1997 as the Pentium II (PII, previously dubbed the "Klamath"). As with the Pentium Pro, the Pentium II is optimized for use with 32-bit operating systems and software (such as Windows 95 or Windows NT), yet the PII also includes the architecture and 57 new instructions needed to handle MMX applications. At 266MHz, the Pentium II processor can provide from 1.6 to over 2 times the performance of a 200MHz Pentium processor.

The Pentium II also uses the dynamic execution technology used in the Pentium Pro. Dynamic execution uses multiple branch prediction to predict the flow of the program through several branches (accelerating the flow of work to the processor). A data-flow analysis then creates an optimized (reordered) schedule of instructions by analyzing the relationships between instructions. And speculative execution finally carries out the instructions "speculatively" (believing the execution order to be correct) based on this optimized schedule. Dynamic execution keeps the processor's superscaler "execution engines" busy and boosts overall performance.

The Pentium II uses a 32KB L1 cache—this allows a 16KB cache for data, and a 16KB cache for instructions. It also provides 512KB of L2 cache right in the CPU package to maximize the processor's performance without relying on the motherboard for cache. The PII supports up to 64GB of physical RAM and allows dual processors; thus, motherboards can be designed for basic symmetric multiprocessing (SMP). A pipelined Floating-Point Unit (FPU) supporting 32-bit, 64-bit, and 80-bit formats is capable of executing two floating-point instructions in a single clock, and sustaining over 300 million floating point instructions per second at 300MHz. Table 11-9 outlines the performance comparison for Pentium II processors at 233MHz, 266MHz, and 300MHz.

One of the most noticeable departures from previous CPUs is the package style. Intel has abandoned the use of Socket 7 (Pentium) and Socket 8 (Pentium Pro) packages, and adopted a "cartridge style" package, known as the *Single-Edge Contact (SEC) cartridge*.

TABLE 11-9   COMPARISON OF PENTIUM II PERFORMANCE RATINGS

FREQUENCY	CACHE SIZE	SPECINT95	SPECFP95	INTELMEDIA BENCHMARK	ICOMP INDEX 2.0
233 MHz	512KB	9.49	6.43	310.40	267
266 MHz	512KB	10.80	6.89	350.77	303
300 MHz	512KB	11.60	7.20	—	—

TABLE 11-10   S-SPEC NUMBERS FOR PENTIUM II PROCESSORS

S-SPEC	MANUFACTURER'S STEP	L2 SIZE (KB)	TAG RAM STEP	MEMORY SUPPORT	SPEED (MHZ) CORE/BUS
SL264	C0	512	B0	non-ECC	233/66
SL265	C0	512	B0	non-ECC	266/66
SL268	C0	512	B0	ECC	233/66
SL269	C0	512	B0	ECC	266/66
SL28R	C0	512	B0	ECC	300/66
SL2HD	C1	512	B0	non-ECC	233/66
SL2HC	C1	512	B0	non-ECC	266/66
SL2HF	C1	512	B0	ECC	233/66
SL2HE	C1	512	B0	ECC	266/66
SL2HA	C1	512	B0	ECC	300/66

Although not nearly as prolific as the "classic" Pentium and Pentium MMX (or even as prolific as the Pentium Pro), there are still a number of Pentium II versions and features to contend with—this can make it difficult to determine the proper motherboard configuration for a given PII. However, you can use the S-spec rating marked on each Pentium II processor to reveal key operating characteristics of the particular CPU. Table 11-10 presents the S-specs for Pentium II processors.

THE AMD CPUs

Advanced Micro Devices (AMD), once Intel's ally, has become its single biggest competitor. AMD is known for providing well-designed and highly compatible "alternative" processors to the PC industry, and has been active in processor manufacturing and marketing since the days of the 386 (such as AMD's Am386). Although AMD tends to lag behind the release of new Intel CPUs, that gap is closing fast—especially with some of AMD's latest products.

AM486DX SERIES (1994–1995)

The Am486 series (see Table 11-3) was AMD's answer to Intel's i486 clock doubling and tripling OverDrive processors of the early 1990s. They incorporate write-back cache and enhanced power-management features; including 3-volt operation, SMM (system management mode), and clock control (appealing for Energy Star-compliant "green" desktop systems and portable PCs). Available as Am486DX4/75, Am486DX4/100, and Am486DX4/120, the AMD 486 line saw service in many late-model 486 platforms.

AM5X86 (1995–CURRENT)

This is really the processor that put AMD "on the map." With the appearance of Intel's Pentium line, PC users were faced with the choice of upgrading their motherboard to accommodate a "true" Pentium CPU, or use a "Pentium OverDrive" processor in a 486 system. AMD rose to the challenge by developing the Am5x86 (or simply 5x86) as an alternative to Intel's Pentium OverDrive processors. The Am5x86 achieves Pentium-level performance by running "clock quadrupled" at 133MHz (using a 33MHz bus speed). This native 33MHz speed also supported the then-emerging 33MHz PCI bus perfectly. Additional features, such as a unified 16KB cache using write-back technology, further improved the 5x86's performance. In operation, Am5x86 microprocessors provided greater performance than a Pentium 75MHz while costing far less than a Pentium at the time. The 5x86 became the standard CPU upgrade for 486 owners who wanted utilize Pentium-class software without a major hardware upgrade.

The 5x86 also offered integrated power-management features: 3-V operation, SMM, and clock control. This allowed the 5x86 to consume less power and run cooler than Pentium 75MHz or i486DX4/100 processors. Both desktop and mobile PCs benefited from these features.

K5 SERIES (1996–CURRENT)

Although the Am5x86 proved to be an extremely popular processor, it was not a "true" Pentium alternative. It was not until 1996 that AMD released its K5 series to the PC industry. As a "true" Pentium alternative, it is fully compatible with Socket 7 (Pentium) motherboards—a drop-in replacement. At most, the K5 might require a motherboard BIOS upgrade for proper identification and support with the motherboard's chipset. But the K5 is fully compatible with all x86 operating systems and software.

The K5 series is rated using the "P-rating" (PR) system (see "The P-rating system" section). Rather than using iCOMP or SPEC benchmarks to categorize the processor's performance, each K5 is assigned a PR number that corresponds to an Intel Pentium operating at the given clock speed. For example, a K5 PR120 performs equivalently to a true Pentium at 120MHz. Table 11-11 lists a comparison of K5 performance figures.

K6 SERIES (1997–CURRENT)

The K6 processor is AMD's most ambitious and timely processor design for the PC. Based on AMD's RISC86 superscalar micro-architecture, the K6 is touted as being competitive with Intel's Pentium II processor in terms of performance. The K6 also incorporates a full suite of support for MMX instructions, and should be fully compatible with all x86 operating systems and software (as well as software designed for MMX enhancements). Because the K6 continues to use the well-established Socket 7 architecture, it

TABLE 11-11 COMPARISON OF AMD K5 PERFORMANCE RATINGS

PROCESSOR	VOLTAGE	BUS SPEED	CLOCK MULTIPLIER PINS
AMD-K5-PR75	3.52 V	50MHz	BF = high
AMD-K5-PR90	3.52 V	60MHz	BF = high
AMD-K5-PR100	3.52 V	66MHz	BF = high
AMD-K5-PR120	3.52 V	60MHz	BF0 = low, BF1 = high
AMD-K5-PR133	3.52 V	66MHz	BF0 = low, BF1 = high
AMD-K5-PR166	3.52 V	66MHz	BF0 = low, BF1 = low

should serve as a drop-in replacement for K5 and Pentium CPUs to provide MMX capability. At most, the K6 might require an upgrade to the motherboard BIOS for proper identification and support with the motherboard chipset.

The K6 incorporates seven parallel "execution engines" and uses two-level branch prediction. When coupled with speculative and full out-of-order execution techniques, the K6 is poised to present a serious challenge to Intel's Pentium MMX and Pentium II processors. A large 64KB L1 cache provides 32KB for data and 32KB for instructions. The IEEE 754-compatible floating-point unit (FPU) should provide performance at least equivalent to the Pentium MMX, and full support for SMM (System Management Mode) should ensure excellent power control.

The Cyrix CPUs

Cyrix emerged as a major "alternative" processor manufacturer in 1992 with their release of the Cyrix 486SLC, and later in 1993 with the 486DX4. By 1995, the Cyrix 5x86 (the M1sc) had presented the only serious competition to the AMD 5x86. Based in no small part on their relationship with IBM, Cyrix has established itself in the PC industry behind Intel and AMD, but they have been working very hard to close the technology and performance gap that seems to have plagued some of the recent Cyrix offerings.

6X86 SERIES (1995–CURRENT)

Cyrix introduced their 6x86 (dubbed the M1—later versions were called *M1R*) in 1995 as an answer to the Intel Pentium optimized for both 16-bit and 32-bit software. The 6x86 Socket 7 processor achieves its performance through the use of two optimized super-pipelined integer units and an on-chip FPU. The integer and floating-point units are tailored for maximum instruction throughput by using register renaming, out-of-order completion, data-dependency removal, branch prediction, and speculative execution. It includes a 16KB unified write-back cache. In most respects, the 6x86 uses many of the same techniques found in other Pentium-class processors.

The 6x86 series uses "P-rating" (or PR) figures instead of iCOMP or SPEC numbers to indicate relative performance. For example, a Cyrix PR150+ processor will perform as well as a Pentium processor running at 150MHz. You'll find PR120+, PR133+, PR150+,

TABLE 11-12 CLOCK SETTINGS FOR THE CYRIX 6X86 FAMILY

PR120+ = 50MHz CPU bus with a 2× clock (50/100MHz)

PR133+ = 55MHz CPU bus with a 2× clock (55/110MHz)

PR150+ = 60MHz CPU bus with a 2× clock (60/120MHz), same as Pentium-120

PR166+ = 66MHz CPU bus with a 2× clock (66/133MHz), same as Pentium-133

PR200+ = 75MHz CPU bus with a 2× clock (75/150MHz)

PR166+, and PR200+ versions of the 6x86 available (the "+" indicates performance better than the corresponding Pentium). Table 11-12 outlines the various clock settings for each version.

The Cyrix 6x86 has two drawbacks. First, the floating-point unit (FPU) does not perform as well as those of similar Intel and AMD processors. Although this does not really affect most basic software and operating systems, math-intensive programs (especially 3D computer games) can suffer reduced performance. Little can be done with this issue in the 6x86 family, although subsequent processors (like the M2) should provide a better FPU. The second drawback to the 6x86 has been excessive heating. In operation, 6x86 processors produce more heat than their AMD or Intel counterparts. Cyrix has addressed this issue by releasing the 6x86L (or M1R) series in 1996. The "L" designation means "low power." More specifically, the 6x86L uses a split voltage of 3.3 V to handle I/O operations with other chips, and 2.8 V to run the core of the CPU itself. Traditional 6x86 processors use 3.3 or 3.52 V only. To support a 6x86L, a motherboard must provide split voltages, or a voltage regulator module must be added between the CPU socket and processor.

The split voltage operation of a 6x86L uses the same voltage levels as an MMX processor. However, the 6x86L is not an MMX processor. These split voltages were chosen so that the 6x86L would be compatible with split-voltage motherboards, and could be later replaced with an MMX-compatible device, such as the 6x86MX (or M2).

MEDIAGX (1996–CURRENT)

Traditional PCs need to use stand-alone media-related devices, such as a video card and a sound card. This increases the overall cost of a PC and opens the opportunity for hardware conflicts. The Cyrix MediaGX processor incorporates the features of audio and video, along with many other conventional motherboard components. This high level of integration provides the basis for low-cost entry-level systems that still offer good performance. The 3.3- to 3.6-V MediaGX system actually consists of two chips—the MediaGX processor itself and the MediaGX Cx5510 companion chip.

The MediaGX processor is a 64-bit device with a proven x86-compatible processor core. The CPU directly interfaces to a PCI bus and DRAM memory. High-quality SVGA graphics are provided by an advanced graphics accelerator right on the MediaGX processor. The graphics frame buffer is stored in main memory without the performance degradation associated with traditional Unified Memory Architecture (UMA) system designs because of Cyrix's Display Compression Technology (DCT) approach. The processor is available at 133, 150, 166, and 180MHz. It includes a 16KB unified L1 cache, a floating-point unit, and enhanced System Management Mode (SMM) features. The PCI controller handles fixed, rotating, hybrid, or ping pong bus arbitration. It supports four masters (three on PCI bus). It uses a synchronous CPU/PCI bus frequency, and supports concurrent CPU and PCI operations. The video system supports up to 1280-x-1024-x-8, and 1024-x-768-x-16 display modes. The MediaGX also works with EDO RAM, and supports up to 128MB of RAM in four banks.

The MediaGX Cx5510 companion chip represents a new generation of integrated, single-chip controllers for Cyrix's line of MediaGX-compatible processors. The Cx5510 bridges the MediaGX processor over the PCI bus to the ISA bus, performs traditional chipset functions, and supports a sound interface compatible with industry-standard sound cards, such as the Creative Labs Sound Blaster.

The key issue with the MediaGX series is that it is not Socket 7 compatible. The MediaGX and companion chip are a surface-mounted solution designed for dedicated motherboards. This means that MediaGX motherboards are not upgradeable to other Socket 7 processors.

6X86MX (M2) (1997-CURRENT)

The 6x86MX (referred to as the *M2*) is the Cyrix response to such MMX processors as the AMD K6 and Intel Pentium MMX. The 6x86MX design quadruples the original 6x86 internal cache size to 64KB, and increases the operating frequency to 200MHz and beyond. Additionally, it features the 57 new MMX instructions that speed up the processing of certain computing-intensive loops used in multimedia and communication applications. The 6x86MX processor also contains a scratch-pad RAM feature, and supports performance monitoring. It delivers optimum 16-bit and 32-bit performance while running Windows 95, Windows NT, OS/2, DOS, UNIX, and other x86 operating systems. The 6x86MX processor features a super-pipelined architecture and advanced techniques, including register renaming, out-of-order completion, data-dependency removal, branch prediction, and speculative execution.

You'll find 6x86MX processors available in 150MHz (PR166), 166MHz (PR200), 188MHz (PR233), 225MHz (PR266), and 250MHz (PR300) versions. As with other Cyrix processors, performance is rated using the P-rating (or PR) nomenclature. For example, a Cyrix 6x86MX at 166MHz performs equally to an Intel Pentium processor at 200MHz.

CPU Overclocking

PC evolution is often a race for performance, and designers are constantly struggling to make the most of every last clock tick. Many factors are involved in computer performance, but CPU speed is one of the most important—faster and better CPUs have been a driving force in computer development, and older CPUs are frequently upgraded to wring ever-more performance from current systems. Although outright CPU replacements are common, they can also be expensive. As an alternative to CPU replacement, PC users and technicians alike are turning to overclocking as a means of maximizing the performance of an existing CPU. This part of the chapter offers comprehensive set of guidelines and procedures that can help you make informed overclocking decisions.

Overclocking is basically reconfiguring a PC to operate a CPU at a higher clock speed (or bus speed) than the particular CPU has been specified for. A system can be reconfigured to overclock a CPU in a matter of minutes, simply by changing one or two jumpers on the motherboard. Ideally, this higher clock speed should increase the CPU's performance without damaging the CPU or reducing its working life. The economics of overclocking can be compelling. In most cases, overclocking can be accomplished with a Pentium-class CPU at less than $30 (U.S.) for a new cooling unit—as opposed to $200 to $500 (U.S.) for a new CPU.

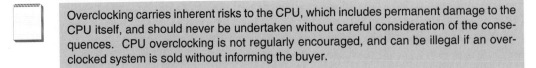

Overclocking carries inherent risks to the CPU, which includes permanent damage to the CPU itself, and should never be undertaken without careful consideration of the consequences. CPU overclocking is not regularly encouraged, and can be illegal if an overclocked system is sold without informing the buyer.

REQUIREMENTS FOR OVERCLOCKING

The most important factor to grasp about CPU overclocking is that it is not a universally successful technique. In many cases, your efforts to overclock a PC will fail. The four critical elements of any PC that influence overclocking are the CPU, the motherboard, system RAM, and CPU cooling. Trouble in any one of those elements will result in overclocking problems.

CPU issues CPUs manufactured by Intel seem to be the most successful at overclocking—usually because AMD and Cyrix/IBM CPUs are often running very close to their rated limits already to compete with their Intel counterparts. However, not all Intel CPUs are so suitable. CPUs marked with the SY022 and SU073 S-spec numbers are often limited to clock multipliers of more than ×2. Also check for "faked" CPUs (which have been remarked and resold at higher clock speeds already). Remarked CPUs are common in Europe, but it's always worth a check of the CPU first before proceeding. As a rule, if you can peel off any stickers underneath the CPU, it is remarked, and most likely running over its originally rated speed anyway.

Motherboard issues Even if your CPU seems perfect for overclocking, the motherboard might not be. Signal reflections and other electrical limitations on the bus can cause the system to crash or hang. Overclocked CPUs are also more sensitive to unstable signals from the bus and will crash if the motherboard can't deliver "clean" signals. Brand-name motherboards, such as Tyan (**http://www.tyan com**) or Supermicro (**http://www.super micro.com**), will tend to support CPU overclocking better than cut-priced no-name motherboards. As a result, you might find that some PCs can be overclocked easily, while others suffer severe performance problems (or will not operate at all after overclocking).

Motherboard bus speeds can present another wrinkle. Most traditional motherboards only support bus speeds up to 66MHz, but more recent motherboard designs can operate at 75MHz or 83MHz. These higher bus speeds will greatly affect the clock multiplier ratio when configuring your overclocking strategy, so be sure to understand the clock speed limits and multipliers for your particular motherboard.

The motherboard should also support a wide range of CPU supply voltages. A STD voltage of 3.3 V and a VRE voltage of 3.45 V are common. If you use an MMX-type CPU (i.e., the P55C, the 6x86MX, or the K6), you'll need access to "split voltage" support (2.8 V and 3.3 V are typical). This might not sound so important because you're not "changing" the CPU, but in some cases, you might need to boost the CPU supply voltage just a bit to support overclocking.

RAM issues System RAM can also be a problem in overclocked systems when the bus speed exceeds 66MHz—you'll require high-end EDO RAM or SDRAM. As a rule, EDO RAM works best with 66MHz motherboards, but SDRAM tends to be best with 75MHz and 83MHz motherboards.

Cooling issues Perhaps the most overlooked problem with CPU overclocking is insufficient cooling. CPUs draw current with each clock tick. The more clock cycles in a given period, the more current is required—and the more heat is generated. Most current CPUs run hot to begin with, but when overclocked, a CPU can easily overheat and crash (or perhaps suffer permanent damage). As a consequence, you should never attempt to overclock a CPU without making accommodations for better cooling. Consider purchasing a high-capacity, top-quality heatsink/fan assembly with a reliable ball-bearing fan with a K/W (Kelvin per Watt) value of 1 K/W or less. You might need to go to a hobby electronics store or full-featured computer store to find a good heatsink/fan. When installing the cooling unit, be sure that it fits to the CPU tightly without any air gaps, and use a thin layer of thermal grease between the CPU and heatsink.

POTENTIAL PITFALLS

Before we actually get into the techniques of CPU overclocking, you should be aware of some potential faults. Three typical failures are associated with CPU overclocking: intermittent operation, shortened life span, and outright failure. All three faults are heat related:

- *Intermittent operation* The added heat produced in the CPU can result in internal signal errors (a lost bit or shift of signal timing), which can easily cause the PC to crash—forcing you to power down the system until the CPU cools.
- *Shortened life span* This is another heat-related problem. Rather than an immediate failure, excessive heat can shorten a CPU's life through a process called "electromigration." Rather than a CPU working for 10 years, it might only work for 2 years or 5 years (it's impossible to say for certain).
- *Outright failure* A CPU is designed to operate from –25 to 80 degrees C. If the CPU is not cooled properly, the CPU die can exceed its maximum working temperature, and the CPU can fail. Although are millions of transistors are in a modern CPU, it only takes the failure of one or two to destroy a CPU.

OVERCLOCKING THE SYSTEM

At this point, you're ready to try some overclocking yourself. Generally speaking, overclocking requires three basic steps: change the bus speed, change the multiplier, and change the supply voltage. Notice that you do not always have to change all three settings

TABLE 11-13 GENERIC 486 OVERCLOCKING SUGGESTIONS

CLOCK RATE (MHZ)	PROBABLE SUCCESS AT: (MHZ)	POSSIBLE SUCCESS AT: (MHZ)
16	20	—
20	25	33
25	33	40 or even 50
33	40	50
40	50	—
66	80	—
100	120	—

TABLE 11-14 GENERIC PENTIUM/6X86 OVERCLOCKING SUGGESTIONS

CLOCK RATE (MHZ)	PROBABLE SUCCESS AT: (MHZ)	POSSIBLE SUCCESS AT: (MHZ)
60	66	—
75	90	100–133
90	100	120–133
100	120	133
120	133	—
133	150	166–180
150	166	—
166	180	187.5
200	225	—

to successfully overclock a CPU. The general steps to overclock a CPU are in the following outline. Tables 11-13 and 11-14 list some generic overclocking suggestions:

1 Turn off the computer. Open it up and get your motherboard manual.

2 Check the markings on the top and bottom of your CPU, write them down, and reinstall the CPU (this helps to ensure that the CPU is "real" and not remarked).

3 Check the current clock speed and multiplier jumper settings on your motherboard, compare them with your manual, and write them down.

4 Check the supply voltage jumper settings on your motherboard, compare them with manual and your CPU marking, and write them down.

5 Inspect the cooling unit on your CPU and upgrade the cooling unit (if necessary).

6 Change the jumper settings for clock speed and/or multiplier, according to your target overclocked level.

7 Double-check that the jumpers are set as expected.

8 Start the computer and allow it to boot.

9 Does it boot or reach the CMOS setup? (If yes, go to step 12).

10 If no, turn off the computer and change CPU voltage jumper to a slightly higher voltage (if possible).

11 If you still can't boot or reach the CMOS setup, return the voltage setting to its original value. You cannot overclock at this desired speed. Return the clock speed and multiplier settings to their original values and quit, or go to step 6.

12 Tweak your CMOS setup settings to optimum performance values, as required (this might not be necessary).

13 Does the system boot to a full working operation system? (If no, go to step 15).

14 If yes, start testing with a utility like Winstone 97 and allow the system to "burn-in" thoroughly. Check for any crashes or other intermittent system operation. If the system proves unstable, you cannot overclock at this level. Return the clock speed and multiplier settings to their original values and quit, or go to step 6.

15 If no, check your cooling unit and go to step 11.

16 If everything works well, congratulations. If not, check your cooling unit and go to step 11.

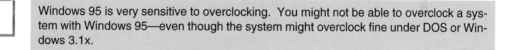

Windows 95 is very sensitive to overclocking. You might not be able to overclock a system with Windows 95—even though the system might overclock fine under DOS or Windows 3.1x.

Change the bus speed The internal clock of a CPU runs at a different speed than the external clock (or "bus speed"). The external clock is the speed at which the cache and the main memory run. When divided by two, it yields the speed of the PCI bus. Only three different "official" bus speeds are used by the Pentium, Pentium Pro, and the AMD K5: 50, 60, and 66MHz. The Cyrix/IBM 6x86 uses five bus speeds: 50, 55, 60, 66, and 75MHz. Also, new motherboards are available that support the unofficial bus speed of 83MHz.

To change the bus speed, look in your motherboard manual for something like "Clock speed" or "CPU external (BUS) frequency selection"—these are the jumpers you will have to change. You will probably have to change several different jumpers to establish each new bus speed. If you are lucky and happen to have a motherboard with "SoftMenu" technology, you can change the bus-speed settings in the CMOS setup menu without even opening the case.

Only increase the bus speed one step at a time (e.g., go from 60MHz to 66MHz, not 60MHz to 75MHz). This is the most successful way to overclock. Using this method, almost every P150 CPU runs at 166MHz and most 6x86 P150+ CPUs run at a P166+ level.

Change the multiplier The CPU's internal clock is controlled by an internal clock multiplier in each CPU that is programmed via CPU pins. Intel Pentium CPUs support the following multipliers: ×1.5, ×2, ×2.5, and ×3. Intel Pentium Pro CPUs support ×2.5, ×3, ×3.5, and ×4. 6x86 CPUs only support ×2 and ×3, but the upcoming M2 will support ×2, ×2.5, ×3, and ×3.5.

To change the multiplier setting, find a set of jumpers marked such as "Clock multiplier" or "CPU-to-bus frequency ratio selection" in your motherboard manual. Usually, two jumpers are used to change these settings. Again, you can do all of this in the CMOS setup menu if you have a SoftMenu motherboard, such as the new Abit motherboards (**http://www.abit.com.tw**).

Change the supply voltage In some circumstances, boosting the CPU supply voltage from 3.3 (STD) to 3.45 V (VRE) might be necessary to make the CPU run reliably at a higher bus speed. This is because of a wider voltage difference between the digital "high" and "low" conditions, which results in "cleaner" signals for the CPU and other motherboard devices. If you can't run your CPU reliably at one particular clock speed, it's always worth considering jumping to the higher supply voltage. However, more voltage will produce more heat, so you must be very careful about cooling.

SPECIAL NOTES FOR 75 AND 83MHZ BUS SPEEDS

Many traditional Pentium-class motherboards handle clock speeds up to 66MHz, but newer motherboards are appearing that operate up to 75MHz, and even 83MHz. There are some precautions to remember when using these faster motherboards:

■ *PCI bus issues* The PCI bus is taken from the clock speed. At 60 or 66MHz, the PCI bus speed is 30 or 33MHz (this is the recommended speed for PCI). However, at 75 or 83 MHz, the PCI bus runs at 37.5 or 41.6MHz, respectively. This can lead to problems with some PCI devices, such as SCSI controllers, video cards, and network cards. Often, SCSI controllers and network cards refuse to work at the faster speed, but some video boards just get much hotter than usual (although some video cards, such as the Diamond Stealth 64, aren't affected by higher bus speeds).
■ *EIDE bus issues* The speed of an EIDE interface is not only determined by the PIO or DMA modes, but it is also highly dependent on the PCI clock. This is one reason why an EIDE interface is always slower in systems with 60MHz bus speeds (or less). However, the EIDE interface will be faster when you are running at 75 or 83MHz bus speeds. This sounds fine at first, but either the interface or the hard disk is often not up to the faster bus speeds. For example, I've seen HDDs work fine at 75MHz bus speeds, but at 83MHz, I've have to scale back to PIO mode 2. This is also true for EIDE CD-ROM drives, and could very well be the culprit if you're running into strange lockups under Windows.
■ *ISA bus issues* In some cases, the ISA bus speed is divided directly from the PCI bus. If the PCI bus is running faster, the ISA bus might also be running faster. This can cause some serious problems for ISA boards (especially older ISA boards). For example, I've heard AWE32 sound boards make strange whistling sounds when being run at a fast bus speed. You can sometimes correct for ISA speed problems by introducing ISA wait states in the CMOS setup.

OVERCLOCKING NOTES FOR THE INTEL PENTIUM

Intel's Pentium and Pentium MMX processors are generally regarded as the easiest CPUs to overclock. This can be attributed to Intel's increased quality demands put in place after their early floating-point flaw disaster with the 60 and 66MHz Pentiums. A Pentium MMX 200 seems to run fine with 2.8 V at 208/83MHz and 225/75MHz. For 250/83MHz, you might need to increase the voltage to 2.9 V. Table 11-15 lists some options for Pentium overclocking.

OVERCLOCKING NOTES FOR THE INTEL PENTIUM PRO

The Pentium Pro is typically not overclocked, but according to the information that's available, you should be able to overclock a Pentium Pro the same as you would a classic

TABLE 11-15   PENTIUM OVERCLOCKING OPTIONS

PENTIUM AT:	1ST CHOICE:	2ND CHOICE:	3RD CHOICE:	4TH CHOICE:
75MHz	112.5MHz (1.5 × 75MHz)	100MHz (1.5 × 66MHz)	90MHz (1.5 × 60MHz)	83MHz (1.5 × 55MHz)
90MHz	125MHz (1.5 × 83MHz)	112.5MHz (1.5 × 75MHz)	100MHz (1.5 × 66MHz)	—
100MHz	125MHz (1.5 × 83 MHz)	112.5MHz (1.5 × 75MHz)	—	—
120MHz	125MHz (1.5 × 83 MHz)	133MHz (2 × 66MHz)	112.5MHz (1.5 × 75MHz)	—
133MHz	166MHz (2 × 83 MHz)	150MHz (2 × 75MHz)	66MHz (2.5 × 66MHz)	—
150MHz	166MHz (2 × 83 MHz)	187.5MHz (2.5 × 75MHz)	200MHz (3 × 66MHz)	150MHz (2 × 75MHz)
166MHz	208MHz (2.5 × 83MHz)	166MHz (2 × 83MHz)	187.5MHz (2.5 × 75MHz)	200MHz (3 × 66MHz)
200MHz	250MHz (3 × 83MHz)	225MHz (3 × 75MHz)	208 MHz (2.5 × 83MHz)	—

TABLE 11-16 PENTIUM PRO OVERCLOCKING OPTIONS

	1ST CHOICE	2ND CHOICE
150MHz	166MHz (2.5 × 66MHz)	
180MHz	233MHz (3.5 × 66 MHz)	200MHz (3 × 66MHz)
200MHz	266MHz (4 × 66MHz)	233MHz (3.5 × 66MHz)

Pentium or Pentium MMX. The main problem seems to be that there are few (if any) motherboards that operate at 75 or 83MHz (leaving only 50, 60, and 66MHz). Table 11-16 lists some overclocking options for the Pentium Pro.

OVERCLOCKING NOTES FOR THE CYRIX/IBM 6X86

The Cyrix/IBM 6x86 CPUs are much more difficult to overclock than comparable Intel CPUs. There are two reasons for this. First, Cyrix CPUs (even the later production steps) produce tremendous amounts of heat. Overclocking them would produce so much heat that it would be difficult to remove it all without huge heatsink/fans or powered Peltier coolers. Second, 6x86 CPUs only support two multiplier settings (×2 and ×3), so far fewer overclocking options are available. Try a Cyrix P120+ (100MHz) as a P133+ (110MHz). Try a P133+ (110MHz) as a P150+ (120MHz). Finally, try a P150+ (120MHz) as a P166+ (133MHz).

You'll generally achieve the best success with 2.7 or 3.7 stepped 6x86 CPUs—they are more stable and produce less heat.

Cooling is crucial for overclocked 6x86 CPUs, so don't even consider overclocking a 6x86 without a very capable heatsink/fan or a powered Peltier cooler.

OVERCLOCKING THE AMD K5

AMD has put itself on the map with its 5x86/133MHz CPU, and earned a lot of respect with the K5. However, the older PR75, PR90, and PR100 versions of the K5 do not seem to tolerate overclocking very well—probably because those CPUs were running at their performance limits already. By comparison, the later K5 versions (such as the PR120, PR133, PR150, and PR166) and the newer K6 seem to be much more tolerant of overclocking. When selecting an overclocking level, choose the next level up. For example, if you have a K5 PR120, try configuring it as a PR133, etc.

TIPS FOR CONTROLLING HEAT

Heat remains the greatest enemy of overclocking, so managing that heat is an important priority. Try some of the following suggestions to help you overcome CPU heating issues:

■ Use a good-quality heatsink/fan which is more than adequately rated for your particular CPU.

- Use a thin layer of heatsink compound to improve heat transfer between the CPU case and heatsink (available at Radio Shack; Cat. No. 276-1372).
- For extremely hot CPUs, try a Peltier cooler or similar refrigeration unit (contact information is listed at the end of this article).
- Select reliable ball-bearing type fans with extended service lifetimes.
- Fold and tie cables away from areas requiring free air circulation (such as the vicinity of the CPU fan). Keep any obstructions clear.
- Be sure that the CPU heatsink/fan is in close thermal contact with the processor surface (using heatsink compound, if needed). It should attach securely to the CPU, or CPU and socket. If not, get a new heatsink/fan.
- Use a CPU cooler with an audio alarm system, which will alert you in case of either fan malfunction or excessive CPU temperature.
- If you are overclocking your CPU, compensate for the increased heat generated by using an "upsized" heatsink/fan or Peltier active cooler.
- Clean fan blades, fan support struts, and power supply louvers of accumulated dirt at least annually. Canned compressed air and vacuum sweeper brushes work well.
- Increase air circulation in and out of your computer case by using an auxiliary fan.

Troubleshooting CPU Problems

The term *microprocessor troubleshooting* is not the misnomer it once was. Early CPUs, such as the 8088, carried only 29,000 transistors. When one of those transistors failed, it would usually result in a complete system failure—the PC would crash or freeze entirely. Further, the system would subsequently fail to boot at all. However, CPUs have become far more complex in the last 15 years or so, and new generations (such as the Pentium) are exceeding 8 million transistors. With so many more transistors, the probability of an immediate catastrophic fault is far less. Of course, any CPU fault is very serious, but there are now many cases where a system might boot, but crash when certain specific CPU functions are attempted (i.e., trying to execute protected-mode instructions). These kinds of errors might give the impression that a piece of software is corrupt or that one or more expansion devices is faulty. This part of the chapter looks at a selection of CPU failure modes and offers some tactics to help resolve the problem.

Your companion CD offers several utilities that can help you identify and quantify you CPU. Use MAXSPEED.EXE to test the clock speed of a system. You can identify processors with general system inspection tools, such as CONF810E.ZIP and SNOOP330.ZIP.

GENERAL SYMPTOMS AND SOLUTIONS

Symptom 11-1. The system is completely dead (the system power LED lights properly) CPU faults are never subtle. When a CPU problem manifests itself, the system will invariably crash. Consequently, systems that do not boot (or freeze without warning during the boot process) stand an excellent chance of suffering from a CPU fault. The frustration with this kind of symptom is that the PC typically does not run long enough to execute its POST diagnostics, nor does the system boot to run any third-party DOS diagnostics. As a result, such "dead" systems require a bit of blind faith on the part of a technician.

Before considering a CPU replacement, you should use a multimeter and check the power supply outputs very carefully. Even though the power LED is lit, one or more outputs might be low or absent. Excessively low outputs can easily result in logic errors that will freeze the system. If this problem occurred after adding an upgrade, the supply might be overloaded—try removing the upgrade. If system operation returns, consider upgrading the power supply. If an output is low or absent and there has been no upgrade (or the problem continues after removing the upgrade), try replacing the power supply.

Next, strip the system of its peripherals and expansion boards, then try the system again. If operation returns, one of the expansion devices is interrupting system operation. Re-install one device at a time and check the system. The last expansion device to be installed when the PC fails is the culprit. Replace the defective device. If the failure persists, try a new CPU.

Remember to shut down and unplug the PC before continuing. When removing the original CPU, be extremely careful to avoid bending any of the pins (you might want to re-install the CPU later). Use care when installing the new CPU as well—bent pins will almost always ruin the IC. If a new CPU fails to correct the problem, replace the motherboard outright.

Symptom 11-2. A beep code or I/O POST code indicates a possible CPU fault The system will almost always fail to boot. When the POST starts, it will test each of the PC's key motherboard components (including the CPU). If a CPU fault is indicated during the POST (usually a single-byte hexadecimal code written to port 80h and read with a POST card), check each output from the system power supply. If one or more outputs is low or absent, a problem might be in the supply. Try a new supply. If all supply outputs measure properly, try a new CPU. If a new CPU does not resolve the problem, replace the motherboard. Refer to Chapter 15 for beep codes and POST code messages.

Symptom 11-3. The system boots with no problem, but crashes or freezes when certain applications are run It might seem as if the application is corrupt, but try a diagnostic (such as AMIDIAG from AMI or The Troubleshooter by AllMicro). Run repetitive tests on the CPU. Although the CPU might work in real-mode, diagnostics can detect errors running protected-mode instructions and perform thorough register checking. AMIDIAG stands out here because of the very specific error codes that are returned. Not only will it tell you if the CPU checks bad, but you will also know the specific reason why. When an error code is returned suggesting a CPU fault, try another CPU. If a CPU fault is not detected, expand the diagnostic to test other portions of the motherboard. If the entire system checks properly, you might indeed have a corrupt file in your application.

Symptom 11-4. The system boots with no problem, but crashes or freezes after several minutes of operation (regardless of the application being run) Also, you will probably notice that no diagnostic indicates a CPU problem. If you shut the system off and wait several minutes, the system will probably boot fine and run for several more minutes before stopping again—this is typical of thermal failure. When the system halts, check the CPU for heat. Use extreme caution when checking for heat—you can be easily burned. An i486-series CPU might not be fitted with a heatsink. As a rule, i486 CPUs below 25MHz are run without a heatsink, and i486 CPUs running at 33MHz and higher do use a heatsink. DX2 and DX4 versions almost certainly use a heatsink. All Pentium processors require a heatsink. Recent Pentium, Pentium MMX, and Pentium Pro processors require a heatsink/fan assembly for adequate cooling.

If the CPU is not fitted with a heatsink, be sure that the system cooling fan is working, and that there is an unobstructed path over the CPU. If not, consider applying a heatsink with a generous helping of thermal compound. If the CPU is already fitted with a heatsink, be sure that there is a ample layer of thermal compound between the CPU case and heatsink base. In many cases, the compound is omitted. This ruins the transfer of heat, and allows the CPU to run much hotter. If you find that there is no thermal compound, allow the PC to cool, then add thermal compound between the CPU case and heatsink.

Symptom 11-5. An older system refuses to run properly when the CPU's internal (L1) cache is enabled This type of symptom occurred frequently with older processors (such as the AMD Am486), and can almost always be traced to a configuration issue. The processor might fail if run at an incorrect bus speed (i.e., overclocking), so check and correct the motherboard bus speed to accommodate the CPU. This symptom can also occur when running the CPU at an incorrect operating voltage. Check the voltage level and reconfigure the motherboard for the correct voltage (if necessary). Finally, the motherboard must be compatible with the L1 cache type on the CPU. For example, installing a CPU with a write-back cache on a motherboard that doesn't support write-back cache can cause problems.

Symptom 11-6. You cannot run a 3.45-V CPU in a 5-V motherboard—even though an appropriate voltage regulator module is being used Double-check the *Voltage-Regulator Module (VRM)*. The VRM must have adequate current-handling capacity to support the CPU's power demands. Otherwise, the VRM will be overloaded and fail to provide adequate power. Check with the CPU manufacturer for their VRM recommendations. You might also try the CPU/VRM in another 5-V motherboard. If the CPU/VRM fails in another 5-V motherboard, chances are that the VRM is underrated or has failed. If the CPU/VRM does work on another 5-V motherboard, it is possible that the original motherboard's BIOS could not support the particular requirements of the new CPU. Check with the motherboard manufacturer to see if an updated BIOS (either flash or ROM IC) is available for the system.

Symptom 11-7. A system malfunctions under HIMEM.SYS or DOS4GW.EXE after installing a new CPU This type of symptom occurred frequently with older CPUs, and could generally be traced to errors in the motherboard CPU voltage and type settings (opposed to the newer bus speed/multiplier configurations). Check the motherboard's CPU configuration jumpers. Also, running a 3.45-V CPU at 5 V, or running a non-SL enhanced CPU as an SL enhanced part can cause these types of problems to occur. So, be sure that the correct part is being used, and see that the CPU voltage is correct (use a voltage regulator module, if necessary).

Symptom 11-8. The system runs fine, but reports the wrong type of CPU In virtually all cases, the motherboard BIOS was not written to support the particular CPU directly. Start by checking the motherboard's CPU configuration jumpers to see that it is set properly for the particular CPU. If the problem persists, you'll probably need a BIOS upgrade (either a flash file or ROM IC) to accommodate the processor. Check with the motherboard or system maker to determine whether an appropriate BIOS upgrade is available.

Symptom 11-9. After reconfiguring a VL motherboard for a faster CPU, the VESA VL video card no longer functions Other VL cards might also malfunction. This frequently occurs on older VL motherboards with support for 40MHz bus speeds. Because the VL bus speed is tied to the motherboard bus speed, setting the motherboard to 40MHz can cause some VL cards to malfunction. Try running the motherboard at 33MHz (the native frequency for VL cards) and set the local bus clock rate jumper for <=33MHz. If the problem disappears, you have an issue with one or more VL cards. Try altering the number of VL bus wait states until the VL devices will support 40MHz (this will compromise system performance). If you cannot resolve the issue, you might not be able to use the motherboard at 40MHz. You could also try finding a VL board that will operate properly at 40MHz.

Symptom 11-10.   Some software locks up on systems running 5x86 processors This is a frequent problem with high-end software, such as AutoDesk's 3D Studio. Often, such programs as 3D Studio use software timing loops in the code. The 5x86 processor executes these loop instructions faster than previous x86 CPUs, which interferes with timing-dependent code inside the program. In most cases, the software manufacturer will offer a patch for the offending program. For 3D Studio, you can download the FSTCPUFX.EXE file from Kinetix (**ftp://ftp.ktx.com/download/patches/3dsr4/ fast_cpu/fstcpufx.exe**). Run the executable patch file and follow the instructions. The patch alters the 3D Studio executable file.

Another prime example of software-related problems is with Clipper applications. Clipper inserts software timing loops into the applications when the code is compiled, which also interferes with timing-dependent code in the program. For Clipper, you can download the PIPELOOP.EXE file (**ftp://ftp.cyrix.com/tech/pipeloop.exe**) and put it in your AUTOEXEC.BAT file.

Symptom 11-11. The Windows 95 Device Manager identifies the CPU incorrectly In many cases, the CPU is misidentified as a 486 or other older CPU. This is caused by an issue with Windows 95. The algorithm used in Windows 95 to detect the CPU was likely completed before the particular CPU was released; therefore, the CPU responds to the algorithm just as a 486 does. Use a diagnostic that will identify your particular CPU correctly or check with the CPU maker for a Windows 95 patch that will support proper identification. This problem happens often with Cyrix 6x86 CPUs, and it can be corrected by downloading a patch, such as 6XOPT074.ZIP (see the "Performance enhancement software" bullet under the "Cyrix 6x86 issues" section).

Symptom 11-12. The heatsink/fan will not secure properly It is not tight against the surface of the CPU. This can be a serious problem for the system because a loose heatsink/fan will not cool the processor correctly. There are three classic solutions to this issue. First, be sure that you have the heatsink/fan model that is recommended for your particular CPU (a common error when building a new PC). Second, be sure that the heatsink attaches to either the CPU chip itself or the ZIF socket that the CPU mounts in. Third, verify that the CPU has not been altered or faked. Faked CPUs are often ground down to remove their original markings, then new markings are placed on the CPU. The grinding process reduces the package thickness, and can prevent the heatsink/fan from being secure (faked CPUs are common in Europe).

CYRIX 6X86 ISSUES

From a technological standpoint, the Cyrix 6x86 (or *M1*, as it used to be called) is a strong competitor to the Intel Pentium. In a properly configured system, the 6x86 can actually out-class the Pentium in some areas. In addition, the 200MHz version of the 6x86 uses a bus speed of 75MHz (replacing the established 66MHz bus speed). However, there are some special circumstances and symptoms to keep in mind when working on Cyrix-based platforms:

- *Bus speed* This is where Cyrix's problems start because the higher bus speeds demand very fast memory technologies and advanced motherboard chipsets. You can't run the P200 chip in a Triton FX or HX motherboard because those chipsets don't support a bus speed of 75MHz. In operation, the 6x86 P200 runs at a clock speed of 150MHz by multiplying the 75MHz motherboard bus speed by 2. If you were to try running the P200 at a bus speed of 50MHz and a multiplier of 3, you would lose any performance benefit because of the slow bus speed. For the P166, P150, and P120 versions, motherboard compatibility is much better.
- *Excess heating* Heat is an important issue with every leading-edge CPU, but although similar Intel and AMD processors will typically run hot, the 6x86 runs extremely hot. Excess heat can cause data corruption and system crashes, and even shorten the working life of the CPU. In the worst cases, excess heat can destroy the CPU. Such reliability issues force the use of good-quality heatsink/fan assemblies with all 6x86 models. The recent release of the 6x86L (low-voltage) versions promise to help combat the issues of heating by using a "split voltage" architecture of 2.8 and 3.3 V—the same voltages used by new MMX processors. Cyrix expects that the "L" series will reduce power demands by more than 25%. If you must replace a 6x86, go for a version 2.7 of the 6x86, or a 6x86L version (with proper voltage regulation) if you can.
- *FPU issues* Another point of contention among 6x86 users is that the floating-point capability of a 6x86 is measurably below that of similar Pentiums. For example, the FPU performance of a 6x86 P166 is only rated equivalent to a Pentium 90MHz unit. There is no real solution for the current 6x86 versions, but the coming M2 from Cyrix is expected to correct these problems.
- *Performance under Windows NT* Here's another serious problem that plagued earlier 6x86 versions. The CPU is so sensitive to signal reflections from the CPU busses that NT would switch off the L1 cache in the 6x86. This, in turn, causes a performance degradation. Cyrix has resolved many of these issues in the version 2.7 releases, as well as in the new 6x86L CPUs, but you might continue to see NT performance problems in systems with older 6x86 versions.
- Performance enhancement software. Given the various limitations of the Cyrix 6x86, a number of utilities are available to enhance the 6x86. You can obtain each utility from the Web resources listed:

    6XOPT074.ZIP This is a 6x86 optimizer written by Mikael Johansson. It configures 6x86 CPU registers to increase performance, and it allows Windows 95 to "see" the 6x86 CPU in the Device manager (**ftp://ftp.sysdoc.pair.com/pub/6xopt074.zip**).

    DIRECTNT.ZIP This utility enables the 6x86 cache under Windows NT 4 (**ftp://ftp. sysdoc.pair.com/pub/directnt.zip**).

    M1OPT.EXE This utility configures the 6x86 for high-performance operation (**ftp: //ftp.hjcomp.cz/pub/support/xyz/cpu/ibm/m1opt.exe**).

M1.EXE This program allows a user to view and edit 6x86 bit settings—advanced users only (**http://www.chips.ibm.com/products/x86/x86dev/appnotes/software/ m1.exe**).

IBMM9.EXE This program allows a user to view and edit 6x86 bit settings similar to M1.EXE—advanced users only (**http://www.chips.ibm.com/products/x86/x86dev/ appnotes/software/ibmm9.exe**).

IBMM1.EXE This program allows a user to view and edit 6x86 bit settings similar to M1.EXE—advanced users only (**ftp://ftp.hjcomp.cz/pub/support/xyz/cpu/ibm/ ibmm1.exe**).

PUZZLE.EXE This utility is designed to enhance 6x86-based PCs (**http://www.chips. ibm.com/products/x86/x86dev/appnotes/software/puzzle.exe**). You can get the manual (in .PDF form) from (**ftp://ftp.hjcomp.cz/pub/support/xyz/cpu/ibm/ puzzle.pdf**).

Symptom 11-13. The Cyrix 6x86 system is crashing or freezing after some period of operation This is almost always a heat-related problem caused by inadequate cooling of the 6x86. If you're not using a heatsink/fan, install one before continuing (be sure to use a thin layer of thermal grease to improve heat transfer between the CPU and heatsink). Use a good-quality heatsink/fan with plenty of capacity and see that it is securely attached to the CPU. Also see that the CPU itself is securely seated in its socket.

You might also consider installing a different 6x86 model. The Type C028 version uses 3.52 V and the Type C016 uses 3.3 V, so just changing models can reduce power demands. You might also try installing a version 2.7 (or later) 6x86, which is better able to deal with heat. Best yet, install a 6x86L CPU (and regulator). A third possible cause of intermittent system operation is a poorly compatible BIOS. Check with the motherboard maker or system manufacturer and see if there is a BIOS upgrade to better support Cyrix CPUs.

Symptom 11-14. The Cyrix 6x86 system crashes and refuses to restart This is another classic heat-related problem, which often indicates that the CPU or its associated voltage regulator has failed. Check the voltage regulator—regulators are more susceptible to failure with Cyrix 6x86 CPUs because of the higher current demands. If the voltage regulator checks out, replace the CPU itself (perhaps with a lower-power model, as mentioned in Symptom 11-13).

Symptom 11-15. The Cyrix 6x86 performs poorly under Windows NT 4.0 In virtually all cases, NT has detected the 6x86 and has elected to shut down the write-back L1 cache completely. This results in the performance hit. Fortunately, there are several ways to address this problem. First, you can download a patch from the Cyrix Web site (**http://www.cyrix.com**), which re-enables the L1 cache under NT 4.0. This brings performance back up, but it also can cause instability for NT. A more practical resolution is to replace the CPU with a 6x86 version 2.7 (or higher) or a 6x86L (and suitable voltage regulator), as mentioned in Symptom 11-13.

Symptom 11-16. Quake (or another graphics-intensive program) doesn't run nearly as well on a Cyrix 6x86 system as it does with a similar Pentium system This is caused by issues with Cyrix FPU performance. There is no real resolution for the problem at this time—later 6x86 versions do not correct the FPU. You can replace the CPU with an AMD or Intel model, or wait to see the performance offered by the Cyrix 6x86MX (M2).

Symptom 11-17. A Cyrix 6x86 CPU won't work on your motherboard Several problems are possible when upgrading to any non-Intel CPU. First, check the motherboard's chipset and be sure that the chipset (and other attributes, such as bus speed) are compatible with the 6x86. As you saw earlier, some 6x86 iterations require unusual bus speeds in order to function.

Motherboard settings are always important when installing a CPU. You will probably need to set a new clock speed to accommodate the 6x86. In some cases, you might also need to specify a CPU type. Finally, you'll need to set the CPU voltage (if your motherboard provides a "switchable" voltage regulator). Otherwise, you'll need to install a voltage regulator with enough power capacity to handle a 6x86 adequately. If you select an underrated regulator, the regulator can overheat and burn out.

The last issue to consider is your BIOS. Often the BIOS must detect a CPU correctly, and make slight variations in BIOS routines to use the new CPU most effectively. If the BIOS does not support your 6x86, you'll need to get a BIOS upgrade from the motherboard maker or system manufacturer.

If all else fails, try slowing down the clock speed to the next slower level. If the CPU runs properly then, there is probably an incompatibility between your motherboard and the 6x86. Check with the motherboard manufacturer (or system maker) and see if any compatibility issues have been identified (and if there is a fix available).

Symptom 11-18. The performance degrades when using a Cyrix 6x86 under Windows 3.1x or Windows 95 In many cases, performance problems when using non-Intel CPUs is related to BIOS support. Often the BIOS must identify a CPU, and adjust to accommodate any particular nuances. If the BIOS is not supporting the CPU correctly, it can result in overall performance problems. Check with the motherboard maker or system manufacturer for any BIOS upgrades that will better support your new CPU.

Clock speed and cache are two other issues that can affect system performance. Check the motherboard jumpers and verify that the clock speed is set correctly for your Cyrix CPU. Also check for cache jumpers and see that any cache settings are correct. You can also verify that Internal (L1) and External (L2) caching are enabled in BIOS.

OVERCLOCKING TROUBLESHOOTING

The process of CPU overclocking is hardly a perfect one. Many variables are involved, such as the CPU type, motherboard quality, available clock speed, and multiplier settings. In many cases, overclocking results in system problems. Some of the more common problems are:

Symptom 11-19. The system does not boot up at all after reconfiguring the system for overclocking This common problem almost always means that you cannot overclock the CPU at the level you have chosen. Scale back the clock speed or the multiplier until the system starts up or return the clock and multiplier to their original values.

Symptom 11-20. The system starts after overclocking, but locks up or crashes after some short period of time Overclocking causes substantial heat dissipation from the CPU, and cooling must be improved to compensate for this additional heat—otherwise, the overheated CPU can lock-up and crash the system. Check the heatsink/fan and see that it is attached correctly with a thin layer of thermal grease between the CPU and heatsink. It might be necessary to "up-size" the heatsink/fan or use a Peltier cooler.

Symptom 11-21. Memory errors occur after increasing the bus speed for overclocking Memory performance is tightly coupled to bus speed (or "clock speed"). Most 60-ns RAM types will work fine up to 66MHz, but you might need high-end 50-ns EDO RAM or 50-ns SDRAM when pushing the bus speed to 75MHz or 83MHz. Try some faster memory in the PC or do not attempt to overclock the system.

Symptom 11-22. After reconfiguring for overclocking, the system works, but you see a rash of CPU failures Chances are that the CPU is running far too hot, resulting in premature CPU failures. Check the cooling unit and see that it is securely attached using a thin layer of thermal grease between the CPU and heatsink. It might be necessary to "up-size" the heatsink/fan or use a Peltier cooler.

Symptom 11-23. After reconfiguring for overclocking, you find that some expansion board or other hardware is no longer recognized or working Because PCI and ISA clocks are typically tied to the system clock speed, increasing the clock speed will also increase the PCI and ISA clocks. This can upset the operation of some sensitive adapter boards. You might be able to replace the suspect hardware with a more tolerant adapter, but it is often safer to return the clock speed and multiplier settings to their original values.

Symptom 11-24. After reconfiguring for overclocking, a number of recent files are corrupt, inaccessible, or missing In effect, the system is not stable Check for excessive heat first (as in Symptom 11-22). Otherwise, you should not overclock this particular system. Try scaling back the overclocking configuration, or return the clock speed and multiplier settings to their original values.

TROUBLESHOOTING A DIAGNOSTIC FAILURE AFTER INSTALLING AN INTEL MATH CO-PROCESSOR

Use the following suggestions if your computer or Intel's diagnostics do not recognize your Intel math co-processor:

■ Check your computer owner's manual for any jumpers or switches that might need to be set.
■ Check your computer owner's manual to see if there is a setup or configuration program that needs to be run once you have installed the math co-processor.
■ Be sure that the math co-processor is completely seated. Look to see if the chip is seated flush in the socket and that one corner is not higher than the others. Try pushing down on each corner.

■ Check that pin 1 on the math co-processor matches pin 1 on the socket and/or the motherboard.

■ If you are experiencing problems with drives or other accessories, check to ensure that all cables and cards are fully seated.

■ If these suggestions don't help, remove the math co-processor and check for any bent or broken pins, and be sure that the socket is clean and free of dust. Then, reseat the math co-processor. If you need a math co-processor extraction tool, contact your local dealer.

■ If you have access to another computer that is compatible with the math co-processor, install the math co-processor in the second computer to determine if the problem is with the math co-processor or with the computer.

The following solutions may help if your Intel math co-processor installation fails a specific diagnostic test:

TROUBLESHOOTING AN ARITHMETIC TEST FAILURE

If your installation fails one or more of the Advanced Diagnostic Arithmetic tests, you might have a defective math co-processor. However, this is very rare. Use the troubleshooting section of your *Intel Math CoProcessor User's Guide* to determine if there are seating or alignment problems that might affect the performance of your math co-processor. If this is not the cause of the problem, check with your dealer, who might be able to test the math co-processor in another computer.

TROUBLESHOOTING AN ENVIRONMENT TEST FAILURE

If your Intel387(TM) SX, Intel387 DX, or Intel487 SX math co-processor installation fails an Advanced Diagnostic environment test, check to ensure the jumpers and/or switches are set correctly. If the error still occurs, remove the math co-processor from the system and contact your system manufacturer. The system might not be compatible with an Intel math co-processor.

INTEL DIAGNOSTICS CONFORMANCE TEST FAILURE WITH INTEL387(TM) SL MATH CO-PROCESSOR

If your Intel386 SL-based system with an Intel387 SL math co-processor fails the Intel Advanced Diagnostics conformance test, but passes all other tests, call the system manufacturer for a BIOS upgrade.

INTEL387 DX MATH CO-PROCESSOR RECOGNIZED AS AN INTEL287TM XL MATH CO-PROCESSOR

On some systems, Intel Advanced Diagnostics might recognize the Intel387 DX math co-processor as an Intel287 XL math co-processor and fail some of the diagnostic tests. In most cases, the system is configured for a Weitek math co-processor, rather than an Intel387 DX math co-processor. Correctly setting jumpers and/or switches usually solves the problem.

INTEL387 MATH CO-PROCESSOR RECOGNIZED AS AN INTEL287 MATH CO-PROCESSOR

On some systems, the Intel Advanced Diagnostics identify an Intel387 math co-processor as an Intel287 math co-processor because the system is using an old BIOS adapted from a 80286 system. In most cases, you can ignore this symptom; the math co-processor runs all floating-point software flawlessly.

SYSTEM INTEGRITY DIAGNOSTIC TEST FAILURE

Some systems with an Intel287 XL math co-processor installed fail the Intel Advanced Diagnostics system integrity test. This condition is caused by a timing problem in all I286 systems. In addition, this problem can be aggravated by excessive noise of the system board and can cause the Intel287 XL math co-processor to fail this test. Replacing the CHMOS 287XL with the less-sensitive 287-10 (an NMOS device) usually resolves the problem.

"CHKCOP HAS FOUND" AND LOCKS UP

When running CHKCOP 2.2, the program might lock up under certain circumstances. These include:

- A poorly seated chip
- Incorrect dipswitch setting
- A conflict with device drivers and/or TSRs
- A bad chip

If CHKCOP locks up, boot to a DOS disk and re-run CHKCOP.

CHKCOP 2.0 FAILS DIVIDE TEST

If the CHKCOP test program intermittently fails the divide test, there might be a timing problem with the system board. Intel has confirmed that Chips and Technologies chipset version 82C211 causes the failure. Version 82C211C of this chipset should work as expected.

The Toshiba T1600 and Dell System 200 both use this chipset. If you experience this problem, examine the system board to see if your computer uses the Chips and Technologies chipset.

CHKCOP SEEMS FASTER ON AN INTEL287 MATH CO-PROCESSOR

You might experience slower execution times when running the CHKCOP test program after replacing an Intel 80287 math co-processor with an Intel287 XL math co-processor.

This condition is caused because the Intel287 math co-processor supports trigonometric functions, but Intel 80287 math co-processor chips (6, 8, and 10MHz) do not. When testing an Intel 80287 math co-processor, CHKCOP skips the transcendental test, but executes it when testing an Intel287 XL math co-processor.

Because CHKCOP runs more tests on the Intel287 XL math co-processor, the total testing time might be longer than when CHKCOP tests an Intel 80287 math co-processor.

SYSTEM DIAGNOSTICS AND THE INTEL287 XL MATH CO-PROCESSOR

Several system diagnostic programs have difficulty properly detecting an Intel287 XL math co-processor. Some programs incorrectly identify the processor as an Intel387 math co-processor, and other programs simply fail some (or all) tests, or lock up during the tests. The following lists system diagnostic programs that Intel has tested and their results:

DIAGNOSTIC PROGRAMS WITH RECOGNITION PROBLEMS

Diagnostic program	Problem	System
PC Consultants V2.02	sees 387	Compuadd 216 & 220
NCR User V1.12	sees 387	NCR PC 810
Epson 80287 V2.02	fails	Epson Equity II+ & III+
IBM 50/60 Ref V1.04	fails	IBM PS/2 mod 50 & 60
IBM Advanced V2.07	fails	IBM AT 339 (5170)
IBM Starter/Ref V1.01	fails	IBM PS/2 mod 30/286 (E-21)

DIAGNOSTIC PROGRAMS WITHOUT PROBLEMS

Diagnostic Program	System
Compaq V4.0 Rev A	Compaq Portable II
Compaq Advanced V5.06	Compaq Portable III
Compaq V6.10 Rev A	Compaq Deskpro 286/12
Epson System V1.01	Epson Equity IIe
Wyse Setup & Test V1.09	Wyse PC 286

INTEL387 DX AND INBOARD INTEL287 MATH MODULE AND IBM ADVANCED DIAGNOSTICS

The Intel387 DX and inboard 80287 math module fail the IBM Advanced Diagnostics. This happens because the diagnostics reinitialize the Intel387 DX or math module after the inboard Intel386 CPU has already initialized it. To test an Intel387 DX or Inboard math module, use the CHKCOP program on the Inboard 386 diskette instead of the IBM diagnostics.

TROUBLESHOOTING FAILURE TO BOOT AFTER INSTALLING AN INTEL MATH CO-PROCESSOR

The following solutions can help you troubleshoot any installation problems with your math co-processor.

There are several immediate troubleshooting solutions you can use if you install your the math co-processor and your computer fails to boot. First, you should:

- Check your manual for any jumpers or switches that might need to be set.
- Check your manual to see if there is a setup or configuration program that needs to be run once you have installed the math co-processor.
- Be sure that the math co-processor is completely seated. Look to see if the chip is seated flush in the socket and that one corner is not higher than the others. Try pushing down on each corner.

■ Check that pin 1 on the math co-processor matches pin 1 on the socket and/or the system board.

■ If these suggestions don't help, remove the math co-processor and check for any bent or broken pins and be sure that the socket is clean and free of dust. Then, reseat the math co-processor.

■ If you have access to another computer that is compatible with this math co-processor, install the math co-processor in the second computer to determine if the problem is with the chip or the computer.

■ If your computer boots partially, but you are experiencing problems with drives or other accessories, check to ensure that you have fully seated all cables and cards.

■ If you need a math co-processor extraction tool, contact your local dealer.

WEITEK CO-PROCESSOR NOT INSTALLED

An error message saying "Weitek co-processor not installed" might appear on some systems after you install an Intel math co-processor. The system passes all Intel diagnostics and runs all applications flawlessly. This error is generated because certain Weitek enabling switches were set by EMM386.

```
EMM386 [on|off|auto] [w=on|w=off]
```

on|off|auto These parameters activate the EMM386.EXE device driver (if set to on), or suspends the driver (if set to off).

```
[w=on|w=off]
```

If the w=on parameter is specified and the off parameter (different from the w=off parameter) is not, EMM386 enables the Weitek co-processor support. The high memory area (HMA) must be available to enable the Weitek co-processor support. If you specify the w=on or w=off parameter and no Weitek co-processor is installed in your computer system, MS-DOS displays the following error message: "Weitek Co-processor not installed."

OS2 1107 ERROR

When you attempt to run the Intel math co-processor diagnostics on a system running OS/2 versions 2.0 or 2.1, the following error message appears:

```
OS2 1107
```

This error occurs because the Intel math co-processor diagnostics do not run under OS/2 versions 2.0 and 2.1. To test the math co-processor, insert the diagnostics diskette into your computer's floppy drive, boot your computer with a DOS system diskette and type the following command:

```
mcpdiags
```

162 ERROR IN IBM PS/2 MODEL 50, 60, AND 70

When you install an Intel math co-processor in an IBM PS/2 Model 50, 60, or 70 system, then boot the system, the following message might appear as the system boots:

```
Error 162
```

The error message occurs because you did not run your computer's reference diskette after the math co-processor was installed in the computer. To eliminate the error message, boot from your IBM reference diskette and run the setup program. Select *Automatic* if you haven't changed the configuration of any add-in cards, and the computer configures itself to run correctly with the math co-processor.

"CONFIGURATION ERROR" AFTER REMOVING 80287 FROM IBM PC/AT

If you remove an Intel math co-processor from an IBM PC/AT computer, do not rerun your computer's SETUP program to show a change has been made, and reboot the system, the following message appears:

```
Configuration Error
```

The error message occurs because the computer cannot find the chip. To solve this problem temporarily, unplug the battery from the system board, run setup, and manually enter all the information about your system. Notice that this process loses all SETUP information, so be sure to write down the hard drive type, floppy drive type, and memory and video configurations before unplugging the battery. This information is crucial in correctly reconfiguring your computer.

Further Study

That concludes Chapter 11. Be sure to review the glossary and chapter questions on the accompanying CD. If you have access to the Internet, take some time to review a few of these CPU manufacturers and other resources:

AMD: **http://www.amd.com**

AMI: **http://www.megatrends.com (AMIDIAG)**

ARM: **http://www.arm.com/**

Cyrix: **http://www.cyrix.com**

DEC Alpha: **http://www.digital.com/info/semiconductor/alpha.htm**

HAL Sparc64 Processor: **http://www.hal.com/docs/**

HP PA-RISC: **http://www.wsg.hp.com/wsg/strategies/strategy.html**

IBM PowerPC: **http://www.chips.ibm.com/products/ppc/**

Intel: **http://www.intel.com**

MIPS: **http://www.sgi.com/MIPS/**

NexGen: **http://www.nexgen.com**

TI: **ftp.ti.com**

NEWSGROUPS

comp.sys.arm

comp.sys.dec

comp.sys.hp.hardware

comp.sys.intel

comp.sys.mips

comp.sys.powerpc

comp.sys.sun.hardware

DISK-COMPRESSION
TROUBLESHOOTING

CONTENTS AT A GLANCE

Concepts of Compression
  Disk space allocation
  Data compression
  The compression system
  Factors that affect compression

Before and After Compresion
  Scan the disk for physical defects
  Defragment the disk and check free
    space
  Check the disk for file defects
  Check the memory
  Install the compression utility
  Create a bootable disk

DBLSPACE.INI and DRVSPACE.INI
  file settings
  Removing DOS Doublespace or
    Drivespace manually

Troubleshooting Compressed Drives
  Troubleshooting Windows 95
    Drivespace

Troubleshooting DOS Doublespace
  and Drivespace
  Troubleshooting DOS stacker

Further Study

It is a weird fact of "PC life" that we never seem to have enough storage space. No matter how large our hard drive is, or how many hard drives are in the system, just about all PC users find themselves removing files and applications at one time or another to make room for new software. Looking back, it is hard to imagine that 10MB and 20MB hard drives were once considered spacious; today, that much space would probably not even cover a single DOS game or application. For many years, overcoming storage limitations has meant replacing the hard drive with a larger model. Given the rate at which hard-drive technology is moving, a new drive generally doubles or triples a system's available space. Although new drive hardware is remarkably inexpensive (typically around 8 cents per MB), the total bill for a 2.5GB to 5.0GB drive is a serious expense for PC owners.

In the late 1980s and early 1990s, companies such as Stac and Microsoft developed an alternative to hard drive swapping known as *disk compression*. Instead of an invasive procedure to upgrade and re-configure a PC's hardware, a software utility re-organizes the drive using compression techniques that can allow a drive to safely store up to 100% or more than its rated capacity. For example, a properly compressed 100MB hard drive would typically be able to offer 200MB or more of effective storage space. Since the initial introduction of disk compression, its acceptance and popularity has soared, and compression is now quite commonplace on DOS and Windows platforms. As you can imagine, however, disk compression is not always flawless—the vast differences between PC designs and the software used on them virtually guarantee problems at some point. This chapter is intended to illustrate the factors that affect disk compression, and show you the symptoms and solutions for a wide variety of compression problems.

> Although disk compression remains widely used in today's DOS and Windows 95 platforms, it seems to slowly be losing popularity because of the huge capacities and low costs of today's hard drives.

Concepts of Compression

To understand some of the problems associated with disk compression, it is important that you be familiar with the basic concepts of compression, and how those concepts are implemented on a typical drive. Disk compression generally achieves its goals through two means: superior disk space allocation and an effective data compression algorithm.

DISK SPACE ALLOCATION

The traditional DOS system of file allocation assigns disk space in terms of clusters (where a cluster can be 4, 8, 16, or more sectors—each sector is 512 bytes long). The larger a drive is, the more sectors are used in each cluster. For example, a 2GB drive typically consumes 64 sectors in each cluster. Each cluster commits (512×64) 32768 bytes per cluster. Because the drive's file allocation table (FAT) works in terms of clusters, a file that only takes 20 bytes, or 1000 bytes, or 20KB will still be given the entire cluster—even though much less than the full cluster might be needed. This is phenomenally wasteful of disk space (the total amount of waste on a disk is referred to as *slack space*). Disk compression forms a barrier between the DOS file system and the drive. This "compression interface" simulates a FAT for the compressed drive, so the compressed drive also allocates space in terms of clusters, but now a compressed cluster can have a variable number of sectors, rather than a fixed number. That way, a file that only needs three sectors has three sectors assigned to the cluster. A file that needs eight sectors has eight sectors assigned to its cluster, and so on.

DATA COMPRESSION

Now that the DOS limitations of file allocation have been overcome, the data that is stored in each sector is compressed as it is written to disk, then decompressed as it is read from the disk into memory. This is known as *on-the-fly compression*. That way, the program that might ordinarily need 20 sectors on a disk can be compressed to only 10 sectors. You can start to see that this combination of "cluster packing" and compression offer some powerful tools for optimizing drive space.

Data compression basically works by locating repetitive data in some given length of data, and replacing the repetitive data with a short representative data fragment (called a *token*). For example, consider any ordinary sentence. In uncompressed form, each text character would require one byte of disk space. On closer inspection, however, you can detect a surprising amount of repetition. In the last sentence alone, the letters "er" were used twice, the letters "on" were used three times, and the letters "tion" were used twice. You can probably find other repetitions as well. If each repetition were replaced by a one byte token, the overall volume of data can be reduced—sometimes significantly. The key to data compression is the ability to search sequences of data and replace repeated sequences with shorter tokens.

The amount of compression then depends on the power of the search and replace algorithm. A more powerful algorithm can search larger amounts of data for larger repeating sequences—replacing larger sequences results in better compression. Unfortunately, more powerful compression algorithms usually require larger commitments of CPU time, which slows down a disk's operations. Of course, any token must be shorter than the sequence it is replacing: otherwise, compression would be pointless. Microsoft's Double-Space looks at data in 8KB blocks, so the chances of finding repetitive data sequences are much higher than that of a single sentence.

The importance of repeating data sequences raises an important question. What happens when a data sequence does not repeat? This is a very real and common possibility in everyday operation. If a data stream has few repeating elements, it cannot be compressed very well (if at all). For example, a graphic image (such as a screen shot) undergoes a certain amount of compression when the screen pixels are saved to a file. The .PCX file format uses an early form of compression called *run-length encoding*, which finds and removes repeating pixels (a much faster and simpler process than looking for repeating pixel sequences). When a compression utility tries to compress that .PCX file, there might be little or no effect on the file because many of the repeating sections have already been replaced with tokens of their own. As a rule, remember that compression is only as good as the data it is compressing. Highly repetitive data will be compressed much better than data with few or no repetitions. Table 12-1 illustrates some typical compression ratios for various file types.

THE COMPRESSION SYSTEM

At this point, you can see how compression is implemented on the system. Traditionally, DOS assigns a logical drive letter to each drive (such as drive C: for the first hard drive). When a compression system is installed on a PC, a portion of your drive is compressed into what is known as the *Compressed Volume File (CVF)*. The CVF effectively becomes the compressed drive. It contains all compressed files, and it is treated by DOS as if it were a separate logical drive. The drive that holds the CVF (e.g., your original C: drive) is known as the *host drive*. Because the vast majority of the drive will be compressed into

TABLE 12-1   TYPICAL COMPRESSION RATIOS

Executable programs	(.EXE and .COM files)	1.4:1
Word-processor documents	(.DOC files)	2.8:1
Spreadsheet files	(.XLS files)	3.3:1
Raw graphic bitmaps	(.BMP files)	4.0:1
Conventional ASCII text	(.TXT or .BAT files)	2.0:1
Sound files	(.WAV files)	1.1:1
Already compressed files	(.ZIP files)	1.0:1 (No subsequent compression)

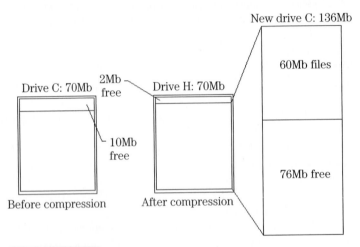

FIGURE 12-1   A hard-disk drive before and after compression.

the CVF, the host drive would have little space left. In actuality, some files (such as the Windows permanent swap file) must be left uncompressed, so you will normally leave 6MB to 10MB uncompressed. The remainder of the drive can be compressed.

Figure 12-1 illustrates the process for a small 70MB drive in a DOS/Windows 3.1x environment. Suppose that your uncompressed drive C: contains 60MB in files throughout various directories. On a 70MB drive, this leaves only 10MB free for your use. When a compression system is installed, the host drive is renamed to another drive letter (in this case, drive H:) and some small amount of space is kept aside as uncompressed space (for example, 2MB). The remaining 68MB of the 70MB drive undergoes compression and becomes the CVF. Even though the CVF is physically located on the same hard drive, the CVF is assigned its own drive letter (in this case, the CVF is "mounted as drive C:"). If you assume that the average compression ratio is 2.0:1, the compressed drive C: now has (68MB × 2.0) 136MB available. Because the original drive C: had 60MB in files, those same files are now available in compressed form. Instead of only 10MB free, the compressed volume now has about 76MB free. As far as DOS is concerned, any access to drive C: will affect the CVF. Any access to drive H: will affect the uncompressed area. The system boot drive is now drive H:.

If you list the directory for a host drive (using the /ah switch to include archive and hidden files), you will see the three DOS files: IO.SYS, MSDOS.SYS, and COMMAND.COM. If you use Windows, you might also find a fairly large file with a .PAR extension (such as 386SPART.PAR). This is the Windows permanent swap file. Also, several files are crucial for compression. For DoubleSpace, three files are needed. DBLSPACE.000 is the CVF file itself—the heart and soul of compression. Microsoft's more recent DriveSpace uses the file DRVSPACE.000. Stacker uses the filename STACVOL.DSK. If you were to erase this file, your compressed drive C: would be gone. DBLSPACE.BIN is the DoubleSpace driver that allows DOS access to the CVF (DRVSPACE.BIN for DriveSpace). DBLSPACE.INI is the DoubleSpace initialization file containing all of the information needed to configure DoubleSpace (DRVSPACE.INI for DriveSpace).

FACTORS THAT AFFECT COMPRESSION

As a technician, you should understand the factors that influence compression performance: the extra space created, the speed of compression/decompression, and the amount of memory needed to support compression/decompression. Of course, the primary purpose of compression is to provide additional disk space, so that is the principal measure of compression performance. Because compression products add a layer of processing between DOS and the disk, reads and writes will take a bit longer. These delays slow down the system—hardly crippling—but it can be annoying. Finally, compression needs memory-resident software to handle compression. Because software consumes conventional memory (often more than 35KB), this puts a serious strain on precious system resources (especially with DOS applications). If possible, you should load compressor software into upper memory rather than conventional memory. If not, there might not be enough conventional memory left to run the applications you need.

Before and After Compression

Whether you are installing a compression system for yourself or a customer, some steps and precautions should be taken in advance of the actual installation. A few minutes of advance planning can make the process much less painful. First, you must realize that the compression process requires about one minute per MB of space. If you are compressing 60MB, the process will take about 60 minutes. Even though the process is automated, the system is going to be on your bench for a while. Do yourself a favor and start the installation in the morning. You will also need to decide in advance how you want to arrange the compressed and uncompressed drives on the system. Do you want a single compressed volume? Do you want two or more compressed volumes? How much uncompressed space is required? Hammer this out with your customer. Finally, backup, backup, backup! Don't even consider installing a compression system unless a complete system backup is performed.

SCAN THE DISK FOR PHYSICAL DEFECTS

Compression problems can arise if the CVF tries to use sectors on the physical drive that are defective. If this occurs, you will not be able to access the file written in the damaged sector. To ensure that no undetected defects are in the drive, run a disk scanning utility such as ScanDisk (included with MS-DOS 6.2x and the Windows 95 Startup Disk), or use the scanning functions included with PC Tools or Norton Utilities. Any sectors that check bad will be marked in the FAT and avoided in the compression process.

DEFRAGMENT THE DISK AND CHECK FREE SPACE

Fragmentation is a common and undesirable by-product of DOS file allocation. The clusters that are used to hold a file become scattered around a disk, rather than positioned contiguously. When clusters become scattered, the drive has to work much harder to locate and reach each part of the file. Defragmentation re-arranges the files on your disk so that the clusters associated with each file are contiguous. You should thoroughly defragment your disk prior to compression. Use DEFRAG (included with MS-DOS 6.x and the Windows 95 Startup Disk) or a third-party defragmentation utility, such as PC Tools or Norton Utilities. After compressing the disk, check that at least 1.5MB of free space is on the disk—some free workspace is needed to perform the compression process.

CHECK THE DISK FOR FILE DEFECTS

It is important to detect any lost clusters or cross-linked files before installing a compression product. Use the DOS CHKDSK utility to find any disk errors. If lost clusters are reported, re-run CHKDSK with the /f (fix) switch to recover the lost clusters. Each lost cluster is recovered as a root directory file with a .CHK extension. You can then simply delete all .CHK files before continuing. If cross-linked files are indicated, note the names of those cross-linked files. Copy those files to new files and delete the originals—this should clear the cross-link conditions, but one or both of those files are now likely to be defective, so restore all cross-linked files from the system backup or original installation disks. If you have MS-DOS 6.2x (or a Windows 95 Startup Disk) available, you can use fix disk errors using ScanDisk instead of CHKDSK.

CHECK THE MEMORY

Remember that a compression package will need to run a TSR or device driver to achieve "on-the-fly" operation. This compression utility should be loaded into the upper memory area (if possible). Otherwise, it will consume precious conventional memory, which might prevent other memory-hungry DOS applications from running. Use the MEM function and look at the report for the "largest free upper memory block." If that number is larger than 45KB, chances are good that you can load the utility into the UMA during system initialization. If little or no upper memory is free, you will have to free sufficient memory by removing other drivers or TSRs, or seriously consider the impact of leaving the compression utility in conventional memory (this is highly undesirable).

INSTALL THE COMPRESSION UTILITY

If everything looks good up to now, you can go ahead and begin installation of the compression product. Both DoubleSpace/DriveSpace and Stacker can be started very simply, and the installation process for each is very automated. For specific installation and operation information, you should refer to the detailed instructions that accompany each product.

CREATE A BOOTABLE DISK

As you will see in Chapter 17, hard disks do fail for a wide variety of reasons. Now that your drive is compressed, you will need to create bootable disks that are "compression-aware." You could certainly boot the system from a conventional boot disk, but you would be unable to access your compressed drive(s). Fortunately, creating a compression-compatible boot disk is a simple matter.

For DoubleSpace/DriveSpace:
1 Format a blank floppy disk using the /s switch (i.e., FORMAT /s).
2 For DOS 6.0 and later, DBLSPACE.BIN (or DRVSPACE.BIN) will be copied along with IO.SYS, MSDOS.SYS, and COMMAND.COM.
3 Copy CONFIG.SYS to the floppy (i.e., COPY CONFIG.SYS A:).
4 Copy AUTOEXEC.BAT to the floppy (COPY AUTOEXEC.BAT A:).
5 Copy needed files referenced by CONFIG.SYS and AUTOEXEC.BAT, such as HIMEM.SYS, EMM386.EXE, MOUSE.COM, MSCDEX.EXE, etc. Check the startup files to find exactly what files are needed. You might have to edit CONFIG.SYS and AUTOEXEC.BAT to change the file paths to the floppy disk.
6 Copy other important DOS utilities, such as FDISK.EXE, FORMAT.COM, CHKDSK .EXE, DBLSPACE.EXE (or DRVSPACE.EXE), SYS.COM, and MEM.EXE.

For Stacker:
1 Format a blank floppy disk using the /s switch (i.e., FORMAT /s).
2 Copy CONFIG.SYS to the floppy (i.e., COPY CONFIG.SYS A:).
3 Copy AUTOEXEC.BAT to the floppy (COPY AUTOEXEC.BAT A:).
4 Copy needed files referenced by CONFIG.SYS and AUTOEXEC.BAT such as HIMEM.SYS, EMM386.EXE, MOUSE.COM, MSCDEX.EXE, etc. Check the startup files to find exactly what files are needed. You might have to edit CONFIG.SYS and AUTOEXEC.BAT to change the file paths to the floppy disk.
5 Copy other important DOS utilities, such as FDISK.EXE, FORMAT.COM, CHKDSK .EXE, STACKER.EXE, SYS.COM, and MEM.EXE.

Test the boot disk and see that no errors occur during initialization. You should also have access to the compressed drive(s) after booting from the compression-aware diskette.

DBLSPACE.INI AND DRVSPACE.INI FILE SETTINGS

Whether operating under DOS or Windows 95, DoubleSpace and DriveSpace disk compression tools record their operating parameters in a file called DBLSPACE.INI (or DRV-SPACE.INI). To successfully troubleshoot these utilities, you'll need to understand the contents of these .INI files and adjust them if necessary. The DBLSPACE.INI (or DRV-SPACE.INI) file might contain any of the following variables:

```
MaxRemovableDrives=
FirstDrive=
```

```
LastDrive=
MaxFileFragments=
ActivateDrive=
Automount=        (MS-DOS 6.2 and Windows 95)
DoubleGuard=      (MS-DOS 6.2 Only)
RomServer=        (MS-DOS 6.2 Only)
Switches=         (MS-DOS 6.2 Only)
```

DBLSPACE.INI and DRVSPACE.INI are text files with Read-Only, Hidden, and System attributes. These files are stored in the root directory of your startup drive (either C: or the host drive for C:). Always make a backup copy of the .INI file before you modify it! To uncover the file, use the ATTRIB command to remove the Read-Only, System, and Hidden attributes on the DBLSPACE.INI or DRVSPACE.INI file. For example:

```
attrib -s -h -r h:\dblspace.ini
```

Although you can change these variables yourself, you should avoid changing settings unless absolutely necessary. When possible, you should let DoubleSpace change the DBLSPACE.INI file for you (or allow DriveSpace to modify DRVSPACE.INI).

```
MaxRemovableDrives=n
```

This entry specifies how many additional drives DoubleSpace (or DriveSpace) should allocate memory for when your computer starts. The compression utility allocates a small amount of memory for each additional drive, and this variable determines how many additional compressed drives you can create or mount without restarting your computer.

To change this setting in DoubleSpace versions up to MS-DOS 6.2, start DBLSPACE and choose *Options* from the *Tools* menu. The *MaxRemovableDrives* setting corresponds to the *Number of removable media drives* option. To change this setting in later versions of DoubleSpace or DriveSpace, edit the DBLSPACE.INI or DRVSPACE.INI file with a text editor.

```
FirstDrive=x
```

This entry specifies the lowest drive letter available for use by DoubleSpace. FirstDrive is set by DBLSPACE.EXE each time it modifies the DBLSPACE.INI file, so do not attempt to change the FirstDrive variable yourself.

```
LastDrive=y
```

This entry specifies the highest drive letter available for use by DoubleSpace or DriveSpace. The compression utility assigns drive letters starting at LastDrive, and works back to FirstDrive. If another program uses one of the drive letters specified for DoubleSpace or DriveSpace, the highest drive letter available to the compression tool will be higher than LastDrive.

To change this entry in versions up to MS-DOS 6.2, run DBLSPACE and choose Options from the Tools menu. The *LastDrive* setting corresponds to the "Last drive reserved for DoubleSpace's use" option. To change this setting in later versions of DoubleSpace or DriveSpace, edit the DBLSPACE.INI or DRVSPACE.INI file with a text editor.

> If you change the DBLSPACE.INI file, do not set FirstDrive to a letter used by a physical or logical drive (such as drive C:). Also, do not set LastDrive and FirstDrive more than 13 letters apart.

```
MaxFileFragments=n
```

This value is set by DoubleSpace or DriveSpace to specify the degree of fragmentation to allow in all mounted compressed volume files (CVFs). After the compression tool is installed, the *MaxFileFragments* setting is changed to reflect the new number of file fragments in all CVFs each time a CVF is changed (i.e., deleted, mounted, or resized). The new value is the sum of file fragments in all mounted CVFs plus 110. For example, if the CVF on drive C has 6 fragments, and the CVF on drive D has three fragments, then MaxFileFragments=119 (110+6+3). The new value is used to allocate memory the next time that a CVF is mounted. Changes to DBLSPACE.INI that affect memory allocation take effect after you restart your computer.

To change this setting, you must edit the DBLSPACE.INI or DRVSPACE.INI file. However, with MS-DOS 6.2 (DoubleSpace), you can use the DBLSPACE /MAXFILE-FRAGMENTS= command. The initial *MaxFileFragments* setting (2600 for MS-DOS 6.0, or 10000 for MS-DOS 6.2) and the number added when a CVF is changed (110) are both read from the DBLSPACE.INF file (this is not the case with Windows 95).

> If you decrease the *MaxFileFragments* setting below the necessary value, DoubleSpace or DriveSpace might not be able to mount your compressed drives.

```
ActivateDrive=X,Yn
```

This specifies a CVF that DoubleSpace or DriveSpace should mount automatically when your computer starts. The DBLSPACE.INI and DRVSPACE.INI files can contain as many ActivateDrive= lines as CVFs, but only the first 15 ActivateDrive= lines are processed by the compression utilities. DoubleSpace and DriveSpace use the *X*, *Y*, and *n* parameters to determine which CVF to mount, and how to assign drive letters. The way these parameters are used depends on whether the specified CVF was created by compressing existing files, or created using free space on a drive, or if both types of CVFs exist on the same drive. The three options are:

- *CVF created by compressing existing files* If the specified CVF was created by compressing existing files, the CVF name is DBLSPACE.000 (or DRVSPACE.000). In this case, *X* specifies the drive letter assigned to the uncompressed (host) drive where the CVF is stored after it is mounted—this is the newly created drive letter. *Y* specifies the drive letter assigned to the compressed drive. *n* specifies the filename extension of the DBLSPACE.00n/DRVSPACE.00n CVF file (which is 0, in most cases). For example,

"ActivateDrive=H,C0" indicates that the CVF filename is DBLSPACE.000. When mounted, the CVF is assigned drive letter C:, and the uncompressed (host) drive (which contains the CVF after startup) is assigned drive letter H:. If the CVF is unmounted, the CVF exists on drive C:, and drive H: does not exist.

■ *CVF created by compressing free space* If the specified CVF was created by compressing free space on an existing drive, the CVF filename is DBLSPACE.001 for the first drive created, DBLSPACE.002 for the second drive created, and so on (substitute DRVSPACE if using DriveSpace). In this case, X specifies the drive letter assigned to the compressed drive—this is the newly created drive letter. Y specifies the drive letter assigned to the uncompressed (host) drive. n specifies the filename extension of the DBLSPACE.00n/DRVSPACE.00n CVF file, which is set to 1 for the first new CVF, 2 for the second new CVF, and so on. For example, "ActivateDrive=G,D2" indicates that the CVF filename is DBLSPACE.002 (the second CVF created by compressing free space). When mounted, the CVF is assigned drive letter G:, and the uncompressed (host) drive which contains the CVF before and after startup is assigned drive letter D:. If not mounted, the CVF exists on drive D:, and drive G: does not exist.

■ *Both types of CVF on the same drive* If the specified CVF was created by compressing free space on an MS-DOS drive that also contains a DBLSPACE.000 or DRV-SPACE.000 CVF (created by compressing existing files), the CVF filename is the same as noted (DBLSPACE.001, DBLSPACE.002, etc.), but it now doesn't matter which CVF was created first. X specifies the drive letter assigned to the compressed drive—this is the newly created drive letter. Y specifies the drive letter of the DBLSPACE.000 or DRVSPACE.000 CVF when mounted on the same MS-DOS drive. If DBL-SPACE.000 is not mounted, this is the drive letter where both the existing CVF and new CVF are stored. n specifies the filename extension of the DBLSPACE.00n or DRVSPACE.00n CVF file.

To change the ActivateDrive= line, edit the DBLSPACE.INI or DRVSPACE.INI file with a text editor. However, with MS-DOS 6.2, you can use the DBLSPACE /HOST command.

AutoMount=0, 1, A...Z (MS-DOS 6.2 and Windows 95 only)

This feature enables or disables the automatic mounting of removable drives (including floppy disk drives). By default, DoubleSpace automatically mounts all removable drives (AutoMount=1), and no entries are required in the DBLSPACE.INI file. DoubleSpace consumes 4K of additional memory with this setting enabled. To disable this setting, you must edit the DBLSPACE.INI file in a text editor. However, in MS-DOS versions you can use the DBLSPACE /AUTOMOUNT=0 command.

DoubleGuard=0, 1   (MS-DOS 6.2 only)

This feature enables or disables DoubleGuard safety checking for older versions of DoubleSpace. When DoubleGuard is enabled, DoubleSpace will constantly check its memory for damage by some other program. DoubleGuard safety-checking detects when another program has violated DoubleSpace's memory, and immediately shuts down your computer to minimize the chance of data loss. If further disk activity were to occur, you could lose some or all of the data on your drive because the data that DoubleSpace has in memory is probably invalid as a result of damage by the other program. By default, Double-

Guard is enabled (DoubleGuard=1), and no entries are required in the DBLSPACE.INI file. To disable this setting, type DBLSPACE /DOUBLEGUARD=0 at the MS-DOS command prompt. As a rule, do not disable DoubleGuard.

`RomServer=0, 1` (MS-DOS 6.2 only)

This feature enables or disables the check for a ROM BIOS Microsoft Real-time Compression Interface (MRCI) server under older versions of DoubleSpace. By default, the ROM MRCI check is disabled (RomServer=0), and no entries are required in the DBLSPACE.INI file. To enable this setting, type DBLSPACE /ROMSERVER=1 at the command prompt.

> You should not enable the ROM MRCI check unless you are certain that your hardware supports this feature.

`Switches=/F, /N, /FN`   (MS-DOS 6.2 only)

This feature controls the way in which the <Ctrl>+<F5> and <Ctrl>+<F8> keys work. Normally, you can press <Ctrl>+<F5> or <Ctrl>+<F8> to bypass older versions of DoubleSpace when your computer starts, and no entries are required in the DBLSPACE.INI file.

REMOVING DOS DOUBLESPACE OR DRIVESPACE MANUALLY

Ideally, the process of removing disk compression should be an automatic one. The maintenance program for DoubleSpace and DriveSpace should allow you to remove compression by choosing the Uncompress feature in the Tools menu. Still, in some situations, automatic decompression will not work, and it might be necessary to remove a compression package manually. The following procedure outlines a method of removing compression while preserving files. If you do not need to preserve your files, DoubleSpace provides a way to delete a compressed drive without manual intervention. You can delete a compressed volume file (CVF) using the DoubleSpace maintenance program interface or the command-line interface. To delete DoubleSpace using the DoubleSpace maintenance program, choose Delete from the Drive menu.

> In this procedure, it is assumed that you have compressed your boot drive (C:), and that your compressed host partition is H:.

> This procedure refers to MS-DOS 6.2 and DoubleSpace. However, if you're using MS-DOS 6.22, the procedure will work just as well. Just substitute DRVSPACE for DBLSPACE commands, DRVSPACE.* for DBLSPACE.*, and DRVSPACE.SYS for DBLSPACE.SYS.

1 Back up all the files you want to preserve from your compressed drive (C:). You can use any suitable backup technique for this.

2 When you finally remove DoubleSpace, what is now drive H: will become drive C:, which means you'll boot from drive H:. To boot from drive H: and restore your backup

files, the DoubleSpace host partition must contain the necessary MS-DOS system files and utilities. Also, if you stored your backup files on a network drive, network redirectors must be available.

3 Use the DIR command to determine how much free space you'll need to copy the MS-DOS files (and network redirectors) on the DoubleSpace host partition (drive H:). For example, to see how much space is needed for your MS-DOS files, type:

```
dir c:\dos
```

You'll see a list of files, then a set of statistics like:

```
194 file(s)          7003143 bytes
12959744 bytes free
```

The next-to-last line shows the number of bytes used by the files in the DOS directory—this is the amount of free disk space needed to store the necessary files and utilities after DoubleSpace is removed.

4 To free unused disk space from the DoubleSpace compressed volume, use the /SIZE switch like:

```
dblspace /size
```

5 Determine how much free space is on the DoubleSpace host partition (drive H:). Change to drive H: and use the DIR /A command. The last line of the report shows the number of bytes free on drive H:. If this number is greater than the number you found in step 3, enough space is available to copy the necessary files and utilities, and you can proceed.

6 If there is not enough space on the DoubleSpace host partition, delete enough files on drive C: to create the needed space (do not delete any MS-DOS or network files: those files must be present during this procedure). You can use the DELTREE command to do this. For example, to remove the WORD directory and all the files and subdirectories it contains, type:

```
deltree /y c:\word
```

After you delete some files, shrink the DoubleSpace volume file again by typing the following:

```
dblspace /size
```

To find out if you've created enough free disk space, change to drive H: and use the DIR command. The bytes in use and bytes free are displayed. If the bytes free line shows enough free disk space, continue on. Otherwise, clear additional space.

7 Copy all the MS-DOS and network files that you need to the DoubleSpace host partition (drive H:). To preserve the file and directory structure, you can use the XCOPY command with the /S switch. For example, to copy all the MS-DOS files into a DOS directory on H:, type:

```
md h:\dos xcopy c:\dos\*.* h:\dos /s
```

Be sure that a copy of COMMAND.COM is in the root of the DoubleSpace host partition (H:):

```
dir h:\command.com
```

If COMMAND.COM is not present, copy it from the boot drive (C:) with the following:

```
copy c:\command.com h:\
```

Repeat this step for AUTOEXEC.BAT and CONFIG.SYS files. These files need to be in the root of the DoubleSpace host partition as well. You now have all the files you need to boot from the uncompressed drive and restore your backup files: you can begin removing the DoubleSpace volume.

8 Switch to the root of the DoubleSpace host partition by typing:

```
h: cd\
```

9 Delete the DoubleSpace files by using the command:

```
deltree /y dblspace.*
```

10 If you are removing DoubleSpace from your boot drive, open the CONFIG.SYS file from the DoubleSpace host partition (H:) in a text editor, such as EDIT. If you are not removing DoubleSpace from your boot drive, open the CONFIG.SYS file for drive C:. Remove any reference to DBLSPACE.SYS. For example, change your DBL-SPACE.SYS DEVICE command to appear as follows:

```
rem device=c:\dos\dblspace.sys
```

11 You can now restart your computer by pressing <Ctrl>+<Alt>+<Del>. Once the system reboots in the uncompressed form, you can restore your backup files.

Troubleshooting Compressed Drives

Disk-compression products are some of the most thoroughly tested and robust computer programs ever released. They have to be—programs that trash a customer's vital data don't last long in the marketplace. However, the bewildering assortment of PC setups and utilities now in service will result in incompatibilities or disk errors somewhere along the line. This part of the chapter takes you through a selection of symptoms and solutions for DriveSpace, DoubleSpace, and Stacker. Remember that a complete system backup should be made (if possible) BEFORE attempting to deal with compression problems.

TROUBLESHOOTING WINDOWS 95 DRIVESPACE

Windows 95 also offers disk compression in the form of DriveSpace 3 which is included in the MS Plus! pack, sold separately. With DriveSpace 3, you can access drives that were compressed using DoubleSpace (included with MS-DOS versions 6.0 and 6.2), as well as DriveSpace for MS-DOS (included in MS-DOS version 6.22). In addition, DriveSpace 3 allows higher compression ratios on drives up to 2GB (earlier versions only support drives up to 512MB).

> DriveSpace 3 only works on FAT16 partitions. Drives that are partitioned as FAT32 (e.g., Windows 95 OSR2) cannot be compressed. Microsoft is considering a FAT32-compatible compression tool, but for now, do not use DriveSpace with OSR2.

Symptom 12-1. A DoubleGuard error code occurs This can occur under any version of DoubleSpace or DriveSpace. DoubleGuard has detected that an application (usually a device driver or TSR) has corrupted memory that DoubleSpace or DriveSpace was using. DoubleGuard halts your computer to prevent any further damage to your data. A typical DoubleGuard alarm message reads like:

```
DoubleGuard Alarm #<nn>
```

where *<nn>* is 13 (BitFAT buffer), 14 (MDFAT buffer), 15 (File Fragment List), or 16 (DBLSPACE.BIN Code Block). DoubleGuard errors are frequently caused by QEMM operating in the "stealth" mode, and Vertisoft SpaceManager 1.53 operating on a 286 machine running MS-DOS 6.2. Restart your computer by turning the power switch off, then on again. Boot to the DOS prompt (do not allow Windows 95 to start). At the DOS command prompt, type:

```
SCANDISK /ALL
```

This runs ScanDisk on all your drives to detect and correct any problems that might have been caused by the program that violated DoubleSpace's memory. Make a note of which program you were running (if any) when the DoubleGuard alarm occurred. That program is probably (but not necessarily) the program that caused the DoubleGuard alarm. If you receive additional DoubleGuard alarms, take notes about what you were doing and see if you can detect a pattern. You'll probably notice that a particular program, or combination of programs, is causing the alarm.

Symptom 12-2. A FAT 32 drive cannot be compressed This error is almost always encountered with DriveSpace and DriveSpace 3. The error appears such as:

```
Drive C cannot be compressed because it is a FAT32 drive.
ID Number: DRVSPACE378
```

This is because DriveSpace and DriveSpace 3 were both designed to work with the FAT12 and FAT16 file systems—they cannot be used with drives using the FAT32 file system implemented with Windows 95 OSR2. This problem has no resolution, except to abandon DriveSpace and use a FAT32-compatible disk-compression tool.

Symptom 12-3. The system is caught in a reboot loop after installing DriveSpace If you press the <F8> key when your computer restarts and then choose Command Prompt Only, your computer reboots again. If you choose Step-By-Step Confirmation, you can start Windows 95. But, when you run DriveSpace, your computer reboots again. Windows 95 must load the real-mode compression drivers into memory. As Windows 95 starts, RESTART.DRV tests for the existence of the real-mode compression drivers. If the real-mode compression drivers have not been loaded, the computer is restarted until the compression drivers have been loaded. If the real-mode compression drivers cannot be loaded, the computer restarts indefinitely. The three potential causes for this problem are:

- A "DRVSpace=0" or "DBLSpace=0" setting is present in the MSDOS.SYS file.
- The DRVSPACE.BIN or DBLSPACE.BIN file is damaged and was not loaded at startup.
- The EMM386 memory manager is using the lower E000h memory range (this is a known problem on Compaq Deskpro 386/20e computers, and may occur elsewhere).

Load the MSDOS.SYS file into a text editor and check for "DRVSpace=0" or "DBL-Space=0" settings. Disable the setting(s) by placing a semicolon at the beginning of the line, such as:

```
;DRVSpace=0
```

If no "DRVSpace=0" or "DBLSpace=0" settings are in the MSDOS.SYS file (or the problem persists), then rename the existing DRVSPACE.BIN and DBLSPACE.BIN files, then extract new copies of the files from your original Windows 95 disks or CD-ROM:

1 Restart the computer. When you see the "Starting Windows 95" message, press the <F8> key and choose *Safe mode command prompt only* from the *Startup* menu.

2 Delete the RESTART.DRV file from the hidden FAILSAFE.DRV folder on the physical boot drive (usually either drive C:, or the host for drive C: if drive C: is compressed), such as:

```
deltree <drive>:\failsafe.drv\restart.drv
```

where <drive> is the physical boot drive.

3 Copy the AUTOEXEC.BAT and CONFIG.SYS files from the hidden FAILSAFE.DRV folder on the physical boot to the root folder of drive C:—replacing the files that are already there, such as:

```
copy <drive>:\failsafe.drv\autoexec.bat c:\ /y
copy <drive>:\failsafe.drv\config.sys c:\ /y
```

where <drive> is the physical boot drive.

4 Remove the read-only, system, and hidden attributes from the DRVSPACE.BIN and DBLSPACE.BIN files in the root folder of the physical boot drive, such as:

```
attrib -r -s -h *.bin
```

5 Rename the DRVSPACE.BIN and DBLSPACE.BIN files in the root folder of the physical boot drive, such as:

```
ren *.bin *.bix
```

6 If you use the Microsoft Plus! pack, extract the DRVSPACE.BIN file from your original Microsoft Plus! disks or CD-ROM to the root folder of the physical boot drive. If you're using the retail version of Windows 95, extract the DRVSPACE.BIN file from your original Windows 95 disks or CD-ROM to the root folder of the physical boot drive. If you use OEM Service Release 2 (OSR2), extract the DRVSPACE.BIN file from your original OEM Service Release 2 disks or CD-ROM to the root folder of the physical boot drive.

7 Copy the DRVSPACE.BIN file in the root folder of the physical boot drive to a file named DBLSPACE.BIN in the root folder of the physical boot drive, such as:

```
copy <drive>:\drvspace.bin c:\dblspace.bin
```

where <drive> is the physical boot drive. If drive C: is compressed, copy the DRV-SPACE.BIN file to the root folder of the host drive such as:

```
copy <drive>:\drvspace.bin <x>:\dblspace.bin
```

where <drive> is the physical boot drive and <x> is the host drive for drive C.

You can now restart your computer normally. If this still does not resolve the problem, you might need to prevent EMM386 from loading. Simply restart your computer, and when you see the "Starting Windows 95" message, press the <F8> key, then choose Step-By-Step Confirmation from the Startup menu. When you are prompted to start EMM386, select No. If the problem disappears, you might need to reconfigure EMM386 to use a different memory range.

Symptom 12-4. The DriveSpace real-mode driver cannot be removed by Windows 95 Normally, the real-mode compression driver is unloaded from memory when the 32-bit DriveSpace driver (DRVSPACX.VXD) is initialized during Windows 95 startup. In this case, the real-mode memory (conventional or upper) used by the real-mode compression driver (DRVSPACE.BIN or DBLSPACE.BIN) cannot be reclaimed when you start Windows 95. This might cause problems with DOS-based programs that require more conventional memory than is available.

This problem can occur if you boot to a command prompt, then start Windows 95 by typing "win." The real-mode memory used by DRVSPACE.BIN (or DBLSPACE.BIN) cannot be reclaimed if you interrupt the normal Windows 95 boot process by pressing <F8> at the "Starting Windows 95" message, select Command Prompt Only from the Windows 95 Startup menu, and then type "win" to start Windows 95. Try starting Windows 95 normally, then exiting to the DOS mode as needed.

Also, the real-mode memory used by the compression drivers cannot be reclaimed if it is loaded into an upper memory block (UMB). If you load DRVSPACE.BIN (or DBL-SPACE.BIN) in upper memory using a command line such as:

```
devicehigh=c:\compres\drvspace.sys /move
```

try loading the driver file into conventional memory instead.

You might be using the "LoadTop=0" line in the MSDOS.SYS file. A setting of 0 does not let Windows 95 load the compression utility at the top of conventional memory (just below 640K). This prevents the unloading of DRVSPACE.BIN (or DBLSPACE.BIN) at Windows startup. Try editing the MSDOS.SYS file and changing the line to "Load-Top=1" or removing the "LoadTop" command line entirely.

Finally, DBLSPACE.BIN remains in memory if you are using a configuration consisting of DRVSPACE.INI and DBLSPACE.BIN. In this configuration, the DBLSPACE.BIN file is loaded as an installable device driver, and is not transitioned to DRVSPACX.VXD. If you use both DBLSPACE.BIN and DRVSPACE.BIN with DRVSPACE.INI, DRV-SPACE.BIN is given priority and this behavior does not occur. Start Windows 95 normally, and change the command in the CONFIG.SYS file from such as:

```
devicehigh=c:\compres\drvspace.sys /move
```

to:

```
device=c:\compres\drvspace.sys /move
```

Remove the "LoadTop=0" command line from the MSDOS.SYS file (if it's there). Rename the DRVSPACX.VXD file in the Windows\System\Iosubsys folder, and reinstall the file. If Microsoft Plus! for Windows 95 is not installed, simply run Windows 95 Setup again, and choose *Restore Windows files that are changed or corrupted* when you are prompted. If Microsoft Plus! for Windows 95 is installed, click *Start*, point to *Settings*, then click *Control Panel*. Double-click the *Add/Remove Programs* icon. On the *Install/Uninstall* tab, click *Microsoft Plus! For Windows 95*, then click *Add/Remove*. When Setup begins, click *Reinstall*. Restart the computer. The real-mode compression utility should now be removed and replaced with the protected-mode version when Windows 95 starts.

Symptom 12-5. DriveSpace does not restart in mini-Windows mode When you perform a DriveSpace operation that requires Windows 95 to restart, you find that Windows 95 is unable to restart in mini-Windows mode, so the operation fails. This problem generally occurs if the files in the hidden FAILSAFE.DRV folder or the Mini.cab file in the Windows\System folder are damaged. These files are required for Windows 95 to restart in mini-Windows mode. The computer might lock up, or generate an error message such as:

```
DrvSpace caused a General Protection Fault in module W31SPACE.EXE
DrvSpace caused a Page Fault in module W31SPACE.EXE
Error Loading PROGMAN.EXE
Error Loading GDI.EXE
Error Loading USER.EXE
Error loading VGA.DRV
Cannot start Windows in standard mode
Segment load failure in W31space.exe
Standard Mode: Bad fault in MSDos Extender
```

Restart your computer and boot to the DOS command prompt (press the <F8> key when you see the "Starting Windows 95" message, then choose *Command Prompt Only* from the Startup menu). Next, copy the AUTOEXEC.BAT and CONFIG.SYS files from the hidden FAILSAFE.DRV folder on the physical boot drive (usually either drive C:, or the host for drive C: if drive C: is compressed) to the root directory of drive C:—replacing the files that are already there:

```
copy <drive>:\failsafe.drv\autoexec.bat c:\ /y
copy <drive>:\failsafe.drv\config.sys c:\ /y
```

where <drive> is the physical boot drive. Now remove the Failsafe.drv folder from the physical boot drive such as:

```
deltree <drive>:\failsafe.drv
```

where <drive> is the physical boot drive. Copy the MINI.CAB file from your original Windows 95 disks or CD-ROM to the \Windows\System folder. The MINI.CAB file is located on disk 1 of the standard 3.5-inch Windows 95 disks, or in the Win95 folder on the Windows 95 CD-ROM. You can copy this file using Windows Explorer or the COPY command. If you are using Microsoft Plus! for Windows 95 and you do not have access to your original Windows 95 disks or CD-ROM, you can extract the MINI.CAB file from the Microsoft Plus! disks or CD-ROM. The MINI.CAB file is located in the PLUS_2.CAB file on the CD-ROM, or in the PLUS_1.CAB file on the disks. Finally, restart Windows 95 normally and run DriveSpace to repeat your operation again.

> The FAILSAFE.DRV folder might contain drivers necessary for troubleshooting if you cannot correct the problem. Copy the FAILSAFE.DRV folder and all its contents to another drive or folder before deleting it.

Symptom 12-6. The MINI.CAB file is missing or corrupt When you are compressing a drive using DriveSpace or DriveSpace 3, you receive one of the following error messages when the operation is about 25% complete:

```
The MINI.CAB file is missing or damaged—ID Number: DRVSPACE331

Windows cannot create the C:\FAILSAFE\FAILSAFE.DRV\W31SPACE.EXE file—ID
Number: DRVSPACE125
```

Either of these error messages might be followed by the error message: "ID Number: DRVSPACE311." These error messages can occur if you are running IBM AntiVirus for Windows 95 with certain virus-protection features enabled. Run the IBM AntiVirus program and disable the "Warn When Viral Activity Occurs" and "Check Files When Opened" options in System Shield (located under the Setup menu item).

> When these two options are enabled, IBM AntiVirus also impairs your ability to create a Startup disk from the Add/Remove Programs tool in Control Panel, and might cause problems with some self-extracting installation programs. When these problems occur, you might receive an error message, such as "File Copying Problem."

Symptom 12-7. A DRVSPACE 125 error occurs when using DriveSpace 3 When you try to compress drive C: with DriveSpace 3, you might receive the following error message when the compression process is 25-percent finished: "Windows cannot create the C:\MSDOSSYS.TMP file. There might not be enough free space on the drive C, the root directory of drive C might be full, or the disk might be write-protected—ID Number: DRVSPACE125." In almost all cases, this error occurs if the root folder on drive C: already contains the maximum allowable number of files (512). When this happens, DriveSpace 3 cannot create the temporary files it needs to finish the compression process.

You'll need to move or delete unnecessary files in the root folder on drive C:, then continue the compression process.

This error might also occur when the compression process is 100% finished if you are compressing a drive that is not the boot drive. The actual filename referenced in the error message can also vary. For example, the error message: "Cannot create the file DRVSPACE.000" is generated when the root folder of the drive being compressed is full. A similar error message might occur if a file is named FAILSAFE.DRV in the root folder of drive C: (or the host for drive C:). If you find this to be the case, remove the FAILSAFE.DRV file and continue the compression operation.

Symptom 12-8. The DriveSpace VxD and real-mode driver are mismatched

If you install, remove, then reinstall Windows 95, you might receive the following error message when you start Windows 95: "DriveSpace Warning—The DriveSpace VxD and the DriveSpace real-mode driver are mismatched. You may need to reinstall them. Press any key to continue." When you press a key, Windows 95 will probably start, but it will likely be unstable. You might see unusual characters on the screen, and you might receive "fatal exception" error messages. This is because DriveSpace 3 (in the Microsoft Plus! pack for Windows 95) places real-mode drivers on the hard disk that are not removed when you delete the Windows folder. When you reinstall Windows 95, Setup places a DriveSpace VxD in the \Iosubsys folder that is incompatible with the DriveSpace 3 drivers. You'll need to replace the DRVSPACX.VXD file in the \Iosubsys folder with the correct version from the original Microsoft Plus! disks or CD-ROM.

Restart your computer normally. When you see the "Starting Windows 95" message, press the <F8> key and choose Command Prompt Only from the Startup menu. Change to the \Windows\System\Iosubsys folder and rename the DRVSPACX.VXD file to DRVSPACX.OLD. Extract the DRVSPACX.VXD file from the Microsoft Plus! CD-ROM or original disks to the \Iosubsys folder (the DRVSPACX.VXD file is located in the PLUS_1.CAB file on both the Microsoft Plus! disks and CD-ROM) such as: "Extract <drive>:\plus_1.cab drvspacx.vxd /L <destination>," where <destination> is the Windows\System\Iosubsys folder and <drive> is the drive containing the Microsoft Plus! disk or CD-ROM. Now restart your computer normally.

If you still receive a "mismatch" error message when the computer starts (and the DRVSPACE.BIN file is the correct version), check for a DBLSPACE.BIN file dated 7/11/95 or earlier (Table 12-2). This file is a hidden file in the root folder of the boot drive. If this file exists, rename it to DBLSPACE.OLD, then restart your computer. DriveSpace 3 does not require DBLSPACE.BIN to mount compressed volumes. This problem can also occur if you reinstall Windows 95 to a different folder than its original folder after you install Microsoft Plus!. If you reinstalled Windows 95 in a different folder, edit the MSDOS.SYS file on both the host drive and the compressed drive. Be sure that the PATH statement points to the correct folder. After you edit the MSDOS.SYS file(s), save the file(s), then restart your computer.

Symptom 12-9. Windows 95 detects a compressed drive access error

This error typically crops up when the system first starts. Windows 95 cannot mount the compressed drive used during startup because the names of the .BIN and the .INI files used for compression do not match. Verify that the versions of the .BIN files match the

TABLE 12-2 DOUBLESPACE FILE VERSIONS WITH AND WITHOUT MICROSOFT PLUS!

Windows 95 without Microsoft Plus!:

FILENAME	DATE/TIME	SIZE	LOCATION
DRVSPACE.BIN	07-11-95 9:50am	71,287	C:\ and root of compressed drive
DBLSPACE.BIN	07-11-95 9:50am	71,287	C:\ and root of compressed drive
DRVSPACX.VXD	07-11-95 9:50am	54,207	C:\windows\system\iosubsys

Windows 95 with Microsoft Plus!:

FILENAME	DATE/TIME	SIZE	LOCATION
DRVSPACE.BIN	07-14-95 12:00am	64,135	C:\ and root of compressed drive
DBLSPACE.BIN	07-14-95 12:00am	64,135	C:\ and root of compressed drive
DRVSPACX.VXD	07-14-95 12:00am	61,719	C:\windows\system\iosubsys

Windows 95 OEM Service Release 2:

FILENAME	DATE/TIME	SIZE	LOCATION
DRVSPACE.BIN	08-24-96 12:00am	65,271	C:\ and root of compressed drive
DBLSPACE.BIN	08-24-96 12:00am	65,271	C:\ and root of compressed drive
DRVSPACX.VXD	07-14-95 12:00am	57,466	C:\windows\system\iosubsys

compression version in use (Table 12-2). DriveSpace for Windows 95 has file dates of 7/11/95. DriveSpace 3 (included with Microsoft Plus!) has file dates of 7/14/95. If the .BIN files do not have the correct date, update the files on the hard disk and the Startup disk (if you do not have a startup disk yet, you should create one).

If the DRVSPACE.BIN file is present and the DBLSPACE.BIN file is not (and there is a DBLSPACE.INI file), create a DBLSPACE.BIN file. Restart your computer—when you see the "Starting Windows 95" message, press the <F8> key, then choose *Safe Mode Command Prompt Only* from the *Startup* menu. At the command prompt, type the following line and then press <Enter>:

```
copy drvspace.bin dblspace.bin
```

Restart your computer normally. If the problem persists, rename the DBLSPACE.INI file to DRVSPACE.INI by rebooting to the *Safe Mode Command Prompt Only* and typing:

```
ren dblspace.ini drvspace.ini
```

Restart your computer normally. If the problem still persists, use ScanDisk to check the compressed volume. Reboot to the *Save Mode Command Prompt Only* and start ScanDisk:

```
scandisk /mount= <yyy> <x>:
```

where <yyy> is the file name extension of the compressed volume file (CVF), and <x> is the drive containing the CVF. ScanDisk creates a DBLSPACE.BIN file and mounts the

CFV. For example, to mount a CVF named DRVSPACE.000 on drive C, type the following line:

```
scandisk /mount=000 c:
```

Symptom 12-10. Windows 95 cannot delete a compressed drive When you attempt to delete a compressed drive under Windows 95, an error message appears, such as: "Windows cannot perform this operation because the enhanced mode disk compression driver could not be loaded. You may need to run setup again to install additional disk components. DRVSPACE 545." This problem occurs if the Windows 95 protected-mode DriveSpace driver (DRVSPACX.VXD) is missing or corrupted. In these cases, Windows 95 loads the real-mode DriveSpace driver for minimum support, but deletion operations are not possible with the real-mode driver. You'll need to reinstall the protected-mode compression driver DRVSPACX.VXD from the original Windows 95 disks or CD-ROM.

Rename the DRVSPACX.VXD file on your hard disk. This file should be located in the \WINDOWS\SYSTEM\IOSUBSYS subdirectory. Click the *Start* button on the Taskbar, and click *Files Or Folders* on the *Find* menu. In the *Find: All Files* dialog box, type: DRVSPACX.VXD in the *Named* box. Click the *Find Now* button. In the file-listing box, use the right mouse button (RMB) to click the file DRVSPACX.VXD, then click *Rename*. Rename the file: DRVSPACX.OLD, then press <Enter>.

If the DRVSPACX.VXD file is missing (not found on the hard disk that contains Windows 95), you'll need to extract DRVSPACX.VXD from the original Windows 95 disk(s) to the \WINDOWS\SYSTEM\IOSUBSYS sub-directory. Insert Disk 11 in the floppy disk drive, or insert the Windows 95 Setup CD in the CD-ROM drive. On the Taskbar, click *Start*, then *Programs*, then click *MS-DOS Prompt*. At the command line, type:

```
extract /l <drive>:\windows\system\iosubsys <drive>:\A drvspacx.vxd
```

where <drive> indicates the letter designating the drive containing the floppy disk or CD-ROM. Now restart the system.

Symptom 12-11 DriveSpace for Windows 95 reports that drive C: contains errors that must be corrected Such problems might occur when upgrading from DriveSpace to DriveSpace 3, when you compress an existing uncompressed drive, when you uncompress a compressed drive, or when you create a new empty compressed drive. You might encounter any of the following error messages: "You cannot upgrade drive X because it contains errors. To upgrade this drive, first run ScanDisk on it, and then try again to upgrade it. ID Number: DRVSPACE 424." "Drive X contains errors that must be corrected before the drive can be compressed. To correct them run ScanDisk. ID Number: DRVSPACE 306." "Drive X contains errors that must be corrected before the drive can be uncompressed. To correct them, run ScanDisk. ID Number: DRVSPACE 307." "Drive C contains errors that must be corrected before the drive can be used to create a new compressed drive. To correct them run ScanDisk. ID Number: DRVSPACE 308."

In virtually all cases, these errors occur if the drive contains a folder with a path that contains more than 66 characters. Fortunately, you can work around the problem. Start the ScanDisk utility. Click the *Automatically fix errors* check box to clear it, then begin checking the drive. When you receive the following error message: "The <path> folder could not be opened in MS-DOS mode because its complete short name was longer than 66 characters."

Make a note of the path that is longer than 66 characters, then click *Ignore*. If you receive more than one such message, note each path. After ScanDisk is finished, move each folder whose path contains more than 66 characters to another location with a shorter path. Now proceed to perform the desired DriveSpace operation. After DriveSpace has finished, move each folder that you just moved back to its original location (path).

Troubleshooting DOS DoubleSpace and DriveSpace

DoubleSpace emerged in the early 1990s with MS-DOS 6.0 as a means of maximizing available drive space. Although early implementations of DoubleSpace suffered from questionable reliability, subsequent patches and releases proved to be adequate. DoubleSpace then came under attack from Stac Electronics (makers of Stacker) who claimed that Microsoft absconded with key DoubleSpace code. In the ensuing litigation, Microsoft dropped DoubleSpace, and replaced it with their own DOS product called *DriveSpace*. Both DoubleSpace and DriveSpace support DOS and Windows 3.1x. The latest version of DriveSpace supports Windows 95 natively.

Symptom 12-12. Some applications do not run properly on a Double-Space-compressed drive A number of DOS games and utilities do not run well (if at all) from a drive compressed with DoubleSpace. The following list highlights some of the more notable products:

- Argus Financial Software
- Complete PC software that uses voice files
- Empire Deluxe
- Epic Megagames' Zone66 and Ken's Labyrinth
- Informix relational database
- Links and Links 386 from Access Software
- Lotus 1-2-3 version 2.01
- Movie Master version 4.0
- MultiMate versions 3.3 and 4.0
- Quicken (MS-DOS-based version)
- Tony LaRussa Baseball II
- Zsoft PhotoFinish

Most DOS and Windows applications should work just fine with DoubleSpace, but with the proliferation of complex software in the marketplace today, some applications might be copy protected, or do not perform well from the compressed state. If such a situation occurs, try moving the application to the uncompressed host drive (or reinstalling it to the uncompressed drive outright). To fit your application into uncompressed space, you might have to resize the CVF to free additional space on the host drive. You can resize the CVF through the DBLSPACE control panel, or directly from the DOS command line. For example:

```
C:\> dblspace /size /reserve=3
```

will change the CVF size so that 3MB are free on the host drive. It might also be that the application needs an unusually large amount of conventional memory. Because DBL-SPACE.BIN needs about 33KB of memory, try loading DBLSPACE.BIN into upper memory by changing the command line in CONFIG.SYS to:

```
devicehigh=c:\dos\dblspace.bin /move
```

Symptom 12-13. A "CVF is damaged" error message appears when the system starts The Compressed Volume File (CVF) is a single file that contains all of the compressed drive's data, which is accessed as a unique logical drive. In effect, the CVF is the compressed drive. The physical hard drive that contains the CVF is the host drive. Under most circumstances, the CVF occupies most of the host drive, except for some area that should not be compressed (such as a Windows permanent swap file).

When DoubleSpace activates on system startup, it performs a check on the CVF's internal data structures that are an equivalent of a DOS CHKDSK. If DoubleSpace detects an error, such as lost allocation units or cross-linked files, the "CVF is damaged" error message appears. The way to correct this type of problem is to run a correction utility. DOS 6.2 offers the ScanDisk utility, but DOS 6.0 and earlier versions of DOS provide you with CHKDSK. Once the disk is corrected, DoubleSpace should work correctly.

Symptom 12-14. A DoubleGuard alert appears in DOS DoubleGuard is a DOS 6.2 utility that helps protect DoubleSpace and DriveSpace from memory conflicts that otherwise might corrupt data on the CVF. If DoubleGuard detects a checksum error in the memory used by disk compression, a rogue program or device driver has probably written in the DoubleSpace memory area. When an error is detected by DoubleGuard, the system simply halts before damage can occur (you'll have to reboot the computer to continue).

Boot the system clean (with no device drivers), then use ScanDisk or CHKDSK to deal with any potential errors on the hard disk. Re-activate one device driver at a time until you can re-create the error. When you find the offending device driver, you can keep it unloaded, or find a way to load it without conflict.

Symptom 12-15. Free space is exhausted on a compressed drive One of the problems with DoubleSpace and DriveSpace is that it is difficult to know how much space is available. Because different files compress differently, there is no way to be absolutely sure just how much space you have to work with. Available disk space must be "predicted" using a compression ratio that you set. By adjusting the predicted compression ratio, you can adjust the amount of reported free space. As a result, MS DOS can "lie." If you seem to be running low on space, try changing the compression ratio from the DOS command line such as:

```
C:\> dblspace /ratio=2.5
```

Ideally, you want to set the compression ratio as close as possible to the actual compression ratio—this will yield the most accurate prediction of available space. If you are unable to change your drive's compression ratio, it might be time to defragment the drive. Disk-compression tools have trouble using highly fragmented drives for file storage. If you are having trouble with drive space, try defragmenting the drive with DOS DEFRAG or another defragmentation utility. If the drive really is out of space, you can increase the size of the CVF by taking space from the uncompressed host (if any more uncompressed space is available). From the DOS command line, start DBLSPACE and use the Change Size function to alter the compressed volume size. You can also adjust the volume size directly from the command line. For example:

```
C:\> dblspace /size /reserve=1.5
```

this command will change the compressed drive size, leaving 1.5MB of uncompressed space on the host drive. If you need to free space on the host drive so that you can increase the size of the CVF, try deleting unneeded files from the uncompressed host drive.

Symptom 12-16. Free space is exhausted on the host drive Under normal use, little free space will be reserved for the host drive anyway—the greatest space advantage with DoubleSpace will be realized when the maximum amount of host drive space is compressed. Only Windows swap files and incompressible applications normally reside outside of the CVF. However, in some occasions, it becomes necessary to place data on the uncompressed drive. Eventually, the host might run out of space. If the files listed in the host directory do not seem large enough to exhaust the space, some hidden files might be on the host drive. Perform a DIR /AH to list all files, including archive and hidden files. The easiest way to correct this problem is to resize the CVF to reserve more free space for the host drive. This can be done from the DBLSPACE control panel or directly from the DOS command line with a command such as:

```
C:\> dblspace /size /reserve=4
```

which would resize the CVF to keep 4MB of uncompressed space on the host drive. Of course, enough free space must on the CVF to be freed to the host drive. If the CVF is very full or is highly fragmented, it might not be possible to resize the CVF.

Symptom 12-17. Estimated compression ratio cannot be changed You might be setting the estimated compression ratio too high. Remember that the amount of free space reported for the CVF is only an estimate based on the compression ratio that you set in DoubleSpace or DriveSpace. If you make the estimated compression ratio larger, more free space is reported, and vise versa. However, DoubleSpace can only work with compressed drive sizes up to 512MB (DriveSpace 3 for Windows 95 can handle up to 2GB). An example will make this clearer.

Assume that you have a compressed drive with 300MB of files and 100MB of true (uncompressed) free space. A compression ratio of 2:1 would cause this 100MB to be reported as 200MB. The 200MB estimated free space plus the 300MB of used space results in total CVF drive space of (300MB + 200MB) = 500MB. If you try adjusting the estimated compression ratio to 2.5:1, that 100MB of true free drive space would be reported as 250MB.

Because 300MB and 250MB add to more than 512MB, an error will be produced. Keep the compression ratio down so that the total CVF drive space does not exceed 512MB.

Symptom 12-18. Compressed drive size cannot be reduced DoubleSpace and DriveSpace are extremely sensitive to file fragmentation because of the way in which disk space is assigned. As a result, it is important to defragment the CVF regularly to keep your compressed drive's performance at an optimum level. You can use DEFRAG or other defragmentation utilities to defragment the drive.

Other factors can also contribute to fragmentation warnings that prevent reducing the CVF size. A delete-tracking program, such as MIRROR, can be saving its MIRORSAV.FIL file at the end of the drive volume—this creates immediate fragmentation of the drive because the file skips all free space to the very end of the volume. The Norton Utilities delete-tracking program IMAGE creates the same problem by saving its IMAGE.IDX file at the end of the CVF. Thus, DoubleSpace cannot reduce the size of the CVF because the tracking file now occupies the highest sectors. Your best tactic here is to disable the delete-tracking utility in CONFIG.SYS or AUTOEXEC.BAT, change the tracking file's attributes with the DOS ATTRIB function, erase the tracking file, and defragment the drive.

```
(for files created by MIRROR)        C:\> attrib mirorsav.fil  -s -h -r
(for files created by IMAGE)         C:\> attrib image.idx  -s -h -r
```

You should then be able to resize the CVF without problems. It might also be impossible to reduce the size of your CVF because a FAT entry for the CVF indicates that an allocation unit is unreadable (including a "bad allocation unit") entry. The CVF can only be reduced to the point at which the bad entry occurs. If you suspect a problem with a bad cluster, it is possible to use a disk editor, such as The Norton Utilities or PC Tools, to change the FAT entry from bad (FFF7h) to unused (0h). Be sure to use extreme caution if you use a disk editor. You can corrupt the entire disk by making erroneous changes to the FAT.

Symptom 12-19. DEFRAG fails to fully defragment the drive DoubleSpace reports that the drive is still fragmented even after performing a full defragmentation procedure. This type of symptom is another manifestation of hidden system delete-tracking files generated by utilities, such as IMAGE or MIRROR. You can see the file by performing a DIR /AH. Because both utilities place hidden system files at the end of the drive volume, DEFRAG cannot move the file. You can delete the offending file:

```
(for files created by MIRROR)        C:\> deltree mirorsav.fil
(for files created by IMAGE)         C:\> deltree image.idx
```

then disable the delete-tracking utility from your AUTOEXEC.BAT or CONFIG.SYS files. You can also change the attributes of the offending file, which will allow DEFRAG to move the file appropriately during the defragmentation process:

```
(for files created by MIRROR)        C:\> attrib mirorsav.fil  -s -h -r
(for files created by IMAGE)         C:\> attrib image.idx  -s -h -r
```

Symptom 12-20. You see a "Swap file is corrupt" error message when starting Windows 3.1x Unless your PC carries more than 16MB of RAM, Windows

3.1x will need supplemental storage space to support the various applications that are loaded and run during normal operation. The hard drive is used to provide this supplemental space in the form of virtual memory—that is, an area of the hard drive is used to hold the contents of RAM. This virtual area is known as the *swap file*. Although you have the choice between a permanent and temporary swap file, most installations of Windows use a *Permanent Swap File (PSF)*. Unfortunately, Windows does not support a compressed permanent swap file under DoubleSpace or DriveSpace. If you compress your drive and include the Windows PSF, the swap file will be reported as corrupt when you try to start Windows. You will need to re-create a PSF on the host (uncompressed) drive.

- Start the *Control Panel* from the Program Manager's *Main* group.
- Doubleclick on the *386 Enhanced* icon to open the *386 Enhanced* dialog box, then click on the *Virtual memory* button to access the *Virtual memory* dialog box.
- Click on the *Change* button.
- Choose an uncompressed drive (usually the host drive) by selecting the drive from the *Drive* pull-down list.
- Choose the *Permanent* file type from the *Type* pull-down list.
- Enter the desired size for the new PSF in the *New Size* box (Windows will suggest a default size based on the amount of memory and disk space available).
- You can select the default or enter a new value.
- Select *OK* to initiate the new PSF.

Symptom 12-21. You cannot access compressed drive(s) after booting from a system disk created by the Windows 3.1x The DoubleSpace or DriveSpace utility has not been copied to the floppy. The Windows 3.1x File Manager allows you to create bootable floppy disks. However, Windows will not copy the vital DBLSPACE.BIN file (or DRVSPACE.BIN) to the floppy—although the *FORMAT /s* command under DOS 6.0 and 6.2 will. If you make a bootable disk from Windows 3.1x, you'll have to complete the process in DOS by copying the DBLSPACE.BIN (or DRVSPACE.BIN) file to the floppy manually using a command such as:

```
C:\> copy \dos\dblspace.bin a:\
```

Symptom 12-22. Compressed drive is too fragmented to resize When you try to resize a DoubleSpace or DriveSpace drive, you receive an error message, such as:

```
Drive <X> is too fragmented to resize.  Before resizing drive <X>, defrag-
ment it by typing DEFRAG.EXE /H /Q <X>: at the DOS command prompt.
```

where <X> is the drive letter of the compressed drive. Try running Defrag, as suggested. If DEFRAG /H /Q <X>: does not correct the problem, you have a system file located at the end of your DoubleSpace or DriveSpace drive (possibly IO.SYS, MSDOS.SYS, or a system file created by a delete-tracking, disk image, erase protect, or format-protection software). You might have a bad sector on your host drive near the end of the *Compressed Volume File (CVF)*. Also, software might be installed on your system that uses a copy-protection scheme with clusters marked as "bad" to store data. The programs in Table 12-3 write system files at the end of a drive and commonly cause the error message noted previously:

TABLE 12-3 PROGRAMS KNOWN TO INTERFERE WITH CVFG OPERATION

PROGRAM NAME	PROGRAM FILE NAME	SYSTEM FILE CREATED
Microsoft MS-DOS Mirror	MIRROR.COM	MIRORSAV.FIL
Central Point Mirror	MIRROR.COM	MIRORSAV.FIL
Symantec Norton Image	IMAGE.EXE	IMAGE.IDX
Symantec Norton Format Recover	FR.EXE	FRECOVER.IDX
Microsoft MS-DOS 5.0 Undelete	MIRROR.COM	PCTRACKR.DEL
MS-DOS 6.0/6.2 Delete Tracker	UNDELETE.EXE	PCTRACKR.DEL
MS-DOS 6.0/6.2 Delete Sentry	UNDELETE.EXE	CONTROL.FIL
Central Point Delete Tracker	UNDELETE.EXE	PCTRACKR.DEL
Central Point Delete Sentry	UNDELETE.EXE	CONTROL.FIL

If you are running MS-DOS 6.2 (and no copy-protected software is on the system), run ScanDisk to perform a surface scan on your host drive. For example, type:

```
scandisk <host drive>: /surface
```

at the MS-DOS command prompt, then press <Enter>. If you are running MS-DOS 6.0, unmount the compressed drive and run a third-party surface scan product, such as Symantec's Norton Utilities Norton Disk Doctor (NDD.EXE) or Central Point Software's DiskFix. If the surface-scan program detects and corrects a bad cluster, you should now be able to resize your drive. If you still cannot resize the drive, use the DIR command to search for hidden system files on the compressed drive. For example, if your compressed drive is drive C:, type:

```
dir c: /s /as /p
```

at the MS-DOS command prompt, then press <Enter>. Use ATTRIB to remove the file attributes on the system files that you found. For example, if you have a Mirror file on drive C:, type the following at the DOS prompt, then press <Enter>:

```
attrib -r -s -h c:\mirorsav.fil
```

If the system files that you detect are used by a delete-tracking program, you need to reboot your computer without loading the corresponding program file before you change the file attributes on the system file.

You should now be able to resize the compressed drive with Defrag. If you can successfully resize the compressed drive, reset the file attributes on the system files that you found. For example, type the following at the DOS prompt and then press <Enter>:

```
attrib +r +s +h c:\mirorsav.fil
```

If you were not able to resize the compressed drive, edit the DBLSPACE.INI file and increase the *MaxFileFragments* entry. Start by removing the read-only, system, and hidden file attributes on the DBLSPACE.INI file. For example, if drive H: is your host drive, type the following at the command prompt and press <Enter>:

```
attrib -r -s -h h:\dblspace.ini
```

Using a text editor, such as EDIT, alter the DBLSPACE.INI file and increase the value for *MaxFileFragments* (2000 is a good number to try). Save the DBLSPACE.INI file and exit the text editor. Restart your computer and try to resize the drive now.

   If you are using copy-protected software, you might be able to work around this problem by using a third-party disk-edit program, such as Symantec's Norton Utilities or Central Point Software's PC Tools, to change the cluster's status from "bad" to "unused" (change the status from FFF7 to 0). However, this usually leaves the copy-protected software unusable. Uninstall the copy-protected software (if possible), resize the compressed drive, then reinstall the copy-protected software.

Symptom 12-23. An error writing to the CVF occurs during defragmenting
If you run Defrag and the *Compressed Volume File (CVF)* is full or nearly full, Defrag might report:

```
Error writing cluster nnn,nnn
Use a disk repair program to fix, then run DEFRAG again.
```

   If CHKDSK shows no problems, and a surface scan utility (such as Symantec's Norton Disk Doctor [NDD.EXE]) shows no problems, the error message is occurring because Defrag is unable to write the information that it has read. Defrag is trying to copy a cluster before moving it, but because the compressed drive is too fragmented or full, no space is large enough to write the cluster. Chances are that the CVF itself is okay. You can work around this issue by increasing the size of your compressed drive, then running Defrag, or simply deleting enough files to allow Defrag to run.

Symptom 12-24. DoubleSpace or DriveSpace does not work properly on systems with Promise Technologies VL IDE controller cards The Promise Technologies (**http://www.promise.com**) model 4030VL VESA local-bus cached IDE controller card and the model DC200 ISA-cached IDE controller card both need a firmware update to run properly with the DoubleSpace and DriveSpace disk-compression programs. Three EPROMs are used for the model 4030VL controller card. Check the last four digits of the EPROM number. If the last four digits are 203E, 203O, or 203X, the card is compatible with DoubleSpace and DriveSpace. The compatible revisions as of June 20, 1993 are P43204-E, P43204-O, and P43204-X. The model DC200 controller card also has three EPROMs. If the number on the EPROMs is P20103E, P20103O, or P20103X, the card is compatible with DoubleSpace and DriveSpace.

Symptom 12-25. The disk-compression program has used all reserved memory When you try to create or mount a DoubleSpace or DriveSpace drive, you might receive an error message such as: "DoubleSpace has used all the memory reserved by the settings in the *Options* dialog box. To enable DoubleSpace to allocate more memory, you should restart your computer now. Do you want to restart your computer now?"

Under MS-DOS 6.22, you might see a DriveSpace error message: "Not enough MEM-ORY to allocate more drives for Dblspace or Drvspace. Reboot and quit other applications?" Chances are that restarting the computer does not help—you still cannot mount the drive. This error occurs if you try to compress or mount more drives than are specified by the *Number of removable-media drives* setting in the DoubleSpace *Options* dialog box, or if the total number of mounted drives is greater than 15. The *Number of removable-media drives* setting specifies how much memory the compression software reserves for mounting additional compressed drives after startup. If you try to mount or create more compressed drives than DoubleSpace has reserved memory for, you receive an error.

You can adjust the *Number of removable-media drives* setting by running DoubleSpace or DriveSpace, choosing *Options* from the *Tools* menu, and changing the setting. This modifies the *MaxRemovableDrives* setting in the DBLSPACE.INI file. If restarting the computer still does not correct this error, you may already have 15 compressed drives mounted. Restarting does not allow you to mount or create any more compressed drives using DoubleSpace or DriveSpace until you have fewer than 15 compressed drives mounted. To mount another compressed drive, you must first unmount one or more of the currently mounted drives. To unmount a compressed drive, start DoubleSpace or Drive-Space and select the drive to unmount, then choose *Unmount* from the *Drive* menu.

> You can create more than 15 compressed drives, but only a maximum of 15 can be mounted at the same time.

Symptom 12-26. A compression error indicates that drive <X> is not available When you use the DBLSPACE /HOST command to change your compression host drive letter, you might receive a message like: "The drive letter <X> is not available for DoubleSpace's use," where <X> is the drive letter you specified. This error might occur when the letter you specify for the new host drive is in use by an existing physical drive (or compressed drive). Also, the drive letter you specified is greater than the "LastDrive=" entry in the DBLSPACE.INI file. Use the DBLSPACE /LASTDRIVE command to increase the "LastDrive=" entry in the DBLSPACE.INI file. For example, type:

```
dblspace /lastdrive=j
```

Restart your computer. You can also use the DBLSPACE /HOST command to change your compressed host drive letter. For example, if your compressed drive is drive C: and you want to change your host drive to drive I:, type the following:

```
dblspace c: /host=i:
```

Now restart your computer.

Symptom 12-27. DIR /C fails to report the file-compression ratio DIR /C won't report a compression ratio if the DoubleSpace FAT (MDFAT) is damaged, if the file is open in another Windows virtual machine (VM), and the MDFAT has not been updated, or if the file was created by Microsoft Backup (or Microsoft Backup for Windows). To work around the problem, check the file-compression ratio in File Manager or run ScanDisk.

Symptom 12-28. FORMAT overwrites the CVF on a floppy disk You might actually see an error message such as: "You must use 'DBLSPACE /FORMAT <drive>:' to format that drive." As a result, you have a freshly formatted non-compressed diskette. This problem occurs if you access an uncompressed floppy disk (for example, DIR A:), remove the uncompressed floppy, insert a compressed floppy, and attempt to format it. When this happens, the DoubleSpace Automount code is never called, and the DoubleSpace-compressed floppy disk is not mounted. This problem might also occur if the Automount feature has been disabled. If you have already formatted over a DoubleSpace-compressed floppy disk, recompress the disk with the DBLSPACE /COMPRESS command. To prevent this problem, access the compressed floppy disks before formatting them. For example, type the following at the command prompt:

```
a:
format a:
```

Symptom 12-29. The system hangs when a SCSI driver is loaded after DBL-SPACE.SYS SCSI device drivers loaded "high" or loaded after MS-DOS 6.2 DBLSPACE.SYS in the CONFIG.SYS file might cause the system to stop hang. To correct this problem, load your SCSI device driver before DBLSPACE.SYS. If your system still hangs, load the device driver "low" (change "DEVICEHIGH=" to "DEVICE=" and remove the /L parameter). For example, change:

```
devicehigh /L:1,1234 =c:\scsi.sys
```

to:

```
device=c:\scsi.sys
```

Symptom 12-30. The compressed disk cannot be mounted in a BackPack drive DoubleSpace and DriveSpace might fail to automatically mount compressed disks in BackPack (**http://www.micro-solutions.com**) drives. This problem occurs when the BACKPACK.SYS device driver is loaded after the DBLSPACE.SYS driver in a CONFIG.SYS file. Because the Automount code works on block device drivers only when they are loaded before DBLSPACE.SYS, load BACKPACK.SYS before DBLSPACE.SYS in the CONFIG.SYS file.

Symptom 12-31. DOS compression restarts the computer and loops endlessly When DoubleSpace or DriveSpace restarts your computer to increase the DBLSPACE.INI *MaxFileFragments* setting (because your DoubleSpace-compressed drive is too fragmented to mount), your computer becomes trapped in an endless loop. This occurs when a compressed drive on your hard disk drive is too fragmented to mount, and you are booting your computer from a floppy disk (typically in drive A). The compression software modifies the DBLSPACE.INI file on the host drive for the overly fragmented compressed drive, but does not consider which drive is the boot drive. Ensure that the floppy disk drives are empty, and reboot your computer. Press <F5> when the "Starting MS-DOS" prompt appears. Run Defrag to defragment the drive, then restart the system.

Symptom 12-32. You cannot use compression on a drive partitioned with Disk Manager If the DMDRVR.BIN command is loaded after SMARTDRV /DOU-BLE_BUFFER in your CONFIG.SYS file (and your hard-disk drive has more than 1024 cylinders), it might appear that your compressed data is lost after you create a new compressed drive. This happens when you have other compressed drives, and you try to create a new compressed drive using the Disk Manager partitioned drive as the host. DMDRVR.BIN should be the first device loaded in the CONFIG.SYS file.

Restart the computer and press <Ctrl>+<F5> when the "Starting MS-DOS" message appears. Delete the C:\DBLSPACE.BIN and C:\DBLSPACE.INI files (you'll probably have to unhide the files first). Restart the computer and edit your CONFIG.SYS file with a text editor. Move the DMDRVR.BIN command to the top of your CONFIG.SYS file. Save the CONFIG.SYS file and exit the text editor, then restart the computer. Run the compression software and create the new compressed drive again.

Symptom 12-33. Compression software mounts a Bernoulli disk as non-removable If you are using Bernoulli Iomega OAD version 1.21 device drivers with MS-DOS 6.2, DoubleSpace creates a permanently mounted drive when you compress existing data on a Bernoulli drive. When you restart your computer, DoubleSpace attempts to mount the newly created compressed disk—even if the Bernoulli drive is empty. To work around this problem, unmount the compressed Bernoulli disk, then reboot your computer. After rebooting your computer, the disk should mount automatically when you access it.

Symptom 12-34. DriveSpace reports an "incompatible version" error Drive-Space might indicate that an incompatible version of DRVSPACE.BIN is running, and that the .BIN file in the root directory must be updated. This error is also displayed if you try to run DoubleSpace (however, the <drive letter> is replaced by an "@" symbol, rather than the actual drive letter). At this point, your compressed volumes are probably inaccessible.

This error occurs after you install MS-DOS 6.22 to a directory other than the one that contains your MS-DOS 6.0 DoubleSpace files (typically, C:\DOS). In this situation, the DBL-SPACE.BIN file has not been properly updated. To correct the problem, uninstall MS-DOS 6.22, then reinstall MS-DOS 6.22 into the directory that contains your MS-DOS files.

Symptom 12-35. DRIVER.SYS causes an "insert diskette" error when compression software is running When you try to create a compressed drive using DoubleSpace or DriveSpace, you might encounter an error like: "Please insert a diskette for drive <x>: and press any key when ready," where <x> is a second logical drive associated with a single physical floppy disk drive. This message occurs when DRIVER.SYS is loading in the CONFIG.SYS file. DRIVER.SYS is a device driver that can be used to create a logical drive that refers to a physical floppy disk drive. When an attempt is made to access the drive through this second logical drive letter, DRIVER.SYS prompts you to insert a disk and press any key before attempting to read the drive. To correct this problem, start MS-DOS by pressing the <F8> key as soon as the "Starting MS-DOS" message appears. When prompted to load DRIVER.SYS, choose *No*. You can then safely restart DoubleSpace or DriveSpace.

Symptom 12-36. A compressed drive refuses to mount after installing RAMDrive If you use compression software with a removable hard drive (such as

Syquest, Bernoulli, or Quatam Passport XL), and later install RAMDrive, DoubleSpace might refuse to mount its compressed drive(s). This is because the RAMDrive DEVICE command in the CONFIG.SYS file precedes the removable hard-drive DEVICE command line. Because RAMDrive might inadvertently use the drive letter of the removable drive, Double-Space or DriveSpace might not find the compressed volume on the expected drive. The same problem might occur if you remove RAMDrive after compressing your removable hard drive.

If this problem was caused by installing RAMDrive, you can simply move the RAM-Drive DEVICE command past the removable drive's DEVICE command in the CON-FIG.SYS file. The advantage of this solution is that the drive letter assignments stay the same. If this problem occurs after removing RAMDrive, run DBLSPACE. From the *Drive* menu, choose *Mount*. DoubleSpace scans all your drives for compressed volumes and reassigns drive letters appropriately. However, this might cause problems for programs configured to specific drive letters.

Symptom 12-37. A compressed SCSI drive doesn't mount at startup DoubleSpace or DriveSpace might not be able to mount the CVF on your SCSI drive when you start your computer if you load SSTOR.SYS into upper memory after DBLSPACE.SYS. Load SSTOR.SYS into upper memory before DBLSPACE.SYS. For example:

```
devicehigh=c:\sstor.sys
devicehigh=c:\dos\dblspace.sys /move
```

Symptom 12-38. DoubleSpace cannot copy the DBLSPACE.INF file This happens because the root directory of the drive contains an excessive number of entries. The root directory of a hard disk can contain up to 512 entries—including both files and directories. You'll need to reduce the number of entries in the root directory.

Symptom 12-39. EZTape hangs or produces an error with a compressed drive When you run Irwin Magnetic Systems' EZTape for MS-DOS (version 2.22 or version 3.1) on a DoubleSpace-compressed drive, EZTape might hang when performing a backup or restore on the DoubleSpace-compressed drive, or EZTape might display one of the following error messages when performing a backup or restore on a compressed drive: "Run-time error R6001 null pointer assignment" or "EMM386 exception error #12, enter to reboot computer."

EZTape for MS-DOS version 2.22 or 3.1 might identify a DoubleSpace-compressed drive as a nonstandard drive and might require that the DOSONLY environment variable is set before you can begin an action on a compressed drive. Set the MS-DOS environment variable to DOSONLY=1 before you use EZTape for MS-DOS. Use a text editor to insert the following statement in the AUTOEXEC.BAT file:

```
SET DOSONLY=1
```

Setting the DOSONLY environment variable forces EZTape for MS-DOS to use standard MS-DOS system calls to access the drive. You must reboot your computer for this change to take effect.

Symptom 12-40. Compression software hangs the system with a DTC 3280 SCSI drive If you install DoubleSpace or DriveSpace on a DTC 3280 SCSI removable drive, your system might stop hang. This problem is almost always caused by the DTC device driver, ASCSI.EXE. You'll need to upgrade the SCSI driver to a newer version, which will co-exist with disk compression. The GSCSI4 driver in your AUTOEXEC.BAT file will also need to be upgraded. You can download the latest drivers from the DTC bulletin board at (408) 942-4010, or from the DTC Web site (**http://www.datatechnology.com**).

Symptom 12-41. A compression error indicates cross-linked files between C: and C: This kind of error suggests a file problem (cross-linked files) on the drive. The reason drive letters are displayed instead of filenames and the two drive letters shown are the same is because entries are cross-linked in the MDFAT. Because these entries (or clusters) are marked as allocated in the MDFAT (but free in the FAT), they are not considered to be parts of any file or files. To correct the cross-linked entries in the MDFAT, run CHKDSK /F. If CHKDSK does not correct the problem, either run ScanDisk (from DOS 6.22 or Windows 95 Startup Disk) on the compressed drive, or obtain a third-party compression-aware surface scan program.

Symptom 12-42. Compression software indicates an "R6003—Integer Divide by Zero" error This error is typically caused by corrupted DoubleSpace or DriveSpace files, or incompatible TSR programs. Copy the DBLSPACE.BIN (or DRVSPACE .BIN) file from Disk 1 of the original MS-DOS Upgrade disk set to the root directory for your host drive. For example, if your compressed drive is C:, and your host drive is H:, type the following at the DOS command prompt, then press <Enter>:

```
copy a:\dblspace.bin h:\
```

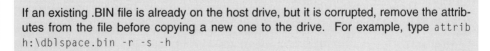

If an existing .BIN file is already on the host drive, but it is corrupted, remove the attributes from the file before copying a new one to the drive. For example, type `attrib h:\dblspace.bin -r -s -h`

DBLSPACE.EX_ is located on Disk 3 of the 1.44MB 3.5" disk set, and on Disk 4 of the 1.2MB 5.25" disk set. Expand the DBLSPACE.EXE files from the original DOS installation disks such as:

```
expand a:\dblspace.ex_ c:\dblspace.exe
```

Now restart the computer by pressing the reset button, or by turning the machine off and then on again.

TROUBLESHOOTING DOS STACKER

Stac, Inc. was once considered to be the leading disk-compression company, and lead the early development of disk-compression technology. However, with the entry of Microsoft into the compression arena, the ensuing litigation over the use of DoubleSpace, and Microsoft's subsequent release and support of DriveSpace with DOS 6.2x and DriveSpace 3 for Windows 95, Stac is no longer a major force in disk compression. Their Stacker 4.1 for Windows 95 uses the real-mode code of their 4.0 version, and did not provide the compression performance demanded by users. No additional compression products are listed or announced on the Stac Web site. Still, there is a broad base of installed Stacker systems, and this part of the chapter outlines many of the important Stacker problems that you might encounter.

Symptom 12-43. An error message appears, indicating "Lost sector groups" You will typically see this error when running the Stacker CHECK utility. This is not nearly as ominous as it might sound—data has not yet been lost or corrupted. A lost sector group can occur on a Stacker drive when data is written to a cluster, but the cluster has not been allocated to a file. Once the operating system does allocate the cluster to a file, the error goes away. In most cases, CHECK will report a lost sector group when a file is extended and truncated without the operating system updating the FAT. For the most part, you can leave lost sector groups alone. If you want to clear any such groups, however, run SDEFRAG or select the Stacker Optimizer in the Stacker Toolbox. You can select Full Optimize, Quick Optimize, or Restack, and any of these choices will completely clear lost sector groups.

Symptom 12-44. The error message "Size mismatch, existing installation" appears This kind of error can result if the STACKVOL.DSK file were corrupted or destroyed (either by a hardware disk fault or software error). When Stacker initializes, it verifies the STACVOL.DSK (the CVF) file before mounting a compressed drive. If the size of the STACVOL.DSK file is incorrect, Stacker pauses the normal startup of your computer with this message until the problem is corrected:

```
E: = C:STACVOL.DSK (Size mismatch)  (Write protected)
Press any key to continue...
```

The solution for this type of fault is rather involved, and you will require the RE-PAIR.EXE utility included with your Stacker disks (or available from the Stac BBS). Notice the compressed and uncompressed volume letters. For this example, the compressed volume is C:, and the host drive (containing STACVOL.DSK) is E:. Next, unmount the Stacker drive by typing *STACKER -d*, where *d* is the compressed drive (C:). Run a disk-repair utility, such as CHKDSK or ScanDisk on the host drive (E:). As the disk utility runs, it will ask if you want to save lost chains as files—do not! Remember, you should not save new files to the disk while this recovery procedure is in progress. If the disk utility indicates that STACVOL is cross-linked with other files, delete the other files and run the disk utility again until the STACVOL file checks clean.

At this point, insert the floppy disk containing REPAIR.EXE and switch to the floppy drive (if REPAIR.EXE is in a floppy sub-directory, switch to that sub-directory as well). Run the REPAIR utility using the syntax: *REPAIR /=U d:\STACVOL.XXX*, where *d:\STACVOL.XXX* is the uncompressed drive letter and STACVOL file name you determined in a previous step. For example:

```
REPAIR /=U E:\STACVOL.DSK                    <Enter>
```

You will see a series of messages as the REPAIR.EXE executes. If the repair process is successful, you will have to remove the REPAIR floppy and reboot the machine for changes to take effect. You should now have access to the compressed volume again.

Symptom 12-45. An error message appears, such as "The drive is too fragmented" You might encounter this kind of message when attempting to upgrade Stacker from a previous version. Abort the upgrade procedure and use the Stacker Optimizer to defragment the drive. You can then re-run the upgrade installation. If the upgrade process introduces additional fragmentation, the upgrade process might fail again. In that event, you can update the Stacker drive manually. Perform a quick optimization by typing SDEFRAG /Q and continue with the procedure—even if the drive reports 0% fragmentation. After optimization, type STACKER and locate the line referring to the drive that failed to update. For example, you might see a line, such as: "Drive C was drive C at boot time [D:\STACVOL.DSK = 115.3MB]" Take note of the drive letter inside the brackets (e.g., D:). Next, start the manual conversion:

```
HCONVERT drive:\STACVOL.DSK /C
```

where *drive:* is the host drive letter (e.g., D:). Once the drive is updated, run the Stacker Optimizer again to take full advantage of Stacker 4.0 compression.

Symptom 12-46. The Stacker drive does not update or HCONVERT hangs up The upgrade to Stacker 4.0 should yield a noticeable gain in drive space over previous versions. If you do not notice an improvement, the update process might not have been successful. In some situations, you do not receive warnings about excessive fragmentation, yet the disk might be too fragmented to sustain an update. The first step here is to determine if the drive has indeed been updated. Switch to the Stacker directory and type SYSINFO to find information concerning your system. Find the area detailing the system's physical drives—the second column of information is labeled "version." Stacker drives will have a version number listed in this column.

A version of 3.0 (or earlier) indicates that the Stacker drive has not been updated. A version of 5.0 indicates that the Stacker drive has been updated, but not recompressed to gain additional space. If this is the case, leave the system information screen and start the Stacker Toolbox. Select *Optimize*, then *Full-MaxSpace*. This should recompress the drive to provide additional space. A version of 5.01 indicates that the drive has been updated and recompressed. When the disk has not been updated, switch to the Stacker directory and type: STACKER. You will see a profile of your Stacker drive(s). For example:

```
Drive C was drive C at boot time [D:\STACVOL.DSK = 112.3MB]
```

this shows drive C: is the Stacker drive and drive D: is the uncompressed drive. Run CHKDSK against the host drive. If errors are reported, run CHKDSK /f to correct the errors. Now, defragment the drive using: SDEFRAG /Q *drive:* where *drive:* is the Stacker drive (e.g., C:). Once the drive is defragmented, update the drive immediately (do not perform any other write operations). Unmount the Stacker drive by typing: STACKER -*drive:* where *drive:* is the Stacker drive (i.e., C:). Next, type:

```
HCONVERT /C drive:\STACVOL.XXX        <Enter>
```

where *drive:* is the host drive (e.g., D:) and *.XXX* is the STACVOL extension (e.g., .DSK). Remove any floppy disks and reboot the PC for changes to take effect. Finally, recompress the drive by entering the Stacker Toolbox, select *Optimize*, then select *Full-MaxSpace*.

Symptom 12-47. "Setup error #2002" appears This error occurs when a floppy drive writes information to the Stacker installation disk improperly. This might be caused by improper floppy drive alignment or floppy drive damage, but chances are that the vital Stacker files on the floppy disk(s) are already corrupted. This is why software manufacturers tell you to make a backup copy of the product, and install from the backup copy. By formatting and copying backup disks on your PC, you compensate for any mild alignment problems. It might not be a bad idea to clean the floppy drive heads. When alignment problems persist, replace the floppy drive. If you have not made a backup copy of your Stacker installation disks, call Stac for a new set of disks. When the new disks arrive, create a backup set and write-protect the master disks.

Symptom 12-48. After converting a DoubleSpace or SuperStor /DS drive to Stacker, no additional space is detected In some cases, drive space will not increase after moving to Stacker 4.0—usually when you are near the DOS limit for a drive. DOS limits refer to the size of clusters on a drive. For example, a 512MB drive uses 8KB clusters, a 1GB drive usually has 16KB clusters, and a 2GB drive offers 32KB clusters. However, the following techniques might draw additional space from a converted drive.

Start by recompressing the drive after Stacker is installed. Open the Stacker Toolbox, select *Optimize*, and select *Full-MaxSpace*. When the drive is recompressed, check the space available on the drive and write it down. Next, uncompress the drive and re-run Stacker Setup. This step allows Stacker to select the optimum cluster size for the drive. As an alternative to removing and re-installing Stacker, try to shrink—then grow—the Stacker drive size. This will not set a new cluster size, but might gain additional space. Remember that you might not have much latitude to change the STACVOL file size if the compressed drive is quite full already.

Symptom 12-49. When using the Stacker CHECK utility, you see an error message indicating that the File Allocation Tables are not identical Normally, a hard drive maintains two copies of the *File Allocation Table (FAT)* in the event of just such an emergency. This is potentially disastrous fault for your hard drive, and you must carefully choose which copy of the FAT to use when repairing the problem. After this initial warning, CHECK will run a second integrity check using the alternate copy of the FAT. After CHECK completes its second examination, you will be presented with three choices: (1) exit and try using the first FAT, (2) exit and try using the second FAT, or (3) copy the first FAT over the second FAT and let CHECK repair any errors. Remember that the FAT currently being tested is considered the first FAT. The objective here is to be sure that the first (the currently tested) FAT is the error-free version. You can then copy that error-free FAT to the second FAT and repair the damage. Here a procedure that will help you.

Select option 1. This will return you to DOS (if you started CHECK from DOS). If you started CHECK from the Stacker Toolbox in Windows, leave Windows and return to the DOS prompt. Run CHECK again, and pay close attention to whether the errors are reported running the first FAT or the second FAT. If the errors are on the first FAT, end

CHECK using menu option 2 (exit and try using the second FAT). If the errors are on the second FAT, end CHECK using menu option 1 (exit and try using the first FAT). At the DOS command line, run: CHECK /f to fix the disk. When presented with the menu options again, select option 3 (copy the first FAT over the second FAT and let CHECK repair the drive).

Symptom 12-50. SDEFRAG errors 109/110, 120, or 170 are encountered A media error has been detected on the disk during the defragmentation process. The 109/110 or 170 errors indicate that SDEFRAG is unable to read, write, or verify a physical cluster on the disk—often the result of a media problem. The 120 error indicates that SDEFRAG is unable to decompress a physical cluster. Either the media is damaged, or the cluster is corrupted. In either case, you are faced with a serious defect. If a physical disk flaw is crippling your Stacker drive, a disk-repair utility can be used to detect and repair the fault. Physical disk utilities can be found in packages, such as Norton Utilities, PC Tools, or SpinRite. Start by locating a file attribute utility, such as ATTRIB. Type STACKER and locate the drive reference line. It should look something like this:

```
Drive C was drive C at boot time [E:\STACVOL.DSK = 173.5MB]
```

The drive letter in brackets is the host drive. The drive outside of brackets is the compressed drive. Go to the DOS sub-directory on your uncompressed drive (or wherever ATTRIB is located). Next, reboot the system with a clean boot disk—do not load any device drivers at all. At the A: prompt, switch to the DOS sub-directory on the host drive and use ATTRIB to unhide STACVOL.DSK, such as:

```
attrib -s -h -r drive:\STACVOL.*      <Enter>
```

where *drive:* is the drive letter you are repairing (e.g., E:). Now that STACVOL is readily available as an ordinary file, run the surface scan on the drive. Be sure to run the surface scan utility from a floppy drive. Use the most rigorous test pattern available, and allow the utility to repair any defective areas. Remember that such a thorough scan might take up to several hours, depending on the size and speed of the drive. After repairs are complete, remove the floppy disk and reboot the PC.

Now, run CHECK /f and allow it to perform a surface check. If CHECK detects ant errors and asks you to delete damaged files, respond YES, and be sure to follow any on-screen instructions that CHECK provides. You are now ready to run SDEFRAG again. If the error code(s) persist, you will need to invoke the special diagnostic mode in CHECK /f, as shown.

For this procedure, you will need to modify your floppy boot disk to disable all device drivers, except for STACKER.COM and SWAP.COM. Use REM statements to remark-out all other device drivers in the CONFIG.SYS file, as shown in Table 12-4. After you complete these modifications, reboot the computer and run CHECK /f. When asked to perform a surface scan test, answer YES. If CHECK detects errors and prompts you to delete damaged files, answer YES, and follow any further instructions provided by CHECK. After CHECK is complete, run SDEFRAG /r again. If SDEFRAG executes without errors, the system is fully optimized, and you can reboot the system from its original configuration files. Otherwise, switch the PC to a slower speed and try running SDEFRAG again.

TABLE 12-4 DISABLING ALL DEVICE DRIVERS EXCEPT FOR STACKER.COM AND SWAP.COM

```
REM device=c:\dos\himem.sys
REM device=c:\dos\emm386.exe noems
REM dos=high,umb
buffers=20
files=30
lastdrive=e
REM devicehigh=c:\mouse\mouse.sys /c1
REM devicehigh=c:\dos\smartdrv.sys 1024
devicehigh=c:\stacker\stacker.com
device=c:\stacker\sswap.com
```

Symptom 12-51. "SDEFRAG/OPTIMIZER error 101" occurs This error indicates that your system does not have enough memory to run the SDEFRAG utility. Increase the conventional memory available to your system (or reduce SDEFRAG's memory requirements). Typical memory requirements depend on cluster size:

- 4KB clusters = 503KB SDEFRAG
- 8KB clusters = 534KB SDEFRAG
- 16KB clusters = 560KB SDEFRAG
- 32KB clusters = 642KB SDEFRAG

To run SDEFRAG, you must increase the amount of conventional memory available, or reduce the memory requirement. If you have access to a memory management tool, such as QEMM, 386MAX, NETROOM, or MemMaker, running such a manager will often increase the available conventional memory and allow SDEFRAG to run successfully. If you cannot use any of these tools, use a boot disk and edit its CONFIG.SYS or AUTOEXEC.BAT file to disable various device drivers and TSRs. This will leave more conventional memory space. Remember, do not disable your memory managers or Stacker command lines. If problems persist, try running SDEFRAG with its */buffer=#* switch, where # is a value between 256 and 4096. Larger numbers save more memory:

- SDEFRAG /buffer=3072 = 21KB of conventional memory saved
- SDEFRAG /buffer=2048 = 42KB of conventional memory saved
- SDEFRAG /buffer=256 = 78KB of conventional memory saved

Some final notes. If you receive these error messages while trying to grow or shrink the Stacker drive, run the Optimizer as: SDEFRAG /buffer=*nnn* /GP, where *nnn* is the memory number. If the errors occur when trying to change the *Expected Compression Ratio (ECR)*, run the Optimizer as: SDEFRAG /buffer=*nnn* /GL, where *nnn* is the memory number.

Symptom 12-52. While running the Stacker CHECK utility, a "Not enough disk space to save header" error appears The header of a STACVOL file contains control information about how and where data is stored, and information relating to the data area in which all of the drive's compressed data is stored. A copy of the STACVOL header is saved every time that CHECK is run. If the STACVOL header is damaged, it can be repaired by using the saved copy. CHECK runs automatically each time the system is started. If not enough space is on the host drive to save the header, you will see an errorx message similar to: "Not enough disk space to save header." Start by determining the host drive letter. Type STACKER and find the information line similar to:

```
Drive D was drive D at boot time [F:\STACVOL.DSK = 123.4MB]
```

The drive letter within brackets (e.g., F:) is the host drive, and the drive outside of the bracket (e.g., D:) is the compressed drive. Also, take note of the STACVOL file extension. Next, find the space needed to store the STACVOL file by switching to the host drive. Take a directory of the drive and notice the amount of free space available. Type DIR /AH to display all hidden or archive files on the drive, then notice the size of the STACVOL file. You should expect the header size to approximate the sizes shown in Table 12-5.

Now that you know approximately the amount of space needed for the header, you can make extra uncompressed space available. Type SDEFRAG /GP, select the host drive, then select the "More Uncompressed Space Available" option. After the drive is defragmented, you will be allowed to enter the desired amount uncompressed space in KB. Add 50KB to the anticipated amount of space needed for a header and enter that value. Select the "Perform changes on Stacker drive" option, and restart the system to allow your changes to take effect. You should now have enough space to store the STACVOL header.

Symptom 12-53. The uncompress process fails UNCOMP.EXE is used to uncompress a Stacker drive. Before uncompressing the drive, SDEFRAG is invoked to defragment the drive. If UNCOMP fails, you will have to determine where the fault occurred, find the specific error message (if possible), and correct the error. First, find where the error occurred. When UNCOMP is running, "UNCOMP" is shown in a title bar at the top of the screen. When SDEFRAG is running, "Stacker Optimizer" is shown in the title bar. Notice which title is shown when the error occurs. Next, denote any SDEFRAG error message. If the process fails without any error message (e.g., the system freezes or

TABLE 12-5 TYPICAL STACVOL HEADER SIZES	
FOR A COMPRESSED DRIVE OF:	**EXPECT A HEADER SIZE OF ABOUT:**
50MB	94KB
120MB	108KB
200MB	171KB
500MB	207KB
1000MB	396KB

drops back to DOS unexpectedly), notice what was happening before the fault. Please read the following procedures carefully before proceeding:

For UNCOMP Problems. If UNCOMP drops back to DOS without uncompressing the Stacker drive, download an updated UNCOMP tool: UNCMP4.EXE from the Stac BBS, America On-Line, or CompuServe. Place the file in a temporary sub-directory and run it. UNCMP4.EXE is a self-extracting file that will make other files available in your sub-directory. Copy the newly generated files, UNCOMP2.EXE and SDEFRAG2.EXE, to the STACKER sub-directory, then run UNCOMP again.

If UNCOMP hangs up while uncompressing files, you will probably have to reboot your system to get control. On reboot, you will likely see the error: "Size Mismatch—Write Protected" (similar to Symptom 2). The Stacker drive is partially uncompressed, and is no longer the size indicated by the header. A write-protect function prevents any further damage. Try running UNCOMP again: in some cases, UNCOMP might start where it left off and begin uncompressing the drive normally. If problems continue, locate and unhide the STACVOL file, unfragment the drive, and run UNCOMP again. This can be accomplished by typing STACKER and noting the drive letter and file name in brackets (e.g., D:\STACVOL.DSK). Use the DOS ATTRIB utility to unhide the STACVOL file (i.e., ATTRIB -S -H -R D:\STACVOL.DSK). From a floppy disk, defragment the host drive (e.g., D:) using a defragmenter, such as Norton Speedisk or MS-DOS DEFRAG. Be sure to do a full optimization. Then, run UNCOMP from a floppy disk.

If UNCOMP still fails, check the available (uncompressed) space on the host drive. If sufficient uncompressed space is available to hold the remaining Stacker files, copy (or XCOPY) the files from the Stacker drive to the uncompressed drive, or floppy disks, then remove the Stacker drive using the REMOVDRV function. Notice that REMOVDRV deletes all data on the Stacker drive, so be sure that you recover any necessary files before deleting the Stacker drive. One way or another, you should be able to recover your vital files prior to deleting the Stacker drive. If you see an error message indicating: "Drive x: is not a Stacker Drive," type STACKER to find the drive descriptions (Stac calls this a drive map), and it appears similar to:

```
Drive C was drive C at boot time [D:\STACVOL.DSK=123.4MB]
```

Remember that the drive letter within the brackets is the host drive, and the drive letter outside of the brackets is the Stacker drive. If you inadvertently tried to UNCOMP the host drive, the process certainly will not work.

If you see a message indicating that "The Stacker drive x: contains more data then will fit on the host drive. You must delete about nnn Kbytes before uncompressing," more data is on the compressed drive than will fit on the physical drive when it is uncompressed. Your only real option here is to backup and delete enough files so that the remainder will fit on the drive when uncompressed. After you off-load or backup a sufficient number of files, run UNCOMP again.

If you see an error message, such as "There is insufficient free space on the uncompressed drive x: to uncompress the drive. You must free up at least nnn Kbytes on the uncompressed drive, or about twice that amount on the Stacker drive, and re-run UNCOMP," not enough working space is on the host drive to uncompress the Stacker drive. Try backing up and deleting the prescribed amount of space—that might clear the problem. Otherwise, type: SDEFRAG /GP at the DOS prompt, and select the "More uncompressed Space Available" option. This will defragment the drive and ask how much space you wish to uncompress. Enter a number larger than the prescribed amount and allow the changes to be made. Restart the system and run UNCOMP.

If you see an error message, such as "There are errors on the Stacker Drive. Please run CHKDSK or another disk repair utility before uncompressing," lost clusters or cross-linked files are on the Stacker drive. Run CHKDSK to determine the nature of any errors. Run CHKDSK /f to fix lost clusters. You can also run disk-repair utilities, such as Norton Disk Doctor or PC Tools DiskFix. When the disk errors are corrected, try running UN-COMP again.

For SDEFRAG Problems. If you see SDEFRAG Error 101, refer to Symptom 12-51. If you see SDEFRAG Error 109/110, 120, or 170, refer to Symptom 12-50. If you see SDE-FRAG Error 157: Internal Error, you might need updated files from the Stac BBS, America On-line, or CompuServe. Download UNCMP4.EXE into a temporary sub-directory and run it. It will self-extract into several new files. Copy the new files UNCOMP2.EXE and SDEFRAG2.EXE into the Stacker sub-directory, and run UNCOMP again.

Symptom 12-54. The error message appears: "Not a Stacker STACVOL file—NOT MOUNTED" or "Invalid # reserved sectors—NOT MOUNTED"
Each Stacker drive is a STACVOL file stored on the uncompressed drive. Each STACVOL file includes a header that contains information on how and where data is stored, and the actual compressed data. Either of the error messages listed indicate that the STACVOL header is damaged or corrupt. Fortunately, a copy of the header is saved for each Stacker drive, and can be used to restore a damaged header. Each time the PC starts, CHECK /WP saves the header as STACSAVQ.nnn. When you start Windows or use the CHECK utility yourself, the header is saved as STACSAVE.nnn. Start by determining which of these saved headers is newest. *Warning:* Do not follow this procedure if you have just run SDEFRAG without running CHECK or restarting your PC.

Start your PC (from a bootable floppy, if necessary) and switch to the root directory of the uncompressed drive and type DIR STACSAV*.* /AH to see the hidden header file(s). Notice the save file with the latest date and time. Now, restore the header. Type DIR /AH to see a directory, including all hidden files, and notice the STACVOL extension (i.e., .DSK). Use the ATTRIB function to unhide the STACVOL file. Type ATTRIB -S -H -R *drive:*\STACVOL.*xxx* where *drive:* is the drive letter containing STACVOL, and *.xxx* is the STACVOL extension. Insert a disk containing the REPAIR.EXE utility. If the newest backup header is a STACSAVE file, type REPAIR /F *drive:*\STACVOL.*xxx*, where *drive:* is the drive containing STACVOL, and *.xxx* is the proper STACVOL extension. If the newest backup header is a STACSAVQ file, type REPAIR /F *drive:*\STACVOL.*xxx* /Q, where *drive:* is the drive containing STACVOL, and *.xxx* is the proper STACVOL extension. Then, remove all disks from the system and restart the computer.

Symptom 12-55. An error message appears: *"CHECK I/O Access Denied: Error 27"* You have corrupt data in the drive's FAT. Such errors might be caused by bad sectors on the physical drive itself, a faulty program or a virus that over-wrote the FAT, or by a program that incorrectly uses EMS (expanded memory). You will have to determine which areas of the hard drive have been damaged, then correct the damaged areas. Boot the system from a clean floppy drive to disable all device drivers and unhide the STACVOL file using the ATTRIB function. Look at the CONFIG.SYS file. If you see a command line that appears similar to:

```
DEVICE=C:\STACKER\STACKER.COM
```

then Stacker does not preload. Otherwise, you have a preloading version of Stacker. For preloading versions of Stacker, type STACKER and note the drive map (e.g., Drive C was drive C at boot time [D:\STACVOL.DSK = 123.4MB]). You need to know the drive letter and STACVOL extension in the brackets. Restart the PC and press F5 when MS-DOS starts. When presented with a command line prompt, unhide the STACVOL file (i.e., AT-TRIB -S -H -R *drive*:\STACVOL.*xxx*, where *drive:* is the drive letter containing STACVOL, and *.xxx* is the STACVOL extension). Change to the Stacker subdirectory and type STACKER -*drive:*, where *drive:* is the letter of the compressed drive.

If Stacker does not preload, type STACKER and note the drive map (i.e., Drive C was drive C at boot time [D:\STACVOL.DSK = 123.4MB]). You need to know the drive letter and STACVOL extension in the brackets. Change to the DOS sub-directory and copy ATTRIB to an uncompressed directory. Clean-boot the system to disable all device drivers, switch to the host drive and sub-directory containing ATTRIB, then unhide the STACVOL file (i.e., ATTRIB -S -H -R *drive*:\STACVOL.*xxx*, where *drive:* is the drive letter containing STACVOL and *.xxx* is the STACVOL extension).

Now that the disk and STACVOL file have been prepared, run a disk repair utility, such as Norton Utilities, PC Tools DiskFix, or Gibson Research SpinRite to detect and correct damaged disk areas. Be sure to run any such utility from a floppy disk. Run a vigorous test (this might take a few hours), and allow the utility to fix any defective areas. When the test is complete, remove any floppy disks and restart the computer. Run CHECK /f to perform a Stacker check of the drive. If no errors are reported, the drive is fixed and normal use can resume. If problems persist, three procedures might allow you to access the damaged drive before having to start from scratch.

First, try removing write protection on the drive by typing CHECK /=W *x:*, where *x:* is the compressed drive. Warning: you must complete this entire procedure before resuming use of the drive. Now, run CHECK /f again, and follow the instructions to repair the drive. When asked to perform a surface test, answer YES and delete any damaged files. When CHECK reports no more errors, the drive should be repaired.

If problems persist, the drive's FAT might be damaged, so try removing the /EMS parameter in the STACKER.INI file. Some programs that use EMS do so improperly, and this can damage a FAT. Further corruption can be prevented by disabling Stacker's use of EMS. Type ED /I and look for an entry similar to /EMS. Delete the line and press <Ctrl>+Z to save the file and exit. Then, restart the system and run CHECK /f to finish the repairs.

If errors continue, try restoring a backup copy of the STACVOL header. If the STACVOL header is error-free, restoring it to the STACVOL file could correct a FAT error. Unhide the STACVOL file as you saw earlier in this procedure. Insert a floppy disk containing REPAIR.EXE, switch to that drive, then type REPAIR /F *drive*:\STACVOL.*xxx*, where *drive:* and *.xxx* are the drive and extension that you used when unhiding STACVOL. Allow REPAIR to replace the STACVOL file header. Restart the system and run CHECK /f to see if the damage was repaired. If the problem persists, the FAT might be damaged beyond repair. You might have to repartition and reformat the drive, then re-install the compression package and restore the most recent system backup.

Further Study

That it for Chapter 12. Be sure to review the glossary and chapter questions on the accompanying CD. If you have access to the Internet, take some time to review these disk-compression resources:

Microsoft Plus! pack: **http://www.microsoft.com/windows/windows95/info/plusdatasheet.htm**

Stacker support: **http://support.stac.com/pssdb3.nsf/webforms/stacker+ibase**

13

DRIVE-ADAPTER

REFERENCE

CONTENTS AT A GLANCE

ST506/412
  ST506/412 features and architecture
  Cabling the ST506/412 interface
  Low-level formatting an ST506/412
   drive
  Partitioning and high-level
   formatting
  The fate of ST506/412

ESDI
  ESDI features and architecture
  Cabling the ESDI drive system
  Low-level formatting an ESDI drive
  Partitioning and high-level
   formatting
  The fate of ESDI

IDE
  IDE features and architecture
  Cabling the IDE/EIDE interface
  Low-level formatting an IDE/EIDE
   drive

BIOS support of IDE
The role of ATAPI

EIDE
  Understanding the 528MB IDE limit
  Understanding LBA
  Drive support
  Data-transfer rates
  Installing an EIDE system
  Adapter configuration jumpers
  Software installation cautions

Ultra-ATA
  Implementing an Ultra-ATA system
  Ultra-ATA compatibility and
   configuration issues

Troubleshooting a Drive Adapter

Further Study

Hard drives and CD-ROM drives are some of the most fundamental and important elements of a PC. The computers we know today would be very different without the fast performance, high reliability, and huge capacity that such drives have come to offer over the last decade. Without large, fast hard drives, much of the complex software so common on current systems (namely Windows 95 and its applications) would simply be impossible. CD-ROMs have made the distribution of large programs and databases practical and inexpensive. However, hard drives and CD-ROM drives must be interfaced to a computer. A drive adapter (or interface) generally consists of two parts: the actual hardware that physically connects the drive and computer, and the firmware (BIOS) that manages the data transfers. As a result, it is the adapter (Fig. 13-1) that defines the way data is stored on a drive—not the drive itself. Although most drive adapters are commonly being fabricated on current PC motherboards, high-performance drive adapters are traditionally implemented in the form of expansion boards. This chapter examines the history, specification, and configuration of three major drive adapters—ST506, ESDI, and IDE/EIDE (SCSI interfaces are detailed in Chapter 39). You'll also find a selection of troubleshooting solutions most commonly related to drive-adapter problems.

ST506/412

The ST506 interface dates back to 1980, when it was developed by Shugart Associates (now Seagate Technologies) to support their ST-506 5MB hard drive. It is largely regarded to be the ancestor of all modern hard-drive interfaces. The serial interface works at 5Mbits/s using MFM encoding, just like floppy drives. In 1981, Seagate revised the 506 interface to support the ST-412 10MB hard drive—thus, the interface was dubbed *ST506/412*. Later versions of ST506/412 use RLL encoding instead of MFM at 17 sectors

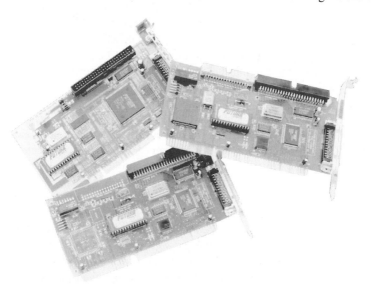

FIGURE 13-1   **A selection of drive adapter boards.** Copyright
©1995 Future Domain Corporation. Reprinted with permission.

per track (512 bytes per sector). This new encoding, combined with a buffered seek feature, achieved 7.5Mbits/s. IBM chose the ST-412 drive as the original hard drive for the PC/XT, so competing drive makers embraced the ST506/412 interface as a de-facto standard. As drive technology pushed beyond 10MB, the interface remained the same. As a result, any hard-drive compatible with the interface became known as an *ST506/412* drive.

> The ST506/412 interface appeared in PC/XT, i286, and early i386 systems. By the late 1980s, it was totally replaced by the IDE interface. You might never encounter ST506/412 drive systems, but this information is provided for your reference.

ST506/412 FEATURES AND ARCHITECTURE

ST506/412 drives are "dumb" devices—like floppy drives, ST506/412 drives must be told explicitly what to do and when to do it. This necessitated a complex and demanding controller residing on a plug-in expansion board (it was impractical to implement ST506/412 adapters on early motherboards). The host computer addressed the controller board through the motherboard's ISA bus, and sent instructions to the controller's on-board registers. The advantage to this kind of architecture is simple modularity—a larger drive can easily be plugged into the original controller, or a defective controller can be quickly replaced.

The only real issue with an ST506/412 interface is the level of BIOS compatibility provided by the host PC. You see, as early ST506/412 hard drives proliferated, each sported a series of parameters (e.g., heads, cylinders, sectors, etc.), which you can see today simply by looking at the system CMOS setup. Although it was a simple matter to plug the new drive into an existing controller, the controller needed to be aware of the drive's particular parameters to ensure that the controller operated the drive properly. When used in XT systems, the BIOS ROM on the controller contained a table of drive parameters—only drives that were listed in the table could be used with the controller. When used in AT systems, the motherboard BIOS contains the hard drive parameters. CMOS setup allowed you to select the proper drive "type" whose parameters matched those in the table. As you might imagine, drives not listed in the table cannot be used, so drive tables evolved along with the BIOS. To accommodate unusual or advanced drive types that might be newer than the BIOS, setup programs in the late 1980s began providing user-definable drive types (e.g., Type 47). All current BIOS supports user-definable drive types.

A typical ST506/412 connector layout is shown in Fig. 13-2. The physical interface for an ST506 drive consists of three cables: a 4-pin power cable, a 34-pin control cable, and a 20-pin data cable. The power cable is a standard, keyed mate-n-lock connector that provides +5 Vdc, +12 Vdc, and ground to the drive. The control cable is responsible for carrying explicit operating signals to the drive, such as Drive Select, Step, Head Select, etc. The data cable supports differential Read and Write lines. Both digital cables are flat or twisted-pair ribbon cable. It is interesting that a set of terminating resistors is mounted to the drive. Although terminating resistors are usually discussed only in relation to SCSI interfaces, the resistors are equally vital for proper signal characteristics in an ST506/412 system. In most cases, terminating resistors can be removed or disabled through a jumper. As you will see later, proper termination is important when more than one drive is attached to the controller. Although many jumpers might be on the drive, a set of drive-select jumpers are usually located between the data and control cables. Drive-select jumpers allow the drive to be set as Drive 0 or Drive 1.

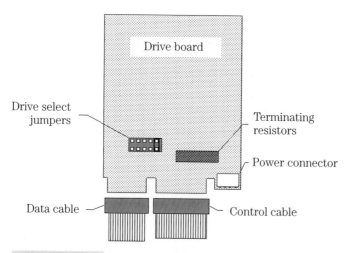

FIGURE 13-2   Connector layout for an ST506/412 drive.

The 34-pin control cable uses 17 single-ended signals (Table 13-1). Single-ended sig-nals are easy to measure with test instruments, and are quite reliable over short distances. You might notice that almost all signals are active-low. The four –*Head select* inputs (pins 14, 18, 4, and 2, respectively) select one of up to 16 R/W heads for reading or writing. The –*Write gate* input (pin 6) is logic 0 during write operations and logic 1 during read opera-tions. A –*Seek complete* output (pin 8) tells the controller when the heads have been moved the desired step distance and settled into their destination track. –*Track 0* (pin 10) is an output informing the controller when the heads move from track 1 to track 0.

> The minus (–) sign preceding many of the signal names (e.g., "–Write Gate") indicates an "active low" logic signal—that is, the signal is "true" when the signal line is at a logic "low" level. You might often see "active low" logic indicated with other symbols or with bars over the signal name.

A –*Write fault* (pin 12) output tells the controller if an error has occurred during the write operation. The number of write faults include:

■ Write current in a head without the –*Write gate* signal true.
■ No write current in the head with –*Write gate* true and the drive selected.
■ –*Write gate* true when heads are off the desired track, or dc power to the drive is out-side of acceptable limits. Writing will be inhibited while the –*Write fault* line is true. An –*Index* output (pin 20) provides a brief active-low pulse whenever a track's index data mark has just passed under the R/W heads. An index pulse appears every 16.6 ms for a disk spinning at 3600 RPM (once per revolution).
■ The –*Ready* output (pin 22) tells the controller when drive speed and dc power are ac-ceptable, and the –*Track 0* signal is true—the drive is considered ready for operation. A pulse on the –*Step* input (pin 24) causes the head stepping motor to move one track position. The direction in which the heads actually step will depend on the –*Direction In* input condition (pin 34). Finally, the four –*Drive select* inputs (pins 26, 28, 30, and 32) are used to identify which drive must be accessed.

PIN	NAME	PIN	NAME
	TABLE 13-1 PINOUT FOR AN ST506/412 CONTROL CABLE		
1	Ground	2	–Head select 8
3	Ground	4	–Head select 4
5	Ground	6	–Write gate
7	Ground	8	–Seek complete
9	Ground	10	–Track 0
11	Ground	12	–Write fault
13	Ground	14	–Head select 1
15	Ground	16	Not connected
17	Ground	18	–Head select 2
19	Ground	20	–Index
21	Ground	22	–Ready
23	Ground	24	–Step
25	Ground	26	–Drive select 1
27	Ground	28	–Drive select 2
29	Ground	30	–Drive select 3
31	Ground	32	–Drive select 4
33	Ground	34	–Direction in

PIN	NAME	PIN	NAME
	TABLE 13-2 PINOUT FOR AN ST506/412 DATA CABLE		
1	Drive selected	2	Ground
3	Reserved	4	Ground
5	Reserved	6	Ground
7	To control cable pin 15	8	Ground
9	Reserved	10	Reserved
11	Ground	12	Ground
13	+Write Data	14	–Write Data
15	Ground	16	Ground
17	+Read Data	18	–Read Data
19	Ground	20	Ground

Although the data cable carries 20 conductors, only three signals are really meaningful (Table 13-2). Four Reserved lines (pins 3, 5, 9, and 10) are not used. The –*Drive select* output (pin 1) acknowledges to the controller when its drive address matches the drive address specified on the control cable's –*Drive select* lines. Differential *Write data* lines (pins 13 and 14) transmit flux reversals (as opposed to "real" digital information—1s and 0s) to the drive from the controller. Differential *Read data* signals (pins 17 and 18) send serial flux reversals from the disk back to the controller, where the reversals are translated back into digital information.

CABLING THE ST506/412 INTERFACE

ST506/412 interfaces are intended to support as many as two drives with the same controller board. You should understand how cable configurations, terminating resistors, and drive jumpers are related. The basic drive system uses a single drive and controller, along with a control cable with one card edge connector (the red or blue wire represents pin 1). It is a simple matter to attach the drive and controller. You should set the only drive as drive 0, and keep the termination resistors in place on the drive.

Many ST506/412 cable assemblies were produced with two drive connectors ganged on the same cable (Fig. 13-3). The end-most card edge connector is always for the first drive, but the drive jumper settings vary. If the cable has no twist, the first drive should be jumpered as drive 0, and the termination resistors should be left in place. When a second drive is added to that untwisted cable, it should be jumpered as drive 1, and its termination resistors should be removed. When the control cable has a twist, things get a bit stickier. The end-most card edge connector is still for the first (or only) drive, but the drive should be jumpered as drive 1, and its termination resistors should be left in place. If a second drive is added to the twisted cable, it should also be jumpered as drive 1, and its termination resistors should be removed. The twist reverses the select pins for the first drive.

> Be very careful that you do not inadvertently use a floppy drive cable in place of an ST506/412 control cable—the twist is in a different place.

LOW-LEVEL FORMATTING AN ST506/412 DRIVE

Preparing a drive for service is typically a three-step process, which includes: low-level formatting, DOS partitioning, and DOS formatting. Formatting is used to organize data on a drive, and each subsequent step refines that organization. When an ST506/412 drive is manufactured, its platters contain absolutely blank media. As a result, an operating system has no idea where to store or locate information. Low-Level (LL) formatting lays down the individual tracks and sectors across the entire drive—this builds a basic foundation for data storage.

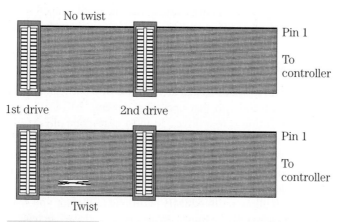

FIGURE 13-3   Control cabling for an ST406/412 drive.

All ST506/412 drives require low-level formatting before using the drive for the first time, or when a serious sector or track failure causes data loss. Low-level formatting is accomplished through the use of a BIOS routine, which can be invoked by a DEBUG command, such as:

```
C:\> debug      ;start DEBUG
- g=c800:5      ;run the LL formatter for the drive controller in use
```

The "5" indicates the type of drive controller being used. Western Digital, DTC, and Seagate controllers work with a "5" suffix, but Adaptec controllers often use a "CCC" suffix, and SMS-OMTI controllers use a "6." If your system BIOS does not provide a LL formatter, it might include a routine in the DOS sub-directory. You can also use a commercial LL formatter, such as DrivePro by MicroHouse. Low-level formatting accomplishes several specific functions. First, it checks for and maps out any defects detected on the drive during manufacture. This is done by placing invalid checksum values in the header of each defective sector. During later formatting steps, DOS will be unable to use the defective sectors as well. LL formatting also sets the drive's interleave factor. Because ST506/412 drives were fast compared to the original circuitry reading the data, the drive had to be delayed by staggering the sector assignments. This forced the drive to rotate several times to read each sector in the track. ST506/412 drives in XT systems often used an interleave of 3:1. In AT systems, this was often set to 2:1. Check the following guidelines before performing a low-level format:

- *Back up a used drive first* Low-level formatting is a destructive and unrecoverable procedure, so any data that was recorded on the drive will be destroyed. Of course, a new drive would contain nothing to backup. Because you will not encounter "new" ST506/412 drives, it is wise to backup whatever you can before committing to a LL format.
- *Format at a running temperature* Let the system warm up for about 30 minutes before attempting a LL format. Because the LL format places tracks and sectors at precise physical locations, the drive should be at a stable running temperature so that the mechanical positioning elements have undergone full expansion from heat. The expansion is only microscopic, but when you realize that the data and positioning is microscopic, formatting a cold drive could cause unusual data errors or positioning problems after the drive warms up.
- *Format in the final position* Mount the drive as it will be used before attempting an LL format. If the drive is formatted in one orientation, then mounted in another, the effects of gravity might throw positioning off enough to cause an unusual number of data errors.

PARTITIONING AND HIGH-LEVEL FORMATTING

Placing a partition on a hard drive allocates that area for use by a particular operating system and allows one partition to boot to that operating system. MS-DOS provides the FDISK utility for assigning partitions to a drive. In most cases, one physical hard drive can be partitioned into four logical drives (or volumes). However, the size of each partition is limited by the DOS version being used. Version 2.0 was limited to a single partition of only 16MB. Versions 2.1 to 3.2x were limited to a single partition size of 32MB. Version 3.3 allowed multiple 32MB partitions. Version 4.xx allowed up to 512MB partitions. Versions 5.xx and 6.0 allow up to 528MB partitions (although you will not find ST506/412 drives that even approach that limit). In all cases, no drive can have over 1024 cylinders in the drive parameters. Remember to set the "boot partition" to *Active*. Once a drive is partitioned, it must be high-level formatted by the operating system. This configures the file-allocation tables and directory structures to be used by the drive. High-level formatting must be repeated for every logical volume that has been partitioned.

THE FATE OF ST506/412

For its day in the early 1980s, the ST506/412 interface was a reliable design—its use of BIOS and flexible parameters also set the stage for future modular drive systems. Unfortunately, the ST506/412 was a slow interface and PC systems quickly outpaced the drive. The nature of the interface also limited the drives to no more than 60MB or so. Additional developments in encoding schemes and drive mechanics demanded a much more efficient interface. By 1984, the ST506/412 interface was considered obsolete; by 1986, virtually no new ST506/412-type drives were being produced. However, you might still encounter these drives in older "hand-me-down" systems.

ESDI

The *Enhanced Small Device Interface (ESDI)* came into being early in 1983 in an effort to replace the already-obsolete ST506/412. Maxtor Corporation (along with a number of other drive and controller manufacturers) led the drive to develop a real drive standard that would extend the speed and capacity of the ST506/412 interface. Originally dubbed the *Enhanced Small Disk Interface*, it was merged with the *Enhanced Small Tape Interface* in October of 1983 to form ESDI. By 1985, a version of ESDI was released that was suitable for optical disks. In 1987, tape support was dropped from the ESDI standard. Today, ESDI exists as an interface standard approved by the *International Standards Organization (ISO)*.

ESDI drives make extensive use of RLL encoding with 34 sectors per track and a direct 1:1 interleave factor. The ESDI scheme uses data separator/encoder circuitry on the drive itself where ST506/412 drives placed the circuitry on a controller card. With data separator/encoder circuitry already on the drive, an ESDI drive need only send straight binary over its data lines (1s and 0s), rather than flux transitions. This approach gives ESDI the potential for serial data rates up to 24Mbits/s, although most transfer occurs at 10Mbits/s. Another improvement to ESDI is the use of buffered seeks, which allows the drive (not the controller) to manage head step movement. The ESDI drive need only receive a single-step command from its controller, which could refer to single or multiple track steps. The capacity and performance advantages provided by ESDI systems made them the preferred drive architecture in high-end PCs into the late 1980s when SCSI and IDE architectures came into common use.

ESDI FEATURES AND ARCHITECTURE

As with ST506/412 drives, ESDI drives are "dumb" devices—the controller must tell the drive explicitly what to do and when to do it. As a consequence, ESDI controllers are equally complicated devices, which reside on a plug-in expansion board. The host computer addresses the controller board through the motherboard's ISA bus and sends instructions to the controller's on-board registers. Like its older cousin, ESDI architecture benefits from this kind of simple modularity. A larger drive can easily be plugged into the original controller or a defective controller can be quickly replaced. In addition, EDSI controllers are virtually register-compatible with ST506/412 controllers, so software written for one type of drive will almost always work on the other. ESDI drives also rely on BIOS drive parameter tables to configure the system for the particular drive. Where a specific drive type is not available, a user-definable drive type (e.g., Type 47) can often be used to ensure ESDI drive support.

The layout for an ESDI drive is identical to the ST506/412 drive shown in Fig. 13-2. The physical interface for an ESDI drive consists of three cables: a 4-pin power cable, a 34-pin control cable, and a 20-pin data cable. The *power cable* is a standard, keyed mate-n-lock connector, which provides +5 Vdc, +12 Vdc, and ground to the drive. The *control cable* is responsible for carrying explicit operating signals to the drive, such as *Drive select*, *Attention*, *Head select*, etc. The *data cable* supports differential *Read* and *Write lines*, along with a series of other signals. Both digital cables are flat or twisted-pair ribbon cable. It is interesting that a set of terminating resistors is mounted to the drive. Although terminating resistors are usually covered only in relation to SCSI interfaces, the resistors are equally vital for proper signal characteristics in an ESDI system. In most cases, terminating resistors can be removed, or disabled through a jumper. As you will see later, proper termination is important when more than one drive is attached to the controller. Although many jumpers might be on the drive, a set of drive-select jumpers are usually located between the data and control cables. Drive select jumpers allow the drive to be set as Drive 0 or Drive 1.

The pinouts for an ESDI control cable are illustrated in Table 13-3. As you look over the pinout labels, you might notice that virtually all of the signals are active-low logic (de-

TABLE 13-3 PINOUT FOR AN ESDI CONTROL CABLE

PIN	NAME	PIN	NAME
1	Ground	2	−Head Select 3
3	Ground	4	−Head Select 2
5	Ground	6	−Write Gate
7	Ground	8	−Config/Status Data
9	Ground	10	−Transfer Acknowledge
11	Ground	12	−Attention
13	Ground	14	−Head Select 0
15	Ground	16	−Sector/Address Mark Found
17	Ground	18	−Head Select 1
19	Ground	20	−Index
21	Ground	22	−Ready
23	Ground	24	−Transfer Request
25	Ground	26	−Drive Select 0
27	Ground	28	−Drive Select 1
29	Ground	30	−Drive Select 2
31	Ground	32	−Read Gate
33	Ground	34	−Command Data

TABLE 13-4 PINOUT FOR AN ESDI DATA CABLE

PIN	NAME	PIN	NAME
1	−Drive Selected	2	−Sector/Address Mark Found
3	−Command Complete	4	−Address Mark Enable
5	Reserved for Step Mode	6	Ground
7	+Write Clock	8	−Write Clock
9	Cartridge Changed	10	+Read/Reference Clock
11	−Read/Reference Clock	12	Ground
13	+Write Data	14	−Write Data
15	Ground	16	Ground
17	+Read Data	18	−Read Data
19	Ground	20	−Index

noted by the minus sign next to their names). Physically, the cable layout is identical to the ST506 approach. The 34-pin control cable uses single-ended signaling, and some of the ESDI signals are the same as those used for ST506. The four *−Head select* lines (pins 2, 4, 14, and 18) select one of up to 16 R/W heads on the drive for reading or writing. The *−Write gate* signal (pin 6) enables the selected head for writing. A *−Config/status data* line (pin 8) responds to the controller's request for information by sending 16 or more serial condition bits back to the controller. A *−Transfer request* input (pin 24) indicates that the host system wants to begin a data transfer, and the *−Transfer acknowledge* output (pin 10) sends a handshaking signal to the controller when a data transfer is permitted to begin. The *−Attention* output (pin 12) is sent by the drive when the controller must read drive status (usually because of a fault).

The *−Sector/address mark found* line (pin 16) outputs a pulse to the controller whenever a sector's address data passes under a head. An *−Index* signal (pin 20) produces a pulse every 16.6 ms, corresponding to a track's index mark data. The drive *−Ready* line (pin 22) outputs a signal to the controller when the drive is at operating speed and is ready to accept commands. A *−Read gate* signal (pin 32) enables the selected R/W head for a read operation. Commands and data can be sent from controller to drive using the 16-bit serial line, called *−Command data* (pin 34). Finally, three *−Drive select* lines (pins 26, 28, and 30, respectively) form a binary value that corresponds to the drive number that the computer wishes to access.

The 20-pin data cable uses a mix of differential and single-ended signals (Table 13-4). A *−Drive select* (pin 1) tells the controller that the selected drive is responding to commands. The *−Sector/address mark found* (pin 2) is essentially the same signal used in the 34-pin cable, but is available at all times. When the ESDI drive has finished its last function, it outputs a *−Command complete* signal (pin 3) to tell the host that a new command can be accepted. An *−Address mark enable* signal (AME, pin 4) causes the drive to search for the next address mark. The AME can also be used to enable writing address marks and sync data fields to the disk during the format process. The +*Write clock* and *−Write clock* (pins 7 and 8) are used to synchronize write data. The +*Read/reference clock* and *−Read/reference clock* (pins 10 and 11) are used to synchronize read data, and to determine the drive's appropriate data-transfer rate. Write data is carried to the drive over the

+*Write data* and –*Write data* lines (pins 13 and 14), and read data is carried to the controller by the +*Read data* and –*Read data* lines (pins 17 and 18). Finally, an –*Index* signal (pin 20) generates a pulse signal each time the platters rotate. This signal serves the same purpose as the index signal in the 34-pin cable, but it is available at all times.

CABLING THE ESDI DRIVE SYSTEM

ESDI systems are cabled almost identically to ST506/412 interfaces—they are intended to support up to two drives with the same controller board. You should understand how cable configurations, terminating resistors, and drive jumpers are related. The basic drive system uses a single drive and controller, along with a control cable with one card edge connector (the red or blue wire represents pin 1). It is a simple matter to attach the drive and controller. You should set the only drive as drive 0 and keep the termination resistors in place on the drive.

Many ESDI cable assemblies were produced with two drive connectors ganged on the same cable (Fig. 13-3). The end-most card edge connector is always for the first drive, but the drive jumper settings vary. If the cable has no twist, the first drive should be jumpered as drive 0 and the termination resistors should be left in place. When a second drive is added to that untwisted cable, it should be jumpered as drive 1, and its termination resistors should be removed. When the control cable has a twist, things are a bit more complicated. The end-most card edge connector is still for the first (or only) drive, but the drive should be jumpered as drive 1, and its termination resistors should be left in place. If a second drive is added to the twisted cable, it should also be jumpered as drive 1, but its termination resistors should be removed. The twist reverses the select pins for the first drive. Be very careful that you do not inadvertently use a floppy drive cable—the twist is in a different place.

LOW-LEVEL FORMATTING AN ESDI DRIVE

Preparing a drive for service is typically a three-step process that includes: low-level formatting, DOS partitioning, and DOS formatting. Formatting is used to organize data on a drive, and each subsequent step refines that organization. When an ESDI drive is manufactured, its platters contain absolutely blank media. As a result, an operating system has no idea where to store or locate information. Low-Level (LL) formatting lays down the individual tracks and sectors across the entire drive—this builds a basic foundation for data storage. All ESDI drives require low-level formatting before using the drive for the first time, or when a serious sector or track failure causes data loss. Low-level formatting is accomplished through the use of a BIOS routine, which can be invoked by a DEBUG command, such as:

```
C:\> debug        ;start DEBUG
- g=c800:5        ;run the LL formatter for the drive controller in use
```

The "5" indicates the type of drive controller being used. Western Digital, DTC, and Seagate controllers work with a "5" suffix, but Adaptec controllers often use a "CCC" suffix, and SMS-OMTI controllers use a "6." If your system BIOS does not provide a LL formatter, it might include a routine in the DOS sub-directory. You can also use a commercial LL formatter, such as DrivePro by MicroHouse. Low-level formatting accomplishes several specific functions. First, it checks for and maps out any defects detected on the drive during manufacture. This is done by placing invalid checksum values in the header of each defective sector. During later formatting steps, DOS will be unable to use the defective sectors as well. LL formatting also sets the drive's interleave factor. Because ESDI drives are later devices, the controller circuitry is typically fast enough to keep pace with the drive, so there is no need to delay the drive. ESDI is not supported in XT systems, but in AT systems, interleave is almost always set to 1:1.

ESDI low-level formatting also handles two advanced-drive features: sector sparing and skewing. *Sector sparing* is a technique of "hiding" one sector per track. This reduces the overall number of sectors, but any bad sector elsewhere in the track is transferred to the hidden sector. This leaves all good sectors in the track. For example, suppose sector 18 of a 36-sector track is bad. Sparing relocates sector 18 to sector 36, and moves sectors 19 to 36 down by one sector. In effect, 35 good sectors will be available and the bad sector will be hidden. Sector skewing is an optimization technique that offsets the first sector of each track. This masks the delay in moving to adjacent tracks; otherwise, the drive might have to make an extra rotation to locate the first sector of a new track. The faster a drive spins, the greater skew value that is required. The outer tracks (which move faster) also use a greater amount of skew. Check the following guidelines before performing a low-level format:

■ *Back up a used drive first* Low-level formatting is a destructive and unrecoverable procedure, so any data that was recorded on the drive will be destroyed. Of course, a new drive would contain nothing to backup. Because you will not encounter "new" ST506/412 drives, it is wise to backup whatever you can before committing to a LL format.

■ *Format at a running temperature* Let the system warm up for about 30 minutes before attempting a LL format. Because the LL format places tracks and sectors at precise physical locations, the drive should be at a stable running temperature so that the mechanical positioning elements have undergone full expansion from heat. The expansion is only microscopic, but when you realize that the data and positioning is microscopic, formatting a cold drive could cause unusual data errors or positioning problems after the drive warms up.

■ *Format in the final position* Mount the drive as it will be used before attempting an LL format. If the drive is formatted in one orientation, then mounted in another, the effects of gravity might throw positioning off enough to cause an unusual number of data errors.

PARTITIONING AND HIGH-LEVEL FORMATTING

Placing a partition on a hard drive allocates that area for use by a particular operating system, and allows one partition to boot to that operating system. MS-DOS provides the FDISK utility for assigning partitions to a drive. In most cases, one physical hard drive can be partitioned into four logical drives (or volumes). However, the size of each partition is limited by the DOS version being used. Version 2.0 was limited to a single partition of only 16MB. Versions 2.1 to 3.2x were limited to a single partition size of 32MB. Version 3.3 allowed multiple 32MB partitions. Version 4.xx allowed up to 512MB partitions. Versions 5.xx and 6.xx allow up to 528MB partitions. In all cases, no drive can have over 1024 cylinders in the drive parameters. Remember to set the "boot partition" as active. Once a drive is partitioned, it must be high-level formatted by the operating system. This configures the file allocation tables and directory structures to be used by the drive. High-level formatting must be repeated for every logical volume that has been partitioned.

THE FATE OF ESDI

ESDI was envisioned and implemented as a high-performance version of ST506/412. Not only does ESDI offer much faster performance, it provides very high storage capacity (as much as a 1GB). These advantages made ESDI the drive architecture of choice for network servers and other high-end systems—a few of which are still in service today. Unfortunately, the full potential of ESDI was never realized, and SCSI systems have moved in to fill the high-end gap. You might encounter ESDI systems at one time or another, but it will be difficult (or impossible) to obtain replacement parts.

IDE

The *Integrated Drive Electronics (IDE)* interface developed in 1988 in response to an industry push to create a standard software interface for SCSI peripherals. The industry consortium, known as the *Common Access Method Committee (CAMC)* attempted to originate an AT Attachment (ATA) interface that could be incorporated into low-cost AT-compatible motherboards. The CAM committee completed its specification, which was later approved by ANSI. The term *ATA Interface* generally refers to the controller interface, and *IDE* refers to the drive. Today, *IDE* can refer to either the drive or controller.

IDE FEATURES AND ARCHITECTURE

IDE drives are typically intelligent—that is, almost all functions relegated to a controller board in older drives are now integrated onto the drive itself. Data is transferred through a single cable attached to a simple *paddle board* (a simple controller board, which is often little more than a buffer) attached to the system's expansion bus. Exterior circuitry is so limited that multiple IDE ports can easily be added to new motherboards. IDE drives are fast, offering short seek times and data-transfer rates easily exceeding 10Mbits/s. IDE also supports reasonably large drives up to 528MB devices (EIDE hard drives break the traditional IDE 528MB barrier and can provide more than 5GB at this time). Although IDE lacks the flexibility and expandability of SCSI, IDE is relatively inexpensive to implement—thus, it is often the choice for simple, inexpensive, mid-range PCs that are not expected to expand much. More recently, the use of an IDE interface has extended beyond just hard drives to include such devices as CD-ROMs and tape drives through the use of the AT Attachment Packet Interface (ATAPI) interface protocol.

A great deal of discussions have concentrated on IDE "intelligence." The intelligence of an IDE system is determined by the capabilities of the on-board controller. For the purposes of this book, intelligent IDE drives are capable of the following functions. First, intelligent IDE drives support *drive translation*—the feature, which allows CMOS drive parameters to be entered in any combination of cylinders, heads, and sectors that add up to equal or less than the true number of sectors on the drive. This is particularly handy when the actual number of cylinders exceeds 1024 (as all modern IDE/EIDE drives do). Nonintelligent IDE drives were limited to physical mode where CMOS parameters were entered to match physical parameters. Intelligent drives also support a number of enhanced commands that are an optional part of the ATA specification.

Another advancement of intelligent IDE technology is zoned recording, which allows a variable number of sectors per track. This allows an overall increase in the number of sectors—and the drive's overall capacity. However, BIOS can only deal with a fixed number of sectors per track, so the zoned IDE drive must always run in translation mode. When running IDE drives in translation mode, you cannot alter interleave or sector skew factors. You also cannot change factory-defect information.

A typical IDE/EIDE layout is shown in Figure 13-4. The physical interface for a standard IDE drive consists of two cables: a 4-pin power cable and a 40-pin data/control cable (IBM uses either a 44-pin or 72-pin cable). The power cable is a standard, keyed mate-n-lock connector, which provides +5 Vdc, +12 Vdc, and ground to the drive. The signal cable is responsible for carrying data and control signals between the drive and paddle board. IDE/EIDE drives also use terminating resistors to ensure reliable signal characteristics, but IDE/EIDE terminating resistors are usually fixed and cannot be removed. In most cases, two IDE/EIDE drives can work together with terminating resistors in place. Although several jumpers are on the drive, a set of drive-select jumpers allow the drive to be set as the primary ("master") or secondary ("slave") drive.

The signal cable for an IDE AT-style drive is typically a 40-pin *Insulation-Displacement Connector (IDC)* cable as shown in Table 13-5. Unlike ST506/412 or ESDI interfaces, IDE/EIDE uses both the even and odd-numbered wires as signal-carrying lines. Also notice that most of the signal labels have dashes beside their names. The dash indicates that the particular signal is active low—that is, the signal is true in the logic 0 state instead of being true in the logic 1 state. All signal lines on the IDE interface are fully TTL-compatible, where a logic 0 is 0.0 to +0.8 Vdc, and a logic 1 is +2.0 to Vcc.

Data points and registers in the hard drive are addressed using *Drive address bus* lines *DA0* to *DA2* (pins 35, 33, and 36, respectively) in conjunction with *–Chip select drive* inputs *–CS1FX* and *–CS3FX* (pins 37 and 38). When a true signal is sent along the *–Drive I/O read* (*–DIOR*, pin 25) line, the drive executes a read cycle, while a true on the *–Drive I/O write* (*–DIOW*, pin 23) line initiates a write cycle. The IDE interface provides TTL-level input and output signals. Where older interfaces were serial, the IDE interface provides 16 bi-directional data lines (*DD0* to *DD15*, pins 3 to 18) to carry data bits into or out of the drive. Once a data transfer is completed, a *–DMA acknowledge* (*–DMACK*, pin 29) signal is provided to the drive from the hard-disk controller IC. Finally, a true signal on

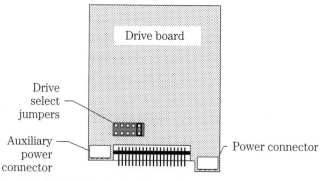

FIGURE 13-4   **Connector layout for an IDE/EIDE drive.**

TABLE 13-5   PINOUT FOR AN IDE/EIDE SIGNAL CABLE

PIN	NAME	PIN	NAME
1	Reset	2	Ground
3	DD7	4	DD8
5	DD6	6	DD9
7	DD5	8	DD10
9	DD4	10	DD11
11	DD3	12	DD12
13	DD2	14	DD13
15	DD1	16	DD14
17	DD0	18	DD15
19	Ground	20	Key (slot only)
21	DMARQ	22	Ground
23	–I/O Write Data (–DIOW)	24	Ground
25	–I/O Read Data (–DIOR)	26	Ground
27	–I/O Channel Ready (–IORDY)	28	unused
29	–DMA Acknowledge (–DMACK)	30	Ground
31	Interrupt Request (INTRQ)	32	–Host 16-bit I/O (–IOCS16)
33	DA1	34	–Passed Diagnostics (–PDIAG)
35	DA0	36	DA2
37	–Host Chip Sel 0 (–CS1FX)	38	–Host Chip Sel 1 (–CS3FX)
39	–Drive Active (–DASP)	40	Ground

the drive's *Reset* line (pin 1) will restore the drive to its original condition at power on. A *Reset* is sent when the computer is first powered on or rebooted.

The IDE/EIDE physical interface also provides a number of outputs back to the motherboard. A *Direct memory access request* (*DMARQ*, pin 21) is used to initiate the transfer of data to or from the drive. The direction of data transfer is dependent on the condition of the –*DIOR* and –*DIOW* inputs. A –*DMACK* signal is generated in response when the *DMARQ* line is asserted (made true). –*IORDY* (pin 27) is an –*I/O channel ready* signal that keeps a system's attention if the drive is not quite ready to respond to a data-transfer request. A drive *Interrupt request* (*INTRQ*, pin 31) is asserted by a drive when a drive interrupt is pending (i.e., the drive is about to transfer information to or from the motherboard). The –*Drive active* line (*DASP*, pin 39) becomes logic 0 when any hard-drive activity is occurring. A –*Passed diagnostic* (*PDIAG*, pin 34) line provides the results of any diagnostic command or reset action. When *PDIAG* is logic 0, the system knows that the drive is ready to use. Finally, the 16-bit –*I/O control* line (*IOCS16*, pin 32) tells the motherboard that the drive is ready to send or receive data. Notice that there are several return (ground) lines (pins 2, 19, 22, 24, 26, 30, and 40), and a key pin (20), which is removed from the male connector.

An older XT variation of the IDE signal cable is outlined in Table 13-6. The first thing you should notice about this setup is that it has much fewer signal lines. Even though the same 40-pin cable is used, all of the even numbered pins are ground lines. There are only eight data signals (*D0* to *D7*). The signals on each odd numbered pin are rearranged a bit, but are identical to those listed for the full AT implementation. The only real exception is the *Address enable* (*AEN*, pin 21) signal, which is asserted during a DMA cycle to disable the processing of I/O port addresses.

CABLING THE IDE/EIDE INTERFACE

The ATA IDE interface is intended to support two drives on the same cable (or channel) in a daisy-chained fashion. A typical IDE controller cable is illustrated in Fig. 13-5. Although tradition dictates that drive 0 be attached to the end connector (as the primary or master drive) and a second drive be attached to the middle connector (as a secondary or slave drive), it is important to note that IDE supports either drive in either location. For the purposes of IDE, you need only set the proper drive jumpers to select a drive as a master or slave. The 40-pin ribbon cable (IBM uses 44-pin or 72-pin cables) should not exceed 61 cm (24") in length. Because IDE drives rely on distributed termination as a means of signal conditioning, it is not necessary to install or remove terminating resistors.

However, you might encounter problems when running two IDE drives together. Older IDE drives did not adhere to the CAMC ATA IDE specification. When trying to run older drives together (especially drives from different manufacturers), they might not respond to their master/slave relationship properly, and conflicts will result—in many cases, such problems will disable both drives. When planning a dual-IDE installation, try to use newer drives that are both from the same manufacturer.

TABLE 13-6	PINOUT FOR AN IDE XT-TYPE SIGNAL CABLE		
PIN	NAME	PIN	NAME
1	Reset	2	Ground
3	DD7	4	Ground
5	DD6	6	Ground
7	DD5	8	Ground
9	DD4	10	Ground
11	DD3	12	Ground
13	DD2	14	Ground
15	DD1	16	Ground
17	DD0	18	Ground
19	Ground	20	Key (slot only)
21	Address Enable (AEN)	22	Ground
23	–I/O Write Data (–DIOW)	24	Ground
25	–I/O Read Data (–DIOR)	26	Ground
27	–DMA Acknowledge (–DMACK)	28	Ground
29	DMA Request (DRQ)	30	Ground
31	Interrupt Request (INTRQ)	32	Ground
33	DA1	34	Ground
35	DA0	36	Ground
37	–Host Chip Sel 0 (–CS1FX)	38	Ground
39	unused	40	Ground

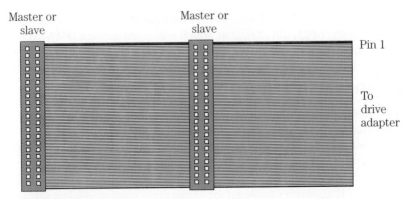

FIGURE 13-5   **Data and control cabling for an IDE/EIDE drive.**

LOW-LEVEL FORMATTING AN IDE/EIDE DRIVE

The question of whether or not to low-level format an IDE drive continues to be a thorn in the side of all technicians. Drive manufacturers claim that low-level formatting can destroy the drive's servo information recorded at the factory. Diagnostic manufacturers claim that their products are smart enough to recognize critical areas of an IDE drive, and perform a safe low-level format. Even today, no single consensus exists on IDE low-level formatting. But you can follow some guidelines.

First, you cannot low-level format an IDE drive using the BIOS formatter at C800h the same way you do with ST506/412 or ESDI drives. Although the heart of an IDE controller is an extension of the basic Western Digital ST506/412 controller architecture, ATA specifications allow for additional commands that are needed to step over servo tracks. However, the fact remains that IDE drives can be low-level formatted—after all, the manufacturers do it. Ultimately, you will need to obtain a low-level formatter routine directly from the drive manufacturer. Seagate, Western Digital, Maxtor, and other drive makers offer LL format and spare-sector defect-management software for their respective drives. In some cases, the LL formatter routine is included on a setup diskette included with many new drives. In the case of Conner drives, you will need a piece of hardware that connects directly to the drive's diagnostic port. TCE makes a Conner hardware formatter. You might also be able to obtain a LL formatter from the manufacturer's technical support department, from their BBS, or from their CompuServe forum.

Some third-party software manufacturers have developed flexible products that recognize the particular drive and use manufacturer-specific commands to achieve proper low-level formatting and defect mapping. Ontrack's *Disk Manager* is perhaps the best-known and most trusted of these third-party products. If you can not obtain a LL formatter from the manufacturer, *Disk Manager* is probably your best second choice. Remember that no LL format software works with every controller.

Of course, low-level formatting has limitations. IDE drives must be running in their physical mode instead of translation mode for a LL format to take place. Zoned IDE drives are even more limited because only the defect map can be updated, and new defective sectors can be spared. Sector headers are almost never rewritten, except to mark bad sectors. Now that you know you can LL format an IDE drive, the question is should you? Notice that you should not have to low-level format a new IDE drive when installing it for the first time. For a technician, LL formatting should be reserved as an emergency measure for drives that have lost track or sector organization data because of defects or age. Remember that low-level formatting is a destructive and unrecoverable process, so make sure to back up as much of the drive as possible before attempting the procedure.

BIOS SUPPORT OF IDE

Unlike SCSI controllers, which use an expansion ROM to provide supplemental BIOS, the firmware needed to provide IDE support is written into the main system BIOS. Although systems manufactured in the last few years (after 1990) are fully compatible with ATA IDE drives, adding an IDE drive to an older PC often resulted in problems. After the broad introduction of IDE, it was discovered that IDE drive operations placed different timing demands on the PC, which frequently caused disk errors, such as data corruption and failure to boot. BIOS makers quickly found a solution to this timing problem, which was incorporated into BIOS that appeared after early 1990. If you encounter a PC with pre-1990 BIOS, you should consider upgrading it before adding an IDE drive or if the current IDE drive is exhibiting problems.

THE ROLE OF ATAPI

Before you go farther, it's necessary to understand the role of the *AT Attachment Packet Interface (ATAPI)* in IDE/EIDE systems. With the broad acceptance and proliferation of IDE in the early 1990s, hard drives finally had a versatile interface, which could support a vast assortment of hard drives using standardized set of BIOS calls. Unfortunately, non-hard drive devices (such as CD-ROMs, tape drives, etc.) could not use the conventional BIOS firmware, etc. could not utilize the IDE/EIDE interface. The PC industry addressed this problem by developing the ATAPI standard. ATAPI is a hardware and software specification that describes the interface between a host computer and other drives using the ATA (IDE) bus. Devices designed to the ATAPI standard can use the IDE interface by simply loading real-mode or protected-mode device drivers at start time. For example, an ATAPI CD-ROM will use an ATAPI driver in the CONFIG.SYS file. For our purposes, any non-hard drive device that uses the IDE/EIDE interface is considered ATAPI.

EIDE

Although IDE offers some compelling advantages, there are three major limitations. First, drive capacities are limited to about 528MB. Second, an IDE interface only supports two drives (almost always hard drives). Third, it does not provide very fast data transfer—about as fast as ESDI. Enhanced IDE (EIDE) is another step in IDE evolution, which addresses these limitations. EIDE interfaces support up to four devices (hard drives as well as ATAPI CD-ROM drives and tape drives, which have traditionally relied on proprietary interfaces). EIDE architecture also increases the 528MB drive capacity limit to 8.4GB. The data-transfer rate for EIDE can approach 16.6MB/s. Yet the physical interface used for EIDE works with the same 40-pin approach now used with the IDE/AT architecture, and EIDE is backwardly compatible with older IDE drives. This part of the chapter examines the improvements that EIDE offers over IDE, and covers the issues involved in implementing EIDE on older PCs.

UNDERSTANDING THE 528MB IDE LIMIT

This is probably the most important and compelling limitation to IDE architecture, and is the result of a simple lack of planning between the developers of BIOS, and the developers of the WD1003 drive controller architecture. To understand the limitations of drive size, you must understand how IDE drives are addressed. The classic addressing scheme is known as *Cylinder Head Sector (CHS)* addressing. Simply stated, you place the cylinder number, head number, and sector number you need to get to into the WD1003 controller registers, then call the Int 13 routine in BIOS, which runs the drive to the desired location for reading or writing.

This works just dynamite in theory, but there is a problem. You see, the limiting values for cylinders, heads, and sectors are not the same in both the BIOS and the WD1003 architecture. Table 13-7 illustrates these values, and you can see their impact on drive size. BIOS specifies a maximum of 1024 cylinders, 255 heads, and 63 sectors per track. If you multiply these together, then multiply 512 bytes/sector, you get 8422686720 bytes (or 8.4GB) of theoretical capacity. For the WD1003 controller, you should be able to have 65536 cylinders, 16 heads, and 255 sectors per track. When this is multiplied by 512 bytes per sector, you get a whopping 1.368991011 bytes (or 136.9GB) of theoretical capacity.

The problem is that you can only use the lowest common number for each approach, so the maximum number of cylinders you can use is 1024, the maximum number of heads is 16, and the maximum number of sectors of 63. When you multiply these out, then multiply times 512 bytes/sector, you only get 528MB. The real tragedy here is that if BIOS designers and WD1003 designers had sat down and come up with the same numbers, we could easily have had IDE drives with capacities up to 136.9GB, and this entire issue would be moot. But instead, an IDE hard drive can only address up to 528MB.

This explains why IDE worked so well with drives up to 528MB, but not more. Of course, there are ways to work around this limitation. Because BIOS is essentially software, the easiest and most economical way to overcome the 528MB barrier is to "augment" the BIOS Int 13 routine by introducing a driver when the PC is initialized. Int 13 enhancements allow the support of drive sizes up to 8.4GB. The *Drive Rocket* and *Disk Manager* by Ontrack are two of the most popular drivers available. They allow the PC to access the entire space of a large IDE drives—not just 528MB.

EIDE can work with such drivers, and *Disk Manager* (or one of its similar cousins) is frequently bundled with large IDE and the new EIDE-compatible hard drives. However,

TABLE 13-7 CHS VALUES VS. DRIVE SIZE

	BIOS	WD1003	RESULTING LIMIT
Cylinders	1024	65536	1024
Heads	255	16	16
Sectors	63	255	63
Max. capacity	8.4GB	136.9GB	528MB

there are some compelling reasons why drivers are not desirable. First, drivers take memory space—typically, precious space within the first 640KB of RAM. Few systems have space remaining in the upper memory area for a disk driver. Second, disk drivers don't always accommodate Windows 3.1x or Windows 95 very well at all, so using large hard drives under Windows has traditionally been a problem. Third, the disk driver might conflict with other device drivers and TSRs that may be on your PC.

Ultimately, the preferred method of large drive support for EIDE is to update the BIOS itself with one that contains the Int 13 enhancements. AMI and Micro Firmware are early entrants into the EIDE-compatible BIOS arena, but today, EIDE support is standard in all BIOS and drive-controller versions. Although upgrading a BIOS is a bit more involved than adding a driver, the rewards (more free memory and better OS compatibility) are almost always worth it. As an effective alternative to the trials of a motherboard BIOS upgrade, you can choose to upgrade your current drive controller with an EIDE adapter with on-board BIOS extensions for Int 13.

UNDERSTANDING LBA

Another great source of confusion in the migration to EIDE is its need for *Logical Block Addressing (LBA)*. Where CHS addressing requires the specification of a discrete cylinder, head, and sector, an LBA address simply requires the specification of a sector (e.g., "go to sector 324534"). The LBA algorithm (implemented in BIOS) will translate the sector to the appropriate CHS equivalent. FAT-based operating systems, such as DOS (and Windows because Windows works on the DOS file system) REQUIRE the use of LBA addressing. As a consequence, you will need to update your motherboard BIOS or use an EIDE controller with on-board BIOS. On the other hand, non-FAT operating systems (such as OS/2 and Novell Netware) do not require LBA addressing. When you actually have an EIDE controller in-hand, you might notice that the controller provides a jumper allowing you to enable or disable LBA addressing. If you are using DOS (or Windows), keep this jumper enabled.

An important consideration in choosing CHS or LBA addressing is the format of your hard drive(s). If you choose to invoke LBA addressing, you will need to reformat your hard drive(s). You must also remember that once a hard drive is formatted for LBA, the drive will only be recognized by PCs that support LBA. As a result, if you take an LBA-formatted drive (EIDE) and install it into a PC whose BIOS does not support LBA (e.g., an older IDE-supported system), the drive will simply not be recognized, and you will have to reformat the drive again. In all cases, remember to perform a complete backup of your hard drive(s) before implementing EIDE on your system.

DRIVE SUPPORT

One of the key advantages of SCSI has traditionally been its ability to support up to seven varied devices on the same bus (hard drives, CD-ROMs, tape drives, etc.). This approach went a long way toward eliminating the proliferation of proprietary controllers and system-configuration problems that remain prevalent in non-SCSI systems. Although IDE allows two drives (master and slave) to reside on the same port (1F0h) and interrupt (IRQ 14), it does not support any other devices. EIDE seeks to overcome this limitation by adding a second "channel" to the EIDE controller.

The "Primary EIDE interface" channel (or simply "primary channel") is intended to handle two EIDE drives in a master/slave relationship. But the "Secondary IDE interface" channel allows up to two additional devices (ideally, an IDE ATAPI-compatible tape drive or IDE CD-ROM drive) to be added. It is important for you to remember that although EIDE marketers tout the ability to support four devices, only two are EIDE drives—the other two are non-hard drive devices. Also, the second channel is located at 170h using IRQ 15, so you will need to check for any hardware conflicts with other devices in your system before installing the EIDE adapter. In fact, the secondary channel is often tied in directly to the ISA bus (although later implementations might tie in to the VL or PCI bus). Because neither a CD-ROM or tape drive exceed maximum ISA-transfer speeds, there is no problem doing this—just don't be misdirected by marketing hype into thinking your new EIDE adapter will support four high-performance EIDE drives.

In theory, an older IDE drive will work on an EIDE channel, but you might run into trouble when "mixing" an EIDE and IDE device on the same EIDE channel. A classic example of this is on systems that use a new fast EIDE hard drive, then add on an IDE ATAPI CD-ROM as the "slave" device. In many cases, the slower CD-ROM interferes with the EIDE drive—reducing the drive's maximum data-transfer rates and slowing drive performance. In more pronounced cases, the CD-ROM might not be recognized. In extreme cases, the hard drive (and perhaps the CD-ROM also) might not be recognized and the system won't even boot. Reconfiguring the hardware to make the CD-ROM a "master" device on the IDE (secondary) controller channel will almost always correct the problem.

As a rule, keep the faster EIDE devices on the EIDE (primary) controller channel and use the slower IDE devices on the IDE (secondary) controller channel.

DATA-TRANSFER RATES

The concept of data-transfer rate has always been a confusing one—especially because the rate can vary tremendously, depending on where you measure it. The rate of data coming off the R/W heads, the rate of data coming across the IDE cable and the rate of data moving across the expansion bus can all be very different numbers. Practically speaking, a hard-drive data transfer is only as fast as its slowest stage, so traditional IDE installations were effectively limited to only 2 to 3 MB/sec. across the ISA bus. It wasn't that the drive itself could not pass data faster, but the practical transfer was limited by the slow ISA bus. As a result, building faster drives offered no real advantage because the faster drives would still be limited by a slow expansion bus architecture.

Two factors have made it possible to enjoy the advantages of high-performance EIDE drives—integrated chipsets, and advanced expansion busses. EIDE controllers are now commonly integrated into motherboard chipsets (refer to Chapter 8) and allow the drive interface to be implemented directly on the motherboard, rather than on an expansion bus adapter. This allows faster data transfer by eliminating the expansion bus bottleneck. The disadvantage here is that you are committed to using the motherboard drive-controller scheme (although the motherboard controller can easily be disabled through a motherboard jumper or CMOS *Setup* entry). An outstanding compromise has been the introduction of EIDE adapters for high-performance bus architectures (VL and PCI). You get the

TABLE 13-8   PIO AND DMA DATA TRANSFER MODES

PIO MODE	CYCLE TIME (NS)	TRANSFER RATE (MB/S)	NOTES
0	600	3.3	These are the old IDE modes
1	383	5.2	
2	240	8.3	
3	180 IORDY	11.1	These are the newer EIDE modes
4	120 IORDY	16.6	

DMA MODE	CYCLE TIME (NS)	TRANSFER RATE (MB/S)	NOTES
Single Word DMA	0 960	2.1	Also in ATA
	1 480	4.2	
	2 240	8.3	
Multiword DMA	0 480	4.2	Also in ATA
	1 150	13.3	
	2 120	16.6	
Ultra-DMA/33	– –	33	Ultra-ATA

speed afforded by a better bus, with the ability to simply plug-in better adapters later as they become available.

These superior hardware schemes provide new data-transfer modes. For example, the PIO Mode 3 scheme allows data transfer up to 11.1MB/sec. across the EIDE interface, although the Multi-word DMA Mode 1 scheme allows up to 13.3MB/sec. across the interface. PIO Mode 4 is also available—allowing interface-transfer rates of 16.6MB/s. To take advantage of these high-performance modes, you need to upgrade your IDE drive adapter to an EIDE drive adapter. When you choose an EIDE adapter, make certain that the adapter supports PIO Mode 3 (as a minimum), and that the IORDY line is being used. This is vital because the faster data-transfer rates require a tight interaction between the adapter and system using the IORDY signal. Table 13-8 compares the popular data-transfer modes for drive controllers—including the newest 33MB/s Ultra-DMA/33, which is outlined later in the chapter.

INSTALLING AN EIDE SYSTEM

To implement true EIDE on your system (or maintain EIDE support during a repair), you need to have three elements in place: the drive, the drive adapter, and a BIOS with the Int 13 extension. The drives and drive adapters are relatively straightforward—they are available off the shelf, and can be installed as quickly and easily as any other drive and controller board. Both must be capable of at least PIO Mode 3 data transfer. The controller board must also use the IORDY signal (as opposed to leaving the signal idle or unconnected). Although there are EIDE adapters for ISA systems, you would be well advised to purchase an adapter for VL or PCI bus operation. As a consequence, EIDE is better suited to newer motherboard designs, which provide several VL or PCI bus slots. However, if you do find yourself limited to an ISA-only motherboard, there are a few ISA-based EIDE controllers (such as the Promise EIDEMAX). The software aspect of EIDE adds a bit of a wrinkle because there are three ways to provide the BIOS Int 13 enhancement. You can add a driver utility (like *EZ-Drive* or *Disk Manager*), you can upgrade your motherboard's BIOS ROM(s), or you can use an EIDE controller with on-board ROM, which provides the Int 13 extension. As it turns out, the supplemental BIOS approach is often the most effective.

EIDE adapter installation issues There is hardly any magic to installing an EIDE drive adapter. Like any controller card, it simply plugs in to an available expansion slot. However, most current EIDE controllers provide a variety of features, which can result in troublesome hardware conflicts unless you deal with them correctly. For example, the VL bus-compatible EIDE2300+ board by Promise Technology provides an on-board BIOS, a primary and secondary controller channel, a floppy controller supporting up to 2.88MB drives, two serial ports, a parallel port, and a game port. When installing such a full-featured board, you must be sure to configure (or disable) each area according to the current configuration of your PC. The following is a checklist for EIDE controller installations (refer to the EIDE adapter's manual for specific instructions and settings):

- *Backup your hard drive(s)* This is perhaps the most important—and understated—part of any PC upgrade. All too often, an installation error, driver conflict, or other oversight can ruin a partition table or FAT. With a complete backup, such problems can be resolved simply by repartitioning and reformatting the drive, then restoring your backup.
- *Remove or disable your existing IDE drive adapter* When the drive adapter has been integrated onto the motherboard, you can almost always disable the controller with a single jumper. Refer to the PC's user manual to determine the correct jumper and position. Things can get a little more complicated when the existing drive adapter is on an expansion board. IDE drive adapters serving that function exclusively (often referred to as *paddle boards*) can just be removed. If the IDE controller handles other integrated functions (e.g., floppy controller, game port, etc.), you will have to either transfer those functions to the EIDE drive adapter or disable the IDE portion of the existing adapter board.
- *Check for conflicts at port 170h and IRQ 15* Although disabling the existing IDE adapter should free port 1F0h and IRQ 14 (the traditional hard drive system resources), EIDE adapters typically provide a secondary IDE channel. Unfortunately, the resources used by that secondary channel might already be in use by other devices in the PC. Before you install the new EIDE drive adapter, run a diagnostic, such as Microsoft's MSD, and determine which IRQs and ports are in use. If IRQ 15 or port 170h are already being used, you might have to remove or reconfigure the device(s) using those resources, or disable the controller's secondary IDE channel. If you do not address this issue during installation, unpredictable hardware conflicts might result.
- *Check for conflicts between the EIDE on-board BIOS and other expansion ROMs in the system* The design of modern PCs allows for the addition of supplemental BIOS—usually from system addresses C800h to DFFFh. However, SCSI adapters, network adapters, and video adapters (as well as some other PC peripherals), also have on-board BIOS. As a consequence, you must check that the default address of the EIDE on-board BIOS does not conflict or overlap any other expansion BIOS in the system. If so, change the EIDE BIOS address to a different (unused) location.

- *Inspect your parallel, floppy, game, and serial ports* Although some low-end EIDE drive adapters simply provide support for EIDE (and IDE) devices, a growing number of EIDE adapters integrate a variety of features in addition to EIDE support. Your new EIDE adapter might offer such added features as a parallel port, serial ports, a game port, and a floppy drive adapter. Although added features are often a welcome enhancement, they are also cumbersome to keep track of. For example, many motherboards provide at least one serial port and parallel port. Most sound boards also integrate a game port. A floppy drive adapter might be on the motherboard or on the old IDE adapter. As you might imagine, many of these added functions will have to be disabled—unless you choose to disable the existing features to migrate them to the new EIDE controller. In either case, you will need to know the configuration and available features of the host PC before installing the new EIDE adapter.
- *Recheck each jumper on the controller board* Although most manufacturers take great pains to pre-configure their devices to reasonable defaults, not all defaults are acceptable in every system. You would also be surprised at how many jumper settings are simply set wrong at the factory. Take a moment and verify that each jumper is where you expect it to be. If you have moved jumpers, take a moment and doublecheck the new configuration. A little time checking the work now can save you hours of troubleshooting time later on.

EIDE drive installation issues Now that you have configured and installed the EIDE controller, the time has come to install the drives. Here are some tips to get an EIDE drive up and running (remember that you do not have to use EIDE drives right away—if you're short on cash, you can use your existing IDE drive(s) with the new controller):

- *LBA and drives* If the current IDE drive(s) are under 528MB, you can use the current drive(s) with the EIDE controller—even in LBA mode—without having to reformat them (this is one of the little-known wrinkles of LBA operation). You can reformat them if you wish, but it is not mandatory. When your new or existing EIDE drives are over 528MB and you wish to use them with the EIDE controller, you do need to repartition and reformat them. New EIDE drives can simply be partitioned and formatted, but if the drive(s) had already been formatted under CHS addressing, you will need to backup, repartition, reformat, and restore the drive(s).
- *Do not mix IDE and EIDE drives* Remember that you generally cannot mix IDE and EIDE drives on the same controller channel. So, if you want to use that old IDE drive with your new EIDE drive and controller, you will need to place the IDE drive (as master) on the "secondary" EIDE channel, and use the EIDE drive by itself (as master) on the "primary" EIDE channel. There are exceptions to this rule—some controllers provide on-board BIOS which, detects the relative speed of each drive on the channel, then controls data transfer speeds to each respective drive. This is typically referred to as *intelligent BIOS*. However, you must not mix radically different drives (e.g., CD-ROM and EIDE drives) on the same cable.

Many current CD-ROM drives (and the new DVD-ROM drives) often use EIDE drive interfaces, rather than IDE interfaces. Check the drive specifications—EIDE devices can co-exist with EIDE hard drives without worrying about performance degradation.

■ *Set CMOS parameters* After the controller and drives are installed and secure, you will need to initialize the PC and enter the CMOS setup routine to configure the CMOS drive geometry. The instruction manual with your controller and drive will tell you the correct drive type to enter. In most cases, the EIDE controller will auto-recognize the drive's optimum geometry anyway, so do not be concerned if the parameters that appear seem inappropriate for the drive. When specific parameters are required, enter the proper geometry for each drive.

ADAPTER CONFIGURATION JUMPERS

When installing a drive controller, you'll typically need to configure one or more jumpers to select the proper system resources. It is important for you to understand the importance of each jumper because incorrect settings can cause resource conflicts and system crashes.

Always refer to the documentation that accompanies your controller for jumper settings and other configuration topics. But if you're stuck with an older or undocumented controller, try the CARDG2.ZIP reference package on the companion CD.

IDE enable This jumper (if present) simply allows you to turn the IDE/EIDE controller port(s) on or off. You'll typically find this feature on multi-I/O controllers, where you might want to use a serial or parallel port only, but continue to use a different drive controller. By default, the drive controller is enabled, so be sure to disable the controller if you don't want to use it.

IDE IRQ setting You'll need to set the controller's interrupt. Drive adapters use IRQ 14 as the standard interrupt for the primary drive-controller channel, and this is almost always the default. IRQ 15 is used for the secondary drive-controller channel. If a tertiary drive controller is needed, you can often use IRQ 12 or IRQ 11.

IDE I/O address The controller port must also use a small amount of I/O space. You'll need to configure the I/O port, depending on the controller's role in your system. The primary drive controller is located at 1F0h–1F7, and this is almost always the default. Secondary drive controllers use 170h–177h. Tertiary drive controllers frequently use 1E8h–1EFh, or 168h–16Fh. You might be able to choose either of these ranges.

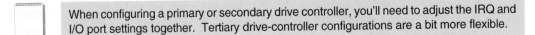

When configuring a primary or secondary drive controller, you'll need to adjust the IRQ and I/O port settings together. Tertiary drive-controller configurations are a bit more flexible.

BIOS address Most drive adapters provide their own on-board BIOS. This is often desirable because it allows newer drive adapters (and drives) to be installed in older PCs whose BIOS might not readily support the features offered by a drive. BIOS uses memory space in the upper memory area (or UMA), so you'll need to set the proper BIOS address, which won't conflict with other adapter ROMs in the system. The four typical addresses are C8000h–CBFFFh, CC000h–DBFFFh, CFFFFh–D8000h, and DC000h–DFFFFh.

BIOS enable This jumper (if present) simply allows you to turn the controller's on-board BIOS on or off. If you do not wish to boot from a drive (i.e., the controller is only supporting CD-ROMs and/or tape drives) or if the motherboard BIOS provides adequate support, you can disable the controller's on-board BIOS. By default, the BIOS is enabled.

"I/O channel ready" enable   This jumper controls the *IORDY* signal. When enabled, the *IORDY* signal is passed to the ISA bus. When disabled, the signal is not passed. By default, the *IORDY* signal is left disabled. However, you might need to enable the signal is you have trouble using high-speed data-transfer rates.

INTx setting   This is usually a series of jumpers used for PCI Plug-and-Play controllers, which configure the board's PCI bus interrupt (#A, #B, #C, or #D). #A and #B are usually the defaults, but other interrupts can be selected as needed.

SOFTWARE INSTALLATION CAUTIONS

Ideally, there should be no device drivers for EIDE operation under DOS—a new or supplemental BIOS should handle that. However, some implementations of EIDE controller do offer a selection of drivers. First, a driver might be required to operate the secondary EIDE channel (to achieve ATAPI-compatibility). You will also find a driver for Windows 3.1x to support 32-bit access—designed to replace the WDCTRL driver typically used for Windows 32-bit access. Full-featured EIDE controllers also provide similar drivers to support OS/2, Windows NT, Novell Netware, etc.

Before installing software drivers, be sure that you have a convenient backup of any system startup and configuration files (e.g., CONFIG.SYS, AUTOEXEC.BAT, SYSTEM.INI, etc.). Also prepare a "clean boot" disk for your preferred operating system. This way, if you find a problem with the new driver(s), you can easily determine if other drivers on the system are causing the trouble, or simply restore the previous system configuration and resume operation until you are able to rectify the driver problem.

Ultra-ATA

EIDE has proven to be a great asset to the PC industry—it supports huge hard drives at relatively fast data-transfer rates, and allows hard drives to be "auto-detected" by the BIOS. However, hard drives are still one of the slowest parts of a PC. If you've ever waited for a program to load or noticed an application hesitate during disk operations, you already have an idea of current drive limits. Designers are always looking for better and faster ways to speed data between the drive and system, and *Ultra-ATA* is the latest effort to reach the PC.

Ultra-ATA (also called *Ultra-DMA/33* or simply *Ultra33*) evolved in early 1997 as a PCI Plug-and-Play bus-master drive controller system that can transfer data between an Ultra-ATA drive and controller at up to 33MB/s. By comparison, EIDE architecture offers speeds up to 16.6MB/s. Ultra-ATA also includes the use of *Cyclic Redundancy Check (CRC)* error protection to ensure the integrity of data.

IMPLEMENTING AN ULTRA-ATA SYSTEM

To use Ultra-ATA on your PC, you'll need three items: an Ultra-ATA hard drive (which are now becoming widely available), an Ultra-ATA drive adapter (motherboard or stand-alone drive controller), and a BIOS (motherboard or controller) that supports Ultra-ATA. Motherboards using the Intel 430TX (or compatible) chipset support Ultra-ATA on-board—including BIOS support—all that's needed is a suitable hard drive. To date, no Pentium Pro or Pentium II motherboards support Ultra-ATA (so a stand-alone Ultra-ATA controller and BIOS is needed), although this is expected to change as PC chipsets continue to evolve.

ULTRA-ATA COMPATIBILITY AND CONFIGURATION ISSUES

One of the advantages touted with stand-alone Ultra-ATA controllers is their ability to co-exist with IDE/EIDE controllers. This is because Ultra-ATA controllers use their own BIOS (the same way SCSI controllers can co-exist with IDE/EIDE controllers). So, you do not have to disable or remove existing IDE/EIDE controllers or drives to install Ultra-ATA. Ultra-ATA is also a bootable system, and an Ultra-ATA drive can be made to boot even if there are prior IDE/EIDE drives. This will require some changes to the CMOS setup, but it can be done. It is interesting that Ultra-ATA also supports drives as large as 12GB (where EIDE supports up to 8.4GB).

Ultra-ATA is also fully backward compatible, so Ultra-ATA controllers will support IDE and EIDE drives (at lower data-transfer rates). Similarly, Ultra-ATA drives will work on EIDE controllers (although also at lower data-transfer rates). You can also "mix and match" EIDE and Ultra-ATA drives without degrading Ultra-ATA controller performance. This is an improvement over EIDE controllers, which could be degraded when mixing slower IDE devices with faster EIDE devices on the same EIDE channel.

Troubleshooting a Drive Adapter

A properly configured drive adapter will rarely cause problems in a PC because BIOS, IRQ, and I/O assignments are very strongly established in the PC industry. However, a variety of problems can plague drive adapter replacements and upgrades. This part of the chapter looks at troubleshooting for ESDI and IDE/EIDE drive systems. SCSI troubleshooting is detailed in Chapter 39.

Symptom 13-1. The drive adapter software will not install properly When installing or upgrading drive-controller software, it is not uncommon to encounter problems—usually because of the many advanced features of the drive controller itself. If you cannot get new software installed, try the following steps to overcome the problem. First, you should start the CMOS setup and disable the high-performance features usually related to drive controllers: "IDE Block Mode," "Multi-Sector Transfer," and "32-bit Disk Access." If there are other options for the secondary drive controller channel, try disabling them as well. You might also try moving the controller BIOS address range (i.e., change the address range from C800h to CF00h).

If you still cannot get the controller software installed, there might also be trouble with "overlay software" (such as Ontrack's Disk Manager or EZ-Drive software) used to partition and format a drive. You might need to uninstall the overlay software and update the CMOS setup by enabling LBA support for the drive. If you can't uninstall the overlay software, you can run FDISK /MBR to overwrite the overlay software. Once the overlay software is removed, repartition and reformat the drive. If you cannot wipe the drive clean, check with the drive manufacturer for such a utility. You should now be able to install the new drive software.

> This step is destructive to any data on the drive. Be sure to make a complete system backup (and have a bootable diskette on hand) before removing the overlay software.

Symptom 13-2. The controller will not support a drive with more than 1024 cylinders. This often happens when building a new system, or piecing together a system from used parts. To support a drive with more than 1024 cylinders, the controller must support a feature called *Logical Block Addressing (LBA)*, and the feature must be enabled. The controller's on-board BIOS should support LBA, but you might need to install a driver for the controller to support LBA (for example, a Promise Technology controller needs the DOSEIDE.SYS driver to support LBA). If the controller is integrated onto the motherboard, the motherboard BIOS must support LBA. If not, you'll need to upgrade the motherboard BIOS or install a drive adapter with an LBA-aware BIOS. Second, the hard drive itself must support LBA. Be sure that the drive is an EIDE hard drive. Finally, check the CMOS setup and verify that the drive is using the LBA mode, rather than the older CHS mode. You might need to repartition and reformat the hard drive.

Symptom 13-3. Loading a disk driver causes the system to hang or generate a "Bad or missing COMMAND.COM" error This is a known problem with some versions of the DTC DTC22XX.SYS or DOSEIDE.SYS drivers, but frequently occurs with other controller makers that use disk drivers. The controller is probably transferring data too fast to the drive. When the disk driver loads, it obtains information from the drive—including drive speed. Sometimes the drive reports that it can support PIO mode 4 or PIO mode 3 when, in actuality, it cannot. In many cases, the original drivers are outdated, and the immediate solution is to slow down the data-transfer rate manually. Download and install the newest drivers—until then, you might be able to add a command line switch to the disk driver. For example, DTC recommends adding a switch to their DOSEIDE.SYS driver, such as:

```
DOSEIDE.SYS /v /dx:m0 /dx:p0
```

where *x* is the drive designation.

If your problems started after loading the disk drivers "high" (into the upper memory area), adjust CONFIG.SYS to load the drivers into conventional memory. Some drive adapters have reported better success with driver software when the "Hidden Refresh" feature is enabled in CMOS setup (in the *Advanced CMOS setup* area). This alters the way in which the system timing refreshes RAM, and it can better support the disk drivers. Also try disabling advanced controller options, such as *IDE block mode*, *Multi-sector transfer*, and *32-bit disk access*. Finally, if you're using overlay software (such as *Disk Manager*), the disk driver might not work with the overlay software. You'll then need to remove the overlay software, and repartition and reformat the drive before the disk driver will work.

Symptom 13-4. Drive performance is poor—data transfer rates are slow This often happens when installing a replacement drive controller. First, be sure that you're not running any anti-virus software. Anti-virus utilities that load at boot time can degrade drive performance. If the controller uses a "speed" jumper, be sure that you have properly configured the jumper settings on card to match speed of the IDE drive and processor (this is a known issue with DTC's 2278VL and 2270 controllers). Also be sure that the highest possible data-transfer rate is selected in the CMOS setup (i.e., PIO Mode 4). If the drive adapter uses a disk driver for optimum performance, be sure that the correct disk driver software is loaded, and enter any necessary command-line switches. Finally, remove any third-party software (such as Disk Manager or EZ-Drive) that might have shipped with the drive itself.

Symptom 13-5. The PC refuses to boot after a drive adapter is installed
There are many possible reasons for this kind of problem. First, be sure that the drive adapter is installed properly and completely into its bus slot, then verify that the drive signal cables are oriented and attached properly. If the drive adapter uses jumpers to match the drive and processor speeds (such as the DTC 2278VL or 2270), be sure that the adapter is configured correctly. Verify that the drive itself is properly jumpered as a "master" or "slave." Finally, check the CMOS setup and confirm that the proper drive parameters are being used. Try disabling such advanced features as *IDE block mode* and *32-bit disk access*. If the problem still persists, try repartitioning and reformatting the drive.

Symptom 13-6. Windows generates a "Validation Failed 03,3F" error This type of problem most frequently occurs after loading the Windows disk driver, and it is almost always caused by a 1024-cylinder limit in the drive system. Be sure that the drive and drive controller are able to support more than 1024 cylinders (both EIDE). Check the CMOS setup and verify that the LBA mode is selected. Once the proper hardware is configured correctly, try reinstalling the disk driver.

Symptom 13-7. Windows hangs or fails to load files after loading the EIDE driver In most cases, Windows hangs, or every file after the offending driver is unable to load. In some cases, you might see an error message, such as: "Can not find KRN.386." Load SYSTEM.INI into a text editor and move the EIDE driver (e.g., WINEIDE.386) to the last line in the [386enh] section. Also be sure that the classic WDCTRL driver is commented out such as:

```
;device=*WDCTRL
```

If problems persist, the EIDE driver might be old or buggy. Download and install the newest disk driver version from the controller maker. If all else fails, disable the block mode and mode speed using the driver's internal switches. For example, the WINEIDE.386 driver provides the switch WINEIDESWITCH, which you can use as:

```
device=wineide.386
wineideswitch= /dx:m0 /dx:p0
```

Symptom 13-8. After replacing a drive adapter with a different model, the hard drive is no longer recognized This can happen frequently with ESDI drives and controllers. You will find that the format tracks are not the same from one drive manufacturer to another. For the new drive adapter card to recognize an existing drive, you'll have to perform a new low-level format of the drive with the new card in place using the DEBUG formatter in BIOS. Afterward, you'll need to repartition and reformat the drive with FDISK and FORMAT. Reinstall the original controller and perform a complete system backup before continuing.

Symptom 13-9. A fatal error is generated when running DEBUG In most cases, you're using disk controllers with older BIOS, which does not support later DOS versions of DEBUG A classic example of this problem is a "Fatal error 01h" when running DOS 5.0 or 6.x DEBUG with a DTC 6280 ESDI disk controller. To resolve this problem, use the DOS DEBUG utility from DOS 3.3 or 4.0. Once this is complete, reboot the system with DOS 5.0 or 6.x and continue on with the DOS FDISK and DOS FORMAT.

Symptom 13-10. Trouble occurs when formatting ESDI drives over 670MB using an older drive adapter Errors are generated during the low-level format process. This is often a limitation of the drive adapter itself. For example, the DTC 6280 only handles drives up to 10Mbits/s, but most ESDI drives over 400MB run faster than 10Mbits/s. If you try a newer controller, or upgrade the controller BIOS, you might be able to overcome this limitation.

Symptom 13-11. When low-level ESDI formatting, a "Fatal error R/W head" message appears You might also encounter a situation where you cannot get the full capacity of the ESDI drive. This common error occurs if the drive has been formatted with another manufacturer's drive controller. You'll need to go back into DEBUG and update the drive's defect table. You'll be asked: "Do you want to update defect table?." Answer "Yes" and delete the defects that are currently in the defect table. Once this is complete, add (Append) two new defects: head 0, cylinder 100, bit length & byte offset = 1, the second defect will be: head 1, cylinder 100, bit length & byte offset = 1. Once this is complete, continue on with the low-level format, then repartition and reformat the drive.

Symptom 13-12. After installing a new ESDI drive adapter, you cannot install Novell When you low-level format the ESDI drive, do not use the "head mapping" mode if your operating system is going to be Novell. Also do not use the "head mapping" mode if your ESDI drive is greater than 528MB. Now under DOS, you won't see the full capacity of the drive, but you're only going to create a small DOS partition anyway—Novell will recognize the full capacity of the hard drive. Use the driver that is built into the Novell operating system (called *ISADISK*, and load it with a "/b" switch). The "/b" tells Novell that the controller card has an on-board BIOS, and Novell will know where to get drive parameters.

Symptom 13-13. System problems occur after installing a VL drive adapter It is quite common for a combination of components on VL-bus systems to exceed the tolerance limits for that specific motherboard. VL-bus noise generated by the motherboard chipset can easily contribute to floppy, floppy tape, and other drive failures. This might cause the system to hang on boot up and render it unable to access the hard drive. VESA video and controller cards also contribute to the load on the VL-bus. If the load on the VL-bus for a given motherboards is too high, then you will see compatibility problems with VESA video cards, intermittent system crashes, and HDD controller failures. System problems can manifest themselves in a wide variety of ways such as:

■ Incompatibility with some VESA video cards (i.e., devices with S3 chipsets).
■ Incompatibility with Colorado floppy tape.
■ Floppy disk failures.
■ System hangs on boot or when trying to access IDE hard drive.
■ Drive won't hold a partition.
■ Performance not improved with new drive adapter.
■ Intermittent system crash in Windows or other graphics program.
■ Modem status failures.

In some cases, upgrading the disk controller to a later revision VL board, which causes less loading and signal issues may provide a proper solution. For an immediate solution, try rearranging the VL devices or slowing the VL bus speed to stabilize VL-bus operation.

Symptom 13-14. You cannot enable 32-bit disk access under Windows 3.1x In most cases, you are using the wrong protected-mode driver, or the driver should be upgraded with a newer version. Download and install the latest disk drivers for your drive adapter. Before installing the new driver(s), be sure to disable advanced data-transfer features, such as *IDE block mode* and *32-bit disk access* (if enabled). Load SYSTEM.INI into a text editor. Be sure that the protected-mode disk driver is installed under the [386enh] section, and verify that the WDCTRL driver is remarked out. Many Windows drivers will not support an IBMSLC2 processor or Ontrack's Disk Manager, and will not work with 32-bit disk access.

Symptom 13-15. The EIDE drive adapter's secondary port refuses to work If the drive adapter has a secondary drive channel, that secondary channel is not working. In many cases, this type of problem occurs when the drive adapter relies on a disk driver for proper operation—often the secondary channel must be enabled specifically through the disk driver's command line in CONFIG.SYS such as:

```
DEVICE=DOSEIDE.SYS /V /2
```

Be sure that the drive attached to the secondary channel is jumpered as the "master" drive, and verify that the signal cable between the drive and controller is oriented properly. Also remember that a secondary drive channel requires a unique interrupt (usually IRQ 15). Be sure that no hardware conflict occurs between the secondary port's IRQ and other devices in the system. Try disabling such advanced data-transfer features as *IDE block mode* and *32-bit disk access*. If your hard drive is an older IDE drive, it might not support Multi-Sector Transfer. Try disabling *Multi-sector transfer* in the CMOS setup, or by adding the necessary command line switch to the disk driver command line in CONFIG.SYS, such as:

```
DEVICE=DOSEIDE.SYS /V /2 /DO:MO
```

Symptom 13-16. The drive adapter's BIOS doesn't load First, be sure that the BIOS is enabled (usually through a jumper on the drive adapter), and see that the BIOS IC is seated correctly and completely in its socket on the drive adapter. If problems persist, try changing the BIOS address—it's probably conflicting with another BIOS in the system. Also check the IRQ and I/O port assignments for the drive adapter for possible conflicts. If all else fails, try another drive controller.

Symptom 13-17. The drive adapter BIOS loads, but the system hangs up First be sure that the drive parameters are set properly in the CMOS setup. Inexperienced users frequently mistake the parameters for a second drive in CMOS with a drive on the secondary channel. When no drive is in the primary *Slave* position, the second drive should be *None* or *Not installed*. If you have an onboard drive controller, be sure to disable it—otherwise, you'll have a hardware conflict between the two drive controllers. Check the individual drives attached to the controller and verify that each drive is jumpered as a unique "master" or "slave" device (try reversing the drive order or working with only one drive). Finally, try disabling some of the advanced drive performance parameters in CMOS, such as *IDE block mode*.

Symptom 13-18. The ATAPI CD-ROM is not recognized as the "slave" device versus an EIDE "master" First, verify that the CD-ROM is ATAPI compatible and suitable for use on an IDE/EIDE interface. Second, be sure that the proper low-level ATAPI driver for the CD-ROM drive is in use. If the driver is old, try downloading and installing the newest version of the driver. If problems persist, the trouble is probably due to a fast EIDE device co-existing with a slower IDE ATAPI device. Reconfigure the CD-ROM as the "master" device on the secondary drive controller channel. You might need to update the ATAPI driver command line.

Symptom 13-19. Hard drives are not recognized on the secondary drive controller channel Be sure that all the hard drives are jumpered correctly. If only one drive is on the secondary channel, it should be configured as the "single" or "master" drive. If two drives are on the secondary channel, verify that the drives are jumpered as "master" and "slave." If the drive adapter uses a disk driver to support EIDE or secondary-channel operation, be sure that the command line in CONFIG.SYS uses the correct switch(es) to enable the secondary drive channel. For example, the Promise Technologies 2300 would add an /S switch to the command line such as:

```
device=c:\eide2300\eide2300.sys /S
```

Check that your system's power-management features are not enabled on IRQ 15 (and confirm that no other devices are conflicting with IRQ 15). If the drive is set to "auto-configure" in the CMOS setup, try entering the drive's parameters specifically (the drive might be too old to understand the *Identify Drive Command (IDC)* needed for auto-configuration. Finally, try booting the system "clean" (with just disk-driver software, if necessary) to see if there are any other driver or TSR conflicts.

Symptom 13-20. The drive adapter can only support 528MB per disk First, be sure that the LBA mode is enabled—this is often accomplished through the CMOS setup, but it may also be necessary to enable an LBA support jumper on some older EIDE drive adapters. If problems, persist, the drive adapter's BIOS is probably too old, and should be upgraded to a new version. If you cannot upgrade the drive-adapter BIOS, install a new drive adapter outright.

Symptom 13-21. You get a "code 10" error relative to the drive adapter You notice that Windows 95 is running in MS-DOS compatibility mode, and the system only boots in *Safe mode*. You'll probably find one or more devices (including the drive adapter) marked with a yellow exclamation. Disk-overlay software (such as Disk Manager, EZ-drive, or MaxBlast) will often cause problems when used in conjunction with drive adapters that use their own disk-driver software. The disk overlay must be removed before installing the adapter's disk drivers. Remove the overlay software or simply repartition and reformat the drive (remember to do a complete backup before repartitioning). Next, remove or disable any 32-bit disk drivers previously installed under Windows. With Promise Technology drive adapters, you'll probably see the following under SYSTEM.INI:

```
[386enh]
device=*int13
;device=*wdctrl
;device=c:\windows\system\eide2300.386 (for eide2300plus)
;device=ontrackw.386
;device=c:\windows\system\pti13.386 (for the 4030)
;device=c:\windows\system\ptictrl.386 (for the 4030)
;device=wdcdrv.386
;device=c:\windows\system\maxi13.386 (for the eidemax)
;device=c:\windows\system\maxctrl.386 (for the eidemax)
32bitdiskaccess=off
```

When first installing the disk driver (such as the Promise Windows 95 driver), follow these steps (notice that some EIDE drive adapters—especially new ones—do not require special drivers):

- Open the *Control panel* and double-click the *System* icon.
- Choose *Device manager* and double-click on *Hard disk controller*.
- Click once on *Driver* (standard IDE/ESDI driver) and click on *Remove*.
- Reboot the computer.
- Reopen the *Control panel* and start the *Add/new hardware* wizard.
- Answer *No* when prompted for Windows 95 to auto-detect the device(s).
- Select *Hard disk controller* and click on *Have disk*.
- Either insert the floppy diskette, or choose *Browse* and move to the sub-directory where the disk drivers are located.
- Follow the prompts and choose *Finish*, but do not reboot the computer yet.
- Open the *Control panel* and doubleclick the *System* icon.
- Choose *Device manager* and doubleclick on *Hard disk controller*. Click once on the installed driver and choose *Properties*. Select the *Resource* tab. If you see Basic configuration of 1, IRQ 15, change this to basic configuration of 0, IRQ 14.
- Now reboot the computer so that your changes can take effect.

There might also be a DMA conflict. Some drive adapters take advantage of DMA when the parallel port is in the ECP mode (the conflict occurs most often with the sound board). To find out which devices use DMA, open the *Control panel*, double-click on the *System* icon, select *Device manager*, and double-click on *Computer*. Choose *Direct memory access*. You can then either switch the controller's use of DMA or disable it altogether. You might need to alter the DMA setting on the drive controller itself, then switch the parallel port's mode to EPP.

Symptom 13-22. You encounter mouse problems after changing the drive adapter This is a known problem with Logitech pointing devices, or standard pointing devices using Logitech drivers. In most cases, you can correct the problem by downloading and installing version 7.0 (or later) Logitech drivers, or switch to the Windows 95 serial mouse driver:

- Open the *Control panel* and double-click on the *System* icon.
- Select *Device manager* and double-click on the *Mouse*.
- Click once on *Logitech* and choose *Remove*.
- Start the *Add/new hardware* wizard in the *Control panel*.
- Choose *No* when Windows prompts to auto-detect the device.
- Select *Mouse*. Click on *Standard serial mouse*. Click on *Finish*.
- Reboot the computer.

Another solution is also to disable the COM port's FIFO buffer. Open the *Control panel* and choose the *System* icon. Click on *Device manager*. Double-click on *Ports* (COM and LPT). Choose the communications port that the mouse uses (i.e., COM 1) by clicking on it once, then click on *Properties*. Select *Port settings* and choose *Advanced*. Uncheck the box next to *Use FIFO buffers*, then click *OK*.

Symptom 13-23. You cannot run Norton Anti-Virus 95 with Promise drive adapters This appears to be an issue with the Norton Anti-Virus (NAV) software itself. According to Symantec (**http://www.symantec.com**), a patch has been released to correct this problem.

Symptom 13-24. The system hangs after counting through system memory You might also receive error messages, such as "Get Configuration Failed!" or "HDD Controller Failure." First, be sure that you have at least one hard drive attached to the controller, and see that the signal cable is oriented properly at both ends. It is also possible that you might have a problem when more than one drive is connected. See that the drives are jumpered in the desired "master" and "slave" relationship. Try working with only one drive or reverse the drive relationship. In all cases, verify that the CMOS setup entries accurately reflect the drives that are connected. If your drive adapter uses on-board RAM, the RAM might be bad. Try replacing the controller's on-board RAM.

Symptom 13-25. After replacing/upgrading a drive adapter, the system hangs intermittently during use This complaint is somewhat common with VL motherboards and drive adapters, and is often caused by bad memory on the drive controller or a bad VL-bus slot. Try replacing the RAM on the drive adapter. If the problem persists, try putting the drive controller in a different VL-bus slot. If you have a VESA VL video card also, try swapping in a 16-bit (ISA) video card. Some motherboards become unstable with two VL cards in the system—especially when the VL bus is being run over 33MHz (there is a great likelihood of this happening at 50MHz)

Symptom 13-26. Errors occur when reading or writing to floppies after re-placing/upgrading a drive adapter This is almost always caused by a hardware conflict between the floppy adapter on the new controller and another floppy adapter else-where in the system. Disable the floppy adapter port on the new drive controller card. If you're using the new floppy port, disable the floppy port already in the system.

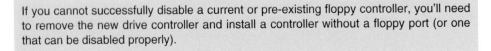

If you cannot successfully disable a current or pre-existing floppy controller, you'll need to remove the new drive controller and install a controller without a floppy port (or one that can be disabled properly).

Further Study

That concludes Chapter 13. Be sure to review the glossary and chapter questions on the accompanying CD. If you have access to the Internet, take a look at some of the drive-adapter manufacturers listed:

DTC: **http://www.datatechnology.com**

Adaptec: **http://www.adaptec.com**

Advansys: **http://www.advansys.com**

Promise Technologies: **http://www.promise.com**

14

DVD DRIVES

CONTENTS AT A GLANCE

The Potential of DVD

Specifications and Standards
 Access Time
 Data-transfer rates
 Books and standards
 Data formats
 Audio and video standards
 CD compatibility

DVD Media
 Caring for a DVD disc

DVD Drives
 Inside the drive
 Region code control

The MPEG-2 Decoder Board
 A look at MPEG-2
 Notes on Dolby AC-3
 Decoder board connections

Basic DVD/MPEG-2 Troubleshooting

Further Study

The compact disc opened up a whole new world of possibilities for the PC. These simple, mass-produced plastic discs could hold up to an hour of stereo music or as much as 650MB of computer programs and data. Software makers quickly found the CD-ROM to be an outstanding medium for all types of multimedia applications, large databases, and interactive games. But today, the CD-ROM is showing its age and a single CD no longer provides enough storage for the increasing demands of data-intensive applications (Table 14-1 illustrates the CD technology timeline). A new generation of high-density optical

TABLE 14-1 CD TECHNOLOGY TIMELINE

YEAR	EVENT
1980	Sony and Philips create the optical disc digital audio standards (now known as *Red Book audio*)
1983	Sony releases the first audio CD player, and music CDs begin to appear
1985	Sony and Philips develop standards for PC-based optical storage (CD-ROM)
1987	The first CD-ROM drives appear for the PC
1994	4× CD-ROM drives appear offering 600KB/s data rates
1995	6× CD-ROM drives appear offering 900KB/s data rates
1996	8× CD-ROM drives appear offering 1.2MB/s data rates. These are quickly followed by 10× and 12× CD-ROM drives.
1997	DVD-ROM drives are released. Initial DVD discs will offer 4.7GB. These are backward compatible with CDs.
1998	Higher-capacity DVD discs (up to 17GB) should become available. DVD-RAM (rewriteable DVD drives) should become available.

FIGURE 14-1   A DVD-ROM drive.

storage, called *DVD*, is now appearing for the desktop PC (Fig. 14-1). The abbreviation *DVD* stands for several different things. In the early phase of DVD development, it stood for *Digital Video Disc*. Later on, it stood for *Digital Versatile Disc* (because it could hold programs and data, as well as video and sound). But regardless of what you call it, DVD technology promises to supply up to 17GB of removable storage on your desktop PC. This chapter explores the background and workings of a DVD package, shows you the steps for DVD installation, and offers some basic troubleshooting that can keep you out of trouble.

The Potential of DVD

The argument for DVD is compelling because gigabytes of removable storage open up some exciting possibilities for entertainment and the development of software. As DVD works its way into the marketplace, you're going to see two designations: *DVD-Video* and *DVD-ROM*. DVD-Video is the approach used to store movies on the disc (analogous to the way audio is placed on CDs). Eventually, DVD-Video is expected to replace videotape players in home entertainment. *DVD-ROM* refers to computer-based software and data recorded on the disc. Where audio CDs can be played on CD-ROM drives, DVD-Video discs will be playable on DVD-ROM drives in your PC. Understandably, a lot of players are trying to make the most of what DVD has to offer:

■ Hollywood has been a major factor in the development of DVD-Video—placing full-length movies, sound tracks, and even multi-lingual sub-titling on a single disc. Because all DVD discs are read by laser, no physical contact occurs between the disc and its player. The result is that the disc won't wear out like VHS video tapes.

■ Business presentations, education, and professional training will also benefit from DVD technology. Animations, charts, and interactive applets can be integrated with real-time video. This offers a truly intensive training experience, where CD-ROM technology has only scratched the surface.

■ Applications for archiving are limitless. Mapping programs, telephone directories, encyclopedias—any software that now spans several CDs can be concentrated on one DVD disc, and dramatically expanded to offer unprecedented detail.

■ Any data-intensive computer software (especially 3D and other interactive games) will get a real boost from the sheer storage volume offered by DVD-ROM.

Specifications and Standards

The next step in exploring DVD is to understand the various specifications "on the box," and becoming familiar with the specifications that make DVD work and what a DVD will support. You don't need a lot of technical details, but you should recognize the most important points that you'll probably run across while reading documentation.

ACCESS TIME

The *access time* is the time required for the drive to locate the required information on a disc. Optical drives such as CD and DVD drives are relatively slow, and can demand up to several hundred milliseconds to access information. For a DVD drive such as the Creative Labs (Matsushita) DVD drive, DVD access time is 470 ms (almost half a second), but access time for an ordinary CD is 180 ms. The reason that DVDs require so much more time is because of the greater density of data. However, not all drives are as slow. The Toshiba DVD drive bundled with Diamond Multimedia's Maximum DVD Kit quotes a DVD access time of only 200 ms (130 ms for CDs).

DATA-TRANSFER RATES

Once data has been accessed, it must be transferred off of the disc to the system. The *data-transfer rate* measures how fast data can be read from the disc. The two typical means of measuring the data rate are the speed at which data is read into the drive's on-board buffer (the "sequential" data-transfer rate), and the speed at which data is transferred across the interface to the drive controller (the "buffered" data-transfer rate). The Creative Labs (Matsushita) DVD drive offers a sequential data-transfer rate of 1.35MB/s, and 900KB/s for an ordinary CD (about equal to a 6× CD-ROM drive). By comparison, the drive can support buffered data-transfer rates of 8.3MB/s (DMA Mode 2), 13.3MB/s (DMA Mode 1), or 11.1MB/s (PIO Mode 3). As a result, the DVD-ROM drive is compatible with most EIDE drive controllers in the marketplace today.

BOOKS AND STANDARDS

CD technology is defined by a set of accepted standards that have become known as *books*. Because each CD "book" was bound in a different color jacket, each standard is dubbed by color. For example, the standard that defines CD audio is called *Red Book*. Similarly, DVD technology is defined by a set of "books." Five books (labeled A through E) relate to different applications:

- Book A defines the format and approach used for DVD-ROM (programs and data)
- Book B defines DVD-Video
- Book C defines DVD-Audio (this specification is still under development)
- Book D defines DVD-WO (write once)
- Book E defines DVD-E (erasable or re-writeable) and DVD-RAM

DATA FORMATS

All DVD discs must use a data format that describes how data is laid out. Data formats are critical because they outline data structures on the disc such as volumes, files, blocks, sectors, CRCs, paths, records, file allocation tables, partitions, character sets, time stamps, as well as methods for reading and writing. The format use by books A, B, and C is called the *UDF bridge*. The UDF bridge is a combination of the *UDF* (*Universal Disk Format* created by *OSTA*, the *Optical Storage Technology Association*) and the established ISO-9660 format used for CDs. You might see the UDF referred to as *standard ISO/IEC 13346*. The UDF is a very flexible format that has been adapted to DVD, and made backward-compatible to existing ISO-9660 operating system software (such as Windows 95). Actual utilization of this disk system on DVD discs will depend in large part on what Microsoft dictates as the future operating system standard. Stand-alone DVD movie players are supposed to use UDF, but computer applications will use the UDF bridge until UDF support becomes universal (possibly as early as Windows 98).

AUDIO AND VIDEO STANDARDS

Even with the huge data capacities offered by DVD, an entire movie's worth of real-time audio and video would never fit on a DVD without some form of compression. Both audio and video must be extensively compressed, and MPEG (Motion Pictures Experts Group) compression has been the scheme of choice. Video compression uses fixed data rate MPEG-1 (ISO/IEC 1117-2) at 30 frames per second with resolutions of 352 × 240, or variable data rate MPEG-2 (ISO/IEC 13818-2) at 60 frames per second with resolutions of 720 × 480. Audio compression uses MPEG-1 (ISO/IEC 1117-3) stereo, MPEG-2 (ISO/IEC 13818-3) 5.1 and 7.1 surround sound, or Dolby AC-3 5.1 surround and stereo. MPEG-2 and AC-3 audio compression allow 48 thousand samples per second, where MPEG-1 allows only 44.1 thousand samples per second. MPEG-2 compression is typically regarded as the preferred scheme for DVD.

> The audio designations "5.1" and "7.1" indicate five (or seven) signal channels, plus one sub-woofer channel.

CD COMPATIBILITY

One of the most important aspects of any technology is "backward compatibility"—how well will the new device support your existing media. The same issue is true for DVD drives. Because DVD technology is designed as an improvement over existing CD-ROMs, the DVD was designed to replace the CD-ROM, rather than co-exist with it. Ideally, you'd remove your CD-ROM and replace it with a DVD-ROM drive. This means that the DVD must be compatible with as many existing CD-ROM standards as possible. A typical DVD-ROM drive will support CD audio, CD-ROM, CD-I, CD Extra, CD-ROM/XA, and Video CD formats. Multi-session formats, such as Photo CD, are not yet supported on all DVD drives.

> One format that is not supported by any DVD drive yet is the CD-R (recordable CD) format. The laser used in a DVD cannot read the CD-R; in some cases, it could even damage the CD-R disc. However, new CD-R blanks are being developed, which should overcome this problem.

At this point, you can talk about what you need to configure DVD on your desktop, and how each part works. To get a DVD setup running on your computer, you need three things: DVD media, a DVD drive, and an MPEG-2 expansion board.

DVD Media

At its core, DVD technology is identical to classic CD-ROMs—data is recorded in a spiral pattern as a series of pits and lands pressed into a plastic substrate. The actual size and dimensions of a DVD are identical to our current compact discs. However, some key differences give DVD its advantages. First, data is highly concentrated on the disc—where classic CDs use spiral tracks that are 1.6 μm apart, DVD tracks are only 0.74 μm apart. A typical pit on a classic CD is 0.83 μm, but DVD pits are just 0.4 μm. Table 14-2 compares the specifications for DVD and CD media. In short, the data on a DVD is much denser than on a regular CD (Figure 14-2 illustrates the differences between DVDs and CDs). To detect these smaller geometries, the laser used in a DVD operates at a much shorter wavelength (a short-wavelength red laser).

Second, DVD can use multiple "layers" of pits and lands (each in their own reflective layer), so one physical disk can hold several layers worth of data. The DVD drive's laser focus control can select which layer to read. Finally, a regular CD only uses one side of the disc, but both sides of the DVD can be used. Combined with this multi-layer

TABLE 14-2 SPECIFICATIONS OF DVD AND CD MEDIA		
SPECIFICATION	DVD	CD-ROM
Diameter (mm)	120	120
Disc thickness (mm)	1.2	1.2
Substrate Thickness (mm)	0.6	1.2
Track pitch (μm)	0.74	1.6
Minimum pit size (μm)	0.4	0.83
Wavelength (nm)	635/650	780
Single-layer capacity (GB)	4.7	0.65

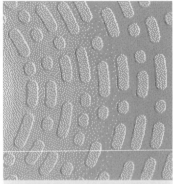

An example of DVD pits and lands

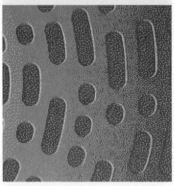

An example of ordinary CD pits and lands

FIGURE 14-2 Comparison of DVD and CD data density.

technique, the DVD can supply up to four "layers" of data to a DVD drive (Fig. 14-3). In actuality, DVD-ROM discs will likely only use one side of the disc—at least for a while. What all this means is that a DVD disc can offer up to 8.5GB of storage for a single-sided double-layer disc, or up to 17GB of storage for a double-sided double-layer disc.

CARING FOR A DVD DISC

As with CDs, a DVD disc is a remarkably reliable long-term storage media (conservative expectations place the life estimates of a DVD disc at about 100 years. However, the longevity of an optical disc is affected by its storage and handling—a faulty CD can cause file and data errors that you might otherwise interpret as a defect in the drive itself. You can get the most life out of your optical disc by obeying the following rules:

- *Don't bend the disc* Polycarbonate is a forgiving material, but you risk cracking or snapping (and thus ruining) the disc.
- *Don't heat the disk* Remember, the disc is plastic. Leaving it by a heater or on the dashboard of your car will cause melting.
- *Don't scratch the disc* Laser wavelengths have a tendency to "look past" minor scratches, but a major scratch can cause problems. Be especially careful of circular scratches (one that follows the spiral track). A circular scratch can easily wipe out entire segments of data that would be unrecoverable.
- *Don't use chemicals on the disc* Chemicals containing solvents, such as ammonia, benzene, acetone, carbon tetrachloride, or chlorinated cleaning solvents, can easily damage the plastic surface.

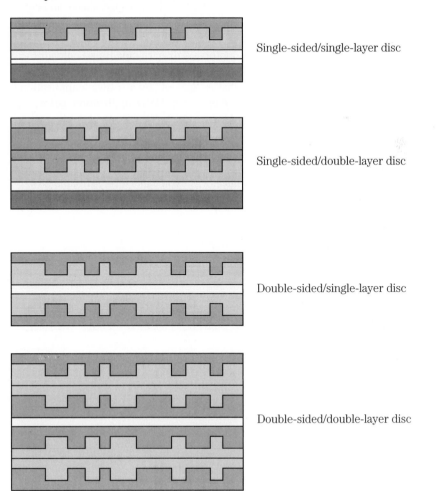

Single-sided/single-layer disc

Single-sided/double-layer disc

Double-sided/single-layer disc

Double-sided/double-layer disc

FIGURE 14-3 Layers and sides in DVD discs.

Eventually, a buildup of excessive dust or fingerprints can interfere with the laser beam enough to cause disc errors. When this happens, the disc can be cleaned easily using a dry, soft, lint-free cloth. Hold the disc from its edges and wipe radially (from hub to edge). Do not wipe in a circular motion. For stubborn stains, moisten the cloth in a bit of fresh isopropyl alcohol (do not use water). Place the cleaned disc in a caddie or jewel case for transport and storage.

> Contrary to popular belief, DVD discs are not more sensitive to scratches or dust than ordinary CDs.

DVD Drives

A DVD drive looks almost identical to a CD-ROM drive in size, shape, and layout. In fact, if not for the "DVD" logo on the tray, you'll probably mistake a DVD-ROM drive for a CD-ROM drive. The front of a DVD drive (Fig. 14-4) carries all of the standard features that you'd find on any CD-ROM. A motorized disc tray loads and unloads the disc. You can close or open the tray by toggling the *Eject* button. It's interesting that the Creative Labs DVD-ROM won't eject a disc that is "locked" by a software application (such as a running movie). You will need to close your DVD application before ejecting the "locked" disc. The *Busy* indicator lights whenever data is being read from the drive. Because the DVD drive also supports CD audio, you can connect headphones to the headphone jack, and adjust volume right from the front panel.

Much of the rear of a DVD-ROM will also probably look familiar (Fig. 14-5). Power is connected through a 4-pin Molex connector, so you can use any suitable power connector from your power supply. The signal connector is typically either EIDE (40 pin) or SCSI

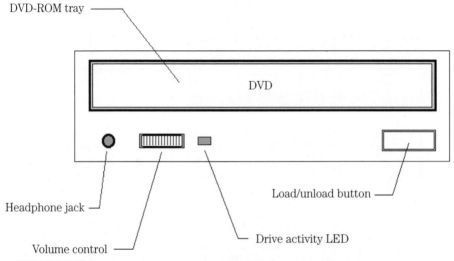

FIGURE 14-4   Front view of a DVD-ROM drive.

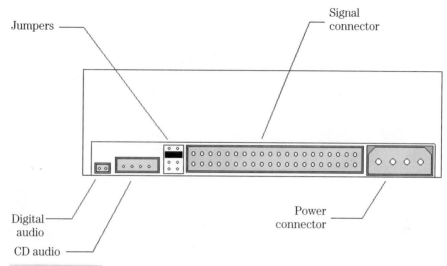

Jumpers

Signal
connector

Digital
audio

CD audio

Power
connector

FIGURE 14-5 Rear view of a DVD-ROM drive.

(50 pin), and connects the drive directly to your existing drive adapter. Unlike early CD-ROM drives, DVD-ROM drives do not use "proprietary" drive controllers. A series of small jumpers allows you to set the drive's identity. For SCSI-type drives, you can set the SCSI ID (usually ID2 through ID6). For EIDE-type drives, you will set the drive as either a primary ("master") or secondary ("slave") drive. If you're running an EIDE DVD-ROM along with a hard drive, the hard drive would typically be the "master" device, and the DVD-ROM drive would be the "slave" device. If you're running the DVD-ROM drive alone, set it as the "master" device. Finally, there are two audio output connectors: a 4-pin CD audio connector that attaches to a sound board, and a 2-pin digital audio connector that supplies sound to a digital audio tape (DAT) or other digital recording system.

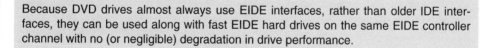

Because DVD drives almost always use EIDE interfaces, rather than older IDE interfaces, they can be used along with fast EIDE hard drives on the same EIDE controller channel with no (or negligible) degradation in drive performance.

INSIDE THE DRIVE

Things get a little more interesting when you look inside the DVD-ROM drive (Fig. 14-6). Looking in from the top of the drive, you'll see the major sub-assemblies needed to operate the drive. That black circular wheel near the tray is the spindle motor that turns the disc. You can also see the laser assembly, and the laser sled that the laser rides back and forth on. A small motor drives a screw, which runs the sled. The load/unload mechanics run the disc tray in and out (though the mechanical parts are obscured below the plastic tray). The main electronics deck is mounted on the underside of the drive (Fig. 14-7). This is a single printed circuit board, which contains all of the circuitry needed to run the drive interface, load/unload motor, audio amplifiers, spindle motor, laser, and laser sled.

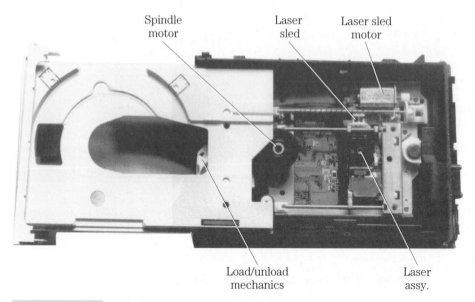

Spindle motor   Laser sled   Laser sled motor

Load/unload mechanics   Laser assy.

FIGURE 14-6 Looking into the tap of a DVD drive.

REGION CODE CONTROL

One item of particular interest in Fig. 14-7 is the removable IC. This chip contains firmware for the drive, as well as the "region codes" for the drive. Motion-picture studios want to control the home release of movies in different countries because theater releases are not simultaneous. Therefore, they have required that the DVD standard include codes that can be used to prevent playback of certain discs in certain geographical regions. Each player is given a code for the region in which it's sold. The player will refuse to play discs that are not allowed in that region. This means that discs bought in one country might not play on players bought in another country. Table 14-3 lists the code numbers and regions that each number covers. Remember that region codes are entirely optional, and discs without codes will play on any player in any country.

The MPEG-2 Decoder Board

Although the DVD drive requires a SCSI or EIDE drive controller for normal program data, DVD video and audio do not use this data path. There are two reasons for this. First, the data required to reproduce real-time video and audio would bog-down even the fastest PC. Second, video and audio data are highly compressed using MPEG standards, so even of the PC bus wasn't bogged down by the compressed data, the decompression process would load down the system with processing overhead. To play DVD audio and video (DVD-Video), DVD-ROM drives require a stand-alone, hardware-based PCI bus MPEG-2 decoder board, such as the one in Fig. 14-8. This MPEG-2 decoder board works independently of the drive-controller system, video system, and sound system.

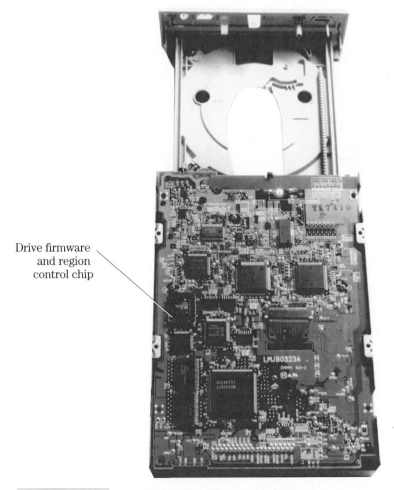

Drive firmware
and region
control chip

FIGURE 14-7   Looking at the bottom of a DVD drive.

TABLE 14-3 DVD REGION CODES	
CODE	**REGION**
1	Canada, U.S., and U.S. territories
2	Japan, Europe, South Africa, Middle East (including Egypt)
3	Southeast Asia, East Asia (including Hong Kong)
4	Australia, New Zealand, Pacific Islands, Central America, South America, Caribbean
5	Former Soviet Union, Indian Subcontinent, Africa (also North Korea, Mongolia)
6	China

FIGURE 14-8   An MPEG-2 board for DVD video and audio playback.

A LOOK AT MPEG-2

When the original video source is recorded for DVD, MPEG-2 analyzes the video picture for redundant data. In fact, more than 95% of the digital data that represents a video signal is "redundant" and can be compressed without visibly harming the picture quality (also referred to as *loss-less compression*). By eliminating redundant data, MPEG-2 achieves excellent video quality at far lower bit rates.

MPEG-2 encoding for DVD is a two-stage process. The original signal is first evaluated for complexity, then higher bit rates are assigned to complex pictures and lower bit rates are assigned to simple pictures. This allows for an "adaptive" variable bit-rate process. The DVD-Video format uses compressed bit rates with a range of up to 10Mbits/s. Although the "average" bit rate for digital video is often quoted as 3.5Mbits/s, the actual figure will vary according to movie length, picture complexity, and the number of audio channels required. With MPEG-2 compression, a single-layer, single-sided DVD disc has enough capacity to hold 2 hours and 13 minutes of video and audio on a 12-cm disc. At the nominal average data rate of 3.5Mbits/s, this still leaves enough capacity for discrete 5.1-channel digital sound in three languages, plus subtitles in four additional languages.

NOTES ON DOLBY AC-3

Dolby AC-3 (also called *Dolby Surround AC-3* or *Dolby Digital*) is another method of encoding DVD audio besides MPEG-2 audio. With five channels and a common sub-woofer channel (known as *5.1*), you get the effects of 3D surround sound with right, left, center, left ear, right ear, and common sub-woofer speakers. AC-3 runs at 384Kbits/s. In actuality, DVD products sold in North America and Japan will include Dolby AC-3 sound on the accompanying MPEG-2 board, and DVD products sold in Europe will likely use the MPEG-2 audio standard.

DECODER BOARD CONNECTIONS

The five major connections on the MPEG-2 decoder board are shown in Fig 14-9: an analog input jack, an analog output jack, a digital output jack, a monitor connector, and a video input connector. The analog input is rarely (if ever) used in normal operations, but it might be handy for mixing-in an auxiliary audio signal to the decoder board. The analog output signal provides the master audio signal, which is fed to the line input of your existing sound board. The advantage of using a line input is that you don't need a volume control on the decoder board. Instead, you can set the line input volume through your sound board's "mixer" applet. When you play a DVD video, any audio will continue to play through your sound board and speakers. The digital output is intended to drive an external Dolby Digital device, so you will probably not be using the digital output in most basic PC setups.

The MPEG-2 decoder board will now drive your VGA/SVGA monitor through the *Monitor* connector. This is important because the decoded video stream is converted to RGB information, and fed to the monitor directly—this avoids having to pass the video data across the PCI bus to your video card. The normal output from your video card is looped from your video board to the decoder card, so while the decoder board is idle, your normal video signal is just "passed through" the MPEG-2 board to the monitor.

Basic DVD/MPEG-2 Troubleshooting

Even though a DVD package should install with an absolute minimum of muss and fuss, and run with all the reliability of a CD-ROM, there are times when things just don't go according

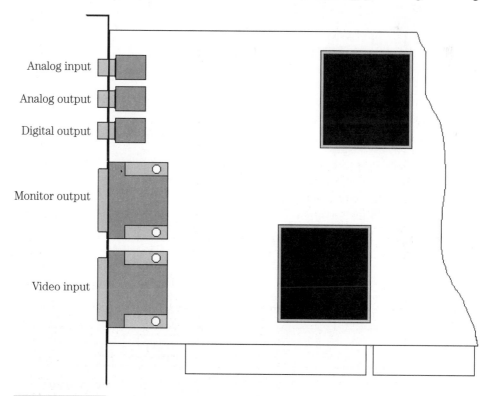

FIGURE 14-9   Decoder board connections.

to plan. Software and hardware problems can both interrupt your DVD system. The following symptoms cover some of the most common troubleshooting issues.

DVD drives use lasers in normal operation. Although these are very low-power semi-conductor lasers, the chances of injury to your eyes is extremely slight, you should still take the proper precautions and not operate a DVD drive with the protective covers open. Turn off and unplug the PC before opening a DVD drive.

Symptom 14-1. The DVD drivers refuse to install This is almost always because Windows 95 is having a problem with one or more .INF files on your driver installation disk(s). Check with your DVD vendor to confirm whether you need to delete one or more entries in your OEMxx.INF file(s), where "xx" is any suffix. You might also need to delete one or more entries from a MKEDVD.INF file. The .INF files are typically con-

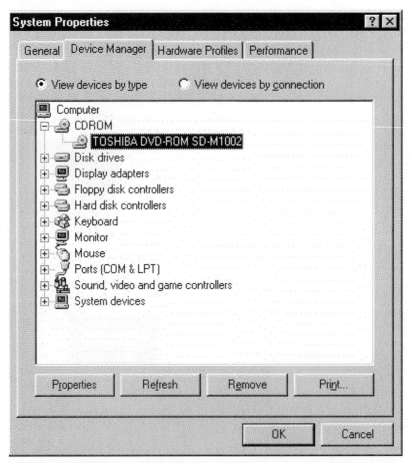

FIGURE 14-10   The DVD-ROM drive entry under the *Device manager.*

tained in the C:\WINDOWS\INF\OTHER directory. Once you've corrected the appropriate .INF file(s), you can re-install the DVD drivers:

■ Click *Start*, select *Settings*, then click on *Control panel*. Double-click on the *System* icon.
■ Click on the *Device manager* tab, then select *Sound, video, and game controllers* or *CD-ROM* (Fig. 14-10).
■ Select the DVD driver(s), then click *Remove*.
■ Exit the *Device manager* and reinstall the drivers again.

Symptom 14-2. The DVD drive isn't detected The DVD drive would not be detected for several possible reasons. Check the power connector attached to the drive, and be sure that the drive isn't being powered from a Y splitter power cable. Check the signal cable next. Both SCSI and EIDE signal cables must be attached securely to the drive. SCSI interfaces are complicated a bit by termination. Be sure that the drive is jumpered properly for its SCSI ID or EIDE "master" or "slave" relationship. Finally, be sure that the DVD drivers are installed and running. Check the drivers under the *Sound, video, and game controllers* (or *CD-ROM*, as in Fig. 14-10) entry of your *Device manager*.

Symptom 14-3. The DVD motorized tray won't open or close The most common issue here is the DVD application itself. Some DVD applications (such as DVD-Video player applications) will "lock" the disc tray closed while a video DVD disc is playing. Try closing all open applications. If the tray still won't open, try restarting the PC. This should clear any "software lock." If the tray still refuses to open or close, the drive itself might be defective—you can "force" the tray open using a straightened paper clip in the emergency eject hole in the front of the drive.

Symptom 14-4. There is no audio when playing an audio CD This is a common problem—especially during new DVD-ROM drive installations. Chances are that you did not connect the CD audio cable between the DVD-ROM drive and the sound board. If so, the cable might be reversed (or defective). Of course, if you're still using your original CD-ROM drive and the CD-ROM is connected to the sound board, there will be no CD audio from the DVD-ROM drive—there is no way to "parallel" or "gang" the sound cable. If the DVD-ROM audio cable is connected to the sound board, be sure that the "CD-audio" input of your sound board's mixer applet is turned up to a reasonable level.

Symptom 14-5. There is no DVD audio while playing a movie or other multimedia presentation Here's another common oversight during new DVD installations. Check the external audio cable attached between the MPEG-2 decoder board and the line input jack of your sound board. The cable might be plugged into the wrong jack(s), or the cable might simply be defective. Also check the sound board's "mixer" applet and see that the *Line input* volume control setting is turned up to an acceptable level.

Symptom 14-6. Video quality appears poor MPEG-2 compression is well-respected for its ability to reproduce high-quality images The problem with "poor" image quality is almost always because of your video configuration—your color depth or resolution are too low. DVD-Video playback is best at resolutions of 800×600 or higher, and color depths of 16-bits (high color) or higher (i.e., 24-bit true color). In most cases, 256 colors will result in a "dithered" image.

Symptom 14-7. The video image is distorted when trying to play an MPEG file Other video operations probably seem fine. A full or partially distorted MPEG image can be the result of two problems. First, the video connections on the back of the card could be loose. Verify that all connections to the MPEG-2 decoder card are secure. Another common cause of distorted playbacks is that the refresh rate on your video card is set too high—it is recommended that the video refresh rate be kept below 85Hz when running MPEG files. Try adjusting the vertical refresh rate to 72Hz, or even 60Hz.

Symptom 14-8.   The picture is beginning to occasionally pixelize or "break apart" The audio might also seem periodically distorted. It is highly likely that the DVD disc needs to be cleaned. Clean the DVD disc properly and try it again, or try another disc. Also try closing any unused applications running in the background. If the problem persists with another DVD disc as well (and if both discs are in good condition), try reinitializing the drive by powering down and rebooting the system. If the problem still persists, the internal optics of the DVD-ROM drive might need to be cleaned with a bit of photography-grade compressed air. Otherwise, try replacing the DVD-ROM drive.

Symptom 14-9.   The DVD-ROM light flashes regularly without a disc inserted System performance might be reduced. This is often because the DVD-ROM drive's properties are set for *Auto insert notification* under Windows 95. Start the *Device Manager*, highlight the DVD-ROM drive, and click the *Properties* button. You'll see the *DVD-ROM properties* dialog (Fig. 14-11). In the *Options* area of the *Properties* dialog, locate the check box that says *Auto insert notification*, and uncheck it. Save your changes (you might need to reboot the system). This should stop the drive's constant checking for a disc.

Symptom 14-10. A "Disk playback unauthorized" error message appears The region code on the DVD disc does not match the code embedded into the drive. Not much can be done when this error occurs. Notice that region code limitations are only applied to DVD-Video movie releases—programs and data discs are generally not marked with region codes.

Symptom 14-11. An error indicates that the DVD device driver could not be loaded You'll need to check the DVD driver installation, or manually install the drivers. To do this, you will need to open the *Control panel*, open *System properties*, then select the *Device manager* tab. In the category of *Other devices*, select *PCI multimedia device* and click on *Properties*. In the *Properties* dialog, select the *Driver* tab and click on *Change* driver. Browse to the *DVD drivers installation disk* and click on *OK*. Click on *OK* again, select the proper MPEG board (such as "MKE DVD-AV Decoder Board"), and click on *OK* again. Exit the *PCI multimedia device properties* by clicking on *OK* again, and Windows 95 will copy over the proper drivers. You will then need to restart the machine.

Symptom 14-12. You see an error, such as "Cannot open <filename>, video and audio glitches might occur" This type of error almost always indicates

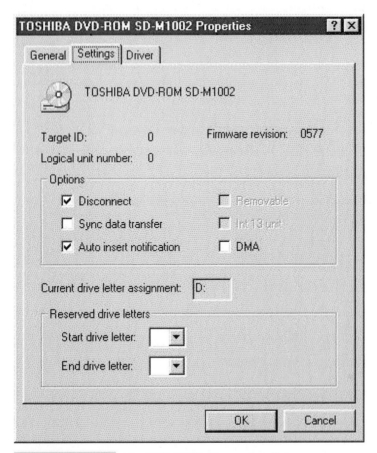

FIGURE 14-11   The DVD-ROM *Properties* dialog.

a fault with the driver installation. You should re-run the "setup" utility, which accompanied your the DVD drive product.

Symptom 14-13. The display turns magenta (red) when attempting to adjust the DVD video overlay feature When adjusting the video overlay, you might have some trouble finding the video window. It often helps to change your background to magenta so you can see where the video window is. To do this, right click on your background, and select *Properties*. Select the *Background* tab and select "none" as both the *Pattern* and the *Wallpaper*. Then select the *Appearance* tab and select *Magenta* as the color of the desktop. Click on *OK* to finish changing your background color to magenta. It should now be easier to locate the video window while adjusting the overlay.

Symptom 14-14. The DVD drive cannot read CD-R or Photo CD discs This is not an error—most first-generation DVD drives will not read CD-recordable or Photo CD (Kodak) disks. In some cases, it is even possible to damage CD recordable disks because of the laser wavelength and energy used in the DVD drive. Do not attempt to read CD-R or Photo CD discs in the DVD unless the drive specifications specifically state that the drive is compatible with those types of discs.

Further Study

That concludes Chapter 14. Be sure to review the glossary and chapter questions on the accompanying CD. If you have access to the Internet, take a look at some of the DVD drive manufacturers listed:

Creative Labs: **http://www-nt-ok.creaf.com/mmuk/pcdvd/**

Diamond Multimedia: **http://www.diamondmm.com**

Toshiba: **http://www.toshiba.com/taisdpd/dvdrom.htm**

Matsushita: **http://www.panasonic.com/PCEC/dvd/index-dvd.html**

ERROR

CODES

CONTENTS AT A GLANCE

IBM Diagnostic Codes
  Reading the codes
  Troubleshooting with diagnostic
    codes

Beep Codes

POST Codes
  Interpreting the post codes

The POST Board
  I/O ports
  Interpreting the LEDs

Beep/POST Troubleshooting

Further Study

In spite of the proliferation of diagnostics and test equipment in the PC industry, most computers are remarkably adept at testing their own hardware and reporting serious errors during start time. This is accomplished through the *Power-On Self-Test (POST)* written into BIOS. Because BIOS is written expressly for a particular processor, chipset, and other motherboard hardware, the BIOS is an ideal choice for startup diagnostics. However, startup diagnostics pose a unique problem—it's hard to report an error when the system isn't fully functional. BIOS reports POST errors through the use of audible signals (called *beep codes*), as well as through hexadecimal codes written to established I/O addresses (called *POST codes*). IBM has also established a standardized set of diagnostic codes for indicating system problems. This chapter explores the IBM diagnostic codes, then presents a compilation of beep and POST codes tracked down from just about every BIOS maker.

IBM Diagnostic Codes

IBM has taken an unusually thorough approach to diagnosing and reporting system errors through the use of their Advanced Diagnostics program (which can be purchased directly from IBM, but is available on many PS/2 reference disks). When the diagnostic is run, it will test and report on every possible sub-system—new or old—that might be in the PC. Unfortunately, IBM has never really done a very good job of documenting their vast array of codes. This section of the chapter is intended as a source of reference to assist you in interpreting these codes and to help you select some repair alternatives.

READING THE CODES

Diagnostic codes are split into two sections: the test code and the fault code. The *test code* is simply the number that corresponds to the particular test being run. The *fault code* is a two-digit decimal number that corresponds to the specific type of error that is identified. A fault code of 00 indicates that no problem was found. For example, the message "100" means that the motherboard was tested (01) and that no errors were detected (00)—thus "0100," or just "100." If a fault code appears other than 00, a problem has been detected that a technician will have to address. System initialization might or might not continue depending on the location and severity of the error. Table 15-1 provides a relatively comprehensive list of diagnostic codes for XT, AT, PS/2 systems.

TABLE 15-1   IBM DIAGNOSTIC CODES

SYSTEM BOARD (01xx)

101	Interrupt failure (unexpected interrupt)
102	BIOS ROM checksum error (PC, XT); timer error (AT, MCA)
103	BASIC ROM checksum error (PC, XT); timer-interrupt error (AT, MCA)
104	Interrupt controller error (PC, XT); protected-mode error (AT, MCA)
105	Timer failure (PC, XT); keyboard-controller failure (MCA)
106	System-board converting-logic test failure
107	System-board adapter-card or math co-processor fault; Hot NMI test failed (MCA)
108	System-board timer bus failure
109	DMA-test memory-select failure
110	PS/2 system-board memory problem (ISA); system-board parity-check error (MCA)
111	PS/2 adapter memory problem (ISA); memory-adapter parity-check error (MCA)
112	PS/2 watchdog time-out error
113	PS/2 DMA arbitration time-out error
114	PS/2 external ROM checksum error
115	Cache parity error, BIOS ROM checksum error, or DMA error
116	System board port R/W error
118	System board L2 cache error
119	2.88MB floppy drive installed but not supported by floppy disk controller
120	CPU self-test error
121	Unexpected hardware interrupt occurred

TABLE 15-1   IBM DIAGNOSTIC CODES (CONTINUED)

131	Cassette wrap test (PC)
132	DMA extended registers error
133	DMA verify logic error
134	DMA arbitration logic error
151	Battery, real-time clock, or CMOS RAM failure
152	Real-time clock or CMOS RAM failure
158	Command Password not set, but Supervisor Password is
159	Command Password set, but not the same as Supervisor Password
160	PS/2 system board ID not recognized
161	CMOS chip lost power—battery dead
162	CMOS checksum or CRC error
163	CMOS error—time and date not set (the clock not updating)
164	Memory-size error—CMOS data does not match system memory found
165	PS/2 adapter ID mismatch
166	PS/2 adapter time-out—card busy
167	PS/2 system clock not updating
168	Math co-processor error in the CMOS configuration
169	System board and processor card configuration mismatch
170	ASCII setup conflict error
171	Rolling bit test failure on CMOS shutdown byte
172	Rolling bit test failure on NVRAM diagnostic byte
173	Bad CMOS/NVRAM checksum
174	Bad system configuration
175	Bad EEPROM CRC
177	Bad password CRC
178	Bad EEPROM
179	NVRAM error log full
180x	Sub-address data error in slot x
181	Unsupported configuration
182	Password switch is not in the writing position
183	System halted—password required
184	Bad power-on password
185	Bad startup sequence
186	Password-protection hardware error
187	Serial-number error
188	Bad EEPROM checksum
189	Too many incorrect password attempts
191	Cache-controller test failure (82385)
194	System-board memory error
195	Configuration read from hibernation area of HDD doesn't match actual configuration
196	Read error occurred in hibernation area of HDD
199	User-indicated device list not correct

SYSTEM MEMORY (02xx)

201	Memory error (physical location will likely be displayed)
202	Memory address line 0–15 error

TABLE 15-1 IBM DIAGNOSTIC CODES (CONTINUED)

203	Memory address line 16–23 error; line 16–31 error (MCA)
204	Memory remapped to compensate for error (PS/2)
205	Error in first 128K (PS/2 ISA) of RAM
207	BIOS ROM failure
210	System-board memory parity error
211	Error in first 64K of RAM (MCA)
212	Watchdog timer error
213	DMA bus arbitration time-out
215	Memory-address error; 64K on daughter/SIP 2 failed (70)
216	Memory-address error; 64K on daughter/SIP 1 failed (70)
221	ROM to RAM copy (shadowing) failed (MCA)
225	Wrong-speed memory on system board (MCA)
230	Memory on motherboard and adapter-board overlaps
231	Non-contiguous adapter memory installed
235	Stuck data line on memory module
241	Memory module 2 failed
251	Memory module 3 failed

KEYBOARD (03xx)

301	Keyboard did not respond correctly (stuck key detected)
302	Keyboard locked (AT, models 25, 30)
303	Keyboard/system-board interface error—keyboard controller fault
304	Keyboard or system unit error (keyboard clock stuck high)
305	Keyboard fuse failed on system board (PS/2 50, 60, 80) or +5 V error (PS/2 70)
306	Unsupported keyboard attached
341	Keyboard error
342	Keyboard cable error
343	Enhancement card or cable error
365	Keyboard failure
366	Interface cable failure
367	Enhancement card or cable failure

MONOCHROME DISPLAY ADAPTER (04xx)

401	Memory, horizontal-sync frequency, or vertical-sync test failure
408	User-indicated display-attribute failure
416	User-indicated character-set failure
424	User-indicated 80-x-25 mode failure
432	MDA-card parallel-port test failure

COLOR GRAPHICS ADAPTER (05xx)

501	Memory, horizontal-sync frequency, or vertical-sync test failure
503	CGA-adapter controller failure
508	User-indicated display-attribute failure
516	User-indicated character-set failure
524	User-indicated 80-x-25 mode failure

TABLE 15-1 IBM DIAGNOSTIC CODES (CONTINUED)

532	User-indicated 40-x-25 mode failure
540	User-indicated 320-x-200 graphics-mode failure
548	User-indicated 640-x-200 graphics-mode failure
556	Light-pen test failed
564	User-indicated screen-paging test failed

FLOPPY DRIVES AND ADAPTERS (06xx)

601	General diskette or adapter-test failure
602	Diskette boot sector is not valid
603	Diskette-size error
604	Media-sense error
605	Diskette drive locked
606	Diskette-verify test failure
607	Write-protect error
608	Drive-command error
610	Diskette-initialization failure
611	Drive time-out error
612	NEC drive-controller IC error
613	Floppy-system DMA error
614	Floppy-system DMA boundary-overrun error
615	Drive index-timing error
616	Drive-speed error
621	Drive-seek error
622	Drive CRC error
623	Sector-not-found error
624	Disk address mark error
625	NEC drive-controller IC seek error
626	Diskette data-compare error
627	Diskette change-line error
628	Diskette removed from drive
630	Drive A: index stuck high
631	Drive A: index stuck low
632	Drive A: track 0 stuck off
633	Drive A: track 0 stuck on
640	Drive B: index stuck high
641	Drive B: index stuck low
642	Drive B: track 0 stuck off
643	Drive B: track 0 stuck on
645	No index pulse
646	Drive track 00 detection failed
647	No transitions on Read Data line
648	Format test failed
649	Incorrect media type in drive
650	Drive speed incorrect

TABLE 15-1   IBM DIAGNOSTIC CODES (CONTINUED)

651	Format failure
652	Verify failure
653	Read failure
654	Write failure
655	Drive-controller error
656	Drive-mechanism failure
657	Write protect stuck in "protected" state
658	Change line stuck in "changed" state
659	Write protect stuck in "unprotected" state
660	Change line stuck in "unchanged" state

MATH CO-PROCESSOR (07xx)

701	MCP presence or initialization error
702	Exception-errors test failure
703	Rounding test failure
704	Arithmetic test 1 failure
705	Arithmetic test 2 failure
706	Arithmetic test 3 (80387 only)
707	Combination test failure
708	Integer load/store test failure
709	Equivalent expressions errors
710	Exception (interrupt) errors
711	Save-state errors
712	Protected-mode test failure
713	Voltage/temperature-sensitivity test failure

PARALLEL PRINTER ADAPTER (09xx)

901	Data-register latch error
902	Control-register latch error
903	Register-address decode error
904	Address decode error
910	Status-line wrap-connector error
911	Status-line bit-8 wrap error
912	Status-line bit-7 wrap error
913	Status-line bit-6 wrap error
914	Status-line bit-5 wrap error
915	Status-line bit-4 wrap error
916	Printer adapter interrupt wrap error
917	Unexpected printer-adapter interrupt
92x	Feature register error

ALTERNATE PRINTER ADAPTER (10xx)

1001	Data-register latch error
1002	Control-register latch error
1003	Register address-decode error

TABLE 15-1   IBM DIAGNOSTIC CODES (CONTINUED)

1004	Address-decode error
1010	Status-line wrap-connector error
1011	Status-line bit-8 wrap error
1012	Status-line bit-7 wrap error
1013	Status-line bit-6 wrap error
1014	Status-line bit-5 wrap error
1015	Status-line bit-4 wrap error
1016	Printer-adapter interrupt-wrap error
1017	Unexpected printer-adapter interrupt
102x	Feature register error

COMMUNICATION DEVICES (11xx)

1101	16450/16550 UART error
1102	Card-selected feedback error
1103	Port 102h register-test failure
1106	Serial option cannot be shut down
1107	Communications-cable or system-board error
1108	IRQ 3 error
1109	IRQ 4 error
1110	16450/16550 chip-register failure
1111	UART control-line internal-wrap test failure
1112	UART control-line external-wrap test failure
1113	UART transmit error
1114	UART receive error
1115	UART transmit and receive data unequal—receive error
1116	UART interrupt function error
1117	UART baud-rate test failure
1118	UART interrupt-driven receive external data-wrap test error
1119	UART FIFO buffer failure
1120	UART interrupt enable register failure: all bits cannot be set
1121	UART interrupt enable register failure: all bits cannot be reset
1122	Interrupt pending—stuck on
1123	Interrupt ID register stuck on
1124	Modem-control register failure: all bits cannot be set
1125	Modem-control register failure: all bits cannot be reset
1126	Modem-status register failure: all bits cannot be set
1127	Modem-status register failure: all bits cannot be reset
1128	Interrupt ID error
1129	Cannot force overrun error
1130	No modem status interrupt
1131	Invalid interrupt pending
1132	No data ready
1133	No data available at interrupt
1134	No transmit holding at interrupt

TABLE 15-1   IBM DIAGNOSTIC CODES (CONTINUED)

1135	No interrupts
1136	No received-line status interrupt
1137	No receive data available
1138	Transmit holding register not empty
1139	No modem status interrupt
1140	Transmit holding register not empty
1141	No interrupts
1142	No IRQ4 interrupt
1143	No IRQ3 interrupt
1144	No data transferred
1145	Maximum baud-rate error
1146	Minimum baud-rate error
1148	Time-out error
1149	Invalid data returned
1150	Modem-status register error
1151	No DSR and delta DSR
1152	No DSR
1153	No delta DSR
1154	Modem-status register not clear
1155	No CTS and delta CTS
1156	No CTS
1157	No delta CTS

ALTERNATE COMMUNICATIONS DEVICES (12xx)

1201	16450/16550 UART error
1202	Card-selected feedback error
1203	Port 102h register-test failure
1206	Serial option cannot be shut down
1207	Communications-cable or system-board error
1208	IRQ 3 error
1209	IRQ 4 error
1210	16450/16550 chip-register failure
1211	UART control-line internal-wrap test failure
1212	UART control-line external-wrap test failure
1213	UART transmit error
1214	UART receive error
1215	UART transmit and receive data unequal—receive error
1216	UART interrupt-function error
1217	UART baud-rate test failure
1218	UART interrupt-driven receive external data-wrap test error
1219	UART FIFO-buffer failure
1220	UART interrupt-enable register failure: all bits cannot be set
1221	UART interrupt-enable register failure: all bits cannot be reset
1222	Interrupt pending—stuck on

TABLE 15-1 IBM DIAGNOSTIC CODES (CONTINUED)

1223	Interrupt ID register stuck on
1224	Modem-control register failure: all bits cannot be set
1225	Modem-control register failure: all bits cannot be reset
1226	Modem-status register failure: all bits cannot be set
1227	Modem-status register failure: all bits cannot be reset
1228	Interrupt ID error
1229	Cannot force overrun error
1230	No-modem status interrupt
1231	Invalid interrupt pending
1232	No data ready
1233	No data available at interrupt
1234	No transmit holding at interrupt
1235	No interrupts
1236	No received-line status interrupt
1237	No receive data available
1238	Transmit-holding register not empty
1239	No-modem status interrupt
1240	Transmit-holding register not empty
1241	No interrupts
1242	No IRQ4 interrupt
1243	No IRQ3 interrupt
1244	No data transferred
1245	Maximum baud-rate error
1246	Minimum baud-rate error
1248	Time-out error
1249	Invalid data returned
1250	Modem-status register error
1251	No DSR and delta DSR
1252	No DSR
1253	No delta DSR
1254	Modem-status register not clear
1255	No CTS and delta CTS
1256	No CTS
1257	No delta CTS

GAME-PORT ADAPTERS (13xx)

1301	Game-port adapter test failure
1302	Joystick test failure

MATRIX PRINTERS (14xx)

1401	Printer test failure
1402	Printer not ready, not on-line, or out of paper
1403	Printer "no paper" error
1404	Matrix-printer test failure; system board time-out
1405	Parallel adapter failure
1406	Printer-presence test failed

TABLE 15-1 IBM DIAGNOSTIC CODES (CONTINUED)

SDLC COMMUNICATIONS ADAPTER (15xx)

1501	SDLC-adapter test failure
1510	8255 port-B failure
1511	8255 port-A failure
1512	8255 port-C failure
1513	8253 timer #1 did not reach terminal count
1514	8253 timer #1 output stuck on
1515	8253 timer #0 did not reach terminal count
1516	8253 timer #0 output stuck on
1517	8253 timer #2 did not reach terminal count
1518	8253 timer #2 output stuck on
1519	8273 port-B error
1520	8273 port-A error
1521	8273 command/read time-out error
1522	Interrupt level-4 error
1523	Ring indicator stuck on
1524	Receive clock stuck on
1525	Transmit clock stuck on
1526	Test Indicate stuck on
1527	Ring Indicate not on
1528	Receive clock not on
1529	Transmit clock not on
1530	Test Indicate not on
1531	Data Set Ready not on
1532	Carrier Detect not on
1533	Clear-To-Send not on
1534	Data Set Ready stuck on
1535	Carrier Detect stuck on
1536	Clear-To-Send stuck on
1537	Interrupt level-3 failure
1538	Receive-interrupt results error
1539	Wrap-data compare error
1540	DMA channel-1 transmit error
1541	DMA channel-1 receive error
1542	8273 error-checking or status-reporting error
1547	Stray-interrupt level-4 error
1548	Stray-interrupt level-3 error
1549	Interrupt presentation sequence time-out

DSEA UNITS (16xx)

1604	DSEA or twinaxial network adapter
1608	DSEA or twinaxial network adapter
1624 through 1658	DSEA system error
1662	DSEA interrupt-level error

TABLE 15-1   IBM DIAGNOSTIC CODES (CONTINUED)

1664	DSEA system error
1668	DSEA interrupt-level error
1669	DSEA diagnostics error
1674	DSEA diagnostics error
1684	DSEA device-address error
1688	DSEA device-address error

HARD DRIVES AND ADAPTERS (17xx)

1701	Fixed-disk or adapter general error
1702	Drive and controller time-out error
1703	Drive-seek error
1704	Drive controller failed
1705	Drive-sector not-found error
1706	Write-fault error
1707	Drive-track 00 error
1708	Head-select error
1709	Bad ECC returned
1710	Sector buffer overrun
1711	Bad-address mark
1712	Internal-controller diagnostics failure
1713	Data-compare error
1714	Drive not ready
1715	Track-00 indicator failure
1716	Diagnostics-cylinder errors
1717	Surface-read errors
1718	Hard-drive error
1720	Bad diagnostics cylinder
1726	Data-compare error
1730	Drive-controller error
1731	Drive-controller error
1732	Drive-controller error
1733	BIOS-undefined error return
1735	Bad-command error
1736	Data-corrected error
1737	Bad drive-track error
1738	Bad-sector error
1739	Bad-initialization error
1740	Bad-sense error
1750	Drive-verify error
1751	Drive-read error
1752	Drive-write error
1753	Drive random-read test failure
1754	Drive-seek test failure
1755	Drive-controller failure
1756	Controller ECC test failure

TABLE 15-1 IBM DIAGNOSTIC CODES (CONTINUED)

1757	Controller head-select failure
1780	Drive-seek failure (Drive 0)
1781	Drive-seek failure (Drive 1)
1782	Hard-disk controller failure
1790	Diagnostic cylinder-read error (Drive 0)
1791	Diagnostic cylinder-read error (Drive 1)

I/O EXPANSION UNIT (18xx)

1801	Expansion Unit POST error
1810	Enable/disable failure
1811	Extender-card wrap-test failure while disabled
1812	High-order address-lines failure while disabled
1813	Wait-state failure while disabled
1814	Enable/disable could not be set on
1815	Wait-state failure while enabled
1816	Extender-card wrap-test failure while enabled
1817	High-order address-lines failure while enabled
1818	Disable not functioning
1819	Wait-request switch not set correctly
1820	Receiver-card wrap test failed
1821	Receiver high-order address-lines failure

BI-SYNCHRONOUS COMMUNICATIONS ADAPTERS (20xx)

2001	BSC adapter-test failure
2010	8255 port-A failure
2011	8255 port-B failure
2012	8255 port-C failure
2013	8253 timer #1 did not reach terminal count
2014	8253 timer #1 output stuck on
2015	8253 timer #2 did not reach terminal count
2016	8253 timer #2 output stuck on
2017	8251 Data-Set-Ready failed to come on
2018	8251 Clear-To-Send not sensed
2019	8251 Data-Set-Ready stuck on
2020	8251 Clear-To-Send stuck on
2021	8251 hardware-reset failure
2022	8251 software-reset command failure
2023	8251 software error-reset command failure
2024	8251 Transmit-Ready did not come on
2025	8251 Receive-Ready did not come on
2026	8251 could not force overrun error status
2027	Interrupt failure—no timer interrupt
2028	Interrupt failure—replace card or planar board
2029	Interrupt failure—replace card only
2030	Interrupt failure—replace card or planar board

TABLE 15-1 IBM DIAGNOSTIC CODES (CONTINUED)

2031	Interrupt failure—replace card only
2033	Ring Indicate signal stuck on
2034	Receive clock stuck on
2035	Transmit clock stuck on
2036	Test Indicate stuck on
2037	Ring Indicate not on
2038	Receive clock not on
2039	Transmit clock not on
2040	Test Indicate not on
2041	Data-Set-Ready stuck on
2042	Carrier Detect not on
2043	Clear-To-Send not on
2044	Data-Set-Ready stuck on
2045	Carrier Detect stuck on
2046	Clear-To-Send stuck on
2047	Unexpected transmit interrupt
2048	Unexpected receive interrupt
2049	Transmit data did not equal receive data
2050	8251 detected overrun error
2051	Lost Data-Set-Ready signal during data wrap
2052	Receive time-out during data wrap

ALTERNATE BI-SYNCHRONOUS COMMUNICATIONS ADAPTERS (21xx)

2101	BSC-adapter test failure
2110	8255 port-A failure
2111	8255 port-B failure
2112	8255 port-C failure
2113	8253 timer #1 did not reach terminal count
2114	8253 timer #1 output stuck on
2115	8253 timer #2 did not reach terminal count
2116	8253 timer #2 output stuck on
2117	8251 Data-Set-Ready failed to come on
2118	8251 Clear-To-Send not sensed
2119	8251 Data-Set-Ready stuck on
2120	8251 Clear-To-Send stuck on
2121	8251 hardware-reset failure
2122	8251 software-reset command failure
2123	8251 software error-reset command failure
2124	8251 Transmit-Ready did not come on
2125	8251 Receive-Ready did not come on
2126	8251 could not force overrun error status
2127	Interrupt failure—no timer interrupt
2128	Interrupt failure—replace card or planar board
2129	Interrupt failure—replace card only
2130	Interrupt failure—replace card or planar board

TABLE 15-1   IBM DIAGNOSTIC CODES (CONTINUED)

2131	Interrupt failure—replace card only
2133	Ring Indicate signal stuck on
2134	Receive clock stuck on
2135	Transmit clock stuck on
2136	Test Indicate stuck on
2137	Ring Indicate not on
2138	Receive clock not on
2139	Transmit clock not on
2140	Test Indicate not on
2141	Data-Set-Ready stuck on
2142	Carrier Detect not on
2143	Clear-To-Send not on
2144	Data-Set-Ready stuck on
2145	Carrier Detect stuck on
2146	Clear-To-Send stuck on
2147	Unexpected transmit interrupt
2148	Unexpected receive interrupt
2149	Transmit data did not equal receive data
2150	8251 detected overrun error
2151	Lost Data-Set-Ready signal during data wrap
2152	Receive time-out during data wrap

CLUSTER ADAPTERS (22xx)

22xx	A cluster-adapter error has been encountered—replace the cluster adapter

PLASMA MONITOR ADAPTER (23xx)

23xx	A plasma-display fault has been detected—replace the plasma-monitor assembly

ENHANCED GRAPHICS ADAPTER (24xx)

2401	Video-adapter test failure
2402	Video-display (monitor) error
2408	User-indicated display-attribute test failed
2409	Video-display (monitor) error
2410	Video-adapter error
2416	User-indicated character-set test failed
2424	User-indicated 80-x-25 mode failure
2432	User-indicated 40-x-25 mode failure
2440	User-indicated 320-x-200 graphics-mode failure
2448	User-indicated 640-x-200 graphics-mode failure
2456	User-indicated light-pen test failure
2464	User-indicated screen-paging test failure

ALTERNATE ENHANCED GRAPHICS ADAPTER (25xx)

2501	Video-adapter test failure
2502	Video-display (monitor) error
2508	User-indicated display-attribute test failed

TABLE 15-1 IBM DIAGNOSTIC CODES (CONTINUED)

2509	Video-display (monitor) error
2510	Video-adapter error
2516	User-indicated character-set test failed
2524	User-indicated 80-x-25 mode failure
2532	User-indicated 40-x-25 mode failure
2540	User-indicated 320-x-200 graphics-mode failure
2548	User-indicated 640-x-200 graphics-mode failure
2556	User-indicated light-pen test failure
2564	User-indicated screen-paging test failure

PC/370-M ADAPTER (26xx)

2601 through 2672	370-M (memory) adapter error
2673 through 2680	370-P (processor) adapter error
2681	370-M (memory) adapter error
2682 through 2697	370-P (processor) adapter error
2698	XT or AT/370 diagnostic diskette error

PC3277 EMULATION ADAPTER (27xx)

2701	3277-EM adapter error
2702	3277-EM adapter error
2703	3277-EM adapter error

3278/3279 EMULATION ADAPTER (28xx)

28xx	An emulation adapter fault has been detected—replace the adapter

COLOR/GRAPHICS PRINTERS (29xx)

29xx	A general fault has been detected with the printer or its printer port—replace the printer or adapter port

PRIMARY PC NETWORK ADAPTER (30xx)

3001	Network-adapter test failure
3002	ROM-checksum test failure
3003	Unit-ID PROM test failure
3004	RAM test failure
3005	Host-Interface Controller (HIC) test failure
3006	+/-12-Vdc test failure
3007	Digital-loopback test failure
3008	Host-detected HIC failure
3009	Sync-signal failure and no-go bit
3010	HIC test OK and no-go bit
3011	Go bit OK, but no command 41
3012	Card not present
3013	Digital failure—fall-through
3015	Analog failure

TABLE 15-1   IBM DIAGNOSTIC CODES (CONTINUED)

3041	Hot carrier—on other card
3042	Hot carrier—on this card

SECONDARY PC NETWORK ADAPTER (31xx)

3101	Network-adapter test failure
3102	ROM-checksum test failure
3103	Unit-ID PROM test failure
3104	RAM test failure
3105	Host-Interface Controller (HIC) test failure
3106	+/–12-Vdc test failure
3107	Digital-loopback test failure
3108	Host-detected HIC failure
3109	Sync signal failure and no-go bit
3110	HIC test OK and no-go bit
3111	Go-bit OK, but no command 41
3112	Card not present
3113	Digital failure—fall-through
3115	Analog failure
3141	Hot carrier—on other card
3142	Hot carrier—on this card

3270 PC/AT DISPLAY (32xx)

32xx	A fault has been detected in the display system—replace the display system

COMPACT PRINTER ERRORS (33xx)

33xx	A fault has been detected in the printer or printer adapter—replace the printer or adapter

ENHANCED DSEA UNITS (35xx)

3504	Adapter connected to twinaxial cable during off-line test
3508	Workstation-address error
3509	Diagnostic-program failure; retry on new diskette
3540	Workstation address invalid
3588	Adapter-address switch error
3599	Diagnostic-program failure; retry on new diskette

IEEE 488 (GPIB) ADAPTER (36xx)

3601	Adapter test failure
3602	Write error at Serial Poll Mode Register (SPMR)
3603	Adapter addressing problems
3610	Adapter cannot be programmed to listen
3611	Adapter cannot be programmed to talk
3612	Adapter-control error
3613	Adapter cannot switch to standby mode
3614	Adapter cannot take control asynchronously
3615	Adapter cannot take control asynchronously
3616	Adapter cannot pass control

TABLE 15-1   IBM DIAGNOSTIC CODES (CONTINUED)

3617	Adapter cannot be addressed to listen
3618	Adapter cannot be un-addressed to listen
3619	Adapter cannot be addressed to talk
3620	Adapter cannot be un-addressed to talk
3621	Adapter cannot be addressed to listen with extended addressing
3622	Adapter cannot be un-addressed to listen with extended addressing
3623	Adapter cannot be addressed to talk with extended addressing
3624	Adapter cannot be un-addressed to talk with extended addressing
3625	Adapter cannot write to self
3626	Adapter error—cannot generate handshake signal
3627	Adapter error—cannot detect Device Clear (DCL) message
3628	Adapter error—cannot detect Selected Device Clear (SDC) message
3629	Adapter error—cannot detect end of transfer with EOI signal
3630	Adapter error—cannot detect end of transmission with EOI signal
3631	Adapter cannot detect END with 0-bit EOS
3632	Adapter cannot detect END with 7-bit EOS
3633	Adapter cannot detect Group Execute Trigger (GET)
3634	Mode 3 addressing not functioning
3635	Adapter cannot recognize undefined command
3636	Adapter error—cannot detect REM, REMC, LOK, or LOKC signals
3637	Adapter error—cannot clear REM or LOK signals
3638	Adapter cannot detect Service Request (SRQ)
3639	Adapter cannot conduct serial poll
3640	Adapter cannot conduct parallel poll
3650	Adapter error—cannot DMA to 7210
3651	Data error on DMA to 7210
3652	Adapter error—cannot DMA from 7210
3653	Data error on DMA from 7210
3658	Un-invoked interrupt received
3659	Adapter cannot interrupt on ADSC signal
3660	Adapter cannot interrupt on ADSC signal
3661	Adapter cannot interrupt on CO
3662	Adapter cannot interrupt on DO
3663	Adapter cannot interrupt on DI
3664	Adapter cannot interrupt on ERR
3665	Adapter cannot interrupt on DEC
3666	Adapter cannot interrupt on END
3667	Adapter cannot interrupt on DET
3668	Adapter cannot interrupt on APT
3669	Adapter cannot interrupt on CPT
3670	Adapter cannot interrupt on REMC
3671	Adapter cannot interrupt on LOKC
3672	Adapter cannot interrupt on SRQI
3673	Adapter cannot interrupt on terminal count on DMA to 7210

TABLE 15-1   IBM DIAGNOSTIC CODES (CONTINUED)

3674	Adapter cannot interrupt on terminal count on DMA from 7210
3675	Spurious DMA terminal-count interrupt
3697	Illegal DMA-configuration setting detected
3698	Illegal interrupt-level configuration setting detected

SYSTEM BOARD SCSI CONTROLLER (37xx)

37xx	The system-board SCSI controller has failed—replace the motherboard

DATA ACQUISITION ADAPTER (38xx)

3801	Adapter test failure
3810	Timer-read test failure
3811	Timer-interrupt test failure
3812	Binary input 13 test failure
3813	Binary input 13 test failure
3814	Binary output 14—interrupt request test failure
3815	Binary output 0, count-in test failure
3816	Binary input strobe (STB), count-out test failure
3817	Binary output 0, Clear-To-Send (CTS) test failure
3818	Binary output 1, binary input 0 test failure
3819	Binary output 2, binary input 1 test failure
3820	Binary output 3, binary input 2 test failure
3821	Binary output 4, binary input 3 test failure
3822	Binary output 5, binary input 4 test failure
3823	Binary output 6, binary input 5 test failure
3824	Binary output 7, binary input 6 test failure
3825	Binary output 8, binary input 7 test failure
3826	Binary output 9, binary input 8 test failure
3827	Binary output 10, binary input 9 test failure
3828	Binary output 11, binary input 10 test failure
3829	Binary output 12, binary input 11 test failure
3830	Binary output 13, binary input 12 test failure
3831	Binary output 15, analog input CE test failure
3832	Binary output strobe (STB), binary output GATE test failure
3833	Binary input Clear-To-Send (CTS), binary input HOLD test failure
3834	Analog input Command Output (CO), binary input 15 test failure
3835	Counter-interrupt test failure
3836	Counter-read test failure
3837	Analog output 0 ranges test failure
3838	Analog output 1 ranges test failure
3839	Analog input 0 values test failure
3840	Analog input 1 values test failure
3841	Analog input 2 values test failure
3842	Analog input 3 values test failure
3843	Analog input interrupt test failure
3844	Analog input 23 address or value test failure

TABLE 15-1   IBM DIAGNOSTIC CODES (CONTINUED)

PROFESSIONAL GRAPHICS ADAPTER (PGA) (39xx)

3901	PGA test failure
3902	ROM1 self-test failure
3903	ROM2 self-test failure
3904	RAM self-test failure
3905	Cold-start-cycle power error
3906	Data error in communications RAM
3907	Address error in communications RAM
3908	Bad data detected while read/write to 6845 register
3909	Bad data detected in lower E0h bytes while read/writing 6845 registers
3910	Display bank output latch error
3911	Basic clock error
3912	Command control error
3913	Vertical-sync scanner error
3914	Horizontal-sync scanner error
3915	Intech error
3916	Lookup Table (LUT) address error
3917	LUT "red" RAM-chip error
3918	LUT "green" RAM-chip error
3919	LUT "blue" RAM-chip error
3920	LUT data-latch error
3921	Horizontal display error
3922	Vertical display error
3923	Light-pen error
3924	Unexpected error
3925	Emulator addressing error
3926	Emulator data-latch error
3927 through 3930	Emulator RAM error
3931	Emulator horizontal/vertical-display problem
3932	Emulator cursor-position error
3933	Emulator attribute-display problem
3934	Emulator cursor-display error
3935	Fundamental-emulation RAM problem
3936	Emulation character-set problem
3937	Emulation graphics-display error
3938	Emulation character-display problem
3939	Emulation bank-select error
3940	Display RAM U2 error
3941	Display RAM U4 error
3942	Display RAM U6 error
3943	Display RAM U8 error
3944	Display RAM U10 error
3945	Display RAM U1 error

TABLE 15-1 IBM DIAGNOSTIC CODES (CONTINUED)

3946	Display RAM U3 error
3947	Display RAM U5 error
3948	Display RAM U7 error
3949	Display RAM U9 error
3950	Display RAM U12 error
3951	Display RAM U14 error
3952	Display RAM U16 error
3953	Display RAM U18 error
3954	Display RAM U20 error
3955	Display RAM U11 error
3956	Display RAM U13 error
3957	Display RAM U15 error
3958	Display RAM U17 error
3959	Display RAM U19 error
3960	Display RAM U22 error
3961	Display RAM U24 error
3962	Display RAM U26 error
3963	Display RAM U28 error
3964	Display RAM U30 error
3965	Display RAM U21 error
3966	Display RAM U23 error
3967	Display RAM U25 error
3968	Display RAM U27 error
3969	Display RAM U29 error
3970	Display RAM U32 error
3971	Display RAM U34 error
3972	Display RAM U36 error
3973	Display RAM U38 error
3974	Display RAM U40 error
3975	Display RAM U31 error
3976	Display RAM U33 error
3977	Display RAM U35 error
3978	Display RAM U37 error
3979	Display RAM U39 error
3980	Graphics-controller RAM-timing error
3981	Graphics-controller read/write latch error
3982	Shift-register bus-output latch error
3983	Addressing error (vertical column of memory; U2 at top)
3984	Addressing error (vertical column of memory; U4 at top)
3985	Addressing error (vertical column of memory; U6 at top)
3986	Addressing error (vertical column of memory; U8 at top)
3987	Addressing error (vertical column of memory; U10 at top)
3988 through 3991	Horizontal bank-latch errors

TABLE 15-1 IBM DIAGNOSTIC CODES (CONTINUED)

3992	RAG/CAG graphics-controller error
3993	Multiple write modes, nibble mask errors
3994	Row nibble (display RAM) error
3995	Graphics-controller addressing error

5278 Display Attachment Unit and 5279 Display (44xx)

44xx	A fault has been detected with the display system—replace the display system

IEEE 488 (GPIB) Interface Adapter (45xx)

45xx	A fault has been detected with the GPIB—replace the adapter

ARTIC Multiport/2 Interface Adapter (46xx)

4611	ARTIC adapter error
4612 or 4613	Memory-module error
4630	ARTIC adapter error
4640 or 4641	Memory-module error
4650	ARTIC interface cable error

Internal Modem (48xx)

48xx	The internal modem has failed—replace the internal modem

Alternate Internal Modem (49xx)

49xx	The alternate internal modem has failed—replace the alternate internal modem

PC CONVERTIBLE LCD (50xx)

5001	LCD-buffer failure
5002	LCD font-buffer failure
5003	LCD-controller failure
5004	User-indicated PEL/drive test failed
5008	User-indicated display-attribute test failed
5016	User-indicated character-set test failed
5020	User-indicated alternate character-set test failure
5024	User-indicated 80-x-25 mode test failure
5032	User-indicated 40-x-25 mode test failure
5040	User-indicated 320-x-200 graphics-test failure
5048	User-indicated 640-x-200 graphics-test failure
5064	User-indicated paging-test failure

PC CONVERTIBLE PORTABLE PRINTER (51xx)

5101	Portable printer-interface failure
5102	Portable printer-busy error
5103	Portable printer-paper or ribbon error
5104	Portable printer time-out
5105	User-indicated print pattern test error

FINANCIAL COMMUNICATION SYSTEM (56xx)

56xx	A fault has been detected in the financial communication system—replace the financial communication system

TABLE 15-1 IBM DIAGNOSTIC CODES (CONTINUED)

PHOENIX BIOS/CHIPSET SPECIFIC ERROR CODES (70xx)

7000	Chipset CMOS failure
7001	Shadow RAM failure (ROM not shadowed to RAM)
7002	Chipset CMOS configuration-data error

VOICE COMMUNICATIONS ADAPTER (VCA) (71xx)

7101	Adapter test failure
7102	Instruction or external-data memory error
7103	PC-to-VCA interrupt error
7104	Internal data memory error
7105	DMA error
7106	Internal registers error
7107	Interactive shared-memory error
7108	VCA-to-PC interrupt error
7109	Dc wrap error
7111	External analog wrap and tone output error
7114	Telephone-attachment test failure

3.5" FLOPPY DISK DRIVE (73xx)

7301	Diskette drive/adapter test failure
7306	Diskette change-line error
7307	Write-protected diskette
7308	Drive-command error
7310	Diskette initialization failure—track 00 error
7311	Drive time-out error
7312	NEC drive-controller IC error
7313	DMA error
7314	DMA boundary-overrun error
7315	Drive index-timing error
7316	Drive-speed error
7321	Drive-seek error
7322	Drive CRC-check error
7323	Sector-not-found error
7324	Address-mark error
7325	NEC-controller IC-seek error

8514/A DISPLAY ADAPTER (74xx)

7426	8514 display error
7440 through 7475	8514/A memory module error

4216 PAGE PRINTER ADAPTER (76xx)

7601	Adapter test failure
7602	Adapter card error
7603	Printer error
7604	Printer cable error

TABLE 15-1   IBM DIAGNOSTIC CODES (CONTINUED)

PCMCIA ADAPTER

8081	Presence test failure (PCMCIA revision number also checked)
8082	PCMCIA register test failure

PS/2 SPEECH ADAPTER (84xx)

84xx	A fault has been detected in the speech adapter—replace the speech adapter

2MB XMA MEMORY ADAPTER (85xx)

85xx	A fault has been detected in the memory adapter—replace the memory adapter

PS/2 POINTING DEVICE (86xx)

8601	Pointing device: mouse time-out error
8602	Pointing device: mouse interface error
8603	System board: mouse interrupt failure
8604	Pointing-device or system-board error
8611	System-bus error
8612	TrackPoint II error
8613	System-bus or TrackPoint II error

MIDI INTERFACE (89xx)

89xx	A fault has been detected in the MIDI adapter—replace the MIDI adapter

3363 WORM OPTICAL DRIVE/ADAPTERS (91xx)

91xx	A fault has been detected in the drive or adapter—replace the adapter and the drive

SCSI ADAPTER (W/32-BIT CACHE) (96xx)

96xx	A fault has been detected in the SCSI adapter—replace the adapter board

MULTIPROTOCOL ADAPTERS (100xx)

10001	Presence-test failure
10002	Card-selected feedback error
10003	Port 102h register-test failure
10004	Port 103h register-test failure
10006	Serial option cannot be disabled
10007	Cable error
10008	IRQ3 error
10009	IRQ4 error
10010	UART register failure
10011	Internal wrap test of UART control line failed
10012	External wrap test of UART control line failed
10013	UART transmit error
10014	UART receive error
10015	UART receive error—data not equal to transmit data
10016	UART interrupt error
10017	UART baud-rate test failure
10018	UART receive external-wrap test failure

TABLE 15-1 IBM DIAGNOSTIC CODES (CONTINUED)

10019	UART FIFO buffer failure
10026	8255 Port-A error
10027	8255 Port-B error
10028	8255 Port-C error
10029	8254 timer-0 error
10030	8254 timer-1 error
10031	8254 timer-2 error
10032	Bi-sync Data-Set-Ready (DSR) response error
10033	Bi-sync Clear-To-Send (CTS) error
10034	8251 hardware reset test failed
10035	8251 function generator
10036	8251 status error
10037	Bi-sync timer-interrupt error
10038	Bi-sync transmit-interrupt error
10039	Bi-sync receive-interrupt error
10040	Stray IRQ3 error
10041	Stray IRQ4 error
10042	Bi-sync external-wrap error
10044	Bi-sync data-wrap error
10045	Bi-sync line-status error
10046	Bi-sync time-out error during wrap test
10050	8273 command acceptance or time-out error
10051	8273 Port-A error
10052	8273 Port-B error
10053	SDLC modem-status logic error
10054	SDLC timer IRQ4 error
10055	SDLC IRQ4 error
10056	SDLC external-wrap error
10057	SDLC interrupt-results error
10058	SDLC data-wrap error
10059	SDLC transmit-interrupt error
10060	SDLC receive-interrupt error
10061	DMA channel-1 transmit error
10062	DMA channel-1 receive error
10063	8273 status-detect failure
10064	8273 error-detect failure

INTERNAL 300/1200BPS MODEM (101xx)

10101	Presence-test failure
10102	Card-selected feedback error
10103	Port 102h register-test error
10106	Serial option cannot be disabled
10108	IRQ3 error
10109	IRQ4 error

TABLE 15-1   IBM DIAGNOSTIC CODES (CONTINUED)

10110	UART chip-register failure
10111	UART control-line internal-wrap test failure
10113	UART transmit error
10114	UART receive error
10115	UART error—transmit and receive data not equal
10116	UART interrupt function error
10117	UART baud-rate test failure
10118	UART interrupt-driven receive external data-wrap test failure
10125	Modem-reset result-code error
10126	Modem general result-code error
10127	Modem S-registers write/read error
10128	Modem echo on/off error
10129	Modem enable/disable result codes error
10130	Modem enable number/word result codes error
10133	Connect results for 300 baud not received
10134	Connect results for 1200 baud not received
10135	Modem fails local analog loopback 300-baud test
10136	Modem fails local analog loopback 1200-baud test
10137	Modem does not respond to escape/reset sequence
10138	S register 13 shows incorrect parity or number of data bits
10139	S register 15 shows incorrect bit rate

ESDI or MCA IDE DRIVE/ADAPTERS (104xx)

10450	Write/read test failed
10451	Read-verify test failed
10452	Seek test failed
10453	Wrong drive type indicated
10454	Controller failed sector-buffer test
10455	Controller failed—invalid
10456	Controller diagnostic command failure
10461	Drive-format error
10462	Controller head-select error
10463	Drive write/read sector error
10464	Drive primary-defect map unreadable
10465	Controller ECC 8-bit error
10466	Controller ECC 9-bit error
10467	Drive soft-seek error
10468	Drive hard-seek error
10469	Drive soft-seek error count exceeded
10470	Controller-attachment diagnostic error
10471	Controller wrap-mode interface error
10472	Controller wrap-mode drive-select error
10473	Error during ESDI read-verify test
10480	Seek failure on drive 0

TABLE 15-1 IBM DIAGNOSTIC CODES (CONTINUED)

10481	Seek failure on drive 1
10482	Controller transfer-acknowledge error
10483	Controller reset error
10484	Controller head select 3 selected bad
10485	Controller head select 2 selected bad
10486	Controller head select 1 selected bad
10487	Controller head select 0 selected bad
10488	Read-gate command error
10489	Read-gate command error
10490	Diagnostic read error on drive 0
10491	Diagnostic read error on drive 1
10492	Drive-1 controller error
10493	Drive-1 reset error
10499	Controller failure

5.25" EXTERNAL DISK DRIVE/ADAPTER (107xx)

107xx	A fault has been detected in the drive or adapter—replace the adapter and drive

SCSI ADAPTER (16-BIT W/O CACHE) (112xx)

112xx	A fault has been detected in the SCSI adapter—replace the SCSI adapter

SYSTEM BOARD SCSI ADAPTER (113xx)

113xx	A fault has been detected in the SCSI adapter—replace the motherboard

CPU BOARD (129xx)

12901	Processor test failed
12902	CPU board cache test failed
12904	Second-level (L2) cache failure
12905	Cache enable/disable errors
12907	Cache fatal error
12908	Cache POST program error
12912	Hardware failure
12913	MCA bus time-out
12914	Software failure
12915	CPU board error
12916	CPU board error
12917	CPU board error
12918	CPU board error
12919	CPU board error
12940	CPU board error
12950	CPU board error
12990	CPU serial number mismatch

P70/P75 PLASMA DISPLAY/ADAPTER (149xx)

14901	Plasma display-adapter failure
14902	Plasma display-adapter failure

TABLE 15-1   IBM DIAGNOSTIC CODES (CONTINUED)

14922	Plasma display failure
14932	External display-device failure

XGA DISPLAY ADAPTER (152xx)

152xx	A fault has been detected in the XGA adapter—replace the adapter

120MB INTERNAL TAPE DRIVE (164xx)

164xx	A fault has been detected in the tape drive—replace the tape drive

6157 STREAMING TAPE DRIVE (165xx)

16520	Streaming tape-drive failure
16540	Tape-attachment adapter failure

PRIMARY TOKEN RING NETWORK ADAPTERS (166xx)

166xx	A fault has been detected with the network adapter—replace the network adapter

SECONDARY TOKEN RING NETWORK ADAPTERS (167xx)

167xx	A fault has been detected with the network adapter—replace the network adapter

PS/2 WIZARD ADAPTER (180xx)

18001	Interrupt-controller failure
18002	Incorrect timer count
18003	Timer-interrupt failure
18004	Sync-check interrupt failure
18005	Parity-check interrupt failure
18006	Access-error interrupt failure
18012	Bad checksum
18013	MCA bus-interface error
18021	Wizard memory-compare or parity error
18022	Wizard memory address-line error
18023	Dynamic RAM controller failure
18029	Wizard memory byte-enable error
18031	Wizard memory expansion-module compare or parity error
18032	Wizard memory expansion-module address-line error
18039	Wizard memory expansion-module byte-enable error

DBCS JAPANESE DISPLAY ADAPTER (185xx)

185xx	A fault has been detected in the display adapter—replace the adapter

80286 MEMORY EXPANSION OPTION MODULE (194xx)

194xx	A fault has been detected in the memory module—replace the memory module

IMAGE ADAPTER (200xx)

200xx	A fault has been detected in the image adapter—replace the image adapter

UNKNOWN SCSI DEVICES (208xx)

208xx	A fault has been detected in an unknown SCSI device—systematically isolate and replace the defective SCSI device

TABLE 15-1   IBM DIAGNOSTIC CODES (CONTINUED)

SCSI REMOVABLE DISK (209xx)

209xx   A fault has been detected in the SCSI removable disk—replace the removable disk

SCSI FIXED DISK (210xx)

210xx   A fault has been detected in the SCSI fixed disk—replace the fixed disk

OTHER ERRORS

I9990301	Hard-disk error
I9990302	Invalid hard-disk boot record
I9990305	No bootable device
I9990303	Bank-2 flash ROM checksum error

TROUBLESHOOTING WITH DIAGNOSTIC CODES

Now that you have an idea of the diagnostic areas that are covered and error codes you can expect to see, you should have an understanding of how to deal with those errors when they occur. Generally speaking, a PC can be divided down into a motherboard, expansion boards, drives, and a power supply—each area can be considered as a replaceable module. When an error code is generated, you can match the code to its description in Table 15-1. You should generally replace the failed module. For example, if a video adapter fails, it should be replaced. If a motherboard fails, it should be replaced; if a hard drive fails, it should be replaced; etc. The following notes will explain some of the finer points.

Motherboard notes   The motherboard manages virtually all of the PC's processing resources (i.e., DMAs, IRQs, memory, etc.). As a consequence, the motherboard is perhaps the most expensive module to replace. Before electing to replace the motherboard, be certain that the faulty component(s) cannot be swapped out. For example, the CPU, BIOS ROM, math co-processor, expansion memory (SIMMs), RTC/CMOS IC, and CMOS backup battery are almost always socket mounted. In fact, when you purchase a new motherboard, it typically comes without those socket-mounted elements. If an error message indicates that the CPU has failed, try another CPU. If the math co-processor appears to be defective, try a new MCP. Of course, if the defective element is hard-soldered to the motherboard, you should probably go ahead and order another motherboard, then simply transfer any of the socket-mounted devices from the old motherboard.

Memory notes   Memory plays a vital role in every PC—the CPU is useless unless memory is available to hold data and program instructions. Because even one bad bit can cause an error that might crash a system, memory is perhaps the most thoroughly tested area of a computer. From a troubleshooting standpoint, memory can often be divided into two areas, the memory located on the motherboard, and the memory added in the form of SIMMs. When a failure occurs in a SIMM, it is a simple matter to locate and replace the SIMM. If the fault is on the motherboard, you are often faced with the prospect of replacing the defective RAM IC(s), or (more frequently) replacing the entire motherboard.

Keyboard notes Not only is the keyboard the most popular and reliable input device for the PC, the keyboard controller IC is also in control of the A20 Gate, which allows the CPU to enter its "protected mode." While in the protected mode, a CPU can address memory above 1MB. When a problem is detected in the keyboard assembly itself, it is usually a quick-and-easy process to replace the keyboard assembly. When a problem is located outside of the keyboard itself (or a protected-mode fault is found), the keyboard controller IC on the motherboard has probably failed. On some motherboards, the keyboard controller is mounted in an IC socket, and can be replaced easily. Where the keyboard controller is hard-soldered to the motherboard, it will probably be easiest to simply replace the motherboard outright.

Video notes As you look over the error codes in Table 15-1, you might notice that sections are dedicated to older video standards, such as MDA and CGA. If you encounter a system with older video adapters that prove to be defective, it will be extremely difficult (if not impossible) to locate new replacement boards. As a result, you should expect to replace an older video board with one of the newer video adapters, such as VGA or SVGA, which offer backward compatibility to the older standards. Unfortunately, older video used TTL monitors, where VGA and SVGA adapters are designed for analog monitors. remember that it might be necessary to upgrade your customer's monitor as well as their video adapter.

Serial/parallel notes Diagnostics typically attempt to test any serial or parallel ports that can be identified. In the early days of PCs, serial and parallel ports were typically added as expansion boards. When such add-on ports fail, it is a simple matter to replace the defective board. With most of today's systems, however, at least one serial and parallel port are integrated right on the motherboard. When these built-in ports check bad, often little can be done, other then replace the motherboard outright. Also, if an error code indicates a fault outside of the port circuit (e.g., the modem or printer), always try a new cable between the port and peripheral first. If a new cable does not correct the problem, try replacing the suspect peripheral. Also remember that some test procedures require you to attach a loop-back plug (rather than connect a live peripheral).

Drive notes Diagnostics typically check the complete suite of floppy drives, hard drives, and even CD-ROM drives. However, you must realize that a drive system includes not only the drive itself, but its controller board. If a drive problem is indicated, you should automatically inspect the signal and power cables at the drive. A loose power connector or frayed signal cable can easily disable the drive. If in doubt, try a new signal cable (much less expensive than replacing a drive).

Of course, if a new cable fails to correct the fault, you must decide whether the drive or controller has failed. Often, the diagnostic error code will pinpoint the fault to either the drive or controller circuit for you. If the drive has failed, replace the drive. If the controller has failed, things can get a bit more complicated. If the controller is implemented as an expansion board, it is easy enough to replace, but be sure that the new controller has any jumpers and DIP switches set similarly to the defective controller. If the controller is incorporated on the motherboard, you might find yourself replacing the entire motherboard.

Beep Codes

When a fault is detected before the video system is initialized, errors are indicated with a series of beeps (or beep codes). Because each BIOS is a bit different, the accuracy, precision, and quality of error detection and reporting varies from BIOS to BIOS. Although most POST routines today follow a remarkably similar pattern, the reporting style can vary greatly. Some routines (such as AMI) generate a continuous string of beeps, and other routines (such as Phoenix) create short beep sequences. This part of the chapter is intended to help you understand and interpret beep codes produced by major BIOS makers:

- AMI (American Megatrends): Table 15-2
- AST: Table 15-3
- Compaq: Table 15-4
- IBM desktop: Table 15-5
- IBM ThinkPad: Table 15-6
- Mylex: Table 15-7
- Mylex 386: Table 15-8
- Phoenix Technologies: Table 15-9
- Quadtel: Table 15-10

TABLE 15-2 AMI BEEP CODES

BEEPS	ERROR MESSAGE
1s	*System RAM refresh failure* The *Programmable Interrupt Timer* (PIT) or *Programmable Interrupt Controller (PIC)* has probably failed. Replace the motherboard.
2s	*Memory parity error* A parity error has been detected in the first 64KB of RAM. The RAM IC is probably defective. Replace the memory or motherboard.
3s	*Base 64KB memory failure* A memory failure has been detected in the first 64KB of RAM. The RAM IC is probably defective. Replace the memory or motherboard.
4s	*System timer failure* The system clock/timer IC has failed.
5s	*CPU failure* The system CPU has failed. Try replacing the CPU or motherboard.
6s	*Gate A20 failure* The keyboard controller IC has failed, so Gate A20 is no longer available to switch the CPU into protected mode. Replace the keyboard controller or motherboard.
7s	*Exception error* The CPU has generated an exception error because of a fault in the CPU or some combination of motherboard conditions. Try replacing the motherboard.
8s	*Video memory read/write error* The system video adapter is missing or defective. Try replacing the video adapter.
9s	*ROM checksum error* The contents of the system BIOS ROM does not match the expected checksum value. The BIOS ROM is probably defective and should be replaced.
10s	*CMOS shutdown register read/write error* The shutdown register for the CMOS memory has failed. Try replacing the RTC/CMOS IC.
1l–3s	*Memory test failure* A fault has been detected in memory over 64KB. Replace the memory or the motherboard.

TABLE 15-2 AMI BEEP CODES (CONTINUED)

BEEPS	ERROR MESSAGE
1l–8s	*Display test failure* The display adapter is missing or defective. Replace the video adapter board. If the video adapter is on the motherboard, try replacing the motherboard.

Legend: l = long s = short

TABLE 15-3 AST BEEP CODES

BEEPS	ERROR MESSAGE
1s	*CPU register test failure* The CPU has failed. Try replacing the CPU or replace the motherboard.
2s	*Keyboard-controller buffer failure* The keyboard-controller IC has failed.
3s	*Keyboard-controller reset failure* The keyboard-controller IC or its associated circuitry has failed.
4s	*Keyboard-communication failure* The keyboard-controller IC or its associated circuitry has failed. Try replacing the keyboard assembly. Try replacing the motherboard.
5s	*Keyboard input port failure* The keyboard-controller IC has failed.
6s	*System-board chipset initialization failure* The chipset(s) used on the motherboard cannot be initialized. Either an element of the chipset(s) or the motherboard has failed.
9s	*BIOS ROM checksum error* The BIOS ROM has failed. Try replacing the BIOS ROM or replace the motherboard.
10s	*System timer test failure* The master system clock IC has failed.
11s	*ASIC register test failure* Motherboard circuitry has failed. Replace the motherboard.
12s	*CMOS RAM shutdown register failure* The RTC/CMOS IC has failed. Try replacing the RTC/CMOS IC or replace the motherboard.
1l	*DMA-controller 0 failure* The DMA-controller IC for channel 0 has failed.
1l–1s	*DMA-controller 1 failure* The DMA-controller IC for channel 1 has failed.
1l–2s	*Video vertical-retrace failure* The video adapter has failed. Replace the video-adapter board.
1l–3s	*Video memory-test failure* A fault has occured in video memory. Replace the video-adapter.
1l–4s	*Video-adapter test failure* The video adapter has failed. Replace the video-adapter board.
1l–5s	*64KB base-memory failure* A failure has occurred in the low 64KB of system RAM. Replace memory or replace the motherboard.
1l–6s	*Unable to load interrupt vectors* BIOS was unable to load interrupt vectors into low memory. Replace the motherboard.
1l–7s	*Unable to initialize video system* There is a defect in the video system. Replace the video adapter board. Replace the motherboard.
1l–8s	*Video memory failure* There is a defect in video memory. Replace the video adapter or replace the motherboard.

TABLE 15-4 COMPAQ BEEP CODES

BEEPS	ERROR MESSAGE
1s	*No error*
1l–1s	*BIOS ROM checksum error*
2s	*General error*
1l–2s	*Video adapter error*

TABLE 15-5 IBM DESKTOP BEEP CODES

BEEPS	ERROR MESSAGE
1s	*Start of test*
2s	*Initialization error*
1l–1s	*System-board error*
1l–2s	*Video-adapter error*
1l–3s	*EGA/VGA adapter error*
3l	*Keyboard-adapter error*
999s	*Power-supply error*

TABLE 15-6 IBM THINKPAD BEEP CODES

BEEPS/ERROR	ERROR MESSAGE
Continuous beeps	*System-board failure*
One beep and a blank, unreadable, or flashing LCD	*LCD connector problem* *LCD backlight inverter problem* *Video-adapter problem* *LCD-assembly failure* *System-board failure* *Power-supply (dc/dc) failure*
One beep, and message "Unable to access boot source"	*Boot-device (drive) failure* *System-board failure*
One long and two short beeps, and a blank or unreadable LCD	*System-board failure* *Video-adapter problem* *LCD-assembly failure*
One long beep followed by four short beeps each time the power switch is operated	*Low battery voltage* Connect the ac adapter or install a fully charged laptop battery
One beep every second (System is shutting down due to low battery voltage)	*Low battery voltage* Connect the ac adapter or install a fully charged battery (Allow the system to completely shut down before changing the battery)
Two short beeps with error codes	*POST error* (refer to Table 19-1 for error-code explanations)
Two short beeps with blank screen	*System-board failure*

TABLE 15-7 MYLEX BEEP CODES

BEEPS	ERROR MESSAGE
1	*Start of test*
2	*Video-adapter error*
3	*Keyboard-controller error*
4	*Keyboard error*
5	*PIC 0 error*
6	*PIC 1 error*
7	*DMA page-register error*
8	*RAM refresh error*
9	*RAM data error*
10	*RAM parity error*
11	*DMA controller-0 error*
12	*CMOS RAM error*
13	*DMA controller-1 error*
14	*CMOS RAM battery error*
15	*CMOS RAM checksum error*
16	*BIOS ROM checksum error*

TABLE 15-8 MYLEX 386 BEEP CODES

BEEPS	ERROR MESSAGE
1l	*Start of test*
2l	*Video-adapter fault (or adapter missing)*
1l–1s–1l	*Keyboard-controller error*
1l–2s–1l	*Keyboard error*
1l–3s–1l	*PIC 0 error*
1l–4s–1l	*PIC 1 error*
1l–5s–1l	*DMA page-register error*
1l–6s–1l	*RAM refresh error*
1l–7s–1l	*RAM data-test error*
1l–8s–1l	*RAM parity error*
1l–9s–1l	*DMA controller-1 error*
1l–10s–1l	*CMOS RAM error*
1l–11s–1l	*DMA controller-2 error*
1l–12s–1l	*CMOS RAM battery failure*
1l–13s–1l	*CMOS checksum failure*
1l–14s–1l	*BIOS ROM checksum failure*
>1l	*Multiple faults detected*

TABLE 15-9 PHOENIX BEEP CODES FOR ISA/MCA/EISA POST

BEEPS	ERROR MESSAGE
1–1–2	*CPU register test failure* The CPU has likely failed. Replace the CPU.
Low 1–1–2	*System board Select failure* The motherboard is suffering from an undetermined fault. Try replacing the motherboard.
1–1–3	*CMOS read/write failure* The RTC/CMOS IC has probably failed. Try replacing the RTC/CMOS IC.
Low 1–1–3	*Extended CMOS RAM failure* The extended portion of the RTC/CMOS IC has failed. Try replcing the RTC/CMOS IC.
1–1–4	BIOS ROM checksum error The BIOS ROM has probably failed.
1–2–1	*Programmable–Interval Timer (PIT) failure* The PIT has probably failed.
1–2–2	DMA initialization failure The DMA controller has probably failed.
1–2–3	DMA page–register read/write failure The DMA controller has probably failed.
1–3–1	*RAM refresh failure* The refresh controller has failed.
1–3–2	*64KB RAM test disabled* The test of the first 64KB of system RAM could not begin. Try replacing the motherboard.
1–3–3	*First 64KB RAM IC or data line failure* The first RAM IC has failed.
1–3–4	*First 64KB odd/even logic failure* The first RAM control logic has failed.
1–4–1	*Address–line failure 64KB of RAM.*
1–4–2	*Parity failure first 64KB or RAM* The first RAM IC has failed.
1–4–3	*EISA failsafe timer test fault* Replace the motherboard.
1–4–4	*EISA NMI port 462 test failure* Replace the motherboard.
2–1–1	*Bit–0 first–64KB RAM failure* This data bit in the first RAM IC has failed.
2–1–2	*Bit–1 first–64KB RAM failure*
2–1–3	*Bit–2 first–64KB RAM failure*
2–1–4	*Bit–3 first–64KB RAM failure*
2–2–1	*Bit–4 first–64KB RAM failure*
2–2–2	*Bit–5 first–64KB RAM failure*
2–2–3	*Bit–6 first–64KB RAM failure*
2–2–4	*Bit–7 first–64KB RAM failure*
2–3–1	*Bit–8 first–64KB RAM failure*
2–3–2	*Bit–9 first–64KB RAM failure*
2–3–3	*Bit–10 first–64KB RAM failure*
2–3–4	*Bit–11 first–64KB RAM failure*
2–4–1	*Bit–12 first–64KB RAM failure*
2–4–2	*Bit–13 first–64KB RAM failure*
2–4–3	*Bit–14 first–64KB RAM failure*
2–4–4	*Bit–15 first–64KB RAM failure*
3–1–1	*Slave DMA–register failure* The DMA controller has probably failed.
3–1–2	*Master DMA–register failure* The DMA controller has probably failed.
3–1–3	*Master–interrupt mask–register failure* The interrupt controller has probably failed.
3–1–4	*Slave–interrupt mask–register failure* The interrupt controller has probably failed.
3–2–2	*Interrupt vector–loading error* BIOS is unable to load the interrupt vectors into low RAM. Replace the motherboard.
3–2–3	Reserved

TABLE 15-9 PHOENIX BEEP CODES FOR ISA/MCA/EISA POST (CONTINUED)

BEEPS	ERROR MESSAGE
3–2–4	*Keyboard–controller test failure* The keyboard controller has failed.
3–3–1	*CMOS RAM power bad* Try replacing the CMOS backup battery. Try replacing the RTC/CMOS IC. Replace the motherboard.
3–3–2	CMOS configuration error The CMOS configuration has failed. Restore the configuration. Replace the CMOS backup battery. Replace the RTC/CMOS IC. Replace the motherboard.
3–3–3	Reserved
3–3–4	*Video–memory test failed* There is a problem with the video memory. Replace video memory or replace the video–adapter board.
3–4–1	*Video–initialization test failure* There is a problem with the video system. Replace the video adapter.
4–2–1	*Timer–tick failure* The system timer IC has failed.
4–2–1	*Shutdown–test failure* The CMOS IC has failed.
4–2–3	*Gate A20 failure* The keyboard controller has probably failed.
4–2–4	*Unexpected interrupt in protected mode* There is a problem with the CPU.
4–3–1	*RAM test–address failure* System RAM addressing circuitry has failed.
4–3–3	*Interval–timer channel–2 failure* The system timer IC has probably failed.
4–3–4	*Time–of–day clock failure* The RTC/CMOS IC has failed.
4–4–1	*Serial–port test failure* A fault has developed in the serial–port circuit.
4–4–2	*Parallel–port test failure* A fault has developed in the parallel–port circuit.
4–4–3	*Math co–processor failure* Try replacing the math co–processor.

TABLE 15-10 QUADTEL BEEP CODES

BEEPS	ERROR MESSAGE
1s	Start of test
2s	CMOS IC error
1l–2s	Video-controller error
1l>2s	Peripheral-controller error

POST Codes

During initialization, the POST performs a self-diagnostic routine designed to check key areas of the PC for major faults. When an error is detected early in the test cycle, you will probably hear a series of beep codes (Tables 15-1 through 15-10). However, BIOS makers soon realized that most beep-code sequences are not terribly specific; a beep code can often represent any one of a number of possible failures. To make more specific information available to technicians, POST procedures are designed to output a single hexadecimal byte to I/O port 80h (or other suitable I/O address) as each step in the initialization is started or completed. If the PC should fail at any point during start-up, the code at port 80h represents the last step to be successfully completed. By knowing the full sequence of I/O POST codes generated by a BIOS, a technician can quickly determine the test step which failed—and thus pinpoint the fault with great accuracy. This part of the chapter presents the POST sequences for popular PC BIOS versions.

If you're looking for a PC-based POST code reference, try the Post Code Master (PCM105.ZIP) on the companion CD.

INTERPRETING THE POST CODES

When working with POST codes, it is important to understand that not all codes are the direct result of a test. Many codes simply indicate that a CPU is attempting to initialize various areas of the PC. These types of codes are known as *checkpoints*, which simply show that certain initialization steps are being completed. Just because you see a hexadecimal code does not necessarily mean that anything has been tested.

Also remember that few listings of BIOS codes are actually complete. With the exception of publicly available code lists (for the IBM PC, XT, and AT), most BIOS manufacturers have been unwilling to release the full context of their POST codes. As a result, POST code indexes (such as those in this book) are often compilations of data extracted from a number of different sources. If you encounter a POST code that is not covered in this book, your best course is usually to contact the BIOS manufacturer directly for specific details (and let Dynamic Learning Systems know so that we can get it into the next update for this book).

Another area of confusion can arise when the POST process starts and ends. This can sometimes confuse a novice technician. When a system is first started with a POST board installed, the POST display is typically blank—this is normal for the initial moments after PC power is applied. After that, codes should begin flashing across the seven-segment LEDs. If the LEDs remain blank, you can assume that no data is reaching the card. In that event, be sure that your system produces POST codes (a few systems do not), and see that the board's I/O address is set properly (some systems use I/O ports other than 80h). After the POST is complete, a system will attempt to boot an operating system. Ordinarily, the last code on the display is 00h or FFh, so don't worry if either of these codes remains on the seven-segment display. In some cases—depending on the particular BIOS—some other code might be left in the display. If the system appears to boot normally, you rarely need to worry about this. Also remember that not all tests are performed in numerical order. You will find that the POST code sequences in many of the following tables are a bit mixed, so look over each table carefully:

- ACER: Table 15-11
- ALR: Table 15-12
- AMI (prior to 04/1990): Table 15-13
- AMI (after 04/1990): Table 15-14
- AMI version 2.2x: Table 15-15
- AMI Plus BIOS: Table 15-16
- AMI Color BIOS: Table 15-17
- AMI EZ-Flex BIOS: Table 15-18
- Arche Legacy: Table 15-19
- AST BIOS: Table 15-20
- AT&T BIOS: Table 15-21

- Award XT BIOS: Table 15-22
- Award XT BIOS 3.1: Table 15-23
- Award AT BIOS 3.0: Table 15-24
- Award AT BIOS 3.1: Table 15-25
- Award AT BIOS 3.3: Table 15-26
- Award AT/EISA BIOS 4.0: Table 15-27
- Award EISA BIOS: Table 15-28
- Award Plug-and-Play BIOS: Table 15-29
- Award EliteBIOS 4.5x: Table 15-30
- Chips & Technologies BIOS: Table 15-31
- Compaq BIOS (general): Table 15-32
- Compaq i286 Deskpro BIOS: Table 15-33
- Compaq i386 Deskpro BIOS: Table 15-34
- Compaq i486 Deskpro BIOS: Table 15-35
- Compaq Video BIOS: Table 15-36
- Dell BIOS: Table 15-37
- DTK BIOS: Table 15-38
- Eurosoft/Mylex BIOS: Table 15-39
- Eurosoft 4.71 BIOS: Table 15-40
- Mylex BIOS: Table 15-41
- Faraday A-Tease BIOS: Table 15-42
- IBM PC/XT BIOS: Table 15-43
- IBM PC/AT BIOS: Table 15-44
- IBM PS/2 BIOS: Table 15-45
- Landmark JumpStart XT BIOS: Table 15-46
- Landmark JumpStart AT BIOS: Table 15-47
- Landmark SuperSoft AT BIOS: Table 15-48
- Microid Research 1.0A BIOS: Table 15-49
- Microid Research (modern): Table 15-50
- Microid Research 3.4x BIOS: Table 15-51
- NCR PC6 (XT) BIOS: Table 15-52
- NCR AT BIOS: Table 15-53
- NCR PC916 BIOS: Table 15-54
- Olivetti 1076/AT&T BIOS: Table 15-55
- Olivetti M20 BIOS: Table 15-56
- Olivetti M24/AT&T BIOS: Table 15-57
- Olivetti PS/2 BIOS: Table 15-58
- Philips BIOS: Table 15-59
- Phoenix XT 2.52 BIOS: Table 15-60
- Phoenix ISA/EISA/MCA BIOS: Table 15-61
- PhoenixBIOS 4.0 BIOS: Table 15-62
- Quadtel XT BIOS: Table 15-63
- Quadtel AT 3.00 BIOS: Table 15-64
- Tandon Type A BIOS: Table 15-65
- Tandon Type B BIOS: Table 15-66
- Tandon i486 EISA BIOS: Table 15-67
- Zenith Orion 4.1E BIOS: Table 15-68

TABLE 15-11 POST CODES FOR ACER BIOS

HEX CODE	DESCRIPTION
04	POST start
08	Shutdown condition 0
0C	Testing the BIOS ROM checksum
10	Testing the CMOS RAM shutdown byte
14	Testing the DMA controller
18	Initializing the system timer
1C	Testing the memory-refresh system
1E	Determining the memory type
20	Testing the low 128KB of memory
24	Testing the 8042 keyboard-controller IC
28	Testing the CPU descriptor instruction
2C	Testing the 8259 interrupt-controller IC
30	Setting up a temporary interrupt
34	Configure the BIOS-interrupt vectors and routines
38	Testing the CMOS RAM
3C	Determining the memory size
40	Shutdown condition 1
44	Initializing the video BIOS ROM
45	Setting up and testing RAM
46	Testing cache memory and controller
48	Testing memory
4C	Shutdown condition 3
50	Shutdown condition 2
54	Shutdown condition 7
58	Shutdown condition 6
5C	Testing the keyboard and auxilliary I/O
60	Setting up BIOS interrupt routines
64	Testing the real-time clock
68	Testing the diskette
6C	Testing the hard drive
70	Testing the parallel port
74	Testing the serial port
78	Setting the time of day
7C	Detect and invoke any optional ROMs
80	Checking for the math co-processor
84	Initializing the keyboard
88	Initializing the system (step 1)
8C	Initializing the system (step 2)
90	Boot the operating system
94	Shutdown condition 5
98	Shutdown condition A
9C	Shutdown condition B

TABLE 15-12 POST CODES FOR ALR BIOS

CODE	DESCRIPTION
01	CPU register test in progress
02	Real-time clock write/read failure
03	ROM BIOS checksum failure
04	Programmable internal timer failure (or no video card)
05	DMA initialization failure
06	DMA page register write/read failure
08	RAM-refresh verification failure
09	1st 64KB RAM test in progress
0A	1st 64KB RAM chip or data line multi-bit failure
0B	1st 64KB RAM odd/even logic failure
0C	Address line failure 1st 64KB RAM
0D	Parity failure 1st 64KB RAM
10–1F	Bit 0–15 64KB RAM failure
20	Slave DMA-register failure
21	Master DMA-register failure
22	Master-interrupt mask-register failure
23	Slave-interrupt mask-register failure
25	Interrupt vector loading in progress
27	Keyboard-controller test failure
28	RTC power failure and checksum calculation in progress
29	Real-time clock-configuration validation in progress
2B	Screen-memory test failure
2C	Screen-initialization failure
2D	Screen-retrace test failure.
2E	Search for video ROM in progress
30	Screen believed operational or screen believed running with video ROM
31	Monochrome display believed operable
32	Color display (40 column) believed operable
33	Color display (80 column) believed operable

TABLE 15-13 POST CODES FOR AMIT BIOS (PRIOR TO APRIL 1990)

CODE	DESCRIPTION
01	NMI is disabled and the i286 register test is about to start
02	i286 register test has passed
03	ROM BIOS checksum test (32KB from F8000h) passed OK
04	8259 PIC has initialized OK
05	CMOS interrupt disabled
06	Video system disabled and the system timer checks OK

TABLE 15-13 POST CODES FOR AMIT BIOS (PRIOR TO APRIL 1990) (CONTINUED)

CODE	DESCRIPTION
07	8253/4 programmable-interval timer test OK
08	Delta counter channel 2 OK
09	Delta counter channel 1 OK
0A	Delta counter channel 0 OK
0B	Parity status cleared
0C	The refresh and system timer check OK
0D	Refresh check OK
0E	Refresh period checks OK
10	Ready to start 64KB base memory test
11	Address-line test OK
12	64KB base memory test OK
13	System-interrupt vectors initialized
14	8042 keyboard controller checks OK
15	CMOS read/write test OK
16	CMOS checksum and battery OK
17	Monochrome video mode OK
18	CGA color mode set OK
19	Attempting to pass control to video ROM at C0000h
1A	Returned from video ROM
1B	Display-memory R/W test OK
1C	Display-memory R/W alternative test OK
1D	Video-retrace test OK
1E	Global equipment byte set for proper video operation
1F	Ready to initialize video system
20	Video test OK
21	Video display OK
22	The power-on message is displayed
30	Ready to start the virtual-mode memory test
31	Virtual memory mode test started
32	CPU has switched to virtual mode
33	Testing the memory address lines
34	Testing the memory address lines
35	Lower 1MB of RAM found
36	Memory-size computation checks OK
37	Memory test in progress
38	Memory below 1MB is initialized
39	Memory above 1MB is initialized
3A	Memory size is displayed
3B	Ready to test the lower 1MB of RAM
3C	Memory test of lower 1MB OK
3D	Memory test above 1MB OK
3E	Ready to shutdown for real-mode testing

TABLE 15-13 POST CODES FOR AMIT BIOS (PRIOR TO APRIL 1990) (CONTINUED)

CODE	DESCRIPTION
3F	Shutdown OK—now in real mode
40	Ready to disable gate A20
41	A20 line disabled successfully
42	Ready to start DMA-controller test
4E	Address line test OK
4F	System still in real mode
50	DMA page-register test OK
51	Starting DMA controller-1 register test
52	DMA controller-1 test passed, starting DMA controller-2 register test
53	DMA controller-2 test passed
54	Ready to test latch on DMA controller 1 and 2
55	DMA controller 1 and 2 latch test OK
56	DMA controller 1 and 2 configured OK
57	8259 PIC initialized OK
58	8259 PIC mask register check OK
59	Master 8259 PIC mask register OK
5A	Ready to check timer interrupts
5B	Timer-interrupt check OK
5C	Ready to test keyboard interrupt
5D	Error detected in timer or keyboard interrupt
5E	8259 PIC-controller error
5F	8259 PIC-controller OK
70	Start of keyboard test
71	Keyboard controller OK
72	Keyboard test OK
73	Keyboard global initialization OK
74	Floppy setup ready to start
75	Floppy-controller setup OK
76	Hard-disk setup ready to start
77	Hard-disk controller setup OK
79	Ready to initialize timer data
7A	Verifying CMOS battery power
7B	CMOS battery verified OK
7D	Analyzing CMOS RAM size
7E	CMOS memory size updated
7F	Send control to adapter ROM
80	Enable the Setup routine if <Delete> is pressed
82	Printer data initialization is OK
83	RS-232 data initialization is OK
84	80x87 check and test OK
85	Display any soft-error message
86	Give control to ROM at E0000h

TABLE 15-13 POST CODES FOR AMIT BIOS (PRIOR TO APRIL 1990) (CONTINUED)

CODE	DESCRIPTION
87	Return from system ROM
00	Call the INT19 boot loader

TABLE 15-14 POST CODES FOR AMI BIOS (AFTER APRIL 1990)

CODE	DESCRIPTION
01	NMI is disabled and the i286 register test is about to start
02	i286 register test has passed
03	ROM BIOS checksum test (32KB from F8000h) passed OK
04	Passed keyboard controller test with and without mouse
05	Chipset initialized . . . DMA and interrupt controller disabled
06	Video system disabled and the system timer checks OK
07	8254 programmable interval timer initialized
08	Delta counter channel-2 initialization complete
09	Delta counter channel-1 initialization complete
0A	Delta counter channel-0 initialization complete
0B	Refresh started
0C	System timer started
0D	Refresh check OK
10	Ready to start 64KB base memory test
11	Address-line test OK
12	64KB base-memory test OK
15	ISA BIOS interrupt vectors initialized
17	Monochrome video mode OK
18	CGA color mode set OK
19	Attempting to pass control to video ROM at C0000h
1A	Returned from video ROM
1B	Shadow RAM enabled
1C	Display-memory R/W test OK
1D	Alternative display-memory R/W test OK
1E	Global equipment byte set for proper video operation
1F	Ready to initialize video system
20	Finished setting video mode
21	ROM type 27256 verified
22	The power-on message is displayed
30	Ready to start the virtual-mode memory test
31	Virtual-memory mode test started
32	CPU has switched to virtual mode
33	Testing the memory address lines
34	Testing the memory address lines

TABLE 15-14 POST CODES FOR AMI BIOS (AFTER APRIL 1990) (CONTINUED)

CODE	DESCRIPTION
35	Lower 1MB of RAM found
36	Memory-size computation checks OK
37	Memory test in progress
38	Memory below 1MB is initialized
39	Memory above 1MB is initialized
3A	Memory size is displayed
3B	Ready to test the lower 1MB of RAM
3C	Memory test of lower 1MB OK
3D	Memory test above 1MB OK
3E	Ready to shutdown for real-mode testing
3F	Shutdown OK—now in real mode
40	Cache memory now on . . . Ready to disable gate A20
41	A20 line disabled successfully
42	i486 internal cache turned on
43	Ready to start DMA controller test
50	DMA page-register test OK
51	Starting DMA controller-1 register test
52	DMA controller-1 test passed, starting DMA controller-2 register test
53	DMA controller-2 test passed
54	Ready to test latch on DMA controller 1 and 2
55	DMA controller 1 and 2 latch test OK
56	DMA controller 1 and 2 configured OK
57	8259 PIC initialized OK
70	Start of keyboard test
71	Keyboard controller OK
72	Keyboard test OK . . . Starting mouse interface test
73	Keyboard and mouse global initialization OK
74	Display Setup prompt . . . Floppy setup ready to start
75	Floppy-controller setup OK
76	Hard-disk setup ready to start
77	Hard-disk controller setup OK
79	Ready to initialize timer data
7A	Timer-data area initialized
7B	CMOS battery verified OK
7D	Analyzing CMOS RAM size
7E	CMOS memory size updated
7F	Enable Setup routine if <Delete> is pressed
80	Send control to adapter ROM at C800h to DE00h
81	Return from adapter ROM
82	Printer data initialization is OK
83	RS-232 data initialization is OK
84	80×87 check and test OK

TABLE 15-14 POST CODES FOR AMI BIOS (AFTER APRIL 1990) (CONTINUED)

CODE	DESCRIPTION
85	Display any soft-error message
86	Give control to ROM at E0000h
A0	Program the cache SRAM
A1	Check for external cache
A2	Initialize EISA adapter card slots
A3	Test extended NMI in EISA system
00	Call the INT19 boot loader

TABLE 15-15 POST CODES FOR AMI BIOS VERSION 2.2X

CODE	DESCRIPTION
00	Flag test (the CPU is being tested)
03	Register test
06	System hardware initialization
09	Test BIOS ROM checksum
0C	Page-register test
0F	8254 timer test
12	Memory-refresh initialization
15	8237 DMA-controller test
18	8237 DMA-controller initialization
1B	8259 PIC initialization
1E	9259 PIC test
21	Memory-refresh test
24	Base 64KB address test
27	Base 64KB memory test
2A	8742 keyboard test
2D	MC145818 CMOS IC test
30	Start the protected-mode test
33	Start the memory-sizing test
36	First protected-mode test passed
39	First protected-mode test failed
3C	CPU-speed calculation
3F	Reading the 8742 hardware switches
42	Initializing the interrupt vector area
45	Verifying the CMOS configuration
48	Testing and initializing the video system
4B	Testing unexpected interrupts
4E	Starting second protected-mode test
51	Verifying the LDT instruction
54	Verifying the TR instruction

TABLE 15-15 POST CODES FOR AMI BIOS VERSION 2.2X (CONTINUED)	
CODE	DESCRIPTION
57	Verifying the LSL instruction
5A	Verifying the LAR instruction
5D	Verifying the VERR instruction
60	Address-line A20 test
63	Testing unexpected exceptions
66	Starting the third protected-mode test
69	Address-line test
6A	Scan DDNIL bits for null pattern
6C	System memory test
6F	Shadow memory test
72	Extended memory test
75	Verify the memory configuration
78	Display configuration error messages
7B	Copy system BIOS to shadow memory
7E	8254 clock test
81	MC46818 real-time clock test
84	Keyboard test
87	Determining the keyboard type
8A	Stuck key test
8D	Initializing hardware interrupt vectors
90	Testing the math co-processor
93	Finding available COM ports
96	Finding available LPT ports
99	Initializing the BIOS data area
9C	Fixed/floppy-disk controller test
9F	Floppy-disk test
A2	Fixed-disk test
A5	Check for external ROMs
A8	System-key lock test
A#	F1 error message test
AE	System boot initialization
B1	Call Int 19 boot loader

TABLE 15-16 POST CODES FOR AMI PLUS BIOS	
CODE	DESCRIPTION
01	NMI disabled
02	CPU register test complete
03	ROM checksum tests OK
04	8259 PIC initialization OK

TABLE 15-16 POST CODES FOR AMI PLUS BIOS (CONTINUED)

CODE	DESCRIPTION
05	CMOS interrupt disabled
06	System timer (PIT) OK
07	PIC channel 0 test OK
08	Delta count channel (DMA) 2 test OK
09	Delta count channel (DMA) 1 test OK
0A	Delta count channel (DMA) 0 test OK
0B	Parity status cleared (DMA/PIT)
0C	Refresh and system time check OK (DMA/PIT)
0D	Refresh link toggling OK (DMA/PIT)
0E	Refresh period on/off 50% OK (RAM IC or address line)
10	Ready to start 64KB base memory test
11	Address-line test OK
12	64KB base memory test OK
13	Interrupt vectors initialized
14	8042 keyboard-controller test
15	CMOS read/write test OK
16	CMOS checksum and battery test
17	Monochrome mode set OK (6845 IC)
18	CGA mode set OK (6845 IC)
19	Checking video ROM
1A	Optional video ROM checks OK
1B	Display memory R/W test OK
1C	Alternate display memory checks OK
1D	Video retrace check OK
1E	Global byte set for video OK (video adapter)
1F	Mode set for mono/color OK (video adapter)
20	Video test OK
21	Video display OK
22	Power-on message display OK
30	Ready for virtual-mode memory test
31	Starting virtual-mode memory test
32	CPU now in virtual mode
33	Memory address-line test
34	Memory address-line test
35	Memory below 1MB calculated
36	Memory-size computation OK
37	Memory test in progress
38	Memory initialization below 1MB complete
39	Memory initialization above 1MB complete
3A	Display memory size
3B	Ready to start memory below 1MB
3C	Memory test below 1MB OK

TABLE 15-16 POST CODES FOR AMI PLUS BIOS (CONTINUED)

CODE	DESCRIPTION
3D	Memory test above 1MB OK
3E	Ready to switch to real mode
3F	Shutdown successful
40	Ready to disable A20 gate (8042 IC)
41	A20 gate disabled (8042 IC)
42	Ready to test DMA controller (8237 DMA IC)
4E	Address-line test OK
4F	CPU now in real mode
50	DMA page-register test OK
51	DMA unit-1 base register OK
52	DMA unit-1 channel OK
53	DMA unit-2 base register OK
54	DMA unit-2 channel OK
55	Latch test for both DMA units OK
56	DMA units 1 and 2 initialized OK
57	8259 PIC initialization complete
58	8259 PIC mask register OK
59	Master 8259 PIC mask register OK
5A	Check timer and keyboard interrupt
5B	PIT timer interrupt OK
5C	Ready to test keyboard interrupt
5D	Error . . . timer/keyboard interrupt
5E	8259 PIC error
5F	8259 PIC test OK
70	Start the keyboard test
71	Keyboard test OK
72	Keyboard test OK
73	Keyboard global data initialized (8042 IC)
74	Ready to start floppy-controller setup
75	Floppy-controller setup OK
76	Ready to start hard-drive controller setup
77	Hard-drive controller setup OK
79	Ready to initialize timer data
7A	Verifying CMOS battery power
7B	CMOS battery verification complete
7D	Analyze test results for memory
7E	CMOS memory-size update OK
7F	Check for optional ROM at C0000h
80	Keyboard checked for Setup keystroke
81	Optional ROM control OK
82	Printer ports initialized OK
83	Serial ports initialized OK

TABLE 15-16 POST CODES FOR AMI PLUS BIOS (CONTINUED)

CODE	DESCRIPTION
84	80×87 test OK
85	Ready to display any soft errors
86	Send control to system ROM E0000h
87	System ROM E0000h check complete
00	Call Int. 19 boot loader

TABLE 15-17 POST CODES FOR AMI COLOR BIOS

CODE	DESCRIPTION
01	CPU flag test
02	Power-on delay
03	Chipset initialization
04	Hard/soft reset
05	ROM enable
06	ROM BIOS checksum
07	8042 KBC test
08	8042 KBC test
09	8042 KBC test
0A	8042 KBC test
0B	8042 protected-mode test
0C	8042 KBC test
0D	8042 KBC test
0E	CMOS checksum test
0F	CMOS initialization
10	CMOS/RTC status OK
11	DMA/PIC disable
12	DMA/PIC initialization
13	Chipset and memory initialization
14	8254 PIT test
15	PIT channel-2 test
16	PIT channel-1 test
17	PIT channel-0 test
18	Memory-refresh test (PIT IC)
19	Memory-refresh test (PIT IC)
1A	Check 15-μs refresh (PIT IC)
1B	Check 30-μs refresh (PIT IC)
20	Base 64KB memory test
21	Base 64KB memory parity test
22	Memory read/write test
23	BIOS vector table initialization

TABLE 15-17 POST CODES FOR AMI COLOR BIOS (CONTINUED)

CODE	DESCRIPTION
24	BIOS vector table initialization
25	Check of 8042 KBC
26	Global data for KBC set
27	Video-mode test
28	Monochrome-mode test
29	CGA-mode test
2A	Parity-enable test
2B	Check for optional ROMs in the system
2C	Check video ROM
2D	Reinitialize the main chipset
2E	Test video memory
2F	Test video memory
30	Test video adapter
31	Test alternate video memory
32	Test alternate video adapter
33	Video-mode test
34	Video-mode set
35	Initialize the BIOS ROM data area
36	Power-on message display
37	Power-on message display
38	Read cursor position
39	Display cursor reference
3A	Display Setup start message
40	Start protected-mode test
41	Build descriptor tables
42	CPU enters protected mode
43	Protected-mode interrupt enable
44	Check descriptor tables
45	Check memory size
46	Memory read/write test
47	Base 640KB memory test
48	Check 640KB memory size
49	Check extended memory size
4A	Verify CMOS extended memory
4B	Check for soft/hard reset
4C	Clear extended memory locations
4D	Update CMOS memory size
4E	Display base RAM size
4F	Perform memory test on base 640KB
50	Update CMOS RAM size
51	Perform extended memory test
52	Resize extended memory

TABLE 15-17 POST CODES FOR AMI COLOR BIOS (CONTINUED)

CODE	DESCRIPTION
53	Return CPU to real mode
54	Restore CPU registers for real mode
55	Disable the A20 gate
56	Recheck the BIOS vectors
57	BIOS vector check complete
58	Display the Setup start message
59	Perform DMA and PIT test
60	Perform DMA page-register test
61	Perform DMA #1 test
62	Perform DMA #2 test
63	Check BIOS data area
64	BIOS data area checked
65	Initialize DMA ICs
66	Perform 8259 PIC initialization
67	Perform keyboard test
80	Keyboard reset
81	Perform stuck key and batch test (keyboard)
82	Run 8042 KBC test
83	Perform lock key check
84	Compare memory size with CMOS
85	Perform password/soft-error check
86	Run CMOS equipment check
87	CMOS setup test
88	Reinitialize the main chipset
89	Display the power-on message
8A	Display the wait and mouse check
8B	Attempt to shadow any option ROMs
8C	Initialize XCMOS settings
8D	Rest hard/floppy disks
8E	Compare floppy setup to CMOS
8F	Initialize the floppy-disk controller
90	Compare hard-disk setup to CMOS
91	Initialize the hard-disk controller
92	Check the BIOS data table
93	BIOS data-table check complete
94	Set memory size
95	Verify the display memory
96	Clear all interrupts
97	Check any optional ROMs
98	Clear all interrupts
99	Setup timer data
9A	Locate and check serial ports

TABLE 15-17 POST CODES FOR AMI COLOR BIOS (CONTINUED)

CODE	DESCRIPTION
99	Setup timer data
9A	Locate and check serial ports
9B	Clear all interrupts
9C	Perform the math co-processor test
9D	Clear all interrupts
9E	Perform an extended keyboard check
9F	Set the NumLock on the keyboard
A0	Keyboard reset
A1	Cache memory test
A2	Display any soft errors
A3	Set typematic rate
A4	Set memory wait states
A5	Clear the display
A6	Enable parity and NMI
A7	Clear all interrupts
A8	Turn over system control to the ROM at E0000
A9	Clear all interrupts
AA	Display configuration
00	Call Int. 19 boot loader

TABLE 15-18 POST CODES FOR AMI EZ-FLEX BIOS

CODE	DESCRIPTION
01	NMI disabled . . . starting CPU flag test
02	Power-on delay
03	Chipset initialization
04	Check keyboard for hard/soft reset
05	ROM enable
06	ROM BIOS checksum
07	8042 KBC test
08	8042 KBC test
09	8042 KBC test
0A	8042 KBC test
0B	8042 protected-mode test
0C	8042 KBC test
0D	Test CMOS RAM shutdown register
0E	CMOS checksum test
0F	CMOS initialization
10	CMOS/RTC status OK

TABLE 15-18 POST CODES FOR AMI EZ-FLEX BIOS (CONTINUED)

CODE	DESCRIPTION
11	DMA/PIC disable
12	Disable video display
13	Chipset and memory initialization
14	8254 PIT test
15	PIT channel-2 test
16	PIT channel-1 test
17	PIT channel-0 test
18	Memory-refresh test (PIT IC)
19	Memory-refresh test (PIT IC)
1A	Check 15-μs refresh (PIT IC)
1B	Test 64KB base memory
20	Test address lines
21	Base 64KB memory parity test
22	Memory read/write test
23	Perform any setups needed prior to vector table initialization
24	BIOS vector table initialization in lower 1KB of system RAM
25	Check of 8042 KBC
26	Global data for KBC set
27	Perform any setups needed after vector table initialization
28	Monochrome-mode test
29	CGA-mode test
2A	Parity-enable test
2B	Check for optional ROMs in the system
2C	Check video ROM
2D	Determine if EGA/VGA is installed
2E	Test video memory (EGA/VGA not installed)
2F	Test video memory
30	Test video adapter
31	Test alternate video memory
32	Test alternate video adapter
33	Video-mode test
34	Video-mode set
35	Initialize the BIOS ROM data area
36	Set cursor for power-on message display
37	Display power-on message
38	Read cursor position
39	Display cursor reference
3A	Display Setup start message
40	Start protected-mode test
41	Build descriptor tables
42	CPU enters protected mode
43	Protected-mode interrupt enable

TABLE 15-18 POST CODES FOR AMI EZ-FLEX BIOS (CONTINUED)

CODE	DESCRIPTION
44	Check descriptor tables
45	Check memory size
46	Memory read/write test
47	Base 640KB memory test
48	Find amount of memory below 1MB
49	Find amount of memory above 1MB
4A	Check ROM BIOS data area
4B	Clear memory below 1MB for soft reset
4C	Clear memory above 1MB for soft reset
4D	Update CMOS memory size
4E	Display base 64KB memory test
4F	Perform memory test on base 640KB
50	Update RAM size for shadow operation
51	Perform extended-memory test
52	Ready to return to real mode
53	Return CPU to real mode
54	Restore CPU registers for real mode
55	Disable the A20 gate
56	Recheck the BIOS data area
57	BIOS data-area check complete
58	Display the Setup start message
59	Perform DMA page-register test
60	Verify display memory
61	Perform DMA #1 test
62	Perform DMA #2 test
63	Check BIOS data area
64	BIOS data area checked
65	Initialize DMA ICs
66	Perform 8259 PIC initialization
67	Perform keyboard test
80	Keyboard reset
81	Perform stuck key and batch test (keyboard)
82	Run 8042 KBC test
83	Perform lock-key check
84	Compare memory size with CMOS
85	Perform password/soft-error check
86	Run CMOS equipment check
87	Run CMOS setup, if selected
88	Reinitialize the main chipset after setup
89	Display the power-on message
8A	Display the wait and mouse check
8B	Attempt to shadow any option ROMs

TABLE 15-18 POST CODES FOR AMI EZ-FLEX BIOS (CONTINUED)

CODE	DESCRIPTION
8C	Initialize system per CMOS settings
8D	Rest hard/floppy disks
8E	Compare floppy setup to CMOS
8F	Initialize the floppy-disk controller
90	Compare hard-disk setup to CMOS
91	Initialize the hard-disk controller
92	Check the BIOS data table
93	BIOS data-table check complete
94	Set memory size
95	Verify the display memory
96	Clear all interrupts
97	Check any optional ROMs
98	Clear all interrupts
99	Setup timer data
9A	Locate and check serial ports
9B	Clear all interrupts
9C	Perform the math co-processor test
9D	Clear all interrupts
9E	Perform an extended keyboard check
9F	Set the NumLock on the keyboard
A0	Keyboard reset
A1	Cache memory test
A2	Display any soft errors
A3	Set typematic rate
A4	Set memory-wait states
A5	Clear the display
A6	Enable parity and NMI
A7	Clear all interrupts
A8	Turn over system control to the ROM at E0000
A9	Clear all interrupts
AA	Display configuration
00	Call Int. 19 boot loader

TABLE 15-19 POST CODES FOR ARCHE LEGACY BIOS

CODE	DESCRIPTION
01	Disable the NMI and test CPU registers
02	Verify the BIOS ROM checksum (32KB at F8000h)
03	Initialize the KBC and CMOS RAM
04	Disable the DMA and PIC . . . est the CMOS RAM interrupt

TABLE 15-19 POST CODES FOR ARCHE LEGACY BIOS (CONTINUED)

CODE	DESCRIPTION
05	Reset the video controller
06	Test the 8254 PIT
07	Test delta-count timer channel 2
08	Test delta-count timer channel 1
09	Test delta-count timer channel 0
0A	Test parity circuit and turn on refresh
0B	Enable parity-check and test system timer
0C	Test refresh trace link toggle
0D	Test refresh timing synchronization
10	Disable cache and shadow memory . . . test the 64KB base memory
11	Perform 64KB memory R/W test
12	Initialize interrupt vector table in lower 1KB of RAM
14	Test CMOS RAM shutdown register . . . disable DMA and interrupt controllers
15	Test CMOS RAM battery and checksum
16	Test for floppy drive, based on CMOS setup . . . initialize monochrome video
17	Initialize CGA video
18	Clear the parity status (if any)
19	Test for EGA/VGA video BIOS at C0000h and pass control
1A	Return from video ROM
1B	Test primary video adapter . . . test video memory
1C	Test secondary video adapter . . . test video memory
1D	Compare CMOS settings to video adapter
1E	Set video mode according to CMOS settings
20	Display CMOS RAM R/W errors and halt
21	Set cursor and call Int. 10 to display status message
22	Display power-on message
23	Read new cursor position
24	Display AMI copyright message at the bottom of the screen
25	Test shadow RAM
F0	Shadow RAM test failed
30	Ready to enter protected mode
31	Enter protected mode (A20 gate) and enable timer interrupt (IRQ0)
32	Get memory size above 1MB
33	Get memory size below 640KB
34	Test memory above 1MB
35	Test memory below 1MB
37	Clear memory below 1MB
38	Clear memory above 1MB
39	Use CMOS shutdown byte and return to real mode
3A	Test 64KB R/W
3B	Test RAM below 1MB and show the area being tested
3C	Test RAM above 1MB and show the area being tested

TABLE 15-19 POST CODES FOR ARCHE LEGACY BIOS (CONTINUED)

CODE	DESCRIPTION
3D	RAM test completed OK
3E	Ready to return to real mode
3F	Back in real mode
40	Disable A20 gate
41	Check for AMI copyright message in ROM
42	Display the AMI copyright message, if found
43	Test cache memory
4E	Process shutdown 1
4F	Restore interrupt vectors and data in BIOS RAM area
50	Test DMA controller
51	Initialize DMA controller
52	Test the DMA controller with patterns
54	Test DMA controller latches
55	Initialize and enable DMA controllers 1 and 2
56	Initialize 8259 PICs
57	Test 8259 PICs and set up interrupt mask registers
61	Check DDNIL status bit and display message
70	Perform keyboard basic assurance test
71	Program keyboard to AT type
72	Disable keyboard and initialize keyboard circular buffer
73	Display message and initialize floppy controller and drive
74	Attempt to access the floppy drive
75	If the CMOS RAM is good, check and initialize the hard-disk controller and drive
76	Attempt to access the hard-disk drive
77	Shuffle any internal error codes
79	Check CMOS RAM battery and checksum . . . clear parity status
7A	Compare size of base/extended memory to CMOS information
7C	Display AMI copyright
7D	Set AT memory expansion bit
7E	Verify the ROM contains an AMI copyright
7F	Clear the <Del> message from the display . . . check if <Del> was pressed
80	Locate option ROM at C800h to DE00h and pass control to any found
81	Return from option ROM and initialize timer and data area
82	Setup parallel and serial ports
83	Test for math co-processor
84	Check if keyboard is locked
85	Display any soft error messages
86	Test for option ROM at E0000h
A0	Error found in 256KB or 1MB RAM IC in lower 640KB
A1	Base 64KB random access and data pattern test
A9	Initialize on-board VGA controller
B0	Error in 256KB RAM IC in lower 640KB

TABLE 15-19 POST CODES FOR ARCHE LEGACY BIOS (CONTINUED)	
CODE	DESCRIPTION
B1	Base 64KB random-access and data-pattern test
E0	Return to real mode and initialize bas 64KB RAM
E1	Initialize 640KB RAM
EF	Configuration memory error—can't find memory
F0	Test shadow RAM from 04000h
00	Call the Int. 19 boot loader

TABLE 15-20 POST CODES FOR AST BIOS	
CODE	DESCRIPTION
01	Test CPU registers
02	Test the 8042 KBC buffer
03	Test the 8042 KBC reset
04	Verify presence of keyboard and check communication
05	Read keyboard input port
06	Initialize system-board support chipset
09	Test BIOS ROM checksum
0D	Test 8254 PIT registers
0E	Test ASIC registers
0F	Test CMOS RAM shutdown byte
10	Test DMA controller 0 registers
11	Test DMA controller 1 registers
12	Test DMA page registers (EGA/VGA vertical retrace failed)
13	EGA/VGA RAM test failed
14	Test memory-refresh toggle (EGA/VGA CRT registers failed)
15	Test base 64KB memory
16	Set interrupt vectors in base memory
17	Initialize video
18	Test display memory
20	EISA bus board power on
30	Test PIC #1 mask register
31	Test PIC #2 mask register
32	Test PICs for stuck interrupts
33	Test for stuck NMI
34	Test for stuck DDINIL status
40	Test CMOS RAM backup battery
41	Calculate and verify CMOS checksum
42	Setup CMOS RAM options
50	Test the protected mode
51	Test protected-mode exceptions
60	Calculate RAM size

TABLE 15-20 POST CODES FOR AST BIOS (CONTINUED)

CODE	DESCRIPTION
60	Calculate RAM size
61	Test RAM
62	Test shadow RAM
63	Test cache memory
64	Copy system BIOS to shadow RAM
65	Copy video BIOS to shadow RAM
66	Test 8254 PIT channel 2
67	Initialize memory

TABLE 15-21 POST CODES FOR AT&T BIOS

CODE	DESCRIPTION
01	CPU test
02	System I/O port test
03	ROM checksum test
05	DMA page-register test
06	Timer 1 test
07	Timer 2 test
08	RAM refresh test
09	8/19-bit bus-conversion check
0A	Interrupt controller 1 test
0B	Interrupt controller 2 test
0C	Keyboard-controller test
0D	CMOS RAM/RTC test
0E	Battery power lost
0F	CMOS RAM checksum test
10	CPU protected-mode test
11	Display-configuration test
12	Display-controller test
13	Primary-display error
14	Extended CMOS test
15	AT-bus reset
16	Initialize chipset registers
17	Check for extension ROMs
18	Internal memory-address test
19	Re-map memory
1A	Memory interleave-mode test
1B	Re-map shadow memory
1C	Setup MRAM
1D	Expanded-memory test

TABLE 15-21 POST CODES FOR AT&T BIOS (CONTINUED)

CODE	DESCRIPTION
1E	AT-memory error
1F	Internal memory error
20	Minimum POST tests complete
21	DMA controller 1 test
22	DMA controller 2 test
23	Timer 0 test
24	Initialize internal controllers
25	Unexpected interrupt
26	Expected interrupt
30	Switch to protected mode
31	Size AT-bus memory or size external memory
32	Address lines A16 to A23 test
33	Internal memory test or conventional memory test
34	AT-bus memory test or external memory test
38	Shadow ROM BIOS to RAM
39	Shadow extension BIOS to RAM
40	Enable/disable keyboard
41	Keyboard clock and data test
42	Keyboard reset
43	Keyboard-controller test
44	A20 gate test
50	Initialize interrupt table
51	Enable timer interrupt
60	Floppy-controller/drive test
61	Hard-disk controller test
62	Initialize floppy drives
63	Initialize hard drives
70	Real-Time Clock (RTC) test
71	Set real-time clock
72	Test parallel interfaces
73	Test serial interfaces
74	Check external ROMs
75	Numeric co-processor test
76	Enable keyboard and RTC interrupts (IRQ9)
F0	Display system startup message
F1	Check for ROM at E000H
F2	Boot from floppy or hard disk
F3	Run setup program
F4	Run password program
FC	DRAM type detection
FD	CPU register test

TABLE 15-22 POST CODES FOR AWARD XT BIOS

CODE	DESCRIPTION
03	Test CPU flag registers
06	Test CPU registers
09	System chipset initialization
0C	Test BIOS checksum
0F	DMA page-register initialization
12	Test DMA address and count registers
15	DMA initialization
18	8253 PIT test
1B	8253 PIT initialization
1E	Start RAM refresh
21	Test base 64KB RAM
24	Setup interrupt vectors and stack
27	Initialize the 8259 PIC
2A	Test PIT interrupt-mask register
2D	Test PIC hot-interrupt test
30	Run V40 DMA test, if present
33	Initialize the system clock
36	Run the keyboard test
39	Setup interrupt vector table
3C	Read system-configuration switches
3F	Run video test
42	Locate and initialize serial ports
45	Locate and initialize parallel ports
48	Locate game port
4B	Display copyright message
4E	Calculation of CPU speed
54	Test of system memory
55	Test floppy drive
57	Finish system initialization before boot
5A	Call Int. 19 boot loader

TABLE 15-23 POST CODES FOR AWARD XT BIOS VERSION 3.1

CODE	DESCRIPTION
01	Test CPU flag registers
02	Determine type of POST and check keyboard buffer
06	Initialize the PIT, PIC, DMA, and 6845
07	Check processor registers
09	ROM checksum
0A	Initialize the video system
15	Test the first 64KB RAM

TABLE 15-23 POST CODES FOR AWARD XT BIOS VERSION 3.1 (CONTINUED)

CODE	DESCRIPTION
16	Setup interrupt tables
17	Setup video system
18	Test video memory
19	Test 8259 PIC mask bits channel 1
1A	Test 8259 PIC mask bits channel 2
1E	Check memory size
1F	Test base memory above 64KB
20	Test stuck interrupts
21	Test stuck NMI
22	Initialize the floppy-drive controller
2C	Locate and initialize COM ports
2D	Locate and initialize LPT ports
2F	Initialize the math co-processor
31	Locate and initialize option ROMs
FF	Call the Int. 19 boot loader

TABLE 15-24 POST CODES FOR AWARD AT BIOS VERSION 3.0

CODE	DESCRIPTION
01	Test CPU flag registers
02	Power-up check . . . initialize motherboard chipset
03	Clear the 8042 KBC
04	Reset the 8042 KBC
05	Test the keyboard
06	Disable video system, parity, and DMA controller
07	Test CPU registers
08	Initialize CMOS/RTC IC
09	Perform BIOS ROM checksum
0A	Initialize the video interface
0B	Test 8254 timer channel 0
0C	Test 8254 timer channel 1
0D	Test 8254 timer channel 2
0E	Test CMOS RAM shutdown byte
0F	Test extended CMOS RAM (if present)
10	Test 8237 DMA-controller channel 0
11	Test 8237 DMA-controller channel 1
12	Test the 8237 DMA-controller page registers
13	Test the 8741 KBC interface
14	Test the memory refresh and toggle circuits
15	Test the first 64KB of system memory
16	Set up the interrupt vector tables in low memory

TABLE 15-24 POST CODES FOR AWARD AT BIOS VERSION 3.0 (CONTINUED)

CODE	DESCRIPTION
17	Set up video I/O operations
18	Test MDA/CGA video memory unless an EGA/VGA adapter is found
19	Test 8259 PIC mask bits channel 1
1A	Test 8259 PIC mask bits channel 2
1B	Test the CMOS RAM battery level
1C	Test the CMOS RAM checksum
1D	Set system memory size from CMOS information
1E	Check base memory size 64KB at a time
1F	Test base memory from 64KB to 640KB
20	Test stuck interrupt lines
21	Test for stuck NMI
22	Test the 8259 PIC
23	Test the protected mode and A20 gate
24	Check the size of extended memory above 1MB
25	Test all base and extended memory found up to 16MB
26	Test protected-mode exceptions
27	Initialize shadow RAM and move system BIOS (and video BIOS) into shadow RAM
28	Detect and initialize 8242 or 8248 IC
2A	Initialize the keyboard
2B	Detect and initialize the floppy drive
2C	Detect and initialize serial ports
2D	Detect and initialize parallel ports
2E	Detect and initialize the hard drive
2F	Detect and initialize the math co-processor
31	Detect and initialize any adapter ROMs
BD	Initialize the cache controller, if present
CA	Initialize cache memory
CC	Shut down the NMI handler
EE	Test for unexpected processor exception
FF	Call the Int. 19 boot loader

TABLE 15-25 POST CODES FOR AWARD AT BIOS VERSION 3.1

CODE	DESCRIPTION
01	Test CPU flag registers
02	Power-up check . . . initialize motherboard chipset
03	Clear the 8042 KBC
04	Reset the 8042 KBC
05	Test the keyboard
06	Disable video system, parity, and DMA controller
07	Test CPU registers
08	Initialize CMOS/RTC IC
09	Perform BIOS ROM checksum

TABLE 15-25 POST CODES FOR AWARD AT BIOS VERSION 3.1 (CONTINUED)

CODE	DESCRIPTION
0A	Initialize the video interface
0B	Test 8254 timer channel 0
0C	Test 8254 timer channel 1
0D	Test 8254 timer channel 2
0E	Test CMOS RAM shutdown byte
0F	Test extended CMOS RAM, if present
10	Test 8237 DMA controller channel 0
11	Test 8237 DMA controller channel 1
12	Test 8237 DMA controller page registers
13	Test 8741 KBC interface
14	Test the memory refresh and toggle circuits
15	Test the first 64KB of system memory
16	Set up the interrupt vector tables in low memory
17	Set up video I/O operations
18	Test MDA/CGA video memory unless an EGA/VGA adapter is found
19	Test 8259 PIC mask bits channel 1
1A	Test 8259 PIC mask bits channel 2
1B	Test the CMOS RAM battery level
1C	Test the CMOS RAM checksum
1D	Set system memory size from CMOS information
1E	Check base memory size 64KB at a time
1F	Test base memory
20	Test stuck interrupt lines
21	Test for stuck NMI
22	Test the 8259 PIC
23	Test the protected mode and A20 gate
24	Check the size of extended memory above 1MB
25	Test all base and extended memory found up to 16MB
26	Test protected-mode exceptions
27	Initialize shadow RAM and move system BIOS (and video BIOS) into shadow RAM
28	Detect and initialize 8242 or 8248 IC
2A	Initialize the keyboard
2B	Detect and initialize the floppy drive
2C	Detect and initialize serial ports
2D	Detect and initialize parallel ports
2E	Detect and initialize the hard drive
2F	Detect and initialize the math co-processor
31	Detect and initialize any adapter ROMs at C8000h to EFFFFh (and F0000h to F7FFFh)
39	Initialize the cache controller, if present
3B	Initialize cache memory
CA	Detect and initialize alternate cache controller
CC	Shut down the NMI handler
EE	Test for unexpected processor exception
FF	Call the Int. 19 boot loader

TABLE 15-26 POST CODES FOR AWARD AT BIOS VERSION 3.3

CODE	DESCRIPTION
01	Test 8042 KBC
02	Test 8042 KBC
03	Test 8042 KBC
04	Test 8042 KBC
05	Test 8042 KBC
06	Initialize any system chipsets
07	Test the CPU flags
08	Calculate the CMOS checksum
09	Initialize the 8254 PIT
0A	Test the 8254 PIT
0B	Test the DMA controller
0C	Initialize the 8259 PIC
0D	Test the 8259 PIC
0E	Test ROM BIOS checksum
0F	Test extended CMOS
10	Test the 8259 PIT IC
11	Test the 8259 PIT IC
12	Test the 8259 PIT IC
13	Test the 8259 PIT IC
14	Test the 8259 PIT IC
15	Test the first 64KB of RAM
16	Initialize the BIOS interrupt vector tables
17	Initialize the video system
18	Check video memory
19	Test 8259 PIC 1 mask
1A	Test 8259 PIC 2 mask
1B	Check CMOS battery level
1C	Verify the CMOS checksum
1D	Verify the CMOS/RTC IC
1E	Check memory size
1F	Verify memory in the system
20	Initialize DMA ICs
21	Initialize PIC ICs
22	Initialize PIT ICs
24	Check extended memory size
25	Test all extended memory detected
26	Enter the protected mode
27	Initialize the shadow RAM and cache controller
28	Test shadow RAM and the cache controller
2A	Initialize the keyboard
2B	Initialize the floppy-drive controller
2C	Check and initialize serial ports

TABLE 15-26 POST CODES FOR AWARD AT BIOS VERSION 3.3 (CONTINUED)

CODE	DESCRIPTION
2D	Check and initialize parallel ports
2E	Initialize the hard-drive controller
2F	Initialize the math co-processor
31	Check for any option ROMs in the system
FF	Call the Int. 19 boot loader

TABLE 15-27 POST CODES FO AWARD AT/EISA BIOS VERSION 4.0

CODE	DESCRIPTION
01	Test the CPU flags
02	Test the CPU registers
03	Check the BIOS ROM checksum
04	Test the CMOS battery level
05	Initialize all system chipsets
06	Test the memory refresh toggle
07	Set up low memory
08	Set up interrupt vector table
09	Test CMOS RAM checksum
0A	Initialize the keyboard
0B	Initialize the video controller
0C	Test video memory
0D	Initialize any specialized chipsets
0F	Test DMA controller 0
10	Test DMA controller 1
11	Test DMA page registers
14	Test 8254 timer
15	Verify 8259 PIC channel 1
16	Verify 8259 PIC channel 2
17	Test for stuck interrupts
18	Test 8259 functions
19	Test for stuck NMI
1F	Initialize EISA mode (for EISA systems)
20	Initialize and enable EISA slot 0
21–2F	Initialize and enable EISA slots 1 to 15
30	Check base memory size
31	Check extended memory size
32	Test any EISA memory found during slot initialization
3C	Enter protected mode
3D	Detect and initialize mouse

TABLE 15-27 POST CODES FO AWARD AT/EISA BIOS VERSION 4.0 (CONTINUED)

CODE	DESCRIPTION
3E	Initialize the cache controller
3F	Enable and test shadow RAM
41	Initialize floppy-disk drive controller
42	Initialize hard-disk drive controller
43	Detect and initialize serial ports
44	Detect and initialize parallel ports
45	Detect and initialize math co-processor
46	Display Setup message
47	Set speed for boot
4E	Display any soft errors
4F	Ask for password, if feature is enabled
50	Check all CMOS RAM values and clear the display
51	Enable parity, NMI, and cache memory
52	Initialize any option ROMs present from C8000h to EFFFFh or F7FFFh
53	Initialize time value at address 40 of BIOS RAM area
55	Initialize DDNIL counter to NULL
63	Call Int. 19 for boot loader

TABLE 15-28 POST CODES FOR AWARD EISA BIOS

CODE	DESCRIPTION
01	Test the CPU flags
02	Test the CPU registers
03	Check the DMA controller, PIC, and PIT
04	Initialize memory refresh
05	Initialize the keyboard
06	Test BIOS ROM checksum
07	Check CMOS battery level
08	Test lower 256KB or RAM
09	Test cache memory
0A	Configure the BIOS interrupt table
0B	Test the CMOS RAM checksum
0C	Initialize the keyboard
0D	Initialize the video adapter
0E	Test video memory
0F	Test DMA controller 0
10	Test DMA controller 0
11	Test page registers
14	Test the 8254 PIT IC
15	Verify 8259 PIC channel 1

TABLE 15-28 POST CODES FOR AWARD EISA BIOS (CONTINUED)

CODE	DESCRIPTION
16	Verify 8259 PIC channel 2
17	Test for stuck interrupts
18	Test 8259 functions
19	Test for stuck NMI
1F	Check extended CMOS RAM, if available
20	Initialize and enable EISA slot 0
21–2F	Initialize and enable EISA slots 1 to 15
30	Check memory size below 256KB
31	Check memory size above 256KB
32	Test any EISA memory found during slot initialization
3C	Enter protected mode
3D	Detect and initialize mouse
3E	Initialize the cache controller
3F	Enable and test shadow RAM
41	Initialize floppy-disk drive controller
42	Initialize hard-disk drive controller
43	Detect and initialize serial ports
45	Detect and initialize math co-processor
47	Set speed for boot
4E	Display any soft errors
4F	Ask for password, if feature is enabled
50	Check all CMOS RAM values and clear the display
51	Enable parity, NMI, and cache memory
52	Initialize any option ROMs present from C8000h to EFFFFh or F7FFFh
53	Initialize time value at address 40 of BIOS RAM area
63	Call Int. 19 for boot loader
B0	NMI still in protected mode (protected mode failed)
B1	Disable NMI
BF	Initialize any system-specific chipsets
C0	Cache memory on/off
C1	Check memory size
C2	Test base 256KB RAM
C3	Test DRAM Page Select
C4	Check video modes
C5	Test shadow RAM
C6	Configure cache memory
C8	Check system speed switch
C9	Test shadow RAM
CA	Initialize OEM chipset
FF	Call Int. 19 boot loader

TABLE 15-29 POST CODES FOR AWARD PLUG-AND-LAY BIOS

CODE	DESCRIPTION
C0	Turn off OEM specific cache, shadow RAM. Initialize all the standard devices with default values.
C1	Auto detection of onboard DRAM and cache.
C3	Test the first 256K DRAM. Expand the compressed codes into temporary DRAM area including the compressed system BIOS and option ROMs.
C5	Copy the BIOS from ROM into E000–FFFF shadow RAM so that POST will go faster.
01–02	Reserved
03	Initialize EISA registers (EISA BIOS only).
04	Reserved
05	Keyboard Controller Self-Test. Enable Keyboard Interface.
06	Reserved
07	Verifies CMOS's basic R/W functionality.
BE	Program defaults values into chipset.
09	Program the configuration register of Cyrix CPU. OEM specific cache initialization.
0A	Initialize the first 32 interrupt vectors. Initialize INTs 33 to 120. Issue CPUID instruction to identify CPU type. Early power-management initialization.
0B	Verify the RTC time is valid or not. Detect bad battery. Read CMOS data into BIOS stack area. Perform PnP initializations (PnP BIOS only). Assign IO and memory for PCI devices (PCI BIOS only).
0C	Initialization of the BIOS data area (40:00–40:FF).
0D	Program some of the chipset's value. Measure CPU speed for display. Video initialization including MDA, CGA, and EGA/VGA.
0E	Initialize the APIC (multi-processor BIOS only). Test video RAM, if monochrome display found. Show startup screen message.
0F	DMA channel-0 test.
10	DMA channel-1 test.
11	DMA page registers test.
12–13	Reserved
14	Test 8254 timer 0 counter 2.
15	Test 8259 interrupt mask bits for channel 1.
16	Test 8259 interrupt mask bits for channel 2.
17	Reserved
19	Test 8259 functionality.
1A–1D	Reserved
1E	If EISA NVM checksum is good, execute EISA initialization (EISA BIOS only).
1F–29	Reserved
30	Get base memory and extended memory size.
31	Test base memory from 256K to 640K. Test extended memory from 1M to the top of memory.
32	Display the Award Plug and Play BIOS extension message (PnP BIOS only). Program all onboard super I/O chips (if any) including COM ports, LPT ports, FDD port, etc.
33–3B	Reserved
3C	Set flag to allow users to enter CMOS setup utility.

TABLE 15-29 POST CODES FOR AWARD PLUG-AND-LAY BIOS (CONTINUED)

CODE	DESCRIPTION
3D	Initialize keyboard. Install PS/2 mouse.
3E	Try to turn on level-2 cache.
3F–40	Reserved
BF	Program the rest of the chipset.
41	Initialize floppy-disk drive controller.
42	Initialize hard-drive controller.
43	If it is a PnP BIOS, initialize serial and parallel ports.
44	Reserved
45	Initialize math coprocessor.
46–4D	Reserved
4E	If there is any error, show all the error messages on the screen and wait for user to press <F1>.
4F	If password is needed, ask for password. Clear the Energy Star logo (Green BIOS only).
50	Write all the CMOS values currently in the BIOS stack areas back into the CMOS.
51	Reserved
52	Initialize all ISA ROMs. Later PCI initializations (PCI BIOS only). PnP initializations (PnP BIOS only). Program shadow RAM according to setup settings. Program parity according to setup setting. Power-management initialization.
53	If it is not a PnP BIOS, initialize serial and parallel ports. Initialize time in BIOS data area.
54–5F	Reserved
60	Setup virus protection (Boot sector protection).
61	Try to turn on level-2 cache. Set the boot up speed according to setup setting. Last chance for chipset initialization. Last chance for power-management initialization. Show the system-configuration table.
62	Setup daylight savings according to setup values. Program the NumLock, type rate and type speed, according to setup setting.
63	If there are any changes in the hardware configuration, update the ESCD information (PnP BIOS only). Clear memory that has been used. Boot system via INT 19h.
FF	System booting. This means that the BIOS already passed control to the operating system.

TABLE 15-30 POST CODES FOR AWARD ELITEBIOS 4.5X

CODE	DESCRIPTION
C0	*Turn off chipset* OEM-specific cache control.
01	*Processor test 1* Processor status (1FLAGS) verification.
02	*Processor test 2* Read/write/verify all CPU registers.
03	*Initialize chipset* Disable NMI, PIE, AIE, UEI, SQWV. Disable video, parity checking, DMA. Reset math co-processor. Clear all page registers and CMOS shutdown byte. Initialize DMA controllers 0 and 1. Initialize interrupt controllers 0 and 1.

TABLE 15-30 POST CODES FOR AWARD ELITEBIOS 4.5X (CONTINUED)

CODE	DESCRIPTION
04	*Test memory refresh toggle* RAM must be periodically refreshed to keep the memory from decaying. This function ensures that the memory refresh function is working properly.
05	*Blank video and initialize keyboard* Keyboard-controller initialization.
06	Reserved
07	*Test CMOS interface and verify battery status* CMOS is working correctly, detects bad battery.
BE	*Chipset default initialization* Program chipset registers with power-on BIOS defaults.
C1	*Memory presence test* OEM specific—Test to size on-board memory.
C5	*Early shadow* OEM specific—Early shadow enable for fast boot.
C6	*Cache presence* External cache-size detection test.
08	*Setup low memory* Early chipset initialization. Memory-presence test. OEM chipset routines. Clear low 64K of memory. Test first 64K memory.
09	*Early cache initialization* Cyrix CPU initialization and cache initialization.
0A	*Setup interrupt vector table* Initialize first 120 interrupt vectors.
0B	*Test CMOS RAM checksum* Test checksum—if bad, or insert key pressed, load defaults.
0C	*Initialize keyboard* Detect type of keyboard controller.
0D	*Initialize video interface* Detect CPU clock. Read CMOS location 14h to find the type of video in use. Detect and initialize video adapter.
0E	*Test video memory* Write sign-on message to screen. Setup shadow RAM.
0F	*Test DMA controller 0* BIOS checksum test. Keyboard detect and initialization.
10	*Test DMA controller 1*
11	*Test DMA page registers*
12–13	Reserved
14	*Test timer counter 2*
15	*Test 8259-1 mask*
16	*Test 8259-2 mask*
17	*Test stuck keys*
18	*Test 8259 interrupt functionality*
19	*Test stuck NMI bits*
1A	*Display CPU clock*
1B–1E	Reserved
1F	*Set EISA mode* If EISA non-volatile memory checksum is good, execute EISA initialization. If not, execute ISA tests an clear EISA mode flag.
20	*Enable slot 0* Initialize slot 0 (system board).
21–2F	*Enable slots 1–15* Initialize slots 1 through 15.
30	*Size base and extended memory* Size base memory from 256K to 640K, and extended memory above 1MB.
31	*Test base and extended memory* Test base memory from 256K to 640K, and extended memory above 1MB, using various bit patterns.
32	*Test EISA extended memory* If EISA flag is set, then test EISA memory found in slots.
33–3B	Reserved

TABLE 15-30   POST CODES FOR AWARD ELITEBIOS 4.5X (CONTINUED)

CODE	DESCRIPTION
3C	*Setup enabled*
3D	*Initialize and install mouse* Detect if mouse is present, initialize and install interrupt vectors.
3E	*Setup cache controller*
3F	Reserved
BF	*Chipset initialization* Program chipset registers with Setup values.
40	*Display "virus protect" disable or enable*
41	*Initialize floppy drive and controller*
42	*Initialize hard drive and controller*
43	*Detect and initialize serial/parallel ports*
44	Reserved
45	*Detect and initialize math co-processor*
46	Reserved
47	Reserved
48–4D	Reserved
4E	*Manufacturing POST loop or display messages*
4F	*Security password*
50	*Write CMOS* Write all CMOS values back to RAM and clear screen.
51	*Pre-boot enable* Enable parity checker. Enable NMI. Enable cache before boot.
52	*Initialize option ROMs* Initialize any option ROMs present from C8000h to EFFFFh.
53	*Initialize time value*
60	*Setup virus protect*
61	*Set boot speed*
62	*Setup NumLock*
63	*Boot attempt*
B0	*Spurious* If interrupt occurs in protected mode.
B1	*Unclaimed NMI* If unmasked NMI occurs, display "Press F1 to disable NMI, F2 re-boot."
E1–EF	*Setup pages*
FF	*Call boot loader*

TABLE 15-31   POST CODES FOR CHIPS & TECHNOLOGIES BIOS

CODE	DESCRIPTION
01	CPU flag test failed
02	CPU register test failed
03	BIOS ROM checksum test failed
04	DMA controller test failed
05	System timer IC failed
06	Base 64KB address-line test failure

TABLE 15-31 POST CODES FOR CHIPS & TECHNOLOGIES BIOS (CONTINUED)

CODE	DESCRIPTION
07	Base 64KB memory-test failure
08	Interrupt controller test failed
09	Hot interrupt occurred
0A	System timer interrupt test failed
0B	CPU won't leave protected mode
0C	DMA page register test failed
0D	Memory refresh fault
0E	Keyboard controller not responding
0F	CPU could not enter protected mode
10	KBC protected-mode test failed
11	KBC protected-mode test failed
12	KBC protected-mode test failed
13	KBC protected-mode test failed
14	KBC protected-mode test failed
15	KBC protected-mode test failed
16	KBC A20 gate failed
17	Exception or unexpected-exception test failed
18	Shutdown during memory-size check
19	BIOS ROM checksum error
1A	BMS checksum error (BIOS, shadow-memory, or memory-controller fault)
50	Initialize system chipsets
51	Initialize system-timer IC
52	Initialize DMA controller
53	Initialize the 8259 PIC
54	Initialize system chipsets
56	Entering protected mode
57	Check memory ICs
58	Configure memory interleave
59	Exit protected mode
5A	Determine system-board memory size
5B	Relocate shadow RAM
5C	Configure possible EMS
5D	Set up wait-state configuration
5E	Retest base 64KB
5F	Test shadow RAM
60	Test CMOS RAM
61	Test the video controller
63	Protected-mode interrupt test
64	Test the A20 line
65	Test the memory-address lines
66	Base 64KB memory test
67	Run extended-memory test

TABLE 15-31 POST CODES FOR CHIPS & TECHNOLOGIES BIOS (CONTINUED)

CODE	DESCRIPTION
68	Run system-timer interrupt test
69	RTC clock test
6A	Keyboard test
6B	Identify and test math co-processor
6C	Locate and initialize serial ports
6D	Locate and initialize parallel ports
6F	Initialize floppy-disk controller
70	Initialize hard-disk controller
71	Check for key lock
72	Mouse test
90	System RAM setup
91	Calculate CPU speed
92	Check system configuration against CMOS data
93	BIOS initialized
94	Power-on diagnostic bootstrap (call Int. 19)
95	Reset ICs
96	Setup cache controller
97	VGA power-on diagnostics

TABLE 15-32 POST CODES FOR GENERAL COMPAQ BIOS

CODE	DESCRIPTION
00	Initialize and test CPU flags
01	Check manufacturing jumper
02	8042 KBC test
03	No response from 8042 KBC
04	Look for ROM at E000h
05	Look for ROM at C800h
06	Normal CMOS reset code
08	Initialize the PIT and math co-processor
09	Jump indexed by CMOS reset code (KBC)
0A	Vector 40:67 reset function (KBC)
0B	Vector 40:67 with E01 function (KBC)
0C	Boot reset function
0D	Test 8254 PIT counter 0
0E	Test 8254 PIT counter 2
0F	Warm boot
10	PPI disabled, test 8254 PIT 0 and 1
11	Initialize video controller
12	Clear display and turn video on

TABLE 15-32 POST CODES FOR GENERAL COMPAQ BIOS (CONTINUED)

CODE	DESCRIPTION
13	Set test time 0
14	Disable RTC interrupts
15	Check battery power levels
16	Battery has lost power
17	Clear CMOS diagnostics
18	Test base memory (first 128KB)
19	Initialize base memory
1A	Initialize video adapter
1B	Check BIOS ROM checksum
1C	Check CMOS checksum
1D	Test DMA-controller page registers
1E	Test the keyboard controller
1F	Test the protected mode
20	Test real and extended memory
21	Initialize the time of day
22	Initialize the math co-processor
23	Test the keyboard and KBC
24	Reset the A20 line and set default CPU speed
25	Test the floppy-disk controller
26	Test the fixed-disk controller
27	Initialize all printer ports
28	Search for optional ROMs
29	Test system configuration against CMOS setup
2A	Clear the screen
2B	Check for invalid time and date
2C	Search for optional ROMs
2D	Test PIT 2
2F	Write to diagnostic byte
30	Clear the first 128KB of RAM
31	Load interrupt vectors 70–77
32	Load interrupt vectors 00–1F
33	Initialize MEMSIZE and RESETWD
34	Verify CMOS checksum
35	CMOS checksum is not valid
36	Check CMOS battery power
37	Check for game adapters
38	Initialize all serial ports
39	Initialize all parallel ports
3A	Initialize Port and Comm timeouts
3B	Flush the keyboard buffer
40	Save the RESETWD value
41	Check RAM refresh

CODE	DESCRIPTION
	TABLE 15-32 POST CODES FOR GENERAL COMPAQ BIOS (CONTINUED)
42	Start write of 128KB RAM
43	Rest parity checks
44	Start verify of 128KB RAM test
45	Check for parity errors
46	NO RAM errors
47	RAM error detected
50	Check for dual frequency in CMOS
51	Check CMOS video configuration
52	Search for video ROM
53	Send control to video option ROM
54	Initialize the first video adapter
55	Initialize the secondary video adapter
56	No display adapters installed
57	Initialize primary video mode
58	Start of video test
59	Check for the presence of a video adapter
5A	Check video registers
5B	Start screen memory test
5C	Stop video test and clear memory
5D	Error detected on adapter
5E	Test the next detected adapter
5F	All found adapters successfully tested
60	Start of memory tests
61	Enter the protected mode
62	Find memory size
63	Get CMOS size
64	Start test of real memory
65	Start test of extended memory
66	Save memory size in CMOS
67	128KB option installed
68	Ready to return to real mode
69	Successful return to real mode
6A	Protected-mode error during test
6B	Display error message
6C	End of memory test
6D	Initialize KB OK string
6E	Determine memory size to test
6F	Start of MEMTEST
70	Display XXXXXKB OK
71	Test each RAM segment
72	High-order address test
73	Exit MEMTEST

TABLE 15-32 POST CODES FOR GENERAL COMPAQ BIOS (CONTINUED)

CODE	DESCRIPTION
74	Parity error on the bus
75	Start protected-mode test
76	Ready to enter protected mode
77	Test software exceptions
78	Prepare to return to real mode
79	Successful return to real mode
7A	Back in real mode (error has been detected)
7B	Exit protected-mode testing
7C	High-order address test failure
7D	Start cache-controller test
7E	Configuring cache memory
7F	Copy system ROM to shadow RAM
80	Start of 8042 KBC test
81	Run 8042 KBC self-test
82	KBC check result received
83	Error returned
84	8042 checks OK
86	Start 8042 test and reset the keyboard
87	Got acknowledge and read the result
88	Got the result and checking it
89	Testing for stuck keys
8A	Key seems to be stuck
8B	Test keyboard interface
8C	Got the result and checking it
8D	End of KBC test—no errors detected
90	Start of CMOS test
91	CMOS checks OK
92	Error in CMOS R/W test
93	Start of DMA-controller test
94	DMA page registers test OK
95	DMA controller tests OK
96	8237 DMA initialization is OK
97	Start of RAM test
A0	Start of diskette tests
A1	FDC reset active
A2	FDC reset inactive
A3	FDC motor on
A4	FDC time-out error
A5	FDC failed reset
A6	FDC passed reset
A8	Determine drive type
A9	Start seek operation

TABLE 15-32 POST CODES FOR GENERAL COMPAQ BIOS (CONTINUED)

CODE	DESCRIPTION
AA	Waiting for FDC seek status
AF	Diskette tests complete
B0	Start of hard drive tests
B1	Controller board not found
B2	Controller test failed
B3	Testing drive 1
B4	Testing drive 2
B5	Drive error
B6	Drive failed
B7	No hard disks detected
B8	Hard-drive tests complete
B9	Attempt to boot diskette
BA	Attempt to boot hard drive
BB	Boot attempt has failed
BC	Jump to boot record
BD	Drive error . . . retry boot
BE	Testing Weitek co-processor
D0	Starting clear memory routine
D1	Ready to switch to protected mode
D2	Ready to clear extended memory
D3	Ready to return to real mode
D4	Successful return to real mode
D5	Clearing base memory
DD	KBC self-test failed
E0	Ready to shadow E000h ROM
E1	Finished shadowing ROM at E000h
E2	Ready to shadow EGA/VGA ROM
E3	Finished shadowing video ROM

TABLE 15-33 POST CODES FOR COMPAQ i286 DESKPRO BIOS

CODE	DESCRIPTION
01	Test the CPU
02	Test the math co-processor
03	Testing 8237 DMA controller
04	Testing 8259 PIC
05	Testing KBC port 61h
06	Testing 8042 KBC
07	CMOS test

TABLE 15-33 POST CODES FOR COMPAQ i286 DESKPRO BIOS (CONTINUED)	
CODE	DESCRIPTION
08	CMOS test
09	CMOS test
10	Testing 8254 PIT
11	Testing 8254 PIT refresh detect
12	System speed test
14	Speaker test
21	Memory R/W test
24	Memory address test
25	Memory walking I/O test
31	Keyboard short test
32	Keyboard long test
33	Keyboard LED test
35	Keyboard lock test
41	Printer test failed
42	Testing printer port
43	Testing printer port
48	Parallel port failure
51	Video-controller test
52	Video-controller test
53	Video-attribute test
54	Video-character set test
55	Video 80×25-mode test
56	Video 80×25-mode test
57	Video 40×25-mode test
60	Floppy-disk ID test
61	Floppy-disk format test
62	Floppy-disk read test
63	Floppy-disk R/W compare test
64	Floppy-disk random-seek test
65	Floppy-disk media ID test
66	Floppy-disk speed test
67	Floppy-disk wrap test
68	Floppy-disk write-protect test
69	Floppy-disk reset-controller test

TABLE 15-34   POST CODES FOR COMPAQ i386 DESKPRO BIOS

CODE	DESCRIPTION
01	I/O ROM checksum error
02	System memory-board failure
12	System option error
13	Time and date not set (not expected from CMOS)
14	Memory-size error (not what was expected from CMOS settings)
21	System-memory error
23	Memory address-line error
25	Memory-test error
26	Keyboard error
33	Keyboard-controller error
34	Keyboard or KBC error
41	Parallel-port error
42	Monochrome video-adapter failure
51	Display-adapter failure
61	Floppy-disk controller error
62	Floppy-disk boot error
65	Floppy-drive error
67	Floppy-disk controller failed
6A	Floppy port-address conflict
6B	Floppy port-address conflict
72	Math co-processor detected

TABLE 15-35   POST CODES FOR COMPAQ i486 DESKPRO BIOS

CODE	DESCRIPTION
01	CPU test failed
02	Math co-processor test failed
03	Testing 8237 DMA page registers
04	Testing 8259 PIC
05	8042 KBC port 61 error
06	8042 KBC self-test error
07	CMOS RAM test failed
08	CMOS interrupt test failed
09	CMOS clock-load data test failed
10	8254 PIT test failed
11	8254 PIT refresh-detect test failed
12	System-speed test mode too slow
13	Protected-mode test failed
14	Speaker test failed

TABLE 15-35 POST CODES FOR COMPAQ i486 DESKPRO BIOS (CONTINUED)

CODE	DESCRIPTION
16	Cache memory configuration failed
19	Testing installed devices
21	Memory configuration test failed
22	BIOS ROM checksum failed
23	Memory R/W test failed
24	Memory address-line test failed
25	Walking I/O test failed
26	Memory-increment pattern test failed
31	Keyboard short test
32	Keyboard long test
33	Keyboard LED test
34	Keyboard typematic test failed
41	Printer test failed or not connected (parallel-port circuits)
42	Printer data register failed (parallel-port circuits)
43	Printer pattern test (parallel-port circuits)
48	Printer not connected (parallel-port circuits)
51	Video-controller test failed
52	Video-memory test failed
53	Video-attribute test failed
54	Video-character set test failed
55	Video 80×25-mode test failed
56	Video 80×25-mode test failed
57	Video 40×25-mode test failed
58	Video 320×200-mode color set 1 test
59	Video 320×200-mode color set 1 test
60	Floppy-disk ID drive types test failed
61	Floppy-disk format failed
62	Floppy-disk read test failed
63	Floppy-disk write, read, seek test failed
65	Floppy-disk ID media failed
66	Floppy-disk speed test failed
67	Floppy-disk wrap test failed
68	Floppy-disk write-protect failed
69	Floppy-disk reset controller test failed
82	Video-memory test failed
84	Video-adapter test failed

TABLE 15-36 POST CODES FOR COMPAQ VIDEO BIOS

CODE	DESCRIPTION
00	Entry into video ROM
01	Test alternate adapters
02	Perform vertical sync tests
03	Perform horizontal sync tests
04	Perform static system tests
05	Perform bug tests
06	Perform configuration tests
07	Perform alternate ROM tests
08	Run color gun off tests
09	Run color gun on tests
0A	Test video memory
0B	Check that adapter board is present
10	Error . . . illegal configuration
20	Error . . . no vertical sync present
21	Error . . . vertical sync out of range
30	Error . . . no horizontal sync present
40	Error . . . color register failure
50	Error . . . slot type conflict error
51	Error . . . video memory conflict error
52	Error . . . ROM conflict error
60	Error . . . red DAC stuck low
61	Error . . . green DAC stuck low
62	Error . . . blue DAC stuck low
63	Error . . . DAC stuck high
64	Error . . . red DAC fault
65	Error . . . green DAC fault
66	Error . . . blue DAC fault
70	Error . . . bad alternate ROM version
80	Error . . . color gun stuck on
90	Error . . . color gun stuck off
A0	Error . . . video memory failure
F0	Error . . . equipment failure
00	Video POST complete

TABLE 15-37 POST CODES FOR DELL BIOS

CODE	DESCRIPTION
01	CPU register test in progress
02	CMOS R/W test failed
03	BIOS ROM checksum bad

TABLE 15-37 POST CODES FOR DELL BIOS (CONTINUED)

CODE	DESCRIPTION
04	8254 PIT test failed
05	DMA controller initialization failed
06	DMA page-register test failed
08	RAM refresh verification failed
09	Starting first-64KB RAM test
0A	First-64KB RAM IC or data line bad
0B	First-64KB RAM odd/even logic bad
0C	First-64KB address line bad
0D	First-64KB parity error
10	Bit 0 bad in first 64KB
11	Bit 1 bad in first 64KB
12	Bit 2 bad in first 64KB
13	Bit 3 bad in first 64KB
14	Bit 4 bad in first 64KB
15	Bit 5 bad in first 64KB
16	Bit 6 bad in first 64KB
17	Bit 7 bad in first 64KB
18	Bit 8 bad in first 64KB
19	Bit 9 bad in first 64KB
1A	Bit 10 bad in first 64KB
1B	Bit 11 bad in first 64KB
1C	Bit 12 bad in first 64KB
1D	Bit 13 bad in first 64KB
1E	Bit 14 bad in first 64KB
1F	Bit 15 bad in first 64KB
20	Slave DMA register bad
21	Master DMA register bad
22	Master interrupt-mask register bad
23	Slave interrupt-mask register bad
25	Loading interrupt vectors
27	Keyboard-controller test failed
28	CMOS RAM battery bad
29	CMOS configuration validation in progress
2B	Video-memory test failed
2C	Video initialization failed
2D	Video-retrace failure
2E	Searching for a video ROM
30	Switching to video ROM
31	Monochrome operation OK
32	Color (CGA) operation OK
33	Color operation OK
34	Timer-tick interrupt in progress (or bad)

TABLE 15-37 POST CODES FOR DELL BIOS (CONTINUED)

CODE	DESCRIPTION
35	CMOS shutdown test in progress (or bad)
36	Gate A20 bad
37	Unexpected interrupt in protected mode
38	RAM test in progress or high address line is bad
3A	Interval timer channel 2 bad
3B	Time-of-day test bad
3C	Serial-port test bad
3D	Parallel-port test bad
3E	Math co-processor test bad
3F	Cache-memory test bad

TABLE 15-38 POST CODES FOR DTK BIOS

CODE	DESCRIPTION
01	Testing the CPU
03	Initialize the 8258 interrupt controller
05	Initialize the video board
0D	Initialize the DMA controller
0E	Initialize the DMA page register
12	Test the 8042 keyboard controller
16	Test the DMA controller and timer
22	Testing DRAM refresh circuitry
25	Base 64KB memory test
30	Set up system stack
33	Read-system configuration through KBC
37	Test keyboard clock and data line
40	Determine video type
44	Locating and testing MDA and CGA video
48	Initialize video 80×25 mode
4D	Display DTK BIOS copyright message
4F	Check serial and parallel ports
50	Check floppy-disk controller
55	Check shadow RAM
58	Display total memory and switch to real mode
5A	Successful switch back to real mode
60	Check hard-disk drive controller
62	Initialize floppy drive
65	Initialize hard drive
67	Initialize the drives
6A	Disable gate A20 and test math co-processor
70	Set system date and time
77	Call Int. 19 boot loader

TABLE 15-39 POST CODES FOR EUROSOFT/MYLEX BIOS

CODE	DESCRIPTION
01	CPU test failed
02	DMA page-register test failed
03	Keyboard-controller test failed
04	BIOS ROM checksum error
05	Keyboard-command test failed
06	CMOS RAM test failed
07	RAM refresh test failed
08	First-64KB memory test failed
09	DMA controller test failed
0A	Initialize DMA controller
0B	Interrupt test failed
0C	Checking RAM size
0D	Initializing video system
0E	Video BIOS checksum failed
10	Search for monochrome video adapter
11	Search for color video adapter
12	Word-splitter and byte-shift test failed (KBC)
13	Keyboard test failed
14	RAM test failed
15	System timer test failed
16	Initialize keyboard-controller output port
17	Keyboard-interrupt test failed
18	Initialize keyboard
19	Real-time clock test failed
1A	Math co-processor test failed
1B	Reset floppy- and hard-drive controllers
1C	Initialize the floppy drive
1D	Initialize the hard drive
1E	Locate adapter ROMs from C800h to DFFFh
1F	Locate and initialize serial and parallel ports
20	Initialize time of day in RTC
21	Locate adapter ROMs from E000h to EFFFh
22	Search for boot device
23	Boot from floppy disk
24	Boot from hard disk
25	Gate A20 enable/disable failure
26	Parity error
30	DDNIL bit-scan failure
FF	Fatal error . . . system halted

TABLE 15-40 POST CODES FOR EUROSOFT 4.71 BIOS

PASS	FAIL	DESCRIPTION
03	04	DMA page-register test
05	06	Keyboard test
07	08	Keyboard self-test
09	0A	8042 KBC checking links
0B	—	RATMOD/DIAG link
0C	0D	Keyboard port 60h test
0E	0F	Keyboard-parameter test
10	11	Keyboard command byte
12	13	Keyboard command-byte return
14	15	RAM-refresh toggle test
16	17	RAM bit test
18	19	RAM parity test
1A	1B	CMOS RAM test
1C	1D	CMOS RAM-battery test
1E	1F	CMOS RAM-checksum test
—	20	CMOS RAM-battery fault-bit set
21	22	Master DMA controller 1 test
21	23	Slave DMA controller 2 test
24	—	Protected mode entered successfully
25	—	RAM test completed
26	27	BIOS RAM checksum test
28	—	Exiting protected mode
29	2A	Keyboard power-up reply received test
2B	2C	Keyboard-disable command test
—	2D	Checking for video system
—	2E	POST errors have been reported
—	2F	About to halt
30	—	Protected mode entered safely
31	—	RAM test complete
32	33	Master interrupt-controller test
34	35	Slave interrupt-controller test
36	37	Chipset initialization
38	39	Shadowing system BIOS
3A	3B	Shadowing video BIOS

TABLE 15-41 POST CODES FOR MYLEX BIOS

CODE	DESCRIPTION
01	CPU test
02	DMA page-register test

TABLE 15-41 POST CODES FOR MYLEX BIOS (CONTINUED)

CODE	DESCRIPTION
03	Keyboard-controller test
04	ROM BIOS checksum
05	Send keyboard-command test
06	CMOS RAM test
08	RAM-refresh test
09	First-64K memory test
0A	DMA controller test
0B	Initialize DMA
0C	Interrupt test
0D	Determine RAM size
0E	Initialize video and verify EGA or VGA checksum
10	Search for monochrome card
11	Search for color card
12	Word-splitter and byte-shifter test
13	Keyboard test
14	RAM test
15	System timer test
16	Initialize keyboard-controller output port
17	Keyboard-interrupt test

TABLE 15-42 POST CODES FOR FARADAY A-TEASE BIOS

CODE	DESCRIPTION
01	CPU test failed
02	BIOS ROM checksum test failed
03	CMOS shutdown byte failed
04	Testing DMA page register
05	Testing system timer (PIT)
06	Testing system refresh
07	Testing 8042 keyboard controller
08	Testing lower 128KB or RAM
09	Testing video controller
0A	Testing RAM 128KB to 640KB
0B	Testing DMA controller #1
0C	Testing DMA controller #2
0D	Testing interrupt controller #1
0E	Testing interrupt controller #2
0F	Testing control port
10	Testing parity

TABLE 15-42 POST CODES FOR FARADAY A-TEASE BIOS (CONTINUED)

CODE	DESCRIPTION
11	Testing CMOS RAM checksum
12	Testing for manufacturing-mode jumper
13	Configure interrupt vectors
14	Testing the keyboard
15	Configuring parallel ports
16	Configuring serial ports
17	Configuring lower 640KB RAM
18	Configuring RAM above 1MB
19	Configuring keyboard
1A	Configuring floppy drive
1B	Configuring hard-disk drive
1C	Configuring game-port adapter
1D	Testing and initializing math co-processor
1E	Checking CMOS real-time clock
1F	Calculate and verify CMOS RAM checksum
21	Initialize PROM drivers
22	Test parallel-port loopback
23	Test serial-port loopback
24	Test CMOS RTC
25	Test the CMOS shutdown
26	Test memory over 1MB
80	Error . . . divide overflow
81	Error . . . single step fault
82	Error . . . NMI stuck or error
83	Error . . . breakpoint fault
84	Error . . . Int. 0 detect fault
85	Error . . . bound error
86	Error . . . invalid opcode (BIOS or CPU fault)
87	Error . . . processor extension not available
88	Error . . . double-exception error
89	Error . . . processor extended-segment error
8A	Error . . . invalid task state segment
8B	Error . . . needed segment not present
8C	Error . . . stack segment not present
8D	Error . . . general-protection error
8E	Error . . . general-protection error
8F	Error . . . general-protection error
90	Error . . . processor-extension error
91–FF	Error . . . spurious interrupts
F3	Error . . . CPU protected-mode fault
F9	Error . . . virtual-block move error

TABLE 15-43 POST CODES FOR IBM XT BIOS

CODE	DESCRIPTION
00 or FF	CPU register test failed
01	BIOS ROM checksum failed
02	System timer 1 failed
03	8237 DMA register R/W failed
04	Base 32KB RAM failed

TABLE 15-44 POST CODES FOR IBM AT BIOS

CODE	DESCRIPTION
01	CPU flag and register test
02	BIOS ROM checksum test
03	CMOS shutdown byte test
04	8254 PIT test—bits on
05	8254 PIT test—bits on
06	8237 DMA initialize registers test 0
07	8237 DMA initialize registers test 1
08	DMA page-register test
09	Memory refresh test
0A	Soft reset test
0B	Reset 8042 KBC
0C	KBC reset OK
0D	Initialize the 8042 KBC
0E	Test memory
0F	Get I/P buffer switch settings
DD	RAM error
11	Initialize protected mode
12	Test protected-mode registers
13	Initialize 8259 PIC #2
14	Setup temporary-interrupt vectors
15	Establish BIOS-interrupt vectors
16	Verify CMOS checksum and battery OK
17	Set the defective CMOS battery flag
18	Ensure CMOS set
19	Set return address byte in CMOS
1A	Set temporary stack
1B	Test segment address 01–0000 (second 64KB)
1C	Decide if 512KB or 640KB installed
1D	Test segment address 10–0000 (over 640KB)
1E	Set expansion memory, as contained in CMOS
1F	Test address lines 19–23

TABLE 15-44 POST CODES FOR IBM AT BIOS (CONTINUED)

CODE	DESCRIPTION
20	Ready to return from protected mode
21	Successful return from protected mode
22	Test video controller
23	Check for EGA/VGA BIOS
24	Test 8259 PIC R/W mask register
25	Test interrupt mask registers
26	Check for hot (unexpected) interrupts
05	Display 101 error (system-board error)
27	Check the POST logic (system-board error)
28	Check unexpected NMI interrupts (system-board error)
29	Test timer 2 (system-board error)
2A	Test 8254 timer
2B	System-board error
2C	System-board error
2D	Check 8042 KBC for last command
2F	Go to next area during a warm boot
30	Set shutdown return 2
31	Switch to protected mode
33	Test next block of 64KB
34	Switch back to real mode
F0	Set data segment
F1	Test interrupts
F2	Test exception interrupts
F3	Verify protected-mode instructions
F4	Verify protected-mode instructions
F5	Verify protected-mode instructions
F6	Verify protected-mode instructions
F7	Verify protected-mode instructions
F8	Verify protected-mode instructions
F9	Verify protected-mode instructions
FA	Verify protected-mode instructions
34	Test keyboard
35	Test keyboard type
36	Check for "AA" scan code
38	Check for stuck key
39	8042 KBC error
3A	Initialize the 8042
3B	Check for expansion ROM in 2KB blocks
40	Enable hardware interrupts
41	Check system code at segment E0000h
42	Exit to system code
43	Call boot loader

TABLE 15-44 POST CODES FOR IBM AT BIOS (CONTINUED)

CODE	DESCRIPTION
3C	Check for initial program load
3D	Initialize floppy for drive type
3E	Initialize hard drive
81	Build descriptor table
82	Switch to virtual mode
90–B6	Memory and bootstrap tests
32	Test address lines 0–15
44	Attempt to boot from fixed disk
45	Unable to boot . . . go to BASIC

TABLE 15-45 POST CODES FOR IBM PX/2 BIOS

CODE	DESCRIPTION
00	CPU flag test
01	32-bit CPU register test
02	Test BIOS ROM checksum
03	Test system enable
04	Test system POS register
05	Test adapter-setup port
06	Test RTC/CMOS RAM shutdown byte
07	Test extended CMOS RAM
08	Test DMA and page-register channels
09	Initialize DMA command and mode registers
0A	Test memory-refresh toggle
0B	Test keyboard-controller buffers
0C	Keyboard-controller self-test
0D	Continue keyboard-controller self-test
0E	Keyboard self-test error
0F	Set up system memory configuration
10	Test first 512KB RAM
11	Halt system if memory test occurs
12	Test protected-mode instructions
13	Initialize interrupt controller 1
14	Initialize interrupt controller 2
15	Initialize 120 interrupt vectors
16	Initialize 16 interrupt vectors
17	Check CMOS/RTC battery
18	Check CMOS/RTC checksum
19	CMOS/RTC battery bad
1A	Skip memory test in protected mode

TABLE 15-45 POST CODES FOR IBM PX/2 BIOS (CONTINUED)

CODE	DESCRIPTION
1B	Prepare for CMOS shutdown
1C	Set up stack pointer to end of first 64KB
1D	Calculate low-memory size in protected mode
1E	Save the memory size detected
1F	Set up system-memory split address
20	Check for extended memory beyond 64MB
21	Test memory-address bus lines
22	Clear parity error and channel lock
23	Initialize interrupt 0
24	Check CMOS RAM validity
25	Write keyboard-controller command byte
40	Check valid CMOS RAM and video system
41	Display error code 160
42	Test registers in both interrupt controllers
43	Test interrupt controller registers
44	Test interrupt mask registers
45	Test NMI
46	NMI error has been detected
47	Test system timer 0
48	Check stuck speaker clock
49	Test system timer 0 count
4A	Test system timer 2 count
4B	Check if timer interrupt occurred
4C	Test timer 0 for improper operation (too fast or too slow)
4D	Verify timer interrupt 0
4E	Check 8042 keyboard controller
4F	Check for soft reset
50	Prepare for shutdown
51	Start protected-mode test
52	Test memory in 64KB increments
53	Check if memory test done
54	Return to real mode
55	Test for regular or manufacturing mode
56	Disable the keyboard
57	Check for keyboard self-test
58	Keyboard test passed
59	Test the keyboard controller
5A	Configure the mouse
5B	Disable the mouse
5C	Initialize interrupt vectors
5D	Initialize interrupt vectors
5E	Initialize interrupt vectors

TABLE 15-45 POST CODES FOR IBM PX/2 BIOS (CONTINUED)

CODE	DESCRIPTION
60	Save DDNIL status
61	Reset floppy drive
62	Test floppy drive
63	Turn floppy-drive motor off
64	Set up serial ports
65	Enable real-time clock interrupt
66	Configure floppy drives
67	Configure hard drives
68	Enable system CPU arbitration
69	Scan for adapter ROMs
6A	Verify serial and parallel ports
6B	Set up equipment byte
6C	Set up configuration
6D	Set keyboard-typematic rate
6E	Call Int. 19 boot loader

TABLE 15-46 POST CODES FOR LANDMARK JUMP-START XT BIOS

CODE	DESCRIPTION
01	Jump to reset area in BIOS ROM
02	Initialize DMA page register
03	Initialize DMA refresh register
04	Clear all RAM
05	Perform RAM test on 1st 64KB
06	Clear first 64KB
07	Initialize BIOS stack to 0FC0h
08	Set the equipment flag based on XT switches
09	Initialize default-interrupt vectors
0A	Initialize the 8255, if it exists
0B	Initialize the 8259 PIT and enable interrupts
0C	Setup adapters and peripherals
0D	Setup video system
0E	Initialize the video system
0F	Initialize the equipment
10	Initialize memory configuration
11	Setup system-timer function
12	Initialize system timer
13	Setup time-of-day function
14	Initialize time of day from RTC data
15	Setup and initialize "print screen" function
16	Setup and initialize cassette interface, if available

TABLE 15-46 POST CODES FOR LANDMARK JUMP-START XT BIOS (CONTINUED)

CODE	DESCRIPTION
17	Setup and initialize bootstrap function
18	Setup and initialize keyboard function
19	Enable speaker
1A	Setup system timer
1B	Enable the RTC
1C	Setup timer 2
1D	Determine memory size
1E	Read first and last word of segment
1F	Compare first and last words
20	Report found memory size to display
21	Perform BIOS ROM checksum test
22	Perform complete RAM testing on cold boot
23	Move system stack to bottom of memory and save pointer
24	Reset parity after RAM sizing
25	Enable timer and keyboard interrupts
26	Setup the serial and parallel ports
27	Setup the game port
28	Setup the floppy-disk controller
29	Scan for optional ROMs in 2KB chunks from C8000h
2A	Call the boot loader

TABLE 15-47 POST CODES FOR LANDMARK JUMPSTART AT BIOS

CODE	DESCRIPTION
03	Sound one short beep
04	Initialize the bell tone
05	Enable CMOS RAM
06	Reset video controller
07	Disable parity checking
08	Start memory refresh
09	Clear the reset flag in RAM
0A	Test DMA page registers
10	Use CMOS to determine if a soft reset has occurred
11	Check BIOS ROM checksum
12	Test system timer A
13	Test DMA channel 0
14	Test DMA channel 1
15	Test memory refresh
16	Flush 8042 KBC input buffer
17	Reset the 8042
18	Get keyboard type

TABLE 15-47   POST CODES FOR LANDMARK JUMPSTART AT BIOS (CONTINUED)

CODE	DESCRIPTION
19	Initialize the keyboard
1A	Clear any existing parity
1B	Enable on-board parity
1C	Test base 64KB memory
1D	Test base 64KB parity
1E	Initialize POST stack
20	Check keyboard type
65	Set video speed
21	Test protected-mode CPU registers
22	Initialize 8259 PIC
23	Initialize all interrupts
24	Test all interrupts
25	Perform DRAM checksum
26	Adjust configuration based on hardware found and CMOS settings
27	Check for presence of manufacturing switch
28	Initialize video controller
2A	Test video memory
2B	Test video sync
2C	Check for auxiliary video controller
2D	Change video configuration
2F	Initialize the video system
30	Change video interrupt
31	Display any POST messages
32	Test memory and calculate size
33	Adjust memory configuration
34	Enable I/O parity
35	Test 8259 PIC
36	Perform byte-swap test
37	Test NMI
38	Perform timer test
39	Initialize system timer A
3A	Protected-mode memory test
3B	Test keyboard
3C	Test keyboard interrupt
3D	Enable A20
3E	Reset hard-disk controller
3F	Setup floppy-disk controller
40	Test floppy-drive system
41	Setup keyboard
42	Enable interrupt timer
43	Check for dual floppy-disk/hard-drive controller
44	Locate floppy drive A
45	Locate floppy drive B

TABLE 15-47   POST CODES FOR LANDMARK JUMPSTART AT BIOS (CONTINUED)

CODE	DESCRIPTION
46	Reset hard-disk controller
47	Enable slave DMA
48	Locate any external ROMs
49	Initialize the parallel port(s)
4A	Initialize the serial port(s)
4B	Initialize the math co-processor
4C	Read CMOS RAM status
4D	Check CMOS configuration against detected hardware
4E	Initialize timer ticks
4F	Enable IRQ9
50	Enable on-board parity
51	Run any add-on ROMs
52	Enable keyboard interrupt
53	Reset the parallel port
60	Check for any errors
61	Sound one short beep
62	Print sign-on message
64	Call Int. 19 boot loader

TABLE 15-48   POST CODES FOR LANDMARK SUPERSOFT AT BIOS

CODE	DESCRIPTION
11	CPU register or logic error
12	ROMPOST A checksum error
13	ROMPOST B checksum error
14	8253 timer channel 0
15	8253 timer channel 1
16	8253 timer channel 2
17	8237 DMA-controller 1 error
18	8237 DMA-controller 2 error
19	DMA page-register error
1A	8042 KBC-parity error
21	Scan 16KB critical RAM error
22	Memory refresh error
23	CPU protected-mode error
24	8259 interrupt-controller 1 error
25	8259 interrupt-controller 2 error
26	Unexpected interrupt detected
27	Interrupt 0 (system timer) error
28	CMOS RTC error

TABLE 15-48 POST CODES FOR LANDMARK SUPERSOFT AT BIOS (CONTINUED)

CODE	DESCRIPTION
29	NMI error
2A	Locate and test math co-processor
31	Keyboard-controller error
32	Stuck key detected or CMOS RAM error
33	Floppy-controller error
34	Floppy-disk read error
35	MDA video-memory error
36	Color video-memory error
37	EGA/VGA RAM error
38	BIOS ROM checksum error
41	Memory error
42	Refresh fault
43-45	Display problem
59	No monitor detected

TABLE 15-49 POST CODES FOR MICROID RESEARCH BIOS 1.0A

CODE	DESCRIPTION
01	Chipset problem
02	Disable NMI and DMA
03	Check BIOS ROM checksum
04	Test DMA page register
05	Keyboard-controller test
06	Initialize the RTC, 8237, 8254, and 8259
07	Check memory refresh
08	DMA master test
09	OEM-specific test
0A	Test memory bank 0
0B	Test PIC units
0C	Test PIC controllers
0D	Initialize PIT channel 0
0E	Initialize PIT channel 2
0F	Test CMOS RAM battery
10	Check video ROM
11	Test RTC
12	Test keyboard controller
13	OEM-specific test
14	Run memory test

TABLE 15-49 POST CODES FOR MICROID RESEARCH BIOS 1.0A (CONTINUED)

CODE	DESCRIPTION
15	Keyboard controller
16	OEM-specific test
17	Test keyboard controller
18	Run memory test
19	Execute OEM memory test
1A	Update RTC contents
1B	Initialize serial ports
1C	Initialize parallel ports
1D	Test math co-processor
1E	Test floppy disk
1F	Test hard disk
20	Validate CMOS contents
21	Check keyboard lock
22	Set Num Lock on keyboard
23	OEM-specific test
29	Test adapter ROMs
2F	Call Int. 19 boot loader

TABLE 15-50 POST AND BEEP CODES FOR CONTEMPORARY MICROID RESEARCH BIOS

BEEP	POST	DESCRIPTION
LH–LLL	03	ROM-BIOS checksum failure
LH–HLL	04	DMA page-register failure
LH–LHL	05	Keyboard-controller selftest failure
LH–HHL	08	Memory-refresh circuitry failure
LH–LLH	09	Master (16 bit) DMA-controller failure
LH–HLH	09	Slave (8 bit) DMA-controller failure
LH–LLLL	0A	Base 64K pattern test failure
LH–HLLL	0A	Base 64K parity circuitry failure
LH–LHLL	0A	Base 64K parity error
LH–HHLL	0A	Base 64K data-bus failure
LH–LLHL	0A	Base 64K address bus failure
LH–HLHL	0A	Base 64K block-access read failure
LH–LHHL	0A	Base 64K block-access write failure
LH–HHHL	0B	Master 8259 failure
LH–LLLH	0B	Slave 8259 failure
LH–HLLH	0C	Master 8259 interrupt-address failure
LH–LHLH	0C	Slave 8259 interrupt-address failure

TABLE 15-50 POST AND BEEP CODES FOR CONTEMPORARY MICROID RESEARCH BIOS (CONTINUED)

BEEP	POST	DESCRIPTION
LH–HHLH	0C	8259 interrupt-address error
LH–LLHH	0C	Master 8259 stuck-interrupt error
LH–HLHH	0C	Slave 8259 stuck-interrupt error
LH–LHHH	0C	System timer 8254 CH0/IRQ0 failure
LH–HHHH	0D	8254 channel-0 (system timer) failure
LH–LLLLH	0E	8254 channel-2 (speaker) failure
LH–HLLLH	0E	8254 OUT2 (speaker detect) failure
LH–LHLLH	0F	CMOS RAM read/write test failure
LH–HHLLH	0F	RTC periodic-interrupt / IRQ8 failure
LH–LLHLH	10	Video ROM checksum failure
None	11	RTC battery discharged or CMOS contents corrupt
LH–HLHLH	12	Keyboard-controller failure
None	12	Keyboard error—stuck key
LH–LHHLH	14	Memory parity error
LH–HHHLH	14	I/O channel error
None	14	RAM pattern test failed
None	15	Keyboard failure or no keyboard present
LH–LLLHH	17	A20 test failure caused by 8042 timeout
LH–HLLHH	17	A20 gate stuck in disabled state
None	17	A20 gate stuck in asserted state
None	18	Parity circuit failure
None	19	Data bus test failed, address-line test failed, block-access read failure, block-access read/write failure, or banks decode to same location
LH–LHLHH	1A	Real-Time Clock (RTC) is not updating
None	1A	RTC settings are invalid
None	1E	Diskette CMOS configuration invalid, diskette-controller failure, or diskette drive A: failure or diskette drive B: failure
None	1F	FDD CMOS configuration invalid, fixed-disk C: failure, or fixed-disk D: failure
None	20	Fixed-disk configuration change, diskette-configuration change, serial-port configuration change, parallel-port configuration change, video-configuration change, memory-configuration change, or co-processor-configuration change
None	21	System key is in locked position
None	29	Adapter ROM Checksum failure

*L = low tone and H = high tone

TABLE 15-51   POST CODES FOR MICROID RESEARCH 3.4X BIOS

CODE	DESCRIPTION
00†	Cold start, output EDX register to I/O ports 85h, 86h, 8Dh, 8Eh for later use
01	Initialize any custom KBD controller, disable CPU cache, cold initialize onboard I/O chipset, size and test RAM, size cache
02	Disable critical IO (monitor, DMA, FDC, I/O ports, speaker, NMI)
03	Checksum the BIOS ROM
04	Test page registers
05	Enable A20 gate, issue 8042 self test
06	Initialize ISA I/O
07	Warm initialize custom KBD controller, warm initialize onboard I/O chipset
08	Refresh toggle test
09	Test DMA master registers, test DMA slave registers
0A	Test 1st 64K of base memory
0B	Test master 8259 mask, test slave 8259 mask
0C	Test 8259 slave, test 8259 slave's interrupt range, initialize interrupt vectors 00–77h, initialize KBD buffer variables
0D	Test Timer 0, 8254 channel 0
0E	Test 8254 Ch2, speaker channel
0F	Test RTC, CMOS RAM read/write test
10	Turn on monitor, show any possible error messages
11	Read and checksum the CMOS
12	Call video ROM initialization routines, show display sign-on message, show ESC delay message
13	Set 8MHz AT-bus
14	Size and test the base memory, stuck NMI check
15	No KB and PowerOn: Retry KB init.
16	Size and test CPU cache
17	Test A20 Off and On states
18	Size and test external memory, stuck NMI check
19	Size and test system memory, stuck NMI check
1A	Test RTC time
1B	Determine serial ports
1C	Determine parallel ports
1D	Initialize numeric co-processor
1E	Determine floppy-diskette controllers
1F	Determine IDE controllers
20	Display CMOS configuration changes
21	Clear screens
22	Set/reset NumLock LED, perform security functions
23	Final determination of on-board serial/parallel ports
24	Set KB typematic rate
25	Initialize floppy controller
26	Initialize ATA discs
27	Set the video mode for primary adapter

TABLE 15-51 POST CODES FOR MICROID RESEARCH 3.4X BIOS (CONTINUED)

CODE	DESCRIPTION
28	Cyrix WB-CPU support, Green PC: purge 8259 slave, relieve any trapped IRRs before enabling PwrMgmt, set 8042 pins, Ctrl-Alt-Del possible now, enable CPU features
29	Reset A20 to Off, install adapter ROMs
2A	Clear primary screen, convert RTC to system ticks, set final DOS timer variables
2B	Enable NMI and latch
2C	Reserved
2D	Reserved
2E	Fast A20: Fix A20
2F	Purge 8259 slave; relieve any trapped IRRs before enabling Green PC; pass control to INT 19 boot
32	Test CPU burst
33	Reserved
34	Determine 8042, set 8042 warm-boot flag STS.2
35	Test HMA wrap, verify A20 enabled via F000:10 HMA
36	Reserved
37	Validate CPU: CPU step NZ, CPUID check; Disable CPU features
38	Set 8042 pins (high-speed, cache off)
39	PCI Bus: Load PCI; processor vector initialized, BIOS vector initialized, OEM vector initialized
3A	Scan PCI bus
3B	Initialize PCI bus with intermediate defaults
3C	Initialize PCI OEM with intermediate defaults, OEM bridge
3D	PCI bus or Plug and Play: Initialize AT slotmap from AT-Bus CDE usage
3E	Find phantom CDE ROM PCI-cards
3F	PCI bus: final fast back-to-back state
40	OEM POST initialization, hook audio
41	Allocate I/O on PCI bus, logs in PCI IDE
42	Hook PCI-ATA chips
43	Allocate IRQs on the PCI bus
44	Allocate/enable PCI memory/ROM space
45	Determine PS/2 mouse
46	Map IRQs to PCI bus per user CMOS, enable ATA IRQs
47	PCI-ROM install, note user CMOS
48	If Setup conditions, execute setup utility
49	Test F000 shadow integrity, transfer EPROM to shadow RAM
4A	Hook VL ATA chip
4B	Identify and spin-up all drives
4C	Detect secondary IRQ, if VL/AT-Bus IDE exists, but its IRQ not known yet, then autodetect it
4D	Detect/log 32-bit I/O ATA devices
4E	ATAPI drive M/S bitmap to shadow RAM, set INT13 vector
4F	Finalize shadow-RAM variables
50	Chain INT 13

TABLE 15-51 POST CODES FOR MICROID RESEARCH 3.4X BIOS (CONTINUED)

CODE	DESCRIPTION
51	Load PnP, processor vector initialized, BIOS vector initialized, OEM vector initialized
52	Scan Plug and Play, update PnP device count
53	Supplement IRQ usage—AT IRQs
54	Conditionally assign everything PnP wants
58	Perform OEM custom boot sequence just prior to INT 19 boot
59	Return from OEM custom boot sequence. Pass control to 1NT 19 boot
5A	Display MR BIOS logo
88	Dead motherboard and/or CPU and/or BIOS ROM
FF	BIOS POST finished

TABLE 15-52 POST CODES FOR NCR PC6 (XT) BIOS

CODE	DESCRIPTION
AA	8088 CPU failure
B1	2764 EPROM-checksum failure
B2	8237 DMA-controller failure
B3	8253 PIT failure
B4	RAM failure
B5	8259 PIC failure
B6	RAM parity error
BB	All tests passed, ready to boot

TABLE 15-53 POST CODES FOR NCR AT BIOS

CODE	DESCRIPTION
01	Test the CPU registers
02	Test system support I/O
03	Test BIOS ROM checksum
04	Test DMA page registers
05	Test timer channel 1
06	Test timer channel 2
07	Test RAM refresh logic
08	Test base 64KB
09	Test 8/16-bit bus conversion
0A	Test interrupt controller 1
0B	Test interrupt controller 2
0C	Test I/O controller
0D	Test CMOS RAM R/W operation
0E	Test battery power

TABLE 15-53 POST CODES FOR NCR AT BIOS (CONTINUED)

CODE	DESCRIPTION
0F	Test CMOS RAM checksum
10	Test CPU protected mode
11	Test video configuration
12	Test primary video controller
13	Test secondary video controller
20	Display results of tests to this point
21	Test DMA controller 1
22	Test DMA controller 2
23	Test system timer channel 0
24	Initialize interrupt controllers
25	Test interrupts
26	Test interrupts
30	Check base 640KB memory
31	Check extended memory size
32	Test higher 8 address lines
33	Test base memory
34	Test extended memory
40	Test keyboard
41	Test keyboard
42	Test keyboard
43	Test keyboard
44	Test A20 gate
50	Set up hardware-interrupt vectors
51	Enable interrupt-timer channel 0
52	Check BIOS ROM
60	Test floppy-disk controller and drive
61	Test hard-drive controller
62	Initialize floppy drives
63	Initialize hard drives
70	Test real-time clock
71	Set time of day in RTC
72	Check parallel-interface port(s)
73	Check serial-interface port(s)
74	Check for any option ROMs
75	Check math co-processors
76	Enable keyboard and RTC interrupts
F0	System not configured properly (or hardware defect)
F1	Scan and execute any option ROMs
F2	Call Int. 19 boot loader

TABLE 15-54 POST CODES FOR NCR PC916 BIOS

CODE	DESCRIPTION
01	Test CPU registers
03	Test BIOS ROM checksum
04	Test DMA page registers
05	Test timer channel 1
06	Test timer channel 2
0C	Test 8042 keyboard controller
14	Test disabling speed stretch at port 69h
15	Start refresh timer 1
16	Enable speed stretch at port 69h
17	Clear write-protect bit
1B	Test 64KB shadow RAM
18	Write and test interrupt descriptor table
19	Verify RAM
02	Verify port 61h
07	Test refresh logic
08	Test base 64KB RAM
09	Test 8/16-bit bus-conversion logic
0A	Test interrupt-mask register A
0B	Test interrupt-mask register B
1A	Check 8042 keyboard controller
0D	Test CMOS RAM shutdown byte
0E	Test CMOS RAM battery power
0F	Test CMOS RAM checksum
10	Test CPU protected mode
11	Test video configuration
12	Initialize and test primary video controller
13	Primary video error
20	Display results of tests to this point
21	Test DMA controller 1
22	Test DMA controller 2
23	Test timer 1 counter 0 840nS clock timer
27	Test timer 2 counter 0 for NMI
28	Test timer 2 counter 1
24	Initialize both interrupt controllers
25	Check for unexpected interrupts
26	Wait for interrupt
30	Check base 640KB memory
31	Check extended-memory size
32	Test higher 8 address lines
33	Test base memory
34	Test extended memory (up to 256MB)
35	Test RAM in segment E000h

TABLE 15-54 POST CODES FOR NCR PC916 BIOS (CONTINUED)

CODE	DESCRIPTION
40	Test keyboard enable/disable
41	Test keyboard-reset command
42	Test keyboard
43	Test keyboard
F4	Display speed setting
45	Initialize the mouse and enable IRQ1
44	Test address-overrun capability
50	Set up hardware-interrupt vectors
51	Enable IRQ0 interval interrupt from timer 0
60	Test for floppy- and hard-disk controllers and drives
61	Test disk controller
62	Initialize floppy drives
63	Initialize hard drives
74	Check and execute option ROMs from C8000h to DFFFFh
70	Test RTC
71	Set interval timer
72	Configure and test parallel interface
73	Configure and test serial interface
75	Test math co-processor, if installed
76	Enable keyboard and RTC
F0	Display any logged errors
F6	Test base memory
F7	Run comprehensive base memory test
F3	Go to setup, if F1 was pressed
F4	Display speed setting
F5	Initialize counter 2 for speed testing
F1	Test system code at E0000h and copy video ROM to shadow memory
F2	Call Int. 19 boot loader
F6	Test base memory
F7	Test extended memory

TABLE 15-55 POST CODES FOR OLIVETTI 1076/AT&T BIOS

PASS	FAIL	DESCRIPTION
41	7F	CPU flag and register test
42	7E	Check and verify CMOS shutdown code
43	7D	BIOS ROM checksum test
44	7C	Test the 8253 timer
45	7B	Start memory refresh
46	7A	Test the 8041 keyboard controller
47	79	Test the first 8KB of RAM

TABLE 15-55 POST CODES FOR OLIVETTI 1076/AT&T BIOS (CONTINUED)

PASS	FAIL	DESCRIPTION
48	78	Test protected-mode operation
49	77	Test CMOS RAM shutdown byte
4A	76	Test protected-mode operation
4B	75	Test RAM from 8KB to 640KB
4C	74	Test all RAM above 1MB
4D	73	Test NMI
4E	72	Test RAM parity system
50	71	Test 8259 PIC 1
51	6F	Test 8259 PIC 2
52	6E	Test DMA page register
53	6D	Test the 8237 DMA controller 1
54	6C	Test the 8237 DMA controller 2
55	6B	Test PIO port 61h
56	6A	Test the keyboard controller
57	69	Test the CMOS clock/calendar IC
59	68	Test the CPU protected mode
5A	66	Test CMOS RAM battery
5B	65	Test CMOS RAM
5C	64	Verify CMOS RAM checksum
5D	63	Test parallel-port configuration
5E	62	Test serial-port configuration
5F	61	Test memory configuration below 640KB
60	60	Test memory configuration above 1MB
61	5F	Detect and test math co-processor
62	5E	Test configuration of game-port adapter
62	5D	Test key-lock switch
63	5D	Test hard-drive configuration
64	5C	Configure floppy drives
66	5B	Test option ROMs
—	—	Call Int. 19 boot loader

TABLE 15-56 POST CODES FOR OLIVETTI M20 BIOS

Note: M20 codes are displayed on the monitor and sent to printer port

CODE	DESCRIPTION
triangle	Test CPU registers and instructions
triangle	Test system RAM
4 vertical lines	Test CPU call and trap instructions
diamond	Initialize screen and printer drivers
EC0	8255 parallel-interface IC test failed

TABLE 15-56 POST CODES FOR OLIVETTI M20 BIOS (CONTINUED)

CODE	DESCRIPTION
EC1	6845 CRT controller IC test failed
EC2	1797 floppy-disk controller chip failed
EC3	8253 timer IC failed
EC4	8251 keyboard interface failed
EC5	8251 keyboard test failed
EC6	8259 PIC IC test failed
EK0	Keyboard did not respond
EK1	Keyboard responds, but self-test failed
ED1	Disk drive 1 test failed
ED0	Disk drive 0 test failed
EI0	Non-vectored interrupt error
E11	Vectored interrupt error

TABLE 15-57 POST CODES FOR OLIVETTI M24/AT&T BIOS

CODE	DESCRIPTION
40	CPU flags and register test failed
41	BIOS ROM checksum test failed
42	Disable 8253 timer channel 1
43	8237 DMA-controller test failed
44	8259 PIC test failed
45	Install the real interrupt vectors
48	Send beep and initialize all basic hardware

TABLE 15-58 POST CODES FOR OLIVETTI PS/2 BIOS

CODE	DESCRIPTION
01	Test CPU
02	Check CMOS shutdown byte
03	Initialize the PIC
04	Test refresh
05	Test CMOS/RTC periodic interrupt
06	Test timer ratio
07	Test first 64KB of RAM
08	Test 8042 keyboard controller
09	Test NMI
0A	Test 8254 PIT
0B	Test port 94h
0C	Test port 103h

TABLE 15-58 POST CODES FOR OLIVETTI PS/2 BIOS (CONTINUED)

CODE	DESCRIPTION
0D	Test port 102h
0E	Test port 96h
0F	Test port 107h
10	Blank the display
11	Check the keyboard
12	Test CMOS RAM battery
13	Verify CMOS RAM checksum
14	Verify extended CMOS RAM checksum
15	Initialize system board and adapter
16	Initialize and test RAM
17	Test protected-mode registers
18	Test CMOS RAM-shutdown byte
19	Test CMOS protected mode
1A	Initiate video-adapter ROM scan
1B	Test BIOS ROM checksum
1C	Test PIC #1
1D	Test PIC #2
1E	Initialize interrupt vectors
1F	Test CMOS RAM
20	Test extended CMOS RAM
21	Test CMOS real-time clock
22	Test clock calendar
23	Dummy checkpoint
24	Test watchdog timer
25	Test 64KB to 640KB RAM
26	Configure lower 640KB RAM
27	Test extended memory
28	Initialize extended BIOS data segment and log POST errors
29	Configure memory above 1MB
2A	Dummy checkpoint
2B	Test RAM parity
2C	Test DMA page registers
2D	Test DMA controller registers
2E	Test DMA transfer-count register
2F	Initialize DMA controller
30	Test PIO 61
31	Test the keyboard
32	Initialize keyboard typematic rate and delay
33	Test auxiliary device
34	Test advanced protected mode
35	Configure parallel ports
36	Configure 8250 serial ports

TABLE 15-58 POST CODES FOR OLIVETTI PS/2 BIOS (CONTINUED)

CODE	DESCRIPTION
37	Test and configure math co-processor
38	Test and configure game-port adapter
39	Configure and initialize hard disk
3A	Floppy-disk configuration
3B	Initialize ROM drivers
3C	Display total memory and hard drives
3D	Final initialization
3E	Detect and initialize parallel ports
3F	Initialize hard drive and controller
40	Initialize math co-processor
42	Initiate adapter ROM scan
CC	Unexpected processor exception occurred
DD	Save DDNIL status
EE	NMI handler shutdown
FF	Call Int. 19 boot loader

TABLE 15-59 POST CODES FOR PHILIPS BIOS

CODE	DESCRIPTION
0A	DMA page-register R/W bad
10	CMOS RAM R/W error
11	System BIOS ROM checksum error
12	Timer A error
13	DMA controller A error
14	DMA controller B error
15	Memory-refresh error
16	Keyboard-controller error
17	Keyboard-controller error
19	Keyboard-controller error
1C	Base 64KB RAM error
1D	Base 64KB RAM parity error
1F	LSI sync missing
21	PVAM register error
25	System-options error
2B	Video sync error
2C	Video BIOS ROM error
2D	Monochrome/color-configuration error
2E	No video memory detected
35	Interrupt controller error

TABLE 15-59 POST CODES FOR PHILIPS BIOS (CONTINUED)

CODE	DESCRIPTION
36	Byte-swapper error
37	NMI error
38	Timer interrupt fault
39	LSI timer halted
3A	Main-memory test error
3B	Keyboard error
3C	Keyboard-interrupt error
3D	DDNIL scan halted and cache disabled
40	Diskette error
48	Adapter card error
4C	CMOS battery/checksum error
4D	System-options error
52	Keyboard-controller error
6A	Failure shadowing BIOS ROM
70	Memory-size configuration error

TABLE 15-60 POST CODES FOR PHOENIX TECHNOLOGIES XT 2.52 BIOS

CODE	DESCRIPTION
01	Test 8253 system timer
02	First 64KB RAM failure
03	First 1KB parity check failed
04	Initialize the 8259 PIC IC
05	Second 1KB RAM (BIOS data area) failed
—	Initialize the display

TABLE 15-61 POST CODES FOR PHOENIX TEXHNOLOGIES ISA/EISA/MAC BIOS

CODE	DESCRIPTION
01	CPU register test
02	CMOS R/W test
03	Testing BIOS ROM checksum
04	Testing 8253 PIT IC
05	Initializing the 8237 DMA controller

TABLE 15-61   POST CODES FOR PHOENIX TEXHNOLOGIES ISA/EISA/MAC BIOS (CONTINUED)

CODE	DESCRIPTION
06	Testing the 8237 DMA page register
08	RAM-refresh circuit test
09	Test first 64KB of RAM
0A	Test first 64KB RAM data lines
0B	Test first 64KB RAM parity
0C	Test first 64KB RAM address lines
0D	Parity failure detected for first 64KB RAM
10–1F	Data bit (0–15) bad in first 64KB RAM
20	Slave DMA register faulty
21	Master DMA register faulty
22	Master PIC register faulty
23	Slave PIC register faulty
25	Initializing interrupt vectors
27	Keyboard-controller test
28	Testing CMOS checksum and battery power
29	Validate CMOS contents
2B	Video initialization faulty
2C	Video retrace test failed
2D	Search for video ROM
2E	Test video ROM
30	Video system checks OK
31	Monochrome video mode detected
32	Color (40 column) mode detected
33	Color (80 column) mode detected
34	Timer-tick interrupt test
35	CMOS shutdown byte test
36	Gate A20 failure (8042 KBC)
37	Unexpected interrupt
38	Extended RAM test
3A	Interval timer channel 2
3B	Test time-of-day clock
3C	Locate and test serial ports
3D	Locate and test parallel ports
3E	Locate and test math co-processor
41	System board select bad
42	Extended CMOS RAM bad

TABLE 15-62 POST CODES FOR PHOENIXBIOS 4.0

BEEP	POST	MEANING
1–1–1–3	02	Verify real-mode operation
1–1–2–1	04	Get the CPU type
1–1–2–3	06	Initialize system hardware
1–1–3–1	08	Initialize chipset registers with POST values
1–1–3–2	09	Set POST flag
1–1–3–3	0A	Initialize CPU registers
1–1–4–1	0C	Initialize cache to initial POST values
1–1–4–3	0E	Initialize I/O
1–2–1–1	10	Initialize power management
1–2–1–2	11	Load alternate registers with POST values
1–2–1–3	12	Jump to UserPatch0
1–2–2–1	14	Initialize keyboard controller
1–2–2–3	16	BIOS ROM checksum
1–2–3–1	18	8254 timer initialization
1–2–3–3	1A	8237 DMA controller initialization
1–2–4–1	1C	Reset programmable interrupt controller
1–3–1–1	20	Test DRAM refresh
1–3–1–3	22	Test 8742 keyboard controller
1–3–2–1	24	Set ES segment to register to 4 GB
1–3–3–1	28	Auto-size DRAM
1–3–3–3	2A	Clear 512K base RAM
1–3–4–1	2C	Test 512 base-address lines
1–3–4–3	2E	Test 512K base memory
1–4–1–3	32	Test CPU bus-clock frequency
1–4–2–4	37	Reinitialize the motherboard chipset
1–4–3–1	38	Shadow system BIOS ROM
1–4–3–2	39	Reinitialize the cache
1–4–3–3	3A	Auto-size cache
1–4–4–1	3C	Configure advanced chipset registers
1–4–4–2	3D	Load alternate registers with CMOS values
2–1–1–1	40	Set initial CPU speed
2–1–1–3	42	Initialize interrupt vectors
2–1–2–1	44	Initialize BIOS interrupts
2–1–2–3	46	Check ROM copyright notice
2–1–2–4	47	Initialize manager for PCI options ROMs
2–1–3–1	48	Check video configuration against CMOS
2–1–3–2	49	Initialize PCI bus and devices
2–1–3–3	4A	Initialize all video adapters in system
2–1–4–1	4C	Shadow video BIOS ROM
2–1–4–3	4E	Display copyright notice
2–2–1–1	50	Display CPU type and speed
2–2–1–3	52	Test keyboard
2–2–2–1	54	Set key click, if enabled

TABLE 15-62 POST CODES FOR PHOENIXBIOS 4.0 (CONTINUED)

BEEP	POST	MEANING
2–2–2–3	56	Enable keyboard
2–2–3–1	58	Test for unexpected interrupts
2–2–3–3	5A	Display prompt "Press F2 to enter Setup"
2–2–4–1	5C	Test RAM between 512 and 640k
2–3–1–1	60	Test expanded memory
2–3–1–3	62	Test extended memory address lines
2–3–2–1	64	Jump to UserPatch1
2–3–2–3	66	Configure advanced cache registers
2–3–3–1	68	Enable external and CPU caches
2–3–3–3	6A	Display external cache size
2–3–4–1	6C	Display shadow message
2–3–4–3	6E	Display non-disposable segments
2–4–1–1	70	Display error messages
2–4–1–3	72	Check for configuration errors
2–4–2–1	74	Test real-time clock
2–4–2–3	76	Check for keyboard errors
2–4–4–1	7C	Set up hardware interrupts vectors
2–4–4–3	7E	Test co-processor, if present
3–1–1–1	80	Disable onboard I/O ports
3–1–1–3	82	Detect and install external RS232 ports
3–1–2–1	84	Detect and install external parallel ports
3–1–2–3	86	Re-initialize onboard I/O ports
3–1–3–1	88	Initialize BIOS data area
3–1–3–3	8A	Initialize Extended BIOS data area
3–1–4–1	8C	Initialize floppy controller
3–2–1–1	90	Initialize hard-disk controller
3–2–1–2	91	Initialize local-bus hard-disk controller
3–2–1–3	92	Jump to UserPatch2
3–2–2–1	94	Disable A20 address line
3–2–2–3	96	Clear huge ES segment register
3–2–3–1	98	Search for option ROMs
3–2–3–3	9A	Shadow option ROMs
3–2–4–1	9C	Set up power management
3–2–4–3	9E	Enable hardware interrupts
3–3–1–1	A0	Set time of day
3–3–1–3	A2	Check key lock
3–3–3–1	A8	Erase F2 prompt
3–3–3–3	AA	Scan for F2 key stroke
3–3–4–1	AC	Enter Setup
3–3–4–3	AE	Clear in–POST flag
3–4–1–1	B0	Check for errors
3–4–1–3	B2	POST done—prepare to boot operating system
3–4–2–1	B4	One beep

TABLE 15-62 POST CODES FOR PHOENIXBIOS 4.0 (CONTINUED)

BEEP	POST	MEANING
3–4–2–3	B6	Check password (optional)
3–4–3–1	B8	Clear global descriptor table
3–4–4–1	BC	Clear parity checkers
3–4–4–3	BE	Clear screen (optional)
3–4–4–4	BF	Check virus and backup reminders
4–1–1–1	C0	Try to boot with INT 19
4–2–1–1	D0	Interrupt-handler error
4–2–1–3	D2	Unknown-interrupt error
4–2–2–1	D4	Pending-interrupt error
4–2–2–3	D6	Initialize option ROM error
4–2–3–1	D8	Shutdown error
4–2–3–3	DA	Extended block move
4–2–4–1	DC	Shutdown 10 error
4–3–1–3	E2	Initialize the motherboard chipset
4–3–1–4	E3	Initialize refresh counter
4–3–2–1	E4	Check for forced flash
4–3–2–2	E5	Check HW status of ROM
4–3–2–3	E6	BIOS ROM is OK
4–3–2–4	E7	Do a complete RAM test
4–3–3–1	E8	Do OEM initialization
4–3–3–2	E9	Initialize interrupt controller
4–3–3–3	EA	Read in bootstrap code
4–3–3–4	EB	Initialize all vectors
4–3–4–1	EC	Boot the Flash program
4–3–4–2	ED	Initialize the boot device
4–3–4–3	EE	Boot code was read OK

TABLE 15-63 POST CODES FOR QUADTEL XT BIOS

CODE	DESCRIPTION
03	Test CPU flags
06	Test CPU registers
09	Initialize any system-specific chipsets
0C	Test BIOS ROM checksum
0F	Initialize 8237 DMA page registers
12	Test 8237 DMA address and count registers
15	Initialize 8237 DMA
18	Test 8253 system timer IC (PIT)
1B	Initialize the 8253 PIT
1E	Start memory refresh test
21	Test the base 64KB RAM

TABLE 15-63 POST CODES FOR QUADTEL XT BIOS

CODE	DESCRIPTION
24	Set up interrupt vectors
27	Initialize 8259 PIC
2A	Test interrupt mask register
2D	Test for unexpected interrupt
30	Test V40 DMA, if present
31	Test for DDNIL bits
33	Verify system-clock interrupt
36	Test the keyboard
39	Set up interrupt table
3C	Read system-configuration switches
3F	Test and initialize video
42	Locate and test COM ports
45	Locate and test LPT ports
48	Locate and test the game-adapter port
4B	Display BIOS copyright message on screen
4E	Calculate CPU speed
54	Test system memory
55	Test floppy drive
57	Initialize system before boot
5A	Call Int. 19 boot loader

TABLE 15-64 POST CODES FOR QUADTEL AT 3.00 BIOS

CODE	DESCRIPTION
02	Test CPU flags
04	Test CPU registers
06	Perform system hardware initialization
08	Initialize specific chipset registers
0A	Test BIOS ROM checksum
0C	Test 8237 DMA page registers
0E	Test 8254 PIT
10	Initialize the 8254 PIT
12	Test 8237 DMA controller
14	Initialize 8237 DMA controller
16	Initialize 8259 PIC
18	Test and set the 8259 PIC
1A	Test memory refresh
1C	Test base 64KB memory
1E	Test base 64KB memory
20	Test base 64KB memory
22	Test keyboard and keyboard controller

TABLE 15-64 POST CODES FOR QUADTEL AT 3.00 BIOS (CONTINUED)

CODE	DESCRIPTION
24	Test CMOS checksum and battery
26	Start first protected-mode test
28	Check memory size
2A	Autosize memory
2C	Set memory IC interleave
2E	Exit first protected-mode test
30	Unexpected shutdown
32	System board memory size
34	Relocate shadow RAM, if available
36	Configure extended memory
38	Configure wait states
3A	Retest 64KB base RAM
3C	Calculate CPU speed
3E	Get configuration from 8042 KBC
40	Configure CPU speed
42	Initialize interrupt vectors
44	Verify video configuration
46	Initialize the video system
48	Test unexpected interrupts
4A	Start second protected-mode test
4B	Verify protected-mode instruction
4D	Verify protected-mode instruction
50	Verify protected-mode instruction
52	Verify protected-mode instruction
54	Verify protected-mode instruction
56	Unexpected exception
58	Test address line A20
5A	Test keyboard
5C	Determine AT or XT keyboard
5E	Start third protected-mode test
60	Test base memory
62	Test base memory address
64	Test shadow memory
66	Test extended memory
68	Test extended-memory addresses
6A	Determine memory size
6C	Display error messages
6E	Copy BIOS to shadow memory
70	Test 8254 PIT
73	Test RTC
74	Test keyboard for stuck keys
76	Initialize system hardware

TABLE 15-64 POST CODES FOR QUADTEL AT 3.00 BIOS (CONTINUED)

CODE	DESCRIPTION
78	Locate and test the math co-processor
7A	Determine COM ports
7C	Determine LPT ports
7E	Initialize the BIOS data area
80	Check for a floppy/hard-drive controller
82	Test floppy disk
84	Test fixed disk
86	Check for option ROMs
88	Check for keyboard lock
8A	Wait for <F1> key pressed
8C	Final system initialization
8E	Call Int. 19 boot loader

TABLE 15-65 POST CODES FOR TANDON TYPE A BIOS

CODE	DESCRIPTION
01	Test CPU flags and registers
02	Test BIOS ROM checksum
03	Test CMOS RAM battery
04	Test 8254 timer
05	8254 timer test failed
06	Test RAM refresh
07	Test first 16KB RAM
08	Initialize interrupt vectors
09	Test 8259 PIC
0A	Configure temporary interrupt vectors
0B	Initialize interrupt-vector table 1
0C	Initialize interrupt-vector table 2
0D	Initialize fixed-disk vector
0E	Interrupt vector test failed
0F	Clear keyboard controller
10	Keyboard-controller test failed
11	Run keyboard-controller self-test
12	Initialize equipment check-data area
13	Check and initialize math co-processor
14	Test CMOS RAM contents
15	Test and configure parallel ports
16	Test and configure serial ports
17	Call Int. 19 boot loader

TABLE 15-66 POST CODES FOR TANDON TYPE B BIOS

CODE	DESCRIPTION
01	Cold boot initialization started
06	Initialize any specialized chipsets
07	Warm reboot starts here
08	Keyboard initialization passed
09	Keyboard self-test finished
0A	Test CMOS RAM battery
0B	Save CMOS RAM battery level in CMOS diagnostic register
0C	Finished saving CMOS battery condition
0D	Test 8254 PIT and disable RAM parity check
0E	8254 PIT test failed
0F	Initialize 8254 PIT channels and start memory-refresh test
10	Refresh test failed
11	Test base 64KB RAM
12	Base 64KB RAM test failed
13	Base 64KB RAM test passed
14	Perform R/W test of CMOS RAM
15	CMOS RAM R/W test complete
16	Calculating CPU speed
18	Test and initialize 8259 PICs
1A	8259 PIC initialization complete
1B	Spurious interrupt detected
1C	Spurious interrupt did not occur
1D	Error . . . timer 0 interrupt failed
1E	8259 PIC tests passed
20	Set up interrupt vectors 02 to 1F
21	Set up interrupt vectors 70 to 77
22	Clear interrupt vectors 41 to 46
23	Read 8042 self-test result
24	Test for proper 8042 KBC self-test
25	Error . . . KBC self-test failed
26	8042 KBC self-test passed
27	Confirm DMA working
28	Initialize video system
29	Set video with cursor off
2A	Video parameters are initialized
2B	Enable NMI and I/O channel check
2C	Run RAM test to check RAM size
2D	RAM sizing complete
2E	Reset keyboard controller
2F	Initialize the CMOS RTC
30	Initialize floppy-drive controller
31	Initialize hard-disk controller
32	Disk controller has been initialized

TABLE 15-66 POST CODES FOR TANDON TYPE B BIOS (CONTINUED)

CODE	DESCRIPTION
33	Perform equipment check and initialize math co-processor
34	Initialize serial and parallel ports
35	Test CMOS RAM battery level
36	Check for keystroke
37	Enable 8254 PIT channel 0
38	Configure cache memory
39	Enable keyboard interface and interrupts
3A	Setup finished . . . clear display
3B	Test the floppy- and hard-disk drives
3C	Scan and run any option BIOS ROMs between C800h and E000h
3D	Disable gate A20
3E	Gate A20 is disabled
3F	Call Int. 19 boot loader

TABLE 15-67 POST CODES FOR TANDON i486 EISA BIOS

CODE	DESCRIPTION
01	Disable cache and EISA NMIs, enable BIOS ROM
05	Initialize address decoder and 640KB RAM
06	Clear CMOS RAM shutdown flag
07	Test 8042 KBC
08	Run 8042 KBC self-test
AA	8042 KBC self-test result
09	Test BIOS ROM checksum
0A	Read CMOS registers three times
0B	Bad CMOS RAM battery
0C	Send command to port 61 to disable speaker
0D	Test 8254 PIT
0E	8254 PIT is faulty
0F	Enable and test memory refresh
10	Memory refresh failed
11	Check and clear first 64KB of RAM
12	First 64KB RAM failed
13	First 64KB memory test passed
14	Test CMOS RAM
15	Shadow BIOS and set system speed high
16	Check CMOS shutdown flag
17	Reset was cold boot
18	Prepare 8259 PICs

TABLE 15-67 POST CODES FOR TANDON i486 EISA BIOS (CONTINUED)

CODE	DESCRIPTION
19	8259 PIC initialization failed
1A	Test 8259 PIC
1B	Check for spurious interrupts
1C	Check system timer IC
1D	PIT failure
1E	Initialize interrupt vectors
1F	Initialize interrupt vectors 00 to 6F
20	Set vectors for interrupt 02–1F
21	Set interrupt vectors for 70–77
22	Clear interrupt vectors for 41 and 46
23	Read 8042 self-test results from DMA page register
24	Test for proper 8042 self-test result
25	8042 self-test failed
26	Initialize the 8042 keyboard controller
27	Check shutdown flag
28	Install video ROM and initialize video
29	Install video ROM, set for mono/color operation, and initialize video
2A	Check for bad CMOS RAM
2B	Check shutdown flag
2C	Test memory for proper size
2D	Display any error messages
2E	Initialize 8042 KBC
2F	Initialize time of day in the RTC
30	Test for and initialize the floppy-disk controller
31	Enable C&T IDE interface and test for hard drive
32	Test and initialize 8259 DMA registers
33	Test and initialize math co-processor
34	Test and initialize parallel and serial ports
35	Check CMOS RAM
36	Check for keyboard lock
37	Enable system clock-tick, keyboard, and interrupt-controller interrupts
38	Initialize RAM variables
39	Enter CMOS Setup mode, if proper keystroke pressed
3A	Clear display
3B	Initialize floppy and fixed disk drives
3C	Scan and run option ROMs
3D	Clear CMOS shutdown flag and turn off gate A20
3E	Set interrupt vectors
3F	Call Int. 19 boot loader

TABLE 15-68 POST CODES FOR ZENITH ORION 4.1E BIOS

CODE	DESCRIPTION
02	Enter protected mode
03	Perform main-board initialization
F0	Start basic hardware initialization
F1	Clear CMOS status locations
F2	Starting CLIO initialization
F3	Initialize SYSCFG register
F4	DXPI initialization for boot block
F5	Turning cache off
F6	Configure CPU socket
F7	Checking for math co-processor
F8	82C206 default initialization
F9	Chipset default initialization
FF	End of machine-specific boot block
04	Check the flash ROM checksum
05	Flash ROM OK
06	Reset or power up
07	CLIO default initialization
08	SYSCFG registers initialized
09	CMOS RAM initialization
10	SCP initialized
11	DRAM autosize detection complete
12	Parity checking enabled
18	Video ROM test at C0000h
19	Internal video ROM checked
1A	Returning to real mode
1B	Internal video hardware enabled
1D	CPU clock frequency detected
1E	BIOS data area cleared
20	Reset
21	Continue after setting memory size
22	Continue after memory test
23	Continue after memory error
24	Continue with boot loader request
25	Jump to user code
26	Continue after protected mode passed
27	Continue after protected mode failed
28	Continue after extended protected-mode test
29	Continue after block move
2A	Jump to user code
30	Exit from protected mode
31	Test/reset passed
32	Check the ROM checksum
33	Clear the video screen

TABLE 15-68   POST CODES FOR ZENITH ORION 4.1E BIOS (CONTINUED)

CODE	DESCRIPTION
34	Check system DRAM configuration
35	Check CMOS contents
36	Turn off the UMB RAM
37	Test parity generation
38	Initialize system variables
39	Check for power errors
3A	Initialize SCP mode
3B	Test CMOS diagnostic power reset
3C	Test CPU reset
3D	Save CPU ID
3E	Initialize the video system
3F	Initialize the DMA controllers
40	System speed error detected
41	Test EEPROM checksum
42	Configure parallel ports, floppy disks, and hard disks
43	Test extended video BIOS
44	Turn cache off
45	Test extended RAM
46	Test base RAM
47	Determine the amount of memory in the system
48	Set warm boot flag
49	Clear 16KB of base RAM
4A	Install BIOS interrupt vector
4B	Test system timer
4C	Initialize interrupt
4D	Enable default hardware initialization
4E	Determine global I/O configuration
4F	Initialize video
50	Initialize WD90C30 scratchpad
51	Check for errors before boot
53	Test system and initialize
55	Initialize the keyboard processor
56	Initialize the PS/2 mouse
57	Configure CLIO for mouse
58	Configure CLIO for LAN
59	Configure CLIO for SCSI
5A	Configure CLIO for WAM
5B	Wait for user to enter password
5C	Initialize and enable system clock
5D	Test and initialize the floppy drive
5E	Check for Z150-type disk
5F	Initialize hard-drive sub-system
60	Set default I/O device parameters

TABLE 15-68 POST CODES FOR ZENITH ORION 4.1E BIOS (CONTINUED)	
CODE	**DESCRIPTION**
61	Get LAN ID from LAN
62	Install option ROM(s) at C8000h
63	Install option ROM(s) at E0000h
64	Initialize the SCSI interface
65	Run with A20 line off
66	Turn off the SCP
67	Set machine speed based on CMOS contents
68	Turn on cache
69	Calibrate 1-ms constants
6A	Enable NMI
6C	Clear warm boot flag
6D	Check for errors before boot
6E	Call Int. 19 boot loader

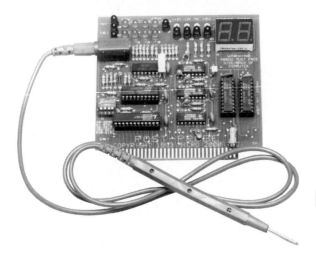

FIGURE 15-1 The Post-Probe from Micro2000.
Micro2000, Inc.

The POST Board

Although virtually all current PC BIOS versions use port 80h, the port itself is merely a repository for that information. For you to read the contents of port 80h, you will need a POST board (such as the Micro2000 Post-Probe shown in Fig. 15-1), which should be installed in an open slot prior to troubleshooting, then removed once troubleshooting is completed. Remember to turn the PC off before installing or removing a POST card. Essentially, the design of a POST board is quite simple. It reads the byte at the POST I/O port and displays the hexadecimal code in the two seven-segment displays. However, many POST boards today provide a technician with a much more powerful troubleshooting tool. As an example, the Post-Probe supplies a series of LEDs that checks for main voltages (+12 Vdc, −12 Vdc, +5 Vdc, and −5 Vdc), and the presence of key signals on the expansion bus (i.e., address latch, I/O read, I/O write, memory read, memory write, system clock, etc.). Even an on-board logic probe attachment is provided.

I/O PORTS

Although most traditional ISA-based PCs use port 80h, not all PCs follow this rule. The Compaq PC outputs codes to port 84h, and PS/2 models 25 and 30 send codes to port 90h. PS/2 model 20-286 sends codes to port 190h. Even most EISA-based PCs use port 80h, but Compaq PCs continue to use port 84h. EISA machines with Award BIOS use port 300h. Systems with a Micro Channel bus Architecture (MCA) use port 680h. Take note that some PS/2 models, Olivetti, early AT&T, some NCR, and a few AT clones will send POST codes to a printer port at 3BCh, 278h, or 378h. The current generation of POST boards typically provides a DIP switch or jumper array for selecting the active port location. Before choosing a POST board, be sure that it can read the proper port address for your system.

Another issue is that not all PCs produce POST codes. The original IBM PC, the AMI XT, and some systems using HP, DTK, and ERSO BIOS do not send out POST codes during initialization. If you are testing such a system, you will be unable to see hexadecimal codes using the POST card (but power and signal indicators should still work).

INTERPRETING THE LEDS

Before discussing the various POST codes in detail, you should have an understanding of the many discrete signal LEDs that accompany current POST boards. These individual signals can be a great asset when interpreted in conjunction with the POST code. Remember that each POST card will offer a different selection of LEDs, so your own POST card might not have all of the indicators shown here:

- *Power LEDs* The PC will not work correctly (if at all) if one or more power supply voltages is low or absent. Typical POST cards provide four LEDs that light when +5 Vdc, +12 Vdc, −5 Vdc, and −12 Vdc are available. If any of those LEDs are dim or out, the problem might be with the power supply or its connection to the motherboard. If problems occur after upgrading the system, the power supply might be overloaded. In any case, power LEDs help you to identify power problems quickly and effectively.
- *ALE* The *Address Latch Enable* signal is generated by the CPU, and is used by virtually all devices in the PC that must capture address signals (such as BIOS). When this LED is on, address generation by the CPU is probably working fine. If this LED is out, there is a problem manipulating addresses in the system. You should then suspect the CPU, DMA controller, bus buffer/controller, or clock generator/system controller IC. This can be very helpful for technicians who choose to troubleshoot to the component level.
- *I/OW* An I/O write LED will generally light whenever BIOS attempts to write data to an I/O device, such as a floppy disk. The BIOS will then attempt to read what was written to confirm that portion of the system is working as expected. If the I/OW LED stays out, you should suspect a fault in either the BIOS or the system's DMA controller IC.
- *I/OR* An I/O read LED will generally light whenever BIOS attempts to read data back from an I/O device after data has been written. If this LED remains out, you should suspect a fault in either the BIOS or the system's DMA controller IC.

- *MR/W* During POST, the BIOS will attempt to write various data patterns into memory, then it will read those patterns back to verify memory integrity. The Memory R/W LED will light during both the read and write operations (it will flicker a bit). If the MW/R LED does not light, the problem is likely with the BIOS, DMA controller, memory controller, or system-controller IC.
- *Reset* When the system is first turned on, the reset line will be asserted. This keeps the CPU neutralized until the *Power good* signal is received from the power supply. At this point, the reset line should be released, the Reset LED should go out, and the initialization process will begin. The reset line should not light again unless the PC's Reset button is pressed. If the Reset LED stays lit, it could indicate a problem with the *Power good* signal at the supply or motherboard. The reset line might also be shorted—in which case you might have to replace the motherboard.
- *CLK* The clock LED(s) light to indicate the presence of synchronizing signals generated by the PC's clock-generator IC. If these signals are not being generated, the CPU simply will not function. If the clock indicator(s) do not light, you should suspect a fault in the system time-base crystal or the clock-generator IC. Remember that micro channel systems do not supply clock signals to the bus.
- *OSC* The oscillator LEDs indicate the presence of a 14.138MHz signal. XT systems used this signal for all internal timing, but AT systems only use the oscillator as a color-burst signal for the video adapter. If the oscillator indicator(s) do not light, you should suspect a fault in the color-burst crystal or the clock-generating circuitry.

Beep/POST Troubleshooting

Generally speaking, a POST board is one of the best all-around PC hardware troubleshooting tools available. It is quick and easy to use, compatible across ISA, EISA, and MCA platforms, and even the simplest POST board can provide you with a remarkable insight into a system's operation. The trouble with POST boards is that every BIOS—although testing virtually the same functions—uses varying codes that are often cryptic and poorly documented (this chapter takes great pains to provide you with fairly comprehensive index of POST codes). Armed with the proper code list, a POST board can often pinpoint a fault to the exact IC—if not to the exact IC, then certainly to the major sub-assembly.

Symptom 15-1. The power and cooling fan(s) are on, but nothing else happens First suspect that incoming ac power is very low, or that the power connector between the supply and motherboard has become loose or disconnected. Start by using a multimeter to check ac power available at the wall outlet. Use extreme caution to protect yourself from accidental electrocution. If the ac level is unusually low, try the PC in an outlet with an adequate voltage level. If the ac level is acceptable, check the power connector at the motherboard. Observe the power LEDs on the POST board. If one or more power LEDs is dim or absent, a fault might be in the power supply. Troubleshoot or replace the supply.

Symptom 15-2. After power-up, you hear the fan change pitch noticeably (a chirping sound might also be coming from the supply) First, be aware that some PCs use a variable-speed fan to optimize cooling. If you hear the fan pitch vary, you should be sure that this is abnormal for your particular system before pursuing a repair. If varying fan pitch is not correct for your system, the ac power level reaching the PC is probably low and allowing the power supply to drop out of regulation. Use a multimeter and check the ac level at the wall outlet. Use extreme caution to protect yourself from accidental electrocution. If the ac level is too low or unsteady, try the PC in a functional ac outlet. If ac levels measure correctly, check the power LEDs on your POST board. If one or more LEDs is dim or out (or if the supply is producing a "chirping" sound), the supply is probably defective. Troubleshoot or repair the power supply.

Symptom 15-3. You see one or more POST board power LEDs off, very dim, or flickering Before suspecting a problem with the supply, try the POST board in a different socket—the expansion bus connector at that location might be bad. If the symptom persists (and the PC is behaving strangely), check the power connector between the supply and motherboard. If the connector is intact, the supply might be defective. Troubleshoot or replace the power supply.

Symptom 15-4. The Reset LED remains on (the POST display will probably remain blank) In most PC designs, the CPU is held in the reset state until a *Power good* signal is received from the power supply. This typically requires no more than a few milliseconds. If the reset LED remains on longer than that, it might be held up by a problem with the *Power good* signal. Use a logic probe (or probe that comes with the POST board) to check the *Power good* signal. If the signal changes state as expected, the reset line might be shorted somewhere on the motherboard—try replacing the motherboard. If the signal does not change as expected, the problem might be in the power supply. Try replacing the power supply.

Symptom 15-5. One or more activity LEDs is out (the POST display will probably remain blank) Most POST boards provide a selection of LEDs that are used to indicate signal activity on major bus lines. If one or more of these LEDs is out, a motherboard fault is probably in the corresponding circuit:

- *ALE* The clock generator, CPU, DMA controller, or bus controller might have failed. Try replacing the motherboard.
- *OSC* The clock-generator IC or time-base crystal might have failed. Replace those components, or replace the motherboard.
- *CLK* Check for excessive ripple in the ac source. Try a clean ac source. There might also be a problem with the clock generator or time-base crystal. Replace those components or replace the motherboard.
- *I/OR, I/OW* Check for excessive ripple or inadequate ground in the system power lines. Try a new power supply, if necessary. There might also be a fault in the DMA controller, CPU, PIT, or PIC devices. Try another motherboard.
- *MR/W* A fault might be in the DMA controller, bus controller, BIOS ROM, PIT, or PIC devices. Try another motherboard.

Symptom. 15-6. You hear a beep code pattern from the system speaker, but no POST codes are displayed Any beep pattern other than a single short beep indicates a serious system problem; however, there might be several reasons why the POST board is not displaying POST codes. First, be sure that the BIOS for your system actually generates POST codes—most do, but a few do not. Also be sure that your POST board is set to read the proper I/O address, which the codes are being written to. Many systems send codes to port 80h, but other ports (such as 1080h, 680h, and 378h) might be used. Configure the POST board to use the proper address. If problems persist, the BIOS itself might be defective. Try a different BIOS, or refer to Chapter 12 to troubleshoot the beep code.

Symptom 15-7. The POST display stops at some code (the system probably hangs up) The CPU and clock systems are probably working to fetch instructions from BIOS, but POST has detected a fault in the system. Use the table for your appropriate manufacturer in this chapter and find the POST code's meaning. If the code refers to a fault on the motherboard, you can either attempt to replace the defective component or replace the motherboard outright. If the code refers to an expansion device, such as a drive or video adapter, take steps to replace the defective device.

Symptom 15-8. A POST or beep code indicates a video problem (there is no monitor display) Chances are that the system was unable to detect video ROM instructions or locate video memory. As a result, no display is available. Try a new video adapter board in the system. If the video adapter is located on the motherboard, try a new motherboard or disable the motherboard video (usually with a jumper) and install an expansion video adapter.

Symptom 15-9. A POST or beep code indicates a drive or controller problem Chances are that the video system is working. If possible, load the CMOS setup program and be sure that the drive selections entered are accurate for your system. An incorrect set of entries can disable your drives. Be sure that the drive being used is properly formatted and partitioned for your system. If the problem persists, either the drive or drive controller has failed. Start by trying an alternative drive controller. If the problem remains, try a new drive.

Further Study

That finishes Chapter 15. Be sure to review the glossary and chapter questions on the accompanying CD. If you have access to the Internet, take a look at some of these diagnostic and information resources:

Data Depot: **http://www.datadepo.com**

ForeFront: **http://www.ffg.com**

Micro2000: **http://www.micro2000.com**

FLOPPY

DRIVES

CONTENTS AT A GLANCE

Magnetic-Storage Concepts
  Media
  Magnetic recording principles
  Data and disk organization
  Media problems

Drive construction
  Drive electronics
  Physical interface

Troubleshooting Floppy Disk Systems
  Repair vs. replace
  Preliminary testing

Further Study

The ability to interchange programs and data between various compatible computers is a fundamental requirement of almost every computer system. This kind of file-exchange compatibility helped rocket IBM PC/XTs into everyday use and spur the personal computer industry into the early 1980s. A standardized operating system, file structure, and recording media also breathed life into the fledgling software industry. With the floppy disk, software developers could finally distribute programs and data to a mass-market of compatible computer users. The mechanism that allowed this quantum leap in compatibility is the *floppy-disk drive* (Fig. 16-1).

A floppy-disk drive (FDD) is one of the least expensive and most reliable forms of mass-storage ever used in computer systems. Virtually every one of the millions of personal computers sold each year incorporates at least one floppy drive. Most notebook and laptop computers also offer a single floppy drive. Not only are FDDs useful for transferring

FIGURE 16-1 **An NEC FD1138H floppy drive.** NEC Technologies, Inc.

files and data between various systems, but the advantage of removable media—the floppy disk itself—make floppy drives an almost intuitive backup system for data files. Although floppy drives have evolved through a number of iterations: from 8" to 5.25" to 3.5", their basic components and operating principles have changed very little.

Magnetic-Storage Concepts

Magnetic-storage media has been attractive to computer designs for many years—long before the personal computer had established itself in homes and offices. This popularity is primarily because magnetic media is non-volatile. Unlike system RAM, no electrical energy is needed to maintain the information once it is stored on magnetic media. Although electrical energy is used to read and write magnetic data, magnetic fields do not change on their own, so data remains intact until "other forces" act upon it (such as another floppy drive). It is this smooth, straightforward translation from electricity to magnetism and back again that has made magnetic storage such a natural choice. To understand how a floppy drive works and why it fails, you should have an understanding of magnetic storage. This part of the chapter shows you the basic storage concepts used for floppy drives.

MEDIA

For the purposes of this book, *media* is the physical material that actually holds recorded information. In a floppy disk, the media is a small mylar disk coated on both sides with a precisely formulated magnetic material, often referred to as the *oxide layer*. Every disk manufacturer uses their own particular formula for magnetic coatings, but most coatings are based on a naturally magnetic element (such as iron, nickel, or cobalt) that has been alloyed with non-magnetic materials or rare earth. This magnetic material is then compounded with plastic, bonding chemicals, and lubricant to form the actual disk media.

The fascinating aspect of these magnetic layers is that each and every particle media acts as a microscopic magnet. Each magnetic particle can be aligned in one orientation or another under the influence of an external magnetic field. If you have ever magnetized a screwdriver's steel shaft by running a permanent magnet along its length, you have already seen this magnetizing process in action. For a floppy disk, microscopic points along the disk's surfaces are magnetized in one alignment or another by the precise forces applied by read/write (R/W) heads. The shifting of alignment polarities would indicate a logic 1, but no change in polarity would indicate a logic 0 (you will see more about data recording and organization later in this chapter).

In analog recording (such as audio tapes), the magnetic field generated by read/write heads varies in direct proportion to the signal being recorded. Such linear variations in field strength cause varying amounts of magnetic particles to align as the media moves. On the other hand, digital recordings, such as floppy disks, save binary 1s and 0s by applying an overwhelming amount of field strength. Very strong magnetic fields saturate the media—that is, so much field strength is applied that any further increase in field strength will not cause a better alignment of magnetic particles at that point on the media. The advantage to operating in saturation is that 1s and 0s are remarkably resistant to the degrading effects of noise that can sometimes appear in analog magnetic recordings.

Although the orientation of magnetic particles on a disk's media can be reversed by using an external magnetic field, particles tend to resist the reversal of polarity. *Coercivity* is the strength with which magnetic particles resist change. More highly coercive material has a greater resistance to change, so a stronger external field will be needed to cause changes. High coercivity is generally considered to be desirable (up to a point) because signals stand out much better against background noise and signals will resist natural degradation because of age, temperature, and random magnetic influences. As you might expect, a highly coercive media requires a more powerful field to record new information.

Another advantage of increased coercivity is greater information density for media. The greater strength of each media particle allows more bits to be packed into less area. The move from 5.25" to 3.5" floppy disks was possible largely because of a superior (more coercive) magnetic layer. This coercivity principle also holds true for hard drives. To pack more information onto ever-smaller platters, the media must be more coercive. Coercivity is a common magnetic measurement with units in *oersteds* (pronounced "or-steds"). The coercivity of a typical floppy disk can range anywhere from 300 to 750 oersteds. By comparison, hard-drive and magneto-optical (MO) media usually offer coercivities up to 6000 oersteds or higher.

The main premise of magnetic storage is that it is static (once recorded, information is retained without any electrical energy). Such stored information is presumed to last forever, but in actuality, magnetic information begins to degrade as soon as it is recorded. A good magnetic media will reliably remember (or retain) the alignment of its particles over a long period of time. The ability of a media to retain its magnetic information is known as *retentivity*. Even the finest, best-formulated floppy disks degrades eventually (although it could take many years before an actual data error materializes).

Ultimately, the ideal answer to media degradation is to refresh (or write over) the data and sector ID information. Data is re-written normally each time a file is saved, but sector IDs are only written once when the disk is formatted. If a sector ID should fail, you will see the dreaded "Sector Not Found" disk error and any data stored in the sector can not be accessed. This failure mode also occurs in hard drives. Little can be done to ensure the integrity of floppy disks, aside from maintaining one or more backups on freshly formatted disks. However, some commercial software is available for restoring disk data (especially hard drives).

MAGNETIC RECORDING PRINCIPLES

The first step in understanding digital recording is to see how binary data is stored on a disk. Binary 1s and 0s are not represented by discrete polarities of magnetic field orientations as

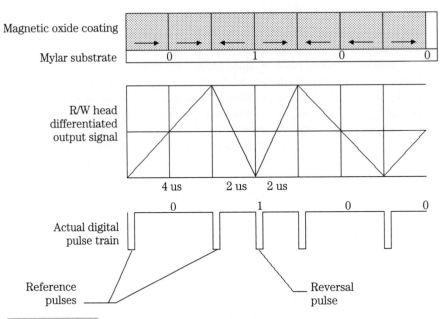

Magnetic oxide coating

Mylar substrate

0   1   0   0

R/W head
differentiated
output signal

4 us   2 us   2 us

0   1   0   0

Actual digital
pulse train

Reference
pulses

Reversal
pulse

FIGURE 16-2   **Flux transitions in floppy disks.**

you might have thought. Instead, binary digits are represented by the presence or absence of flux transitions (Fig. 16-2). By detecting the change from one polarity to another, instead of simply detecting a discrete polarity itself, maximum sensitivity can be achieved with very simple circuitry.

In its simplest form, a *logic 1* is indicated by the presence of a *flux reversal* within a fixed time frame, but a *logic 0* is indicated by the absence of a flux reversal. Most floppy-drive systems insert artificial flux reversals between consecutive 0s to prevent reversals from occurring at great intervals. You can see some example magnetic states recorded on the media of Fig. 16-2. Notice that the direction of reversal does not matter—it is the reversal event that defines a 1 or 0. For example, the first 0 uses left-to-right orientation, the second 0 uses a right-to-left orientation, but both can represent 0s.

The second trace in Fig. 16-2 represents an amplified output signal from a typical read/write head. Notice that the analog signal peaks wherever there is a flux transition—long slopes indicate a 0 and short slopes indicate a 1. When such peaks are encountered, peak-detection circuits in the floppy drive cause marking pulses in the ultimate data signal. Each bit is usually encoded in about 4 µs.

Often, the most confusing aspect to flux transitions is the artificial reversals. Why reverse the polarities for consecutive 0s? Artificial reversals are added to guarantee synchronization in the floppy-disk circuitry. Remember that data read or written to a floppy disk is serial; without any clock signal, such serial data is asynchronous of the drive's circuitry. Regular flux reversals (even if added artificially) create reference pulses that help to synchronize the drive and data without use of clocks or other timing signals. This approach is loosely referred to as the *Modified Frequency Modulation (MFM)* recording technique. Early hard drives (e.g. ST506/412 drives) also used MFM recording.

The ability of floppy disks to store information depends upon being able to write new magnetic field polarities on top of old or existing orientations. A drive must also be able to sense the existing polarities on a disk during read operations. The mechanism responsible for translating electrical signals into magnetic signals (and vice versa) is the *read/write head (R/W head)*. In principle, a head is little more than a coil of very fine wire wrapped around a soft, highly permeable core material (Fig. 16-3).

When the head is energized with current flow from a driver IC, a path of magnetic flux is established in the head core. The direction (or orientation) of flux depends on the direction of energizing current. To reverse a head's magnetic orientation, the direction of energizing current must be reversed. The small head size and low current levels needed to energize a head allow very high-frequency flux reversals. As magnetic flux is generated in a head, the resulting, tightly focused magnetic field aligns the floppy disk's particles at that point. In general, the current signal magnetizes an almost microscopic area on the media. R/W heads actually contact the media while a disk is inserted into a drive.

During a read operation, the heads are left unenergized while the disk spins. Just as varying current produces magnetism in a head, the reverse is also true—varying magnetic influences cause currents to be developed in the head(s). As the spinning media moves across a R/W head, a current is produced in the head coil. The direction of induced current depends on the polarity of each flux orientation. Induced current is proportional to the flux density (how closely each flux transition is placed) and the velocity of the media across each head. In other words, signal strength depends on the rate of change of flux versus time.

DATA AND DISK ORGANIZATION

Another important aspect of drive troubleshooting is to understand how data is arranged on the disk. You cannot place data just anywhere—the drive would have no idea where to look for the data later on, or even if the data is valid. In order for a disk to be of use, information must be sorted and organized into known, standard locations. Standardized organization ensures that a disk written by one drive will be readable by another drive in a different machine. Table 16-1 compares the major specifications of today's popular drive types.

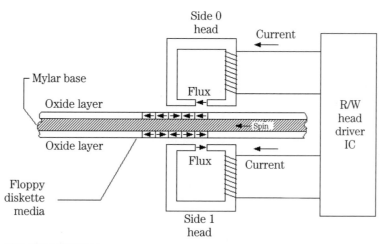

FIGURE 16-3   Floppy-drive recording principles.

TABLE 16-1 COMPARISON OF FLOPPY DISK DRIVE SPECIFICATIONS

SPECIFICATION	5.25" (360KB)	5.25" (1.2MB)	3.5" (720KB)	3.5" (1.44MB)	3.5" (2.88MB)
Bytes per Sector	512	512	512	512	512
Sectors per Track	9	15	9	18	36
Tracks per Side	40	80	80	80	80
Sectors per Cluster	2	1	2	1	2
FAT Length (sectors)	2	7	3	9	9
Number of FATs	2	2	2	2	2
Root Dir. Length	7 sectors	14 sectors	7 sectors	14 sectors	15 sectors
Max. Root Entries	112	224	112	224	240
Total Sectors on Disk	708	2371	1426	2847	5726
Media Base	Ferrite	Ferrite	Cobalt	Cobalt	Cobalt
Coercitivity (oersteds)	300	300	600	600	720
Media Descriptor Byte	FDh	F9h	F9h	F0h	F0h
Encoding Format	MFM or FM	MFM or FM	MFM	MFM	MFM
Data Rate (KB/sec)	250 or 125	500 or 250	500	500	500

It is important to note that a floppy disk is a two-dimensional entity possessing both height and width (depth is irrelevant here). This two-dimensional characteristic allows disk information to be recorded in concentric circles, which creates a random-access type of media. *Random access* means that it is possible to move around the disk almost instantly to obtain a desired piece of information. This is a much faster and more convenient approach than a sequential recording medium, such as magnetic tape.

Floppy-disk organization is not terribly complicated, but you must be familiar with several important concepts. The disk itself is rotated in one direction (usually clockwise) under read/write heads, which are perpendicular (at right angles) to the disk's plane. The path of the disk beneath a head describes a circle. As a head steps in and out along a disk's radius, each step describes a circle with a different circumference—rather like lanes on a roadway. Each of these concentric "lanes" is known as a *track*. A typical 8.89-cm disk offers 160 tracks—80 tracks on each side of the media. Tracks have a finite width, which is defined largely by the drive size, head size, and media. When a R/W head jumps from track to track, it must jump precisely the correct distance to position itself in the middle of another track. If positioning is not correct, the head might encounter data signals from two adjacent tracks. Faulty positioning almost invariably results in disk errors. Also notice that the circumference of each track drops as the head moves toward the disk's center. With less space and a constant rate of spin, data is densest on the innermost tracks (79 or 159, depending on the disk side) and least dense on the outermost tracks (0 or 80). A track is also known as a *cylinder*.

Every cylinder is divided into smaller units called *sectors*. There are 18 sectors on every track of an 8.89-cm disk. Sectors serve two purposes. First, a sector stores 512 bytes of data. With 18 sectors per track and 160 tracks per disk, an 8.89-cm disk holds 2880 sectors (18 × 160). At 512 bytes per sector, a formatted disk can handle about (2880 × 512) = 1,474,560 bytes of data. In actuality, this amount is often slightly less to allow for boot sector and file allocation information. Sectors are referenced in groups called *clusters* or *allocation units*. Although hard drives can group 16 or more sectors into a cluster, floppy drives only use 1 or 2 sectors in a cluster.

Second, and perhaps more important, a sector provides housekeeping data that identifies the sector, the track, and error checking results from *Cyclical Redundancy Check (CRC)* calculations. The location of each sector and housekeeping information is set down during the format process. Once formatted, only the sector data and CRC results are updated when a disk is written. Sector ID and synchronization data is never re-written unless the disk is reformatted. This extra information means that each sector actually holds more than 512 bytes, but you only have access to the 512 data bytes in a sector during normal disk read/write operations. If sector ID data is accidentally overwritten or corrupted, the user-data in the afflicted sector becomes unreadable.

The format process also writes a bit of other important information to the disk. The boot record is the first sector on a disk (sector 0). It contains several key parameters that describe the characteristics of the disk. If the disk is "bootable" the boot sector will also run the files (e.g., IO.SYS and MSDOS.SYS) that load DOS. In addition to the boot record, a *File Allocation Table (FAT)* is placed on track 00. The FAT acts as a table of contents for the disk. As files are added and erased, the FAT is updated to reflect the contents of each cluster. As you might imagine, a working FAT is critical to the proper operation of a disk. If the FAT is accidentally overwritten or corrupted, the entire disk can become useless. Without a viable FAT, the computer has no other way to determine what files are available or where they are spread throughout the disk. The very first byte in a FAT is the media descriptor byte, which allows the drive to recognize the type of disk that is inserted.

MEDIA PROBLEMS

Magnetic media has come a long way in the last decade or so. Today's high-quality magnetic materials, combined with the benefits of precise, high-volume production equipment, produce disks that are exceptionally reliable over normal long-term use in a floppy-disk drive. However, floppy disks are removable items. The care they receive in physical handling and the storage environment where they are kept will greatly impact a disk's life span.

The most troubling and insidious problem plaguing floppy-disk media is the accidental influence of magnetic fields. Any magnetized item in close proximity to a floppy disk poses a potential threat. Permanent magnets, such as refrigerator magnets or magnetic paper clips, are prime sources of stray fields. Electromagnetic sources (such as telephone ringers, monitor or TV degaussing coils, and all types of motors) will corrupt data if the media is close enough. The best policy is to keep all floppy disks in a dedicated container, placed well away from stray magnetic fields.

Disks and magnetic media are also subject to a wide variety of physical damage. Substrates and media are manufactured to very tight tolerances, so anything at all that alters the precise surface features of a floppy disk can cause problems. The introduction of hair, dirt, or dust through the disk's head-access aperture, wild temperature variations, fingerprints on the media, or any substantial impact or flexing of the media can cause temporary loss of contact between media and head. When loss of contact occurs, data is lost and a number of disk errors can occur. Head wear and the accumulation of worn oxides also affects head contact. Once again, storing disks in a dedicated container located well out of harm's way is often the best means of protection.

Drive Construction

At the core of a floppy drive (Fig. 16-4) is a *frame assembly* (15). It is the single, main structure for mounting the drive's mechanisms and electronics. Frames are typically made from die-cast aluminum to provide a strong, rigid foundation for the drive. The *front bezel*

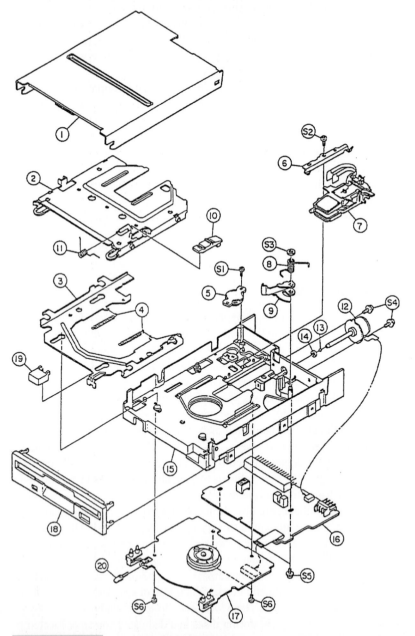

FIGURE 16-4   **An exploded diagram of a floppy disk-drive assembly.** Teac America, Inc.

Fixing screws

PCBA spindle motor servo

Connector J5 (CN61)

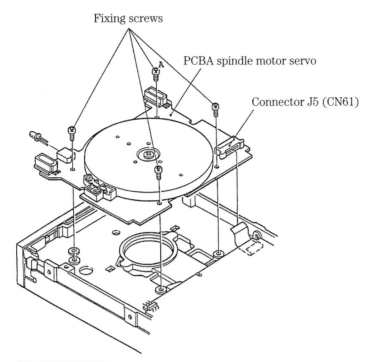

FIGURE 16-5   **Underside view of a floppy drive spindle motor assembly.** Teac America, Inc.

(18) attaches to the frame to provide a clean, cosmetic appearance, and to offer a fixed slot for disk insertion or removal. For 8.89-cm drives, bezels often include a small colored lens, a disk-ejection button hole, and a flap to cover the disk slot when the drive is empty. A *spindle motor assembly* (17) uses an outer-rotor dc motor fabricated onto a small PC board. The motor's shaft is inserted into that large hole in the frame. A disk's metal drive hub automatically interlocks to the spindle. For 13.34-cm disks, the center hole is clamped between two halves of a spindle assembly. The halves clamp the disk when the drive lever is locked down. Figure 16-5 shows the spindle motor assembly from the underside of the drive. The *disk-activity LED* (20) illuminates through the bezel's colored lens whenever spindle motor activity is in progress.

Just behind the spindle motor is the drive's *control electronics* (16). It contains the circuitry needed to operate the drive's motors, R/W heads, and sensors. A standardized interface is used to connect the drive to a floppy-drive controller. Figure 16-6 shows you a close-up view of a drive's control board (notice the optoisolator just below U1). The *read/write head assembly* (7) (also sometimes called a *head carriage assembly*), holds a set of two R/W heads. Head 0 is the lower head (underside of the disk), and head 1 is on top. A *head stepping motor* (12) is added to ensure even and consistent movement between tracks. A threaded rod at the motor end is what actually moves the heads. A *mechanical damper* (5) helps to smooth the disk's travel into or out of the 8.89-cm drive. Figure 16-7 shows a close-up view of the R/W heads and stepping motor.

When a disk is inserted through the bezel, the disk is restrained by a *diskette clamp assembly* (2). To eject the disk, you would press the *ejector button* (19), which pushes a *slider*

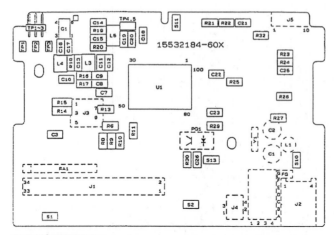

FIGURE 16-6 **A typical floppy drive mail logic/interface board.** Teac America, Inc.

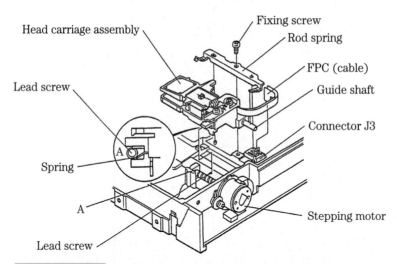

FIGURE 16-7 **Detailed view of a R/W head and stepping motor.** Teac America, Inc.

mechanism (3). When the ejector button is fully depressed, the disk will disengage from the spindle and pop out of the drive. For 13.34-cm drives, the disk is released whenever the drive door is opened. Your particular drive might contain other miscellaneous components. Finally, the entire upper portion of a drive can be covered by a *metal shield* (1).

DRIVE ELECTRONICS

Proper drive operation depends on the intimate cooperation between magnetic media, electromechanical devices, and dedicated electronics. Floppy-drive electronics are responsible for two major tasks: controlling the drive's physical operations and managing the flow of data in or out of the drive. These tasks are not nearly as simple as they sound, but the sleek, low-profile drives in today's computer systems are a far cry from the clunky, full-height drives used in early systems. Older drives needed a large number of ICs spanning several boards that had to be fitted to the chassis. However, the drive in your computer right now is probably implemented with only a few highly integrated ICs that are neatly surface-mounted on two small, opposing PC boards. This part of the chapter covers the drive's operating circuits. A complete block diagram for a Teac 8.89-cm (3.5") floppy drive is illustrated in Fig. 16-8. The figure is shown with a floppy disk inserted.

Write-protect sensors are used to detect the position of a disk's file-protect tab. For 8.89-cm disks, the write-protect notch must be covered to allow both read and write operations. If the notch is open, the disk can only be read. Optoisolators are commonly used as write-protect sensors because an open notch will easily allow light through, but a closed notch will cut off the light path.

Before the drive is allowed to operate at all, a disk must be inserted properly and interlocked with the spindle. A disk-in-place sensor detects the presence or absence of a disk. Like the write-protect sensor, disk sensors are often mechanical switches that are activated by disk contact. If drive access is attempted without a disk in place, the sensor causes the drive's logic to induce a DOS "Disk Not Ready" error code. It is not unusual to find an optoisolator acting as a disk-in-place sensor.

The electronics of an 8.89-cm drive must be able to differentiate whether the disk contains normal (double) density or high-density media. A high-density sensor looks for the hole that is found near the top of all high-density disk bodies. A mechanical switch is typically used to detect the high-density hole, but a separate LED/detector pair might also be used. When the hole is absent (a double-density disk), the switch is activated upon disk insertion.

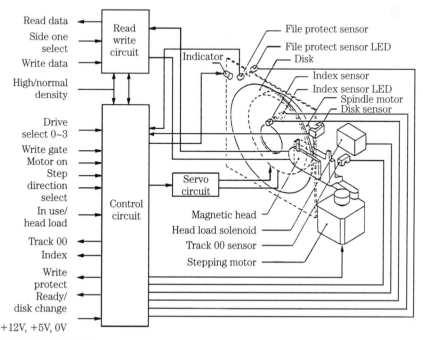

FIGURE 16-8 Block diagram of a floppy drive.

If the hole is present (a high-density disk), the switch is not actuated. All switch conditions are translated into logic signals used by the drive electronics.

Before disk data can be read or written, the system must read the disk's boot sector information and FAT. Although programs and data can be broken up and scattered all over a disk, the FAT must always be located at a known location so that the drive knows where to look for it. The FAT is always located on track 00—the first track of disk side 0. A track 00 sensor provides a logic signal when the heads are positioned over track 00. Each time that a read or write is ordered, the head assembly is stepped to track 00. Although a drive "remembers" how many steps should be needed to position the heads precisely over track 00, an optoisolator or switch senses the head carriage assembly position. At track 00, the head carriage should interrupt the optoisolator or actuate the switch. If the drive supposedly steps to track 00 and there is no sensor signal to confirm the position (or the signal occurs before the drive has finished stepping), the drive assumes that a head positioning error has occurred. Head step counts and sensor outputs virtually always agree unless the sensor has failed or the drive has been physically damaged.

Spindle speed is a critically important drive parameter. Once the disk has reached its running velocity (300 or 360 RPM), the drive must maintain that velocity for the duration of the disk-access process. Unfortunately, simply telling the spindle motor to move is no guarantee that the motor is turning—a sensor is required to measure the motor's speed. This is the index sensor. Signals from an index sensor are fed back to the drive electronics, which adjust spindle speed in order to maintain a constant rotation. Most drives use optoisolators as index sensors, which detect the motion of small slots cut in a template or the spindle rotor itself. When a disk is spinning, the output from an index sensor is a fast logic pulse sent along to the drive electronics. Remember that some index sensors are magnetic. A magnetic sensor typically operates by detecting the proximity of small slots in a template or the spindle rotor, but the pulse output is essentially identical to that of the optoisolator.

PHYSICAL INTERFACE

The drive must receive control and data signals from the computer, and deliver status and data signals back to the computer, as required. The series of connections between a floppy-disk PC board and the floppy-disk controller circuit is known as the *physical interface*. The advantage to using a standard interface is that various drives made by different manufacturers can be "mixed and matched" by computer designers. A floppy drive working in one computer will operate properly in another computer, regardless of the manufacturer as long as the same physical interface scheme is being used.

Floppy drives use a physical interface that includes two cables: a power cable and a signal cable. Both cable pinouts are illustrated in Fig. 16-9. The classic power connector is a 4-pin "mate-n-lock" connector, although many low-profile drives used in mobile computers (e.g., laptops or notebooks) might use much smaller connector designs. Floppy drives require two voltage levels: +5.0 Vdc for logic, and +12.0 Vdc for motors. The return (ground) for each supply is also provided at the connector. The signal connector is typically a 34-pin Insulation-Displacement Connector (IDC) cable. Notice that all odd-numbered pins are ground lines, but the even-numbered pins carry active signals. Logic signals are all TTL-level signals.

In a system with more than one floppy drive, the particular destination drive must be selected before any read or write is attempted. A drive is selected using the appropriate

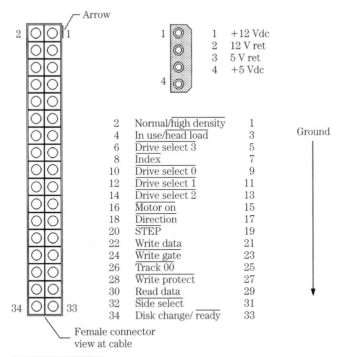

FIGURE 16-9   Diagram of a standard 34-pin floppy-
drive interface.

Drive select line (Drive select 0 to 3) on pins 10, 12, 14, and 6, respectively. For notebook or sub-notebook systems where only one floppy drive is used, only Drive Select 0 is used—the remaining select inputs might simply be disconnected. The spindle motor servo circuit is controlled through the *Motor on* signal (pin 16). When pin 16 is logic 0, the spindle motor should spinup (approach a stable operating speed). The media must be spinning at the proper rate before reading or writing can occur.

To move the R/W heads, the host computer must specify the number of steps that a head carriage assembly must move, and the direction in which steps must occur. A *Direction select* signal (pin 18) tells the coil driver circuit whether the heads should be moved inward (toward the spindle) or outward (away from the spindle). The *Step* signal (pin 20) provides the pulse sequence that actually steps the head motor in the desired direction. The combination of *Step* and *Direction select* controls can position the R/W heads over the disk very precisely. The *Side select* control pin (pin 32) determines whether head 0 or head 1 is active for reading or writing—only one side of the disk can be manipulated at a time.

Two signals are needed to write data to a disk. The *Write gate* signal (pin 24) is logic 0 when writing is to occur, and logic 1 when writing is inhibited (or reading). After the *Write gate* is asserted, data can be written to the disk over the *Write data* line (pin 22). When reading, the data that is extracted from the disk is delivered from the *Read data* line (pin 30).

Each of the drive's sensor conditions are sent over the physical interface. The *Track 00* signal (pin 26) is logic 0 whenever the head carriage assembly is positioned over track 00. The *Write protect* line (pin 28) is logic 0 whenever the disk's *Write protect* notch is in place. Writing is inhibited whenever the *Write protect* signal is asserted. The *Index* signal (pin 8) supplies a chain of pulses from the index sensor. Media type is indicated by the *Normal/high-density* sensor (pin 2). The status of the disk-in-place sensor is indicated over the *Disk change ready* line (pin 34).

Troubleshooting Floppy Disk Systems

This section of the chapter is concerned with drive problems that cannot be corrected with cleaning or mechanical adjustments. To perform some of the following tests, you should have a known-good diskette that has been properly formatted. The disk might contain files, but be certain that any such files are backed up properly on a hard drive or another floppy disk—if you can't afford to lose the files on a disk, don't use the disk.

REPAIR VS. REPLACE

As with so many other PC assemblies, the price of floppy drives has dropped tremendously over the last few years. Now that the price of a standard 8.89-cm drive is roughly that of two hours of labor, most technicians ask whether it is better to simply replace a floppy drive outright, rather than attempt a repair. Ultimately, the decision should depend on volume. Clearly, it makes little sense for a anyone to invest valuable time in repairing a single drive. If a large number of drives are to be repaired, however, an enterprising technician who chooses to deal in floppy-drive service can effectively provide rebuilt or refurbished drives to their customers.

PRELIMINARY TESTING

Proper testing is essential for any type of drive repair. Most drive-alignment packages, such as DriveProbe by Accurite Technologies or AlignIt by Landmark Research, measure and display a drive's parameters (Fig. 16-10). When floppy drive trouble occurs, running a diagnostic can help determine whether the drive mechanics or electronics are at fault. Although you can swap a drive symptomatically, thorough testing is an inexpensive means to verify your suspicions before spending money to replace sub-assemblies.

For cleaning and testing your floppy drive, check out AUTOTEST.ZIP, CHKDRV.ZIP, CLEAN4.ZIP, and DFR.ZIP on the companion CD.

Symptom 16-1. The floppy drive is completely dead The disk does not even initialize when inserted. Begin troubleshooting by inspecting the diskette itself. When a 3.5" disk is inserted into a drive, a mechanism should pull the disk's metal shroud away and briefly rotate the spindle motor to ensure positive engagement. Be sure that the disk is properly inserted into the floppy-drive assembly. If the diskette does not enter and seat just right within the drive, disk access will be impossible. Try several different diskettes to ensure that the test diskette is not defective. It might be necessary to partially disassemble the computer to access the drive and allow you to see the overall assembly. Free or adjust any jammed assemblies or linkages to correct disk insertion. If you cannot get diskettes to insert properly, change the floppy drive.

AUTOMATIC Drive Test   'Esc'- For Previous Menu

Test	Track	Head 0 Data	Head 1 Data	Test Limits	Results	
Speed	NA	300 RPM / 199.7 mS		300 ± 6 RPM	Pass	NA
Eccentricity	44	100 uI	NA	0 ± 300 uI	Pass	NA
Radial	0	96% 50 uI	100% 0 uI	60 - 100 %	Pass	Pass
Radial	40	93% -100 uI	90% -150 uI	60 - 100 %	Pass	Pass
Radial	79	96% 50 uI	90% -150 uI	60 - 100 %	Pass	Pass
Azimuth	76	6 Min	4 Min	0 ± 30 Min	Pass	Pass
Index	0	414 uS	407 uS	400 ± 600 uS	Pass	Pass
Index	79	397 uS	380 uS	400 ± 600 uS	Pass	Pass
Hysteresis	40	100 uI	NA	0 ± 250 uI	Pass	NA

```
uI = Micro-inches      uS = Microsecond      mS = Millisecond
Min = Minutes          NA = Not Applicable   NT = Not Tested
```

Note: Radial is expressed as LOBE RATIO and OFFSET from track center line.
Auto Test Completed 'Esc' For Previous Menu

FIGURE 16-10 A DriveProbe screen display for automatic drive testing. Accurite Technologies, Inc.

If the diskette inserts properly but fails to initialize, carefully inspect the drive's physical interface cabling. Loose connectors or faulty cable wiring can easily disable a floppy drive. Use your multimeter to measure dc voltages at the power connector. Place your meter's ground lead on pin 2 and measure +12 Vdc at pin 1. Ground your meter on pin 3 and measure +5 Vdc at pin 4. If either or both of these voltages is low or missing, troubleshoot your computer power supply.

Before disk activity can begin, the drive must sense a disk in the drive. Locate the disk-in-place sensor and use your multimeter to measure voltage across the sensor. When a disk is out of the drive, you should read a logic 1 voltage across the sensor output. When a disk is in place, you should read a logic 0 voltage across the sensor (this convention might be reversed in some drive designs). If the sensor does not register the presence of a disk, replace the sensor. If the sensor does seem to register the presence of a disk, use your logic probe to check the *Disk change/ready* signal (pin 34) of the physical interface. If the interface signal does not agree with the sensor signal, replace the control-circuit IC on the drive PC board. You can also replace the entire drive-control PC board, or replace the entire drive outright.

At this point, the trouble is probably in the floppy-drive PC board, or the floppy-drive controller board. Try replacing the floppy-drive PC board assembly. This is not the least expensive avenue in terms of materials, but it is fast and simple. If a new floppy-drive PC board corrects the problem, re-assemble the computer and return it to service. You could retain the old floppy-drive board for parts. If a new drive PC board does not correct the problem (or is not available), replace the entire drive. You could retain the old floppy drive for parts. If a new floppy-drive assembly fails to correct the problem, replace the floppy-controller board. You will have to disassemble your computer to expose the motherboard and expansion boards.

Symptom 16-2. The floppy drive rotates a disk, but will not seek to the desired track This type of symptom generally suggests that the head-positioning stepping motor is inhibited or defective, but all other floppy-drive functions are working properly. Begin by disassembling your computer and removing the floppy drive. Carefully inspect the head-positioning assembly to be certain that no broken parts or obstructions could jam the read/write heads. You might wish to examine the mechanical system with a disk inserted to be certain that the trouble is not a disk-alignment problem, which might be interfering with head movement. Gently remove any obstructions that you might find. Be careful not to accidentally misalign any linkages or mechanical components in the process of clearing an obstruction.

Remove any diskette from the drive and re-connect the drive's signal and power cables. Apply power to the computer and measure drive voltages with your multimeter. Ground your multimeter on pin 2 of the power connector and measure +12 Vdc at pin 1. Move the meter ground to pin 3 and measure +5 Vdc on pin 4. If either voltage is low or absent, troubleshoot your computer power supply.

Once confident that the drive's mechanics are intact and appropriate power is available, you must determine whether the trouble is in your floppy drive PC board or floppy-drive controller IC on the motherboard. Use your logic probe to measure the STEP signal in the physical interface (pin 20). When drive access is requested, you should find a pulse signal as the floppy controller attempts to position the R/W heads. If STEP pulses are missing, the floppy-drive controller board is probably defective and should be replaced.

If STEP pulses are present at the interface, check the pulses into the coil driver circuit. An absence of pulses into the coil driver circuit indicates a faulty control-circuit IC. If pulses reach the coil driver, measure pulses to the stepping motor. If no pulses leave the coil driver, replace the coil driver IC. When pulses are correct to the stepping motor but no motion is taking place, replace the defective stepping motor. If you do not have the tools or inclination to replace surface-mount ICs, you can replace the drive PC board. You can also replace the entire drive outright.

Symptom 16-3. The floppy drive heads seek properly, but the spindle does not turn This symptom suggests that the spindle motor is inhibited or defective, but all other functions are working properly. Remove all power from the computer. Disassemble the system enough to remove the floppy drive. Carefully inspect the spindle motor, drive belt (if used), and spindle assembly. Be certain that no broken parts or obstructions could jam the spindle. If a belt is between the motor and spindle, be sure that the belt is reasonably tight—it should not slip. You should also examine the floppy drive with a diskette inserted to be certain that the disk's insertion or alignment is not causing the problem. You can double-check your observations using several different diskettes. Gently remove any obstruction(s) that you might find. Be careful not to cause any accidental damage in the process of clearing an obstruction. Do not add any lubricating agents to the assembly, but gently vacuum or wipe away any significant accumulations of dust or dirt.

Remove any diskette from the drive and re-connect the floppy drive's signal and power cables. Restore power to the computer and measure drive voltages with your multimeter. Ground your multimeter on pin 2 and measure +12 Vdc on pin 1. Move the meter ground to pin 3 and measure +5 Vdc on pin 4. If either voltage is low or absent, troubleshoot your computer power supply.

Once you are confident that the floppy drive is mechanically sound and appropriate power is available, you must determine whether the trouble is in the floppy drive PC board or the floppy drive controller board. Use your logic probe to measure the *Motor on* signal in the physical interface (pin 16). When drive access is requested, the *Motor on* signal should become true (in most cases an active low). If the *Motor on* signal is missing, the floppy drive-controller board is probably defective and should be replaced.

If the *Motor on* signal is present at the interface, check the signal driving the servo circuit. A missing *Motor on* signal at the servo circuit suggests a faulty control-circuit IC. If the signal reaches the servo circuit, the servo IC is probably defective. You can replace the servo IC, but your best course is usually to replace the spindle motor/PC board assembly as a unit. If you are unable to replace the spindle motor PC board, you can replace the floppy drive outright.

Symptom 16-4.   The floppy drive will not read from/write to the diskette
All other operations appear normal. This type of problem can manifest itself in several ways, but your computer's operating system will usually inform you when a disk read or write error has occurred. Begin by trying a known-good, properly formatted diskette in the drive. A faulty diskette can generate some very perplexing read/write problems. If a known-good diskette does not resolve the problem, try cleaning the read/write heads, as described in the previous section. Do not run the drive with a head-cleaning disk inserted for more than 30 seconds at a time, or you risk damaging the heads with excessive friction.

When a fresh diskette and clean R/W heads do not correct the problem, you must determine whether the trouble exists in the floppy-drive assembly or the floppy-controller IC. If you cannot read data from the floppy drive, use your logic probe to measure the *Read data* signal (pin 30). When the disk is idle, the *Read data* line should read as a constant logic 1 or logic 0. During a read cycle, you should measure a pulse signal as data moves from the drive to the floppy-controller board. If no pulse signal appears on the *Read data* line during a read cycle, use your oscilloscope to measure analog signals from the R/W heads. If there are no signals from the R/W heads, replace the head or head carriage assembly. When signals are available from the R/W heads, the control-circuit IC is probably defective and should be replaced. If you are unable to replace the IC, you can replace the drive's control PC board. You can also replace the entire drive outright. If a pulse signal does exist during a read cycle, the floppy-disk controller board is probably defective and should be replaced.

When you cannot write data to the floppy drive, use your logic probe to measure the *Write gate* and *Write data* lines (pins 24 and 22, respectively). During a write cycle, the *Write gate* should be logic 0 and you should read a pulse signal as data flows from the floppy controller IC to the drive. If the *Write gate* remains logic 1 or no pulse is on the *Write data* line, replace the defective floppy controller board. When the two *Write* signals appear as expected, check the analog signal to the R/W heads with your oscilloscope. If you do not find analog write signals, replace the defective control-circuit IC. If analog signals are present to the heads, try replacing the heads or the entire head carriage assembly. You can also replace the entire drive outright.

Symptom 16-5.   The drive is able to write to a write-protected disk Before concluding that there is a drive problem, remove and examine the disk itself to ensure that it is actually write protected. If the disk is not write protected, write protect it appropriately and try the disk again. If the disk is already protected, use your multimeter to check the drive's write-protect sensor. For an unprotected disk, the sensor output should be a logic 1; a protected disk should generate a logic 0 (some drives might reverse this convention).

If there is no change in logic level across the sensor for a protected or unprotected disk, try a new write-protect sensor.

If the sensor itself appears to function properly, check the *Write protect* signal at the physical interface (pin 28). A write protected disk should cause a logic 0 on the *Write protect* line. If the signal remains logic 1 regardless of whether the disk is write protected or not, the control-circuit IC in the drive is probably defective. If you are unable to replace the IC, change the drive PC board or replace the entire floppy drive outright.

Symptom 16-6. The drive can only recognize either high- or double-density media, but not both This problem usually appears in 8.89-cm drives during the disk format process when the drive must check the media type. In most cases, the normal/high-density sensor is jammed or defective. Remove the disk and use your multimeter to measure across the sensor. You should be able to actuate the sensor by hand (either by pressing a switch or interrupting a light path) and watch the output display change accordingly on your multimeter. If the sensor does not respond, it is probably defective and should be replaced.

If the sensor itself responds as expected, check the *Normal/high-density* signal at the physical interface (pin 2). A double-density disk should cause a logic 1 output, but a high-density disk should cause a logic 0 signal. If the signal at the physical interface does not respond to changes in the density sensor, the control-circuit IC on the drive PC board is probably defective. If you are unable to replace the control-circuit IC, you can replace the drive PC board or the entire floppy drive outright.

Symptom 16-7. Double-density (720KB) 3.5" disks are not working properly when formatted as high-density (1.44MB) disks This is common when double-density diskettes are pressed into service as high-density disks. Double-density disks use a lower-grade media than high-density disks—this makes double-density disks unreliable when used in high-density mode. Some good-quality diskettes will tolerate this misuse better than other lower-quality diskettes. In general, do not use double-density diskettes as high-density disks.

Symptom 16-8. DOS reports an error, such as "Cannot Read From Drive A:" even though a diskette is fully inserted in the drive, and the drive LED indicates that access is being attempted Start by trying a known-good diskette in the drive (a faulty diskette can cause some perplexing R/W problems). If the diskette is working properly, take a few minutes to clean the drive. Oxides and debris on the R/W heads can interfere with head contact. Do not run the drive with a head-cleaning disk inserted for more than 30 seconds at a time or you risk damaging the heads with excessive friction.

Next, remove the floppy drive and check the assembly for visible damage or obstructions. Insert a diskette and see that the disk is clamped properly. Clear any obstructions that might prevent the disk from seating properly. Also inspect the 34-pin signal cable for obvious damage, and see that it is connected properly at both the drive and the drive controller. Try a new signal cable. If problems persist, the drive itself is probably defective. Try replacing the floppy drive. In most cases, this should correct the problem. If not, replace the floppy-drive controller.

Symptom 16-9.   When a new diskette is inserted in the drive, a directory from a previous diskette appears You might have to reset the system to get the new diskette to be recognized. This is the classic "phantom directory" problem, and is usually caused by a drive or cable fault. Check the 34-pin signal cable first. In most cases, the cable is damaged, or is not inserted properly at either end. Try a new signal cable. If this is a new drive installation, check the floppy-drive jumpers. Some floppy drives allow the *Disk change* signal to be enabled or disabled. Be sure that the *Disk change* signal is enabled. If problems persist, the floppy drive itself is probably defective, so try replacing the floppy drive. In the unlikely event that problems remain, try replacing the drive-controller board (phantom directory problems are rare in the drive controller itself).

> If you suspect a phantom directory, do not initiate any writing to the diskette—its FAT table and directories could be overwritten, rendering the disks's contents inaccessible without careful data-recovery procedures.

Symptom 16-10.   The 3.5" high-density floppy disk cannot format high-density diskettes (but can read and write to them just fine) This problem plagues older computers (i286 and i386 systems), where after-market high-density drives were added. The problem is a lack of BIOS support for high-density formatting—the system is just too old. In such a case, you have a choice. First, you can upgrade your motherboard BIOS to a version that directly supports 3.5" high-density diskettes. You could also use the DRIVER.SYS utility—a DOS driver that allows an existing 3.5" to be "redefined" as a new logical drive providing high-density support. A typical DRIVER.SYS command line would appear in CONFIG.SYS such as:

```
device = c:\dos\driver.sys /D:1
```

Symptom 16-11.   An XT-class PC cannot be upgraded with a 3.5" floppy disk XT systems support up to four double-density 5.25" floppy-disk drives. It will not support 3.5" floppy diskettes at all. To install 3.5" floppy disks, check your DOS version (you need to have DOS 3.3 or later installed). Next, you'll need to install an 8-bit floppy drive controller board (remember to disable any existing floppy controller in the system first). The floppy controller will have its own on-board BIOS to support floppy-disk operations. Finally, take a look at the XT configuration switches and see that any entries for your floppy drives are set correctly. If you're using a stand-alone floppy controller, you might need to set the motherboard jumpers to "no floppy drives."

Symptom 16-12.   The floppy drives cannot be "swapped" so that A: becomes B: and B: becomes A: This often happens on older systems when users want to make their 3.5" after-market B: drive into their A: drive, and relegate their aging 5.25" drive to B: instead. First, check your signal cable. For floppy cables with a wire twist, the end-most connector is A:, and the connector prior to the twist is B:. Reverse the connectors at each floppy drive to reverse their identities. If the cable has no twist (this is rare), reset the jumper ID on each drive so that your desired A: drive is set to DS0 (Drive Select 0), and your desired B: drive is jumpered to DS1. If you accomplish this exchange, but one drive is not recognized, try a new floppy signal cable. Also remember to check your

CMOS settings—you'll need to reverse the floppy drive entries for your A: and B: drives, then reboot the system.

Symptom 16-13. When using a combination floppy drive (called a *combo drive*), one of the drives does not work, but the other works fine This problem is often caused by a drive fault. First, be sure to check the power connector—be sure that both +5 V and +12 V are adequately provided to the drive through the 4-pin "mate-n-lock" connector. If the drive is receiving the proper power, the drive itself has almost certainly failed—try a new drive.

Symptom 16-14. No jumpers are available on the floppy disk, so it is impossible to change settings This is not a problem as much as it is an inconvenience. Typically, you can expect "un-jumpered" floppy disks to be set to the following specifications: *Drive select* 1, *Disk change* (pin 34) enabled, and *Frame ground* enabled. This configuration supports dual drive systems with twisted floppy cables.

Symptom 16-15. The floppy-drive activity LED stays on as soon as the computer is powered up This is a classic signaling problem which occurs after changing or upgrading a drive system. In virtually all cases, one end of the drive cable has been inserted backwards. Be sure that pin 1 on the 34-pin cable is aligned properly with the connector on both the drive and controller. If problems remain, the drive controller might have failed. This is rare, but try a new drive controller.

Further Study

That finishes Chapter 16. Be sure to review the glossary and chapter questions on the accompanying CD. If you have access to the Internet, take a look at some of these floppy-drive manufacturers:

Mitsumi: **http://www.mitsumi.com**

Teac: **http://www.teac.com**

Sony: **http://www.ita.sel.sony.com/products/storage**

HARD

DRIVES

CONTENTS AT A GLANCE

Drive Concepts
  Platters and media
  Air flow and head flight
  Data-density characteristics
  Latency
  Tracks, sectors, and cylinders
  Zoned recording
  Sector sparing (defect management)
  Landing zone
  Interleave
  Write precompensation
  Drive parameters and translation
  Start time
  Power-mode definitions
  Smart command set
  IDE/EIDE hard-drive concepts
  Data-transfer rates
  Block-mode transfers
  Bus mastering
  Drive caching

Drive Construction
  Frame
  Platters
  Read/write heads
  Head actuators
  Spindle motor
  Drive electronics

Concepts of Drive Formatting
  Low-level formatting
  Partitioning
  High-level (DOS) formatting

File Systems and Tips
  FAT basics
  FAT 16
  Partitioning large hard drives
  FAT 32
  Partitioning and formatting for FAT 32

Understanding Drive-Capacity Limits
  Cylinder limits in BIOS
  Partition limits in the operating
    system
  Overcoming capacity limits

Drive Testing and Troubleshooting
  HDD-controller BIOS error codes
  Troubleshooting "DOS compatibility
    mode" problems
  Symptoms and solutions

Further Study
  USENET FAQ

The *hard-disk drive (HDD)* evolved to answer the incessant demands for permanent high-volume file and data storage in the PC. Early floppy disks provided simple and inexpensive storage, but they were slow and programs quickly became far too large to store adequately on diskettes. Switching between multiple diskettes also proved to be a cumbersome proposition. By the early 1980s, hard drives had become an important part of PC architecture (Fig. 17-1) and helped to fuel further OS and applications development. Today, the hard drive is an indispensable element of the modern PC. The hard drive holds the operating system, which boots the system, stores the multi-megabyte applications and files that we rely on, and even provides "virtual memory" for systems lean on RAM. Hard-drive performance also has a profound effect on overall system performance. As you might imagine, hard-drive problems can easily cripple a system. This chapter presents the technology and principles of hard-disk drives, and provides you with some solutions for drive testing and troubleshooting.

Drive Concepts

The first step in understanding hard drives is to learn the basic concepts involved. Many of the terms covered in Chapter 16 also apply to hard drives, but the additional performance requirements and operating demands placed on hard drives have resulted in an array of important new ideas. In principle, a hard-disk drive is very similar to a floppy drive—a magnetic recording media is applied to a substrate material, which is then spun at a high rate of speed. Magnetic read/write heads in close proximity to the media can step rapidly across the spinning media to detect or create flux transistions, as required. When you look closely, however, you can see that there are some major physical differences between floppy and hard drives.

PLATTERS AND MEDIA

Where floppy disks use magnetic material applied over a thin, flexible substrate of mylar (or some other plastic), hard drives use rugged, solid substrates, called *platters*. You can clearly view the platters of a hard drive in Fig. 17-2. A platter is traditionally made of alu-

FIGURE 17-1 A contemporary hard-drive unit.
NEC Techologies, Inc.

FIGURE 17-2   **A Maxtor hard drive.** Maxtor Corporation

minum because aluminum is a light material, it is easy to machine to desired tolerances, and it holds its shape under the high centrifugal forces that occur at high rotation rates. But today, most platters are made from materials like glass or ceramic composites, which have very low thermal expansion rates (so there are fewer media problems and can withstand higher centrifugal forces than aluminum. Because a major advantage of a hard drive is speed, platters are rotated from about 7600 RPM to as much as 10,000 RPM (compared to older hard drives, which ran at 3600 to 5200 RPM). A hard drive generally uses two or more platters, although extremely small drive assemblies might use only one platter.

Hard drives must be capable of tremendous recording densities—well over 10,000 *Bits Per Inch (BPI)*. To achieve such substantial recording densities, platter media is far superior to the oxide media used for floppy disks. First, the media must possess a high coercitivity so that each flux transition is well defined and easily discernible from every other flux transition. Coercitivity of hard drive media typically exceeds 1,400 oersteds. Second, the media must be extremely flat across the entire platter surface to within just a few microinches. Hard-drive R/W heads do not actually contact their platters, but ride within a few microinches over the platter surfaces. A surface defect of only a few microinches can collide with a head and destroy it. Such a "head crash" is often a catastrophic defect that requires hard-drive replacement. Floppy drive heads do contact the media, so minor surface defects are not a major concern. You will see more about head flight and surface defects later in this chapter.

Media today is a "thin-film," which has long since replaced magnetic oxides. Thin-film media is a microscopic layer of pure metal (or a metal compound), which is bonded to the substrate surface through an interim layer. The media is then coated with a protective layer to help survive head crashing. Thin-film media also tends to be very flat, so R/W heads can be run at microscopic distances from the platter surfaces.

AIR FLOW AND HEAD FLIGHT

Read/write heads in a hard-disk drive must travel extremely close to the surface of each platter, but can never actually contact the media while the drive is running. The heads could be mechanically fixed, but fixed-altitude flight does not allow for shock or natural vibration that is always present in a drive assembly. Instead, R/W heads are made to float within microinches of a platter surface by suspending the heads on a layer of moving air.

Figure 17-3 illustrates the typical air flow in a hard drive. Disk (platter) rotation creates a slight cushion that elevates the heads. You might also notice that some air is channeled through a fine filter that helps to remove any particles from the drive's enclosure.

It is important that all hard drives seal their platter assemblies into an air-tight chamber. The reason for such a seal is to prevent contamination from dust, dirt, spills, or strands of hair. Contamination that lands on a platter's surface can easily result in a head crash. A head crash can damage the head, the media, or both—and any physical damage can result in an unusable drive. Consider the comparison shown in Fig. 17-4. During normal operation, a hard drive's R/W head flies above the media at a distance of only about 10 microns (microinches). Many technical professionals relate that specification to a jumbo jet flying 30 feet above the ground at 600 miles per hour. It follows then that any variation in surface flatness because of platter defects or contaminates can have catastrophic effects on head height. Even an average particle of smoke is 10 times wider than the flying height.

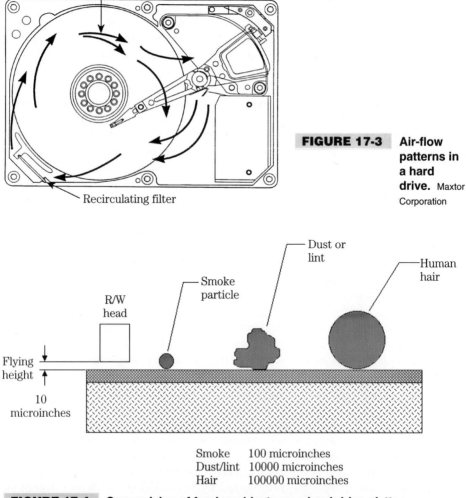

FIGURE 17-3 Air-flow patterns in a hard drive. Maxtor Corporation

Smoke   100 microinches
Dust/lint   10000 microinches
Hair   100000 microinches

FIGURE 17-4   Comparision of foreign objects on a hard-drive platter.

With such proportions, you can understand why it is critically important that the platter compartment remain sealed at all times. The platter compartment can only be opened in a *cleanroom environment*. A cleanroom is a small, enclosed room where the air is filtered to remove any contaminants larger than 3 microns. Hard-drive assemblers wear gloves and cleanroom suits that cover all but their faces—masks cover their mouth and nose to prevent breath vapor from contaminating the platters.

DATA-DENSITY CHARACTERISTICS

It is desirable to pack as much information as possible in the media of hard-drive platters. The *areal density* of a media describes this maximum amount of capacity in terms of megabytes per square inch (sometimes noted *MBSI* or *MB/in²*). Today's hard drives used in most computers use media supporting 1500 MBSI or more (several years ago, this figure was more like 400 to 800 MBSI). As you might imagine, physically smaller platters must hold media with a higher areal density to offer storage capacities similar to larger drives.

Several major factors affect areal density. First, the actual size of magnetic particles in the media places an upper barrier on areal density—smaller particles allow higher areal densities. Larger coercitivity of the media and smaller R/W heads with tighter magnetization fields allow higher areal densities. Finally, head height—the altitude of a R/W head over the platter surface—controls density. The closer a R/W head passes to its media, the higher areal densities can be. As heads fly further away, magnetic fields spread out, resulting in lower densities. Surface smoothness is then a major limiting factor in areal density because smoother surfaces allow R/W heads to fly closer to the media.

Other factors define the way that data can be packed onto a drive—most of which are related to areal density. *Track density* indicates the number of *Tracks Per Inch (TPI)*. Current hard drives commonly run faster than 7000 TPI. The track density is also influenced by the precision of the R/W head-positioning system—finer precision allows more tracks to be defined. Flux density highlights the number of individual magnetic flux transitions per linear inch of track space rated as *flux changes per inch* (*FCI*, or *KFCI* for "thousands of FCI"). Typical hard drives now offer flux densities between 160 and more than 210 KFCI. Finally, you'll probably see references to *recording density*, which is basically the number of bits per linear inch of track space listed as *bits per inch* (*BPI*, or *KBPI* for "thousands of BPI"). Current recording densities range from 150 to 200 KBPI.

LATENCY

As fast as a hard drive is, it cannot work instantaneously. A finite period of delay occurs between the moment that a read or write command is initiated over the drive's physical interface and the moment that desired information is available (or placed). This delay is known as *latency*. More specifically, latency refers to the time it takes for needed bytes to pass under a R/W head. If the head has not quite reached the desired location yet, latency can be quite short. If the head has just missed the desired location, the head must wait almost a full rotation before the needed bits are available again, so latency can be rather long. In general, a disk drive is specified with average latency, which (statistically) is time for the spindle to make half of a full rotation. For a disk rotating at 3600 RPM (60 rotations per second), a full rotation is completed in $(1/60) = 16.7$ ms. Average latency would then be $(16.7/2) = 8.3$ ms. Disks spinning at 5200 RPM offer an average latency of 5.8 ms, etc.

As a rule, the faster a disk spins, the lower its latency will be. Ultimately, disk speed is limited by centrifugal forces acting on the platters.

TRACKS, SECTORS, AND CYLINDERS

As with floppy drives, you cannot simply place data anywhere on a hard-drive platter—the drive would have no idea where to look for data, or if the data is even valid. The information on each platter must be sorted and organized into a series of known, standard locations. Each platter side can be considered as a two-dimensional field possessing length and width. With this sort of geometry, data is recorded in sets of concentric circles running from the disk spindle to the platter edge. A drive can move its R/W heads over the spinning media to locate needed data or programs in a matter of milliseconds. Every concentric circle on a platter is known as a *track*. A current platter generally contains 2048 to more than 16278 tracks. You can see a comparison of tracks vs. drive capacity for several current Maxtor hard drives outlined in Table 17-1. Figure 17-5 shows data organization on a simple platter assembly. Notice that only one side of the three platters is shown.

TABLE 17-1 COMPARISON OF DRIVE PARAMETERS VS. CAPACITY				
MODEL	TRACKS (CYLINDERS)	HEADS	SECTORS	CAPACITY
88400D8	16278	16	63	8400MB
86480D6	13395	15	63	6480MB
84320D4	8930	15	63	4320MB
83240D3	6697	15	63	3240MB
82160D2	4465	15	63	2160MB

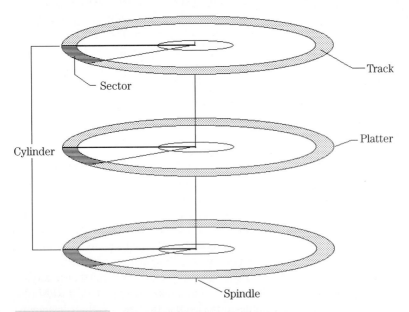

FIGURE 17-5 Data organization on a hard drive.

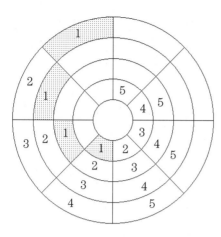

FIGURE 17-6 An example of cylinder skewing.

Although each surface of a platter is a two-dimensional area, the number of platter surfaces involved in a hard drive (4, 6, 8, or more) bring a third dimension (height) into play. Because each track is located directly over the same tracks on subsequent platters, each track in a platter assembly can be visualized as a "cylinder" that passes through every platter. The number of cylinders is equal to the number of tracks on one side of a platter.

Once a R/W head finishes reading one track, the head must be stepped to another (usually adjacent) track. This stepping process, no matter how rapid, does require some finite amount of time. This is called *seek time* and it is often less than 1 ms for track-to-track seeks. When the head tries to step directly from the end of one track to the beginning of another, the head will arrive too late to catch the new track's index pulse(s), so the drive will have to wait almost an entire rotation to synchronize with the track index pulse. By offsetting the start points of each track (Fig. 17-6), head travel time can be compensated for. This cylinder-skewing technique is intended to improve hard-drive performance by reducing the disk time lost during normal head steps. A head should be able to identify and read the desired information from a track within one disk rotation.

Tracks are broken down even further into small segments called *sectors*. As with DOS floppy disks, a sector holds 512 bytes of data, along with error-checking and housekeeping data that identifies the sector, track, and results calculated by *Cyclical Redundancy Checking (CRC)*. The location and ID information for each sector is developed when the drive is low-level formatted at the factory. After formatting, only sector data and CRC bytes are updated during writing. If sector ID information is accidentally overwritten or corrupted, the data recorded in the afflicted sector becomes unreadable.

Figure 17-7 shows the layout for a typical sector on a Maxtor SCSI drive. As you can see, there is much more than just 512 bytes of data. The start of every sector is marked with a pulse. The pulse signaling the first sector of a track is called the *index pulse*. Every sector has two portions: an address area and data area. The address area is used to identify the sector. This is critically important because the drive must be able to identify precisely which cylinder, head, and sector is about to be read or written. This location information is recorded in the "address field," and is followed by two bytes of *Cyclical Redundancy Check (CRC)* data. When a drive identifies a location, it generates a CRC code, which it compares to the CRC code recorded on the disk. If the two CRC codes match, the address is assumed to be valid, and disk operation can continue. Otherwise, an error has occurred

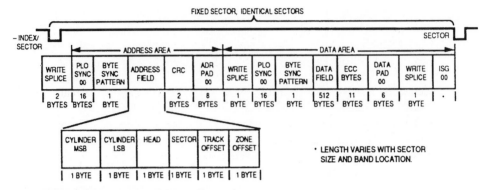

FIGURE 17-7   A typical hard-drive sector layout. Maxtor Corporation

and the entire sector is considered invalid. This failure usually precipitates a catastrophic DOS error message.

After a number of bytes are encountered for drive timing and synchronization, up to 512 bytes can be read or written to the "data field." The data is processed to derive 11 bytes of ECC error checking code using Reed Solomon encoding. If data is being read, the derived ECC is compared to the recorded ECC. When the codes match, data is assumed to be valid and drive operation continues. Otherwise, a data read error is assumed. During writing, the old ECC data is replaced with the new ECC data derived for the current data. It is interesting that only the data and ECC fields of a sector are written after formatting. All other sector data remains untouched until the drive is reformatted. If a retentivity problem should eventually allow one or more bits to become corrupt in the address area, the sector will fail.

ZONED RECORDING

In the early days of hard drives, every track had the same number of sectors (i.e., 64, or 0 through 63). This worked well, but designers realized that for a *Constant Angular Velocity (CAV)* drive, the data was recorded more densely on the inner tracks, where the circumference is lower, and less densely on the outer tracks, where the circumference is higher. A feature known as *zoned recording* was added to the drive, which allows a variable number of tracks. The total number of tracks is divided up into a number of "zones" (i.e., 16 zones). All of the tracks within a zone use the same number of sectors, but inner zones use fewer sectors, and outer zones use more sectors. Zoned recording lets hard drives make the most efficient use of their storage space. Zoned recording is managed by the drive itself, so you might still be able to enter a fixed number in the "Sectors per Track" entry under the CMOS Setup. Current hard drives can run from 195 to 312 physical sectors per track.

SECTOR SPARING (DEFECT MANAGEMENT)

Not all sectors on a hard drive are usable. When a drive is formatted, bad sectors must be removed from normal use. The *sparing* process works to ensure that each track has access to the appropriate number of working sectors. When sparing is performed in-line (as a drive is being formatted), faulty sectors cause all subsequent sectors to be shifted up one sector. *In-line sparing* is not widely used. *Field-defect sparing* (after the format process is complete) assigns (or "remaps") faulty sectors to other working sectors located in spare disk tracks that are reserved for that purpose. For example, most EIDE hard drives use field-defect sparing. It reserves a full 16 tracks for spare sectors (often referred to as the defect management zone). Faulty sectors are typically marked for reallocation when the disk is formatted.

The only place where faulty sectors are absolutely not permitted is on track 00. Track 00 is used to hold a hard drive's partition and FAT information. If a drive cannot read or write to track 00, the entire drive is rendered unusable. If a sector in track 00 should fail during operation, reformatting the drive to lockout the bad sector will not necessarily recover the drive's operation. Track 00 failures usually necessitates reformatting the drive from scratch or replacing it entirely.

LANDING ZONE

The R/W heads of a hard drive fly within microinches of their respective platter surfaces—held aloft with air currents produced by the spinning platters. When the drive is turned off, however, the platters slow to a halt. During this spindown period, air flow falls rapidly, and heads can literally "crash" into the platter surfaces. Whenever a head touches a platter surface, data can be irretrievably destroyed. Even during normal operation, a sudden shock or bump can cause one or more heads to skid across their surfaces. Although a drive can usually be reformatted after a head crash, data and programs would have to be reloaded from scratch.

To avoid a head crash during normal spindown, a cylinder is reserved (either the innermost or outermost cylinder) as a *Landing Zone (LZ)*. No data is stored on the landing zone, so any surface problems caused by head landings are harmless. Virtually all hard drives today will automatically move the head assembly over the landing zone before spindown, then gently lock the heads into place until power is restored. Locking helps to ensure that random shocks and vibrations do not shake the heads onto adjacent data-carrying tracks and cause damage while the power is off. Older hard drives required a specific "landing zone" entry in the CMOS setup. But today, the process is automatic, so you can usually just enter "0" for the LZ, or allow the system to auto-detect the LZ.

INTERLEAVE

The *interleave* of a hard drive refers to the order in which sectors are numbered on a platter. Interleave was a critical factor in older desktop computer systems, where the core logic (i.e., CPU and memory) was relatively slow compared to drive performance. It was necessary to create artificial delays in the drive to allow core logic to catch up. Delays were accomplished by physically separating the sectors (numbering contiguous sectors out of order). This ordering forced the drive to read a sector, then skip one or more sectors (1, 2, 3, or more) to reach the next subsequent sector. Effectively, the "interleaved" drive would have to make several rotations before all sectors on a track could be read.

The ratio of a sector's length versus the distance between two subsequent sectors is known as the *interleave factor*. For example, if a drive reads a sector and skips a sector to reach the next sequential sector, interleave factor would be 1:3, etc. The greater the interleave, the more rotations that would be needed to read all the sectors on a track, and the slower the drive would be. To achieve highest disk performance, interleave should be eliminated. Because drive and interface logic today is so much faster than even the fastest hard drive, the issue of interleave is largely irrelevant now. Drives no longer interleave their sectors, so all sectors are in sequential order around the track, and the interleave factor is 1:1—all data on a track can be read in one disk rotation (minus latency). An interleave factor of 1:1 yields optimal drive performance.

> As a rule, do not allow any drive utility to adjust or "optimize" the drive interleave. Changing the interleave not only destroys existing data, but it can also seriously impair drive performance.

WRITE PRECOMPENSATION

As you have already seen, a hard drive spins its platter(s) at a constant rate. This is known as *Constant Angular Velocity (CAV)*. Although constant rotation requires only a very simple motor circuit, extra demands are placed on the media. Tracks closer to the spindle are physically shorter than tracks toward the platter's outer edge. Shorter tracks result in shorter sectors. For inner sectors to hold the same amount of data as outer sectors, data must be packed more densely on the inner sectors—each magnetic flux reversal is actually closer together. Unfortunately, smaller flux reversals produce weaker magnetic fields in the R/W heads during reading.

If the inner sectors are written with a stronger magnetic field, flux transitions stored in the media will be stronger. When the inner sectors are then read, a clearer, more well-defined signal will result. The use of increased writing current to compensate for diminished disk response is known as *Write Precompensation (WP)*. The track where write precompensation is expected to begin is specified in the drive's parameter table in CMOS setup. Write precompensation filled an important role in early drives that used older, oxide-based media. Today's thin-film media and very small drive geometries (combined with Zoned Recording techniques) result in low signal differences across the platter area, so write precompensation (although still specified) is rarely meaningful anymore. In most cases, you can enter "0" for WP or allow the system to auto-detect the WP.

DRIVE PARAMETERS AND TRANSLATION

A host computer must know the key parameters of its installed hard drive before the drive can be used. A system must know six parameters: the number of cylinders, heads, and sectors; the track where write precompensation begins; what track the landing zone is on; and the drive's total formatted capacity. These parameters are stored in the computer's CMOS RAM and configured with the CMOS setup utility. If a new drive is installed, the CMOS setup can easily be updated to show the changes. You can tell a lot about a drive by reviewing its parameters. Consider the Maxtor 88400D8 shown in Table 17-1. With 16 heads, 63 sectors per track, and 16278 tracks (cylinders), the capacity works out as $(16278 \times 16 \times 63 \times 512) = 8,401,010,688$ bytes (or 8.4GB).

There are two interesting things about the drives of Table 17-1. First, the write precompensation and landing-zone entries are essentially unused. In most cases, the landing zone is now an automated feature of the particular drive. The second issue to consider is that these numbers are logical, not physical. Just imagine that with two heads per platter, you'd need 8 platters to support 16 heads—not too likely in today's small form-factor drives. Also, the number of sectors per track can differ because of zoned recording techniques. This means that the drive parameters you are entering into CMOS are "translation parameters." The electronics on the drive itself actually converts (or translates) those parameters into actual physical drive locations.

This is also a good time to discuss the way in which drive sizes are measured. There are two means of "measuring" a megabyte—some manufacturers use 106 (1,000,000) bytes (a "straight megabyte") and others use 220 (1,048,576) bytes (this is also called a *binary megabyte*). Similarly, some manufacturers use 109 (100,0000,000) bytes (a *straight gigabyte*), but others use 230 (1,073,741,824) bytes (called a *binary gigabyte*). This can cause confusion when checking your drive space. Drive manufacturers and the CHKDSK utility typically use "straight" megabytes and gigabytes in their drive-size numbers. But many software makers (i.e., FDISK and the CMOS setup routine) use "binary" megabytes and gigabytes. This can make drive sizes seem unusually low.

Table 17-2 compares typical variations in drive size reporting. There is a quick way to check the drive size—take the manufacturer's "formatted capacity" megabyte number and divide by 1.0485. The resulting number is what will probably be reported by CMOS, FDISK, and other utilities that use "binary" megabytes or gigabytes. For example, the 2.1GB drive in Table 17-2 has a "formatted capacity" of 2111.8MB (2.11GB). If you divide this by 1.0485, you'll get (2111.8/1.0485) = 2014.1MB—this is what will probably be reported by CMOS or FDISK. If the reported number is significantly lower, you're probably losing drive capacity somewhere (probably through incomplete partitioning).

START TIME

Booting a computer can take up to 30 seconds—often more. Some of this time is an artificial delay needed to initialize the hard drive. From the moment that power is applied to the hard drive, it can take anywhere from 7 to 10 seconds for the drive's on-board controller to

TABLE 17-2 TYPICAL REPORTED DRIVE CAPACITIES			
DRIVE	CAPACITY (MB)	CMOS (MB)	CHKDSK (MB)
850MB	853.6	814.1	853.6
1.2GB	1291.9	1232.1	1281.9
1.6GB	1624.6	1549.4	1624.6
2.0GB	2000.3	1907.7	2000.3
2.1GB	2111.8	2014.1	2111.8
2.5GB	2559.8	2441.2	2559.8
3.1GB	3166.7	3020.2	3166.7
4.0GB	4000.7	3815.4	4000.7

start and initialize the drive where it can be recognized by the system POST. This is known as the drive's *start time*. Boot problems with a new hard drive are frequently caused by an insufficient delay at boot time. The BIOS attempts to check for the presence of a hard drive, which has not yet had time to initialize.

POWER-MODE DEFINITIONS

Modern hard drives are not simply "on" or "off." They operate in any one of several modes, and each mode makes different power demands on the host system. This is particularly important because today's PCs are becoming ever-more power conscious, so the ability to control drive power is an integral part of PC power-conservation systems. Typical hard drives operate in any of five different power modes:

- *Spin-up* The drive is spinning up following initial application of power and has not yet reached full speed. This demands about 14 W and is particularly demanding of the power supply (if the supply is marginal or overloaded, the hard drive might not spin-up properly).
- *Seek* This is a random-access operation by the disk drive as it tries to locate the required track for reading or writing. This demands about 8.5- to 9.0 W.
- *Read/write* A seek has been completed, and data is being read from or written to the drive. This uses about 5.0 W.
- *Idle* This is a basic power-conservation mode, where the drive is spinning and all other circuitry is powered on, but the head actuator is parked and powered off. This drops power demands to about 4 W, yet the drive is capable of responding to read commands within 40 ms.
- *Standby* The spindle motor is not running (the drive "spins down"). This is the main power-conservation mode, and it requires just 1 W. It might require up to several seconds for the drive will leave this mode (or spin-up) upon receipt of a command that requires disk access.

SMART COMMAND SET

Some of the newest hard drives use the *Self-Monitoring Analysis and Reporting Technology (SMART)* command set. SMART-compliant drives improve the data integrity and data availability of hard-disk drives by regularly checking for potential drive problems. In some cases, a SMART-compliant device will predict an impending failure with sufficient time to allow users to backup their data and replace the drive before data loss occurs.

IDE/EIDE HARD-DRIVE CONCEPTS

IDE hard drives have come a long way since their introduction in the late 1980s. In fact, IDE technology has come so far that it's difficult to keep all of the concepts straight. This part of the chapter recaps the important concepts and attributes of IDE and its successors.

IDE/ATA   *Integrated Drive Electronics (IDE)* and *AT Attachment (ATA)* are basically one and the same thing—a disk-drive scheme designed to integrate the controller onto the drive itself, instead of relying on a stand-alone controller board. This approach reduces interface costs and makes drive firmware implementations easier. IDE proved to be a low-cost, easily configured system—so much so that it created a boom in the disk-drive industry. Although *IDE* and *ATA* are sometimes used interchangeably, ATA is the formal standard that defines the drive and how it operates, but IDE is really the "trade name" that refers to the 40-pin interface and drive-controller architecture designed to implement the ATA standard.

ATAPI   One of the major disadvantages of ATA is that it was designed for hard drives only. With the broad introduction of CD-ROM drives, designers needed a means of attaching CD-ROMs (and other devices, such as tape drives) to the existing ATA (IDE) interface, rather than using a stand-alone controller card. The *ATA Packet Interface (ATAPI)* is a standard based on the ATA (IDE) interface designed to allow non-hard drive devices to plug into an ordinary ATA (IDE) port. Hard drives enjoy ATA (IDE) support through BIOS, but ATAPI devices require a device driver to support them. Booting from an ATAPI CD-ROM is only possible with an "El Torito" CD-ROM and the latest BIOS.

ATA-2, Fast-ATA, and EIDE   By the early 1990s, it became clear that ATA architecture would soon be overwhelmed by advances in hard-drive technology. The hard-drive industry responded by developing the ATA-2 standard as an extension of ATA. ATA-2 is largely regarded as a significant improvement to ATA. It defines faster PIO and DMA data-transfer modes, adds more powerful drive commands (such as the *Identify drive* command to support auto-identification in CMOS), adds support for a second drive channel, handles block data transfers (*Block transfer mode*), and defines a new means of addressing sectors on the hard drive using *Logical Block Addressing (LBA)*. LBA has proven to be a very effective vehicle for overcoming the traditional 528MB hard-drive size limit. Yet ATA-2 continues to use the same 40-pin physical interface used by ATA and is backward compatible with ATA (IDE) drives.

Along with ATA-2, you'll probably find two additional terms: *Enhanced IDE (EIDE)* and *Fast-ATA*. These are not standards—merely different implementations of the ATA-2 standard. EIDE represents the Western Digital implementation of ATA-2, which builds upon both the ATA-2 and ATAPI standards. This has been so effective that EIDE has become the "generic" term. Seagate and Quantum have thrown their support behind the Fast-ATA implementation of the ATA-2 standard. However, Fast-ATA builds on ATA-2 only. For all practical purposes, there is no significant difference between ATA-2, EIDE, and Fast-ATA, and you'll probably see these three terms used interchangeably (although this is not technically correct).

ATA-3   The latest official implementation of the ATA standard is ATA-3. It does not define any new data-transfer modes, but it does improve the reliability of PIO Mode 4. It also offers a simple password-based security scheme, more sophisticated power-management features, and *Self-Monitoring Analysis and Reporting Technology (SMART)*. ATA-3 is also backward compatible with ATA-2, ATAPI, and ATA devices. Because no new data-transfer modes are defined by ATA-3, you might also see the generic term "EIDE" used interchangeably (although this is also not technically correct).

Ultra-ATA   The push for ever-faster data-transfer rates is never-ending, and the Ultra-ATA standard represents an extension to ATA-3 by providing a high-performance 33MB/s

DMA data-transfer rate. The implementation of Ultra-ATA is usually called *Ultra-DMA/33*. You'll need an Ultra-ATA drive, controller, and BIOS to support an Ultra-ATA drive system, but it is fully backward compatible with previous ATA standards.

ATA-4   The next generation of ATA standards is still on the drawing boards. The most important issue with ATA-4 will be to effectively merge ATA-3, Ultra-ATA, and ATAPI all into one coherent standard, and probably add some even faster data-transfer rates. Unfortunately, ATA-4 has met with some resistance in its present form, and is not complete as of this writing.

DATA-TRANSFER RATES

Data-transfer rates play a major role in drive performance. In operation, the two measures of data transfer are: the rate at which data is taken from the platters, and the rate at which data is passed between the drive and controller. The internal data transfer between the platters and drive buffer is typically the slower rate. Older drives could run at about 5MB/sec, but newer Ultra-ATA drives (such as the Maxtor DiamondMax 2160) runs at 14MB/s. The external data transfer between the drive and controller (the *interface rate*) is often the faster rate. Older drives provided between 5 and 8MB/sec, but ATA-2 (EIDE) drives can operate up to 16MB/sec. Ultra-ATA drives can run at 33MB/s. The modern standards of IDE/EIDE external data transfer are listed as *Programmed I/O (PIO)* and *Direct Memory Access (DMA)* modes. The PIO mode specifies how fast data is transferred to and from the drive (Table 17-3).

You might notice that the EIDE-specific modes (PIO-3 and PIO-4) use the IORDY hardware flow control line. This means that the drive can use the IORDY line to slow down the interface when necessary. Interfaces without proper IORDY support might cause data corruption in the fast PIO modes (so you'd be stuck with the slower modes). When choosing an EIDE drive and controller, always be sure to check that the IORDY line is being used.

DMA data transfers mean that the data is transferred directly between the drive and memory without using the CPU as an intermediary (as is the case with PIO). In true multitasking operating systems (such as OS/2, Windows NT, or Linux), DMA leaves the CPU free to do something useful during disk transfers. In a DOS or Windows environment, the CPU will have to wait for the transfer to finish anyway. In these cases, DMA transfers don't offer that much of a multitasking advantage. The two distinct types of direct memory access are *ordinary DMA* and *bus-mastering DMA*. Ordinary DMA uses the DMA controller on the system's motherboard to perform the complex task of arbitration, grab-

TABLE 17-3 DATA TRANSFER SPEEDS VS. PIO MODES

PIO MODE	CYCLE TIME (NS)	TRANSFER RATE (MB/S)	NOTES
0	600	3.3	These are the old ATA (IDE) modes
1	383	5.2	
2	240	8.3	
3	180 IORDY	11.1	These are the newer ATA-2 (EIDE) modes
4	120 IORDY	16.6	

TABLE 17-4 DATA TRANSFER SPEEDS VS. DMA MODES

DMA MODE	CYCLE TIME (NS)		TRANSFER RATE (MB/S)	NOTES
Single Word	0	960	2.1	Also in ATA
	1	480	4.2	
	2	240	8.3	
Multiword	0	480	4.2	Also in ATA
	1	150	13.3	
	2	120	16.6	
	3	—	33.0	Ultra-ATA

bing the system bus, and transferring the data. With bus-mastering DMA, all this is done by logic on the drive-controller card itself (this adds considerably to the complexity and the price of a bus-mastering interface).

Unfortunately, the DMA controller on traditional ISA bus systems is slow—and out of the question for use with a modern hard disk. VLB cards cannot be used as DMA targets at all, and can only do bus-mastering DMA. Only EISA and PCI-based interfaces make non-bus-mastering DMA viable: EISA type "B" DMA will transfer 4MB/s and PCI type "F" DMA will transfer between 6 and 8MB/s. Today, the proper software support for DMA is relatively rare (as well as the interfaces supporting it). Still, the DMA data-transfer modes are listed in Table 17-4.

BLOCK-MODE TRANSFERS

Traditionally, an interrupt (IRQ) is generated each time that a read or write command is passed to the drive. This causes a certain amount of overhead work for the host system and CPU. If it were possible to transfer multiple sectors of data between the drive and host without generating an IRQ, data transfer could be accomplished much more efficiently. Block-mode transfers allow up to 128 sectors of data to be transferred at a single time, and can improve transfers by as much as 30%. However, block-mode transfers are not terribly effective on single-tasking operating systems, such as DOS—any improvement over a few percent usually indicates bad buffer cache management on the part of the drive. Finally, the block size that is optimal for drive throughput isn't always the best for system performance. For example, the DOS FAT file system tends to favor a block size equal to the cluster size.

BUS MASTERING

Bus mastering is a high-performance enhancement to the ATA-2/3 interface on your drive controller (you might see some motherboards or chipsets mention bus master support as *BM-IDE*). When configured properly, bus mastering uses *Direct Memory Access (DMA)* data transfers to reduce the CPU's workload when it comes to saving or recalling data from the EIDE/IDE drive (such as a hard drive or ATAPI CD-ROM). By comparison, *Programmed I/O (PIO)* data-transfer modes are very CPU-intensive. Bus mastering is particularly useful if you have multiple disk-intensive applications running simultaneously. Many modern PCs support bus mastering, but to make the most of bus master performance, your system must have all of the following elements:

■ The motherboard (drive controller) must be bus master IDE compliant.
■ The motherboard BIOS must support bus mastering.
■ You need a multitasking operating system (OS), such as Windows 95.
■ A bus-mastering device driver is needed for the operating system.
■ And you need an EIDE/IDE device (disk drive or CD-ROM) that is bus-mastering compatible and supports "DMA multi-word" modes.

    You can use bus-master IDE and non-bus master IDE devices in the same system, but the non-bus-master IDE devices will reduce the overall performance of the bus mastering devices. However, bus-mastering IDE is not a cure-all for system performance problems. In fact, bus mastering will probably not benefit the system at all if you run DOS games, work with only single applications at a time, or use multiple applications that are not disk-intensive.

> SCSI devices are not supported by bus-master IDE.

Windows 95 IDE bus master drivers As stated, you'll need a bus-master driver to support your operating system (namely Windows 95). The commercial release of Windows 95 offers only a generic solution (ESDI_506.PDR), and the version released with OSR2 is still quite basic. For top performance, you should use the bus-master driver that accompanies your motherboard or another compliant bus-master drive controller. You can check some of the following sources for current bus-master drivers:

■ Drivers Headquarters: **http://www.drivershq.com/**
■ Intel Bus-Master Driver 3.0: **http://web2.iadfw.net/ksm/drivers/bmide_95.exe**
■ Intel Bus-Master Driver 2.85: **http://web2.iadfw.net/ksm/drivers/bmide285.exe**
■ ASUS Bus-Master Driver: **ftp://ftp1.asus.com.tw/pub/ASUS/Drivers/bmide_95.exe**
■ Elitegroup (ECS) Bus-Master Driver: **ftp://ftp.ecs.com.tw/pub/ide/triton/430v17.exe**
■ Tyan Bus-Master Driver 2.0: **ftp://204.156.147.247:21/pub/motherboard/tynbm20.zip**

Bus-master driver problems under Windows 95 Although bus mastering can clearly enhance the drive performance of a busy multitasking system, it is not without its problems. As it turns out, bus-master driver issues are the most prevalent problems. The two most common issues are: (1) The CD-ROM or IDE HDD on the secondary drive channel disappear after installing bus-master driver, and (2) Windows 95 takes a long time to boot after bus-master drivers are installed.
    In both cases, you'll notice that the secondary controller channel (IDE) no longer appears in the *Device manager*. This is because bus-master drivers do not support ATA (IDE) controllers correctly. You'll need to install the bus-master driver for the primary (EIDE) drive channel, and leave the PIO driver in place to support the secondary (IDE) drive channel. Install the bus master driver, then alter the *Registry* to manually redirect the secondary IDE drive channel to use a standard IDE driver again:

Altering the Windows 95 *Registry* can have a profound effect on your system or even prevent the system from booting. Always make a backup copy of the original *Registry* files (SYSTEM.DAT and USER.DAT) before attempting to edit them.

1 Start REGEDIT, load the *Registry* file, and find the entry: HKEY_LOCAL_MA-CHINE/System/CurrentControlSet/control/Services/Class/hdc.

2 There should be four sub-directories: 0000 to 0003.

3 Find the one where *DriverDesc* reads something like "Primary Bus Master IDE controller" or "Secondary Bus Master IDE controller," according to the port you want to change (it should be 0002 or 0003). You'd most likely want to change the secondary entry.

4 In this sub-directory, change *PortDriver* from "ESDI_506.PDR" (or whatever bus-master driver you're using) to "IDEATAPI.MPD."

5 You can also change the *DriverDesc* to something like "Standard IDE/ESDI controller"—this will produce a more familiar entry when viewed in the *System manager*.

6 Save your changes and reboot the computer.

Your secondary (IDE) drive-controller channel should now be using a standard IDE driver, and the IDE devices on that channel (i.e., the CD-ROM) should now appear normally. Here's another trick that might shorten the startup time—start Windows 95 in *Safe mode* and delete all drives in *System manager*. Then, reboot the PC and allow Windows 95 to re-detect all the drives automatically.

Some technicians have suggested that configuring an ATAPI CD-ROM as the "slave" device when it's the only device on the secondary (IDE) drive channel might work when using bus-master drivers. Normally, the only IDE device would be jumpered as the "master." Please notice that this suggestion won't damage the CD-ROM or drive controller, but it has not been tested to verify whether it actually works. Given the proliferation of bus-master hardware and software, there might circumstances where this suggestion might not work. Consider this as a last resort.

DRIVE CACHING

Ideally, a drive should respond instantaneously—data should be available the moment it is requested. Unfortunately, the instant access and transfer of data is impossible with even today's magnetic (and optical) storage technologies. The inescapable laws of physics govern the limitations of mechanical systems, such as spindles and head stepping, and mechanical delays will always be present (to some extent) in drive systems. The problem now facing computer designers is that mechanical drive systems—as fast and precise as they are—still lag far behind the computer circuitry handling the information. In the world of personal computers, a millisecond is a very long time. For DOS-based systems, you often must wait for disk access to be completed before DOS allows another operation to begin. Such delays can be quite irritating when the drive is accessing huge programs and data files typical of current software packages. Drives use a technique called *drive caching* to increase the apparent speed of drive systems.

Caching basically allocates a small amount of solid-state memory, which acts as an interim storage area (or buffer) located right on the drive. A cache is typically loaded with information that is anticipated to be required by the system. When a disk read is initiated, the cache is checked for desired information. If the desired information is actually in the cache (a cache hit), that information is transferred from the cache buffer to the core logic at electronic rates— no disk access occurs, and very fast data transfer is achieved. If the desired information is not in the cache (a cache miss), the data is taken from the hard disk at normal drive speeds with no improvement in performance. Today's hard drives use as much as 256KB of modern high-performance memory, such as EDO RAM (the same type of RAM used on many Pentium motherboards) for on-board drive cache. A variety of complex software algorithms are used to predict what disk information to load and save in a cache. Figure 17-8 illustrates the caching algorithm used by Quantum Corporation for some of their ProDrive hard drives.

Although the majority of caches are intended to buffer read operations, some caches also buffer write operations. A write cache accepts the data to be saved from core logic, then returns system control while the drive works separately to save the information. Remember that a cache does not accelerate the drive itself. A cache merely helps to move your system along so that you need not wait for drive delays. In terms of general implementation, a cache can be located on the hard drive itself or on the drive-controller board. For most computers using system-level hard-drive interfaces (EIDE or SCSI), any cache is usually located on the drive itself.

Drive Construction

Now that you have a background in major hard-drive concepts and operations, it is time to take a drive apart and show you how all the key pieces fit together. Although it is somewhat rare that you should ever need to disassemble a hard drive, the understanding of each part and its placement will help you to appreciate drive testing and the various hard-drive failure modes. An exploded diagram for a Quantum hard drive is illustrated in Figure 17-9. This book concentrates on the frame, platters, R/W heads, head actuators, spindle motor, and electronics package.

FRAME

The mechanical *frame* or *chassis* (1) is remarkably important to the successful operation of a hard drive. The frame affects a drive's structural, thermal, and electrical integrity. A frame must be rigid and provide a steady platform for mounting the working components. Larger drives typically use a chassis of cast aluminum, but the small drive in your notebook or sub-notebook computer might use a plastic frame. The particular frame material really depends on the form factor (dimensions) of your drive. Table 17-5 compares the form factors of several drive generations.

PLATTERS

As you probably read early in this chapter, *platters* (2) are relatively heavy-duty disks of aluminum, glass, or ceramic composite material. Platters are then coated on both sides

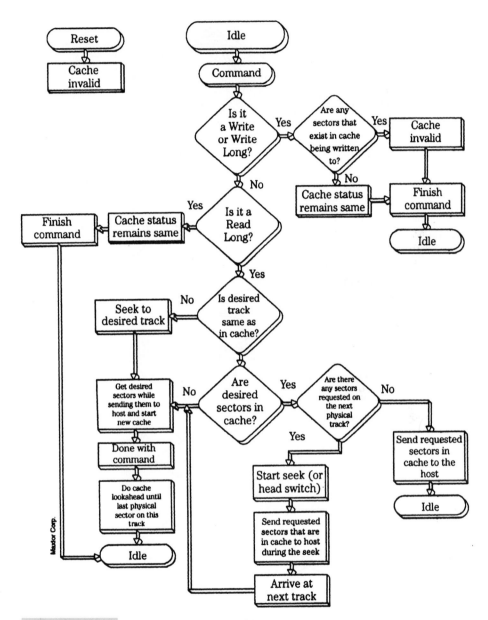

FIGURE 17-8 **A cache control algorithm.** Maxtor Corporation

with a layer of magnetic material (the actual media) and covered with a protective layer. Finished and polished platters are then stacked and coupled to the *spindle motor* (3). Some drives might only use one platter. Before the platter stack is fixed to the chassis, the *R/W head assembly* (4) is fitted in between each disk. There is usually one head per platter side, so a drive with two platters should have three or four heads. During drive operation, the platter stack spins at a speed from 5200 RPM to 10,000 RPM.

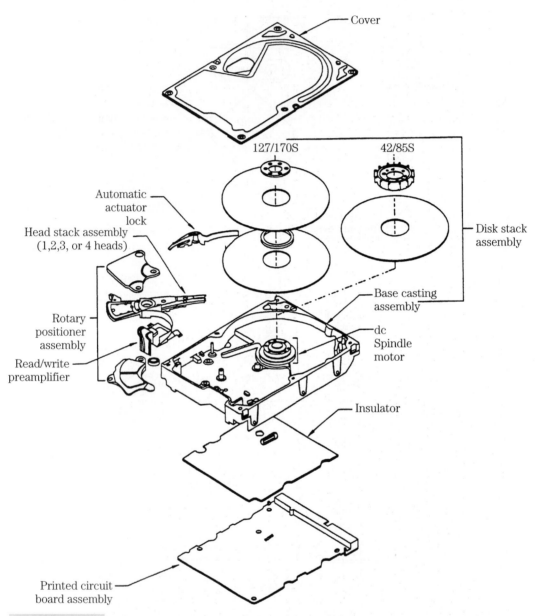

FIGURE 17-9 **An exploded diagram of a Quantum hard drive.** Quantum Corporation

READ/WRITE HEADS

As with floppy drives, read/write (R/W) heads form the interface between a drive's electronic circuitry and magnetic media. During writing, a head translates electronic signals into magnetic-flux transitions that saturate points on the media, where those transitions occur. A read operation works roughly in reverse. Flux transitions along the disk induce electrical signals in the head, which are amplified, filtered, and translated into corresponding logic signals. It is up to the drive's electronics to determine whether a head is reading or writing.

Early hard drive R/W heads generally resembled floppy-drive heads—soft iron cores with a core of 8 to 34 turns of fine copper wire. Such heads were physically large and relatively heavy, which limited the number of tracks available on a platter surface, and presented more inertia to be overcome by the head-positioning system. Virtually all current hard-drive designs have abandoned classic "wound coil" heads in favor of thin-film R/W heads. Thin-film heads are fabricated in much the same way as ICs or platter media using photochemical processes. The result is a very flat, sensitive, small, and durable R/W head, but even thin-film heads use an air gap and 8 to 34 turns of copper wire. Small size and light weight allow for smaller track widths (large drives today can use more than 16,000 tracks) and faster head travel time. The inherent flatness of thin-film heads helps to reduce flying height to only about 5 microns.

In assemblies, the heads themselves are attached to long metal arms that are moved by the head actuator motor(s), as shown in Fig. 17-10. Read/write preamp ICs are typically mounted on a small PC board that is attached to the head/actuator assembly. The entire subassembly is sealed in the platter compartment, and is generally inaccessible, unless it is opened in a cleanroom environment. The compartment is sealed with a *metal lid/gasket assembly* (6).

TABLE 17-5 COMPARISON OF FORM FACTOR TO ACTUAL DRIVE DIMENSIONS				
		APPROXIMATE DIMENSIONS		
FORM FACTOR NOMENCLATURE		HEIGHT	WIDTH	DEPTH
5.25" Full-Height*	mm	82.60	145.54	202.69
	in	3.25	5.73	7.98
5.25" Half-Height*	mm	41.28	145.54	202.68
	in	1.63	5.73	7.98
3.5" Half-Height**	mm	41.28	106.60	146.05
	in	1.63	4.00	5.75
3.5" Low-Profile**	mm	25.40	101.60	146.05
	in	1.00	4.00	5.75
2.5" Low-Profile	mm	19.05	70.10	101.85
	in	0.75	2.76	4.01
1.8" Low-Profile	mm	15.00	51.00	77.00
	in	0.59	2.00	3.03
1.3" Low-Profile	mm	10.50	36.50	50.8
	in	0.41	1.44	2.00

* Used in desktop systems ONLY
** Used in desktops and some older laptops

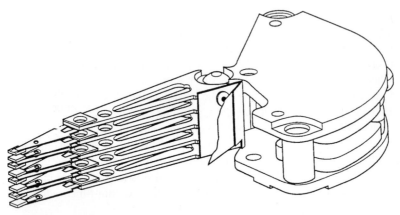

FIGURE 17-10   **Close-up view of a head-actuator assembly.** Maxtor Corporation

HEAD ACTUATORS

Unlike floppy motors that step their R/W heads in and out, hard drives swing the heads along a slight arc to achieve radial travel from edge to spindle. Many hard drives use *voice-coil motors* (also called *rotary coil motors* or *servos*) to actuate head movement. Voice-coil motors (5) work using the same principle as analog meter movements: a permanent magnet is enclosed within two opposing coils. As current flows through the coils, a magnetic field is produced that opposes the permanent magnet. Head arms are attached to the rotating magnet, so the force of opposition causes a deflection that is directly proportional to the amount of driving current. Greater current signals result in greater opposition and greater deflection. Cylinders are selected by incrementing the servo signal and maintaining the signal at the desired level. Voice-coil motors are very small and light assemblies that are well suited to fast access times and small hard-drive assemblies.

The greatest challenge to head movement is to keep the heads centered on the desired track. Otherwise, aerodynamic disturbances, thermal effects in the platters, and variations in voice-coil driver signals can cause head-positioning error. Head position must be constantly checked and adjusted in real time to ensure that desired tracks are followed exactly. The process of track following is called *servoing the heads*. Information is required to compare the head's expected position to their actual position—any resulting difference can then be corrected by adjusting the voice-coil signal. Servo information is located somewhere on the platters using a variety of techniques.

Dedicated servo information is recorded on a reserved platter side. For example, a two-platter drive using dedicated servo tracking might use three sides for data, but use a fourth surface exclusively for track locating information. Because all heads are positioned along the same track (a cylinder), a single surface can provide data that is needed to correct all heads simultaneously. Embedded servo information, however, is encoded as short bursts of data placed between every sector. All surfaces then can hold data and provide tracking information. The servo system uses the phase shift of pulses between adjacent tracks to determine whether heads are centered on the desired track, or are drifting to one side or another. For the purposes of this book, don't be concerned with the particular tracking techniques—only that tracking information must be provided to keep the heads in proper alignment.

SPINDLE MOTOR

One of the major factors that contribute to hard-drive performance is the speed at which the media passes under the R/W heads. Media is passed under the R/W heads by spinning the platter(s) at a high rate of speed (at least 3600 RPM, to as high as 10,000 RPM). The spindle motor is responsible for spinning the platter(s). A spindle motor is typically a brushless, low-profile dc motor (similar in principle to the spindle motors used in floppy-disk drives).

An *index sensor* (10) provides a feedback pulse signal that detects the spindle as it rotates. The drive's *control electronics* (8) uses the index signal to regulate spindle speed as precisely as possible. Today's drives typically use magnetic sensors, which detect iron tabs on the spindle shaft, or optoisolators, which monitor holes or tabs rotating along the spindle. The spindle motor and index sensor are also sealed in the platter compartment.

Older hard drives used a rubber or cork pad to slow the spindle to a stop after drive power is removed, but virtually all IDE drives use a technique called *dynamic braking*. When power is applied to a spindle motor, a magnetic field is developed in the motor coils. When power is removed, the magnetic energy stored in the coils is released as a reverse voltage pulse. Dynamic braking channels the energy of that reverse voltage to stop the drive faster and more reliably than physical braking.

DRIVE ELECTRONICS

Hard drives are controlled by a suite of remarkably sophisticated circuitry. The drive electronics board mounted below the chassis contains all of the circuitry necessary to communicate control and data signals with the particular physical interface, maneuver the R/W heads, read or write (as required), and spin the platter(s). Each of these functions must be accomplished to high levels of precision. In spite of the demands and complexity involved in drive electronics, the entire circuit can be fabricated on a single PC board.

A practical hard disk is illustrated in the block diagram of Fig. 17-11. You should understand the purpose of each part. The heart of this drive is a microcontroller (μC). A μC is basically a customized version of a microprocessor that can process program instructions, as well as provide a selection of specialized control signals that are not available from ordinary microprocessors. A μC can be considered an application-specific IC (ASIC). The program that operates this drive is stored in a small, programmable read-only memory (PROM). The microcontroller provides enable signals to the voice-coil driver IC, read/write preamplifier IC, read/write ASIC, and disk controller/interface ASIC. A controller/interface ASIC works in conjunction with the μC by managing data and control signals on the physical interface. For the drive shown, the ASIC is designed to support an SCSI interface, but variations of this model can use interface ASICs that support IDE interfaces.

The primary activity of the controller/interface ASIC is to coordinate the flow of data into or out of the drive. The controller determines read or write operations, handles clock synchronization, and organizes data flow to the read/write ASIC. The controller also manages the local cache memory (located on the drive itself). Commands received over the physical interface are passed on to the μC for processing and response. The frequency synthesizer helps to synchronize the controller and read/write ASIC. Finally, the disk-controller ASIC is responsible for selecting the head position and controlling the spindle and motor driver.

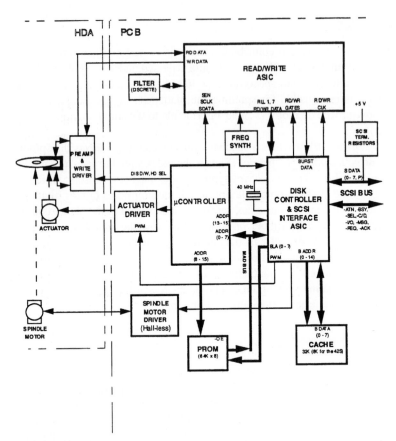

FIGURE 17-11 Block diagram of a high-performance Quantum drive system.
Quantum Corporation

The read/write ASIC is another major IC on the drive's PC board. A R/W ASIC accepts data from the controller IC and translates data into serial signals that are sent to the write driver for writing. The R/W ASIC also receives signals amplified by the read preamp and translates serial signals into parallel digital information available to the controller ASIC. A discrete filter affects the way in which analog signals are handled. R/W heads are connected directly to the read preamplifier/write driver IC, which is little more than a bi-directional amplifier IC.

The actuator driver accepts a logic enable signal from the μC and a proportional logic signal from the controller ASIC. The actuator driver then produces an analog output current that positions the R/W heads by driving a voice-coil motor. The spindle motor driver is turned on and off by a logic-enable signal from the controller ASIC. Once the spindle motor driver is enabled, it will self-regulate its own speed using feedback from an index sensor. All components within the dotted area marked *HDA* are located within the sealed platter compartment, and other components in the area marked *PCB* are located on the drive PC board. Most of the drive's intelligence is contained in the μC, controller ASIC, and R/W ASIC.

Concepts of Drive Formatting

You can imagine a disk drive as being a big file cabinet. When the drive is first installed, the file cabinet is completely empty—there are no dividers or folders or labels of any kind to organize information. To make the drive useful, it must be formatted and partitioned. There are basically three steps to the format process: a low-level format, partitioning, and a high-level format. Each of these steps are crucially important for the proper operation of a drive.

LOW-LEVEL FORMATTING

The low-level format is perhaps the most important step (and is responsible for most of a drive's long-term problems). Sector header and trailer information is written (refer to Fig. 17-7) along with dummy data. Inter-sector and inter-track gaps are also created. As you might imagine, the low-level format forms the foundation of a hard drive's organization. Because this information is only written once, age and wear can allow sector information to eventually fail. When this happens, the failed sector(s) are unreadable. Advanced drive features, such as translation, defect management, and zoned recording also complicate a proper low-level format.

This problem is further compounded by the fact that low-level formatting is hardware-specific, and most current drive makers low-level format their drives at the factory—those routines are rarely made available to technicians and end users. If you determine that an IDE or SCSI drive must be low-level formatted, contact the drive manufacturer and obtain a proper low-level format utility written expressly for that particular drive model. Even leading professional utilities, such as DrivePro strongly urge against low-level formats for IDE/EIDE drives, except as a last resort. If you attempt to invoke low-level IDE/EIDE formatting with a DOS DEBUG sequence or software utility, one of four things might happen:

- The drive will ignore the low-level formatter entirely.
- The drive will accept the formatter, but only erase areas containing data (and fail to rewrite sector ID information).
- The drive will accept the formatter and erase vital servo information and other sector information. Thus, the drive will be rendered completely unusable.
- The drive will accept the formatter and perform a correct low-level format. This is highly unlikely.

Any low-level format process will completely destroy all data on a drive. Backup as much of the drive as possible before attempting a low-level format. Do not attempt to low-level format a hard drive unless you have an appropriate utility from the drive maker—and then only as a last resort.

PARTITIONING

Where low-level formatting is a hardware-specific process, *partitioning* is an operating system-specific process. After low-level formatting is complete, the drive must be partitioned before an OS file system or boot information is written to the drive. Also, partitioning allows a large physical drive to be divided up into several smaller logical drives. Several file systems are in service today, but DOS, Windows 3.1x, and Windows 95 continue to use the *File Allocation Table (FAT)* system. The main criticism of the FAT is that sectors are grouped and assigned as clusters. This is a wasteful use of drive space (especially for large drives, where up to 64 sectors—32KB—might be in a single cluster). One of the newly created partitions will be assigned as the boot partition, and a *Master Boot Sector (MBS)* containing a special boot program and partition table will be written to the first sector. The MBS is often referred to as the *Master Boot Record (MBR)*. FDISK is the DOS utility used for drive partitioning.

HIGH-LEVEL (DOS) FORMATTING

Even after partitioning, an operating system cannot store files on a drive. A series of data structures must be written to the drive. A *Volume Boot Sector (VBS)*, two copies of the *File Allocation Table (FAT)*, and a root directory are written to each logical partition. High-level formatting also checks and locks out bad sectors so that they will not be used during normal operation. FORMAT is the DOS utility used for high-level formatting. It is interesting that the FORMAT utility will perform both low-level and high-level formatting for a floppy disk, but not for a hard drive.

File Systems and Tips

When you purchase an IDE/EIDE or SCSI hard drive today, it is already low-level formatted; the cylinder, track, and sector information is already written onto the drive. This means you can partition the drive with FDISK and format the drive with FORMAT right "out of the box." The process of FDISK and FORMAT prepare the drive for a particular file system. We won't talk much about file systems in this edition, but you should understand the basic FAT system, and know some implications of FAT 16 and FAT 32.

FAT BASICS

Microsoft DOS, Windows 3.1x, and Windows 95 use a File Allocation Table (FAT) to organize files on the drive. Sectors are organized into groups called *clusters*, and each cluster is assigned a number. Early drives used a 12-bit number (known as *FAT 12*), but drives today use a 16-bit number (called *FAT 16*). The newest releases of Windows 95 (OSR2) assign a 32-bit number to each cluster (called *FAT 32*). By assigning each cluster with its own number, it is possible to store files in any available (unused) clusters throughout the drive without worrying about the file's size. As files are erased, those clusters become available for re-use. Overall, the FAT system has proven to be a versatile and reliable file-management system.

The problem with the FAT system is that you can only have as many clusters as can be specified by the number of bits available. For a 12-bit FAT, you can only have 4096 (2^{12}) clusters. For a 16-bit FAT, you can have 65,536 (2^{16}) clusters. If the drive is 120MB, each cluster must then be about (120MB/65,536) 1.8KB (2KB, in actuality). If the drive was 500MB, each cluster must be about (540MB/65,536) 7.6KB (8KB, in actuality). Because only one file can be assigned to any given cluster, the entire space for that cluster is assigned (even if the file is very small). So, if you were to store a 2KB file in an 8KB cluster, you'd waste (8KB – 2KB) = 6KB! This wasted space is known as *slack space*. Of course, the FAT 12 system was long since abandoned while drives were still about 32MB, but you get the idea that very large drives can waste a serious amount of space when using a FAT system.

Another frequent complaint about the FAT file system is the phenomenon of "file fragmentation." Because clusters are all independent, and assigned wherever they can be found, a file requiring more than one cluster can be scattered anywhere on the disk. For example, suppose that you're editing a large image (it can take several MB). The file might use the 20 available clusters on track 345, two more available clusters on track 1012, 50 available clusters on track 2011, etc. In theory, fragmentation is simply a harmless side-effect of the FAT system. But, in actuality, badly fragmented files can force the hard drive to work unusually hard chasing down the various clusters associated with the file. Not only does this slow drive performance, but the extra work required of the drive might ultimately shorten its working life. The best way to correct this issue is to periodically "defragment" the disk with a utility, such as Defrag. Defragmenting the disk will rearrange all the clusters so that all of the clusters for any given file will be contiguous.

FAT 16

DOS (including DOS 7.0 of Windows 95) uses the FAT 16 file system to store data. The FAT 16 system uses 16-bit-cluster address numbers, which allow up to 65,536 clusters. Under FAT 16, a cluster can be as big as 32KB, which translates into a maximum partition size of $(65,536 \times 32,768)$ 2,147,483,648 bytes (2.1GB). Although a 16-bit cluster number is much more efficient than a 12-bit cluster number, every file must take up at least one cluster—even if the file size is much smaller than the cluster. For today's very large drives, the correspondingly large clusters can result in a significant amount of slack space. If the physical drive is larger than 2.1GB, you must create subsequent logical partitions to utilize the additional space. For example, if you have a 3.1GB drive, you can create one 2.1GB partition and a second 1.0GB partition. One way to reduce slack space is to create a larger number of smaller logical partitions—this results in smaller clusters. Table 17-6 illustrates the relationship between partition size and cluster size.

TABLE 17-6 PARTITION SIZE VS. CLUSTER SIZE FOR FAT 16 PARTITIONS	
PARTITION SIZE	CLUSTER SIZE
1024–2047MB	32KB
512–1023MB	16KB
256–511MB	8KB
128–255MB	4KB
0–127MB	2KB

* These figures are for a FAT 16-file system.

PARTITIONING LARGE HARD DRIVES

Chances are that you're already familiar with the DOS FDISK partitioning utility and have used it at one time or another to partition older hard drives. However, large hard drives (over 2GB) present an unusual wrinkle for technicians—DOS and Windows 95 only support partitions up to 2GB. When you install a hard drive that's larger than 2GB, you need to create multiple partitions on the drive—otherwise, you won't be able to take advantage of the full drive capacity. The following procedure offers a step-by-step guide for partitioning large drives.

Partitioning a large hard drive with FAT 16 FDISK

1 At the *FDISK options* menu, select *4. Display partition information* and hit <Enter>. If the partition-information display indicates that there are existing partition(s) on the drive, these partitions must be deleted before proceeding (select *3. Delete partition information* on the *FDISK options* menu to remove any existing partitions).

2 At the *FDISK options* menu, select *1. Create DOS partition or Logical DOS drive* and hit <Enter>. The *Create DOS partition or logical DOS drive* menu is displayed. Select *1. Create primary DOS partition* and hit <Enter>.

3 The message: "Do you wish to use the maximum available size for a Primary DOS Partition and make the Partition active(Y/N)" is displayed. Type *N* and press <Enter>.

> When this message is displayed, you must respond with *N*. If you reply *Y*, a primary partition of 2.048GB will be created, and the system will not be able to access the remainder of the drive's capacity unless the partition is deleted.

4 Type in the size of the primary partition (in MB). This value can be anywhere from 1 to 2048MB (default). Then press the <Enter> key. The message "Primary DOS Partition created" is displayed. Press <Esc> to continue.

5 At the *FDISK options* menu, select *1. Create DOS partition or logical DOS drive* and press <Enter>. The *Create DOS partition or logical DOS drive* menu is displayed. Select *2. Create extended DOS partition* and press <Enter>.

6 The *Create extended DOS partition* screen is displayed. Press <Enter> to place the remaining available space on the drive into the extended DOS partition.

> If all of the remaining drive space is not placed into the extended DOS partition, the total capacity of the hard drive will not be available to the system.

7 Press <Esc> to continue when the FDISK message "Extended DOS partition created" appears on the monitor. FDISK will now prompt you to create logical drives for the extended DOS partition. The message "Enter logical drive size in megabytes or percent of disk space (%) . . ." is displayed.

8 Type the value desired for the capacity value of the logical drive size (up to 2048MB) and press <Enter>. If you choose a value less than the displayed total size, you must continue entering drive sizes until all of the available space has been assigned logical drive letters.

Remember that each logical DOS drive created represents a drive letter (i.e., C:, D:, E:, or F:).

9 Press <Esc> to continue when the FDISK message "All available space in the extended DOS partition is assigned to logical drives" appears.

10 If the drive is going to be the primary boot drive, select *2. Set active partition* and press <Enter> at the *FDISK options* menu. The *Set active partition* screen is displayed and the message "Enter the number of the partition you want to make active" is displayed. Press *1*, then press <Enter>. The message "Partition 1 made active" is displayed. Press <Esc>.

11 Press <Esc> to exit FDISK. Exiting FDISK under DOS will cause the system to re-boot. Under Windows 95, the system will return to the "C:\WINDOWS\COMMAND>" prompt, and the user will have to manually re-boot the system.

12 After the system re-boots, each drive letter assigned to the partitioned hard drive must be formatted with FORMAT. You should now be able to use the drive.

A number of problems have been reported with the Windows 95 version of FDISK. As a rule, use the DOS 6.22 version of FDISK or the 16-bit version of FDISK included with OSR2.

FAT 32

Obviously, the limitations of FAT 16 are presenting a serious issue as hard drives reach 6GB and beyond. Microsoft has responded by developing a 32-bit FAT system to implement in a service release of Windows 95 (called *OSR2*)—also implementing DOS 7.1. The upper 4 bits are reserved, so the system will actually access (228) 268,435,456 clusters (over 256 million clusters). This allows single partitions of 8GB with clusters only 4KB in size—the maximum size of any given partition is 2TB (yes, Terrabytes—thousands of gigabytes). Table 17-7 compares cluster sizes under FAT 32. FAT 32 also eliminates the fixed size for a root directory, so you can have as many files and directories in the root as you want.

On the surface, this probably sounds like a great deal, but there are some major problems that you'll need to consider before updating to FAT 32. First, DOS applications (without being rewritten) can only access files up to 2GB, and Win32 applications can work with

TABLE 17-7 PARTITION SIZE VS. CLUSTER SIZE FOR FAT 32 PARTITIONS	
GIGABYTES (GB)	**CLUSTER SIZE**
0.512GB to 8GB	4KB
16GB	8KB
32GB	16KB
>32GB	32KB

files up to 4GB. By itself, that's not so bad, but FAT 32 partitions are only accessible through the OSR 2-enhanced Windows 95 and DOS 7.1—no other operating system can read the partitions (including Windows NT). Also, any disk utilities written for FAT 16 won't work for FAT 32 (and can seriously damage your data).

Even though the OSR 2 release ships with FAT 32 versions of FDISK, FORMAT, SCANDISK, and DEFRAG, the version of DriveSpace 3 will not support FAT 32. So if you're using drive compression, you're out of luck. Further, some *Application Programming Interfaces (APIs)* simply won't support FAT 32, so some programs might refuse to work outright until the software is recompiled with FAT 32-compliant APIs. And MS-DOS device drivers (such as those needed to support SCSI devices) will have to be updated for FAT 32. In other words, you'll lose your SCSI drives until suitable drivers become available. Finally, the OSR 2 version of Windows 95 appears to decrease FAT 32 drive performance. Hard numbers are not yet available, but initial figures suggest a performance penalty of as much as 10% below FAT 16 drives. In short, FAT 32 is an idea whose time has come, but it will take more work from Microsoft before FAT 32 takes over our drives.

PARTITIONING AND FORMATTING FOR FAT 32

Before you make the decision to use FAT 32, you'll need to be familiar with the issues involved in partitioning and formatting. The basic steps in drive preparation are the same as FAT 16, but FAT 32 introduces a few wrinkles that you should understand. This part of the chapter describes the general process used to partition and format the drive under FAT 32. First, a FAT 32 partition can only be created (with Windows 95 OSR2) under the following circumstances:

- The hard drive must be greater than 528MB in total capacity.
- The partition size must be greater than 528MB.
- You need an OSR2 setup disk or OSR2 startup disk made from another OSR2-configured PC.
- When the OSR2 FDISK prompts: "Do you wish to enable large disk support? Y or N," you'll need to answer *Y*. If you answer *N*, a FAT 16 partition will be created.

Partitioning a large hard drive with FAT 32 (OSR2) FDISK

1 Boot the PC with the Windows 95 OSR2 setup diskette.
2 At the *Welcome to setup* screen, press the <F3> key twice—this will terminate the execution of the Setup program, and take you to the A: prompt.

> If you have an OSR2 startup disk from another PC, you can boot from that diskette instead and avoid the hassle of exiting the OSR2 "Setup" routine.

3 Type *FDISK* and press <Enter>. You'll be prompted with: "Do you wish to enable large disk support? Y or N."
4 Type *Y* to create a FAT 32 partition and press <Enter>. At this point, the *FDISK options* menu will appear on the screen. If more than one hard drive is in the system, use option

"5" ("Change current fixed drive") to select the desired drive to partition. Careful—partitioning the wrong drive will render any existing data on that drive inaccessible.

5 Select option *4* for "Display partition information" and press <Enter>. For a brand new hard drive, FDISK should respond: "No Partitions Defined." Any pre-existing partitions (i.e., FAT 16 partitions) must be deleted before continuing. Remember, this will delete all existing data on the hard drive. Press the <Esc> key to return to the *FDISK options* menu, then select option *1* for "Create DOS partition or logical DOS drive" and press <Enter>. Next, select option *1* for "Create primary DOS partition" and press <Enter>.

6 After FDISK verifies the drive integrity, it will prompt you with: "Do you wish to use the maximum available size for a primary DOS partition and make the partition active (Y/N)?" Type *Y* and press <Enter>.

7 Exit FDISK by pressing the <Esc> key until you see the message: "You must restart the system for changes to take effect." Press the <Esc> key to exit FDISK, and remove the floppy diskette in drive A:. Reboot the computer using <Ctrl>+<Alt>+<Del>.

Formatting a large hard drive with FAT32 (OSR2) FORMAT

1 Boot the PC with the Windows 95 OSR2 setup diskette.
2 At the *Welcome to setup* screen, press the <F3> key twice—this will terminate the execution of the setup program, and take you to the A: prompt.

> If you have an OSR2 startup disk from another PC, you can boot from that diskette instead and avoid the hassle of exiting the OSR2 "Setup" routine.

3 Type *FORMAT <insert your drive letter: here>* and press <Enter> to start formatting (i.e., *FORMAT D:*). After FORMAT starts, you'll see the message: "WARNING all data on non removable disk drive <letter:> will be lost proceed with format? Y/N."
4 Type *Y* and press <Enter>. The OSR2 FORMAT utility will then prepare the hard drive for use with FAT 32.

Understanding Drive-Capacity Limits

Capacity limitations are encountered whenever a computer system BIOS (and operating system) is unable to identify (or address) physical locations on a hard drive. This is not a problem with the design or structure of the hard drive itself, but rather a limitation of the system's BIOS or operating system. For the BIOS, it is not capable of translating the addresses of the sectors beyond a certain number of cylinders—thus limiting the capacity of the hard drive to less than its full amount. For the operating system, the file structure (File Allocation Table, FAT) is limited in the number of physical locations (or addresses) that can be entered in the FAT. Drive manufacturers first encountered BIOS limitations in 1994 with the release of 540MB (ATA-2/EIDE) hard drives. Operating-system limitations were discovered with the release of hard drives larger than 2.1GB. Your exact limitations vary depending on your BIOS version and the operating system. Today, newer

BIOS typically experiences limitations at 2.1 and 4.2GB levels. Operating systems, such as DOS and Windows 95, have a 2.1GB partition size limitation, and Windows NT has a 4.2GB partition-size limit. This part of the chapter is intended to help you understand and correct these drive-size limitations.

CYLINDER LIMITS IN BIOS

BIOS is the key to hard-drive addressing through the use of Int. 13 services. Today, you'll find three major BIOS limitations:

- BIOS versions dated prior to July of 1994 will typically experience a 528MB drive size limit. BIOS cannot support more than 1024 cylinders. *Logical Block Addressing (LBA)* mode capability did not become widely accepted until after this point.
- BIOS versions dated after July 1994 will typically experience a 2.1GB drive-size limit. BIOS cannot support more than 4093 to 4096 cylinders. Even though LBA is being used correctly, the BIOS makers simply imposed an artificial limit on the number of addressable cylinders.
- BIOS versions dated after 1996 can support drives over 528MB, and support drives over 2.1GB, but might experience a 4.2GB drive-size limit. Once again, the BIOS cannot support the number of cylinders (around 8190) needed to handle these larger drives—even though LBA is being used correctly.

PARTITION LIMITS IN THE OPERATING SYSTEM

File systems used by various operating systems are also subject to drive-size limits. FAT 16-type operating systems (DOS, the commercial release of Windows 95, Windows NT with FAT 16, and OS/2 with FAT 16) are typically limited to 2.1GB drive sizes. Windows NT using NTFS suffers a 4GB drive-size limit. When using a physical hard drive that is larger than these limits, you'll need to create multiple partitions on the drive to access all of the available space.

OVERCOMING CAPACITY LIMITS

Since 1994, the PC industry has been working hard to overcome the drive-size limits imposed by BIOS and operating systems. Unfortunately, drive-size limits still plague older systems. This is particularly prevalent because many systems a few years old are now being upgraded with the huge hard drives that are on the market. As a result, drive-size support problems are the most-frequent issues encountered during drive upgrades. Still, several tactics have become available for technicians.

The 528MB limit Supporting large (EIDE) hard drives over 528MB will clearly require a system upgrade. The three possible solutions to the problem are: upgrade the motherboard BIOS to support LBA, upgrade the drive controller with one using an on-board BIOS that supports LBA, or partition the drive with a "drive overlay" utility, such as Disk Manager or EZ-Drive. If the system is older than 1994, a new drive controller and on-board BIOS will probably yield a noticeable drive system performance improvement.

If price is the primary concern, drive overlay software is free (included with most new hard drives) and requires no invasive hardware upgrade.

2.1GB and 4.2GB limits   The difficulty with these limits is that several possible symptoms can crop up:

- *Truncation of cylinders* Cylinder truncation is when the BIOS limits the number of cylinders reported to the operating system to 4095. The BIOS might display the drive as having more than 4095 cylinders, but it still only reports a total of 4095.
- *System hang-up at POST* A system hang-up occurs when the BIOS has a problem truncating the cylinders and locks the system up during power on self test (POST). This is most frequently caused by the auto-detect feature some BIOS versions have implemented.
- *Cylinder wrap* Cylinder wrapping is when the BIOS takes the remaining number of cylinders from the maximum allowed (4095) and reports it to the operating system. For example, if the drive listed 4096 cylinders, the BIOS would report only 1 cylinder to the operating system.
- *System hangs at boot time* This usually occurs for drives larger than 4.2GB. A system hang is when the operating system hangs-up during initial loading (either from floppy diskette or existing hard drives). This can be caused by the BIOS reporting the number of heads to the operating system as 256 (100h). The register size DOS/Windows 95 used for the head count has a capacity of two hex digits (equivalent to decimal values 255).

In virtually all cases, this is a BIOS problem, and can be corrected by a BIOS upgrade. You should contact the system or motherboard maker to inquire if a BIOS update is available. If you cannot upgrade the motherboard BIOS directly, you can install a new drive controller with an LBA-compatible BIOS that will support additional cylinders.

You might also be able to adjust the drive's "translation" to overcome BIOS cylinder limits. You might find that these "huge" hard drives seem to "auto-detect" correctly in BIOS, and the problem crops up when trying to partition the drive. The partition might seem to be created properly through FDISK, but the system hangs when rebooting. Although this is an operating system limitation, it appears that the appropriate way to deal with this problem is to account for it in the system BIOS. Fortunately, there is a temporary workaround to the problem (until you get the BIOS upgraded).

> You should first verify that you have a new enough BIOS to handle drives over 2GB correctly.

To setup a drive over 4GB (under an older BIOS):

1 "Auto-detect" the drive in CMOS setup.
2 Manually adjust the number of heads from 16 to 15.
3 Multiply the number of cylinders by 16/15 (rounded down to whole number). Because 16/15 is 1.06667, the simplest way to multiply by 16/15 would be to multiply by 1.06667 (then round down to a whole number).
4 Adjust the number of cylinders to this larger amount.

TABLE 17-8 POSSIBLE CMOS WORKAROUNDS FOR HUGE HARD DRIVES		
MODEL	FACTORY CHS VALUES	WORKAROUND CHS VALUES
Maxtor 85120A	9924 × 16 × 63	10585 × 15 × 63
Micropolis 4550A	9692 × 16 × 63	10338 × 15 × 63

5 Write down these adjusted values for cylinders, heads, and sectors.

6 Save changes to CMOS, then partition and format the drive.

As an example, Table 17-8 illustrates some workaround parameters that can be used with popular models of hard drives over 4GB. Although this can be considered a temporary workaround, there should be no problem with continuing to use a hard drive set up this way. If an updated BIOS version becomes available at a later date, it should not be necessary to repartition and reformat the drive.

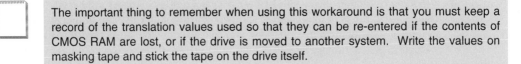

The important thing to remember when using this workaround is that you must keep a record of the translation values used so that they can be re-entered if the contents of CMOS RAM are lost, or if the drive is moved to another system. Write the values on masking tape and stick the tape on the drive itself.

Operating system limits   You basically have two solutions for overcoming drive-size limits through an operating system. If you continue to use FAT 16, you'll need to create partitions equal to or smaller than 2GB. If the drive is larger than 2GB, you can make multiple partitions on the drive. This makes more than one "logical drive" for the system to deal with, but it will allow you to use the entire drive capacity. As an alternative, you can upgrade to a FAT 32 system, such as the OSR2 version of Windows 95, which should easily handle partitions over 32GB.

Drive Testing and Troubleshooting

Hard-disk drives present some perplexing challenges for computer technicians and every day users alike. The problem with hard drives is that they are inaccessible devices. Unless you have the cleanroom environment to open the sealed drive platters, it is pointless to even consider replacing failed drive mechanics. Even if you could open a drive safely, the advances in hard-drive technology have been so fast and furious that no spare parts market has ever developed. Drive manufacturers themselves rarely bother to repair faulty drives or invest in specialized drive-testing equipment. Clearly, the course for hard-drive repair is to identify defective drives and replace faulty units with new (usually better) ones.

Fortunately, not all hard-drive problems are necessarily fatal. True, you might lose some programs and data (backup your hard drive frequently), but many drive problems are recoverable without resorting to drive replacement. Instead of focusing on repairing a hard drive's electronics or mechanics, today's repair tactics focus on repairing a drive's data. By reconstructing or relocating faulty drive information, it is often possible to re-

cover from a wide variety of drive problems. Before you begin any sort of drive troubleshooting, you should take the following steps:

■ Gather a DOS boot disk or Windows 95 startup disk (refer to the end of Chapter 3). If
you don't have a boot disk on hand, you should make one before continuing.
■ Gather your DOS installation disk(s) or Windows 95 CD-ROM—if you need to reinstall the operating system, these will be invaluable.
■ Gather any hard drive/controller diagnostics that you'll need.
■ Backup as much as you can from your hard drive(s) before attempting any sort of drive
service.

This book's companion CD offers a selection of hard-drive diagnostics and utilities. Check
out DUGIDE.ZIP, FIPS10.ZIP, and HDINFO.ZIP, as well as other related utilities on the CD.

HDD-CONTROLLER BIOS ERROR CODES

There might be times when your hard-drive controller fails or cannot communicate
properly with the hard drive. When this occurs, you'll often find that the controller returns an error code. Table 17-9 lists a selection of HDD controller error codes that are

TABLE 17-9 COMMON HDD CONTROLLER ERROR CODES	
CODE	DESCRIPTION
00h	No error
01h	Bad command
02h	Address mark not found
03h	Write protect
04h	Request sector not found
05h	Reset failed
06h	Media change
07h	Initialization failed
09h	Cross 64K DMA boundary
0Ah	Bad sector flag detected
0Bh	Bad track flag detected
10h	Bad ECC on disk read
11h	ECC corrected data error
20h	Controller has failed
40h	Seek operation failed
80h	Drive failed to respond
AAh	Drive not ready
BBh	Undefined error
CCh	Write fault
0EH	Register error
FFh	Sense operation failed

most commonly encountered during low-level formatting, DOS installation, or other software installations.

TROUBLESHOOTING "DOS COMPATIBILITY MODE" PROBLEMS

One of the great advantages enjoyed by Windows 95 is that it operates in the "protected-mode"—that is, drivers and software can be executed beyond the traditional "real-mode" RAM limit of 1MB. By comparison, DOS is a real-mode environment. DOS programs and drivers can only be executed within the first 640KB of RAM (the "conventional memory" area). If Windows 95 cannot establish protected-mode operation for a drive, it will fall back to real-mode driver support. This is known as *DOS compatibility mode*. Unfortunately, real-mode support often impairs system performance. If you notice that one or more of the hard drives in a system is using DOS compatibility mode (there might be an error message such as: "Compatibility mode paging reduces overall system performance"), you'll need to track down and correct the cause. In general, Windows 95 might invoke the DOS compatibility mode for any of the following reasons:

■ A questionable device driver, TSR, or computer virus has hooked the INT 21h or INT 13h chain before Windows 95 loaded.
■ The hard-disk controller in your computer was not detected by Windows 95.
■ The hard-disk controller was removed from the current configuration in *Device manager*.
■ There is a resource conflict between the hard-disk controller and another hardware device.
■ The Windows 95 protected-mode driver is missing or damaged.
■ The Windows 95 protected-mode driver detected incompatible or unsupportable hardware.

You can use the following procedure to isolate and correct the cause of DOS compatibility mode problems:

1 Open the *Control panel*, double-click the *System* icon, then choose the *Performance* tab in the *System properties* dialog. You can identify which drive is using DOS compatibility mode and why.
2 If the driver name listed as causing the DOS compatibility mode is: MBRINT13.SYS, your computer might be infected with a boot-sector virus or you are running real-mode disk overlay software (for an IDE hard disk with more than 1024 cylinders) that is not compatible with Windows 95 protected-mode disk drivers.
  • Run a recent anti-virus program to detect and remove boot-sector viruses (such as Norton Anti-Virus, NAV). You might need to rewrite your boot sector using a DOS command, such as *FDISK /MBR*.
  • If you cannot detect any virus activity, check the disk-management software. Be sure that you're using Disk Manager 7.0 or later (use Disk Manager 7.04 if you're running DriveSpace 3, included with the Microsoft Plus! pack).
3 If the driver name that is listed is in the CONFIG.SYS file, contact the driver's manufacturer to determine whether there is a more recent version of the driver that allows protected-mode operation in Windows 95. You might be able to download the latest driver version from the driver manufacturer's Web site.

4 If no driver is listed on the *Performance* tab, check that the hard-disk controller is listed in the *Device manager*. If not, install it through the *Add new hardware* wizard. If the wizard cannot detect the controller automatically, run the wizard again, but do not let it attempt to detect the hardware in your computer—instead, select the controller specifically from the hardware list. If your particular controller is not listed, contact the manufacturer of the disk controller to obtain a Windows 95 protected-mode disk driver (or a Windows 3.1x 32-bit disk access (FastDisk) driver, if available).

> If the hard-disk controller is listed in *Device manager*, but has a red "X" over it, it has been removed from the current hardware profile. Click *Properties* for the controller in *Device manager*, then click the check box that corresponds to the current hardware profile under *Device usage*.

5 If the hard-disk controller is listed in the *Device manager*, but has a yellow "!" over it, there is a resource conflict (IRQ, I/O, DMA, or BIOS address range) with another device, the protected-mode driver is missing or damaged, or the *Disable all 32-bit protected-mode disk drivers* check box has been selected in *File system* properties.
- Doubleclick the *System* icon in the *Control panel*, click the *Performance* tab, then click *File system*. Select the *Troubleshooting* tab and see that the *Disable all 32-bit protected-mode disk drivers* check box has not been selected.
- Resolve any resource conflicts with other devices in the system (refer to Chapter 10).
- Check that the protected-mode driver is in the Windows\SYSTEM\IOSUBSYS directory and is loading properly. To find which driver is providing 32-bit disk access, click *Properties* for the disk controller in *Device manager* and click the *Driver* tab to see which driver files are associated with the controller. For most IDE, EIDE, and ESDI disk controllers, 32-bit disk access is provided by the ESDI_506.PDR driver. For SCSI controllers, Windows 95 often uses SCSIPORT.PDR and a "mini port" (or .MPD) driver. Restart Windows 95, press <F8> when the "Starting Windows 95" message appears, then select a "Logged" (BOOTLOG.TXT) start. If the 32-bit driver is listed as loading properly, you're all set. Otherwise, the driver might be missing or damaged—try reinstalling the respective 32-bit drivers.
6 Load SYSTEM.INI into a text editor and check to see if the MH32BIT.386 driver is being loaded (check for a line that reads: "device=mh32bit.386"). This driver is installed by MicroHouse EZ-Drive software, and is not compatible with the Windows 95 protected-mode disk drivers. Unfortunately, this driver is not removed by Windows 95 Setup, so you'll need to disable the line manually, save your changes, and reboot the PC.
7 If all else fails, you might be able to achieve protected-mode support from the disk controller by disabling any of the controller's advanced features (i.e., caching, fast or "turbo" modes), or reducing data-transfer rates. You might also try systematically disabling advanced IDE controller features in the CMOS setup.
8 If problems persist, you might have to replace the drive controller with a model that better supports protected-mode operation.

SYMPTOMS AND SOLUTIONS

Now it's time to take a look at some problems and solutions. The important concept here is that a hard-drive problem does not necessarily mean a hard-drive failure. The failure of a sector or track does not automatically indicate physical head or platter damage—that is why software tools have been so successful. Even if one or more sectors are physically damaged, millions of sectors are on a hard drive. A few bad sectors do not render a drive faulty. One of the only times that a drive is truly irreparable is when physical media damage occurs on track 00, but software tools will help you to identify the scope of the problem.

> Drive troubleshooting has the potential of destroying any data on the drive(s). Before attempting to troubleshoot hard-disk problems, be sure to back up as much of the drive as possible. If no backup is available, do not repartition or reformat the drive unless absolutely necessary, and all other possible alternatives have been exhausted.

Symptom 17-1. The hard drive is completely dead   The drive does not spin up, the drive light doesn't illuminate during power-up, or you see an error message indicating that the drive is not found or ready. In most cases, you should suspect a power problem first. Be sure that the 4-pin power connector is inserted properly and completely. If the drive is being powered by a "Y-connector," be sure any interim connections are secure. Use a voltmeter and measure the +5-V (pin 4) and +12-V (pin 1) levels. If either voltage (especially the +12-V supply) is unusually low or absent, replace the power supply. Also check your signal cable. See that the drive's signal interface cable is connected securely at both the drive and controller ends. For IDE/EIDE drives, this is the 40-pin ribbon cable. If the cable is visibly worn or damaged, try a new cable.

The PC cannot use a hard drive that it can't recognize, so enter the CMOS setup routine and see that all of the parameters entered for the drive are correct. Heads, cylinders, sectors per track, landing zone, and write precompensation must all be correct—otherwise, POST will not recognize the drive. If you have an "auto-detect" option available, try that also. Remember to save your changes in CMOS and reboot the system.

If problems continue, the hard drive itself might be defective. Try a known-good hard drive. If a known-good drive works as expected, your original drive is probably defective, and should be replaced. If a known-good hard drive fails to operate, replace the drive controller board.

Symptom 17-2. You see drive activity, but the computer will not boot from the hard drive   In most cases, there is a drive failure, boot-sector failure, or DOS/Windows file corruption. Check the signal cable first. Be sure that the drive's signal interface cable is connected securely at both the drive and controller. If the cable is visibly worn or damaged, try a new one. You should check the CMOS setup next—see that all of the parameters entered for the drive are correct. Heads, cylinders, sectors per track, landing zone, and write precompensation must all correct. Otherwise, POST will not recognize the drive. If it has an option to "auto-detect" the drive, try that as well.

The boot sector might also be defective. Boot from a floppy disk and try accessing the hard drive. If the hard drive is accessible, chances are that the boot files are missing or corrupt. Try a utility, such as DrivePro's Drive Boot Fixer or DISKFIX with PC Tools. You might also try running "FDISK /MBR," which will rebuild the drive's master boot record. Careful: the FDISK /MBR command might render the files on your drive inaccessible.

Finally, you might have a problem with your drive-system hardware. If you cannot access the hard drive, run a diagnostic such as Windsor Technologies' PC Technician. Test the drive and drive controller. If the controller responds, but the drive does not, try repartitioning and reformatting the hard drive. If the drive still doesn't respond, replace the hard drive outright. If the controller doesn't respond, replace the hard-drive controller.

Symptom 17-3. One or more sub-directories appear lost or damaged
Both the root directory of a drive and its FAT contain references to sub-directories. If data in either the root directory or file allocation table is corrupt, one or more sub-directories might be inaccessible by the drive. Try repairing the drive's directory structure. Use DISKFIX (with PC Tools) or SCANDISK (with DOS 6.2 or later) to check the disk's directory structure for problems.

Symptom 17-4. Errors occur during drive reads or writes Magnetic information does not last forever, and sector ID information can gradually degrade to a point where you encounter file errors. Start by checking for file structure problems on the drive. Use a utility, such as DISKFIX or SCANDISK, to examine the drive and search for bad sectors. If a failed sector contains part of an .EXE or .COM file, that file is now corrupt and should be restored from a backup. If you cannot isolate file problems, you might need to consider a *Low-Level (LL)* format. This is an ideal solution because LL formatting rewrites sector ID information, but the sophistication of today's drives makes LL formatting almost impossible. If the drive manufacturer provides a "drive preparation" utility, you should backup the drive, run the utility, FDISK, FORMAT, and restore the drive.

Symptom 17-5. The hard drive was formatted accidentally A high-level format does not actually destroy data, but rather it clears the file names and locations kept in the root directory and FAT—this prevents DOS from finding those files. You will need to recover those files. Use a utility, such as UNFORMAT (with PC Tools), which can reconstruct root directory and FAT data contained in a MIRROR file. This is not always a perfect process and you might not be able to recover all files.

> In order for MIRROR data to be useful, do not save new files before running UNFORMAT.

Symptom 17-6. A file has been deleted accidentally Mis-typing or forgetting to add a drive specification can accidentally erase files from places you did not intend to erase. You can often recover those files if you act quickly. Use a utility, such as UNDELETE (with PC Tools and DOS), to restore the deleted file. This is not always a perfect process and you might not be able to recover every file.

> In order for UNDELETE to be useful, do NOT save new files before running UNDELETE.

Symptom 17-7. The hard drive's root directory is damaged A faulty root directory can cripple the entire disk, rendering all sub-directories inaccessible. You might be able to recover the root directory structure. Use a utility, such as DISKFIX (with PC Tools), to reconstruct the damaged FATs and directories. If you have been running MIRROR, DISKFIX should be able to perform a very reliable recovery. You might also try other recovery utilities, such as DrivePro or ScanDisk. However, if you cannot recover the root directory reliably, you will need to reformat the drive, then restore its contents from a backup.

Symptom 17-8. Hard drive performance appears to be slowing down over time In virtually all cases, diminishing drive performance can be caused by file fragmentation. To a far lesser extent, you might be faced with a computer virus. Start the PC with a "clean" boot disk and be sure that no TSRs or drivers are being loaded. After a clean boot, run your anti-virus checker and be sure that there are no memory-resident or file-based viruses.

If the system checks clean for computer viruses, you should check for file fragmentation next. Start your defragmentation utility (such as COMPRESS with PC Tools or DEFRAG with DOS) and check to see the percentage of file fragmentation. If it has more than 10% fragmentation, you should consider running the defragmentation utility after preparing Windows. Before defragmenting a drive, reboot the system normally, start Windows, access the *Virtual memory* controls for your version of Windows, and shut down virtual memory. Then leave Windows and boot the system "clean" again. Restart your defragmentation utility and proceed to defragment the disk. This process might take several minutes, depending on the size of your drive. Once defragmentation is complete, reboot the system normally, start Windows, access the *Virtual memory* controls for your version of Windows, and recreate a permanent swap file to support virtual memory. You should now notice a performance improvement.

Symptom 17-9.   The hard drive accesses correctly, but the drive light stays on continuously A continuous LED indication is not necessarily a problem as long as the drive seems to be operating properly. Check the drive and drive controller for drive "light jumpers"—examine the drive itself for any jumper that might select *Latched* mode vs. *Activity* mode. If no such jumpers are on the drive, check the drive controller or motherboard. Set the jumper to *Activity* mode to see the drive light during access only. Next, consider the possibility of drive-light error messages. Some drive types (especially SCSI drives) use the drive-activity light to signal drive and controller errors. Check the drive and controller documents and see if any error is indicated by the light remaining on.

Symptom 17-10. The hard drive is not accessible and the drive light stays on continuously This usually indicates a reversed signal cable, which is most common when upgrading or replacing a drive system. In virtually all cases, one end of the signal cable is reversed. Be sure that both ends of the cable are installed properly (remember that the red or blue stripe on one side of the cable represents pin 1). If problems persist, replace the drive controller. It is rare for a fault in the drive controller to cause this type of problem, but if trouble persists, try a known-good drive controller board.

Symptom 17-11. A "No fixed disk present" error message appears on the monitor This kind of problem can occur during installation, or at any point in the PC's working life. Check the power connector first, and be sure the 4-pin power connector is inserted properly and completely. If the drive is being powered by a Y-connector, be sure any interim connections are secure. Use a voltmeter and measure the +5-V (pin 4) and +12-V (pin 1) levels. If either voltage (especially the +12-V supply) is unusually low or absent, replace the power supply. Next, check the signal connector. Be sure that the drive's signal cable is connected securely at both the drive and controller. If the cable is visibly worn or damaged, try a new one.

If problems persist, check the CMOS setup—enter the CMOS setup routine and see that all of the parameters entered for the drive are correct. Heads, cylinders, sectors per track, landing zone, and write precompensation must all correct—otherwise, POST will not recognize the drive. You might also try "auto-detecting" the drive. Also check for hardware conflicts. Be sure that no other expansion devices in the system use the same IRQs or I/O addresses used by your drive controller. If so, change the resources used by the conflicting device. If your drive system uses a SCSI interface, be sure that the SCSI cable is terminated properly.

If problems continue, try a known-good hard drive. If a known-good drive works as expected, your original drive is probably defective. If problems persist with a known-good hard drive, replace the drive-controller board.

Symptom 17-12. The drive spins up, but the system fails to recognize it
Your computer might flag this as a "Hard-disk error" or "Hard-disk controller failure" during system initialization. Start by checking the signal connector. Be sure that the interface signal cable is inserted properly and completely at the drive and controller. Try a new signal cable. Next, check any drive jumpers, and see that a primary (master) drive is configured as primary, and a secondary (slave) drive is configured as secondary. For SCSI drives, see that each drive has a unique ID setting and check that the SCSI bus is terminated properly.

Enter the CMOS setup routine and see that all of the parameters entered for the drive are correct. Heads, cylinders, sectors per track, landing zone, and write precompensation must all correct—otherwise, POST will not recognize the drive. Try using the "auto-detect" feature if it is available. If the CMOS is configured properly, you should suspect a problem with the partition. Boot from a floppy disk and run FDISK to check the partitions on your hard drive. Be sure that there is at least one DOS partition. If the drive is to be your boot drive, the primary partition must be active and bootable. Repartition and reformat the drive, if necessary.

If problems persist, try a known-good hard drive. If a known-good drive works as expected, your original drive is probably defective. If a known-good hard drive fails to work as expected, replace the drive controller. If problems persist with a known-good floppy drive, replace the drive-controller board.

Symptom 17-13. The IDE drive spins up when power is applied, then rapidly spins down again The drive is defective, or it is not communicating properly with its host system. Check the power connector first. Be sure that the 4-pin power connector is inserted properly and completely into the drive. Always check the signal connector next, and see that the interface signal cable is inserted properly and completely at the drive and controller. Try a new signal cable.

Inspect the drive jumpers—the primary (master) drive should be configured as primary, and a secondary (slave) drive should be configured as secondary. For SCSI drives, see that each drive has a unique ID setting, and check that the SCSI bus is terminated properly. If problems persist, try a known-good hard drive. If a known-good drive works as expected, your original drive is probably defective.

Symptom 17-14. A "Sector not found" error message appears on the monitor This problem usually occurs after the drive has been in operation for quite some time, and is typically the result of a media failure. Fortunately, a bad sector will only affect one file. Try recovering the file. Use a utility, such as SpinRite (from Gibson Research) or another data-recovery utility, and attempt to recover the damaged file. Notice that you might be unsuccessful, and have to restore the file from a backup later. Check the media itself. Use a disk utility, such as ScanDisk, to evaluate the drive, then locate and map out any bad sectors that are located on the drive.

If problems persist, perform a low-level format (if possible). Lost sectors often occur as drives age and sector ID information degrades. LL formatting restores the sector IDs, but LL formatting is performed at the factory for IDE/EIDE and SCSI drives. If an LL formatting utility is available for your particular drive (available right from the drive manufacturer), and ScanDisk reveals a large number of bad sectors, you might consider backing up the drive completely, running the LL utility, repartitioning, reformatting, then restoring the drive. Finally, if ScanDisk maps out bad sectors, you might need to restore those files from a backup.

Symptom 17-15. A "1780 or 1781 ERROR" appears on the monitor The classic 1780 error code indicates a "Hard disk 0 failure," and the 1781 error code marks a "Hard disk 1 failure." Start the PC with a "clean" boot disk and be sure that no TSRs or drivers are being loaded. If you haven't done so already, run your anti-virus checker and be sure that there are no memory-resident or file-based viruses. Next, if you can access the hard drive once your system is booted, chances are that the boot files are missing or corrupt. Try a utility, such as DrivePro's Drive Boot Fixer or DISKFIX with PC Tools. Otherwise, you will need to repartition and reformat the disk, then restore disk files from a backup.

Check the hardware next—if you cannot access the hard drive, run a diagnostic such as Windsor Technologies' PC Technician. Test the drive and drive controller. If the controller responds but the drive does not, try repartitioning and reformatting the hard drive. If the drive still doesn't respond, replace the hard drive outright. If the controller doesn't respond, replace the hard-drive controller.

Symptom 17-16. A "1790 or 1791 ERROR" appears on the monitor The classic 1790 error code indicates a "Hard Disk 0 Error," although the 1791 error code marks a "Hard Disk 1 Error." Check the signal connector first. Be sure that the interface signal cable is inserted properly and completely at the drive and controller. Try a new signal cable. There might also be a problem with the drive's partition. Boot from a floppy disk and run FDISK to check the partitions on your hard drive. Be sure that there is at least one DOS partition. If the drive is to be your boot drive, the primary partition must be active and bootable. Repartition and reformat the drive, if necessary.

If problems persist, replace the hard drive. If a known-good drive works as expected, your original drive is probably defective. If problems persist with a known-good floppy drive, replace the drive-controller board.

Symptom 17-17. A "1701 ERROR" appears on the monitor The 1701 error code indicates a hard-drive POST error—the drive did not pass its POST test. Check the power connector first, and be sure that the 4-pin power connector is inserted properly and completely. If the drive is being powered by a Y connector, be sure that any interim connections are secure. Use a voltmeter and measure the +5-V (pin 4) and +12-V (pin 1) levels. If either voltage (especially the +12-V supply) is unusually low or absent, replace the power supply.

Enter the CMOS setup routine and see that all of the parameters entered for the drive are correct. Heads, cylinders, sectors per track, landing zone, and write precompensation must all correct; otherwise, POST will not recognize the drive. Try "auto-detecting" the drive.

If problems persist, perform a low-level format (if possible). ST506/412 and ESDI drives might require LL formatting, but LL formatting is performed at the factory for IDE/EIDE and SCSI drives. If an LL-formatting utility is available for your particular drive (available right from the drive manufacturer), you might consider backing up the drive completely, running the LL utility, repartitioning, reformatting, then restoring the drive.

Symptom 17-18. The system reports random data, seek, or format errors
Random errors rarely indicate a permanent problem, but identifying the problem source can be a time-consuming task. Check the power connector first. Be sure that the 4-pin power connector is inserted properly and completely. If the drive is being powered by a "Y-connector," be sure that any interim connections are secure. Use a voltmeter and measure the +5-V (pin 4) and +12-V (pin 1) levels. If either voltage (especially the +12-V supply) is unusually low, replace the power supply.

Check the signal connector next. Be sure that the interface signal cable is inserted properly and completely at the drive and controller. Try a new signal cable. Also try re-routing the signal cable away from the power-supply or "noisy" expansion devices. Check the drive orientation. If problems occur after remounting the drive in a different orientation, you might need to repartition and reformat the drive, or return it to its original orientation. Try relocating the drive-controller away from cables and "noisy" expansion devices. If your system has a "turbo" mode, your ISA drive controller might have trouble operating while the system is in turbo mode. Take the system out of turbo mode. If the problem disappears, try a new drive controller. The media might also be defective. Use a utility, such as ScanDisk, to check for and map out any bad sectors. Once bad sectors are mapped out, you might need to restore some files from your backup.

Try the hard drive and controller in another system. If the drive and controller work in another system, excessive noise or grounding problems are probably in the original system. Reinstall the drive and controller in the original system and remove all extra expansion boards. If the problem goes away, replace one board at a time and retest the system until the problem returns. The last board you inserted when the problem returned is probably the culprit. If the problem persists, there might be a ground problem on the motherboard. Try replacing the motherboard as an absolute last effort.

Symptom 17-19. A "Bad or Missing Command Interpreter" error message appears This is a typical error that appears when a drive is formatted in one DOS version, but loaded with another. Compatibility problems occur when you mix DOS versions. Start by booting the PC with a "clean" boot disk, and be sure no TSRs or drivers are being loaded. If you haven't done so already, run your anti-virus checker and be sure that there are no memory-resident or file-based viruses. Finally, be sure that the drive is partitioned and formatted with the version of DOS that you intend to use. Also be sure to use FORMAT with the /S switch, or SYS C: to transfer system files to the drive.

Symptom 17-20. An "Error reading drive C:" error message appears Read errors in a hard drive typically indicate problems with the disk media, but might also indicate viruses or signaling problems. Check the signal connector first. Be sure that the interface signal cable is inserted properly and completely at the drive and controller. Try a new signal cable. Next, start the PC with a "clean" boot disk and be sure that no TSRs or drivers are being loaded. If you haven't done so already, run your anti-virus checker and be sure that there are no memory-resident or file-based viruses.

Consider the drive's orientation. If problems occur after remounting the drive in a different orientation, you might need to repartition and reformat the drive, or return it to its original orientation. Also check the media—use a utility, such as ScanDisk, to check for and map out any bad sectors. Once bad sectors are mapped out, you might need to restore some files from your backup. Try a known-good hard drive. If a known-good drive works as expected, your original drive is probably defective.

Symptom 17-21. A "Track 0 not found" error message appears A fault on track 00 can disable the entire drive because track 00 contains the drive's *File Allocation Table (FAT)*. This can be a serious error, which might require you to replace the drive. Before going too far with this type of problem, check the signal connector and see that the interface signal cable is inserted properly and completely at the drive and controller. Try a new signal cable.

Boot from a floppy disk and run FDISK to check the partitions on your hard drive. Be sure that there is at least one DOS partition. If the drive is to be your boot drive, the primary partition must be active and bootable. Repartition and reformat the drive, if necessary. Try a known-good hard drive. If a known-good drive works as expected, your original drive is probably defective.

Symptom 17-22. Software diagnostics indicate an average access time that is longer than specified for the drive The average access time is the average amount of time needed for a drive to reach the track and sector, where a needed file begins. Before you do anything else, check the drive specifications and verify the timing specifications for your particular drive. Start your defragmentation utility (such as COMPRESS with PC Tools or DEFRAG with DOS) and check to see the percentage of file fragmentation. If there is more than 10% fragmentation, you should consider running the defragmentation utility after preparing Windows (see Symptom 8).

Also remember that different software packages measure access time differently. Be sure that the diagnostic subtracts system overhead processing from the access-time calculation. Try one or two other diagnostics to confirm the measurement. Before you panic and replace a drive, try testing several similar drives for comparison. If only the suspect drive measures incorrectly, you might not need to replace the drive itself just yet, but you should at least maintain frequent backups in case the drive is near failure.

Symptom 17-23. Software diagnostics indicate a slower data transfer rate than specified This is often because of "less-than-ideal" data-transfer rates, rather than an actual hardware failure. Enter the CMOS setup routine and verify that any enhanced data-transfer modes are enabled (such as PIO Mode 3). This can increase data-transfer rate substantially. Also check the drive specifications, and verify the timing specifications for your particular drive.

Check for fragmentation next. Start your defragmentation utility (such as COMPRESS with PC Tools or DEFRAG with DOS), and check to see the percentage of file fragmentation. If there is more than 10% fragmentation, you should consider running the defragmentation utility after preparing Windows (see Symptom 8). Also remember that different software packages measure access time differently. Be sure that the diagnostic subtracts system overhead processing from the access-time calculation. Try one or two other diagnostics to confirm the measurement.

If the drive is an IDE/EIDE type, be sure that the original user did not perform a low-level format—this might remove head and cylinder skewing optimization and result in a degradation of data transfer. This error cannot be corrected by end-user software. Finally, if the drive is a SCSI type, be sure that the SCSI bus is terminated properly—poor termination can cause data errors and result in re-transmissions that degrade overall data-transfer rates.

Symptom 17-24. The low-level format operation is taking too long or it hangs up the system Notice that this procedure does not apply to IDE/EIDE or SCSI drives. You probably see a large number of format errors, such as code 20 or 80. You might also see "Unsuccessful Format" error messages. Check the low-level format DEBUG string and be sure that your specific DEBUG command is correct for the ST506/412 or ESDI drive being used. A list of typical DEBUG strings are shown in Table 17-7.

If the ST506/412 or ESDI drive is installed on an i286 or later system, be sure that the drive parameters entered for the drive in CMOS are correct. When working on an XT (without CMOS), check that the drive-controller board is set correctly for the drive. Also check the signal connector and see that the interface signal cables are inserted properly and completely at the drive and controller. Try some new signal cables. Finally, check the turbo mode—your ISA drive controller might have trouble operating while the system is in turbo mode. Take the system out of turbo mode. If the problem disappears, try a new drive controller.

Symptom 17-25. The low-level format utility is not accessible from the DEBUG address This procedure does not apply to IDE/EIDE or SCSI drives. First, check the low-level format DEBUG string and be sure that your DEBUG command is correct for the ST506/412 or ESDI drive being used. A list of typical DEBUG strings are shown in Table 10-7. Examine the CMOS setup next—some systems will not low-level format a drive while its parameters are entered in the CMOS setup, so enter your CMOS

TABLE 17-10 TYPICAL DEBUG COMMAND STRINGS FOR LL FORMATTING

G=C800:5
G=CC00:5
G=C800:CCC
G=C800:6
G=D800:5
G=DC00:5

setup menu and remove the drive-type entries (remember to record them first). If that fails to clear the problem, return to the CMOS setup again and restore the drive parameters. Be sure that the drive controller's on-board BIOS is fully enabled. Otherwise, the DEBUG command might not be interpreted properly. Also be sure that the controller's base address matches with the DEBUG command.

Symptom 17-26. The low-level format process regularly hangs up on a specific head/cylinder/sector Notice that this procedure does not apply to IDE/EIDE or SCSI drives. Check the hard error list. Not all portions of an ST506/412 or ESDI drive are usable. These are called *hard errors* and the low-level format procedure must recognize and avoid these hard errors. Some low-level format procedures require you to enter these hard errors manually. If you forget to enter a hard error (or enter the wrong location), the format process will stop when the hard error is encountered. Try low-level formatting the drive again, but be sure to enter the proper hard error locations. Also check the CMOS setup and be sure that the drive parameters entered for the drive in CMOS are correct. When working on an XT (without CMOS), check that the drive-controller board is set correctly for the drive.

Symptom 17-27. The FDISK procedure hangs up or fails to create or save partition record for the drive(s) You might also see an error message, such as "Runtime error." This type of problem often indicates a problem with track 00 on the drive. Before you do anything else, check the signal connector—be sure that the interface signal cables are inserted properly and completely at the drive and controller. Try some new signal cables.

Enter the CMOS setup routine and see that all of the parameters entered for the drive are correct. Heads, cylinders, sectors per track, landing zone, and write precompensation must all be appropriate. Check with the drive maker and see if there is an alternate "translation geometry" that you can enter instead. If the BIOS supports auto-detection, try "auto-detecting" the drive.

Check your version of FDISK. The version of FDISK you are using must be the same as the DOS version on your boot diskette—older versions might not work. Next, run FDISK and see if any partitions are already on the drive. If so, you might need to erase any existing partitions, then create your new partition from scratch. Remember that erasing a partition will destroy any data already on the drive. Use a utility, such as DrivePro (from MicroHouse) or ScanDisk, to check the media for physical defects—especially at track 00. If the boot sector is physically damaged, you should replace the drive.

Finally, check for emergency drive utilities. Some drive makers provide low-level preparation utilities, which can rewrite track 00. For example, Western Digital provides the WD_CLEAR.EXE utility. If problems still persist, replace the defective hard drive.

Symptom 17-28. A "Hard disk controller failure" message appears or a large number of defects occur in the last logical partition This is typically a CMOS setup or drive-controller problem. Enter the CMOS setup routine and see that all of the parameters entered for the drive are correct. If the geometry specifies a larger drive, the system will attempt to format areas of the drive that don't exist—resulting in a large number of errors. If CMOS is configured correctly, the problem might be with the hard-drive controller. Try a new hard-drive controller. If a new drive controller does not correct the problem, the drive itself is probably defective and should be replaced.

Symptom 17-29. The high-level (DOS) format process takes too long In almost all cases, long formats are the result of older DOS versions. Check your DOS version. MS-DOS version 4.x tries to recover hard errors, which can consume quite a bit of extra time. You will probably see a number of "Attempting to recover allocation units" messages. Your best course is to upgrade the MS-DOS version to 6.22 (or MS-DOS 7.0 with Windows 95). Later versions of DOS abandon hard-error retries.

Symptom 17-30. The IDE drive (<528MB) does not partition or format to full capacity When relatively small hard drives do not realize their full capacity, the CMOS setup is usually at fault. The drive parameters entered into CMOS must specify the full capacity of the drive—using a geometry setup that is acceptable. If you use parameters that specify a smaller drive, any extra capacity will be ignored. If there are more than 1024 cylinders, you must use an alternate "translation geometry" to realize the full drive potential. The drive maker can provide you with the right translation geometry. Also check your DOS version—older versions of DOS use a partition limit of 32MB. Upgrade your older version of DOS to 6.22 (or MS-DOS 7.0 with Windows 95).

Symptom 17-31. The EIDE drive (>528MB) does not partition or format to full capacity This type of problem might also be caused by a CMOS setup error, but is almost always caused by poor system configuration. Check the CMOS setup for drive geometry—the drive parameters entered into CMOS must specify the full capacity of the drive. If you use parameters that specify a smaller drive, any extra capacity will be ignored. If there are more than 1024 cylinders, you must use an alternate "translation geometry" to realize the full drive potential. The drive maker can provide you with the right translation geometry. Also check the CMOS setup for LBA. EIDE drives need Logical Block Addressing to access over 528MB. Be sure that there is an entry such as "LBA mode" in CMOS. Otherwise, you might need to upgrade your motherboard BIOS to have full drive capacity.

Check the drive controller. If you cannot upgrade an older motherboard BIOS, install an EIDE drive controller with its own controller BIOS—this will supplement the motherboard BIOS. Finally, check the drive-management software. If neither the motherboard or controller BIOS will support LBA mode, you will need to install drive-management software, such as EZ-Drive or Drive Manager from Ontrack.

Symptom 17-32. "Disk boot failure," "non system disk," or "No ROM basic—SYSTEM HALTED" error messages appear There are several possible reasons for these errors. Start by checking the signal connector. Be sure that the interface signal cables are inserted properly and completely at the drive and controller. Try some new signal cables. Boot the PC with a "clean" boot disk and be sure that no TSRs or drivers are being loaded that interfere with drive operation. If you haven't done so already, run your anti-virus checker and be sure that there are no memory-resident or file-based viruses.

Next, enter the CMOS setup routine and see that all of the parameters entered for the drive are correct. Heads, cylinders, sectors per track, landing zone, and write precompensation must all be entered. Boot from a floppy disk and run FDISK to check the partitions on your hard drive. Be sure that there is at least one DOS partition. If the drive is to be your boot drive, the primary partition must be active and bootable.

It is also possible that the hard drive itself is defective. Try a known-good hard drive. If a known-good drive works as expected, your original drive is probably defective. If problems persist with a known-good floppy drive, replace the drive controller.

Symptom 17-33. The hard drive in a PC is suffering frequent breakdowns (i.e., between 6 to 12 months) When drives tend to fail within a few months, there are some factors to consider. Check the PC power first. If the ac power supplying your PC is "dirty" (i.e., lots of spikes and surges), power anomalies can often make it through the power supply and damage other components. Remove any high-load devices, such as air conditioners, motors, or coffee makers from the same ac circuit used by the PC, or try the PC on a known-good ac circuit. You might also consider a good-quality UPS to power your PC.

Drive utilization might be another factor. If the drive is being worked hard by applications and swap files, consider upgrading RAM or adding cache to reduce dependency on the drive. Keep the drive defragmented. Periodically run a utility, such as DEFRAG, to reorganize the files. This reduces the amount of "drive thrashing" that occurs when loading and saving files.

Finally, check the environment. Constant, low-level vibrations, such as those in an industrial environment, can kill a hard drive. Smoke (even cigarette smoke), high humidity, very low humidity, and caustic vapors can ruin drives. Be sure that the system is used in a stable office-type environment.

Symptom 17-34. A hard-drive controller is replaced, but during initialization, the system displays error messages, such as "Hard disk failure" or "Not a recognized drive type" The PC might also lock-up. Some drive controllers might be incompatible in some systems. Check with the controller manufacturer and see if there have been any reports of incompatibilities with your PC. If so, try a different drive-controller board.

Symptom 17-35. A new hard drive is installed, but it will not boot, or a message appears, such as: "HDD controller failure" The new drive has probably not been installed or prepared properly. Check the power connector first. Be sure that the 4-pin power connector is inserted properly and completely. If the drive is being powered by a Y-connector, be sure that any interim connections are secure. Use a voltmeter and measure the +5-V (pin 4) and +12-V (pin 1) levels. If either voltage (especially the +12-V supply) is unusually low or absent, replace the power supply.

Next, be sure that the drive's signal interface cable is connected securely at both the drive and controller. If the cable is visibly worn or damaged, try a new one. Enter the CMOS setup routine and see that all of the parameters entered for the drive are correct. Heads, cylinders, sectors per track, landing zone, and write precompensation must all correct; otherwise, POST will not recognize the drive. Finally, the drive might not be prepared properly. Run FDISK from a bootable diskette to partition the drive, then run FORMAT to initialize the drive. Then, run SYS C: to make the drive bootable.

Symptom 17-36. Disk Manager is installed to a hard drive, but is formatted back to 528 MB when DOS is reinstalled After *Disk manager* is installed, you must create a "rescue disk" to use in conjunction with your DOS installation. There are two means of accomplishing this. First:

- Create a "clean" DOS bootable disk.
- Copy two files from the original *Disk manager* disk to your bootable disk: XBIOS.OVL and DMDRVR.BIN.
- Create a CONFIG.SYS file on this bootable disk with these three lines:
```
DEVICE=DMDRVR.BIN
FILES=35
BUFFERS=35
```
- Remove the bootable diskette and reboot the system.
- When you see "Press space bar to boot from diskette," do so—the system will halt.
- Insert the rescue disk in drive A: and press any key to resume the boot process.
- At the A: prompt, remove your rescue disk, insert the DOS installation disk, then type *SETUP*.
- You will now install DOS files without overwriting the *Disk manager* files.

or:

- Create a "clean" DOS bootable disk.
- Insert the original *Disk manager* diskette in the A: drive and type:
```
DMCFIG/D=A:
```
- You will prompted to inert a bootable floppy in drive A:.
- You will need to remove and insert the bootable disk a few times as *Drive manager* files are copied.
- Remove the floppy and reboot the system.
- When you see "Press space bar to boot from diskette," do so—the system will halt.
- Insert the rescue disk in drive A: and press any key to resume the boot process.
- At the A: prompt, remove your rescue disk, insert the DOS installation disk, then type *SETUP*.
- You will now install DOS files without overwriting the *Disk manager* files.

Symptom 17-37. ScanDisk reports some bad sectors, but cannot map them out during a surface analysis You might need a surface-analysis utility (provided by the drive maker) for your particular drive. For example, Western Digital provides the WDATIDE.EXE utility for its Caviar series of drives. It will mark all "grown" defects, and compensate for lost capacity by utilizing spare tracks.

These types of surface-analysis utilities are typically destructive. Be sure to have a complete backup of the drive before proceeding. Also, the utility might take a very long time to run, depending on your drive's capacity.

Symptom 17-38. The drive will work as a primary drive, but not as a secondary (or vice versa) In most cases, the drive is simply jumpered incorrectly, but it might also have timing problems. Check the drive jumpers first. Be sure that the drive is jumpered properly as a primary (single drive), primary (dual drive), or secondary drive.

The drive-signal timing might also be off. Some IDE/EIDE drives do not work as primary or secondary drives with certain other drives in the system. Reverse the primary/secondary relationship. If the problem persists, try the drives separately. If the drives work individually, there is probably a timing problem, so try a different drive as the primary or secondary.

Symptom 17-39. 32-bit access does not work under Windows 3.1x You are probably not using the correct hard drive driver. Check your EIDE BIOS. If your motherboard (or drive controller) BIOS supports LBA, obtaining a driver should be easy. The drive maker either provides a 32-bit driver on a diskette accompanying the drive or a driver can be downloaded from the drive maker's BBS or Internet Web site. If the motherboard (or drive controller) does not support LBA directly, you can install Ontrack's Disk Manager (6.03 or later) and run DMCFIG to install the 32-bit driver software.

Symptom 17-40. Drive diagnostics reveal a great deal of wasted space on the drive You probably have a large drive partitioned as a single large logical volume. Check the cluster size (Table 6-6 shows a comparison of partition size vs. cluster size). If you deal with large numbers of small files, it might be more efficient to create multiple smaller partitions utilizing smaller clusters.

Symptom 17-41. A Y-adapter fails to work Some Y-adapters are incorrectly wired, and can cause severe damage to any device attached to it. Examine the power connector first. Be certain that both of the female connectors are lined up with the two chamfered (rounded) corners facing up and both of the squared corners facing down. The four wires attached to the female connectors should now be in the following order from left to right: Yellow (12 V), Black (ground), Black (ground), and Red (5 V). If this order is reversed on one of the connectors, then your Y power adapter is faulty and should not be used.

Symptom 17-42. During the POST, the drive begins to spin-up and produces a sharp noise This problem has been encountered with some combinations of drives, motherboards, and motherboard BIOS. This type of problem can easily result in data loss (and media damage). Check the motherboard BIOS version first, then contact the PC system manufacturer and see if a BIOS upgrade is necessary. Try a BIOS upgrade. Otherwise, replace the drive controller. Often, a new drive controller might resolve the problem if the motherboard BIOS cannot be replaced.

Symptom 17-43. Opening a folder under Windows 95 seems to take a long time When you open a folder in Microsoft Explorer on a drive using the FAT32 file system, it might seem to take an unusually long time before the window is accessible or the "working in the background" pointer might appear for prolonged periods. This is a typical sign of FAT 32 problems under Windows 95, and is usually because the total space used by all directory entries in the particular folder exceeds 32KB. Until Microsoft provides a fix for their service release, you should simply move some files in the overloaded folder to a different folder.

Symptom 17-44. The hard drive is infected by a bootblock virus You might detect the presence of a bootblock virus (a virus that infects the MBR) by running an anti-virus utility, or receiving a warning from the BIOS bootblock-protection feature. In every case, you should attempt to use the anti-virus utility to eradicate the virus. You might also remove a bootblock virus by using "FDISK /MBR" (although that could render the contents of your disk inaccessible). If you're using drive overlay software, such as Disk Manager, you can usually re-write the code through the "Maintenance Menu" within the *Disk manager* program itself.

Symptom 17-45. An "Incorrect DOS version" error appears You attempted to execute an external DOS command (i.e., FORMAT) using a version of the utility, which is not from the same DOS version as the COMMAND.COM file, which is currently running. Reboot with a corresponding version of COMMAND.COM, or get a version of the utility, which matches the current version of COMMAND.COM.

Symptom 17-46. A "File allocation table bad" error appears The operating system has encountered a problem with the FAT. Normally, two copies of the FAT are on a drive—chances are that one of the copies has become damaged. It might also be possible that no partition is on the drive to begin with. Run ScanDisk—this might be able to correct the problem by allowing you to select which copy of the FAT you wish to use. If the problem continues, you'll need to back up as many files as possible and reformat the drive.

Symptom 17-47. DOS requires a "volume label," but the label is corrupt Some versions of DOS (i.e., DOS 3.x) require you to enter the volume label when formatting a hard drive or deleting a logical drive partition using the FDISK command. However, if the volume label is corrupted (or was changed by a third-party utility to contain lowercase letters), this is impossible. To correct this problem, use the *Label* command to delete the volume label, then use FORMAT or FDISK. When you are prompted for the volume label, press <Enter> (which indicates no volume label). If *Label* doesn't successfully delete the volume label, you can use the following debug script to erase the first sector of the drive and make it appear unformatted, then repartition and reformat the drive. Start DEBUG, then type the following:

```
-  F 100 L 200 0 ;Create a sector of zeros at address 100.
-  W 100 2 0 1   ;Write information at address 100 to sector 0 of drive 2*
-  Q             ;Quit DEBUG.
```

For DOS versions 5.x and later, you can use the following command to resolve this issue:

```
format /q /v:VOLUME x:
```

where "VOLUME" is the new volume name you want to assign to the hard-disk drive, and "x:" is the drive letter you want to format.

Further Study

That's all for Chapter 17. Be sure to review the glossary and chapter questions on the accompanying CD. If you have access to the Internet, take a look at some of the hard-drive manufacturers listed:

MicroHouse: **http://www.microhouse.com**

Symantec: **http://www.symantec.com**

Maxtor: **http://www.maxtor.com**

Quantum: **http://www.quantum.com**

Seagate: **http://www.seagate.com**

Western Digital: **http://www.wdc.com**

Windows 95 Emergency Recover Utility: **http://www.microsoft.com/windows/download/eruzip.exe**

USENET FAQ

http://www.cis.ohio-state.edu/hypertext/faq/bngusenet/comp/sys/ibm/pc/hardware/storage/top.html

18

ISA/EISA
BUS
OPERATIONS

CONTENTS AT A GLANCE

Industry-Standard Architecture (ISA)
  8-bit ISA
  Knowing the XT signals
  16-bit ISA
  Knowing the AT signals
  Potential problems mixing 8-bit and
    16-bit ISA boards

**Extended Industry-Standard
Architecture (EISA)**
  Knowing the EISA signals
  Configuring an EISA system

General Bus Troubleshooting

Further Study

When it was first introduced, the IBM PC was no gem. It was a slow, clunky contraption with virtually no system resources (memory, interrupts, DMA channels, etc.). Yet, the IBM PC ushered in the personal computer era that we know today. Certainly, it was not speed or efficiency that brought IBM systems to the forefront of technology. Instead, it was a revolutionary (and rather risky) concept called *open architecture*. Rather than designing a computer and being the sole developer of proprietary add-on devices (as so many other computer manufacturers were at the time), IBM chose to incorporate only the essential processing elements on the motherboard, and leave many of the other functions to expansion boards that could be plugged into "standard" bus connectors.

By publishing the specifications of this "standard" expansion bus and making it available to the industry as a whole, any company was then able to develop IBM-compatible adapters and add-ons. Those adapters would also work on "clone" PCs, which used the same expansion bus. As a result, the PC became a processing platform for some of the most creative video, drive, and communication devices ever devised. As you might suspect, the key to an open architecture is the bus connector itself. By understanding the location and purpose of each bus signal, you can follow the operations and limitations of the bus. This chapter is intended to provide you with background information on the two classic bus architectures used in modern PCs—ISA and EISA.

Industry-Standard Architecture (ISA)

The venerable *Industry Standard Architecture (ISA)* shown in Fig. 18-1 is the first open system bus architecture used for personal computers—any manufacturer was welcome to use the architecture for a small licensing fee. Because there were no restrictions placed on the use of ISA busses (also referred to simply as *PC busses*), they were duplicated in every IBM-compatible clone that followed. Not only did the use of a standard bus pave the way for thousands of manufacturers to produce compatible PCs and expansion devices, but it also allowed the use of standardized operating systems and applications software. Both an 8-bit and 16-bit version of the ISA bus are available, although current motherboards have essentially abandoned the 8-bit XT version in favor of the faster, more flexible 16-bit AT version.

8-BIT ISA

Use of the 8-bit XT bus started in 1982. The 8-bit ISA bus consists of a single card-edge connector with 62 contacts. The bus provides eight data lines and 20 address lines, which allow the board to reside within the XT's 1MB of conventional memory. The bus also supports connections for six interrupts (IRQ2 to IRQ7) and three DMA channels. The XT bus runs at the system speed of 4.77MHz. Although the bus itself is relatively simple, IBM failed to publish specific timing relationships for data, address, and control signals. This ambiguity left early manufacturers to find the proper timing relationships by trial and error.

Although each connector on the bus is supposed to work the same way, early PCs designed with eight expansion slots required any card inserted in the eighth slot (the slot

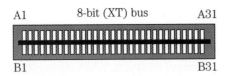

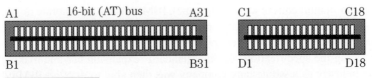

FIGURE 18-1   Diagram of 8-bit and 16-bit ISA slots.

TABLE 18-1   ISA 8-BIT (XT) BUS PINOUT

SIGNAL	PIN	PIN	SIGNAL
Ground	B1	A1	−I/O channel check
Reset	B2	A2	Data bit 7
+5 Vdc	B3	A3	Data bit 6
IRQ 2	B4	A4	Data bit 5
−5 Vdc	B5	A5	Data bit 4
DRQ 2	B6	A6	Data bit 3
−12 Vdc	B7	A7	Data bit 2
−Card selected	B8	A8	Data bit 1
+12 Vdc	B9	A9	Data bit 0
Ground	B10	A10	I/O channel ready
−SMEMW	B11	A11	AEN
−SMEMR	B12	A12	Address bit 19
−I/O W	B13	A13	Address bit 18
−I/O R	B14	A14	Address bit 17
−DACK 3	B15	A15	Address bit 16
DRQ 3	B16	A16	Address bit 15
−DACK 1	B17	A17	Address bit 14
DRQ 1	B18	A18	Address bit 13
−Refresh	B19	A19	Address bit 12
Clock (4.77 MHz)	B20	A20	Address bit 11
IRQ 7	B21	A21	Address bit 10
IRQ 6	B22	A22	Address bit 9
IRQ 5	B23	A23	Address bit 8
IRQ 4	B24	A24	Address bit 7
IRQ3	B25	A25	Address bit 6
−DACK 2	B26	A26	Address bit 5
T/C	B27	A27	Address bit 4
BALE	B28	A28	Address bit 3
+5 Vdc	B29	A29	Address bit 2
Oscillator (14.3 MHz)	B30	A30	Address bit 1
Ground	B31	A31	Address bit 0

closest to the power supply) to provide a special "card selected" signal on pin B8. Timing requirements for the eighth slot are also tighter. Contrary to popular belief, the eighth slot has nothing to do with the IBM expansion chassis. The demands of slot 8 were to support a keyboard/timer adapter board for IBM's special configuration called the *3270PC*. Most XT clones did not adhere to this "eighth slot" peculiarity.

KNOWING THE XT SIGNALS

Table 18-1 shows the pinout for an XT bus configuration. The *Oscillator* pin provides the 14.3MHz system oscillator signal to the expansion bus, and the *Clock* pin supplies the

4.77MHz system clock signal. When the PC needs to be reset, the *RESET DRV* pin drives the whole system into a reset state. The 20 address pins (0 to 19) connect an expansion board to the system's address bus, when address signals are valid, the *Address Latch Enable (ALE)* signal indicates that the address can now be decoded. The eight data lines (0 to 7) connect the board to the system's data bus.

The *–I/O channel check (–IOCHCK)* line flags the motherboard when errors occur on the expansion board. Notice that the minus sign (–) preceding the signal indicates that the signal uses active-low logic. The *I/O channel ready* is active when an addressed expansion board is ready. If this pin is logic 0, the CPU will extend the bus cycle by inserting wait states. The six hardware *interrupts* (IRQ2 to IRQ7) are used by the expansion board to demand the CPU's attention. Interrupts 0 and 1 are not available to the bus because they handle the highest priorities of the timer chip and keyboard. The *–I/O read (–I/O R)* and *–I/O write (– I/O W)* lines indicate that the CPU or DMA controller want to transfer data to or from the data bus. The *–Memory read (– MEMR)* and *–Memory write (–MEMW)* signals tells the expansion board that the CPU or DMA controller is going to read or write data to main memory.

The XT bus supplies three *DMA requests (DRQ1 to DRQ3)* so that an expansion board can transfer data to or from memory. DMA requests must be held until the corresponding *–DMA acknowledge (–DACK1 to –DACK3)* signals become true. If the *Address enable (AEN)* signal is true, the DMA controller is controlling the bus for a data transfer. Finally, the *Terminal count (T/C)* signal provides a pulse when the DMA transfer is completed.

16-BIT ISA

The limitations of the 8-bit ISA bus were soon obvious. With a floppy drive and hard drive taking up two of the six available interrupts, COM 3 and COM 4 taking up another two interrupts (IRQ 3 and IRQ 4), and an LPT port taking up IRQ 7, competition for the remaining interrupt was fierce. Of the three DMA channels available, the floppy and hard drives take two, so only one DMA channel remains available. Only 1MB of address space is addressable, and 8 data bits form a serious bottleneck for data transfers. It would have been a simple matter to start from scratch and design an entirely new bus, but that would have obsoleted the entire installed base of XT owners.

The next logical step in bus evolution came in 1984/85 with the introduction of the 80286 in IBM's PC/AT. System resources were added to the bus while still allowing XT boards to function in the expanded bus. The result became what we know today as the 16-bit AT bus. Instead of a different bus connector, the original 62-pin connector was left intact and an extra 36-pin connector was added, as shown in Table 18-2, designated *C* and *D*. An extra eight data bits are added to bring the total data bus to 16 bits. Five interrupts and four DMA channels are included. Four more address lines are also provided, in addition to several more control signals. Clock speed is increased on the AT bus to 8.33MHz. It is important to note that although XT boards should theoretically work with an AT bus, not all older XT expansion boards will work on the AT bus.

KNOWING THE AT SIGNALS

The *–System Bus High Enable (–SBHE)* is active when the upper eight data bits are being used. If the upper eight bits are not being used (i.e., an XT board in the AT slot), –SBHE will be inactive. If the expansion board requires 16 bit access to memory locations, it must

TABLE 18-2 ISA 16-BIT (AT) BUS PINOUT

SIGNAL	PIN	PIN	SIGNAL
Ground	B1	A1	−I/O channel check
Reset	B2	A2	Data bit 7
+5 Vdc	B3	A3	Data bit 6
IRQ 9	B4	A4	Data bit 5
−5 Vdc	B5	A5	Data bit 4
DRQ 2	B6	A6	Data bit 3
−12 Vdc	B7	A7	Data bit 2
−0 WAIT	B8	A8	Data bit 1
+12 Vdc	B9	A9	Data bit 0
Ground	B10	A10	−I/O channel ready
−SMEMW	B11	A11	AEN
−SMEMR	B12	A12	Address bit 19
−I/O W	B13	A13	Address bit 18
−I/O R	B14	A14	Address bit 17
−DACK 3	B15	A15	Address bit 16
DRQ 3	B16	A16	Address bit 15
−DACK 1	B17	A17	Address bit 14
DRQ 1	B18	A18	Address bit 13
−Refresh	B19	A19	Address bit 12
Clock (8.33 MHz)	B20	A20	Address bit 11
IRQ 7	B21	A21	Address bit 10
IRQ 6	B22	A22	Address bit 9
IRQ 5	B23	A23	Address bit 8
IRQ 4	B24	A24	Address bit 7
IRQ 3	B25	A25	Address bit 6
−DACK 2	B26	A26	Address bit 5
T/C	B27	A27	Address bit 4
BALE	B28	A28	Address bit 3
+5 Vdc	B29	A29	Address bit 2
Oscillator (14.3 MHz)	B30	A30	Address bit 1
Ground	B31	A31	Address bit 0
Key	Key	Key	Key
−MEM CS16	D1	C1	−SBHE
−I/O CS16	D2	C2	Address bit 23
IRQ 10	D3	C3	Address bit 22
IRQ 11	D4	C4	Address bit 21
IRQ 12	D5	C5	Address bit 20
IRQ 15	D6	C6	Address bit 19
IRQ 14	D7	C7	Address bit 18
−DACK 0	D8	C8	Address bit 17
DRQ 0	D9	C9	−MEM R
−DACK 5	D10	C10	−MEM W
DRQ 5	D11	C11	Data bit 8

TABLE 18-2 ISA 16-BIT (AT) BUS PINOUT (CONTINUED)			
SIGNAL	PIN	PIN	SIGNAL
–DACK 6	D12	C12	Data bit 9
DRQ 6	D13	C13	Data bit 10
–DACK 7	D14	C14	Data bit 11
DRQ 7	D15	C15	Data bit 12
+5 Vdc	D16	C16	Data bit 13
–Master	D17	C17	Data bit 14
Ground	D18	C18	Data bit 15

return an active –EM CS16 signal. If the expansion board requires 16-bit access to an I/O location, it must make the –I/O CS16 signal active. The *–Memory read (–MEMR)* and *–Memory write (–MEMW)* signals provided by an expansion board tell the CPU or DMA controller that memory access is needed up to 16MB. The –SMEMR and –SMEMW signals only indicate memory access for the first 1MB. The –MASTER signal can be used by expansion boards that are able to take control of the bus through use of a DMA channel. It is interesting that small, highly integrated AT systems are available for embedded systems and dedicated applications.

POTENTIAL PROBLEMS MIXING 8-BIT AND 16-BIT ISA BOARDS

ISA 16-bit architecture that was developed on the foundation of IBM's original 8-bit XT bus. By extending the original XT bus, rather than redesigning an expansion bus from scratch, IBM was able to develop their AT to accommodate new, more sophisticated 16-bit expansion boards while still being backwardly compatible with the installed base of 8-bit boards. For the most part, this strategy worked quite well—the ISA bus remains a prominent feature of today's PCs. However, there is a potential problem with the ISA bus when inserting an 8-bit and 16-bit adapter that both use ROM residing in the same memory vicinity. Such a problem generally results in trouble with the 8-bit board.

To understand where this problem arises from, you should be familiar with the ISA bus pinout, as shown in Table 18-2. There is an initial 62-pin connector (A1 through A31 and B1 through B31), followed by the extended 36-pin connector (C1 through C18 and D1 through D18). Notice that Address Bits 17, 18, and 19 are repeated on pins C8, C7, and C6. When a 16-bit board is inserted in the system, those repeated address lines indicate that a memory access is about to occur somewhere within 128KB of the address signals on A17, A18, and A19 (the lower 17 address lines—A0 to A16—specify exactly where in that 128KB range the access will take place). If an 16-bit expansion board has memory (such as a Video BIOS ROM or hard-drive controller ROM) within the 128KB range about to be accessed, it responds to the system using the –MEM CS16 or –I/O CS16 lines that its memory is ready for access in 16-bit transfers. If the system receives no response from either of these lines, data is transferred in 8-bit sections.

The problem here is that 8-bit boards may also have memory within that 128KB range, but because they cannot detect the three extra address lines, the board cannot respond to the system. If a 16-bit board tells the system to proceed with a 16-bit data transfer, but there is also an 8-bit board in that same address range, the 8-bit board will be forced to receive 16-bit data transfers. As you might expect, this is quite impossible for an 8-bit board, so the 8-bit board will appear to malfunction. Because most expansion boards reserve their ROM addresses for the 128KB block between 768KB to 896KB (C0000h to DBFFFh, sometimes called the *ROM Reserve*), this is where most problems reside.

It is important for you to understand that this problem does not refer to a hardware conflict. The ROM locations of the 8-bit and 16-bit boards can certainly not overlap at any point. As you might realize, however, it is possible to have several different ROMs contained within the same 128KB of system memory. If one such ROM is on a 16-bit board and one is on an 8-bit board, the 8-bit board will likely malfunction because of the way in which 16-bit boards handle ISA bus operation. Correcting such a problem is generally a matter of replacing the 8-bit board with a 16-bit version. It might also be possible to disable the 8-bit ROM using an on-board jumper, then use the motherboard BIOS ROM instead.

Extended Industry-Standard Architecture (EISA)

The *Extended ISA (EISA)* bus (Fig. 18-2) is a 32-bit bus developed in 1988/89 to address the continuing need for greater speed and performance from expansion peripherals caused by the use of 80386 and 80486 CPUs. It also did not make sense to leave the entire 32-bit bus market to IBM's MCA bus. Even though the bus works at 8.33MHz, the 32-bit data path doubles data throughput between motherboard and expansion board. Unlike the MCA bus, however, EISA ensures backward compatibility with existing ISA peripherals and PC software. The EISA bus is designed to be fully compatible with ISA boards, as shown in the pinout of Table 18-3. The EISA bus switches automatically between 16-bit ISA and 32-bit EISA operation using a second row of card-edge connectors and the −EX32 and −EX16 lines. Thus, EISA boards have access to all of the signals available to ISA boards, as well as the second row of EISA signals.

As with the MCA bus, EISA supports arbitration for bus mastering and automatic board configuration, which simplifies the installation of new boards. The EISA bus can access 15 interrupt levels and 7 DMA channels. To maintain backward compatibility with ISA expansion boards, however, there is no direct bus support for video or audio as there is with the MCA bus. Because the EISA bus clock runs at the same 8.33MHz rate as ISA, the potential data throughput of an EISA board is roughly twice that of ISA boards. EISA

16-bit ISA/32-bit EISA bus

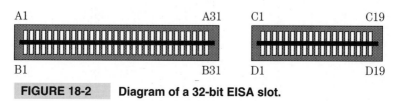

FIGURE 18-2   Diagram of a 32-bit EISA slot.

TABLE 18-3   EISA 16/32-BIT BUS PINOUT

32 BIT	16 BIT	PIN	PIN	16 BIT	32 BIT
Ground	Ground	B1	A1	−I/O channel check	−CMD
+5 Vdc	Reset	B2	A2	Data bit 7	−START
+5 Vdc	+5 Vdc	B3	A3	Data bit 6	EXRDY
Reserved	IRQ 9	B4	A4	Data bit 5	− EX32
Reserved	−5 Vdc	B5	A5	Data bit 4	Ground
Key	DRQ 2	B6	A6	Data bit 3	Key
Reserved	−12 Vdc	B7	A7	Data bit 2	−EX16
Reserved	−0 WAIT	B8	A8	Data bit 1	−SLBURST
+12 Vdc	+12 Vdc	B9	A9	Data bit 0	−MSBURST
M −I/O	Ground	B10	A10	−I/O channel ready	W −R
−LOCK	−SMEMW	B11	A11	AEN	Ground
Reserved	−SMEMR	B12	A12	Address bit 19	Reserved
Ground	−I/O W	B13	A13	Address bit 18	Reserved
Reserved	−I/O R	B14	A14	Address bit 17	Reserved
−BE3	−DACK 3	B15	A15	Address bit 16	Ground
Key	DRQ3	B16	A16	Address bit 15	Key
−BE2	−DACK 1	B17	A17	Address bit 14	−BE1
−BE0	DRQ 1	B18	A18	Address bit 13	−Addr. 31
Ground	−Refresh	B19	A19	Address bit 12	Ground
+5 Vdc	Clock (8.33 MHz)	B20	A20	Address bit 11	−Addr. 30
−Addr. 29	IRQ 7	B21	A21	Address bit 10	−Addr. 28
Ground	IRQ 6	B22	A22	Address btit 9	−Addr. 27
−Addr. 26	IRQ 5	B23	A23	Address bit 8	−Addr. 25
−Addr. 24	IRQ4	B24	A24	Address bit 7	Ground
Key	IRQ3	B25	A25	Address bit 6	Key
Addr. 16	−DACK 2	B26	A26	Address bit 5	Addr. 15
Addr. 14	T/C	B27	A27	Address bit 4	Addr. 13
+5 Vdc	BALE	B28	A28	Address bit 3	Addr. 12
+5 Vdc	+5 Vdc	B29	A29	Address bit 2	Addr. 11
Ground	Osc. (14.3 MHz)	B30	A30	Address bit 1	Ground
Addr. 10	Ground	B31	A31	Address bit 0	Addr. 9
Key	Key	Key	Key	Key	Key
Addr. 8	−MEM CS16	D1	C1	−SBHE	Addr. 7
Addr. 6	−I/O CS16	D2	C2	Address bit 23	Ground
Addr. 5	IRQ 10	D3	C3	Address bit 22	Addr. 4
+5 Vdc	IRQ11	D4	C4	Address bit 21	Addr. 3
Addr. 2	IRQ 12	D5	C5	Address bit 20	Ground
Key	IRQ 15	D6	C6	Address bit 19	Key
Data 16	IRQ 14	D7	C7	Address bit 18	Data 17
Data 18	−DACK 0	D8	C8	Address bit 17	Data 19
Ground	DRQ 0	D9	C9	−MEM R	Data 20
Data 21	−DACK 5	D10	C10	−MEM W	Data 22
Data 23	DRQ 5	D11	C11	Data bit 8	Ground

TABLE 18-3 EISA 16/32-BIT BUS PINOUT (CONTINUED)

32 BIT	16 BIT	PIN	PIN	16 BIT	32 BIT
Data 24	–DACK 6	D12	C12	Data bit 9	Data 25
Ground	DRQ 6	D13	C13	Data bit 10	Data 26
Data 27	–DACK 7	D14	C14	Data bit 11	Data 28
Key	DRQ 7	D15	C15	Data bit 12	Key
Data 29	+5 Vdc	D16	C16	Data bit 13	Ground
+5 Vdc	–MASTER	D17	C17	Data bit 14	Data 30
+5 Vdc	Ground	D18	C18	Data bit 15	Data 31
–MAKx	——	D19	C19	——	–MREQx

systems are used as network servers, workstations, and high-end PCs. Although EISA systems have proliferated farther than MCA systems, EISA remains a high-end standard—never really filtering down to low-cost consumer systems.

KNOWING THE EISA SIGNALS

The EISA bus uses 30 *address lines* (Addr. 2 to Addr. 31). The lower two address lines (A0 and A1) are decoded by the *Byte enable* lines (–BE0 to –BE3). Data bits 0 to 15 are taken from the ISA portion of the bus, but the upper 16 *data lines* are provided by (Data 16 to Data 31). The *Memory/ –I/O (M/ –I/O)* signal determines whether a memory or I/O bus cycle is being performed, while the *Write/ –Read (W/ –R)* line defines whether the access is for reading or writing. When an EISA device is allowed to complete a bus cycle, the *EISA ready (EXRDY)* line is used to insert wait states. When the motherboard is providing exclusive access to an EISA board, the *–Locked cycle (–LOCK)* signal is true. If an EISA board can run in 32-bit mode, the *–EISA 32-bit device (–EX32)* signal is true, but if the board can only run in 16-bit mode, the *–EISA 16-bit device (–EX16)* signal is true.

The *–Master burst (–MSBURST)* signal is activated by the EISA bus master, which informs the EISA bus controller that a burst-transfer cycle will commence—thus doubling the bus-transfer rate. When an external device must send a data burst, it activates the *–Slave burst (–SLBURST)* line. An external device requests control of the EISA bus using the *–Master request (–MREQ)* line. If the bus arbitrator decides that the requester can control the bus, a *–Master acknowledge (–MACK)* signal is sent to the requesting device. A *–Command (–CMD)* signal is sent to synchronize the EISA bus cycle with the system clock, and the *–Start (–START)* signal helps to coordinate the system clock with the beginning of an EISA bus cycle. Finally, the *Bus clock (BCLK)* is provided at 8.33MHz.

CONFIGURING AN EISA SYSTEM

There's an added wrinkle when working with EISA systems—each EISA slot must be configured through software. Whenever adding, removing, or upgrading an EISA device, you'll need to run an *EISA Configuration Utility (ECU)* to configure each EISA slot. If you don't have an ECU handy, you can download ECU v.3 from Micro Computer Systems at: **http://www.mcsdallas.com/mcs/ecuv3.htm.**

General Bus Troubleshooting

In most cases, you will not be troubleshooting a bus—after all, the bus is little more than a passive connector. However, the major signals that exist on an ISA or EISA bus can provide you with important clues about the system's operation. The most effective bus troubleshooting tool available to you is a POST board (such as the ones covered in Chapter 22). Many POST boards are equipped with a number of LEDs that display power status, along with important timing and control signals. If one or more of those LEDs is missing, a fault has likely occurred somewhere on the motherboard. Refer to Chapter 15 for detailed POST board instructions.

Another point to consider is that bus connectors are mechanical devices—as a result, they do not last forever. If you or your customer are in the habit of removing and inserting boards frequently, it is likely that the metal "fingers" providing contact will wear and result in unreliable connections. Similarly, inserting a board improperly (or with excessive force) can break the connector. In extreme cases, even the motherboard can be damaged. The first rule of board replacement is: always try removing and re-inserting the suspect board. It is not uncommon for oxides to develop on board and slot contacts that could eventually degrade signal quality. By removing the board and re-inserting it, you can wipe off any oxides or dust and possible improve the connections.

The second rule of board replacement is: always try a board in another expansion slot before replacing it. This way, a faulty bus slot can be ruled out before suffering the expense of a new board. If a bus slot proves defective, there is little that a technician can do, except:

1 Block the slot and inform the customer that it is damaged and should not be used.
2 Replace the damaged bus slot connector (a tedious and time-consuming task) and pass the labor expense on to the customer.
3 Replace the motherboard outright (also a rather expensive option).

Further Study

That's it for Chapter 18. Be sure to review the glossary and chapter questions on the accompanying CD. If you have access to the Internet, take a look at some of the resources listed:

Micro Computer Systems: **http://www.mcsdallas.com/mcs/ecuv3.htm** (ECU—EISA Configuration Utility v.3)

JOYSTICKS

AND

GAME PORTS

CONTENTS AT A GLANCE

Understanding the Game-Port System
   Inside the joystick
   Adapting a second joystick
   Digital joysticks (game pads)
   Joystick calibration
   Joystick drift

Cleaning Joysticks

Joysticks and Windows 95

Troubleshooting Joysticks and Game Ports
   Joystick eliminator plug
   Adapting IDC connectors
   Sound cards and Y-adapter
    problems

Further Study

Few peripheral devices have come to represent PC entertainment like the joystick (Fig. 19-1). Although it is one of the simplest peripherals available for a PC, the joystick allows a user to bring an element of hand-eye coordination to interactive programs (i.e., flight simulators and 3D "walk through" games) that would simply be impossible with a keyboard or mouse. The joystick interfaces to the host PC through a board called the *game-port adapter* (or simply the *game port*). This chapter covers the joystick and game port, then covers a selection of service issues.

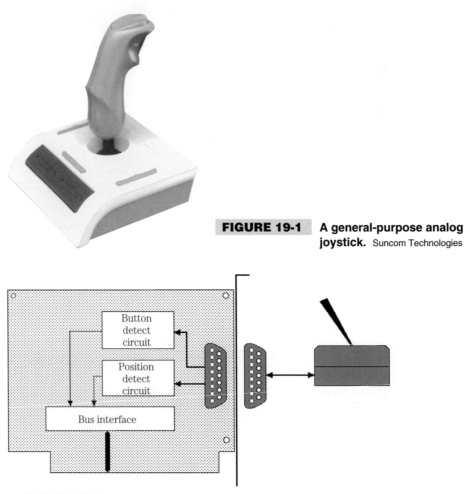

FIGURE 19-1   **A general-purpose analog joystick.** Suncom Technologies

FIGURE 19-2   **Simplified diagram of a game-port system.**

Understanding the Game-Port System

The typical game port uses a relatively simple interface to the PC. Only the lower 8 data bits are used (which explains why so many game ports still use the older 8-bit "XT" card style, rather than switching to a 16-bit "AT" card type). Also, only the lower 10 address bits are needed. Because the game port is an I/O device, the card uses I/OR and I/OR control signals. On virtually all PCs, port 201h is reserved for the game port. Figure 19-2 illustrates a typical game-port system.

INSIDE THE JOYSTICK

Each analog joystick is assembled with two separate potentiometers (typically 100 kΩ) arranged perpendicularly to one another—one potentiometer represents the X axis, and the other potentiometer represents the Y axis. Both potentiometers are linked together mechanically and attached to a movable stick. As the stick is moved left or right, one potentiometer is moved. As the stick moves up or down, the other potentiometer is moved. Of course, the stick can be moved in both the X and Y axis simultaneously, with the proportions of resistance reflecting the stick's position. You can see the wiring scheme for a standard 15-pin dual joystick port in Fig. 19-3. The pinout for a standard joystick port is listed in Table 19-1.

Detecting the stick's X and Y position is not an intuitively obvious process. Ultimately, the analog value of each potentiometer must be converted to a digital value that is read by the application software. This is an important wrinkle—because the game port does not generate an interrupt, it is up to the particular application to interrogate the joystick port

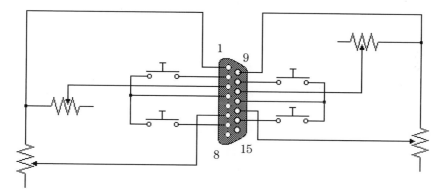

FIGURE 19-3   Wiring diagram for a dual joystick port.

TABLE 194-1	PINOUT FOR A STANDARD JOYSTICK PORT
1	XY1 (Joystick 1 +5-V supply)
2	Switch 1
3	Potentiometer X1
4	Ground (for switch 1&2)
5	Ground (for switch 2)
6	Potentiometer Y1 signal
7	Switch 2
8	N.C. (or +5 V)
9	XY2 (Joystick 2 +5-V supply)
10	Switch 3
11	Potentiometer X2 signal
12	Ground (for switch 3&4)
13	Potentiometer Y2 signal
14	Switch 4
15	N.C. (or +5 V)

* The standard game port uses a DB-15 female connector.

regularly. You might imagine that such a conversion would use an *Analog-to-Digital Converter (ADC)*. However, an ADC provides much greater resolution than is needed and its conversions require a relatively long time. Current game-port conversion circuits use a multivibrator element.

Ultimately, the resistance of each potentiometer is determined indirectly by measuring amount of time required for a charged capacitor to discharge through the particular potentiometer. If a certain axis is at 0 Ω, the multivibrator's internal capacitor will discharge in about 24.2 μs, and at 100 kΩ, the multivibrator's capacitor will discharge in about 1124 μs. Because this is a relatively linear relationship, the discharge time can easily be equated to potentiometer position (an actual routine to accomplish this requires only about 16 lines of assembler code). The multivibrator technique also simplifies the circuitry needed on the game-port adapter—it is really the application that is doing the work.

A joystick also has one or two buttons. As you see from Fig. 19-3, the buttons are typically open, and their closed state can be detected by reading the byte at 201h. Because the game port is capable of supporting two joysticks simultaneously (each with two buttons), the upper four bits of 201h indicate the on/off status of all four buttons.

ADAPTING A SECOND JOYSTICK

Although the typical game port is capable of supporting two joysticks, most joystick products only connect a single joystick. This means that only "half" the game port is being utilized. You can purchase a joystick Y-adapter from any computer store or construct a Y-adapter using the pinout in Table 19-2. You'll need a DB-15 male connector to attach to the game port and two DB-15 female connectors to attach to each of the two joysticks.

TABLE 19-2 PINOUT FOR A JOYSTICK "Y" ADAPTER			
GAME PORT DB-15 MALE		**JOYSTICK 1 DB-15 FEMALE**	**JOYSTICK 2 DB-15 FEMALE**
1	XY1 (joystick 1 +5-V supply)	1	
2	Switch 1	2	
3	Potentiometer X1 signal	3	
4	Ground (for switch 1&2)	4	
5	Ground (for switch 2)	5	
6	Potentiometer Y1 signal	6	
7	Switch 2	7	
8	N.C. (or +5 V)	8	
9	XY2 (Joystick 2 +5-V supply)		1
10	Switch 3		2
11	Potentiometer X2 signal		3
12	Ground (for switch 3&4)		4 and 5
13	Potentiometer Y2 signal		6
14	Switch 4		7
15	N.C. (or +5 V)		8

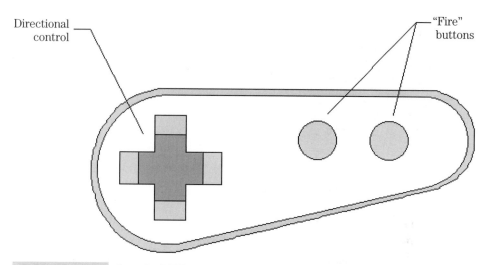

FIGURE 19-4   A typical "Nintendo-style" digital joystick.

Some types of game-port boards provide a separate 15-pin connector for each joystick. Some cut-price game-port boards only provide one connector and the circuitry for one joystick. Verify the capabilities of your game port before using or replacing a joystick Y-adapter.

DIGITAL JOYSTICKS (GAME PADS)

Where an "analog" joystick uses two potentiometers to provide linear information about the joystick's relative position, a "digital" joystick (also called a *game pad*) simply uses an array of switches to indicate absolute direction—usually up, down, left, right, and fire (Fig. 19-4). The game pad actually pre-dates the analog joystick a bit and uses a 9-pin TTL interface as illustrated in the Amiga-style game pad (Table 19-3). Current versions of the digital joystick (such as the Gravis GamePad Pro) use a 15-pin PC game-port interface. This book will not go farther with game-pad control devices, but you should at least understand how they compare to analog joysticks.

9-pin "game pad-type" joysticks are not directly compatible with the PC analog game port, and you should not attempt to adapt a 9-pin game pad to a 15-pin PC game port without some appropriate interface circuitry. Game pads specifically marked as PC joystick compatible (using 15-pin connectors) can usually be attached to ordinary game ports without problems.

JOYSTICK CALIBRATION

Unfortunately, these values of time versus resistance are not the same for every system. Variations in joystick potentiometers, game-port adapter circuits and computer speed will all affect the relationship of time-vs.-resistance value. Even variations in component temperature as the PC warms up can cause changes in resistance interpretation. This is why

TABLE 19-3 PINOUT FOR AN AMIGA-TYPE GAME PAD	
PIN	GAME PAD
1	Forward
2	Back
3	Left
4	Right
5	n/c
6	Button (fire) 1
7	+5 V
8	Ground
9	Button (fire) 2

* Game pads often use a
DB-9 female connector.

each application program that uses a joystick comes with a calibration routine. Calibration allows the application to measure values for center and corner positions. With this data as a base, the application can extrapolate all other joystick positions.

JOYSTICK DRIFT

The term *drift* (*rolling*) is used to indicate a loss of control by the joystick. There are several possible reasons for this. As a technician, you should understand the reasons why drift occurs, and how to correct such problems. First, drift might be the result of a system conflict. Because the game port does not generate an interrupt, conflicts rarely result in system crashes or lockups, but another device feeding data to port 201h can easily upset joystick operation. If you have sound boards or multi-port I/O boards in your system equipped with game ports, be sure to disable any unused ports (check with the user instructions for individual boards to disable extra game ports).

Another possible cause of drift is heat. Once PCs are started up, it is natural for the power used by most components to be dissipated as heat. Unfortunately, heating tends to change the value of components. For logic circuits, this is typically not a problem, but for analog circuits, the consequences can be much more pronounced. As heat changes the values of a multivibrator circuit, timing (and thus positional values) will shift. As the circuit warms up, an error creeps into the joystick. Well-designed game-port adapters will use high-quality, low-drift components that minimize the affects of heat-related drift. It is interesting that the joystick itself is rarely the cause of drift. If you can compensate for drift by periodically re-calibrating the joystick, try a better-quality game-port adapter board.

Finally, the quality of calibration is only as good as the calibration routine itself. A poor or inaccurate routine will tend to calibrate the joystick incorrectly. Try another application. If another application can calibrate and use the joystick properly, you should suspect a bug in the particular application. Try contacting the application manufacturer to find if there is a patch or fix available.

Cleaning Joysticks

Ordinarily, the typical joystick should not require routine cleaning or maintenance. Most joysticks use reasonably reliable potentiometers that should last for the life of the joystick. The two major enemies of a joystick are wear and dust. Wear occurs during normal use as potentiometer sliders move across the resistive surface—it can't be avoided. Over time, wear will effect the contact resistance values of both potentiometers. Uneven wear will result in uneven performance. When this becomes noticeable, it is time to buy a new joystick.

Dust presents another problem. The open aperture at the top of a joystick is an invitation for dust and other debris. Because dust is conductive, it can adversely affect potentiometer values and interfere with slider contacts. If the joystick seems to produce a jumpy or non-linear response to the application, it might be worth trying to clean the joystick, rather than scrapping it. Turn off the computer and disconnect the joystick. Open the joystick that is usually held together by two screws in the bottom housing. Remove the bottom housing and locate the two potentiometers. Most potentiometers have small openings somewhere around their circumference. Dust out the joystick area with compressed air and spray a small quantity of good-quality electrical contact cleaner into each potentiometer. Move the potentiometer through its complete range of motion a few times and allow several minutes for the cleaner to dry. Re-assemble the housing and try the joystick again. If problems persist, replace the joystick.

Joysticks and Windows 95

Games have traditionally been a domain of DOS, so there has been little support for joysticks under Windows. However, now that games are routinely using Windows 95 (taking advantage of such features DirectX and Direct3D), you can now install and calibrate a variety of joysticks under Windows 95. Open your *Control panel* and look for the *Joystick* icon. If the *Joystick* icon appears in your *Control panel*, joystick support is already installed and you can skip to the *Game controller setup*. If you have not yet added your PC game port as *New hardware* in the Windows 95 *Control panel*, you should do this first:

1 Click the *Start* button.

2 Select *Settings*, then *Control panel*.

3 In the *Control panel*, look for a *Joystick* icon. If it's there, skip to the *Game controller setup*. If not, doubleclick the *Add new hardware* icon to start the *Add new hardware* wizard.

4 When prompted to have Windows search for new hardware, select *No*. Click *Next* to continue.

5 Select *Sound, video and game controllers*, then click *Next*.

6 Select the *Manufacturer and game port joystick* (or other appropriate model). This will add the game port as a device. Click *Next*.

7 If resource settings are given as 0201-0201, click *Next*. Windows will look for the required files. If it can't find these files, it will ask you to insert your Windows 95 CD or disk.

8 When the files have been installed, click *Finished*.

9 Shut down your computer and restart Windows 95 to enable your game-port support.

Once your game-port driver has been added, a joystick icon appears in your *Control panel*. Use this to set up and calibrate your joystick:

1 Doubleclick the *Joystick* icon in the *Control panel*.

2 In the *Joystick configuration* section, choose the appropriate joystick type from the list.

3 After selecting your joystick configuration, click the *Calibration* button and carefully follow the onscreen instructions.

You should not be able to use the joystick under any Windows 95 game or other joystick-aware application.

Troubleshooting Joysticks and Game Ports

The unique advantage to troubleshooting this area of a PC is that there is surprisingly little to actually go wrong. In virtually all cases, problems reside in either the joystick, the game-port adapter, or the application software. This part of the chapter provides you with some handy troubleshooting issues and examines a suite of perplexing joystick problems.

You can use the CALJOY22.ZIP and JOY2.EXE programs on the companion CD to aid you with testing and calibrating joysticks.

JOYSTICK ELIMINATOR PLUG

From time to time, you might find yourself testing a game port, but have no joystick handy (or it might be too much of a hassle to "borrow" a joystick already connected to a working PC). You can construct a very simple circuit with two resistors (Fig. 19-5) that can "fool" the game port into thinking that a real joystick is attached. This "joystick eliminator" plug simply places the cursor in a far corner of the display.

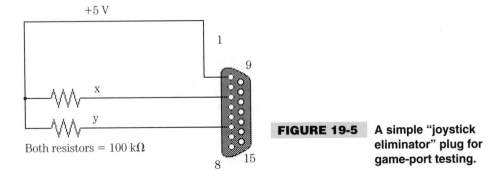

FIGURE 19-5   A simple "joystick eliminator" plug for game-port testing.

TABLE 19-4 PINOUT FOR A SOUND BOARD JOYSTICK CABLE ADAPTER	
DB-15 MALE (TO GAME PORT)	**DB-15 FEMALE (TO JOYSTICK "Y-ADAPTER")**
Wire pin . . .	to pin(s) . . .
1	1
2	2
3	3
4	4
5	5 and 12
6	6
7	7
8	8
9	9 and 15
10	10
11	11
12 unused	to pin 5
13	13
14	14
15 unused	to pin 9

ADAPTING IDC CONNECTORS

Some multi-I/O boards implement the game port as a 16-pin IDC (ribbon cable) connector—assuming that you'll use a DB-15 connector "plate" in another open card slot and simply connect the DB-15 "plate" to the multi-I/O card using a 16-pin ribbon cable. The pin assignments are all identical (pin 16 of the IDC connector is just left unused), but remember that the pin order is different between IDC and DB-style connectors. For example, the top row of a DB-15 connector runs pins 9 through 15, but the top row of an IDC cable uses pins 2, 4, 5, 6, 10, 12, 14, and 16.

SOUND CARDS AND Y-ADAPTER PROBLEMS

You will probably encounter difficulties when connecting commercial joystick Y-adapters to the game port on a sound board. This is because many sound-card manufacturers (such as Creative Labs) have replaced pins 12 (ground for joystick 2 switches 3 and 4) and 15 (N.C. or +5 V) with specialized MIDI interface pins. The problem doesn't surface using a single joystick because pins 12 and 15 are normally unused. But when a second joystick is added through a Y-adapter, the second joystick will probably fail to function. Table 19-4 illustrates a simple correction to enable a commercial Y-adapter. Essentially, you must disconnect pins 12 and 15 at the game-port (sound board) end, then cross-wire pin 12 to pin 5 (ground), and cross-wire pin 15 to pin 9 (+5V). If you want to make your own sound-board compatible Y-adapter, follow the pinout in Table 19-5.

TABLE 19-5 PINOUT FOR A SOUND BOARD COMPATIBLE JOYSTICK "Y-ADAPTER"

GAME PORT DB-15 MALE		JOYSTICK 1 DB-15 FEMALE	JOYSTICK 2 DB-15 FEMALE
Wire pin . . .		To pin . . .	And to pin . . .
1	XY1 (Joystick 1 +5-V supply)	1	1
2	Switch 1	2	
3	Potentiometer X1 signal	3	
4	Ground (for switch 1&2)	4	4
5	Ground (for switch 2)	5	5
6	Potentiometer Y1 signal	6	
7	Switch 2	7	
8	N.C. (or +5V)	8	
9	XY2 (Joystick 2 +5-V supply)		8
10	Switch 3		2
11	Potentiometer X2 signal		3
12	MIDI		unused
13	Potentiometer Y2 signal		6
14	Switch 4		7
15	MIDI		unused

Do not attempt to connect a MIDI device to the sound card while this modified Y-adapter is in place. Doing so can easily damage the MIDI device or the sound card's MIDI/game port.

Symptom 19-1. The joystick does not respond Be sure that the joystick is plugged into the game port correctly. When the game port has more than one connector, be sure that the joystick is plugged into the correct connector (joystick 1 or joystick 2). If the game port is running through a sound board, be sure that the sound board is configured to use the port as a game port instead of a MIDI port and see that any joystick Y-adapter is wired properly. Refer to the application and see that it is configured to run from the joystick (if mouse or keyboard control is selected, the joystick will not function). Now that many new joysticks are appearing with supplemental functions (i.e., hat switches, throttle controls, etc.), be sure that the application is written to take advantage of the particular joystick. If problems persist, be sure that the game port is set for the proper I/O address (most are fixed at 210h, but check the user documentation to be sure). Try a known-good joystick with the game port. If a known-good joystick works, the original joystick is defective and should be replaced. If another joystick is not the problem, try a different game-port board.

Symptom 19-2. Joystick performance is erratic or choppy Start by checking the joystick to be sure that it is connected properly. Try another joystick. When a new joystick works properly, the original joystick is probably damaged and should be replaced. If a new joystick fails to solve the problem, the game-port board might be too slow for the system. Remember that many game ports still use XT board types. An older board design might not be able to process joystick signals fast enough to provide adequate signaling to the system. Not only should you try another game-port adapter, but you should use a speed-adjusting game port.

Symptom 19-3. The joystick is sending incorrect information to the system—the joystick appears to be drifting First, check the application to be sure that the joystick is calibrated correctly. If you cannot calibrate the joystick, the application might not support the joystick properly—try another application. Be sure that there are no other active devices in the system (such as other game ports) using I/O port 201h. If this happens, data produced on those other boards will adversely affect the game port that you are using. If all unused game ports are disabled, check the active game port. Poor-quality game ports can drift. Try a newer, low-drift or speed-adjusting game-port board.

Symptom 19-4. The basic X/Y, two-button features of the joystick work, but the hat switch, throttle controls, and supplemental buttons do not seem to respond In virtually all cases, the joystick is configured wrong. Check the application first—many new applications provide several different joystick options, and even allow you to define the particular use of each feature from within the application itself.

Check the joystick definition files next. Your joystick probably requires a supplemental definition file (i.e., an .FCS file) to use all of the joystick's particular features. Finally, check the game-port type. You might need a "dual-port" game-port adapter, rather than an inexpensive "single-port" game-port adapter. Some enhanced joysticks use both joystick positions (i.e., the XY axis and fire buttons make up one joystick, and the throttle and other buttons take up the other position). You might need to install a dual-port game-port card.

Symptom 19-5. A "Joystick not connected" error appears under Windows 95 Windows 95 does not recognize the game-port hardware. Check the game-port driver first. Use the *Device manager* under Windows 95 to examine the resources assigned to the game-port driver. Typically, the resource range should be set to 201h through 201h (only one address location). If the game-port entry has a yellow icon next to it, there is a hardware conflict in the system, and other hardware is also trying to use the same I/O location.

Next, check the game-port hardware for proper configuration. The game-port card should be installed properly into its bus slot. Be sure that the game port is enabled (this is typical of game ports integrated onto sound cards or multi-I/O cards). If a sound card enables you to switch a 15-pin port between MIDI and joystick, see that the jumper is set to the "joystick" position. Be sure that the joystick cable is not cut or damaged anywhere, and see that it is attached securely to the game port. Finally, test a known-good joystick on the system. If a new joystick works as expected, the original joystick is probably suffering from internal wiring damage.

Symptom 19-6. The joystick drifts frequently and requires recalibration This type of symptom is usually the result of problems with the game-port adapter. Try a different game-port adapter and see if the problem persists. If problems disappear, you simply need a better-quality or speed-adjusting game port. Otherwise, test a known-good joystick on the system. If a new joystick works as expected, the original joystick is probably suffering from internal wiring damage and should be replaced.

Symptom 19-7. The joystick handle has lost tension—it no longer "snaps" back to the center This problem might be accompanied by a rattling sound within the joystick. In most cases, a spring has popped out of place inside the joystick. Check the joystick for internal damage. Open the joystick and see if any springs or clips have slipped out of place. Replace any springs or clips (if possible). Some joysticks also use mechanical latches that can enable or disable the "spring action" of the X and Y axis. Check to see that any such latches are enabled. If you cannot locate or correct the problem, simply replace the joystick outright.

Symptom 19-8. The joystick responds, but refuses to accept a calibration In virtually all cases, the problem is with your game-port adapter. Check the hardware setup—be sure that there are no other devices in the system using the I/O address assigned to your game port (i.e., 201h). If more than one adapter in your system has game-port capability, see that only one game port is enabled. Replace the game port, or enable a different game port in the system. If drift issues continue with different applications, you might need to replace the game-port adapter with a "low drift" or speed-adjusting model.

Symptom 19-9. The hat switch and buttons on a joystick work only intermittently (if at all) This problem also applies to stand-alone pedals. In most cases, erratic behavior of a joystick's "enhanced features" is a symptom of game-port speed problems. Check the joystick first. Try a known-good joystick. If the problems disappear, the original joystick might in fact be defective. If the problems persist, you have a game-port problem. Be sure that there are no other devices in the system using the I/O address assigned to your game port (i.e., 201h). If more than one adapter in your system has game-port capability, see that only one game port is enabled. If drift issues continue with different applications, you might need to replace the game-port adapter with a "low drift" or speed-adjusting model.

Symptom 19-10. When downloading FCS (or calibration) files to a joystick, the line saying: "Put switch into calibrate" doesn't change when the download switch is moved" This is a typical problem with advanced joysticks. In most cases, the joystick needs to be "cleared." Clear the joystick—rock the download switch back to "analog," then to "calibrate"—this should clear the joystick for a new calibration download. Try downloading the FCS file again. If problems persist, the actual switch might be defective. Try a known-good joystick instead.

Symptom 19-11. To download a calibration file, you need to rock the red switch back and forth a number of times (or hit the <Enter> key a number of times) to get it to 100% This is virtually always the result of a keyboard-controller (keyboard BIOS) compatibility problem. Upgrade the keyboard controller (keyboard BIOS). Some advanced joystick products do not interact well with the host computer's keyboard controller. For example, Thrustmaster's Mark II experiences known microcode problems with a few of keyboard controller chips on the market. These include AMI versions (D, B, 8, 0), Acer, and Phoenix. You might need to replace the keyboard controller with a later version.

Symptom 19-12.   A joystick cannot be used with a PC using a sound card with an ESS or OPTi chipset The joystick might stop responding while using an application or report a "not connected" status in the game controller's area of the *Control panel*. This is a known problem with the ESS and OPTi sound chipsets. You'll need to set *Single-mode DMA* to use the joystick:

1 *Start*, select *Settings*, then click *Control panel*.
2 Doubleclick *Multimedia*.
3 On the *Advanced* tab, doubleclick the *Audio devices* entry to expand it.
4 Click the *Audio for...* entry that corresponds to your particular sound card, the click *Properties*.
5 Click *Settings*.
6 Click the *Use single-mode DMA* check box to select it.
7 Click *OK* until you return to Windows, then restart the PC.

Symptom 19-13.   The joystick port is not removed when the sound card is removed The entry for your game port will still be visible in the Windows 95 *Device manager*. This is not really a problem—Windows 95 does not recognize the game port as being part of the sound card, so removing the sound card doesn't automatically disable the game port. Also, the virtual joystick device driver (VJOYD.VXD) cannot detect whether the game port or joystick is installed so that the driver is always active. You'll need to manually remove the game port in *Device manager*:

1 Use the right mouse button to click *My computer*, then click *Properties* on the menu.
2 Click the *Device manager* tab.
3 Doubleclick the *Sound, video, and game controllers* entry to expand it.
4 Click the joystick port, then click *Remove*.
5 Return to Windows 95 and restart the system.

Symptom 19-14.   The "jumperless" joystick port cannot be disabled This issue frequently crops up with newer sound cards, such as the Ensoniq VIVO, and jumperless boards are controlled exclusively through drivers. The VIVO also uses drivers to disable certain functions, such as the joystick port. Use the following steps to disable the VIVO's joystick port (the specific command lines for your own sound board might be different, but the idea is very similar):

1 Leave Windows 95 and enter the MS-DOS mode.
2 Edit the SNDSCAPE.INI file in the \Windows directory. Change the line JSEnable =true to JSEnable=false (check your particular sound board's documentation for the correct command line).
3 Save the file and reboot the system. The joystick will now be disabled.

Further Study

That's all for Chapter 19. Be sure to review the glossary and chapter questions on the accompanying CD. If you have access to the Internet, take a look at some of these joystick and game-port resources:

Advanced Gravis: **http://www.gravis.com**

Logitech: **http://www.logitech.com**

Thrustmaster: **http://www.thrustmaster.com**

CH Products: **http://www.chproducts.com**

KEYBOARDS

CONTENTS AT A GLANCE

Keyboard Construction
  Key codes
  Keyboard interfaces

Dvorak Keyboards
  Converting to Dvorak keyboards

Keyboard Cleaning and Maintenance
  Correcting problem keyboards
  Vacuum cleaners and keyboards

Replacing the <space bar>
Preventing the problems
Dealing with large objects
Dealing with spills
Disabling a keyboard

Keyboard Troubleshooting

Further Study

Keyboards (Fig. 20-1) are the classic input device. By manipulating a matrix of individual electrical switches, commands, and instructions can be entered into the computer one character at a time. If you've used computers or typewriters to any extent, you already have an excellent grasp of keyboard handling. However, keyboards are not without their share of drawbacks and limitations. Although today's keyboard switches are not mechanically complex, there are a number of important moving parts. When you multiply this number of moving parts times the 80 to 100+ keys on a typical keyboard, you are faced with a substantial number of moving parts. A jam or failure in any one of these many mechanical parts results in a keyboard problem. Most keyboard failures are hardly

FIGURE 20-1   A Cherry G83-3000 keyboard. Cherry Electrical Products

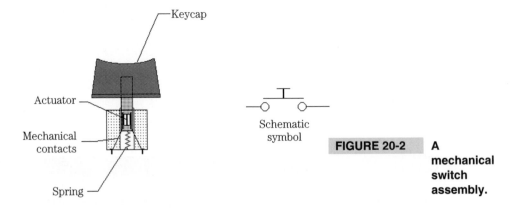

FIGURE 20-2   A mechanical switch assembly.

catastrophic, but they can certainly be inconvenient. This chapter gives you the information needed to understand and repair computer keyboards.

Keyboard Construction

To understand a keyboard, you must first understand the kinds of switches that are used. In general, you should be concerned with two types of switches: mechanical switches and membrane switches. Both switches are used extensively through out the computer industry, but any single keyboard will use only one type of switch.

A mechanical key switch is shown in Fig. 20-2. Two tempered bronze contacts are separated by a plastic actuator bar. The bar is pushed up by a spring in the switch base. When the key cap is pressed, the actuator bar slides down. This action compresses the spring and allows the gold-plated contacts to touch. Because gold is a soft metal and an excellent conductor, a good, low-resistance electrical contact is developed. When the key cap is released, the compressed spring expands and drives the plastic actuator bar between the contacts once again. The entire stroke of travel on a mechanical switch is little more than 3.56 mm (0.140"), but an electrical contact (a *make* condition) can be established in as little as 1.78 mm (0.070"). Mechanical switches are typically quite rugged—many are rated for 100 million cycles or more.

A diagram of a membrane key switch is illustrated in Fig. 20-3. A plastic actuator rests on top of a soft rubber boot. The inside of the rubber boot is coated with a conductive silver-carbon compound. Beneath the rubber boot are two open PC board contacts. When the key cap is pressed, the plastic actuator collapses the rubber boot. Collapse forces the conductive material across both PC board contacts to complete the switch. When the key cap is released, the compressed rubber boot breaks its contact on the PC board returns to its original shape. The full travel stroke of a membrane key switch is about 3.56 mm (0.140")—roughly the same as a mechanical switch. An electrical contact is established in about 2.29 mm (0.090"). Membrane switches are not quite as durable as mechanical switches. Most switches are rated for 20 million cycles or less.

Mechanical and membrane switches offer a number of unique advantages and disadvantages. Mechanical switches tend to be highly reliable and provide a good tactile feedback when typing (that "clicking" noise we usually associate with offices). On the other hand, mechanical keyboards are more expensive to manufacture, and can be extremely sensitive to spills and foreign matter. Membrane switches are not quite as reliable, and tend to offer a softer, "mushier" feel when typing (some people prefer this feel). Because of the membrane cover used in the keyboard, membrane switches seem to withstand spills and foreign matter better than mechanical switches.

The next step in understanding a keyboard is to learn about the key matrix. Keys are not interpreted individually—that is, each switch is not wired directly to the motherboard. Instead, keys are arranged in a matrix of rows and columns (Fig. 20-4). When a key is pressed, a unique row (top to bottom) and column (left to right) signal is generated to represent the corresponding key. The great advantage of a matrix approach is that a huge array of keys can be identified using only a few row and column signals. Wiring from the keyboard is vastly simplified. An 84-key keyboard can be identified using only 12 column signals and 8 row signals.

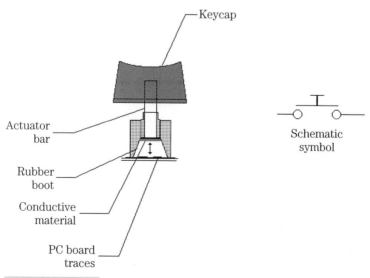

FIGURE 20-3   **A membrane switch assembly.**

Column signals

Row signals

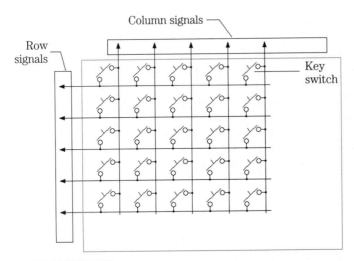

Key switch

FIGURE 20-4   Simplified diagram of a keyboard matrix.

KEY CODES

When a key is pressed, the row and column signals that are generated are interpreted by a keyboard-interface IC (typically located on the keyboard assembly itself). The keyboard interface converts the row and column signals into a single-byte code (called a *key code* or *scan code*). Two unique scan codes are produced during a key-stroke cycle. When the key is pressed, a *make* code byte is sent along to the system. When the key is released, a *break* code byte is generated. Both codes are transmitted to the host computer in a serial fashion. For example, a make code of 1Eh is sent when the "A" key is pressed. A 9Eh code is sent when the "A" key is subsequently released. By using two individual codes, the computer can determine when a key is held down, or when keys are held in combinations. Just about every key on a keyboard is typematic—that is, it will repeat automatically if it is held down for more than 500 ms or so. Typematic settings can usually be adjusted in the CMOS advanced settings for your system.

Most computers today are prepared for multinational operation. To accommodate the special characters and punctuation used in various different countries, keyboard controllers can be configured to provide scan codes for different languages. Table 20-1 illustrates the make and break codes for conventional keyboards used in the domestic United States.

KEYBOARD INTERFACES

Once a key is pressed and the keyboard interface converts the key-matrix signals into a suitable scan code, that code must be transmitted to the *KeyBoard Controller (KBC)* on the host computer motherboard. Once key data reaches the keyboard controller, it is converted to parallel data by the KBC, which in turn generates an interrupt that forces the system to handle the key. The actual transfer of scan codes between the keyboard and PC is accomplished serially using one of the interfaces shown in Figure 20-5.

Notice that three important signals are really in a keyboard interface: the keyboard clock (KBCLOCK), the keyboard data (KBDATA), and the signal ground. Unlike most serial communication, which is asynchronous, the transfer of data from keyboard to controller is

TABLE 20-1 STANDARD SCAN CODES FOR US KEYBOARDS

KEY	MAKE CODE	BREAK CODE	KEY	MAKECODE	BREAK CODE
A	1E	9E	B	30	B0
C	2E	AE	D	20	A0
E	12	92	F	21	A1
G	22	A2	H	23	A3
I	17	97	J	24	A4
K	25	A5	L	26	A6
M	32	B2	N	31	B1
O	18	98	P	19	99
Q	10	90	R	13	93
S	1F	9F	T	14	94
U	16	96	V	2F	AF
W	11	91	X	2D	AD
Y	15	95	Z	2C	AC
0 /)	0B	8B	1 / !	02	82
2 / @	03	83	3 / #	04	84
4 / $	05	85	5 / %	06	86
6 / ^	07	87	7 / &	08	88
8 / *	09	89	9 / (	0A	8A
. / >	29	A9	– / _	0C	8C
= / +	0D	8D	[	1A	9A
]	1B	9B	; / :	27	A7
' / "	28	A8	, / <	33	B3
/ / ?	35	B5	L Sh	2A	AA
L Ctrl	1D	9D	L Alt	38	B8
R Sh	36	B6	R Alt	E0 38	E0 B8
R Ctrl	E0 1D	E0 9D	Caps	3A	BA
BK SP	0E	8E	Tab	0F	8F
Space	39	B9	Enter	1C	9C
ESC	01	81	F1	3B	BB
F2	3C	BC	F3	3D	BD
F4	3E	BE	F5	3F	BF
F6	40	C0	F7	41	C1
F8	42	C2	F9	43	C3
F10	44	C4	F11	57	D7
F12	58	D8	Up Ar	E0 48	E0 C8
Dn Ar	E0 50	E0 D0	Lt Ar	E0 4B	E0 CB
Rt Ar	E0 4D	E0 CD	Ins	E0 52	E0 D2
Home	E0 47	E0 C7	Pg Up	E0 49	E0 C9
Del	E0 53	E0 D3	End	E0 4F	E0 CF
Pg Dn	E0 51	E0 D1	ScrLk	46	C6

* All MAKE and BREAK codes are given in hexidecimal (*hex) values.
* Alphabetic characters represent both upper and lower case.

IBM PC/XT/AT configuration

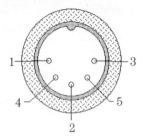

6 pin mini-DIN connector

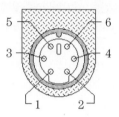

1	KBCLOCK		1	KBDATA
2	KBDATA		2	nc
3	nc		3	Ground
4	Ground		4	+5 Vdc (or +3.0 or +3.3 Vdc)
5	+5 Vdc (or +3.0 or +3.3 Vdc)		5	KBCLOCK
			6	nc

FIGURE 20-5   **Keyboard interface connectors.**

accomplished synchronously—data bits are returned in sync with the clock signals. As you might expect, the signal ground provides a common reference for the keyboard and system. The keyboard is powered by +5 Vdc, which is also provided through the keyboard interface. It is also important that you notice that most XT-style systems are designed with a unidirectional data path (from keyboard to system). AT-style keyboard interfaces are bi-directional. This feature allows AT keyboards to be controlled and programmed from the PC.

Dvorak Keyboards

Most technicians are familiar with QWERTY-style keyboards—this standard format for typewriters was adopted in the late 1800s. A popular alternative to the QWERTY keyboard is the *Dvorak keyboard*. Mechanically and electronically, the Dvorak keyboard is identical to conventional keyboards. Only the key order is different—all of the vowels are located on the left side of your home row (the middle row of letters) in the pattern: AOEUIDHTNS.

Dvorak keyboards claim several advantages over QWERTY models. Most letters typed (~70%) are on the home row, so finger (and wrist strain) can be reduced. With less reach to deal with, typing can be accomplished faster, and with fewer errors. The vast majority of Dvorak words use both hands for typing, but thousands of words demand one-handed typing for QWERTY keyboards—this spreads out the strain on your hands more evenly.

CONVERTING TO DVORAK KEYBOARDS

There are two classic methods of implementing Dvorak keyboards: *dedicated keyboards* and *keyboard conversions*. Dedicated keyboards are just as the name implies—you buy a ready-made Dvorak keyboard and plug it in. Although the keys are located in different places, the key codes are the same, so your PC doesn't know the difference. As a result, you can interchange QWERTY and Dvorak keyboards at will without any changes to the

PC or operating system. You can also convert your existing QWERTY keyboard to Dvorak under Windows 95:

- Open the *Control panel* and doubleclick on the *Keyboard* icon.
- Select the *Language* page and doubleclick on the *English (United States)* entry (or your own default entry for countries outside of the U.S.).
- Select *United States (Dvorak)* from the list that appears.
- Save your changes—you might need to install a diskette with the proper drivers.
- It might be necessary to reboot the system.

Under DOS, you will need a DOS TSR to handle the conversion. For MS-DOS 5.0 through 6.22, you can find the Dvorak TSR on the *MS-DOS Supplemental Disk*. You can obtain the driver files from Microsoft's FTP or Web site (**http://www.microsoft.com**), or from the Microsoft forum on CompuServe (GO MSDOS). Download the file DOS62S.EXE.

> If you do download and extract these supplemental DOS files, be very sure to extract them to a new or temporary directory. Under no circumstances should you allow DOS files to overwrite files in the DOS directory or anywhere in your Windows directories.

Once the software conversion is made, you will need to exchange the keys on your QWERTY keyboard. Figure 20-6 illustrates the comparison between a QWERTY key layout and a Dvorak key layout. You can use a key pulling tool to physically exchange the key caps, or use key stickers or overlays from Hooleon Corporation at (602)-634-7515 or Keytime at (206)-522-8973. You can also obtain more detailed information directly from Dvorak International at (802)-287-2434.

Keyboard Cleaning and Maintenance

Keyboards are perhaps the most abused part of any computer, yet they are often ignored until serious problems develop. With some regular cleaning and maintenance, however, a

```
QWERTY

- - - - - - - - - - -

Q   W   E   R   T   Y   U   I   O   P

A   S   D   F   G   H   J   K   L   ;   '

Z   X   C   V   B   N   M   ,   .   /

Dvoark

- - - - - - - - -

"   ,   .   P   Y   F   G   C   R   L   /

A   O   E   U   I   D   H   T   N   S   -

;   Q   J   K   X   B   M   W   V   Z
```

FIGURE 20-6   **QWERTY vs. Dvorak keyboards.**

keyboard can easily last for the lifetime of a computer. This part of the chapter shows you some practical techniques for keyboard service.

CORRECTING PROBLEM KEYBOARDS

Virtually all computer keyboards are open to the air. Over time, everyday dust, pet hair, air vapor, cigar/cigarette smoke, and debris from hands and ordinary use will settle into the keyboard. Eventually, accumulations of this foreign matter will cause keys to stick, or will prevent keys from making proper contact (i.e., a key does not work every time it is pressed). In either case, keyboard problems will develop. Fortunately, correcting a finicky keyboard is a relatively straightforward process. Start by removing the key caps of the offending keys. Be sure to note where each key is placed before starting your disassembly—especially if the keyboard is a DVORAK-type or unusual ergonomic design. To remove a key cap, bend an ordinary paper clip into the shape of a narrow "U", and bend-in small tabs at the tip of the "U" shape. Slip the small tabs under the key cap and pull up gently. Do not struggle with the key cap. If a cap will not come off, remove one or more adjacent caps. If there is a substantial accumulation of foreign matter in the keyboard, you should consider removing all of the key caps for a thorough cleaning, but this requires more time.

> Avoid removing the <Space Bar> unless it is absolutely necessary because the space bar is often much more difficult to replace than ordinary keys.

Flip the keyboard upside down and rap gently on the case. This will loosen and dislodge any larger, heavier foreign matter, and allow it to fall out of the keyboard. A soft-bristled brush will help loosen the debris. Return the keyboard to an upright position. Use a can of compressed air (available from almost any electronics or photography store) to blow out the remainder of foreign matter. Because this tends to blow dust and debris in all directions, you might wish to use the compressed air outside or in an area away from your workbench. A medium- or firm-bristled brush will help loosen any stubborn debris.

Now that the keyboard is cleaned out, squirt a small amount of good-quality electronics-grade contact cleaner (also available from almost any electronics store) into each key contact, and work the key to distribute the cleaner evenly. Allow a few minutes for the contact cleaner to dry completely and test the keyboard again before reinstalling the key caps. If the problems persist, the keyboard might be damaged or the individual key(s) might simply be worn out beyond recovery. In such an event, replace the keyboard outright.

VACUUM CLEANERS AND KEYBOARDS

There is an ongoing debate as to the safety of vacuum cleaners with computer equipment. The problem is static discharge. Many vacuum cleaners—especially small, inexpensive models—use cheap plastic and synthetic fabrics in their construction. When a fast air flow passes over those materials, a static charge is developed (just like combing your hair with a plastic comb). If the charged vacuum touches the keyboard, a static discharge might have enough potential to damage the keyboard-controller IC, or even travel back into the motherboard for more serious damage.

FIGURE 20-7   **A Curtis anti-static keyboard mat.** Curtis, a division of Rolodex, Secaucus, NJ 07094

If you do choose to use a vacuum for keyboard cleaning, take these two steps to prevent damage. First, be sure that the computer is powered down and disconnect the keyboard from the computer before starting service. If a static discharge does occur, the most that would be damaged is the keyboard itself. Second, use a vacuum cleaner that is made for electronics work and certified as "static-safe." Third, try working on an anti-static mat (such as the mat in Fig. 20-7), which is properly grounded. This will tend to "bleed-off" static charges before they can enter the keyboard or PC.

REPLACING THE <SPACE BAR>

Of all the keys on the keyboard, replacing the <Space Bar> is probably the most difficult. The <Space Bar> is kept even by a metal wire that is inserted into slots on each leg of the plastic bar key. However, you have to get the wire into the slots without pressing the wire. If you push the wire down, you compress the wire and installation becomes impossible. As a general rule, do not remove the <Space Bar> unless absolutely necessary. If you must remove the <Space Bar>, remove several surrounding key caps also. This will let you get some tools under the <Space Bar> wire later on. Once the <Space Bar> is re-inserted, you can easily replace any of the other key caps.

PREVENTING THE PROBLEMS

Keyboard problems do not happen suddenly (unless the keyboard is dropped or physically abused). The accumulation of dust and debris is a slow process that can take months (sometimes years) to produce serious, repetitive keyboard problems. By following a regimen of regular cleaning, you can stop problems before they manifest themselves in your keyboard. In normal office environments, keyboards should be cleaned once every four months. Keyboards in home environments should be cleaned every two months. Keyboards in harsh or industrial environments should be cleaned even more frequently.

Turn your keyboard upside-down and use a soft-bristled brush to clean between the keys. This prevents debris that might already be on the keys from entering the keyboard. Next, run the long, thin nozzle of your compressed air can between the key spaces to blow out any accumulations of dust. Because compressed air will tend to blow dust in all directions, you might consider "blowing down" the keyboard outside, or in an area away from your workbench. Instead of compressed air, you might use a "static-safe" vacuum cleaner to remove dust and debris.

DEALING WITH LARGE OBJECTS

Staples and paper clips pose a clear and present danger to keyboards. Although the odds of a staple or paper clip finding its way into a keyboard are generally slight, foreign objects can jam the key or short it out. If the keyboard is moved, the object can wind up in the keyboard's circuitry where serious damage can occur. When a foreign object falls into the keyboard, do not move the keyboard. Power down the PC, then locate the object and find the nearest key. Use a paper clip bent in a "U" shape with the ends of the "U" angled inward to remove the nearest key cap. Use a pair of non-conductive tweezers or needle-nose pliers to remove the object. Replace the key cap.

DEALING WITH SPILLS

Accidental spills are probably the most serious and dangerous keyboard problem. Coffee, soda pop, and even tap water is highly conductive (even corrosive). Your keyboard will almost certainly short circuit. Immediately shut down your computer (you might be able to exit your application using a mouse) and disconnect the keyboard. The popular tactic is to simply let the liquid dry. The problem with this tactic is that most liquids contain minerals and materials that are corrosive to metals—your keyboard will never be the same unless the offending liquid is removed before it dries. Also, liquids tend to turn any dust and smoke film into a sticky glue that will just jam the keys when dry (not even considering the sticky sugar in most soda pop).

Disassemble the keyboard's main housings and remove the keyboard printed-circuit assembly. As quickly as you can after the incident, rinse the assembly thoroughly in clean, room-temperature, de-mineralized water (available from any pharmacy for contact lens maintenance). You can clean the plastic housings separately. Do not use tap water. Let the assembly drip dry in air. Do not attempt to accelerate the drying process with a hair dryer or other such heat source. The de-mineralized water should dry clean without mineral deposits or any sticky, conductive residue. Once the assembly is dry, you might wish to squirt a small amount of good-quality, electronics-grade contact cleaner into each key switch to ensure that no residue is on the contacts. Assuming that the keyboard's circuitry was not damaged by the initial spill, you should be able to reassemble the keyboard and continue using it without problems. If the keyboard behaves erratically (or not at all), replace the keyboard outright.

DISABLING A KEYBOARD

Keyboards are an essential peripheral for all computers, except servers. In many cases, network administrators would prefer to restrict direct access to the server, and prevent potential tampering. Traditional PCs did not allow you disable the keyboard, but newer systems do offer a CMOS setup entry that can enable or disable the keyboard. When the keyboard is disabled through CMOS, the PC will boot without suffering "Keyboard not found" errors. Before starting service on a server, it might be necessary to reattach and re-enable the keyboard.

Keyboard Troubleshooting

Although their appearance might seem daunting at first glance, keyboard systems are not terribly difficult to troubleshoot. This ease is primarily because of the keyboard's modularity—if all else fails, it's a simple matter to replace a keyboard outright. The keyboard's great weakness, however, is its vulnerability to the elements. Spills, dust, and any other foreign matter that finds its way between the key caps can easily ruin a keyboard. The keyboard's PC board is also a likely candidate to be damaged by impacts or other physical abuse. The following procedures address many of the most troublesome keyboard problems.

You can use the SCODE22.ZIP utility on the Companion CD to examine the scan codes for each key. You can use this utility to determine which keys (if any) are not working.

Symptom 20-1.   During initialization, an error message indicates that no keyboard is connected   Check your keyboard cable and see that it is inserted properly and completely into the PC connector. Remember that you will have to reboot your system to clear this error message. Try another compatible keyboard. If a new keyboard assembly works properly, there is probably a wiring fault in the original keyboard. Given the very low price of new keyboards, it is usually most economical to simply replace a defective keyboard. If you're working on a file or network server, see that the CMOS setup has enabled the keyboard.

If a known-good keyboard fails to function, try the original keyboard on a known-good PC to verify that the keyboard itself is indeed operational. If so, your trouble now lies in the PC. Check the wiring between the PC keyboard connector and the motherboard. Check the connector pins to be sure that none of them have been bent or pushed in (resulting in a bad connection). You might also want to check the soldering connections where the keyboard connector attaches to the motherboard. Repeated removals and insertions of the keyboard might have fatigued the solder joints. Reheat any defective solder joints. If the keyboard connector is intact, it is likely that the keyboard controller IC (KBC) has failed. Try booting the PC with a POST board installed (as covered in Chapter 15). A KBC failure will usually be indicated by the system stopping on the appropriate POST code. You can attempt to replace the KBC or replace the motherboard outright. If a POST board indicates a fault other than a KBC (such as the programmable interrupt controller, which manages the KBC's interrupt), you can attempt to replace that component, or simply exchange the motherboard anyway.

Symptom 20-2.   During initialization, an error message indicates that the keyboard lock is on   In many cases, the detection of a locked keyboard will halt system initialization. Be sure that the keyboard lock switch is set completely to the "unlocked" position. If the switch is unlocked, but the system detects it as locked. The switch might be defective. Turn off and unplug the system, then use a multimeter to measure continuity across the lock switch (you might need to disconnect the lock switch cable from the motherboard. In one position, the switch should measure as an open circuit. In the opposing position, the switch should measure as a short circuit. If this is not the case, the lock switch is probably bad and should be replaced. If the switch measures properly, there is probably a logic fault on the motherboard (perhaps the keyboard controller). Your best course is to try another motherboard.

Symptom 20-3.   The keyboard is completely dead—no keys appear to function at all   All other computer operations are normal. In this symptom, it is assumed that your computer initializes and boots to its DOS prompt or other operating system as expected, but the keyboard does not respond when touched. Keyboard-status LEDs might not be working properly. Your first step in such a situation is to try a known-good keyboard in the system. Notice that you should reboot the system when a keyboard is replaced. If a known-good keyboard works, the fault is probably on the keyboard-interface IC. You can attempt to replace this IC if you wish, but it is often most economical to simply replace the keyboard outright.

If another keyboard fails to correct the problem, use a multimeter and check the +5-V supply at the keyboard connector (refer to Fig. 20-5). If the +5-V signal is missing, the female connector might be broken. Check the connector's soldering junctions on the motherboard. Reheat any connectors that appear fatigued or intermittent. Many motherboards also use a "pico-fuse" to protect the +5-V supply feeding the keyboard connector. If your +5 V is lost, locate and check the keyboard-connector fuse. If problems continue, replace the motherboard.

Symptom 20-4.   The keyboard is acting erratically   One or more keys appear to work intermittently, or it is inoperative. The computer operates normally and most keys work just fine, but one or more keys do not respond when pressed. Extra force or repeated strikes might be needed to operate the key. This type of problem can usually range from a minor nuisance to a major headache. Chances are that your key contacts are dirty. Sooner or later, dust and debris works into all key switches. Electrical contacts eventually become coated and fail to make contact reliably. This symptom is typical of older keyboards, or keyboards that have been in service for prolonged periods of time. In many cases, you need only vacuum the keyboard and clean the suspect contacts with a good-quality electronic contact cleaner.

Begin by disconnecting the keyboard. Use a static-safe, fine-tipped vacuum to remove any accumulations of dust or debris that might have accumulated on the keyboard PC board. You might wish to vacuum your keyboard regularly as preventive maintenance. Once the keyboard is clean, gently remove the plastic key cap from the offending key(s). The use of a keycap-removal tool is highly recommended, but you might also use a modified set of blunt-ended tweezers with their flat ends (just the tips) bent inward. Grasp the key cap and pull up evenly. You can expect the cap to slide off with little resistance. Do not rip the key cap off—you stand a good chance of marring the cap and causing permanent key switch damage.

Use a can of good-quality electronics-grade contact cleaner and spray a little bit of cleaner into the switch assembly. When spraying, attach the long, narrow tube to the spray nozzle—this directs cleaner into the switch. Work the switch in and out to distribute the cleaner. Repeat this maintenance once or twice to clean the switch thoroughly. Allow residual cleaner to dry thoroughly before re-testing the keyboard. Never use harsh cleaners or solvents. Industrial-strength chemicals can easily ruin plastic components and housings. Reapply power and retest the system. If the suspect key(s) respond normally again, install the removed key caps and return the system to service. As a preventive measure, you might wish to go through the process of cleaning every key.

Membrane keys must be cleaned somewhat differently from mechanical keys. It is necessary for you to remove the rubber or plastic boot to clean the PC board contacts. Depending on the design of your particular membrane switch, this might not be an easy task. If you are able to see the contact boot, use a pick or tweezers to gently lift the boot. Spray a bit of cleaner under the boot, then work the key to distribute the cleaner. If the boot is confined within the individual key, you might have to remove the suspect key before applying cleaner.

If cleaning does not work, your next step should be to disassemble the keyboard and replace the defective key switch(es). Observe the board closely for cracks or fractures. Many key-switch designs still utilize through-hole technology, but you should exercise extreme care when desoldering and resoldering. Extra care helps prevent accidental damage to the PC keyboard. You also have the more economical option of replacing the entire keyboard assembly outright.

Symptom 20-5. The keyboard is acting erratically One or more keys might be stuck or repeating. Suspect a shorted or jammed key. Short circuits can be caused by conductive foreign objects (e.g., staples, paper clips) falling into the keyboard and landing across PC board contacts. Remove all power and disassemble the keyboard housing assembly. Once the keyboard is exposed, shake out the foreign object or remove it with a pair of long needle-nose pliers or sharp tweezers.

Accumulations of dirt or debris can work into the key actuator shaft and restrict its movement. Apply good-quality electronics-grade cleaners to the key, and work the key in and out to distribute cleaner evenly. If the key returns to normal, you can re-assemble the computer and return it to service. Keys that remain jammed should be replaced. If you can not clear the jammed key, simply replace the entire keyboard assembly outright. If you elect to replace the keyboard assembly, retain the old assembly for parts—key caps, good switches, and cable assemblies can be scavenged for use in future repairs.

Symptom 20-6. A "KBC Error" (or similar) is displayed during system startup When your computer initializes (either from a warm or cold start) it executes a comprehensive self-test routine that checks the key ICs in the system (e.g., the CPU, memory, drive controllers, and so on). As part of this power-on self-test (POST) routine, the computer looks for the KBCLK signal, along with a series of test scan codes generated by the KB controller IC—you can see the keyboard LEDs flash as the controller sequences through its codes. If either the keyboard clock or keyboard data signals are missing, the POST knows that either the keyboard is disconnected or that the keyboard controller has failed. If you are using a POST board, it will probably be displaying a code corresponding to a KBC error. Unless you have the tools and inclination to replace a KBC controller IC, your best course is simply to replace the motherboard outright.

Symptom 20-7. Macros cannot be cleared from a programmable keyboard In most cases, you need to use the right key combination to clear the macros. If the keyboard has a <Remap> key, press that first (a *Program* light or other LED will start blinking). Press the <Ctrl> key twice to map the key to itself. Press <Alt> twice to map the key to itself. Press the <Suspend Macro> key (the *Program* light should stop blinking). Press the <Ctrl> and <Alt> keys while pressing <Suspend Macro>—this will clear all of the keyboard's programming. The key sequence used for your keyboard might be different, so be sure to check the procedure for your own keyboard. If problems persist, replace the keyboard.

Symptom 20-8. The keyboard keys are not functioning as expected Pressing a key causes unexpected results or a series of operations that would ordinarily not be attributed to that key. Chances are that the keyboard has been programmed with macros, and you'll need to clear those macros to restore normal keyboard operation. If the keyboard has a <Remap> key, press that first (a *Program* light or other LED will start blinking). Press the <Ctrl> key twice to map the key to itself. Press <Alt> twice to map the key to itself. Press the <Suspend Macro> key (the *Program* light should stop blinking). Press the <Ctrl> and <Alt> keys while pressing <Suspend Macro>—this will clear all of the keyboard's programming. The key sequence used for your keyboard might be different, so be sure to check the procedure for your own keyboard. If problems persist, replace the keyboard.

Symptom 20-9.   Some keys on a programmable keyboard will not remap to their default state   This can happen with some Gateway 2000 (AnyKey) keyboards—as well as other programmable keyboards—and you might have to "force clear" the keyboard at boot time. Power down the system. While holding down the <Suspend Macro> key, turn the system power back on. Continue booting with the <Suspend Macro> key pressed until the *Program* light (or similar LED) quits flashing. This light will stay lit until you press and release it.

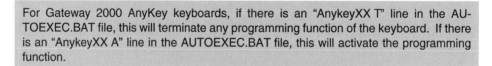

For Gateway 2000 AnyKey keyboards, if there is an "AnykeyXX T" line in the AUTOEXEC.BAT file, this will terminate any programming function of the keyboard. If there is an "AnykeyXX A" line in the AUTOEXEC.BAT file, this will activate the programming function.

Symptom 20-10.   A wireless keyboard types random characters   You'll need to reset both ends of the wireless system. First, take a look at the DIP switch settings that control the RF channel for the wireless transmitter and receiver (usually under the battery cover at the keyboard). Be sure that the transmitter and receiver are both set for the same channel. Find the "Reset" button on both the transmitter and receiver. Press the RF receiver reset button first, then press the RF transmitter button immediately after (usually within 15 seconds of one another). If the problem persists, reboot the system and try the reset process again.

Symptom 20-11.   The wireless keyboard beeps while typing   In virtually all cases, the batteries in the wireless keyboard are running low. Replace the batteries and try the wireless keyboard again—the beeping should stop.

Symptom 20-12.   Typed characters do not appear, but the cursor moves   This issue is a result of the color scheme being used. Some of the applications reported as suffering this problem are MSWORKS 4.0, CASHGRAF, MSBOB (address book and letter writer), and MSPUBLISHER. Check the color scheme selected by right clicking on the desktop. Click on *Properties*, then the *Appearance* tab. Set the scheme to *Windows standard*. Click on *OK* to return to the desktop. The text should now appear normal. This solution can generally be attempted with any application.

Symptom 20-13.   Some function keys and Windows keys might not work some PC configurations   For example, this is a known problem with Toshiba 8500 desktop systems and the Microsoft Natural Keyboard. In virtually all cases (including the

Toshiba 8500), the PC keyboard controller BIOS recognizes the keyboard during the *Power-On Self Test (POST)*, but it does not recognize some of the keys—including certain function keys and Windows-specific keys. You'll need to try a generic keyboard or upgrade the system's keyboard controller BIOS.

Symptom 20-14.   One or more Windows-specific keys don't work This is almost always a limitation of the keyboard-controller BIOS. For example, a Jetkey keyboard controller BIOS (v.3.0) will not recognize the right Windows key on a Microsoft Natural Keyboard. You'll need to try a generic keyboard or upgrade the system's keyboard-controller BIOS.

Symptom 20-15.   Remote-control programs don't work after installing keyboard drivers Many PC "remote-control" programs (e.g., PC Anywhere, ReachOut, and Carbon Copy) use keyboard and mouse drivers that are simply not compatible with the keyboard's specific drivers. For example, the remote-control programs listed will not work when IntelliType software is installed for the Microsoft Natural Keyboard. You'll need to disable the remote-control software, install patches for the remote-control software that will properly support the keyboard or replace the keyboard with a more generic model.

Symptom 20-16.   On a PS/2 system, you encounter keyboard errors, even though the keyboard driver loads successfully Often, you'll see an error like: "Keyboard error: keyboard not found," and you cannot access the keyboard. This type of problem is known to occur on PS/2 systems when the IBM ROM BIOS patch file (DASDDRVR.SYS) is loaded after the keyboard driver in CONFIG.SYS. Rearrange the CONFIG.SYS file to load the DASDDRVR.SYS file before the keyboard driver. Be sure that you are loading the patch driver (DASDDRVR.SYS) that is designed for your specific computer (for example, you cannot use the DASDDRVR.SYS file that ships with an IBM PS/2 Model 80 on a PS/2 Model 70 computer). This device driver can normally be found on the SETUP disk that you received with your IBM PS/2. Otherwise, you can obtain it from IBM (**http://www.ibm.com**).

Symptom 20-17.   Assigned key sounds do not work When you assign sounds to keystrokes (under the *Options* tab in the *Keyboard* tool in your *Control panel*), the sounds might play when you press the assigned keys. This problem is known to occur with some programmable keyboards when HiJaak Pro or HiJaak 95 Graphics Suite installed on your computer. These products might load a device driver named "Runner" that disables programmable keyboard sounds. You might be able to work around the problem by closing the "Runner" task:

■ Press <Ctrl>+<Alt>+<Del> to open the *Close program* dialog box.
■ If "Runner" is listed, click *Runner*, then click *End task*.

Symptom 20-18.   You cannot use Windows-specific keys to start task switching software other than TASKSW16.EXE You can start the desired task switching software using <Ctrl>+<Esc>, or by doubleclicking the desktop. Chances are that your Windows-specific key will not start any other task switching utility if

TASKSW16.EXE can be found on the path. You'll need to update the task switching program reference in SYSTEM.INI. Load SYSTEM.INI into any text editor, and modify the line that reads:

```
TASKMAN=TASKSW16.EXE
```

to read

```
TASKMAN=<task manager>
```

where <task manager> is the name of the executable file that you want to start when you press the Windows key. Rename the TASKSW16.EXE file (e.g., TASKSW16.OLD) or move it to a directory that is not in the path. Save and close the SYSTEM.INI file, then restart the computer.

Symptom 20-19. The NumLock feature might not activate when the NumLock key is pressed This can happen with some programmable keyboards when pen software is installed on the system. You should be able to correct the problem by disabling the pen device:

1 Click *Start*, select *Settings*, then click *Control panel*.
2 Doubleclick the *System* icon and select the *Device manager* tab.
3 Doubleclick the *Ports* entry to expand it.
4 Doubleclick the port to which the pen (or touch-screen) device is connected.
5 In the *Device usage* area on the *General* tab, click the *Original configuration (current)* check box to clear it (if you're using OSR2, click the *Disable in this hardware profile* check box to select it).
6 Click *OK*, then restart the system when prompted.

> To enable your pen device again, repeat these steps, but re-select (or re-clear) the check box in step 5.

Further Study

That's all for Chapter 20. Be sure to review the glossary and chapter questions on the accompanying CD. If you have access to the Internet, take a look at some of the keyboard resources listed:

NMB Technologies: **http://www.nmbtech.com/**

Keytronic: **http://www.keytronic.com**

Mitsumi: **http://www.mitsumi.com**

Microsoft: **http://www.microsoft.com/products/prodref/310_ov.htm (Natural Keyboard)**

Chicony: **http://www.chicony.com/**

LASER/LED

PRINTERS

CONTENTS AT A GLANCE

Understanding EP Operation
  Cleaning
  Charging
  Writing
  Developing
  Transfer
  Fusing

Understanding Writing Mechanisms
  Lasers
  LEDs

The EP Cartridge
  Protecting an EP cartridge

Laser/LED Printer Troubleshooting
  Controller (logic) symptoms
  Registration symptoms
  Laser/scanner symptoms
  Drive and transmission symptoms
  HVPS symptoms
  Fusing symptoms
  Corona (charge roller) symptoms
  Miscellaneous symptoms

Further Study
  Webpages
  Usenet newsgroups

*E*lectrophotographic (EP) printers are fundamentally different from traditional moving-carriage printers (such as ink jet or dot matrix). Those conventional printers develop dots as a one-step process, moving a discrete print head across a page surface. EP printers are not nearly as simple. EP images are formed by a complex and delicate interaction of light, static electricity, chemistry, pressure, and heat—all guided by a sophisticated *Electronic*

Control Unit (ECU). This chapter details the background of EP technology and provides you with a series of image formation troubleshooting procedures.

Understanding EP Operation

Electrophotographic printing is accomplished through a "process," rather than a "print head". The collection of components that performs the EP printing process is called an *Image Formation System (IFS).* An IFS is made up of eight distinctive areas: a photosensitive drum (#14), cleaning blade, erasure lamp (#3), primary corona (#4), writing mechanism (#5 & 6), toner, transfer corona (#13), and fusing rollers (#18 and #19). Each of these parts, as shown in Fig. 21-1, play an important role in the proper operation of an IFS.

A photosensitive drum is generally considered to be the heart of any IFS. An extruded aluminum cylinder is coated with a non-toxic organic compound that exhibits photoconductive properties. That is, the coating will conduct electricity when exposed to light. The

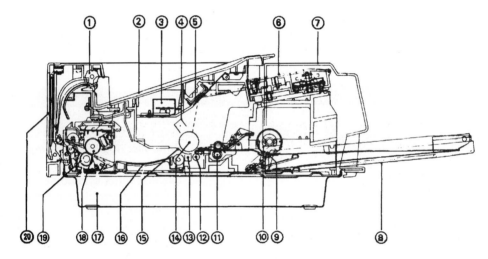

1. Delivery Assembly	11. Registration Rollers
2. Face-Down Tray	12. Transfer Corona Roller
3. Erase Lamp Assembly	13. Transfer Corona Assembly
4. Primary Corona	14. Photosensitive EP Drum
5. Beam-to-Drum Mirror	15. EP Drum Protective Shield
6. Laser/Scanning Assembly	16. Feed Guide Assembly
7. Main Body Covers	17. Lower Main Body
8. Paper Tray	18. Upper Fusing Roller
9. Separation Pad	19. Lower Pressure Roller
10. Feed Roller Assembly	20. Face-Up Output Tray (Closed)

FIGURE 21-1   **Cross-section of an HP LaserJet-type printer.** Hewlett-Packard Company

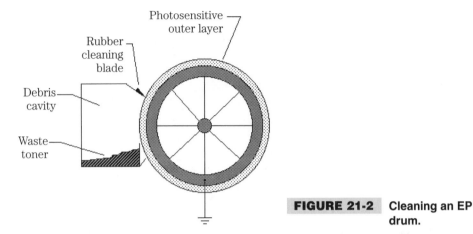

FIGURE 21-2 Cleaning an EP drum.

aluminum base cylinder is connected to ground of the high-voltage power supply. The drum receives an image from a "writing mechanism," develops the image with toner, then transfers the developed image to paper. Although you might think that this constitutes a print head because it delivers an image to paper, the image is not yet permanent—other operations must be performed by the IFS. Complete image development is a six-step process that involves all eight IFS components: cleaning, charging, writing, developing, transfer, and fusing. To really understand the IFS, you should know each of these steps in detail.

Later CX-type EP engines use superior EP drum coatings that are more resistant to nicks and scratches, and offer much longer working life.

CLEANING

Before a new printing cycle can begin, the photosensitive drum must be physically cleaned and electrically erased. Cleaning might sound like a rather unimportant step, but not even the best drum will transfer every microscopic granule of toner to a page every time. A rubber "cleaning blade" is applied across the entire length of the drum to gently scrape away any residual toner that might remain from a previous image. If residual toner were not cleaned, it could adhere to subsequent pages and appear as random black speckles. Toner that is removed from the drum is deposited into a debris cavity (Fig. 21-2). Remember that cleaning must be accomplished without scratching or nicking the drum. Any damage to the drum's photosensitive surface would leave a permanent mark on every subsequent page. Some EP printer designs actually return scrap toner back to the supply for re-use. This kind of recycling technique can extend the life of your electrophotographic (EP) cartridge and eliminate the need for a large debris cavity.

Images are written to a drum's surface as horizontal rows of electrical charges that correspond to the image being printed. A dot of light causes a relatively positive charge at that point. This corresponds to a visual dot in the completed image. Absence of light allows a relatively negative charge to remain and no dots are generated. The charges caused by light must be removed before any new images can be written—otherwise, images would overwrite and superimpose on one another. A series of erase lamps are placed in

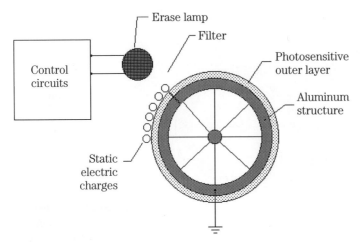

FIGURE 21-3   Erasing all charges on the EP drum.

close proximity to the drum's surface. Their light is filtered to allow only effective wavelengths to pass. Erase light bleeds away any charges along the drum. Charges are carried to ground through the aluminum cylinder (Fig. 21-3). After erasure, the drum's surface is completely neutral—it contains no charges at all.

CHARGING

A neutral drum surface is no longer receptive to light from the writing mechanism. New images cannot be written until the drum is charged again. To charge (or condition) the drum, a uniform electrical charge must be applied evenly across its entire surface. Surface charging is accomplished by applying a tremendous negative voltage (often more than –6000 volts) to a solid wire, called a *primary corona*, located close to the drum. Because the drum and high-voltage power supply share the same ground, an electrical field is established between the corona wire and drum (Fig. 21-4).

For low voltages, the air gap between a corona wire and drum would act as an insulator. With thousands of volts of potential, however, the insulating strength of air breaks down and an electric "corona" forms. A corona ionizes any air molecules surrounding the wire, so negative charges migrate to the drum's surface. The trouble with ionized gas is that it exhibits a very low resistance to current flow. Once a corona is established, there is essentially a short-circuit between the wire and drum. This is not good for a high-voltage power supply. A primary grid (part of the primary corona assembly) is added between the wire and drum. By applying a negative voltage to the grid, charging voltage and current to the drum can be carefully regulated. This "regulating grid voltage" (often –600 to –1000 V) sets the charge level actually applied to the drum, which is typically equal to the regulating voltage (–600 to –1000 volts). The drum is now ready to receive a new image.

Later CX-type EP engines replace the primary corona with a charging roller. The charging roller handles erasure also, and allows charging at a much lower voltage than corona wires.

WRITING

To form a latent image on a drum surface, the uniform charge that has conditioned the drum must be discharged in the precise points where images are to be produced. Images are written using light. Any points on the drum exposed to light will discharge to a very low level (about −100 V), while any areas left unexposed retain their conditioning charge (−600 to −1000 V). The device that produces and directs light to the drum surface is called a *writing mechanism*. Because images are formed as a series of individual dots, a larger number of dots per area will allow finer resolution (and higher quality) of the image.

For example, suppose a writing mechanism can place 300 dots per inch along a single horizontal line on the drum, and the drum can rotate in increments of ⅟₃₀₀ of an inch. This means that your printer can develop images with a resolution of 300 × 300 *Dots Per Inch (DPI)*. Current EP printers are reaching 1200 × 1200 DPI. Lasers have been traditionally used as writing mechanisms (thus the name *Laser Printer*), and are still used in many EP printer designs, but many new printers are replacing lasers with bars of microscopic light-emitting diodes (LEDs) to direct light as needed. Once an image has been written to a drum, that image must be developed.

DEVELOPING

Images written to the drum by laser or LED are initially invisible—merely an array of electrostatic charges on the drum's surface. There are low charges (where the light strikes) and high charges (where the light skips). The latent image must be developed into a visible one before it can be transferred to paper. *Toner* is used for this purpose. Toner itself is an extremely fine powder of plastic resin and organic compounds bonded to iron particles. Individual granules can be seen under extreme magnification of a microscope.

Toner is applied using a *toner cylinder* (also known as *developer roller*) as shown in Fig. 21-5. A toner cylinder is basically a long metal sleeve containing a permanent magnet. It is mounted inside the toner supply trough. When the cylinder turns, iron in the

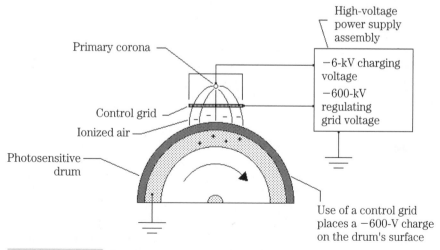

FIGURE 21-4   Placing a uniform charge on the EP drum.

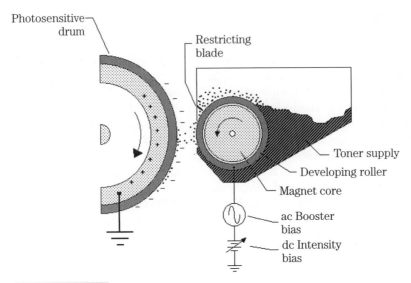

FIGURE 21-5   Developing the latent drum image with toner.

toner attracts it to the cylinder. Once attracted, toner acquires a negative static charge provided by the high-voltage power supply. This static charge level falls between the photosensitive drum's exposed and unexposed charge levels (anywhere from –200 to –500 V, depending on the intensity-control setting). A restricting blade limits toner on the cylinder to just a single layer.

Charged toner on the cylinder now rotates into close proximity with the exposed drum. Any points on the drum that are not exposed will have a strong negative charge. This repels toner that remains on the toner cylinder and is returned to the supply. Any points on the drum that are exposed now have a much lower charge than the toner particles. This attracts toner from the cylinder to corresponding points on the drum. Toner "fills-in" the latent image to form a visible (or developed) image.

Notice that an ac booster bias (more than 1500 V_{pp}) is added in series to the dc-intensity bias. Ac causes strong but brief fluctuations in the toner's charge level. As the ac signal goes positive, the intensity level increases to help toner particles overcome attraction of the cylinder's permanent magnet. As the ac signal goes negative, intensity levels decrease to pull back any toner particles that might have falsely jumped to unexposed areas. This technique greatly improves print density and image contrast. The developed image can now be applied to paper.

TRANSFER

At this point, the developed toner image on the drum must be transferred onto paper. Because toner is now attracted to the drum, it must be pried away by applying an even larger attractive charge to the page. A transfer corona wire charges the page (Fig. 21-6). The theory behind the operation of a transfer corona is exactly the same as that for a primary corona, except that the potential is now positive. This places a powerful positive charge onto paper, which attracts the negatively charged toner particles. Remember that this is not a perfect process—not all toner is transferred to paper. This is why a cleaning process is needed.

Caution is needed here. Because the negatively charged drum and positively charged paper tend to attract each other, it is possible that paper could wrap around the drum. Even though the small-diameter drum and natural stiffness of paper tend to prevent wrapping, a *static-charge eliminator* (or *static-eliminator comb*) is included to counteract positive charges and remove the attractive force between paper and drum immediately after toner is transferred. Paper now has no net charge. The drum can be cleaned and prepared for a new image.

> Later CX-type EP engines replace the transfer corona with a transfer roller. The transfer roller allows transfer to paper at lower voltages than corona wires.

FUSING

Once the toner image has reached paper, it is only held to the page by gravity and weak electrostatic attraction—toner is still in its powder form. Toner must be fixed permanently (or fused) to the page before it can be handled. Fusing is accomplished with a heat and pressure assembly (Fig. 21-7). A high-intensity quartz lamp heats a non-stick roller to about 180 degrees C. Pressure is applied with a pliable rubber roller. When a developed page is passed between these two rollers, heat from the top roller melts the toner, and pressure from the bottom roller squeezes molten toner into the paper fibers, where it cools and adheres permanently. The finished page is then fed to an output tray. Notice that both rollers are referred to as *fusing rollers*, even though only the heated top roller actually fuses. To prevent toner particles from sticking to a fusing roller, it is coated with a non-stick material, such as Teflon. A cleaning pad is added to wipe away any toner that might yet adhere. The pad also applies a thin coating of silicon oil to prevent further sticking.

Fusing temperature must be carefully controlled. Often a thermistor is used to regulate current through the quartz lamp to maintain a constant temperature. A snap-action thermal

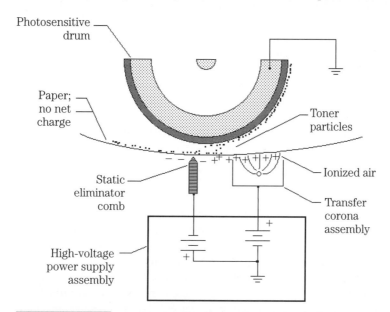

FIGURE 21-6   Transferring the developed image to paper.

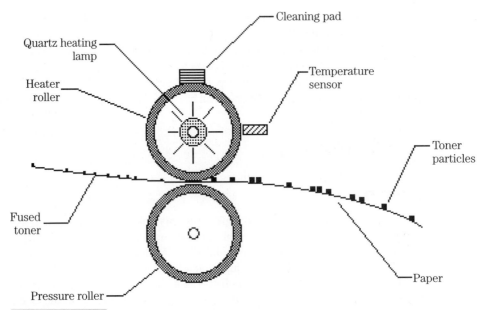

FIGURE 21-7 Fusing the toner image to the page.

switch is also included as a safety interlock in the event that lamp temperature should rise out of control. If temperature is not controlled carefully, a failure could result in printer damage, or even a fire hazard.

Understanding Writing Mechanisms

After charging, the photosensitive drum contains a uniform electrostatic charge across its surface. To form a latent image, the drum must be discharged at any points that comprise the image. Light is used to discharge the drum as needed. Such a "writing mechanism" is illustrated in Fig. 21-8. Images are scanned onto the drum one horizontal line at a time. A single pass across the drum is called a *trace* or *scan line*. Light is directed to any points along the scan line where dots are required. When a scan line is completed, the drum increments in preparation for another scan line. It is up to the printer's control circuits to break down an image into individual scan lines, then direct the writing mechanism accordingly.

LASERS

Lasers have been around since the early 1960s, and have developed to the point where they can be manufactured in a great variety of shapes, sizes, and power outputs. To understand why lasers make such a useful writing mechanism, you must understand the difference between laser light and ordinary "white" light. Ordinary white light is actually not white. The light you see is composed of many different wavelengths, each traveling in their own directions. When these various wavelengths combine, they do so virtually at random. This makes everyday light very difficult to direct and almost impossible to control as a fine beam. As an example, take a flashlight and direct it at a far wall. You will see just how much white light can scatter and disperse over a relatively small distance.

The nature of laser light, however, is much different. A laser beam contains only one major wavelength of light (it is monochromatic). Each ray travels in the same direction and combines in an additive fashion (known as *coherence*). These characteristics make laser light easy to direct at a target as a hair-thin beam, with almost no scatter (or divergence). Older EP printers used Helium-Neon (HeNe) gas lasers, but strong semiconductor laser diodes have essentially replaced gas lasers in just about all laser-printing applications.

Laser diodes appear very similar to ordinary light-emitting diodes. When the appropriate amount of voltage and current is applied to a laser diode, photons of light will be liberated that have the characteristics of laser light (coherent, monochromatic, and low divergence). A small lens window (or "laser aperture" allows light to escape, and helps to focus the beam. Laser diodes are not very efficient devices—a great deal of power is required to generate a much smaller amount of light power, but this trade-off is usually worthwhile for the small size, light weight, and high reliability of a semiconductor laser.

Generating a laser beam is only the beginning. The beam must be modulated (turned on and off) while being swept across the drum's surface. Beam modulation can be accomplished by turning the laser on and off, as needed (usually done with semiconductor laser diodes), as shown in Fig. 21-9, or by interrupting a continuous beam with an electro-optical switch (typically used with gas lasers, which are difficult to switch on and off rapidly). Mirrors are used to alter the direction of the laser beam, and lenses are used to focus the beam and maintain a low divergence at all points along the beam path. Figure 21-9 is just one illustration of a laser-writing mechanism, but it shows some of the complexity that is involved. The weight of glass lenses, mirrors, and their shock mountings have kept EP laser printers bulky and expensive.

Alignment has always been an unavoidable problem in complex optical systems, such as Fig. 21-9. Consider what might happen to the beam if any optical component should become

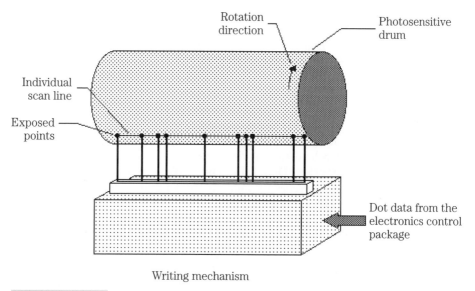

FIGURE 21-8   Simplified diagram of a generic writing mechanism.

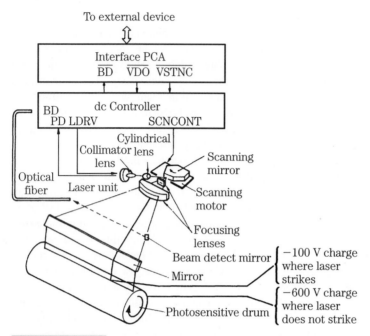

To external device

Interface PCA
$\overline{BD}$ $\overline{VDO}$ $\overline{VSTNC}$

dc Controller
BD
PD LDRV   SCNCONT

Cylindrical
Collimator lens
lens

Scanning
mirror

Optical
fiber   Laser unit

Scanning
motor

Focusing
lenses

Beam detect mirror

Mirror

Photosensitive drum

$\begin{cases} -100 \text{ V charge} \\ \text{where laser} \\ \text{strikes} \end{cases}$

$\begin{cases} -600 \text{ V charge} \\ \text{where laser} \\ \text{does not strike} \end{cases}$

FIGURE 21-9   **A LaserJet-type laser scanning assembly.**

damaged or fall out of alignment—focus and direction problems could render a drum image unintelligible. Realignment of optical systems is virtually impossible without special alignment tools, and is beyond the scope of this book. Finally, printing speed is limited by the speed of moving parts, and the rate at which the laser beam can be modulated and moved.

LEDS

Fortunately, a laser printer's photosensitive drum is receptive to light from many different sources. Even light from *Light-Emitting Diodes (LEDs)* can expose the drum. By fabricating a series of microscopic LEDs into a single scan line, an LED can be provided for every possible dot in a scan line. For example, the ROHM JE3008SS02 is an LED print bar containing 2560 microscopic LEDs over 8.53 inches. This equates to 300 dots per inch. Each LED is just 50×65 micrometers (μm) and they are spaced 84.6 μm apart. The operation of an LED print bar is remarkably straightforward. An entire series of data bits, corresponding to each possible dot in a horizontal line, is shifted into internal digital circuitry within the print bar. Dots that will be visible are represented by a logic "1," and dots that are not visible will remain at logic "0." For a device, such as the JE3008SS02, 2560 bits must be entered for each scan line.

You can probably see the advantages of an LED print-bar system over a laser approach. There are no moving parts involved in light delivery—no mirror motor to jam or wear out. The printer can operate at much higher speeds because it does not have to overcome the dynamic limitations of moving parts. There is only one focusing lens between the print bar and drum. This greatly simplifies the optics assembly, and removes substantial weight and bulk from the printer. An LED system overcomes almost all alignment problems, so a defective assembly can be replaced or aligned quickly and easily.

The EP Cartridge

Electrostatic printers mandate the use of extremely tight manufacturing tolerances to ensure precise, consistent operation. A defect of even a few thousandths of an inch could cause unacceptable image formation. Even normal mechanical wear can have an adverse affect on print quality. Many key IFS components would have to be replaced every 5000 to 10,000 pages to maintain acceptable performance. Clearly, it would be undesirable to send your printer away for a complete (and time-consuming) overhaul every 10,000 pages.

To ease manufacturing difficulties and provide fast, affordable maintenance to every EP printer user, crucial components of the IFS, as well as a supply of toner, are assembled into a replaceable electrophotographic (or EP) cartridge. As Fig. 21-10 shows, a typical EP cartridge contains the toner roller, toner supply, debris cavity, primary corona (and primary grid), photosensitive drum, and cleaning blade assembly. All necessary electrical connectors and drive gears are included. By assembling sensitive components into a single replaceable cartridge, printer reliability is substantially improved by preventing problems before they ever become noticeable. The cost of an EP cartridge is low enough to consider it a disposable (or recyclable) part.

A typical EP cartridge is capable of producing 200 to 5000 printed pages. The exact number varies, depending upon just how much toner is available, and which crucial parts

FIGURE 21-10   **An exploded view of an HP EP cartridge.** Hewlett-Packard Company

are placed in the cartridge—highly integrated EP cartridges will last longer than simple toner cartridges. Because toner is comprised partially of organic materials, it has a limited useful life (often six months after the cartridge is removed from its sealed container). Later "high-volume" engines can support 7000 to 10,000 pages.

PROTECTING AN EP CARTRIDGE

As you might imagine, the precision components in an EP cartridge are sensitive and delicate. The photosensitive drum and toner supply are particularly sensitive to light and environmental conditions, so it is important to follow several handling and storage guidelines:

■ *Keep light away from the drum* The photosensitive drum is coated with an organic material that is extremely sensitive to light. Although a metal shroud covers the drum when the cartridge is exposed, light might still penetrate the shroud and cause exposure (also known as *fogging*). Deactivating the printer for a time will often eliminate mild fogging. Do not defeat the shroud in open light unless absolutely necessary, and then only for short periods. This will certainly fog the drum. A seriously fogged cartridge might have to be placed in a dark area for several days. Never expose the drum to direct sunlight—direct sunlight can permanently damage the drum's coating.

■ *Avoid extremes of temperature and humidity* Temperatures exceeding 40 degrees C can permanently damage an EP cartridge. Extreme humidity is just about as dangerous. Do not allow the cartridge to become exposed to ammonia vapors or other organic solvent vapors—they break down the drum's coating very quickly. Finally, keep a cartridge secure and level. Never allow it to be dropped or abused in any way.

■ *Redistribute toner regularly* As the toner supply diminishes, it might be necessary to redistribute remaining toner so that it reaches the toner roller. Because toner is available along the entire cartridge, it must be redistributed by rocking the cartridge back and forth along its long axis. If you tip a cartridge upright, remaining toner will fall to one end and cause uneven distribution.

Laser/LED Printer Troubleshooting

Now that you have an understanding of EP technology, the following sections of the chapter will present a series of printer problems and solutions. Given the proliferation of printer manufacturers—each requiring drivers and support, Table 21-1 lists an index of printer manufacturers for your reference. Before you begin troubleshooting, however, two important cautions are in order:

Shock warning: Be sure to unplug the printer and allow ample time for the power supply (or supplies) to discharge before attempting to open the enclosure. High-voltage supplies are especially dangerous, and can result in a nasty shock if they are not allowed to discharge.

Burn warning: Fusing assemblies in EP printers also reach more than 200 degrees F during normal operation. Even when opening the EP printer for routine maintenance, allow ample time for the fuser to cool (at least 10 minutes) before reaching inside.

TABLE 21-1 INDEX OF PRINTER MANUFACTURERS

Alps Electric Inc.	www.alpsusa.com
Apple	www.apple.com
Brother	www.brother.com
C. Itoh	www.citoh.com
CalComp	www.calcomp.com
Canon	www.usa.canon.com
Casio	www.casio-usa.com
Citizen America	www.citizen-america.com
CoStar	www.costar.com
Dataproducts	www.dataproducts.com
Digital (DEC)	www.digital.com
Eastman Kodak	www.kodak.com
Epson	www.epson.com
Fargo	www.fargo.com
Fujitsu	www.fujitsu.com
Ganson Engineering	www.ganson.com
Genicom	www.genicom.com
Hewlett-Packard	www.hp.com
IBM	www.ibm.com
JetFax	www.jetfax.com
Konica	www.konica.com
Kyocera	www.kyocera.com
LaserMaster	www.lasermaster.com
Lexmark	www.lexmark.com
Mannesmann Tally	www.tally.com
Mita	www.mita.com
NEC	www.nec.com
Okidata	www.okidata.com
Olivetti	www.olivettipc.com
Panasonic	www.panasonic.com
Printronix	www.printronix.com
QMS	www.qms.com
Radio Shack	www.radioshack.com
Ricoh	www.ricoh.com
Samsung	www.sosimple.com
Seikosha	www.seikosha.com
ServiceWorks	www.serviceworks.com
Sharp	www.sharp-usa.com
Star Micronics	www.starmicronics.com
Sun Microsystems	www.sun.com
Talaris	www.talaris.com
Tandy Corporation	www.tandy.com
Tektronix	www.tektronix.com
Texas Instruments	www.ti.com
Toshiba	www.toshiba.com

TABLE 21-1 INDEX OF PRINTER MANUFACTURERS (CONTINUED)	
Unisys	**www.unisys.com**
Verifone	**www.verifone.com**
Westrex International	**www.westrex.com**
Xante Corporation	**www.xante.com**
Xerox	**www.xerox.com**

You'll also get a great deal of troubleshooting information from the diagnostics built into your EP printer. Many messages and codes displayed to the printer's LCD panel are simply status indicators or reminders, but some printers (such as Hewlett-Packard's line of LaserJet printers) use the LCD panel extensively for diagnostics. Table 21-2 presents the operating and error codes for the HP LaserJet family.

CONTROLLER (LOGIC) SYMPTOMS

Most EP printers use an ECU consisting of two parts: a main board and a mechanical controller. The main board provides the core logic for the printer—CPU, memory, an interface for the control panel, the communication circuits, and other processing elements. The mechanical controller provides an interface between the pure logic and the electro-mechanical components of the printer. For example, a mechanical controller holds the driver circuitry controlling the printer's motors and solenoids. Some printers integrate these functions onto a single PC board, but other printer designs use two separate boards. Although controller circuitry is generally quite reliable, it does fail from time to time, so it is important that you recognize the signs of trouble.

Symptom 21-1. The printer's LCD shows a "CPU error"   Some printer designs might show this error as a series of blinking LEDs or as a sequence of beeps. The CPU is the heart of your printer's logical operation. When you first start the printer the CPU and its associated core logic is tested, much like the BIOS of a computer, it will execute a self test (you can see the CPU in Fig. 21-11). If the CPU fails to pass all of its test requirements, an error will be generated. Unlike the CISC-type (Complex Instruction Set Computing) CPUs used in PC motherboards, the CPUs used in EP printers are typically RISC-based (Reduced Instruction Set Computing) for added printer performance.

As you might imagine, a CPU failure is catastrophic—that is, the printer simply will not work without it. Start by turning off and unplugging the printer, then examine each of the connectors on the main controller. Each connector should be installed properly and completely. If problems persist, you will have to replace the CPU. Replacing the CPU can be either cheap or expensive, depending on how it is mounted. If the CPU is socket-mounted on the main controller, you can often just remove the old CPU and plug in a new one. However, if the CPU is soldered to the main controller board, you will have to desolder and resolder the CPU (if you have the proper surface-mount soldering tools), or replace the entire main controller board.

Symptom 21-2. The printer's LCD shows a "ROM checksum error"   Your particular printer might use an error number (i.e., ERROR 11) to represent the condition.

TABLE 21-2 HP LASERJET FAMILY MESSAGES AND ERROR CODES

00 PCL Ready (HP LaserJet IIISi) The printer is ready to use in PCL mode. An asterisk (*) indicates that Sys Switch = Off.

00 PS Ready (HP LaserJet IIISi) The printer is ready to use in PostScript mode. An asterisk (*) indicates that Sys Switch = Off.

02 Warming Up (All HP LaserJet printers) Wait until the printer has initialized. Prolonged display of this message indicates a defective interface cable or poor interface connection. Check the printer cable and LPT port. If the problem persists, check the printer's interface circuit.

04 Self-Test (HP LaserJet II, IID, IIP, IIP+,III, IIID, IIIP, IIISi, 4, 4Si, 4P) The printer is printing a continuous self-test. A self test will empty the paper tray unless the printer is turned off or put back on-line. If the printer is put back on-line to clear the 04 Self Test, an additional one to three sheets can be printed before the test is complete.

05 Self-Test (HP LaserJet II, IID, IIP, IIP+,III, IIID, IIIP, IIISi, 4, 4Si, 4P, 500 Series) A printer self-test is in progress. If the printer remains on the "05 Self-Test," the printer might have a problem with its internal circuitry.

06 Config Page (HP LaserJet 4, 4M, 4Si, 4SiMx, 4P, 4MP) The printer is printing a PostScript configuration page. No action is needed.

06 Demo Page (HP LaserJet 4, 4M, 4Si, 4SiMX, 4P, 4MP) The printer is printing a PCL demonstration page or PostScript demonstration page. No action is needed.

06 Font Printout (HP LaserJet II, IID, IIP, IIP+ III, IIID, IIIP, IIISi) The printer is printing sample characters from available downloaded soft fonts, internal fonts, and installed cartridge fonts along with their respective escape characters (Series II font printouts do not show escape sequence characters).

06 Printing Test (HP LaserJet II, IID, IIP, IIP+, III, IIID, IIIP, IIISi, 4, 4M, 4Si, 4SiMX, 4P, 4MP) The printer self-test is printing a single output sheet titled "Self Test."

06 Typeface List (HP LaserJet 4, 4M, 4Si, 4SiMX, 4P, 4MP) The printer is printing a typeface list.

07 Reset (All HP LaserJet printers, except 2686A) Reset returns all printing menu items to selected settings, then clears buffer pages, temporary soft fonts, and temporary macros.

08 Cold Reset (HP LaserJet II, IID, IIP, IIP+ III, IIID, IIIP, IIISi, 4, 4Si, 4P) Reset returns all configuration and printing menu selections to the factory-default settings. This is performed by holding down the <On-Line> key while turning the printer on. This is a "last resort" option to clear the printer of any suspected glitches. Run a "05 Self Test" before the reset to retain a hard copy of all the current printer settings. Some variables are not reset:
- HP LaserJet 4 Page count, MP tray size, envelope feeder size, and display language are not reset.
- HP LaserJet 4Si Page count and display language are not reset.
- HP LaserJet 4P Page count and display language are not reset.

09 Menu Reset (HP LaserJet II, IID,IIP, IIP+, IID, III, IIID, IIIP, IIISi, 4, 4Si, 4P) This reset returns all printing menu settings back to the factory default settings and clears all buffered pages, temporary soft fonts, and temporary macros.

09 Reset All I/O (HP LaserJet 4, 4M, 4Si, 4P) This clears the page buffer, removing all perishable personality data (such as temporary typefaces), and clears the input and output buffer for all I/Os.

10 Reset To Save (HP LaserJet IID, IIP, IIP+, III, IIID, IIIP, IIISi, 4, 4M, 4Si, 4P) Changes in the menu were made with data present in the print buffer. Press and hold <Continue/Reset> until 07 Reset appears to confirm the selections (temporary macros and temporary fonts will be deleted) or press <Continue/Reset> or <On-Line> so that no changes to any menu selections will be made.

11 Paper Out (HP LaserJet, Plus, 500 Plus, II) The paper tray is empty. If paper is in the tray and the printer still displays 11, verify that the tray is inserted completely. Try another tray.

12 Printer Open (HP LaserJet II, IID, III, IIID, IIISI, 4, 4M, 4Si, 4P) The printer's top cover is not correctly closed or the toner cartridge is not correctly installed. Check the toner cartridge seating and close the printer firmly. Plugging a 220-V printer model into a 120-V power source can also result in this message.

TABLE 21-2 HP LASERJET FAMILY MESSAGES AND ERROR CODES (CONTINUED)

12 Printer Open Or No EP (HP LaserJet IIP, IIP Plus, IIIP) The printer is not closed properly, the EP/toner cartridge is missing, broken, or defective, or the cooling fan is not working. Check the EP/toner cartridge and close the printer firmly. Try another EP/toner cartridge. Plugging a 220-V printer model into a 120-V power source can also result in this message.

13 Paper Jam (HP LaserJet 4, 4M) Paper is jammed somewhere along the paper path or the paper jam sensor at the rear of the fusing assembly might be stuck (causing a false paper jam warning). Remove any jammed paper, and be sure to open and close the top cover—or the rear cover must be opened and closed firmly. If problems persist, check the paper-jam sensor.

13 Paper Jam (HP LaserJet 4P, 4MP) Paper is jammed in the top or rear of the printer. Clear the jam and press <Continue> or <On-Line> to resume printing. Verify that all doors are closed securely. A false paper-jam message can occur if the printer's back door is open. If the problem persists, check the paper-jam sensor.

13 Paper Jam (HP LaserJet II, IIP, IIIP, IID, IIP+, IIID) There is a paper jam. Remove jammed paper. The top cover must be opened and closed (the front cover on an IIP, IIP+, IIIP) to clear this message. Check the duplexing paper path on the IID and IIID (left side door) and the optional duplexing paper path on the IIISi and the HP LaserJet 4Si. Jams can also occur with IID and IIID printers when operating in an "automatic manual feed" mode. If the message persists, the paper-path sensor might need to be serviced.

13.X Paper Jam (HP LaserJet IIISi, 4Si) Paper is jammed somewhere along the paper path. The value of *X* that follows the "13" in the message window specifies which part of the paper path the paper is jammed at ("1" internal, "2" input, "3" duplex, "4" output). Also, the paper-jam sensor at the rear of the fusing assembly might have become stuck.

14 No EP Cart (HP LaserJet II, IID, III, IIID, 4, 4M, IIISi) No EP/toner cartridge is in the printer, or the EP/toner cartridge might be broken or damaged. Turn the printer off and back on. Try a new EP/toner cartridge.

14 No Toner Cart (HP LaserJet II, IID, III, IIID, 4, 4M, IIISi) See 14 No EP Cart.

15 Engine Test (All except HP LaserJet IIP, IIP Plus, IIIP, 4P) This EP engine test prints a single sheet of vertical line printout (also known as a *skewing test*).

16 Toner Low (HP LaserJet II, IID, III, IIID, 4, 4M) The EP/toner cartridge is low on toner. The message might also indicate that the EP cartridge is not making good contact with the printer's internal circuitry. Gently shake and reinstall the EP/toner cartridge. Replace the EP/toner cartridge, if necessary. You might need to press the <Continue> button to clear the message.

16 Toner Low 1, 2, 3 (HP LaserJet IIISi, 4Si) "Toner Low 1" indicates that the 8000-page toner cartridge is approximately 200 pages from depletion. "Toner Low 2" and "Toner Low 3" messages are indications of further exhaustion ("Toner Low 3" indicates a nearly illegible page). Replace the toner cartridge.

17 Mem Config (HP LaserJet IIIP, III, IIID, IIISi) This status message indicates that it is reconfiguring internal and expanded memory for page protection. You might lose the optional setting in the configuration menu. If this error occurs after page protection is turned on, cycle the printer power and re-select the optional I/O in the Configuration menu.

18 Aux I/O Init (HP LaserJet 4, 4M) The modular I/O (MIO) card is initializing. This message will automatically stop after the card is initialized (usually less than 60 seconds).

18 Aux I/O Nt Rdy (HP LaserJet 4, 4M) The modular I/O (MIO) card is not ready. The printer will continue to display this message until the problem with the card is corrected or the card is removed. Always turn off and unplug the printer when removing I/O cards.

18 Lower MIO (HP LaserJet 4Si) The upper MIO card is initializing. During initialization, the MIO is not active, but the printer remains on-line and displays this message. The message will clear after the card is initialized.

18 Skip Self Test (HP LaserJet III, IIID, IIISi) This status message indicates that the "minus" key was held down while powering up the printer. If the printer is stuck in this mode, the minus key is probably stuck.

18 Upper MIO (HP LaserJet 4Si) See *18 Lower MIO*.

TABLE 21-2 HP LASERJET FAMILY MESSAGES AND ERROR CODES (CONTINUED)

19 Add Memory (HP LaserJet IIP, IIP Plus) This message appears if the PCL 5 Cartridge is installed without adding optional memory.

20 Error (HP LaserJet 4, 4M, 4Si, 4P) See *20 Mem Overflow*.

20 Mem Overflow (HP LaserJet 4, 4M, 4Si, 4P) This error indicates a memory overflow. Too much data has been sent to the printer and it has run out of memory. Pressing <Continue> will print only what the printer has received. If the error persists, add memory or "simplify" the print job.

21 Error (All HP LaserJet printers) The printer is unable to process very complex data fast enough for the print engine. Reduce the document's complexity by using fewer fonts and remove such enhancements as bolding, shading, or underlining. Reduce the document's graphics resolution. For the LaserJet III or 4 family, try selecting the printer's Page-protect option (Letter, A4, Legal).

22 Error (All HP LaserJet printers) This represents a serial buffer overflow error. If you're running a parallel port printer, the printer interface cable is defective. For serial printers, check the protocol (data frame). For parallel printers, check/replace the cable.

25 XXX Mem Full (HP LaserJet 4Si) "XXX" is the name of the printer personality (i.e., PCL or PS) and the personality-environment save area is full. To continue printing, press <Continue> (but some data is lost).

40 Error (All HP LaserJet printers) This message indicates that a protocol error occurred during the transfer of data from the computer to the printer. This error can be caused by a loose or damaged cable, loss of power to the computer while the printer is on-line, or incompatible serial data frame (if the printer is configured for serial operation). For modular I/O (MIO) cards, this means that there was an abnormal connection break. Press *Continue* to clear the error message. Check that the printer and computer are configured for the same baud rate (typically 9600).

41 Error (HP LaserJet IIP) This error might indicate that a ground-loop problem is causing static build up on the fuser assembly (causing the "41 Error"). Turn the printer off. If dense media is being used, decrease the amount of pages sitting in the multi-purpose (MP) tray or lower cassette. Do not refill the tray with paper until it runs out and prompts for more paper. "41 Errors" can also be caused by adding paper to the top of the MP tray while the printer is in the printing process.

41.1 Error (HP LaserJet 4, 4M, 4Si, 4P) See 41.5 Error.

41.2 Error (All HP LaserJet printers) See 51 Error.

41.2 Error (HP LaserJet 4, 4M, 4Si, 4P) See 41.5 Error.

41.3 Error (HP LaserJet 4, 4M, 4Si, 4P) See 41.5 Error.

41.4 Error (HP LaserJet 4, 4M, 4Si, 4P) See 41.5 Error.

41.5 Error (HP LaserJet 4, 4M, 4Si, 4P) A temporary error occurred while printing. This error most commonly occurs when the wrong-size media is loaded into the tray or when the printer picks two sheets of paper at once. Remove the page from the printer's output tray and press <Continue>. The printer will automatically reprint the page and resume printing.

48 Invalid (HP LaserJet IIISi) This message will be displayed if the wrong printer language (i.e., PCL5 or PostScript) is being used, or if a language other than PCL5 or Postscript is being used. The message will disappear when a valid language switching sequence is received or when a printer reset occurs. Check the printing software to see that the correct language was chosen.

49 Remove Page (HP LaserJet IIISi, 4Si) A sheet of paper was in the manual-feed guides when the printer powered on, or a paper tray with a sheet of paper in its manual-feed guides was inserted while the printer was powering on. Remove the sheets or the tray until the printer has initialized.

49 Remv Pg (HP LaserJet IIISi) There was paper in one or both of the manual paper-feed slots when the printer was turned on, or when a paper tray with paper in the manual feed slot was installed.

50 Needs Service (HP LaserJet IIP) The fusing assembly is not functioning. Turn the printer off for 10 to 15 minutes. If the message persists, service/replace the fusing assembly.

50 Service Error (All HP LaserJet printers) This error indicates a possible malfunction in the fusing assembly. Turn the printer off for 10 to 15 minutes (30 minutes for HP LaserJet IIISi or 4Si) and restart. If the message persists, service/replace the fusing assembly.

TABLE 21-2 HP LASERJET FAMILY MESSAGES AND ERROR CODES (CONTINUED)

51 Error   (All HP LaserJet printers) This indicates a beam-detect error. Press the <Continue> key, and the printer will repeat the page. If the printer cannot correct the error after two seconds, a beam-detect "51 Error" will occur. Replace the EP/toner cartridge and retest the printer. If the printer was just moved from a cold to warm environment, condensation might have formed inside the printer. Allow the printer to stand for up to six hours, until any condensation has dissipated.

52 Error   (All HP LaserJet printers) The printer has detected a temporary error. Press <Continue> to resume operation.

53 Error   (HP LaserJet 4, 4M, 4Si, 4P) See 53.XY.ZZ.

53 Error   (HP LaserJet IID, IIP, IIP Plus, IIIP) This error indicates that the optional memory installed in the printer is not compatible with the interface control circuit. Verify that the memory is compatible—HP supports HP memory only.

53 Error   (HP LaserJet IIISi) This error indicates an internal service error. Turn the printer off for 10 minutes and turn back on. If the error persists, replace the main controller board.

53 Error   (HP LaserJet, Plus, 500 plus) This error indicates an internal service malfunction. Press <Continue> to resume operation.

53.XY.ZZ   (HP LaserJet 4, 4M, 4Si, 4P) An error occurred during the configuration and validation of SIMM memory inside the printer. Verify that all SIMMs are installed correctly. Identify and replace the SIMM that caused the error:

- X "Hardware type"
  0 = ROM
  1 = RAM

- Y "Hardware device"
  0 = Internal memory
  1 = SIMM slot 1
  2 = SIMM slot 2
  3 = SIMM slot 3
  4 = SIMM slot 4 (HP LaserJet 4 and HP LaserJet 4Si only)

- ZZ "Error number"
  1 = Unsupported memory
  2 = Unrecognized memory
  3 = Failed RAM test
  4 = Exceeded max. RAM size
  5 = Exceeded max. ROM size
  6 = Invalid SIMM speed
  7 = SIMM reporting info incorrectly.
  8 = SIMM RAM parity error
  9 = SIMM ROM needs mapped to an unsupported address.
  10 = SIMM address conflict.
  11 = SIMM ROM located in illegal address range (HP LaserJet 4Si only)
  12 = SIMM is too large for available memory (HP LaserJet 4Si only).

53-1 Error   (HP LaserJet IIP, IIP Plus, III, IIID, IIIP) An error was detected in the optional memory card installed in the front memory-card slot. Turn off and unplug the printer, re-seat the memory card in the slot, then turn the printer back on. Try a new memory card.

53-2 Error   (HP LaserJet IIP, IIP Plus, III, IIID, IIIP) An error was detected on the optional memory card installed in the rear memory card slot. Turn off and unplug the printer, re-seat the memory card in the slot, then power the printer back on. Try a new memory card.

54 Error   (HP LaserJet IIP, IIP Plus, III, IIIP, IIISi) This error indicates an internal service error. Turn the printer off for 10 minutes, then turn it back on. If the error persists, replace the main controller.

54 Error   (HP LaserJet, Plus, 500 Plus, II) This message indicates a main motor overload. The most common cause is a paper tray that is too full or simultaneous paper feeds because of paper friction or static "cling." Check the paper tray for an "over-full" condition. Remove excess paper and press <Continue>. If the problem persists, you may need to replace the main motor.

TABLE 21-2   HP LASERJET FAMILY MESSAGES AND ERROR CODES (CONTINUED)

54 Service   (HP LaserJet IID, IIID) An error occurred while the printer was duplexing. Verify that the paper is the correct size.

54 Service   (HP LaserJet IIISi, 4Si) A problem occurred with the duplex-unit shift plate. Switch off the printer, then switch it on again. If the error persists, replace the duplex unit.

55 Error   (All HP LaserJet printers) This error indicates an internal service error. Turn the printer off for 10 minutes, then turn it back on. If the message persists, replace the main controller.

56 Error   (HP LaserJet IID, IIID) A duplex job was sent to the printer with the rear-output selector knob in the wrong position. Adjust the output knob to the correct position and press <Continue> to resume operation.

56 Error   (HP LaserJet IIISi, 4Si) This message indicates that the optional envelope feeder was selected while the printer's duplex feature was enabled. Either remove the envelope feeder or disable the duplex feature.

57 Service   (HP LaserJet IIISi, 4, 4M, 4Si, 4P) The printer has identified an internal service error. Turn the printer off and then back on again. If the message persists, replace the main controller.

57.1 Error   (HP LaserJet IIISi, 4, 4M, 4Si, 4P) See 57 Service.

57.1 Error   (HP LaserJet IIP, IIP Plus, III, IIID, IIIP) The memory card in the front slot cannot be configured because it exceeds memory capacity (the printer reads a maximum 2MB per memory slot). Install a properly sized memory card.

57.2 Error   (HP LaserJet IIISi, 4, 4M, 4Si, 4P) See 57 Service.

57.2 Error   (HP LaserJet IIP, IIP Plus, III, IIID, IIIP) The memory card in the rear slot cannot be configured because it exceeds memory capacity (the printer reads a maximum two megabytes per memory slot). Install a properly sized memory card.

57.3 Error   (HP LaserJet IIISi, 4, 4M, 4Si, 4P) See 57 Service.

57.4 Error   (HP LaserJet IIISi, 4, 4M, 4Si, 4P) See 57 Service.

58 Service   (HP LaserJet 4, 4M, 4P, 4MP) The printer has detected an exhaust-fan failure. Replace the defective fan assembly.

58.1 Error   (HP LaserJet 4Si) The lifter mechanism of the upper paper tray has failed. Press <Continue> to have the printer print from the other tray.

58.2 Error   (HP LaserJet 4Si) The lifter mechanism of the lower paper tray has failed. Press <Continue> to have the printer print from the other tray.

59 Add Mem   (HP LaserJet 4Si, 4SiMX) The PostScript option is installed without enough memory to support the application (the Postscript option requires a minimum of 4MB for proper operation). Disable the PostScript option or install enough suitable printer memory to support it.

60 Error   (HP LaserJet, Plus, 500 Plus) The printer's interface board has detected an internal error. Check for an improperly seated font cartridge or data cable. Turn printer off and back on. If the message persists, replace the interface board or main controller.

60.1 Error   (HP LaserJet IIISi) See 60.4 Error.

60.2 Error   (HP LaserJet IIISi) See 60.4 Error.

60.3 Error   (HP LaserJet IIISi) See 60.4 Error.

60.4 Error   (HP LaserJet IIISi) An expansion memory card has been installed incorrectly (out of sequence) into the slot indicated by the error code (.1–.4). The printer will still be able to print, but will only be able to use the memory below the faulty card. Four-megabyte cards go in first from the bottom slot up, then one-megabyte cards. Turn the printer off and reorganize the memory cards into their correct slots.

61 Service   (All HP LaserJet printers) See 67 Service.

61.1 Error   (HP LaserJet 4, 4M, 4Si) See 61.4 Error.

61.1 Error   (HP LaserJet IIISi) See 61.4 Error.

61.2 Error   (HP LaserJet 4, 4M, 4Si) See 61.4 Error.

TABLE 21-2 HP LASERJET FAMILY MESSAGES AND ERROR CODES (CONTINUED)

61.2 Error (HP LaserJet IIISi) See 61.4 Error.

61.3 Error (HP LaserJet 4, 4M, 4Si) See 61.4 Error.

61.3 Error (HP LaserJet IIISi) See 61.4 Error.

61.4 Error (HP LaserJet 4, 4M, 4Si) The printer encountered a parity error when accessing the RAM memory SIMM in slot "X" (slot .1–.4). If X=.0, the slot with the defective SIMM could not be determined. Switch the printer off, then back on. Verify that the SIMM board is installed correctly. If the error persists, power down and remove the indicated SIMM board. If the error message does not reappear, the problem is on the SIMM you just removed. If the message *still* appears, the problem is in the printer's internal memory and you'll need to replace the main controller.

61.4 Error (HP LaserJet IIISi) An expansion SIMM of the wrong size or speed has been installed in the slot indicated by the error code (.1–.4). The printer will still print, but will only be able to use the memory installed below the faulty SIMM.

62 Service (All HP LaserJet printers) See 67 Service.

62.1 Error (HP LaserJet 4, 4M, 4MP, 4P, 4Si, 4SiMX) See 62.5 Error.

62.2 Error (HP LaserJet 4, 4M, 4MP, 4P, 4Si, 4SiMX) See 62.5 Error.

62.3 Error (HP LaserJet 4, 4M, 4MP, 4P, 4Si, 4SiMX) See 62.5 Error.

62.4 Error (HP LaserJet 4, 4M, 4MP, 4P, 4Si, 4SiMX) See 62.5 Error.

62.5 Error (HP LaserJet 4, 4M, 4MP, 4P, 4Si, 4SiMX) The printer identified a problem while checking its memory. If the printer contains a SIMM memory board or a typeface cartridge, switch the printer off, then back on. Verify that the SIMM board is installed correctly. If the error persists, power down and remove the indicated SIMM board. If the error message does not reappear, the problem is on the SIMM you just removed. If the message still appears, the problem is in the printer's internal memory and you'll need to replace the main controller. X refers to the device the printer was checking when it encountered the error:
- 0 = Internal memory
- 0 = Internal Memory (HP LaserJet 4P and 4MP)
- 1–3 = SIMM Slot (HP LaserJet 4P and 4MP)
- 1–4 = SIMM slot
- 4 = Cartridge (HP LaserJet 4P and 4MP)
- 5 = Font cartridge (upper on HP LaserJet 4Si)
- 6 = Lower cartridge (HP LaserJet 4Si only)

63 Needs Service (HP LaserJet 4Si) The printer identified a problem while checking its internal RAM. Remove any expanded memory boards and reboot the printer. If message persists, replace the main controller. If message clears, then the problem is with the expanded memory.

63 Service (HP LaserJet 4Si) See 63 Needs Service.

63.1 Error (HP LaserJet IIISi) See 63.4 Error.

63.2 Error (HP LaserJet IIISi) See 63.4 Error.

63.3 Error (HP LaserJet IIISi) See 63.4 Error.

63.4 Error (HP LaserJet IIISi) This error indicates a possible faulty expansion SIMM. The printer will still print, but will only be able to use the expansion memory below the faulty SIMM. Turn the printer off and verify that the SIMM is installed correctly, then turn the printer back on. If the error continues, turn the printer off and remove the SIMM. If the message clears, the problem is on the SIMM. If the message appears, the problem is in the base printer memory or SIMM socket.

63.5 Service (HP LaserJet 4Si) See 63 Needs Service.

64 Service (All HP LaserJet printers) See 67 Service.

65 Service (All HP LaserJet printers) See 67 Service.

67 Service (All HP LaserJet printers) The printer has identified an internal service error. Turn the printer off, remove any font cartridges from the printer, and turn the printer back on. If the message persists, replace the main controller.

TABLE 21-2   HP LASERJET FAMILY MESSAGES AND ERROR CODES (CONTINUED)

68 Cold Reset   (HP LaserJet IIISi) The printer's non-volatile memory is new or the battery is dead. The printer returns all printing and configuration menu selections to factory default. If the printer is set up as a PostScript printer, the 68 reset will return it to PCL status. If the message always appears when the printer is turned on, the printer will still operate, but it should be serviced (replace the NVRAM or battery) to correct the problem.

68 Error   (HP LaserJet 4, 4SI, 4P) This is a recoverable NVRAM error. Press <Continue> to clear the error.

68 Service   (HP LaserJet II, IID, IIP, IIP+ III, IIID, IIIP, IIISi, 4, 4Si, 4P) The printer has detected a non-volatile RAM failure. The printer can be operated until the NVRAM is replaced (all control-panel settings return to factory default until serviced).

69 Service   (HP LaserJet II, IID, III, IIID) This error indicates an optional I/O interface error. The printer has found a problem on the optional interface card. Turn the printer off and verify that the optional interface card is installed correctly. Turn printer on and verify that the optional interface card is configured correctly. If the error persists, replace the I/O interface card.

70 Error   (HP LaserJet II, IID, IIP, IIP Plus, II, IIID, IIIP, 4Si) This error indicates an incompatibility between the printer and the installed font cartridge. Turn the printer off and then back on. Verify that the cartridge was designed for use with that model printer.

71 Error   (HP LaserJet II, IID, IIP, IIP Plus, IIID, IIIP) This error indicates an incompatibility between the printer and the installed font cartridge. Turn the printer off, then back on. Verify that the installed cartridge was designed for use with that model printer.

71 Error   (HP LaserJet IIISi, 4Si) An attempt was made to use a "personality" firmware cartridge. Personality cartridges are not supported on the HP LaserJet IIISi or HP LaserJet 4Si printers.

72 Service   (HP LaserJet IIISi, 4Si, 4SiMX) A font cartridge was removed while the printer was trying to access it —this causes a misread by the printer, and produces the error code. Turn the printer off and back on, then try the font cartridge again.

72 Service   (LaserJet II, IID, IIP, IIP Plus, III, IIID, IIIP) The font cartridge was removed too quickly after it was inserted, causing a misread by the printer. Turn the printer off and back on, then try the font cartridge again.

79 01bb   (HP LaserJet IIP Plus) There are incompatibilities between the printer and software. Check the memory indicated by the software ("XXXX" or "bb") and verify that it is what is in the printer.

79 Service XXXX   (HP LaserJet IIP Plus) See 79 01bb.

80 Service XXXX   (HP LaserJet IIISi, 4, 4M, 4Si) A modular I/O interface error has occurred. Replace the I/O interface.

81 Service XXXX   (HP LaserJet 4, 4M) The printer has detected a problem with an internal controller. The numbers following the message ("XXXX") indicate the specific type of error. If the problem doesn't clear by cycling the printer's power, replace the main controller.

89 Service   (HP LaserJet IIISi) A PostScript internal controller error occurred.

Blank LCD   (HP LaserJet SII, IIP, IIP Plus, IID, III, IIID, IIIP, IIISi, 4, 4M, 4P, 4MP, 4Si, 4SiMX) Printer cannot generate sufficient voltages to activate the display panel or the display panel and/or its related circuitry is defective. Verify that the ac power supply and cord are OK. Turn the printer off and wait 10 to 15 minutes, then turn it back on. If the display remains blank, it will have to be serviced.

Blank LED   (HP LaserJet, Plus, and 500 Plus) The printer cannot generate sufficient voltages to activate the display panel or the display panel and/or its related circuitry is defective. Verify ac power supply and cord are OK. Turn the printer off and wait 10 to 15 minutes, then turn it back on. If the display remains blank, it will have to be serviced.

Config Lang.   (HP LaserJet IIP, IIP+, IID, III, IIIP, IIID, IIISi) The printer was turned on while holding down the <Enter> key. This allows the operator to select a local language for display. See the Language= message.

TABLE 21-2 HP LASERJET FAMILY MESSAGES AND ERROR CODES (CONTINUED)

EE Load (envelope) (HP LaserJet 4, 4M, 4Si, 4SiMX) The printer received a request for an envelope size that is not currently loaded in the envelope feeder (or the feeder is empty). Load the correct envelope size into the feeder, or press <Continue> to use the media currently loaded in the feeder.

FC bottom (All HP LaserJet printers) See FC top.

FC left (All HP LaserJet printers) See FC top.

FC No Font (HP LaserJet IIISi) The font cartridge (FC) could not be read by the printer. Reinsert the cartridge and press <Continue> or <On-Line> to resume operation. If the error persists, replace the font cartridge.

FC right (All HP LaserJet printers) See FC top.

FC top (All HP LaserJet printers) The font cartridge (FC) was removed while the printer was offline and contained buffered print data. Re-insert font cartridge(s) and press <Continue>.

FE Font Cart Err (All HP LaserJet printers) The font cartridge (FC) was removed or installed while the printer was on-line. Turn the printer off and back on to clear the message.

FI Insert Btm (HP LaserJet 4, 4M, 4P, 4Si) See FI Insert Cart.

FI Insert Cart (HP LaserJet 4, 4M, 4P, 4Si) An accessory cartridge was removed while the printer was in an error state. Insert the accessory cartridge and clear any pending error conditions before removing the cartridge.

FI Insert Top (HP LaserJet 4, 4M, 4P, 4Si) See FI Insert Cart.

FR Remove Btm (HP LaserJet 4, 4M, 4Si, 4P) See FR Remove Cart.

FR Remove Cart (HP LaserJet 4, 4M, 4Si, 4P) An accessory cartridge was inserted while the printer was in an error state. Remove the accessory cartridge and clear any pending error condition before inserting the cartridge.

FR Remove Top (HP LaserJet 4, 4M, 4Si, 4P) See FR Remove Cart.

Language= (HP LaserJet IIP, IIP+, IID, III, IIIP, IIID, IIISi) This status message will default to: Language=Eng. Press the + (plus) or − (minus) key to select an appropriate language. Press the <Enter> key once to select the language, then put the printer back on-line.

LC Empty (HP LaserJet IIP, IIP+, IIIP) This message appears when the lower cassette (LC) tray is empty and is not the selected paper tray. Because the message refers to a non-selected paper tray, it does not require the tray to be filled for the printer to function—it is merely a reminder that the tray is empty.

LC Load (HP LaserJet IIP, IIP+, IIIP) This message appears when the lower cassette (LC) tray is empty, and has been chosen by the front panel as the selected paper tray. Load the correct paper size and put the printer back on-line. Verify that the page size has been properly set.

LE Empty (HP LaserJet IIP, IIP+, IIIP) This message appears when the lower envelope (LE) tray is empty and is not the selected paper tray. Because the message refers to a non-selected paper tray, it does not require the tray to filled for the printer to function—it is merely a reminder that the tray is empty.

LE Load (HP LaserJet IIP, IIP+, IIIP) This message appears when the lower envelope (LE) tray is empty and has been chosen by the front panel as the selected paper tray. Load the correct envelope size and put the printer back on-line. Verify that the envelope size has been properly set.

ME Feed (envelope) (HP LaserJet 4, 4M, 4Si, 4SiMX, 4P, 4MP) The printer requested that an envelope be manually fed. Insert the appropriate envelope size (#10, Monarch, DL, C5, B5, or Envelope) into the tray (manual feed guides for the HP LaserJet 4Si) and press <On-Line> to print. On the HP LaserJet 4P, insert the appropriate media in the manual-feed slot and it will automatically pull the envelope.

MF Feed (paper size) (HP LaserJet 4, 4M 4Si, 4P, 4MP) The printer requested that media be manually fed (MF). Insert the appropriate media size (Letter, Legal, Exec, or A4) into the MP tray (or manual feed guides for the HP LaserJet 4Si), and press <On-Line> to print, or press <Continue> to feed from the Paper Cassette. On the HP LaserJet 4P, insert the appropriate media into the manual feed slot, and it will automatically pull the paper.

TABLE 21-2 HP LASERJET FAMILY MESSAGES AND ERROR CODES (CONTINUED)

MF Ready   (HP LaserJet IIP, IIP+, IIIP) The printer is displaying a status message indicating that the front-panel selection of manual feed (MF) has been turned on. Insert paper into the multi-purpose tray and continue.

MP Empty   (HP LaserJet IIP, IIP+, IIIP) This message appears when the multi-purpose (MP) tray is empty and is not the selected paper tray. Because the message refers to a non-selected paper tray, it does not require the tray to filled for the printer to function—it is merely a reminder that the tray is empty.

MP Load   (HP LaserJet IIP, IIP+, IIIP) This message appears when the multi-purpose (MP) tray has been chosen by the front panel as the selected paper tray. Load the correct paper size and put the printer back on-line. Verify that the page size has been properly set.

PC Install   (HP LaserJet 4, 4M) The printer has detected that the paper cassette (PC), which serves as a paper guide for the lower cassette (LC), is not installed. Install or reseat the paper cassette.

PC-65   (HP LaserJet, Plus, 500 Plus) This is a printer message related to the paper cassette (PC). The printer is asking for the same paper length (size) that was requested by the printing software.

PCL Config   (HP LaserJet IIISi) In PCL mode, this message appears for one second before the PCL Configuration Menu appears after the Menu key is pressed and held for about five seconds.

PCL Print Menu   (HP LaserJet IIISi) In PCL mode, this message appears for one second before the PCL Printing Menu appears after the Menu key is pressed once.

Switching To   (HP LaserJet IIISi) This message indicates that the printer's language is in the process of being changed from PCL to PostScript, or from PostScript to PCL.

W0 Job 600/A4   (HP LaserJet 4, 4M, 4SI, 4P) The job was printed at 600 dpi with page-protection set to A4. To print the job as requested, install additional memory.

W1 Image Adapt   (HP LaserJet 4, 4M, 4SI, 4P) The printer received a graphics print file that was too complex to print at the requested resolution. The printer automatically processes the file in the highest resolution possible with the memory installed. Add additional memory to print the file at full resolution.

W2 Invalid Pers   (HP LaserJet 4, 4M, 4SI, 4P) The job was not printed because the requested "personality" (such as PostScript) was not installed. Install the proper "personality."

W3 Job Aborted   (HP LaserJet 4, 4M, 4SI, 4P) The printer was forced to abort the print job because there was not enough memory to support the printer language used. Add more memory.

W4 Job 300/Off   (HP LaserJet 4, 4M, 4SI, 4P) The job was printed at 300 dpi with page protection set to off. To print the job as requested, install additional memory.

W5 Job 300/Ltr   (HP LaserJet 4, 4M, 4SI, 4P) The job was printed at 300 dpi with page protection set to letter. To print the job as requested, install additional memory.

W6 Job 300/A4   (HP LaserJet 4, 4M, 4SI, 4P) The job was printed at 300 dpi with page protection set to A4. To print the job as requested, install additional memory.

W7 Job 300/Lgl   (HP LaserJet 4, 4M, 4SI, 4P) The job was printed at 300 dpi with page protection set to legal. To print the job as requested, install additional memory.

W8 Job 600/Off   (HP LaserJet 4, 4M, 4SI, 4P) The job was printed at 600 dpi with page protection off. To print the job as requested, install additional memory.

W9 Job 600/Ltr   (HP LaserJet 4, 4M, 4SI, 4P) The job was printed at 600 dpi with page protection set to letter. To print the job as requested, install additional memory.

Wm Check Mem Mgt   (HP LaserJet 4Si, 4SiMX) There is still sufficient memory to accommodate resource saving, but the current setting cannot be satisfied by the available memory. Reconfigure the "resource saving" feature for the current personality.

Wm Mem Cnfig N/A   (HP LaserJet 4Si, 4SiMX) Because of configuration changes, resource saving is no longer available. If resource saving is desired, print a self-test page. Check the configuration settings, then reconfigure resource saving.

XX Load (paper size)   (HP LaserJet 4, 4M, 4Si, and 4SiMX) The printer received a request for a paper or envelope size not available in the printer (or the tray is empty). The "XX" will be "MP" (Multi-Purpose), "PC" (Paper Cassette), or "LC" (Lower Cassette). 4Si and 4SiMX printers might also use "UC" (Upper Cassette). Load the correct paper tray and media, and press <Continue> to use the media in the selected tray.

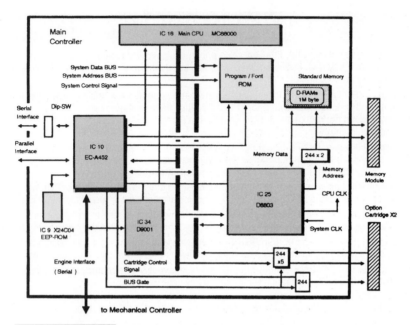

FIGURE 21-11   **Diagram of an EP main controller board.** Tandy
Corporation

As in a computer, all of the printer's on-board instructions and programming are held in a
ROM on the main controller board. The ROM provides the internal instructions and data
(the "firmware") needed by the CPU for processing. When the printer starts, a checksum
test is run on the ROM to verify the integrity of its contents. If the resulting checksum
does not match the checksum reference number stored in the ROM, an error is generated.
You can see the "program/font ROM" in Fig. 21-11.

First, check to see that any supplemental font or option cartridges are installed properly—you might try removing the cartridge(s) to find if the problem disappears. If there
are no option cartridges, check to see that the ROM IC is installed securely. If the problem persists, you must replace the ROM IC. In many cases, ROM ICs are socket-mounted
devices because they must be programmed outside of the logic board's assembly process.
When this is the case, you might be able to replace the ROM IC directly. If the ROM IC
is soldered to the main logic board (or a replacement ROM IC is simply not available), you
will have to replace the entire main logic board.

**Symptom 21-3. The printer's LCD shows a "RAM R/W error," a "Memory er-
ror," or another memory defect**   Your particular printer might use an error number
(i.e., Error 12 or Error 30) to represent the condition. Dynamic RAM (DRAM) serves as
the workspace for an EP printer. Where moving-carriage printers typically offer buffers
of 8KB or 16KB, the EP printer can easily offer 4MB or more—some high-end printers
can accommodate 48MB or more. This volume of memory is necessary because the EP
printer must be able to construct the data needed to form an entire page at a time. For an
8.5"-×-11" page at high resolutions, this can be a phenomenal volume of data. Unfortunately, trouble in any part of the DRAM can adversely affect the image—especially Post-

Script images. Memory is tested when the printer is first initialized. Like PCs, the more memory that is installed, the longer it takes the printer to initialize. A typical test involves writing a known byte to each address, then reading those bytes back. If the read byte matches the written byte, the address is considered good—otherwise, a RAM error is reported. You can see the default 1MB of DRAM in Fig. 21-11.

It is rare that a RAM error message will indicate the specific location of the error, but you can easily isolate the fault to a bad memory module or to the standard (resident) memory. Turn off and unplug the printer, then remove any expansion memory modules that might be installed. You might have to set jumpers or DIP switches to tell the printer that memory has been removed. If the problem disappears, one or more of your expansion memory modules has failed. Try re-installing one module at a time until the problem reoccurs—the last module to be installed when the error surfaced is the faulty module. If the problem persists when memory modules are removed, you can be confident that the fault is in your resident memory. Although memory modules often take the form of SIMMs or other plug-in modules, resident RAM is typically hard-soldered to the main controller board. You might attempt to replace the RAM if you have the proper desoldering tools and replacement RAM ICs on hand. Otherwise, simply replace the main controller board.

Symptom 21-4. Your printer's LCD shows a "Memory overflow" error Your particular printer might use an error code (i.e., Error 20) to represent the condition. When data is sent from the computer to the printer, part of that data consists of "user information," such as soft-fonts and macro commands. If the amount of "user information" exceeds the amount of RAM set aside for it, a "Memory overflow" (or similar error) will be generated. Although this error is not directly related to the image size or complexity, complex images typically carry a larger overhead of "user information"—so you might find that "simplifying" the image can sometimes clear the problem—even though the image itself is not really at fault. Generally speaking, you can eliminate this error by adding optional memory, or reducing the amount of data that must be downloaded to the printer (such as reducing the image's resolution or size—these are often functions of the application doing the printing).

Symptom 21-5. Your printer's LCD shows a "Print overrun" error Your particular printer might use an error code (i.e., Error 21) to represent the condition. Unlike the last error, "print overrun" problems almost always indicate that the page to be printed is too complicated for the printer—there is just not enough memory to hold all of the data required to form the image. To overcome this type of problem, try simplifying the image (i.e., use fewer fonts or try using solid shading instead of dithering). You might also try making the printed area smaller. For example, instead of printing an image at 8" × 8", try printing it at 5" × 5". The smaller image requires less raw data. The ideal way to correct this problem over the long term is to add memory to the printer.

Symptom 21-6. The printer reports an "I/O protocol error" Your particular printer might use an error code (i.e., Error 22) to represent the condition. This is a communication fault. The term *protocol* basically means "agreement" or "rules." So, when a protocol error arises, it suggests that the computer and printer are not communicating "by the rules." The most blatant protocol error is connecting a serial port to a parallel printer, or a parallel port to a serial printer—but this extremely rare oversight usually only occurs when a printer is first installed. Protocol errors among parallel ports are also very rare because parallel-port operation is very well defined with handshaking designed right into the signal layout. The most likely protocol problems can arise with serial communication—there are so many variables in the serial process (which must be matched between the printer and computer) that even the slightest error can cause problems.

Start by checking the connections between the computer and printer. See that the communication link is parallel-to-parallel or serial-to-serial. Also try a new, high-quality cable (serial or parallel, as appropriate) between the printer and computer. When parallel communication is being used, a protocol error is suggestive of a failure in the communication-interface IC (IC10 in Fig. 21-11). You can try replacing the communication IC or replace the main controller board entirely. When serial communication is being used, you should examine any DIP switches or jumpers inside the printer. Check to see that the communication speed and framing bits are all set as expected, then see that the corresponding COM port in the PC is configured similarly (through the printing application or the Windows Printer control panel). If problems persist—even when the serial communication link is set properly—suspect that trouble is in the communication interface IC. You can try replacing the communication IC or replace the main controller outright.

Symptom 21-7. The image is composed of "garbage" and disassociated symbols Your printer might also generate a "Parity/framing error" or use an error code (i.e., Error 40) to represent the condition. This error indicates that there is a problem with serial data framing. Serial data must be "framed" with the proper number of start, data, parity, and stop bits. These bits must be set the same way at the printer and the computer's COM port. If either end of the communication link is set improperly, data passed from the computer to the printer will be misinterpreted (resulting in highly distorted printout). Check the printer first and note any DIP switch or jumper settings that affect the data frame. Next, check the COM-port settings at the computer (under the printing application or the Windows Printer control panel). The COM port's start, data, parity, and stop-bit configuration should all match the printer's settings. If not, adjust either the COM-port parameters or the printer DIP switch settings so that both ends of the communication link are set the same way. If problems persist, there might be a fault in the printer's communication IC (i.e., IC10 in Fig. 21-11). You might try replacing the IC or the main controller entirely.

Symptom 21-8. The image appears to be "stitched" *Stitching* is an image distortion, where points in the image appear to have been "pulled" in the horizontal direction (typically to the right). Figure 21-12 illustrates the "stitching" effect, along with some manifestations of other controller errors. Images are formed by scanning a laser beam repetitively across the drum. Pixels are formed by turning the laser beam on and off while scanning—a function performed by the mechanical controller board (Fig. 21-13). If there is an intermittent fault in the mechanical controller logic, beam modulation might fail during one or more scanning passes—resulting in random "pulls" in the image.

Start your examination by checking all of the cables between the laser/scanner assembly and the mechanical controller. Loose wiring might result in intermittent laser fire. Turn off and unplug the printer, then try removing and reinstalling each of the connectors. Check any other wiring on the mechanical controller as well. If problems persist, chances are very good that the mechanical controller has failed. You might attempt to troubleshoot

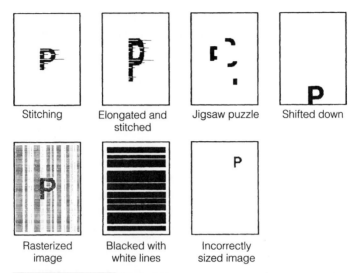

| Stitching | Elongated and stitched | Jigsaw puzzle | Shifted down |

| Rasterized image | Blacked with white lines | Incorrectly sized image |

FIGURE 21-12   Recognizing main controller board faults.

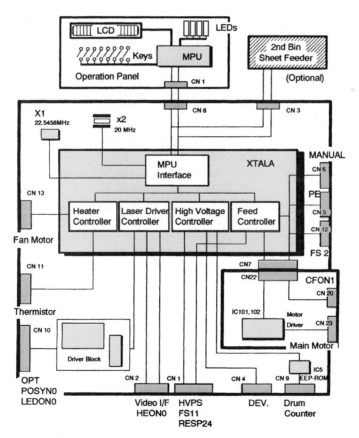

FIGURE 21-13   Diagram of an EP mechanical controller board. Tandy Corporation

the mechanical controller, but it is often more efficient to simply replace the mechanical controller board outright. If a new mechanical controller fails to resolve the problem, replace the laser/scanner assembly.

Symptom 21-9. The image appears elongated and "stitched" This is a variation of Symptom 21-8. Not only is the laser beam misfiring intermittently, but the image is being "stretched" along the page. Under most circumstances, there has been a logic failure on the mechanical controller. Before you attempt work on the controller, however, try reseating each of the connectors on the mechanical controller. Be sure to turn off and unplug the printer before fiddling with any connectors. If problems persist, there is a serious fault in the printer's ECU. You might attempt to troubleshoot the ECU, but this type of fault can be very difficult to track down. As a result, it is often better to replace the mechanical controller board first. If that fails to correct the problem, try a new main logic board. If your particular printer design integrates all of the logic and controlling circuitry on a single ECU board, replace that board outright.

Symptom 21-10. Portions of the image are disassociated like a "jigsaw puzzle" Of all the controller failures, this is perhaps one of the most perplexing. You might notice that some elements of the printed image are just fine, but other (larger) areas of print seem jumbled around. To make matters worse, the problem is often intermittent, so some printed pages might appear just fine. Under most circumstances, there has been a logic failure on the main controller board. Before you attempt work on the main controller, however, try reseating each of the connectors on the main and mechanical controller boards. Be sure to turn off and unplug the printer before working with any connectors. If problems persist, there is a serious fault in the printer's ECU. You might attempt to troubleshoot the ECU, but this type of "jigsaw puzzle" operation can be very difficult to track down. As a result, it is often better to replace the main controller board first. If that fails to correct the problem, try a new mechanical controller board. If your particular printer design integrates all of the logic and controlling circuitry on a single ECU board, replace that board outright.

Symptom 21-11. The image appears to be shifted down very significantly This type of problem is illustrated in Fig. 21-12. At first glance, you might be tempted to think that this is a registration problem (and that cannot be ruled out), but it is also possible that fault on the mechanical controller (probably the "feed control" circuit, as in Fig. 21-13) is passing the page through far too soon before the developed image is aligned. Chances are that the pickup and registration mechanics are working correctly; otherwise, the page would likely lose its top margin or appear smudged. When the top margin is excessive, suspect a logic fault. Specifically, you should suspect that a logic error is firing the registration system too soon after a printing cycle starts. You should address this type of problem by troubleshooting or replacing the mechanical controller board.

Symptom 21-12. The image appears "rasterized" with no intelligible information A "rasterized" image is a complete distortion—there is rarely any discernible information in the printed page. Instead, the image is composed of broken horizontal lines (Fig. 21-12). The trick with this type of fault is that it is not always easy to determine the problem origin. Turn off and unplug the printer. Open the printer and check each cable and wiring harness at the controller board(s) and laser/scanning assembly. Try reseating each of the connectors. If the problem persists, the fault is almost certainly in the main controller board. You might be able to troubleshoot the ECU, but this type of logical troubleshooting can be extremely challenging and time consuming. So, it is often easier to just replace the main controller board and re-test the printer. If a new controller board fails to correct the problem, you should troubleshoot or replace the mechanical controller board.

Symptom 21-13. The image is blacked out with white horizontal lines

This type of problem creates a page that is blacked out, except for a series of white horizontal bars, and will typically eradicate any discernible image on the page. As it turns out, connector problems can readily cause this type of problem, so start your examination there. Turn off and unplug the printer, then check the wiring harnesses and reseat each connector on the main and mechanical controller boards. Be extremely careful to replace each connector carefully, and avoid bending any of the connector pins.

   If the problem continues, your fault is likely to be in the main controller board. You might be able to troubleshoot the ECU, but this type of logical troubleshooting can be extremely challenging and time consuming—especially under these symptoms. So, it is often easier to just replace the main controller board and re-test the printer. If a new controller board fails to correct the problem, you should troubleshoot or replace the mechanical controller board.

Symptom 21-14. The image is incorrectly sized along the vertical axis

Ideally, an image should be sized according the size of whatever paper tray is installed. If the image size is significantly smaller than expected, you should first check to see that the proper paper tray is installed, and that the printing application is set to use the correct paper size (especially under Windows). If everything is configured properly, you should examine the paper-tray sensors, as described in Chapter 9. Replace any defective tray sensor microswitches. If problems persist, you should also inspect any wiring harnesses and connectors at the mechanical controller. Loose or defective wiring can cause erroneous page sizing. If the connectors check properly, you should suspect a logical problem in the mechanical controller board. You might attempt to troubleshoot the mechanical controller if you wish or you might simply choose to replace the mechanical controller outright. If that should fail to resolve the problem, try a new main controller board.

REGISTRATION SYMPTOMS

The "registration" process involves picking up a sheet of paper and positioning it for use. As a result, any problems in the paper tray, pickup roller, separation pad, registration rollers, or the related drive train can result in any one of the following problems. Registration problems are really quite common—especially in older printers, where age and wear can affect the rollers, gears, and crucial mechanical spacing. In very mild cases, you might be able to correct a registration problem with careful cleaning and a bit of re-adjustment. For most situations, however, you will need to replace a defective mechanical assembly or a failing electromechanical device (such as a clutch).

Symptom 21-15. The print contains lines of print—usually in the lower half of the page—that appear smudged

A simple example of this problem is shown in Fig. 21-14. This symptom is almost always the result of a problem with your registration rollers. Uneven wear can allow the registration rollers to grip the page firmly at one point,

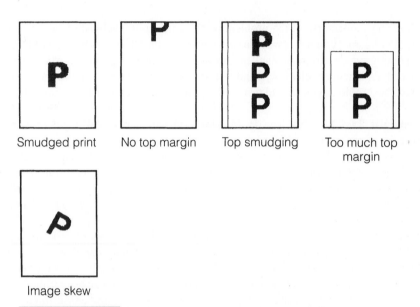

Smudged print   No top margin   Top smudging   Too much top margin

Image skew

FIGURE 21-14   **Recognizing pickup/registration faults.**

then loosely at another point. When the grip tightens up, the page jerks forward just a fraction—but enough to smudge (or "blur") the print at that point. Turn off and unplug the printer, then expose the registration assembly and examine it closely. Look for any accumulations of debris or obstructions that might force the registration rollers apart at different points. Remove any obstructions and try cleaning the roller pair. Examine the registration drive train and look for any gears that might be damaged or obstructed. Clean the drive train and replace any damaged gears. If the problem persists, consider replacing the registration assembly.

Symptom 21-16. There is no apparent top margin The image might run off the top of the page (Fig. 21-14). In just about every case, there is a fault in the pickup assembly. As a consequence, the page is not being passed to the registration assembly in time to be aligned with the leading edge of the drum image, so the image appears cut off at the page top. Start by examining your paper tray. Be sure that the "lift mechanism" is not jammed or otherwise interfering with paper leaving the tray. If you're not sure, try a different paper tray. Also consider paper problems. Unusually light or specially coated papers might simply not be picked up properly. Try a standard 20-lb. bond xerography-grade paper. If problems persist at this point, chances are that your pickup assembly is failing. Turn off and unplug the printer, then examine your pickup system closely. Check for any accumulations of debris or obstructions that might interfere with the pickup sequence. Remove any obstructions, then clean the pickup roller and separation pad. Also examine the pickup drive train and clutch. Any jammed or damaged gears should be replaced. If the solenoid clutch is sticking or failing, you should replace the solenoid clutch or clutch PC board. If that fails to resolve the problem, you will have little alternative but to replace the pickup assembly and separation pad.

Symptom 21-17. Pronounced smudging is at the top of the image (generally near the top margin) This symptom suggests that the registration assembly is failing or has not been installed correctly. Turn off and unplug the printer, then expose the registration system. Carefully inspect the system to see that the rollers and drive drain are installed properly. Try re-installing the registration assembly. If problems persist, try a new registration assembly.

Symptom 21-18. Too much margin space is on top of the image If excessive margin space is at the top of the image, it generally indicates that the paper has been allowed into the IFS too soon—paper is traveling through the printer before the drum image was ready. This fault is usually related to the registration roller clutch. You see, the registration rollers are supposed to hold the page until the drum image is aligned properly. This means that the registrations rollers must be engaged or disengaged, as required—typically through a clutch mechanism. If the clutch is jammed in the engaged position, the registration rollers will always run (passing each new page through immediately). Turn off and unplug the printer, then examine your registration clutch closely. If the clutch is jammed, try to free it and clean surrounding mechanics to remove any accumulations of debris. If the clutch fails to re-engage or remains jammed, replace the registration clutch entirely or replace the clutch solenoid PC board.

Symptom 21-19. The image is "skewed" (not square with the page) Skew occurs when the page is passed through the printer at an angle (rather than straight). Typically, paper must enter the printer straight because of the paper tray, so the page must shift because of a mechanical problem. In actuality, however, a loose or bent paper guide tab can often shift the paper as it enters the printer. Start your examination by checking the paper tray—specifically the paper cassette guide tab. If the tab is loose or bent, replace it or try a new paper tray. If the paper tray is intact, consider the paper itself. Unusually light or specially coated papers can skew in the pickup and registration mechanics. If you are using an unusual paper, try some standard 20-lb. xerography-grade paper. If the problem continues, turn off and unplug the printer, then examine the pickup and registration mechanics. Check for obstructions or any accumulations of foreign matter that might interfere with the paper path and cause the page to skew. If there is nothing conclusive, try replacing the pickup assembly and separation pad, then the registration assembly (in that order).

LASER/SCANNER SYMPTOMS

A laser beam must be modulated (turned on and off, corresponding to the presence or absence of a dot) and scanned across the conditioned drum. Both modulation and scanning must occur at a fairly high rate to form an image—up to 24 pages per minute and more in some high-end models. However, the process of writing with a laser beam is not so simple a task, as you see in Fig. 21-15. Variations in laser output power (often because of age), variations in polygon motor speed (also caused by age and wear), and the accumulation of dust and debris on the polygon mirror and other optical components will all have an adverse impact on the final image. Faults can even creep into the laser sensor and affect beam detection and alignment. EP printer designers responded to the problems associated with such a delicate assembly by placing all of the laser, control, and scanning components into a single "laser/scanner" assembly. Today, the laser/scanner is an easily replaceable module—and that is how you should treat it.

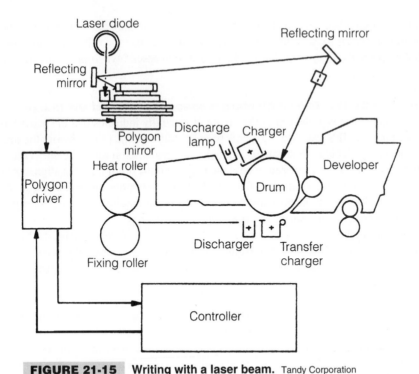

FIGURE 21-15   **Writing with a laser beam.** Tandy Corporation

Symptom 21-20 Right-hand text appears missing or distorted Figure 21-16 illustrates a typical example. In many cases, this is simply a manifestation of low toner in your EP/toner cartridge. If any area of the development roller receives insufficient toner, it will result in very light or missing image areas. Turn off and unplug the printer, remove the EP/toner cartridge, and re-distribute the toner. Follow your manufacturer's recommendations for toner redistribution. If you see an improvement in image quality (at least temporarily), replace the EP/toner cartridge.

Examine the shock mountings that support your laser/scanner assembly. If the laser/scanner assembly is loose or not mounted correctly, scan lines might not be delivered to the proper drum locations. Try re-mounting the laser/scanner assembly. If the problem persists, replace the writing mechanism entirely. If you are using a laser-writing mechanism, pay special attention to the installation and alignment of the laser-beam sensor.

Symptom 21-21 Horizontal black lines are spaced randomly through the print Remember that black areas are the result of light striking the drum. If your printer uses a laser/scanner assembly, a defective or improperly seated beam detector could send false scan timing signals to the main logic. The laser would then make its scan line while main logic waits to send its data. At the beginning of each scan cycle, the laser beam strikes a detector. The detector carries laser light through an optical fiber to a circuit, which converts light into an electronic logic signal that is compatible with the mechanical controller's logic. Circuitry interprets this "beam-detect signal" and knows the polygon mirror is properly aligned to begin a new scan. The mechanical controller then modulates the laser beam on and off, corresponding to the presence or absence of dots in the scan line.

Positioning and alignment are crucial here. If the beam detector is misaligned or loose, the printer's motor vibrations might cause the detector to occasionally miss the beam. Printer circuitry responds to this by activating the laser full-duty in an effort to synchronize itself again. Re-seat the laser/scanner assembly, or try re-seating the beam detector and optical fiber. If the problem persists, replace the beam detector and cable, or replace the laser/scanner unit outright.

Symptom 21-22 The printer's LCD reports a "polygon motor synchronization error" The printer might also display an error code (i.e., Error 31) to represent the condition. The polygon mirror is the heart of the laser scanning system. The motor's speed must be absolutely steady. If the motor fails to rotate or fails to synchronize at a constant rate within a few seconds of power-up, scanning will fail. In early EP printers, the polygon motor and mirror were implemented as discrete devices. In today's EP printers, however, the laser, scanner motor, and polygon mirror are all integrated into a replaceable laser/scanner assembly. If a scanner error is reported, you should first shut down the entire printer, let it rest for several minutes, then turn it back on to see if the error clears. If the fault persists, your best course is simply to replace the laser/scanner assembly entirely.

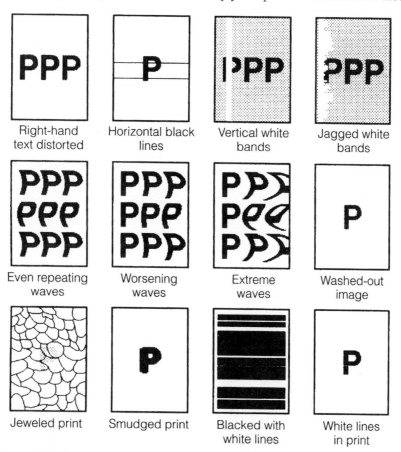

Right-hand text distorted	Horizontal black lines	Vertical white bands	Jagged white bands
Even repeating waves	Worsening waves	Extreme waves	Washed-out image
Jeweled print	Smudged print	Blacked with white lines	White lines in print

FIGURE 21-16 Recognizing laser/scanner faults. Tandy Corporation

Symptom 21-23. One or more vertical white bands is in the image At first glance, this symptom might appear to be a problem with the transfer corona. However, you will notice that the white band(s) appearing here are thick and well-defined (and cleaning the transfer corona will have no effect). A hard white band, such as this, suggests that the laser beam (or LED light) is being blocked. This is not as uncommon as you might imagine. Dust, foreign matter, and debris can accumulate on the focusing lens and obstruct the light path. It is also possible that a chip or scratch is in the lens.

Turn off and unplug the printer. Start your examination by checking and cleaning the transfer corona—the trouble is probably not here, but perform a quick check just to eliminate that possibility. If the transfer corona is dirty, certainly retest the printer. If the problem persists, expose the "beam-to-drum" mirror and focusing lens, and examine both closely. Look for dust, dirt, toner, paper fragments, or any other foreign matter that might have accumulated on the optics. If you find foreign matter, you should not just blow it out with compressed air—it will make a mess, and the dust will eventually resettle somewhere else. Take the nozzle of a vacuum cleaner and hold it in proximity of the optical area, then blow the optics clean with a canister of compressed air. This way, the foreign matter loosened by the compressed air will be vacuumed away, rather than re-settle in the printer. The key idea to remember here is: Do not touch the optics!

For stains or stubborn debris, clean the afflicted optics gently with a high-quality lens-cleaner fluid and wipes from any photography store. Be very careful not to dislodge the "beam-to-drum" mirror or lens from its mounting. Never blow on a lens or mirror yourself—breath vapor and particles can condense and dry on a lens to cause even more problems in the future. Allow any cleaner residue to dry completely before re-assembling and re-testing the printer.

If the problem persists, suspect a problem with the laser/scanner assembly. Some foreign matter, which would block the scanned beam as it leaves the scanner, might be on the laser aperture. Check the laser/scanner's beam aperture and clean away any foreign matter. If the material is inside the laser/scanner assembly, it should be replaced.

Symptom 21-24. A white, jagged band is in the image This symptom is similar in nature to the previous symptom—foreign matter is interfering with the laser beam path. The major difference is that instead of a solid white band, you see a random, jagged white band. A major difference, however, is that the obstruction is random (drifting in and out of the laser path unpredictably). This suggests that you are dealing with a loose obstruction, such as a paper fragment, which is able to move freely. Turn off and unplug the printer, then check for obstructions around the transfer corona. Although the transfer corona itself is probably not fouled, a paper fragment stuck on the monofilament line can flutter back and forth resulting in the same jagged appearance.

Next, check the optical path for any loose material that could obstruct the laser beam. Be particularly concerned with paper fragments or peeling labels. Fortunately, such obstructions are relatively easy to spot and remove. When removing an obstruction, be careful to avoid scratching or moving any of the optical components. If the problem persists, you might have an obstruction inside of the laser/scanner assembly, so it should be replaced.

Symptom 21-25. Repetitive waves are in the image You can see a simple example of this fault in Fig. 21-16. All of the image elements are printed, but there is a regular "wave" in the image. This kind of distortion is typically referred to as *scanner modulation*, where scanner speed oscillates up and down just a bit during the scanning process. In virtually all cases, the fault lies in your laser/scanner assembly. Turn off and unplug the printer, then try re-seating the cables and wiring harnesses connected to the laser/scanner unit. Try the printer again. If problems persist, replace the laser/scanner assembly.

Symptom 21-26. Worsening waves are in the image This type of problem is a variation of the "scanner modulation" fault shown in the previous symptom. In this case, however, the modulation is relatively mild on the left side of the page, and gradually increases in magnitude toward the right side. These "worsening waves" can take several forms (Fig. 21-16): typical manifestations can be heavy or light. Regardless of the modulation intensity, all of these symptoms can often be traced to a connector problem at the laser/scanner assembly. Turn off and unplug the printer, then carefully re-seat each connector and wiring harness between the laser/scanner unit and the mechanical controller board. If problems persist, replace the laser/scanner assembly.

Symptom 21-27. The image appears washed out—little or no intelligible information is in the image Typically, you will see random dots appearing over the page, but there are not enough dots to form a coherent image. Now, you might recall that light images might suggest a problem with the high-voltage power supply or the transfer system, but in many such circumstances, some hint of an image is visible. You might also suspect the toner supply, but toner that is too low to form an image will register a "low toner" error. Still, a quick check is always advisable. Remove the EP cartridge and try re-distributing the toner, then try darkening the print-density wheel setting. If the image improves, check the EP/toner cartridge and suspect the HVPS. Otherwise, you should suspect a failure at the laser diode itself. Although solid-state lasers do tend to run for long periods with little real degradation in power, an aging laser diode might produce enough energy to satisfy the laser sensor, but not nearly enough to discharge the EP drum. Try replacing the laser/scanner assembly.

Symptom 21-28. The print appears "jeweled" You can see this kind of print in Fig. 21-16. This is caused when the laser beam is totally unable to synchronize with the printer—the laser sensor is failing to detect the beam. In many cases, the fiber-optic cable carrying the laser signal has been detached or broken. If the optical cable is a stand-alone component, it is a relatively easy matter to replace the cable and sensor. If the cable and sensor are integrated into the laser/scanner assembly, your best course is to re-seat the cables and wiring harnesses between the laser/scanner and the mechanical controller board. If problems persist, replace the laser/scanner assembly outright.

Symptom 21-29. The print regularly "smudges" When dirt, dust, and other foreign matter accumulate on the "beam-to-drum" mirror or compensating lens, they tend to block laser light at those points—resulting in vertical white bars or lines down the image. However, mild accumulations of dust or debris, which might not be heavy enough to block laser light, might be enough to "scatter" some of the light. This "scattered light" spreads like shrapnel, resulting in unwanted exposures. Because each point of exposure becomes dark, this often manifests itself as a "dirty" or "smudged" appearance in the print. Your best course is to clean the printer's optical deck. Turn off and unplug the printer, the expose the optical area. Place the nozzle from your vacuum cleaner in the immediate area, and blow away any dust and debris with a can of photography-grade compressed air. Do not attempt to vacuum inside of the printer! Just let it remove any airborne contaminants dislodged by the compressed air.

Symptom 21-30. The print is blacked out with white horizontal lines To modulate the laser beam to form dots, the data must be synchronized with the position of the laser beam. This synchronization is accomplished by the beam detector, which is typically located in the contemporary laser/scanner assembly. If the detector fails to detect the laser beam, it will fire full duty in an attempt to re-establish synchronization. When the beam fires, it will produce a black line across the page. Multiple subsequent black lines will effectively black-out the image. The white gaps occur if the beam is sensed or if a time-out/retry period has elapsed. In most cases, the beam sensor in the laser/scanner assembly has failed or become intermittent. Turn off and unplug the printer, then try re-seating each of the cables from the laser/scanner. If the problem persists, your best course is simply to replace the laser/scanner assembly entirely.

Symptom 21-31. The image forms correctly, except for random white gaps that appear horizontally across the page This is another manifestation of trouble in the laser-beam detection process. A kink in the fiber-optic cable can result in intermittent losses of laser power. In older printers with a discrete fiber-optic cable, it was simple to replace the cable outright. Now that beam detection is accomplished in the laser/scanner assembly itself, your best course is simply to replace the unit outright.

DRIVE AND TRANSMISSION SYMPTOMS

With so much emphasis placed on the key electronic and mechanical sub-assemblies of an EP printer, it can be easy to forget that each of those mechanical assemblies are coupled together with a comprehensive drive train of motors, gears, and (sometimes) pulleys. A failure—even an intermittent one—at any point in the drive or transmission will have some serious consequences in the printed image. Figure 21-17 outlines the printer's mechanical system.

The mechanical controller (sometimes referred to as the *dc controller*) starts the main motor. Once the main motor starts, a gear train will operate the EP drum, the transfer (or "feed") roller(s), and the fusing rollers. In some designs, the main motor will also operate a set of exit rollers, which direct the page to an output tray. Of course, there must also be a provision to pickup and register each page, but those assemblies cannot run "full-duty." Instead, they must be switched on and off at the proper time. To accomplish this timing, a solenoid-driven clutch (marked *solenoid*) is added to the pickup roller and registration roller assemblies. For the system in Fig. 21-17, a separate motor (marked *magnetic motor*) is used to drive the development system.

Symptom 21-32. Gaps and overlaps are in the print Figure 21-18 shows an example of this symptom. The problem here is a slipping gear or failing drive motor. Unfortunately, this is not so simple a problem to spot—gear assemblies are generally quite fine, and an intermittent gear movement can easily go unnoticed. Start with a careful inspection of the gear train. Be sure that all gears are attached and meshed securely. It is not

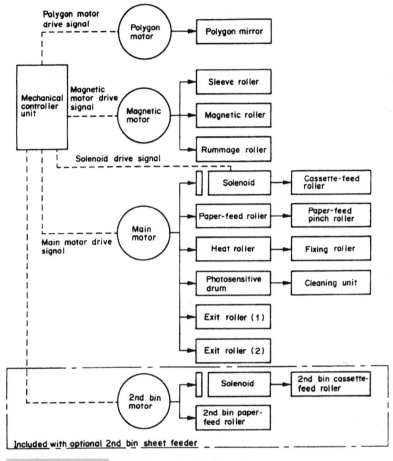

FIGURE 21-17   An EP mechanical system. Tandy Corporation

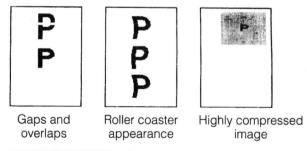

Gaps and overlaps

Roller coaster appearance

Highly compressed image

FIGURE 21-18   Recognizing drive or transmission problems.

uncommon for older gear assemblies to loosen with wear. Also check that the main motor is mounted securely and meshed properly with other gears. Be especially careful to check for obstructions or foreign matter that might be lodged in the gear train. Finally, you will need to check each gear for broken teeth—a time-consuming and tedious process to be sure, but it is preferable to dismantling the entire drive train. A high-intensity pen light will help to highlight broken gear teeth. Replace any gears that might be damaged. If the problem persists and the drive train is flawless, try replacing the main motor assembly.

Symptom 21-33. The print has a "roller-coaster" appearance This type of roller-coaster distortion is typically the result of a fault in the gear train. Start with a careful inspection of the gear train. Be sure that all gears are attached and meshed securely. It is not uncommon for older gear assemblies to loosen with wear. Also check that the main motor is mounted securely and meshed properly with other gears. Be especially careful to check for obstructions or foreign matter that might be lodged in the gear train. Finally, you will need to check each gear for broken teeth—a time-consuming and tedious process to be sure, but preferable to dismantling the entire drive train. A high-intensity pen light will help to highlight broken gear teeth. Replace any gears that might be damaged.

Symptom 21-34. The image is highly compressed in the vertical axis A highly compressed image can indicate a failing main motor—especially when the amount of "compression" varies randomly from page to page. Because the main motor is responsible for driving the entire system, a fault can interrupt the page transport. Check the main motor to see that it is mounted securely to the frame and meshed properly with other gears. Also check the connector and wiring harness at the main motor and mechanical controller board to be sure that everything is attached properly. If problems persist, try replacing the main motor. If that fails to correct the problem, replace the mechanical controller board.

HVPS SYMPTOMS

High voltage is the key to the electrophotographic process. Huge electrical charges must be established to condition the EP drum, develop a latent image, and transfer that image to a page. An HVPS for the classic "SX-type" engine develops –6000, +6000, and –600 V. The newer "CX-type" engine requires far less voltage (–1000, +1000, and –400 V). Still, high voltages impose some important demands on the power supply and its associated wiring. First, high-voltage supplies require precise component values that are rated for high-voltage operation. Although ordinary circuits might easily tolerate a "close" component value, HV supplies demand direct replacements. Installing a "close" value (or a part with a loose tolerance) in an HVPS can throw the output(s) way off. The other factor to consider is the wiring. Most commercial wire is only insulated to 600 V or so—higher voltages can jump the inexpensive commercial insulation and arc or short-circuit—even electrocute you. So, HVPS wiring harnesses and connectors are specially designed to operate safely at high voltages.

As a technician, these factors present some special problems. Replacement components are expensive and often difficult to find. Installing those components can be tedious and time consuming. Even when things are working perfectly, you can not measure the outputs directly without specialized test leads and equipment. When all of this is taken into account, it is almost always preferable to replace a suspect HVPS outright, rather than attempt to troubleshoot it.

Symptom 21-35. The printer's LCD displays a "high-voltage error" The printer might also use an error code (i.e., Error 35) to represent the condition. This indicates that one or more outputs from the HVPS are low or absent. The preferred technique is to replace the HVPS outright. Before replacing an HVPS, turn off and unplug the printer, and allow at least 15 minutes for charges in the HVPS to dissipate. When replacing the HVPS, be very careful to route any wiring away from logic circuitry, and pay close attention when installing new connectors. It is also important that you bolt the new HVPS securely into place to ensure proper grounding.

Symptom 21-36. The image is visible, but the printout is darkened You can see this type of symptom in Fig. 21-19. For an image to be developed, the EP drum must be discharged. This can also happen if the primary corona fails to place a conditioning charge on the drum. At first, you might suspect that the –6000-V source is low, but in actuality, this type of symptom is typically the result of bad HVPS grounding. Turn off and unplug the printer, then allow at least 15 minutes for the HVPS to discharge. Open the printer and inspect the mounting bolts holding the HVPS in place. Chances are that you'll find one or more grounding screws loose. Gently tighten each of the mounting/grounding hardware (you don't want to strip any of the mounting holes). Secure the printer and re-test it.

Symptom 21-37. Random black splotches are in the image Generally, the image will appear, but it will contain a series of small black marks spaced randomly throughout the page. This type of image problem suggests that the HVPS is arcing internally (and is probably close to failure). Turn off and unplug the printer, then allow at least 15 minutes for charges in the HVPS to dissipate. Check the high-voltage connectors and high-voltage wiring harness. Try re-seating the connectors to check for failing contacts. If problems persist, replace the HVPS.

Symptom 21-38. "Graping" is in the image The "graping" effect places small, dark, oval-shaped marks on the page—usually along one side of the page. Graping is often

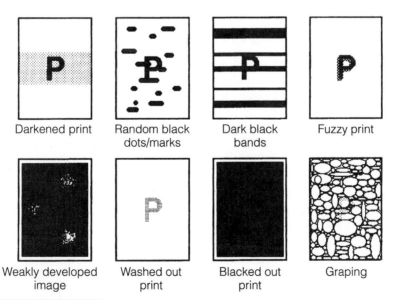

Darkened print   Random black dots/marks   Dark black bands   Fuzzy print

Weakly developed image   Washed out print   Blacked out print   Graping

FIGURE 21-19 Recognizing high-voltage power-supply problems.

caused by a short-circuit in the primary corona HV connector—HV is arcing out. Turn off and unplug the printer, then allow at least 15 minutes for any charges in the HVPS to dissipate. Inspect the primary corona wiring, and check for any shorts along the corona, or along the HV lead from the HVPS. Try re-seating the HV connectors and wiring. If problems persist, replace the primary corona HV lead (if possible)—otherwise, replace the HVPS.

Symptom 21-39. The image appears, but it contains heavy black bands
You can see an example of this in Fig. 21-19. Although this symptom might look quite different from Symptom 21-2, it is really quite similar. If the HVPS ground is loose, the image can be darkened, but if the HVPS ground is simply intermittent, portions of the image might be exposed just fine. As the grounding cuts out, however, primary voltage fails, and the lack of conditioning voltage causes a black band to form. When the ground kicks in again, the image formation resumes—and so on. Turn off and unplug the printer, and allow at least 15 minutes for the HVPS to discharge. Gently tighten or re-seat each of the grounding screws holding the HVPS in place (be careful not to strip the threaded holes). Also check the HV wiring harness to see that it is not crimped or shorted by other assemblies. If problems persist, replace the HVPS.

Symptom 21-40. The image appears fuzzy—letters and graphics appear "smudged" or "out of focus" This type of problem is suggestive of a fault in the ac bias voltage. You see, toner is heavily attracted to the exposed drum. Then toner jumps to the drum, some toner lands in non-exposed areas near the exposed points. By using an ac developer bias, the developer voltage varies up and down. As developer voltage increases, more toner is passed to the exposed drum areas. As developer voltage decreases, toner is pulled back from the non-exposed drum areas. This action increases image contrast while cleaning up any "collateral" toner that might have landed improperly. If the ac component of your developer voltage fails, that contrast-enhancing feature will go away—resulting in fuzzy print. Because developer voltage is generated in the HVPS, try replacing the HVPS outright.

Symptom 21-41. Weakly developed areas are in the image The image appears, but various areas are unusually light. This can be attributed to moisture in the paper. Try a supply of fresh, dry paper in the paper cassette. Also be sure that the paper does not have a specialized coating. If the problem persists, you should suspect that the HVPS is weak and nearing failure. For a symptom such as this, your best course is usually just to replace the HVPS outright. Be sure to turn off and unplug the printer, and allow at least 15 minutes for the HVPS to discharge before attempting replacement.

Symptom 21-42. The image appears washed out This type of symptom can often be the result of several causes. Before proceeding, check the print-density wheel and try increasing the density setting. If problems continue, check your paper supply. Specially or chemically coated papers might not transfer very well. If the problem continues, you should suspect that the transfer voltage is weak or absent, or that the primary grid voltage might be failing. In either case, you should replace the HVPS. Be sure to turn off and unplug the printer, and allow at least 15 minutes for the HVPS to discharge before attempting replacement.

Symptom 21-43. The page is blacked out This symptom suggests that the primary corona voltage has failed. Without a conditioning charge, the EP drum will remain completely discharged—this will attract full toner, which will result in a black page. Before attempting to replace the HVPS, check the primary corona to see that it is still intact, and check the wiring between the primary corona and the HVPS. If the primary corona is damaged, replace the EP/toner cartridge. Otherwise, replace the HVPS. Be sure to turn off and unplug the printer, and allow at least 15 minutes for the HVPS to discharge before attempting replacement.

FUSING SYMPTOMS

The fusing assembly is another focal point for many printer problems. To fix toner to the page surface, a combination of heat and pressure is applied with a set of fusing rollers. The upper roller provides heat while the lower roller provides pressure. For the fusing assembly to work properly, several factors must be in place. First, the heating roller must reach and maintain a constant temperature—that temperature must be consistent across the roller's surface. Second, pressure must be constant all the way across the two rollers, so the two rollers must be aligned properly. Third, not all melted toner will stick to the page—some will adhere to the heating roller. So there must be some provision for cleaning the heating roller. Finally, there must be a reliable method for protecting the printer from overheating.

The fusing unit design shown in Fig. 21-20 addresses these concerns. Heat is generated by a bar heater or a long quartz lamp mounted inside of the upper fusing roller. Power to operate the heater is provided from the dc power supply (typically, 24 V). A separate thermistor in the roller changes resistance versus temperature, so it acts as a temperature detector. The thermistor's resistance is measured by a circuit on the mechanical controller board, which, in turn, modulates the power feeding the heater. This process "closes the loop" to achieve a stable operating temperature. If a failure should occur that allows the heater to run continuously, a thermal fuse will open and cut off voltage to the heater above a given limit. Although Fig. 21-20 does not show it, the upper and lower fusing rollers are held together with torsion springs—the springs keep both rollers together with the right amount of compression, and can adjust for slight variations in paper weight and system wear. Toner that sticks to the upper fusing roller can transfer off the roller elsewhere on the page—resulting in a "speckled" appearance. So, the upper roller is coated with Teflon to reduce sticking, and a cleaning pad rubs any toner off the roller. You will find that temperature, alignment, and cleaning problems are the cause of some of the most frequent fusing troubles.

Symptom 21-44. The printer's LCD indicates a "heater error" or other type of fusing temperature malfunction Your particular printer might use an error number (i.e., Error 32) to represent the condition. Fusing is integral to the successful operation of any EP printer. Toner that is not fused successfully remains a powder or crust that can flake or rub off onto your hands or other pages. Mechanical controller logic interprets the temperature signal developed by the thermistor and modulates power to the quartz lamp. Three conditions will generate a fusing malfunction error: the fusing-roller temperature falls below about 140 degrees C, the fusing-roller temperature climbs above 230 degrees C, or the fusing-roller temperature does not reach 165 degrees C in 90 seconds after the printer is powered up. Your particular printer might utilize slightly different temperature and timing

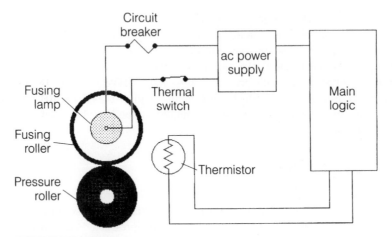

FIGURE 21-20   Fusing-unit temperature-control loop.

parameters. Also notice that a fusing error will often remain with a printer for 10 minutes or so after it is powered down, so be sure to allow plenty of time for the system to cool before examining the fusing system.

Begin by examining the installation of your fusing assembly. Check to see that all wiring and connectors are tight and seated properly. The quartz heater power supply is often equipped with a fuse or circuit breaker that protects the printer (this is not the thermal switch shown in Fig. 21-20). If this fuse or circuit breaker is open, replace your fuse or reset your circuit breaker, then retest the printer. Remember to clear the error or allow enough time for the error to clear by itself. If the fuse or breaker trips again during retest, you have a serious short circuit in your fusing assembly or power supply. You can attempt to isolate the short circuit, or simply replace your suspected assemblies—fusing assembly first, then the dc power supply.

Turn off and unplug the printer, allow it to cool, and check your temperature-sensing thermistor by measuring its resistance with a multimeter. At room temperature, the thermistor should read about 1 kΩ (depending on the particular thermistor). If the printer has been at running temperature, thermistor resistance might be much lower. If the thermistor appears open or shorted, replace it with an exact replacement part and retest the printer.

A thermal switch (sometimes called a *thermoprotector*) is added in series with the fusing lamp. If a thermistor or main logic failure should allow temperature to climb out of control, the thermal switch will open and break the circuit once it senses temperatures over its preset threshold. This protects the printer from severe damage—and possibly a fire hazard. Unplug the printer, disconnect the thermal switch from the fusing lamp circuit, and measure its continuity with a multimeter. The switch should normally be closed. If you find an open switch, it should be replaced. Check the quartz lamp next by measuring continuity across the bulb itself. If you read an open circuit, replace the quartz lamp (or the entire fusing assembly). Be sure to secure any disconnected wires. If the printer still does not reach its desired temperature, or if it continuously opens the thermal switch, troubleshoot your thermistor signal-conditioning circuit and the fusing-lamp control signal from the mechanical controller, or replace the mechanical controller board entirely.

Symptom 21-45. Print appears smeared or fused improperly Temperature and pressure are two key variables of the EP printing process. Toner must be melted and bonded to a page to fix an image permanently. If fusing temperature or roller pressure is too low during the fusing operation, toner might remain in its powder form. Resulting images can be smeared or smudged with a touch. You can run the Printers fusing test to check fusing quality by running a series of continuous prints. Place the first and last printout on a firm surface and rub both surfaces with your fingertips. No smearing should occur. If your fusing level varies between pages (one page might smear while another might not), clean the thermistor temperature sensor and repeat this test. Remember to wait 10 minutes or so before working on the fusing assembly. If fusing performance does not improve, replace the thermistor and troubleshoot its signal-conditioning circuit at the mechanical controller. If smearing persists, replace the fusing assembly and cleaning pad.

Static teeth just beyond the transfer corona are used to discharge the paper once toner has been attracted away from the EP drum. This helps paper to clear the drum without being attracted to it. An even charge is needed to discharge paper evenly; otherwise, some portions of the page might retain a local charge. As paper moves toward the fusing assembly, remaining charge forces might shift some toner resulting in an image that does not smear to the touch, but has a smeared or pulled appearance. Examine the static discharge comb once the printer is unplugged and discharged. If any of its teeth are bent or missing, replace the comb.

A cleaning pad rubs against the fusing roller to wipe away any accumulations of toner particles or dust. If this cleaning pad is worn out or missing, contamination on the fusing roller can be transferred to the page, resulting in smeared print. Check your cleaning pad in the fusing assembly. Worn out or missing pads should be replaced immediately.

Inspect your drive train for any gears that show signs of damage or excessive wear. Slipping gears could allow the EP drum and paper to move at different speeds. This can easily cause portions of an image to appear smudged—such areas would appear bolder or darker than other portions of the image. Replace any gears that you find to be defective. If you do not find any defective drive-train components, try replacing the EP cartridge. Finally, a foreign object in the paper path can rub against a toner powder image and smudge it before fusing. Check the paper path and remove any debris or paper fragments that might be interfering with the image.

Symptom 21-46. The print is smudged in narrow, horizontal bands Figure 21-21 shows an example of this problem. Although smudging is usually suggestive of a

 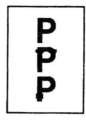  

Smudged print   Smudged zones   Pencil line(s)   No fusing on part of page

FIGURE 21-21   **Recognizing fusing system faults.**

fusing problem, its occurrence in relatively narrow bands actually points to a problem with the paper feed—the registration or transfer rollers are not moving evenly, so they are jerking the paper. When the paper jerks, the toner immediately being transferred from the EP drum becomes smudged.

Check your paper stock first. Unusually light or specially coated papers might slip periodically—resulting in a slight jerking motion. Try a standard 20-lb. xerography-grade paper. If the paper is appropriate, there are three causes for this kind of "paper jerk"—either your rollers are worn (allowing loose contact at some point in their rotation), the rollers are obstructed (effectively jamming the paper at some point in their rotation) or a fault is in the drive train. Unfortunately, observing the paper path while the printer is running will rarely reveal subtle mechanical defects, so turn off and unplug the printer, then inspect your registration rollers for signs of wear or accumulations of foreign matter. If the registration rollers appear to be damaged or worn, replace the registration assembly. If there is a buildup of foreign matter, carefully clean the registration rollers.

If the problem persists, inspect the drive train carefully. Check each gear to see that they are meshed properly, and see if there are any broken gear teeth. A small, high-intensity pen light will make this inspection easier. Replace any gears that are worn or damaged. If obstructions are in the gear train, clean them away carefully with a cotton swab, lightly dampened in isopropyl alcohol. If this still fails to correct the problem, the fault is probably in the EP engine mechanics. Try replacing the EP/toner cartridge (the "engine").

Symptom 21-47. Wide, horizontal areas of print are smudged You can see this type of symptom in Fig. 21-21. Although this problem might sound quite similar to the previous symptom, the fault is almost always in the fusing assembly. Excessive pressure from the lower fusing roller squeezes the page so tightly that the print is smudged—typically, across a wide area. Turn off and unplug the printer, and allow 15 minutes (or so) for the fusing assembly to cool. Inspect the fusing assembly carefully. If torsion springs hold the upper and lower fusing rollers together, you can probably reduce the tension to relieve some of the pressure. You might have to work in small increments to get the best results. Also check the lower fusing roller itself—if the roller is worn or damaged, it should be replaced. As an alternative, you can replace the entire fusing assembly outright.

Symptom 21-48. Dark creases are in the print These visible creases (also referred to as *pencil lines*) are in the page itself—not just in the printed image. In virtually all cases, "pencil lines" are the result of a bloated lower fusing roller. The way in which it applies pressure on the page causes a crease in the page. First, check your paper supply. Light bond or specially coated papers are especially susceptible to this kind of problem. Try a standard 20-lb. xerography-grade paper. If the problem persists, you will need to inspect the fusing assembly. Turn off and unplug the printer, and allow 15 minutes for the fusing system to cool before opening the printer. Check the lower fusing roller for signs of bloating, excessive wear, or other damage. Try replacing the lower fusing roller. Otherwise, you should replace the entire fusing assembly.

Symptom 21-49. Little or no fusing is on one side of the image However, the other half is fused properly. This problem occurs when there is a gap in the fusing rollers. Even if the upper fusing roller is producing the correct amount of heat, it will not fuse toner without pressure from the lower fusing roller. Gaps are often caused from physical damage to the fusing assembly or by an accumulation of foreign matter that forces the rollers apart. Turn off and unplug the printer, then wait about 15 minutes for the fusing assembly to cool. Inspect the rollers carefully. You can expect to find your problem on the side that does not fuse. For example, if the right side of the page is not fusing, the problem is likely on the right side of the fusing rollers. Check for mechanical alignment of the rollers. You might be able to restore operation by adjusting the torsion-spring tension. If problems continue, you should replace the entire fusing assembly.

CORONA (CHARGE ROLLER) SYMPTOMS

The two high-voltage charge areas in the EP printer are: the primary area and the transfer area. Classic "SX-type" engines use corona wires, so the primary area will use a *primary corona* and the transfer area will use a *transfer corona*. The newer "CX-type" engines replace the corona wires with charge rollers, so the primary area will use a *primary charge roller* and the transfer area will use a *transfer charge roller*. Although these areas very rarely fail, a suite of problems plague the coronas. This part of the chapter shows you some of the more pervasive faults.

Symptom 21-50. Pages are completely blacked out, and might appear blotched with an undefined border An example of this problem is shown in Fig. 21-22. Turn off and unplug the printer, remove the EP cartridge, and examine its primary corona wire. Remember that a primary corona applies an even charge across a drum surface. This charge readily repels toner—except at those points exposed to light by the writing mechanism, which discharges those points and attracts toner. A failure in the primary corona will prevent charge development on the drum. As a result, the entire drum surface will tend to attract toner (even if your writing mechanism works perfectly). This creates a totally black image. If you find a broken or fouled corona wire, clean the wire or replace the EP cartridge.

If your blacked-out page shows print with sharp, clearly defined borders, your writing mechanism might be running out of control. LEDs in a solid-state print bar or laser beam might be shorted in an On condition, or receiving erroneous data bits from its control circuitry (all logic 1s). In this case, the primary corona is working just fine, but a writing mechanism that is always on will effectively expose the entire drum and discharge whatever charge was applied by the primary corona. The net result of attracting toner would be the same, but whatever image is formed would probably appear crisper, more deliberate.

Use your oscilloscope to measure the data signals reaching your writing mechanism during a print cycle. You should find a semi-random square wave representing the 1s and 0s composing the image. If you find only one logic state, troubleshoot your main logic and driving circuits handling the data, or replace the mechanical controller board. If data entering the writing mechanism appears normal, replace your writing mechanism (LED bar or laser/scanner assembly). You might wish to cross-reference this symptom with an HVPS problem earlier in this chapter.

Symptom 21-51. Print is very faint Turn off and unplug the printer, remove the EP cartridge, and try re-distributing toner in the cartridge. Your user's manual probably offers preferred instructions for re-distributing toner. Remember that toner is largely organic—as such, it has only a limited shelf and useful life. If re-distribution temporarily or partially improves the image, or if the EP cartridge has been in service for more than six

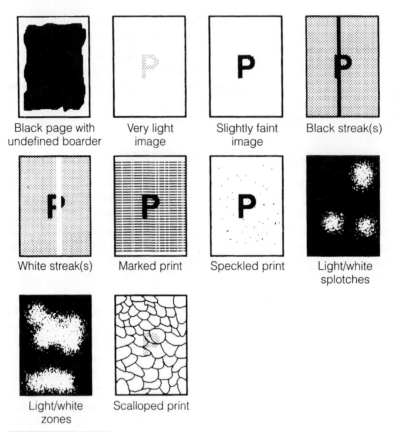

Black page with undefined boarder	Very light image	Slightly faint image	Black streak(s)
White streak(s)	Marked print	Speckled print	Light/white splotches
Light/white zones	Scalloped print		

FIGURE 21-22   **Recognizing a corona-or charge-roller fault.**

months, replace the EP cartridge. If you are using a paper with a moisture content, finish, or conductivity that is not acceptable, image formation might not take place properly. Try a standard 20-lb xerography-grade paper.

Check your transfer corona or transfer-charge roller. The transfer corona applies a charge to paper that pulls toner off the drum. A weak transfer corona or charge roller might not apply enough charge to attract all the toner in a drum image. This can result in very faint images. Turn off and unplug the printer, allow ample time for the high-voltage power supply to discharge completely, then inspect all wiring and connections at the transfer corona. If the monofilament line encircling the transfer corona is damaged, replace the transfer corona assembly, or attempt to re-thread the monofilament line. If faint images persist, repair or replace the high-voltage power-supply assembly.

Finally, check the drum ground contacts to be sure that they are secure. Dirty or damaged ground contacts will not readily allow exposed drum areas to discharge. As a result, very little toner will be attracted and only faint images will result. If the problem persists, replace the EP engine.

Symptom 21-52. Print is just slightly faint   Print that is only slightly faint does not necessarily suggest a serious problem. There are a series of fairly simple checks that can narrow down the problem. Check the print-density control dial. Turn the dial to a lower setting to increase contrast (or whatever darker setting there is for your particular printer). Check your paper supply next. Unusual or specially coated paper might cause fused toner images to appear faint. If you are unsure about the paper currently in the printer, insert a good-quality, standard-weight xerographic paper and test the printer again.

Over time, natural dust particles in the air will be attracted to the transfer corona and accumulate there. This eventually causes a layer of debris to form on the wire. This type of accumulation cuts down on transfer corona effectiveness, which places less of a charge on paper. Less toner is pulled from the drum, so the resulting image appears fainter. Turn off and unplug the printer, allow ample time for the high-voltage power supply to discharge, then gently clean the transfer corona with a clean cotton swab or a corona cleaning tool. Be very careful not to break the monofilament line wrapped about the transfer corona assembly. If this line does break, the transfer corona assembly will have to be re-wrapped or replaced.

Check your toner level. Unplug the printer, remove the EP cartridge and re-distribute toner. Follow all manufacturer's recommendations when it comes to re-distributing toner. The toner supply might just be slightly low at the developing roller. Unplug your printer and examine the EP cartridge-sensitivity switch settings. These microswitches are actuated by molded tabs attached to your EP cartridge. This tab configuration represents the relative sensitivity of the drum. Main logic uses this code to set the power level of its writing mechanism to ensure optimum print quality. These switches also tell main logic whether an EP cartridge is installed. If one of these tabs are broken or if a switch has failed, the drum might not be receiving enough light energy to achieve proper contrast. Check your sensitivity switches as outlined for a "No EP cartridge" error, shown later in this chapter. If the problem persists, your high-voltage power supply is probably failing. Replace your high-voltage power supply.

Symptom 21-53. One or more vertical black streaks are in the print Black streaks might range from narrow lines to wide bands, depending on the severity of the problem. In most cases, this fault is caused by foreign matter accumulating on the primary corona. Foreign matter will prevent charges from forming on the drum. In turn, this will invariably attract toner, which creates black streaks. Typically, the edges of these streaks are fuzzy and ill-defined. Your best course is simply to clean the primary corona—most printers enclose a cleaning tool for just this purpose. The process takes no more than a minute. If the problem persists (very unlikely), replace the EP engine.

Symptom 21-54. One or more vertical white streaks are in the print Begin by checking your toner level. Toner might be distributed unevenly along the cartridge's length. Turn off and unplug the printer, remove the EP cartridge, and re-distribute the toner. Follow your manufacturer's recommendations when handling the EP cartridge. If this improves your print quality (at least temporarily), replace the nearly exhausted EP cartridge.

Next, examine your transfer corona for areas of blockage or extreme contamination. Such faults would prevent the transfer corona from generating an even charge along its length—corrosion acts as an insulator that reduces the corona's electric field. Uncharged page areas will not attract toner from the drum, so those page areas will remain white. Clean the transfer corona very carefully with a clean cotton swab. If your printer comes with a corona-cleaning tool, use that instead. When cleaning, be sure to avoid the monofilament line wrapped around the transfer corona assembly. If the line breaks, it will have to be re-wrapped or the entire transfer corona assembly will have to be replaced.

Check the optical assembly for any accumulation of dust or debris that could block out sections of light. Because EP drums are only scanned as fine horizontal lines, it would take little more than a fragment of debris to block light through a focusing lens. Gently blow off any dust or debris with a can of high-quality, optical-grade compressed air available from any photography store. For stains or stubborn debris, clean the afflicted lens gently with a high-quality lens cleaner and wipes from any photography store. Be very careful not to dislodge the lens from its mounting. Never blow on a lens or mirror—breath vapor and particles can condense and dry on a lens to cause even more problems in the future.

Symptom 21-55.   The print appears "scalloped"   You can see an example of "scalloping" in Fig. 21-22. The scalloping effect has a unique and unmistakable appearance, which almost always indicates that the primary corona has broken. The image that forms is then expressly the result of random discharge from the erase lamps. In many cases, the failure of a primary corona will simply blacken the page. In some circumstances, however, the erase lamps will leave a latent image that is developed into the scalloped pattern. You should immediately suspect a failure in the primary corona. Your best course is simply to replace the primary corona by exchanging the EP/toner cartridge.

Symptom 21-56.   The print contains columns of horizontal "tic" marks   An image appears as expected, but it is marked vertical swatches of small horizontal tics. Experience has demonstrated that this type of symptom is frequently caused by a short-circuited transfer corona. Turn off and unplug the printer, then allow at least 15 minutes for the printer to cool and discharge. Inspect the transfer corona carefully, as well as any wiring at the corona. Gently clear away any foreign material (especially conductive material) from the transfer area and try the printer again. If the problem persists, try replacing the transfer corona assembly.

Symptom 21-57.   Print appears speckled   In almost all cases, speckled print is the result of a fault in your primary corona grid. A *grid* is essentially a fine wire mesh between the primary corona and drum surface. A constant voltage applied across the grid regulates the charge applied to the drum to establish a more consistent charge distribution. Grid failure will allow much higher charge levels to be applied unevenly. A higher conditioning charge might not be discharged sufficiently by the writing mechanism; toner might not be attracted to the drum—even though the writing is working as expected. This results in a very light image (almost absent, except for some light speckles across the page). Because the primary grid assembly is part of the EP cartridge, replace the EP/toner cartridge and retest the printer. If speckled print persists, you should suspect a fault in the HVPS.

Symptom 21-58.   Light/white splotches are in the image   When you see a symptom such as this, your first suspicion should be moisture in the paper supply—a common occurrence in humid summer months. When the paper becomes damp (even just from the air's humidity), charges do not distribute properly across the page. As a result, paper will not charge in the damp areas, so toner is not attracted from the drum. Damp areas then remain very light or white. Paper that is unusually coated can have similar problems. In virtually all cases, a supply of fresh, dry, 20-lb, xerography-grade paper should correct the problem. To correct the problem over the long term, consider adding a dehumidifier or air-conditioner in the work area to keep paper dry.

Symptom 21-59. Light/white zones are spread through the image At first glance, you might think that this symptom is similar to the previous one. However, random white zones in the printed page are much larger and more distinct than simple light splotches—in effect, the white areas have just disappeared. This symptom is indigenous to the CX-type EP engine, which uses charge rollers, rather than coronas. In most cases, you will find that the transfer charge roller has failed or is missing. Even without a working transfer corona, the CX engine can transfer portions of the latent image to the page, but you can see from Fig. 21-22 that the transfer is very unstable. Check and replace the transfer charge roller—or replace the EP engine outright.

MISCELLANEOUS SYMPTOMS

This chapter has focused on problems that plague key areas of the EP printer. However, some symptoms cannot easily be associated with any particular area of the printer. As a consequence, these problems can be difficult to track down and correct. This part of the chapter illustrates some of the printer's miscellaneous problems.

Symptom 21-60. The printer never leaves its warm-up mode There is a continuous "Warming up" status code. EP printers must perform two important tasks during initialization. First, a self-test is performed to check the printer's logic circuits and electromechanical components. This usually takes no more than 10 seconds from the time that power is first applied. Second, its fusing rollers must warm up to a working temperature. Fusing temperature is typically acceptable within 90 seconds from a cold start. At that point, the printer will establish communication with the host computer and stand by to accept data, so its "Warming up" code should change to an "On-line" or "Ready" code.

If the printer fails to go on-line, it might be the result of a faulty communication interface, or a control panel problem. Turn the printer off, disconnect its communication cable, and restore power. If the printer finally becomes ready without its communication cable, check the cable itself and its connection at the computer. You might have plugged a parallel printer into the computer's serial port, or vice versa. A faulty communication interface might be in your host computer.

If the printer still fails to become ready, unplug the printer and check that the control-panel cables or interconnecting wiring is attached properly. Check the control panel to see that it is operating correctly. Also check the control-panel interface circuit (sometimes called an "interface/formatter" circuit). Repair or replace your faulty control panel or interface/formatter circuit. Depending on the complexity of your particular printer, the interface/formatter might be a separate printed circuit plugged into the main logic board, or its functions might be incorporated right into the main logic board itself.

Symptom 21-61. A "Paper out" message appears If the printer generates a "Paper out" message, either the paper is exhausted or the paper tray has been removed. When a paper tray is inserted, a series of metal or plastic tabs make contact with a set of

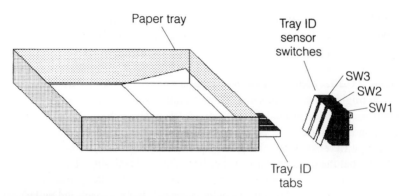

FIGURE 21-23   Paper-tray ID switch system.

TABLE 26-3 TYPICAL TABLE OF TRAY SWITCH CONFIGURATIONS			
PAPER TRAY	**SW1**	**SW2**	**SW3**
Executive	1	1	1
A4	1	1	0
Legal	0	0	1
Envelope	0	1	1
Letter	1	0	0
* No Tray	0	0	0

1 = on (engaged)
0 = off (disengaged)

microswitches (Fig. 21-23). The presence or absence of tabs will form a code that is unique to that particular paper size. Microswitches are activated by the presence or tabs. Main logic interprets this paper-type code, and it knows automatically what kind of media (paper, envelopes, etc.) it is working with. This allows the printer to automatically scale the image, according to the paper size. Table 21-3 shows a typical paper-code table.

The presence of paper is detected by a mechanical sensing lever (Fig. 21-24). If paper is available, a lever rests on the paper. A metal or plastic shaft links this lever to a thin plastic flag. While paper is available, this flag is clear of the paper-out sensor. If the tray becomes empty, this lever falls through a slot in the tray, which rotates its flag into the paper out sensor. This indicates that paper is exhausted. The paper-out sensor is usually mounted on an auxiliary PC board (known as the *paper-control board*), and its signal is typically interpreted by the mechanical controller board. Begin your check by removing the paper tray. Be sure that there is paper in the tray, and that any ID tabs are intact—especially if you have just recently dropped the tray. Re-insert the filled paper tray carefully and completely. If the "Paper out" message continues, then there is either a problem with your paper-ID microswitches, paper-sensing lever, or the paper-out optoisolator.

You can check the paper-ID microswitches by removing the paper tray and actuating the paper-sensing lever by hand (so the printer thinks that paper is available). Refer to Table

21-3 and actuate each switch in turn using the eraser of pencil. Actuate one switch at a time and observe the printer's display. The "Paper out" error should go away whenever at least one microswitch is pressed. If the error remains when a switch is pressed, that switch is probably defective. Unplug the printer and use your multimeter to check continuity across the suspect switch as you actuate it. Replace any defective switch. If the switches work electrically, but the printer does not register them, troubleshoot or replace the main logic board. Inspect the paper-out lever and optoisolator next.

When paper is available, the paper-out lever should move its plastic flag clear of the optoisolator. When paper is empty, the lever should place its flag into the optoisolator slot. Notice that this logic might be reversed, depending on the particular logic of the printer. This check confirms that the paper-sensing arm works properly. If the lever mechanism is jammed or bent, repair or replace the mechanism. Check the paper-out optoisolator, and replace the optoisolator if it appears to be defective. If the sensors appear to be operational, replace the mechanical controller board.

Symptom 21-62. A "Printer open" message appears Printers can be opened to perform routine cleaning and EP cartridge replacement. The cover(s) that can be opened to access your printer are usually interlocked with the writing mechanism and high-voltage power supply to prevent possible injury from laser light or high-voltages while the printer is opened. The top cover (or some other cover assembly) uses a pushrod to actuate a simple electrical switch. When the top cover is opened, the interlock switch opens, and the printer's driver voltage (+24 Vdc is shown) is cutoff from all other circuits. This effectively

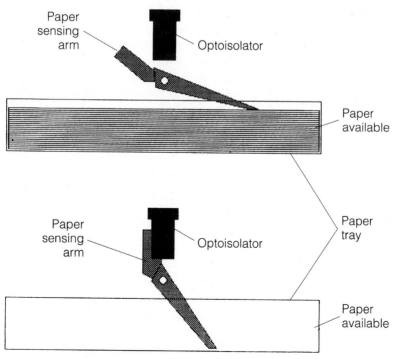

FIGURE 21-24 Operation of a paper-sensing arm.

disables the printer's operation. When the top cover is closed again, the interlock switch is reactivated, and printer operation is restored.

Be sure that the cover(s) are all shut securely (try opening and re-closing each cover). Inspect any actuating levers or pushrods carefully. Replace any bent, broken, or missing mechanical levers. Unplug the printer and observe how each interlock is actuated (it might be necessary to disassemble other covers to observe interlock operation). Adjust the pushrods or switch positions, if necessary, to ensure firm contact.

Turn off and unplug the printer, then use your multimeter to measure continuity across any questionable interlock switches. It might be necessary to remove at least one wire from the switch to prevent false readings. Actuate the switch by hand to be sure that it works properly. Replace any defective interlock switches, re-attach all connectors and interconnecting wiring, and retest the printer. If the switch itself works correctly, check the signals feeding the switch. Check the dc voltage at the switch. If the voltage is low or absent, trace the voltage back to the power supply or other signal source. If signals are behaving as expected but a "Printer open" message remains, trace the interlock signal into the mechanical controller board and troubleshoot your electronics, or replace the mechanical controller outright.

Symptom 21-63. A "No EP cartridge" message appears An electrophotographic engine assembly uses several tabs (known as *sensitivity tabs*) to register its presence, as well as to inform the printer about the drum's relative sensitivity level. The ECU regulates the output power of its writing mechanism based on these tab arrangements (i.e., high-power, medium-power, low-power, or no-power—No cartridge). Sensitivity tabs are used to actuate microswitches located on a secondary PC board. The sequence of switch contacts forms a "sensitivity" code that is interpreted by the mechanical controller.

Begin by checking the installation of your current EP engine. Be sure that it is in place and seated properly. Check that at least one sensitivity tab is actuating a sensor switch. If no tabs are on the EP engine, replace it with a new or correct-model EP engine that has at least one tab. Retest the printer. If your "No EP cartridge" error persists, check all sensitivity switches in the printer. Turn off and unplug the printer, then use your multimeter to measure continuity across each sensitivity switch. It might be necessary to remove at least one wire from each switch to prevent false continuity readings. Actuate each switch by hand and see that each one works properly. Replace any microswitch that appears to be defective or intermittent. Replace any connectors or interconnecting wiring, and retest the printer. If the sensitivity switches are working properly, troubleshoot or replace the mechanical controller board, or replace it outright.

Symptom 21-64. A "Toner low" message appears constantly or the error never appears A toner sensor is located within the EP/toner cartridge itself. Functionally, the sensor is little more than an antenna that receives a signal from the high-voltage ac developer bias (Fig. 21-25). When toner is plentiful, much of the electromagnetic field generated by the presence of high-voltage ac is blocked. As a result, the toner sensor only generates a small voltage. This weak signal is often conditioned in the mechanical controller by an amplifier that uses some type of operational-amplifier circuit, which compares sensed voltage to a preset reference voltage. For the sensor in Fig. 21-25, sensed voltage is normally below the reference voltage, its output is a logic 0. Main logic would interpret this signal as a satisfactory toner supply. As toner volume decreases, more high-

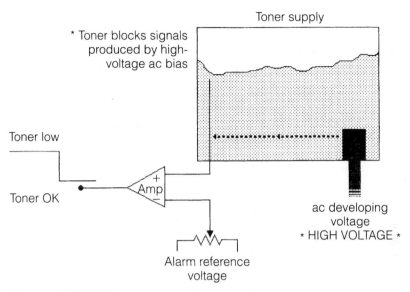

FIGURE 21-25 Operation of a low-toner sensor.

voltage energy is picked up by the toner sensor, in turn developing a higher-voltage signal. When toner is too low, sensed voltage will exceed the reference, and the comparator's output will switch to a logic 1. This is handled in main logic and a "Toner low" warning is produced.

Unfortunately, there is no good way to test the toner sensor. High voltage is very dangerous to measure directly without the appropriate test probes, and the signal picked up at the receiving wire are too small to measure without a sensitive meter or an oscilloscope. Turn off and unplug the printer and begin your check by shaking the toner to re-distribute the toner supply (or insert a fresh EP/toner cartridge). Refer to the user's manual for your particular printer to find the recommended procedure for re-distributing toner, then retest the printer. If the problem persists, a fault might be in the mechanical controller board's detection circuit. Troubleshoot the mechanical controller or replace it entirely.

Symptom 21-65. The printer's LCD displays a "fan motor error" or similar fault The printer might also use an error code (i.e., Error 34) to represent the condition. The typical EP printer uses two fans: a high-voltage cooling fan and an ozone-venting fan. In most cases, the ozone-venting fan runs off-line and is not detected by the printer. The power-supply cooling fan, however, is vital for the supply's reliability—if the cooling fan fails, the power supply will quickly overheat and fail. To prevent this from happening, the fan's operation is often monitored. If the fan quits, an error will be produced. In most cases, the fan is simply defective and should be replaced. Check the voltage available at the fan. If fan voltage is available (but the fan does not spin), the fan is defective and should be replaced. If fan voltage is missing, you will need to work back into the printer to find where fan power was lost—check any loose wiring or connectors.

Symptom 21-66. Ghosting is in the image The expected image prints normally, but upon inspection, you can see faint traces of previous image portions (Fig. 21-26). This

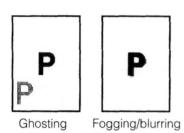

Ghosting   Fogging/blurring

FIGURE 21-26   Recognizing miscellaneous faults.

is a case of poor housekeeping—ordinarily, a cleaning blade should scrape away any residual toner remaining on the EP drum prior to erasing and conditioning. If the cleaning blade is worn out or if the scrap toner reservoir is full, cleaning might not occur as expected, and toner will remain on the EP drum for one or more subsequent rotations. If the residual toner comes off on another rotation, it will often appear as the "ghost" of a previous image. Unfortunately, the only way to really correct this problem is to replace the entire EP engine. Cleaning blades are hardly replaceable parts, and if the scrap toner bin is full, there is no way to recycle the toner back into the reservoir. Turn off and unplug the printer, replace the EP engine, and try the printer again.

Symptom 21-67. The print appears fogged or blurred This might appear somewhat like smudging in previous symptoms, but where smudging was generally limited in other symptoms, it occurs throughout the page here. This is a situation where you should examine the paper-transfer guide—the passage between the static-discharge comb (the transfer area) and the fusing assembly. Most transfer guides are coated with Teflon or a similar material to reduce static. Over time and use, the anti-static coating can wear off, revealing the static-prone plastic below the coating. If the plastic of the transfer guide causes a static charge, it might be strong enough to "drag" the toner image just slightly, resulting in a blurred of fogged image. If you find wear in the transfer guide, replace the transfer-guide assembly.

Symptom 21-68. Nothing happens when power is turned on You should hear the printer respond as soon as power is turned on. You should see a power indicator on the control panel (alphanumeric displays will typically read "Self-test"). You should also hear and feel the printer's cooling fan(s) in operation. If the printer remains dead, the trouble is probably with the ac power. Check the ac line cord for proper connection with the printer and wall outlet. Try the printer in a known-good ac outlet. Also check the printer's main ac fuse. If the ac and fuse check properly, the problem is probably with the printer's power supply.

If the printer's fan(s) and power indicator operate, you can be confident that the printer is receiving power. If the control panel remains blank, there might be a problem with the dc power supply or ECU. You can troubleshoot or replace the dc power supply at your discretion. If the power supply checks properly, the trouble is likely somewhere in the ECU or in the control-panel assembly itself. Remove power from the printer and check the control-panel cable. If there are no indicators at all on the control panel, replace the control panel cable. If problems remain, try replacing the ECU. If only one or a few indicators appear on the control panel, try replacing the control-panel cable. If problems remain, replace the control panel.

Further Study

That's all for Chapter 21. Be sure to review the glossary and chapter questions on the accompanying CD. If you have access to the Internet, take a look at some of these laser/LED printer resources (in addition to the printer manufacturers listed in Table 21-1):

WEBPAGES

Environmental Laser: **http://www.toners.com/welcome.html**

Laser Pros International: **http://www.laserpros.com/**

~Laser Saver: **http://rampages.onramp.net/~laser/**

Laser Supplies: **http://www.mind.net/laser/**

~Printer Drivers Page: **http://www.primenet.com/~penguink/printers.html**

The Printer Works: **http://www.printerworks.com/index.html**

USENET NEWSGROUPS

comp.periphs.printers (general printer newsgroup)

comp.periphs (general peripheral newsgroup)

22

MCA BUS
OPERATIONS

CONTENTS AT A GLANCE

MCA Bus Configuration and Signals
  MCA layout
  Knowing the MCA signals

PS/2 Reference and Diagnostic Disks
  Clearing a 55SX password
  Dealing with PS/2 "165" errors
   (.ADF files)

General Bus Troubleshooting

Further Study
  Usenet newsgroup

With the introduction and widespread use of 32-bit microprocessors, such as the Intel 80386 and 80486, the 16-bit ISA bus faced a serious data throughput bottleneck. Passing a 32-bit word across the expansion bus in two 16-bit halves presented a serious waste of valuable processing time. Not only was data and CPU speed an issue, but video and audio systems in PCs had also been improving—and demanding an increasing share of bus bandwidth. By early 1987, IBM concluded that it was time to lay the ISA bus to rest and unleash an entirely new bus structure, which it dubbed the *MicroChannel Architecture (MCA)*. IBM incorporated the MCA bus into their PS/2 series of personal computers and also in their System/6000 workstations. This chapter shows you the layout and operations of the MCA bus.

MCA Bus Configuration and Signals

All things considered, the MCA bus was a revolutionary—and superior—design. One of the most substantial advantages is a reduction in electrical noise because of a radical re-arrangement of bus signals. Unlike the ISA or EISA bus (which had only a few ground lines), the MCA bus provides an electrical ground every fourth pin. Superior grounding and the corresponding reduction in electrical interference also means that the MCA bus can operate at higher frequencies than XT or AT busses (10MHz, as opposed to the ISA/EISA 8.33MHz). The MCA bus also offers extended performance in data and ad-dressing. You already know that an MCA bus can work with up to 32-bits of data. How-ever, the bus also has an increased number of address lines (32 instead of 24). This increases the amount of directly addressable memory from 16MB to 4GB.

The MCA also brings sound and video to the bus. A single analog audio channel is added to the 8-bit bus segment. The audio channel can handle voice and music, and is in-tended to be almost as good as FM radio (roughly about 50Hz to 10kHz). Because the au-dio channel is available to all expansion devices, the signal can be exchanged and processed among each device independently. A VGA video extension is also provided with the MCA bus. This allows expansion video boards to be installed and work in con-cert with the VGA circuitry already existing on the MCA motherboard. An 8-bit video data bus and all necessary synchronization signals are available to an expansion board. Typically, only one video extension connector is included on an MCA motherboard.

Still more advances include such features as matched memory cycles, burst and stream-ing data modes, data multiplexing, and bus mastering. A matched memory cycle is sup-ported with a small expansion connector. When a device is capable of sustaining matched memory transfers, the typical memory transfer cycle of 250 ns is increased 25% to only 187 ns. The burst data-transfer mode allows data to be transferred in blocks without the intervention of a CPU (unlike ordinary data transfers, which require multiple CPU cycles for each transfer). The streaming data-transfer mode allows even faster transfers during bus-mastering operation. Using a data multiplexing technique, the MCA bus can accom-plish 64-bit data transfers by multiplexing the upper 32 data bits on the 32 idle address lines. Finally, the MCA bus supports bus mastering—a technique that allows other de-vices besides the main CPU to take control of the system busses to accomplish their re-spective tasks.

Although MCA offers many tangible enhancements over the ISA bus, computer users refused to abandon their hardware and software investment in order to scramble for lim-ited MCA-compatible peripherals to fill their needs. As a result, the MCA bus has never become the new standard that IBM hoped it would be. Although the number of PS/2 sys-tems still in service are dwindling rapidly, you might still encounter PS/2s in many home and school environments.

MCA LAYOUT

The layout for an MCA bus slot is shown in Fig. 22-1. Notice that up to three segments are on the bus connector: an 8-bit portion, a 16-bit portion, and a 32-bit portion. Also, an auxiliary video extension connector is usually available on only one slot. The first thing

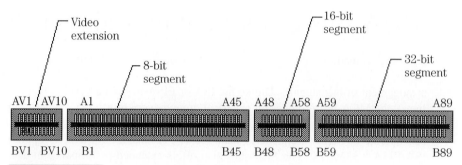

FIGURE 22-1   The various elements of an MCA bus.

you should realize about the MCA bus is that it is physically much smaller than an ISA or EISA bus—as a result, it is totally incompatible with ISA or EISA expansion products.

The pinout for a 16-bit MCA slot is shown in Table 22-1. This primary type of MCA connector combines video and audio signals in the expansion bus. The connection itself can be divided into three sections: the video section (pins xV00 to xV10), the 8-bit section (pins 1 through 45), and the 16-bit section (pins 48 to 58). Power, ground, and interrupt lines are easy to spot, but most other signals are new. The signal pinout for a 32-bit MCA slot is shown in Table 22-2. The 32-bit bus replaces the video section with a smaller matched memory control section (pins xM4 to xM1), but 8-bit and 16-bit sections remain the same. The 32-bit MCA slot also includes a 32-bit section (pins 59 to 89).

KNOWING THE MCA SIGNALS

Enable Synchronization (ESYNC) controls VGA signals (VSYNC, HSYNC, and BLANK) on the motherboard. When ESYNC is true, the *Vertical Synchronization (VSYNC)* pulses, *Horizontal Synchronization (HSYNC)*, and *Blanking (BLANK)* signals control the display. An independent 8-bit video data bus (P0 to P7) support 256 colors on the VGA display. VGA timing signals are controlled by the *Enable Data Clock (EDCLK)* and *Data Clock (DCLK)* signals. The *Enable Video (EVIDEO)* signal switches control of the palette bus allowing an external video adapter to provide signals on P0 to P7. *Audio (Audio)* and *Audio Signal Ground (Audio GROUND)* allow the expansion board to send tone signals to the motherboard speaker.

There are 32 *address bits (Address bit 0 to Address bit 31)*, 11 interrupts, and 32 data bits (Data bit 0 to Data bit 31). The *–Address Latch (–ADL)* signal is true when a valid address exists on the address lines. A *–Channel Check (–CHCK)* signal flags the motherboard when an error is detected on the expansion board. When data on the data bus is valid, the *–Command (–CMD)* is true. The *Channel Ready Return (CHRDYRTN)* signal is sent to the motherboard when the addressed expansion board I/O channel is ready. A *Channel Reset (CHRESET)* signal can be used to reset all expansion boards. The *–Card Setup (–CDSETUP)* instructs an addressed board to perform a setup. The *Memory Address Enable 24 (MADE24)* line activates address line 24. The *Channel Ready (CHRDY)* line that the addressed board is idle after completing its access. When *–Burst (–BURST)* is true, the system bus will execute a burst cycle.

The *–Data Size 16 Return (–DS16RTN)* and *–Data Size 32 Return (–DS32RTN)* tell the motherboard whether the board is running at a 16- or 32-bit bus width. The *System Byte*

TABLE 22-1 MCA 16 BIT BUS PINOUT

SIGNAL	PIN	PIN	SIGNAL
ESYNC	BV10	AV10	VSYNC
Ground	BV9	AV9	HSYNC
P5	BV8	AV8	BLANK
P4	BV7	AV7	Ground
P3	BV6	AV6	P6
Ground	BV5	AV5	EDCLK
P2	BV4	AV4	DCLK
P1	BV3	AV3	Ground
P0	BV2	AV2	P7
Ground	BV1	AV1	EVIDEO
Key	Key	Key	Key
AUDIO Ground	B1	A1	- CD setup
AUDIO	B2	A2	MADE 24
Ground	B3	A3	Ground
Oscillator (14.3MHz)	B4	A4	Address bit 11
Ground	B5	A5	Address bit 10
Address Bit 23	B6	A6	Address bit 9
Address bit 22	B7	A7	+5 Vdc
Address bit 21	B8	A8	Address bit 8
Ground	B9	A9	Address bit 7
Address bit 20	B10	A10	Address bit 6
Address bit 19	B11	A11	+5 Vdc
Address bit 18	B12	A12	Address bit 5
Ground	B13	A13	Address bit 4
Address bit 17	B14	A14	Address bit 3
Address bit 16	B15	A15	+5 Vdc
Address bit 15	B16	A16	Address bit 2
Ground	B17	A17	Address bit 1
Address bit 14	B18	A18	Address bit 0
Address bit 13	B19	A19	+12 Vdc
Address bit 12	B20	A20	- ADL
Ground	B21	A21	- Preempt
- IRQ 9	B22	A22	- Burst
- IRQ 3	B23	A23	-12 Vdc
- IRQ 4	B24	A24	ARB 00
Ground	B25	A25	ARB 01
- IRQ 5	B26	A26	ARB 02
- IRQ 6	B27	A27	-12 Vdc
- IRQ 7	B28	A28	ARB 03
Ground	B29	A29	ARB/ - GNT
Reserved	B30	A30	- TC
Reserved	B31	A31	+5 Vdc

TABLE 22-1   MCA 16 BIT BUS PINOUT (CONTINUED)

SIGNAL	PIN	PIN	SIGNAL
- CHCK	B32	A32	- S0
Ground	B33	A33	- S1
- CMD	B34	A34	M/ - I/O
CHRDYRTN	B35	A35	+12 Vdc
- CD SFDBK	B36	A36	CD CHRDY
Ground	B37	A37	Data bit 0
Data bit 1	B38	A38	Data bit 2
Data bit 3	B39	A39	+5 Vdc
Data bit 4	B40	A40	Data bit 5
Ground	B41	A41	Data bit 6
CHRESET	B42	A42	Data bit 7
Reserved	B43	A43	Ground
Reserved	B44	A44	- DS 16 RTN
Ground	B45	A45	- Refresh
Key	Key	Key	Key
Key	Key	Key	Key
Data bit 8	B48	A48	+5 Vdc
Data bit 9	B49	A49	Data bit 10
Ground	B50	A50	Data bit 11
Data bit 12	B51	A51	Data bit 13
Data bit 14	B52	A52	+12 Vdc
Data bit 15	B53	A53	Reserved
Ground	B54	A54	- SBHE
- IRQ 10	B55	A55	- CD DS 16
- IRQ 11	B56	A56	+5 Vdc
- IRQ 12	B57	A57	- IRQ 14
Ground	B58	A58	- IRQ 15
Reserved	B59	A59	Reserved
Reserved	B60	A60	Reserved

TABLE 22-2   MCA 32 BIT BUS PINOUT

SIGNAL	PIN	PIN	SIGNAL
Ground	BM4	AM4	Reserved
Reserved	BM3	AM3	- MMC CMD
- MMCR	BM2	AM2	Ground
Reserved	BM1	AM1	- MMC
Audio ground	B1	A1	-CD setup
Audio	B2	A2	MADE 24
Ground	B3	A3	Ground
Oscillator (14.3 MHz)	B4	A4	Address bit 11

TABLE 22-2   MCA 32 BIT BUS PINOUT (CONTINUED)

SIGNAL	PIN	PIN	SIGNAL
Ground	B5	A5	Address bit 10
Address bit 23	B6	A6	Address bit 9
Address bit 22	B7	A7	+5 Vdc
Address bit 21	B8	A8	Address bit 8
Ground	B9	A9	Address bit 7
Address bit 20	B10	A10	Address bit 6
Address bit 19	B11	A11	+5 Vdc
Address bit 18	B12	A12	Address bit 5
Ground	B13	A13	Address bit 4
Address bit 17	B14	A14	Address bit 3
Address bit 16	B15	A15	+5 Vdc
Address bit 15	B16	A16	Address bit 2
Ground	B17	A17	Address bit 1
Address bit 14	B18	A18	Address bit 0
Address bit 13	B19	A19	+12 Vdc
Address bit 12	B20	A20	- ADL
Ground	B21	A21	- Preempt
- IRQ 9	B22	A22	- Burst
- IRQ 3	B23	A23	-12 Vdc
- IRQ 4	B24	A24	ARB 00
Ground	B25	A25	ARB 01
- IRQ 5	B26	A26	ARB 02
- IRQ 6	B27	A27	-12 Vdc
- IRQ 7	B28	A28	ARB 03
Ground	B29	A29	ARB/ - GNT
Reserved	B30	A30	- TC
Reserved	B31	A31	+5 Vdc
- CHCK	B32	A32	- SO
Ground	B33	A33	- S1
- CMD	B34	A34	M/ - I/O
CHRDYRTN	B35	A35	+12 Vdc
- CD SFDBK	B36	A36	CD CHRDY
Ground	B37	A37	Data bit 0
Data bit 1	B38	A38	Data bit 2
Data bit 3	B39	A39	+5 Vdc
Data bit 4	B40	A40	Data bit 5
Ground	B41	A41	Data bit 6
CHRESET	B42	A42	Data bit 7
Reserved	B43	A43	Ground
Reserved	B44	A44	- DS 16 RTN
Ground	B45	A45	- Refresh
Key	Key	Key	Key

TABLE 22-2   MCA 32 BIT BUS PINOUT (CONTINUED)

SIGNAL	PIN	PIN	SIGNAL
Key	Key	Key	Key
Data bit 8	B48	A48	+5 Vdc
Data bit 9	B49	A49	Data bit 10
Ground	B50	A50	Data bit 11
Data bit 12	B51	A51	Data bit 13
Data bit 14	B52	A52	+12 Vdc
Data bit 15	B53	A53	Reserved
Ground	B54	A54	- SBHE
- IRQ 10	B55	A55	- CD DS 16
- IRQ 11	B56	A56	+5 Vdc
- IRQ 12	B57	A57	- IRQ 14
Ground	B58	A58	- IRQ 15
Reserved	B59	A59	Reserved
Reserved	B60	A60	Reserved
Reserved	B61	A61	Ground
Reserved	B62	A62	Reserved
Ground	B63	A63	Reserved
Data bit 16	B64	A64	Reserved
Data bit 17	B65	A65	+12 Vdc
Data bit 18	B66	A66	Data bit 19
Ground	B67	A67	Data bit 20
Data bit 22	B68	A68	Data bit 21
Data bit 23	B69	A69	+5 Vdc
Reserved	B70	A70	Data bit 24
Ground	B71	A71	Data bit 25
Data bit 27	B72	A72	Data bit 26
Data bit 28	B73	A73	+5 Vdc
Data bit 29	B74	A74	Data bit 30
Ground	B75	A75	Data bit 31
- BE 0	B76	A76	Reserved
- BE 1	B77	A77	+12 Vdc
- BE 2	B78	A78	- BE 3
Ground	B79	A79	- DC 32 RTN
TR 32	B80	A80	- CD DS 32
Address bit 24	B81	A81	+5 Vdc
Address bit 25	B82	A82	Address bit 26
Ground	B83	A83	Address bit 27
Address bit 29	B84	A84	Address bit 28
Address bit 30	B85	A85	+5 Vdc
Address bit 31	B86	A86	Reserved
Ground	B87	A87	Reserved
Reserved	B88	A88	Reserved
Reserved	B89	A89	Ground

High Enable (SBHE) signal is true when the upper 16 data bits are being used, but the Card Data Size 16 (CDDS16) signal is true when only 16 data bits are being used. If all 32 bits of data are being transferred, the –Card Data Size 32 (–CDDS32) signal is true. When the main memory is being refreshed, the –Refresh (–REF) line is true. This allows any dynamic memory on expansion boards to be refreshed as well. The Memory/–I/O (M/–I/O) signal defines whether the expansion board is accessing a memory or I/O location. Signals –S0 and –S1 carry the status of a MicroChannel bus.

The -Preempt (-PREEMPT) signal is true when a bus arbitration cycle begins. Arbitration signals ARB00 to ARB03 indicate (in BCD) which of the 16 possible bus masters has won arbitration. The Arbitration/–Grant (ARB/–GNT) is high when the bus is in arbitration, and low when bus control has been granted. When a DMA transfer has finished, the Terminal Count (TC) signal is true. –Byte Enable signals 0 to 3 (–BE0 to –BE3) indicate which four bytes of a 32-bit data bus are transferring data. When an external bus master is a 32-bit device, the Translate 32 (TR32) line is true. The –MMCR, –MMCCMD, and –MMC lines are matched memory-control signals.

PS/2 Reference and Diagnostic Disks

MicroChannel (PS/2) computers require the use of a "reference" (or "startup") disk whenever configuring the system, or exchanging MCA cards in their bus slots. Each time you add, remove, or exchange an MCA card, you'll need to run the reference disk. However, reference disks are often among the first items to be misplaced as a PC is sold or passed from owner to owner. When servicing a PS/2 system, you might easily find yourself without a reference disk. Fortunately, the reference disks for many PS/2 systems (along with a variety of diagnostic disks) can be downloaded from the IBM FTP site. Table 22-3 highlights the most popular FTP download addresses. Download the file to an empty directory on the hard drive, then decompress the file. This will usually result in several individual files, with specific instructions for creating a reference/startup disk.

> For files with a .TG0 extension, you will also need to download Teleget—a utility that extracts .TG0 files: **ftp://ftp.pc.ibm.com/pub/pccbbs/os2_fixes/tgsfx.com**

CLEARING A 55SX PASSWORD

For PS/2 55sx systems, a password will prevent the reference disk from running. You'll need to clear the CMOS RAM (including the password). Ordinarily, you can remove the CMOS backup battery and allow the memory to clear. But for 55sx systems, you can use the speaker cable to clear the CMOS RAM:

- Turn off your system.
- Unplug the speaker cable from the riser card and plug it in upside down.
- Turn it back on, wait for memory to count, and listen for the beep.
- Turn the system off, and plug the speaker cable right side up again.
- The password will be cleared when you power the system up again.

TABLE 22-3 PS/2 REFERENCE AND DIAGNOSTIC DISK FTP ADDRESSES

PS/2 25:	**ftp://ftp.pc.ibm.com/pub/pccbbs/refdisks/25start.tg0**
PS/2 25 - 286:	**ftp://ftp.pc.ibm.com/pub/pccbbs/refdisks/rs25286a.tg0**
PS/2 30:	**ftp://ftp.pc.ibm.com/pub/pccbbs/refdisks/30start.exe**
PS/2 30 - 286:	**ftp://ftp.pc.ibm.com/pub/pccbbs/refdisks/mod30286.exe**
PS/2 35/40:	**ftp://ftp.pc.ibm.com/pub/pccbbs/refdisks/3540st.exe**
PS/2 50/50z/60:	**ftp://ftp.pc.ibm.com/pub/pccbbs/refdisks/rf5060a.exe**
PS/2 53:	**ftp://ftp.pc.ibm.com/pub/pccbbs/refdisks/rf9553a.exe** (reference disk)
PS/2 53:	**ftp://ftp.pc.ibm.com/pub/pccbbs/refdisks/rd9553a.exe** (diagnostic disk)
PS/2 55sx/65sx:	**ftp://ftp.pc.ibm.com/pub/pccbbs/refdisks/rf5565a.exe**
PS/2 56/57 - 386:	**ftp://ftp.pc.ibm.com/pub/pccbbs/refdisks/rf855657.exe**
PS/2 56/57 - 486:	**ftp://ftp.pc.ibm.com/pub/pccbbs/refdisks/rf955657.exe**
PS/2 P70 (portable):	**ftp://ftp.pc.ibm.com/pub/pccbbs/refdisks/rfp70a.exe**
PS/2 70/80:	**ftp://ftp.pc.ibm.com/pub/pccbbs/refdisks/rf7080a.exe**
PS/2 P75 (portable):	**ftp://ftp.pc.ibm.com/pub/pccbbs/refdisks/rfp75a.exe**
PS/2 76/77:	**ftp://ftp.pc.ibm.com/pub/pccbbs/refdisks/rf7677a.exe** (reference disk)
PS/2 76/77:	**ftp://ftp.pc.ibm.com/pub/pccbbs/refdisks/rd7677a.exe** (diagnostic disk)
PS/2 76/77 (I or S):	**ftp://ftp.pc.ibm.com/pub/pccbbs/refdisks/7677ref.exe** (reference disk)
PS/2 76/77 (I or S):	**ftp://ftp.pc.ibm.com/pub/pccbbs/refdisks/7677diag.exe** (diagnostic disk)
PS/2 85 (9585):	**ftp://ftp.pc.ibm.com/pub/pccbbs/pc_servers/9585rf.exe** (reference disk)
PS/2 85 (9585):	**ftp://ftp.pc.ibm.com/pub/pccbbs/pc_servers/9585rd.exe** (diagnostic disk)
PS/2 90/95 (type 1):	**ftp://ftp.pc.ibm.com/pub/pccbbs/pc_servers/rf90951a.exe**
PS/2 90/95 (type 2):	**ftp://ftp.pc.ibm.com/pub/pccbbs/pc_servers/rf90952a.exe**
PS/2 90/95 (type 3):	**ftp://ftp.pc.ibm.com/pub/pccbbs/pc_servers/rf90953a.exe**
PS/2 90/95 (type 4):	**ftp://ftp.pc.ibm.com/pub/pccbbs/pc_servers/rf90954a.exe**
PS/2 90/95 (all):	**ftp://ftp.pc.ibm.com/pub/pccbbs/pc_servers/rd9095a.exe** (diagnostic disk)

DEALING WITH PS/2 "165" ERRORS (.ADF FILES)

When running the PS/2 reference disk, you'll need to have an .ADF file for each MCA board in the system. If you encounter a "165" error when running "autoconfigure" with the reference disk, chances are that the .ADF file for one or more MCA devices in the system is missing from the reference disk. Check with the driver software that came with the particular MCA card (its diskette might contain the needed .ADF file).

If you've got IBM-brand MCA cards in the system, you can obtain current .ADFs (Adapter Description Files) directly from IBM. Download the ALLFILES.TXT file from: **ftp://ftp.pc.ibm.com/pub/pccbbs/allfiles.txt** and locate the .ADF file for your particular device(s). You can then navigate the FTP site and obtain the .ADF file (usually somewhere under **ftp://ftp.pc.ibm.com/pub/pccbbs/**).

If you're using third-party MicroChannel cards, you'll need to contact each particular manufacturer and download the current .ADF file from their "tech support" areas or FTP sites. One very good source for .ADF files for older, non-IBM MicroChannel cards is at NCR's Web site (**http://www.ncr.com/support/pc/pcdesc/library/adfs.shtml**). You should also check Peter H. Wendt's Web site (**http://members.aol.com/phwimage1/mcaindex.htm**) for free software that will identify MicroChannel controllers and give you the ADF file name. The site also has a large library of .ADF files for download.

General Bus Troubleshooting

In most cases, you will not be troubleshooting a bus—after all, the bus is little more than a passive connector. However, the major signals that exist on an MCA bus can provide you with important clues about the system's operation. The most effective bus troubleshooting tool available to you is a POST board. Many POST boards are equipped with a number of LEDs that display power status, along with important timing and control signals. If one or more of those LEDs is missing, a fault has likely occurred somewhere on the motherboard. Although most POST boards are designed for ISA bus work, Micro2000 provides an MCA adapter for their POST-Probe.

Another point to consider is that bus connectors are mechanical devices—as a result, they do not last forever. If you or your customer are in the habit of removing and inserting boards frequently, it is likely that the metal "fingers" providing contact will wear and result in unreliable connections. Similarly, inserting a board improperly (or with excessive force) can break the connector. In extreme cases, even the motherboard can be damaged. The first rule of board replacement is: always try removing and re-inserting the suspect board. It is not uncommon for oxides to develop on board and slot contacts that might eventually degrade signal quality. By removing the board and re-inserting it, you can wipe off any oxides or dust and possible improve the connections.

The second rule of board replacement is: always try a board in another expansion slot before replacing it. This way, a faulty bus slot can be ruled out before suffering the expense of a new board. If a bus slot is defective, a technician can do little, except:

1 Block the slot and inform the customer that it is damaged and should not be used.
2 Replace the damaged bus slot connector (a tedious and time-consuming task) and pass the labor expense on to the customer.
3 Replace the motherboard outright (also a rather expensive option).

Further Study

That's it for Chapter 22. Be sure to review the glossary and chapter questions on the accompanying CD. If you have access to the Internet, take a look at some of these MCA (or PS/2) resources (in addition to the FTP references in Table 22-3):

General Technics: **http://gtweb.net/mi151.html** (MicroChannel Sound Card)

IBM PS/2 Reference Disks: **ftp://ftp.pc.ibm.com/pub/pccbbs/refdisks/**

Indelible Blue: **http://www.indelible-blue.com/** (MicroChannel add-on boards)

PS/2 Parts: **http://www.can.ibm.com/parts/catalogue/indexes/ps2indx.htm**

Vintage PCs: **http://www.can.ibm.com/helpware/vintage.html**

USENET NEWSGROUP

comp.sys.ibm.ps2.hardware

23

MEMORY

TROUBLESHOOTING

CONTENTS AT A GLANCE

Essential Memory Concepts
  Memory organization
  Memory signals

Memory Package Styles and Structures
  Add-on memory devices
  Megabytes and memory layout

Memory Organization
  Conventional memory
  Extended memory
  Expanded memory
  Upper memory area (UMA)
  High memory

Memory Considerations
  Memory speed and wait states
  Determining memory speed
  Presence detect (PD)
  Understanding memory "refresh"
  Memory types
  Memory techniques

The Issue of Parity
  The parity principle
  Even vs. odd
  The problems with parity

  Circumventing parity
  Abuse and detection of fake memory
  Alternative error correction

Memory Installation and Options
  Getting the right amount
  Filling banks
  Bank requirements

Recycling Older Memory Devices
  Memory speed
  Memory type
  SIMM stackers
  Mixing "composite" and
   "non-composite" SIMMS
  Remounting and rebuilding memory

Memory Troubleshooting
  Memory test equipment
  Repairing SIMM sockets
  Contact corrosion
  Parity errors
  Troubleshooting classic XT memory
  Troubleshooting classic at memory
  Troubleshooting contemporary
   memory errors

Further Study

Memory is a cornerstone of the modern PC. Memory that holds the program code and data that is processed by the CPU—and it is this intimate relationship between memory and the CPU that forms the basis of computer performance. With larger and faster CPUs constantly being introduced, and more complex software is developed to take advantage of the processing power. In turn, the more complex software demands larger amounts of faster memory. With the explosive growth of Windows (and more recently, Windows 95) the demands made on memory performance are more acute than ever. These demands have resulted in a proliferation of memory types that go far beyond the simple, traditional DRAM. Cache (SRAM), fast page-mode (FPM) memory, extended data output (EDO) memory, video memory (VRAM), synchronous DRAM (SDRAM), flash BIOS, and other exotic memory types (such as RAMBUS) now compete for the attention of PC technicians. These new forms of memory also present some new problems. This chapter will provide you an understanding of memory types, configurations, installation concerns, and troubleshooting options.

Essential Memory Concepts

The first step in any discussion of memory is to understand basically how memory works.
If you already have a good grasp of memory basics, feel free to skip this part of the chapter.

MEMORY ORGANIZATION

All memory is basically an array organized as rows and columns (Fig. 23-1). Each row is
known as an *address*—one million or more addresses might be on a single memory IC.
The columns represent data bits—a typical high-density memory IC has 1 bit, but might
have 2 or 4 bits, depending on the overall amount of memory required.

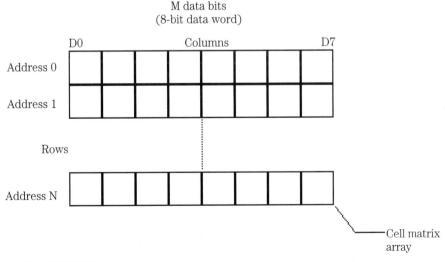

FIGURE 23-1   Simplified diagram of a memory array.

As you probably see in Fig. 23-1, the intersection of each column and row is an individual memory bit (known as a *cell*). This is important because the number of components in a cell—and the way those components are fabricated onto the memory IC—will have a profound impact on memory performance. For example, a classic DRAM cell is a single MOS transistor, and static RAM (or SRAM) cells often pack several transistors and other components onto the IC die. Although you do not have to be an expert on IC design, you should realize that the internal fabrication of a memory IC has more to do with its performance than just the way it is soldered into your computer.

MEMORY SIGNALS

A memory IC communicates with the "outside world" through three sets of signals: address lines, data lines, and control lines. Figure 23-2 illustrates these signal types. *Address lines* define which row of the memory array will be active. In actuality, the address is specified as a binary number, and conversion circuitry inside the memory IC translates the binary number into a specific row signal. Data lines pass binary values back and forth to the defined address. Control lines are used to operate the memory IC. A Read/–Write (R/–W) line defines whether data is being read from the specified address or written to it. A –Chip Select (–CS) signal makes a memory IC active or inactive (this ability to "disconnect" from a circuit is what allows a myriad of memory ICs to all share common address and data signals in the computer). Some memory types require additional signals, such as Row Address-Select (RAS) and Column Address-Select (CAS), for refresh operations. More exotic memory types might require additional control signals.

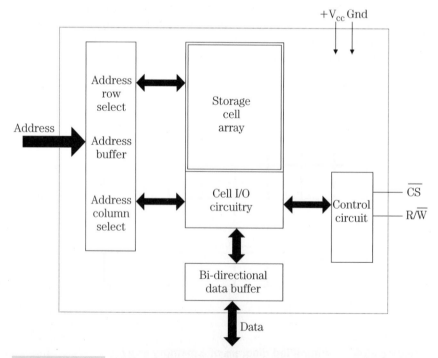

FIGURE 23-2   Diagram of a typical memory IC.

Memory Package Styles and Structures

Ultimately, the memory die is mounted in a package just like any other IC. The completed memory packages can then be soldered to your motherboard or attached to plug-in structures, such as SIMMs, DIMMs, and memory cards. Only four package styles are normally used for memory devices:

- *DIP (Dual In-line Package)* This classic IC package is used for through-hole mounting (prior to surface-mount technology). The advantage of DIP ICs is their compatibility with IC sockets, which allows ICs to be inserted or removed as required. Unfortunately, the long metal pins can bend and break if the IC is inserted or removed incorrectly. Also, the overall size of the package demands extra space. DIP ICs were used in older PCs (286 and earlier systems) and older VGA/SVGA video boards. DIPs are still sometimes used on motherboards to provide cache RAM.
- *SIP (Single In-line Package)* This type of IC package is rarely used today—there are simply not enough pins. However, they did make a short appearance with memory devices in late-model 286 and early 386 systems, which flirted with proprietary memory expansions. I remember NEC using such devices in a 2MB add-on for their 386SX/20— and you needed to add that module before you added even more memory in the form of proprietary SIMMs. SIPs can be troublesome because they are difficult to find replacements for, so expect replacement memory modules using them to cost a premium.
- *SOJ (Small-Outline "J" Lead)* This is the contemporary package style for surface-mount circuits. The leads protrude from the package like a DIP, but are bent around just under the package in the form of a "j". Sockets for SOJ packages are often used for replaceable memory ICs, such as the BIOS ROM, but most RAM devices are soldered directly to the motherboard as system memory (or a video board as video RAM). SIMMs often use SOJ memory components.
- *TSOP (Thin, Small-Outline Package)* Like the SOJ, a TSOP is also a surface-mount package style. However, its small, thin body makes TSOP memory ideal for narrow spaces. Expect to find such devices serving as memory in notebook/sub-notebook systems or PCMCIA cards (a.k.a., PC Cards).

ADD-ON MEMORY DEVICES

Memory has always pushed the envelope of IC design. This trend has given us tremendous amounts of memory in very small packages, but it also has kept memory relatively expensive. Manufacturers responded by providing a minimum amount of memory with the system, then selling more memory as an add-on option—this keeps the cost of a basic machine down and increases profit through add-on sales. As a technician, you should understand the three basic types of add-on memory.

Proprietary add-on modules Once the Intel i286 opened the door for more than 1MB of memory, PC makers scrambled to fill the void. However, the rush to more memory resulted in a proliferation of non-standard (and incompatible) memory modules. Each new motherboard came with a new add-on memory scheme—this invariably led to a great deal of confusion among PC users and makers alike. You will likely find proprietary memory modules in 286 and early 386 systems.

SIMMs and DIMMs   By the time 386 systems took hold in the PC industry, proprietary memory modules had been largely abandoned in favor of the "Memory Module" (Fig. 23-3). A SIMM (Single In-line Memory Module) is light, small, and contains a relatively large block of memory, but perhaps the greatest advantage of a SIMM is standardization. Using a standard pin layout, a SIMM from one PC can be installed in any other PC. The 30-pin SIMM (Table 23-1) provides 8 data bits, and generally holds up to 4MB of RAM. The 30-

A 72-pin SIMM

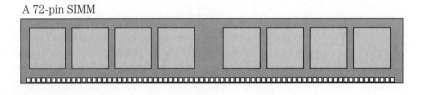

A 168-pin DIMM

FIGURE 23-3   Comparison of SIMMs and DIMMs.

TABLE 23-1 PINOUT OF A STANDARD 30-PIN SIMM	
PIN NAME	**DESCRIPTION**
1 VCC	+5 VDC
2 –CAS	–Column address strobe
3 DQ0	Data 0
4 A0	Address 0
5 A1	Address 1
6 DQ1	Data 1
7 A2	Address 2
8 A3	Address 3
9 GND	Ground
10 DQ2	Data 2
11 A4	Address 4
12 A5	Address 5
13 DQ3	Data 3
14 A6	Address 6
15 A7	Address 7
16 DQ4	Data 4
17 A8	Address 8
18 A9	Address 9
19 A10	Address 10
20 DQ5	Data 5

TABLE 23-1	PINOUT OF A STANDARD 30-PIN SIMM (CONTINUED)	
PIN NAME		**DESCRIPTION**
21	–WE	–Write enable
22	GND	Ground
23	DQ6	Data 6
24	n/c	Not connected
25	DQ7	Data 7
26	QP	Data parity out
27	–RAS	–Row address strobe
28	–CASP	–Parity control
29	DP	Data parity in
30	VCC	+5 Vdc

pin SIMM proved its worth in 386 and early 486 systems, but fell short when providing more memory to later-model PCs. The 72-pin SIMM (Table 23-2) supplanted the 30-pin version by providing 32 data bits, and it could hold up to 32MB (or more). Table 23-3 outlines a variation of the standard 72-pin SIMM highlighting the use of *Error-Correction Code (ECC)* instead of parity.

You might also find such structures referred to as *DIMMs (Dual In-Line Memory Modules)*. DIMMs appear virtually identical to SIMMs, but they are larger. And where each electrical contact on the SIMM is tied together between the front and back, the DIMM keeps front and back contacts separate—effectively doubling the number of contacts available on the device. For example, if you look at a 72-pin SIMM, you will see 72 electrical contacts on both sides of the device (144 contacts total)—but these are tied together, so there are only 72 signals (even with 144 contacts). On the other hand, a DIMM keeps the front and back contacts electrically separate (and usually adds some additional pins to keep SIMMs and DIMMs from accidentally being mixed). Table 23-4 outlines a 144-pin DIMM. Today, virtually all DIMM versions provide 168 pins (84 pins on each side). DIMMs are appearing in high-end 64-bit data-bus PCs (such as Pentiums and PowerPC RISC workstations). As PCs move from 64 to 128 bits over the next few years, DIMMs will likely replace SIMMs as the preferred memory-expansion device. Table 23-5 lists the pinout for an unbuffered DRAM DIMM and Table 23-6 presents the pinout for an unbuffered SDRAM DIMM.

Finally, you might see SIMMs and DIMMs referred to as *composite* or *non-composite modules*. These terms are used infrequently to describe the technology level of the memory module. For example, a composite module uses older, lower-density memory, so more ICs are required to achieve the required storage capacity. Conversely, a non-composite module uses newer memory technology, so fewer ICs are needed to reach the same storage capacity. In other words, if you encounter a high-density SIMM with only a few ICs on it, chances are that the SIMM is non-composite.

MEGABYTES AND MEMORY LAYOUT

Now is a good time to explain the idea of "bytes" and "megabytes." Very simply, a byte is 8 bits (binary 1s and 0s), and a megabyte is one million of those bytes (1,048,576 bytes

TABLE 23-2 PINOUT OF A STANDARD 72-PIN SIMM

PIN	NON-PARITY	PARITY	DESCRIPTION
1	VSS	VSS	Ground
2	DQ0	DQ0	Data 0
3	DQ18	DQ18	Data 18
4	DQ1	DQ1	Data 1
5	DQ19	DQ19	Data 19
6	DQ2	DQ2	Data 2
7	DQ20	DQ20	Data 20
8	DQ3	DQ3	Data 3
9	DQ21	DQ21	Data 21
10	VCC	VCC	+5 Vdc
11	n/c	n/c	Not connected
12	A0	A0	Address 0
13	A1	A1	Address 1
14	A2	A2	Address 2
15	A3	A3	Address 3
16	A4	A4	Address 4
17	A5	A5	Address 5
18	A6	A6	Address 6
19	A10	A10	Address 10
20	DQ4	DQ4	Data 4
21	DQ22	DQ22	Data 22
22	DQ5	DQ5	Data 5
23	DQ23	DQ23	Data 23
24	DQ6	DQ6	Data 6
25	DQ24	DQ24	Data 24
26	DQ7	DQ7	Data 7
27	DQ25	DQ25	Data 25
28	A7	A7	Address 7
29	A11	A11	Address 11
30	VCC	VCC	+5 VDC
31	A8	A8	Address 8
32	A9	A9	Address 9
33	−RAS3	−RAS3	−Row address strobe 3
34	−RAS2	−RAS2	−Row address strobe 2
35	n/c	PQ26	Parity 26 (3rd)
36	n/c	PQ8	Parity 8 (1st)
37	n/c	PQ17	Parity 26 (3rd)
38	n/c	PQ35	Parity 35 (4th)
39	VSS	VSS	Ground
40	−CAS0	−CAS0	−Column address strobe 0
41	−CAS2	−CAS2	−Column address strobe 2
42	−CAS3	−CAS3	−Column address strobe 3
43	−CAS1	−CAS1	−Column address strobe 1

TABLE 23-2 PINOUT OF A STANDARD 72-PIN SIMM (CONTINUED)

PIN NON-PARITY	PARITY	DESCRIPTION
44 –RAS0	–RAS0	–Row address strobe 0
45 –RAS1	–RAS1	–Row address strobe 1
46 n/c	n/c	Not connected
47 –WE	–WE	Read/-write
48 n/c	n/c	Not connected
49 DQ9	DQ9	Data 9
50 DQ27	DQ27	Data 27
51 DQ10	DQ10	Data 10
52 DQ28	DQ28	Data 28
53 DQ11	DQ11	Data 11
54 DQ29	DQ29	Data 29
55 DQ12	DQ12	Data 12
56 DQ30	DQ30	Data 30
57 DQ13	DQ13	Data 13
58 DQ31	DQ31	Data 31
59 VCC	VCC	+5 Vdc
60 DQ32	DQ32	Data 32
61 DQ14	DQ14	Data 14
62 DQ33	DQ33	Data 33
63 DQ15	DQ15	Data 15
64 DQ34	DQ34	Data 34
65 DQ16	DQ16	Data 16
66 n/c	n/c	Not connected
67 PD1	PD1	Presence detect 1
68 PD2	PD2	Presence detect 2
69 PD3	PD3	Presence detect 3
70 PD4	PD4	Presence detect 4
71 n/c	n/c	Not connected
72 VSS	VSS	Ground

SIZE: (PRESENCE DETECT LINES)

PD2	PD1	SIZE
GND	GND	4 or 64MB
GND	NC	2 or 32MB
NC	GND	1 or 16MB
NC	NC	8 MB

ACCESSTIME: (PRESENCE DETECT LINES)

PD4	PD3	ACCESSTIME
GND	GND	50, 100 ns
GND	NC	80 ns
NC	GND	70 ns
NC	NC	60 ns

TABLE 23-3 PINOUT OF A 72-PIN ECC SIMM

PIN ECC	OPTIMIZED	DESCRIPTION
1 VSS	VSS	Ground
2 DQ0	DQ0	Data 0
3 DQ1	DQ1	Data 1
4 DQ2	DQ2	Data 2
5 DQ3	DQ3	Data 3
6 DQ4	DQ4	Data 4
7 DQ5	DQ5	Data 5
8 DQ6	DQ6	Data 6
9 DQ7	DQ7	Data 7
10 VCC	VCC	+5 Vdc
11 PD5	PD5	Presence detect 5
12 A0	A0	Address 0
13 A1	A1	Address 1
14 A2	A2	Address 2
15 A3	A3	Address 3
16 A4	A4	Address 4
17 A5	A5	Address 5
18 A6	A6	Address 6
19 n/c	n/c	Not connected
20 DQ8	DQ8	Data 8
21 DQ9	DQ9	Data 9
22 DQ10	DQ10	Data 10
23 DQ11	DQ11	Data 11
24 DQ12	DQ12	Data 12
25 DQ13	DQ13	Data 13
26 DQ14	DQ14	Data 14
27 DQ15	DQ15	Data 15
28 A7	A7	Address 7
29 DQ16	DQ16	Data 16
30 VCC	VCC	+5 Vdc
31 A8	A8	Address 8
32 A9	A9	Address 9
33 n/c	n/c	Not connected
34 −RAS1	−RAS1	−Row address strobe 1
35 DQ17	DQ17	Data 17
36 DQ18	DQ18	Data 18
37 DQ19	DQ19	Data 19
38 DQ20	DQ20	Data 20
39 VSS	VSS	Ground
40 −CAS0	−CAS0	−Column address strobe 0
41 A10	A10	Address 10
42 A11	A11	Address 11
43 −CAS1	−CAS1	−Column address strobe 1
44 −RAS0	−RAS0	−Row Address Strobe 0

TABLE 23-3   PINOUT OF A 72-PIN ECC SIMM (CONTINUED)

PIN	ECC	OPTIMIZED	DESCRIPTION
45	–RAS1	–RAS1	–Row address strobe 1
46	DQ21	DQ21	Data 21
47	–WE	–WE	Read/-write
48	–ECC	–ECC	–Error-correction control
49	DQ22	DQ22	Data 22
50	DQ23	DQ23	Data 23
51	DQ24	DQ24	Data 24
52	DQ25	DQ25	Data 25
53	DQ26	DQ26	Data 26
54	DQ27	DQ27	Data 27
55	DQ28	DQ28	Data 28
56	DQ29	DQ29	Data 29
57	DQ30	DQ30	Data 30
58	DQ31	DQ31	Data 31
59	VCC	VCC	+5 Vdc
60	DQ32	DQ32	Data 32
61	DQ33	DQ33	Data 33
62	DQ34	DQ34	Data 34
63	DQ35	DQ35	Data 35
64	n/c	DQ36	Data 36
65	n/c	DQ37	Data 37
66	n/c	DQ38	Data 38
67	PD1	PD1	Presence detect 1
68	PD2	PD2	Presence detect 2
69	PD3	PD3	Presence detect 3
70	PD4	PD4	Presence detect 4
71	n/c	DQ39	Data 39
72	VSS	VSS	Ground

TABLE 23-4   PINOUT FOR AN OLDER 144-PIN SMALL-OUTLINE (SO) DIMM

PIN	NORMAL	ECC	DESCRIPTION
1	VSS	VSS	Ground
2	VSS	VSS	Ground
3	DQ0	DQ0	Data 0
4	DQ32	DQ32	Data 32
5	DQ1	DQ1	Data 1
6	DQ33	DQ33	Data 33
7	DQ2	DQ2	Data 2
8	DQ34	DQ34	Data 34
9	DQ3	DQ3	Data 3
10	DQ35	DQ35	Data 35

TABLE 23-4   PINOUT FOR AN OLDER 144-PIN SMALL-OUTLINE (SO) DIMM (CONTINUED)

PIN	NORMAL	ECC	DESCRIPTION
11	VCC	VCC	+5 Vdc
12	VCC	VCC	+5 Vdc
13	DQ4	DQ4	Data 4
14	DQ36	DQ36	Data 36
15	DQ5	DQ5	Data 5
16	DQ37	DQ37	Data 37
17	DQ6	DQ6	Data 6
18	DQ38	DQ38	Data 38
19	DQ7	DQ7	Data 7
20	DQ39	DQ39	Data 39
21	VSS	VSS	Ground
22	VSS	VSS	Ground
23	−CAS0	−CAS0	−Column address strobe 0
24	−CAS4	−CAS4	−Column address strobe 4
25	−CAS1	−CAS1	−Column address strobe 1
26	−CAS5	−CAS5	−Column address strobe 5
27	VCC	VCC	+5 Vdc
28	VCC	VCC	+5 Vdc
29	A0	A0	Address 0
30	A3	A3	Address 3
31	A1	A1	Address 1
32	A4	A4	Address 4
33	A2	A2	Address 2
34	A5	A5	Address 5
35	VSS	VSS	Ground
36	VSS	VSS	Ground
37	DQ8	DQ8	Data 8
38	DQ40	DQ40	Data 40
39	DQ9	DQ9	Data 9
40	DQ41	DQ41	Data 41
41	DQ10	DQ10	Data 10
42	DQ42	DQ42	Data 42
43	DQ11	DQ11	Data 11
44	DQ43	DQ43	Data 43
45	VCC	VCC	+5 Vdc
46	VCC	VCC	+5 Vdc
47	DQ12	DQ12	Data 12
48	DQ44	DQ44	Data 44
49	DQ13	DQ13	Data 13
50	DQ45	DQ45	Data 45
51	DQ14	DQ14	Data 14
52	DQ46	DQ46	Data 46
53	DQ15	DQ15	Data 15
54	DQ47	DQ47	Data 47

PIN	NORMAL	ECC	DESCRIPTION
TABLE 23-4 PINOUT FOR AN OLDER 144-PIN SMALL-OUTLINE (SO) DIMM (CONTINUED)			
55	VSS	VSS	Ground
56	VSS	VSS	Ground
57	n/c	CB0	
58	n/c	CB4	
59	n/c	CB1	
60	n/c	CB5	
61	DU	DU	Don't use
62	DU	DU	Don't use
63	VCC	VCC	+5 Vdc
64	VCC	VCC	+5 Vdc
65	DU	DU	Don't use
66	DU	DU	Don't use
67	−WE	−WE	Read/-write
68	n/c	n/c	Not connected
69	−RAS0	−RAS0	−Row address strobe 0
70	n/c	n/c	Not connected
71	−RAS1	−RAS1	−Row address strobe 1
72	n/c	n/c	Not connected
73	−OE	−OE	−Output enable
74	n/c	n/c	Not connected
75	VSS	VSS	Ground
76	VSS	VSS	Ground
77	n/c	CB2	
78	n/c	CB6	
79	n/c	CB3	
80	n/c	CB7	
81	VCC	VCC	+5 Vdc
82	VCC	VCC	+5 Vdc
83	DQ16	DQ16	Data 16
84	DQ48	DQ48	Data 48
85	DQ17	DQ17	Data 17
86	DQ49	DQ49	Data 49
87	DQ18	DQ18	Data 18
88	DQ50	DQ50	Data 50
89	DQ19	DQ19	Data 19
90	DQ51	DQ51	Data 51
91	VSS	VSS	Ground
92	VSS	VSS	Ground
93	DQ20	DQ20	Data 20
94	DQ52	DQ52	Data 52
95	DQ21	DQ21	Data 21
96	DQ53	DQ53	Data 53
97	DQ22	DQ22	Data 22
98	DQ54	DQ54	Data 54
99	DQ23	DQ23	Data 23

PIN	NORMAL	ECC	DESCRIPTION
	**TABLE 23-4 PINOUT FOR AN OLDER 144-PIN SMALL-OUTLINE (SO) DIMM (CONTINUED)**		
100	DQ55	DQ55	Data 55
101	VCC	VCC	+5 Vdc
102	VCC	VCC	+5 Vdc
103	A6	A6	Address 6
104	A7	A7	Address 7
105	A8	A8	Address 8
106	A11	A11	Address 11
107	VSS	VSS	Ground
108	VSS	VSS	Ground
109	A9	A9	Address 9
110	A12	A12	Address 12
111	A10	A10	Address 10
112	A13	A13	Address 13
113	VCC	VCC	+5 Vdc
114	VCC	VCC	+5 Vdc
115	−CAS2	−CAS2	−Column address strobe 2
116	−CAS6	−CAS6	−Column address strobe 6
117	−CAS3	−CAS3	−Column address strobe 3
118	−CAS7	−CAS7	−Column address strobe 7
119	VSS	VSS	Ground
120	VSS	VSS	Ground
121	DQ24	DQ24	Data 24
122	DQ56	DQ56	Data 56
123	DQ25	DQ25	Data 25
124	DQ57	DQ57	Data 57
125	DQ26	DQ26	Data 26
126	DQ58	DQ58	Data 58
127	DQ27	DQ27	Data 27
128	DQ59	DQ59	Data 59
129	VCC	VCC	+5 Vdc
130	VCC	VCC	+5 Vdc
131	DQ28	DQ28	Data 28
132	DQ60	DQ60	Data 60
133	DQ29	DQ29	Data 29
134	DQ61	DQ61	Data 61
135	DQ30	DQ30	Data 30
136	DQ62	DQ62	Data 62
137	DQ31	DQ31	Data 31
138	DQ63	DQ63	Data 63
139	VSS	VSS	Ground
140	VSS	VSS	Ground
141	SDA	SDA	
142	SCL	SCL	
143	VCC	VCC	+5 Vdc
144	VCC	VCC	+5 Vdc

TABLE 23-5 PINOUT OF A 168-PIN UNBUFFERED DRAM DIMM

PIN	NON-PARITY	PARITY	72 ECC	80 ECC	DESCRIPTION
1	VSS	VSS	VSS	VSS	Ground
2	DQ0	DQ0	DQ0	DQ0	Data 0
3	DQ1	DQ1	DQ1	DQ1	Data 1
4	DQ2	DQ2	DQ2	DQ2	Data 2
5	DQ3	DQ3	DQ3	DQ3	Data 3
6	VCC	VCC	VCC	VCC	+5 Vdc or +3.3 Vdc
7	DQ4	DQ4	DQ4	DQ4	Data 4
8	DQ5	DQ5	DQ5	DQ5	Data 5
9	DQ6	DQ6	DQ6	DQ6	Data 6
10	DQ7	DQ7	DQ7	DQ7	Data 7
11	DQ8	DQ8	DQ8	DQ8	Data 8
12	VSS	VSS	VSS	VSS	Ground
13	DQ9	DQ9	DQ9	DQ9	Data 9
14	DQ10	DQ10	DQ10	DQ10	Data 10
15	DQ11	DQ11	DQ11	DQ11	Data 11
16	DQ12	DQ12	DQ12	DQ12	Data 12
17	DQ13	DQ13	DQ13	DQ13	Data 13
18	VCC	VCC	VCC	VCC	+5 Vdc or +3.3 Vdc
19	DQ14	DQ14	DQ14	DQ14	Data 14
20	DQ15	DQ15	DQ15	DQ15	Data 15
21	n/c	CB0	CB0	CB0	Parity/check-bit input/output 0
22	n/c	CB1	CB1	CB1	Parity/check-bit input/output 1
23	VSS	VSS	VSS	VSS	Ground
24	n/c	n/c	n/c	CB8	Parity/check-bit input/output 8
25	n/c	n/c	n/c	CB9	Parity/check-bit input/output 9
26	VCC	VCC	VCC	VCC	+5 Vdc or +3.3 Vdc
27	−WE0	−WE0	−WE0	−WE0	Read/−write input
28	−CAS0	−CAS0	−CAS0	−CAS0	−Column address strobe 0
29	−CAS1	−CAS1	−CAS1	−CAS1	−Column address strobe 1
30	−RAS0	−RAS0	−RAS0	−RAS0	−Row address strobe 0
31	−OE0	−OE0	−OE0	−OE0	−Output enable
32	VSS	VSS	VSS	VSS	Ground
33	A0	A0	A0	A0	Address 0
34	A2	A2	A2	A2	Address 2
35	A4	A4	A4	A4	Address 4
36	A6	A6	A6	A6	Address 6
37	A8	A8	A8	A8	Address 8
38	A10	A10	A10	A10	Address 10
39	A12	A12	A12	A12	Address 12
40	VCC	VCC	VCC	VCC	+5 Vdc or +3.3 Vdc
41	VCC	VCC	VCC	VCC	+5 Vdc or +3.3 Vdc
42	DU	DU	DU	DU	Don't use
43	VSS	VSS	VSS	VSS	Ground
44	−OE2	−OE2	−OE2	−OE2	−Output enable 2

TABLE 23-5   PINOUT OF A 168-PIN UNBUFFERED DRAM DIMM (CONTINUED)

PIN	NON-PARITY	PARITY	72 ECC	80 ECC	DESCRIPTION
45	–RAS2	–RAS2	–RAS2	–RAS2	–Row address strobe 2
46	–CAS2	–CAS2	–CAS2	–CAS2	–Column address strobe 2
47	–CAS3	–CAS3	–CAS3	–CAS3	–Column address strobe 3
48	–WE2	–WE2	–WE2	–WE2	Read/–write Input 2
49	VCC	VCC	VCC	VCC	+5 Vdc or +3.3 Vdc
50	n/c	n/c	n/c	CB10	Parity/check bit input/output 10
51	n/c	n/c	n/c	CB11	Parity/check bit input/output 11
52	n/c	CB2	CB2	CB2	Parity/check bit input/output 2
53	n/c	CB3	CB3	CB3	Parity/check bit input/output 3
54	VSS	VSS	VSS	VSS	Ground
55	DQ16	DQ16	DQ16	DQ16	Data 16
56	DQ17	DQ17	DQ17	DQ17	Data 17
57	DQ18	DQ18	DQ18	DQ18	Data 18
58	DQ19	DQ19	DQ19	DQ19	Data 19
59	VCC	VCC	VCC	VCC	+5 Vdc or +3.3 Vdc
60	DQ20	DQ20	DQ20	DQ20	Data 20
61	n/c	n/c	n/c	n/c	Not connected
62	DU	DU	DU	DU	Don't use
63	n/c	n/c	n/c	n/c	Not connected
64	VSS	VSS	VSS	VSS	Ground
65	DQ21	DQ21	DQ21	DQ21	Data 21
66	DQ22	DQ22	DQ22	DQ22	Data 22
67	DQ23	DQ23	DQ23	DQ23	Data 23
68	VSS	VSS	VSS	VSS	Ground
69	DQ24	DQ24	DQ24	DQ24	Data 24
70	DQ25	DQ25	DQ25	DQ25	Data 25
71	DQ26	DQ26	DQ26	DQ26	Data 26
72	DQ27	DQ27	DQ27	DQ27	Data 27
73	VCC	VCC	VCC	VCC	+5 Vdc or +3.3 Vdc
74	DQ28	DQ28	DQ28	DQ28	Data 28
75	DQ29	DQ29	DQ29	DQ29	Data 29
76	DQ30	DQ30	DQ30	DQ30	Data 30
77	DQ31	DQ31	DQ31	DQ31	Data 31
78	VSS	VSS	VSS	VSS	Ground
79	n/c	n/c	n/c	n/c	Not connected
80	n/c	n/c	n/c	n/c	Not connected
81	n/c	n/c	n/c	n/c	Not connected
82	SDA	SDA	SDA	SDA	Serial data
83	SCL	SCL	SCL	SCL	Serial clock
84	VCC	VCC	VCC	VCC	+5 Vdc or +3.3 Vdc
85	VSS	VSS	VSS	VSS	Ground
86	DQ32	DQ32	DQ32	DQ32	Data 32
87	DQ33	DQ33	DQ33	DQ33	Data 33
88	DQ34	DQ34	DQ34	DQ34	Data 34

TABLE 23-5 PINOUT OF A 168-PIN UNBUFFERED DRAM DIMM (CONTINUED)

PIN	NON-PARITY	PARITY	72 ECC	80 ECC	DESCRIPTION
89	DQ35	DQ35	DQ35	DQ35	Data 35
90	VCC	VCC	VCC	VCC	+5 Vdc or +3.3 Vdc
91	DQ36	DQ36	DQ36	DQ36	Data 36
92	DQ37	DQ37	DQ37	DQ37	Data 37
93	DQ38	DQ38	DQ38	DQ38	Data 38
94	DQ39	DQ39	DQ39	DQ39	Data 39
95	DQ40	DQ40	DQ40	DQ40	Data 40
96	VSS	VSS	VSS	VSS	Ground
97	DQ41	DQ41	DQ41	DQ41	Data 41
98	DQ42	DQ42	DQ42	DQ42	Data 42
99	DQ43	DQ43	DQ43	DQ43	Data 43
100	DQ44	DQ44	DQ44	DQ44	Data 44
101	DQ45	DQ45	DQ45	DQ45	Data 45
102	VCC	VCC	VCC	VCC	+5 Vdc or +3.3 Vdc
103	DQ46	DQ46	DQ46	DQ46	Data 46
104	DQ47	DQ47	DQ47	DQ47	Data 47
105	n/c	CB4	CB4	CB4	Parity/check bit input/output 4
106	n/c	CB5	CB5	CB5	Parity/check bit input/output 5
107	VSS	VSS	VSS	VSS	Ground
108	n/c	n/c	n/c	CB12	Parity/check bit input/output 12
109	n/c	n/c	n/c	CB13	Parity/check bit input/output 13
110	VCC	VCC	VCC	VCC	+5 Vdc or +3.3 Vdc
111	DU	DU	DU	DU	Don't use
112	−CAS4	−CAS4	−CAS4	−CAS4	−Column address strobe 4
113	−CAS5	−CAS5	−CAS5	−CAS5	−Column address strobe 5
114	−RAS1	−RAS1	−RAS1	−RAS1	−Row address strobe 1
115	DU	DU	DU	DU	Don't use
116	VSS	VSS	VSS	VSS	Ground
117	A1	A1	A1	A1	Address 1
118	A3	A3	A3	A3	Address 3
119	A5	A5	A5	A5	Address 5
120	A7	A7	A7	A7	Address 7
121	A9	A9	A9	A9	Address 9
122	A11	A11	A11	A11	Address 11
123	A13	A13	A13	A13	Address 13
124	VCC	VCC	VCC	VCC	+5 Vdc or +3.3 Vdc
125	DU	DU	DU	DU	Don't use
126	DU	DU	DU	DU	Don't use
127	VSS	VSS	VSS	VSS	Ground
128	DU	DU	DU	DU	Don't use
129	−RAS3	−RAS3	−RAS3	−RAS3	−Column address strobe 3
130	−CAS6	−CAS6	−CAS6	−CAS6	−Column address strobe 6
131	−CAS7	−CAS7	−CAS7	−CAS7	−Column address strobe 7
132	DU	DU	DU	DU	Don't use

TABLE 23-5 PINOUT OF A 168-PIN UNBUFFERED DRAM DIMM (CONTINUED)

PIN	NON-PARITY	PARITY	72 ECC	80 ECC	DESCRIPTION
133	VCC	VCC	VCC	VCC	+5 Vdc or +3.3 Vdc
134	n/c	n/c	n/c	CB14	Parity/check bit input/output 14
135	n/c	n/c	n/c	CB15	Parity/check bit input/output 15
136	n/c	CB6	CB6	CB6	Parity/check bit input/output 6
137	n/c	CB7	CB7	CB7	Parity/check bit input/output 7
138	VSS	VSS	VSS	VSS	Ground
139	DQ48	DQ48	DQ48	DQ48	Data 48
140	DQ49	DQ49	DQ49	DQ49	Data 49
141	DQ50	DQ50	DQ50	DQ50	Data 50
142	DQ51	DQ51	DQ51	DQ51	Data 51
143	VCC	VCC	VCC	VCC	+5 Vdc or +3.3 Vdc
144	DQ52	DQ52	DQ52	DQ52	Data 52
145	n/c	n/c	n/c	n/c	Not connected
146	DU	DU	DU	DU	Don't use
147	n/c	n/c	n/c	n/c	Not connected
148	VSS	VSS	VSS	VSS	Ground
149	DQ53	DQ53	DQ53	DQ53	Data 53
150	DQ54	DQ54	DQ54	DQ54	Data 54
151	DQ55	DQ55	DQ55	DQ55	Data 55
152	VSS	VSS	VSS	VSS	Ground
153	DQ56	DQ56	DQ56	DQ56	Data 56
154	DQ57	DQ57	DQ57	DQ57	Data 57
155	DQ58	DQ58	DQ58	DQ58	Data 58
156	DQ59	DQ59	DQ59	DQ59	Data 59
157	VCC	VCC	VCC	VCC	+5 Vdc or +3.3 Vdc
158	DQ60	DQ60	DQ60	DQ60	Data 60
159	DQ61	DQ61	DQ61	DQ61	Data 61
160	DQ62	DQ62	DQ62	DQ62	Data 62
161	DQ63	DQ63	DQ63	DQ63	Data 63
162	VSS	VSS	VSS	VSS	Ground
163	CK3	CK3	CK3	CK3	
164	n/c	n/c	n/c	n/c	Not connected
165	SA0	SA0	SA0	SA0	Serial address 0
166	SA1	SA1	SA1	SA1	Serial address 1
167	SA2	SA2	SA2	SA2	Serial address 2
168	VCC	VCC	VCC	VCC	+5 Vdc or +3.3 Vdc

TABLE 23-6 PINOUT OF A 168-PIN UNBUFFERED SDRAM DIMM

PIN	NON-PARITY	72 ECC	80 ECC	DESCRIPTION
1	VSS	VSS	VSS	Ground
2	DQ0	DQ0	DQ0	Data 0
3	DQ1	DQ1	DQ1	Data 1

TABLE 23-6   PINOUT OF A 168-PIN UNBUFFERED SDRAM DIMM (CONTINUED)

PIN	NON-PARITY	72 ECC	80 ECC	DESCRIPTION
4	DQ2	DQ2	DQ2	Data 2
5	DQ3	DQ3	DQ3	Data 3
6	VDD	VDD	VDD	+5 Vdc or +3.3 Vdc
7	DQ4	DQ4	DQ4	Data 4
8	DQ5	DQ5	DQ5	Data 5
9	DQ6	DQ6	DQ6	Data 6
10	DQ7	DQ7	DQ7	Data 7
11	DQ8	DQ8	DQ8	Data 8
12	VSS	VSS	VSS	Ground
13	DQ9	DQ9	DQ9	Data 9
14	DQ10	DQ10	DQ10	Data 10
15	DQ11	DQ11	DQ11	Data 11
16	DQ12	DQ12	DQ12	Data 12
17	DQ13	DQ13	DQ13	Data 13
18	VDD	VDD	VDD	+5 Vdc or +3.3 Vdc
19	DQ14	DQ14	DQ14	Data 14
20	DQ15	DQ15	DQ15	Data 15
21	n/c	CB0	CB0	Parity/check-bit input/output 0
22	n/c	CB1	CB1	Parity/check-bit input/output 1
23	VSS	VSS	VSS	Ground
24	n/c	n/c	CB8	Parity/check-bit input/output 8
25	n/c	n/c	CB9	Parity/check-bit input/output 9
26	VDD	VDD	VDD	+5 Vdc or +3.3 Vdc
27	−WE	−WE	−WE	Read/-write
28	DQMB0	DQMB0	DQMB0	Byte mask signal 0
29	DQMB1	DQMB1	DQMB1	Byte mask signal 1
30	−S0	−S0	−S0	−Chip select
31	DU	DU	DU	Don't use
32	VSS	VSS	VSS	Ground
33	A0	A0	A0	Address 0
34	A2	A2	A2	Address 2
35	A4	A4	A4	Address 4
36	A6	A6	A6	Address 6
37	A8	A8	A8	Address 8
38	A10/AP	A10/AP	A10/AP	Address 10
39	BA1	BA1	BA1	Bank address 1
40	VDD	VDD	VDD	+5 Vdc or +3.3 Vdc
41	VDD	VDD	VDD	+5 Vdc or +3.3 Vdc
42	CK0	CK0	CK0	Clock signal 0
43	VSS	VSS	VSS	Ground
44	DU	DU	DU	Don't use
45	−S2	−S2	−S2	−Chip select 2
46	DQMB2	DQMB2	DQMB2	Byte mask signal 2
47	DQMB3	DQMB3	DQMB3	Byte mask signal 3

TABLE 23-6 PINOUT OF A 168-PIN UNBUFFERED SDRAM DIMM (CONTINUED)

PIN	NON-PARITY	72 ECC	80 ECC	DESCRIPTION
48	DU	DU	DU	Don't use
49	VDD	VDD	VDD	+5 Vdc or +3.3 Vdc
50	n/c	n/c	CB10	Parity/check-bit input/output 10
51	n/c	n/c	CB11	Parity/check-bit input/output 11
52	n/c	CB2	CB2	Parity/check-bit input/output 2
53	n/c	CB3	CB3	Parity/check-bit input/output 3
54	VSS	VSS	VSS	Ground
55	DQ16	DQ16	DQ16	Data 16
56	DQ17	DQ17	DQ17	Data 17
57	DQ18	DQ18	DQ18	Data 18
58	DQ19	DQ19	DQ19	Data 19
59	VDD	VDD	VDD	+5 Vdc or +3.3 Vdc
60	DQ20	DQ20	DQ20	Data 20
61	n/c	n/c	n/c	Not connected
62	Vref,NC	Vref,NC	Vref,NC	
63	CKE1	CKE1	CKE1	Clock enable signal 1
64	VSS	VSS	VSS	Ground
65	DQ21	DQ21	DQ21	Data 21
66	DQ22	DQ22	DQ22	Data 22
67	DQ23	DQ23	DQ23	Data 23
68	VSS	VSS	VSS	Ground
69	DQ24	DQ24	DQ24	Data 24
70	DQ25	DQ25	DQ25	Data 25
71	DQ26	DQ26	DQ26	Data 26
72	DQ27	DQ27	DQ27	Data 27
73	VDD	VDD	VDD	+5 Vdc or +3.3 Vdc
74	DQ28	DQ28	DQ28	Data 28
75	DQ29	DQ29	DQ29	Data 29
76	DQ30	DQ30	DQ30	Data 30
77	DQ31	DQ31	DQ31	Data 31
78	VSS	VSS	VSS	Ground
79	CK2	CK2	CK2	Clock signal 2
80	n/c	n/c	n/c	Not connected
81	n/c	n/c	n/c	Not connected
82S	DAS	DAS	DAS	Serial data
83S	CLS	CLS	CLS	Serial clock
84	VDD	VDD	VDD	+5 Vdc or +3.3 Vdc
85	VSS	VSS	VSS	Ground
86	DQ32	DQ32	DQ32	Data 32
87	DQ33	DQ33	DQ33	Data 33
88	DQ34	DQ34	DQ34	Data 34
89	DQ35	DQ35	DQ35	Data 35
90	VDD	VDD	VDD	+5 Vdc or +3.3 Vdc
91	DQ36	DQ36	DQ36	Data 36
92	DQ37	DQ37	DQ37	Data 37

TABLE 23-6 PINOUT OF A 168-PIN UNBUFFERED SDRAM DIMM (CONTINUED)

PIN	NON-PARITY	72 ECC	80 ECC	DESCRIPTION
93	DQ38	DQ38	DQ38	Data 38
94	DQ39	DQ39	DQ39	Data 39
95	DQ40	DQ40	DQ40	Data 40
96	VSS	VSS	VSS	Ground
97	DQ41	DQ41	DQ41	Data 41
98	DQ42	DQ42	DQ42	Data 42
99	DQ43	DQ43	DQ43	Data 43
100	DQ44	DQ44	DQ44	Data 44
101	DQ45	DQ45	DQ45	Data 45
102	VDD	VDD	VDD	+5 Vdc or +3.3 Vdc
103	DQ46	DQ46	DQ46	Data 46
104	DQ47	DQ47	DQ47	Data 47
105	n/c	CB4	CB4	Parity/check-bit input/output 4
106	n/c	CB5	CB5	Parity/check-bit input/output 5
107	VSS	VSS	VSS	Ground
108	n/c	n/c	CB12	Parity/check-bit input/output 12
109	n/c	n/c	CB13	Parity/check-bit input/output 13
110	VDD	VDD	VDD	+5 Vdc or +3.3 Vdc
111	−CAS	−CAS	−CAS	−Column address strobe
112	DQMB4	DQMB4	DQMB4	Byte mask signal 4
113	DQMB5	DQMB5	DQMB5	Byte mask signal 5
114	−S1	−S1	−S1	−Chip select 1
115	−RAS	−RAS	−RAS	−Row address strobe
116	VSS	VSS	VSS	Ground
117	A1	A1	A1	Address 1
118	A3	A3	A3	Address 3
119	A5	A5	A5	Address 5
120	A7	A7	A7	Address 7
121	A9	A9	A9	Address 9
122	BA0	BA0	BA0	Bank address 0
123	A11	A11	A11	Address 11
124	VDD	VDD	VDD	+5 Vdc or +3.3 Vdc
125	CK1	CK1	CK1	Clock signal 1
126	A12	A12	A12	Address 12
127	VSS	VSS	VSS	Ground
128	CKE0	CKE0	CKE0	Clock enable signal 0
129	−S3	−S3	−S3	−Chip Select 3
130	DQMB6	DQMB6	DQMB6	Byte mask signal 6
131	DQMB7	DQMB7	DQMB7	Byte mask signal 7
132	A13	A13	A13	Address 13
133	VDD	VDD	VDD	+5 Vdc or +3.3 Vdc
134	n/c	n/c	CB14	Parity/check-bit input/output 14
135	n/c	n/c	CB15	Parity/check-bit input/output 15
136	n/c	CB6	CB6	Parity/check-bit input/output 6
137	n/c	CB7	CB7	Parity/check-bit input/output 7

TABLE 23-6 PINOUT OF A 168-PIN UNBUFFERED SDRAM DIMM (CONTINUED)

PIN	NON-PARITY	72 ECC	80 ECC	DESCRIPTION
138	VSS	VSS	VSS	Ground
139	DQ48	DQ48	DQ48	Data 48
140	DQ49	DQ49	DQ49	Data 49
141	DQ50	DQ50	DQ50	Data 50
142	DQ51	DQ51	DQ51	Data 51
143	VDD	VDD	VDD	+5 Vdc or +3.3 Vdc
144	DQ52	DQ52	DQ52	Data 52
145	n/c	n/c	n/c	Not connected
146	Vref,NC	Vref,NC	Vref,NC	
147	n/c	n/c	n/c	Not connected
148	VSS	VSS	VSS	Ground
149	DQ53	DQ53	DQ53	Data 53
150	DQ54	DQ54	DQ54	Data 54
151	DQ55	DQ55	DQ55	Data 55
152	VSS	VSS	VSS	Ground
153	DQ56	DQ56	DQ56	Data 56
154	DQ57	DQ57	DQ57	Data 57
155	DQ58	DQ58	DQ58	Data 58
156	DQ59	DQ59	DQ59	Data 59
157	VDD	VDD	VDD	+5 Vdc or +3.3 Vdc
158	DQ60	DQ60	DQ60	Data 60
159	DQ61	DQ61	DQ61	Data 61
160	DQ62	DQ62	DQ62	Data 62
161	DQ63	DQ63	DQ63	Data 63
162	VSS	VSS	VSS	Ground
163	CK3	CK3	CK3	Clock signal 3
164	n/c	n/c	n/c	Not connected
165	SA0	SA0	SA0	Serial address 0
166	SA1	SA1	SA1	Serial address 1
167	SA2	SA2	SA2	Serial address 2
168	VDD	VDD	VDD	+5 Vdc or +3.3 Vdc

to be exact—but manufacturers often round down to the nearest million or so). The idea of megabytes (MB) is important when measuring memory in your PC. For example, if a SIMM is laid out as 1M by 8 bits, it has 1MB. If the SIMM is laid out as 4M by 8 bits, it has 4MB. Unfortunately, memory has not been laid out as 8 bits since the IBM XT.

More practical memory layouts involve 32-bit memory (for 486 and OverDrive processors) or 64-bit memory (for Pentium processors). When memory is "wider" than one byte, it is still measured in MB. For example, a 1M × 32-bit (4 bytes) SIMM would be 4MB (that is, the capacity of the device is 4MB), and a 4M × 32-bit SIMM would be 16MB. So when you go shopping for an 8MB 72-pin SIMM, chances are that you're getting a 2M × 32-bit memory module. Table 23-7 provides you with an index to help identify common 72-pin SIMMs. You can see the relationship between memory layout and overall capacity.

TABLE 23-7 72-PIN SIMM IDENTIFICATION GUIDELINES

CONFIGURATION	DESCRIPTION	CAPACITY	TYPE
36 chips: (36) 16 × 1 SOJs or 12 chips: (8) 16 × 4, (4) 16 × 1 SOJs	Parity SIMM, usually double sided	64MB	16 × 36
24 chips: (16) 4 × 4 SOJs, (8) 4 × 1 SOJs	Parity SIMM, usually double sided	32MB	8 × 36
12 chips: (8) 4 × 4 SOJs, (4) 4 × 1 SOJs	Parity SIMM, double or single sided	16MB	4 × 36
24 chips: (16) 1 × 4 SOJs, (8) 1 × 1 SOJs	Parity SIMM, usually double sided	8MB	2 × 36
12 chips: (8) 1 × 4 SOJs, (4) 1 × 1 SOJs	Parity SIMM, double or single sided	4MB	1 × 36
4 chips: (4) 256 × 18 SOJs or 24 chips: (16) 256 × 4 SOJs, & (8) 256 × 1 PLCC	Parity SIMM, usually double sided	2MB	512 × 36
12 chips: (8) 256 × 4 SOJs, & (4) 256 × 1 PLCC	Parity SIMM	1MB	256 × 36
32 chips: (32) 16 × 1 SOJs or 8 chips: (8) 16 × 4 SOJs	Non-parity SIMM, usually double sided	64MB	16 × 32
16 chips: (16) 4 × 4 SOJs	Non-parity SIMM, usually double sided	32MB	8 × 32
8 chips: (8) 4 × 4 SOJs	Non-parity SIMM, usually single sided	16MB	4 × 32
16 chips: (16) 1 × 4 SOJs or 4 chips: (4) 1 × 16 SOJs	Non-parity SIMM, usually double sided	8MB	2 × 32
8 chips: (8) 1 × 4 SOJs or 2 chips: (2) 1 × 16 SOJs	Non-parity SIMM, usually single sided	4MB	1 × 32
16 chips: (16) 256 × 4 SOJs	Non-parity SIMM, usually double sided	2MB	512 × 32
8 chips: (8) 256 × 4 SOJs	Non-parity SIMM	1MB	256 × 32

Memory Organization

The memory in your computer represents the result of evolution over several computer generations. Memory operation and handling is taken care of by your system's microprocessor. As CPUs improved, memory-handling capabilities have improved as well. Today's microprocessors, such as the Intel Pentium or Pentium Pro, are capable of addressing more than 4GB of system memory—well beyond the levels of contemporary software applications. Unfortunately, the early PCs were not nearly so powerful. Older PCs could only address 1MB of memory because of the limitations of the 8088 microprocessor.

Because backward compatibility is so important to computer users, the drawbacks and limitations of older systems had to be carried forward into newer computers, instead of being eliminated. Newer systems overcome their inherent limitations by adding different "types" of memory, along with the hardware and software to access the memory. This part of the chapter describes the typical classifications of computer memory: conventional, extended, and expanded memory. This chapter also describes high memory concepts. Notice that these memory types have nothing to do with the actual ICs in your system, but the way in which software uses the memory.

CONVENTIONAL MEMORY

Conventional memory is the traditional 640KB assigned to the DOS Memory Area (10000h to 9FFFFh, as shown in Fig. 23-4). The original PCs used microprocessors that

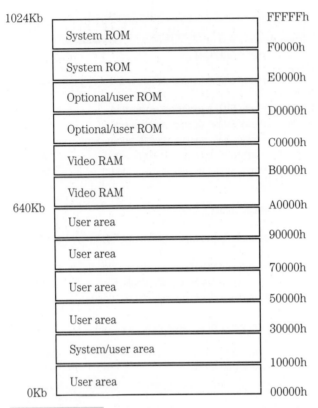

FIGURE 23-4   Conventional and upper memory in
a typical PC.

could only address 1MB of memory (called *real-mode memory* or *base memory*). Out of
that 1MB, portions of the memory must be set aside for basic system functions. BIOS
code, video memory, interrupt vectors, and BIOS data are only some of the areas that require reserved memory. The remaining 640KB became available to load and run your application, which can be any combination of executable code and data. The original PC
only provided 512KB for the DOS program area, but computer designers quickly learned
that another 128KB could be added to the DOS area while still retaining enough memory
for overhead functions, so 512KB became 640KB.

Every IBM-compatible PC still provides a 640KB "base memory" range, and most DOS
application programs continue to fit within that limit to ensure backward compatibility to
older systems. However, the drawbacks to the 8088 CPU were soon apparent. More
memory had to added to the computer for its evolution to continue. Yet, memory had to
be added in a way that did not interfere with the conventional memory area. Table 23-8 illustrates a comprehensive memory map for a typical PC.

EXTENDED MEMORY

The 80286 introduced in IBM's PC/AT was envisioned to overcome the 640KB barrier by
incorporating a protected mode of addressing. The 80286 can address up to 16MB of memory in protected mode, and its successors (the 80386 and later) can handle 4GB of protected-

TABLE 23-8   REAL-MODE MEMORY MAP OF A TYPICAL PC

ADDRESS RANGE (H)	DESCRIPTION	
00000–003FF	**Interrupt Vector Table (256 double words):**	
00000	INT 00H Divide-by-zero interrupt handler	
00004	INT 01H Single-step interrupt handler	
00008	INT 02H Non-maskable interrupt (memory parity or I/O error)	
0000C	INT 03H Breakpoint	
00010	INT 04H Arithmetic overflow interrupt handler	
00014	INT 05H Print screen	
00018	INT 06H Reserved	
0001C	INT 07H Reserved	
00020	INT 08H Timer-interrupt routine (18.21590 /sec)	IRQ0
00024	INT 09H Keyboard service routine	IRQ1
00028	INT 0AH VGA retrace (and AT slave interrupts)	IRQ2
0002C	INT 0BH Serial device 2 service routine	IRQ3
00030	INT 0CH Serial device 1 service routine	IRQ4
00034	INT 0DH Hard-disk interrupt routine	IRQ5
00038	INT 0EH Diskette interrupt routine	IRQ6
0003C	INT 0FH Parallel-port service routine	IRQ7
00040	INT 10H Video services	
00044	INT 11H Equipment check	
00048	INT 12H Memory-size check	
0004C	INT 13H Diskette and hard disk I/O	
00050	INT 14H RS-232 service call	
00054	INT 15H System services calls	
00058	INT 16H Keyboard call	
0005C	INT 17H Printer I/O call	
00060	INT 18H Basic ROM entry (startup)	
00064	INT 19H Boot loader: implement system (IPL) from disk	
00068	INT 1AH Time-of-day call	
0006C	INT 1BH Keyboard break address	
00070	INT 1CH User timer interrupt	
00074	INT 1DH Monitor ROM—for 6845 video inititialization	
00078	INT 1EH Disk-control table pointer	
0007C	INT 1FH Alphanumeric character pattern table pointer	
00080	INT 20H DOS terminate program	
00084	INT 21H Microsoft DOS function calls	
00088	INT 22H DOS terminate address (not a callable function)	
0008C	INT 23H DOS Ctrl-break exit address (not a callable function)	
00090	INT 24H DOS fatal-error exit address (not a callable function)	
00094	INT 25H DOS absolute disk read	
00098	INT 26H DOS absolute disk write	
0009C	INT 27H Terminate and stay resident (control passes to COMMAND.COM)	
000A0	INT 28H Idle loop, spooler waiting; issued by DOS when waiting	

TABLE 23-8 REAL-MODE MEMORY MAP OF A TYPICAL PC (CONTINUED)

ADDRESS RANGE (H)	DESCRIPTION	
000A4	INT 29H CON device raw output handler	
000A8	INT 2AH 3.x Network communications	
000AC	INT 2BH-2DH reserved for DOS	
000B8	INT 2EH Execute DOS command (undocumented)	
000BC	INT 2FH Print spool control (Multiplex Interrupt)	
000C0	INT 30H-31H Internal use	
000C8	INT 32H Reserved for DOS	
000CC	INT 33H Microsoft mouse-driver calls	
000D0	INT 34H-3EH Reserved for DOS	
000FC	INT 3FH Used by LINK to manage overlay segments	
00100	INT 40H Fixed-disk/floppy-disk handler	
00104	INT 41H ROM pointer; fixed-disk parameters	
00108	INT 42H EGA: video vector screen BIOS entry	
0010C	INT 43H EGA: Initialization parameters	
00100	INT 44H EGA: Graphics-character patterns	
00114	INT 45H Reserved	
00118	INT 46H AT: Pointer to second fixed disk parameters	
0011C	INT 47H Reserved	
00120	INT 48H PCjr cordless-keyboard Xlat routine	
00124	INT 49H PCjr non-keyboard scan-code Xlat table	
00128	INT 4AH AT, PS/2 user alarm routine	
0012C	INT 4BH-4FH Reserved	
00140	INT 50H Periodic alarm interrupt from timer	
00144	INT 51H-59H Reserved	
00168	INT 5AH Cluster adapter BIOS-entry address	
0016C	INT 5BH Cluster boot	
00170	INT 5CH NETBIOS entry point	
00174	INT 5DH-5FH Reserved	
00180	INT 60H-66H Reserved for user program interrupts	
0019C	INT 67H EMM: Expanded memory manager routines	
001A0	INT 68H-6BH Unused	
001B0	INT 6CH System-resume vector	
001B4	INT 6DH-6FH Unused	
001C0	INT 70H Real-time clock	IRQ8
001C4	INT 71H LAN adapter	IRQ9
001C8	INT 72H Reserved	IRQ10
001CC	INT 73H Reserved	IRQ11
001D0	INT 74H Mouse interrupt	IRQ12
001D4	INT 75H 80287 NMI Error	IRQ13
001D8	INT 76H Fixed disk controller	IRQ14
001DC	INT 77H Reserved	IRQ15
001E0	INT 78H-7FH Unused	

TABLE 23-8 REAL-MODE MEMORY MAP OF A TYPICAL PC (CONTINUED)

ADDRESS RANGE (H)	DESCRIPTION
00200	INT 80H-85H Reserved for BASIC
00218	INT 86H AT: NetBIOS relocated INT 18H
0021C	INT 87H-F0H Reserved for BASIC interpreter
003C4	INT F1H-FFH Reserved for user program interrupts
003FF	Used for power-on and initial boot stack
00400-004FF	**BIOS Data Area:**
00400	COM1: to COM4: port addresses
00408	LPT1: to LPT3: port addresses
0040E	LPT4: address except PS/2 reserved
00410	Equipment flag
	bits: 15–14 Number of LPTs attached
	13 Internal modem (CVT) or reserved
	12 Joystick
	11–9 Number of COMs
	8 Unused (jr: DMS chip present)
	7–6 Number of disk drives
	5 $1 = 80 \times 25 \; 0 = 40 \times 25$ screen
	4 1 = color 0 = monochrome
	3–2 00 = 64K chips; 11 = 256K chips (PC,XT,AT)
	1 Math coprocessor installed
	0 IPL disk installed
00412	Init. flag; reserved (CVT self-test status)
00413	Memory size in K bytes
00415	Reserved
00416	Reserved
00417	Keyboard monitor flag bytes 0 and 1:
	bit: 7 ins lock 7 ins pressed
	6 caps lock 6 caps pressed
	5 num lock 5 num lock pressed
	4 scroll lock 4 scroll pressed
	3 alt pressed 3 pause locked
	2 crtl pressed 2 sysreq pressed
	1 <shift press 1 <alt pressed
	0 >shift press 0 >alt pressed
00419	Alternate keypad entry
0041A	Keyboard buffer head pointer
0041C	Keyboard buffer tail pointer
0041E	Keyboard buffer
0043E	Drive recalibration status
	bit: 7 Interrupt flag
	6–4 Reserved
	3 Recalibrate drive 3
	2 Recalibrate drive 2
	1 Recalibrate drive 1
	0 Recalibrate drive 0

TABLE 23-8 REAL-MODE MEMORY MAP OF A TYPICAL PC (CONTINUED)

ADDRESS RANGE (H)	DESCRIPTION
0043F	Motor status
	bit: 7 Currently reading or writing
	6 Reserved
	5–4 00 Drive 0 Selected
	01 Drive 1 Selected
	10 Drive 2 Selected
	11 Drive 3 Selected
	3-0 Drive 3-0 motor on status
00440	Motor-control time-out counter
00441	Diskette Status Return Code
	00H No error
	01H Invalid diskette drive parameter
	02H Address mark not found
	03H Write-protect error
	04H Requested sector not found
	05H Reserved
	06H Diskette change line active
	07H Reserved
	08H DMA overrun on operation
	09H Attempt to DMA across a 64K boundary
	0AH Reserved
	0BH Reserved
	0CH Media type not found
	0DH Reserved
	0EH Reserved
	0FH Reserved
	10H CRC error on diskette read
	20H General controller failure
	40H Seek operation failed
	80H Diskette drive not ready
00442	Diskette drive controller status bytes (NEC)
00449	CRT_MODE
	bit: 7 Text 80 × 25 mono on mono card
	6 Graphics 640 × 200 mono on color card
	5 Graphics 320 × 200 mono on color card
	4 Graphics 320 × 200 on color card
	3 Text 80 × 25 color
	2 Text 80 × 25 mono on color
	1 Text 40 × 25 color
	0 Text 40 × 25 mono on color card
0044A	CRT_COLS Number of columns (80)
0044C	CRT_LEN Length of regen buffer in bytes
0044E	CRT_START Starting address in regen buffer
00450	Cursor position on each of eight pages
00460	CURSOR_MODE top-bottom line of cursor (cursor type)
00462	ACTIVE_PAGE index
00463	ADDR_6845 Base address for 6845 display chip
	3B4H for monochrome
	3D4H for color

TABLE 23-8   REAL-MODE MEMORY MAP OF A TYPICAL PC (CONTINUED)

ADDRESS RANGE (H)	DESCRIPTION
00465	CRT_MODE_SETTING for 3 x 8 register 3B8H for MDA 3D8H for CGA
00466	CRT_PALLETTE setting register (3D9H) on color card
00467	Temporary storage for SS:SP during shutdown
0046B	Flag to indicate interrupt
0046C	Timer counter (timer low, timer high words)
00470	Timer overflow (24-hour roll-over flag byte)
00471	Break key state (bit 7 = 1 if break key pressed)
00472	Reset flag word: 1234 bypass memory test 4321 preserve memory 5678 system suspend 9ABC manufacturing test ABCD system POST loop (CVT)
00474	Hard-disk status or reserved for ESDI Adapter/A 00H No error 01H Invalid function request 02H Address mark not found 03H Write protect error 04H Requested sector not found 05H Reset failed 06H Reserved 07H Drive parameter activity failed 08H DMA overrun on operation 09H Data boundary error 0AH Bad sector flag detected 0BH Bad track detected 0CH Reserved 0DH Invalid number of sectors on format 0EH Control data address mark detected 0FH DMA arbitration level out of range 10H Uncorrectable ECC or CRC error 20H General controller failure 40H Seek operation failed 80H Time out AAH Drive not ready BBH Undefined error occurred CCH Write fault on selected drive E0H Status error/error register 0 FFH Sense operation failed
00475	Number of hard-disk drives
00476	Fixed disk-drive control byte (PC XT)
00477	Fixed disk-drive controller port (PC XT)
00478	LPT1: to LPT4: time-out byte values (PS/2 has no LPT4:)
0047C	COM1: to COM4: timeout byte values
00480	Keyboard buffer start pointer (word)
00482	Keyboard buffer end pointer (word)

TABLE 23-8   REAL-MODE MEMORY MAP OF A TYPICAL PC (CONTINUED)

ADDRESS RANGE (H)	DESCRIPTION
00484	ROWS video character Rows - 1
00485	POINTS Height of character matrix-bytes per character
00487	INFO byte:
	bit: 7 Video mode number (of INT 10H funct.0)
	6–5 Size of video RAM 00–64K
	10–192K
	01–128K
	11–256K
	4 reserved
	3 (1) video subsystem is inactive
	2 reserved
	1 (1) video subsystem on monochrome
	0 (1) alphanumeric cursor emulation enabled
00488	INFO_3 byte:
	bit: 7 Input FEAT1 (bit 6 of ISR0 (Input Status Reg.)
	6 Input FEAT1 (bit 5 of ISR0)
	5 Input FEAT0 (bit 6 of ISR0)
	4 Input FEAT0 (bit 5 of ISR0)
	3 EGA config. switch 4 (1=off)
	2 EGA config. switch 3
	1 EGA config. switch 2
	0 EGA config. switch 1
00489	Flags
	bit: 7 bit 4 Alphanumeric scan lines:
	00 350-line mode
	01 400
	10 200
	11 Reserved
	6 (1) Display switching enabled
	5 Reserved
	3 (1) Default palett loading is disabled
	2 (1) Using monochrome monitor
	1 (1) Gray scale is enabled
	0 (1) VGA is active
0048A	DCC Display combination code table index (VGA)
0048B	Media control
	bit: 7–6 Last diskette drive data rate selected
	00–500Kb per second
	01–300Kb per second
	10–250Kb per second
	11–reserved
	5–4 Last diskette drive step rate selected
	3–0 reserved
0048C	Hard-disk status register
0048D	Hard-disk error register
0048E	Hard-disk interrupt control flag
0048F	Combination hard disk/floppy card (bit 0=1)
00490	Drive-0 media-state byte
00491	Drive-1 media-state byte

TABLE 23-8 REAL-MODE MEMORY MAP OF A TYPICAL PC (CONTINUED)

ADDRESS RANGE (H)	DESCRIPTION
00492	Drive 2 media state byte
00493	Drive 3 media state byte
	bit: 7–6 Diskette drive date rate
	00–500Kb per second
	01–300Kb per second
	10–250Kb per second
	11–Reserved
	5 Double stepping required
	4 Media established
	3 Reserved
	2–0 Drive/media state
	000 360Kb diskette/360Kb drive not established
	001 360Kb diskette/1.2Mb drive not established
	010 1.2Mb diskette/1.2Mb drive not established
	011 360Kb diskette/360Kb drive established
	100 360Kb diskette/1.2Mb drive established
	101 1.2Mb diskette/1.2Mb drive established
	110 Reserved
	111 None of the above
00494	Drive 0 track currently selected
00495	Drive 1 track currently selected
00496	Keyboard mode state and type flags
	bit: 7 Read ID in progress
	6 Last character was first ID character
	5 Force NumLock if read ID and KBX
	4 101/102 keyboard installed
	3 Right Alt key pressed
	2 Right Ctrl key pressed
	1 Last code was E0 hidden code
	0 Last code was E1 hidden code
00497	Keyboard LED flags
	bit: 7 Keyboard transmit error flag
	6 Mode-indicator update
	5 Cancel receive flag
	4 Acknowledgment received
	3 = 0 reserved
	2-0 Keyboard LED state bits
00498	Offset address to user wait complete flag
0049A	Segment to user wait complete flag
0049C	User wait count, microseconds low word
0049E	User wait count, microseconds high word
004A0	Wait active flag
	bit: 7 Wait-time elapse and post flag
	6–1 Reserved
004A1	LANA DMA channel flags
004A2	LANA 0 status
004A3	LANA 1 status
004A4	Saved hardfile interrupt vector

TABLE 23-8 REAL-MODE MEMORY MAP OF A TYPICAL PC (CONTINUED)

ADDRESS RANGE (H)	DESCRIPTION
004A8	BIOS video save table and overrides
004AC	Reserved
004B4	Keyboard NMI control flags (CVT)
004B5	Keyboard break-pending flags (CVT)
004B9	Port-60 single-byte queue (CVT)
004BA	Scan code of last key (CVT)
004BB	Pointer-to-NMI buffer head (CVT)
004BC	Pointer-to-NMI buffer tail (CVT)
004BD	NMI scan-code buffer (CVT)
004CE	Day counter (CVT and after)
004D0	Reserved
004F0	Application program communication area
00500–005FF	**DOS Data Area:**
00500	Print-screen status flag 1 = printer active 0FFH = printer fault
00501	Reserved for BASIC and POST work area
00504	Single-drive mode-status byte 0 = drive A 1 = drive B
00505	Reserved POST work area
00510	Reserved for BASIC
0050F	BASIC Shell Flag = 2 if current shell
00510	BASIC segment address storage set with DEF SEG
00512	BASIC int 1Ch clock-interrupt vector
00516	BASIC int 23h ctrl-break interrupt vector
0051A	BASIC int 24h disk-error interrupt vector
0051B	BASIC dynamic storage
00520	DOS dynamic storage
00522	Used by DOS for diskette initialization
00530	Used by MODE command
00534	Reserved for DOS data
00600	Reserved for DOS
00700	I/O drivers from xIO.SYS
00847–0FFFF	xIO.SYS IRET for interrupts 1, 3, and 0FH during POST
	MS-DOS kernel from xDOS.SYS: Interrupt handlers and routines
	MS-DOS disk-buffer cache, FCBs and installable device drivers
	MCB (Memory control block, 16 bytes, paragraph aligned)
	Start of transient program

TABLE 23-8 REAL-MODE MEMORY MAP OF A TYPICAL PC (CONTINUED)

ADDRESS RANGE (H)	DESCRIPTION
10000–9FFFF	**User Data Area (programs and data)**
A0000–AFFFF	Start of EGA and VGA graphics-display RAM modes 0Dh and above
B0000–B3FFF	Start of MDPA and Hercules graphics-display RAM
B4000–B7FFF	Reserved for graphics-display RAM
B8000–BBFFF	Start of CGA color graphics-display RAM
BC000–BFFFF	Reserved for graphics-display RAM
C0000–C3FFF	EGA BIOS ROM
C4000–C5FFF	Video-adapter ROM space
C6000–C63FF	256 bytes of PGA communication area
C6400–C7FFF	Last 7Kb of video adapter ROM space
C8000–CBFFF	16K of hard-disk BIOS adapter ROM space
CC000–CFFFF	
D0000–D7FFF	32K cluster-adapter BIOS ROM
D8000–DBFFF	
DC000–DFFFF	Last 16Kb of adapter ROM space
E0000–EFFFF	64K expansion ROM space (AT, PS/2)
F0000–F3FFF	System-monitor ROM
F4000–F7FFF	System-expansion ROMs
F8000–FBFFF	
FC000–FEFFF	BIOS ROM, BASIC, and simple BIOS
FF000–FFFEF	System ROM
FFFF0–FFFF3	Hardware boot far jump vector

mode memory. Today, virtually all computer systems provide several MB of extended memory. Besides an advanced microprocessor, another key element for extended memory is software. Memory-management software must be loaded in advance for the computer to access its extended memory. Microsoft's DOS 5.0 provides an extended memory manager utility (HIMEM.SYS), but other off-the-shelf utilities are available as well.

Unfortunately, DOS itself cannot use extended memory. You might fill the extended memory with data, but the executable code comprising the program remains limited to the original 640KB of base memory. Some programs written with DOS extenders can overcome the 640KB limit, but the additional code needed for the extenders can make such programs a bit clunky. A DOS extender is basically a software module containing its own memory-management code, which is compiled into the final application program.

The DOS extender loads a program in real-mode memory. After the program is loaded, it switches program control to the protected-mode memory. When the program in protected mode needs to execute a DOS (real mode) function, the DOS extender converts protected-mode addresses into real-mode addresses, copies any necessary program data from protected to real-mode locations, switches the CPU to real-mode addressing, and carries out the function. The DOS extender then copies any results (if necessary) back to protected-mode addresses, switches the system to protected-mode once again, and the program continues to run. This back-and-forth conversion overhead results in less-than-optimum performance, compared to strictly real-mode programs or true "protected-mode" programs.

With multiple megabytes of extended memory typically available, it is possible (but unlikely) that any one program will utilize all of the extended memory. Multiple programs that use extended memory must not attempt to utilize the same memory locations. If conflicts occur, a catastrophic system crash is almost inevitable. To prevent conflicts in extended memory, memory-manager software can make use of three major industry standards: the *Extended Memory Specification (XMS)*, the *Virtual Control Program Interface (VCPI)*, or the *DOS Protected-Mode Interface (DPMI)*. This chapter does not detail these standards, but you should know where they are used.

EXPANDED MEMORY

Expanded memory is another popular technique used to overcome the traditional 640KB limit of real-mode addressing. Expanded memory uses the same "physical" RAM chips, but differs from extended memory in the way that physical memory is used. Instead of trying to address physical memory locations outside of the conventional memory range, as extended memory does, expanded memory blocks are switched into the base memory range, where the CPU can access it in real mode. The original expanded memory specification (called the *Lotus-Intel-Microsoft LIM* or *EMS* specification) used 16KB banks of memory which were mapped into a 64KB range of real-mode memory existing just above the video memory range. Thus, four "blocks" of expanded memory could be dealt with simultaneously in the real mode.

Early implementations of expanded memory utilized special expansion boards that switched blocks of memory, but later CPUs that support memory mapping allowed expanded memory managers (EMMs or LIMs) to supply software-only solutions for i386, i486, and Pentium-based machines. EMS/LIM 4.0 is the latest version of the expanded memory standard which handles up to 32MB of memory. An expanded memory manager (such as the DOS utility EMM386.EXE) allows the extended memory sitting in your computer to emulate expanded memory. For most practical purposes, expanded memory is more useful than extended memory because its ability to map directly to the real mode allows support for program multi-tasking. To use expanded memory, programs must be written specifically to take advantage of the function calls and subroutines needed to switch memory blocks. Functions are completely specified in the LIM/EMS 4.0 standard.

UPPER MEMORY AREA (UMA)

The upper 384KB of real-mode memory is not available to DOS because it is dedicated to handling memory requirements of the physical computer system. This is called the *High DOS Memory Range* or *Upper Memory Area (UMA)*. However, even the most advanced PCs do not use the entire 384KB, so there is often a substantial amount of unused memory existing in your system's real-mode range. Late-model CPUs, such as the i386 and i486 can remap extended memory into the range unused by your system. Because this "found" memory space is not contiguous with your 640KB DOS space, DOS application programs cannot use the space, but small independent drivers and TSRs can be loaded and run from this UMA. The advantage to using high DOS memory is that more of the 640KB DOS range remains available for your application program. Memory-management programs (such as the utilities found with DOS 5.0 and higher) are needed to locate and remap these memory "blocks."

HIGH MEMORY

A peculiar anomaly occurs with CPUs that support extended memory—they can access one segment (about 64KB) of extended memory beyond the real-mode area. This capability arises because of the address line layout on late-model CPUs. As a result, the real-mode operation can access roughly 64KB above the 1MB limit. Like high DOS memory, this "found" 64KB is not contiguous with the normal 640KB DOS memory range, so DOS cannot use this high memory to load a DOS application, but device drivers and TSRs can be placed in high memory. DOS 5.0 is intentionally designed so that its 40 to 50KB of code can be easily moved into this high memory area. With DOS loaded into high memory, an extra 40 to 50KB or so will be available within the 640KB DOS range.

Memory Considerations

Memory has become far more important than just a place to store bits for the microprocessor. It has proliferated and specialized to the point where it is difficult to keep track of all the memory options and architectures that are available. This part of the chapter reviews established memory types, and explains some of the current memory architectures.

MEMORY SPEED AND WAIT STATES

The PC industry is constantly struggling with the balance between price and performance. Higher prices usually bring higher performance, but low cost makes the PC appealing to more people. In terms of memory, cost-cutting typically involves using cheaper (slower) memory devices. Unfortunately, slow memory cannot deliver data to the CPU quickly enough, so the CPU must be made to wait until memory can catch up. All memory is rated in terms of speed—specifically, *access time*. Access time is the delay between the time data in memory is successfully addressed, to the point at which the data has been successfully delivered to the data bus. For PC memory, access time is measured in nanoseconds (ns), and current memory offers access times of 50 to 60 ns. 70-ns memory is extremely common.

The question often arises: "Can I use faster memory than the manufacturer recommends?" The answer to this question is almost always "Yes," but rarely does performance benefit. As you will see in the following sections, memory and architectures are typically tailored for specific performance. Using memory that is faster should not hurt the memory or impair system performance, but it costs more and will not produce a noticeable performance improvement. The only time such a tactic would be advised is when your current system is almost obsolete, and you would want the new memory to be useable on a new, faster motherboard if you choose to upgrade the motherboard later on.

A wait state orders the CPU to pause for one clock cycle to give memory additional time to operate. Typical PCs use one wait state, although very old systems might require two or three. The latest PC designs with high-end memory or aggressive caching might be able to operate with no (zero) wait states. As you might imagine, a wait state is basically a waste of time, so more wait states result in lower system performance. Zero wait states allow optimum system performance. Table 23-9 illustrates the general relationship between CPUs, wait states, and memory speed. It is interesting to note that some of the fastest systems allow the most wait states. This flexibility lets the system support old, slow memory,

TABLE 23-9 CPUS, WAIT STATES, AND MEMORY SPEED

CPU	WAIT STATES	MEMORY ACCESS
8088	1	200 ns
8086	0	150 ns
80286	1	150 ns
80286	1	120 ns
80286	0	85 ns
80386SX	0–2	100 ns
80386SX/DX	0–2	85 ns
80386SX	0–2	80 ns
80386DX	0–5	80 ns
80386SX	0–2	70 ns
80486DX	0–5	80 ns
80486DX	0–5	70 ns
80486SLC2	0–2	70 ns
80486SLC3	0–2	70 ns
80486SX	0–2	70 ns
80486DX4	0–2	70 ns
80486DX2	0–2	70 ns
Pentium	0–5	60 ns
Pentium	0–2	50 ns

but the resulting system performance would be so poor that there would be little point in using the system in the first place.

There are three classic means of selecting wait states. First, the number of wait states might be fixed (common in old XT systems). Wait states might be selected with one or more jumpers on the motherboard (typical of i286 and early i386 systems). Current systems, such as i486 and Pentium computers, place the wait state control in the CMOS setup routine. You might have to look in an "advanced settings" area to find the entry. When optimizing a computer, you should be sure to set the minimum number of wait states.

Setting too few wait states can cause the PC to behave erratically.

DETERMINING MEMORY SPEED

It is often necessary to check SIMMs or DIMMs for proper memory speed during troubleshooting, or when selecting replacement parts. Unfortunately, it can be very difficult to determine memory speed accurately based on part markings. Speeds are normally marked cryptically by adding a number to the end of the part number. For example, a part number ending in -6 often means 60 ns, a –7 is usually 70 ns, and a –8 can be 80 ns. Still, the only way to be absolutely certain of the memory speed is to cross reference the memory part number with a manufacturer's catalog, and read the speed from the catalog's description (i.e., *4M × 32 50 ns EDO*).

PRESENCE DETECT (PD)

Another feature of modern memory devices is a series of signals known as the *Presence Detect lines* (you'll see these as *PDx* signals in 72-pin pinouts, such as Table 23-2 and 23-3). By setting the appropriate conditions of the PD signals, it is possible for a computer to immediately recognize the characteristics of the installed memory devices, and configure itself accordingly. Presence detect lines typically specify three operating characteristics of memory: size (device layout) and speed. Table 23-10 highlights many of the most commonly used signal combinations.

UNDERSTANDING MEMORY "REFRESH"

The electrical signals placed in each DRAM storage cell must be replenished (or refreshed) periodically every few milliseconds. Without refresh, DRAM data will be lost. In principle, refresh requires that each storage cell be read and re-written to the memory array. This is typically accomplished by reading and re-writing an entire row of the array at one time. Each row of bits is sequentially read into a sense/refresh amplifier (part of the DRAM IC), which basically recharges the appropriate storage capacitors, then re-writes each row bit to the array. In actual operation, a row of bits is automatically refreshed whenever an array row is selected. Thus, the entire memory array can be refreshed by reading each row in the array every few milliseconds.

The key to refresh is in the way DRAM is addressed. Unlike other memory ICs that supply all address signals to the IC simultaneously, a DRAM is addressed in a two-step sequence. The overall address is separated into a row (low) address and a column (high) address. Row

TABLE 23-10 INDEX OF PRESENCE DETECT (PD) SIGNALS

	72-PIN SIMM	PIN 67 (PD1)	PIN 68 (PD2)	PIN 69 (PD3)	PIN 70 (PD4)	PIN 71 (PD5)
Size (parity pinout)	256K × 32/36	GND	N/C	—	—	—
	512K × 32/36	N/C	GND	—	—	—
	1M × 32/36	GND	GND	—	—	—
	2M × 32/36	N/C	N/C	—	—	—
	4M × 32/36	GND	N/C	—	—	N/C
	8M × 32/36	N/C	GND	—	—	N/C
Size (ECC pinout)	256K × 32/36	GND	N/C	—	—	N/C
	512K × 32/36	N/C	GND	—	—	N/C
	1M × 32/36	GND	GND	—	—	N/C
	2M × 32/36	N/C	N/C	—	—	N/C
	4M × 32/36	GND	N/C	—	—	GND
	8M × 32/36	N/C	GND	—	—	GND
Speed (parity/ECC pinout)	60 ns	—	—	N/C	N/C	—
	70 ns	—	—	GND	N/C	—
	80 ns	—	—	N/C	GND	—
	100 ns	—	—	GND	GND	—
	120 ns	—	—	N/C	N/C	—

GND = Jumper installed
N/C = No jumper installed

address bits are placed on the DRAM address bus first, and the –Row Address Select (–RAS) line is pulsed logic 0 to multiplex the bits into the IC's address decoding circuitry. The low portion of the address activates an entire array row and causes each bit in the row to be sensed and refreshed. Logic 0s remain logic 0s and logic 1s are recharged to their full value.

Column address bits are then placed on the DRAM address bus, and the –Column Address Select (–CAS) is pulsed to logic 0. The column portion of the address selects the appropriate bits within the chosen row. If a read operation is taking place, the selected bits pass through the data buffer to the data bus. During a Write operation, the Read/Write line must be logic 0, and valid data must be available to the IC before –CAS is strobed. New data bits are then placed in their corresponding locations in the memory array.

Even if the IC is not being accessed for reading or writing, the memory must still be refreshed to ensure data integrity. Fortunately, refresh can be accomplished by interrupting the microprocessor to run a refresh routine that simply steps through every row address in sequence (column addresses need not be selected for simple refresh). This row-only (or -RAS only) refresh technique speeds the refresh process. Although refreshing DRAM every few milliseconds might seem like a constant aggravation, the computer can execute quite a few instructions before being interrupted for refresh. Refresh operations are generally handled by the chipset on your motherboard. Often, memory problems (especially "parity errors") that cannot be resolved by replacing a SIMM can be traced to a refresh fault on the motherboard.

MEMORY TYPES

For a computer to work, the CPU must take program instructions and exchange data directly with memory. As a consequence, memory must keep pace with the CPU (or make the CPU wait for it to catch up). Now that processors are so incredibly fast (and getting faster), traditional memory architectures are being replaced by specialized memory devices that have been tailored to serve specific functions in the PC. As you upgrade and repair various systems, you will undoubtedly encounter some of the following memory designations:

- *DRAM (Dynamic Random-Access Memory)* This remains the most recognized and common form of computer memory. DRAM achieves a good mix of speed and density, while being relatively simple and inexpensive to produce—only a single transistor and capacitor is needed to hold a bit. Unfortunately, DRAM contents must be refreshed every few milliseconds or the contents of each bit location will decay. DRAM performance is also limited because of relatively long access times. Today, many video boards are using DRAM SIMMs to supply video memory.
- *SRAM (Static Random-Access Memory)* The SRAM is also a classic memory design— it is even older than DRAM. SRAM does not require regular refresh operations, and can be made to operate at access speeds that are much faster than DRAM. However, SRAM uses six transistors (or more) to hold a single bit. This reduces the density of SRAM and increases power demands (which is why SRAM was never adopted for general PC use in the first place). Still, the high speed of SRAM has earned it a place as the PC's L2 (or external) cache. You'll probably encounter three types of SRAM cache schemes: asynchronous, synchronous burst, and pipeline burst.
- *Asynchronous Static RAM (Async SRAM or ASRAM)* This is the traditional form of L2 cache, introduced with i386 systems. There's really nothing too special about AS-RAM, except that its contents can be accessed much faster (20 ns, 15 ns, or 12 ns) than

DRAM. ASRAM does not have enough performance to be accessed synchronously, and has long since been replaced by better types of cache.

■ *Synchronous-Burst Static RAM (Sync SRAM or SBSRAM)* This is largely regarded as the best type of L2 cache for intermediate-speed motherboards (~60 to 66MHz). With access times of 8.5 ns and 12 ns, the SBSRAM can provide synchronous bursts of cache information in 2-1-1-1 cycles (i.e., 2 clock cycles for the first access, then 1 cycles per access—in time with the CPU clock). However, as motherboards pass 66MHz (i.e., 75 and 83MHz designs), SBSRAM loses its advantage to Pipelined Burst SRAM.

■ *Pipelined-Burst Static RAM (PB SRAM)* At 4.5 to 8 ns, this is the fastest form of high-performance cache now available for 75MHz+ motherboards. PBSRAM requires an extra clock cycle for "lead off," but then can sync with the motherboard clock (with timing such as 3-1-1-1) across a wide range of motherboard frequencies. If you're interested in more technical details about PBSRAM, check out the ASUS site at:

http://asustek.asus.com.tw/Products/TB/mem-0001.html.

■ *VRAM (Video Random-Access Memory)* DRAM has been the traditional choice for video memory, but the ever-increasing demand for fast video information (i.e., high-resolution SVGA displays) requires a more efficient means of transferring data to and from video memory. Originally developed by Samsung Electronics, video RAM achieves speed improvements by using a "dual data bus" scheme. Ordinary RAM uses a single data bus—data enters or leaves the RAM through a single set of signals. Video RAM provides an "input" data bus and an "output" data bus. This allows data to be read from video RAM at the same time new information is being written to it. You should realize that the advantages of VRAM will only be realized on high-end video systems, such as $1024 \times 768 \times 256$ (or higher), where you can get up to 40% more performance than a DRAM video adapter. Below that, you will see no perceivable improvement with a VRAM video adapter.

■ *FPM DRAM (Fast-Page Mode DRAM)* This is a popular twist on conventional DRAM. Typical DRAM access is accomplished in a fashion similar to reading from a book—a memory "page" is accessed first, then the contents of that "page" can be located. The problem is that every access requires the DRAM to re-locate the "page." Fast-page mode operation overcomes this delay by allowing the CPU to access multiple pieces of data on the same "page" without having to "re-locate" the "page" every time—as long as the subsequent read or write cycle is on the previously located "page," the FPDRAM can access the specific location on that "page" directly.

■ *EDRAM (Enhanced DRAM)* This is another, lesser-known variation of the classic DRAM developed by Ramtron International and United Memories. First demonstrated in August 1994, the EDRAM eliminates an external cache by placing a small amount of static RAM (cache) into each EDRAM device itself. In essence, the cache is distributed within the system RAM; as more memory is added to the PC, more cache is effectively added as well. The internal construction of an EDRAM allows it to act like page-mode memory—if a subsequent read requests data that is in the EDRAM's cache (known as a *hit*), the data is made available in about 15 ns—roughly equal to the speed of a fair external cache. If the subsequent read requests data that is not in the cache (called a *miss*), the data is accessed from the DRAM portion of memory in about 35 ns, which is still much faster than ordinary DRAM.

■ *EDO RAM (Extended Data Output RAM)* EDO RAM is a relatively well-established variation to DRAM, which extends the time that output data is valid—thus the word's presence on the data bus is "extended." This is accomplished by modifying the DRAM's output buffer, which prolongs the time where read data is valid. The data will remain valid until a motherboard signal is received to release it. This eases timing constraints on the memory and allows a 15 to 30% improvement in memory performance with little real increase in cost. Because a new external signal is needed to operate EDO RAM, the motherboard must use a chipset designed to accommodate EDO. Intel's Triton chipset was one of the first to support EDO, although now most chipsets (and most current motherboards) currently support EDO. EDO RAM can be used in non-EDO motherboards, but there will be no performance improvement.

■ *BEDO (Burst Extended Data Output RAM)* This powerful variation of EDO RAM reads data in a burst, which means that after a valid address has been provided, the next three data addresses can be read in only one clock cycle each. The CPU can read BEDO data in a 5-1-1-1 pattern (5 clock cycles for the first address, then one clock cycle for the next three addresses. Although BEDO offers an advantage over EDO, it is only supported currently by the VIA chipsets: 580VP, 590VP, 680VP. Also, BEDO seems to have difficulty supporting motherboards over 66MHz.

■ *SDRAM (Synchronous or Synchronized DRAM)* Typical memory can only transfer data during certain portions of a clock cycle. The SDRAM modifies memory operation so that outputs can be valid at any point in the clock cycle. By itself, this is not really significant, but SDRAM also provides a "pipeline burst" mode that allows a second access to begin before the current access is complete. This "continuous" memory access offers effective access speeds as fast as 10 ns, and can transfer data at up to 100MB/s. SDRAM is becoming quite popular on current motherboard designs, and is supported by the Intel VX chipset, and VIA 580VP, 590VP, and 680VP chipsets. Like BEDO, SDRAM can transfer data in a 5-1-1-1 pattern, but it can support motherboard speeds up to 100MHz, which is ideal for the 75MHz and 82MHz motherboards now becoming so vital for Pentium II systems. Check out the following references for more information on SDRAM:
~http://www.chips.ibm.com/products/memory/sdramart/sdramart.html
~http://www.fujitsu-ede.com/sdram/index.html
~http://www.ti.com/sc/docs/memory/brief.htm

■ *CDRAM (Cached DRAM)* Like EDRAM, the CDRAM from Mitsubishi incorporates cache and DRAM on the same IC. This eliminates the need for an external (or L2) cache, and has the extra benefit of adding cache whenever RAM is added to the system. The difference is that CDRAM uses a "set-associative" cache approach that can be 15 to 20% more efficient than the EDRAM cache scheme. On the other hand, EDRAM appears to offer better overall performance.

■ *RDRAM (Rambus DRAM)* Most of the memory alternatives so far have been variations of the same basic architecture. Rambus, Inc. (joint developers of EDRAM) has created a new memory architecture called the *Rambus Channel*. A CPU or specialized IC is used as the "master" device and the RDRAMs are used as "slave" devices. Data is then sent back and forth across the Rambus channel in 256-byte blocks. With a dual 250MHz clock, the Rambus Channel can transfer data based on the timing of both clocks—this results in data-transfer rates approaching 500MB/s (roughly equivalent to 2-ns access time). The problem with RDRAM is that a Rambus Channel would require an extensive re-design to the current PC memory architecture—a move that most PC makers strenuously resist. As a result, you are most likely to see RDRAM in high-end, specialized computing systems. Still, as memory struggles to match the microprocessor, PC makers might yet embrace the Rambus approach for commercial systems.

■ *WRAM (Windows RAM)* Samsung Electronics has recently introduced WRAM as a new video-specific memory device. WRAM uses multiple-bit arrays connected with an extensive internal bus and high-speed registers that can transfer data almost continuously. Other specialized registers support attributes, such as foreground color, background color, write-block control bits, and true-byte masking. Samsung claims data-transfer rates of up to 640MB/s—about 50% faster than VRAM—yet WRAM devices are cheaper than their VRAM counterparts. It is likely that WRAM will receive some serious consideration in the next few years.

MEMORY TECHNIQUES

Rather than incur the added expense of specialized memory devices, PC makers often use inexpensive, well-established memory types in unique architectures designed to make the most of low-end memory. The three most-popular architectures are: paged memory, interleaved memory, and memory caching.

Paged memory This approach basically divides system RAM into small groups (or "pages") from 512 bytes to several KB long. Memory-management circuitry on the motherboard allows subsequent memory accesses on the same "page" to be accomplished with zero wait states. If the subsequent access occurs outside of the current "page," one or more wait states might be added while the new "page" is found. This is identical in principle to fast-page mode DRAM. You will find page-mode architectures implemented on high-end i286, PS/2 (model 70 and 80), and many i386 systems.

Interleaved memory This technique provides better performance than paged memory. Simply put, interleaved memory combines two banks of memory into one. The first portion is "even," while the second portion is "odd"—so memory contents are alternated between these two areas. This allows a memory access in the second portion to begin before the memory access in the first portion has finished. In effect, interleaving can double memory performance. The problem with interleaving is that you must provide twice the amount of memory as matched pairs. Most PCs that use interleaving will allow you to add memory one bank at a time, but interleaving will be disabled and system performance will suffer.

Memory caching This is perhaps the most recognized form of memory-enhancement architecture (Fig. 23-5). Cache is a small amount (anywhere from 8KB to 1MB) of very fast SRAM, which forms an interface between the CPU and ordinary DRAM. The SRAM typically operates on the order of 5 to 15 ns, which is fast enough to keep pace with a CPU using zero wait states. A cache-controller IC on the motherboard keeps track of frequently accessed memory locations (as well as predicted memory locations), and copies those contents into cache. When a CPU reads from memory, it checks the cache first. If the needed contents are present in cache (called a cache hit), the data is read at zero wait states. If the needed contents are not present in the cache (known as a cache miss), the data must be read directly from DRAM at a penalty of one or more wait states. A small quantity of very fast

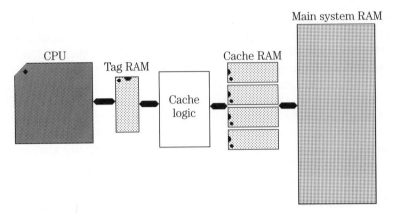

Main system RAM

CPU   Tag RAM   Cache RAM

Cache
logic

FIGURE 23-5   Major cache system components.

cache (called Tag RAM) acts as an index, recording the various locations of data stored in cache. A well-designed caching system can achieve a hit ratio of 95% or more—in other words, memory can run without wait states 95% of the time.

Two levels of cache are in the contemporary PC. CPUs from the i486 onward have a small internal cache (known as *L1 cache*) and external cache (SRAM installed as DIPs or COAST modules on the motherboard) is referred to as *L2 cache*. The i386 CPUs have no internal cache (although IBM's 386SLC offered 8KB of L1 cache). Most i486 CPUs provide an 8KB internal cache. Early Pentium processors were fitted with two 8KB internal caches—one for data and one for instructions. Today's Pentium II Slot 1 CPU incorporates 256 to 512KB of L2 cache into the processor cartridge itself.

Shadow memory ROM devices (whether the BIOS ROM on your motherboard or a ROM IC on an expansion board) are frustratingly slow with access times often exceeding several hundred nanoseconds. ROM access then requires a large number of wait states, which slow down the system's performance. This problem is compounded because the routines stored in BIOS (especially the video BIOS ROM on the video board) are some of the most frequently accessed memory in your computer.

Beginning with the i386-class computers, some designs used a memory technique called *shadowing*. ROM contents are loaded into an area of fast RAM during system initialization, then the computer maps the fast RAM into memory locations used by the ROM devices. Whenever ROM routines must be accessed during run time, information is taken from the "shadowed ROM" instead of the actual ROM IC. The ROM performance can be improved by at least 300%.

Shadow memory is also useful for ROM devices that do not use the full available data bus width. For example, a 16-bit computer system might hold an expansion board that contains an 8-bit ROM IC. The system would have to access the ROM not once, but twice, to extract a single 16-bit word. If the computer is a 32-bit machine, that 8-bit ROM would have to be addressed four times to make a complete 32-bit word. You might imagine the hideous system delays that can be encountered. Loading the ROM to shadow memory in advance virtually eliminates such delays. Shadowing can usually be turned on or off through the system's CMOS Setup routines.

The Issue of Parity

As you might imagine, it is vital that data and program instructions remain error-free. Even one incorrect bit because of electrical noise or a component failure can crash the PC, corrupt drive information, cause video problems, or result in a myriad of other faults. PC designers approached the issue of memory integrity by using a technique known as *parity* (the same technique used to check serial data integrity).

THE PARITY PRINCIPLE

The basic idea behind parity is simple—each byte written to memory is checked, and a 9th bit is added to the byte as a checking (or "parity") bit. When a memory address is later read by the CPU, memory-checking circuitry on the motherboard will calculate the expected parity bit and compare it to the bit actually read from memory. In this fashion, the PC can continuously diagnose system memory by checking the integrity of its data. If the read parity bit matches the expected parity bit, the data (and, indirectly, the RAM) is assumed to be valid, and the CPU can go on its way. If the read and expected parity bits do not match, the system registers an error and halts. Every byte is given a parity bit, so for a 32-bit PC, there will be 4 parity bits for every address. A 64-bit PC, has 8 parity bits, etc.

EVEN VS. ODD

The two types of parity are even and odd. With even parity, the parity bit is set to 0 if an even number of 1s are already in the corresponding byte (keeping the number of 1s even). If an even number of 1s is not in the byte, the even parity bit will be 1 (making the number of 1s even).

With odd parity, the parity bit is set to 0 if an odd number of 1s is already in the corresponding byte (keeping the number of 1s odd). If an odd number of 1s is not in the byte, the odd parity bit will be 1 (making the number of 1s odd).

Although even and odd parity work opposite of one another, both schemes serve exactly the same purpose and have the same probability of catching a bad bit. The memory device itself does not care at all about what type of parity is being used—it just needs to have the parity bits available. The use of parity (and the choice of even or odd) is left up to the motherboard's memory-control circuit.

THE PROBLEMS WITH PARITY

Although parity has proven to be a simple and cost-effective means of continuously checking memory, there are two significant limitations. First, although parity can detect an error, it cannot correct the error because there is no way to tell which bit has gone bad. This is why a system simply halts when a parity error is detected. Second, parity is unable to detect multi-bit errors. For example, if a 1 accidentally becomes a 0 and a 0 accidentally becomes a 1 within the same byte, parity conditions will still be satisfied. Fortunately, the probability of a multi-bit error in the same byte is extremely remote.

CIRCUMVENTING PARITY

Over the last few years, parity has come under fire from PC makers and memory manufacturers alike. Opponents claim that the rate of parity errors because of hardware (RAM) faults is very small and that the expense of providing parity bits in a memory-hungry marketplace just isn't justified anymore. There is some truth to this argument, considering that the parity technique is more than 15 years old and has serious limitations.

As a consequence, a few motherboard makers have begun removing parity support from their low-end motherboards, and others are providing motherboards that will function with or without parity (usually set in CMOS or with a motherboard jumper). Similarly, some memory makers are now providing non-parity and "fake" parity memory as cheaper alternatives to conventional parity memory. Non-parity memory simply foregoes the 9th bit. For example, a non-parity SIMM would be designated ×8 or ×32 (i.e., *4M × 8* or *4M × 32*). If the SIMM supports parity, it will be designated ×9 or ×36 (i.e., *4M × 9* or *4M × 36*). Fake parity is a bit more devious—the 9th bit is replaced by a simple (and dirt cheap) parity-generator chip that "looks" like a normal DRAM IC. When a read cycle occurs, the parity chip on the SIMM provides the proper parity bit to the motherboard all the time. In effect, your memory is "lying" to the motherboard.

Although there is a cost savings, your memory is left with no means of error checking at all. It's a little like driving a car without a speedometer—you could go for miles without a problem, but sooner or later you'll cross a speed trap. You can go indefinitely without parity, but when an error does occur, having parity in place can save you immeasurable frustration. Unless the "lowest cost" is your absolute highest priority, it is recommended that you spend the extra few dollars for parity RAM.

> Most motherboards can be operated with non-parity RAM. It is also usually possible to mix parity and non-parity memory in the same system. In either case, you will need to disable all parity-checking features for the RAM.

ABUSE AND DETECTION OF FAKE MEMORY

Another potential problem with "fake" parity memory is fraud. There have already been reported instances where memory was purchased as "parity" at full price—only to find that the parity ICs were actually parity generators. This was determined by dissecting the IC packages and finding that the IC die in the parity position did not match the IC dies in the other bit positions. The buyer doesn't know because parity generators are packaged to look just like DRAM ICs, and there is no other obvious way to tell, just by looking at the SIMM or other memory device. System diagnostic software also cannot detect the presence of parity memory vs. fake memory.

There are really only two ways to protect yourself from fake memory fraud. First, industry experts indicate that many fake-parity ICs (the parity generators) are marked with designations such as "BP," "VT," "GSM," or "MPEC." If you find that 1 out of every 9 ICs on your SIMM carries such a designation (or any other designation not matching the first 8), you might have a fraud situation. Of course, the first step in all justice is a "benefit of the doubt," so contact the organization you purchased the memory from—they might simply have sent the wrong SIMMs.

Second, you can check the IC dies themselves. Unfortunately, this requires that you to carefully dissect several IC packages on the SIMM and compare the IC dies under a microscope—resulting in the destruction of the memory device(s). If the 9th die looks radically different (usually much simpler) than the other 8, you've likely got fake parity. A non-destructive way to check the SIMM is to use a SIMM checker (if you have access to one) with a testing routine specially written to test parity memory. If the SIMM works, but the parity IC test fails (i.e., the tester cannot write to the parity memory), chances are you've got fake parity.

If you determine that you have been sold fake parity memory in place of real parity memory and you cannot get any satisfaction from the seller, you are encouraged to contact the Attorney General in the seller's state, and convey your information to them. After all, if you're being stiffed, chances are a lot of other people are too—and they probably don't even know it.

ALTERNATIVE ERROR CORRECTION

Although this book supports the use of parity, it is also quick to recognize its old age. In the world of personal computing, parity is an ancient technique. Frankly, it could easily be replaced by more sophisticated techniques, such as *Error-Correction Code (ECC)* or *ECC on SIMM (EOS)*. ECC (which is already being used in high-end PCs and file servers) uses a mathematical process in conjunction with the motherboard's memory controller, and appends a number of ECC bits to the data bits. When data is read back from memory, the ECC memory controller checks the ECC data read back as well.

ECC has two important advantages over parity. It can actually correct single-bit errors "on-the-fly" without the user ever knowing there's been a problem. In addition, ECC can successfully detect 2-bit, 3-bit, and 4-bit errors, which makes it an incredibly powerful error-detection tool. If a rare multi-bit error is detected, ECC is unable to correct it, but it will be reported and the system will halt.

It takes 7 or 8 bits at each address to successfully implement ECC. For a 32-bit system, you will need to use $\times 39$ or $\times 40$ SIMMs (i.e., 8M $\times$ 39 or 8M $\times$ 40). These are relatively new designations, so you should at least recognize them as ECC SIMMs if you encounter them. As an alternative, some 64-bit systems use two 36-bit SIMMs for a total of 72 bits—64 bits for data and 8 bits (which would otherwise be for parity) for ECC information.

EOS is a relatively new (and rather expensive) technology that places ECC functions on the memory module itself, but it provides ECC results as parity. While the memory module runs ECC, the motherboard continues to see parity. This is an interesting experiment, but it is unlikely that EOS will gain significant market share. Systems that use parity can be fitted with parity memory much more cheaply than EOS memory.

Memory Installation and Options

Installing memory is not nearly as easy as it used to be. Certainly, today's memory modules just plug right in, but deciding which memory to buy, how much (or how little) to buy, and how to use existing memory in new systems, presents technicians with a bewildering variety of choices. This part of the chapter illustrates the important ideas behind choosing and using memory.

GETTING THE RIGHT AMOUNT

"How much memory do I need?" This age-old question has plagued the PC industry ever since the 80286 CPU broke the 1MB memory barrier. With more memory, additional programs and data can be run by the CPU at any given time—which indirectly helps to improve the productivity of the particular PC. The problem is cost. Typical DRAM is running around $15/MB (U.S.)—compared to about $0.50/MB (U.S.) for hard-drive space. The goal of good system configuration is to install enough memory to support the PC's routine tasks. Installing too much memory means that you've spent money for PC resources that just remain idle. Installing too little memory results in programs that will not run (typical under DOS) or poor system performance because of extensive swap-file use (typical under Windows).

So how much memory is enough? The fact of the matter is that "enough" is an ever-changing figure. DOS systems of the early 1980s (8088/8086) worked just fine with 1MB. By the mid-1980s (80286), DOS systems with 2MB were adequate. Into the late 1980s (80386), Windows 3.0 and 3.1 needed 4MB. As the 1990s got underway (80486), Windows systems with 8MB were common (even DOS applications were using 4 to 6MB). Today, with Pentium systems and Windows 95, 16MB is considered to be a minimum requirement, and 32MB systems are readily available. For today, this is the benchmark that you should use for general-purpose home and office systems. But by the end of the decade, 48 to 64MB systems will probably be the norm. And this is not to say that 32MB systems are the pinnacle of performance. Today's file servers and industrial-strength design packages are using 64MB to 128MB of RAM—motherboard chipsets can often support up to 512MB of RAM or more.

FILLING BANKS

Another point of confusion is the idea of a "memory bank." Most memory devices are installed in sets (or banks). The amount of memory in the bank can vary, depending on how much you wish to add, but there must always be enough data bits in the bank to fill each bit position. Table 23-11 illustrates a relationship between data bits and banks for the range of typical CPUs. For example, the 8086 is a 16-bit microprocessor (two bytes). This means that two extra bits are required for parity, providing a total of 18 bits. Thus, one bank is 18 bits wide. You might fill the bank by adding eighteen 1-bit DIPs or two 30-pin SIMMs. As another example, an 80486DX is a 32-bit CPU, so 36 bits are needed to fill a

CPU	DATA WIDTH (W/PARITY)	XMB BY 1 DIPS	30-PIN SIMMS	72-PIN SIMMS
8088	9 bits	9	1	—
8086	18 bits	18	2	—
80286	18 bits	—	2	1 (2 banks)
80386SX, SL, SLC	18 bits	—	2	1 (2 banks)
80386DX	36 bits	—	4	1
80486SLC, SLC2	18 bits	—	2	1 (2 banks)
80486DX, SX, DX2, DX4	36 bits	—	4	1
Pentium	64 bits	—	8	2

TABLE 23-11 CPUS VS. MEMORY BANK SIZE

bank (32 bits plus 4 parity bits). If you use 30-pin SIMMs, you will need four to fill a bank. If you use 72-pin SIMMs, only one is needed. Notice that the size of the memory in MB does not really matter, so long as the entire bank is filled.

BANK REQUIREMENTS

There is more to filling a memory bank than just installing the right number of bits. Memory amount, memory matching, and bank order are three additional considerations. First, you must use the proper memory amount that will bring you to the expected volume of total memory. Suppose a Pentium system has 8MB already installed in Bank 0, and you need to put another 8MB into the system in Bank 1. Table 23-11 shows that two 72-pin SIMMs are needed to fill a bank, but each SIMM need only be 1M. Remember that a $1M \times 36$-bit (with parity) device is 4MB. Because two such SIMMs are needed to fill a bank, the total would be 8MB. When added to the 8MB already in the system, the total would be 16MB.

How about another example? Suppose that the same 8MB is already installed in your Pentium system and you want to add 16MB to Bank 1, rather than 8MB (bringing the total system memory to 24MB). In that case, you could use two 2M 72-pin SIMMs, where $2M \times 36$ is 8MB (with parity) per SIMM. Two 8MB SIMMs yield 16MB, bringing the system total to (16MB + 8MB) = 24MB.

Now for a curve. Suppose you want to outfit that Pentium as a network server with 128MB of RAM. Remember that 8MB is already in Bank 0, which means that only Bank 1 is available. Because the largest commercially available SIMMs are $8M \times 36$ (32MB with parity), you can only add up to 64MB to Bank 1 (for a system total of 72MB. To get around this, you should remove the existing $1M \times 36$ SIMMs in Bank 0, and fill both Bank 0 and Bank 1 with $8M \times 36$ SIMMs, which would put 64MB in Bank 0, and 64MB in Bank 1—yielding 128MB in total. You can review many of the recommended SIMM/DIMM combinations for a typical Pentium motherboard in Table 23-12.

TABLE 23-12 MEMORY COMBINATIONS FOR A TYPICAL MOTHERBOARD								
MEMORY SIZE	SIMM 1	SIMM 2	SIMM 3	SIMM 4	SIMM 5	SIMM 6	DIMM 1	DIMM 2
8MB	$1M \times 32$	$1M \times 32$	—	—	—	—	—	—
8MB	—	—	—	—	—	—	$1M \times 64$	—
16MB	$2M \times 32$	$2M \times 32$	—	—	—	—	—	—
16MB	$1M \times 32$	$1M \times 32$	$1M \times 32$	$1M \times 32$	—	—	—	—
16MB	—	—	—	—	—	—	$2M \times 64$	—
16MB	—	—	—	—	—	—	$1M \times 64$	$1M \times 64$
24MB	$1M \times 32$	$1M \times 32$	$2M \times 32$	$2M \times 32$	—	—	—	—
24MB	$1M \times 32$	$1M \times 32$	$1M \times 32$	$1M \times 32$	$1M \times 32$	1Mx32	—	—
24MB	—	—	—	—	—	—	$1M \times 64$	$2M \times 64$
32MB	$4M \times 32$	$4M \times 32$	—	—	—	—	—	—
32MB	$2M \times 32$	$2M \times 32$	$2M \times 32$	$2M \times 32$	—	—	—	—
32MB	$1M \times 32$	$1M \times 32$	$1M \times 32$	$1M \times 32$	$2M \times 32$	2Mx32	—	—
32MB	—	—	—	—	—	—	$4M \times 64$	—
32MB	—	—	—	—	—	—	$2M \times 64$	$2M \times 64$

TABLE 23-12 MEMORY COMBINATIONS FOR A TYPICAL MOTHERBOARD (CONTINUED)

MEMORY SIZE	SIMM 1	SIMM 2	SIMM 3	SIMM 4	SIMM 5	SIMM 6	DIMM 1	DIMM 2
40MB	1M × 32	1M × 32	4M × 32	4M × 32	—	—	—	—
40MB	—	—	—	—	—	—	1M × 64	4M × 64
48MB	2M × 32	2M × 32	4M × 32	4M × 32	—	—	—	—
48MB	1M × 32	1M × 32	1M × 32	1M × 32	4M × 32	4M × 32	—	—
48MB	2M × 32	2M × 32	2M × 32	2M × 32	2M × 32	2M × 32	—	—
48MB	—	—	—	—	—	—	2M × 64	4M × 64
64MB	8M × 32	8M × 32	—	—	—	—	—	—
64MB	4M × 32	4M × 32	4M × 32	4M × 32	—	—	—	—
64MB	2M × 32	2M × 32	2M × 32	2M × 32	4M × 32	4Mx32	—	—
64MB	—	—	—	—	—	—	8M × 64	—
64MB	—	—	—	—	—	—	4M × 64	4M × 64
72MB	1M × 32	1M × 32	8M × 32	8M × 32	—	—	—	—
72MB	—	—	—	—	—	—	1M × 64	8M × 64
80MB	2M × 32	2M × 32	8M × 32	8M × 32	—	—	—	—
80MB	1M × 32	1M × 32	1M × 32	1M × 32	8M × 32	8M × 32	—	—
80MB	—	—	—	—	—	—	2M × 64	8M × 64
96MB	4M × 32	4M × 32	8M × 32	8M × 32	—	—	—	—
96MB	2M × 32	2M × 32	2M × 32	2M × 32	8M × 32	8M × 32	—	—
96MB	4M × 32	4M × 32	4M × 32	4M × 32	4M × 32	4M × 32	—	—
96MB	—	—	—	—	—	—	4M × 64	8M × 64
128MB	16M × 32	16M × 32	—	—	—	—	—	—
128MB	8M × 32	8M × 32	8M × 32	8M × 32	—	—	—	—
128MB	4M × 32	4M × 32	4M × 32	4M × 32	8M × 32	8Mx32	—	—
128MB	—	—	—	—	—	—	8M × 64	8M × 64
136MB	1M × 32	1M × 32	16M × 32	16M × 32	—	—	—	—
144MB	2M × 32	2M × 32	16M × 32	16M × 32	—	—	—	—
144MB	1M × 32	1M × 32	1M × 32	1M × 32	16M × 32	16M × 32	—	—
160MB	4M × 32	4M × 32	16M × 32	16M × 32	—	—	—	—
160MB	2M × 32	2M × 32	2M × 32	2M × 32	16M × 32	16M × 32	—	—
192MB	8M × 32	8M × 32	16M × 32	16M × 32	—	—	—	—
192MB	4M × 32	4M × 32	4M × 32	4M × 32	16M × 32	16M × 32	—	—
192MB	8M × 32	8M × 32	8M × 32	8M × 32	8M × 32	8M × 32	—	—
256MB	32M × 32	32M × 32	—	—	—	—	—	—
256MB	16M × 32	16M × 32	16M × 32	16M × 32	—	—	—	—
256MB	8M × 32	8M × 32	8M × 32	8M × 32	16M × 32	16M × 32	—	—
256MB	—	—	—	—	—	—	16M × 64	16M x 64

Another bank requirement demands memory matching—using SIMMs of the same size and speed within a bank. For example, when adding multiple SIMMs to a bank, each SIMM must be rated for the same access speed and share the same memory configuration (i.e., 2M × 36).

Finally, you must follow the bank order. For example, fill Bank 0 first, then Bank 1, then Bank 2, etc. Otherwise, memory will not be contiguous within the PC and CMOS will not recognize the additional RAM.

Recycling Older Memory Devices

Given the relatively high cost of PC memory, it is only natural that users and technicians alike would choose to re-use memory as much as possible when systems are upgraded or replaced. It is a simple matter to re-use memory—just as you would re-use hard drives or video boards. But consider some special issues before you make plans to transfer memory from one system to another.

MEMORY SPEED

The goal of memory is to keep pace with the microprocessor using a minimum of wait states. It is possible to place a 100-ns SIMM in a Pentium system, but the wait states required to allow this awful mis-match would negate any benefits from the advanced microprocessor. As a consequence, it is most effective to use memory that is fast enough to handle the CPU in the system that will be receiving the memory. Table 23-10 shows typical memory speeds for various microprocessors. It is possible to use memory if the speed is faster than the minimum requirement, but all the memory in the bank should be the same speed. Ordinarily, there is no reason to buy memory that is faster than necessary—no additional benefit is realized by the system. The only time it might be advisable to invest in faster memory is if you know in advance that the memory will eventually be transferred to another system.

MEMORY TYPE

You should also be sure to use the same type of memory (i.e., EDO, FPM, SDRAM, etc.). For example, if your motherboard is designed to use EDO RAM, and you have EDO RAM already installed, you should be sure to install more EDO RAM. Some motherboard designs allow you to mix memory types, but mixing memory types on other (especially older) motherboards might cause the system to malfunction.

SIMM STACKERS

Although your memory type should be able to fit into the new computer, there are ways to make it fit. One of the most popular memory adapters is the "SIMM stacker." The devices are known by a variety of trade names, but all allow you to convert four 30-pin SIMMs into a 72-pin SIMM frame. However, with SIMM Stackers have two drawbacks:

- *Cramped quarters* SIMM adapter products require serious amounts of space. Remember that the adapter snaps into the SIMM socket and SIMMs attach to the adapter. As a result, the filled SIMM adapter looks a bit like a tree with branches. This is rarely a problem when SIMM sockets are placed side-to-side, but with several banks close together, multiple SIMM sockets might interfere with one another.
- *Timing penalty* Timing is everything for memory, and with signals traveling on the order of nanoseconds, the very length of a printed signal run can adversely impact system performance. Generally speaking, you can expect access times to be increased by 10 ns or so when using a SIMM adapter. This is not a problem when the memory is measurably faster than needed. But if your memory speed is on the border, a SIMM adapter might necessitate an additional wait state.

MIXING "COMPOSITE" AND "NON-COMPOSITE" SIMMS

Most ordinary 30-pin SIMMs use nine ICs (eight for data and one for parity). From time to time, you might encounter SIMMs with just a few ICs (usually three). The composite SIMM (with nine ICs) is older—using less-dense memory. The non-composite SIMM (with three or so ICs) generally uses newer memory devices. In theory, it should be possible to mix composite and non-composite SIMMs together in the same bank or in the same system. However, system problems have been reported when this happens. As a rule, you can try mixing these two generations of memory, but if you encounter memory problems with the system later on, remove either memory type and see if the problem goes away.

REMOUNTING AND REBUILDING MEMORY

Memory "recycling" has taken another more unexpected turn—some small companies are actually taking older memory devices and re-mounting them on SIMMs and other memory structures. In this way, you can use DIPs that are re-mounted on a SIMM. For example, a company called Autotime (**http://www.autotime.com**) in Portland, OR will remove memory devices from one SIMM and install them on a SIMM that you need (i.e., remove the ICs from four 1MB 30-pin SIMMs and install and test them on one 4MB 72-pin SIMM).

Memory Troubleshooting

Unfortunately, even the best memory devices fail from time to time. An accidental static discharge during installation, incorrect installation, a poor system configuration, operating system problems, and even outright failures because of old age or poor manufacture can cause memory problems. This part of the chapter looks at some of the troubles that plague memory devices, and offers advise on how to deal with them.

A selection of tools are on the Companion CD, which can aid you in testing and troubleshooting PC memory. Check out CACHECHK.ZIP for cache testing, MEMSCAN.ZIP and RAMMAP.ZIP for general testing, and SHADTEST.ZIP for shadow RAM-performance testing.

MEMORY TEST EQUIPMENT

If you are working in a repair-shop environment or plan to be testing a substantial number of memory devices, you should consider acquiring some specialized test equipment. A memory tester, such as the SIMCHECK from Innoventions, Inc. (Fig. 23-6), is a modular microprocessor-based system that can perform a thorough, comprehensive test of various SIMMs and indicate the specific IC that has failed (if any). The system can be configured to work with specific SIMMs by installing an appropriate adapter module (Fig. 23-7). Intelligent testers work automatically, and show the progress and results of their examinations on a multi-line LCD Guesswork is totally eliminated from memory testing.

Single ICs, such as DIPs and SIPs, can be tested using a single-chip plug-in module. The static RAM checker (Fig. 23-8) is another test bed for checking high-performance static RAM components in a DIP package. Both Innoventions test devices work together to provide a full-featured test system. Specialized tools can be an added expense—but no more

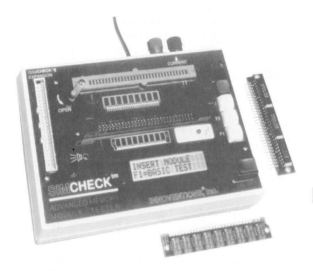

FIGURE 23-6 The SIMCHECK main unit. Innoventions, Inc.

FIGURE 23-7 The SIM-CHECK PS/2 SIMM adapter. Innoventions, Inc.

FIGURE 23-8 The SIMCHECK static RAM unit. Innoventions, Inc.

so than an oscilloscope or other piece of useful test equipment. The return on your investment is less time wasted in the repair and fewer parts to replace.

REPAIRING SIMM SOCKETS

If there is one weak link in the architecture of a SIMM, it is the socket that connects it to the motherboard. Ideally, the SIMM should sit comfortably in the SIMM socket, then gently snap back—held in place by two clips on either side of the socket. In actuality, you really have to push that SIMM to get it into place. Taking it out again is just as tricky. As a result, it is not uncommon for a SIMM socket to break and render your extra memory unusable.

The best ("textbook") solution is to remove the SIMM socket and install a new one. Clearly, this tactic has some problems. First, removing the old socket will require you to remove the motherboard, desolder the broken socket, then solder in a new socket (which you can buy from a full-feature electronics store, such as DigiKey). In the hands of a skilled technician with the right tools, this is not so hard. But the printed circuit runs of a computer motherboard are extremely delicate, and the slightest amount of excess heat can easily destroy the sensitive, multi-layer connections.

Fortunately, there are some tricks that might help you. If either of the SIMM clips have bent or broken, you can usually use a medium-weight rubber band that is about 1" shorter than the SIMM. Wrap the rubber band around the SIMM and socket, and the rubber band should do a fair job holding the SIMM in place. If any part of the socket should crack or break, it can be repaired (or at least reinforced) with a good-quality epoxy. If you choose to use epoxy, be sure to work in a ventilated area and allow plenty of time for the epoxy to dry.

CONTACT CORROSION

Here's one to tuck away for future reference. Corrosion can occur on SIMM contacts if the SIMM contact metal is not the same as the socket—this will eventually cause contact (and memory) problems. As a rule, check that the metal on the socket contact is the same as the SIMM contacts (usually tin or gold). You might be able get around the problem in the short term by cleaning corrosion off the contacts manually using a cotton swab and good electronics-grade contact cleaner. In the mean time, if you discover that your memory and connectors have dissimilar metals, you might be able to get the memory seller to exchange the SIMMs.

PARITY ERRORS

Parity errors constitute many of the memory faults that you will see as a technician. As you saw earlier in this chapter, parity is an important part of a computer's self-checking capability. Errors in memory will cause the system to halt—rather than continue blindly along with a potentially catastrophic error. But not just faulty memory that causes parity errors. Parity can also be influenced by your system's configuration. Here are the major causes of parity problems:

- One or more memory bits is intermittent or has failed entirely.
- Poor connections between the SIMM and socket.
- Too few wait states entered in BIOS (memory is too slow for the CPU).
- An intermittent failure or other fault has occurred in the power supply.

■ A bug, computer virus, or other rogue software is operating.
■ A fault has occurred in the memory-controller IC or BIOS.

When you are faced with a parity error after an upgrade, you should suspect a problem with wait states, so check that first. If the wait states are correct, systematically remove each SIMM, clean the contacts, and re-seat each SIMM. If the errors continue, try removing one bank of SIMMs at a time (chances are that the memory is bad). You might have to relocate memory so that Bank 0 remains filled. When the error disappears, the memory you removed is likely defective.

If parity errors occur spontaneously (with no apparent cause), you should clean and re-install each SIMM first to eliminate the possibility of bad contacts. Next, check the power-supply outputs—low or noisy outputs might allow random bit errors. You might have to upgrade the supply if it is overloaded. Try booting the system "clean" from a write-protected floppy disk to eliminate the possibility of buggy software or computer viruses. If the problem persists, suspect a memory defect.

TROUBLESHOOTING CLASSIC XT MEMORY

It seems only fitting to start an examination of memory problems with a brief overview of the original IBM PC/XT computer. In the "good old days" of personal computing, when only one or two commercial computers were on the market, there were few memory arrangements. POST could be written very specifically, and errors could be correlated directly to memory IC location. The POST routine in an XT's BIOS ROM is designed to identify the exact bank and bit where a memory error is detected, and display that information on the computer's monitor.

IBM PC/XT computers classify a memory (RAM) failure as error code 201. In actual operation, a RAM error would appear as "XXYY 201," where "XX" is the bank, and "YY" is the bit where the fault is detected. As a result, it was often a simple matter to locate and replace a defective RAM IC. An XT is built with four RAM banks—each with nine bits (parity plus eight bits). Table 23-13 shows some bank and bit error codes for XT-

TABLE 23-13 INDEX OF IBM PC/XT ERROR CODES			
"XXYY 201": MEMORY FAILURE			
XX	BANK	YY	BIT
00	0	00	Parity bit
04	1	01	D0
08	2	02	D1
0C	3	04	D2
		08	D3
		10	D4
		20	D5
		40	D6
		80	D7

class computers. As an example, suppose that an XT system displayed 0002 201. This would indicate a memory failure in bank 0 at data bit D1. You need only replace the DIP memory IC residing at that location.

Symptom 23-1. You see a "1055 201" or "2055 201" error message Both of these error codes indicate a problem with the system's DIP switch settings. Remember that XTs do not use CMOS RAM to contain a system setup configuration, so DIP switches are used to tell the system how much memory should be present. If memory is added or removed, the appropriate switches in switch bank 2 (bits 1 to 8) and switch bank 1 (bits 3 and 4) must be set properly. Turn off the computer, check your switch settings and reboot the computer.

Symptom 23-2. You see a "PARITY CHECK 1" error message This error typically suggests a power-supply problem—RAM ICs are not receiving the proper voltage levels, so their contents are being lost or corrupted. When this happens, parity errors will be produced. Remove all power from the computer, and repair or replace the power supply.

Symptom 23-3. You see a "XXYY 201" error message This is a general RAM failure format for XT computers, which indicates the bank and bit where the fault is located. XX is the faulty bank, and YY is the faulty bit. See Table 23-13 to decipher the specific bank and bit in an XT. For example, an error code of 0004 201 indicates a memory fault in bank 0 (00) and bit D2 (04). Replace the defective IC or bank of ICs.

Symptom 23-4. You see a "PARITY ERROR 1" error message Multiple addresses or multiple data bits are detected as faulty in the XT. In some cases, one or more ICs might be loose or inserted incorrectly in their sockets. Remove power from the system and reseat all RAM ICs. If all RAM ICs are inserted correctly, rotate a new DRAM IC through each occupied IC location until the defective IC is located.

TROUBLESHOOTING CLASSIC AT MEMORY

Like the XT, IBM's PC/AT was the leader of the 80286 generation. Because there was only one model (at the time), ATs use some specific error messages to pinpoint memory (RAM or ROM) problems on the motherboard, as well as in its standard memory-expansion devices. The 200 series error codes represent system memory errors (Table 23-14). ATs present memory failures in the format: "AAXXXX YYYY 20x." The 10-digit code can be broken down to indicate the specific system bank and IC number, although the particular bit failure is not indicated. The first two digits ("AA") represent the defective bank, and the last four digits ("YYYY") show the defective IC number. It is then a matter of finding and replacing the faulty DIP IC. Table 23-15 shows a set of error codes for early AT-class computers. For example, suppose that an IBM PC/AT displayed the error message: "05xxxxxx 0001 201" (we don't care about the x's). That message would place the error in IC 0 of bank 1 on the AT's system memory.

TROUBLESHOOTING CONTEMPORARY MEMORY ERRORS

Since the introduction of 286-class computers, the competition among motherboard manufacturers, as well as the rapid advances in memory technology, has resulted in a tremendous

TABLE 23-14 200-SERIES ERROR CODES

201	Memory error (physical location will likely be displayed)
202	Memory address line 0–15 error
203	Memory address line 16–23 error; line 16–31 error (MCA)
204	Memory remapped to compensate for error (PS/2)
205	Error in first 128K (PS/2 ISA) of RAM
207	BIOS ROM failure
210	System-board memory-parity error
211	Error in first 64K of RAM (MCA)
212	Watchdog timer error
213	DMA bus-arbitration time out
215	Memory address error; 64K on daughter/SIP 2 failed (70)
216	Memory address error; 64K on daughter/SIP 1 failed (70)
221	ROM to RAM copy (shadowing) failed (MCA)
225	Wrong speed memory on system board (MCA)
230	Memory on motherboard and adapter board overlaps
231	Non-contiguous adapter memory installed
235	Stuck data line on memory module
241	Memory module 2 failed
251	Memory module 3 failed

TABLE 23-15 CLASSIC AT ERROR CODES

"AAXXXXYYYY 20X": MEMORY FAILURE

AA	BOARD	BANK
00 01 02 03	Motherboard	0
04 05 06 07	Motherboard	1
08 09	128KB memory expansion	n/a
10 11 12 13	1st 512KB memory adapter	0
14 15 16 17	1st 512KB memory adapter	1
18 19 1A 1B	2nd 512KB memory adapter	0
1C 1D 1E 1F	2nd 512KB memory adapter	1
20 21 22 23	3rd 512KB memory adapter	0
24 25 26 27	3rd 512KB memory adapter	1
28 29 2A 2B	4th 512KB memory adapter	0
2C 2D 2E 2F	4th 512KB memory adapter	1
30 31 32 33	5th 512KB memory adapter	0
34 35 36 37	5th 512KB memory adapter	1

YYYY	FAILED IC	YYYY	FAILED IC
0000	Parity IC	0100	8
0001	0	0200	9
0002	1	0400	10

TABLE 23-15 CLASSIC AT ERROR CODES			
YYYY	FAILED IC	YYYY	FAILED IC
0004	2	0800	11
0008	3	1000	12
0010	4	2000	13
0020	5	4000	14
0040	6	8000	15
0080	7		

amount of diversity in the design and layout of memory systems. Although the basic concepts of memory operation remain unchanged, every one of the hundreds of computer models manufactured today use slightly different memory arrangements. Today's PCs also hold much more RAM than XT and early AT systems.

As a consequence of this trend, specific numerical (bank and bit) error codes have long-since been rendered impractical in newer systems, where megabytes can be stored in just a few ICs. The i386, i486, and today's Pentium/Pentium II computers use a series of generic error codes. The address of a fault is always presented, but no attempt is made to correlate the fault's address to a physical IC. Fortunately, today's memory systems are so small and modular that trial-and-error isolation can often be performed rapidly. Let's look at some typical errors.

Symptom 23-5. The number "164" is displayed on the monitor This is a generic memory-size error—the amount of memory found during the POST does not match the amount of memory listed in the system's CMOS setup. Run the CMOS setup routine and be sure that the listed memory amount matches the actual memory amount. If memory has been added or removed from the system, you will have to adjust the figure in the CMOS setup to reflect that configuration change. If CMOS setup parameters do not remain in the system after power is removed, try replacing the battery or CMOS/RTC IC.

> The latest CMOS setup routines do not list the amount of RAM—it is detected automatically. However, you might simply have to enter the CMOS setup, then immediately save changes and exit to "recalibrate" the amount of detected RAM.

Symptom 23-6. You see an "Incorrect Memory Size" error message This message might be displayed if the CMOS system setup is incorrect, or if there is an actual memory failure that is not caught with a numerical 200-series code. Check your CMOS setup, as described in Symptom 23-5 and correct it, if necessary. If the error persists, there is probably a failure in some portion of RAM.

Without a numerical code, it can be difficult to find the exact problem location, so adopt a divide-and-conquer strategy. Remove all expansion memory from the system, alter the CMOS setup to reflect base memory (system board) only, and retest the system. If the problem disappears, the fault is in some portion of expansion memory. If the problem still persists, you know the trouble is likely in your base (system board) memory. Take a known-good SIMM or DIMM and systematically swap devices until you locate the defective device. If you have access to a memory tester, the process will be much faster.

If you successfully isolate the problem to a memory expansion board (often found in older proprietary PCs), you can adopt the same strategy for the board(s). Return one board at a time to the system (and update the CMOS setup to keep track of available memory). When the error message reappears, you will have found the defective board. Use a known-good RAM IC, SIMM, or DIMM, and begin a systematic swapping process until you have found the defective memory device.

Symptom 23-7. You see a "ROM Error" message displayed on the monitor
To guarantee the integrity of system ROM, a checksum error test is performed as part of the POST. If this error occurs, one or more ROM locations might be faulty. Your only alternative here is to replace the system BIOS ROM(s) and retest the system.

Symptom 23-8. New memory is installed, but the system refuses to recognize it New memory installation has always presented some unique problems because different generations of PC deal with new memory differently. The oldest PCs require you to set jumpers or DIP switches for the computer to recognize new blocks of memory. The vintage i286 and i386 systems (i.e., a PS/2) use a setup diskette to tell CMOS about the PC's configuration (including new memory). More recent i386 and i486 systems incorporate an "installed memory" setting into a CMOS setup utility in BIOS. Late-model i486 and Pentium systems actually "auto-detect" installed memory each time the system is booted (so it need not be entered in the CMOS setup).

Also check that an correct bank has been filled properly. The PC might not recognize any additional memory, unless an entire bank has been filled and the bank is next in order (i.e., Bank 0, then Bank 1, etc.). You might wish to check the PC's user manual for any unique rules or limitations in the particular motherboard.

> Some late-model Pentium/Pentium II motherboards do not need banks filled in order, although that's usually the safest policy to follow when upgrading or troubleshooting any PC.

Symptom 23-9. New memory has been installed or replaced, and the system refuses to boot When faced with complete boot failures, always start by checking ac power, the system power switch, and power connections to the motherboard. Also see that all expansion boards are inserted evenly and completely in their expansion slots (flexing the motherboard during memory installation might have pried one or more boards out of their slots). Your memory modules might not be inserted correctly. Take the modules out and seat them again, making sure the locking arm is holding the module securely in place. If the problem continues, you probably do not have the right memory module for that particular computer. Be sure that the memory module (SIMM or DIMM) is compatible with your PC. Finally, check for any particular "device order" that might be required by the motherboard. Certain systems require that memory be installed in pairs or in descending order by size.

Symptom 23-10. You see an "XXXX Optional ROM Bad, Checksum = YYYY" error message Part of the POST sequence checks for the presence of any other ROMs in the system. When another ROM is located, a checksum test is performed to check its integrity. This error message indicates that the external ROM (such as a SCSI adapter or Video BIOS) has checked bad or its address conflicts with another device in the system. In either case, system initialization cannot continue.

If you have just installed a new peripheral device when this error occurs (i.e., a SCSI controller board), try changing the device's ROM address jumpers to resolve the conflict. If the problem remains, remove the peripheral board—the fault should disappear. Try the board on another PC. If the problem continues on another PC, the adapter (or its ROM) might be defective. If this error has occurred spontaneously, remove one peripheral board at a time and retest the system until you isolate the faulty board, then replace the faulty board (or just replace its ROM if possible).

Symptom 23-11. You see a general RAM error with fault addresses listed In actuality, the error message might appear as any of the following examples, depending on the specific fault, where the fault was detected, and the BIOS version reporting the error:

■ Memory address line failure at XXXX, read YYYY, expecting ZZZZ
■ Memory data line failure at XXXX, read YYYY, expecting ZZZZ
■ Memory high address failure at XXXX, read YYYY, expecting ZZZZ
■ Memory logic failure at XXXX, read YYYY, expecting ZZZZ
■ Memory odd/even logic failure at XXXX, read YYYY, expecting ZZZZ
■ Memory parity failure at XXXX, read YYYY, expecting ZZZZ
■ Memory read/write failure at XXXX, read YYYY, expecting ZZZZ

Each of these errors are general RAM error messages indicating a problem in base or extended/expanded RAM. The code "XXXX" is the failure segment address—an offset address might be included. The word "YYYY" is what was read back from the address, and "ZZZZ" is the word that was expected. The difference between these read and expected words is what precipitated the error. In general, these errors indicate that at least one base RAM IC (if you have RAM soldered to the motherboard) or at least one SIMM/DIMM has failed. A trial-and-error approach is usually the least expensive route in finding the problem. First, re-seat each SIMM or DIMM and retest the system to be sure that each SIMM/DIMM is inserted and secured properly. Rotate a known-good SIMM/DIMM through each occupied SIMM/DIMM socket in sequence. If the error disappears when the known-good SIMM or DIMM is in a slot, the old device that had been displaced is probably the faulty one. You can go on to use specialized SIMM troubleshooting equipment to identify the defective IC, but such equipment is rather expensive unless you intend to repair a large volume of SIMMs/DIMMs to the IC level.

If the problem remains unchanged—even though every SIMM has been checked, the error is probably in the motherboard RAM or RAM support circuitry. Run a thorough system diagnostic, if possible, and check for failures in other areas of the motherboard that affect memory (such as the interrupt controller, cache controller, DMA controller, or memory-management chips). If the problem prohibits a software diagnostic, use a POST board and try identifying any hexadecimal error code. If a support IC is identified, you can replace the defective IC or replace the motherboard outright. If RAM continues to be the problem, try replacing the motherboard RAM (or replace the entire motherboard), and retest the system.

Symptom 23-12. You see a "Cache Memory Failure—Disabling Cache" error The cache system has failed. The tag RAM, cache logic, or cache memory on your motherboard is defective. Your best course is to replace the cache RAM IC(s) or COAST (Cache-on-a-Stick) module. If the problem persists, try replacing the cache logic or tag RAM (or replace the entire motherboard). You will probably need a schematic diagram or a detailed block diagram of your system in order to locate the cache memory IC(s).

Symptom 23-13. You see a "Decreasing Available Memory" error message This is basically a confirmation message that indicates a failure has been detected in extended or expanded memory, and that all memory after the failure has been disabled to allow the system to continue operating (although at a substantially reduced level). Your first step should be to re-seat each SIMM/DIMM and ensure that they are properly inserted and secured. Next, take a known-good SIMM or DIMM and step through each occupied SIMM/DIMM slot until the problem disappears—the device that had been removed is probably the faulty one. Keep in mind that you might have to alter the system's CMOS setup parameters as you move memory around the machine (an incorrect setup can cause problems during system initialization).

Symptom 23-14. You are encountering a memory error with HIMEM.SYS under DOS In many cases, this is a compatibility problem with system memory. For example, the Intel Advanced/AS motherboard is incompatible with two specific Texas Instruments EDO SIMMs (part numbers TM124FBK32S-60 and TM248GBK32S-60). Other EDO SIMMs from TI and other vendors will not cause this error. Try a SIMM from a different manufacturer. Also be sure that you're using the latest version of HIMEM.SYS.

Symptom 23-15. Memory devices from various vendors refuse to work together The system experiences a "Memory failure" during the memory count at start time. This is a very "machine-specific" problem. For example, Gateway Solo PCs can suffer this problem when customers use the same-size memory modules (4MB, 8MB, or 16MB) made from different vendors. Try matching the memory modules from the same manufacturer (including part number and speed).

Symptom 23-16. Windows 95 "Protection" errors occur after adding SIMMs/DIMMs Windows 95 stalls with "Windows Protection Errors" during boot or randomly crashes with "Fatal Exception Errors" when opening applications. This is a known problem with the Intel Thor motherboard using the 1.00.01.CNOT BIOS after installing 32MB of RAM. This issue is usually caused by certain third-party SIMMs operating at speeds faster or slower than 60 ns. The motherboard probably has tight memory specifications, and SIMMs that operate at correct speed are required (not faster or slower—even though the SIMMs are "marked" properly). Some SIMM manufacturers mark the SIMMs at 60 ns, but the SIMMs actually run at 45 ns. Try some SIMMs from a different manufacturer. It is also possible that a BIOS upgrade might loosen timing enough to make the SIMMs usable.

Further Study

That's it for Chapter 23. Be sure to review the glossary and chapter questions on the accompanying CD. If you have access to the Internet, take a look at some of these memory resources:

Autotime: **http://www.autotime.com**

Cameleon Technology: **http://www.camusa.com/**

CST, Inc: **http://www.simmtester.com/**

Innoventions: **http://www.simcheck.com/**

Jaguar Marketing Group: **http://www2.inow.com/~degeorge/jaguar.htm**

Kingston: **http://www.kingston.com**

PNY: **http://www.pny.com**

Simmsaver Technology, Inc.: **http://www.simmsaver.com/**

24

MEMORY

MANAGERS

CONTENTS AT A GLANCE

Making the Most of Conventional
  Memory
  Protect the configuration
  Optimizations for config.sys
  Optimizations for autoexec.bat
  Reviewing your results with MEM
  Mix and match
  Adjusting the memory environment
    for DOS programs under
    Windows 95

Troubleshooting typical
  optimization problems

Troubleshooting QEMM

Troubleshooting HIMEM/EMM386

Troubleshooting 386MAX

Further Study

As personal computers broke the 1MB mark, the problem became utilizing memory over 640KB (conventional memory). For application programs to utilize memory beyond 640KB, a *memory manager* is required to support the physical RAM present in the system and configure the RAM as "extended" (XMS) or "expanded" (EMS) memory. In general, memory managers provide a series of crucial services to a modern PC:

- It allows the operating system and applications to access to extended memory (XMS) over 1MB.
- It allows extended memory (XMS) to simulate expanded memory (EMS), which otherwise would require specialized hardware support.

- It locates and frees unused memory in the upper memory area (UMA) to make it available for use.
- It utilizes the high memory area (HMA)—that 64KB segment just above the 1MB mark.
- It supports the use of shadow RAM, where slower ROM contents are copied to faster RAM to provide faster system performance.
- It can rearrange the address order of physical memory in the PC so that faster memory appears in the lower addresses, a technique known as *memory sorting*.
- It can fill in empty addresses below 640KB with memory contents from extended memory (XMS) to utilize the entire 640KB at all times, a technique called *backfilling*.

As a consequence of these features, use of memory managers offers some significant advantages for a computer; larger applications (or applications with huge volumes of data) and more sophisticated operating systems can be created; extended memory supports the execution of code beyond 1MB, so programs can be run outside of conventional memory; multiple programs can be loaded into the available RAM space for more effective multitasking; and unused space in the UMA and HMA can be loaded with DOS or real-mode device drivers—freeing more conventional memory for DOS applications. The current generation of memory managers also offer a suite of advanced features and conveniences, such as accelerating software loading and execution times, better memory utilization and performance reporting, and more aggressive location of unused memory.

Although the current memory managers are compatible with Windows 95, memory managers are not as vital as they once were. Windows 95 now incorporates many of the memory-management functions needed by the PC—relegating MS-DOS and third-party memory managers to DOS platforms or "game machines," as well as DOS applications running in a Windows 95 "window." Although memory managers are well-developed pieces of software, they are not always as well-behaved as they should be. This chapter presents some tips for optimizing your use of memory, and examines a selection of symptoms and solutions for the three major memory manager families: QEMM, HIMEM/EMM386, and 386MAX.

Making the Most of Conventional Memory

Even under DOS 7.x of Windows 95, DOS applications still depend on an ample amount of conventional memory for proper operation. Freeing conventional memory and loading real-mode drivers and DOS into upper memory are still two key objectives of memory management. The memory-management process usually consists of enabling the memory managers, then rearranging real-mode software in an optimum fashion. Because every PC configuration is different, and can use an incredibly diverse array of software, no single set of rules can ensure optimum memory utilization (even such memory optimizers as DOS MEMMAKER are known to fail under some circumstances). As a consequence, optimizing a PC's memory is sometimes more of an art than a science. This part of the chapter outlines the essential concepts of using memory managers, and offers some tips to help you utilize memory better.

PROTECT THE CONFIGURATION

Optimizing memory is largely a matter of tweaking a system's CONFIG.SYS and AU-TOEXEC.BAT files. Although Windows 95 tries to eliminate them, these startup files are still the only way to configure a PC for real-mode (DOS) operation. Before you attempt to modify the startup files, you should always make it a point to backup the startup files by copying CONFIG.SYS and AUTOEXEC.BAT to different file names such as:

```
C:\> copy config.sys config.bak
C:\> copy autoexec.bat autoexec.bak
```

This creates two "backup" files and allows you to modify the original startup files. If you make a mistake modifying the startup files, you can always restore the original CON-FIG.SYS and AUTOEXEC.BAT files by re-copying the backup files to the original file names, such as:

```
C:\> copy config.bak config.sys
C:\> copy autoexec.bak autoexec.bat
```

Once the files have been restored, you can resume modifying them. If you have a boot diskette, you should also consider placing a copy of the original startup files on it.

Also make it a point to know the <F8> key. When you see the message: "Starting Windows 95," press <F8> to load a Startup menu. From here, you can control the ways in which your system starts. This can be a valuable tool when checking to see just which drivers or utilities load (or not). If you're working on an older DOS/Windows 3.1x platform, use the <F5> key to bypass CONFIG.SYS when the "Starting MS-DOS" message appears, or use <F8> to step through each line in the startup files.

OPTIMIZATIONS FOR CONFIG.SYS

The first step in optimizing your system's memory is to enable your high memory area. To do this, you will need to place HIMEM.SYS and EMM386.EXE into your CONFIG.SYS startup file. From the DOS prompt, start a text editor, such as DOS EDIT, and load your CONFIG.SYS file. One of the first things that CONFIG.SYS should do is load HIMEM and EMM386, as shown in Fig. 24-1 (this is shown as an example only—your CON-FIG.SYS file might be radically different). Remember that there are a number of command line switches for both HIMEM and EMM386. Depending on the vintage and particular configuration of your PC, you might need to add one or more switches to achieve proper driver operation. Table 24-1 lists the syntax and command line switches for HIMEM, and Table 24-2 lists the syntax and command line switches for EMM386. If you intend to make use of both high memory and any available UMAs, you should use the RAM switch with EMM386.

When MEM /C is run with the CONFIG.SYS file shown in Fig. 24-1, only 441KB of the total 640KB conventional memory space is available. Large DOS applications might fail to function with so little conventional memory. Now that you know the high memory is active (thanks to HIMEM and EMM386), you can optimize CONFIG.SYS to free as much conventional memory as possible.

```
device = c:\dos\himem.sys
device = c:\dos\setver.exe
device = c:\dos\emm386.exe
stacks = 9,256
files = 80
buffers = 50
lastdrive = Z
device = c:\sb16\drv\sbcd.sys /D:mscd001 /P:220
device = c:\rodent\oldmouse.exe
```

FIGURE 24-1   A simple, but inefficient, CONFIG. SYS file.

TABLE 24-1 SYNTAX AND COMMAND LINE SWITCHES FOR HIMEM

SYNTAX

device=[drive:][path]himem.sys [/hmamin=m] [/numhandles=n] [/int15=xxxx] [/machine:g] [/a2Ocontrol:onloff] [/shadowram:onloff] [/cpuclock:onloff]

Parameters

[drive:][path]	Specifies the location of the HIMEM.SYS file.
/hmamin=m	Specifies the amount of memory (in kilobytes) that a program must use before HIMEM.SYS permits the program to use the high-memory area. Valid values for *m* are 0–63. The default value is 0.
/numhandles=n	Specifies the maximum number of *Extended Memory Block (EMB)* handles that can be used simultaneously. Valid values for *n* are 1–128. The default value is 32. Each additional handle requires an additional six bytes of resident memory.
/int15=xxxx	Allocates the specified amount of extended memory (in kilobytes) for the Interrupt 15h interface. Some older programs use a conflicting extended memory scheme. To use memory allocated by this switch, programs must recognize VDisk headers. To ensure enough memory is available, add 64 to the value you want to specify for *xxxx*. Valid values for *xxxx* are 64–65535. If you specify a value less than 64, the value becomes 0. The default value is 0.
/machine:xxxx	Specifies the A20 handler to be used. An A20 handler is a part of your computer that gives it access to the high-memory area. The *xxxx* value can be any of the following codes or their equivalent numbers:

Code	Number	A20 handler
at	1	IBM PC/AT or COMPUADD 386 or JDR 386/33
ps2	2	IBM PS/2 or Datamedia 386/486 or UNISYS PowerPort
ptlcascade	3	Phoenix Cascade BIOS
hpvectra	4	HP Vectra (A and A+)
att6300plus	5	AT&T 6300 Plus
acer1100	6	Acer 1100
toshiba	7	Toshiba 1600 and 1200XE or Toshiba 5100
wyse	8	Wyse 12.5MHz i286 or COMPUADD 386 or Hitachi HL500C or Intel 301z or 302
tulip	9	Tulip SX
zenith	10	Zenith ZBIOS
at	11	IBM PC/AT
at2	12	IBM PC/AT (alternative delay)
css	12	CSS Labs

TABLE 24-1   SYNTAX AND COMMAND LINE SWITCHES FOR HIMEM (CONTINUED)

SYNTAX

Code	Number	A20 handler
at3	13	IBM PC/AT (alternative delay)
philips	13	Philips
fasthp	14	HP Vectra
ibm7552	15	IBM 7552 Industrial Computer
bullmicral	16	Bull Micral 60
dell	17	Dell XBIOS

/a20control:onloff	Specifies whether HIMEM.SYS is to take control of the A20 line—even if A20 was on when HIMEM.SYS was loaded. If you specify /a20control:off, HIMEM.SYS takes control of the A20 line only if A20 was off when HIMEM.SYS was loaded. The default setting is /a20control:on.
/shadowram:onloff	Specifies whether HIMEM.SYS is to switch off shadow RAM used for read-only memory, and add that RAM to its memory pool. If your computer has less than 2MB of RAM, the default setting is /shadowram:off. This parameter is supported only on some computers.
/cpuclock:onloff	Specifies whether HIMEM.SYS is to affect the clock speed of your computer. If your computer's speed changes when you install HIMEM.SYS, specifying /cpuclock:on might correct the problem. Enabling this switch slows down HIMEM.SYS.

TABLE 24-2   SYNTAX AND COMMAND LINE SWITCHES FOR EMM386

SYNTAX

device=[drive:][path]emm386.exe [onlofflauto] [memory] [w=onlw=off] [mxlframe=addressl/pm-mmm] [pn=address] [x=mmmm-nnnn] [i=mmmm-nnnn] [b=address] [L=minXMS] [a=altregs] [h=handles] [d=nnn] [ram] [noems]

Parameters

[drive:l[path]	Specifies the location of the EMM386.EXE file.
[onlofflauto]	Activates the EMM386.EXE device driver (if set to *On*), or suspends the EMM386.EXE device driver (if set to *Off*), or places the EMM386.EXE device driver in auto mode (if set to *Auto*). Auto mode enables expanded memory support only when a program calls for it. The default value is on. Use the emm386 command to change this value after EMM386 has started.
memory	Specifies the amount of memory (in kilobytes) that you want to allocate to EMM386.EXE. Values for memory are 16–32768. The default value is 256. EMM386.EXE rounds the value down to the nearest multiple of 16. If you are using expanded memory, this value is in addition to the memory used for low-memory backfilling.
w=onlw=off	Enables or disables support for the Weitek coprocessor. The default setting is w=off.

TABLE 24-2 SYNTAX AND COMMAND LINE SWITCHES FOR EMM386 (CONTINUED)

SYNTAX	
mx	Specifies the address of the page frame. Valid values for x are 1–14. The following list shows each value and its associated base address in hexadecimal format (values 10–14 should be used only on old computers with 512KB of memory): 1 => C000h 8 => DC00h 2 => C400h 9 => E000h 3 => C800h 10 => 8000h 4 => CC00h 11 => 8400h 5 => D000h 12 => 8800h 6 => D400h 13 => 8C00h 7 => D800h 14 => 9000h
frame=address	Specifies the page-frame segment base directly. To specify a specific segment-base address for the page frame, use the frame switch and specify the address you want. Valid values for address are 8000h-9000h and C000h-E000h, in increments of 400h.
/pmmmm	Specifies the address of the page frame. Valid values for mmmm are 8000h, 9000h, and C000h-E000h, in increments of 400h.
pn=address	Specifies the segment address of a specific page, where n is the number of the page you are specifying and address is the segment address you want. Valid values for n are 0-255. Valid values for address are 8000h-9C00h and C000h-EC00h, in increments of 400h. The addresses for pages 0 through 3 must be contiguous in order to maintain compatibility with version 3.2 of the Lotus/Intel/Microsoft Expanded Memory Specification (LIM EMS). If you use the mx switch, the frame switch, or the /pmmmm switch, you cannot specify the addresses for pages 0 through 3 for the /pmmmm switch.
x=mmmm-nnnn	Prevents EMM386.EXE from using a particular range of segment addresses for an EMS page. Valid values for mmmm and nnnn are A000h–FFFFh and are rounded down to the nearest 4KB boundary. The x switch takes precedence over the i switch if the two ranges overlap.
i=mmmm-nnnn	Specifies a range of segment addresses to be used (included) for an EMS page or for RAM. Valid values for *mmmm* and *nnnn* are A000h–FFFFh and are rounded down to the nearest 4KB boundary. The x switch takes precedence over the i switch if the two ranges overlap.
b=address	Specifies the lowest segment address available for EMS "banking" (swapping of 16KB pages). Valid values are 1000h–4000h. The default value is 4000h.
L=minXMS	Ensures that the specified amount (in kilobytes) of extended memory will still be available after you load EMM386.EXE. The default value is 0.
a=altregs	Specifies how many fast alternate register sets (used for multitasking) you want to allocate to EMM386.EXE. Valid values are 0–254. The default value is 7. Every alternate register set adds about 200 bytes to the size in memory of EMM386.EXE.
h=handles	Specifies how many handles EMM386.EXE can use. Valid values are 2–255. The default value is 64.
d=nnn	Specifies how many kilobytes of memory should be reserved for buffered direct memory access (DMA). Discounting floppy-disk DMA, this value should reflect the largest DMA transfer that will occur while EMM386.EXE is active. Valid values for *nnn* are 16–256. The default value is 16.
ram	Provides access to both expanded memory and the upper memory area.
noems	Provides access to upper memory area, but prevents access to expanded memory.

Eliminate or disable unnecessary entries The first and simplest step in freeing conventional memory is to remove any entries that are no longer being used. For example, when old peripherals are upgraded, the old device driver should be removed and the new one loaded. Look through the CONFIG.SYS file and erase any obsolete entries. Suppose for Fig. 24-1 that the file oldmouse.exe was an old mouse driver that was no longer needed. You can simply erase the entry. If you are not certain whether the entry is needed or not, you can disable the entry (rather than remove it) by adding the term *REM* before the entry, such as:

```
REM device = c:\rodent\oldmouse.exe
```

This effectively REMarks-out the entry. If you find that you need the entry after all, you can remove the REM statement later and re-enable the entry without having to type it in again from scratch (this feature goes a long way toward minimizing typing errors).

Allocate files and buffers sparingly The FILES entry defines how many files MS-DOS can have open at one time. The BUFFERS entry sets the number of 500-byte buffers that MS-DOS reserves for data transfer to and from disk. Large numbers of FILES and BUFFERS wastes conventional memory.   Be sure that the number of FILES and BUFFERS allocated for your system are sufficient without being excessive. For example, if you have been using a complex application that required 80 files and 50 buffers, but the application has been removed from your system, you can return the number of FILES and buffers to a lower level (60 FILES and 40 BUFFERS are usually typical for most Windows 95-configured systems) like:

```
files = 60
buffers = 40
```

Tighten the "LASTDRIVE=" entry DOS allows up to 26 letters to be used as logical drive references. In many cases, the "LASTDRIVE=" function is set to Z: (as in Fig. 24-1), but the actual last drive to be enabled might only be E:, H:, or K:. Each letter requires about 100 bytes. Use a smaller letter that more closely reflects the true last drive. For this example, you might change the LASTDRIVE reference to M:, such as:

```
lastdrive = M
```

Set the stacks properly If you are running DOS only, you can usually remove the interrupt stack reference entirely or set it to 0,0. For Windows and Windows 95 systems, however, the setting of 9,256 is adequate for most systems.

Relocate DOS MS-DOS is one of the largest files to occupy conventional memory, so one of your priorities in optimizing conventional memory should be to move DOS to either an available part of the upper memory area (UMA), or to the high memory area (HMA) using the "dos=" command in CONFIG.SYS. Remember that you will first need to load HIMEM in order to load DOS into high memory, and use the RAM switch with EMM386 if you plan to try DOS in the UMA. Be sure the following line is added after the EMM386.EXE entry in CONFIG.SYS:

```
dos=umb,high
```

```
device = c:\dos\himem.sys
device = c:\dos\emm386.exe ram
dos = umb,high
stacks = 9,256
files = 60
buffers = 40
lastdrive = M
devicehigh = c:\sb16\drv\sbcd.sys /D:mscd001 /P:220
devicehigh = c:\dos\setver.exe
```

FIGURE 24-2   A reasonably optimized CONFIG.SYS file.

If you do not wish to try putting DOS in the UMA, you can omit the "umb" portion of the line. Figure 24-2 shows our refined CONFIG.SYS file beginning to take shape.

Make use of DEVICEHIGH The "DEVICEHIGH=" function allows you to place most device drivers into the UMA where otherwise they would be loaded into conventional memory. There are only a few rules to keep in mind when using DEVICEHIGH. First, you must add the "umb" reference to the "dos=" function in order to use DEVICEHIGH at all. Second, you cannot use DEVICEHIGH until your memory managers are loaded, so HIMEM and EMM386 must always be loaded in conventional memory with the ordinary DEVICE function (Fig. 24-2). Third, if you have any DEVICE references placed before your memory managers (such as the SETVER.EXE reference placed before EMM386.EXE in Fig. 24-1), relocate the statement(s) after the memory managers (Fig. 24-2).

You can then use the DOS MEM function to check the new amount of free conventional memory. After booting a system using the CONFIG.SYS file of Fig. 24-2, free conventional memory reported by MEM (the "Largest executable program size" entry) rose to 555KB. For only a few minutes worth of work, the system picked up over 114KB of conventional memory.

OPTIMIZATIONS FOR AUTOEXEC.BAT

Working with the AUTOEXEC.BAT system startup file is a bit easier than dealing with CONFIG.SYS. AUTOEXEC.BAT is used to set system variables and to start any non-crucial device drivers or TSRs (such as mouse drivers and caching programs) that might be needed to streamline the system. Before you attempt to work with the AUTOEXEC.BAT file, remember to make a backup of the original file, just in case you get into trouble. If you need guidance making a backup of AUTOEXEC.BAT, see the section "Protect the configuration." Start a text editor and load the AUTOEXEC.BAT file.

Eliminate unnecessary entries This is the most common method of streamlining an AUTOEXEC file. As applications come and go on your system, you will likely be left with a number of system variables that are no longer used, as well as very long PATH statements that you probably do not need. You might also find obsolete or unused drivers and TSRs in AUTOEXEC.BAT that can be removed without problems. If you are not sure whether an entry can be removed safely, place a REM statement in front of the entry. This effectively REMarks-out (disables) the entry without removing it. If you find that you need the entry after all, you can simply remove the REM statement later to re-enable the entry.

Make use of LOADHIGH The "LOADHIGH=" function is used to load a program into the UMA; otherwise, it would be loaded into conventional memory. As with DEVICEHIGH, there are some rules that must be followed in order to use LOADHIGH successfully. The "umb" reference must be added to the "dos=" statement in CONFIG.SYS, and the LOADHIGH function can not be used until the memory managers are loaded in CONFIG.SYS. A typical application of LOADHIGH is shown in the sample AUTOEXEC.BAT file of Fig. 24-3. It is important to note that DOS does not report whether a LOADHIGH was successful or not. If a file cannot be loaded into upper memory, it will be loaded into conventional memory. Keep in mind that you can use the letters "lh" instead of LOADHIGH.

REVIEWING YOUR RESULTS WITH MEM

DOS offers the MEM function, which provides a comprehensive breakdown of memory in the system and how it is used. You can use the MEM function before and after an optimization to see the results of your work. Figure 24-4 illustrates a typical memory report using the /C switch. Because this chapter is primarily concerned with freeing as much conventional memory as possible, you should be most concerned with the third line from the bottom: "Largest executable program size." The objective is to make this number as large (as close to 640KB) as possible.

MIX AND MATCH

Chances are that not all of the drivers or TSRs you've attempted to load high (with DEVICEHIGH or LOADHIGH) will actually fit into the available space in the UMA. The trick to "optimizing" memory is to fit "as much as possible" into the UMA. Once you review the status of your memory with MEM (as in Fig. 24-4), you can then return to your text editor and continue tweaking the CONFIG.SYS and AUTOEXEC.BAT files to load other drivers high. For Fig. 24-4, the MEM report indicates that a total of 59KB of "Upper" memory is available. It also reports that 57KB of that space has been utilized by DOS and other drivers—specifically SBDC (a Sound Blaster CD driver), SETVER, and MSCDEX. This leaves only 2KB (1744 bytes) available. If you find a utility in the MEM report that uses less than 1744 bytes, you might also be able to load that driver high, and use the remainder of free upper memory.

```
set blaster = A220 I5 D1 H5 P330 T6
set sound = c:\sb16
prompt $p$g
loadhigh c:\sb16\sb16set /M:220 /VOC:220 /CD:220 /MIDI:220 /LINE:220 /TREBLE:0
loadhigh c:\sb16\sbconfig.exe /S
loadhigh c:\sb16\drv\mscdex.exe /D:MSCD001 /V /M:15
loadhigh c:\dos\smartdrv.exe
loadhigh c:\mouse\mouse.com
loadhigh c:\dos\share.exe /L:100
```

FIGURE 24-3   A typical AUTOEXEC. BAT file using the LOADHIGH command.

```
Name        Total     =   Conventional    +    Upper Memory
-------    ----------      ----------------      ----------------
MSDOS      17149  (17K)     17149  (17K)             0   (0K)
HIMEM       1168   (1K)      1168   (1K)             0   (0K)
EMM386      4144   (4K)      4144   (4K)             0   (0K)
COMMAND     2912   (2K)      2912   (2K)             0   (0K)
SMARTDRV   28816  (28K)     28816  (28K)             0   (0K)
MOUSE      24560  (24K)     24560  (24K)             0   (0K)
SHARE       7648   (7K)      7648   (7K)             0   (0K)
SBCD       11584  (11K)         0   (0K)         11584  (11K)
SETVER       640   (1K)         0   (0K)           640   (1K)
MSCDEX     46576  (45K)         0   (0K)         46576  (45K)
Free      570432 (557K)    568688 (555K)          1744   (2K)

Memory Summary:

Type of Memory         Total      =      Used      +      Free
--------------       -------------     -------------     -------------
Conventional          655360  (640K)     86672  (85K)     568688  (555K)
Upper                  60544  (59K)      58800  (57K)       1744   (2K)
Adapter RAM/ROM       393216 (384K)     393216 (384K)          0   (0K)
Extended (XMS)*     15668096 (15310K)  2610048 (2549K)  13058048(12752K)
--------------       -------------     -------------     -------------
Total Memory        16777216 (1638K)   3148736 (3075K)  13628480(13309K)

Total under 1MB       715904  (699K)    145472 (142K)     570432  (557K)

Total Expanded (EMS)           16056320 (15680K)
Free Expanded (EMS)*           13303808 (12992K)
```

* EMM386 is using XMS memory to simulate EMS memory as needed.
  Free EMS memory may change as free XMS memory changes.

```
Largest executable program size    568592   (555K)
Largest free upper memory block      1296    (1K)
MS-DOS is resident in the high memory area.
```

FIGURE 24-4 **A breakdown of memory utilization using the DOS MEM /C function.**

ADJUSTING THE MEMORY ENVIRONMENT FOR DOS PROGRAMS UNDER WINDOWS 95

Windows 95 provides the ability to run MS-DOS programs in a "DOS window." This requires you to configure a suitable environment for the DOS program. You can modify the DOS environment using the following steps:

1 On the desktop, right-click the *MS-DOS* icon, then select *Properties*.
2 Click the *Program* tab, then click the *Advanced* button.
3 The *Advanced program settings* dialog appears (Figure 24-5).
4 Now you can adjust the CONFIG.SYS and AUTOEXEC.BAT attributes that you want to use when running the MS-DOS window.

TROUBLESHOOTING TYPICAL OPTIMIZATION PROBLEMS

In an ideal world, you should be able to load DOS, TSRs, and device drivers into the UMA and high memory without any difficulty. But in the practical PC world, many situations can prevent a program from being relocated out of conventional memory. In many cases, the result is harmless—the program will simply load into conventional memory as it had before. In other cases, however, system operation can be adversely affected when programs are relocated. The following symptoms explain a number of common problems related to memory optimization.

Symptom 24-1. You see an error message from a driver or TSR when attempting to relocate it This is not necessarily a problem. It might simply be that not enough memory is available in the UMA to handle the program you are trying to relocate. Try re-arranging the order in which the drivers or TSRs are loaded. Also, the available space in the upper memory area will vary, depending on how the PC is configured. A PC with a great many expansion boards and expansion BIOS ROMs might not leave enough upper memory to hold more than a couple of drivers or TSRs. Little else can be done with such a problem.

Symptom 24-2. The system locks up when a program is relocated Not all software is suitable for operation in the UMA. Check the screen messages carefully as the PC initializes and attempt to determine the last program to load successfully before a fault occurs. If you can find the fault, it is a simple matter to remove the DEVICEHIGH= statement and replace it with the DEVICE statement. This will load the uncooperative program

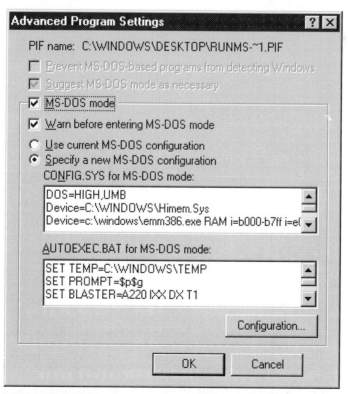

FIGURE 24-5 The *Advanced Program Settings dialog.*

in conventional memory. Remember that it might be necessary to boot the system from a backup or alternate boot disk so that you are able to use a text editor to make and save such a correction.

If you are unable to determine the point at which the system locks up, start with the last DEVICEHIGH statement in the CONFIG.SYS file and change each one to DEVICE. Reboot the PC after each change is made. The last line to be changed before system operation returns is the problem. You can then leave that line (to load into conventional memory) and return all subsequent lines to the DEVICEHIGH function.

Symptom 24-3. A device driver small enough for the available UMA fails to load there Some device drivers expand when they are loaded into memory. In most cases, the program will be loaded into conventional memory. You can find the actual amount of space a driver needs by allowing the driver to load into conventional memory, then using the MEM /C command to see the file and its corresponding file size—this will be the true amount of memory needed by the driver. You can then try loading the driver with DEVICEHIGH using its "size=" switch.

Symptom 24-4. A program works erratically or improperly when loaded into the UMA Some device drivers simply do not work well (or at all) in the UMA. It could be that the program needs a certain amount of memory above it or the driver does not recognize addresses in the UMA. In either case, the offending program should be loaded into conventional memory. If the offending program is being loaded from CONFIG.SYS, change its DEVICEHIGH statement to DEVICE. If the problem is occurring in AUTOEXEC.BAT, remove the LOADHIGH (or "lh") statement.

Symptom 24-5. Nothing is being loaded into the UMA You can see this by looking at the MEM report. Chances are that you have missed a configuration step, which is preventing your system from using the UMA. Check the following items. First, check CONFIG.SYS to see that the "dos=umb" or "dos=umb,high" statement is included after the memory managers are loaded. Second, check that HIMEM and EMM386 are loaded using the DEVICE statement, rather than the DEVICEHIGH statement. HIMEM should be loaded before EMM386. Also see that the EMM386 entry is using the "noems" or "ram" switch. This configuration should enable use of the UMA. At this point, simply be sure that you are using DEVICEHIGH statements for any CONFIG.SYS device drivers to be loaded in the UMA, and LOADHIGH statements for any AUTOEXEC.BAT device drivers.

Troubleshooting QEMM

Symptom 24-6. The message appears: "Address wrap at xxxx" This message is not really an error, but it means that QEMM's SCANMEM feature has detected that your PC's address space is smaller than the 4GB that the processor can address.

Symptom 24-7. The error appears: "NOUSERAM=xxxxx-yyyyy" This error indicates that QEMM's SCANMEM feature does not detect physical memory in the address range "xxxxx-yyyyy"—even though your system's BIOS has reported enough extended memory (XMS) to fill these addresses. If you see this message, use your PC's CMOS setup to reconfigure the machine so that the BIOS reports extended memory properly.

Symptom 24-8.   The error appears: "Invalid USERAM due to memory cache!" This error means that QEMM's SCANMEM feature has detected that the "USERAM=xxxxx-yyyyy" parameter that it last printed to the display is invalid and should not be used. You should ignore only the last USERAM message printed to the screen—previous USERAM messages are valid. This error might occur if an unusual memory cache architecture makes the contents of memory appear to be variable to SCANMEM.

Symptom 24-9. QEMM 8.0x refuses to function properly under Windows 95 on an IBM ThinkPad The problem is with the BIOS on IBM ThinkPads running Windows 95. Call the IBM BBS at 919-517-0001 to download TPWIN95.EXE. This file explains the solution, and provides a patch for the IBM BIOS problem.

Symptom 24-10.   The error appears: "QEMM386: Cannot load because there is not enough memory" This error message can appear for several different reasons, but it often occurs on machines with a total of 1MB of RAM (640K conventional + 384K extended). When QEMM386 starts, it finds all of the memory in your system and puts it into one big pool. Then it checks the parameters that were specified in the QEMM386 command line in the CONFIG.SYS file. If not enough memory is available to provide all of the services requested by the user (as well as those that QEMM386 performs by default), QEMM386 will terminate with this error message.

Remove any EXTMEM (EXT) or MEMORY (MEM) parameters that might exist on the QEMM386.SYS command line (these parameters can easily prevent QEMM from loading when set incorrectly). Supply QEMM386 with parameters that will cause it to use less memory—these include NOFILL (NO), NOROM (NR), and MAPS=0. If you have specified the ROM parameter, remove it. Also, you might need to exclude some of your usable high RAM areas. On an EGA/VGA system, try X=B000-B7FF. On a Hercules system, the NV parameter should be sufficient. If your system uses shadow RAM, QEMM386 can usually use it also, so enabling the shadow RAM is a good idea when this message appears. Of course, the preferable solution to this problem is to install more memory in the computer. This allows QEMM386 to perform all of its requested functions, while also providing more expanded memory for applications that need it.

Symptom 24-11. The error appears: "QEMM386: Cannot load because the processor is already in Virtual 86 mode" The Intel i386 and later processors can run in one of three different modes: real-mode, protected mode, and virtual 8086 mode. When QEMM386 starts up, its default settings tell it to place the processor in Virtual 86 mode. However, QEMM386 will not load if some other program (i.e., some other memory manager) has already done this.

Check to be sure that QEMM386 is the first line in your CONFIG.SYS file. If not, move the QEMM386 command line to the beginning of the CONFIG.SYS file, and see if QEMM386 will load. If QEMM386 still refuses to load (or it was already the first program to load in CONFIG.SYS), then you should check your machine's BIOS settings for memory-management features that might have to be disabled.

Symptom 24-12. The error appears: "QEMM386: Cannot load because an expanded memory manager is already loaded" Only one expanded memory manager can be running on the computer at any given time. When QEMM386 initializes, it checks to see if another expanded memory manager has already been loaded into the system. If it detects the presence of such a memory manager, it will abort with this error message, rather than attempt to install itself. Because QEMM386 is designed to provide all of the features you need in an expanded memory manager, the old expanded memory manager is no longer needed. Check your CONFIG.SYS for another expanded memory manager or place QEMM386 on the first line of the CONFIG.SYS (expanded memory managers tend to have the letters "EMM" or "EMS" in their names). If you see a line that appears such as:

```
DEVICE=C:\DOS\EMM386.EXE
DEVICE=C:\REMM.SYS
DEVICE=C:\EMM.SYS
DEVICE=C:\EMS.SYS
DEVICE=C:\CEMM.EXE
```

remove or "REMark-out" the line from the CONFIG.SYS file.

Symptom 24-13. The error appears: "QEMM386: Unknown Microchannel Adapter ID: XXXX" On MicroChannel (MCA) computers, each installed adapter has its own ID number. This number is a four-digit alphanumeric code ("XXXX"). When QEMM386 initializes during boot-up, it notes the names of all of the adapters that are present and compares them to a list of adapters contained in its MCA.ADL file. If an adapter is present that is not listed in the MCA.ADL file, QEMM386 will display the error message. You'll need to add the adapter ID information to your existing .ADL file or update the .ADL file by downloading the latest version from Quarterdeck's BBS (573-875-0503) or Web site (**http://www.quarterdeck.com**).

Symptom 24-14. The error appears: "QEMM386: Cannot find file MCA.ADL" The QEMM386.SYS device driver is reporting that it cannot find the MCA.ADL file that it uses to determine memory locations used by adapter cards in MicroChannel (MCA) machines. QEMM386.SYS looks for MCA.ADL in the directory from which it was loaded in the CONFIG.SYS file. For example, if your CONFIG.SYS contains a line that reads:

```
device=c:\qemm\qemm386.sys
```

QEMM will look in the C:directory for the MCA.ADL file. Ensure that the MCA.ADL file is located in the directory that is specified on the QEMM386.SYS device line in your CONFIG.SYS file.

Symptom 24-15. The error appears: "QEMM38452 Cannot load because this is not an 80386" When QEMM386 initializes, it checks the machine to ensure that a 386/486 processor is present. QEMM386 cannot run on 80286, 8088, or 8086 machines. If QEMM386 displays this error on a 386/486 machine, you should re-install QEMM386. If the message still appears, you should obtain a new copy of QEMM386 and try again. If you have a 386 add-in board, this error message might appear if QEMM386.SYS appears in the CONFIG.SYS file before the driver for your particular 386 add-in board. Put the add-in board's driver before QEMM386.SYS in the CONFIG.SYS and the problem should go away.

Symptom 24-16. The error appears: "QEMM386: Cannot load because there is no room for a page frame" To create and utilize expanded memory, QEMM386 must create a page frame that is 64K in size. By default, QEMM386 attempts to put the page frame between A000h (640K) and F000h (960K). However, some configurations prevent QEMM386 from placing a page frame above A000h by splitting or fragmenting the unused areas above A000h into chunks that are less than 64K in size. If QEMM386 cannot place the page frame above A000h, it will attempt to place it in conventional memory. When it cannot create a page frame at all, QEMM386 will display this error message.

Try re-arranging any adapters so that a 64K area above A000h is unused. This might involve changing physical switch settings on the adapters (reconfiguring the adapter ROMs). On PS/2 and other MicroChannel (MCA) machines, this will entail using the reference diskette. If rearranging the adapter locations above A000h is not possible, remove any exclusions (X=xxxx-xxxx) statements that reference areas between 0000h and 9FFFh.

Symptom 24-17. The error appears: "QEMM386: Cannot load because QEMM is already loaded" QEMM386 is a "control program"—that is, software which oversees virtually all aspects of the computer's operation. By definition, only one control program can be in charge of the system at any given time. As a result, QEMM386 cannot be loaded on top of itself. QEMM386 is intelligent enough to detect its own presence while loading. If it sees that it has already been loaded, it will abort with this error message. This error will only result if you have multiple lines in your CONFIG.SYS file that load the QEMM386.SYS device file. By removing all but one of these lines, you should correct the problem.

Symptom 24-18. The error appears: "QEMM386: Disabling StealthROM:F because the page frame does not overlap any ROM" QEMM's "stealth technology" (introduced with QEMM386 version 6.0) effectively "hides" ROM areas above 640K and allows them to be used as either high RAM or part of the EMS page frame. To use the STEALTHROM:F feature, the page frame must be located atop a "stealthed" ROM area. By default, QEMM will do its best to place the page frame properly. However, if the page frame has been explicitly set (by using QEMM's FRAME= parameter) at an address that is not occupied by a ROM (or if all ROMS have been excluded with the X= parameter), QEMM will disable ST:F and continue. This might result in an overall reduction of the amount high RAM created by QEMM386. Remove the FRAME= parameter from your QEMM386.SYS command line in your CONFIG.SYS file. If no FRAME= parameters are in the command line, check for exclusions (EXCLUDE= or X= parameters) that might be "covering" ROM areas. Remove the exclusions and try again.

Symptom 24-19. The error appears: "QEMM386: Disabling StealthROM:M because there is no page frame" A "page frame" is required to use the ST:M parameter and take full advantage of QEMM's stealth feature. Check your QEMM386.SYS device line in your CONFIG.SYS file for the following parameters:

```
FRAME=NONE     (or FR=NONE)
NOEMS
FRAMELENGTH=x (or FL=x)—where "x" is a value less than 4
```

If your QEMM386.SYS device line contains any of these parameters, Stealth will be automatically disabled. To use Stealth, remove the appropriate parameters, save your changes to CONFIG.SYS, and try again.

Symptom 24-20.   The error appears: "QEMM386: Disabling stealth because QEMM could not locate the ROM handler for INT xx" When using stealth features, QEMM386 must monitor some interrupts at all times. When these interrupts have been diverted by another program, QEMM386 will disable stealth features. As a result, QEMM386 should usually be loaded on the first line of your machine's CONFIG.SYS file. This is practical in the vast majority of system configurations. However, it is sometimes desirable to load other device drivers before QEMM386.SYS. When doing this, some device drivers might make it impossible for stealth to "see" all of the activity in the machine—and problems can result.

   If possible, place the QEMM386.SYS device line at the beginning of your CONFIG.SYS file. If this is not possible, use HOOKROM.SYS (included with QEMM386 version 6.0 and later). This device driver must be placed at the beginning of the CONFIG.SYS file. HOOKROM.SYS acts as a secretary for QEMM386, noting the state of the machine as CONFIG.SYS is processed, then passing these notes to QEMM386 so that it can operate properly with stealth features active.

Symptom 24-21.   The error appears: "Cannot load because QEMM is not registered Run the INSTALL program to register" The files on the QEMM386 product diskette must be installed by running the INSTALL program—they will not function properly when copied over by the DOS COPY command. Run the INSTALL program from the original QEMM386 product-distribution diskette.

Symptom 24-22. You see the errors: "CONTEXTS is no longer a QEMM parameter!," or "NAMES is no longer a QEMM parameter!" QEMM386 versions 4.23 and earlier featured a CONTEXTS parameter that allowed users to specify the maximum number of mapping contexts that QEMM386 could save at one time. Mapping contexts are now determined by the number of HANDLES provided by QEMM386 (ranging from 16 to 255—64 by default). Similarly, it was determined that the function of the NAMES parameter (also from QEMM386 versions 4.23 and earlier), which specified the maximum number of named handles, could be included into the HANDLES parameter. As a result, the CONTEXTS and NAMES parameters were abandoned in QEMM386 version 5.0 and later. Remove the CONTEXTS=xxx and NAMES=xxx parameters from your QEMM386.SYS command line in the CONFIG.SYS file.

Symptom 24-23. The error appears: "LOADHI: The high memory chain is corrupted" QEMM386 uses a collection of high memory areas called a *memory chain* to keep track of the TSRs and device drivers that are loaded high by the LOADHI programs. If the conflict is in high memory, this chain can become corrupted. This error message is usually accompanied by an address (e.g., C800h). You can frequently resolve the conflict with an exclusion on the QEMM386 command line in the CONFIG.SYS file. It is also possible that other drivers or programs that are being loaded in the CONFIG.SYS or AUTOEXEC.BAT might be corrupting the high memory chain—in which case you should disable all device drivers or TSRs that aren't absolutely vital to your machine's operation, then re-enable each line—one at a time—rebooting each time you make a change, until the conflicting driver or TSR is discovered.

Symptom 24-24. The error appears: "LOADHI: Cannot write to log file"
This error usually appears when a copy of the QEMM386.SYS device driver is in the root directory of the hard drive, as well as in the sub-directory. This can cause confusion when loading high. Be sure that QEMM386.SYS is only found in the sub-directory, and that the QEMM386 device line in the CONFIG.SYS file specifically points to that sub-directory such as:

```
device=c:\qemm\qemm386.sys
```

Symptom 24-25. The error appears: "Stealth ROM is being disabled because it cannot find ROM handler 05 76" This error indicates a stealth-compatibility problem with QEMM 8.0x. To work around this problem, exclude stealth features from the indicated memory area or turn off stealth features entirely.

Symptom 24-26. The system will hang when attempting to use Colorado Tape Backup Some implementations of shadow RAM do not allow QEMM to reclaim them properly. This can manifest itself in a number of ways—including the tape backup working perfectly with QEMM 7.0x, but failing with QEMM 7.5x. Add the SH:N switch to the QEMM386.SYS command line in the CONFIG.SYS.

Symptom 24-27. There is no specific error message, but Optimize won't complete You are running Ontrack's Disk Manager overlay program with QEMM 8.0x. To work around this problem, move the DMDRVR.BIN file in CONFIG.SYS so it directly precedes the QEMM386.SYS command line. Optimize should now complete normally.

Symptom 24-28. After Optimize is complete, you see the error: "Fixed disk parameter error or BIOS error" This type of problem often occurs when using QEMM 8.0x on Compaq Prolinea 5120 systems. You can usually work around this problem by adding the CF:N and BE:N switches to the QEMM386.SYS command line in your CONFIG.SYS (you can do this using QSETUP), then re-run Optimize.

Symptom 24-29. Optimize won't complete on a PC with a Plextor 6X CD-ROM and Adaptec 1515 SCSI controller This is a known problem with QEMM 8.0x and the ASPI2DOS.SYS SCSI driver. This adapter's drivers will only work with the following configurations: (1) with the ST:M switch, load the ASPI driver after QEMM—in this configuration, QEMM will optimize and load the driver high: (2) with the ST:F switch, load the ASPI driver before QEMM with the /u and /p140 switches added to the ASPI2DOS.SYS driver line.

Symptom 24-30. An NEC UltraLite Versa PC suffers Exception 13 errors in the Exxxh range You might also find that Windows 3.1x loads PROGMAN, then drops back to the "C:" prompt and hangs up. The problem is caused by a memory conflict, and can usually be corrected by adding an exclusion (X=E000-EFFF) on the QEMM 7.0 command line.

> The NEC UltraLite Versa has the video ROM in E000h-E7FFh. It has additional ROM in E800h-EFFFh (power-management code). QEMM detects the video ROM properly and requires no exclusion for it, but QEMM maps over E800h-EFFFh. So, this does require an exclusion if you wish to use the power-management features of the system.

Symptom 24-31. A Philips CD Recorder (i.e., CDD200) fails to function if you put the USERAM=1M:32M parameter on the QEMM386.SYS line in CONFIG.SYS You find this problem most readily with Compaq systems. Apparently, the Corel CD Creator software (provided by Adaptec) is not compatible with Compaq's CPQCFG Plug-and-Play (PnP) configuration manager. You need to turn off the PnP switch on the Adaptec SCSI (AHA1535) board and run the CMOS configuration editor. You'll need to specify the exact parameters (addresses) for your Adaptec SCSI board.

Symptom 24-32. QEMM 8.0x refuses to complete an optimization on a Compaq computer You are possibly having a conflict with some of the built-in Compaq BIOS features. Use the following switches in the QEMM command line in CONFIG.SYS to get around the problems:

- CF:Y or :N This enables or disables all three Compaq features: Compaq EGA ROM, Compaq Half ROM, and Compaq ROM Memory. By default, all are enabled. CF:Y enables all features and CF:N disables all features.
- CER:Y or :N This enables or disables Compaq EGA ROM. Disabling this can require 32KB of upper memory addresses on some Compaq computers. However, QEMM cannot be turned off if this feature is enabled.
- CHR:Y or :N This enables or disables Compaq Half ROM. Disabling this can require 32KB of upper memory addresses on some Compaq computers.
- CRM:Y or :N This enables or disables the Compaq Memory ROM. QEMM cannot be turned off if this feature is enabled.

Symptom 24-33. XtraDrive cannot be installed on the desired drive The error appears: "Drive 1 is being controlled by a program that appropriates INT13." This often occurs when using QEMM386 in the stealth mode. Try removing the ST:M or ST:F parameters from the QEMM386 command line, and try to install it again (this only needs to be removed during the installation of XtraDrive).

Symptom 24-34. QEMM cannot be installed on a system with XtraDrive When you install QEMM386 on a system that has XtraDrive already installed, you get a system lockup or Exception 13 error when you reboot the machine (and the QEMM386 loading process starts). You need to add an exception to the QEMM command line. Simply reboot without QEMM, edit the CONFIG.SYS file and add X=9000-9FFF to the QEMM command line. Save your changes and restart the system again.

Symptom 24-35. The XtraDrive device driver cannot be installed into high RAM This is a known problem with SCSI bus mastering controllers and XtraDrive. Even with double-buffering, you will not be able to load XtraDrive into high RAM when using a SCSI bus-mastering device. This is not really a QEMM memory-manager issue, but a problem with XtraDrive.

Symptom 24-36. The error appears: "This program is attempting to access the disk via the page frame" This is often a problem with the EMS XtraDrive disk cache when using QEMM in the stealth mode. You cannot use the XtraDrive EMS cache with QEMM. You must disable the XtraDrive cache (a DBF=2 parameter will not work on the QEMM command line).

Symptom 24-37. Windows 95 hangs on the opening logo screen or your video display appears distorted This usually happens after installing QEMM 8.0x. In virtually all cases, this type of problem is caused by QEMM mapping program memory across some portion of the video memory area. A memory exclusion is required to correct the issue. Start by excluding the address range A000-C7FF. If the problem is solved, you can try reducing the exclude-statement range to further pinpoint the exact video range.

Symptom 24-38. After accepting the Optimize results, the system gets caught in a loop and eventually stops in Windows-protection fault 14 This kind of problem can occur with QEMM 8.0x, which is Windows 95 compliant. To work around this problem, add SH:N and RH:N switches to the QEMM386.SYS command line in CONFIG.SYS and reboot the system. After rebooting, check the Startup group and remove all programs from the Startup group. Rebooting the system again should now take care of the looping and protection fault.

Symptom 24-39. An error appears: "Configuration too large for memory" while running *Optimize under Windows 95* This also typically occurs with a standard QEMM installation. You'll need to modify the configuration of your CONFIG.SYS file. Open the CONFIG.SYS file in a text editor and add the following lines to the end of the file:

```
device=c:\windows\setver.exe
device=c:\windows\ifshlp.sys
dos=noumb
```

If you are loading any ASPI drivers (e.g., ASPI2DOS.SYS or ASPI4DOS.SYS) or have a SCSI CD-ROM or SCSI hard disk, add this line also:

```
device=c:\windows\aspi2hlp.sys
```

Save this modified file, then run the QEMM Optimize feature. If the problem continues, open a DOS prompt and switch to your QEMM directory. Type `OPTIMIZE /NH`, then select the *OPTIMIZE Custom* feature (Option F3). At the beginning of the "software detection" (when it says "Starting Windows 95"), hit <Shift>+<F8>. You'll be prompted to load each driver. Respond "Yes" to each line and watch what is loading. Look for any line that begins with the command: "DEVICEHIGH=." If you find one, write this line down, and then reboot the system. When you see "Starting Windows 95" again, press <Shift>+<F5>. Switch to your QEMM directory and type `UNOPT <Enter>`. Now edit your CONFIG.SYS file and replace the "DEVICEHIGH=" with "DEVICE=" line. Run Optimize again and repeat your search and replace of DEVICEHIGH= lines.

Symptom 24-40. Floppy-drive problems occur after installing QEMM
QEMM is generally regarded as an "aggressive" memory manager because it can seek out areas of memory that can be utilized—rather than simply use the memory that is readily available. As a result, it is possible that QEMM can impair some system functions under the right conditions (usually from using the stealth or ROM hole-detection features). Start by editing the CONFIG.SYS file and add the XST=F000 switch to the QEMM386.SYS command line. The new command line will appear like:

```
device=c:\qemm\qemm386.sys ram st:m xst=f000
```

Save your changes, then reboot the system and test your floppy drive(s). If the problem persists, you'll need to troubleshoot the ROM hole. Re-open the CONFIG.SYS file in a text editor and remove the "XST" switch you added, then add the exclusion: "X=F400-FFFF" such as:

```
device=c:\qemm\qemm386.sys ram x=f400-ffff
```

Save your changes, then reboot the system and test your floppy drive(s). Once the problem is fixed, Quarterdeck suggests that you re-Optimize QEMM by typing: C:/Q at the DOS prompt.

If the problem persists, chances are that the floppy problem is not because of QEMM. You can test this by rebooting the machine. After the machine beeps, press and hold the <Alt> key. You should see a message telling you to press <Esc> to unload DOS-DATA.SYS. Press <Esc>, then immediately press and hold <Alt> key again. You will see a message telling you to press <Esc> to unload QEMM. Press <Esc>. If QDPMI is normally loaded after QEMM, a message will indicate that it cannot load without a memory manager—press any key to bypass this message. LOADHI entries will warn about drivers not loading high (this is normal when testing). Once the system finishes booting, try the floppy drive(s) again. If the problem continues, it is resulting from something other than QEMM. If the problem disappears, you might need to remove QEMM from the system.

Symptom 24-41. Using the RAM parameter with QEMM causes an IBM ThinkPad to hang In most cases, the ThinkPad will hang after 10 to 15 seconds. The extended BIOS Data Area (XBDA) is a data area normally located at the top of conventional memory—just below 640KB. This memory is used to hold BIOS-specific information. By default, QEMM will relocate this XBDA, reclaiming the conventional memory it uses and allowing programs, such as VIDRAM to extend conventional memory past 640K. On the IBM ThinkPad, this relocation can result in a crash when the ThinkPad operating system writes data intended for the XBDA into the wrong place (usually around 10 to 15 seconds after loading QEMM). Add the XBDA:L switch to the QEMM386.SYS command line. This will tell QEMM to move the XBDA to low conventional memory (but demands 1KB of conventional memory).

Symptom 24-42. Problems occur when loading programs high, the system hangs, or there is other odd behavior from TSRs, device drivers, or PC cards This often happens when QEMM is loaded onto an IBM ThinkPad and cannot determine which addresses the ThinkPad's PC card(s) are using. Each PC card will demand from 0 to 64KB of upper memory addressing space, which must be excluded from QEMM—there is no guarantee that QEMM can auto-detect the region. You'll need to specifically exclude the upper memory range where the PCMCIA card is mapped.

If your PCMCIA card is properly configured, a line should be in your CONFIG.SYS that loads the DICRMU01.SYS driver. This driver is the PC-card resource-map utility, which tells the card what area of memory it is supposed to use. Check that command line for an "/MA=" parameter. This parameter will be followed by the ranges of memory to exclude with the X= parameter on the QEMM386.SYS line. For example, if your CONFIG.SYS file has a DICRMU01.SYS line with /MA=D000-D3FF, you would need to add X=D000-D3FF to the end of your QEMM386.SYS command line in the CONFIG.SYS file.

Symptom 24-43. QEMM generates an Exception 6, 12, or 13 error Generally speaking, an "exception error" indicates a programming fault that the CPU cannot deal with. An exception error can be caused by a problem with QEMM itself (corruption in the QEMM files) or an application (caused by a software bug or simple incompatibility running under QEMM). Run a virus checker to scan for any possible virus activity on disk or in memory. Run ScanDisk to check and correct any file problems on the disk. Check with the application's maker to see if there are known incompatibilities with QEMM, and if there are any workarounds or patches to the application. Finally, try booting without QEMM or use another memory manager to correct the problem.

Symptom 24-44. Systems with Disk Manager fail to Optimize properly This often happens with Disk Manager and QEMM 8.00 (dated 11/4/95). Optimize hangs during the software detection phase. With QEMM 8.00, the XBIOS.OVL overlay file could not be loaded high successfully during the Optimize process. This file does not appear in CONFIG.SYS or AUTOEXEC.BAT—it is loaded automatically and invisibly by Disk Manager at start time. Contact Quarterdeck and obtain the patch for QEMM 8.01. Until you can obtain QEMM 8.01, you might work around the problem using a text editor to add the line: XBIOS to the end of the OPTIMIZE.NOT file in your QEMM directory.

Troubleshooting HIMEM/EMM386

Symptom 24-45. System hangs using HIMEM /TESTMEM The memory test performed by HIMEM.SYS (version 3.10) might fail—possibly causing your system to hang up—if your machine uses a hardware cache controller. This is because some hardware cache controllers do not handle 16MB and 32MB memory boundaries well. As a result, the HIMEM.SYS memory test fails. To work around this problem, disable the hardware cache controller in your system or remove the /TESTMEM switch from the HIMEM command line.

Symptom 24-46. A20 gate problems occur when installing HIMEM The selection of A20 gate handlers is accomplished automatically—HIMEM runs through a series of auto-detection schemes trying to find a match. When a match is found, the particular A20 handler is installed. If no match is found, the default A20 handler is installed. Because of the diverse and non-standard nature of today's PCs, HIMEM auto-detection fails and the default handler is installed. Unfortunately, the default handler might not work too well. In this case, you should use the /A20 switch, along with the corresponding machine designation number (Table 24-1) to select the proper A20 handler for your particular PC.

Symptom 24-47. A general error or system problem occurs with EMM386 In most cases, you'll notice that the system or an application will lock up when using EMM386. Table 24-3 lists the version designations for EMM386. Fully reinitialize the system: turn your machine off, then turn it back on (a.k.a. "cold boot"). When the message "Starting MS-DOS" appears, press <F8> and elect to start the system interactively. When prompted to load EMM386.EXE, choose "N" for no. If the problem persists when EMM386.EXE is not loaded, something other than EMM386.EXE is causing the problem. If the problem disappears when EMM386.EXE is not loaded, edit the CONFIG.SYS file as follows using an ASCII text editor:

```
device=c:\dos\emm386.exe x=a000-f7ff nohi noems novcpi nomovexbda notr
```

Cold boot the machine again. If the problem still persists, the system might have faulty RAM or might require a special machine switch for HIMEM.SYS. Also, advanced memory-related

TABLE 24-3 VERSION DESIGNATIONS FOR EMM386

MS-DOS VERSION	EMM386 VERSION
MS-DOS 5.0	4.20
MS-DOS 5.00a	4.33
MS-DOS 6.0	4.45
MS-DOS 6.2	4.48
MS-DOS 6.21	4.48
MS-DOS 6.22	4.49
Windows 3.1	4.44
Windows 3.11	4.44
Windows for Workgroups 3.1	4.44
Windows for Workgroups 3.11	4.48
Windows 95	4.95

CMOS settings (such as shadow RAM) might need to be disabled. The system BIOS might also need to be upgraded. If the problem disappears after loading the modified EMM386 command line, the problem is probably related to some service that EMM386 provides.

Try removing the X=A000-F7FF switch. If the problem reappears, EMM386.EXE might be scanning memory too aggressively and configuring upper memory blocks on top of some adapter ROM or RAM. Restore the exclusion, but try narrowing the exclusion range. Try removing the NOHI switch. If the problem reappears, EMM386.EXE might be loading into an occupied UMB. If all such regions are excluded, EMM386.EXE cannot be loaded high on the system and NOHI must be used. Try removing the NOEMS switch. If the problem reappears, EMM386.EXE might be conflicting with some hardware ROM or RAM address in the UMA when attempting to establish an expanded memory (EMS) page frame. If EMS is required to run MS-DOS-based applications, use the parameter FRAME=. The angle brackets should appear in both places>> (where × is the defined hexadecimal address) to explicitly specify placement of the EMS page frame in a non-conflicting region. If no applications require EMS, simply continue to use the NOEMS parameter.

Next, try removing the NOVCPI switch. The NOVCPI switch disables *Virtual Control Program Interface (VCPI)* support and can be used only in conjunction with the NOEMS parameter. If the problem reappears, the application might not be fully compatible with the EMM386.EXE VCPI allocation scheme. Either continue using the NOVCPI parameter or do not load EMM386.EXE when using the application. Remove the NOMOVEXBDA switch. Some machines use the last 1KB of conventional memory for an *eXtended BIOS Data Area (XBDA)*. By default, EMM386.EXE remaps this memory area into the UMA instead of conventional memory. If this causes unexpected system behavior, the NOMOVEXBDA parameter must be used. Finally, try removing the NOTR switch. EMM386.EXE has a detection code to search for the presence of a token-ring network adapter—this detection code might cause some computers to hang. The NOTR switch can be used to disable this search.

Symptom 24-48. An error appears: "Unable to set page frame base address—EMS unavailable" This error message is displayed if EMM386 cannot locate a 64KB contiguous "hole" in the UMA for the EMS page frame. According to the LIM 3.2 specification, a *page frame* consists of four contiguous 16KB pages, and a LIM provider (EMM386) must set the page frame. According to the LIM 4.0 specification, an EMS provider need not set a 64KB page frame, but it should set a 16KB page at the minimum.

Although EMM386 conforms to the LIM 4.0 specification, it does not load as an EMS provider if it cannot find a 64KB contiguous hole that can be used for the page frame. This is because the majority of LIM 3.2 applications assume the existence of a page frame. EMM386 can be forced to load without a LIM 3.2 (64KB) page frame by using the Pn parameters (see Table 24-2). If you force EMM386 to load as a LIM 4.0 provider, do not attempt to run LIM 3.2 applications. The best solution is to free a 64KB block of memory in the UMA so that EMM386 can support LIM 3.2 and higher.

Symptom 24-49. An error appears: "Size of expanded memory pool adjusted" This message is displayed if EMM386 cannot provide all the EMS memory requested on the command line. For example, if you use the command line:

```
device=emm386.exe 2048
```

and your computer only has 1024KB of XMS memory, EMM386 displays this error message and provides as much EMS as possible (notice that EMM386 uses some XMS memory for its own code and data, which reduces the amount of XMS memory available for EMS simulation). Little can be done to correct this error, except to reduce the EMS called for on the EMM386 command line or add more physical memory to the PC.

Symptom 24-50.   Windows 3.x cannot provide EMS when using the NOEMS switch   According to the LIM 4.0 specification, an EMS page can also reside in conventional memory (0 to 640KB). The EMM386 EMS line starts at 256KB by default. If the NOEMS switch is added to the command line, all the holes in the adapter region A000h-FFFFh are used for UMBs, and EMM386 cannot provide any EMS. If Windows 3.0 is started and an MS-DOS session are started, EMM386 might not be able to provide EMS. If Windows 3.0 is running in "386 Enhanced" mode, EMM386 can provide EMS within an MS-DOS session. However, the EMS pages are in conventional memory, which can cause problems because of the behavior of LIM 3.2 applications. In a Windows 3.1 "386 Enhanced" mode MS-DOS session, EMS is not provided. Your best course here is to remove the NOEMS switch from the EMM386 command line.

Symptom 24-51.   EMM386 locks up the computer   Although EMM386 is generally considered to be a basic and robust memory manager, there are some conditions where its use might result in a system crash. The /HIGHSCAN feature cannot be used on some computers. If the EMM386 command line in the CONFIG.SYS file contains the /HIGHSCAN parameter, remove /HIGHSCAN from the command line, save the CONFIG.SYS file, and restart your computer.

Next, use excludes to isolate potential EMM386 memory conflicts. EMM386 might have incorrectly identified an area being used by the system as a "hole" (a region that can be used as a UMB or an EMS page frame). As a result, EMM386 accidentally overwrites a portion of memory that is used by a hardware adapter in your computer. Start by excluding addresses in the range A000-EFFF. EMM386 does not use any part of the excluded region for a UMB or EMS page frame. If the problem disappears, you might be able to identify the correct region(s) with some experimentation. Start by excluding a large region, then reducing the size of the region. For example, start with:

```
device=emm386.exe noems x=a000-efff
```

If that works, try narrowing the range to:

```
device=emm386.exe noems x=c000-dfff
```

If that works too, try narrowing the range further to:

```
device=emm386.exe noems x=c800-cfff
```

Remember that you can use multiple exclusions on the same EMM386 command line, such as:

```
device=emm386.exe noems x=c000-c7ff x=e000-efff
```

If the computer has a SCSI disk controller and requires a device driver to operate the SCSI adapter, be sure that the DEVICE= line for the SCSI driver appears before the EMM386 command line. Examples of SCSI device drivers include ASPI4DOS.SYS and USPI14.SYS.

If problems continue, try loading the SmartDrive double buffer driver. The driver should appear before the EMM386 command line in CONFIG.SYS. If you're using DOS 6.0 (or later), Windows 3.1 (or later), or Windows for Workgroups, the SmartDrive double buffer driver is loaded from the CONFIG.SYS file, such as:

```
device=c:\windows\smartdrv.exe /double_buffer
```

In the AUTOEXEC.BAT file, add a /L to the end of the SMARTDRV.EXE line, such as:

```
c:\windows\smartdrv.exe /L
```

If the problems persist, add a plus sign (+) to the end of the double buffer device line:

```
device=c:\dos\smartdrv.exe /double_buffer+
```

If you use the SMARTDRV.SYS driver included with MS-DOS 5.x, the SmartDrive double buffer driver is loaded in the CONFIG.SYS:

```
device=c:\dos\smartdrv.sys /b+
```

If the problem with EMM386 continues, experiment with different HIMEM.SYS A20 handlers. This is done using the /MACHINE: switch on the HIMEM.SYS device line (see Table 24-1).

Symptom 24-52. An error appears: "Insufficient memory for UMBs or virtual HMA" This can often happen when using an AMI or Phoenix BIOS. EMM386 might provide this message—even though there is more than 384KB of extended memory. To work around this problem, modify your CMOS RAM settings to disable the "Fast A20 Gating" feature. You might also be able to update your motherboard's BIOS. This message might also appear on systems with only 384K of extended memory if MS-DOS is loaded high. The solution is to exclude 64KB from EMM386 in order to accommodate loading MS-DOS high.

Symptom 24-53. An error appears: "Unable to create page frame" If EMM386 is unable to find 64KB of contiguous memory in the upper memory area, it cannot create an expanded memory page frame. If you don't want expanded memory for your system, you can substitute the NOEMS switch for the RAM switch in your EMM386 command line in CONFIG.SYS. If you do want expanded memory, you can try establishing a page frame in a portion of the upper memory area not normally used by EMM386. You can try putting the page frame in the E000h memory block by modifying the EMM386 command line:

```
device=c:\dos\emm386 m9 ram
```

Do not try this procedure on an IBM model PS/2 computer. Always remember to backup your existing copy of CONFIG.SYS and AUTOEXEC.BAT (preferably to a bootable floppy disk) before attempting any modifications to your startup file.

Symptom 24-54. An error appears: "EMM386 Privileged Operation Error #01" The problem is with EMM386 and the AST 386 FastBoard. AST Research has confirmed that loading EMM386 (MS-DOS 5.0 and later versions) on an AST Premium 286 computer with an AST 386 FastBoard upgrade might cause the error. The AST 386 FastBoard is an 80386 upgrade for AST 80286 motherboards. This error might occur if the 386 FastBoard driver (FB386.SYS) is not loaded before EMM386 in the CONFIG.SYS file. Load the 386 FastBoard device driver (FB386.SYS) before EMM386:

```
device=c:\fb386.sys
device=c:\dos\himem.sys
device=c:\dos\emm386.exe
```

Symptom 24-55. An error appears: "EMM386 Not Installed—Unable to set page frame base address" This message indicates that EMM386 was unable to find 64KB of contiguous space needed for the expanded memory page frame. When you specify the RAM switch (or no switch at all), EMM386 attempts to create a 64KB page frame in the *Upper Memory Area (UMA)*. The actual amount of extended memory used will be 108KB (64KB + 44KB = 108KB). The extra 44KB is used for tables that EMM386 sets up to emulate expanded memory. This 64KB of space acts as a window into expanded memory—allowing programs to see all the available expanded memory 64KB at a time. Try using the NOEMS switch if expanded memory is not needed. Next, be sure HIMEM is installed above EMM386 in the CONFIG.SYS file (other devices should be loaded after EMM386, except for such drivers as DMDRVR.BIN, EMM.SYS, or ADAPTEC.SYS). If you're not working on an IBM machine, add the following switches to the EMM386 command line in the CONFIG.SYS file:

```
device=c:\dos\emm386.exe i=e000-efff (m9 or frame=e000) ram
```

The "included" E000h-EFFFh memory range is generally not used by non-IBM machines, and including this range can allow you to find 64KB of free contiguous memory. The "mx" switch also allows you to specify different locations for the page frame to begin (see Table 24-2). For m9, the page frame will attempt to begin at E000h.

If the program requiring expanded memory can use the LIM 4.0 specification, then the 64KB page frame can be set non-contiguously. Add the "Pn=address" parameter to the EMM386 command line in CONFIG.SYS:

```
device=c:\dos\emm886.exe p0=c800 p1=d400 p2=e000 p3=d000 ram
```

Symptom 24-56. An AT&T 6386E system hangs with a RAM option in EMM386 An expanded-memory page frame set to DC00h or higher on a AT&T 6386E causes the system to hang up. For example, the following DEVICE= statement hangs the system:

```
device=emm386.exe m8 ram
```

The AT&T 6386E has a ROM option at address E800h that is used during system operations. Setting a page frame to DC00h or higher overlaps with the ROM option, resulting in a system lockup. Alter the "mx" switch to start the page frame at an address that avoids the conflict.

Symptom 24-57. A Plus Hardcard II is very slow with EMM386 You might need to exclude the Hardcard XL BIOS from the EMM386 command line:

```
device=c:\dos\emm386.exe x=c000-c800
```

Notice that the exclusion range is only an example—the exact addresses to exclude will depend on your configuration. If you are not using UMBs, use the "frame=" parameter to set the address of the page frame so that the page frame will not conflict with the addresses being used by the Hardcard. For example, if the Hardcard is using addresses C000-C800, you might use:

```
device=c:\dos\emm386.exe frame=d000
```

This sets the page frame for the D000-DFFF range of memory.

Symptom 24-58. Exception errors occur with EMM386 This kind of error means that the CPU has encountered a general-protection violation. Because the EMM386 driver operates the CPU in virtual real mode, the CPU checks for valid memory accesses. If a program tries to access memory that it is not allowed to access, the CPU generates an exception fault error, which is detected by EMM386. In effect, EMM386 is reporting a program error detected by the CPU. In general, this error should not occur on PCs that are 100% IBM compatible. Machines that are not might require an OEM version of EMM386. Table 24-4 is a list of protected-mode exception errors and their names:

Troubleshooting 386MAX

Symptom 24-59. The Qualitas DOSMAX utility doesn't function as expected DOSMAX for Windows won't work if software is loaded at the top of conventional memory (near 640KB). Most resident programs load into the lowest address memory available. If the software loads into the top of low DOS memory, DOSMAX for Windows won't work. Disk-controller software is the most common software that uses memory at the top of low DOS, but CD-ROM device drivers sometimes configure a buffer in this area as well. Certain viruses have also been known to attach themselves to this area of memory.

DOSMAX also won't work if the system's Qualitas MAX profile includes the option "NOXBIOS" (Qualitas MAX is not relocating the extended BIOS into high DOS)—DOSMAX is disabled. The extended BIOS normally resides at the top of conventional memory. A problem can also occur if you have a system with less than 640KB base memory. Qualitas MAX backfills this memory to 640KB, but these systems aren't compatible with Windows 3.x.

TABLE 24-4 PROTECTED MODE
EXCEPTION ERRORS
FOR EMM386

CODE	MEANING
0	Divide error
1	Debugger interrupt
2	Nonmaskable interrupt
3	Breakpoint
4	Overflow interrupt
5	Array-boundary violation
6	Invalid opcode
7	Co-processor not available
8	Double fault
9	Co-processor-segment overrun
10	Invalid task state segment
11	Segment not present
12	Stack exception
13	General-protection violation
14	Page fault
16	Coprocessor error

If you're still having problems with DOSMAX, exit Windows and add the "DOSMAX-Mono=OFF" switch to the [Qualitas] section of SYSTEM.INI. Add the line (and the section if it doesn't already exist). Restart Windows and retry DOSMAX. You might also try exiting Windows and editing your 386MAX.PRO file—using a semicolon, comment-out the "VGASWAP" and "USE=B000-B800" options. Re-run Maximize and see if DOSMAX works properly. If problems persist, check to see that you have the most current version of your video drivers (try the standard VGA drivers that come with Windows).

Symptom 24-60. The error appears: "Error 1014: Disk cache or other file I/O software using EMS memory" Qualitas MAX has detected EMS memory in use by a disk cache or other resident file I/O software (the other software might be a disk-compression utility or a network). It is recommended that these programs use extended (XMS) memory when operating in a Windows environment. Check EMS memory usage by typing "386util /e" in the Qualitas MAX directory to determine which programs are using EMS memory. If you must run Windows with this type of software, you might override the error message by editing your AUTOEXEC.BAT file and adding the DOS command: "SET EMSCACHE=OK."

Symptom 24-61. The error appears: "VxD Error: Unable to provide DOSMAX features" DOSMAX has detected that your system has less than 640KB of conventional memory. Because the top of conventional memory does not correspond to the bottom of graphics memory (as it does on a system with 640KB) DOSMAX features are unavailable. Most resident programs load into the lowest address memory available. If the software loads into the top of low DOS memory, DOSMAX for Windows won't work. The most common software that loads in this manner is software that is necessary for certain hard-disk controllers and some CD-ROM buffers. The best way to overcome this kind of problem is to bring conventional memory to 640KB or to disable software that loads at the top of DOS memory.

Symptom 24-62. The error appears: "VxD Error: Qpopup is not running" The Qualitas MAX device driver will not be able to protect this DOSMAX window from programs attempting to enter graphics mode. QPOPUP.EXE is not loading from the WIN.INI file or the Startup group. Without this file, Qualitas MAX can't protect DOSMAX windows from programs that attempt to enter graphics mode. Check the "LOAD=" line in the WIN.INI file. You can also try to reinstall DOSMAX by using the DOSMAX entry on the *Startup* tab of the Toolbox (Windows 95).

Symptom 24-63. The error appears: "Error 1021: Qualitas MAX stacks required for DOSMAX support" There is a problem with the assignment of stacks in MAX. Qualitas MAX stacks must be enabled to use the DOSMAX feature. Click *Load DOS stacks high* on the *Startup* tab of Toolbox (Windows 95) or remove the STACKS=0 option from the 386MAX.PRO file and reboot your system.

Symptom 24-64. The error appears: "Error 1011: Bus master disk subsystem detected that requires Qcache or other compliant disk cache to be loaded" Qualitas MAX detected a bus-mastering hard-disk controller that does not support VDS. Also, your 386MAX.PRO file might contain the NOSCSI option. In either case, 386MAX.VXD expects to find a VDS-compliant disk cache program in memory. You'll need to update the bus mastering driver.

Symptom 24-65. The error appears: "Error 2035: V86 RAM page(s) in use" The error message might also ask you to modify "RAM=" statement(s) in the 386MAX.PRO file to remove one or more memory regions. Windows 95 is attempting to use RAM pages that are already in use by Qualitas MAX. Remove the overlapping portion of the "RAM=" statement from the 386MAX.PRO file and reboot the system.

Symptom 24-66. The error appears: "Error 1020: 386MAX.SYS version mismatch" The versions of 386MAX.SYS and 386MAX.VXD that are in use do not match. Check that the current version of each file is in the Qualitas MAX sub-directory. You might need to reinstall MAX from scratch.

Symptom 24-67. Video problems or conflicts occur while using MAX Common video symptoms include a blank screen on entering or exiting a program, spontaneous system reboots, strange graphics or characters appearing on the screen, or the system hangs after the Qualitas MAX initialization screen. Several regions in the high DOS area have predetermined uses. The first 128KB (between addresses A000h and C000h) is for memory on video boards. Each kind of video display uses a different amount of address space. Just above the video RAM area is a 32KB area (C000h-C800h) for the ROM on many VGA video adapters. In most cases, 386MAX automatically identifies used memory, and does not map into the appropriate video regions of most systems. However, under some circumstances, video cannot be accurately identified.

If you experience any odd video symptoms, Qualitas MAX might have re-mapped high DOS memory into a region that the video adapter needs, or might have unsuccessfully relocated the video ROMs via the VGASWAP option. To correct this conflict, disable VGASWAP and USE=B000-B800 in the 386MAX.PRO file. You can do this in Windows 95 by using the *UMB/Adapters* tab in Toolbox to deactivate use of the *Monochrome Display Area (MDA)* and VGASWAP. When you make these changes, Toolbox displays a message suggesting that you run Maximize. Choose *Exit*, then reboot the system to activate your changes, which result in a change to the configuration of high DOS memory. If the problem is resolved, it is important to re-run Maximize at this time to re-optimize your memory configuration.

In a DOS environment, edit the 386MAX.PRO file to make the changes. Use any text editor to look at the profile located in the Qualitas MAX directory (QMAX is the default directory). If there is a "USE=B000-B800" or any "USE=" statement in the B000h range, comment that line out of the profile by placing a semicolon (;) in front of the line. Repeat the process for the keyword VGASWAP. Reboot the system to activate the changes. Again, if the problem is resolved, it is important to re-run Maximize at this time to re-optimize your memory configuration.

Further Study

That's it for Chapter 24. Be sure to review the glossary and chapter questions on the accompanying CD. If you have access to the Internet, take a look at some of these memory-manager resources:

Microsoft (HIMEM and EMM386): **http://www.microsoft.com**

Qualitas (386MAX and BlueMAX): **http://www.qualitas.com**

Quarterdeck (QEMM): **http://www.qdeck.com**

MICE AND
TRACKBALLS

CONTENTS AT A GLANCE

The Mouse
Mouse gestures
Mouse construction
Mechanical sensors
Opto-mechanical sensors

The Trackball
Trackball construction

Cleaning a Pointing Device

Troubleshooting a Pointing Device
Mouse/trackball interfaces
Mouse driver software issues
Mousekeys under Windows 95
Symptoms

Further Study

As software packages evolved beyond simple menus and began to make use of the powerful graphics systems coming into popular use during the mid-1980s (i.e., EGA and VGA graphics), ever-larger amounts of information were presented in the display. Simple, multi-layered text menus were aggressively replaced with striking graphic user interfaces (GUIs). System options and selections were soon represented with symbols (graphic "buttons" or "icons"), instead of plain text. Using a keyboard to maneuver through such visual software soon became a cumbersome (if not impossible) chore.

Peripherals designers responded to this situation by developing a family of *pointing devices* (Fig. 25-1). Pointing devices use a combination of hardware and software to produce

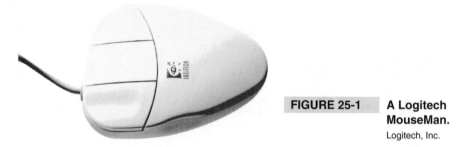

FIGURE 25-1   **A Logitech MouseMan.**
Logitech, Inc.

and control a graphical screen *cursor*. A software device driver generates the cursor and reports its position. As the pointing device is moved around, hardware signals from the pointing device are interpreted by the device driver, which moves the cursor in a similar manner. By positioning the cursor over a graphic symbol and activating one, two, or three of the buttons on the pointing device, it is now possible to select (i.e., "click" or "doubleclick") and manipulate (i.e., "drag") options in the application program instead of using a keyboard.

Three factors are needed to make pointing devices work: the physical signal-generating hardware itself, a software driver (the "device driver"), and the application program must be written to make use of the device driver. If any of these three items are missing, the pointing device will not work. This chapter looks at the technology, maintenance, and troubleshooting of two popular pointing devices: the mouse and the trackball.

The Mouse

Although the development of computer pointing devices has been ongoing since the early 1970s, the first commercial pointing devices for IBM-compatible systems were widely introduced in the early 1980s. The device was small enough to be held under your palm, and your fingertips rested on its button(s). A small, thin cord connected the device to its host computer. The device's small size, long tail-like cord, and quick scurrying movements immediately earned it the label of *mouse*.

Every mouse needs at least one button. By pressing the button, you indicate that a selection is being made at the current cursor location. Many mouse-compatible software packages only use a single mouse button even to this day. A two-button mouse is more popular (reflecting the endurance of the mouse design) because a second button can add more flexibility to the mouse. For example, one button can work to "select" an item; the second button can be used to "deselect" that item again or to activate other menus and options. A few mouse designs use three buttons, but the third button is rarely supported by application programs, aside from CAD or high-end art applications.

MOUSE GESTURES

The first mouse "gesture" is called *clicking*, which is little more than a single momentary press of the left mouse button (on a two-button mouse). Clicking is the primary means of making a selection in the particular application program. The second common gesture is *doubleclicking*, which is simply two single clicks in immediate succession. A doubleclick also represents selection, but its exact use depends upon the application program. The third type of mouse gesture is the *drag*, where a graphical item can literally be moved around the display. Dragging is almost always accomplished by pressing the left mouse button over the desired item, then (without releasing the button) moving the item to its new location. When the item moved to its new position, releasing the left mouse button will "drop" the item in that location.

It is interesting that pen gestures are interpreted by the computer's operating system, but mouse movements and button conditions are handled by the actual application program (such as a word processor or game). Thus, the same mouse gestures can be made to represent different actions, depending on which program is executing.

MOUSE CONSTRUCTION

A mouse is a relatively straightforward device, consisting of four major parts: the plastic housing, the mouse ball, the electronics PC board, and the signal cable. Figure 25-2 illustrates a typical mouse assembly. The housing assembly will vary a little, depending on the manufacturer and vintage of your particular mouse (just walk through a computer store and look at the variety of mouse styles available), but the overall scheme is almost always identical. The mouse ball is a hard rubber ball situated inside the mouse body, just below a small PC board. When the mouse is positioned on a desktop, the ball contacts two actuators that register the mouse ball's movement in the X (left-to-right) and Y (up-to-down)

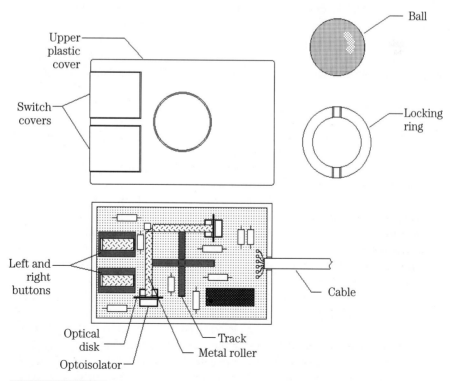

FIGURE 25-2   The internal construction of a basic mouse.

FIGURE 25-3   **The Crystal Mouse from Suncom Technologies.** Suncom Technologies

directions. Both sensors generate a series of pulses that represent movement in both axis. Pulses equate to mouse movement—more pulses mean more movement. The pulses from both axis are amplified by the PC board and sent back to the computer along with information on the condition of each mouse button. Figure 25-3 shows a Suncom Crystal mouse, which allows you to see the internal mouse construction.

The mouse device driver already running in your computer (most systems load the mouse's device driver, such as Microsoft's MOUSE.COM, during computer initialization) interprets the pulses generated by the mouse and translates them into X and Y screen locations where the visible mouse cursor is positioned. As the mouse moves left and right or up and down, pulses are added or subtracted from the cursor's X and Y screen coordinates by the device driver. The application program can then call for the X and Y coordinates, as well as button states. The key to a working mouse is its sensor devices. Sensors (or actuators) must be responsive enough to detect minute shifts in mouse position and generate pulses accordingly, yet be reliable enough to withstand wear, abuse, and environmental effects. The two general types of sensors are mechanical and opto-mechanical.

MECHANICAL SENSORS

The greatest challenge in mouse design (and the largest cause of failures) is the reliable and repeatable conversion of mouse movement into serial electrical pulses. Early mouse versions used purely mechanical sensors to encode the mouse ball's movements. As the mouse ball turned against a roller (or shaft), copper contacts on the shaft would sweep across contacts on the mouse PC board—much like commutating rings and brushes on a dc motor. Each time that a roller contact touches a corresponding contact in the mouse, an electrical pulse is generated. Because a mouse must typically generate hundreds of pulses for every linear inch of mouse movement, there are several sets of contacts for each axis.

It is important that mouse pulses can be positive or negative, depending on the relative direction of the mouse in an axis. For example, moving the mouse right produces positive pulses, and moving the mouse left produces negative pulses. Similarly, moving the mouse down along its Y axis produces positive pulses, and moving the mouse up might produce negative pulses. All pulses are then interpreted and tracked by the host computer.

Although mechanical sensors are simple, straightforward, and very inexpensive to produce, some significant problems can plague the mechanical mouse. Mechanical mouse designs are not terribly reliable. The metal-on-metal contact sets used to generate pulses are prone to wear and breakage. Dust, dirt, hair, and any other foreign matter carried into the mouse by the ball can also interfere with contacts. Any contact interference prevents pulses from being generated. This condition results in a frustratingly intermittent "skip" or "stall" of the cursor while you move the mouse. Fortunately, it is often a simple matter to disassemble and clean the contacts.

OPTO-MECHANICAL SENSORS

The next generation of mouse designs replaced the mechanical contacts with an optoisolator arrangement (Fig. 25-4). A hard rubber mouse ball still rests against two perpendicularly opposed metal actuator rollers, but instead of each roller driving an array of contacts, the rollers rotate slotted wheels, which are inserted into optoisolators. An optoisolator shines LED light across an air gap where it is detected by a photodiode or phototransistor. When a roller (and slotted wheel) spins, the light path between LED and detector is alternated or "chopped." This causes the detector's output signal to oscillate; thus, pulses are generated. The pulse frequency is dependent upon mouse speed. As with the mechanical mouse, the opto-mechanical mouse produces both positive and negative serial pulses, depending on the direction of mouse movement.

The opto-mechanical mouse is a great improvement over the plain mechanical approach. By eliminating mechanical contacts, wear and tear on the mouse is significantly reduced, resulting in much longer life and higher reliability. However, the mouse is still subject to the interference of dust and other foreign matter that invariably finds its way into the mouse housing. Regular cleaning and internal dusting can prevent or correct instances of cursor skip or stall. Most mouse models use opto-mechanical sensors.

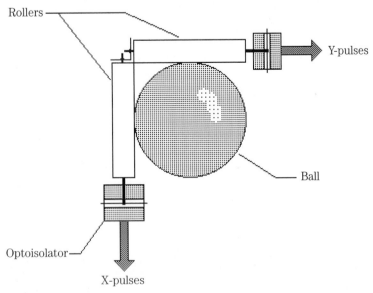

FIGURE 25-4   **Sensor layout for an opto-mechanical mouse or trackball.**

The Trackball

The *trackball* is basically an inverted mouse. Instead of using your hand to move a mouse body around on a desk surface, a trackball remains stationary. Your hand or fingertips move the ball itself, which is mounted through the top of the device. The advantage to a trackball is that it does not move. As a result, trackballs can be incorporated into desktop keyboards, or added to your work area with a minimum of required space. Such characteristics have made trackballs extremely popular with laptop and notebook computers. Today, most notebook computers incorporate pointing devices directly.

In spite of their advantages, however, a trackball is not quite as easy to use as a mouse. The successful use of a mouse is largely a matter of hand-eye coordination—a flick of the wrist and a click or two can maneuver you through a program at an impressive rate. Because you can move the mouse and manipulate its buttons simultaneously, dragging is a very intuitive gesture. Trackballs are usually turned with only your thumb. This positions the rest of your hand so that you can only reach one trackball button. That is a fine arrangement as long as you are only clicking a single button, but you often have to move your hand around completely to get to the second button (or you must at least let go of the ball). Dragging is also typically a cumbersome effort. Even a clumsy trackball is better than none at all, so you should be as familiar with trackballs as with a mouse.

TRACKBALL CONSTRUCTION

Virtually all trackballs use the same opto-mechanical sensor technology that is used with mice. Instead of the mouse PC board resting over the ball, a trackball sits on top of a PC board. The hard rubber ball sits at the intersection of a set of small plastic rails (or tracks)—thus, the term "track-ball." This positions the ball between two perpendicularly oriented metal rollers. Each roller drives a slotted wheel, which, in turn, runs between the LED and detector of an optoisolator. As the ball and rollers are made to turn, the slotted wheels cause the respective optoisolator's light path to alternate and generate signal pulses. Pulse frequency is dependent on the relative movements of each roller. Pulses are read and interpreted just like a mouse.

During initialization, your computer must load a device driver designed to read the proper port, interpret any signals generated by the trackball, and make switch and roller information available to whatever program calls for it. Given the similarities of mice and trackballs, many mouse-compatible applications are capable of accessing trackball data and responding just like a mouse—even the trackball device driver is virtually identical to a mouse driver (trackball drivers are usually "adopted" mouse drivers that simply compensate for the inversion of the ball). Because the technologies and construction techniques of mice and trackballs are essentially the same, the remainder of this chapter will treat a mouse and trackball as interchangeable devices.

Cleaning a Pointing Device

Pointing devices are perhaps the simplest peripheral available for your computer. Although they are reasonably forgiving to wear and tear, trackballs and mice can easily be fouled by dust, debris, and foreign matter introduced from the ball. Contamination of this

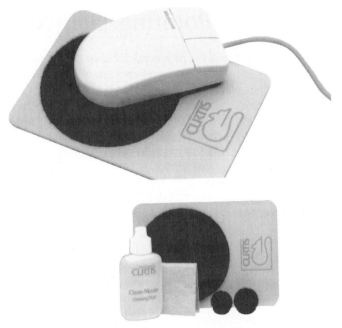

FIGURE 25-5   **A Curtis mouse-cleaning kit.** Curtis, a division of Rolodex, Secaucus, NJ 07094

sort is almost never damaging, but it can cause some maddening problems when using the pointing device. A regimen of routine cleaning will help to prevent contamination problems. You can use pre-fabricated mouse cleaning kits (Fig. 25-5) to speed the cleaning process. Turn your small-computer off before performing any cleaning procedures:

- *Remove the ball* A ball is held in place by a retaining ring. For a mouse, the retaining ring is on the bottom. For a trackball, the ring is in the top. Rotate the ring and remove it gently—the ball will fall out. Place the retaining ring in a safe place.
- *Clean the ball* Wash the ball in warm, soapy water, then dry it thoroughly with a clean, lint-free towel. Place the ball in a safe place.
- *Blow out the dust* Use a can of photography-grade compressed air to blow out any dust or debris that has accumulated inside the pointing device. You might want to do this in an open or outdoor area.
- *Clean the rollers* Notice that the mouse has three rollers: an X roller, a Y roller, and a small pressure roller that keeps the ball pressed against the X and Y rollers. Use a cotton swab dipped in isopropyl alcohol to clean off any layers of gunk that might have accumulated on the rollers.
- *Reassemble and test* Allow everything to dry completely, then replace the ball and retaining ring. Then test the pointing device to be sure that it is performing as expected.

Do not use harsh solvents, wood alcohol, or chemicals inside the pointing device or on the ball. Chemicals can easily melt the plastic and result in permanent damage to the pointing device.

Troubleshooting a Pointing Device

The weakest link in a pointing system is the peripheral pointing device itself. Few peripheral devices are subjected to the wear and general abuse seen by trackballs or mice. They are dropped, yanked, and moved constantly from place to place. Damage to the device's PC board, cabling, and connector is extremely common because of abuse. Accumulations of dust and debris can easily work into the housing and create havoc with the rubber ball, tracks, and rollers. Hardware conflicts and driver-configuration issues can also result in limitless problems. This part of the chapter guides you through some simple troubleshooting techniques for your trackball and mouse.

MOUSE/TRACKBALL INTERFACES

From time to time, you might need to check the physical interface on a mouse or trackball. At its core, the mouse uses a simple serial device—that is, it can pass serial data back and forth with the host computer using communication protocols managed by the mouse driver. Three types of mouse interfaces are common in the field: serial mice, bus mice, and PS/2 mice. This part of the chapter highlights the pinouts for each interface type.

Serial mice A "serial" mouse connects to an existing RS232 serial port at the PC (usually COM1 or COM2) using a standard DB-9F (9-pin female) or DB-25F (25-pin female) connector. Table 25-1 lists the pinout for a Logitech Type M, V, or W serial mouse connector.

Bus mice In many circumstances, it is not possible to use a serial mouse on an open COM port, and the PC is not fitted with a PS/2 port. In this case, it might be necessary to use a "bus mouse," which basically involves using a stand-alone mouse-controller board (a bus mouse controller) and a mouse fitted with a bus mouse connector—usually a male sub-miniature "D"-type connector or a miniature male DIN (circular) connector. Be careful not to mistake the 9-pin DIN connector of a bus mouse for the 6-pin circular connector of a PS/2 mouse. Table 25-2 lists the pinout for a Logitech bus mouse.

TABLE 25-1	PINOUT OF A SERIAL MOUSE PORT (LOGITECH)		
DB-9F 9 PIN	**DB-25F 25 PIN**	**WIRE NAME**	**COMMENTS**
Shell	1	Protective ground	
3	2	Receive data	Serial data from host to mouse
2	3	Transmit data	Serial data from mouse to host (for power only)
7	5	RTS	Request to send
8	5	CTS	Clear to send
6	6	DSR	Data set ready
5	7	Signal ground	
4	20	DTR	Data terminal ready

TABLE 25-2 PINOUT OF A BUS MOUSE PORT (LOGITECH)

WIRE COLOR	MINI-DIN PIN	LOGITECH P-SERIES SIGNAL	MICROSOFT INPORT SIGNAL
Black	1	+5 V	+5 V
Brown	2	X2	XA
Red	3	X1	XB
Orange	4	Y1	YA
Yellow	5	Y2	YB
Green	6	Left	SW1
Violet	7	Middle	SW2
Gray	8	Right	SW3
White	9	GND	Logic GND
SHIELD	shell	Chassis	Chassis

TABLE 25-3 PINOUT OF A PS/2 MOUSE PORT (LOGITECH)

PIN	WIRE NAME
1	Data
2	Reserved
3	Ground
4	+5-V Supply
5	CLK
6	Reserved
Shield	Chassis

PS/2 mice Most current computers are fitted with one or two PS/2 ports (these are often called *PIX ports* because the motherboard's PIX controller(s) can manage the ports directly. PS/2 ports are basic serial interfaces that are ideal for keyboards and mice. PS/2 mice use a 6-pin DIN (barrel) connector (Table 25-3). Bi-directional data transmission is controlled by the CLK and DATA lines—both are fed by an "open collector" device that lets either the host or mouse control the lines. During non-transmission, CLK is at logic "1" and DATA is at logic "0" or "1." The PC can inhibit mouse transmission by forcing CLK to logic "0."

MOUSE DRIVER SOFTWARE ISSUES

Device drivers are often underrated when it comes to mouse/trackball troubleshooting. The driver plays a vital role in mouse performance, and any driver bugs or incompatibilities will have direct consequences on mouse operation. Mouse drivers are also surprisingly versatile programs that can be extensively configured through the use of command

TABLE 25-4 COMMAND LINE SWITCHES FOR MICROSOFT MOUSE DRIVER 9.0X

SWITCH	EXPLANATION
ON	Enable mouse
OFF	Disable mouse
/B	Bus mouse type
/C<n>	Serial mouse on COM1 or COM2
/E	Load mouse in low memory
/F	Find pointing device
/H<n>	Horizontal sensitivity (5–100)
/I<n>	InPort mouse type (1 or 2)
/KP<n>	Small button selection (P = primary, S = secondary)
/K<n>	ClickLock (/KC = ON, /K = Off)
/M<n>	Enable default cursor (/M1 = ON, /M = Off)
/N<n>	Cursor delay (0–10)
/O<n>	Rotation angle (0–359)
/P<n>	Active acceleration profile
/Q	Load mouse quietly (no startup messages; only in 9.01)
/R<n>	Interrupt rate
/S<n>	Horizontal and vertical sensitivity (5–100)
/V<n>	Vertical sensitivity (5–100)
/Y	Disables hardware cursor
/Z	PS/2 mouse type

Note: The /E and /F switches are new in version 9.0; /Q is new in 9.01.

line switches. Table 25-4 lists the command-line switches for Microsoft's Mouse driver 9.0x. When dealing with any kind of mouse issue, always start by checking that the correct driver is installed, that the driver is the latest version, and that it is using any necessary command line switches to adapt itself to the particular PC (default settings are not always adequate).

MOUSEKEYS UNDER WINDOWS 95

Windows 95 traditionally relies on a mouse for clicking and dragging, but a little-known feature of Windows 95, called *MouseKeys*, allows you to use the numeric keypad to move the mouse around the screen, click, doubleclick, and drag. MouseKeys can be helpful if you're caught without a mouse (or troubleshooting a defective mouse system), and you need to navigate the Windows 95 environment.

The MouseKeys feature is activated through the *Accessibility* properties under the Control panel. Click on *Start*, select *Settings*, then open the Control panel. Doubleclick on the *Accessibility* icon and select the *Mouse* tab (Fig. 25-6). You can enable or disable MouseKeys by checking or clearing the check box. Once MouseKeys is enabled, you can further optimize its settings by clicking the *Settings* button (Fig. 25-7). If you check the

"Use Shortcut" box, you can turn MouseKeys on and off by toggling the <Left Alt>+<Left Shift>+<Num Lock> keys.

Once the MouseKeys feature is turned on, move the cursor by pressing the arrow keys on the numeric keypad. Use the <Home>, <End>, <PageUp>, and <PageDown> keys to move the mouse cursor diagonally.

You can "left click" by pressing the <5> key on the numeric keypad. To "left doubleclick," press the <+> key on the numeric keypad. To "right click," press the <-> button on the numeric keypad first, then press <5> to "click" or <+> to "doubleclick." To click as if you were using both mouse buttons at once, press the <*> key on your numeric keypad, then press <5> "click" or <+> to "doubleclick." If you want to switch back to standard clicking, press </> on your numeric keypad. You'll also need to be able to drag using MouseKeys. Be sure that the MouseKeys feature is turned on, then move the mouse pointer over the desired object. Press <Ins> on the numeric keypad to "hold down" the mouse button and "grab" the object. Move the mouse pointer over the new desired area, then press <Del> on the numeric keypad to "drop" the object.

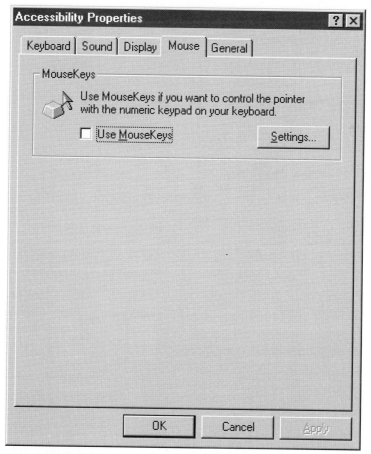

FIGURE 25-6   **Controlling the Windows 95 MouseKeys feature.**

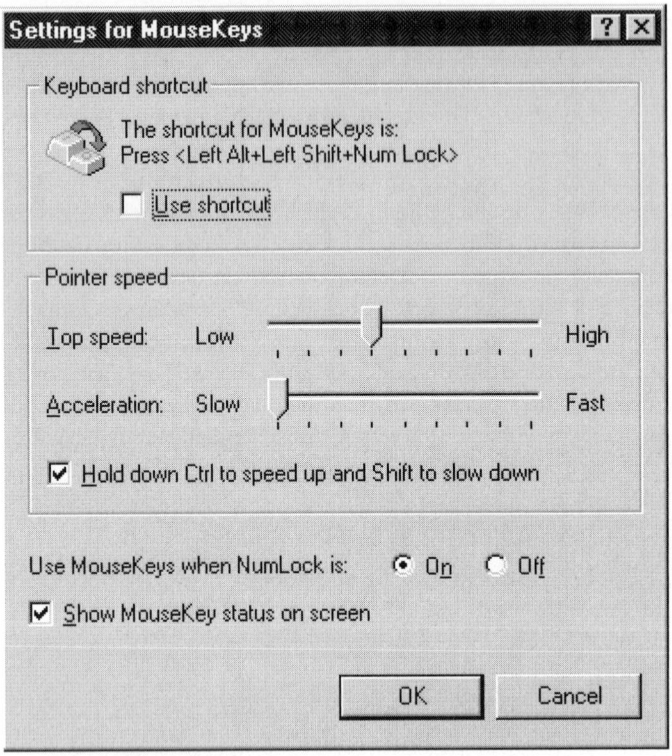

FIGURE 25-7   Configuring MouseKeys operation.

SYMPTOMS

Symptom 25-1. The mouse cursor appears, but it only moves erratically as the ball moves (if at all) This symptom might occur in either the horizontal or vertical axis. This symptom suggests that an intermittent condition is occurring somewhere in the pointing device. You should not have to disassemble your computer during this procedure. Start your investigation by powering down the computer. Check the device's cable connector at the computer. Be sure that the connector is tight and inserted properly. If you are in the habit of continually plugging and unplugging the mouse/trackball, excessive wear can develop in the connector pins over time. If the connector does not seem to fit tightly in the computer, try a new pointing device.

More likely, the device's rollers are not turning, or are turning only intermittently. In most cases, roller stall is caused by a dirty or damaged ball, or an accumulation of dirt blocking one or both sensors. Clean the ball and blow out any dust or debris that might have settled into the mouse/trackball housing. Refer to the preceding section on cleaning and attempt to clean the device thoroughly. Never use harsh solvents or chemicals to clean the housings or ball.

If you have the mouse connected to a standard serial communication port (a COM port), you should check that no other devices are using the same interrupt (IRQ). For example, COM1 and COM3 use the same IRQ, while COM2 and COM4 share another IRQ. If you have a mouse on COM1 and a modem on COM3, there will almost invariably be a hardware conflict. If possible, switch the mouse (or conflicting device) to another port and try the system again.

If no hardware conflict occurs, and cleaning does not correct an intermittent condition, remove the device's upper housing to expose the PC board, and use your multimeter to check continuity across each wire in the connecting cable. Because you probably will not know which connector pins correspond to which wires at the sensor PC board, place one meter probe on a device's wire and "ring-out" each connector pin until you find continuity. Make a wiring chart as you go. Each time you find a wire path, wiggle the cable to stimulate any possible intermittent wiring. Repair any intermittent wiring, if possible. If you cannot find continuity or repair faulty wiring, simply replace the pointing device.

Symptom 25-2. One or both buttons function erratically (if at all) Buttons are prone to problems from dust accumulation and general contact corrosion. Your first step should be power down your computer and disconnect the pointing device. Remove the ball and upper housing to expose the PC board and switches. Spray a small amount of electronics-grade contact cleaner into each switch, then work each switch to circulate the cleaner.

If cleaning does not improve intermittent switch contacts, you might wish to check continuity across the connecting cable. With the ball and housing cover removed, use your multimeter to check continuity across each wire in the connecting cable. Because you probably do not know which connector pins correspond to which wires at the device, place one meter lead on a device wire and "ring-out" each connector pin until you find continuity. Once you find continuity, wiggle the cable to stimulate any possible intermittent wiring. Repair any intermittent wiring if you can, or simply replace the pointing device.

Symptom 25-3. The screen cursor appears on the display, but it does not move If the cursor appears, the device driver has loaded correctly and the application program is communicating with the driver. Your first step should be to suspect the serial connection. If there is no serial connection, however, no pulses will modify the cursor's position. If you find a bad connection, power down your computer before reattaching the device's serial connector, then restore power and allow the system to reinitialize.

If the device is attached correctly to its proper serial port, the problem probably exists in the pointing device's wiring. Remove the ball and upper housing to expose the PC board, then use your multimeter to check continuity across each wire in the connecting cable. Because you probably do not know which connector pins correspond to which wires in the device, place one meter lead on a device wire and "ring-out" each connector pin until you find continuity. Once you find continuity, wiggle the cable to stimulate any possible intermittent wiring. Repair any intermittent or open wiring if you can, or simply replace the pointing device.

Symptom 25-4. The mouse/trackball device driver fails to load The device driver is a short program that allows an application program to access information from a pointing device. Most computer users prefer to load their device drivers during system initialization by invoking the drivers in the CONFIG.SYS or AUTOEXEC.BAT files. Most drivers are written to check for the presence of their respective device first—if the expected device does not respond, the driver will not be loaded into memory. Other drivers load blindly, regardless of whether the expected device is present or not.

If the device driver fails to load during initialization, your pointing device might not have been detected. Power down your computer and check the connection of your pointing device. Ensure the device is securely plugged into the proper serial port (or other

mouse port). If the device is missing or incorrectly inserted, install or re-secure the pointing device and allow the system to re-initialize. If you see a "File not found" error message displayed at the point your device driver was supposed to load, the driver might have
been accidentally erased, might be corrupted, or might be located in a sub-directory where
the CONFIG.SYS or AUTOEXEC.BAT files are not looking. Try re-installing a valid
copy of your mouse device driver and ensure that the driver is located where your calling
batch file can access it. Reboot your system.

Most well-designed application programs check for the presence of a pointing device
through the device driver during initial program execution. If the application program
aborts or fails to execute because of a "No mouse found" or "No mouse driver" error, return to the preceding paragraphs and recheck the device and driver installation.

**Symptom 25-5. You see a "General protection fault" after installing a new
mouse and driver under Windows** First, this is probably not a hardware fault (although
it would be helpful to check any mouse driver command line switches in CONFIG.SYS or
AUTOEXEC.BAT). It is more likely that the new mouse driver is conflicting with one or
more applications. Try several different applications—most will probably work just fine.
Check with the mouse manufacturer to see if there are any other reported problems, and
find if any patches are planned. If you have an older version of the mouse driver available,
try replacing that one. An older driver might not work as well as a newer one, but it might
not suffer from this kind of compatibility problem. If no patches or older drivers are available, you might be forced to change the mouse and mouse driver to something completely
different to eliminate the problem.

**Symptom 25-6. You see an error: "This pointer device requires a newer ver-
sion"** In virtually all cases, you have the wrong driver installed on the system for your driver. Check the driver and be sure that the driver you are using is appropriate for the particular
mouse. For example, a Logitech or Genius mouse selected in Windows setup can cause this
kind of problem if you have a Microsoft mouse on the system. Change the mouse type under Windows. Under Windows 95, you'll need to remove the old mouse reference from the
Device manager, then use the *Add new hardware* wizard to install the new mouse manually.

**Symptom 25-7. You see an error: "Mouse port disabled or mouse not pre-
sent"** This is almost always a connection or setup problem. Check the signal connector
first. Be sure the mouse cable is not cut or damaged anywhere, and see that it is attached
securely to the serial or PS/2 port. Many newer system BIOS versions now provide an option in the CMOS setup for a mouse port. Check the CMOS setup and see that any entries
for your mouse are enabled properly.

Symptom 25-8. The mouse works for a few minutes, then stops When the
computer is rebooted, the mouse starts working again. This problem often plagues cut-
price mice, and is almost always caused by buildups of static in the mouse. The static
charges are interfering with the mouse circuitry, causing the mouse to stop responding
(though charges are not enough to actually damage the mouse). There are generally three
ways to resolve the problem: (1) spray the surrounding carpet and upholstery with a very
dilute fabric softener to dissipate static buildup, (2) hire an electrician to ensure that the

computer and house wiring are grounded properly, or (3) replace the mouse with a more static-resistant model.

Symptom 25-9. You attempt a doubleclick but get quadrupleclick, or you attempt a singleclick and get a doubleclick This is a phenomenon called "button bounce," and is the result of a hardware defect (broken or poorly buffered mouse buttons). You might be able to clean the mouse buttons by spraying in some good-quality electronic-grade contact cleaner. Otherwise, you'll need to replace the mouse outright.

Symptom 25-10. A single mouse click works, but doubleclick doesn't When this problem occurs, it is almost always because the "doubleclick speed" is set too high in the Windows 95 mouse control panel. Try setting it lower. Click *Start*, select *Settings*, then open the *Control panel*. Doubleclick the *Mouse* icon and adjust the *Doubleclick speed* slider under the *Buttons* tab.

Symptom 25-11. A PS/2 mouse is not detected by a notebook PC under Windows 95 There is a known problem with PS/2 mouse detection on a Toshiba portable computer under Windows 95. You can usually correct the problem by taking the following steps:

1 Shut down the computer entirely and physically disconnect the PS/2 mouse from the PS/2 port.
2 Restart the PC to the DOS mode and create backup copies of your CONFIG.SYS and AUTOEXEC.BAT files.
3 Restart Windows 95 (reboot the PC, if necessary).
4 Click *Start*, select *Settings*, open the *Control panel*, and doubleclick on the *System* icon.
5 Select the *Device manager* tab and doubleclick the *Mouse* entry.
6 Select the mouse entry that is not being detected (i.e., "Toshiba AccuPoint"), and click *Remove*.
7 Select and remove any other mouse entries.
8 Shut down the computer and reconnect the mouse, then turn the PC back on.
9 When the system reboots, it should detect the mouse and attempt to reinstall the appropriate drivers.

If this doesn't fix the problem, a hardware issue could exist. Try a different PS/2 mouse (preferably from a manufacturer different than the current one). If a different make and model PS/2 mouse does not work, the PS/2 port might require service.

Symptom 25-12. Mouse pointer options are not saved This is a known problem when you use the "extra points" features in the Mouse Manager program included with the Microsoft Mouse driver. The pointer options are not saved or written to the MOUSE.INI file when you are running a virus-protection program, such as Microsoft Anti-Virus (MSAV) or Norton Anti-Virus (NAV). To correct this problem, remove the CHKLIST.MS or CHKLIST.CPS file in the directory, which contains the mouse files. To determine the location of that directory, type "set" at the MS-DOS command prompt—it will return a list of locations of various files and memory strings. Look for the MOUSE=

line, then go to that directory and delete the CHKLIST.MS or CHKLIST.CPS file. Reboot the system and try saving options again.

Symptom 25-13. Clicking the right mouse button doesn't start the default context menus of Windows 95 If the Mouse Manager software you're running is using an assignment set for the right button, this assignment will override the Windows 95 default setting of "context menus." Open the Mouse Management software utility and change the assignment for the right button to "Unassigned." Save your changes. The right mouse button will now access the default context menus.

Symptom 25-14. The modem won't start after installing new mouse software For example, this is a known problem when installing Logitech's MouseWare 6.60 (or later) under Windows 95. Sometimes the mouse drivers might detect the modem as a second mouse and try to initialize it. This can cause the modem to go into a busy state. However, you can prevent the mouse drivers from searching the serial port that the modem is using:

1 Download the current mouse driver for Windows 95.
2 Edit the Windows 95 registry by clicking on the *Start* menu and selecting *Run*.
3 Type "C:.EXE" on the *Open* line.
4 Click *OK*. The Registry Editor program will start.
5 Doubleclick on the *HKEY_LOCAL_MACHINE* folder.
6 Doubleclick on the *Software* folder.
7 Doubleclick on the manufacturer's folder (i.e., Logitech).
8 Doubleclick on the manufacturer's driver folder (i.e., MouseWare).
9 Doubleclick on the *CurrentVersion* folder.
10 Click on the *Global* folder.
11 Let's assume the mouse is on COM1 and the modem is on COM2. On the right side of the screen will be a list of value data strings. Doubleclick on the *PortSearchOrder* string. An *Edit string* dialogue box will appear. The *Value data* line will read:

```
COM1, COM2
```

12 Remove the space, the comma, and "COM2," so the line reads:

```
COM1
```

13 If you only plan to use one mouse on the system, change the *MaximumDevices* value data line to "1" using the same steps. This will tell the driver to stop searching for additional mice after the primary mouse has been found.

> If you are not using a serial mouse, remove "Serial" from the "SearchOrder" value data line so that no serial devices are searched for at all. In general, remove any reference to the port that the modem is using.

14 Now click *OK*, and the values under the data value section on the right side of the screen should change. Exit the registry editor (saving is automatic). Shut down the computer and reboot from a cold start so that your changes can take effect.

Symptom 25-15. A two-button "First Mouse" refuses to work on a Packard Bell system The pointer doesn't move, but Windows 95 did not report any problem detecting the mouse. This is a known problem with some Packard Bell computers and the two-button "First Mouse" serial version (M/N: M34). It might be possible to work around the problem by pressing <Ctrl>+<Esc> to open the *Start* menu. Using the arrow keys, highlight *Settings*, then *Control panel*, and press the <Enter> key. Select the *Mouse* icon with the arrow keys, and press the <Enter> key. This will open the *Mouse properties* dialog box. "Tab over" to the *Quick setup* tab. Then, (using the right arrow key) open the *Devices* tab. Once on the *Devices* tab, "Tab over" to the *Add mouse* button and press the <Enter> key. The mouse-control software should now detect the two-button serial mouse, and the pointer should now move properly. Unfortunately, you'll need to perform this procedure each time you restart the system. Otherwise, you should try disabling the built-in serial port and install a different serial card.

You might also exchange the serial version for a PS/2 version, if your system has a dedicated PS/2 style mouse port (be sure to uninstall the mouse software if you plan to exchange the mouse). Go to the Windows 95 *Control panel* and launch the *Add/remove programs* icon. Select the mouse product (i.e., "Logitech MouseWare") and click on the *Add/remove* button. When the message "Uninstall Completed" appears, reboot the system.

Symptom 25-16. A Logitech three-button mouse refuses to work on a Packard Bell computer You install a Logitech three-button mouse on a Packard Bell computer, and when you open the *Enhanced mouse control center* on the *Devices* tab, it states: "Pointing device on unknown port." It also shows only a two-button mouse. In virtually all cases, you'll need to tweak the Registry:

1 Click on the *Start* menu and select *Run*.
2 Type "C:.EXE" on the *Open* line.
3 Click *OK*. The *Registry editor* program will start.
4 Open the *Hkey_Local_Machinennnn>* folder (where *<nnnn>* is an incremental four-digit number starting at 0000).
5 Click on each folder under the *Mouse* folder and delete them until no 000X folders remain.
6 Exit the Registry (saving is automatic) and reboot the system from a cold start.
7 Open the *Enhanced mouse control center* to verify the correct detection of the pointing device.

Symptom 25-17. The mouse pointer moves only vertically The mouse is connected to a PS/2 port under Windows 95. If the mouse works along one axis but not the other, it's usually because of a hardware problem—either the mouse needs to be cleaned or repaired. However, in some cases a software-configuration problem can occur when the mouse driver (i.e., Mouse Power v9.5) is installed on a system with Plug-and-Play BIOS running Windows 95, and the mouse is connected to the PS/2-style mouse port. As soon as you touch the mouse, the pointer darts over the right edge of the screen, and then will move only up and down.

1 To regain control over your computer, reboot in *Safe* mode.
2 Click *Start*, then *Run*, then type "REGEDIT" and press <Enter>.

3 Open the *HKEY_LOCAL_MACHINE* folder and see if "BIOS" is listed under Enum. If it is, then you know the software configuration is causing the problem.

4 Open *HKEY_LOCAL_MACHINEPNP0F13*, and look for a key (usually "05" or "07") under "*PNP0F13." Click on this key to highlight it. The key under "*PNP0F13" should now be highlighted, and the corresponding values should be displayed on the right side of the window. Notice that "string values" have an "ab" icon next to them and "binary values" have a "011" icon next to them.

5 Compare your values to those shown. Edit your entries until all your values shown on the screen match these values:

```
ab    Class         "Mouse"
011   ConfigFlags   00 00 00 00
ab    DeviceDesc    "Mouse Systems v2.18"
ab    Driver        "Mouse\0000"
ab    HardwareID    "*PNP0F0C"
ab    Mfg           "Mouse Systems"
```

6 Open HKEY_LOCAL_MACHINE. There should be multiple keys under Mouse (such as "0000" and "0001"). All but one are to be deleted. Carefully determine which one pertains to your current mouse (by looking at the values associated with each key), and delete all keys under Mouse, except the related one.

7 Be sure that the one remaining key under Mouse is labelled "0000" (rename it, if necessary).

8 Click on the *X* box in the far upper-right corner of the Registry editor to close it.

9 Reboot the computer from a cold start. The computer should reboot in normal mode, and the problem with the mouse and keyboard should be gone.

Further Study

That concludes the material for Chapter 25. Be sure to review the glossary and chapter questions on the accompanying CD. If you have access to the Internet, take a look at some of these mouse and trackball resources:

Microsoft: **http://www.microsoft.com**

Logitech: **http://www.logitech.com**

Genius: **http://www.genius-kye.com/**

Mitsumi: **http://www.mitsumi.com**

Mouse Systems: **http://www.mousesystems.com/**

Mouse Trak: **http://www.mousetrak.com/**

No Hands Mouse: **http://www.footmouse.com/**

26

MODEMS AND

FAX CARDS

CONTENTS AT A GLANCE

**Basic Modem Construction and
Operation**
The internal modem
The external modem
Advanced modem features
Modem commands
Modem initialization strings
Modem modes
Modem negotiation
Reading the lights

Understanding Signal Modulation
BPS vs. baud rate
Modulation schemes

Signaling Standards
Bell standards
ITU (CCITT) standards
MNP standards
File-transfer protocols

Modem Troubleshooting
Checking the command processor
Checking the dialer and telephone
line
Typical communication problems
Symptoms

Further Study

Long before computers ever became "personal," the mainframe and mini computers of the 1960s and 1970s needed to communicate over large geographic distances, which could sometimes stretch across town or around the world. Designers faced the problem of wiring the computers together—stringing a cable across even a few miles represents a serious logistical challenge. Instead of installing a network of new cabling, computer designers realized that they already had a sophisticated, world-wide wiring system in place: the *Public Switched Telephone Network (PSTN)*. By enabling one computer to "call" another and exchange data, computers could communicate over telephone lines as-needed—anywhere a telephone jack is available (even using cellular facilities).

Of course, computers cannot work directly on your telephone line. The digital information processed by computers must be translated (*modulated*) into audible sounds that are carried across telephone lines to a remote location. Sound signals returning over the telephone lines must be converted back into digital information (or demodulated) for the computer. This continuous process of modulation and demodulation between a computer and telephone line is performed by a device called a *MOdulator/DEModulator (MODEM)*. As the number of personal computers has grown into the millions, the demand for faster and more reliable modem communications has resulted in impressive speed and performance. Today's modems have also enabled entirely new developments, such as fax and voice capabilities. This chapter is intended to explain the operations, standards, and connections of today's modems, as well as provide you with a compendium of modem symptoms and solutions.

Basic Modem Construction and Operation

To understand how a modem works and how to react when things go wrong, you should be familiar with the typical sections of a modem circuit. Although most modems today can be fabricated with only a few ASICs and discrete parts, virtually all computer communication systems contain the same essential parts. First, data must be translated from parallel into serial form and back again. Serial data being transmitted must be converted into an audio signal, then placed on an ordinary telephone circuit. Audio signals received from the telephone line must be separated from transmitted signals, then converted back into serial data. All of these activities must occur under the direction of a controller circuit. Finally, a modem uses *Non-Volatile RAM (NVRAM)* to maintain a lengthy list of setup parameters (*S registers*). For the purposes of this book, the two types of modems are: internal and external.

THE INTERNAL MODEM

The internal modem is fabricated as a stand-alone board, which plugs directly into the PC expansion bus. You can see each major modem function detailed in the block diagram of Fig. 26-1. The internal modem contains its own *Universal Asynchronous Receiver/Transmitter (UART)*, which is responsible for manipulating data into and out of serial form. A UART forms the foundation of a serial port. This can represent a serious hardware conflict for your PC—when installing an internal modem, be sure that the IRQ line and I/O address chosen for the UART "serial port" does not conflict with other serial ports (a.k.a. COM ports) already in the system. It might be necessary to disable conflicting ports.

Before being transmitted over telephone lines, serial data must be converted into audio signals. This process is carried out by a modulator circuit. The modulated audio is then coupled to the telephone line using a circuit very similar to that used by ordinary telephones to couple voice. Audio signals are made available to a single RJ11-type (telephone

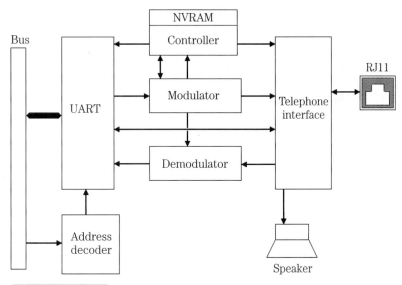

FIGURE 26-1 **Block diagram of an internal modem.**

line) connector at the rear of the modem. Many modems provide a second RJ11 jack for a telephone—this allows you to check the line and make calls while the modem is idle. Signals received from the telephone line must be translated back into serial data. The telephone interface separates received signals and passes them to the demodulator. After demodulation, the resulting serial data is passed to the UART, which converts the serial bits into parallel words that are placed on the system's data bus.

Besides combining and separating modulated audio data, the telephone interface generates the *Dual-Tone Multi-Frequency (DTMF)* dialing signals needed to reach a remote modem—much the same way as a touch-tone telephone. When a remote modem dials in, the telephone interface detects the incoming ring, and alerts the UART to begin negotiating a connection. Finally, the telephone interface drives a small speaker. During the first stages of modem operation, the speaker is often used to hear dial tone, dialing signals, and audio negotiation between the two modems. Once a connection is established, the speaker is usually disabled.

A controller circuit manages the overall operation of the modem, but in a more general sense, it switches the modem between its control and data operating modes. The controller accepts commands from the modulator, which allows modem characteristics and operating parameters to be changed. In the event of power loss or reset conditions, default modem parameters can be loaded from NVRAM. Permanent changes to modem parameters are stored in NVRAM.

THE EXTERNAL MODEM

For all practical intents and purposes, the external modem provides virtually all of the essential functions offered by an internal modem. As you can see by the block diagram of Fig. 26-2, many of the external functions are identical to those of an internal modem. The major difference between modems is that the external modem does not include a built-in UART to provide a serial port. Instead, the external modem relies on a serial port (or

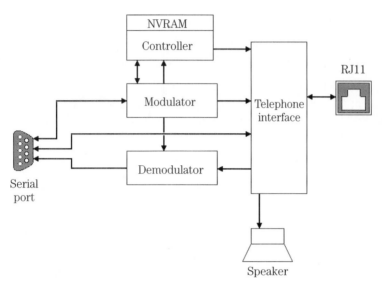

FIGURE 26-2   **Block diagram of an external modem.**

COM port) already configured in the PC. A 9-pin or 25-pin serial cable connects the PC
serial port to the modem. This often makes external modem setup faster and easier than
internal modems because you need not worry about interrupt lines and I/O address settings—hardware conflicts are rare with external modems.

The other practical differences in an external modem is the way it is powered. Where internal modems are powered from the expansion bus, external modems must be powered
from a small ac adapter. In locations where ac outlets are scarce, this might be a problem.
On the other hand, external modems provide a series of signal-status LEDs. The LEDs allow you to easily check the state of serial communications.

ADVANCED MODEM FEATURES

Today's modems do far more than just exchange data between computers. A myriad of
advanced features are built into current modems that you should be aware of—a few of the
more notable advancements are:

x2 technology Although *x2* is trademarked by US Robotics, it is often used generically
to refer to high-speed modem technology used for 56KB modems. x2 technology is a new
method developed for 56KB downloads from the Internet, corporate networks and on-line
services over regular phone lines. Although x2 doesn't support 56KB uploads or 56KB
transfers between modems, it does offer a powerful enhancement for PC users seeking
more speed from the Internet or other online services. You need three elements to support
x2 at 56KB downloads: an ISP or other remote x2-compatible server, an "analog loop" between your home/office and the local central office, and an x2 modem (such as a US Robotics Sportster). However, x2 technology is very sensitive to telephone-line issues, and
must have close to ideal conditions to achieve top-speed downloads. When uploading or
communicating with other modems, an x2 modem typically runs at 28.8KB.

DSVD In addition to simply sending and receiving data, some modern modems incorporate a feature called *Dual Simultaneous Voice and Data (DSVD)*. The modem can carry your analog voice as well as computer data. In effect, the modem becomes a "speakerphone," able to transfer real-time voice and data at the same time (though the bandwidth needed to transfer voice information reduces the available bandwidth for data transfers). Notice that the DSVD feature can only be used between two DSVD modems. To use DSVD, you need a sound board with a microphone (to digitize your voice), as well as a set of speakers (to play the voice from the other end). DSVD has found a small, but powerful, niche among on-line computer gamers who wish to communicate in real-time as they play.

Voice mail Some modern modems are providing advanced voice-mail features that essentially allow the modem (and PC) to serve as an intelligent answering machine or digital information system. When installed and configured properly, voice mail allows you to create "mailboxes," record voice greetings/announcements for each mail box, record messages to each "mailbox," access each "mailbox" remotely, and even support "fax on demand." Voice-mail features are particularly popular with small businesses and *Small-Office Home-Office (SOHO)* environments, looking to automate messaging and information distribution.

Auto-detection/auto-switching Virtually all current modems can detect the difference between a voice call, a modem call, and an incoming fax, and can automatically use the proper software tools to record the voice message (used with voice mail systems), start BBS or other electronic-messaging software to communicate with the calling modem (ideal for remote-access software), or record the fax image to the hard drive.

Distinctive ring Many local phone service areas now support the "distinctive ring" feature, which allows several phone numbers to be assigned to the same physical telephone line—each assigned number rings with a different ringing pattern. Modems that are compatible with "distinctive ring" can be placed on the same physical phone line with other devices, but will only answer when a certain ringing pattern is detected.

Caller ID Modern modems are also able to detect the caller's originating telephone number, which is transmitted to the receiving end of the communications link. In its simplest form, caller ID simply provides an "on-screen" display of the caller's telephone number (used most often when you're receiving calls with the modem in "speakerphone" mode). In its most enhanced form, database software can trap the caller ID number, then automatically pull up contact information, notes of past phone conversations, or a wide range of other caller-related information. This feature is ideal for sales or help-desk services.

MODEM COMMANDS

Modems used to be "dumb" devices. It was almost impossible for them to do such things as answer the ringing telephone line, dial a number, set speaker volume, etc. Hayes Microcomputer Products developed a product called a "Smartmodem," which accepted high-level commands in the form of ASCII text strings. This was dubbed the *Hayes AT command set*, which has been the de-facto standard for modem commands ever since. As a consequence, virtually every modem that is Hayes-compatible is capable of using the AT command set. Ultimately, the AT commands go a long way to simplify the interface between a modem and communication software. Table 26-1 provides an extensive index of the AT commands—this can be particularly helpful when trying to interpret command strings.

TABLE 26-1   INDEX OF THE AT COMMAND SET

Basic AT commands

Note: Settings with an underline (i.e., *F0*) are the default settings for an entry.

(A/) *Repeat Last Command*

(A) *Answer*

(Bx) *CCITT or Bell Modulation*
- **B0** CCITT operation at 300 or 1200bps.
- **B1** BELL operation at 300 or 1200bps.
- **B2** V.23 originate mode: receive 1200bps, transmit 75bps; answer mode: receive 75bps, transmit 1200bps.
- **B3** V.23 originate mode: receive 75bps, transmit 1200bps; answer mode: receive 1200bps, transmit 75bps.

(Dx) *Dial* The valid dial string parameters are described below. Punctuation characters may be used for clarity, with parentheses, hyphen, and spaces being ignored:

0–9	*DTMF digits:* the numbers 0 to 9.
*	*The "star" digit:* (tone dialing only).
#	*The "pound" digit:* (tone dialing only).
!	*Flash:* The modem will go on-hook for a time defined by the value of S29.
,	*Dial pause:* The modem will pause for a time specified by S8 before dialing the digits following ",".
;	*Return to command state:* Added to the end of a dial string, this causes the modem to return to the command state after it processes the portion of the dial string preceding the ";". This allows the user to issue additional AT commands while remaining off-hook. The additional AT commands may be placed in the original command line following the ";" or may be entered on subsequent command lines. The modem will enter call progress only after an additional dial command is issued without the ";" terminator. Use "H" to abort the dial in progress and go back on-hook.
^	*Enable calling tone:* Applicable to current dial attempt only. The calling tone is a 1800-Hz tone every 3–4 seconds that alerts recipient of automatic-calling equipment (as defined in CCITT V.25).
>	*Ground pulse:* If enabled by country specific parameter, the modem will generate a grounding pulse on the Earth relay output.
@	*Wait for silence:* The modem will wait for at least 5 seconds of silence in the call-progress frequency band before continuing with the next dial-string parameter. If the modem does not detect these 5 seconds of silence before the expiration of the call abort timer (S7), the modem will terminate the call attempt with a No answer message. If busy detection is enabled, the modem may terminate the call with the Busy result code. If answer tone arrives during execution of this parameter, the modem handshakes.
A–D	*DTMF letters:* A, B, C, and D.
J	*Fastest speed:* Perform MNP 10 link negotiation at the highest supported speed for this call only.
K	*Power adjustment:* Enable power-level adjustment during MNP 10 link negotiation for this call only.
L	*Re-dial last number:* The modem will re-dial the last valid telephone number. This command must be immediately after the "D," with all the following characters ignored.
P	*Select pulse dialing:* Pulse dial the numbers that follow until a "T" is encountered. Affects current and subsequent dialing.

TABLE 26-1 INDEX OF THE AT COMMAND SET (CONTINUED)

R   *Delay:* This command will cause the modem to wait 10 seconds after dialing, then go into answer mode. This command must be placed at the end of the dial string.

T   *Select tone dialing:* Tone dial the numbers that follow until a "P" is encountered. Affects current and subsequent dialing.

W   *Wait for dial tone:* The modem will wait for a dial tone before dialing the digits following "W". If no dial tone is detected within the time specified by S6, the modem will abort the rest of the sequence, return on-hook, and generate an error message.

(Ex) *Command Echo*
- **E0** Disables command echo.
- **E1** Enables command echo.

(Fx) *Select Line Modulation*
- **F0** Selects auto-detect mode—all connect speeds are possible.
- **F1** Selects V.21 or Bell 103 according to the "B" setting.
- **F2** *Not supported* (some modems use this setting for 600bps).
- **F3** Originator is at 75bps and answerer is at 1200bps.
- **F4** Selects V.22 1200bps or Bell 212A, according to the "B" setting.
- **F5** Selects V.22bis as the only acceptable line modulation.
- **F6** Select V.32bis 4800bps or V.32 4800bps as the only acceptable line modulation.
- **F7** Selects V.32bis 7200bps as the only acceptable line modulation.
- **F8** Selects V.32bis 9600bps or V.32 9600bps as the only acceptable line modulation.
- **F9** Selects V.32bis 12,000bps as the only acceptable line modulation.
- **F10** Selects V.32bis 14,400bps as the only acceptable line modulation.

(Hx) *Disconnect [Hangup]*
- **H0** The modem will release the line if the modem is currently on-line, and will terminate any test (AT&T) that is in progress.
- **H1** If on-hook, the modem will go off-hook and enter the Command mode. The modem will return on-hook after a period of time determined by S7.

(Ix) *Identification*
- **I0** Reports product code.
- **I1** Reports pre-computed checksum from ROM.
- **I2** The modem will respond OK.
- **I3** Reports firmware revision.
- **I4** Reports modem identifier string.
- **I5** Reports Country-code parameter (e.g., "022").
- **I6** Reports modem data pump model and internal code revision.

(Lx) *Speaker Volume*
- **L0** Low speaker volume.
- **L1** Low speaker volume.
- **L2** Medium speaker volume.
- **L3** High speaker volume.

(Mx) *Speaker Control*
- **M0** Speaker is always off.
- **M1** Speaker is on during call establishment, but off when receiving carrier.
- **M2** Speaker is always on.
- **M3** Speaker is off when receiving carrier and during dialing, but on during answering.

(Nx) *Automode Enable*
- **N0** Automode detection is disabled.
- **N1** Automode detection is enabled.

(Ox) *Return to On-Line Data Mode*
- **O0** Enters on-line data mode without a retrain.
- **O1** Enters on-line data mode with a retrain before returning to on-line data mode.
- **O3–14** Forces the modem to a new rate that is user defined (defined in S62).

TABLE 26-1 INDEX OF THE AT COMMAND SET (CONTINUED)

(P) *Set Pulse Dial Default*

(Qx) *Quiet Results Codes*
- **Q0** Enables result codes to the DTE.
- **Q1** Disables result codes to the DTE.

(Sn) *Read/Write S-Registers*
- **n=v** Sets S-register *n* to value *v*.
- **n?** Reports the value of S-register n.

(T) *Set Tone Dial Default*

(Vx) *Result Code Form*
- **V0** Enables short-form (terse) result codes.
- **V1** Enables long-form (verbose) result codes.

(Wx) *Error-Correction Message Control*
- **W0** Upon connection, the modem reports only the DTE speed.
- **W1** Upon connection, the modem reports the line speed, the error-correction protocol, and the DTE speed respectively.
- **W2** Upon connection, the modem reports the DCE speed.

(Xx) *Extended Result Codes*
- **X0** Sends only OK, CONNECT, RING, NO CARRIER, ERROR, and NO ANSWER result codes.
- **X1** Sends only OK, CONNECT, RING, NO CARRIER, ERROR, NO ANSWER, and CONNECT XXXX.
- **X2** Sends only OK, CONNECT, RING, NO CARRIER, ERROR, NO DIAL TONE, NO ANSWER, and CONNECT XXXX.
- **X3** Sends only OK, CONNECT, RING, NO CARRIER, ERROR, NO ANSWER, CONNECT XXXX and BUSY.
- **X4** Enables monitoring of busy tones; sends all messages.

(Yx) *Long-Space Disconnect*
- **Y0** Disables long-space disconnect.
- **Y1** Enables long-space disconnect.

(Zx) *Soft Reset and Restore Profile*
- **Z0** Soft reset and restore stored profile 0.
- **Z1** Soft reset and restore stored profile 1.

AT "&" commands

(&Bx) *Autoretrain*
- **&B0** Hang up on a poorly received signal.
- **&B1** Retrain on a poorly received signal. Hang up if the condition persists.
- **&B2** Do not hang up; do not retrain (i.e., tolerate any line).

(&Cx) *RLSD (DCD) Option*
- **&C0** RLSD remains on at all times.
- **&C1** RLSD follows the state of the carrier.

(&Dx) *DTR Option*
- **&D0** DTR drop is interpreted according to the current &Q setting as follows:
  (&Q0, 5, 6) DTR is ignored (assumed on). Allows operation with DTE's that don't provide DTR.
  (&Q1, 4) DTR drop causes the modem to hang up. Auto-answer is not affected.
  (&Q2, 3) DTR drop causes the modem to hang up. Auto-answer is inhibited.
- **&D1** DTR drop is interpreted according to the current &Q setting as follows:
  (&Q0, 1, 4, 5, 6) DTR drop is interpreted by the modem as if the asynchronous escape sequence had been entered. The modem returns to asynchronous command state without disconnecting.
  (&Q2, 3) DTR drop causes the modem to hang up. Auto-answer is inhibited.

TABLE 26-1   INDEX OF THE AT COMMAND SET (CONTINUED)

- **&D2** DTR drop is interpreted according to the current &Q setting as follows:
  (&Q0–6) DTR drop causes the modem to hang up. Auto-answer is inhibited.
- **&D3** DTR drop is interpreted according to the current &Q setting as follows:
  (&Q0, 1, 4, 5, 6) DTR drop causes the modem to perform a soft reset as if the "Z" command were received. The &Y setting determines which profile is loaded.
  (&Q2, 3) DTR drop causes the modem to hang up. Auto-answer is inhibited.

(&Fx) _Restore Factory Configuration_
- **&F0** Restore factory configuration 0.
- **&F1** Restore factory configuration 1.

(&Gx) _Select Guard Tone_
- **&G0** Disables guard tone.
- **&G1** Disables guard tone.
- **&G2** Selects 1800Hz guard tone.

(&Hn) _Sets Transmit Data (TD) flow control (see also &Rn)_
- **&H0** Flow control disabled
- **&H1** Hardware flow control, Clear to Send (CTS) (default)
- **&H2** Software flow control, XON/XOFF
- **&H3** Hardware and software flow control

(&In) _Sets Receive Data (RD) software flow control (see also &Rn)_
- **&I0** Software flow control disabled (default)
- **&I1** XON/XOFF signals to your modem and remote system
- **&I2** XON/XOFF signals to your modem only

(&Jx) _Telephone Jack Type_
- **&J0** RJ11 telephone jack.
- **&J1** RJ12 or RJ13 telephone jack.

(&Kx) _Flow Control_
- **&K0** Disables flow control.
- **&K3** Enables RTS/CTS flow control.
- **&K4** Enables XON/XOFF flow control.
- **&K5** Enables transparent XON/XOFF flow control.
- **&K6** Enables both RTS/CTS and XON/XOFF flow control.

(&Lx) _Dial Up/Lease Line Option_
- **&L0** Dial line.
- **&L1** Leased line.

(&Mx) _Asynchronous/Synchronous Mode Selection_
- **&M0** Selects direct asynchronous operation.
- **&M1** Selects synchronous connect mode with asynchronous off-line command mode.
- **&M2** Selects synchronous connect mode with asynchronous off-line command mode.
- **&M3** Selects synchronous connect mode.
- **&M4** Hayes AutoSync mode.

(&Nn) _Sets connect speed_
- **&N0** Variable rate (default)
- **&N1** 300bps
- **&N2** 1200bps
- **&N3** 2400bps
- **&N4** 4800bps
- **&N5** 7200bps
- **&N6** 9600bps
- **&N7** 12,000bps
- **&N8** 14,400bps
- **&N9** 16,800bps
- **&N10** 19,200bps
- **&N11** 21,600bps

TABLE 26-1   INDEX OF THE AT COMMAND SET (CONTINUED)

- **&N12** 24,000bps
- **&N13** 26,400bps
- **&N14** 28,800bps
- **&N15** 31,200bps
- **&N16** 33,600bps
- **&N17** 33,333bps
- **&N18** 37,333bps
- **&N19** 41,333bps
- **&N20** 42,666bps
- **&N21** 44,000bps
- **&N22** 45,333bps
- **&N23** 46,666bps
- **&N24** 48,000bps
- **&N25** 49,333bps
- **&N26** 50,666bps
- **&N27** 52,000bps
- **&N28** 53,333bps
- **&N29** 54,666bps
- **&N30** 56,000bps
- **&N31** 57,333bps

(&Px) *Dial Pulse Ratio*
- **&P0** Make=39%, break=61% (at 10pps for the US).
- **&P1** Make=33%, break=67% (at 10pps for Europe).
- **&P2** Make=33%, break=67% (at 20pps for Japan).

(&Qx) *Sync/Async Mode*
- **&Q0** Selects direct asynchronous operation.
- **&Q1** Selects Synchronous connect mode with Async off-line command mode.
- **&Q2** Selects Synchronous connect mode with Async off-line command mode.
- **&Q3** Selects Synchronous connect mode.
- **&Q4** Select AutoSync operation.
- **&Q5** The modem will try to negotiate an error-corrected link.
- **&Q6** Selects asynchronous operation in normal mode (speed buffering).

Starting AutoSync. *Set registers S19, S20, and S25 to the desired values before selecting AutoSync operation with &Q4. After the Connect message is issued, the modem waits the period of time specified by S25 before examining DTR. If DTR is on, the modem enters the synchronous operating state; if DTR is off, the modem terminates the line connection and returns to the asynchronous command state.*

Stopping AutoSync. *AutoSync operation is stopped upon loss of carrier or the on-to-off transition of DTR. Loss of carrier will cause the modem to return to the asynchronous command state. An on-to-off transition of DTR will cause the modem to return to the asynchronous command state and either not terminate the line connection (&D1 active) or terminate the line connection (any other &Dn command active).*

(&Rx) *RTS/CTS Option*
- **&R0** In Sync mode, CTS tracks the state of RTS; the RTS-to-CTS delay is defined by S26. In Async mode, CTS acts according to V.25bis handshake.
- **&R1** In Sync mode, CTS is always ON (RTS transitions are ignored). In Async, CTS will drop only if required by flow control.

(&Sx) *DSR Override*
- **&S0** DSR will remain on at all times.
- **&S1** DSR will become active after answer tone has been detected and inactive after the carrier has been lost.

TABLE 26-1   INDEX OF THE AT COMMAND SET (CONTINUED)

(&Tx) *Test and Diagnostics*
- **&T0** Terminates the test in progress. Clears S16.
- **&T1** Initiates local analog loopback, V.54 Loop 3.
- **&T2** Returns an Error message.
- **&T3** Initiates local digital loopback, V.54 Loop 2.
- **&T4** Enables digital loopback acknowledgment for remote request.
- **&T5** Disables digital loopback acknowledgement for remote request.
- **&T8** Initiates local analog loopback, V.54 Loop 3, with self test.

(&Un) *Sets floor connect speed.*
- **&U0** Disabled (the default)
- **&U1** 300bps
- **&U2** 1200bps
- **&U3** 2400bps
- **&U4** 4800bps
- **&U5** 7200bps
- **&U6** 9600bps
- **&U7** 12,000bps
- **&U8** 14,400bps
- **&U9** 16,800bps
- **&U10** 19,200bps
- **&U11** 21,600bps
- **&U12** 24,000bps
- **&U13** 26,400bps
- **&U14** 28,800bps
- **&U15** 31,200bps
- **&U16** 33,600bps
- **&U17** 33,333bps
- **&U18** 37,333bps
- **&U19** 41,333bps
- **&U20** 42,666bps
- **&U21** 44,000bps
- **&U22** 45,333bps
- **&U23** 46,666bps
- **&U24** 48,000bps
- **&U25** 49,333bps
- **&U26** 50,666bps
- **&U27** 52,000bps
- **&U28** 53,333bps
- **&U29** 54,666bps
- **&U30** 56,000bps
- **&U31** 57,333bps

(&Vx) *Display Current Configuration and Stored Profiles*
- **&V0** View active file, stored Profile 0, and stored phone numbers.
- **&V0** View active file, stored Profile 1, and stored phone numbers.

(&Wx) *Store Current Configuration*
- **&W0** Store the current configuration as Profile 0.
- **&W1** Store the current configuration as Profile 1.

(&Xx) *Sync Transmit Clock Source Option*
- **&X0** The modem generates the transmit clock.
- **&X1** The DTE generates the transmit clock.
- **&X2** The modem derives the transmit clock.

(&Yx) *Designate a Default Reset Profile*
- **&Y0** The modem will use Profile 0.
- **&Y1** The modem will use Profile 1.

TABLE 26-1 INDEX OF THE AT COMMAND SET (CONTINUED)

(&ZL?) *Displays the last executed dial string*

(&Zn?) *Displays the phone number stored at position "n" (n = 0-3)*

(&Zn=x) *Store Telephone Number*
- **&Zn=x** (*n* = 0 to 3, and *x* = dial string)

AT "%" commands

(%BAUD) *Bit Rate Multiplier*

(%Cx) *Enable/Disable Data Compression*
- **%C0** Disables data compression. Resets S46 bit 1.
- **%C1** Enables MNP 5 data-compression negotiation. Resets S46 bit 1.
- **%C2** Enables V.42bis data compression. Sets S46 bit 1.
- **%C3** Enables both V.42bis and MNP 5 data compression. Sets S46 bit 1.

(%CCID) *Enable Caller ID*

(%CD) *Carrier Detect Lamp*

(%CDIA) *Display last DIAG*

(%CIDS) *Store ID Numbers*

(%CRID) *Repeat Last ID*

(%CSIG) *Store SIG Numbers*

(%CXID) *XID Enable*

(%Dx) *V.42bis Dictionary Size*
- **%D0** Dictionary set to 512.
- **%D1** Dictionary set to 1024.
- **%D2** Dictionary set to 2048.
- **%D3** Dictionary set to 4096.

(%Ex) *Enable/Disable Line Quality Monitor and Auto-Retrain Fallback/Fall Forward*
- **%E0** Disable line-quality monitor and auto-retrain.
- **%E1** Enable line-quality monitor and auto-retrain.
- **%E2** Enable line-quality monitor and fallback/fall forward.
- **%E3** Enable line-quality monitor and auto-retrain, but hang up when EQM reaches threshold.

(%Gx) *Auto Fall Forward/Fallback Enable*
- **%G0** Disabled.
- **%G1** Enabled.

(%L) *Line Signal Level*

(%Mx) *Compression Type*
- **%M0** Compression disabled.
- **%M1** Transmit compression only.
- **%M2** Receive compression only.
- **%M3** Two-way compression.

(%P) *Clear Encoder Dictionary*

(%Q) *Line Signal Quality*

(%Sx) *Set Maximum String Length in V.42bis*

(%SCBR) *Call Back Reference Outgoing Calls*

(%SKEY) *Store Authentication Key Outgoing Call*

(%SPRT) *Security Mode—Outgoing Calls*

(%SPNP) *Serial Plug-and-Play Control*

(%SPWD) *Password Outgoing Calls*

(%SSPW) *Supervisor Password Outgoing Calls*

TABLE 26-1 INDEX OF THE AT COMMAND SET (CONTINUED)

(%SUID) *User ID Outgoing Calls*

(%TTx) *PTT Testing Utilities*
- **%TT00–%TT09** DTMF tone dial digits 0 to 9.
- **%TT0A** DTMF digit *.
- **%TT0B** DTMF digit A.
- **%TT0C** DTMF digit B.
- **%TT0D** DTMF digit C.
- **%TT0E** DTMF digit #.
- **%TT0F** DTMF digit D.
- **%TT10** V.21 channel 1 mark (originate) symbol.
- **%TT11** V.21 channel 2 mark symbol.
- **%TT12** V.23 backward channel mark symbol.
- **%TT13** V.23 forward channel mark symbol.
- **%TT14** V.22 originate (call mark) signalling at 600bps (not supported).
- **%TT15** V.22 originate (call mark) signalling at 1200bps.
- **%TT16** V.22bis originate (call mark) signalling at 2400bps.
- **%TT17** V.22 answer signalling (guard tone, if PTT required).
- **%TT18** V.22bis answer signalling (guard tone, if required).
- **%TT19** V.21 channel 1 space symbol.
- **%TT20** V.32 9600bps.
- **%TT21** V.32bis 14,400bps.
- **%TT1A** V.21 channel 2 space symbol.
- **%TT1B** V.23 backward-channel space symbol.
- **%TT1C** V.23 forward-channel space symbol.
- **%TT30** Silence (on-line), i.e., go off-hook.
- **%TT31** V.25 answer tone.
- **%TT32** 1800-Hz guard tone.
- **%TT33** V.25 calling tone (1300Hz).
- **%TT34** Fax calling tone (1100Hz).
- **%TT40** V.21 channel 2.
- **%TT41** V.27ter 2400bps.
- **%TT42** V.27ter 4800bps.
- **%TT43** V.29 7200bps.
- **%TT44** V.29 9600bps.
- **%TT45** V.17 7200bps long train.
- **%TT46** V.17 7200bps short train.
- **%TT47** V.17 9600bps long train.
- **%TT48** V.17 9600bps short train.
- **%TT49** V.17 12,000bps long train.
- **%TT4A** V.17 12,000bps short train.
- **%TT4B** V.17 14,400bps long train.
- **%TT4C** V.17 14,400bps short train.

AT "\" commands

(\Ax) *Select Maximum MNP Block Size*
- **\A0** 64 characters
- **\A1** 128 characters
- **\A2** 192 characters
- **\A3** 256 characters
- **\A4** Max 32 characters (for ETC enhanced-throughput cellular).

(\Bx) *Transmit Break to Remote*
- **\B1–\B9** Break length in 100-ms units (default = 3 non-error-corrected mode only)

TABLE 26-1 INDEX OF THE AT COMMAND SET (CONTINUED)

(\Cx) *Set Autoreliable Buffer*
- **\C0** Does not buffer data.
- **\C1** Buffers data on the answering modem for 4 seconds.
- **\C2** Does not buffer data on the answering modem.

(\Ex) *Optimize Local Echo*

(\Gx) *Modem-to-Modem Flow Control (XON/XOFF)*
- **\G0** Disables modem-to-modem XON/XOFF flow control.
- **\G1** Enables modem-to-modem XON/XOFF flow control.

(\Jx) *Constant DTE Speed Option*
- **\J0** DCE and DTE rates are independent.
- **\J1** DTE rate adjusts to DCE connection rate after on-line.

(\Kx) *Break Control* If the modem receives a break from the DTE when the modem is operating in data transfer mode:
- **\K0** Enter on-line command mode, no break sent to the remote modem.
- **\K1** Clear data buffers and send break to remote modem.
- **\K2** Same as \K0.
- **\K3** Send break to remote modem immediately.
- **\K4** Same as \K0.
- **\K5** Send break to remote modem in sequence with transmitted data.

If the modem is in the On-line command state (waiting for AT commands) during a data connection, and the \B command is received in order to send a break to the remote modem:
- **\K0** Clear data buffers and send break to remote modem.
- **\K1** Clear data buffers and send break to remote modem (same as \K0).
- **\K2** Send break to remote modem immediately.
- **\K3** Send break to remote modem immediately (same as \K2).
- **\K4** Send break to remote modem in sequence with data.
- **\K5** Send break to remote modem in sequence with data (same as \K4).

If there is a break received from a remote modem during a non-error-corrected connection:
- **\K0** Clears data buffers and sends break to the DTE.
- **\K1** Clears data buffers and sends break to the DTE (same as \K0).
- **\K2** Send a break immediately to DTE.
- **\K3** Send a break immediately to DTE (same as \K2).
- **\K4** Send a break in sequence with received data to DTE.
- **\K5** Send a break in sequence with received data to DTE (same as \K4).

(\Lx) *MNP Block/Stream Mode Select*
- **\L0** Use stream mode for MNP connection.
- **\L1** Use interactive block mode for MNP connection.

(\Nx) *Operating Mode*
- **\N0** Selects normal-speed buffered mode.
- **\N1** Selects direct mode.
- **\N2** Selects reliable (error correction) mode.
- **\N3** Selects auto reliable mode.
- **\N4** Selects LAPM error-correction mode.
- **\N5** Selects MNP error-correction mode.

(\O) *Originate Reliable Link Control*

(\Qx) *DTE Flow Control Options*
- **\Q0** Disables flow control.
- **\Q1** XON/XOFF software flow control.
- **\Q2** CTS flow control to the DTE.
- **\Q3** RTS/CTS hardware flow control.

(\S) *Report Active Configuration*

TABLE 26-1   INDEX OF THE AT COMMAND SET (CONTINUED)

(\Tx) *Set Inactivity Timer*
- **n=0** Disable the inactivity timer.
- **n=1–90** Length in minutes.

(\U) *Accept Reliable Link Control*

(\Vx) *Protocol Result Code*
- **\V0** Disable protocol result code (i.e., CONNECT 9600).
- **\V1** Enable protocol result code (i.e., CONNECT 9600/LAPM).

(\Xx) *Set XON/XOFF Pass-through Option*
- **\X0** If XON/XOFF flow control enabled, do not pass XON/XOFF to remote modem or local DTE.
- **\X1** Always pass XON/XOFF to the remote modem or local DTE.

(\Y) *Switch to Reliable Operation*

(\Z) *Switch to Normal Operation*

AT "-" commands

(–Jx) *Set V.42 Detection Phase*
- **–J0** Disables the V.42 detection phase.
- **–J1** Enables the V.42 detection phase.

(–Kx) *MNP Extended Services*
- **–K0** Disables V.42 LAPM to MNP 10 conversion.
- **–K1** Enables V.42 LAPM to MNP 10 conversion.
- **–K2** Enables V.42 LAPM to MNP 10 conversion; inhibits MNP Extended Services.

(–Qx) *Enable Fallback to V.22 bis/V.22*
- **–Q0** Disables fallback to 2400bps (V.22bis) and 1200bps (V.22). Fallback only to 4800bps.
- **–Q1** Enables fallback to 2400bps (V.22bis) and 1200bps (V.22).

(–SDR=n) *Distinctive Ring Reporting*
- **–SDR=1** Type 1 Distinctive ring detect
- **–SDR=2** Type 2 Distinctive ring detect
- **–SDR=3** Type 1 and Type 2 Distinctive ring detect
- **–SDR=4** Type 3 Distinctive ring detect
- **–SDR=5** Type 1 and Type 3 Distinctive ring detect
- **–SDR=6** Type 2 and Type 3 Distinctive ring detect
- **–SDR=7** Types 1, 2, and 3 Distinctive ring detect

Distinctive Ring Types

Type	On	Off	On	Off	On	Off	Sound
1	2.0	4.0					Rinnnnnnnnnng
2	0.8	0.4	0.8	4.0			Ring Ring
3	0.4	0.2	0.4	0.2	0.8	4.0	Ring Ring Rinnng

(–SEC=n) *LAPM and MNP Link Control*
- **–SEC=0** Disable LAPM or MNP10. EC transmit level set in register S91.
- **–SEC=1, 0–30** Enable LAPM or MNP10. EC transmit level set to value after comma (0 to 30).

(–SKEY) *Program Key*

(–SPRT) *Remote Security Mode*

(–SPWD) *Program Password*

(–SSE) *Simultaneous Voice Data*

(–SSG) *Set DSVD Receive Gain*

(–SSKY) *Program Supervisor Key*

TABLE 26-1   INDEX OF THE AT COMMAND SET (CONTINUED)

(–SSP) *Select DVSD Port*

(–SSPW) *Supervisor Password*

(–SUID) *Program User ID*

(–V) *Display Root Firmware Version Number*

AT " commands

("Hx) *V.42bis Compression Control*
- "H0 Disable V.42bis.
- "H1 Enable V.42bis only when transmitting data.
- "H2 Enable V.42bis only when receiving data.
- "H3 Enable V.42bis for both directions.

("Nx) *V.42bis Dictionary Size*
- "N0 512bytes.
- "N1 1024bytes.
- "N2 1536bytes.

("Ox) *Select V.42bis Maximum String Length*
- n=6–64
- n=32

AT "~" commands

(~Dx) *Factory Configured Operating Profile*
- ~D0 Disable (No error correction, no data compression)
- ~D1 MNP4
- ~D2 MNP5
- ~D3 V.42
- ~D4 V.42bis

AT "~~" commands

(~~Lx) *Digital Line Current Sensing On/Off*
- ~~L0 Turn off digital line-current sensing.
- ~~L1 Turn on digital line current sensing.

(~~S=m) *Digital Line Over-Current Sense Time Set*
- m=0 through 9
- m=4

(~~S?) *Display Line Over-Current Sense Time Display*

AT "+" fax commands

Some modems support fax commands conforming to EIA standard 578. These commands are given here with short descriptions - they also typically support error correction and V.17terbo at 19.2KB.

(+FAA) *Auto Answer Mode Parameter*

(+FAXERR=x) *Fax Error Value Parameter*

(+FBOR=x) *Phase C Data Bit Order Parameter*

(+FBUF?) *Read the Buffer Size*

(+FCLASS?) *Service Class Indication*
- +FCLASS? 000 if in data mode; 001 if in fax class 1.

(+FCLASS=x) *Service Class Capabilities*
- +FCLASS? 0 - modem is set up for data mode.
    0,1 - modem is capable of data and fax class I services.

TABLE 26-1 INDEX OF THE AT COMMAND SET (CONTINUED)

(+FCLASS=n) *Service Class Selection*
- **+FCLASS=0** Select data mode
- **+FCLASS=1** Select fax class 1

(+FCR) *Capability to Receive*

(+FDCC=x) *Modem Capabilities Parameter*

(+FDCS=x) *Current Session Results*

(+FDIS=x) *Current Session Negotiation Parameters*

(+FDR) *Begin or Continue Phase C Receive Data*

(+FDT=x) *Data Transmission*

(+FET=x) *Transmit Page Punctuation*

(+FK) *Terminate Session*

(+FLID=x) *Local ID String Parameter*

(+FMDL?) *Request Modem Model*

(+FMFR?) *Request Modem IC Manufacturer*

(+FPHCTO) *Phase C Time Out*

(+FPTS=x) *Page Transfer Status*

(+FREV?) *Request Modem Revision*

(+FRH=?) *FAX SDLC Receive Capabilities*

(+FRH=n) *Modem Accept Training (SDLC)*

(+FRM=?) *FAX Normal Mode Receive Capabilities*

(+FRM=n) *Modem Accept Training*

(+FRS=?) *FRS Range Capabilities*

(+FRS=n) *Receive Silence*
- **+FRS=4** i.e., Wait 40 ms for silence.

(+FTH=?) *FAX SDLC Mode Transmit Capabilities*

(+FTH=n) *Modem Initiate Training (SDLC)*

(+FTM=?) *FAX Normal Mode Transmit Capabilities*

(+FTM=n) *Modem Initiate Training*

(+FTS=?) *FTS Range Capabilities*

(+FTS=n) *Transmission Silence*
- **+FTS=5** i.e., Fax transmission silence for 50 ms.

(+VCID) *Caller ID Service*

Other AT commands

(_+BRC+_) *Remote Escape into BRC State (from Host Online Data Mode)*

($BRC) *Enable/Disable Host*

(#CID) *Enable Caller ID Detection*

(:E) *Compromise Equalizer Enable*
- **:E0** Disables the equalizer.
- **:E1** Enables the equalizer.

($GIVEBRC) *Enter BRC State (from Target Online Command State)*

(*Hx) *Link Negotiation Speed*
- ***H0** Link negotiation occurs at the highest supported speed.
- ***H1** Link negotiation occurs at 1200bps.
- ***H2** Link negotiation occurs at 4800bps.

TABLE 26-1 INDEX OF THE AT COMMAND SET (CONTINUED)

()Mx) *Enable Cellular Power Level Adjustment*
- **)M0** Disables power level adjustment during MNP 10 link negotiation.
- **)M1** Enables power level adjustment during MNP 10 link negotiation.

(@Mx) *Initial Cellular Power Level Setting*

- **@M0** −26 dBm
- **@M1** −30 dBm
- **@M2** −10 dBm
- **@M26** −26 dBm

Virtually all AT command strings start with the prefix "AT" (Attention). For example, the command string: "ATZE1Q0V1" contains five separate commands: attention (AT), reset the modem to its power-up defaults (Z), enable the command echo to send command characters back to the sender (E1), send command result codes back to the PC (Q0), and select text result codes, which causes words to be used as result codes (V1). Although this might seem like a mouthful, a typical modem can accept command strings up to 40 characters long. The term *result codes* are the messages that the modem generates when a command string is processed. Table 26-2 outlines a series of typical result codes. Either numbers (default) or words (using the V1 command) can be returned. When a command is processed correctly, a result code OK is produced, or CONNECT, when a successful connection is established.

Many attributes of the Hayes-compatible modem are programmable. To accommodate this feature, each parameter must be held in a series of memory locations (called *S-registers*). Each S-register is described in Table 26-3. For example, the default escape sequence for the AT command set is a series of three plusses: "+++." You could change this character by writing a new ASCII character to register S2. For the most part, default S-register values are fine for most work, but you can often optimize the modem's operation by experimenting with the register values. Because S-register contents must be maintained after power is removed from the modem, the registers are stored in non-volatile RAM (NVRAM).

MODEM INITIALIZATION STRINGS

One of the most difficult steps to configuring a new modem (or new modem software) is the proper use of *initialization strings*. Initialization strings (or *init strings*, as they are sometimes called) are vital to set up the modem properly before each use; otherwise, the modem will not behave as expected (if it works at all). There are strings for CCITT and ISDN modems. Keep in mind that these initialization strings are not absolute—except for the "AT" at the start of each line, you can modify each string as required for your own system and telephone line.

TABLE 26-2 LIST OF TYPICAL MODEM RESULT CODES

RESPONSE CODE #	VERBOSE	DEFINITION
0	OK	The OK code is returned by the modem to acknowledge execution of a command line.
1	CONNECT	Sent alone when speed is 300bps.
2	RING	The modem sends this result code when incoming ringing is detected on the line.
3	NO CARRIER	No modem carrier signal is detected.
4	ERROR	Generated from AT command string errors, if a command cannot be executed, or if a parameter is outside of range.
5	CONNECT 1200	Connection at 1200bps.
6	NO DIAL TONE	No dial tone was received from the local line.
7	BUSY	A busy tone has been detected.
8	NO ANSWER	The remote modem does not answer properly.
9	CONNECT 600	Connection at 600bps.
10	CONNECT 2400	Connection at 2400bps.
11	CONNECT 4800	Connection at 4800bps.
12	CONNECT 9600	Connection at 9600bps.
13	CONNECT 14400	Connection at 14,400bps.
14	CONNECT 19200	Connection at 19,200bps.
15	CONNECT 16800	Connection at 16,800bps.
16	CONNECT 19200	Connection at 19,200bps.
17	CONNECT 38400	Connection at 38,400bps.
18	CONNECT 57600	Connection at 57,600bps.
22	CONNECT 1200TX/75RX	Connection at 1200bps/75bps.
23	CONNECT 75TX/1200RX	Connection at 75bps/1200bps.
24	CONNECT 7200	Connection at 7200bps.
25	CONNECT 12000	Connection at 12,000bps.
26	CONNECT 1200/75	Connection at 1200bps/75bps (V.23).
27	CONNECT 75/1200	Connection at 75bps/1200bps (V.23).
28	CONNECT 38400	Connection at 38,400bps.
29	CONNECT 21600	Connection at 21,600bps.
30	CONNECT 24000	Connection at 24,000bps.
31	CONNECT 26400	Connection at 26,400bps.
32	CONNECT 28800	Connection at 28,800bps.
33	CONNECT 115200	Connection at 115.2 Kbps.
35	DATA	Modem data is present.
40	CARRIER 300	A V.21 or Bell 103 carrier has been detected on the line.
42	CARRIER 75/1200	A V.23 backward-channel carrier has been detected on the line.
43	CARRIER 1200/75	A V.23 forward-channel carrier has been detected on the line.
44	CARRIER 1200/75	A V.23 forward-channel carrier has been detected on the line.

TABLE 26-2 LIST OF TYPICAL MODEM RESULT CODES (CONTINUED)

RESPONSE CODE #	VERBOSE	DEFINITION
45	CARRIER 75/1200	A V.23 backward-channel carrier has been detected on the line.
46	CARRIER 1200	The high- or low-channel carrier in either V.22 or Bell 212 mode has been detected on the line.
47	CARRIER 2400	The high- or low-channel carrier in V.22bis or V.34 mode has been detected on the line.
48	CARRIER 4800	The channel carrier in V.32, V.32bis, or V.34 has been detected on the line.
49	CARRIER 7200	The channel carrier in V.32bis or V.34 has been detected.
50	CARRIER 9600	The channel carrier in V.32, V.32bis, or V.34 mode has been detected on the line.
51	CARRIER 12,000	The channel carrier in V.32bis or V.34 mode has been detected.
52	CARRIER 14,400	The channel carrier in V.32bis or V.34 mode has been detected.
53	CARRIER 16,800	The channel carrier in V.32terbo or V.34 mode has been detected on the line.
54	CARRIER 19,200	The channel carrier in V.32terbo or V.34 mode has been detected on the line.
55	CARRIER 21,600	The channel carrier in V.34 mode has been detected on the line.
56	CARRIER 24,000	The channel carrier in V.34 mode has been detected on the line.
57	CARRIER 26,400	The channel carrier in V.34 mode has been detected on the line.
58	CARRIER 28,800	The channel carrier in V.34 mode has been detected on the line.
66	COMPRESSION: CLASS 5	The modem has connected with MNP Class-5 data compression.
67	COMPRESSION: V.42bis	The modem has connected with V.42bis data compression.
69	COMPRESSION: NONE	The modem has connected without data compression.
70	PROTOCOL: NONE	The modem has connected without any form of error correction.
76	PROTOCOL: NONE	The modem has connected without any form of error correction.
77	PROTOCOL: LAP-M	The modem has connected with V.42 LAPM error correction.
80	PROTOCOL: MNP	The modem has connected with MNP error correction.
81	PROTOCOL: MNP 2	The modem has connected with MNP error correction.

TABLE 26-2 LIST OF TYPICAL MODEM RESULT CODES (CONTINUED)

RESPONSE CODE #	VERBOSE	DEFINITION
82	PROTOCOL: MNP 3	The modem has connected with MNP error correction.
83	PROTOCOL: MNP 2, 4	The modem has connected with MNP error correction.
84	PROTOCOL: MNP 3, 4	The modem has connected with MNP error correction.
151	CONNECT 31,200	Connection at 31,200bps.
152	CONNECT 31,200/ARQ	Connection at 31,200bps with Automatic Repeat Request.
153	CONNECT 31,200/V34	Connection at 31,200bps with fallback to 28.8KB (V.34).
154	CONNECT 31,200/ARQ/V34	Connection at 31,200bps with ARQ and fallback to 28.8KB.
155	CONNECT 33,600	Connection at 33,600bps.
156	CONNECT 33,600/ARQ	Connection at 33,600bps with Automatic Repeat Request.
157	CONNECT 33,600/V34	Connection at 33,600bps with fallback to 28.8KB (V.34).
158	CONNECT 33,600/ARQ/V34	Connection at 33,600bps with ARQ and fallback to 28.8KB.

TABLE 26-3 INDEX OF S-REGISTER ASSIGNMENTS

REGISTER	FUNCTION	RANGE	UNITS	DEFAULT
S0	Rings to auto-answer	0–255	Rings	0
S1	Ring counter	0–255	Rings	0
S2	Escape character	0–255	ASCII	43
S3	Carriage-return character	0–127	ASCII	13
S4	Line-feed character	0–127	ASCII	10
S5	Backspace character	0–255	ASCII	8
S6	Wait time for dial tone	2–255	seconds	4
S7	Wait for carrier	1–255	seconds	50
S8	Pause time for (,) comma	0–255	seconds	2
S9	Carrier-detect response time	1–255	$\frac{1}{10}$ sec	6
S10	Carrier-loss disconnect time	1–255	$\frac{1}{10}$ sec	14
S11	Touch-tone (DTMF) duration	50–255	$\frac{1}{1000}$ sec	95
S12	Escape-code guard time	0–255	$\frac{2}{100}$ sec	50
S13	Reserved	—	—	—
S14	General bit-mapped options	—	—	138 (8Ah)
S15	Reserved	—	—	—
S16	Test-mode bit-map options (&T)	—	—	0

TABLE 26-3 INDEX OF S-REGISTER ASSIGNMENTS (CONTINUED)

REGISTER	FUNCTION	RANGE	UNITS	DEFAULT
S17	Reserved	—	—	—
S18	Test timer	0-255	seconds	0
S19	Auto-sync bit-map register	—	—	0
S20	AutoSync HDLC address or BSC sync character	0–255	—	0
S21	V.24/General bit-map options	—	—	4 (04h)
S22	Speaker/Results bit-map options	—	—	118 (76h)
S23	General bit-map options	—	—	55 (37h)
S24	Sleep inactivity timer	0–255	seconds	1
S25	Delay to DTR off	0–255	$\frac{1}{100}$ sec	5
S26	RTS-to-CTS delay	0–255	$\frac{1}{100}$ sec	1
S27	General bit-map options	—	—	73 (49h) with ECC 74 (4Ah) without ECC
S28	General bit-map options	—	—	0
S29	Flash-dial modifier time	0–255	10 ms	70
S30	Disconnect activity timer	0–255	10 sec	0
S31	General bit-map options	—	—	194 (C2h)
S32	XON character	0–255	ASCII	17 (11h)
S33	XOFF character	0–255	ASCII	19 (13h)
S34	Reserved	—	—	—
S35	Reserved	—	—	—
S36	LAPM failure control	—	—	7
S37	Line-connection speed	—	—	0
S38	Delay before forced hangup	0–255	seconds	20
S39	Flow control	—	—	3
S40	General bit-map options	—	—	105 (69h) No MNP 10 107 (6Bh) MNP 10
S41	General bit-mapped options	—	—	131 (83h)
S43	Auto fallback character for MNP negotiation	0–255	—	13
S44	Data framing	—	—	—
S46	Data compression control	—	—	136 (no compression) 138 (with compression)
S46*	Automatic sleep timer	0–255	100 ms	100
S47	Forced sleep timer with Powerdown mode in PCMCIA	0–255	100 ms	10
S48	V.42 Negotiation control	—	—	7
S49	Buffer low limit	—	—	—
S50	Buffer high limit	—	—	—
S50*	FAX/Data-mode selection	—	—	0 (data mode) 1 (fax mode)
S53	Global PAD configuration	—	—	—
S55	AutoStream protocol request	—	—	—

TABLE 26-3 INDEX OF S-REGISTER ASSIGNMENTS (CONTINUED)

REGISTER	FUNCTION	RANGE	UNITS	DEFAULT
S56	AutoStream protocol status	—	—	—
S57	Network options register	—	—	—
S58	BTLZ string length	6–64	bytes	32
S59	Leased-line failure alarm	—	—	—
S60	Leased-line failure action	—	—	—
S61	Leased-line retry number	—	—	—
S62	Leased-line restoral options	—	—	—
S62*	DTE rate status	0–17	—	16 (57600bps)
S63	Leased-line transmit level	—	—	—
S64	Leased-line receive level	—	—	—
S69	Link layer k protocol	—	—	—
S70	Max. number of retransmissions	—	—	—
S71	Link layer timeout	—	—	—
S72	Loss of flag idle timeout	—	—	—
S72*	DTE speed select	0–18	—	0 (last autobaud)
S73	No activity timeout	—	—	—
S74	Minimum incoming LCN	—	—	—
S75	Minimum incoming LCN	—	—	—
S76	Maximum incoming LCN	—	—	—
S77	Maximum incoming LCN	—	—	—
S78	Outgoing LCN	—	—	—
S79	Outgoing LCN	—	—	—
S80	X.25 packet-level N20 parameter	—	—	—
S80*	Soft switch functions	—	—	1
S81	X.25 packet-level T20 parameter	—	—	—
S82	LAPM break control	—	—	128 (40h)
S84	ASU negotiation	—	—	—
S85	ASU negotiation status	—	—	—
S86	Call failure reason code	0–255	—	—
S87	Fixed-speed DTE interface	—	—	—
S91	PSTN transmit attenuation level	0–15	-dBm	10
S92	Fax transmit attenuation level	0–15	-dBm	10
S92*	MI/MIC options	—	—	—
S93	V.25bis async interface speed	—	—	—
S94	V.25bis mode control	—	—	—
S95	Result-code messages control	—	—	0
S97	V.32 late connecting handshake timing	—	—	—
S99	Leased-line transmit level	0–15	-dBm	10
S101	Distinctive ring reporting	0–63	—	0
S105	Frame size	—	—	—
S108	Signal-quality selector	—	—	—

TABLE 26-3 INDEX OF S-REGISTER ASSIGNMENTS (CONTINUED)

REGISTER	FUNCTION	RANGE	UNITS	DEFAULT
S109	Carrier-speed selector	—	—	—
S110	V.32/V.32bis selector	—	—	—
S113	Calling tone control	—	—	—
S116	Connection timeout	—	—	—
S121	Use of DTR	—	—	—
S122	V.13 selection	—	—	—
S141	Detection phase timer	—	—	—
S142	Online character format	—	—	—
S143	KDS handshake mode	—	—	—
S144	Autobaud group selection	—	—	—
S150	V.42 options	—	—	—
S151	Simultaneous voice data control	—	—	—
S154	Force port speed	—	—	—
S157	Timeout result code	—	—	—
S201	Cellular transmit level (MNP 10)	10–63	—	58 (3Ah)
S202	Remote-access escape character	0–255	ASCII	170

* The register might be used for different purposes by some modems.

MODEM MODES

The modem is always in one of two primary modes: the command mode or the data mode. When first switched on (or reset), the modem starts up in *command mode*. In this mode, the controller circuit (sometimes called a *command processor*) is constantly checking to see if you have typed a valid AT command. When the modem receives a valid command, it executes that command for you. While your modem is in the command mode, you can instruct it to answer the telephone, change an S-Register value, hang up or dial the telephone, and perform any number of other command functions.

The other mode is the *data mode*. In the data mode, your modem is transmitting all of the data it receives from your computer or terminal along the telephone line to the remote modem. Your modem is constantly checking the state of the *Data Carrier Detect (DCD)* and *Data Terminal Ready (DTR)* signals (depending on the system configuration). It is also watching the local data stream for a command-mode escape sequence. The default escape sequence the AT command set is: "+++." When the proper escape sequence or a change in the state of the DCD or DTR signal occurs, the modem returns to a command mode, where it waits for the next AT command.

MODEM NEGOTIATION

Now that you have seen the essential elements of a modem and learned about modem signaling, you can use that background to form a picture of how the modem actually works. You see, modem communication is not an event—it is a process whose success depends on not only your modem, but on the modem and PC you are trying to communicate with.

This part of the chapter is intended to familiarize you with an operating session for a typical modem.

Communication begins when you instruct the communication software to establish a connection. Control signals sent to the selected serial port causes the UART to assert the *Data Terminal Ready (DTR) signal*. This tells the attached modem that the PC is turned on and ready to transmit. The modem responds by asserting the *Data Set Ready (DSR) line*. The serial port receives this signal and tells the software that the modem is ready—both DTR and DSR must be present for communication to take place.

The communication software then sends an AT initialization string to the COM port (which forwards the string to the modem). In the command mode, the controller circuit interprets the initialization string, which tells the modem to go off hook (get dial tone), then dial the telephone number of the destination modem. Dialing can occur in pulse (rotary) or tone mode, depending on the initialization string. The modem transmits an acknowledgment back to the COM port—this is often displayed right on the communication software window. The line at the destination end begins to ring. If configured properly, and running communication software of its own, the remote modem will pick up the ringing line and a complete wiring path will be established between the two modems.

When the destination modem picks up the line, your local modem sends out a standard tone (a carrier tone)—this lets the remote modem know it's being called by another modem. If the remote modem recognizes the carrier, it sends out an even higher-pitched tone. You can often hear these tones when your modem is equipped with a speaker. Once your modem recognizes the remote modem, it sends a *Carrier Detect (CD) signal* to the serial port. These mutual carriers will be modulated to exchange data.

OK, both modems know they are talking to other modems, but now there has to be a mutual agreement on how they'll exchange data. They must agree on transmission speed, the proper size of a data packet, the signaling bits on each end of the data packet, whether or not parity will be used, and if the modems will operate in half- or full-duplex mode—both modems must settle on these parameters or the data exchanged between them will make no sense. This process is known as *negotiation*. Assuming that the negotiation process is successful, both modems can now exchange data.

When the communication software attempts to send data, it tells the serial port to assert the *Request-to-Send (RTS) signal*. This checks to see if your modem is free to receive data. If the PC is busy doing something else (such as disk access), it will disable the RTS signal until it is ready to resume sending. When the modem is ready for data, it will return a *Clear-to-Send (CTS) signal* to the serial port. The PC can then begin sending data to the modem, and receiving data returned from the remote end. If the modem gets backed up with work, it will drop the CTS line until it is ready to resume communication. Because a standard system of tones is used, both modems can exchange data simultaneously. Data can now be exchanged between the two systems simultaneously.

When the time comes to terminate the connection, the communication software will send another AT command string to the serial port that causes it to break the connection. If the connection is broken by the remote modem, the local modem will drop the Carrier-Detect line. The communication software will interpret this as a "Dropped Carrier" condition. That is basically all the phases involved in modem communication. If you're looking for more details on modem connections, Table 26-4 highlights the specific connect-sequences for V.22bis and V.32 modems.

TABLE 26-4 CONNECT SEQUENCES FOR V.22BIS AND V.32 MODEMS

V.22bis

- **Step 1:** _Pickup_ The receiving modem picks up the ringing line (goes "off-hook"). It then waits at least two seconds. This is known as a _billing delay_, and is required by the telephone company to ensure that the connection has been properly established. No data transfer is allowed during the billing delay.
- **Step 2:** _Answer Tone_ The receiving modem transmits an answer tone back to the network. A 2100Hz tone lasts for about 3.3 seconds. An answer tone serves two purposes. First, you can hear this tone in the receiving modem's speaker, so manual modem users know when to place their modem into data mode. Even more important, the answer tone is used by the telephone network to disable echo suppressers in the connection in order to allow optimum data through-put. If echo suppressers remain active, data transfer will be half-duplex (one direction at a time). The answering modem then goes silent for about 75 ms to separate the answer tone from data.
- **Step 3:** _The USB1 Signal_ The receiving modem then transmits alternating binary 1 s at 1200 bps (known as the USB1 signal). This results in the static sound you hear just after the answer tone. The sending modem detects the USB1 signal in about 155 ms, then falls silent for about 456 ms.
- **Step 4:** _The S1 Signal_ After the 456-ms silence, the sending modem transmits double digits (i.e., 00 and 11) at 1200bps for 100 ms (the _S1_ signal). An older Bell 212 or V.22 modem does not send the S1 signal, so if the S1 signal is absent, the receiving V.22bis modem will fall back to 1200bps. The receiving modem (still generating a USB1 signal) receives the S1 signal. It responds by sending a 100 ms burst of S1 signal so that the sending modem knows the receiving modem can handle 2400bps operation. At this point, both modems know whether they will be operating in 1200bps or 2400bps mode.
- **Step 5:** _The SB1 Signal_ At this point, the sending modem sends scrambled 1 s at 1200bps (the SB1 signal). The "scrambling" creates white noise, which checks power across the whole audio bandwidth. The receiving modem then replies with the SB1 signal for 500 ms.
- **Step 6:** _Ready to Answer_ After 500 ms, the receiving modem switches starts sending scrambled 1 s at 2400bps for 200 ms. A full 600 ms after getting the SB1 signal from the receiving modem, the sending modem also sends scrambled 1 s at 2400bps for 200 ms. After both modems have finished their final 200-ms transmissions, they are ready to pass data.

V.32

- **Step 1:** _Pickup_ The receiving modem picks up the ringing line (goes "off-hook"). It then waits at least 2 seconds. This is known as a _billing delay_, and is required by the telephone company to ensure that the connection has been properly established. As with the V.22bis modem, no data transfer is allowed during the billing delay.
- **Step 2:** _Answer Tone_ The receiving modem transmits an answer tone back to the network. A V.25 answer tone (a 2100Hz tone with a duration of about 3.3 seconds) is returned to the calling modem. However, the V.32 modem uses a modified answer tone where the signal phase is reversed every 450 ms—this sounds like little "clicks" in the signal. An answer tone serves two purposes. First, you can _hear_ this tone in the receiving modem's speaker, so manual modem users know when to place their modem into "data mode." Even more important, the answer tone is used by the telephone network to disable echo suppressers in the connection in order to allow optimum data throughput. The modems themselves will handle echo suppression.
- **Step 3:** _Signal AA_ The sending modem waits about 1 second after receiving the answer tone, then generates an 1800Hz tone (known as _Signal AA_). When the receiving modem interprets this signal, it knows (quite early on) that it is communicating with another V.32 modem.
- **Step 4:** _The USB1 Fall Back_ If the answering modem heard signal AA, it will immediately try establishing a connection; otherwise, it will reply to the sending modem with a USB1 signal (alternating binary 1 s at 1200bps). This causes the connection to "fall back" to a V.22bis connection. This fall back attempt will continue for 3 seconds. If the sending modem does not respond to the USB1 signal within 3 seconds, the receiving modem will continue trying the connection as a V.32.
- **Step 5:** _Signal AC and CA_ During a V.32 connection, the receiving modem sends Signal AC (a mixed 600Hz and 3000Hz tone signal) for at least 1/2400th of a second, then it reverses the signal phase, creating Signal CA.

TABLE 26-4 CONNECT SEQUENCES FOR V.22BIS AND V.32 MODEMS (CONTINUED)

- **Step 6:** *Signal CC* When the sending modem detects the phase change in Signal AC/CA, it reverses the phase of its own Signal AA, creating a new signal (called *Signal CC*).
- **Step 7:** *Echo Canceller Configuration* Once the answering modem receives the phase-changed signal CC, it again changes the phase of CA, returning it to signal AC. This multitude of phase changes might seem like a ridiculous waste of time, but this exchange between the two modems is vital for approximating the round-trip (propogation) delay of the communication circuit so that the modem's echo-canceller circuitry can be set properly.
- **Step 8:** *Agreeing on Specifics* Once the exchange of phase changes sets the echo cancellers, both modems exchange data in half-duplex mode in order to set up adaptive equalizers, test the phone line quality, and agree on an acceptable data rate. In actuality, the answering modem sends first (from 650 ms to 3525 ms). The sending modem responds, but leaves the signal on while the answering modem sends another burst of signals (this is when the final data rate is established).
- **Step 9:** *Passing Data* Once the data rate is established, both modems proceed to send scrambled binary 1 s for at least $\frac{1}{200}$ of a second (a brief white-noise sound), then they are ready to pass data.

READING THE LIGHTS

One of the appealing attributes of external modems is the series of lights that typically adorns the front face. By observing each light and the sequence in which they light, you can often follow the progress of a communication—or quickly discern the cause of a communication failure. The following markings are typical of many modems, but remember that your particular modem might use fewer indicators (or be marked differently):

- **HS** *(High Speed)* When this indicator is lit, the modem is operating at its very highest transfer rate.
- **AA** *(Auto Answer)* When illuminated, your modem will answer any incoming calls automatically. This feature is vital for unattended systems, such as bulletin boards.
- **CD** *(Carrier Detect)* This lights whenever the modem detects a carrier signal. This means it has successfully connected to a remote computer. This LED will go out when either one of the modems drops the line.
- **OH** *(Off Hook)* This LED lights any time that the modem takes control of the telephone line—equivalent to taking the telephone off-hook.
- **RD** *(Receive Data)* Also marked *Rx*. This LED flickers as data is received by the modem from a remote modem.
- **SD** *(Send Data)* Also marked *Tx*. This LED flickers as data is sent from your modem to the remote modem.
- **TR** *(Terminal Ready)* This light illuminates when the modem detects a DTR signal from the communication software.
- **MR** *(Modem Ready)* A simple power-on light that indicates the modem is turned on and is ready to operate.

Understanding Signal Modulation

Once the modem accepts a bipolar signal from an RS-232 port, the carrier signal being generated on the telephone line must be modulated to reflect the logic levels being transmitted. Several different means of signal modulation have been developed through the years to improve the efficiency of data transfers. This part of the chapter gives you a brief explanation of each scheme. As you would expect, both modems must be capable of the same modulation scheme.

BPS VS. BAUD RATE

In the early days of modem communication, each audio signal *transition* represented a single bit. Each audio signal is known as a *baud*, and the baud rate naturally equaled the transmission rate in bps (or bits-per-second). Unlike those early modems, newer modem schemes can encode 2, 3, 4, or more bits into every audio signal transition (or baud). This means that modem throughput now equals 2×, 3×, or 4× the baud rate being carried across the telephone line.

For example, a modem operating at 2400baud (2400 audio signal transitions per second) can carry 4800bps if two bits are encoded onto every baud. The same 2400baud modem could also carry 9600bps if 4 bits are encoded onto every baud. Today, the modem's baud rate rarely matches the modem's throughput in bps, unless a very old signaling standard is being used. If the modem were operating at 4800baud and used 3-bit encoding, the modem would be handling 14,400bps (14.4Kbps), etc. The concept of *encoding* is different from *data compression* because encoding transfers all original data bits from system to system, but data compression replaces repeating sequences of bits with much shorter bit sequences (known as *symbols* or *tokens*). Much more about encoding schemes and data compression is included later in this chapter.

MODULATION SCHEMES

To discuss modulation, you must first understand a sinusoidal waveform. The three basic physical characteristics of any waveform are: amplitude, frequency, and phase. Each of these characteristics can be adjusted to represent a bit. *Amplitude* is simply the magnitude of the wave (usually measured in volts peak-to-peak or volts RMS). Amplitude represents how far above and below the zero axis that waveform travels. *Frequency* indicates the number of times that a single wave will repeat over any period of time (measured as cycles-per-second, Hertz, Hz). An 1800Hz signal repeats 1800 times per second. The signal also has a time reference known as *phase*. Phase is measured in degrees where 90 degrees is the time to travel 25% of a wave, 180 degrees is the time to travel 50% of the wave, 270 degrees is the time to travel 75% of a wave, etc. Because phase can take on any one of four states (degrees), phase shifts can be made to represent two bits simultaneously. Data between modems is modulated by altering the amplitude, frequency, and phase of a carrier signal.

Frequency Shift Keying (FSK) is very similar to *Frequency Modulation (FM)*. In FM, only the frequency of a carrier is changed, and it is one of the oldest modulation schemes still in service. FSK sends a logic 1 as one particular frequency (usually 1750Hz), and a logic 0 is sent as another discrete frequency (often 1080Hz). Frequencies are typically sent at 300 baud and each baud can carry 1 bit, so FSK can send 300bps. This early technique resulted in the classic "baud=bps" confusion, which is still prevalent today.

Phase Shift Keying (PSK) is a close cousin of FSK, but the phase timing of a carrier wave is altered while the carrier's frequency stays the same. By altering the carrier's

phase, a logic 1 or 0 is represented. Because phase can be shifted in several precise increments (e.g., 0, 90, 180, or 270 degrees), PSK can encode 1, 2, 3, or more bits bit per baud.
For example, a 1200baud modem using PSK can transmit 2400bps over an 1800Hz carrier. PSK can also be used in conjunction with FSK to encode even more bits per baud.

Quadrature Amplitude Modulation (QAM) uses both phase and amplitude modulation to encode up to six bits onto every baud, although four bits are usually reserved for
data. Not only can four phase states represent two bits, but four levels of amplitude can
represent another two bits. Most QAM modems use a 1700 or 1800Hz carrier and a
base rate of 2400baud, so they carry up to 9600bps.

Trellis-Coded Quadrature Amplitude Modulation (TCQAM or TCM) also uses an
1800Hz carrier at a 2400baud base rate, but uses the full six-bit encoding capability of
QAM to handle 14,400bps. Most newer modems using TCM offer high speed and excellent echo-cancellation circuitry. TCM is currently the most popular modulation scheme
for high-performance modems because data can be checked on-the-fly with much better
reliability than using a parity bit.

Signaling Standards

Now that you have covered serial concepts and modulation techniques, you can see how
modulation is used in conjunction with the many communications standards (or protocols)
that have appeared. This part of the chapter details each of the major standards for
modems, data compression, and error correction that are now in force today. In addition
to simply transferring data, however, current modem standards embrace two other facets
of data communication: data compression and error correction.

Most data sent between modems contains some amount of repetitive or redundant information. If the redundant information is located and replaced by a small token during transmission—the data is compressed. A token could be passed much faster than the redundant
data, and the receiving modem accurately recreates the original data based on the token.
Data compression has become an important technique that allows modems to increase
their data throughput without increasing the baud rate or bps. Data compression can occur
only when the two communicating modems support the same compression protocol. If
modems support more than one type of compression, the communicating modems will use
the most powerful technique common to both.

Modem error correction is the ability of some modems to detect data errors that might
have occurred in transit between modems, then automatically resend the faulty data until
a correct copy is received. As with modulation standards, both modems must be using
the same error-correction standard to operate together. However, there are few error-correction standards, and most modem manufacturers adhere closely to the few that are
available.

BELL STANDARDS

The old "Bell System" largely dictated North American telecommunications standards
before it was broken up into AT&T and seven regional operating companies in 1984.

Before that time, two major standards were developed that set the stage for future modem development:

- *BELL103* This was the first widely accepted modem standard using simple FSK modulation at 300baud. This is the only standard where the data rate matches the baud rate. It is interesting that some modems today still support BELL103 as a lowest common denominator when all other modulation techniques fail.
- *BELL212A* This represents a second widely accepted modem standard in North America using PSK modulation at 600baud to transmit 1200bps. Many European countries ignored BELL212A in favor of the similar (but not entirely identical) European standard, called *V.22*.

ITU (CCITT) STANDARDS

After the "Bell System" breakup, AT&T no longer wielded enough clout to dictate standards in North America—and certainly not to the international community, which had developed serious computing interest. At this time, the *ITU (International Telecommunications Union*, formally the *CCITT)* gained prominence and acceptance in the U.S. All U.S. modems have been built to ITU standards ever since. ITU specifications are characterized by the symbol *V* (e.g., V.17). The term *V* simply means *standard* (rather like the "RS" in RS-232). The subsequent number simply denotes the particular standard. Some standards also add the term *bis*, which means the second version of a particular standard. You might also soon see the terms *ter* or *terbo*, which is the third version of a standard. The following list provides a comprehensive look at ITU standards. Only the bolded standards relate to modems in particular, but all are related to communications. This index might help you to understand the broad specifications that are required to fully characterize the computer communications environment:

- *V.1* This is a very early standard that defines binary 0/1 bits as space/mark line conditions and voltage levels.
- *V.2* This limits the power levels (in decibels, dB) of modems used on phone lines.
- *V.4* This describes the sequence of bits within a character, as transmitted (the data frame).
- *V.5* This describes the standard synchronous signaling rates for dialup lines.
- *V.6* This describes the standard synchronous signaling rates for leased lines.
- *V.7* This provides a list of modem terms in English, Spanish, French.
- *V.8* This describes the initial handshaking (negotiation) process between modems, and it forms the basis for call "auto-detection" or "auto-switching" (voice/fax/modem).
- *V.10* This describes unbalanced high-speed electrical interface characteristics (RS-423)
- *V.11* This describes balanced high-speed electrical characteristics (RS-422)
- *V.13* This explains simulated carrier control (with a full-duplex modem used as half-duplex modem).
- *V.14* This explains the procedure for asynchronous to synchronous conversion.
- *V.15* This describes the requirements and designs for telephone acoustic couplers. This is largely unused today because most telephone equipment is modular and can be

plugged into telephone adapters directly, rather than loosely attached to the telephone handset.

- *V.17* This describes an application-specific modulation scheme for Group 3 fax, which provides two-wire half-duplex trellis-coded transmission at 7200, 9600, 12,000, and 14,400bps. In spite of the low numbers, this is a fairly recent standard.

- *V.19* This describes early DTMF modems using low-speed parallel transmission. This standard is largely obsolete.

- *V.20* This explains modems with parallel data transmission. This standard is largely obsolete.

- *V.21* This provides the specifications for 300bps FSK serial modems (based upon BELL103).

- *V.22* This provides the specifications for 1200bps (600baud) PSK modems (similar to BELL212A).

- *V.22bis* This describes 2400bps modems operating at 600baud using QAM.

- *V.23* This describes the operation of a rather unusual type of FM modem working at 1200/75bps. That is, the host transmits at 1200bps and receives at 75bps. The remote modem transmits at 75bps and receives at 1200bps. V.23 is used in Europe to support some videotext applications.

- *V.24* This is known as EIA RS-232 in the U.S. V.24 defines only the functions of the serial-port circuits. EIA-232-E (the current version of the standard) also defines electrical characteristics and connectors.

- *V.25* This defines automatic answering equipment and parallel automatic dialing. It also defines the answer tone that modems send.

- *V.25bis* This defines serial automatic calling and answering, which is the ITU (CCITT) equivalent of AT commands. This is the current ITU standard for modem control by computers via serial interface. The Hayes AT command set is used primarily in the U.S.

- *V.26* This defines a 2400bps PSK full-duplex modem operating at 1200baud.

- *V.26bis* This defines a 2400bps PSK half-duplex modem operating at 1200baud.

- *V.26terbo* This defines a 2400/1200bps switchable PSK full-duplex modem operating at 1200baud.

- *V.27* This defines a 4800bps PSK modem operating at 1600baud.

- *V.27bis* This defines a more-advanced 4800/2400bps switchable PSK modem operating at 1600/1200baud.

- *V.27terbo* This defines a 4800/2400bps switchable PSK modem, commonly used in half-duplex mode at 1600/1200baud to handle Group 3 fax, rather than computer modems.

- *V.28* This defines the electrical characteristics and connections for V.24 (RS-232). Where the RS-232 specification defines all necessary parameters, the ITU (CCITT) breaks the specifications down into two separate documents.

- *V.29* This defines a 9600/7200/4800bps switchable PSK/QAM modem operating at 2400baud. This type of modem is often used to implement Group 3 fax, rather than computer modems.

- *V.32* This defines the first of the truly modern modems as a 9600/4800bps switchable QAM full-duplex modem operating at 2400baud. This standard also incorporates trellis coding and echo cancellation to produce a stable, reliable, high-speed modem.

- *V.32bis* This fairly new standard extends the V.32 specification to define a 4800/ 7200/9600/12,000/14,400bps switchable TCQAM full-duplex modem operating at

2400baud. Trellis coding, automatic-transfer-rate negotiation, and echo cancellation make this type of modem one of the most popular and least expensive for everyday PC communication.

■ *V.32terbo* This continues to extend the V.32 specification by using advanced techniques to implement a 14,400/16,800/19,200bps switchable TCQAM full-duplex modem operating at 2400baud. Unlike V.32bis, V.32terbo is not widely used because of the rather high cost of components.

■ *V.32fast* This is the informal name to a standard that the ITU (CCITT) has not yet completed. When finished, a V.32fast modem will likely replace V.32bis with speeds up to 28,800bps. It is anticipated that this will be the last analog protocol—eventually giving way to all-digital protocols as local telephone services become entirely digital. V.32fast will probably be renamed V.34 on completion and acceptance.

■ *V.33* This defines a specialized 14,400bps TCQAM full-duplex modem operating at 2400baud.

■ *V.34* This defines the standard for modem communications at 2400 through 28,800bps.

■ *V.34+* An update to V.34, which outlines the enhancements needed for modem communication at 33,600bps.

■ *V.36* This defines a specialized 48,000bps "group" modem, which is rarely (if ever) used commercially. This type of modem uses several conventional telephone lines.

■ *V.37* This defines a specialized 72,000bps "group" modem, which combines several telephone channels.

■ *V.42* This is the only ITU error-correcting procedure for modems using V.22, V.22bis, V.26ter, V.32, and V.32bis protocols. The standard is also defined as a *Link-Access Procedure for Modems (LAPM)* protocol. ITU V.42 is considered very efficient, and is about 20% faster than MNP4. If a V.42 connection cannot be established between modems, V.42 automatically provides fallback to the MNP4 error-correction standard.

■ *V.42bis* This uses a Lempel-Ziv-based data-compression scheme for use in conjunction with V.42 LAPM (error correction). V.42bis is a data-compression standard for high-speed modems, which can compress data by as much as 4:1 (depending on the type of file you send). Thus, a 9600baud modem can transmit data at up to 38,400bps using V.42bis. A 14.4kbps modem can transmit up to a startling 57,600bps.

■ *V.50* This sets standard telephony limits for modem transmission quality.

■ *V.51* This outlines required maintenance of international data circuits.

■ *V.52* This describes apparatus for measuring data-transmission distortion and error rates.

■ *V.53* This outlines impairment limits for data circuits.

■ *V.54* This describes loop test devices for modem testing.

■ *V.55* This describes impulse noise-measuring equipment for line testing.

■ *V.56* This outlines the comparative testing of modems.

■ *V.57* This describes comprehensive test equipment for high-speed data transmission.

■ *V.100* This describes the interconnection techniques between *PDNs (Public Data Networks)* and *PSTNs (Public Switched Telephone Networks)*.

MNP STANDARDS

The *Microcom Networking Protocol (MNP)* is a complete hierarchy of standards developed during the mid 1980s, which are designed to work with other modem technologies for error correction and data compression. Although most ITU standards refer to modem data transfer, MNP standards concentrate on providing error correction and data compression when your modem is communicating with another modem that supports MNP. For example, MNP class 4 is specified by ITU V.42 as a backup error control scheme for LAPM in the event that V.24 cannot be invoked. Out of nine recognized MNP levels, your modem probably supports the first five. Each MNP class has all the features of the previous class plus its own:

- *MNP class 1 (block mode)* An old data-transfer mode that sends data in only one direction at a time—about 70 percent as fast as data transmissions using no error correction. This level is now virtually obsolete.
- *MNP class 2 (stream mode)* An older data-transfer mode that sends data in both directions at the same time—about 84 percent as fast as data transmissions using no error correction.
- *MNP class 3* The sending modem strips start and stop bits from the data block before sending it, while the receiving modem adds start and stop bits before passing the data to the receiving computer. About 8 percent faster than data transmissions using no error correction. The increased throughput is realized only if modems on both ends of the connection are operating in a split speed (or locked COM port) fashion—that is, the rate of data transfer from computer to modem is higher than the data-transfer rate from modem to modem. Also, data is being transferred in big blocks (e.g., 1KB) or continuously (i.e., using the Zmodem file-transfer protocol).
- *MNP class 4* A protocol (with limited data compression) that checks telephone-connection quality and uses a transfer technique called *Adaptive Packet Assembly*. On a noise-free line, the modem sends larger blocks of data. If the line is noisy, the modem sends smaller blocks of data (less data will have to be resent). This means more successful transmissions on the first try. This standard is about 20 percent faster than data transmissions using no error correction at all, so most current modems are MNP4 compatible.
- *MNP class 5* Classic MNP data compression. MNP5 provides data compression by detecting redundant data and recoding it to fewer bits, thus increasing effective data throughput. A receiving modem decompresses the data before passing it to the receiving computer. MNP5 can speed data transmissions up to 2× over using no data compression or error correction (depending on the kind of data transmitted). In effect, MNP5 gives a 2400bps modem and effective data throughput of as much as 4800bps, and a 9600bps system as much as 19,200bps.
- *MNP class 6* This uses *Universal Link Negotiation* to let modems get maximum performance out of a line. Modems start at low speeds, then move to higher speeds until the best speed is found. MNP6 also provides *Statistical Duplexing* to help half-duplex modems simulate full-duplex modems.
- *MNP class 7* This offers a much more powerful data-compression process (Huffman encoding) than MNP5. MNP7 modems can increase the data throughput by as much as 3×, in some cases. Although more efficient than MNP5, not all modems are designed to handle the MNP7 protocol. Also, MNP7 is faster than MNP5, but MNP7 is still generally considered slower than the ITU's V.42bis.
- *MNP class 9* This reduces the data overhead (the "housekeeping bits") encountered with each data packet. MNP9 also improves error-correction performance because

only the data that was in error has to be resent instead of resending the entire data packet.

■ *MNP class 10* This uses a set of protocols, known as *Adverse Channel Enhancements*, to help modems overcome poor telephone connections by adjusting data packet size and transmission speed until the most reliable transmission is established. This is a more powerful version of MNP4.

FILE-TRANSFER PROTOCOLS

Even with powerful data transfer, compression, and correction protocols, the way in which data is packaged and exchanged is still largely undefined by ITU and MNP standards. You see, a typical modem has no way of knowing the difference between a keyboard stroke or data being downloaded from a hard drive—the modem does not understand a file. Instead, it only works with bytes, bits, timing, and tones. As a consequence, the modem relies on communications software to manage file characteristics, such as filename, file size, and content. The software routines that bundle and organize data between modems are called *file-transfer protocols*. Errors that occur during file transfer are automatically detected and corrected by file-transfer protocols. If a block of data is received incorrectly, the receiving system sends a message to the sending system and requests the re-transmission. This process is automatic, and is essentially transparent to the computer users (except perhaps for a display in the communication software's file-transfer status window). The following are some of the more common transfer protocols:

■ *ASCII* This protocol is designed to work with ASCII text files only. Notice that you do not have to use this protocol when transferring text files. The ASCII protocol is useful for uploading a text file when you are composing e-mail on-line.

■ *Xmodem* This is one of the most widely used file-transfer protocols. Introduced in 1977 by Ward Christensen, this protocol is slow, but reliable. The original Xmodem protocol used 128-byte packets and a simple checksum method of error detection. A later enhancement, Xmodem-CRC, uses a more secure *Cyclic Redundancy Check (CRC)* method for error detection. Xmodem protocols always attempt to use CRC first. If the sender does not acknowledge the requests for CRC, the receiver shifts to the checksum mode and continues its request for transmission. Mismatching the two variants of Xmodem during file transfers is usually the reason for transfer problems, although many communication systems can now detect the differences automatically.

■ *Xmodem-1K* The Xmodem-1K protocol is essentially Xmodem CRC with 1KB (1024 byte) packets. On some systems and bulletin boards, it is referred to as *Ymodem*. Some communication software programs (most notably Procomm Plus 1.x) also list Xmodem-1K as Ymodem, but Procomm Plus 2.0 refers it as *Xmodem-1K*.

■ *Ymodem* A Ymodem protocol is little more than a version of Xmodem-1K that allows multiple batch-file transfer (sending/receiving several files one after another unattended). On some systems, it is listed as *Ymodem Batch* (and is sometimes called *true Ymodem*). Ymodem offers a faster transmission rate than Xmodem, and better data security through a refined CRC checksum method.

■ *Ymodem-g* The Ymodem-g protocol is a variant of basic Ymodem. It is designed to be used with modems that support error correction. This protocol does not provide software error correction or recovery itself, but expects the modem to provide the service. It is a streaming protocol that sends and receives 1K packets in a continuous stream until it is instructed to stop. It does not wait for positive acknowledgment after each block is sent, but rather sends blocks in rapid succession. If any block is unsuccessfully transferred, the entire transfer is canceled.

- *Zmodem* This is generally the best protocol to use if the electronic service you are calling supports it. Zmodem has two significant features: it is extremely efficient and it provides automatic "crash" recovery. Like Ymodem-g, Zmodem does not wait for positive acknowledgment after each block is sent, but rather sends blocks in rapid succession. If a Zmodem transfer "crashes" (is canceled or interrupted for any reason), the transfer can be resurrected later and the previously transferred information need not be re-sent. Zmodem can detect excessive line noise and automatically drop to a shorter, more reliable data packet size when necessary. Data integrity and accuracy is ensured by the use of reliable 16-bit *CRC (Cyclic Redundancy Check)* methods, rather than less-reliable CRC checking of Ymodem and Xmodem.
- *Kermit* The Kermit protocol was developed at Columbia University. It was designed to facilitate the exchange of data among very different types of computers (mainly minicomputers and mainframes). You probably will not need to use Kermit unless you are calling a minicomputer or mainframe at an educational institution.
- *Sealink* The Sealink protocol is a variant of Xmodem. It was developed to overcome the transmission delays caused by satellite relays or packet-switching networks.

Modem Troubleshooting

The modem is installed (or replaced), the communication software is loaded, the telephone line is connected—and nothing happens. This is an all too-common theme for today's technicians and computer users. Although the actual failure rate among ordinary modems is quite small, it turns out that modems (and serial ports, as you will see later in the book) are some of the most difficult and time-consuming devices to setup and configure. As a consequence, proper setup initially can simplify troubleshooting significantly. If a modem fails to work properly, there are a number of conditions to explore:

- *Incorrect hardware resources* An internal modem must be set with a unique IRQ line and I/O port. If the assigned resources are also used by another serial device in the system (such as a mouse), the modem and the conflicting device (or perhaps both) will not function properly. Remove the modem and use a diagnostic to check available resources. Under Windows 95, you can use the *Device manager* to investigate devices and examine their configurations. Reconfigure the internal modem to clear the conflict. External modems make use of existing COM ports.
- *Defective telecommunication resources* All modems need access to a telephone line to establish connections with other modems. If the telephone jack is defective or hooked up improperly, the modem might work fine, but no connection is possible. Remove the telephone cord from the modem and try the line cord on an ordinary telephone. When you lift the receiver, you should draw the dial tone. Try dialing a local number—if the

line rings, chances are good that the telephone line is working. Check the RJ11 jack on the modem. One or more bent connector pins can break the line—even though the line cord is inserted properly.

■ *Improper cabling* An external modem must be connected to the PC serial port with a cable. Traditional serial cables were 25-pin assemblies. Later, 9-pin serial connectors and cables became common—out of those nine wires, only three are really vital. As a result, quite a few cable assemblies might be incorrect or otherwise specialized. Be sure that the serial cable between the PC and modem is a "straight-through" cable. Also check that both ends of the cable are intact (i.e., installed evenly, no bent pins, etc.). Try a new cable, if necessary.

■ *Improper power* External modems must receive power from batteries or from an ac eliminator. Be sure that any batteries are fresh and installed completely. If an ac adapter is used, see that it is connected to the modem properly.

Incorrect software settings—both internal and external modems must be initialized with an AT ASCII command string before a connection is established. If these settings are absent or incorrect, the modem will not respond as expected (if at all). Check the communication software and be sure that the AT command strings are appropriate for the modem being used—different modems often require slightly different command strings.

■ *Suspect the modem itself* Modems are typically quite reliable in everyday use. If jumpers or DIP switches are on the modem, check that each setting is placed correctly. Perhaps their most vulnerable point is the telephone interface, which is particularly susceptible to high-voltage spikes that might enter through the telephone line. If all else fails, try another modem.

CHECKING THE COMMAND PROCESSOR

The *command processor* is the controller that manages the modem's operation in the command mode, and it is the command processor which interprets AT command strings. If the new modem fails to behave as it should, first check the modem command processor using the following procedure. Before going too far with this, be sure you have the modem's user guide on hand (if possible). When the command processor checks out, but the modem refuses to work under normal communication software operations, the software might be refusing to save such settings as COM port selection, speed, and character format:

1 Be sure that the modem is installed properly and connected to the desired PC serial port. Of course, if the modem is internal, you will only need to worry about IRQ and I/O port settings.

2 Start the communication software and select a "direct connection" to establish a path from your keyboard to the modem (this is sometimes referred to as *terminal mode*). You will probably see a dialog box appear with a blinking cursor. If the modem is working and installed properly, you should now be able to send commands directly to the modem.

Under Windows 95, you can use the HyperTerminal applet under Start, Programs, Accessories, and HyperTerminal. Once the HyperTerminal folder opens, doubleclick the

Hypertrm icon, and type "Test1" in the *Connection description* dialog. Click *OK*. When you're asked to enter a phone number, enter your own number and click *OK*. When the *Connect* dialog asks to dial the number, just click *Cancel*. A text window appears (Fig. 26-3). Type "AT" and press <Enter>. You should see an "OK" response.

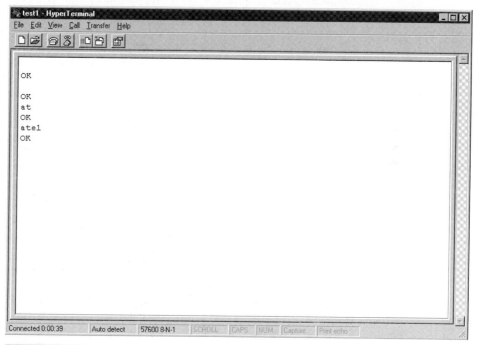

FIGURE 26-3   **Testing the command processor in the terminal window.**

3 Type the command "AT" and then press the <Enter> key. The modem should return an "OK" result code. When an "OK" is returned, chances are that the modem is working correctly. If you see double characters being displayed, try the command "ATE0" to disable the command mode echo. If you do not see an "OK," try issuing an "ATE1" command to enable the command mode echo. If there is still no response, commands are not reaching the modem or the modem is defective. Check the connections between the modem and serial port. If the modem is internal, check that it is installed correctly and that all jumpers are placed properly.

4 Try resetting the modem with the "ATZ" command and the <Enter> key. This should reset the modem. If the modem now responds with "OK," you might have to adjust the initialization command string in the communication software.

5 Try factory-default settings by typing the command "AT&F" then pressing the <Enter> key. This should restore the factory-default values for each S-register. You might also try the command "AT&Q0" and <Enter> to deliberately place the modem into asynchronous mode. You should see "OK" responses to each attempt, which indicates that the modem is responding as expected—it might be necessary to update the modem's initialization command string. If the modem still does not respond, the communication software might be incompatible or the modem is defective.

CHECKING THE DIALER AND TELEPHONE LINE

After you are confident that the modem's command processor is responding properly, you can also check the "telephone interface" by attempting a call—this also can verify an active telephone line. If the telephone interface checks out, but the modem refuses to work under normal communication software operations, the software might be refusing to save settings, such as COM port selection, speed, and character format:

1 Be sure that the modem is installed properly and connected to the desired PC serial port. Of course, if the modem is internal, you will only need to worry about IRQ and I/O port settings.

2 Start the communication software and select a "direct connection" to establish a path from your keyboard to the modem (this is sometimes referred to as *terminal mode*). You will probably see a dialog box appear with a blinking cursor. If the modem is working and installed properly, you should now be able to send commands directly to the modem.

3 Dial a number by using the DT (dial using tones) command followed by the full number being called—for example, "ATDT15083667683" followed by the <Enter> key. If your local telephone line only supports rotary dialing, use the modifier R after the D. If calling from a PBX, be sure to dial 9 or other outside-access codes. Listen for a dial tone, followed by the tone dialing beeps. You should also hear the destination phone ringing. These occur to ensure that your telephone interface dials correctly and that the local phone line is responding properly.

4 If there is no dial tone, check the phone line by dialing with an ordinary phone. Some PBX systems must be modified to produce at least 48 Vdc for the modem to work. If there is no dial tone, but the modem attempts to dial, the telephone interface is not grabbing the telephone line correctly (the dialer is working). If the modem draws dial tone, but no digits are generated, the dialer might be defective. In either case, try another modem.

TYPICAL COMMUNICATION PROBLEMS

Even when the modem hardware is working perfectly, the serial communication process is anything but flawless. Problems ranging from accidental loss of carrier to a catastrophic loss of data regularly plague computer communication. To make your on-line time as fool-proof as possible, this section of the chapter shows you how to deal with some of the most pernicious communication problems.

Modem settings Modem settings are crucially important to inter-modem communication. The number of data bits, use of parity, number of stop bits, and data transfer speed must be set precisely the same way on both modems. Otherwise, the valid data leaving one modem will be interpreted as complete "junk" at the receiving end. Normally, this should not happen when modems are set to auto-answer—negotiation should allow both modems to settle at the same parameters. The time that incompatible settings really become a factor is when negotiation is unsuccessful or when communication is being established manually. A typical example is an avid BBS user with communication software set to eight data bits, no parity bit, and one stop bit, trying to use a network that runs at seven data bits, even parity, and two stop bits. The aspect that stands out with incompatible settings is that virtually nothing is intelligible—and the connection is typically lost.

Modems and UART types   Whether internal or external, the UART is clearly the heart of a modem system. The modem converts bus data into serial data (and vice versa), but the UART must be able to keep pace with the modem's data-transfer rate. As modem speeds have increased, UARTs have become faster also. When installing a new external modem on an older PC, the PC's serial port might simply not be fast enough to deal with the modem. The result is often limited modem performance (if the modem works at all). Today, the 16550A UART is the device of choice. Table 26-5 compares the major UART types. When faced with an older UART, it is often possible to replace the UART IC outright. Otherwise, it is a simple matter to disable the existing serial port, and install a newer serial adapter using a new UART.

Line noise   Where faulty settings can load the display with trash, even a properly established connection can lose integrity periodically. Remember that serial communication is made possible by a global network of switched telephone wiring. Each time you dial the same number, you typically get a different set of wiring. Faulty wiring at any point along the network, from electrical storms, wet or snowy weather, and other natural or man-made disasters, can interrupt the network momentarily or cut communication entirely. Most of the time, brief interruptions can result in small patches of garbled text. This type of behavior is most prominent in real-time on-line sessions (such as typing in a "chat" message). When uploading or downloading files, file-transfer protocols can usually catch such anomalies and correct errors or request new data packets to overcome the errors. When you have trouble moving files or notice a high level of "junk" on-line, try calling back—when a new telephone line is established, the connection might be better.

TABLE 26-5 COMPARISON OF POPULAR UARTS	
UART	**DESCRIPTION**
8250	This is the original PC/XT serial port UART. Several minor bugs are in the UART, but the original PC/XT BIOS corrected for them. The 8250 was replaced by the 8250B.
8250A	This slightly updated UART fixed many of the issues in the 8250, but would not work in PC/XT systems because the BIOS was written to circumvent the 8250's problems. In either case, the 8250A will not work adequately at speeds faster than 9600bps.
8250B	The last of the 8250 series re-inserted the bugs that existed in the original 8250 so that PC/XT BIOS would function properly. The 8250B also does not run at speeds faster than 9600bps.
16450	This higher-speed UART was the desired choice for AT (i286) systems. Stable at 9600bps, the 16450 laid the groundwork for the first "high-speed" modems. However, the 16450 will not work in PC/XT systems. This IC should be replaced by the 16550A.
16550	The 16550 was faster than the 16450 allowing operation at speeds faster than 9600bps, but its performance was still limited by internal design problems. This IC should be replaced by the 16550A.
16550A	The fastest of the UARTs, a 16550A eliminates many of the serial-port problems encountered when using a fast modem.

Transmit and receive levels Other factors that affect both leased and dial-up telephone lines are the transmit and receive levels. These settings determine the signal levels used by the modem in each direction. Some Hayes-compatible modems permit these levels to be adjusted. The range and availability of these adjustments is, in large part, controlled by the local telephone system. For example, the recommended settings and ranges are different for modems sold in the U.K. than for those sold in the U.S. See the documentation accompanying the modem to determine whether this capability is supported.

System processor limitations Some multi-tasking operating systems can occasionally lose small amounts of data if the computer is heavily loaded and cannot allocate processing time to the communications task frequently enough. In this case, the data is corrupted by the host computer itself. This could also cause incomplete data transmission to the remote system. Host processor capabilities should be a concern when choosing software for data communications when the line speed is greater than 9600bps and the modem-to-DTE connection is 19,200bps or higher (for example, when data compression is used). The modem will provide exact transmission of the data it receives, but if the host PC cannot "keep up" with the modem because of other tasks or speed restrictions, precautions should be taken when writing software or when adding modems with extra high-speed capabilities. One way to avoid the problem of data loss caused by the host PC is the use of an upgraded serial port, such as a Hayes Enhanced Serial-Port card or a newer modem with a 16550 UART. Such advanced modems are powerful enough to take some of the load off the PC processor. When processor time is stretched to the limit, try shutting down any unnecessary applications to reduce load on the system.

Call waiting The "call waiting" feature, now available on most dial-up lines, momentarily interrupts a call. This interruption causes a click that informs voice-call users that another call is coming through. Although this technique is dynamite for voice communication, it is also quite effective at interrupting a modem's carrier signal—and might cause some modems to drop the connection. One way around this is to set S-register S10 to a higher value so that the modem tolerates a fairly long loss of carrier signal. Data loss might still occur, but the connection will not drop. Of course, the remote modem must be similarly configured. When originating the call, a special prefix can be issued as part of the dialing string to disable call waiting for the duration of the call. The exact procedure varies from area to area, so contact your local telephone system for details.

Automatic timeout Some Hayes-compatible modems offer an automatic *timeout* feature. Automatic timeout prevents an inactive connection from being maintained. This "watchdog" feature prevents undesired long-distance charges for a connection that was maintained for too long. This inactivity delay can be set or disabled with S-register S30.

System lock up In some situations, host systems do lock up, but in many cases, it is simply that one or the other of the computers has been *flowed off*—that is, the character that stops data transfer has been inadvertently sent. This can happen during error-control connections if the wrong kind of local flow control has been selected. In addition, the problem could be the result of incompatible EIA 232-D/ITU V.24 signaling. If systems seem to cease transmitting or receiving without warning, but do not disconnect, perform a thorough examination of flow control.

Modem initialization strings Modems rely on initialization strings for proper configuration at start time or when new communication software is initialized. The initialization string must be correct for your particular modem to utilize all of the modem's features or achieve optimum performance. You might be able to use "generic" initialization strings, but might not be able to get full functionality from the modem (e.g., you might be able to use a Hayes-compatible initialization string, but caller ID might not work).

SYMPTOMS

Many of the problems that you will encounter with modem/fax boards are related to its physical and software configuration. The host PC also plays an important role in the modem's overall performance and reliability. Modems themselves are rarely at fault—although they are hardly invulnerable. This part of the chapter presents you with an index of potential troubleshooting problems and solutions. If you determine that the modem itself is at fault, you should replace the modem outright. When replacing the modem, remember that the initialization and operating strings often vary slightly between modem manufacturers—be sure to alter AT command strings in the communication software to accommodate the new modem.

Symptom 26-1. The PC (or communication software) refuses to recognize the modem First, verify that the modem is turned on (external modems only). For internal modems, see that the modem is installed correctly and completely in its expansion slot. Check your CMOS settings and verify that the COM port for your external modem is even enabled. There might be a COM port (IRQ) conflict in the system. Check the configuration of your internal modem (try the Windows 95 *Device manager*) and verify that there are no hardware conflicts. If you have trouble running the modem in "terminal mode" (the modem doesn't respond to AT commands), be sure that you're entering everything in either upper-case (AT) or lower-case (at) format—mixing cases can sometimes confuse a modem.

Symptom 26-2. The modem appears to be functioning properly, but you can't see what you are typing The two types of duplex are full and half. Half-duplex systems simply transmit to and receive from each other. Full-duplex systems do that, plus they "receive" what they transmit—echoing the data back to the sender. Because half-duplex systems do not echo, what is being sent is typically not shown on the screen. Most terminal programs have an option to enable local echo so that what is transmitted is also displayed. You can often enable the modem's local echo by typing the "ATE1" command during a direct connection, or add the "E1" entry to the modem's initialization string. When local echo is not an option, switching to full-duplex mode will often do the same thing. Customer complaints that they can't see what they are typing are solved by turning on local echo or by switching to full-duplex.

Symptom 26-3. The modem appears to be functioning properly, but you see double characters print while typing By their nature, full-duplex modem connections produce an echo. If local echo is enabled in addition, you'll see not only what you are transmitting, but also that character being echoed, creating a double display—for example, when you hit "A," you'll see "AA." This can be annoying, but is totally harmless.

Customer complaints of double letters are solved by turning off local echo by entering the "ATE0" command during direct connection or by adding the "E0" command to the modem's initialization string.

Symptom 26-4. The modem will not answer at the customer's site, but it works fine in the shop Since deregulation of the original "Bell Telephone" company, customers have been allowed to attach devices to phone lines with the proviso that they notify the phone company of each device's FCC registration and Ringer Equivalence Number (REN). Although few customers make it a point of informing their local telephone company how many phones and gadgets are connected to the telephone line, there is a good reason for having it—you see, the amount of ringing voltage supplied to a site is fixed. If you load down the line beyond its maximum rating, not enough voltage will be available to ring all of the bells. The ringer equivalence is the amount of load that the device will place on the line. Modems have to be able to detect a ring signal before they know to pick up. If the ringing signal is too weak, the modem will not detect it properly and initiate an answer sequence.

Have the customer remove some other equipment from their phone lines and see if the problem disappears. With today's fax machines, modems, multiple extension phones and answering machines all plugged into the same line, it would be easy to overload the ringing voltage. The customer should also take a listing of the registration numbers and ringer-equivalence numbers on all devices connected to phone lines and notify the local phone company of them. The phone company can then boost the ringer voltage to compensate for the added loads.

As a precaution, be sure that your customer is starting the communication software properly before attempting to receive a modem call—the modem will not pick up a ringing line unless the proper software is running and the modem is in an "auto-answer" mode.

Symptom 26-5. Your modem is receiving or transmitting garbage, or is having great difficulty displaying anything at all Serial communication is totally dependent on the data frame settings and transfer rate of the receiver and the transmitter being an exact match. The baud rate, word bits, stop bits and parity must all match exactly or errors will show up. These errors can show as either no data, or as incorrect data (garbage) on screen. You'll see this one crop up a lot when customers switch from calling a local BBS to CompuServe. Local BBS's are usually set for eight-bit words, no parity and one stop bit. CompuServe, on the other hand, uses seven-bit words, even parity and two stop bits. The terminal software must be reconfigured to match the settings of each service being called. Most programs allow for these differences by letting you specify a configuration for each entry in the dialing directory. Also check the method of flow control being used (e.g., XOFF/XON, DTR/DSR, CTS/RTS) and be sure that it is set properly.

Baud-rate mismatches most often result in what looks like a dead modem—often, nothing is displayed on either end. Modems will automatically negotiate a common baud rate to connect at, without regard to the terminal settings. The modems will normally connect at the highest baud rate available to the slowest modem, so if a 14,400bps modem connects to a 2400bps modem, both will set themselves to 2400bps. If the software on the higher-speed modem is still set for the higher speed, you'll typically get large amounts of garbage or nothing at all.

If the problem results from being connected to a service, such as a BBS, call the sysop and find out the settings. You can also let the modem tell you what transfer rate it connects at. Before dialing, set a direct connection and send the command "ATQ0V1" to the modem. This tells the modem to send result codes in plain English. When connected, you'll see a message similar to "Connect 2400." The actual number you see is the bps rate, and you can reconfigure your software accordingly. Working out the word, stop and parity bits might be a process of trial and error, but almost all BBS installations use eight data bits, no parity, and one stop bit. If you are forced to attempt trial and error, target one, item to get right at a time. First, get the baud rates to match. Next, get word bits settled down and then go for parity and stop bits. If you make more than one change, you'll never know which change made the difference. It might seem slower, but your overall service time will be cut.

Symptom 26-6. The modem is connected and turned on, but the modem is not responding The communication software's configuration must match the port settings of the modem. Check to be sure that any modem parameters are entered and saved properly. Establish a direct connection with the modem and enter the "ATZ" command. This will reset the modem. The modem should respond "OK" or "0" (the numerical equivalent of OK). If that doesn't work, change to COM2 and try again, then COM3 and COM4. If none of the combinations work, check the DIP switches or jumpers on the modem for the correct configuration.

Symptom 26-7. The modem will not pick up phone line The modem is not able to initiate a call or answer an incoming call. Most modems today come with two RJ11 telephone line connectors for the phone lines: one labeled *Line* (where the outside line enters the modem) and the other labeled *Phone* (where an extension telephone can be plugged in). Check that the outgoing telephone line is plugged into the line jack. Leave the phone connector disconnected while the modem is in use.

Test the modem manually by establishing a direct connection and typing a dial command, such as "ATDT15083667683." When you enter this command string, the modem should go off hook, draw dial tone, and dial the numbers. If this happens as expected, you can be reasonably sure that the modem is working properly, and that the communication software is at fault. Check the modem initialization strings or try a new communication package. If the modem does not respond during a direct connection, check that the modem is installed and configured properly. You might need to try a new modem.

Symptom 26-8. The modem appears to work fine, but prints garbage whenever it's supposed to show IBM text graphics, such as boxes or ANSI graphics The communication software is probably set for seven-bit words. The IBM text graphic character set starts at ASCII 128 and has to have the eighth bit. Adjust the communication software configuration to handle eight-bit words. You might also be using an unusual ASCII character set during the connection—try setting the character-set emulation to ANSI BBS or TTY.

Symptom 26-9. Strange character groups, such as "[0m," frequently appear in the text These ANSI control codes are attempting to control your display. Popular among BBS software, ANSI codes can be used to set colors, draw ASCII boxes, clear the screen, move the cursor, etc. DOS provides an ANSI screen driver called *ANSI.SYS* that can be loaded into the CONFIG.SYS when the computer is rebooted. Most of today's terminal software will offer a setting for this as well. If you are able to select character-set emulation in your communication software, try setting to ANSI BBS.

Symptom 26-10.   The modem makes audible "clicking" noises when hooked to the phone line A short is probably in the phone line. The "clicking" is the noise of the modem trying to pick up when it sees the short and hang up when the short clears. Try replacing the line cord going from the modem to the telephone wall jack; line cords don't last very long under constant use and abuse. If problems continue, try using a different telephone line—the physical wiring might be defective between the wall jack and telephone pole. Contact your local telephone company if you suspect this to be the case. Next, try establishing a direct connection to the modem and enter an "AT&F" command, which will restore the modem's factory-default settings. If that clears the problem, the modem's initialized state might not be fully compatible with the current telephone-line characteristics. Check each modem setting carefully and adjust parameters to try and settle its operation down. If factory-default settings do not help and the telephone line seems reliable, the problem might be in the modem's telephone interface circuit—try replacing the modem.

Symptom 26-11.   The modem is having difficulty connecting to another modem The modem is powered and connected properly. It dials the desired number and you can hear the modems negotiating, but they never quite seem to make a connection. This is a classic software-configuration problem. You might often see a "No carrier" message associated with this problem. Check each parameter in your communication software—especially the modem's AT initialization string. Be sure that each entry in the string is appropriate for your modem. If the string looks correct, try disabling the modem's MNP5 protocol. You will have to refer to the modem's manual to find the exact command, but many modems use "AT." If your modem is using MNP5 and the destination modem does not support it, the negotiation can hang up. If problems persist, try lowering the modem's data transfer rate. Although most modems can set the proper transfer rate automatically, some modems that do not support it might also cause the negotiation to freeze.

Another problem might be that your modem is not configured to wait long enough for carrier from the remote modem. You can adjust this delay by entering a larger number for S-register S7. Start the communication software, establish a direct connection (terminal mode), and type "ATS7?" followed by the <Enter> key. This will return the current value of register S7. You can then use the command "ATS7=10" to enter a larger delay (in this case, 10 seconds). That should give the destination modem more time to respond. If all else fails, try a modem from a different manufacturer.

Symptom 26-12.   The modem starts dialing before it draws dialtone As a result, one or more of the numbers are lost during dialing, making it difficult to establish a connection. Chances are that the modem is working just fine, but the modem does not wait long enough for dial tone to be present once it goes off hook. The solution is to increase the time delay before the modem starts dialing. This can be done by changing the value in S-register S6. To find the current value, start the communication software and establish a direct connection (terminal mode), then type "ATS6?" followed by the <Enter> key. This queries the S-register. You can then enter a new value (such as "ATS6=10") to provide a 10-second delay.

Symptom 26-13. The modem has trouble sending or receiving when the system's power-saving features are turned on This type of problem is most prevalent with PCMCIA modems running on a notebook PC. The power-conservation features on many notebook systems often interfere with the modem's operation—proper modem operation typically relies on full processing speed, which is often scaled back when power conservation is turned on. Ultimately, the most-effective resolution to this problem is simply to turn the power-conservation features off while you use the modem (you can reset the power features later). However, it might be possible to correct these types of problems using a BIOS upgrade for the mobile PC or an updated modem driver.

Symptom 26-14. You see an error, such as: "Already on line" or "Carrier already established" These types of errors often arise when you start a communications package while the modem is already on-line. You might also find this problem when the *Carrier Detect (CD)* signal is set to "always on" (using a command string, such as "AT&C0"). To be sure that the CD signal is on only when the modem makes a connection, use a command string, such as "AT&C1&D2&W." The &W suffix loads the settings into non-volatile RAM. If this problem arises when you hang up the connection without signing off the modem, you will have to reboot the system to clear CD—"AT&F" and "ATZ" will not clear the signal.

Symptom 26-15. The modem refuses to answer the incoming line First, be sure to set the communication software to answer the calling modem—or set the modem to auto-answer mode (set S-register S0 to 1 or more). On external modems, you will see the "AA" LED lit when the auto-answer mode is active. Problems can also occur if your external modem does not recognize the DTR signal generated by the host PC. The command "AT&D" controls how the modem responds to the computer's DTR signal. An external modem turns on the TR light when it is set to see the DTR signal. If the TR light is out, the modem will not answer (regardless of whether the auto-answer mode is enabled or not). Use the "AT&D0" command if your serial port does not support the DTR signal or if your modem cable does not connect to it. Otherwise, you should use the "AT&D2" command.

Symptom 26-16. The modem switches into the command mode intermittently When this problem develops, you might have to tweak the DTR arrangement. To correct this fault, try changing the modem's DTR setting using the "AT&D2&W" command.

Symptom 26-17. Your current modem won't connect at 2400bps with a 2400bps modem This is a compatibility issue between vastly different generations of hardware. The modem you're trying to connect with is almost certainly an older model that doesn't support error control (e.g., MNP protocols). You can disable error control on your modem with the command "AT&M0" <Enter> and try placing the call to the modem again. When you're finished, reset your modem with "ATZ" to re-enable the error-control features.

Symptom 26-18. The communications software is reporting many Cyclic Redundancy Check (CRC) errors and low Characters Per Second (CPS) transfers This might simply be a matter of a poor phone connection established through the telephone network. Try making the call again—chances are that the call will be routed differently, and result in a more reliable connection. Next, check the flow-control scheme (e.g., XOFF/XON, CTS/RTS, etc.) to verify that it is optimum. Or type "AT&F1" from the terminal mode to load the optimum flow control setting. The serial-port rate in your communications software might be set too high for your modem's UART or your area's phone lines. Try lowering the serial port rate in your communications software to 38,400bps or 19,200bps (or lower for slower modems). The remote site you are dialing into might have trouble with the file-transfer protocol that you've selected. Try using a different file-transfer protocol (such as Ymodem-g, rather than Zmodem). Do not use Xmodem if other protocols are available. Finally, a TSR program might be running in the background and interfering with data communications. Disable any TSR programs running in the background and try the communication again.

Symptom 26-19. Errors are constantly occurring in your V.17 fax transmissions As a rule, sending fax transmissions over a modem should present no special problems for a PC, but there are some issues to keep in mind. First, your modem initialization string could be insufficient or incomplete for fax transmissions. Enter the correct initialization string for fax support (e.g., "AT&H3&I2&R2S7=90"). You could also have a disruptive TSR program running in the background. Disable any TSR programs and try the communication again. An outdated comdriver could be on your system. Load the comdriver that came with your fax software (this might require you to re-install your internal modem). Finally, your baud rate might be set too high. Try a lower baud rate of 9600bps.

Symptom 26-20. During installation, a modem setup program cannot find the internal modem In virtually all cases, you have a hardware conflict between the modem and another device in the system. Check the hardware installation first. For internal modems, be sure that the IRQ and I/O address are set correctly, and see that no other devices are using the same IRQ or I/O space as your modem. Under Windows 95, the *Device manager* can usually display any conflicting devices with yellow icons (exclamation marks). Next, be sure that the modem is inserted properly into its bus slot. If any of the card's gold "fingers" appear corroded or soiled, clean the fingers gently with a pencil eraser. Try the modem in another bus slot. Finally, check the modem switches. Most external modems use a series of DIP switches to configure its various features. Refer to the modem's documentation and see that any modem switches are set properly.

Symptom 26-21. After installing a new internal modem, the system mouse driver no longer loads or the mouse behaves erratically In virtually all cases, a hardware conflict is between the new modem and the existing mouse port. Check the hardware installation. If the mouse is connected to a COM port, be sure that your internal modem is set to use a different COM port. You might need to disable COM2 on the motherboard or I/O controller and set up the modem as COM2. Under Windows 95, the *Device manager* can usually display any conflicting devices with a yellow icon (exclamation mark).

Symptom 26-22. After installing modem driver software, Windows locks up or crashes This is almost always the result of a defective or outdated modem driver. Check the software installation. Be sure that the modem driver software you have installed is the proper version for the particular modem, and your version of Windows (i.e., 3.1, 3.11, or 95). You can usually check the driver version on the modem's manufacturer's BBS, CompuServe forum, or Internet Web site. If you do find that the modem driver is incorrect, run any "uninstall" utility that accompanied the software to remove the driver cleanly—otherwise, you'll have to remove the modem driver references from SYSTEM.INI manually. Under Windows 95, you can often *Remove* a device from the *Device manager*, then allow Windows to re-detect the modem during the next boot (and reinstall the new drivers at that point).

Symptom 26-23. DOS communication software works fine, but Windows communication software will not You might also see Windows error messages suggesting that certain files are missing. In most cases, the modem drivers (and any required parameters) have not been loaded properly. Check the software installation and be sure that the modem driver software you have installed is the proper version for the particular modem, and your version of Windows (i.e., 3.1, 3.11, or 95). Try uninstalling the modem drivers (if possible), then reload the drivers from scratch—being sure that they are set up properly for your system configuration. Next, check the manufacturer's BBS, CompuServe forum, or Internet Web site for any adjustments or workarounds that might be required for your particular modem and drivers. You might need to make manual adjustments to SYSTEM.INI and WIN.INI files, as well as to the Windows 95 Registry files.

Symptom 26-24. You cannot get the modem's "distinctive-ring" feature to work Some new modems support the *distinctive-ring service* provided by many telephone companies. This allows the modem to reside on the same physical telephone line as other devices, but only answer when the proper ringing pattern is received. Improper modem configuration is the most common problem. Try calling the distinctive ring numbers associated to your telephone line and see that each number rings with the required pattern. Notice that the distinctive-ring service is not available from all telephone companies and service areas. Next, check the initialization string for S101. Modems supporting distinctive ring usually control the feature through register S101. A typical AT command string might appear, such as "AT&FS101=60." A typical settings list is:

- S101=0 Detects all ringing cadences and report them with RING result code.
- S101=1 Enables the RING result codes: all ringing types will be reported.
- S101=30 Reports only unidentified ring types.
- S101=46 Reports only ring type D.
- S101=54 Reports only ring type C.
- S101=58 Reports only ring type B.
- S101=60 Reports only ring type A.
- S101=62 Disables all ringing detection—the modem will not answer any ring.

> To specify a particular ring type, you must disable the other ring types with this register.

Next, check the initialization string for –SDR. Rather than using S-register 101, some modems use the –SDR command to configure "distinctive ring" operation. A typical AT command string might appear, such as "AT&F-SDR=1." A setting list is shown:

- -SDR=0 Disables the distinctive-ring function.
- -SDR=1 Enables distinctive-ring type 1.
- -SDR=2 Enables distinctive-ring type 2.
- -SDR=3 Enables distinctive-ring type 1 and 2.
- -SDR=4 Enables distinctive-ring type 3.
- -SDR=5 Enables distinctive-ring type 1 and 3.
- -SDR=6 Enables distinctive-ring type 2 and 3.
- -SDR=7 Enables distinctive-ring type 1, 2, and 3.

Symptom 26-25. You cannot get the modem's Caller ID feature to work
Some new modems support the Caller ID service provided by many telephone companies. This allows the modem to identify the telephone number and caller to the computer's communication software when the ringing line is answered. Improper modem configuration is the most common problem. Before you do anything else, check the Caller ID service. Connect any Caller ID-compatible telephone or phone box to the telephone line and be sure that the ID service is working properly. Remember that the Caller ID service is not available from all telephone companies and service areas. Also, remove other Caller ID devices. It is possible that other Caller ID-compatible telephones or phone boxes might be interfering with the modem. Try removing any other devices from the phone line. Check the initialization string for "%CCID." Modems supporting Caller ID usually control the feature through a %CCID command. A typical AT command string might appear, such as "AT&F%CCID=1." A setting list is shown:

- %CCID=0 Turns Caller ID off.
- %CCID=1 Gives Caller ID data using a formatted output.
- %CCID=2 Gives Caller ID data using an unformatted output.

Finally, check the initialization string for #CID. Rather than using the %CCID command, some modems support Caller ID using the #CID command. A typical command string might appear, such as "AT&F#CID=1." A setting list is shown:

- AT#CID=0 Turns Caller ID off.
- AT#CID=1 Gives Caller ID data using a formatted output.
- AT#CID=2 Gives Caller ID data using an unformatted output.

Two special messages might be sent instead of Caller ID information. "O" means that the caller is *Out* of the Caller ID service area—usually a long distance call. "P" is for *Private* and will be displayed for callers who have made arrangements with their phone company to have their numbers blocked.

Symptom 26-26. You cannot recall previous Caller ID data This assumes that normal Caller ID features are working correctly. In most cases, your communication software is not sending the correct AT command to your modem. Check the Caller ID feature and be sure that Caller ID is enabled using the "%CCID" or "#CID" commands, as in Symptom 26-25. Caller ID must be enabled first before data can be recalled. Check the initialization string for "%CRID." Caller ID data can typically be recalled using the "%CRID" command, such as "AT%CRID=0" (recall formatted data) or "AT%CRID=1" (recall unformatted data).

Symptom 26-27. The modem will not provide synchronous communication Modems are typically asynchronous devices, but most can be configured for synchronous communication with host systems, such as mainframe computers. If your modem will not work in synchronous mode, chances are that the modem is not configured properly. You must configure both the originating modem and the answering modem. The originating modem will be configured for synchronous originate mode and will dial a stored number when a connection is attempted. You will need a dumb terminal or terminal-emulation software to configure the modem:

1 Attach the modem to a serial port on a PC or dumb terminal using a standard RS-232 cable.
2 Configure the port-speed setting in the dumb terminal or the terminal-emulation software to match the speed that will be used on the synchronous port.
3 Configure the software for direct connect or terminal mode and open the connection to the port.
4 Type "AT&F&W" and press <Enter>. The modem should respond with "OK." If double characters appear, type "ATE0" and press <Enter> to disable local character echo.
5 Type "AT&Q2&S2&W" and press <Enter>. The modem should respond with "OK."
6 Type "AT&Z0=T[phone number to store]" and press <Enter>. The modem should respond with "OK."
7 Type "AT&D2&W" and press <Enter>. The modem should respond with "OK."
8 Type "AT&C1E0Q1&W" and press <Enter>. The modem should not respond with "OK" because character echo and result code reporting have been disabled.

Next, configure the answering modem. The answering modem must be configured for synchronous answer mode. Although the answering modem is usually attached to the mainframe host system, you will first need to connect it to a dumb terminal for configuration. To configure the answering modem:

1 Attach the modem to a serial port on a PC or dumb terminal using a standard RS-232 cable.
2 Configure the port-speed setting in the dumb terminal or the terminal-emulation software to match the speed that will be used on the synchronous port.
3 Type "AT" and press <Enter>. The modem should respond with "OK." If double characters appear, type "ATE0" and press <Enter> to disable local character echo.
4 Type "AT&F&W" and press <Enter>. The modem should respond with "OK."
5 Type "AT&Q1&S2&W" and press <Enter>. The modem should respond with "OK."
6 Type "ATS0=1" (or the number of rings you want the modem to answer on) and press <Enter>. The modem should respond with OK.

7 Type "AT&D2&W" and press <Enter>. The modem should respond with "OK."

8 Type "AT&C1E0Q1&W" and press <Enter>. The modem should not respond with "OK" because character echo and result-code reporting have been disabled.

Now, disable command recognition. After each modem has been configured properly, the command recognition should be disabled as follows:

1 Turn the modems off.

2 Locate the DIP switches that define modem operations.

3 Move the proper DIP switch to turn command recognition off. If the modem is internal, move the appropriate jumper. The particular DIP switch or jumper will depend on your specific modem, so check with the modem's documentation.

4 Turn the modems on.

Finally, establish a synchronous connection. Attach the originating modem to the SDLC or synchronous port and turn the power on. When a connection is attempted, the modem will automatically dial the stored number and attempt to connect to the other modem. Attach the answering modem to the synchronous port on the host system. The modem will answer incoming calls in "&Q1" synchronous mode.

Symptom 26-28. The modem appears to be set up and configured properly, but it is experiencing data loss Such symptoms might appear as excessive file-transfer errors, missing text or characters, and jumbled ASCII text. Although modern modems are capable of data rates up to 230,400bps, data rates faster than 19,200bps can cause problems for older PCs because of inadequate serial port hardware. Check the UART first—your serial ports should be using 16,550A UARTs for optimum performance. If the UART is older, data throughput will be limited. If you cannot upgrade the UART IC directly, you can often disable the existing serial port and install an upgraded I/O board. Any diagnostic program, such as MSD, can identify the UARTs in your system. Check your modem drivers and be sure that the modem-driver software is up to date and optimized for your particular version of Windows (i.e., 3.1, 3.11, or 95). Finally, reduce your data rates. If you cannot resolve the problem through a driver or new UART, try reducing the modem's data rate in your communication software.

Symptom 26-29. When running modem software, an error appears, such as: "Can't run on a Plug-and-Play ready system" In most cases, the PCMCIA modem is incompatible with a PC's PnP architecture. Check your PnP driver. You might need to load an alternative PnP driver for your modem. Check with the modem manufacturer's BBS, CompuServe forum, or Internet Web site to obtain any updated driver software. You might need to disable the existing DOS PnP driver in CONFIG.SYS.

Symptom 26-30. The modem appears to be set up and configured properly, but it regularly connects at slower speeds than it is capable of Several different factors can account for such a problem. First, modems can only connect at the maximum speed of the slowest modem. If the remote modem is slower than yours, your connection speed will be limited. Try connecting to a faster BBS or another online connection. Check the modem initialization string next—one or more important commands might be missing from the command string. Look for the recommended initialization string in the modem's documentation. Also see that the correct modem is selected in the communication software. Check the modem's firmware version. Use the ATI3 command to check the modem's ID information (including the firmware revision). If the firmware is old, it might need to be updated. If the firmware is very new, it might contain a bug that the manufacturer should be made aware of. Finally, try a different phone line. Faulty noisy telephone connections can reduce effective communication speed. Try the call at an "off time" or try calling on a different phone line.

Symptom 26-31. Windows 95 insists on assigning the modem to COM5
You will need to reconfigure the modem's port assignment through the *Control panel*. First, you'll need to remove any unused modem entries. Software that has been loaded for previous modems might interfere with the current modem's software. Remove unused modem hardware references through the *Device manager*:

1 Select *My computer*, doubleclick on *Control panel*, then choose *Modems*.
2 Highlight any modems that are no longer in the system, then press the *Remove* button.
3 If multiple entries are for the same modem, remove all entries for the modem, restart the system, then reinstall the software.

Next, verify that the modem is on COM5. Check to see that the modem is identified and checks properly before continuing:

1 Select *My computer*, doubleclick on *Control panel*, then choose *Modems*.
2 Select the *Diagnostics* tab.
3 Highlight *COM5* and press the *More info . . .* button.
4 Verify that the modem responds to the "ATI3" command with its proper ID information.
5 Click *OK*.

Now find an unused COM port. Check the *Diagnostics* screen and examine the COM ports in use—any ports not in use are available. Next, use REGEDIT.EXE to edit the Windows 95 *Registry*. You can change the COM port assignment by adjusting the *Registry*:

1 Click on the *Start* button, then select *Run*.
2 Type "REGEDIT" and click *OK*.
3 Select the *Edit/Find* option, then type "COM5."
4 Click *Find next*—this should highlight *Portname* under a *Registry* key.
5 Doubleclick on *Portname*.
6 Enter the new COM port, such as "COM2."
7 Click *OK*, then close REGEDIT.
8 Shut down and restart Windows 95.

Before attempting to edit a Windows 95 *Registry* file, be sure to have a complete backup of the registry files SYSTEM.DAT and USER.DAT.

Finally, check the updated configuration and verify that modem now works on new COM port:

1 Select *My computer*, doubleclick on *Control panel*, then choose *Modems*.
2 Select the *Diagnostics* tab.
3 Select the new COM port that you selected for the modem.
4 Press the *More info . . .* button.
5 Verify that the modem responds to the "ATI3" command with its proper ID information.
6 Click *OK*.

Symptom 26-32. You cannot get the modem to work with a Winsock, but conventional BBS or CompuServe connections work fine In almost all cases, one or more command strings in your Internet connection configuration files is causing an error with the modem. First, be sure that you are using the Winsock version that is appropriate for your particular Internet connection software. Next, check the configuration file. Contact your modem manufacturer to check on any fixes or workarounds, but some modems might not work with the default command strings provided with their Internet software. For example, the Motorola Power 14.4 PCMCIA modem will not work with Trumpet Winsock because of an error in the LOGIN.CMD file—the "$modemsetup=" string is wrong.

Symptom 26-33. You are having trouble configuring the modem for hardware and software flow control This is usually caused by invalid command strings. Try some generic command strings. The following two AT command strings can configure most Hayes-compatible modems for hardware or software flow control. Remember that you might need to add additional commands to configure the modem completely:

- Software flow control (XON/XOFF)   AT&F1&C1&D2
- Hardware flow control (CTS/RTS)   AT&F1&C1&D2\Q3

Symptom 26-34. The modem will not establish a connection through a cellular telephone In most cases, the modem is not configured properly. Check the SCM setting first—be sure that the Station Class Mark (SCM) level is set correctly. Try resetting the modem with an "AT&F1" command. Check the phone type. Be sure that the telephone is set to analog mode—the digital mode might interfere with modem operation.

Symptom 26-35. The modem will not fax properly through a cellular telephone In most cases, the modem is not configured properly. Check the modem's initialization string first, and be sure that the initialization string is set correctly. A basic command string might be "AT&F1E1V1&C1&D2\Q3S7=90S10=60" (although this will not work on all modems). Check the data rate next. For faxing, see that the data rate is set to 4800. You can use the command "AT%B4800."

Symptom 26-36. Windows 95 recognizes the modem, but 16-bit communications software will not see it Windows 95 might not have updated the SYS-

TEM.INI file to reflect changes to the COM port settings. Check the SYSTEM.INI file. Your COM port base address and IRQs are defined in the [386Enh] section of your SYS-TEM.INI file. Check these settings to be sure that they match your modem's settings. The following lines need to be added to your SYSTEM.INI file in the [386enh] section:

```
com1irq=4
com1base=03f8
com2irq=3
com2base=02f8
com3irq=4
com3base=03e8
com4irq=3
com4base=02e8
```

Symptom 26-37. DOS ICU software is installed, but it will not allow the modem to be configured on COM1 or COM2 The ICU software might be inappropriate for your particular modem and system configuration. Check with the modem manufacturer and see if there is a replacement DOS PnP driver or other workaround. If an alternate PnP software is available, you might need to remove the installation of ICU before proceeding:

1 Delete the ESCD.RF file from the root directory of c:\.
2 In the CONFIG.SYS file, delete the line that says: device=c:\plugplay\ . . . , then save your changes.
3 In the [386Enh] section of SYSTEM.INI, delete the lines that start with "device=c: \plug play . . .," then save your changes.
4 In the [windows] section of WIN.INI, the "RUN=" entry should have no reference to ICU or PLUGPLAY after the equal sign. Save your changes, if any were made.
5 Delete the c:\plugplay directory.
6 Exit Windows and reboot your system.

Symptom 26-38. The modem's flash ROM update will not install because it cannot recognize the modem's current firmware version This is invariably a problem with the flash ROM update software itself. Check the software source. Contact the manufacturer to see if a corrected update is available, or see if there is a workaround to the problem. One or more command-line switches can override the update's firmware auto-detection.

Symptom 26-39. The modem establishes connections properly, but it frequently drops connections Both hardware and software issues can cause this kind of trouble. Problems with the telephone connection itself can cause connection problems. Try connecting to various different places. If problems seem to occur more frequently in one connection over another, the remote location might be suffering from communications problems. Also try using a different local telephone line. Next, check the modem's initialization string and be sure that the modem is set up properly for data compression and error correction. Finally, check the Windows driver. If you are using Windows-based communications software, it must be able to support high speed. Standard Windows drivers will not support 28.8KB operation unless third-party communications software modifies it (although Windows 95 drivers are more current). To find out what communications driver you are currently using, review the [Boot] section of your SYSTEM.INI file.

Symptom 26-40. When selecting a modem in your communication software, your particular modem is not listed You will need to obtain the proper driver supplements from the modem manufacturer (or software maker). Try running the modem as a Hayes-compatible—virtually all modems will function as generic Hayes-compatible modems, "AT&F&C1&D2."

Symptom 26-41. It seems to take the modem an unusually long time to hang up The carrier delay time is probably set too long. Check the carrier delay time. Modems can be set to wait (often as long as 25 seconds) after a carrier is lost to see whether it comes back—if you frequently encounter poor signal quality, this can be quite convenient. After a legitimate hang-up, however, the modem might continue to wait. In this case, you might want to set the value of the S10 register to a low number—10 or less.

Symptom 26-42. The modem is configured as COM4 (IRQ3) under Windows 95, but the modem refuses to work There might be a hardware acceleration issue. Go into the Windows 95 *Control panel*, doubleclick the *System* icon, select *Performance*, then click *Graphics*. Set *Hardware acceleration* to "None" and try the modem again. Some advanced modem manufacturers have found an addressing conflict with certain graphic-accelerator cards. If you configure your Windows 95 graphic driver to basic VGA, and find that the modem now works at that setting, then the problem is probably an addressing conflict with your graphics card. You might want to try using one of the more commonly used COM port and IRQ settings, such as:

- COM 1   IRQ 4
- COM 2   IRQ 3
- COM 3   IRQ 5 (if not used by your sound card)

Symptom 26-43. When auto-detect tries to add a new modem at COM2, Windows 95 locks up Open the *Control panel* (*System settings*) and deselect COM2. This can be accomplished by selecting COM2 under *System settings*, then choosing *Properties*. A red "X" in a box should be toward the bottom of the *Properties* screen. Click once on the red "X" and it should clear. This disables the COM port in Windows 95. Click *OK*, then restart the machine. When Windows 95 restarts, it should now find the COM port. This technique applies to all available COM ports.

Symptom 26-44. HyperTerminal works using PCMCIA support under Windows 95, but no 16-bit communication programs work Using a text editor, edit the SYSTEM.INI file in your Windows directory. Under the [386Enh] section of your SYSTEM.INI file, change the COMM.DRV line back to its original COMM.DRV. This line should read comm.drv=comm.drv. Also check that there is a line that states "device=*vcd." If your SYSTEM.INI has a line that reads "device=*vrdd," place a semicolon in front of it. Your 16-bit applications should now work.

Symptom 26-45.   A Winmodem installed correctly and responds to AT commands fine, but whenever you call out, the modem makes a 9600 V.34 connection This is typically caused by a problem with the current communications driver. Adding the following line:

```
ForceBridgeOrRouter=TRUE
```

to the SYSTEM.INI file. It might correct this problem by bypassing the current communications driver and going directly to the Winmodem driver. Also be sure that the *Port rate* is set to 19,200 in the *Control panel* (*Port settings*) in Windows 3.1x, and that it is set to 38,400 (or faster) under Windows 95.

Symptom 26-46. Windows 95 never detected the Winmodem First, be sure that the system has a free COM port or IRQ to use. If the Winmodem was previously installed on the system with Windows 3.1x running, you'll need to search the SYSTEM.INI and WIN.INI files and remove all Winmodem settings so that Windows 95 can detect the Winmodem properly. Under Windows 95, be sure that the modem is not listed in the *Device manager* under *Other devices*. If it is, delete it and reinstall. Next, be sure the Winmodem's key ("USR1001" for the USR Winmodem) is not in the *Registry*.

Further Study

That's all for Chapter 26. Be sure to review the glossary and chapter questions on the accompanying CD. If you have access to the Internet, take a look at some of these modem/fax card resources:

Boca Research: **http://www.bocaresearch.com**

Cardinal: **http://www.cardtech.com/**

Diamond Multimedia: **http://www.diamondmm.com**

Hayes: **http://www.hayes.com/**

ITU: **http://www.itu.com**

Motorola: **http://www.mot.com**

Practical Peripherals: **http://www.practinet.com/**

US Robotics: **http://x2.usr.com/**

Zoom Telephonics: **http://www.zoomtel.com/**

27

MONITOR

TROUBLESHOOTING

CONTENTS AT A GLANCE

Monitor Specifications
and Characteristics
 CRT
 Pixels and resolution
 Triads and dot pitch
 Shadow and slot masks
 Convergence
 Pincushion and barrel distortion
 Horizontal scanning, vertical
  scanning, raster, and retrace
 Interlacing
 Bandwidth
 Swim, jitter, and drift
 Video signal
 Synchronization and polarity

The Color Circuits
 Video drive circuits
 Vertical drive circuit

Horizontal drive circuit
The flyback circuit
Construction

Troubleshooting a CRT
 Inside the CRT
 Identifying CRT problems
 Correcting shorts
 CRT testers/rejuvenators

Troubleshooting a Color Monitor
 Wrapping it up
 Post-repair testing and alignment
 Symptoms

Further Study

From their humble beginnings as basic monochrome text displays, the *monitor* (Fig. 27-1) has grown to provide real-time photo-realistic images of unprecedented quality and color. Monitors have allowed real-time video playback, stunning graphics, and information-filled illustrations to replace the generic "command line" user interface of just a few years ago. In effect, monitors have become our "virtual window" into the modern computer. With many millions of computers now in service, the economical maintenance and repair of computer monitors represents a serious challenge to technicians and hobbyists alike. Fortunately, the basic principles and operations of a computer monitor have changed very little since the days of "terminal displays." This chapter explains the basic concepts behind today's computer monitors, and provides a cross-section of troubleshooting procedures.

Monitor Specifications and Characteristics

Although PCs are defined by a set of fairly well-understood specifications, such as RAM size, hard drive space, and clock speed, monitor specifications describe a whole series of physical properties that PCs never deal with. With this in mind, perhaps the

FIGURE 27-1   A CTX EX910 color monitor. CTX International, Inc.

best introduction to monitor troubleshooting is to cover each specification in detail and show you how each specification and characteristic affects a monitor's performance.

CRT

The *Cathode-Ray Tube (CRT)* is essentially a large vacuum tube. One end of the CRT is formed as a long, narrow neck, and the other end is a broad, almost-flat surface. A coating of colored phosphors is applied inside the CRT, along the front face. The neck end of the CRT contains an element (called the *cathode*), which is energized and heated to very high temperatures (much like an incandescent lamp). At high temperatures, the cathode liberates electrons. When a very high positive voltage potential is applied at the front face of the CRT, electrons liberated by the cathode (which are negatively charged) are accelerated toward the front face. When the electrons strike the phosphor on the front face, light is produced. By directing the stream of electrons across the front face, a visible image is produced. Of course, other elements are needed to control and direct the electron stream, but this is CRT operation in a nutshell. CRT face size (or screen size) is generally measured as a diagonal dimension—that is, a 43.2-cm (17") CRT is 43.2 cm (17") between opposing corners. Larger CRTs are more expensive, but produce larger images, which are usually easier on the eyes.

PIXELS AND RESOLUTION

The picture element (or pixel) is the very smallest point that can be controlled on a CRT. For monochrome displays, a pixel can simply be turned on or off. For a color display, a pixel could assume any of a number of different colors. Pixels are combined in the form of an array (rows and columns). The size of the pixel array defines the display's resolution. Thus, resolution is the total number of pixels in width by the total number of pixels in height. For example, a typical EGA resolution is 640 pixels wide by 350 pixels high (a total of 224,000 pixels), and a typical VGA resolution is 640 pixels wide by 480 pixels high (a total of 307,200 pixels). Typical Super VGA (SVGA) resolution is 800 pixels wide by 600 pixels high. Resolution is important for computer monitors because higher resolutions allow finer image detail.

TRIADS AND DOT PITCH

Although monochrome CRTs use a single, uniform phosphor coating (usually white, amber, or green), color CRTs use three color phosphors (red, green, and blue) arranged as triangles (or triads). Figure 27-2 illustrates a series of color phosphor triads. On a color monitor, each triad represents one pixel (even though three dots are in the pixel). By using the electron streams from three electron guns (one gun for red, one for blue, and another for green) to excite each dot, a broad spectrum of colors can be produced. The three dots are placed so close together that they appear as a single point to the unaided eye.

The quality of a color image is related to just how close each of the three dots are to one another. The closer together they are, the purer the image appears. As the dots are spaced further apart, the image quality degrades because the eye can begin to discern the individual dots in each pixel. This results in lines that no longer appear straight and colors are no longer

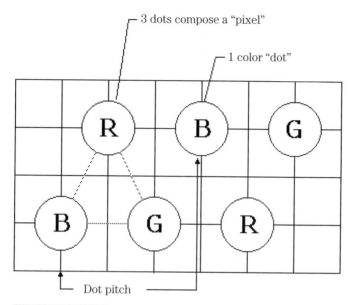

FIGURE 27-2   **Arranging color phosphors in a triad.**

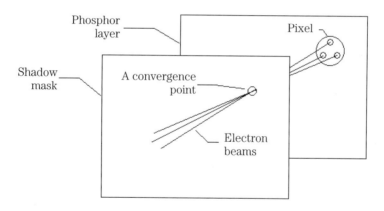

*Sizes and distances are NOT shown to scale.

FIGURE 27-3   **The importance of convergence in a color monitor.**

pure. Dot pitch is a measure of the distance between two adjacent phosphor dots on the display. This is also the same dimension for the distance between openings in a "shadow mask." Displays with a dot pitch of 0.31 mm (or less) generally provide adequate image quality.

SHADOW AND SLOT MASKS

The shadow mask is a thin sheet of perforated metal that is placed in the color CRT just behind the phosphor coating. Electron beams from each of the three "electron guns" are focused to converge at each hole in the mask—not at the phosphor screen (Fig. 27-3). The microscopic holes act as apertures that let the electron beams through only to their corresponding color phosphors. In this way, any stray electrons are masked and color is kept pure. Some CRT designs substitute a shadow mask with a slot mask (or aperture grille), which is made up of vertical wires behind the phosphor screen. The "dot pitch" for CRTs with slot masks is defined as the distance between each slot. Remember that monochrome CRTs do not need a shadow mask at all because the entire phosphor surface is the same color.

CONVERGENCE

Remember that three electron guns are used in a color monitor—the electrons themselves are invisible, but each gun excites a particular color phosphor. All three electron beams are tracking around the screen simultaneously and the beams converge at holes in the shadow mask. This convergence of electron beams is closely related to color purity in the screen image. Ideally, the three beams converge perfectly at all points on the display and the resulting color is perfectly pure throughout (i.e., pure white). If one or more beams do not converge properly, the image color will not be pure. In most cases, poor convergence will result in colored shadows. For example, you might see a red, green, or blue shadow when looking at a white line. Serious convergence problems can result in a blurred or distorted image. Monitor specifications usually list typical convergence error as *misconvergence* at both the display center and the overall display area. Typical center misconvergence runs approximately 0.45 mm, and overall display area misconvergence is about 0.65 mm. Larger numbers result in poorer convergence. Fortunately, monitor convergence can be calibrated (see Chapter 57: "Monitor testing and alignment").

PINCUSHION AND BARREL DISTORTION

The front face of most CRTs is slightly convex (bulging outward). However, digital images are perfectly square (that is, two dimensional). When a flat (2D) image is projected onto a curved (3D) surface, distortion results. Ideally, a monitor's raster circuits will compensate for this screen shape so that the image appears flat when viewed at normal distances. In actuality, however, the image is rarely flat. The sides of the image (top-to-bottom) and (left-to-right) might be bent slightly inward or slightly outward. Figure 27-4 illustrates an exaggerated view of these effects. *Pincushioning* occurs when sides are bent inward, making the image's border appear concave. *Barreling* occurs when the sides are bent outward making the image's border appear convex. In most cases, these distortions should be just barely noticeable (no more than 2.0 or 3.0 mm). Many technicians refer to barrel distortion as pincushioning as well, although this is not technically correct.

HORIZONTAL SCANNING, VERTICAL SCANNING, RASTER, AND RETRACE

To understand what scanning is, you must first understand how a monitor's image is formed. A monitor's image is generated one horizontal line of pixels at a time, starting from the upper left corner of the display (Fig. 27-5). As the beams travel horizontally across the line, each pixel in the line is excited, based on the video data contained in the corresponding location of video RAM on the video adapter board. When a line is com-

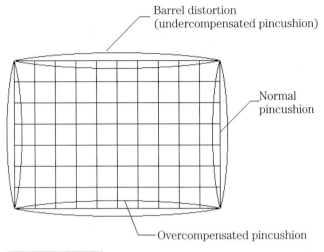

FIGURE 27-4   **The effects of pincushion and barrel distortion.**

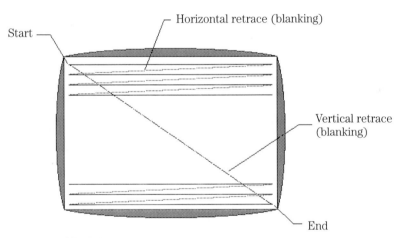

FIGURE 27-5   **Forming a screen image on a CRT.**

plete, the beam turns off (known as *horizontal blanking*). The beam is then directed horizontally (and slightly lower vertically) to the beginning of the next subsequent line. A new horizontal line can then be drawn. This process continues until all horizontal lines are drawn and the beam is in the lower right corner of the display. When this image "page" is complete, the beam turns off (called *vertical blanking*) and is redirected back to the upper left corner of the display to start all over again.

The rate at which horizontal lines are drawn is known as the *horizontal scanning rate* (sometimes called *horizontal sync*). The rate at which a complete "page" of horizontal lines is generated is known as the *vertical scanning rate* (*vertical sync*). Both the horizontal and vertical blanking lines are known as *retrace lines* because the deactivated beams are "retracing" their path before starting a new trace. A typical horizontal retrace time is 5 s, and the typical vertical retrace time is 700 s. This continuous horizontal and

TABLE 27-1   SCAN RATES VS. MONITOR RESOLUTION

MONITOR	RESOLUTION	HORIZONTAL SCAN	VERTICAL SCAN	
MDA	720 × 348	18.43kHz	50Hz	
CGA	320 × 200	15.85kHz	60.5Hz	
EGA	640 × 350	21.8kHz	60Hz	
VGA	640 × 350	31.5kHz	70.1Hz	Alternate config.
VGA	640 × 480	31.47kHz	60Hz	
VGA	640 × 480	37.9kHz	72Hz	VESA config.
SVGA	800 × 600	38.0kHz	60Hz	
"	800 × 600	35.16kHz	56Hz	
"	800 × 600	37.60kHz	72Hz	
"	1024 × 768	35.52kHz	87Hz	Interlaced (8514A)
"	1024 × 768	48.8kHz	60Hz	Sony config.
"	1024 × 864	54kHz	60Hz	DEC config.
"	1006 × 1048	62.8kHz	59.8Hz	Samsung config.
"	1280 × 1024	70.7kHz	66.5Hz	DEC config.
"	1600 × 1280	89.2kHz	66.9Hz	Sun config.

vertical scanning action is generally referred to as *raster*. Numbers can easily be applied to scanning rates to give you an even better idea of their relationship. A typical VGA monitor with a resolution of 640 × 480 pixels uses a horizontal scanning rate of 31.5kHz. This means that 31,500 lines can be drawn in one second or a single line of 640 pixels can be drawn in 31.7 s. Because 480 horizontal lines are drawn in one "page," a complete page can be drawn in (480 × 31.7 s) 15.2 ms. If a single page can be drawn in 15.2 ms, the screen can be refreshed 65.7 times per second (65.7Hz)—this is roughly the vertical rate that will be set for VGA operation at 640-×-480 resolution. In actuality, the vertical scanning rate will be set to a whole number, such as 60Hz, which leaves a lot of spare time for blanking and synchronization. It was discovered early in TV design that vertical scanning rates less than 60Hz resulted in perceivable flicker that causes eye strain and fatigue. You can start to see now that horizontal scanning rates are not chosen arbitrarily. The objective is to select a horizontal frequency that will cover a page's worth of horizontal pixel lines for any given resolution at about 60 times per second (or even higher for reduced flicker). Table 27-1 compares typical monitor resolutions and scan rates.

INTERLACING

Images are "painted" onto a display one horizontal row at a time, but the sequence in which those lines are drawn can be *non-interlaced* or *interlaced*. As you see in Fig. 27-6, a non-interlaced monitor draws all of the lines that compose an image in one pass. This is preferable because a non-interlaced image is easier on your eyes—the entire image is refreshed at the vertical scanning frequency, so a 60Hz vertical scanning rate will update the entire image 60 times in one second. A non-interlaced display draws an image as two passes. Once the first pass is complete, a second pass fills in the rest of the image. The effective image-refresh rate is only half the stated vertical scanning rate. The typical 1024-×-768 SVGA monitor offers a vertical scanning rate of 87Hz, but because the monitor is "interlaced," effective refresh is only 43.5Hz—screen flicker is much more noticeable.

BANDWIDTH

In the very simplest terms, the *bandwidth* of a monitor is the absolute maximum rate at which pixels can be sent to the monitor. Typical VGA displays offer a bandwidth of 30MHz. That is, the monitor could generate up to 30 million pixels per second on the display. Consider that each scan line of a VGA display uses 640 pixels and the horizontal scan rate of 31.45kHz allows 31,450 scan lines per second to be written. At that rate, the monitor is processing (640 pixels/scan line × 31,450 scan lines/second) 20,128,000 pixels/second—well within the monitor's 30MHz bandwidth. The very newest color monitors offer bandwidths of 135MHz. Such high-resolution 1280-×-1024 monitors with scanning rates of 79kHz would need to process at least (1280 pixels/scan line × 79,000 scan lines/second) 101,120,000 pixels/second (101.12MHz), so enhanced bandwidth is truly a necessity for high resolutions.

SWIM, JITTER, AND DRIFT

The electron beam(s) that form an image are directed around a display using variable magnetic fields generated by separate vertical and horizontal deflection coils mounted around the CRT's neck. The analog signals that drive each deflection coil are produced by horizontal and vertical deflection circuitry. Ideally, deflection circuitry should steer the electron beam(s) precisely the same way in each pass. This would result in an absolutely rock-solid image on the display. In the real world, however, there are minute variations in the placement of images over any given period of time. *Jitter* is a term used to measure such variation over a 15-second period. *Swim* (sometimes called *wave*) is a measure of position variation over a 30-second period. *Drift* is a measure of position variation over a one-minute period. Notice that all three terms represent essentially the same problem over different amounts of time. Swim, jitter, and drift can be expressed as fractions of a pixel or as physical measurements, such as millimeters.

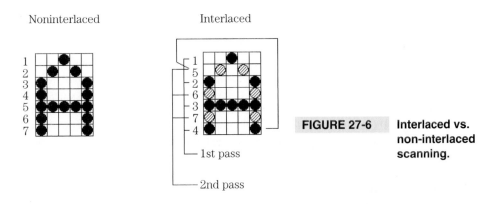

FIGURE 27-6   Interlaced vs. non-interlaced scanning.

VIDEO SIGNAL

This specification lists signal levels and characteristics of the analog video input channel(s). In most cases, a video signal in the 0.7-Vpp (peak to peak) range is used. Circuitry inside the monitor amplifies and manipulates these relatively small signals. A related specification is *input impedance*, which is often at 75 ohms. Older monitors using digital (on/off) video signals typically operate up to 1.5 V.

SYNCHRONIZATION AND POLARITY

After a line is drawn on the display, the electron beams are turned off (blanked) and repositioned to start the next horizontal line. However, no data is contained in the retrace line. For the new line to be "in sync" with the data for that line, a *synchronization pulse* is sent from the video adapter to the monitor. There is a separate pulse for horizontal synchronization and vertical synchronization. In most current monitors, synchronization signals are edge-triggered TTL (transistor-transistor logic) signals. *Polarity* refers to the edge that triggers the synchronization. A falling trigger (marked "-" or "positive/negative") indicates that synchronization occurs at the high-to-low transition of the sync signal. A leading trigger (marked "+" or "negative/positive") indicates that synchronization occurs on the low-to-high transition of the sync signal.

The Color Circuits

To have a full understanding of color monitors, it is best to start with a block diagram. The block diagram for a VGA monitor is shown in Fig. 27-7. Three complete video drive circuits are needed (one for each primary color—red, green, and blue). Although early color monitors used logic levels to represent video signals, current monitors use analog signals that allow the intensity of each color to be varied. The CRT is designed to provide three electron beams that are directed at corresponding color phosphors. By varying the intensity of each electron beam, virtually any color can be produced. For all practical purposes, the color monitor can be considered in three sub-sections: the video drive circuits, the vertical drive circuit, and the horizontal drive circuit (including the high-voltage system).

VIDEO DRIVE CIRCUITS

The schematic diagram for a typical *RGB (Red, Green, and Blue)* drive circuit is shown in Fig. 27-8. This schematic is actually part of a Tandy VGM-220 analog color monitor. You will see that there are three separate video drive circuits. Components with a 5xx designation (e.g., IC501) are part of the red video drive circuit. The 6xx designation (e.g., Q602) shows a part in the green video drive circuit. A 7xx marking (e.g., C704) indicates a component in the blue video drive circuit. Other components marked with 8xx designations (e.g., Q803) are included to operate the CRT control grid. Let's walk through the operation of one of these video circuits.

The red analog signal is filtered by the small array of F501. The ferrite beads on either side of the small filter capacitor serve to reduce noise that might otherwise interfere with the weak analog signal. The video signal is amplified by transistor Q501. Potentiometer

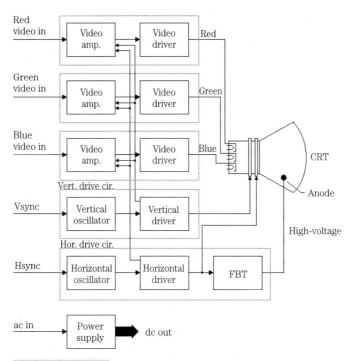

FIGURE 27-7   Block diagram of a color (VGA) monitor.

VR501 adjusts the signal gain (the amount of amplification applied to the video signal). Collector signals are then passed to the differential amplifier circuit in IC501. Once again, noise is a major concern in color signals, and differential amplifiers help to improve signal strength while eliminating noise. The resulting video signal is applied to a "push-pull" amplifier circuit consisting of Q503 and Q504, then fed to a subsequent "push-pull" amplifier pair of Q505 and Q506. Potentiometer VR502 controls the amount of dc bias used to generate the final output signal. The output from this final amplifier stage is coupled directly to the corresponding CRT video control grid. The remaining two drive circuits both work the same way.

Problems with the video circuits in color monitors rarely disable the image entirely. Even if one video drive circuit should fail, two others are still left to drive the CRT. Of course, the loss of one primary color will severely distort the image colors, but the image should still be visible. You can tell when one of the video drive circuits fails: the faulty circuit will either saturate the display with that color or cut that color out completely. For example, if the red video drive circuit should fail, the resulting screen image will either be saturated with red, or red will be absent (leaving a greenish-blue or cyan image).

VERTICAL DRIVE CIRCUIT

The vertical drive circuit is designed to operate the monitor's vertical deflection yoke (dubbed V-DY). To give you a broad perspective of vertical drive operation and its inter-relation to other important monitor circuits, Fig. 27-9 illustrates the vertical drive, horizontal drive, high-voltage, and power-supply circuits—all combined together in the same schematic. This

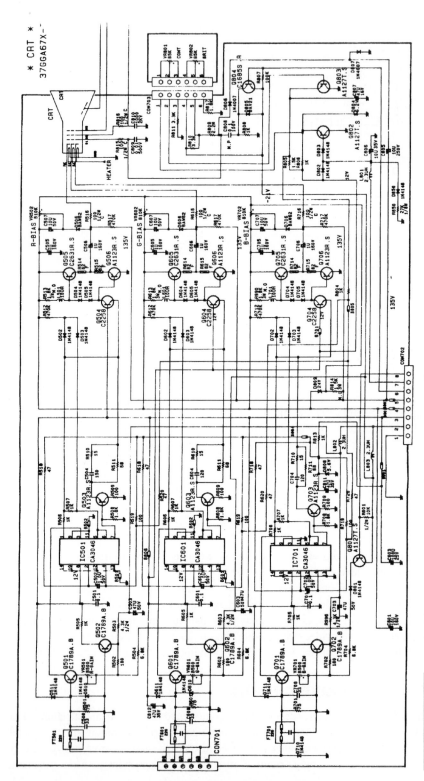

FIGURE 27-8   Schematic of a VGM-220 video circuit. Tandy Corporation

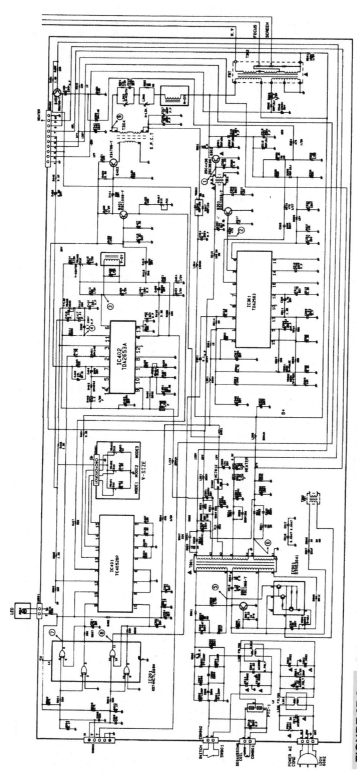

FIGURE 27-9   Schematic of a VGM-220 main (raster) circuit. Tandy Corporation

schematic is essentially the main PC board for the Tandy VGM-220 monitor. Components marked with 4xx numbers (e.g., IC401) are part of the vertical drive system.

The vertical sync pulses enter the monitor at connector CH202 (the line marked V). A simple exclusive-OR gate (IC201) is used to condition the sync pulses and select the video mode being used. Because the polarity of horizontal and vertical sync pulses will be different for each video mode, IC201 detects those polarities and causes the digitally controlled analog switch (IC401) to select one of three vertical size (V-SIZE) control sets, which is connected to the vertical sawtooth oscillator (IC402). This mode-switching circuit allows the monitor to auto-size the display.

The vertical sync pulse fires the vertical sawtooth oscillator on pin 2 of IC402. The frequency of the vertical sweep is set to 60Hz, but it can be optimized by adjusting the vertical frequency control, (V-FREQ) VR404. It is highly recommended that you do not attempt to adjust the vertical frequency unless you have an oscilloscope available. Vertical linearity (V-LIN) is adjusted through potentiometer VR405. Vertical centering (V-CENTER) is controlled through VR406. Linearity and centering adjustments should only be made while displaying an appropriate test pattern. It is interesting that no discrete power amplifiers are needed to drive the vertical deflection yoke—IC402 pin 6 drives the deflection yoke directly through an internal power amplifier.

The pincushion circuit forms a link between the vertical and horizontal deflection systems through the pincushion transformer (T304). Transistors Q401 and Q402 form a compensator circuit that slightly modulates horizontal deflection. This prevents distortion in the image when projecting a flat, two-dimensional image onto a curved surface (the CRT). Potentiometer VR407 provides the pincushion control (PCC). As with other alignments, you should not attempt to adjust the pincushion unless an appropriate test pattern is displayed.

Problems that develop in the vertical amplifier will invariably effect the appearance of the CRT image. A catastrophic fault in the vertical oscillator or amplifier will leave a narrow horizontal line in the display. The likeliest cause is the vertical drive IC (IC402) because that component handles both sawtooth generation and amplification. If only the upper or lower half of an image disappears, only one part of the vertical amplifier in IC402 might have failed. However, any fault on the PC board that interrupts the vertical sawtooth will disable vertical deflection entirely. When the vertical deflection is marginal (too expanded or too compressed), suspect a fault in IC402, but its related components might also be breaking down. An image that is over-expanded will usually appear "folded over" with a whitish haze along the bottom. It might also be interesting to note that vertical drive problems do not affect display colors.

HORIZONTAL DRIVE CIRCUIT

The horizontal drive circuit is responsible for operating the horizontal deflection yoke (H-DY). This circuit sweeps the electron beams left and right across the display. To understand how the horizontal drive works, you should again refer to the schematic of Fig. 27-9. All components marked 3xx numbers (e.g., IC301) relate to the horizontal drive circuit. Horizontal sync signals enter the monitor at connector CH202 (the line marked "H") and are conditioned by the executive-OR gates of IC201. Conditioned sync pulses fire the horizontal oscillator (IC301). Horizontal frequency should be locked at 31.5kHz, but potentiometer VR302 can be used to optimize the frequency. Do not attempt to adjust horizontal frequency, unless you have an oscilloscope available. Horizontal phase can be adjusted with VR301. You should avoid altering any alignments until a suitable test pattern is displayed, as covered in Chapter 57.

IC301 is a highly integrated device that is designed to provide precision horizontal square-wave pulses to the driver transistors Q301 and Q302. IC301 pin 3 provides the horizontal pulses to Q301. Transistor Q301 switches on and off, causing current pulses in the horizontal output transformer (T303). Current pulses produced by the secondary winding of T303 fire the horizontal output transistor (Q302). Output from the HOT drives the horizontal deflection yoke (H-DY). The deflection circuit includes two adjustable coils to control horizontal linearity (H-LIN: L302) and horizontal width (H-WIDTH: L303). You will also notice that the collector signal from Q302 is directly connected to the flyback transformer (FBT). Operation of the high-voltage system is covered in the next section.

Problems in the horizontal drive circuit can take several forms. One common manifestation is the loss of horizontal sweep, leaving a vertical line in the center of the display. This is generally caused by a fault in the horizontal oscillator (IC301), rather than the horizontal driver transistors. The second common symptom is a loss of image (including raster), and is almost always the result of a failure in the *HOT (High-voltage Output Transistor circuit)*. Because the HOT also operates the flyback transformer, a loss of horizontal output will disrupt high-voltage generation—the image will disappear.

THE FLYBACK CIRCUIT

The presence of a large positive potential on the CRT's anode is needed in order to accelerate an electron beam across the distance between the cathode and CRT phosphor. Electrons must strike the phosphor hard enough to liberate visible light. Under normal circumstances, this requires a potential of 15,000 to 30,000 V. Larger CRTs need higher voltages because a greater physical distance must be overcome. Monitors generate high-voltage through the flyback circuit.

The heart of the high-voltage circuit is the *flyback transformer (FBT)*, as shown in Fig. 27-9. The FBT's primary winding is directly coupled to the horizontal output transistor (Q302). Another primary winding is used to compensate the high-voltage level for changes in brightness and contrast. Flyback voltage is generated during the horizontal retrace (the time between the end of one scan line and the beginning of another), when the sudden drop in deflection signal causes a strong voltage spike on the FBT secondary windings. You will notice that the FBT in Fig. 27-9 provides one multi-tapped secondary winding. The top-most tap from the FBT secondary provides high-voltage to the CRT anode. A high-voltage rectifier diode added to the FBT assembly forms a half-wave rectifier—only positive voltages reach the CRT anode. The effective capacitance of the CRT anode will act to filter the high-voltage spikes into dc. You can read the high-voltage level with a high-voltage probe. The CRT needs additional voltages in order to function. The lower tap from the FBT secondary supplies voltage to the focus and screen-grid adjustments. These adjustments, in turn, drive the CRT directly.

Trouble in the high-voltage circuit can render the monitor inoperative. Typically, a high-voltage fault manifests itself as a loss of image and raster. In many cases where the HOT and deflection signals are intact, the flyback transformer has probably failed, causing a loss of output in one or more of the three FBT secondary windings. The troubleshooting procedures in the next section of this chapter will cover high-voltage symptoms and solutions in more detail.

CONSTRUCTION

Before jumping right into troubleshooting, it would be helpful to understand how the circuits shown in Fig. 27-9 are assembled. A wiring diagram for the Tandy VGM-220 is shown in Fig. 27-10. The two PC boards are the video drive PC board and the main PC board. The main PC board contains the raster circuits, power supply, and high-voltage cir-

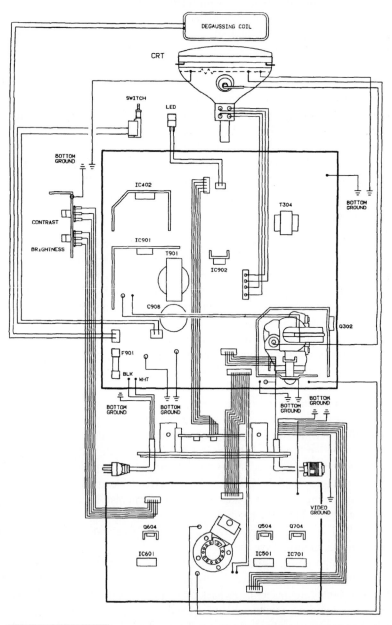

FIGURE 27-10   **A wiring diagram for the VGM-220.** Tandy Corporation

cuitry. The video drive PC board contains red, green, and blue video circuits. Video signals, focus grid voltage, screen grid voltage, and brightness and contrast controls connect to the video drive board. The video PC board plugs in to the CRT at its neck (although the diagram of Fig. 27-10 might not show this clearly). A power switch, power LED, and CRT degaussing coil plug into the main PC board. There are also connections at the main PC board for the ac line cord and video sync signals.

Troubleshooting a CRT

In spite of its age, the *Cathode-Ray Tube (CRT)* continues to play an important role in modern computer monitors. There are some very important reasons for this longevity. First, the CRT is relatively inexpensive to make, and it requires only simple circuitry. Second, the CRT is extremely reliable. Typical working lives can extend to 10 years or longer. This combination of low-cost, ease of operation, and long-term reliability has allowed the CRT to keep pace with today's personal computers. However, CRTs are certainly not perfect devices—the delicate assemblies within the CRT used to generate and direct electron beams can eventually open, short-circuit, or wear out. Like most classic vacuum tubes, CRT failures often occur slowly over a period of weeks or months. This part of the chapter shows you the assemblies in a typical color CRT, explains the faults that often occur, and offer some alternatives for dealing with CRT problems.

INSIDE THE CRT

Before reading about CRT problems, you should have an understanding of the color CRT itself. Figure 27-11 shows a cross-section of a typical color CRT. To produce an image, electron beams are generated, concentrated, and directed across a phosphor-coated face. When electron beams (which are invisible) strike phosphor, light is liberated—this is the light you see from the CRT. The color of light is determined by the particular phosphor chemistry. Notice that there are three electron "guns" in the color CRT: a beam for red, a beam for green, and a beam for blue.

Electron beams start with a heater wire. When energized, the heater becomes extremely hot (this is the glow you see in the CRT neck). The heat from a heater warms its corresponding cathode, and a barium tip on the cathode begins "boiling off" electrons. Ordinarily, electrons would simply boil off into a big, clumsy cloud. But because electrons are negatively charged, they will be attracted to any large positive potential. A moderate positive potential (+500 V or so) on the screen grid starts accelerating the electrons down the CRT's neck, while the control grid voltage limits the electrons—effectively forcing the unruly cloud into a beam. Once electrons pass the screen grid, a high positive potential on the CRT anode (anywhere from 15 to 30 kV) rockets the electrons toward the CRT face. The beam is still rather wide, so a focus grid applies another potential that concentrates the beam.

All this is very effective at generating narrow, high-velocity electron beams. But unless you want to watch a big, bright spot in the middle of the CRT, there has to be some method of tracing the beams around the CRT face. *Beam tracing* is accomplished through the use

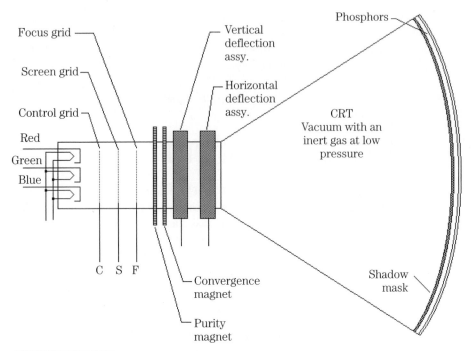

Focus grid

Screen grid

Control grid

Red

Green

Blue

Vertical
deflection
assy.

Horizontal
deflection
assy.

C S F

Convergence
magnet

Purity
magnet

Phosphors

CRT
Vacuum with an
inert gas at low
pressure

Shadow
mask

FIGURE 27-11   **Cross-section of a color CRT.**

of deflection magnets placed around the CRT neck—these magnets (actually electromagnets) are heavy coils of wire where the CRT funnel meets the neck. Four electromagnets are in this "deflection assembly": two opposing electromagnets direct the beam in the vertical direction, and another set of opposing magnets direct the beam in the horizontal direction. Using electrical signals from the monitor's raster circuits, an electron beam can trace across the entire CRT face.

Another element of the CRT that you should understand is called the *shadow mask*. A shadow mask is basically a thin metal sheet with a series of small holes punched into it. Some CRTs use a mask of rectangular openings referred to as an *aperture grille* or *slot mask*. Both types of mask perform the same purpose—to ensure that electron beams strike only the color phosphors of the intended pixel. This is a vital element of a color monitor. In a monochrome monitor, the CRT is coated with a single homogeneous layer of phosphor—if stray electrons strike nearby phosphor particles, a letter or line might simply appear to be a bit out of focus. For a color CRT, however, stray electrons can cause incorrect colors to appear on nearby pixels. Masks help to preserve color purity. Color purity is also aided by a *purity magnet*, which helps correct fine beam positioning. A *convergence magnet* helps ensure that all three electron beams meet (or converge) at the shadow mask.

Of course, grids, heaters, and cathodes are all located inside the glass CRT vessel. Electrical connections are made through a circular arrangement of sealed pins in the neck. Table 27-2 explains the designations for each pin. Remember that the high-voltage anode is attached directly to the CRT in the top right part of the glass funnel. Also remember that some CRT designs might use additional pins.

IDENTIFYING CRT PROBLEMS

CRTs enjoy a long, reliable working life because there are really no moving parts—merely a set of stationary metal elements. However, the arrangement of grids and cathodes are located in very close proximity to one another. Physical shocks can dislodge elements and cause sudden short circuits. Eventually, regular use will alter the physical dimensions of cathodes and grids (resulting in the development of a slower, more gradual short-circuit). The stress of regular wear can also cause open circuits in the heater, cathode, or grid.

When considering a CRT replacement, you should remember that the CRT is typically the most expensive part of the monitor. For larger monitors, the CRT becomes an even larger percentage of the monitor's overall cost. In many cases, the cost for a replacement CRT approaches the original cost of the entire monitor. As a consequence, you should carefully evaluate the economics of replacing the CRT versus buying a new monitor outright.

Symptom 27-1. Heater opens in the CRT Each time the heater runs, it expands. When the CRT turns off, the heater cools and contracts again. This regular thermal expansion and contraction might eventually fatigue the heater and cause it to open. You will see this as a complete loss of the corresponding color. Because heaters are all tied together electrically, there is no way to measure a particular heater directly, but you might see only two glowing heaters in the CRT neck, instead of three. An open heater cannot be recovered, and the only available alternative is to replace the CRT itself.

Symptom 27-2. Heater shorts to a cathode in the CRT This is not as strange as it might seem at first. To heat a cathode effectively, the heater must be extremely close to the cathode—especially to the barium element that actually liberates the electrons. Over time, the heater might develop accumulations of corrosion, which might eventually cause the heater to contact the cathode. In theory, this should never happen because the inert low-pressure gasses inside the CRT should prevent this. But in actuality, some small amount of oxygen will still be present in the CRT, and oxidation might occur. A shorted heater will cause the electron gun to fire at full power—in effect, the electron gun will be stuck "on." The image will appear saturated with the color of the defective electron gun.

TABLE 27-2 TYPICAL CRT PIN DESIGNATIONS	
DESIGNATION	**DESCRIPTION**
G1	Control grid voltage
G2	Screen grid voltage
G3 or F	Focus grid voltage
KG	Green video signal
KR	Red video signal
KB	Blue video signal
H1	Heater voltage in
H2	Heater voltage out

For example, if the blue heater shorts to the cathode, the image will appear to be saturated with blue. You will also likely see visible retrace lines in the image.

You can verify this problem by removing all power from the monitor, removing the video drive board from the CRT's neck, and measuring the resistance between a heater wire and the suspect cathode. For the CRT pinout listed in Table 27-2, you could check the blue cathode by measuring resistance between the KB and H1 (or H2) pins. Ideally, an infinite resistance should be between the heaters and cathodes. If there is measurable resistance (or a direct short-circuit), you have found the problem. If the resistance measures infinity, as expected, you might have a defect on the video drive board.

Symptom 27-3. Cathode shorts to the control grid in the CRT A cathode can also short-circuit to the control grid. Often, corrosion flakes off the cathode and contacts the control grid. When this happens, the control grid loses its effectiveness, and the corresponding color will appear saturated. This symptom will appear very much like a heater short. Fortunately, you should be able to verify this problem with your meter by measuring resistance between the control grid and the suspect cathode. Ideally, an infinite resistance should be between the control grid and all cathodes. If you read a measurable resistance (or a direct short-circuit), chances are good that you're facing a cathode-to-control grid short.

Symptom 27-4. One or more colors appear weak This is a common symptom in many older CRTs. Over time, the barium emitter in your cathodes will wear out or develop a layer of ions (referred to as *cathode poisoning*), which inhibit the release of electrons. In either case, the afflicted cathode will lose efficiency, resulting in weakened screen colors. Typically, you might expect all three cathodes to degrade evenly over time—and they will—but by the time the problem becomes serious enough for service, you will usually notice one color weaker than the others. Try increasing the gain of the afflicted signal on the video drive board. If the cathode is indeed afflicted, increasing signal gain should not have a substantial effect on the color brightness, and you should consider replacing the CRT.

Symptom 27-5. CRT phosphors appear aged or worn *Phosphors* are specially formulated chemicals that glow in a particular color when excited by a high-energy electron beam. Typically, phosphors will last for the lifetime of the monitor, but age and normal use will eventually reduce the sensitivity of the phosphors—for old CRTs, you might see this as dull, low-contrast colors. Perhaps a more dramatic problem occurs with "phosphor burn," which occurs when a monitor is left on displaying the same image for a very long period of time. If you turn the monitor off, you can see the latent image burned onto the CRT as a dark shadow. In both cases, there is no way to rejuvenate phosphors, so the CRT will have to be replaced. You can advise customers to prolong the life of their CRT by keeping the brightness at a minimum and using a screen-saver utility, if an image will sit unchanging for a long time.

Symptom 27-6. The CRT suffers from bad cutoff (a.k.a. bad gamma) On a CRT, color linearity is a function of the cathode's ability to adjust the level of electron emission—in other words, beam intensity must be linear across the entire range of the video signal (e.g., 0 to 20 V or 0 to 50 V). As cathodes age, however, they tend to become non-linear. When this happens, images tend to be too "black and white," rather than display a smooth transition of colors. Technicians often refer to this as a "gassy" CRT, which is actually a CRT gamma problem. In addition to cathode wear, control grid failure can adversely affect beam intensity.

Symptom 27-7. The control grid in the CRT is open The control grid is used to limit the beam intensity produced by a cathode by applying a potential on the grid. Occasionally, you will find that a control grid might open. In that case, there is no longer a potential available to control the beam intensity, and the beam will fire at full intensity. At first glance, you might think this is a cathode-to-control grid short or a heater-to-cathode short. But if you can't find a short with your multimeter, the control grid is probably open, and the CRT will have to be replaced.

Symptom 27-8. The CRT screen grid is open The screen grid plays an important role in image brightness by accelerating the electron beam toward the CRT phosphors. If the screen grid opens, no potential will be available to begin accelerating the beam. This will result in a very dark image—even with the screen voltage at maximum. You might think this is a control-to-screen grid short, but if you can't find the short with your multimeter, the screen grid is probably open, and the CRT will have to be replaced.

Symptom 27-9. The CRT focus grid is open A focus grid assembly concentrates electron beams into narrow pinpoints by the time the beam reaches the shadow mask. Typically, a focus control is located around the flyback transformer. If the focus grid fails, the image will appear highly distorted, and the focus adjustment will have no effect. When a focus grid fails, the entire CRT will have to be replaced.

Symptom 27-10. The control grid shorts to the screen grid in the CRT The same flakes of oxidation that can short a cathode to the control grid can also short the control grid to the screen grid. The screen grid starts accelerating the electrons toward the CRT face. If the screen grid is shorted, it will reduce the energy imparted to the electrons—in effect, a shorted screen grid will significantly reduce the overall image brightness (even with the brightness at maximum). In extreme cases, the image might disappear entirely. You can measure the screen grid voltage at G2, which typically runs from 250 to 750 V in normal operation. If the voltage is low (even with the screen grid control at maximum), power down the monitor, remove the video drive board from the monitor's neck, restart the monitor, and measure the screen voltage again. If the screen voltage returns to normal, you can be confident that the screen grid is shorted. If screen voltage remains low, you might have a fault in the screen voltage circuit. You can also verify a short between the control and screen grids by powering down the monitor and measuring resistance between the G1 and G2 pins on the CRT neck. Ideally, it should be an infinite resistance.

CORRECTING SHORTS

You can probably guess that short circuits within a CRT can be maddening—there is just no way to get to them. However, most shorts are not held in place by anything more than gravity, or a slight arc during contact. As a result, it might be possible to dislodge the short by turning the monitor over and gently rapping on the CRT neck with the plastic end of a screwdriver. Obviously, this is also a prime way to shatter the CRT, so be very careful if you attempt to dislodge a suspected short. If a few light taps don't do the job, quit while the CRT is still in one piece.

CRT TESTERS/REJUVENATORS

Because shorts are small fragments of conductive material, they can be "burned" away using a surge of electricity—this is much safer than the "tap-and-pray" method mentioned previously. Such devices as Sencore's CR70 Universal CRT Restorer/Analyzer can help check the CRT for shorts and opens, burn out a wide variety of shorts, and (in many cases) rejuvenate weak elements. As another advantage, a tester can usually check and rejuvenate a CRT without having the whole monitor available. Most CRT test equipment can perform four major operations: color balance testing, emission testing, removing shorts, and beam rejuvenation:

■ *Color-balance testing* To produce pure white (and all other true colors), all three electron guns must be able to run at the same intensity. A color-balance test can compare the strongest gun to the weakest gun. If the variation is greater than 55%, the weakest gun will be displayed as "bad." But it is possible to recover a portion of the weaker beam's operation through a "Beam builder" or "Beam rejuvenator" function on the tester.

■ *Emission testing* A cathode must be able to "emit" electrons—that is the basis of all vacuum tubes. As the cathode ages, ions generated from air in the CRT gradually block the cathode's ability to produce electrons. This is "ion poisoning," which results in weakened electron beams. A rejuvenator function can usually overcome low-emission problems.

■ *Removing shorts* Generally speaking, a decent CRT tester/rejuvenator can remove shorts between the control grid and the cathode or the screen grid. In actuality, you might see such a function marked "Remove G1 short" or some similar nomenclature. However, few testers attempt to remove heater-to-cathode shorts because the energy needed to clear a short there would usually burn out the heater element entirely.

■ *Beam rejuvenation* The purpose of rejuvenation is basically to restore the emission of weak electron guns. This is usually accomplished by boosting the heater voltage (making the cathode extremely hot), then passing a 100- to 150-mA current through the cathode. The effect of rejuvenation exposes fresh emitting material, which, in turn, adds new life to weakened guns. A current meter measures beam current; when beam current reaches its nominal range during rejuvenation, the electron gun is restored.

Troubleshooting a Color Monitor

Any chapter about monitor troubleshooting must start with a reminder of the dangers involved. Computer monitors use very high voltages for proper operation. Potentially lethal shock hazards exist within the monitor assembly—both from ordinary ac line voltage, as well as from the CRT anode voltage developed by the flyback transformer. You must use extreme caution whenever a monitor's outer housings are removed. If you are uncomfortable with the idea of working around high voltages, defer your troubleshooting to an experienced technician.

WRAPPING IT UP

When you finally get your monitor working again and are ready to reassemble it, be very careful to see that all wiring and connectors are routed properly. No wires should be pinched or lodged between the chassis or other metal parts (especially sharp edges). After the wiring is secure, be sure that any insulators, shielding, or protective enclosures are installed. This is even more important for larger monitors with supplemental X-ray shielding. Replace all plastic enclosures and secure them with their full complement of screws.

POST-REPAIR TESTING AND ALIGNMENT

Regardless of the problem with your monitor or how you go about repairing it, a check of the monitor's alignment is always worthwhile before returning the unit to service. Your first procedure after a repair is complete should be to ensure that the high-voltage level does not exceed the maximum specified value. Excessive high-voltage can liberate X-radiation from the CRT. Over prolonged exposure, X-rays can present a serious biohazard. The high-voltage value is usually marked on the specification plate glued to the outer housing, or recorded on a sticker placed somewhere inside the housing. If you cannot find the high-voltage level, refer to service data from the monitor's manufacturer. Once high-voltage is correct, you can proceed with other alignment tests. Refer to Chapter 57 for testing and alignment procedures. When testing (and realignment) is complete, it is wise to let the monitor run for 24 hours or so (called a *burn-in test*) before returning it to service. Running the monitor for a prolonged period helps ensure that the original problem has indeed been resolved. This is a form of quality control. If the problem resurfaces, a more serious problem might be elsewhere in the monitor.

SYMPTOMS

Symptom 27-11. The image is saturated with red or appears greenish-blue (cyan) If any user color controls are available from the front or rear housings, be sure that those controls have not been accidentally adjusted. If color controls are set properly (or not available externally), the red video drive circuit has probably failed. Refer to the example circuit of Fig. 27-8. Use your oscilloscope to trace the video signal from its initial input to the final output. If no red video signal is at the amplifier input (i.e., the base of Q501), check the connection between the monitor and the video adapter board. If the connection is intact, try a known-good monitor. If the problem persists on a known-good monitor, replace the video adapter board. As you trace the video signal, you can compare the signal to characteristics at the corresponding points in the green or blue video circuits. The point at which the signal disappears is probably the point of failure, and the offending component should be replaced. If you do not have the tools or inclination to perform component-level troubleshooting, try replacing the video drive PC board entirely.

   If the video signal measures properly all the way to the CRT (or a new video drive PC board does not correct the problem), suspect a fault in the CRT itself—the corresponding cathode or video control grid might have failed. If you have access to a CRT tester/rejuvenator, test the CRT. If the CRT measures bad (and cannot be recovered through any available rejuvenation procedure), it should be replaced. A color CRT is usually the most expensive component in the monitor. As with any CRT replacement, you should carefully consider the economics of the repair versus buying a new or rebuilt monitor.

Symptom 27-12. The image is saturated with blue or appears yellow If any user color controls are available from the front or rear housings, be sure that those controls have not been accidentally adjusted. If color controls are set properly (or are not available externally), the blue video drive circuit has probably failed. Refer to the example circuit of Fig. 27-8. Use your oscilloscope to trace the video signal from its initial input to the final output. If no blue video signal is at the amplifier input (i.e., the base of Q701), check the connection between the monitor and the video adapter board. If the connection is intact, try a known-good monitor. If the problem persists on a known-good monitor, replace the video adapter board. As you trace the video signal, you can compare the signal to characteristics at the corresponding points in the green or red video circuits. The point at which the signal disappears is probably the point of failure, and the offending component should be replaced. If you do not have the tools or inclination to perform component-level troubleshooting, try replacing the video drive PC board entirely.

If the video signal measures properly all the way to the CRT (or a new video drive PC board does not correct the problem), suspect that a fault is in the CRT itself—the corresponding cathode or video control grid might have failed. If you have access to a CRT tester/rejuvenator, test the CRT. If the CRT measures bad (and cannot be recovered through any available rejuvenation procedure), it should be replaced. A color CRT is usually the most expensive component in the monitor. As with any CRT replacement, you should carefully consider the economics of the repair versus buying a new or rebuilt monitor.

Symptom 27-13. The image is saturated with green, or appears bluish-red (magenta) If any user color controls are available from the front or rear housings, be sure that those controls have not been accidentally adjusted. If color controls are set properly (or not available externally), the green video drive circuit has probably failed. Refer to the example circuit of Fig. 27-8. Use your oscilloscope to trace the video signal from its initial input to the final output. If no green video signal is at the amplifier input (i.e., the base of Q601), check the connection between the monitor and the video adapter board. If the connection is intact, try a known-good monitor. If the problem persists on a known-good monitor, replace the video adapter board. As you trace the video signal, you can compare the signal to characteristics at the corresponding points in the red or blue video circuits. The point at which the signal disappears is probably the point of failure, and the offending component should be replaced. If you do not have the tools or inclination to perform component-level troubleshooting, try replacing the video drive PC board entirely.

If the video signal measures properly all the way to the CRT (or a new video drive PC board does not correct the problem), suspect a fault in the CRT itself—the corresponding cathode or video control grid might have failed. If you have access to a CRT tester/rejuvenator, test the CRT. If the CRT measures bad (and cannot be recovered through any available rejuvenation procedure), it should be replaced. A color CRT is usually the most expensive component in the monitor. As with any CRT replacement, you should carefully consider the economics of the repair versus buying a new or rebuilt monitor.

Symptom 27-14. Raster is present, but there is no image When the monitor is properly connected to a PC, a series of text information should appear as the PC initializes. You can use this as your baseline image. Isolate the monitor by trying a known-good monitor on your host PC. If the known-good monitor works, you prove that the PC and video adapter are working properly. Reconnect the suspect monitor to the PC and turn up the brightness (and contrast if necessary). You should see a faint white haze covering the display. This raster is generated by the normal sweep of an electron beam. Remember that the PC must be on and running. Without the horizontal and vertical retrace signals provided by the video adapter, there will be no raster.

For a color image to fail completely, all three video drive circuits will have to be disabled. You should check all connectors between the video adapter board and the monitor's main PC board. A loose or severed wire can interrupt the voltage(s) powering the board. You should also check each output from your power supply. A low or missing voltage can disable your video circuits as effectively as a loose connector. If you find a faulty supply output, you can attempt to troubleshoot the supply, or you can replace the power supply outright. For monitors that incorporate the power supply onto the main PC board, the entire main PC board would have to be replaced.

If supply voltage levels and connections are intact, use an oscilloscope to trace the video signals through their respective amplifier circuits. Chances are that you will see all three video signals fail at the same location of each circuit. This is usually because of a problem in common parts of the video circuits. In the example video drive board of Fig. 27-8, such common circuitry involves the components marked with 8xx numbers (e.g., Q801). If you do not have the tools or inclination to perform such component-level troubleshooting, replace the video drive PC board.

You should also suspect a problem with the raster-blanking circuits. During horizontal- and vertical-retrace periods, video signals are cut off. If visible raster lines appear in your image, check the blanking signals. If you are unable to check the blanking signals, try replacing the video drive PC board. If a new video drive board fails to correct the problem, replace the main PC board.

If you should find that all three video signals check correctly all the way to the CRT (or replacing the video drive circuit does not restore the image), you should suspect a major fault in the CRT itself—little else can fail. If you have a CRT tester/rejuvenator available, you should test the CRT thoroughly for shorted grids or a weak cathode. If the problem cannot be rectified through rejuvenation (or you do not have access to a CRT tester), try replacing the CRT. A CRT is usually the most expensive part of the monochrome monitor. If each step up to now has not restored your image, you should weigh the economics of replacing the CRT versus scrapping it in favor of a new or rebuilt unit.

Symptom 27-15. A single horizontal line appears in the middle of the display The horizontal sweep is working properly, but there is no vertical deflection. A fault has almost certainly developed in the vertical drive circuit (refer to Fig. 27-9). Use your oscilloscope to check the sawtooth wave being generated by the vertical oscillator/amplifier IC (pin 6 of IC402). If the sawtooth wave is missing, the fault is almost certainly in the IC. For the circuit of Fig. 27-9, try replacing IC402. If the sawtooth wave is available on IC402 pin 6, suspect that a defect is in the horizontal deflection yoke itself or in one of its related components. If you are not able to check signals to the component level, simply replace the monitor's main PC board.

Symptom 27-16. Only the upper or lower half of an image appears In most cases, a problem is in the vertical amplifier. For the example circuit of Fig. 27-9, the trouble is likely in the vertical oscillator/amplifier (IC402). Use your oscilloscope to check the sawtooth waveform leaving IC402 pin 6. If the sawtooth is distorted, replace IC402. If the sawtooth signal reads properly, check for other faulty components in the vertical deflection yoke circuit. If you do not have the tools or inclination to check and replace devices at the component level, replace the monitor's main PC board. When the image is restored, be sure to check vertical linearity (Chapter 57).

Symptom 27-17. A single vertical line appears along the middle of the display The vertical sweep is working properly, but there is no horizontal deflection. However, to even see the display at normal brightness, high-voltage must be present in the monitor—the horizontal drive circuit must be working (refer to Fig. 27-9). The fault probably lies in the horizontal deflection yoke. Check the yoke and all wiring connected to it. It might be necessary to replace the horizontal deflection yoke or the entire yoke assembly.

If horizontal deflection is lost, as well as substantial screen brightness, a marginal fault might be in the horizontal drive circuit. If the problem is with the horizontal oscillator pulses, the switching characteristics of the horizontal amplifier will change. In turn, this affects high-voltage development and horizontal deflection. Use your oscilloscope to check the square wave generated by the horizontal oscillator IC301 pin 3 (Fig. 27-9). You should see a square wave. If the square wave is distorted, replace the oscillator IC (IC301). If the horizontal pulse is correct, check the horizontal switching transistors (Q301 and Q302). Replace any transistor that appears defective. If the collector signal at the HOT is low or distorted, a short circuit might be in the flyback transformer primary winding. Try replacing the FBT. If you do not have the tools or inclination to check components to the component level (or the problem persists), replace the monitor's main PC board. When the repair is complete, check the horizontal linearity and size (Chapter 57).

Symptom 27-18. There is no image and no raster When the monitor is properly connected to a PC, a series of text information should appear as the PC initializes. You can use this as our baseline image. Isolate the monitor by trying a known-good monitor on your host PC. If the known-good monitor works, you prove that the PC and video adapter are working properly. Reconnect the suspect monitor to the PC and turn up the brightness (and contrast, if necessary). Start by checking for the presence of horizontal and vertical synchronization pulses. If pulses are absent, no raster will be generated. If sync pulses are present, the problem is probably somewhere in the horizontal drive or high-voltage circuits.

Always suspect a power supply problem, so check every output from the supply (especially the 20- and 135-Vdc outputs, as shown in Fig. 27-9). A low or absent supply voltage will disable the horizontal deflection and high-voltage circuits. If one or more supply outputs are low or absent, you can troubleshoot the power-supply circuit or replace the power supply outright (if the power circuit is combined on the monitor's main PC board, the entire main PC board would have to be replaced).

If the supply outputs read correctly, suspect your horizontal drive circuit. Use your oscilloscope to check the horizontal oscillator output at the base of Q301 (Fig. 27-9). You should see a square wave. If the square wave is low, distorted, or absent, replace the horizontal oscillator IC (IC301). If a regular pulse is present, the horizontal oscillator is working. Because Q301 is intended to act as a switch, you should also find a pulse at the collector of Q301. If the pulse output is severely distorted or absent, Q301 is probably damaged (remove Q301 and test it). If Q301 reads as faulty, it should be replaced. If Q301 reads good, check the horizontal coupling transformer (T303) for shorted or open windings. Try replacing T303 (little else can go wrong in this part of the circuit).

Check the HOT (Q302) next by removing it from the circuit and testing it. If Q302 reads faulty, it should be replaced with an exact replacement part. If Q302 reads good, the fault probably lies in the flyback transformer. Try replacing the FBT. If you do not have the tools or inclination to perform these component-level checks, simply replace the monitor's main PC board outright.

If these steps fail to restore the image, the CRT has probably failed. If you have access to a CRT tester/rejuvenator, you can test the CRT. If the CRT measures as bad (and can not be restored through rejuvenation), it should be replaced. If you do not have a CRT test instrument, you can simply replace the CRT. A CRT is usually the most expensive part of a color monitor. If each step up to now has not restored your image, you should weigh the economics of replacing the CRT versus scrapping it in favor of a new or rebuilt unit. If you choose to replace the CRT, you should perform a full set of alignments (Chapter 57).

Symptom 27-19. The image is too compressed or too expanded A whitish haze might appear along the bottom of the image. Start by checking your vertical size control to be sure that it was not adjusted accidentally. Because vertical size is a function of the vertical sawtooth oscillator, you should suspect that a problem is in the vertical oscillator circuit. A sawtooth signal that is too large will result in an over-expanded image, but a signal that is too small will appear to compress the image. Use your oscilloscope to check the vertical sawtooth signal. For the vertical drive circuit of Fig. 27-9, you should find a sawtooth signal on IC402 pin 6. If the signal is incorrect, try replacing IC402. You might also wish to check the PC board for any cracks or faulty soldering connections around the vertical oscillator circuit. If the problem persists, or you do not have the tools or inclination to perform component-level troubleshooting, simply replace the monitor's main PC board outright.

Symptom 27-20. The displayed characters appear to be distorted The term *distortion* can be interpreted in many different ways. For the purposes of this book, the definition is simply that the image (usually text) is difficult to read. Before even opening your toolbox, check the monitor's location. The presence of stray magnetic fields in close proximity to the monitor can cause bizarre forms of distortion. Try moving the monitor to another location. Remove any electromagnetic or magnetic objects (such as motors or refrigerator magnets) from the area. If the problem persists, it is likely that the monitor is at fault.

If only certain areas of the display appear affected (or affected worse than other areas), the trouble is probably caused by poor linearity (either horizontal, vertical, or both). If raster speed varies across the display, the pixels in some areas of the image might appear too close together, although the pixels in other areas of the image might appear too far apart. You can check and correct horizontal and vertical linearity using a test pattern, such as the one described in Chapter 57. If alignment fails to correct poor linearity, your best course is often simply to replace the monitor's main PC board. If the image is difficult to read because it is out of focus, you should check the focus alignment. If you cannot achieve a sharp focus using controls either on the front panel of the monitor or on the fly-back transformer assembly, a fault is probably in the flyback transformer. Try replacing the FBT. If the problem persists, your best course is often simply to replace the monitor's main PC board.

Symptom 27-21. The display appears wavy Waves appear along the edges of the display as the image sways back and forth. This is almost always the result of a power-supply problem—one or more outputs is failing. Use your multimeter and check each supply output. If you find a low or absent output, you can proceed to troubleshoot the supply or you can simply replace the supply outright. If the power supply is integrated onto the main PC board, you will have to replace the entire main PC board.

Symptom 27-22. The display is too bright or too dim Before opening the monitor, be sure to check the brightness and contrast controls. If the controls had been accidentally adjusted, set contrast to maximum, and adjust the brightness level until a clear, crisp display is produced. If the front-panel controls fail to provide the proper display (but focus seems steady), suspect that a fault is in the monitor's power supply. Refer to the example schematic of Fig. 27-9. If the 135-Vdc supply is too low or too high, brightness levels controlling the CRT screen grid will shift. If you find one or more incorrect outputs from the power supply, you can troubleshoot the supply or replace the supply outright. For those monitors that incorporate the power supply on the main PC board, the entire main PC board will have to be replaced.

Symptom 27-23. Visible raster scan lines are in the display The very first places that you should check are the front-panel brightness and contrast controls. If contrast is set too low and/or brightness is set too high, raster will be visible on top of the image. This will tend to make the image appear a bit fuzzy. If the front-panel controls cannot eliminate visible raster from the image, chances are that you have a problem with the power supply. Use your multimeter and check each output from the supply. If one or more outputs appear too high (or too low), you can troubleshoot the supply or replace the supply outright. If the supply is integrated with the monitor's main PC board, the entire PC board will have to be replaced.

If the power supply is intact, you should suspect that a problem is in the raster blanking circuits. During horizontal and vertical retrace periods, video signals are cut off. If visible raster lines appear in your image, check the blanking signals. If you are unable to check the blanking signals, try replacing the video drive PC board. If a new video drive board fails to correct the problem, replace the main PC board.

Symptom 27-24. Colors bleed or smear Ultimately, this symptom occurs when unwanted pixels are excited in the CRT. However, this can be caused by several different problems. Perhaps the most common problem is a fault in the video cable between the video board and the monitor. Electrical noise (sometimes called *crosstalk*) in the cable might allow signals representing one color to accidentally be picked up in another color-signal wire. This can easily cause unwanted colors to appear in the display. Although the video cable is designed to be shielded and carefully filtered, age or poor installation can precipitate this type of problem. Try wiggling the cable. If the problem stops, appears intermittent, or shifts around, you have likely found the source of the problem—replace the cable with a proper replacement assembly.

If the video cable appears intact, suspect failing capacitors in the video amplifier circuits. You can see these capacitors in the schematic of Fig. 27-8. Such capacitors as C505 and C506 are typically low-value, high-voltage components, so they tend to degrade rather quickly. Fortunately, such capacitors are easy to spot on the video amplifier board. If the color problem appears intermittent (or occurs when the monitor warms up), try a bit of liquid refrigerant on each capacitor. If the problem disappears, the one you froze is probably defective. Otherwise, you can turn off and unplug the monitor, then check each capacitor individually. When replacing capacitors in the video amplifier circuit, be sure to replace them with those of the same type and voltage rating.

If capacitors are not at fault, suspect a problem in the amplifier transistors on the video amplifier board (i.e., Q504, Q505, or Q506). Turn off and unplug the monitor, then check each of the transistors. Chances are that your readings will be inconclusive, so try comparing readings from each transistor to find a device that gives the most unusual readings. Replace any defective or questionable amplifier transistors. If you do not have the time or inclination to troubleshoot the video amplifier board, try replacing the board outright.

Symptom 27-25. Colors appear to change when the monitor is warm Either colors will appear correctly when the monitor is cold, then change as the monitor warms up, or vice versa. In both cases, there is likely to be some kind of thermal problem in the video amplifier circuits. Turn off and unplug the monitor, then start by checking the video cable—especially its connection to the raster board inside the monitor. If this connection is loose, it might be intermittent or unreliable. Tighten any loose connections and try the monitor again. Also check the cable that connects the video amplifier board to the raster board.

If the connections appear tight, your best course of action is often to remove the video amplifier board and try re-soldering each of the junctions. Chances are that age or thermal stress has fatigued one or more connections. By re-soldering the connections, you should be able to correct any potential connection problems. You might also try re-soldering the connector which passes video data from the raster board to the video amplifier board. If your problems persist, try replacing the video amplifier board.

Symptom 27-26. An image appears distorted in 350- or 400-line mode In most cases, the "distortion" is an image that appears excessively compressed. As you probably read earlier in this book, different screen modes have a different number of horizontal lines (e.g., a 640-×-480 display offers 480 horizontal traces of 640 pixels each). When the screen mode changes, the number of lines changes as well (i.e., to a 320-×-200 mode). As you might expect, the "size" of each pixel has to be adjusted when the screen mode changes to keep the image roughly square—otherwise the image simply "shrinks." Monitors detect the screen mode by checking the polarity of the sync signals. You can see this function in the schematic of Fig. 27-9.

Typically, each screen mode size can be optimized by an adjustment on the raster board. However, if a mode adjustment is thrown off (or the sync-sensing circuit fails), an image can easily appear with an incorrect size. If you notice this kind of distortion without warning, suspect a problem with the sync-sensing circuit. If the sync-sensing circuit is incorporated into a single IC (such as IC201), replace the IC outright. If you notice a size problem after aligning the monitor, you might have accidentally upset a size adjustment. Re-adjust the size controls to restore proper image dimensions.

Symptom 27-27.   The fine detail of high-resolution graphic images appears a bit fuzzy   At best, this kind of symptom might not appear noticeable without careful inspection, but it might signal a serious problem in the video amplifier circuit. High resolutions demand high bandwidth—a video amplifier must respond quickly to the rapid variations between pixels. If a weakness in the video amplifier(s) occurs, it can limit bandwidth and degrade video performance at high resolutions. The problem will likely disappear at lower resolutions.

The particular problem with this symptom is that it is almost impossible to isolate a defective component—the video amplifier board is working. As a result, your best course of action is to first check all connectors for secure installation. Nicked or frayed video cables can also contribute to the problem. If the problem remains, replace the video amplifier board.

Symptom 27-28.   The display changes color, flickers, or cuts out when the video cable is moved   Check the video cable's connection to the video adapter at the PC—a loose connection will almost certainly result in such intermittent problems. If the connection is secure, an intermittent connection is in the video cable. Before replacing the cable, check its connections within the monitor itself. If connections are intact, replace the intermittent video cable outright. Do not bother cutting or splicing the cable—any breaks in the signal shielding will cause crosstalk, which will result in color bleeding.

Symptom 27-29.   The image expands in the horizontal direction when the monitor gets warm   One or more components in the horizontal retrace circuit are weak—and changing value a bit once the monitor gets warm. Turn off and unplug the monitor. You should inspect any capacitors located around the *Horizontal Output Transistor (HOT)*. The problem is that thermal problems, such as this, can be extremely difficult to isolate because you can't measure capacitor values while the monitor is running; after the monitor is turned off, the parts will cool too quickly to catch a thermal problem. It is often most effective to simply replace several of the key capacitors around the HOT outright. If you don't want to bother with individual components, replace the raster board.

Symptom 27-30.   The image shrinks in the horizontal direction when the monitor gets warm   This is another thermal-related problem that indicates either a weakness in one or more components or a mild soldering-related problem. Turn off and unplug the monitor. Start by checking for a poor solder connection—especially around the horizontal deflection yoke wiring, the *Horizontal Output Transistor (HOT)*, and the flyback transformer. If nothing appears obvious, consider resoldering all of the components in the HOT area of the raster board. If problems continue, suspect that a failure is in the HOT itself. Semiconductors rarely become marginal—they either work or they don't. Still, semiconductor junctions can become unstable when temperatures change, and result in circuit characteristic changes. You could also try replacing the HOT outright.

It is also possible that one or more mid-range power-supply outputs (i.e., 12 or 20 V) are sagging when the monitor warms up. Use a voltmeter and measure the outputs from your power supply. If the 12- or 20-V outputs appear to drop a little once the monitor has been running for a bit, you should troubleshoot the power supply.

Symptom 27-31. High-voltage fails after the monitor is warm A large number of possible causes are behind this problem, but no matter what permutation you find, you will likely be dealing with soldering problems or thermal-related failures. Turn off and unplug the monitor. Inspect the HOT's heatsink assembly—a bad solder connection might be on the heatsink ground. An open solder connection might be on one or more of the flyback transformer pins. If you cannot locate a faulty soldering connection, you might simply choose to re-solder all of the connections in the flyback area.

If the problem persists, suspect that either your HOT or flyback transformer is failing under load (after the monitor warms up). One possible means of isolating the problem is to measure pulses from the HOT output with your oscilloscope. If the pulses stop at the same time your high-voltage fails, you can suspect that the problem is with your HOT or other horizontal components. Try replacing the HOT. If high-voltage fails but the HOT pulses remain, your flyback transformer has likely failed. Replace the flyback transformer. If you do not have an oscilloscope, try replacing the HOT first because that is the least-expensive part, then replace the flyback transformer, if necessary.

In the unlikely event that both a new HOT and flyback transformer do not correct the problem, carefully inspect the capacitors in the HOT circuit. One or more might be failing. Unfortunately, it is very difficult to identify a marginal capacitor (especially one that is suffering from a thermal failure). You might try replacing the major capacitors in the HOT circuit or replace the raster board entirely.

Symptom 27-32. The image blooms intermittently The amount of high voltage driving the CRT is varying intermittently. Because high voltage is related to the HOT circuit and flyback transformer, concentrate your search in those two areas of the raster board. Examine the soldering of your HOT and FBT connections—especially the ground connections, if you can identify them. You might try resoldering all of the connections in those areas (remember to turn off and unplug the monitor before soldering). A ground problem might also be on the video amplifier board, which allows all three color signals to vary in amplitude. If this happens, the overall brightness of the image changes, and the image might grow or shrink a bit in response. Try resoldering connections on the video amplifier board.

If the problem remains (even after soldering), your FBT might be failing—probably because of an age-related internal short. High-end test equipment, such as Sencore's monitor test station provides the instrumentation to test a flyback transformer. If you do not have access to such dedicated test equipment, however, try replacing the FBT assembly. If you do not have the time or inclination to deal with component replacement, replace the raster board outright. In the unlikely event that your problem persists, suspect a fault in the CRT itself. If you have access to a CRT tester/rejuvenator, you can check the CRT's operation. Some weaknesses in the CRT might be corrected (at least temporarily) by rejuvenation. If the fault cannot be corrected, you might have to replace the CRT.

Symptom 27-33. The image appears out of focus Before suspecting a component failure, try adjusting the focus control. In most cases, the focus control is located adjacent to the flyback transformer. Remember that the focus control should be adjusted with brightness and contrast set to optimum values—excessively bright images might lose focus naturally. If the focus control is unable to restore a proper image, check the CRT focus voltage. In Fig. 27-9, you can find the focus voltage off a flyback transformer tap. If the focus voltage is low (often combined with a dim image), you might have a failing FBT.

It is possible to test the FBT if you have the specialized test instrumentation; otherwise, you should just replace the FBT outright. If you lack the time or inclination to replace the FBT, you can simply replace the raster board.

If a new FBT does not resolve your focus problem, suspect that a fault is in the CRT— probably in the focus grid. You can use a CRT tester/rejuvenator to examine the CRT, and it might be possible to restore normal operation (at least temporarily). If you do not have such equipment, you will simply have to try a new CRT.

Symptom 27-34. The image appears to flip or scroll horizontally A synchronization problem is in your horizontal raster circuit. Begin by checking the video cable to be sure that it is installed and connected securely. Cables that behave intermittently (or that appear frayed or nicked) should be replaced. If the cable is intact, suspect a problem in your horizontal circuit. If a horizontal-sync (or "horizontal hold") adjustment is on the raster board, adjust it in small increments until the image snaps back into sync. If no such adjustment is on your particular monitor, try resoldering all of the connections in the horizontal-processing circuit. If the problem persists, replace the horizontal oscillator IC or replace the entire raster board.

Symptom 27-35. The image appears to flip or scroll vertically A synchronization problem is in your vertical raster circuit. Begin by checking the video cable to be sure that it is installed and connected securely. Cables that behave intermittently (or that appear frayed or nicked) should be replaced. If the cable is intact, suspect that the problem is in your vertical circuit. If a vertical-sync (or "vertical hold") adjustment is on the raster board, adjust it in small increments until the image snaps back into sync. If no such adjustment is on your particular monitor, try resoldering all of the connections in the vertical-processing circuit. If the problem persists, replace the vertical oscillator IC or replace the entire raster board.

Symptom 27-36. The image appears to shake or oscillate in size This might occur in bursts, but it typically occurs constantly. In most cases, this is caused by a fault in the power supply—usually the 135-V (B+) output. Try measuring your power-supply outputs with an oscilloscope and see if an output is varying along with the screen-size changes. If you locate such an output, the filtering portion of that output might be malfunctioning. Track the output back into the supply and replace any defective components. If you are unable to isolate a faulty component, replace the power supply. If the power supply is integrated onto the raster board, you might have to replace the raster board entirely.

If the outputs from your power supply appear to be stable, you should suspect that a weak capacitor is in your horizontal circuit. Try resoldering the FBT, HOT, and other horizontal circuit components to eliminate the possibility of a soldering problem. If the problem remains, you will have to systematically replace the capacitors in the horizontal circuit. If you do not have the time or inclination to replace individual components, replace the raster board outright.

Here's an unusual problem. The shaking you see might be related to a problem in the degaussing coil located around the CRT funnel. Ordinarily, the degaussing coil should unleash the most of its energy in the initial moments after monitor power is turned on. Thermistors (or posistors) in the power supply quickly diminish coil voltage—effectively cutting off the degaussing coil's operation. A fault in the degaussing-coil circuit (in the power supply) might continue to allow enough power to the coil to affect the image's stability. Try disconnecting the degaussing coil. If the problem remains, the degaussing coil is probably operating properly. If the problem disappears, a fault is in the degaussing-coil circuit.

Further Study

That concludes Chapter 27. Be sure to review the glossary and chapter questions on the accompanying CD. If you have access to the Internet, take a look at some of these monitor resources:

Acer: **http://www.aci.acer.com.tw**

CTX: **http://www.ctxintl.com**

Hitachi: **http://www.hitachi.com**

Magnavox: **http://www.magnavox.com**

Nanao: **http://www.traveller.com/nanao/**

NEC: **http://webserver.nectech.com/textgraph/tocmon.htm**

Sony: **http://www.sel.sony.com/SEL/ccpg/index.html**

Viewsonic: **http://www.viewsonic.com**

28

MOTHERBOARD
TROUBLESHOOTING

CONTENTS AT A GLANCE

Active, Passive, and Modular

Understanding the Motherboard
Socket 7, Socket 8, or Slot 1
AT, ATX, and NLX
Learning your way around

Troubleshooting a Motherboard
Repair vs. replace
Start with the basics
Symptoms

Further Study

The motherboard is the heart of any personal computer. It provides system resources (i.e., IRQ lines, DMA channels, I/O locations), as well as "core" components, such as the CPU, chipset(s), *Real-Time Clock (RTC)*, and all system memory—including RAM, BIOS ROM, and CMOS RAM. Indeed, most of a PC's capabilities are defined by motherboard components. This chapter is intended to provide a guided tour of contemporary motherboards and show you how to translate error information and symptoms into motherboard repairs.

Active, Passive, and Modular

Before going any further, you should understand the difference between a motherboard and a backplane. For the purposes of this book, a *motherboard* is a printed circuit board that contains most of the processing components required by the computer. PC purists often refer to a motherboard as an *active backplane*. The term *active* is used because ICs are running on the board. The advantage of a motherboard is its simplicity—the motherboard virtually is the PC. Unfortunately, the motherboard has disadvantages. Namely, it is difficult to upgrade. Aside from plugging in an upgraded CPU or adding RAM, the only real way to upgrade a motherboard is to replace it outright with a newer one. For example, the only way to add PCI bus slots to an all-ISA motherboard is to replace the motherboard with one that contains PCI slots.

On the other hand, a backplane (also referred to as a *passive backplane*) is little more than a board containing interconnecting slots—no ICs are on the backplane (except perhaps some power-supply regulating circuitry). The CPU, DRAM, BIOS ROM, and other central-processing components are fabricated onto a board that simply plugs into one of the backplane slots. Other expansion devices (e.g., video board, drive controller, sound board, etc.) just plug into adjacent slots. The PS/2 was one of the first PCs to use a backplane design. Backplane systems are easy to troubleshoot. Unlike traditional motherboards, which require the entire system to be disassembled, a processor board can be removed and replaced as easily as any other board, so it is also a simple matter to upgrade the PC by installing a new processor board. The great limitation to backplanes is the bus. Where traditional motherboards can optimize a system with different busses, the backplane is limited to a single bus style (usually ISA or MCA). High-performance bus architectures, such as VL or PCI, are not readily available.

In an effort to provide a motherboard that is more upgradeable and serviceable, manufacturers are experimenting with modular motherboards. The modular motherboard places the CPU, math co-processor, and key support ICs on a replaceable card that plugs into a motherboard. This, in turn, holds BIOS ROM, CMOS RAM, DRAM, other system controllers, and bus interfaces. The modular approach allows a motherboard to be upgraded far more than a traditional motherboard, without having to replace it outright—the replacement processing card is then much cheaper than a new motherboard. However, today's PC architectures can usually support a variety of CPU versions and an extensive amount of RAM on the original motherboard, so "modularity" has never become a very popular approach.

Contrary to popular belief, expansion bus connectors are not needed to make a motherboard. You can see this in any laptop or notebook computer motherboard (Fig. 28-1). The devices that traditionally demanded expansion slots (video and drive controllers) are easily fabricated directly onto the motherboard. Even the motherboards used in most desktop and tower PCs over the last few years integrate video- and drive-controller circuits. If upgrades are needed in the future, the motherboard-based circuits can be disabled with jumpers, and replacement sub-systems are plugged into expansion slots.

Understanding the Motherboard

Before you can troubleshoot a motherboard effectively, it is important that you know your way around and be able to identify at least most of the available components. Although each motherboard is designed differently, this process of identification is not nearly as difficult as it might sound. This part of the chapter will familiarize you with the essential functions and components that you'll find on a modern motherboard.

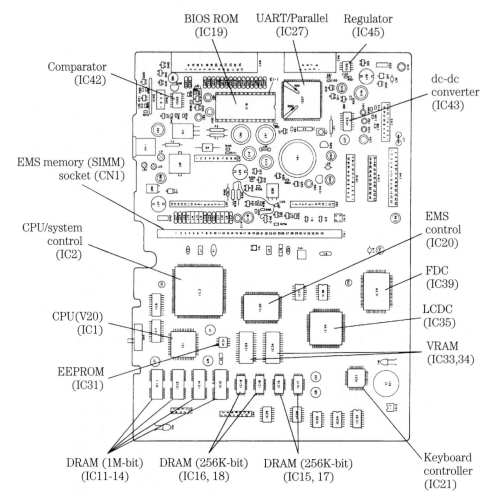

Comparator (IC42)

BIOS ROM (IC19)

UART/Parallel (IC27)

Regulator (IC45)

dc-dc converter (IC43)

EMS memory (SIMM) socket (CN1)

EMS control (IC20)

CPU/system control (IC2)

FDC (IC39)

CPU(V20) (IC1)

LCDC (IC35)

EEPROM (IC31)

VRAM (IC33,34)

DRAM (1M-bit) (IC11-14)

DRAM (256K-bit) (IC16, 18)

DRAM (256K-bit) (IC15, 17)

Keyboard controller (IC21)

FIGURE 28-1   **Motherboard assembly for a Tandy 1500HD laptop.**   Tandy Corporation

SOCKET 7, SOCKET 8, OR SLOT 1

When examining a motherboard, you'll probably find it designated as "Socket 7," "Socket 8," or "Slot 1." These classifications refer to the type of CPU that the motherboard can support: *Socket-7 motherboards* are generally designed for Pentium and Pentium MMX CPUs, *Socket-8 motherboards* are made for PentiumPro CPUs, and *Slot-1 motherboards* are slated for Pentium II systems. This does not mean that a motherboard can support ANY such processor, only that the motherboard supports a given "class" of processor. For example, older Pentium motherboards can only support Pentium CPUs up to 120MHz, but newer Pentium motherboards can support Pentium (or Pentium MMX) processors up to 200MHz—but all would be categorized as "Socket 7" motherboards. You can find a complete breakdown of socket/slot designations in Chapter 11.

AT, ATX, AND NLX

Another important classification that you must be familiar with is the motherboard's *form factor*. In simplest terms, the form factor is little more than the dimensions of the board and its mounting-hole positions, as well as the general layout and placement of key components such as the CPU, SIMMs, and expansion slots. Today, the three major form factors to consider are: AT, ATX, and NLX. It is important for you to understand that form factors do not directly influence performance—a "baby AT" motherboard and an NLX motherboard can offer exactly the same performance characteristics. Form factor is most important in system assembly and access for service.

AT-style motherboards The "AT-style" motherboards really represent the classic approach to component placement (Fig. 28-2). AT-style motherboards are typically available in two variations: the "Baby AT" and the "Full AT." Both variations simply affect the overall dimensions of the motherboard (Full AT motherboards are larger). You can usually identify an AT-style motherboard based upon two distinctions. First, look at the power connectors where the power supply attaches. An AT-style motherboard uses two sets of 6-pin in-line connectors. Second, the CPU is usually positioned in line with the ISA bus slots (almost always obstructing full-length ISA cards).

The Socket-5 connector shown in Fig. 34-2 indicates an i486 motherboard.

ATX-style motherboards "ATX-style" motherboards are the result of the first serious industry push to "standardize" the dimensions and connections of a PC motherboard, such as the ATX Slot 1 motherboard (Fig. 28-3). An ATX motherboard is distinguished by three points. First, all I/O port connectors are concentrated into a single "I/O panel" at the rear of the motherboard. Second, the ATX motherboard uses a 20-pin PS/2-style power connection from the power supply. Third, the CPU is located clear and away from all expansion bus slots—eliminating any interference with full-slot expansion cards. ATX motherboards can be found supporting Socket 7, Socket 8, and Slot 1 CPUs.

NLX-style motherboards Although ATX motherboards represented a good effort at standardization, they still retain all the assembly problems of AT-style motherboards—namely that the motherboard is cumbersome to install and time-consuming to upgrade or replace. The "NLX-style" motherboards (Fig. 28-4) overcome this disadvantage by making the motherboard a replaceable "card," and moving all expansion slots and connection headers (e.g., speaker connector, power-switch connector, etc.) to a "riser card." The NLX motherboard itself then plugs into the riser card. In this fashion, the motherboard can quickly and easily be removed from the system to change jumpers, add memory, or install a replacement motherboard.

LEARNING YOUR WAY AROUND

Now that you've seen some essential motherboard classifications, it's time to actually look at a motherboard up close, and identify the crucial parts. For the purposes of this book, the

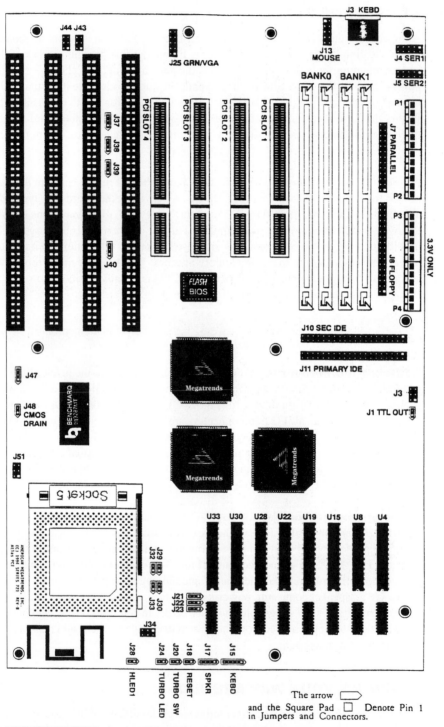

FIGURE 28-2   **The AMI Atlas PCI motherboard.** American Megatrends, Inc.

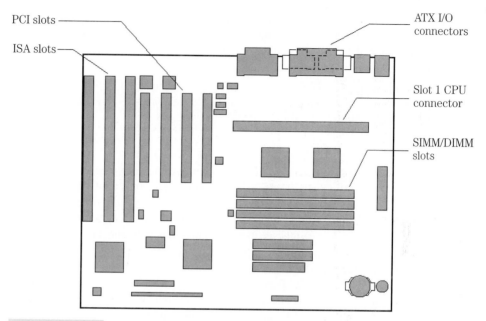

PCI slots

ISA slots

ATX I/O connectors

Slot 1 CPU connector

SIMM/DIMM slots

FIGURE 28-3   **An Intel ATX Slot 1 motherboard.** Intel Corporation

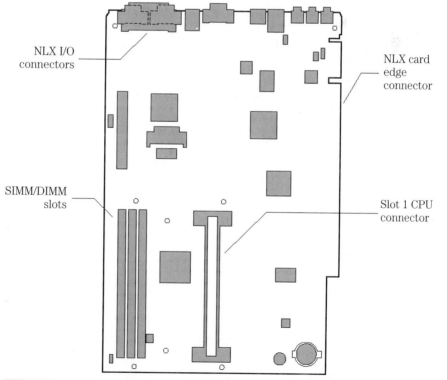

NLX I/O connectors

NLX card edge connector

SIMM/DIMM slots

Slot 1 CPU connector

FIGURE 28-4   **An Intel NLX Slot 1 motherboard.** Intel Corporation

Intel PD440FX ATX Slot 1 motherboard (Fig. 28-5) is used as a model. Other mother-boards and form factors will appear a bit different, but the basic key parts are all the same. The pinouts of each major connector are illustrated in Fig. 28-6.

The following chipset components are presented for example purposes only. Your moth-erboard will undoubtedly use different chips (and chipsets)—each offering their own set of characteristics.

1 *ISA bus slots* For ISA adapter boards.
2 *Yamaha OPL4-ML* This optional on-board wavetable synthesizer features the single-chip OPL4-ML (YMF704) IC. The OPL4-ML integrates the OPL3 audio system, gen-eral MIDI processor, and wavetable ROM into a single component. The features include: general MIDI system-1 compliance, an interface compatible with MPU-401 UART mode, FM synthesis that is compatible with the OPL3 audio system, and wavetable synthesis generates up to 24 voices simultaneously.
3 *Yamaha OPL3-SA3* This optional on-board audio subsystem features the Yamaha OPL3-SA3 (YMF715) IC. The features include: a 16-bit audio CODEC and OPL3 FM synthe-sis; an integrated 3-D enhanced stereo controller including all required analog components; an interface for MPU-401 and a joystick (game port); stereo analog-to-digital and digital-

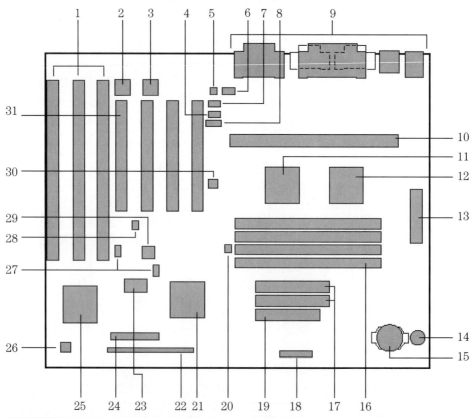

FIGURE 28-5   **An Intel PD440FX motherboard layout.** Intel Corporation

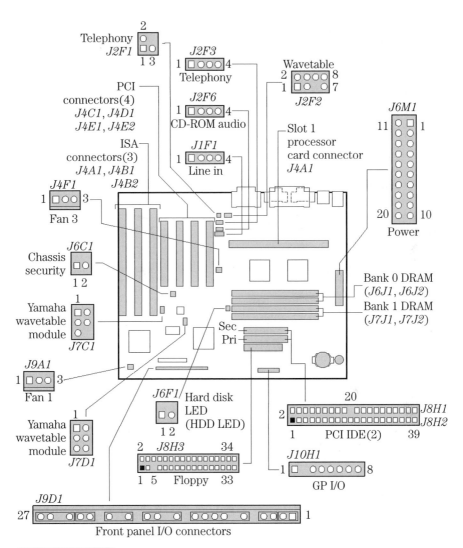

FIGURE 28-6   **Connector pinouts of an Intel PD440FX motherboard.** Intel
Corporation

to-analog converters; analog mixing, anti-aliasing, and reconstruction filters for sound reproduction; line, microphone, and monaural inputs; ADPCM, A-law, or M-law digital audio compression and decompression; full digital control of all mixer and volume-control
functions; software switching between rear-panel mic-in and line-in connectors; Plug-and-
Play compatibility; and Sound Blaster Pro and Windows Sound System compatibility.

4 *CD-ROM audio connector* This is necessary to play CD audio through the motherboard's sound system (used in conjunction with on-board sound). It is a 4-pin header
and the pinout is shown in Table 28-1.

5 *Telephony connector* Telephony support is available on some motherboards for connecting the monaural audio signals of an "internal telephony device" to the motherboard's
audio subsystem. A monaural audio-in and audio-out signal interface is necessary for

TABLE 28-1	CD-ROM AUDIO CONNECTOR PINOUT
PIN	SIGNAL NAME
1	Ground
2	CD Left
3	Ground
4	CD Right

TABLE 28-2	TELEPHONY CONNECTOR PINOUTS
1X4 ATAPI CONNECTOR	
PIN	SIGNAL NAME
1	MONO IN (from external device)
2	Ground
3	Ground
4	MONO OUT (to external device)
2X2 CONNECTOR	
PIN	SIGNAL NAME
1	Ground
2	MONO IN (from external device)
3	MONO OUT (to external device)
4	Key

telephony applications, such as speakerphones, fax/modems, and answering machines. Two different interface headers are available for this application: a general telephony interface with a 1- × 4-pin ATAPI-type connector (Table 28-2), and a telephony interface with a 2- × 2-pin header (same function as #7).

6 *Wavetable header* This 2- × 4-pin header supports wavetable add-in cards. Most wavetable add-in cards are installed in an ISA slot, and a cable is routed from the card to this header. Compatible wavetable cards include the ICS WaveFront and the Crysta-Lake Series 2000 wavetable product.

8 *Line-in connector* The line-in connector is available for connecting left and right channel signals of an internal audio device to the motherboard's audio subsystem. An audio-in signal interface of this type is necessary for such applications as TV tuner boards. A general audio interface is provided with a 1- × 4-pin ATAPI-type connector (Table 28-4).

9 *Back-panel I/O connectors* These are the group of I/O connectors that reside on the back panel. These include serial ports, parallel ports, USB ports, keyboard and mouse ports, game/MIDI ports, and sound connections. Figure 28-7 illustrates a typical ATX back panel.

10 *Slot-1 processor connector* The processor connects to the motherboard through the Slot-1 processor connector, a 242-pin edge connector. When the processor is mounted in Slot 1, it is secured by a "retention mechanism" attached to the motherboard. The processor's heatsink is stabilized by a heatsink support that is attached to the motherboard.

11 *Intel SB82442FX Data Bus Xccelerator (DBX)* This is part of 440FX chipset, which controls the memory operations of the motherboard. The DBX connects to 64-bit processor data bus, the 64- or 72-bit memory data bus, and the 16-bit PMC chip's private-data bus. The DBX works in parallel with the PMC chip to provide a high-performance memory subsystem.

12 *Intel SB82441FX PCI Bridge and Memory Controller (PMC)* This is part of 440FX chipset. The PMC chip provides bus-control signals and address paths for

TABLE 28-3 WAVETABLE CONNECTOR PINOUT

PIN	SIGNAL NAME	PIN	SIGNAL NAME
1	Wave In Right	2	Ground
3	Wave In Left	4	Ground
5	Key	6	Ground
7	Not connected	8	MIDI Out (from host)

TABLE 28-4 LINE IN CONNECTOR PINOUT

PIN	SIGNAL NAME
1	Left Line In
2	Ground
3	Ground
4	Right Line In (monaural)

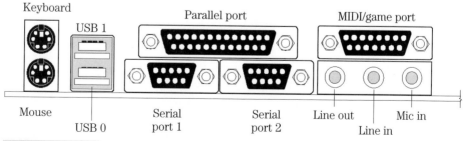

FIGURE 28-7   Connector layout of a typical ATX back panel.

data transfers between the host bus, PCI bus, and main memory. The 82441FX provides the following features:

- Microprocessor interface control, including processor host bus speeds up to 66 MHz and 32-bit addressing.
- An integrated DRAM controller providing a 64- or 72-bit non-interleaved path to memory with ECC support, support for EDO DRAM, and support for 8MB to 256MB of main memory.
- A fully synchronous PCI bus interface that is compliant with the PCI specification revision 2.1 and operating at 33MHz PCI-bus speed for PCI-to-DRAM speed greater than 100MB/sec.

13 *Power connector* This is a 20-pin PS/2-type power connector that supplies +5, -5, +12, -12, and +3.3 V to the ATX motherboard. Table 28-5 lists the pinout for this power connector.

14 *Speaker* This is a small integrated general-purpose speaker. Some motherboards might replace an integrated speaker with a 2-pin header for an external speaker in the case.

15 *Battery* The CMOS RAM backup battery.

16 *SIMM sockets* The sockets for 72-pin SIMMs—later motherboards use 168-pin DIMMs.

17 *IDE connectors* The 40-pin primary and secondary drive-controller channels for ATA (IDE), ATA-2 (EIDE), and ATAPI devices (such as CD-ROM drives).

18 *GP I/O header* A general-purpose I/O connector. Table 28-6 lists the pinout for a GP I/O connector.

19 *Floppy-drive connector* The 28-pin floppy-drive channel.

20 *Intel SB82371SB PCI/ISA IDE Xccelerator (PIIX3)*

21 *Front-panel header* The group of connectors used to connect front-panel switches and indicators, such as the speaker, reset switch, power LED, hard-drive activity LED (HDD LED—same as #20), infrared (IrDA) port, sleep switch, or power switch. Figure 28-8 shows a typical header arrangement for an ATX motherboard. Table 28-7 lists the pinout the header connectors.

22 *TSOP flash device* The BIOS ROM IC.

TABLE 28-5 ATX POWER CONNECTOR PINOUT

CONNECTOR	SIGNAL NAME	CONNECTOR	SIGNAL NAME
1	+3.3 V	11	+3.3 V
2	+3.3 V	12	−12 V
3	Ground	13	Ground
4	+5 V	14	PW_ON#
5	Ground	15	Ground
6	+5 V	16	Ground
7	Ground	17	Ground
8	PWRGD (power good)	18	−5 V
9	+5 VSB (standby for real-time clock)	19	+5 V
10	+12 V	20	+5 V

TABLE 28-6	GP I/O CONNECTOR PINOUT
PIN	SIGNAL NAME
1	Vcc
2	Key
3	GP1 7
4	Ground
5	GP1 2
6	Ground
7	GP1 1
8	Ground

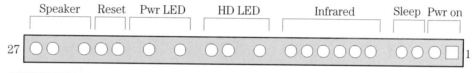

FIGURE 28-8   Front-panel header layout for a typical ATX motherboard.

TABLE 28-7	FRONT PANEL HEADER ASSIGNMENTS	
PIN	SIGNAL NAME	
1	SW_ON#	(power-on connector)
2	Ground	
3	SLEEP	(sleep/resume switch)
4	Sleep Pullup (SLEEP_PU)	
5	No connect	
6	+5 V	(IrDA connector)
7	Key	
8	IrRX	
9	Ground	
10	IrTX	
11	Consumer IR (CONIR)	
12	No connect	
13	HD_PWR +5 V	(HDD LED connector)
14	Key	
15	HD Active#	
16	HD_PWR	
17	No connect	
18	Ground	(sleep/power LED)
19	Key	
20	PWR_LED	
21	No connect	

TABLE 28-7 FRONT PANEL HEADER ASSIGNMENTS (CONTINUED)	
PIN	**SIGNAL NAME**
22	Ground (Reset switch)
23	SW_RST
24	Ground (Speaker)
25	Key
26	PIEZO_IN
27	SPKR_HDR

23 *Configuration jumper block* The group of jumpers used to configure the motherboard. Typical configuration jumpers can include (but are not limited to):

■ *Bus speed* One or more jumpers used to set the motherboard bus speed.

■ *Clock multiplier* One or more jumpers used to multiply the bus speed for the given CPU.

■ *CPU type* One or more jumpers used to define the presence of an Intel, AMD, or Cyrix CPU.

■ *CPU voltage(s)* One or more jumpers used to select the particular operating voltage(s) for a given CPU.

■ *Video port* If the motherboard offers on-board video, this jumper enables or disables it.

■ *Hard drives* If the motherboard offers on-board hard-drive ports, this jumper enables or disables it.

■ *Floppy drives* If the motherboard offers an on-board floppy-drive port, this jumper enables or disables it.

■ *CMOS clear* This jumper can be used to clear the CMOS (NVRAM and ESCD).

■ *Clear password* This jumper can be used to erase the CMOS password(s) without clearing the CMOS.

■ *CMOS access* This jumper can be used to prevent access to the CMOS setup routine.

■ *BIOS recovery* This jumper can be used to invoke BIOS boot block recovery if a BIOS flash upgrade fails.

24 *National PC87307VUL I/O controller* The PC87307 super I/O controller from National Semiconductor is an ISA Plug-and-Play compatible, multifunction I/O device that provides the following features:

■ *Two serial ports* Including two 16450/16550A-software compatible UARTs, an internal send/receive 16-byte FIFO buffer, and four internal 8-bit DMA options for the UART with SIR support (USI).

■ A multimode bi-directional parallel port that can operate in Standard mode (IBM and Centronics compatible), Enhanced Parallel Port (EPP) mode with BIOS and driver support, or high-speed Extended Capabilities Port (ECP) mode.

■ A floppy-disk controller that is DP8473 and N82077 compatible.

■ A keyboard and mouse controller that is industry-standard 8042A compatible.

■ A real-time clock that is DS1287 and MC146818 compatible, and is accurate within ±13 minutes/year at 25°C with 5 V applied.

TABLE 28-8 YAMAHA WAVETABLE MODULE CONNECTOR PINOUTS			
PIN	SIGNAL NAME	PIN	SIGNAL NAME
1	EXTEN#	1	RSTDRV
2	SIN	2	VCC
3	VCC	3	AUD33MHZ
4	Ground	4	MIDI Out
5	BCK	5	Ground
6	LACK	6	Key

■ Support for Advanced Power Control (APC).

■ Support for an IrDA and consumer IR-compliant infrared interface.

25 *Fan 1 header* A connector used to power a fan in the system and detect its operation (same function as #30). Pin 1 is ground, pin 2 is +12 V, and pin 3 is a "fan sense" line, which can be monitored by the management-extension hardware (#29).

26 *Yamaha wavetable module headers* Two optional 2- × 3-pin connections are used for Yamaha wavetable cards (Table 28-8). These connectors are not identical, and the one you use will depend on the particular wavetable card installed.

27 *Chassis security header* A "tamper" switch contact used in conjunction with management-extension hardware (#29).

28 *Management-extension hardware* This optional management-extension hardware provides low-cost instrumentation capabilities that are designed to reduce the total cost of owning a PC. The hardware implementation is a single-chip ASIC, which includes such features as: an integrated temperature sensor, fan speed sensors for up to three fans, power-supply voltage monitoring to detect levels above or below acceptable values, and a header for an external chassis-security switch feature.

29 *PCI connectors* For PCI adapter boards.

Troubleshooting a Motherboard

Because motherboards contain the majority of system processing components, it is likely that you will encounter a faulty motherboard sooner or later. The BIOS POST is written to test each sub-section of the motherboard each time the PC is powered up, so most problems are detected well before you ever see the DOS prompt. Errors are reported in a myriad of ways. Beep codes and POST codes (Chapter 19) provide indications of fatal errors that occur before the video system is initialized. Still, plenty of symptoms can elude the initial testing at start time. This part of the chapter digs in and presents a lengthy selection of motherboard symptoms for you to reference.

REPAIR VS. REPLACE

This is the perennial troubleshooting dilemma. The problem with motherboard repair is not so much the availability of replacement parts (although that can be a challenge) as is the use of *surface-mount soldering (SMT)*. You see, a surface-mounted IC cannot be desoldered with conventional tools. To successfully desolder a surface-mounted IC, you need to heat each of the IC's pins (often in excess of 100) simultaneously, then lift the IC off the board. It is then a simple matter to clean up any residual solder. Unfortunately, specialized surface-mount soldering equipment is required to do this. The equipment is readily available commercially, so it is easy to buy—but you can invest $1000 to $2000 to equip your work bench properly.

As you can imagine, the "repair vs. replace" decision is an economic one. It makes little sense for the part-time PC enthusiast to make such a substantial investment to exchange a defective IC (which are usually under $30). It is generally better to replace the motherboard outright, which is only a fraction of the cost of such SMT equipment. On the other hand, professionals who intend to pursue PC repair as a living are well served with surface-mount equipment. The customer's cost for labor, the part(s), and markup is typically much less than purchasing a new motherboard (especially the high-end boards such as i486/66 and Pentium motherboards).

START WITH THE BASICS

Because motherboard troubleshooting represents a significant expense, be sure to start any motherboard repair by inspecting the following points in the PC. Remember to turn all power off before performing these inspections:

- *Check all connectors* This can happen easily when the PC is serviced or upgraded, and you accidentally forget to replace every cable (or the cable is installed incorrectly). Start with the power connector, and inspect each cable and connector attached to the motherboard. Frayed cables should be replaced. Loose or detached cables should be reattached properly.
- *Check all socket-mounted ICs* Some ICs in the computer (especially the CPU) get hot during normal operation. It is not unheard of for the repetitive expansion and contraction encountered with everyday use to eventually "rock" an IC out of its socket. The CPU, math-co-processor (on older motherboards), BIOS ROM, and often the CMOS/RTC module are socket mounted, so check them carefully.
- *Check power levels* Low or erratic ac power levels can cause problems in the PC. Use a multimeter and check ac at the wall outlet. Be very careful whenever dealing with ac. Take all precautions to protect yourself from injury. If the ac is low or is heavily loaded by motors, coffee pots, or other highly inductive loads, try the PC in another outlet running from a different circuit. If ac checks properly, use your multimeter (or a measurement tool, such as PC Power Check from Data Depot) to check the power supply outputs. If one or more outputs is low or absent, you should repair or replace the supply.
- *Check the motherboard for foreign objects* A screw, paper clip, or free strand of wire can cause a short circuit that might disable the motherboard. Examine the motherboard carefully and use ample lighting.
- *Check that all motherboard DIP switches and jumpers are correct* For example, if the motherboard provides a video port and you have a video board plugged into the expansion bus, the motherboard's video circuit will have to be disabled through a switch or jumper. Otherwise, a hardware conflict can result that might interfere with mother-

board operation. You will need the user manual for the PC to identify and check each jumper or switch.

■ *Check for intermittent connections and accidental grounding* Inspect each of the motherboard's mounting screws, and see that they are not touching nearby printed traces. Also check the space under the motherboard and see that nothing that is grounding the motherboard and chassis. As an experiment, you might try loosening the motherboard mounting screws. If the fault goes away, the motherboard might be suffering from an intermittent connection—when all screws are tight, the board is bent just enough to let the intermittent appear. Unfortunately, intermittent connections are almost impossible to find.

SYMPTOMS

Symptom 28-1. A motherboard failure is reported, but goes away when the PC's outer cover is removed An intermittent connection is on the motherboard. When the housing is secured, the PC chassis warps just slightly—this might be enough to precipitate an intermittent contact. When the housing is removed, the chassis relaxes and hides the intermittent connection. Replace the outer cover and gently re-tighten each screw with the system running. Chances are that you will find one screw that triggers the problem. You can leave that screw out, but it is advisable to replace the motherboard as a long-term fix.

Symptom 28-2. The POST (or your software diagnostic) reports a CPU fault This is a fatal error, and chances are that system initialization has halted. CPU problems are generally reported when one or more CPU registers do not respond as expected, or has trouble switching to the protected mode. In either case, the CPU is probably at fault. Fortunately, the CPU is socket mounted and should be very straightforward to replace. Be sure to remove all power to the PC and make careful use of static controls when replacing a CPU. Mark the questionable CPU with indelible ink before replacing it.

Zero-Insertion Force (ZIF) sockets are easiest because the IC will be released simply by lifting the metal lever at the socket's side. Slide out the original CPU and insert a new one. Secure the metal lever and try the PC again. However, many CPUs are mounted in *Pin-Grid Array (PGA)* sockets, and a specialized PGA-removal tool is strongly suggested for proper removal. You should also be able to use a small, regular screwdriver to gently pry up each of the four sides of the CPU, but be very careful to avoid cracking the IC, the socket, or the motherboard—never use excessive force. If the IC is free, install the new CPU with close attention to pin alignment, then gently press the new CPU into place.

A word about heatsink/fans. Most i486 (and later) CPUs are equipped with a metal heatsink (or heatsink/fan) assembly. It is vital to the proper operation of your system that the heatsink be re-installed correctly. Otherwise, the new CPU will eventually overheat and lock up or fail. Be sure to use good-quality thermal compound to ensure proper heat transfer to the heatsink (remember that a sound mechanical connection does not guarantee a good thermal connection).

Symptom 28-3. The POST (or your software diagnostic) reports a problem with the floating-point unit Math co-processor (also called the *Floating-Point Unit, FPU*) problems are generally reported when one or more MPC registers do not respond as expected. Fortunately, MCP faults are not always fatal. It is often possible to remove the

MCP or disable the MCP availability through the CMOS setup. Of course, programs that depend on the MCP will no longer run, but at least the system can be used until a new one is installed. On older systems that use separate MCPs, the device is socket mounted, and should be very straightforward to replace. Be sure to remove all power to the PC, and make careful use of static controls when replacing an MPC. Mark the questionable MPC with indelible ink before replacing it. If the MCP is integrated into the CPU (i386DX, i486DX, Pentium, and later CPUs) are a bit more expensive because you'll need to replace the entire CPU, but the replacement process is no more difficult (remember to remount any heatsink/fan assembly properly).

Symptom 28-4. The POST (or your software diagnostic) reports a BIOS ROM checksum error The integrity of your system BIOS ROM is verified after the CPU is tested. This is necessary to ensure that no unwanted instructions or data could easily crash the system during POST or normal operation. A checksum is performed on the ROM contents, and that value is compared with the value stored in the ROM itself. If the two values are equal, the ROM is considered good and initialization continues. Otherwise, the BIOS is considered defective and should be replaced. Chapter 6 provides an index of major BIOS manufacturers.

Traditionally, BIOS ROM is implemented as one or two ICs that are plugged into DIP sockets. They can be removed easily with the blade of a regular screwdriver, as long as you pry the IC up slowly and gently (be sure to pry the IC evenly from both ends). When installing new DIP ICs, you might have to straighten their pins against the surface of a table or use a DIP pin-straightening tool. Ultimately, the IC pins will fit nicely into each receptacle in the DIP socket. You can then ease the IC evenly into the socket. Alignment is crucial to ensure that all pins are inserted. If not, one or more pins might be bent under the IC and ruin the new ROM. Also, be sure to insert the new IC(s) in the proper orientation. If they are accidentally installed backward, they might be damaged.

Newer BIOS ICs use flash EEPROM technology, which allows the device to be erased and reprogrammed in the field without having to replace the entire BIOS ROM IC. When a flash BIOS fails its checksum test, it also has probably failed. Because flash BIOS devices are often fabricated as PLCC ICs, it is a bit easier to replace them, but you will need a PLCC-removal tool to take the original IC out of its socket—there simply is not enough room for a screwdriver.

Symptom 28-5. The POST (or software diagnostic) reports a timer (PIT) failure, an RTC update problem, or a refresh failure The PIT is often an 8254 or compatible device. Ultimately, one or more of its three channels might have failed and the PIT should be replaced. It is important to realize that many modern motherboards incorporate the PIT functions into a system controller or other chipset IC (refer to Chapter 8 for a listing of chipsets and functions). Because the PIT is typically surface mounted, you can attempt to replace the device or replace the motherboard entirely.

Symptom 28-6. The POST (or software diagnostic) reports an interrupt controller (PIC) failure The PIC is often an 8259 or compatible device, and two PICs are on the typical AT motherboard (PIC#1 handles IRQ0 through IRQ7, and PIC#2 handles IRQ8 through IRQ15). Of the two, PIC#1 is more important because the lower interrupts have a higher priority, and the lowest channels handle crucial low-level functions, such as the system timer and keyboard interface. Generally, a diagnostic will reveal which of the two PICs have failed. Be sure that no interrupt conflicts are between two or more system devices. You can then replace the defective PIC. In many current systems, both PICs are integrated into a system controller or chipset IC. You can replace the defective IC if you have the appropriate surface-mount equipment available, or replace the motherboard entirely.

Symptom 28-7. The POST (or software diagnostic) reports a DMA controller (DMAC) failure The DMAC is often an 8237 or compatible device, and two DMACs are on the typical AT motherboard (DMAC#1 handles channel 0 through channel 3 and DMAC#2 handles channel 4 through channel 7). Of the two, DMAC#1 is more important because channel 2 runs the floppy-disk controller. Generally, a diagnostic will reveal which of the two DMACs have failed. Be sure that no DMA conflicts are between two or more system devices. You can then replace the defective DMAC. In many current systems, both DMACs are integrated into a system controller or chipset IC. You can replace the defective IC if you have the appropriate surface-mount equipment available, or replace the motherboard entirely.

Symptom 28-8. The POST (or software diagnostic) reports a KBC fault The *KeyBoard controller (KBC)* is often either an 8042 or an 8742. Because the KBC is a microcontroller in its own right, diagnostics can usually detect a KBC fault with great accuracy. The KBC might either be a socket-mounted PLCC device, or (in rare cases) a surface-mounted IC. Remember, remove all power and mark the old KBC before you remove it from the PC. You will probably need a PLCC-removal tool to take out the old KBC. If you cannot exchange a defective KBC, you'll need to replace the motherboard.

Symptom 28-9. A keyboard error is reported, but a new keyboard has no effect The keyboard fuse on the motherboard might have failed. Many motherboard designs incorporate a small fuse (called a *pico-fuse*) in the +5-Vdc line that drives the keyboard. If this fuse fails, the keyboard will be dead. Use your multimeter and measure the +5-Vdc line at the keyboard connector. If this reads 0 Vdc, locate the keyboard fuse on the motherboard and replace it (you might have to trace the line back to the fuse, which looks almost exactly like a resistor).

Symptom 28-10. The POST (or software diagnostic) reports a CMOS or RTC fault With either error, the same device is usually at fault. The CMOS RAM and RTC are generally fabricated onto the sane device. RTC problems indicate that the real-time clock portion of the IC has failed or is not being updated. CMOS RAM failure can be caused by a dead backup battery or by the failure of the IC itself. When dealing with a CMOS or setup problem, try the following protocol. First, try a new backup battery and reload the CMOS setup variables. If a new battery does not resolve the problem, the CMOS/RTC IC should be replaced. Often, the CMOS/RTC IC is surface mounted, and will have to be replaced (or the motherboard will have to be replaced). However, the growing trend is toward making the IC socket mounted and including the battery into a single replaceable module (such as the Dallas Semiconductor-type devices). Modules are typically replaceable DIP devices.

Symptom 28-11. The POST (or software diagnostic) reports a fault in the first 64KB of RAM The first RAM page is important because it holds the *BIOS Data*

Area (BDA) and interrupt vectors—the system will not work without it. When a RAM error is indicated, your only real recourse is to replace the motherboard RAM. On older motherboards, if the diagnostic indicates which bit has failed and you can correlate the bit to a specific IC, you can sometimes replace the defective IC (typically, surface mounted). Otherwise, you will need to locate and replace all of the motherboard RAM, or replace the motherboard entirely. Newer motherboards utilize SIMMs or DIMMs for all system memory, so it should be relatively simple to cycle through each SIMM or DIMM with a known-good unit and isolate the defective memory.

Symptom 28-12. The MCP does not work properly when installed on a motherboard when external caching is enabled Some non-Intel math co-processors or FPUs work in areas that must be non-cached. For example, a Cyrix EMC87 MCP with an AMI Mark IV i386 motherboard has been known to cause these types of problems. When MCP problems arise (especially during upgrades), try disabling the external cache through CMOS setup. As another alternative, try a different math co-processor.

Symptom 28-13. A "jumperless motherboard" receives incorrect CPU Soft Menu settings and now refuses to boot This might occur on a motherboard, such as the Abit IT5V, and is usually caused by accidental settings during system configuration. Fortunately, this type of problem can be corrected by removing power from the motherboard—try turning off the system and unplugging it for several minutes. When you restore power to the system, the CPU soft menu will automatically reset the CPU frequency for the lowest setting and allow the motherboard to boot. You can then go back into the CPU soft menu and correct any speed-setting errors. If this were a jumpered motherboard, you would need to find the CPU speed jumper and set it correctly.

Symptom 28-14. When installing two 64MB SIMMS, only 32MB of RAM are displayed when the computer is turned on The motherboard is probably using a 430VX chipset that (although supporting 128MB of RAM) will not support 64MB memory devices. The 430VX only supports the following memory devices:

- 512K × 32 bit (2MB)
- 1M × 32 bit (4MB)
- 2M × 32 bit (8MB)
- 4M × 32 bit (16MB)

The layout for a 64MB SIMM is 16M × 32 bit, which isn't in the preceding list. When you install two 64MB SIMMs, the system will use the 4M- × 32-bit specification to calculate the memory, thus displaying 32MB. Unfortunately, this limitation of the motherboard cannot be corrected without upgrading the motherboard.

Symptom 28-15. A Creative Labs PnP sound board refuses to work on one motherboard, but the board works just fine on another motherboard In this issue, the PnP BIOS is usually at fault. Check with the motherboard manufacturer to see if a BIOS update is available to correct PnP problems.

Symptom 28-16. The system CD-ROM drive refuses to work once an IDE bus master driver is installed This is almost always a driver problem, which is not interacting properly with the IDE/EIDE bus controller on the motherboard. In almost all cases, you should update the IDE bus master driver or disable bus mastering completely.

Symptom 28-17. You cannot get an AMD 5x86 133MHz CPU to run on your motherboard Check your voltage first. The AMD 5x86 runs on 3.3 V, so you might need a voltage regulator in the CPU socket (the AMD CPU might already be damaged). Also check your BIOS version—you might need an updated BIOS to support the AMD CPU properly. Check your jumper settings next—the speed or CPU type selection is almost always set wrong. If you cannot jumper the motherboard correctly (i.e., 33MHz bus speed), then the motherboard itself is limited—it cannot enable the 4× internal CPU clock for the AMD 5x86. In this case, you will need to use a different CPU or replace the motherboard outright.

Symptom 28-18. You cannot get a Cyrix 5x86 CPU to run on your motherboard Check your voltage first. The Cyrix 5x86 uses 3.3 V, so you might need a voltage regulator in the CPU socket (the Cyrix CPU might already be damaged). Also check your BIOS version—you might need an updated BIOS to support the Cyrix CPU properly. Check your jumper settings next—the speed (33MHz) or CPU-type selection is almost always set wrong. If problems persist, you might need a different CPU or motherboard.

Symptom 28-19. You see the error message "System Resource Conflict" on the AMI BIOS POST display This error is generated by AMI PnP BIOS (although other PnP BIOS might produce similar errors) when the BIOS detects a resource conflict during initialization. You might try to force the BIOS to reconfigure the conflicting resource by pressing the <Insert> key during POST. If problems continue, you might need a BIOS update, which might be able to resolve assignment conflicts more intelligently. Otherwise, you might need to try to reconfigure the conflicting resource manually (disabling its PnP support), or remove the offending device entirely.

Symptom 28-20. The system hangs after using MEMMAKER under DOS This is most prevalent with AMI's WinBIOS, which cannot support the "highscan" option used with EMM386.EXE. Be sure to disable the "highscan" option from EMM386 before running MEMMAKER. You might also choose to upgrade the system BIOS to a more recent version, which might be more robust when testing memory.

Symptom 28-21. The *Power management* icon does not appear in the Windows 95 *Control panel* This occurs even though the APM parameter under the BIOS power-management setup is enabled. This problem occurs if you do not enable the APM function before you install Windows 95. If you have already installed Windows 95, you must re-install it. Before doing so, however, be sure that the APM function is enabled.

Symptom 28-22. Systems with a Western Digital 1.6GB HDD fail to boot even though BIOS recognized the presence of HDD This is a typical problem with large hard drives, which often need additional time to start up after powering the system. Check your BIOS advanced setup and increase the "Power-on Delay" time. This should correct the problem. This problem might reoccur if CMOS default values are re-loaded or if CMOS contents are lost.

Symptom 28-23. After installing Windows 95, the system can no longer find the CD-ROM drive on the secondary IDE channel You might also find that the IDE drives are running in MS-DOS "compatibility mode." This problem occurs often with motherboards using the Intel 430HX chipset—Windows 95 is not recognizing the Intel 82371SB drive controller on the motherboard, which causes BIOS to disable the secondary IDE channel—devices on the secondary channel are not being detected after the system is rebooted. In most cases, you can upgrade the BIOS to correct this problem or move the IDE devices to a separate IDE controller. You might also be able to find an update to the MSHDC.INF file, which will force Windows 95 to recognize the 82371SB controller.

Symptom 28-24. The system hangs up or crashes when the chipset-specific PCI-IDE DOS driver is loaded This is a known problem with Micro-Star motherboards using a VIA VP1 chipset and Award BIOS 4.50PG. The problem is with the BIOS version and its interaction with the PCI controller portion of the VIA chipset. Upgrading the BIOS version should resolve the problem.

Symptom 28-25. The Pentium motherboard is unusually picky about which SIMMs it will accept This occurs even though the SIMMs are all within the proper type and rating. Consider several possible problems. First, Intel chipsets are very discriminating when it comes to memory speed, so be sure that the memory speed is well within the required range (usually 70 ns or faster). Second, try changing the wait states in the CMOS setup to a lower speed (e.g., 4-4-4-4). If your system works under this low speed, then increase the speed (e.g., 3-3-3-3, 3-2-2-2, 3-1-1-1, etc.) and keep trying until the best number has reached. Finally, the memory itself might be of questionable quality—try good-quality memory, bought from a reputable vendor. Be sure that the vendor offers a liberal return policy so that you can return questionable memory easily.

Symptom 28-26. You experience a problem with pipeline burst cache This is a recognized problem with UMC pipeline burst cache (especially on an Amptron motherboard). The problem can usually be solved by adjusting the cache control to 4-4-4-4 (the default in CMOS is typically 2-3-3-3). This will reduce performance, but it should stabilize cache operations.

Symptom 28-27. You get no display, or the system refuses to boot because of the keyboard controller Notice that the video adapter proves out fine in another system. This is a problem with the VIA 82C41 24-pin keyboard controller (especially on the Amptron PM-7600 motherboard). A fault with the KBC might cause a "no display" or "fail to boot" condition. The VIA 82C41 is extremely sensitive to damage from power-supply surges/spikes, and ESD damage. Replace the KBC or replace the motherboard with a more robust model.

Symptom 28-28. Your customer forgets their password The PC password is stored in the CMOS RAM, which is located in either the motherboard chipset or the real-time clock chip. If it is stored in the chipset, the CMOS memory is backed up by a coin-shaped lithium battery (or other battery). If it is stored in the RTC chip, it has an internal battery to back up the CMOS RAM. For the external battery, follow these steps: First, make a complete backup of the CMOS settings. Turn off the system, and remove the battery for at least two hours. This should clear the CMOS setting and erase the password. For the RTC battery, follow these steps: Determine which RTC chip you have—the five different kinds of real-time clock CMOS chips are:

- Dallas DS 12887 real time
- Benchmarc
- Dallas DS 12B887
- Dallas DS 12887A
- BQ3287A

For the Dallas DS 12887 and Benchmarc RTC chips, if you can boot to the A: prompt, flash the BIOS chip with the same boot block record, but different BIOS revision. For example, if you have a P/I P55TP4XE motherboard with BIOS revision 0202, flash the BIOS chip to BIOS revision 0115. A BIOS checksum error will be generated. Enter the CMOS setup screen, reload setup defaults, then save and exit. At this point, the password has been cleared. You can flash the BIOS back to the original revision. If you can't boot to the A: prompt, turn off the system, remove the BIOS chip, and insert another with the same boot block record but different BIOS revision. Power on the system. A BIOS checksum error will be generated. Turn off the system. Reinstall the original BIOS. Power on the system again, and hit <Del> to enter the BIOS setup screen. Reload the setup defaults, then save and exit.

For the Dallas DS 12887A, a jumper is on the motherboard, which clears the CMOS. Please check your manual for the location of this jumper (it will vary between motherboards). Shorting this jumper should erase the system-configuration information (including password) stored in the CMOS. To clear the CMOS, be sure that the system is off. Short the jumper for a moment and then remove it. Do not leave this jumper shorted. After clearing the CMOS, the password should be erased. For the BQ3287A and Dallas DS12B887 RTC chips, short the same jumper (as in the previous section), but be sure to power the system on and off before removing the jumper.

Symptom 28-29. You encounter problems with Western Digital hard drives (the drives work on other systems) This type of problem has been identified with Asus motherboards using Award BIOS with older Western Digital (~1.6GB) drives. Notice that problems do not appear in newer Western Digital drives. There are several means of addressing the problems: First, disable the "Quick Power-on Self Test" in your CMOS setup, and enable the "floppy seek" option. This will increase the time that the drive gets to spinup. If your CMOS offers a "Power-on Delay Time" instead, try increasing that time. Also avoid using DEFRAG, or the "disk surface scan" feature of ScanDisk with Western Digital drives—both have been reported to increase the number of bad blocks on the disk.

Next, consider a BIOS upgrade (especially if you're using a motherboard with the Intel 430FX chipset). Some BIOS versions use a "park head" command that can cause problems with Western Digital hard drives. Finally, check the Western Digital Web site (**http://www.wdc.com**) for any drive patches that might be currently available. If all else fails, you can replace the drive outright.

Symptom 28-30. You encounter memory parity errors at bootup If you're using non-parity memory devices (e.g., a 32-bit device instead of a 36-bit device), you will need to disable DRAM ECC or parity checking through the CMOS chipset features settings. This problem can occur if you reload default CMOS settings, which restores parity/ECC on a system with non-parity memory. Also, the Triton chipset does not support parity, so even if you use parity RAM, you should try disabling parity checking. If the system is configured properly, you might actually have a memory failure, and you'll need to isolate the memory fault.

Symptom 28-31. You flash a BIOS, but now you get no video When you flash a BIOS, the CMOS settings are left useless. This means you will have to restore the proper CMOS settings before the system might run properly. Clear your CMOS and reload the proper settings. The BIOS IC itself might also be troublesome. There are some problems when flashing an Intel flash ROM IC. Be sure that no warnings or cautions are in the system documentation or from the manufacturer's Web site before flashing a particular BIOS IC. Try restoring the original BIOS, if possible, or contact the manufacturer for a replacement BIOS.

Symptom 28-32. You are trying to use a PnP sound card and PnP modem together on the same system, but you're getting hardware conflicts This is an all-too-common problem with PnP systems. In general, the modem should take COM2 (2F8h and IRQ3), and the sound card should take 220h, IRQ5, and DMA 1. Try adding the cards one at a time—install the sound card first and let Windows 95 detect it. Add the modem next. If problems persist, configure the cards manually (disable their PnP support), if possible.

Symptom 28-33. After setting the DRAM speed to 70 ns in the Advanced chipset setup, the system crashes or refuses to boot Chances are that you have the incorrect number of wait states set for your memory configuration—70-ns RAM typically requires at least one wait state. Disable any "Auto configure DRAM timing" feature, then set the number of wait states to 1. That should clear up the problem.

Symptom 28-34. 32MB (or more) of memory is installed, and the BIOS counts it all during POST, but you only see 16MB in the CMOS setup screen This problem has been identified with some Award BIOS versions. To correct the problem, be sure that the "memory hole" option in the Advanced chipset setup area is disabled. The "memory hole" option assumes that a maximum of 16MB of physical RAM is in the system.

Symptom 28-35. You move a working IDE drive from an older 386/486 system to your new Pentium system, but the system no longer works In most cases, the data-transfer mode is set improperly for the old IDE hard drive (e.g., using LBA mode when the IDE drive requires CHS mode). Find the *Peripheral setup* screen in your CMOS setup and be sure to change all the PIO mode settings to Mode 0 (chances are the settings are currently at Automatic, and are configuring the data transfer incorrectly). In some cases, you might need to repartition and reformat the drive to use it on a different (older) controller.

Symptom 28-36. Windows 95 locks up when you install a Diamond Stealth Video 3200 board and an Intel EtherExpress Pro 10/100 network card However, you verify that both cards work fine on other systems. Problems begin when you load the Intel network driver. This is a problem that has been identified with Premio motherboards and is caused by a problem in the system BIOS. Upgrade the Premio BIOS to the latest version.

Symptom 28-37. You install an Intel Pentium P55C (MMX) 200MHz CPU, and you set the CPU speed jumper(s) for 200MHz, but the system still reports 166MHz In virtually all cases, you have set the speed jumper(s) incorrectly. Take another look at the documentation for your motherboard and see that the speed is indeed set correctly. If problems persist, the BIOS might not recognize the higher CPU speed correctly, so try upgrading the motherboard BIOS.

Symptom 28-38. The system frequently locks up or crashes after installing a Cyrix 6x86 CPU In most cases, the Cyrix 6x86 is not being cooled properly and is overheating. Be sure that you have a heatsink/fan assembly attached properly to the Cyrix chip, and see that the fan is running. Also, the Cyrix 6x86 P166+ is a 3.52-V CPU. Check your voltage regulator and see that it is set to provide 3.45 to 3.6 V.

Symptom 28-39. After installing a Pentium 120MHz motherboard, you get "registry corruption" or "out of memory" errors from Windows 95 This happens most often with slightly older Pentium motherboards (~100 to 120MHz), and is almost always a BIOS version problem, which causes the motherboard to misbehave under Windows 95. You will need to update the BIOS version for your particular motherboard.

Symptom 28-40. The motherboard fails to "auto-detect" the hard drive parameters This is a known problem on Dataexpert EXP8551S motherboards, and is caused by a problem with Windows 95 in recognizing the PCI/ISA/I/O controller portion of the chipset. You can use the following procedure to force Windows 95 to recognize the chipset properly:

1 Boot up the Windows 95 system normally
2 Change the directory to /WINDOWS/INF
3 Edit the hidden file MSHDC.INF
4 Search for all lines with the "1230" device ID. Copy the lines and replace "1230" with "7010" (the correct device ID)
5 Save the file MSHDC.INF
6 Remove the "Standard IDE/ESDI hard-disk controller" entry from the *Device manager*.
7 Restart the computer, then choose the Windows default driver following the instructions shown on the screen.

> You should make a backup copy of the MSHDC.INF file before proceeding to edit the file. That way, you can easily restore the original file, if necessary.

If the problem persists, you should try entering the specific hard-drive parameters for your particular drive into the CMOS setup.

Symptom 28-41. The motherboard refuses to detect the SCSI controller during bootup This problem has been identified with the Dataexpert EXP8551 motherboard, but it might occur on many different types of PCI motherboards. In most cases, you will have to change the configuration of your PCI slots on the motherboard. For example, if the SCSI controller is installed on slot 2, you will need to configure the PCI slot 2 in CMOS setup.

Symptom 28-42. A Cyrix 6x86 CPU will not run on a particular motherboard This is a problem has been identified on Eurone/Matsonic motherboards, and is usually the result of an incompatible motherboard clock generator. Some clock generators support the Cyrix 120, 133, and 166MHz models, but exempt the 200MHz model. Other clock generators support the 120, 150, 166, and 200MHz models, but exempt the 133MHz model. So, if you're using a 133MHz or 200MHz Cyrix CPU, you might be using the "wrong" clock generator. You will have to replace the CPU with a speed that is suitable to the particular clock generator, or change the motherboard to one that will accommodate the particular CPU speed.

Symptom 28-43. The system can only count up to and recognize 8MB of RAM, although the system can accommodate even more This problem is often identified with Freetech 586F61x motherboards using Award BIOS version D or earlier. You can duplicate the problem by initiating a software reset with <Ctrl>+<Alt>+<Del>, then hitting the hardware reset—BIOS will only count memory up to 8MB. You will need to update the Award BIOS to version E or later. Freetech provides the BIOS patch on their Web site.

Symptom 28-44. When four 8MB SIMMs are installed in the system (32MB), the system only counts up to 24MB This is a known problem with gigabyte motherboards (typically the GA-586ATE, ATM, and AP version 1.x). The motherboard does not support "double-sided" SIMMs (i.e., 2MB, 8MB, 32MB, or 128MB) in the center bank. Install the SIMMs in bank 0 and bank 2—leaving bank 1 empty.

> Some motherboards require the banks to be filled in sequential order or allow you to change the bank order with jumpers.

Symptom 28-45. Gold-plated SIMMs do not work properly in tin-plated sockets As a general rule, you should avoid mixing metal types when choosing SIMMs—the metal in the SIMM socket must be the same as the metal on the SIMM itself. Otherwise, tin debris will transfer to the gold surface and oxidize. This will eventually result in memory failures, which suggests faulty SIMMs.

Symptom 28-46. Even though all peripherals in the system are SCSI, Windows 95 will continue to detect the PCI IDE controller You notice that this occurs even though the controller was disabled in CMOS. This is a known problem with the Iwill P54TS motherboard. Normally, Windows 95 will try to recognize and try to enable I/O devices, but should not enable devices that are deliberately disabled in CMOS. This is typically a BIOS problem, so try upgrading your BIOS to the latest version.

Symptom 28-47. An "EISA CMOS configuration error" occurs when the system starts For EISA systems, you must run the EISA configuration utility to properly set up the system. Without this step, the system will not be able to detect any possible resource conflicts. This type of problem is most common when installing a new EISA motherboard, when CMOS contents are lost, or when devices (such as memory) are added or removed.

Symptom 28-48. The SMP (dual processor) mode refuses to run in Windows NT The most common problem is an incompatibility with the SMP HAL shipped with Windows NT (versions prior to 3.51) and the motherboard's chipset. If you are upgrading from an older version of NT (prior to 3.51), first install NT as a standard PC (single-processor kernel), then install NT with the default multi-processor kernel that it provides (NT will not recognize your dual CPUs if you upgrade straight to a multi-processor configuration).

Symptom 28-49. When attempting to upgrade your flash BIOS, an "insufficient memory" error occurs In most cases, you simply don't have enough conventional memory available to execute the flash program. Most flash programs require about 560KB or conventional RAM. Try booting "clean" with a DOS diskette, then run the flash upgrade.

Symptom 28-50. A prolonged "Updating ESCD" message appears each time that the system boots The *Extended System Configuration Data (ESCD)* area is part of a PnP system. One or more PnP devices are attempting to update your BIOS settings. To stop this from occurring, set the BIOS to "program" mode.

Symptom 28-51. A yellow (!) sign appears over the USB port in the *Device manager* Windows 95 indicates that it has detected an unknown PCI device. In virtually all cases, the proper driver for the USB on your system has not been installed, and Windows 95 cannot recognize the USB hardware. You can usually correct this problem by updating your system BIOS to a newer version that supports the USB under Windows 95.

Symptom 28-52. The *Device manager* under Windows 95 indicates four COM ports (at unusual IRQs and I/O addresses), but only two physical ports are on the motherboard This problem has been identified with the Ocean Rhino motherboard, which is running a very old Award BIOS. The Award BIOS has since been upgraded to provide full support for Windows 95, so download the newest BIOS version from the motherboard manufacturer.

Symptom 28-53. The performance of a motherboard with an AMD K5 CPU seems extremely poor This is almost always because of the motherboard BIOS—chances are the BIOS was released before the AMD K5 was widely introduced, so there might be problems providing proper AMD support. Be sure that you are using the very latest BIOS that supplies adequate AMD support.

Symptom 28-54. The system hangs up after installing a Cyrix 6x86 CPU The problem is probably with the utilization of system cache, which is causing the system to hang up. Try disabling the internal (L1) and external (L2) cache.

Symptom 28-55. When attempting to upgrade the BIOS version, a key sequence, such as <Ctrl>+<Home>, cannot be used to reboot the PC in order to start the flash process The current BIOS version does not support such key sequences. To flash the BIOS, start the flash program manually from the DOS prompt. For example:

```
A:\> AMIFL PAIV17.ROM        <Enter>
```

Symptom 28-56. A particular SVGA board refuses to work on a particular motherboard However, the video board proves out fine on other systems. In most cases, this is a compatibility problem between the video chipset and the motherboard. A BIOS upgrade for the motherboard or video board can overcome the problem. You might simply have to use a different video board.

Symptom 28-57. When the on-board printer port is set to 3BCh (and EPP/ SPP mode) and another parallel port add-on card is set to 378h or 278h, the BIOS only recognizes the add-on card Port 3BCh seems to disappear. This might be a configuration problem with the Winbond chipset, which specifies that LPT1 on the motherboard should be set at 378h (EPP or SPP), and add-on parallel ports should be set at 278h or 3BCh. The Winbond chip was designed this way for Windows 95. Check with the motherboard manufacturer for any available BIOS upgrades that can correct this issue.

Symptom 28-58. With 32MB of RAM on the motherboard, Checkit 3.0 causes the system to reboot when performing DRAM tests This is because Checkit 3.0 will not perform memory testing over 16MB. This is an issue with Checkit— not the motherboard. Upgrade to a later version of Checkit.

Symptom 28-59. The IBM Blue Lighting CPU will not run on a motherboard that should support it In most cases, the problem is an older BIOS version. Be sure that you are running the latest version of BIOS before installing the IBM Blue Lightning. Also check to be sure that any CPU type and speed jumpers are set properly for the CPU.

Symptom 28-60. When using a benchmark program, such as SYSINFO, the "Overall Performance" rating of a Pentium 100 system marks better than a Pentium-120 system This is because of the PCI bus speed. For a 100MHz system, the PCI bus speed is 33MHz. For a 120MHz system, the bus speed is 30MHz. The slightly faster PCI system will register a bit better performance.

Always be sure that your benchmark and diagnostic programs are updated for the CPUs and other hardware that you are testing.

Symptom 28-61. Parallel-port devices do not work on your motherboard In most cases, you must set the proper parallel-port mode (i.e., SPP/ECP/EPP) for the particular device you plan to use. Often, setting the port to Compatibility mode will work for many common peripherals. Parallel-port modes are selected through the CMOS setup— usually under "Integrated peripherals" or some similar heading.

Symptom 28-62. Some configurations of memory provide less performance than others This type of problem is most noted on motherboards with 440FX chipsets, and is usually the result of a BIOS problem. Try updating your BIOS to the latest available version.

Symptom 28-63. The performance does not improve when enabling PCI/IDE bus mastering The problem is often that you are using an older (or buggy) driver. Be sure that you have installed the most recent bus-mastering driver file (Triton I, Triton II and Natoma chipsets might use the same driver).

Symptom 28-64. The BIOS banner displayed at power-on is showing the wrong motherboard model In virtually all cases, this is a problem with the BIOS version. Get the latest update for your motherboard BIOS.

Symptom 28-65. The Pentium P55CM BIOS shows a 150MHz CPU—even though the CPU is a 166MHz model This is almost always due to a BIOS fault. You should upgrade to the very latest BIOS version for your particular motherboard. If you cannot flash the BIOS, replace the BIOS IC outright.

Symptom 28-66. "Static device resource conflict" error message occurs after the system memory count when using the P55CM CPU This problem is usually in the PCI bus system. Press and hold the <Insert> key before turning on the computer. Release the <Insert> key when the video comes up. This forces the system to reassign PCI resources. If the error message still appears, remove all PCI cards (except for the video card) and try again. Reinsert one PCI card at a time until the problem returns—that is where the problem is.

Further Study

That's all for Chapter 28. Be sure to review the glossary and chapter questions on the accompanying CD. If you have access to the Internet, take a look at some of these motherboard resources:

Abit Computer Corp.: **http://www.abit.com.tw/html/emain.htm**

Acer America Corp.: **http://www.acer.com**

American Megatrends (AMI): **http://www.megatrends.com**

American Predator Corp.: **http://www.americanpredator.com**

ASUS: **http://www.asus.com**

Biostar Microtech Intl.: **http://www.biostar.net**

CompuTrend Systems, Inc. (Premio): **http://www.premiopc.com**

Data Expert Corp.: http://www.dataexpert.com

Diamond Flower, Inc. (DFI): **http://www.dfiusa.com**

Elitegroup Computers, Ltd. (ECS): **http://www.ecs.com.tw**

Famous Technology Co., Ltd.: **http://www1.magic-pro.com.hk/famous/index.html**

First International Computer, Inc. (FIC): **http://www.fica.com**

Fong Kai Industrial Co. (FKI): **http://www.fkusa.com**

Gemlight Computer Ltd.: **http://www.gemlight.com.hk**

Genoa Systems Corp.: **http://www.genoasys.com**

Giga-Byte Technology Co., Ltd.: **http://www.giga-byte.com**

Intel Corp.: **http://www.intel.com**

Iwill Computer: **http://www.iwill.com.tw**

Jbond: **http://www.jbond.com**

J-Mark Computer Corp.: **http://www.j-mark.com**

Kam-Tronic Computer Co., Ltd.: **http://megastar.kamtronic.com**

Micronics Computers, Inc.: **http://www.micronics.com**

Microway: **http://www.microway.com**

Micro Star International Co., Ltd. (MSI): **http://www.msi.com.tw**

PC Chips Manufacturing Ltd.: **http://www.pcchips.com**

Pine Technology Ltd.: **http://www.pinegroup.com**

Shuttle Computer International: **http://www.shuttlegroup.com**

Soyo Computer Inc.: **http://www.soyo.com.tw**

Supermicro Computer Inc.: **http://www.supermicro.com**

Tekram Technology: **http://www.tekram.com**

Tyan Computer: **http://www.tyan.com**

29

OVERLAY SOFTWARE

TROUBLESHOOTING

CONTENTS AT A GLANCE

Disk Manager Troubleshooting

EZ-Drive Troubleshooting

Drive Rocket Troubleshooting

Further Study

Hard drives have undergone phenomenal growth. 250MB drives that were considered spacious just a few years ago are now considered insignificant against the 3GB, 4GB, and 5GB+ drives that are now on store shelves. Although the battle for ever-larger drives has been waged relentlessly by drive manufacturers, the struggle to actually use those massive drives has rested squarely on the shoulders of computer users. Because traditional BIOS calls for ATA drives limit drive sizes to 528MB, making use of space beyond the 528MB mark has required PC users to use several different tactics. Updated motherboard BIOS and ATA-2 (Enhanced IDE or EIDE) controllers have been two popular solutions, but the drive-overlay software from manufacturers, such as Ontrack, has proven to be particularly useful.

Software solutions, such as Disk Manager or EZ-Drive, allow older systems to access the full capacity of a drive without ever touching the PC's hardware. Still, software solutions are not always as elegant and reliable as we would like to believe, and overlay software is certainly subject to a range of performance and compatibility problems under the wrong circumstances. This chapter provides symptoms and solutions for three premier drive-overlay software products: Disk Manager, EZ-Drive, and Drive Rocket.

Disk Manager Troubleshooting

Ontrack's Disk Manager is a utility that partitions and formats a hard drive, and allows you to access the full capacity of the drive (even when your system BIOS is unable to do so). Current versions of Disk Manager are fully compatible with 32-bit disk and file access under Windows 3.1x and Windows 95. The Disk Manager driver is loaded from the Master Boot Record (MBR) when the drive is set up as a primary ("master") drive. When the drive is set up as a secondary ("slave") drive, Disk Manager is called by the CONFIG.SYS file.

Symptom 29-1. You are having difficulty installing Ontrack's Disk Manager software from the B: drive Ontrack software must be installed from the A: drive. If your A: drive is the wrong size for your Ontrack distribution diskette, copy the diskette to a floppy disk that has been sized properly for drive A:, then try reinstalling Disk Manager.

Symptom 29-2. Windows 95 reports that the system is operating in "DOS Compatibility Mode" This type of problem is not necessarily related to Disk Manager (although older versions or poorly configured installations can cause the problem). The "DOS compatibility mode" is invoked by Windows 95 whenever the system loads a real-mode driver. This would happen when Windows 95 does not have an equivalent 32-bit protected-mode driver to replace a real-mode driver. Click on the *Performance* page under the *System* icon for details on what devices are causing the problem. Often, this problem is triggered when real-mode drivers for a device are loaded in CONFIG.SYS and AUTOEXEC.BAT. Try disabling any such real-mode entries, then restart the system. If the problem persists, be sure that you are using the latest protected-mode driver version for each device.

Symptom 29-3. Disk Manager does not appear to function properly with Windows 95 In virtually all cases, you are using an older version of Disk Manager. Version 6.0 or higher is known to work with Windows 95. It might be necessary to download the patch file (DMPATCH.EXE) from the Ontrack Internet Web site (*http://www.ontrack.com*), which will update the Dynamic Drive Overlay (DDO) to 6.03d.

Symptom 29-4. When using Disk Manager 6.0x, Windows 95 reports operating in the "DOS compatibility mode" Although Disk Manager version 6.0x is supported by Windows 95, some factors can keep the utility from running properly with Windows 95. First, be sure that the number of cylinders set for the drive under CMOS setup is 1024 or less—often, "translation geometries" are available from the drive maker that provide alternate entries for heads, sectors, cylinders, etc.

Next, be sure that any 32-bit disk-access drivers (such as WDCDRV.386) loaded in the Windows 3.1x SYSTEM.INI file are disabled prior to installing Windows 95 in the first place. Otherwise, you will need to edit the [386Enh] portion of your SYSTEM.INI file and disable 32-bit disk access by inserting a semicolon before the driver entry such as:

```
;32Bit DiskAccess=On
```

You could also simply change *on* to *off* on this line. Windows 95 provides its own 32-bit protected-mode drivers for the support of your IDE drives. Finally, check once again to be sure that you are, in fact, using the latest version of Disk Manager. If not, you can download the 6.03 patch file (DMPATCH.EXE) from the Ontrack Internet Web site.

Symptom 29-5. You encounter trouble with the disk driver (such as WDC-DRV.386) for 32-bit disk access in Windows 95 Don't use any third-party disk drivers under Windows 95, which provides its own native IDE protected-mode drivers. If references to third-party disk drivers are still in SYSTEM.INI, you will need to edit those references out manually, as noted in Symptom 29-4.

Symptom 29-6. When installing a new, large drive (and reinstalling Disk Manager to the new drive), you encounter errors with cluster sizes In virtually all cases, you are using an older version of Disk Manager, which does not support cluster sizes over 8KB. Be sure to obtain the very latest version of Disk Manager, which will support larger cluster sizes.

Symptom 29-7. Disk Manager fails to identify the hard drive correctly Some OEM versions of Disk Manager (such as the version distributed by Western Digital) check for the presence of a particular hard drive. Disk Manager starts by sending a query to the drive. If the response is anything other than the expected ID, Disk Manager will produce an error message. Some sophisticated IDE cards will intercept queries and commands sent to the drive. This will cause Disk Manager to believe there is no expected drive—even if there is. You should try to disable the BIOS on your controller, or format the drive using another controller card to avoid this problem (or use a generic commercial version of Disk Manager).

Symptom 29-8. You have problems removing Disk Manager Disk Manager installs itself in the *Master Boot Record (MBR)* of your primary ("master") hard drive. To eliminate Disk Manager, simply boot from a bootable diskette, repartition the hard drive with FDISK, then reformat the drive. Keep in mind that this process is destructive to your data—be sure to perform a complete backup of the drive before proceeding.

Symptom 29-9. You find "Out of disk space" errors after loading as little as 800MB of data onto a 1GB drive This is not a direct effect of Disk Manager (although it might appear so). In reality, you are seeing a limitation of the FAT 16 (DOS) file allocation system, which is based in clusters. In DOS, every file that is stored gets at least one cluster (or "allocation unit"), no matter what the size of the file is. The size of the cluster grows incrementally with the size of the partition. For example, if you have a 1.08GB partition, the cluster size will be 32KB; this means that even a 62-byte batch file consumes 32KB of storage space (the difference between the 32KB cluster size and the 62 bytes that the file really needs is called *slack space*). The only feasible way to reduce the cluster size is to reduce the partition size. To utilize drives larger than 2.1GB under FAT 16, you need to create additional partitions.

Symptom 29-10. Disk Manager appears to conflict with other programs in conventional memory The *Dynamic Drive Overlay (DDO)* used by Disk Manager first loads into conventional memory, where it takes 6KB. It then moves into 4KB of upper memory. When the program code leaves conventional memory, it leaves a 62-byte "footprint" at the top of conventional memory. This "footprint" can sometimes conflict with other programs. You might have to change how Disk Manager loads. During the boot process, when you see the message that tells you to press the space bar to boot from a floppy disk, press the "S" key instead, then answer "Y" to the next question. This will cause Disk Manager to stay in conventional memory, rather than moving to high memory, and might resolve the conflict you are experiencing.

If this does resolve the problem, a special version of Disk Manager (LOADLOW.ZIP) can prevent you from having to hit the "S" key every time you boot. You can obtain the file from the Ontrack BBS at (612)-937-0860, or from the Ontrack Web site (*http://www.ontrack.com*).

Symptom 29-11. Disk Manager installed properly and responded as expected, but after installing DOS 6.2, the drive ended up at 504MB To install DOS properly, you must load the *Dynamic Drive Overlay (DDO)* before running the DOS installation floppy. Start by booting from the hard drive. When you see the message: "Press spacebar to boot from diskette", press the <Space Bar>, insert the DOS startup diskette, and press any key to continue. The boot process will proceed from the floppy, but the DDO will have had a chance to load into memory first—the partitions will now make sense, so the DOS installation will not overwrite the partition information.

Symptom 29-12. Disk Manager installed and ran properly, but now you get a "DDO integrity error" and cannot access the hard drive This very serious error indicates that the hard-drive sector containing the DDO information has become corrupted. Such problems can be caused by:

- Infection by a boot or partition sector virus (boot from a clean DOS diskette and run virus-scan software).
- A power surge.
- A hardware failure (usually the controller card).
- Shutting the computer down in the middle of a write process.

Unfortunately, little can be done to correct the problem. If a virus is found and eliminated, you can re-install Disk Manager. If hardware is at fault, you will have to replace the hardware. In either case, any data on the drive that is not backed up will be lost.

Symptom 29-13. You can only get 16-bit file access on the secondary ("slave") drive formatted with Disk Manager When Disk Manager is used to format the primary ("master") drive, the DDO is loaded during the boot process. In this situation, no device=dmdrvr.bin line is in the CONFIG.SYS file. When Disk Manager is used to prepare the secondary ("slave") drive and the primary drive was prepared without Disk Manager, a driver will be loaded in the CONFIG.SYS file and the DDO is loaded differently. This difference in how the DDO is loaded that is causing the 16-bit file access on the secondary drive. The only solution here is to back up all the data on the primary drive and prepare it also with Disk Manager. This causes the DDO to be loaded during the boot process and allow 32-bit file access on both drives.

Symptom 29-14. Drive letters are all switched around when booting from a bootable diskette DOS allocates drive letters every time you boot. It starts first on cylinder 1, then goes on to subsequent cylinders, looking first for primary DOS partitions, then for DOS extended partitions. When this allocation is complete, DOS then proceeds to allocate drive letters, as requested by drivers loaded in CONFIG.SYS (e.g., CD-ROMs, hardcards, etc.). When you boot from a hard drive, the *Dynamic Drive Overlay (DDO)* is loaded before DOS. This means that when DOS looks at cylinder 1, it can identify that primary DOS partition, and assigns it to C:. It then goes to the second drive and allocates D:. When you boot from a floppy, the driver line in CONFIG.SYS (dmdrvr.bin) starts the DDO—but not until after DOS has already assigned drive letters. Because the DDO wasn't in memory when it looked at cylinder 1, it did not see that partition. It did see the partition on the non-Disk Manager cylinder and that became C:. When CONFIG.SYS loaded the driver which started the DDO and asked for drive letters, DOS saw the partition on cylinder 1 and gave it the next drive letter—D:.

An easy way to avoid this problem is to start the boot from the hard drive. When you see the "Press spacebar to boot from diskette" message, press the spacebar to halt the boot process and insert your boot floppy. The boot will continue on the floppy, but DDO will have loaded and the drive letters will be allocated as usual.

Symptom 29-15. You have trouble creating a floppy so that you can boot from a diskette and still have the DDO load You should insert a floppy disk and use the DMCFIG utility, such as:

```
DMCFIG /d=a:
```

You will need to answer a series of questions as DMCFIG runs.

Symptom 29-16. You encounter problems using certain utilities on your hard drive Generally speaking, utilities that use interrupt 13 for communicating with drive hardware will be compatible with Disk Manager. Utilities that attempt to communicate with drive hardware directly might encounter some problems and data corruption. Be suspicious of any disk utility that claims high performance by communicating directly with drive hardware.

EZ-Drive Troubleshooting

EZ-Drive is very similar in nature to Disk Manager—it provides large-drive support for older BIOS. It also works around problems with BIOS versions that hang on drives larger than 2.1GB. As with Disk Manager, however, EZ-Drive also suffers from its share of problems under the wrong conditions.

Symptom 29-17. EZ-Drive refuses to work properly with the system's VLB IDE controller EZ-Drive has a number of compatibility problems with some VL bus drive controllers. Fortunately, there is a workaround in most cases:

■ *Appian ADI2* This is fully compatible. The HVLIDE.SYS driver is fully compatible with EZ-Drive. The ADI2C143.SYS driver is also fully compatible with EZ-Drive. Install EZ-Drive, then install one of these drivers into your CONFIG.SYS file.

■ *CMD640x* This is fully compatible. The CMD640X.SYS driver is fully compatible with EZ-Drive. Install EZ-Drive, then install the driver into your CONFIG.SYS file.

■ *PC Tech RZ1000* This is not supported. The ZEOS/Phoenix BIOS does not need EZ-Drive as it natively supports large drives. If EZ-Drive sets up a large drive, it will take over from the BIOS and the drive will be slower than with native BIOS support. Set up the drive through BIOS and not EZ-Drive.

■ *Opti 611A and 621A* This is not supported by any product or hardware. The OP-TIVIC.SYS driver (dated 5-11-94) is incompatible with large drives—with and without EZ-Drive. An updated driver is under development by Opti.

Symptom 29-18. The keyboard or mouse does not function normally after exiting Windows on an EZ-Drive system This is almost always caused by a problem with the mouse driver installation. Some mouse drivers change a line in the SYSTEM.INI file to:

```
Keyboard=C:\MOUSE\mousevkd.386
```

To correct the problem, change that line in the SYSTEM.INI file back to:

```
Keyboard=*vkd
```

Symptom 29-19. With EZ-Drive installed on the system, QEMM 7.5 will not load in stealth mode This is often a problem with QEMM related to the way in which QEMM processes software interrupt 76. Add the following switch to the QEMM command line in CONFIG.SYS which will force QEMM to ignore software interrupt 76:

```
XSTI=76
```

Symptom 29-20. Windows crashes with EZ-Drive installed on my drive This problem has been reported on systems using Award BIOS version 4.50G. A patch file is available from MicroHouse (EZPCH502.EXE) that can update the EZ-Drive MBR. You can download the patch file from the MicroHouse BBS at (303)-443-9957 or from the web (*http://www.microhouse.com*).

Symptom 29-21. You have trouble removing EZ-Drive from the system You will need to re-write the drive's Master Boot Record (MBR). Disable any BIOS MBR virus protection that might be enabled through the CMOS setup. Boot the system from a floppy diskette containing FDISK, then run FDISK /MBR. This will overwrite the MBR and effectively remove EZ-Drive.

The FDISK /MBR command is very powerful, and data on the drive might be lost. Be sure to make a complete backup of the drive's contents before performing this procedure.

Symptom 29-22. You see an error message, such as: "No IDE drive installed" EZ-Drive might not be reading the particular drive properly. Normally, EZ-

Drive identifies an IDE drive even though the CMOS setup might have no drive geometry information entered (or set to "auto-detect"). Occasionally, EZ-Drive reports that no IDE drive is installed—even when a drive is present. If CMOS has no values for the drive, it might inhibit the EZ-Drive setup. You should simply run the "auto-detect" feature of the BIOS before running EZ-Drive. A more reliable solution is often to insert the proper drive parameters into the CMOS setup (e.g., heads, cylinders, sectors, etc.).

Symptom 29-23. You have trouble removing EZ-Drive from a system with available LBA support You can eliminate EZ-Drive from an LBA-compatible system via two methods. Before attempting either of these methods, be sure that you are using EZ-Drive 5.00 or later:

- Insert the EZ-Drive diskette.
- Run EZ.
- Pick *Change installed* features.
- Enable Windows NT compatibility mode for 5.00.

or:

- Disable floppy boot protection for EZ 5.02 and later.
- Pick *Save changes*.
- Exit EZ-Drive.
- Boot system and enter CMOS setup.
- "Auto-detect" hard drive or enter cylinders, sector, and heads under *User definable type*.
- Enable LBA mode.
- Save changes and exit CMOS setup.
- Boot system from a bootable floppy diskette (by-passing EZ-Drive).
- If all drives/directories are accessible, run the command FDISK/MBR to remove EZ-Drive MBR.
- If all drives/directories are not accessible, the BIOS LBA translation is different from the translation EZ-Drive used (in this case, the data must be backed up before proceeding).
- Boot directly from a floppy disk, run FDISK /MBR, then re-partition the drive with FDISK. Format the drive using FORMAT, then restore your data.

The FDISK /MBR command is very powerful, and data on the drive might be lost. Be sure to make a complete backup of the drive's contents before performing this procedure.

Symptom 29-24. You keep getting the message "Hold down the CTRL key . . ." In virtually all cases, the system has been infected with the "Ripper" virus. To correct the problem, try the following procedure (you will need EZ-Drive 5.00 or later):

- Boot directly from a floppy diskette.
- Insert the EZ-Drive diskette.
- Type "EZ /MBR" and press <Enter>.
- Run EZ.

- Pick *Change installed* features.
- Enable Windows NT compatibility mode for 5.00.

or:

- Disable floppy boot protection for EZ 5.02 and later.
- Pick *Save changes*.
- Run virus-scan software.

Symptom 29-25. The system hangs after booting directly from non-system disk A user turns on the machine with a diskette in the floppy drive that does not contain bootable system files. The message: "Non-system disk or disk error" is displayed on the screen. After the user removes the floppy and re-boots the system, it hangs and will not boot. All cases of this error have been linked to the "Antiexe" virus. To correct the problem, try the following procedure (you will need EZ-Drive 5.00 or later):

- Boot directly from a floppy diskette.
- Insert the EZ-Drive diskette.
- Type "EZ/MBR" and press <Enter>.
- Run EZ.
- Pick *Change installed* features.
- Enable Windows NT compatibility mode for 5.00.

or:

- Disable floppy boot protection for EZ 5.02 and later.
- Pick *Save changes*.
- Run virus-scan software.

Symptom 29-26. You encounter an: "Unrecognized DBR" message from EZ-Drive An unrecognized *Disk Boot Record (DBR)* message might mean that the DBR on the floppy diskette has been corrupted or simply is not one that is easily recognized by the program (i.e., a language-specific version of DOS). If the DBR is on a bootable floppy someone else has created, the first recommendation is to abort the boot process and SYS the diskette again such as:

SYS a:

   If the DBR is on a DOS diskette, such as DOS Disk1, answer *Yes* to complete the system transfer. If the hard drive refuses to boot (with a "Non-system disk error," reset the system and hold down the <Space> key. Insert a bootable floppy when prompted and press a key to get to an A: prompt. Then, SYS the hard drive to transfer the bootable files. At that point, the hard drive should be able to boot without any problems.

Symptom 29-27. You cannot get EZ-Drive to work on some PS/1 and PS/2 systems EZ-Drive will not work on micro-channel PCs.

Symptom 29-28. Windows 95 reports a problem with the MH32BIT.386 driver   The MH32BIT.386 driver should not be used with Windows 95, which already has all the support needed for EZ-Drive. Open the SYSTEM.INI file and comment out any references to the MH32BIT.386 driver.

Symptom 29-29. After removing EZ-Drive, the data on a hard drive is inaccessible   That is because: the drive controller does not support large hard drives, or the drive geometry entered into CMOS setup is different than the configuration EZ-Drive had used. If the drive system does not support large hard drives, you must upgrade the drive controller or motherboard BIOS to support EIDE drives. If the drive system already supports EIDE, check the drive parameters entered in CMOS setup, or try using the "auto-detect" feature in CMOS. If both of these options fail, you will need to repartition and re-format the drive, then restore the drive files from a backup.

Symptom 29-30. The <Alt> + <T> function was accidentally invoked under Disk Manager, and the DDO could not be recovered through EZ-Drive   Unfortunately, once the partition data on the first cylinder is wiped out, it cannot be recovered. You will have to reinstall the *Dynamic Drive Overlay (DDO)* and restore the drive files from a backup.

Drive Rocket Troubleshooting

Unlike Disk Manager or EZ-Drive, which allow a system to use EIDE hard drives, Ontrack's Drive Rocket is disk-enhancement software, which allows an IDE drive to transfer data in large "chunks." This speeds the transfer of data, and improves drive performance. Today's hard drives allow for very fast and efficient data transfer, so Drive Rocket is no longer in popular use, but older systems and drives might still utilize Drive Rocket.

Symptom 29-31. When running Drive Rocket, the QEMM Stealth ROM feature indicates: "Disabling Stealth ROM," then reports a reference to INT 76   The Stealth ROM feature is monitoring interrupts, and is disabling itself when Drive Rocket uses INT 13. You can disable the interrupt detection by adding the XSTI switch to the QEMM386 command line, such as:

```
XSTI=76
```

This switch forces QEMM's Stealth mode to ignore INT 76.

Symptom 29-32. During installation, Drive Rocket produces an error, which says that it can't recognize the driver   Some machines simply will not support the Drive Rocket software because of the way that Drive Rocket interacts with PC hardware. Do not manually over-ride a failed installation. Specific areas where Drive Rocket might fail are machines that already have a number of performance enhancement in place (i.e., a Pentium with PCI, LBA, or some other technology that is translating the drive parameters). When you see such an error, do not proceed with the Drive Rocket installation.

Symptom 29-33. Drive Rocket cannot be removed Drive Rocket is called as a command line in CONFIG.SYS, such as:

```
device=rocket.bin
```

To remove Drive Rocket, simply disable the command line. You should also delete the ROCKET.BIN file from the hard drive's root directory.

Symptom 29-34. Drive Rocket refuses to identify the hard drive correctly
Some OEM versions of Drive Rocket (such as the version distributed by Western Digital) check for the presence of a particular hard drive. Drive Rocket starts by sending a query to the drive. If the response is anything other than the expected ID, Drive Rocket will produce an error message. Some sophisticated IDE cards will intercept queries and commands sent to the drive. This will cause Drive Rocket to believe there is no expected drive—even if there is. You should try to disable the BIOS on your controller or format the drive using another controller card to avoid this problem. You could also install a non-OEM version of Drive Rocket.

Symptom 29-35. You have trouble loading Drive Rocket into high memory
Ideally, Drive Rocket can be loaded into the *Upper Memory Area (UMA)*. However, there are reports of problems with the QEMM LOADHI statement loading Drive Rocket. Try using a different memory manager, such as EMM386, or try loading other drivers into the UMA to free space in conventional memory for Drive Rocket.

Symptom 29-36. Drive Rocket reports a –35% increase This typically occurs in contemporary, high-performance systems. It means that Drive Rocket is conflicting with some other driver or device, and is probably not a good choice for that particular computer. Remove the Drive Rocket command line from CONFIG.SYS and delete ROCKET.BIN from the root directory.

Symptom 29-37. You encounter a GPF when working with the Control Panel in Windows 3.1x You need to define the drives that contain Drive Rocket. Add a command line switch to the end of the line in CONFIG.SYS that calls the Drive Rocket driver. Add the following switch if Drive Rocket is on a primary and secondary drive:

```
/w=1,1
```

If Drive Rocket is only on the primary drive, use the command:

```
/w=1,
```

If Drive Rocket is only on the secondary drive, use the command:

```
/w=,1
```

Further Study

That's all for Chapter 29. Be sure to review the glossary and chapter questions on the accompanying CD. If you have access to the Internet, take a look at some of these resources:

MicroHouse: **http://www.microhouse.com**

Ontrack: **http://www.ontrack.com**

30

OTHER INTERFACES

AND TECHNOLOGIES

CONTENTS AT A GLANCE

ACPI (Advanced Configuration and
Power Interface)
  Implementing ACPI

AGP (Accelerated Graphics Port)
  AGP and PCI
  Implementing AGP

APM (Advanced Power Management)
  The parts of APM
  Implementing APM

Device Bay
  Implementing device bay

DMI (Desktop Management Interface)
  Each device is identified
  Implementing DMI

I²O (Intelligent I/O)
  I²O in operation
  Implementing I²O

Instant ON
  Implementing instant ON

IrDA (Infrared Data Association)
  IrDA standards
  Limitations to IrDA
  Implementing IrDA

SMBus (System Management Bus)
and Smart Battery
  The "smart battery"
  Implementing SMBus

USB (Universal Serial Bus)
  USB operations
  Implementing USB

Further Study

Although this book presents many important PC technologies and bus schemes, there are always a number of emerging interfaces—both software and hardware based—designed to streamline the performance and usability of the personal computer. Most new interfaces and technologies are designed around four key areas of the PC: improving graphics performance (AGP), improving power management (ACPI, APM, Instant ON, SMBus), simplifying connections and improving the performance of peripheral devices (Device Bay, I²O, USB), and improving the utilization of PCs (DMI, IrDA). Many of these emerging standards come from the PC industry leaders, such as Intel, Compaq, and Microsoft, but other standards are evolving from industry *Special Interest Groups (SIGs)*, such as the *Desktop Management Task Force (DTMF)*. Virtually all current PCs support one or more of these new standards to some degree, so as a technician, you should at least be familiar with the benefits and features that each one offers. This chapter presents an overview of these new interfaces and technologies, and offers some resources for more detailed study.

ACPI (Advanced Configuration and Power Interface)

One of the major drawbacks to older power management schemes has been that "system events" (i.e., Plug-and-Play events) are largely overlooked if the system happens to be in a power-saving mode while the event occurs. In many cases, this could also result in a system crash or other system problem. Intel, Microsoft, and Toshiba have banded together to develop *ACPI (Advanced Configuration and Power Interface)* standard. The ACPI interface is largely a software feature incorporated into new operating systems (e.g., Windows 95) that gives the operating system direct control over both the power-management and Plug-and-Play functions of a computer. When the operating system loads, the ACPI feature takes over the power-management functions (such as APM) and PnP functions from the existing BIOS. Once the OS takes over, it handles all the PnP events, power-management, and thermal states (based on user settings and requests made by individual applications). The ACPI interface affects many areas of the contemporary PC:

- *System power management* ACPI defines the techniques for putting the whole computer into and out of system "sleeping" states. It also provides a general mechanism for any device to "wake" the computer, as needed.
- *Device power management* ACPI tables describe motherboard devices, their power states, the power planes the devices are connected to, and controls for putting devices into different power states. This enables the OS to put various devices into low-power states, based on application usage. In other words, devices that are not being used by an application can be placed into low-power states, and devices that are being used can be kept active.
- *Processor power management* While the OS is idle (but not sleeping), it will use commands described by the ACPI standard to put processors in low-power states.
- *Plug-and-Play* ACPI specifies the techniques used to enumerate and configure motherboard devices. This information is arranged hierarchically, so when events, such as

docking and undocking, occur, the operating system has precise knowledge of which devices are affected by the event.

■ *System events* ACPI provides a "general event" mechanism that can be used to keep track of thermal events, power-management events, docking, device insertion and removal, etc. This mechanism is very flexible in that it does not define specifically how events are routed to the core logic chipset. This allows individual device makers to incorporate their own responses to system events.

■ *Battery management* For portable computers, battery-management policy moves from the APM BIOS to the ACPI operating system. The OS determines the "low battery" and "battery warning" points, and the OS also calculates the remaining battery capacity and remaining battery life. An ACPI-compatible battery device needs either a *Smart Battery subsystem interface (SMbus)*, which is controlled by the OS directly through the embedded controller interface or a *Control Method Battery (CMBatt)* interface.

■ *Thermal management* Because the ACPI OS controls the power states of devices and processors, ACPI also addresses system thermal management. It provides a simple, direct approach that allows manufacturers to define thermal zones, thermal indicators, and methods for cooling thermal zones.

■ *Embedded controller* ACPI defines a standard hardware and software communications interface between an OS bus enumerator and an embedded controller. This allows any OS to provide a standard bus enumerator that can directly communicate with an embedded controller in the system, thus allowing other drivers within the system to communicate with and use the resources of system embedded controllers. This then enables an OEM to provide platform features that the OS and applications can use.

■ *System-management bus controller* ACPI defines a standard hardware and software communications interface between an OS bus driver and an SMBus controller. This allows any OS to provide a standard bus driver that can directly communicate with SMBus devices in the system. This then enables an OEM to provide platform features that the OS and applications can use.

IMPLEMENTING ACPI

ACPI support is provided at the hardware and software level in a PC. At the hardware level, you'll need a motherboard with an ACPI-compliant chipset, as well as ACPI compliant devices. For software, you'll need an ACPI operating system (such as Windows 95) and perhaps an ACPI driver. Many of the newest PCs are now supporting ACPI. Keep in mind that using "legacy" devices might sometimes result in power-management or Plug-and-Play problems under ACPI.

AGP (Accelerated Graphics Port)

Today, 3D rendering is considered to be more of a necessity than an option, and it is used extensively in games and all types of presentation and CAD software. The problems with

3D technology is that it requires intensive processing and lots of memory. This places a lot of strain on ordinary 3D video cards that use the PCI bus—their performance is often limited because of the massive amounts of data that must be passed between the video card and main memory. The *AGP (Accelerated Graphics Port)* developed by Intel uses a variation of the PCI bus slot to provide a high-speed data pathway between the 3D video card and main memory, and it allows the AGP video card to utilize main memory for graphics purposes.

A prime example of AGPs potential is in the use of "surface textures." Ordinarily, textures (the "painted" surfaces you see in so many 3D walk-through games, such as Quake II) are stored in the memory on a video card. This demands a lot of memory because texture maps are basically images, and textures are usually drawn in low-resolution to save space (which explains why so many scenes appear grainy when you get close to them). By moving the texture maps to main system RAM and accessing them across the AGP, it is possible to accelerate graphics performance because the 3D-rendering engine can focus on rendering, rather than patching in textures. The textures can also be made larger and at higher resolutions because there is typically much more main RAM available than graphics card memory. In actuality, other graphics-related data can also be moved to main memory through the AGP.

AGP AND PCI

The AGP interface specification uses the 66MHz PCI specification (Revision 2.1) as a baseline, and adds three significant performance extensions (or enhancements), which are intended to optimize the AGP for high-performance 3D graphics applications (these AGP extensions are not described in, or required by, the PCI specification 2.1). These extensions are:

■ Deeply pipelined memory read and write operations, which fully hide memory-access latency.
■ Demultiplexing of address and data on the bus, allowing almost 100% bus efficiency.
■ Timing for 133MHz data-transfer rates, allowing for real-data throughput in excess of 500MB/sec.

The high-speed AGP is physically, logically, and electrically independent of the PCI bus. It is an additional expansion bus in the system (Fig. 30-1), which is intended for the exclusive use of visual display devices—all other I/O devices (such as drive controllers) will remain on the PCI bus. The add-in slot defined for AGP uses a new connector body (for electrical signaling reasons) which is not compatible with the PCI connector, so PCI and AGP boards are not mechanically interchangeable. The pinout for an AGP slot is listed in Table 30-1.

Although the AGP interface is based on the PCI bus, it was developed by Intel (independent of the PCI Special Interest Group) and has neither been reviewed nor endorsed by that group.

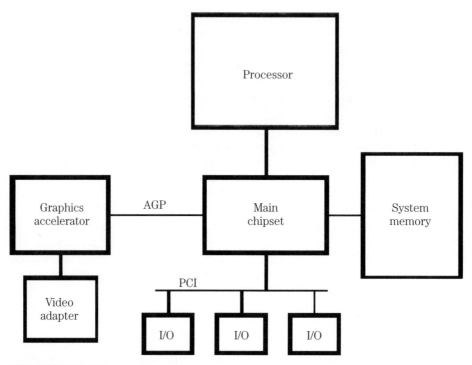

FIGURE 30-1   Basic block diagram of an AGP implementation.

TABLE 30-1 PINOUT FOR AN AGP SLOT		
PIN	SIDE B	SIDE A
1	Spare	12 V
2	5.0 V	Spare
3	5.0 V	Reserved
4	USB+	USB-
5	GND	GND
6	INTB#	INTA#
7	CLK	RST#
8	REQ#	GNT#
9	VCC (3.3)	VCC (3.3)
10	ST0	ST1
11	ST2	Reserved
12	RBF#	PIPE#
13	GND	GND
14	Spare	Spare
15	SBA0	SBA1
16	VCC (3.3)	VCC (3.3)
17	SBA2	SBA3
18	SB_STB	Reserved

PIN	SIDE B	SIDE A
TABLE 30-1 PINOUT FOR AN AGP SLOT (CONTINUED)		
19	GND	GND
20	SBA4	SBA5
21	SBA6	SBA7
22	Key	Key
23	Key	Key
24	Key	Key
25	Key	Key
26	AD31	AD30
27	AD29	AD28
28	VCC (3.3)	VCC (3.3)
29	AD27	AD26
30	AD25	AD24
31	GND	GND
32	AD_STB1	Reserved
33	AD23	C/BE3#
34	Vddq (3.3)	Vddq (3.3)
35	AD21	AD22
36	AD19	AD20
37	GND	GND
38	AD17	AD18
39	C/BE2#	AD16
40	Vddq (3.3)	Vddq (3.3)
41	IRDY#	FRAME#
42	—	—
43	GND	GND
44	—	—
45	VCC (3.3)	VCC (3.3)
46	DEVSEL#	TRDY#
47	Vddq (3.3)	STOP#
48	PERR#	Spare
49	GND	GND
50	SERR#	PAR
51	C/BE1#	AD15
52	Vddq (3.3)	Vddq (3.3)
53	AD14	AD13
54	AD12	AD11
55	GND	GND
56	AD10	AD9
57	AD8	C/BE0#
58	Vddq (3.3)	Vddq (3.3)
59	AD_STB0	Reserved
60	AD7	AD6

TABLE 30-1	PINOUT FOR AN AGP SLOT (CONTINUED)	
PIN	SIDE B	SIDE A
61	GND	GND
62	AD5	AD4
63	AD3	AD2
64	Vddq (3.3)	Vddq (3.3)
65	AD1	AD0
66	SMB0	SMB1

IMPLEMENTING AGP

Implementing AGP on the desktop requires support from the latest hardware. You'll need a motherboard (often a Pentium II ATX or NLX motherboard) with a recent chipset that supports an AGP slot, as well as an AGP video adapter (e.g., one of the Matrox AGP video cards). With the suitable hardware available, you'll need a video driver for Windows 95.

APM (Advanced Power Management)

Power management has become a serious concern for both desktop and mobile computers alike. The sheer volume of desktop PCs in service today accounts for a substantial percentage of all energy consumption, so power-management techniques can reduce those energy demands (and costs). For mobile PCs, power management helps to extend battery life by powering down idle systems. The *APM (Advanced Power Management)* specification authored by Intel and Microsoft represents the first concerted effort to define the role and actions of system-wide power management in the PC. APM is a software approach involving BIOS, the operating system, device drivers, and the devices themselves. When properly implemented, APM can control the system through five power modes: on, enabled, standby, suspend, and off. Table 30-2 outlines the system conditions in each APM state.

THE PARTS OF APM

For APM to function properly, three essential elements are needed (as shown in Fig. 30-2): the BIOS layer, the operating system layer, and the application layer. The following sections outline the operation of each element.

The BIOS layer The APM BIOS is the lowest level of power-management software in the PC, and it interfaces directly to suitable "power-managed" system motherboard hardware. The APM BIOS is supplied by the OEM and is specific to the hardware platform. An APM BIOS might provide some degree of power-management functionality without any support from operating system or application software (the OEM or BIOS provider determines just how much power-management functionality is implemented by the APM

BIOS in a stand-alone configuration). The APM BIOS stand-alone power-management functions are enhanced once an APM driver establishes a "connection" with the APM BIOS. Once made, this "connection" establishes a protocol that allows the firmware to communicate power-management events to the APM driver, and to wait for APM driver acknowledgment, if necessary.

The operating system layer The APM driver has three primary power-management functions: (1) passing calls and information between the application and APM BIOS layers, (2) arbitrating application power-management calls in a multitasking environment, and (3) identifying power-saving opportunities not apparent at the application or BIOS layer. An APM "connection" must be established between the APM BIOS and an APM driver for optimum system power management.

TABLE 30-2 APM SYSTEM CONDITIONS

APM STATE	SYSTEM CONDITIONS
Full On	System is working. System is not power managed. All devices are on.
APM Enabled	System is working. System is power managed. The CPU clock is slowed or stopped as needed. Devices are power managed as needed.
APM Standby	System might not be working. System is in a low-power state with some power savings. Most devices are in a low-power mode. The CPU clock is slowed or stopped. Operational parameters are retained. System returns quickly to the APM-enabled state. The Resume timer event must return the system to the APM-enabled state. User might be required to return the system to the APM-enabled state. The operating system is notified after the system shifts to the Enabled state. Prior operation resumes after returning to the APM-enabled state. Interrupts must be processed normally (this might require waking up the CPU temporarily if it was stopped, but the CPU might be stopped again by the APM driver).
APM Suspend	System is not working. System is in a low-power state with maximum power savings. Most power-managed devices are not powered. The CPU clock is stopped. The CPU core is in its minimum-power state. Operational parameters are saved to be restored later when resuming. System takes a relatively long time to return to the APM-enabled state. Wakeup events can return the system to the APM-enabled state. The Resume timer event must be one of the wakeup events. The OS is notified after the system shifts to the Enabled state. Prior operation resumes after returning to the APM-enabled state.
Off	System is not working. The power supply is off. Operational parameters are not saved. System resets and initializes when shifting to the Full-on state.

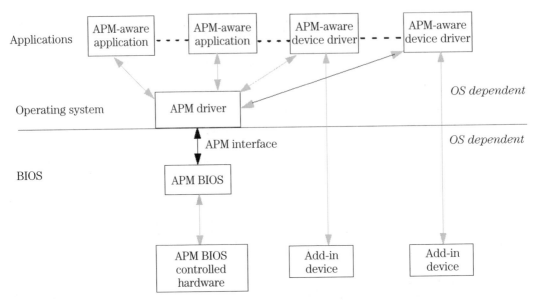

FIGURE 30-2   Block diagram of an APM configuration.

By regularly polling the APM BIOS, the APM driver will determine whether the APM BIOS wants a power-saving state to occur. In the case of a Standby or Suspend request, the APM driver is expected to do the appropriate processing to prepare for the state change, then call the APM BIOS to actually execute the power-state change in hardware. Because only one APM driver can exist in the system (and there might be many APM applications), the APM driver must provide an interface between the APM BIOS and APM-aware applications. This interface should pass the application's APM requests to the APM BIOS, and send any APM BIOS-generated events back to the applications. Each APM driver should specify a power-management application-to-OS interface.

The application layer   APM-aware applications assist in power management by providing information that only the application is in a position to know (or easily determine). Similarly, device drivers for add-in devices that are not under direct control of the BIOS (such as PCMCIA cards or ISA video adapters) might be able to manage power on their device, given suitable information about the overall system state, or by monitoring usage of their own hardware. Applications and device drivers are not required to be APM-aware, but they can greatly increase APM effectiveness—particularly on less-sophisticated operating systems. Under DOS, the application or device driver is often in the best position to know when the application or an add-in device is idle and awaiting further activity.

APM-aware applications register with the APM driver using an OS-dependent mechanism. The APM driver notifies registered applications and device drivers when system power-management events occur, and the applications and device drivers then take suitable action. For example, when an APM-aware device driver learns from the APM driver that the system will be suspended, it saves device information to be restored when the system resumes. When an APM-aware device driver is notified that the system has resumed, it restores the add-in device to its previous operating state.

IMPLEMENTING APM

APM requires four elements to function properly: an APM BIOS, an APM operating system (i.e., Windows 95), power-manageable devices, and APM device drivers to operate those devices. Most Pentium and Pentium MMX PCs support APM, although the very newest PCs (e.g., Pentium II systems) are implementing ACPI support instead of APM.

Now in version 1.2, it is unlikely that the APM specification will continue to develop as a stand-alone technology. The reason for this is that APM techniques are known to interfere with some Plug-and-Play devices (especially PC Card swapping and mobile PC docking and undocking operations). Rather than continue developing APM, the role of APM has been expanded and combined with PnP operations in the ACPI standard (see the ACPI section in this chapter).

Device Bay

Adding or replacing a drive on a PC continues to be a fairly labor-intensive process. Even with the benefits of automated device detection and driver installation offered by Windows 95, it is still necessary for users or technicians to physically open the system and manually install or replace any given device. To simplify system assembly, maintenance, and expansion, designers have introduced the *Device Bay*—an industry specification for interchangeable peripheral devices (such as hard-disk drives, modems, network adapters, CD-ROM drives, DVD-ROM drives, and a variety of other electronic devices). When fully implemented, you should simply insert a peripheral (e.g., a DVD-ROM) into the PC without opening, rebooting, or even powering down the PC. The system would then recognize the new or replaced device, and automatically reconfigure the system to accommodate it. Device Bay is expected to use a combination of USB port for hot-swappable, medium-speed serial data, and IEEE 1394 "Fire Wire" for high-speed serial data. In addition, the Device Bay will accommodate staged power management (compatible with ACPI).

IMPLEMENTING DEVICE BAY

To implement the Device Bay, you'll need a Device Bay-compliant operating system, Device Bay devices, and a Device Bay-compliant motherboard, BIOS, and chipset. You'll also need a case that provides Device Bay slots and connectors. As of this edition, the Device Bay specification is finalized, but actual Device Bay systems are not yet available—largely because of the slow adoption of IEEE 1394 and the poor industry response to USB (both of which have delayed the appearance of Device Bay-compliant drives). Intel has yet to release a Device Bay-compliant chipset, and Microsoft has not yet released the next version of Windows (i.e., Windows 98), which should include support needed for Device Bay operation.

DMI (Desktop Management Interface)

If you've been in the PC industry for any period of time, you know how much PC hardware has proliferated. Just take a stroll through any computer superstore, such as Comp-USA or Computer City, and you'll see a vast array of devices. There are literally dozens of options to choose from in everything from cases to CD-ROM drives and sound cards. You can also see this range of products in the myriad of PCs now in the market. Unfortunately, the problem with all of this diversity is that it is very difficult to manage from the technical standpoint. In other words, it's hard to find out about what's inside any given PC. Diagnostics can identify some parts, but diagnostics are not always reliable, and they are obsolete soon after new products arrive. Diagnostics also don't provide useful information about when products were installed or upgraded, or what versions of drivers are in use. This often means that a technician must work "in the dark." Some corporate environments might have hundreds (perhaps thousands) of computers that must be networked and supported, so you can imagine how daunting the task of equipment management can be for managers and technicians alike.

The *Desktop Management Task Force (DTMF)* has developed the *Desktop Management Interface (DMI)* as a solution to this "information gap." The DMI is a software standard for describing and accessing information about all types of PCs and PC components. The DMI standard provides a common resource for tech support, IT managers, and individual users to access information about all aspects of a given PC, including processor type, installation date, attached printers and other peripherals, power sources, and maintenance history. The DMI provides support for describing the more than 80,000 PC products in the marketplace today, allowing more cost-effective (and less "crisis-driven") PC management and support. Current versions of DMI also allow technicians to troubleshoot remote PCs right over a network from their own desktop PC.

EACH DEVICE IS IDENTIFIED

DMTF working committees create standardized DMI data-models in the .MIF (Management Information Format) file format to make it easier for vendors to implement the DMI standard in different product categories. For example, DMTF working committees have described standard sets of manageable attributes in model .MIF files for products, such as PC systems, servers, printers, LAN adapters, modems, software applications, and mobile devices. To make a product DMI-enabled, vendors can code in the appropriate .MIF file with information about their specific product and create "instrumentation code" to handle DMI information.

IMPLEMENTING DMI

Now at version 2.0, the DMI is a software standard requires a "service layer" of software under the operating system, as well as DMI-enabled products (devices with .MIF files already prepared). DMI will work under Windows 95, and many major system manufacturers (such as Compaq, Dell, HP, IBM, NEC, and Sun) are now producing DMI-compliant systems. There are now about 200 to 300 DMI-enabled devices. As more devices are "instrumented" for DMI, it is very probable that DMI-enabled systems will become more popular.

For an individual end-user, DMI has little direct impact on your system. It does not improve performance in any way—it simply provides a standard suite of information about what's inside the machine. Such information has little value for end users, but might be handy when troubleshooting or upgrading a system. As a consequence, you will probably encounter DMI-enabled systems, but it is unlikely that you would "upgrade" a system to support DMI. However, such standards as DMI might eventually make "remote troubleshooting" services feasible for end-user systems.

I²O (Intelligent I/O)

One of the most common activities of the computer is "input/output" (I/O)—that is, moving data into the system from a device (such as a drive controller) or putting data out to a device (like writing image data to a video adapter). Ordinarily, most I/O operations are handled through the CPU. This is perfectly normal, and modern CPUs are quite adept at managing I/O operations. The problem with CPU-based I/O is processing overhead. Every time an I/O process is handled, the CPU must stop its other, usually more important, tasks, such as calculating or logical comparison, and so on. This slows down the computer's overall processing performance—especially for calculation-intensive tasks.

If I/O processes could be handled "outside" of the CPU, the CPU could then focus on its more important tasks. This is hardly a new idea—*Direct Memory Access (DMA)* is the traditional means of channeling data without direct intervention by the CPU. However, DMA is an old and relatively slow technology, which is really only useful for "low-bandwidth" data, such as handling floppy drive or sound card data. For more complex systems (network servers, for example), DMA is totally inadequate. Designers have developed an improved means of "off-loading" I/O operations with the introduction of *Intelligent I/O (I²O)*.

But there's another, even more compelling advantage to I²O: device and OS independence. We've all experienced driver problems for devices, such as sound cards. For example, a Sound Blaster card uses different drivers for DOS, Windows 3.1x, Windows 95, Windows NT, OS/2, etc. A Sound Blaster 16 card uses an entirely different suite of drivers. A Gravis sound card uses its own suite of drivers, and on it goes. Upgrading the device or operating system demands the installation of a new driver. Of course, drivers must be kept up to date. This often places a great burden on device manufacturers, and continues to present a daunting problem for technicians. I²O offers both device and operating system independence. Ideally, any sound card would use a single I²O driver, which would work on any sound card from any I²O device manufacturer under any popular OS. Other I/O devices, such as modems, drive controllers, etc., would have their own "universal" cross-platform I²O driver.

I²O IN OPERATION

I²O defines a standard architecture for "intelligent I/O"—an approach to I/O in which low-level interrupts are off-loaded from the CPU to I/O sub-processors (IOPs) designed specifically to handle I/O processing. There is support for message-passing between multiple independent I/O processors, so the I²O architecture relieves the host of interrupt-intensive I/O tasks, greatly improving I/O performance in high-bandwidth applications, such as networked video, "groupware," and client/server processing. I²O also provides support for single-processor, multiprocessor, and clustered systems.

The I²O specification also defines a "universal driver" approach for creating drivers that are portable across multiple operating systems and host PC platforms. With the proliferation of *Network Operating Systems (NOSs)*, most notably NetWare 4, Windows NT

Server, and UnixWare, the number of drivers that must be written, tested, integrated and supported has escalated (one for every unique combination of OS and device). Using the universal driver approach, I²O significantly decreases the number of drivers required. OS vendors write a single I²O-ready driver for each class of device (such as disk adapter), known as the *OS Services Module (OSM)* and device manufacturers write a single I²O-ready driver for each device, known as the *Hardware Device Module (HDM)*, which will work for any OS that supports I²O. This two-driver model ensures that the OS does not have to be aware of every device—only classes of devices, and each particular device will offer its own I²O driver, which will interface to the OS's I²O "device class driver."

IMPLEMENTING I²O

Although I²O was developed by the I²O SIG in 1996, the actual implementation of I²O on desktop systems has been slow—largely because the I²O API needed for operating system support has not yet appeared for Windows 95 or Windows NT 4.0 (although it might appear in Windows 98 or Windows NT 5.0), and I²O-compliant devices are slow in appearing. Also, although chipsets are now available to support I²O, few desktop-class motherboards are incorporating the I/O sub-processors and PCI bridge needed to bring intelligent I/O to a PCI bus. It is possible to provide the I/O sub-processor(s) on a PCI expansion card (making it possible to add I²O support by adding the expansion card), but PCI slots are often too scarce for this tactic. Finally, few existing devices in the field actually support I²O at this time (the drivers are also limited). The I²O SIG expects general implementation of I²O by mid-1998.

Instant ON

One of the problems with power conservation has traditionally been "connectivity"—the PC cannot respond to the outside world while in a power-saving mode, and any network or dial-up connection already in service is usually severed. Another problem has often been that power recovery after being in a power-saving state is often a slow and convoluted process. *Instant ON* (a part of the APM and broad ACPI standards) resolves these issues by allowing fast recovery of the system when needed, and support for "remote waking" by external events (such as incoming faxes) or scheduled events (such as backups or defragmenting the hard drive). This improved functionality allows you to keep the PC turned on at all times and be responsive to real-world events, yet provide excellent power conservation. Instant ON provides three key features:

■ *Schedule automated tasks* With Instant ON, you no longer need to be present for your PC to be productive. Programs can be run whether you are at the machine or not (and whether the machine is in use or not). Schedule disk maintenance, phone calls, and other routine tasks whenever they are most convenient. Leave your Windows 95 system powered up at all times, and the Instant ON scheduler will run the tasks you've specified. You can set up applications to run at particular times or on particular days. You can run programs repeatedly (e.g., once each week on Mondays or once a month on the first of the month). You can schedule programs to run several times a day if needed. They can also be scheduled to run after another application has finished a scheduled task. Instant ON also switches your PC to low-power mode to save energy and wear. If the machine is in low power, Instant ON powers it up in time to run a scheduled task.

■ *Unattended operation* Automating tasks also makes it possible for a computer to run in an unattended mode. For instance, you do not need to be present for your fax/modem software to receive an incoming fax, so it can run without you. The disk utilities supplied with the Microsoft Plus Pack are also designed to run using settings determined in advance. The program should also be able to stop without requiring confirmation or other input from you.

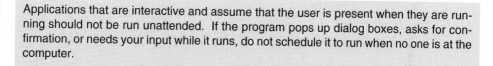

Applications that are interactive and assume that the user is present when they are running should not be run unattended. If the program pops up dialog boxes, asks for confirmation, or needs your input while it runs, do not schedule it to run when no one is at the computer.

■ *Energy efficient, yet available* With Instant ON, you never need to turn off the PC, so you don't have to wait for it to boot. Instant ON allows a power-managed PC to enter a low-power state when application and user activity cease, or when you choose to switch the PC to its low-power mode from the Instant ON scheduler. The system comes out of low-power mode when a scheduled task is to be run or when activity resumes (such as when the mouse is moved). The low-power state provides energy savings while allowing the system to return immediately to full power whenever necessary.

IMPLEMENTING INSTANT ON

Instant ON is actually a software application developed by Intel to enhance PCs with APM or ACPI power-conservation schemes in place. To use Instant ON, you'll need the Instant ON applet (available from **http://www.intel.com**), a PC platform that supports APM or ACPI power management, and power-managed devices (such as a modem).

IrDA (Infrared Data Association)

One of the persistent problems for technicians is the issue of "connectivity"—connecting one device to another. This is most pronounced when connecting peripheral devices, such as printers. Cabling is always a hassle—especially for mobile PCs and stationary printers. Another connectivity issue occurs with PC-to-PC file exchanges using tools, such as Windows 95's Direct Connect feature. Rather than deal with the physical connection of systems or serial devices, the *Infrared Data Association (IrDA)* has developed the IrDA port for serial communication over an optical (infrared) link. Just a few applications for IrDA ports include:

■ Printing from a desktop or notebook PC without cables.
■ Synchronizing files between PCs, or between hand-held PCs and desktop systems.

- Sending faxes/e-mail from a notebook PC through an IrDA-equipped telephone.
- Banking using a mobile PC and IrDA-equipped ATM.
- Accessing a network with a mobile PC using an IrDA-equipped node.

IrDA STANDARDS

In September 1993, IrDA outlined the basis for the IrDA SIR Data Link Standards. In June 1994, IrDA published the IrDA standards, which includes *Serial Infrared (SIR) Link* specification, *Link Access Protocol (IrLAP)* specification, and *Link Management Protocol (IrLMP)* specification. IrDA released extensions to SIR standard (including 4Mb/s) in October 1995. The IrDA standard specification has been expanded to include high-speed extensions from 1.152 Mb/s and 4.0 Mb/s. This extension will require an add-in card to retrofit existing PCs with high-speed IR and synchronous communications controllers (or equivalent).

LIMITATIONS TO IrDA

Although the IR serial port offers some serious advantages to PC users, IR technology has some limitations that you should keep in mind before using or upgrading to an IrDA port:

- IR working range is limited from 1 m to about 3 m.
- You need a direct line of site between two IR ports.
- The two IR ports must be directly facing one another (an angle of no more than 30 degrees).
- IrDA drivers and software further complicate an already crowded Windows 95 platform.

IMPLEMENTING IrDA

IrDA ports are now being incorporated into many new mobile computers and peripherals (especially printers). If you already have IrDA-enabled devices, you just need IrDA software and drivers for Windows 95. If you want to upgrade existing desktop systems, mobile systems, or peripherals, you can purchase and install IrDA adapters for existing serial ports (including the software and drivers needed to operate the IrDA adapters).

SMBus (System Management Bus) and Smart Battery

Battery-operated equipment (namely mobile PCs) presents some perplexing challenges to end users. In many cases, it is difficult (if not impossible) to accurately determine how much of a charge remains on the battery, how long it will take for the battery to charge, or how the insertion or removal of devices (e.g., PC Cards) will affect the remaining battery life. Intel has addressed this problem with the introduction of the *System Management Bus (SMBus)*, which is designed to operate in conjunction with "smart batteries" (Fig. 30-3).

SMBus support starts in the PC chipset, and is most often included with current mobile PC chipsets (such as Intel's 430MX). The "smart battery" can be connected directly to the

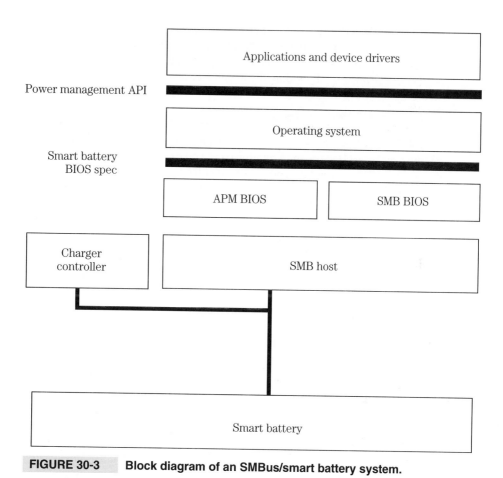

FIGURE 30-3   Block diagram of an SMBus/smart battery system.

SMBus host over a two-wire serial interface. SMBus BIOS provides the low-level BIOS support needed to operate the SMBus host, and an SMBus API provides the high-level operating-system support and dialog boxes used to configure and operate the SMBus.

THE "SMART BATTERY"

The key to a successful SMBus is the "smart battery" itself. In addition to the electrochemical components of a traditional battery, the "smart battery" incorporates active circuitry, which adds a level of intelligence to the battery. The battery can then pass messages about its status and respond to queries from the system. The smart battery's software API was designed to meet stringent requirements for data from the battery. The data that a smart battery must report falls into several general categories:

■ *Alarms* The battery is about to run out.
■ *Control/Status/Error* To control the battery's operating mode.
■ *Predictive functions* Indicating how long will the battery will supply power at a given rate.
■ *Measured data* Indicting how much current the battery is supplying.

- *Battery state of charge* The fuel gauge information.
- *Charging information* Indicating how to properly charge the battery.
- *Battery characteristics* Outlining the design capacity and cell chemistry of the battery.
- *Manufacturing data* Providing the manufacturer's name and serial number.

IMPLEMENTING SMBUS

Because the SMBus was designed primarily for mobile PCs, you will probably encounter SMBus and Smart Battery configurations, but you cannot add SMBus support to an existing system. The most important impact you'll have on smart battery operations is the proper configuration of Smart Battery software.

USB (Universal Serial Bus)

Connecting devices to a computer continues to be a problem for technicians. The PC must be powered down (and usually opened) before new devices or peripherals can be added or replaced. The system must then be rebooted to recognize the new device. Then the drivers must be loaded, and the device must be prepared for service. Designers have long sought to develop an interface that is simple, robust, and provides "hot swappable" connectivity so that devices can be attached and removed with power applied. This vision not only requires a fundamental shift in the way devices are designed, but it also demands changes to the operating system for "as needed" device recognition and handling. The *Universal Serial Bus (USB)* is the first step toward realizing these goals for low-to-medium bandwidth peripheral devices, such as monitors, printers, digital speakers, modems, graphics tablets, scanners, digital cameras, joysticks, etc. You can find the "first wave" of USB products highlighted at: **http://developer.intel.com/design/usb/frstwave.htm**.

USB OPERATIONS

USB has two data rates: a 12Mbps rate for devices requiring increased bandwidth, and a 1.5Mbps rate for lower-speed devices, such as joysticks and game pads. USB uses a "tiered star topology," which means that some USB devices (called *USB hubs*) can serve as connection ports for other USB peripherals. Only one device needs to be plugged into the PC. Other devices can then be plugged into the hub. USB hubs can be embedded in such key devices as monitors, printers and keyboards. Stand-alone hubs can also be made available. Hubs feature an upstream connection (pointed toward the PC), as well as multiple downstream ports to allow the connection of additional peripheral devices. Up to 127 USB devices can be connected together in this way. Industry pundits often refer to this as "plug and play outside of the box."

USB host controllers (which are available as part of several Intel PCI chip sets) manage and control the driver software and data flow required by each peripheral connected to the bus. Users don't need to take any specific configuration action because all the configuration steps happen automatically—the USB host controller even allocates electrical power to the USB devices. USB hubs and host controllers can detect attachments and detachments of peripherals occurring downstream and supply appropriate levels of power to downstream devices, as needed. Figure 30-4 illustrates a typical USB connector and pinout.

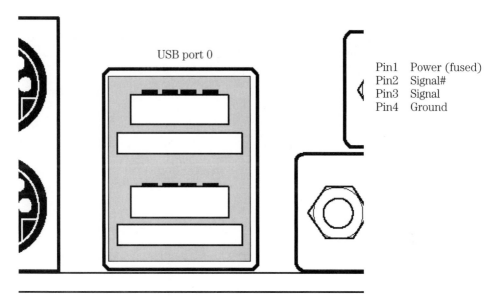

USB port 0

Pin1   Power (fused)
Pin2   Signal#
Pin3   Signal
Pin4   Ground

USB port 1

FIGURE 30-4   **A typical USB port layout.**

IMPLEMENTING USB

Most new systems are equipped with one or two USB ports (usually located in the area of COM or LPT ports). In this case, it is simply a matter of attaching a USB hub (such as a USB keyboard), then attaching USB devices to the hub. For systems without USB, you'll need a motherboard upgrade, which contains a USB-compliant chipset and port(s). Most current ATX and NLX motherboards will sport a USB port. Once the new motherboard is in place, USB devices can be attached.

Further Study

That concludes the material for Chapter 30. Be sure to review the glossary and chapter questions on the accompanying CD. If you have access to the Internet, take a look at some of these resources:

ACPI: **http://www.teleport.com/~acpi/**

APM: **http://www.intel.com/IAL/powermgm/**

AGP: **http://www.agpforum.org/**

ATX: **http://www.teleport.com/~atx**

Device Bay: **http://www.device-bay.org**

DMI: **http://www.dmtf.org/**

I^{2}O: **http://www.i2osig.org/**

IrDA: **http://www.irda.org/**

Smart Battery and SMBus: **http://www.sbs-forum.org/**

Instant ON Scheduler: **http://developer.intel.com/ial/inston/install.htm**

USB: **http://www.usb.org/**

31

PARALLEL-PORT
(CENTRONICS) TROUBLESHOOTING

CONTENTS AT A GLANCE

Understanding the Parallel Port
  Addresses and interrupts
  Parallel-port signals
  Port operation
  Advanced parallel ports
  IEEE 1284 modes
  ECP/EPP cable quality
  IEEE 1284 issues

Troubleshooting the Parallel Port
  Tips to fix parallel ports
  Symptoms

Further Study

Even after more than a decade of intense computer development, the *parallel port* (also called the *LPT port* or *printer port*) remains the fastest and most reliable printer-connection technique in the computer industry. By sending an entire byte of data from computer to printer simultaneously, and managing the flow of data with discrete handshaking signals, the circuitry required to bundle and decode data and control signals (such as that needed by serial ports) is virtually eliminated. The longevity of parallel ports has been largely because of their simplicity and good overall performance, but today's parallel ports are not invulnerable to failure. Cable problems, static discharge damage, and spontaneous IC faults can easily disable printer communication. Additional parallel-port problems can arise from the new generation of high-performance printers and other parallel-port devices. This chapter explains the pinout and operation of conventional parallel ports, explains the advances that have occurred, and present a series of troubleshooting procedures intended to help you isolate and correct port problems.

Understanding the Parallel Port

The parallel-port interface is one of the simplest and most straightforward circuits that you will encounter in a PC. Figure 31-1 illustrates a typical bi-directional port. A parallel port is composed of three separate registers: the data register, the status register, and the control register. Address bits A0 to A9 are decoded to determine which of the three registers are active. The use of –I/OR (–I/O Read) and –I/OW (–I/O Write) lines determine whether signals on the data bus (D0 to D7) are being read from or written to the respective register. When the port is ready to accept another character, handshaking line conditions will trigger an interrupt to request a new character.

The heart of a parallel port is the data register. In older PCs, the data register could only be written to (which renders the port unidirectional). But virtually all PCs since the release of i386 systems provide data registers that can be read and written (which makes the port bi-directional). To access a printer, the system CPU simply loads the port data register with the value to be passed. The bi-directional control register manages the behavior of the port, and affects the conditions under which new characters are requested from the CPU. For example, the control register is typically set up to generate an interrupt whenever the printer is ready to accept another character (i.e., IRQ7 for LPT1, and IRQ5 for LPT2). Finally, the status register is read to determine the printer's status (extracted from the logic conditions of several printer handshaking lines). All that remains is the port connector itself, which is a female 25-pin sub-miniature D-type connector.

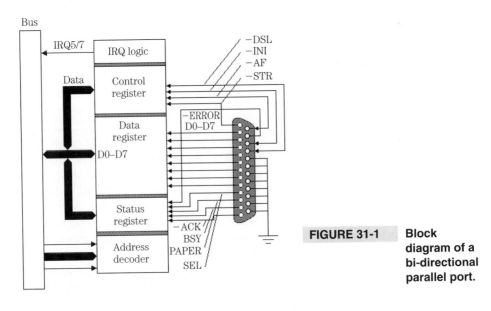

FIGURE 31-1   Block diagram of a bi-directional parallel port.

ADDRESSES AND INTERRUPTS

As you saw above, the conventional parallel port in a PC is implemented through a series of three registers—one register simply buffers the 8 data bits while the other two registers handle the port's handshaking lines. Although older BIOS versions only supported two or three parallel ports, today's PCs use BIOS written to support up to four complete parallel ports designated: *LPT1, LPT2, LPT3,* and *LPT4.* The base addresses allocated for each port are 0378h (LPT1), 0278h (LPT2), 03BCh (LPT3), and 02BCh (LPT4). The base address of each port corresponds to the data register. The status register of a respective port is accessed from the base address with an offset of 01h (i.e., 0379h, 0279h, 03BDh, and 02BDh), and the control register is accessed with an offset of 02h (i.e., 037Ah, 027Ah, 03BEh, and 02BEh).

> Although a typical PC can theoretically support four LPT ports, it is extremely rare for a PC to offer more than two ports. Even then, the IRQ for LPT2 (IRQ5) often conflicts with the IRQ assigned to Sound Blaster-type sound boards.

During initialization, ports are checked in the following order: 03BCh, 0378h, 0278h, and 02BCh, and LPT designations are assigned depending on what ports are found, so LPT addresses might be exchanged, depending on your particular system. The specific I/O addresses for each port are kept in the BIOS data area of RAM starting at 0408h (see Table 23-8). As you might expect, only one LPT port can be assigned to a base address. If more than one parallel port is assigned to the same address, system problems will almost certainly occur.

The use of interrupts gets a bit complicated. There are basically two modes of requesting new characters for the printer: polling and interrupt-driven. Polling is the most popular method where BIOS "polls" (or checks) the respective port's status register to see if it is ready to accept another character—no interrupts are generated. An interrupt-driven interface is much more efficient, but can bog down other important operations during printing.

For technicians who work on older machines, remember that address 03BCh was originally reserved for a parallel port located on the IBM *Monochrome Display Adapter (MDA).* If you are servicing an older system with no video support on the motherboard, the address 03BCh might be reserved in the event you (for some reason) want to install an IBM MDA card. For newer systems with video support located on the motherboard, address 03BCh might be the first parallel port address.

Always begin your service examination by checking the number of parallel ports in your system. Parallel ports are so simple and easy to add to various expansion cards, you can exceed the limit of four parallel ports without even knowing it. If more than four ports are active, a hardware conflict can result and crash the system—you will have to remove or disable the extra ports.

PARALLEL-PORT SIGNALS

IBM and compatible PCs implement a parallel port as a 25 pin sub-miniature D-type female connector, similar to the one shown in Fig. 31-2. The parallel connection at the printer uses a 36-pin "Centronics-type" connector (Amphenol type 57-30360). The exact reasoning for this rather specialized connector is not clear because 11 pins of the Centronics connector

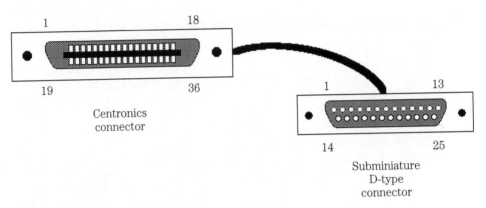

1   18

19   36

Centronics
connector

1   13

14   25

Subminiature
D-type
connector

FIGURE 31-2   A typical parallel cable assembly.

TABLE 31-1 PINOUTS FOR A CENTRONICS-TYPE PARALLEL CABLE

COMPUTER END	PRINTER END	DESIGNATION	DESCRIPTION	
1	1	–STR	–Strobe	(send character)
2	2	D0	Data bit 0	
3	3	D1	Data bit 1	
4	4	D2	Data bit 2	
5	5	D3	Data bit 3	
6	6	D4	Data bit 4	
7	7	D5	Data bit 5	
8	8	D6	Data bit 6	
9	9	D7	Data bit 7	
10	10	–ACK	–Acknowledge	(character received)
11	11	BSY	Busy	(processing character)
12	12	PAPER	Paper out	(out of paper)
13	13	SEL	Select	(printer is on/off line)
14	14	–AF	–Auto feed	(line feed manual/automatic)
15	32	–ERROR	–Error	(printer error)
16	31	–INI	–Initialize	(reset the printer)
17	36	–DSL	–Device select	(master printer control)
18–25	19–30, 33	Ground	Common electrical ground	
n/a	16	0 V	Open	
n/a	17	Frame	Frame electrical ground	
n/a	18	+5 Vdc	Remote voltage source	
n/a	34, 35	n/a	Unused	

will remain unused. Be concerned with three types of signals in parallel connections: data
lines, control (or handshaking) lines, and ground lines. Table 31-1 identifies the name and
description of each pin. The following section describes each signal. The pin numbers at
both the PC and printer ends are listed for your reference. Also remember that all signals
on the parallel port are compatible with TTL signal levels.

Data lines   The data lines are conductors that carry information from the parallel port to (or from) the printer (or other peripheral). The eight data lines (D0 to D7) are located on pins 2 through 9. To reduce the effects of signal noise on parallel cables, each data line is given a corresponding data ground line (pins 18 to 25). Ground lines also provide a common electrical reference between the computer and peripheral. The remainder of a parallel port is devoted to handshaking.

Initialize and select   To ensure that the printer starts in a known initialized state, an *–Initialize* signal (–INI on pin 16) sent from the computer is used to reset a printer to the state it powered up in. Initializing the peripheral has the same effect as turning it off, then turning it on again. The –Initialize line is active-low, so the printer must apply a logic 0 to trigger an initialization.

The *select line* (SEL on pin 13) tells the waiting computer that the peripheral is "on-line" and ready to receive data. Select is an active-high logic signal, so a logic 1 indicates that a device is on-line and ready, and a logic 0 indicates that the printer is not ready to receive data. The computer will not send data when the select line is logic 0. You can usually determine the select line's general condition from the printer's front-panel "on-line" light.

Strobe, busy, and acknowledge   Once a computer has placed eight valid bits on the parallel data lines, the peripheral must be told that the data is ready. A *–Strobe* signal (–STR on pin 1) is applied to the peripheral from the computer just after data is valid. The brief –Strobe signal causes the peripheral to accept the byte and store it in the printer's internal buffer for processing.

Under ideal circumstances, parallel ports can achieve data rates of up to 500,000 characters per second. With such a tremendous throughput, the printer needs some method of coordinating data transfer—the computer must wait between characters until the printer is ready to resume accepting new characters. Printers use the *Busy* signal (BSY on pin 11) to delay the computer until the printer is ready. Peripherals drive the Busy line to logic 1 any time a –Strobe signal is received. The Busy signal remains logic 1 for as long as it takes the peripheral to prepare for the next byte. Notice that a Busy signal can delay the computer indefinitely if a serious peripheral error has occurred (e.g., paper exhausted or ribbon jammed).

When the peripheral has received a byte and dealt with it, the peripheral must then request another character from the waiting computer. The printer drops the Busy line and initiates a brief *–Acknowledge* pulse (–ACK on pin 10). –Acknowledge signals are always active-low logic signals, and a typical acknowledge pulse lasts about 8 seconds. This interaction of data, –Strobe, Busy, and –Acknowledge signals handles the bulk of data transfer in a parallel port.

Auto feed   Some printers make the assumption that a carriage return signal (<CR>) will automatically advance the paper to the next line, while other printers simply return the carriage to the beginning of the existing line without advancing the paper. Many printers make this feature selectable through the use of a DIP switch in the printer, but an *–Auto Feed* signal (–AF on pin 14) from the computer can control that feature. A TTL logic 0 from the computer causes the printer to feed one line of paper automatically when a carriage return command is detected. A TTL logic 1 from the computer allows only a carriage return (paper would have to be fed manually). Most computer parallel ports keep this line at logic 0.

Device select The *–Device Select* line (–DSL on pin 17) allows the computer to bring the peripheral on and off-line remotely. Many parallel ports leave this signal as a logic 0 so that peripherals will automatically accept data. A logic 1 on this line would inhibit printer operation.

Error The *–Error* signal (–Error on pin 15) generated by a printer (or other peripheral) tells the computer that trouble has occurred, but is not specific about the exact problem. A variety of problems can cause an error—it depends on your particular peripheral and what it is capable of detecting. The error line uses active-low logic, so it is normally logic 1 until an error has occurred. An –Error signal can typically indicate an "out of paper," "printer offline," or "general printer fault" error condition.

PORT OPERATION

This part of the chapter describes a standard sequence of events in a parallel port. The parallel data transfer begins by placing the printer on-line. –Strobe and –Acknowledge must be TTL logic 1, while Busy must be logic 0. In this state, the peripheral can now accept a byte of data. When printing is attempted, the CPU polls the desired LPT port and checks its status register. If the post is ready, a byte is written to the data register, and passed to the peripheral.

   Data must be valid for at least 0.5 seconds before the computer initiates a logic 0 –Strobe. The printer responds by returning a logic 1 Busy signal, which changes the port's status. Subsequent polling of the status register will indicate that the port is unavailable. The –Strobe pulse must last at least 1.0 s. Data must be held valid at least 0.5 s after the –Strobe pulse passes. This timing ensures that the peripheral has enough time to receive the data. Because Busy is now logic 1, communication stops until the data byte has been processed. Processing can take 1 ms if the printer's buffer is not full. If the printer's buffer is full, communication might be halted for one second or longer. After the data byte has been processed, Busy is dropped to logic 0 and the printer sends a 5.0-s logic 0 –Acknowledge pulse to request another data byte from the waiting computer. Once the –Acknowledge line returns to a TTL logic 1 condition, the interface is ready to begin a new transfer. The status register then indicates the port is ready. When the port is next polled, a new byte can be written. Figure 31-3 illustrates this relationship—one complete cycle can take a bit longer than 1 ms.

ADVANCED PARALLEL PORTS

The appeal of a parallel port is easy to understand—it is simple. While serial devices struggle with baud rates, stop bits, and parity (problems that continue to this day), parallel devices just plug into the 25-pin D-type connector, and away you go. The parallel port offered "Plug-and-Play" capability before the term ever became vogue. Although the parallel port has been a staple of PC communication, it certainly has not gone unchanged over the last 15 years. If you've been shopping for new computers or I/O boards over the last year or two, you've probably noticed the terms *Enhanced Parallel Port (EPP)* or *Enhanced Capabilities Port (ECP)* associated with the parallel port. With a recent IEEE 1284 parallel-port standard developed by the *Institute of Electrical and Electronic Engi-*

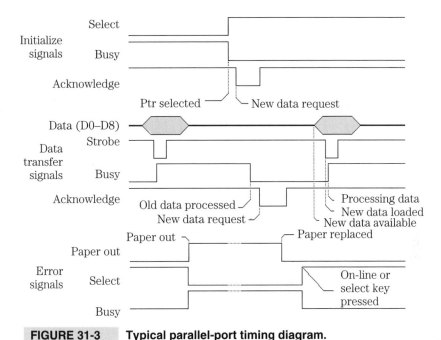

FIGURE 31-3   Typical parallel-port timing diagram.

neers (IEEE), the PC industry has finally moved past the parallel-port architecture, and embraced a truly improved parallel port. This part of the chapter compares the various parallel port "modes."

Unidirectional ports The original PC utilized a unidirectional parallel port. That is, the port sent data only one way (from the PC to the peripheral device, which was almost always a printer). For the time, unidirectional communication was adequate for general-purpose PCs, and the parallel port became synonymous with "printer port." Unidirectional ports reigned in the PC market until 1987 (around the time of the i386).

"Type 1" bi-directional ports By 1987, IBM had launched its PS/2 line. Among the other technological advances in the PS/2, IBM incorporated a bi-directional parallel port. Now, bi-directional ports were hardly a breakthrough (older hobby-type PCs had used similar ports), but IBM was really the first to use a bi-directional port in a commercial PC. The bi-directional port was really not any faster or better than a uni-directional port, but the ability to send data back to the PC opened up the parallel port to other devices besides printers. Clone PC manufacturers jumped on the improvement, and bi-directional ports became common in almost all subsequent clones.

"Type 3" bi-directional ports One of the problems with bi-directional parallel ports is that they are CPU-intensive, requiring relatively large amounts of CPU attention to manage the transfer of data. Later models of the PS/2 (the 57, 90, and 95) made an attempt to increase the throughput of a parallel port by using *Direct Memory Access (DMA)* techniques. The DMA approach allows the CPU to define a block of memory (e.g., printer ASCII characters) to be sent. A DMA controller takes over control from the CPU and transfers the data without CPU intervention—generally resulting in faster data transfer. This approach also worked when receiving data. Currently, Type 3 bi-directional ports are rarely used because today's high-performance CPUs can transfer data much faster than a DMA process.

IEEE 1284 MODES

By the end of the 1980s, it was becoming clear that "conventional" bi-directional parallel ports were simply not adequate to handle the new generations of faster peripherals that were appearing for the parallel port (e.g., CD-ROMs, tape drives, and laser printers). The 150KB/s parallel transfer rates that were once considered speedy were now severely limiting the new peripherals. In 1991, a group of major PC manufacturers (including IBM, Lexmark, and Texas Instruments) formed the *Network Printing Alliance (NPA)* in an attempt to develop a new parallel-port architecture. In 1994, the IEEE (in conjunction with the NPA) released the *Standard Signaling Method for a Bi-Directional Parallel Peripheral Interface*, also known as *IEEE standard 1284*.

The IEEE 1284 does not define a single parallel approach, but instead outlines five different operational modes for the parallel port: compatibility mode, nibble mode, byte mode, ECP mode, and EPP mode. All four modes offer some amount of bi-directional capability (known under IEEE 1284 as back channel communication). When the 1284-compliant parallel port is initialized, it checks to see which operating mode is most appropriate.

Compatibility mode IEEE 1284 is fully backward-compatible with conventional parallel-port technologies, where data is sent along eight data lines, the status lines are checked for errors and to see that the device is not busy, then a Strobe signal is generated to "push" the data into the device. As with ordinary parallel ports, the output of a single byte requires at least four I/O instructions. Data bandwidth is limited to 150KB/s.

> Whenever problems are encountered operating parallel-port devices, try setting the parallel port to Compatibility Mode in the CMOS setup.

Nibble mode The *nibble mode* (four bits at a time) is a simple means of receiving data back from a peripheral device in fewer I/O instructions, although it is very inefficient. When used by itself, the nibble mode is limited to about 50KB/s. In most practical implementations of IEEE 1284, the nibble mode will rarely be used for more than gathering brief diagnostic or status information about the peripheral.

Byte mode The byte mode allows the PC to disable the hardware drivers normally used to operate parallel data lines, which allows the data lines to be used as an input port to the PC. When in the byte mode, a peripheral can send a full byte to the PC in only one I/O cycle. Thus, it is possible to acquire data from a peripheral much faster than would be possible in the nibble mode.

ECP mode The *Enhanced Capabilities Port (ECP)* allows bi-directional data transfer within a single I/O cycle. When a transfer is requested, the port's hardware will automatically perform all of the port synchronization and handshaking operations formally handled by software-driven I/O cycles in the compatibility mode. When properly implemented, an ECP port can run from 800KB/s to 2MB/s, depending on the device at the port and the cable quality between them.

EPP mode   The *Enhanced Parallel Port (EPP)* is the apex of IEEE standard 1284. Like the ECP mode, EPP operation facilitated bi-directional data transfer in a single I/O cycle with the port hardware itself handling all synchronization and handshaking. EPP operation also can run from 800KB/s to 2MB/s. However, EPP operation takes another step forward by treating the parallel port as an extension of the system bus—this allows multiple EPP devices to exist on the same port, while still remaining uniquely addressable (similar to a SCSI bus, where multiple devices can exist on the same bus).

ECP/EPP CABLE QUALITY

Conventional parallel ports are limited to cable lengths of about 10 feet (about 3 meters). Beyond that, cross-talk in the parallel cable can result in data errors. Ideally, high-quality, well-shielded cable assemblies can extend that range even more, but the cheap, mass-produced cable assemblies that you often find in stores are rarely suited to support communication over more than six feet (about two meters). To support the high-speed communication promised by IEEE 1284, a new cable specification also had to be devised. This is hardly a trivial concern—especially considering that IEEE 1284 seeks to extend parallel-port operation to as much as 30 feet (about 10 meters). Be sure to use an appropriate cable when configuring a parallel port in ECP or EPP modes.

IEEE 1284 ISSUES

Unfortunately, although the potential and promise of IEEE 1284 offers a lot of appeal, some serious considerations are involved in configuring an enhanced port arrangement. Specifically, you will need an IEEE 1284-compliant parallel port, cable, and peripheral (e.g., printer, tape drive, hard drive, etc.) to take full advantage of enhanced capabilities.

Installing an IEEE 1284 parallel port is certainly not a problem—most current multi-I/O boards and late-model motherboards are now providing IEEE 1284-compliant ports. The trouble is that using a $5 printer cable with your old Panasonic KX-P1124 dot-matrix printer will just not provide any advantages. To start benefiting from an IEEE 1284 port, you will need at least an IEEE 1284 cable and a device with significant memory capacity (such as a laser printer). At that point, you might start to see some speed improvements, but the additional speed will still fall far short of the projected figures. Ultimately, you will need to install IEEE 1284-compliant peripherals that will provide ID information to the port and allow optimum performance.

Troubleshooting the Parallel Port

Although the typical parallel port is a rather simple I/O device, it presents some special challenges for the technician. Older PCs provided their parallel ports in the form of 8-bit expansion boards—when a port failed, it was a simple matter to replace the board outright.

Today, however, virtually all PCs provide at least one parallel port directly on the motherboard—the feature usually supported by an "I/O Controller" component of the motherboard's main chipset. When a problem is detected with a motherboard parallel port, a technician often has three choices:

- Replace the chipset IC that supports the parallel port(s). This requires access to surface-mount soldering tools and replacement ICs, and can be quite economical in volume. But this is a totally impractical solution for end-user troubleshooting.
- Set the motherboard jumpers (if possible) to disable the defective parallel port and install an expansion "multi-I/O" board to take the place of the defective port. This assumes there is an available expansion slot. This uses an expansion slot, but offers a cheap, fast fix for a defective parallel port. Remember to disable all other unused ports of the multi-I/O board.
- Replace the motherboard outright. This simple tactic requires little overhead equipment, but can be rather expensive—a general solution of last resort if you can confirm the parallel port to be defective.

If a diagnostic cannot identify the presence of a physical parallel port (a loopback plug might need to be attached), chances are that the port is defective.

TIPS TO FIX PARALLEL PORTS

Parallel ports are generally not complex devices, but some common issues show up regularly. Before you check out the symptoms later in this chapter, take a look at some of these points:

- *Check the cable* You'd be surprised how many LPT problems are caused by loose, cheap, or damaged printer cables. Be sure that the cable is 6' or less in length, see that it is secure at both ends, and try a different cable (or try the cable in place of a known-good one).
- *Beware of the port mode* Remember that modern parallel ports can operate in several different modes such as "compatibility," "ECP," or "EPP." Not all devices work properly with ECP or EPP modes. If you have trouble with a printer or other parallel-port device, try setting the parallel port to "compatibility mode" in the CMOS setup.
- *Beware of hardware conflicts* LPT ports use IRQ7 and IRQ5. For systems with a second LPT port (LPT2), it is common for IRQ5 to conflict with IRQ5, which is almost always used by sound boards. It might be necessary to reconfigure the sound board to use another IRQ or remove the sound board entirely.
- *Careful for printer-driver conflicts* This problem often arises with parallel-port devices, such as Iomega Zip drives or SyQuest SyJet drives. The drive software sends special reserved non-printable characters to the parallel port—this signals the drive to know the next data being placed on the parallel-port cable is for that drive (not the printer). Color printers and multiple-font printers can also be using some of these special characters for their printer setups. This can cause conflicts between the two drivers and make each unit (the printer and the parallel-port drive) look defective to the system.

Many printer companies, such as HP, are in the process of rewriting printer drivers to stay clear of these reserved non-printable characters, but some drivers still use these characters and will cause conflicts that cannot be resolved. The only way to correct this problem is to use one LPT port for the parallel-port drive and another LPT port for the printer. You should contact the printer manufacturer to see if they have updated drivers that will not interfere with the parallel-port device.

■ *Problems with printer-monitoring software* Another form of driver conflicts happens with printer-monitoring software. Some companies, such as HP, have status drivers that monitor the printer's status. If these printers are connected to the pass-through port of a parallel-port drive, the printer-monitoring drivers should be disabled. These drivers can also cause data corruption and system problems. Disabling status communications does not affect the printing.

SYMPTOMS

Symptom 31-1. You hear a beep code or see a POST error, indicating a parallel-port error The system initialization might not halt, depending on how the BIOS is written. Low-level initialization problems generally indicate trouble in the computer's hardware. If the computer's beep-code sequence is indistinct, you could try re-booting the computer with a POST analyzer card installed. The BIOS POST code displayed on the card could be matched to a specific error explanation in the POST card's documentation. Once you have clearly identified the error as a parallel-port fault, you can proceed with troubleshooting.

Start with the system as a whole and remove any expansion boards that have parallel ports available. Retest the computer after removing each board. If the error disappears after removing a particular card, then that card is likely at fault. You can simply replace the card with a new one, or attempt to repair the card to the component level. If there is only one parallel port in the system, it is most likely built into the motherboard.

For older systems, the fault is probably in one or more of the discrete I/O ICs or latches directing the port's operation. You will need to refer to the schematic(s) for your particular system motherboard to determine exact signal flows and component locations. Newer system motherboards enjoy a far lower component count, so all parallel port circuitry is usually integrated onto the same application-specific IC (ASIC). A schematic would still be valuable to determine signal paths, but you could probably trace the parallel port connector directly to its controlling IC. Replace any defective components, or replace the motherboard outright.

Symptom 31-2. A 9xx parallel adapter displayed on the XT or early AT system BIOS has not located any parallel-circuit defects on initialization, but has been unable to map LPT labels to the appropriate hardware-level ports. As in Symptom 31-1, the 9xx-series error codes usually indicate a hardware fault in the computer. Follow the procedures in Symptom 31-1 to isolate and resolve the problem.

Symptom 31-3. The computer initializes properly, but the peripheral (printer) does not work Your applications software might indicate a "printer time-out" or "general printer" error. Before you even open your tool kit, you must determine whether the trouble lies in your computer or your peripheral. When your printer stops working, run a self test to ensure the device is at least operational. Check all cables and connectors (perhaps try a different cable). If the peripheral offers multiple interfaces, such as serial and parallel, be sure that the parallel interface is activated in the peripheral. Also be sure to check the software package being used (e.g., word processor, painting package, system diagnostic, etc.) to operate the printer. Ensure that the software is configured properly to use the appropriate LPT port, and that any necessary printer driver is selected. If no software is available, you can try printing from the DOS command line using the <Shift> and <Print Screen> keys. This key sequence will dump the screen contents to a printer.

Disconnect the printer at the computer and install a parallel loopback plug. Run a diagnostic to inspect each available parallel port. Take note of any port(s) that register as defective. Locate the corresponding parallel port. If the port is installed as an expansion board, replace the defective expansion board. If the port is on the motherboard, you can replace the defective port-controller IC, install an alternate expansion board, or replace the motherboard outright.

Symptom 31-4. The peripheral (printer) will not go on-line Before data can be transferred across a parallel port, proper handshaking conditions must exist: the Busy (pin 11) and Paper Out (pin 12) lines must be TTL logic 0, and the Select (pin 13) and –Error (pin 15) lines must be TTL logic 1. All four signals are outputs from the peripheral. You can examine these levels with an ordinary logic probe. If any of these signals is incorrect, the peripheral will not be on-line. First, try a new communication cable. An old or worn cable might have developed a fault in one or more connections. Next, try the computer with a different peripheral. If a new peripheral does come on-line, the error exists in the original peripheral's parallel-port circuitry.

If a different peripheral does not operate properly, the problem is with the computer's parallel port. Examine and alter the computer configuration to ensure that there is no conflict between multiple parallel ports. Disconnect the printer at the computer and install a parallel loopback plug. Run a diagnostic to inspect each available parallel port. Take note of any port(s) that register as defective. Locate the corresponding parallel port. If the port is installed as an expansion board, replace the defective expansion board. If the port is on the motherboard, you can replace the defective port-controller IC, install an alternate expansion board, or replace the motherboard outright.

Symptom 31-5. Data is randomly lost or garbled Your first step should be to check the communication cable. Be sure that the cable is intact and properly secured at both ends. The cable should also be less than six feet (about two meters) long. Very long cables can allow crosstalk to generate erroneous signals. If the cable checks properly, either the port or peripheral is at fault. Start by suspecting the parallel port. Disconnect the printer at the computer and install a parallel loopback plug. Run a diagnostic to inspect each available parallel port. Take note of any port(s) that register as defective. Locate the corresponding parallel port. If the port is installed as an expansion board, replace the defective expansion board. If the port is on the motherboard, you can replace the defective port controller IC, install an alternate expansion board, or replace the motherboard outright.

If you cannot test the computer's parallel port directly, test the port indirectly by trying the peripheral on another known-good computer. If the peripheral works properly on another computer, the trouble is probably in the original computer's parallel-port circuitry. Replace any defective circuitry or replace the motherboard. If the peripheral remains defective on another computer, the peripheral itself is probably faulty.

Symptom 31-6. You see a continuous "paper out" error—even though paper is available and the printer's paper sensor works properly Plenty of paper is installed in the printer and you have already checked the paper sensor. Try another printer. If another printer works, the problem is in your original printer, not in the parallel port. Use a logic probe and check the Paper Out signal at the computer. Try removing and re-inserting paper while the printer is running. You should see the Paper Out signal vary between a TTL logic 0 (paper available) and a TTL logic 1 (paper missing). If the signal remains TTL logic 1, regardless of paper availability, the printer's sensor or communication circuits are probably defective. If the Paper Out signal correctly follows the paper availability, the trouble is probably in your computer's communication circuitry.

If you suspect that the problem is in the parallel port, disconnect the printer at the computer and install a parallel loopback plug. Run a diagnostic to inspect each available parallel port. Take note of any port(s) that register as defective. Locate the corresponding parallel port. If the port is installed as an expansion board, replace the defective expansion board. If the port is on the motherboard, you can replace the defective port-controller IC, install an alternate expansion board, or replace the motherboard outright.

Further Study

That's all for Chapter 31. Be sure to review the glossary and chapter questions on the accompanying CD. If you have access to the Internet, take a look at some of these parallel-port resources:

LPT Ports and Parallel Drives: **http://syquest.com/support/papers.html**

HP: **http://www.hp.com**

32

PC CARDS
AND PERIPHERALS

CONTENTS AT A GLANCE

Understanding the PC Card
  Making it work
  Enablers
  Card types
  Cardbus and zoomed video
  Inside the card
  Hot insertion and removal
  Understanding attribute memory
  Connections

PC Card Applications
  PC card problems
  Today's cards
  Installing a PC card

Optimizing Memory in PC Card Systems
  Remove any unnecessary drivers
  Recover unused memory areas
  Utilize any PCMCIA reserved window
  Change the driver loading order

Troubleshooting PC Card Problems

Further Study
  Newsgroup

Desktop computers have always provided a standardized interface—the expansion bus. On the other hand, mobile computers have traditionally lacked all the most basic upgrade potential. By the late 1980s, it was clear that a standard would be needed to allow rapid and convenient upgrades for the exploding field of mobile computing. Neil Chandra of Poquet Computer (now part of Fujitsu) took a vision originally conceived to provide memory for the hand-held Poquet computer, and brought together industry leaders to forge a

FIGURE 32-1   A PC-card SCSI adapter for mobile computers. Copyright © 1995 Future Domain Corporation. Reprinted with permission.

standard. In 1989, Chandra's brainchild, the *Personal Computer Memory Card International Association (PCMCIA)*, was formed as a standards body and trade association. The objective of the PCMCIA is to provide universal, non-proprietary expansion capability for mobile computer systems (Fig. 32-1). More than 500 organizations are affiliated with the PCMCIA, which also works very closely with other major standards organizations, such as the *Japan Electronics Industry Development Association (JEIDA)*, the *Electronics Industries Association (EIA)*, the *Joint Electron Device Engineering Council (JEDEC)*, and the *International Standards Organization (ISO)*. This chapter explains the inner workings of a PCMCIA interface and cards that use it. You will also find a broad selection of troubleshooting procedures intended to help you overcome many of the problems attributed to the PCMCIA interface, and the difficulties it can encounter under Windows 95.

Understanding the PC Card

Ultimately, the universal expansion standard envisioned by the PCMCIA has taken the form of a "card" (called a *PC Card*), which is roughly the length and width of a credit card (Fig. 32-2). This basic shape has remained virtually unchanged since the initial release of PCMCIA standards (version 1.0) in September 1990. The original specification (reflecting the original Poquet vision) defined an interface that was intended exclusively for memory cards, such as DRAM, flash EEPROM, and ROM. However, a memory-only interface

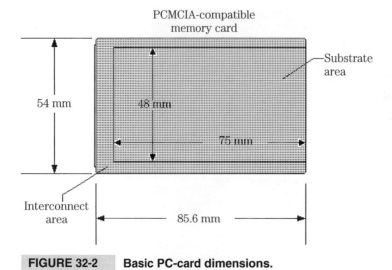

PCMCIA-compatible
memory card

Substrate
area

54 mm

48 mm

75 mm

Interconnect
area

85.6 mm

FIGURE 32-2   Basic PC-card dimensions.

did not even come close to fulfilling the promise of mobile-expansion capability—PCs are
much more than memory.

PCMCIA release 2.0 followed a year later in September 1991. Version 2.0 took the quantum leap that version 1.0 ignored and incorporated I/O capability and software support into
the PC Card. It was this addition of I/O capability that PC Card technology finally began
to attract serious attention from mobile computer manufacturers. PC Card makers could
now move past memory products and offer a wealth of other expansion products, such as
LAN cards, fax/modems, and disk drives. Release 2.1 followed in July of 1993, which
specifies software support and BIOS card and socket services. The newest set of PCMCIA
standards appeared in February of 1995 (loosely referred to as *PCMCIA '95* or *Release
3.0*). Release 3.0 added support for "multi-function" PC Cards, such as modem/LAN cards,
as well as support for 3.3-V operation, DMA handling, and 32-bit CardBus bus-mastering.

Since February of 1995, there have been some important revisions of the PCMCIA standards, but no "new" revision levels. In May of 1995, the second printing of PCMCIA standards addressed timing problems during card power-up/power-down sequences. In
November of 1995, the third printing of PCMCIA standards included provisions for custom card interfaces and indirect CIS addressing. The latest standards update in July of
1996 provided for a *Zoomed Video (ZV)* interface for fast video systems, and a *Flash
Translation Layer (FTL)* for card reprogramability.

MAKING IT WORK

Of course, integrating a PC Card into a computer is not as easy as just attaching a connec-
tor to the PC busses. A selection of system hardware and software is needed (Fig. 32-3).
This multi-layered approach is typical of most PC peripherals—if you've ever installed a
CD-ROM drive before, this type of diagram probably looks very familiar.

At the foundation of PC Card architecture is the hardware layer. This represents the
physical card itself, its connectors, and the circuitry needed to interface the card to the PC
buses. In most cases, PC Card support can be added to a computer with one or two *Very*

Large Scale Integration (VLSI) ICs and a bit of "glue" logic. You can see this hardware implemented for a desktop or tower PC in the PC Card drive shown in Fig. 32-4.

The next layer above hardware is called the *Socket Services layer*. Socket Services act as a supplement for system BIOS by providing the low-level routines needed to access the card hardware. Socket Services software is frequently implemented as firmware—either in the system BIOS itself (often in new BIOS versions) or on an expansion ROM included

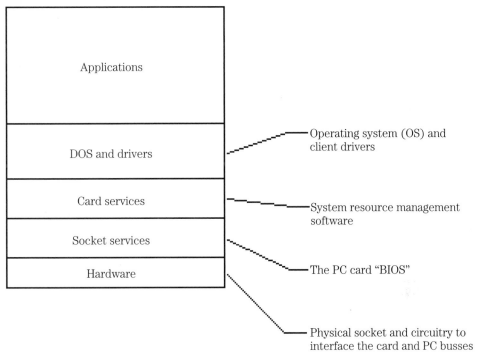

| Applications |
DOS and drivers	—— Operating system (OS) and client drivers
Card services	—— System resource management software
Socket services	—— The PC card "BIOS"
Hardware	—— Physical socket and circuitry to interface the card and PC busses

FIGURE 32-3   **Simplified PC-card architecture.**

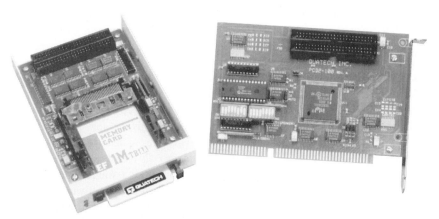

FIGURE 32-4   **A commercial PC-card drive for desktop or tower PCs.**
Quatech

on the PC Card reader's adapter board. Socket Services are used by the computer to identify how many sockets are in the system and whether cards are inserted or removed while system power is applied.

The Card Services layer forms the interface between the operating system and Socket Services. When Socket Services detects the presence of a card, Card Services allocates and manages the system resources (interrupts, DMA channels, and addressing) needed by the card(s). When a card is removed, Card Services will free those system resources again. This unique ability to find, use, then free system resources gives PC Cards their powerful I/O capability and Plug-and-Play flexibility. Because Card Services software is universal across hardware platforms, it can be loaded either as a DOS or Windows device driver or it might be an integral part of the operating system, such as IBM's DOS 6.22 and OS/2 4.0.

Unfortunately, not all notebook and sub-notebook systems use Socket and Card Services—this is a major reason for PC Card compatibility problems. Some PC Cards come with software device drivers that attempt to communicate directly with the system hardware. These cards were developed prior to the release of the PCMCIA Card Services standard, and such cards will only work on certain hardware platforms. Also, not all notebooks provide PCMCIA Socket Services. Some vendors provide proprietary BIOS firmware that supports a specific, limited set of PC Cards. Just recently, some vendors have begun bundling compatible Card and Socket Services with their systems. These card support device drivers are loosely termed "enablers."

Above Card Services, you see the familiar DOS and Application layers. Specialized (client) device drivers that might be needed for particular cards (such as an ATA card driver or flash file driver) are considered as part of the DOS layer.

ENABLERS

Many PC Cards offer an additional wrinkle before they work on your system—they need an *enabler*. While Socket Services interface the card to your hardware and Card Services provide resource management, the PC Card is still not always fully configured. An enabler is often required to place the PC Card at a particular I/O address, memory address, or IRQ. The three types of enabler software are: generic enablers, specific enablers, and point enablers.

Perhaps the most common type of enabler is called a *generic enabler* (some vendors also refer to these as *super client drivers*). Generic enablers are capable of configuring a wide range of the most common card types, such as modems and network adapters, and are usually provided with PCMCIA system software. Generic enablers typically require Socket Services and Card Services to be loaded before it can run. The problem with generic enablers is their demand on conventional memory—it is not uncommon for a generic enabler to demand 40 to 50KB. Along with Socket and Card Services, the memory requirements to support a PC Card can easily reach over 100KB. This memory problem is most acute when running large native DOS applications. However, unless you're running more than one type of PC Card, you might be able to use a *specific enabler*.

A specific enabler is a program designed to configure a single type of PC Card, and might be provided by the PC Card maker (or by a third-party software company). There are two compelling advantages to specific enablers. First, a specific enabler demands only a fraction of the memory used by generic enablers. If you use only one specific type of card, a specific enabler can save up to 40KB of memory. Second, your generic enabler might not support a particular type of PC Card, so a specific enabler can be used to supplement a generic enabler using a minimum amount of additional RAM.

There is the potential for some problems when both a generic enabler and specific enabler are loaded—and both recognize and configure a particular type of I/O card. An oversight in the PCMCIA specification allows the first enabler to be loaded and configure the card if the card is installed when the machine is booted; if the card is inserted after the machine is booted, however, the last enabler loaded will configure the card. This can create serious problems if the two enablers have different ideas about how the card should be configured, or if the application software depends on a particular enabler to configure the card. Here are the rules for loading generic and specific enablers together:

■ If you have the need for a generic enabler to configure your modem or another device that doesn't have a specific enabler, load it.
■ If the only PC Card you use has a specific enabler, load the specific enabler instead of the generic one.
■ If you have one or more cards that are configured by the generic enabler and a card that needs a specific enabler, first see if the generic enabler can handle the particular card (or a new version is available that can handle the specific card). If the generic enabler (or its updated version) can handle all of the cards, don't load the specific enabler. Otherwise, load both.

A third type of enabler is called a *point enabler*. This is similar to a specific enabler in that it is designed to configure a single type of PC Card. Unlike generic or specific enablers, however, point enablers do not require Socket Services or Card Services to be loaded. Instead, they talk directly to the PCMCIA adapter hardware. This has both advantages and drawbacks. The most compelling advantage is memory. Because Socket and Card Services are not needed, a point enabler takes up very little memory. Unfortunately, that is where the advantages end. To communicate with hardware directly, a point enabler must be designed for specific hardware. As a result, a point enabler usually doesn't work on all PC Card systems. Also, the point enabler will bypass the socket and card services if they are loaded. This can be a real problem if you want to use other cards at the same time. Generally speaking, bypassing your socket and card services is not a good idea, so reserve point enablers as a last resort (and only if you use no other PC Cards in the system at the same time).

CARD TYPES

PCMCIA standards also define the physical dimensions that a PC Card is limited to. The three types of cards are: Type I, Type II, and Type III. Although the length and width of each card remains the same, the thickness of their substrate area can vary (Fig. 32-5) to accommodate different applications. The classic Type-I card is only 3.3-mm thick. Although this is too thin for mechanical assemblies, it is ideal for most types of memory enhancements. Type II cards run 5.0-mm thick, which make them ideal for larger memory enhancements and most I/O cards, such as modems or LAN adapters. Notice in Fig. 32-5 that the edges and connector area (the interconnect area) of the card remain at 3.3 mm to fit the card's slide rails. The Type III card is a full 10.5-mm thick, which is large enough to accommodate the components for a complete hard drive or radio-communication device,

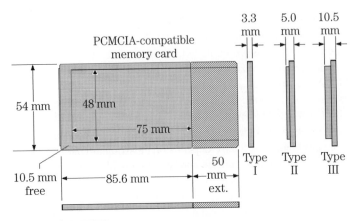

FIGURE 32-5   Comparison of PC-card thicknesses.

such as a cellular modem. Like Type II cards, the interconnect area remains 3.3 mm. This 3.3-mm rail height permits thinner cards to be inserted into thicker slots (but not vice versa).

CARDBUS AND ZOOMED VIDEO

If you work with PC Cards at all, chances are that you're going to encounter CardBus and Zoomed Video architectures. The *CardBus* is a 32-bit implementation of the PC Card, which appeared as part of the PCMCIA standard in February of 1995. The CardBus supports bus-mastering data transfers up to 133Mbps at 33MHz. In short, the CardBus is PCMCIA's answer to the PCI interface used on modern motherboards. Of course, CardBus is not identical to PCI, but it is as close as PC Cards have been able to come.

Zoomed Video (ZV) is another enhancement to the PC Card, which supports a high-speed connection between a PC Card and host computer system. This connection allows the card to write video data directly to the system's VGA controller. The data is transferred with no buffering requirements because it is transferred over the ZV bus, not the system bus. As a result, ZV cards are ideal for video capture, PC/TV applications.

INSIDE THE CARD

You can develop a tremendous respect for PC Cards by understanding the fragile and compact assemblies that are inside them. Consider the Maxtor MobileMax Lite (Fig. 32-6). The drive contains a single platter, upper and lower R/W heads, a voice-coil servo motor to position the heads, a spindle motor to spin the platters, and the circuitry required to handle all drive functions and interfacing. As you might imagine, each element of the PC card must be kept extremely thin—still, it is sometimes difficult to believe that the assembly actually fits into a shell only 0.5-cm thick (Type II). Another important consideration in PC card design is the control and suppression of *ElectroStatic Discharge (ESD)*. Static electricity must be prevented from reaching the card's PC board, where IC damage can occur. Once a card is inserted into a system, a discharge tab at the physical interface connector carries away any accumulation of charges to system ground. Until a card is inserted, a card protects its circuitry from damage using the Faraday cage principle—the same principle used by anti-static bags to protect their contents. The shell of most PC cards is either constructed of a metal (such as stainless steel) or some sort of metalized plastic. Both shell halves are bonded together by a small spring. Any charge introduced to the card is quickly dispersed over the entire shell surface, instead of being allowed to enter the card.

HOT INSERTION AND REMOVAL

One of the great disadvantages to most expansion devices is that computer power must be completely off before the device can be installed or removed. Not only is this necessary to prevent accidental damage from improper insertion, but the traditional BIOS and DOS only allocate system resources when the system is first initialized—they were not designed to accommodate allocating system resources "on-the-fly." Even "Plug-and-Play" devices only allocate resources during initialization. PC Cards take a major step toward this type of "dynamic resource allocation" with the support of hot swapping. *Hot swapping* (or *hot insertion and removal*) refers to the ability to insert and remove cards while the PC power is still on, without any degradation or damage to the system or card. Ideally, software applications can recognize the card's function and adjust accordingly.

Although PC Cards supports hot swapping, and can be inserted or removed without fear of damaging the card itself, very few operating systems or application programs are currently "PC Card aware." That is, they do not automatically recognize when cards have been inserted or removed. Therefore, users of any computer with PC Card slots should close any open application programs before inserting or removing a PC Card. Otherwise, the application might not initialize a card that has been inserted and might lock up when a card is removed.

> When working with PC Cards, always be sure to close any open applications before inserting or removing cards from the system. If possible, shut the system down entirely.

UNDERSTANDING ATTRIBUTE MEMORY

One of the greatest challenges facing PC Cards is cross-compatibility—the ability to use various card species from diverse manufacturers in the same card slot. Quite a few card sizes and types are currently in production, and many more card models will be available by the time

FIGURE 32-6   **Internal view of PC-card ATA drive.**

Maxtor Corporation

you read this book. How does the computer "know" when you have replaced your 2MB SRAM card with a 20MB Flash card or a 100MB PCMCIA hard drive? A computer capable of accepting PC Cards must be able to detect and adjust to the diverse attributes of each card it might encounter—even though each card might utilize the same physical card interface.

The best analogy to this are hard drives that are available in a staggering array of capacities, heads, cylinders, sectors, etc., but all those drives can use the same physical interface (e.g., ATA-2). A computer interacts properly with a hard drive because you enter the drive's key parameters in the computer's CMOS setup routine. The same basic problem exists for PC Cards. However, memory cards are intended to be transient items—inserted and removed at will. Imagine the inconvenience of having to re-enter a card's key parameters each time that a new card is inserted. Even a single typing error can be disastrous for some cards and their contents.

The PCMCIA has supported a standard for memory-card services that defines the software interface for accessing cards. The interface can either be a device driver loaded when the computer boots or be designed directly into BIOS ROM or the operating system. For this driver system to work, each card must be able to identify itself to the computer. The complete characteristic and ID data for a memory card is held in the *attribute memory* area of each individual card. Attribute memory contains a surprising amount of information—it must, considering the huge number of potential differences in card layout and features. Attribute memory tells the computer how much storage a card contains, the particular device type (memory, disk, I/O, etc.), the card's data format, speed capabilities, and many other variables.

The contents of attribute memory is typically setup information that falls into one of four categories of PCMCIA's *Card Identification System (CIS)*—otherwise known as the card's *meta-format*. Those four layers are: the basic compatibility layer, indicating how the card's storage is organized; the data recording format layer, specifying how blocks of card information are to be stored; the data organization layer, defining the card's operating system format (e.g., DOS, Microsoft's FlashFile system, PCMCIA's XIP, etc.), and any specific standards (or system-specific standards) needed to support an operating system.

The CIS data contained in attribute memory is a collection of related data blocks, which are interlinked rather like a chain. Each "link" in this chain (a data block) is called a *tuple*, and it can be up to 128 bytes long. The first byte of a tuple encodes the function of that tuple and its parameters. The second byte in a tuple links to the next tuple (if any) and specifies the precise number of bytes in that tuple. Because you know how long the present tuple is, you know exactly where the next tuple begins. In addition to standard tuples, individual card manufacturers are also free to add their own unique tuples to support proprietary features. It is not necessary for you to know the precise operation of each tuple, but it can help you to be familiar with their nomenclature and general purpose. One of the most important tuples is the Function ID entry, called CISTPL_FUNCID. This tuple tells the host computer exactly what kind of card is installed. Table 32-1 shows typical entries for the most popular PC Card types.

CONNECTIONS

The standard PC Card is connected to a PC through a 68-pin header arranged in two rows of 34 pins (Fig. 32-7). If you look at the header pins closely, you will notice that several of the pins are longer than the others—these are ground pins. By making them longer, a card will be attached to ground first when inserted. Figure 32-8 clearly illustrates how a

TABLE 32-1 TYPICAL FUNCTION ID ENTRIES FOR CISTPL_FUNCID

CISTPL_FUNCID: FUNCTION IDENTIFICATION TUPLE

CODE	NAME
0	Multi-function
1	Memory
2	Serial port
3	Parallel port
4	Fixed disk
5	Video adapter
6	Network adapter
7	AIMS (auto-indexing mass-storage)
8	SCSI
9	Security
A–FD	Reserved (allocated as new devices are introduced)
FE	Vendor-specific
FF	Do not use

34   1

68   PC MCIA 68-pin connector   35

FIGURE 32-7   PCMCIA header diagram.

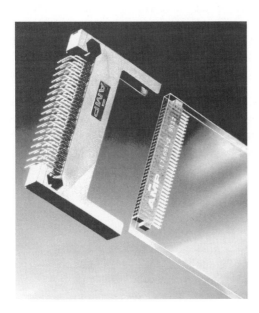

FIGURE 32-8   Typical PC-card connector products.

AMP Inc.

PC Card interfaces to its mating connector. When the card is removed, the ground will still be attached after the power pins have been disconnected. Good grounding helps to ensure the card's reliability, and permit "hot" insertion and removal. When you look at the assignment of each pin in Table 32-2, you will see that there are basically four types of signals at the PCMCIA interface: data pins, address pins, power (and ground), and control signals. This healthy mix of signals makes it possible to support many of the PC Card applications that are available today. Also notice that the CardBus PC Cards use the same 68-pin connector, but their signal assignments are vastly different.

TABLE 32-2 PIN ASSIGNMENTS FOR PC CARD AND CARDBUS INTERFACES

16-BIT PIN	MEMORY	32-BIT I/O+MEM	CARDBUS	16-BIT PIN	MEMORY	32-BIT I/O+MEM	CARDBUS
1	GND	GND	GND	35	GND	GND	GND
2	D3	D3	CAD0	36	CD1#	CD1#	CCD1#
3	D4	D4	CAD1	37	D11	D11	CAD2
4	D5	D5	CAD3	38	D12	D12	CAD4
5	D6	D6	CAD5	39	D13	D13	CAD6
6	D7	D7	CAD7	40	D14	D14	RSRVD
7	CE1#	CE1#	CCBE0#	41	D15	D15	CAD8
8	A10	A10	CAD9	42	CE2#	CE2#	CAD10
9	OE#	OE#	CAD11	43	VS1#	VS1#	CVS1
10	A11	A11	CAD12	44	RSRVD	IORD#	CAD13
11	A9	A9	CAD14	45	RSRVD	IOWR#	CAD15
12	A8	A8	CCBE1#	46	A17	A17	CAD16
13	A13	A13	CPAR	47	A18	A18	RSRVD
14	A14	A14	CPERR#	48	A19	A19	CBLOCK#
15	WE#	WE#	CGNT#	49	A20	A20	CSTOP#
16	READY	IREQ#	CINT#	50	A21	A21	CDEVSEL#
17	Vcc	Vcc	Vcc	51	Vcc	Vcc	Vcc
18	Vpp1	Vpp1	Vpp1	52	Vpp2	Vpp2	Vpp2
19	A16	A16	CCLK	53	A22	A22	CTRDY#
20	A15	A15	CIRDY#	54	A23	A23	CFRAME#
21	A12	A12	CCBE2#	55	A24	A24	CAD17
22	A7	A7	CAD18	56	A25	A25	CAD19
23	A6	A6	CAD20	57	VS2#	VS2#	CVS2
24	A5	A5	CAD21	58	RESET	RESET	CRST#
25	A4	A4	CAD22	59	WAIT#	WAIT#	CSERR#
26	A3	A3	CAD23	60	RSRVD	INPACK#	CREQ#
27	A2	A2	CAD24	61	REG#	REG#	CCBE3#
28	A1	A1	CAD25	62	BVD2	SPKR#	CAUDIO
29	A0	A0	CAD26	63	BVD1	STSCHG#	CSTSCHG
30	D0	D0	CAD27	64	D8	D8	CAD28
31	D1	D1	CAD29	65	D9	D9	CAD30

TABLE 32-2   PIN ASSIGNMENTS FOR PC CARD AND CARDBUS INTERFACES (CONTINUED)

16-BIT PIN	MEMORY	32-BIT I/O+MEM	CARDBUS	16-BIT PIN	MEMORY	32-BIT I/O+MEM	CARDBUS
32	D2	D2	RSRVD	66	D10	D10	CAD31
33	WP	IOIS16#	CCLKRUN#	67	CD2#	CD2#	CCD2#
34	GND	GND	GND	68	GND	GND	GND

Legend:

Ax or CAx	An address line
BVDx	Battery-voltage detect line
CADx	Multiplexed address/data line
CAUDIO	Audio line
CBEx or CCBEx	Command byte enable
CCLK	System clock
CCLKRUN	Clock status
CDEVSEL	Device select
CDx or CCDx	Card-detect line
CEx	Card-enable line
CFRAME	Address or data phase
CGNT	Grant line
CINT	Interrupt
CIRDY	Initiator ready
CPAR	Parity line
CPERR	Parity error
CREQ	System request
CRST	Reset
CSERR	System error
CSTOP	Stop transfer cycle
CTRDY	Target ready
Dx or CDx	A data line
IREQ	Interrupt request
OE	Output enable
RSRVDIORD	Reserved/IO read line
RSRVDIOWR	Reserved/IO write line
VSx	Refresh line
Vpp	Programming voltage
WE	Write enable

PC Card Applications

Now that PC Cards are being developed according to release 2.1, they offer a series of compelling advantages for mobile computer users:

■ The I/O support offered by PCMCIA specifications allows virtually any product to be incorporated into a PC card. Modems, network adapters, video capture modules, audio cards, and hard drives are just some of the devices that PCMCIA standards now embrace.
■ PC Cards can be made to operate in a dual-voltage mode (either 5.0 V or 3.3 V), depending on the design of the mobile PC. Low-voltage compatibility saves power and extends battery life.

■ The programs and applications stored on PC Cards can now be executed in place, rather than having to load the card's contents into main memory. This *eXecute-In-Place (XIP)* technology reduces the demand for large amounts of on-board RAM.

■ The Socket Services software defined by release 2.1 describes a BIOS-level interface that allows applications to access the card's hardware. The device drivers written to operate specific PC cards will run on any PC that supports Socket Services.

■ The Card Services software automatically allocates system resources (e.g., memory and IRQs) once a PC Card is inserted into a system (referred to as *dynamic resource allocation*). Information (called *tuple information*) contained in the *Card Information Structure (CIS)* of a card describes the characteristics and abilities of that card. In turn, the host system can automatically configure the card for proper operation. This type of operation is the earliest implementation of a "Plug and Play" architecture.

PC CARD PROBLEMS

Like all new PC technologies, however, there are some disappointing problems with the early implementations of PC Cards. Before you decide to buy that next "PC Card-compatible" system, you should understand some of the factors that have contributed to PCMCIA's poor early showing. When the PCMCIA issued release 1.0 in 1990, socket and card services did not exist—card makers had to supply their own specific drivers, which had to be tested on each specific computer. If the host computer were updated or upgraded, the cards that worked on the older systems would probably not work on the newer ones. This resulted in perplexing compatibility problems.

Socket and card services were added in 1991 with PCMCIA release 2.0, but the release also brought I/O devices into the PC Card picture. Although this made PCMCIA much more versatile, I/O brought in a host of new problems. Although all I/O cards are supposed to be treated as a generic device, an operating system does not see all devices the same way. For example, an operating system does not treat a hard drive and a modem the same way, but card makers did not take that into account, so compatibility between systems is still an issue. Also, most operating systems are designed to work with resources that are present when a system is booted, so although you might be able to insert and remove cards safely, the operating system can rarely adjust the system resources properly. As a result, many cards have to be installed before the system boots.

Today, most PCMCIA cards work in most systems, and can be inserted and removed without rebooting the computer—but there are no guarantees. The situation has gotten much better over the last year or so, but beware of older PCMCIA systems.

TODAY'S CARDS

PCMCIA cards have come a long way since the early memory cards of 1990. Virtually any device that can be implemented on an expansion card can be fabricated as a PC Card. As a technician, you should understand the range of devices that you might encounter when servicing notebook and sun-notebook systems:

■ *Memory cards* Memory-expansion devices continue to be popular PC Card devices—not so much for added system memory, but to run pre-fabricated applications directly off the card.

■ *Modem cards* PCMCIA modems are rapidly replacing proprietary modems as internal communication devices. PCMCIA modems are easily matching the speed and performance of stand-alone modems, and are even being equipped with cellular connections for true mobile operation.

■ *LAN cards* Local-area networks are becoming more popular as businesses integrate their operations and add connections to such resources as the Internet. LAN cards allow mobile computers to play a constructive role on networks using topologies, such as Ethernet, Token Ring, and 3270 Emulation.

■ *Digital video cards* The soaring popularity of multimedia applications has dramatically increased the demand for video and still-frame capture products. PCMCIA technology allows video and audio capture capability in PC Card products for high-quality multimedia "on-the-road."

■ *Hard-drive cards* Until the advent of PCMCIA, it was virtually impossible to add a second hard drive to a portable PC. Fortunately, the use of PCMCIA combined with the stunning advances in hard-drive technology allow substantial hard-drive capacities in a Type-III form factor.

■ *Audio cards* Games and music composition software demands high-quality sound reproduction. PCMCIA audio cards provide SoundBlaster-compatible sound to external speakers. The trend toward mobile multimedia is integrating sound systems and speakers right into the mobile PC, but stand-alone sound cards are available.

■ *SCSI adapter cards* The *Small Computer System Interface (SCSI)* is a system-level interface scheme that allows a multitude of devices (e.g., CD-ROM, scanners, tape drives, etc.) to be connected to a system. A PCMCIA SCSI adapter card opens a whole new level of compatibility for a mobile computer.

■ *Floppy drive cards* The recent trend among sub-notebook and palmtop computers has been to forego the floppy drive in favor of a PCMCIA slot. However, PCMCIA floppy-disk adapters, such as the Accurite Technologies PassportCard, bring a standard floppy drive to any mobile PC that lacks an internal floppy drive.

INSTALLING A PC CARD

Like so many things in PC service, proper installation can avoid a round of troubleshooting later on. This is particularly true for PC Cards because they are completely dependent on software for proper configuration and operation. This part of the chapter describes the general steps involved in setting up a typical PC Card. Of course, always be sure to read the manual that accompanies your card for specific instructions or caveats. Most PC Cards require access to four different pieces of software: the socket services, the card services, the enabler (or super client driver), and a resource manager (usually a high-level driver). Table 32-3 lists some typical PC card drivers for DOS, and Table 32-4 lists the PC card drivers for use under Windows.

The file names shown in Tables 32-3 and 32-4 are examples often used in Compaq laptops. Your own system might utilize entirely different file names, but their purpose and loading order will almost always remain the same.

TABLE 32-3   DOS PC CARD DRIVERS

FULL NAME	FILENAME	FUNCTION	MEMORY	NOTES
Socket Services	SSVLSI.EXE SCIRRUS.EXE	Provides a standard software interface to PCMCIA host controller chips and isolates the socket hardware from higher level software	3,760 (4K)	Must be loaded first
Card Services	CS.EXE	Manages system resources and configuration conflict issues	39,392 (38K)	Requires socket services
Card Services Resource Allocation	CSALLOC.EXE	Initializes Card Services resource table at boot time	—	Requires Socket and Card Services
Card Services Super Client	CARDID.EXE	Configures PC Cards that do not have CS client drivers and "exception" cases	20,320 (20K)	Requires Socket and Card Services
Memory Card Driver	MEMDRV.EXE	Block device driver for memory cards	17,184 (17K)	Required for SRAM or Flash card support
ATA Card Driver Support	ATADRV.EXE	Provides support for ATA/ IDE mass-storage cards, such as rotation media or Sundisk-style cards	6,496 (6K)	Relies on CARDID to configure ATA cards
Microsoft Flash File System	MS-FLASH.SYS	Provides file system support for flash memory cards	70,240 (69K)	Requires MEMDRV.EXE
DoubleSpace for Flash File System	DBLFLASH.EXE	Provides DoubleSpace data-compression support for the Microsoft Flash File System	13,504 (13K)	Req. MS-FLASH.SYS
Power Management Driver	PCMSMIX.EXE	Provides support for standby hibernation and ring resume for certain PCs	—	—

TABLE 32-4 WINDOWS PC CARD DRIVERS

FULL NAME	FILENAME	FUNCTION	NOTES
Communications driver	SSCOMM.DRV	Card Services-aware version of Windows COMM.DRV	Replaces COMM.DRV
Card Services Serial Port Virtual Driver	CSVCD.386	Card Services-aware version of standard Windows VCD.386	Replaces *vcd
Card Services Windows API	SSWINCS.DLL	Provides the Card Services interface to Windows applications	—
Card Services Virtual Driver	CS.386	Provides the Card Services interface to Windows virtual sessions library (DLL) required to support hot plugability	—
Card Event Monitor	CPQEVENT.EXE	Displays pop-ups on insertion/ removal of PC Card	—

If your system does not yet support PC Cards (or if you are restoring a failed hard drive), you will need to install the socket and card services first. This should usually be done before installing the card itself. However, most mobile computers come with card and socket services installed already, so you should not re-install those applications because they might be optimized for your particular hardware. Power-up the PC and read the driver banners. If you see mention of card and socket services, that software is probably installed already. Windows 95 has a small suite of card and socket service drivers (refer to the *PCMCIA Plug-and-Play* card wizard under your *Control panel*).

Next, you will need to install the PC Card enabler (you might also see this grouped with Card Services software). In many cases, the diskette accompanying the PC Card will have an installation routine that will add the enabler's command line to CONFIG.SYS. Otherwise, you will have to add the enabler's command line manually by editing the CONFIG.SYS file. Once the enabler is added to CONFIG.SYS, save the file and turn off the PC. Insert the card in its card slot, then restart the PC. If the software is installed correctly so far, you should hear a beep as the card is recognized. You will hear two beeps if the card is not recognized (check the card and software installation).

Finally, you will need to install the "resource manager" (or client driver) that accompanies the particular card. For example, a PC Card fax/modem usually requires a fax/modem client driver, or a PC Card hard drive requires an ATA IDE client driver, etc. Client drivers are often card-specific, so be sure to install the client driver that accompanies your particular card.

You can see an example of how this works by looking at the combination of software in Table 32-5. The program names are examples only (your particular software will use different names). Notice that PC Card support requires several different pieces of software—and the software varies, depending on the particular cards that you need to support. For example, an ATA IDE card and a fax/modem card use the same socket services, card services, and enabler, but require two different client drivers. With this type of relationship, you can load only the drivers that are needed to support specific card types.

TABLE 32-5 PC-CARD SOFTWARE VS. APPLICATION

FILENAME	ATA IDE	FLASH MEMORY	LAN	FAX/ MODEM	SRAM MEMORY
PCMSS.EXE (Socket Services)	Yes	Yes	Yes	Yes	Yes
PCMCS.EXE (Card Services)	Yes	No	Yes	Yes	Yes
PCMCSFUL.EXE (Card Enabler)	Yes	Yes	Yes	Yes	Yes
PCMSCD.EXE (Comm. Client)	No	No	Yes	Yes	No
PCMATA.EXE (HDD Client)	Yes	No	No	No	Yes
PCMFFCS.EXE (Flash Client)	No	Yes	No	No	Yes

Optimizing Memory in PC Card Systems

PC cards are very demanding of conventional memory. For example, a typical PC Card-equipped PC must allocate almost 180KB of conventional memory to support the PCMCIA slot and PC Card devices. Although this is not so much of a problem in Windows 95, DOS and Windows 3.1x environments can experience severe memory shortages. Fortunately, it is often possible to reclaim some conventional memory (sometimes as much as 115KB). The actual amount depends on the number of drivers required for proper PC Card support, and the size of each respective driver, but the process needed to reclaim memory often breaks down into four steps:

■ Remove any unnecessary drivers
■ Recover unused memory areas
■ Utilize any PCMCIA reserved memory
■ Change the driver loading order

REMOVE ANY UNNECESSARY DRIVERS

The first step in regaining the memory normally used by PCMCIA drivers is to remove (or disable) any drivers that are not required in your configuration. If there are PCMCIA drivers that are not currently being used by the particular PC Card, remove them by inserting the word REM (which stands for "REMark") or a single semi-colon (";") at the beginning of the appropriate statement in your CONFIG.SYS file. This will prevent the driver(s) from being loaded the next time the system is booted, and will, therefore, reclaim the memory that the driver(s) would have used.

> If you are not currently using PC Cards, you can add a REMark to all PCMCIA driver references and delete the X=D000-DFFF exclusion on the EMM386 command line in your CONFIG.SYS file—this disables PCMCIA support entirely. You will regain all the upper memory usually available in non-PCMCIA based PCs, but you will not have access to PCMCIA capabilities.

For example, remarking-out the PCMCIA files ATADRV.EXE and MEMDRV.EXE will recover a bit more than 20KB of memory. Remarking-out the files MS-FLASH.SYS and DBLFLASH.EXE will recover 83KB of memory. Just keep in mind that these drivers must be loaded later if you add an ATA, SRAM, or flash-memory card to the PC.

RECOVER UNUSED MEMORY AREAS

Take control of the memory regions in the UMA that you know are not being used. For example, Compaq recommends that if you are not using a monochrome controller in an expansion base, you can recover the monochrome region (B000h-B7FFh) to gain 32KB. To accomplish this, you'd use the "Include" statement in your EMM386 command line, such as:

```
I=B000-B7FF
```

Remember that you will lose the ability to utilize devices that need that memory region. For the Compaq example, you'd lose the ability to use monochrome cards in an Elite SmartStation.

> If you have any problems entering Windows after making this change you might need to add the following to the [386enh] section of the SYSTEM.INI file:
> ```
> DEVICE=C:\DOS\MONOUMB.386
> ```

UTILIZE ANY PCMCIA RESERVED WINDOW

The next step is to use any reserved memory in the UMA not being used by PCMCIA cards. As an example, new Compaq PCMCIA-based PCs reserve a 64KB window of memory in the UMA from D000h through DFFFh for PC Cards to reside in. Card services requires 4KB of that memory, but most cards that you install do not require the balance of 60KB. In fact, some cards do not require any memory in this area, other than the 4KB required by card services (to determine how much memory your PC Cards require, consult the card's user guide or call the manufacturer).

First, determine how much memory each of your PCMCIA cards require to initialize. For example, PCMCIA modems usually do not require any memory, and most PCMCIA Ethernet adapters require only 8 to 12KB. If your memory requirements are relatively small, you can usually move the PCMCIA window out of the D000h range, allowing for larger contiguous UMBs. A good place to move this range to is the C800h area (as long as no other devices have BIOS residing in this area).

Modify your CONFIG.SYS file by moving the PCMCIA card initialization area out of the D000h range and reducing the amount of memory used from 64KB to a smaller amount.

As an example, a modem (with the 4KB card services overhead) and Ethernet card will usually only require 16KB or less, so you can change the default EMM386.EXE statement of:

```
X=D000-DFFF
```

to

```
X=C800-CBFF
```

This example will yield a 48KB gain in the UMA. If you are unable to determine just how much memory your card requires to initialize, it might take several trial-and-error attempts to assess how much memory it requires. In this example, you might even be able to recover more memory because some Ethernet PCMCIA cards require less than 12KB. You will also need to modify the card services .INI file (i.e., CSALLOC.INI) by adding or editing the MEMEXCLUDE entry to exclude the newly defined C800-CBFF range, such as:

```
MEMEXCLUDE=CC00-EFFF
```

This will tell Card Services to avoid using any memory above CC00h to configure PCMCIA cards. Finally, modify the [386Enh] section of your SYSTEM.INI file to include an EMMEXCLUDE statement that matches the range excluded on the EMM386.EXE line in the CONFIG.SYS file. For this example, the line must read:

```
EMMEXCLUDE=C800-CBFF
```

> Whenever you alter the exclusion range in your EMM386 line, be sure to modify the MEMEXCLUDE statement in your card services .INI file and the EMMEXCLUDE statement in the SYSTEM.INI file to match.

CHANGE THE DRIVER LOADING ORDER

Shifting the load order of your specific drivers (but not the PCMCIA drivers themselves—they must remain in the same order) might allow you to load more drivers into upper memory. To do this, you can manually adjust the driver order by trial-and-error changing the execution order in the CONFIG.SYS file. Alternatively, you can try to force specific drivers into desired regions of upper memory by using the /L: option for DEVICEHIGH (CONFIG.SYS) and LOADHIGH (AUTOEXEC.BAT).

> The load order of PCMCIA drivers themselves should not be modified.

Example: IBM Token-Ring PC Card   As an example, look at some typical configuration files for an IBM Token-Ring PC Card on a Compaq laptop. You'll need to attack the memory problem in four steps: optimize the card's resource assignments (the IBM Token-Ring adapter uses utility called PCCARD to change the card's I/O, IRQ, and memory assignments), modify CONFIG.SYS, modify SYSTEM.INI, and modify the card services .INI file (i.e., CSALLOC.INI).

CONFIG.SYS example

```
DEVICE=C:\DOS\HIMEM.SYS
DEVICE=C:\DOS\EMM386.EXE NOEMS I=B000-B7FF X=C800-D0FF I=D100-EFFF
DEVICEHIGH=C:\DOS\SETVER.EXE
FILES=60
BUFFERS=20
DOS=HIGH,UMB
LASTDRIVE=E
FCBS=4,0
STACKS=9,256
SHELL:C:\DOS\COMMAND.COM C:\DOS\ /E:512 /p
REM *** Begin PCMCIA Drivers, DO NOT Change Order ***
DEVICEHIGH=C:\CPQDOS\SSVLSI.EXE
DEVICEHIGH=C:\CPQDOS\CS.EXE /IRQ A
DEVICE=C:\CPQDOS\CSALLOC.EXE
REM DEVICEHIGH=C:\CPQDOS\ATADRV.EXE
DEVICEHIGH=C\CPQDOS\CARDID.EXE C:\CPQDOS\CARDID.INI
REM DEVICEHIGH=C:\CPQDOS\MEMDRV.EXE
REM DEVICEHIGH=C:\CPQDOS\DBLFLASH.EXE
REM DEVICEHIGH=C:\CPQDOS\MS-FLASH.SYS
REM *** End PCMCIA Drivers ***
DEVICEHIGH=C:\DOS\POWER.EXE
DEVICEHIGH=C:\DXM\DXMA0MOD.SYS
DEVICEHIGH=C:\DXM\DXMC0MOD.SYS ,CC00
```

SYSTEM.INI example [386ENH]

Add the entry:

```
DEVICE=C:\DOS\MONOUMB.386
```

and change the entry:

```
EMMEXCLUDE=D000-DFFF
```

to:

```
EMMEXCLUDE= C800-D0FF
```

This range should reflect the exclude statement on the EMM386 line in your CONFIG.SYS file.

CSALLOC.INI example

```
MEM=C800-D0FF
RIO=170-177,2E8-2EF,370-377,3E8-3F7,3F0-3F7
IOINCLUDE=3F0-3F7
MEMEXCLUDE=B000-B7FF,C000-C7FF,D100-EFFF
```

Troubleshooting PC Card Problems

The PCMCIA represents an interface, not a particular card. As a consequence, PC Card troubleshooting is rather like solving problems with any other type of bus interface (SCSI,

ISA, VL, etc.). The objective is not to repair a PC Card itself, but rather to isolate a functional problem to the card, the interface itself, or some portion of the host system's driver configuration and operating system. When you determine a PC Card to be defective, your best course is to replace the card outright or to return it to the manufacturer for repair.

Symptom 32-1. The SRAM or flash card loses its memory when powered down or removed from the system Because flash cards use advanced EEPROMs, you might wonder why batteries would be incorporated. Some flash cards use a small amount of SRAM to speed the transfer of data to or from the card. Batteries would be needed to backup the SRAM only. If your memory card does not appear to hold its memory, you should start your investigation by removing the memory card and testing its batteries. Be sure that the card's batteries are inserted properly. Use your multimeter to check the battery voltage(s). Replace any memory card batteries that appear to be marginal or low. You should expect a two- to five-year backup life from your memory card batteries, depending on the amount of card memory—more memory results in shorter battery life. All battery contacts should be clean and bright, and the contacts should make firm connections with the battery terminals.

Try a known-good working card in your system. You might verify a new or known-good memory card on another computer with a compatible card slot. If another card works properly, your original memory card is probably defective and should be replaced. Under no circumstances should you actually open the card.

Symptom 32-2. You are unable to access a memory card for reading You might not be able to write to the card either. Begin troubleshooting by checking memory-card compatibility (programmed OTPROM cards and Mask ROM cards cannot be written to). If a memory card is not compatible with the interface used by your small-computer, the interface might not access the card. For example, a PCMCIA-compatible 68-pin card will probably not work in a 68-pin card slot that is not 100% PCMCIA compatible. Try a known-good compatible card in the suspect card slot. Also check your CONFIG.SYS or AUTOEXEC.BAT files to be sure that any required device drivers have been installed during system initialization. If you are having difficulty writing to an SRAM or flash card, take a moment and inspect the card's write-protect switch. A switch left in the "protected" position prevents new information from being written to the card. Move the switch to the "unprotected" position and try the memory card again.

If you are having difficulty writing to EEPROM or Flash EEPROM cards, check your programming voltages (V_{pp1} and V_{pp2}). Without high-voltage pulses, new data cannot be written to such cards. Measure V_{pp1} and V_{pp2} with your oscilloscope, with the card removed from your system (it might be necessary to ground the card-detect lines (CD1 and CD2) to fool the host system into believing that a card is actually installed. You will probably have to disassemble your small-computer's housing to gain easy access to the motherboard's card connector. If one or both programming pulses are missing during a write operation, check your power-supply output(s). When high-voltage supplies are missing, troubleshoot your computer's power supply. If programming voltage(s) are present, a defect might be in the card controller IC or board, or any discrete switching circuitry that is designed to produce the programming pulses. Try replacing the card controller (or motherboard).

The memory card might be inserted incorrectly. Two card-detect signals are needed from a PCMCIA-compatible card to ensure proper insertion. If the card is not inserted properly, the host system will inhibit all card activities. Remove the card and re-insert it completely. Be sure that the card is straight, even, and fully inserted. Try accessing the card again.

If trouble remains, remove the card and inspect the connector on the card and inside the computer. Check for any contacts that might be loose, bent, or broken. It might be necessary to disassemble the mobile computer in order to inspect its connector, but a clear view with a small flashlight will show you all you need to know. Connections in the computer that are damaged or extremely worn should be replaced with a new connector assembly. If a memory-card connector is worn or damaged, the memory card should be replaced.

If your results are still inconclusive, try a known-good memory card in the system. Remember that the new card must be fully compatible with the original one. Be sure that there are no valuable or irreplaceable files on the known-good card before you try it in a suspect system. If a known-good card works properly, then the old memory card is probably damaged and should be replaced. If a known-good card also does not work, the original card is probably working properly. Your final step is to disassemble your computer and replace the memory-card controller or motherboard. A defective controller can prevent all data and control signals from reaching the card.

Symptom 32-3. You see an error message, indicating that a PCMCIA card will not install or is not recognized Chances are that one or more device drivers in the system are interfering with the offending PCMCIA card. Load your CONFIG.SYS file into an ordinary text editor and systematically edit out any other PCMCIA drivers. Try re-initializing the system after each change. Once you locate the offending driver, try reconfiguring the driver so that it will not interfere (maybe a new driver or patch is available).

Symptom 32-4. Even though a desired card is installed, an error message or warning is displayed asking you to insert the card The PCMCIA card might not be installed properly. Try removing the card, then re-insert it carefully. The card socket might not be enabled, so the application might not be able to see it. Be sure that the card socket is enabled. For most systems (such as the Canon NoteJet 486, which ships with the PCMCIA socket turned off), the solution is to get into the BIOS setup for the computer, and to enable the PCMCIA socket. Check the documentation for your system to find out how to get into the BIOS setup. Sometimes this feature is located in the *Advanced settings* or in the *Power-management* area of the BIOS settings. After you have changed the settings, save the changes and restart your system. In more advanced systems (such as the Compaq Concerto), you can turn the PCMCIA socket off and on with the computer's setup utility under Windows. After changing the settings, save the changes and restart your system.

Another possibility might be that the application program interacting with the PCMCIA slot is addressing the wrong interrupt line for insertion or removal. Check for any card-socket diagnostics and determine which interrupt(s) the application is trying to use for card-status change. Check the device driver for the card and add an explicit command-line switch to specify the desired interrupt. If an interrupt is already specified, be sure that this is the correct one.

Symptom 32-5. You encounter a number of card-service errors or other problems when anti-virus programs are used Such errors include "Card services allocation error," "Error: Configuration file not found," "Error: Could not open configuration file," or "Error using card services." Under some circumstances, an anti-virus program can interfere with PCMCIA card services. The Norton anti-virus program NAV&.SYS is known to cause this sort of problem if it is loaded before the card services software. There are typically three ways around this type of problem. First, re-arrange the order of drivers called in your CONFIG.SYS file so that NAV&.SYS comes after the card services software. Second, use NAV_.SYS instead of NAV&.SYS. Although NAV_.SYS requires more space than NAV&.SYS, it is better at co-existing with other memory-resident programs. Third, remove NAV&.SYS and use NAVTSR instead. If you are using anti-virus programs, try remarking them out of CONFIG.SYS or AUTOEXEC.BAT.

Symptom 32-6. There are no pop-up displays when a PC card is inserted or removed Normally, when a card is installed or removed, a dialog box will appear, indicating that the card that has been inserted or removed. However, there are three reasons why this might happen. First, the DOS pop-up function (also called a *card-event manager*) is disabled under DOS (but still works under Windows). Check the card services software and be sure that the proper command line switches are set to enable the DOS pop-up. Second, there might be an *Upper Memory Area (UMA)* conflict. Many card managers require 10KB or more of UMA (each). If no free UMA is available, the card manager cannot read the card's attribute memory to install the card. Be sure that plenty of UMA space is available for the card-services software and check that it loads properly. Third, the PCMCIA card might not be supported by the card services software—the two might not be fully compatible. Try a different card or update the card-services software.

Symptom 32-7. The application locks up when a PC card is inserted or removed Not all applications are fully PCMCIA-aware—that is, they do not recognize card insertion and removal properly. If your application crashes or locks up when a card is inserted or removed, chances are that the application is not written to handle hot insertion or removal with the card-services software being used. Try inserting the card before starting the application or close the application before removing it.

Symptom 32-8. The fax/modem card works fine in DOS, but refuses to work in Windows 95 In virtually all cases, the port addresses and IRQ assigned by Windows 95 do not match the assignments that the card is expecting. Go to the *Control panel*, doubleclick on *Ports*, and doubleclick on the COM port that you are assigning to your fax/modem. Then go to *Advanced* and check to see if the Port Address and IRQ match your fax/modem settings. If they don't, put in the proper settings and restart Windows 95.

Symptom 32-9. The mouse/trackball locks up or acts strangely after a fax/modem card is installed Chances are that the pointing device is sharing the same IRQ as the fax/modem card. In most cases, changing the fax/modem IRQ assignments will correct the problem (although you could change the pointing device IRQ instead).

Symptom 32-10. My peripheral (e.g., sound card, scanner, etc.) no longer works now that the PC Card is installed This type of problem almost always indicates a hardware conflict. In most cases, the IRQ assigned to the PC Card is conflicting with the IRQ assigned to the malfunctioning device. Survey your system and determine the IRQs used by every device. You can change the IRQ of the PC Card or change the IRQ of the other conflicting device. In either case, you'll need to restart the PC after you make those changes.

Symptom 32-11. The PCMCIA CardSoft enabler software won't install You probably have a PCMCIA enabler already installed on the system. If enabler software is already installed, it might support your card. If so, you can skip the new enabler software. If not, you need to remove the current enabler software, then install the new enabler software.

Symptom 32-12. When installing a PC Card (such as a fax/modem card), you find that the desired COM port or IRQ is not available In virtually all cases, the needed COM port or IRQ is being used by another device. Check for hardware conflicts, then reset the PC Card to use different resources.

Symptom 32-13. You don't hear the proper number of beeps when inserting a PCMCIA card When the PC Card is inserted into a slot properly, you should hear a certain number of beeps. In most cases, this will be either one or two beeps (depending on your particular card software). If you don't hear the correct number of beeps, chances are that the card has not been inserted properly into its socket.

Symptom 32-14. The card's configuration refuses to accept memory addresses (if needed) Some PC Cards require certain memory resources for proper operation. If you are prohibited from assigning those addresses to the PC Card, chances are that those memory locations are being used by another device in the system. Check for resource conflicts. You can usually resolve memory conflicts by changing the address assigned to the PC Card or by changing the address assigned to the conflicting device.

Symptom 32-15. Other programs stop working or change their behavior after the card software is installed In most cases, new .DLL files installed to support the PC Card have changed shared files used by other programs. Check with the technical support for your particular PC Card maker and see if any problem files are identified. If so, see if any updated files are available. You can usually download the corrected file and copy it to the /windows/system directory (or other suitable directory). If no corrected file is available, you will need to un-install the PC Card, and restore the original shared files from installation disks or tape backups.

Symptom 32-16. When starting a client driver under Windows 95, the message "Client registration failed" appears In most cases, the client driver is not installed or not installed properly. In principle, you'll need to remove any traces of the client driver, then reinstall the client driver from scratch. You might also have resource conflicts that prevent the client driver from loading. For example, consider problems with Nogatech's CaptureVision 95 client driver:

- Open the *Control panel*, then doubleclick on the *System* icon.
- Click the *Device manager* tab and select *View devices by type*.

- If you have the line "Other devices," and under it you see "NOGATECH NOGAVI-SION," do the following:

  1 Highlight the "NOGATECH NOGAVISION" entry and click the *Remove* button. Now, remove the card from your computer.

  2 Go to the Windowsdirectory.

  3 Look for an "OEMx.INF" file (where *x* can be any digit) Don't worry if you can't find any OEMx.INF files.

  4 Rename the file(s) to OEMx.BAK (where *x* is the digit).

  5 Look for a NOGATECH.INF file and delete the file. Don't worry if you can't find the file.

  6 Now go to the Windowsdirectory.

  7 Look for any files starting with "noga." Delete any files starting with "noga."

  8 Now, reinstall the software and start CaptureVision 95 when finished with the setup.

- If you do not have the line "Unknown Device," continue with the following:

  1 Doubleclick the line "Sound, Video, and Game Controllers."

  2 You should see the line "Nogatech Nogavision Video Capture."

  3 If you do not get this line, try to install the software once again.

  4 If you see an exclamation mark in front of the line "Nogatech Nogavision Video Capture," you have resource problems and the drivers have not been loaded.

Symptom 32-17. The PC Card will not configure properly. An I/O Address conflict message is displayed A resource conflict is between several PC Cards. For example, network and SCSI PC Cards often require the same I/O addresses. You will need to find available I/O space, then reconfigure one of the conflicting devices to use that available space.

Check for point enablers. Most PC Cards depend on card and socket services software, as well as generic enablers, for proper configuration. However, point enablers bypass card and socket services. If you can use a generic enabler instead of a point enabler, try removing the point enabler. As a rule, point enablers should not be used when more than one PC Card is in the system.

Check for I/O resources using a program, such as MSD (Microsoft Diagnostics), and note any regions of I/O space that are unused. If the cards provide several different "prefabricated" configurations, try each of those configurations—chances are that one of those configurations will work on your computer. If none of the "prefabricated" configurations will resolve the problem, you will need to manually change one of the cards to use free space available in the system. In many cases, this can be accomplished by making command-line changes to the card's enabler or client driver. Once you finish making changes, you'll need to reboot the computer for your changes to take effect.

Symptom 32-18. My system hangs when card services loads First, check to see that you are only loading one copy of card-services software; attempting to load a second copy can sometimes hang the system. It is also possible that the PC Card software-configuration file (typically, an .INI file, such as PCM.INI) might be set up improperly. You might need to modify the configuration file to place the card services software in the "poll" mode (i.e., /POLL). Refer to the documentation that accompanied your software or system for more information on configuration modes.

Symptom 32-19. An "Invalid command-line switch" message is displayed when loading services or client drivers You might be placing command-line switches in the wrong places. Traditionally, command-line switches are placed on the actual command lines in CONFIG.SYS or AUTOEXEC.BAT. For some PC Card installations, however, command-line switches must be entered in the PC Card configuration file (an .INI file, such as PCM.INI). In some cases, switches must be entered in the configuration file instead of the actual command-line entry.

Symptom 32-20. You have a Xircom Combo card (i.e., fax/modem and LAN) and cannot get it to work with standard card-manager software This is typically because Xircom developed a non-PCMCIA compliant combo card (marked "Combo Card") prior to the ratification of the new PCMCIA standards. As a consequence, the card is supported with proprietary software. You will have to install proprietary software to use the Xircom Combo Cards. Only cards marked "PC Card-compliant multifunction cards" are supported by standard software.

Symptom 32-21. You get an "Abort, Retry, Ignore" message when accessing an ATA PC Card In most cases, you are missing the client driver for your ATA PC Card (in CONFIG.SYS), or the wrong client driver is installed. You will need to install the proper client driver for your ATA PC Card, then reboot the system and watch for the drive letter assigned to the socket.

Symptom 32-22. You can't get any sound from the PC Card sound device or you get an error message saying that it can't talk to card services As with many network cards, most PC Card sound devices have their own client driver software, which configures the card. If you try to use the card with standard card-management software, you will need to remove the sound device from that software, then install the PC Card-specific software after socket and card services (or other card-management software) has been loaded.

Symptom 32-23. When you insert a Practical Peripherals PractiCard 14,400bps modem (revision A) in a PCMCIA slot, the modem might not be initialized This is a hardware problem with older Practical Peripherals PC Card modems. You will need to upgrade the modem to revision B or later to correct the problem.

Symptom 32-24. The SRAM card refuses to work In many cases, this is a software problem. SRAM cards are supported by an ATA PC Card driver; in effect, the SRAM card is treated like a drive. Be sure that the proper client driver is installed for your particular SRAM card. Also make note of the drive letter assigned to the SRAM card during system initialization. Point enablers for an SRAM card can also cause problems when other cards are in the system being supported with socket and card services or other enablers.

Symptom 32-25. When you first install your PC Card software, you get the error message: "No PCMCIA controller found" In virtually all cases, the software version that you are using does not support the PCMCIA controller used in your system.

You will need to contact the software maker (or the system maker) and see if an updated version or patch is available for the PC Card software. It is also possible that the system's PCMCIA controller is disabled (in CMOS) or that it is defective.

Symptom 32-26. When a program attempts to identify or check the status of a PC Card modem, the program might stop responding (or cause the computer to hang) if the modem has been powered off using power-management features The problem occurs when the program makes calls to the modem, but the modem had been powered off with power-management features. Ideally, you should not be able to make calls to a device while it is in idle or power-down mode, but some programs allow this to happen. In turn, the program making the calls can crash or take the system with it. This is a known problem in Microsoft's OSR2 for Windows 95. For now, the only way around the problem is to disable power-save functions on the PC Card or shut down the offending program before allowing the PC Card to go idle.

Symptom 32-27. When you eject a PC Card network adapter from a CardBus socket without stopping the card in PC Card properties, your computer might restart This software-related problem is encountered under Windows 95. The PC Card network adapter is removed from the CardBus socket without properly notifying VMM (the software that controls the resources used by the PC Card). The software continues to "think" that the PC Card is installed—even after the card is removed; subsequent access causes the system to crash. The only workaround at this time is to stop the PC Card network adapter using the PC Card tool in your *Control panel* (or the *PC Card* icon on the taskbar) before you remove the network-adapter PC Card.

Symptom 32-28. After a multi-function PCMCIA adapter is installed, the adapter might appear as a "parent" node below a "child" node in the Windows 95 *Device manager* In almost all cases, this is caused by a problem during device installation—the .INF file used to install the device has been processed incorrectly. Unfortunately, this is not a Windows 95 problem, but a manufacturer-specific .INF file problem. Contact the PC Card manufacturer and see if an updated .INF file or other workaround is available for the problem.

Symptom 32-29. After a second boot with a CardBus PCMCIA controller installed in your computer, the *Device manager* might display a red "X" for one or more PCMCIA sockets on your system Red "X"s mean that the sockets are disabled. CardBus controllers are dynamically enabled during the first boot after installation (even though they are installed disabled). On the second boot, Windows 95 recognizes that the device is disabled and reports this to the *Device manager*. Enable the PCMCIA CardBus controller:

- Open the *Control panel* and doubleclick the *System* icon.
- Click the PCMCIA controller, then click *Properties*.
- In the *Device usage* box, click the "(Current)" check box to select it, then click *OK*.
- Click *Close*, then restart the computer when prompted.

When Windows 95 restarts, the PCMCIA Wizard runs to help you configure the PCMCIA controller. CardBus controllers must be explicitly enabled to start the PCMCIA wizard on the second boot.

Symptom 32-30. After installing Windows 95 OSR2, the *Device manager* might display a PCIC-compatible PCMCIA controller as a conflicting resource (an exclamation point in a yellow circle) This typically happens with CardBus PCMCIA controllers. CardBus controllers had been initialized by BIOS into the PCIC-compatible mode for backward compatibility. Unfortunately, OSR2 disables the PCIC compatibility mode in BIOS and configures the controller straight to CardBus mode. However, it neglects to remove the PCIC-compatible controller entry from your *Device manager*. You will have to remove the PCIC-compatible entry from your *Device manager* manually:

- In the *Device manager*, click the PCIC-compatible controller to select it.
- Click *Remove,* then select *Yes.*
- Click *OK* to save your changes.

Symptom 32-31. When using a 3COM Elnk3 PCMCIA network card and a Xircom CE2ps PCMCIA network card together on a DEC HiNote Ultra CT475 computer, the Xircom card is not recognized You'll find that the Xircom card does not appear in the *Device manager* or the PCMCIA tool in your *Control panel*. This system-specific problem can be rectified by inserting the Xircom CE2ps card first, then inserting the 3COM Elink3 card.

Symptom 32-32. When you use the Suspend command on certain Gateway laptop computers, battery power continues to drain This is a known problem with Gateway ColorBook 4SX25, ColorBook 4SX33, ColorBook 4DX33, Liberty, and Solo systems, and is caused by a BIOS bug. When the Suspend mode is implemented, the PCMCIA slots should receive 0.0 V. Instead, the slots are receiving 2.5 V. This continues to drain the battery. Upgrade the BIOS on those systems to correct the problem.

Symptom 32-33. When you insert a Hayes Optima 14.4 PCMCIA modem into a PC Card socket, you hear a single (low) tone (or other indication) that the PCMCIA modem has not been recognized This is typically a modem hardware problem—versions of the Hayes Optima PCMCIA 14.4 modem before version 2.6H do not work with Windows 95 PC Card socket services. These older modems can be easily identified by their beige color (later modems are silver). In a situation like this, there is no workaround; you must upgrade the PCMCIA modem to a later version.

Symptom 32-34. When you use the Windows 95 Compression Agent with a removable PCMCIA hard disk, the Compression Agent might restart continuously at 10% finished This can occur if the drive is marked as *removable* in the *Device manager*. Fortunately, there is a workaround:

- In the *Control panel*, doubleclick the *System* icon.
- Click the *Device manager* tab, and then doubleclick *Disk drives.*

■ Doubleclick the appropriate drive to display its properties.
■ Click the *Settings* tab, and then click the *Removable* check box to clear it.
■ Click *OK* to save your changes, then restart the PC when prompted.

Unfortunately, once the PCMCIA drive is no longer marked as *removable*, you might no longer be able to swap drives on the fly.

Symptom 32-35. When you start Windows 95 with a PCMCIA hard disk inserted in the computer's PCMCIA slot, the hard disk seems to be recognized, but might not be available in Windows 95 This problem with Windows 95 can occur if your computer does not have an IDE hard-disk controller installed. If no IDE hard-disk controller is installed, the PCMCIA hard disk is assigned IDE port 1F0h. Because this port is normally associated with the primary hard-disk controller, Windows 95 treats it differently from other IDE ports and does not assign it a drive letter. To get around this problem, remove the PCMCIA hard disk after Windows 95 starts, then insert the disk into the PCMCIA slot again.

Symptom 32-36. When you insert a PCMCIA disk drive into a PCMCIA slot, your computer beeps (indicating that the PCMCIA card is recognized), but the disk drive is unavailable in Windows 95 This is often caused by a hardware conflict—the PCMCIA disk controller might be configured to use I/O ports 170 to 177 and your computer might use the same ports for other purposes. Check the resource settings in *Device manager*. If the PCMCIA disk controller is using ports 170 to 177, you can try reserving I/O ports 170 to 177 (forcing Windows 95 to configure the PCMCIA disk controller at another I/O address):

■ In the *Control panel*, doubleclick the *System* icon.
■ On the *Device manager* tab, click *Properties*.
■ On the *Reserve resources* tab, click the *Input/Output (I/O)* option button, and then click *Add*.
■ In the *Start value* box, enter 170.
■ In the *End value* box, enter 177.
■ Click *OK* to save your changes.
■ Restart the computer.

As an alternative, try disabling any secondary disk controller that uses I/O ports 170 to 177 in the computer's CMOS settings.

Symptom 32-37. When you attempt to dial under Windows 95 using an *Integrated Services Digital Network (ISDN)* connection, your computer might hang This hardware-specific problem has been known to occur with Eicon PCMCIA ISDN adapters. The hardware version of the adapter does not support dialing under Windows 95 properly. Unfortunately, you will have to correct this hardware problem by updating to a new ISDN adapter.

Symptom 32-38. When you try to send a fax from a cellular phone using Microsoft Exchange and a Motorola Power 14.4 PCMCIA modem, your fax

feature might not work This is a problem with Microsoft Exchange—the default initialization string sent to the modem from Microsoft Exchange initializes the modem for non-cellular calls only (regardless of the status of the *Use cellular protocol* option in *Modems* properties). You will need to edit your Windows 95 Registry with REGEDIT.EXE to correct the problem.

> Altering Registry values can have devastating effects on your Windows 95 system. Always make a backup copy of the Registry files (SYSTEM.DAT and USER.DAT) before starting your edit.

   The following registry key contains the initialization strings for installed modems (where <xxxx> is the modem ID number). To determine which ID is the correct modem, see the DriverDesc key.

```
HKEY_LOCAL_MACHINE\System\CurrentControlSet\Services\Class\Modem\<xxxx>\Init
```

Use the following value to use the modem with a cellular phone:

```
"2"="AT&F1&D2&C1\V1S0=0E0V1<cr>"
```

To return the initialization string to normal (land use), change the key to:

```
"2"="AT&F&D2&C1\V1S0=0E0V1<cr>"
```

> You can reset these values to their default values by removing the modem in *Device manager*, then reinstalling it.

Symptom 32-39. When you run Windows 95 on a Dell Latitude XP Notebook computer with a port replicator, PC Card services might not be available There will probably be no listing for the PC Card socket in the *Device manager*, and the PC Card icon might be missing in your *Control panel*. The Dell port replicator is fitted with a SCSI adapter, but by default, both the PC Card socket and the SCSI port use the same IRQ (often IRQ 11). You will have to change the setting for the PC Card socket:

- Detach the port replicator from the computer, then use the *Add new hardware* wizard in your *Control panel* to search for new hardware.
- After the PC Card socket is detected and installed, restart the computer when you are prompted to do so.
- In *Control panel*, doubleclick the *System* icon, then click the *Device manager* tab.
- Doubleclick the PCMCIA Socket entry, doubleclick the PCMCIA controller, then click the *Resources* tab.
- Click the *Use automatic settings* check box to clear it, click *Interrupt request*, then click *Change settings*.
- In the *Value* box, click an available IRQ setting.
- Click *OK* to save your changes.

■ Shut down Windows 95, then turn your computer off and back on (cold boot).
■ Reattach the port-replicator unit.

Symptom 32-40. When you try to undock a laptop computer with a PCM-CIA card installed in a Databook PCMCIA controller socket, you might receive the following error message: "The computer failed to undock" In this problem, the PC Card adapter is probably interfering with the docking port adapter. The only known workaround is to remove all PC Cards from their sockets before undocking the mobile computer. Afterward, the *Eject* command on your *Start* menu should work correctly.

Symptom 32-41. When you insert a PCMCIA SRAM or flash memory card into a Windows 95 computer that has been configured to use protected-mode PCMCIA card drivers, there might be no drive letter in My Computer or Windows Explorer associated with the PCMCIA card This can occur even though the card seems to be recognized properly and the appropriate driver appears to be installed. The problem is often that although the drivers might be installed, they are not installed correctly; the protected-mode drivers for SRAM and flash PC Cards must be installed differently than drivers for other cards. To install a PCMCIA SRAM card in Windows 95, you must place one or more entries in the CONFIG.SYS file, such as:

```
device=c:\windows\system\csmapper.sys
device=c:\windows\system\carddrv.exe /slot=<x>
```

where <windows> is the Windows folder and × indicates the number of PCMCIA card slots in the computer. To install a PCMCIA flash memory card in Windows 95, you must also place some driver entries in CONFIG.SYS, such as:

```
device=c:\windows\system\csmapper.sys
device=c:\windows\system\carddrive.exe /slot<x>
device=c:\windows\ms-flash.sys
```

where <windows> is the Windows folder and × indicates the number of PCMCIA slots in the computer.

> Not all SRAM and flash card drivers are included with Windows 95. In many cases, you will need to use drivers provided with the particular cards.

> If you use only protected-mode drivers for SRAM and flash cards, you will not have access to the cards if you boot your computer to a command prompt.

Symptom 32-42. You are logged on without a password When you remove a Plug-and-Play network adapter in *Device manager*, then restart your computer, the network adapter is redetected, and you are logged on to the network and validated by a Microsoft Windows NT server without entering a password. This problem also manifests itself when you remove a PCMCIA network adapter from the PCMCIA socket in your computer, restart your computer, then reinsert the PCMCIA network adapter, you are logged on to the network and validated by a Windows NT server without entering a password. This can occur under three circumstances: you have a null Windows password, password caching is enabled, or user profiles are enabled.

To correct these problems, configure Windows 95 so that your Windows password is not null or use the System Policy Editor to disable password caching. To configure Windows 95 so that your Windows password is not null, follow these steps:

■ In the *Control panel*, doubleclick on *Passwords*.
■ Click *Change Windows password*.
■ If you want your network password to be the same as your Windows password, click the *Microsoft networking* check box to select it, then click *OK*. If you do not want your network password to be the same as your Windows password, verify that the *Microsoft networking* check box is not selected, then click *OK*.
■ Type your new password in the *New password* and *Confirm new password* boxes, then click *OK*.

Use the following steps to edit the registry with System Policy Editor and disable password caching in Windows 95:

■ Click the *Start* button, then click *Run*.
■ Type POLEDIT in the *Open* box, then click *OK*.
■ On the *File* menu, click *Open registry*, then doubleclick *Local computer*.
■ Click the plus sign (+) next to *Network*, then click the plus sign next to *Passwords*.
■ Click the *Disable password caching* check box to select it, then click *OK*.
■ Save the changes to the *Registry*, exit the *System policy editor*, then restart Windows 95.

Symptom 32-43. You have trouble with incompatible NDIS driver versions
When you are using a portable computer with a PCMCIA network adapter that uses NDIS 2.0 (16-bit) drivers, the computer might stop responding (hang) or reboot when you try to start it while it is not docked in its docking station if the docking station contains a network card that is capable of using NDIS 3.x (32-bit) network adapter drivers. This happens because Windows 95 detects the NDIS 2.0 drivers for the PCMCIA network adapter and forces the loading of NDIS 2.0 drivers for the other network adapter (which is not currently present because the computer is undocked). Because one of the network adapters is not present, an incomplete binding occurs, which can cause the computer to hang or reboot. To enable Windows 95 to start whether the computer is docked or undocked, create a multiple-boot configuration.

Before you attempt to create a multi-boot configuration, be sure that you have a docked state that requires an NDIS 3.x driver to be loaded and an undocked state that requires an NDIS 2.0 driver to be loaded (or vice versa).

Symptom 32-44. You can't set up the PCMCIA slot in an AT&T Globalyst 130 laptop This is because the Globalyst 130 requires an unusual PCMCIA card setup, compared to other Globalyst laptops. The AT&T Globalyst 130 does not have any options in the BIOS for enabling/disabling the PCMCIA socket services on the laptop. Instead, the socket must be enabled by loading the device driver, SS365SL.EXE, in the CONFIG.SYS file. This file is a socket enabler, and must be loaded for protected-mode socket services to initialize in Windows 95. Without this file, the PCMCIA socket services are disabled.

Symptom 32-45. When you are using a Motorola Power 14.4 cellular modem with Windows 95, you might not be able to dial the second time you try to use the modem The initialization string used for this modem in Windows 95 enables a *dial suffix*. The dial suffix (also known as *staged dialing*) enables transmission of tones after the connection has been made, without breaking the connection. This feature is often used in such applications as electronic banking. With staged dialing enabled, you must remove and reinsert the PC Card modem each time you want to dial. You can disable staged dialing by editing the MDMMOTO.INF file:

■ Use any text editor to open the MDMMOTO.INF file in the Windowsfolder (this is a hidden folder).
■ Add the following line to the end of the [Modem16.AddReg] section of the file:

```
HKR, Settings, DialSuffix,, ""
```

■ Save, then close the file.
■ Remove the Motorola Power 14.4 modem using the *Modems* tool in *Control panel*.
■ Remove and reinsert the modem.

Be sure to make a backup of the .INF file before beginning you edit.

Symptom 32-46. A PCMCIA token-ring network adapter refuses to work in the computer This type of problem can occur when the following combination of conditions exist. First, the token-ring network adapter uses an address range of A20h to A2Fh. Second, the PC has a sound board or other device in the address range of 220h to 22Fh. And third, only the 10 least-significant digits are used to resolve I/O addresses. Because the Windows 95 I/O arbitrator only pays attention to the first 10 bits of any I/O allocation, devices that have I/O allocations that conflict in a 10-bit decode are registered by the system as having an I/O address conflict. As a consequence, this is a problem with Windows 95. You can work around this problem by manually configuring both devices:

■ In the *Control panel*, doubleclick the *System* icon.
■ On the *Device manager* tab, doubleclick *IBM token-ring credit-card adapter II or compatibles*.
■ Click the *Resources* tab and note the resources that the network adapter is using. To change a resource, click the *Use automatic settings* check box to clear it, click the resource, and then click *Change setting*.
■ Change the *Interrupt request (IRQ)* setting so that it does not conflict with the IRQ used by any other device.
■ Change the first memory range to D4000–D5FFF. Change the second memory range to E0000–EFFFF.

If these values continue to conflict with other devices, you might have to use different values.

- Click *OK* to save those resource changes.
- Doubleclick *Sound, video, and game controllers*, then doubleclick the sound card or the conflicting device.
- Be sure that the *Use automatic settings* check box is clear.
- Click *OK* and return to the *Control panel*.
- Restart the computer.

Symptom 32-47. You restart the computer improperly after installing PCMCIA drivers After you run the PCMCIA Wizard to install protected-mode socket services for a PC Card, you are instructed to shut down Windows 95 and then turn your computer off and back on. If you restart your computer by pressing <Ctrl>+<Alt>+<Del> instead of turning the computer off and back on, you might receive an error message stating that the PCMCIA drivers are not working correctly. The problem is that the protected-mode drivers for the PCMCIA controller might not initialize correctly when you perform a warm boot because the real-mode drivers still have control of the device. Correct the problem by performing a cold reboot of the system.

Symptom 32-48. In System Agent, the Last Result column for a ScanDisk task might report "Check was stopped because of an error" However, the SCANDISK.LOG file does not list any errors, and you do not encounter any errors if you run ScanDisk manually. This problem might be caused by an invalid drive in ScanDisk's DrivesToCheck registry setting—the setting can become invalid if a drive that existed when the ScanDisk task was created is subsequently removed. For example, this problem can occur when you remove a PCMCIA drive, uncompress or unmount a compressed drive, or remove a laptop computer from its docking station. The way around this problem is to delete the existing ScanDisk task and schedule a new task—or run ScanDisk manually.

Symptom 32-49. When you start Windows 95 on a Zenith ZDS 1762 laptop computer, the computer might stop responding (hang) while Windows 95 is running the CONFIG.SYS file This problem occurs if PCENABLE.EXE (Zenith's PCMCIA driver) is loaded before MZTINIT.SYS (Zenith's Mozart sound system driver) in the CONFIG.SYS file. When this occurs, PCENABLE.EXE installs a hook for IRQ 7, which MZTINIT.SYS also tries to use. Edit the CONFIG.SYS file and move the Mozart sound driver above any PC Card drivers. Save your changes, then restart the computer.

Symptom 32-50. When you use the Suspend feature on a Dell Latitude XP laptop computer connected to a port replicator, your PCMCIA devices might not reactivate when you exit the Suspend mode This problem can occur with BIOS version A05 or earlier. BIOS versions A05 and earlier do not send an *Advanced Power Management (APM)* "resume" event to reactivate PCMCIA devices when the computer is connected to a port replicator. You might avoid this problem by not using the *Suspend* feature while the laptop is connected to a port replicator. To resolve the problem on a more permanent basis, you will need to update the laptop's BIOS version.

Symptom 32-51. You have trouble using similar cards simultaneously For example, if you start Windows 95 with one Xircom PCMCIA network card inserted in the computer, the card works correctly until you insert a second Xircom PCMCIA network card. When you insert the second card, the second card works correctly and the first stops working. If you remove and reinsert the first card, it works correctly and the second card stops working. This happens because both cards have the same PCMCIA ID, but different checksums—the cards both appear to be the same card to Windows 95, so Windows 95 switches system resources from one card to the other. Ultimately, if you must run two network cards at the same time, they cannot both be Xircom network cards.

Symptom 32-52. The Zenith Zplayer PCMCIA CD-ROM adapter does not function correctly using Windows 95 32-bit drivers In virtually all cases, the 32-bit PCMCIA drivers included with Windows 95 are not compatible with the Zenith Zplayer PCMCIA adapter. You will need to disable the 32-bit PCMCIA drivers:

■ In the *Control panel*, doubleclick the *System* icon.
■ On the *Device manager* tab, doubleclick the PCMCIA adapter.
■ Click the check box for the current configuration to clear it.
■ Click *OK* or *Close* until you return to *Control panel*, then restart your computer.
■ To use the PCMCIA adapter with real-mode drivers, use the installation program included with the adapter.

Do not run the *PCMCIA* wizard to install the 32-bit PCMCIA drivers.

Symptom 32-53. On a computer with only one PCMCIA socket, Windows 95 cannot set up a new PCMCIA card if the original PCMCIA card is being used to access the Windows 95 source files If you remove the PCMCIA card that is providing access to Windows 95 source files to set up a new card, Windows 95 cannot access the source files. When you are prompted to provide the source files, you cannot remove the new card and insert the original card because Windows 95 does not detect the removal and insertion of PCMCIA cards during the configuration of the new card. To get around this problem, use the *Add new hardware* wizard to manually install the new PCMCIA card. This process pre-installs the necessary driver files so that you can set up the new card without accessing Windows 95 source files.

Symptom 32-54. You cannot format an SRAM card using the Windows 95 graphical user interface because the *Full and quick* format options are not available In almost all cases, the problem is with the device driver for the SRAM card. The device driver is probably returning device parameters for a 128KB SRAM card, regardless of what card is actually inserted in the PC Card slot. You will need to contact the SRAM card maker to obtain an updated driver, which corrects the problem.

Symptom 32-55. After you dock or undock a Compaq Elite laptop computer, the computer's PCMCIA devices might stop working Also, multiple disabled PCMCIA controllers might appear in *Device manager*. This is a problem with early versions of Compaq Elite PnP BIOS—some versions report incorrect PCMCIA resources. When this happens, Windows 95 disables the PCMCIA controller. To correct this problem on a permanent basis, you'll need to update the Compaq BIOS with a current version (5/95 or later). To remove incorrect PCMCIA devices in the meantime:

- In the *Control panel*, doubleclick the *System* icon.
- On the *Device manager* tab, click each PCMCIA device, then click *Remove* (remove all the PCMCIA devices).
- Click *Computer*, then click *Refresh* (this will re-detect the correct PCMCIA device).
- Click *OK* to save your changes.

Symptom 32-56. When you set up Windows 95, it will not install more than one PCMCIA network adapter correctly This is because the Windows 95 32-bit socket drivers are not enabled. To install the Windows 95 32-bit PCMCIA socket drivers:

- Doubleclick on *My computer*.
- Doubleclick the *Control panel*.
- Start the 32-bit PCMCIA wizard and follow the instructions on the screen.

Windows 95 is specifically designed to detect and install only one PCMCIA network card during setup.

Symptom 32-57. When you try to connect to a network using an IBM token-ring PCMCIA network card on an Omnibook 600 computer, you are unable to view any resources A resource conflict is between the Omnibook's proprietary PCMCIA controller and the IBM Token Ring PCMCIA network card. The Omnibook's proprietary PCMCIA controller supports I/O ranges up to 3FFh. The IBM token-ring PCMCIA network card can only reside at I/O address A20h. There is no solution to this problem—the IBM token-ring PCMCIA network card cannot be used on an Omnibook 600 computer.

Symptom 32-58. When you run ScanDisk, the "Select the drive you want to check for errors" box might or might not show drives that exist In most cases, you have removed or inserted an ATA PC Card. Unfortunately, the drive list in ScanDisk is static. That list is generated when you start ScanDisk and it is not updated while ScanDisk is running. If you add or remove drives (such as PCMCIA drives or Drive-Space-compressed drives) while ScanDisk is running, the list is not updated to reflect the changes. You must update the drive list by exiting and restarting ScanDisk.

Symptom 32-59. When you insert a Xircom CE2 PCMCIA network adapter card, the card might not work and the computer might not be connected to the network When this occurs, your computer might stop responding. The network adapter might require a real-mode enabler or different client drivers to work properly. To correct this problem, load the real-mode card and socket services drivers in the CON-FIG.SYS file. The actual drivers that are required vary from one system to another, but they typically look like:

```
device=cs.exe
device=sscirrus.exe
```

Symptom 32-60. PCMCIA cards are not configuring properly on your Compaq computer In many cases, you have an outdated or buggy BIOS in the system. You can usually correct this kind of problem by updating the BIOS version.

Symptom 32-61. When the system boots up, you see the error message "Divide overflow" before entering Windows 95—this forces you to boot Windows 95 in safe mode The drivers installed for the PCMCIA card are obsolete or are otherwise incompatible with Windows 95. You will need to disable those real-mode drivers in CONFIG.SYS and AUTOEXEC.BAT, and ultimately install the current drivers for Windows 95.

Symptom 32-62. Your PC Card client drivers refuse to load and an error message appears when starting Windows 95 In most cases, you have real-mode PCMCIA drivers starting in CONFIG.SYS and AUTOEXEC.BAT, which are causing problems for Windows 95. Try disabling those real-mode PC Card drivers in CONFIG.SYS and AUTOEXEC.BAT first. Turn off the PC and remove the PC Card. Boot to Windows 95 normally, then insert the card—you might need to run the *PCMCIA* wizard to install the proper card drivers. You might also need to download the latest protected-mode drivers from the PC Card maker, then install the new drivers with the *Have disk* option.

Symptom 32-63. PCMCIA cards are not configuring properly on IBM Thinkpads This is because you must run a specific IBM utility to update the BIOS on IBM Thinkpads first. Install "IBM WIN95SETUP" before installing Windows 95—this utility updates the BIOS, which has several Plug-and-Play fixes. This utility can be obtained from: **http://www.pc.ibm.com** or IBM's BBS. You can then install Windows 95 and proceed to re-install your PCMCIA cards.

Symptom 32-64. The computer produces a single, low beep when the PCMCIA card is inserted, but the *PC Card icon shows no information about the socket, and the* Stop feature shows the "Device cannot be removed" error In almost all cases, the PC Card has not been assigned the proper memory exclusion, and is experiencing a memory conflict with another device in the system. Go into the Control Panel, then select the "PC Card" icon. Choose *Global settings* and be sure that the *Automatic setting* check box is checked. Then restart Windows 95. This should clear the problem.

Symptom 32-65. Windows 95 does not recognize the parameters of the PCMCIA note disk You will have to perform a hard-disk drive setup for an unformatted drive. Before proceeding, be sure to backup any vital information on the PC Card disk—it will be erased:

- Choose *My computer* and select the *Control panel* icon.
- Choose the *System* icon and select the *Device manager* tab.
- Select *Disk drives*, then choose the *Settings* tab.
- Select *Int. 13* unit.
- Save your changes and restart the system when prompted.
- When Windows 95 has fully rebooted, choose the *Start*, then *Run*.
- Type in FDISK and choose *OK*.
- When you start FDISK, be sure to choose Disk 2 before partitioning the drive.
- Create partition(s) as required.

- Repeat the first four steps and remove the checkmark from *Int. 13* unit.
- Save your changes and restart the system when prompted.
- When Windows 95 is fully rebooted, choose *My computer*.
- Click the right mouse button on the D: drive, then select *Format*.
- After formatting the drive, run ScanDisk.
- The PCMCIA disk should now be ready for use.

Further Study

That's all for Chapter 32. Be sure to review the glossary and chapter questions on the accompanying CD. If you have access to the Internet, take a look at some of these PC Card resources:

General PC Card information: **http://beta.missilab.com/readertest/pcmcia.html**

PC Card Frame Grabbers: **http://www.ct-oy.com/artsi/pcmcia.html**

PC Card information: **http://login.eunet.no/~sverream/pcmcia.htm**

PC Card Links: **http://www.cybersim.com/kats/pcmcia/**

PC Card suppliers: **http://www.apresearch.com/databaselist.htm**

PCMCIA: **http://www.pc-card.com/**

NEWSGROUP

alt.periphs.pcmcia

33

PCI BUS

OPERATIONS

CONTENTS AT A GLANCE

PCI Bus Configuration and Signals
   PCI Bus layout
   Knowing the PCI signals

General Bus Troubleshooting

Further Study

By the late 1980s, the proliferation of 32-bit CPUs and graphics-intensive operating systems made it painfully obvious that the 8.33MHz ISA bus was no longer satisfactory. The PC industry began to develop alternative architectures for improved performance. Two architectures are now prominent: VL and PCI. Although the VL bus seems ideal, some serious limitations must be overcome. Perhaps most important is the VL bus dependence on CPU speed—fast computers must use wait states with the VL bus, and the VL bus only supports one or two slots (maximum). Another problem is that the VL standard is voluntary, and not all manufacturers adhere to VESA specifications completely. In mid-1992, Intel Corporation and a comprehensive consortium of manufacturers introduced the *Peripheral Component Interconnect (PCI) bus*. Where the VL bus was designed specifically to enhance PC video systems, the 188-pin PCI bus looks to the future of CPUs (and PCs in general) by providing a bus architecture that also supports peripherals, such as hard drives, networks, etc. This chapter shows you the layout and operations of the PCI bus.

PCI Bus Configuration and Signals

The PCI architecture is capable of transferring data at 132MB/sec—a great improvement over the 5MB/sec transfer rate of the standard ISA bus. Another key advantage of the PCI bus is that it will have automatic configuration capabilities for switchless/jumperless peripherals. Auto-configuration (the heart of Plug and Play) will take care of all addresses, interrupt requests, and DMA used by a PCI peripheral. Table 33-1 lists the features for a PCI bus.

The PCI bus supports *linear bursts*, which is a method of transferring data that ensures that the bus is continually filled with data. The peripheral devices expect to receive data from the system main memory in a linear address order. This means that large amounts of data is read from or written to a single address, which is then incremented for the next byte in the stream. The linear burst is one of the unique aspects of the PCI bus because it will perform both burst reads and burst writes. In short, it will transfer data on the bus every clock cycle—this doubles the PCI throughput compared to buses without linear burst capabilities. The devices designed to support PCI have low access latency, reducing the time required for a peripheral to be granted control of the bus after requesting access. For example, an Ethernet controller card connected to a LAN has large data files from the network coming into its buffer. Waiting for access to the bus, the Ethernet is unable to transfer the data to the CPU quickly enough to avoid a buffer overflow—forcing it to temporarily store the file's contents in extra RAM. Because PCI-compliant devices support faster access times, the Ethernet card can promptly send data to the CPU.

**TABLE 33-1   FEATURES OF A
PCI BUS ARCHITECTURE**

Performance features include:

- Data bursting as normal operating mode—both read and write
- Linear burst ordering
- Concurrency support (deadlock, buffering solutions)
- Low latency guarantees for real-time devices
- Access-oriented arbitration (not time slice)
- Supports multiple loads (PCI boards) at 33MHz
- Error detection and reporting
- Multimaster; peer-to-peer communication
- 32-bit multiplexed, processor independent
- Synchronous, 8–33MHz (132MB/sec) operation
- Variable length, linear bursting (both read and write)
- Parity on address, data, command signals
- Concurrency/pipelining support
- Initialization hooks for auto-configuration
- Arbitration supported
- 64-bit extension transparently compatible with 32-bit
- CMOS drivers; TTL voltage levels
- 5-V and 3.3-V compatible

The PCI bus supports bus mastering, which allows one of a number of intelligent peripherals to take control of the bus to accelerate a high-throughput, high-priority task. PCI architecture also supports concurrency—a technique that ensures that the microprocessor operates simultaneously with these masters, instead of waiting for them. As one example, concurrency allows the CPU to perform floating-point calculations on a spreadsheet while an Ethernet card and the LAN have control of the bus. Finally, PCI was developed as a dual-voltage architecture. Normally, the bus is a +5-Vdc system, like other busses. However, the bus can also operate in a +3.3-Vdc (low-voltage) mode.

PCI BUS LAYOUT

The layout for a PCI bus slot is shown in Fig. 33-1. Notice that there are two major segments to the +5-Vdc connector. A +3.3-Vdc connector adds a key in the 12/13 positions to prevent accidental insertion of a +5-Vdc PCI board into a +3.3-Vdc slot. Similarly, the +5-Vdc slot is keyed in the 50/51 position to prevent placing a +3.3-Vdc board into a +5-Vdc slot. The pinout for a PCI bus is shown in Table 33-2.

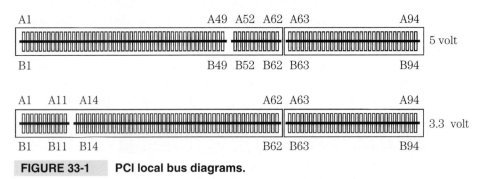

FIGURE 33-1 PCI local bus diagrams.

TABLE 33-2 PCI BUS PINOUT—5 VOLT AND 3.3 VOLT (REV. 2.0)					
5 VOLT	**3.3 VOLT**	**PIN**	**PIN**	**3.3 VOLT**	**5 VOLT**
−12 Vdc	−12 Vdc	B1	A1	−TRST	−TRST
TCK	TCK	B2	A2	+12 Vdc	+12 Vdc
Ground	Ground	B3	A3	TMS	TMS
TDO	TDO	B4	A4	TDI	TDI
+5 Vdc	+5 Vdc	B5	A5	+5 Vdc	+5 Vdc
+5 Vdc	+5 Vdc	B6	A6	−INTA	−INTA
−INTB	−INTB	B7	A7	−INTC	−INTC
−INTD	−INTD	B8	A8	+5 Vdc	+5 Vdc
−PRSNT1	−PRSNT1	B9	A9	Reserved	Reserved
Reserved	Reserved	B10	A10	+3.3 Vdc (I/O)	+5 Vdc
−PRSNT2	−PRSNT2	B11	A11	Reserved	Reserved
Ground	Key	B12	A12	Key	Ground
Ground	Key	B13	A13	Key	Ground

TABLE 33-2	PCI BUS PINOUT—5 VOLT AND 3.3 VOLT (REV. 2.0) (CONTINUED)				
5 VOLT	**3.3 VOLT**	**PIN**	**PIN**	**3.3 VOLT**	**5 VOLT**
Reserved	Reserved	B14	A14	Reserved	Reserved
Ground	Ground	B15	A15	−RST	−RST
Clock	Clock	B16	A16	+3.3 Vdc	+5 Vdc
Ground	Ground	B17	A17	−GNT	−GNT
−REQ	−REQ	B18	A18	Ground	Ground
+5 Vdc	+3.3 Vdc	B19	A19	Reserved	Reserved
Adr/Dat 31	Adr/Dat 31	B20	A20	Adr/Dat 30	Adr/Dat 30
Adr/Dat 29	Adr/Dat 29	B21	A21	+3.3 Vdc	+5 Vdc
Ground	Ground	B22	A22	Adr/Dat 28	Adr/Dat 28
Adr/Dat 27	Adr/Dat 27	B23	A23	Adr/Dat 26	Adr/Dat 26
Adr/Dat 25	Adr/Dat 25	B24	A24	Ground	Ground
+5 Vdc	+3.3 Vdc	B25	A25	Adr/Dat 24	Adr/Dat 24
C/ −BE3	C/ −BE3	B26	A26	IDSEL	IDSEL
Adr/Dat 23	Adr/Dat 23	B27	A27	+3.3 Vdc	+5 Vdc
Ground	Ground	B28	A28	Adr/Dat 22	Adr/Dat 22
Adr/Dat 21	Adr/Dat 21	B29	A29	Adr/Dat 20	Adr/Dat 20
Adr/Dat 19	Adr/Dat 19	B30	A30	Ground	Ground
+5 Vdc	+3.3 Vdc	B31	A31	Adr/Dat 18	Adr/Dat 18
Adr/Dat 17	Adr/Dat 17	B32	A32	Adr/Dat 16	Adr/Dat 16
C/ −BE2	C/ −BE2	B33	A33	+3.3 Vdc	+5 Vdc
Ground	Ground	B34	A34	−FRAME	−FRAME
−IRDY	−IRDY	B35	A35	Ground	Ground
+5 Vdc	+3.3 Vdc	B36	A36	−TRDY	−TRDY
−DEVSEL	−DEVSEL	B37	A37	Ground	Ground
Ground	Ground	B38	A38	−STOP	−STOP
−LOCK	−LOCK	B39	A39	+3.3 Vdc	+5 Vdc
−PERR	−PERR	B40	A40	SDONE	SDONE
+5 Vdc	+3.3 Vdc	B41	A41	−SBO	−SBO
−SERR	−SERR	B42	A42	Ground	Ground
+5 Vdc	+3.3 Vdc	B43	A43	PAR	PAR
C/ −BE1	C/ −BE1	B44	A44	Adr/Dat 15	Adr/Dat 15
Adr/Dat 14	Adr/Dat 14	B45	A45	+3.3 Vdc	+5 Vdc
Ground	Ground	B46	A46	Adr/Dat 13	Adr/Dat 13
Adr/Dat 12	Adr/Dat 12	B47	A47	Adr/Dat 11	Adr/Dat 11
Adr/Dat 10	Adr/Dat 10	B48	A48	Ground	Ground
Ground	Ground	B49	A49	Adr/Dat 9	Adr/Dat 9
Key	Ground	B50	A50	Ground	Key
Key	Ground	B51	A51	Ground	Key
Adr/Dat 8	Adr/Dat 8	B52	A52	C/ −BE0	C/ −BE0
Adr/Dat 7	Adr/Dat 7	B53	A53	+3.3 Vdc	+5 Vdc
+5 Vdc	+3.3 Vdc	B54	A54	Adr/Dat 6	Adr/Dat 6
Adr/Dat 5	Adr/Dat 5	B55	A55	Adr/Dat 4	Adr/Dat 4

TABLE 33-2   PCI BUS PINOUT—5 VOLT AND 3.3 VOLT (REV. 2.0) (CONTINUED)

5 VOLT	3.3 VOLT	PIN	PIN	3.3 VOLT	5 VOLT
Adr/Dat 3	Adr/Dat 3	B56	A56	Ground	Ground
Ground	Ground	B57	A57	Adr/Dat 2	Adr/Dat 2
Adr/Dat 1	Adr/Dat 1	B58	A58	Adr/Dat 0	Adr/Dat 0
+5 Vdc	+3.3 Vdc	B59	A59	+3.3 Vdc	+5 Vdc
−ACK64	−ACK64	B60	A60	−REQ64	−REQ64
+5 Vdc	+5 Vdc	B61	A61	+5 Vdc	+5 Vdc
+5 Vdc	+5 Vdc	B62	A62	+5 Vdc	+5 Vdc
Key	Key	Key	Key	Key	Key
Key	Key	Key	Key	Key	Key
Reserved	Reserved	B63	A63	Ground	Ground
Ground	Ground	B64	A64	C/ −BE7	C/ −BE7
C/ −BE6	C/ −BE6	B65	A65	C/ −BE5	C/ −BE5
C/ −BE4	C/ −BE4	B66	A66	+3.3 Vdc	+5 Vdc
Ground	Ground	B67	A67	PAR64	PAR64
Adr/Dat 63	Adr/Dat 63	B68	A68	Adr/Dat 62	Adr/Dat 62
Adr/Dat 61	Adr/Dat 61	B69	A69	Ground	Ground
+5 Vdc	+3.3 Vdc	B70	A70	Adr/Dat 60	Adr/Dat 60
Adr/Dat 59	Adr/Dat 59	B71	A71	Adr/Dat 58	Adr/Dat 58
Adr/Dat 57	Adr/Dat 57	B72	A72	Ground	Ground
Ground	Ground	B73	A73	Adr/Dat 56	Adr/Dat 56
Adr/Dat 55	Adr/Dat 55	B74	A74	Adr/Dat 54	Adr/Dat 54
Adr/Dat 53	Adr/Dat 53	B75	A75	+3.3 Vdc	+5 Vdc
Ground	Ground	B76	A76	Adr/Dat 52	Adr/Dat 52
Adr/Dat 51	Adr/Dat 51	B77	A77	Adr/Dat 50	Adr/Dat 50
Adr/Dat 49	Adr/Dat 49	B78	A78	Ground	Ground
+5 Vdc	+3.3 Vdc	B79	A79	Adr/Dat 48	Adr/Dat 48
Adr/Dat 47	Adr/Dat 47	B80	A80	Adr/Dat 46	Adr/Dat 46
Adr/Dat 45	Adr/Dat 45	B81	A81	Ground	Ground
Ground	Ground	B82	A82	Adr/Dat 44	Adr/Dat 44
Adr/Dat 43	Adr/Dat 43	B83	A83	Adr/Dat 42	Adr/Dat 42
Adr/Dat 41	Adr/Dat 41	B84	A84	+3.3 Vdc	+5 Vdc
Ground	Ground	B85	A85	Adr/Dat 40	Adr/Dat 40
Adr/Dat 39	Adr/Dat 39	B86	A86	Adr/Dat 38	Adr/Dat 38
Adr/Dat 37	Adr/Dat 37	B87	A87	Ground	Ground
+5 Vdc	+3.3 Vdc	B88	A88	Adr/Dat 36	Adr/Dat 36
Adr/Dat 35	Adr/Dat 35	B89	A89	Adr/Dat 34	Adr/Dat 34
Adr/Dat 33	Adr/Dat 33	B90	A90	Ground	Ground
Ground	Ground	B91	A91	Adr/Dat 32	Adr/Dat 32
Reserved	Reserved	B92	A92	Reserved	Reserved
Reserved	Reserved	B93	A93	Ground	Ground
Ground	Ground	B94	A94	Reserved	Reserved

KNOWING THE PCI SIGNALS

To reduce the number of pins needed in the PCI bus, data and address lines are multiplexed together (Adr./Dat 0 to Adr./Dat 63). It is also interesting to note that PCI is the first bus standard designed to support a low-voltage (+3.3 Vdc) logic implementation. On inspection, you will see that +5-Vdc and +3.3-Vdc implementations of the PCI bus place their physical key slots in different places so that the two implementations are not interchangeable. The *Clock (CLOCK)* signal provides timing for the PCI bus only, and can be adjusted from dc (0Hz) to 33MHz. Asserting the *–Reset (–RST)* signal will reset all PCI devices. Because the 64-bit data path uses eight bytes, the *Command/ –Byte Enable (C/ –BE0 to C/ –BE7)* signals define which bytes are transferred. Parity across the Address/Data and Byte Enable lines is represented with a *Parity (PAR)* or *64-Bit Parity (PAR64)* signal. Bus mastering is initiated by the *–Request (–REQ)* line and granted after approval using the *–Grant (–GNT)* line.

When a valid PCI bus cycle is in progress, the *–Frame (–FRAME)* signal is true. If the PCI bus cycle is in its final phase, –Frame will be released. The *–Target Ready (–TRDY)* line is true when an addressed device is able to complete the data phase of its bus cycle. An *–Initiator Ready (–IRDY)* signal indicates that valid data is present on the bus (or the bus is ready to accept data). The –FRAME, –TARGET READY, and –INITIATOR READY signals are all used together. A *–Stop (–STOP)* signal is asserted by a target asking a master to halt the current data transfer. The *ID Select (IDSEL)* signal is used as a chip-select signal during board configuration read and write cycles. The *–Device Select (–DEVSEL)* line is both an input and an output. As an input, –DEVSEL indicates if a device has assumed control of the current bus transfer. As an output, –DEVSEL shows that a device has identified itself as the target for the current bus transfer.

The four interrupt lines are labeled –INTA to –INTD. When the full 64-bit data mode is being used, an expansion device will initiate a *–64-Bit Bus Request (–REQ 64)* and await a *–64-Bit Bus Acknowledge (–ACK64)* signal from the bus controller. The *–Bus Lock (–LOCK)* signal is an interface control used to ensure use of the bus by a selected expansion device. Error reporting is performed by *–Primary Error (–PERR)* and *–Secondary Error (–SERR)* lines. Cache memory and JTAG support are also provided on the PCI bus.

General Bus Troubleshooting

In most cases, you will not be troubleshooting a bus—after all, the bus is little more than a passive connector. However, the major signals that exist on an PCI bus can provide you with important clues about the system's operation. The most effective bus troubleshooting tool available to you is a POST board (such as the ones covered in Chapter 15). Many POST boards are equipped with a number of LEDs that display power status, along with important timing and control signals. If one or more of those LEDs is missing, a fault has likely occurred somewhere on the motherboard. Remember that the vast majority of POST boards are designed for the ISA bus. You can plug a POST board (with a built-in logic probe capable of 33MHz operation) into an ISA connector, then use the logic probe to test key signals. Because the signals on a PCI bus are quite different than those on an ISA bus, try the following signals:

■ *Voltage* Use your multimeter and check each voltage level on the PCI bus. You should be able to find –12 Vdc and +5 Vdc, regardless of whether the bus is standard or low-voltage.

For a low-voltage bus, you should also be able to find a +3.3-Vdc supply. If any of these supply levels are low or are absent, troubleshoot or replace the power supply.

- *CLOCK (pin B16)* The Clock signal provides timing signals for the expansion device. It can be adjusted between DC (0Hz) and 33MHz. If this signal is absent, the expansion board will probably not run. Check the clock-generating circuitry on the motherboard or replace the motherboard outright.
- *RST (pin B18)* The Reset line can be used to re-initialize the PCI expansion device. This line should not be active for more than a few moments after power is applied or after a warm reset is initiated.

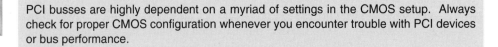

PCI busses are highly dependent on a myriad of settings in the CMOS setup. Always check for proper CMOS configuration whenever you encounter trouble with PCI devices or bus performance.

Another point to consider is that bus connectors are mechanical devices. As a result, they do not last forever. If you or your customer are in the habit of removing and inserting boards frequently, it is likely that the metal "fingers" providing contact will wear, resulting in unreliable connections. Similarly, inserting a board improperly (or with excessive force) can break the connector. In extreme cases, even the motherboard can be damaged. The first rule of board replacement is: always remove and re-insert the suspect board. It is not uncommon for oxides to develop on board and slot contacts that may eventually degrade signal quality. By removing the board and re-inserting it, you can wipe off any oxides or dust and possibly improve the connections.

The second rule of board replacement is: always try a board in another expansion slot before replacing it. This way, a faulty bus slot can be ruled out before suffering the expense of a new board. Keep in mind that many current PCI motherboards have only one or two PCI slots—the remainder are ISA slots. If a bus slot is defective, a technician can do little, except:

1 Block the slot and inform the customer that it is damaged and should not be used.
2 Replace the damaged bus slot connector (a tedious and time-consuming task) and pass the labor expense on to the customer.
3 Replace the motherboard outright (also a rather expensive option).

Further Study

That's it for Chapter 33. Be sure to review the glossary and chapter questions on the accompanying CD. If you have access to the Internet, take a look at some of these various PCI resources:

PCI Special Interest Group Home Page: **http://www.pcisig.com/**

PC2 Consulting: **http://www.pc2.com/**

CompactPCI Home Page: **http://www.compactpci.com/**

Small PCI: **http://www.pcisig.com/current/smallpci/**

34

PEN SYSTEMS
AND TOUCHPADS

CONTENTS AT A GLANCE

Understanding Pen Digitizers
   Resistive digitizers
   Capacitive pen digitizers
   Capacitive touchpad digitizers
   Electromagnetic digitizers

A Pen Environment
   Gestures
   Glyphs

Troubleshooting Pen Systems
   Cleaning a pen-tablet or touchpad
   Ink and video drivers
   Pen tips and batteries
   Pen-tablet symptoms
   Touchpad symptoms

Further Study

One of the greatest complaints about personal computers has been their input devices. Keyboards and mice are remarkably effective at entering text or making selections, but these are not "natural" for humans to use. Keyboards and mice often intimidate many novice PC users, and many veteran PC users suffer from repetitive stress injuries as a result of odd finger and wrist motion. PC designers have responded to these problems by developing new input devices, such as pen-based tablets and touchpads. *Pen tablets* (Fig. 34-1) replace the mouse with a pointing "pen" (or stylus), which is used against a sensitive electronic tablet in just the same way that we would use a pen against a sheet of paper. Pen-tablets can work just like a mouse, but they can also be used as very versatile "brushes" in painting and other graphic design/editing software. Pen-based input also provides a means for basic handwriting and signature recognition. The newest generations of

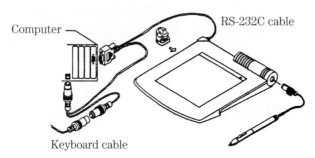

FIGURE 34-1   **A popular pen-based tablet.** AceCAD

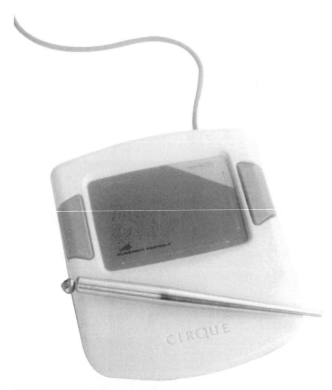

FIGURE 34-2   **A popular touchpad assembly.** Cirque

personal digital assistants and super-small mobile computers are made possible by the use of pen-tablets integrated into the LCD assembly. By contrast, *touchpads* (Fig. 34-2) are small, low-resolution tablets that are used almost exclusively to replace the mouse. By running your finger along the touchpad, you can move the mouse and perform other mouse-type gestures, such as clicking, doubleclicking, and dragging. Touchpads are most popular in new mobile computers, although some high-end keyboards are also incorporating a touchpad instead of a trackball. This chapter explains the basic operation of pen-tablet and touchpad technologies, and examines a series of related symptoms.

Understanding Pen Digitizers

The key to any pen tablet or touchpad is the hardware system itself, which is referred to as the *digitizer*. A digitizer converts the analog position of a pen (or finger contact in the case of a touchpad) on the contact surface into a set of horizontal (X) and vertical (Y) coordinate data. In most cases, this position data is passed to the host computer through an ordinary serial (COM) port. The operating system and drivers interpret those coordinates and will either activate pixels on the display, which echo the pen's position (called the *ink*), or respond to a gesture according to the rules of an operating system. To interpret cursive (handwritten) characters or gestures drawn with a pen, the operating system compares the size, direction, and sequence of each stroke against information contained in a database. When a match occurs, the computer responds accordingly. For instance, the pen computer might interpret a "cross-out" pen motion as a delete command, or as an upper or lower case "x". This chapter covers three major digitizer technologies: resistive, capacitive, and electromagnetic.

RESISTIVE DIGITIZERS

Resistive digitizers are the simplest and least-expensive type of digitizer. They are applied in older low-end pen-computer (PDA) systems. You might encounter two varieties of resistive digitizer: single-layer digitizers and double-layer digitizers. The diagram for a single-layer resistive digitizer is illustrated in Fig. 34-3. A layer of conductive transparent film is applied over a protective glass cover. For a pen computer, the film and glass are then

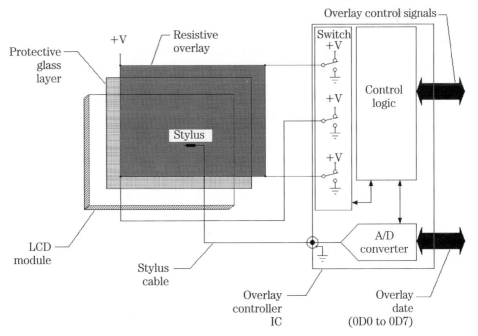

FIGURE 34-3   A single-layer resistive digitizer.

mounted in position over a LCD module. Notice how the film's four corners are attached to voltage sources switched by the tablet controller IC. In the idle state, all four corners of the film are held at +5 Vdc (low-voltage systems might use +3.0 or +3.3 Vdc).

X and Y coordinates are read in sequence. The tablet controller IC sets up to measure the Y coordinate by switching controls B and C to the ground position. This configuration keeps the top two corners of the conductive tablet at $+V$, and places the two lower corners at ground. Because the tablet film has a known resistance (per square area), linear voltage gradients are setup from top to bottom. When a pen is applied against the conductive tablet, the pen cable carries a voltage to an analog-to-digital (A/D) converter. As the pen nears the tablet top, its terminal voltage nears $+V$. As the pen nears the tablet bottom, its terminal voltage approaches 0 V (ground). The A/D converter translates the analog pen voltage into an 8-, 12-, or 16-bit data word. An 8-bit A/D converter allows the tablet to resolve 256 (2^8) distinct positions in the vertical (Y) direction, but a 12-bit A/D converter lets the tablet resolve 4096 (2^{12}) Y locations. As you might see, more bits used in a conversion allow the computer to resolve finer pen positions.

Once the Y coordinate is generated, the tablet controller sets up to measure the horizontal (X) coordinate by switching control C to $+V$ and switching controls A and B to ground. This configuration raises the two left corners of the conductive tablet to $+V$, and places the two right corners at 0 V (ground). Linear voltage gradients then develop from left to right. Assuming the pen has not been moved since the Y coordinate was just taken, its output voltage now represents the X location. As the pen nears the left of the tablet, its output voltage to the A/D converter approaches $+V$. As the pen nears the right side of the tablet, its voltage nears 0 V.

Double-layer resistive digitizers are a bit more involved (Fig. 34-4). The upper conductive layer and controller IC are virtually identical to the components shown already, but the transparent conductive film is laminated to a substrate of clear, flexible polyester. The lower conductive layer is highly conductive—virtually zero resistance. The lower layer is bonded to a sheet of protective glass. Upper and lower conductive layers are separated by a series of carefully placed flexible spacers. When a pen pushes the two layers into contact, the lower conductive layer (not the pen) conducts the analog position voltage to the A/D converter. Because no cabled pen is needed, almost any pointing device will suffice. You could even use your finger as the pen. The basic methodology of determining X and Y coordinates is very much the same for two-layer digitizers as for single-layer digitizers.

Resistive digitizers are not without their drawbacks. First, the glass and conductive film(s) placed over the LCD take away from the pen computer's display visibility. A single-layer digitizer can reduce optical transmission by 15%. Two layers can reduce a display's optical transmission by 30% or more. Such substantial reductions in visibility can make LCDs unacceptably dark. Additional backlighting can be used to counter the optical reduction, but only at the cost of shorter battery life or heavier systems. Also, resistive digitizers only measure position, not contact pressure. Intuitive pen-based systems should ideally leave darker "ink" when the pen is under strong pressure, and should leave lighter "ink" when a light touch is used. Because a resistive digitizer simply makes contact (or not), there is little interest in resistive digitizers for pen-centric (character recognition-oriented) pen systems. Finally, resistive material tends to drift with temperature, humidity, and wear. Drift can cause inaccuracies that carry over into the digitizer's output.

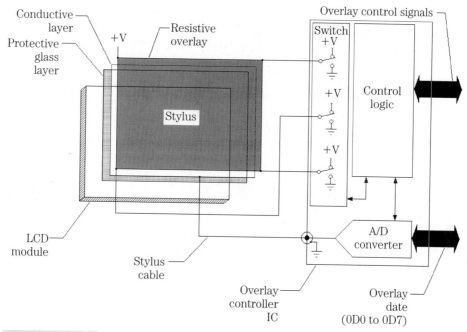

FIGURE 34-4 A dual-layer resistive digitizer.

CAPACITIVE PEN DIGITIZERS

A *capacitive digitizer* (also called an *electrostatic digitizer*) uses a single protective layer of glass with a layer of conductive film bonded underneath (Fig. 34-5). The digitizer controller IC generates a low-power, high-frequency signal, which is conducted down the tether wire to the pen tip. As the pen nears the glass, the conductive layer bonded underneath the glass picks up this signal and generates a voltage at that point. This tablet voltage is proportional to pen proximity. The closer the pen is to the glass, the larger the signal will be on the conductive layer, and vice versa. By comparing signal amplitudes from top to bottom and left to right, the digitizer controller IC can extrapolate the pen X and Y coordinates, as well as its proximity to the glass. Because the pattern of capacitive coupling changes as pen orientation changes, the digitizer controller IC can also detect pen tilt and accent the "ink" feedback to show that tilt.

Capacitive digitizers are an improvement over resistive digitizers because the capacitive approach allows the pen-tablet to sense pen proximity as well as X and Y position. The front glass used in capacitive digitizers makes the tablet virtually immune to wear. On the down side, the tablet must be positioned in front of the LCD, which can reduce the display's visible output by up to 15% (for pen computers only—not for stand-alone pen tablets). The pen must also be cabled to the system by a wire.

CAPACITIVE TOUCHPAD DIGITIZERS

Many older touchpads use resistive digitizer techniques to detect finger position, but resistive touchpads are often imprecise, and suffer from wear. More recent PC touchpads

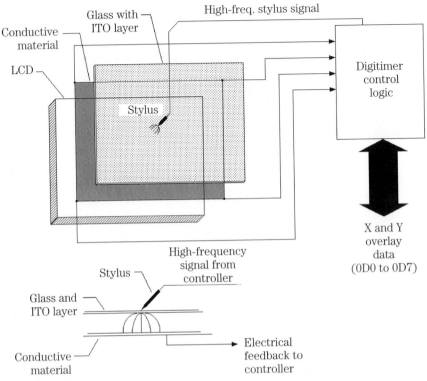

FIGURE 34-5   A capacitive (electrostatic) digitzer.

(such as the Cirque "Cat" family) use a variation of capacitive digitizer technology to de-tect finger position. The Cirque touchpad contains a two-layer grid of electrodes that are driven by a custom ASIC mounted on the underside of the touchpad. The upper layer con-tains vertical electrode strips while the lower layer is composed of horizontal electrode strips. The ASIC measures the "mutual capacitance" from each of the horizontal elec-trodes to each of the vertical electrodes. A human finger near the intersection of two elec-trodes modifies the mutual capacitance between them (because a finger has very different dielectric properties than air). The position of a finger can then be precisely determined based on these mutual capacitance changes at various locations—and can even be detected before a finger actually touches the pad. This means that the wear and tear on a capacitive touchpad is significantly reduced.

ELECTROMAGNETIC DIGITIZERS

An *electromagnetic digitizer* (*RF digitizer*) is generally considered to be the top-of-the-line digitizer technique for pen computers. For a pen computer, a thin glass sheet is placed over the top of a standard LCD and backlight assembly (Fig. 34-6). The glass provides a wear-resistant writing surface for a pen. Glass is also treated with an anti-reflective coat-ing on its bottom surface (LCD-side), and the upper surface is gently etched with mild acid to provide paper-like friction for writing utensils. An RF pen is designed to produce a very low-power, high-frequency RF signal. The transmitter circuit might be entirely self-contained in a free pen, or contained in the computer and wired to the pen through a tether cable (depending on the designer's particular preference).

The central element in an RF digitizer is the "sensor" PC board. Signals generated by the pen must be detected and converted to X and Y coordinates. The pen transmitter itself is usually powered by one or more batteries, but the very low transmission power allows hundreds of operating hours. Sensor PC boards are five-layer boards fabricated as multi-layer PC boards. Four board layers are dedicated to signal detection, and one layer serves as the ground plane. A ground plane is needed to prevent pen signals from causing interference with motherboard circuitry.

Each board layer is etched with sensing coils—two layers sense in the X direction, and two layers sense in the Y orientation. The actual patterns and physical layout of these copper trace loops are patented because they define the performance characteristics of the digitizer module. Whenever pen transmissions are detected, the digitizer is activated, and it scans across the active digitizing area to determine pen position. The pen also transmits serial pulses that indicate its switch positions and battery level(s). The 3D sensing structure developed in an RF digitizer can also detect pen proximity and tilt (usually up to 45 degrees from perpendicular).

Sensor PC boards must be mounted within 13 mm (0.5") below the writing surface. Because the digitizer PC board is the last part of the display section (below the LCD and backlight), you can count on a very dense, precise assembly. It is crucially important that you are cautious when disassembling and reassembling the digitizer. Be certain to maintain all mounting positions and clearances. Erroneous reassembly can easily upset the digitizer's operation. The digitizer can detect the pen transmitter up to 25 mm (1.0") above the writing surface.

Electromagnetic shielding and the placement of metals are also important concerns in RF digitizer systems. Be sure to replace any and all ground planes or shields before testing a

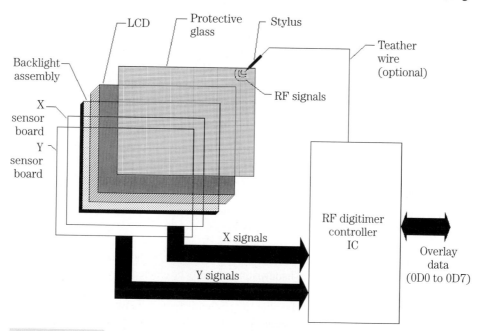

FIGURE 34-6   An electromagnetic (RF) digitizer.

reassembled digitizer. Not only is it necessary to replace shields around and behind the digitizer, it is not allowed to add any metal within the digitizer assembly. Metals between the writing surface and sensor PC board will interfere with the pen signal and cause erroneous operation. Even the step-up transformer used in a CCFT backlight power supply must be shielded to prevent unwanted electromagnetic signals from causing faulty operation. Now that you have a basic understanding of the major pen digitizer techniques, you should learn a few details about pen/panel interaction.

A Pen Environment

The pen environment is almost entirely software dependent. It is the computer's operating system that provides the driver programs and routines for writing and working with the pen. Experienced Windows or PenPoint programmers can also write application programs that recognize and utilize the pen. Of course, a pen computer will usually run software that does not use the pen. Such programs are known as *pen-oblivious applications*. To make the program useful, however, input will have to be provided from elsewhere (i.e., an external keyboard or mouse). The next level of software is capable of checking for and using a pen, if one is available, but will run with external input if a pen is not available—much the same way that many DOS programs check for the presence of a mouse and use it, if available. These are *pen-enhanced programs*. The highest level of pen software supports all pen functions and gestures, as well as the capture and recognition of written input. Such pen-dependent applications are called *pen-centric programs*. As a technician, you should expect to see several different layers of software, depending on the ways that a pen-tablet (or touchpad) is being used:

- If the pen tablet or touchpad is being used simply as a mouse replacement, chances are that you'll only need a low-level DOS or Windows 95 mouse-emulation driver. In some cases (depending in the format of serial data), an ordinary serial mouse driver will work just as well. For a touchpad, this is about all you'll need.
- If your pen tablet or touchpad unit supports multiple input devices simultaneously, you'll also find a WINTAB driver in the system to support multiple input devices.
- The pen tablet or touchpad might support signature capture/security software.
- Pen tablets often include a type of *Control-panel* applet used to adjust the tablet's features and sensitivity settings, as well as low-level diagnostic to test the tablet's output.
- Handwriting recognition requires additional software for the pen tablet. You'll need handwriting-recognition software (drivers) for the operating system, as well as an operating system extension, such as Windows for Pen Computing (3.1, 3.11, or 95) or CIC PenDOS under MS-DOS or PC-DOS.

Just how a pen's movements are interpreted depend on how the program divides the screen graphically. For example, handwriting can only be entered into certain, pre-defined areas of the display, and gestures can only be interpreted outside of those handwriting areas—how else would the computer be able to tell the difference between the two? To understand why this is important, you should see a bit more about the two major pen input modes: gestures and glyphs.

GESTURES

For anyone who has never worked with pen computers or pen tablets before, the change from keyboards to pens requires somewhat of a mental jump backwards. Instead of interacting with the computer by entering text or individual keystrokes, or using a mouse to "click" and "drag" items around the screen, pen systems rely on a series of movements (called *gestures*). A gesture is a type of motion or sequence of subsequent motions that the computer's operating system recognizes and uses. Gestures can be used for two general purposes: editing and navigation. *Editing* gestures affect information. For example, an "X" motion made through a word can delete that word, while drawing a line under a word or sentence can select the text for character enhancement (i.e., italic, bold, etc.). *Navigation* gestures are used primarily to interact with the pen operating system. As an example, *tapping* on a menu choice might cause a new option bar to be displayed, but tapping and *holding* a screen item can allow you to move an item around the screen—rather like the "click" and "drag" of a mouse or trackball. Figure 34-7 illustrates the suite of pen gestures for both the Windows for Pen Computing (PenWindows) and PenPoint pen-based operating systems.

The variations in gestures between operating systems might prove to be a source of some confusion, so you should always be aware of your computer's operating system before beginning a repair. Remember, just because a gesture does not work does not indicate a fault in the computer—you might be performing the gesture incorrectly. Even though pen-computers and their operating systems strive to be intuitive, their tolerance in accepting gestures is limited.

GLYPHS

The process of acquiring a handwritten image, translating the image into individual characters or commands, and sending the translated image to an actual application program

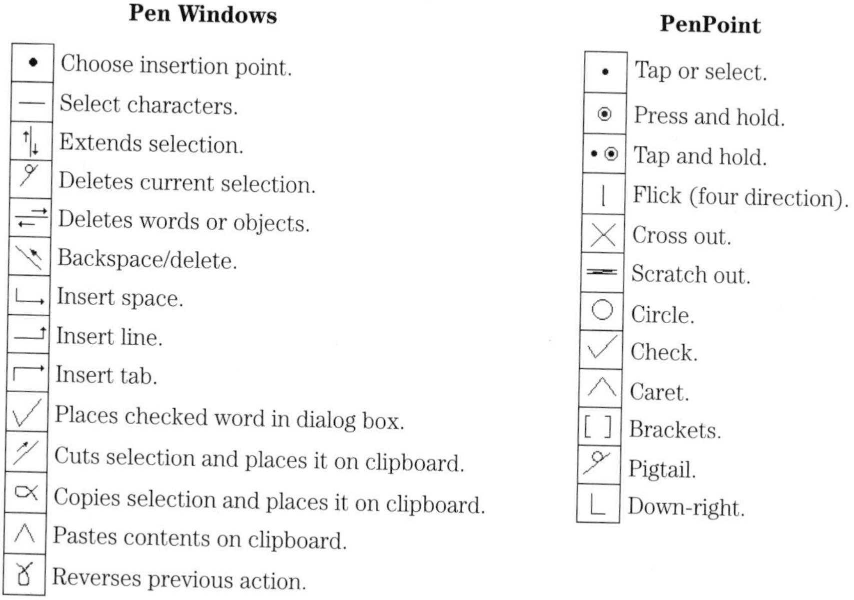

Pen Windows

•	Choose insertion point.
—	Select characters.
↑↓	Extends selection.
℘	Deletes current selection.
⇌	Deletes words or objects.
↘	Backspace/delete.
⌞→	Insert space.
⌐↑	Insert line.
⌐→	Insert tab.
√	Places checked word in dialog box.
∥	Cuts selection and places it on clipboard.
∝	Copies selection and places it on clipboard.
∧	Pastes contents on clipboard.
ඊ	Reverses previous action.

PenPoint

•	Tap or select.
⊙	Press and hold.
• ⊙	Tap and hold.
|	Flick (four direction).
✕	Cross out.
══	Scratch out.
○	Circle.
✓	Check.
∧	Caret.
[ ]	Brackets.
℘	Pigtail.
∟	Down-right.

FIGURE 34-7 Comparison of typical pen gestures.

(such as a word processor) is an unbelievably involved and complex software process, which is well beyond the scope of this book. However, you should have some understanding of the basic steps involved. The algorithms used to evaluate handwritten input are improving constantly.

The first step is to provide a known, rectangular area of the display, where handwriting can be entered. In the PenWindows environment, this is usually accomplished by opening a small working window. Whenever pen contact is registered within the handwriting window, the master pen device driver software tracks the pen's motion. As it tracks, the device driver calls a display driver program, which echoes the pen's path—this is the "ink" that you see on the display. The pen driver then stores the X and Y coordinates at the beginning and end of each pen stroke. Every alphanumeric character is composed of one or more unique strokes.

A recognition program organizes each set of strokes into an item called a *glyph*. Glyphs are then matched against a set of prototype glyphs, and every possible corresponding character for a glyph is recorded as a symbol graph. The symbol graph is passed along to another program that adds extra information about the glyph (i.e., text in a word processor, numbers in a spreadsheet, etc.) and a customized dictionary evaluates the enhanced symbol graph and determines the likeliest translation, which is finally passed to the actual application program (i.e., the word processor) utilizing the handwriting feature. The processing overhead required to handle handwriting recognition is quite demanding, so it is not yet possible to recognize written characters in real time. There will be delays between the writing and the result (though improved computer power is speeding this process considerably). This section is certainly not comprehensive, but perhaps you will have an appreciation for pen software, and how important it is for hardware and software to work together.

Troubleshooting Pen Systems

The great advantage to pen systems is modularity. Only four components are in a digitizer: the tablet, the pen, the tablet controller, and the bus-interface ASIC. When trouble occurs in the pen system, your problem is almost always located in at least one of these four operating areas. For resistive digitizers, most of the wear and tear in a pen digitizer occurs in the pen and tablet, so you will probably find that most problems occur there. Other digitizer technologies, however, have virtually no wear between the pen and glass writing surface. Typical problems with electrostatic and RF digitizers involve the pen and its cable (if a cable is used). The following notes and symptoms will give you some additional insights.

CLEANING A PEN-TABLET OR TOUCHPAD

Pen tablets and touchpads are both solid-state devices, and there are virtually no moving parts (other than a few buttons). Tablet and touchpad surfaces are extremely durable, and should require no maintenance, but it is important to keep the working surface clean. In most cases, you can clean a touchpad or pen tablet by dampening a clean lint-free cloth with demineralized water or isopropyl alcohol, then gently wiping the working surface clean (be sure to turn off the PC first). See that the working surface is completely dry before restoring power to the PC. Under no circumstances should you ever use harsh chemicals or cleansers to clean a pen-tablet or touchpad.

Do not soak the pen tablet or touchpad surface.

INK AND VIDEO DRIVERS

Pen systems echo the position of a pen by displaying pixels on the screen that mark the pen's travel. This is known as the *ink*. In some cases, you'll notice that the pen's cursor moves, and handwriting recognition proceeds properly, but no "ink trails" are left behind as you move the pen. This is almost always because of an issue with the video driver. Be sure that your video driver is compatible with pen tablets. It might be necessary to download and install an updated video driver from the video board manufacturer.

PEN TIPS AND BATTERIES

Pen issues make up a surprising number of pen-tablet problems. Although pen surfaces generate little wear and tear on the tip, wear is a factor in pen maintenance. The constant clicking and doubleclicking can also wear the tip shaft within the pen. Wear can make it difficult to click and drag with the pen. Always be sure that the pen contains a fresh tip, and is responsive to basic "clicking" and "dragging" gestures.

Many capacitive and RF digitizers incorporate active circuitry in the pen (or pen), and this circuitry is run by batteries in the pen. When these batteries approach exhaustion, the pen's signals weaken, which can result in all manner of erratic pen-tablet behavior. Always see that the pen contains fresh batteries (or try a new pen).

If the pen is tethered to a tablet via a cable, pen problems can often be traced to cable wear and intermittent contacts. The constant bending and flexing of a cable can eventually result in wiring faults. In this case, try a new pen-tablet to correct the pen problems.

PEN-TABLET SYMPTOMS

Symptom 34-1. The pen seems to operate intermittently as it moves along the surface When you slide a pen across the tablet, some portions of the stroke might not be visible as ink feedback on the display. In other cases, entire strokes might be missing while other strokes are fully visible. Fortunately, the ink that does appear shows up in the right places. This problem can be maddening—especially when attempting to write cursive characters. Resistive digitizers are extremely sensitive to pen contact. Be certain to hold the pen gently, but firmly, in contact. A careless touch might allow bad contact between the tablet and pen.

Such a symptom is almost always the result of a faulty pen cable. Remove your pen from its input jack, open the pen body and jack (if possible), and use your multimeter to check the continuity along each cable wire. Once your multimeter is connected, wiggle the cable to stimulate any intermittent wiring. If your pen cable is hard wired into the tablet, you should remove the tablet's outer housing to expose the cable wiring. If you encounter a faulty pen, repair or replace the defective wiring, or replace the pen altogether.

If your pen checks out properly (or is not cabled to begin with), check the pen batteries, replace the pen tip, or try a new pen entirely. Next, suspect that a fault is in your resistive tablet. Both single-layer and double-layer resistive digitizers are extremely prone to wear. As the pen wears out, tablet resistance and surface features might become irregular. Your pen might not make proper contact at all points of a worn surface. Try replacing the resistive tablet. Some small-computer manufacturers sell tablet assemblies as component parts. Use extreme caution when replacing an tablet to avoid accidental damage to the LCD or backlight assemblies. Take careful notes and pay close attention to maintain proper assembly dimensions.

For capacitive or RF digitizers, the sensing assembly is very rarely at fault because writing occurs against a sheet of thin, tempered glass. Intermittent writing performance with a capacitive or RF digitizer is usually the result of a faulty pen transmitter. Check or replace the pen batteries and try the system again. If the problem persists, try a new pen.

Symptom 34-2. The pen or tablet does not appear to respond at all Other computer functions seem normal. The external keyboard adapter (if available) appears to work properly. Before you check anything else, be sure that the pen or tablet is properly connected to the computer. Also be sure that the pen tip is in good contact with the tablet surface. Good contact is crucial for resistive digitizers. A careless touch might allow bad contact between an tablet and pen—especially when the tablet surface is worn. For RF digitizers, you should suspect the pen transmitter first. Check the batteries or cabling to your pen. Replace the batteries (if necessary) and try the system again. Otherwise, try a new pen.

An open pen cable wire can easily disable your pen input (if the pen is tethered). Remove your pen from its input jack, open the pen body and jack (if possible), and use your multimeter to measure continuity along each cable wire. Once your multimeter is connected, wiggle the cable to stimulate any possible intermittent wiring. Repair or replace any faulty wiring or replace the defective pen outright. If your pen cable is hard-wired into the computer, remove the pen computer's housing to expose the cable wires.

If the digitizer still does not function, suspect that the problem is in your tablet or tablet controller IC. For a stand-alone pen tablet, you can usually replace the entire tablet outright. For a pen computer, disassemble the unit to expose the motherboard, and check any cabling between the tablet and motherboard. Try replacing the tablet controller IC. If you lack the tools or inclination to perform surface-mount work, try replacing the entire motherboard. If the problem persists, try another tablet assembly.

Symptom 34-3. Ink appears on the LCD as the pen moves, but ink is not exactly under the pen This symptom occurs with older pen computers, and is much more of a nuisance than an actual defect in resistive digitizers. You might assume that the pen is working adequately. The trouble is most likely in the resistive tablet material itself. Resistance is extremely dependent on temperature and humidity. Variations in an tablet's temperature or humidity can introduce small analog voltage errors when a pen passes over the resistive surface. The net result is a small shift in the visual feedback that appears on the LCD. You can do little with temperature or humidity problems, except to keep the pen computer in a stable, consistent room environment. If the tablet is damp for any reason, be certain to dry its surface very carefully.

Problems can also occur when the tablet is extremely worn. As resistive material becomes thinner, its resistance at the thinner areas becomes greater. Worn areas can upset the overall resistance of the tablet and result in erroneous voltage signals at the pen. Again, such errors are digitized and appear somewhere in the display. Your best course of action with a worn resistive tablet is simply to replace it entirely. Use extreme caution when replacing an tablet to avoid accidental damage to the LCD or backlight, and to maintain all dimensional tolerances in the assembly.

Symptom 34-4. The pen-computer locks up or suffers other strange problems once the RF digitizer has been repaired or replaced This kind of a follow-up problem is not unusual for pen computers using RF digitizers. The RF sensor PC board located behind the backlight must be re-installed exactly as it was removed. No metal objects can be added or removed. Be sure that any and all shielding is installed properly. Missing or damaged shields can allow stray RF signals to reach the motherboard and cause peculiar EMI problems that result in system crashes and intermittent bad data. It only takes one bad bit to crash a computer. Also inspect the way in which the display and digitizer arrangement has been reassembled. Missing spacers or loose screws can change the physical spacing of the display components and also result in system problems.

It is important that no metal objects be added to the display/digitizer assembly as well. Metal acts as a shield that can interfere with RF signals. The presence of unwanted metal might cause trouble in pen tracking and system operation. Remove any metal that might have been added to the system or digitizer. It is worthwhile to keep thorough notes when working on a display/digitizer system. Notes help to ensure that you reassemble the small-computer exactly as it should be.

Symptom 34-5. As you write, no "ink" appears on the display, but the characters are recognized and translated properly This is almost invariably a problem with the Windows/Windows 95 video driver. When the pen operating system is installed—especially as an extension, such as Microsoft Pen Extensions for Windows (there are versions for 3.1, 3.11, and 95), the video driver will be required to produce the "ink." Unfortunately, not all video drivers interact so smoothly with pen-enhanced or pen-centric applications, and an "ink" trail is not left under the pen. Although hardly damaging, it can be a significant nuisance. Try a video driver that is designed to deal with pen operations. In actuality, this might be difficult because many pen-compatible video drivers do not provide extended color depths or resolutions that many Windows users have come to expect. Check with the pen-tablet vendor and video-adapter manufacturer for a "pen aware" video driver.

Symptom 34-6. The DOS pen driver(s) will not load as the system initializes This is typical of external, stand-alone tablets, and is often indicated by an error code or message when the PC initializes—usually because the tablet hardware cannot be located. First, be sure that the tablet is turned on (if necessary) and receiving power. Next, check that the tablet is connected properly to its serial port, and that the COM number and IRQ number correspond to any command-line settings used to execute the driver. For example, suppose the tablet driver is being started in your CONFIG.SYS file and its command line says that the driver should be installed for COM1 using IRQ3. If the tablet is plugged into COM2, the driver will probably not be able to load.

Symptom 34-7. The pen buttons do not work correctly in your software Button assignments for a stand-alone pen tablet are typically made in the tablet device driver's command line (in CONFIG.SYS or AUTOEXEC.BAT). Check the command line against your pen tablet's documentation and be sure that any button assignments are correct. Check your particular application as well to see if any options control button functions. If your application allows you to select a pointing device, you can usually keep the Microsoft Mouse selection.

Symptom 34-8. The pen tablet does not work in Windows   This problem often surfaces with stand-alone pen tablets. If the tablet works with DOS applications (or its diagnostic), the problem is likely caused by a Windows driver conflict. Check the device driver used in Windows setup (or the Windows 95 *Device manager*) and verify that the appropriate driver is selected to support the tablet. Many tablets give you the option of using the tablet as the sole pointing device, or using both the tablet and mouse together (you might also need a WINTAB driver to support multiple simultaneous input devices). The driver used with the tablet will depend on whether the tablet is used alone or with a mouse.

Symptom 34-9. Windows locks-up or the tablet fails to respond   This type of problem might show up intermittently and is generally related to the cursor speed that is set through the Windows *Control panel*. When the tablet is set to work in relative mode and the cursor speed is set to fast, older PCs might not be able to respond to button clicks or pen movement fast enough under some circumstances. This condition almost always results in a fault that can crash Windows or its application. The easiest way to correct this type of problem is to reduce the cursor sensitivity to a low level (50% or so) when working in the relative mode. Most pen tablets designed to work with Windows/Windows 95 provide a Windows utility (i.e., a *Tablet control panel*), which allows you to adjust the tablet parameters.

Symptom 34-10. The cursor is too sensitive or not sensitive enough to pen movement   When operating a stand-alone tablet in the "relative" mode, you might need to reduce the cursor-sensitivity parameter. When working in the "absolute" mode, you can adjust sensitivity by altering the size of the cursor's active area. Most stand-alone pen tablets designed to work in Windows/Windows 95 provide a Windows adjustment utility (i.e., *Tablet control panel*), which allows you to adjust the tablet parameters, such as sensitivity and active area.

Symptom 34-11. The cursor seems to "jitter" or leave spikes when drawing   This type of problem is usually related to the serial port (COM port) being used with the stand-alone pen tablet. Older serial ports using the 8250 or 8250A UARTs have a subtle bug that the Windows/Windows 95 environments tend to find. The older serial port does not support current tablets as well as current serial ports. Running Windows 3.1x in the "standard" mode can sometimes improve the situation, but the very best solution is to replace the older UART (or entire serial port) with a current version (you can usually install a new multi-I/O board with high-speed serial ports, but remember to disable the older existing serial ports).

Symptom 34-12. No matter what "stroke width" is chosen in the drawing application, only thin, narrow lines appear when drawing on the pen tablet   This type of issue arises most often with "pressure sensitive" applications like PhotoShop 4, and non-pressure-sensitive tablets like AceCAD tablets. In many cases, the drawing application assumes that your tablet/digitizer is "pressure sensitive" by default—when in fact the pen tablet is not. If the tablet is not pressure sensitive, be sure to turn off the pressure-sensitivity feature in the drawing application (you'll need to select line widths manually). If the tablet is supposed to be pressure sensitive, verify that the tablet and its drivers are configured properly for pressure-sensitive operation. Also check the pen for proper operation.

Symptom 34-13. After installing the latest pen tablet drivers for Windows 95, you get an: "Invalid Dynamic Link call to a .DLL file" error once the PC restarts In many cases, this kind of error message is generated as the result of a conflict between the WINTAB driver for your pen tablet and the "video capture" driver for your video board (i.e., these problems often crop up with Diamond Stealth 64 PCI video cards). You must remove the offending video capture driver. For the example of a Diamond video capture driver:

- Open your *Control panel*, then select *Multimedia*.
- Under *Multimedia*, select *Advanced*, then click the "plus sign" just to the left of *Video-capture devices*.
- Highlight the *Diamond video capture* entry (or the capture device for your particular video board), then click *Properties*.
- Under *Properties*, click *Remove* to remove the driver.

If you get the error message again, simply go back through the process one more time (the second time around, it should let you remove the driver without incident). Restart Windows 95 and the problem should be gone.

Symptom 34-14. Installing the pen tablet on a Packard Bell PC results in various errors Error messages often start out, such as: "While initializing device PBCIR . . .", and the system winds up starting in safe mode. Such problems are almost always the result of Packard Bell's "Remote Media Card." The following workaround will often get the pen tablet up and running, but it will disable the IrDA ("infra-red") functionality of this card—you can restore the card by just reversing this process:

1 Shut down the computer and turn it off.
2 Restart the computer. When you see the message: "Starting Windows 95," press the <F8> key.
3 When you see the Windows 95 startup menu, select *Command prompt only* and press the <Enter> key.
4 At the C: \> prompt, type CD WINDOWS and press the <Enter> key.
5 At the C:\WINDOWS\> prompt, type EDIT SYSTEM.INI and press the <Enter> key.
6 You will now be looking at the [boot] section of your Windows 95 system.ini file. Find the section entitled [386Enh].
7 Look for a line in the [386Enh] section that says DEVICE=PBEWD01S.VXD. When you find this line, type a semicolon (;) in front of the line. The line should then read ;DEVICE=PBEWD01S.VXD
8 Save the changes to the SYSTEM.INI file and exit.
9 You should now be back at the C:\WINDOWS\> prompt. Type: edit win.ini and press the <Enter> key.

10 You will now be looking at the [windows] section of your Windows 95 win.ini file.

11 Look for a line in the [Windows] section that says RUN=C:\FMEDIA\FMEDIA.EXE. When you find this line, type a semicolon (;) in front of the line. The line should then read ;RUN=C:\FMEDIA\FMEDIA.EXE (it might be necessary to delete this line entirely).

12 Save the changes to the WIN.INI file and exit.

13 You should now be back at the C:\WINDOWS\> prompt. Type WIN and press the <Enter> key to return to Windows.

At this point, your pen tablet should be working. However, it might be necessary to re-install the pen tablet drivers (be sure to use the most recent pen tablet drivers).

Always create backup copies of your .INI files before attempting to edit them.

Symptom 34-15. The pen cursor moves, but everything is reversed For example, when the pen moves up, the cursor moves down. The tablet also "thinks" it's the wrong size (i.e., 12" × 12" instead of 5" × 5"). This is usually because you're running a tablet-sizing utility when you shouldn't be. For example, AceCAD tablets can suffer this problem when mistakenly running the ACE12 utility. Open your AUTOEXEC.BAT file and verify that the proper command line switches are in place. For the AceCAD example, copy ACE12.COM from the ACE12 sub-directory on your drivers/utilities diskette to your C:directory, then add/modify the following line to your AUTOEXEC.BAT file:

```
C:\WINDOWS\COMMAND\ACE12.COM U     (If your tablet is on COM1)
C:\WINDOWS\COMMAND\ACE12.COM U2    (If your tablet is on COM2)
```

Reboot your computer—the problem should be gone.

Symptom 34-16. The pen is not "selecting" or "inking" In virtually all cases, the fault is with the pen. If the pen is tethered to the tablet, check the pen wiring. If the pen is "free," try replacing the pen batteries. Also check the pen tip, and be sure that the pen tip is not sticking out or is loose inside the pen. Carefully unscrew the pen cap and inspect the battery casing for cracks. If the problem persists, try another pen.

Symptom 34-17. The cursor flickers in Windows 95 Handwriting recognition works, but the "ink" often gets cut off. This problem sometimes occurs when 16-bit applications (written for Windows 3.1x) are running under Windows 95. The cause is a minor incompatibility between the 16-bit application and Microsoft's Pen Services 2.0 for Windows 95. Turn off any 16-bit applications. If possible, upgrade the application from the 16-bit version to the 32-bit equivalent.

Symptom 34-18. The cursor is moving, selecting items, or otherwise behaving strangely—even though the pen is not touching the tablet Chances are that the tablet and pen operate at a frequency that might be shared by some monitors—this can cause the tablet to become "confused" if it is placed too close to the monitor. Be sure that the tablet is not physically located too close to the monitor (keep it at least 12 inches away). Another possible cause for odd cursor behavior is weak pen batteries. Try replacing the batteries.

Symptom 34-19. There is no "inking" and handwriting recognition doesn't work If you cannot see ink on the screen, or if you cannot get handwriting recognition to work, check the following points:

■ In Windows 95, click *Start*, then *Run*. Point to the *Open* edit box. If you do not see a pen pointer, you need to install the operating system pen extensions (e.g., Microsoft Pen Extensions for Windows 95).

■ Try writing in the *Open* edit box. If you do not see "ink," try writing in Notepad or WordPad. If you still do not get "inking" in these apps, reinstall the operating system pen extensions.

■ If you see a pen pointer, try selecting text in the edit box. If the pen pointer does not change to an inverted arrow pointer, reinstall the operating system pen extensions.

■ Check your video driver and notice the driver you are using (some drivers do not support pen environments well). Set your video to VGA, 16 colors. Try inking and/or handwriting-recognition again. If it works, update your video driver with a version that will support "ink."

■ If you are still not getting handwriting recognition and/or "inking," try uninstalling the pen tablet's low-level software. Disable all TSRs (virus checkers, etc.) and reinstall the pen tablet's low-level software again.

Symptom 34-20. The pen does not work properly in Microsoft Word using Windows 95 Pen Computing A number of known problems occur with Windows 95 for Pen Computing and MS Word for Windows 95 (v 7.0a) and MS Word 97. Check with Microsoft (**http://www.microsoft.com**) for updates to either Word or the operating system that might overcome these problems. The following gestures do not work:

■ Edit Text (check mark circled)
■ Insert Text (caret circled)
■ Context Menu (M circled) or can't right-click for Context menus (to work around this problem, press <Shift>+<F10> with the pen at the point you want a context menu).
■ Select (lasso tap)

In addition, the following symptoms and problems might be experienced:

■ The Pen Windows display does not refresh correctly when the pen is near the digitizer pad. To work around this problem, keep the pen away from the digitizer pad when not in use.

■ When the pen is near the digitizer pad and the pen barrel button is pressed, the insertion point changes to an I-beam.

■ The pen "drag handle" is not shown. This is a small button that floats along with the insertion point, allowing access to a context menu and easier access with a pen.

Symptom 34-21. An "Invalid VxD dynamic link call" error occurs when trying to install pen-tablet software under Windows 95 For example, such problems might cause an error, such as "Invalid VxD dynamic link call from CICPEN(01) + 0000431D to device 'VCD', service 4" while trying to install CIC Handwriter software under Windows 95." Normally, an Invalid Dynamic Link Call error message is the result of an incompatibility between driver versions, or a damaged or missing driver. Try uninstalling, then reinstalling any programs or components that you installed recently. You might also workaround this problem by bypassing the VCD (creating an additional binary entry in your Win95 Registry):

■ Run the Regedit utility.
■ Select HKEY_LOCAL_MACHINE
■ Create a new binary entry.
■ Enter "PORTPROTECTION."
■ Assign a value of "0."
■ Save the changes and reboot.

> Always make a backup copy of your Registry files before attempting to edit them.

Symptom 34-22. An error appears: "VxD not present: either Windows 95 is running in safe mode or xxx.VxD is not installed correctly" This .VxD file is not loaded if you are running Windows 95 in safe mode. If you are not in safe mode, be sure that the named driver (i.e., CICPenC.VxD) is present in your directory. Try reinstalling the pen-tablet software.

Symptom 34-23. The pen tablet works intermittently on a laptop If your particular pen tablet (such as the CIC Handwriter Manta) has been designed to draw power from the serial port (RS232), the port might have a power-draw limitation (desktop PCs do not suffer this problem). For example, CIC has encountered some laptops that have power draw problems with their Manta. To conserve power, the laptop's current draw is reduced to the load so that the tablet stops working after a certain time. The following lists the laptops CIC has identified as having this power-draw issue:

■ IBM 750cs
■ Gateway 2000 SOLO (REV 3)
■ Samsung Sens Pro
■ Winbook Fx
■ Hitachi Mx
■ Dell Latitude

Check with the pen tablet maker to see if a supplemental power supply or other patch might alleviate this problem.

Symptom 34-24. After installing a pen tablet driver, the cursor moves very slowly This is an issue with some Wacom drivers and it is almost always caused by problems with the video driver. Many of the current video drivers have cursor problems in high-resolution modes because of the amount of data that is being produced by the pen tablet. For example, a Wacom tablet produces approximately four times more data than a standard mouse, and the video drivers cannot keep up with the amount of data being transmitted. You should try to update your video driver to a version that is more compatible with high-resolution pen tablets. In the mean time, do not run with an enlarged or animated cursor. If cursor performance is still slow, reduce the color palette to 256 colors or less until the video driver can be updated.

Symptom 34-25. After installing a pen tablet driver, SCSI devices are no longer present This is almost always a pen-tablet driver problem, and it is a known problem with Wacom pen tablet drivers prior to version 2.44. Try installing the latest version of the pen-tablet driver (check with the pen-tablet manufacturer for the latest version). For the Wacom pen tablets, install the v.2.44 driver, then restart to MS-DOS mode. From the Wacom 2.44 driver disk, copy the SCSI.FIX file such as:

```
c:\XXXXX\win\3195\>copy scsi.fix c:\windows\system\wacom.vxd
```

where *XXXXX* is the directory where the Wacom driver was extracted. You should be prompted to replace the WACOM.VXD file. Select *Yes* to replace the file. Restart Windows and try the SCSI devices again. If you expanded the patch file to a floppy disk, restart to MS-DOS mode, place the floppy in the floppy drive, and from the c:\windows> prompt type:

```
c:\windows>copy a:\win\3195\scsi.fix c:\windows\system\wacom.vxd
```

You should be prompted to replace the WACOM.VXD file. Select *Yes* to replace the file.

Symptom 34-26. When you place a pen against the tablet surface, the cursor jumps to the top left corner of the screen You also might see an error, such as: "unable to implement function." In most cases, this occurs after upgrading pen tablet hardware, and is caused by "leftover" pen-tablet drivers from other manufacturers. You'll need to remove the "leftover" driver(s):

■ *Removing ACECAT drivers* Edit your SYSTEM.INI file, go to the drivers= line in the [boot] section and remove AWINTAB, then go to the [drivers] section and remove the line that reads: AWINTAB=AWINTAB.DRV. Also look for any reference to "Virtual Tablet" and remove it. Save the changes to SYSTEM.INI and restart Windows 95.
■ *Removing KURTA drivers* Edit your SYSTEM.INI, look for references to WTKURTA, and remove them. Save your changes to SYSTEM.INI and restart Windows 95.

Symptom 34-27. After installing a pen-tablet driver, .AVI files do not open This sometimes occurs with Wacom drivers, and is caused by a module in DirectX v.2.0. You should remove this module and install a newer version of DirectX. To remove the module, open the *Multimedia* control panel, select *Advanced*, then open the *Video-compression codecs* folder, highlight the *DirectVideo driver* [Draw] entry and click on the *Properties* button. Select the *Remove* button, close the *Control panel*, and restart Windows 95.

TOUCHPAD SYMPTOMS

Symptom 34-28. You notice that the system slows after installing touchpad drivers in Windows 95 In almost all cases, this is caused by a conflict between touchpad drivers and older (pre-existing) mouse drivers. You'll need to isolate and remove the older mouse drivers:

- Shut down the PC (you might need to just turn the PC off, if you can't exit normally).
- Reboot the PC and press <F8> when you see "Starting Windows 95".
- You should now see the "Windows 95 Start-up Menu".
- Start the PC in the safe mode.
- Open the Windows 95 *Control panel*.
- With the *Control panel* open, doubleclick on the *Add/Remove programs* icon.
- In the list of programs available for removal, find the reference to the old mouse software (e.g., Mouseware or Logitech Mouseware) and highlight it by clicking on it once.
- Click on the *Add/Remove* button.
- The old software should uninstall (e.g., Mouseware Setup will initialize and prompt you to confirm removal).
- Windows should uninstall the software and prompt you that the computer needs to be restarted. Click the *Restart* button.
- The computer will restart and begin loading Windows 95 (you might see added information about the software's removal—this is normal).
- The system will boot into normal mode and should be functioning normally.

Symptom 34-29. The touchpad cursor freezes in the center of the screen after installing the driver(s) You might also see this as a "Windows protection error" after installing the driver(s) under Windows 95. This is usually caused by an improper mouse driver reference in SYSTEM.INI. You'll need to edit SYSTEM.INI manually without the benefit of the mouse:

- Press <Ctrl> and <Esc> together to bring up your Windows 95 *Start menu*.
- Use your arrow keys to move the highlight to *Run*, then press <Enter>.
- In the text box next to *Open*, type `SYSEDIT` and press <Enter>.
- The *Sysedit* window will appear, displaying your system files.
- Press <Alt> and <W> together to display a menu listing your system files.
- Use your arrow keys to move the highlight down to the line that has SYSTEM.INI in it, then press <Enter>.
- Use your arrow keys to scroll through the system.ini file until you find a line reading: [386enh].
- Find the line that reads `mouse=c:\glide\xmvmd.386`.
- Change this line to read `mouse=*vmd`.
- After you have made this change to the system.ini file, press the <Alt> and <F> keys together. This will bring down the *File* menu.
- Use your arrow keys to move the highlight down to *Exit*, then press <Enter>.
- Windows will display a dialog box stating that the SYSTEM.INI file has been changed and will ask if you want to save these changes. Select *Yes*.
- After the *Sysedit* window has closed, press <Ctrl> and <Esc> together to bring up the Windows 95 *Start menu*.
- Use your arrow keys to move the highlight up to *Shut down*, then press <Enter>.

- Use your arrow keys to select *Restart the computer* from the *Shut down* dialog, then press <Enter>.
- Windows will restart the system and the cursor should now move with the touchpad.

Symptom 34-30. The touchpad and software were installed, but it refuses to operate—the mouse continues to operate Most touchpad drivers (such as for the Cirque GlidePoint) only accommodate one pointing device. If you still have an external mouse connected, unplug it and reboot your computer. If your computer has a built-in pointing device, consult your computer manual for instructions on disabling the device.

   If you have no way to disable the existing mouse, you might also be able to edit the touchpad's .INI file to specify how the touchpad is connected. For example, a Cirque touchpad uses the GLIDE.INI (or MOUSE.INI) file in the Cirque GlidePoint directory. The line that reads MOUSETYPE= should be changed to indicate the port in which the touchpad is installed. If the touchpad is on a serial port, the line should read MOUSE-TYPE=SERIAL1 or MOUSETYPE=SERIAL2. If the touchpad is on a PS/2 port, the line would read MOUSETYPE=PS2.

Further Study

That's it for Chapter 34. Be sure to review the glossary and chapter questions on the accompanying CD. If you have access to the Internet, take a look at some of these pen and tablet resources:

AceCAD: **http://www.acecad.com**

CCI: **http://www.cic.com**

Cirque: **http://www.cirque.com**

Glidepoint: **http://www.glidepoint.com**

Kurta/Mutoh: **http://www.mutoh.com**

Pen Computing Magazine: **http://www.pencomputing.com/**

35

PLUG-AND-PLAY CONFIGURATION

AND TROUBLESHOOTING

CONTENTS AT A GLANCE

Understanding PnP under Windows 95
  PnP devices
  PnP BIOS
  PnP operating system
  An overview of PnP behavior
  Device types and identification
  Detection vs. enumeration
  Legacy devices

Enabling PnP Under DOS
  The PnP configuraton driver
  The PnP configuration utility
  Blaster variables
  Potential problems with generic
   PnP configuration software

Potential problems with
  manufacturer's PnP software
Handling PnP configuraiton issues
  under DOS

Managing and Troubleshooting PnP Devices
  Installing PnP devices
  Installing legacy devices
  Updating device drivers
  Installing modems manually
  Installing printers manually
  Disabling a device
  Removing a device
  Symptoms

Further Study

One of the key appeals to the IBM-type personal computer architecture is its functional modularity—its ability to accept a variety of expansion devices, such as modems, video controllers, drive adapters, video capture/TV boards, etc. Each device added to a system needs to be "configured" to utilize unique IRQ, DMA, and I/O resources. Traditionally, devices were configured manually using a series of jumpers on the device. Although this proved to be a straightforward approach, it also opened the way for many configuration conflicts (devices accidentally configured to use overlapping resources). Reporting utilities are also imprecise, making conflict resolution somewhat of a tedious, "hit-or-miss" process. Current operating systems typically provide better tools for conflict resolution (see Chapter 10), but resolving conflicts still demands a certain amount of patience and expertise.

Designers have long sought to "automate" this device-configuration process, removing the error-prone task of device configuration from the hands of end users and busy technicians. The results of this "automatic configuration" technology has become known as *Plug-and-Play (PnP)*. First introduced with late-model i486 systems, PnP is now a standard technology implemented in all current PCs. Although PnP simplifies much of the configuration problems with new systems, there are still many situations where PnP doesn't work perfectly (especially when running devices under DOS, or using pre-PnP devices in a PnP system). This chapter describes the requirements for PnP, outlines the special requirements for implementing PnP under DOS, and provides a series of troubleshooting points.

Understanding PnP under Windows 95

The first step in troubleshooting Plug and Play is to understand the issues involved in making it run. PnP is not one particular technology, but rather it is a combination of features all brought together. The three components are involved in a PnP system are: PnP devices, PnP BIOS, and a PnP-compliant operating system—each part must be PnP-compatible.

PNP DEVICES

A PnP system requires one or more "devices:" the modems, video adapters, chipsets, drive adapters, and a myriad of other hardware elements in the PC. Ideally, every device in the PC will be PnP-compatible, and today's systems do contain virtually all PnP devices. PnP devices are capable of identifying themselves and their resource requirements to the rest of the system. The only wrinkles occur when non-PnP (or "legacy") devices are mixed into the system hardware.

PNP BIOS

A PnP system requires a PnP BIOS—especially at boot time. Because PnP devices initialize in the inactive state by default, the PnP BIOS is needed to initialize the core PnP devices (i.e., the video adapter and boot drive) to complete the POST and launch the operating system. Also note that the original version of PnP BIOS (version 1.0) was finalized in May 1994. By October 1994, additional clarifications were added. As a consequence, older PnP systems are not fully compliant with the current specification. PnP support problems on older systems can usually be corrected with a BIOS upgrade. System PnP support can typically be enabled or disabled through the CMOS setup routine.

PNP OPERATING SYSTEM

The PnP OS takes over where the PnP BIOS leaves off by identifying and configuring the remaining PnP devices in the system, then loading the appropriate drivers needed to initialize and operate each respective device. The OS also must keep resources aside for non-PnP ("legacy") devices, and report any changes to the hardware complement in the system. Windows 95 is generally regarded as the premier PnP operating system for end-users and general-purpose PCs, but Windows NT provides PnP support for networked and business systems.

AN OVERVIEW OF PNP BEHAVIOR

Now that you've seen the essential elements of PnP, it's time to look at how it all works. A PnP system must be robust enough to handle several important functions. The major functions that must be handled by these three PnP components can be summarized as:

- *Identification of installed devices* The PnP system must be able to identify each installed device. This requires the device to have a certain amount of on-board intelligence.
- *Determination of device resource requirements* Based on the device identification, the PnP system must be able to determine the kinds of resources (IRQ, DMA, I/O addresses, or BIOS space) required to support the device.
- *Creation of a complete system configuration, eliminating all resource conflicts* After all devices have been identified, and their resource needs evaluated, the PnP system must then allocate the required resources to each device every time the system initializes (without causing a resource conflict).
- *Loading of device drivers* After the operating system starts, it then must load the appropriate device drivers needed to support every device in the system.
- *Notification of configuration changes* Each time that a PnP device is added or removed from the PC, the PnP system reports the configuration change. When a device is added, the PnP system attempts to identify it and install the appropriate device drivers. When a device is removed, the PnP system attempts to remove all traces of the device and its drivers.

The PnP system starts with the BIOS at boot time—a certain amount of configuration must first be performed by the system BIOS during system initialization. In order for the system to boot, the PnP BIOS must configure a display device, input device, and initial boot device (i.e., video adapter, keyboard, and floppy/hard drives). Then, the PnP BIOS must pass the information about each of these devices to the operating system (i.e., Windows 95) for additional configuration of the remaining system devices.

The operating system then continues the configuration process by identifying every device in the system, and gathering their respective resource requirements. Each non-boot device (i.e., modems, video capture devices) must be inactive upon power-up so that the operating system can identify any conflicts between the resource requirements of different devices before configuring them. When different devices require the same resources, the devices must be able to provide information to the operating system about alternative resource requirements. The operating system then uses initial or alternative requirements to assemble a working system configuration. Once any resource conflicts have been resolved, the operating system automatically programs each hardware device with its working configuration, then stores all configuration information in the central database contained in *ESCD (Extended System Configuration Data)* memory, which is part of CMOS RAM space. Finally, the operating system loads the device drivers for each device and notifies these drivers of each resource assignment.

If a change occurs to the system configuration during operation (for example, a device is installed or removed), the hardware must be able to notify the operating system of the event so that the operating system can configure the new device. Additionally, applications must be able to respond to configuration changes to take advantage of new devices and to cease calling devices that have been removed. Such dynamic configuration events might include the insertion of a PC Card, the addition or removal of a peripheral, such as a mouse, CD-ROM drive, printer, or a docking/undocking event for a notebook computer.

> In most cases, configuration changes are made before boot time while system power is off. Only PC card and laptop designs support "hot" insertion and removal.

DEVICE TYPES AND IDENTIFICATION

The PnP system is designed to support a wide variety of devices across a number of different bus architectures. The nine general classifications of PnP devices:

- ISA bus cards
- PCI bus cards
- Microchannel (MCA) bus cards
- VESA local bus (VLB) cards
- IDE devices (for hard drives and CD-ROM drives)
- SCSI controllers and devices
- PC Card devices
- Serial-port devices (such as modems)
- Parallel-port devices (such as printers and parallel-port drives)

For the PC to recognize and configure a PnP device, each and every device must be able to identify itself and its resource requirements to the system—even motherboard busses and devices must be able to identify themselves. Identification is accomplished through a seven-character code. Each manufacturer is assigned a three-character prefix, the following character identifies the device type, and the remaining three characters identify the particular device. For example, the PnP code PNP0907 identifies a "Western Digital VGA" device adapter. Microsoft reserves the code "PNP" for itself, but other manufacturers are assigned their own codes (e.g., Creative Labs uses the "CTL" prefix). The advantage of Microsoft's prefixes is that they are "generic," and you can usually identify a device adequately by utilizing the Microsoft generic equivalent. Table 35-1 lists the generic PnP identification categories and codes used by Microsoft.

DETECTION VS. ENUMERATION

Detection is the process Windows 95 uses during its search for legacy (non-Plug and Play) devices on a computer. Detection is used during Windows 95 setup and any time you use

TABLE 35-1   MICROSOFT PNP DEVICE IDENTIFICATION CODES

DEVICE CATEGORIES

PNP0xxx	System devices
PNP8xxx	Network adapters
PNPAxxx	SCSI, proprietary CD adapters
PNPBxxx	Sound, video capture, multimedia
PNPCxxx–Dxxx	Modems

DEVICE ID CODES

DEVICE ID	DESCRIPTION

System Devices - PNP0xxx - *Interrupt Controllers*

PNP0000	AT interrupt controller
PNP0001	EISA interrupt controller
PNP0002	MCA interrupt controller
PNP0003	APIC
PNP0004	Cyrix SLiC MP interrupt controller

System Devices - PNP0xxx - *Timers*

PNP0100	AT timer
PNP0101	EISA timer
PNP0102	MCA timer

System Devices - PNP0xxx - *DMA*

PNP0200	AT DMA controller
PNP0201	EISA DMA controller
PNP0202	MCA DMA controller

System Devices - PNP0xxx - *Keyboards*

PNP0300	IBM PC/XT keyboard controller (83-key)
PNP0301	IBM PC/AT keyboard controller (86-key)
PNP0302	IBM PC/XT keyboard controller (84-key)
PNP0303	IBM Enhanced (101/102-key, PS/2 mouse support)
PNP0304	Olivetti keyboard (83-key)
PNP0305	Olivetti keyboard (102-key)
PNP0306	Olivetti keyboard (86-key)
PNP0307	Microsoft Windows keyboard
PNP0308	General Input Device Emulation Interface (GIDEI) legacy
PNP0309	Olivetti keyboard (A101/102 key)
PNP030A	AT&T 302 keyboard
PNP030B	Reserved (by Microsoft)
PNP0320	Japanese 106-key keyboard A01
PNP0321	Japanese 101-key keyboard
PNP0322	Japanese AX keyboard
PNP0323	Japanese 106-key keyboard 002/003
PNP0324	Japanese 106-key keyboard 001
PNP0325	Japanese Toshiba desktop keyboard
PNP0326	Japanese Toshiba laptop keyboard
PNP0327	Japanese Toshiba notebook keyboard
PNP0340	Korean 84-key keyboard
PNP0341	Korean 86-key keyboard
PNP0342	Korean enhanced keyboard
PNP0343	Korean enhanced keyboard 101b
PNP0343	Korean enhanced keyboard 101c
PNP0344	Korean enhanced keyboard 103

TABLE 35-1   MICROSOFT PNP DEVICE IDENTIFICATION CODES (CONTINUED)

System Devices - PNP0xxx - *Parallel Devices*

PNP0400	Standard LPT printer port
PNP0401	ECP printer port

System Devices - PNP0xxx - *Serial Devices*

PNP0500	Standard PC COM port
PNP0501	16550A-compatible COM port
PNP0502	Multiport serial device (non-intelligent 16550)
PNP0510	Generic IRDA-compatible device

System Devices - PNP0xxx - *Disk Controllers*

PNP0600	Generic ESDI/IDE/ATA compatible hard-disk controller
PNP0601	Plus Hardcard II
PNP0602	Plus Hardcard IIXL/EZ
PNP0603	Generic IDE supporting Microsoft device bay specification
PNP0700	PC standard floppy-disk controller
PNP0701	Standard floppy controller supporting Microsoft device bay spec.

System Devices - PNP0xxx - *Early Sound Systems*

PNP0802	Microsoft Sound System device (now obsolete—use PNPB0xx instead)

System Devices - PNP0xxx - *Display Adapters*

PNP0900	VGA compatible
PNP0901	Video Seven VRAM/VRAM II/1024i
PNP0902	8514/A compatible
PNP0903	Trident VGA
PNP0904	Cirrus Logic laptop VGA
PNP0905	Cirrus Logic VGA
PNP0906	Tseng ET4000
PNP0907	Western Digital VGA
PNP0908	Western Digital laptop VGA
PNP0909	S3 Inc. 911/924
PNP090A	ATI Ultra Pro/Plus (Mach 32)
PNP090B	ATI Ultra (Mach 8)
PNP090C	XGA compatible
PNP090D	ATI VGA Wonder
PNP090E	Weitek P9000 graphics adapter
PNP090F	Oak Technology VGA
PNP0910	Compaq QVision
PNP0911	XGA/2
PNP0912	Tseng Labs W32/W32i/W32p
PNP0913	S3 Inc. 801/928/964
PNP0914	Cirrus Logic 5429/5434 (memory mapped)
PNP0915	Compaq Advanced VGA (AVGA)
PNP0916	ATI Ultra Pro Turbo (Mach64)
PNP0917	Reserved (by Microsoft)
PNP0918	Matrox MGA
PNP0919	Compaq QVision 2000
PNP091A	Tseng W128
PNP0930	Chips & Technologies Super VGA
PNP0931	Chips & Technologies Accelerator
PNP0940	NCR 77c22e Super VGA
PNP0941	NCR 77c32blt
PNP09FF	Plug and Play Monitors (VESA DDC)

System Devices - PNP0xxx - *Peripheral Buses*

PNP0A00	ISA bus
PNP0A01	EISA bus

TABLE 35-1   MICROSOFT PNP DEVICE IDENTIFICATION CODES (CONTINUED)

PNP0A02	MCA bus
PNP0A03	PCI bus
PNP0A04	VESA/VL bus
PNP0A05	Generic ACPI bus
PNP0A06	Generic ACPI Extended-IO bus (EIO bus)

System Devices - PNP0xxx - *Real-Time Clock, BIOS, Motherboard devices*

PNP0800	AT-style speaker sound
PNP0B00	AT real-time clock
PNP0C00	Plug and Play BIOS
PNP0C01	System board
PNP0C02	General ID for reserving resources required by Plug and Play motherboard registers.
PNP0C03	Plug and Play BIOS Event Notification Interrupt
PNP0C04	Math Coprocessor
PNP0C05	APM BIOS (Version independent)
PNP0C06	Reserved for identification of early Plug and Play BIOS implementation.
PNP0C07	Reserved for identification of early Plug and Play BIOS implementation.
PNP0C08	ACPI system board hardware
PNP0C09	ACPI embedded controller
PNP0C0A	ACPI control method battery
PNP0C0B	ACPI fan
PNP0C0C	ACPI power-button device
PNP0C0D	ACPI lid device
PNP0C0E	ACPI sleep-button device
PNP0C0F	PCI interrupt link device
PNP0C10	ACPI system-indicator device
PNP0C11	ACPI thermal zone
PNP0C12	Device bay controller

System Devices - PNP0xxx - *PCMCIA Controller Chipsets*

PNP0E00	Intel 82365-compatible PCMCIA controller
PNP0E01	Cirrus Logic CL-PD6720 PCMCIA controller
PNP0E02	VLSI VL82C146 PCMCIA controller
PNP0E03	Intel 82365-compatible CardBus controller

System Devices - PNP0xxx - *Mice*

PNP0F00	Microsoft bus mouse
PNP0F01	Microsoft serial mouse
PNP0F02	Microsoft InPort mouse
PNP0F03	Microsoft PS/2-style mouse
PNP0F04	Mouse Systems Mouse
PNP0F05	Mouse Systems 3-button mouse (COM2)
PNP0F06	Genius mouse (COM1)
PNP0F07	Genius mouse (COM2)
PNP0F08	Logitech serial mouse
PNP0F09	Microsoft BallPoint serial mouse
PNP0F0A	Microsoft Plug and Play mouse
PNP0F0B	Microsoft Plug and Play BallPoint mouse
PNP0F0C	Microsoft-compatible serial mouse
PNP0F0D	Microsoft-compatible InPort-compatible mouse
PNP0F0E	Microsoft-compatible PS/2-style mouse
PNP0F0F	Microsoft-compatible serial BallPoint-compatible mouse
PNP0F10	Texas Instruments QuickPort mouse
PNP0F11	Microsoft-compatible bus mouse
PNP0F12	Logitech PS/2-style mouse
PNP0F13	PS/2 port for PS/2-style mice

TABLE 35-1   MICROSOFT PNP DEVICE IDENTIFICATION CODES (CONTINUED)

PNP0F14	Microsoft Kids mouse
PNP0F15	Logitech bus mouse
PNP0F16	Logitech SWIFT device
PNP0F17	Logitech-compatible serial mouse
PNP0F18	Logitech-compatible bus mouse
PNP0F19	Logitech-compatible PS/2-style mouse
PNP0F1A	Logitech-compatible SWIFT device
PNP0F1B	HP Omnibook mouse
PNP0F1C	Compaq LTE trackball PS/2-style mouse
PNP0F1D	Compaq LTE trackball serial mouse
PNP0F1E	Microsoft Kids trackball mouse
PNP0F1F	Reserved (by Microsoft Input Device Group)
PNP0F20	Reserved (by Microsoft Input Device Group)
PNP0F21	Reserved (by Microsoft Input Device Group)
PNP0F22	Reserved (by Microsoft Input Device Group)
PNP0F23	Reserved (by Microsoft Input Device Group)
PNP0FFF	Reserved (by Microsoft Systems)

System Devices - PNP8xxx - *Network Adapters*

PNP8001	Novell/Anthem NE3200
PNP8004	Compaq NE3200
PNP8006	Intel EtherExpress/32
PNP8008	HP EtherTwist EISA LAN Adapter/32 (HP27248A)
PNP8065	Ungermann-Bass NIUps or NIUps/EOTP
PNP8072	DEC (DE211) EtherWorks MC/TP
PNP8073	DEC (DE212) EtherWorks MC/TP_BNC
PNP8078	DCA 10Mb MCA
PNP8074	HP MC LAN adapter/16 TP (PC27246)
PNP80C9	IBM token ring
PNP80CA	IBM token ring II
PNP80CB	IBM token ring II/short
PNP80CC	IBM token ring 4/16Mbs
PNP80D3	Novell/Anthem NE1000
PNP80D4	Novell/Anthem NE2000
PNP80D5	NE1000 compatible
PNP80D6	NE2000 compatible
PNP80D7	Novell/Anthem NE1500T
PNP80D8	Novell/Anthem NE2100
PNP80DD	SMC ARCNETPC
PNP80DE	SMC ARCNET PC100, PC200
PNP80DF	SMC ARCNET PC110, PC210, PC250
PNP80E0	SMC ARCNET PC130/E
PNP80E1	SMC ARCNET PC120, PC220, PC260
PNP80E2	SMC ARCNET PC270/E
PNP80E5	SMC ARCNET PC600W, PC650W
PNP80E7	DEC DEPCA
PNP80E8	DEC (DE100) EtherWorks LC
PNP80E9	DEC (DE200) EtherWorks Turbo
PNP80EA	DEC (DE101) EtherWorks LC/TP
PNP80EB	DEC (DE201) EtherWorks Turbo/TP
PNP80EC	DEC (DE202) EtherWorks Turbo/TP_BNC
PNP80ED	DEC (DE102) EtherWorks LC/TP_BNC
PNP80EE	DEC EE101 (Built-In)
PNP80EF	DECpc 433 WS (Built-In)
PNP80F1	3Com EtherLink Plus
PNP80F3	3Com EtherLink II or IITP (8 or 16-bit)

TABLE 35-1 MICROSOFT PNP DEVICE IDENTIFICATION CODES (CONTINUED)

PNP80F4	3Com TokenLink
PNP80F6	3Com EtherLink 16
PNP80F7	3Com EtherLink III
PNP80F8	3Com Generic Etherlink Plug and Play device
PNP80FB	Thomas Conrad TC6045
PNP80FC	Thomas Conrad TC6042
PNP80FD	Thomas Conrad TC6142
PNP80FE	Thomas Conrad TC6145
PNP80FF	Thomas Conrad TC6242
PNP8100	Thomas Conrad TC6245
PNP8105	DCA 10MB
PNP8106	DCA 10MB fiber optic
PNP8107	DCA 10MB twisted pair
PNP8113	Racal NI6510
PNP811C	Ungermann-Bass NIUpc
PNP8120	Ungermann-Bass NIUpc/EOTP
PNP8123	SMC StarCard PLUS (WD/8003S)
PNP8124	SMC StarCard PLUS with on-board hub (WD/8003SH)
PNP8125	SMC EtherCard PLUS (WD/8003E)
PNP8126	SMC EtherCard PLUS with boot ROM socket (WD/8003EBT)
PNP8127	SMC EtherCard PLUS with boot ROM socket (WD/8003EB)
PNP8128	SMC EtherCard PLUS TP (WD/8003WT)
PNP812A	SMC EtherCard PLUS 16 with boot ROM socket (WD/8013EBT)
PNP812D	Intel EtherExpress 16 or 16TP
PNP812F	Intel TokenExpress 16/4
PNP8130	Intel TokenExpress MCA 16/4
PNP8132	Intel EtherExpress 16 (MCA)
PNP8137	Artisoft AE-1
PNP8138	Artisoft AE-2 or AE-3
PNP8141	Amplicard AC 210/XT
PNP8142	Amplicard AC 210/AT
PNP814B	Everex SpeedLink /PC16 (EV2027)
PNP8155	HP PC LAN adapter/8 TP (HP27245)
PNP8156	HP PC LAN adapter/16 TP (HP27247A)
PNP8157	HP PC LAN adapter/8 TL (HP27250)
PNP8158	HP PC LAN adapter/16 TP Plus (HP27247B)
PNP8159	HP PC LAN adapter/16 TL Plus (HP27252)
PNP815F	National Semiconductor Ethernode *16AT
PNP8160	National Semiconductor AT/LANTIC EtherNODE 16-AT3
PNP816A	NCR token-ring 4Mbs ISA
PNP816D	NCR token-ring 16/4Mbs ISA
PNP8191	Olicom 16/4 token-ring adapter
PNP81C3	SMC EtherCard PLUS Elite (WD/8003EP)
PNP81C4	SMC EtherCard PLUS 10T (WD/8003W)
PNP81C5	SMC EtherCard PLUS Elite 16 (WD/8013EP)
PNP81C6	SMC EtherCard PLUS Elite 16T (WD/8013W)
PNP81C7	SMC EtherCard PLUS Elite 16 Combo (WD/8013EW or 8013EWC)
PNP81C8	SMC EtherElite Ultra 16
PNP81E4	Pure Data PDI9025-32 (token ring)
PNP81E6	Pure Data PDI508+ (ArcNet)
PNP81E7	Pure Data PDI516+ (ArcNet)
PNP81EB	Proteon token ring (P1390)
PNP81EC	Proteon token ring (P1392)
PNP81ED	Proteon ISA token ring (1340)
PNP81EE	Proteon ISA token ring (1342)

TABLE 35-1 MICROSOFT PNP DEVICE IDENTIFICATION CODES (CONTINUED)

PNP81EF	Proteon ISA token ring (1346)
PNP81F0	Proteon ISA token ring (1347)
PNP81FF	Cabletron E2000 Series DNI
PNP8200	Cabletron E2100 Series DNI
PNP8209	Zenith Data Systems Z-Note
PNP820A	Zenith Data Systems NE2000-Compatible
PNP8213	Xircom Pocket Ethernet II
PNP8214	Xircom Pocket Ethernet I
PNP821D	RadiSys EXM-10
PNP8227	SMC 3000 series
PNP8228	SMC 91C2 controller
PNP8231	Advanced Micro Devices AM2100/AM1500T
PNP8263	Tulip NCC-16
PNP8277	Exos 105
PNP828A	Intel '595 based ethernet
PNP828B	TI2000-style token ring
PNP828C	AMD PCNet family cards
PNP828D	AMD PCNet32 (VL version)
PNP8294	IrDA Infrared NDIS driver (Microsoft-supplied)
PNP82BD	IBM PCMCIA-NIC
PNP82C2	Xircom CE10
PNP82C3	Xircom CEM2
PNP8321	DEC ethernet (all types)
PNP8323	SMC EtherCard (all types, except 8013/A)
PNP8324	ARCNET compatible
PNP8326	Thomas Conrad (all Arcnet types)
PNP8327	IBM token ring (all types)
PNP8385	Remote network access driver
PNP8387	RNA point-to-point protocol driver
PNP8388	Reserved (for Microsoft networking components)
PNP8389	Peer IrLAN infrared driver (Microsoft-supplied)
PNP8390	Generic network adapter

System Devices - PNPAxxx - *SCSI and Proprietary CD Adapters*

PNPA002	Future Domain 16-700 compatible controller
PNPA003	Panasonic proprietary CD-ROM adapter (SBPro/SB16)
PNPA01B	Trantor 128 SCSI controller
PNPA01D	Trantor T160 SCSI controller
PNPA01E	Trantor T338 parallel SCSI controller
PNPA01F	Trantor T348 parallel SCSI controller
PNPA020	Trantor Media Vision SCSI controller
PNPA022	Always IN-2000 SCSI controller
PNPA02B	Sony proprietary CD-ROM controller
PNPA02D	Trantor T13b 8-bit SCSI controller
PNPA02F	Trantor T358 parallel SCSI controller
PNPA030	Mitsumi LU-005 single-speed CD-ROM controller + drive
PNPA031	Mitsumi FX-001 single-speed CD-ROM controller + drive
PNPA032	Mitsumi FX-001 double-speed CD-ROM controller + drive

System Devices - PNPBxxx - *Sound, Video Capture, and Multimedia*

PNPB000	Sound Blaster 1.5-compatible sound device
PNPB001	Sound Blaster 2.0-compatible sound device
PNPB002	Sound Blaster Pro-compatible sound device
PNPB003	Sound Blaster 16-compatible sound device
PNPB004	Thunderboard-compatible sound device
PNPB005	Adlib-compatible FM synthesizer device
PNPB006	MPU401 compatible

TABLE 35-1   MICROSOFT PNP DEVICE IDENTIFICATION CODES (CONTINUED)

PNPB007	Microsoft Windows Sound System-compatible sound device
PNPB008	Compaq Business Audio
PNPB009	Plug and Play Microsoft Windows Sound System device
PNPB00A	MediaVision Pro Audio Spectrum (Trantor SCSI enabled, Thunder Chip disabled)
PNPB00B	MediaVision Pro Audio 3D
PNPB00C	MusicQuest MQX-32M
PNPB00D	MediaVision Pro Audio Spectrum basic (No Trantor SCSI, Thunder Chip enabled)
PNPB00E	MediaVision Pro Audio Spectrum (Trantor SCSI enabled, Thunder Chip enabled)
PNPB00F	MediaVision Jazz-16 chipset (OEM versions)
PNPB010	Auravision VxP500 chipset—Orchid Videola
PNPB018	MediaVision Pro Audio Spectrum 8-bit
PNPB019	MediaVision Pro Audio Spectrum basic (no Trantor SCSI, Thunder Chip disabled)
PNPB020	Yamaha OPL3-compatible FM synthesizer device
PNPB02F	Joystick/game port
System Devices - PNPCxxx-Dxxx - *Modems*	
PNPC000	Compaq 14400 modem
PNPC001	Compaq 2400/9600 modem

the *Add new hardware* Wizard to search for new hardware installed in your computer. Detection does not run each time you start Windows 95. During the detection process, Windows 95 creates a file called DETLOG.TXT in the root directory of the boot drive. This file exists primarily as a troubleshooting tool.

Enumeration is the process Windows 95 uses to identify Plug-and-Play devices in your computer, including those devices on Plug-and-Play busses, such as ISAPNP, PCI, and PCMCIA (PC card) devices. Enumeration occurs each time Windows 95 starts and whenever Windows 95 receives notification that a change has occurred in the computer's hardware configuration, such as when you remove a PCMCIA card.

LEGACY DEVICES

Another issue to consider when working with PnP systems is the support of pre-PnP devices (called *legacy devices*). These are the traditional "jumpered" devices, which need to be configured manually. Under DOS, legacy devices run just fine and require no special support, but they can cause a problem under Windows 95. Remember that a PnP system relies on the ability to automatically identify each and every device in the system. Because legacy devices are not designed to communicate their configuration to the operating system, there is no way for Windows 95 to detect the device—much less assign resources for it. This means Windows 95 can assign resources to a PnP device that are already in use by a legacy device. Windows 95 circumvents this problem by requiring you to "register" legacy devices using the *Add new hardware* wizard under the *Control panel*. Once a legacy device is installed and the system is rebooted, use the *Add new hardware* wizard to "tell" Windows 95 about the new device, and install the proper drivers for it.

Enabling PnP under DOS

Now that so many PnP devices are becoming available, a new problem is developing for technicians—PnP support under DOS. Windows 95 was designed to be a platform for PnP devices, but DOS cannot automatically identify and configure PnP devices without additional software drivers. This makes it difficult to use many PnP devices under DOS, but with the proliferation of DOS games and other applications still being developed, PnP support is unquestionably a necessity. In other cases, older hardware platforms might lack the support to fully implement a PnP system (such as older BIOS). This part of the chapter examines the techniques used to implement PnP support under DOS and Windows 3.1x.

If you do not have access to a PnP operating system (i.e., you're using DOS or Windows 3.1x), you will need to install a PnP *configuration driver* in CONFIG.SYS that will perform resource allocation and configuration for a PnP device. A PnP configuration driver determines the resource settings of all your system devices and legacy cards, configures PnP cards, and provides relevant configuration information to other drivers or applications that access your PnP cards. By contrast, a PnP *configuration utility* allows you to view, enter, or change the resource settings of the PnP and legacy cards in your system—the new or changed settings are then used by the PnP configuration driver to configure new PnP cards. For example, the PnP driver for an Ensonique SoundScape board is DW-CFGMG.SYS entered into a CONFIG.SYS command line. The corresponding PnP utility for that Ensonique board is SSINIT.EXE, which is entered into an AUTOEXEC.BAT command line.

THE PNP CONFIGURATION DRIVER

A PnP driver is loaded in the CONFIG.SYS file. For example, the Creative Labs PnP Configuration Manager (for Creative Labs PnP devices) would load the driver CTCM.EXE in a command line, such as:

```
device=c:\pnp\ctcm.exe
```

where C:is the directory where you have installed CTCM. This CTCM statement will be placed before all the statements that load other low-level device drivers (such as CTSB16.SYS and SBIDE.SYS) so that your Creative PnP cards will be configured before these device drivers try to use them. For an Ensonique SoundScape sound board, the PnP driver would be installed, such as:

```
device=c:\pnp\soundscp.sys
```

In most cases, an automated installation routine will copy the PnP files to your hard drive, and make any necessary changes to your CONFIG.SYS file. But if you have to install the software manually, be sure to place the driver command lines for each PnP device after the PnP configuration manager.

THE PNP CONFIGURATION UTILITY

A PnP utility is loaded in the AUTOEXEC.BAT file. This utility actually configures and initializes the PnP device. For Creative Labs PnP devices, the utility CTCU is entered in AUTOEXEC.BAT command line(s), such as:

```
set CTCM=C:
C:\ctcmdir\CTCU /S /W=C:\windows
```

where C:and C:are the directories where your CTCM, CTCU, and Windows 3.x files are installed, respectively. For an Ensonique SoundScape sound board, a typical entry would appear similar to:

```
set sndscape=c:
lh c:sndscape\ssinit /I
```

Once again, most PnP products will come with an automated installation routine on diskette. But when you are troubleshooting a defective installation or performing a manual installation, this can help you avoid problems.

BLASTER VARIABLES

When configuring a PnP sound board, you will usually have to deal with a BLASTER variable in the AUTOEXEC.BAT file. For legacy sound cards, the BLASTER variable includes fixed settings for address, interrupt, and DMA information, such as:

```
set BLASTER=A220 I5 D1 T1
```

With a PnP installation, however, the BLASTER variable is re-defined to "X-out" the interrupt and DMA entries:

```
set BLASTER=A220 IXX DX T1
```

The actual values for interrupt and DMA will be entered when the PnP configuration utility runs.

POTENTIAL PROBLEMS WITH GENERIC PNP CONFIGURATION SOFTWARE

A number of "generic" PnP driver/utility sets designed to support a wide range of PnP devices under DOS or Windows 3.1x. Two of the most popular are the *Intel Configuration Manager (ICM)* and *ISA Configuration Utility (ICU)*—both developed by Intel Corporation. In fact, this software might already be installed on your PC (or bundled with PnP cards). Although the idea of generic PnP software is appealing, such generic software is not necessarily compatible with all types of PnP boards. When the software and hardware is incompatible, you will see one of the following error messages:

- Failed NVS write.
- Failure to detect PnP BIOS machine.
- Failure to assign new configuration to PnP card.
- ICM might not be able to configure your PnP card properly.

In general, you should use the manufacturer-specific software that accompanies a PnP device, rather than generic PnP software.

POTENTIAL PROBLEMS WITH MANUFACTURER'S PNP SOFTWARE

Although manufacturer-specific PnP software will generally provide excellent service, it has some potential limitations. When you use a non-PnP operating system, such as DOS or Windows 3.1x (and you do not have a PnP BIOS), your PnP card works like a software-configurable card. In such a situation, the PnP driver needs to know which resources have been reserved by all the legacy cards, PnP cards, and system devices in your system before it can allocate conflict-free resources to your new PnP card. Normally, the PnP driver can "see" all the resource settings, but you might need to use the PnP utility to enter the resource settings of all the legacy cards in your PC.

You might still encounter hardware conflicts if the resource settings specified through a PnP utility are incomplete or wrong. If this happens, use the configuration utility to select a different group of resources for the PnP card that caused the conflict. You might need to try a few combinations until you find one that works. This can be tedious, but it is easier than the traditional method of changing DIP switches or jumpers.

HANDLING PNP CONFIGURATION ISSUES UNDER DOS

DOS PnP software allows you to use PnP devices in the DOS environment. In many cases, DOS support for PnP works adequately, but several issues can arise that you should know how to deal with:

Choosing between the PnP BIOS, PnP software, or PnP OS A number of PC setups allow you to configure a PnP device, based on the PnP BIOS, the PnP driver/utility software, or the PnP operating system. When you are faced with such a choice, it is often better to use the PnP software or operating system, rather than the BIOS. Set the BIOS so that it will not configure PnP devices. The reason is that a BIOS does not have any way of knowing how legacy devices are configured, so allowing the BIOS to configure a "mixed" system (with legacy and PnP devices) introduces an excellent chance for hardware conflicts.

For "pure" system configurations (containing all PnP devices), you can choose to let the PnP BIOS configure PnP devices.

Upgrading a PnP system to Windows 95 You might have a system with PnP devices that is running with PnP driver and utility software under DOS or Windows 3.1x.

When Windows 95 is installed, it should recognize the PnP device(s) during the hardware-detection phase of the installation, then install the proper software for dealing with the device(s) under Windows 95. At the same time, Windows 95 should remark-out the real-mode driver and utility software entries under CONFIG.SYS and AUTOEXEC.BAT. This loss of real-mode drivers can cause a problem when returning to the DOS mode later.

Replacing generic PnP software with manufacturer-specific software   If generic software is already used to initialize and run your PnP device(s), that software should be disabled before installing manufacturer-specific software. You can do this by placing the REM statement before the generic software's command lines in CONFIG.SYS and AUTOEXEC.BAT. It is not necessary to remove generic PnP software files from the system.

The system hangs or reboots whenever the driver software loads   The upper memory area of your PnP BIOS machine is probably mapped by EMM386 using the HIGHSCAN option (and thus can get corrupted easily). When it does, CTCM (or other DOS PnP software) will not work properly. Your system might then hang or reboot whenever you load CTCM. To resolve this problem, remove the HIGHSCAN option in the EMM386 statement in the CONFIG.SYS file. For example, change the statement:

```
device=c:\dir\emm386.exe highscan
```

to

```
device=c:\dir\emm386.exe
```

where C:\dir is the directory in which your EMM386 utility is installed.

Managing and Troubleshooting PnP Devices

Plug-and-Play technology provides technicians and end-users with a powerful configuration tool that takes much of the guesswork and trial and error out of hardware installations and upgrades. Still, PnP platforms are far from perfect, and managing the mix of PnP and legacy devices in today's systems takes a bit of care. This part of the chapter provides some tips for working with PnP and legacy devices under Windows 95, then examines a series of PnP troubleshooting procedures.

INSTALLING PNP DEVICES

Ideally, you simply need to install the physical device in the system. When Windows 95 starts, it should recognize the new device automatically, and install the appropriate drivers for it. If Windows 95 cannot locate an appropriate driver already "on-board," it will prompt you to provide a diskette containing the correct driver.

INSTALLING LEGACY DEVICES

Remember that "legacy" devices are configured manually, and cannot report their configuration to Windows 95 automatically. When installing new legacy hardware in the system, you must run the *Add new hardware* wizard to register the device with Windows 95 and add the appropriate driver:

1 In the *Control panel*, doubleclick the *Add new hardware* icon.
2 In the *Add new hardware* wizard, click *Next*, then select *Automatically detect installed hardware*.
3 Allow Windows 95 to detect the new device, then follow the instructions to configure the driver.

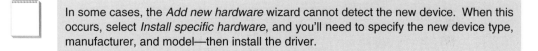

> In some cases, the *Add new hardware* wizard cannot detect the new device. When this occurs, select *Install specific hardware*, and you'll need to specify the new device type, manufacturer, and model—then install the driver.

UPDATING DEVICE DRIVERS

All devices installed under Windows 95 (both PnP and legacy) are heavily dependent on drivers. Over time, drivers often need to be updated to resolve bugs with the driver, streamline the performance of the particular device, or overcome incompatibilities with other devices or drivers. An important part of device management under Windows 95 involves driver updates. In some cases, new drivers are provided on a "maintenance diskette" sent by the manufacturer. In other cases, the new driver is downloaded from the manufacturer's tech support Web site. But in either case, all drivers must be properly installed—usually through the *Add new hardware* wizard. The following steps outline the process for installing a new driver:

1 In the *Control panel*, doubleclick the *Add new hardware* icon.
2 Click *Next*, click *No*, then click *Next* (do not let the wizard "auto-detect" devices).
3 Click the type of hardware for which you are installing the driver, then click *Next*.
4 Click *Have disk*.
5 Type the path for the driver you are installing and click *OK*, or click *Browse* and locate the driver manually. You must type the path for or locate the OEMSETUP.INF file from the manufacturer.
6 In the dialog box listing the .INF file, click *OK*. Click *OK* to continue.
7 Click the correct driver and then click *OK*.
8 Click *Finish*.

INSTALLING MODEMS MANUALLY

With the popularity of on-line resources, such as AOL and the Internet, most current PCs are equipped with a modem. Although modem installation is very similar to other device installations, modems offer some peculiar wrinkles that often demand a slightly different installation approach (they are also not always detected with 100% reliability). The following steps outline a modem installation:

1 In the *Control panel*, double-click the Modems icon.
2 If this is to be the first modem installed in the computer, the Install New Modem wizard starts automatically. If not, click *Add*.
3 If you want Windows 95 to "auto-detect" your modem, click *Next*. If not, click the "Don't detect my modem..." check box to select it, then click *Next*.
4 If you chose to have Windows 95 detect your modem, Windows 95 queries the serial ports on your computer looking for a modem. If Windows 95 detects an incorrect modem, click *Change*, and select the appropriate manufacturer and model. Click *Next*, then continue with step 7.
5 If you chose to select your modem manually, click the appropriate manufacturer and model, then click *Next*.
6 Click the appropriate communications port, then click *Next*.
7 Click *Finish*.

INSTALLING PRINTERS MANUALLY

Although the newest generation of printers are PnP compatible and can be identified automatically, most "traditional" printers must be specified under Windows 95 manually. This is accomplished through the *Printers* icon:

1 Click the *Start* button, point to *Settings*, then click *Printers*.
2 Doubleclick *Add printer*, then click *Next*.
3 Click *Local printer* or *Network printer*, as appropriate, then click *Next*.

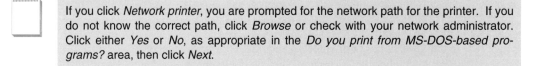

If you click *Network printer*, you are prompted for the network path for the printer. If you do not know the correct path, click *Browse* or check with your network administrator. Click either *Yes* or *No*, as appropriate in the *Do you print from MS-DOS-based programs?* area, then click *Next*.

4 Click the appropriate manufacturer and model for your printer, then click *Next*.
5 If you chose to install a local printer, click the correct port, then click *Next*.
6 Type a name for the printer (or accept the default name), then click either *Yes* or *No* in the *Do you want your Windows-based programs to use this printer as the default printer?* area. Click *Next*.
7 To print a test page, click *Yes*, then click *Finish*.

DISABLING A DEVICE

Ordinarily, Windows 95 identifies devices, assigns resources, and loads drivers for all the devices it finds. From time to time (especially during troubleshooting), it might be necessary to "disable" a device. In effect, "disabling" a device prevents Windows 95 from loading drivers or allocating resources associated with the device, but it does not "remove" the device from the system. This is particularly handy when checking for resource assignment problems:

1 Click the *Start* button, point to *Settings*, then click *Control panel*.
2 Doubleclick the *System* icon.
3 On the *Device manager* tab, click the device you want, and then click *Properties*.
4 On the *General* tab, click the *Original configuration (current)* check box to clear it, then click *OK*.

You might need to reboot the system to free the resources, but the neutralized device should no longer be available.

REMOVING A DEVICE

At times (especially during troubleshooting), it might be necessary to remove a device entirely from the Windows 95 platform to free resources otherwise assigned to the device. Normally, Windows 95 should free the resources of a PnP device simply by "disabling" it (see "Disabling a device"), or when the device is physically removed. But legacy cards might need to be "removed" manually before their assigned resources can be freed. To free resource settings used by disabled hardware:

1 Click *Start*, *Settings*, and *Control panel*. Click the *System* icon and select the *Device manager* tab.
2 In the hardware list, click the plus sign next to the type of hardware, then click the device that is disabled.
3 Click *Remove*, then click *OK*.
4 Click the *Start* button, then click *Shut down*. Click *OK*. When the message appears saying it is safe to do so, turn off and unplug your computer, then remove the physical hardware device from inside the computer.

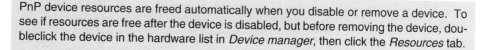

PnP device resources are freed automatically when you disable or remove a device. To see if resources are free after the device is disabled, but before removing the device, doubleclick the device in the hardware list in *Device manager*, then click the *Resources* tab.

SYMPTOMS

Symptom 35-1. Windows 95 fails to recognize the computer as "Plug and Play" This type of problem often occurs with Intel OEM motherboards. Windows 95 does not recognize the computer as a Plug-and-Play platform—even though you receive a message during startup, such as: "Intel PnP BIOS Extensions Installed." Intel has developed some OEM motherboards that are equipped with a Plug-and-Play BIOS that does not contain the run-time services necessary to configure motherboard devices. An example of such a motherboard is the Intel P5/90. Gateway 2000 (and possibly other OEMs) ship computers with the P5/90 motherboard. You'll need to upgrade the system BIOS to comply with the Plug-and-Play BIOS version 1.0a specification (or later).

Symptom 35-2. The IRQ conflicts with PCI display adapters When you install a PCI video adapter that is configured to use a particular interrupt (IRQ), Windows 95 might configure it to use another IRQ that is already in use by another device. Although PCI devices can share PCI IRQs, Windows 95 does not support sharing PCI IRQs with other non-PCI devices (such as an IDE controller). Use the *Device manager* to resolve the conflict by assigning a different IRQ to one of the conflicting devices (usually the new PCI video adapter).

> This kind of behavior does not occur with ISA or VESA Local Bus VLB display adapters.

Symptom 35-3. The resources for disabled devices are not freed Even though you disable a device in your computer's CMOS setup, Windows 95 re-enables the device and allocates its resources. Windows 95 might also reinstall a device that is removed from *Device manager*. This happens because Windows 95 detects Plug-and-Play devices, regardless of the CMOS setup. To prevent Windows 95 from re-activating disabled hardware, you must disable the hardware in the computer's CMOS setup and remove it from the current configuration in Windows 95. This frees the device's resources for other devices to use:

1 Click the *Start* button, point to *Settings*, then click *Control panel*.
2 Doubleclick the *System* icon.
3 Click the *Device manager* tab, then doubleclick the device you want to disable.
4 Click the *General* tab, then click the *Original configuration (current)* check box to clear it.
5 Click the *OK* button.
6 Restart Windows 95 when prompted.
7 Immediately start the CMOS setup routine and disable the device in the CMOS setup.
8 Save the changes to CMOS, and allow the system to boot normally.

> When you disable a device in *Device manager*, you must restart your computer before you can reassign the device's resources to another device.

Symptom 35-4. An AST PnP BIOS is not registered as PnP The AST Plug-and-Play BIOS is not registered as being Plug-and-Play capable under Windows 95. This is usually because the AST PnP BIOS contains incorrect information in its 16-bit protected-mode entry point. When Windows 95 detects this incorrect code in the AST BIOS it will not recognize the BIOS as being Plug-and-Play capable. You will need to contact AST for a BIOS upgrade.

Symptom 35-5. A PnP ISA adapter is not recognized automatically If you insert a PnP ISA adapter in a computer whose motherboard does not contain PCI slots, Windows 95 might not recognize the new ISA adapter automatically. The *Device manager* might also display a "PCI bus" entry with an exclamation point in a yellow circle, with the status "No Plug-and-Play ISA bus was found. (Code 29)." This problem is typically caused by a PnP BIOS that is not supported by Windows 95 on computers that have a PCI BIOS, but not a PCI bus. On PCI computers, usually the PCI driver starts the PnP

ISA driver. If the PCI driver fails, the ISA driver is not loaded; therefore, PnP ISA adapters are not automatically recognized or configured. To add a PnP adapter so that Windows 95 automatically recognizes it, enable the ISA PnP bus manually:

1 In *Control panel*, doubleclick the *Add new hardware* icon, then click *Next*.
2 Click *No*, then click *Next*.
3 Click *System devices*, then click *Next*.
4 Click *ISA Plug-And-Play bus*, then click *Next*.
5 Click *Finish*.
6 Restart your computer when you are prompted to do so.

You might also want to contact your computer manufacturer to see about obtaining an updated PnP BIOS that is supported by Windows 95.

Symptom 35-6. The computer no longer operates properly after docking or undocking As an example, the keyboard or mouse might stop working. *Hot docking* and *hot undocking* refer to inserting the computer in a docking station or removing it from the docking station while the computer is running at full power. By contrast, *warm docking* refers to docking or undocking the computer while it is in suspend mode. Laptop or portable computers with a PnP BIOS can be hot or warm docked or undocked. In virtually all cases, the computer does not have a suitable PnP BIOS (this is mandatory for hot or warm docking and undocking). To correct this problem on a permanent basis, you'll need to upgrade the laptop's BIOS to a version that supports PnP. In the mean time, you can work around this problem by turning the computer off before you dock or undock it.

Symptom 35-7. Serial PnP devices are not recognized when an adapter is used to connect them For example, when you use a 9-pin to 25-pin serial adapter with a serial PnP device, the device might not be enumerated by the configuration manager at startup. This is caused by the adapter—some 9-pin to 25-pin serial adapters do not connect the lines that pass the PnP initialization string (including adapters made by Microsoft before the release of Windows 95). Try another (more current) serial adapter. If the problem persists, add the device manually using the *Add new hardware* wizard in the *Control panel*.

Symptom 35-8. Windows 95 *Setup* hangs up when detecting SCSI controllers This often happens with Adaptec SCSI controllers on the first reboot while PnP devices are being detected, and is known to happen when a SCSI hard disk is supported by an Adaptec AHA 2940, Adaptec 2940AU, or Adaptec 2940W controller. You can work around this problem by disabling the SCSI controller and allowing *Setup* to finish the PnP device detection:

1 Enable PnP SCAM support in the Adaptec SCSI controller BIOS setup.
2 Disable *BIOS Support For Int13 Extension* in the Adaptec SCSI controller BIOS setup.
3 Restart Windows 95, press the <F8> key when you see the "Starting Windows 95" message, then choose *Safe mode* from the *Startup* menu.
4 In *Control panel*, doubleclick the *System* icon, click the *Performance* tab, click *File system*, then click the *Troubleshooting* tab.

5 Enable the following two options: "Disable protect-mode hard-disk interrupt handling" and "Disable all 32-bit protected-mode disk drivers."

6 Click *OK*, then click *OK* again.

7 When you are prompted to restart your computer, click *Yes* to continue with *Setup*.

8 After Windows 95 is installed, disable the options you enabled in step 5.

Symptom 35-9. After installing an HP OfficeJet 300 printer, a "Fatal exception error" occurs each time you run the *Add new hardware* wizard You'll typically see Exception Errors 06, 0E, 0C, or 0D. This is because the HP OfficeJet Series 300 *Device manager* contends with Windows 95 for control of PnP. The HP installation process sets up a shortcut in the *Startup* folder that runs "HPOJDMAN.EXE /AUTOPROMPT." This causes HPOJDMAN.EXE to run in the background. Start the *Close program* dialog box by pressing <Ctrl>+<Alt>+<Delete>. Click *HPOJDMAN* in the list of tasks, then click *End task*. Check with HP (**http://www.hp.com**) for updated printer software utilities.

Symptom 35-10. The PS/2 mouse is disabled after installing an ISA PnP device For example, installing a SoundBlaster 16 "value" sound card disables the PS/2 mouse. This problem can occur on computers where the PnP BIOS (rather than Windows 95) assigns resources to ISA PnP devices. The PnP BIOS might assign IRQ 12 to the IDE drive and disable the mouse port. To correct this problem, disable the BIOS PnP support in the computer's CMOS setup to allow Windows 95 to configure the hardware instead.

Symptom 35-11. When running the *Add new hardware* wizard, it doesn't detect a device that has been removed in *Device manager* on a multiple-profile system This is because removing a PnP device from one profile and leaving it in another causes a flag to be set in the registry to prevent the device from being enumerated on the next startup. This might also cause the *Add new hardware* wizard to bypass the device. The flag exists only in the profile in which the device was removed. To prevent this type of problem from occurring, disable the device in *Device manager* instead of removing it. To disable a device, click the *Disable in this hardware profile* check box for the device in *Device manager*. To restore (or re-detect) the device, remove it from all profiles, then run the *Add new hardware* wizard.

Symptom 35-12. An extra serial port is displayed in the *Device manager* When you are using Windows 95 OSR 2 or 2.1, you might see an extra communications port in *Device manager*. An exclamation point is in a yellow circle next to the port. If you remove the port, it is re-detected again the next time you restart your computer. The computer's PnP BIOS is probably reporting (incorrectly) that the COM ports are not using resources—although they were detected during *Setup*. This is a problem with Windows 95. Check with Microsoft (**http://www.microsoft.com**) for any available upgrades or patches.

Symptom 35-13. Windows 95 cannot setup with a PnP program active When you try to install Windows 95, you might receive the following error message:

```
A fatal exception 0E has occurred at 0028:xxxxxxxx in VxD VMM(06) + xxxxxxxx
```

Or, you might receive a Vwin32 error message displayed on a blue screen, a registry error message, or a *general-protection (GP) fault* error message. This problem can occur if you have a PnP program active in memory when you try to install Windows 95. To work around this issue, install Windows 95 from a command prompt. Restart the computer. When you see the "Starting Windows 95" message, press the <F8> key, then choose *Command prompt only* from the *Startup* menu. At the command prompt, type:

```
<drive>:\setup.exe
```

where <drive> is the drive containing your original Windows 95 setup disk or CD-ROM.

Symptom 35-14. An IBM ThinkPad doesn't support PnP under Windows 95

Chances are that the ThinkPad required a BIOS update. The following IBM ThinkPad models are known to need specific BIOS versions:

- ThinkPad 750 family: 750/360/755 System Program Service Diskette version 1.20 (or later).
- ThinkPad 755C/Cs and 360/355 family: 750/360/755 System Program Service Diskette version 1.20 (or later).
- ThinkPad 755CE/CD, ThinkPad 755CX/CV, ThinkPad 755CDV: 755 System Program Service Diskette version 1.30 (or later).
- ThinkPad 701C: 701C System Program Service Diskette version 3H (or later).
- ThinkPad 340CSE and 370C: 340 System Program Service Diskette version 1.10 (or later).

The following ThinkPad models require APM BIOS 1.1 (or later) and PnP BIOS 1.0a (or later) for these features to work correctly with Windows 95:

- ThinkPad 755C/Cs
- ThinkPad 360/355 family
- ThinkPad 755CE/CD/CX/CV/CDV
- ThinkPad 340CSE
- ThinkPad 370C
- ThinkPad 701C
- ThinkPad 530CS

The following ThinkPad models require APM BIOS version 1.0 to work correctly with Windows 95. There is no PnP BIOS support for these models:

- ThinkPad 750 family
- ThinkPad 340 monochrome display system
- ThinkPad 230Cs

To obtain an updated BIOS or System Program Service Diskette for an IBM ThinkPad computer, contact IBM (**http://www.ibm.com**).

Symptom 35-15. A PnP pointing device is not detected When you connect a PnP pointing device (e.g., Microsoft PnP serial mouse, Microsoft EasyBall, or Microsoft IntelliMouse), the new device might not be detected by Windows 95. Running the *Add new hardware* wizard does not correct the problem. This is almost always because the registry entries for your previous pointing device were not properly removed from the registry. This problem is known to occur when your previous pointing device was a Microsoft, Microsoft-compatible, or Logitech mouse. To work around this problem, use the registry editor (REGEDIT) to remove the registry entries for your previous pointing device. Remove the following registry keys:

```
Hkey_Local_Machine\System\CurrentControlSet\Services\Class\Mouse\<nnnn>
```

where *<nnnn>* is an incremental four-digit number starting at 0000. Also remove the following registry keys (if they exist):

```
Hkey_Local_Machine\Enum\Root\Mouse\<nnnn>
```

where *<nnnn>* in an incremental four-digit number starting at 0000. Remove all registry keys under the following registry key (if they exist):

```
Hkey_Local_Machine\Enum\Serenum
```

Remove the following registry key (if it exists):

```
Hkey_Local_Machine\Software\Logitech\Mouseware
```

Use the right mouse button to click *My computer*, then click *Properties* on the menu that appears. Click the *Device manager* tab. Click each serial pointing device, then click *Remove*. Click *OK*, then restart Windows 95. When you restart Windows, the attached pointing device will be detected and the appropriate drivers will be installed.

> Before you edit the registry, first make a backup copy of the registry files (SYSTEM.DAT and USER.DAT). Both are hidden in the folder.

Symptom 35-16. The PnP printer is re-detected every time Windows 95 starts This occurs even when the printer is already installed. When you start Windows 95, the following message might be displayed:

```
New Hardware Found
<device>
Windows has found new hardware and is installing the software for it
```

This problem is known to occur with Hewlett-Packard 4L and Hewlett-Packard DeskJet 660C PnP printers, and is usually caused by damage to the following registry key:

```
Hkey_Local_Machine\Enum\Lptenum
```

Remove the registry key, then restart your computer. When Windows 95 starts, it will detect the printer and install support for it. Once the printer is installed, it will no longer be detected each time you start Windows 95.

> Before you edit the registry, first make a backup copy of the registry files (SYSTEM.DAT and USER.DAT). Both are hidden in the folder.

Symptom 35-17. After installing Windows 95, none of the APM features were installed You might also notice that there is no "battery meter" for laptops. Some computers and BIOS revisions have known incompatibilities with the APM 1.1 specification. You are probably running Windows 95 on such a computer. As a result, the hardware "suspend" functions of your computer should still function correctly, but you cannot use the Windows 95 APM features. Windows 95 turns off APM support completely on the following computers:

- AMIBIOS 07/08/1994
- AMIBIOS 07/08/94
- Any Gateway ColorBook >1.0 w/SystemSoft BIOS
- Any Gateway ColorBook with APM 1.0
- AST Ascentia 900N
- Canon Innova 150C
- DECpc LPv+ 1.00
- DECpc LPv+ 1.01
- DECpc LPv+ 1.02
- NCR/AT&T 3150
- Ultra laptop 486sx33
- Wyse Forte GSV 486/66
- Zenon P5/90

Windows 95 turns off power status polling (so you do not see a battery meter) on the following computers:

- IBM ThinkPad 500
- LexBook
- WinBook

Windows 95 uses APM 1.0 mode on NEC Versa and AT&T Globalyst systems with APM 1.1 BIOS and no Plug-and-Play BIOS. The following IBM ThinkPad computers support APM 1.1:

- ThinkPad 755C
- ThinkPad 360/355 Family
- ThinkPad 755CE/CD/CX/CV/CDV

- ThinkPad 340CSE
- ThinkPad 370C
- ThinkPad 701C
- ThinkPad 530CS

The following IBM ThinkPad computers work with Windows 95, but only APM BIOS 1.0 is supported:

- ThinkPad 750 family
- ThinkPad 340 (monochrome)
- ThinkPad 230Cs

The ASUS PCI/I P55SP4 motherboard with a SiS 5511/5512/5513 chipset and an Award BIOS has been known to exhibit similar problems (the battery meter might appear on the *Taskbar* when it should not). This problem should be fixed with PnP BIOS version 0110 (11/21/95) for revision 1.2 and 1.3 motherboards. Revision 1.4 motherboards have this fix using PnP BIOS version 0303 (11/21/95).

Symptom 35-18. The *Device manager* reports a "PCI-to-ISA bridge conflict" The *Device manager* displays a PCI-to-ISA bridge entry with an exclamation point in a yellow circle, indicating a resource conflict. This problem is typically caused by a PnP BIOS that reports both a PCI and an ISA bus, but only an ISA bus is present, so there is no actual conflict. You'll need to update the PnP BIOS to a version with better detection and reporting capability.

Symptom 35-19. The PnP BIOS is disabled on a laptop or notebook computer When you install Windows 95 on a dockable notebook computer with a PnP BIOS, you see no "Eject PC" command on the *Start* menu when the notebook computer is docked in a docking station. Also, no PnP BIOS node is displayed in *System devices* under the *Device manager*. This problem was known to occur on IBM ThinkPad (360/750/755 series) dockable notebook computers with a PnP BIOS; it occurs because early versions of dockable notebook computers with PnP BIOS are not fully compatible with Windows 95. When a PnP BIOS is disabled in Windows 95, certain features (such as warm docking) no longer work. To make your dockable notebook computer compatible with Windows 95, contact the manufacturer of your notebook computer and obtain the most recent PnP BIOS.

In general, a PnP BIOS dated after 7/1/95 is compatible with Windows 95.

Symptom 35-20. The sound device on a DEC HiNote Ultra isn't working When you install Windows 95 over an existing Windows for Workgroups 3.1x or Windows 3.1x installation on a DEC HiNote Ultra computer with a PnP BIOS, the sound device no longer works properly. Also, the wrong sound device is installed in Windows 95. This is a PnP BIOS problem—early versions of the DEC HiNote Ultra shipped with a PnP

BIOS are not compatible with Windows 95. Contact DEC and obtain the most recent PnP BIOS for the DEC HiNote Ultra.

Symptom 35-21. Device resources are not updated in a "forced" configuration You'll notice that an exclamation point appears over a resource icon in *Computer properties* in *Device manager*, or that changes you make to the resources assigned to a PnP device in the computer's CMOS setup are not reflected in the *Settings* column in *Computer properties* under *Device manager*. This is because the device is using a "forced" configuration instead of an automatic configuration. To remove a "forced" configuration and allow the PnP device to be fully configurable by the computer's BIOS and Windows 95, set the device to use automatic settings:

1 Doubleclick the *System* icon in *Control panel*.
2 Click the *Device manager* tab.
3 Doubleclick the device, then click the *Resources* tab.
4 Click the *Use automatic settings* check box to select it.
5 Click *OK*.

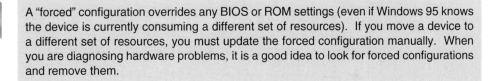

A "forced" configuration overrides any BIOS or ROM settings (even if Windows 95 knows the device is currently consuming a different set of resources). If you move a device to a different set of resources, you must update the forced configuration manually. When you are diagnosing hardware problems, it is a good idea to look for forced configurations and remove them.

Symptom 35-22. Restarting the computer causes the PC to hang This often happens when you try to restart your computer using the *Restart the computer* option in the *Shut down windows* dialog box. This problem can occur on computers with a BIOS that expects IRQ 12 to be used by a PS/2-style mouse port, but instead have a software-configurable hardware device (such as a PnP adapter) using IRQ 12. To work around this problem, reserve IRQ 12 in *Device manager* or change the IRQ for the software-configurable device in *Device manager*. You might also want to consider upgrading the BIOS in the computer to a later version. To reserve an IRQ with *Device manager*:

1 In the *Control panel*, doubleclick the *System* icon.
2 On the *Device manager* tab, doubleclick *Computer*.
3 On the *Reserve resources* tab, click the *Interrupt Request (IRQ)* option, then click *Add*.
4 In the *Value* box, click the IRQ that you want to reserve.
5 Click *OK* until you return to *Control panel*.

Symptom 35-23. Adding a PCI device to a Dell Dimension causes the system to hang in Windows 95 The BIOS in the Dell computer has probably configured the new PCI device to use IRQ 10, but another legacy device installed in the system is already configured to use IRQ 10. Although Windows 95 is designed to recognize resource conflicts such as this, this particular conflict causes the computer to hang before the Windows 95 *Configuration manager* recognizes that the conflict exists. Although the PCI bus is normally a PnP-compatible bus, the BIOS in Dell Dimension computers statically allocates IRQ 10 to a new PCI device—there is no way to disable this behavior. To work around this problem, configure the existing legacy device to use an IRQ other than IRQ 10.

Symptom 35-24.   You cannot configure disabled devices in the *Device manager* When you're using a PnP BIOS, you might not be able to configure (through *Device manager*) a device that has been disabled in the BIOS—even though the BIOS supports configuring devices for the next time the computer starts. When you click the device in *Device manager*, then click *Properties*, you see a message, such as:

```
The device has been disabled in the hardware.  In order to use this device,
you must re-enable the hardware.  See your hardware documentation for de-
tails (Code 29).
```

This is a problem with Windows 95. You'll need to enable the device in the BIOS before you try to configure it in *Device manager*.

Symptom 35-25.   A Toshiba T4900 laptop doesn't switch from LCD to external monitor If you place a Toshiba T4900 computer into its docking station while Windows 95 is running (a "warm dock" operation), the display might not switch from the LCD screen to the external monitor. Toshiba's PnP BIOS does not switch the display properly between the LCD screen and an external monitor. For a short-term work around, press the <F5> key to manually toggle the display between the LCD screen and the external monitor. In the mean time, contact Toshiba for a PnP BIOS upgrade.

Symptom 35-26.   A third port is detected with a CMD PCI dual-port IDE controller When using a CMD PCI Dual Port IDE controller (with at least one device on both the primary and secondary port), the *Device manager* displays a third port. This "false" third port is displayed with an exclamation point inside a yellow circle. This happens because the PnP BIOS in your computer is erroneously reporting that a third port is present. Windows 95 does not allocate any resources to the third port, and the existence of the third port in *Device manager* should not cause any problems. However, if you want to disable the third port, follow these steps:

1 Use the right mouse button to click *My computer*, then click *Properties* on the menu that appears.
2 Click the *Device manager* tab.
3 Click the third port, then click *Properties*. You might need to expand a branch of the hardware tree by doubleclicking the branch, or by clicking the plus sign (+) to the left of the branch, before you can click the port.
4 Click the *Original configuration (current)* check box to clear it, then click *OK*.

Further Study

That's all for Chapter 35. Be sure to review the glossary and chapter questions on the accompanying CD. If you have access to the Internet, take a look at some of these PnP resources:

Microsoft's PnP page: **http://www.microsoft.com/hwdev/specs/pnpspecs.htm**

Microsoft PnP technology: **http://www.microsoft.com/win32dev/base/pnp.htm**

Intel's PnP page: **http://www.intel.com/IAL/plugplay/index.htm**

36

SWITCHING

POWER SUPPLIES

CONTENTS AT A GLANCE

Understanding Switching Supplies
Concepts of switching regulation

Connecting the Power Supply
AT-style power connections
Drive power connections
ATX/NLX-style power connections
Optional ATX/NLX power connector
Voltage tolerances

Troubleshooting Switching Power Supplies
Tips for power-supply service
An example power supply
Symptoms

Further Study

Power supplies play a vital role in the operation of PCs and their peripherals—a supply converts commercial ac into various levels of dc that can be used by electronic and electro-mechanical devices. For the purposes of this book, power supplies are broken into three classes: linear (dc) supplies, switching (dc) supplies, and high-voltage supplies. Although linear power supplies are popular because of their simplicity, they are inefficient. As a result, linear supplies are typically relegated to low-end applications, such as ac adapters and battery eliminators, and are not covered in this edition of the book. On the other hand, switching power supplies are well-entrenched as the primary power source in PC applications. Virtually all PC and peripheral designs incorporate a switching supply. This chapter illustrates the operation and troubleshooting approaches for a switching power supply.

Understanding Switching Supplies

The great disadvantage to linear power supplies is their tremendous waste. At least half of all power provided to a linear supply is literally "thrown away" as heat—most of this waste occurs in the regulator. Ideally, if just enough energy was supplied to the regulator to achieve a stable output voltage, regulator waste could be reduced almost entirely and supply efficiency would be vastly improved.

CONCEPTS OF SWITCHING REGULATION

Instead of throwing away extra input energy, a switching power supply creates a *feedback loop*. Feedback senses the output voltage provided to a load, then switches the ac primary (or secondary) voltage on or off (as needed) to maintain steady levels at the output. In effect, a switching power supply is constantly turning on and off to keep the output voltage(s) steady. A block diagram of a typical switching power supply is shown in Fig. 36-1. A variety of configurations are possible, but Fig. 36-1 illustrates one classic design.

Raw ac line voltage entering the supply is immediately converted to pulsating dc, then filtered to provide a primary dc voltage. Notice that unlike a linear supply, ac is not transformed before rectification, so primary dc can easily reach levels that exceed 170 V. Remember that ac is 120 V RMS. Because capacitors charge to the peak voltage (*peak = RMS* (1.414), dc levels can be higher than your ac voltmeter readings.

> Remember that high-voltage pulsating dc can be as dangerous as ac line voltage, so treat it with extreme caution.

On start-up, the switching transistor is turned on and off at a high frequency (usually 20kHz to 40kHz), and a long duty cycle. The switching transistor acts as a *chopper*, which

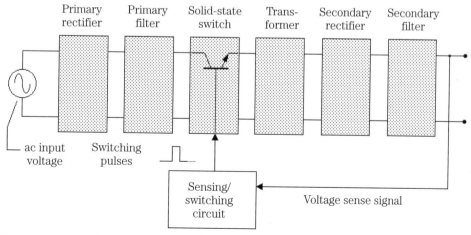

FIGURE 36-1   **Block diagram of a switching power supply.**

breaks up this primary dc to form *chopped dc*, which can now be used as the primary signal for a step-down transformer. The duty cycle of chopped dc will affect the ac voltage level generated on the transformer's secondary. A *long duty cycle* means a larger output voltage (for heavy loads) and a *short duty cycle* means lower output voltage (for light loads). *Duty cycle* itself refers to the amount of time that a signal is "on," compared to its overall cycle. The duty cycle is continuously adjusted by the sensing/switching circuit. You can use an oscilloscope to view switching and chopped dc signals. Figure 36-2 illustrates a more practical representation for a switching supply.

Ac voltage produced on the transformer's secondary winding (typically a step-down transformer) is not a pure sine wave, but it alternates regularly enough to be treated as ac by the remainder of the supply. Secondary voltage is re-rectified and re-filtered to form a secondary dc voltage that is actually applied to the load. Output voltage is sensed by the sensing/switching circuit, which constantly adjusts the chopped dc duty cycle. As load increases on the secondary circuit (more current is drawn by the load), output voltage tends to drop. This is perfectly normal, and the same thing happens in every unregulated supply. However, a sensing circuit detects this voltage drop and increases the switching duty cycle. In turn, the duty cycle for chopped dc increases, which increases the voltage produced by the secondary winding. Output voltage climbs back up again to its desired value. The output voltage is regulated.

The reverse will happen as load decreases on the secondary circuit (less current is drawn by the load). A smaller load will tend to make output voltage climb. Again, the same actions happen in an unregulated supply. The sensing/switching circuit detects this increase in voltage and reduces the switching duty cycle. As a result, the duty cycle for chopped dc decreases and transformer secondary voltage decreases. Output voltage drops back to its desired value. The output voltage remains regulated.

Consider the advantages of a switching power circuit. Current is only drawn in the primary circuit when its switching transistor is on, so very little power is wasted in the primary circuit. The secondary circuit will supply just enough power to keep the load voltage constant (regulated), but very little power is wasted by the secondary rectifier, filter, or switching circuit. Switching power supplies can reach efficiencies higher than 85% (35%

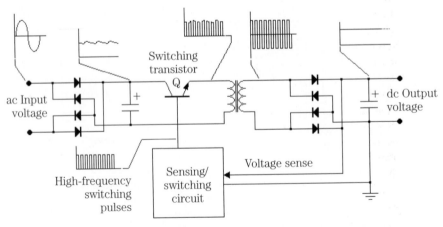

FIGURE 36-2   Simplified diagram of a switching power supply.

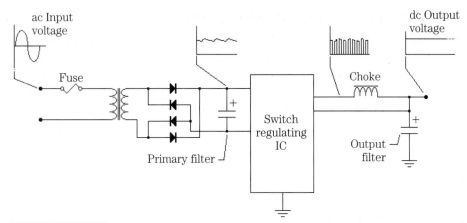

FIGURE 36-3   **Simplified schematic of an IC-based switching power supply.**

more efficient than most comparable linear supplies). More efficiency means less heat is generated by the supply, so components can be smaller and packaged more tightly.

Unfortunately, switching supplies have several disadvantages. First, switching supplies tend to act as radio transmitters. Their 20kHz to 40kHz operating frequencies can wreak havoc radio and television reception, not to mention the circuitry within the PC or peripheral itself. This is why you will see most switching supplies somehow covered or shielded in a metal casing. It is crucially important that you replace any shielding removed during your repair. Strong *ElectroMagnetic Interference (EMI)* can easily disturb the operation of a logic circuit.

Second, the output voltage will always contain some amount of high-frequency ripple. In many applications, this is not enough noise to present interference to the load. In fact, most of the noise is filtered out in a carefully designed supply. Finally, a switching supply often contains more components and is more difficult to troubleshoot than a linear supply. This is often outweighed by the smaller, lighter packaging of switching supplies.

Today, sensing and switching functions can be fabricated right onto an integrated circuit. IC-based switching circuits allow simple, inexpensive circuits to be built (Fig. 36-3). Notice how similar this looks versus a linear supply. Ac line voltage is transformed (usually stepped down), then it is rectified and filtered before reaching a switch-regulating IC. The IC chops dc voltage at a duty cycle that will provide adequate power to the load. Chopped dc from the switching regulator is filtered by the combination of choke and output filter capacitor to reform a steady dc signal at the output. The output voltage is sampled back at the IC, which constantly adjusts the chopped dc duty cycle.

Connecting the Power Supply

PC power supplies operate the motherboard directly, as well as a number of internal drives. This part of the chapter presents the typical connection schemes for AT, ATX, and NLX power supplies, and highlights the major signals.

AT-STYLE POWER CONNECTIONS

The AT-style power supply is largely considered to be the classic connection scheme for IBM-compatible PCs. An AT-style supply provides four voltages to the motherboard (+5 Vdc, –5 Vdc, +12 Vdc, and –12 Vdc) through a series of two 6-pin connectors (Fig. 36-4). You might notice that several wires are used for Ground and other voltage signals, such as +5 Vdc. There is no difference between these similarly colored wires—the extra wires are provided simply because the additional wire is needed to help carry the required current.

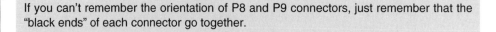

If you can't remember the orientation of P8 and P9 connectors, just remember that the "black ends" of each connector go together.

The only discrete "signal" in the AT-style power connector is the *Power Good (Pwr-Good or PG)* signal. This signal is typically tied to the CPU's Reset pin. When the PC is first powered up, this signal is logic 0 and the CPU is forced into a continuous reset mode. After the power supply is stable (usually about 0.5 seconds from the time you flip the power switch), this signal rises to a logic 1. This releases the Reset, and the CPU can begin processing, which starts the boot process.

DRIVE POWER CONNECTIONS

The internal drives of the PC (e.g., floppy drives, hard drives, CD-ROM drives, etc.) must also be powered. Because drives are electromechanical devices that typically demand a substantial amount of current, they are powered directly from the power supply, rather than from their respective interfaces. Drives traditionally use a heavy-duty four-wire connector to provide

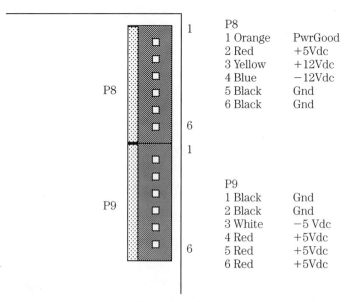

FIGURE 36-4   AT-style motherboard power connections.

+12 Vdc and +5 Vdc to each drive. The +12-Vdc signal powers the drive's motor(s), while the +5-Vdc signal operates the drive's logic circuits. The wire colors are identified as follows:

- Yellow   +12 Vdc
- Black   Ground
- Black   Ground
- Red   +5 Vdc

As a rule, one drive power connector should be available for each drive in the system. Higher-capacity power supplies typically offer more drive power connectors. If you do not have enough drive power connectors to power all of the drives in your system, you might be able to use a Y splitter to transform one power connector into two. However, you should be extremely judicious in the use of Y splitters. The use of inadequate power connectors might indicate that you're pushing the power supply beyond its capacity, and erratic system behavior can result (if the system boots at all). Also, never split the power connector operating a hard drive—the power diverted from a hard drive might result in erratic HDD performance and data corruption.

ATX/NLX-STYLE POWER CONNECTIONS

Although ATX and NLX form-factor systems now constitute the majority of new systems entering service, their power requirements are remarkably similar. The ATX/NLX power supply provides five voltages to the motherboard (+5 Vdc, −5 Vdc, +12 Vdc, −12 Vdc, and +3.3 Vdc) through a 20-pin connector (Fig. 36-5). The +3.3-Vdc supply is added to support the growing base of "low-voltage logic" appearing in the PC. Older AT-style motherboards also incorporate low-voltage logic, but require an on-board voltage regulator to supply the +3.3 Vdc, rather than the power supply. The signals can be identified by their colors:

- Black   Gnd
- Blue   −12 Vdc
- Brown   3.3 V sense
- Gray   Power OK
- Green   PS-ON
- Orange   +3.3 Vdc
- Purple   5 VSB
- Red   +5 Vdc
- White   −5 Vdc
- Yellow   +12 Vdc

In addition to the actual voltages feeding the motherboard, several logic signals are used to control power:

PS-ON   PS-ON is an active-low signal that turns on all of the main power outputs (+3.3 Vdc, +5 Vdc, −5 Vdc, +12 Vdc, and −12 Vdc). When this signal is held high (logic 1) or left open-circuited, the power-supply outputs should be off. In effect, this is the signal that allows "soft control" of the system power.

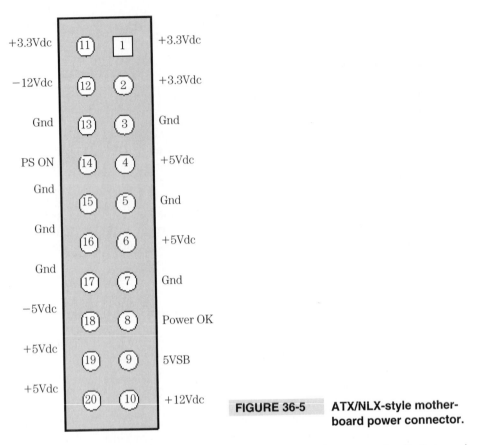

+3.3Vdc	11 1	+3.3Vdc
−12Vdc	12 2	+3.3Vdc
Gnd	13 3	Gnd
PS ON	14 4	+5Vdc
Gnd	15 5	Gnd
Gnd	16 6	+5Vdc
Gnd	17 7	Gnd
−5Vdc	18 8	Power OK
+5Vdc	19 9	5VSB
+5Vdc	20 10	+12Vdc

FIGURE 36-5   ATX/NLX-style mother-board power connector.

5VSB 5VSB is a "standby voltage" source that can be used to power circuits that require power input during the powered-down state. The 5VSB pin should deliver 5 Vdc (+/- 5%) at a minimum of 10 mA for PC board circuits to operate.

PW-OK PW-OK (Power OK) is a "power good" signal and should be set at logic 1 by the power supply to indicate that the +5-Vdc and +3.3-Vdc outputs are above the undervoltage thresholds of the power supply.

OPTIONAL ATX/NLX POWER CONNECTOR

The ATX and NLX form-factor specifications also provide for an optional 6-pin power connector (Fig. 36-6). Each signal adds a certain amount of versatility to the ATX/NLX system. You can identify the optional power connector signals by their wire colors:

- White   FanM
- White/blue stripe   FanC
- White/brown stripe   3.3-V sense
- White/red stripe   1394V
- White/black stripe   1394R

FanM signal The FanM signal is an open collector, 2-pulse per revolution tachometer signal from the power-supply fan. This signal allows the system to monitor the power supply for fan speed or failures. If this signal is not implemented on the motherboard, it should not impact the power-supply function.

FanC signal The FanC signal is an optional fan-speed and shutdown-control signal. The fan speed and shutdown are controlled by a variable voltage on this pin. This signal allows the system to request control of the power supply fan from full speed to off. The control circuit on the motherboard should supply voltage to this pin from +12 Vdc to 0 Vdc for the fan-control request.

3.3-V sense line A remote 3.3-V sense line can be added to the optional connector to allow for accurate control of the 3.3-Vdc line directly at motherboard loads.

1394V pin This pin on the optional connector allows for implementation of a segregated voltage supply rail for use with unpowered IEEE-1394 ("fire wire") solutions. The power derived from this pin should be used to power only 1394 connectors (unregulated anywhere from 8 to 40 V).

1394R pin The 1394R pin provides an isolated ground path for unpowered IEEE-1394 ("fire wire") implementations. This ground should be used only for 1394 connections, and should be fully isolated from other ground planes in the system.

VOLTAGE TOLERANCES

If you pursue power-supply testing or troubleshooting at any level, you're going to need to test the output voltages. One important aspect of voltage measurements that are often overlooked by novice technicians is the idea of "voltage tolerance." Voltage outputs are rarely exact, and might vary from their rated value by as much as 5% (often 3 to 4% for the +3.3-Vdc output). For example, a +5-Vdc output might actually read between +4.75 Vdc and +5.25 Vdc, and a +12-Vdc output might read from +11.4 Vdc to +12.6 Vdc. As long as the measured voltage is within a reasonable tolerance, the output should be considered good. If the measured voltage strays outside of this reasonable tolerance (usually to the

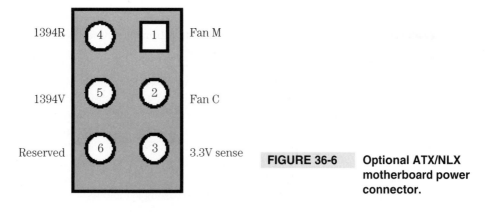

FIGURE 36-6   Optional ATX/NLX motherboard power connector.

low side), chances are that the output is being overloaded by excessive devices. If the output measures extremely low (or is absent) chances are that the output (and the power supply) is defective. You can then choose to repair or replace the power supply.

Troubleshooting Switching Power Supplies

Troubleshooting a switching power supply can be a complex and time-consuming task. Although the operation of rectifier and filter sections are reasonably straightforward, sensing/switching circuits can be complex oscillators that are difficult to follow without a schematic. Sub-assembly replacement of dc switching supplies is quite common.

TIPS FOR POWER-SUPPLY SERVICE

Power and power-supply problems can manifest themselves in a stunning variety of ways, but the following tips should help you to stay out of trouble:

- Power-supply cooling is important—keep the vent openings and fan blades clean.
- Be sure that the line-voltage switch (120/220 Vac) is set correctly for your region.
- Verify that the power-supply connectors are attached to the motherboard and drives securely.
- Remember that for AT-style power connections, the "black wires go together."
- Do not use a Y splitter to split power from a HDD (avoid Y splitters entirely, if possible).
- Some Y splitters are wired improperly. If you have trouble with a device after installing a Y splitter, check the splitter or try powering the device directly.
- Voltage tolerances are usually ±5% (±4% for 3.3 Vdc), so be sure that each output is within tolerance.
- If you experience erratic system behavior after adding a new device, this can be the result of an overload. Try removing the device.

AN EXAMPLE POWER SUPPLY

For the purposes of this troubleshooting section, consider the IC-based switching supply of Fig. 36-7. The STK7554 is a switching regulator IC manufactured as a 16-pin SIP (single in-line package). It offers a dual output of 24 Vdc and 5 Vdc. Notice that both output waveforms from the STK7554 are 38-V square waves, but the duty cycle of those square waves sets the desired output levels. The square wave's amplitude simply provides energy to the filter circuits. Filters made from coils ("chokes") and high-value polarized capacitors smooth the square-wave input (actually a form of pulsating dc) into a steady source of dc. Some small amount of high-frequency ripple will be on each dc output. Smaller, non-polarized capacitors on each output act to filter out high-frequency components of the dc output. Finally, notice the resistor-capacitor-diode combinations on each output. These form a surge and flyback protector, which prevents energy stored in the choke from re-entering the IC and damaging it. Refer to Fig. 36-7 for the following symptoms.

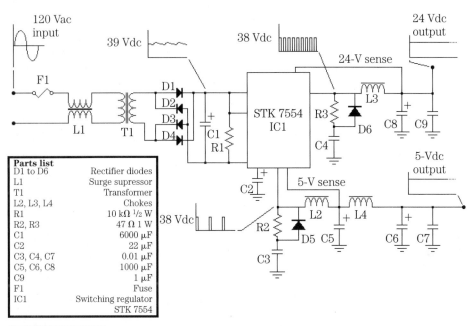

FIGURE 36-7   A complete IC-based switching power supply.

SYMPTOMS

Symptom 36-1. The PC or peripheral is completely dead—no power indicators are lit As with linear supplies, check the ac line voltage entering the PC before beginning any major repair work. Use your multimeter to measure the ac line voltage available at the wall outlet that is powering your computer or peripheral. Be extremely cautious whenever measuring ac line-voltage levels. Normally, you should read between 105 and 130 Vac to ensure proper-supply operation. If you find either very high or low ac voltage, try the device in an outlet that provides the correct amount of ac voltage. Unusual line voltage levels might damage your power supply, so proceed cautiously.

If ac line voltage is normal, suspect that the main power fuse in the supply has failed. Most power fuses are accessible from the rear of the computer near the ac line cord, but some fuses might only be accessible by disassembling the device and opening the supply. Unplug the device and remove the fuse from its holder. You should find the fusible link intact, but use your multimeter to measure continuity across the fuse. A good fuse should measure as a short circuit (0 ohms), but a failed fuse will measure as an open circuit (infinity). Replace any failed fuse and re-test the PC. If the fuse continually fails, a serious defect is elsewhere within the power supply or other computer/peripheral circuits. If your supply has an ac selector switch that sets the supply for 120-Vac or 240-Vac operation, be sure that switch is in the proper position for your region of the world (an improperly set ac switch can disable the entire system).

Unplug the computer and disassemble it enough to expose the power supply clearly. Restore power to the PC and measure each dc output with your multimeter or oscilloscope (you can usually find a power connector at the motherboard or other main board). Be sure that any power cables are securely attached. If each output measures correctly, then your trouble lies outside of the supply—a key circuit has failed elsewhere in the device. You can try a POST board or diagnostic to trace the specific problem further. A low output voltage is suggestive of a problem within the supply itself. Check each connector and all interconnecting wiring leading to or from the supply. Remember that many switching supplies must be attached to a load for proper switching to occur. If the load circuit is disconnected from its supply, the voltage signal could shutdown or oscillate wildly.

If the supply outputs continue to measure incorrectly with all connectors and wiring intact, chances are that your problem is inside the supply. With a linear supply, begin testing at the output, then work back toward the ac input. For a switching supply, you should begin testing at the ac input, then work toward the defective output.

Measure the primary ac voltage applied across the transformer (T1). Use extreme caution when measuring high-voltage ac. You should read approximately 120 Vac for Fig. 36-7. If voltage has been interrupted in that primary circuit, the meter will read 0 Vac. Check the primary circuit for any fault that might interrupt power. Measure secondary ac voltage supplying the rectifier stage. It should read higher than the highest output voltage that you expect. For the example of Fig. 36-7, the highest expected dc output is 24 V, so ac secondary voltage should be several volts higher than this. The example shows this as 28 Vac. If primary voltage reads correctly and secondary voltage does not, an open circuit might be in the primary or secondary transformer winding. Try replacing the transformer.

Next, check the pre-switched dc voltage supplying the switching IC. Use your multimeter or oscilloscope to measure this dc level. You should read approximately the peak value of whatever secondary ac voltage you just measured. For Fig. 36-7, a secondary voltage of 28 Vac should yield a dc voltage of about (28 Vac RMS (1.414) 39 Vdc. If this voltage is low or non-existent, unplug ac from the supply and check each rectifier diode, then inspect the filter capacitor.

Use your oscilloscope to measure each chopped dc output signal. You should find a high-frequency square wave at each output (20kHz to 40kHz) with an amplitude approximately equal to the pre-switched dc level (38 to 39 volts in this case). Set your oscilloscope to a time base of 5 or 10 S/DIV and start your VOLTS/DIV setting at 10 VOLTS/DIV. Once you have established a clear trace, adjust the time base and vertical sensitivity to optimize the display.

If you do not read a chopped dc output from the switching IC, either the IC is defective or one (or more) of the polarized output filter capacitors might be shorted. Unplug the PC and inspect each questionable filter capacitor. Replace any capacitors that appear shorted. As a general rule, filter capacitors tend to fail more readily in switching supplies than in linear supplies because of high-frequency electrical stress and the smaller physical size of most switching-supply components. If all filter capacitors check out correctly, replace the switching IC. Use care when desoldering the old regulator. Install an IC socket (if possible) to prevent repeat soldering work, then just plug in the new IC. If you do not have the tools to perform this work (or the problem persists), replace the power supply outright.

Symptom 36-2. Supply operation is intermittent—device operation cuts in and out with the supply Inspect the ac line voltage into your printer. Be sure that the ac line cord is secured properly at the wall outlet and printer. Be sure that the power fuse is installed securely. If the PC/peripheral comes on at all, the fuse has to be intact. Unplug the device and expose your power supply. Inspect every connector or interconnecting wire leading into or out of the supply. A loose or improperly installed connector can play havoc with the system's operation. Pay particular attention to any output connections. In almost all cases, a switching power supply must be connected to its load circuit in order to operate. Without a load, the supply might cut out or oscillate wildly.

In many cases, intermittent operation might be the result of a PC board problem. PC board problems are often the result of physical abuse or impact, but they can also be caused by accidental damage during a repair. Lead pull-through occurs when a wire or component lead is pulled away from its solder joint, usually through its hole in the PC board. This type of defect can easily be repaired by re-inserting the pulled lead and properly re-soldering the defective joint. Trace breaks are hairline fractures between a solder pad and its printed trace. Such breaks can usually render a circuit inoperative, and they are almost impossible to spot without a careful visual inspection. Board cracks can sever any number of printed traces, but they are often very easy to spot. The best method for repairing trace breaks and board cracks is to solder jumper wires across the damage between two adjacent solder pads. You could also simply replace the power supply outright.

Some forms of intermittent failures are time or temperature related. If your system works just fine when first turned on, but fails only after a period of use, then spontaneously returns to operation later on (or after it has been off for a while), you might be faced with a thermally intermittent component—a component might work when cool, but fail later on after reaching or exceeding its working temperature. After a system quits under such circumstances, check for any unusually hot components. Never touch an operating circuit with your fingers—injury is almost certain. Instead, smell around the circuit for any trace of burning semiconductor or unusually heated air. If you detect an overheated component, spray it with a liquid refrigerant. Spray in short bursts for the best cooling. If normal operation returns, then you have isolated the defective component. Replace any components that behave intermittently. If operation does not return, test any other unusually warm components. If problems persist, replace the entire power supply outright.

Further Study

This concludes the material for Chapter 36. Be sure to review the glossary and chapter questions on the accompanying CD. If you have access to the Internet, take a look at some of these power-supply resources:

UL (Underwriter's Laboratories): **http://www.ul.com/**

TUV (German Standards): **http://www.tuv.com/**

Astec: **http://www.astec.com/**

PC Power and Cooling: **http://www.pcpowercooling.com**

Amtrade: **http://www.amtrade.com**

37

HIGH-VOLTAGE
POWER SUPPLIES

CONTENTS AT A GLANCE

Backlight Power Supplies
   Inverter principles
   Troubleshooting backlight supplies

CRT Flyback Supplies
   Troubleshooting flyback supplies

Further Study

Although switching power supplies provide the conventional dc voltage levels needed for PC and peripheral operation, they are not well suited for high-voltage applications. To power specialized devices, such as CRTs and LCD backlights, the ordinary power supply is supplemented by high-voltage supply circuits, which can turn relatively low voltages into high voltages that range anywhere from several hundred volts to tens of thousands of volts, depending on the particular need. This chapter illustrates the operation and troubleshooting approaches two important high-voltage circuits: the backlight supply and the CRT flyback supply.

Backlight Power Supplies

Today's notebook and sub-notebook LCDs are almost always based on a transmissive light design; the light that you see from the display is generated entirely from behind the

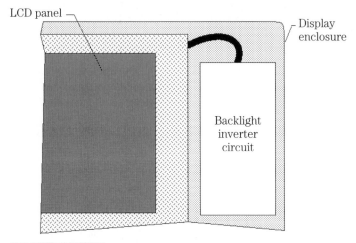

FIGURE 37-1   Locating the LCD backlight inverter.

LCD by a backlight assembly. Whatever light emanates from the display is interpreted as being transparent (or colored). Light that is absorbed by energized liquid crystal material appears opaque. To run a *CCFT (Cold-Cathode Fluorescent Tube)* or *EL (ElectroLuminescent)* backlight, a source of several hundred volts is needed (often 200 V or more). Because the battery pack in a mobile computer is certainly not capable of sourcing that much voltage, it must be created on the fly. If you remove the front housing from an LCD panel, you can locate the backlight supply right next to the LCD (Fig. 37-1).

INVERTER PRINCIPLES

The key to a backlight power supply is the principle of *inversion*—converting ("chopping") dc into an ac signal. A simple inverter circuit is shown in the illustration of Fig. 37-2. Dc from the battery pack is fed to an oscillator. The oscillator chops the dc into low-voltage pulsating dc. In turn, the pulsating dc is applied across a small, high-ratio step-up transformer, which multiplies the pulsating dc into a rough ac signal. This high-voltage ac signal can then be used to run a CCFT or EL backlight. As you might notice, the conversion of dc into ac is virtually opposite of the process used in linear or switching power supplies (thus, the term *inverter*), where a relatively high ac voltage is transformed into a low dc voltage(s). If dc is required from the inverter, rather than ac, a rectifier and filter will follow the transformer output.

TROUBLESHOOTING BACKLIGHT SUPPLIES

Backlight problems usually manifest themselves in the LCD itself. Without proper backlighting, the contrast and brightness of a display will be extremely poor. The display might appear clearly in strong daylight, but might disappear in low light or darkness. When backlight problems occur, investigate the inverter supply, as well as the particular mechanism (e.g., CCFT or EL panel) producing the light.

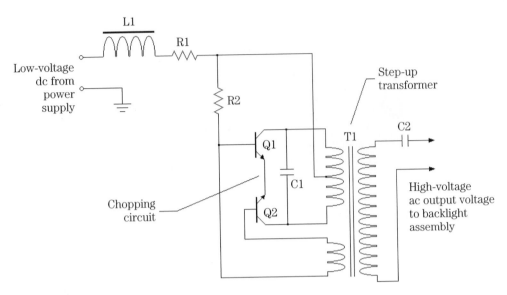

FIGURE 37-2 A basic backlight inverter circuit.

Symptom 37-1. The backlight appears to be inoperative The LCD might seem washed out or invisible in low light. Remember that virtually all notebook and sub-notebook computers are designed to shut down the backlight after some period of inactivity, regardless of whether the system is being powered by battery or line voltage. Backlights, such as CCFTs and EL panels, do not last forever, so disabling the backlight not only saves power during battery operation, but saves the backlight itself. If the backlight cuts out suddenly, it might simply have timed out. Try pressing a key or moving the mouse to restore backlight power. You can usually select the backlight timeout period through the system setup software.

Disassemble the display portion of your display to expose the inverter board (typically located behind or next to the LCD). Apply power to the system, then use your multimeter to measure the inverter's dc input voltage. The input voltage usually runs anywhere from 6 to 32 Vdc, depending on your particular system and backlight type. In any case, you would expect to measure a strong, steady dc voltage. If input voltage is low or absent, the connection to the system motherboard might be faulty.

Next, use your multimeter to measure the inverter's ac output voltage. Fluorescent tubes and electroluminescent panels typically require 200 to 600 Vac for starting and running illumination. Warning: the insulation of ordinary test leads might break down while measuring voltages higher than 600 V. If you will be measuring voltages over 500 or 600 V, be sure to use better-insulated test probes. If output voltage is low or absent, the inverter circuit is probably defective. You could simply replace the inverter circuit outright or attempt to troubleshoot the inverter to the component level. If output voltage measures an acceptable level, your inverter board is probably working correctly—the trouble might exist in the light source itself. For example, a CCFT might have failed or an EL panel might be damaged. Try replacing the suspect light source.

If you elect to troubleshoot the inverter board itself, you can see from Fig. 37-2 that little can fail. Remove all power from the computer and check the oscillator transistors. A faulty transistor can stop your inverter from oscillating so that no ac voltage will be produced. Replace any defective transistors. Beyond faulty transistors, inspect any electrolytic capacitors on the inverter board. A shorted or open tantalum or aluminum electrolytic capacitor might prevent the oscillator from functioning. The transformer might also fail, but these specialized components are often difficult to find replacements for. If you are unable to locate any obvious component failures, replace the inverter board.

CRT Flyback Supplies

High-voltage is perhaps the most crucial (and dangerous) aspect of any computer monitor. A CRT requires an extremely high potential to accelerate an electron beam from the cathode to its phosphor-coated face (easily a distance of 12" to 14" or more). To accomplish this feat of physics, a positive voltage of 15,000 to 30,000 Vdc is applied to the CRT's face through a connection known as the *anode*. It is easy to identify the anode connection—it is underneath the thick red rubber cap on the upper right corner of the CRT (with the neck toward you). Fortunately, the high-voltage system is relatively easy to understand.

A typical high-voltage system is illustrated in the schematic fragment of Fig. 37-3. The only one crucial part is the *FlyBack Transformer (FBT)*, marked *T302*. The horizontal output transistor (Q302) generate high-current pulses that control the horizontal deflection yoke (H-DY). Horizontal output signals are also fed to the FBT, which boosts the signal to its final high-voltage level. The lower primary winding is connected back to the video circuit and acts as an "error amplifier." This allows the high-voltage level to vary as contrast and brightness are adjusted. The FBT assembly produces three outputs. The high-voltage output is connected directly to the CRT anode through a well-insulated, high-voltage cable. A supplemental output of several hundred volts feeds a small voltage-divider network, consisting of two potentiometers and a fixed resistor. The top potentiometer controls the higher voltages and is used to drive the CRT's focus electrode(s). The second potentiometer drives the CRT's screen electrode(s).

The voltages generated by a FBT are all pulsating dc signals. Because all transformers work with ac, rather than dc, there is always a question of how dc is produced by an ac device. The answer is in the small diode located between the top and middle coils of the FBT secondary. This diode forms a half-wave rectifier built right into the FBT. Pulsating high-voltage is smoothed by the characteristic capacitance of the CRT. The pulsating focus and screen voltages are smoothed by filtering components located on the video board attached to the CRT.

TROUBLESHOOTING FLYBACK SUPPLIES

The loss of high-voltage can manifest itself in several ways, depending on exactly where the fault occurs, but in virtually all cases, the screen image and raster will be disturbed or disappear completely. Whenever a screen image disappears, you should first suspect a fault in the conventional power supply. By measuring each available output with a multimeter, you can often determine whether the problem is inside or outside of the power supply. If one or more conventional power output levels appear low or absent, concentrate

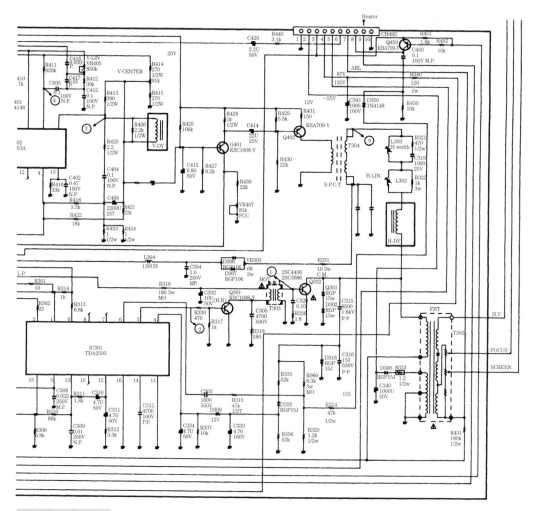

FIGURE 37-3 **High-voltage schematic fragment from Tandy VGM-220 monitor.** Tandy Corporation

your troubleshooting on the conventional supply. If all outputs appear normal, the problem is likely in the high-voltage system. Refer to Fig. 37-3.

Symptom 37-2. Anode high-voltage measures very low—it has no raster and no picture, or a vertical line is against the raster The power LED appears steadily lit, and all conventional power-supply outputs measure correctly. Be sure that the display contrast and brightness controls are set to acceptable levels. Also check that the video signal cable from the video adapter is connected properly. Use your oscilloscope and measure the horizontal pulse at the collector of the horizontal output transistor (Q302). If the pulse is present, the fault is likely in the flyback transformer assembly. Try replacing the FBT. Remember that the FBT must be replaced with an identical type of part. If the problem persists, suspect that the problem is in the CRT. Use a CRT analyzer/rejuvenator (if possible) to check the CRT. If the CRT checks bad or if the equipment is not available, replace the CRT. Note that the CRT is often the most expensive part of a monitor. Before replacing the CRT, you should carefully weigh the cost of another CRT against the cost of another monitor.

If the horizontal pulse is missing from the collector, use your oscilloscope to check the input at the base of Q302. You should find approximately a 5-V pulse. If the pulse is present, Q302 has failed and should be replaced with an exact replacement part. If the pulse is missing from the base, check the collector of the horizontal switching transistor (Q301). If the pulse is present at the collector of Q301, but missing from the base of Q302, the fault is likely in the horizontal output transformer (T303). Try replacing T303. If you find that the pulse signal is missing from the collector of Q301, check for the pulse at the base of Q301. If the pulse is present, Q301 is defective and should be replaced. If the pulse is still missing from the base of Q301, the problem is likely in the horizontal output controller. Try replacing the horizontal controller IC. If you are unable to follow trace the circuit or locate the defect, you can simply replace the main monitor PC board.

Further Study

That's all for Chapter 37. Be sure to review the glossary and chapter questions on the accompanying CD (no Internet references are in this chapter).

38

REMOVABLE

MEDIA DRIVES

CONTENTS AT A GLANCE

Iomega Zip Drive
  Zip drive troubleshooting

Iomega Ditto Drive
  Ditto demands
  Ditto drive troubleshooting

Iomega Bernoulli Drives
  Bernoulli notes
  Bernoulli drive troubleshooting

SyQuest Drives
  SyQuest drive troubleshooting

Further Study

When you think about "PC drives", you probably think about the four classic types of drives: floppy drives, hard drives, tape drives, and CD-ROM drives. These are the most widely accepted and supported drives available today. However, drive designers are always looking for ways to provide better and faster storage solutions, and pack ever-more data onto smaller, more efficient media. As a result, the PC industry often deals with a number of "non-standard" drives—devices that utilize existing magnetic and optical technologies, but do not easily fit the mold of other drives. "Non-standard" drives are also traditionally after-market or add-on devices that are attached through a parallel port, a SCSI interface, or some other proprietary type of drive adapter. Iomega and SyQuest are perhaps the two largest and best-respected makers of "non-standard" drives, and this chapter looks at the background and troubleshooting of the four most popular "non-standard" drives: the Iomega Zip drive, the Iomega Ditto drive, the Iomega Bernoulli drive, and the SyQuest drive.

Iomega Zip Drive

For "removable media" to be popular, it must follow three basic guidelines: it must record quickly, it must hold a lot of data on a single cartridge (or other media), and it must be portable between drives. Floppy drives are very portable, but they hold only a little data. Tapes hold a lot of data, but they are slow and are not very portable between drives. Hard drives are quite fast and hold a great deal of data, but they are simply not portable. CD-ROM drives are relatively fast, they also hold a lot of data, and the CDs themselves are very portable, but you need specialized drives to "burn" a CD—and the disc can be used only once. The search for reusable, high-capacity media that is transportable between inexpensive, readily available drives has led Iomega to produce their Zip drive.

The Zip drive has become perhaps the single most popular "non-standard" drive in production today. In fact, the Zip drive is so popular that some PC makers include them as standard equipment in new systems. Zip drives offer relatively fast seek times at 29 ms, and can sustain data rates of 300KB/s across the parallel port (or 1MB/s via SCSI or IDE interfaces). Each cartridge can hold up to 100MB, which is large enough to hold huge illustrations, CAD layouts, and even small multimedia presentations. When used with a SCSI interface and a properly configured Adaptec SCSI controller, you can even boot from the Zip drive. Zip drives are available in both internal and external versions.

ZIP DRIVE TROUBLESHOOTING

Symptom 38-1. An Iomega Zip drive displays a *Floppy-disk* icon under Windows 95 However, the drive appears to operate properly. This is almost always because of the use of a real-mode DOS driver to support the Iomega drive and adapter. You will need to update the real-mode driver to an appropriate protected-mode driver for Windows 95. For SCSI adapters, you need to find the protected-mode SCSI driver for your particular SCSI adapter and install it through the *Add new hardware* wizard in the *Control panel*. After the protected-mode driver is installed, you can remove the obsolete real-mode driver from CONFIG.SYS. For native Iomega SCSI adapters, get the protected-mode drivers directly from Iomega. For parallel-port Zip drives, uninstall the old drive software and install the new Windows 95 driver software.

Symptom 38-2. The SCSI Zip drive has no drive letter under Windows 95 The drive does not appear to respond. In virtually all cases, the SCSI driver has not loaded properly. First, open the *Device manager* and expand the *SCSI controllers* entry, then check the *Iomega adapter* line beneath it. If there is a yellow symbol with an exclamation mark on it, the Windows 95 driver did not load. Check the controller next by highlighting that *Iomega adapter* line, then select *Properties*. Click on the *Resources* page, then verify that your I/O range and IRQ options are set correctly—they must match the jumper settings on your adapter board. If you must update the resource settings manually, be sure that the *Automatic settings* box is not checked (and remember to save any changes). If you allocated new resources, you might have to shut off the PC and change jumper settings on the controller board itself to match the resources allocated in the *Device manager*. Restart the computer—once the system reboots, the Windows 95 driver should load normally.

If problems persist, check the signal connector (especially for SCSI adapters). Be sure that the SCSI cable is intact and connected to the drive properly. If problems continue, your SCSI adapter is probably installed correctly, but the bus might be terminated improperly. Be sure that you terminate both ends of the SCSI bus properly.

Symptom 38-3. The parallel-port Zip drive has no drive letter under Windows 95 Parallel-port drive problems can almost always be traced to faulty connections, port-configuration issues, or driver problems. Check the external power connector first. Parallel-port drives are powered externally. Be sure that the power pack is working, and see that the power cable is connected properly to the drive. If the drive does not appear to power up, try a different power pack or drive. Check the signal cable next and be sure that you are using a good-quality, known-good parallel-port cable that is attached securely at the PC and drive. The Zip drive is very sensitive to devices, such as copy-protection modules (*dongles*), and other "pass-through" devices. Try connecting the drive directly to the parallel port. Also disconnect any printers on the parallel port.

The parallel-port setup might be incorrect. Reboot the PC and enter CMOS setup. Check to see that the parallel port is configured in EPP or bi-directional mode. If the problem continues in the EPP mode, try configuring the parallel port for "compatibility mode." For SCSI installations, check the SCSI host controller. There is a known incompatibility between the Iomega Zip drive and the Adaptec 284x adapter—the Iomega PPA3 driver does not work with the Adaptec 284x controller. Check with Iomega for an updated driver.

The problem might be with your driver(s). Open the *Device manager* and find the *SCSI controllers* entry (even though it is a parallel-port device). If there is no such entry, the driver is not installed. If you expand the *SCSI controllers* section, there should be an entry for the Iomega parallel-port Zip interface. If not, the driver is not installed. Check for hardware conflicts. If the *Device manager* entry for the Iomega parallel-port Zip interface has a yellow circle with an exclamation mark on it, the interface is configured improperly and is conflicting with other devices. Also check for device properties. Highlight the *Iomega parallel-port Zip interface* entry, click on *Properties*, then select the *Settings* page. Find the box marked *Adapter settings*, then type:

```
/mode:nibble /speed:1
```

Save your changes and reboot the system. If that fails, try reinstalling the drivers. Highlight the *Iomega parallel-port Zip interface* and select *Remove*. Then reinstall the drivers from scratch. Next, try running in DOS. Start the PC in DOS mode (command prompt only), then install the Iomega installation disk and type:

```
a:\guest        <Enter>
```

If the Zip drive still does not receive a drive letter, the parallel port might be faulty or incompatible with the drive. Try the drive on another system. If this tactic works on another system, the problem is definitely related to your original PC hardware. If the problem follows the drive, the fault is likely in the drive. Try another drive.

Symptom 38-4. The system hangs when installing drivers for Windows 95
System hangups during installation are usually the result of hardware conflicts or problems. Check the signal cable first and be sure that you are using a good-quality, known-good cable, which is attached securely at the PC and drive. Open the *Device manager* and find the *SCSI controllers*. If there is no such entry, the driver is not installed. If you expand the *SCSI controllers* section, an entry should be listed for the *Iomega parallel-port Zip interface*. If not, the driver is not installed.

Check for hardware conflicts. If the *Device manager* entry for the Iomega parallel-port Zip interface has a yellow circle with an exclamation mark on it, the interface is configured improperly and is conflicting with other devices. Highlight the *Iomega parallel-port Zip interface* entry, click on *Properties*, then select the *Settings* page. Find the box marked *Adapter settings*, then type:

```
/mode:nibble /speed:1
```

Save your changes and reboot the system. If problems continue, try running in DOS. Start the PC in DOS mode (command prompt only), then install the Iomega installation disk and type:

```
a:\guest        <Enter>
```

If the Zip drive still does not receive a drive letter, the parallel port might be faulty or incompatible with the drive. Try the drive on another system. If this tactic works on another system, the problem is definitely related to your original PC hardware. If the problem follows the drive, the fault is likely in the drive. Try another drive.

Symptom 38-5. After installing a Zip drive, you find the other drives in the system are using the DOS-compatibility mode
This is almost always the result of the GUEST.EXE program. The real-mode GUEST.EXE program supplied by Iomega is designed to allow you to access the Zip drive in DOS and Windows 95, and this causes the other drives in your system to use the DOS-compatibility mode (you might also notice a decline in drive or system performance). Try installing the protected-mode drivers for the Iomega drive:

- In the *Control panel*, doubleclick the *Add new hardware* icon.
- Click *Next*, click the *No* button, then click *Next*.
- Click *Other devices*, then click *Next*.
- In the *Manufacturers* box, click *Iomega*, then click *Have disk*.
- Install the files from the Windows 95 CD-ROM by inserting the CD-ROM in the drive, typing the following line in the *Copy manufacturer's files from* box, then clicking *Next*:

```
<drive>:\drivers\storage\iomega
```

where <drive> is the drive letter of the CD-ROM drive.

■ After the files are copied, click *Finish*.

■ Restart the computer when prompted to do so.

Symptom 38-6. The Zip drive takes over the CD-ROM drive letter in Windows 95 You might simply need to switch drive letters between the Zip drive and CD-ROM drive:

■ Open *Device manager* and doubleclick on the *Disk drives* entry.

■ Highlight the *Iomega Zip* drive entry and click on *Properties*.

■ Click on the *Settings* page.

■ In the *Reserved drive letters* section, there is a *Start drive letter* and an *End drive letter* setting. Enter the desired drive letter for the Zip drive in both start and end drive entries (be sure to use the same drive letter for both start and end). Click on *OK*.

■ Doubleclick on the CD-ROM entry.

■ Highlight your *CD-ROM drive* entry and click on *Properties*.

■ Click on the *Settings* page.

■ The *Reserved drive letters* section has a *Start drive letter* and an *End drive letter* setting. Enter the desired drive letter for the CD-ROM drive in both start and end entries (be sure to use the same drive letter for both start and end). Click on *OK*.

■ Click on *OK* to close *Device manager*, then shut down and restart the computer.

Symptom 38-7. Duplicate ZIP drive letters appear You notice that the Zip drive (or another drive) has been assigned a duplicate drive letter. In most cases, the problem can be traced to a third-party SCSI adapter and drivers, which conflict with Iomega SCSI drivers. Do not use any drive before correcting this problem. Open your CONFIG.SYS file and examine each driver that scans the SCSI bus to assign drive letters. Chances are very good that you have a third-party driver, which is assigning a letter to the Zip drive, as well as an Iomega-specific driver assigning another letter to the Zip drive. Use a command-line switch with the third-party SCSI driver to limit the number of IDs that will be assigned.

Symptom 38-8. A Zip guest locks up or cannot locate the drive or adapter Chances are that an ASPI manager referenced in the GUEST.INI file is conflicting with hardware in the PC. This often happens in systems with two SCSI adapters (and parallel ports). Try editing the GUEST.INI file. Open the GUEST.INI file on your Iomega install disk and specify which ASPI manager needs to load in order to access the Zip drive. Remember to make a backup copy of the GUEST.INI file before editing it. As an alternative, choose the Iomega SCSI adapter driver. If you are using a native Iomega SCSI adapter, choose the ASPI manager that applies to the adapter as shown in Table 38-1. Once you have identified the proper ASPI manager for your adapter, REMark-out all of the other ASPI lines in GUEST.INI, except for the one that you need.

If you are using a non-Iomega SCSI adapter, you will need to add the complete path and filename for the driver to GUEST.INI, and REMark-out all of the other ASPI drivers. Once the GUEST.INI file is updated, save your changes and reboot the system, then run GUEST from the drive and directory containing the updated GUEST.INI file. If problems persist, try the drive on another system or try a new drive on the suspect system.

TABLE 38-1 A LISTING OF NATIVE IOMEGA ASPI DRIVERS	
IOMEGA ADAPTER	**ASPI MANAGER**
Zip Zoom SCSI accelerator	ASPIPC16.SYS
Jaz Jet SCSI accelerator	ASPI2930.SYS
Parallel-Port Zip drive	ASPIPPA3.SYS or ASPIPPM1.SYS
PPA-3 adapter	ASPIPPA3.SYS
PC1616	ASPIPC16.SYS
PC800	ASPIPC8.SYS
PC2	ASPIPC2.SYS
PC4	ASPIPC4.SYS

Symptom 38-9. You encounter Zip drive letter problems under DOS The drive letters following C: might change unexpectedly when Iomega drivers are installed to support a new device. This can interfere with applications that look at specific drives, or access to network resources. You will need to relocate the drives before installing Iomega software. Because the GUEST.EXE utility loads at the end of AUTOEXEC.BAT, the Iomega drive will be assigned the last drive letter. DOS assigns letters to network drives alphabetically after assigning letters to any internal or external drives connected to the computer. When a new drive is added, the network drive might be "pushed down" one letter (i.e., from E: to F:). Applications that reference specific drive letters might then fail to work correctly unless they are reinstalled or adjusted for the drive letter change. If you use a batch file to connect to a network, it will need to be updated to the new drive letter. A network log-in script might also need to be revised.

Use the DOS LASTDRIVE= command to relocate your first network drive letter further down the alphabet—this insulates your network drive letter assignment from future changes should you add other drives to your system. For example, you can make your network drive N: by adding the following line to the end of CONFIG.SYS. This would allow you to add 10 drives (D: through M:) to a system without pushing down your network drive letter:

```
LASTDRIVE=M
```

Do not set your last drive to Z: or you will be unable to access any network drive. If you use multiple network drives, do not set your last drive to a letter late in the alphabet (such as X: or Y) because that will limit the number of network drives that you can use simultaneously.

Check your CD-ROM drive letters. CD-ROM drives have a specific drive letter determined by the /L option of MSCDEX in AUTOEXEC.BAT (for example, /L:E assigns the CD-ROM as drive E:). When a new drive is installed, DOS might assign the CD-ROM drive letter to the new drive and the CD-ROM drive might seem to disappear. Change the drive letter for the CD-ROM to a letter not assigned to another drive. You might want to relocate your CD-ROM drive several letters down the alphabet so that you do not have to relocate it each time you add a new drive to your system. You must have a LASTDRIVE statement in CONFIG.SYS, which sets the last drive equal to or later than the CD-ROM letter. Finally, check the overall system configuration. When DOS does reassign drive letters, be sure to check each of these points:

■ Edit the PATH statement in AUTOEXEC.BAT to correctly reference new drive letter.
■ Edit any batch files (including AUTOEXEC.BAT) to correctly reference new drive letters.
■ Edit all Windows .INI files and Windows groups to correctly reference new drive letters.
■ Check other application setup files and rerun the application's setup if the drive letters cannot be edited.
■ For networks, check your user log-in script for references to specific network drive letters.
■ Reboot the computer and check major applications—those that do not work with the new drive letter might need to be reinstalled.

Symptom 38-10. The GUEST utility cannot find an available drive letter If all drive letters are in use, GUEST will not be able to assign a drive letter to the Zip drive. Change the last drive designation. Use the DOS LASTDRIVE command in the end of CONFIG.SYS to increase the number of available drive letters. Do not use a letter near the end of the alphabet.

Symptom 38-11. System recovery fails after the Zip Tools setup process is complete If the Zip Tools software for your Zip drive fails to install properly (or if the system hangs or was powered down), the Windows *Startup* group will have a *Zip setup* icon that will attempt to run each time Windows is started. Delete the *Zip* icon in your *Startup* group, then reinstall the Zip software.

Symptom 38-12. Error messages, such as: "Can't find Zip tools disk" or "No drive letters added," appear when using Zip parallel-port drives In most cases, you will have to manually assign the proper ASPI driver by editing your GUEST.INI file. Open the GUEST.INI file on your Iomega install disk. Highlight the ASPI driver line that reads ASPIPPA3.SYS, then add the following commands: /MODE=1 /SPEED=1. Remember to make a backup copy of the GUEST.INI file before editing it. The final command line should appear, such as:

```
ASPI=ASPIPPA3.SYS SCAN /INFO SL360=NO SMC=NO /MODE=1 /SPEED=1
```

Save your changes to GUEST.INI, then run GUEST from the drive and directory that contains your edited GUEST.INI file. GUEST should now assign a drive letter to the Zip drive. Reboot the PC, start Windows, then run the Iomega setup routine from the drive and directory, which contains your edited GUEST.INI file. The Windows installation should now proceed normally.

Next, check the signal connector and be sure that the parallel-port or SCSI cable is connected properly between the drive and system. Try a known-good working signal cable. If problems persist, boot the system from a "clean" diskette and try running GUEST. If a drive letter is assigned properly, then a driver loading in CONFIG.SYS or AUTOEXEC.BAT is conflicting with the Zip drive. You will have to systematically locate the offending driver. Finally, try the Zip drive on another PC. If GUEST works on another PC, the original PC is using an incompatible parallel port. If the drive still refuses to work, try another Zip drive.

Symptom 38-13. Windows 3.11 allows network drive letter to conflict with Zip drive letter You might see this as a "No Zip Tools disk detected" message. The drive might also no longer be accessible from the *File manager* or DOS prompt. The problem is that Windows for Workgroups allows GUEST to assign a drive letter that is already used by a network drive. Remap the shared volume. Because GUEST is typically run first, you will need to alter the network drive letter under Windows for Workgroups.

Symptom 38-14. The Zip drive setup could not find a Zip Tools disk for Zip parallel-port drives This is usually an issue with the GUEST.INI file, which needs to be edited for proper operation. Start the system from a clean floppy diskette, insert the Iomega installation disk, then try running the GUEST utility. If a drive letter is assigned, a driver in CONFIG.SYS or AUTOEXEC.BAT might be conflicting with the Zip drive. If GUEST fails to assign a Zip drive letter from a clean boot, open the GUEST.INI file in a text editor, locate the ASPI=ASPIPPA3.SYS line, then add the switches: /MODE=1 /SPEED=1, which makes the complete command line appear like:

```
ASPI=ASPIPPA3.SYS SCAN /INFO SL360=NO SMC=NO /MODE=1 /SPEED=1
```

Reboot the PC and run the GUEST utility again. If GUEST does run, but you still cannot read the Zip Tools disk, be sure that the signal cables are secure between the drive and system. If problems persist, try the Zip drive on another PC. If GUEST works on another PC, the original PC is using an incompatible parallel port. If the drive still refuses to work, try another Zip drive.

Symptom 38-15. You cannot print while using a ZIP drive The Iomega parallel-port Zip drive works as a "pass-through" device, and the software allows the drive to share a parallel port with printers. However, some printers require two-way communication between the printer and parallel port, which conflicts with the Zip software. This can cause data corruption and system lockups. In many cases, disabling the bi-directional communication features of the printer will clear the problem.

Canon BJ-610/Canon BJC 610 These printers use drivers that are incompatible with the Zip drive—the drivers reserve the parallel port exclusively for the operation of the printer, and the Zip drive is unable to access the port (and will usually result in a system lock-up when the drive is accessed). The drivers for the Canon printers must be removed. The installation program for the printers will add the following lines to the [386Enh] section of your SYSTEM.INI file. These entries must be removed:

```
DEVICE=WPSRCOM.386
DEVICE=WPSCREM.386
DEVICE=WPSRBND.386
```

The following line in WIN.INI will also have to be removed:

```
LOAD=WPSLOAD.EXE
```

At this point, the Zip drive will function, but the printer will not (at least not in its high-resolution modes). To restore full printer operation, you will need to re-install the Canon drivers.

Canon Multi-Pass 1000   You cannot use this printer and the parallel-port Zip drive at the same time. The only way to make this printer and drive compatible is to change the output of the printer to *File* when you need to use the Zip drive, then back to *LPT1* when you want to use the printer. Use the following procedure to toggle the output from *File* to *LPT1* under Windows 95:

- Doubleclick on *My computer*.
- Doubleclick on *Properties*.
- Right mouse button click on the *Canon Printer*.
- Click on *Details*.
- Click the down arrow button in the window labeled *Print to the following port*.
- Click on *File* (to switch back, choose LPT1).
- Click on *OK* at the bottom of your screen.

Hewlett Packard 4S, 4+, 4V, 4SI, 4L, 4P, and 5P   You need to disable the bi-directional communication between the printer and system. This can be accomplished by executing the following command from the *Run* command line:

```
c:\windows\dinstall -fdinstall.ins
```

You can also use the following procedure:

- Bring up the WIN.INI file through either SYSEDIT (in Windows) or EDIT (in DOS).
- In the first section of this file, you should see a line that reads: LOAD=HPSW.EXE. You need to disable this line by inserting a semi-colon (;) at the beginning of the line.
- Now scroll down to the section labeled *[Spooler]* and insert a semi-colon (;) at the beginning of the line that reads: QP.LPT1=HPLJ4QP.DLL.
- Save the WIN.INI file, exit Windows, and restart the system.

You can now use the HP printer and Zip drive together. These changes will not affect the printer—they just disable the status windows that might pop up, showing the current status of the printer.

Hewlett Packard 5L   If you installed your printer using the HOST option, you will need to un-install the printer then re-install it using the PCL option. In your WIN.INI file, disable the line that reads: LOAD=HPLJSW.EXE by placing a semi-colon at the beginning of the line. You will need to do the same with the line that reads: QP.LPT1=??? in the [Spooler] section of your WIN.INI file.

Symptom 38-16. Problems occur while installing a Zip SCSI drive   In virtually all cases, SCSI problems can be traced to hardware problems or driver issues. Be sure that power is provided to the drive (see that the drive power light comes on). See that the

SCSI signal cable is intact, and connected securely between the drive and SCSI adapter. Try a new signal cable. Both ends of the SCSI bus must be terminated properly. Be sure that terminators are installed in the correct places. Ensure that the Zip SCSI drive is assigned to a SCSI ID that is not in use by any other SCSI device. Finally, check the drivers—the drivers for your SCSI adapter and drive must be correct. Use the right command-line switches and be the very latest versions. Also check for conflicts between SCSI drivers or other drivers in the system.

Symptom 38-17. The drive letter is lost each time the PC is turned off In many cases, the GUEST utility does not load properly because it is at the end of AUTOEXEC.BAT. Relocate the GUEST command line—open the AUTOEXEC.BAT file and move the GUEST command line to a point earlier in the file. Ideally, the GUEST command line should immediately follow the MSCDEX command line. Save your changes and reboot the computer. The GUEST utility should now load each time the system is rebooted.

Iomega Ditto Drive

Tape drives have generally come to be seen as a necessary evil in the computer industry. We all know that backups are vitally important to protect our valuable data and system setups, yet we cringe when considering the effort required to configure and execute a backup. As a result, Iomega has taken great lengths to develop a tape drive that can be set up and used as quickly and easily as possible. The result is their Ditto drive. There are several versions of the Ditto, providing 420MB, 800MB, and 2GB backups, respectively. According to Iomega, the Ditto can be installed in just five minutes and the Ditto software makes backup operations almost intuitive (it will even accomplish backups in the background while you work on other things).

DITTO DEMANDS

The Ditto tape drive is included in this chapter (instead of Chapter 42) for two reasons. First, the Ditto 2GB drive requires a high-performance floppy-drive interface to function properly. If you are using an ordinary 500KB/s floppy interface, you will need to install the Ditto Dash accelerator card. Second, the 2GB tape is a proprietary tape, manufactured exclusively for Iomega. The Ditto 2GB tape cartridge uses a slightly wider tape (0.315") than the QIC-80 and QIC-40 minicartridges (the uncompressed capacity for Ditto 2GB tapes is only 1GB). The 2GB tape drive can read and write to the 2GB cartridge, but cannot format this cartridge, so all Ditto 2GB tapes are pre-formatted.

DITTO DRIVE TROUBLESHOOTING

Symptom 38-18. The internal Ditto tape drive is not detected when running from a floppy-disk controller In most cases, the drive is not powered or is not connected properly. Check the power connector first. Internal drives are powered by a standard 4-pin mate-n-lock type connector. Be sure that +5- and +1-V supply levels are adequate and see that the connector is securely attached to the drive. Next, be sure that the signal cable is attached properly to the drive and that the orientation of pin 1 is correct at the drive and controller. Try a new signal cable, if possible.

Check the tape cartridge itself. Be sure that you have inserted a known-good tape properly into the drive. If the tape does not initialize after it is inserted, the drive might be defective. Try a new drive. Be sure that the backup software is installed and configured properly on your system. Try reinstalling the software. Finally, try the drive on another computer. If the drive works on another computer, the original floppy-drive controller might be inadequate. Try the Ditto Dash accelerator card. If the drive does not work on another computer (or does not work properly with the accelerator card), the drive might be defective. Try a new drive.

Symptom 38-19. The internal Ditto drive is not detected when running from a Ditto Dash accelerator card In most cases, the drive is not powered or is not connected properly. Check the power connector first. Internal drives are powered by a standard four-pin mate-n-lock type connector. Be sure that +5- and +12-V supply levels are adequate and see that the power connector is securely attached to the drive. Be sure that the signal cable is attached properly to the drive and see that the orientation of pin 1 is correct at the drive and controller. Try a new signal cable.

Check the tape cartridge next and see that you have inserted a known-good tape properly into the drive. If the tape does not initialize after it is inserted, the drive might be defective. Try a new drive. Check for hardware conflicts—the Ditto Dash accelerator board might be using an IRQ, DMA, or I/O setting in use by another device in the system. Reconfigure the accelerator card, if necessary. Be sure that the backup software is installed and configured properly. Try reinstalling the software. Finally, you should be concerned with the card slot. Be sure that the Ditto Dash accelerator card is located in a slot away from modem/fax boards or video boards. Try the accelerator in a new slot.

Symptom 38-20. The internal Ditto drive takes longer to backup than expected and the drive regularly spins back and forth Regular "back and forth" movement is known as *shoeshining* and is usually accompanied by several corrected errors. The drive is probably running from a floppy controller and the data transfer rate of your backup software is set too high. Check for any backup software settings that control the data-transfer rate, and set the rate to 500KB/s. Save the changes and try another backup—you should see an improvement. If the PC is in its turbo mode, try disabling the turbo mode and try another backup. Finally, try a different drive controller, such as a Tape Accelerator II card (or a Parallel Port II tape drive) to improve data-transfer rates.

Symptom 38-21. The Ditto parallel-port drive is not detected under DOS or Windows 3.1x This is usually caused by interference with the parallel port. Check the power connector first—parallel-port drives are powered externally. Be sure that the power pack is working, and see that the power cable is connected properly to the drive. If the drive does not appear to power up, try a different power pack or drive. Check the signal cable next, and be sure that you are using a good-quality, known-good parallel-port cable, which is attached securely at the PC and drive. Parallel-port drives are very sensitive to devices, such as copy-protection modules (*dongles*), and other "pass-through" devices.

Try connecting the drive directly to the parallel port. Also disconnect any printers on the parallel port.

Reboot the PC and enter CMOS setup. Check to see that the parallel port is configured in EPP or bi-directional mode. As a rule, do not set the port for ECP mode. Hardware conflicts can also present a problem. Be sure that no other device in the system is using IRQ 7 (for LPT1) or IRQ 5 (for LPT2). If your sound board is using IRQ 7 or IRQ 5, you might need to reconfigure the device. Be sure that you have inserted a known-good tape properly into the drive. If the tape does not initialize after it is inserted, the drive might be defective. Try a new drive. If problems persist, add the following two lines to AUTOEXEC.BAT:

```
set port_delay=20
set ppt_flags=16
```

Try the drive on another system. If it works on another system, the original parallel port cannot support the Ditto drive. Try adding a second parallel port to the system. If the drive does not work on another PC, the drive is probably defective and should be replaced.

Symptom 38-22. The internal Ditto drive does not find any catalogs during a restore The tape's "catalog" has been lost or corrupted. Use the steps below to rebuild a tape catalog with Iomega backup software:

■ Choose the *Restore* option from the main menu.
■ Choose the *Catalog* pull down menu, then click on *Rebuild*.
■ A screen will appear listing all the catalogs on the tape. Choose the catalog that you wish to rebuild, then choose the *OK* button (in DOS) or start *Rebuild* (in Windows).
■ The software will then rebuild the catalog and write it automatically to the hard disk. The catalog will then appear in the appropriate box to select files to restore.

Symptom 38-23. The Ditto drive encounters many corrected errors during a compare If a tape file does not match the same file on a hard disk, the backup software logs a read error. The software then performs a series of re-reads to compare the file. If the re-reads match, the software corrects the logged error. If a full tape backup exceeds 50 corrected errors, there might be a system configuration problem.

First, the drive might be dirty. Clean the R/W tape heads and try the tape again. You can also use the backup software to retension the tape. The tape itself might also be bad. Try a known-good tape. If a known-good tape works properly, the original tape might need to be reformatted. If problems persist, try another tape.

Try booting from a "clean" diskette, then try the DOS backup software again. If the problem disappears, a driver or TSR might be interfering with the Ditto drive's operation. Check the signal connector. Try a new parallel port (or internal floppy drive) cable to connect the drive and system. Also check for local electrical interference—the parallel-port drive might be positioned too close to monitors or high-power multimedia speakers. Try moving the drive away from strong magnetic sources. Internal drives might be positioned too close to CD-ROM drives or hard drives. Try relocating the internal Ditto drive to a more remote drive bay. Finally, the DMA operation of your computer might be too fast. Try slowing down DMA operation through the Iomega software.

Symptom 38-24. A "Fatal exception error" occurs with the Ditto drive The configuration files for the drive are set up incorrectly. You will need to correct the proper entries.

Internal Ditto configurations For the internal Ditto drive, you will need to edit the TAPECTRL.CFG file located in the QBWIN directory. Delete the following lines:

```
DRIVER_TYPE:5,1 "PARALLEL Port Tape Drive," "qbwppqt.dll"
MANUFACTURER: "IOMEGA"
MODEL: "PARALLEL PORT TAPE DRIVE,"FFFF
DRIVER: 5
FEATURES: 0
I/O ADDRESS: 278, *378, 3bc
IRQ NUMBER: 5, *7
DMA NUMBER:
```

and:

```
MANUFACTURER: "IOMEGA"
MODEL: "PPT (MSO chip),"FFFF
DRIVER: 5
FEATURES: 0
I/O ADDRESS: 278, *378, 3bc
IRQ NUMBER: 5, *7, 10, 11, 12, 15
DMA NUMBER:
```

Save your changes, restart the system, then run the tape backup software again.

External Ditto configurations For the external Ditto drive, you will need to add the following two lines to the AUTOEXEC.BAT file:

```
set port_delay=20
set ppt_flags=16
```

Save your changes, restart the system, then run the tape backup software again.

Symptom 38-25. The Ditto drive is not restoring selected files The backup software is probably claiming that no files are selected—even though you have selected files. Take the following steps with Iomega backup software:

■ Be sure that marks are next to the files listed.
■ Select all files (go to the *File* command and use the *Select all files* option).
■ If the backup software still claims that no files are selected, go back into the *Select files* option, then select the *Special* option and take the check mark out of the box that says *Exclude read-only files*.
■ Read only files are excluded by default. This should solve the problem.

It is very important that you perform a "compare" after a backup. This ensures that the data on your tape is intact. If you do not compare, data integrity cannot be guaranteed (and a restore might not be possible).

Symptom 38-26. The error: "The drive received an invalid command" appears when using a Ditto drive In most cases, the drive is experiencing communication problems with the controller. Change the backup software configuration. Go into the *Configure* menu of the Iomega backup software. Click on the *Settings* button, then change the *Transfer rate* option to 500KB/s. Press <Alt> + <F10> and set the option *Cntr card* to "bi-directional." Click on the *OK* button, and run another backup. If problems persist, add the following line to AUTOEXEC.BAT:

```
set port_delay=20
```

Restart the system and try another backup.

Iomega Bernoulli Drives

Perhaps the single most important complaint about hard drives has been that they are not portable—you can't just slide out one drive and pop in a new one. Hard drives are traditionally permanent installations. When that drive fills up, you must physically add another hard drive or replace the existing hard drive with a larger model. Both options require an invasive and time-consuming upgrade procedure. The idea of high-capacity removable media overcomes this limitation. With a removable media drive, such as the Iomega Bernoulli (or their current Jaz) drive, you can finally achieve limitless storage simply by exchanging data cartridges. If you need to use files on another PC, you can just pop out a cartridge, then take it with you to another PC with a Bernoulli (or Jaz) drive. Bernoulli drives are not quite as fast as hard drives, but they are close, and you can usually start programs right from the drive.

BERNOULLI NOTES

The Bernoulli disk is a variation of fixed disk technology. Conventional hard drives rotate rigid disks, which force read/write heads to ride on the resulting cushion of air. By comparison, the Bernoulli disk uses a flexible platter, which is forced to flex beneath a fixed read/write head. At first glance, you probably would not know the difference between a fixed-platter cartridge (such as a SyQuest cartridge), and a Bernoulli cartridge.

Bernoulli disks have been around for years, and have been through 20MB, 35MB, 44MB, 65MB, 90MB, 105MB, 150MB, and 230MB incarnations. The Iomega Bernoulli 230 drive will operate with all of the previous disk sizes (except 20MB and 44MB) with only a negligible performance hit. Bernoulli drives are traditionally SCSI devices, but Iomega offers a parallel port-to-SCSI adapter to allow operation with a PC parallel port. When used on a SCSI system, you can use the Iomega PC2x, PC4x, PC90, PC800, PC1600, and PC1616 SCSI adapters. Other SCSI adapters can also be used as long as they are ASPI-compatible and an ASPI driver is provided by the adapter vendor.

BERNOULLI DRIVE TROUBLESHOOTING

Symptom 38-27. The Iomega Bernoulli drive has a floppy icon in Windows 95 This is usually the result of running a real-mode driver to support the Iomega drive and adapter under Windows 95. Check the Iomega driver; you might need to disable the real-mode driver and install the protected-mode driver under Windows 95. The Iomega software provides protected-mode drivers for Jaz Jet, Zip Zoom, PC1600, PC1616, PC800, PC2x, PPA-3, and parallel-port devices. If you are using a different adapter, you might need to upgrade and update the driver accordingly. If you are using a non-Iomega adapter (such as a SCSI adapter), you will need protected-mode drivers from the particular SCSI vendor. However, Windows 95 does have a comprehensive library of protected-mode drivers already available.

Symptom 38-28. The Iomega Bernoulli SCSI drive does not have a drive letter in Windows 95 The drive does not appear to respond. In virtually all cases, the SCSI driver has failed to load. Check the driver first. Open the *Device manager* and expand the *SCSI controllers* entry, then check the *Iomega adapter* line beneath it. If a yellow symbol with an exclamation mark is on it, the Windows 95 driver did not load. Highlight that *Iomega adapter* line and select *Properties*. Click on the *Resources* page, then verify that your I/O range and IRQ options are set correctly—they must match the jumper settings on your adapter board. If you must update the resource settings manually, be sure that the *Automatic settings* box is not checked. Remember to save any changes. If you allocated new resources, you might have to shut off the PC and change jumper settings on the controller to match the resources allocated in the *Device manager*. Restart the computer—once the system reboots, the Windows 95 driver should load normally.

If the driver checks out properly, you'll need to check the device connections. Check the SCSI signal connector first, and be sure that the SCSI cable is intact and connected to the drive properly. If problems persist, the SCSI adapter is probably installed correctly, but the bus might be terminated improperly. Terminate both ends of the SCSI bus properly. Finally, be sure that the SCSI ID for your drive does not conflict with the ID of other SCSI devices in the system.

Symptom 38-29. The parallel-port (or PPA-3) adapter does not have a drive letter in Windows 95 Parallel-port drive problems can almost always be traced to faulty connections, port-configuration issues, or driver problems. Check the power connector first. Parallel-port drives are powered externally, so ensure that the power pack is working and that the power cable is connected properly to the drive. If the drive does not appear to power up, try a different power pack or drive. Also be sure that you are using a good-quality, known-good parallel-port cable, which is attached securely at the PC and drive.

Remove any other devices on the parallel port. Parallel-port drives are often very sensitive to devices, such as copy-protection modules (*dongles*), and other "pass-through" devices. Try connecting the drive directly to the parallel port. Also disconnect any printers on the parallel port. Reboot the PC and enter CMOS setup. Check to see that the parallel port is configured in EPP or bi-directional mode. The controller might also be presenting a problem. There is a known incompatibility between the Iomega Bernoulli drive and the Adaptec 284x adapter—the Iomega PPA3 driver does not work with the Adaptec 284x controller. Check with Iomega for an updated SCSI driver.

Open the *Device manager* and find the *SCSI controllers* entry (even though it is a parallel-port device). If there is no such entry, the driver is not installed. If you expand the *SCSI controllers* section, an entry for the Iomega adapter should be listed. If not, the driver is not installed. If the *Device manager* entry for the Iomega adapter has a yellow circle with an exclamation mark on it, the interface is configured improperly and is conflicting with other devices in the system. Device properties might also be a problem. Highlight the *Iomega adapter* entry, click on *Properties*, then select the *Settings* page. Find the box marked *Adapter settings*, then type:

```
/mode:nibble /speed:1
```

Save your changes and reboot the system. You could also try reinstalling the drivers. Highlight the *Iomega adapter* and select *Remove*. Then reinstall the drivers from scratch. Finally, consider the drive itself. Try the drive on another PC. If the drive works on another system, the parallel port is incompatible (or the PPA3 is not configured properly). If the drive does not work on another PC, try a new Bernoulli drive.

Symptom 38-30. The Bernoulli drive takes over the CD-ROM's drive letter in Windows 95 You might simply need to switch drive letters between the Bernoulli drive and CD-ROM drive:

- Open *Device manager* and doubleclick on the *Disk drives* entry.
- Highlight the *Iomega Bernoulli drive* entry and click on *Properties*.
- Click on the *Settings* page.
- The *Reserved drive letters* section has a *Start drive letter* and an *End drive letter* setting. Enter the desired drive letter for the Bernoulli drive in both start and end drive entries (be sure to use the same drive letter for both start and end). Click on *OK*.
- Doubleclick on the *CD-ROM* entry.
- Highlight your *CD-ROM drive* entry and click on *Properties*.
- Click on the *Settings* page.
- The *Reserved drive letters* section has a *Start drive letter* and an *End drive letter* setting. Enter the desired drive letter for the CD-ROM drive in both start and end entries (be sure to use the same drive letter for both start and end). Click on OK.
- Click on *OK* to close *Device manager*, then shut down and restart the computer.

Symptom 38-31. An "Invalid drive specification" error occurs after installing an Iomega SCSI drive Your system automatically boots into Windows, and it will not return to the installation program. The error occurs when you try to access the Iomega drive. In most cases, you need to install the Iomega SCSI software from the DOS prompt. Boot the system from a "clean" diskette, then try installing the Iomega SCSI software again.

Symptom 38-32. An "Invalid Unit Reading Drive <x>" error occurs Software drivers appear to load fine and the Bernoulli drive is assigned a drive letter, as expected. In virtually all cases, the problem is with the SMARTDRV statement in AUTOEXEC.BAT. Check the drive-controller BIOS first—the conflict might be with the BIOS on your PC1616 controller card. If you are NOT booting from the PC1616, try disabling the PC1616 BIOS with the ISACFG.COM utility accompanying the PC1616 adapter (you can also obtain the utility from Iomega at **http://www.iomega.com**). Reboot the PC—the error should be corrected.

If you are booting from the PC1616 controller (the Bernoulli drive), leave the controller's BIOS enabled, but try loading SMARTDRV high (i.e., into the upper memory area). If you cannot load SMARTDRV high, disable its command line in AU-TOEXEC.BAT and reboot the system, then load SMARTDRV from the DOS command line once the PC initializes. If problems persist, try the new GUEST program from Iomega (be sure that you're using the latest version). Once you install the GUEST.EXE and GUEST.INI files to your PC, enter the path and command line for GUEST near the end of AUTOEXEC.BAT (before Windows starts), such as:

```
c:\zinstall\guest.exe
```

If these solutions fail to correct the error, then SMARTDRV cannot be loaded and will need to be remarked out of the AUTOEXEC.BAT file entirely.

> If you use the GUEST program, you cannot compress the disks using DISKSPACE. Also, GUEST does not support the PC80 or PC90 adapter cards.

Symptom 38-33. Problems occur when using the Iomega parallel-port interface (PPA-3) with a Bernoulli drive Problems with the PPA3 are usually related to installation issues, but drivers can also prevent the PPA3 from responding. Check the power connector first—the external device must be turned on before powering up the computer. If the device refuses to power up, check the power pack and its connection to the Bernoulli drive. Be sure that the signal cable is the proper length and is connected securely to the drive and system. Unusually long cables might cause read/write errors. Try disconnecting the printer or other parallel-port device from the system, then try the PPA3 as the only parallel-port device attached to the parallel port. Check the drive termination next. The PPA3 board is terminated, and the last drive attached to the PPA3 cable must also be terminated. If the Bernoulli drive is the last device attached to the PPA3, be sure that it is terminated properly.

Check the driver installation. You need either OAD 1.3 (and higher) or Iomega SCSI 2.0 (and higher) to use the PPA3 board. Once the drivers are installed, you should see several lines in CONFIG.SYS, such as:

```
REM OAD 1.3 or later:
DEVICE=C:\OADDOS\ASPIPPA3.SYS /L=001
DEVICE=C:\OADDOS\DOSCFG.EXE /M1 /V /L=001
DEVICE=C:\OADDOS\DOSOAD.SYS /L=001
```

or:

```
REM Iomega SCSI 2.0 or later:
DEVICE=C:\IOMEGA\ASPIPPA3.SYS /L=001
DEVICE=C:\IOMEGA\SCSICFG.EXE /V /L=001
DEVICE=C:\IOMEGA\SCSIDRVR.SYS /L=001
```

Try some ASPIPPA3.SYS command-line options. The ASPIPPA3.SYS driver provides several important command-line options in Table 38-2 that can be used to streamline its

TABLE 38-2 COMMAND LINE OPTIONS FOR ASPIPPA3.SYS

/MODE=n

/MODE=1 is the most compatible mode.
/MODE=2 is the Bi-directional transfer mode—your PC must have a bi-directional parallel port.
/MODE=3 is Enhanced mode, which requires an Intel SL series microprocessor (e..g., 80386SL, 80486SL, or 82360SL).

/SL360=Yes/No

This tells the ASPIPPA3.SYS driver whether or not the computer uses an Intel SL microprocessor chipset. If you're not sure (or if a divide overflow occurs during loading), set to /SL360=No

/SPEED=n

Values 1 to 10 are available. Start by setting /SPEED=1. If that solves the problem, continue to increase the value until the problem recurs, then use highest value that functioned properly. If you are still not sure which value to use, set /SPEED=1

/SCAN

Forces the ASPIPPA3.SYS driver to check all parallel-port addresses—three addresses are possible: 278h, 378h, and 3BCh.

/Busy_Retry=Yes

This option forces the driver to retry several times when a device is busy (instead of just reporting an error).

/Port=<Address>

Used to manually specify the port address of the parallel port.

TABLE 38-3 ASPIPPA3.SYS ERROR MESSAGES

ERROR CODE	POSSIBLE CAUSE
4001	Command-line syntax error.
4002	Adapter initialization failed—possible problem with the adapter or the parallel port.
4003	User specified a port address and there was no adapter there.
4004	No adapter found.
4005	User pressed both Shift keys to bypass this driver.
4006	Current DOS version is not supported by this driver.
4100	Conflicting port address was detected in command line.
4107	Improper speed value. Acceptable range is 0 to 10 decimal.
4108	Bad value—value outside limits.

operation. If the ASPIPPA3.SYS command line generates any errors, you can decipher the errors with Table 38-3.

Symptom 38-34. The Iomega PPA3 locks up on installation Chances are that the ASPIPPA3.SYS driver is causing the computer to lock up or is causing a "Divide by zero overflow" error. Check the power connector first. The external device must be turned on before powering up the computer. If the device refuses to power up, check the power pack and its connection to the Bernoulli drive. Also be sure that the signal cable is the proper length and is connected securely to the drive and system. Unusually long cables might cause read/write errors. Termination might be an issue—the PPA3 board is terminated, and the last drive attached to the PPA3 board must also be terminated. If the Bernoulli drive is the last device attached to the PPA3, be sure that it is terminated properly by setting the termination switch on the back of the drive to "I." If the switch is set to "O," turn off the drive, set the switch to "I," turn the drive on, and reboot the PC. Update the ASPIPPA3.SYS driver. Try adding the /SL360=NO switch to the command line, such as:

```
DEVICE=C:\IOMEGA\ASPIPPA3.SYS /SL360=NO
```

Save your changes to CONFIG.SYS and reboot the computer. Try the PPA3 board and Bernoulli drive on another PC. If they work on another system, the original parallel port is probably incompatible. If the PPA3 and drive do not work on another system, try another set of cables. If problems persist, try the Bernoulli drive directly on a SCSI adapter. If the drive works directly, the PPA3 has probably failed. If the drive does not work, it has probably failed.

Symptom 38-35. SCSI communication problems occur In virtually all cases, SCSI problems can be traced to hardware problems or driver issues. Check the power connector first and see that power is provided to the drive (the drive power light should be on). Be sure that the SCSI cable is intact, and connected securely between the drive and SCSI adapter. Try a new signal cable, if possible. Termination might also be a problem. Both ends of the SCSI bus must be terminated properly. Be sure that the terminators are installed in the correct places on your SCSI chain. The Bernoulli SCSI drive must be assigned to a SCSI ID that is not in use by any other SCSI device. Finally, check the drivers. Be sure that the drivers for your SCSI adapter and drive are correct, use the right command-line switches, and that you are using the very latest versions. Also check for conflicts between SCSI drivers or other drivers in the system.

Symptom 38-36. The IDE Bernoulli drive receives two drive letters Your Plug-and-Play (PnP) BIOS is detecting the Bernoulli drive as a fixed drive and one drive letter is assigned, but the Iomega drivers detect the Bernoulli drive again—assigning a second drive letter. PnP support for the Bernoulli drive might be a problem. Enter your system CMOS setup and disable the PnP support for the Bernoulli drive. Save your changes and reboot the system. If you cannot disable BIOS support for the Bernoulli drive, power up the system with the Bernoulli disk removed—this causes BIOS to overlook the drive, but the Iomega drivers will still assign the drive letter properly.

Symptom 38-37. Using an Iomega PC2X 8-bit Bernoulli controller might cause the system to crash According to Iomega, their PC2X 8-bit Bernoulli controller cards might not function properly on 486/33MHz (and faster) computers. For Windows 95, you might need to run *Setup* with the "ignore hardware detection" parameter, such as:

```
SETUP /I
```

To correct this problem, you'll need to use the controller on a slower computer (rarely a practical option) or install a better Bernoulli controller card in the existing system.

Symptom 38-38. The compressed removable-media drive(s) are not auto-matically mounted on startup This problem can occur under Windows 95 if the computer has two floppy-disk drives and the following settings exist in the DRV-SPACE.INI file:

```
MaxRemovableDrives=2
AutoMount=1
```

To resolve this issue, you'll need to increase the value of the "MaxRemovableDrives=" setting to match the total number of removable-media drives in the computer. For exam-ple, if your computer has two floppy-disk drives and a double Bernoulli drive, use "MaxRemovableDrives=4" (two floppy-disk drives plus two Bernoulli drives). Edit the DRVSPACE.INI file as follows:

1 Locate the DRVSPACE.INI file using Windows Explorer (it should be in the root di-rectory). Right-click the file, then click *Properties*.
2 Click the *Read-only* check box to clear it, then click *OK*.
3 Doubleclick the DRVSPACE.INI file to open it.
4 Change the value of the MaxRemovableDrives= setting to match the total number of re-movable-media drives, or set the AutoMount= entry to the drive letters assigned to the removable-media drives. For example, if you have a double Bernoulli drive with drive letters D and E assigned to the drive, use the setting "AutoMount=DE."
5 Save, then close the file. Reboot Windows 95.

When you use an Iomega RCD driver with a double Bernoulli drive, you might receive a "General failure" error message the first time that you access the second drive. This causes automatic activation and automatic mounting to fail. Use an Iomega OAD or SCSI driver to resolve the problem.

Symptom 38-39. Problems occur when running Iomega Jaz Tools under Windows 95 When Iomega Tools for Windows 95 is installed on your computer, the system might crash (or you might receive an error message referencing the IOMEGA.VXD file) when you attempt to use the Iomega Jaz Tools. This occurs espe-cially under FAT32 partitions of OSR2. Chances are that you're using an older version of Jaz Tools for Windows 95 (earlier than version 5.0). Earlier versions of Jaz Tools are not compatible with FAT32 (OSR2). You'll need to uninstall the Jaz Tools package, then in-stall version 5.0 (or later), which is FAT32 aware.

SyQuest Drives

SyQuest is another drive manufacturer that has capitalized on the popularity for removable media drives. Rather than using the flexible disk media of Bernoulli technology, SyQuest chose to exploit the rigid platter/floating head approach used by more conventional hard drives. As a result, SyQuest drives are a bit closer to being "real" hard drives than Bernoulli drives. The traditional 44MB and 88MB SyQuest drives of years past have been replaced by such products as the EZ-Drive (135MB) and EZ-Flyer (230MB) drives. SyQuest has just recently released the dual-platter 1.5GB SyJet drive, which places the SyJet in direct contention with Iomega's 1.0GB Jaz drive.

SYQUEST DRIVE TROUBLESHOOTING

Symptom 38-40. Removable-media IDE drives have problems in Windows 95 The potential problems are: The removable drive is not detected or not accessible within Windows 95, media changes (such as removing a disk and inserting a new disk) are not detected, or the removable drive appears as a non-removable hard disk in Windows Explorer or *Device manager*. This happens because removable-media IDE drives are not fully supported by the IDE drivers included with Windows 95. You'll need to install the following patch files for Windows 95: ESDI_506.PDR (version 4.00.1116 dated 8/25/97, or later) and VOLTRACK.VXD (version 4.00.954 dated 3/6/96, or later). Both of these files are available in the REMIDEUP.EXE file available from the Microsoft Software Library (**http://www.microsoft.com**). Once downloaded, find the file in Windows Explorer and doubleclick on it, then follow the on-screen instructions. The new files will be patched to the Windowsdirectory.

The VOLTRACK.VXD file is installed on Windows 95a computers only—this file is not installed on computers running OSR2.

Symptom 38-41. Problems are encountered with SyQuest drives and Future Domain SCSI adapters Although SyQuest drives should perform properly with Future Domain SCSI adapters, some issues might cause problems. Inspect the SCSI ID first. Future Domain SCSI adapters install drives from the higher SCSI ID (6) to the lowest (0)—this is opposite from the majority of HBA manufacturers, which assign drives from ID 0. Be sure that any hard-disk drives have a higher SCSI ID number than the SyQuest drives when you install a removable drive on the SCSI bus. That way, the hard drives will be assigned the lower DOS drive letter (e.g., C: then D:).

Future Domain controllers will not allow the SyQuest drive to serve as a boot device. If you must make the SyQuest drive bootable, contact Future Domain for a firmware upgrade. Cartridge preparation can also be a problem. Future Domain PowerSCSI software works with cartridges prepared and used on the same PC. When exchanging the cartridge with one of a different format, size, or partition, the PowerSCSI driver will not handle the new cartridge properly. You might need different SCSI drivers. Check your SCSI drivers. For the SyQuest utilities to work properly with Future Domain adapters (and handle nonnative cartridges), the CONFIG.SYS file must contain the following drivers:

```
DEVICE=C:\PWRSCSI!\DCAM18XX.EXE
DEVICE=C:\PWRSCSI!\ASPIFCAM.SYS
DEVICE=C:\SYQUEST\SCSI\SQDRIVER.SYS
```

The correct CAM.EXE driver for your particular adapter must be used in the CONFIG.SYS file (such as CAM950.EXE). Do not use FDBIOS.SYS or INT4BCAM.SYS with SQDRIVER.SYS (only one driver can be used to control the SyQuest drive). The

SyQuest DOS formatting program SQPREP will partition and format DOS cartridges with Future Domain adapters if the drivers are correctly installed in CONFIG.SYS.

Symptom 38-42. Problems are encountered with SyQuest drives and NCR SCSI adapters SyQuest drives work well with NCR (now part of AT&T Global Systems) adapters, but you must be using version 3.12 (or later) SyQuest utilities. The SCSI drivers might be causing problems. To make the SyQuest cartridges removable under DOS, the following three entries must be present in CONFIG.SYS:

```
DEVICE=C:\SDMS\DOSCAM.SYS            (10-08-93 or later)
DEVICE=C:\SDMS\ASPICAM.SYS          (10-08-93 or later)
DEVICE=C:\SyQuest\SCSI\SQDRIVER.SYS
```

If you choose to use the NCR driver SCSIDISK.SYS instead of SQDRIVER.SYS, the ability to remove cartridges and use non-native cartridges will be lost. Be sure that both drivers are not loaded together or data corruption will result. Also suspect a problem with the SCSI ID. Typical NCR SCSI priority is from lowest (0) to highest (6), and the NCR adapter is SCSI ID 7. The SyQuest DOS partition and format utility (SQPREP) works well with NCR adapters as long as the drivers are loaded in CONFIG.SYS (as shown).

Symptom 38-43. Problems are encountered with SyQuest drives and Rancho Technology SCSI adapters SyQuest SCSI drives work properly with Rancho Technology SCSI adapters, you must be aware of some issues. First, Rancho Technology SCSI BIOS requires that a cartridge be installed in the SyQuest drive at boot time (the Rancho Technology BIOS will hang if no cartridge is installed and the drive is ready). SCSI drivers can also be an issue. SyQuest utilities will work through the ASPICAM driver supplied with Rancho Technology adapters. To make the cartridges removable under DOS, the CONFIG.SYS file must have drivers loaded in this order:

```
REM For the Rancho Technology 1600:
DEVICE=C:\RT1600\DOSCAM.SYS          (12-14-94 or later)
DEVICE=C:\RT1600\ASPICAM.SYS         (12-14-94 or later)
DEVICE=C:\SyQuest\SCSI\SQDRIVER.SYS
```

or:

```
REM For the Rancho Technology 1000:
DEVICE=C:\RT1000\RTASPI10.SYS        (01-26-93 or later)
DEVICE=C:\SyQuest\SCSI\SQDRIVER.SYS
```

If you choose to use the Rancho Technology driver SCSIDISK.SYS instead of SQ-DRIVER.SYS, the ability to remove cartridges and use non-native cartridges will be lost. Be sure that both drivers are not loaded together, or data corruption will result. Check the SCSI ID—typical Rancho Technology SCSI priority is from lowest (0) to highest (6), and the Rancho Technology adapter is SCSI ID 7. The SyQuest DOS partition and format utility (SQPREP) works well with Rancho Technology adapters as long as the drivers are loaded in CONFIG.SYS.

Symptom 38-44. Problems occur with Packard-Bell multimedia PCs and SyQuest drives Packard Bell systems often use unusual IRQ assignments that might interfere with the default settings of many SCSI adapters. Check the hardware settings—many Packard Bell PCs use IRQ 11 and IRQ 12 for the CD-ROM drive, sound board, and mouse. When installing a SCSI adapter, be sure to use IRQ 10 and the I/O address of 340h. If any other 16-bit card (especially a network card) is in the system, use IRQ 15 instead.

Symptom 38-45.   Problems occur using BusLogic SCSI adapters and SyQuest drives The BusLogic ASPI driver (BTDOSM.SYS) will operate with the SyQuest device driver SQDRIVER.SYS, but the order of installation can be very important. Install the BusLogic driver first, then install the SyQuest software. Once the drivers are installed, the CONFIG.SYS file should be in this order:

```
DEVICE=C:\BUSLOGIC\BTDOSM.SYS /D
DEVICE=C:\SYQUEST\SCSI\SQDRIVER.SYS
```

Remove the BusLogic disk driver BTMDISK.SYS:

```
REM DEVICE=C:\BUSLOGIC\BTMDISK.SYS
```

Relocate any other Buslogic device drivers after SQDRIVER.SYS. Reboot the system after making any changes to CONFIG.SYS. Finally, check the driver dates. Be sure that you are using SQDRIVER.SYS version 7.72 (or higher) or SyQuest software release 3.12 (or higher, 01-27-95 or later).

Symptom 38-46. Problems occur when using Qlogic SCSI adapters and SyQuest drives Although SyQuest SCSI drives will operate properly with Qlogic SCSI adapters, some issues can cause problems. First, Qlogic FastSCSI software does not support SyQuest cartridge exchange without installing the SyQuest SQDRIVER.SYS driver. Install the two Qlogic drivers, then install the SyQuest drivers. Be sure that the QL00DISK.SYS driver is not installed in CONFIG.SYS. A typical CONFIG.SYS file will appear, such as:

```
DEVICE=C:\QLOGIC\QL41DOS.SYS
DEVICE=C:\QLOGIC\QL00ASPI.SYS
DEVICE=C:\SyQuest\SCSI\SQDRIVER.SYS
```

Be sure to use the correct QLxxDOS.SYS driver for your particular Qlogic SCSI adapter. CorelSCSI software is often shipped with Qlogic SCSI adapters. If a CorelSCSI driver is installed to support a SyQuest drive, do not install the SQDRIVER.SYS driver. Finally, disable or REMark out the QL00DISK.SYS driver if it is entered in the CONFIG.SYS file. If the QL00DISK.SYS driver is allowed to coexist with SQDRIVER.SYS, data corruption will result.

Symptom 38-47. Problems occur when using an IBM MicroChannel SCSI controller and SyQuest drive This applies to the /A and /2A MicroChannel SCSI adapters. The IBM ASPI driver (ASPI4B.SYS) will only operate with the SyQuest driver

SQDRIVER.SYS under DOS—not under Windows. The MSDRVR.ZIP shareware has been known to circumvent this incompatibility. For current pricing and availability, contact the shareware maker:

Micro Staff Co., Ltd.
1-46-9 Matsubara, Setagaya-ku, Tokyo, Japan 156
Tel: 011-81-3-3325-8128
Fax: 011-81-3-3327-7037
CompuServe ID: 100157,1053

Symptom 38-48. Problems occur when using Data Technology Corporation (DTC) SCSI adapters and SyQuest drives The DTC SCSI adapters will operate with SyQuest drives, but several problems can occur. Install the DTC ASPI driver first, then install the SyQuest utility software. Once all the drivers are installed, the CONFIG.SYS file should appear in this order:

```
REM For the DTC 3280AS ISA version and the DTC 3290AS EISA version:
DEVICE=C:\DTC\ASPI3xxx.SYS
DEVICE=C:\SYQUEST\SCSI\SQDRIVER.SYS
```

Remember to remove the DTC device driver ASCSI.SYS in the CONFIG.SYS file:

```
REM DEVICE=C:\DTC\ASCI.SYS
```

Also, in the AUTOEXEC.BAT file:

```
REM C:\DTC\ASCSI.EXE
```

Load any other DTC device drivers after SQDRIVER.SYS, or:

```
REM For the DTC 3130 PCI version:
DEVICE=C:\DTC\DOSCAM.SYS
DEVICE=C:\DTC\ASPICAM.SYS
DEVICE=C:\SYQUEST\SCSI\SQDRIVER.SYS
```

Remember to remove the DTC device driver SCSIDISK.SYS in the CONFIG.SYS file:

```
REM DEVICE=C:\DTC\SCSIDISK.SYS
```

Load any other DTC device drivers after SQDRIVER.SYS. Remember to reboot the PC after making any changes to your CONFIG.SYS or AUTOEXEC.BAT files. Finally, check the driver dates. Be sure that you are using SQDRIVER.SYS version 7.72 (or higher) or the SyQuest software release 3.12 (or higher, 01-27-95, or later).

Symptom 38-49. The lights on the SyQuest drive are blinking in a regular pattern The drive has suffered a fault and generally must be replaced. Use Table 38-4 to find the specific error code. In most cases, you will have to replace the drive outright.

TABLE 38-4 SYQUEST ERROR CODES FOR SQ555, SQ5110C, AND 5200C DRIVES

GREEN FLASHES	AMBER FLASHES	PROBLEM	ACTION
0	3	Microprocessor problems	Replace drive
1	1, 2, 3	PCBA (drive circuitry) failure	Replace drive
2	1, 2, 3, 4, 5, 6	PCBA (drive circuitry) failure	Replace drive
3	0, 3	Microprocessor problems	Replace drive
3	1, 2, 4, 5	PCBA (drive circuitry) failure	Replace drive
4	1, 2, 3	Drive motor problem	Replace drive
4	4, 5	Drive motor speed problem	Replace cartridge
4	6	Cannot find servo	Reinsert cartridge
5	1	Power failure	Check power supply
5	2	Drive motor speed problem	Replace cartridge
5	3, 4, 5, 6, 7, 8, 9	Power-up initialization incomp.	Reinsert cartridge Replace cartridge
6	0, 1, 2, 3	PCBA (drive circuitry) failure	Replace drive
6	4	Drive motor-speed problem	Replace cartridge
6	5	Excessive run-out failure	Reinsert cartridge Clean spindle motor Replace cartridge
6	6	Incompatible cartridge	Use proper cartridge
6	7	PCBA (drive circuitry) failure	Replace drive
7	1, 2, 3, 4, 5	PCBA (drive circuitry) failure	Replace drive
Off	Solid On or flashing light	Power fault Defective cartridge Head loading failure	Replace drive Replace cartridge Replace drive
Solid On	Solid On	Microprocessor problem	Reinitialize the drive Replace the drive

Further Study

This concludes the material for Chapter 38. Be sure to review the glossary and chapter questions on the accompanying CD. If you have access to the Internet, take a look at some of these removable-media drive makers:

Iomega: **http://www.iomega.com**

SyQuest: **http://www.syquest.com**

SCSI SYSTEMS
AND TROUBLESHOOTING

CONTENTS AT A GLANCE

Understanding SCSI Concepts
Device independence
SCSI variations
Initiators and targets
Synchronous and asynchronous
Disconnect and reconnect
Single-ended and differential
Terminators
SCSI IDS
Bus configurations

Understanding SCSI Bus Operation
Negotiation
Information

Upgrading a PC for SCSI
SCSI peripherals
SCSI host adapter

SCSI cables and terminators
SCSI drivers
Tips for a smooth upgrade
Configure and install the SCSI
  adapter
Configure and install the SCSI
  peripheral
Cabling and termination
Real-mode SCSI driver issues
Tips for Windows 95 SCSI drivers

Troubleshooting the SCSI System
Isolating trouble spots
General troubleshooting tips
Symptoms

Further Study

PC designers have always sought ways to connect more devices to fewer cables. This reduces the amount of adapter card hardware in the system, so power, space, cost, and maintenance demands are also lowered. In the early 1980s, it became clear that a more versatile and intelligent interface would be needed to overcome the myriad of proprietary interfaces appearing at the time. By 1986, PC designers responded with the introduction of the *Small Computer System Interface* (*SCSI*, pronounced "scuzzy"). SCSI proved to be a revolution for PC "power-users"—a single adapter could operate a number of unique devices simultaneously—all "daisy-chained" to the same cable. Where other "low-end" PCs needed one adapter for hard drives, one adapter for the CD-ROM, another adapter for a tape drive, etc., a system fitted with a SCSI adapter could handle all of these devices and achieve data throughputs that other interfaces of the day couldn't even dream of.

Today's PC industry has changed. Proprietary interfaces are largely discouraged and the "standardized" interfaces (such as *ATA-2*, also known as *EIDE*) now support a variety of devices while offering low cost and performance levels rivaling SCSI. Yet, SCSI has endured and evolved, and it remains the interface of choice for multitasking and high-end systems. This chapter examines the inner workings of the SCSI interface, and shows you how to deal with installation and troubleshooting problems.

Understanding SCSI Concepts

Ideally, peripherals should be independent of the microprocessor's operation. The computer should only have to send commands and data to the peripheral, and wait for the peripheral to respond. Printers work this way. The parallel and serial ports are actually "device-level" interfaces. The computer is unconcerned with what device is attached to the port. In other words, you can take a printer built 12 years ago and connect it to a new Pentium-based system—and the printer will work just fine because only data and commands are being sent across the interface. Very simply put, this is the concept behind SCSI. Computers and peripherals can be designed, developed, and integrated without worrying about hardware compatibility. Such compatibility is established entirely by the SCSI interface.

DEVICE INDEPENDENCE

From a practical standpoint, SCSI is a bus—an organization of physical wires and terminations, where each wire has its own name and purpose. SCSI also consists of a command set—a limited set of instructions that allow the computer and peripherals to communicate over the physical bus. The SCSI bus is used in systems that want to achieve device independence. For example, all hard-disk drives look alike to the SCSI interface (except for their total capacity), all optical drives look alike, all printers look alike, etc. For any particular type of SCSI device, you should be able to replace an existing device with another device, without any system modifications. New SCSI devices can often be added to the bus with little more than a driver upgrade. Because the intelligence of SCSI resides in the peripheral device itself and not in the computer, the computer is able to use a small set of standard commands to accomplish data transfer back and forth to the peripheral. Now that you understand a bit about the nature of the SCSI interface, the following sections explain some of the important terms and concepts you'll need to know.

SCSI VARIATIONS

This section covers at the evolution of the SCSI interface and the ways in which it has evolved and proliferated. SCSI began life in 1979 when Shugart Associates (you might remember them as one of the first PC hard drive makers) released their "Shugart Associates Systems Interface" (or SASI) standard. The X3T9.2 committee was formed by ANSI in 1982 to develop the SASI standard, which was renamed SCSI. SCSI drives and interfaces that were developed under the evolving X3T9.2 SCSI standard were known as *SCSI-1*, although the actual SCSI-1 standard (ANSI X3.131-1986) didn't become official until 1986. SCSI-1 provided a system-level 8-bit bus that could operate up to eight devices and transfer data at up to 5MB/s. However, the delay in standardization lead to a lot of configuration and compatibility problems with SCSI-1 setups. Table 39-1 compares SCSI-1 specs to other versions.

> Although SCSI-1 was supposed to support all SCSI devices, manufacturers took liberties with the evolving standard. This frequently led to installation and compatibility problems between SCSI-1 devices which "theoretically" should have worked together perfectly. Today, all existing SCSI-1 adapters should be upgraded to SCSI-2 installations.

Earlier in 1986 (even before the SCSI-1 standard was ratified), work started on the SCSI-2 standard, which was intended to overcome many of the speed and compatibility problems encountered with SCSI-1. By 1994, ANSI blessed the SCSI-2 standard (X3.131-1994). SCSI-2 was designed to be backwardly compatible with SCSI-1, but SCSI-2 also provided for several variations. Fast SCSI-2 (or "Fast SCSI") doubles the SCSI bus clock speed and allows 10MB/s data transfers across the 8-bit SCSI data bus. Wide SCSI-2 (or "Wide SCSI") also doubles the original data-transfer rate to 10MB/s by using a 16-bit data bus instead of the original 8-bit data bus (the SCSI clock is left unchanged). To support the larger data bus, Wide SCSI uses a 68-pin cable instead of the traditional 50-pin cable. Wide SCSI can also support up to 16 SCSI devices. Designers then combined the attributes of fast and wide operation to create Fast Wide SCSI-2 ("Fast Wide

TABLE 39-1 COMPARISON OF SCSI VARIATIONS

TERM	BUS SPEED (MB/S)	BUS WIDTH (BITS)	BUS LENGTH (METERS)	DEVICES SUPPORTED
SCSI-1				
SCSI-1	5	8	6	8
SCSI-2				
Fast SCSI	10	8	3	8
Wide SCSI	10	16	3	16
Fast Wide SCSI	20	16	3	16
SCSI-3				
Fast-20 SCSI	20	8	1.5	8
Wide Fast-20 SCSI	40	16	3	4
*Fast-40 SCSI	40	8	n/d	8
*Wide Fast-40 SCSI	80	16	n/d	16

* These standards are still in development, and their full specifications are still being determined.

SCSI"), which supports 20MB/s data transfers across a 16-bit data bus. Whenever you see references to "Fast SCSI," "Wide SCSI," or "Fast Wide SCSI," you're always dealing with a SCSI-2 implementation.

But SCSI advancement hasn't stopped there. ANSI began development of the SCSI-3 standard in 1993 (even before SCSI-2 was adopted). SCSI-3 is intended to be backwardly compatible with SCSI-2 and SCSI-1 devices. Although SCSI-3 is still not finalized, many SCSI devices and controllers are using the advances offered by SCSI-3 development. These early SCSI-3 devices are generally known as *Fast-20 SCSI* (or *Ultra SCSI-3*, also termed *Ultra SCSI*). Ultra SCSI uses a 20MHz SCSI bus clock with an 8-bit data bus to achieve 20MB/s data transfers. By using a 16-bit data bus, SCSI-3 offers *Wide Fast-20 SCSI* (*Wide Ultra SCSI-3*, also termed *Wide Ultra SCSI*) which handles 40MB/s data transfers.

For the future, the SCSI-3 standard is also proposing *Fast-40 SCSI* (called *Ultra2 SCSI-3* and *Ultra2 SCSI*), using a 40MHz bus clock to provide 40MB/s data transfers with an 8-bit data bus. The 16-bit data bus version is known as *Wide Fast-40 SCSI* (called *Wide Ultra2 SCSI-3* or *Wide Ultra2 SCSI*), which is supposed to support 80MB/s data transfers. Whenever you see references to "Ultra," "Fast-20," "Ultra2," or "Fast-40," you're almost certain to be faced with a SCSI-3 setup.

> You'll probably encounter a lot of literature using the term *Ultra SCSI*, but the use of *Ultra* as a SCSI-3 designator is being actively discouraged because of legal disputes with companies using the term *Ultra* in their SCSI-2 (yes, SCSI-2) devices. As a rule, use the *Fast* or *Wide Fast* terms instead of the *Ultra* terms.

SCSI has traditionally been a "parallel" bus; that is, 8 or 16 bits of data are transferred at a time across parallel data lines. SCSI-3 is proposing three new serial connection schemes. You'll see these noted as *Serial Storage Architecture (SSA)*, *Fibre Channel*, and *IEEE P1394* (a.k.a. *Fire Wire*). These serial schemes will offer faster data transfers than their parallel-bus cousins, but are not backward compatible with SCSI-2 or SCSI-1.

INITIATORS AND TARGETS

Basically two types of devices are on the SCSI bus: *initiators* and *targets*. An initiator starts communication when something has to be done and a target responds to the initiator's commands. The important thing for you to understand here is that this "master/slave" relationship is not a one-way arrangement—an initiator might become a target at some points in the data-transfer cycle, and the target might become the initiator at other points. You will see more about this role duality later in this chapter. A SCSI bus can support up to eight devices simultaneously, but at least one initiator and one target must be in the system. An SCSI host adapter (the expansion card installed in one of the computer's expansion slots) is typically the initiator, and all other devices (e.g., hard drives or CD-ROMs) are usually targets, but that is not necessarily the only possible case.

Many kinds of computer peripherals are candidates for the SCSI bus. Each peripheral offers unique characteristics and applications, but each also requires different methods of control. By adding SCSI "intelligence" to these devices, they can all be made to share the same bus together. The SCSI nomenclature groups similar devices together into specific "device types." The original SCSI standard defines six devices:

- Random-access devices (e.g., hard drives)
- Sequential access (e.g., tape drives)
- Printers
- Processors
- WORM (write-once read-many) drives
- Read-only random-access devices

The SCSI-2 interface adds five more devices to the specification:

- CD-ROM drives
- Scanners
- Magneto-optical drives
- Media changer (jukebox)
- Communication devices

SYNCHRONOUS AND ASYNCHRONOUS

As a system-level interface, SCSI requires an operating "handshaking protocol" that organizes the transfer of data from a sending point to a requesting point. The three typical handshaking protocols for SCSI are: asynchronous, synchronous, and fast synchronous. The *asynchronous* protocol works rather like a parallel port. Each byte must be requested and acknowledged before the next byte can be sent. Asynchronous operation generally results in very reliable (but slow) performance. *Synchronous* and *fast synchronous* operation both ignore the request/acknowledge handshake for data transfer only. This allows slightly faster operation than an asynchronous protocol, but a certain fixed amount of time delay (sometimes called an *offset*) must be allowed for request and acknowledge effects. The fast synchronous protocol uses slightly shorter signals, resulting in even faster speed. An important point to remember is that SCSI systems can typically use any of these three protocols, as desired. The actual protocol that is used must be mutually agreed to by the initiator and the target through their communications. SCSI systems normally initialize in an asynchronous protocol.

DISCONNECT AND RECONNECT

In a number of instances, it would be desirable to allow a target to operate off-line while the initiator is occupied elsewhere. Tape rewind time is just one example. An important feature of SCSI is the ability to disconnect two communicating devices, then reconnect them again later. Disconnect and reconnect operations allow several different operations to occur simultaneously in the system. This is the main reason why SCSI architecture is so desirable in a multitasking environment. It is up to the initiator to grant a disconnect privilege to a target.

SINGLE-ENDED AND DIFFERENTIAL

The signal wiring used in an SCSI bus has a definite impact on bus performance. The two generally used wiring techniques for SCSI are: single-ended and differential. Both wiring schemes have advantages and disadvantages.

The *single-ended (SE)* wiring technique is just as the name implies—a single wire carries the particular signal from initiator to target. Each signal requires only one wire. Terminating resistors at each end of the cable help to maintain acceptable signal levels. A common ground (return) provides the reference for all single-ended signals. Unfortunately, single-ended circuitry is not very noise resistant, so single-ended cabling is generally limited to about six meters at data transfer speeds of 5MHz or less. At higher data-transfer speeds, cable length can be as short as 1.5 meters. In spite of the disadvantages, single-ended operation is simple and popular because of its simplicity.

The *differential (DIF)* wiring approach uses two wires for each signal (instead of one wire referenced to a common ground). A differential signal offers excellent noise resistance because it does not rely on a common ground. This allows much longer cables (up to 25 meters) and higher-speed operation (10 MHz). An array of pull-up resistors at each end of the cable help to ensure signal integrity. The problem with differential wiring is that it is more complicated than single-ended interfaces.

TERMINATORS

When high-frequency signals are transmitted over adjacent wires, signals tend to degrade and interfere with one another over the length of the cable. This is a very natural and relatively well-understood electrical phenomenon. In the PC, SCSI signal integrity is enhanced by using powered resistors at each end of the data cable to "pull up" active signals. Most high-frequency signal cables in the PC are already terminated by pull-up resistors at drives and controller cards. The small resistor array is known as a *terminator*. Because the number of devices that can be added to a floppy drive or IDE cable is limited, designers have never made a big deal about termination—they just added the resistors and that was it. With SCSI, however, up to eight devices can be added to the bus cable. The SCSI cable also must be terminated, but the location of terminating resistors depends on which devices are added to the bus and where they are placed. As a result, termination is a much more vital element of SCSI setup and troubleshooting. As you will see later in this chapter, poor or incorrect termination can cause intermittent signal problems. Later on, you will see how to determine the proper placement of terminating resistors.

Termination is typically either active or passive. Basically, *passive termination* is simply plugging a resistor pack into a SCSI device. Passive resistors are powered by the TERMPWR line. Passive termination is simple and effective over short distances (up to about 1 meter) and usually works just fine for the cable lengths inside a PC, but can be a drawback over longer distances. *Active terminators* provide their own regulated power sources, which makes them most effective for longer cables (such as those in external SCSI devices, such as page scanners) or Wide SCSI systems. Most SCSI-2 implementations use active terminators. A variation on active termination is *forced perfect termination (FPT)*. FPT includes diode clamps, which prevent signal overshoot and undershoot. This makes FPT effective for long SCSI cable lengths.

SCSI IDS

A SCSI bus will support up to eight devices. This means that each device on the bus must have its own unique ID number (0 to 7)—if two devices use the same ID, there will be a conflict. IDs are typically set on the SCSI adapter and each SCSI device using jumpers or DIP switches. Typically, the SCSI adapter is set for ID 7, the primary SCSI hard drive is set to ID 0, and a second SCSI hard drive is ID 1. Other devices can usually be placed anywhere from ID 2 to ID 6.

BUS CONFIGURATIONS

Most of the SCSI implementations currently available use single-ended cabling that supports an 8-bit data bus (known as an *A-cable*). An A-cable is a 50-pin assembly outlined in Table 39-2. The three major sections to the 50-pin single-ended SCSI cable are: ground wires, data signals, and control signals. You will notice that at least half of the single-ended interface carries ground lines. There are eight data lines (D0 to D7) and a data parity bit (DPAR). Notice that SCSI parity is always odd. There are four terminator power lines (TERMPWR) and nine control-signal wires. Each signal is explained:

- −C/D *Control/Data (driven by target)* Allows the target device to select whether it will be returning a command or data to the initiator.
- −I/O *Input/Output (driven by target)* Allows the target device to determine whether it will be receiving or sending information along the data bus.
- −MSG *Message (driven by target)* Allows the target device to send coded status or error messages back to the initiator during the "message" portion of the SCSI bus cycle.
- −REQ *Request (driven by target)* A data strobe signal that allows a potential target device to obtain data on the bus.

TABLE 39-2 PINOUT OF A STANDARD SINGLE-ENDED A-CABLE

SIGNAL	PIN	PIN	SIGNAL	
Ground	1	2	Data 0	
Ground	3	4	Data 1	
Ground	5	6	Data 2	
Ground	7	8	Data 3	
Ground	9	10	Data 4	
Ground	11	12	Data 5	
Ground	13	14	Data 6	
Ground	15	16	Data 7	
Ground	17	18	Data parity	
Ground	19	20	Ground	
Ground	21	22	Ground	
reserved	23	24	reserved	
open	25	26	TERMPWR	
reserved	27	28	reserved	
Ground	29	30	Ground	
Ground	31	32	−ATN	(−Attention)
Ground	33	34	Ground	
Ground	35	36	−BSY	(−Busy)
Ground	37	38	−ACK	(−Acknowledge)

SIGNAL	PIN	PIN	SIGNAL	
TABLE 39-2 PINOUT OF A STANDARD SINGLE-ENDED A-CABLE (CONTINUED)				
Ground	39	40	–RST	(–Reset)
Ground	41	42	–MSG	(–Message)
Ground	43	44	–SEL	(–Select)
Ground	45	46	–C/D	(–Control/Data)
Ground	47	48	–REQ	(–Request)
Ground	49	50	–I/O	(–Input/Output)

- –ACK *Acknowledge (driven by initiator)* A data strobe signal sent in response to the target's REQ signal, which informs the target device that it has gained use of the bus.
- –BSY *Busy (driven by initiator or target)* Allows a device to inform the bus that the device is currently busy.
- –SEL *Select (driven by initiator or target)* A signal used by an initiator to select a target device.
- –ATN *Attention (driven by initiator)* A signal produced by the initiator that informs the target that the initiator has a message ready. The target should switch to the "message" phase.
- –RST *Reset (driven by initiator or target)* A strobe signal that triggers a bus-wide reset of all devices. Usually, only one device produces a Reset signal.

The differential SCSI interface replaces most of the ground wires with +signal leads. For example, pin 2 represents +D0, while pin 27 is -D0. These + and - signal pairs are the differential signals. Notice that there are still a few ground wires, but the grounds are not related to differential signals as they are to single-ended signals. Just about all of the data and control signals in the differential interface serve an identical purpose in the single-ended interface, but the signal locations have been rearranged (Table 39-3). The one additional differential signal is the DIFFSENS (Differential Sense) line, which provides an active high enable for differential drivers. Remember that plugging a differential cable into a single-ended interface (or vice versa) can damage the device, the SCSI adapter, or both.

As you might imagine, wide SCSI implementations will not work with A-cables. A 16-bit cable is needed. Early implementations of wide SCSI used a second cable to provide the extra signal lines, but was quickly abandoned for a single cable assembly (called a P-cable). The single-ended P-cable is shown in Table 39-4. Although many of the signals might look familiar, you will notice that it has 68 pins instead of 50—primarily to support the eight additional data lines (D8 to D15). Control lines are identical to those in the A-cable. Table 39-5 shows the pinout for a differential 68-pin P-cable.

Understanding SCSI Bus Operation

Now that you have learned about SCSI bus concepts and structure, you can see how the interface behaves during normal operation. Because bus wires are common to every device

TABLE 39-3 PINOUT OF A STANDARD DIFFERENTIAL A-CABLE

SIGNAL	PIN	PIN	SIGNAL	
Ground	1	2	Ground	
+Data 0	3	4	−Data 0	
+Data 1	5	6	−Data 1	
+Data 2	7	8	−Data 2	
+Data 3	9	10	−Data 3	
+Data 4	11	12	−Data 4	
+Data 5	13	14	−Data 5	
+Data 6	15	16	−Data 6	
+Data 7	17	18	−Data 7	
+Data parity	19	20	−Data parity	
DIFFSENS	21	22	Ground	
Reserved	23	24	Reserved	
TERMPWR	25	26	TERMPWR	
Reserved	27	28	Reserved	
+ATN	29	30	−ATN	(Attention)
Ground	31	32	Ground	
+BSY	33	34	−BSY	(Busy)
+ACK	35	36	−ACK	(Acknowledge)
+RST	37	38	−RST	(Reset)
+MSG	39	40	−MSG	(Message)
+SEL	41	42	−SEL	(Select)
+C/D	43	44	−C/D	(Control/Data)
+REQ	45	46	−REQ	(Request)
+I/O	47	48	−I/O	(Input/Output)
Ground	49	50	Ground	

TABLE 39-4 PINOUT OF A STANDARD SINGLE-ENDED P-CABLE

SIGNAL	PIN	PIN	SIGNAL
Ground	1	35	Data 12
Ground	2	36	Data 13
Ground	3	37	Data 14
Ground	4	38	Data 15
Ground	5	39	Data parity 1
Ground	6	40	Data 0
Ground	7	41	Data 1
Ground	8	42	Data 2
Ground	9	43	Data 3
Ground	10	44	Data 4

TABLE 39-4   PINOUT OF A STANDARD SINGLE-ENDED P-CABLE (CONTINUED)

SIGNAL	PIN	PIN	SIGNAL	
Ground	11	45	Data 5	
Ground	12	46	Data 6	
Ground	13	47	Data 7	
Ground	14	48	Data parity 0	
Ground	15	49	Ground	
Ground	16	50	Ground	
TERMPWR	17	51	TERMPWR	
TERMPWR	18	52	TERMPWR	
Reserved	19	53	Reserved	
Ground	20	54	Ground	
Ground	21	55	−ATN	(−Attention)
Ground	22	56	Ground	
Ground	23	57	−BSY	(−Busy)
Ground	24	58	−ACK	(−Acknowledge)
Ground	25	59	−RST	(−Reset)
Ground	26	60	−MSG	(−Message)
Ground	27	61	−SEL	(−Select)
Ground	28	62	−C/D	(−Control/Data)
Ground	29	63	−REQ	(−Request)
Ground	30	64	−I/O	(−Input/Output)
Ground	31	65	Data 8	
Ground	32	66	Data 9	
Ground	33	67	Data 10	
Ground	34	68	Data 11	

TABLE 39-5   PINOUT OF A STANDARD DIFFERENTIAL P-CABLE

SIGNAL	PIN	PIN	SIGNAL
+Data 12	1	35	−Data 12
+Data 13	2	36	−Data 13
+Data 14	3	37	−Data 14
+Data 15	4	38	−Data 15
+Data parity 1	5	39	−Data parity 1
Ground	6	40	Ground
+Data 0	7	41	−Data 0
+Data 1	8	42	−Data 1
+Data 2	9	43	−Data 2
+Data 3	10	44	−Data 3
+Data 4	11	45	−Data 4
+Data 5	12	46	−Data 5

TABLE 39-5	PINOUT OF A STANDARD DIFFERENTIAL P-CABLE (CONTINUED)		
SIGNAL	PIN	PIN	SIGNAL
+Data 6	13	47	−Data 6	
+Data 7	14	48	−Data 7	
+Data parity 0	15	49	−Data parity 0	
DIFFSENS	16	50	Ground	
TERMPWR	17	51	TERMPWR	
TERMPWR	18	52	TERMPWR	
Reserved	19	53	Reserved	
+ATN	20	54	−ATN	(Attention)
Ground	21	55	Ground	
+BSY	22	56	+BSY	(Busy)
+ACK	23	57	−ACK	(Acknowledge)
+RST	24	58	−RST	(Reset)
+MSG	25	59	−MSG	(Message)
+SEL	26	60	−SEL	(Select)
+C/D	27	61	−C/D	(Control/Data)
+REQ	28	62	−REQ	(Request)
+I/O	29	63	−I/O	(Input/Output)
Ground	30	64	Ground	
+Data 8	31	65	−Data 8	
+Data 9	32	66	−Data 9	
+Data 10	33	67	−Data 10	
+Data 11	34	68	−Data 11	

attached to the bus, a device must obtain permission from all other devices before it can take control of the bus. This attempt to access the bus is called the *arbitration phase*. Once a device (such as the SCSI controller) has won the bus arbitration, it must then make contact with the device to be communicated with. This device selection is known as the *selection phase*. When this contact is established, data transfer can occur. This part of the chapter details negotiation and information transfer over the SCSI bus.

NEGOTIATION

Devices must negotiate to access and use an SCSI bus. Negotiation begins when the bus is free (BSY and SEL lines are idle). A device begins arbitration by activating the BSY line and its own data ID line (data bit D0 to D7, depending on the device). If more than one device tries to control the bus simultaneously, the device with the higher ID line wins. The winning device (an initiator) attempts to acquire a target device by asserting the SEL line and the data ID line (data bit D0 to D7) of the desired device. The BSY line is then released by the initiator and the desired target device asserts the BSY line to confirm that it has been selected. The initiator then releases the SEL and data bus lines. Information transfer can now take place.

INFORMATION

The selected target controls the data being transferred and the direction of transfer. Information transfer lasts until the target device releases the BSY line, thus returning the bus to the idle state. If a piece of information requires a long time for preparation, the target can end the connection by issuing a disconnect message. It will try to re-establish the connection later with a new arbitration and selection procedure.

During information transfer, the initiator tells its target how to act on a command and establishes the mode of data transfer during the message-out phase. A specific SCSI command follows the message during the command phase. After a command is sent, data transfer occurs during the data-in and/or data-out phases. The target relinquishes control to the initiator during the command phase. For example, the command itself might ask that more information be transferred. The target then tells the initiator whether the command was successfully completed or not by returning status information during a status phase. Finally, the command is finished when the target sends a progress report to the initiator during the message in phase. Consider this simple SCSI communication example:

1	Bus Free Phase	System is idle
2	Arbitration Phase	A device takes control of the bus
3	Select Phase	The desired device is selected
4	Message-Out Phase	Target sets up data transfer
5	Command Phase	send Command
6	Data-In Phase	Exchange data
7	Status Phase	Indicate the results of the exchange
8	Message-In Phase	Indicate exchange is complete
9	Bus Free Phase	System is idle

Upgrading a PC for SCSI

Whether you are considering adding SCSI support to your own computer or are planning an upgrade for a customer, four essential elements must be considered: the SCSI peripheral, the SCSI host adapter, the SCSI cable assembly, and the SCSI software driver(s). If any one of these four elements is missing or ill-planned, your installation is going to run into problems.

SCSI PERIPHERALS

The first item to be considered is the SCSI peripheral itself. You first need to know what type of device is needed (such as a SCSI hard drive or CD-ROM). The peripheral should be compatible with SCSI-2 architecture. You might also find a growing base of SCSI-3 compliant adapters and peripherals. Each SCSI peripheral device should also have a wide range of available SCSI ID settings. SCSI typically handles eight IDs (0 to 7) and the peripheral should have the flexibility to run on virtually any ID. If only a few IDs are available, you might be limited when it comes time to add other SCSI devices. Peripherals should support SCSI parity.

Ideally, a SCSI-3 host adapter should support SCSI-2 devices. If you have any intention of using SCSI-3 (Wide/Fast 20 SCSI) devices, be sure to use a SCSI-3 adapter.

SCSI devices are available in both internal and external versions. If you consider an internal peripheral, be sure that there is adequate drive space in the PC to accommodate the new peripheral. Either there is a drive bay available, or an existing device might be removed to make room. If the peripheral is to be an external device (such as a printer or scanner), there should be two SCSI connectors on the device to allow for daisy-chaining additional devices later. All SCSI peripherals other than hard drives will require device drivers. Be sure that the device driver is compatible with the same standard protocol used by the adapter (i.e., ASPI, CAM, or LADDR). This is a serious consideration because peripherals using incompatible device driver standards will not work properly. Finally, try to choose SCSI peripherals that offer built-in cable termination.

SCSI HOST ADAPTER

The next item to be considered is the SCSI host adapter (often just called a *host* or *HA*) that fits in the PC expansion bus (Fig. 39-1). Be sure to choose an adapter that is compatible with the PC bus in use (e.g., ISA, EISA, MCA, PCI, etc.). Bus-mastering 32-/64-bit PCI SCSI adapters will provide superior performance if your system will support them. Like

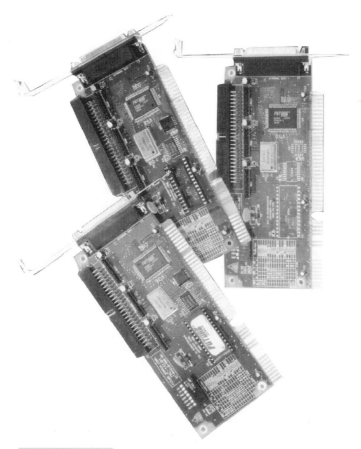

FIGURE 39-1 **SCSI adapter boards.** Copyright © 1995 Future
Domain Corporation. Reprinted with permission

the peripheral itself, the adapter should also be designed to support the SCSI-2 standard (or SCSI-3, if possible). Although most adapters are assigned a SCSI ID of 7, the adapter should be flexible enough to work with any ID from 0 to 7. The host adapter will also require a device driver for using devices other than hard drives. Be sure that the host device driver uses the same standard as the peripheral(s) (ASPI, CAM, or LADDR). It is important to note here that the driver standard has nothing to do with the choice of SCSI, SCSI-2, or SCSI-3. It is only important that the peripherals and the adapter use the same driver standard.

SCSI CABLES AND TERMINATORS

Check that you select the proper cabling for the SCSI level you are using. Although SCSI cabling is now highly standardized, some older cables might use slight modifications for particular peripherals (a typical trick used with SCSI-1 devices. Be certain that you know of any specialized cabling requirements when choosing peripherals. Try to avoid specialized cabling, if at all possible. But if you must use specialized cabling, you should determine what impact the cabling will have on any other SCSI peripherals that might be installed (or might be installed later). Use good-quality SCSI cables, specifically intended for the SCSI level you are using (probably SCSI-2), and keep the cables short to minimize signal degradation.

SCSI cables must be terminated at the beginning (host adapter) and end (after the last device) of the SCSI chain. Try to choose internal peripherals that have built-in terminators. Also try to select a host adapter and peripherals that use the same type of terminator resistor network. SCSI-2 systems use active terminator networks. Much more about cabling and termination is included a bit later in this chapter.

SCSI DRIVERS

Device drivers provide the instructions that allow the SCSI host adapter to communicate with the PC, as well as the peripherals in the SCSI chain (or the SCSI bus). The host adapter itself requires a device driver, as will every peripheral that is added. For example, a SCSI system with one CD-ROM will need a driver for the host adapter and a driver for the CD-ROM. Be sure that driver standards (ASPI, CAM, or LADDR) are the SAME for the host adapter and peripherals. The only exception to the device-driver requirement (at this time) is the SCSI hard drive, which might be supported by the SCSI adapter's BIOS ROM.

Real-mode device drivers are added by including them in your PC's CONFIG.SYS and AUTOEXEC.BAT files. One issue to remember when adding device drivers is that drivers use conventional memory (unless you successfully load the drivers into high memory). The more drivers that are added, the more memory will be consumed. It is possible that a large number of device drivers might prevent certain memory-demanding DOS applications from running. To keep as much conventional memory (the first 640KB in RAM) free as possible, use the DOS devicehigh and loadhigh features to load the drivers into upper memory (from 640KB to 1MB in RAM). Windows 95 uses protected-mode drivers for the host adapter and devices.

TIPS FOR A SMOOTH UPGRADE

SCSI upgrades are not terribly difficult to perform properly, but the subtle considerations and inconsistencies that have always been a part of SCSI implementations can result in confusion and serious delays for you and your customer. The following tips should help to ease your upgrades:

■ *Add only add one SCSI device at a time* By adding one device at a time and testing the system after each installation, it becomes much easier to determine the point where problems occur. Suppose what happens when you add an adapter, hard drive, and CD-ROM. If the system fails to function, you will have to isolate and check each item to locate the fault. On the other hand, by adding the adapter and testing it, then adding the hard drive and testing it, then adding the CD-ROM and testing it, installation troubleshooting becomes a much simpler matter (although it might take a bit more time overall).

■ *Record the host adapter's resources* One of the most difficult aspects of troubleshooting is determining what the configuration of a system is. This is especially important during an upgrade because you must know the interrupts (IRQs), DMA channel(s), and I/O ranges used by other expansion devices in the PC. Any overlap in the use of these system resources will eventually result in a hardware conflict. When you install a SCSI host adapter, make it a point to record its IRQ, DMA, and I/O settings along with the SCSI ID settings of all devices that are installed. Tape the record to the inside of the PC's cover. The next time the PC returns for service or upgrade, you'll have the information right at your fingertips.

■ *Use good-quality cabling* Using the correct terminators and cables can have a profound effect on the performance of your SCSI installation. Good-quality cables and terminators provide electrical characteristics that support good signal transfer. This results in good data reliability between the host controller and peripherals. If the cable quality is sub-standard or terminator networks are not correct for the SCSI level being used, the cable's electrical characteristics and data transfer will be degraded.

CONFIGURE AND INSTALL THE SCSI ADAPTER

The SCSI adapter is an expansion board—much like any other expansion board in your PC. You will need to configure the adapter before installing it. Most SCSI adapters need four system resources: an IRQ, a DMA channel, an I/O range, and ROM addresses. Settings are typically made by changing jumper placement. The user's manual for your particular adapter will outline precisely what selections are available, and how to change each one. When choosing system resources, be very careful to avoid conflicts with other adapters in your system. Although manufacturers try to avoid conflicts by "pre-setting" the adapter to rarely used settings, you should check for possible conflicts anyway.

You can also set the adapter's SCSI ID and the SCSI parity. In almost all circumstances, the adapter will use a SCSI ID of 7. Parity is a means of error checking the data passed along a SCSI data path. The problem with parity is that all installed SCSI devices must support it or parity should be disabled. If you select only peripheral devices that support SCSI parity, you can enable it on the adapter. Record the settings on paper and tape the paper inside the PC's cover. Insert the adapter into an available expansion slot and secure the board properly.

New SCSI host adapters (mainly PCI boards) are often Plug-and-Play (PnP) devices, and are configured through the SCSI BIOS and host adapter driver(s) at startup.

CONFIGURE AND INSTALL THE SCSI PERIPHERAL

It should not be difficult to configure a SCSI peripheral. You should be concerned with set-ting the SCSI ID and SCSI parity. The ID (also called *Target ID* or *Target SCSI ID*) can range from 0 to 7. Because the adapter is almost always set at 7, only 0 through 6 remain. However, SCSI hard drives for AT-compatible machines should be issued IDs of 0 or 1. As a general rule, do not use ID 0 or ID 1 for any devices but hard drives. If you intend to boot your PC from the SCSI hard disk, assign it an ID of 0. PS/2 machines place the bootable hard drive on SCSI ID 6. When assigning IDs in systems with more than one SCSI periph-eral, be careful not to use duplicate IDs. Each device must have its own unique ID number.

If the device supports SCSI parity, the setting should be enabled. Remember that to use SCSI parity, all SCSI devices in the system must support it. If even one device does not support it, parity must be disabled system-wide. If another device already in the system relies on SCSI parity (such as a CD-ROM drive), disabling parity to accommodate a new device can render an existing device inoperative. You might need to change your selec-tion of peripheral to one that supports SCSI parity.

Depending on the SCSI device being installed, you might also need to set a *Start-on command* jumper. Drives draw a serious amount of power during startup. If a large num-ber of devices are trying to draw power, the power supply can be overloaded. A Start-on command option (if available on your peripheral) will keep the device idle until a Start command is sent from the SCSI adapter. This way, multiple SCSI devices can be started in a staggered fashion to "spread out" the power load. For external SCSI devices, situate the device close to the computer—SCSI cables tend to be kept short. If the peripheral is an internal device, you should now mount it in an available drive bay.

CABLING AND TERMINATION

Once the host adapter and peripheral are configured and installed, you must connect them with a cable. Internal devices are typically connected with a 50-pin *Insulation Displacement Connector (IDC)* ribbon cable (an A-cable). By placing multiple con-nectors along the length of cable, daisy chaining can be achieved with a single connec-tor on each internal device. External devices typically connect to an external 50-pin connector on the rear of the SCSI adapter, and each device offers two connectors, which allows daisy chaining to additional devices. Most commercial adapter and drive "kits" are packed with an appropriate cable.

The cable(s) must be terminated. Internal and external SCSI cable terminators are avail-able, along with SCSI devices that have terminating resistor networks already built in. The concept of termination is reasonably simple—achieve the desired signal-cable characteris-tics by loading each end of the SCSI "chain" with resistors. If the chain is not terminated properly, signals will not be carried reliably (which invariably results in system errors). For technicians and end-users alike, the trouble usually arises in determining where the "ends" are. A number of examples clarify how to determine the chain "ends."

For a single SCSI drive and adapter (Fig. 39-2), the "ends" are easy to see. One end should be terminated at the host adapter (which usually has terminating resistors built in). The other end should be terminated at the SCSI hard drive (which also usually has termi-nating resistors built in). In this type of situation, you need only connect the cable between both devices and verify that the terminators are in place.

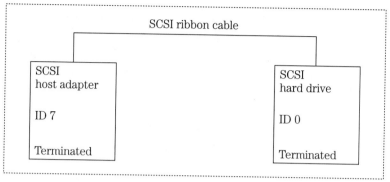

FIGURE 39-2   **Terminating an internal SCSI adapter and hard drive.**

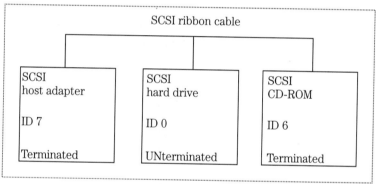

FIGURE 39-3   **Terminating an internal SCSI adapter, HDD, and CD-ROM.**

When a second SCSI peripheral is added (Fig. 39-3), termination becomes a bit more complex. Suppose that a CD-ROM is added with a SCSI ID of 6. The terminator on the existing SCSI hard drive is no longer appropriate; it should be removed, and the termination should be made on the CD-ROM, which is now the last device in the SCSI chain. In most cases, a terminator network can be deactivated by flipping a DIP switch or changing a jumper on the peripheral itself. If the terminator can not be "shut off," it can almost always be removed by gently easing the resistor network out of its holder using needle-nose pliers. If you remove a terminator, place it in an envelope and tape it to the inside of the PC enclosure. If it is simply impossible to remove the existing terminator on the hard drive, place the CD-ROM between the adapter and hard drive and remove the CD-ROM's terminator (re-arrange the chain). The SCSI host adapter must remain terminated.

So what happens if an external device is used (such as a scanner), as in Fig. 39-4? An external cable connects the adapter to the scanner. Because the scanner (ID 6) and adapter (ID 7) are the only two points in the chain, both are terminated. Most external devices designed for SCSI-2 compatibility allow the active terminator built into the peripheral to be switched off, if necessary.

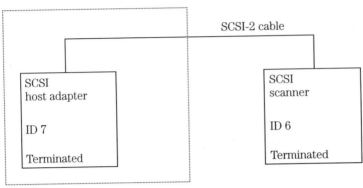

FIGURE 39-4 **Terminating an external SCSI device.**

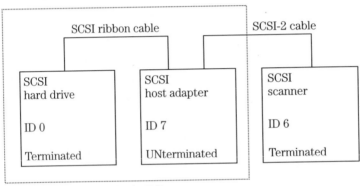

FIGURE 39-5 **Terminating mixed internal and external SCSI devices.**

Suppose that both an internal and an external SCSI device are being used (Fig. 39-5). The SCSI host adapter (ID 7) is no longer at an end of the chain, so its terminator should be switched off or removed. The internal hard drive (ID 0) and external scanner (ID 6) now form the ends, so both devices should be terminated. Because both peripherals should ideally support internal termination, nothing needs to be done, except to confirm that the terminators are in place and switched on.

REAL-MODE SCSI DRIVER ISSUES

Hardware configuration and installation is only one part of the SCSI installation. Software needs to be installed to allow the hardware to interact with your system. The problem with SCSI drivers is that prior to 1991, various drivers were rarely compatible. For example, an adapter and hard drive might have worked fine, but adding a CD-ROM would create havoc because the CD-ROM driver was not compatible with the hard drive or the host adapter driver (or both). After 1991, a set of "universal" driver standards appeared, which created a "buffer" between the operating system and hardware, which isolated each particular driver from one another. Drivers can now be written for each peripheral without worry of incompatibility so long as the drivers are written to be compatible with the standard.

Three SCSI standards are now competing: ASPI (Advanced SCSI Programming Interface), CAM (Common Access Method), and LADDR (Layered Device Driver Architecture). ASPI is the most popular of the three standards. The idea for compatibility is to select a host adapter and peripherals that support the same standard. For example, if you select a host adapter that uses an ASPI driver, each of the peripherals that you choose must also use ASPI drivers. If you upgrade the host adapter later, you also upgrade the host's ASPI driver—full compatibility should be maintained.

The actual installation process varies little from other software installations. The real-mode driver files for your adapter and peripheral(s) are copied to a sub-directory on the hard drive, then the CONFIG.SYS and AUTOEXEC.BAT files are updated to load the appropriate drivers on system startup. If your particular system commits too much conventional memory to drivers, you can manually optimize your startup files later to load as many drivers as possible into upper memory.

TIPS FOR WINDOWS 95 SCSI DRIVERS

If you intend to use your SCSI system under Windows 95, you'll need to install protected-mode drivers for the host adapter and devices. Contemporary SCSI host adapters (and many SCSI devices) are compliant with Plug-and-Play operation under Windows 95—this means Windows 95 should typically be able to identify the SCSI adapter (or newly installed devices) and install the appropriate protected-mode drivers for it. Ordinarily, this process should be automatic, but the following tips might help you handle Windows 95 installations:

■ Verify the SCSI adapter and devices in DOS first with its real-mode drivers.
■ If Windows 95 does not automatically identify the SCSI hardware, run the *Add new hardware* wizard to register the device(s) and install the protected-mode drivers (remember not to let Windows 95 detect devices itself).
■ You can use the Add New Hardware wizard to update existing SCSI drivers if new versions become available.
■ If your SCSI hardware is not listed in the *Add new hardware* wizard, you'll need to contact the hardware manufacturer(s) and download the correct .INF file and protected-mode drivers. If no protected-mode drivers are available for your SCSI hardware (that would be rare today), you'll need to use the real-mode (DOS) drivers—this might result in all system drives running in DOS compatibility mode and impairing system performance.

Troubleshooting the SCSI System

As far as the bus is concerned, very little can go "wrong"—wires and connectors do not fail spontaneously. However, it never hurts to examine the wiring, connectors, and terminator network(s) to ensure that the physical connections are intact (especially after installing or configuring new devices). The most likely areas of trouble are in the installation, setup, and operation of the devices residing on the bus.

ISOLATING TROUBLE SPOTS

Assuming that your SCSI devices have been installed correctly, problem scenarios can occur during normal operation. The first indication of a problem usually comes in the form of an error message from your operating system or application program. For example, your SCSI hard drive might not be responding, or the host PC might not be able to identify the SCSI host controller board, etc.

The advantage to SCSI architecture is that it is reasonably easy to determine problem locations using intuitive deduction. Consider a typical SCSI system with one initiator (a host controller) and one target (e.g., a hard drive). If the hard drive fails to function, the trouble is either in the host controller or the drive itself. If drive access is attempted, but an error is generated, the trouble is probably in the drive. If no drive access is attempted before an error is generated, the error is likely in the host controller. As another example, consider a setup with one initiator and two or more targets (e.g., a hard drive and CD-ROM). If both the hard drive and CD-ROM become inoperative, the problem is likely in the host controller card because the host adapter controls both targets. If only one of the devices becomes inoperative (and the other device works just fine), the trouble is likely in the particular device itself.

Of course, these are only common isolation methods, and their effectiveness will depend on the sophistication of the particular system that you are working with. There is always some amount of uncertainty in the intuitive approach because it is not quantitative. You can suspect where the trouble is coming from, but you can not prove it. Given the great expense of many SCSI peripherals, it is often unwise to purchase replacement parts based solely on intuitive techniques. To prove the problem's source, you can track communication along the SCSI bus using a specialized SCSI tester. If you perform extensive SCSI testing on a professional level, you might wish to invest in an SCSI bus tester, such as Ancot's DSC-216 portable SCSI bus analyzer. An analyzer can let you track the communication process along the SCSI bus, as well as provide bus-speed calculations and command profiling. Once you have located the problem device, you can deal with that device specifically through replacement or repair.

However, specialized test equipment carries a significant price tag—a worthy investment if you have the service volume to justify it, but hardly a reasonable outlay for the casual PC hobbyist. Fortunately, a growing number of contemporary diagnostic software packages are being upgraded with SCSI test capabilities. For example, the PC Technician software by Windsor Technologies can test a limited number of SCSI adapters (such as Western Digital, Adaptec, and NCR) and associated peripherals. SCSIDiag by AMI is a diagnostic specifically designed for SCSI system testing.

The reason for this lack of broad diagnostic software support is simple—SCSI is not supported by the PC motherboard BIOS (where IDE and EIDE are supported). As a result, the diagnostic must be written to handle specific SCSI controllers. The issue to remember when selecting a diagnostic for SCSI testing is that the software must be compatible with the SCSI adapter in your system—just because a diagnostic says "SCSI-compatible" does not necessarily make it so for the PC setup you are faced with. As an alternative to commercial diagnostics, you might be able to find small controller diagnostics right on the software disks that accompany the SCSI adapter. You would run the test routine after installation to see that the controller is working, but you can also use it in a pinch for "as-needed" troubleshooting for that particular controller. Check with the manufacturer's BBS or CompuServe forum to find up-to-date test routines for various controllers.

GENERAL TROUBLESHOOTING TIPS

No matter how many precautions you take, you cannot always prevent problems from striking during a SCSI installations or replacements. Fortunately, if you are installing devices one-by-one, as suggested, you will have far fewer problem areas to check. Your first diagnostic for a SCSI installation should be the host adapter's SCSI BIOS initialization message. If you see no initialization message when the system powers up, the problem is likely with the adapter itself. Either it is not installed properly or it is defective. Be sure that the adapter is set to the desired ID (usually 7). Try a new or alternate SCSI adapter. If the adapter provides its initialization message as expected, the problem is probably related to driver installation. Check the installation and any command-line switches for each device driver. When installing a SCSI hard drive instead of IDE/EIDE hard drives, you must ensure that any previous hard-drive references are "mapped out" of the CMOS setup by entering "none" or "not installed." If pre-existing drive references are not removed, the system will try to boot from IDE/EIDE drives, which aren't there.

Be aware that faulty SCSI ID settings can result in system problems, such as "ghost" disks—disks that the system says are there, but that cannot be read from or written to. Some peripherals might also not work properly with the ID that has been assigned. If you have problems interacting with an installed device, try the device with a different ID, and be sure that no two devices are using the same ID. Don't be surprised to find that certain types of cables don't work properly with SCSI installations. Be sure that everything is terminated correctly. Also be sure that any external SCSI devices are powered up (if possible) before the PC is initialized. If problems persist, try different cables. An quick-reference checklist is shown:

- Check the power to all SCSI devices (be sure that the power supply has enough capacity to handle all of your attached SCSI devices).
- Check the cable to all SCSI devices. A good-quality cable should be attached securely to each device.
- Check the orientation of each connector on the SCSI cable. Pin 1 must always be in the proper orientation.
- Check the SCSI ID of each device. Duplicate IDs are not allowed.
- Check that both ends of the SCSI cable are properly terminated and that the terminators are active.
- Check the SCSI controller configuration (IRQQ, I/O, BIOS addresses, etc.).
- Verify that the SCSI controller is not conflicting with other devices in the system.
- Check SCSI host adapter BIOS. If you're not booting from SCSI hard drives, you can often leave the SCSI BIOS disabled. This will also simplify the device configuration.
- Check the CMOS setup for drive configurations. When SCSI drives are in the system and IDE/EIDE drives are not, be sure that the drive entries under CMOS are set for *None* or *Not installed*.
- Check the PCI bus configuration in the CMOS setup. See that the PCI slot containing the SCSI host adapter is active and is using a unique IRQ (usually named *IRQ A*).

- Check for the real-mode drivers under DOS. If you're working under DOS, see that any needed driver(s) for the host adapter and non-HDD device(s) are installed in the CONFIG.SYS and AUTOEXEC.BAT files.
- Check for the protected-mode drivers under Windows 95. If you're working under Windows 95, see that any needed protected-mode drivers for the host adapter and SCSI devices are installed.
- Try remarking-out real-mode drivers if problems occur only under Windows 95. Real-mode SCSI drivers can sometimes interfere with protected-mode SCSI drivers. If the SCSI system works fine in DOS, but not in Windows 95, try temporarily disabling the DOS drivers in your startup files.

SYMPTOMS

Even the best-planned SCSI setups go wrong from time to time, and SCSI systems already in the field will not run forever. Sooner or later, you will have to deal with a SCSI problem. This part of the chapter is intended to show you a variety of symptoms and solutions for many of the problems that you will likely encounter.

Symptom 39-1. After initial SCSI installation, the system will not boot from the floppy drive You might see an error code corresponding to this problem. Suspect the SCSI host adapter first. An internal fault with the adapter might be interfering with system operation. Check that all of the adapter's settings are correct and that all jumpers are intact. If the adapter is equipped with any diagnostic LEDs, check for any problem indications. When adapter problems are indicated, replace the adapter board. If a SCSI hard drive has been installed and the drive light is always on, the SCSI signal cable has probably been reversed between the drive and adapter. Be sure to install the drive cable properly.

Check for the SCSI-adapter BIOS message generated when the system starts. If the message does not appear, check for the presence of a ROM-address conflict between the SCSI adapter and ROMs on other expansion boards. Try a new address setting for the SCSI adapter. If a BIOS wait-state jumper is on the adapter, try changing its setting. If you see an error message indicating that the SCSI host adapter was not found at a particular address, check the I/O setting for the adapter.

Some more-recent SCSI host adapters incorporate a floppy controller. This can cause a conflict with an existing floppy controller. If you choose to continue using the existing floppy controller, be sure to disable the host adapter's floppy controller. If you'd prefer to use the host adapter's floppy controller, remember to disable the pre-existing floppy controller port.

Symptom 39-2. The system will not boot from the SCSI hard drive Start by checking the system's CMOS setup. When SCSI drives are installed in a PC, the corresponding hard-drive reference in the CMOS setup must be changed to "none" or "not installed" (this assumes that you will not be using IDE/EIDE hard drives in the system). If previous hard-drive references have not been "mapped out," do so now, save the CMOS setup, and reboot the PC. If the problem persists, check that the SCSI boot drive is set to ID 0. You will need to refer to the user manual for your particular drive to find how the ID is set.

Next, check the SCSI parity to be sure that it is selected consistently among all SCSI devices. Remember that all SCSI devices must have SCSI parity enabled or disabled—if even one device in the SCSI chain does not support parity, it must be disabled on all devices. Check the SCSI cabling to be sure that all cables are installed and terminated properly. Finally, be sure that the hard drive has been partitioned and formatted properly. If not, boot from a floppy disk and prepare the hard drive, as required, using FDISK and FORMAT.

Symptom 39-3. The SCSI drive fails to respond with an alternate HDD as the boot drive Technically, you should be able to use a SCSI drive as a non-boot drive (e.g., drive D:) while using an IDE/EIDE drive as the boot device. If the SCSI drive fails to respond in this kind of arrangement, check the CMOS setting to be sure that drive 1 (the SCSI drive) is "mapped out" (or set to *None* or *Not installed*). Save the CMOS setup and reboot the PC. If the problem persists, check that the SCSI drive is set to SCSI ID 1 (the non-boot ID). Next, be sure that the SCSI parity is enabled or disabled consistently throughout the SCSI installation. If the SCSI parity is enabled for some devices and disabled for others, the SCSI system might function erratically. Finally, check that the SCSI cabling is installed and terminated properly. Faulty cables or termination can easily interrupt a SCSI system. If the problem persists, try another hard drive.

> Later SCSI host adapters use BIOS that allows SCSI drives to boot—even with IDE/EIDE drives in the system. In such a configuration, the "Boot order" entry in CMOS setup will determine whether A:, C:, or SCSI will be the boot device.

Symptom 39-4. The SCSI drive fails to respond with another SCSI drive as the boot drive This typically occurs in a dual-drive system using two SCSI drives. Check the CMOS setup and be sure that both drive entries in the setup are set to "none" or "not installed." Save the CMOS setup. The boot drive should be set to SCSI ID 0 while the supplemental drive should be set to SCSI ID 1 (you will probably have to refer to the manual for the drives to determine how to select a SCSI ID). The hard drives should have a DOS partition and format. If not, create the partitions (FDISK) and format the drives (FORMAT) as required. Check to be sure that SCSI parity is enabled or disabled consistently throughout the SCSI system. If some devices use parity and other devices do not, the SCSI system might not function properly. Be sure that all SCSI cables are installed and terminated properly. If the problem persists, try systematically exchanging each hard drive.

Symptom 39-5. The system works erratically The PC hangs or the SCSI adapter cannot find the drive(s). Such intermittent operation can be the result of several different SCSI factors. Before taking any action, be sure that the application software you were running when the fault occurred did not cause the problem. Unstable or buggy software can seriously interfere with system operation. Try different applications and see if the system still hangs up (you might also try any DOS diagnostic utilities that accompanied the host adapter). Check each SCSI device and be sure that parity is enabled or disabled consistently throughout the SCSI system. If parity is enabled in some devices and disabled in others, erratic operation can result. Be sure that no two SCSI devices are using the same

ID. Cabling problems are another common source of erratic behavior. Be sure that all SCSI cables are attached correctly and completely. Also check that the cabling is properly terminated.

Next, suspect that a resource conflict might be between the SCSI host adapter and another board in the system. Check each expansion board in the system to be sure that nothing is using the same IRQ, DMA, or I/O address as the host adapter (or check the *Device manager* under Windows 95). If you find a conflict, you should alter the most recently installed adapter board. If problems persist, try a new drive adapter board.

Symptom 39-6. A 096xxxx error code appears This diagnostic error code indicates a problem in a 32-bit SCSI host adapter board. Check the board to be sure that it is installed correctly and completely. The board should not be shorted against any other board or cable. Try disabling one SCSI device at a time. If normal operation returns, the last device to be removed is responsible for the problem (you might need to disable drivers and reconfigure termination when isolating problems in this fashion). If the problem persists, remove and re-install all SCSI devices from scratch, or try a new SCSI adapter board.

Symptom 39-7. A 112xxxx error code appears This diagnostic error code indicates that a problem is in a 16-bit SCSI adapter board. Check the board to be sure that it is installed correctly and completely. The board should not be shorted against any other board or cable. Try disabling one SCSI device at a time. If normal operation returns, the last device to be removed is responsible for the problem (you might need to disable drivers and reconfigure termination when isolating problems in this fashion). Try a new SCSI host-adapter board.

Symptom 39-8. A 113xxxx error code appears This diagnostic code indicates that a problem is in a system (motherboard) SCSI adapter configuration. If a SCSI BIOS ROM is installed on the motherboard, be sure that it is up-to-date and installed correctly and completely. If problems persist, replace the motherboard's SCSI controller IC or replace the system board. It might be possible to circumvent a damaged motherboard SCSI controller by disabling the motherboard's controller, then installing a SCSI host adapter card.

Symptom 39-9. A 210xxxx error code appears A fault is in a SCSI hard disk. Check that the power and signal cables to the disk are connected properly. Be sure that the SCSI cable is correctly terminated. Try repartitioning and reformatting the SCSI hard disk. Finally, try a new SCSI hard disk.

Symptom 39-10.   A SCSI device refuses to function with the SCSI adapter—even though both the adapter and device check properly This is often a classic case of basic incompatibility between the device and host adapter. Even though SCSI-2 helps to streamline compatibility between devices and controllers, the two just don't work together in some situations. Check the literature included with the finicky device and see if any notices of compatibility problems are included with the controller (perhaps the particular controller brand) you are using. If warnings are included, alternative jumpers or DIP switch settings might be included to compensate for the problem and allow you to use the device after all. A call to technical support at the device's manufacturer might help shed light on any recently discovered bugs or fixes (e.g., an updated SCSI

BIOS, SCSI device driver, or host adapter driver). If problems remain, try using a similar device from a different manufacturer (e.g., try a Connor tape drive instead of a Mountain tape drive).

Symptom 39-11. A "No SCSI controller present" error message appears
Immediately suspect that the controller is defective or installed improperly. Check the host adapter installation (including IRQ, DMA, and I/O settings) and see that the proper suite of device drivers have been installed correctly. If the system still refuses to recognize the controller, try installing it in a different PC. If the controller also fails in a different PC, the controller is probably bad and should be replaced. However, if the controller works in a different PC, your original PC might not support all the functions under the interrupt 15h call required to configure SCSI adapters (such as an AMI SCSI host adapter). Consider upgrading the PC BIOS ROM to a new version—especially if the PC BIOS is older. An upgraded SCSI BIOS or host adapter driver might be available to compensate for this problem.

Symptom 39-12. The PCI SCSI host adapter is not recognized and the SCSI BIOS banner is not displayed This often occurs when installing new PCI SCSI host adapters. The host computer must be PCI REV. 2.0 compliant and the motherboard BIOS must support PCI-to-PCI Bridges (PPB) and bus mastering. This is typically a problem (or limitation) with some older PCI motherboard chipsets, and you'll probably find that the PCI SCSI adapter board works just fine on newer systems. If the system doesn't support PPB, it might not be possible to use the PCI SCSI adapter. You can try an ISA SCSI adapter instead or upgrade the motherboard to one with a more recent chipset.

If the system hardware does offer PPB support and the problem persists, the motherboard BIOS might still not support PPB features as required by the PCI 2.0 standard. In this case, try a motherboard BIOS upgrade if one is available. If the problem continues, either the board is not in a bus-mastering slot, or the PCI slot is not enabled for bus mastering. Configure the PCI slot for bus mastering through CMOS setup or through a jumper on the motherboard (check your system's documentation to see exactly how).

Symptom 39-13.   During boot-up, a "Host-adapter configuration error" message appears In virtually all cases, the problem is with the PCI slot configuration for the SCSI host adapter. Try enabling a IRQ for the SCSI adapter's PCI slot (usually accomplished through the CMOS setup). Be sure that any IRQ being assigned to the SCSI adapter PCI slot is not conflicting with other devices in the system.

Symptom 39-14. An error message, such as "No SCSI functions in use," appears Even when a SCSI adapter and devices are installed and configured properly, there are several possible causes for this kind of an error. First, be sure that no hard-disk drivers are installed when no physical SCSI hard disks are in the system. Also be sure that there are no hard disk drivers installed (i.e., in CONFIG.SYS) when the SCSI host-adapter BIOS is enabled. HDD drivers aren't needed then, but you could leave the drivers in place and disable the SCSI BIOS. Finally, this error can occur if the HDD was formatted on another SCSI controller that does not support ASPI, or uses a specialized format. For example, Western Digital controllers only work with Western Digital HDDs. In this case, you should try a more generic controller.

Symptom 39-15.   An error message, such as "No boot record found," appears   This generally simple problem can be traced to several possible issues. First, chances are that the drive has never been partitioned (FDISK) or formatted as a bootable drive (FORMAT). Repartition and reformat the hard drive. If you partitioned and formatted the drive with a third-party utility (e.g., TFORMAT), be sure to answer *Y*, if asked to make the disk bootable. A third possibility can occur if the disk was formatted on another manufacturer's controller. If this is the case, the only alternative might be to repartition and reformat the drive again on your current controller.

Symptom 39-16.   An error, such as "Device fails to respond—No devices in use.   Driver load aborted," appears   In most cases, the problem is something simple, such as the SCSI device not being turned on or cabled correctly. Verify that the SCSI devices are on and connected correctly. In other cases, the SCSI device is on, but fails the INQUIRY command—this happens when the SCSI device is defective or not supported by the host adapter. The device might need default jumper settings changed (i.e., the drive should spin up and come ready on its own). You might find that the SCSI device is sharing the same SCSI ID with another device. Check all SCSI devices to verify that each device has separate SCSI ID. You might have the wrong device driver loaded for your particular device type. Check config.sys to be sure the correct driver is loaded for the drive type (e.g., TSCSI.SYS for a hard disk, not a CD-ROM).

Symptom 39-17.   An error, such as "Unknown SCSI device" or "Waiting for SCSI device," appears   The SCSI hard disk has failed to boot as the primary drive— check that the primary hard disk is set at SCSI ID 0. Be sure that the drive is partitioned and formatted as the primary drive. If necessary, boot from a floppy with just the ASPI manager loaded in CONFIG.SYS (and no other drivers), then format the drive. It might also be that the SCSI cable termination is not correct (or TERMPWR is not provided by the hard disk for the host adapter). Verify the cable terminations and the TERMPWR signal.

Symptom 39-18.   An error, such as "CMD failure XX," appears   This typically occurs during the format process—the "XX" is a vendor-specific code (and you'll need to contact the vendor to determine what the error means). The most common problem is trying to partition a drive that is not low-level formatted. If this is the case, run the low-level format utility that accompanied the SCSI drive, then try partitioning again. If you're suffering a different error, you might need to take other action, depending on the nature of the error.

Symptom 39-19.   After the SCSI adapter BIOS header appears, a message, such as "Checking for SCSI target 0 LUN 0," appears   The system pauses about 30 seconds, then reports "BIOS not installed, no INT 13h device found." The system then boots normally. In most cases, the BIOS is trying to find a hard drive at SCSI ID 0 or 1, but no hard drive is available. If you do not have a SCSI hard drive attached to the host adapter, then it is recommended that the SCSI BIOS be disabled.

Symptom 39-20.   The system hangs up when the SCSI BIOS header appears   This is usually caused by a terminator problem. Be sure that the SCSI devices at the end of the SCSI chain (either internally or externally) are terminated. Check all device IDs to be sure that they are unique, and also check for system resource conflicts (e.g.,

BIOS address, I/O address, and interrupts). You might also need to disable the Shadow RAM feature in the CMOS setup.

Symptom 39-21. The SCSI BIOS header is displayed during system startup, then the message appears: "Host adapter diagnostic error" The card either has a port-address conflict with another card or the card has been changed to port address 140h and the BIOS is enabled. Some SCSI host adapters are able to use the BIOS under port address 140h, so check for I/O conflicts. You might need to reconfigure the SCSI host adapter.

Symptom 39-22.   When a VL bus SCSI adapter is installed, the system hangs at startup Chances are that the VL SCSI adapter is a bus-mastering device and requires that the VL slot support full 32-bit bus mastering. Most VL bus systems have either "slave" slots and/or "master" slots. The SCSI adapter must be inserted into a "master" slot. If you are not sure if the system supports bus mastering or if you have a master slot, contact the system manufacturer.

Also, the slot that the SCSI VL card is inserted into must be a 5-Vdc slot that operates at 33MHz or less. The VL bus speed is typically set through a jumper on the motherboard. It should be set in the *<=33MHz* position. The motherboard might also need to be set for write-through caching. This might be set in the motherboard's CMOS setup utility or it might be configured via a jumper on the motherboard (if both a CMOS setting and a jumper are used, be sure that both are set the same way).

Symptom 39-23. When upgrading a VL bus system CPU to a faster model, the system locks up with a SCSI VL card installed, or it won't boot from the SCSI HDD Most likely a DMA or other timing discrepancy is between the SCSI adapter and the VL local bus. The SCSI adapter probably works fine on VL bus systems running up to 33MHz. Faster CPUs can increase the VL bus speed beyond 33MHz. Above this 33MHz speed, variations in motherboard, chipset, or CPU design might cause the SCSI adapter to function intermittently or to fail. In some cases, this problem can be resolved:

- The motherboard might have jumpers that govern the VL bus speed—be sure that the VL bus-speed jumper is set in the *<=33MHz* position.
- This might also be set in the motherboard's CMOS setup.
- In the CMOS setup, you can disable the CPU external cache or change the caching method to write-through instead of write-back.
- The internal cache on some CPUs might also cause the VL SCSI adapter to hang. Try disabling the CPU's internal cache.
- Reducing the CPU speed might be necessary to allow the SCSI adapter to function reliably.
- Try disabling the system's "turbo setting" during the boot-up sequence, then re-enable the turbo setting after the system has booted.

Symptom 39-24. The VL SCSI adapter won't work with an "SLC" type CPU VL SCSI adapters often refuse to run with "SLC" type CPUs because the SLC uses 16-bit architecture, rather than 32-bit at the VL bus. Some VL SCSI adapters will run in this configuration, but it is rare. Use an ISA SCSI adapter instead of an VL adapter in this circumstance.

Symptom 39-25. When running the Qualitas 386MAX memory-manager software on ISA or VL systems with an SCSI host adapter, the system crashes when booting 386MAX is known to cause problems with SCSI systems, and you'll need to adjust the 386MAX command line. Do not allow 386MAX to load during boot up, then include the key NOIOWRAP on the 386MAX command line. This will allow you to boot with 386MAX loaded.

Symptom 39-26. When installing an EISA SCSI adapter and running the EISA configuration utility, you see an "EISA configuration slot mismatch" or "board not found in slot x" error This error occurs because your board is not completely seated in the EISA slot. You can verify this by booting to a floppy diskette, and running the DOS Debug command. After typing Debug, you will receive the debug prompt (a dash). Then type "i (space) Xc80" where "X" is the EISA slot where your board is physically installed. If a "04" is returned, the board is correctly seated and the problem lies elsewhere. If "FF" is returned, the board needs to be pushed down further. Power down your system before re-seating your board.

Symptom 39-27. An EISA SCSI adapter can't be configured in enhanced mode You get the error: "Unable to initialize Host Adapter" or the system hangs after the SCSI BIOS scans the SCSI devices. These errors are usually limited to motherboards that do not support LEVEL INT triggering. These chipsets (such as the Hint and SIS) require a few modifications be made to the host adapter's EISA configuration (.CFG) file. Make the following changes to the !ADP000X.CFG file:

```
CHOICE = "Enhanced Mode"
FREE
INT=IOPORT(1) LOC (7 6 2 1 0) 10000B
LINK
IRQ=11|12|10|15|14|9
SHARE = "AHA-1740"      (Change to: SHARE = NO)
TRIGGER = LEVEL(Change to: TRIGGER = EDGE)
INIT=IOPORT(3) LOC(4 3 2 1 0) 10010B | 10011B | 10001B | 1010B | 10101B |
10000B
(Change first zero in each binary number to a one: Example: 10010B = 11010B)
```

Another option is to download the latest .CFG file for your SCSI adapter card (i.e., ASWC174.EXE). Reconfigure the card with new .CFG file and select edge-triggered IRQ.

Further Study

This concludes the material for Chapter 39. Be sure to review the glossary and chapter questions on the accompanying CD. If you have access to the Internet, take a look at some of these SCSI system resources:

Adaptec: **http://www.adaptec.com**

AMI: **http://www.megatrends.com**

Ancot: **http://www.ancot.com/**

Fibre Channel Association: **http://www.Amdahl.com/ext/CARP/FCA/FCA.html**

Quantum: **http://www.quantum.com/src/**

SCSI FAQ: **http://www.cis.ohio-state.edu/hypertext/faq/usenet/scsi-faq/top.html**

SCSI guide: **http://www.delec.com/Tech_Links/SCSIGuide/**

SCSI Trade Association: **http://www.scsita.org/**

SCSI-2 spec: **http://abekas.com:8080/SCSI2/**

Symbios articles: **http://www.symbios.com/articles/articles.htm**

Symbios specs: **http://www.symbios.com/x3t10**

Western Digital: **http://www.wdc.com**

40

SERIAL (RS232)
PORT TROUBLESHOOTING

CONTENTS AT A GLANCE

Understanding Asynchronous
Communication
  The data frame
  Signal levels
  Baud vs. bps

Understanding the Serial Port
  Addresses and interrupts
  DTE vs. DCE

Serial-Port Signals
  TX and RX
  RTS and CTS
  DTR and DSR
  DCD
  RI

IrDA Port Issues
  Installing the IrDA driver(s)
  Removing the IrDA driver(s)
  IrDA tips

Troubleshooting the Serial Port
  Serial-port conflicts
  Match the settings
  Frame it right
  Finding a port address with debug
  General symptoms

Further Study

Although the parallel port is slowly gaining acceptance as a peripheral communication port, early PCs used the parallel port almost exclusively for local printers. As more and more peripherals became available for the PC, alternative methods of communication were required that were ill-suited for parallel connections at the time. The Electronics Industry Association (EIA) developed a standard for serial communication. Instead of sending eight bits at a time over a set of data lines, only two data lines were used: one to transmit data and one to receive data. The EIA denoted its serial standard as *RS-232* (or simply the *serial port*). A serial port offers several distinct advantages over early parallel ports. First, the serial port was designed to be bi-directional, right from the start. This made serial the preferred method for interactive devices, such as modems, mice, etc. Second, the serial port used fewer physical signal lines than the parallel port. This made cabling less expensive and reduced potential connector problems. Where a printer cable is generally limited to two meters in length, a serial cable can easily exceed 60 meters. This difference opened the way for basic local networking. This chapter shows you the essential concepts of serial communication and port operation, then guides you through a series of troubleshooting procedures.

Understanding Asynchronous Communication

The serial port is not terribly difficult to grasp, but its operation is a bit more involved than that of a parallel port. To appreciate the operations and signals of a typical serial port, you should be familiar with a variety of concepts. When a parallel port strobes a printer, the printer "knows" that all eight bits of data are available and valid. However, a serial port must send or receive eight data bits one at a time over a single data line. As you might imagine, this presents some serious challenges for the receiving device which must determine where the data stream starts and ends—hardly a simple task. It is certainly possible to send a synchronizing clock signal along with the data wire. The receiving device could easily use the clock to detect each data bit. This technique is known as *synchronous serial communication*. It is reliable, but rarely used in PCs (other than the keyboard interface).

Instead of using a discrete clock signal to accompany the data, it is possible to eliminate the clock by embedding synchronization information along with the data bits. Thus, when a data stream reaches a receiving device, it can strip away the synchronization bits, leaving the original data. As a result, serial communication is not constrained by a clock. This is *asynchronous communication*—a popular and inexpensive serial technique. The remainder of this chapter deals with asynchronous communication.

THE DATA FRAME

Asynchronous communication requires that data bits be combined with synchronization bits before transmission. Synchronization bits provide three important pieces of information to the receiving device: where the data starts, where the data ends, and if the data is correct. These bits, combined with the data byte, form the data frame (Fig. 40-1). The first thing you should notice about serial data is that it is bi-polar—that is, there are both positive and negative voltages. Contrary to what you might guess, a + voltage represents a logical 0 (called a *space*), and a -voltage represents a logical 1 (called a *mark*). The next thing you should note is that the serial signal line is normally idle in the logic 0 (space) state.

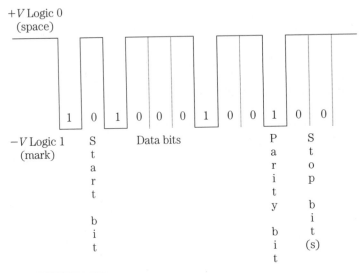

+V Logic 0
(space)

| | 1 | 0 | 1 | 0 | 0 | 0 | 1 | 0 | 0 | 1 | 0 | 0 | |

−V Logic 1   S   Data bits   P   S
(mark)   t   a   t
                   a   r   o
                   r   i   p
                   t   t
                                                            y   b
                   b   i
                   i   b   t
                   t   i   (s)
                                                            t

FIGURE 40-1   A typical data frame.

The first element of all asynchronous data frames is a single start bit, which is always a logic 1 (mark). When the receiver detects a logic 1, it "knows" the data frame has started. The next five to eight bits are always the data bits. The exact number of bits (usually eight) can be set by the communication software, but must be the same at both the transmitting and receiving ends. After data, a single error-checking bit (called a *parity bit*) can be included, if desired. Parity is calculated at the sending device and sent with the word. Parity is also calculated at the receiving device and checked against the received parity bit. If the two match, the data is assumed to be correct. If the two do not match, an error is flagged. There are five classes of parity:

■ *None* No parity bit is added to the word. This is typical for much of today's serial communication.
■ *Even* If the number of 1s in the data word is odd, parity is set to 1 to make the number of 1s even.
■ *Odd* If the number of 1s in the data word is even, parity is set to 1 to make the number of 1s odd.
■ *Mark* Parity is always set to 1.
■ *Space* Parity is always set to 0.

Many communication connections today abandon the use of parity in favor of the more reliable and sophisticated *Cyclical Redundancy Check (CRC)*. A CRC has the same effect as a parity check, but instead of checking one byte at a time, an entire block of data is checked.

The last part of the data frame is the stop bit(s)—typically only one, but two can be used. Stop bits are always logic 0 (space). After the receiving device detects the stop bit(s), the line remains idle in the space condition, awaiting the next subsequent start bit. Framing is usually denoted as data/parity/stop. For example, the connection to a BBS typically uses 8/N/1 framing (8 data bits/no parity bit/1 stop bit).

> One of the most important aspects of serial communication is that both the receiving and transmitting ends must be configured for the exact same data frame. If both ends are not configured identically, serial data will misinterpreted as meaningless garbage.

SIGNAL LEVELS

Where the parallel port uses TTL-compatible logic signals in its communication, a serial port uses bi-polar signaling (both positive and negative voltages). The advantage of bi-polar signaling is that it supports very long cabling with minimum noise. A logic 0 (space) condition is represented by a positive voltage between +3 Vdc and +15 Vdc. A logic 1 (mark) condition is represented by a negative voltage between –3 Vdc and –15 Vdc. On the average, you can expect to see serial ports using ±5 Vdc or ±12 Vdc because those voltages are already produced by the PC power supply.

BAUD VS. BPS

Another key concept of asynchronous communication is the idea of *rate*. Because data is traveling across a serial link versus time, the rate at which that data passes becomes an important variable. Although rate is not a literal part of the data frame, it is every bit as important. Simply stated, data rates are measured in *Bits Per Second (bps)*. This is a simple and intuitive measurement. If the serial port is delivering 2400bits in one second, it is working at 2400bps. At that rate, the average bit is (1/2400bps) = 417 s. When you are dealing with a serial port, you are dealing with bps.

Traditionally, when the bits from a serial port are processed through a modem, a modem will modulate the data through a series of phase, frequency, or amplitude transitions. A *transition* is referred to as a *baud* (named for French mathematician J.M.E. Baudot). Older modems that were designed to operate with signal rates of 2400bps or less could modulate the telephone line at the bit rate—thus, baud would be the same as bps. However, this is a faulty comparison. Because later modems were restricted by the limited bandwidth of a telephone line, modems had to encode more than one bit in every transition. As a result, the effective bps of a modern modem usually exceeds its baud rate by several times. For example, a modem that can encode 4bits in every transition can work at 2400baud, yet be sending the equivalent of 9600bps. See the difference? As modems evolved to encompass data compression standards, effective bps has been increased even more (yet the modem still only works at a relatively low baud rate). When you are dealing with modems, you are usually talking about baud rates.

You need to be aware of another catch. Because baud refers to any transition (Baudot never said a word about modems), it is technically valid to measure serial port speed in baud, although it can be terribly confusing. For example, today's serial-port circuits can sustain data rates of 115,200bps. Now, because every bit from the serial port is treated as a "transition" by local devices, such as printers, it becomes just as correct to say 115,200baud. The thing to remember here is that most modems don't operate over

2400baud. The telephone line just cannot handle faster signal rates. So, if you see high baud rates quoted in books or specifications, it probably refers to the performance of the serial port, not the modem.

Understanding the Serial Port

A serial port must be capable of several important operations. It must convert parallel data from the PC system bus into a sequence of serial bits, add the appropriate framing bits (which might be changed for different serial connections), then provide each if those bits to the data line at the proper rate. The serial port must also work in reverse, accepting serial data at a known rate, stripping off the framing bits, converting the serial data bits back into bus form, and checking blocks of data for accuracy. The heart of the serial port is a single IC—the *Universal Asynchronous Receiver/Transmitter (UART)*. A simplified block diagram for a serial port is illustrated in Fig. 40-2.

The UART connects directly to the PC bus architecture—either added to the motherboard or incorporated on an expansion board. A UART IC contains all of the internal circuitry necessary to process, transmit, and receive data between the serial line and the PC bus. Since the UART is programmable, its configuration (i.e., framing format and baud rate) can be set through DOS or Windows communication software. All data output, data input, and handshaking signals needed by the serial port are generated within the UART itself. It is interesting that the UART is powered by +5 Vdc only, just like any other ASIC in the system. This means that data and handshaking signals entering and leaving the UART are all TTL-compatible. Transmitted data is converted to bi-polar signals through a line-driver IC. Bi-

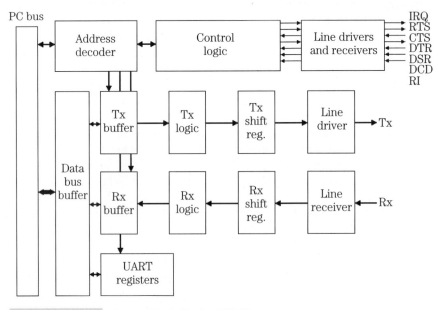

FIGURE 40-2   **Block diagram of a UART.**

polar data that appears on the receive line is converted back to TTL levels through a line-receiver IC. All that remains is the port connector itself. The original serial-port design used a 25-pin male sub-miniature D-type connector, but newer ports have abandoned the extra handshaking signals to accommodate a 9-pin male sub-miniature D-type connector.

ADDRESSES AND INTERRUPTS

The UART is controlled through a series of important registers that allow the serial-port characteristics to be programmed, channel transmitted, and received data, as required. Older BIOS versions supported only two serial (or COM) ports, but newer BIOS releases support four COM ports (designated COM1, COM2, COM3, and COM4). MicroChannel bus systems can support up to eight COM ports (COM1 through COM8). The typical base addresses for the COM ports are shown in Table 40-1. When a new COM port is installed in the system, it must be assigned to a valid base address and interrupt (IRQ). During actual operation, communication software deals with each port register individually. Table 40-2 lists the standard base address offsets for UART registers. With no offset, both transmit and receive registers are available.

During system initialization, COM ports are checked in the following order: 03F8h, 02F8h, 03E8h, 02E8h, 03E0h, 02E0h, 0338h, and 0238h (MicroChannel systems use a different order), and COM designations are assigned, depending on what ports are actually found. The COM addresses might be exchanged, depending on your particular system. In virtually all cases, COM1 is available at 03F8h. The specific I/O addresses for each COM port are kept in the BIOS data area of RAM, starting at 0400h. As you might expect, only one COM port can be assigned to a base address. If more than one COM port is assigned to the same base address, system problems will almost certainly occur.

TABLE 40-1 TYPICAL SERIAL PORT ADDRESSES AND IRQ ASSIGNMENTS			
BUS ARCHITECTURE	PORT	ADDRESS	IRQ
All Systems	COM1	03F8h	IRQ4
All Systems	COM2	02F8h	IRQ3
ISA*	COM3	03E8h	IRQ4
ISA	COM4	02E8h	IRQ3
ISA	COM3	03E0h	IRQ4
ISA	COM4	02E0h	IRQ3
ISA	COM3	0338h	IRQ4
ISA	COM4	0238h	IRQ3
MCA	COM3	3220h	IRQ3
MCA	COM4	3228h	IRQ3
MCA	COM5	4220h	IRQ3
MCA	COM6	4228h	IRQ3
MCA	COM7	5220h	IRQ3
MCA	COM8	5228h	IRQ3

* Systems with DOS 3.3 and later

TABLE 40-2 TYPICAL UART REGISTER ADDRESS OFFSETS	
REGISTER	**OFFSET**
Receive register	00h
Transmit register	00h
Interrupt enable register	01h
Interrupt ID register	02h
Data frame register	03h
UART control register	04h
Serialization status register	05h
UART status register	06h
General-purpose register	07h

The use of interrupts in conjunction with COM ports can easily be confusing. Unlike parallel ports, which can be polled by BIOS, a serial port demands the use of interrupts. Because early PCs allocated space for two COM ports, only two IRQ lines were reserved (IRQ4 for COM1 and IRQ3 for COM2). Unfortunately, when PC BIOS expanded its support for additional COM ports, no extra IRQ lines were available to assign. Thus, COM ports had to "share" interrupts. For example, COM1 and COM3 must share IRQ4, while COM2 and COM4 must share IRQ3. The problem is that no two devices can use the same IRQ at the same time—otherwise, a system conflict will result. Ultimately, though, a typical PC can use four COM ports, only two of the four can be used at any one time (i.e., COM1 and COM2, COM3 and COM4, COM1 and COM4, or COM2 and COM3). Further, the assignment of COM port address and IRQ lines must match. Although COM3 and COM4 can be polled by BIOS, the speed and asynchronous nature of contemporary data transmission make polling very unreliable for serial ports.

Always begin a service examination by checking the number of serial ports in your system. Serial ports are so simple and easy to add to various expansion cards that you might exceed the maximum number of ports or allow two ports to conflict without even realizing it. Be sure to remove or disable any unused or conflicting COM ports by removing the offending port or disabling it through jumpers or DIP switches.

DTE VS. DCE

As you work with serial ports and peripherals, you will often see the acronyms DTE and DCE used very frequently. *DTE* represents *Data Terminal Equipment*, which is typically the computer containing the serial port. The modem, serial printer, or other serial peripheral is referred to as the *Data Carrier Equipment (DCE)*. The distinction becomes important because the data and handshaking signals are swapped at the DCE end. For example, the Tx pin (usually on pin 3 of a 9-pin DTE) cannot connect directly to the same pin on the DCE—it must route to the Rx pin instead. The DCE connector makes those swaps, so pin 3 of the DCE would be the Rx pin, and a straight-through cable can be used without difficulty.

However, suppose that two DTEs had to be connected. Because both devices carry the same signals on the same pins, a straight-through cable would cause confusion (e.g., the Tx line would connect to the Tx line on the other device, Rx would connect to Rx, etc.). As you can imagine, two DTEs can not be connected with a straight-through cable. Of course, a specialized cable can be built containing the proper wire swaps, but an easier alternative is simply to use a null-modem, which plugs into one end of the straight-through cable. The null-modem is little more than a jumper box that contains all of the proper swaps. This allows two DTEs to work as if one were a DTE and one were a DCE.

Serial-Port Signals

IBM and compatible PCs implement a serial port as either a 25-pin or 9-pin sub-miniature D-type connector (Fig. 40-3). Both ends of the serial cable are identical. Be concerned with three types of signals in a serial connection: data lines, control (or handshaking) lines, and ground lines. Table 40-3 identifies the name and description of each conductor for both 25-pin and 9-pin serial connections. Remember that all data and control signals on the serial port are bi-polar.

25-pin M   9-pin M   **FIGURE 40-3**   **Serial port connectors.**

TABLE 40-3 SERIAL PORT CONNECTOR PINOUTS (AT THE PC END)			
25-PIN CONNECTOR	**9-PIN CONNECTOR**	**SIGNAL**	**DIRECTION**
1	n/a	Protective ground	n/a
2	3	Tx Transmit data	Output
3	2	Rx Receive data	Input
4	7	RTS Request to send	Output
5	8	CTS Clear to send	Input
6	6	DSR Data set ready	Input
7	5	Signal ground	n/a
8	1	DCD Data carrier detect	Input
9	n/a	+ Transmit current loop	Output
11	n/a	− Transmit current loop	Output
18	n/a	+ Receive current loop	Input
20	4	DTR Data terminal ready	Output
22	9	RI Ring indicator	Input
23	n/a	DSRD Data signal-rate indicator	I/O
25	n/a	− Receive current loop	Input

TX AND RX

Rx and Tx are simply the data lines into and out of the port. *Tx* is the *Transmit* line, which outputs serial data from the PC, and *Rx* is the *Receive* line, which accepts serial data from the serial peripheral.

RTS AND CTS

The *RTS (Request to Send)* signal is generated by the DTE. When asserted, it tells the DCE (i.e., the modem) to expect to receive data. However, the DTE can't just dump data to DCE. The DCE must be ready to receive the data, so after the RTS line is asserted, the DTE waits for the *CTS (Clear to Send)* signal back from the DCE. Once the DTE receives a valid CTS signal, it can begin transferring data. This RTS/CTS handshake forms the basis for data flow control.

DTR AND DSR

When the DTE is turned on or initialized and ready to begin serial operation, the DTR (Data Terminal Ready) line is asserted. This tells the DCE (i.e., modem) that the DTE (i.e., computer) is ready to establish a connection. When the DCE has initialized and is ready for a connection, it will assert the DSR (Data Set Ready) line back to the DTE. Once the DTE is ready and recognizes the DSR signal, a connection is established. This DTR/DSR handshake is established only once when the DTE and DCE devices are first initialized, and it must remain active throughout the connection. If either the DTR or DSR signal should fall, the communication channel will be interrupted (and the RTS/CTS handshake will no longer have any effect).

DCD

The *DCD (Data Carrier Detect)* signal is particularly useful with modems. It is produced by the DCE when a carrier is detected from a remote target, and the DCE is ready to establish a communications pathway. The DCD signal is then sent back to the DTE. Once the DCD line is asserted, it will remain so as long as a connection is established.

RI

The *RI (Ring Indicator)* signal is asserted by the DCE, and is also particularly useful with modems. It is produced by the DCE when a telephone ring is detected. This becomes a vital signal if it is necessary for a remote user to call in and access your computer (i.e., a BBS configuration).

IrDA Port Issues

A growing number of desktop and laptop PCs (and their peripherals) are being equipped with infrared ports (dubbed "IrDA" by the Infrared Desktop Association). IrDA ports allow PCs and peripherals to communicate serially over an infrared link, rather than going through the hassle of using cables. For example, you can type a document on a laptop, then move the laptop into the vicinity of an IrDA printer and print the document without ever attaching a cable. Although IrDA ports offer some real connectivity benefits to PC users, they also present some problems with installation and configuration. Windows 95 requires IrDA drivers to be loaded on the system.

INSTALLING THE IRDA DRIVER(S)

If you already have a PC fitted with IrDA support, you simply need to use the *Add new hardware* wizard to install a new set of drivers, or use the *Add infrared device* wizard from the IR icon in the *Control panel*. If you'll be installing IrDA support for the first time, download the newest IR drivers from the Microsoft Web site (**http://www.microsoft.com**), and run SETUP.EXE:

- When the *Add infrared device* wizard prompts to choose a manufacturer's name for the IR device, choose *Standard infrared devices* if the computer has a built-in device or choose the name of the manufacturer and the model of the adapter if an IR adapter is attached to the computer. Click the *Next* button.
- When the *Add infrared device* wizard prompts to choose the communications port that the IR device is physically connected to, click the port from the list. If you're uncertain which physical communications port the IR device is using, select the first COM port in the list (for example, COM1), then click the *Next* button.
- When the *Add infrared device* wizard prompts to select the virtual COM and LPT ports, accept the default values by clicking the *Next* button. After the wizard copies the IR communications driver files to the hard disk, watch for the wizard to display two *New hardware found* messages.
- When prompted by the *Add infrared device* wizard, click the *Finish* button to complete the IR device installation (if the wizard did not display *New hardware found* messages, then restart the computer).
- Activate the IR device by doubleclicking the *Infrared* icon in the *Control panel*. If no *Infrared* icon is in the *Control panel*, select the *Refresh* option from the *Control panel view* menu (or press the <F5> function key) to make the *Infrared* icon appear.

The next step is to test the IR device. The easiest and quickest way to do this is to print over an IrDA link to an IR printer or exchange data between two computers using the IR link (and a communications application, such as LapLink).

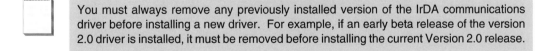

You must always remove any previously installed version of the IrDA communications driver before installing a new driver. For example, if an early beta release of the version 2.0 driver is installed, it must be removed before installing the current Version 2.0 release.

REMOVING THE IRDA DRIVER(S)

In some instances, it might be necessary to remove the IR communication drivers (most often when upgrading the drivers or IR adapter hardware). The IR communication drivers can be removed either by using *Add/remove programs* in the *Control panel* or by using the *Device manager*. Using *Add/remove programs* in the *Control panel*:

■ Click the *Start* button and select the *Settings* option, then select *Control panel*.
■ Doubleclick *Add/remove programs* in the *Control panel*.
■ When a list of software components is displayed, select the *Infrared support for Windows 95* entry and click the *Add/remove* button.
■ Restart the system when prompted to do so.

  Using *Device manager*:

■ Right-click on the *My computer* icon, select the *Properties* option from the popup menu, then click the *Device manager* tab in the *System properties* dialog.
■ To display the name of the infrared device installed on the computer, be sure that the "View devices by type" option is selected in the *System properties* dialog. Then click the plus sign to the left of the *Infrared device* class label. Select the infrared device name, then click the *Remove* button.
■ Click *OK* to confirm the device removal. After the *Device manager* has successfully removed the infrared device installation from the computer, the *Infrared device* class label will disappear from the *System properties* dialog.
■ Click the *Close* button.

> The *Infrared monitor* icon might still be displayed in the Windows 95 status bar (even after the infrared device is removed). Ignore it—the infrared monitor cannot be used to establish an IR link after the infrared device is removed.

IRDA TIPS

Although IR support is reasonably automatic under Windows 95, a number of tips can make your troubleshooting a bit easier:

■ Always remove the existing IR drivers before installing new IR drivers (or upgrading the IR adapter hardware). Pre-existing drivers can sometimes interfere with new IR drivers.
■ If you upgrade the IR adapter hardware on your system, you must remove the IR drivers and install new drivers.
■ Be sure to select the proper COM port for the IR adapter. If you select the wrong COM port during installation, the system will be unable to use the IR adapter.
■ IR communication problems might require you to realign the IR devices so that they are closer together (usually 3' or less), and in a direct line of sight. You might need to try new batteries in the IR adapter.
■ If an IR adapter is attached to a COM port that is using an older 8250 UART instead of a 16550A UART (or if an IR adapter is connected to a relatively slow computer, such as a 386 running at 20MHz), you might need to use the *Limit connection speed to* option in the *Infrared monitor options* tab to limit the connection speed to 19.2kbps. After establishing a successful IR connection at this speed, you can use the *Limit connection speed to* option to experiment with higher-speed connections.

- Communication over a virtual COM port link between two computers might not be reliable if a printer's IR adapter is also within range. Be sure to move the printer's IR adapter (or any other non-essential IR adapter) out of range.
- Do not suspend a Windows 95 computer while an IR connection is established. Wait until the IR link is disconnected (or force a disconnection) before putting the computer in suspend mode. For example, if an IrLan connection is established on a laptop, you must always move the laptop out of range of the IrLan access point before suspending the system or closing the laptop lid. Otherwise, the connection remains active and can drain the battery over time.
- Connecting and disconnecting over a low-speed IR link (or over a poor-quality link) can take a few seconds—during which time the screen will appear to be frozen. To work around this, you should use a higher-speed connection and take steps to improve the quality of the connection.

Troubleshooting the Serial Port

Although the typical serial port is a rather simple I/O device, it presents some special challenges for the technician. Older PCs provided their serial ports in the form of 8-bit expansion boards. When a port failed, it was a simple matter to replace the board outright. Today, however, virtually all PCs provide at least one serial port directly on the motherboard—usually integrated into a component of the main chipset. When a problem is detected with a motherboard serial port, a technician often has three choices:

- Replace the UART (responsible for virtually all serial port failures) on the motherboard. This requires access to surface-mount soldering tools and replacement ICs, and can be quite economical in volume.
- Set the motherboard jumpers (if possible) to disable the defective serial port, and install an expansion board (such as a "multi-I/O" board) to take the place of the defective port. This assumes that there is an available expansion slot.
- Replace the motherboard outright. This simple tactic requires little overhead equipment, but can be rather expensive.

Virtually all commercial diagnostics are capable of locating any installed serial ports, and testing the ports thoroughly through a loopback plug. Now that you have reviewed the layout, signals, and operation of a typical serial port, you can take a clear look at port-troubleshooting procedures.

SERIAL-PORT CONFLICTS

Hardware and software conflicts with a system's serial ports are some of the most recurring and perplexing problems in PC troubleshooting. Although PC purists are pleased that current operating systems and BIOS supports four COM ports, they cannot overcome the fact that there are still only two interrupts available to run the ports from. Technicians trying to upgrade a PC often encounter problems adding I/O adapters because many current PC motherboards already provide two COM ports right out of the factory. If a PC offers only one COM port (e.g., COM1) and another serial port is placed in the system (by accident or on purpose), be aware that you must choose a port and IRQ that does not conflict with the existing port (i.e., COM 2 or COM4). If the PC already provides two COM ports (i.e., COM1 and COM2), adding a third COM port to the system will cause a hardware conflict. You can rectify the conflict by disabling the new COM port, or by disabling one of the two existing COM ports and jumpering the new COM port to those settings.

Serial device drivers can also be a source of problems for COM ports. Incorrectly written mouse drivers, printer drivers, or third-party interrupt handlers can leave a port inoperative or erratic. If problems develop after a new driver is installed, disable the driver's reference in CONFIG.SYS or install an updated protected-mode driver under Windows 95 using the *Add new hardware* wizard. TSRs (often loaded in AUTOEXEC.BAT) can cause problems as well. If problems develop after a new TSR is installed, disable the offending TSR and try the system again. Remember that drivers and TSRs can easily be disabled by adding the REM statement before the command line in CONFIG.SYS or AUTOEXEC.BAT. If the communication trouble is under Windows 95, strongly suspect the Windows communication package, or the *Registry* might need to be adjusted for an optimum modem-initialization string.

MATCH THE SETTINGS

It's bad enough that you can only (practically) use two COM ports, but you also have to be sure that the port addresses and IRQ assignments match (Table 40-1). For example, suppose that no COM1 is at 03F8h, but a COM port is at 02F8h. During system initialization, BIOS locates each available port and assigns a COM designation, so because no port is at 03F8h, the port at 02F8h (normally COM2) is the first port detected, and is assigned as COM1. However, DOS and BIOS expect COM1 to use IRQ4, but the port at 02F8h uses IRQ3. If you attempt to use BASIC or DOS for COM1, the standard interrupt handlers will not work. You would have to use communication software that talks to the port directly (thus avoiding using DOS-interrupt handlers) and can be assigned with the address and IRQ setting of your choosing. As an alternative, you can switch the COM port to 03F8h and set the interrupt to IRQ4—that should restore normal COM1 operation through DOS.

FRAME IT RIGHT

The data frame and rate play very important roles in serial communication. The sending and receiving ends of the serial link must be set to the same configuration. Otherwise, the received data will be interpreted as garbage. If you encounter such troubles, be sure to check the settings for data bits, parity bit, stop bits, and baud rate. Change the data frame at either end of the serial link so that all devices are running with the same parameters.

FINDING A PORT ADDRESS WITH DEBUG

You can use the DOS Debug utility to determine the I/O addresses of a serial port. Be sure that you boot the computer in the DOS mode, then switch to the directory containing the Debug utility (such as C:). Type:

```
C:\DOS\> debug    <Enter>
```

A hyphen will appear. This is the Debug prompt. At the debug prompt, type:

```
D 40:00 09
```

A single line of text appears, such as:

```
0040:0000   F8 03 F8 02 00 00 00 00-78 03
```

To exit Debug, press *Q* (to quit), then press <Enter> to leave Debug and return to the DOS prompt. The line of interest begins 0040:0000. In this example, the F8 03 (read 03F8h) and F8 02 (read 02F8h) indicate two serial ports (COM1 and COM2). Other possibilities include E8 03 (read 03E8) and E8 02 (read 02E8)—these are COM3 and COM4, respectively. A machine with four serial ports should read:

```
0040:0000   F8 03 F8 02 E8 03 E8 02-78 03
```

A machine with no serial ports should read:

```
0040:0000   00 00 00 00 00 00 00 00-78 03
```

The –78 03 entry is the address of the first parallel port (read 0378h).

GENERAL SYMPTOMS

Your companion CD contains a variety of tools for identifying and diagnosing COM ports. The BBX201.ZIP utility offers a "breakout box" type of display, and you will find CTSSPU22.ZIP to be an excellent all-around utility. Other serial utilities include: COMPRT25.ZIP, COMRESET.ZIP, COMTAP21.ZIP, COMTEST.ZIP, SIMTRM.ZIP, and UARTTS.ZIP.

Symptom 40-1. You hear a beep code or see a POST error, which indicates a serial-port fault The system initialization might or might not halt, depending on how the BIOS is written. Low-level initialization problems generally indicate trouble in the computer's hardware. If the computer's beep code sequence is indistinct, you could try rebooting the computer with a POST analyzer card installed. The BIOS POST code displayed on the card could be matched to a specific error explanation in the POST card's documentation. Once you have clearly identified the error as a serial-port fault, you can proceed with troubleshooting.

Start with the system as a whole and remove any expansion boards that have serial ports available. Retest the computer after removing each board. If the error disappears after removing a particular card, then that card is likely at fault. You can simply replace the card with a new one or attempt to repair the card to the component level. If only one serial port is in the system, it is most likely built into the motherboard. Again, you can replace the defective UART, replace the motherboard or disable the defective motherboard port.

Symptom 40-2. An 11xx or 12xx serial adapter error is displayed A hardware fault has been detected in one of the COM ports. The 11xx errors typically indicate a fault in COM1, while 12xx errors suggest a problem with COM2, COM3, or COM4. In most cases, the fault is in the UART. You have the option whether to replace the UART IC, replace the motherboard, or disable the defective COM port and replace it with an expansion board.

Symptom 40-3. The computer initializes properly, but the serial peripheral does not work Your applications software might indicate that no device is connected. Before you even open your tool kit, you must determine whether the trouble lies in your computer or your peripheral. When your modem or printer stops working, run a self test to ensure the device is at least operational. Check all cables and connectors (perhaps try a different cable). Also be sure to check the software package being used to operate the serial port. Ensure that the software is configured properly to use the appropriate COM port and that any necessary drivers are selected.

   Disconnect the peripheral at the computer and install a serial loopback plug. Run a diagnostic to inspect each available serial port. Take note of any port(s) that register as defective. Locate the corresponding serial port. If the port is installed as an expansion board, replace the defective expansion board. If the port is on the motherboard, you can replace the defective UART IC, install an alternate expansion board or replace the motherboard outright.

Symptom 40-4. Data is randomly lost or garbled Your first step should be to check the communication cable. Be sure that the cable is intact and properly secured at both ends. Try a different cable. If the cable checks properly, either the port or peripheral is at fault. Start by suspecting the serial port. Be sure that the DTE and DCE are both set to use the same data frame and data rate. Incorrect settings can easily garble data. If problems persist, disconnect the printer at the computer and install a serial loopback plug. Run a diagnostic to inspect each available serial port. Take note of any port(s) that register as defective. Locate the corresponding serial port(s). If the port is installed as an expansion board, replace the defective expansion board. If the port is on the motherboard, you can replace the defective port-controller IC, install an alternate expansion board, or replace the motherboard outright.

   If you can not test the computer's serial port directly, test the port indirectly by trying the peripheral on another known-good computer. If the peripheral works properly on another computer, the trouble is probably in the original computer's serial-port circuitry. Replace any defective circuitry or replace the motherboard. If the peripheral remains defective on another computer, the peripheral itself (i.e., printer or modem) is probably faulty.

Symptom 40-5. LapLink does not recognize the IR COM port When you attempt to use LapLink with virtual COM ports created by an infrared adapter, you might receive the following error message:

```
This port is unavailable: it might not be physically present in this com-
puter.  If no other communications program is currently running, check for
a mouse or other serial device on this port.
```

This problem occurs because LapLink accesses the hardware directly to determine the status of the COM port and does not recognize virtual COM ports created using the infrared adapter. To work around this problem, you'll need to contact Traveling Software for a possible patch for LapLink or discard the use of LapLink in favor of the *Direct Cable Connection (DCC)* tool included with Windows 95.

Symptom 40-6. Problems occur when maintaining an IR connection in the daylight This problem is common with all infrared devices, and is usually caused by "interference" from the natural IR component of ordinary sunlight. Try shortening the transmission distance between the transmitter and receiver, and be sure that the path between the two is as straight as possible.

Further Study

This concludes the material for Chapter 40. Be sure to review the glossary and chapter questions on the accompanying CD. If you have access to the Internet, take a look at some of these serial-port resources:

Adaptec: **http://www.adaptec.com**

ActiSys: **http://www.actisys.com**

TI: **http://www.ti.com**

Sharp: **http://www.sharp.com**

HP: **http://www.hp.com**

41

SOUND
BOARDS

CONTENTS AT A GLANCE

Understanding Sound Boards
   The recording process
   The playback process
   The concept of "sampling"
   Data bits vs. sound quality
   The role of MIDI
   Inside a sound board

Knowing the Benchmarks
   Decibels
   Frequency response
   Signal-to-noise ratio
   Total harmonic distortion
   Intermodulation distortion
   Sensitivity
   Gain

Using Microphones
   Microphone types
   Phantom power
   Choosing a microphone

Troubleshooting a Sound Board
   Drivers and driver order
   Full-duplex drivers
   .WAV playback problems under
      Windows 95
   Symptoms

Further Study

Sound is an area of the PC that has been largely overlooked in early systems. Aside from a simple, oscillator-driven speaker, the early PCs were mute. Driven largely by the demand for better PC games, designers developed stand-alone sound boards that could read sound data recorded in separate files, then reconstruct those files into basic sound, music,

FIGURE 41-1   **A Logitech SoundMan Wave sound board.** Copyright
© 1995 Logitech Corporation

and speech. Since the beginning of the decade, those early sound boards have blossomed into an array of powerful, high-fidelity sound products, capable of duplicating voice, orchestral soundtracks, and real-life sounds with uncanny realism (Fig. 41-1). Not only have sound products helped the game industry to mature, but they have been instrumental in the development of multimedia technology (the integration of sound and picture), as well as Internet Web phones and other communication tools. This chapter is intended to explain the essential ideas and operations of a contemporary sound board, and show you how to isolate a defective sound board when problems arise.

Understanding Sound Boards

Before you attempt to troubleshoot a problem with a sound board, you should have an understanding of how the board works and what it must accomplish. This type of background helps you when recommending a sound board to a customer or choosing a compatible card as a replacement. If you already have a strong background in digital sound concepts and software, feel free to skip directly to the troubleshooting portion of this chapter.

THE RECORDING PROCESS

All sound starts as *pressure variations* traveling through the air. Sound can come from almost anywhere—a barking dog, a laughing child, a fire engine's siren, a person speaking. You get the idea. The process of recording sound to a hard drive requires sound to be carried through several manipulations (Fig. 41-2). First, sound must be translated from pressure variations in the air to analog electrical signals. This is accomplished by a microphone. These analog signals are amplified by the sound card, then digitized (converted to a series of representative digital words each taken at a fixed time interval). The resulting stream of data is processed and organized through the use of software, which places the

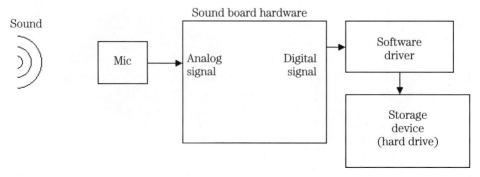

FIGURE 41-2 **The sound-board recording process.**

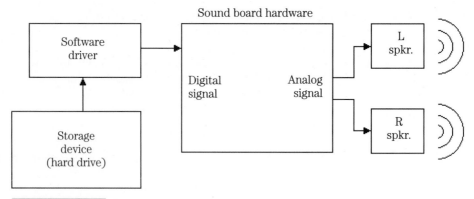

FIGURE 41-3 **The sound-board playback process.**

data (as well as any overhead or housekeeping data) into a standard file format. The file is saved to the drive of choice (typically, a hard drive).

THE PLAYBACK PROCESS

Simply speaking, the playback process is virtually the reverse of recording (Fig. 41-3). A software application opens a sound file on the hard drive, then passes the digital data back to the sound card. Data is translated back into equivalent analog levels—ideally, the re-constructed shape of the analog signal closely mimics the original digitized signal. The analog signal is amplified, then passed to a speaker. If the sound was recorded in stereo, the data is divided into two channels that are separately converted back to analog signals, amplified, and sent to their corresponding speakers. Speakers convert the analog signal back into traveling pressure waves that you can hear.

THE CONCEPT OF "SAMPLING"

To appreciate the intricacies of a sound card's operation, you must understand the concept of *digitization* (otherwise known as *sampling*). In principle, sampling is a very straight-forward concept; an analog signal is measured periodically, and its voltage at each point in time is converted to a digital number. The device that performs this conversion is known as an *Analog-to-Digital Converter (ADC)*. It sounds simple enough in principle, but it has some important wrinkles.

The problem with sampling is that a digitizer circuit has to capture enough points of an analog waveform to reproduce it faithfully. The example in Fig. 41-4 illustrates the importance of sampling rate. Waveforms A and B represent the same original signal. Waveform A is sampled at a relatively slow rate—only a few samples are taken. The problem comes when the signal is reconstructed with a *Digital-to-Analog Converter (DAC)*. As you see, there are not enough sample points to reconstruct the original signal. As a result, some of the information in the original signal is lost. This form of distortion is known as *aliasing*. Waveform B is the same signal, but it is sampled at a much higher rate. When that data is reconstructed, the resulting signal is a much more faithful reproduction of the original.

As a rule, a signal should be sampled at least twice as fast as the highest frequency contained in the signal—this is known as *Nyquist's Sampling Theorem*. The lowest standard sampling rate used with today's sound boards is 11kHz—this allows fair reproduction of normal speech and vocalization (up to about 5.5kHz). However, most low-end sound boards can digitize signals up to 22kHz. Unfortunately, the human range of hearing is about 22kHz. To capture sounds reasonably well throughout the entire range of hearing, you would need a sampling rate of 44kHz—often known as *CD-quality sampling* because it is the same rate used to record audio on CDs. The disadvantage to high sampling rates is disk space (and sound file size). Each sample is a piece of data, so the more samples taken each second, the larger and faster a file grows.

DATA BITS VS. SOUND QUALITY

Not only does the number of samples affect sound quality, but also the precision (or number of bits) of each sample. Suppose that each sample is converted to a 4-bit number. That means each point can be represented by a number from 0 to 15—not much precision there.

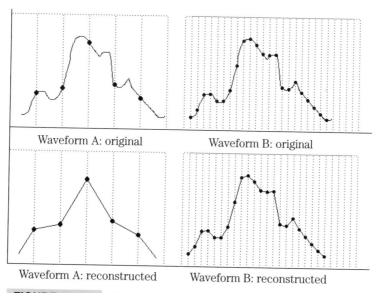

Waveform A: original   Waveform B: original

Waveform A: reconstructed   Waveform B: reconstructed

FIGURE 41-4   **The concept of *sampling rate*.**

If 8 bits are used for each sample, 256 discrete levels can be supported. But the most popular configuration is 16-bit conversion, which allows a sample to be represented by one of 65,536 levels. At that level of resolution, samples form a very close replica of the original signal. Many of today's sound boards are 16-bit.

THE ROLE OF MIDI

Although the majority of a sound card is geared toward handling the recording and playback of sound files, the *Musical Instrument Digital Interface (MIDI)* port has become an inexpensive and popular addition to many sound-card designs. The MIDI standard is defined by hardware, software, and electrical interconnections. At the core of a MIDI interface is a synthesizer IC. Unlike a sound file, which basically contains the digital equivalent of an analog waveform, a MIDI file is a set of instructions for playing musical notes. Each note is sent to the synthesizer, along with duration, pitch, and timing specifications. The synthesizer can be made to replicate a variety of musical instruments, such as a piano, guitar, harmonica, flute—you name it. The high-end sound boards are capable of synthesizing a small orchestra. Because most synthesizers can process several channels simultaneously, the MIDI standard supports playing a number of "instruments" (or voices) at the same time. Thus, very high-quality music can be produced with MIDI on a PC. The two most common synthesizer types are FM and Wavetable.

Figure 41-5 illustrates the kinds of things that MIDI is capable of. Pre-recorded MIDI files can be read from a storage device, such as a hard-drive file, or from CD-ROM (many games include an orchestral-quality MIDI soundtrack on the CD). The MIDI data is passed through to the sound board's synthesizer which reproduces the sound, and out to the amplified speakers. If you plan to compose music yourself, you can interface a MIDI instrument to the sound board's MIDI port. Using MIDI sequencer software, the notes played on the instrument will be heard through the speaker, as well as recorded to the MIDI file on the hard drive. Notice that you do not need a MIDI instrument to playback a MIDI file, but you need an instrument and sequencer software to create a MIDI file. Also,

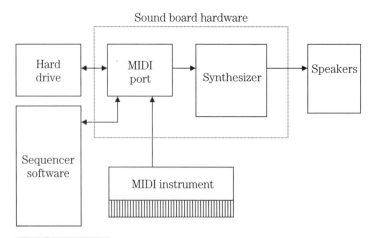

FIGURE 41-5   The path of MIDI signals through the PC.

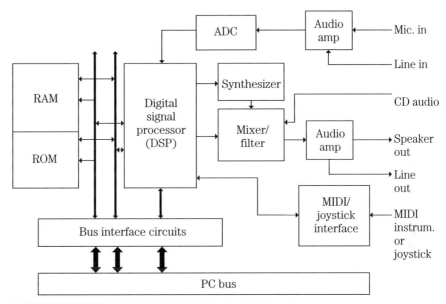

FIGURE 41-6   **Simplified block diagram of a sound board.**

because MIDI is not sound (but rather sound "blueprints"), the same MIDI composition entered on a keyboard can be played back as a harp, or a guitar, or a flute.

INSIDE A SOUND BOARD

Now that you are aware of the major functions a sound board must perform, you can see those functions in the context of a complete board. Figure 41-6 shows a simplified block diagram of a sound board. It is important that your own particular sound board might differ somewhat, but all contemporary boards should contain these subsections.

The core element of a sound board is the *Digital Signal Processor (DSP)*. A DSP is a variation of a microprocessor that is specially designed to manipulate large volumes of digital data. Like all processor components, the DSP requires memory. A ROM contains all of the instructions needed to operate the DSP and direct the board's major operations. A small quantity of RAM serves two purposes: it provides a "scratch pad" area for the DSP's calculations and it serves as a buffer for data traveling to or from the PC bus.

Signals entering the sound board are passed through an amplifier stage and provided to an A/D converter. When recording occurs, the DSP runs the A/D converter and accepts the resulting conversions for processing and storage. Signals delivered by a microphone are typically quite faint, so they are amplified significantly. Signals delivered to the "line" input are often much stronger (such as the output from a CD player or stereo preamp), so it receives less amplification.

For signals leaving the sound board, the first (and often most important) stop is the *mixer*. The mixer combines CD-audio, DSP sound output, and synthesizer output into a single analog channel. Because most sound boards now operate in a stereo mode, most have two mixer channels and amplifier stages. The audio amplifier stage(s) boost the analogs signal for delivery to stereo speakers. If the sound will be driving a stereo system, a "line" output provides a separate output. Amplifier output can be adjusted by a single master volume control located on the rear of the board.

Finally, a MIDI controller is provided to accommodate the interface of a MIDI instrument to the sound board. In many cases, the interface can be jumpered to switch the controller to serve as a joystick port. That way, the sound board can support a single joystick if the MIDI instrument will not be used. MIDI information processed by the DSP will be output to the on-board synthesizer.

Knowing the Benchmarks

An important aspect of sound boards is their audio benchmarks. Unlike logic and processing circuitry, which is measured in terms of millions of operations per second, the benchmarks that define a sound card are very much analog. If you are an audiophile, many of the following terms might already be familiar. If most of your experience has been with logic systems, however, these concepts will appear very different than many of the other sections in this book.

DECIBELS

No discussion of sound concepts is complete without an understanding of the *decibel (dB)*. Decibels are used because they are logarithmic. Human hearing is not a linear response. If you increase the power of your stereo output from 4 W to 16 W, the sound is not 4 times louder—it is only twice as loud. If you increase the power from 4 W to 64 W, the sound is only three times as loud. In human terms, *amplitude perception* is measured logarithmically. As a result, very small decibel values actually relate to substantial amounts of power. The accepted formula for decibels is:

$$gain \ (in \ dB) = 10 \log 10 \ \frac{P_{out}}{P_{in}}$$

Don't worry if this formula looks intimidating. Chances are that you will not need to use it, but consider what happens when output power is greater than input power. Suppose that a 1-mW signal is applied to a circuit and a 2-mW signal leaves. The circuit provides a gain of +3 dB. Suppose that the situation was reversed, where a 2-mW signal is applied to the circuit and a 1-mW signal leaves it. The circuit would then have a gain of -3 dB. *Negative gain* is a loss, also called *attenuation*. As you see, a small dB number represents a large change in signal levels.

FREQUENCY RESPONSE

Expressed simply, the frequency response of a sound board is the range of frequencies that the board will handle uniformly. Examine the sample graph of Fig. 41-7. Ideally, a sound board should be able to produce the same amount of power (0 dB) across the entire work-

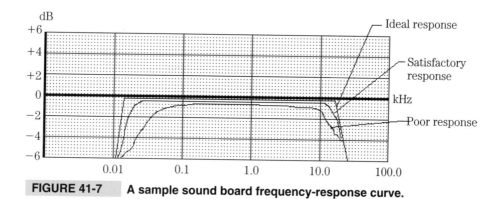

FIGURE 41-7   A sample sound board frequency-response curve.

ing frequency range (usually 20Hz to 20kHz). This would show up as a flat line across the graph. In actuality, however, this is not practical; invariably a rolloff of signal strength will be at both ends of the operating range. A good-quality sound board will demonstrate sharp, steep rolloffs. As the rolloffs get longer and more shallow at high and low frequencies, the board has difficulty producing sound power at those frequencies. The result is that bass and treble ranges might sound weak, which affects the sound's overall fidelity. By looking at a frequency-response curve, you can anticipate the frequency ranges where a sound board might sound weak.

SIGNAL-TO-NOISE RATIO

The *signal-to-noise ratio (SNR)* of a sound board is basically the ratio of maximum undistorted signal power to the accompanying electronic noise being generated by the board (primarily hum and hiss), expressed in decibels. Ideally, this will be a very large dB number, which would indicate that the output signal is so much stronger than the noise signal that for all intents and purposes the noise is imperceptible. In actuality, a good-quality sound board will enjoy an SNR of 85 dB or higher—but these are difficult to find. For most current sound boards with SNR levels below 75 dB, hum and hiss are audible during silent periods, as well as a certain amount of sound "grit" underlying sound and music reproduction. Some very inexpensive sound boards are on the market with SNR levels as low as 41 dB (noise might be noticeable and actually annoying).

You might also find the SNR value expressed as an "A-weighted" decibel number. The reason for this is that human hearing is not equal at all frequencies, so we cannot hear all noise equally. The process of "A-weighting" emphasizes the noise levels at frequencies that we are most sensitive to. Resulting SNR values are often several dB higher (better) than non-weighted SNR values. Be careful here; a sound board with a low SNR might use the A-weighted value in the specification sheet. If this is the case, subtract about 3 or 4 dB for the actual SNR figure.

TOTAL HARMONIC DISTORTION

Sound and music are rich in harmonics (overtones) that are basically integer multiples of an original frequency signal (although at much lower levels). As a consequence, harmonics are a valuable attribute of sound. The number and amplitude of harmonics provide the sound characteristics that allow you to distinguish between a guitar, flute, piano, or any other musical instrument played at the same note—without harmonics, every instrument would just produce flat tones, and every instrument would sound exactly the same.

However, when sound is produced in an electronic circuit, other unwanted harmonics are generated that can alter the sound of the music being produced (thus the term *harmonic distortion*). The *total harmonic distortion (THD)* of a sound board is the *root-mean squared (RMS)* sum of all unwanted harmonic frequencies produced, expressed as a percentage of the total undistorted output signal level. In many cases, the RMS value of noise is added to THD (expressed as *THD+N*). The lower this percentage is, the better. *THD+N* values over 0.1% can often be heard, and suggest a less-than-adequate sound-board design.

INTERMODULATION DISTORTION

This figure is related to harmonics. When two or more tones are generated together, amplifiers create harmonics, as well as tone combinations. For example, if a 1kHz and 60Hz tone are mixed together, *intermodulation harmonics* will be generated (e.g., 940Hz, 880Hz, 1060Hz, 1120Hz, etc.). This intermodulation gives sound a harsh overtone. Because intermodulation is not related to sound quality, it is a form of distortion that should be kept to a very low level. Like THD, *Intermodulation Distortion (IMD)* is the RMS sum of all unwanted harmonic frequencies expressed as a percentage of the total undistorted output signal level. IMD should be under 0.1% on a well-designed board.

SENSITIVITY

Although it does not directly affect the fidelity of sound reproduction, sensitivity can be an important specification. *Sensitivity* is basically the amplitude of an input signal (such as a microphone signal) that will produce the maximum undistorted signal at the output(s) with volume at maximum.

GAIN

By itself, sensitivity is hard to apply to a sound board, but if you consider the board's output power versus its input signal power and express the ratio as a decibel, you would have the gain of the sound board. Many sound boards offer a potential gain of up to 6dB. However, it is important that not all sound boards provide positive gain—some boards actually attenuate the signal even with the volume at maximum. In practical terms, this usually forces you to keep the volume control at maximum.

Using Microphones

An ever-growing number of sound card owners are using their sound cards to record sound or broadcast sound over the Internet through such applications as WebPhone. Sound recording demands the use of microphones, and not all microphones work properly with every sound board. Often, the user mistakes a poor microphone response as being a problem with the sound card. This part of the chapter looks at some important considerations for choosing and using a microphone.

MICROPHONE TYPES

The three types of microphones are: dynamic, condenser, and electret condenser. All three microphone types are available for sound boards:

- *Dynamic* Dynamic microphones are typically hand-held or desktop units. They have a larger response range and usually sound better than condenser microphones. A dynamic microphone does not require phantom power because the diaphragm element in the microphone can create enough electric current for the sound board to use.
- *Condenser* Condenser microphones are the small multimedia microphones that are typically sold with computers. When you open a new sound board and take the microphone out of the box, it is almost always a condenser microphone. They do not have as good a response range as dynamic microphones, and they also have a smaller diaphragm—this demands phantom power from the sound board.
- *Electret condenser* Electret condenser microphones are basically condenser microphones with a built-in battery for power. They have the same response as a condenser microphone, but they do not require phantom power to operate. Some electret condenser microphones will allow you to remove this internal battery. With the battery not installed, phantom power would be required.

PHANTOM POWER

The next question is "What is phantom power?" *Phantom power* is simply a small, low-current power supply on the sound board, which is used to power some microphones. Such devices as dynamic microphones can produce enough current on their own to avoid the use of phantom power, but condenser microphones demand phantom power as a current source.

Here's the main problem with today's sound boards—not all of them provide switchable phantom power. Ideally, sound boards (such as the Ensoniq Soundscape) would provide phantom power and allow you to jumper the phantom power on or off, depending on which microphone you plan to use. If you use a dynamic microphone, you'd switch phantom power off. If you use a condenser microphone, you'd switch phantom power on. If a sound board does not provide phantom power at all, you're stuck using a dynamic microphone or a powered electret condenser microphone. If a sound board provides full-time phantom power (and you cannot turn it off), you'll need to stay with a condenser microphone.

You can probably see the potential for trouble here. If you use a condenser microphone on an unpowered sound board, the microphone will not work at all (or generate little more than faint noise). On the other hand, plugging a dynamic or electret microphone into a powered sound board will usually result in severe clipping—once again, you'll capture little more than noise.

CHOOSING A MICROPHONE

Whether you're choosing a microphone for yourself or recommending one to someone else, remember some considerations. Perhaps the most important issue is the application.

If you just need a basic, inexpensive microphone to record a few simple voice notes, a condenser or electret microphone would work just fine and your sound board will require a phantom power supply. If you want to record more professional vocals or if you are preparing a presentation, a dynamic microphone will generally provide the best results (and no phantom power is needed).

Troubleshooting a Sound Board

Traditionally, sound boards use many of the same chipsets and basic components, but because each board is designed a bit differently, it is very difficult for commercial diagnostic products to identify failed IC functions. For the most part, commercial and shareware diagnostics can only identify whether a brand-compatible board is responding or not. As a result, this chapter will take the sub-assembly replacement approach. When a sound board is judged to be defective, it should be replaced outright. This part of the chapter reviews the problems and solutions for sound boards under both DOS and Windows. The following tips might help you nail down a sound problem most efficiently:

- Check to see that your speakers are connected, powered, and turned on.
- Check that the speaker volume and sound card master volume are turned up.
- Check to see that the mixer volume and master volume are set properly.
- Be sure that the music or sound file(s) are installed properly.
- Check that all sound card and multimedia drivers are installed.
- Be sure that the drivers are up to date.
- Check for resource conflicts between the sound card and other devices in the system.
- Be sure that the sound card is selected and configured properly (especially for DOS apps).
- The sound device should be enabled and configured under CMOS (for sound functions incorporated on the motherboard).

DRIVERS AND DRIVER ORDER

Unlike most other expansion devices that are driven by system or supplemental BIOS, sound boards use small device drivers to set up their operations. These drivers are generally included in CONFIG.SYS and AUTOEXEC.BAT, and are called when the system is first initialized. Most sound-board drivers are only used to initialize and set up the board, so they do not remain resident—this is good because it would reduce the load on conventional and upper memory. However, these initialization routines vary from board to board. For example, the files installed for a Creative Labs Sound Blaster will not support a Turtle Beach MultiSound board. If you elect to replace a sound board, you must also disable any current sound-board drivers, and include any new supporting driver files. The process is not difficult—just follow the installation instructions for the board. But the software consideration does add another wrinkle to the replacement process.

   When there are problems installing or upgrading a sound board, one of the first issues to suspect is the driver loading order. Sound boards are typically multi-function devices that require several drivers in CONFIG.SYS and AUTOEXEC.BAT. If the drivers are installed in the wrong order, the sound board (or other features of the board) might not function. As a rule, the drivers should be loaded in the following order after your memory managers:

■ The sound board's device driver:

```
DEVICE=C:\SB16\DRV\SB16.SYS /A:220
```

■ The CD-ROM port setup driver (if the sound board is equipped):

```
DEVICE=C:\SB16\DRV\CDSETUP.SYS /P:340
```

■ The CD-ROM driver (if the sound board is equipped):

```
DEVICE=C:\SB16\DRV\MTMCDAE.SYS /D:MSCD001 /P:340 /A:0 /T:5 /I:11
```

FULL-DUPLEX DRIVERS

Many current sound boards are compatible with "multimedia communication" technologies, such as Internet Phone, Webphone, and communication tools. These tools require full-duplex operation; that is, sound is digitized with the microphone and received sound is played through the speakers simultaneously. This demands full-duplex drivers. If you plan to use communication tools, you'll need to install full-duplex sound-card drivers that are appropriate for your particular sound board and operating system. For example, the Creative Labs SB32, AWE32, and AWE64 require the Windows 95 full-duplex driver file (SBW95UP.EXE) available from the Creative Labs Web site (**http:\www.creaf.com**). To use those same devices for full-duplex under Windows NT 4.0, you'd need the AWENT40.EXE driver file. As a rule, always check with the sound board maker for current full-duplex drivers.

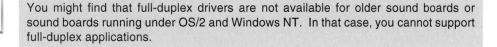

You might find that full-duplex drivers are not available for older sound boards or sound boards running under OS/2 and Windows NT. In that case, you cannot support full-duplex applications.

.WAV PLAYBACK PROBLEMS UNDER WINDOWS 95

Of all the sound-board problems reported, perhaps the most common is the failure to play wave files (ordinary sound files with the .WAV extension) under Windows 95. This problem usually manifests itself during the Windows startup or shutdown when the accompanying sounds are not played. A variety of issues can prevent .WAV files from playing.

Program-specific problems If you cannot play .WAV files from a specific program that you use in Windows 95, check to see if the same problem occurs when you play the file from another program. If the problem occurs only with one particular program, the files associated with that program might be damaged or that program might not be configured correctly under Windows 95. If you cannot get .WAV files to play under any application, chances are that another issue is responsible.

Sound device is not configured properly   If you cannot play any .WAV files in
Windows 95 (or if .WAV files are not played at the proper volume), you might not have a
sound device selected or the sound device that you have selected might not be configured
properly. To select and configure a sound device in Windows 95:

■ Open the *Control panel* and doubleclick the *Multimedia* icon.
■ In the *Playback* area under the *Audio* tab (Fig. 41-8), click the playback device that you
  want to use in the *Preferred device* list, then move the *Volume* slider to the value you
  want (usually 50 to 75% volume is adequate).
■ In the *Recording* area under the *Audio* tab, click the playback device that you want to
  use in the *Preferred device* list, then move the *Volume* slider to the value you want.
■ Be sure that the speakers are properly connected to the sound card and that the speakers are turned on.

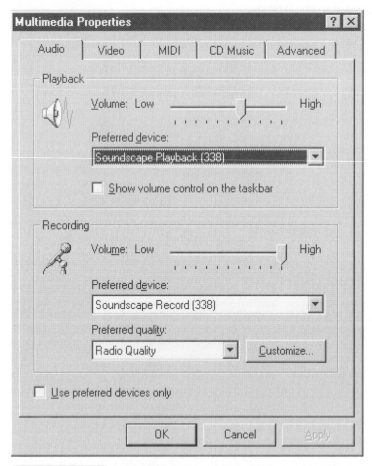

FIGURE 41-8   The *Audio* tab under the *Multimedia properties* dialog.

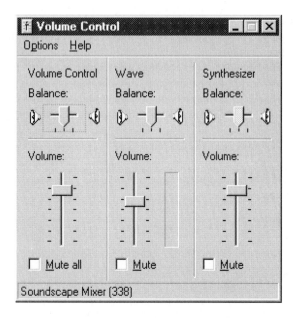

FIGURE 41-9   The multimedia *Volume control* applet.

Mixer settings are not configured properly If you cannot play any .WAV files under Windows 95 (or if .WAV files are not played at the proper volume), the mixer control settings might not be configured properly. You can use the mixer-control program included with Windows 95 to adjust the volume for playback, recording, and voice commands. To configure mixer control settings for Windows 95:

- Click the *Start* button, point to *Programs*, point to *Accessories*, point to *Multimedia*, then click *Volume control* (Fig. 41-9).
- Be sure that the *Mute all* check box below the *Volume control* slider and the "Mute" check box below the *Wave* slider are not selected, and that the *Balance* sliders for *Volume control* and *Wave* are in the center of the scale.
- Move the *Volume control* and *Wave* sliders at least halfway to the top of the scale. You might need to adjust the current *Volume control* or *Wave* settings to play .WAV files at the volume level you want.

> If the *Volume control* and *Wave* sliders do not appear, click *Properties* on the *Options* menu, then click the *Volume control* and *Wave* check boxes in the "Show the following volume controls" box to select them.

The sound hardware is not configured properly It is possible that your sound card might not be compatible with the type of .WAV file you are attempting to play, or a resource conflict might be between your sound card and another device installed in your computer. Check the *Device manager* to see if your sound board has any resource conflicts. To determine whether your sound card supports the .WAV file format you are attempting to play, contact the sound card's manufacturer.

The sound files are damaged If you cannot play certain .WAV files in Windows 95 (or if the .WAV files are not played properly), the .WAV files themselves might be damaged. To check if a .WAV file is damaged, use the right mouse button to click the .WAV file in Windows Explorer, click *Properties* on the menu, then click the *Details* tab. The *Audio format* line should contain information about the type of compression used to compress the file, the sound quality of the file, and whether or not the file is in stereo. If this information is missing, the .WAV file is probably damaged and should be reinstalled or re-copied to the drive.

If you can play other .WAV files of a similar format, chances are good that the suspect file is indeed damaged. If you can play .WAV files of different formats, but not .WAV files of a particular format, it might be that your sound board does not support the particular format.

Compression-related problems Windows 95 includes 32-bit versions of several common CODECS including *Adaptive Delta Pulse Code Modulation (ADPCM), Interactive Multimedia Association (IMA) ADPCM, Group Special Mobile (GSM) 6.10, Consultative Committee for International Telephone and Telegraph (CCITT) G.711 A-Law and u-Law,* and *Truespeech* from DSP. These 32-bit CODECS are installed by default during Windows 95 setup, and are used by multimedia programs—even if a 16-bit version of the same CODEC is available. Be sure that .WAV file format is supported by an available CODEC. Otherwise, you might need to install an appropriate CODEC.

SYMPTOMS

Symptom 41-1. A noticeable buzz or hum is being produced in one or both speakers Low-cost speakers use unshielded cables. Unfortunately, strong signals from ac cords and other signal-carrying conductors can easily induce interference in the speaker wires. Try rerouting speaker cables clear of other cables in the system. If problems persist, try using higher-quality speakers with shielded cables and enclosures. In most cases, that should resolve everyday noise problems. If the noise continues, regardless of what you do, the fault might be in the sound-board amplifier. Try moving the sound board to another bus slot away from other boards or the power supply. If that does not resolve the problem, try a new sound board.

Symptom 41-2. No sound is produced by the speaker(s) The lack of sound from a sound board can be caused by any one of a wide range of potential problems. If the sound board works with some applications, but not with others, it is likely that the problem is caused by an improperly installed or configured application. See that the offending application is set up properly (and be sure it is even capable of using the sound card). Also check that the proper sound driver files (if any) are loaded into CONFIG.SYS and AUTOEXEC.BAT, as required. In many cases, one or two sound-related environment variables that are set in AUTOEXEC.BAT. Be sure that your startup files are configured properly.

Check your speakers next. See that they are turned on and set to a normal volume level. The speakers should be receiving adequate power and should be plugged properly into the correct output jack—if speakers have been plugged into the wrong jack, no sound will be produced. If the cable is broken or questionable, try a new set of speakers. Also see that the master volume control on the sound board is turned up most (or all) of the way.

If problems continue, a resource conflict might be occurring between the sound board and another device in the system. Examine the IRQ, DMA, and I/O settings of each device in the system. Be sure that no two devices are using the same resources. You might like to use the PC Configuration Form at the end of this book to record your settings. If problems persist, and no conflict is present, try another sound board.

Symptom 41-3. CD audio will not play through the sound card This problem can occur under both DOS and Windows. First, be sure that the sound board is actually capable of playing CD audio (older boards might not be compatible). If the sound card is playing sound files, but is not playing CD audio, check several things. First, open the PC and be sure that the CD-audio cable (a thin, 4-wire cable) is attached from the CD-ROM drive to the sound board. If this cable is broken, disconnected, or absent, CD audio will not be passed to the sound board. If the cable is intact, be sure that the CD audio player is configured properly for the sound board you are using, and check the startup files to see that any drivers and environment variables needed by CONFIG.SYS and AUTOEXEC.BAT are available. If CD audio fails to play under Windows, be sure that an *MCI (Multimedia Control Interface)* CD Audio driver is included in the *Drivers* dialog box under Windows *Control panel.*

Symptom 41-4. An error, such as "No interrupt vector available" appears The DOS interrupt vectors used by the sound board's setup drivers (usually INT 80h to BFh) are being used by one or more other drivers in the system. As a consequence, there is a software conflict. Try disabling other drivers in the system one at a time until you see the conflict disappear. Once you have isolated the offending driver(s), you can leave them disabled, or (if possible) alter their command-line settings so that they no longer conflict with the sound board's software.

Symptom 41-5. It has no MIDI output Be sure that the file you are trying to play is a valid MIDI file (usually with a .MID extension). In most cases, you will find that the *MIDI mapper* under Windows is not set up properly for the sound board. Load the Windows *MIDI mapper* applet from the *Control panel*, and set it properly to accommodate your sound board.

Symptom 41-6. Sound play is jerky Choppy or jerky sound playback is typically the result of a hard drive problem—more specifically, the drive cannot read the sound file to a buffer fast enough. In most cases, the reason for this slow drive performance is excessive disk fragmentation. Under DOS, the sound file(s) might be highly fragmented. Under Windows, the permanent or temporary swap files might be highly fragmented. In either case, use a reliable DOS defragmenter, such as PC Tools or Norton Utilities (leave Windows before defragmenting the disk), and defragment the disk thoroughly.

Symptom 41-7. An error, such as "Out of environment space" appears The system is out of environment space. You will need to increase the system's environment space by adding the following line to your CONFIG.SYS file:

```
shell=c:\command.com /E:512 /P
```

This command line sets the environment space to 512 bytes. If you still encounter the error message, change the E entry to 1024.

Symptom 41-8. Regular "clicks," "stutters," or "hiccups" occur during the playback of speech This might also be heard as a "garbled" sound in speech or sound effects. In virtually all cases, the system CPU is simply not fast enough to permit buffering without dropping sound data. Systems with i286 and slower i386 CPUs typically suffer with this kind of problem. This is often compounded by insufficient memory (especially under Windows), which automatically resorts to virtual memory. Because virtual memory is delivered by the hard drive and the hard drive is much slower than RAM anyway, the hard drive simply can't provide data fast enough. Unfortunately, little can be done in this kind of situation (aside from adding RAM, upgrading the CPU, or changing the motherboard). If it is possible to shut off various sound features (i.e., music, voice, effects, etc.), try shutting down any extra sound features that you can live without. Be sure that no TSRs or other applications are running in the background.

Symptom 41-9. The joystick is not working or is not working properly on all systems This problem only applies to sound boards with a multi-function MIDI/joystick port being used in the joystick mode. Chances are that the joystick is conflicting with another joystick port in the system. Disable the original joystick port or the new joystick port—only one joystick port (game adapter) can be active at any one time in the system. Because joystick performance depends on CPU speed, the CPU might actually be too fast for the joystick port. Disable the joystick port or try slowing the CPU down.

Symptom 41-10. The sound board is installed and everything works properly, but now the printer does not seem to work An interrupt conflict is between the sound board and an IRQ line used by the printer. Although parallel printers are often polled, they can also be driven by an IRQ line (IRQ5 or IRQ7). If the sound board is using either one of these interrupts, try changing to an alternative IRQ line. When changing an IRQ line, be sure to reflect the changes in any sound board files called by CONFIG.SYS or AUTOEXEC.BAT.

Symptom 41-11. The following error message appears: "Error MMSYSTEM 337: The specified MIDI device is already in use" This problem often occurs with high-end sound boards, such as the Creative Labs AWE64. This error is often caused by having the sound board's mixer display on with the wavetable synthesizer selected (i.e., the LED display in the Creative Mixer turned on and Creative Wave Synthesizer selected as the MIDI playback device). You can usually correct the problem by turning the mixer display off.

Symptom 41-12. The following error message appears: "Error: Wave device already in use when trying to play wave files while a MIDI file is playing" This problem often occurs with high-end sound boards, such as the Creative Labs AWE64, and it is usually the result of a device configuration problem. If "full-duplex" is turned on and you try to play a .WAV file and a MIDI file at the same time with the wavetable synthesizer (e.g., the Creative Wave Synthesizer) selected as the MIDI playback device, an error will occur. To resolve this problem, you need to turn off the full-duplex mode:

- Hold down <Alt>key and doubleclick on *My computer*.
- Select the *Device manager* tab. A listing for *Sound, video, game controllers* should be included in the *Device manager*, doubleclick on the listing to expand it.
- You should now see a listing for the sound board (e.g., Creative AWE32 16-Bit Audio). Doubleclick on the listing, then select the *Settings* tab. Un-check the box labeled *Allow full-duplex operation*. Click *OK* until you are back to the *Control panel*.
- Now try to play a .WAV and MIDI file at the same time.

Symptom 41-13. You hear "pops" and "clicks" when recording sound under Windows 95 Cache is insufficient to adequately support the recording process (or cache is improperly configured). Try the following procedure to alter the way cache is allocated:

- Open *Notepad* and load SYSTEM.INI
- Locate the area of SYSTEM.INI labeled [vcache].
- Add the following line [vcache]:

```
maxfilecache=2048
```

- Save your changes to the SYSTEM.INI file.
- From the desktop, right-click on *My computer*, then select *Properties*.
- Select the *Performance* page, then click on *File system*.
- Find the slider marked *Read-ahead optimization*, then pull the slider to *None*.
- Save your changes and restart Windows 95.

Symptom 41-14. You notice high frequency distortion in one or possibly in both channels In many cases, the AT bus clock is set faster than 8MHz and data is being randomly lost. This problem usually occurs in very fast systems using an ISA sound board. Enter the system's CMOS setup and check the AT bus clock under the *Advanced chipset setup* area. See that the bus clock is set as close as possible to 8MHz. If the bus clock is derived as a divisor of the CPU clock, you might see an entry, such as /4. Be sure that divisor results in a clock speed as close to 8MHz as possible. If problems still persist, try increasing the divisor to drop the bus speed below 8MHz (this might have an adverse effect on other ISA peripherals).

Symptom 41-15. You hear "pops" and "clicks" when playing back prerecorded files under Windows 95 An excessive processing load is on the system, which is often caused by virtual memory and/or 32-bit access. Start by disabling virtual memory: Open the *Control panel* and doubleclick on the *System* icon. Select the *Performance* page and click on *Virtual memory*. Set the swap file to *None* and save your changes. Try the file playback again. If problems persist, try disabling 32-bit file access. If that still does not resolve the problem, try disabling 32-bit disk access.

Symptom 41-16. "Pops" and "clicks" are audible on new recordings only, pre-existing files sound clean This is often caused by issues with software caching.

If you are using DOS or Windows 3.1, disable SmartDrive from both CONFIG.SYS and AUTOEXEC.BAT, then restart the computer for your changes to take effect. If problems continue (or you are using Windows 95), an excessive processing load on the system might be caused by virtual memory or 32-bit access. Follow the recommendations under Symptom 41-15.

Symptom 41-17. "Pops" and "clicks" occur when playing back or recording any sound file In most cases, there is a wiring problem with the speaker system. Check all of your cabling between the sound board and speakers. If the speakers are powered by ac, be sure that the power jack is inserted properly. If the speakers are powered by battery, be sure that the batteries are fresh. Check for loose connections. If you cannot resolve the problem, try some new speakers. If the problem persists, replace the sound board.

Symptom 41-18. The sound board plays back fine, but it will not record The board probably records fine in DOS, but not in Windows. If the sound board is using 16-bit DMA transfer (typical under Windows), two DMA channels are in use. Chances are that one of those two DMA channels are conflicting with another device in the system. Determine the DMA channels being used under Windows, then check other devices for DMA conflicts. If you are using Windows 95, check the *Device manager* and look for entries marked with a yellow icon.

Symptom 41-19. A DMA error is produced when using a sound board with an Adaptec 2842 controller in the system This is a known problem with the Digital Audio Labs "DOC" product and the Adaptec 2842. You will need to alter the controller's FIFO buffer. Go in the controller's Setup by hitting <Ctrl>+<A> Open prompted during system startup. Select the *Advanced Configuration* option, then select the FIFO threshold—chances are that it will be set to 100%. Try setting the FIFO threshold to 0% and see if this makes a difference.

Symptom 41-20. A DMA error is produced when using a sound board with an Adaptec 1542 controller in the system This is a known problem with the Digital Audio Labs "DOC" sound product and the Adaptec 1542. The problem can usually be resolved by rearranging the DMA channels. Place the Adaptec controller on DMA 7, then place the sound board on DMA 5 for playback and DMA 6 for recording.

Symptom 41-21. The sound card will not play or record—the system just locks up when either is attempted The board will probably not play in either DOS or Windows, but might run fine on other systems. This is a problem that has been identified with some sound boards and ATI video boards. ATI video boards use unusual address ranges, which sometimes overlap the I/O address used by the sound board. Change the sound board to another I/O address.

Symptom 41-22. The sound card will record, but will not playback Assuming that the sound board and its drivers are installed and configured properly, chances are that a playback oscillator on the sound board has failed. Try replacing the sound board outright.

Symptom 41-23. The sound application or editor produces a significant number of DMA errors This type of problem is known to occur frequently when using the standard VGA driver that accompanies Windows—the driver is poorly written and cannot keep up with screen draws. Try updating your video driver to a later, more efficient version. If the driver is known to contain bugs, try using a generic video driver that is written for the video board's chipset.

Symptom 41-24. The sound board will not record in DOS Several possible problems can account for this behavior. First, suspect a hardware conflict between the sound board and other devices in the system. Be sure that the IRQs, DMA channels, and I/O port addresses used by the sound board are not used by other devices.

If the hardware setup appears correct, suspect a problem between DOS drivers. Try a clean boot of the system (with no CONFIG.SYS or AUTOEXEC.BAT). If sound can be run properly now, there is a driver conflict. Examine your entries in CONFIG.SYS or AUTOEXEC.BAT for possible conflicts or for older drivers that might still be loading to support hardware that is no longer in the system.

Finally, suspect the hard-drive controller. Try setting up a RAM drive with RAMDRIVE.SYS. You can install a RAMdrive on your system by adding the line:

```
device=c:\dos\ramdrive.sys /e 8000
```

The 8000 is for 8MB worth of RAM—be sure that enough RAM is in the PC. Once the RAMdrive is setup, try recording and playing from the RAMdrive (you might have to specify a new path in the sound-recorder program). If that works, the hard-drive controller might simply be too slow to support the sound board, and you might need to consider upgrading the drive system.

Symptom 41-25. When recording sound, the system locks up if a key other than the recorder's "hot-keys" are pushed This is a frequent problem under Windows 3.1x. The system sounds (generated under Windows) might be interfering with the sound recorder. Try turning off system sounds. Go to the *Main* icon, choose the *Control panel*, then select *Sounds*. A box will appear in the lower left corner marked *Enable system sounds*. Click on this box to remove the check mark, then click *OK*.

Symptom 41-26. After the sound-board driver is loaded, Windows locks up when starting or exiting In virtually all cases, you have a hardware conflict between the sound board and another device in the system. Be sure that the IRQs, DMA channels, and I/O port addressed used by the sound board are not used by other devices.

Symptom 41-27. When using Windows sound-editing software, the sound board refuses to enter the "digital" mode—always switching back to the analog mode Generally speaking, this is a software-configuration issue. Be sure that your editing (or other sound) software is set for the correct type of sound board (i.e., an AWE32 instead of a Sound Blaster 16/Pro). If problems persist, the issue is with your sound drivers. Check the [drivers] section of the Windows SYSTEM.INI file for your sound-board driver entries. If more than one entry is listed, you might need to disable the competing driver. This is a known problem with the Digital Audio Labs CardDplus, and it is caused by incorrect driver listings. For example, the proper CardDplus driver must be entered as:

```
Wave=cardp.drv
```

and the companion driver must be listed as:

```
Wave1=tahiti.drv
```

You will need to be sure that the proper driver(s) for your sound board are entered in SYS-TEM.INI. You might also need to restart the system after making any changes.

Symptom 41-28. The microphone records at very low levels (or not at all)
Suspect that the problem is in your microphone. Most sound boards demand the use of a good-quality dynamic microphone. Also, Creative Labs and Labtec microphones are not always compatible with sound boards from other manufacturers. Try a generic dynamic microphone. If problems persist, chances are that your recording software is not config-ured properly for the microphone input. Try the following procedure to set up the record-ing application properly under Windows 95:

- Open your *Control panel* and doubleclick on the *Multimedia* icon.
- The *Multimedia properties* dialog will open. Select the *Audio* page.
- In the *Recording* area, be sure to set the *Volume* slider all the way up.
- Also see that the *Preferred device* and *Preferred quality* settings are correct.
- Save your changes and try the microphone again.

Symptom 41-29. The sound card isn't working in full-duplex mode Virtu-ally all current sound boards are capable of full-duplex operation for such applications as Internet phones. Check the specifications for your sound board and see that the board is, in fact, capable of full-duplex operation. If it is, and full-duplex isn't working, your audio properties might be set up incorrectly:

- Open your *Control panel* and doubleclick on the *Multimedia* icon.
- The *Multimedia properties* dialog will open. Select the *Audio* page.
- If the *Playback* device and the *Record* device are set to the same I/O address, this is only half duplex.
- Change the *Playback device* I/O address, so it is different from the *Record* device.
- Hit the *Apply* button, then hit the *OK* button.
- You should now be in *Full duplex* mode.

Some of the very latest sound boards (such as the Ensoniq SoundscapeVIVO 90) will carry full duplex operation with the same *Playback* and *Record* device selected.

Symptom 41-30. DMA errors occur using an older sound board and an Adaptec 1542 In many cases, you can clear DMA issues by slowing down the 1542 using the /n switch. Add the /n switch to the ASPI4DOS command line in CONFIG.SYS, such as:

```
device=c:\aspi4dos.sys /n2
```

If slowing the 1542 down with an /n2 switch doesn't fix the problem, then you should strongly consider upgrading the sound board. This is a known problem with the older Digital Audio Labs CardD sound board.

Symptom 41-31. Hard-disk recording problems occur under Windows 95 Recorded audio is saved to your hard drive. For most systems, sound data can be transferred to the HDD fast enough to avoid any problems—if data transfer is interrupted, your recorded sound might "pop" or break up. Many factors affect HDD data-transfer speed. The following sections outline a number of procedures that might help you optimize a system for sound recording. First, try disabling the *CD auto insert notification* feature:

- Go to the *Device manager*
- Open the *CD-ROM* entry
- Select your CD-ROM drive, and click *Properties*
- Go to the *Settings* page
- Uncheck the *Auto insert notification* box
- Select *OK*

Next, try turning down the level of graphics acceleration:

- Right-click on the *My computer* icon
- Left-click on *Properties*
- Select the *Performance* page
- Select the button labeled *Graphics*
- Start by turning down the acceleration one notch (you can return later to turn it down further if more performance is required)
- Select *OK*

It might also be necessary to adjust the size of your virtual memory swap file:

- Right-click on the *My computer* icon
- Left-click on *Properties*
- Select the *Performance* page
- Select the button labeled *Virtual memory*
- Choose *Let me specify my own virtual memory settings*
- If your PC has 16MB of RAM, set the minimum and maximum at 40MB. If you have 32MB of RAM, set the minimum and maximum at 64MB.
- Select *OK*

Try removing any active items from your Startup group:

- Click the *Start* button
- Go to the *Programs* menu, then select *Startup*. If you see anything here, it might be hurting your system performance. Eliminate anything that is not absolutely necessary.
- To remove items, click the *Start* button, go to *Settings*, then select *Taskbar*
- Choose the page labeled *Start menu programs*
- Click the *Remove* button
- Open the *Startup* group by doubleclicking it
- Remove any items that you feel are not necessary and are wasting resources
- Select the *Close* button when finished

Clear any indexes of the Find Fast utility:

- Click the *Start* button
- Go to *Settings*, then choose the *Control panel*
- Open the *Find Fast* utility
- Go to the *Index* menu
- Select *Delete index*
- Select an index in the *In and below* drop box
- Select the *OK* button
- Repeat steps 5 through 7 until all indexes are removed

Try defragmenting the hard drive:

- Click the *Start* button
- Go to *Programs*, *Accessories*, and *System tools*
- Choose *Disk defragmenter*
- Select the drive to defragment and click *OK*
- Click the *Start* button to begin defragmentation

Finally, you might want to suspend the System Agent (if installed):

- If System Agent is installed, open it by doubleclicking its icon in the taskbar
- Go to the *Advanced* menu
- Choose *Suspend system agent*
- Close the *System agent* window.

Symptom 41-32. The microphone records only at very low levels or not at all Check your phantom power settings first. In many cases, the microphone's gain is set too low in the sound board's mixer applet. Start the sound board's mixer, be sure that the microphone input is turned on, then raise the microphone's level control. Remember to save the mixer settings before exiting the mixer. You should not have to restart the system.

Symptom 41-33. The dynamic microphone clips terribly, and recordings are noisy and faint This is probably caused by phantom power being switched on in your sound board. Try turning the phantom power off. If you cannot turn phantom power off, try plugging the dynamic microphone into the sound board line input jack. Remember to start the sound board mixer applet and set the line input level properly.

Symptom 41-34. Trouble occurs when using Creative Labs or Labtec microphones with your (non-Creative Labs) sound board This is a common complaint among Ensoniq sound board users. It turns out that Ensoniq sound boards are not compatible with Creative Labs or Labtec microphones. Try a generic microphone instead.

Symptom 41-35. Static is at the remote end when talking through a voice application, such as WebPhone Noise is occurring at the line input or microphone input, which is being transmitted to the remote listener. Check the line input signal. You might try reducing or turning off the line input mixer level. If the problem persists, check your phantom power setting and your microphone. Try reducing the microphone level in the sound board's mixer. Try a different microphone.

Further Study

This concludes the material for Chapter 41. Be sure to review the glossary and chapter questions on the accompanying CD. If you have access to the Internet, take a look at some of these sound-board resources:

Creative Labs: **http://www.creaf.com**

Turtle Beach: **http://www.tbeach.com/**

Frontier Design Group: **http://www.frontierdesign.com/**

Ensoniq: **http://www.ensoniq.com**

SIC Resource: **http://www.sicresource.com/**

Star Multimedia: **http://www.starusa.com/**

42

TAPE

DRIVES

CONTENTS AT A GLANCE

Understanding Tape Media
  Quarter-inch cartridge
  QIC cartridge details
  QIC minicartridge details
  QIC tape compatibility
  Travan tape cartridges
  Helical-scan tapes

Tape Drive Construction
  Mechanical construction
  Electronic circuitry

Drive and Tape Maintenance
  Drive cleaning
  Autoloader cleaning

Tape maintenance
Errors because of cleaning neglect
Media problems and DAT drives
Recommended cleaning frequency
  for DAT drives

Freeing Caught Tapes
  The power trick
  Rescuing the tape

Tape-Drive Troubleshooting
  Sense codes and tape drives
  Symptoms

Further Study

The single most pervasive problem with magnetic media (such as floppy drives and hard drives) is that, sooner or later, the drive is going to fail. Old age, media problems, and even rogue software (such as computer viruses) can render your valuable data useless. When a problem arises, you're going to have to restore your data (regardless of whether you replace the drive itself). Unfortunately, restoring data is not always as simple and straight-

FIGURE 42-1   **Typical internal and external tape drives.**
Copyright © 1995 Mountain Network Solutions, Inc.

forward a process as you might think. When a drive fails, it can take hours (if not days) to restore your operating system and applications—then tweak them to work together correctly. Even more frightening is the threat of files you can't restore, like those important documents, drawings, databases, etc. Without a system of backups, your business could be crippled or shut down entirely. Tape drives (Fig. 42-1) have long been a popular means of backup because of their capacity—tape drives are the only mechanisms with the capacity to backup multi-gigabyte hard drives onto a single, relatively inexpensive, data cartridge. However, tape drives are not without their unique problems. This chapter explains the construction and operation of typical tape drives, and offers some maintenance and troubleshooting procedures that can help you resolve tape drive problems.

Understanding Tape Media

Magnetic tape is the oldest form of magnetic mass storage. Tape systems served as the primary mass-storage technique for older mainframes (obsoleting the aging punched card and punched paper tape environment of the day). Tape systems proved to be inexpensive and reliable—so much so that even the original IBM PC was outfitted with a drive port for cassette-tape storage. With the development of floppy and hard drives, tape systems became obsolete as a primary storage method, but retain a valuable role as backup systems.

Although the size, shape, and standards used for tape packaging and recording has advanced, the tape itself is virtually unchanged in principle from the very first incarnation. Figure 42-2 illustrates a tape cartridge used in a minicartridge tape backup system. A tape is a long, slender length of polyester substrate, which is much more flexible than the mylar substrate used in floppy disks. Polyester also sustains a bit of stretch to help the tape negotiate the high tensions and sharp turns encountered in today's tape cartridge assemblies. As with all other magnetic storage media, the substrate is coated with a layer of magnetic material, which is actually magnetized to retain digital information. Many different coatings have been tried through the years, but tapes still use coatings of conventional

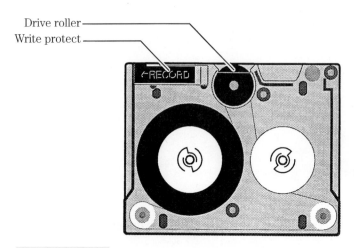

Drive roller ⎯⎯⎯⎯⎯⎯⎯⎯⎯⎯⎯⎯
Write protect ⎯⎯⎯⎯⎯⎯⎯⎯⎯⎯

FIGURE 42-2   **A typical tape minicartridge.**

magnetic oxides similar to older floppy-disk coatings. More exotic coatings, such as metal films and pure metal particles suspended in a binder material, have also been used.

Unlike floppy disks and hard drive platters, which are "random-access" media, tapes represent a sequential (or "serial") type of storage media—that is, a tape drive stores its data sequentially along the length of its media. Where floppy and hard disks store bits along a two-dimensional plane that read/write heads can access in a matter of milliseconds, tapes must be searched bit-by-bit from beginning to end to locate a desired file. A tape search can take minutes—totally impractical for use as primary storage today. The three major types of tape drives to consider are: quarter-inch cartridges, Travan tape cartridges, and helical-scan cartridges.

QUARTER-INCH CARTRIDGE

The concept of the quarter-inch tape cartridge is identical to the compact cassette tape: a plastic shell contains two spools that hold a length of tape. Enclosing the tape supply in a pre-fabricated shell eliminates the need for handling open reel tape or threading the tape through the labyrinth of a mechanical handling system. The original QIC was introduced by 3M in the early 1970s as a recording medium for telecommunication system programming and high-volume data acquisition.

Although QIC and cassette tapes might appear similar by outward appearances, the means used to drive both tapes is radically different. Cassette tapes are driven using a capstan drive system, where the tape is pulled by a take-up reel as it winds across a R/W head. A QIC (Fig. 42-3) uses a small belt that loops around and contacts both the supply and take-up spools, as well as a rubber drive wheel. The capstan in a QIC system contacts the drive wheel (but not the tape), so only the belt's contact friction is used to drive the tape. Drive forces are spread evenly over a long length of tape, so the tape can be moved faster and sustain more direction reversals than a cassette, so tape reliability and working life are greatly improved. Because the components needed to handle the tape are already contained in the QIC shell, the drive mechanism is simple because only a motor and R/W head is required.

With the introduction of personal computers and the subsequent discard of audio cassettes as mass-storage devices, the quarter-inch cartridges emerged as the premier tape mechanism, but early QIC systems were riddled with incompatibilities—each manufacturer had their own ideas about how QIC systems should work. A number of tape drive companies met in the early 1980s to decide on a set of standards for the new QIC devices. In 1982, this group of industrial manufacturers formed an organization called the *QIC Committee*. The QIC Committee is responsible for developing standards for all aspects of tape drive construction and application.

QIC CARTRIDGE DETAILS

A classic (or "full-size") QIC can be identified by its general dimensions. The cartridge is 15.24 cm (6") wide, 10.16 cm (4") long, and 1.59 cm (⅝") deep—somewhat smaller than a VHS video cassette. Although dimensions have not changed significantly through the years, several iterations of "standard" quarter-inch cartridges have been developed. The earliest type of QIC tape was the DC300 cartridge produced by 3M Company, named for the 300' (91.44 m) of tape that it contained. However, the DC300 cartridge proved limited, so the tape length was increased to 600' (181.88 m) and renamed as the *DC600 cartridge* (although the designation was later changed to *DC6000*). For this purpose, all current QIC drives will be using DC6000 cartridges. Storage capacities for the DC6000 cartridge vary from 60MB at the low end, to 2.1GB at the high end. Many notable QIC standards are used for full-size cartridges (Table 42-1). For ordinary end-user PCs, you probably will not encounter these QIC designations too often—the full-size cartridges are usually reserved for file servers and high-end systems with SCSI-2 interfaces.

QIC MINICARTRIDGE DETAILS

The major drawback to standard QICs is their overall large size—they do not fit well into today's small drive bays, so most QIC systems are external desktop devices. To address

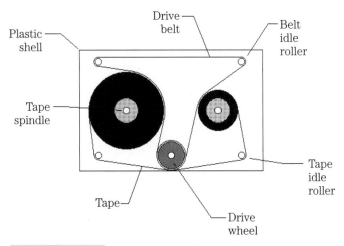

FIGURE 42-3   A typical QIC tape cartridge.

TABLE 42-1 QIC STANDARDS FOR FULL-SIZE CARTRIDGES

QIC STANDARD	CAPACITY	TRACKS	DATA TRANSFER RATE	INTERFACE
QIC-11	45MB	9	n/a	QIC-02
QIC-24	45MB/60MB	9	n/a	SCSI/QIC-02
QIC-120	125MB	15	n/a	SCSI/QIC-02
QIC-150	150MB/250MB	18	n/a	SCSI/QIC-02
QIC-525	320MB/525MB	26	12MB/min	SCSI/SCSI-2
QIC-1000	1.0GB	30	18MB/min	SCSI/SCSI-2
QIC-1350	1.35GB	30	18MB/min	SCSI-2
QIC-2100	2.1GB	30	18MB/min	SCSI-2
QIC-2GB	2.0GB	42	18MB/min	SCSI-2
QIC-5GB	5.0GB	44	18MB/min	SCSI-2
QIC-5010	13GB	144	18MB/min	SCSI-2

TABLE 42-2 QIC STANDARDS FOR MINICARTRIDGES

QIC STANDARD	CAPACITY	TRACKS	DATA TRANSFER RATE	INTERFACE
QIC-40	40MB/60MB	20	2-8MB/min	Floppy/proprietary
QIC-80	80MB/120MB	28	3-9MB/min	Floppy/proprietary
QIC-100	20MB/40MB	12/24	n/a	SCSI/QIC
QIC-128	86MB/128MB	32	n/a	SCSI/QIC
QIC-3010	255MB	40	9MB/min	Floppy/IDE
QIC-3020	500MB	40	9MB/min	Floppy/IDE
QIC-3030	555MB	40	n/a	SCSI-2/QIC
QIC-3040	840MB	42/52	n/a	SCSI-2/QIC
QIC-3050	750MB	40	n/a	SCSI-2/QIC
QIC-3060	875MB	38	n/a	SCSI-2/QIC
QIC-3070	4.0GB	144	n/a	SCSI-2/QIC
QIC-3080	1.6GB	50	n/a	SCSI-2/QIC
QIC-3110	2.0GB	48	n/a	SCSI-2/QIC
QIC-5010	13.0GB	144	n/a	SCSI-2/QIC

the need for smaller-sized QIC systems, the QIC Committee created the minicartridge: an 8.26-cm (3.25") × 6.35-cm (2.5") × 1.59-cm (⅝") assembly holding about 62.48 m (205') of quarter-inch tape. Minicartridges use a DC2000 designation, where the last three digits in the number reflect the cartridge's capacity. For example, a DC2080 minicartridge is designated to hold 80 MB, etc. Any time you see a tape or tape drive associated with a DC2000 designation, you know you must use a minicartridge. There are also many differing QIC designations for today's minicartridges. Table 42-2 outlines the major minicartridge standards.

QIC TAPE COMPATIBILITY

One of the problems with tape drives has been the lack of compatibility—not all tapes work in all drives. For example, the QIC-5010 tape will not work in a QIC-80 drive—even though both are based on the same minicartridge design. In actuality, most drives are capable of reading several different classes of tape, but can write to only a few specific tape versions. Table 42-3 lists the compatibility specifications between the most popular tape standards. The issue of compatibility can have a profound impact when choosing to add or update an existing tape drive. For example, suppose you have a large number of QIC-80 backup tapes, but you need to increase your backup capacity with a larger drive. You can get up to 4GB of storage by choosing a QIC-3070 drive, but it will not read QIC-80 tapes, so your existing backups will be rendered inaccessible. You might be better off choosing a QIC-3010 2GB drive. It has less capacity, but its backward compatibility might be well worth the tradeoff.

TRAVAN TAPE CARTRIDGES

By the early 1990s, tape drives had simply not kept pace with the explosive growth of hard drives. Large tape drives were available, but they cost a premium and were not always easy to interface to every-day PCs. By late 1994, 3M and several other key manufacturers had developed and introduced a new, high-density tape technology, called *Travan*. Travan technology allows much higher recording densities on a tape, and Travan tapes are now readily available with recording capacities from 400MB to 4GB (although many tape drive manufacturers factor in 2:1 data compression when quoting high capacities, such as 8GB).

TABLE 42-3 QIC TAPE COMPATIBILITY	
THE FOLLOWING DRIVE . . .	**. . . WILL *READ* THE FOLLOWING TAPE(S):**
QIC-24	n/a
QIC-40	n/a
QIC-80	QIC-40
QIC-100	n/a
QIC-120	QIC-24
QIC-128	QIC-100
QIC-150	QIC-24 and QIC-120
QIC-525	QIC-24, QIC-120, and QIC-150
QIC-1000	QIC-120, QIC-150, and QIC-525
QIC-1350	QIC-525 and QIC-1000
QIC-2GB	QIC-120, QIC-150, QIC-525, and QIC-1000
QIC-2100	QIC-525 and QIC-1000
QIC-3010	QIC-40 and QIC-80
QIC-3030	QIC-3010
QIC-3070	QIC-3030
QIC-5GB	QIC-24, QIC-120, QIC-150, QIC-525, and QIC-1000
QIC-5010	QIC-150, QIC-525, and QIC-1000

TABLE 42-4 TRAVAN TAPE SPECIFICATIONS*				
	TR-1	**TR-2**	**TR-3**	**TR-4**
Capacity**	400MB	800MB	1.6GB	4.0GB
Data Rate	62.5KB/s	62.5–125KB/s	125–250KB/s	567KB/s
Tracks	36	50	50	72
Interface	Floppy	Floppy	Floppy	SCSI/EIDE

* All Travan tapes are 750' long and 0.315" wide
** All capacities are shown uncompressed

Another attribute to Travan drives is that the larger drives are highly backward compatible with smaller Travan tapes and QIC tapes. Table 42-4 illustrates the relationship between the four available Traven tapes.

HELICAL-SCAN TAPES

The rate at which data is transferred in tape systems has long been an issue. Transfer rates of 250 or 500 KB/s per second can seem extraordinarily slow when gigabytes worth of data are to be moved onto a tape. Because the conventional tape systems included thus far move tape across stationary heads, data-transfer rates are ultimately limited by the tape speed—and a tape can only be moved so fast. Data transfer is also affected by the drive electronics, but even new encoding techniques are of limited utility. Tape-drive designers realized that the head and tape can be moved together to increase the relative speed between the two, while allowing the tape-transport mechanism itself to continue operating at a normal speed.

It was discovered that a set of R/W heads mounted on a cylindrical drum could be spun across a length of moving tape wrapped about 90 degrees around the drum's circumference (Fig. 42-4). The drum itself would be offset (or cantered) at a slight angle relative to the tape's path of travel. During normal operation, the spinning drum describes a helical path (thus the term *helical scan*) across the tape (Fig. 42-5). Such a helical pattern allows more information to be written to the tape faster than conventional stationary head systems. Two major helical recording systems are available: 4-mm digital audio tape (DAT) and 8-mm tape. DAT heads are cantered about 6 degrees, and 8-mm tape heads use a 5-degree tilt. DAT heads spin at 2000 RPM and lay down 1869 tracks (traces) per linear inch (2.54 cm) of tape. Each trace is only 4-mm wide.

Data can be packed very tightly on DAT tapes because each trace (or scan line) is recorded at a unique azimuth angle. Each head in the drum is skewed slightly from the perpendicular so that the data on adjacent traces is oriented very differently. During playback, a head responds well to signals written in the same orientation, but it responds poorly to signals written in the other orientation, so blank space between each signal is not required. Another advantage to helical scan is data integrity. By adding two more heads to the rotating drum (total of four heads), data can be read immediately after writing. Any errors that are detected can be corrected by repeating the data on subsequent traces until data is valid. Physically, helical scan DAT tape is about 4 mm wide and wound into a plastic cartridge roughly the size of a credit card. A DAT usually packs 2.0GB to 4.0GB of data in up to 90 m of 1450-oersted tape. Probably the greatest disadvantage to helical-scan tape systems is the additional mechanical complexity required to wrap the tape around a spinning drum. Where cassettes, QICs, and minicartridges allow only a single point of contact with a stationary R/W head, helical-scan tapes must be pulled out and away from its shell and wrapped around the rotating drum (Fig. 42-6). Notice the series of rollers and guides that are needed to properly position and tension the tape.

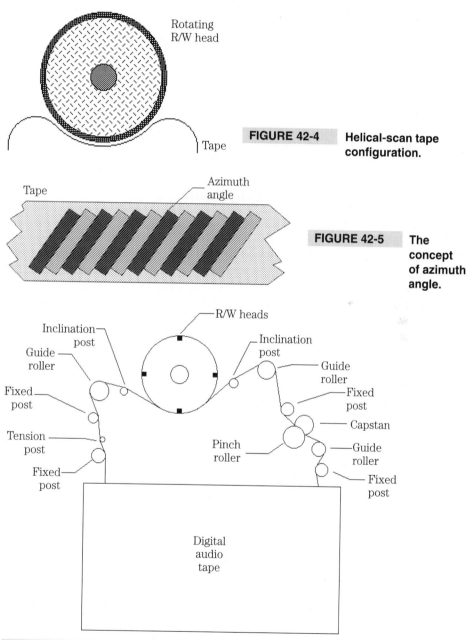

Rotating
R/W head

Tape

FIGURE 42-4   **Helical-scan tape configuration.**

Tape

Azimuth angle

FIGURE 42-5   **The concept of azimuth angle.**

R/W heads

Inclination post

Guide roller

Fixed post

Tension post

Fixed post

Inclination post

Guide roller

Fixed post

Capstan

Pinch roller

Guide roller

Fixed post

Digital audio tape

FIGURE 42-6   **Example of a helical-scan tape path.**

Eight millimeter tape is twice as wide as DAT media in a 9.53-cm (3.75") × 6.35-cm (2.5") × 1.27-cm (0.5") cassette that appears rather like a VHS cassette. In actuality, 8-mm systems can store up to 10.0GB (uncompressed) on a single cassette. The high cost of helical-tape backup systems are well beyond the means of most hobbyists and enthusiasts (even some small companies). Still, costs are continuing to fall.

Tape Drive Construction

Now that you have an understanding of basic tape styles and drive standards, this part of the chapter will show you how tape drives are physically assembled. Figure 42-7 shows an exploded diagram for a Teac D/CAS tape-drive mechanism. Although the construction of most fixed-head tape drives is not incredibly complex, it is rather involved and delicate. Helical-scan tape drives, however, can offer significant technical challenges because of the added heads and tape-handling mechanisms.

MECHANICAL CONSTRUCTION

At the core of the mechanical assembly is the *drive chassis* (1), also called the *transport sub-assembly*. This chassis forms the foundation for all other drive components, including two PC boards. The chassis is built with four assemblies already in place (two *loading-base assemblies*, a *lever-base assembly*, and a *loading-arm assembly*). These mechanical assemblies are responsible for loading and ejecting the tape. When you encounter difficulties with tape loading or unloading, you should suspect a problem in one or more of these mechanical areas. The chassis mechanics are also responsible for allowing tapes to be inserted on one side only (side A). If the tape is inserted with side B up, the mechanics will not allow the tape to seat in the drive. A *front bezel/door assembly* (28) and an *eject button* (29) give the drive its cosmetic appearance once the completed drive is mounted in its drive bay.

A D/CAS tape is transported through the drive using two reel motors: a *forward reel motor* (9) and a *reverse reel motor* (10). These are both dc motors, which are driven by control circuitry on the *drive-control PC board* (26). Ideally, these reel motors should turn at a constant rate of speed, but tape speed tends to vary as tape is unwound from one spool and wound onto another. To keep tape velocity constant, the tape contacts an *encoder roller* (15), which drives an *encoder assembly* (12). Data generated by the encoder is used to regulate reel motor speed—much the same way that an index sensor is used to regulate spindle speed in a floppy or hard drive. Tension on the encoder roller is maintained and adjusted by tweaking the *encoder spring* (13) and *pin spring* (14) with a screw.

D/CAS tape is separated into individual tracks along the tape's width. The *read/write head assembly* (22) is actually composed of five separate magnetic heads: two read heads, two write heads, and an erase head. During a write operation, the erase head erases any previous data that might have existed on the tape, the write head(s) then lay down new flux transitions, and the read head(s) immediately re-read the written data to ensure its integrity. During a read operation, the erase and write heads are idle, and only the read(s) respond. The head assembly is held in place with a *head mounting screw* (24). A *clamp* (25) holds the head's flat cable.

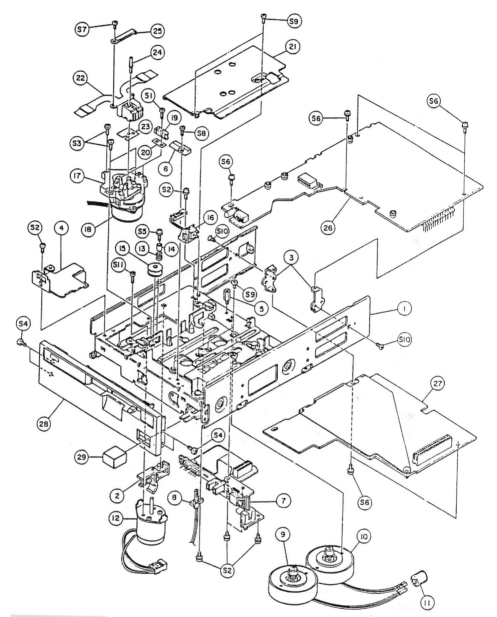

FIGURE 42-7   Exploded diagram of a Teac tape drive. Teac America, Inc.

The head assembly is mounted to a *head-seek assembly* (17) through an *electrical-isolation sheet* (23). A *head-seek unit* raises or lowers the head to the desired track as the tape moves past. A *stepping motor* (18) drives the head-seek assembly using a lead screw. As the stepping motor turns in one direction, the force of rotation is translated to linear motion by the lead screw—the head moves in a fashion similar to head stepping in a floppy drive. It also has several tape guides (6 and 19). The remainder of mechanical parts are generally brackets and screws. Always make it a point to note the locations of all screws and brackets during disassembly.

ELECTRONIC CIRCUITRY

The electronics involved in the Teac D/CAS drive are also called out in the exploded view of Fig. 42-7. The two PC boards are: the *drive-control PC board* (26) and the *drive-interface PC board* (27). The drive-control board contains all the circuitry necessary for operating the drive's physical devices, such as the R/W head(s), the reel motors, the stepping motor, reading the encoder, and reading the other drive sensor elements. A drive-interface board contains the high-level processing circuitry needed to communicate with a host computer and operate the drive control board.

Three discrete sensors are in the drive (not counting the encoder): a *cassette load sensor* (7), a *file-protect sensor* (7), an *LED hole sensor* (8), and a *sensor guide pair* (16). Notice that cassette and file sensors are both held on the same sub PC board. The cassette load sensor is an optoisolator that produces a logic 0 when a tape is absent and a logic 1 when a tape is present (similar to the disk-in-place sensor of a floppy drive). The file-protect sensor produces a logic 0 when the tape is protected (writing is inhibited) and a logic 1 when writing is allowed (similar to a floppy drive's write-protect sensor). All sensors are important parts of the drive and its ability to interact with the outside world.

Figure 42-8 presents these major electronic sections as a block diagram. The left portion of the diagram shows you how a D/CAS tape will interact with the R/W head and system

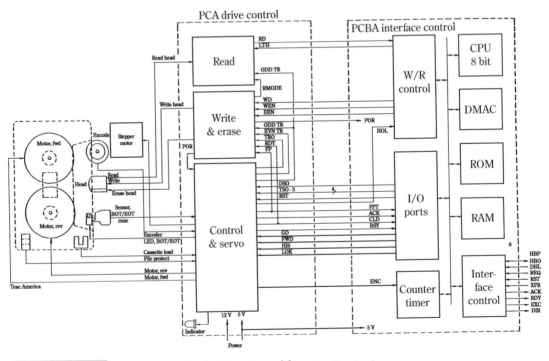

FIGURE 42-8   **Block diagram of a Teac tape drive.** Teac America, Inc.

sensors. When the cassette is inserted properly, it will engage into the forward and reverse reel motors. A properly inserted tape also asserts the cassette load sensor. The signal being generated by a file-protect sensor depends on whether the cassette's write-protect notch is exposed or covered. The *Beginning Of Tape (BOT)* and *End Of Tape (EOT)* contain a short series of holes. An LED source is placed on one side of the tape, and a sensor is placed on the other side. When EOT and BOT holes are encountered, a pulse signal is returned to drive-control circuitry. During reading or writing, a R/W head assembly is engaged to contact the tape. The encoder wheel also contacts the tape. Resulting encoder signals are used by drive control circuits to regulate tape speed by adjusting reel speed. The head is mounted to its track-seeking stepping motor, which is also operated by drive-control circuits.

The tape drive-control PC board handles the drive's physical operations and processes all sensor readings. Analog head signals are processed through a read circuit, where they are converted into logic signals and sent along to the R/W head control circuit on the drive's interface control PC board. Write signals leave the R/W control circuit in logic form and are sent to the write/erase circuit on the drive-control PC board. Logic write signals are converted to analog signals and sent to the R/W head. During writing, the write/erase circuit also actuates the erase head to clear any previous data before new data is written. The drive-control board is managed by the control/servo circuit, which communicates with I/O ports on the drive interface board. The control/servo circuit also lights an LED on the drive's front panel when any drive activity occurs.

The tape-drive interface-control PC board is a microprocessor-driven system that handles high-level drive operations. A CPU is responsible for processing system instructions provided by an on-board ROM, as well as any variables or data information held in RAM. The CPU handles the physical interface through the interface control circuit, and directs the drive's control board utilizing I/O circuits. Data flowing into or out of the drive is processed through a write/read control circuit. System synchronization is maintained by reading the counter/timer circuit being driven by the control/servo circuit. The layout and control structure of your particular tape drive might vary quite a bit from the Teac system illustrated here, but all major operating areas should be present to one extent or another. You might also encounter several functions integrated into a single high-density ASIC, so you should regard Fig. 42-8 as more of a conceptual guideline than an absolute rule.

Drive and Tape Maintenance

Tape drives require periodic maintenance for proper operation. In general, you will need to handle two types of maintenance: drive cleaning and tape maintenance. Although these hardly sound like exciting procedures, they can have profound effects on your drive's overall performance and the reliability of your backups.

DRIVE CLEANING

As with floppy-disk drives, tape drives bring magnetic media directly into contact with magnetic R/W heads. Over time and use, magnetic oxides from the tape rub off onto the head surface. Oxides (combined with dust particles and smoke contamination) accumulate and act as a wedge that forces the tape away from the head surface. Even if you never have cause to actually disassemble your tape drive, you should make it a point to perform routine cleaning. Regular cleaning improves the working life of your recording media and can significantly reduce the occurrence of data errors—especially during file restores, where problems can keep you shut down.

The objective of drive cleaning is remarkably simple: remove any buildup of foreign material that might have accumulated on the R/W head. The most common cleaning method uses a pre-packaged cleaning cartridge. The cartridge contains a length of slightly abrasive cleaning material. When cleaning tape is run through the drive, any foreign matter on the head is rubbed away. The cleaning tape can often be used for several cleanings before being discarded. Some cleaning tapes can be run dry, and others might have to be dampened with an alcohol-based cleaning solution. The advantage to a cleaning cartridge is simplicity—the procedure is quick and you never have to disassemble the drive. Because QIC and Travan-type tape moves much more slowly across a R/W head than floppy media does, you need not worry about damaging the R/W head because of friction. DAT and 8-mm (helical) heads do move across the tape quickly, so you must be cautious about cleaning times. You will likely have better results over the long term using dry cleaning cartridges that are impregnated with a lubricating agent to reduce friction.

> Cleaning cartridges are typically not rewindable—once they have been run through the drive once, they are simply discarded. However, many tape drives do not detect the "end" of a cleaning tape. Be sure to inspect the cleaning cartridge regularly and discard it after it is exhausted.

You can also clean R/W heads manually, which can be convenient during a repair when the drive is already opened. Start by vacuuming away any dust, debris, or pet hair that might be in the drive. Use a small, hand-held vacuum to reach tight spots. Heads and capstans can be cleaned with a fresh, lint-free swab, dipped lightly in a head cleaning solution (Fig. 42-9). If no head-cleaning solution is available, use fresh ethyl or isopropyl alcohol. Rub the head gently, but firmly, to remove any debris. You might wish to use several swabs to ensure a thorough cleaning. Allow the head to dry completely before running a tape.

> Remember that these are only general guidelines. Refer to the user's manual or reference manual for your particular drive to find the specific cleaning recommendations, procedures, and cautions listed by the manufacturer. Every drive has slightly different cleaning and preventive maintenance procedures. Some drives might also require periodic lubrication.

> Some tape drives—especially DAT drives recommend against the use of alcohol, alcohol-based cleaning solutions, or cotton swabs when cleaning a drive.

AUTOLOADER CLEANING

The *autoloader* feature loads and unloads helical-scan DAT tapes (in much the same way that VCRs use automatic loaders and unloaders). In some DAT drives, the loader mecha-

Capstan   Tape head

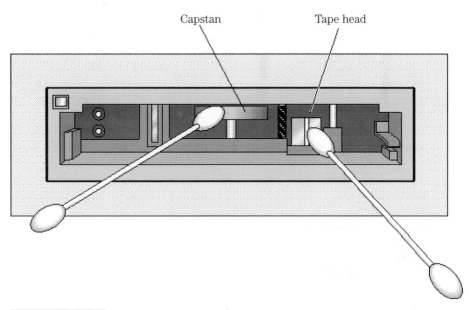

FIGURE 42-9   **Manually cleaning a tape drive.**

nism retrieves cartridges from a magazine, inserts them in the DAT drive inside the autoloader, and returns them to the magazine when the cartridges are unloaded and ejected by the internal drive. Autoloader mechanisms and guide paths should also be cleaned (and lubricated, if necessary) on a regular basis—often once a month or when an autoloader front panel error is displayed.

TAPE MAINTENANCE

Tape cartridges are one of the more rugged items in the PC world—tape is contained in a hard plastic shell, and the R/W head aperture is usually guarded by a metal or plastic shroud. However, tapes are certainly not indestructible. They must be handled with care to ensure the integrity of their data. The following guidelines will help you get the most from your tapes:

- *Avoid fingerprinting the tape* Do not open the tape-access door of the cartridges or touch the tape itself. Fingerprints can prevent the drive from reading the tape and result in errors.
- *Set the write-protect switch* Be sure to set the write-protect switch after backing up your data—this will reduce the possibility of accidentally overwriting crucial data if you forget to label the tape.
- *Be careful of magnetic fields* Tapes are sensitive to magnetic fields from monitors, electromechanical telephone ringers, fans, etc. Keep the tape away from sources of magnetic fields.
- *Be careful of toner* The toner used by laser printers and photocopiers is a micro-fine dust, which might filter out of the device in small quantities. Keep your tapes away from printers and copiers to avoid accidental contamination by toner dust.

- *Be careful of the tape environment* Keep the tape out of direct sunlight, keep the tape dry, and keep the tape safe from temperature extremes (sudden hot-to-cold or cold-to-hot transitions). Before using a tape, allow it to slowly assume the current room temperature.
- *Retention your tapes regularly* Before using a tape that has been idle for a month or more, use your backup software to retention the tape first. This removes any "tight spots" that often develop on the tape.

You've probably noticed that if you play a video tape often, the picture and sound quality on the tape will begin to degrade. This is a natural effect of wear as the media passes repeatedly over the R/W heads. Data tapes do not last forever; after a period of use, they should be destroyed before their reliability deteriorates to a point where your data is not safe. Tape life is generally rated in terms of passes. But passes are difficult to track because a single backup or restore operation might involve many passes. Tape life also depends on how the tape is used. For example, a nightly backup to an 8-mm tape might use only the first half or the tape, but leave the last half of the tape almost unused. As a rule, follow the "20-use" rule: If a tape is used daily, replace the tape every month. If a tape is used weekly, replace the tape every 6 months. If a tape is only used monthly, replace it every 18 to 24 months.

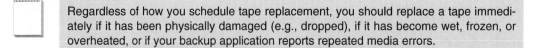

Regardless of how you schedule tape replacement, you should replace a tape immediately if it has been physically damaged (e.g., dropped), if it has become wet, frozen, or overheated, or if your backup application reports repeated media errors.

ERRORS BECAUSE OF CLEANING NEGLECT

Tape drives are some of the most susceptible to the buildup of contaminants. If a tape drive is not kept clean, increased dropouts will occur where the drive cannot read or write to the tape (you might lose as much as 20% of backup capacity and performance if the recommended head-cleaning schedule is not followed). High-end tape drives typically monitor the total number of dropouts. When the number reaches a predetermined threshold (defined in the drive's firmware), an LED on the drive will slowly flash, indicating that the tape drive needs cleaning. These are some of the errors that can result from failure to observe routine tape-drive maintenance and cleaning:

- *Dropouts* A dropout is caused by weak signal strength from dirty read/write heads, and can result in reduced tape capacity and backup performance.
- *Media errors* The backup tapes can be jammed, torn, or otherwise damaged by a dirty read/write head. This might require you to replace the affected tape cartridge.
- *Read or write errors* Data might not be recorded on the tape during backup because of a dirty read/write head. Even if the data is on the backup tape, retrieval might not be possible if the dirty head cannot read the data.
- *Format failures* During backup, data is laid on the tape in a certain format for easy retrieval. A dirty write head can cause format failures, which means that data can be lost or impossible to retrieve.
- *Bad blocks* The tape might not accept backup data because of media damage. Also, the read/write head might be unable to retrieve data from bad blocks that have been caused by tape failures.

MEDIA PROBLEMS AND DAT DRIVES

DAT drives are particularly sensitive to contaminants and media problems. If the DAT media is marginal or defective, it will cause the drive to report an error. Several characteristics of a DAT tape cartridge can cause DAT drives to fail:

■ Head clogs are the most common media problem, and are caused by loose particles that are deposited on the read/write heads. These deposits prevent the drive from reading or writing to the tape. Head clogs are reported in several ways (depending on the firmware version in use). If a head clog occurs, clean the drive at least four times to ensure the heads are clean. The "sense codes" that report head clogs are typically 03/03/02, and any sense code starting with 03 and ending with either BE or BF (for example, 03/3B/BE is a head clog). Tape media problems can also result in head clogs. Keep track of when tapes fail and when they are successful for the first three uses—if a tape fails 2 out of 3 times, the tape is failing and must be replaced.

■ High-torque cartridges might be wound incorrectly during manufacturing (the tape rubs against the top and/or bottom of the inside of the tape cartridge shell). This creates enough resistance to prevent the DAT drive from moving the tape consistently. High-torque cartridges are always reported with a "sense code" of 04/44/AF. Autoloaders will display the message "BAD TPE #," where # is the slot number of the tape (so you can find it in the autoloader magazine). High-torque tapes must be replaced.

■ BOT/EOT prism problems are caused by bad cartridges. These problems are not common, but when they happen, they will intermittently prevent the drive from sensing the end or beginning of tape. This causes the motors that move the tape to stop suddenly, resulting in an error message. BOT/EOT prism failures are either reported as "sense codes" 04/44/AF or 04/44/B9. In either case, the cartridge must be replaced.

■ Physical tape damage might be caused by the drive or might occur during tape manufacturing. This problem always occurs on the exact same location on tape. Physical damage is reported as "sense codes" 03/31/00 or 03/3b/00 in the exact same location on tape. This problem can only be verified by testing with a special debug tool that can eject the tape without rewinding so that the damage is visible. It is generally recommended that tapes reporting these errors be replaced.

■ Tape hub-alignment problems typically cause noise during high-speed tape motion, such as a "rewind." When this occurs, it is recommended to replace the tape.

RECOMMENDED CLEANING FREQUENCY FOR DAT DRIVES

To optimize the performance and reliability of DAT drives, follow these recommendations for cleaning:

■ When using new tape media for backups, DAT drives need to be cleaned after each eight hours of read/write operation until the entire data cartridge has been used five times.

■ When using data cartridges that have already been used five times or more, clean DAT drives after each 25 hours of read/write operation.

■ Clean DAT drives before performing a complete server (or major system) backup.

- Clean only once for routine cleaning to minimize head wear. Occasionally, a single cleaning cycle will not fully clean read/write heads on a DAT drive. If the backup software reports errors, clean the drive again to eliminate the possibility that dirty heads are causing the error.
- Clean the drive four times after a failure to ensure the heads are cleaned. A single cleaning cycle might not remove a head clog adequately.
- When using an autoloader, keep a cleaning cartridge in the last slot. Refer to your software user manual for instructions on how to schedule and perform automatic cleaning operations using the backup software.
- DAT cleaning cartridges typically last 30 cleaning cycles (passes). Remember to replace the cleaning cartridge after it has been exhausted.

Freeing Caught Tapes

One of the worse times for a tape drive to fail is while a tape is actually installed. For mini-cartridges tape drives (such as the Colorado Trakker series), this is not so serious, because the tape never leaves its cartridge—you can simply pull the tape cartridge out. But with helical-scan tape drives (such as Exabyte EXB-series drives), the implications are much more serious. As with ordinary video tapes, helical-scan tape is pulled from the cartridge and wound around a complex series of rollers and capstans. Under normal operation, the tape is released and withdrawn back into the cartridge during the ejection process. Unfortunately, if the tape drive fails (and the tape remains wound in the drive), you cannot remove the tape without ruining it. But you might be able to rescue a helical-scan tape while preserving the maximum amount of data.

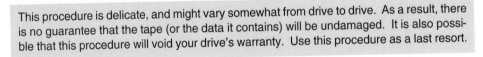

This procedure is delicate, and might vary somewhat from drive to drive. As a result, there is no guarantee that the tape (or the data it contains) will be undamaged. It is also possible that this procedure will void your drive's warranty. Use this procedure as a last resort.

THE POWER TRICK

On very rare occasions, a helical-scan tape drive might "hang-up" (rather than suffer a hard failure). This might be caused by a hardware or software conflict in the computer, intermittent cabling, a bad driver (or backup software), or a signal glitch in the drive or its controller. Before attempting an invasive procedure, try powering the PC down, waiting several moments, and power the system up again. If an error has occurred, cycling the power might clear it and restore drive operation. If the drive's ready light is lit, press the Eject or Unload button and see if the tape will eject of its own accord. If so, you have saved yourself a great deal of time and effort.

RESCUING THE TAPE

The objective of this procedure is to preserve your tape. This is accomplished by removing the drive, opening it up, and temporarily disabling some of the drive mechanics to free the tape from its tape path and wind it safely back into the cartridge. Before proceeding, you will need a selection of tools, including a small regular and Phillips screwdriver, adhesive tape, and a non-conductive tool, such as a molded potentiometer adjustment tool. Depending on the design of your particular tape drive, you might need some Torx drivers (often T-10 and T-8 sizes), and perhaps even a Torque-limiting screwdriver (3.4 to 5.0 inch-pounds, or 3.9 to 5.8 kg-cm).

Disconnect your power   Power down the PC and disconnect the ac cord to ensure the maximum amount of safety while working inside the computer. Remove the computer's enclosure to expose the tape drive assembly and its cabling.

Remove the drive   Your first goal is to remove the tape drive so that you can work on it without the obstructions of the PC. In most cases, your tape drive will be internal, so disconnect the power and signal cabling from the drive. You might wish to use masking tape to note the position of signal pin 1. The drive is probably held in its drive bay with four small Phillips screws, so remove them, and slide the drive (with the tape still inserted) from the computer. You can then rest the drive on a comfortable work surface—preferably a static-safe surface.

Remove the drive cover   Once the drive is free, you need to remove the top cover to expose the inner-workings. This is where those Torx drivers will come in handy. If the top cover is held in place by conventional screws, you only need screwdrivers of the appropriate size. Under no circumstances should you force the cover—if it is not free after removing the screws, check for additional screws or tabs that you might have to disengage.

Check the tape path   You should now have a clear view of the tape path inside the drive. You will find one of two conditions—either the tape has been unloaded from its tape path (and simply has not ejected), or the tape is still wound in its tape path. If the tape has already unloaded, you might skip the following steps by using a thin, non-conductive tool to move the door release lever. The release lever is typically located on the left side of the drive chassis, and it can be actuated by moving the lever toward the front of the machine (although this might not be the case for all drives). Keep in mind that you need very little force to actuate the door release lever, and it should move no more than $\frac{1}{8}$" (about 3 mm). This should successfully eject the tape cartridge, and you can then just replace the top cover.

Remove the "deck hanger"   To rescue your tape, you will need to access all of the elements of your tape path. If any supplemental support or guard hardware covers the tape path (sometimes referred to as a *deck hanger*), you will also need to remove that hardware before continuing. In some cases, this "deck hangar" might be bolted into place—in other cases, it can be removed simply by popping out several clips.

Tape the cartridge door open   Use some adhesive tape to hold the tape cartridge door open—this is only temporary, and will be removed when the cartridge is free.

Remove the erase-head bracket and tape guide   The tape is being held under a tape guide. Before you can remove the tape from its path, you must remove the tape guide, and the erase-head bracket, which is holding the tape guide in place. Once you find the erase-head bracket, it is usually held in place by a single Phillips screw. Remove the screw and ease the erase-head bracket straight off its post (you might wish to mark the starting position with a marker so that you can easily replace the bracket later). Once the erase-head bracket is free, ease the tape guide from all three of its posts and set the guide aside. You are now ready to free the tape from its path.

Removing the tape Using your non-conductive tool (do not use your fingers or metal objects), pull the tape gently to establish some slack in the tape. Use your finger to move the pinch-roller flange toward the left, then hold the flange in that position. Do not release the pinch roller until the tape is completely removed from around the pinch roller and capstan. Otherwise, the tape might be damaged. Insert the non-conductive tool into the tape loop and gently lift the tape from around the pinch roller and capstan. Once the tape is completely clear, you can release the pinch-roller flange.

Next, gently remove the tape from around the guide posts and rollers. Remember to use the non-conductive tool from inside the loop to avoid touching the tape-recording surface or head assembly. Position the non-conductive tool inside the loop. You'll see an "L"-shaped black part that prevents the tape from riding up over the drum. Gently move the tape up so that it passes between the "L" and the edges of the head assembly. Finally, lift the tape from around the guide posts and roller. Once again, remember to place the tool inside the tape loop to avoid damaging the tape.

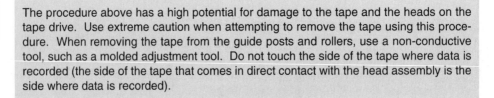

The procedure above has a high potential for damage to the tape and the heads on the tape drive. Use extreme caution when attempting to remove the tape using this procedure. When removing the tape from the guide posts and rollers, use a non-conductive tool, such as a molded adjustment tool. Do not touch the side of the tape where data is recorded (the side of the tape that comes in direct contact with the head assembly is the side where data is recorded).

Remove the cartridge and wind the tape Now that the tape is free, you need to free the cartridge without damaging the tape loose inside the drive. Use a thin, non-conductive tool to move the door release lever. The release lever is typically located on the left side of the drive chassis, and can be actuated by moving the lever toward the front of the machine (although this might not be the case for all drives). Keep in mind that you need very little force to actuate the door release lever, and it should move no more than ⅛" (about 3 mm).

You should now be able to remove the cartridge, but pull the cartridge out just enough to see the cartridge spindles (you don't want to pull the cartridge all the way out and have loose tape flapping around). Place the drive on its left side with the cartridge exposed enough to see the two tape spindles. The upper spindle is the takeup reel. Insert a screwdriver into the takeup reel and slowly turn the reel counter-clockwise to wind the loose tape into the cartridge. Keep an eye on the loose tape to be sure that it doesn't catch on anything as you wind it into the cartridge. Do not over-wind the tape! At this point, you can remove the adhesive tape holding the cartridge door open and gently close the cartridge door (be sure that the tape is taunt enough to that it will not contact the door when it is closed. You can then remove the tape cartridge.

When opening the drive door, hold the door gently so that it opens slowly—this will prevent the data cartridge from ejecting suddenly and damaging the tape.

Replace the tape guide and erase-head bracket Now that the tape is successfully free and removed from the drive, you must re-assemble the components that you removed earlier. The first order of business should be to replace the tape guide, which simply fits onto the three guide posts where you removed it from. Once the tape guide is in place, replace the erase-head bracket. If you had made a reference mark before removal, replacing the bracket should be a simple matter. Secure the bracket with its screw (remember not to over-tighten the screw).

Replace the "deck hanger" If you have removed any supplementary guards or shields during the disassembly procedure, you should replace them now. Be especially careful not to pinch any wiring or cables running through the drive. Be sure that nothing interferes with the tape path.

Replace the cover Finally, you must replace the drive cover. If there are any tabs or clips holding the cover in place, engage them first, then install any screws to secure the cover. In most cases, these screws will be quite small, so be sure to avoid over-tightening any of the screws.

Service the drive, as necessary At this point, the drive should be fully re-assembled and ready to re-install in the computer. However, you might take this opportunity to package the drive in its original container (or other suitable container), and send it to the manufacturer for repair.

Tape-Drive Troubleshooting

The motors, sensors, and mechanisms in a typical tape drive are all prone to eventual failure. Even the natural wear that occurs in mechanical systems has an impact on drive performance and data-error rates. This part of the chapter is intended to provide some general service guidelines and basic troubleshooting procedures. Bear in mind that tape drives (especially helical drives, such as DAT drives) contain a substantial amount of mechanical and electro-mechanical components. Given the nature of mechanical parts, many of your problems will be mechanically oriented. The following tips might help resolve some basic problems:

- Be sure that the tape drive's firmware is upgraded to the latest revision. This is especially important with more "intelligent" drives, such as DAT drives.
- Be sure that you're using the very latest drivers and tape-drive application software.
- Keep the drive clean by following the routine cleaning procedures for the drive. This is especially important after heavy usage or when "breaking in" new media.
- Poor media is often a source of errors. Identify and remove questionable media as soon as possible. Rotate aging media out of service regularly.
- Be sure that any tape-drive controller is installed and configured properly.

■ Verify the drive-signal cabling is correct and intact.

■ Check drive power. Do not "split" power from a hard drive or other crucial drive.

■ Drives often use LEDs to indicate errors. Check any drive LED signals against the drive's user manual.

SENSE CODES AND TAPE DRIVES

SCSI "sense codes" indicate status or error information, and are normally returned from SCSI devices, such as CD-ROM drives, hard drives, and tape drives. Sense codes are composed of three 8-bit hexadecimal numbers. The first number indicates the type of sense code and are listed as categories in Table 42-5. The last two numbers provide more specific error information. Table 42-6 provides a listing of important media and hardware errors returned by SCSI tape drives. You'll find that sense codes are essential in troubleshooting SCSI DAT drives. Here are some important points:

■ SCSI devices return sense codes whenever a recoverable or non-recoverable error occurs. Codes 01 indicate a recoverable error—an error occurred, but the drive was able to recover from the error. Codes 03 (media errors) and 04 (hardware errors) indicate an unrecoverable error. Codes 05 indicate an illegal command (usually caused by an application issue).

■ Sense codes isolate the problem because they originate from the device. It does not mean that the drive itself is the cause of the problem—just that the drive generated the sense code. A sense code indicates either a firmware, hardware, or media issue.

■ Sense codes can be used to resolve DAT drive issues in all operating systems and backup applications that record these sense codes to log files.

■ If sense codes are not returned, you'll know the problem can be diagnosed as a software or driver issue, the drive is not responding, or the drive's time-out values are set too low.

TABLE 42-5 INDEX OF SCSI TAPE DRIVE SENSE CODES

01 (*Recovered Error*) Indicates that the last command completed successfully with some recovery action performed by the tape drive.

02 (*Not Ready*) The drive is busy, and operator intervention might be required to correct this condition.

03 (*Media Error*) This is an unrecoverable error occurred that might have been caused by defective media.

04 (*Hardware Error*) The drive detected an unrecoverable failure that might have been caused by the drive's hardware. The drive will continue to return this sense code until the cartridge is ejected or the drive is reset.

05 (*Illegal Request*) This indicates that an illegal parameter was sent to the drive (such as to eject a tape after it is already ejected). This code is usually returned by the application.

06 (*Unit Attention*) This code is returned under several conditions; the drive is reset, the firmware is upgraded, the media is changed, or the drive is turned off, then on again.

07 (*Data Protect*) The tape cartridge is write-protected.

08 (*Blank Check*) This code is returned if the tape is blank or when the tape cannot be read because it has an unknown format.

Note: This table describes **tape drive** sense codes. Sense codes returned from other SCSI devices may have very different meanings and corrective actions.

TABLE 42-6 INDEX OF MEDIA AND HARDWARE ERROR SENSE CODES

03/00/02 (*Reached EOT*) The EOD marker was not written to the tape, and the drive unexpectedly reached end-of-tape (EOT). You should reformat the tape unless a previous error is known.

03/03/02 (*Excessive write errors*) This indicates a head clog. Clean the drive four times and record the failure on the label of the cartridge that was inside the drive when the error was reported. Replace any cartridges that fail two out of three times (or three out of five times).

03/03/BE (*Excessive write errors*) This indicates a head clog. Clean the drive four times and record the failure on the label of the cartridge that was inside the drive when the error was reported. Replace any cartridges that fail two out of three times (or three out of five times).

03/31/00 (*Media format is corrupt*) This error might be caused by a head clog, physical damage (e.g., vertical creases in the media), or an alignment problem. Be sure that the drive's firmware is up to date to ensure that the drive is capable of isolating media problems from other potential problems. Otherwise, the media is probably defective and should be replaced.

03/31/BE (*Media format is corrupt while writing*) The error always indicates a head clog. Clean the drive four times and record the failure on the label of the cartridge that was inside the drive when the error was reported. Replace any cartridges that fail two out of three times (or three out of five times).

03/31/BF (*Media format is corrupt while reading*) The error always indicates a head clog. Clean the drive four times and record the failure on the label of the cartridge that was inside the drive when the error was reported. Replace any cartridges that fail two out of three times (or three out of five times).

03/3B/00 (*Sequential positioning error*) There is a head clog problem or you're using a 120m DDS2 tape in a 2/8Gb DAT drive. Be sure that the drive's firmware is up to date. This helps ensure that head clogs are most accurately detected, and might also prevent 120m tapes from being used by immediately ejecting them once detected. Also, the tape might be physically damaged. When this occurs, the tape will fail consistently in the exact same location on tape. Replace the media immediately and try again.

03/3B/BE (*Sequential positioning error while writing*) This indicates a head clog. Clean the drive four times and record the failure on the label of the cartridge that was inside the drive when the error was reported. Replace any cartridges that fail two out of three times (or three out of five times).

03/3B/BF (*Sequential positioning error while reading*) This indicates a head clog. Clean the drive four times and record the failure on the label of the cartridge that was inside the drive when the error was reported. Replace any cartridges that fail two out of three times (or three out of five times).

03/XX/BE (*Error while writing*) "XX" indicates any number. This indicates a head clog. Clean the drive four times and record the failure on the label of the cartridge that was inside the drive when the error was reported. Replace any cartridges that fail two out of three times (or three out of five times).

03/XX/BF (*Error while reading*) "XX" indicates any number. This indicates a head clog. Clean the drive four times and record the failure on the label of the cartridge that was inside the drive when the error was reported. Replace any cartridges that fail two out of three times (or three out of five times).

04/44/80 (*Hardware compression fault*) This indicates a head clog. Upgrade the firmware and clean the drive four times and record the failure on the label of the cartridge that was inside the drive when the error was reported. Replace any cartridges that fail two out of three times (or three out of five times). This sense code might also indicate a firmware error. Be sure that the drive's firmware is the very latest revision.

04/44/A0 (*Unknown error*) The error always indicates a head clog. Clean the drive four times and record the failure on the label of the cartridge that was inside the drive when the error was reported. Replace any cartridges that fail two out of three times (or three out of five times).

04/44/A1 (*Unknown error*) This error is typically reported after an 04/44/A0 error and indicates a head clog. Upgrade the drive's firmware to the latest version, which will usually detect an error more accurately.

TABLE 42-6   INDEX OF MEDIA AND HARDWARE ERROR SENSE CODES (CONTINUED)

04/44/AF (*Tape reel error*) There is a media or drive-tape reel error. If this sense code is reported only intermittently, replace the defective tape cartridge. If this sense code is reported on every tape (even after a power reset to the drive), the motors that turn the reels on the tape cartridge are not working and the drive must be replaced.

04/44/B4 (*Tape process internal error*) This is a general tape error, and it can usually be detailed by upgrading the drive's firmware (the latest versions of firmware expand this error into multiple codes). Upgrade the drive's firmware to the latest version.

04/44/B9 (*Erase failure*) There is a potential marginal prism issue. Replace the tape cartridge. This may be a falsely reported dew sensor error. Replace the drive.

04/46/00 (*Unsuccessful soft reset*) This is a firmware error usually seen with 4mm DAT drivers for Windows NT). Upgrade the drive's firmware to the latest version.

04/82/80 (*Dew indicator*) This error indicates that moisture has condensed in the drive. Replace the drive.

05/3B/0D (*Destination element is full*) This means that the software issued a command to the drive to move a cartridge into either the drive or a slot in the magazine that is full or already has a cartridge in that particular location. This usually occurs if the application lost track of where the cartridges are located. Re-inventory the cartridge magazine.

05/3B/0E (*Source element empty*) This means that the software issued a command to the drive to eject the tape cartridge, but no cartridge is currently inside the drive. On the autoloader, the software might be requesting to move a cartridge from the magazine to the drive and the magazine slot is empty. This is usually reported after automating cleaning. The drive automatically ejects the cartridge after it is finished cleaning, but the application still issues the Eject command. This error message can often be disregarded.

SYMPTOMS

Symptom 42-1.   The tape drive does not work at all   Begin your repair by checking for obvious setup-and-configuration errors. First, be sure that power is available to the drive (a power indicator will usually be lit on the drive). An internal tape drive is usually powered from the host computer, so be sure that the internal 4-pin power connector is correctly attached. External drives are almost always powered from a separate ac adapter or power supply, but a few proprietary drives can be powered through their interface cables. Check the output of any external ac adapter or power supply. If the ac adapter output is low or non-existent, replace the ac adapter.

Check that the interface cable between drive and tape-controller card is connected properly. Also check that your backup software is running and properly configured to your particular drive. If you are troubleshooting a new, unproved installation, inspect the tape-controller board address, interrupt, and DMA settings as necessary—configuration conflicts can lock up a software package or render a drive inoperative. Check the tape itself to be sure it is inserted properly and completely.

If power, interface cables, and software setup check properly, your trouble is likely in your drive or host controller. Ideally, your next step would be to isolate further by substitution. Try a known-good tape drive and/or controller card in your system. For most of us, however, tape drives are few and far between, so simply "plugging in" a compatible system from a friend or colleague is not nearly as likely as it would be with floppy or even hard drives.

If your tape drive is being controlled by an ordinary floppy-drive controller board, turn system power off and try disconnecting your tape drive and plugging in a floppy drive. When power is restored, you might have to disable any TSRs installed (to manage the tape drive) and change the CMOS system setup so that the floppy drive will be recognized. If your test floppy drive works properly, you can be confident that the controller board works properly. The problem is then likely in your tape drive or the problem is still in your tape system setup. If you cannot get the test floppy drive to work, the floppy-controller board might be defective, so try a new controller board. If a new controller board supports the test floppy drive, return the floppy drive to its original port, re-install the tape drive, restore the system setup for the tape drive, and try the tape drive again.

As an alternative to hardware swapping, many drives are now shipped with a simple diagnostic routine on the installation disk. Try a diagnostic if it is available. If a diagnostic recognizes the controller, but not the drive, the drive is either defective, or is connected or setup incorrectly. You might see an error message, such as "No tape drive found." If the diagnostic does not recognize the tape controller at all, the controller is probably defective, or the controller is configured improperly. A typical error message might be something like "No tape controller found."

Symptom 42-2. The tape does not read or write, but the tape and head seem to move properly You will probably find read/write errors indicated by your backup software. Start your repair by inspecting the tape cartridge itself. The cartridge should be inserted completely and properly into the drive, and sit firmly over the reel (Fig. 42-10). If the current tape is inserted properly, try loading from another tape. Old tapes might have degraded to a point where data can no longer be read or written reliably. If an

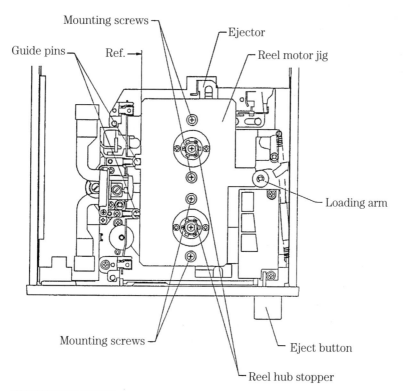

FIGURE 42-10   **Carriage view of a Teac tape drive.** Teac America, Inc.

alternate tape works properly, discard and replace the old tape. If problems persist, try cleaning the tape drive's R/W heads. Excessive buildups of dust or residual oxides can easily interfere with normal tape recording/playback operations. If you still encounter R/W trouble, the R/W heads or their associated circuitry has probably failed. Try replacing the tape drive.

Symptom 42-3. The R/W head does not step from track to track The remainder of the drive appears to work properly. This problem might also result in tape read or write errors. The head assembly must step across very small tracks laid out along the width of the tape. Depending on the vintage of tape and drive you are faced with, the tape might have 9 to 144 tracks. When the tape reaches its end, the head is positioned to another track, tape direction reverses, and reading or writing continues. Two physical elements are responsible for positioning a R/W head: a head-stepping motor and a mechanism called the *head-seek assembly*. A defect or jam in either one of these components can prevent the head from moving. You can see the stepping motor in the underside view of Fig. 42-11.

Check the LED/sensor pair that detect the EOT/BOT holes. If the LED transmitter or phototransistor receiver is defective, the drive will not know when to switch tracks. Remove the tape and place your multimeter across the receiving sensor. As you alternately pass and interrupt the light path from transmitter to receiver, you should see the logic output from the detector sensor switch from logic 1 to logic 0 (or vice versa). If the sensor does not work, replace the LED and phototransistor, and try the sensor pair again. If the sensor pair still malfunctions, replace the drive's control PC board, or replace the entire drive. If problems persist, the drive's control circuitry has probably failed. Try replacing the drive.

Symptom 42-4. The tape does not move or its speed does not remain constant When a tape is set into motion for reading or writing, it is vitally important that

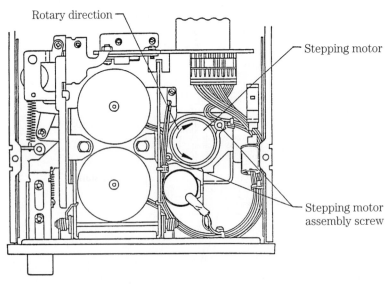

FIGURE 42-11   **Underside view of a tape-drive mechanism.** Teac America, Inc.

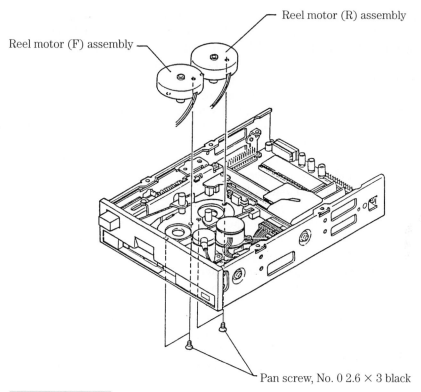

Reel motor (R) assembly

Reel motor (F) assembly

Pan screw, No. 0 2.6 × 3 black

FIGURE 42-12 **A Teac tape drive with drive motors removed.** Teac
America, Inc.

tape speed remain constant. Tape speed is a function of the reel motors and the encoder,
which produces speed feedback signals. Begin by removing the tape and check for any accumulation of dust and debris that might be interfering with drive operation. Carefully
clear away any obstruction that you might find.

If the tape does not move, check the dc motor signal across the reel motor(s) with your
multimeter. When activated, about +12 Vdc should be across the appropriate motor (forward or reverse motor, depending on the tape's initial direction). If no excitation voltage
is present, a fault is probably in the drive's control PC board. Try replacing the drive-control PC board or replace the entire drive. If drive voltage is present, but the tape does not
turn, replace both reel motors as in Fig. 42-12 or replace the drive.

If the reel motors turn as expected, but their speed is not constant, the problem might be
in the encoder. Tape is normally kept in contact with a rubber encoder roller. As a tape
moves, the encoder roller turns and spins the encoder. Pulse signals from the encoder are
used by the drive-control PC board to regulate reel motor speed. Check the encoder roller.
Tighten the encoder roller if it is loose or worn. A heavily worn encoder roller should be
replaced. Be sure that one roller turn results in one encoder turn—the roller must not slip
on the encoder shaft. Place your logic probe on the encoder output and check for pulses as
the tape moves. If there are no pulses, replace the defective encoder or replace the drive.
If pulses are present, replace the drive's control PC board or replace the entire drive.

Symptom 42-5. There are problems in loading or ejecting the tape Most of the mechanisms for loading or unloading a tape are incorporated directly into the drive chassis itself. Physical abuse and the accumulation of dust and debris can eventually cause problems in your tape-handling mechanisms. Before you disassemble your drive, however, check your tape very carefully. Old tapes can jam or wear out, and some tapes (such as Teac's digital cassette) can only be inserted into the drive in one orientation. Try a fresh tape and be sure that the tape is inserted properly into the drive.

If the tape continues to load or unload with resistance, expose the drive's mechanical assemblies and inspect all levers and linkages (such as in Fig. 42-13) for any signs of obstruction or damage. Gently clear away any obstructions that you might find. You might wish to use a fresh, dry cotton swab to wipe away any accumulations of debris. Do not add any lubricant to the load/unload mechanism, unless lubricant was there to begin with. Then, use only the same type of lubricant. Replace any components that show signs of unusual wear. Use extreme caution when working with tape assemblies. Mechanical systems are very precisely designed, so make careful notes and assembly diagrams during disassembly. An improperly reassembled mechanical system might damage the tape or hold the tape in an improper position, resulting in read/write or motor-speed errors. If you cannot rectify the problem, replace the drive outright.

Symptom 42-6. The drive writes to write-protected tapes When a tape is write protected, the drive should not be able to write to that protected tape. Your first step should be to remove and inspect the tape itself. Check to be sure that the write-protect lever is in the "protect" position. If the protect lever is not in the right place, the tape is

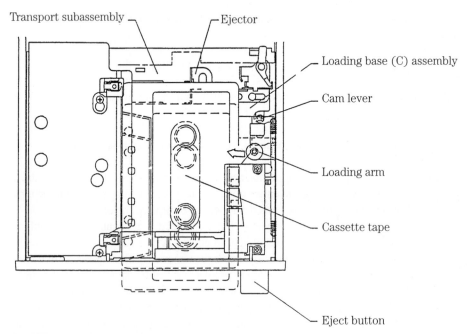

FIGURE 42-13   Close-up view of a carriage load/unload mechanism. Teac America, Inc.

vulnerable to writing. If the tape-protect lever is set properly, expose the drive mechanism and place your voltmeter across the sensor's output. Alternately, interrupt and free the optoisolator beam by hand and watch the sensor's output on your multimeter. If the output switches logic levels as you actuate the sensor manually, the trouble is probably in your drive's control PC board. Replace the drive-control PC board or replace the entire drive. If the output does not shift logic levels as expected, the sensor might be defective. Replace the write-protect sensor and repeat your test. If the sensor remains inoperative, replace the drive-control PC board or replace the entire drive.

Symptom 42-7. The drive does not recognize the beginning or end of the tape A tape drive must know when the end or beginning of a tape has been reached. The majority of tapes use a series of small holes at each end of the tape. An optoisolator provides a pulse signal to the drive-control PC board when holes pass by. Begin by removing the tape and checking for the presence of end holes. The wrong type of tape (i.e., a tape without holes) can cause problems for the drive. If the wrong type of tape is being used, retry the system using the correct type of tape.

Focus next on the BOT/EOT sensor, which is an optoisolator located across the tape path (an LED on one side and a detector on the other). Remove the tape, expose the system, and place your multimeter across the detector's output. Alternately, interrupt and free the light path by hand and watch the detector's output on your multimeter. If the output switches logic levels as expected, the trouble is probably in your drive's control PC board. Replace the drive-control PC board, or replace the entire drive. If the output does not shift as expected, replace the LED source and detector elements together, then retest the sensor pair. If the sensor remains inoperative, replace the drive-control PC board or replace the entire drive.

Symptom 42-8. A software program using a hardware copy-protection device on the parallel port locks up This symptom is typical of parallel-port tape drives. The backup software attempts to communicate with the tape drive, but it winds up communicating with the copy-protection device (a.k.a. dongle) instead. You can either switch the tape to a free parallel port or remove the copy-protection device.

Symptom 42-9. The backup software indicates "Too many bad sectors" on the tape You might also see an error such as "Error correction failed." This type of error generally indicates that more than 5% of the sectors on a tape are unreadable. In many cases, this is caused by dirty R/W heads. Try cleaning the R/W head assembly. If problems continue, try a new tape cartridge. If problems persist, check the drive's power and signal cables and be sure that they are installed properly and completely.

Symptom 42-10. The tape backup software produces a "Tape drive error XX," where XX is a specific fault type The fault type will depend on the particular drive and tape backup software you are using, so refer to the user manual for exact code meanings. The following code examples are for Colorado tape-backup software:

■ **0Ah** *Broken or dirty tape* Clean the R/W heads carefully and replace the tape (if broken).
■ **0Bh** *Gain error* Reformat the tape before attempting a backup.

■ **1Ah** *Power-on reset occurred* Check the drive's power and signal connections and try again.

■ **1Bh** *Software reset occurred* Shut down any application that might be conflicting with the tape-backup software.

■ **04h** *Drive motor jammed* Remove the tape and be sure that nothing (including the tape) is blocking the motor(s). Insert a new tape and try the system again.

Symptom 42-11. The tape drive is not found by the backup software There are several possible reasons for this problem. First, the tape backup software must be compatible with the particular tape drive and operating system. For example, the Micro Solutions Backpack tape drive is only supported by the BPBackup Windows 95 software program that is packaged with the drive itself. If you're using the Windows 95 native backup utility, you might not be able to access the drive. If you know the backup software is correct for your drive, the drive (or its controller board) might not be installed or configured properly.

When using a parallel-port tape drive, you might encounter such "Not detected" or "Not found" errors because of an IRQ conflict between the parallel port and other devices in the system. LPT1 typically uses IRQ7, and LPT2 often uses IRQ5. However, sound boards often use IRQ5 also. If you lose tape drive capability after installing new hardware, check the configuration of your new hardware. "Not Found/Not Detected" errors could also indicate that the parallel port is using a non-standard parallel-port data-transfer mode. Most parallel-port backup software will automatically detect and utilize IEEE-1284 compatible *Enhanced Parallel Ports (EPP)*. Some non-standard EPP ports (or parallel ports configured for other types of high-speed data transfer) might cause the backup software to report problems. Try changing the port mode in CMOS setup.

Some notebook and desktop computers with multimedia sound chips integrated onto the motherboard must be reconfigured in the Windows *Control panel* under *Drivers—Setup*. Change *ESS audio driver* or *Microsoft Windows sound system* to IRQ5 or IRQ10, then re-start Windows.

Symptom 42-12. The tape drive works in DOS, but refuses to work in Windows 95 First, be sure that the backup software you're using under Windows 95 is able to detect the tape drive. If the backup software is working properly, chances are that one or more Windows 95 drivers are interfering with the tape drive. Try starting Windows 95 in the safe mode and try your tape access again. If the tape drive is accessible now, you're going to have to check for driver conflicts. This often happens with parallel-port tape backups when Windows 95 drivers block parallel-port access using third-party printer drivers loaded by SYSTEM.INI. You should check the [386Enh] section of SYSTEM.INI and use semi-colons to "remark out" any offending "device=" lines.

Symptom 42-13. The backup software generates an overlay error, such as "Could not open file: QBACKUP.OVL" Failure to open overlay files are often caused by insufficient buffers. For example, you should usually have a BUFFERS=30 or higher entry in your CONFIG.SYS file. Otherwise, the backup utility might not function properly. If you do edit changes to your CONFIG.SYS file, remember to save your changes before rebooting the computer.

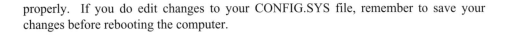

Always have backup copies of your CONFIG.SYS and AUTOEXEC.BAT files available before making changes to them. That way, you can easily restore your original startup files, if necessary, without having to re-edit the files.

Symptom 42-14. An error occurs when using older versions of backup software (e.g., "General tape failure: 187") This was a common problem with older parallel-port tape-backup systems, and was usually caused by timing problems in the parallel-port signals—the software was unable to utilize the parallel port at its proper timing. In virtually all cases, such problems are eliminated in new versions of backup software. Check the backup software version. Update older software as appropriate.

Symptom 42-15. "Media errors," "bad block errors," "system errors," or "lock-ups" occur These types of problems are known to occur with Travan tapes. Consider several possible problems. First, try removing and reinserting the Travan data cartridge. In many cases, this allows the drive mechanism to clear any errors. If problems continue, try reinitializing the data cartridge (typically handled through the backup software, such as: "Tools" and "Initialize"). Notice that reinitializing the cartridge will render all data on it unusable. Finally, try disabling data compression—especially if you notice a high frequency of "shoe shining," which often results in error messages.

All TR-4 data cartridges are pre-formatted, and these TR-4 tapes cannot be re-formatted unless your tape-drive mechanism is designed to format TR-4 tapes. As a consequence, do not "bulk erase" a TR-4 cartridge using an electromagnet or similar device.

Symptom 42-16. During initialization under DOS or Windows, the SCSI tape driver (e.g., BPASPI.SYS) reports the error: "An ASPI drive was not found" In many cases, the driver's test for enhanced parallel ports is causing the problem, so try disabling the EPP test by adding a command line switch to the ASPI tape driver. For example:

```
device=\bpaspi\bpaspi.sys NOEPP
```

Notice that your particular drive mechanism and driver might use different command-line switches. Once you make the changes to CONFIG.SYS, save your changes, then turn off the tape drive and computer before rebooting the system.

Symptom 42-17. When using a Colorado Trakker tape drive, you cannot get the drive to save or restore files reliably You will probably see error messages, such as "Unable to transfer data properly. Retry the operation," "Tape header contains unexpected or invalid values," "Microsoft Backup encountered an error reading this tape. This error might be caused by an unformatted or incorrectly formatted tape. Reformat the tape, and then try again." In virtually all cases, the drive (or backup software) does not function with EPP or ECP parallel ports. You should enter the CMOS setup and change the parallel-port mode to "Compatibility Mode."

> You might not receive any error messages when you back up files, but you might then be unable to compare or restore the files. If you can restore the files, the data that is restored to your hard disk might be damaged.

Symptom 42-18. It takes much longer than you expect to perform a backup This poor backup performance might also be accompanied by poor hard-disk performance while you perform other tasks in Windows 95. A number of problems can cause this poor performance. First, it might lack available RAM—you might have too many programs open at the same time or not have enough physical RAM installed in the computer. Try closing all programs before starting the backup process. If performance does not improve, remove all programs from the *Startup* folder, and from the "load=" and "run=" lines in WIN.INI, then restart Windows 95. If performance is still poor, you might need to add more physical RAM to your computer to improve performance.

One or more of your hard disks might be running in the "Compatibility Mode." If the *Performance* tab in *System* properties shows that one or more of the hard disks in your computer is using the MS-DOS *Compatibility* mode, resolving this problem should improve performance in *Backup*. You might need a new protected-mode driver for the hard drive. Even if your hard disks are not using MS-DOS *Compatibility* mode, the speed of your backup might be affected by the overall performance of your hard disks. For example, if you are using an IDE hard disk, the performance of the hard disk might be affected by another device that is connected to the same IDE controller channel (such as CD-ROM drives). Try moving the slower device to a separate IDE controller or to the second IDE channel on an EIDE dual-port controller.

If you are using disk compression on a computer with an older CPU, hard-disk performance might not be as good as if you were not using disk compression. If you are using third-party disk compression software that uses a real-mode driver to access your compressed drives, you might be able to improve performance by replacing the real-mode driver with a protected-mode driver (contact the maker of your compression software).

Check the file fragmentation on your hard drive. Badly fragmented hard disks can affect the performance of backup software, as well as the performance of other tasks in Windows 95. Run DEFRAG to defragment your hard disks. Finally, backup software can often detect and avoid unusable sectors on a tape, but the process that it uses to do so can be time consuming. If you suspect that performance problems are caused by unusable sectors on a tape, try using a new tape or a tape that you know does not contain unusable sectors.

Symptom 42-19. When you try to format a DT-350 tape in a Conner 250 tape drive, the following message appears: "Errors occurred during this operation" In virtually all cases, this is a limitation of the tape drive itself. Most 250 tape drives cannot format DT-350 tapes. Try a tape that is compatible with the drive.

Symptom 42-20. When you try to perform a backup, restore, or compare operation in Microsoft Backup, or close Backup after performing one of

these operations, the following error message appears: "Microsoft Backup has encountered a serious error in the Memory Manager. Quit and restart Backup, and then try again" Several possible problems can cause this behavior. First, an incompatible device driver or TSR might be running on the system, which is interfering with the backup software. Try running backup from the Windows 95 safe mode. You might have trouble with your swap file. Try disabling the swap file, then restoring it. The files for your backup software might be damaged or corrupted. Try removing Backup from your Windows 95 installation, then reinstall it to ensure a fresh set of files. It is also possible that you have a damaged tape drive or tape cartridge. Try a new tape cartridge. If problems persist, try a new tape drive. Finally, you might have a fault in RAM. Run a DOS diagnostic with an aggressive RAM test and see if you can identify any failed memory. Replace defective RAM as necessary. If the defective RAM is hard-soldered to your motherboard, you might have to replace the motherboard.

Symptom 42-21. The QIC-3020 formatted tape is not recognized by tape drive for writing This is often an issue with tape controllers. Some floppy-based tape drives require a floppy controller operating at 1Mbit/s to support writing on all compatible tapes. If the floppy controller does not support at least 1Mbit/s, the drive might not be able to write to larger tapes. Try a high-speed floppy-controller board. It is probably more cost-effective to use a high-performance drive controller than to reformat the larger tape for the smaller format (which can take up to 18 hours).

Symptom 42-22. The backup software does not auto-skip busy files This is almost always a limitation of the particular backup software. You might consider upgrading to the latest version of your backup software for best performance.

Symptom 42-23. The floppy-port tape drive cannot be connected to a floppy controller This often happens with Compaq systems because Compaq floppy-controller cables are keyed differently than ordinary floppy-drive cables. Try a generic floppy-drive cable that will connect the drive to the controller.

Symptom 42-24. An error message, such as: "DMA setting specified for this device might be incorrect" appears This problem is common when using floppy-based drive accelerator controllers. First, be sure that the accelerator controller uses the same setting for DRQ and DACK signals. Next, try a different DMA setting—if necessary, try sharing DMA 2 with the floppy-drive controller. There might be a driver or TSR conflict, so shut down any screen savers or TSRs on the system. Try disabling the "high-speed burst mode" feature of the controller through Windows 95 in the *Device manager*. Finally, be sure that your SYSTEM.INI file is not loading other tape drivers (or device drivers that might be conflicting with your tape drive).

Symptom 42-25. The tape drive makes no sound when a minicartridge is inserted In virtually all cases, the tape drive is not receiving power. Check the power to your tape drive. If problems continue, it is likely to be in the drive itself. Try replacing the tape drive.

Symptom 42-26. An error message such as: "File not found in file set directory" appears This is almost always a problem with the backup software itself, rather than the drive. Try downloading and installing the latest version of the backup software. If no later version is available, try the following:

■ Deselect the backup software directory during a backup.
■ Turn off file compression.
■ Deselect the registry.

Symptom 42-27. Formatting the minicartridge lasts from 7 to 18 hours This is not necessarily a problem. The time it takes to format a data cartridge depends on the length of the tape and the mode of your controller. In QIC-3020 mode (using a 1Mbit/s or 2Mbit/s controller), it might take seven to nine hours to completely format a tape. In QIC-3010 mode (using a 500Kbit/s controller), it can last up to 18 hours. You might need to install a drive-accelerator card to use QIC-3020 pre-formatted cartridges. Try retensioning the cartridge.

Symptom 42-28. You experience low capacity, or slow read and writes to your tape drive If you connect the tape drive to a floppy controller, you might experience slower transfer rates and lower capacities than expected—transfer rates and capacities are affected by the speed of the controller. Many ordinary floppy controllers operate at 500Kbit/s, but the accelerated controller cards operate at 1Mbit/s or 2Mbit/s. At 500Kbit/s, 680MB of data can take up to 2.5 hours to back up. A 1Mbit/s accelerator card can back up that amount of data in 1.25 hours. A 2Mbit/s card takes 40 minutes. Most 386 and 486 systems will operate at 500Kbit/s, and newer 486 and Pentium systems contain floppy-controller cards that offer 1Mbit/s and 2Mbit/s speeds. Try cleaning the tape drive.

> If your minicartridge was formatted in QIC-3010 format (using a 500Kbit/s controller), you will achieve only half the capacity of a minicartridge formatted in QIC-3020 format (using a 1Mbit/s or 2Mbit/s controller). This is so—even if you are currently running off a high-speed controller.

Consider other issues. Run CHKDSK or ScanDisk to clean up any bad files or lost clusters, then defragment the disk with DEFRAG. Be sure that you are using the latest version of your backup software. You might try removing any screen savers or TSRs that might be putting an unusual load on the computer's resources. Finally, try minimizing the backup application's window under Windows 95.

Symptom 42-29. A parsing or logic error occurs This type of problem is almost always related to the backup software itself. Be sure to use the very latest version of the backup software, and be sure that the software is directly compatible with your specific tape drive and operating system.

Symptom 42-30. Space runs out during DOS backups This is almost always caused by a lack of conventional memory space, and it can happen quite frequently when using a DOS program under a window. Be sure that you have the minimum conventional memory available to run the DOS backup utility. You should also have some limited amount of hard-drive space available for creating temporary files or buffering the file transfer. Finally, be sure that you have the minimum number of buffers required in CONFIG.SYS for the backup program (often BUFFERS=40).

Symptom 42-31. Excessive "shoe shining" occurs during backups In normal tape-drive operations, the tape drive writes data to a single track from one end of the tape to another: it then writes data in a parallel data track back to the beginning of the tape, etc., until the tape is full. *Shoe shining* refers to frequent back-and-forth tape motion. If you have the backup window open, minimize it. With the window open, the system has to continually update the screen, which this takes resources away from the software sending data to the tape drive. If the PC offers a turbo mode, try disabling the turbo mode (especially when using parallel-port tape drives).

Further Study

That concludes the material for Chapter 42. Be sure to review the glossary and chapter questions on the accompanying CD. If you have access to the Internet, take a look at some of these tape-drive resources:

Computer Peripherals: **http://www.cpuinc.com/**

Exabyte: **http://www.exabyte.com/**

Seagate: **http://www.seagate.com**

Tandberg Data: **http://www.tandberg.com/**

Overland Data: **http://www.ovrland.com/**

Hewlett-Packard: **http://www.hp.com/go/colorado/**

Valitek: **http://www.valitek.com/**

43

VIDEO ADAPTERS
AND ACCELERATORS

CONTENTS AT A GLANCE

Understanding Conventional Video Adapters
  Text vs. graphics
  ROM BIOS (video bios)

Reviewing Video Display Hardware
  MDA
  CGA
  EGA
  PGA
  MCGA
  VGA
  8514
  SVGA
  XGA

Understanding Graphics Accelerators
  Key 3D-speed issues
  Video speed factors

3D Graphics-Accelerator Issues
  The 3D process
  Key 3D-speed issues
  Improving 3D performance through
    hardware

Understanding DirectX
  Pieces of a puzzle
  More on DirectDraw
  More on DirectSound
  More on DirectInput
  More on Direct3D
  More on DirectPlay
  Determining the installed version of
    DirectX

Video Feature Connectors
  AMI multimedia channel

Troubleshooting Video Adapters
  Isolating the problem area

Unusual Hardware Issues
  Clock speed and the VL bus
  "SLC" motherboards and the VL bus
  8514/A and COM4 conflicts
  ATI mach, S3 vision/trio, and COM4
    conflicts
  Award video BIOS glitch
  Symptoms

Further Study

The monitor itself is merely an output device (a peripheral) that translates synchronized analog or TTL video signals into a visual image. Of course, a monitor alone is not good for very much—except perhaps as a conversation piece or a room heater. The next logical question is: "where does the video signal come from?" All video signals displayed on a monitor are produced by a video-adapter circuit (Fig. 43-1). The term *adapter* is often used because the PC is "adapted" to the particular monitor through this circuit. In most cases, the video adapter is an expansion board that plugs into the PC's available bus slots. The video adapter that converts raw data from the PC into image data, is stored in the adapter's video memory. The exact amount of memory available depends on the particular adapter and the video modes that the adapter is designed to support. Simple adapters offer as little as 256KB, and the latest adapters provide 4MB or more. The video adapter then translates the contents of video memory into corresponding video signals that drive a monitor.

The actual operations of a video adapter are certainly more involved than described, but you can begin to appreciate the crucial role that the video adapter plays in a PC. If a video adapter fails, the monitor will display gibberish (or nothing at all). To complicate matters even further, many current software applications require small device drivers (called *video drivers*). A video driver is a rather small program that allows an application to access a video adapter's high-resolution or high-color video modes (usually for SVGA operation) with little or no interaction from the system BIOS. During troubleshooting, it will be necessary for you to isolate display problems to either the monitor, the video adapter, or the driver software before a solution can be found. This chapter explains the operation and troubleshooting of typical 2D and 3D video adapters.

Understanding Conventional Video Adapters

The conventional frame buffer is the oldest and most well-established type of video adapter. The term *frame buffer* refers to the adapter's operation—image data is loaded and

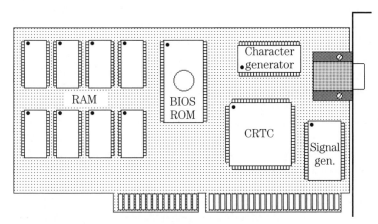

FIGURE 43-1   **A typical video-adapter board.**

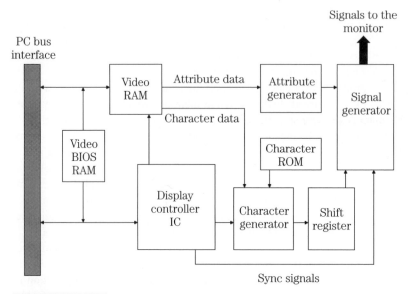

FIGURE 43-2   **Block diagram of a frame-buffer video adapter.**

stored in video memory one "frame" at a time. Frame buffer architecture (Fig. 43-2) has changed very little since PCs first started displaying text and graphics. The heart of the frame-buffer video adapter is the highly integrated display controller IC (sometimes called a *CRTC, Cathode-Ray Tube Controller*). The CRTC generates control signals and supervises adapter operation. The CRTC reads *Video RAM (VRAM)* contents and passes those contents along for further processing. Many new video boards use specially designed IC groups (*chipsets*) that are intended to work together. Chipsets provide fast, efficient video performance while minimizing the amount of circuitry needed on a video adapter.

TEXT VS. GRAPHICS

Video RAM also plays a vital role because the RAM holds the image data to be displayed. The video adapter can operate in two modes: text and graphic. In the text mode, ASCII characters are stored in video RAM. A character ROM, character generator, and shift register produce the pixel patterns that form ASCII screen characters. The character ROM holds a pixel pattern for every possible ASCII character (including letters, numbers, and punctuation). The character generator converts ROM data into a sequence of pixel bits and transfers them to a shift register. The shift register produces a bit stream. At the same time, an attribute decoder determines whether the defined ASCII character is to be displayed as blinking, inverted, high-intensity, standard text, or a text color (for color monitors). The signal generator is responsible for turning the ASCII serial-bit stream from the shift register into the video and synchronization signals that actually drive the monitor. The signal generator might produce either analog or TTL video signals, depending on how the particular monitor is to be operated. Today, virtually all color graphic monitors operate from analog video signals.

In the graphic mode, video RAM locations contain the color/gray-scale information for each screen pixel, rather than ASCII characters, so the character ROM and character-generating circuitry used in text mode is bypassed. For example, monochrome graphics use a single bit per pixel, 16-color graphics use 4 bits per pixel, 256 color graphics use 8 bits per pixel, etc. Pixel data taken from VRAM by the CRTC is passed through the character generator without any changes. Data is then sent directly to the shift register and on to the signal generator. The signal generator produces analog or TTL video signals along with sync signals, as dictated by the CRTC.

ROM BIOS (VIDEO BIOS)

One part of the classic video adapter has not been mentioned, the video BIOS. The display controller requires substantial instruction changes when it is switched from text mode to any one of its available graphics modes. Because the instructions required to re-configure and direct the CRTC depend on its particular design (and the video-board design, in general), it is impossible to rely on the software application or the PC's BIOS to provide the required software. As a result, all video adapters from EGA on use local BIOS ROM to hold the firmware needed by the particular display controller. Current PC architecture allocates about 128KB of space from C0000h to DFFFFh within the upper memory area. This space is reserved for devices with expansion ROMs, such as hard-drive controllers and video adapters. Motherboard BIOS works in conjunction with the video BIOS, which is detected during the POST.

Reviewing Video Display Hardware

The early days of PC development left users with a simple choice between monochrome or color graphics (all video adapters support text modes). In the years that followed, however, the proliferation of video adapters have brought an array of video modes and standards that you should be familiar with before upgrading a PC or attempting to troubleshoot a video system. This part of the chapter explains each of the video standards that have been developed in the last 15 years and shows you the video modes that each standard offers. Table 43-1 provides a comprehensive listing of the standard hardware-supported video modes, along with the most popular software-supported (i.e., video-driver supported) video modes.

TABLE 43-1 INDEX OF VIDEO MODES

MODE	RESOLUTION	COLORS	HORZ. (KHZ)	VERT. (HZ)
00h	40 × 25	16	31.5	70
01h	40 × 25	16	31.5	70
02h	80 × 25	16	31.5	70
03h	80 × 25	16	31.5	70
04h	320 × 200	4	31.5	70
05h	320 × 200	4	31.5	70
06h	640 × 200	2	31.5	70
07h	80 × 25	Mono	31.5	70
0Dh	320 × 200	16	31.5	70
0Eh	640 × 200	16	31.5	70
0Fh	640 × 350	Mono	31.5	70

TABLE 43-1 INDEX OF VIDEO MODES (CONTINUED)

MODE	RESOLUTION	COLORS	HORZ. (KHZ)	VERT. (HZ)
10h	640 × 350	16	31.5	70
11h	640 × 480	2	31.5	60
12h	640 × 480	16	31.5	60
13h	320 × 200	256	31.5	70
54h	132 × 43	16	31.5	70
55h	132 × 25	16	31.5	70
100h	640 × 480	256	31.3	70
101h	640 × 480	256	31.3	60
101h	640 × 480	256	38.0	72
101h	640 × 480	256	37.6	75
102h	800 × 600	16	35.3	56
102h	800 × 600	16	37.8	60
102h	800 × 600	16	48.1	72
102h	800 × 600	16	47.4	75
103h	800 × 600	256	35.3	56
103h	800 × 600	256	37.8	60
103h	800 × 600	256	48.1	72
103h	800 × 600	256	47.4	75
104h	1024 × 768	16	35.1	43.5 interlaced
104h	1024 × 768	16	48.1	60
104h	1024 × 768	16	56.2	70
104h	1024 × 768	16	59.8	75
105h	1024 × 768	256	35.1	43.5 interlaced
105h	1024 × 768	256	48.1	60
105h	1024 × 768	256	56.2	70
105h	1024 × 768	256	59.8	75
106h	1280 × 1024	16	47.7	43.5 interlaced
107h	1280 × 1024	256	47.7	43.5 interlaced
107h	1280 × 1024	256	63.1	60
107h	1280 × 1024	256	77.7	72
107h	1280 × 1024	256	79.7	75
110h	640 × 480	32K	31.4	60
110h	640 × 480	32K	37.8	72
110h	640 × 480	32K	37.2	75
111h	640 × 480	64K	31.4	60
111h	640 × 480	64K	37.8	72
111h	640 × 480	64K	37.2	75
112h	640 × 480	16.8M	31.4	60
112h	640 × 480	16.8M	37.8	72
112h	640 × 480	16.8M	37.5	75
113h	800 × 600	32K	37.8	60
113h	800 × 600	32K	48.0	72
113h	800 × 600	32K	47.2	76
114h	800 × 600	64K	37.8	60

TABLE 43-1   INDEX OF VIDEO MODES (CONTINUED)

MODE	RESOLUTION	COLORS	HORZ. (KHZ)	VERT. (HZ)
114h	800 × 600	64K	48.0	72
114h	800 × 600	64K	47.2	76
115h	800 × 600	16.8M	37.8	60
116h	1024 × 768	32K	35.2	43.5 interlaced
116h	1024 × 768	32K	48.1	60
116h	1024 × 768	32K	56.2	70
116h	1024 × 768	32K	60.0	75
117h	1024 × 768	64K	35.2	43.5 interlaced
117h	1024 × 768	64K	48.1	60
117h	1024 × 768	64K	56.2	70
117h	1024 × 768	64K	60.0	75
201h	640 × 480	256	31.3	60
201h	640 × 480	256	38.0	72
201h	640 × 480	256	37.6	75
203h	800 × 600	256	36.1	56
203h	800 × 600	256	37.8	60
203h	800 × 600	256	48.1	72
203h	800 × 600	256	47.4	75
205h	1024 × 768	256	35.1	43.5 interlaced
205h	1024 × 768	256	48.1	60
205h	1024 × 768	256	56.2	70
205h	1024 × 768	256	59.8	75
207h	1152 × 864	256	54.9	60
208h	1280 × 1024	16	47.7	43.5 interlaced
208h	1280 × 1024	16	63.1	60
208h	1280 × 1024	16	77.9	72
208h	1280 × 1024	16	79.7	75

MDA (MONOCHROME DISPLAY ADAPTER—1981)

The *Monochrome Display Adapter (MDA)* is the oldest video adapter available for the PC. Text is available in 80-column × 25-row format using 9- × 14-pixel characters. Being a text-only system, MDA offered no graphics capability, but it achieved popularity because of its relatively low cost, good text-display quality, and integrated printer (LPT) port. Figure 43-3 shows the video connector pinout for an MDA board. The 9-pin monitor connection uses four active TTL signals: intensity, video, horizontal, and vertical. Video and intensity signals provide the on/off and high/low intensity information for each pixel. The horizontal and vertical signals control the monitor's synchronization. MDA boards have long been obsolete and the probability of your encountering one is remote at best.

CGA (COLOR GRAPHICS ADAPTER—1981)

The *Color Graphics Adapter (CGA)* was the first to offer color text and graphics modes for the PC. A 160-x-200 low-resolution mode offered 16 colors, but such low resolution received

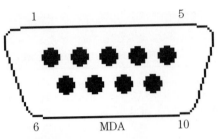

1. Ground
2. Ground
3. n/a
4. n/a
5. n/a
6. (+) Intensity
7. (+) video
8. (+) Horizontal sync
9. (−) Vertical sync

FIGURE 43-3   **Pinout of an MDA video connector.**

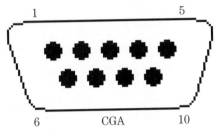

1. Ground
2. Ground
3. Red
4. Green
5. Blue
6. Intensity
7. n/a
8. Horizontal sync
9. Vertical sync

FIGURE 43-4   **Pinout of a CGA video connector.**

very little attention. A 320-×-200 medium-resolution graphics mode allowed finer graphic detail, but with only four colors. The highest-resolution mode provided 640×200 at two colors (usually black and one other color). The relationship between resolution and colors is important because a CGA frame requires 16KB of video RAM. 640-×-200 resolution results in 128,000 pixels. With eight bits able to represent eight pixels, $(128,000/8) = 16,000$ bytes are adequate. 320-×-200 resolution results in 64,000 pixels, but with two bits needed to represent one pixel (four pixels/byte), $(64,000/4) = 16,000$ bytes are still enough. You can see that video RAM is directly related to video capacity. Because typically much more video RAM is available than is needed for an image, video boards support multiple video pages. Figure 43-4 shows the pinout for a typical CGA video connector. As with the earlier MDA design, CGA video signals reserve pins 1 and 2 as ground lines, while the horizontal sync signal is produced on pin 8 and the vertical sync signal is produced on pin 9. CGA is strictly a digital display system with TTL signals used on the Red (3), Green (4), Blue (5), and Intensity (6) lines.

EGA (ENHANCED GRAPHICS ADAPTER—1984)

It was not long before the limitations of CGA became painfully apparent. The demand for higher resolutions and color depths drove designers to introduce the next generation of video adapter, known as the *Enhanced Graphics Adapter (EGA)*. One of the unique appeals of EGA was its backward compatibility—an EGA board would emulate CGA and MDA modes on the proper monitor, as well as its native resolutions and color depths when using an EGA monitor. EGA is known for its 320-× 200-×-16, 640-×-200-×-16, and 640-× -350-×-16 video modes. More memory is needed for EGA and 128KB is common for EGA boards (although many boards could be expanded to 256KB).

The EGA connector pinout is illustrated in Fig. 43-5. TTL signals are used to provide Primary Red (3), Primary Green (4), and Primary Blue (5) color signals. By adding a set of secondary color signals (or color-intensity signals), such as Red Intensity (2), Green Intensity (6), and Blue Intensity (7), the total of six color-control signals allow the EGA to produce up to 64 possible colors. Although 64 colors are possible, only 16 of those colors are available in the palette at any one time. Pin 8 carries the horizontal sync signal, pin 9 carries the vertical sync signal, and pin 1 remains ground.

PGA (PROFESSIONAL GRAPHICS ADAPTER—1984)

The *Professional Graphics Adapter (PGA)* was also introduced in 1984. This system offered a then-revolutionary display capability of $640 \times 480 \times 256$. Three-dimensional rotation and graphic clipping was included as a hardware function, and the adapter could update the display at 60 frames per second. The PGA was incredibly expensive and beyond reach of all but the most serious business user. In actual operation, a PGA system required two or three expansion boards, so it also represented a serious commitment of limited system space. Ultimately, PGA failed to capture any significant market acceptance. It is unlikely that you will ever encounter a PGA board—most that ever saw service in PCs have long since been upgraded.

MCGA (MULTI-COLOR GRAPHICS ARRAY—1987)

The *Multi-Color Graphics Array (MCGA)* had originally been integrated into the motherboard of IBM's PS/2-25 and PS/2-30. MCGA supports all of the CGA video modes, and also offers several new video modes, including a 320-x-200-x-256 mode that had become a preferred mode for game software of the day. MCGA was one of the first graphic systems to use analog color signals, rather than TTL signals. Analog signals were necessary to allow MCGA to produce its 256 colors using only three primary color lines (red, green, and blue, "RGB").

IBM also took used a new, high-density 15-pin sub-miniature "D-type" connector as shown in Fig. 43-6. One of the striking differences between the "analog" connector and older TTL connectors is the use of individual ground lines for each color. Careful grounding is vital because any signal noise on the analog lines will result in color anomalies. If you inspect a video cable closely, you will find that one or both ends are terminated with a square metal box, which actually contains a noise filter. It is important to

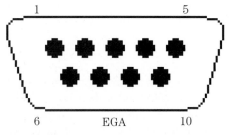

1.	Ground
2.	Red intensity
3.	Primary red
4.	Primary green
5.	Primary blue
6.	Green intensity
7.	Blue intensity
8.	Horizontal sync
9.	Vertical sync

FIGURE 43-5   Pinout of an EGA video connector.

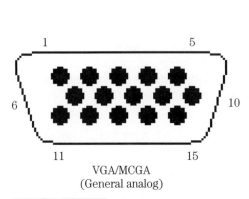

1. Red
2. Green
3. Blue
4. Ground
5. Ground
6. Red ground
7. Green ground
8. Blue ground
9. n/a
10. Ground
11. Ground
12. n/a
13. Horizontal sync
14. Vertical sync
15. n/a

VGA/MCGA
(General analog)

FIGURE 43-6   Pinout of a VGA/MCGA/SVGA video connector.

realize that although the MCGA could emulate CGA modes, older TTL monitors were no longer compatible with analog RGB signal levels.

Although a number of notable technical improvements went into the PS/2 design, none of them could assure broad acceptance of the PS/2 series. However, the MCGA ushered in a new age of analog display technology, and virtually all subsequent video adapters now use the 15-pin analog format (Fig. 43-6). Although MCGA adapters are also (technically) obsolete, the standard lives on in MCGA's cousins, VGA and SVGA.

VGA (VIDEO GRAPHICS ARRAY—1987)

The *Video Graphics Array (VGA)* was introduced along with MCGA and implemented in other members of IBM's PS/2 series. The line between MCGA and VGA has always been a bit fuzzy because both were introduced simultaneously (both using the same 15-pin video connector), and VGA can handle every mode that MCGA could. For all practical purposes, we can say that MCGA is a subset of VGA.

VGA provides the familiar 640-×-480-×-16 screen mode, which has become the baseline for Microsoft Windows 95 "SafeMode" displays. The use of analog color signals allow VGA systems to produce a palette of 16 colors from 262,144 possible colors. VGA also provides backward compatibility for all older screen modes. Although the PS/2 line has been discontinued, the flexibility and backward compatibility of VGA proved so successful that VGA adapters were soon developed for the PC. For a time, VGA support was considered to be "standard equipment" for all new PCs sold, but SVGA boards are rapidly replacing VGA systems, and most SVGA adapters offer full VGA support.

8514 (1987)

The 8514/A video adapter is a high-resolution system also developed for the PS/2. In addition to full support for MDA, CGA, EGA, and VGA modes, the 8514/A can display 256 colors at 640 × 480 and 1024 × 768 (interlaced) resolutions. Unfortunately, the 8514/A was a standard ahead of its time. The lack of available software and the demise of the PS/2 line doomed the 8514/A to extinction before it could become an accepted standard. Today, the XGA is rapidly becoming the PC standard for high-resolution/high-color display systems on MicroChannel PC platforms.

SVGA (SUPER VIDEO GRAPHICS ARRAY)

Ever since VGA became the de-facto standard for PC graphics, there has been a strong demand from PC users to move beyond the 640-x-480-x-16 limit imposed by "conventional" VGA to provide higher resolutions and color depths. As a result, a new generation of extended or super VGA (SVGA) adapters have moved into the PC market. Unlike VGA, which adhered to strict hardware configurations, there is no generally accepted standard on which to develop an SVGA board—each manufacturer makes an SVGA board that supports a variety of different (not necessarily compatible) video modes. For example, one manufacturer might produce an SVGA board capable of $1024 \times 768 \times 65,000$, and another manufacturer might produce a board that only reaches $640 \times 480 \times 16,000,000$ (more than 16 million colors).

This mixing and matching of resolutions and color depths has resulted in a very fractured market—no two SVGA boards are necessarily capable of the same things. This proliferation of video hardware also makes it impossible for applications software to take advantage of super video modes without supplemental software, called *video drivers*. Video drivers are device drivers (loaded before an application program is started) that allow the particular program to work with the SVGA board hardware. Video drivers are typically developed by the board manufacturer and shipped on a floppy disk with the board. Windows and Windows 95 takes particular advantage of video drivers because the Windows interface allows all Windows applications to use the same graphics system, rather than having to write a driver for every application as DOS drivers must be. Using an incorrect, obsolete, or corrupted video driver can be a serious source of problems for SVGA installations. The one common attribute of SVGA boards is that most offer full support for conventional VGA (which requires no video drivers), so Windows can always be started in the conventional 640-x-480-x-16 VGA mode. Only a handful of SVGA board manufacturers abandon conventional VGA support.

Today, most SVGA boards offer terrific video performance, a wide selection of modes, and extremely reasonable prices. If it were not for the lack of standardization in SVGA adapters, VGA would likely be considered obsolete already. The *Video Electronics Standards Association (VESA)* has started the push for SVGA standards by proposing and supporting the VESA BIOS Extension—a universal video driver. The extension (now at version 2.0) provides a uniform set of functions that allow application programs to detect a card's capabilities and use the optimum adapter configuration, regardless of how the particular board's hardware is designed. Virtually all of the SVGA boards in production today support the VESA BIOS Extensions, and it is worthwhile to recommend boards that support VESA SVGA. Some SVGA boards even incorporate the extensions into the video BIOS ROM, which saves the RAM space that would otherwise be needed by a video driver.

XGA (1990)

The XGA and XGA/2 are 32-bit high-performance video adapters developed by IBM to support MicroChannel-based PCs. XGA design with MicroChannel architecture allows the adapter to take control of the system for rapid data transfers. MDA, CGA, EGA, and

VGA modes are all supported for backward compatibility. In addition, several color depths are available at 1024-x-768 resolution, and a photo-realistic 65,536 colors are available at 640-x-480 resolution. To improve performance even further, fast video RAM and a graphics co-processor are added to the XGA design. For the time being, XGA is limited to high-performance applications in MicroChannel systems. The migration to ISA-based PCs has been slow because the ISA bus is limited to 16 bits and does not support bus-mastering as micro-channel busses do. For PCs, SVGA adapters using the high-performance PCI (or even the AGP) bus will likely provide extended screen modes as they continue to grow in sophistication as graphics accelerators.

Understanding Graphics Accelerators

When screen resolutions approach or surpass 640×480, the data needed to form a single screen image can be substantial. Consider a single 640-x-480-x-256 image. There are $(640 \times 480) = 307,200$ pixels. Because it has 256 colors, eight bits are needed to define the color for each pixel. Thus, 307,200 bytes are needed for every frame. If the frame must be updated 10 times per second, $(307,200 \times 10) = 3,072,000$ bytes per second (3.072MB/sec) must be moved across the bus (i.e., PCI or ISA bus). If a 65,536 color mode is being used, two bytes are needed for each pixel, so $(307,200 \times 2) = 614,400$ bytes are needed for a frame. At 10 frames per second, $(614,400 \times 10) = 6,144,000$ bytes per second (6.144MB/sec) must be moved across the bus—this is just for video information and it does not consider the needs of system overhead operations, such as memory refresh, keyboard and mouse handling, drive access, and other data-intensive system operations. When such volumes of information must be moved across an ISA bus limited at 8.33 MHz, you can see how a serious data-transfer bottleneck develops. Even the PCI bus can be strained by higher video modes. This results in painfully slow screen refreshes—especially under Windows, which requires frequent refreshes.

Video designers seek to overcome the limitations of conventional video adapters by incorporating processing power onto the video board itself, rather than relying on the system CPU for graphic processing. By off-loading work from the system CPU and assigning the graphics processing to local processing components, graphics performance can be improved by a factor of three or more. Several means of acceleration are possible, depending on the sophistication of the board (Fig. 43-7). *Fixed-function acceleration* relieves load on the system CPU by providing adapter support for a limited number of specific functions, such as BitBlt or line draws. Fixed-function accelerators were an improvement over frame buffers, but they do not offer the performance of more-sophisticated accelerators. A graphics accelerator uses an *Application-Specific IC (ASIC)*, which intercepts graphics tasks and processes them without the intervention of the system CPU. Graphics accelerators are perhaps the most cost-effective type of accelerator. Graphics co-processors are the most sophisticated type of accelerator. The co-processor acts as a CPU, which is dedicated to handling image data. Older graphics co-processors, such as the TMS34010 and TMS34020, represent the Texas Instruments Graphical Architecture (TIGA), which is broadly used for high-end accelerators. Unfortunately, not all graphics co-processors provide increased performance to warrant the higher cost.

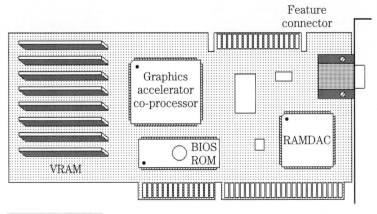

FIGURE 43-7   A typical video accelerator board.

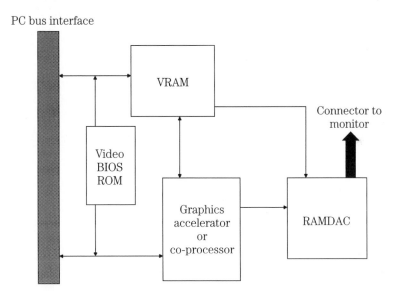

FIGURE 43-8   Block diagram of a video-accelerator board.

Figure 43-8 shows the block diagram for a typical graphics accelerator. The core of the accelerator is the graphics IC (or video chipset). The graphics IC connects directly with the PC expansion bus. Graphics commands and data are translated into pixel data, which is stored in video RAM. High-performance video memory offers a second data bus, which is routed directly to the video board's *RAMDAC (random access memory video-to-analog converter)*. The graphics IC directs RAMDAC operation and ensures that VRAM data is available. The RAMDAC then translates video data into red, green, and blue analog signals, along with horizontal and vertical synchronization signals. Output signals generated by the RAMDAC drive the monitor. This architecture might appear simple, but that is because of the extremely high level of integration of ICs and chipsets being used. Table 43-2 provides a listing of many 2D and 3D graphics chipsets in use today.

TABLE 43-2   LISTING OR POPULAR 2D AND 3D VIDEO CHIPSETS

MANUFACTURER	PRODUCT	
3DLabs	Permedia	http://www.3dlabs.com/3dlabs
3Dlabs	GLINT 300SX	
Acer Labs	ALI-M3145	
Acer Labs	ALI CAT-32/64	
Alliance Semiconductor	ProMotion-3210	
Alliance Semiconductor	ProMotion-6410	
Alliance Semiconductor	ProMotion-6422	
Alliance Semiconductor	ProMotion-AT24	
ARK Logic	ARK1000PV	
ARK Logic	ARK2000PV	
Artist Graphics	3GA Graphics Processor	http://www.artgraphics.com/
Artist Graphics	Artist 3GA	
Artist Graphics	Artist GPX	
ATI	264VT	http://www.atitech.ca/
ATI	3D RAGE	
ATI	Mach32	
ATI	Mach64	
ATI	Mach64CT	
ATI	Mach8	
Avance Logic	ALG 2032	http://www.avance.com
Avance Logic	ALG 2064	
Avance Logic	ALG 2302	
Avance Logic	ALG 2308	
Avance Logic	ALG 2364	
Avance Logic	ALG 2401	
Avance Logic	ALG 25128	
Avance Logic	ALG 2564	
Avance Logic	ALG 27000	
Avance Logic	ALG 2101	
Avance Logic	ALG 2228	
Avance Logic	ALG 2301	
Chips and Technologies	64300	http://www.chips.com
Chips and Technologies	82c455/6	
Chips and Technologies	82c452	
Chromatic Research	Mpact	http://www.mpact.com/
Cirrus Logic, Inc.	CL-GD5420	http://www.cirrus.com
Cirrus Logic, Inc.	CL-GD5421	
Cirrus Logic, Inc.	CL-GD5422	
Cirrus Logic, Inc.	CL-GD5424	
Cirrus Logic, Inc.	CL-GD5425	
Cirrus Logic, Inc.	CL-GD5426	
Cirrus Logic, Inc.	CL-GD5428	

TABLE 43-2 LISTING OR POPULAR 2D AND 3D VIDEO CHIPSETS (CONTINUED)		
MANUFACTURER	**PRODUCT**	
Cirrus Logic, Inc.	CL-GD5429	
Cirrus Logic, Inc.	CL-GD5430	
Cirrus Logic, Inc.	CL-GD5434	
Cirrus Logic, Inc.	CL-GD5434-E	
Cirrus Logic, Inc.	CL-GD5436	
Cirrus Logic, Inc.	CL-GD5440	
Cirrus Logic, Inc.	CL-GD5446	
Cirrus Logic, Inc.	CL-GD5462	
Cirrus Logic, Inc.	CL-GD54M40	
IIT (AGX)	AGX-015	
IIT (AGX)	AGX-016	
Lockheed Martin	Real3D	http://www.mmc.com/real3d/
Matrox	MGA-1064SG	http://www.matrox.com
Matrox	MGA-2064W	
NCR	77C22E+	
NCR	77C32BLT	
NVidia/SGS-THOMSON	NV1/STG-2000	http://www.nvidia.com/
Oak Technologies Inc.	OTI-057/67	http://www.oaktech.com
Oak Technologies Inc.	OTI-077	
Oak Technologies Inc.	OTI-087	
Oak Technologies Inc.	OTI-64105/107	
Oak Technologies Inc.	OTI-64111	
Oak Technologies Inc.	OTI-64217	
Realtek Semiconductor Corp.	RTG3105I	http://www.realtek.com.tw
Rendition	Vèritè	http://www.rendition.com/
S3, Inc.	Aurora64V+	http://www.s3.com
S3, Inc.	S3-801	
S3, Inc.	S3-805/805p	
S3, Inc.	S3-805i	
S3, Inc.	S3-864	
S3, Inc.	S3-868	
S3, Inc.	S3-911	
S3, Inc.	S3-924	
S3, Inc.	S3-928	
S3, Inc.	S3-964	
S3, Inc.	S3-968	
S3, Inc.	S3-ViRGE	
S3, Inc.	S3-ViRGE/VX	
S3, Inc.	Scenic/MX2	
S3, Inc.	Trio32 (732)	
S3, Inc.	Trio64 (764)	
S3, Inc.	Trio64UV+	
S3, Inc.	Trio64V+	
Sierra Semiconductor	Falcon/64	

TABLE 43-2 LISTING OR POPULAR 2D AND 3D VIDEO CHIPSETS (CONTINUED)		
MANUFACTURER	**PRODUCT**	
Sierra Semiconductor	SC15064	
S-MOS	SPC1500	http://www.smos.com/
Trident Microsystems	TGUI9420/30	http://www.trid.com
Trident Microsystems	TGUI9440AGi	
Trident Microsystems	TGUI9660/968x	
Trident Microsystems	TVGA8900CL	
Trident Microsystems	TVGA9000	
Trident Microsystems	TVGA9200Cxr	
Trident Microsystems	TVGA9400CXi	
Trident Microsystems	TVGA8900C	
Tseng Labs, Inc.	ET4000/W32	http://www.tseng.com
Tseng Labs, Inc.	ET4000/W32i	
Tseng Labs, Inc.	ET4000/W32p	
Tseng Labs, Inc.	ET4000AX	
Tseng Labs, Inc.	ET6000	
Tseng Labs, Inc.	VIPeR	
Tseng Labs, Inc.	VPR6000	
UMC	UMC 86C408	
UMC	UMC 86C418	
UMC	UMC 8710	
Weitek	P9000	
Weitek	P9100	
Western Digital (Paradise)	WD90C30	http://www.wdc.com
Western Digital (Paradise)	WD90C31	
Western Digital (Paradise)	WD90C33	
Western Digital	RocketCHIP	

VIDEO SPEED FACTORS

No one element defines the performance of an accelerator board. Overall performance is actually a combination of five major factors: the video accelerator IC (a.k.a. the "chipset"), the video RAM, the video BIOS/drivers, the RAMDAC, and the expansion bus architecture. By understanding how each of these factors relate to performance, you can make the best recommendations for system upgrades or replacement boards.

The commercial MONITORS software encrypted on the companion CD provides a utility that checks the specifications of your particular video adapter.

Video accelerator   Of course, the video-accelerator IC itself (usually the graphics chipset being used) is at the core of the accelerator board. The type of IC (fixed function, graphics accelerator, or graphics co-processor) loosely defines the board's capabilities. All other factors being equal, a board with a graphics accelerator will certainly perform better than a fixed-function accelerator. Such companies like ATI, Advance Logic, Chips & Technologies, Matrox, and Oak have developed many of the video-accelerator ICs in use today. Many of the ICs provide a 32-bit data bus (although even newer designs are providing a 64-bit or 128-bit data bus), and they sustain very high data rates, but a data bottleneck across a 16-bit (e.g., ISA) expansion bus can seriously degrade the IC's effectiveness. This means you should match the recommended board to the particular system—a state-of-the-art graphics accelerator will not necessarily make your old i286 shine.

Video RAM   Video adapters rely on RAM to hold image data, and video-accelerator boards are no exception. Although the current amount of video RAM typically varies from 1MB to 4MB (some late-mode video adapters offer as much as 8MB), the amount of RAM is not so important to a video accelerator as the RAM's speed. Faster memory is able to read and write image data faster, so adapter performance is improved. The introduction of specialized *Video RAM (VRAM)*—memory devices with two separate data busses that can be read from and written to simultaneously—is reputed to be superior to conventional dynamic RAM (DRAM) or EDO RAM, such as the kind used for ordinary PC memory. Recent advances in DRAM speed have narrowed that gap while still remaining very economical. At this point, adapters with fast DRAM or EDO RAM are just about as fast as adapters with specialized video RAM for video modes up to $1024 \times 768 \times 256$. For higher modes and color depths found on high-end accelerators, specialized video RAM is still the way to go for optimum performance.

Video BIOS and drivers   Software is often considered as an after-thought to adapter design, yet it plays a surprisingly important role in accelerator performance. Even the finest accelerator board hardware can bog-down when run with careless, loosely written code. You must be concerned with two classes of software: video BIOS and drivers. The video BIOS is firmware (software that is permanently recorded on a memory device, such as a ROM). Video BIOS holds the programming that allows the accelerator to interact with DOS applications software. VESA BIOS extensions are now being used almost universally as part of the video BIOS for many accelerators, as well as conventional frame-buffer adapters. By adding VESA BIOS extensions to video BIOS, it eliminates the need to load another device driver under DOS.

However, video drivers have compelling advantages. Windows 95 works quite well with drivers (and generally ignores video BIOS entirely). Unlike BIOS ROMs, which can never change once programmed, a video driver can change very quickly as bugs are corrected and enhancements are made. The driver can be downloaded from a manufacturer's BBS or their Web site on the Internet (or other on-line information service, such as AOL) and installed on your system in a matter of minutes without ever having to disassemble the PC. It is also possible for you to use third-party video drivers. Hardware manufacturers are not always adept at writing efficient software, and a third-party driver developed by an organization that specializes in software might actually let your accelerator perform better than the original driver shipped from the manufacturer.

The RAMDAC   Just about every analog video system in service today is modeled after the 15-pin VGA scheme, which uses three separate analog signals to represent the three primary colors. The color for each pixel must be broken down into component red, green, and blue levels, and those levels must be converted into analog equivalents. The conversion from digital values to analog levels is handled by a *Digital-to-Analog Converter (DAC)*. Each conversion also requires a certain amount of time. Faster DACs are needed to support faster horizontal refresh rates. Remember that each video adapter uses a palette that is a subset of the colors that can possibly be produced. Even though a monitor might be able to produce "unlimited" colors, a VGA board can only produce 256 of those colors in any 256-color mode. Older video boards stored the palette entries in registers, but the large-palette video modes now available (64K colors through 16 million colors) require the use of RAM. Boards that incorporate a *RAMDAC (Random Access Memory Digital-to-Analog Converter)* are preferred because memory integrated with DACs tends to be much faster than accessing discrete RAM elsewhere on the board. Keep in mind that the RAM on a RAMDAC is used for holding palette information—not for the actual image.

The expansion bus architecture   Finally, graphic data must be transferred between the PC motherboard and the adapter as you saw early in this section. Such transfer occurs across the PC's expansion bus. If data can be transferred between the PC and adapter at a faster rate, video performance should improve. Consequently, the choice of bus architecture has a significant impact on video performance. Video accelerators are available to support three bus architectures: ISA, VL, and PCI.

The venerable *Industry Standard Architecture (ISA)* has remained virtually unchanged since its introduction with the PC/AT in the early 1980s. The ISA continues to be a mature interface standard for most IBM-compatible expansion devices. The sheer volume of ISA systems currently in service guarantees to keep the ISA on desktops for at least another 10 years. However, ISA's 16-bit data bus width, its lack of advanced features (such as interrupt sharing or bus mastering), and its relatively slow 8.33MHz operating speed form a serious bottleneck to the incredible volume of video data demanded by Windows 95 and most graphics-intensive DOS applications. ISA works, but it is no longer the interface of choice to achieve optimum video performance. When recommending an accelerator product, look to the newer busses for best results.

By the early 1990s, the *Video Electronics Standards Association (VESA)* had invested a great deal of time and effort to develop a standard bus interface, which has been optimized for video operation. In essence, this video bus is "local" to the system CPU, which allows faster access without the 8.33MHz limitation imposed by ISA. The actual bus speed is limited by the system clock speed. The VESA Local bus (VL bus, VLB) achieved a remarkable level of industry acceptance and success in boosting video performance—especially when used with a high-quality graphics accelerator board. However, the 32-bit VL bus is generally limited to video systems. Other peripherals, such as IDE hard-drive controllers have been built for the VL bus, but VL bus limitations frequently interfere with multiple VL cards in the same system (especially with faster motherboards). As a result, existing VL-compatible PCs typically offer only one or two VL expansion slots—the other expansion slots are ISA. Some video accelerators are still manufactured for the VL bus, but virtually all high-performance video boards today are designed for the PCI bus.

Intel's *Peripheral Component Interconnect (PCI)* bus is one of the newest and most exciting bus architectures to reach the PC. The PCI bus runs at a fixed frequency of 30 or 33MHz, and offers a full 64-bit data bus, which can take advantage of new 64-bit CPUs, such as Intel's Pentium (although most implementations of the PCI bus are designed for a

32-bit implementation). The PCI bus overcomes the speed and functional limitations of ISA, and the PCI architecture is intended to support all types of PC peripherals (not just video boards). Current PCI video boards now clearly out-perform ISA and VL bus-type video adapters.

3D Graphics-Accelerator Issues

Technically speaking, "3D graphics" is the graphical representation of a scene or object along three axes of reference (height, width, and depth) to make the scene look more realistic. This technique "tricks" the PC user into seeing a 3D image on a flat (a "2D") screen. The demand for 3D video has dramatically increased from all parts of the PC industry. 3D rendering has proven to be the technique of choice for many types of high-end games, business presentations, computer-aided designs, and multimedia applications. However, the use of 3D demands more of a PC than simply passing huge volumes of data across an expansion bus—3D rendering requires complex mathematical calculations, determinations of coloring, the inclusion of special effects, and conversion of the rendered scene to a 2D plane (the display). In many cases, all this must be accomplished in real-time (15+ frames per second). Today, most video systems are upgraded for express purpose of supporting 3D animation (usually in 3D computer games, such as Quake II). This part of the chapter examines some of the key factors involved on 3D rendering and acceleration.

THE 3D PROCESS

To display a 3D object in real time, an object is first represented as a set of points (or vertices) in a 3D coordinate system (i.e., x, y, and z coordinates). The vertices of the given object (the "object" might be a car, a fighter plane, or a complete 3D world) are stored in system RAM and completely define the object. To display this object on the flat 2D monitor, the object must then be *rendered*.

Rendering is the act of calculating, on a "per pixel" basis, the different color and position information, which tricks the viewer into perceiving depth on the 2D screen. Rendering also "fills in" the points on the surface of the object that were previously stored only as a set of vertices. In this way, a solid object can be drawn (even shaded with shadows and fog for 3D effect) can be drawn on the screen. To render an object, it is necessary to determine the color and position information. To accomplish this efficiently, the vertices of the object are segmented into triangles, and these triangles (a set of three vertices) are then passed down the "3D processing pipeline" one at a time. The actual steps are:

- ■ *Triangularize the 3D object* This process divides the 3D object into triangles (sets of three vertices).
- ■ *Transformation* Translates, rotates, zooms, the object (as necessary), based on the "camera angle." This is a mathematically intensive part of the rendering process.
- ■ *Clipping* Eliminates any portions of the object that fall outside of the "window" of the viewer's line of sight. Clipping also demands a fair amount of mathematical processing.
- ■ *Lighting* Calculates shadow or light information, depending on where light sources in the world are positioned. Other effects, such as "fog," can also be included.

■ *Map triangles to screen* The triangularized, transformed, clipped, and illuminated object must then be "mapped" to the 2D screen. Triangles that are farther away from the viewer's viewpoint will be smaller than those triangles that are closer.

■ *Draw the triangles* The triangles are then drawn to the screen using a variety of shading or texture mapping techniques. This time-intensive process completes the scene that you see; the entire process must be repeated for every frame generated by the game or other application.

KEY 3D-SPEED ISSUES

Higher frame rates create realism and true-to-life atmosphere in 3D games. Speed is the main factor in providing faster frame rates. If the frame rate of a game is too slow, the game becomes unplayable because the time needed to react to an action in the game will be far too long. Consider playing a flight simulator if the display was only updated once or twice per second. Frame rate is entirely dependent on the speed of a graphics accelerator. The speed of a 3D graphics engine is typically rated in terms of "millions of texels (textured pixels) per second" or Mtexels/sec. It is also frequently rated in polygons (e.g., triangles) per second. Current 3D graphics accelerators can provide several million texels per second.

The speed of a 3D application depends on many tasks, but the most daunting tasks are 3D geometry and rendering. Geometry is the calculations used to determine an object's position and color on the screen. Rendering is the actual drawing of the object on the screen. A typical graphics accelerator takes the load of the CPU so that the CPU can devote more processing power to other functions. More advanced CPUs (such as the Pentium MMX or Pentium II with MMX technology) incorporate additional instructions, which aid many of the calculation-intensive work needed in 3D environments. Three features that most often affect 3D speed are bus mastering, resolution, and color depth.

Bus mastering With PCI bus master graphics accelerator, a 3D graphics engine will never incur latency (delays) during the rendering process because once the CPU has prepared all of the triangles for rendering, the bus master will fetch the list of triangles asynchronously without requiring the CPU to wait. The two different implementations of bus mastering are: the basic bus master and the scatter gather bus master. A basic bus master is capable of operating independently from the host CPU for short periods of time before it interrupts the host to ask for direction. During data-intensive operations, such as 3D, this minimizes the advantages of bus mastering. By contrast, a scatter-gather bus master is able to operate almost independently from the host CPU, achieving serious performance benefits.

Resolutions Because of limitations in operating systems and graphics accelerators, most games and multimedia applications have been developed for low resolutions (such as 320×200) to achieve high-performance. Increasing resolution means displaying more pixels on the screen with every frame—which places more demand on the monitor and graphics board. Some applications developed in 320×200 can be played at 640×400, but the extra pixels are simply a replication of existing ones, which makes the image appear "blocky."

With today's standards in software and fast hardware accelerators, developers can include more unique pixel information in each frame, effectively increasing graphics detail at resolutions as high as 640×400 or 800×600. Thus, gamers can play in high resolutions without any performance loss.

Color depth Using extra colors in 3D games makes the scenes much richer and more life-like. The more colors used in a scene, the more detailed and realistic it looks, but the more calculations are needed to determine the color of each rendered pixel. With the new generation of 3D graphics accelerators, higher color depths are supported without dramatic performance loss, and developers can now use more colors in each scene. For example, developers can now use 16-bit (65K) or 24-bit (16.7M) color, instead of the traditional 8-bit (256) color.

IMPROVING 3D PERFORMANCE THROUGH HARDWARE

A 3D graphics accelerator improves 3D performance by relieving the host CPU of many of the computation-intensive tasks needed to render a scene. In most cases, these tasks are performed by graphics processors on the 3D video accelerator itself. Today's 3D graphics accelerators are capable of an astonishing array of features—some of which are:

Perspective-correct texture mapping In real life, objects have details that allow us to recognize them. For example, an object made of wood is granular, but steel is smooth and shimmering. In 3D applications, this detail is called *texture*. Applying two-dimensional texture images to 3D objects or scenes make them appear more realistic. In the real world, our perspective relative to an object changes as our position changes. For example, when you are walking along the side of a house, the house will have a different perspective which each step. To create this experience in a 3D application, texture maps must be "corrected" to fit the changing perspective. If the texture mapping is not perspective-correct, the image will be visually incorrect and filled with artifacts from previous frames. Although older 3D graphics accelerators only provided non-perspective correct texture mapping in hardware, many of the newest 3D graphics engines offer perspective correct textures at full rendering speed.

Lighting For greater realism in a scene, lighting is applied to objects to accentuate curves or create ambiance (such as shadows). Lighting effects are limited in software (otherwise, this degrades the frame rate). A key advantage of performing hardware-based 3D rendering is the ability to apply lighting effects to polygons while maintaining full rendering speed.

Texture transparency The technique of texture transparency is similar to "chroma-keying" in video. This technique draws one image on top of another—while appearing to fit there naturally. Mapping complicated objects in a 3D scene (such as trees) is a challenge for the software developer. They must be able to map the tree on a transparent polygon so that the background of the scene will be shown through the "branches." Objects like trees might not be essential, but they significantly improve the overall realism of a scene. Without texture transparency, these objects are typically left out or simplified. New 3D graphics chips support texture transparency in hardware, allowing developers to add a higher level of detail while maintaining graphics performance.

Hardware z-buffering The use of a "z-buffer" (or "depth buffer") is necessary when two objects are intersecting each other. The z-buffer determines which portions of the intersecting objects are visible. However, many software developers do not use a z-buffer for all objects in the scene. This is because the z-buffer takes up space in the off-screen memory that could be used instead to store extra source textures for greater detail. For this reason, many 3D graphics chips provide an optional z-buffer allowing the developer to decide whether to use the off-screen memory for z-buffering or texture storage. If a game using a z-buffer (such as Quake II) is played on a graphics accelerator that does not allow for a hardware z-buffer, the game will not run (or will run at very low frame rates) because all z-buffering will need to be done in software.

Palletized textures Storing source textures of 3D games in off-screen memory is very taxing on the graphics frame buffer. Each time a new scene is created, all of its source textures need to be loaded in off-screen memory for use by the graphics chip. Memory available to store textures is limited because a 3D game accelerator generally has about 2MB of memory. This restricts the number of textures, effectively reducing the detail and quality of the scene. To compensate for this, developers can use a method of palletized textures that assigns a *Color Look-Up Table (CLUT)* to each texture in the scene. This technique allows the developer to use a smaller amount of colors for each texture, instead of the normal 16-bit color values (65K colors). This smaller color format (CLUT) requires less memory space than the true 65K colors, which means that more colors can be saved in memory to add detail to a scene.

However, most older 3D graphics accelerators do not support palletized textures, which means the information can only be stored in full 16-bit color format in the frame buffer, utilizing all of the available off-screen memory. In that case, the extra textures will have to be stored and retrieved from system memory, resulting in a serious hit on performance. Alternately, textures can be dropped from the scene by the graphics accelerator to maintain performance. Newer 3D graphics accelerators do provide full hardware support for palletized textures, and they allow developers to create very detailed scenes with two to four times as many textures. This gives 3D applications a significant performance boost because the applications do not rely on the speed of the system to convert the information to 16-bit colors.

Texture-mapping methods Texture mapping is a data-intensive operation—a bitmap is wrapped onto a 3D object or polygon to add more visual details (thus enhancing realism). The original bitmap used as the texture to be mapped is also called the *source texture*. Textures can be mapped onto a 3D object with perspective correction:

- *Point sampling* This is the most common way to map a texture on a given polygon. Point sampling allows the 3D graphics engine to approximate the color value of a given pixel on the resulting texture map by replicating the value of the closest existing pixel on the source texture. Point sampling provides very good results when used in conjunction with tile-based MIP mapping, and it maintains high-performance levels at a low cost.
- *Filtering* Some source textures might need a considerable amount of warping, which might lead to a "blocky" appearance. Some graphics-accelerator manufacturers use a

technique called *bilinear filtering* to make the textures appear smoother. In bilinear filtering, four-source texel values are read, and their color values are then blended together, based on proximity. The resulting values will be used for the texel to be drawn. Although this technique is useful, the resulting quality is not comparable to using high-resolution source textures. 3D graphics accelerators without support for palletized textures have to scale down the textures to store them, and apply filtering to map them onto polygons. This results in poor-quality rendering.

■ *MIP mapping* Mip-mapping is another way to improve the quality of the 3D texture mapped object. The more alterations made to a texture to "fit" an object, the less it will resemble the source texture. One way to avoid this severe deviation from the original texture is to create three copies (MIP levels) of the same source texture (each in different sizes). MIP-mapping can be implemented in three ways: tile-based MIP mapping, per-pixel MIP mapping, and tri-linear MIP mapping.

Fogging   To maintain high performance, developers created "tricks" to reduce the amount of rendering needed for a scene. One of these tricks is called *fogging*. It is mostly used in landscape scenes, such as flight simulators. Fogging allows the developer to "hide" the background of a scene behind a layer of "fog"—mixing the textures' color values with a monochrome color, such as white. Some newer 3D graphics chips support fogging in hardware.

Alpha-Blending   Blending is a visual effect that mixes two textures on the same object. Different levels of blending can be implemented to create visual effects. The simplest method is called *screen door* or *stippling*. Only some pixels making up the object are rendered to produce a "see-through" effect. For example, the developer would decide that an object would be 50% transparent. The graphics accelerator would then draw the background image, then write only every second pixel of the object. This approach is easy to implement in hardware and delivers a reasonable quality at a low cost. By contrast, true alpha blending is a data-intensive operation that involves reading the values of two source textures and performing the perspective calculations on both textures simultaneously. This effect is very taxing on performance and costly to implement. Only high-end 3D graphics cards use true alpha-blending in hardware.

Gouraud shading   Gouraud shading (or smooth shading) draws smooth shadows across the face of an object. This causes the viewer's eyes to perceive depth and curvature information from the surface of the object. Gouraud shading works by reading the color information at the three vertices of a triangle and interpolating the intensities in red, green, and blue smoothly between the three vertices. Gouraud shading is the most popular algorithm used to draw 3D objects on a 2D screen. Most objects can be rendered with amazing realism in 3D by using Gouraud shading, and this feature is often available in 3D graphics-accelerator hardware.

Double buffering   Everyone has seen the old animation trick of drawing a cartoon character on the corner of a page of paper, and altering the drawing slightly on following pages of paper. When the sheaf of paper is complete and the pages flipped rapidly, the cartoon character appears to move smoothly. Double-buffered 3D animation on the PC works in the same way—the next position of the character is being drawn before the page is flipped. Viewing 3D animation without double buffering would be like looking at the animated cartoon if the character were being redrawn with every flip of the page (the animation would appear to "flicker").

Double buffering requires having two areas reserved on the frame buffer of the 3D graphics card. Both regions need to be the size of the visible screen, and one buffer is used to render the next frame of the animation while the other displays the previously rendered animation frame on the monitor. Under Windows, double buffering requires bit-blitting to copy the animation from buffer to buffer.

Color dithering The number of colors that can be drawn to the visible screen depends on the number of bits per pixel that carry color information. For instance, with eight bits per pixel of color information, only 256 colors can exist on the desktop at any one time. *Color dithering* is the process of mixing these defined colors into small patterns to produce a wider spectrum of color without requiring extra video memory. This is especially important in 3D because such techniques as Gouraud shading require many shades of each color used in each scene. If dithering were not handled in hardware, a 3D scene could only contain eight different main colors in 256-color mode (because each color would require 32 shades to be programmed into the color lookup table to roughly approximate Gouraud shading). With hardware support for color dithering, a scene with many more colors might be rendered without requiring extra video RAM.

Understanding DirectX

When Windows first emerged as a major operating system, its focus was primarily on file management and utilities. High-performance graphics and other forms of multimedia were barely even dreamed of. This made it very difficult for Windows to support graphics-intensive applications, such as games, PC-TV, or MPEG video (and is largely the reason why DOS support continues to be an important issue on PC platforms). Developers realized that for Windows to finally become independent of DOS, a means of supporting high-performance multimedia functions would be required—and DirectX technology was born. With Windows 95, DirectX has emerged as a key element in graphics, sound, and interaction for multimedia. This part of the chapter offers a basic overview of DirectX and its components.

PIECES OF A PUZZLE

Contrary to popular belief, DirectX is not one single piece of software. Instead, DirectX is actually a comprehensive collection of Windows 95 *APIs (Application Programming Interfaces)* that provide a standardized set of features for graphics, sound, input devices, multi-player interaction, and application setup. DirectX software is categorized into three layers: a foundation layer, a media layer, and a components layer.

Foundation The "foundation" layer forms the heart and soul of DirectX. It is a set of low-level APIs that are the basis for all high-performance multimedia under Windows 95.

DirectX foundation APIs provide direct access to hardware acceleration, such as 3D graphics-acceleration chips (in effect, allowing Windows 95 to "talk" directly to hardware). The foundation layer uses the following APIs:

- *DirectDraw* Provides graphics "surface" management.
- *Direct3D (Immediate Mode)* Supplies low-level 3D features used in conjunction with DirectDraw.
- *DirectInput* Supports a rich selection of input devices (including new "force feedback" joysticks).
- *DirectSound* Provides sound and mixer effects.
- *DirectSound 3D* Offers 3D sound effects from ordinary 2D speaker arrangements.
- *DirectSetup* Installs software and drivers automatically.

Media The DirectX "media" layer consists of application-level APIs that take advantage of the system-level services provided by the DirectX foundation. The media-level services are device independent and include features, such as animation, behaviors, and video streaming. The DirectX media layer includes five APIs:

- *Direct3D (Retained Mode)* Offers a collection of 3D scene features.
- *DirectPlay* Supports multi-player/network play.
- *DirectShow* Handles slide-show-type operation and features.
- *DirectAnimation* Supplies animation support.
- *DirectModel* Supplies 3D modeling support.

Components The "components" layer makes up the top level of the DirectX hierarchy. This group of application-specific modules can draw on all features available in the media and foundation layers. DirectX components include NetMeeting (an on-line white-board for real-time group collaboration), ActiveMovie (a set of tools for rendering full-screen MPEG video and supporting playback of a wide range of audio and video formats), and Netshow (enabling live broadcast of multimedia content over the Internet, along with the compelling 3D worlds of VRML).

MORE ON DIRECTDRAW

Most Windows programs access "drawing surfaces" indirectly through Win32 device context functions, such as GetDC. The application then writes indirectly to the device through the *Graphics Device Interface (GDI)* system. The GDI is the Windows component that provides an abstraction layer that enables all standard Windows applications to draw to the screen. The disadvantage of GDI is that it was not designed for high-performance graphics software. It was made to be used by business applications, such as word processors and spreadsheet applications. The GDI provides access to a video buffer in system memory (not video memory) and does not take advantage of special features that some video cards provide. As a result, GDI is great for most types of business software, but is far too slow for multimedia or game software.

DirectDraw circumvents this limitation by providing drawing surfaces that represent actual video memory. This means that with DirectDraw, an application can write directly to the memory on the video card—making your graphics routines extremely fast. Surfaces are represented as contiguous blocks of memory, making it easy to perform addressing within them. DirectDraw also supports hardware-accelerated functions, such as bit-blitting and overlays. DirectDraw works with a wide variety of display hardware. It is designed so that applications can determine the capabilities of the underlying display hardware, and then use any supported hardware-accelerated features. Any features that are not supported in hardware can then be emulated in software.

In actuality, DirectDraw is not a high-level graphics API that draws graphics "primitives," such as lines and rectangles. Instead, DirectDraw is a low-level API that operates at the graphics "surface" level—providing the essential support for higher-level 2D and 3D graphics APIs that do draw and render.

MORE ON DIRECTSOUND

DirectSound is the audio component of DirectX. DirectSound enables hardware and software sound mixing, capture, and effects, such as 3D positioning and panning. In operation, DirectSound is essentially a sound mixing engine—the application places a set of sounds in buffers (called *secondary buffers*). DirectSound then combines these sounds and writes them into a primary buffer, which holds the sound that the listener actually hears. DirectSound automatically creates a primary buffer that typically resides in memory on the sound card itself. The application creates the secondary buffers either in system memory or directly on the sound card. DirectSound supports *Pulse-Code Modulation (PCM)* sound data, but does not currently support compressed wave formats. DirectSound does not include functions for parsing a sound file (it is the responsibility of the developer to stream data in the correct format into the secondary sound buffers).

The DirectSound mixing engine does not simply mix several sounds together. It can also apply effects to a sound as it is written from a secondary buffer into the primary buffer. Although these effects are audible using standard loudspeakers, they are more obvious and compelling when the user wears headphones. Basic effects are volume/frequency control and panning (changing the relative volume between the left and right audio channels), but DirectSound can also simulate 3D positional effects through the following techniques:

- *Rolloff* The further an object is from the listener, the quieter it sounds. This phenomenon is known as *rolloff*.
- *Arrival offset* A sound emitted by a source to the listener's right will arrive at the right ear slightly before it arrives at the left ear (the duration of this offset is approximately a millisecond).
- *Muffling* The orientation of the ears ensures that sounds coming from behind the listener are slightly muffled, compared with sounds coming from in front. In addition, if a sound is coming from the right, the sounds reaching the left ear will be muffled by the mass of the listener's head and by the orientation of the left ear.
- *Doppler shift* DirectSound automatically creates Doppler shift effects for any buffer or listener that has a velocity. Effects are cumulative—if the listener and the sound source are both moving, the system automatically calculates the relationship between their velocities and adjusts the Doppler effect accordingly.

MORE ON DIRECTINPUT

DirectInput provides high-performance access to input devices including the mouse, keyboard, joystick, and the new force-feedback (input/output) devices that are arriving on the market. DirectInput offers generalized device interfaces that support a much wider range of input and output devices than the standard Win32 API functions. DirectInput works directly with device drivers—bypassing the Windows message system. This results in faster and more responsive access to input devices. DirectInput also supports *force-feedback* devices. Force-feedback devices "respond" to an application with physical effects, such as kick-back (when a trigger is fired), vibration, and resistance. Force-feedback devices make many game and entertainment experiences much more realistic and engaging. DirectInput also supports the Universal Serial Bus for access to USB input devices.

MORE ON DIRECT3D

Direct3D is a drawing interface for 3D hardware. Using DirectDraw as a base, Direct3D actually draws and renders the 3D scenes. You can use Direct3D in either immediate mode or retained mode. The Direct3D "immediate mode" was developed as a low-level 3D API, and is ideal for developers who need to port games and other high-performance multimedia applications to the Microsoft Windows operating system. It is a device-independent way for applications to communicate with accelerator hardware at a low level. By contrast, "retained mode" is a high-level 3D *Application Programmer Interface (API)* for programmers who require rapid development or who want the support for hierarchies and animations. Direct3D retained mode is built "on top" of immediate mode. The three components of the Direct3D device are: the transform (formulas describing how to convert a coordinate in 3D space into 2D display coordinates), the state variables (defining the styles for drawing operations), and the draw engine that actually generate the object.

MORE ON DIRECTPLAY

Applications (especially games) can be more compelling if they can be played against real players, and the PC provides a versatile platform for connections over networks or the Internet. Instead of forcing the developer to deal with the differences that each connection scheme represents, DirectPlay provides well-defined, generalized communication capabilities. DirectPlay is a software interface that simplifies an application's access to communication services.

A DirectPlay "session" is a communications channel between several machines. Before an application can start communicating with other machines, it must "join a session." An application can do this in two ways: it can identify all the existing sessions on a network and join one of them, or it can create a new session and wait for other machines to join it. Once the application has joined a session, it can create a player and exchange messages with all the other players in the session. Each session has one machine that is designated as the host. The host is the owner of the session and is the only machine that can change the properties of the session.

The most essential entity within a DirectPlay session is a player. A *player* represents a logical object within the session that can send and receive messages. DirectPlay does not have any representation of a physical machine in the session. Each player is identified as being either a *local player* (one that exists on your machine) or a *remote player* (one that exists on another machine), and each machine must have at least one local player before it can start sending and receiving messages. DirectPlay supports the concepts of groups within a session. A "group" is a logical collection of players. By creating a group of players, an application can send a single message to the group and all the players in the group will receive a copy of the message.

DETERMINING THE INSTALLED VERSION OF DIRECTX

Because DirectX is a collection of APIs, each application that uses DirectX is written to use a particular version of DirectX—the application needs the correct version of DirectX components installed under Windows 95. Otherwise, the application will not work. In most cases, DirectX is backward compatible, so an application written for DirectX 3.x should work on a system with DirectX 5.x installed. But an application written for DirectX 5.x won't work on a system with DirectX 3.x. As a technician, you'll need to spot DirectX version issues. You can use the following procedure to check the current version of DirectX installed on a given system:

1 Using Windows Explorer or *My computer*, locate the DDRAW.DLL file in the *Windows* folder.

2 Use the right mouse button to click the DDRAW.DLL file, then click *Properties* on the menu that appears.

3 Click the *Version* tab.

4 Compare the version number on the *File version* line with the following list:

- 4.02.0095   DirectX 1
- 4.03.00.1096   DirectX 2
- 4.04.00.0068   DirectX 3 or 3a
- 4.05.00.0155   DirectX 5

DirectX versions 3 and 3a use the same version of the Ddraw.dll file. To determine whether you are using version 3 or 3a of DirectX, use this procedure to check the version of the D3DRGBXF.DLL file:

- 4.04.00.0068   DirectX 3
- 4.04.00.0070   DirectX 3a

If the DDRAW.DLL file does not exist in the Windowsfolder, DirectX is probably not installed on your computer.

Video Feature Connectors

In most cases, a video adapter is a single, self-contained piece of PC hardware. However, some video add-on devices require access to video signals or the video-adapter hardware.

FIGURE 43-9   A typical video-feature connector.

TABLE 43-3 PINOUT FOR A VIDEO FEATURE CONNECTOR

PIN (COMPONENT SIDE)	FUNCTION	PIN (SOLDER SIDE)	FUNCTION
Y1	PD0 (DAC pixel data)	Z1	Ground
Y2	PD1	Z2	Ground
Y3	PD2	Z3	Ground
Y4	PD3	Z4	Select internal video
Y5	PD4	Z5	Select internal syncs
Y6	PD5	Z6	Select internal DAC
Y7	PD6	Z7	Not used
Y8	PD7	Z8	Ground
Y9	DAC clock	Z9	Ground
Y10	DAC blanking	Z10	Ground
Y11	Ext. horiz. sync	Z11	Ground
Y12	Ext. vert. sync	Z12	Not used
Y13	Ground	Z13	Not used

A typical example of this might be a 3D graphics accelerator board, which works in conjunction with the existing video adapter. To access video signals or the video-adapter hardware, the video adapter provides a *Video Feature Connector (VFC)* similar to the 26-pin card-edge connector shown in Fig. 43-9 (although many video adapters now use an IDC "ribbon" cable header). The pinout for a "classic" 26-pin VFC is shown in Table 43-3.

AMI MULTIMEDIA CHANNEL

In addition to the "classic" VFC found on many video boards, some current motherboards are incorporating advanced feature connectors to complement the on-board video system. American Megatrends (AMI) provides an AMI Multimedia Channel VFC (AMI/VFC) on some of its motherboards. These connectors are designed to maximize multimedia performance with the motherboard's video system, and a connector is available for connecting multimedia building components (such as MPEG or video-capture modules) to the system board. Multiple protocols are supported through the same connector as follows:

■ Standard VFC mode
■ *Digital Video Stream (DVS)* mode.
■ *MPEG Data Port (MDP)* mode or *Multimedia Peripheral Port (MPP)* mode.

TABLE 43-4 AMI MULTIMEDIA CHANNEL PINOUT (STANDARD VFC MODE)			
PIN	DESCRIPTION	PIN	DESCRIPTION
Y1	DATA0	Z1	DGND
Y2	DATA1	Z2	DGND
Y3	DATA2	Z3	DGND
Y4	DATA3	Z4	EVIDEO
Y5	DATA4	Z5	ESYNC
Y6	DATA5	Z6	EDCLK
Y7	DATA6	Z7	Not used
Y8	DATA7	Z8	DGND
Y9	DCLK	Z9	DGND
Y10	BLK#	Z10	DGND
Y11	HSYNC	Z11	VFSENSE#
Y12	VSYNC	Z12	Not used
Y13	DGND	Z13	Key
Y14	Not used	Z14	Not used
Y15	Not used	Z15	Not used
Y16	Not used	Z16	Not used
Y17	Not used	Z17	Not used
Y18	Not used	Z18	Not used
Y19	Not used	Z19	Not used
Y20	Not used	Z20	Not used

Standard VFC mode This VESA-compliant video feature connector interface synchronizes graphics output, and lets pass-through signals from a video add-in board use the motherboard's video circuits. Table 43-4 lists the pinout for a 40-pin AMI/VFC in the "standard" mode. Notice the similarities between the first 13 pins of the "classic" VFC and the standard AMI VFC.

DVS mode In *Digital Video Stream (DVS)* mode, the interface is configured as a synchronous input port—this allows the graphics controllers to be directly connected to certain video decoders through the VFC interface. Some video decoders might require additional logic to encode the synchronization information within the data stream. In DVS mode, the AMI/VFC consists of three independent signal groups: an 8-bit data bus, a two-wire serial bus, and an audio interface. The pinout for a 40-pin AMI/VFC in the "DVS" mode is shown in Table 43-5.

MDP/MPP mode The *MPEG Data Port (MDP)* and *Multimedia Peripheral Port (MPP)* modes are mutually exclusive of each other—the support for a particular mode is determined by the revision of the graphics controller in use. MPP provides a direct connection to an MPEG decoder. It adds an additional multiplexed address/data bus (which can be used to connect a range of third-party devices, such as MPEG2 decoders or audio processors). This bus uses ISA type control and either an 8-bit or 16-bit protocol. The fully programmable control signals allow it to interface to a variety of devices with minimal external logic. Table 43-6 illustrates the pinout for an AMI/VFC in MDP mode, while Table 43-7 shows the pinout for an AMI/VFC in the MPP mode.

TABLE 43-5 AMI MULTIMEDIA CHANNEL PINOUT (DVS MODE)

PIN	DESCRIPTION	PIN	DESCRIPTION
Y1	DATA0	Z1	DGND
Y2	DATA1	Z2	DGND
Y3	DATA2	Z3	DGND
Y4	DATA3	Z4	BS#1
Y5	DATA4	Z5	CONTRL
Y6	DATA5	Z6	SB#
Y7	DATA6	Z7	SDA
Y8	DATA7	Z8	DGND
Y9	CLK	Z9	DGND
Y10	BS#0	Z10	DGND
Y11	Not used	Z11	VFSENSE#
Y12	Not used	Z12	SCL
Y13	DGND	Z13	Key
Y14	Key	Z14	Key
Y15	SA#	Z15	+5V
Y16	SNRDY#	Z16	RESET#
Y17	MASK0	Z17	Not used
Y18	REV	Z18	RESVD
Y19	+12V	Z19	AGND
Y20	AUDL	Z20	AUDR

TABLE 43-6 AMI MULTIMEDIA CHANNEL PINOUT (MDP MODE)

PIN	DESCRIPTION	PIN	DESCRIPTION
Y1	DATA0	Z1	DGND
Y2	DATA1	Z2	DGND
Y3	DATA2	Z3	DGND
Y4	DATA3	Z4	IOR
Y5	DATA4	Z5	IOW
Y6	DATA5	Z6	RDY/INT
Y7	DATA6	Z7	SDA/SAD4
Y8	DATA7	Z8	DGND
Y9	DCLK	Z9	DGND
Y10	SAD0	Z10	DGND
Y11	SAD1	Z11	VFSENSE#
Y12	SAD2	Z12	SCL

TABLE 43-6	AMI MULTIMEDIA CHANNEL PINOUT (MDP MODE) (CONTINUED)		
PIN	**DESCRIPTION**	**PIN**	**DESCRIPTION**
Y13	DGND	Z13	Key
Y14	Key	Z14	Key
Y15	SAD3	Z15	+5V
Y16	SAD7	Z16	RESET#
Y17	SAD5	Z17	SAD6
Y18	REV	Z18	RESVD
Y19	+12 V	Z19	AGND
Y20	AUDL	Z20	AUDR

TABLE 43-7	AMI MULTIMEDIA CHANNEL PINOUT (MPP MODE)		
PIN	**DESCRIPTION**	**PIN**	**DESCRIPTION**
Y1	DATA0	Z1	DGND
Y2	DATA1	Z2	DGND
Y3	DATA2	Z3	DGND
Y4	DATA3	Z4	IOR
Y5	DATA4	Z5	IOW
Y6	DATA5	Z6	RDY/INT
Y7	DATA6	Z7	SDA
Y8	DATA7	Z8	DGND
Y9	DCLK	Z9	DGND
Y10	SAD0	Z10	DGND
Y11	SAD1	Z11	VFSENSE#
Y12	SAD2	Z12	SCL
Y13	DGND	Z13	Key
Y14	Key	Z14	Key
Y15	SAD3	Z15	+5 V
Y16	SAD7	Z16	RESET#
Y17	SAD5	Z17	SAD6
Y18	REV	Z18	SAD4
Y19	+12 V	Z19	AGND
Y20	AUDL	Z20	AUDR

Troubleshooting Video Adapters

A PC video system consists of four parts: the host PC itself, the video adapter/accelerator, the monitor, and the software (video BIOS and drivers). To deal with a failure in the video system, you must be able to isolate the problem to one of these four areas. When isolating the problem, your best tool is a working (or testbed) PC. With another PC, you can systematically exchange hardware to verify each element of the video system.

The companion CD provides several tools for helping to troubleshoot video issues and return video BIOS information. Try ATMEM10.ZIP, IS_VID.EXE, or PSV10.ZIP.

ISOLATING THE PROBLEM AREA

The first step is to verify the monitor by testing it on a known-good working PC. Keep in mind that the monitor must be compatible with the video adapter on which it is being tested. If the monitor works on another PC, the fault lies in one of the three remaining areas. If the monitor fails on a known-good machine, try the known-good monitor on the questionable machine. If the known-good monitor then works on your questionable machine, you can be certain that the fault lies in your monitor, and you can refer to the appropriate chapter here for detailed troubleshooting if you wish. If the monitor checks out, suspect the video adapter. Follow the same process to check the video adapter. Try the suspect video adapter on a known-good PC. If the problem follows the video adapter, you can replace the video adapter. If the suspected video adapter works in a known-good system, the adapter is probably good. Replace the adapter in the suspect machine, but try another expansion slot and be sure that the monitor cable is attached securely.

If both the monitor and the video adapter work in a known-good PC, but the video problem persists in the original machine, suspect a problem with the PC motherboard. Try the working video adapter in another expansion slot. Either the expansion slot is faulty, or a fault has occurred on the motherboard. Run some PC diagnostics if you have some available. Diagnostics might help to pinpoint motherboard problems. You might then choose to troubleshoot the motherboard further or replace the motherboard outright at your discretion.

If the video system appears to work properly during system initialization, but fails with a particular application (or in Windows/Windows 95), strongly suspect a problem with the selected video driver. Because almost all video adapters support VGA at the hardware level, set your application (or change the Windows setup) to run in standard VGA mode (for Windows 95, you can start the PC in the safe mode). If the display functions properly at that point, you can be confident that the problem is driver related. Check with the manufacturer to see that you have the latest video driver available. Reload the driver from its original disk (or a new disk) or select a new driver. If the problem persists in VGA mode, the trouble might be in the video adapter. Problem isolation can be summarized with these points:

- *Check the driver(s)* Video drivers are crucially important in Windows 3.1x and 95. Older drivers might contain bugs or be incompatible with certain applications. This accounts for the majority of all video problems. Obtain the latest video driver release, and be sure that it is properly installed on the system. If the driver is most current, try a generic video driver (usually available from the video chipset manufacturer).
- *Check the physical installation* See that the video board is installed properly in its expansion slot, and make sure that any jumpers are set properly for the particular system.
- *Check for memory conflicts* The memory space used by video adapters is hotly contested territory in the upper memory area. Printer drivers, sound cards, tape backups, SCSI adapters, and scanners are just some of the devices that can step all over the memory space needed by a video board. Many of today's video boards require you to exclude

a range of upper memory through your memory manager (often A000h through C7FFh, though your particular video board might be different). Be sure that any necessary memory exclusions are made in CONFIG.SYS at the memory manager's command line. You might also have to add an EMMExclude=A000-C7FF line to the [386enh] section of your SYSTEM.INI file.

■ *Suspect your memory manager* Advanced memory managers, such as QEMM or Netroom, use very aggressive techniques to "find" memory. Often, this interferes with video operation. Try disabling any stealth or cloaking mode.

■ *Check your system CMOS setup* Today's motherboards sport all manner of advanced features. Try systematically disabling such attributes as: video cache, video RAM shadow, byte-merge, palette snoop, or decouple/hidden refresh. If "PCI bus bursting" is used on the video bus, try disabling that also. If the video system requires the use of an interrupt, be sure that the IRQ is not being used by another device.

Unusual Hardware Issues

A lot of emphasis is placed on drivers and software configurations, but also quite a few unique hardware problems can affect your video system. Some of the most frequent oversights are outlined in the following sections.

CLOCK SPEED AND THE VL BUS

Video boards that use the VL bus are very sensitive to motherboard clock speeds over 40MHz. If your motherboard runs the VL bus at over 40MHz, it's quite possible that you will have trouble with VL bus video boards. The VESA specification states that one card can operate at 40MHz, or two can operate at up to 33MHz (a best-case scenario). Some manufacturers don't even guarantee that their cards will run at 40MHz—preferring to support bus speeds of 33MHz or less. So, if your VL bus video board is running at over 40MHz, and it refuses to run properly, your best option is usually to step your bus speed down. Bus speeds can usually be controlled by a motherboard jumper or an entry in CMOS. If you cannot change bus speed for any reason, try a different brand of VL card.

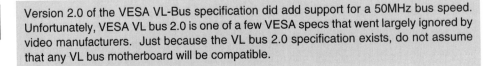

Version 2.0 of the VESA VL-Bus specification did add support for a 50MHz bus speed. Unfortunately, VESA VL bus 2.0 is one of a few VESA specs that went largely ignored by video manufacturers. Just because the VL bus 2.0 specification exists, do not assume that any VL bus motherboard will be compatible.

"SLC" MOTHERBOARDS AND THE VL BUS

If you have an older motherboard using an i486SLC-type CPU, some VL bus video boards will not operate properly when used with that particular motherboard. This is because the 32-bit VL bus was not implemented properly in conjunction with the 16-bit data path of the i486SLC. This is a problem with the motherboard's design, not the particular video boards. Later-model motherboards with the i486SLC CPU largely overcame this problem, but take care when using any VL bus video board on i486SLC motherboards. Chances are that an older ISA video board will work just fine.

8514/A AND COM4 CONFLICTS

The 8514/a video adapter was designed to coexist with a VGA adapter. To achieve this, the 8514/a uses a different range of addresses. Some of these are 16-bit addresses, which are located at 42E8h, 82E8h, 92E8h, A2E8h, and E2E8h. Unfortunately, many serial controllers only decode the first 12-bits of the I/O port address, and assume that calls to x2E8h (such as all of those listed) are intended for the serial port (e.g., 2E8h), rather than the video card. This means that COM4 cannot be used on most machines with an 8514/a compatible video card, unless the address of COM4 can be changed on the serial card (usually via jumpers), or the serial controller decodes all 16-bits of the I/O port addresses. There is no other way to get COM4 and any 8514/a compatible display adapter to coexist. Keep in mind that this is an issue with the serial controller, rather than the 8514/a video adapter.

ATI MACH, S3 VISION/TRIO, AND COM4 CONFLICTS

As you saw in the last section, 8514/a video adapters will often conflict with COM4 because of poor I/O address decoding. ATI's Mach chipsets and S3's chipsets are based on IBM's 8514/a standard, and frequently suffer the same problems as the 8514/a video adapters.

AWARD VIDEO BIOS GLITCH

Motherboards using the Award Modular BIOS 4.50G series with Matrox video cards might have problems loading drivers under Windows 95. This is because the 4.50G series of Award BIOS is not Plug-and-Play compliant, and cannot work under Windows 95. Upgrade the BIOS version on the motherboard to fix this problem, and set the following CMOS configuration under the PCI configuration setup:

■ PCI IRQ Activated By: Level
■ If no other PCI devices are used in the system, set the "Slot X Using INT#" to: AUTO
■ Be sure that the PCI IRQ is assigned to the slot the video card is in.

SYMPTOMS

Symptom 43-1. The computer is on, but there is no display The PC seems to initialize properly. If you hear a series of beeps during system initialization, refer to Chapter 15 to determine the error. Be sure that the monitor is turned on and plugged into the video adapter properly. Also check that the monitor's brightness and contrast controls are turned up enough (it sounds silly, but it really does happen). Try the monitor on a known-good PC. If the monitor works properly, suspect the video adapter. Power down the PC and be sure the video adapter is seated properly in its expansion slot. If any of the board contacts are dirty or corroded, clean the contacts by rubbing them with an eraser. You can also use any electronics-grade contact cleaner. You might want to try the video board in another expansion slot.

Chances are that the video adapter has at least one hardware jumper or DIP switch setting. Contact the manufacturer or refer to the owner's manual for the board and check that any jumpers or DIP switch settings on the board are configured properly. If this is a new installation, check the adapter-board settings against the configuration of other expansion boards in the system. When the hardware settings of one board overlap the settings of another, a hardware conflict can result. When you suspect a conflict, adjust the settings of the video adapter (or another newly installed device) to eliminate the conflict. There might also be a memory conflict. Some video adapters make unusual demands of upper system memory (the area between 640KB and 1MB). It is possible that an Exclude switch must be added to the EMM386.EXE entry in a CONFIG.SYS file. Check with the adapter's instruction manual to see if any memory configuration changes or optimizations are required.

Symptom 43-2. There is no display, and you hear a series of beeps when the PC initializes The video adapter failed to initialize during the system's POST. Because the video adapter is not responding, it is impossible to display information—that is why a series of beeps are used. Remember that the actual beep sequence might vary from system to system depending on the type of BIOS being used. You can probably find the beep code for your BIOS in Chapter 15. In actuality, the video adapter could fail for several different reasons. Power down the PC and check that the video adapter is installed properly and securely in an expansion slot. Be sure that the video adapter is not touching any exposed wiring or any other expansion board.

Isolate the video adapter by trying another adapter in the system. If the display works properly with another adapter installed, check the original adapter to see that all settings and jumpers are correct. If the problem persists, the original adapter is probably defective and should be replaced. If a new adapter fails to resolve the problem, a fault might be elsewhere on the motherboard. Install a POST board in the PC and allow the system to initialize. Each step of the initialization procedure corresponds to a two-digit hexadecimal code shown on the POST card indicators. The last code to be displayed is the point at which the failure occurred. POST cards are handy for checking the motherboard when a low-level fault has occurred. If a motherboard fault is detected, you might troubleshoot the motherboard or replace it outright at your discretion.

Symptom 43-3. Large, blank bands are at the top and bottom of the display in some screen modes, but not in others Multi-frequency and multi-mode monitors sometimes behave this way. This is not necessarily a defect, but it can cause some confusion unless you understand what is going on. When screen resolution changes, the overall number of pixels being displayed also changes. Ideally, a multi-frequency monitor should detect the mode change and adjust the vertical screen size to compensate (a feature called *auto-sizing*). However, not all multi-frequency monitors have this feature. When video modes change, you are left to adjust the vertical size manually. Of course, if information is missing from the display, a serious problem might be in the VRAM or the adapter's graphics-controller IC. In this event, try another video adapter board.

Symptom 43-4. The display image rolls Vertical synchronization is not keeping the image steady (horizontal sync might also be affected). This problem is typical of a monitor that cannot display a particular screen mode. Mode incompatibility is most common with fixed-frequency monitors, but it can also appear in multi-frequency monitors that are being pushed beyond their specifications. The best course of action here is to simply re-configure your software to use a compatible video mode (or reduce the vertical refresh rate). If that is an unsatisfactory solution, you will have to upgrade to a monitor that will support the desired video mode.

If the monitor and video board are compatible, the problem is synchronization. Try the monitor on a known-good PC. If the monitor also fails on a known-good PC, try the known-good monitor on original PC. If the known-good monitor works on the suspect PC, the sync circuits in your original monitor have almost certainly failed. If the suspect monitor works on a known-good PC, the trouble is likely in the original video adapter. Try replacing the video adapter.

Symptom 43-5. An error message appears on system startup indicating an invalid system configuration The system CMOS backup battery has probably failed, and the video type might have defaulted to "EGA" or "MCA" instead of "VGA"— resulting in the error. This is typically a symptom that occurs in older systems. If you enter your system setup (either through a BIOS routine or through a disk-based setup utility) and examine each entry, you will probably find that all entries have returned to a default setting—including the video system setting. Your best course is to replace the CMOS backup battery and enter each configuration setting again (hopefully, you have recorded each setting on paper already, or saved the CMOS contents to floppy disk using a CMOS backup utility). Once new settings are entered and saved, the system should operate properly. If the CMOS still will not retain system configuration information, the CMOS RAM itself is probably defective. Use a software diagnostic to check the RTC/CMOS IC (and the rest of the motherboard) thoroughly. If a motherboard fault is detected, you can troubleshoot the motherboard or replace it outright at your discretion.

Symptom 43-6. Garbage appears on the screen or the system hangs up The display might be distorted for a variety of reasons. One potential problem is a monitor mismatch. Check the video adapter jumpers and DIP switch settings and be sure that the video board will support the type of monitor you are using. It is possible that the video mode being used is not supported by your monitor (the display might also roll as described in Symptom 43-4). Try re-configuring your application software to use a compatible video mode. The problem should disappear. If that is unsatisfactory, you will have to upgrade to a monitor that will support the desired video mode.

Some older multi-frequency monitors are unable to switch video modes without being turned off, then turned on again. If such monitors experience a change in video mode, they will respond by displaying a distorted image until the monitor is reset. If you have an older monitor, try turning it off, wait several minutes, then turn it on again.

Conflicts between device drivers and *Terminate-and-Stay-Resident (TSR)* programs will upset the display, and are particularly effective at crashing the computer. The most effective way to check for conflicts is to create a backup copy of your system startup files CONFIG.SYS and AUTOEXEC.BAT. From the root directory (or directory that contains your startup files), type:

```
copy autoexec.bat autoexec.xyz
copy config.sys config.xyz
```

The extensions "xyz" suggest that you use any three letters, but avoid using "bak" because many ASCII text editors create backup files with this extension.

Now that you have backup files, go ahead and use an ASCII text editor (such as the text editor included with DOS) to REM-out each driver or TSR command line. Reboot the computer. If the problem disappears, use the ASCII text editor to re-enable one REMed-out command at a time. Reboot and check the system after each command line is re-enabled. If the problem occurs again, the last command you re-enabled is the cause of the conflict. Check that command line carefully. There might be command line switches that you can add to the startup file, which will load the driver or TSR without causing a conflict. Otherwise, you would be wise to leave the offending command line REMed-out. If you encounter serious trouble in editing the startup files, you can simply re-copy the backup files to the working file names and start again.

Video drivers also play a big part in Windows. If your display problems are occurring in Windows, be sure that you have loaded the proper video driver, and that the driver is compatible with the video board being used. If problems persist in Windows, load the standard generic VGA driver. The generic VGA driver should function properly with virtually every video board and VGA (or SVGA) monitor available. If the problem disappears when using the generic driver setup, the original driver is incorrect, corrupt, or obsolete. Contact the driver manufacturer to obtain a copy of the latest driver version. If the problem persists, the video adapter board might be defective or incompatible with Windows. Try another video adapter.

Symptom 43-7. When returning to Windows from a DOS application, the Windows screen "splits" from top-to-bottom This is a DOS problem that is seen under Windows, which indicates an obsolete or corrupted video driver (for example, using a Windows 3.0 video driver under Windows 3.1). Chances are that the video adapter is running just fine. Be sure that the proper DOS "grabber" file is installed and specified in the SYSTEM.INI file. Check with the video-board manufacturer to obtain the latest assortment of drivers and grabber files. Try re-installing the drivers from their master disk. If you do not have current drivers available, try switching to the generic VGA driver.

Symptom 43-8. The system hangs up during initialization, some characters might be missing from the display, or the screen colors might be incorrect These are classic symptoms of a hardware conflict between the video adapter and one or more cards in the system, or an area of memory. Some video boards use an area of upper memory that is larger than the "classic" video area. For example, the Impact SVGA board imposes itself on the entire address range between A0000h and DFFFFh. In this kind of situation, any other device using an address in this range will conflict with the video board. A conflict might occur when the video board is first installed, or the board might work fine until another device is added or modified.

Resolving a hardware conflict basically means that something has to give—one of the conflicting elements (i.e., IRQ lines, DMA channels, or I/O addresses) must be adjusted to use unique system resources. As a technician, it rarely matters which of the conflicting devices you change, but remember that system startup files, device drivers, and application settings might also have to change to reflect newly selected resources. You might also be able to resolve some memory conflicts by adding the EXCLUDE switch to

EMM386.EXE. The video adapter manual will indicate when an EXCLUDE switch is necessary.

Symptom 43-9. Your system is generating DMA errors with a VGA board in the system, and video BIOS shadowing disabled This is a fairly rare symptom that develops only on some older i486 systems, and is usually caused by an 8-bit VGA board in a system equipped with a slower version of the i486 CPU (in the 25MHz range). Eight-bit access takes so long that some DMA requests are ignored—thus, an error is generated. If you find such a problem, try enabling video ROM shadowing through the CMOS setup to allow faster access to video instructions. Also, you might try a newer revision of the i486 CPU.

Symptom 43-10. The system hangs up using a 16-bit VGA board and one or more 8-bit controllers This is typically a problem that arises when 8-bit and 16-bit ISA boards are used in the same system. Because of the way that an ISA bus separates the 8-bit and 16-bit segments, accessing an 8-bit board when 16-bit boards are in the system might cause the CPU to (falsely) determine that it is accessing a 16-bit board. When this occurs, the system will almost invariably crash. Try removing any 8-bit boards from the system. If the crashes cease, you have probably nailed down the error. Unfortunately, the only real correction is to either remove the 8-bit board(s) or reconfigure the board(s) to use a higher area of memory.

Symptom 43-11. You have trouble sizing or positioning the display, or you see error messages, such as "Mode not supported" or "Insufficient memory" These kinds of errors might occur in newer or high-end video boards if the board is not set up properly for the monitor it is being used with. Most new video boards include an installation routine that records the monitor's maximum specifications, such as resolution (and refresh frequencies), horizontal scanning frequencies, and vertical scanning frequencies. If such data is entered incorrectly (or the monitor is changed), certain screen modes might no longer work properly. Check the video adapter's installation parameters and correct its setup, if necessary.

Symptom 43-12. You frequently encounter GPFs when using QuickTime for Windows 1.1 This is a notable problem with ATI Mach64 cards, but it has been known to occur with other advanced video boards. Often, the problem can be corrected by making a change in the Windows SYSTEM.INI file. For the ATI Mach64, you must turn DeviceBitmaps=off under the [macx] section. As an alternative, start the ATI FlexDesk, type OPT (this starts a "hidden" window), then uncheck the DeviceBitmap entry.

Symptom 43-13. The video board will not boot up when used in a particular motherboard Generally speaking, cases of hardware incompatibility occur between certain video boards and motherboards. This usually causes a great deal of confusion because the video board might work just fine when tested in a different motherboard, and other video boards might work well in the original motherboard—the technician simply winds up chasing ghosts. A noted example of this problem is the Boca Research VGAXL1/2 refusing to work in a Micronics 486DX2/66 motherboard. The solution to this problem demands that U13 on the video board be a Texas Instruments TI-74F04. If U13 is a Motorola IC, you will need to send the board back for rework—strange but true. For general troubleshooting purposes, if a certain video board and motherboard refuse to work together, don't waste your time chasing ghosts—contact both the board maker and PC (or motherboard) maker, and see if there are any reports of incompatibilities.

Symptom 43-14. Diagnostics refuse to show all of the available video modes for a particular board—even though all video RAM was properly detected, or the board refuses to operate in some video modes If a video board does not respond to certain video modes (usually the higher video modes), it is because a conflict is in the upper memory area and a memory range needs to be excluded. If a memory manager is at work (e.g., QEMM, 386MAX, or EMM386), try disabling the memory manager in CONFIG.SYS, or boot the system from a clean floppy. Try your diagnostic(s) again—chances are that the problem has disappeared. To fix this problem on a more permanent basis, re-enable the memory manager using an exclude command. Try x=B100h-B1FFh as the first parameter on the memory manager's command line. If that does not work, try x=A000h-BFFFh. Finally, try x=A000h-C7FF.

Symptom 43-15. The characters shown in the display appear fuzzy This is often the result of a speed problem, where the system is running too fast for the VL bus video board. In virtually all cases, you will find the VL bus to be running over 33MHz. Try slowing down the VL bus speed. This will sacrifice video performance, but should stabilize the system. Chances are also very good that the system has been locking up frequently—slowing down the video board should also correct such lock-ups.

Symptom 43-16. Pixels appear "dropped" behind the mouse cursor and graphic images appear to break up under Windows The two major causes for this type of problem are: bad video RAM or the system bus speed is too fast. Check the CMOS setup for an entry in Advanced Setup, such as "AT Bus Clock," "ISA Bus Speed," "AT Bus Speed." The corresponding entry should be set to 8.33MHz. Otherwise, excessive speed might result in "lost" video data. If the bus speed is set properly, run a diagnostic to check the integrity of video RAM (you might have to replace the video RAM or replace the video board entirely).

Symptom 43-17. Video-related conflicts occur in Packard Bell systems The system refuses to boot or starts with "garbage" and erratic screen displays. This symptom is encountered most frequently with Boca video boards on Packard Bell systems with video circuits already on the motherboard. Even when the on-board video has been disabled, reports indicate that the video circuitry remains active, then conflicts with the add-on video board. Packard Bell indicates that their Vxxx.16 BIOS will correct this problem, so contact Packard Bell for an appropriate BIOS upgrade.

Symptom 43-18. Text appears in an odd color For example, text that should be green appears black. This is almost always the result of a problem with the palette decoding registers on the particular video board, and will typically appear when using higher color modes (e.g., 64k or 16M colors). Be sure that the video drivers are correct, complete, and up-to-date. If the problem persists, you might need to replace the video board outright.

Symptom 43-19.   When an application is started (under Windows), the opening display appears "scrambled" Although this might appear to be a video memory problem at first glance, it is actually more likely to be related to a buggy video driver. Upgrade the video driver to the latest version or try a generic video driver that is compatible with your video chipset.

Symptom 43-20.   The display colors change when exiting from a DOS shell under Windows This problem has been noted with video boards, such as the Diamond SpeedStar Pro, and is almost always the result of a video board defect (usually a palette problem). For the Diamond board, the product must be replaced with revision A2. For other video boards, such problems can usually be corrected by replacing the video board outright.

Symptom 43-21. The computer locks up or crashes when starting an .AVI file This problem is encountered frequently as computer users first begin to try multimedia applications. Rather than being a problem with the video board specifically, the trouble is often from using an outdated version of Video for Windows. Be sure to use Video for Windows 1.1E or later. Video for Windows can be downloaded from the Diamond Multimedia FTP site at: **ftp://ftp.diamondmm.com/pub/misc/vfw11e.exe**. You might also need to edit the [DrawDib] section of the WIN.INI file and add an entry that says: DVA=0. If no [DrawDib] section is present, you can add it. Remember to restart Windows after making any changes.

Symptom 43-22. The computer is running very slowly (poor performance), and the hard drive light is continuously lit This problem is particularly apparent with Diamond Edge 3D video boards on systems with more than 16MB of RAM. The Diamond Edge 3D board comes with both 1MB and 6MB MIDI bank files. Diamond recommends that you use only the 6MB bank file on systems with more than 16MB of RAM. To change the size of the MIDI bank file being used, right-click on *My computer* and choose *Properties*. Open the *System control panel* and click on the *Device manager* tab. Click on the (+) symbol beside the *Sound, video, and game controller* line, then highlight the *Diamond EDGE 3D PCI multimedia device*, and click on *Properties*. Click on *Settings*. You will then see the 1MB and 6MB MIDI bank selection. Select the 6MB option and choose *OK*. Restart your computer when prompted.

Symptom 43-23. The .AVI files have distorted colors or "grainy" playback This usually occurs when playing 8-bit .AVI files that are not supported by DCI, and can usually be corrected by disabling the accelerated video playback features of the video board. For example, the Diamond ViperPro Video board is noted for this problem; you would need to edit the COPRO.INI file located in the directory. In the [VCP] area, change the VCPEnable= line to OFF. Save the .INI file and restart Windows.

Symptom 43-24. The PCI video board will not work under Windows unless the system's PCI SCSI devices are disconnected This type of problem occurs only on certain combinations of PCI system hardware. For example, this type of symptom has been documented using Phoenix BIOS 4.04 and a UMC8810P-AIO motherboard on systems with an NCR SCSI controller and SCSI devices. You can often correct such

problems by correcting the *Advanced system setup* in CMOS. Start the CMOS setup, go
to the *Advanced system setup*, and select *PCI devices*. Setup the PCI slot for the SCSI controller as IRQ9 and Level edge select. The slot for the video board should have the IRQ
set to *None* and *Level edge select*. Change the Base Memory Address from 0080000000
to 0081000000.

**Symptom 43-25. Boot problems occur after a new video board has been
installed** Typical problems include no video or eight beeps when the system is turned
on. This is usually the result of an outdated system BIOS, which is not capable of detecting the particular video chipset in use. The BIOS interprets this as meaning that no video
board is in the system, and an error is generated accordingly. Contact the motherboard
manufacturer (or PC maker) for an updated system BIOS. Most BIOS versions dated after the fall of 1994 should be able to detect most modern video chipsets.

Symptom 43-26. Boot problems occur when a PCI video board is installed
Two common problems account for this. First, the system BIOS did not complete the configuration of the video board correctly and the board has not been enabled onto the PCI
bus. The video board manufacturer might have a utility available that can "remap" the
video card to a new address outside of physical memory. For the Matrox Millennium, use
the PCIMAP.EXE utility. Other Matrox boards use the MGABASE.EXE utility. Other
PCI video board manufacturers probably offer their own utilities. The second problem is
that the system BIOS has assigned a base memory address to the video board, which is
used by another device or is reserved for use by the motherboard chipset. Although the
utilities mentioned might often help to correct this problem, a more permanent fix is usually to update the system BIOS. Investigate a BIOS upgrade from the motherboard (or PC)
manufacturer.

**Symptom 43-27. The monitor overscans when entering a DOS shell from
Windows** This creates a highly distorted image, and it can (if left for prolonged periods)
damage the monitor circuitry. The cause of this problem is usually a bug in the video driver.
For example, this type of problem is known to happen when using the Diamond SpeedStar
Pro with drivers prior to version 1.06. Obtain the latest video driver from the video-board
maker or try a generic video driver written by the video chipset maker.

Symptom 43-28. An intermittent "Divide by zero" error occurs Although
this type of error has several possible causes, they are all related to flaws in software—in
this case, problems with the video driver or video "toolkit" that is installed with the particular video board. Often, upgrading the driver or video support tools will eliminate this
problem. For example, "Divide by zero" errors can be corrected with the Diamond Stealth
64 Video 2001 series by opening the InControl Tools package, and changing a "Center to
viewport" selection to "Center to desktop." Similarly, the "Maximize to viewport" selection should be changed to "Maximize to desktop."

**Symptom 43-29. During MPEG playback, the display flickers, shows low
refresh rates, or appears to be in an interlaced mode** This is not necessarily
an error. With some video boards (such as the Diamond MVP1100), MPEG files cannot

play correctly at high refresh rates—typically over 72Hz. When an MPEG file is played, the driver will automatically switch to a 72Hz vertical refresh rate. This might result in an unexpected change of display quality during playback. After exiting from the MPEG player, the original (higher) refresh rate will be restored. If a vertical refresh rate lower than 72Hz was originally selected, then the vertical refresh rate will not change during MPEG playback, so you should see no difference in the display.

Symptom 43-30. An error, such as "There is an undetectable problem in loading the specified device driver" occurs when starting an MPEG player or other video tool In almost all cases, the related driver is missing, installed improperly, or corrupted. Reinstall the MPEG playback driver(s) for your particular video board and be sure to use the latest version. If problems persist, check for the driver under the WIN.INI or SYSTEM.INI file and see that it contains only one load= reference to the particular driver(s)—repeated references can cause conflicts or other loading problems.

Symptom 43-31. On video boards with TV tuners, the TV window is blurry or fuzzy at 1024-x-768 (or higher) resolutions This symptom is particularly noted with the Diamond DVV1100. Unfortunately, this type of symptom is usually the result of limited bandwidth of the particular video board—specifically of the video chipset. The only real option is to reduce the resolution to 800×600 or 640×480 when running the TV, and lower the refresh rate to 60Hz. Contact your video board's manufacturer—an RMA or other replacement/upgrade program might be available to correct the issue.

Symptom 43-32. On video boards with TV tuners, the reception does not appear as good as that of an ordinary TV This problem has been noted in conjunction with Matrox Media-TV boards, and is usually caused by the local cable company using the HRC carrier frequency instead of the standard carrier frequency. For Matrox boards, you can correct the problem by modifying the DVMCIMIL.INI file in the directory. Under the [Carrier] section, change the CarrierType=0 entry to CarrierType=1. Other video/TV boards might utilize different .INI entries, or allow carrier selection through the use of an onboard jumper, but poor reception is almost always the result of an unusual cable carrier.

Symptom 43-33. Errors appear, such as "Insufficient video memory" Not enough video memory is on the board to handle screen images at the resolution and color depth you have selected. In most cases, the system might crash outright. Your immediate solution should be to select a lower resolution or a smaller color palette. If you are encountering such problems when attempting to play .AVI or MPEG files, you should be able to select smaller video windows and lower color depth without altering your Windows setup. As a more long-term solution, you should consider adding more video memory or replacing the video board with one that contains more video memory.

Symptom 43-34. The PCI video board is not working properly. A BIOS conflict is occurring with PCI interrupt 1Ah The lower 32KB of the ROM BIOS has been redirected for high memory use. Disable this memory with your memory manager by adding an exclude command, such as: x=f000-f7ff.

Symptom 43-35. Video corruption or sporadic system rebooting occurs when using an SLC-type motherboard This particular symptom has been most noted when using Number Nine video boards with Alaris SLC2 motherboards. The SLC2 microprocessor uses a 32-bit internal data bus, but the external data bus (seen by the motherboard) is 16 bit. Most of the registers on contemporary VL and PCI video boards are mapped as 32 bits, and cannot be accessed as two 16-bit registers. As a result, the video board simply cannot be used together with the particular motherboard. You will have to upgrade the motherboard or use a different video board.

Symptom 43-36. Video playback experiences long pauses while the hard drive thrashes excessively This problem appears under Windows 95, and it is almost always the result of disk-caching problems. Start Windows Explorer and highlight the drivers responsible for video playback (for a Motion Pixels video board, highlight MPXPLAY.EXE and MPXPLAY.PIF). Click the right mouse button and select *Properties*. In the *Memory* page, be sure that the "Protected" option has been set. Restart the video clip or restart Windows 95, if necessary.

Symptom 43-37. The loop-through feature of your video board cannot be used Typical examples include the Number Nine 9FX Motion 771 VGA loop through connector with a Reel Magic board and a Number Nine driver. Unfortunately, this is often the result of a limitation with the video board's graphics processor IC (refusing to support loop-through functionality). To use loop-through, try the standard VGA driver.

Symptom 43-38. Windows appears with a "black box" cursor and/or icons that fail to appear on the screen In most cases, the problem is caused by an incompatibility with the motherboard's non-compliant PCI BIOS (the motherboard's BIOS does not comply with the PCI backward-compatibility requirement). To overcome this problem, set the video board's memory aperture manually by editing the SYSTEM.INI file located in the directory. For example, when working with a Number Nine 9GXE, find the [#9GXE] section of SYSTEM.INI, then add a command line, such as: APERTURE-BASE=0x8800 or APERTURE-BASE=31. Save the file and restart Windows. The actual section for your particular video board might be different.

Symptom 43-39. Video problems occur or the system locks up while using an anti-virus program This error occurs frequently when using memory-resident virus checking. Some video boards allow you to compensate for this by editing the SYSTEM.INI file. For the Number Nine 9GXE board, find the [#9GXE] area in SYSTEM.INI, then set the FastMMIO= entry to *Off*. Remember to save the .INI file and restart Windows. The actual section for your particular video board might be different. As an alternative, you could also disable or remove the anti-virus program.

Symptom 43-40. An error indicates that not enough memory is available for playback or re-sizing of the playback window This type of program is directly caused by a lack of system (not video) memory in the PC. If your system uses SMARTDRV (Windows 3.1x), try reducing the memory used for caching. Try unloading various unneeded programs from memory, and consider disabling any RAM drives that might be active. Finally, consider adding more system RAM to the PC.

Symptom 43-41. The video board refuses to accept a particular video mode Mode problems are most frequent when attempting to use unusual palette sizes, such as 32,000 or 64,000 colors. Try setting the video board to 256 colors. If a higher color depth is needed, it might be possible to run the video board in a palletized mode or gray-scale mode by adding command-line switches to the video driver. Refer to the instructions that accompany the particular video board for detailed information. You might also consider a video BIOS upgrade or try using an upgraded VESA driver (such as UNI-VBE 5.3 from SciTech Software).

Symptom 43-42. The video system cannot lock memory using QEMM and linear video memory This is often a DOS problem with Motion Pixels video boards when using QEMM 7.04 and earlier versions. The DPMI has a bug when accessing physical memory above the DPMI's host memory. Upgrade the version of QEMM to 7.5 (or later) or play video under Windows instead.

Symptom 43-43. The video system cannot lock memory under Windows or the system hangs This is also a problem noted most often with Motion Pixels video boards, and is almost always related to the use of a WINDPMI.386 DPMI driver loaded through SYSTEM.INI. WINDPMI.386 reports the wrong amount of free lockable DPMI memory. If your Windows platform is using Borland's WINDPMI.386, manually reduce the cache size with the /c option or remove (or disable) the driver from SYSTEM.INI entirely. You might also consider upgrading WINDPMI.386 to a later version. Contact Borland technical support or contact the technical support department of the video board maker.

Symptom 43-44. Other devices don't work properly after the PCI video card is installed For example, the sound card output is distorted or a fast modem loses data. This can happen often with newer video adapters. Some computers require that software wait for the hardware to be ready to receive new data. Newer video board drivers are not normally set do this because it slows them down slightly (and it's not necessary for most current computers). Under Windows 95, right-click on the Windows 95 desktop background. Click the *Properties* menu item, select the video board's *Settings* tab. Select the *Advanced* button, then click the *Performance* tab. Clear the "Use automatic PCI bus retry" check box. Finally, accept your changes and reboot the computer when instructed to do so. Under Windows 3.1x, edit the SYSTEM.INI file in your directory to add the line PciChipSet=1 to the particular video board's section (e.g., [mga.drv]).

Symptom 43-45. A Windows 95 game doesn't start or runs slower than normal The program uses the Microsoft DirectX interface. DirectX might not be installed or an older version of DirectX is installed. Most programs that use DirectX install it as part of their installation, but some do not. Also, some older programs might install an earlier version of DirectX (overwriting a later version). To see if DirectX is installed:

- Right-click on the Windows 95 desktop.
- Click the *Properties* menu item and select the video adapter's *Settings* tab.
- Click the *Advanced* button and click the *Information* tab.
- Look at the Microsoft DirectX Version label. DirectX 5.x should be the current version.

If the current version of DirectX is installed, you're finished. Otherwise, you'll need to install DirectX:

> If the DirectX setup program asks if you want to replace the existing display drivers, click *No.*

Further Study

That concludes the material for Chapter 43. Be sure to review the glossary and chapter questions on the accompanying CD. If you have access to the Internet, take a look at some of these video adapter resources:

ATI: **http://www.atitech.ca**

Data Expert: **http://www.dataexpert.com**

Diamond Multimedia: **http://www.diamondmm.com**

Genoa: **http://www.genoasys.com**

Hercules: **http://www.hercules.com**

Matrox: **http://www.matrox.com**

Number Nine: **http://www.nine.com**

Oak: **http://www.oaktech.com**

Orchid: **http://www.orchid.com**

STB: **http://www.stb.com**

Trident: **http://www.trid.com**

Video Logic: **http://www.videologic.com**

VIDEO CAPTURE/
PC-TV BOARDS

CONTENTS AT A GLANCE

Understanding Video-Capture
Boards
  How a capture board works
  The capture process
  The role of a CODEC
  Intel indeo video

Making the Most of Video Capture
  Image window size
  Image frame rate
  Video source quality
  Color
  Lighting
  Camera techniques

Understanding PC-TV Boards
  Displaying TV video in a window
  Video overlay mode

  Primary surface mode
  Decoding intercast broadcasts

Troubleshooting Video Capture and
PC-TV Boards
  Effects of hardware conflicts in
    video capture
  Troubleshooting tips
  Installation symptoms
  Video-capture symptoms
  Capture/TV application symptoms
  Video playback symptoms
  MPEG/PC-TV board troubleshooting

Further Study

Of all the expansion devices that have become available for PCs over the last decade, video capture and PC-TV boards (Fig. 44-1) are probably the most exciting. The ability to record sound and video on a PC has been an important element in the push toward desktop multimedia PCs. The captured data can then be edited, enhanced, and incorporated into any manner of computerized presentation. Such potential makes the video-capture board ideal for applications ranging from real-estate to business to medicine. PC-TV boards bring television and Intercast broadcasts to your desktop. Not only does this open another avenue of entertainment for the PC, but it also takes another step toward the "convergence" of PC, TV, and the Internet. In many cases, a single device can play TV, capture audio and video, or playback MPEG files. This chapter introduces you to basic video recorder and PC-TV concepts, and shows you how to deal with a wide range of problems that can accompany the hardware.

Understanding Video-Capture Boards

The first step in dealing with video-capture problems is to understand the processes that make the board work in the first place. Figure 44-2 illustrates a multi-function video board that doubles as a capture board, a VGA video adapter, and a video output system (to drive things such as a TV monitor or VCR). The capture board plugs right into any available ISA slot. Remember that this is only one type of video-capture product. Many of the newest video capture-type products use the PCI bus for high-performance data transfer.

HOW A CAPTURE BOARD WORKS

The heart of the board is a microcontroller that directly operates the video-decoder and image-controller ICs. Video signals entering the decoder are converted to analog RGB (red,

FIGURE 44-1   A typical PC-TV/video-capture board.
Intel Corporation

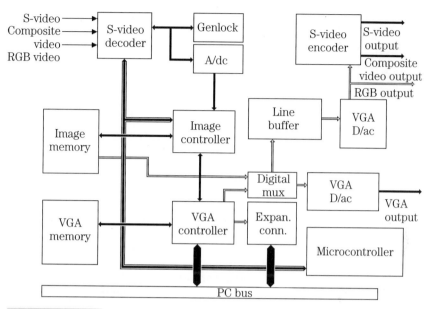

FIGURE 44-2   Block diagram of an integrated video-capture/VGA board.

green, and blue) data. The genlock circuit is a high-frequency clock source that is phase-locked to the horizontal sync signal of the video source. The *Analog-to-Digital Converter (ADC)* circuits use the "genlock" signal as a basis for digitizing the video (not all video-capture products offer a genlock feature). The image controller (which can be set to operate in several different color modes, such as 15-bit, 16-bit, and 24-bit modes) directs the transfer of digitized image data into image memory. Image memory can then be read from a second data bus directly to a digital multiplexer. The multiplexer selects data from either the image memory or the VGA controller to be passed on to the VGA *Digital-to-Analog Converter (DAC)*, where data is converted into analog form to drive the monitor. Thus, you can see the digitized video image on the monitor while it is being recorded.

The capture board also contains a standard VGA sub-system, which provides a VGA video adapter for the PC on the same board. The VGA controller IC manages the video adapter operations, and stores graphic information in the VGA memory. The VGA controller can be addressed directly from the expansion bus. When the capture circuit is idle, the VGA controller passes data from the VGA memory on to the data multiplexer, where it is converted to analog RGB monitor signals. Not all video-capture devices include an on-board video adapter—many only capture video, and use the existing video adapter for "preview" and "playback."

The capture board in Fig. 44-2 offers an added bonus—a video drive sub-system. Video data is passed through a line buffer. The line buffer converts data to NTSC data rates, then passes the data on to a stand-alone VGA DAC. The analog RGB signals are sent to an output port, as well as processed through an S-video encoder, which provides an independent video source. This is ideal for observing the VGA image on a TV or recording it to a VCR. Figure 44-3 shows you the typical connector arrangement for such a multi-function capture board. As a technician, you should realize that only a few video-capture boards provide built-in VGA adapter support or an independent video output.

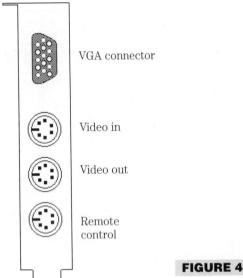

VGA connector

Video in

Video out

Remote
control

FIGURE 44-3 Typical video-capture board
connections.

THE CAPTURE PROCESS

Now that you have some insight into how a video-capture board works, you can understand how the video-capture process works in the PC as a whole. Figure 44-4 shows you
a "roadmap" of audio and video data through the PC. As with all capture systems, the
process begins with a video source. In today's PCs, the source can be any S-video device,
such as a camcorder, VCR, or laserdisk player. Video signals are sent to the capture board,
but sound is sent to the PC sound board.

The video-capture board digitizes the video signal. Some boards, such as Intel's Smart
Video Recorder (SVR), will process and compress the video data "on-the-fly" (also known
as *hardware-based compression*). Data is then stored in system RAM. Audio is digitized
by the sound board, and that audio data is also placed in system RAM. Under software tools,
such as Microsoft Video for Windows, sound and video data are synchronized together, then
stored on the hard drive in a standard file format, such as *Audio-Video Interleave (.AVI)*.
While data is being moved to the hard drive, additional data-compression techniques (or
software-based compression) can be applied to reduce the overall resulting file size.

During the playback process, files are read from the hard drive and expanded (if necessary, with software-decompression techniques) into system RAM. Sound and video data
are separated. Video data is sent to the display adapter and on to the monitor. Sound data
is sent to the sound board, where it is processed and passed to the speakers. Thus, sound
and video can be repeated (as required) or used in conjunction with other computer packages, such as presentation packages.

THE ROLE OF A CODEC

Video capture produces a tremendous amount of data. Just consider a single 320-x-200
frame that is made up of 64,000 pixels (320 × 200). If you are using a color depth of
65,536 colors, each pixel would need 16 bits (2 bytes) or 128KB per frame. If you are trying to capture 10 complete frames per second, more than 1.28MB per second will have to

be channeled into system RAM. As you might imagine, it would not take more than a few seconds to use up all the available RAM in a PC. However, much of the video data captured in each frame is repetitive—it can be compressed before storing data in RAM or on the hard drive, then decompressed during playback. As a result, the actual data stored in the system can be much less than it would be otherwise.

The *Compressor/Decompressor (CODEC)* is responsible for reducing this data load. A well-designed CODEC can reduce data without measurably reducing the quality of an image. CODEC functions can be implemented in hardware (as a digital signal processor) or in software (as a driver). Today, the four major CODEC techniques are: Cinepack, Indeo, Video 1, and RLE. Cinepack is perhaps the best codec, offering very good compression for fast-action sequences (where data changes rapidly) with little loss of image quality. However, Cinepack compression is a very slow process—certainly not appropriate for "on-the-fly" compression. Intel's Indeo video is much faster than Cinepack, but is not well-suited for quickly changing data, such as that found in fast-action sequences. Video 1 and RLE are generally used only for slow animation or palletized video.

INTEL INDEO VIDEO

Indeo video is Intel's digital video capture, compression, and decompression software. The technology revolves around a software-based CODEC (a driver) that compresses digital video data for storage, and decompresses it for playback on a multimedia PC. For a computer to play files compressed with Indeo video, the Indeo video codec must be installed on the computer, using the setup program provided by Intel. You can check for the presence of Indeo video drivers using the following steps:

- Click *Start*, select *Settings*, then open the *Control panel*.
- Doubleclick on *Multimedia*.
- Select the *Advanced* tab.

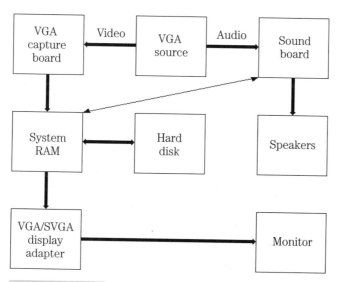

FIGURE 44-4   The audio/video capture and playback map.

- Doubleclick on *Video compression codecs*.
- Doubleclick on the Indeo video drivers you see listed.
- Click *Settings*. An *About* box appears containing the version number.

If no Indeo video drivers are listed, they are not installed.

Making the Most of Video Capture

Even under the best of circumstances, video capture presents a serious challenge to system processing. The challenge of video capture is to record an image of adequate quality at a window size large enough to be meaningful, while maintaining a frame rate high-enough to reproduce smooth motion. Quality video capture requires a careful balance of processing power with window size, frame rate, and original image quality. This part of the chapter outlines some issues to consider when capturing video.

IMAGE WINDOW SIZE

A finite amount of time is required to put a pixel on the screen; the more pixels that must be generated, the more time is required. Because larger playback windows contain more pixels, more time is necessary to "draw" each playback frame. This, in turn, reduces the frame rate. Larger playback windows also result in larger video files. Faster machines can support larger playback windows for any given frame rate. The three typical playback window sizes are:

- 320×240 is considered ideal for many multimedia applications, but is limited to slower frame rates.
- 240×180 is regarded as a good intermediate window size across a range of frame rates.
- 160×120 is the smallest commonly used video window size, but it allows the fastest frame rates.

IMAGE FRAME RATE

Frame rate has a profound influence on playback quality. Faster frame rates provide smoother images (especially for moving images or action shots), but requires more data. Smaller playback windows can usually sustain a higher frame rate and vice versa. Faster machines can support faster frame rates for any given playback window size. The most common frame rates are:

- 5–10fps Used for low data rate applications, such as video conferencing or Internet video.
- 15fps Considered satisfactory for most multimedia presentation applications.
- 24fps The frame rate at which motion pictures are projected in theaters.
- 25fps PAL (Europe) broadcast television frame rate.
- 30fps NTSC (USA, Japan) broadcast television frame rate.

VIDEO SOURCE QUALITY

The most important factor affecting the quality of your final video-capture file is the quality of the original source video. Compression cannot recreate detail that wasn't present in the original image, but it can take artifacts present in the original video (such as static) and potentially make them worse. So, it is important that the best video source possible be used to create compressed video files.

Compression algorithms (such as Indeo) analyze the digitized video input stream searching for redundant or predictable data patterns that can be compressed and reconstructed later. The CODEC compressor interprets noise or artifacts digitized from the analog source as non-redundant, unpredictable data; it wastes valuable CPU time and file space attempting to accurately compress and store these deficiencies. That's why the quality of the original source video is so crucial to the quality of the resulting compressed digital video file. Video artifacts can also look worse after compression than they did originally.

Capture your source video using a high-quality video tape format. The best source video uses S-Video, rather than composite formats. S-Video signals carry separate signals for luminance (brightness) and chrominance (color), resulting in higher bandwidth and an improved signal-to-noise ratio. Composite video sources modulate the luminance and chrominance together on one signal, which lowers both the bandwidth and the signal-to-noise ratio. Composite video signals are also subject to video artifacts, such as color bleeding. The available formats are:

- *D1 and Digital Betacam* D1 and Digital Betacam actually store video information digitally (rather like an audio CD). Both formats are broadcast-quality, but expensive even for a professional's budget.
- *D2* D2 is the digital composite cousin of D1 and is similar to D1 in both quality and expense.
- *Betacam SP* Betacam SP is the most widely used analog recording format for video creation and post production. Its high quality makes it an ideal choice for professional and semiprofessional multimedia authoring.
- *1" Type C, _" U-Matic* 1" and _" literally refer to the width of the recording tape used in each format. 1" is an open reel-to-reel format, and _" is a cartridge format. Both are older professional studio formats. Both produce better results than consumer formats, but they have been almost entirely supplanted by the newer and better Betacam SP format.
- *Videodisc* Despite being a composite format, videodisc (also known as "laserdisc") still provides good overall quality. Some videodisc players provide S-Video outputs, though the original signal is still composite, and low-cost electronics can sometimes make these S-Video outputs worse than the composite.
- *Hi-8, Super-VHS* Hi-8 and S-VHS are consumer formats, so they're inexpensive and easily available. Both produce good results for desktop and consumer use.
- *VHS* VHS is the familiar home consumer format. Its composite signal and low-cost recording and playback mechanisms make it the lowest in quality of any available format, and it is not suitable for commercial multimedia.

COLOR

As with lighting, selecting colors and arranging color in a scene can affect the overall quality of your video source. Use the points below to optimize your use of color:

- *Avoid saturated colors in the scene* Video with highly saturated colors (especially red) can bleed or appear blocky—particularly when viewed on 8-bit (256 color) displays.
- *Avoid adjacent areas of high contrast* For example, a white shirt with black stripes is a poor choice. Sudden changes in brightness levels can emphasize color bleeding and create edges that are more difficult to compress.
- *Avoid extremely thin horizontal or vertical lines* Areas of fine detail are not always particularly visible after compression—especially when displayed in a multimedia application window. Extremely fine lines or patterns (such as those that are one pixel wide) can distort the source video image. Such distortion looks bad and is extremely difficult to compress successfully.

LIGHTING

If you've ever snapped a photo, you've probably been concerned with lighting. Lighting is just as important with video, and it can affect the overall image quality used during the capture. The following points offer some lighting tips to produce the clearest images and minimize the noise often produced in poor-lighting environments:

- *Use ample light* Adequate lighting is vital for creating high-quality video. Most consumer video cameras generate noise in low light. Random noise in an image decreases the redundant information and leads to poor compressed video quality and larger image files.
- *Avoid fluorescent light* The "color temperature" of fluorescent light makes videos look blue-green. If you're in an office, shoot near windows to use the natural light. Place the camera between the windows and the subject (don't use the windows as a background—this would place your subject in a shadow).
- *Use natural light wherever possible* The best light occurs outside on a cloudy or overcast day because the light is evenly diffused. Direct sunlight can create areas of deep shadow where video noise can be prominent.
- *Use a reflector to bounce light onto your subject* Reflectors produce more even lighting and can also reduce areas of deep shadow.

CAMERA TECHNIQUES

The way in which you use the camera to record original video will also have a profound impact on the way in which the CODEC can compress the video during capture. The following tips can help you get the most compression potential from your camera techniques:

- *Use a tripod* Even the best hand-held video camera moves, and this movement is always noticed by the viewer. Also, because a camera on a tripod is steadier, more information is redundant between frames—yielding better compression.

- *Use close-ups* Remember that your video will probably be played within a relatively small window on a computer monitor. Close-ups work well to emphasize your visual message in this medium and reduce the small detail, which might be lost during compression anyway.
- *Don't overuse pans and zooms* Pans and zooms limit how much can be compressed because nearly every pixel can change between frames. Rather than zooming, break the action up into two static shots (i.e. one close-up and one long shot). Use other techniques to create visual excitement. For example, instead of centering your subject in the frame, create a more dynamic shot by placing the subject to one side of center and directing her attention to the other side of the frame.
- *Use auto-focus wisely* The auto-focus feature of most modern video cameras works well for most medium and wide shots, but don't use it in close-ups, where the subject is moving, or when zooming in on a subject. The entire image gets blurry for a moment, then it becomes sharp, as the camera attempts to stay focused on the object in the center of the frame. This is distracting and it limits the effectiveness of compression because every pixel changes as the camera refocuses. Instead, lock your camera on non-auto focus, zoom in tight on the subject, then manually focus and zoom back out to frame the shot before you shoot.

Understanding PC-TV Boards

Television has always been a popular medium for information, education, and entertainment. With the introduction of PC-TV boards, television programs can now be presented on your monitor directly in a window—even while you do other work, such as working on a spreadsheet or in a word processor. Now that many urban and suburban areas are wired for cable service, a PC-TV board can display dozens of channels of clean, clear programming. Many PC-TV boards also provide a means of capturing still or moving images from any valid NTSC or PAL signal, so live television signals can be captured, or the signals can be taken from recorded sources, such as VCRs. In addition, PC-TV boards can access Intercast broadcasting (mixing Internet Web content and live TV programming). This combination of features makes PC-TV boards particularly handy tools for low-end multimedia creation. A typical PC-TV board is illustrated in Fig. 44-5.

The heart of the PC-TV card is the *TV tuner*. As with any ordinary TV, the tuner isolates particular channels from a cable or antenna signal source. A dbx TV-stereo decoder separates video and audio components of the channel. An audio jack provides sound from the tuned channel (and is ideal for headphones), and a CD-audio pass-through connector allows the sound to be passed through to the sound card, just like CD audio. At the same time, video data is digitized through a video-digitizer IC and is formatted to cross the PCI bus to the video adapter board. A set of auxiliary video and audio inputs allow the PC-TV board to play or capture signals from other video sources, such as VCRs.

DISPLAYING TV VIDEO IN A WINDOW

To display live video on your PC monitor, many current PC-TV boards (such as Hauppague's WinCast/TV board) use a technique called *PCI Push*. With this technique, the

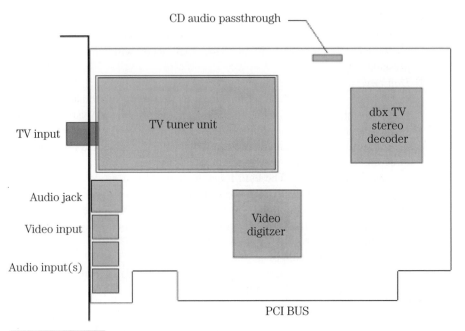

FIGURE 44-5 A typical TV board.

live video is digitized by the PC-TV board itself, then is moved over the PCI bus directly into the memory of your video display adapter. The advantage of this process is a significant reduction in processing overhead—video data does not need to be stored in main RAM. Here are the basic steps involved in getting live TV onto your video screen:

- The TV tuner is controlled by software to tune to a specified TV channel (antenna or local cable). The tuner takes a modulated television broadcast signal and turns it into demodulated video and audio signals.
- The demodulated video from the TV tuner goes directly into the video digitizer, where it is converted into a digital form using YUV 4:2:2 sampling. This high-quality sampling scheme results in resolution equivalent to 24-bits of RGB per video pixel (a "true-color" video mode).
- The demodulated audio goes into an on-board audio switcher, which can receive audio from the TV tuner or the audio-in jack. The output of this audio switcher goes to both the audio out jack and the CD-audio pass-through connector for connection to a sound card.
- The video digitizer is also a PCI master-mode device. After the video pixels are digitized, the video digitizer "pushes" them over the PCI bus into the memory of the PC's video display adapter. It does this without requiring the processor to do any work.
- Using PC-TV software, the video adapter receives the TV information and displays the selected channel in a window.

VIDEO OVERLAY MODE

Live TV can be displayed on your monitor using either "video overlay" or the "primary surface" mode (the actual mode used depends on the PC's hardware and software). If you have a video-display adapter that supports Windows 95 DirectDraw, a video adapter with a "video port" (designed to accept digital video), and enough video-adapter display memory to hold the digitized video image, then the PC-TV board's video digitizer moves YUV 4:2:2 video pixels for temporary storage into an off-screen part of the video memory, called a *secondary surface*. This method is called *video overlay*. The video display adapter will then convert the video image from YUV 4:2:2 into RGB video and continuously overlay the display screen with the video image. Using video overlay, the video controller treats the live TV image just like any other window, which results in a 24-bit video image on your VGA screen. You will also see closed captioning on-screen and you can display full-screen TV at all video resolutions.

> Video chips that can support "Video Overlay" include the S3 Trio 64V+, S3 ViRGE 3D, Cirrus Logic 5446, and ATI Rage II.

PRIMARY SURFACE MODE

If your VGA display adapter has a DirectDraw driver, but does not have either a video port or enough memory to hold the video image off-screen, then the PC-TV board will likely convert the YUV 4:2:2 video pixels into an RGB format that is compatible with your video display adapter's current operating mode (8 bits per pixel, 16 bits per pixel, or 24 bits per pixel) and then moves the pixels directly into the memory (or "primary surface") of your video adapter. This results in a video image whose color depth depends on your video adapter's operating mode. For example, the TV image will not be as good when running in a 8-bit (per pixel) mode as when running your video system in 16-bit (per pixel) mode. Also, because the video is moved directly onto the primary surface, features such as closed captioning and full-screen TV (in resolutions greater than 640 × 480) will be disabled.

> Video chips that can support "Primary Surface" mode include the S3 Trio 64, S3 Vision 968, Matrox Millenium, Matrox Mystique, and Tseng ET6000.

DECODING INTERCAST BROADCASTS

Intel Intercast technology is a relatively new feature for television broadcasts, which merges television broadcasts with the Internet's World Wide Web (WWW, or simply "the Web"). With the Intel Intercast, broadcasters can combine the television signal with Web data that includes information, such as details about the current broadcast, links to other Web pages, or advertising. With a PC that has a PC-TV board (such as the WinCast/TV board), a Pentium processor, and the Intel Intercast viewer software, you can:

- Watch television
- View Web pages received over the airwaves
- Connect to the Internet
- Capture video images
- Track mutual funds or stocks

With the viewer, you can get more information on programs as you're watching them, or "surf" to other related Web information available through the Intercast.

Intercast content is transmitted by a TV broadcaster in a common part of the ordinary TV signal, called the *Vertical Blanking Interval (VBI)*. The VBI can contain up to 10 lines of Intercast content, plus one line of closed-captioning data. The data consists of a series of 1s and 0s, and would show up on your TV screen (if you could see it) as a series of black and white dots on each line in the VBI. The PC-TV board digitizes the video lines in the VBI, which are used for Intercast Web pages (the Hauppauge WinCast/TV board uses 5× oversampling to digitize the video).

Because each line in the VBI has 35 bytes of data, each line contains 1400 samples. This digitizing is very similar to the digitizing used for TV video, but instead of using the PCI bus to move digitized video into VGA display memory, the PC-TV board moves the digitized lines from the VBI into main system memory. Once in system RAM, your processor can take the digitized line and extract the Intercast content. The method of extracting the 35 bytes of Intercast content in each VBI line uses such techniques as noise reduction and echo cancellation to extract valid Intercast content (even when given a noisy TV signal). Intel's Intercast viewer then displays the data in the Intercast viewer window.

Troubleshooting Video Capture and PC-TV Boards

Like most other expansion boards, video-capture products generally use highly integrated, proprietary ICs. As a result, it can be extremely difficult to troubleshoot the capture board to the component level. Fortunately, a large number of capture problems can be tracked to installation, setup, and operational errors. When the use of diagnostics allow problems to be isolated to the capture board itself, it is a simple matter to replace the capture board outright.

EFFECTS OF HARDWARE CONFLICTS IN VIDEO CAPTURE

Hardware conflicts are much more prevalent in today's systems than in systems only a few years ago. Sound boards, CD-ROM interfaces, modems, drive controllers, network interface cards (NICs), and video-capture boards all contribute to the congestion that fills up a system and demands its available resources. Most devices require an interrupt (IRQ), one or more I/O address settings, an occasional *Direct Memory Access (DMA)* channel, and possibly some small amount of memory for a BIOS. Unfortunately, those resources are scarce in most PCs, and you must be aware of what resources are available and what is being used before adding new devices to your system. When configuring a system from scratch, it is a simple matter to make a written record of each device setting. But with so many new upgrade options, keeping a written list up to date can be a difficult effort. The use of Plug and Play also makes "presetting" a device's resources difficult. As a technician servicing and upgrading customer's systems, you will rarely have the luxury to perform such a thorough analysis. Your most effective course is to use a diagnostic tool (such as Microsoft's MSD) or a hardware tool (such as the Discovery Card by AllMicro) to quickly check your system and report on the resources being used.

All CPUs operate linearly—that is, they only tackle one task at a time. When a device, such as the keyboard, needs the CPU to perform important work that cannot wait for free

CPU time, an interrupt signal is generated that forces the CPU to put aside whatever it was doing and respond to the interrupt immediately. When the device requesting the interrupt has been taken care of, the CPU can return to whatever it was doing until the next interrupt comes along. The problem is that only one device can use any one interrupt. If two or more devices try to use the same interrupt at the same time, one of those conflicting devices will not operate properly. In mild cases, this might appear simply as system hesitation. In serious cases, IRQ conflicts can crash your system. If you find that more than one device is using an interrupt, you must place one of those conflicting devices on an unused IRQ. IRQs can usually be changed by altering a jumper or DIP switch on the expansion board. You can recognize the effects of IRQ conflicts between a video-capture board and other devices in your system from the following symptoms:

- Video frames are dropped during video capture or playback.
- The video capture or playback process is slow or jumpy.
- The system hesitates or hangs up (crashes) completely.
- The display or data file generated during capture is corrupt.
- Audio is not captured or played back properly (if at all).

An I/O address works a bit differently. Most devices require one or more addresses to exchange data and instructions between its "registers" and the system. This I/O address works in conjunction with an IRQ, although an IRQ can be changed without changing the I/O address. All devices must use a unique I/O address. Otherwise, one device might try writing data while another device tries to read data, and the operation of both devices will be effected. I/O conflicts might also result in system crashes. Like IRQs, it is important that each device be assigned to its own unique I/O address. If more than one address is needed, there can be NO overlap of addresses at all. When more than one device attempts to use the same address(es), you must move one of the devices to an unused area. I/O settings can usually be changed by altering hardware jumpers or DIP switch settings on the expansion board. You can recognize the effects of I/O conflicts between a video-capture board and other devices in your system from the following symptoms:

- The video-capture board installation program or device driver refuses to recognize or initialize the capture board.
- Microsoft Video for Windows (or other capture application) can't initialize the capture device.
- The video-capture board works erratically or fails to respond at all.

TROUBLESHOOTING TIPS

Although video capture and playback devices can sometimes be daunting, a series of fairly "standard" troubleshooting policies can help you track down potential problem areas quickly:

- Use the latest drivers. Video capture, MPEG, and PC-TV devices depend on drivers. Buggy or outdated drivers can easily result in errors and poor performance.
- Run in the 8-bit (256 color) graphics mode. Running in any "lower" mode will result in extremely poor image quality. If you have sufficient video memory and PC processing power, you should run in the 16-bit (high color) video mode.

■ Use care in the installation of drivers—especially with PC-TV drivers, which depend on DirectDraw and ActiveX resources under Windows 95. You might need to update or reinstall these resources after the device is installed.

■ Be sure to use a strong and clean signal for recording. Your capture is only as good as the original signal.

■ Be sure to use good-quality cabling. Poor cabling and connectors can easily degrade even strong video signals. Check that all of your video/audio cables are secure.

■ When using MPEG and PC-TV devices, use moderate video resolutions and refresh rates. These devices normally "downshift" higher refresh rates during play, and the flicker can be quite noticeable at high resolutions.

■ Don't shift video modes while MPEG or PC-TV devices are in use. The change in the video drivers can crash the computer.

■ Disable power-management features, such as APM, when using video capture, MPEG, and playback devices. The computer can crash if the system shuts down into suspend mode while these devices are in operation.

■ PCI video devices often depend on the correct configuration of a PCI bus slot. Check the slot's configuration under your CMOS setup.

INSTALLATION SYMPTOMS

Symptom 44-1. Problems occur when installing the S-Video cable Most video-capture boards are designed to accept composite audio/video signals from either a single RCA connector or an S-Video connector. Unfortunately, the S-Video connector is not keyed to prevent incorrect insertion. This generally means that signals will not reach the capture board. It is possible to install the S-Video cable rotated 90 degrees from where it should be. Be sure that the arrow on the cable matches the marking on the capture board.

Symptom 44-2. Even though a valid video source is available, vertical multi-colored lines appear in the capture application window This is a problem particular to capture boards when the board itself is loose or installed improperly, or if the signal cabling is not secure. Check the capture board to see that it is fully inserted in the expansion slot. If any modules or sub-boards are attached to the capture board, see that they are secure and inserted properly. Also check any connectors and cables to be sure that they are all installed correctly.

Symptom 44-3. Even though a valid video source is available, only black appears in the capture application window There are several possible reasons for this symptom. First, check the video signal being fed to the capture board. With no signal, the video-capture window (i.e., the Video for Windows VIDCAP window) will be dark. You can test the video signal by disconnecting the video cable from the capture board and connecting it to a stand-alone monitor, such as a TV set. Damaged or defective video cables and connectors should be replaced. If you are using a camcorder as a real-time video source, be sure that the camera is turned on, the lens cover is off, and that you have selected the correct video source (i.e., composite or S-Video). Also check that the capture board is inserted in the system properly and completely. Any sub-modules should be attached securely to the main expansion board.

Finally, an IRQ conflict might be between your video-capture board and another device in your system. If you attempt to capture a video file while the capture window is dark and receive an error, such as "Wave input device not responding," it is almost certainly an IRQ problem. Run a diagnostic such as Microsoft's MSD (or use a hardware tool, such as AllMicro's Discovery Card) to identify unused IRQs, then set the video-capture board to use an available IRQ. In some cases, you must run an installation routine for the capture board when changing settings. If problems persist, the capture board might have failed.

Symptom 44-4. During installation, the error "Unable to locate an available interrupt" appears This type of symptom occurs with an IRQ conflict, or when a device driver or TSR interferes with the installation. Be sure that the capture board is configured to use an available IRQ (i.e., 9, 10, 11, or 12). You might have to use a diagnostic (such as Microsoft's MSD or the Discovery Card by AllMicro) to locate available interrupts. Try booting the system from a clean DOS disk to prevent any TSRs or device drivers from interfering with installation.

Unfortunately, if a conflict occurs during installation, it will also probably occur during actual use. So, if you suspect a TSR or device-driver conflict, you will have to disable TSRs and device drivers one by one until the conflict disappears, then work with the offending TSR or device-driver configuration to eliminate the conflict.

Symptom 44-5. The capture board cannot be initialized because of a lack of available IRQs On some systems, the capture board fails to initialize when launching the capture application. This is usually because of the lack of an available interrupt request (IRQ) for the capture board to use. To check the IRQs on your system:

1 Go to the Windows 95 desktop.
2 Right-click the *My computer* icon and select *Properties*.
3 Click the *Device manager* tab.
4 Doubleclick on *Computer* to display all IRQ resources.

You see each of your system's interrupts and which devices are using them. If all IRQs are already assigned to other devices, you'll need to free an IRQ for the video-capture board. You can usually free an IRQ by removing a device no longer in use or by disabling the IRQ on a feature not being used (e.g., if you're not using the MIDI port of a sound board, disable it to free the IRQ).

Symptom 44-6. When starting the capture utility, the error "Unable to initialize a capture device" appears This error message is produced by the capture utility (i.e., the Video for Windows VIDCAP utility) when the capture board cannot be located. For most capture boards, an IRQ conflict is probably occuring with one or more devices in the system. This can happen easily when new devices are added to the system after the capture board has been installed. Use a diagnostic (such as Microsoft's MSD or the Discovery Card by AllMicro) to locate unused IRQs. If new equipment has been added, change the new equipment to relieve the conflict. If the error manifested itself when the capture board was installed, change the board's IRQ to an available setting.

If interrupts check out properly, be sure that the capture board is inserted properly and completely into the motherboard. If any modules or sub-boards are attached to the capture board, see that they are inserted and secured properly. You might also have installed the capture software in the wrong order. Some boards require that DOS software be installed first, then Windows software drivers must be installed. If this process is reversed, the capture board's Windows drivers might not install properly. Try reinstalling the capture software. If software is correct, try another capture board.

VIDEO-CAPTURE SYMPTOMS

Symptom 44-7. Colors appear washed out or bleeding This can occur while viewing the video image before capture or during the actual playback of an image file. If the problem is manifesting itself before capture, begin by checking the signal quality from your video source, such as a VCR or video camera. A loose or damaged cable, or a poor-quality video source can result in signal degradation at the video-capture board.

If the video signal and connections are intact (and the signal looks good on a monitor, such as a TV), the problem might be in the Windows video driver being used. Better color depth in the video driver will result in better color quality in the video capture. In virtually all cases, a 16-color video driver (generic VGA) is totally inappropriate for video-capture applications—a 256-color driver is considered to be the minimum. If you are already using a 256-color video driver, try an upgrade to a 32K, 64K, or 16M color driver. You might have to contact the manufacturer of the particular video board to obtain an advanced video driver for Windows 3.1x or Windows 95.

Symptom 44-8. The video signal appears to be weak or washed out even though the video signal source is acceptable This is typical when a composite video signal output is being sent to the video-capture board as well as to a stand-alone monitor through a Y-connector. Composite output signals are usually power balanced for one connection load only. If the load on a composite output is not balanced properly, the video signal at your capture board will not contain enough power (signal degradation will occur). Try connecting the video signal directly to the video-capture board.

Symptom 44-9. "Vertical sync" error appears when trying to capture Chances are that your computer has an IRQ conflict. Check the IRQ assigned to the video card's PCI slot in the *Device manager* under Windows 95. If this PCI slot the video card is in is being used by another device, you will need to reassign the PCI slot for the video board a different IRQ. This can be done through your system's CMOS setup. If no IRQ is being assigned to the PCI slot the video card is in, that can also be a problem. Once again, you can assign an IRQ to the PCI slot through the CMOS setup. There could also be an IRQ conflict with the video capture driver. To check this, look in the *Control panel* under *Multimedia*. Click on the *Advanced* tab, then look under *Video capture drivers*. There, you'll see an entry, such as *Diamond Multimedia Capture Driver*. Doubleclick on it, then click on the *Settings* option. There, you can change the IRQ of the capture driver. Try a free IRQ or free an IRQ.

Symptom 44-10. Up to 50% of small frames are being dropped (large frames appear to capture properly) This symptom might occur in systems using fast 32-bit SCSI adapter boards, and is almost always caused by the effects of double buffering in the SMARTDRV.EXE utility. If possible, try to disable SmartDrive in the CONFIG.SYS file. If SmartDrive cannot be disabled (usually because it would have adverse side-effects on other devices that rely on SmartDrive's caching), try capturing video at a larger frame size, such as 320×240 before capturing at a small frame size. This lets SmartDrive adjust to the data needs of the larger frame size, so subsequent captures at a smaller frame size should work correctly until the system is rebooted. An updated video capture driver might also provide better performance.

Symptom 44-11. When capturing video, the corresponding screen image appears broken-up or jerky If the image being previewed on the screen prior to capture looks smooth and the captured video looks smooth when played back, you should suspect that the customer's hardware platform is not quite fast enough to update the screen while capturing. This is not necessarily a problem because many video capture applications (e.g., Video for Windows) is designed to sacrifice screen updates for the sake of smooth captures. If you need a smooth display during capture, start by relieving any unnecessary processing loads from the system:

- Close other Windows 95 applications running in the background.
- Close any DOS applications running through a window.
- Be sure that the Windows disk cache is set to at least 2MB (4MB, if possible).
- Set audio capture specifications to 8-bit, mono, 11kHz sample frequency for the lowest audio processing overhead.

Symptom 44-12. The video-capture board is working, but captures are occurring very slowly In most cases, very slow recording performance is caused as the result of an IRQ conflict between the capture board and another device on the system. Evaluate the components in your system or run a diagnostic (such as Microsoft's MSD) to locate and identify any unused interrupts in your system. If you are faced with a jumper-only capture board, set the jumper(s) to use a free valid IRQ. If your capture board requires a software setup, run its setup utility and choose another valid interrupt (e.g., 9, 10, 11, or 15).

Symptom 44-13. The Super Compressor option cannot be used in Video for Windows This is not an actual user problem. The Super Compressor is an off-line compression utility that compresses and stores video files captured at 320×240, 15 frames per second (fps) at the same data rate as CD-ROM (150KB/sec). Video for Windows version 1.0 does not support the Super Compressor function when used with Indeo 3.0 device drivers. Only the Quick Compressor in the VIDEDIT utility is available. Later versions of Video for Windows make use of this function, and you should upgrade your version of Video for Windows at your earliest convenience.

Symptom 44-14. More than one frame of motion video can't be captured This problem is reported with the Intel SVR III. While trying to capture video, the capture process stops after one frame, but the capture application acts as if it is still capturing and you must click *Stop* to exit. The YUV9 video format always seems to exhibit this problem. The RGB24 video format seems to work at lower window sizes. There are no problems capturing still images or sequences of still images. This problem appears to be related to an improper or incomplete installation of Windows 95 Direct Draw drivers. You can download and install the latest DirectX drivers from Microsoft's Website at: **http://www.microsoft.com/directx/default.asp**.

Symptom 44-15. The color video being captured is shown as black and white There are two possible causes for this. First, the capture window (e.g., the Video for Windows VIDCAP utility) is set to receive a composite video source, but the video signal being fed to the capture board through its S-Video cable. Check the configuration settings under your *Video capture* options. Be sure that the correct input type (*Composite* or *S-Video*) is selected in the video capture utility.

Another possible source of problems is a bad connection. Check that the video signal is indeed color and that a good cable is securely attached to the capture board. Try a different video source. Next, check that the capture board is inserted properly and completely in the expansion slot. If any modules or sub-boards are attached to the capture board, see that they are secured correctly. If problems persist, try another capture board.

Symptom 44-16. The video image shown in the VIDCAP capture window appears torn or bent at the top This symptom is typical of signals being supplied by VCRs (or camcorders used as VCRs), and is almost always the result of a weak video synchronization signal from the signal source. The problem can often be rectified by using a different (stronger) signal source (e.g., another camcorder or VCR). If you are using a VCR signal source, be sure that the Video for Windows *VCR* box is checked.

Use the S-Video signal source, if possible, because S-Video signals are less prone to noise and losses than composite signals. Also be sure that the video cable feeding your capture board is not lying parallel to power cables because the power cable can induce unwanted noise into the video signal. Try placing the video-capture board in another expansion slot as far as possible from the system power supply and other expansion boards because electrical signals generated by other boards might cause interference with the video data. As a sanity check, be sure that any modules or sub-boards for the video-capture device are attached properly.

Symptom 44-17. When capturing video, an error appears: "No frames captured. Confirm that vertical sync interrupts are configured and enabled" Some issues are known to occur with the Intel SVR III, but these might also affect other capture devices:

■ The Adaptec 1542B and 1542C 16-Bit ISA SCSI controllers were tested with the SVR III using IRQ 11 and I/O address 330h. When the SVR III was also set to IRQ 11, the VidCap utility in Video for Windows returned blank video, and no frames were captured, then returned the error message.
■ Reconfigure the system devices to avoid IRQ conflicts.
■ The Media Vision Pro Audio Spectrum 16 16-bit sound board was tested with the SVR III using IRQ 5, IRQ 15, and I/O addresses 220h and 388h. When the SVR III and the Pro Audio Spectrum 16 were both set to IRQ 11, the SVR III software detected a conflict, and Video for Windows returned the error message. Reconfigure the system devices to avoid IRQ conflicts.

■ This fault can also be caused by a Diamond VLB Speedstar Pro Video board using IRQ 2 by default. Disable the use of IRQ 2 on the Diamond Video Board.
■ SiS FI2 P54C motherboards using an Award BIOS also have been known to suffer this problem. You'll need to go into BIOS and tweak the chipset configuration. Change the *ISA BUS Clk Frequency* entry from *PCI Clk divided by 3* to *PCI Clk divided by 4*.

> This changes numerous settings in the chipset configuration (e.g., SRAM, Read Pulse, SRAM Burst, and Refresh) all of which go to slower value.

Symptom 44-18. Artifacts appear when capturing video at high data rates

When capturing at high data rates (such as when using 640-×-480 resolutions and 30fps frame rates), occasional problems have been noted on some PCs—most notably with Intel SVR III or Pro capture products. *Artifacts*, which resemble black horizontal lines, might appear in your preview or capture window. Try repeating the capture (best if the problem only occurs infrequently). If the artifacts occur too frequently for you to recapture, you're probably trying to capture at too high a data rate for your computer's PCI bus to handle. Reduce PCI bus traffic by lowering the data rate of the video you're capturing:

■ Use a lower frame rate.
■ Use a lower window resolution.
■ If you're using RGB24 as the video format, try using YUV9 instead.
■ Use more compression (a lower-quality setting).
■ Turn off the preview mode.

If you continue to find horizontal black lines in both preview and captured video (even at 320-×-240 resolution) when using the YUV9 video format, your computer's PCI chipset might be programmed to disable a featured called *host memory write posting*. When enabled, this feature allows your PCI chipset to write to memory at its maximum speed. When write posting is disabled, your PCI bus performance can be significantly reduced. Write posting is enabled in different ways on different systems. Some computers might permit this feature to be controlled through the CMOS setup, but other computers might require a BIOS upgrade from the system manufacturer.

Symptom 44-19. Artifacts appear when capturing video using certain PCI graphics cards

The method used by some graphics cards and their drivers to utilize the PCI bus can sometimes cause horizontal line artifacts. For example, Intel has verified a problem using the Number Nine 9FX Motion 771 graphics card (which uses the S3 Vision968 graphics chipset) together with the SVR III. The following problems seem to occur when the display color depth is 16 bit or 32 bit, and when *Preview* is on during the capture process. This also seems to occur in files captured at 320-×-240 resolution at 15 fps using either the YUV9 or RGB24 video format. Try setting the graphics display to 8-bit (256 color) mode (this has no effect on the quality of the captured video—only on the previewed video). You might also try disabling "preview" during the capture process.

Symptom 44-20. Systems with SiS 5596 or 5511 PCI chipsets lock up when using a video-capture device

This issue is known with the Video Logic Captivator

PCI board. SiS has identified the problem and a fix is available through a BIOS update. Contact the system maker or motherboard manufacturer for a BIOS update.

Symptom 44-21. Systems lockup when running video-capture devices on PCs with Phoenix BIOS Some PCs are known to lock up with the Video Logic Captivator PCI card installed (such as members of the DEC Venturis family). This has been traced to a problem to the Phoenix v.1.6 BIOS. All PCs using Phoenix v.1.6 BIOS should be upgraded to Phoenix BIOS v.1.9 (or later).

Symptom 44-22. You cannot use the capture device on a system with a SiS PCI chipset This problem is known with the Intel SVR III, and is caused by a driver-compatibility issue. The SVR III driver 1.2 will cause the system to lock up when launching the capture utility. You can determine the current driver version by opening the README.TXT file on the SVR III CD-ROM. Download and install the version 1.3 driver or later (SVR3-14.EXE from Intel at **http:\www.intel.com**). You can find out which PCI chipset is in your system by checking the PCI chipset in the *Device manager*:

- Click *Start*, Settings, and *Control panel*.
- Doubleclick the *System* icon.
- Go to the *Device manager* tab.
- Click the + in front of *System devices*, and look for a reference to the "PCI to ISA bridge," as in Fig. 44-6.

Symptom 44-23. The capture device cannot be used on a system with an S3 chipset-based video card If your system uses: an Award BIOS version 4.51pg, Windows 95 Release 2 (OSR2), and an S3 968-based video graphics card, you might experience system lockups when trying to launch your capture program. This problem has occurred with the Intel SVR III and the Diamond Stealth 64, as well as the Number Nine Motion 771). It arises from a memory-address conflict between the Intel SVR III and the S3-based video-graphics card. According to Intel, it appears that the S3 only requests 32MB of virtual memory, rather than the 64MB it actually requires. If the BIOS allocates the memory for the capture device (such as the SVR III) right above the S3 board's range, the system will lockup. To correct this problem, you'll need to change the memory address range used by the video capture device:

- Open the *Device manager* and doubleclick on the capture device (e.g., the Intel Smart Video Recorder III). Ignore the exclamation point next to it, if it has one.
- Click on the *Resources* tab, then un-check the box titled *Use automatic settings*.
- Doubleclick on the memory range and enter an address of FFFBF000–FFFBFFFF (the spaces on each side of the "–" symbol are needed). Click on *OK*.
- If Windows 95 returns the message: "The setting you have chosen conflicts with another device," click on *No*, then scroll with the up and down arrows next to the address range until no conflict is noted. Click on *OK*.

This device conflict is not apparent in *Device manager*.

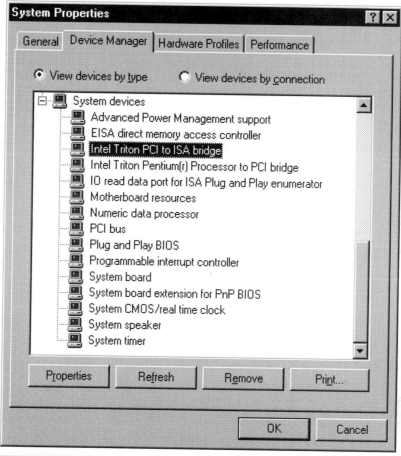

FIGURE 44-6   Locating *PCI to ISA bridge* in the Device manager.

Some installations have also noted that reinstalling Windows 95a or installing a video graphics card not based on the S3 968 chipset might also correct this problem.

Symptom 44-24. A gray background is in the live video window display
This sometimes happens with the Video Logic Captivator family. Some PCs have a problem displaying live video using Captivator Pro/TV and instead show a gray background. If the window is moved around or covered by another window, then the Windows background might show through—it's as though the live video is "transparent." Verify that all cabling and software for the video/MPEG device is installed properly.

PCs using the VIA VT481/495 chipset on the motherboard are known to have this problem (such as Unisys MPI46664-540 model 486/66MHz). The problem is caused by nonstandard ISA bus timing used by the motherboard, so sending data to the video/MPEG device (e.g., the Captivator Pro/TV) registers results in the card being reset by accident. No workaround or patch is known, except to use a different video/MPEG device.

Symptom 44-25. The video device locks up in 8-bit (256 color) display modes This problem is known to occur with Prolab VideoWorks, but it can also occur with other video/MPEG devices. You might experience system lock-ups on PCs when displaying live video in 8-bit display modes with DirectX 5 installed. This problem occurs only with graphics cards that use color keying, rather than hardware overlay to display live video (for example S3 Vision 968 based graphics cards). The only known workaround at this time is to run in 16-bit display mode.

CAPTURE/TV APPLICATION SYMPTOMS

Symptom 44-26. Bitmap or still-image files can't be imported into the Intel DVP 4.0 application If you can import .WAV and .AVI files, but can't import .BMP and other static-image files, you need to move three files from the DVP 4.0 directory to the directory. The names of the files are: DSEQFI40.DLL, TGAFIL40.DLL, and FLIFIL40.DLL. These .DLL files are copied to the DVP 4.0 directory by the DVP 4.0 setup program. In very rare cases, the location of the files results in the error: "Can't import this media type" when trying to import single-image file formats. Manually moving these .DLL files to the directory should fix the problem.

Symptom 44-27. Intercast viewer can't be started If the viewer can't detect a valid signal source, it tries to locate one. If a valid signal exists, the software asks if you want to make it permanent. Click *OK* to make the setting permanent, or click *No* to repeat the same process the next time you run the program. If no valid signal exists, an error message appears and the software shuts down. To correct the problem, ensure that the cable or antenna connection to the PC-TV card is secure, and have the local cable company check the signal quality.

Symptom 44-28. You only receive incomplete Intercast broadcast Web page displays on the PC-TV card This happens most often when you change channels quickly—you might interrupt the reception of "billboards" and Web pages sent by the broadcaster. In those instances, the default billboard or a partial Web page might display. Be sure that you remain on any given channel for a few minutes to allow enough time to receive complete Web pages or billboards.

Symptom 44-29. Intercast broadcast Web pages are missing When tuned to a channel that broadcasts Intercast content, the Intercast channel indicator animates. If no Web page displays (even with the animated channel indicator), be sure that you are not actively browsing (using the Web browser). Doubleclick the desired Web page title or icon in the *Media library*. The broadcaster might send many Web pages connected by hypertext links before signaling the main Web page to display. If part or all of the pages are missing, you can still view the existing pages through the *Media library*. Unless the broadcaster resends the pages, you cannot view pages sent before you tuned to the channel—any links referring to those pages are also not valid. Finally, check with your local cable company. The cable company might have blocked the portion of the signal that sends Intercast content.

Symptom 44-30. An error indicates that the computer can't find a .DLL file when trying to run the PC-TV application This problem frequently arises with Diamond Multimedia DTV devices and Stealth 64 drivers. This error usually means that the Diamond Stealth 64 drivers aren't installed properly, or that wrong drivers are installed. Be sure that you're using the newest drivers available from the video-board manufacturer. You can tell which driver is loaded by looking in the *Device manager* in Windows 95. You can update the video driver through the *Add new hardware* wizard, or remove the existing video device through the *Device manager*, and let Windows 95 re-detect and reinstall it.

Symptom 44-31. An error appears, such as: "The following entry should be in your system.ini file: [drivers] Msvideo=stlthcap.drv" You are then asked to press *OK* to add, or *Cancel* to exit. This means that, for some reason, the capture driver for the PC-TV card was not installed in the SYSTEM.INI file. You would only need to click *OK* to have the software add it for you. The driver might have been replaced if you have had another capture driver (e.g., from a different video-capture board) installed recently. Click *OK* to re-install the current PC-TV software.

VIDEO PLAYBACK SYMPTOMS

Symptom 44-32. The error "MMTASK ERROR >> GPF IR30.DLL 0003:0B85" appears when trying to play a captured file You encounter this error when trying to play a captured file with a utility, such as Media Player or VIDEDIT, and video and sound is in the same file (it does not occur if audio is not captured). The audio track can be played if video is not played. This problem is known to occur because of drive overlay software. For example, a Western Digital 1GB drive using an overlay software was known to conflict with the IR30.DLL file. Drive-overlay software is used so that DOS can read a drive with more than 1024 cylinders. If you upgrade the motherboard BIOS or drive controller to support LBA mode operation, you can eliminate the use of overlay software and the error should disappear.

Symptom 44-33. The video playback is choppy or contains dropped frames This is typically not related to the video-capture board. For most video-capture systems, playback speed and quality is very dependent on machine speed—faster machines with higher-performance equipment will play back video files better than slower, simpler systems. Be sure that your customer's system is equipped with at least the minimum amount of hardware to ensure a proper playback. If playback performance still seems choppy, your customer might have to upgrade their hardware platform. If a platform upgrade is out of the question, try reducing the system load during capture and playback. For example, close all unused Windows and DOS applications, close any unused data files, and select a larger virtual memory size.

This symptom appears frequently in EISA systems—even on fast EISA systems up to 50 MHz. In many cases, the afflicted EISA system CMOS was not reconfigured properly after adding memory. An EISA configuration diskette might have to be run in order to cache new memory—even though the new memory might be recognized correctly. Try booting the EISA system from its configuration disk and adjust the system from there.

Symptom 44-34. An initial flash of color appears when playing back video files Chances are that your customer is trying to play video files using an older version of VIDEDIT or VIDCAP utilities in Video for Windows. This is a known problem with these older utilities, and current versions of the software should correct the problem (**http://www.microsoft.com**). Until you can download and install updated versions of Video for Windows, you can do little other than play back video clips using the Windows Media Player or Media Browser.

Symptom 44-35. No sound is heard during playback Not all video-capture products capture sound at the same time video is captured. If no sound was captured (intentionally), no sound will be heard when the video clip is played back through Video for Windows. Some capture boards (such as Intel's SVR family) do capture sound and video simultaneously as long as audio is made available on the composite or S-Video signal cables, and the *Audio* box is checked in the *Video capture* options dialog. Also check the *Audio setup* and *Audio level* settings in Video for Windows before proceeding.

If all is well with Video for Windows, check to be sure that sound was provided to the SVR during capture. If sound was recorded, you should check the configuration of your sound board. The sound board should contain appropriate hardware settings (such as I/O, IRQ, and DMA). The proper Windows device drivers for the sound board must also be installed, and the driver must be loaded with other Windows drivers. Missing Windows sound drivers will inhibit sound. If the system is configured properly and sound is available, but no sound is recorded, the capture board might be defective—try another capture board. If sound is being captured by the sound card, the sound card might be defective.

Symptom 44-36. When playing video, the system locks up when power-management features are enabled This typically required a cold reboot. Unfortunately, video playback is often incompatible with a PC's power-management features, such as APM (even screen savers can cause this problem). For the immediate future, disable all APM or screen savers when using video-playback features. For the long term, check with the PC-TV maker and see if new drivers or playback software is available that can support APM or screen savers.

Symptom 44-37. The system locks up when changing resolutions or color depths while using MPEG playback or video-capture functions This common problem is typically caused by the behavior of the MPEG or capture software. You must close all MPEG and capture functions prior to changing resolutions or color depths.

Symptom 44-38. Sound gaps occur and the image appears choppy during playback This symptom is particular to capture boards (such as Intel's SVR family), and audio and video are integrated into a single .AVI capture file. The integrated file prevents audio and video from slipping out of sync. However, playing synchronized capture files requires substantial processing power. If a system is not fast enough, sound can "hiccup" and the video can be choppy. Unfortunately, this kind of playback problem is not a fault or defect—it is a limitation of slower PC systems (usually i486-class systems).

First, remove any Windows or DOS applications running in the background so that Windows can concentrate on Video for Windows or another playback application. If playback does not improve enough, try running the playback in a smaller window. For example, try playing back in a 160-x-120 window instead of a 320-x-240 window. Smaller windows require less processing overhead for each frame. Beyond that, the hardware platform might need to be upgraded.

Symptom 44-39. Blue or green flesh tones are in the live video and MPEG playback This corruption is often caused when an MPEG player application (e.g., MPEG Player 4.0) is loaded on a system that already has a video/MPEG player installed. This problem has been reported with the Captivator Pro/TV by Video Logic. You can correct the problem by reinstalling the video/MPEG driver for the particular device:

■ Close down all MPEG and live windows.
■ Start a DOS window.
■ Select the directory where the video/MPEG driver file resides (for the *Captivator*, the driver is PSTREAM.DRV normally in the VLPOWER directory).
■ Rename this driver file to something else.
■ Expand the driver file from your original MPEG player installation disk into your current directory, such as: EXPAND A:.DR_PSTREAM.DRV (This assumes that the Microsoft EXPAND utility is on the path).
■ Exit DOS and Windows.
■ Restart Windows and check the video again.

Symptom 44-40. An MPEG movie clip cannot be scaled to full screen when using 16.7 million colors This kind of problem is known with the Diamond MVP 2000, but can occur on other video-capture/playback platforms. You are usually missing an entry from the video device's .INI file. For the MVP 2000, you can add the following line to the [System] section of your STLTHMVP.INI file if you wish to playback MPEG full-screen in 16M color mode:

```
NoVideoSizeLimit=1
```

If you are experiencing lockups when playing MPEG clips full-screen in a 16M color mode, your system might be encountering bandwidth limitations. If you encounter this problem, you should change the following line to the [System] section of your STLTH-MVP.INI file:

```
NoVideoSizeLimit=0
```

Symptom 44-41. The video looks grainy (or otherwise poor quality) when playing back or recording This is a symptom that can occur across all video capture devices. Image quality is closely related to the color depth of your Windows video driver. Many older Windows 3.1x installations and some low-end Windows 95 platforms use the default 16-color VGA video driver supplied with the Windows operating system. 16 colors are almost never adequate to define a video image, so the image will look washed out or very grainy. You must install a 256-color (or higher) video driver written for the video board in your system. Contact the video-board manufacturer for their latest Windows 3.1/Windows 95 drivers. Most manufacturers will send a driver for free, or place the driver on a BBS or on-line service for free downloading.

Symptom 44-42. With Active Movie installed, the MPEG options do not show up as a device under Media Player If you install the MPEG video playback drivers while ActiveX (Active Movie) is installed on your system, you will not see the correct menu options in the Media Player. To correct this, uninstall the ActiveX software and reinstall the MPEG video playback drivers. To remove the Active Movie portion of ActiveX:

1 Click the *Start* button, then select *Settings*.
2 From *Settings*, choose *Control panel*.
3 Once in *Control panel*, choose and open the *Multimedia* icon.
4 Click on the *Advanced* tab.
5 Click on the "+" symbol next to the *Video compression codecs*.
6 Once a list of Codecs appears, select the *Intel Indeo (R) video interactive 32-bit driver [IV41]*.
7 Once highlighted, select the *Properties* button.
8 Click on the *Remove* button.
9 Apply or *OK* the selection.

You are now ready to install the MPEG video player drivers, then reinstall the ActiveX software later.

> ActiveX (Active Movie) is included with most versions of Microsoft Internet Explorer 3.xx. If you install the ActiveX software before installing the MPEG video playback drivers, you will not have the option to use the MPEG video player for hardware MPEG playback.

MPEG/PC-TV BOARD TROUBLESHOOTING

Symptom 44-43. The error: "No suitable DirectDraw provider" appears PC-TV boards (such as WinCast/TV) typically require a Windows 95 DirectDraw driver for your PCs video accelerator to provide "TV-in-a-window" or to extract Intercast content from the TV signal. The error message appears when the PC-TV application(s) cannot find the DirectDraw driver. You'll need to install a DirectDraw driver for your particular video board or upgrade the DirectDraw video driver. Check with the video-board manufacturer for updated video drivers with DirectDraw support.

> If your video adapter was sold before Windows 95 was introduced in August 1995, it is possible that your video chipset does not (and will not) have a DirectDraw driver. In this case, you'll need to upgrade the video adapter.

Symptom 44-44. The PC locks up when using the PC-TV in full-screen mode This is known to occur with some PC-TV boards (such as the Happauge Win-Cast/TV) when using older video adapters based on the S3 Trio64V+ chipset and running the TV in full-screen mode. For the WinCast/TV board, you will need to use an update that is found in the Filesdirectory on your PC. To install this update so that it takes effect every time you turn your system on, add the following line to your AUTOEXEC.BAT file (found in the root directory):

c:65

For other PC-TV boards, you might need to contact the individual manufacturer and obtain a driver update to correct the S3 issue or replace the video adapter with one using other than an S3 chipset.

Symptom 44-45. TV images move only very slowly in an Intercast viewer
This will occur without an updated DirectDraw driver in the PC. If an updated DirectDraw driver is not installed, the Intercast viewer will still work with some VGA video adapters, but the video image is moved to the Intercast viewer window through a Video for Windows preview window (which displays at roughly 4fps). This problem can be fixed by installing an updated Direct Draw driver—usually along with updated video adapter drivers.

Symptom 44-46. Bad or improper colors appear in the PC-TV window If your video display is running in 256 color mode, the TV picture will be displayed with only 256 colors. This compares with the 16 million different colors in the original TV image. The color palette in the TV window will change, depending upon which Windows programs are being run, and what color palettes are being used. This causes a "shortage" of colors, which can result in the wrong colors displayed. To fix this problem, first try running your video adapter at a minimum of 16 bits per pixel (a "high-color" mode). If you do not have enough memory on your video adapter to run at 16 bits per pixel at your current resolution, either lower the resolution (e.g., from 1024 × 768 to 800 × 600) or add more memory to your video display adapter.

Symptom 44-47. The system locks up when using S3 Vision 968 or 868-based video adapters System lockups occur randomly and shortly after starting the PC-TV application. This is caused by a PnP resource-allocation problem (typically memory allocation) between the S3 video adapter and the PC-TV board. To correct this problem, you'll need to manually readjust the memory address of the PC-TV board:

■ Click on the *Start* button, then *Settings* then *Control panel*.
■ Doubleclick on the *System* icon, then the *Device manager* tab.
■ Double click on *Sound, video and game controllers*, then doubleclick on the PC-TV card (i.e., "Hauppauge WinCast/TV").
■ This brings up the TV card's *Properties* window. Click on the *Resources* tab.
■ Uncheck the "Use automatic settings" box. Highlight *Memory range* and click on *Change setting*.
■ The memory address range of the PC-TV card is a set of two 8-digit hexadecimal numbers, such as: FFFA0000–FFFA0FFF

To eliminate the memory overlap, either increase the second digit by four or decrease it by eight (remember to use hexadecimal arithmetic). This changes the memory space between the video adapter and the PC-TV to 64MB. Table 44-1 illustrates two examples.

Symptom 44-48. You cannot tune the PC-TV card above channel 13 This is almost always a card setup oversight. Check the video source setting in the video property dialog(s). When connecting local cable to your PC-TV card, you must set the video source setting for *Cable*. If you select *Antenna*, the tuner stops at channel 13.

TABLE 44-1 ALTERING MEMORY ALLOCATION FOR A PC-TV BOARD

ORIGINAL CONFIGURATION	INCREASE BY 4	DECREASE BY 8
80000000–80000FFF	84000000–84000FFF	78000000–78000FFF
FFFA0000–FFFA0FFF	can't do	F8FA0000–F8FA0FFF

Symptom 44-49. The PC-TV picture suffers from poor quality This is usually because of inadequate video board support. A poor TV image is usually caused when your video adapter does not have enough video RAM to hold the TV image. In this case, the PC-TV board will usually resorts to a lower-quality mode (such as Primary Surface mode), which lowers image quality. A memory upgrade on your video display adapter might fix this problem. Another possible cause of this problem could be that your video adapter does not support Windows 95 DirectDraw. In this case, you should consider an upgrade to a new video accelerator that has DirectDraw support.

A poor video picture might also indicate a bad signal. To verify a bad signal, move the antenna or check your local cable connection. Move possible interference sources (such as other computers or television sets) away from your PC. Contact the cable company to check your signal quality.

Symptom 44-50. The TV picture displays a blue screen In several conditions, the TV picture might display a blue screen, a momentary loss of signal, a weak video signal, changing the channel, or a scrambled channel. A momentary loss of signal is beyond your control and sometimes cannot be avoided. A weak video signal can be caused by weak reception from a distant station while using the antenna. Weak cable signals should be addressed by the local cable company. Changing channels can sometimes cause momentary blue screens (switch the channel up or down, then return to the original channel). A scrambled channel is not a valid channel—you'll need to contact your local cable company and obtain a descrambler (and pay a premium for the channel).

Symptom 44-51. Snapshots taken from a PC-TV board don't display correctly This usually occurs when using a 256-color mode in the video adapter. Colors often corrupt when displaying an image with 16 or 24 bits per pixel. Try changing the Windows video mode to 16-bit color. Otherwise, copy the image to a third-party graphics program and re-save it as a 24-bit image, then display the image again.

Symptom 44-52. The display flickers when using a PC-TV device This often occurs with devices such as the Diamond DTV 1100. The DTV 1100 is designed to run at a 60Hz refresh rate, so your graphics card will automatically switch its refresh rate to 60Hz, no matter what you have currently set under Windows 95. The refresh rate is then switched back to the original setting once the DTV 1100 is no longer in use (you might see your screen might go blank momentarily while this happens). Also, you'll notice that the flickering will probably be more noticeable at higher resolutions. Unfortunately, little can be done about this because TV signals must be reproduced at their natural frequency of 60 frames per second (60Hz). The best way to get around this problem is to lower the display resolution.

Symptom 44-53. Only channels 5 and 6 are available, and they are only in black and white This problem is with the PC-TV software. You're using an old version of the PC-TV software. Contact the PC-TV device maker and obtain a patch or update driver that will correct this problem. For example, this is a known problem with the Diamond DTV 1100 when using driver versions prior to 1.02.

Symptom 44-54. The television picture is green This sometimes happens with PC-TV cards like the Diamond DTV 1100 card, and is usually the result of poor or faulty cabling. For the DTV 1100, be sure that the ribbon cable is connected between the Scenic Highway local peripheral bus connector on the video card and the DTV1100 Scenic Highway local peripheral bus connector. Also be sure that pin one (usually designated by a red stripe or dots at the edge of the cable) is connected to pin one on the video hardware.

Symptom 44-55. All channels are available, but 14 and 15 This is a problem with the PC-TV software. You're using an old version of the PC-TV software. Contact the PC-TV device maker and obtain a patch or update driver that will correct this problem. For example, this is a known problem with the Diamond DTV 1100 when using driver versions prior to 1.02.

Further Study

That concludes Chapter 44. Be sure to review the glossary and chapter questions on the accompanying CD. If you have access to the Internet, take some time to review a few of these video capture/PC-TV resources:

Aitech: **http://www.aitech.com**

Creative Labs: **http://www.creaf.com**

Hauppauge: **http://www.hauppauge.com**

Intel: **http://www.intel.com**

Matrox: **http://www.matrox.com**

Video for Windows: **http://www.microsoft.com**

Video Logic: **http://www.videologic.com/**

45

VIRUS SYMPTOMS
AND COUNTERMEASURES

CONTENTS AT A GLANCE

Understanding Virulent Software
Software bugs
Trojan horses
Software chameleons
Software bombs
Logic bombs
Time bombs
Replicators
Worms
Viruses

Types of Viruses
Command processor infection
Boot sector infection
Executable-file infection
File-specific infection
Memory-resident infection
Multipartite infection
Macro viruses

Virus Myths

Protecting the PC

Recognizing an Infection
Dealing with an infection
Learning about specific viruses

Understanding Anti-Virus Tools
Vaccines
File comparisons
Antidotes
Signature scanners
Memory-resident utilities
Disk mappers

Troubleshooting Anti-Virus Tools
Preventing macro viruses
Symptoms

Further Study

Although most of the software products in the marketplace today are useful, constructive, and beneficial, other software serves a darker purpose. The computer "virus" is designed to load and run without the user's knowledge, often hiding in normal programs. Viruses also execute their functions without prompting users for permission, they do not warn of potential dangers to the system, and they do not produce error messages when problems are encountered. Essentially, a computer "virus" is a fragment of executable code that runs secretly and is capable of cloning itself in other programs.

Technically, nothing in this definition can indicate that a virus is necessarily destructive— that's a twist added by the virus programmers themselves. But legitimate software does not need to run secretly, hide itself in other programs, or duplicate itself without a user's knowledge or permission. The very nature of a computer virus makes it an ideal vehicle for spreading computer chaos. This chapter is intended to explain the nature and operations of computer viruses, show you how they spread and manifest themselves, and explain some procedures you can take to protect yourself and your customer from their effects.

Understanding Virulent Software

The term *virus* is used to describe virtually any type of destructive software. Although this is a good, general term, it is also a misnomer—a virus is actually only one of many destructive software types. At least nine types of rogue software are recognized, and most are considered every bit as deadly as a virus. Each type of software has a different mode of operation. As a technician, you should understand how these software types operate.

SOFTWARE BUGS

Simply speaking, a *software bug* is an error in program coding or logic that results in faulty or unexpected operation. Bugs are rarely intentional, but the vast majority of serious system-crippling bugs are caught during the developer's alpha and beta testing processes. For serious bugs to get through into a finished product (the kind of bugs that can cause serious memory errors of damage hard-drive files), the developer would have to do little (if any) testing on various PC platforms. Serious bugs are typically not intended as malicious, but they suggest a dangerous lack of concern on the part of the software developer. Two clues suggest the presence of software bugs: only a single program (usually the one you just installed or started using) causes the problem and the problem will not be detected by any anti-virus tool (the application will be reported as clean). Software containing serious or persistent bugs is often referred to as *bug ware*.

TROJAN HORSES

The Trojan horse is largely considered to be the grandparent of today's virulent software. Basically, the Trojan horse is a destructive computer program concealed in the guise of a useful, run-of-the-mill program, such as word processor or graphics program. Well-developed user shells or seemingly normal operations trick the user into believing that the program is harmless—until the virulent code is triggered—then the program's true nature is revealed.

The Trojan horse tactic is the most popular means of introducing viruses by distributing seemingly harmless software, which actually contains virulent code. Fortunately, most virulent code can be detected by scanning new software before it is executed for the first time. To prevent the spread of Trojan horses, be suspicious of unwanted or unsolicited software arriving through the mail or as e-mail attachments. Also beware of software that sounds too good to be true (e.g., a TSR that will increase Windows performance by 100X, get SVGA graphics on an EGA video adapter, use AOL for free, etc.)

SOFTWARE CHAMELEONS

Just as a chameleon hides itself by mimicking its background, *software chameleons* mask virulent code with an image of a legitimate application. Of course, the mask is just a facade—like a demonstration program or a simulation. What makes a chameleon different from a Trojan horse is that it almost never causes system damage. Instead, it generally makes a modification to a program. In one classic case, a chameleon was introduced to a large multi-user platform. When the user typed in their name and password, it was recorded to a secret file. The chameleon's author later accessed the system, entered their own code, and downloaded the accumulated list of passwords. Thus, the author now had access to various user data for their own illegal purposes. In another case, a chameleon was planted into a banking program, which automatically diverted a few tenths of a cent (round-offs) off every transaction into a secret account. Ultimately, the chameleon's author had amassed hundreds of thousands of dollars in the secret account.

SOFTWARE BOMBS

The *software bomb* is just what the name implies—when the infected program is launched, the virulent "bomb" code executes almost immediately and does its damage. Software bombs typically contain no bells or whistles—they also make little effort to cloak themselves, and almost no effort to replicate. As a consequence, the software bomb is quick and easy to develop. Its somewhat clumsy nature also make them fairly easy to spot with anti-virus tools.

LOGIC BOMBS

Where the software bomb is used for immediate and indiscriminate destruction, a *logic bomb* is set to go off when a particular logical condition is met. For example, the logic bomb might "detonate" (erase files, calculate subsequent payroll records incorrectly, reformat the disk, etc.) if payroll records indicate that the bomb's author is fired or laid off, or if their payroll statements do not appear for over four weeks. A logic bomb can be triggered by virtually any system condition. However, the "bomb" approach is fairly easy to spot with anti-virus techniques.

TIME BOMBS

Instead of triggering a bomb immediately or through system-status conditions, a time bomb uses time or repetition conditionals. For example, a time bomb can be set to "detonate" after some number of program runs, on a particular day (e.g., April 1st or Friday 13th), or at a certain time (i.e., midnight). Time bombs are often used as a means of "making a statement" about a particular date and time. This kind of bomb architecture is relatively easy to spot with anti-virus tools. Table 45-1 lists the activation dates of many known computer viruses.

TABLE 45-1 ACTIVATION DATES OF MANY KNOWN COMPUTER VIRUSES	
ACTIVATION DATE/DAY	**VIRUS NAME**
Sundays (any)	Mindless
	Sunday
	Sunday-2
	Witcode
Sundays After 9th (Apr–Dec)	Doctor Qumak 2
Mondays (any)	Carfield
	I-B (BadGuy)
	I-B (BadGuy 2)
	I-B (Exterminator)
	Immolation
	Kalah (Kalah-499)
	Witcode
Mondays (starting in 1993)	VirDem (VirDem-833)
Monday first of month	Beware
Mondays the 28ths	Crazy Eddie
Tuesdays (any)	Ah
	Emo-899
	I-B (Demon)
	I-B (Demon-B)
	Murphy (Kamasya)
Tuesday The 1st	Jerusalem (JVT1)
Tuesday The 13th	Jerusalem (Anarkia)
Wednesdays (any)	PS-MPC (No Wednesday)
	VCL (Red Team)
	Victor
Thursdays (any)	TPE (Girafe)
Thursday The 12ths	CD
Fridays (any)	Bryansk
	Immolation
	Frere Jacques
	PS-MPC (Mimic-Den Zuk)
	PS-MPC (Mimic-Jerusalem)
	Murphy (Smack)
	NaziPhobia
	TalkingHeads
	VCL (Diarrhea)
	Wild Thing 2
Friday Not The 13ths	Jerusalem (Payday)
Friday The 11ths	VCL (Kinison)
Friday The 13ths	1720
	Friday 13th
	Jerusalem
	RAM Virus
	Suriv 3.00
	Westwood
	Witcode

TABLE 45-1 ACTIVATION DATES OF MANY KNOWN COMPUTER VIRUSES (CONTINUED)	
ACTIVATION DATE/DAY	**VIRUS NAME**
Friday The 13ths (starting in 1992)	Hybryd
Fridays After 15th of month	Jerusalem (Skism)
	Jerusalem (Skism-1)
Fridays last of month	Jerusalem (Sub-Zero B)
Saturdays (any)	Murphy (Finger)
	Jerusalem (Phenome)
	Murphy (Migram)
Saturday the 14ths	Saturday The 14th
1st day of any month	10 Past 3
	Pinworm
2nd day of any month	Flip
	Tormentor (Nuke)
3rd day of any month	VCL (Miles)
5th day of any month	Frogs
7th day of any month	Bones
8th day of any month	Taiwan
10th day of any month	Day10
	Leprosy (Leprosy-664A)
13th day of any month	NPox (NPox 2.1)
	Monxla
	Rocko
16th day of any month	10 Past 3
18th day of any month	Npox
	FORM-Virus (Form-18)
20th day of any month	Day10
22nd day of any month	10 Past 3
	VCL (Beva 32)
24th day of any month	FORM-Virus
	Rocko (Mutating Rocko)
29th day of any month	10 Past 3
	Geek
	Highlander
30th day of any month	Day10
31st day of any month	Tormentor (Lixo Nuke)
	VCL (Diogenes)
January 1st	Big Bang
	VCL (Beva 33)
January 1st - September 21st	Plastique (COBOL)
January 5th	Barrotes
	Joshi
January 15th	Casino
January 25th	Jerusalem (January 25th)
February 1st - February 29th	Vienna (Beta Boys)
February 2nd	Dark Avenger (Amilia)
	Marauder

TABLE 45-1 ACTIVATION DATES OF MANY KNOWN COMPUTER VIRUSES (CONTINUED)

ACTIVATION DATE/DAY	VIRUS NAME
February 23rd	Swedish Boys (Why Windows)
February 24th	Swedish Boys (Why Windows)
February 25th	Swedish Boys (Why Windows)
February 28th	Zaphod
March 1st - March 31st	Fich
	Micropox
March 5th	X-2 (X-1 & X-1B)
March 6th	Mich II
	Michelangelo
	RIP-699
March 14th	Arale
March 15th	Maltese Amoeba
March 25th	March 25th
March 31st - April 30th	Mordor.1110
April 1st	Casper
	Christmas Tree
	Suriv 1.01
	Suriv 2.01
	Suriv 4.02
	Tchantches
April 1st - April 30th	Akuku (Wilbur 3)
	Death Dragon
April 1st - June 30th	Month 4-6
April 3rd - December 31st	Italian Boy
April 12th	ARCV Friends
April 15th	Casino
	Murphy (Swami)
April 28th	Arale
May 1st - May 4th	1210
May 1st - May 31st	Kthulhu
May 5th	PS-MPC (Cinco de Mayo)
May 13th & May 17th	Arale
May 26th	Find_Me
June 6th	Jerusalem (Sub-Zero B)
	Psychosis
	Tiny Virus (Kennedy)
June 12th	Arale
	June 12th
June 14th	Gremlin
June 16th	June 16th
June 17th - December 31st	Jerusalem (June 17th)
June 26th	DOSHunter
June 28th	Crazy Eddie
July 1st - July 31st	ARCV 330

TABLE 45-1 ACTIVATION DATES OF MANY KNOWN COMPUTER VIRUSES (CONTINUED)	
ACTIVATION DATE/DAY	**VIRUS NAME**
July 1st - December 31st	Got-You
	Jerusalem (Jerusalem-PLO)
	Jerusalem (Mendoza)
July 4th	VCL (Beva 96)
July 13th	July 13th
July 15th	Arale
July 26th	July 26th
August 15th	Casino
August 16th	August 16th
August 22nd	Hare
August 31st	Bomber
September 1st–September 30th	AirCop (AirCop-B)
	Cascade
	Sad
	TenBytes
September 4th	Violator (Violator B1)
September 8th	RIP-699
September 16th	It (Viva Mexico)
September 20th–December 31st	Plastique
	Plastique-B
September 22nd	Hare
September 22nd–December 31st	4096
October 1st - December 31st	4096
	Cascade
	TenBytes
	Violator (Violator-C)
October 4th	Violator (Violator B1)
October 12th	Akuku (Columbus)
	Jerusalem (Anarkia-B)
October 13th–December 31st	Datacrime
October 15th	Dark End
October 23rd	Karin
October 28th	Aragorn
October 30th	Gotcha (Gotcha-Mut4)
October 31st	Halloween
	Violator (Violator B2)
November, first Tuesday of	Little Brother (LB-349)
November 1st	Maltese Amoeba
November 4th	Violator (Violator B1)
November 11th	Flower
November 12th	Timor
November 17th	November 17th
November 17th–December 31st	November 17th (Nov 17-880)
November 18th	Tiny Virus (Kennedy)

TABLE 45-1 ACTIVATION DATES OF MANY KNOWN COMPUTER VIRUSES (CONTINUED)	
ACTIVATION DATE/DAY	**VIRUS NAME**
November 22nd	Tiny Virus (Kennedy)
November 24th	PS-MPC (Love Bink)
November 30th	Jerusalem 11-30
	Sampo
December 1st–December 31st	1253
	Int10
December 1st	Ant
December 4th	Violator (Violator B1)
December 7th	VCL (Pearl Harbor)
December 12th	Arale
December 19th–December 31st	Father Christmas
December 20th–December 25th	ARCV Xmas
December 21st	Poem
December 24th	Icelandic (Icelandic-III)
December 24th–December 31st	Witcode
December 24th–January 1st	Christmas Tree
	Merry Xmas
December 25th	Black Hawk
	Japanese Christmas
	Violator (Violator B3)
December 26th	Find_Me
December 28th	Ash (Ash.546)
	Spanish April Fools
December 31st	Violator (Violator B2)
After August 1, 1989	Fu Manchu
After June, 1990	Flash
After August, 1990	DataLock
After August 14, 1990	Violator
After November 11, 1990	Fingers
After December 31, 1991	Sicilian Mob
After December 31, 1992	CyberTech
	OMT
After January 1, 1993	Grunt-1
After December 31, 1993	CyberTech (CyberTech-B)

REPLICATORS

The purpose of a *replicator* (also called a *rabbit*) is to drain system resources. It accomplishes this function by cloning copies of itself. Each clone copy is launched by the parent that created it. Before long, the multitude of copies on disk and in memory soak up so many resources that the system can no longer function In effect, the system is crippled until the copies are removed and the replicating virus is eliminated. This type of behavior is particularly effective at shutting down large, multi-user systems or networks. Because the virulent code is self-replicating, it is easy to spot with anti-virus tools.

WORMS

Unlike most other types of virulent code, the *worm* travels through a network computer system. The worm travels from computer to computer—usually without doing any real damage. Worms rarely replicate, except in cases where it is absolutely necessary to continue traveling through the system, and delete all traces of their presence. A worm is another typical network presence used to seek out and selectively alter or destroy a limited number of files or programs. For example, a worm can be used to enter a network and alter or erase passwords. Because worms can be tailored for specific jobs, they are often difficult to spot unless the worm is known.

VIRUSES

The most recognized and dynamic of the rogue software is the *virus*. A virus modifies other programs to include executable virulent code. In some cases, the virulent code mutates and changes as it is copied. Expertly engineered viruses do not change the infected file date, time stamps, file size, its attributes, or its checksums. As a result, viruses can be extremely difficult to detect and even harder to erase—and the task becomes even more difficult as viruses become increasingly powerful and sophisticated. With today's "high overhead" operating systems, such as Windows 95 or Windows NT, viruses can usually hide and replicate quite easily in any of the numerous .DLL files, .VXD files, or other modules normally in operation. Given their predilection toward stealth and replication, viruses tend to linger in systems to spread themselves between hard drives and floppy disks, and network connections, where they disrupt data, cause system errors, and generally degrade system performance. Eventually, most viruses will self-destruct, typically taking the hard-drive files with it.

Types of Viruses

As you might have suspected, all virulent code is not created equal. Viruses are as varied as legitimate application software—each technique provides the virus author with an array of advantages and disadvantages. Some viral techniques are preferred because they are more difficult to detect and remove, but require extra resources to develop. Other viral techniques are easier to develop, but lack the stealth and sophistication that more powerful viruses demand. Still other viral techniques stand a better chance of infecting multiple systems. This part of the chapter explains the major infection modes used by modern viruses.

COMMAND PROCESSOR INFECTION

DOS relies on a series of hidden files (i.e., IO.SYS and MSDOS.SYS). The files are hidden, they cannot be directly executed, and they are not easily deleted, renamed, or copied. Thus, it is necessary to have a command processor that allows the user to interact with the operating system. For DOS, the command processor is COMMAND.COM. When you see the command line prompt (e.g., A:\> or C:\>), you know that COMMAND.COM is loaded and active. When you enter a command line, the processor parses (interprets) the command and attempts to determine a proper response.

By placing a virus in the command processor (infecting the COMMAND.COM), the virus has access to a large number of DOS facilities—especially user interface and disk access. Consider the DIR command used to produce a disk directory. An infected COMMAND.COM can allow its virus to search for and infect other files before running the actual directory function (thus, the virus is concealed). The function might take a bit longer to execute, but most users barely notice. If you insert a floppy disk in drive A: and take a directory, you risk infecting files on the floppy disk. By making a bootable floppy disk, that disk will likely contain an infected COMMAND.COM file as well. Because viruses are active once a program is started, and COMMAND.COM is started every time DOS is loaded, command-processor infections are serious, and they can be spread very quickly.

BOOT SECTOR INFECTION

Every PC ever made requires a "bootable" disk, which has access to DOS. When the PC boots (starts up), the computer automatically attempts to load the operating system files from the boot disk. Startup files are typically kept in the disk boot sector (sometimes referred to as the *master boot record*). If a virus is able to infiltrate the boot sector and interfere with the loading process, it can very effectively cripple the entire computer. Viruses that infect the boot sector, but do not shut the boot disk down, are often capable of remaining resident in memory—even during a warm boot. When bootable floppy disks are used during the warm boot, boot-sector viruses can easily infect the bootable floppy. Top boot-sector viruses include:

- *NYB* (Alias *B1*)
- *AntiEXE* (Alias *Newbug*) Can cause file damage.
- *AntiCMOS* (Alias *LENART*) Can blank CMOS/BIOS values.
- *Monkey A or B* Encrypts the partition table upon infection and causes "Invalid drive specification" errors when booting the computer from a clean floppy.
- *Form_A* Infects boot sectors only, but doesn't infect the MBR.
- *Da'Boys* Like Form_A, but works with GoldBug virus to cause damage.
- *WelcomB* (Alias *BUPT.9146*) Mostly found in Southeast Asia.
- *Stoned* most MBR/BS viruses are based on the original Stoned.
- *Michelangelo* Reformats the hard drive on March 6.

Because boot-sector viruses are loaded along with the DOS kernel and command processor, they are typically active before a user ever has a chance to launch an anti-virus application. With access to all of DOS's resources, the boot-sector virus can alter directory listings to show an expected file date, size, and attributes when in fact such files have been infected—a tactic that can render some anti-virus packages useless.

EXECUTABLE-FILE INFECTION

Unlike command-processor or boot-sector infections, which target a limited number of low-level operating system files, many viral strains today simply focus on the infection of any executable file (.EXE or .COM files). Because COMMAND.COM is executable, it can also be infected by these "general-purpose" viruses, but not as deeply or cleverly as viruses specially designed for that purpose. Often, general file infections are loaded into memory once an infected application is started. Afterward, the virus can easily spread to other executable files any time other executable files are listed (e.g., open file, save file, etc.). This type of infection proliferates very quickly within the infected PC. Because disks are often shared between various computers, general infections also stand a good chance of infecting multiple machines—creating an "epidemic." The problem with such proliferation is that you must locate and disinfect every copy of the virus (on common floppies as well) to remove it. If you miss a copy and run that infected application later, the whole cycle can start all over again. Under Windows 95, viruses can also infect other executable code, such as .DLL and .VXD files. Top file-infecting viruses include:

- *Jerusalem* Many variants, many names, multiple infections of the same file.
- *Die Hard 2* (Alias *DH2*) Very stealthy.
- *BUA.2263* Displays an obscene graphic. Original distribution via Internet. Mildly polymorphic.
- *Green Caterpillar* Displays a caterpillar like the Centipede arcade game.
- *Screaming Fist* Several variants, some polymorphic.
- *Little Red* Polymorphic.
- *DAME, PS-MPC, MTE, VCL, TRIDENT* These mutation/polymorphism engines enable a novice virus writer to create a nasty virus.
- *Natas* Origin in Mexico. A polymorphic multipartite virus widespread in the U.S. Southwest.
- *Digress* Drops MusicBug.MBR on boot record.
- *OneHalf* Extremely polymorphic multipartite virus. Requires special handling.

Multi-purpose infections are a more potent form of general-purpose virus, which combines two or more virus techniques. For example, a multi-purpose virus can infiltrate a system's boot sector, then move on to the command processor, then spawn parasitic viruses that infect ordinary executable files. Because the virus finds its way into so many areas of the PC, it is very difficult to remove completely. If the virus changes or morphs as it works, it might be virtually impossible to spot with anti-virus tools. As a consequence, multi-purpose infections are particularly pernicious.

FILE-SPECIFIC INFECTION

The *file-specific infection* is generally a type of worm that is specifically designed to seek out and corrupt specific files or types of files. Often, the file-specific infection is created and introduced by someone with a score to settle—perhaps an ex-employee or competitor. Because an outright search for the desired file(s) would take some time (and almost certainly be noticed), the file-specific infection latches onto a variety of files throughout the system, spreading its search capability without attracting attention. If the desired files are located, the virus either erases them outright or it corrupts them over time, resulting in application or data corruption. Another advantage of infecting multiple files is that the damaged file(s) will invariably be reloaded, so the virus is able to "hang around" in the system to continue harassing the target file(s).

MEMORY-RESIDENT INFECTION

Although many viruses are loaded and active only while the infected file is running, the *memory-resident infection* remains active in memory throughout the entire computing session. The advantage to memory-resident viruses is that, like ordinary TSRs, the virus can continue infecting other files and corrupting data throughout the system, regardless of which application is running.

MULTIPARTITE INFECTION

In an effort to spread infection even faster, *multipartite viruses* target both file and boot sectors. Multipartite infections usually enter the system through either an infected executable file and wind up copying themselves to the boot sector and load each time the system starts—subsequently infecting files in the system.

MACRO VIRUSES

A *macro* is little more than a simple programming language that is embedded into documents and spreadsheets. When used properly, a macro can automate many of the time-consuming and redundant tasks related to document/spreadsheet processing or formatting. The problem is that macros are so powerful that they can be written to actually cause havoc on the PC. Because macros are typically started automatically when a document or spreadsheet is opened, damage usually occurs immediately. In other cases, the template is altered—infecting subsequent documents or spreadsheets. New anti-virus tools are being designed to check for macro viruses.

Virus Myths

Computer viruses are a real threat that should always be taken seriously, But in most cases, computer viruses are rarely the harbingers of doom and gloom that many novices (and much of the PC media) perceive them to be. Now that you have an idea of the nature of viruses and other rogue software, it's time to dispel some persistent myths surrounding viruses:

- *No anti-virus software is 100% effective* Although anti-virus products are constantly being updated to protect against the latest virus threats, no virus-protection program is foolproof. New viruses are constantly being designed to bypass them. The best protection is to scan for viruses regularly using a current anti-virus tool, and always keep your vital files backed up.
- *A virus cannot hide inside a data file* Data files (such as images) cannot spread a virus on your computer. Only executable program files (and files containing executable macros) can spread viruses. A computer virus could infect a data file, but it would be a useless effort—because a data file is not executed, only loaded, the virus would not be able run or to replicate itself.

> Text and spreadsheet files supporting macros can be "infected" with destructive macros. Scan text and spreadsheet files for macro viruses before loading them.

- *Viruses cannot spread to all types of computers* Viruses are limited to a given family of computers. For example, a virus designed to spread on IBM PCs cannot infect an IBM 4300 series mainframe, infect a Commodore C64, or infect an Apple Macintosh. However, cross-platform software can spread on any system capable of opening and reading the infected file(s). Word macro viruses can spread on any platform that reads Word files.

- *A computer cannot be infected by calling an infected BBS, FTP, or Web site* BBS and FTP sites containing infected files cannot write information onto your computer under its own direction. Your communications software (or Web browser) performs this task. You can only transfer an infected file to your computer if you let your software do it. If an infected file is transferred to your computer, it cannot spread until you execute the downloaded file. If a file is scanned after being downloaded (and found to be infected), it can be safely deleted before infecting other components of the computer.

- *Compressed file archives can be infected* Although an "archive" file (e.g., a .ZIP file) cannot be infected itself, the executable files contained in the archive can be infected. You can decompress the archive without executing any of the files in the archive, then scan the files with an anti-virus tool before installing the software or running any of the executable files in the archive.

- *A boot-sector virus cannot travel in downloaded software* BBS and Internet download sites deal only in program files and do not pass along copies of disk boot sectors. Because boot-sector viruses can only spread by "booting" (or attempting to boot the computer from an infected diskette), downloading is generally immune to boot-sector viruses. However, you should still scan all downloaded files before executing them for the first time.

- *Damaged files do not always indicate a virus attack* This is a very common misconception about viruses. Damaged files can be caused by many things (including the result of a power surge, power drop-off, static electricity, magnetic forces, failing hardware components, a bug in another software package, dust, fingerprints, spilled coffee, etc.). Power failures and spilled cups of coffee have destroyed more data than any viruses. Still, you should run your virus checker just to be sure.

- *Backups are still valuable—even with a virus* Suppose a virus is backed up with your files. It could not be a boot-infecting virus because the back-up software will not back up the boot sector. If you had a file-infecting virus, you could restore important documents, databases, and your data, without restoring an infected program—or delete the infected program(s) and restore them specifically from the original installation disks.

- *Read-only files are not immune to infection* Some computer users believe you can protect yourself by using the DOS ATTRIB command to set the read-only attribute on program files. However, ATTRIB is software, and what it can do, a virus can easily undo. Although this tactic might be marginally successful at halting very old or simple viruses, the ATTRIB command very rarely halts the spread of viruses.

- *Viruses cannot infect write-protected disks* Because viruses can modify read-only files, people tend to believe that can also modify write-protected floppy diskettes. The disk drive senses a protected diskette and refuses to write on it. This is controlled by the hardware—not software. You can physically disable a floppy drive's write-protect sensor, but you cannot override it with a software command. Write protecting your diskettes are a free and easy means of halting the spread of viruses—especially boot-sector viruses.

Protecting the PC

Even with the most comprehensive, accurate, aggressive, up-to-the-minute anti-virus package available, anti-virus tools alone will not always protect a PC from the ravages of a virus or other rogue software. Trying a suspicious piece of software without testing it first, forgetting to virus scan the system regularly, and even intentional sabotage can render an anti-virus tool useless. Before trouble strikes, you can take some pro-active steps to prevent the spread of viruses, and ease your recovery should a virus actually strike:

- *Check for viruses regularly* You would be surprised how many people buy anti-virus products—only to use them sporadically, or leave them sitting unused until it is too late. Remember that anti-virus tools are always behind viruses—you need to use your anti-virus tools consistently and aggressively in order to catch viruses before they do their damage. If you are regularly trying new shareware or commercial products, you should be sure to check for viruses religiously. Also check for viruses if you routinely swap disks between home and work PCs or a variety of different computers.
- *Backup your data* This might sound a bit cliché, but frequent, complete backups are one of the most foolproof and reliable means of protecting your vital data. No virus can destroy the backup. Even though the backup might contain a virus, it is better to restore an infected backup (then clean it immediately) than to forego the backup entirely. The problem with backups is frequency—how often should it be done? That really depends on how often you use your system. Businesses with active, rapidly changing databases should back up their data at least daily. Casual home users who use only a few utilities infrequently would probably receive little benefit from frequent backups. Most small offices and home offices would be well-served to back up every month or so. If new applications or data files are changed dramatically in the mean time, the backup can be updated, as needed. The yardstick is simple enough: "If my hard drive were erased now, would I be able to restore it and move on?" If the answer to that question is "no," it's time to back up the system. If the contents of your system changes frequently, it might make sense to keep several generations of backup. That way, if Thursday's backup doesn't have the files you need, maybe Monday's will.
- *Keep your original disks write-protected* Although write protection is not foolproof, it can prevent an infected system from spreading its infection to the diskettes—and thereby proliferating to other systems. This can be doubly important for original program distribution disks.
- *Keep an eye out for mysterious or hidden files* Although most modern drive utilities have no trouble revealing hidden files, some virulent code might indeed be saved with hidden file attributes. Also check batch files before running them to be sure that there are no destructive commands (such as FORMAT C:).

- *Beware of famous dates* Time bombs often trigger on holidays, such as Christmas, New Year, July 4th, or other famous holidays or dates. The day before a special day, set the system clock to the day after. For example, on July 3rd, set the system calendar to July 5th. After the holiday has passed, you can easily reset the clock to the correct date.
- *Keep a bootable diskette on-hand* Before trouble strikes, invest about five minutes and make a clean bootable floppy disk. The disk should also have a copy of FORMAT, FDISK, DEBUG, PKUNZIP (or your favorite decompression utility), and any other DOS utilities that you need during startup. Be sure to write protect the floppy disk and keep it in a safe place.

Recognizing an Infection

As any doctor will tell you, the first step toward recovery is diagnosis—recognizing the subtle (and not so subtle) signs of viral activity can give you an edge in stopping the activities of a virus, and save you a substantial amount of time in needless hardware troubleshooting. The following part of this chapter illustrates some of the more important signs of virus activity:

- *A warning is generated by a virus scanner* Your anti-virus package has detected a virus either in memory or in one (or more) executable files. Once the anti-virus package has completed its infection report, go ahead and attempt to disinfect as many files as possible. Many of today's viruses cannot be removed without damaging the executable file, so be prepared to restore the infected files from a backup or original installation disks. After the system is cleaned (and damaged files restored), go ahead and check for viruses again. Repeat this procedure until the entire system is clear.
- *A bizarre message appears (e.g., "legalize marijuana" or "your computer is stoned")* Unfortunately, when a virus reveals itself in this way, it has probably already done its damage to your system. Launch your anti-virus software as soon as possible and remove any occurrences of the virus. Be prepared to restore damaged executable files and corrupted data files.
- *The computer is acting strangely for no apparent reason* This might happen especially on holidays and other important days of the year. Applications might freeze, crash, or produce unusual error messages without warning. You might notice excessive or random disk access where there was none before. The system might behave unusually slowly. Files and programs might take a long time to load. Familiar applications might not respond to the keyboard or mouse properly. Leave the application as soon as possible and run your anti-virus tools.
- *The computer starts to boot, but freezes before displaying a DOS prompt* Chances are that you've got a command-processor infection. Boot the system from a clean, write-protected floppy disk, then try switching to the infected hard drive. If you cannot access the hard drive, it might be defective or the virus might have affected the drive's partition table. Run an anti-virus package to check the system and eliminate any virulent code. When the system is clean, try a drive maintenance package, such as Drive-Pro from MicroHouse to check and rebuild any corrupted boot sector/partition table data.

■ *Programs and data files become erased or corrupted without warning* This is a classic sign of a virus at work. It is highly unlikely that the random loss of a single file is caused by a hardware defect. DOS drive access works in terms of clusters, and most files require several clusters. If a cluster—or a sector within that cluster—were to fail, the file would still appear in the directory. Run your anti-virus package and check for viruses in memory as well as on disk.

■ *An error message indicates a problem with the file allocation table or the partition table* Although this might indeed be the result of a hard-drive fault, you should boot the system from a write-protected floppy disk and check for viruses. If the system checks clear, go ahead and try a package, such as Drive Pro by MicroHouse, to check and reconstruct the damaged boot areas.

■ *Programs access more than one disk drive, where they did not before* It is exceptionally rare for a program to try accessing more than one drive, unless it is explicitly instructed to do so by you. For example, if you save your new word-processing document to drive C:, there will be no reason for the program to access drive A:. This kind of behavior suggests that a virus is attempting to slip its operations into normal disk-access activities. Leave your application and run a virus checker.

■ *The number of bad disk sectors increases steadily* It is not uncommon for viruses to create bad disk sectors and hide within them to escape detection. Because DOS is designed to step over bad sectors, some anti-virus programs will not detect viruses using that tactic, leaving you to back up as much of the drive as possible and perform a new low-level format of the drive. Before resorting to that tactic, however, try a different anti-virus package.

■ *The amount of available system RAM suddenly or steadily decreases* DOS provides the MEM function, which allows you to peek at conventional, upper, extended, and expanded memory. If you find that certain programs no longer have enough memory to run, consider the possibility that the computer is infected with a memory-resident virus or replicator or some sort. Try your anti-virus package. If you have a memory-resident anti-virus product available, try loading that on the system for a while.

■ *Memory maps (such as the DOS MEM function) reveal strange TSRs not loaded by CONFIG.SYS or AUTOEXEC.BAT* You can use the MEM function to reveal any drivers or TSRs loaded in the system. If you see a strange or unexpected TSR, you might be faced with a memory-resident virus. Run your anti-virus package. If you have a memory-resident anti-virus product available, try loading that on the system for a while.

■ *File names, extensions, attributes, or date codes are changed unexpectedly* This is another classic sign of viral activity, which is usually attributable to older virulent code that lacked the sophistication to hide its own actions. A reliable anti-virus program should be able to deal with any viruses effectively.

■ *Unknown files mysteriously appear* This is a tough call for technicians new to a system, but as a computer user, you are generally pretty aware when a new data file is created on your own system (e.g., a new word-processor document or a new spreadsheet). However, when unknown executable files are created, a virus might be at work. Newly created files might be hidden, so use a directory tool that displays hidden files (such as Windows Explorer). Try your anti-virus software to locate and eliminate potential viruses.

DEALING WITH AN INFECTION

Even with the best anti-virus tools, regular testing, and consistent backups, systems can still be susceptible to the ravages of computer viruses. When dealing with viruses, you must understand what can and cannot be infected. Programs can be infected—that's all. Programs are any file that has an extension of: .EXE, .COM, .BAT, .SYS, .BIN, .DRV, .OVL, .DLL, .VXD, and, of course the two hidden system files that compose the DOS kernel. With the rise of macro viruses, data files, such as Microsoft Word and Excel files, can also be infected—spreading their havoc with the file's macro is run. Other data files, such as images, certainly can be corrupted, damaged, or completely destroyed, but they cannot be infected. For example, if you download an Internet image (i.e., a .JPG file), it cannot contain a virus. It is not impossible to infect programs inside an archive (such as .ZIP, .ARC, .ARJ, .LZH, or .ZOO), but it is extremely unlikely since a virus does not want you to know it's there—but the programs might have been contaminated before being placed in the archive. If you suspect the presence of a virus in the system, the following procedures can help you optimize the "damage control":

1 *Boot from a clean, write-protected floppy disk* One of the most fundamental rules of virus defense is that a virus is harmless until it is launched by the boot sector, command processor, or application. If you can prevent the virus from loading in the first place, you stand a good chance of running an anti-virus tool successfully. Be sure that the boot disk is prepared on a virus-free PC. The disk should also contain a copy of your anti-virus package (most are designed to run from a floppy disk). Do not attempt to launch applications from the questionable hard drive until it has been checked and cleaned.

2 *Use your anti-virus tools* If the system booted properly from your write-protected floppy disk, the virus(es) in your system should now be neutralized. Start the anti-virus tool contained on your floppy disk and run a comprehensive test of all system files. Also make it a point to check the boot sector and command processor. If your current tool does not support boot-sector or command-processor testing, consider using a second tool that does. If viruses are detected (chances are that more than one file will be infected), attempt to remove as many instances as possible. With luck, you can remove viruses without damaging the infected file, but this is often not possible with today's viruses. If a file cannot be "cleaned," it should be erased. Be sure to log each erased file and directory path so that you can replace only those files, rather than restore entire sub-directories.

3 *Start a quarantine on your computer* Because many viruses propagate by infecting floppy disks, any disks that have been in your computer should be assumed to have the virus on them. By assuming the worst-case situation, you are possibly saving many others from getting and spreading the virus even further. Gather up as many disks as you can find and check each for viruses. Also, do not share disks between other systems until your system has run for a while and proven itself to be virus-free.

4 *Restore the backups* It is very likely that you had to destroy one or more executable files. Systematically re-load any files that were erased during the cleaning process. In most cases, you can restore the damaged files from their original, write-protected installation disks. A tape backup is another popular backup source. Try to avoid re-installing the entire application unless there is no other alternative.

5 *Recheck the backup* After the deleted files have been destroyed, it is vitally important to restart your anti-virus tool and check the suspect disk again. It is not uncommon for recent backups to be contaminated as well. Verify that the drive is still virus-free. If you locate new viruses introduced in the restored files, remove the viruses again and re-store the files from original, write-protected floppy disks.

6 *Minimize the collateral damage* Immediately notify anybody who you have given any software, bootable disks, or even read their disks on your computer. If you have up-loaded any programs to a BBS or the Internet, notify the sysop or webmaster of that system immediately.

LEARNING ABOUT SPECIFIC VIRUSES

Thousands of computer viruses are in the field today—each with its own aliases, modes of infection, and techniques for removal. It would be impractical to index all of that information here. Fortunately, most major anti-virus makers provide extensive virus "encyclo-pedias" over their Internet Web sites. If you can get on-line, you can easily find detailed information on just about any virus or strain.

Understanding Anti-Virus Tools

As the awareness of computer viruses grew through the last decade, so did the prolifera-tion of anti-virus tools designed to combat the threat. However, you should understand that every anti-virus tool is created as a response to viruses that have already penetrated the PC environment. As a result, anti-virus products are forever playing "catch-up" with ever-more sophisticated virus programmers. No anti-virus product is 100% effective in all forms of detection. The one rule to remember with all anti-virus tools is that they become outdated very quickly. As a technician, you must make it a point to keep your anti-virus tools current. In the perpetual virus "arms race," you should seriously consider updating any product over 6 months old. This part of the chapter examines the major anti-virus tac-tics and explains the limitations of each approach.

VACCINES

This is the earliest form of virus protection, which appended small programs and check-sums to various executable files. When the modified program is run, the anti-virus vac-cine calculates the program's checksum and compares it to the appended checksum. If the two checksums match, control is returned to the executable file and it runs normally. If the comparison fails because of file damage or the presence of a virus, a warning is generated and corrective action can be taken. You should be familiar with the number of serious drawbacks to the vaccine technique:

■ The vaccine (or *antigen*, as it was called) is little more than a virus itself. Although it does not reproduce without permission or harm files, many users felt uncomfortable "inoculating" their files intentionally.

   If the system has a large number of executable files, the increased disk space needed for each appended vaccine can become significant.

- Device drivers, overlay files, packed .EXE files, and executable data files cannot be vaccinated.
- False alarms are typical—especially for self-modifying programs, such as Borland's SideKick—which force users to remove vaccine protection.
- In some cases, the modifications to an executable file to vaccinate it can cause unpredictable program operation—some programs simply do not work with vaccine-based viral defense.
- The virus-type behavior of vaccines often cause false alarms with other non-vaccine anti-virus programs.
- Because vaccine techniques are the same for every files, it is a simple matter for a virus to bypass the vaccine's loading checksum test, so vaccines provided limited viral protection.

FILE COMPARISONS

A plain and simple technique utilized byte-by-byte comparisons between known-good files and potentially infected files. Any variation between the two signaled the possibility of a virus. *File-comparison techniques* were initially embraced because they were easy to develop and quick to document, so they were an inexpensive option for anti-virus developers. However, file comparison presents some serious disadvantages in the marketplace:

- The most crucial problem is the need for known-good files to be added to the disk (in addition to the normal operating files). Even for large drives, this is a hideous waste of valuable disk space.
- File comparison anti-virus tools often lack the typical resources that are considered to be standard equipment for virus management (i.e., activity logs, data encryption, comprehensive warnings indicating which virus is at work, system lockouts, and wildcard file searches).
- It is a simple matter for viruses to search a disk looking for multiple copies of a file, and infect both copies—rendering the file-comparison technique useless.

ANTIDOTES

Software antidotes (sometimes called *disinfectors* or *eradicators*) are a close cousin to vaccines, where the antidote "surgically removes" the virus. But antidotes are designed specifically to deal with a limited set of viral strains within a small group of program types. Often, an antidote is designed to check and remove a particular virus. For example, the media scare surrounding the Michaelangelo virus some years back resulted in a number of related "antidote" products developed specifically to check for and eradicate the virus. Such limited operation presents several serious limitations:

- The limited nature of antidotes makes them unsuited for general, system-wide use. Viruses not specifically addressed by the antidote remain totally untouched.
- Because viruses are constantly changing, antidotes must continuously be updated and expanded; otherwise, the antidotes quickly become useless. The constant expense of regular updates is often too much for the average computer user.

■ Antidotes often destroy program files while trying to remove virulent code. They are reputed to suffer frequent false alarms that cause the antidote to alter good files in an attempt to remove a virus that is not there. Effectively, this destroys good files as well.

■ Each executable file has its own particular characteristics and internal structure. As a result, it is virtually impossible for any one infection antidote to remove a virus from every possible file type.

■ Generally, it is safer and more reliable to recover an infected file by overwriting it with an uninfected copy rather than trust an antidote to surgically remove the virus.

SIGNATURE SCANNERS

Currently, the virus scanner is the most widely accepted type of anti-virus tool. Scanning basically checks each executable file against a fixed set of virus "signatures"—tell-tale fragments of code that indicate the presence of particular viruses. When the virulent code is identified, it can be removed fairly accurately, but many executable files are still destroyed. The technique is fast and flexible, viruses can be identified very accurately. Few instances of false alarms or incompatibilities occur, which plague older techniques. However, there are still limitations to virus scanning:

■ Scanners rely on a fixed set of signatures. If a signature is not in the database, it is not checked. Signature databases are easy to update, but the updates can often be costly (although updates can now be downloaded easily from the Internet). Because viruses are constantly changing, signature databases become outdated quickly.

■ Virus scanners cannot detect signatures that change or mutate as the infection propagates through the system. As a result, scanners are largely ineffective against stealth or polymorphic viruses.

MEMORY-RESIDENT UTILITIES

One breed of anti-virus tool can be loaded into memory where it will remain resident (TSR) and provide "last-minute" protection against viral infiltration of disk commands and viral activity. Unfortunately, this class of anti-virus tool suffers from a set of very serious problems:

■ As a TSR, the program must remain in memory. This consumes valuable memory (often significant amounts of memory), which are needed by other applications. It is not uncommon to eventually disable TSRs to free extra memory for large applications.

■ False alarms are commonplace with anti-virus TSRs, which mistake disk caching or normal system activity with virus activity. Even communication functions, such as e-mail downloads, are often interrupted as virus attacks.

■ Many systems respond poorly to TSRs. If you consider that TSR technology is intended to coerce DOS to perform multitasking—a feature it was not intended to do—it is no wonder that TSR development is non-standardized. As a consequence, TSRs are often quite troublesome. When used with combinations of other device drivers and TSRs, anti-viral TSRs can present a serious problem.

■ Viruses can circumvent anti-virus TSRs by accessing PC hardware directly (such as direct access of disk controllers).

DISK MAPPERS

The disk-mapping technique is similar to the file-comparison process. A mapper maintains a single data file which contains a coded "snapshot" of the protected disk. Each time a mapper is run, it notifies you about any variations between the protected disk files and the "key map." Ideally, these variations will alert you to the possibility of a virus. Many later disk-mapping schemes allow users to specify exactly which files (or file types) must be monitored. However, this is not enough to overcome some inherent problems:

- Creating a "key map" of the disk can require a substantial amount of space. The space demand increases along with the number of files that must be "mapped".
- For most professional users, the state of a PC is changing constantly as files are created, modified, and deleted. This demands regular maintenance of the "key map." Such maintenance is often cumbersome and time consuming because disk mappers are typically complex systems to use.
- Disk mappers are typically tied into the boot process to ensure regular "key map" checks and updates. This results in longer (sometimes much longer) boot times.
- Disk mappers are not immune to infiltration and damage by viruses. Some viruses seek out and destroy "key map" files.

Troubleshooting Anti-Virus Tools

The key to dealing with computer viruses is the proper use of anti-virus tools. A quick walk through almost any software store will show you just how many anti-virus products are available. Being able to use those products properly and successfully is not always a simple task. This part of the chapter offers some guidelines to help you handle problems with the tools themselves.

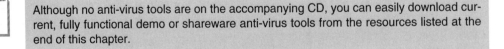

Although no anti-virus tools are on the accompanying CD, you can easily download current, fully functional demo or shareware anti-virus tools from the resources listed at the end of this chapter.

PREVENTING MACRO VIRUSES

Macro viruses can be detected by most of the current anti-virus tools now available (and you should regularly scan documents for macro viruses), but you might be able to reduce the risk of macro virus effects with the following tips:

- Mark the NORMAL.DOT template file as "read-only." This generally protects the NORMAL.DOT file from infection.
- Use Word 7.0a or Word97 from Microsoft. These versions present an *Alert* box if the file you are going to open contains macros or customization information. You also have the opportunity to disable unknown macros.

SYMPTOMS

Symptom 45-1.   You cannot run more than one anti-virus product at a time   This problem is not uncommon, and it occurs most frequently when memory-resident virus protectors conflict with file-based anti-virus tools. When you run more than one anti-virus program, there is always the risk of strange results and false alarms. For example, some anti-virus programs store their "virus signature strings" unprotected in memory. Running incompatible or conflicting anti-virus tools might detect other signature strings or memory-resident activity as a virus. Run only one anti-virus program at a time.

Symptom 45-2.   Your anti-virus tool does not function or causes other drivers to malfunction   Some TSR software might conflict with some anti-virus programs—especially memory-resident anti-virus programs. If problems occur, try booting the system from a clean bootable disk so that no other drivers or TSRs are in the system, aside from the anti-virus tool.

Symptom 45-3.   You notice that your anti-virus tool is slowing disk access dramatically or it locks up under Windows   Normally, many anti-virus tools (especially memory-resident tools) will slow disk access a bit. If the disk performance is tremendously reduced, or if the tool freezes during operation, the disk cache being used might conflict with the anti-virus product. Try increasing the number of buffers in the CONFIG.SYS file. If problems continue, try disabling the disk-caching software while running the anti-virus product.

Symptom 45-4.   The anti-virus tool is reporting false alarms   It is not uncommon for anti-virus products to report false alarms. This problem is most often caused by conflicts with other memory-resident software running in the system. Try running the software from a clean boot disk. The nature of anti-viral detection techniques also plays a role in reporting false errors. For example, file comparison is a typical technique, but files can be changed for many reasons other than a virus, so false alarms are a strong possibility. Other techniques also have flaws that might result in false alarms.

Symptom 45-5.   The memory-resident anti-virus tool cannot be removed   Probably another TSR is running in the system and is conflicting with the anti-virus tool. You might have to reboot the system to clear the anti-virus tool. In the future, try loading the anti-virus tool last—after all other drivers and TSRs are loaded.

Symptom 45-6.   The virus scanner is only scanning files very slowly   This is usually an issue with certain older virus-scanning software. Ideally, you should be able to correct this problem by upgrading to the latest patch or version of the virus scanner. If you cannot patch or update the program, try scanning only the program files, not all files or compressed files.

Symptom 45-7.   The virus scanner seems to conflict with the boot sector when it scans   If the virus scanner is conflicting with your boot sector (either upon installation or after installing), choose the *Custom* setup feature and disable the initial system scan during installation. Then edit the scanner's configuration to skip the boot scan. As an example for McAfee's VirusScan product, edit your DEFAULT.VSC file and under the [Scan Options] section, change bSkipBootScan=0 to bSkip-BootScan=1. This will skip the boot sector scan when you run VirusScan. Thus, the boot sector will not be scanned for viruses.

Symptom 45-8. You receive a "Cannot load device drivers error" from the virus scanner This error typically occurs on platforms that have been upgraded from Windows 3.1 to Windows 95, but have not completely uninstalled the 3.1 version of virus scanner (or a previous installation of a Windows 95 virus scanner was not completely removed from the system). You'll need to remove all traces of the virus scanner manually from SYSTEM.INI and WIN.INI. Using McAfee's VirusScan as an example, open the SYSTEM.INI file and remove:

```
device=MCSCAN32.386
device=MCUTIL.386
device=mCKRNL.386
device=MCFSHOOK.386
device=vshield.386
```

Open the WIN.INI file and remove:

```
load = C:\MCAFEE\VIRUSCAN\VSHWIN.EXE
```

And remove the section:

```
[VIRUSCAN]
WSCAN=C:\McAfee\VIRUSCAN\WSCAN.EXE
```

Of course, you should be sure to remove the correct entries for your particular virus scanner.

Symptom 45-9. An "Insufficient memory" message appears when the virus scanner is loading under Windows 95 This error is usually caused when Windows 95 uses a DOS version of a virus scanner to scan the root directory of C: at startup, and not enough conventional memory is available to run the DOS virus scanner. Try updating the virus scanner program or patching it to a later version, if possible, or disable virus scanning on Windows 95 startup.

Symptom 45-10. A "Cannot create events" error appears when the virus scanner is loading This is usually caused by an improperly located KERNEL32.DLL file. Search your computer for the file KERNEL32.DLL on the root of your hard drive (C:). If you move this file to C:\Windows\System where it belongs, this should resolve this issue. Some new systems are shipped with the KERNEL32.DLL file improperly located in the root directory.

Further Study

That's all for Chapter 45. Be sure to review the glossary and chapter questions on the accompanying CD. If you have access to the Internet, take some time to review these antivirus resources:

Command Software Systems: **http://www.commandcom.com/**

IBM: **http://www.av.ibm.com/**

McAfee: **http://www.mcafee.com** or **http://www.networkassociate.com/**

NCSA: **http://www.ncsa.com/**

S&S Software International: **http://www.drsolomon.com/**

Symantec: **http://www.symantec.com/avcenter**

VSUM: **http://www.vsum.com**

46

VL BUS
OPERATIONS

CONTENTS AT A GLANCE

VL Bus Configuraton and Signals
   VL bus layout
   Knowing the VL signals

General Bus Troubleshooting
   VL-specific issues

Further Study

The demands of data transfer across the expansion bus have continued to evolve faster than the throughput of classic ISA/EISA bus architectures allow. The volumes of data required by graphic user interfaces (such as Microsoft's Windows) present serious challenges to conventional video adapter and memory design. Early in 1992, the *Video Electronics Standards Association (VESA)* proposed a new local bus standard called the *VESA Local bus* (*VL bus*, also dubbed the *Video Local bus*) intended to improve the performance of graphics and video sub-systems. In general terms, a "local bus" is a pathway that allows peripherals to access the system's main memory quickly. For the VL bus, such improved access means higher data throughput and performance for video information at the speed of the CPU itself. By using a stand-alone bus for video, ISA or EISA busses can be implemented for backward system compatibility. That is, users can upgrade to a new motherboard and graphics card, but all other peripherals and software remain compatible.

VL Bus Configuration and Signals

Of course, the path to a "standard" local bus was not an easy one. In 1991 and 1992, a few chip set suppliers and manufacturers implemented non-standard high-performance I/O buses. For example, some OPTi chip sets were designed to support an OPTi local bus. Unfortunately, the OPTi local bus was supported by only a small handful of manufacturers, and because the OPTi approach was specific to their chip sets, few (if any) I/O cards were ever actually developed for these buses and few manufacturers provided them. Thus, OPTi and other proprietary buses met the same fate as all other non-standardized approaches in the PC industry—they disappeared. However, the failure of proprietary local bus designs did not prevent industry acceptance of a "standard" VL bus design developed by *VESA (Video Electronics Standards Association)* in late 1992. By placing the VL extension connectors in-line with standard ISA connectors, the VL board can also serve as an ISA board—only with far higher data throughput.

The essential advantage of a VL bus is direct access to the CPU's main busses. This allows a VL device to rapidly transfer the large quantities of data that are vital for high-performance video under Windows (and now Windows 95). Further, the VL bus operates at the motherboard's bus speed, rather than a fixed 8.3MHz, like the ISA bus. As a result, faster CPU speed will result in faster bus speed. Unfortunately, this is where the advantages end.

Although virtually direct connection to the CPU might seem like a real asset, you should understand the serious drawbacks. Processor dependence can ultimately become a disadvantage for the VL bus. Because higher processor speed results in higher bus capacitance, VL signals can lose reliability at high CPU clock frequencies. Further, the processor signals were intended to attach to only a few chips (such as the RAM controller) and have very precise timing rules. In fact, each type of Intel i486 chip (i.e., i486SX, i486DX, and i486DX/2) has slightly different timing requirements. When additional capacitance loads are added by adding multiple connectors and multiple local-bus chips, all sorts of undesirable things can happen. The two most likely problems are: data "glitches" caused by slowed processor bus signals and out-of-spec timing for different I/O cards with different loading characteristics.

> i486-type CPUs are listed in this paragraph because the VL bus had largely fallen into disuse by the time Pentium processors arrived. You will only rarely (if ever) find a Pentium motherboard fitted with VL bus slots.

Although the VL specification does not list an upper frequency limit, the potential load problems dictate a practical limit. With a clock speed of 33MHz, a VL motherboard should be able to support two VL devices reliably. At 40MHz, only one VL device should be used. Above 40MHz, the chances of unreliable operation with even one VL device become substantial. If you find yourself working on a fast VL system with random system errors, see if the problem goes away when the VL device(s) are removed (and replaced with ISA equivalents, if necessary).

Another problem is the lack of concurrency. For a PCI bus, the CPU can continue operating when a PCI device takes control of the system busses. VL architecture also allows for bus-mastering operation, but when a VL device takes control of the bus, the CPU must be stopped. Although this is technically not a defect, it clearly limits the performance of high-end devices (e.g., SCSI controllers) that might attempt to use a VL architecture. Finally, the VL bus has several other disadvantages. It is a +5-Vdc architecture (where PCI can support +3.3-Vdc). Unlike PCI, no "auto-configuration" capability is in the VL bus (jumpers and DIP switches are required), so Plug-and-Play operation is not supported.

VL BUS LAYOUT

The VL bus uses a 116-pin card edge connector with small contacts (similar in appearance to MicroChannel contacts), as shown in Fig. 46-1. The most recent VL bus release (2.0) offers a 32-bit data path with a maximum data throughput of about 130MB/sec. The pinout for a VL bus is illustrated in Table 46-1. Interestingly, the VL bus has an extension to the standard ISA/EISA bus. The two right connectors are standard 16-bit ISA bus connectors. The two right-most connectors provide the VL compatibility. The long VL connector portion provides the 32-bit VL support. This is different than the PCI bus, which does not use any part of the ISA bus.

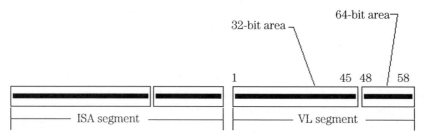

FIGURE 46-1   **A simplified drawing of a VL card and bus.**

TABLE 46-1 VL BUS PINOUT (REV. 2.0)			
PIN	DESCRIPTION	PIN	DESCRIPTION
A01	Data 00	B01	Data 01
A02	Data 02	B02	Data 03
A03	Data 04	B03	Ground
A04	Data 06	B04	Data 05
A05	Data 08	B05	Data 07
A06	Ground	B06	Data 09
A07	Data 10	B07	Data 11
A08	Data 12	B08	Data 13
A09	+VCC	B09	Data 15
A10	Data 14	B10	Ground
A11	Data 16	B11	Data 17
A12	Data 18	B12	+VCC
A13	Data 20	B13	Data 19
A14	Ground	B14	Data 21

PIN	DESCRIPTION	PIN	DESCRIPTION
TABLE 46-1 VL BUS PINOUT (REV. 2.0) (CONTINUED)			
A15	Data 22	B15	Data 23
A16	Data 24	B16	Data 25
A17	Data 26	B17	Ground
A18	Data 28	B18	Data 27
A19	Data 30	B19	Data 29
A20	+VCC	B20	Data 31
A21	Address 31	B21	Address 30
A22	Ground	B22	Address 28
A23	Address 29	B23	Address 26
A24	Address 27	B24	Ground
A25	Address 25	B25	Address 24
A26	Address 23	B26	Address 22
A27	Address 21	B27	+VCC
A28	Address 19	B28	Address 20
A29	Ground	B29	Address 18
A30	Address 17	B30	Address 16
A31	Address 15	B31	Address 14
A32	+VCC	B32	Address 12
A33	Address 13	B33	Address 10
A34	Address 11	B34	Address 8
A35	Address 9	B35	Ground
A36	Address 7	B36	Address 6
A37	Address 5	B37	Address 4
A38	Ground	B38	−WBAK
A39	Address 3	B39	−BE 0
A40	Address 2	B40	+VCC
A41	n/c	B41	−BE 1
A42	−RESET	B42	−BE 2
A43	D/ −C	B43	Ground
A44	M/ −I/O	B44	−BE 3
A45	W/ −R	B45	−ADS
Key		Key	
Key		Key	
A48	−RDYRTN	B48	−LRDY
A49	Ground	B49	−LDEV
A50	IRQ 9	B50	−LREQ
A51	−BRDY	B51	Ground
A52	−BLAST	B52	−LGNT
A53	ID 0	B53	+VCC
A54	ID 1	B54	ID 2
A55	Ground	B55	ID 3
A56	LCLK	B56	ID 4
A57	+VCC	B57	n/c
A58	−LBS16	B58	−LEADS

KNOWING THE VL SIGNALS

The *Data/-Command (D/–C)* signal tells whether information on the bus is data or a command. Clock signals from the CPU are provided through the *Local Bus Clock (LCLK)* line. *Memory/–I/O (M/–I/O)* distinguishes between memory and I/O access, while the *Write/–Read (W/–R)* signal differentiates between read or write operations. The *–Byte Enable* lines *(–BE0 to –BE7)* indicate which eight bit bytes of the data bus are being transferred. A *–Reset* signal *(–RESET)* will initialize the VL device. The *–Ready Return (–RDYRTN)* line indicates that the VL bus is free for access. Data bus width is determined by the *–Local Bus Size 16 (–LBS16)* signal.

Accessing the VL bus is a process of arbitration—much like the arbitration that takes place on an MCA or EISA bus. Each VL device is defined by its own ID number (ID0 to ID4). The *-Local Bus Ready (–LRDY)*, *–Local Bus Device (–LDEV)*, *–Local Bus Request (–LREQ)*, and *–Local Bus Grant (–LGNT)* lines are used to negotiate for control of the VL bus. In most cases, only one VL device is on the bus, but arbitration must be performed to ensure proper access to memory.

General Bus Troubleshooting

In most cases, you will not be troubleshooting a bus. After all, the bus is little more than a passive connector. However, the major signals that exist on a VL bus can provide you with important clues about the system's operation. The most effective bus troubleshooting tool available to you is a POST board (such as the ones covered in Chapter 15). Many POST boards are equipped with a number of LEDs that display power status, along with important timing and control signals. If one or more of those LEDs is missing, a fault has likely occurred somewhere on the motherboard. Keep in mind that the vast majority of POST boards are designed for the ISA bus. You can plug a POST board (with a built-in logic probe capable of 33MHz operation) into an ISA connector (which will check the ISA portion of the VL connector arrangement), then use the logic probe to test key signals on the VL extension. Because the signals on a VL extension are quite different than those on an ISA bus, try the following signals:

- *Voltage* Use your multimeter and check each voltage level on the VL bus. You should be able to find +5 Vdc. If any of these supply levels are low or absent, troubleshoot or replace the power supply.
- *LCLK (pin A56)* The Local Bus Clock signal provides timing signals for the expansion device. It will typically be at the processor frequency. If this signal is absent, the expansion board will probably not run. Check the clock-generating circuitry on the motherboard, or replace the motherboard outright.
- *–RESET (pin A42)* The Reset line can be used to re-initialize the VL expansion device. This line should not be active for more than a few moments after power is applied or after a warm reset is initiated.
- *M/–I/O (pin A44)* The Memory/–I/O line indicates whether memory or I/O locations are being accessed. You can expect this signal to flicker or remain dim because it should switch modes very regularly. A problem here usually indicates trouble with the CPU or intervening logic. Try replacing the motherboard.

■ *W/–R (pin A45)* The Write/–Read line defines whether data is being read or written across the bus. This signal should also flicker or remain dim because it should switch modes regularly. Problems with this signal usually indicate trouble with the CPU or intervening logic. Try replacing the motherboard.

■ –LRDY (pin B48)—the Local Bus Ready signal tells VL devices that the bus is ready for use. If this signal is frozen at logic 1, the VL device might not be releasing the bus or a problem with motherboard logic might be disabling the bus. Try removing the VL device or moving it to another slot. If that fails, try replacing the motherboard.

Another point to consider is that bus connectors are mechanical devices—as a result, they do not last forever. If you or your customer are in the habit of removing and inserting boards frequently, it is likely that the metal "fingers" providing contact will wear and result in unreliable connections. Similarly, inserting a board improperly (or with excessive force) can break the connector. In extreme cases, even the motherboard can be damaged. The first rule of board replacement is: Always try removing and re-inserting the suspect board. It is not uncommon for oxides to develop on board and slot contacts that might eventually degrade signal quality. By removing the board and re-inserting it, you can wipe off any oxides or dust and possible improve the connections.

The second rule of board replacement is: Always try a board in another expansion slot before replacing it. This way, a faulty bus slot can be ruled out before suffering the expense of a new board. Remember that many current VL motherboards have only one or two VL slots—the remainder are ISA slots. If a bus slot is defective, a technician can do little, except:

1 Block the slot and inform the customer that it is damaged and should not be used.
2 Replace the damaged bus slot connector (a tedious and time-consuming task) and pass the labor expense on to the customer.
3 Replace the motherboard outright (also a rather expensive option).

VL-SPECIFIC ISSUES

Although the VL-bus is generally considered to be a sound (but dated) bus architecture, some perplexing issues sometimes crop up on the workbench. The two major issues to contend with are bus speed and VL device types.

■ *Bus speed* The VL bus is linked to the CPU clock speed. This was fine when CPUs ran at 33MHz or less, but the VL bus wasn't intended to support higher clock speeds. Clock speeds higher than 33MHz (often activated when a late-model i486 motherboard was upgraded with an OverDrive processor), could cause signal degradation—the VL device(s) would malfunction. Whenever you encounter difficulty on a VL motherboard, always verify that the bus speed is 33MHz or less. Notice that a single well-designed VL board can often run up to 40MHz (sometimes 50MHz), but this is extremely rare and should never be expected.

■ *Multiple VL devices* The VL bus was originally intended as a single-slot architecture (primarily for high-performance graphic accelerators of the day). When designers expanded the role of VL and added more VL slots, the potential for signal degradation increased. More than two VL devices often cause problems on VL motherboards (especially at clock speeds over 33MHz).

Further Study

That's it for Chapter 46. Be sure to review the glossary and chapter questions on the ac-companying CD. If you have access to the Internet, take some time to review this VL bus resource:

VESA (Video Electronics Standards Organization): **http://www.vesa.org**

FLOPPY DRIVE

TESTING AND ALIGNMENT

CONTENTS AT A GLANCE

Understanding Alignment Problems
  Recognizing the problems
  Repair vs. replace
  Tips to reduce floppy-drive problems

Using Alignment Tools
  Advanced tools

Aligning the Drive
  Drive cleaning
  Clamping

Spindle speed
Track 00 test
Radial alignment
Azimuth alignment
Head step
Hysteresis
Head width

Further Study

Floppy disk drives (Fig. 47-1) are basically electromechanical devices. Their motors, lead screws, sliders, levers, and linkages are all subject to eventual wear and tear. As a result, a drive can develop problems that are caused by mechanical defects instead of electronic problems. Fortunately, few mechanical problems are fatal to a drive. With the proper software tools, you can test a troublesome drive and often correct problems simply through careful cleaning and alignment. This chapter explains the concepts and procedures for floppy drive testing and alignment.

FIGURE 47-1   **A Teac FD-235 3.5" floppy drive.** Teac
America, Inc.

Understanding Alignment Problems

The causes behind floppy-drive alignment problems will vary somewhat depending on the
design of the drive itself, but some common causes can crop up time after time:

- Wear in the drive's head positioning mechanism can eventually cause the radial alignment to drift out of specification.
- Various forms of debris often find their way into the drive's mechanical parts and will
  often accelerate wear in the drive—and in some cases, affect alignment directly by
  changing the way that the drive's sensors and mechanisms respond.
- Dirt and normal wear might cause the head mechanism to not slide as easily as it
  should. This puts an excessive load on the small stepper motor used to position the
  heads.
- The read/write head assembly itself can become bent or otherwise damaged from accidental abuse—often not enough to cause a complete failure, but enough to significantly
  affect the alignment and cause problems when reading a diskette recorded by another
  drive.
- Drive alignment problems might also be revealed by marginal diskettes. If a drive is
  slightly out of alignment, it might work with a good data diskette, but not with a marginal "cut priced" one.

RECOGNIZING THE PROBLEMS

As a technician, you will need to understand when a floppy drive is showing signs that
might be related to alignment errors. In general, you should always respond to a chronic
drive error by examining the disk media itself. Slowly spin the disk and observe both sides
of the oxide layer. The layer should be smooth and even throughout—like the smooth surface of a quiet pond. If you see any marks or scratches on the disk, you should suspect that
either the R/W heads are misaligned or that a significant buildup of oxides are on the R/W

head(s). If you have not already cleaned the R/W heads as part of your regular repair practices, clean them now. If the problem persists, the head assembly is probably severely misaligned and you should replace the drive or re-align it as you see fit.

Other classic indicators of alignment trouble are reading and writing errors. Data is checked when it is read from or written to a drive. When you encounter a drive that has difficulty reading diskettes that were written on another PC (or writes diskettes that other PCs have difficulty reading), the drive's alignment is in serious doubt. Fortunately, alignment software can test the drive and report on its specifications, allowing you to see any unacceptable performance characteristics. If you find that the drive is faulty, you can then decide to replace or re-align the drive at your discretion.

REPAIR VS. REPLACE

Floppy-drive alignment continues to be a matter of debate. The cost of a floppy-drive alignment package is often higher than the cost of a new drive. When compared with the rising costs of labor and alignment packages, many technicians question the practice of drive alignment when new drives are readily available. True, most casual PC enthusiasts would not choose to align a misbehaving drive. However, testing software has an important place in any toolbox. At the very least, test software can confirm the faulty alignment of a drive and eliminate the guesswork involved in drive replacement. For enthusiasts and technicians who have a volume of drives to service, alignment tools offer a relatively efficient means of recovering drives that might otherwise be discarded. Ultimately, one of a technician's most vital tools is an open mind—you can repair or replace the drive, depending on what makes the most economic sense in your particular situation.

TIPS TO REDUCE FLOPPY-DRIVE PROBLEMS

Now that you've seen the most common causes of floppy-drive problems, you can recommend some pro-active steps to avoid or reduce problems in the future:

- *Keep the floppy drives clean* Not only is it important to keep the drive's R/W heads clean, but it is also important to keep dust and debris from accumulating inside the drive's mechanisms. A static-safe vacuum cleaner can usually remove unwanted dust or the debris can be removed by "blowing down" the drive with a can of electronics-grade compressed air and a long, thin nozzle.
- *Do not force disks in or out* This is a classic cause of drive problems. Disks that become stuck in the floppy drive (usually because the drive does not release the 3.5" disk's protective shroud properly) should be removed with the utmost care.
- *Keep air from circulating through the drive* Floppy drives should generally be installed outside of the normal air flow in a PC. This will reduce the amount of dust and debris that normally flows around and through the drive.
- *Use good-quality diskettes* "Bargain" diskettes often use inferior oxides, which tend to rub off and accumulate on the R/W heads. If you encounter an unusual number of failures with "bargain" diskettes, you should clean the R/W heads and switch to a better brand of diskettes.

Using Alignment Tools

Drive alignment is not a new concept. Technicians have tested and aligned floppy drives for years using oscilloscopes and test disks containing precise, specially recorded data patterns. You might already be familiar with the classic "cat's eye" or "index burst" alignment patterns on oscilloscopes. This kind of manual alignment required you to find the right test point on your particular drive's PC board, locate the proper adjustment in the drive assembly, and interpret complex (sometimes rather confusing) oscilloscope displays. Traditionally, manual alignment required a substantial investment in an oscilloscope, test disk, and stand-alone drive exerciser equipment to run a drive outside of the computer.

Although manual drive-alignment techniques are still used today, they are being largely replaced by automatic alignment techniques. Software developers have created interactive control programs to operate with their specially-recorded data disks. These software tool kits provide all the features necessary to operate a suspected drive through a wide variety of tests while displaying the results numerically or graphically right on a computer monitor (Fig. 47-2). As you make adjustments, you can see real-time results displayed on the monitor. Software-based testing eliminates the need for an oscilloscope and ancillary test equipment. You also do not need to know the specific signal test points for every possible drive. Several popular tool kits are on the market, including FloppyTune by Data Depot, Inc. and DriveProbe (Fig. 47-3) by Accurite Technologies Inc. The contact information for both manufacturers is listed at the end of the chapter.

ADVANCED TOOLS

Although software tools make up a majority of the typical floppy-drive service options, the tools available to serious floppy-drive service technicians do not stop at software. With the proper supplemental test hardware (such as the Drive Probe Advanced Edition from Accurite Technologies, Fig. 47-3), a PC can be turned into a comprehensive floppy-drive

AUTOMATIC Drive Test   'Esc'- For Previous Menu

Test	Track	Head 0 Data		Head 1 Data		Test Limits	Results	
Speed	NA	300 RPM	/ 199.7 mS			300 ± 6 RPM	Pass	NA
Eccentricity	44	100 uI		NA		0 ± 300 uI	Pass	NA
Radial	0	96%	50 uI	100%	0 uI	60 - 100 %	Pass	Pass
Radial	40	93%	-100 uI	90%	-150 uI	60 - 100 %	Pass	Pass
Radial	79	96%	50 uI	90%	-150 uI	60 - 100 %	Pass	Pass
Azimuth	76	6 Min		4 Min		0 ± 30 Min	Pass	Pass
Index	0	414 uS		407 uS		400 ± 600 uS	Pass	Pass
Index	79	397 uS		380 uS		400 ± 600 uS	Pass	Pass
Hysteresis	40	100 uI		NA		0 ± 250 uI	Pass	NA

```
uI = Micro-inches        uS = Microsecond       mS = Millisecond
Min = Minutes            NA = Not Applicable     NT = Not Tested
```

Note: Radial is expressed as LOBE RATIO and OFFSET from track center line.
Auto Test Completed   'Esc' For Previous Menu

FIGURE 47-2   **The DriveProbe automatic drive-test display.**

Accurite Technologies, Inc.

FIGURE 47-3   **DriveProbe: the advanced edition.** Accurite
Technologies, Inc.

test bed that supports all types of standard PC drives, as well as Macintosh drives and many types of floppy-disk duplicator drives.

Aligning the Drive

At this point in the chapter, you are ready to start the testing/alignment software and go to work. Before starting your software, however, you should disable any caching software that will cache your floppy drive(s). Because caching software affects the way in which data is read or written to the floppy disk, caching will adversely affect the measurements produced by the alignment software. To ensure the truest transfer of data to or from the floppy disk, boot the PC from a "clean" boot disk to disable all TSRs or device drivers in the system. Once the alignment software is started, eight major tests gauge the performance of a floppy drive: clamping, spindle speed, track 00, radial alignment, azimuth alignment, head step, hysteresis, and head width. Remember that not all tests have adjustments that can correct the corresponding fault.

DRIVE CLEANING

Floppy-drive R/W heads are not terribly complex devices, but they do require precision positioning. Heads must contact the disk media to read or write information reliably. As the disk spins, particles from the disk's magnetic coating wear off and form a deposit on the heads. Accumulations of everyday contaminants, such as dust and cigarette smoke, also contribute to deposits on the heads. Head deposits present several serious problems. First, deposits act as a wedge—forcing heads away from the disk surface, resulting in lost data and read/write errors, and generally unreliable and intermittent operation. Deposits tend to be more abrasive than the head itself, so dirty heads can generally reduce a disk's working life. Finally, dirty heads can cause erroneous readings during testing and alignment. Because alignment disks are specially recorded in a very precise fashion, faulty readings will yield erroneous information that can actually cause you to improperly adjust the drive. As a general procedure, clean the drive thoroughly before you test or align it.

R/W heads can also be cleaned manually or automatically. The manual method is just as the name implies. Use a high-quality head cleaner on a soft, lint-free, anti-static swab, and scrub both head surfaces by hand. Wet the swab, but do not soak it. You might need to repeat the cleaning with fresh swabs to ensure that all residual deposits are removed. Be certain that all computer power is off before manual cleaning and allow a few minutes for the cleaner to dry completely before restoring power. If you do not have head-cleaning chemicals on-hand, you can use fresh ethyl or isopropyl alcohol. The advantage to manual cleaning is thoroughness—heads can be cleaned very well with no chance of damage from friction.

Most software tool kits provide a cleaning disk and software option that allows you to clean the disk automatically. With computer power on and the software tool kit loaded and running, insert the cleaning disk and choose the cleaning option from your software menu. Software will then spin the drive for some period of time—10 to 30 seconds should be adequate, but do not exceed 60 seconds of continuous cleaning. Choose high-quality cleaning disks that are impregnated with a lubricant. Avoid "bargain" off-the-shelf cleaning disks that force you to wet the disk. Wetted cleaning disks are often harsh and prolonged use can actually damage the heads from excessive friction. Once the drive is clean, it can be tested and aligned.

CLAMPING

A floppy disk is formatted into individual tracks laid down in concentric circles along the media. Because each track is ideally a perfect circle, it is crucial that the disk rotate evenly in a drive. If the disk is not on-center for any reason, it will not spin evenly. If a disk is not clamped evenly, the eccentricity introduced into the spin might be enough to allow heads to read or write data to adjoining tracks. A clamping test should be performed first, after the drive is cleaned because high eccentricity can adversely effect disk tests. Clamping problems are more pronounced on 5.25" drives, where the soft mylar hub ring is vulnerable to damage from the clamping mechanism.

Start your software tool kit from your computer's hard drive, then insert the alignment disk containing test patterns into the questionable drive. Select a clamping or eccentricity test and allow the test to run a bit. You will probably see a display similar to the one shown in Fig. 47-4. Typical software tool kits can measure eccentricity in terms of microinches-from true center. If clamping is off by more than a few hundred microinches, the spindle or clamping mechanisms should be replaced (be sure the diskette itself is not damaged). You can also simply replace the floppy drive. Try reinserting and retesting the disk several times to confirm your results. Repeated failures confirm a faulty spindle system.

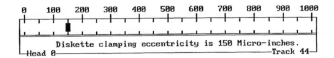

DISKETTE ECCENTRICITY test   'Esc'- For Previous Menu

```
     0    100   200   300   400   500   600   700   800   900   1000
```
        Diskette clamping eccentricity is 150 Micro-inches.
    └Head 0─   ─Track 44─┘

Drive 1 Selected as [3 1/2" 1.4Mb 300 RPM]   Location: Track 44 Head 0

FIGURE 47-4   **Screen display from a DriveProbe eccentricity test.** Accurite Technologies, Inc.

SPINDLE SPEED

Media must be rotated at a fixed rate in order for data to be read or written properly. A drive that is too fast or too slow might be able to read files that it has written at that wrong speed without error, but the disk might not be readable in other drives operating at a normal speed. Files recorded at a normal speed also might not be readable in drives that are too fast or too slow. Such transfer problems between drives is a classic sign of speed trouble (usually signaled as "general disk read/write errors"). Drive speeds should be accurate to within ±1.5%, so a drive running at 300 RPM should be accurate to ±4.5 RPM (295.5 to 304.5 RPM), and a drive running at 360 RPM should be accurate to within ±5.4 RPM (354.6 RPM to 365.4 RPM).

After cleaning the R/W heads and testing disk eccentricity, select the spindle speed test from your software menu. The display will probably appear much like the one in Fig. 47-5. Today's floppy drives rarely drift out of alignment because rotational speed is regulated by feedback from the spindle's index sensor. The servo circuit is constantly adjusting motor torque to achieve optimal spindle speed. If a self-compensating drive is out of tolerance, excess motor wear, mechanical obstructions, or index-sensor failure is indicated. Check and replace the index sensor or the entire spindle-motor assembly. You can also replace the entire floppy drive outright.

TRACK 00 TEST

The first track on any floppy disk is the outermost track of side 0, which is track 00. Track 00 is important because it contains the boot record and file-allocation information vital for finding disk files. The particular files saved on a disk can be broken up and spread out all over the disk, but the FAT data must always be in a known location. If the drive cannot find track 00 reliably, the system might not be able to boot from the floppy drive or even use disks. Floppy drives utilize a sensor, such as an optoisolator, to physically determine when the R/W heads are over the outermost track.

Select the track 00 test from your software menu and allow the test to run. A track 00 test measures the difference between the actual location of track 00 versus the point at which the track 00 sensor indicates that track 00 is reached. The difference should be less than ±1.5 mils (one-thousandths of an inch). A larger error might cause the drive to encounter problems reading or writing to the disk. The easiest and quickest fix is to alter the track 00 sensor position. This adjustment usually involves loosening the sensor and moving it until the monitor display indicates an acceptable reading. Remember that you only need to move the sensor a small fraction, so a patient, steady hand is required. The track 00 sensor is almost always located along the head-carriage lead screw. Mark the original position of the sensor with indelible ink so that you can return it to its original position if you get in trouble.

RADIAL ALIGNMENT

The alignment of a drive's R/W heads versus the disk is crucial to reliable drive operation because alignment directly affects contact between heads and media. If head contact is not precise, data read or written to the disk might be vulnerable. The radial alignment test measures the head's actual position versus the precise center of the outer, middle, and inner tracks (as established by ANSI standards). Ideally, R/W heads should be centered perfectly when positioned over any track, but any differences are measured in microinches. A radial alignment error more than several hundred microinches might suggest a head-alignment error.

Select the radial alignment test from your software tool kit and allow the test to run. A typical radial alignment test display is illustrated in Fig. 47-6. If you must perform an adjustment, you can start by loosening the slotted screws that secure the stepping motor, and gently rotate the motor to alter lead screw position. As you make adjustments with the test in progress, watch the display for the middle track. When error is minimized on the inner track, secure the stepping motor carefully to keep the assembly from shifting position. Use

MOTOR SPEED Test   'Esc'- For Previous Menu

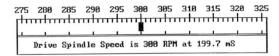

Drive 1 Selected as [3 1/2" 1.4Mb 300 RPM]   Location: Track 0   Head 0

FIGURE 47-5   **Screen display from a DriveProbe motor-speed test.** Accurite Technologies, Inc.

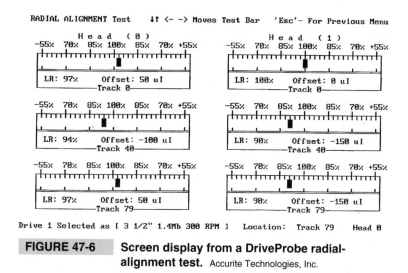

Head (0)

-55% 70% 85% 100% 85% 70% +55%

LR: 97%   Offset: 50 uI
————Track 0————

-55% 70% 85% 100% 85% 70% +55%

LR: 94%   Offset: -100 uI
————Track 40————

-55% 70% 85% 100% 85% 70% +55%

LR: 97%   Offset: 50 uI
————Track 79————

Head (1)

-55% 70% 85% 100% 85% 70% +55%

LR: 100%   Offset: 0 uI
————Track 0————

-55% 70% 85% 100% 85% 70% +55%

LR: 90%   Offset: -150 uI
————Track 40————

-55% 70% 85% 100% 85% 70% +55%

LR: 90%   Offset: -150 uI
————Track 79————

Drive 1 Selected as [3 1/2" 1.4Mb 300 RPM]   Location: Track 79   Head 0

FIGURE 47-6   **Screen display from a DriveProbe radial-alignment test.** Accurite Technologies, Inc.

extreme caution when adjusting radial head position—you only need to move the head a fraction, so a very steady hand is needed. You should also re-check the track 00 sensor to be sure the sensor position is acceptable. If you are unable to affect radial head alignment, the drive should be replaced.

AZIMUTH ALIGNMENT

Not only must the heads be centered perfectly along a disk's radius, but the heads must also be perfectly perpendicular to the disk plane. If the head azimuth is off by more than a few minutes (1/60 of a degree), data integrity can be compromised and disk interchangeability between drives—especially high-density drives—might become unreliable. When the heads are perfectly perpendicular to the disk (at 90 degrees), the azimuth should be 0 minutes.

Select the azimuth test from your software tool kit and allow the test to run. Figure 47-7 shows an azimuth-alignment test display. An azimuth-alignment test measures the rotation (or twist) of R/W heads in terms of + or – minutes. A clockwise twist is expressed as a plus (+) number, and a counterclockwise twist is expressed as a negative (–) number. Heads should be perpendicular to within about ±10 minutes. It is important to note that most floppy drives do not allow azimuth adjustments easily. Unless you want to experiment with the adjustment, it is often easiest to replace a severely misaligned drive.

HEAD STEP

The head step (or index step) test measures the amount of time between a step pulse from the coil-driver circuits and a set of timing mark data recorded on the test disk. In manual oscilloscope adjustments, this would be seen as the "index burst." Average index time is typically 200 s for 5.25" drives, and 400 s for 3.5" drives. In automatic testing with your software tool kit, you will see time measurements for both heads on the inner and outer tracks (Fig. 47-8). The actual range of acceptable time depends on your particular drive, but variations of ±100 s or more is not unusual.

If the head step timing is off too far, you can adjust timing by moving the index sensor. As with all other drive adjustments, you need only move the sensor a small fraction, so be extremely careful about moving the sensor. A steady hand is very important here. Be sure to secure the sensor when you are done with your timing adjustments.

HYSTERESIS

It is natural for wear and debris in the mechanical head-positioning system to result in some "play"—that is, the head will not wind up in the exact same position moving from outside in, as moving from the inside out. Excessive play, however, will make it difficult to find the correct track reliably. Testing is accomplished by starting the heads at a known track, stepping the heads out to track 00, then stepping back to the starting track. Head position is then measured and recorded. The heads are then stepped in to the innermost track, then back to

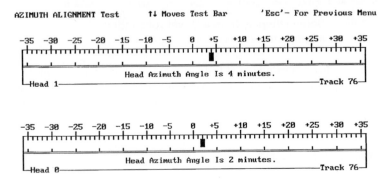

FIGURE 47-7 Screen display from a DriveProbe azimuth-alignment test. Accurite Technologies, Inc.

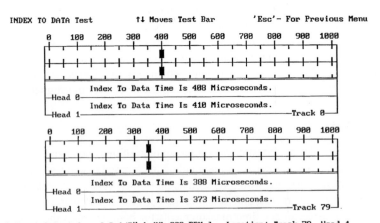

FIGURE 47-8 Screen display from a DriveProbe index-to-data test. Accurite Technologies, Inc.

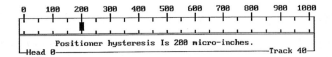

POSITIONER HYSTERESIS Test   'Esc'- For Previous Menu

Drive 1 Selected as [3 1/2" 1.4Mb 300 RPM]   Location: Track 1 Head 0

FIGURE 47-9   Screen display from a DriveProbe hystersis test. Accurite Technologies, Inc.

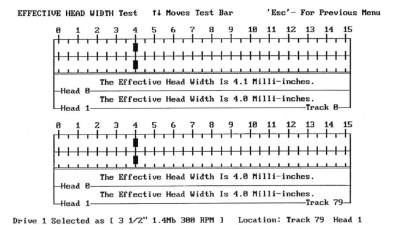

Drive 1 Selected as [3 1/2" 1.4Mb 300 RPM]   Location: Track 79 Head 1

FIGURE 47-10   Screen display from a DriveProbe head-width test. Accurite Technologies, Inc.

the starting track. Head position is measured and recorded again. Under ideal conditions, the head carriage should wind up in precisely the same place (zero hysteresis), but natural play almost guarantees some minor difference. A typical hysteresis test-measurement display is shown in Fig. 47-9. If excessive hysteresis is encountered, the drive should be replaced because it is difficult to determine exactly where the excess play is causes in the drive.

HEAD WIDTH

Another test of a drive's R/W heads is the measurement of their effective width. Effective head widths are 12 or 13 mils for 5.25" double-density drives, 5 or 6 mils for 5.25" high-density drives, and 4 or 5 mils for all 3.5" drives. As you run the head-width test with your software tool kit, you will see effective width displayed on the monitor (Fig. 47-10). As R/W heads wear down, their effective width increases. If the effective width is too low, the heads might be contaminated with oxide buildup. When small head widths are detected, try cleaning the drive again to remove any remaining contaminates. If the width reading remains too small (or measures too large), the heads or head carriage might be damaged. You can replace the R/W head assembly, but often the best course is simply to replace the drive outright.

Further Study

That's all for Chapter 47. Be sure to review the glossary and chapter questions on the accompanying CD. If you have access to the Internet, take a look at some of these floppy-drive maintenance resources:

Accurite Technologies: **http://www.accurite.com**

Data Depot: **http://www.datadepo.com**

NEC: **http://www.nec.com**

48

MONITOR TESTING
AND ALIGNMENT

CONTENTS AT A GLANCE

Before You Begin
   Testing vs. alignment
   Know the warranty
   Getting from here to there
   High-voltage cautions
   The mirror trick
   Making an adjustment

Test and Procedures
   High-voltage test and regulation
   Screen control
   Focus
   Dynamic pincushion

Horizontal phase
Horizontal and vertical centering
Horizontal and vertical size (height
   and width)
Horizontal and vertical linearity
Static convergence
Dynamic convergence
Color purity
Color drive
Cleaning and vacuuming

Further Study

When set-up and ventilated properly, computer monitors are notoriously rugged devices. The CRT itself enjoys a reasonably long life span. By their very nature, CRTs are remarkably tolerant to physical abuse and can withstand wide variations in power and signal voltages. However, even the best CRT and its associated circuitry suffers eventual degradation with age and use. Monitor operation can also be upset when major sub-assemblies are replaced, such as circuit boards or deflection assemblies. Maintenance and alignment procedures are available to evaluate a monitor's performance and allow you to keep it working within its specifications. This chapter illustrates a comprehensive set of procedures that can be performed to test and adjust the monitor's performance. Keep in mind that this chapter uses test patterns generated with the commercial utility "MONITORS" available on the companion CD.

> The MONITORS utility is commercial software that is included on the companion CD in encrypted format. To use MONITORS, you'll need to purchase the unlock code. See the order form at the back of this book for more ordering information.

Before You Begin

Adjusting a monitor is a serious matter and it should not be undertaken without careful consideration. A myriad of adjustments are found on the main circuit board—any of which can render a screen image unviewable if adjusted improperly. The delicate magnets and deflection assemblies around the CRT's neck can easily be damaged or knocked out of alignment by careless handling. In short, aligning a monitor can do more harm than good unless you have the patience to understand the purpose of each procedure. You also need to have a calm, methodical approach. The following points might help to keep you out of trouble.

TESTING VS. ALIGNMENT

The difference between monitor testing and monitor alignment is distinct. Testing is a low-level operation. Testing is also unobtrusive, so you can test a monitor at any point in the repair process. By using the companion software with your PC, you can test any monitor that is compatible with your video adapter. Testing is accomplished by displaying a test pattern on the monitor. After observing the condition of the pattern, you can usually deduce the monitor's fault area very quickly. Once the monitor is working (able to display a steady, full-screen image), you can also use test patterns to evaluate the monitor's current state of alignment.

Alignment is a high-level operation—a task that is performed only after the monitor has been completely repaired. Because alignment requires you to make adjustments to the monitor circuits, the monitor circuits must be working properly. After all, alignment does no good if a fault is preventing the monitor from displaying an image in the first place. Proper alignment is important to ensure that the monitor is displaying images as accurately as possible.

KNOW THE WARRANTY

A warranty is a written promise made by a manufacturer that their product will be free of most problems for some period of time. For monitors, typical warranties cover parts and labor for a period of one year from the date of purchase. The CRT itself is often covered up to three years. Before even touching the monitor, you should check to see if the warranty is still in force. Monitors that are still under warranty should be sent back to the manufacturer for repair. This book does not advocate voiding any warranty and the reasoning is very simple—why spend your time and effort to do a job that the manufacturer will do for free?

You paid for that warranty when you bought the monitor. Of course, most monitors in need of service are already out of warranty.

Only three exceptions might prompt you to ignore a warranty. First, the warranty might already be void if you purchased the monitor used. Manufacturers typically support the warranty only for the original purchaser (the individual that returns the warranty card). Third-party claims are often refused, but it might still be worth a call to the manufacturer's service manager just to be sure. Second, any warranty is only as good as the manufacturer. A manufacturer that goes out of business is not concerned with supporting your monitor, although reputable manufacturers that close their doors will turn over their service operations to an independent repair house. Again, a bit of detective work might be required to find out if the ultimate service provider will honor the unit's warranty. Finally, you might choose to ignore a warranty for organizations with poor or unclear service performance. Call the service provider and ask about the turn-around time and return procedures. If they "don't know" or you can't get a straight answer, chances are that your monitor is going to sit untouched for quite a while.

GETTING FROM HERE TO THERE

Monitors require special care in moving and handling. A monitor is typically a heavy device (most of the weight being contributed by the CRT and chassis). Back injury is a serious concern. If you must move the monitor between locations, remember to lift from the knees and not from the back—it's hard to fix a monitor while you're in traction. When carrying the monitor, keep the CRT screen toward your chest with your arms wrapped carefully around the enclosure to support the weight. Large monitors (larger than 17") are particularly unwieldy. You are wise to get another person's help when moving such bulky, expensive devices. If the monitor is to be used in-house, keep it on a roll-around cart so that you will not have to carry it.

When transporting a monitor from place to place in an automobile, the monitor should be sealed in a well-cushioned box. If an appropriate box is not to be had, place the monitor on a car seat that is well-cushioned with soft foam or blankets—even an old pillow or two will do. Sit the monitor on its cushioning face down because that will lower the monitor's center of gravity and make it as stable as possible. Use twine or thin rope to secure the monitor so it will not shift in transit.

When shipping the monitor to a distant location, the monitor should be shipped in its original container and packing materials. If the original shipping material has been discarded, purchase a heavy-gauge cardboard box. The box dimensions should be at least 4" to 6" bigger in every dimension than the monitor. Fill the empty space with plenty of foam padding or "bubble-wrap" that can be obtained from any full-service stationary store. The box should be sealed and reinforced with heavy-gauge box tape. It does not pay to skimp here—a monitor's weight demands a serious level of protection.

HIGH-VOLTAGE CAUTIONS

It is also important to remind you that a computer monitor uses very high voltages for proper operation. Potentially lethal shock hazards exist within the monitor assembly—both from ordinary ac line voltage, as well as from the CRT anode voltage developed by the flyback transformer. You must exercise extreme caution whenever the monitor's outer housings are removed.

THE MIRROR TRICK

Monitor alignment poses a special problem for technicians—you must watch the adjustment that you are moving while also watching the display to see what effect the adjustment is having. Sure, you could watch the display and reach around the back of the monitor, but given the serious shock hazards that exist with exposed monitor circuitry, that is a very unwise tactic (you would place your personal safety at risk). Monitor technicians use an ordinary mirror placed several feet in front of the CRT. That way, you can watch inside the monitor as you make an adjustment, then glance up to see the display reflected in the mirror. If a suitable mirror is not to be found, ask someone to watch the display for you and relate what is happening. Ultimately, the idea is that you should never take your eyes off of your hand(s) while making an adjustment.

MAKING AN ADJUSTMENT

Monitor adjustments are not difficult to make, but each adjustment should be the result of careful consideration rather than a random, haphazard "shot in the dark." The reason for this concern is simple—it is just as easy to make the display worse. Changing adjustments indiscriminately can quickly ruin display quality beyond your ability to correct it. The following three guidelines will help you make the most effective adjustments with the greatest probability of improving image quality.

First, mark your adjustment (Fig. 48-1). Use a narrow-tip indelible marker to make a reference mark along the body of the adjustment. It does not have to be anything fancy. By making a reference mark, you can quickly return the adjustment to the exact place it started. A reference mark can really save the day if you get lost or move the wrong adjustment.

Second, concentrate on only one adjustment for any one alignment procedure. For example, if you are trying to optimize horizontal linearity, you should only be concerned with the horizontal linearity adjustment. If you do not have documentation that describes the location of each control, check the silk-screen labels on the PC board. If you absolutely cannot locate the needed adjustment point, skip the alignment and move on to the next test. When you do move an adjustment, move it slowly and in very small increments (perhaps

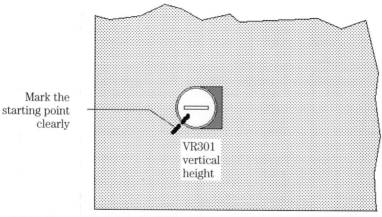

Mark the
starting point
clearly

VR301
vertical
height

FIGURE 48-1 Mark a starting point before starting an adjustment.

⅛ to ¼ turn). Check the display after each step. If the display fails to improve, return the control to its original location (a snap to do if you've made a reference mark) and try it in the opposite direction.

Finally, avoid using metal tools (such as screwdrivers) to make your adjustments. Some of the controls in a monitor are based on coils with permeable cores. Inserting steel tools to make an adjustment will throw the setting off—the display might look fine with the tool inserted, but degrade when the tool is removed. As a general rule, use plastic tools (such as TV-alignment tools) that are available from almost any electronics store.

Tests and Procedures

Testing a computer monitor is easy and it can be accomplished through the use of relatively standard test patterns. Once the companion alignment software is started, you can select the test pattern for the specific test you wish to run, Each of the following procedures covers how to interpret the pattern, and provides a step-by-step procedure for making adjustments. For the purposes of this section, you should refer to the sample main board shown in Fig. 48-2. Remember that the PC board(s) used in your particular monitor might be quite different, so examine your own PC board very closely before attempting an adjustment.

Many newer monitors forego the use of discrete adjustments in favor of electronic "on-screen" controls. Before opening a monitor for alignment, check for on-screen controls, as described in Chapter 2.

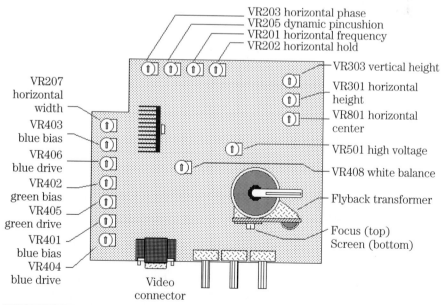

FIGURE 48-2   A typical main PC board for a monitor.

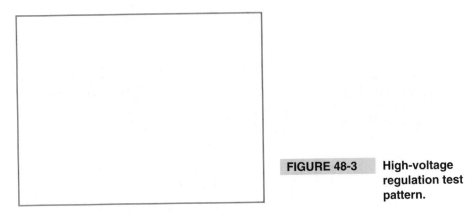

FIGURE 48-3 High-voltage regulation test pattern.

HIGH-VOLTAGE TEST AND REGULATION

The high-voltage test is one of the more important tests that you will perform on computer monitors. Excessive high-voltage levels can allow X-radiation to escape the CRT. Over long-term exposure, X-rays pose a serious biohazard. Your first check should be to use a high-voltage probe. Ground the probe appropriately and insert the metal test tip under the rubber CRT anode cap. You can then read the high-voltage level directly from the probe's meter. Be certain to refer to any particular operating and safety instructions that accompany your high-voltage probe. If the high-voltage level is unusually high or unusually low, carefully adjust the level using a high-voltage control (Fig. 48-2 shows VR501 as the high-voltage control), which is usually located near the flyback transformer.

Regulation is the ability of a power supply to provide a constant output as the load's demands change. The high-voltage supply must also provide regulation within specified limits. As the display image changes, high-voltage levels should remain relatively steady. If not, the display image will flinch as image brightness changes. Select the *High-voltage test pattern* (Fig. 48-3) from the alignment-software main menu. This is a narrow white double border with a solid white center. Watch the border as the center switches on and off at two-second intervals. A well-regulated high-voltage system set at the correct level will keep the white border reasonably steady—there should be very little variation in image height or width. If the image flinches significantly, the high-voltage system might be damaged or failing.

SCREEN CONTROL

The CRT screen grid provides a form of master control over the electron beam(s), which affects the display's overall brightness. A proper screen grid setting is important so that the brightness and contrast controls work within an appropriate range. Select the *Blank raster test* from the alignment software main menu. Adjust the monitor's brightness and contrast controls to their maximum levels—the background raster should be plainly visible.

Locate the *screen voltage control*. In Fig. 48-2, the screen voltage control is located just below the focus control on the flyback transformer assembly. Slowly adjust the screen voltage control until the background raster is just barely visible. Set the monitor's brightness control to its middle (detent) position. The background raster should now be invisible. Press any key to return to the main menu. You might reduce the monitor's contrast control to achieve a clear image.

FOCUS

When an electron beam is first generated in a CRT, electrons are not directed very well. A focus electrode in the CRT's neck acts to narrow the electron stream. An improperly focused image is difficult to see and can lead to excessive eye strain, resulting in headaches, fatigue, etc. The Focus test pattern allows you to check the image clarity and optimize the focus, if necessary. Focus is a subjective measurement—it depends on your perception. You would be wise to confer with another person while making focus adjustments because their perception of the display might be different than yours.

Because focus is indirectly related to screen brightness and contrast, you should set the screen controls for an optimum display. An image that is too bright or has poor contrast might adversely affect your perception of focus. Start the companion software if it is not running already. Select the *Blank raster test* from the alignment software main menu. Adjust the screen brightness to its middle (detent) position or until the display's background raster disappears (the screen should be perfectly dark). Press any key to return to the main menu, then select the *White purity test*. The display should be filled with a solid white box. Adjust screen contrast to its maximum position, or until a good white image is achieved. Once the display conditions are set properly, press any key to return to the main menu.

Now, select the *Focus test pattern* (Fig. 48-4) from the main menu. You will see a screen filled with the letter "m." Review the entire screen carefully to determine if the image is out of focus. Again, it is wise to get a second opinion before altering the focus. If the image requires a focus adjustment, gently and slowly alter the focus control. For the sample main board shown in Fig. 48-2, the focus control is located on the flyback transformer assembly. Once you are satisfied with the focus, press any key to return to the main menu.

DYNAMIC PINCUSHION

A computer-generated image is produced in two dimensions—it is essentially flat. Unfortunately, the traditional CRT face is not flat (although some new CRT designs use an extremely flat face). When a flat image is projected onto a curved surface, the image becomes distorted. Typically, the edges of the image bow outward making straight lines appear *convex* (barrel distortion). Monitor raster circuitry is designed to compensate for

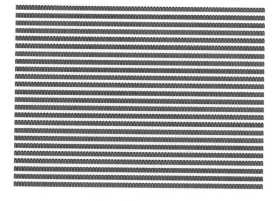

FIGURE 48-4   Screen-focus test pattern.

this distortion and allows the image to "appear" flat—even though it is being projected onto a slightly curved surface. This is known as the *dynamic pincushion circuit* (or just the "pincushion"). However, if the pincushion circuit overcompensates for curvature, the edges of an image will appear to bow inward, making straight lines appear concave.

It is a simple matter to check the dynamic pincushion. Select the *Convergence test (crosshatch) pattern* from the main menu. A white grid will appear in the display. Inspect the outer border of the grid pattern. If the edges of the border appear straight and true, the dynamic pincushion is set properly and no further action is needed. If the edges appear to bow outward, the pincushion is undercompensated. If the edges appear to bow inward, the pincushion is overcompensated. In either case, you will need to make a minor adjustment to the dynamic pincushion control. Figure 48-2 lists VR205 as the dynamic pincushion control, but your monitor probably uses different nomenclature. Before making such an adjustment, you might wish to confer with another individual because their perception of the display might be different from yours. If you cannot locate the dynamic pincushion control, simply move on to the next test.

HORIZONTAL PHASE

When brightness and contrast are set to their maximum levels, you will see a dim, dark gray rectangle formed around the screen image. This border is part of the raster—the over-all area of the screen, which is hit by the electron beam(s). Ideally, the raster is just slightly larger than the typical image. You are able to control the position of an image within this raster area. This is known as *horizontal phase*. The image should be horizontally centered within the raster area. The term *phase* is used because it refers to the amount of delay be-tween the time the horizontal scan (raster) starts and the time where pixel data starts. By adjusting this delay, you effectively shift the image left or right in the raster area (which should remain perfectly still).

Select the *Phase test pattern* from the alignment software main menu. A phase pattern will appear (Fig. 48-5). Set the monitor's brightness and contrast controls to their maxi-mum values—the raster should now be visible around the image. Locate the horizontal phase control. The sample main board shown in Fig. 48-2 indicates VR203 as the hori-zontal phase control. Carefully adjust the horizontal phase control until the image is ap-proximately centered in the raster. This need not be a precise adjustment, but a bit of

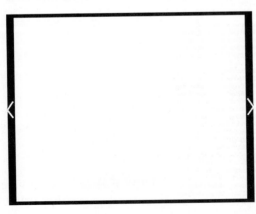

FIGURE 48-5   **Phase test pattern.**

raster should be visible all around the image. Return the monitor brightness control to its middle (detent) position and reduce the monitor contrast control, if necessary, to achieve a crisp, clear image.

HORIZONTAL AND VERTICAL CENTERING

Now that the image has been centered in the raster, it is time to center the image in the display. Centering ensures that the image is shown evenly so that you can check and adjust linearity later on without the added distortion of an off-center image. Select the *Convergence test (crosshatch) pattern* from the alignment software main menu. If the image appears well-centered, no further action is required.

The sample main PC board shown in Fig. 48-2 indicates VR801 as the horizontal centering control. Adjust the centering control so that the image is centered horizontally in the display. Figure 48-2 also shows VR303 as the vertical centering control. Adjust this centering control so that the image is centered vertically in the display. These need not be precise adjustments. Many monitors make their centering controls "user-accessible" from the front or rear housings (along with brightness and contrast).

HORIZONTAL AND VERTICAL SIZE (HEIGHT AND WIDTH)

Many monitors are capable of displaying more than one video mode. Unless the monitor offers an auto-sizing feature, however, the image will shift in size (especially vertical height) for each different video mode. Now that you have a focused, centered image, it should be set to the proper width and height. Remember that image size depends on the CRT size, so you will have to check the specifications for your particular monitor. If you do not have specifications available (or they do not specify image dimensions), you can at least approach a properly proportioned image using alignment software.

Select the *Convergence test (crosshatch) pattern* from the main menu. This pattern produces a grid, and each square of the grid should be roughly square. If the image is proportioned correctly, no further action is needed. Figure 48-2 uses VR301 to control vertical height. Slowly adjust the vertical height until the grid squares are actually about square. The entire grid will be a rectangle that is wider than it is high. If the overall image is too small, you can adjust the horizontal width (VR207 is shown in Fig. 48-2) to make the grid wider, then adjust the vertical height again to keep the grid squares in a square shape. Of course, if the image is too large, you can reverse this procedure to shrink the image.

If your monitor is a multi-mode design and is able to display images in several different graphics modes, there might be several independent vertical height adjustments—one for each available mode. You will have to check the test mode that you have selected against the vertical control to be sure that the vertical height control you are changing is appropriate for the test mode being used. If you are using a 640-x-480 graphics mode, for example, you should be adjusting the vertical height control for the monitor's 640-x-480 mode. If the monitor offers an auto-sizing feature that automatically compensates image size for changes in screen mode, a vertical height adjustment might not be available on the main PC board.

HORIZONTAL AND VERTICAL LINEARITY

The concept of linearity is often difficult to grasp because there are so few real-life examples for us to draw from. Linearity is best related to consistency—everything should be the same as everything else. For a computer monitor, there must be both horizontal and vertical linearity for an image to appear properly. An image is formed as a series of horizontally scanned lines. Each line should be scanned at the same speed from start to finish. If horizontal scanning speed fluctuates, vertical lines will appear closer together (or farther apart) than they actually are. Circles will appear compressed (or elongated) in the horizontal direction. Each horizontal line should be spaced exactly the same vertical distance apart. If the spacing between scanned lines should vary, horizontal lines will appear closer together (or farther apart) than they actually are. Circles will appear compressed (or elongated) in the vertical direction. Any "non-linearity" will result in distortion to the image.

Before testing, you should understand that the screen mode will have an effect on the test pattern. When screen modes change, the vertical height of the image will also change. This is especially prevalent in multi-frequency and multi-mode monitor designs, which can display images in more than one graphics mode. Before testing for linearity, the height and width of the image should be set properly for the selected screen mode, as described in the previous procedures. Otherwise, the image might appear compressed or elongated, resulting in a false diagnosis.

Select the *Linearity test (lines and circles test)* from the alignment software main menu. A grid will appear with an array of five circles (Fig. 48-6). Observe the test pattern carefully. The spacing between each horizontal line should be equal. The spacing between each vertical line should be equal. Assuming the vertical height and horizontal width are set properly, each of the five circles should appear round and even. Each grid square should appear square. If the image appears correct, no further action is needed.

If the vertical lines are not spaced evenly apart, there might be a horizontal linearity problem. Find the horizontal linearity adjustment (Fig. 48-2 shows VR202). Be sure to mark the starting point, then slowly adjust the control until the horizontal linearity improves. If there is no improvement in one direction (or linearity worsens), return to the starting point and try the adjustment in the opposite direction. If there is still no improvement (or linearity worsens again), return the control to its starting position and take no further action—the fault might be in the horizontal drive circuit.

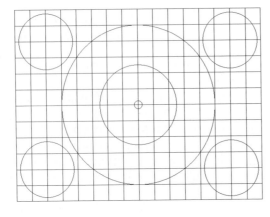

FIGURE 48-6   **Linearity test pattern.**

If the horizontal lines are not spaced evenly apart, there might be a vertical linearity problem. Find the vertical linearity adjustment (Fig. 48-2 shows VR201). Mark the starting point, then slowly adjust the control until the vertical linearity improves. If there is no improvement in one direction (or linearity worsens), return to the starting point and try the adjustment in the opposite direction. If there is still no improvement (or linearity worsens again), return the control to its starting position and take no further action—the fault might be in the vertical drive circuit. Refer to Chapter 27 on monitor troubleshooting for detailed service procedures.

STATIC CONVERGENCE

Convergence is a concept that relates expressly to color CRTs. A color CRT produces three electron beams—one for each of the primary colors (red, green, and blue). These electron beams strike color phosphors on the CRT face. By adjusting the intensity of each electron beam, any color can be produced—including white. The three electron beams must converge at the *shadow mask*, which is mounted just behind the phosphor layer. The shadow mask maintains color purity by allowing the beams to impinge only where needed (any stray or misdirected electrons are physically blocked). Without the shadow mask, stray electrons could excite adjacent color phosphors and result in strange or unsteady colors. If the beams are not aligned properly, a beam might pass through an adjacent mask aperture and excite an undesired color dot. Proper convergence is important for a quality color display.

It is simple matter to check convergence. Be certain to allow at least 15 minutes for the monitor to warm up. Select the *Convergence test (dots)* from the alignment software main menu. An array of white dots should appear on the display. Observe the dots carefully. If you can see any "shadows" of red, green, or blue around the dots, convergence alignment might be necessary. If the dot pattern looks good, then select *Convergence test (crosshatch) pattern* from the main menu. A white grid should appear. Once again, observe the display carefully to locate any primary color "shadows" that might appear around the white lines. If the crosshatch pattern looks good, no further action is necessary, so press any key to return to the main menu.

If you determine that a convergence alignment is necessary, be sure to select the *Convergence test (crosshatch)* from the main menu. Locate the convergence rings located on the CRT's neck, just behind the deflection yokes (Fig. 48-7). Using a fine-tip black marker, mark the starting position of each convergence ring, relative to the glass CRT neck. This is a vital step because it will allow you to quickly return the rings to their original positions if you run into trouble. Convergence alignment is delicate, so it is easy to make the display much worse if you are not very careful. Also, this alignment must be performed with monitor power applied, so be extremely careful to protect yourself from shock hazards. The alignment process is not difficult, but requires a bit of practice and patience to become proficient. As the following procedure shows, you will align the red and blue electron beams to make "magenta," then you will align the green electron beam over the magenta pattern to make "white." Keep in mind that this procedure uses the monitor alignment software (MONITORS) included on the Companion CD.

While the crosshatch pattern is displayed, press the letter "M" on the keyboard which will switch the crosshatch pattern to a magenta color. Magenta is a combination of blue

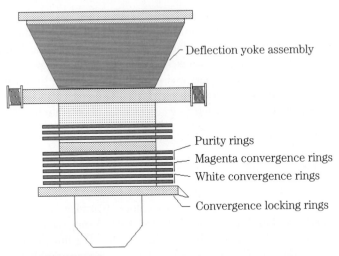

Deflection yoke assembly

Purity rings
Magenta convergence rings
White convergence rings

Convergence locking rings

FIGURE 48-7   A typical convergence-ring assembly.

and red (by choosing magenta, the green electron beam is effectively shut down, so there is less clutter in the display). Loosen the metal band holding the rings in place. Do not remove the band. You might also have to loosen a locking ring before moving the convergence rings. Move the magenta convergence rings together or separately until the blue and red shadows overlap to form a uniform magenta crosshatch pattern. Be sure to move these rings only in small, careful steps. By moving the rings together, you adjust red and blue overlap in the vertical lines. By moving the rings separately, you adjust red and blue overlap in the horizontal lines. If you get into trouble, use the starting marks to return the rings to their original locations and start again.

Once the magenta pattern is aligned, press the letter "W" on the keyboard, which will switch the crosshatch pattern to its original white color (thus activating the green electron beam). Adjust the white convergence rings until any green shadows overlap the crosshatch to form a uniform white grid, as desired. As with the magenta rings, moving the white convergence rings together will adjust green overlap in the vertical lines. Moving the white convergence rings separately will adjust green overlap in the horizontal lines. If the image appears white, carefully secure the locking ring and setup band. Recheck the convergence as you tighten the assembly to be sure nothing has shifted. Do not overtighten the setup band—you stand a good chance of damaging the CRT.

DYNAMIC CONVERGENCE

You will probably hear convergence referred to as being *static* and *dynamic*. These terms refer to the convergence in different areas of the display. *Static* refers to the convergence in the center area of the display. *Dynamic* refers to the convergence around the perimeter of the display. Although static convergence provides a good overall alignment with a minimum of fuss, dynamic convergence is a more difficult alignment because it requires inserting rubber wedges between the edge of the deflection yoke(s) and the CRT funnel—touchy procedures even for a practiced hand. If a visible misconvergence is around the display perimeter—even after a careful static convergence alignment, you will have to consider a dynamic convergence procedure.

As you might expect, dynamic convergence is perhaps the most unforgiving alignment procedure—once you remove the wedges or alter their positions, it is extremely difficult to restore them (even with alignment marks). Unfortunately, there are no formal procedures for positioning the wedges, so you are often left to your own trial-and-error calls. In the end, you should avoid dynamic convergence adjustments, if possible.

Dynamic convergence alignment requires several important steps. First, start the white convergence (crosshatch) pattern and allow the monitor to warm up for at least 15 minutes. Then, mark and remove all three wedges (be sure they are free to move). When you tilt the deflection yoke up and down, you will see distortion (as illustrated in the "A" portion of Fig. 48-8). As you see, misconvergence increases near the screen edge. Use the first two wedges to align the up/down positioning of the deflection yoke—the distortion shown in Fig. 48-8 should disappear. Next, when you tilt the deflection yoke right and left, you will see distortion (as illustrated in the "B" portion of Fig. 48-8). Use the third wedge to eliminate that distortion. You might have to tweak the three wedges to optimize the dynamic convergence. Finally, you should secure the wedges in place with a dab of high-temperature/high-voltage epoxy.

The problem with dynamic convergence is that you often make the display worse when removing the wedges (even with installation marks) because you typically have to break the hold of any epoxy and wrench the wedges free. As a consequence, it is extremely dif-

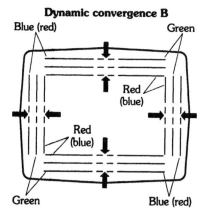

FIGURE 48-8 Calibrating dynamic convergence.

ficult to just "tweak" an existing dynamic convergence calibration—in virtually all cases, it is an all-or-nothing proposition. With this in mind, you should evaluate the need for dynamic convergence very carefully before proceeding. If you do choose to proceed, be sure to leave yourself plenty of time.

COLOR PURITY

Another concern is color purity—that is, a solid color should have the same hue across the entire display. If discoloration develops in the display, purity might need to be restored by degaussing (demagnetizing) the monitor. Typically, the discoloration follows a semicircular pattern around one side or corner with several bands of different color distortions (Fig. 48-9)—the color banding appears almost like a rainbow. Sometimes the discoloration involves the entire screen, but that is rare.

Such discoloration might be caused by an externally induced magnetic field that has permanently magnetized some material in the monitor. The three CRT electron beams are guided to their appropriate phosphor dots by a magnetic deflection system. The beams converge and pass through a shadow mask near the phosphor surface, ensuring that the red beam hits the red phosphor, the blue beam hits the blue phosphor, and the green beam hits the green phosphor. If some component within the CRT (frequently, it is the shadow mask itself) has become sufficiently magnetized, the beams receive an undesired deflection and will not land on the appropriate phosphor (or will land partly on one color and partly on another). The result is an impure color that arcs around the magnetized area.

Location is an important clue to this problem. If the discoloration moves or disappears when the monitor is moved, it is not being caused by a permanent magnetization, but by some magnetic interference in or near the monitor. Placing a highly magnetic or electromagnetic source (such as a strong industrial magnet or power supply) on or near the monitor can cause such discoloration. If the discoloration does not move when the monitor is moved, it might be caused by permanent magnetization in the shadow mask. In that case, degaussing is necessary.

Checking color purity is a straightforward procedure. Select the *White purity test* from the main menu. A white box will fill the entire screen. If there are any areas of discoloration, degaussing is probably necessary. Degaussing removes permanent magnetization by introducing an alternating magnetic field that is stronger than the offending permanent

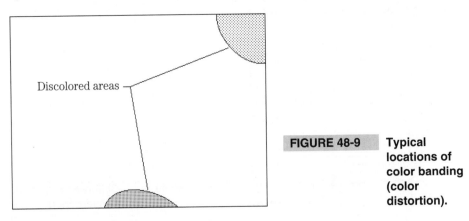

FIGURE 48-9 Typical locations of color banding (color distortion).

magnetization. This field will energize the magnetic domains of the material and induce an alternating magnetic field. Then, if the amplitude of the alternating magnetic field is gradually reduced to zero, the magnetic domains in the material will be left disorganized and scrambled. This effectively demagnetizes the monitor.

The easiest way to degauss a monitor is often to let the monitor do it. All modern color monitors have built-in degaussing coils and circuits. There will be a thick, black coil of wire wrapped in tape or other insulation surrounding the CRT face plate. Usually, it is coiled around the CRT behind its mounting ears. That is the internal degaussing coil. The coil is connected to the ac supply through a thermistor current-limiting circuit. The thermistor has a low resistance when cold and a higher resistance when warm (typically a 10:1 ratio). It is in series with the degaussing coil so that when started cold, a large current will flow through the coil, then will decrease to a low value. The internal degaussing coil thus automatically degausses the monitor every time it is turned on. This degaussing occurs while the monitor screen is blank (the video system has not yet initialized) so that the resulting discoloration during auto-degaussing is not visible. Unfortunately, design limitations reduce the magnetic field strength available from internal degaussing coils. That limits the amount of permanent magnetization that can be neutralized by internal degaussing. If a monitor has been strongly magnetized, internal degaussing might not be enough and discoloration eventually results.

Manual degaussing requires a hand-held degaussing coil. You might have to search a bit to find one, but they are available. The basic principle involved in operating a manual degaussing coil is the same as the auto-degaussing assemblies already in place on color monitors—introduce a strong alternating magnetic field, then slowly reduce its amplitude to zero. Start the companion software (if it is not already running) and select the *White purity test* from the main menu. A white rectangle should fill the entire image. Discoloration should be visible. Hold the degaussing coil near the monitor, flip the degaussing coil switch on and slowly move the coil away from the monitor as smoothly as you can. The image will discolor drastically when the degaussing coil is activated. When the coil is at arm's length from the monitor flip the degaussing switch off. You might need to repeat this procedure several times. When the monitor is degaussed properly, the white image should be consistent at all points on the display.

> Excessive degaussing can damage the monitor. Wait between 15 to 30 minutes before repeating a degaussing procedure.

COLOR DRIVE

Once color convergence and purity are set correctly, you should turn your attention to the color drive levels (also known as *white balance*). Select the *White purity test* from the alignment software main menu. A white box will fill the entire screen. Set the screen contrast to its highest level and reduce brightness to its middle (detent) position. The background raster should disappear. Ideally, all three color signal levels should be equal and the resulting image should be a pure white—rather like a blank piece of white photocopier paper. However, judging the quality of a display color is largely a subjective evaluation. You will need an oscilloscope to measure the actual voltage level of each color signal in order to set them equally. If you do not have an oscilloscope (or do not have access to one), do not attempt to adjust the color drive settings "by-eye."

Use your oscilloscope to measure the signal levels being generated by the red, green, and blue video drivers. These three color signals are actually driving the CRT. With the full white pattern being displayed, all three color signals should be equal (probably around 30 volts, although your own monitor might use slightly different signal levels). Even if you are not quite sure what the level should be, all three signals must be set to the same level to ensure a white image. If you do not know what the level should be, find the highest of the three color signals and use that as a reference. Adjust the gain levels of the other two colors until both levels match the reference. Reduce contrast and inspect the image again. It should remain white (and all three signals should be equal). Disconnect your oscilloscope and press any key to return to the main menu.

CLEANING AND VACUUMING

Once the monitor is checked and aligned, your final step before returning the unit to service should be to inspect the housings and PC boards for accumulations of dust and debris. Look for dust accumulating in the housing vents. A monitor is typically cooled by convection (hot air rises, drawing in cooler air from the lower vents). If these vents become clogged, heat will build up inside the monitor and lead to operational problems and perhaps even cause a premature breakdown. Dust is also conductive. If enough dust builds up within the monitor, the dust might short circuit two or more components and cause operational problems. Vacuum away any dust or debris that might have accumulated in the outer housing. When you see dust buildup around the monitor PC boards and CRT, turn off and unplug the monitor, then vacuum away any buildups. Carefully re-assemble the monitor's housing(s) and return it to service.

Further Study

That concludes Chapter 48. Be sure to review the glossary and chapter questions on the accompanying CD. If you have access to the Internet, take a look at some of these monitor maintenance resources:

AnaTek: **http://www.anatekcorp.com**

Repair World: **http://www.repairworld.com**

49

PREVENTIVE

MAINTENANCE

CONTENTS AT A GLANCE

Protecting Your Data
  Step 1: File backups
  Step 2: CMOS backups

Cleaning
  Step 3: Clean the case
  Step 4: Clean the air intake
  Step 5: Clean the speakers
  Step 6: Clean the keyboard
  Step 7: Clean the monitor
  Step 8: Clean the mouse

External Check
  Step 9: Check external cables
  Step 10: Clean the floppy drive
  Step 11: Clean the tape drive
  Step 12: Check the CD tray
  Step 13: Check the sound system
  Step 14: Check color purity

Internal Check
  Step 15: Check the fans
  Step 16: Clean fans and filters
  Step 17: Check expansion boards
  Step 18: Check internal cables
  Step 19: Check memory
  Step 20: Check the CPU
  Step 21: Check drive mounting

Drive Check
  Step 22: Update the boot disk
  Step 23: Run ScanDisk
  Step 24: Run Defrag

**Preventive Maintenance
Troubleshooting**

Further Study

For most end-users, the purchase of a PC is a substantial investment of both time and money. For corporations and organizations with hundreds (even thousands) of PCs, this investment is that much higher. But after the money is spent and the PC is in our home or office, few PC users ever take the time to maintain their PC. Routine maintenance is an important part of PC ownership, and can go a long way toward keeping your computer's hardware and software error-free. Proper routine maintenance can also help to avoid costly visits to the repair shop (U.S. \$50 to \$70/hour). Businesses can save a substantial amount of money by assigning technicians to perform regular maintenance. If you're in business for yourself, offering "preventive maintenance" services as part of a normal repair or as seasonal "specials" can provide you with an added income stream. This chapter provides you with a comprehensive, step-by-step procedure for protecting and maintaining a personal computer investment.

> This chapter is geared primarily for novices, although experienced technicians might also get some helpful tips and pointers. If you're comfortable with practical routine maintenance procedures, feel free to skip this chapter.

Protecting Your Data

It's interesting that the data recorded on our computer is often far more valuable than the actual cost of a new drive. But if the drive fails, that precious data is usually lost along with the hardware. Months (perhaps years) of records and data could be irretrievably lost. One of the first steps in any routine maintenance plan is to make regular backups of the system's contents—as well as the system's configuration. Backups ensure that you can recover from any hardware glitch, accidental file erasure, or virus attack.

STEP 1: FILE BACKUPS

File backups are important for all types of PC user from major corporations to occasional home users. By creating a "copy" of your system files (or even just a part of them), you can restore the copy and continue working in the event of a disaster. Before you proceed with any type of system checks, consider performing a file backup (see Chapter 52 for more detailed information on backups).

What you need You're going to need two items to backup your files: a "backup drive" and backup software. The actual choice of backup drive is really quite open. Tape drives, such as the Iomega Ditto drive (**http://www.iomega.com**) or the MicroSolutions 8000t 8GB "Backpack" drive (**http://www.micro-solutions.com**), are the traditional choice, but other high-volume removable media drives, such as Iomega's 100MB Zip drive, their 1GB Jaz drive, or the SyQuest 1.5GB SyJet drive (**http://www.syquest.com**) are very popular. You might choose an internal or external version of a drive, but you might consider an external parallel-port drive because it is portable—it can be shared between any PCs.

You'll also need some backup software to format the media, and handle your backup and restore operations. If you're using Windows 95, try the native Backup applet (click on

Start, Programs, Accessories, System tools, and *Backup*). If Backup doesn't suit your needs (or doesn't support your choice for a backup drive), many drives ship with a backup utility on diskette. Just be sure that the backup drive and backup software are compatible with one another.

Types of backups Backups generally fall into two categories: incremental and complete. Both types of backups offer unique advantages and disadvantages. An incremental backup only records the "differences" from the last backup. This usually results in a faster backup procedure and uses less tape (or other media), but restores take longer because you need to walk through each "increment" in order. A complete backup records the drive's full contents. This takes much longer and uses a lot more media, but restores are easier. Many PC users use a combination of complete and incremental backups. For example, you might start with a complete backup on January 1, then make incremental backups each week until the end of February. By March 1, you'd make another complete backup, and start the incremental backup process again.

Backup frequency Perhaps the most overlooked issue with backups is the frequency—how often should backups be performed? The answer to that question is not always simple because everyone's needs are different. Major corporations with busy order-entry systems might backup several times each day, but individual home users might not even consider backups to be necessary. The standard that I use is this: Can you afford to lose the data on this drive? If the answer is "no," it's time to back up. Table 49-1 summarizes the recommended periods for preventive maintenance procedures.

File backup tips Regardless of how you choose to handle file backups, some tips will help you get the most from your backup efforts:

■ Keep the backup(s) in a secure location (such as a fire-proof safe or cabinet).
■ Back up consistently—backups are useless if they are out of date.

TABLE 49-1 SUMMARY OF PC PREVENTIVE-MAINTENANCE PERIODS

PROCEDURE	FREQUENCY

File Backup	Whenever important data cannot be recreated:
	    Order entry (daily)
	    Business/art/multimedia (weekly)
	    SOHO/accounting (bi-weekly or monthly)
	    Home use (every several months)

CMOS Backup	Whenever changes are made to the system's configuration
Cleaning	Every 4 months or as required Vacuum clear accumulations of dust and debris, as required
External Check	Every 4 months CRT degauss only if necessary
Internal Check	Every 6 months
Drive Check	Monthly or when major files are added/deleted from the system Boot disk: update disk whenever hardware changes are made to the system

■ If time is a factor, start with a complete backup, then use incremental backups.
■ Use a parallel-port tape drive (or other "backup" drive) for maximum portability between PCs.

STEP 2: CMOS BACKUPS

All PCs use a sophisticated set of configuration settings (everything from "Date" and "Time" to "Video Palette Snoop" and "Memory Hole") which define how the system should be operated. These settings are stored in a small amount of very low-power memory, called *CMOS RAM*. Each time the PC starts, motherboard BIOS reads the CMOS RAM and copies the contents into low system memory (the BIOS Data Area, BDA. See Chapter 9 for more information on CMOS or Chapter 6 for more details on BIOS). While the system power is off, CMOS RAM contents are maintained with a small battery. If this battery goes dead, CMOS contents can be lost. In most cases, this will prevent the system from even starting until you reconfigure the CMOS setup from scratch. By making a backup of the CMOS setup, you can restore lost settings in a matter of minutes. CMOS backups are simply printed screens of your CMOS setup pages.

What you need The one item that you'll need to perform a CMOS backup is a printer—it really doesn't matter what kind of printer (e.g., dot-matrix, ink jet, or laser). The printer should be attached to the PC's parallel port. After starting the CMOS setup routine, visit each page of the setup and use the <Print Screen> key to "capture" each page to the printer. Because every BIOS is written differently, be sure to check for sub-menus that might be buried under each main menu option.

Several CMOS backup/restore tools are on the companion CD. Try CMOS.ZIP or CMOSRAM2.ZIP.

CMOS backup tips CMOS backups are quick and simple, but you'll get the most benefit from a CMOS backup by following these pointers:

■ Print out every CMOS setup page.
■ Keep the printed pages taped to the PC's housing or with the system's original documentation.
■ You should backup the CMOS setup whenever you make a change to the system's configuration.

Cleaning

Now that you've backed up the system's vital information, you can proceed with the actual maintenance procedures. The first set of procedures involve exterior cleaning. This might hardly sound like a glamorous process, but you'd be surprised how quickly dust, pet hair, and other debris can accumulate around a computer. You'll need four items for cleaning: a supply of Windex or another mild ammonia-based cleaner (a little ordinary ammonia in demineralized water will work just as well), a supply of paper towels or clean lint-free cloths, a canister of electronics-grade compressed air, which can be obtained from any electronics store, and a small static-safe vacuum cleaner.

Avoid the use of ordinary household vacuum cleaners. The rush of air tends to generate significant amounts of static electricity along plastic hoses and tubes, which can accidentally damage the sensitive electronics in a PC.

Never use harsh or industrial-grade cleaners around a PC. Harsh cleaners often contain chemicals that can damage the finish of (or even melt) the plastics used in PC housings. Use a highly diluted ammonia solution only.

As a rule, exterior cleaning can be performed every four months (three times per year) or as required. If the PC is operating in dusty, industrial, or other adverse environments, you might need to clean the system more frequently. Systems operating in clean office environments might only need to be cleaned once or twice each year. Always remember to turn off the computer and unplug the ac cord from the wall outlet before cleaning.

STEP 3: CLEAN THE CASE

Use a clean cloth lightly dampened with ammonia cleaner to remove dust, dirt, or stains from the exterior of the PC. Start at the top and work down. Add a little bit of extra cleaner to remove stubborn stains. You'll find that the housing base is typically the dirtiest (especially for tower systems). When cleaning, be careful not to accidentally alter the CD-ROM volume or sound card master volume controls. Also, do not dislodge any cables or connectors behind the PC.

Always dampen a clean towel with cleaner. Never spray cleaner directly onto any part of the computer.

STEP 4: CLEAN THE AIR INTAKE

While cleaning the case, pay particular attention to the air intake(s), which are usually located in the front (or front sides) of the housing. Check for accumulations of dust or debris around the intakes, or caught in an intake filter. Clean away any accumulations from the intake area, then use your static-safe vacuum to clean the intake filter, if possible. You might need to remove the intake filter for better access. If the intake filter is washable, you might choose to rinse the filter in simple soap and water for best cleaning (remember to dry the filter thoroughly before replacing it). Of course, if there is no intake filter, simply clean around the intake area.

STEP 5: CLEAN THE SPEAKERS

Multimedia speakers offer a countless number of ridges and openings that are just perfect for accumulating dust and debris. Use your can of compressed air to gently dust-out the speaker's openings. Do not insert the long, thin air nozzle into the speaker—you can easily puncture the speaker cone and ruin it. Instead, remove the long nozzle and spray air directly from the can. Afterward, use a clean cloth lightly dampened with ammonia solution to remove any dirt or stains from the speaker housings.

STEP 6: CLEAN THE KEYBOARD

Keyboards are open to the environment, so dust and debris readily settle between the keys. Over time, these accumulations can jam keys or cause repeated keystrokes. Attach the long, thin nozzle to your can of compressed air and use the air to blow through the horizontal gaps between key rows. Be careful. This will kick up a lot of dust, so keep the keyboard away from your face. Afterward, use a clean cloth lightly dampened with ammonia solution to remove dirt or stains from the keys and keyboard housing. If any keys seem unresponsive or "sticky," you can remove the corresponding keycap (see Chapter 20) and spray a bit of good-quality electronic contact cleaner into the key assembly, then gently replace the keycap.

Do not remove the <Enter> key or <Space Bar>. These keys are held in place by metal brackets that are extremely difficult to re-attach once the key is removed. Only the most experienced technicians should work with these keys.

STEP 7: CLEAN THE MONITOR

Several issues are important when cleaning a monitor: ventilation, case, and CRT. Monitors rely on vent openings for proper cooling. Use your vacuum cleaner and carefully remove any accumulations of dust and debris from the vents underneath the case, as well as those on top of the case. Be sure that none of the vent openings are blocked by paper or other objects (this can restrict ventilation and force the monitor to run hot).

Next, use a clean cloth, lightly dampened with ammonia solution, to clean the monitor's plastic case. Active circuitry is directly under the top vents, so under no circumstances should you spray cleaner directly onto the monitor housings. Do not use ammonia or any chemicals to clean the CRT face. The CRT is often treated with anti-glare and other coatings, and even mild chemicals can react with some coatings. Instead, use clean tap water only to clean the CRT face. Be sure to dry the CRT face completely.

STEP 8: CLEAN THE MOUSE

Like the keyboard, a mouse is particularly susceptible to dust and debris, which are carried from the mouse pad up into the mouse ball and rollers. When enough foreign matter has accumulated, you'll find that the mouse cursor hesitates or refuses to move completely. Loosen the retaining ring and remove the mouse ball. Clean the mouse ball using a clean cloth and an ammonia solution. Dry the mouse ball thoroughly and set it aside with the retaining ring. Next, locate three rollers inside the mouse (an "X" roller, a "Y" roller, and a small "pressure" roller, as shown Chapter 25). Use a clean cloth, dampened with ammonia solution, to clean all of the rollers completely. Use your can of compressed air to blow out any remaining dust or debris that might still be inside the mouse. Finally, replace the mouse ball and secure it into place with its retaining ring.

External Check

Now that the system is clean, it's time to perform a few practical checks of the system interconnections, and take care of some basic drive maintenance. Gather a small regular screwdriver (i.e., a "jewler's" screwdriver), along with a commercial floppy-drive cleaning kit. If your system uses a tape drive, arrange to have a tape-drive cleaning kit also. If you cannot locate the appropriate cleaning kits, you can use isopropyl alcohol and long electronics-grade swabs. A hand-held degaussing coil is recommended, but might not be necessary. For this part of the chapter, you'll need to power up the PC.

These checks should be performed every four months (three times per year) or as required. If the PC is operating in dusty, industrial, or other adverse environments, you might need to check the system more frequently. Systems operating in clean office environments might only need to be checked once or twice each year.

STEP 9: CHECK EXTERNAL CABLES

A myriad of external cables interconnect the computer to its peripheral devices. You should examine each cable and verify that it is securely connected. If the cable can be secured to its connector with screws, be sure that the cable is secured properly. As a minimum, check for the following cables:

- Ac power cable for the PC
- Ac power cable for the monitor
- Ac power cable for the printer
- Ac/dc power pack for an external modem (if used)
- Keyboard cable
- Mouse cable
- Joystick cable (if used)
- Video cable to the monitor
- Speaker cable(s) from the sound board
- Microphone cable to the sound board (if used)
- Serial port cable to external modem (if used)
- Parallel-port cable to printer
- RJ11 telephone-line cable to internal or external modem (if used)

STEP 10: CLEAN THE FLOPPY DRIVE

In spite of their age, floppy disks remain a reliable and highly standardized media, and every new PC sold today still carries a 3.5" 1.44MB floppy drive. However, floppy disks are a "contact" media—the read/write heads of the floppy drive actually contact the floppy disk. This contact transfers some of the magnetic oxides from the floppy disk to the

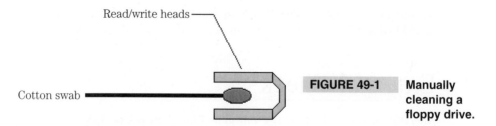

Read/write heads

Cotton swab

FIGURE 49-1   Manually cleaning a floppy drive.

drive's read/write heads. Eventually, enough oxides can accumulate on the read/write heads to cause reading or writing problems with the floppy drive. Periodically clean the floppy drive to remove any excess oxides.

Cleaning can be accomplished in several ways—you can use a pre-packaged "cleaning kit" or swab the read/write heads with fresh isopropyl alcohol. You can obtain pre-packaged cleaning kits from almost any store with a computer or consumer electronics department. With a cleaning kit, simply dampen a mildly abrasive "cleaning diskette" with cleaning solution (typically alcohol-based), then run the cleaning diskette in the drive for 15 to 30 seconds. You can often get 10 to 20 cleanings from a cleaning diskette before discarding it.

If you don't have a cleaning kit handy, you can use a thin fabric swab dampened in fresh isopropyl alcohol, and gently scrub between the read/write heads (Fig. 49-1). Remember to turn off and unplug the PC before attempting a manual cleaning. Repeat the scrubbing with several fresh swabs, then use a dry swab to gently dry the heads. Allow several minutes for any residual alcohol to dry before turning the PC back on.

STEP 11: CLEAN THE TAPE DRIVE

As with floppy drives, tape drives are also a "contact" media and the tape head is in constant contact with the moving tape. This causes oxides from the tape to transfer to the tape head and capstans, which can ultimately result in reading or writing errors from the tape drive. If a tape drive is present with your system, you should periodically clean the tape head(s) and capstans to remove any dust and excess oxides. You might be able to find a pre-packaged drive cleaning kit for your particular tape drive. Otherwise, you'll need to clean the tape drive manually.

Turn off and unplug the PC. Use a thin fabric swab dampened in fresh isopropyl alcohol to gently scrub the tape head(s) and capstan (see Chapter 42 for tape-drive maintenance). Repeat the scrubbing with several fresh swabs, then use a dry swab to gently dry the tape head(s). Allow several minutes for any residual alcohol to dry before turning the computer back on.

> This step is only needed if you have an internal or external tape drive with your system. If not, you can omit this step.

STEP 12: CHECK THE CD TRAY

Most CD-ROM drives operate using a "tray" to hold the CD. Try ejecting and closing the tray several times—be sure that the motion is smooth and that there is no hesitation or grinding, which might suggest a problem with the drive mechanism (you do not need a CD in the drive for this). While the tray is open, check for any accumulations of dust, pet hair, or other debris in the tray that might interfere with a CD. Clean the tray with a cloth lightly dampened in water only. Be sure that the tray is completely dry before closing it again. Do not use ammonia or ammonia-based cleaners around the CD-ROM—prolonged exposure to ammonia vapors can damage a CD.

STEP 13: CHECK THE SOUND SYSTEM

Next, you should be sure that your sound system is set properly. Begin playing an ordinary audio CD in the CD-ROM drive. Check the sound board itself and locate the master volume control (not all sound boards have a physical volume knob). Be sure that the master volume is set at 75% or higher. If not, you might need to keep the speaker volume abnormally high, which can result in a hum or other noise in the speakers. If the sound board does not have a master volume control, check the board's "mixer" applet and see that the master volume is set properly. Once the sound board is set, you can adjust the speaker volume to achieve the best sound quality.

> Speakers are magnetic devices that can interfere with the color purity of a monitor. Keep unshielded speakers at least six inches away from your monitor.

STEP 14: CHECK COLOR PURITY

Color monitors use a fine metal screen located just behind the CRT face to isolate the individual color pixels in the display. This ensures that stray electrons don't strike adjacent phosphors and cause incorrect colors. If part or all of this metal screen becomes magnetized, it will deflect the electron beams and cause color distortion. Normally, a color CRT is demagnetized ("degaussed") each time the monitor is turned on. This is accomplished through a "degaussing coil" located around the perimeter of the CRT face. However, if the CRT is subjected to external magnetic fields (such as unshielded speakers, motors, or other strong magnets), it might cause color problems across the entire CRT, or in small localized areas (see Chapter 57 for more information on monitor testing and alignment).

Check the CRT for color purity by displaying an image of a known color (preferably white). Examine the image for discoloration or discolored areas. For example, if you display an image that you know is white and it appears bluish (or there are bluish patches), chances are that you've got color-purity problems.

There are three means of correcting color-purity problems. First, try moving anything that might be magnetic (such as speakers) away from the monitor. Second, try degaussing the monitor by turning it off, waiting 30 seconds, then turning it on again. This allows the monitor's built-in degaussing coil to cycle. If the problem persists, wait 20 to 30 minutes and try cycling the monitor again. Finally, if the image is still discolored, you should use a hand-held degaussing coil to demagnetize the CRT.

> When degaussing "by hand," remember to wait 20 to 30 minutes before repeating the degaussing procedure. Excessive degaussing can damage the CRT.

Internal Check

At this point, move into the PC and perform some internal checks to verify that crucial parts and cables are secure, and that all cooling systems are working. Internal checks can usually be performed every six months (twice per year). Gather a small Philips screwdriver and an anti-static wrist strap. Use your screwdriver to unbolt the outer cover. Remove the outer cover and set it aside (be careful of the sharp edges on the cover and in the case). Attach the wrist strap from your wrist to a good earth ground—this allows you to work safely inside the PC without the risk of accidental damage from electrostatic discharge.

STEP 15: CHECK THE FANS

PCs tend to generate a substantial amount of heat during normal operation and this heat must be ventilated with fans. If one or more fans fail, excess heat can build up in the PC enclosure and result in system crashes or premature system failures. Now that the cover is off, your first check should be to see that all the fans are running. As a minimum, check the power-supply fan, the case exhaust fan (both usually located at the rear of the enclosure), and the CPU heatsink/fan. Other PCs, such as tower systems, might sport even more fans. If any fans are not running, they should be replaced—or the power supply driving the fans should be checked.

Pay particular attention to the CPU heatsink/fan. Virtually all Intel Pentium/Pentium MMX, AMD K5/K6, and Cyrix 6x86/M2 CPUs are fitted with a heatsink/fan (Pentium II CPU assemblies use their own internal fan). This fan must be running, or the CPU runs a very real risk of overheating and failing. If you notice that the fan has stopped, you should replace the heatsink/fan assembly as soon as possible.

STEP 16: CLEAN FANS AND FILTERS

Turn off and unplug the PC, then examine the fans and exhaust filters for accumulations of dust or other debris. Use your static-safe vacuum to clean the fan blades. Clean away any accumulations from the exhaust area, then clean the exhaust filter, if possible. You might need to remove the exhaust filter for better access. If the exhaust filter is washable, you might choose to rinse the filter in simple soap and water for best cleaning (remember to dry the filter thoroughly before replacing it). Of course, if there is no exhaust filter, simply clean around the exhaust area. Also vacuum away any other accumulations of dust that you might find on the motherboard or around the drives, but be very careful to avoid vacuuming up the little jumpers on the motherboard.

> Remember that PC electronics are extremely sensitive to ESD, so be sure to use a static-safe vacuum inside the PC.

STEP 17: CHECK EXPANSION BOARDS

Most PCs use several expansion boards that are plugged into expansion slots on the motherboard. Internal modems, video boards, SCSI adapters, and network cards are just a few types of expansion boards that you might encounter. Each expansion board must be inserted completely into their corresponding slot, and the metal mounting bracket on the board should be secured to the chassis with a single screw. Be sure that every board is installed evenly and completely, and see that the mounting bolts are snugged down. Pay particular attention to any expansion board that might be inserted unevenly or incompletely.

STEP 18: CHECK INTERNAL CABLES

You'll notice a large number of cables are inside the PC. Each cable must be installed securely—especially the wide ribbon cable connectors that can easily be tugged off. Take a moment to check any wiring between the case and the motherboard such as the keyboard connector, power LED, on/off switch, drive activity LED, turbo switch, turbo LED, etc. Next, check the following cables:

- Motherboard power connector(s)
- All 4-pin drive power cables
- Floppy-drive ribbon cable
- Hard-drive ribbon cable
- CD-ROM ribbon cable (usually separate from the hard drive cable)
- CD four-wire audio cable (between the CD-ROM and sound board)
- SCSI ribbon cable (if used)
- SCSI terminating resistors (if used)

STEP 19: CHECK MEMORY

Most modern PC memory is provided in the form of *SIMMs (single in-line memory modules)* or *DIMMs (dual in-line memory modules)*, which simply clip into sockets on the motherboard. Loose SIMMs or DIMMs can cause serious startup problems for the PC. Examine each SIMM/DIMM. Verify that they are inserted properly into each socket and that both ends of each SIMM/DIMM are clipped into place.

STEP 20: CHECK THE CPU

The CPU is the single largest IC on the motherboard, and it is installed into a *ZIF (Zero Insertion Force)* socket for easy replacement or upgrade. Examine the CPU and see that it is inserted evenly into its socket. The ZIF socket lever should be in the "closed" position and locked down at the socket itself. Check the CPU's heatsink/fan next—it should sit flush against the top of the CPU. It should not slide around or be loose. If it is, the heatsink/fan should be secured or replaced.

Slot 1 CPUs, such as the Pentium II, are installed into a slot on the motherboard and are held in place by a retaining clip. When working with a Pentium II system, see that the CPU is installed evenly and completely, and that the retaining clip is secure.

STEP 21: CHECK DRIVE MOUNTING

The final step in your internal check should be to inspect the drive mountings. Each drive should be mounted in place with four screws—fewer screws might allow excessive vibration in the drive, which can lead to vibration noise from the chassis or premature failure of the drive itself. Be sure that each drive has four mounting bolts and use your Philips screwdriver to snug down each bolt.

> Do not overtighten the bolts. This can actually warp the drive frame and cause errors or drive failure.

Drive Check

After the PC has been cleaned and checked inside and out, it's time to check the hard drive for potential problems. This involves checking the drive's file system, reorganizing files, and creating an updated boot disk. To perform a drive check, you'll need a copy of Scan-Disk and Defrag. Because these utilities are already built into Windows 95, you can re-boot the system and use those utilities directly. If you are more comfortable with running these utilities from DOS, create a startup disk from within Windows 95 and boot from that diskette. Then run ScanDisk and Defrag right from the startup disk. You should perform the drive check very regularly—once a month is usually recommended, or whenever you make major additions or deletions of files from your system.

STEP 22: UPDATE THE BOOT DISK

Your PC should always have a boot disk, which can start the system from a floppy drive in the event of an emergency. Windows 95 has the ability to create a startup disk automatically. If you have access to a Windows 95 system, use the following procedure to create a DOS 7.x startup disk:

- Label a blank pre-formatted diskette and insert it into your floppy drive.
- Click on *Start*, *Settings*, and *Control panel*.
- Doubleclick on the *Add/remove programs* icon.
- Select the *Startup disk* tab.
- Click on *Create disk*.
- The utility will remind you to insert a diskette, then prepare the disk automatically. When the preparation is complete, test the diskette.

The preparation process takes several minutes and will copy the following files to your diskette: ATTRIB, CHKDSK, COMMAND, DEBUG, DRVSPACE.BIN, EDIT, FDISK, FORMAT, REGEDIT, SCANDISK, SYS, and UNINSTAL. All of these files are DOS 7.x-based files, so you can run them from the A: prompt.

STEP 23: RUN SCANDISK

The ScanDisk utility is designed to check your drive for file problems (such as lost or cross-linked clusters), then correct those problems. ScanDisk is also particularly useful for testing for potential media (surface) errors on a disk. If you're running from the startup disk, start ScanDisk by typing:

```
A:\> scandisk  <Enter>
```

If you're running from Windows 95, click *Start*, *Programs*, *Accessories*, *System tools*, and *ScanDisk*. Select the drive to be tested, and start the test cycle. ScanDisk will report any problems and give you the option of repairing the problems.

STEP 24: RUN DEFRAG

Operating systems like DOS and Windows 95 segregate drive space into groups of sectors called *clusters*. Clusters are used on an "as found" basis, so it is possible for the clusters that compose a file to be scattered across a drive. This forces the drive to work harder (and take longer) to read or write the complete file because a lot of time is wasted moving around the drive. The Defrag utility allows related file clusters to be relocated together. If you're running from the startup disk, start Defrag by typing:

```
A:\> defrag   <Enter>
```

If you're running from Windows 95, click *Start*, *Programs*, *Accessories*, *System tools*, and *Disk defragmenter*. Select the drive to be tested and start the cycle. Defrag will relocate every file on the disk so that all their clusters are positioned together (contiguous).

You can run Defrag any time, but you do not need to run Defrag until your disk is more than 10% fragmented.

Preventive Maintenance Troubleshooting

Ideally, the preventive maintenance process is designed to prevent problems—not cause them. However, at times, an accidental oversight or careless effort can result in problems. Fortunately, most maintenance-related issues are easy to spot and resolve.

Symptom 49-1. No CD audio is audible through the CD-ROM headphone jack or no sound is emanating from the system speakers The sound might also be too high now. In virtually all cases, you accidentally changed a volume control when wiping-down the exterior of the PC. Your cloth might have rubbed across the CD-ROM or sound-board master volume controls. You might also have changed the speaker volume control. Recheck all of your system volume controls and re-adjust the sound volume.

Symptom 49-2. The system no longer boots correctly or key feature(s) no longer work correctly This is typical after an internal check and it is almost always because of an oversight in checking or seating a cable or expansion board inside the PC. Recheck the seating of all power and signal cables, recheck the seating of all expansion devices and recheck the CPU and SIMM/DIMM seating on the motherboard.

Further Study

That concludes Chapter 49. Be sure to review the glossary and chapter questions on the accompanying CD. If you have access to the Internet, take a look at some of these PC preventive maintenance resources:

CompUSA: **http://www.compusa.com**   (cleaning kits and supplies)

Iomega: **http://www.iomega.com**

MicroSolutions: **http://www.micro-solutions.com**

SyQuest: **http://www.syquest.com**

APPENDICES

APPENDICES

MPC STANDARDS
FOR THE PC

COMPONENT	MPC LEVEL 1	MPC LEVEL 2	MPC LEVEL 3
The CPU chip and speed	386SX at 16MHz	486SX at 25MHz	Pentium at 75MHz
Main System RAM	2MB	4MB	8MB
Video adapter and resolution	VGA graphics**	1.2 million pixels/sec at 40% of CPU capacity	Color space conversion and capability; direct access to frame buffer for video graphics sub-system with a resolution of 352×240 @ 30 fps, or 352×288 @ 25 fps—both at 15 bits/pixel unscaled, without cropping.
Video playback capability	N/A	N/A	MPEG 1

COMPONENT	MPC LEVEL 1	MPC LEVEL 2	MPC LEVEL 3
Audio	8-bit DAC and ADC linear PCM sampling 22-kHz rate for DAC 11-kHz rate for ADC Microphone input Synthesizer Multivoice Multitimbral 6 melody/2 percussive 3-channel mixer Stereo output	16-bit DAC and ADC linear PCM sampling 44.1-kHz rate for DAC 44.1-kHz rate for ADC Stereo input and output Microphone input Synthesizer Multivoice Multitimbral 3-channel mixer 6 melody/2 percussive Stereo output	16-bit DAC and ADC linear PCM sampling 44.1-kHz rate for DAC 44.1-kHz rate for ADC Stereo input and output Microphone input MIDI playback Multivoice Multitimbral 3-channel mixer 6 melody/2 percussive Stereo output
Data-input options	101 keyboard Two-button mouse	101 keyboard Two-button mouse	101 keyboard Two-button mouse
Input/Output	9600 baud serial port Bidirectional parallel port Joystick port MIDI I/O port	9600 baud serial port Bidirectional parallel port Joystick port MIDI I/O port	9600 baud serial port Bidirectional parallel port Joystick port MIDI I/O port
Main storage (hard disk)	30MB hard disk	160MB hard disk	540MB hard disk
Floppy disk	1.44MB 3.5" floppy	1.44MB 3.5" floppy	1.44MB 3.5" floppy
CD-ROM or Optical audio/ video storage removable)	150KB/second data transfer 1-sec. maximum seek time	Double-speed 300KB/sec. data transfer 400-ms maximum seektime multisession, CD-DA and XA capability	Quad-speed 600KB/sec data transfer 250-ms maximum seek time multisession, CD-DA and XA capability

** 640-x-480 resolution with 16 colors

STANDARD ASCII

CHART (0 TO 127)

CHARACTER	DECIMAL	HEX	CHARACTER	DECIMAL	HEX
NUL	0	00h	SOH	1	01h
STX	2	02h	ETX	3	03h
EOT	4	04h	ENQ	5	05h
ACK	6	06h	BEL	7	07h
BS	8	08h	HT	9	09h
LF	10	0Ah	VT	11	0Bh
FF	12	0Ch	CR	13	0Dh
SO	14	0Eh	SI	15	0Fh
DLE	16	10h	DC1	17	11h
DC2	18	12h	DC3	19	13h
DC4	20	14h	NAK	21	15h
SYN	22	16h	ETB	23	17h
CAN	24	18h	EM	25	19h
SUB	26	1Ah	ESC	27	1Bh
FS	28	1Ch	GS	29	1Dh
RS	30	1Eh	US	31	1Fh
SP	32	20h	!	33	21h
"	34	22h	#	35	23h

CHARACTER	DECIMAL	HEX	CHARACTER	DECIMAL	HEX
$	36	24h	%	37	25h
&	38	26h	'	39	27h
(	40	28h	)	41	29h
*	42	2Ah	+	43	2Bh
,	44	2Ch	-	45	2Dh
.	46	2Eh	/	47	2Fh
0	48	30h	1	49	31h
2	50	32h	3	51	33h
4	52	34h	5	53	35h
6	54	36h	7	55	37h
8	56	38h	9	57	39h
:	58	3Ah	;	59	3Bh
<	60	3Ch	=	61	3Dh
>	62	3Eh	?	63	3Fh
	66	42h	C	67	43h
B	64	40h	A	65	41h
D	68	44h	E	69	45h
F	70	46h	G	71	47h
H	72	48h	I	73	49h
J	74	4Ah	K	75	4Bh
L	76	4Ch	M	77	4Dh
N	78	4Eh	O	79	4Fh
P	80	50h	Q	81	51h
R	82	52h	S	83	53h
T	84	54h	U	85	55h
V	86	56h	W	87	57h
X	88	58h	Y	89	59h
Z	90	5Ah	[	91	5Bh
\	92	5Ch	]	93	5Dh
^	94	5Eh	_	95	5Fh
`	96	60h	a	97	61h
b	98	62h	c	99	63h
d	100	64h	e	101	65h
f	102	66h	g	103	67h

CHARACTER	DECIMAL	HEX	CHARACTER	DECIMAL	HEX
h	104	68h	i	105	69h
j	106	6Ah	k	107	6Bh
l	108	6Ch	m	109	6Dh
n	110	6Eh	o	111	6Fh
p	112	70h	q	113	71h
r	114	72h	s	115	73h
t	116	74h	u	117	75h
v	118	76h	w	119	77h
x	120	78h	y	121	79h
z	122	7Ah	{	123	7Bh
l	124	7Ch	}	125	7Dh
~	126	7Eh	DEL	127	7Fh

DOS ERROR
MESSAGES

DOS provides a myriad of error messages to indicate problems or issues that we should be aware of. Unfortunately, DOS error messages are cryptic at best, and precious little documentation explains the causes of these errors (and even less help in correcting these errors). The following list provides a general index of DOS error messages, explains the potential causes of the error, and offers some practical solutions.

> The exact wording of these errors might vary slightly between DOS versions and not all errors might be reported in all DOS versions.

Abort, retry, fail There are several causes for this message, but they all mean a problem with the disk(ette) that DOS is trying to access. The drive is not reading a disk in the drive that you've instructed DOS to check. First, see that you typed the correct drive letter in the command line and that the diskette is in the correct drive (if you have more than one diskette drive). Next, check that the diskette is fully inserted into the drive (label side up), and that the drive door is closed properly. Then press <R> to retry. This message also could mean that the disk you're using is damaged. Try the diskette in a different drive or try a different diskette.

Access denied You just tried to change a file that is: (1) on a write-protected diskette, (2) locked, or (3) a read-only file. Write-protected diskettes can be read, but not written to (e.g., some commercial software is write-protected). A "locked" file is one that can't be altered in a common way (such as adding or deleting data, moving the file, or changing the name of the file). A read-only file is one to which a programmer has added a command so that users might only view the information or one that resides in *Read-Only Memory (ROM)*. There's usually a good reason why you aren't allowed to change the file. You might need to change the attributes of the file before you're allowed to modify it.

Bad command or file name DOS didn't recognize the command you just typed or can't find a file you referred to in the command-line entry. The most likely problem is that you misspelled either the command or the file name. Another possibility is that you haven't established the right path to a file. Re-check the location of the file and be sure to enter the path correctly when you retype the command. Finally, it might be possible that the version of DOS you're running doesn't recognize this command. You'll need to see if your version has an equivalent command or update the DOS version.

Bad or missing command interpreter This means DOS can't find COMMAND.COM and your CONFIG.SYS file doesn't have a SHELL statement telling DOS where to look for COMMAND.COM. Your COMMAND.COM file might have been damaged or deleted, or your SHELL command was removed from the CONFIG.SYS file. It might also be that the wrong version of COMMAND.COM is copied to the disk. Your hard drive might also be damaged (or infected with a virus), preventing DOS from accessing the DOS directory. Boot from an emergency bootable diskette that contains the same version of COMMAND.COM that should be on the hard drive, then copy the COMMAND.COM file to the root directory of your hard drive and reboot. You might wish to add a SHELL statement to the CONFIG.SYS file, indicating the exact location of the COMMAND.COM file. You might also wish to reinstall DOS (or Windows 95) outright.

Bad or missing file name A command in your CONFIG.SYS file is entered incorrectly. You should get this message only if you recently changed something in this file. Go back and check to be sure you typed the recent addition or change correctly. If you have not made changes to the file, the file(s) being referred to in CONFIG.SYS might be corrupt or deleted. Verify that any files referred to in CONFIG.SYS are present.

> Any time you make a change to your CONFIG.SYS or AUTOEXEC.BAT file, make a backup copy of the original file(s) prior to making the changes.

Cannot find a device file that may be needed to run Windows The error also goes on to say: "Make sure that the PATH line in your AUTOEXEC.BAT points to the directory that contains the file and that it exists on your hard disk. If the file does not exist, try running Setup to install it or remove any references in your SYSTEM.INI file. C:\directory\filename. Press a key to continue." Although this message does tell you what to do to fix the problem, it is still largely unclear. It means a given file that might or might not be necessary to run Windows isn't where DOS thinks it should be.

The offending file is listed in the second to last sentence of the error message and the path given is the location where DOS expected to find the file. It might be a file that was installed with an application you've since removed (when you remove an application from your system, a reference to a file from that program often remains in your SYSTEM.INI file). You might be able to simply press a key to continue and experience no difficulty. To be sure you don't encounter a more serious problem, however, you'll want to either install the offending file in the location DOS specified, point DOS to the real location of the file, or remove mention of the file from your SYSTEM.INI file so that DOS won't try to look for it anymore.

Cannot find system files This message appears when you try to make a bootable diskette, but DOS can't find the necessary system files. Be sure that you're in the directory containing these files (which is usually your C:\ root directory). Switch drives and/or directories, if necessary, then try making the system diskette again.

Directory already exists You've tried to create a directory with the same name as one that already exists. Just choose a different name for the new directory or use the existing directory, if it's appropriate.

Disk full This message appears during a copy operation when the destination diskette is full. Remove some unneeded files from the diskette to make room for the full copy to fit, or use another diskette to receive the additional files.

Drive A: does not exist This message can be caused by a dirty diskette drive (the diskette cannot be read). Get a diskette drive cleaner kit and follow its instructions to clean the drive. If this doesn't solve the problem, you might have a bad floppy-disk drive or floppy-disk controller.

Duplicate file name or file(s) not found This message occurs when you try to use the REN command to rename a file. It means that either you're trying to rename the file using a name that is already in use, or the file you want to rename couldn't be found. Check your spelling and check whether the new name is already in use in the directory. Then, try the REN command again, typing carefully and using a new name.

Existing format differs from that specified If you're reformatting a disk or diskette to a different capacity, you actually want to see this message. It means you're doing the right thing, however, you'll need to tell DOS that it's OK to continue. The reason to reformat a diskette to a different capacity is to make it match the capacity of the drive. You can use a low-capacity diskette in a high-capacity drive, but not the other way around. It's best to match the capacity of the diskette to the maximum drive capacity.

File cannot be copied onto itself This message probably means you forgot to give a destination location for a file you're trying to copy. Type the COPY command again (be sure to include the destination). If you're unsure how to use the COPY command correctly, type: HELP COPY and press <Enter> for more information.

File creation error This means one of two things: either you're trying to create a file with the same name as an existing file or the disk you're using is write-protected. Check the tab on the diskette to be sure it isn't in the write-protected position. If it isn't, try using a different file name. If neither of these solutions work, try using another diskette with the new file name.

File exists You're trying to name your new file with a file name already in use. Choose another name. If you're unsure what names you've used before, use the DIR command to check out the files in the current directory.

File not found You've typed a file name in a command incorrectly, the file doesn't exist, or the file is in a location other than the one you specified. Check for accuracy and enter the command again.

Formatting while copying This DOS message is more informational. It's telling you that the diskette you're using needs to be formatted to hold the information you're copying to it. You should be aware, however, that formatting a diskette takes longer while copying than if you're just formatting it.

Help not available for this command Either you've asked for help with a command or utility program for which there is no help in the version of DOS you're running or you typed the command incorrectly.

Incorrect DOS version The program you're trying to run has found a version of COMMAND.COM other than the one it expected. You probably upgraded DOS versions at some point and now have more than one version of some DOS files on your system (and the program found an older or newer one than it wanted). You might need to re-install DOS to fix this problem.

Insert system disk This just means you need to insert your bootable diskette into a diskette drive—usually when installing or repartitioning a hard drive.

Insufficient disk space You don't have enough room on your hard disk or diskette to complete the command. Use another diskette or delete some files to make more space available.

Insufficient memory This message means that you don't have enough memory available to complete the command. Remove any unnecessary *Terminate-and-Stay-Resident (TSR)* programs and try the command again. TSRs (also known as *memory-resident programs*) remain loaded in memory (even when they're not running) so they can be quickly activated for specific tasks while you're running other applications.

Invalid date/invalid time You've used an improper format for a date/time. To check the proper format, use the DATE/TIME command. Make note of the correct format and try again.

Invalid directory DOS can't find the directory you specified. Either you typed the directory's name incorrectly or it doesn't exist (at least not on the drive you specified). Check your typing and the location of the directory—it might be in a sub-directory.

Invalid drive in search path This probably means that you have made a hardware change and haven't updated the PATH command in your AUTOEXEC.BAT file to reflect the drives that are now in your computer. Update the PATH command and try again.

Invalid drive specification DOS can't find the drive you tried to switch to. Either you made a typing error (asking your computer to find a drive that doesn't exist) or the drive you asked for is not working. If you get this message when trying to switch to your hard drive, the drive might be suffering from corrupted partition information, or the drive might be defective.

Invalid filename DOS can't find the file you're looking for. Check the name and location of the file and try again (be sure to check your typing).

Invalid media type The diskette you're trying to use is defective or not formatted properly for the particular floppy drive. Reformat the floppy disk or try a different one.

Invalid parameter You've entered a command parameter incorrectly. A "parameter" is something you add to the end of a command to tell it what to operate on (also called a "command line switch"). For example, in the command: dir a:, the "a:" tells DOS you want a list of the contents of the A: drive, regardless of which drive you're currently in. Check the format of the command and re-enter it. The other possibility is that you're using a parameter not used in the utility program you're trying to use.

Non-system disk or disk error—replace and strike any key Before computers had hard drives, the operating system was stored on a diskette called the *system diskette*, *bootable diskette*, or *DOS disk*. That diskette was kept in the A: drive, where the computer would look for it when it was started. Although operating systems are now on the hard drive, most computers still look at the diskette drive before checking the hard drive. If they don't find anything in the A: drive, they check the hard drive, usually the C: drive. If they find a non-system diskette in the A: drive, you'll get this message. The most common reason for this message is that you forgot to remove a diskette from the A: drive when you last used it. Remove the diskette and strike any key to continue. Another possibility is that you have a computer (probably an old one) that boots from a system diskette. In that case, this message means you need to put a bootable diskette in the A: drive and continue.

The last scenario is a bit more serious. If neither of these situations applies, the first step is to get a DOS system diskette and try booting the computer from it. This should get you to an A:\> prompt. At the A:\> prompt, type C: and press <Enter>. If you get a C:\> prompt, the drive is running, but your operating system is lost. Type: CD DOS at the prompt and press <Enter>, then type: SYS C: and press <Enter> again. That should replace the operating system. On the other hand, if you get a message saying: "Invalid drive specification" when you try to switch to the C: drive, your hard drive is not working properly. The drive will have to be replaced.

Out of memory This means a program can't complete its task because you don't have enough free memory. Close some other running programs and try again. If no other programs are running, you might need to add memory to your computer. Before buying more memory, you might want to try EMM386 (a driver included with DOS 6.0 that provides expanded memory), or a memory manager, such as Quarterdeck's QEMM.

Path not found A path is the set of directions you give DOS to tell it how to find something. For example, the path: C:\DOS\EDIT.HLP tells DOS to find the file EDIT.HLP in the DOS directory on your C: drive. If you get this message, DOS couldn't find the path you entered. Check your typing and re-enter the path carefully. If that doesn't work, it means the path doesn't exist.

Proceed with format (Y/N)? This message means you will lose any information that is on the diskette when you format it. Press Y to continue with the format, if you're sure that you won't lose any important information, or N to stop the process, if you want to check the contents of the diskette before formatting it.

Read error DOS has found a problem with a sector of your disk. There was either damage during the formatting process or a fault in one of the sectors. Run ScanDisk (version 6.2 or newer) to find the bad spot and rescue as much data as possible. If the error occurs on a floppy diskette, you should reformat or discard the diskette.

Stack overflow—system halted Reboot your system and edit your CONFIG.SYS file so the value of stacks= is increased to 10 or more, then try again.

Syntax error You've either made a typing error in a command or you've used terminology DOS doesn't recognize (or at least your version of DOS). Check your typing for accuracy and try again.

Terminate batch job (Y/N)? Either you've interrupted a batch file in progress, or the batch file is incomplete or incorrect. If you didn't mean to interrupt the batch job, type N to let DOS return to work. If the batch file is defective, type Y to return to the DOS prompt.

This disk cannot be unformatted UNFORMAT is a command that can sometimes save data if you accidentally format a disk or diskette containing data you didn't mean to eliminate. Depending on the type of format you performed, and whether you've written new data to the location, UNFORMAT might not work. If it does not, try again. If you get the same message, your data is irretrievable.

Too many open files You've tried to open too many files at one time. Open your CONFIG.SYS file and increase the number of files specified in the Files= command. Restart your system and try again. You should now be able to have more files open at a time.

Write-protect error You've tried to format a diskette that is write-protected. Remove the write protection from the disk and try again.

D

PC

NEWSGROUPS

The Internet has become a uniquely effective resource for technical support issues. A myriad of newsgroups are dedicated to very specific PC issues. These groups are frequented by many experienced professionals, and can be of great assistance in tracking down solutions to problems or obtaining additional information. You should be able to access these newsgroups with any recent newsreader utility.

FOR QUESTIONS ON...	POST THE MESSAGE TO...
Acer users & support	alt.sys.pc-clone.acer
CD-ROM drives	comp.sys.ibm.pc.hardware.cd-rom
Chips, RAM & cache	comp.sys.ibm.pc.hardware.chips
Dell users & support	alt.sys.pc-clone.dell
Gateway users & support	alt.sys.pc-clone.gateway2000
Hardware for sale	misc.forsale.computers.discussion
Home-built PCs	alt.comp.hardware.pc-homebuilt
Laptops & notebooks	comp.sys.laptops
Magnetic drives	comp.sys.ibm.pc.hardware.storage
Memory for sale	misc.forsale.computers.memory
Micron users & support	alt.sys.pc-clone.micron
Modems	comp.sys.ibm.pc.hardware.comm comp.dcom.modems
Monitors & video cards	comp.sys.ibm.pc.hardware.video

Networking, hardware	**comp.sys.ibm.pc.hardware.networking**
Networking, networks	**comp.os.netware.announce**
	comp.os.netware.connectivity
	comp.os.netware.misc
	comp.os.netware.security
	comp.dcom.lans.ethernet
	comp.dcom.lans.fddi
	comp.dcom.lans.misc
	comp.dcom.lans.token-ring
	comp.protocols.tcp-ip.ibmpc
	comp.os.os2.networking.misc
	comp.os.os2.networking.tcp-ip
	comp.os.ms-windows.networking.misc
	comp.os.ms-windows.networking.ras
	comp.os.ms-windows.networking.tcp-ip
	comp.os.ms-windows.networking.windows
Networking, NSF-based	**comp.protocols.nfs**
Networking, SMB-based	**comp.protocols.smb**
Palmtops	**comp.sys.palmtops**
PCMCIA devices	**alt.periphs.pcmcia**
PC-specific for-sale	**misc.forsale.computers.pc-specific.audio**
	misc.forsale.computers.pc-specific.cards.misc
	misc.forsale.computers.pc-specific.cards.video
	misc.forsale.computers.pc-specific.misc
	misc.forsale.computers.pc-specific.motherboards
	misc.forsale.computers.pc-specific.portables
	misc.forsale.computers.pc-specific.software
	misc.forsale.computers.pc-specific.systems
Printers	**comp.periphs.printers**
SCSI devices	**comp.periphs.scsi**
Servers	**comp.dcom.servers**
Sound card topics	**comp.sys.ibm.pc.soundcard.tech**
	comp.sys.ibm.pc.soundcard.advocacy
	comp.sys.ibm.pc.soundcard.games
	comp.sys.ibm.pc.soundcard.music
	comp.sys.ibm.pc.soundcard.misc
Other for-sale	**misc.forsale.computers.other.misc**
	misc.forsale.computers.other.software
	misc.forsale.computers.other.systems
Other hardware questions	**comp.sys.ibm.pc.hardware.misc**
Other peripherals	**comp.periphs**
Vendors & specific systems	**comp.sys.ibm.pc.hardware.systems**
Zenith users & support	**comp.sys.zenith**
Zeos users & support	**alt.sys.pc-clone.zeos**

E

WINDOWS
SHORTCUT KEYS

As a technician, there are many times when you'll need to navigate in the Windows 95 environment without the benefit of a working mouse or another pointing device. When this happens, you'll need to rely on the keyboard equivalents or shortcuts.

GENERAL WINDOWS KEYS

F1	See *Help* on the selected dialog box item
ALT+F4	Quit a program
SHIFT+F10	View the shortcut menu for the selected item
CTRL+ESC	Display the *Start* menu
ALT+TAB	Switch to the window you last used or switch to the next window by pressing ALT while repeatedly pressing TAB.
CTRL+X	Cut
CTRL+C	Copy
CTRL+V	Paste
DEL	Delete
CTRL+Z	Undo
SHIFT (while inserting the CD-ROM)	Bypass AutoPlay when inserting a compact disc

KEYS FOR MY COMPUTER AND WINDOWS EXPLORER

CTRL+A	Select all
F5	Refresh a window

BACKSPACE   View the folder one level up
SHIFT (while clicking the *Close* button)   Close the selected folder and all its parent
                                                 folders

KEYS FOR *OPEN* AND *SAVE AS* DIALOG BOXES

F4   Open the *Save in* or *Look in* list
F5   Refresh
BACKSPACE   Open folder one level up, if a folder is selected

KEYS FOR *PROPERTIES* DIALOG BOXES

TAB   Move forward through options
SHIFT+TAB   Move backward through options
CTRL+TAB   Move forward through tabs
CTRL+SHIFT+TAB   Move backward through tabs

FOR THE DESKTOP, MY COMPUTER, AND WINDOWS EXPLORER"

F2   Rename an item
F3   Find a folder or file
SHIFT+DEL   Delete immediately without placing the item in
                                           the Recycle Bin
ALT+ENTER or ALT+doubleclick   View item properties
CTRL (while dragging the file)   Copy a file
CTRL+SHIFT (while dragging the file)   Create a shortcut

KEYS FOR WINDOWS EXPLORER ONLY

CTRL+G   Go to
F6   Switch between left and right panes
NUMLOCK+ASTERISK   Expand all subfolders under the selected folder
NUMLOCK+PLUS SIGN   Expand the selected folder
NUMLOCK+MINUS SIGN   Collapse the selected folder
RIGHT ARROW   Expand current selection if it's collapsed; otherwise, se-
                          lect first subfolder
LEFT ARROW   Collapse current selection if it's expanded; otherwise, se
                          lect parent folder

ACCESSIBILITY KEY SHORTCUTS

SHIFT 5 times   Toggle StickyKeys on and off
RIGHT SHIFT for 8 seconds   Toggle FilterKeys on and off
NUMLOCK for 5 seconds   Toggle ToggleKeys on and off

LEFT ALT+LEFT SHIFT+NUMLOCK   Toggle MouseKeys on and off
LEFT ALT+LEFT SHIFT+PRINT SCREEN   Toggle High Contrast on and off

> To use Accessibility shortcut keys, the shortcut keys must be enabled. For more information, look up "Accessibility, shortcut keys" in the Help index.

WINDOWS NATURAL KEYBOARD KEYS

WIN+R   Display *Run* dialog box
WIN+M   Minimize all
SHIFT+WIN+M   Undo Minimize all
WIN+F1   Start Help
WIN+E   Start Windows Explorer
WIN+F   Find files or folders
CTRL+WIN+F   Find computer
WIN+TAB   Cycle through *Taskbar* buttons
WIN+BREAK   *System Properties* dialog box

F

FORMS

The forms in this appendix are provided for your convenience and use. You may tear these forms out or photocopy them as required. As the purchaser of this book, you have non-exclusive rights to photocopy the following forms so long as you do so only for your own use or use within your own organization. Duplication, copying, or other distribution of these forms for sale or use by others is strictly prohibited.

1 *PC configuration form* Use this form when installing or configuring the PC and its expansion boards.
2 *System CMOS sheet* Use this form to record system parameters (as shown in the system SETUP screens).
3 *BIOS upgrade* Use this form when planning a BIOS upgrade for your PC.
4 *Customer billing* A simple time and material form for beginning technicians.

PC Configuration Form

System: _____

Serial #: _____ Mfg. Date: _____

Customer: _____

_____

Phone: _____ Fax: _____

Notes: _____

_____

_____

Power Supply Mfg: _____ Wattage: _____W

Motherboard Mfg: _____ Part: _____

CPU: _____ BIOS: _____

RAM: _____

EBoard Description	IRQ	DMA	I/O	Misc

System CMOS Setup

System: _____

Serial #: _____   Mfg. Date: _____

BIOS Mfg.: _____   Version: _____

BIOS Date: _____

Notes: _____

_____

Base Memory: _____ KB   Ext. Memory: _____ KB

FDD A: _____   FDD B: _____

DRIVE	TYPE	CYL	HEADS	SECTORS	SIZE (MB)
C:					
D:					
E:					
F:					
G:					
H:					
I:					

Typematic Rate Programming: _____   Typematic Rate Delay: _____ mS

Typematic Rate (char/Sec): _____   Setup Message Disp.: _____

Num Lock on Boot: _____   Boot Sequence: _____   CPU Speed: _____

Cache Memory: _____   Password: _____   ISA Buffer: _____

ISA Buf. Addr.: _____   Enhanced ISA Timing: _____

Shadow Memory Size: _____   Shadow Memory Base: _____

IDE DMA Xfer Mode: _____   IDE Multiple Sector Mode: _____

IRQ 9 State: _____   IRQ 10 State: _____   IRQ 11 State: _____

BIOS Upgrade Data

PC Mfg.: _____   PC Model: _____

Motherboard Mrg.: _____   CPU: _____

BIOS Mfg.: _____   BIOS Ver.: _____

BIOS Date: _____   BIOS Part Number: _____

Number of BIOS ICs: _____   Main Chipset: _____

Notes: _____

_____

_____

BIOS Upgrade Data

PC Mfg.: _____   PC Model: _____

Motherboard Mrg.: _____   CPU: _____

BIOS Mfg.: _____   BIOS Ver.: _____

BIOS Date: _____   BIOS Part Number: _____

Number of BIOS ICs: _____   Main Chipset: _____

Notes: _____

_____

_____

Customer Billing Sheet

Customer: _____ Cust#: _____

Address: _____

City, State, Postal Code: _____

Telephone: _____ Fax: _____

System: _____

Serial #: _____

Description of Work: _____

_____

_____

_____

PART NUMBER	DESCRIPTION	QUAN	COST	TOTAL

Notes:

SUBTOTAL	
SALES TAX	
SHIPPING/MISC.	
>>> TOTAL	

G

THE A+
CHECKLIST

With the explosive growth in computer service needs, The *Computing Technology Industry Association (CompTIA*, formerly known as *ABCD: The Microcomputer Industry Association*) sponsored and worked with industry to develop the A+ Certification for Computer Service Technicians (Figure G-1). What makes A+ Certification different from other credentials is the strong support that it has received from the computer industry. More than 37 corporations—some of the largest PC makers in the world—have backed A+ Certification as a requirement for their service staff, as well as the technical staff of other companies that they do business with.

The test itself focuses on all major aspects of PC maintenance and repair, and a wide range of hardware and software is covered. Unlike other exams (such as the CET exam), an A+ exam can be taken by anyone interested in the test. There are no educational or experience pre-requisites. Although the CompTIA is responsible for developing the test, it is implemented nation-wide (and in most Canadian provinces) by Sylvan Prometric. The test is given on computer that will actually compile your scores and grade the test before you leave the test room. Some readers might consider the A+ certification a bit pricey at $165.00 (U.S.), but few can argue that it's a small price for your professional development. Contact data for CompTIA and Drake is:

Computing Technology Industry Association (CompTIA)
450 East 22nd Street, Suite 230
Lombard, IL 60148-6158
Tel: 800-333-9532
Fax: 708-268-1384

The Computing
Technology
Industry
Association

FIGURE G-1 Official logo of the A+
Certification Program. A+ is
a program of the Computing
Technology Industry
Association.

Sylvan Prometric
Tel: 800-77MICRO   (registrar)

Eventually, you're going to need A+ certification to pursue professional employment in
the PC service field. To help you prepare for the A+ exam, the following checklist provides you with a series of important test points for every major area tested: installation and
setup, configuration, upgrading, diagnosis, repairing, preventive maintenance, and safety.
Once you feel comfortable with each of these topic areas, you should be able to pass the
A+ exam satisfactorily.

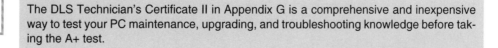

The DLS Technician's Certificate II in Appendix G is a comprehensive and inexpensive
way to test your PC maintenance, upgrading, and troubleshooting knowledge before taking the A+ test.

INSTALLATION AND SETUP

You must be able to add new equipment to a computer, integrate the new hardware and software into the existing system, then prepare the new equipment for service without interfering with the operation of existing equipment. To pass the A+ exam, you must be able to:

- inspect all of the sub-assemblies of a system.
- connect new peripheral devices to the system—on your bench, as well as at a customer's site.
- perform a complete system checkout after the equipment has been installed.
- explain the basic functions of the newly installed equipment and any changes that have
  been made to the system.
- connect the system to a network and verify the network's operation.
- tune the system's operation for optimal performance.
- perform machine moves at the customer site.

CONFIGURATION

You must demonstrate a knowledge of the internal subassemblies in a typical computer,
then demonstrate an understanding of the proper procedures for system setup, prepara-

tion, and configuration, according to a customer's specifications. Ideally, you should be able to:

- identify each of the major assemblies in a modern computer and understand the functions of each.
- identify the major components in a display.
- identify major storage devices and their functions (including SCSI devices).
- indentify the major assemblies of modern printers and understand the functions of each.
- identify the major components of a basic LAN.
- identify the major elements of operating systems, such as Windows, DOS, System 7, and OS/2.
- identify a system's RAM and ROM, and understand the functions of each.
- take the necessary steps required to setup and initialize a system.
- identify external connectors and ports, such as serial ports, keyboard ports, printer ports, etc.
- understand how to test each part connected to the system.
- configure a system according to specification.
- verify that a system is properly setup and configured.
- boot the system from diskette.
- prepare, format, and backup the floppy and hard disks.
- disassemble the system for shipment to the customer.

UPGRADING

As a technician, you must also be able to replace existing equipment with new and improved equipment, then update the system software and operating system drivers to accommodate the new equipment. All of this must be accomplished without interfering with other devices in the system. You should be able to:

- install operating system and driver versions to a system.
- replace memory and drives (including SCSI drives).
- replace existing display subassemblies.
- replace new printers and other peripheral devices.
- maintain an awareness of existing and potential customers, and possible system problems.
- verify the newly upgraded system's operation.

DIAGNOSIS

The art of diagnosis is the first critical step toward resolving problems. When a system malfunctions, you must be able to track down and isolate the problem area as quickly and accurately as possible. This includes considerations, such as any changes made to the system hardware or software. To pass the diagnosis portion of the A+ exam, you must be able to:

- question the customer to exact specific fault details.
- use visual and audible indications to identify possible problems.
- recreate the problem as the customer describes it.

- determine the hardware and software related to the fault area.
- use the appropriate tools, test equipment, and diagnostic software needed to isolate the fault.
- identify faulty hardware or software.
- take the appropriate steps needed to correct the system fault.

REPAIRING

Once the diagnosis is accomplished, you will need to take the proper steps to correct the fault that you have identified. In most cases, this will involve the replacement of one or more hardware devices. In other cases, you might have to install (or reinstall) software. On rare instances, you might need to perform some soldering. To master the repair part of the A+ exam, you must be able to:

- understand and follow a modular (sub-assembly) repair strategy.
- understand the function of each system sub-assembly.
- take the corrective steps needed to resolve a fault.
- repair basic printer failures.
- reassemble, clean, and optimize the system.
- prepare the system for shipping.
- perform basic soldering (if necessary)

PREVENTIVE MAINTENANCE

It is often not enough to simply take a "reactive" roll in repairing faulty systems. A good technician should be able to understand and implement a "proactive" strategy of preventive maintenance to maximize a system's working life. For the preventive maintenance part of an A+ exam, you should be able to:

- inspect, test, clean, and adjust the system to keep the system running properly, while still having the minimum impact on the system's operation.

SAFETY

Finally, a technician must be able to work safely with high-energy electricity, static-sensitive devices, and soldering tools. For the A+ exam, you should be able to:

- recognize the danger posed by ac, and take the proper steps to protect yourself.
- recognize the danger posed by ESD and take the proper steps to protect the equipment.
- use tools and test equipment properly.

PC STANDARDS
CHART

SPECIFICATION	DESCRIPTION	REVISION LEVEL
APM	Advanced Power Management BIOS interface specification	Revision 1.2, February, 1996 Intel, Microsoft
ATA-3	Information Technology—AT Attachment-3 Interface	X3T10/2008D Revision 6 ATA Anonymous FTP Site: fission.dt.wdc.com
ATA-33	Synchronous DMA Transfer Protocol specification (to be proposed as Ultra DMA/33 standard)	Revision 0.7, May 21, 1996 Quantum document no. 70-108412-1
ATAPI	ATA Packet Interface	SFF-8020i Revision 2.5 (SFF) Fax Access: (408) 741-1600
ATX	ATX form factor specification	Revision 2.01, February 1997
DDC	Display Data Channel standard	Version 2, Revision 0, April 9, 1996 Video Electronics Standards Association
DMI	Desktop Management Interface BIOS specification	Version 2.0, October 16, 1995 American Megatrends Inc., Award Software International Inc., Dell Computer Corporation, Intel, Phoenix Technologies Ltd, SystemSoft Corporation
DPMS	Display Power Management Signaling	Revision 1.0 Video Electronics Standards Association

SPECIFICATION	DESCRIPTION	REVISION LEVEL
"El Torito"	Bootable CD-ROM format specification	Version 1.0, January 25, 1995 Phoenix Technologies, IBM Corporation
EPP	Enhanced Parallel Port	IEEE 1284 standard, Mode (1 or 2)
Feature Connector	Advanced Feature Connector (VAFC)	Version 1.0, March 1994 Video Electronics Standards Association
IrDA	Serial Infrared Physical Layer Link specification	Version 1.1, October 17, 1995 Infrared Data Association
Management extension hardware	LM78 Microprocessor System Hardware Monitor	Current Web site: http://www.national.com/pf/LM/LM78.html
PCI	PCI Local Bus specification	Revision 2.1, June 1, 1995 PCI Special Interest Group
Plug and Play	Plug and Play BIOS specification	Version 1.0a, May 5, 1994 Compaq Computer, Phoenix Technologies, Intel
UHCI	Universal Host Controller Interface	Revision 1.0
USB	Universal Serial Bus specification	Revision 1.0, January 15, 1996 Compaq, Digital Equipment Corporation, IBM PC Company, Intel Microsoft, NEC, Northern Telecom

INDEX

244PC cards, Windows 95/98 problems, 1038
386MAX, 798, 823–826
3D graphics accelerators, 1261–1266

A
A+ checklist, 1414–1417
accelerated graphics port (AGP), 25, 974–978, **976**
accelerators, 941
access time, 215, 419, 624, 771–772
Acer chipsets, 198–199
Acer POST codes, 471
active low logic, 385
adapters, drive (*see* drive adapters), 13
adapters, joystick (*see* joysticks/game ports), 19
adaptive delta pulse code modulation (ADPCM), 1200
address latch enable (ALE), CMOS setup, 223
addressing, 239, 396–397, 412, 738–739, **738, 739**
  cylinder head sector (CHS) addressing, 400
  logical block addressing (LBA), 401, 405, 593, 612
  modes, 288
advanced configuration power interface (ACPI), 116, 973–974
advanced power control (APC), 945
advanced power management (APM), 951, 978–981
air flow, hard drive, 583–585, **584**
A-Law codec, 1200
allocation units, 567

alpha blending, 1265
ALR BIOS POST codes, 472
AMD chipsets, 181–185, 289
American Megatrends BIOS, 121–122
AMI BIOS, 119, 120, 464, 475–487
AMI Multimedia channel, 1271, 1272
amplitude, 872
amplitude modulation (AM), 872
analog-to-digital conversions, 1189, 1291
antidotes (*see also* viruses/antivirals), 1336–1337
anti-static precautions, 2–4
anti-virus software (*see also* viruses), 81, 83, 1318
Apollo (VIA) chipsets P6 through Master chipsets, 191–195
application specific IC (ASIC), 180, 603–604, 1254
applications, 46
  problems after upgrades, 89
arbiter mode, 235
arbitrate priority rotation, 237, 240
Arche Legacy BIOS POST codes, 487–490
arithmetic test failure, 333
ASCII, 878, 1246, 1395–1397
assembly (*see* disassembly/assembly tips)
AST beep/POST codes, 465, 491
asynchronous communications, 1145, 1171–1174
asynchronous static RAM (ASRAM), 774–775
AT attachment (ATA) interface, 394, 592–594

Illustrations are in **boldface**.

AT attachment packet interface (ATAPI), 394, 399, 413, 593, 597
AT form factor motherboards, 935
AT&T BIOS POST codes, 492–493, 538–539, 540
ATA 3 drives, 593
ATA 4 drives, 594
attenuation, 1192
attribute memory, 1011–1012
ATX form factor components, 22–25, 935, **937**
audio standards, 420–421
audio video interleave (AVI), 1292
auto park feature, 216
autoconfiguration, 222, 243, 278
AUTOEXEC.BAT, 66, 263, 799, 804–805, 808, 1081, 1196–1197
automation for computers, Instant On, 984–985
Award BIOS codes, 117–118, 493–505

B

back-to-back memory, 235, 238
backfilling, 798
backlight power supplies, 1110–1115, **1114**
BackPack drives, compressed disks, 368
backplane board (*see* motherboards)
backup strategies, 19, 404, 1378–1380
  CMOS backups, 243–244, 1380
  frequency of backups, 1379
  incremental vs complete, 1379
  tape drives, 1210–1243, **1211**
bandwidth, 907
banks of memory, 782–784
barrel distortion, 904, **905**
basic input/output system (*see* BIOS ROM)
batteries (*see also* power supplies), 6, 94–110, 942
  advanced configuration power interface (ACPI), 973–974
  backup batteries, 97–102
  BIOS error message, 128, 129
  cell voltage, 95
  CMOS backup batteries, 97–102, 208, 250
  conserving battery power, portable PCs, 105–106
  constant-current chargers, 96–97
  electrodes, 95
  electrolytes, 95
  life span of batteries in portable PCs, 104
  lithium backup batteries, 97–102, **98**
  lithium ion (Li ion) batteries, 105
  memory capacity with NiCad batteries, 103
  memory effect in NiCad batteries, 103
  mobile (notebook, laptop) batteries, 102–110
  nickel cadmium (NiCad), 96, 102–104, **103**
  nickel metal hydride (NiMH), 96, 104
  non rechargeable (primary) batteries, 95
  pen input systems, touchpads, 1059
  power management, 215, 242–243, 245–246
  ratings, 95
  rechargeable (secondary) batteries, 95, 105, 106–110
  recharging process, 95–97
  recycling used batteries, 110
  replacing backup batteries, 99–100
  slow or trickle charge, 96
  Smart Battery, 986–988
  system management bus (SMBus), 986–988
  voltage memory in NiCad batteries, 103
  watt-hours per kilogram or pound(Wh/kg or lb), 95
  zinc air batteries, 105
BatteryMark, 78
baud rate, 872, 1173–1174
BCLK divider, 231
beep codes, 326, 435, 464–465, 558–560, 1027, 1040, 1278
Bell modem signaling standards, 873–874
bench testing techniques, 83–92
benchmarking, 73–77, 289, 958
Bernoulli drives, 369, 1129–1135
bi-directional ports, type 1, 3, 997–998
billing sheet, 1413
binary data, 563–564
binary gigabytes, 591
binary megabytes, 591
BIOS/BIOS ROM (*see also* POST codes), 6, 9, 45, 111–137, 224–245, 611, 932, 1412
  adapter or expansion BIOS, 112
  advanced configuration power interface (ACPI), 116
  advanced power management (APM), 978–979, 978
  American Megatrends BIOS, boot sequence, 121–122
  AMI BIOS, 119–120
  autoconfiguration, 243
  Award EliteBIOS features, 117–118
  battery failures, 128
  boot process, 63–68, 116, 121–124, 133, 137
  bootable media message, 131
  bugs errors in, 126
  cache memory errors, 128
  checksum errors, 128, 136
  chipsets, 116
  clock/timing circuit errors, 133, 135
  CMOS setup, 208, 238–239
  configuration errors, 131
  CPU, 115–116, 129, 131, 327
  cylinder limit, hard disk drives, 612
  data error, 129
  defaults, 243
  device driver compatibility, 124, 129–130
  direct control of hardware vs., 125–126
  direct memory access (DMA) error, 130
  display errors, 130
  error codes, 128–135, 136, 435–560, 456
  flash memory compatibility, 125
  gate A20 error, 128
  hard disk drive setting, 116, 399, 401, 406–407, 413, 613–614, 639
  hard disk errors, 130–131, 134–135

I/O errors, 131, 136
ID strings, determining features present,
    118–120
IDE controller errors, 137
initialization stalled, 86–87
input device errors, 137
intelligent BIOS, 405
intelligent I/O (I2O), 116
interrupts, 113–115, 135, 136
IO.SYS files, 55–56
keyboard errors, 131–132
main sections of, **112**
memory errors, 116, 129, 133–134, 136
Microid Research Mr. BIOS, 117–118
motherboard, 948, 949–950, 957, 958
non-system disk errors, 133
NVRAM errors, 136
overlay software, 961–971
override errors, 134
parity errors, 131, 133–134
password access, 953
PCI error messages, 136–137
peripheral component interconnect (PCI), 116
Phoenix Technologies BIOS, boot sequence,
    122–124
plug-and- play devices, 116, 134, 1071, 1088,
    1094
port errors, 136
POST codes, 112, 113, 128, 134, 435, 469–486
real time clock (RTC), 126–127
SCSI devices, 1166–1167
seek error message, 129
setup routines, 113
shadowing, ROM shadowing, 125
shutdown failure, 135
system option error messages, 129
system service routines, 113–115
temperature warnings, 135–136
terminator/processor card errors, 135
thermal probe warning, 135
time wrong error message, 129
universal standards (USB), 116
upper memory area (UMA), 112
video adapters, 1285–1286
video BIOS/ROM, 227, 1247, 1259
Year 2000 (Y2K) problems, 126–127
bits per inch (BPI), 583, 585
bits per second (bps), 1173–1174
Blue Book standard, CD-ROM, 145
bombs, software, 1320
Books A through E, DVD standards, 420
boot delay, 237
boot disks, 67–69, 1388
  BIOS messages, 131
  boots from hard drive, bootable disk
      present, 245
  CD-ROMs as bootable discs, 147, 154–159
  disk compression, 345
  El Torito, 147, 154–159
boot process, 63–68, 592

American Megatrends BIOS, sequence,
    121–122
AUTOEXEC.BAT files, 66
BIOS, 116, 121–124, 133, 137
boot delay, 237
boot disks 67–69, 131, 147, 154–159, 1388
boot sequences, 219
boots from hard drive, bootable disk
    present, 245
bootstrap operation, 63
CMOS setup, 219
COMMAND.COM, 66
CONFIG.SYS files, 56–57, 66
core tests in POST sequence, 63–65
CPU speed, 219
crashes/reboots intermittently, 87–88
dead system, 84
environment configuration, 66–67
error/failure messages, 65–66, 462
finding operating system, 65–66
hard disk drive problems, 618–619, 627–628
initialization stalled, 86–87
IO.SYS files, 56–57, 66
loading operating system, 66
lock up/freezes at boot, 88, 631
MSDOS.SYS files, 56–57, 66
new memory installation problems, 793
PC cards, 1037, 1040
Phoenix Technologies BIOS, sequence,
    122–124
POST, 63–65
power up, 63
problems, 410, 613
registry files (SYSTEM.DAT), 66
SCSI devices, 1162–1163, 1165, 1166
troubleshooting, 1390
turbo mode, 219, 220
video adapters, 1281–1282
video/monitor problems, 1284, 1286
viral infection, 1327
volume boot sector (VBS), 65
WINBOOT.SYS files, 56, 66
Windows 95, 89–92
boot volume descriptor (BVD), CD-ROM, 156
booting catalog (BC), CD-ROM, 156, 157
bootstrap operation, 63
branch prediction, 291
buffer settings, 232, 233, 235, 237, 240, 803
bugs, software, 45, 1319
burn-in, 72
BURNIN43.ZIP, 72
burst extended data output (BEDO RAM), 776
burst length, 232
burst mode, 237, 238, 239, 240, 241, 242
bus mastering, 594, 595–597, 1262
busses, 287–288
  AT bus setup, CMOS, 225
  bus mastering, 594, 595–597, 1262
  bus mode, CMOS setup, 224
  control signals, 288

busses, *continued*
  data lines, 287
  data volume (bits), 287
  extended ISA (EISA) busses, 253–254,
    633–642
  industry standard architecture (ISA),
    633–642, **634**
  master setting, 233
  mastering, 594, 595–597
  micro channel architecture (MCA) bus, 253,
    728–737, **730**
  overclocking CPUs, 317–325
  PC busses (*see also* industry standard archi-
    tecture), 634
  peripheral component interconnect (PCI), 235,
    241, 1042–1048, **1044,** 1260–1261, 1287
  read operations, 288
  size, 287–288
  system management bus (SMBus), 986–988
  troubleshooting, 642
  universal serial bus (USB), 988–989, **989**
  VL bus, 235, 237, 1042, 1260, 1276–1277,
    1342–1348
  write operations, 288
byte merge, 234
byte mode, 998
bytes, 591

C
cables, 21
cabling and connectors, 1383, 1387
  ATX form factor, 24, **24**
  NLX form factor, 26–27
cache memory, 6, 8, 215, 232, 738, 777–778,
    778, 795, 950, 952
  BIOS error message, 128, 129
  CD-ROM, 147, 162
  CMOS setup, 219, 226–227, 232
cached DRAM (CDRAM), 776
caching, drive, 597–598, **599**
calibrating joysticks, 647–648
caller ID, 849, 892–893
camera techniques, capture, 1296–1297
capture, video, 1292, 1294–1297, 1304–1311
CardBus, 1010
cases (*see* enclosures)
cathode ray tube (*see also* monitors/video
    adapters), 31–33, **32,** 902, 915–920, **916,**
    1113–1116
  CRT controller (CRTC), 1246
  discharging, 39–40, **40**
CCITT G.711 CODECS, 1200
CD-R drives (*see also* CD-ROM drives), 11
  absorption control error, 173
  application code error, 173
  ASPI driver problems, 173
  buffer underrun error, 173
  buffer, recorder, 171
  can't find CD-R drive letter, 175
  closed audio session errors, 173, 174

compatibility problems, 172
data block problems, 175
dead unit, 177
error codes, 174
file size, 170
fragmentation, 170
full disc errors, 174
general protection faults, 175
gold discs won't read, 177
hard disk drives, 170
image file problems, 176
indicator light problems, 176
MSCDEX, 175
multisession CD problems, 172
overrun/underrun problems, 174
QEMM problems, 814
read file errors, 176
read problems, 172, 174, 177
recorder, 171
recording process, 170–171
speed, 170
symptoms, 172–177
system interrupts, 170
thermal calibration, 171
TOC or PMA errors, 175
troubleshooting, 169–177
write problems, 175–177
write protected errors, 174
CD-ROM drives (*see also* CD-R drives; DVD
    drives), 10, 14, 138–178, 413, 939, 951
  audio problems, 161, 168, 169
  block diagram, electronics, **152**
  Blue Book standard, 145
  boot volume descriptor (BVD), 156
  bootable CD-ROMs (El Torito), 147, 154–159
  booting catalog (BC), 156, 157
  burning files onto CD-R discs, 158
  caching, 147, 162–163
  care of discs, 143
  CD Plus or Enhanced problems, 169
  chemicals/solvent damage, 143
  cleaning discs, 143
  Compact Disc Digital Audio Standard CEI
    IEC 908, 145
  compact disc interactive (CD I), 145
  conflicts, 264
  constant angular velocity (CAV), 149
  constant linear velocity (CLV), 149, 160
  construction details of, 149–153
  controls don't work, 166
  cross interleaved Reed Solomon Code
    (CIRC), 152
  data transfer rates, 145–146
  developmental timeline, 418
  Device Bay, 981
  device drivers, 153–154, 162–165, 167
  disc at once write mode, 148
  disc stuck, 160
  disc won't read, 160
  door stuck, 166

drive adapters, 382–416, **383**
drive engine, 150, **151**
drive letter problems, 162, 166
drive problems, 162, 163–165, 167
drives not detected, 245
DVD compatiblity, 421
EIDE/IDE interface for, 153, 405
eight-to-fourteen modulation (EFM), 141, 142–143, **143**, 152
electronics in, 152–153, **152**
error correction (EC) symbols, 142
exploded view, **150**
finalization, 148
fixation, 148
focus problems, 160–161
frames, 142
Green Book standard, 145
heat damage to, 143
High Sierra standard, 144
IDE interface problems, 168–169
image files, bootable CD-ROMs, 156, 157–158
incremental write mode, 149
indicator light stays on, 169
ISO 10149, 1989 standard, 145
ISO 9660 standard, 145
Kodak Photo CDs, 144
labels/writing on discs, 144
load/unload problems, 159
magneto-optical (MO) drives, 145
media, 139–140, 147–148
motherboard, 952
MSCDEX.EXE, 154, 155, 161–162
multi spin drives, 145–146
multimedia personal computer (MPC) standard, 146–147
multisession capability, 148
no access to directories or computer data, 166
no sound, 1389–1390
Orange Book standard, 145, 147–148
packet write mode, 149
pits lands in media, 139, 140, 421, **422**
playback process, 140–141, **141**
port problems, 164, 167–168
protected real mode drivers, 168
recordable (see CD-R)
Recordable Compact Disc Standard, 145
recording process, 140–141
Red Book standard, 145
scratches, 143
SCSI interface, 154, 164–165, 167–168
seek inoperative, 159–160
sled, 150–151, **151**
software, 153–154
sound boards & cards/audio systems:, 1201
standards, 144–149
stepping motors, 151–152
substrates, 139
symbols, 142
track at once write mode, 149

tray operation test, 1384–1385
troubleshooting, 159–169
underside view, **151**
upper memory area (UMA) use, 153
vertical mount problems, 164
video CD I problems, 168
video problems, 168
volume table of contents (VTOC), 144
White Book standard, 145
write-once CD-R drives, 145
Wrong DOS version error message, 161–162
XA format, 145
Yellow Book standard, 145
central processing unit (see CPU)
Centronics ports, 991–1003, **992**
chameleons, software, 1320
Chandra, Neil, 1004
charging, in laser/LED printer, 676, **677**
chassis, 21
checkpoints (see also POST codes), 236, 470
checksum errors, 128, 136, 248, 948
Chips & Technologies chipsets, 199–200
Chips & Technologies POST codes, 505–507
chipsets, 8–9, 179–206, 932, 938, 952
    Acer chipsets, 198–199
    address latch enable (ALE) setup, 223
    AMD 640 chipset, 182–184
    AMD chipsets, 181–185
    application specific ICs (ASICs), 180
    AT bus setup, 225
    automatic configuration, 222
    BIOS, 116
    bus mode setup, 224
    cache memory setup, 226–227
    Chips & Technologies chipsets, 199–200
    clock/timing circuit setup, 223–224, 225
    CMOS setup, 222–229
    component/function list, 182–184
    core logic, 181
    direct memory access (DMA)setup, 226
    dirty bit RAM, 227
    DRAM setup, 228, 229
    error codes, 456
    ETEQ Microsystems chipsets, 201
    Faraday chipsets, 201
    fast AT cycle, 224
    fast decode enable, 225
    I/O setup, 224, 225–226
    IDE setup, 226
    Integrated Technology chipsets, 201
    Intel chipsets, 185–191
    interleave mode, 228
    interrupt setup, 224
    legacy chips, 198–206
    list of, 181
    memory remapping, 225
    Northbridge controller (AMD 640 chipset), 184
    OPTi chipsets, 195, 197–198, 202–203
    refresh memory setup, 222–223

chipsets, *continued*
  row address strobe (RAS) setup, 228
  SiS chipsets, 195, 196–197, 203
  Southbridge controller (AMD 645 chipset),
    184–185
  Suntec chipsets, 203
  support ICs, 198–206
  Symphony Labs chipsets, 204
  Triton chipset, 187–188
  VIA Apollo P6 through Master chipsets,
    191–195
  VIA legacy chips, 204–205
  video BIOS setup, 227
  VLSI Technology chipsets, 205
  wait state setup, 224, 225, 227–228
  Western Digital chipsets, 204
  video, 1256–1258
  Zilog chipsets, 206
  Zymos chipsets, 206
CHKCOP, 334
cleaning computer systems, 1377–1390
clicking/doubleclicking, 828–829
CLK/PCI CLK divider, 231
clock speed, 771–772
clock/timing circuits, 6, 233, 240, 944
  BIOS, 126–127, 129, 133, 135
  CMOS setup, 223–224, 225, 233, 240
  latency timer, 232
  overclocking CPUs, 317–325
  PCI CLK setting, 242
  poor time keeping, 247
  preempt timer, 241–242
  real time clock (RTC), 126–127, 932
  retry timer, 241
  setting, 215–216, 240
  speed, 771–772
  time outs, 238
  timing modes, 237
  Year 2000 (Y2K) problems, 126–127
cluster adapters, error codes, 448
clusters, 340, 566–567, 606, 1389
CMOS, 207–250, 932, 1411
  address latch enable (ALE) setup, 223
  advanced chipset setup, 222–229
  advanced CMOS Setup, 217–222
  AT bus setup, 225
  automatic configuration, 222, 243
  backing up CMOS RAM, 243–244, 1380
  backup batteries for, 97–102, 208, 250, 942
  BIOS, 208
  boot process, 219, 245
  bus mode setup, 224
  cache memory, 215, 219, 226–227
  changes not saved, 244
  checksum errors, 248
  clock/timing circuit setup, 223–224, 225, 247
  configuring CMOS setup, 213–243
  crashes or lockups, 246–247
  date/time setting, 215–216
  devices not recognized, 246

direct memory access (DMA) setup, 226
dirty bit RAM setup, 227
disabled Setup, 214
DRAM setup, 228, 229
drive access, 215
drive letter designation, 216
drives not detected, 245
error messages, 86, 218, 248
fast AT cycle, 224
fast decode enable, 225
floppy disk drive setup, 217, 219
hard disk drive setup, 216, 406
high memory area (HMA) setup, 219–220
I/O setup, 224, 225–226
IDE setup, 226
interleave mode, 228
interrupt setup, 224
invalid system configuration data error,
  247–248
keyboard setup, 217, 222
launching/entering Setup utility, 213–214
map of, 208–213
math (numeric) co processor test, 218–219
memory remapping, 225
memory setup, 217–218, 225
mismatch errors, 245
monitor setup, 217
motherboard, 949, 957
NumLock setting, 218
optimization, 215
parity error, 218
password access, 220, 248–249, 952–953
plug-and-play configuration, 229–242, 246
poor performance, 244–245
port problems, 247
power management, 215, 242–243, 245–246
refresh memory setup, 222–223
ROM shadowing, 215
row address strobe (RAS) setup, 228
setup disks, 214
setup problems, 246
shadow memory setup, 220–221
test tick, 218
troubleshooting, 244–249
turbo mode setting, 219, 220
Type 47 HDD data area, 218
typematic rate, 217
video BIOS setup, 227
video ROM shadow, 220
video settings, 1279
virus protection setup, 221–222
wait state setup, 215, 224, 225, 233–234
CODECS, 1200
coercivity, 563, 583
coherence of light, lasers, 681
color graphics adapter (CGA), 12, 1249–1250
color look up tables (CLUT), 1264
color purity, 32, **33**
COM/serial port, 6, 15, 247, 1170–1185
  addresses interrupts, 1175–1176, 1181–1183

asynchronous communication, 1171–1174
baud vs. bps, 1173–1174
conflicts, 1181–1183
data carrier equipment (DCE), 1176–1177
data terminal equipment (DTE), 1176–1177
error codes, POST/beep codes, 1183–1184
garbled communications, 1184
Infrared Data Association (IrDA), 985–986,
    1178–1181, 1184–1185
initialization problems, 1184
modems, 846, 847–848, 897, 898
motherboard connection, 944
RS–232 ports, 1170–1185
signals, 1177–1178
troubleshooting, 1181–1185
universal asynchronous receiver/transmitter
    (UART), 1174–1175, **1175**
video adapter conflicts, 1277
command processors/COMMAND.COM, 59–62,
    66, 1326–1327
common access method committee (CAMC)
    (*see* IDE), 394
communications error codes, 441–443, 444,
    446–448, 455–456, 458–459
Compact Disc Digital Audio Standard CEI IEC
    908, CD-ROM, 145
compact disc interactive (CD I), 145
Compaq beep/POST codes, 465, 507–515
compatibility (*see* conflict resolution)
complementary metal–oxide semiconductor
    (*see* CMOS)
complex instruction set computing (CISC),
    291
compressed volume file (CVF), 341–343, 361,
    366, 368
compression, CODECS, 1200, 1292–1293
compression, data (*see also* disk
    compression), 872
CompTIA, 1414
concurrency, 240
CONFIG.SYS, 56–57, 66, 263, 799–800, 805,
    1081, 1196–1197
  BUFFERS setting, 803
  DEVICEHIGH setting, 804, 805, 807–808
  DOS location, 803–804
  editing for memory performance, 803–804
  FILES setting, 803
  LASTDRIVE setting, 803
configuration, 66–67, 1410
  autoconfiguration, 222, 243, 278
  BIOS error messages, 131
  CMOS setup, 213–243
  environment test failure, 333
  launching/entering Setup utility, 213–214
  plug-and-play (PNP) devices, 278
configuration mode, 230
conflict resolution (*see also* devices/device
    drivers; interrupts), 251–278, 404
  AUTOEXEC.BAT files, 263
  CD-ROM drives, 264

CONFIG.SYS files, 263
  crashes, 262
  device drivers, 263–264
  device/port assignments, typical, 261–262
  direct memory access (DMA), 254–255
  Discovery Card testing tool, 264
  extended ISA (EISA) busses, 253–254
  hardware conflicts, 264
  I/O area assignments, 255–260
  interrupts, 252–254
  keeping notes of settings, 278
  last in first out (LIFO) conflict resolution,
    263
  lockups, 262
  memory assignments, 255, 260
  micro channel architecture (MCA) bus, 253
  open architectures, 251
  plug-and-play (PNP) devices, 277–278
  popup utilities, 263
  recognizing conflicts, 262–263
  software conflicts, 263–264
  system reporting tools, 263
  terminate stay resident (TSR), 263
  Windows 95/98 troubleshooting, 264–277
connectors (*see* cabling and connectors)
constant angular velocity (CAV), CD-ROM,
    149, 590
constant linear velocity (CLV), CD-ROM, 149,
    160
control grid, 32
control signals, busses, 288
controllers, 13
  floppy disk drives, 572
  hard disk drives, 603–604, 626–627
  Northbridge controller (AMD 640 chipset),
    184
  Southbridge controller (AMD 645 chipset),
    184–185
conventional memory, 759–760, **760,** 798–808
convergence, 33, 904, 1368, 1369, 1371–1374
cooling (*see* fans/cooling)
core logic, 181
core tests in POST sequence, 63–64
corona, in laser/LED printer, 676, 717–721
CPPU, 932
CPU, 6, 7–8, 22, 947, 951
  addressing modes, 288
  AMD CPUs, 313–315
  arithmetic test failure, 333
  beep codes, 326
  benchmarking, 289
  BIOS, 115–116, 129, 131, 327
  branch prediction, 291
  busses, 287–288
  cache enabled causes problems, 327
  CHKCOP fails divide test, 334
  CHKCOP Has Found locks up, 334
  CHKCOP slow, 334
  CMOS setup, 219, 236
  comparison chart, 293–297

CPU, *continued*
  complex instruction set computing (CISC), 291
  crashes, 326–327
  Cyrix CPUs, 315–317
  dead system, 325–326
  diagram of generic CPU, **287**
  direct memory access (DMA), 254–255
  DOS4GW.EXE malfunction, 327
  dynamic execution, 292
  environment test failure, 333
  error codes, 460
  execution, superscalar vs. dynamic, 292
  general symptoms/solutions, 325–328
  heatsink/fan is loose, 328
  HIMEM.SYS malfunction, 327
  historical index of CPUs/MCPs, list, 282–287
  Intel CPUs, 292, 298–313
  lockups, 326–327, 328, 334
  math co processor (MCP), 281, 333–336
  motherboad, 957–958
  numerical processing unit (NPU), 281
  overclocking, 317–325, 331–332
  P rating (PR) system, 289
  performance (*see also* overclocking), 281, 317
  pipelining, 291
  POST codes, 326
  processor interrupts, 115
  protected mode operation, 288
  reduced instruction set computing (RISC), 291
  sockets, 289–291, **291**
  speed (*see also* overclocking), 8, 236, 281, 317
  superscalar execution, 292
  system diagnostics, math co processors, 335
  system integrity diagnostic test failure, 334
  testing, 1387
  troubleshooting, 325–338
  turbo mode, 219, 220
  upgrading, 8
  VESA bus, 328
  voltage mismatch, voltage regulator module (VRM), 327
  Winstone 96 benchmark, 289
  wrong CPU reported, 327, 328
crashes, 87–88, 135, 246–247, 262, 326–327, 332
cross interleaved Reed Solomon Code (CIRC), CD-ROM, 152
cursor, 828
cyclic redundancy check (CRC), 407, 567, 587, 879, 890, 1172
cylinder head sector (CHS) addressing, 400
cylinders, 566, 586–588, **586, 587**
Cyrix (*see* chipsets; CPU)

D
data acquisition adapter, error codes, 452
data bus Xccelerator (DBX), 941

data carrier equipment (DCE), 1176–1177
data compression, 341, 872
data error, BIOS error messages, 129
data frames, 1171–1172, **1172**
data lines, busses, 287
data terminal equipment (DTE), 1176–1177
data transfer rates
  CD-ROM, 145–146
  DVD drives, 419–420
  EIDE drives, 402–403
  hard disk drives, 402–403, 594–595
dates for virus activation, 1321–1325
DEC Alpha (*see* chipsets; CPU)
decibels, 1192
decoder boards, MPEG, 16, **17,** 18
DEFRAG, 68
defragmentation, 170, 363, 364–366, 368, 375–376, 1389
degaussing, 1375, 1385
Dell BIOS POST codes, 515–517
desktop management interface (DMI), 981–983
Device Bay, 981
DEVICEHIGH setting, 804, 805, 807–808
devices/device drivers (*see also* plug-and-play), 124, 251, 263–264
  advanced configuration power interface (ACPI), 973–974
  advanced power management (APM), 978–981
  arbitrate priority rotation, 237, 240
  BIOS compatibility, 124
  CD-ROM, 153–154
  conflict resolution, 251–278, 404
  desktop management interface (DMI), 981–983
  Device Bay, 981
  device/port assignments, typical, 261–262
  DEVICEHIGH setting, 804–805, 807–808
  devices not recognized, overclocked CPU, 332
  EIDE drive support, 401–402
  failure after upgrade, 88–89
  hot insertion/removal, hot swapping, 1011
  independence, 1142
  Intelligent I/O (I2O), 983–984
  IO.SYS files, 55–56
  legacy devices, 1080, 1085
  not recognized, 246, 332
  PC cards, 1017–1020, 1026–1027
  peripheral component interconnect (PCI), 1042–1048, **1044**
  plug-and-play (*see also* plug-and-play), 277, 1070–1097
  SCSI, 1141–1169
  sound boards & cards, 1196–1197
  universal serial bus (USB), 988–989, **989**
  video drivers, 1245
  Windows 95/98 conflict resolution, 264–277
  wrong CPU reported, Win95, 328

diagnostics, 73
differential SCSI, 1145–1146
digital audio tape (DAT) drives (*see also* tape drives), 1225–1226
digital signal processor (DSP), 1191–1192
digital to analog conversion, 1291
digital video cards, 1017
digital video stream (DVS) mode, 1272, 1273
digital video/versatile disk (*see* DVD drives)
digital-to-analog conversions, 1189
digitization of sound, 1188–1189
digitizers (*see* pen input systems; touchpads)
DIP switches, 946–947
direct memory access (DMA), 64, 254–255, 395–396, 415, 594, 595–597, 932, 949, 983
  BIOS error message, 130
  CMOS setup, 226
  conflicts after upgrade, 88
  device/port assignments, 261–262
  sound boards & cards/audio systems:, 1204, 1205, 1207
  video, 1281, 1300
DirectX technology, 1266–1270, 1287–1288
dirty bit RAM, 227
disassembly/assembly tips, 19–22
  backing up data, 19
  closing the system, 20–21
  monitors, 39–41
  opening the system, 19–20
  safety precautions, 21–22
  work orders, 19
disc-at-once write mode, CD-ROM, 148
Discovery Card testing tool, 264
disk compression, 339–381
  backing up data before compression, 343
  BackPack drives, 368
  Bernoulli drives, 369
  bootable disk creation, 345
  compressed volume file (CVF), 341–343, 361, 366, 368
  compression utility installation, 344–345
  data compression, 341
  DBLSPACE. INI file settings, 345–351, 360–371
  defragmentation, 344, 363–368, 375–376
  disk space allocation, 340
  DOS DoubleSpace, troubleshooting, 360–371
  DOS DriveSpace, troubleshooting, 360–371
  DOS Stacker troubleshooting, 371–381
  DoubleGuard, DOS, 361
  DRVSPACE.INI file settings, 345–371
  factors affecting, 343
  file allocation table (FAT), 340, 374–375
  file defects, 344
  free space available, 344, 361, 362
  graphic demonstration of, **342**
  host drives, 341
  looping problems, 368
  memory check, 344
  on-the-fly compression, 341
  physical defects on disk, 343–344
  preparing for compression, 343–351
  RAMDrive, 369–370
  ratio of compression, 342, 362, 367
  run length encoding (RLE), 341
  slack space, 340
  swap files, 363–364
  system for compression, 341–343
  tape drives, 370
  tracks, sectors, clusters, 340
  troubleshooting compressed drives, 351–381
  Windows 95/98 DriveSpace, troubleshooting, 351–360
Disk Manager, 398, 400, 404, 961–965
disk mapper (*see also* viruses/antivirals), 1338
distortion, 1194
dithering, 1266
Ditto drive (Iomega), 1125–1129
divide by zero errors, 1284
Dolby, 420, 428
DOS, 45
  DoubleGuard, 361
  DoubleSpace, disk compression, 360–371
  DriveSpace, disk compression, 360–371
  error messages, 1398–1403
  memory location of, 803–804
  MS DOS, 48–49
  PC DOS, 49–50
  plug-and-play configuration, 1081–1084
  sound boards & cards/audio systems:, 1205
  Stacker troubleshooting, 371–381
  tape drives:, 1238
DOS extenders, 769–770
DOS protected mode interface (DPMI), 770
DOSMAX, 823–835
dot pitch, 902–903
dots per inch (DPI), 677
double buffering, 1265–1266
DoubleGuard, DOS, 361
DoubleSpace (DBLSPACE.INI) settings, 345–351, 360–371
Drake, 1414
drift, in monitors, 907
drive adapters (*see also* hard disks), 13–14, 382–416, **383**
  error codes, 449, 450–452, 457–458
  troubleshooting, 408–416
drive board for CRT, 33–34
Drive Rocket, 400, 961, 969–970
drive translation, 394, 590–591, 613
DriveSpace (DRVSPACE.INI) settings, 345–360
DSEA units, error codes, 444–445, 450
DTK BIOS POST codes, 517
dual inline memory modules (DIMMs), 8, 742–743, **742,** 747–758, 1387
dual inline package (DIP), 741
dual simultaneous voice data (DSVD), 849
dual tone multi frequency (DTMF) signals, 847
duty cycles, power supplies, 1100

DVD drives (*see also* CD-ROM), 11, 417–434, **418**
  access time, 419
  audio out, 431
  audio standards, 420–421
  Books A through E, standards, 420
  care of discs, 422–424
  CD-R/Photo CD problems, 433
  CD-ROM compatibility, 421
  data formats, 420
  data transfer rates, 419–420
  decoder board connections, 428–429, **429**
  Device Bay, 981
  Dolby, 420, 428
  drive mechanics, 424–426, 424–**426, 427**
  DVD–ROM, 418–419
  DVD–Video, 418–419
  indicator light flashing, 432
  installation problems, 430–433
  laser safety, 430
  media, 421–424, **422, 423**
  motors, 425, **426**
  MPEG compression, 420–421, 426, 428–429
  playback errors, 432
  region code control, 426, 427
  specifications/standards, 419–421
  stuck tray, 431
  troubleshooting, 429–433
  universal disk format (UDF), 420
  video quality problems, 431–433
  video standards, 420–421
Dvorak keyboards, 662–663
dynamic convergence, 33
dynamic decode, 241
dynamic execution, 292
dynamic RAM (DRAM), 228, 229, 738, 774

E

8086/8088 CPUs, 292, 298
8514/A adapter (PS/2), 1252–1253
ECC on SIMM (EOS), 781
EDIT, 68
eight-to-fourteen modulation (EFM), 141, 142–143, **143,** 152
El Torito standard, 9, 147
electrodes, battery, 95
electrolytes, battery, 95
electromagnetic interference (EMI), 1101
electronic control unit (ECU), 673–674
Electronics Industries Association (EIA), 1005
electrophotographic (EP) printers (*see* laser/LED printers)
electrostatic discharge (ESD), 2–4, 1010
EMM386, 68, 798, 799, 800–801, 808, 817–823
emulation adapters, error codes, 449
enablers, PC card, 1008–1009, 1027
enclosures, 19–20, 25, 27, 30–31
encoding/decoding, 872
enhanced capabilities port (ECP), 996, 998–999

enhanced DRAM (EDRAM), 775
enhanced graphics adapter (EGA), 12–13, 1250–1251
enhanced IDE (EIDE), 399–407, 592–594, 961
  528 Mb limit, 400–401
  BIOS settings, 401, 406–407
  CD-ROM, 153, 405
  CMOS settings, 406
  conflicts, 404
  cylinder head sector (CHS) addressing, 400
  data transfer rates, 402–403
  device/drive support, 401–402
  file allocation tables (FAT), 401
  installation, 403–406
  IORDY signal, 403–404, 407
  jumpers, 405, 406–407
  logical block addressing (LBA), 401, 405
  mixing IDE EIDE drives, 405
  translation modes, 216–217
  Ultra ATA compatiblity, 408
enhanced ISA (EISA), SCSI devices, 1168
enhanced parallel port (EPP), 996, 999
enhanced small device interface (ESDI), 389–394
Ensoniq sound boards, 1209
environment test failure, 333
error correction (EC) symbols, CD-ROM, 142
error correction code (ECC), 743, 781
error codes/messages, 435–560, 1164
  BIOS, 128–135, 136
  CD-R drives, 174
  CD-ROM, 161–162
  CMOS, 86
  DOS, 1398–1403
  interrupt errors, 115
  PCI error messages, 136–137
  setting, CMOS, 218
errors/bugs in software, 264
ETEQ Microsystems chipsets, 201
Eurosoft/Mylex BIOS POST codes, 518–520
executable files, viral infection, 1327–1328
execution, superscalar vs. dynamic, 292
expanded memory, 770, 797
expansion boards, 11–19, 22, 642
  controllers, drive controllers, 13
  decoder boards, MPEG, 16, **17,** 18
  drive adapters, 13–14, 382–416, **383**
  joystick adapters, 18–19, **18**
  modems, 14–16
  ports, 14–16
  SCSI adapters, 14, **15**
  sound boards, 16, **17**
  testing, 1386–1387
  video boards, 12–13, **12**
expansion busses (*see also* extended ISA; industry standard architecture), 633–634, 1005, 1260–1261
expansion slots, 4–5, 6–7, 9, 938
extended data output (EDO RAM), 738, 775–776

extended ISA (EISA) busses, 253–254,
633–642
16-, 32-bit bus pinout, 640–641
configuration, 641
diagram of 32–bit EISA slot, **639**
extended memory (XMS), 760, 769–770, 797,
798
extended system configuration (ESCD), 957
external commands, 59–62
EZ Drive, 404, 961, 965–969

F

486TST.ZIP, 72
fake memory (*see also* parity), 780–781
fans/cooling (*see also* heatsinks), 6, 21, 22,
558–560, 945
cleaning, 1381, 1386
fan runs/no system activity, 84
loose fan, 328
overclocking CPUs, 319, 324–325
testing, 1386
Faraday A–Tease BIOS POST codes, 520–521
Faraday chipsets, 201
Fast ATA drives, 593
fast decode enable, 225
fast page mode (FPM) memory, 738, 775
fault codes (*see also* error codes; IBM diagnos-
tic/error codes), 436
fax modem (*see* modems/fax cards)
FDISK, 68, 626
feedback loops, power supplies, 1099
file allocation table (FAT), 340, 374–375, 401,
567, 572, 606–607, 608–611, 631
file comparison (*see also* viruses/antivirals),
1336
file transfer protocols, modems, 878–879
FILES setting, 803
files, viral infection, 1328
finalization, CD-ROM, 148
firmware, 45
fixation, CD-ROM, 148
flash memory, 125, 738, 942
floating point math (*see* math co processor;
numerical processing unit (NPU)
floating point unit (FPU), 947–948
floppy disk drives (FDD), 9, 561–580, **562,**
1349–1360
access problems, 578
activity LED light, 580
alignment, 1349–1360
allocation units, 567
azimuth alignment, 1357
clamping/eccentricity test, 1354, **1355**
cleaning, 1353–1354, 1383–1384
CMOS setup, 217, 219
combo drive problems, 580
controllers, 572
cyclical redundancy check (CRC), 567
damage to disks, 567
data disk organization, 565–567

dead unit, 574–575
density of disks, 578, 579
drive designation letter, 217, 572–573,
579–580
drives not detected, 245
electronic components, 570–572, **571**
error codes, 439–440, 456, 463
exploded view, **568**
file allocation table (FAT), 567, 572
floppy drive cards, 1017
formatting disks, 579, 1354
head step, 1357–1358
head width test, 1359–1360, **1359**
hysteresis, 1358–1359, **1359**
insulation displacement connector (IDC)
cable, 572
jumper settings, 580
logic/interface board, 569, **570**
magnetic media, 562–567
maintenance, 1351
mechanical components, 568–570, **568, 569**
modified frequency modulation (MFM), 564
motherboard connection, 944
motors, 569–570, **570**
mounting, 1388
phantom directory problems, 579
physical interface, 572–574, **571**
pin outs for interface, **573**
QEMM problems, 816
radial alignment, 1356–1357, **1357**
read/write heads, 563, 565, 573, 577–578
recording principles, 565–567, **575**
refresh, 563
repair vs. replacement, 574, 1351
seek problems, 219, 575–576
speed of operation, 572
spindle speed test, 1355
stuck drive, 576–577
swapping drives, 579–580
tape drives:, 1241
testing, 574, 1349–1360
Track 00 signal, 573–574, 1355–1356
tracks, cylinders, sectors, clusters, 566–567
troubleshooting, 574–580
upgrading, 579
Write protect, 573–574, 577–578
flux changes per inch (FCI or KFCI), 585
flux reversal, 564
flyback transformer (FBT), 35, 913,
1113–1116
focus grid, 32
fogging effects, 1265
forced perfect termination (FPT), SCSI, 1146
form factors/standards, 22–27, 935
FORMAT, 68
formatting hard disks, 387–389
ragmentation (*see* defragmentation)
frame buffers, 1245–1246, **1246**
frame rate, video capture, 1294
frames, CD-ROM, 142

free space available, 361, 362
freezes (*see* lockups)
frequency, 872
frequency modulation, 872
frequency response, 1192–1193, **1193**
frequency shift keying (FSK), 872
fuses, 84

G

gain, 1192, 1194
game ports
game ports (*see* joysticks/game ports), 18–19, **18,** 18
general protection faults (GPF), 1281
gestures glyphs, pen systems, 1057–1058
gigabytes, 591
glyphs, pen systems, 1057–1058
Gouraud shading, 1265
graphical user interface (GUI), 46
graphics (*see* monitors/video)
graphics accelerators (*see* monitors/video)
graphics device interface (GDI), 1267–1268
Green Book standard, CD-ROM, 145
green PCs (*see also* power management), 242–243
grounds, enclosure as ground, 2–4
group special mobile (GSM) 6.10, 1200

H

handshaking, 1145
hard disk drives (HDD), 10, 581–632, **582, 583**
  32-bit access, 630
  528 Mb limit, 414, 612–614
  access time, 624
  accidental format/deletion, 619
  addressing, 396–397, 412
  air flow, 583–585, **584**
  allocation of space, 340
  application specific IC (ASIC), 603–604
  AT attachment (ATA) interface, 394, 592–594
  AT attachment packet interface (ATAPI), 394, 399, 413, 593, 597
  ATA 3 drives, 593
  ATA 4 drives, 594
  auto park feature, 216
  backups, 404
  bad sectors, 629
  Bernoulli drives, 369, 1129–1135
  BIOS error messages, 130–131, 134–135
  BIOS settings, 399, 406–407, 413, 613–614, 630
  bits per inch (BPI), 583, 585
  block diagram, **604**
  block transfer mode, 593, 595
  boot disks, 1388
  boot problems, 410, 613, 618–619, 627–628
  bus mastering, 594, 595–597
  cabling, IDE/EIDE, 397, **398**

caching, 597–598, **599**
capacity (in bytes), 591, 611–614
CD-R drives
CD-ROM
clusters, 340, 606, 1389
CMOS settings, 216–217, 406
code 10 error, 414–415
coercivity, 583
command interpreter errors, 623
compression (*see* disk compression)
conflicts, 404
constant angular velocity (CAV), 590
contaminants on disc, 584–585, **586**
controllers, 394, 409, 603–604, 626–627
crashes/fatal errors, 411, 583, 622, 628
cyclic redundancy check (CRC), 407, 587
cylinder head sector (CHS) addressing, 400
cylinder wrapping, 613
cylinders, 216, 612
data transfer rates, 402–403, 594–595
dead unit, 618
defragmentation, 344, 363, 364–366, 368, 375–376, 1389
density of recording, 583, 585
Device Bay, 981
direct memory access (DMA), 395–396, 415, 594, 595–597
directory problems, 619–620
Disk Manager, 961–965
Ditto drive (Iomega), 1125–1129
DOS compatibility problems, 616–617, 628–629, 631
drive adapters, 382–416, **383**
drive letter designation, 629–630
drive not recognized errors, 245, 410–411, 413, 620–621, 628, 955–956
Drive Rocket, 961, 969–970
drive translation, 394, 590–591, 613
electronic components, 603–604
enhanced IDE (EIDE), 399–407, 592–594, 961
enhanced small device interface (ESDI), 389–394
error codes, 463, 445–446, 459–460, 615–616, 622–623
exploded view, **600**
EZ–Drive, 961, 965–969
Fast ATA drives, 593
FDISK, 626
file allocation table (FAT), 340, 374–375, 401, 606– 611, 631
file defects, 344
flux changes per inch (FCI or KFCI), 585
form factors, 601
format errors, 411, 623, 627
frame, 598
free space available, 344, 361, 362
hard–drive cards, 1017
HDD controller error codes, 615–616
head actuators, 602

head flight, 583–585
heads, 216
high level formatting, 388–389, 393, 606, 627
IDE drives, 592–594, 942, 951, 954
index pulse, 587
indicator light always on, 620
installation, EIDE, 403–406
insulation–displacement connector (IDC), 395, 396
integrated drive electronics (IDE) interface, 394–399
interface rates, 594
interleave, 589–590
intermittent operation, 621
interrupts, 396–397, 412, 595
jumpers, 405, 406–407
landing zone (LZ), 216, 589
latency, 585–586
lock ups, 409, 410, 415–516, 613, 631
logical block addressing (LBA), 401, 409, 593, 612
logical drives, 614
low level format, 387, 392–394, 398–399, 605, 625–626
master boot record/sector (MBR/MBS), 606
master/slave drives, 134–135, 413, 595–597
mechanical components, 598–603
media, 582
mixing IDE EIDE drives, 405
motherboard, 953–954
mounting, 1388
mouse problems, 415
Norton Anti Virus problems, 415
Novell compatiblity, 411
overlay software, 961–971
paddle board controller, 394
parameters, 216, 590–591
partitioning, 388–389, 393, 605–612, 626, 627, 630
physical defects, 343–344
platters, 582–583, 586–588, **586, 587,** 598–599
port failures, 412
POST codes, 630
power modes, 592
primary (master) drives, 216
programmable I/O (PIO), 594, 595–597
Promise drive adapters, 415
RAMDrive, 369–370
random data errors, 623
read/write errors, 416, 619, 623–624
read/write heads, 601–602, **603**
recording density, 585
registry for Windows95, 597
removable, 1116–1140
SCANDISK, 1389
secondary (slave) drives, 216
sector not found error, 621–622
sector sparing (defect management), 588–589

sectors, 340, 629
sectors per track (SPT), 216
seek errors, 623
seek time, 587
servoing the heads, 602
size of drive, 216
slack space, 340
slow performance, 409–410, 620, 624–625, 630
SMART command set, 592
spindle motors, 603
ST506/412, 383–389, **385**
start time, 591–592
SyQuest removable drives, 1135–1140
testing, 1388–1389
thin–film media, 583
thrashing, 628, 1286
Track 00 signal, 624
track density/tracks per inch (TPI), 585
tracks, sectors, cylinders, 340, 586–588, **586, 587**
translation modes, 216–217
troubleshooting, 408–416, 614–631
truncation of cylinders, 613
Type 47 HDD data area, 218
Ultra ATA drives, 407–408, 593–594
virtual memory, 620
viruses, 631
VL drive adapters, 411–412
volume lables, 631
Windows errors, 410, 412
WPcom (compensated cylinders) setting, 216
write precompensation (WP), 590
Y adapters, 630
Zip drive (Iomega), 1117–1125
zoned recording, 395, 588
hard–drive cards, 1017
hardware conflicts, 44–45, 264, 280
harmonic distortion, total (THD), 1193–1194
Hayes compatibility, 849, 862, 898
head flight, 583–585
heatsinks (see also fans/cooling), 22
helical scan tapes, 1216–1218, **1217**
high level formatting, 388–389, 393, 606, 627
high memory area (HMA), 219–220, 798, 806–808
High Sierra standard, CD-ROM, 144
high voltage power supplies, 1110–1115, **1114**
HIMEM.SYS, 68, 769, 795, 798, 799, 800–801, 817–823
horizontal drive circuits, 34–35
horizontal scan/sync, 904–906
host adapters for SCSI devices, 1152–1160, **1153,** 1164
host drives, disk compression, 341
hot swapping, 1011

I
I/O, 235, 240, 932, 940–941, 942, 944
  addressing, 396–397
  area assignments, 255–260

I/O, *continued*
  BIOS error messages, 131, 136
  CMOS setup, 225–226, 235
  COM/serial port addresses, 1175–1176,
    1181–1183
  conflicts after upgrade, 88
  device/port assignments, typical, 261–262
  DIP switch settings, 255–260
  DirectInput, 1269
  error codes, 446
  Intelligent I/O (I2O), 116, 983–984
  jumper settings, 255–260
  POST codes, 557
  recovery time, 224, 225, 240
  video, 1300–1301
  wait states, 224
IBM diagnostic/error codes, 436–462, 466,
    522–526
IBM Microelectronics (*see* chipsets; CPU)
identifying problems, 71
image files, bootable CD-ROMs, 156, 157–158
incremental write mode, CD-ROM, 149
Indeo video codec (Intel), 1293–1294
independence of devices, 1142
index pulse, 587
industry standard architecture (ISA) busses,
    633–642, **634**
  AT 16–bit signals/pinouts, 636–638
  diagram of 8- and 16-bit ISA slots, **634**
  mixing 8- and 16-bit ISA boards, 638–639
  plug-and-play devices, 1088–1089
  XT 8–bit signals/pinouts, 635–636, **635**
Infrared Data Association (IrDA), 985–986,
    1178–1181, 1184–1185
initialization (*see* boot process),
initiators, SCSI, 1144–1145
input devices/device drivers, BIOS error mes-
    sages, 137
Instant On, 984–985
instruction pipelining (*see* pipelining)
insulation-displacement connector (IDC), 395,
    396, 572
integrated drive electronics (IDE) interface,
    13–14, 231, 394–399, 592–594, 942, 951,
    954
  528 Mb limit, 400–401
  AT Attachment interface (ATA), 394
  AT attachment packet interface (ATAPI),
    394, 399
  BIOS settings, 137, 399
  cabling, 397, **398**
  CD-ROM, 153
  CMOS setup, 226, 231
  controllers, paddle board, 394
  cylinder head sector (CHS) addressing, 400
  direct memory access (DMA), 395–396
  drive translation, 394
  error codes, 459–460
  insulation–displacement connector (IDC),
    395, 396

  interrupts/addressing, 396–397
  jumpers, 406–407
  low level formatting, Disk Manager, 398–399
  mixing IDE EIDE drives, 405
  translation modes, 216–217
  Ultra ATA compatiblity, 408
  zoned recording, 395
  PCI IDE setup, 230–231
Integrated Technology chipsets, 201
Intel chipsets, 185–191, 201–202
intelligent BIOS, 405
intelligent I/O (I2O), 116, 983–984
interactive multimedia association (IMA)
    ADPCM, 1200
intercast broadcasts, 1299–1300, 1310–1311
interlace, 906–907, **907,** 1284–1285
interleave memory, 777
interleave mode, 228, 589–590
intermodulation distortion (IMD), 1194
internal commands, 59
International Standards Organization (ISO),
    1005
interrupts (IRQ), 64, 113–115, 229, 230, 238,
    252–254, 396–397, 412, 932, 948–949
  BIOS error messages, 135, 136
  CD-R drives, 170
  Centronics ports, 993
  CMOS setup, 224, 229, 230, 238
  COM/serial ports, 1175–1176, 1181–1183
  conflicts, 404
  device/port assignments, typical, 261–262
  error messages, 115
  extended ISA (EISA) busses, 253
  Intelligent I/O (I2O), 983–984
  micro channel architecture (MCA) bus, 253
  modems, 1175–1176, 1181–1183
  PC cards, 1027
  plug-and-play devices, 1088
  printers, 993, 1202
  processor interrupts, 115
  sound boards & cards/audio systems:, 1201
  stacks, 252
  video, 1300–1301
invalid system configuration data error,
    247–248
IO.SYS files, 55–57, 66
Iomega (*see* Bernoulli drives; Ditto drives; Zip
    drive)
IORDY signal, 403–404, 407
ISO 10149, 1989 standard, CD-ROM, 145
ISO 9660 standard, CD-ROM, 145
isolating problem areas, 71
ITU (CCITT) modem signal standards,
    874–876

J

Japan Electronics Industry Development As-
    soc. (JEIDA), 1005
jitter, in monitors, 907

JMark, 78
Joint Electron Device Engineering Council
    (JEDEC), 1005
joysticks/game ports, 643–656, **644**
    adapter, 18–19, **18**
    calibration, 647–648
    cleaning, 649
    digital (game pad) joysticks, 647, 648
    drift or rolling, 648
    eliminator plug, 650, **650**
    error codes, 443
    IDC ribbon cable connectors, 651
    internal components, 644–646, **646**
    MIDI devices, 651, 652, 1202
    second joystick adapter, 646
    sound cards, 651
    symptoms/solutions, 652–655
    troubleshooting, 650–655
    Windows 95/98 use, 649–650
    Y adapters, 651, 652
jumpers, 405, 944, 946–947, 950, 955

K
Kermit, 879
key codes, 660–661
keyboard settings, 241
keyboards (*see also* pen input systems; touch-
        pads), 657–672, **658**
    BIOS error messages, 131–132
    cleaning/maintenance, 663–666, 1382
    CMOS setup, 217, 222, 241
    conflicts, 671
    dead/erratic keyboard, 668–669
    Dvorak keyboards, 662–663
    error codes, 438, 463, 669, 671
    function keys, 670–671
    initialization errors, 667
    interfaces/controllers (KBC), 660, **662**
    key codes/scan codes, 660–661
    macro/programmable keys, 669–670
    make/break connections, 658, 660–661
    matrix of keys, 659, **660**
    mechanical switch assembly, 657–658, **667**
    membrane switch assembly, 659, **659**
    motherboard connection, 944, 949, 952
    NumLock, 218, 672
    sounds to keystrokes, 671
    stuck cursor, 670
    troubleshooting, 667–673
    typematic rate, 217
    Windows specific keys, 670–671
    wireless keyboards, 670
Kodak Photo CDs, 144

L
LAN cards, 1017
landing zone (LZ), 216, 589
Landmark BIOS POST codes, 526–530
lands, CD-ROM media, 139, 140, 421, **422**
laptop computers (*see* portable PCs),

laser/LED printers, 673–727
    alignment or focus of laser, 681–682
    black image, 701
    black lines on page, 704–705, 712, 716, 719
    blacked out image, 711, 713, 717
    broken jigsaw puzzle image, 700
    cartridge, EP cartridge, 683–684, **683,** 724
    charging drum, 676, **677**
    charging process, 717–721
    checksum errors, 686
    cleaning/maintenance, 675–676, **675, 676**
    controller (logic) symptoms, 686, 696–697,
        696
    corona, 676, 717–721
    CPU errors, 686
    cross section view, **674**
    dead printer, 726
    developing mechanism, 677–678, **677**
    dots per inch (DPI), 677
    drive/transmission system, 708–710, **709**
    drum cartridge replacement, 683–684
    electronic control unit (ECU), 673–674
    error codes, 687–695
    fan errors, 725
    fusing process, 679–680, **680,** 713–717, **714**
    fuzzy image, 712
    gaps in print, 708–709
    garbage/symbols in image, 698
    ghosting in image, 725–726
    graping in image, 711–712
    half of image missing, 716–717
    high temperature errors, 713–714
    high voltage power supply (HVPS), 710–713
    I/O errors, 697–698
    image formation system (IFS), 674
    jeweled image, 707
    laser assembly, 680–682, **682,** 703–708, **704**
    LEDs, 682
    manufacturers listing, web sites, 685–686
    memory/RAM error, 696–697
    opening the printer, 723–724
    overlapped print, 708–709
    overrun error, 697
    paper feed, 721–723, **722, 729**
    polygon motor errors, 705
    processes involved in printing, 674–675
    rasterized image, 700–701
    registration problems/symptoms, 701–703,
        702
    resolution, 677
    right hand text distorted, 704
    sample image problems, **699, 702, 705, 709,**
        711, 715, 718, 726
    scalloping, 720
    scanner assembly, 703–708, **704**
    shock/burn hazards, 684
    size wrong, 701
    skewed image, 703
    smudged/blurred image, 701–703, 707–708,
        715–716, 726

laser/LED printers, *continued*
splotches, 711, 720–721
squashed image, 710
static–charge eliminator, 679
stitching in image, 698, **699, 700**
tic marks on page, 720
toner developer, 677–678, 724–725, **725**
top margin too big/too small, 702, 703
trace/scan line, 680
transfer process/mechanism, 678–679, **679**
troubleshooting, 684–727
warm up mode stuck, 721
washed out/faded image, 707, 712, 717–719
waves in image, 706–707, 710
white bands on page, 706, 708, 719–720, **721**
writing mechanism, 677, 680–682, **681**
wrong position on page, 700
lasers, 430, 680–682, **682**
last in first out (LIFO) conflict resolution, 263
LASTDRIVE setting, 803
latency, 232, 585–586
legacy devices, 1080, 1085
light emitting diode (LED), 682
lighting, 1263
line in line out systems, 940
lithium backup batteries, 97–102, **98**
lithium ion (Li ion) batteries, 105
LOADHIGH setting, 805, 808
logic, 385, 564
logic bombs, 1320
logical block addressing (LBA), 401, 405, 409,
    593, 612
loop through, 1286
lossless compression, 428
Lotus Intel Microsoft (LIM or EMS)
    specification, 770
low level format, 387–388, 392–393, 398–399,
    605, 625–626

M
macro viruses, 1329–1330, 1338–1340
magnetic storage, 562–567
allocation units, 567
binary data, 563–564
coercivity, 563, 583
density of recording, 583, 585
disk organization, 565–567
flux reversal, 564
logic 1/logic 0 in binary data, 564
modified frequency modulation (MFM), 564
oxide layer of magnetic media, 562
problems with media, 567
random access media, 566
refresh, 563
retentitivity, 563
tape, 563
thin–film media, 583
tracks, cylinders, sectors, clusters, 566–567
magneto–optical (MO) drives, 145
main board (*see* motherboards)

maintenance, preventive, 1377–1390
make/break connections, 658, 660–661
management extension hardware, 945
mapping memory, 1338
mask, shadow mask, 903–904, 1371–1372
master boot record/sector (MBR/MBS), 606
master/slave drives, 134–135, 413, 595–597
mastering, bus, 594, 595–597, 1262
math co processors, 6, 281
162 error, IBM PS/2 50,60, 70, 337
arithmetic test failure, 333
error codes, 440
CHKCOP fails divide test, 334
CHKCOP Has Found locks up, 334
CHKCOP slow, 334
Configuration Error message, 337
failure to boot after install, 335–336
OS2 1107 error, 336
system diagnostics, 335
test, CMOS setup, 218–219
troubleshooting, 333–336
Weitek not installed message, 336
matrix of keys, keyboard, 659, **660**
MCA bus (*see* micro channel architecture)
mechanical switch assembly, 657–658, **667**
MEM, 68, 805, 806
membrane switch assembly, 659, **659**
memory and memory managers, 22, 230, 233,
    234, 239, 738–826, 932, 954, 956
386MAX, 798, 823–826
access time, 771–772
add on memory, 741
addressing, 288, 738–739, **738, 739**
assigning memory, 255, 260
asynchronous static RAM (ASRAM), 774–775
AT memory troubleshooting, 790
attribute memory, 1011–1012
AUTOEXEC.BAT, 799, 804–805
back-to-back, 235, 238
backfilling, 798
backup batteries for, 97–102
banks of memory, 782–784
BIOS error messages, 129, 133–134, 136
BIOS ROM, 6, 9, 45, 116
boot problems, 793
BUFFERS setting, 803
burst extended data output (BEDO RAM),
    776
burst length, 232
burst mode, 237, 238, 239, 240, 241, 242
cache memory, 8, 147, 162, 215, 219, 226–227,
    232, 738, 777–778, **778**, 795, 950, 952
cached DRAM (CDRAM), 776
checksum errors, 793–794
CMOS, 97, 208–213, 217–218, 230, 233, 234,
    239
compatibility problems, 795
complementary metal–oxide semiconductor
    (*see* CMOS)
compression (*see* disk compression)

compression memory check, 344
CONFIG.SYS, 799–800, 805
conflicts after upgrade, 88
conventional memory, 759–760, **760,** 798–808
corrosion on contacts, 788
DEVICEHIGH setting, 804, 805, 807–808
diagnostic/error codes, 462
direct memory access (DMA), 64, 130, 226, 254–255, 395–396, 415, 949
dirty bit RAM, 227
DOS extenders, 769–770
DOS location, 803–804
DOS protected mode interface (DPMI), 770
DOSMAX, 823–835
dual inline memory module (DIMM), 8, 742–743, **742,** 747–758, 1387
dual inline package (DIP), 741
dynamic RAM (DRAM), 8, 228, 229, 774
ECC on SIMM (EOS), 781
EDO RAM, 8
EMM386, 798, 799, 800–801, 808, 817–823
enhanced DRAM (EDRAM), 775
error codes, 437–438, 457, 461, 789–795, 808–817
error correction code (ECC), 743, 781
expanded memory, 770, 797
extended data output (EDO RAM), 738, 775–776
extended memory (XMS), 760, 769–770, 797, 798
fake memory, 780–781
fast page mode (FPM) memory, 738, 775
fault addresses error, 794–795
FILES setting, 803
flash memory, 125, 738, 942
high memory, 771
high memory area (HMA), 219–220, 798, 806–808
HIMEM.SYS, 769, 795, 798, 799, 800–801, 817–823
I/O area assignments, 255–260
installing memory, 781–784
interleave memory, 777
LASTDRIVE setting, 803
LOADHIGH setting, 805, 808
Lotus Intel Microsoft (LIM or EMS) specification, 770
low memory errors, 795
managers (*see* memory managers), 797–826
mapping memory, 1338
megabyte sizes, 743, 758
MEM function, 805, 806
modem use, 846, 847, 862, 897
motherboards, 958
new memory doesn't work, 793
NiCad batteries in portable PCs, problems, 103
overclocking CPUs, 319, 332
overlay software, 961–971
packages, 741–759

pages, 775, 777
parity, 218, 743, 775, 777, 779–781, 788–789, 954
PC card problems, 1020–1023, 1024–1025, 1027, 1029
pipelined burst static RAM (PB SRAM), 775
pipelining, 235, 241, 952
presence detect (PD), 773
protected mode, 288, 770
protection errors, 795
QEMM, 798, 808–817
RAM, 6, 8
RAMBUS, 738, 776–777
RAMDAC, 1255, 1259–1260
RDRAM, 8
real mode or base memory, 760, 761–769
recycling old memory devices, 785–786
refresh memory, 222–223, 773–774
remapping, 225
ROM, 6, 45
SDRAM, 8, 9
shadow memory, 125, 215, 220–221, 233, 778, 798
SIMCHECK equipment, 786–788, **787**
single inline memory module (SIMM), 8, 88, 742–743, **742,** 744–747, 759, 785–788, 942, 950, 952, 956, 1387
single inline package (SIP), 741
small outline J leads memory package, 741
snoop/snoop filters, 234–235, 240, 241
sorting, memory sorting, 798
speed of memory, 771–772, 785
stacks, 252
static RAM (SRAM), 738, 774
streaming, 240
synchronous burst static RAM (SBSRAM), 775
synchronous DRAM (SDRAM), 738, 776
terminate stay resident (TSR) programs, 807
test tick, 218
testing, 786–788, 1387
thin small outline package (TSOP), 741
troubleshooting, 786–795
Type 47 HDD data area, 218
upgrading, 8
upper memory area (UMA), 112, 153, 235, 770, 798, 803, 805, 806–808
video memory (VRAM), 738, 775
video problems, 1286, 1287
video RAM (VRAM), 738, 775, 825–826, 1246–1247, 1285
video ROM (VROM), 220, 814
viral infection, 1329–1330
virtual control program interface (VCPI), 770
virtual memory, 620
wait states, 8, 215, 224, 225, 227–228, 771–772
Windows 95/98 memory, 806, 815–816
Windows RAM (WRAM), 777
XT memory troubleshooting, 789–790
memory cards, 1016

Memphis (*see* Windows 95/98)

micro channel architecture (MCA) bus, 253, 728–737, **730**

Microcom Networking Protocol (MNP) standard, 876–878

Microid Research BIOS, 117–118, 530–535

microphones (*see also* sound boards & cards), 1194–1196, 1206, 1208–1209

microprocessors (*see* chipsets; CPU)

Microsoft, 44

MIDI (*see also* sound boards & cards), 457, 651, 652, 1190–1191, **1190,** 1201, 1202

MIPS Orion (*see* chipsets; CPU)

mixers, 1191–1192

modems/fax cards (*see also* COM/serial ports), 14–16, 845–899, 1017

 asynchronous communication, 1171–1174

 auto detection/switching, 849

 automatic timeout/watchdog, 884

 baud rate, 1173–1174

 bit/baud rate, 872

 bits per second (bps), 1173–1174

 cabling, 880

 call waiting, 884

 caller ID, 849, 892–893

 COM (COM/serial port) connection, 846, 847–848, 897, 898, 1170–1185

 command processor, 880–882

 command set, 849–862, 869

 computer, 884

 connect sequences for V.22bis/V.32, 869, 870–871

 connection problems, 888–889, 896, 897–898

 cyclic redundancy check (CRC), 879, 890, 1172

 data carrier equipment (DCE), 1176–1177

 data frames, 1171–1172, **1172**

 data terminal equipment (DTE), 1176–1177

 dead unit, 887

 distinctive ring, 849, 891–892

 dual simultaneous voice data (DSVD), 849

 dual tone multi frequency (DTMF) signals, 847

 duplexing, 885

 error codes, 455, 458–459

 escape sequence, 868

 external modems, 847–848, **848**

 fax transmission, 890, 896

 file transfer protocols, 878–879

 garbage, 886–888

 hardware problems, 879

 Hayes compatibility, 849, 862, 898

 Infrared Data Association (IrDA), 985–986, 1178–1181, 1184–1185

 initialization (init) strings, 862, 885

 intermittent operation, 886

 internal modems, 846–847, **847**

 interrupts, 1175–1176, 1181–1183

 Kermit, 879

 lock up, 884, 891, 898

 memory use, nonvolatile RAM (NVRAM), 846, 847, 862, 897

 modem cards, 1017

 modes, 868, 889

 modulation/demodulation, 846, 871–873

 mouse problems, 842, 890

 negotiation, 868–869

 no answer, 887

 noise, 883, 888

 not recognized, 885

 on–screen text wrong, 885–886

 PC card problems, 1030, 1032–1033, 1036

 plug-and-play, 1085–1086

 PnP errors, 894

 power save feature, 889

 power supplies, 880

 result codes, 862, 865–868

 Sealink, 879

 setup parameters (S registers), 846, 862, 865–868, 882, 890

 signal level, 884

 signaling standards, Bell, ITU/CCITT (V), MNP, 873–878

 slow operation, 894–895, 898

 state–checking, 868

 status lights, 871

 sychronous communication, 893–894

 telephone equipment, 879–880, 882

 troubleshooting, 879–889

 universal asynchronous receiver/transmitter (UART), 846–847, 883, 1174–1175, **1175**

 voice mail, 849

 Windows errors, 891, 895–899

 X-, Y-, ZModem, 878–879

 x2 technology, 848

modified frequency modulation (MFM), 564

modulation, 141, 142–143, **143,** 152, 871–873

monitors/video, 12–13, **13,** 29–42, **30, 31,** 900–931, **901,** 954, 1244–1288, 1361–1376

 3D graphics accelerators, 1261–1266

 8514/A adapter (PS/2), 1252–1253

 accelerated graphics port (AGP), 974–978, **976**

 accelerator, video, 1258–1259

 alignment/adjustment, 921, 1361–1376

 alpha blending, 1265

 AMI Multimedia channel, 1271, 1272

 bandwidth, 907

 barrel distortion, 904, **905**

 beam tracing, 915–916

 beep codes, 1278

 BIOS error messages, 130

 BIOS settings, 1285–1286

 bloom, 929

 boot problems, 1281–1282, 1284, 1286

 brightness control, 35, 926

 bus mastering, 1262

 cathode ray tube (CRT), 31–33, **32,** 39–40, **40,** 902, 915–920, **916**

cathode ray tube controller (CRTC), 1246
center balance, 38, 1369
center pincushion (center PCC) adjustment, 38
chipsets, video, 1256–1258
clamp pulse position, 39
cleaning, 1376, 1382
clock speed, 1276
CMOS settings, 217, 1279
color alignment (horizontal static) adjustment, 37
color depth, 1263
color drive, 1375–1376
color graphics adapter (CGA), 12, 1249–1250
color look up tables (CLUT), 1264
color problems, 918, 921–922, 926–928, 1280, 1282
COM4 conflicts, 1277
compressed/expanded image, 925, 928
configuration problems, 1279
connectors, 1270–1274
contrast control, 35
control, screen, focus grids, 32, 919
convergence, 33, 904, 916, 1368, 1369, 1371–1374
corner balance, 38
corner pincushion (corner PCC) adjustment, 38
cursor looks wrong, 1286
curvature (pin balance) adjustment, 37
degaussing, 1375, 1385
digital video cards, 1017
digital video stream (DVS) mode, 1272, 1273
DirectX technology, 1266–1270, 1287–1288
disassembly/assembly tips, 39–41
discharging the CRT, 39–40, **40**
distorted image, 925–926, 927–928, 1284
dithering, 1266
divide by zero errors, 1284
DMA errors, 1281
dot pitch, 902–903
double buffering, 1265–1266
drift, 907
drive board for monitor, 33–34
drivers, video drivers, 1245
dynamic convergence, 33, 1371–1374
enclosure, 30–31
enhanced graphics adapter (EGA), 12–13, 1250–1251
error codes, 438–439, 448–450, 455, 456, 460–461, 463
expanded/shrunken display, 1281
expansion bus architecture, 1260–1261
exploded view, **31**
flickering, intermittent images, 928
flipping, scrolling image, 930
flyback circuit, 913
flyback transformer (FBT), 35
focus grid, 32, 929–930, 1367
fogging effects, 1265
frame buffers, 1245–1246, **1246**

fuzzy picture, 1282, 1285
gamma/cutoff problems, 918–919
garbage display, 1279–1280, 1282, 1283
general protection faults (GPF), 1281
Gouraud shading, 1265
graphics accelerators, 1254–1266
graphics, 1246–1247
half, cut, shrunk screen, 924
hangs or locks up, 1280, 1281, 1286
height, width of image, 1369
high output transistor (HOT), 913
high voltage test/regulation, 1366
horizontal adjustment/control, 36, 37, 1368–1369
horizontal drive circuits, 34–35, 904–906, 912–913
horizontal output transistor (HOT), 928–929
hot operation, 917, 929
interlacing, 906–907, **907**, 1284–1285
jitter, 907
key balance adjustment, 37
lighting, 1263
line across screen, 923–924, 926, 1278
linearity, 1370–1371
loop through, 1286
memory problems, 1285, 1286, 1287
mirror for testing, 1364
missing information in picture, 1282
modes of operation, 1247–1249, 1287
moire level, 37
monochrome display adapter (MDA), 12, 1249
MPEG data port (MDP) mode, 1272–1274, 1285
multicolor graphics array (MCGA), 1251–1252
multimedia peripheral port (MPP) mode, 1272–1274
no display, 1277–1278
no video, normal system activity, 87
not recognized, 1282
on-screen controls, 35–39
overscanning, 1284
palette snoop, 234
palletized textures, 1264
PC board, **1365**
PCI bus, 1260–1261, 1287
phase, 1368–1369
phosphor triads (RGB, etc.), 32
phosphors, 918
pin balance adjustment, 37
pincushion (PCC amp) adjustment, 37
pincushion distortion, 904, **905,** 1367–1368
pixel depth, chart, 13
pixels, 902
polarity, 908
power supplies, 35
professional graphics adapter (PGA), 1251
purity, 32, **33,** 37, 39, 916, 1367, 1374–1375, 1385
radiation from screen, 1366

monitors/video, *continued*
RAMDAC, 1255, 1259–1260
raster, 33, 34–35, 904–906, **911,** 922, 924–925, 1367
reassembly tips, 921
refresh, 1284–1285
rejuvenators for CRT, 920
rendering, 1261–1262
resolution, 13, 902, 1262–1263
retrace, 904
rolling image, 1278–1279
rotation adjustment, 37
screen control, 1366–1367
screen door/stippling effect, 1265
screen grid, 32
SCSI device problems, 1283–1284
shadow or slot masks, 32–33, **33,** 903–904, 916, 1371–1372
shaky image, 930–931
shock hazards, 39–40, **40,** 1363
shorts, 917–918, 919–920
slant or tilt (key balance) adjustment, 37
SLC motherboards, 1276
slow performance, 1283
speed of video, 1258–1261, 1262–1263
split screen, 1280
standard mode operation, 1272
starting point for adjustment, 1364–1365, **1364**
static convergence, 33, 1371–1374
sub–assembly removal/replacement, 40–41
super VGA (SVGA), 13, 1253
swim, 907
synchronization, 908
testers for CRT, 920
testing, 921, 1361–1376
Texas Instruments Graphical Architecture (TIGA), 1254
text, 1246–1247
texture mapping, 1263, 1264–1265
thrashing, 1286
transparency, 1263
trapezoidal (PCC phase) adjustment, 37
triads, color palettes, 902–903, **903**
troubleshooting, 33–34, 915–931, 1274–1288
twist (rotation) adjustment, 37
vertical adjustment/control, 35–37, 38, 904–906, 912, 1369
vertical drive circuits, 34–35
video BIOS/video ROM, 1247, 1259
video drive circuits (RGB), 908–909, **909, 910**
video graphics array (VGA), 13, 1252
video RAM, 1246–1247, 1259
video signal, 908
VL bus, 1260, 1276–1277, 1342–1348
warranties, 1362–1363
Windows 95/98 problems, 1287–1288
wiring diagrams, **914**

XGA XGA/2, 1253–1254
z-buffering, 1264
Zoomed Video (ZV), 1010
monochrome display adapter (MDA), 12, 1249
motherboards, 6–9, **7,** 932–960, **934, 936, 937, 938**
accelerators, 941
active, passive, modular, 932–933
advanced power control (APC), 945
advanced power management (APM), 951
AT Attachment interface (ATA), 394
AT form factor, 935
ATX form factor, 22–24, **23,** 935, **937**
battery, 942
benchmarking, 958
BIOS, 6, 9, 948, 949–950, 957, 958, 959
bus mastering, 959
cache, 6, 8, 950, 952
CD-ROM drives, 939, 951, 952
checksum errors, 948
chipsets, 8–9, 938, 952, 956
clock/timing circuits, 6, 944
CMOS, 949, 957
COM/serial ports, 6
compatibility problems, 950–954, 956–958
connections, **939,** 946, 947
core logic, 181
CPU, 6, 7–8, 947, 951, 958, 959, 963–964
crashes/locks up, 954, 955, 957–958
data bus Xccelerator (DBX), 941
diagnostic/error codes, 462
DIP switch settings, 946–947
direct memory access (DMA), 64, 949
error codes, 436–437
expansion slots, 6–7, 9
extended system configuration (ESCD), 957
fans/cooling, 945
flash memory, 942
floating point unit (FPU), 947–948
floppy disk drive, 944
foreign objects, 946
form factors, 935
front panel connections, 942, **943**
grounding, 947
hard disk drives, 953–954, 955–956
I/O, 940–942, 944
IDE drives, 942, 951, 954
intermittent problems, 947
interrupts (IRQ), 64, 948–949
jumperless motherboard, 950
jumpers, 944, 946–947, 950, 955
keyboard connections, 944, 949, 952
management extension hardware, 945
math co processor, 6
MEMMAKER problems, 951
memory, 8, 954, 956, 958, 959
monitors, video adapters, 958, 1276
mounting, 21
NLX form factor, 25–27, **25,** 935, **937**

overclocking CPUs, 318–319
parallel ports, 6
parity errors, 954
password access, 958–959
PCI bridge memory controller (PMC),
    941–942
PCI connectors, 945
pipelined memory, 952
ports, 944, 958
POST test, 947–949, 951
power supplies, 942, 946
printer ports, 958
RAM, 6, 949
refresh, 948
repair vs. replace, 945–946
SCSI, 956
single inline memory module (SIMM), 942,
    950, 952, 956
Slot–1 connectors, 941
slots, 938
Socket 7–, Socket 8–, or Slot 1–, 934
socket mounted ICs, 946
sockets, CPU, 289–291, **291**
sound cards/audio systems, 938, 940, 954
speakers, 942
static device errors, 959
telephone support, 939–940
troubleshooting, 945–959
upgrading, 957, 958
video, 954, 958
VL bus, 1342–1348
wavetable cards, 940, 945
Windows problems, 952, 955, 957
mouse (*see also* pen input systems; touch-
    pads), 827–831, **843**
cleaning, 832–833, 1382–1383
clicking/doubleclicking, 828–829, 841
cursor position, 828, 839, 843–844
dead unit, 843
drivers, 835–836, 839–840
erratic performance, 838–839, 840–851
error codes, 840
general protection faults, 840
hard drive compatibility, 415
interfaces, 834
mechanical construction, 829–830, **829**
modem problems, 842, 890
motherboard connection, 944
options for pointer, 841–842
PC card problems, 1026
plug-and-play devices, 1090, 1092
port settings, 835
PS/2 mouse, 835, 841
right button features, 842
sensors, 830–831, **831**
serial vs. bus mouse, 834
troubleshooting, 834–844
Windows 95, 836–383, 842
MPC (*see* multimedia PC)

MPEG compression, 420–421, 426, 428–429,
    1314–1317
MPEG data port (MDP) mode, 1272–1274,
    1285
MPEG decoder boards, 16, **17,** 18
MS DOS 6.2, 48–49, 67–69
MS DOS 7.x, 57–59
MS DOS, 55–63
MSCDEX.EXE, 154, 155
MSDOS.SYS files, 56–57, 66
multi spin CD-ROM, 145–146
multicolor graphics array (MCGA), 1251–1252
multimedia extension (MMX) processors,
    Pentium, 311
multimedia mode, 234
multimedia PC (MPC), 146–147, 311,
    1393–1394
multimedia peripheral port (MPP) mode,
    1272–1274
multipartite viral infection, 1329
multipliers, overclocking CPUs, 321
multisession capability, CD-ROM, 148
musical instrument digital interface (*see* MIDI)
Mylex BIOS, 467, 518–520

N
NCR BIOS POST codes, 535–538
NetBench, 78
network adapters, 449–450, 461
network operating systems (NOS), 983–984
networks
    Infrared Data Association (IrDA), 985–986,
        1178–1181, 1184–1185
    LAN cards, 1017
    optical networks, 985–986, 1178–1181,
        1184–1185
    PC cards, 1027–1028, 1036–1037, 1039
    peripheral component interconnect (PCI),
        1049–1054, **1050**
    wireless networks, 985–986, 1178–1181,
        1184–1185
newsgroups, PC related, 1404–1405
nibble mode, 998
nickel cadmium (NiCad) batteries, 96,
    102–104, **103**
nickel metal hydride (NiMH) batteries, 96, 104
NLX form factor motherboards, 25–27, 935,
    937
non–system disk error, BIOS, 133
Northbridge controller (AMD 640 chipset),
    184
Norton Anti Virus, 415
notebook computers (*see* portable PCs)
Novell compatibility issues, 411
NTSC standards, 1297
numerical processing unit (NPU), 281
NumLock setting, CMOS, 218
NVRAM errors, BIOS, 136

Nyquist Sampling Theorem, 1189

O

offset, 1145
Olivetti BIOS POST codes, 538–542
on-the-fly compression, 341
open architectures, 251, 633
operating systems, 43–68, 611
  adjusting MS DOS for upgrades, 57–59
  advanced power management (APM), 979–980
  AUTOEXEC.BAT files, 66
  boot disk creation, 67–69
  boot process, 63–68
  bugs or errors in, 62–63
  COMMAND.COM files, 59–62, 66
  CONFIG.SYS files, 56–57, 66
  disk operating system (DOS), 45
  environment configuration, 66–67
  features of, 46–48
  graphical user interface (GUI), 46
  initialization (*see* boot process), 63
  installing/using multiple versions of MS DOS,
    59
  IO.SYS files, 55–57, 66
  limitations, 614
  list of popular OSs, 46–48
  loading, 66
  MS DOS 6.2, 48–49
  MS DOS 7.x, 57–59
  MS DOS, 55–63
  MSDOS.SYS files, 56–57, 66
  OS 2 Warp 4.x, 50–51
  partitioning limits, 612
  PC DOS 7.0, 49–50
  plug-and-play devices, 1072
  registry files (SYSTEM.DAT), 66
  troubleshooting, 62–63
  upgrading, 63
  WINBOOT.SYS files, 56, 66
  Windows 95/98, 50, 53–57
  Windows CE, 51
  Windows NT (Workstation), 51–53
OPTi chipsets, 195, 197–198, 202–203
optical networks, Infrared Data Association
    (IrDA), 985–986, 1178–1181, 1184–1185
optical storage technology association
    (OSTA), 420
optimization, CMOS, 215
Orange Book standard, CD-ROM, 145, 147–148
OS 2 Warp 4.x, 50–51
overclocking CPUs, 317–325
  75 and 83 MHz bus speeds, 322
  AMD K5 series, 324
  bus speed, 321, 322
  corrupted/missing files, 332
  CPU issues, 318, 332
  crashes, 332
  Cyrix/IBM 6X86, 324
  devices not recognized, 332
  heat/cooling, 319, 324–325

Intel Pentium CPUs, 322, 323
  lockups, 332
  memory errors, 332
  motherboards, 318–319
  multiplier setting, 321
  no boot up, 331
  pitfalls of, 319
  RAM, 319
  requirements for, 318–319
  steps to overclock the system, 319–320
  supply voltages, 321–322
  troubleshooting, 331–332
  Windows 95/98 caveat, 321
overlay mode, PC TV, 1298–1299
overlay software, 961–971
override errors, BIOS, 134
overscanning, 1284

P

P rating (PR) system, 289
packet write mode, CD-ROM, 149
paddle board, 394
pages, in memory, 775, 777
PAL standards, 1297
palletized textures, 1264
parallel ports (*see also* printers), 6, 14,
    958–959
  bi–directional ports, type 1 3, 997–998
  BIOS error messages, 136
  Centronics ports, 991–1003, **992**
  enhanced capabilities port (ECP), 996,
    998–999
  enhanced parallel port (EPP), 996, 999
  motherboard connection, 944
  unidirectional ports, 997
parity, 131, 133–134, 218, 233, 743, 779–781,
    788–789, 954
partitioning, 388–389, 393, 605–612
password access, 220, 248–249, 952–953
PC busses (*see also* industry standard archi-
    tecture), 634
PC cards, 11, 1004–1041, **1005**
  anti-virus program problems, 1025–1026
  architecture, 1006–1008, **1007**
  attribute memory, 1011–1012
  audio system problems, 1029
  beep codes, 1027, 1040
  boot problems, 1037, 1040
  CardBus, 1010
  configuration/compatibility problems, 1027,
    1028, 1029, 1030, 1031, 1035, 1037–1040
  connections/interfaces, 1012–1015
  device/device driver incompatibility,
    1026–1027
  drivers, 1017–1020
  enablers, 1008–1009, 1027
  hot insertion/removal, hot swapping, 1011
  installation, 1017–1020
  interrupts, 1027
  lock ups, 1026, 1028

logon problems, 1034–1035
memory optimization, 1020–1023
memory problems, 1024–1025, 1027, 1029,
    1034
modem problems, 1030, 1032–1033, 1036
mouse problems, 1026
network problems, 1027–1028, 1036–1037,
    1039
no display, 1026
not recognized, 1025, 1029–1030, 1031
other types of PC cards, 1016–1017
parent/child nodes, 1030
portable PCs, 1036, 1038–1039
power problems, 1031
socket disabled (red X), 1030–1031
troubleshooting, 1016, 1023–1041
types I, II, III, 1009–1010
Windows 95/98 problems, 1026, 1031–1033,
    1036, 1037, 1039, 1040–1041
Zoomed Video (ZV), 1010
PC DOS 7.0, 49–50
PC TV boards, 1289, 1297–1300, **1298,**
    1310–1311
PCI bridge memory controller (PMC), 941–942
PCI IDE setup, 230–231
PCI push, PC TV boards, 1297–1298
PCMCIA (*see* PC card)
PCs, basic layout/components, 4–8, **5–7**
pen input systems, 1049–1069
  batteries, 1059
  capacitive type, 1053–1054, **1054**
  cleaning/maintenance, 1058
  electromagnetic type, 1054–1056, **1055**
  environment, software, applications,
    1056–1058
  gestures glyphs, 1057–1058
  resistive type, 1051–1052, **1052, 1053**
  troubleshooting, 1058–1068
Pentium (*see* CPU)
peripheral component interconnect (PCI),
    116, 136–137, 235, 241, 1042–1048, **1044,**
    1260–1261, 1287
peripherals (*see* devices/device drivers; plug-
    and-play devices), 1070
phantom power, microphones, 1195
phase shift keying (PSK), 872–873
phase, in modulation, 872
Philips BIOS POST codes, 542–543
Phoenix BIOS, 122–124, 456, 468–469, 543–547
phosphor triads (RGB, etc.), 32
Photo CDs, Kodak, 144
pincushion distortion, 904, **905,** 1367–1368
pipelined burst static RAM (PB SRAM), 775
pipelining, 235, 241, 291, 952
pits, CD-ROM media, 139, 140, 421, **422**
pixel depth, 13
pixels, 902
planar board (*see* motherboards)
platters, 582–583, 586–588, **586, 587,**
    598–599

playback, audio, 1188, **1188,** 1204–1205
playback, video, 1311–1314
plug-and-play (PNP) devices, drivers,
    1070–1097
  autoconfiguration, 278
  BIOS, 116, 134, 1071, 1088, 1094
  BLASTER variable, DOS, 1082
  bridge conflicts, 1094
  CMOS configuration/setup, 229–242
  conflict resolution, 277–278, 1082–1084, 1095
  detection vs enumeration, 1073, 1080
  disabling, 1086–1087, 1088, 1096
  DOS, 1081–1084
  extra port displayed, 1090, 1096
  hot insertion/removal, hot swapping, 1011
  identification codes, 1073–1080
  improper function, 246
  installation, 1084–1087
  interrupts, 1088
  ISA adapters, 1088–1089
  legacy devices, 1080, 1085
  locks/hangs up, 1089–1090, 1095–1096
  modems, 1085–1086
  mouse, 1090, 1092
  not recognized, 1089
  operating systems, 1072
  portable PCs, 1089, 1096
  printers, 1086, 1090, 1092–1093
  removal, 1087, 1090
  SCSI, 1089–1090
  sound devices, 1094–1095
  troubleshooting, 1087–1097
  Windows 95/98, 1071–1080, 1087, 1089,
    1090–1091, 1093–1096
pointing devices, 457, 827–828
polarity, in monitors, 908
popup utilities, 263
portable PCs
  backlight power supplies, 1110–1115, **1114**
  batteries, 102–110
  conserving battery power, 105–106
  PC card problems, 1036, 1038–1039
  plug-and-play devices, 1089, 1096
  Smart Battery, 986–988
  Suspend or Hibernation mode, 105
  system management bus (SMBus), 986–988
ports (*see also* COM/serial ports; parallel
    ports), 14–16, 247, 958
  ATX form factor, 22–24, **23**
  BIOS error messages, 136
  Centronics ports, 991–1003, **992**
  COM/serial ports, 1170–1185
  device/port assignments, typical, 261–262
  error codes, 440–441, 463
  I/O port assignments, 255–260
  motherboard connection, 944
  parallel, 14
  serial, 14
POST, 45, 63–65, 86, 112–113, 128, 134, 326,
    435, 469–486, 556–560, 630, 947–949, 951

POST boards/cards, 556–560, 642
Post Probe, 556–558, **558**
power management (*see also* power supplies),
    215, 242–243, 245–246, 984
power on defaults, 243
power supplies (*see also* batteries)
    advanced configuration power interface
        (ACPI), 973–974
    advanced power control (APC), 945
    advanced power management (APM), 951,
        978–981
    ATX form factor, 24–25
    backlight power supplies, 1110–1115, **1114**
    CPU, 327
    CRT flyback supplies, 1113–1116
    dead system, 84
    duty cycles, 1100
    electromagnetic interference (EMI), 1101
    fan runs/no system activity, 84
    feedback loops, 1099
    flyback transformer (FBT), 35, 1113–1116
    high voltage power supplies, 1110–1115,
        1114
    high voltage test/regulation, 1366
    Instant On, 984–985
    monitors, 35
    motherboard, 942, 946
    NLX form factor, 27
    overclocking CPUs, supply voltages, 321
    phantom power, microphones, 1195
    power managemement, 215, 242–243, 245–246
    Smart Battery, 986–988
    switching power supplies, 1098–1109, **1100,
        1101**
    transformers, 1100
    voltage output by pin, 84, 85
    voltage regulator module (VRM), 327
prediction, branch, 291
preempt timer, 241–242
prefetch, 239
presence detect (PD) in memory, 773
preventive maintenance, 1377–1390
primary (master) drives, 216
primary surface mode, PC TV, 1299
printers (*see also* parallel ports)
    Centronics ports, 991–1003, **992**
    error codes, 440–441, 443, 449, 450, 455, 456,
        463, 687–695
    interrupts, 993, 1202
    laser/LED printers, 673–727
    motherboards, 958
    plug-and-play, 1086, 1090, 1092–1093
    sound card conflicts, 1202
professional graphics adapter (PGA), 1251
programmable I/O (PIO), 594, 595–597
programs (*see* applications)
Promise drive adapter, 415
protected mode, 288, 770
protection errors, 795

public switched telephone network (PSTN),
    846
purity, 32, 1367, 1374–1375, 1385

Q
QEMM, 798, 808–817
quadrature amplitude modulation (QAM), 873
Quadtel BIOS, 469, 547–550
quarter inch cartridge (QIC), 1212–1215

R
rabbit, virus, 1325
RAM, 6, 8, 932, 949–950, 1259
RAMBUS, 738, 776–777
RAMDAC, 1255, 1259–1260
RAMDrive, 369–370
random access, 566
raster, 33, 904–906, **911**, 922, 924–925, 1367
raster drive board, 34–35
read operations, 288
read settings, 231, 237, 239
real mode or base memory, 760, 761–769
real time clock (RTC) (*see also* clock/timer
    circuits), 126–127, 944
rechargeable batteries (*see* batteries
Recordable Compact Disc Standard, CD-ROM,
    145
recording density, 585
recording process, sound boards, 1187–1188,
    1188, 1204–1205
Red Book standard, CD-ROM, 145
reduced instruction set computing (RISC),
    291
refresh, 222–223, 563, 773–774, 948,
    1284–1285
region codes, DVD drives, 426, 427
registry files (SYSTEM.DAT), 66, 90–91, 597
removable drives, 1116–1140
    Bernoulli drives (Iomega), 1129–1135
    Ditto drive (Iomega), 1125–1129
    SyQuest drives, 1135–1140
    Zip drive (Iomega), 1117–1125
rendering, 1261–1262
replacement parts, 71–73
replicators, virus, 1325
resolution, laser/LED printers, 677
resolution, monitors, 13, 902, 1262–1263
retentitivity, 563
retesting, 72
retrace, 904
retry timer, 241
ROM, 45, 1247, 1259
row address strobe (RAS) setup, 228
RS–232 port (*see* COM/serial ports)
run length encoding (RLE), 341

S
safety precautions, 21–22
sampling, 1188–1189

scan codes, keyboard, 660–661
scan line, in laser/LED printer, 680
SCANDISK, 68, 1389
screen door/stippling effect, 1265
screen grid, 32
SCSI, 14–15, 1141–1169
 adapter cards, 1017
 BIOS, 1166–1167
 boot problems, 1162–1163, 1165, 1166
 cables terminators, 1146, 1154, 1156–1158, **1157, 1158**
 CD-ROM, 154
 configuration, bus pinouts, 1147–1152, 1155, 1156
 device independence, 1142
 differential, 1145–1146
 disconnect/reconnect, 1145
 drivers, 1154, 1158–1159
 EISA drives, 1168
 erratic operation, 1163–1164
 error codes, 452, 457, 460, 461–462, 1164
 hangs up, 1166–1167
 host adapters for SCSI devices, 1152–1160, **1153,** 1164
 ID numbers, 1146–1147
 initiators, 1144–1145
 installation, 1156
 motherboard, 956
 negotiation, 1151
 not recognized, 1165, 1166
 plug-and-play devices, 1089–1090
 sense codes, 1230–1232
 single–ended, 1145–1146
 synchronous, asychronous communications, 1145
 tape drives, 1230–1232
 targets, 1144–1145, 1166
 troubleshooting, 1159–1168
 upgrading for SCSI, 1152–1159
 variations, SCSI 1, Fast– Wide–, etc. 1143–1144
 video adapters, 1283–1284
 VL bus/card use, 1167–1168
 Windows 95, 1159
SDRAM, 9
Sealink, 879
secondary (slave) drives, 216
sector sparing (defect management), 588–589
sectors per track (SPT), 216
sectors, 566, 586–588, **586,** 587
sectors, hard disk drives, 340
seek time, 587
self monitoring analysis reporting technology (see SMART)
sense codes, tape drives, 1230–1232
sensitiviy, 1194
serial ports (see COM/serial ports)
ServerBench, 78
setup routines, BIOS, 113

Setup utility, CMOS, 213–243
SGS Thomson (see chipsets; CPU)
shadow or slot masks, 32–33, **33,** 903–904, 1371–1372
shadow memory, 125, 215, 220–221, 233, 778, 798
shoe shining, tape drives, 1243
signal to noise ratio (SNR), 1193
signature scanners (see also viruses/ antivirals), 1337
SIMCHECK equipment, 786–788, **787**
single inline memory module (SIMM), 8, 88, 742–743, **742,** 744–747, 759, 785–786, 788, 942, 950, 952, 956, 1387
single inline package (SIP), 741
single–ended SCSI, 1145–1146
SiS chipsets, 195, 196–197, 203
slack space, 340
Slot 1 motherboards, 934
slots, expansion, 229, 938
small computer system interface (see SCSI)
small outline J leads memory package, 741
Smart Battery, 986–988
SMART command set, 592
snoop/snoop filters, 240, 241, 234–235
Socket 7/8 motherboards, 934
sockets, CPU, 289–291, **291**
software, 45, 80, 263–264, 981–983
sorting, memory sorting, 798
sound boards & cards, 16, **17,** 938, 954, 1186–1209, **1187, 1191**
 analog-to-digital/digital-to-analog conversions, 1189
 attenuation, 1192
 audio cards, 1017
 buzz or hum, 1200
 CD problems, 1201
 CODECS, compression, 1200
 CONFIG.SYS AUTOEXEC.BAT, 1196–1197
 data bits, 1189–1190
 decibels, 1192
 digital signal processor (DSP), 1191–1192
 digitization of sound, 1188–1189
 direct memory access (DMA), 1204, 1205, 1207
 DirectSound, 1268
 distortion, 1194, 1203
 DOS, 1205
 drivers, 1196–1197
 Ensoniq sound boards, 1209
 frequency response, 1192–1193, **1193**
 full-duplex operation, 1206
 gain, 1192, 1194
 harmonic distortion, total (THD), 1193–1194
 intermodulation distortion (IMD), 1194
 interrupts, 1201
 joystick problems, 651, 1202
 line-in line-out systems, 940
 lock ups, 1204, 1205

sound boards & cards, *continued*
memory/environment space, 1201–1202, 1204, 1205
microphones, 1194–1196, 1206, 1208–1209
MIDI, 1190–1191, **1190,** 1201
mixers, 1191–1192
Nyquist Sampling Theorem, 1189
PC card problems, 1029
playback process, 1188, **1188,** 1204–1205
plug-and-play devices, 1094–1095
poor sound, 1200, 1201, 1202, 1203–1204
printer problems, 1202
quality of sound, 1189–1190
recording process, 1187–1188, **1188,** 1204, 1205
sampling, 1188–1189
sensitivy, 1194
signal to noise ratio (SNR), 1193
speakers, 942, 1200–1201
stereo receiver connections, 940
testing, 1385
troubleshooting, 1196–1209
WAV files, Windows 95/98 problems, 1197–1200, 1202–1203
WebPhone, 1209
Windows 95, 1205, 1207–1208
Southbridge controller (AMD 645 chipset), 1184–185
speakers, 942, 1200–1201, 1381–1382
speech adapters, error codes, 457
speed of processor, 8, 771–772
ST506/412 drive adapter, 383–389, **385**
Stacker, DOS disk compression, 371–381
stacks, 252
standard mode operation, 1272
standards, form factors for components, 22–27, 1418–1419
state machine settings, 238
static convergence, 33, 1371–1374
static RAM (SRAM), 738, 774
stereo receiver connections, 940
sterilizing the shop, 81–83
storage (*see* disk compression; magnetic storage)
streaming, 240
Suntec chipsets, 203
super VGA (SVGA), 13, 1253
superscalar execution, 292
surface mounted devices (SMD), 946
swap files, 363–364
swim, in monitors, 907
switching power supplies, 1098–1109, **1100, 1101**
sychronous communication, 893–894
symbols, CD-ROM, 142
symbols, tokens, 872
Symphony Labs chipsets, 204
synchronization, in monitors, 908
synchronous burst static RAM (SBSRAM), 775

synchronous communications, 1145
synchronous DRAM (SDRAM), 738, 776
SyQuest removable drives, 1135–1140
SYS, 68
system BIOS (*see* BIOS ROM)
system board (*see* motherboards)
system integrity diagnostic test failure, 334
system management bus (SMBus), 986–988
system options, BIOS error message, 129
system reporting tools, 263
system resources, 252–262
conflict resolution, 251–278
device/port assignments, typical, 261–262
direct memory access (DMA), 254–255
extended ISA (EISA) busses, 253–254
I/O area assignments, 255–260
interrupts, 252–254
memory assignments, 255, 260
micro channel architecture (MCA) bus, 253
plug-and-play (PNP) settings, 277–278
stacks, 252
system reporting tools, 263
Windows 95/98 conflict resolution, 264–277
system service routines, BIOS, 113–115

T
3D WinBench 97, 77
Tandon BIOS POST codes, 550–553
tape, 563
tape drives, 10, 370, 1210–1243, **1211**
autoloaders, 1222–1223
auto–skip, 1241
bad blocks, 1224, 1237, 1239
beginning/end of tape, 1237
capacity, 1242–1243
caught tapes, freeing, 1226–1229
cleaning tapes/drives, 1221–1226, 1384
compatibility issues, 1215, 1239
dead unit, 1232–1233
digital audio tape (DAT) drives, 1225–1226
DOS, 1238
dropout errors, 1224
electronic circuitry, 1220–1221, **1221**
error codes, 461
exploded view, **1219**
fault type errors, 1237–1238
floppy drives, 1241
format errors, 1224, 1240, 1241, 1242
handling tape, 1221–1226
helical scan tapes, 1216–1218, **1217**
load/eject problems, 1236, 1241
locks up, 1237
logic errors, 1242
maintenance, 1221–1226
mechanical components, 1218–1220, **1233, 1234, 1235**
media errors, 1224, 1225, 1239
memory errors, 1240–1241
not recognized, 1238

overlay errors, 1238–1239
quarter inch cartridge (QIC), 1212–1215
read/write errors, 1224, 1233–1234
sense codes, 1230–1232
shoe shining errors, 1243
speed problems, 1234–1235, 1240, 1242
tape properties, 1211–1212
Travan tape cartridges, 1215–1216
troubleshooting, 1229–1243
Windows 95, 1238
write protected tapes, 1236–1237
targets, SCSI, 1144–1145
temperature warnings, 135–136
terminate stay resident (TSR) (*see also*
   virus/antivirals), 251, 263, 807, 1337
terminators, BIOS error messages, 135
test codes (*see also* error codes; IBM
   diagnostic/error codes)
test tick, memory, 218
Texas Instruments Graphical Architecture
   (TIGA), 1254
texture mapping, 1263, 1264–1265
thermal calibration, CD-R drives, 171
thermal probe warning, BIOS, 135
thin small outline package (TSOP), 741
thin–film media, 583
ThinkPad, QEMM problems, 816–817
thrashing, 628, 1286
time bombs, 1320–1325
time outs, 238
timing modes, 237
toner developer, 677–678
total harmonic distortion (THD), 1193–1194
touchpads (*see* pen input systems)
tower enclosures (*see also* enclosures), 5–6
trace, in laser/LED printer, 680
track at once write mode, CD-ROM, 149
track density/tracks per inch (TPI), 585
trackballs, 827, 832
   cleaning, 832–833
   drivers, 839–840
   error codes, 840
   interfaces, 834
   troubleshooting, 834–844
tracks, 340, 566, 586–588, **586, 587**
transformers, 913, 1100, 1113–1116
transient commands (*see* external
   commands)
translation modes, hard drives, 216–217, 394,
   613
transparency, 1263
Travan tape cartridges, 1215–1216
trellis coded quadrature amplitude modulation
   (TCQAM), 873
triads, color palettes, 902–903, **903**
Trojan horses, 1319–1320
Truespeech codec, 1200
truncation of cylinders, 613
turbo mode, 219, 220

TV (*see* PC TV boards)
Type 47 HDD data area, 218
typematic rate, 217

U
u–Law codec, 1200
Ultra ATA drives, 407–408, 593–594
unidirectional ports, 997
universal asynchronous receiver/transmitter
   (UART), 846–847, 883, 1174–1175, **1175**
universal disk format (UDF), 420
universal serial bus (USB), 116, 988–989, **989**
upgrading
   benchmarks, 73
   conflicts after upgrade, 88
   CPU upgrades, 8
   memory, 8
   operating system adjustments, 57–59, 63
   SCSI upgrades, 1152–1159
   troubleshooting problems, 88–89
upper memory area (UMA), 112, 153, 235,
   770, 798, 803, 805, 806–808

V
vaccines (*see also* viruses/antivirals),
   1335–1336
vertical drive circuits, 34–35
vertical scan/sync, 904–906
VESA (*see* VL bus), 1342
VIA Apollo chipsets, 191–195, 204–205
video (*see* monitors and video)
video capture boards (*see also* PC TV boards),
   1289–1297, **1290, 1291**
   analog to digital/digital to analog conversion,
      1291
   audio video interleave (AVI), 1292
   camera techniques, capture, 1296–1297
   capture process, 1292, 1294–1297,
      1304–1311
   CODECs, 1292–1293
   color, 1296
   direct memory access (DMA), 1300
   frame rate, 1294
   I/O addresses, 1300–1301
   image window size for capture, 1294
   Indeo video codec (Intel), 1293–1294
   installing video capture boards, 1302–1304
   intercast broadcasts, 1299–1300, 1310–1311
   interrupts, 1300–1301
   lighting, 1296
   MPEG compression, 1314–1317
   overlay mode, PC TV, 1298–1299
   playback process, 1311–1314
   primary surface mode, PC TV, 1299
   quality of video source for capture, 1295
   troubleshooting, 1300–1317
   vertical sync/blanking, 1300
video electronics standards association (*see*
   VESA; VL bus)

video graphics array (VGA), 13, 234, 237, 239, 1252
video memory (VRAM), 738, 775
video palette snoop, 234
video RAM (VRAM), 825–826
video ROM (VROM), 220, 227, 814, 1247
video standards, 420–421
virtual control program interface (VCPI), 770
virtual memory, 620
virus/antivirals, 79–83, 631, 1318–1341
  antiviral tools, 81, 83, 1335–1338
  CMOS protection setup, 221–222
  curing infections, 1334–1335
  identifying, 79–81
  myths, 1329–1331
  protection, 1331–1332
  sterilizing the shop, 81–83
  symptoms, 1332–1333
  types of virus, 1326–1329
  virulent code, 1318–1326
VL bus, 235, 237, 328, 411–412, 1042, 1167–1168, 1260, 1276–1277, 1342–1348
VLSI Technology chipsets, 205
voice mail, 849
voltage regulator module (VRM), 327
volume boot sector (VBS), 65
volume lables, 631
volume table of contents (VTOC), CD-ROM, 144
Vxx modem signal standards, 874–876

W

wait states, 8, 215, 224, 225, 227–228, 771–772
Warp (OS2) 4.x, 50–51
WAV files, 1197–1200, 1202–1203
WebBench, 78
WebPhone (*see also* sound boards & cards), 1209
Western Digital chipsets, 204
White Book standard, CD-ROM, 145
WinBench 97, 77
WINBOOT.SYS files, 56, 66
Windows 95/98, 50, 53–55, 56–57
  boot disk creation, 67–69
  boot process, problems, 89–92
  conflict resolution, 264–277
  DriveSpace disk compression, 351–360
  memory, 806, 815–816
  motherboard, 952, 955, 957
  mouse, 836–838, 842
  overclocking CPUs, 321
  PC card problems, 1026, 1031–1034, 1036–1041
  plug-and-play devices, 1071–1080, 1087, 1089, 1090–1091, 1093–1096
  registry files, missing, 90–91
  resource settings, 264–277
  SCSI devices, 1159
  shortcut keys, 1406–1408
  sound boards & cards, 1197–1200, 1205, 1207–1208
  tape drives:, 1238
  video adapters, 1287–1288
  WAV file problems, 1197–1200
  WINBOOT.SYS files, 56, 66
  wrong CPU reported, 328
Windows CE, 51
Windows NT (Workstation), 51–53, 957
Windows RAM (WRAM), 777
Winstone 97, 77
Wintune 97, 78
wireless communications, Infrared Data Association (IrDA), 985–986, 1178–1181, 1184–1185
wireless keyboards, 670
Wizard adapter, error codes, 461
work orders, 19
worms, 1326
wrapping, cylinder wrapping, 613
write operations, 288
write precompensation (WP), 590
write settings, 231, 232, 233, 236–237, 239, 241
write-once CD-R drives, 145

X

X- Y- ZModem, 878–879
XA format, CD-ROM, 145
XGA XGA/2 video adapter, 1253–1254
XtraDrive systems, QEMM problems, 814–815

Y

Y adapters, joysticks, 651, 652
Year 2000 (Y2K) problems, 126–127
Yellow Book standard, CD-ROM, 145

Z

z-buffering, 1264
Zenith BIOS POST codes, 554–555
Zilog chipsets, 206
zinc air batteries, 105
Zip drive (Iomega), 9–10, 1117–1125
zoned recording, 395, 588
Zoomed Video (ZV), 1010
Zymos chipsets, 206

ABOUT THE AUTHOR

Stephen J. Bigelow is the founder and president of Dynamic Learning Systems—a technical writing, research, and publishing company specializing in electronic and PC service topics. Bigelow is the author of twelve feature-length books for TAB/McGraw-Hill, and almost 100 major articles for mainstream electronics magazines such as *Popular Electronics*, *Electronics NOW*, *Circuit Cellar INK*, and *Electronic Service & Technology*. Bigelow is a contributing columnist for Computer Currents (the "Computer Advisor": column) and Computer Connections ("The Computer Guy" column). Bigelow is also the editor and publisher of *The PC Toolbox*™—a premier PC service newsletter for computer enthusiasts and technicians. He is an Electrical Engineer with a BS EE from Central New England College in Worcester, MA. Before contacting the author with questions about the book, be sure to read the *FAQ—"Getting the most from this book."*

Dynamic Learning Systems
PO Box 282
Jefferson, MA 01522-0282 USA
Internet: sbigelow@cerfnet.com

Or visit the Dynamic Learning Systems web site at; **http://www.dlspubs.com**

DLS Order Form

Use this form when subscribing to *The PC Toolbox*™ or when ordering the unlock codes for MONITORS and/or PRINTERS. You may tear out or photocopy this order form.

YES! Please accept my order as shown below: (check any one)

_____ Send me the unlock code for the commercial version of **MONITORS** for **$30** (US)
Massachusetts residents please add $1 sales tax.

_____ Send me the unlock code for the commercial version of **PRINTERS** for **$30** (US)
Massachusetts residents please add $1 sales tax.

Start my 1 year subscription (6 issues) to *The PC Toolbox*™ for **$39** (US).
_____ I understand that I have an unconditional 90 day money-back guarantee
with the newsletter.

A special offer! Give me a 1 year subscription to *The PC Toolbox*™, as well as the
_____ **unlock codes for MONITORS and PRINTERS for just $70 (US).** I understand that I
have an unconditional 90 day money-back guarantee with the newsletter.
Massachusetts residents please add $2 sales tax.

PRINT YOUR MAILING INFORMATION HERE:

Name: Company:

Address:

City, State, Zip:

Country:

Telephone: (   )   Fax: (   )

PLACING YOUR ORDER:

By FAX: Fax this completed order form (24 hrs/day, 7 days/week) to **508-829-6819**

By Phone: Phone in your order (Mon-Fri; 9am-4pm EST) to **508-829-6744**

___ MasterCard   Card: ___ ___ ___ ___ ___ ___ ___ ___ ___ ___ ___ ___ ___ ___ ___ ___

___ VISA   Exp: ___/___   Sig: _____

Or by Mail: Mail this completed form, along with your check, money order, PO, or credit card info to:
***Dynamic Learning Systems*, P.O. Box 282, Jefferson, MA 01522-0282 USA**

Please allow 2-4 weeks for order processing. Returned checks are subject to a $15 charge.

SOFTWARE AND INFORMATION LICENSE